CW00485284
Dreamcast
DRAPER
TOOLS
DANKA
Auto

The PFA
Premier

Football League
Players' Records
1946 – 2005

Edited And Compiled By Barry J. Hugman

Assistant Editors
Michael Featherstone, Michael Joyce
and Alan Platt

QUEEN ANNE PRESS

Queen Anne Press
is a division of
Lennard Associates Limited
Mackerye End, Harpenden
AL5 5DR

First published in Great Britain in 2005

A CIP catalogue record for this book
is available from the British Library

ISBN 1 85291 665 6

Cover design by Design2Print

Typesetting and internal design by
Typecast, Yeovil

Printed and bound in Great Britain by
Bath Press

ENDPAPERS

The photos on the front and back endpapers are of players who, to the end of the 2004-05 season, had made more than 650 league appearances.

Left to right and by horizontal rows, top to bottom

Front endpaper

Lefthand page:
Peter Shilton, Tony Ford, Terry Paine, Tommy Hutchison; Neil Redfearn, Robbie James, Alan Oakes, Dave Beasant; John Trollope, Jimmy Dickinson, Roy Sproson; Mick Tait; Billy Bonds, Ray Clemence, Pat Jennings, Frank Worthington; Ernie Moss, Les Chapman, Asa Hartford, Alan Ball.

Righthand page:
John Hollins, Phil Parkes, Steve Bruce, Mick Mills; Ian Callaghan, David Seaman, Steve Perryman, Martin Peters; Mike Channon, Ron Harris, Mike Summerbee, Glenn Cockerill; Keith Curle, John Wile, Andy Melville, Phil Neal; Neville Southall, Mick Gooding, Paul Futcher, Stanley Matthews.

Back endpaper

Lefthand page:
Roy Tunks, Roger Jones, Derek Fazackerley, Ivor Allchurch; John Burridge, Nigel Winterburn, Alan Knight, Denis Irwin; Trevor Cherry, Norman Hunter, Alan Mullery, Paul Stancliffe; Wayne Allison, Alec Chamberlain, Rob Newman, Bryan 'Pop' Robson; Geraint Williams, Rob Lee, Teddy Sheringham, Steve Foster.

Righthand page:
Bobby Moore, Mike Keen, Kevin Hector, Paul Simpson; Martin Dobson, Gary McAllister, Dave Watson, Marco Gabbiadini; Colin Greenall, Peter Beardsley, John Jackson, Leighton James; Mike Walker, Steve Thompson, Mike Flynn, Ian McDonald; Billy Bremner, Phil Brown, Peter Jackson, Peter Downsborough.

All photographs supplied by Colorsport

CONTENTS

PROFESSIONAL FOOTBALLERS' ASSOCIATION
PFA
ACCIDENT INSURANCE
EDUCATION
YOUTH TRAINING
PERSONAL REPRESENTATION
COMMERCIAL AFFAIRS
PENSIONS
TRANSFERS
LEGAL ADVICE
FINANCIAL HELP
CONTRACTS
PLAYERS UNITED
THE OUTCASTS F.C.
TEN DECADES' SERVICE TO FOOTBALL
FOUNDED AT THE IMPERIAL HOTEL, MANCHESTER IN 1907, THE PROFESSIONAL FOOTBALLERS' ASSOCIATION TODAY COMMANDS AN ENVIABLE REPUTATION AS THE WORLD'S LONGEST ESTABLISHED PROFESSIONAL SPORTSMEN'S UNION.
This status stands as testament to the unswerving determination, dedication and commitment of all its contributors, from its earliest forefathers such as Billy Meredith right through to its current Management Committee.
The result is that the PFA is now involved in every aspect of a player's career from financial management and pensions, to education and training, coaching, commercial, accident insurance, medical and benevolent assistance.
The PFA plays a key role in both the Football Scholarship Scheme and Football in the Community Programme, ensuring that the players of tomorrow receive the best possible start to their careers and that football clubs are a focal point in their communities for all age groups and cultures promoting anti-racism and social awareness.
THE PFA - PROTECTING THE PLAYERS, PROTECTING THE GAME.
PROFESSIONAL FOOTBALLERS ASSOCIATION
20 Oxford Court, Bishopsgate, Manchester M2 3WQ
THE PFA SAYS LET'S KICK RACISM OUT OF FOOTBALL
it's only
the colou
of the shirt
that counts
adidas

FOREWORD

'A definitive record of all our professional (and a few amateur) players who have graced the Football and Premier Leagues': that's the proud boast of the PFA and the publishers of this unique book. And it's no idle boast either.

Barry Hugman and his team of enthusiasts have again worked tirelessly to compile a list of every footballer to have played in the Football League since the Second World War – a thankless task you might think, but one which has been carried out and completed with all the professionalism of those contained within.

So, here then is the official list of all those who actually wore their club colours in League battle. And, of course, this book also shows the transfers, plus the career records of every single player. All of these players have been members of the Professional Footballers' Association and we at the PFA are proud to see such a magnificently produced record of the careers of so many members, past and present.

In my opinion, this book will not only give hours and hours of pleasure to football fans throughout the country, but to ex-players who love reminiscing, love comparing records, and who love following the modern game and the fortunes of today's stars. It is a veritable 'who's who' of all the players who have brought so much pleasure to so many people over the last 60 years.

We are delighted to be involved with this publication and anticipate referring to it time and time again, and our thanks go to Barry and his team for all their dedicated hard work.

Gordon Taylor
Chief Executive
Professional Footballers' Association

INTRODUCTION
by Barry J. Hugman
(Editor & Compiler)

Since the first edition of *(Premier &) Football League Players' Records* appeared in 1980, published by Rothmans, I have striven to improve this now well-established work of reference on post-war footballers' accuracy, not only by updating the statistics and listing new entries for players who made their Premier and Football League debuts since the last edition, but also correcting, where necessary, the details of players long since retired.

When I first started this compendium in the mid-1970s, the only source of data were the hardy football perennials – the *News of the World* and *News Chronicle* (*later Playfair*) *Football Annuals* – which listed each player's appearances and goals for the previous season. During the 1980s, a number of football statisticians began to chronicle the detailed history of their favourite clubs, match by match, with reference to Football League archives and local newspapers. Much of their research has since come to fruition in the shape of club histories, initially published by Breedon Books, which include line-ups for every match played, and, at the time of going to press, many clubs are now covered. A big thank you should also be given to Tony Brown of SoccerData Publications, who continues to publish the definitive histories of clubs yet to be dealt with, and Dave Twydell of Yore Publications.

All their researches have been cross-referenced with the data contained in previous editions of this book and many discrepancies in appearances and goals have been noted. In most cases the discrepancies were trivial, a question of one or two appearances or goals difference. In a few cases they were significant, usually when players with the same (or similar) surname played in the same season for the same club. If the P&FLPR's team are satisfied that the research has been done correctly and that the statistics continued in these books are more reliable than the figures in by-gone football annuals, we have corrected our records accordingly.

It should be noted, however, that while an appearance in a particular match is a matter of fact, goalscorers are often a matter of opinions. In a goalmouth scramble, a goal may be credited to one player by the assembled journalists sitting 100 yards from the action and reported as such by the press the following day, whilst the club, following a post-mortem, credits the goal to another of its players. In such cases we accept the opinion of the club rather than the press. However, there are other cases where the club is anxious to credit a goal to one of its own players when it is quite manifestly an own goal. For example, the misjudged back pass, the misdirected shot deflected into goal by an opposing defender, or the goalkeeper stepping over the line after safely catching a high ball. Such examples we consider as 'own goals' and not credited to any player. More recently, the Premier League has set up a panel to deal with disputed goals and it's their decision that we accept. As a result of these differences of interpretation, there are inevitably some small discrepancies between the goalscoring figures of some players in this book and those logged by other sources.

Players Names: As far as is humanly possible, we have listed players in alphabetic order, firstly by surname and then by christian names. However, in cases where players are better known by their second or third christian name, we have listed them under their commonly used name. For example Mark Hughes of Manchester United was christened 'Leslie Mark' but will be found under 'Mark'. Philip Lee Jones of Liverpool will be found under 'Lee'. To do otherwise could cause confusion to the reader searching for the entry of a player with a very common surname. Other players are not recorded under the family surname. For example, the Brazilian, Mirandinha, of Newcastle United, is in fact 'Francisco da Silva', but is listed under his adopted moniker rather than his family name. In the case of double-barrelled surnames we have taken a pragmatic view, according to the name most commonly used by themselves or the media. Thus, Ian Storey-Moore and Forbes Phillipson-Masters will be found under their full names while the Martin-Chambers brothers, David and Philip, will be found under 'Chambers' and Jeffrey Thompson-Minton will be found under 'Minton'. In many cases players were known by a corruption of their christian names or by a totally different nickname, such as the Brentford goalkeeper, 'Sonny' Feehan, christened Ignatius. In these cases, players are listed under their christened name with their familiar moniker shown in brackets afterwards.

Birthplaces: The purpose of showing birthplaces is to indicate the area of the British Isles a player originates from. However, this is frequently misleading. Many players were born overseas, either as sons of fathers serving in the armed forces stationed in West Germany, or in further flung former colonies. Their birthplace does not, however, indicate their nationality, which is conferred on them by their parentage. A player may be born in one area, but grow up in another. In such cases the place of education is more meaningful than place of birth. Some players were born while their parents were on holiday, such as the Kimble brothers, Alan and Garry, in Poole (Dorset). In their particular case, as it was known to us, the birthplace is shown as the family home of Dagenham. Whenever possible, birthplaces are taken from birth certificates, which may only indicate an area, such as a county or the birth registration district with an antiquated name, often not stating the town or village of birth. All persons born in the counties of Gloucestershire and Worcestershire are registered as born in the county town. Those born in County Durham are shown by obscure registration districts such as 'Central South-East' and 'North-West', which do not indicate the town of origin. Most players shown with their birthplace as 'Ormskirk' were almost certainly born in the neighbouring new town of Skelmersdale. Some players were born in maternity hospitals located in different administrative areas from the parential home, such as Rochford (for Southend) and Orsett (for Grays and Thurrock). In cases where the actual birthplace is known to the authors, the original information as shown in earlier editions has been corrected. In some cases where the birthplace was an obscure country village, or suburb of a large city, the name of the nearest market town or city has been substituted. However, in the case of mining villages which produced many fine players, we have taken care to preserve their identity.

Birthdate: For recent players, we have checked our data against the PFA's records and although some discrepancies with club histories have been noted against older players, mainly in the year of birth, when we are satisfied that a transcribing error has occurred we have corrected the original birthdate.

International Appearances: Levels covered are (Amat) Amateur; B; (Sch) School; SemiPro; u20; u21; u23; War; (Yth) Youth. The number of full caps, where known, appear besides the country or country code. If the number of caps are not known, the player in question is shown, for example, as French int. Representative levels include: (FLge) Football League; (IrLge) Irish League; (LoI) League of Ireland; (NIRL) Northern Ireland Regional League; (SLge) Scottish League; (WLge) Welsh League. For codes relating to other countries see under Source.

League Clubs: During the post-war period, several clubs have changed their name and in this edition we have gone to great lengths to show those changes. For example, Hartlepool United began 1946-47 as Hartlepools United, became Hartlepool in 1968-69 and Hartlepool United in 1977-78. Thus the players who overlapped those years are shown under the club name when first appearing. However, where the club name changes dramatically such as Wimbledon to Milton Keynes Dons, both names are shown against any player who has appeared during the transition.

Source (or Previous Club): This column indicates a player's origins, whether from outside the P/FL or within the ranks of the Leagues. For the latter the following code is used:

- Jnrs = Junior players signed from school/college, without serving an apprenticeship or trainee period.
- App = Apprentice signing prior to 1986.
- YT = Trainee. This rank was introduced in 1986 and includes players sponsored by the Government's Youth Training Scheme.
- Sch = Scholar. From 1999-2000 trainees were gradually superseded by scholars under the new scholarship scheme and, for our purposes, we have shown players who turned pro after July 2002, having come through their club's youth scheme, as being scholars.
- Tr = Transfers (including free transfers).
- L = Loan signing, or temporary transfer, shown only when the player made an appearance.

For players signed from overseas clubs, where space allows the name of the country in question is spelt out. However, where space is at a premium, the following country codes are employed:
(Ar or Arg) Argentina; (Au or Aus) Australia; (Aut) Austria; (Bar) Barbados; (Bs) Belarus; (Be or Bel) Belgium; (Ber) Bermuda; (Bol) Bolivia; (Br) Brazil; (Bul) Bulgaria; (Ca or Can) Canada; (Cm) Cameroon; (Ch) Chile; (Col) Colombia; (CR) Costa Rica; (Cro) Croatia; (Cyp) Cyprus; (Cz) Czechoslovakia; (CzR) Czech Republic; (De or Den) Denmark; (Ec) Ecuador; (Est) Estonia; (Fi or Fin) Finland; (Fr) France; (Ge or Ger) Germany; (Geo) Georgia; (Gr or Gre) Greece; (Ho or Holl) Holland; (Hon) Honduras; (HK) Hong Kong; (Hu or Hun) Hungary; (Ic or Ice) Iceland; (IC) Ivory Coast; (Ind) India; (Isr) Israel; (It) Italy; (Ja or Jam) Jamaica; (Jap) Japan; (Lat) Latvia; (Lit) Lithuania; (Mal) Malaysia; (Mex) Mexico; (Mol) Moldova; (Mor) Morocco; (Nz) New Zealand; (Ng or Nig) Nigeria; (No or Nor) Norway; (Par) Paraguay; (Pol) Poland; (Por) Portugal; (Ro or Rom) Romania; (Rus) Russia; (St V) St Vincent; (Sau) Saudi Arabia; (Sl) Slovenia; (Slo) Slovakia; (SA) South Africa; (SK) South Korea; (Sp) Spain; (Sw or Swe) Sweden; (Swi or Swit) Switzerland; (Tr) Trinidad; (Tun) Tunisia; (Tu) Turkey; (Uk) Ukraine; (Ur) Uruguay; (Us) USA; (Ven) Venezuela; (Yu or Yug) Yugoslavia; (Zim) Zimbabwe.

Date Signed: The date given by month/year is when the player signed professional or non-contract forms. In the case of amateurs, the date of their initial signing is indicated, while trainees who made an appearance but did not sign professional forms are shown by the use of •. For players first signed on loan, before a permanent transfer was arranged, the date of signing is that of the loan transfer, except when the player returned to his former club and made further appearances. Non-League (N/L) is only shown where the compilers have not been able to find the necessary date in question.

Seasons Played: The year shown is the first year of the season played. Thus, 1997 indicates the season 1997-98, '1979-85' means that the player made his debut in 1979-80 and his last appearance in 1985-86, but does not necessarily mean that he played in every intervening season.

Appearances, Subs and Goals: The statistics shown are for Premiership and Football League matches only. Cup games and end of season play-offs are not included, nor are appearances made for League clubs before they entered the League or in temporary absence (e.g. Lincoln City 1987-88 and Darlington 1989-90). Whilst other sources have aggregated full and substitute appearances into a single total, we consider it important to maintain the distinction. Most substitutions occur in the final quarter of the game and we feel that one full appearance, plus 17 substitute appearances, is not the same as 18 full appearances.

Positions:

(G)	Goalkeeper
(FB)	Full Back
(CD)	Central Defender
(WH)	Wing Half
(W)	Winger
(IF)	Inside Forward
(CF)	Centre Forward
(M)	Midfielder
(F)	Forward

The position shown for each player is that in which he played most frequently, or is most commonly associated. This, despite many of the more recent players frequently switching between defence and midfield, or between defence and attack. Only where there has been a marked change in position, in cases such as Tony Read or John Charles, is more than one position listed for a player. Otherwise the position is the one in which a player appeared most throughout his career. Thus Tom Smalley, who was a post-war full-back with Northampton Town, appeared mostly as a wing-half in an extensive pre-war career with Wolverhampton Wanderers, and is listed as such. One must also take into account that several more recent players have yet to settle into a regular position. The nomenclature of playing positions has changed considerably since the last war. From 1946 to the early 1960s it was widely assumed that teams played a 2-3-5 formation with two full backs, three half backs and five forwards. In fact, after the change to the offside law in 1925 the true formation was usually 3-2-2-3, with the centre half converted to a centre back, or even 3-3-4, with one of the inside forwards withdrawn to a deeper position. Despite all the changes, the term 'full back' still persists up to the present day, whilst, until the invention of the term 'midfielder' in the mid 1960s, inside forwards could be either deep lying schemers such as Johnny Haynes (Fulham), or lethal goalscorers such as Ted Phillips (Ipswich Town). In 1958 Brazil introduced 4-2-4 to the world, when winning the World Cup in Sweden. Under this system, one wing half was converted to twin centre back, while the other wing half, plus an inside forward, patrolled the middle of the park. Although this system was copied by many English clubs, it was not entirely successful since it required two talented and hard-working players in the central positions. After Alf Ramsey won the 1966 World Cup for England with a 4-3-3 system, with one winger withdrawn to augment the midfield, most English clubs adopted the same system and when Ramsey dispensed with wingers altogether with a 4-4-2 system for the 1970 World Cup in Mexico, the orthodox attacking winger disappeared for several years from the English game, to be replaced by workaholic midfielders. By 1970 the terms 'centre half', 'wing half', 'inside forward' and 'centre forward', 'outside right' and 'outside left' were virtually obsolescent, to be replaced by 'central defenders', 'midfielders', 'twin strikers' and, occasionally, 'wingers'. Happily, the orthodox winger returned to favour in the 1980s with a corresponding increase in the goal rate, as some clubs reverted to 4-3-3 instead of 4-4-2. Since the late 1980s many teams have played with three central defenders, with one deployed behind the other two as a 'sweeper' and the two full backs pushed forward into midfield as auxiliary wingers. The result has been the emergence of a 3-5-2 formation, with overcrowded midfield areas, or a more fluid 3-4-3 system with one winger deployed as an auxiliary forward.

Since the first edition we have implemented several changes, including that of listing the complete career record of all players who played in the Football League prior to the last war. This takes into account famous players like Sir Stanley Matthews, who played for eight seasons before the outbreak of war and for nearly 20 after, and also many other stars whose careers ran parallel with a man such as Stan Cullis. These are the players who had lost the best years of their football life because of hostilities and retired early into the post-war period. Early editions showed Cullis as having played only 37 games for 'Wolves', whereas, in fact, he played 152 times between 1934-35 and 1946-47. Since the last edition, we have carried out further research into players whose careers were interrupted by the Second World War. The tale of the three (yes three) Harry Toppings, all full backs, all from Lancashire, and all playing league football in the 1930s, is worth a chapter on its own. Only one of them played post-war league football and his record appears here, having been revised from what has been published before. Similar stories could be told about the two James Henry Clarkes and the two goalkeepers called John Daniels. Even in the early 1960s, Stockport County had two wingers – Michael Connolly and Michael Connelly – who were originally confused. We have also introduced full christian names, along with many additional notifications of players who have unfortunately deceased, provided by Michael Featherstone, and will continue to bring on board relevant information as and when it becomes available.

As we have stated in previous editions, one thing is for sure . . . if they have played in the post-war Football League and Premiership, they are included within the pages of this book and somebody, somewhere, sometime, will look them up. *Premier & Football League Players' Records* is a testament to all of the men who have donned the colours of their specific side since 1946-47 and to the Professional Footballers' Association, who have magnificently supported their members throughout that period.

Finally, we have tried without success to trace birth and birthplace details for the following:- Michael Connelly (Stockport), Len Davies (Southend), William E. Davies (Crewe), David Ellis (Bury, Halifax and Barrow), James Grant (Brighton), Michael Gray (Aldershot and Watford), Leslie James (Darlington), William Johnston (Barrow), Stan J. Jones (Crewe), James J. Kelly (Barrow), Michael J. Kelly (Wolves and Crewe), William McLean (New Brighton), Alf Morris (Accrington), John Peat (Workington), Joe Riley (Darlington), Alex Shaw (Crewe), Alan Smith (Hull), Alf Smith (Walsall), George T. Smith (Walsall), John Smith (Ipswich), Tommy Teasdale (Hull), Adam Wasilewski (Rochdale), Ken Williams (Watford), and Robert Wilson (Workington).

If anyone can help with details, additonal to what we already have within the pages of this book, please write to Michael Featherstone, c/o The Fuchsias, Cromer Road, Trimingham, Norfolk NR11 8HT.

ACKNOWLEDGEMENTS

With *Football League Players' Records* now in its sixth edition, the editor would once again like to thank the many experts without whose help this book would not have been updated as effectively.

The assistant editor, Alan Platt, who by profession is a freelance transport planner, first introduced himself to me as long ago as 1981, following the release of the first edition. His help on the ever continuing project has been invaluable, especially in the area of players birthplaces, which he researches diligently. Unlike many schoolboys he did not take an interest in soccer until reaching the age of 14, but from that moment he was hooked and from 1960 onwards he has kept detailed records on all Football League clubs and their players.

Another important member of the production team, and also an assistant editor, is Michael Featherstone. Michael was a willing helper when I first perceived the idea for such a book way back in 1975. His speciality is in researching births and deaths, something he also does for the various cricketing societies and the new wave of soccer histories that have begun to be produced over the last 20 years or so. He started out by collecting both cricket and football information, often topping up with visits to the Colindale National Newspaper Library. Eventually, he joined Ray Spiller's Association of Football Statisticians after being introduced by his good friend, the late Morley Farror. He has also contributed to the *British Boxing Yearbook*, *The Olympic Games: Complete Track & Field Results 1896-1988*, *Cricket Who's Who*, *The Official Football League Yearbook*, *PFA Footballers' Who's Who*, and many other publications.

For the past few years it has been my pleasure to work with Michael Joyce on the statistical side of both the *PFA Who's Who* and this publication. Also an assistant editor, Michael is the author of *Football League Players' Records, 1888 to 1939*, which is still available from SoccerData, 4 Adrian Close, Beeston, Nottingham NG9 6FL. He has accumulated data for a complete Football League database over many years and used it to produce the player indexes for the Definitive series of club histories and several other publications. Michael also provides statistical information for the website: www.since1888.co.uk.

Also, I would like to place on record my thanks to all the editors of the various club histories that have been published since the first edition of *Premier and Football League Players Records*. My gratitude is also extended to all the contributors of the *PFA Footballers Who's Who*, an annual work which went much of the way in updating this edition. For example, a few years ago, Gareth Davies, the Wrexham contributor for the *Who's Who*, advised me that after all these years he had discovered a new player. It transpired that Derek Hughes, an amateur who played one game for Wrexham in 1961-62, had long been confused with David, who later played for Tranmere. This then is one of the delights of such a work and something that makes it so rewarding.

Among those who have been of great help during this update, were Peter Holme, the research officer at the National Football Museum in Preston, who was extremely helpful when it came to identifying wartime clubs for certain players who played both before and after the war. Ian Nannestad, the assistant editor of the *Who's Who* and publisher of *Soccer History*, kindly provided obituaries relevant to the past 12 months and other football people such as Leigh Edwards, Garth Dykes, Gerry Somerton, Mike Davage and Derek Hyde, to name a few, also provided useful information.

Once again I would like to show my appreciation for the support given by Gordon Taylor, the chief executive of the Professional Footballers' Association, who has always recognised that this book is a testament to their members, both past and present. I would also like to thank Carol Brown, Gordon's personal assistant, for her generous help.

Finally, I must thank Adrian Stephenson, the publisher, for his continued faith in *Premier & Football League Players' Records*, Jean Bastin, the typesetter, and Jennifer Hugman, my wife, for reading and correcting many hours worth of galleys.

Barry J. Hugman

League Club	Source	Date Signed	Seasons Played	Career Record Apps	Subs	Gls

AAS Einar Jan
Moss, Norway, 12 October, 1955 Norway int (CD)

Nottingham F	Bayern Munich (Ger)	03.81	80-81	20	1	1

ABBEY Benjamin (Ben) Charles
London, 13 May, 1978 (F)

Oxford U	Crawley T	09.99	99	0	10	0

ABBEY George Peterson
Port Harcourt, Nigeria, 20 October, 1978 Nigeria 16 (FB)

Macclesfield T	Sharks	08.99	99-03	79	21	1
Port Vale	Tr	12.04	04	16	2	0

ABBEY Nathanael (Nathan)
Islington, 11 July, 1978 (G)

Luton T	YT	05.96	98-00	54	1	0
Chesterfield	Tr	06.01	01	46	0	0
Northampton T	Tr	08.02	02	4	1	0
Boston U	St Albans C	07.04	04	44	0	0

ABBEY Zema
Luton, 17 April, 1977 (F)

Cambridge U	Hitchin T	02.00	99-00	16	6	5
Norwich C	Tr	12.00	00-03	30	29	7
Boston U	L	08.04	04	3	2	1
Wycombe W	Tr	10.04	04	3	2	0
Bradford C	Tr	11.04	04	6	0	1
Torquay U	Tr	03.05	04	2	4	1

ABBIS Keith Douglas
Hatfield, 26 April, 1932 (WH)

Brighton & Hove A	Hitchin T	10.57	59-60	19	-	3

ABBLEY Stephen (Steve) George
Liverpool, 19 March, 1957 (W)

Swindon T	Parks	10.79	79-81	14	9	0

ABBOTT Gregory (Greg) Stephen
Coventry, 14 December, 1963 (M)

Coventry C	App	01.82				
Bradford C	Tr	09.82	82-90	256	25	38
Halifax T	Tr	07.91	91	24	4	1
Hull C	Guiseley	12.92	92-95	120	4	16

ABBOTT John
Winsford, 25 May, 1943 (CD)

Crewe Alex	Winsford U	06.61	61-64	2	-	0

ABBOTT Pawel Tadeusz Howard
York, 2 December, 1981 Poland u21 (F)

Preston NE	LKS Lodz (Poland)	02.01	02-03	8	17	6
Bury	L	08.02	02	13	0	5
Bury	L	03.03	02	4	0	1
Huddersfield T	Tr	02.04	03-04	48	9	31

ABBOTT Peter Ashley
Rotherham, 1 October, 1953 (F)

Manchester U	App	10.70				
Swansea C	Tr	02.74	73-75	35	7	3
Crewe Alex	Hartford (USA)	08.76	76	27	4	8
Southend U	Tr	07.77	77-78	26	1	4

ABBOTT Ronald (Ron) Frederick
Lambeth, 2 August, 1953 (CD)

Queens Park Rgrs	App	07.71	73-78	32	14	4

ABBOTTS John
Stoke-on-Trent, 10 October, 1924 (CD)

Port Vale	Ravenscliffe	05.49	50	3	-	0

ABEL Graham
Runcorn, 17 September, 1960 (CD)

Chester C	Northwich Vic	10.85	85-92	287	9	29
Crewe Alex	Tr	08.93	93	18	2	1

ABIDALLAH Nabil
Amsterdam, Holland, 5 August, 1982 Morocco Yth (M)

Ipswich T	Ajax (Holl)	07.00	00	0	2	0
Northampton T	L	01.04	03	0	1	0

ABIODUN Ayodeji **Opeyemi (Yemi)**
Clapton, 29 December, 1980 (F)

Southend U	YT	07.99	99	1	2	0

League Club	Source	Date Signed	Seasons Played	Career Record Apps	Subs	Gls

ABLETT Gary Ian
Liverpool, 19 November, 1965 Eu21-1/EB-1 (CD)

Liverpool	App	11.83	86-91	103	6	1
Derby Co	L	01.85	84	3	3	0
Hull C	L	09.86	86	5	0	0
Everton	Tr	01.92	91-95	128	0	5
Sheffield U	L	03.96	95	12	0	0
Birmingham C	Tr	07.96	96-98	96	8	1
Wycombe W	L	12.99	99	4	0	0
Blackpool	Tr	01.00	99	9	1	1

ABOU Samassi
Gagnoa, Ivory Coast, 4 April, 1973 Fru21 (F)

West Ham U	AS Cannes (Fr)	11.97	97-98	14	8	5
Ipswich T	L	12.98	98	5	0	1
Walsall	L	10.99	99	7	1	0

ABRAHAM Gareth John
Aberfan, 13 February, 1969 (CD)

Cardiff C	YT	07.87	87-91	82	5	4
Hereford U	Tr	01.93	92-93	48	1	2

ABRAHAMS Lawrence (Lawrie) Adam Michael
Stepney, 3 April, 1953 (F)

Charlton Ath	Barking	05.77	77	12	4	2

ABRAHAMS Paul
Colchester, 31 October, 1973 (F)

Colchester U	YT	08.92	92-94	30	25	8
Brentford	Tr	03.95	94-96	26	9	8
Colchester U	L	12.95	95	8	0	2
Colchester U	Tr	10.96	96-98	56	25	16

ABREY Brian Anthony
Hendon, 25 April, 1939 (CD)

Chelsea	Jnrs	10.56				
Colchester U	Tr	05.61	61	38	-	2

ABRUZZESE David John
Aberdare, 8 October, 1969 WYth (FB)

Newport Co	App	08.86	86-87	24	1	0

ABTHORPE John
Mansfield, 19 January, 1933 (CF)

Notts Co (Am)	Wolverhampton W (Am)	09.55	55	5	-	3

ACHAMPONG Kenneth (Kenny)
Kilburn, 26 June, 1966 (W)

Fulham	App	06.84	84-87	68	13	15
Charlton Ath	Tr	08.89	89	2	8	0
Leyton Orient	Tr	08.90	90-92	64	19	7

ACHTERBERG John
Utrecht, Holland, 8 July, 1971 (G)

Tranmere Rov	FC Eindhoven (Holl)	09.98	98-04	219	3	0

ACIMOVIC Milenko
Ljubljana, Slovenia, 15 February, 1977 Slovenia 52 (M)

Tottenham H	Red Star Belgrade (Yug)	05.02	02	4	13	0

ACKERLEY Ernest (Ernie) Nicol
Manchester, 23 September, 1943 (CF)

Manchester U	Jnrs	10.60				
Barrow	Tr	04.63	62-63	53	-	12

ACKERLEY Stanley (Stan)
Manchester, 12 July, 1942 Australia int (FB)

Manchester U	Jnrs	11.59				
Oldham Ath	Tr	06.61	61	2	-	0

ACKERMAN Alfred (Alf) Arthur Eric
Daspoort, South Africa, 5 January, 1929 Died 1988 (CF)

Hull C	Clyde	07.50	50	34	-	21
Norwich C	Tr	08.51	51-53	66	-	31
Hull C	Tr	10.53	53-54	58	-	28
Derby Co	Tr	03.55	54-56	36	-	21
Carlisle U	Tr	11.56	56-58	97	-	61
Millwall	Tr	01.59	58-60	81	-	35

ACKERMAN Anthony (Tony) Alan
Islington, 20 February, 1948 (CD)

Leyton Orient	West Ham U (Am)	10.66	66-67	4	0	0

ACKLAND Michael (Mike) Edward
Sidcup, 4 June, 1935 (CF)

Gillingham	Harland Social	08.55	56	2	-	0

A'COURT Alan
Rainhill, 30 September, 1934 Eu23-7/FLge-2/E-5 (W)

Liverpool	Prescot Cables	09.52	52-62	355	-	61
Tranmere Rov	Tr	10.64	64-65	50	0	11

ACRES Basil Derek John
Brantham, 27 October, 1926 Died 2000 (FB)

League Club	Source	Date Signed	Seasons Played	Apps	Subs	Gls
Ipswich T	Brantham	09.50	51-59	217	-	6

ACTON Alec Edward
Billesdon, 12 November, 1938 Died 1994 (WH)

League Club	Source	Date Signed	Seasons Played	Apps	Subs	Gls
Stoke C	Leicester C (Am)	01.56				
Stockport Co	Brush Sports	08.58	58-59	9	-	0

ACUNA Donoso **Clarence** Williams
Coya Rancagua, Chile, 8 February, 1975 ChileYth/Chile 58 (M)

League Club	Source	Date Signed	Seasons Played	Apps	Subs	Gls
Newcastle U	Univ de Chile (Ch)	10.00	00-02	35	11	6

ADAGGIO Marco
Malaga, Spain, 6 October, 1987 (F)

League Club	Source	Date Signed	Seasons Played	Apps	Subs	Gls
Shrewsbury T	Jnrs	03.05	04	0	5	0

ADAM Charles (Charlie)
Glasgow, 22 March, 1919 Died 1996 (W)

League Club	Source	Date Signed	Seasons Played	Apps	Subs	Gls
Leicester C	Strathclyde	09.38	46-50	158	-	22
Mansfield T	Tr	07.52	52-54	93	-	6

ADAM James (Jimmy)
Blantyre, 13 May, 1931 (W)

League Club	Source	Date Signed	Seasons Played	Apps	Subs	Gls
Luton T	Spennymoor U	07.53	53-58	137	-	22
Aston Villa	Tr	08.59	59-60	24	-	3
Stoke C	Tr	07.61	61	22	-	7

ADAM James (Jimmy)
Paisley, 22 April, 1931 (IF)

League Club	Source	Date Signed	Seasons Played	Apps	Subs	Gls
Leeds U	Penilee U	06.51				
Mansfield T	Tr	08.54	54	39	-	10

ADAMCZUK Dariusz
Szczecin, Poland, 20 October, 1969 Poland 11 (M)

League Club	Source	Date Signed	Seasons Played	Apps	Subs	Gls
Wigan Ath (L)	Glasgow Rgrs	08.01	01	3	0	0

ADAMS Brian Thomas
Tottenham, 18 May, 1947 (M)

League Club	Source	Date Signed	Seasons Played	Apps	Subs	Gls
Millwall	Chelsea (App)	08.64	64-65	15	0	0

ADAMS Christopher (Chris) James
Hornchurch, 6 September, 1927 (W)

League Club	Source	Date Signed	Seasons Played	Apps	Subs	Gls
Tottenham H	Leytonstone	11.48	51-52	6	-	1
Norwich C	Tr	12.52	52-53	29	-	3
Watford	Tr	03.54	53-55	75	-	5

ADAMS Craig John
Northampton, 9 November, 1974 (CD)

League Club	Source	Date Signed	Seasons Played	Apps	Subs	Gls
Northampton T	YT	•	91	0	1	0

ADAMS Daniel (Danny) Benjamin
Manchester, 3 January, 1976 (FB)

League Club	Source	Date Signed	Seasons Played	Apps	Subs	Gls
Macclesfield T	Altrincham	08.00	00-03	146	2	1
Stockport Co	Tr	03.04	03-04	39	0	1
Huddersfield T	Tr	03.05	04	5	0	0

ADAMS Darren Steven
Bromley, 12 January, 1974 (F)

League Club	Source	Date Signed	Seasons Played	Apps	Subs	Gls
Cardiff C	Danson Furnace	01.94	93-95	21	13	4

ADAMS Derek Watt
Aberdeen, 25 June, 1975 (M)

League Club	Source	Date Signed	Seasons Played	Apps	Subs	Gls
Burnley	Aberdeen	01.95	95	0	2	0

ADAMS Donald (Don) Frederick
Northampton, 15 February, 1931 Died 1993 (CF)

League Club	Source	Date Signed	Seasons Played	Apps	Subs	Gls
Northampton T		05.51	51-55	23	-	7

ADAMS Ernest (Ernie) Robert
Hackney, 17 January, 1948 (G)

League Club	Source	Date Signed	Seasons Played	Apps	Subs	Gls
Arsenal	App	01.65				
Colchester U	Tr	07.67	67-68	48	0	0
Crewe Alex	Tr	07.69	69-71	112	0	0
Darlington	Tr	07.72	72	25	0	0

ADAMS Ernest (Ernie) William
Willesden, 3 April, 1922 (W)

League Club	Source	Date Signed	Seasons Played	Apps	Subs	Gls
Preston NE		01.45				
Queens Park Rgrs	Tr	09.47	47-49	5	-	0

ADAMS Francis (Frank) Nicholas
Liverpool, 8 February, 1933 (G)

League Club	Source	Date Signed	Seasons Played	Apps	Subs	Gls
Bury	Bury Amats	01.56	56-61	169	-	0
Chester	Tr	07.63	63	8	-	0

ADAMS George
Falkirk, 16 October, 1926 (WH)

League Club	Source	Date Signed	Seasons Played	Apps	Subs	Gls
Leyton Orient	Chelmsford C	05.49	49	4	-	0

ADAMS George Robert
Shoreditch, 28 September, 1947 (M)

League Club	Source	Date Signed	Seasons Played	Apps	Subs	Gls
Chelsea	Jnrs	09.65				
Peterborough U	Tr	07.66	66-67	13	3	2

ADAMS Graham Wallace
Torrington, 1 March, 1933 (FB)

League Club	Source	Date Signed	Seasons Played	Apps	Subs	Gls
Plymouth Arg		01.58	57	1	-	0

ADAMS James (Jim) Arthur
Stoke-on-Trent, 2 August, 1937 (FB)

League Club	Source	Date Signed	Seasons Played	Apps	Subs	Gls
Port Vale		06.56	57	1	-	0

ADAMS Kieran Charles
St Ives, Cambridgeshire, 20 October, 1977 (M)

League Club	Source	Date Signed	Seasons Played	Apps	Subs	Gls
Barnet	YT	07.96	94-97	8	11	1

ADAMS Laurence (Laurie) Edward
Barnet, 14 February, 1931 (IF)

League Club	Source	Date Signed	Seasons Played	Apps	Subs	Gls
Watford (Am)		01.52	51	1	-	0

ADAMS Michael (Mike) Alan
Banwell, 20 February, 1965 (M)

League Club	Source	Date Signed	Seasons Played	Apps	Subs	Gls
Bristol Rov	App	02.83	82	0	1	0

ADAMS Michael (Micky) Richard
Sheffield, 8 November, 1961 EYth (FB)

League Club	Source	Date Signed	Seasons Played	Apps	Subs	Gls
Gillingham	App	11.79	79-82	85	7	4
Coventry C	Tr	07.83	83-86	85	5	9
Leeds U	Tr	01.87	86-88	72	1	2
Southampton	Tr	03.89	88-93	141	3	7
Stoke C	Tr	03.94	93	10	0	3
Fulham	Tr	07.94	94-96	25	4	9

ADAMS Neil James
Stoke-on-Trent, 23 November, 1965 Eu21-1 (W)

League Club	Source	Date Signed	Seasons Played	Apps	Subs	Gls
Stoke C	QM Rgrs	07.85	85	31	1	4
Everton	Tr	07.86	86-87	17	3	0
Oldham Ath	L	01.89	88	9	0	0
Oldham Ath	Tr	06.89	89-93	93	36	23
Norwich C	Tr	02.94	93-98	164	18	25
Oldham Ath	Tr	07.99	99-00	47	0	4

ADAMS Rex Malcolm
Oxford, 13 February, 1928 (W)

League Club	Source	Date Signed	Seasons Played	Apps	Subs	Gls
Blackpool	Oxford C	06.48	48-50	16	-	1
Oldham Ath	Worcester C	06.53	53	23	-	1

ADAMS Rodney Leslie
Bath, 15 September, 1945 (W)

League Club	Source	Date Signed	Seasons Played	Apps	Subs	Gls
Bournemouth	Frome T	06.66	66-68	15	2	4

ADAMS Stephen (Steve)
Sheffield, 7 September, 1959 (W)

League Club	Source	Date Signed	Seasons Played	Apps	Subs	Gls
Scarborough	Worksop T	09.87	87-88	25	23	5
Doncaster Rov	Tr	10.89	89-90	25	10	2

ADAMS Stephen (Steve) Marc
Plymouth, 25 September, 1980 (M)

League Club	Source	Date Signed	Seasons Played	Apps	Subs	Gls
Plymouth Arg	YT	07.99	99-04	131	26	7
Sheffield Wed	Tr	03.05	04	8	1	0

ADAMS Stephen (Steve) Thomas
Windsor, 18 June, 1958 (M)

League Club	Source	Date Signed	Seasons Played	Apps	Subs	Gls
Queens Park Rgrs	App	07.75				
Millwall	Tr	07.77	77	1	0	0
Cambridge U	Windsor & Eton	03.78	77-78	1	2	0

ADAMS Tony Alexander
Romford, 10 October, 1966 EYth/Eu21-5/EB-4/E-66 (CD)

League Club	Source	Date Signed	Seasons Played	Apps	Subs	Gls
Arsenal	App	01.84	83-01	500	4	32

ADAMS Vincent (Vince)
Chesterfield, 16 October, 1946 ESch (M)

League Club	Source	Date Signed	Seasons Played	Apps	Subs	Gls
Arsenal	App	10.63				
Chesterfield	Tr	11.65	65-66	15	2	1

ADAMS William (Billy) Henry
Arlecdon, 8 January, 1919 Died 1989 (FB)

League Club	Source	Date Signed	Seasons Played	Apps	Subs	Gls
Tottenham H	Hartlepools U (Am)	05.39				
Carlisle U	Tr	06.46	46	33	-	1
Workington	Chelmsford C	(N/L)	51	3	-	0

ADAMS William (Bill) Victor
Plymouth, 10 May, 1921 Died 1997 (FB)

League Club	Source	Date Signed	Seasons Played	Apps	Subs	Gls
Plymouth Arg	Plymouth U	04.45	46	1	-	0

ADAMSON Christopher (Chris)
Ashington, 4 November, 1978 (G)

League Club	Source	Date Signed	Seasons Played	Apps	Subs	Gls
West Bromwich A	YT	07.97	97-99	12	0	0
Mansfield T	L	04.99	98	2	0	0
Halifax T	L	07.99	99	7	0	0
Plymouth Arg	L	01.02	01	1	0	0
Sheffield Wed	St Patrick's Ath	01.05	04	1	1	0

ADAMSON David (Dave) Henry
Chester-le-Street, 7 May, 1951 ESemiPro (FB)

League Club	Source	Date Signed	Seasons Played	Apps	Subs	Gls
Doncaster Rov	Durham C	07.70	70-71	28	0	0

ADAMSON Henry (Harry)
Kelty, 27 June, 1924 Died 1997 (WH)

League Club	Source	Date Signed	Seasons Played	Apps	Subs	Gls
Notts Co	Jeanfield Swifts	08.46	47-55	233	-	5

ADAMSON James (Jimmy)
Ashington, 4 April, 1929 FLge-1 (WH)

League Club	Source	Date Signed	Seasons Played	Apps	Subs	Gls
Burnley	Ashington	01.47	50-63	426	-	17

ADAMSON Keith Brian
Houghton-le-Spring, 3 July, 1945 (F)

League Club	Source	Date Signed	Seasons Played	Apps	Subs	Gls
Barnsley	Tow Law T	03.66	65-66	7	0	0

ADAMSON Terence (Terry)
Houghton-le-Spring, 15 October, 1948 (FB)

League Club	Source	Date Signed	Seasons Played	Apps	Subs	Gls
Sunderland	App	11.65				
Luton T	Tr	07.66	66	2	0	0
Hartlepools U	Tr	07.67	67	1	0	0

ADCOCK Anthony (Tony) Charles
Bethnal Green, 27 March, 1963 (F)

League Club	Source	Date Signed	Seasons Played	Apps	Subs	Gls
Colchester U	App	03.81	80-86	192	18	98
Manchester C	Tr	06.87	87	12	3	5
Northampton T	Tr	01.88	87-89	72	0	30
Bradford C	Tr	10.89	89-90	33	5	6
Northampton T	Tr	01.91	90-91	34	1	10
Peterborough U	Tr	12.91	91-93	107	4	35
Luton T	Tr	08.94	94	0	2	0
Colchester U	Tr	08.95	95-98	86	22	28

ADCOCK Paul Malcolm
Ilminster, 2 May, 1972 (F)

League Club	Source	Date Signed	Seasons Played	Apps	Subs	Gls
Plymouth Arg	YT	08.90	90-92	11	10	2
Torquay U	Bath C	08.95	96	0	1	0

ADDINALL Albert (Bert) William
Paddington, 30 January, 1921 (CF)

League Club	Source	Date Signed	Seasons Played	Apps	Subs	Gls
Queens Park Rgrs	British Oxygen	04.45	46-52	150	-	59
Brighton & Hove A	Tr	01.53	52-53	60	-	31
Crystal Palace	Tr	07.54	54	12	-	2

ADDISON Colin
Taunton, 18 May, 1940 (M)

League Club	Source	Date Signed	Seasons Played	Apps	Subs	Gls
York C	Jnrs	05.57	57-60	87	-	28
Nottingham F	Tr	01.61	60-66	160	0	62
Arsenal	Tr	09.66	66-67	27	1	9
Sheffield U	Tr	12.67	67-70	93	1	22
Hereford U	Tr	10.71	72-73	23	0	1

ADDY Michael (Mike)
Knottingley, 20 February, 1943 (M)

League Club	Source	Date Signed	Seasons Played	Apps	Subs	Gls
Leeds U	Jnrs	05.62	62	2	-	0
Barnsley	Tr	06.64	64-66	50	1	5

ADEBOLA Bamderdele (Dele)
Lagos, Nigeria, 23 June, 1975 (F)

League Club	Source	Date Signed	Seasons Played	Apps	Subs	Gls
Crewe Alex	YT	06.93	92-97	98	26	39
Birmingham C	Tr	02.98	97-00	86	43	31
Oldham Ath	L	03.02	01	5	0	0
Crystal Palace	Tr	08.02	02	32	7	5
Coventry C	Tr	07.03	03-04	33	20	7
Burnley	L	03.04	03	0	3	1
Bradford C	L	08.04	04	14	1	3

ADEKOLA David Adeolu
Lagos, Nigeria, 19 May, 1968 (F)

League Club	Source	Date Signed	Seasons Played	Apps	Subs	Gls
Bury	AS Cannes (Fr)	01.93	92-93	21	14	12
Exeter C	L	02.94	93	1	2	1
Wigan Ath	Bournemouth (N/C)	10.94	94	1	3	0
Hereford U	Tr	02.95				
Cambridge U	Bath C	08.95	95	1	4	1
Brighton & Hove A	Preussen Munster (Ger)	10.96	96	1	0	0

ADEY Arthur Lewis
Glasgow, 1 March, 1930 (CF)

League Club	Source	Date Signed	Seasons Played	Apps	Subs	Gls
Doncaster Rov	Bishop Auckland	09.50	50-53	48	-	9
Gillingham	Tr	07.54	54	7	-	1
Bradford PA	Tr	10.54	54	13	-	4

ADKINS Nigel Howard
Birkenhead, 11 March, 1965 ESch (G)

League Club	Source	Date Signed	Seasons Played	Apps	Subs	Gls
Tranmere Rov	App	03.83	82-85	86	0	0
Wigan Ath	Tr	07.86	86-92	155	0	0

ADLINGTON Terence (Terry)
Blackwell, Derbyshire, 21 November, 1935 Died 1994 (G)

League Club	Source	Date Signed	Seasons Played	Apps	Subs	Gls
Derby Co	Blackwell Colliery	12.55	56-60	36	-	0
Torquay U	Tr	06.62	62-65	148	0	0

ADVICE-DESRUISSEAUX Frederic
Paris, France, 12 January, 1983 (M)

League Club	Source	Date Signed	Seasons Played	Apps	Subs	Gls
Kidderminster Hrs	OSC Lille (Fr)	07.04	04	9	0	0

AFFOR Louis Kofi Jeffrey
Ghana, 29 August, 1972 (W)

League Club	Source	Date Signed	Seasons Played	Apps	Subs	Gls
Barnet		08.93	93	0	3	0

AFFUL Leslie Samuel
Liverpool, 4 February, 1984 (M)

League Club	Source	Date Signed	Seasons Played	Apps	Subs	Gls
Exeter C	YT	08.02	01	0	2	0

AGANA Patrick Anthony (Tony) Olozinka
Bromley, 2 October, 1963 ESemiPro (F)

League Club	Source	Date Signed	Seasons Played	Apps	Subs	Gls
Watford	Weymouth	08.87	87	12	3	1
Sheffield U	Tr	02.88	87-91	105	13	42
Notts Co	Tr	11.91	91-96	114	31	15
Leeds U	L	02.92	91	1	1	0
Hereford U	Tr	03.97	96	3	2	2

AGAR Roy
Islington, 1 April, 1936 EAmat (IF)

League Club	Source	Date Signed	Seasons Played	Apps	Subs	Gls
Swindon T (Am)	Barnet	12.55	55-56	12	-	0

AGBOOLA Reuben Omajola Folasanje
Camden, 30 May, 1962 (FB)

League Club	Source	Date Signed	Seasons Played	Apps	Subs	Gls
Southampton	App	04.80	80-84	89	1	0
Sunderland	Tr	01.85	84-91	129	11	0
Charlton Ath	L	10.86	86	1	0	0
Port Vale	L	11.90	90	9	0	0
Swansea C	Tr	11.91	91-92	26	2	0

AGGREY James (Jimmy) Emmanuel
Hammersmith, 26 October, 1978 (CD)

League Club	Source	Date Signed	Seasons Played	Apps	Subs	Gls
Fulham	Chelsea (YT)	07.97				
Torquay U	Airdrie	10.98	98-01	87	8	2

AGNEW David George
Belfast, 31 March, 1925 NIAmat (G)

League Club	Source	Date Signed	Seasons Played	Apps	Subs	Gls
Sunderland	Crusaders	01.50	50	1	-	0

AGNEW David Young
Kilwinning, 4 August, 1939 (FB)

League Club	Source	Date Signed	Seasons Played	Apps	Subs	Gls
Leicester C	Jnrs	08.58				
Scunthorpe U	Tr	06.61	61	1	-	0
Notts Co	Tr	06.62	62-66	85	0	1

AGNEW John Terence
Stockton, 27 June, 1935 (W)

League Club	Source	Date Signed	Seasons Played	Apps	Subs	Gls
Sheffield Wed		11.53				
Darlington	Tr	08.54	54-55	25	-	4

AGNEW Paul
Lisburn, 15 August, 1965 NISch/NIYth/NIu23-1 (FB)

League Club	Source	Date Signed	Seasons Played	Apps	Subs	Gls
Grimsby T	Cliftonville	02.84	83-94	219	24	3
West Bromwich A	Tr	02.95	94-96	38	1	1
Swansea C	Ilkeston T	09.97	97	7	0	0

AGNEW Stephen (Steve) Mark
Shipley, 9 November, 1965 (M)

League Club	Source	Date Signed	Seasons Played	Apps	Subs	Gls
Barnsley	App	11.83	83-90	185	9	29
Blackburn Rov	Tr	06.91	91	2	0	0
Portsmouth	L	11.92	92	3	2	0
Leicester C	Tr	02.93	92-94	52	4	4
Sunderland	Tr	01.95	94-97	56	7	9
York C	Tr	07.98	98-00	76	5	4

AGOGO Manuel (Junior)
Accra, Ghana, 1 August, 1979 ESemiPro-3 (F)

League Club	Source	Date Signed	Seasons Played	Apps	Subs	Gls
Sheffield Wed	Willesden Constantine	10.96	97-98	0	2	0
Oldham Ath	L	07.99	99	2	0	0
Chester C	L	09.99	99	10	0	6
Chesterfield	L	11.99	99	3	1	0
Lincoln C	L	12.99	99	3	0	1
Queens Park Rgrs	San Jose (USA)	03.02	01	0	2	0
Bristol Rov	Barnet	07.03	03-04	65	16	25

AGOSTINO Paul
Woodville, Australia, 9 June, 1975 Australia int (F)

League Club	Source	Date Signed	Seasons Played	Apps	Subs	Gls
Bristol C	Young Boys Berne (Swi)	07.95	95-96	63	21	19

AGYEMANG Patrick
Walthamstow, 29 September, 1980 Ghana1 (F)

League Club	Source	Date Signed	Seasons Played	Apps	Subs	Gls
Wimbledon	YT	05.99	00-03	68	53	20
Brentford	L	10.99	99	3	9	0
Gillingham	Tr	01.04	03-04	29	4	8
Preston NE	Tr	11.04	04	15	12	4

AHERNE Thomas (Tom)
Limerick, 26 January, 1919 Died 1999 LoI-4/NIRL-2/IrLge-4/IWar-2/I-4/IR-16 (FB)

League Club	Source	Date Signed	Seasons Played	Apps	Subs	Gls
Luton T	Belfast Celtic	03.49	48-56	267	-	0

AHMED Adnan Farooq
Burnley, 7 June, 1984 (M)

League Club	Source	Date Signed	Seasons Played	Apps	Subs	Gls
Huddersfield T	Sch	08.03	03-04	16	3	1

AHMED Shahed
East Ham, 13 September, 1985 (F)

League Club	Source	Date Signed	Seasons Played	Apps	Subs	Gls
Wycombe W	Wimbledon (YT)	07.04	04	0	4	1

AIKEN Thomas (Tommy)
Ballymena, 18 March, 1946 NIAmat (W)

League Club	Source	Date Signed	Seasons Played	Apps	Subs	Gls
Doncaster Rov	Ballymena U	11.67	67-68	12	1	1

AIMSON Paul Edward
Macclesfield, 3 August, 1943 (F)

League Club	Source	Date Signed	Seasons Played	Apps	Subs	Gls
Manchester C	Jnrs	08.60	61-63	16	-	4
York C	Tr	07.64	64-65	77	0	43
Bury	Tr	03.66	65-66	30	1	11
Bradford C	Tr	09.67	67	23	0	11
Huddersfield T	Tr	03.68	67-68	34	4	13
York C	Tr	08.69	69-72	133	8	55
Bournemouth	Tr	03.73	72	7	2	2
Colchester U	Tr	08.73	73	3	1	2

AINDOW Roger Allan
Seaforth, 23 October, 1946 (CD)

League Club	Source	Date Signed	Seasons Played	Apps	Subs	Gls
Southport	Formby	10.67	68-70	52	6	4

AINGE Ronald (Ron) Percy
Pontardawe, 5 August, 1920 (W)

League Club	Source	Date Signed	Seasons Played	Apps	Subs	Gls
Newport Co	Llanelli	10.46	46	5	-	0

AINSCOUGH John (Jack)
Adlington, 26 March, 1926 Died 2004 (CD)

League Club	Source	Date Signed	Seasons Played	Apps	Subs	Gls
Blackpool	Astley Bridge	08.49	50-53	7	-	0

AINSCOW Alan
Bolton, 15 July, 1953 EYth (M)

League Club	Source	Date Signed	Seasons Played	Apps	Subs	Gls
Blackpool	App	07.71	71-77	178	14	28
Birmingham C	Tr	07.78	78-80	104	4	16
Everton	Tr	08.81	81-82	24	4	3
Barnsley	L	11.82	82	2	0	0
Wolverhampton W	Eastern Ath (HK)	08.84	84-85	56	2	5
Blackburn Rov	Tr	12.85	85-88	42	23	5
Rochdale	Tr	07.89	89	19	1	0

AINSCOW Andrew (Andy) Paul
Orrell, 1 October, 1968 EYth (F)

League Club	Source	Date Signed	Seasons Played	Apps	Subs	Gls
Wigan Ath	App	10.86	87-88	14	8	4
Rotherham U	Tr	08.89	89	0	1	0

AINSLEY George Edward
South Shields, 15 April, 1915 Died 1985 (CF)

League Club	Source	Date Signed	Seasons Played	Apps	Subs	Gls
Sunderland	South Shields St A	04.32	32-33	4	-	0
Bolton W	Tr	08.36	36	7	-	0
Leeds U	Tr	12.36	36-47	89	-	30
Bradford PA	Tr	11.47	47-48	44	-	29

AINSLEY Jason
Stockton, 30 July, 1970 (M)

League Club	Source	Date Signed	Seasons Played	Apps	Subs	Gls
Hartlepool U	Spennymoor U	07.94	94	14	1	1

AINSWORTH Alphonso (Alf)
Manchester, 31 July, 1913 Died 1975 (IF)

League Club	Source	Date Signed	Seasons Played	Apps	Subs	Gls
Manchester U	Ashton Ath	02.34	33	2	-	0
New Brighton	Tr	09.35	35-38	150	-	39
New Brighton		08.46	46-47	28	-	9

AINSWORTH David
Bolton, 28 January, 1958 (F)

League Club	Source	Date Signed	Seasons Played	Apps	Subs	Gls
Rochdale	App	01.76	75	0	2	0

AINSWORTH Gareth
Blackburn, 10 May, 1973 (W)

League Club	Source	Date Signed	Seasons Played	Apps	Subs	Gls
Preston NE	Northwich Vic	01.92	91	2	3	0
Cambridge U	Tr	08.92	92	1	3	1
Preston NE	Tr	12.92	92-95	76	6	12
Lincoln C	Tr	10.95	95-97	83	0	37
Port Vale	Tr	09.97	97-98	53	2	10
Wimbledon	Tr	11.98	98-02	21	15	6
Preston NE	L	03.02	01	3	2	1
Walsall	L	12.02	02	2	3	1
Cardiff C	Tr	03.03	02	9	0	0
Queens Park Rgrs	Tr	07.03	03-04	35	16	8

AINSWORTH John (Jack)
Wallasey, 20 September, 1922 Died 1981 (CF)

League Club	Source	Date Signed	Seasons Played	Apps	Subs	Gls
New Brighton (Am)		03.47	46-47	14	-	3

AIRD John (Jock) Rae
Glencraig, 18 February, 1926 S-4 (FB)

League Club	Source	Date Signed	Seasons Played	Apps	Subs	Gls
Burnley	Jeanfield Swifts	08.48	49-54	132	-	0

AIREY Carl
Wakefield, 6 February, 1965 (F)

League Club	Source	Date Signed	Seasons Played	Apps	Subs	Gls
Barnsley	App	02.83	82-83	30	8	5
Bradford C	L	10.83	83	4	1	0
Darlington	Tr	08.84	84-85	72	3	28
Chesterfield (L)	RSC Charleroi (Bel)	12.86	86	24	2	4
Rotherham U	Tr	08.87	87	25	7	11
Torquay U	RSC Charleroi (Bel)	01.89	88-89	21	8	11

AIREY John (Jack)
Bedford, 28 November, 1937 (W)

League Club	Source	Date Signed	Seasons Played	Apps	Subs	Gls
Blackburn Rov		01.59	58-59	3	-	1

AISTON Samuel (Sam) James
Newcastle, 21 November, 1976 ESch (M)

League Club	Source	Date Signed	Seasons Played	Apps	Subs	Gls
Sunderland	Newcastle U (YT)	07.95	95-98	5	15	0
Chester C	L	02.97	96	14	0	0
Chester C	L	11.98	98	11	0	0
Stoke C	L	08.99	99	2	4	0
Shrewsbury T	L	12.99	99	10	0	0
Shrewsbury T	Tr	07.00	00-04	99	34	7

AITCHISON Barrie George
Colchester, 15 November, 1937 (W)

League Club	Source	Date Signed	Seasons Played	Apps	Subs	Gls
Tottenham H	Jnrs	01.55				
Colchester U	Tr	08.64	64-65	49	1	6

AITCHISON Peter Munro
Harlow, 19 September, 1931 (W)

League Club	Source	Date Signed	Seasons Played	Apps	Subs	Gls
Colchester U		10.51	51-54	18	-	2

AITKEN Andrew (Andy) Fox Scott
Craigmillar, 21 August, 1934 Died 2005 (W)

League Club	Source	Date Signed	Seasons Played	Apps	Subs	Gls
West Bromwich A	Hibernian	09.59	59-60	22	-	2

AITKEN Charles (Charlie) Alexander
Edinburgh, 1 May, 1942 Su23-3 (FB)

League Club	Source	Date Signed	Seasons Played	Apps	Subs	Gls
Aston Villa	Edinburgh Thistle	08.59	60-75	559	2	14

AITKEN George Bruce
Dalkeith, 13 August, 1928 (CD)

League Club	Source	Date Signed	Seasons Played	Apps	Subs	Gls
Middlesbrough	Edinburgh Thistle	06.46	51-52	17	-	0
Workington	Tr	07.53	53-59	262	-	3

AITKEN George Graham
Lochgelly, 28 May, 1925 Died 2003 S-8 (WH)

League Club	Source	Date Signed	Seasons Played	Apps	Subs	Gls
Sunderland	Third Lanark	11.51	51-58	245	-	3
Gateshead	Tr	03.59	58-59	58	-	0

AITKEN Glenn Leslie
Woolwich, 30 September, 1952 EYth (FB)

League Club	Source	Date Signed	Seasons Played	Apps	Subs	Gls
Gillingham	Chelsea (Am)	12.72	72-74	19	4	0
Wimbledon	Tr	09.74	77	11	0	1

AITKEN Peter Gerald
Cardiff, 30 June, 1954 (CD)

League Club	Source	Date Signed	Seasons Played	Apps	Subs	Gls
Bristol Rov	App	07.72	72-79	230	4	3
Bristol C	Tr	11.80	80-81	41	0	1
York C	Tr	02.82	81	18	0	2
Bournemouth	Forest Green Rov	11.82	82	1	0	0

AITKEN Robert (Roy) Sime
Irvine, 24 November, 1958 SSch/Su21-16/S-57 (M)

League Club	Source	Date Signed	Seasons Played	Apps	Subs	Gls
Newcastle U	Glasgow Celtic	01.90	89-90	54	0	1

AITKEN William (Billy) Robert Crawford
Dumfries, 11 January, 1951 (M)

League Club	Source	Date Signed	Seasons Played	Apps	Subs	Gls
Oldham Ath	App	01.68	68	1	0	0

AIZLEWOOD Mark
Newport, 1 October, 1959 WSch/Wu21-2/W-39 (M)

League Club	Source	Date Signed	Seasons Played	Apps	Subs	Gls
Newport Co	App	10.77	75-77	35	3	1
Luton T	Tr	04.78	78-81	90	8	3
Charlton Ath	Tr	11.82	82-86	152	0	9
Leeds U	Tr	02.87	86-88	65	5	3
Bradford C	Tr	08.89	89	39	0	1
Bristol C	Tr	08.90	90-93	99	2	3
Cardiff C	Tr	10.93	93-94	39	0	3

AIZLEWOOD Steven (Steve)
Newport, 9 October, 1952 WSch (CD)

League Club	Source	Date Signed	Seasons Played	Apps	Subs	Gls
Newport Co	Jnrs	01.70	68-75	191	5	18
Swindon T	Tr	03.76	75-78	111	1	10
Portsmouth	Tr	07.79	79-83	175	0	13

AKERS Victor (Vic) David
Islington, 24 August, 1946 (FB)

League Club	Source	Date Signed	Seasons Played	Apps	Subs	Gls
Cambridge U	Bexley U	07.71	71-74	122	7	5
Watford	Tooting & Mitcham	07.75	75	22	0	0

League Club	Source	Date Signed	Seasons Played	Apps	Subs	Gls
AKIN Bulent						
Brussels, Belgium, 28 August, 1979 Tuu21-6						(M)
Bolton W	Galatasaray (Tu)	08.02	02	0	1	0
AKINBIYI Adeola (Ade) Oluwatoyin						
Hackney, 10 October, 1974 Nigeria 1						(F)
Norwich C	YT	02.93	93-96	22	27	3
Hereford U	L	01.94	93	3	1	2
Brighton & Hove A	L	11.94	94	7	0	4
Gillingham	Tr	01.97	96-97	63	0	28
Bristol C	Tr	05.98	98-99	47	0	21
Wolverhampton W	Tr	09.99	99	36	1	16
Leicester C	Tr	07.00	00-01	49	9	11
Crystal Palace	Tr	02.02	01-02	11	13	3
Stoke C	L	03.03	02	4	0	2
Stoke C	Tr	09.03	03-04	52	7	17
Burnley	Tr	02.05	04	9	1	4
AKINFENWA Saheed **Adebayo**						
Nigeria, 10 May, 1982						(F)
Boston U	Barry T	10.03	03	2	1	0
Leyton Orient	Tr	10.03	03	0	1	0
Rushden & Diamonds	Tr	12.03				
Doncaster Rov	Tr	02.04	03	4	5	4
Torquay U	Tr	07.04	04	28	9	14
ALBERRY William **Edward (Ted)**						
Doncaster, 21 July, 1922 Died 1978						(CF)
Leeds U	Doncaster Rov (Am)	05.46				
Hull C	Tr	04.47	46	1	-	0
ALBERT Philippe						
Bouillon, Belgium, 10 August, 1967 Belgium 41						(CD)
Newcastle U	Anderlecht (Bel)	08.94	94-98	87	9	8
Fulham	L	01.99	98	12	1	2
ALBESON Brian						
Oldham, 14 December, 1946 Died 2003 EYth						(CD)
Bury	Jnrs	05.65	65	0	1	0
Darlington	Tr	07.67	67-70	134	2	2
Southend U	Tr	07.71	71-73	109	1	9
Stockport Co	Tr	03.74	73-74	54	0	1
ALBISTON Arthur Richard						
Edinburgh, 14 July, 1957 SSch/Su21-5/S-14						(FB)
Manchester U	App	07.74	74-87	364	15	6
West Bromwich A	Tr	08.88	88	43	0	2
Chesterfield (L)	Dundee	11.90	90	3	0	1
Chester C	Dundee	08.91	91	44	0	0
Chester C	Molde FK	11.92	92	23	1	0
ALBRECHTSEN Martin						
Copenhagen, Denmark, 31 March, 1980 DeYth/Deu21-14/De-3						(CD)
West Bromwich A	FC Copenhagen (Den)	06.04	04	20	4	0
ALBRIGHTON Mark Christopher						
Nuneaton, 6 March, 1976						(CD)
Doncaster Rov	Telford U	07.02	03-04	42	3	4
ALBURY William (Bill) Frederick						
Portsmouth, 10 August, 1933						(IF)
Portsmouth	Jnrs	10.51	56-57	23	-	0
Gillingham	Tr	07.59	59	38	-	12
ALCIDE Colin James						
Huddersfield, 14 April, 1972						(F)
Lincoln C	Emley	12.95	95-98	105	16	26
Hull C	L	02.99	98	5	0	1
Hull C	Tr	03.99	98-99	22	2	3
York C	Tr	11.99	99-00	33	20	7
Cambridge U	Tr	06.01	01	7	1	0
Exeter C	Gainsborough Trinity	11.02	02	1	0	0
ALCOCK Daniel (Danny) James						
Salford, 15 February, 1984						(G)
Barnsley	Stoke C (YT)	10.03	03	0	1	0
ALCOCK Terence (Terry)						
Hanley, 9 December, 1946						(CD)
Port Vale	App	09.64	63-66	112	0	0
Blackpool	Tr	08.67	67-75	185	6	21
Bury	L	02.72	71	6	0	1
Blackburn Rov	L	12.76	76	3	0	1
Port Vale	Tr	02.77	76-77	4	0	0
Halifax T	Tr	09.77	77	14	0	2
ALDECOA Emilio Gomez						
Bilbao, Spain, 30 November, 1922 Died 1999 Spain int						(W)
Wolverhampton W		12.43				
Coventry C	Tr	12.45	46	29	-	0

League Club	Source	Date Signed	Seasons Played	Apps	Subs	Gls
ALDERSON Brian Roderick						
Dundee, 5 May, 1950 Died 1997 Su23-1						(W)
Coventry C	Lochee Harp	07.70	70-74	116	11	29
Leicester C	Tr	07.75	75-77	87	3	9
ALDERSON Kevin						
Shildon, 21 August, 1953						(W)
Darlington	App	•	70	2	0	0
ALDERSON Richard						
Durham, 27 January, 1975						(W)
York C	Spennymoor U	12.97	97	0	1	0
ALDERSON Stuart						
Bishop Auckland, 15 August, 1948						(W)
Newcastle U	Evenwood T	08.65	66	3	0	0
York C	Tr	06.67	67	17	2	5
ALDERTON James (Jim) Harris						
Wingate, 6 December, 1924 Died 1998						(WH)
Wolverhampton W	Jnrs	12.41	46	11	-	0
Coventry C	Tr	10.47	47-51	62	-	0
ALDERTON Rio Kevin						
Colchester, 12 August, 1982						(M)
Millwall	YT	07.01				
Southend U	Tr	03.02	01	0	2	0
ALDIS Basil **Peter**						
King's Norton, 11 April, 1927						(FB)
Aston Villa	Hay Green	05.49	50-58	262	-	1
ALDOUS Stanley (Stan) Elvey Reginald						
Northfleet, 10 February, 1923 Died 1995						(CD)
Leyton Orient	Gravesend & Northfleet	07.50	50-57	302	-	3
ALDREAD Paul						
Mansfield, 6 November, 1946						(F)
Mansfield T	Jnrs	12.63	65-66	11	1	3
ALDRED Arthur						
Atherton, 27 August, 1919 Died 2002						(W)
Aston Villa	Hereford U	07.46				
Walsall	Tr	05.48	48	11	-	1
ALDRED Graeme						
Ferryhill, 11 September, 1966 Died 1987						(FB)
Darlington	Newcastle U (YT)	09.84	84-85	30	14	0
ALDRIDGE John William						
Liverpool, 18 September, 1958 IR-69						(F)
Newport Co	South Liverpool	05.79	79-83	159	11	69
Oxford U	Tr	01.84	83-86	111	3	72
Liverpool	Tr	01.87	86-89	69	14	50
Tranmere Rov	Real Sociedad (Sp)	07.91	91-97	221	21	138
ALDRIDGE Martin James						
Northampton, 6 December, 1974 Died 2000						(F)
Northampton T	YT	08.93	91-94	50	20	17
Oxford U	Tr	12.95	95-97	46	26	19
Southend U	L	02.98	97	7	4	1
Blackpool	Tr	08.98	98-99	19	8	7
Port Vale	L	09.99	99	0	3	0
ALDRIDGE Neil Robert						
Manchester, 10 January, 1966 ESch/EYth						(FB)
Manchester C	App	11.83				
Crewe Alex	Tr	07.84	84	12	3	0
ALDRIDGE Norman Hubert						
Coventry, 23 February, 1921						(FB)
West Bromwich A	Foxford	05.46	46	1	-	0
Northampton T	Tr	06.48	48	2	-	0
ALDRIDGE Paul John						
Liverpool, 2 December, 1981						(M)
Tranmere Rov	YT	03.00	99-00	0	6	0
Macclesfield T	Tr	03.02	02	0	1	0
ALDRIDGE Stephen (Steve) Paul						
Armthorpe, 2 November, 1957						(F)
Sheffield U	App	12.75				
Doncaster Rov		02.81	80	1	0	0
ALEKSIC Milija Antony						
Newcastle-under-Lyme, 14 April, 1951						(G)
Plymouth Arg	Stafford Rgrs	02.73	73-75	32	0	0
Luton T	Tr	12.76	76-78	77	0	0
Tottenham H	Tr	12.78	78-81	25	0	0
Luton T	L	11.81	81	4	0	0

ALEKSIDZE Rati
Tbilisi, Georgia, 6 August, 1978 Georgia 10 (F)

League Club	Source	Date Signed	Seasons Played	Apps	Subs	Gls
Chelsea	Dynamo Tbilisi (Geo)	02.00	00	0	2	0

ALESINOYE Martin
Middlesbrough, 1 October, 1955 (M)

League Club	Source	Date Signed	Seasons Played	Apps	Subs	Gls
Doncaster Rov	Barnsley (Am)	10.75	75	13	1	1

ALEXANDER Alan
Cumbernauld, 1 November, 1941 (G)

League Club	Source	Date Signed	Seasons Played	Apps	Subs	Gls
Bradford PA		07.59	61	5	-	0

ALEXANDER Alexander (Alex)
Glasgow, 28 September, 1924 (W)

League Club	Source	Date Signed	Seasons Played	Apps	Subs	Gls
Tranmere Rov	New Brighton (Am)	10.47	46-48	23	-	3

ALEXANDER Angus (Gus) Charles
Arbroath, 10 January, 1934 (WH)

League Club	Source	Date Signed	Seasons Played	Apps	Subs	Gls
Burnley	Arbroath YC	01.51				
Southport	Tr	07.57	57	14	-	1
Workington	Tr	02.58	57-58	49	-	4
York C	Tr	06.59	59	7	-	0

ALEXANDER Anthony (Tony) Alan
Reading, 8 February, 1935 (IF)

League Club	Source	Date Signed	Seasons Played	Apps	Subs	Gls
Reading	Jnrs	08.52	52-55	11	-	2

ALEXANDER Dennis Leslie
Nottingham, 19 February, 1935 (IF)

League Club	Source	Date Signed	Seasons Played	Apps	Subs	Gls
Nottingham F	Jnrs	06.55	55-56	20	-	4
Brighton & Hove A	Tr	03.58				
Gateshead	Tr	10.58	58	17	-	1

ALEXANDER Gary George
Lambeth, 15 August, 1979 (F)

League Club	Source	Date Signed	Seasons Played	Apps	Subs	Gls
West Ham U	YT	07.98				
Exeter C	L	08.99	99	37	0	16
Swindon T	Tr	08.00	00	30	7	7
Hull C	Tr	06.01	01-02	64	4	23
Leyton Orient	Tr	01.03	02-04	81	8	26

ALEXANDER Graham
Coventry, 10 October, 1971 SB-1/S-16 (FB)

League Club	Source	Date Signed	Seasons Played	Apps	Subs	Gls
Scunthorpe U	YT	03.90	90-94	149	10	18
Luton T	Tr	07.95	95-98	146	4	15
Preston NE	Tr	03.99	98-04	266	1	43

ALEXANDER Ian
Glasgow, 26 January, 1963 (FB)

League Club	Source	Date Signed	Seasons Played	Apps	Subs	Gls
Rotherham U	Leicester Juv	10.81	81-82	5	6	0
Bristol Rov	Pez Larnaca (Cyp)	08.86	86-93	284	7	6

ALEXANDER John David
Middlesbrough, 24 September, 1985 (F)

League Club	Source	Date Signed	Seasons Played	Apps	Subs	Gls
Darlington	Sch	•	02-03	0	4	0

ALEXANDER John Eric
Liverpool, 5 October, 1955 (F)

League Club	Source	Date Signed	Seasons Played	Apps	Subs	Gls
Millwall	Ulysses	07.77	76-77	10	5	2
Reading	Tr	10.78	78-80	22	3	9
Northampton T	Tr	08.81	81	21	1	4

ALEXANDER Keith
Nottingham, 14 November, 1956 St Lucia int (F)

League Club	Source	Date Signed	Seasons Played	Apps	Subs	Gls
Grimsby T	Barnet	07.88	88-90	64	19	26
Stockport Co	Tr	09.90	90	9	2	0
Lincoln C	Tr	12.90	90-92	26	19	4
Mansfield T	Tr	08.94	94	0	2	0
Mansfield T	Cliftonville	01.96	95	0	1	0

ALEXANDER Neil
Edinburgh, 10 March, 1978 Su21-10/SB-1 (G)

League Club	Source	Date Signed	Seasons Played	Apps	Subs	Gls
Cardiff C	Livingston	08.01	01-04	127	1	0

ALEXANDER Philip (Phil) James
Slough, 4 September, 1962 ESch (CD)

League Club	Source	Date Signed	Seasons Played	Apps	Subs	Gls
Norwich C	Wokingham T	08.81	82	0	1	0

ALEXANDER Rowan Samuel
Ayr, 28 January, 1961 (F)

League Club	Source	Date Signed	Seasons Played	Apps	Subs	Gls
Brentford	St Mirren	09.84	84-85	41	6	6

ALEXANDER Timothy (Tim) Mark
Chertsey, 29 March, 1974 (CD)

League Club	Source	Date Signed	Seasons Played	Apps	Subs	Gls
Barnet	Wimbledon (YT)	08.92	93-94	29	7	0

ALEXANDERSSON Niclas
Halmstad, Sweden, 29 December, 1971 Sweden 68 (M)

League Club	Source	Date Signed	Seasons Played	Apps	Subs	Gls
Sheffield Wed	IFK Gothenburg (Swe)	12.97	97-99	73	2	8
Everton	Tr	07.00	00-02	49	9	4
West Ham U	L	09.03	03	5	3	0

ALFORD Carl Peter
Denton, 11 February, 1972 (F)

League Club	Source	Date Signed	Seasons Played	Apps	Subs	Gls
Rochdale	YT	•	88	0	4	0

ALIADIERE Jeremie
Rambouillet, France, 30 March, 1983 FrYth/Fru21 (F)

League Club	Source	Date Signed	Seasons Played	Apps	Subs	Gls
Arsenal	YT	04.00	01-04	3	15	1

ALISON James (Jimmy)
Peebles, 11 October, 1923 Died 1998 (WH)

League Club	Source	Date Signed	Seasons Played	Apps	Subs	Gls
Manchester C	Falkirk	12.49	49-50	19	-	0
Aldershot	Tr	07.52	52-56	171	-	8

AL-JABER Sami Abdullah
Riyadh, Saudi Arabia, 11 December, 1972 Saudi int (M)

League Club	Source	Date Signed	Seasons Played	Apps	Subs	Gls
Wolverhampton W (L)	Al-Hilal (Sau)	09.00	00	0	4	0

ALJOFREE Hasney
Manchester, 11 July, 1978 EYth (FB)

League Club	Source	Date Signed	Seasons Played	Apps	Subs	Gls
Bolton W	YT	07.96	97-99	6	8	0
Plymouth Arg	Dundee U	08.02	02-04	51	4	2
Sheffield Wed	L	09.04	04	2	0	0

ALLAN Alexander (Sandy) Begg
Forfar, 29 October, 1947 (F)

League Club	Source	Date Signed	Seasons Played	Apps	Subs	Gls
Cardiff C	Rhyl	03.67	67-69	8	1	1
Bristol Rov	Tr	03.70	69-72	51	6	18
Swansea C	L	03.73	72	6	1	1

ALLAN Derek Thomas
Irvine, 24 December, 1974 SYth (CD)

League Club	Source	Date Signed	Seasons Played	Apps	Subs	Gls
Southampton	Ayr U	03.93	92	0	1	0
Brighton & Hove A	Tr	03.96	95-98	77	3	2

ALLAN James (Jimmy)
Inverness, 10 November, 1953 (G)

League Club	Source	Date Signed	Seasons Played	Apps	Subs	Gls
Swindon T	App	07.71	71-83	371	0	0

ALLAN John
Amble, 26 September, 1931 (G)

League Club	Source	Date Signed	Seasons Played	Apps	Subs	Gls
Barnsley	Amble Welfare	01.49	51-52	11	-	0

ALLAN John
Stirling, 22 March, 1931 (CF)

League Club	Source	Date Signed	Seasons Played	Apps	Subs	Gls
Bradford PA	Third Lanark	02.59	58-60	70	-	51
Halifax T	Tr	03.61	60	10	-	1

ALLAN Jonathan (Jonny) Michael
Carlisle, 24 May, 1983 (F)

League Club	Source	Date Signed	Seasons Played	Apps	Subs	Gls
Carlisle U	YT	05.00	01	10	19	2

ALLANSON Gary Ernest
Hull, 6 March, 1965 (FB)

League Club	Source	Date Signed	Seasons Played	Apps	Subs	Gls
Doncaster Rov	App	03.83	81-83	11	2	0

ALLARDYCE Craig Samuel
Bolton, 9 June, 1975 (CD)

League Club	Source	Date Signed	Seasons Played	Apps	Subs	Gls
Preston NE	YT	07.93	92	0	1	0
Blackpool	Northwich Vic	09.94	95	0	1	0
Chesterfield	Chorley	03.98	97	0	1	0
Peterborough U	Tr	08.98	98	4	0	0
Mansfield T	Welling U	12.98	98-99	7	3	0

ALLARDYCE Samuel (Sam)
Dudley, 19 October, 1954 (CD)

League Club	Source	Date Signed	Seasons Played	Apps	Subs	Gls
Bolton W	App	11.71	73-79	180	4	21
Sunderland	Tr	07.80	80	24	1	2
Millwall	Tr	09.81	81-82	63	0	2
Coventry C	Tampa Bay (USA)	09.83	83	28	0	1
Huddersfield T	Tr	07.84	84	37	0	0
Bolton W	Tr	07.85	85	14	0	0
Preston NE	Tr	08.86	86-88	88	2	2
West Bromwich A	Tr	06.89	89	0	1	0
Preston NE	(Retired)	08.92	92	1	2	0

ALLATT Vernon
Cannock, 28 May, 1959 (F)

League Club	Source	Date Signed	Seasons Played	Apps	Subs	Gls
Halifax T	Hednesford T	11.79	79-81	66	4	7
Halifax T		11.82	82	27	1	7
Rochdale	Tr	08.83	83	40	0	8
Crewe Alex	Tr	06.84	84-85	36	3	8
Preston NE	Tr	11.85	85	17	2	3
Stockport Co	Tr	10.86	86	23	1	10
Crewe Alex	Hednesford T	12.87	87	4	1	2

ALLAWAY James (Jim) Frederick
Bristol, 23 April, 1922 Died 1991 (IF)

League Club	Source	Date Signed	Seasons Played	Apps	Subs	Gls
Bristol Rov		12.46	46	4	-	0

ALLBACK Marcus
Gothenburg, Sweden, 5 July, 1973 Sweden 42 (F)

League Club	Source	Date Signed	Seasons Played	Apps	Subs	Gls
Aston Villa	SC Heerenveen (Holl)	05.02	02-03	16	19	6

ALLCHURCH Ivor John
Swansea, 16 December, 1929 Died 1997 WLge-4/W-68 (IF)

League Club	Source	Date Signed	Seasons Played	Apps	Subs	Gls
Swansea T	Plasmarl	05.47	49-58	327	-	124
Newcastle U	Tr	10.58	58-61	143	-	46
Cardiff C	Tr	08.62	62-64	103	-	39
Swansea T	Tr	07.65	65-67	116	2	40

ALLCHURCH Leonard (Len)
Swansea, 12 September, 1933 WSch/W-11 (W)

League Club	Source	Date Signed	Seasons Played	Apps	Subs	Gls
Swansea T	Jnrs	10.50	50-60	276	-	49
Sheffield U	Tr	03.61	60-64	123	-	32
Stockport Co	Tr	09.65	65-68	131	0	16
Swansea C	Tr	07.69	69-70	70	1	11

ALLCOCK Frank Edward
Beeston, 7 September, 1925 (FB)

League Club	Source	Date Signed	Seasons Played	Apps	Subs	Gls
Nottingham F	Beeston BC	03.45				
Aston Villa	Tr	08.46				
Bristol Rov	Cheltenham T	06.52	53-55	59	-	0

ALLCOCK Kenneth (Ken)
Kirkby-in-Ashfield, 24 April, 1921 Died 1996 (CF)

League Club	Source	Date Signed	Seasons Played	Apps	Subs	Gls
Mansfield T	Notts Co (Am)	04.47	47	1	-	0

ALLCOCK Terence (Terry)
Leeds, 10 December, 1935 (IF)

League Club	Source	Date Signed	Seasons Played	Apps	Subs	Gls
Bolton W	Jnrs	12.52	53-57	31	-	9
Norwich C	Tr	03.58	57-68	334	5	106

ALLDER Douglas (Doug) Stewart
Hammersmith, 30 December, 1951 EYth (W)

League Club	Source	Date Signed	Seasons Played	Apps	Subs	Gls
Millwall	App	10.69	69-74	191	11	10
Orient	Tr	07.75	75-76	34	7	0
Watford	Torquay U (N/C)	09.77	77	1	0	0
Brentford	Tr	10.77	77-79	68	20	2

ALLDIS Gilbert (Gillie) John
Birkenhead, 26 January, 1920 Died 1998 (WH)

League Club	Source	Date Signed	Seasons Played	Apps	Subs	Gls
Tranmere Rov		10.38	38-48	75	-	4
New Brighton	Tr	07.50	50	12	-	0

ALLEN Adrian
Preston, 23 March, 1934 (W)

League Club	Source	Date Signed	Seasons Played	Apps	Subs	Gls
Southport	Preston NE (Am)	05.54	54	6	-	0

ALLEN Andrew (Andy)
Liverpool, 4 September, 1974 (W)

League Club	Source	Date Signed	Seasons Played	Apps	Subs	Gls
Chester C	YT	●	91	0	1	0

ALLEN Anthony (Tony)
Stoke-on-Trent, 27 November, 1939 EYth/Eu23-3/FLge-2/E-3 (FB)

League Club	Source	Date Signed	Seasons Played	Apps	Subs	Gls
Stoke C	Jnrs	11.56	57-69	414	3	2
Bury	Tr	10.70	70-71	29	0	0

ALLEN Herbert **Anthony**
Beeston, 27 October, 1924 (FB)

League Club	Source	Date Signed	Seasons Played	Apps	Subs	Gls
Nottingham F	Beeston BC	01.46	47	1	-	0
Notts Co	Tr	08.49	51-53	30	-	0

ALLEN Bradley James
Harold Wood, 13 September, 1971 EYth/Eu21-8 (F)

League Club	Source	Date Signed	Seasons Played	Apps	Subs	Gls
Queens Park Rgrs	Jnrs	09.88	88-95	56	25	27
Charlton Ath	Tr	03.96	95-97	30	10	9
Colchester U	L	02.99	98	4	0	1
Grimsby T	Tr	07.99	99-01	46	34	15
Peterborough U	Tr	08.02	02	10	3	3
Bristol Rov	Tr	11.02	02	5	3	1

ALLEN Brynley (Bryn) William
Gilfach Goch, 23 March, 1921 Died 2005 W-2 (IF)

League Club	Source	Date Signed	Seasons Played	Apps	Subs	Gls
Swansea T	Gilfach Welfare	03.39				
Cardiff C	Tr	12.45	46-47	41	-	17
Newport Co	Tr	10.47	47	26	-	8
Cardiff C	Tr	08.48	48	17	-	4
Reading	Tr	05.49	49	26	-	12
Coventry C	Tr	02.50	49-52	88	-	26

ALLEN Christopher (Chris) Anthony
Oxford, 18 November, 1972 Eu21-2 (W)

League Club	Source	Date Signed	Seasons Played	Apps	Subs	Gls
Oxford U	YT	05.91	91-95	110	40	12
Nottingham F	L	02.96	95	1	2	1
Nottingham F	Tr	07.96	96-97	17	8	0
Luton T	L	11.97	97	14	0	1
Cardiff C	L	10.98	98	3	1	0
Port Vale	Tr	03.99	98	2	3	1
Stockport Co	Tr	10.99	99	10	6	0

ALLEN Clive Darren
Stepney, 20 May, 1961 ESch/EYth/Eu21-3/FLge/E-5 (F)

League Club	Source	Date Signed	Seasons Played	Apps	Subs	Gls
Queens Park Rgrs	App	09.78	78-79	43	6	32
Arsenal	Tr	06.80				
Crystal Palace	Tr	08.80	80	25	0	9
Queens Park Rgrs	Tr	06.81	81-83	83	4	40
Tottenham H	Tr	08.84	84-87	97	8	60
Manchester C	Bordeaux (Fr)	08.89	89-91	31	22	16
Chelsea	Tr	12.91	91	15	1	7
West Ham U	Tr	03.92	91-93	36	2	17
Millwall	Tr	03.94	93	11	1	0
Carlisle U	Tr	09.95	95	3	0	0

ALLEN Damien Samuel
Cheadle, 1 August, 1986 (M)

League Club	Source	Date Signed	Seasons Played	Apps	Subs	Gls
Stockport Co	Sch	07.04	04	14	7	1

ALLEN Dennis James
Dagenham, 2 March, 1939 Died 1995 (M)

League Club	Source	Date Signed	Seasons Played	Apps	Subs	Gls
Charlton Ath	Jnrs	08.56	57-60	5	-	1
Reading	Tr	06.61	61-69	331	4	84
Bournemouth	Tr	08.70	70	17	0	3

ALLEN Derrick
Wombwell, 14 July, 1946 (M)

League Club	Source	Date Signed	Seasons Played	Apps	Subs	Gls
Rotherham U	Jnrs	11.65	65	1	0	0

ALLEN Derrick Sydney
Luton, 18 April, 1930 Died 1978 (W)

League Club	Source	Date Signed	Seasons Played	Apps	Subs	Gls
Luton T	Alton T	01.52	54	1	-	0
Watford	Tr	06.56	56	6	-	1

ALLEN Frank
Shirebrook, 28 June, 1927 (WH)

League Club	Source	Date Signed	Seasons Played	Apps	Subs	Gls
Chesterfield	Langwith Imperial	03.51	51-52	3	-	0
Mansfield T	Tr	07.53	53-54	6	-	0

ALLEN Geoffrey (Geoff) Barry
Newcastle, 10 November, 1946 EYth (W)

League Club	Source	Date Signed	Seasons Played	Apps	Subs	Gls
Newcastle U	Jnrs	02.64	63-68	22	0	1

ALLEN George Henry
Birmingham, 23 January, 1932 (FB)

League Club	Source	Date Signed	Seasons Played	Apps	Subs	Gls
Birmingham C	Coventry C (Am)	11.52	53-61	135	-	0
Torquay U	Tr	01.62	61-64	134	-	0

ALLEN Graham
Bolton, 8 April, 1977 EYth (CD)

League Club	Source	Date Signed	Seasons Played	Apps	Subs	Gls
Everton	YT	12.94	96-97	2	4	0
Tranmere Rov	Tr	08.98	98-03	193	7	10
Rushden & Diamonds	Tr	06.04	04	25	1	1

ALLEN Graham Frederick
Walsall, 30 August, 1932 (IF)

League Club	Source	Date Signed	Seasons Played	Apps	Subs	Gls
Walsall (Am)		04.54	53	2	-	1

ALLEN Gregory (Greg) Frank
West Ham, 18 October, 1967 (M)

League Club	Source	Date Signed	Seasons Played	Apps	Subs	Gls
Arsenal	App	07.85				
Cambridge U	Dagenham	08.88	88	4	0	0

ALLEN John
Coventry, 24 April, 1955 (F)

League Club	Source	Date Signed	Seasons Played	Apps	Subs	Gls
Leicester C	Hinckley Ath	08.78				
Port Vale	Tr	06.80	80	18	0	4

ALLEN John
Mancot, 14 November, 1964 WSch/WYth (M)

League Club	Source	Date Signed	Seasons Played	Apps	Subs	Gls
Chester	App	11.81	81-83	67	12	5
Mansfield T	Tr	08.84	84	1	1	0

ALLEN John (Ian) Craig
Johnstone, 27 January, 1932 (W)

League Club	Source	Date Signed	Seasons Played	Apps	Subs	Gls
Queens Park Rgrs	Beith Jnrs	09.52	53	1	-	0
Bournemouth	Tr	07.54	54-55	52	-	11

ALLEN Keith
Newport, Isle of Wight, 9 November, 1943 (F)

League Club	Source	Date Signed	Seasons Played	Apps	Subs	Gls
Portsmouth	Ryde	12.62				
Grimsby T	Tr	05.64	64	6	-	1
Stockport Co	Tr	06.65	65-66	49	0	15
Luton T	Tr	03.67	66-69	128	9	36
Plymouth Arg	Tr	07.70	70-72	74	5	10

ALLEN Kenneth (Kenny) Richard
Thornaby, 12 January, 1948 (G)

League Club	Source	Date Signed	Seasons Played	Apps	Subs	Gls
Hartlepool (Am)	Tow Law	08.68	68	7	0	0
West Bromwich A	Hellenic (SA)	12.72				
Bournemouth	Bath C	08.78	78-82	152	0	0
Peterborough U	Bury (N/C)	12.83				
Torquay U	Tr	03.84	83-85	58	0	0
Swindon T	Tr	09.85	85-86	45	0	0
Torquay U	Tr	12.86	86-87	74	0	0

ALLEN Kevin
Ryde, 22 March, 1961 (FB)

League Club	Source	Date Signed	Seasons Played	Apps	Subs	Gls
Bournemouth	Jnrs	08.79	79	1	0	0

League Club	Source	Date Signed	Seasons Played	Apps	Subs	Gls
ALLEN Leighton Gary						
Brighton, 22 November, 1973						(F)
Wimbledon	YT	07.92				
Colchester U	Tr	08.94	94	0	2	0
ALLEN Leslie (Les) William						
Dagenham, 4 September, 1937 Eu23-1/FLge-1						(F)
Chelsea	Briggs Sports	09.54	56-59	44	-	11
Tottenham H	Tr	12.59	59-64	119	-	47
Queens Park Rgrs	Tr	07.65	65-68	123	5	55
ALLEN Malcolm						
Deiniolen, 21 March, 1967 WYth/WB/W-14						(F)
Watford	App	03.85	85-87	27	12	5
Aston Villa	L	09.87	87	4	0	0
Norwich C	Tr	08.88	88-89	24	11	8
Millwall	Tr	03.90	89-92	64	17	24
Newcastle U	Tr	08.93	93-94	9	1	5
ALLEN Mark Stephen						
Newcastle, 18 December, 1963						(F)
Burnley	App	12.81	81	0	2	1
Tranmere Rov	Tr	08.83	83	6	4	0
ALLEN Martin James						
Reading, 14 August, 1965 EYth/Eu21-2						(M)
Queens Park Rgrs	App	05.83	84-89	128	8	16
West Ham U	Tr	08.89	89-95	163	27	25
Portsmouth	Tr	09.95	95-97	34	11	4
Southend U	L	09.97	97	5	0	0
ALLEN Michael (Mike)						
South Shields, 30 March, 1949						(FB)
Middlesbrough	App	05.66	67-71	32	2	0
Brentford	Tr	10.71	71-78	223	10	11
ALLEN Paul Kevin						
Aveley, 28 August, 1962 EYth/Eu21-3						(M)
West Ham U	App	08.79	79-84	149	3	6
Tottenham H	Tr	06.85	85-93	276	16	23
Southampton	Tr	09.93	93-94	40	3	1
Luton T	L	12.94	94	4	0	0
Stoke C	L	01.95	94	17	0	1
Swindon T	Tr	10.95	95-96	30	7	1
Bristol C	Tr	01.97	96	13	1	0
Millwall	Tr	08.97	97	21	7	0
ALLEN Paul Michael						
Leeds, 30 July, 1967						(G)
Doncaster Rov	Bradford C (YT)	10.84	84-85	4	0	0
ALLEN Paul Robert						
Bury, 13 March, 1968						(M)
Bolton W	App	07.86	86	0	1	0
ALLEN Peter Charles						
Hove, 1 November, 1946						(M)
Leyton Orient	Tottenham H (Am)	07.65	65-77	424	8	27
Millwall	Tr	03.78	77-78	16	2	0
ALLEN Peter Michael						
Bristol, 8 October, 1934						(CD)
Bristol C		07.53	54	1	-	0
ALLEN Arthur **Reginald (Reg)**						
Marylebone, 3 May, 1919 Died 1976 FLge-2						(G)
Queens Park Rgrs	Corona	05.38	38-49	183	-	0
Manchester U	Tr	06.50	50-52	75	-	0
ALLEN Robert (Bob)						
Belfast, 16 January, 1939						(WH)
Wolverhampton W	Denbigh T	09.57				
Coventry C	Tr	06.59	60-61	25	-	2
ALLEN Albert **Robert (Bob)**						
Bromley-by-Bow, 11 October, 1916 Died 1992 ESch						(W)
Clapton Orient	Leytonstone (Am)	12.33	33	1	-	0
Fulham	Tr	05.34	34-36	11	-	0
Doncaster Rov	Tr	06.37	37	31	-	6
Brentford	Tr	06.38				
Northampton T	Dartford	09.45	46	5	-	0
Colchester U	Tr	08.47	50	29	-	1
ALLEN Robert Howard Allen						
Shepton Mallet, 5 December, 1916						(FB)
Notts Co		02.45	46	1	-	0
Bristol C	Tr	11.46	46	1	-	0
ALLEN Ronald (Ronnie)						
Fenton, 15 January, 1929 Died 2001 FLge-1/EB/E-5						(CF)
Port Vale	Jnrs	04.46	46-49	123	-	34
West Bromwich A	Tr	03.50	49-60	415	-	208
Crystal Palace	Tr	05.61	61-64	100	-	34

League Club	Source	Date Signed	Seasons Played	Apps	Subs	Gls
ALLEN Ronald (Ron) Leslie						
Birmingham, 22 April, 1935						(FB)
Birmingham C	Ladywood Jnrs	05.53				
Lincoln C	Tr	07.58	58-60	60	-	1
ALLEN Rory William						
Beckenham, 17 October, 1977 Eu21-3						(F)
Tottenham H	YT	03.96	96-98	10	11	2
Luton T	L	03.98	97	8	0	6
Portsmouth	Tr	07.99	99	10	5	3
ALLEN Russell Philip						
Smethwick, 9 January, 1954						(F)
West Bromwich A	Arsenal (App)	05.71				
Tranmere Rov	Tr	07.73	73-77	137	19	42
Mansfield T	Tr	07.78	78-80	99	17	18
ALLEN William (Bill)						
Newburn, 22 October, 1917 Died 1981						(WH)
Chesterfield		11.37	38	2	-	0
York C	Tr	05.39	46-49	130	-	23
Scunthorpe U	Tr	06.50	50-51	64	-	1
ALLEYNE Andrew (Andy) McArthur						
Springtown, Barbados, 19 May, 1951						(FB)
Reading	Newbury T	11.72	72-75	46	2	2
ALLEYNE Robert Anthony						
Dudley, 27 September, 1968						(F)
Leicester C	Jnrs	01.87	86	1	2	0
Wrexham	L	10.87	87	7	3	2
Chesterfield	Tr	03.88	87-88	32	8	5
ALLINSON Ian James Robert						
Hitchin, 1 October, 1957						(W)
Colchester U	App	10.75	74-82	291	17	69
Arsenal	Tr	08.83	83-86	60	23	16
Stoke C	Tr	06.87	87	6	3	0
Luton T	Tr	10.87	87-88	24	8	3
Colchester U	Tr	12.88	88-89	36	2	10
ALLINSON Jamie						
Stockton, 15 June, 1978						(CD)
Hartlepool U	YT	07.96	95	3	1	0
ALLISON John (Jack)						
Stannington, 31 July, 1922 Died 1985						(W)
Chesterfield	West Sleekburn	04.47				
Reading	Blyth Spartans	01.49	48-49	29	-	4
Walsall	Tr	06.50	50-51	47	-	1
ALLISON John Alfred						
Cramlington, 9 August, 1932						(CD)
Chesterfield	Blyth Spartans	05.55	57-60	32	-	0
ALLISON John Joseph						
Consett, 17 November, 1913 Died 1971						(WH)
Barnsley	Workington	05.39				
Hartlepools U	Tr	09.46	46	13	-	0
ALLISON Kenneth (Kenny)						
Edinburgh, 6 January, 1937						(F)
Darlington	Cowdenbeath	07.63	63-65	74	0	40
Lincoln C	Tr	02.66	65-66	41	1	13
ALLISON Malcolm Alexander						
Dartford, 5 September, 1927						(CD)
Charlton Ath	Erith & Belvedere	02.45	49	2	-	0
West Ham U	Tr	02.51	50-57	238	-	10
ALLISON Michael (Mike)						
Bolton, 17 March, 1966						(G)
Chesterfield	Horwich RMI	07.89	90	16	0	0
ALLISON Neil James						
Hull, 20 October, 1973						(CD)
Hull C	YT	07.92	90-96	95	11	3
Chesterfield	North Ferriby U	03.97	96	0	2	0
ALLISON Thomas (Tom)						
Fencehouses, 20 February, 1921						(IF)
Darlington	South Hetton	09.46	46	6	-	0
ALLISON Wayne Anthony						
Huddersfield, 16 October, 1968						(F)
Halifax T	YT	07.87	86-88	74	10	23
Watford	Tr	07.89	89	6	1	0
Bristol C	Tr	08.90	90-94	149	46	48
Swindon T	Tr	07.95	95-97	98	3	31
Huddersfield T	Tr	11.97	97-99	71	3	15
Tranmere Rov	Tr	09.99	99-01	85	18	26
Sheffield U	Tr	07.02	02-03	29	44	7
Chesterfield	Tr	07.04	04	27	11	6

ALLISTER John (Jack) Grandison
Edinburgh, 30 June, 1927 Died 1999 (CF)

League Club	Source	Date Signed	Seasons Played	Apps	Subs	Gls
Chelsea	Tranent Jnrs	07.49	51-52	4	-	1

ALLMAN George
Stockport, 23 July, 1930 (CF)

League Club	Source	Date Signed	Seasons Played	Apps	Subs	Gls
Stockport Co		05.50	50-51	7	-	1
Chester	Holywell T	07.55	55-56	49	-	13

ALLON Joseph (Joe) Ball
Gateshead, 12 November, 1966 EYth (F)

League Club	Source	Date Signed	Seasons Played	Apps	Subs	Gls
Newcastle U	App	11.84	84-86	9	0	2
Swansea C	Tr	08.87	87-88	27	7	12
Hartlepool U	Tr	11.88	88-90	112	0	48
Chelsea	Tr	08.91	91-92	3	11	2
Port Vale	L	02.92	91	2	4	0
Brentford	Tr	11.92	92-93	38	7	19
Southend U	L	09.93	93	2	1	0
Port Vale	Tr	03.94	93-94	13	10	9
Lincoln C	Tr	07.95	95	3	1	0
Hartlepool U	Tr	10.95	95-97	52	4	19

ALLOTT Mark Stephen
Manchester, 3 October, 1977 (F)

League Club	Source	Date Signed	Seasons Played	Apps	Subs	Gls
Oldham Ath	YT	10.95	96-01	105	49	31
Chesterfield	Tr	12.01	01-04	123	16	8

ALLOU Anoh **Bernard**
Cocody, Ivory Coast, 19 June, 1975 Fru21-24 (M)

League Club	Source	Date Signed	Seasons Played	Apps	Subs	Gls
Nottingham F	Grampus 8 (Japan)	03.99	98-99	1	5	1

ALLPRESS Timothy (Tim) John
Hitchin, 27 January, 1971 (FB)

League Club	Source	Date Signed	Seasons Played	Apps	Subs	Gls
Luton T	YT	07.89	89	1	0	0
Preston NE	L	10.91	91	7	2	0
Colchester U	Bayer Uerdingen (Ger)	08.93	93-94	24	10	0

ALLSOP Norman
West Bromwich, 1 November, 1930 (IF)

League Club	Source	Date Signed	Seasons Played	Apps	Subs	Gls
West Bromwich A	Hednesford T	05.48				
Walsall	Worcester C	10.53	53	9	-	0

ALLSOP William (Bill) Henry
Ripley, 29 January, 1912 Died 1997 (FB)

League Club	Source	Date Signed	Seasons Played	Apps	Subs	Gls
Port Vale	Bolton W (Am)	08.31	31-32	6	-	0
Halifax T	Tr	05.34	34-46	239	-	1

ALLSOPP Daniel (Danny)
Melbourne, Australia, 10 August, 1978 AuYth/Auu23-7 (F)

League Club	Source	Date Signed	Seasons Played	Apps	Subs	Gls
Manchester C	Carlton (Aus)	08.98	98-00	3	26	4
Notts Co	L	11.99	99	3	0	1
Wrexham	L	02.00	99	3	0	4
Bristol Rov	L	10.00	00	4	2	0
Notts Co	Tr	11.00	00-02	97	8	42
Hull C	Tr	05.03	03-04	45	19	22

ALLUM Albert (Bert) Edward
Notting Hill, 15 October, 1930 (W)

League Club	Source	Date Signed	Seasons Played	Apps	Subs	Gls
Queens Park Rgrs	Dover	06.57	57	1	-	0

ALMEIDA Marco Antonio
Lisbon, Portugal, 4 April, 1977 Portugal u21-1 (CD)

League Club	Source	Date Signed	Seasons Played	Apps	Subs	Gls
Southampton (L)	Sporting Lisbon (Por)	07.99	99	0	1	0

ALMUNIA Manuel
Pamplona, Spain, 19 May, 1977 (G)

League Club	Source	Date Signed	Seasons Played	Apps	Subs	Gls
Arsenal	Celta Vigo (Sp)	07.04	04	10	0	0

ALNWICK Benjamin (Ben) Robert
Prudhoe, 1 January, 1987 EYth (G)

League Club	Source	Date Signed	Seasons Played	Apps	Subs	Gls
Sunderland	Sch	03.04	04	3	0	0

ALOISI John
Adelaide, Australia, 5 February, 1976 AuYth/Auu21 (F)

League Club	Source	Date Signed	Seasons Played	Apps	Subs	Gls
Portsmouth	Cremonese (It)	08.97	97-98	55	5	25
Coventry C	Tr	12.98	98-00	18	24	10

ALONSO Xabi
Tolosa, Spain, 25 November, 1981 Spain 17 (M)

League Club	Source	Date Signed	Seasons Played	Apps	Subs	Gls
Liverpool	Real Sociedad (Sp)	08.04	04	20	4	2

[ALPAY] OZALAN Fehmi
Karisyaled, Turkey, 29 May, 1973 Turkey 84 (CD)

League Club	Source	Date Signed	Seasons Played	Apps	Subs	Gls
Aston Villa	Fenerbahce (Tu)	07.00	00-03	56	2	1

ALSAKER Paul Christian
Stord, Norway, 6 November, 1973 (M)

League Club	Source	Date Signed	Seasons Played	Apps	Subs	Gls
Stockport Co	Flora Tallin (Est)	08.98	98	1	0	0

ALSFORD Julian
Poole, 24 December, 1972 (CD)

League Club	Source	Date Signed	Seasons Played	Apps	Subs	Gls
Watford	YT	04.91	92-93	9	4	1
Chester C	Tr	08.94	94-97	136	5	6
Barnet (L)	Dundee U	09.98	98	9	0	1
Chester C	Dundee U	02.99	98	9	1	1

ALSOP Gilbert Arthur
Frampton Cotterell, 10 September, 1908 Died 1992 (CF)

League Club	Source	Date Signed	Seasons Played	Apps	Subs	Gls
Coventry C	Bath C	12.29	29-30	16	-	4
Walsall	Tr	10.31	31-35	160	-	126
West Bromwich A	Tr	11.35	35	1	-	0
Ipswich T	Tr	06.37	38	9	-	2
Walsall	Tr	11.38	38-46	35	-	25

ALSOP Julian Mark
Nuneaton, 28 May, 1973 (F)

League Club	Source	Date Signed	Seasons Played	Apps	Subs	Gls
Bristol Rov	Halesowen T	02.97	96-97	20	13	4
Swansea C	L	01.98	97	5	0	2
Swansea C	Tr	03.98	97-99	73	12	14
Cheltenham T	Tr	07.00	00-02	99	18	35
Oxford U	Tr	07.03	03-04	29	5	5
Northampton T	Tr	10.04	04	1	6	1

ALSTON Adrian
Preston, 6 February, 1949 Australia int (F)

League Club	Source	Date Signed	Seasons Played	Apps	Subs	Gls
Luton T	South Coast U (Aus)	08.74	74-75	26	3	8
Cardiff C	Tr	10.75	75-76	44	4	16

ALSTON Alexander (Alec) George
Preston, 26 February, 1937 (F)

League Club	Source	Date Signed	Seasons Played	Apps	Subs	Gls
Preston NE	Netherfield	05.55	57-62	102	-	26
Bury	Tr	03.63	62-65	85	0	22
Barrow	Tr	09.65	65-66	46	1	13

ALTY Colin
Birkdale, 23 October, 1944 (CD)

League Club	Source	Date Signed	Seasons Played	Apps	Subs	Gls
Preston NE	Jnrs	10.61				
Southport	Tr	06.64	64-69	184	6	22

ALVES Paulo Laurenco
Mateus Villareal, Portugal, 10 December, 1969 Portugal int (F)

League Club	Source	Date Signed	Seasons Played	Apps	Subs	Gls
West Ham U (L)	Sporting Lisbon (Por)	11.97	97	0	4	0

AMANKWAAH Kevin Osei-Kuffour
Harrow, 19 May, 1982 EYth (FB)

League Club	Source	Date Signed	Seasons Played	Apps	Subs	Gls
Bristol C	YT	06.00	99-04	35	19	1
Torquay U	L	01.03	02	6	0	0
Cheltenham T	L	08.03	03	11	1	0
Yeovil T	Tr	02.05	04	10	5	0

AMBLER Roy
Wakefield, 2 December, 1937 (CF)

League Club	Source	Date Signed	Seasons Played	Apps	Subs	Gls
Leeds U	Outwood Stormcocks	12.54				
Shrewsbury T	Tr	01.59	58-60	29	-	8
Wrexham	Tr	05.61	61-62	21	-	13
York C	Tr	11.62	62	12	-	3
Southport	Tr	07.63	63	11	-	0

AMBROSE Darren Paul
Harlow, 29 February, 1984 EYth/Eu21-5 (M)

League Club	Source	Date Signed	Seasons Played	Apps	Subs	Gls
Ipswich T	YT	07.01	01-02	20	10	8
Newcastle U	Tr	03.03	02-04	18	19	5

AMBROSE Anthony **Leroy**
St Vincent, 22 June, 1960 (M)

League Club	Source	Date Signed	Seasons Played	Apps	Subs	Gls
Charlton Ath	Croydon	08.79	79-81	28	5	1

AMBROSETTI Gabriele
Varese, Italy, 7 August, 1973 (M)

League Club	Source	Date Signed	Seasons Played	Apps	Subs	Gls
Chelsea	Vicenza (It)	08.99	99	9	7	0

AMBROSIO Marco
Brescia, Italy, 30 May, 1973 (G)

League Club	Source	Date Signed	Seasons Played	Apps	Subs	Gls
Chelsea	Chievo (It)	07.03	03	8	0	0

AMEOBI Foluwashola (Shola)
Zaria, Nigeria, 12 October, 1981 Eu21-21 (F)

League Club	Source	Date Signed	Seasons Played	Apps	Subs	Gls
Newcastle U	YT	10.98	00-04	59	61	16

AMES Kenneth (Ken) George
Canford, 17 September, 1933 ESch (CF)

League Club	Source	Date Signed	Seasons Played	Apps	Subs	Gls
Portsmouth	Jnrs	09.50	53	2	-	0

AMES Percy Talbot
Bedford, 13 December, 1931 Died 1998 (G)

League Club	Source	Date Signed	Seasons Played	Apps	Subs	Gls
Tottenham H	Bedford Avenue	05.51				
Colchester U	Tr	05.55	55-64	397	-	0

AMES Trevor
Poole, 14 December, 1962 (F)

League Club	Source	Date Signed	Seasons Played	Apps	Subs	Gls
Hereford U	Ason Villa (App)	10.80	80-81	5	3	0

AMMANN Michael (Mike) Anton
California, USA, 8 February, 1971 (G)

League Club	Source	Date Signed	Seasons Played	Apps	Subs	Gls
Charlton Ath	Los Angeles (USA)	07.94	94-95	28	2	0

AMOKACHI Daniel Owofen
Kaduna, Nigeria, 30 December, 1972 Nigeria int (F)

League Club	Source	Date Signed	Seasons Played	Apps	Subs	Gls
Everton	FC Bruges (Bel)	08.94	94-95	34	9	10

AMOO Ryan Lee
Leicester, 11 October, 1983 (M)

League Club	Source	Date Signed	Seasons Played	Apps	Subs	Gls
Aston Villa	YT	07.01				
Northampton T	Tr	03.04	03-04	2	4	0

AMOR William (Bill) George
Pewsey, 6 November, 1919 Died 1988 EAmat (W)

League Club	Source	Date Signed	Seasons Played	Apps	Subs	Gls
Reading (Am)	Huntley & Palmers	12.47	47-51	66	-	12

AMORUSO Lorenzo
Bari, Italy, 28 June, 1971 (CD)

League Club	Source	Date Signed	Seasons Played	Apps	Subs	Gls
Blackburn Rov	Glasgow Rgrs	07.03	03-04	16	2	3

AMOS Keith James
Walton-on-Thames, 13 January, 1932 (G)

League Club	Source	Date Signed	Seasons Played	Apps	Subs	Gls
Arsenal	Jnrs	05.52				
Aldershot	Tr	08.54	55-57	77	-	0

AMPADU Patrick **Kwame**
Bradford, 20 December, 1970 IRYth/IRu21-4 (M)

League Club	Source	Date Signed	Seasons Played	Apps	Subs	Gls
Arsenal	YT	11.88	89	0	2	0
Plymouth Arg	L	10.90	90	6	0	1
West Bromwich A	Tr	06.91	90-93	27	22	4
Swansea C	Tr	02.94	93-97	128	19	12
Leyton Orient	Tr	07.98	98-99	69	3	1
Exeter C	Tr	07.00	00-02	80	15	0

AMPHLETT Raymond (Ray) Henry
Manchester, 25 September, 1922 (FB)

League Club	Source	Date Signed	Seasons Played	Apps	Subs	Gls
Cardiff C	Guildford C	04.48				
Newport Co	Tr	04.49	49	13	-	0

AMPOFO Christopher (Chris) John Kwasi
Paddington, 6 October, 1963 (CD)

League Club	Source	Date Signed	Seasons Played	Apps	Subs	Gls
West Ham U	App	10.81				
Aldershot	Tr	08.83	83	4	0	0

AMSALEM David
Israel, 4 September, 1971 Israel 1 (CD)

League Club	Source	Date Signed	Seasons Played	Apps	Subs	Gls
Crystal Palace	Beitar Jerusalem (Isr)	08.98	98	6	4	0

ANDERS Henry (Harry)
St Helens, 28 November, 1926 Died 1994 (W)

League Club	Source	Date Signed	Seasons Played	Apps	Subs	Gls
Preston NE	St Helens	08.45	47-52	69	-	4
Manchester C	Tr	03.53	52-54	32	-	4
Port Vale	Tr	07.56	56	3	-	0
Accrington St	Tr	06.57	57-59	114	-	18
Workington	Tr	07.60	60	7	-	1

ANDERS James (Jimmy)
St Helens, 8 March, 1928 Died 2002 (W)

League Club	Source	Date Signed	Seasons Played	Apps	Subs	Gls
Preston NE	St Helens	08.45				
Brentford	Tr	09.48	49-50	12	-	0
Bradford C	Tr	06.51	51-52	51	-	11
Rochdale	Tr	07.53	53-56	123	-	28
Bradford PA	Tr	09.56	56	20	-	4
Accrington St	Tr	01.57	56-59	129	-	29
Bradford PA	Buxton	09.60	60-61	39	-	8
Tranmere Rov	Tr	11.61	61	8	-	1

ANDERS Jason Stuart
Littleborough, 13 March, 1974 (F)

League Club	Source	Date Signed	Seasons Played	Apps	Subs	Gls
Rochdale	YT	07.90	90-92	2	15	1

ANDERSEN Braastrup (Bo)
Slagelse, Denmark, 26 March, 1976 (G)

League Club	Source	Date Signed	Seasons Played	Apps	Subs	Gls
Bristol C	Lyngby (Den)	12.98	98	10	0	0

ANDERSEN Leif Erik
Fredrikstad, Norway, 19 April, 1971 (CD)

League Club	Source	Date Signed	Seasons Played	Apps	Subs	Gls
Crystal Palace	Moss FK (Nor)	01.96	95-96	19	11	1

ANDERSEN Nicholas (Nicky) John
Lincoln, 29 March, 1969 (FB)

League Club	Source	Date Signed	Seasons Played	Apps	Subs	Gls
Mansfield T	YT	01.87	86-88	9	11	0
Lincoln C	Tr	08.89	89	1	0	0

ANDERSEN Soren
Aarhus, Denmark, 31 January, 1970 Denmark 10 (F)

League Club	Source	Date Signed	Seasons Played	Apps	Subs	Gls
Bristol C	Aalborg BK (Den)	07.98	98	26	13	10

ANDERSEN Stephan Maigaard
Copenhagen, Denmark, 26 November, 1981 DeYth/Deu21-21/De-1 (G)

League Club	Source	Date Signed	Seasons Played	Apps	Subs	Gls
Charlton Ath	AB Copenhagen (Den)	05.04	04	2	0	0

ANDERSEN Trond
Kristiansand, Norway, 6 January, 1975 NoYth/Nou21/NoB-1/No-29 (M)

League Club	Source	Date Signed	Seasons Played	Apps	Subs	Gls
Wimbledon	Molde FK (Nor)	08.99	99-02	136	10	6

ANDERSEN Vetle Gregle
Kristiansand, Norway, 20 April, 1964 (CD)

League Club	Source	Date Signed	Seasons Played	Apps	Subs	Gls
West Bromwich A	Lyngby (Den)	12.89	89	0	1	0

ANDERSON Arthur **Alan** Duncan
Edinburgh, 21 December, 1939 (WH)

League Club	Source	Date Signed	Seasons Played	Apps	Subs	Gls
Millwall	Falkirk	09.59	60-61	74	-	0
Scunthorpe U	Tr	07.62	62	6	-	0

ANDERSON Alexander (Alex)
Gorbals, 8 January, 1922 Died 1984 LoI-1 (G)

League Club	Source	Date Signed	Seasons Played	Apps	Subs	Gls
Rochdale	Third Lanark	02.48	47	4	-	0
Southport	Dundalk	11.49	49-50	21	-	0

ANDERSON Alexander (Alex) Ferguson
Monifieth, 15 November, 1921 Died 1999 (FB)

League Club	Source	Date Signed	Seasons Played	Apps	Subs	Gls
Southampton	Forfar Ath	11.49	49-51	20	-	0
Exeter C	Tr	06.52	52	6	-	0

ANDERSON Alexander (Sandy) Ogilvie Walker
Auchtermuchty, 20 February, 1930 (FB)

League Club	Source	Date Signed	Seasons Played	Apps	Subs	Gls
Southend U	Newburgh Jnrs	04.50	50-62	452	-	8

ANDERSON Benjamin (Ben) Cummings
Aberdeen, 18 February, 1946 (CD)

League Club	Source	Date Signed	Seasons Played	Apps	Subs	Gls
Blackburn Rov	Peterlee Jnrs	03.64	64-67	21	7	7
Bury	Tr	07.68	68-69	52	2	6
Crystal Palace	Cape Town C (SA)	11.73	73	11	0	1

ANDERSON Christopher (Chris)
Aberdeen, 30 August, 1925 Died 1986 (WH)

League Club	Source	Date Signed	Seasons Played	Apps	Subs	Gls
Hartlepools U	Aberdeen	09.46	46	2	-	0

ANDERSON Christopher (Chris) Shelley Inglis
East Wemyss, 28 November, 1928 Died 1996 (W)

League Club	Source	Date Signed	Seasons Played	Apps	Subs	Gls
Blackburn Rov	Lochore Welfare	08.50	50-51	13	-	1
Stockport Co	Nelson	06.53	53	34	-	0
Southport	Tr	07.54	54	28	-	0

ANDERSON Colin Russell
Newcastle, 26 April, 1962 (M)

League Club	Source	Date Signed	Seasons Played	Apps	Subs	Gls
Burnley	App	04.80	80-81	3	3	0
Torquay U	North Shields	09.82	82-84	107	2	10
West Bromwich A	Tr	03.85	85-90	131	9	10
Walsall	Tr	08.91	91	25	1	2
Hereford U	Tr	08.92	92-93	67	3	1
Exeter C	Tr	07.94	94-95	26	8	1

ANDERSON Dale
Newton Aycliffe, 23 August, 1970 (F)

League Club	Source	Date Signed	Seasons Played	Apps	Subs	Gls
Darlington	YT	09.88	86-88	4	11	0

ANDERSON Darren Irwin
Merton, 6 September, 1966 EYth (CD)

League Club	Source	Date Signed	Seasons Played	Apps	Subs	Gls
Charlton Ath	Coventry C (App)	03.84	83-84	10	0	1
Crewe Alex	L	10.85	85	5	0	0
Aldershot	Tr	07.86	86-89	69	29	4

ANDERSON Desmond (Des)
Edinburgh, 9 January, 1938 SSch (WH)

League Club	Source	Date Signed	Seasons Played	Apps	Subs	Gls
Millwall	Morton	06.61	61-63	46	-	1

ANDERSON John **Desmond (Des)**
Downpatrick, 11 September, 1940 (CD)

League Club	Source	Date Signed	Seasons Played	Apps	Subs	Gls
Exeter C	Glenavon	08.62	62-65	142	2	1
Chesterfield	Tr	07.66	66-67	8	0	0

ANDERSON Douglas (Doug) Eric
Hong Kong, 29 August, 1963 (W)

League Club	Source	Date Signed	Seasons Played	Apps	Subs	Gls
Oldham Ath	Port Glasgow Rgrs	09.80	81-83	4	5	0
Tranmere Rov	Tr	08.84	84-86	125	1	15
Plymouth Arg	Tr	08.87	87	17	2	1
Cambridge U	L	09.88	88	8	0	2
Northampton T	L	12.88	88	4	1	0

ANDERSON Edward (Eddie)
Glasgow, 23 September, 1917 Died 1999 (FB)

League Club	Source	Date Signed	Seasons Played	Apps	Subs	Gls
Rochdale	Stirling A	03.48	47	1	-	0

ANDERSON Edward (Ted) Walton
Dudley, Northumberland, 17 July, 1911 Died 1979 (WH)

League Club	Source	Date Signed	Seasons Played	Apps	Subs	Gls
Wolverhampton W	Worksop T	12.29	30	3	-	0
Torquay U	Tr	12.31	31-32	61	-	2
West Ham U	Tr	06.33	33-34	26	-	0
Chester	Tr	06.35	35-36	23	-	0
Tranmere Rov	Tr	07.37	37-47	73	-	0

League Club	Source	Date Signed	Seasons Played	Apps	Subs	Gls
ANDERSON Eric						
Manchester, 7 December, 1931 Died 1990						(IF)
Liverpool		12.51	52-56	73	-	21
Barnsley	Tr	07.57	57	9	-	1
ANDERSON Gary Leslie						
Bow, 20 October, 1955						(FB)
Tottenham H	App	12.72				
Northampton T	Tr	03.75	74-75	14	0	0
ANDERSON Geoffrey (Geoff) Thomas						
Sheerness, 26 November, 1944						(W)
Birmingham C	App	12.62	63	1	-	0
Mansfield T	Tr	05.64	64-65	43	0	13
Lincoln C	Tr	07.66	66	44	0	6
ANDERSON Iain						
Glasgow, 23 July, 1977 Su21-15						(M)
Preston NE	Toulouse (Fr)	02.00	99-02	46	36	13
Tranmere Rov	L	03.03	02	7	0	2
Grimsby T	Tr	07.03	03	24	5	5
ANDERSON Ijah Massai						
Hackney, 30 December, 1975						(FB)
Southend U	Tottenham H (YT)	08.94				
Brentford	Tr	07.95	95-02	196	6	4
Wycombe W	L	11.02	02	5	0	0
Bristol Rov	Tr	02.03	02-03	51	2	0
Swansea C	Tr	11.04	04	8	5	0
ANDERSON James (Jimmy)						
Pelaw, 23 July, 1913						(FB)
Brentford	Blyth Spartans	07.39				
Carlisle U	Tr	09.46	46	11	-	0
ANDERSON James (Jimmy) McFarland						
Glasgow, 25 December, 1932						(WH)
Bristol Rov	RAOC Hilsea	04.53	54-56	24	-	0
Chester	Tr	06.57	57-59	62	-	0
ANDERSON John (Johnny)						
Salford, 11 October, 1921						(WH)
Manchester U	Jnrs	11.38	47-48	33	-	1
Nottingham F	Tr	10.49	49-50	40	-	1
ANDERSON John (Johnny)						
Barrhead, 8 December, 1929 Died 2001 SB/S-1						(G)
Leicester C	Arthurlie	12.48	48-58	261	-	0
ANDERSON John						
Greenock, 2 October, 1972						(CD)
Hull C	Livingston	06.02	02	42	1	1
Bristol Rov	Tr	03.04	03-04	36	6	1
ANDERSON John Christopher Patrick						
Dublin, 7 November, 1959 IRYth/IRu21-1/IR-16						(FB)
West Bromwich A	App	11.77				
Preston NE	Tr	08.79	79-81	47	4	0
Newcastle U	Tr	09.82	82-90	283	16	14
ANDERSON John (Jock) Curr						
Dundee, 8 May, 1915 Died 1987						(IF)
Portsmouth	Stobswell	01.33	33-38	81	-	33
Aldershot	Tr	06.46	46	4	-	1
ANDERSON John Ephraim						
Ridsdale, 7 June, 1931 Died 2003						(FB)
Grimsby T	Langold CW	05.54	55	3	-	0
ANDERSON John Hugh Todd						
Johnstone, 11 January, 1937						(W)
Stoke C	Johnstone Burgh	01.57	57-60	24	-	2
ANDERSON John (Johnny) Lochart						
Glasgow, 5 April, 1928 Died 2001						(IF)
Northampton T	Partick Th	06.53	53	14	-	5
Exeter C	Tr	07.54	54	7	-	0
Wrexham	Dundee	06.56	56-58	98	-	27
Rochdale	Tr	07.59	59	28	-	5
Chester	Tr	07.60	60	17	-	2
Wrexham	Tr	08.61	61	1	-	0
ANDERSON Lee Charles						
Tottington, 4 October, 1973						(FB)
Bury	YT	10.91	91-93	27	2	0
Doncaster Rov	Altrincham	03.97	96	6	0	0
ANDERSON Mark James						
Scunthorpe, 7 October, 1981						(F)
Scunthorpe U	YT	07.01	01	0	1	0

League Club	Source	Date Signed	Seasons Played	Apps	Subs	Gls
ANDERSON Norman Hindmarsh						
Hebburn, 30 November, 1930						(IF)
Gateshead	Reyrolles	03.51	53-55	21	-	2
ANDERSON Percy Archibald						
Cambridge, 22 September, 1930						(WH)
West Bromwich A	Cambridge U	09.51				
Stockport Co	Tr	07.53	53	1	-	0
ANDERSON Peter Dennis						
Devonport, 11 September, 1932						(W)
Plymouth Arg	Oak Villa	07.50	52-62	241	-	41
Torquay U	Tr	12.62	62-64	77	-	18
ANDERSON Peter Thomas						
Hendon, 31 May, 1949						(M)
Luton T	Hendon	02.71	70-75	178	3	34
Sheffield U	Tampa Bay (USA)	09.78	78	28	2	12
Millwall	Tampa Bay (USA)	12.80	80-82	30	2	4
ANDERSON Philip (Phil) Oswald						
Portadown, 5 January, 1948						(W)
Bury	Portadown	05.66	66-68	4	3	1
ANDERSON Robert (Bobby)						
Newton Mearns, 11 August, 1928 Died 2000						(W)
Leicester C	Mearns Amats	01.46	46-47	19	-	2
ANDERSON Robert						
Aberdeen, 21 January, 1937						(W)
Chesterfield	Partick Th	08.59	59	4	-	0
ANDERSON John **Robert (Bob)**						
Prestwick, 9 November, 1924 Died 1994						(G)
Middlesbrough	Blackhall CW	11.45	47	1	-	0
Crystal Palace	Blackhall CW	10.51	51-52	38	-	0
Bristol Rov	Tr	03.53	52-53	10	-	0
Bristol C	Tr	04.54	54-58	106	-	0
ANDERSON Robert John						
Portsmouth, 23 February, 1936 Died 1996						(W)
Mansfield T	Chesterfield Tube Wks	09.56	56-59	40	-	4
ANDERSON Robert (Bert) Lymbun						
Derry, 23 April, 1926 Died 1986						(FB)
Doncaster Rov	Ulsterville	11.49	50-51	3	-	0
ANDERSON Ronald (Ron) James						
Gateshead, 3 July, 1922 Died 1984						(IF)
Bury	Newcastle YMCA	08.39	46	2	-	0
ANDERSON William **Ronald (Ron)**						
Ponteland, 20 September, 1927 Died 1995						(G)
Newcastle U	Throckley CW	02.47	46	1	-	0
ANDERSON Samuel (Sammy)						
Manchester, 11 January, 1936						(FB)
Oldham Ath	Oldham Amats	08.54	55-56	6	-	0
ANDERSON Stanley (Stan)						
Horden, 27 February, 1934 ESch/Eu23-4/E-2						(WH)
Sunderland	Jnrs	03.51	52-63	402	-	31
Newcastle U	Tr	11.63	63-65	81	0	13
Middlesbrough	Tr	11.65	65	21	0	2
ANDERSON Stuart						
Banff, 22 April, 1986 SYth						(M)
Southampton	Sch	04.04				
Blackpool	Tr	12.04	04	1	3	0
ANDERSON Terence (Terry) Keith						
Woking, 11 March, 1944 Died 1980 EYth						(W)
Arsenal	App	08.61	62-64	25	-	6
Norwich C	Tr	02.65	64-73	218	18	16
Colchester U	L	02.74	73	4	0	0
Scunthorpe U	Baltimore (USA)	09.74	74	10	0	0
Crewe Alex	Tr	11.74	74	4	0	0
Colchester U	Baltimore (USA)	08.75	75	13	3	0
ANDERSON Thomas (Tommy) Cowan						
Haddington, 24 September, 1934 SSch						(IF)
Watford	Ayr U	12.56	56-57	52	-	12
Bournemouth	Tr	06.58	58	5	-	1
Queens Park Rgrs	Tr	11.58	58	10	-	3
Torquay U	Tr	07.59	59	9	-	4
Stockport Co	Tr	06.60	60-61	60	-	17
Doncaster Rov	Tr	11.61	61	16	-	3
Wrexham	Tr	03.62	61-62	12	-	3
Barrow	Hellas (Aus)	12.63	63	11	-	3
Watford	Hellas (Aus)	12.64	64-65	21	0	2
Orient	George Cross (Aus)	07.67	67	8	1	0

League Club	Source	Date Signed	Seasons Played	Career Record Apps	Subs	Gls
ANDERSON Trevor						
Belfast, 3 March, 1951 NIu21-1/IrLge-1/NI-22 (W)						
Manchester U	Portadown	10.72	72-73	13	6	2
Swindon T	Tr	11.74	74-77	128	3	34
Peterborough U	Tr	12.77	77-78	49	0	6
ANDERSON Vivian (Viv) Alexander						
Nottingham, 29 August, 1956 Eu21-1/EB/E-30 (FB)						
Nottingham F	App	08.74	74-83	323	5	15
Arsenal	Tr	07.84	84-86	120	0	9
Manchester U	Tr	05.87	87-90	50	4	2
Sheffield Wed	Tr	01.91	90-92	60	10	8
Barnsley	Tr	07.93	93	20	0	3
Middlesbrough	Tr	07.94	94	2	0	0
ANDERSON William (Bill)						
Lochore, 6 November, 1926 (IF)						
Southend U	Hibernian	05.54	54-55	16	-	1
ANDERSON William (Billy) Boston						
Sunderland, 28 March, 1935 (WH)						
Barnsley	Silksworth Jnrs	09.52	55	6	-	0
Hartlepools U	Tr	02.56	55-60	179	-	11
ANDERSON William (Willie) John						
Liverpool, 24 January, 1947 (W)						
Manchester U	App	02.64	63-66	7	2	0
Aston Villa	Tr	01.67	66-72	229	2	36
Cardiff C	Tr	02.73	72-76	122	4	12
ANDERSON William Ross						
Kilmarnock, 13 November, 1917 Died 1981 (CF)						
Millwall	Dundee	07.44	46-47	32	-	6
ANDERSSON Anders Per						
Tomelilla, Sweden, 15 March, 1974 Sweden int (M)						
Blackburn Rov	FF Malmo (Swe)	06.97	97	1	3	0
ANDERSSON Andreas Claes						
Osterhoninge, Sweden, 10 April, 1974 Sweden 23 (F)						
Newcastle U	AC Milan (It)	01.98	97-98	21	6	4
ANDERSSON Patrik Jonas						
Borgeby, Sweden, 18 August, 1971 Sweden int (CD)						
Blackburn Rov	FF Malmo (Swe)	12.92	92-93	7	5	0
ANDERTON Darren Robert						
Southampton, 3 March, 1972 EYth/Eu21-12/EB-1/E-30 (M)						
Portsmouth	YT	02.90	90-91	53	9	7
Tottenham H	Tr	06.92	92-03	273	26	34
Birmingham C	Tr	08.04	04	9	11	3
ANDERTON John						
Skelmersdale, 7 February, 1933 (FB)						
Everton	Jnrs	03.51				
Torquay U	Tr	07.54	54-57	40	-	2
ANDERTON Steven David						
Lancaster, 2 October, 1969 (M)						
Preston NE	YT	07.88	89	0	1	0
ANDERTON Sylvan James						
Reading, 23 November, 1934 (WH)						
Reading	Jnrs	06.52	52-58	155	-	18
Chelsea	Tr	03.59	58-61	76	-	2
Queens Park Rgrs	Tr	01.62	61	4	-	0
ANDRADE Jose Manuel						
Cape Verde Islands, 1 June, 1970 (F)						
Stoke C (L)	Acad de Futbol (Por)	03.95	94	2	2	1
Stoke C (L)	Academica Viscu (Por)	08.97	97	4	8	1
ANDRE Carlos Paulino de Oli						
Lisbon, Portugal, 28 November, 1971 (M)						
Walsall	Vitoria Guimaraes (Por)	12.01	01	5	0	0
ANDRE Pierre-Yves						
Lannion, France, 14 May, 1974 (F)						
Bolton W (L)	Nantes (Fr)	01.03	02	0	9	0
ANDREASSEN Svein Are						
Hadsel, Norway, 3 July, 1968 (M)						
Portsmouth (L)	Lillestrom (Nor)	12.98	98	0	2	0
ANDREASSON Marcus						
Monrovia, Liberia, 13 July, 1978 (CD)						
Bristol Rov	Osters IF (Swe)	07.98	98-99	5	1	0
Bristol Rov	Kalmar FF (Swe)	03.00	99-00	9	0	1
ANDRESEN Martin						
Oslo, Norway, 2 February, 1977 NoYth/Nou21/No-12 (M)						
Wimbledon	Stabaek (Nor)	10.99	99	4	10	1
Blackburn Rov (L)	Stabaek (Nor)	01.04	03	11	0	0
ANDREW Calvin						
Luton, 19 December, 1986 (F)						
Luton T	Sch	09.04	04	2	6	0
ANDREW George						
Glasgow, 24 November, 1945 Died 1993 (CD)						
West Ham U	Possilpark Jnrs	09.63	66	2	0	0
ANDREW Matthew (Matt)						
Johnstone, 5 January, 1922 Died 1999 (WH)						
Bristol C		10.47				
Swansea T	Tr	08.48	48-50	4	-	0
Workington	Tr	06.51	51	22	-	0
ANDREW Ronald (Ron) Edward Harold						
Bebington, 5 January, 1936 (CD)						
Stoke C	Ellesmere Port T	05.54	57-63	115	-	1
Port Vale	Tr	06.64	64	8	-	1
ANDREWS Benjamin (Ben) Philip						
Burton-on-Trent, 18 November, 1980 (FB)						
Brighton & Hove A	YT	03.98	97-98	2	2	0
ANDREWS Bradley James						
Bristol, 8 December, 1979 (M)						
Norwich C	YT	07.98				
Bristol Rov	Tr	03.99	98	3	0	0
ANDREWS Cecil (Archie) James						
Alton, 1 November, 1930 Died 1986 (WH)						
Portsmouth		01.49				
Crystal Palace	Tr	06.52	52-55	104	-	12
Queens Park Rgrs	Tr	06.56	56-57	58	-	1
ANDREWS Derek						
Bury, 14 December, 1934 (IF)						
Rochdale		03.55	55	22	-	4
ANDREWS Gary Michael						
Nottingham, 12 May, 1968 (FB)						
Nottingham F	App	09.85				
Peterborough U	Tr	08.88	88-89	42	1	0
ANDREWS George						
Dudley, 23 April, 1942 (F)						
Luton T	Vono Sports	01.60				
Cardiff C	Lower Gornal Ath	10.65	65-66	43	0	21
Southport	Tr	02.67	66-69	115	2	41
Shrewsbury T	Tr	11.69	69-72	123	1	49
Walsall	Tr	01.73	72-76	156	3	38
ANDREWS Glendon (Glen)						
Dudley, 11 February, 1945 (FB)						
Manchester U	Jnrs	09.63				
Wolverhampton W	Tr	07.66				
Bradford PA	Tr	09.67	67-68	47	1	6
ANDREWS Ian Edmund						
Nottingham, 1 December, 1964 EYth/Eu21-1 (G)						
Leicester C	App	12.82	83-87	126	0	0
Swindon T	L	01.84	83	1	0	0
Leeds U (L)	Glasgow Celtic	12.88	88	1	0	0
Southampton	Glasgow Celtic	12.89	89-93	10	0	0
Bournemouth	Tr	09.94	94-95	64	0	0
ANDREWS James (Jimmy) Patrick						
Invergordon, 1 February, 1927 (W)						
West Ham U	Dundee	11.51	51-55	114	-	21
Leyton Orient	Tr	06.56	56-58	36	-	8
Queens Park Rgrs	Tr	06.59	59-61	82	-	16
ANDREWS John Edward						
York, 3 February, 1950 (G)						
York C (Am)	Moor Lane YC	08.68	68	11	0	0
ANDREWS John Henry						
Cork, 27 September, 1978 (FB)						
Coventry C	YT	05.97				
Mansfield T	Grantham T	10.99	99-00	34	4	1
ANDREWS Keith Joseph						
Dublin, 13 September, 1980 (M)						
Wolverhampton W	YT	09.97	99-04	41	24	0
Oxford U	L	11.00	00	4	0	1
Stoke C	L	08.03	03	16	0	0
Walsall	L	03.04	03	10	0	2

League Club	Source	Date Signed	Seasons Played	Career Record Apps	Subs	Gls
ANDREWS Keri Anthony						
Swansea, 28 April, 1968 WYth						(W)
Swansea C	App	04.86	84-87	32	9	3
ANDREWS Lee David						
Carlisle, 23 April, 1983						(CD)
Carlisle U	YT	06.01	01-03	81	10	0
Rochdale	L	02.03	02	8	0	0
ANDREWS Leslie (Les) Lindon						
Dudley, 29 October, 1953						(F)
Wolverhampton W	Jnrs	09.72				
Scunthorpe U	L	03.74	73	7	2	1
ANDREWS Arthur **Percy**						
Alton, 12 June, 1922 Died 1985						(FB)
York C	Portsmouth (Am)	09.47	47-54	176	-	0
ANDREWS Philip (Phil) Donald						
Andover, 14 September, 1976						(F)
Brighton & Hove A	YT	05.95	93-96	2	23	1
ANDREWS Wayne Michael Hill						
Paddington, 25 November, 1977						(F)
Watford	YT	07.96	95-97	16	12	4
Cambridge U	L	10.98	98	1	1	0
Peterborough U	L	02.99	98	8	2	5
Oldham Ath	Chesham U	05.02	02	28	9	11
Colchester U	Tr	08.03	03-04	36	10	14
Crystal Palace	Tr	09.04	04	0	9	0
ANDRUSZEWSKI Emanuel (Manny) Franciszek						
Eastleigh, 4 October, 1955						(FB)
Southampton	App	10.73	74-79	82	1	3
Aldershot	Tampa Bay (USA)	08.82	82	25	2	0
ANELKA Nicolas						
Versailles, France, 14 March, 1979 FrYth/Fru21/Fr-28						(F)
Arsenal	Paris St Germain (Fr)	03.97	96-98	50	15	23
Liverpool (L)	Paris St Germain (Fr)	12.01	01	13	7	4
Manchester C	Paris St Germain (Fr)	07.02	02-04	87	2	37
ANGEL Juan Pablo						
Medellin, Colombia, 24 October, 1975 ColombiaYth/Colombia 30						(F)
Aston Villa	River Plate (Arg)	01.01	00-04	104	17	37
ANGEL Mark						
Newcastle, 23 August, 1975 ESemiPro-3						(W)
Sunderland	Walker Central	12.93				
Oxford U	Tr	08.95	95-97	40	33	4
West Bromwich A	Tr	07.98	98-99	4	21	1
Darlington	Tr	08.00	00	1	4	0
Boston U	Tr	06.01	02-03	36	18	6
ANGELL Brett Ashley Mark						
Marlborough, 20 August, 1968						(F)
Portsmouth	YT	08.86				
Derby Co	Cheltenham T	02.88				
Stockport Co	Tr	10.88	88-89	60	10	28
Southend U	Tr	08.90	90-93	109	6	47
Everton	L	09.93	93	0	1	0
Everton	Tr	01.94	93-94	16	3	1
Sunderland	Tr	03.95	94-95	10	0	0
Sheffield U	L	01.96	95	6	0	2
West Bromwich A	L	03.96	95	0	3	0
Stockport Co	Tr	08.96	96-99	122	4	50
Notts Co	L	12.99	99	6	0	5
Preston NE	L	02.00	99	9	6	8
Walsall	Tr	07.00	00-01	36	25	16
Rushden & Diamonds	Tr	02.02	01	3	2	2
Port Vale	Tr	08.02	02	13	2	5
Queens Park Rgrs	Tr	11.02	02	8	5	0
ANGELL Darren James						
Marlborough, 19 January, 1967						(CD)
Portsmouth	Newbury T	06.85				
Colchester U	L	12.87	87	1	0	0
ANGELL Peter Frank						
Eton, 11 January, 1932 Died 1979						(WH)
Queens Park Rgrs	Slough T	07.53	53-64	417	-	37
ANGUS John (Jack)						
Amble, 12 March, 1909 Died 1965						(CD)
Wolverhampton W	Amble Welfare	09.28				
Exeter C	Scunthorpe & Lindsey U	05.30	30-47	246	-	1
ANGUS John						
Warkworth, 2 September, 1938 EYth/Eu23-7/FLge-1/E-1						(FB)
Burnley	Amble BC	09.55	56-71	438	1	4

League Club	Source	Date Signed	Seasons Played	Career Record Apps	Subs	Gls
ANGUS Michael (Mike) Anthony						
Middlesbrough, 28 October, 1960						(M)
Middlesbrough	Jnrs	08.78	79-81	35	2	1
Scunthorpe U	L	09.82	82	20	0	2
Southend U	Tr	08.83				
Darlington	Tr	03.84	83-84	18	0	7
ANGUS Stevland (Stev) Dennis						
Westminster, 16 September, 1980						(CD)
West Ham U	YT	07.99				
Bournemouth	L	08.00	00	7	2	0
Cambridge U	Tr	07.01	01-04	134	1	1
Hull C	L	12.04	04	1	1	0
Scunthorpe U	L	01.05	04	9	0	0
ANGUS Terence (Terry) Norman						
Coventry, 14 January, 1966						(CD)
Northampton T	VS Rugby	08.90	90-92	115	1	6
Fulham	Tr	07.93	93-96	107	15	5
ANNAN Richard Amondo						
Leeds, 4 December, 1968						(FB)
Leeds U	App	12.86				
Doncaster Rov	Tr	10.87				
Crewe Alex	Guiseley	05.92	92-93	17	2	1
ANNON Darren Carlton						
Chelsea, 17 February, 1972						(W)
Brentford	Carshalton Ath	03.94	93-95	14	6	2
ANSAH Andrew (Andy)						
Lewisham, 19 March, 1969						(F)
Brentford	Dorking	03.89	88-89	3	5	2
Southend U	Tr	03.90	89-95	141	16	33
Brentford	L	11.94	94	2	1	1
Brentford	L	11.95	95	6	0	1
Peterborough U	Tr	03.96	95	0	2	1
Gillingham	Tr	03.96	95	0	2	0
Leyton Orient	Tr	12.96	96	0	2	0
Brighton & Hove A	Heybridge Swifts	11.97	97-98	10	15	3
ANSELIN Cedric						
Lens, France, 24 July, 1977 FrYth						(M)
Norwich C	Bordeaux (Fr)	03.99	98-99	22	4	1
Cambridge U	Mildenhall T	11.04	04	2	0	0
ANSELL Barry						
Birmingham, 29 September, 1947						(FB)
Aston Villa	Jnrs	10.67	67	1	0	0
ANSELL Gary Scott						
Ilford, 8 November, 1978						(M)
Barnet	Barking	08.99	99	0	3	0
ANSELL William **John (Jack)**						
Newport Pagnell, 4 August, 1921						(G)
Northampton T	Bletchley Brick Works	03.48	47-51	131	-	0
ANSLOW Stanley (Stan) Thomas						
Hackney, 5 May, 1931						(FB)
Millwall	Eton Manor	03.51	51-58	131	-	13
ANTHONY Graham John						
Jarrow, 9 August, 1975						(M)
Sheffield U	YT	07.93	94-96	0	3	0
Scarborough	L	03.96	95	2	0	0
Swindon T	Tr	03.97	96	3	0	0
Plymouth Arg	Tr	08.97	97	5	0	0
Carlisle U	Tr	11.97	97-99	58	11	3
ANTHONY Thomas (Tom) Henry						
Hounslow, 16 August, 1943						(FB)
Brentford	Jnrs	12.61	62	33	-	1
ANTHROBUS Stephen (Steve) Anthony						
Lewisham, 10 November, 1968						(F)
Millwall	Jnrs	08.86	87-89	19	2	4
Wimbledon	Tr	02.90	89-92	27	1	0
Peterborough U	L	01.94	93	2	0	0
Chester C	L	08.94	94	7	0	0
Shrewsbury T	Tr	08.95	95-96	60	12	16
Crewe Alex	Tr	03.97	96-98	53	8	9
Oxford U	Tr	07.99	99-00	38	18	3
ANTIC Radomir (Raddy)						
Zitiste, Yugoslavia, 22 November, 1949 Yugoslavia int						(M)
Luton T	Real Zaragoza (Sp)	07.80	80-83	54	40	9
ANTOINE-CURIER Mickael						
Orsay, France, 5 March, 1983						(F)
Preston NE	Nancy (Fr)	11.00				

League Club	Source	Date Signed	Seasons Played	Career Record Apps	Subs	Gls
Nottingham F	Tr	06.01				
Brentford	L	03.03	02	11	0	3
Oldham Ath	Tr	08.03	03	5	3	2
Kidderminster Hrs	Tr	09.03	03	0	1	0
Rochdale	Tr	09.03	03	5	3	1
Sheffield Wed	Tr	11.03	03	0	1	0
Notts Co	Tr	02.04	03	4	0	1
Grimsby T	Tr	03.04	03	3	2	0
ANTONIO George Rowlands						
Whitchurch, 20 October, 1914 Died 1997						(IF)
Stoke C	Oswestry T	02.36	35-46	84	-	13
Derby Co	Tr	03.47	46-47	18	-	2
Doncaster Rov	Tr	10.48	48-49	34	-	7
Mansfield T	Tr	10.49	49-50	67	-	2
ANTWI Agyei **William (Will)** Kwabena						
Epsom, 19 October, 1982						(CD)
Crystal Palace	Sch	07.02	02	0	4	0
ANYA Ikechi						
Glasgow, 3 January, 1988						(M)
Wycombe W	Sch	●	04	0	3	0
ANYINSAH Joseph (Joe) Greene						
Bristol, 8 October, 1984						(M)
Bristol C	YT	10.01	04	2	5	0
APPLEBY Andrew (Andy)						
Seaham, 11 October, 1985						(F)
Hartlepool U	Sch	●	04	0	15	2
APPLEBY James (Jim) Park						
Shotton Colliery, 15 June, 1934						(CD)
Burnley	Wingate CW	02.53	56	1	-	0
Blackburn Rov	Tr	02.58	58-61	2	-	0
Southport	Tr	10.61	61	13	-	0
Chester	Tr	06.62	62	1	-	0
APPLEBY Matthew (Matty) Wilfred						
Middlesbrough, 16 April, 1972						(M)
Newcastle U	YT	05.90	90-93	18	2	0
Darlington	L	11.93	93	10	0	1
Darlington	Tr	06.94	94-95	77	2	7
Barnsley	Tr	07.96	96-00	131	8	7
Oldham Ath	Tr	01.02	01-04	36	10	2
Darlington	Tr	03.05	04	10	0	0
APPLEBY Richard (Richie) Dean						
Middlesbrough, 18 September, 1975 EYth						(M)
Newcastle U	YT	08.93				
Ipswich T	Tr	12.95	95	0	3	0
Swansea C	Tr	08.96	96-01	90	30	11
Kidderminster Hrs	Tr	11.01	01	18	1	4
Hull C	Tr	07.02	02	6	0	0
Kidderminster Hrs	Tr	07.04	04	6	3	1
APPLEBY Robert (Bob)						
Warkworth, 15 January, 1940						(G)
Middlesbrough	Amble Welfare	05.57	59-66	99	0	0
APPLETON Colin Harry						
Scarborough, 7 March, 1936 FLge-1						(WH)
Leicester C	Scarborough	03.54	54-65	277	0	19
Charlton Ath	Tr	06.66	66	28	0	1
Barrow	Tr	08.67	67-68	39	4	1
APPLETON Michael Antony						
Salford, 4 December, 1975						(M)
Manchester U	YT	07.94				
Lincoln C	L	09.95	95	4	0	0
Grimsby T	L	01.97	96	10	0	3
Preston NE	Tr	08.97	97-00	90	25	12
West Bromwich A	Tr	01.01	00-01	33	0	0
APPLETON Ronald (Ron)						
Cleator Moor, 24 September, 1932						(W)
Workington	Frizington	02.53	52	3	-	0
APPLETON Stephen (Steve)						
Liverpool, 27 July, 1973						(FB)
Wigan Ath	YT	09.90	90-92	31	17	1
APPLETON Thomas (Tom) Henry						
Stanley, 9 June, 1936						(WH)
Burnley	Annfield Plain	08.54				
Gateshead	Tr	08.58	58	26	-	0
ARANALDE Zigor						
Guipuzcoa, Spain, 28 February, 1973						(FB)
Walsall	CD Logrones (Sp)	08.00	00-04	183	12	5
Sheffield Wed	Tr	03.05	04	1	1	0
ARBER Mark Andrew						
Johannesburg, South Africa, 9 October, 1977						(CD)
Tottenham H	YT	03.96				
Barnet	Tr	09.98	98-00	123	2	15
Peterborough U	Tr	12.02	02-03	67	2	5
Oldham Ath	Tr	07.04	04	13	1	1
Peterborough U	Tr	12.04	04	21	0	0
ARBER Robert (Bobby) Leonard						
Poplar, 13 January, 1951						(FB)
Arsenal	App	03.68				
Orient	Tr	07.70	71-72	31	0	0
ARBLASTER Michael **Brian**						
Kensington, 6 June, 1943						(G)
Sheffield U	Mosborough Trinity	07.62				
Chesterfield	Tr	12.64	64-66	55	0	0
Scunthorpe U	Tr	06.67	67	10	0	0
Barnsley	Tr	05.68	67-73	111	0	0
ARCA Julio Andres						
Quilmes Bernal, Argentina, 31 January, 1981 ArYth						(M)
Sunderland	Argentinos Jnrs (Arg)	08.00	00-04	123	10	16
ARCHDEACON Owen Duncan						
Greenock, 4 March, 1966 SYth/Su21-1						(W)
Barnsley	Glasgow Celtic	07.89	89-95	222	11	22
Carlisle U	Tr	07.96	96-97	64	0	10
ARCHELL Graham Leonard						
Islington, 8 February, 1950						(W)
Orient	Jnrs	11.67	67-68	5	2	0
ARCHER John						
Biddulph, 18 June, 1941						(M)
Port Vale	Jnrs	07.58	59-60	10	-	3
Bournemouth	Tr	07.61	61-65	139	0	37
Crewe Alex	Tr	09.66	66-67	59	1	16
Huddersfield T	Tr	01.68	67	7	2	0
Chesterfield	Tr	05.69	69-71	116	0	24
ARCHER John George						
Whitstable, 9 April, 1936 Died 1987						(G)
Grimsby T	Whitstable T	04.54	54	10	-	0
ARCHER Lee						
Bristol, 6 November, 1972						(M)
Bristol Rov	YT	07.91	91-96	104	22	15
ARCHER Philip (Phil)						
Rotherham, 25 August, 1952						(FB)
Reading	Sheffield U (App)	09.70	71	12	5	0
ARCHER Ronald (Ron)						
Barnsley, 3 September, 1933 ESch						(WH)
Barnsley	Jnrs	09.50	51-55	29	-	0
ARCHER William (Bill) Henry						
Scunthorpe, 5 February, 1914 Died 1992						(CD)
Lincoln C	Grantham	06.39				
Doncaster Rov	Tr	10.45	46-47	14	-	0
ARCHIBALD John **Murray**						
Carron, 19 March, 1917						(CF)
Wrexham		03.46	46	1	-	0
ARCHIBALD Steven (Steve)						
Glasgow, 27 September, 1956 Su21-5/S-27						(F)
Tottenham H	Aberdeen	05.80	80-83	128	3	58
Blackburn Rov (L)	Barcelona (Sp)	12.87	87	20	0	6
Reading	St Mirren	01.92	91	1	0	0
Fulham	Clyde	09.92	92	2	0	0
ARDILES Osvaldo (Ossie) Cesar						
Cordoba, Argentina, 3 August, 1952 Argentina int						(M)
Tottenham H	Huracan (Arg)	07.78	78-87	221	16	16
Blackburn Rov	L	03.88	87	5	0	0
Queens Park Rgrs	Tr	08.88	88	4	4	0
Swindon T	Fort Lauderdale (USA)	07.89	89	0	2	0
ARDLEY Neal Christopher						
Epsom, 1 September, 1972 Eu21-10						(M)
Wimbledon	YT	07.91	90-01	212	33	18
Watford	Tr	08.02	02-04	105	6	7
Cardiff C	Tr	03.05	04	8	0	1
ARDRON Walter (Wally)						
Rotherham, 19 September, 1918 Died 1978						(CF)
Rotherham U	Denaby U	12.38	38-48	123	-	98
Nottingham F	Tr	07.49	49-54	182	-	123

ARENDSE Andre
Cape Town, South Africa, 27 June, 1967 South Africa 38 (G)

League Club	Source	Date Signed	Seasons Played	Apps	Subs	Gls
Fulham	Cape Town Spurs (SA)	08.97	97	6	0	0
Oxford U	Tr	07.99	99	13	0	0

ARENTOFT Preben (Ben)
Copenhagen, Denmark, 1 November, 1942 Denmark int (M)

League Club	Source	Date Signed	Seasons Played	Apps	Subs	Gls
Newcastle U	Morton	03.69	68-70	46	4	2
Blackburn Rov	Tr	09.71	71-73	94	0	3

ARGUE James (Jimmy)
Glasgow, 26 November, 1911 Died 1978 (IF)

League Club	Source	Date Signed	Seasons Played	Apps	Subs	Gls
Birmingham	St Roch's	12.31				
Chelsea	Tr	05.33	33-46	118	-	30

ARINS Anthony (Tony) Francis
Chesterfield, 26 October, 1958 (FB)

League Club	Source	Date Signed	Seasons Played	Apps	Subs	Gls
Burnley	App	07.76	78-79	29	0	2
Leeds U	Tr	05.80	81	0	1	0
Scunthorpe U	Tr	11.81	81	20	0	1

ARKINS Vincent (Vinny) Thomas
Dublin, 18 September, 1970 IRYth/IRu21-8/IRB (F)

League Club	Source	Date Signed	Seasons Played	Apps	Subs	Gls
Notts Co	Shelbourne	09.95	95-96	30	8	8

ARKWRIGHT Ian
Shafton, 18 September, 1959 (W)

League Club	Source	Date Signed	Seasons Played	Apps	Subs	Gls
Wolverhampton W	App	09.77	78	3	1	0
Wrexham	Tr	03.80	79-83	102	2	10
Torquay U	L	03.84	83	2	0	0

ARMES Ivan William
Lowestoft, 6 April, 1924 (WH)

League Club	Source	Date Signed	Seasons Played	Apps	Subs	Gls
Norwich C	Brooke Marine	11.46	46-49	61	-	1
Exeter C	Tr	12.51	51-52	14	-	2

ARMFIELD James (Jimmy) Christopher
Denton, 21 September, 1935 Eu23-9/FLge-12/E-43 (FB)

League Club	Source	Date Signed	Seasons Played	Apps	Subs	Gls
Blackpool	Jnrs	09.54	54-70	568	0	6

ARMITAGE Andrew (Andy) Mark
Leeds, 17 October, 1968 (FB)

League Club	Source	Date Signed	Seasons Played	Apps	Subs	Gls
Leeds U	YT	08.87				
Rochdale	Tr	07.88	88	33	3	0

ARMITAGE (FENTON) Kenneth (Ken) James
Sheffield, 23 October, 1920 Died 1952 (CD)

League Club	Source	Date Signed	Seasons Played	Apps	Subs	Gls
Leyton Orient	Gainsborough Trinity	04.46	46	7	-	0
Oldham Ath	Tr	07.47	47	5	-	0

ARMITAGE Louis Greaves
Hull, 15 December, 1921 Died 2000 (IF)

League Club	Source	Date Signed	Seasons Played	Apps	Subs	Gls
Rotherham U		12.40	46-47	15	-	9
Grimsby T	Tr	01.48	47	8	-	2

ARMITAGE Stanley (Stan) Albert
Woolwich, 5 June, 1919 Died 1997 (IF)

League Club	Source	Date Signed	Seasons Played	Apps	Subs	Gls
Queens Park Rgrs		06.46	46	2	-	0

ARMSTRONG Alun
Gateshead, 22 February, 1975 (F)

League Club	Source	Date Signed	Seasons Played	Apps	Subs	Gls
Newcastle U	YT	10.93				
Stockport Co	Tr	06.94	94-97	151	8	48
Middlesbrough	Tr	02.98	97-99	10	19	9
Huddersfield T	L	03.00	99	4	2	0
Ipswich T	Tr	12.00	00-03	50	29	14
Bradford C	L	12.03	03	6	0	1
Darlington	Tr	09.04	04	31	1	9

ARMSTRONG Christopher (Chris)
Newcastle, 5 August, 1982 EYth/Eu20 (FB)

League Club	Source	Date Signed	Seasons Played	Apps	Subs	Gls
Bury	YT	03.01	00-01	33	0	1
Oldham Ath	Tr	10.01	01-02	64	1	1
Sheffield U	Tr	08.03	03	4	8	1

ARMSTRONG Christopher (Chris) David
Ripon, 8 November, 1984 (F)

League Club	Source	Date Signed	Seasons Played	Apps	Subs	Gls
Leeds U	YT	11.01				
Stockport Co	Queen of the South	01.05	04	9	2	1

ARMSTRONG Christopher (Chris) Peter
Newcastle, 19 June, 1971 EB-1 (F)

League Club	Source	Date Signed	Seasons Played	Apps	Subs	Gls
Wrexham	Llay Welfare	03.89	89-90	40	20	13
Millwall	Tr	08.91	91-92	11	17	5
Crystal Palace	Tr	09.92	92-94	118	0	45
Tottenham H	Tr	06.95	95-00	117	24	48
Bolton W	Tr	08.02				
Wrexham	Tr	07.03	03-04	37	22	13

ARMSTRONG Steven **Craig**
South Shields, 23 May, 1975 (CD)

League Club	Source	Date Signed	Seasons Played	Apps	Subs	Gls
Nottingham F	YT	06.92	97-98	24	16	0
Burnley	L	12.94	94	4	0	0
Bristol Rov	L	01.96	95	4	1	0
Bristol Rov	L	03.96	95	9	0	0
Gillingham	L	10.96	96	10	0	0
Watford	L	01.97	96	3	0	0
Watford	L	03.97	96	12	0	0
Huddersfield T	Tr	02.99	98-01	101	6	5
Sheffield Wed	Tr	02.02	01-03	29	6	1
Grimsby T	L	02.04	03	9	0	1
Bradford C	Tr	01.05	04	4	3	0

ARMSTRONG David
Durham, 26 December, 1954 Eu23-4/EB/E-3 (M)

League Club	Source	Date Signed	Seasons Played	Apps	Subs	Gls
Middlesbrough	App	01.72	71-80	357	2	59
Southampton	Tr	08.81	81-86	222	0	59
Bournemouth	Tr	07.87	87	6	3	2

ARMSTRONG David (Dave) Thomas
Mile End, 9 November, 1942 (W)

League Club	Source	Date Signed	Seasons Played	Apps	Subs	Gls
Millwall	Hornchurch	12.65	65-67	14	6	1
Brighton & Hove A	Tr	09.68	68-69	38	6	6

ARMSTRONG Derek James
Carlisle, 16 March, 1939 (IF)

League Club	Source	Date Signed	Seasons Played	Apps	Subs	Gls
Blackpool		08.58	58	1	-	0
Carlisle U	Morecambe	08.61	61	1	-	0

ARMSTRONG Eric
Hebburn, 25 May, 1921 Died 1975 (WH)

League Club	Source	Date Signed	Seasons Played	Apps	Subs	Gls
West Ham U	Cramlington Welfare	01.47	47	1	-	0

ARMSTRONG Gary Stephen
West Ham, 2 January, 1958 (FB)

League Club	Source	Date Signed	Seasons Played	Apps	Subs	Gls
Gillingham	Jnrs	01.76	75-79	82	4	2
Wimbledon	Tr	03.80	79-81	71	0	0
Gillingham	Barnet	11.83	83	7	1	0
Crewe Alex	Tr	08.84	84	31	0	0

ARMSTRONG George
Hebburn, 9 August, 1944 Died 2000 EYth/Eu23-5 (W)

League Club	Source	Date Signed	Seasons Played	Apps	Subs	Gls
Arsenal	Jnrs	08.61	61-76	490	10	53
Leicester C	Tr	09.77	77-78	14	1	0
Stockport Co	Tr	09.78	78	34	0	0

ARMSTRONG Gerard (Gerry) Joseph
Belfast, 23 May, 1954 NI-63 (F)

League Club	Source	Date Signed	Seasons Played	Apps	Subs	Gls
Tottenham H	Bangor	11.75	76-80	65	19	10
Watford	Tr	11.80	80-82	50	26	12
West Bromwich A	Real Malorca (Sp)	08.85	85	7	1	0
Chesterfield	L	01.86	85	12	0	1
Brighton & Hove A	Tr	07.86	86-88	30	17	6
Millwall	L	01.87	86	7	0	0

ARMSTRONG Gordon Ian
Newcastle, 15 July, 1967 (M)

League Club	Source	Date Signed	Seasons Played	Apps	Subs	Gls
Sunderland	App	07.85	84-95	331	18	50
Bristol C	L	08.95	95	6	0	0
Northampton T	L	01.96	95	4	0	1
Bury	Tr	07.96	96-98	49	22	4
Burnley	Tr	08.98	98-02	88	17	5

ARMSTRONG Ian
Kirkby, 16 November, 1981 ESch/EYth (M)

League Club	Source	Date Signed	Seasons Played	Apps	Subs	Gls
Liverpool	YT	12.98				
Port Vale	Tr	07.01	01-04	50	39	14

ARMSTRONG James (Jimmy)
Ulverston, 14 September, 1943 (W)

League Club	Source	Date Signed	Seasons Played	Apps	Subs	Gls
Barrow	App	01.61	60-62	17	-	3
Chesterfield	Tr	07.63	63	7	-	0

ARMSTRONG Joel
Chesterfield, 25 September, 1981 (G)

League Club	Source	Date Signed	Seasons Played	Apps	Subs	Gls
Chesterfield	YT	07.01	99-00	3	1	0

ARMSTRONG John
Airdrie, 5 September, 1936 (G)

League Club	Source	Date Signed	Seasons Played	Apps	Subs	Gls
Barrow	Bellshill Ath	03.58	57-58	21	-	0
Nottingham F	Tr	11.58	58-62	20	-	0
Portsmouth	Tr	02.63	62-66	79	0	0
Southport	Tr	08.67	67-70	86	0	0

ARMSTRONG Adam **John (Johnny)**
Blackpool, 6 June, 1925 Died 2004 LoI-2 (W)

League Club	Source	Date Signed	Seasons Played	Apps	Subs	Gls
Chesterfield	Petershill Jnrs	09.49	49	1	-	0

ARMSTRONG Joseph (Joe)
Brighton, 16 November, 1931 Died 1986 (IF)

League Club	Source	Date Signed	Seasons Played	Apps	Subs	Gls
Southend U		11.52				
Barrow	Tr	07.53	53-57	103	-	33
Workington	Tr	03.58	57-58	25	-	10

League Club	Source	Date Signed	Seasons Played	Career Record Apps	Subs	Gls
ARMSTRONG Joseph (Joe) Michael						
Newcastle, 29 January, 1939						(IF)
Leeds U	Leslie BC	05.57				
Gateshead	Tr	07.59	59	22	-	9
ARMSTRONG Keith Thomas						
Corbridge, 11 October, 1957						(W)
Sunderland	Jnrs	01.75	77	7	4	0
Newport Co	L	08.78	78	3	1	0
Scunthorpe U	L	10.78	78	0	1	0
ARMSTRONG Kenneth (Ken)						
Bradford, 3 June, 1924 Died 1984 FLge/EB/E-1						(WH)
Chelsea	Bradford Rov	12.46	47-56	362	-	25
ARMSTRONG Kenneth (Ken) Charles						
Bridgnorth, 31 January, 1959						(CD)
Southampton	Kilmarnock	06.83	83	26	0	0
Notts Co	L	03.84	83	10	0	0
Birmingham C	Tr	08.84	84-85	58	0	2
ARMSTRONG Lee William						
Cockermouth, 19 October, 1972						(FB)
Carlisle U	YT	01.90	90-91	12	8	0
ARMSTRONG Paul George						
Dublin, 5 October, 1978 IRu21-2						(M)
Brighton & Hove A	YT	07.97	97-99	33	20	2
ARMSTRONG John **Robert**						
Newcastle, 1 November, 1938						(IF)
Darlington		07.59	59	1	-	0
ARMSTRONG Stephen Mark						
Birkenhead, 23 July, 1976						(F)
Watford	Vastra Frolunda (Swe)	10.00	00	0	3	0
ARMSTRONG Terence (Terry)						
Barnsley, 10 July, 1958						(M)
Huddersfield T	App	07.76	76-78	36	4	2
Port Vale	Tr	02.81	80-84	113	3	12
ARMSTRONG Thomas (Tom)						
Carlisle, 27 February, 1920 Died 1985						(WH)
Carlisle U	Holme Head	08.46	46	4	-	0
ARNDALE Neil Darren						
Bristol, 26 April, 1984 EYth						(FB)
Bristol Rov	Sch	07.03	01-03	2	3	0
ARNELL Alan Jack						
Chichester, 25 November, 1933						(IF)
Liverpool	Worthing	03.54	53-60	69	-	33
Tranmere Rov	Tr	02.61	60-62	68	-	34
Halifax T	Tr	07.63	63	14	-	6
ARNISON Paul Simon						
Hartlepool, 18 September, 1977						(FB)
Newcastle U	YT	03.96				
Hartlepool U	Tr	03.00	99-03	53	24	3
Carlisle U	Tr	10.03	03	20	6	1
ARNISON Joseph **William (Billy)**						
Johannesburg, South Africa, 27 June, 1924 Died 1996						(CF)
Luton T	Glasgow Rgrs	08.48	48-50	44	-	19
ARNOLD Eric Arthur						
Kessingland, 13 September, 1922 Died 2002						(FB)
Norwich C	Lowestoft T	09.47	47-51	13	-	0
ARNOLD Ian						
Durham, 4 July, 1972						(F)
Middlesbrough	YT	01.90	90-91	0	3	0
Carlisle U	Tr	08.92	92-94	34	13	11
ARNOLD James (Jim) Alexander						
Stafford, 6 August, 1950 ESemiPro						(G)
Blackburn Rov	Stafford Rgrs	06.79	79-80	58	0	0
Everton	Tr	08.81	81-83	48	0	0
Preston NE	L	10.82	82	6	0	0
Port Vale	Tr	08.85	85-86	53	0	0
ARNOLD John Walter Leonard						
Southwark, 6 December, 1954						(F)
Charlton Ath	App	12.72	72-73	1	4	0
ARNOLD Roderick (Rod) James						
Wolverhampton, 3 June, 1952						(G)
Wolverhampton W	App	06.70				
Mansfield T	L	02.71	70	17	0	0
Mansfield T	Tr	03.73	72-83	423	0	0

League Club	Source	Date Signed	Seasons Played	Career Record Apps	Subs	Gls
ARNOLD Stephen (Steve) Frank						
Crewe, 5 January, 1951						(M)
Crewe Alex	App	01.69	68-70	13	2	0
Liverpool	Tr	09.70	70	1	0	0
Southport	L	01.72	71	16	0	3
Torquay U	L	09.72	72	2	1	1
Rochdale	Tr	06.73	73	37	3	1
ARNOTT Andrew (Andy) John						
Chatham, 18 October, 1973						(M)
Gillingham	YT	05.91	91-95	50	23	12
Leyton Orient	Tr	01.96	95-96	47	3	6
Fulham	Tr	06.97	97	0	1	0
Brighton & Hove A	Tr	10.98	98-99	27	1	2
Colchester U	Tr	09.99	99-00	5	10	0
ARNOTT John Henry						
Sydenham, 6 September, 1932						(WH)
West Ham U	Churchfield OB	07.54	53-54	6	-	2
Shrewsbury T	Tr	08.55	55	30	-	6
Bournemouth	Tr	07.56	56-61	173	-	21
Gillingham	Tr	08.62	62-67	183	2	2
ARNOTT Kevin William						
Gateshead, 28 September, 1958						(M)
Sunderland	App	09.76	76-81	132	1	16
Blackburn Rov	L	11.81	81	17	0	2
Sheffield U	Tr	06.82	82-86	120	1	11
Blackburn Rov	L	11.82	82	11	1	1
Rotherham U	L	03.83	82	9	0	2
Chesterfield	Vasalund (Swe)	11.87	87-89	67	4	4
ARNOTT George **William**						
Edinburgh, 29 May, 1935						(WH)
Crewe Alex	Berwick Rgrs	12.57	57	8	-	0
ARPHEXAD Pegguy Michel						
Les Abymes, Guadeloupe, 18 May, 1973						(G)
Leicester C	RC Lens (Fr)	08.97	97-99	17	4	0
Liverpool	Tr	07.00	01	1	1	0
Stockport Co	L	09.01	01	3	0	0
Coventry C	Tr	08.03	03	5	0	0
Notts Co	L	03.04	03	3	0	0
ARROWSMITH Alfred (Alf) William						
Manchester, 11 December, 1942 Died 2005						(F)
Liverpool	Ashton U	09.60	61-67	43	4	20
Bury	Tr	12.68	68-69	45	3	11
Rochdale	Tr	06.70	70-71	40	4	14
ARROWSMITH Brian William						
Barrow, 2 July, 1940						(CD)
Barrow	Vickers Sports	10.61	61-70	376	2	3
ARTELL David (Dave) John						
Rotherham, 22 November, 1980						(CD)
Rotherham U	YT	07.99	99-00	35	2	4
Shrewsbury T	L	09.02	02	27	1	1
Mansfield T	Tr	08.03	03-04	43	2	5
ARTETA Mikel						
San Sebastian, Spain, 26 March, 1982						(M)
Everton (L)	Real Sociedad (Sp)	01.05	04	10	2	1
ARTHUR Adam Joseph						
Nottingham, 27 October, 1985						(M)
York C	Sch	●	03	2	1	0
ARTHUR David Robert						
Bushbury, 9 March, 1960						(FB)
West Bromwich A	App	03.78	81	2	1	0
Walsall	Tr	08.82	82	8	1	0
ARTHUR John (Jackie)						
Edenfield, 14 December, 1917 Died 1986						(W)
Everton	Blackburn Rov (Am)	09.36				
Stockport Co	Tr	05.38	38	2	-	0
Chester	Tr	05.46	46	24	-	3
Rochdale	Tr	04.47	46-53	170	-	25
ARUNDEL Frank William						
Plymouth, 20 February, 1939 Died 1994						(W)
Plymouth Arg	Oak Villa	08.56	56	4	-	0
Torquay U	Tr	07.59	59-60	6	-	0
ASABA Carl Edward						
Westminster, 28 January, 1973						(F)
Brentford	Dulwich Hamlet	08.94	95-96	49	5	25
Colchester U	L	02.95	94	9	3	2
Reading	Tr	08.97	97-98	31	2	8
Gillingham	Tr	08.98	98-00	65	12	36

League Club	Source	Date Signed	Seasons Played	Career Record Apps	Subs	Gls
Sheffield U	Tr	03.01	00-02	52	15	23
Stoke C	Tr	08.03	03-04	40	30	9

ASAMOAH Derek
Accra, Ghana, 1 May, 1981 (F)

League Club	Source	Date Signed	Seasons Played	Apps	Subs	Gls
Northampton T	Slough T	07.01	01-03	27	86	10
Mansfield T	Tr	08.04	04	24	6	5
Lincoln C	Tr	03.05	04	8	2	0

ASANOVIC Aljosa
Split, Croatia, 14 December, 1965 Croatia int (M)

League Club	Source	Date Signed	Seasons Played	Apps	Subs	Gls
Derby Co	Real Valladolid (Sp)	06.96	96-97	37	1	7

ASH Mark Christian
Sheffield, 22 January, 1968 (FB)

League Club	Source	Date Signed	Seasons Played	Apps	Subs	Gls
Rotherham U	App	01.86	86-88	14	6	0
Scarborough	Tr	08.89	89-91	32	7	0

ASH Michael (Micky)
Sheffield, 4 September, 1943 ESch/EYth (M)

League Club	Source	Date Signed	Seasons Played	Apps	Subs	Gls
Sheffield U	App	11.60	63	3	-	1
Scunthorpe U	Tr	09.65	65-66	48	1	7

ASHALL George Henry
Killamarsh, 29 September, 1911 Died 1998 FLge-1 (W)

League Club	Source	Date Signed	Seasons Played	Apps	Subs	Gls
Wolverhampton W	Frickley Colliery	02.36	35-37	84	-	14
Coventry C	Tr	07.38	38-47	62	-	10

ASHALL James (Jimmy)
Temple Normanton, 13 December, 1933 (FB)

League Club	Source	Date Signed	Seasons Played	Apps	Subs	Gls
Leeds U	Hasland OB	10.51	55-60	89	-	0

ASHBEE Ian
Birmingham, 6 September, 1976 EYth (M)

League Club	Source	Date Signed	Seasons Played	Apps	Subs	Gls
Derby Co	YT	11.94	94	1	0	0
Cambridge U	Tr	12.96	96-01	192	11	11
Hull C	Tr	07.02	02-04	110	0	4

ASHBY Barry John
Park Royal, 2 November, 1970 (CD)

League Club	Source	Date Signed	Seasons Played	Apps	Subs	Gls
Watford	YT	12.88	89-93	101	13	3
Brentford	Tr	03.94	93-96	119	2	4
Gillingham	Tr	08.97	97-04	270	3	7

ASHCROFT Charles (Charlie) Thomas
Chorley, 3 July, 1926 EB (G)

League Club	Source	Date Signed	Seasons Played	Apps	Subs	Gls
Liverpool	Eccleston Jnrs	05.46	46-54	87	-	0
Ipswich T	Tr	06.55	55	7	-	0
Coventry C	Tr	06.57	57	19	-	0

ASHCROFT Kane John
Leeds, 19 March, 1986 (M)

League Club	Source	Date Signed	Seasons Played	Apps	Subs	Gls
York C	Sch	•	03	1	1	0

ASHCROFT Lee
Preston, 7 September, 1972 Eu21-1 (W)

League Club	Source	Date Signed	Seasons Played	Apps	Subs	Gls
Preston NE	YT	07.91	90-92	78	13	13
West Bromwich A	Tr	08.93	93-96	66	24	17
Notts Co	L	03.96	95	4	2	0
Preston NE	L	09.96	96	7	0	3
Preston NE	Tr	11.96	96-97	56	1	19
Grimsby T	Tr	08.98	98-99	52	9	15
Wigan Ath	Tr	08.00	00-01	37	9	8
Port Vale	L	10.02	02	3	0	0
Huddersfield T	L	12.02	02	4	0	0

ASHCROFT Llewellyn (Llew) Lloyd
Flint, 10 July, 1921 (W)

League Club	Source	Date Signed	Seasons Played	Apps	Subs	Gls
Tranmere Rov	Flint T	08.45	46	20	-	4

ASHCROFT William (Billy)
Liverpool, 1 October, 1952 (F)

League Club	Source	Date Signed	Seasons Played	Apps	Subs	Gls
Wrexham	Jnrs	10.70	70-77	196	23	72
Middlesbrough	Tr	09.77	77-81	139	20	21
Tranmere Rov	Twente Enschede (Holl)	08.85	85	16	7	2

ASHDJIAN John Anthony
Hackney, 13 September, 1972 (W)

League Club	Source	Date Signed	Seasons Played	Apps	Subs	Gls
Scarborough	Northampton T (YT)	07.91	91-93	40	27	14

ASHDOWN Jamie Lawrence
Wokingham, 30 November, 1980 (G)

League Club	Source	Date Signed	Seasons Played	Apps	Subs	Gls
Reading	YT	11.99	00-03	12	1	0
Bournemouth	L	08.02	02	2	0	0
Rushden & Diamonds	L	11.03	03	19	0	0
Portsmouth	Tr	07.04	04	16	0	0

ASHE Armour Donald
Paisley, 14 October, 1925 Died 1968 (FB)

League Club	Source	Date Signed	Seasons Played	Apps	Subs	Gls
Stockport Co	St Mirren	06.53	53	2	-	0
Accrington St	Tr	09.53	53-57	162	-	0
Gateshead	Tr	11.57	57-58	54	-	1
Southport	Tr	07.59	59	14	-	2

ASHE Norman James
Bloxwich, 16 November, 1943 ESch/EYth (W)

League Club	Source	Date Signed	Seasons Played	Apps	Subs	Gls
Aston Villa	App	05.61	59-61	5	-	0
Rotherham U	Tr	03.63	62	6	-	1

ASHENDEN Russell Edward
South Ockendon, 4 February, 1961 (M)

League Club	Source	Date Signed	Seasons Played	Apps	Subs	Gls
Northampton T	App	02.79	78-79	6	12	0

ASHENDEN Scott
Basildon, 3 February, 1974 (W)

League Club	Source	Date Signed	Seasons Played	Apps	Subs	Gls
Southend U	YT	07.92	92	4	1	0

ASHER Alistair Andrew
Leicester, 14 October, 1980 (FB)

League Club	Source	Date Signed	Seasons Played	Apps	Subs	Gls
Mansfield T	YT	06.99	99-01	53	20	0

ASHER Sydney (Syd) James
Portsmouth, 24 December, 1930 Died 1994 (CF)

League Club	Source	Date Signed	Seasons Played	Apps	Subs	Gls
Portsmouth	Jnrs	08.48				
Northampton T	Hastings U	11.56	56	21	-	11

ASHER Thomas (Tommy)
Dunscroft, 21 December, 1936 ESch (IF)

League Club	Source	Date Signed	Seasons Played	Apps	Subs	Gls
Notts Co	Ilkeston T	07.54	57-58	31	-	4

ASHFIELD George Owen
Manchester, 7 April, 1934 Died 1985 (FB)

League Club	Source	Date Signed	Seasons Played	Apps	Subs	Gls
Stockport Co	Jnrs	09.51				
Aston Villa	Tr	03.54	55-57	9	-	0
Chester	Tr	02.59	58	5	-	0

ASHFORD Ryan Marc
Honiton, 13 October, 1981 (FB)

League Club	Source	Date Signed	Seasons Played	Apps	Subs	Gls
Southampton	YT	01.01				
Torquay U	Tr	03.02	01	1	1	1

ASHIKODI Moses
Lagos, Nigeria, 27 June, 1987 EYth (M)

League Club	Source	Date Signed	Seasons Played	Apps	Subs	Gls
Millwall	Sch	•	02	0	5	0

ASHINGTON Ryan David
Torbay, 28 March, 1983 (F)

League Club	Source	Date Signed	Seasons Played	Apps	Subs	Gls
Torquay U	YT	07.01	00-02	9	7	0

ASHLEY John (Joe)
Clowne, 10 June, 1931 (G)

League Club	Source	Date Signed	Seasons Played	Apps	Subs	Gls
York C	Frickley Colliery	10.50	50	9	-	0

ASHLEY Kevin Mark
Birmingham, 31 December, 1968 (FB)

League Club	Source	Date Signed	Seasons Played	Apps	Subs	Gls
Birmingham C	App	01.87	86-90	56	1	1
Wolverhampton W	Tr	09.90	90-92	87	1	1
Peterborough U	Tr	08.94	94-95	36	0	0
Doncaster Rov	L	03.96	95	3	0	0

ASHMAN George **Allan**
Rotherham, 30 May, 1928 Died 2002 (CF)

League Club	Source	Date Signed	Seasons Played	Apps	Subs	Gls
Nottingham F	Sheffield U (Am)	04.46	48-49	13	-	3
Carlisle U	Tr	06.51	51-57	206	-	99

ASHMAN Ronald (Ron) George
Whittlesey, 19 May, 1926 Died 2004 (WH)

League Club	Source	Date Signed	Seasons Played	Apps	Subs	Gls
Norwich C	Whittlesey	05.44	47-63	592	-	55

ASHMORE George **Arthur**
Swadlincote, 11 August, 1946 (M)

League Club	Source	Date Signed	Seasons Played	Apps	Subs	Gls
Doncaster Rov	Frickley Colliery	11.66	66-67	3	0	0

ASHMORE Alfred **Maxwell (Max)**
Sheffield, 11 September, 1937 (G)

League Club	Source	Date Signed	Seasons Played	Apps	Subs	Gls
Sheffield U		08.57	57	1	-	0
Bradford C	Tr	07.61	61	9	-	0
Chesterfield	Tr	10.62	62	2	-	0

ASHTON Dean
Crewe, 24 November, 1983 EYth/Eu20/Eu21-6 (F)

League Club	Source	Date Signed	Seasons Played	Apps	Subs	Gls
Crewe Alex	YT	02.01	00-04	131	28	60
Norwich C	Tr	01.05	04	16	0	7

ASHTON Derrick
Worksop, 4 July, 1922 Died 1997 (FB)

League Club	Source	Date Signed	Seasons Played	Apps	Subs	Gls
Wolverhampton W		09.41				
Aston Villa	Tr	05.46	46-48	8	-	0

ASHTON John
Reading, 4 July, 1954 (F)

League Club	Source	Date Signed	Seasons Played	Apps	Subs	Gls
Reading	Jnrs	04.72	71-74	10	3	1

ASHTON Jonathan (Jon) Frank
Plymouth, 4 August, 1979 (FB)

League Club	Source	Date Signed	Seasons Played	Apps	Subs	Gls
Plymouth Arg	YT	07.97	98-99	27	7	0
Exeter C	Tr	07.00	00	7	6	0

ASHTON Jonathan (Jon) James
Nuneaton, 4 October, 1982 (CD)

League Club	Source	Date Signed	Seasons Played	Apps	Subs	Gls
Leicester C	YT	01.01	01-02	3	6	0
Notts Co	L	11.02	02	4	0	0
Oxford U	Tr	08.03	03-04	60	4	0

ASHTON Kenneth (Ken) James
Irlam, 12 December, 1936 (FB)

League Club	Source	Date Signed	Seasons Played	Apps	Subs	Gls
Stockport Co	Bolton W (Am)	09.56	57-61	39	-	0

ASHTON Neil John
Liverpool, 15 January, 1985 (M)

League Club	Source	Date Signed	Seasons Played	Apps	Subs	Gls
Tranmere Rov	Sch	04.03	03	0	1	0
Shrewsbury T	L	12.04	04	22	2	0

ASHTON Roger William
Llanidloes, 16 August, 1921 Died 1985 (G)

League Club	Source	Date Signed	Seasons Played	Apps	Subs	Gls
Wrexham		12.45				
Cardiff C		04.48	47	1	-	0
Newport Co	Bath C	12.49	49	10	-	0
Newport Co	Merthyr Tydfil	12.50	50	1	-	0

ASHURST John (Jackie)
Coatbridge, 12 October, 1954 (CD)

League Club	Source	Date Signed	Seasons Played	Apps	Subs	Gls
Sunderland	App	10.71	72-79	129	11	4
Blackpool	Tr	10.79	79-80	53	0	3
Carlisle U	Tr	08.81	81-85	194	0	2
Leeds U	Tr	07.86	86-88	88	1	1
Doncaster Rov	Tr	11.88	88-89	73	0	1
Doncaster Rov	Bridlington T	11.90	90-91	66	0	1
Rochdale	Tr	08.92	92	1	0	0

ASHURST Leonard (Len)
Liverpool, 10 March, 1939 EYth/Eu23-1 (FB)

League Club	Source	Date Signed	Seasons Played	Apps	Subs	Gls
Sunderland	Prescot Cables	12.57	58-69	403	5	4
Hartlepool	Tr	03.71	70-72	42	4	2

ASHWORTH Alec
Southport, 1 October, 1939 Died 1995 (IF)

League Club	Source	Date Signed	Seasons Played	Apps	Subs	Gls
Everton	Jnrs	05.57	57-59	12	-	3
Luton T	Tr	10.60	60-61	63	-	20
Northampton T	Tr	07.62	62	30	-	25
Preston NE	Tr	06.63	63-65	42	1	14

ASHWORTH Barry
Stockport, 18 August, 1942 (M)

League Club	Source	Date Signed	Seasons Played	Apps	Subs	Gls
Southend U	Bangor C	07.63	63-64	31	-	5
Hartlepools U	Tr	03.65	64-65	45	0	4
Tranmere Rov	Tr	07.66	66	21	0	3
Chester	Tr	08.67	67-69	116	3	12

ASHWORTH Frederick (Fred)
Oldham, 26 January, 1928 (CD)

League Club	Source	Date Signed	Seasons Played	Apps	Subs	Gls
Blackburn Rov		10.48				
Shrewsbury T	Tr	11.51	51-52	56	-	1

ASHWORTH Ian
Blackburn, 17 December, 1958 (W)

League Club	Source	Date Signed	Seasons Played	Apps	Subs	Gls
Manchester U	App	12.75				
Crewe Alex	Tr	07.79	79	7	6	0

ASHWORTH John
Nottingham, 4 July, 1937 EAmat (CD)

League Club	Source	Date Signed	Seasons Played	Apps	Subs	Gls
Portsmouth (Am)	Wealdstone	08.62	62	1	-	0

ASHWORTH Joseph (Joe) Matthew
Huddersfield, 6 January, 1943 Died 2002 (CD)

League Club	Source	Date Signed	Seasons Played	Apps	Subs	Gls
Bradford PA	Jnrs	01.60	61	3	-	0
York C	Tr	05.62	62-64	57	-	0
Bournemouth	Tr	06.65	65-66	60	0	2
Southend U	Tr	07.67	67	36	0	2
Rochdale	Tr	07.68	68-71	132	0	3
Chester	Tr	12.71	71	5	0	0
Stockport Co	Tr	06.72	72	14	0	0

ASHWORTH Neil
Southend-on-Sea, 16 January, 1968 (M)

League Club	Source	Date Signed	Seasons Played	Apps	Subs	Gls
Rochdale	App	07.85	84	1	0	0

ASHWORTH Philip (Phil) Anthony
Burnley, 4 April, 1953 (F)

League Club	Source	Date Signed	Seasons Played	Apps	Subs	Gls
Blackburn Rov	Nelson	01.75				
Bournemouth	Tr	09.75	75	30	1	2
Workington	Tr	07.76	76	38	1	7
Southport	Tr	08.77	77	22	2	9
Rochdale	Tr	07.78	78	9	2	0
Portsmouth	Tr	09.79	79	3	1	4
Scunthorpe U	Tr	07.80	80	14	9	3

ASKEW William (Billy)
Great Lumley, 2 October, 1959 (M)

League Club	Source	Date Signed	Seasons Played	Apps	Subs	Gls
Middlesbrough	App	10.77	79-81	10	2	0
Hull C	Gateshead	09.82	82-89	247	6	19
Newcastle U	Tr	03.90	89-90	5	1	0
Shrewsbury T	L	01.91	90	5	0	0

ASKEY Colin
Stoke-on-Trent, 3 October, 1932 (W)

League Club	Source	Date Signed	Seasons Played	Apps	Subs	Gls
Port Vale	Jnrs	10.49	49-57	200	-	21
Walsall	Tr	07.58	58-61	83	-	12
Mansfield T	Tr	06.62	62-63	30	-	2

ASKEY John Colin
Stoke-on-Trent, 4 November, 1964 ESemiPro-1 (F)

League Club	Source	Date Signed	Seasons Played	Apps	Subs	Gls
Macclesfield T	Milton U	01.86	97-02	136	45	31

ASPDEN John Raymond (Ray)
Horwich, 6 February, 1938 (CD)

League Club	Source	Date Signed	Seasons Played	Apps	Subs	Gls
Rochdale	Bolton W (Am)	05.55	55-65	297	0	2

ASPIN Neil
Gateshead, 12 April, 1965 (CD)

League Club	Source	Date Signed	Seasons Played	Apps	Subs	Gls
Leeds U	App	10.82	81-88	203	4	5
Port Vale	Tr	07.89	89-98	343	5	3
Darlington	Tr	07.99	99-00	50	0	0
Hartlepool U	Tr	01.01	00	5	5	0

ASPINALL Brendan James
Johannesburg, South Africa, 22 July, 1975 (CD)

League Club	Source	Date Signed	Seasons Played	Apps	Subs	Gls
Mansfield T	Huddersfield T (Jnrs)	07.94	94	13	7	0

ASPINALL John
Ashton-under-Lyne, 27 April, 1916 Died 1996 (WH)

League Club	Source	Date Signed	Seasons Played	Apps	Subs	Gls
Oldham Ath	Stalybridge Celtic	05.36	36-38	11	-	0
Bolton W	Ashton National	09.45	46-49	14	-	0

ASPINALL John Joseph
Birkenhead, 15 March, 1959 (W)

League Club	Source	Date Signed	Seasons Played	Apps	Subs	Gls
Tranmere Rov	Cammell Laird	10.82	82-84	100	7	25
Tranmere Rov	Bangor C	07.87	87	11	1	1

ASPINALL Warren
Wigan, 13 September, 1967 EYth (M)

League Club	Source	Date Signed	Seasons Played	Apps	Subs	Gls
Wigan Ath	App	08.85	84-85	21	12	10
Everton	Tr	02.86	85-86	0	7	0
Wigan Ath	L	02.86	85	18	0	12
Aston Villa	Tr	02.87	86-87	40	4	14
Portsmouth	Tr	08.88	88-93	97	35	21
Bournemouth	L	08.93	93	4	2	1
Swansea C	L	10.93	93	5	0	0
Bournemouth	Tr	12.93	93-94	26	1	8
Carlisle U	Tr	03.95	94-97	99	8	12
Brentford	Tr	11.97	97-98	41	2	5
Colchester U	Tr	02.99	98-99	22	0	5
Brighton & Hove A	Tr	09.99	99-00	19	13	3

ASPINALL Wayne
Wigan, 10 December, 1964 (FB)

League Club	Source	Date Signed	Seasons Played	Apps	Subs	Gls
Wigan Ath	Atherton Collieries	06.83	83-84	8	0	0

ASPREY William (Bill)
Wolverhampton, 11 September, 1936 (WH)

League Club	Source	Date Signed	Seasons Played	Apps	Subs	Gls
Stoke C	Jnrs	09.53	53-65	304	0	23
Oldham Ath	Tr	01.66	65-67	80	0	4
Port Vale	Tr	12.67	67-68	30	1	0

ASPRILLA Hinestroza Faustino Hernan
Cali, Colombia, 10 November, 1969 Colombia int (F)

League Club	Source	Date Signed	Seasons Played	Apps	Subs	Gls
Newcastle U	Parma (It)	02.96	95-97	36	12	9

ASQUITH Beaumont
Painthorpe, 16 September, 1910 Died 1977 (IF)

League Club	Source	Date Signed	Seasons Played	Apps	Subs	Gls
Barnsley	Painthorpe A	07.33	34-38	105	-	40
Manchester U	Tr	05.39				
Barnsley	Tr	07.42	46-47	40	-	5
Bradford C	Tr	09.48	48-49	31	-	4

ASTAFJEVS Vitalis
Riga, Latvia, 3 April, 1971 Latvia 93 (M)

League Club	Source	Date Signed	Seasons Played	Apps	Subs	Gls
Bristol Rov	Skonto Riga (Lat)	01.00	99-02	87	22	16

ASTALL Gordon
Horwich, 22 September, 1927 EB/FLge-1/E-2 (W)

League Club	Source	Date Signed	Seasons Played	Apps	Subs	Gls
Plymouth Arg	Southampton (Am)	11.47	47-53	188	-	42
Birmingham C	Tr	10.53	53-60	235	-	59
Torquay U	Tr	07.61	61-62	33	-	10

ASTBURY Michael (Mike) John
Kippax, 22 January, 1964 (G)

League Club	Source	Date Signed	Seasons Played	Apps	Subs	Gls
York C	App	01.82	80-85	48	0	0
Peterborough U	L	01.86	85	4	0	0
Darlington	Tr	03.86	85-86	38	0	0
Chester C	Tr	07.87	87	5	0	0
Chesterfield	Tr	07.88	88	8	0	0

ASTBURY Thomas (Tommy) Arthur
Buckley, 9 February, 1920 Died 1993 WWar-2 (WH)

League Club	Source	Date Signed	Seasons Played	Apps	Subs	Gls
Chester	Mold Alexandra	05.38	46-54	303	-	38

ASTLE Jeffrey (Jeff)
Eastwood, 13 May, 1942 Died 2002 FLge-2/E-5 (F)

League Club	Source	Date Signed	Seasons Played	Apps	Subs	Gls
Notts Co	John Player	10.59	61-64	103	-	31
West Bromwich A	Tr	09.64	64-73	290	2	137

ASTON John
Prestwich, 3 September, 1921 Died 2003 FLge-2/E-17 (FB)

League Club	Source	Date Signed	Seasons Played	Apps	Subs	Gls
Manchester U	Jnrs	04.46	46-53	253	-	29

ASTON John
Manchester, 28 June, 1947 Eu23-1 (W)

League Club	Source	Date Signed	Seasons Played	Apps	Subs	Gls
Manchester U	App	06.63	64-71	139	16	25
Luton T	Tr	07.72	72-77	171	3	31
Mansfield T	Tr	09.77	77	24	7	4
Blackburn Rov	Tr	07.78	78-79	12	3	2

ASTON Alfred **John**
Newport, 29 July, 1930 Died 1992 (W)

League Club	Source	Date Signed	Seasons Played	Apps	Subs	Gls
Newport Co	Newport YMCA	04.48	47-50	6	-	1

ASTON Philip Thomas
Measham, 13 May, 1924 (WH)

League Club	Source	Date Signed	Seasons Played	Apps	Subs	Gls
Walsall	Measham Imperial	12.51	51	10	-	0

ASTON Stanley (Stan)
Nuneaton, 10 May, 1940 (CD)

League Club	Source	Date Signed	Seasons Played	Apps	Subs	Gls
Hartlepools U	Burton A	12.66	66-67	20	1	0

ASTON Walter **Vivien (Viv)**
Coseley, 16 October, 1918 Died 1999 (FB)

League Club	Source	Date Signed	Seasons Played	Apps	Subs	Gls
Bury		12.36	38-47	23	-	0
Oldham Ath	Tr	07.48	48-51	30	-	1

ATANGANA Simon Pierre **Mvondo**
Yaounde, Cameroon, 10 July, 1979 Cameroon int (F)

League Club	Source	Date Signed	Seasons Played	Apps	Subs	Gls
Port Vale (L)	Dundee U	01.02	01	1	1	0
Colchester U	Dundee U	11.02	02	1	5	0

ATHERSYCH Russell (Russ)
Sheffield, 21 September, 1962 (M)

League Club	Source	Date Signed	Seasons Played	Apps	Subs	Gls
Chesterfield	App	09.80	81-82	11	9	0

ATHERTON Dewi Lewis
Bangor, 6 July, 1951 (M)

League Club	Source	Date Signed	Seasons Played	Apps	Subs	Gls
Blackburn Rov	Jnrs	07.68	68-70	9	1	0

ATHERTON Francis **Gordon**
Horwich, 18 June, 1934 (WH)

League Club	Source	Date Signed	Seasons Played	Apps	Subs	Gls
Bury	Bury Amats	09.55	55-64	327	-	14
Swindon T	Tr	12.64	64-65	31	0	0
Bury	Tr	01.66	65	7	0	0

ATHERTON James (Jim) Geoffrey
Queensferry, 2 April, 1923 WAmat (G)

League Club	Source	Date Signed	Seasons Played	Apps	Subs	Gls
Wrexham (Am)		07.47	47-48	18	-	0

ATHERTON Peter
Orrell, 6 April, 1970 ESch/Eu21-1 (CD)

League Club	Source	Date Signed	Seasons Played	Apps	Subs	Gls
Wigan Ath	YT	02.88	87-91	145	4	1
Coventry C	Tr	08.91	91-93	113	1	0
Sheffield Wed	Tr	06.94	94-99	214	0	9
Bradford C	Tr	07.00	00-04	90	4	3
Birmingham C	L	02.01	00	10	0	0

ATIENO Taiwo Leo
Brixton, 6 August, 1985 (F)

League Club	Source	Date Signed	Seasons Played	Apps	Subs	Gls
Walsall	Tr	07.04	04	0	3	0
Rochdale	L	10.04	04	6	7	2
Chester C	L	02.05	04	3	1	1

ATKIN John Michael
Scunthorpe, 14 February, 1948 (CD)

League Club	Source	Date Signed	Seasons Played	Apps	Subs	Gls
Scunthorpe U		09.69	69-74	115	4	0

ATKIN Paul Anthony
Nottingham, 3 September, 1969 ESch/EYth (CD)

League Club	Source	Date Signed	Seasons Played	Apps	Subs	Gls
Notts Co	YT	07.87				
Bury	Tr	03.89	88-90	14	7	1
York C	Tr	07.91	91-96	131	22	3
Leyton Orient	L	03.97	96	5	0	0
Scarborough	Tr	08.97	97	26	8	1

ATKINS Arthur Walter
Tokyo, Japan, 21 February, 1925 Died 1988 (CD)

League Club	Source	Date Signed	Seasons Played	Apps	Subs	Gls
Birmingham C	Paget Rgrs	11.48	49-53	97	-	0
Shrewsbury T	Tr	06.54	54	16	-	0

ATKINS Dennis
Bradford Moor, 8 November, 1938 (FB)

League Club	Source	Date Signed	Seasons Played	Apps	Subs	Gls
Huddersfield T	Jnrs	12.55	59-66	194	0	0
Bradford C	Tr	05.68	67-70	108	0	0

ATKINS Ian Leslie
Birmingham, 16 January, 1957 (M)

League Club	Source	Date Signed	Seasons Played	Apps	Subs	Gls
Shrewsbury T	App	01.75	75-81	273	5	58
Sunderland	Tr	08.82	82-83	76	1	6
Everton	Tr	11.84	84-85	6	1	1
Ipswich T	Tr	09.85	85-87	73	4	4
Birmingham C	Tr	03.88	87-89	93	0	6
Birmingham C	Colchester U	09.91	91	5	3	0
Cambridge U	Tr	12.92	92	1	1	0
Doncaster Rov	Sunderland (N/C)	01.94	93	7	0	0

ATKINS Mark Nigel
Doncaster, 14 August, 1968 ESch (M)

League Club	Source	Date Signed	Seasons Played	Apps	Subs	Gls
Scunthorpe U	Jnrs	07.86	84-87	45	5	2
Blackburn Rov	Tr	06.88	88-95	224	33	35
Wolverhampton W	Tr	09.95	95-98	115	11	9
York C	Tr	08.99	99	10	0	2
Hull C	Doncaster Rov	03.01	00	8	0	0
Shrewsbury T	Tr	07.01	01-02	71	1	3

ATKINS Robert (Bob) Gary
Leicester, 16 October, 1962 (CD)

League Club	Source	Date Signed	Seasons Played	Apps	Subs	Gls
Sheffield U	Enderby T	07.82	82-84	36	4	3
Preston NE	Tr	02.85	84-89	198	2	5

ATKINS Alfred James **Trevor**
Exeter, 17 August, 1941 (W)

League Club	Source	Date Signed	Seasons Played	Apps	Subs	Gls
Exeter C	Jnrs	08.58	57-59	3	-	3

ATKINS William (Bill) Mark
Solihull, 9 May, 1939 (F)

League Club	Source	Date Signed	Seasons Played	Apps	Subs	Gls
Aston Villa	Birmingham GPO	05.58				
Swindon T	Tr	06.59	59-64	75	-	28
Halifax T	Tr	08.65	65-66	74	0	33
Stockport Co	Tr	03.67	66-68	92	0	37
Portsmouth	Tr	04.69	68-69	11	0	2
Halifax T	Tr	11.69	69-72	123	2	37
Rochdale	Tr	12.72	72-73	25	0	7
Darlington	Tr	09.73	73-74	41	3	12

ATKINSON Brian
Sheffield, 16 November, 1934 (WH)

League Club	Source	Date Signed	Seasons Played	Apps	Subs	Gls
Sheffield U		06.53				
Halifax T	Tr	06.56	56-58	67	-	0

ATKINSON Brian
Darlington, 19 January, 1971 Eu21-6 (M)

League Club	Source	Date Signed	Seasons Played	Apps	Subs	Gls
Sunderland	YT	07.89	88-95	119	22	4
Carlisle U	L	01.96	95	2	0	0
Darlington	Tr	08.96	96-01	174	19	12

ATKINSON Bryan Herbert
Saffron Walden, 15 April, 1934 Died 1989 (WH)

League Club	Source	Date Signed	Seasons Played	Apps	Subs	Gls
Watford	Bishops Stortford	06.54	55-56	20	-	0

ATKINSON Charles (Charlie)
Hull, 17 December, 1932 (WH)

League Club	Source	Date Signed	Seasons Played	Apps	Subs	Gls
Hull C	Marist OB	05.50	53-55	37	-	2
Bradford PA	Tr	07.56	56-63	339	-	50
Bradford C	Tr	06.64	64	16	-	1

ATKINSON Charles (Charlie) Brown Clayton
Haswell, 5 May, 1938 (CD)

League Club	Source	Date Signed	Seasons Played	Apps	Subs	Gls
Hartlepools U	Eppleton CW	12.58	59-63	47	-	0

ATKINSON Dalian Robert
Shrewsbury, 21 March, 1968 EB (F)

League Club	Source	Date Signed	Seasons Played	Apps	Subs	Gls
Ipswich T	App	06.85	85-88	49	11	18
Sheffield Wed	Tr	07.89	89	38	0	10
Aston Villa	Real Sociedad (Sp)	09.91	91-94	79	8	23
Manchester C (L)	Fenerbahce (Tu)	03.97	96	7	1	2

ATKINSON David John
Hull, 3 April, 1951 (W)

League Club	Source	Date Signed	Seasons Played	Apps	Subs	Gls
Hartlepool	App	●	68	8	0	1

ATKINSON Frederick (Fred) James
Newcastle, 24 August, 1919 Died 1991 (WH)

League Club	Source	Date Signed	Seasons Played	Apps	Subs	Gls
Gateshead		12.45	46-48	32	-	6

League Club	Source	Date Signed	Seasons Played	Career Record Apps	Subs	Gls
ATKINSON Graeme						
Hull, 11 November, 1971						(W)
Hull C	YT	05.90	89-94	129	20	23
Preston NE	Tr	10.94	94-97	63	16	6
Rochdale	L	12.97	97	5	1	0
Brighton & Hove A	Tr	03.98	97-98	16	0	0
Scunthorpe U	Tr	11.98	98	0	1	0
Scarborough	Tr	02.99	98	15	0	1
Rochdale	Tr	07.99	99-01	40	11	5
ATKINSON Graham James						
Liverpool, 17 May, 1943						(M)
Oxford U	Aston Villa (Am)	02.60	62	18	-	4
Oxford U	Cambridge U	12.64	64-73	303	4	73
ATKINSON Harold						
Liverpool, 28 July, 1925 Died 2003						(CF)
Tranmere Rov	Carlton	03.45	46-54	185	-	91
ATKINSON Hugh Anthony						
Dublin, 8 November, 1960 IRu21-1						(M)
Wolverhampton W	App	11.78	79-81	38	8	3
Exeter C	Tr	10.83	83	28	0	1
York C	Tr	07.84	84	3	4	0
Darlington	L	03.85	84	7	0	0
ATKINSON Arthur **Ian**						
Carlisle, 19 December, 1932 Died 1995						(IF)
Carlisle U		06.51	52-56	123	-	54
Exeter C	Tr	07.57	57	8	-	2
ATKINSON John (Jack) Edward						
New Washington, 20 December, 1913 Died 1977 ESch						(CD)
Bolton W	Washington Colliery	09.31	32-47	240	-	4
New Brighton	Tr	05.48	48-49	52	-	0
ATKINSON Jonathan (Jon) David						
Ashington, 18 September, 1972						(F)
Darlington	Morpeth T	03.97	96	2	3	0
ATKINSON Patrick (Paddy) Darren						
Singapore, 22 May, 1970						(FB)
Hartlepool U	Sheffield U (YT)	08.88	88-89	9	12	3
York C	Workington	11.95	95-97	36	5	0
Scarborough	Tr	08.98	98	23	4	0
ATKINSON Paul						
Chester-le-Street, 19 January, 1966 EYth						(W)
Sunderland	App	11.83	83-87	46	14	5
Port Vale	Tr	06.88	88	4	0	3
Hartlepool U	L	03.90	89	5	6	1
ATKINSON Paul Graham						
Pudsey, 14 August, 1961						(W)
Oldham Ath	App	08.79	79-82	139	4	11
Watford	Tr	07.83	83	8	3	0
Oldham Ath	Tr	08.85	85-87	29	4	1
Swansea C	L	12.86	86	6	0	1
Bolton W	L	02.87	86	2	1	0
Swansea C	L	03.87	86	12	0	2
Burnley	Tr	07.88	88-89	18	4	1
ATKINSON Peter						
Middlesbrough, 13 September, 1924 Died 1972						(G)
Hull C	Billingham Synthonia	04.47	46-47	6	-	0
ATKINSON Peter						
Gainsborough, 14 December, 1949						(M)
Rotherham U		05.69	69	3	0	0
ATKINSON Peter Maurice Carl						
Spilsby, 20 September, 1929 Died 2000						(G)
Walsall	Walsall YMCA	11.49	49-51	2	-	0
ATKINSON Robert (Rob) Guy						
Beverley, 29 April, 1987						(FB)
Barnsley	Sch	●	03-04	0	2	0
ATKINSON Ronald (Ron) Frederick						
Liverpool, 18 March, 1939						(M)
Aston Villa	BSA Tools	05.56				
Oxford U	Tr	07.59	62-71	383	1	14
ATKINSON Trevor						
Barnsley, 19 November, 1928 Died 1992						(W)
Hull C	Hull Amats	05.46	46	2	-	0
ATKINSON Trevor						
Bishop Auckland, 23 November, 1942						(CD)
Darlington	Spennymoor U	11.63	63-68	135	4	3
Bradford PA	Tr	01.69	68-69	59	1	6

League Club	Source	Date Signed	Seasons Played	Career Record Apps	Subs	Gls
ATKINSON Walter						
Ryton-on-Tyne, 31 August, 1920						(WH)
Norwich C	Hexham Hearts	01.49	51	1	-	0
ATKINSON William (Bill)						
Sunderland, 21 December, 1944 ESch						(W)
Birmingham C	App	03.62				
Torquay U	Tr	06.64	64	19	-	7
ATOUBA Thimothee Essama						
Douala, Cameroon, 17 February, 1982 Cameroon 23						(M)
Tottenham H	FC Basle (Swi)	08.04	04	15	3	1
ATTEVELD Raymond (Ray)						
Amsterdam, Holland, 8 September, 1966						(FB)
Everton	Haarlem (Holl)	08.89	89-91	41	10	1
West Ham U	L	02.92	91	1	0	0
Bristol C	Tr	03.92	91-92	9	5	1
ATTHEY Nicholas (Nick)						
Tantobie, 8 May, 1946						(M)
Walsall	App	07.63	63-76	429	10	17
ATTLEY Brian Robert						
Cardiff, 23 August, 1955						(FB)
Cardiff C	App	08.73	74-78	73	6	1
Swansea C	Tr	02.79	78-81	83	6	6
Derby Co	Tr	02.82	81-83	54	1	1
Oxford U	L	03.83	82	5	0	0
ATTWELL Jamie Wayne						
Bristol, 8 June, 1982						(G)
Bristol C	Tottenham H (YT)	08.01				
Torquay U	Tr	07.02	02	2	2	0
ATTWELL Frederick **Reginald (Reg)**						
Shifnal, 23 March, 1920 Died 1986 FLge-1						(WH)
West Ham U	Denaby U	04.38	37-46	5	-	0
Burnley	Tr	10.46	46-54	244	-	9
Bradford C	Tr	10.54	54	24	-	0
ATYEO Peter **John** Walter						
Dilton, 7 February, 1932 Died 1993 EYth/Eu23-2/FLge-2/EB/E-6						(IF)
Portsmouth (Am)	Westbury U	09.50	50	1	-	0
Bristol C	Tr	06.51	51-65	596	0	315
AUGUSTE Joseph (Joe)						
Trinidad, 24 November, 1955						(F)
Exeter C	Hounslow	09.83	83	7	3	0
AULD Robert (Bertie)						
Maryhill, 23 March, 1938 SLge-2/S-3						(W)
Birmingham C	Glasgow Celtic	05.61	61-64	126	-	26
AULD Walter Bottomley						
Bellshill, 9 July, 1929 Died 1988						(W)
Middlesbrough	Bellshill Ath	12.50	50	2	-	1
AUNGER Geoffrey (Geoff) Edward Ramer						
Red Deer, Alberta, Canada, 4 February, 1968 Canada int						(F)
Luton T	Vancouver (Can)	09.93	93	5	0	1
Chester C	Tr	12.94	94	1	4	0
Stockport Co	Seattle (USA)	12.97	97	0	1	0
AUSTIN Dean Barry						
Hemel Hempstead, 26 April, 1970						(FB)
Southend U	St Albans C	03.90	89-91	96	0	2
Tottenham H	Tr	06.92	92-96	117	7	0
Crystal Palace	Tr	07.98	98-02	127	15	6
AUSTIN John **Frank**						
Stoke-on-Trent, 6 July, 1933 Died 2004 ESch						(FB)
Coventry C	Toton	07.50	52-62	302	-	2
Torquay U	Tr	01.63	62-63	24	-	0
AUSTIN Karl						
Stoke-on-Trent, 7 August, 1961						(G)
Port Vale	Stafford Rgrs	02.85	84	1	0	0
AUSTIN Kevin Levi						
Hackney, 12 February, 1973 Trinidad 1						(CD)
Leyton Orient	Saffron Walden T	08.93	93-95	101	8	3
Lincoln C	Tr	07.96	96-98	128	1	2
Barnsley	Tr	07.99	99	3	0	0
Brentford	L	10.00	00	3	0	0
Cambridge U	Tr	11.01	01	4	2	0
Bristol Rov	Tr	07.02	02-03	52	4	0
Swansea C	Tr	07.04	04	41	1	0
AUSTIN Neil Jeffrey						
Barnsley, 26 April, 1983 EYth/Eu20						(CD)
Barnsley	YT	04.00	02-04	73	13	0

League Club	Source	Date Signed	Seasons Played	Career Record Apps	Subs	Gls
AUSTIN Roy Leonard						
Islington, 26 March, 1960						(F)
Doncaster Rov	Millwall (App)	08.78	78	3	0	0
AUSTIN Terence (Terry) Willis						
Isleworth, 1 February, 1954						(F)
Crystal Palace	Jnrs	06.72				
Ipswich T	Tr	05.73	74-75	10	9	1
Plymouth Arg	Tr	10.76	76-77	58	0	18
Walsall	Tr	03.78	77-78	44	3	19
Mansfield T	Tr	03.79	78-80	84	0	31
Huddersfield T	Tr	12.80	80-82	39	3	10
Doncaster Rov	Tr	09.82	82	30	4	5
Northampton T	Tr	08.83	83	42	1	10
AVDIU Kemajl						
Kosovo, Yugoslavia, 22 December, 1976						(M)
Bury	Esbjerg (Den)	08.98	98-99	8	19	1
AVERY Roger Joseph						
Cambridge, 17 February, 1961						(F)
Cambridge U	App	02.79	77	0	1	0
AVEYARD Walter						
Thurnscoe, 11 June, 1918 Died 1985						(CF)
Sheffield Wed	Denaby U	10.38	46	4	-	3
Birmingham C	Tr	04.47	47	7	-	3
Port Vale	Tr	06.48	48-51	103	-	26
Accrington St	Tr	03.52	51-52	24	-	4
AVIS Vernon Charles Sidney						
Marylebone, 24 October, 1935 Died 1996						(FB)
Brentford	Jnrs	11.52	53-60	19	-	0
AVRAMOVIC Radojko (Raddy)						
Rijeka, Croatia, 29 November, 1949 Yugoslavia int						(G)
Notts Co	NK Rijeka (Cro)	08.79	79-82	149	0	0
Coventry C	Inter Montreal (Can)	09.83	83	18	0	0
AWFORD Andrew (Andy) Terence						
Worcester, 14 July, 1972 ESch/EYth/Eu21-9						(CD)
Portsmouth	YT	07.89	88-00	293	20	3
AWUAH Jones						
Ghana, 10 July, 1983						(M)
Gillingham	Sch	07.03	02	1	3	0
AXELDAHL Jonas Michael						
Holm, Sweden, 2 September, 1970						(F)
Ipswich T	Foggia (It)	07.99	99	1	15	0
Cambridge U	Tr	08.00	00	12	6	2
AYLOTT Stephen (Steve) John						
Ilford, 3 September, 1951						(M)
West Ham U	App	08.69				
Oxford U	Tr	04.71	71-75	143	11	8
Brentford	Tr	07.76	76-77	6	1	0
AYLOTT Trevor Keith Charles						
Bermondsey, 26 November, 1957						(F)
Chelsea	App	11.75	77-79	26	3	2
Barnsley	Tr	11.79	79-81	93	3	26
Millwall	Tr	08.82	82	32	0	5
Luton T	Tr	03.83	82-83	32	0	10
Crystal Palace	Tr	07.84	84-85	50	3	12
Barnsley	L	02.86	85	9	0	0
Bournemouth	Tr	08.86	86-90	137	10	27
Birmingham C	Tr	10.90	90-91	25	2	0
Oxford U	Tr	09.91	91	35	2	6
Gillingham	Tr	07.92	92	8	2	2
AYORINDE Samuel (Sammy) Tayo						
Lagos, Nigeria, 20 October, 1974 Ngu21/Ngu23/Ng						(F)
Leyton Orient	Sturm Graz (Aut)	04.96	95-96	7	6	2
AYRE Colin						
Ashington, 14 March, 1956						(W)
Newcastle U	App	09.73				
Torquay U	Telstar	09.76	76	2	0	0
AYRE Robert (Bobby) William						
Berwick-on-Tweed, 26 March, 1932 Eu23-2						(CF)
Charlton Ath	Chippenham T	07.52	52-57	109	-	48
Reading	Tr	05.58	58-59	57	-	24
AYRE William (Billy)						
Crookhill, 7 May, 1952 Died 2002						(CD)
Hartlepool U	Scarborough	08.77	77-80	141	0	27
Halifax T	Tr	01.81	80-81	63	0	5
Mansfield T	Tr	08.82	82-83	67	0	7
Halifax T	Tr	07.84	84-85	32	0	2

League Club	Source	Date Signed	Seasons Played	Career Record Apps	Subs	Gls
AYRES Frederick (Fred) Edward						
Stoke-on-Trent, 17 July, 1926						(W)
Crewe Alex		11.48	48	3	-	0
AYRES Harold (Harry)						
Redcar, 10 March, 1920 Died 2002						(WH)
Fulham	Clapton	07.46	46-48	38	-	8
Gillingham	Tr	06.50	50-54	136	-	2
AYRES Kenneth (Ken) Edward						
Oxford, 15 May, 1956 ESch						(F)
Manchester U	App	06.73				
Crystal Palace	Tr	11.73	74	3	3	0
AYRES Lee Terence						
Birmingham, 28 August, 1982						(CD)
Kidderminster Hrs	Evesham U	06.01	01-02	27	8	2
AYRIS John (Johnny) Patrick						
Wapping, 8 January, 1953 EYth						(W)
West Ham U	App	10.70	70-76	41	16	1
AYRTON Neil John						
Lewisham, 11 February, 1962						(F)
Portsmouth	Maidstone U	12.79	80	1	1	0
AYTON James (Jimmy)						
Barrhead, 15 October, 1923 Died 1988						(IF)
Leicester C	Third Lanark	10.48	48-50	8	-	1
Shrewsbury T	Tr	06.51	51	25	-	1

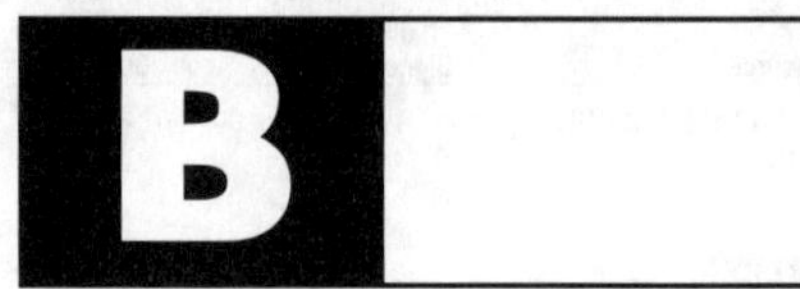

BA Ibrahim
Dakar, Senegal, 12 November, 1973 France 8 (M)

League Club	Source	Date Signed	Seasons Played	Apps	Subs	Gls
Bolton W	AC Milan (It)	09.03	03	0	9	0

BAAH Peter Hayford
Littleborough, 1 May, 1973 (W)

League Club	Source	Date Signed	Seasons Played	Apps	Subs	Gls
Blackburn Rov	YT	06.91	91	1	0	0
Fulham	Tr	07.92	92-93	38	11	4

BAARDSEN Per Espen
San Rafael, Texas, USA, 7 December, 1977 UsYth/NoYth/Nou21-31/No-4 (G)

League Club	Source	Date Signed	Seasons Played	Apps	Subs	Gls
Tottenham H	San Francisco (USA)	07.96	96-98	22	1	0
Watford	Tr	08.00	00-01	41	0	0
Everton	Tr	12.02	02	1	0	0

BABAYARO Celestine
Kaduna, Nigeria, 29 August, 1978 NgYth/Ngu23/Ng-26 (FB)

League Club	Source	Date Signed	Seasons Played	Apps	Subs	Gls
Chelsea	Anderlecht (Holl)	06.97	97-04	118	14	5
Newcastle U	Tr	01.05	04	7	0	0

BABB Philip (Phil) Andrew
Lambeth, 30 November, 1970 IR 'B'-1/IR-35 (CD)

League Club	Source	Date Signed	Seasons Played	Apps	Subs	Gls
Millwall	YT	04.89				
Bradford C	Tr	08.90	90-91	73	7	14
Coventry C	Tr	07.92	92-94	70	7	3
Liverpool	Tr	09.94	94-98	124	4	1
Tranmere Rov	L	01.00	99	4	0	0
Sunderland	Sporting Lisbon (Por)	06.02	02-03	48	0	0

BABBEL Markus
Munich, Germany, 8 September, 1972 Germany 51 (FB)

League Club	Source	Date Signed	Seasons Played	Apps	Subs	Gls
Liverpool	Bayern Munich (Ger)	07.00	00-02	42	0	3
Blackburn Rov	L	08.03	03	23	2	3

BABER John Michael
Lambeth, 10 October, 1947 (W)

League Club	Source	Date Signed	Seasons Played	Apps	Subs	Gls
Southend U	Charlton Ath (App)	09.66	66-70	72	10	18

BABES John
Lurgan, 20 November, 1929 (FB)

League Club	Source	Date Signed	Seasons Played	Apps	Subs	Gls
Arsenal	Glentoran	01.48				
Scunthorpe U	Tr	09.50	50-51	9	-	0

BACCI Alfredo (Alf) Giovanni
Bedlington, 15 July, 1922 Died 1993 (IF)

League Club	Source	Date Signed	Seasons Played	Apps	Subs	Gls
Chesterfield	West Sleekburn Jnrs	08.50	50-51	6	-	2

BACKOS Desmond (Des) Patrick
Wynberg, South Africa, 13 November, 1950 (F)

League Club	Source	Date Signed	Seasons Played	Apps	Subs	Gls
Stoke C	Los Angeles (USA)	10.77	77	1	1	0

BACON Cyril William
Hammersmith, 9 November, 1919 (WH)

League Club	Source	Date Signed	Seasons Played	Apps	Subs	Gls
Leyton Orient	Hayes	06.46	46-49	118	-	3

BACON Daniel (Danny) Stephen
Mansfield, 20 September, 1980 (F)

League Club	Source	Date Signed	Seasons Played	Apps	Subs	Gls
Mansfield T	YT	01.00	99-02	14	30	4

BACON Paul Darren
Forest Gate, 20 December, 1970 (M)

League Club	Source	Date Signed	Seasons Played	Apps	Subs	Gls
Charlton Ath	YT	01.89	90-92	25	8	0

BACON Ronald (Ron) Alfred Sydney
Fakenham, 4 March, 1935 (W)

League Club	Source	Date Signed	Seasons Played	Apps	Subs	Gls
Norwich C	Holt	12.55	55-57	42	-	6
Gillingham	Tr	05.58	58-60	128	-	15

BACQUE Herve
Bordeaux, France, 13 July, 1976 (F)

League Club	Source	Date Signed	Seasons Played	Apps	Subs	Gls
Luton T	AS Monaco (Fr)	08.98	98	2	5	0

BACUZZI Reno David (Dave)
Islington, 12 October, 1940 EYth/Lol-2 (FB)

League Club	Source	Date Signed	Seasons Played	Apps	Subs	Gls
Arsenal	Eastbourne U	05.59	60-63	46	-	0
Manchester C	Tr	04.64	64-65	56	1	0
Reading	Tr	09.66	66-69	107	0	1

BACUZZI Giuseppe (Joe) Luigi Davide
Holborn, 25 September, 1916 Died 1995 FLge-1/EWar-13 (FB)

League Club	Source	Date Signed	Seasons Played	Apps	Subs	Gls
Fulham	Tufnell Park	04.36	36-55	283	-	2

BADCOCK Stephen (Steve) William
Kensington, 10 September, 1958 (W)

League Club	Source	Date Signed	Seasons Played	Apps	Subs	Gls
Bristol Rov	Bristol Portway	07.85	85	14	3	3

BADDELEY Kevin Stuart
Swindon, 12 March, 1962 (FB)

League Club	Source	Date Signed	Seasons Played	Apps	Subs	Gls
Bristol C	App	03.80	80	1	0	0
Swindon T	Tr	06.81	81-84	94	1	2

BADDELEY Lee Matthew
Cardiff, 12 July, 1974 W Yth/Wu21-2 (CD)

League Club	Source	Date Signed	Seasons Played	Apps	Subs	Gls
Cardiff C	YT	08.91	90-96	112	21	1
Exeter C	Tr	02.97	96-98	60	6	1

BADES Brian Lawrence
Farnworth, 3 July, 1939 (IF)

League Club	Source	Date Signed	Seasons Played	Apps	Subs	Gls
Accrington St		02.60				
Chester		08.63	63	15	-	1

BADGER Colin Albert
Rotherham, 16 June, 1930 Died 1985 (W)

League Club	Source	Date Signed	Seasons Played	Apps	Subs	Gls
Rotherham U		11.50	50	2	-	0

BADGER Leonard (Len)
Sheffield, 8 June, 1945 E Sch/E Yth/Eu23-13/FLge-3 (FB)

League Club	Source	Date Signed	Seasons Played	Apps	Subs	Gls
Sheffield U	App	08.62	62-75	457	1	7
Chesterfield	Tr	01.76	75-77	46	0	0

BADHAM John (Jack)
Birmingham, 31 January, 1919 Died 1992 (FB)

League Club	Source	Date Signed	Seasons Played	Apps	Subs	Gls
Birmingham C	Muntz Street YC	05.46	47-56	175	-	4

BADIR Walid
Kafr Kasm, Israel, 12 March, 1974 Israel 23 (M)

League Club	Source	Date Signed	Seasons Played	Apps	Subs	Gls
Wimbledon	Hapoel Petach T (Isr)	08.99	99	12	9	1

BADMINTON Roger Geoffrey
Portsmouth, 15 September, 1947 (FB)

League Club	Source	Date Signed	Seasons Played	Apps	Subs	Gls
Brighton & Hove A	Jnrs	07.66	66	1	0	0

BAGGIO Dino
Camposampiero, Italy, 24 July, 1971 Italy 60 (M)

League Club	Source	Date Signed	Seasons Played	Apps	Subs	Gls
Blackburn Rov	SS Lazio (It)	09.03	03	0	9	1

BAGHERI Karim
Abbasi, Iran, 20 February, 1974 Iran int (M)

League Club	Source	Date Signed	Seasons Played	Apps	Subs	Gls
Charlton Ath	Pirouzi (Iran)	08.00	00	0	1	0

BAGNALL Reginald (Reg)
Brinsworth, 22 November, 1926 (FB)

League Club	Source	Date Signed	Seasons Played	Apps	Subs	Gls
Notts Co	Rotherham U (Am)	06.45	46-47	9	-	0

BAGSHAW Paul John
Sheffield, 29 May, 1979 (M)

League Club	Source	Date Signed	Seasons Played	Apps	Subs	Gls
Barnsley	YT	07.97	98	0	1	0
Carlisle U	L	03.99	98	5	4	0

BAIANO Francesco
Naples, Italy, 24 February, 1968 Italy 2 (F)

League Club	Source	Date Signed	Seasons Played	Apps	Subs	Gls
Derby Co	Fiorentina (It)	08.97	97-99	52	12	16

BAIDOO Shabazz Kwame
Hackney, 13 April, 1988 EYth (F)

League Club	Source	Date Signed	Seasons Played	Apps	Subs	Gls
Queens Park Rgrs	Sch	•	04	2	2	0

BAILEY Alan
Macclesfield, 1 November, 1978 (F)

League Club	Source	Date Signed	Seasons Played	Apps	Subs	Gls
Manchester C	YT	07.97				
Macclesfield T	L	01.99	98	5	5	1
Stockport Co	Tr	08.99	99-00	6	12	1

BAILEY Alexander (Alex) Christopher
Newham, 21 September, 1983 EYth (FB)

League Club	Source	Date Signed	Seasons Played	Apps	Subs	Gls
Arsenal	YT	07.01				
Chesterfield	Tr	07.04	04	45	0	1

BAILEY Alfred (Alf) Benjamin
West Bromwich, 16 December, 1927 Died 1978 (CF)

League Club	Source	Date Signed	Seasons Played	Apps	Subs	Gls
Walsall (Am)	Darwen	09.53	53	1	-	0

BAILEY Anthony (Tony)
Winsford, 3 December, 1939 (W)

League Club	Source	Date Signed	Seasons Played	Apps	Subs	Gls
Crewe Alex (Am)		05.59	59	2	-	0

BAILEY Anthony (Tony) David
Burton-on-Trent, 23 September, 1946 (CD)

League Club	Source	Date Signed	Seasons Played	Apps	Subs	Gls
Derby Co	Burton A	09.70	71	1	0	0
Oldham Ath	Tr	01.74	73-74	26	0	1
Bury	Tr	12.74	74-78	124	7	1

BAILEY William **Craig**
Airdrie, 6 July, 1944 (CF)

League Club	Source	Date Signed	Seasons Played	Apps	Subs	Gls
Brighton & Hove A	Kirkintilloch Rob Roy	12.61	62	4	-	1

BAILEY Danny Stephen
Leyton, 21 May, 1964 (M)

League Club	Source	Date Signed	Seasons Played	Apps	Subs	Gls
Bournemouth	App	•	80	1	1	0
Torquay U	Walthamstow Ave	03.84	83	1	0	0
Exeter C	Wealdstone	08.89	89-90	63	1	2
Reading	Tr	12.90	90-91	49	1	2
Fulham	L	07.92	92	2	1	0
Exeter C	Tr	12.92	92-96	143	9	4

BAILEY David
Worksop, 11 January, 1957 (F)

League Club	Source	Date Signed	Seasons Played	Apps	Subs	Gls
Chesterfield	Jnrs	01.76	75	1	0	1

BAILEY Dennis
Church Hulme, 24 September, 1935 (W)

League Club	Source	Date Signed	Seasons Played	Apps	Subs	Gls
Bolton W	Jnrs	09.53	56	1	-	0
Port Vale	Tr	08.58	58	1	-	0

BAILEY Dennis Lincoln
Lambeth, 13 November, 1965 (F)

League Club	Source	Date Signed	Seasons Played	Apps	Subs	Gls
Fulham	Barking	11.86				
Crystal Palace	Farnborough T	12.87	87	0	5	1
Bristol Rov	L	02.89	88	17	0	9
Birmingham C	Tr	08.89	89-90	65	10	23
Bristol Rov	L	03.91	90	6	0	1
Queens Park Rgrs	Tr	07.91	91-92	32	7	10
Charlton Ath	L	10.93	93	0	4	0
Watford	L	03.94	93	2	6	4
Brentford	L	01.95	94	6	0	3
Gillingham	Tr	08.95	95-97	63	25	11
Lincoln C	Tr	03.98	97	1	4	1

BAILEY Gary Richard
Ipswich, 9 August, 1958 Eu21-14/EB/E-2 (G)

League Club	Source	Date Signed	Seasons Played	Apps	Subs	Gls
Manchester U	Wits Univ (SA)	01.78	78-86	294	0	0

BAILEY George Ernest
Doncaster, 31 October, 1958 ESch (W)

League Club	Source	Date Signed	Seasons Played	Apps	Subs	Gls
Manchester U	App	11.75				
Doncaster Rov	L	02.78	77	3	0	0

BAILEY Thomas **Graham**
Dawley, 22 March, 1920 (FB)

League Club	Source	Date Signed	Seasons Played	Apps	Subs	Gls
Huddersfield T	Donnington Wood	03.37	46	33		0
Sheffield U	Tr	03.48	47-48	20	-	0

BAILEY Ian Craig
Middlesbrough, 20 October, 1956 (FB)

League Club	Source	Date Signed	Seasons Played	Apps	Subs	Gls
Middlesbrough	App	10.74	75-81	140	4	1
Doncaster Rov	L	11.76	76	9	0	0
Carlisle U	L	02.77	76	7	0	1
Bolton W	L	11.81	81	5	0	0
Sheffield Wed	Tr	08.82	82	35	0	0
Blackpool	L	10.84	84	3	0	0
Bolton W	Tr	03.85	84	10	0	0

BAILEY John Andrew
Lambeth, 6 May, 1969 (M)

League Club	Source	Date Signed	Seasons Played	Apps	Subs	Gls
Bournemouth	Enfield	07.95	95-99	136	13	6

BAILEY John Anthony
Liverpool, 1 April, 1957 (FB)

League Club	Source	Date Signed	Seasons Played	Apps	Subs	Gls
Blackburn Rov	App	04.75	75-78	115	5	1
Everton	Tr	07.79	79-85	171	0	3
Newcastle U	Tr	10.85	85-87	39	1	0
Bristol C	Tr	09.88	88-90	79	1	1

BAILEY John Anthony Kenneth
Manchester, 2 July, 1984 EYth (M)

League Club	Source	Date Signed	Seasons Played	Apps	Subs	Gls
Preston NE	YT	07.01	02	0	1	0

BAILEY Ernest **John (Jack)**
Bristol, 17 June, 1921 Died 1986 (FB)

League Club	Source	Date Signed	Seasons Played	Apps	Subs	Gls
Bristol C	BAC	05.45	46-57	347	-	0

BAILEY John Stephen
Oxford, 30 July, 1950 (M)

League Club	Source	Date Signed	Seasons Played	Apps	Subs	Gls
Swindon T	App	08.68	67	0	2	0

BAILEY Malcolm
Halifax, 7 May, 1937 (W)

League Club	Source	Date Signed	Seasons Played	Apps	Subs	Gls
Bradford PA	Luddendenfoot	04.58	57-58	10	-	1
Accrington St	Tr	10.60	60	2	-	0

BAILEY Malcolm Roy
Biddulph, 14 April, 1950 (M)

League Club	Source	Date Signed	Seasons Played	Apps	Subs	Gls
Port Vale	Jnrs	05.67	68	2	0	0

BAILEY Mark
Stoke-on-Trent, 12 August, 1976 (FB)

League Club	Source	Date Signed	Seasons Played	Apps	Subs	Gls
Stoke C	YT	07.94				
Rochdale	Tr	10.96	96-98	49	18	1
Lincoln C	Northwich Vic	10.01	01-03	97	1	1
Macclesfield T	Tr	07.04	04	20	1	2

BAILEY Matthew (Matt) John
Crewe, 12 March, 1986 (F)

League Club	Source	Date Signed	Seasons Played	Apps	Subs	Gls
Stockport Co	Sch	07.03	04	0	1	0
Scunthorpe U	L	08.04	04	2	2	0

BAILEY Michael (Mike) Alfred
Wisbech, 27 February, 1942 Eu23-5/FLge-3/E-2 (M)

League Club	Source	Date Signed	Seasons Played	Apps	Subs	Gls
Charlton Ath	Jnrs	03.59	60-65	151	0	20
Wolverhampton W	Tr	03.66	65-76	360	1	19
Hereford U	Minnesota (USA)	08.78	78	13	3	1

BAILEY Neil
Billinge, 26 September, 1958 (M)

League Club	Source	Date Signed	Seasons Played	Apps	Subs	Gls
Burnley	App	07.76				
Newport Co	Ashton U	09.78	78-83	129	5	7
Wigan Ath	Tr	10.83	83-85	31	10	2
Stockport Co	Tr	07.86	86-87	50	1	0
Newport Co	L	03.87	86	7	1	1
Blackpool	(Retired)	09.92	92-93	8	1	0

BAILEY Raymond (Ray) Reginald
Bedford, 16 May, 1944 (CD)

League Club	Source	Date Signed	Seasons Played	Apps	Subs	Gls
Gillingham	Bedford T	05.66	66-70	154	6	7
Northampton T	L	10.71	71	1	0	0

BAILEY Roy Norman
Epsom, 26 May, 1932 Died 1993 (G)

League Club	Source	Date Signed	Seasons Played	Apps	Subs	Gls
Crystal Palace	Jnrs	06.49	49-55	118	-	0
Ipswich T	Tr	03.56	55-64	315	-	0

BAILEY Stefan Kyon Lloyd
London, 10 November, 1987 (M)

League Club	Source	Date Signed	Seasons Played	Apps	Subs	Gls
Queens Park Rgrs	Sch	•	04	1	1	0

BAILEY Steven (Steve) John
Bristol, 12 March, 1964 (M)

League Club	Source	Date Signed	Seasons Played	Apps	Subs	Gls
Bristol Rov	App	03.82	81	15	1	1

BAILEY Terence (Terry)
Stoke-on-Trent, 18 December, 1947 (M)

League Club	Source	Date Signed	Seasons Played	Apps	Subs	Gls
Port Vale	Stafford Rgrs	08.74	74-77	161	4	26

BAILIE Colin James
Belfast, 31 March, 1964 (FB)

League Club	Source	Date Signed	Seasons Played	Apps	Subs	Gls
Swindon T	App	03.82	81-84	105	2	4
Reading	Tr	07.85	85-87	83	1	1
Cambridge U	Tr	08.88	88-91	104	15	3

BAILLIE Douglas (Doug)
Drycross, 27 January, 1937 SSch/Su23-2 (CF)

League Club	Source	Date Signed	Seasons Played	Apps	Subs	Gls
Swindon T	Airdrie	03.56	55	1	-	0

BAILLIE Joseph (Joe)
Dumfries, 26 February, 1929 Died 1966 SLge-3/SB (FB)

League Club	Source	Date Signed	Seasons Played	Apps	Subs	Gls
Wolverhampton W	Glasgow Celtic	12.54	54	1	-	0
Bristol C	Tr	06.56	56	10	-	0
Leicester C	Tr	06.57	57-59	75	-	0
Bradford PA	Tr	06.60	60	7	-	1

BAILY Edward (Eddie) Francis
Clapton, 6 August, 1925 FLge-6/EB/E-9 (IF)

League Club	Source	Date Signed	Seasons Played	Apps	Subs	Gls
Tottenham H	Finchley	02.46	46-55	296	-	64
Port Vale	Tr	01.56	55-56	26	-	8
Nottingham F	Tr	10.56	56-58	68	-	14
Leyton Orient	Tr	12.58	58-59	29	-	3

BAIN Alexander (Alex) Edward
Edinburgh, 22 January, 1936 (CF)

League Club	Source	Date Signed	Seasons Played	Apps	Subs	Gls
Huddersfield T	Motherwell	08.57	57-58	29	-	11
Chesterfield	Tr	02.60	59	18	-	9
Bournemouth	Falkirk	08.61	61	8	-	4

BAIN James (Jimmy) Alistair
Blairgowrie, 14 December, 1919 (W)

League Club	Source	Date Signed	Seasons Played	Apps	Subs	Gls
Chelsea	Gillingham	05.45	46	9	-	1
Swindon T	Tr	05.47	47-53	235	-	40

BAIN John
Falkirk, 23 June, 1957 (M)

League Club	Source	Date Signed	Seasons Played	Apps	Subs	Gls
Bristol C	App	07.74	76-78	5	1	0
Brentford	L	02.77	76	17	1	1

BAIN John Shanks
Calderbank, 20 July, 1946 (FB)

League Club	Source	Date Signed	Seasons Played	Apps	Subs	Gls
Bury	Clarkston	07.63	64-66	9	3	0

BAIN Kevin
Kirkcaldy, 19 September, 1972 SSch/SYth/Su21-4 (M)

League Club	Source	Date Signed	Seasons Played	Apps	Subs	Gls
Rotherham U (L)	Dundee	03.97	96	10	2	0

BAIN William (Billy) Clark
Alloa, 16 November, 1924 (CF)

League Club	Source	Date Signed	Seasons Played	Apps	Subs	Gls
Hartlepools U	Dunfermline Ath	08.50	50	2	-	0

BAINBRIDGE Kenneth (Ken) Victor
Barking, 15 January, 1921 (W)

League Club	Source	Date Signed	Seasons Played	Apps	Subs	Gls
West Ham U	Leyton	11.44	46-49	80	-	16
Reading	Tr	06.50	50-52	89	-	32
Southend U	Tr	02.53	52-54	78	-	25

BAINBRIDGE Peter Edgar
Newton-on-Ouse, 30 January, 1958 (CD)

League Club	Source	Date Signed	Seasons Played	Apps	Subs	Gls
York C	Middlesbrough (App)	11.77	77-78	9	0	0
Darlington	Tr	08.79	79	16	0	0

BAINBRIDGE Robert Esmond
York, 22 February, 1931 (CF)

League Club	Source	Date Signed	Seasons Played	Apps	Subs	Gls
York C	Terry's	04.54	53-54	4	-	0

BAINBRIDGE Terence (Terry)
Hartlepool, 23 December, 1962 (CD)

League Club	Source	Date Signed	Seasons Played	Apps	Subs	Gls
Hartlepool U	Henry Smith's BC	12.81	81-83	34	3	1

BAINBRIDGE William (Bill)
Gateshead, 9 March, 1922 (IF)

League Club	Source	Date Signed	Seasons Played	Apps	Subs	Gls
Manchester U	Ashington	12.45				
Bury	Tr	05.46	46	2	-	1
Tranmere Rov	Tr	11.48	48-53	168	-	64

BAINES John Robert
Colchester, 25 September, 1937 (CF)

League Club	Source	Date Signed	Seasons Played	Apps	Subs	Gls
Colchester U	Colchester Casuals	01.60	60-62	4	-	0

BAINES Leighton John
Liverpool, 11 December, 1984 Eu21-3 (FB)

League Club	Source	Date Signed	Seasons Played	Apps	Subs	Gls
Wigan Ath	Sch	01.03	02-04	70	3	1

BAINES Paul
Burton-on-Trent, 15 January, 1972 (W)

League Club	Source	Date Signed	Seasons Played	Apps	Subs	Gls
Stoke C	YT	07.90	90	1	1	0

BAINES Cecil **Peter**
Australia, 11 September, 1919 Died 1997 (IF)

League Club	Source	Date Signed	Seasons Played	Apps	Subs	Gls
Wrexham	Oldham Ath (Am)	04.43	46	6	-	2
Crewe Alex	Tr	11.46	46	8	-	0
Hartlepools U	Tr	06.47	47	9	-	1
New Brighton	Tr	10.47	47	2	-	0

BAINES Stanley (Stan) Norman
Syston, 28 July, 1920 Died 1990 (W)

League Club	Source	Date Signed	Seasons Played	Apps	Subs	Gls
Leicester C	Coalville T	11.37	38	7	-	1
Northampton T	Tr	07.46	46	1	-	0

BAINES Stephen (Steve) John
Newark, 23 June, 1954 (CD)

League Club	Source	Date Signed	Seasons Played	Apps	Subs	Gls
Nottingham F	App	07.72	72	2	0	0
Huddersfield T	Tr	07.75	75-77	113	1	10
Bradford C	Tr	03.78	77-79	98	1	17
Walsall	Tr	07.80	80-81	47	1	5
Bury	L	12.81	81	7	0	0
Scunthorpe U	Tr	08.82	82	37	1	1
Chesterfield	Tr	07.83	83-86	132	1	9

BAIRD Andrew (Andy) Crawford
East Kilbride, 18 January, 1979 (F)

League Club	Source	Date Signed	Seasons Played	Apps	Subs	Gls
Wycombe W	YT	03.98	97-01	55	24	13

BAIRD Christopher (Chris) Patrick
Ballymoney, 25 February, 1982 NIYth/NIu21-6/NI-11 (FB)

League Club	Source	Date Signed	Seasons Played	Apps	Subs	Gls
Southampton	YT	01.01	02-03	2	5	0
Walsall	L	09.03	03	10	0	0
Watford	L	03.04	03	8	0	0

BAIRD Douglas (Doug) Francis Hogg
Falkirk, 26 November, 1935 Su23-1/SLge-1 (FB)

League Club	Source	Date Signed	Seasons Played	Apps	Subs	Gls
Nottingham F	Partick Th	09.60	60-62	32	-	0
Plymouth Arg	Tr	10.63	63-67	147	1	1

BAIRD John Alfred **Gordon**
Nottingham, 14 January, 1924 Died 1999 (WH)

League Club	Source	Date Signed	Seasons Played	Apps	Subs	Gls
Mansfield T	New Houghton	11.46	46-47	9	-	0

BAIRD Henry (Harry)
Belfast, 17 August, 1913 Died 1973 IrLge-2/I-1 (WH)

League Club	Source	Date Signed	Seasons Played	Apps	Subs	Gls
Manchester U	Linfield	01.37	36-37	49	-	15
Huddersfield T	Tr	09.38	38	19	-	4
Ipswich T	Linfield	06.46	46-51	216	-	6

BAIRD Hugh
New Monkland, 14 March, 1930 S-1 (CF)

League Club	Source	Date Signed	Seasons Played	Apps	Subs	Gls
Leeds U	Airdrie	06.57	57-58	45	-	22

BAIRD Ian James
Rotherham, 1 April, 1964 ESch (F)

League Club	Source	Date Signed	Seasons Played	Apps	Subs	Gls
Southampton	App	04.82	82-84	20	2	5
Cardiff C	L	11.83	83	12	0	6
Newcastle U	L	12.84	84	4	1	1
Leeds U	Tr	03.85	84-86	84	1	33
Portsmouth	Tr	08.87	87	20	0	1
Leeds U	Tr	03.88	87-89	76	1	17
Middlesbrough	Tr	01.90	89-90	60	3	19
Bristol C	Heart of Midlothian	07.93	93-95	45	12	11
Plymouth Arg	Tr	09.95	95	24	3	5
Brighton & Hove A	Tr	07.96	96-97	43	1	14

BAIRD Samuel (Sammy)
Denny, 13 May, 1930 SLge-5/S-7 (IF)

League Club	Source	Date Signed	Seasons Played	Apps	Subs	Gls
Preston NE	Clyde	06.54	54	15	-	2

BAIRSTOW David Leslie
Bradford, 1 September, 1951 Died 1998 (F)

League Club	Source	Date Signed	Seasons Played	Apps	Subs	Gls
Bradford C	Jnrs	12.71	71-72	10	7	1

BAK Arkadiusz
Szczecin, Poland, 6 January, 1974 Poland 14 (M)

League Club	Source	Date Signed	Seasons Played	Apps	Subs	Gls
Birmingham C (L)	Polonia Warsaw (Pol)	12.01	01	2	2	0

BAKALLI Adrian
Brussels, Belgium, 22 November, 1976 (F)

League Club	Source	Date Signed	Seasons Played	Apps	Subs	Gls
Watford	RWD Molenbeek (Bel)	01.99	99	0	2	0
Swindon T	Tr	03.01	00	1	0	0

BAKAYOKO Ibrahima
Seguela, Ivory Coast, 31 December, 1976 Ivory Coast 17 (F)

League Club	Source	Date Signed	Seasons Played	Apps	Subs	Gls
Everton	Montpellier (Fr)	10.98	98	17	6	4

BAKER Alan Reeves
Tipton, 22 June, 1944 ESch/EYth (M)

League Club	Source	Date Signed	Seasons Played	Apps	Subs	Gls
Aston Villa	App	07.61	60-65	92	1	13
Walsall	Tr	07.66	66-70	128	9	31

BAKER Charles (Charlie) Joseph
Turner's Hill, 6 January, 1936 (G)

League Club	Source	Date Signed	Seasons Played	Apps	Subs	Gls
Brighton & Hove A	Horsham	05.60	60-62	81	-	0
Aldershot	Tr	07.64	64-65	28	0	0

BAKER Christopher (Chris)
Maltby, 2 February, 1952 (F)

League Club	Source	Date Signed	Seasons Played	Apps	Subs	Gls
Barnsley (Am)		11.70	71	0	1	0

BAKER Clifford (Cliff) Henry
Bristol, 11 January, 1924 (IF)

League Club	Source	Date Signed	Seasons Played	Apps	Subs	Gls
Bristol Rov	Coalpit Heath	01.47	46	5	-	2

BAKER Clive
Adwick-le-Street, 5 July, 1934 (IF)

League Club	Source	Date Signed	Seasons Played	Apps	Subs	Gls
Doncaster Rov		08.52				
Halifax T	Tr	08.55	55-58	58	-	22

BAKER Clive Edward
North Walsham, 14 March, 1959 (G)

League Club	Source	Date Signed	Seasons Played	Apps	Subs	Gls
Norwich C	Jnrs	07.77	77-80	14	0	0
Barnsley	Tr	08.84	84-90	291	0	0
Coventry C	Tr	08.91				
Ipswich T	Tr	08.92	92-94	47	1	0

BAKER Colin Walter
Cardiff, 18 December, 1934 Wu23-1/W-7 (WH)

League Club	Source	Date Signed	Seasons Played	Apps	Subs	Gls
Cardiff C	Cardiff Nomads	03.53	53-65	297	1	18

BAKER Darren Spencer
Wednesbury, 28 June, 1965 WSch (M)

League Club	Source	Date Signed	Seasons Played	Apps	Subs	Gls
Wrexham	Jnrs	08.83	82-83	18	6	1

BAKER David Henry
Penzance, 21 October, 1928 (CD)

League Club	Source	Date Signed	Seasons Played	Apps	Subs	Gls
Nottingham F	Brush Sports	10.49	49	3	-	0

BAKER Douglas (Doug) Graham
Lewisham, 8 April, 1947 (F)

League Club	Source	Date Signed	Seasons Played	Apps	Subs	Gls
Arsenal	App	05.64				
Millwall	Tr	06.66	66	4	1	1

BAKER Frank
Stoke-on-Trent, 22 October, 1918 Died 1989 (W)

League Club	Source	Date Signed	Seasons Played	Apps	Subs	Gls
Stoke C	Port Vale (Am)	06.36	36-49	162	-	32

BAKER Thomas **George**
Maerdy, 6 April, 1936 Wu23-2 (CF)

League Club	Source	Date Signed	Seasons Played	Apps	Subs	Gls
Plymouth Arg	Maerdy	10.53	54-59	78	-	16
Shrewsbury T	Tr	06.60	60-61	52	-	5

League Club	Source	Date Signed	Seasons Played	Apps	Subs	Gls
BAKER Gerald (Gerry)						
South Hiendley, 22 April, 1939						(FB)
Bradford PA	Jnrs	01.57	57-60	16	-	0
BAKER Gerard (Gerry)						
Wigan, 16 September, 1938						(FB)
Nottingham F	Wigan Ath	12.59				
York C	Tr	07.63	63-68	214	0	7
BAKER Gerard (Gerry) Austin						
New York, USA, 11 April, 1938						(F)
Chelsea	Larkhall Thistle	06.55				
Manchester C	St Mirren	11.60	60-61	37	-	14
Ipswich T	Hibernian	12.63	63-67	135	0	58
Coventry C	Tr	11.67	67-69	27	4	5
Brentford	L	10.69	69	8	0	2
BAKER Graham Edgar						
Southampton, 3 December, 1958 Eu21-2						(M)
Southampton	App	12.76	77-81	111	2	22
Manchester C	Tr	08.82	82-86	114	3	19
Southampton	Tr	06.87	87-89	57	3	9
Aldershot	L	03.90	89	7	0	2
Fulham	Tr	07.90	90-91	8	2	1
BAKER Joseph (Joe) Henry						
Liverpool, 17 July, 1940 Died 2003 SSch/Eu23-6/E-8						(F)
Arsenal	Torino (It)	08.62	62-65	144	0	93
Nottingham F	Tr	03.66	65-68	117	1	41
Sunderland	Tr	07.69	69-70	39	1	12
BAKER Joseph (Joe) Philip						
Kentish Town, 19 April, 1977						(W)
Leyton Orient	Charlton Ath (YT)	05.95	95-98	23	52	3
BAKER Keith						
Oxford, 15 October, 1956 ESch						(G)
Oxford U	App	11.74				
Grimsby T	L	08.75	75	1	0	0
BAKER Kieron Richard						
Ryde, 29 October, 1949						(G)
Bournemouth	Fulham (Am)	07.67	69-77	217	0	0
Brentford	L	02.73	72	6	0	0
BAKER Mark						
Swansea, 26 April, 1961						(F)
Swansea C	Jnrs	09.78	78-79	3	8	2
BAKER Matthew (Matt) Christopher						
Harrogate, 18 December, 1979 ESemiPro-4						(G)
Hull C	YT	07.98	99	0	2	0
Wrexham	Hereford U	07.04	04	11	2	0
MK Dons	Tr	12.04	04	20	0	0
BAKER David **Paul**						
Newcastle, 5 January, 1963						(F)
Southampton	Bishop Auckland	07.84				
Carlisle U	Tr	07.85	85-86	66	5	11
Hartlepool U	Tr	07.87	87-91	192	5	67
Gillingham	Motherwell	01.93	92-94	58	4	16
York C	Tr	10.94	94-95	36	12	18
Torquay U	Tr	01.96	95-96	30	0	8
Scunthorpe U	Tr	10.96	96	21	0	9
Hartlepool U	Tr	03.97	96-98	25	10	9
Carlisle U	Tr	08.99	99	12	5	2
BAKER Peter Robert						
West Ham, 24 August, 1934						(FB)
Sheffield Wed	Tottenham H (Am)	11.54	57	11	-	0
Queens Park Rgrs	Tr	03.61	60-62	27	-	0
BAKER Peter Russell Barker						
Hampstead, 10 December, 1931 EYth						(FB)
Tottenham H	Enfield	10.52	52-64	299	-	3
BAKER Philip (Phil)						
Birkenhead, 4 November, 1982						(FB)
Tranmere Rov	YT	05.02				
Exeter C	Bangor C	03.03	02	5	1	0
BAKER Roy Vincent						
Bradford, 8 June, 1954						(F)
Bradford C		07.72	72-74	39	7	11
BAKER Stephen (Steve)						
Wallsend, 2 December, 1961						(FB)
Southampton	App	12.79	80-87	61	12	0
Burnley	L	02.84	83	10	0	0
Leyton Orient	Tr	03.88	87-90	105	7	5
Bournemouth	Tr	08.91	91	5	1	0

League Club	Source	Date Signed	Seasons Played	Apps	Subs	Gls
BAKER Steven (Steve) Richard						
Pontefract, 8 September, 1978 IRu21-4						(FB)
Middlesbrough	YT	07.97	97-98	6	2	0
Huddersfield T	L	08.99	99	3	0	0
Darlington	L	03.00	99	4	1	0
Hartlepool U	L	09.00	00	9	0	0
BAKER Terence (Terry)						
Rochford, 13 November, 1965						(CD)
West Ham U	App	11.83				
Colchester U	Billericay T	11.85	85-87	55	0	2
BAKER Thomas (Tom)						
Salford, 28 March, 1985						(M)
Barnsley	Sch	07.04	03-04	0	4	0
BAKER Thomas (Tom) Arthur						
Stepney, 9 August, 1939						(IF)
Bristol Rov		10.56	62	1	-	0
BAKER Wayne Robert						
Leeds, 4 December, 1965						(G)
Sheffield Wed	App	12.83				
Darlington	Whitby T	11.86	86	5	0	0
BAKER William (Billy) George						
Penrhiwceiber, 3 October, 1920 Died 2005 WSch/WLge-4/W-1						(WH)
Cardiff C	Troedyrhiw	01.38	38-54	292	-	5
Ipswich T	Tr	06.55	55	20	-	0
BAKES Martin Stansfield						
Bradford, 8 February, 1937						(W)
Bradford C	Jnrs	02.54	53-58	72	-	7
Scunthorpe U	Tr	06.59	59-62	77	-	5
BAKEWELL Herbert						
Barnsley, 8 March, 1921 Died 1998						(G)
Barnsley	Jnrs	02.39				
Newport Co	Tr	09.46	46	8	-	0
BAKHOLT Kurt						
Odense, Denmark, 12 August, 1963						(M)
Queens Park Rgrs	Vejle BK (Den)	01.86	85	0	1	0
BAKKE Eirik						
Sogndal, Norway, 13 September, 1977 NoYth/Nou21-34/No-25						(M)
Leeds U	Sogndal IF (Nor)	07.99	99-04	107	23	8
BALABAN Bosko						
Rijeka, Croatia, 15 October, 1978 Croatia 13						(F)
Aston Villa	Dynamo Zagreb (Cro)	08.01	01	0	8	0
B'ALAC Peta John						
Exeter, 9 December, 1953						(G)
Plymouth Arg	App	12.71	71-72	40	0	0
Hereford U	L	08.73	73	2	0	0
Swansea C	L	09.73	73	4	0	0
BALCOMBE Stephen (Steve) William						
Bangor, 2 September, 1961 Wu21-1						(F)
Leeds U	App	06.79	81	1	0	1
BALDACCHINO Ryan Lee						
Leicester, 13 January, 1981						(M)
Blackburn Rov	YT	02.99				
Bolton W	Tr	03.01				
Carlisle U	Tr	08.02	02-03	11	12	0
BALDERSTONE John **Christopher (Chris)**						
Huddersfield, 16 November, 1940 Died 2000						(M)
Huddersfield T	Jnrs	05.58	59-64	117	-	24
Carlisle U	Tr	06.65	65-74	368	7	66
Doncaster Rov	Tr	07.75	75	38	1	1
BALDIE Douglas Wilson						
Scone, 16 April, 1921 Died 1998						(IF)
Bristol Rov	Luton T (Am)	04.46	46-47	8	-	4
BALDRIDGE Robert William						
Sunderland, 26 November, 1932						(CF)
Gateshead	Hendon Social	02.57	56-59	59	-	21
BALDRY Simon Jonathan						
Huddersfield, 12 February, 1976						(W)
Huddersfield T	YT	07.94	93-02	87	59	8
Bury	L	09.98	98	0	5	0
Notts Co	Tr	08.03	03	32	3	1
BALDRY William (Bill) Joseph						
Luton, 9 July, 1956						(FB)
Cambridge U	Luton T (Am)	03.76	75-77	27	0	0

BALDWIN Joseph George
Islington, 26 July, 1921 Died 1976 (WH)

League Club	Source	Date Signed	Seasons Played	Apps	Subs	Gls
Gillingham	Gravesend & Northfleet	08.51	51	1	-	0

BALDWIN Harold (Harry)
Saltley, 17 July, 1920 (G)

League Club	Source	Date Signed	Seasons Played	Apps	Subs	Gls
West Bromwich A	Sutton T	04.38	37	5	-	0
Brighton & Hove A	Tr	05.39	46-51	164	-	0
Walsall	Kettering T	12.53	53-54	37	-	0

BALDWIN James (Jimmy)
Blackburn, 12 January, 1922 Died 1985 (WH)

League Club	Source	Date Signed	Seasons Played	Apps	Subs	Gls
Blackburn Rov	Mill Hill St Peter's	12.45	46-49	88	-	0
Leicester C	Tr	02.50	49-55	180	-	4

BALDWIN Patrick (Pat) Michael
City of London, 12 November, 1982 (CD)

League Club	Source	Date Signed	Seasons Played	Apps	Subs	Gls
Colchester U	Chelsea (YT)	08.02	02-04	49	12	0

BALDWIN Thomas (Tommy)
Gateshead, 10 June, 1945 Eu23-2 (F)

League Club	Source	Date Signed	Seasons Played	Apps	Subs	Gls
Arsenal	Wrekenton Jnrs	12.62	64-66	17	0	7
Chelsea	Tr	09.66	66-74	182	5	74
Millwall	L	11.74	74	6	0	1
Manchester U	L	01.75	74	2	0	0
Brentford	Gravesend & N (N/C)	10.77	77	4	0	1

BALIS Igor
Zalozinik, Slovakia, 5 January, 1970 Slovakia 41 (FB)

League Club	Source	Date Signed	Seasons Played	Apps	Subs	Gls
West Bromwich A	Slovan Bratislava (Slo)	12.00	00-02	60	9	4

BALL Alan James
Farnworth, 12 May, 1945 Eu23-8/FLge-6/E-72 (M)

League Club	Source	Date Signed	Seasons Played	Apps	Subs	Gls
Blackpool	App	05.62	62-65	116	0	40
Everton	Tr	08.66	66-71	208	0	66
Arsenal	Tr	12.71	71-76	177	0	45
Southampton	Tr	12.76	76-79	132	0	9
Blackpool	Vancouver (Can)	07.80	80	30	0	5
Southampton	Tr	03.81	80-82	63	0	2
Bristol Rov	Eastern Ath (HK)	01.83	82	17	0	2

BALL James Alan
Farnworth, 23 September, 1924 Died 1982 (IF)

League Club	Source	Date Signed	Seasons Played	Apps	Subs	Gls
Southport	Bolton Boys Federation	03.46	46	2	-	0
Birmingham C	Tr	05.47				
Southport	Tr	02.48	47-49	39	-	9
Oldham Ath	Tr	07.50	50	7	-	1
Rochdale	Tr	02.52	51	5	-	1

BALL Donald
Barnard Castle, 14 June, 1962 (CD)

League Club	Source	Date Signed	Seasons Played	Apps	Subs	Gls
Darlington	App	06.80	79-81	57	3	2

BALL Stephen Gary
St Austell, 15 December, 1959 (M)

League Club	Source	Date Signed	Seasons Played	Apps	Subs	Gls
Plymouth Arg	App	12.77	79	0	1	0
Lincoln C	Tr	10.79	79	3	0	0

BALL Geoffrey (Geoff) Hudson
Nottingham, 2 November, 1944 (FB)

League Club	Source	Date Signed	Seasons Played	Apps	Subs	Gls
Nottingham F	Ericsson's Electronic	02.63	64-65	3	0	0
Notts Co	Tr	11.67	67-71	111	1	0

BALL John
Ince, 13 March, 1925 FLge-2/EB (FB)

League Club	Source	Date Signed	Seasons Played	Apps	Subs	Gls
Manchester U	Wigan Ath	03.48	47-49	22	-	0
Bolton W	Tr	09.50	50-57	200	-	2

BALL John (Jack) Albert
Brighton, 16 July, 1923 Died 1999 (G)

League Club	Source	Date Signed	Seasons Played	Apps	Subs	Gls
Brighton & Hove A	Vernon Ath	02.43	46-52	113	-	0

BALL Joseph (Joe) Howard
Walsall, 4 April, 1931 Died 1974 (W)

League Club	Source	Date Signed	Seasons Played	Apps	Subs	Gls
Ipswich T	Banbury Spencer	08.51	51-52	32	-	2
Aldershot	Tr	06.54	54-55	31	-	5

BALL Keith
Walsall, 26 October, 1940 (G)

League Club	Source	Date Signed	Seasons Played	Apps	Subs	Gls
Walsall	Jnrs	01.59	58-61	11	-	0
Walsall	Worcester C	05.65	66-67	34	0	0
Port Vale	Tr	11.68	68-71	130	0	0
Walsall	Stourbridge	11.72	72	2	0	0

BALL Kevin Anthony
Hastings, 12 November, 1964 (M)

League Club	Source	Date Signed	Seasons Played	Apps	Subs	Gls
Portsmouth	Coventry C (App)	10.82	83-89	96	9	4
Sunderland	Tr	07.90	90-99	329	10	21
Fulham	Tr	12.99	99	15	3	0
Burnley	Tr	07.00	00-01	77	5	2

BALL Michael John
Liverpool, 2 October, 1979 ESch/EYth/Eu21-7/E-1 (FB)

League Club	Source	Date Signed	Seasons Played	Apps	Subs	Gls
Everton	YT	10.96	96-00	102	19	8

BALL Stephen (Steve)
Leeds, 22 November, 1973 (M)

League Club	Source	Date Signed	Seasons Played	Apps	Subs	Gls
Darlington	Leeds U (YT)	08.92	92-93	30	12	3

BALL Steven (Steve) James
Colchester, 2 September, 1969 (M)

League Club	Source	Date Signed	Seasons Played	Apps	Subs	Gls
Arsenal	YT	09.87				
Colchester U	Tr	12.89	89	3	1	0
Norwich C	Tr	09.90	91	0	2	0
Colchester U	Cambridge U (N/C)	09.92	92-95	52	12	7

BALLAGHER John
Ashton-under-Lyne, 21 March, 1936 (IF)

League Club	Source	Date Signed	Seasons Played	Apps	Subs	Gls
Sheffield Wed	Dukinfield T	02.57	58	3	-	0
Doncaster Rov	Tr	02.61	60-61	41	-	13
Gillingham	Tr	08.62	62-63	41	-	10

BALLANTYNE John Dixon (Dick)
Newburn, 16 September, 1927 (FB)

League Club	Source	Date Signed	Seasons Played	Apps	Subs	Gls
West Ham U		05.46				
Hartlepools U	Tr	07.50	50-51	13	-	0

BALLARD Edgar (Ted) Albert
Brentford, 16 June, 1920 (FB)

League Club	Source	Date Signed	Seasons Played	Apps	Subs	Gls
Leyton Orient	Hayes	04.46	46	26	-	1
Southampton	Tr	06.47	47-50	45	-	0

BALMER John (Jack)
Liverpool, 6 February, 1916 Died 1984 EWar-1 (IF)

League Club	Source	Date Signed	Seasons Played	Apps	Subs	Gls
Liverpool	Collegiate OB	08.35	35-51	289	-	98

BALMER John Michael (Mike)
Hexham, 25 May, 1946 (CF)

League Club	Source	Date Signed	Seasons Played	Apps	Subs	Gls
Leicester C	App	01.64				
Halifax T	Tr	05.65	65-66	28	0	9

BALMER Stuart Murray
Falkirk, 20 September, 1969 SSch/SYth (CD)

League Club	Source	Date Signed	Seasons Played	Apps	Subs	Gls
Charlton Ath	Glasgow Celtic	08.90	90-97	201	26	8
Wigan Ath	Tr	09.98	98-00	99	2	4
Oldham Ath	Tr	07.01	01	35	1	6
Scunthorpe U	L	10.02	02	6	0	0
Boston U	Tr	12.02	02-03	46	1	3

BALOGUN Teslim Ayinde
Lagos, Nigeria, 27 March, 1931 (CF)

League Club	Source	Date Signed	Seasons Played	Apps	Subs	Gls
Queens Park Rgrs	Skegness T	09.56	56	13	-	3

BALSOM Clifford (Cliff) Gene
Torquay, 25 March, 1946 (FB)

League Club	Source	Date Signed	Seasons Played	Apps	Subs	Gls
Torquay U	App	03.64	63	4	-	0

BALSON Michael (Mike) John Charles
Bridport, 9 September, 1947 (CD)

League Club	Source	Date Signed	Seasons Played	Apps	Subs	Gls
Exeter C	Jnrs	08.65	66-73	273	3	9

BALTACHA Sergei Pavlovich
Kiev, Ukraine, 17 February, 1958 USSR int (M)

League Club	Source	Date Signed	Seasons Played	Apps	Subs	Gls
Ipswich T	Dynamo Kiev (Ukr)	01.89	88-89	22	6	1

BALTACHA Sergei Sergeivich
Kiev, Ukraine, 28 July, 1979 Su21-3 (FB)

League Club	Source	Date Signed	Seasons Played	Apps	Subs	Gls
Millwall	St Mirren	10.02	02	1	1	0

BAMBER John David (Dave)
Prescot, 1 February, 1959 (F)

League Club	Source	Date Signed	Seasons Played	Apps	Subs	Gls
Blackpool	St Helens T	09.79	79-82	81	5	29
Coventry C	Tr	06.83	83	18	1	3
Walsall	Tr	03.84	83-84	17	3	7
Portsmouth	Tr	12.84	84	4	0	1
Swindon T	Tr	11.85	85-87	103	3	31
Watford	Tr	06.88	88	16	2	3
Stoke C	Tr	12.88	88-89	43	0	8
Hull C	Tr	02.90	89-90	25	3	5
Blackpool	Tr	11.90	90-94	111	2	60

BAMBER Lee
Burnley, 31 October, 1968 (G)

League Club	Source	Date Signed	Seasons Played	Apps	Subs	Gls
Preston NE	Chorley	08.93	93	0	1	0

BAMBER Michael (Mike) John
Preston, 1 October, 1980 (FB)

League Club	Source	Date Signed	Seasons Played	Apps	Subs	Gls
Macclesfield T	Blackpool (YT)	12.99	99-00	2	4	0

BAMBRIDGE Keith Graham
Rawmarsh, 1 September, 1935 (W)

League Club	Source	Date Signed	Seasons Played	Apps	Subs	Gls
Rotherham U	Masborough St Paul's	02.55	55-62	162	-	15
Darlington	Tr	12.64	64	6	-	0
Halifax T	Tr	03.65	64-65	8	1	1

BAMBRIDGE Stephen (Steve) Martin
Marylebone, 27 May, 1960 (F)

League Club	Source	Date Signed	Seasons Played	Apps	Subs	Gls
Aldershot	App	05.78	76	0	2	0

BAMFORD Harry Frank Ernest
Kingston, 8 April, 1914 Died 1949 (FB)

League Club	Source	Date Signed	Seasons Played	Apps	Subs	Gls
Brentford	Ealing YC	05.39				
Brighton & Hove A	Tr	06.46	46	8	-	0

BAMFORD Henry (Harry) Charles
Bristol, 8 February, 1920 Died 1958 (FB)

League Club	Source	Date Signed	Seasons Played	Apps	Subs	Gls
Bristol Rov	Ipswich T (Am)	01.46	46-58	486	-	5

BAMPTON David (Dave) Peter
Swindon, 5 May, 1985 (M)

League Club	Source	Date Signed	Seasons Played	Apps	Subs	Gls
Swindon T	Sch	•	02	0	3	0

BANCE Daniel (Danny) Robert
Plymouth, 27 September, 1982 (FB)

League Club	Source	Date Signed	Seasons Played	Apps	Subs	Gls
Plymouth Arg	YT	•	00	1	0	0

BANCROFT Paul Andrew
Derby, 10 September, 1964 (M)

League Club	Source	Date Signed	Seasons Played	Apps	Subs	Gls
Derby Co	App	09.82				
Crewe Alex	L	01.83	82	21	0	3
Northampton T	Tr	07.84	84	15	1	0

BANFIELD Neil Anthony
Poplar, 20 January, 1962 ESch/EYth (CD)

League Club	Source	Date Signed	Seasons Played	Apps	Subs	Gls
Crystal Palace	App	08.79	80	2	1	0
Orient	Adelaide City Fce (Aus)	12.83	83-84	30	1	0

BANGER Nicholas (Nicky) Lee
Southampton, 25 February, 1971 (F)

League Club	Source	Date Signed	Seasons Played	Apps	Subs	Gls
Southampton	YT	04.89	90-94	18	37	8
Oldham Ath	Tr	10.94	94-96	44	20	10
Oxford U	Tr	07.97	97-99	41	22	8
Scunthorpe U (L)	Dundee	11.00	00	0	1	0
Plymouth Arg	Dundee	08.01	01	3	7	2
Torquay U	Tr	03.02	01	1	0	0

BANGURA Alhassan (Al)
Sierra Leone, 24 January, 1988 (M)

League Club	Source	Date Signed	Seasons Played	Apps	Subs	Gls
Watford	Sch	•	04	1	1	0

BANHAM Roy
Nottingham, 30 October, 1936 (CD)

League Club	Source	Date Signed	Seasons Played	Apps	Subs	Gls
Nottingham F	Hyson Green BC	11.53	55-56	2	-	0
Peterborough U	Tr	07.58	60-61	16	-	0

BANJO Tunji Babajide
Kennington, 19 February, 1960 Nigeria 7 (M)

League Club	Source	Date Signed	Seasons Played	Apps	Subs	Gls
Orient	App	03.77	77-81	20	7	1

BANKOLE Ademola (Ade)
Abeokuta, Nigeria, 9 September, 1969 (G)

League Club	Source	Date Signed	Seasons Played	Apps	Subs	Gls
Crewe Alex	Shooting Stars (Nig)	09.96	96-97	6	0	0
Queens Park Rgrs	Tr	07.98	99	0	1	0
Crewe Alex	Tr	07.00	00-02	51	1	0
Brentford	Maidenhead U	02.05	04	3	0	0

BANKS Alan
Liverpool, 5 October, 1938 (F)

League Club	Source	Date Signed	Seasons Played	Apps	Subs	Gls
Liverpool	Rankin Boys	05.58	58-60	8	-	6
Exeter C	Cambridge C	10.63	63-65	85	0	43
Plymouth Arg	Tr	06.66	66-67	19	0	5
Exeter C	Tr	11.67	67-72	160	13	58

BANKS Christopher (Chris) Noel
Stone, 12 November, 1965 ESemiPro-2 (CD)

League Club	Source	Date Signed	Seasons Played	Apps	Subs	Gls
Port Vale	Jnrs	12.82	84-87	50	15	1
Exeter C	Tr	06.88	88	43	2	1
Cheltenham T	Bath C	08.94	99-01	119	1	1

BANKS Eric
Workington, 7 April, 1950 (W)

League Club	Source	Date Signed	Seasons Played	Apps	Subs	Gls
Workington	Jnrs	09.68	67-72	26	4	1

BANKS Francis (Frank) Stanley
Hull, 21 August, 1945 (FB)

League Club	Source	Date Signed	Seasons Played	Apps	Subs	Gls
Southend U	Jnrs	10.62	63-65	4	0	0
Hull C	Tr	09.66	67-75	284	4	6
Southend U	Tr	03.76	75-77	75	0	0

BANKS George Ernest
Wednesbury, 28 March, 1919 Died 1991 (CF)

League Club	Source	Date Signed	Seasons Played	Apps	Subs	Gls
West Bromwich A	Brownhills Ath	06.38	38	1	-	2
Mansfield T	Tr	11.47	47-48	63	-	21

BANKS Gordon
Sheffield, 30 December, 1937 Eu23-2/FLge-6/E-73 (G)

League Club	Source	Date Signed	Seasons Played	Apps	Subs	Gls
Chesterfield	Rawmarsh CW	09.55	58	23	-	0
Leicester C	Tr	05.59	59-66	293	0	0
Stoke C	Tr	04.67	66-72	194	0	0

BANKS Ian Frederick
Mexborough, 9 January, 1961 (M)

League Club	Source	Date Signed	Seasons Played	Apps	Subs	Gls
Barnsley	App	01.79	78-82	158	6	37
Leicester C	Tr	06.83	83-86	78	15	14
Huddersfield T	Tr	09.86	86-87	78	0	17
Bradford C	Tr	07.88	88	26	4	3
West Bromwich A	Tr	03.89	88	2	2	0
Barnsley	Tr	07.89	89-91	87	9	7
Rotherham U	Tr	07.92	92-93	76	0	8
Darlington	Tr	08.94	94	39	0	1

BANKS Jason Mark
Farnworth, 16 November, 1968 (FB)

League Club	Source	Date Signed	Seasons Played	Apps	Subs	Gls
Wigan Ath	App	11.86				
Chester C	Atherton Colliery	10.87	87	1	1	0

BANKS Kenneth (Kenny)
Wigan, 19 October, 1923 Died 1994 (WH)

League Club	Source	Date Signed	Seasons Played	Apps	Subs	Gls
Southport	Wigan BC	08.45	46-51	118	-	5

BANKS Ralph
Farnworth, 28 June, 1920 Died 1993 (FB)

League Club	Source	Date Signed	Seasons Played	Apps	Subs	Gls
Bolton W	South Liverpool	12.40	46-52	104	-	0
Aldershot	Tr	01.54	53-54	44	-	1

BANKS Steven (Steve)
Hillingdon, 9 February, 1972 (G)

League Club	Source	Date Signed	Seasons Played	Apps	Subs	Gls
West Ham U	YT	03.90				
Gillingham	Tr	03.93	93-94	67	0	0
Blackpool	Tr	08.95	95-98	150	0	0
Bolton W	Tr	03.99	98-01	20	1	0
Rochdale	L	12.01	01	15	0	0
Bradford C	L	08.02	02	8	1	0
Stoke C	Tr	12.02	02	14	0	0
Wimbledon	Tr	08.03	03	24	0	0
Gillingham	Tr	03.04	03-04	39	0	0

BANKS Thomas (Tommy)
Farnworth, 10 November, 1929 FLge-1/E-6 (FB)

League Club	Source	Date Signed	Seasons Played	Apps	Subs	Gls
Bolton W	Partridges (Bolton)	10.47	47-60	233	-	2

BANNAN Thomas (Tommy) Neilson
Darngavel, 13 April, 1930 Died 2003 (CF)

League Club	Source	Date Signed	Seasons Played	Apps	Subs	Gls
Wrexham	Airdrie	06.51	51-54	158	-	60
Lincoln C	Tr	06.55	55-56	67	-	19
Wrexham	Tr	08.57	57-58	68	-	23
Barrow	Tr	08.59	59-60	45	-	15

BANNER Arthur
Sheffield, 28 June, 1918 Died 1980 (FB)

League Club	Source	Date Signed	Seasons Played	Apps	Subs	Gls
Doncaster Rov	Lopham Street	03.37				
West Ham U	Tr	05.38	38-47	27	-	0
Leyton Orient	Tr	02.48	47-52	164	-	1

BANNERMAN Telford Gordon
Coupar Angus, 17 September, 1924 (W)

League Club	Source	Date Signed	Seasons Played	Apps	Subs	Gls
New Brighton	Blairgowrie Jnrs	01.49	48-50	35	-	3

BANNISTER Bruce Ian
Bradford, 14 April, 1947 ESch (F)

League Club	Source	Date Signed	Seasons Played	Apps	Subs	Gls
Bradford C	Leeds U (Jnrs)	08.65	65-71	199	9	60
Bristol Rov	Tr	11.71	71-76	202	4	80
Plymouth Arg	Tr	12.76	76	24	0	7
Hull C	Tr	06.77	77-79	79	6	20

BANNISTER Edward (Eddie)
Leyland, 2 June, 1920 Died 1991 (FB)

League Club	Source	Date Signed	Seasons Played	Apps	Subs	Gls
Leeds U	Oaks Fold	05.46	46-49	44	-	1
Barnsley	Tr	07.50	50	32	-	0

BANNISTER Gary
Warrington, 22 July, 1960 Eu21-1 (F)

League Club	Source	Date Signed	Seasons Played	Apps	Subs	Gls
Coventry C	App	05.78	78-80	17	5	3
Sheffield Wed	Tr	08.81	81-83	117	1	55
Queens Park Rgrs	Tr	08.84	84-87	136	0	56
Coventry C	Tr	03.88	87-89	39	4	11
West Bromwich A	Tr	03.90	89-91	62	10	18
Oxford U	L	03.92	91	7	3	2
Nottingham F	Tr	08.92	92	27	4	8
Stoke C	Tr	05.93	93	10	5	2
Lincoln C	Hong Kong Rgrs (HK)	09.94	94	25	4	7
Darlington	Tr	08.95	95	39	2	10

BANNISTER Jack
Chesterfield, 26 January, 1942 (FB)

League Club	Source	Date Signed	Seasons Played	Apps	Subs	Gls
West Bromwich A	Jnrs	08.59	59-62	9	-	0
Scunthorpe U	Tr	06.64	64	9	-	0
Crystal Palace	Tr	07.65	65-68	117	3	7
Luton T	Tr	10.68	68-70	79	4	0
Cambridge U	Tr	05.71	71-73	28	4	0

BANNISTER James (Jimmy) Henry
Chesterfield, 1 February, 1929 (FB)

League Club	Source	Date Signed	Seasons Played	Apps	Subs	Gls
Chesterfield		12.50				
Shrewsbury T	Tr	06.52	52-57	238	-	6
Northampton T	Tr	07.58	58	24	-	0
Aldershot	Tr	08.59	59-60	85	-	0

BANNISTER Keith
Sheffield, 27 January, 1923 (FB)

League Club	Source	Date Signed	Seasons Played	Apps	Subs	Gls
Sheffield Wed	Sheffield YMCA	02.45	46-52	75	-	0
Chesterfield	Tr	06.53	53	17	-	0

BANNISTER Keith
Sheffield, 13 November, 1930 EYth (WH)

League Club	Source	Date Signed	Seasons Played	Apps	Subs	Gls
Sheffield U	Jnrs	05.48				
Birmingham C	Tr	08.50	52-53	22	-	0
Wrexham	King's Lynn	07.55	55	14	-	0
Chesterfield	Tr	12.55	55	21	-	1
Norwich C	Tr	07.56	56	7	-	0

BANNISTER Neville
Brierfield, 21 July, 1937 (W)

League Club	Source	Date Signed	Seasons Played	Apps	Subs	Gls
Bolton W	Jnrs	07.54	55-60	26	-	4
Lincoln C	Tr	03.61	60-63	68	-	16
Hartlepools U	Tr	08.64	64	41	-	8
Rochdale	Tr	07.65	65	18	1	2

BANNISTER Paul Francis
Stoke-on-Trent, 11 October, 1947 (F)

League Club	Source	Date Signed	Seasons Played	Apps	Subs	Gls
Port Vale	Jnrs	04.65	64-67	12	0	2

BANNON Eamonn John Peter
Edinburgh, 18 April, 1958 SSch/Su21-7/SLge-1/S-11 (M)

League Club	Source	Date Signed	Seasons Played	Apps	Subs	Gls
Chelsea	Heart of Midlothian	01.79	78-79	25	0	1

BANNON Ian
Bury, 3 September, 1959 (CD)

League Club	Source	Date Signed	Seasons Played	Apps	Subs	Gls
Rochdale	App	09.77	76-79	112	10	0

BANNON Paul Anthony
Dublin, 15 November, 1956 (F)

League Club	Source	Date Signed	Seasons Played	Apps	Subs	Gls
Nottingham F	Jnrs	06.75				
Carlisle U	Everwarm (Bridgend)	02.79	78-83	127	13	45
Darlington	L	10.83	83	2	0	0
Bristol Rov	Tr	01.84	83-84	27	2	8
Cardiff C	L	08.84	84	3	1	0
Plymouth Arg	L	11.84	84	0	2	0

BANOVIC Vjekoslav (Yakka)
Bihac, Bosnia, 12 November, 1956 Yugoslavia int (G)

League Club	Source	Date Signed	Seasons Played	Apps	Subs	Gls
Derby Co	Heidelberg U (Aus)	09.80	81-83	35	0	0

BANTON Dale Conrad
Kensington, 15 May, 1961 (F)

League Club	Source	Date Signed	Seasons Played	Apps	Subs	Gls
West Ham U	App	05.79	79-81	2	3	0
Aldershot	Tr	08.82	82-84	105	1	47
York C	Tr	11.84	84-88	129	9	49
Walsall	Tr	10.88	88	9	1	0
Grimsby T	Tr	03.89	88	3	5	1
Aldershot	Tr	08.89	89-90	29	15	3

BANTON Geoffrey (Geoff)
Ashton-under-Lyne, 16 March, 1957 (CD)

League Club	Source	Date Signed	Seasons Played	Apps	Subs	Gls
Plymouth Arg	Bolton W (App)	05.75	76-77	6	1	0
Fulham	Tr	07.78	78-81	37	1	3

BAPTISTE Jairzinho **Rocky** Alon
Lambeth, 7 August, 1972 (F)

League Club	Source	Date Signed	Seasons Played	Apps	Subs	Gls
Luton T	Hayes	10.00	00	0	3	0

BARACLOUGH Ian Robert
Leicester, 4 December, 1970 EYth (FB)

League Club	Source	Date Signed	Seasons Played	Apps	Subs	Gls
Leicester C	YT	12.88				
Wigan Ath	L	03.90	89	8	1	2
Grimsby T	L	12.90	90	1	3	0
Grimsby T	Tr	08.91	92	1	0	0
Lincoln C	Tr	08.92	92-93	68	5	10
Mansfield T	Tr	06.94	94-95	47	0	5
Notts Co	Tr	10.95	95-97	107	4	10
Queens Park Rgrs	Tr	03.98	97-00	120	5	1
Notts Co	Tr	07.01	01-03	93	8	5
Scunthorpe U	Tr	08.04	04	45	0	3

BARADA Taylor
Charlottesville, Virginia, USA, 14 August, 1972 (G)

League Club	Source	Date Signed	Seasons Played	Apps	Subs	Gls
Colchester U	Notts Co (N/C)	03.94	93	1	0	0

BARBARA Daniel
France, 12 October, 1974 (F)

League Club	Source	Date Signed	Seasons Played	Apps	Subs	Gls
Darlington	FC Lourosa (Por)	12.96	96	1	5	1

BARBER David (Dave) Eric
Wombwell, 6 December, 1939 EYth (WH)

League Club	Source	Date Signed	Seasons Played	Apps	Subs	Gls
Barnsley	Jnrs	06.58	57-60	83	-	4
Preston NE	Tr	06.61	61-63	37	-	2

BARBER Eric
Stockport, 25 March, 1926 (W)

League Club	Source	Date Signed	Seasons Played	Apps	Subs	Gls
Sheffield U		02.47				
Bolton W	Macclesfield T	03.50				
Rochdale	Tr	04.51	50-51	17	-	2

BARBER Eric
Dublin, 18 January, 1942 LoI-3/IR-2 (IF)

League Club	Source	Date Signed	Seasons Played	Apps	Subs	Gls
Birmingham C	Shelbourne	03.66	65-66	3	1	1

BARBER Frederick (Fred)
Ferryhill, 26 August, 1963 (G)

League Club	Source	Date Signed	Seasons Played	Apps	Subs	Gls
Darlington	App	08.81	82-85	135	0	0
Everton	Tr	04.86				
Walsall	Tr	10.86	86-90	153	0	0
Peterborough U	L	10.89	89	6	0	0
Chester C	L	10.90	90	3	0	0
Blackpool	L	11.90	90	2	0	0
Chester C	L	03.91	90	5	0	0
Peterborough U	Tr	08.91	91-93	63	0	0
Colchester U	L	03.93	92	10	0	0
Luton T	Tr	08.94				
Peterborough U	L	12.94	94	5	0	0
Ipswich T	L	11.95	95	1	0	0
Blackpool	L	12.95	95	1	0	0
Birmingham C	Tr	01.96	95	1	0	0

BARBER John Nathaniel
Lichfield, 9 October, 1929 Died 2002 (W)

League Club	Source	Date Signed	Seasons Played	Apps	Subs	Gls
Swansea T	Arsenal (Am)	08.50	50	4	-	0
Walsall	Tr	07.51	51	6	-	0

BARBER Keith
Luton, 21 September, 1947 (G)

League Club	Source	Date Signed	Seasons Played	Apps	Subs	Gls
Luton T	Dunstable T	04.71	70-76	142	0	0
Swansea C	Tr	07.77	77	42	0	0
Cardiff C	L	09.78	78	2	0	0

BARBER Leonard (Len)
Stoke-on-Trent, 3 July, 1929 Died 1988 (CF)

League Club	Source	Date Signed	Seasons Played	Apps	Subs	Gls
Port Vale	Bury (Am)	06.47	49-54	47	-	12

BARBER Michael (Mike) James
Kensington, 24 August, 1941 (WH)

League Club	Source	Date Signed	Seasons Played	Apps	Subs	Gls
Queens Park Rgrs	Arsenal (Am)	12.59	60-62	63	-	11
Notts Co	Tr	07.63	63-64	33	-	3

BARBER Philip (Phil) Andrew
Tring, 10 June, 1965 (M)

League Club	Source	Date Signed	Seasons Played	Apps	Subs	Gls
Crystal Palace	Aylesbury U	02.84	83-90	207	27	35
Millwall	Tr	07.91	91-93	104	6	12
Plymouth Arg	L	12.94	94	4	0	0
Bristol C	Tr	07.95	95	3	0	0
Mansfield T	L	11.95	95	4	0	1
Fulham	L	01.96	95	13	0	1

BARBER William (Billy) George
Bushey, 19 September, 1939 (WH)

League Club	Source	Date Signed	Seasons Played	Apps	Subs	Gls
Watford	Jnrs	03.57	56-59	25	-	0
Aldershot	Tr	08.62	62	1	-	0

BARCLAY Dominic Alexander
Bristol, 5 September, 1976 (F)

League Club	Source	Date Signed	Seasons Played	Apps	Subs	Gls
Bristol C	YT	07.95	93-97	2	10	0
Macclesfield T	Tr	07.98	98	3	6	1

BARCLAY John Mitchell
Mid Calder, 8 September, 1921 Died 1996 (CF)

League Club	Source	Date Signed	Seasons Played	Apps	Subs	Gls
Bournemouth	Haddington Ath	12.47	47-48	5	-	2

BARCLAY Robert Lindsay Guthrie
Perth, 13 November, 1922 Died 1991 (CF)

League Club	Source	Date Signed	Seasons Played	Apps	Subs	Gls
Preston NE		10.45				
Stockport Co	Alloa Ath	08.48	48	1	-	0

BARCLAY William (Willie) Wood
Larkhall, 11 July, 1924 (W)

League Club	Source	Date Signed	Seasons Played	Apps	Subs	Gls
Bury	Motherwell	03.49	48-49	17	-	1

BARDSLEY David John
Manchester, 11 September, 1964 EYth/E-2 (FB)

League Club	Source	Date Signed	Seasons Played	Apps	Subs	Gls
Blackpool	App	11.82	81-83	45	0	0
Watford	Tr	11.83	83-87	97	3	7
Oxford U	Tr	09.87	87-89	74	0	7
Queens Park Rgrs	Tr	09.89	89-97	252	1	4
Blackpool	Tr	07.98	98-99	64	0	0

BARDSLEY Leslie (Les)
Stockport, 18 August, 1925 (WH)

League Club	Source	Date Signed	Seasons Played	Apps	Subs	Gls
Manchester C	Jnrs	01.45				
Bury	Linfield	04.48	47-54	200	-	2
Barrow	Tr	09.55	55	22	-	0

BARFOOT Stuart John
Southampton, 10 December, 1975 (FB)

League Club	Source	Date Signed	Seasons Played	Apps	Subs	Gls
Bournemouth	YT	07.94	94	0	2	0

BARGH George Wolfenden
Bilsborrow, 27 May, 1910 Died 1995 (IF)

League Club	Source	Date Signed	Seasons Played	Apps	Subs	Gls
Preston NE	Garstang	02.28	28-34	142	-	42
Sheffield Wed	Tr	09.35	35	5	-	0
Bury	Tr	05.36	36-38	90	-	13
Chesterfield	Tr	06.39				
Bury	Tr	09.46	46	1	-	0

BARHAM Mark Francis
Folkestone, 12 July, 1962 EYth/E-2 (W)

League Club	Source	Date Signed	Seasons Played	Apps	Subs	Gls
Norwich C	App	04.80	79-86	169	8	23
Huddersfield T	Tr	07.87	87-88	25	2	1
Middlesbrough	Tr	11.88	88	3	1	0
West Bromwich A	Tr	09.89	89	4	0	0
Brighton & Hove A	Millwall (N/C)	12.89	89-91	70	3	8
Shrewsbury T	Tr	09.92	92	7	1	1

BARK Robert (Bobby)
Stranraer, 27 January, 1926 (W)

League Club	Source	Date Signed	Seasons Played	Apps	Subs	Gls
Barrow	Queen of the South	04.48	48	1	-	0

BARKAS Samuel (Sam)
Wardley Colliery, 29 December, 1909 Died 1989 FLge-3/E-5 (FB)

League Club	Source	Date Signed	Seasons Played	Apps	Subs	Gls
Bradford C	Middle Dock	08.27	27-33	202	-	8
Manchester C	Tr	04.34	33-46	175	-	1

BARKAS Thomas (Tommy)
Gateshead, 27 March, 1912 Died 1991 (IF)

League Club	Source	Date Signed	Seasons Played	Apps	Subs	Gls
Bradford C	Washington Colliery	09.32	32-34	16	-	2
Halifax T	Tr	12.34	34-38	169	-	35
Rochdale	Tr	09.46	46-47	44	-	17
Stockport Co	Tr	11.47	47-48	44	-	18
Carlisle U	Tr	02.49	48	14	-	5

BARKE John **Lloyd**
Nuncargate, 16 December, 1912 Died 1976 (CD)

League Club	Source	Date Signed	Seasons Played	Apps	Subs	Gls
Sheffield U	Scunthorpe & Lindsey U	05.33	34-36	6	-	0
Mansfield T	Tr	06.37	37-46	114	-	0

BARKE (NAYLOR) William (Bill) Henry
Sheffield, 23 November, 1919 Died 1989 (IF)

League Club	Source	Date Signed	Seasons Played	Apps	Subs	Gls
Crystal Palace	Hampton Sports	01.39	46	18	-	9
Brentford	Tr	02.47	46	11	-	2
Leyton Orient	Tr	06.47	47-49	64	-	14

BARKER Christopher (Chris) Andrew
Sheffield, 2 March, 1980 (FB)

League Club	Source	Date Signed	Seasons Played	Apps	Subs	Gls
Barnsley	Alfreton T	08.98	99-01	110	3	3
Cardiff C	Tr	07.02	02-04	103	15	0
Stoke C	L	08.04	04	4	0	0

BARKER Donald (Don)
Long Eaton, 17 June, 1911 Died 1979 (IF)

League Club	Source	Date Signed	Seasons Played	Apps	Subs	Gls
Bradford PA	Johnson & Barnes	01.34	33-36	55	-	15
Millwall	Tr	01.37	36-38	62	-	18
Brighton & Hove A	Tr	07.46	46	14	-	4

BARKER Geoffrey (Geoff) Arthur
Hull, 7 February, 1949 (CD)

League Club	Source	Date Signed	Seasons Played	Apps	Subs	Gls
Hull C	Jnrs	03.67	68-70	29	1	2
Southend U	L	12.70	70	25	0	0
Darlington	Tr	07.71	71-74	151	0	6
Reading	Tr	02.75	74-76	51	1	2
Grimsby T	Tr	07.77	77-78	66	0	1

BARKER Gordon
Bramley, 6 July, 1931 (W)

League Club	Source	Date Signed	Seasons Played	Apps	Subs	Gls
Southend U	Bishop Auckland	12.54	54-58	57	-	9

BARKER Thomas **Haydn**
Astley, 12 January, 1936 (IF)

League Club	Source	Date Signed	Seasons Played	Apps	Subs	Gls
Southport	Holy Family	12.57	57-58	35	-	4

BARKER Jeffrey (Jeff)
Scunthorpe, 16 October, 1915 Died 1985 (FB)

League Club	Source	Date Signed	Seasons Played	Apps	Subs	Gls
Aston Villa	Scunthorpe & Lindsey U	11.36	37	3	-	0
Huddersfield T	Tr	11.45	46-47	67	-	0
Scunthorpe U	Tr	08.48	50-51	73	-	1

BARKER John
Huddersfield, 4 July, 1948 Died 2004 (FB)

League Club	Source	Date Signed	Seasons Played	Apps	Subs	Gls
Scunthorpe U	App	07.66	65-74	261	2	6

BARKER Keith
Stoke-on-Trent, 22 February, 1949 (G)

League Club	Source	Date Signed	Seasons Played	Apps	Subs	Gls
Barnsley	Cambridge U	03.71	71	9	0	0

BARKER Leonard (Len)
Salford, 26 March, 1924 Died 1991 (W)

League Club	Source	Date Signed	Seasons Played	Apps	Subs	Gls
Stockport Co		01.48	48-50	40	-	12

BARKER Allan **Michael (Mickey)**
Bishop Auckland, 23 February, 1956 (FB)

League Club	Source	Date Signed	Seasons Played	Apps	Subs	Gls
Newcastle U	App	03.73	74-78	21	2	0
Gillingham	Tr	01.79	78-79	64	0	2
Hartlepool U	(USA)	09.82	82-83	59	1	1

BARKER Richard (Richie) Ian
Sheffield, 30 May, 1975 ESch/EYth (F)

League Club	Source	Date Signed	Seasons Played	Apps	Subs	Gls
Sheffield Wed	Jnrs	07.93				
Doncaster Rov	L	09.95	95	5	1	0
Brighton & Hove A	Linfield	12.97	97-98	48	12	12
Macclesfield T	Tr	07.99	99-00	58	0	23
Rotherham U	Tr	01.01	00-04	69	71	12
Mansfield T	Tr	11.04	04	28	0	10

BARKER Richard (Richie) Joseph
Loughborough, 23 November, 1939 (F)

League Club	Source	Date Signed	Seasons Played	Apps	Subs	Gls
Derby Co	Burton A	10.67	67-68	30	8	12
Notts Co	Tr	12.68	68-71	99	12	37
Peterborough U	Tr	09.71	71	36	0	9

BARKER Robert (Bobby) Campbell
Kinglassie, 1 December, 1927 (W)

League Club	Source	Date Signed	Seasons Played	Apps	Subs	Gls
West Bromwich A	Kelty Rgrs	09.45	48	14	-	2
Shrewsbury T	Tr	08.50	50	25	-	1

BARKER Shaun
Nottingham, 19 September, 1982 (FB)

League Club	Source	Date Signed	Seasons Played	Apps	Subs	Gls
Rotherham U	Sch	07.02	02-04	77	3	4

BARKER Simon
Farnworth, 4 November, 1964 Eu21-4 (M)

League Club	Source	Date Signed	Seasons Played	Apps	Subs	Gls
Blackburn Rov	App	11.82	83-87	180	2	35
Queens Park Rgrs	Tr	07.88	88-97	291	24	33
Port Vale	Tr	09.98	98-99	26	6	2

BARKER William (Bill)
Stoke-on-Trent, 31 May, 1924 Died 2002 (CF)

League Club	Source	Date Signed	Seasons Played	Apps	Subs	Gls
Stoke C		10.48	49	1	-	0

BARKS Edwin (Eddie)
Ilkeston, 1 September, 1921 Died 1989 (WH)

League Club	Source	Date Signed	Seasons Played	Apps	Subs	Gls
Nottingham F	Heanor T	04.39	46-48	66	-	5
Mansfield T	Tr	01.49	48-54	213	-	6

BARKUS Lea Paul
Reading, 7 December, 1974 (F)

League Club	Source	Date Signed	Seasons Played	Apps	Subs	Gls
Reading	YT	08.92	91-92	8	7	1
Fulham	Tr	07.95	95	3	6	1

BARLEY Charles (Charlie) Derek
Highbury, 20 March, 1932 Died 1994 EYth (CF)

League Club	Source	Date Signed	Seasons Played	Apps	Subs	Gls
Arsenal	Maidenhead U	12.51				
Queens Park Rgrs	Tr	05.53	53	4	-	0
Aldershot	Tr	07.54	54	2	-	0

BARLEY Peter James
Scunthorpe, 25 April, 1936 (G)

League Club	Source	Date Signed	Seasons Played	Apps	Subs	Gls
Scunthorpe U	Leeds U (Am)	10.53	53	5	-	0

BARLOW Andrew (Andy) John
Oldham, 24 November, 1965 (FB)

League Club	Source	Date Signed	Seasons Played	Apps	Subs	Gls
Oldham Ath	Jnrs	07.84	84-94	245	16	5
Bradford C	L	11.93	93	2	0	0
Blackpool	Tr	07.95	95-96	77	3	2
Rochdale	Tr	07.97	97-98	60	7	1

BARLOW Colin James
Manchester, 14 November, 1935 (W)

League Club	Source	Date Signed	Seasons Played	Apps	Subs	Gls
Manchester C	Tarporley BC	12.56	57-62	179	-	78
Oldham Ath	Tr	08.63	63	6	-	1
Doncaster Rov	Tr	08.64	64	3	-	0

BARLOW Frank Charles
Mexborough, 15 October, 1946 ESch (CD)

League Club	Source	Date Signed	Seasons Played	Apps	Subs	Gls
Sheffield U	Jnrs	09.65	65-71	116	5	2
Chesterfield	Tr	08.72	72-75	140	1	3

BARLOW Harold (Harry)
Manchester, 25 October, 1925 (WH)

League Club	Source	Date Signed	Seasons Played	Apps	Subs	Gls
Crewe Alex	Manchester C (Am)	02.46	46-50	27	-	1

BARLOW Herbert (Bert)
Kilnhurst, 22 July, 1916 Died 2004 (IF)

League Club	Source	Date Signed	Seasons Played	Apps	Subs	Gls
Barnsley	Silverwood Colliery	07.35	35-37	58	-	12
Wolverhampton W	Tr	06.38	38	3	-	1
Portsmouth	Tr	02.39	38-49	104	-	34
Leicester C	Tr	12.49	49-51	42	-	9
Colchester U	Tr	07.52	52-53	60	-	16

BARLOW Martin David
Barnstaple, 25 June, 1971 (W)

League Club	Source	Date Signed	Seasons Played	Apps	Subs	Gls
Plymouth Arg	YT	07.89	88-00	294	35	24
Exeter C	Tr	07.01	01	26	4	0

BARLOW Matthew (Matty) John
Oldham, 25 June, 1987 (F)

League Club	Source	Date Signed	Seasons Played	Apps	Subs	Gls
Oldham Ath	Sch	●	03-04	1	9	0

BARLOW Neil Keith
Bury, 24 March, 1978 (CD)

League Club	Source	Date Signed	Seasons Played	Apps	Subs	Gls
Rochdale	YT	07.96	95	1	1	0

BARLOW Peter
Portsmouth, 9 January, 1950 (F)

League Club	Source	Date Signed	Seasons Played	Apps	Subs	Gls
Colchester U	App	01.68	66-68	18	3	4
Workington	Tr	02.69	68-69	41	1	11
Hartlepool	Tr	07.70	70	8	3	0

BARLOW Philip (Phil) Douglas
Shipley, 19 December, 1946 (CD)

League Club	Source	Date Signed	Seasons Played	Apps	Subs	Gls
Bradford C	Guiseley	07.66	66	15	1	0
Lincoln C	Tr	08.67	67	5	0	0

BARLOW Raymond (Ray) John
Swindon, 17 August, 1926 FLge-4/E-1 (WH)

League Club	Source	Date Signed	Seasons Played	Apps	Subs	Gls
West Bromwich A	Garrards	06.44	46-59	403	-	31
Birmingham C	Tr	08.60	60	5	-	0

BARLOW Stuart
Liverpool, 16 July, 1968 (F)

League Club	Source	Date Signed	Seasons Played	Apps	Subs	Gls
Everton	Sherwood Park	06.90	90-95	24	47	10
Oldham Ath	Tr	11.95	95-97	78	15	31
Wigan Ath	Tr	03.98	97-99	72	11	40
Tranmere Rov	Tr	07.00	00-02	62	32	19
Stockport Co	Tr	08.03	03-04	26	35	11

BARMBY Jeffrey (Jeff)
Hull, 15 January, 1943 (CF)

League Club	Source	Date Signed	Seasons Played	Apps	Subs	Gls
York C (Am)	Selby T	03.63	62-63	2	-	0

BARMBY Nicholas (Nick) Jonathan
Hull, 11 February, 1974 ESch/EYth/Eu21-4/EB-2/E-23 (M)

League Club	Source	Date Signed	Seasons Played	Apps	Subs	Gls
Tottenham H	YT	04.91	92-94	81	6	20
Middlesbrough	Tr	08.95	95-96	42	0	8
Everton	Tr	11.96	96-99	105	11	18
Liverpool	Tr	07.00	00-01	23	9	2
Leeds U	Tr	08.02	02-03	17	8	4
Nottingham F	L	02.04	03	6	0	1
Hull C	Tr	07.04	04	38	1	9

BARNARD Arthur
Boothstown, 20 June, 1932 (G)

League Club	Source	Date Signed	Seasons Played	Apps	Subs	Gls
Bolton W	Astley & Tyldesley	11.51	54-55	2	-	0
Stockport Co	Tr	07.56	56-58	53	-	0
Southport	Tr	09.59	59	42	-	0

BARNARD Christopher (Chris) Leslie
Cardiff, 1 August, 1947 (M)

League Club	Source	Date Signed	Seasons Played	Apps	Subs	Gls
Southend U	App	08.65	65	4	4	0
Ipswich T	Tr	07.66	66-70	18	3	0
Torquay U	Tr	10.70	70-71	29	3	3
Charlton Ath	Tr	01.72	71	0	1	0

BARNARD Darren Sean
Rinteln, Germany, 30 November, 1971 ESch/EYth/W-22 (FB)

League Club	Source	Date Signed	Seasons Played	Apps	Subs	Gls
Chelsea	Wokingham T	07.90	91-93	18	11	2
Reading	L	11.94	94	3	1	0
Bristol C	Tr	10.95	95-96	77	1	15
Barnsley	Tr	08.97	97-01	151	19	28
Grimsby T	Tr	08.02	02-03	55	8	4

BARNARD Donny Gary
Forest Gate, 1 July, 1984 (FB)

League Club	Source	Date Signed	Seasons Played	Apps	Subs	Gls
Leyton Orient	Sch	03.03	01-04	67	28	1

BARNARD Geoffrey (Geoff)
Southend-on-Sea, 23 March, 1946 (G)

League Club	Source	Date Signed	Seasons Played	Apps	Subs	Gls
Norwich C	Jnrs	09.63	64-66	6	0	0
Scunthorpe U	Tr	07.68	68-74	265	0	0
Scunthorpe U	Scarborough	09.76	76	6	0	0

BARNARD Lee James
Romford, 18 July, 1984 EYth (F)

League Club	Source	Date Signed	Seasons Played	Apps	Subs	Gls
Tottenham H	Sch	07.02				
Exeter C	L	11.02	02	3	0	0
Leyton Orient	L	11.04	04	3	5	0
Northampton T	L	03.05	04	3	2	0

BARNARD Leigh Kenneth
Worsley, 29 October, 1958 (M)

League Club	Source	Date Signed	Seasons Played	Apps	Subs	Gls
Portsmouth	App	10.76	77-81	71	8	8
Peterborough U	L	03.82	81	1	3	0
Swindon T	Tr	07.82	82-89	212	5	22
Exeter C	L	02.85	84	6	0	2
Cardiff C	Tr	10.89	89-90	61	2	9

BARNARD Mark
Sheffield, 27 November, 1975 (FB)

League Club	Source	Date Signed	Seasons Played	Apps	Subs	Gls
Rotherham U	YT	07.94				
Darlington	Worksop T	09.95	95-98	131	12	4

BARNARD Henry Michael (Mike)
Portsmouth, 18 July, 1933 (IF)

League Club	Source	Date Signed	Seasons Played	Apps	Subs	Gls
Portsmouth	Gosport Borough	08.51	53-58	116	-	25

BARNARD Raymond (Ray) Scholey
Middlesbrough, 16 April, 1933 ESch (FB)

League Club	Source	Date Signed	Seasons Played	Apps	Subs	Gls
Middlesbrough	Jnrs	04.50	51-59	113	-	0
Lincoln C	Tr	06.60	60-62	43	-	0

BARNES Andrew (Andy) John
Croydon, 31 March, 1967 (F)

League Club	Source	Date Signed	Seasons Played	Apps	Subs	Gls
Crystal Palace	Sutton U	09.91	91	0	1	0
Carlisle U	L	12.93	93	2	0	0

BARNES Bernard Noel Preston
Plymouth, 25 December, 1937 Died 2004 (CF)

League Club	Source	Date Signed	Seasons Played	Apps	Subs	Gls
Plymouth Arg	Bideford T	01.55	56-57	4	-	1

BARNES Colin
Notting Hill, 28 May, 1957 (F)

League Club	Source	Date Signed	Seasons Played	Apps	Subs	Gls
Torquay U	Barnet	08.83	83-84	42	1	11

BARNES David
Paddington, 16 November, 1961 EYth (FB)

League Club	Source	Date Signed	Seasons Played	Apps	Subs	Gls
Coventry C	App	05.79	79-81	9	0	0
Ipswich T	Tr	04.82	82-83	16	1	0
Wolverhampton W	Tr	10.84	84-87	86	2	4
Aldershot	Tr	08.87	87-88	68	1	1
Sheffield U	Tr	07.89	89-93	82	0	1
Watford	Tr	01.94	93-95	16	0	0
Colchester U	Tr	08.96	96	11	0	0

BARNES David (Bobby) Oswald
Kingston, 17 December, 1962 EYth (W)

League Club	Source	Date Signed	Seasons Played	Apps	Subs	Gls
West Ham U	App	09.80	80-85	31	12	5
Scunthorpe U	L	11.85	85	6	0	0
Aldershot	Tr	03.86	85-87	49	0	26
Swindon T	Tr	10.87	87-88	43	2	13
Bournemouth	Tr	03.89	88-89	11	3	0
Northampton T	Tr	10.89	89-91	97	1	37
Peterborough U	Tr	02.92	91-93	42	7	9
Torquay U	(Hong Kong)	09.95	95	0	1	0

BARNES Eric
Wythenshawe, 29 November, 1937 (CD)

League Club	Source	Date Signed	Seasons Played	Apps	Subs	Gls
Crewe Alex		01.58	57-69	352	2	1

BARNES John Charles Bryan
Kingston, Jamaica, 7 November, 1963 Eu21-3/FLge/E-79 (W)

League Club	Source	Date Signed	Seasons Played	Apps	Subs	Gls
Watford	Sudbury Court	07.81	81-86	232	1	65
Liverpool	Tr	06.87	87-96	310	4	84
Newcastle U	Tr	08.97	97-98	22	5	6
Charlton Ath	Tr	02.99	98	2	10	0

BARNES Kenneth (Ken) Herbert
Birmingham, 16 March, 1929 (WH)

League Club	Source	Date Signed	Seasons Played	Apps	Subs	Gls
Manchester C	Stafford Rgrs	05.50	51-60	258	-	18
Wrexham	Tr	05.61	61-64	132	-	24

BARNES Kevin
Fleetwood, 12 September, 1975 (F)

League Club	Source	Date Signed	Seasons Played	Apps	Subs	Gls
Blackpool	Lancaster C	03.99	98	2	2	0

BARNES Michael Frederick
Reading, 17 September, 1963 (CD)

League Club	Source	Date Signed	Seasons Played	Apps	Subs	Gls
Reading	App	09.81	80-83	29	5	2
Northampton T	Tr	08.84	84	19	0	1

BARNES Paul Lance
Leicester, 16 November, 1967 (F)

League Club	Source	Date Signed	Seasons Played	Apps	Subs	Gls
Notts Co	App	11.85	85-89	36	17	14

League Club	Source	Date Signed	Seasons Played	Apps	Subs	Gls
Stoke C	Tr	03.90	89-91	10	14	3
Chesterfield	L	11.90	90	1	0	0
York C	Tr	07.92	92-95	147	1	76
Birmingham C	Tr	03.96	95	15	0	7
Burnley	Tr	09.96	96-97	63	2	30
Huddersfield T	Tr	01.98	97-98	13	17	2
Bury	Tr	03.99	98-00	31	23	8
Doncaster Rov	Tr	07.01	03	2	5	0

BARNES Peter
St Albans, 29 June, 1938 (WH)

League Club	Source	Date Signed	Seasons Played	Apps	Subs	Gls
Watford	Jnrs	03.57	60-61	10	-	0

BARNES Peter Simon
Manchester, 10 June, 1957 EYth/Eu21-9/FLge/E-22 (W)

League Club	Source	Date Signed	Seasons Played	Apps	Subs	Gls
Manchester C	App	08.74	74-78	108	7	15
West Bromwich A	Tr	07.79	79-80	76	1	23
Leeds U	Tr	08.81	81	31	0	1
Leeds U	Real Betis (Sp)	08.83	83	25	2	4
Coventry C	Tr	10.84	84	18	0	2
Manchester U	Tr	07.85	85-86	19	1	2
Manchester C	Tr	01.87	86	8	0	0
Bolton W	L	10.87	87	2	0	0
Port Vale	L	12.87	87	3	0	0
Hull C	Tr	03.88	87	11	0	0
Bolton W	Deportivo Farense (Por)	11.88	88	2	1	0
Sunderland	Tr	02.89	88	1	0	0

BARNES Philip (Phil) Kenneth
Sheffield, 2 March, 1979 (G)

League Club	Source	Date Signed	Seasons Played	Apps	Subs	Gls
Rotherham U	YT	06.97	96	2	0	0
Blackpool	Tr	07.97	97-03	141	0	0
Sheffield U	Tr	07.04	04	1	0	0
Torquay U	L	02.05	04	5	0	0

BARNES Richard Ian
Wrexham, 6 September, 1975 (FB)

League Club	Source	Date Signed	Seasons Played	Apps	Subs	Gls
Wrexham	YT	05.94	94	0	1	0

BARNES Robert Alan
Stoke-on-Trent, 26 November, 1969 (FB)

League Club	Source	Date Signed	Seasons Played	Apps	Subs	Gls
Manchester C	YT	07.88				
Wrexham	Tr	06.89	89-90	8	1	0

BARNES Charles **Ronald (Ron)**
Bolton, 21 February, 1936 Died 1991 (W)

League Club	Source	Date Signed	Seasons Played	Apps	Subs	Gls
Blackpool	Jnrs	05.54	56-58	9	-	0
Rochdale	Tr	06.59	59-60	91	-	7
Wrexham	Tr	07.61	61-63	88	-	24
Norwich C	Tr	08.63	63	21	-	1
Peterborough U	Tr	07.64	64-65	39	0	6
Torquay U	Tr	01.66	65-68	110	4	25

BARNES Steven (Steve) Leslie
Harrow, 5 January, 1976 (W)

League Club	Source	Date Signed	Seasons Played	Apps	Subs	Gls
Birmingham C	Welling U	10.95	95	0	3	0
Brighton & Hove A	L	01.98	97	12	0	0
Barnet	Tr	10.98	98-99	4	11	0

BARNES Walley
Brecon, 16 January, 1920 Died 1972 WWar-2/W-22 (FB)

League Club	Source	Date Signed	Seasons Played	Apps	Subs	Gls
Arsenal	Southampton (Am)	09.43	46-55	267	-	11

BARNES William (Billy)
Dumbarton, 16 March, 1939 (FB)

League Club	Source	Date Signed	Seasons Played	Apps	Subs	Gls
Bradford C	Rutherglen Glencairn	04.58	58-60	59	-	0
Bradford PA	Scarborough	09.66	66-67	53	0	0

BARNESS Anthony
Lewisham, 25 March, 1973 (FB)

League Club	Source	Date Signed	Seasons Played	Apps	Subs	Gls
Charlton Ath	YT	03.91	91-92	21	6	1
Chelsea	Tr	09.92	92-94	12	2	0
Southend U	L	02.96	95	5	0	0
Charlton Ath	Tr	08.96	96-99	83	13	3
Bolton W	Tr	07.00	00-04	73	20	0

BARNETT George **Alan** Samuel
Croydon, 4 November, 1934 (G)

League Club	Source	Date Signed	Seasons Played	Apps	Subs	Gls
Portsmouth	Croydon Amats	09.55	55-57	25	-	0
Grimsby T	Tr	12.58	58-62	116	-	0
Exeter C	Tr	07.63	63-65	57	0	0

BARNETT Benjamin (Ben) James
Islington, 18 December, 1969 (F)

League Club	Source	Date Signed	Seasons Played	Apps	Subs	Gls
Barnet	Heybridge Swifts	08.93	93	0	2	0

BARNETT David (Dave)
Lambeth, 24 September, 1951 (CD)

League Club	Source	Date Signed	Seasons Played	Apps	Subs	Gls
Southend U	App	09.69	68-72	48	9	0

BARNETT David (Dave) Kwame
Birmingham, 16 April, 1967 (CD)

League Club	Source	Date Signed	Seasons Played	Apps	Subs	Gls
Colchester U	Windsor & Eton	08.88	88	19	1	0
West Bromwich A	Edmonton (Can)	10.89				
Walsall	Tr	07.90	90	4	1	0
Barnet	Kidderminster Hrs	02.92	91-93	58	1	3
Birmingham C	L	12.93	93	2	1	0
Birmingham C	Tr	02.94	93-96	43	0	0
Port Vale	Dunfermline Ath	03.98	97-97	34	2	1
Lincoln C	Tr	07.99	99	20	2	3

BARNETT Gary Lloyd
Stratford-on-Avon, 11 March, 1963 (W)

League Club	Source	Date Signed	Seasons Played	Apps	Subs	Gls
Coventry C	App	01.81				
Oxford U	Tr	07.82	82-85	37	8	9
Wimbledon	L	02.83	82	5	0	1
Fulham	L	12.84	84	0	2	1
Fulham	Tr	09.85	85-89	167	13	30
Huddersfield T	Tr	07.90	90-93	92	8	11
Leyton Orient	Tr	08.93	93-94	47	16	7
Kidderminster Hrs	Barry T	08.99	00	2	0	0

BARNETT Geoffrey (Geoff) Colin
Northwich, 16 October, 1946 ESch/EYth (G)

League Club	Source	Date Signed	Seasons Played	Apps	Subs	Gls
Everton	App	05.64	65-67	10	0	0
Arsenal	Tr	10.69	69-75	39	0	0

BARNETT Graham
Stoke-on-Trent, 17 May, 1936 (IF)

League Club	Source	Date Signed	Seasons Played	Apps	Subs	Gls
Port Vale	Jnrs	06.56	58-59	49	-	34
Tranmere Rov	Tr	03.60	59-60	32	-	11
Halifax T	Tr	08.61	61	32	-	10

BARNETT Jason Vincent
Shrewsbury, 21 April, 1976 (FB)

League Club	Source	Date Signed	Seasons Played	Apps	Subs	Gls
Wolverhampton W	YT	07.94				
Lincoln C	Tr	10.95	95-01	189	18	6

BARNETT Thomas (Tommy) Andrew
Muswell Hill, 12 October, 1936 (CF)

League Club	Source	Date Signed	Seasons Played	Apps	Subs	Gls
Crystal Palace	Chatham	12.58	58-60	14	-	2

BARNEY Victor (Vic) Charles
Stepney, 3 April, 1922 (IF)

League Club	Source	Date Signed	Seasons Played	Apps	Subs	Gls
Reading	Oxford C	09.46	46-48	45	-	12
Bristol C	Tr	10.48	48	28	-	4
Grimsby T	Tr	06.49	49	7	-	0

BARNEY Victor (Vic) Roy
Shipton, 18 November, 1947 (M)

League Club	Source	Date Signed	Seasons Played	Apps	Subs	Gls
Bristol Rov	App	12.65	66-69	30	1	3

BARNHOUSE David John
Swansea, 19 March, 1975 WSch/WYth/Wu21-3 (FB)

League Club	Source	Date Signed	Seasons Played	Apps	Subs	Gls
Swansea C	YT	07.93	91-95	18	5	0

BARNSLEY Andrew (Andy)
Sheffield, 9 June, 1962 (FB)

League Club	Source	Date Signed	Seasons Played	Apps	Subs	Gls
Rotherham U	Denaby U	06.85	85	28	0	0
Sheffield U	Tr	07.86	86-88	73	4	0
Rotherham U	Tr	12.88	88-90	77	6	3
Carlisle U	Tr	08.91	91-92	53	2	5

BARNSLEY Geoffrey (Geoff) Robert
Bilston, 9 December, 1935 (G)

League Club	Source	Date Signed	Seasons Played	Apps	Subs	Gls
West Bromwich A	Jnrs	12.52	54	1	-	0
Plymouth Arg	Tr	06.57	57-60	131	-	0
Norwich C	Tr	05.61	61	8	-	0
Torquay U	Tr	12.62	63	6	-	0

BARNWELL John
Newcastle, 24 December, 1938 EYth/Eu23-1 (M)

League Club	Source	Date Signed	Seasons Played	Apps	Subs	Gls
Arsenal	Bishop Auckland	11.56	56-63	138	-	23
Nottingham F	Tr	03.64	63-69	172	8	22
Sheffield U	Tr	04.70	70	9	0	2

BARNWELL-EDINBORO Jamie
Hull, 26 December, 1975 (F)

League Club	Source	Date Signed	Seasons Played	Apps	Subs	Gls
Coventry C	YT	07.94	95	0	1	0
Swansea C	L	12.95	95	2	2	0
Wigan Ath	L	02.96	95	2	8	1
Cambridge U	Tr	03.96	95-97	53	10	12

BARON Kevin Mark Patrick
Preston, 19 July, 1926 Died 1971 (IF)

League Club	Source	Date Signed	Seasons Played	Apps	Subs	Gls
Liverpool	Preston NE (Am)	08.45	47-53	140	-	32
Southend U	Tr	05.54	54-58	138	-	45
Northampton T	Tr	09.58	58	25	-	4
Aldershot	Wisbech T	07.60	60	6	-	0

BAROS Milan (F)
Valasske Mezirici,Czech Rep, 28 October,1981 CzRYth/CzRu21-19/CzR-39

League Club	Source	Date Signed	Seasons Played	Apps	Subs	Gls
Liverpool	Banik Ostrava (Cz)	12.01	02-04	45	21	19

BARR Hugh Henry (IF)
Ballymena, 17 May, 1935 NISch/IrLge-6/NI-3

League Club	Source	Date Signed	Seasons Played	Apps	Subs	Gls
Coventry C	Linfield	07.62	62-63	47	-	15

BARR John Millar (CD)
Bridge of Weir, 9 September, 1917 Died 1997

League Club	Source	Date Signed	Seasons Played	Apps	Subs	Gls
Queens Park Rgrs	Third Lanark	05.39	46	4	-	0

BARR Robert (Bobbie) Andrew (CD)
Halifax, 5 December, 1969

League Club	Source	Date Signed	Seasons Played	Apps	Subs	Gls
Halifax T	YT	06.88	86-88	4	1	0

BARR William (Billy) Joseph (FB)
Halifax, 21 January, 1969

League Club	Source	Date Signed	Seasons Played	Apps	Subs	Gls
Halifax T	YT	07.87	87-92	178	18	13
Crewe Alex	Tr	06.94	94-96	73	12	7
Carlisle U	Tr	07.97	97-99	88	3	3

BARRAS Anthony (Tony) (CD)
Billingham, 29 March, 1971

League Club	Source	Date Signed	Seasons Played	Apps	Subs	Gls
Hartlepool U	YT	07.89	88-89	9	3	0
Stockport Co	Tr	07.90	90-93	94	5	5
Rotherham U	L	02.94	93	5	0	1
York C	Tr	07.94	94-98	167	4	11
Reading	Tr	03.99	98	4	2	1
Walsall	Tr	07.99	99-02	91	14	9
Plymouth Arg	L	11.02	02	4	0	0
Notts Co	Tr	08.03	03	38	2	2
Macclesfield T	Tr	07.04	04	22	2	1

BARRASS Malcolm Williamson (CD)
Blackpool, 15 December, 1924 FLge-2/EWar-1/E-3

League Club	Source	Date Signed	Seasons Played	Apps	Subs	Gls
Bolton W	Ford Motors	11.44	46-56	329	-	25
Sheffield U	Tr	09.56	56	18	-	0

BARRASS Matthew (Matt) Robert (FB)
Bury, 28 February, 1980

League Club	Source	Date Signed	Seasons Played	Apps	Subs	Gls
Bury	YT	05.99	99-04	77	7	2

BARRATT Alfred (Alf) George (CD)
Weldon, 13 April, 1920 Died 2001

League Club	Source	Date Signed	Seasons Played	Apps	Subs	Gls
Northampton T	Kettering T	07.38	38	1	-	0
Leicester C	Corby T	09.46	47-48	4	-	0
Grimsby T	Tr	07.50	50	23	-	0
Southport	Tr	07.51	51-55	198	-	0

BARRATT Anthony (Tony) (FB)
Salford, 18 October, 1965

League Club	Source	Date Signed	Seasons Played	Apps	Subs	Gls
Grimsby T	Billingham T	08.85	85	20	2	0
Hartlepool U	Billingham T	12.86	86-88	93	5	4
York C	Tr	03.89	88-94	116	31	10

BARRATT Harold (Harry) (FB)
Headington, 25 December, 1918 Died 1989

League Club	Source	Date Signed	Seasons Played	Apps	Subs	Gls
Coventry C	Herberts Ath	12.35	37-51	170	-	12

BARRATT Leslie (Les) Edwin (IF)
Nuneaton, 13 August, 1945

League Club	Source	Date Signed	Seasons Played	Apps	Subs	Gls
Barrow	App	08.62	62-63	10	-	0
Grimsby T	Tr	07.64	64	4	-	1
Southport	Tr	07.65	65	9	1	0

BARRELL Leslie (Les) Peter (W)
Colchester, 30 August, 1932

League Club	Source	Date Signed	Seasons Played	Apps	Subs	Gls
Colchester U	Lexden W	12.56	56	4	-	1

BARRETT Adam Nicholas (CD)
Dagenham, 29 November, 1979

League Club	Source	Date Signed	Seasons Played	Apps	Subs	Gls
Plymouth Arg	(USA)	01.99	98-00	47	5	3
Mansfield T	Tr	12.00	00-01	34	3	1
Bristol Rov	Tr	07.02	02-03	90	0	5
Southend U	Tr	07.04	04	42	1	11

BARRETT Arthur Henry (WH)
Liverpool, 21 December, 1927

League Club	Source	Date Signed	Seasons Played	Apps	Subs	Gls
Tranmere Rov	Jnrs	03.45	46	1	-	0

BARRETT Colin (FB)
Stockport, 3 August, 1952

League Club	Source	Date Signed	Seasons Played	Apps	Subs	Gls
Manchester C	Cheadle Heath	05.70	72-75	50	3	0
Nottingham F	Tr	03.76	75-78	64	5	4
Swindon T	Tr	06.80	80	3	0	0

BARRETT Daniel (Danny) Thomas (M)
Bradford, 25 September, 1980

League Club	Source	Date Signed	Seasons Played	Apps	Subs	Gls
Chesterfield	YT	07.99	99-00	0	3	0

BARRETT Earl Delisser (FB)
Rochdale, 28 April, 1967 Eu21-4/EB/FLge/E-3

League Club	Source	Date Signed	Seasons Played	Apps	Subs	Gls
Manchester C	App	04.85	85-86	2	1	0
Chester C	L	03.86	85	12	0	0
Oldham Ath	Tr	11.87	87-91	181	2	7
Aston Villa	Tr	02.92	91-94	118	1	1
Everton	Tr	01.95	94-97	73	1	0
Sheffield U	L	01.98	97	5	0	0
Sheffield Wed	Tr	02.98	97-98	10	5	0

BARRETT Graham (F)
Dublin, 6 October, 1981 IRSch/IRYth/IRu21-24/IR-6

League Club	Source	Date Signed	Seasons Played	Apps	Subs	Gls
Arsenal	YT	10.98	99	0	2	0
Bristol Rov	L	12.00	00	0	1	0
Crewe Alex	L	09.01	01	2	1	0
Colchester U	L	12.01	01	19	1	4
Brighton & Hove A	L	08.02	02	20	10	1
Coventry C	Tr	07.03	03-04	32	23	6
Sheffield Wed	L	03.05	04	5	1	1

BARRETT James (Jimmy) Guy (IF)
West Ham, 5 November, 1930

League Club	Source	Date Signed	Seasons Played	Apps	Subs	Gls
West Ham U	Jnrs	02.49	49-54	85	-	24
Nottingham F	Tr	12.54	54-58	105	-	64
Birmingham C	Tr	10.59	59	10	-	4

BARRETT John (WH)
Birmingham, 26 March, 1931 Died 2002 EYth

League Club	Source	Date Signed	Seasons Played	Apps	Subs	Gls
Aston Villa	Jnrs	07.49				
Scunthorpe U	Tr	06.54	54-55	17	-	0

BARRETT Kenneth (Ken) Brian (W)
Bromsgrove, 5 May, 1938

League Club	Source	Date Signed	Seasons Played	Apps	Subs	Gls
Aston Villa	Stoke Works	02.57	58	5	-	3
Lincoln C	Tr	06.59	59-62	17	-	4

BARRETT Leslie (Les) (W)
Chelsea, 22 October, 1947 Eu23-1

League Club	Source	Date Signed	Seasons Played	Apps	Subs	Gls
Fulham	Jnrs	10.65	65-76	421	3	74
Millwall	Tr	10.77	77	8	0	1

BARRETT Michael (Mike) John (W)
Bristol, 12 September, 1959 Died 1984

League Club	Source	Date Signed	Seasons Played	Apps	Subs	Gls
Bristol Rov	Portway	10.79	79-83	119	10	18

BARRETT Michael (Mike) John (G)
Exeter, 20 October, 1963

League Club	Source	Date Signed	Seasons Played	Apps	Subs	Gls
Exeter C	Liskeard Ath	12.94	94	4	0	0

BARRETT Neil William (M)
Tooting, 24 December, 1981 ESch

League Club	Source	Date Signed	Seasons Played	Apps	Subs	Gls
Portsmouth	Chelsea (Jnrs)	07.01	01	23	3	2

BARRETT Paul David (M)
Newcastle, 13 April, 1978 EYth

League Club	Source	Date Signed	Seasons Played	Apps	Subs	Gls
Newcastle U	YT	06.96				
Wrexham	Tr	03.99	98-03	98	22	5

BARRETT Charles **Roger** (F)
Doncaster, 19 October, 1946

League Club	Source	Date Signed	Seasons Played	Apps	Subs	Gls
Doncaster Rov	Doncaster U	10.68	68	1	0	0

BARRETT Ronald (Ron) Harold (CF)
Reading, 22 July, 1939

League Club	Source	Date Signed	Seasons Played	Apps	Subs	Gls
Grimsby T	Maidenhead U	08.58	58	3	-	0

BARRETT Scott (G)
Alvaston, 2 April, 1963

League Club	Source	Date Signed	Seasons Played	Apps	Subs	Gls
Wolverhampton W	Ilkeston T	09.84	84-86	30	0	0
Stoke C	Tr	07.87	87-89	51	0	0
Colchester U	L	01.90	89	13	0	0
Stockport Co	L	03.90	89	10	0	0
Gillingham	Colchester U	08.92	92-94	51	0	0
Cambridge U	Tr	08.95	95-97	119	0	0
Leyton Orient	Tr	01.99	98-02	99	0	0

BARRETT George **Thomas (Tom)** (CD)
Salford, 16 March, 1934

League Club	Source	Date Signed	Seasons Played	Apps	Subs	Gls
Manchester U	Jnrs	08.52				
Plymouth Arg	Tr	07.57	57-58	26	-	1
Chester	Tr	07.60	60	39	-	2

BARRICK Dean (FB)
Hemsworth, 30 September, 1969

League Club	Source	Date Signed	Seasons Played	Apps	Subs	Gls
Sheffield Wed	YT	05.88	88-89	11	0	2
Rotherham U	Tr	02.91	90-92	96	3	7
Cambridge U	Tr	08.93	93-95	90	1	3
Preston NE	Tr	09.95	95-97	98	11	1
Bury	Tr	07.98	98-00	37	10	1

BARRIE John
Hamilton, 17 May, 1925 (CF)

League Club	Source	Date Signed	Seasons Played	Apps	Subs	Gls
Cardiff C	Thorniewood Ath	07.48				
Tranmere Rov	Tr	11.48	48-50	14	-	3

BARRITT Ronald (Ron)
Huddersfield, 15 April, 1919 (CF)

League Club	Source	Date Signed	Seasons Played	Apps	Subs	Gls
Doncaster Rov	Wombwell	01.49	48-49	13	-	5
Leeds U	Frickley Colliery	04.51	51	6	-	1
York C	Tr	07.52	52	5	-	0

BARRON James (Jim)
Burnhope, 19 July, 1913 Died 1969 (G)

League Club	Source	Date Signed	Seasons Played	Apps	Subs	Gls
Blackburn Rov	Blyth Spartans	03.35	35-38	76	-	0
Darlington	Tr	06.46	46	23	-	0

BARRON James (Jim)
Tantobie, 19 October, 1943 (G)

League Club	Source	Date Signed	Seasons Played	Apps	Subs	Gls
Wolverhampton W	Newcastle West End	11.61	63-64	8	-	0
Chelsea	Tr	04.65	65	1	0	0
Oxford U	Tr	03.66	65-69	152	0	0
Nottingham F	Tr	07.70	70-73	155	0	0
Swindon T	Tr	08.74	74-76	79	0	0
Peterborough U	Connecticut (USA)	08.77	77-80	21	0	0

BARRON Michael (Mike) James
Chester-le-Street, 22 December, 1974 (CD)

League Club	Source	Date Signed	Seasons Played	Apps	Subs	Gls
Middlesbrough	YT	02.93	93-95	2	1	0
Hartlepool U	L	09.96	96	16	0	0
Hartlepool U	Tr	07.97	97-04	260	5	3

BARRON Paul George
Woolwich, 16 September, 1953 (G)

League Club	Source	Date Signed	Seasons Played	Apps	Subs	Gls
Plymouth Arg	Slough T	07.76	76-77	44	0	0
Arsenal	Tr	07.78	78-79	8	0	0
Crystal Palace	Tr	08.80	80-82	90	0	0
West Bromwich A	Tr	12.82	82-84	63	0	0
Stoke C	L	01.85	84	1	0	0
Queens Park Rgrs	Tr	03.85	85-86	32	0	0
Reading	L	12.86	86	4	0	0

BARRON Roger William
Northampton, 30 June, 1947 (G)

League Club	Source	Date Signed	Seasons Played	Apps	Subs	Gls
Northampton T	App	07.65	67-68	17	0	0

BARRON William (Bill)
Houghton-le-Spring, 26 October, 1917 (FB)

League Club	Source	Date Signed	Seasons Played	Apps	Subs	Gls
Charlton Ath	Annfield Plain	10.37	37	3	-	2
Northampton T	Tr	05.38	38-50	166	-	4

BARROW Graham
Chorley, 13 June, 1954 (M)

League Club	Source	Date Signed	Seasons Played	Apps	Subs	Gls
Wigan Ath	Altrincham	07.81	81-85	173	6	35
Chester C	Tr	07.86	86-93	244	4	17

BARROW Lee Alexander
Belper, 1 May, 1973 (CD)

League Club	Source	Date Signed	Seasons Played	Apps	Subs	Gls
Notts Co	YT	07.91				
Scarborough	Tr	08.92	92	11	0	0
Torquay U	Tr	02.93	92-97	154	10	5

BARROWCLIFF Paul Joseph
Hillingdon, 15 June, 1969 (M)

League Club	Source	Date Signed	Seasons Played	Apps	Subs	Gls
Brentford	Stevenage Borough	08.97	97	5	6	0

BARROWCLIFFE Geoffrey (Geoff)
Ilkeston, 18 October, 1931 (FB)

League Club	Source	Date Signed	Seasons Played	Apps	Subs	Gls
Derby Co	Ilkeston T	10.50	51-65	475	0	37

BARROWCLOUGH Carl William
Doncaster, 25 September, 1981 (F)

League Club	Source	Date Signed	Seasons Played	Apps	Subs	Gls
Barnsley	YT	03.01	00-02	2	10	0

BARROWCLOUGH Stewart James
Barnsley, 29 October, 1951 Eu23-5 (W)

League Club	Source	Date Signed	Seasons Played	Apps	Subs	Gls
Barnsley	App	11.69	69	9	0	0
Newcastle U	Tr	08.70	70-77	201	18	21
Birmingham C	Tr	05.78	78	26	3	2
Bristol Rov	Tr	07.79	79-80	60	1	14
Barnsley	Tr	02.81	80-82	46	6	1
Mansfield T	Tr	08.83	83-84	50	4	10

BARROWMAN Andrew
Wishaw, 27 November, 1984 SYth (F)

League Club	Source	Date Signed	Seasons Played	Apps	Subs	Gls
Birmingham C	YT	12.01	03	0	1	0
Crewe Alex	L	10.03	03	3	1	1
Blackpool	L	08.04	04	0	2	0
Mansfield T	L	03.05	04	1	2	0

BARRY Gareth
Hastings, 23 February, 1981 EYth/Eu21-27/E-8 (M)

League Club	Source	Date Signed	Seasons Played	Apps	Subs	Gls
Aston Villa	YT	02.98	97-04	207	12	16

BARRY George
Islington, 19 September, 1967 (FB)

League Club	Source	Date Signed	Seasons Played	Apps	Subs	Gls
Leyton Orient	Fisher Ath	03.95	94	5	1	0

BARRY Kevin Anthony
Woolwich, 13 September, 1930 (W)

League Club	Source	Date Signed	Seasons Played	Apps	Subs	Gls
Charlton Ath	Jnrs	12.47	52	3	-	0

BARRY Kevin Thomas
Newcastle, 9 January, 1961 (G)

League Club	Source	Date Signed	Seasons Played	Apps	Subs	Gls
Darlington	Nottingham F (App)	09.79	79-80	18	0	0

BARRY Michael (Mike) James
Hull, 22 May, 1953 Wu23-1 (W)

League Club	Source	Date Signed	Seasons Played	Apps	Subs	Gls
Huddersfield T	App	06.70	70-72	21	5	0
Carlisle U	Tr	05.73	73-76	73	8	10
Bristol Rov	Tr	09.77	77-78	46	1	3

BARRY Patrick (Pat) Percival
Southampton, 25 October, 1920 Died 1994 (FB)

League Club	Source	Date Signed	Seasons Played	Apps	Subs	Gls
Southampton		02.40				
Blackburn Rov	Hyde U	05.48				
Bournemouth	Tr	05.50	50	4	-	0

BARRY Roy Alexander
Edinburgh, 19 September, 1942 (FB)

League Club	Source	Date Signed	Seasons Played	Apps	Subs	Gls
Coventry C	Dunfermline Ath	10.69	69-72	82	1	2
Crystal Palace	Tr	09.73	73-74	41	1	1

BARRY-MURPHY Brian
Cork, 27 July, 1978 IRYth/IRu21-6 (FB)

League Club	Source	Date Signed	Seasons Played	Apps	Subs	Gls
Preston NE	Cork C	08.99	99-02	6	15	0
Southend U	L	02.02	01	8	0	1
Hartlepool U	L	10.02	02	7	0	0
Sheffield Wed	Tr	01.03	02-03	55	3	0
Bury	Tr	08.04	04	43	2	6

BARTHEZ Fabien Alain
Lavelanet, France, 28 June, 1971 France 59 (G)

League Club	Source	Date Signed	Seasons Played	Apps	Subs	Gls
Manchester U	AS Monaco (Fr)	06.00	00-02	92	0	0

BARTHOLOMEW Henry (Harry)
Motherwell, 18 January, 1920 Died 2001 (WH)

League Club	Source	Date Signed	Seasons Played	Apps	Subs	Gls
Exeter C	Motherwell	05.47	47-48	66	-	6
Bournemouth	Tr	08.49				
Newport Co	Tr	06.50	50	3	-	0

BARTLETT Frank
Chester-le-Street, 8 November, 1930 (WH)

League Club	Source	Date Signed	Seasons Played	Apps	Subs	Gls
Barnsley	Blackhall CW	08.50	52-62	297	-	68
Halifax T	Tr	07.63	63	21	-	4

BARTLETT Frederick (Fred) Leslie
Reading, 5 March, 1913 Died 1968 (CD)

League Club	Source	Date Signed	Seasons Played	Apps	Subs	Gls
Queens Park Rgrs		10.32	34-36	48	-	0
Clapton Orient	Tr	05.37	37-47	96	-	0

BARTLETT Gordon
Chiswick, 3 December, 1955 (F)

League Club	Source	Date Signed	Seasons Played	Apps	Subs	Gls
Portsmouth	App	12.73	74	0	2	1

BARTLETT Kevin Francis
Portsmouth, 12 October, 1962 (F)

League Club	Source	Date Signed	Seasons Played	Apps	Subs	Gls
Portsmouth	App	10.80	80-81	0	3	0
Cardiff C	Fareham T	09.86	86-88	60	21	25
West Bromwich A	Tr	02.89	88-89	25	12	10
Notts Co	Tr	03.90	89-92	86	13	33
Port Vale	L	09.92	92	5	0	1
Cambridge U	Tr	03.93	92	3	5	1

BARTLETT Neal James
Southampton, 7 April, 1975 ESch (M)

League Club	Source	Date Signed	Seasons Played	Apps	Subs	Gls
Southampton	YT	07.93	92-93	4	4	0
Hereford U	BK Hacken (Swe)	09.96	96	0	3	0

BARTLETT Paul John
Grimsby, 17 January, 1960 (W)

League Club	Source	Date Signed	Seasons Played	Apps	Subs	Gls
Derby Co	App	12.77	77-79	7	6	0

BARTLETT Thurston Shaun
Cape Town, South Africa, 31 October, 1972 South Africa 72 (F)

League Club	Source	Date Signed	Seasons Played	Apps	Subs	Gls
Charlton Ath	FC Zurich (Swi)	12.00	00-04	89	18	23

BARTLETT Terence (Terry) Richard
Cleethorpes, 28 August, 1948 (W)

League Club	Source	Date Signed	Seasons Played	Apps	Subs	Gls
Grimsby T (Am)	Jnrs	08.67	67	1	0	0

BARTLEY Anthony (Tony)
Stalybridge, 8 March, 1938 (W)

League Club	Source	Date Signed	Seasons Played	Apps	Subs	Gls
Bolton W	Stalybridge Celtic	09.56				
Bury	Stalybridge Celtic	11.58	58-64	116	-	24

League Club	Source	Date Signed	Seasons Played	Career Record Apps	Subs	Gls
Oldham Ath	Tr	09.64	64-65	48	2	13
Chesterfield	Tr	07.66	66	12	0	2

BARTLEY Carl Alexander
Lambeth, 6 October, 1976 (F)

League Club	Source	Date Signed	Seasons Played	Apps	Subs	Gls
Fulham	YT	07.95	94	1	0	0

BARTLEY Daniel (Danny) Robert
Paulton, 3 October, 1947 EYth (W)

League Club	Source	Date Signed	Seasons Played	Apps	Subs	Gls
Bristol C	App	10.64	65-72	92	8	7
Swansea C	Tr	08.73	73-79	195	4	8
Hereford U	Tr	03.80	79-82	112	2	7

BARTLEY John Reginald
Camberwell, 15 September, 1958 (F)

League Club	Source	Date Signed	Seasons Played	Apps	Subs	Gls
Millwall	Welling U	10.80	80-81	39	1	8

BARTON Anthony (Tony) Edward
Sutton, 8 April, 1937 Died 1993 ESch (W)

League Club	Source	Date Signed	Seasons Played	Apps	Subs	Gls
Fulham	Sutton U	05.54	53-58	49	-	8
Nottingham F	Tr	12.59	59-61	22	-	1
Portsmouth	Tr	12.61	61-66	129	1	34

BARTON David
Bishop Auckland, 9 May, 1959 (CD)

League Club	Source	Date Signed	Seasons Played	Apps	Subs	Gls
Newcastle U	App	05.77	77-81	101	1	5
Blackburn Rov	L	08.82	82	8	0	1
Darlington	Tr	02.83	82-83	49	0	3

BARTON Douglas (Dougie) Joseph
Islington, 31 July, 1927 Died 2002 (FB)

League Club	Source	Date Signed	Seasons Played	Apps	Subs	Gls
Reading	Ford Sports	02.49	50-52	10	-	0
Newport Co	Tr	01.53	52-53	23	-	0

BARTON Frank
Barton-on-Humber, 22 October, 1947 EYth (M)

League Club	Source	Date Signed	Seasons Played	Apps	Subs	Gls
Scunthorpe U	App	08.65	64-67	93	0	26
Carlisle U	Tr	01.68	67-71	161	4	22
Blackpool	Tr	07.72	72	18	0	1
Grimsby T	Tr	06.73	73-75	123	0	15
Bournemouth	Tr	06.76	76-77	66	0	13
Hereford U	Tr	01.78	77-78	22	0	3
Bournemouth	Tr	09.78	78	22	0	2

BARTON John Birchall
Orrell, 27 April, 1942 (G)

League Club	Source	Date Signed	Seasons Played	Apps	Subs	Gls
Preston NE	Jnrs	05.59	58-65	48	0	0
Blackburn Rov	Tr	06.66	66-71	68	0	0

BARTON John Stanley
Birmingham, 24 October, 1953 (FB)

League Club	Source	Date Signed	Seasons Played	Apps	Subs	Gls
Everton	Worcester C	12.78	78-80	18	2	0
Derby Co	Tr	03.82	81-83	68	1	1

BARTON Joseph (Joey) Anthony
Huyton, 2 September, 1982 Eu21-2 (M)

League Club	Source	Date Signed	Seasons Played	Apps	Subs	Gls
Manchester C	YT	07.01	02-04	59	7	3

BARTON Kenneth (Ken) Rees
Caernarfon, 20 September, 1937 Died 1982 WSch (FB)

League Club	Source	Date Signed	Seasons Played	Apps	Subs	Gls
Tottenham H	Jnrs	10.56	60-63	4	-	0
Millwall	Tr	09.64				
Luton T	Tr	12.64	64	11	-	0

BARTON Leslie (Les)
Rochdale, 20 March, 1920 Died 2002 (FB)

League Club	Source	Date Signed	Seasons Played	Apps	Subs	Gls
Bolton W		09.46				
New Brighton	Tr	08.49	49-50	64	-	1

BARTON Michael Geoffrey
Gainsborough, 23 September, 1973 (G)

League Club	Source	Date Signed	Seasons Played	Apps	Subs	Gls
Shrewsbury T	YT	07.90	91	1	0	0

BARTON Peter
Barrow, 3 April, 1951 (G)

League Club	Source	Date Signed	Seasons Played	Apps	Subs	Gls
Barrow	App	04.69	68	2	0	0

BARTON Charles **Reginald (Reg)**
Chester, 4 March, 1942 (G)

League Club	Source	Date Signed	Seasons Played	Apps	Subs	Gls
Chester	Jnrs	06.61	61-64	14	-	0

BARTON David **Roger**
Jump, 25 September, 1946 (M)

League Club	Source	Date Signed	Seasons Played	Apps	Subs	Gls
Wolverhampton W	App	10.63				
Lincoln C	Tr	07.64	64-65	28	0	1
Barnsley	Tr	07.66	66-68	52	3	3

BARTON Warren Dean
Stoke Newington, 19 March, 1969 EB-3/E-3 (FB)

League Club	Source	Date Signed	Seasons Played	Apps	Subs	Gls
Maidstone U	Leytonstone & Ilford	07.89	89	41	1	0
Wimbledon	Tr	06.90	90-94	178	2	10
Newcastle U	Tr	06.95	95-01	142	22	4
Derby Co	Tr	02.02	01-02	53	0	0
Queens Park Rgrs	Tr	10.03	03	2	1	0
Wimbledon	Tr	02.04	03	5	0	0

BARTRAM Andreas **Per**
Odense, Denmark, 8 January, 1944 (F)

League Club	Source	Date Signed	Seasons Played	Apps	Subs	Gls
Crystal Palace	Morton	08.69	69	8	2	2

BARTRAM Samuel (Sam)
Simonside, 22 January, 1914 Died 1981 EWar-3 (G)

League Club	Source	Date Signed	Seasons Played	Apps	Subs	Gls
Charlton Ath	Boldon Villa	09.34	34-55	579	-	0

BARTRAM Vincent (Vince) Lee
Birmingham, 7 August, 1968 (G)

League Club	Source	Date Signed	Seasons Played	Apps	Subs	Gls
Wolverhampton W	Jnrs	08.85	86-90	5	0	0
Blackpool	L	10.89	89	9	0	0
Bournemouth	Tr	07.91	91-93	132	0	0
Arsenal	Tr	08.94	94	11	0	0
Huddersfield T	L	10.97	97	12	0	0
Gillingham	Tr	03.98	97-03	186	1	0

BART-WILLIAMS Christopher (Chris) Gerald
Freetown, Sierra Leone, 16 June, 1974 EYth/Eu21-16/EB-1 (M)

League Club	Source	Date Signed	Seasons Played	Apps	Subs	Gls
Leyton Orient	YT	07.91	90-91	34	2	2
Sheffield Wed	Tr	11.91	91-94	95	29	16
Nottingham F	Tr	07.95	95-01	200	7	30
Charlton Ath	Tr	12.01	01-02	17	12	2
Ipswich T	Tr	09.03	03	23	3	2

BARWICK Terence (Terry) Patrick
Doncaster, 11 January, 1983 (M)

League Club	Source	Date Signed	Seasons Played	Apps	Subs	Gls
Scunthorpe U	Sch	07.02	99-03	35	11	1

BARWOOD Daniel (Danny) David
Caerphilly, 25 February, 1981 WYth (W)

League Club	Source	Date Signed	Seasons Played	Apps	Subs	Gls
Swansea C	YT	07.99	97	1	2	1

BASEY Philip (Phil) John
Cardiff, 27 August, 1948 (W)

League Club	Source	Date Signed	Seasons Played	Apps	Subs	Gls
Brentford	Jnrs	06.66	66	2	0	0

BASFORD John (Jack)
Crewe, 24 July, 1925 Died 1998 (CF)

League Club	Source	Date Signed	Seasons Played	Apps	Subs	Gls
Crewe Alex	Wolverhampton W (Am)	04.48	47-53	144	-	58
Chester	Tr	01.54	53	10	-	1

BASFORD Luke William
Croydon, 6 January, 1980 (FB)

League Club	Source	Date Signed	Seasons Played	Apps	Subs	Gls
Bristol Rov	YT	07.98	97-98	11	5	0

BASHAM Michael (Mike)
Barking, 27 September, 1973 ESch/EYth (CD)

League Club	Source	Date Signed	Seasons Played	Apps	Subs	Gls
West Ham U	YT	07.92				
Colchester U	L	11.93	93	1	0	0
Swansea C	Tr	03.94	93-95	27	2	1
Peterborough U	Tr	12.95	95-96	17	2	1
Barnet	Tr	08.97	97-00	74	1	2
York C	Tr	03.01	00-01	32	4	3

BASHAM Steven (Steve) Brian
Southampton, 2 December, 1977 (F)

League Club	Source	Date Signed	Seasons Played	Apps	Subs	Gls
Southampton	YT	05.96	96-98	1	18	1
Wrexham	L	02.98	97	4	1	0
Preston NE	Tr	02.99	98-01	37	31	15
Oxford U	Tr	08.02	02-04	92	16	31

BASHIR Naseem
Amersham, 12 September, 1969 (M)

League Club	Source	Date Signed	Seasons Played	Apps	Subs	Gls
Reading	Jnrs	06.88	89	1	2	1

BASON Brian
Epsom, 3 September, 1955 ESch (M)

League Club	Source	Date Signed	Seasons Played	Apps	Subs	Gls
Chelsea	App	09.72	72-76	18	1	1
Plymouth Arg	Tr	09.77	77-80	127	3	10
Crystal Palace	Tr	03.81	80-81	25	2	0
Portsmouth	L	01.82	81	9	0	0
Reading	Tr	08.82	82	41	0	0

BASS David
Frimley, 29 November, 1974 (M)

League Club	Source	Date Signed	Seasons Played	Apps	Subs	Gls
Reading	YT	07.93	91-96	7	4	0
Rotherham U	Tr	07.97	97	13	5	0
Carlisle U	Tr	03.99	98	8	1	0

BASS Jonathan (Jon) David
Weston-super-Mare, 1 January, 1976 ESch (FB)

League Club	Source	Date Signed	Seasons Played	Apps	Subs	Gls
Birmingham C	Jnrs	06.94	95-00	60	8	0
Carlisle U	L	10.96	96	3	0	0
Gillingham	L	03.00	99	4	3	0
Hartlepool U	Tr	07.01	01-02	21	3	1
Bristol Rov	Pahang FA (Mal)	03.05	04	3	0	0

BASSEDAS Christian Gustavo
Buenos Aires, Argentina, 16 February, 1973 Argentina 23 (M)

League Club	Source	Date Signed	Seasons Played	Apps	Subs	Gls
Newcastle U	Velez Sarsfield (Arg)	07.00	00-01	18	6	1

BASSETT David (Dave)
Hendon, 4 September, 1944 EAmat (CD)

League Club	Source	Date Signed	Seasons Played	Apps	Subs	Gls
Wimbledon	Walton & Hersham	08.74	77	35	0	0

BASSETT George Raymond
Birmingham, 12 May, 1943 (W)

League Club	Source	Date Signed	Seasons Played	Apps	Subs	Gls
Coventry C	Jnrs	08.61	61	1	-	0

BASSETT Graham Raymond
Sunderland, 6 October, 1964 (F)

League Club	Source	Date Signed	Seasons Played	Apps	Subs	Gls
Hartlepool U	Sunderland (App)	08.83	83	4	3	0

BASSETT William (Billy) Edward George
Brithdir, 8 June, 1912 Died 1977 (CD)

League Club	Source	Date Signed	Seasons Played	Apps	Subs	Gls
Cardiff C	Aberaman Ath	08.34	34-38	154	-	2
Crystal Palace	Tr	09.42	46-48	70	-	0

BASSHAM Alan John
Kensington, 3 October, 1933 ESch (FB)

League Club	Source	Date Signed	Seasons Played	Apps	Subs	Gls
Brentford	Jnrs	10.51	53-57	43	-	0

BASSILA Christian
Paris, France, 5 October, 1977 Fru21 (FB)

League Club	Source	Date Signed	Seasons Played	Apps	Subs	Gls
West Ham U (L)	Rennes (Fr)	08.00	00	0	3	0

BASSINDER Gavin David
Mexborough, 24 September, 1979 (CD)

League Club	Source	Date Signed	Seasons Played	Apps	Subs	Gls
Barnsley	YT	07.98				
Mansfield T	Tr	03.00	99	1	3	0

BASTIN Clifford (Cliff) Sydney
Exeter, 14 March, 1912 Died 1991 ESch/FLge-4/E-21 (W)

League Club	Source	Date Signed	Seasons Played	Apps	Subs	Gls
Exeter C	Jnrs	03.29	27-28	17	-	6
Arsenal	Tr	05.29	29-46	350	-	150

BASTOCK Paul Anthony
Leamington Spa, 19 May, 1970 (G)

League Club	Source	Date Signed	Seasons Played	Apps	Subs	Gls
Cambridge U	Coventry C (YT)	03.88	87-88	12	0	0
Boston U	Kettering T	08.92	02-03	92	0	0

BASTOW Darren John
Torquay, 22 December, 1981 (M)

League Club	Source	Date Signed	Seasons Played	Apps	Subs	Gls
Plymouth Arg	YT	01.99	98-99	28	14	3

BASTOW Ian John
Torquay, 12 August, 1971 (W)

League Club	Source	Date Signed	Seasons Played	Apps	Subs	Gls
Torquay U	YT	03.89	88-89	7	4	0

BATCH Nigel Anthony
Huddersfield, 9 September, 1957 (G)

League Club	Source	Date Signed	Seasons Played	Apps	Subs	Gls
Grimsby T	Derby Co (App)	07.76	76-86	348	0	0
Darlington	Lincoln C	09.88	88	30	0	0
Stockport Co	Tr	03.89	88	12	0	0
Scunthorpe U	(Retired)	08.91	91	1	0	0

BATCHELOR Edward
Rugby, 4 August, 1930 (WH)

League Club	Source	Date Signed	Seasons Played	Apps	Subs	Gls
Wolverhampton W	Jnrs	10.47				
Swindon T	Tr	08.50	50-54	91	-	0

BATEMAN Albert
Stocksbridge, 13 June, 1924 (W)

League Club	Source	Date Signed	Seasons Played	Apps	Subs	Gls
Huddersfield T	Yorkshire Iron & Steel	09.43	46-48	73	-	14

BATEMAN Arthur
Audley, 12 June, 1918 Died 1984 (FB)

League Club	Source	Date Signed	Seasons Played	Apps	Subs	Gls
Crewe Alex	Rolls Royce	11.42	46	4	-	0

BATEMAN Colin
Hemel Hempstead, 22 October, 1930 (FB)

League Club	Source	Date Signed	Seasons Played	Apps	Subs	Gls
Watford	Hemel Hempstead	03.53	54-57	50	-	0

BATEMAN Ernest (Ernie)
Hemel Hempstead, 5 April, 1929 (CD)

League Club	Source	Date Signed	Seasons Played	Apps	Subs	Gls
Watford	Hemel Hempstead	03.52	55-56	23	-	0

BATER Philip (Phil) Thomas
Cardiff, 26 October, 1955 Wu21-2 (FB)

League Club	Source	Date Signed	Seasons Played	Apps	Subs	Gls
Bristol Rov	App	10.73	74-80	211	1	2
Wrexham	Tr	09.81	81-82	73	0	1
Bristol Rov	Tr	09.83	83-85	90	8	1
Brentford	Tr	05.86	86	19	0	2
Cardiff C	Tr	07.87	87-88	67	9	0

BATES Anthony (Tony) Norman
Blidworth, 6 April, 1938 (CF)

League Club	Source	Date Signed	Seasons Played	Apps	Subs	Gls
Notts Co	Blidworth Colliery	07.59	58	1	-	0

BATES Brian Frederick
Beeston, 4 December, 1944 (W)

League Club	Source	Date Signed	Seasons Played	Apps	Subs	Gls
Notts Co	Loughborough College	07.63	63-68	125	3	24
Mansfield T	Tr	07.69	69	20	0	3

BATES Donald (Don) Lawson
Brighton, 10 May, 1933 Died 2005 (WH)

League Club	Source	Date Signed	Seasons Played	Apps	Subs	Gls
Brighton & Hove A	Lewes	11.50	57	21	-	1

BATES Edric (Ted) Thornton
Thetford, 3 May, 1918 Died 2003 (IF)

League Club	Source	Date Signed	Seasons Played	Apps	Subs	Gls
Norwich C	Thetford T	09.36				
Southampton	Tr	05.37	37-52	202	-	65

BATES Ernest (Ernie)
Huddersfield, 10 June, 1935 Died 1995 (FB)

League Club	Source	Date Signed	Seasons Played	Apps	Subs	Gls
Huddersfield T	Deighton YMCA	08.55				
Bradford PA	Tr	05.57	57-58	44	-	0

BATES George Reginald
Sheffield, 21 November, 1923 Died 1995 (W)

League Club	Source	Date Signed	Seasons Played	Apps	Subs	Gls
Sheffield Wed	Shardlows	03.45				
Darlington	Tr	07.46	46	3	-	0

BATES James (Jamie) Alan
Croydon, 24 February, 1968 (CD)

League Club	Source	Date Signed	Seasons Played	Apps	Subs	Gls
Brentford	App	08.86	86-98	399	20	18
Wycombe W	Tr	03.99	98-00	76	4	4

BATES John Wilfred
Newcastle, 28 April, 1942 (W)

League Club	Source	Date Signed	Seasons Played	Apps	Subs	Gls
Hartlepools U	Consett	03.66	65	11	0	0

BATES Keith
Huddersfield, 1 September, 1933 (IF)

League Club	Source	Date Signed	Seasons Played	Apps	Subs	Gls
Halifax T (Am)	Bradley Rgrs	11.56	56	1	-	0

BATES Mark
Walsall, 25 April, 1965 (FB)

League Club	Source	Date Signed	Seasons Played	Apps	Subs	Gls
Walsall	App	04.83	82-83	6	0	0
Shrewsbury T	Tr	07.84	84	7	1	0

BATES Matthew David
Stockton, 10 December, 1986 EYth (CD)

League Club	Source	Date Signed	Seasons Played	Apps	Subs	Gls
Middlesbrough	Sch	01.05	04	0	2	0
Darlington	L	03.05	04	4	0	0

BATES Michael (Mick) John
Armthorpe, 19 September, 1947 (M)

League Club	Source	Date Signed	Seasons Played	Apps	Subs	Gls
Leeds U	App	09.64	66-75	106	15	4
Walsall	Tr	06.76	76-77	84	1	4
Bradford C	Tr	06.78	78-79	54	2	1
Doncaster Rov	Tr	06.80	80	3	1	0

BATES Philip (Chic) Desmond
West Bromwich, 28 November, 1949 (F)

League Club	Source	Date Signed	Seasons Played	Apps	Subs	Gls
Shrewsbury T	Stourbridge	05.74	74-77	160	0	45
Swindon T	Tr	01.78	77-79	50	13	15
Bristol Rov	Tr	03.80	79-80	26	3	4
Shrewsbury T	Tr	12.80	80-85	114	20	19

BATES Thomas (Tom)
Coventry, 31 October, 1985 (M)

League Club	Source	Date Signed	Seasons Played	Apps	Subs	Gls
Coventry C	Bedworth U	01.03	02	0	1	0

BATES William (Billy) Henry
Eaton Bray, 13 January, 1922 Died 1997 (W)

League Club	Source	Date Signed	Seasons Played	Apps	Subs	Gls
Luton T	Waterlows	09.41	46	1	-	0
Watford	Tr	07.48	48	13	-	1

BATEY Norman **Robert (Bob)**
Greenhead, 18 October, 1912 Died 1988 (CD)

League Club	Source	Date Signed	Seasons Played	Apps	Subs	Gls
Carlisle U	Greenhead S Tyne Rgrs	09.32	32-33	23	-	0
Preston NE	Tr	03.34	34-38	90	-	0
Leeds U	Tr	04.46	46	8	-	0
Southport	Tr	06.47	47	29	-	0

BATHGATE Sidney (Syd)
Aberdeen, 20 December, 1919 Died 1962 (FB)

League Club	Source	Date Signed	Seasons Played	Apps	Subs	Gls
Chelsea	Parkvale Jnrs	09.46	46-52	135	-	0

BATSON Brendan Martin
St George's, Grenada, 6 February, 1953 EB (FB)

League Club	Source	Date Signed	Seasons Played	Apps	Subs	Gls
Arsenal	App	06.71	71-73	6	4	0
Cambridge U	Tr	01.74	73-77	162	1	6
West Bromwich A	Tr	02.78	77-82	172	0	1

BATT Victor (Vic) Thomas
Dorking, 13 March, 1943 (W)

League Club	Source	Date Signed	Seasons Played	Apps	Subs	Gls
Reading	Jnrs	08.61	61-62	15	-	0

League Club	Source	Date Signed	Seasons Played	Career Record Apps	Subs	Gls
BATTERSBY Anthony (Tony)						
Doncaster, 30 August, 1975						(F)
Sheffield U	YT	07.93	95	3	7	1
Southend U	L	03.95	94	6	2	1
Notts Co	Tr	01.96	95-96	20	19	8
Bury	Tr	03.97	96-97	37	11	8
Lincoln C	Tr	08.98	98-02	95	35	21
Northampton T	L	09.99	99	0	3	1
Boston U	Tr	10.02	02	7	4	1
Rushden & Diamonds	Tr	02.03	02	2	3	0
BATTY David						
Leeds, 2 December, 1968 Eu21-7/EB-5/E-42						(M)
Leeds U	YT	08.87	87-93	201	10	4
Blackburn Rov	Tr	10.93	93-95	53	1	1
Newcastle U	Tr	03.96	95-98	81	2	3
Leeds U	Tr	12.98	98-03	79	11	0
BATTY Frederick (Fred) Robson						
Stanley, 20 December, 1934						(CD)
Bradford PA	Stanley U	01.56	55-58	56	-	0
BATTY Laurence William						
Westminster, 15 February, 1964						(G)
Fulham	Deportivo Farense (Por)	08.84	85-90	9	0	0
BATTY Michael (Mike)						
Manchester, 10 July, 1944						(CD)
Manchester C	App	07.61	62-64	13	-	0
BATTY Paul William						
Edington, 9 January, 1964						(M)
Swindon T	App	01.82	82-84	102	6	7
Chesterfield	Tr	07.85	85	24	2	0
Exeter C	Tr	07.86	86-90	98	13	11
BATTY Ronald (Ron) Robson						
Lanchester, 5 October, 1925 Died 1971						(FB)
Newcastle U	Quaking Houses	10.45	48-57	161	-	1
Gateshead	Tr	03.58	57-58	40	-	0
BATTY Stanley (Stan) George						
Tottenham, 14 February, 1913 Died 1998						(WH)
Aston Villa	Finchley	11.37				
Newport Co	Tr	12.45	46-47	60	-	3
BATTYE John Edward						
Scissett, 19 May, 1926						(WH)
Huddersfield T	Shepley Jnrs	12.43	49-57	71	-	1
York C	Tr	07.59	59	17	-	0
BAUDET Julien						
Grenoble, France, 13 January, 1979						(CD)
Oldham Ath	Toulouse (Fr)	10.01	01-02	34	10	3
Rotherham U	Tr	08.03	03	8	3	0
Notts Co	Tr	07.04	04	38	1	5
BAUGH John Robert						
Uganda, 23 February, 1956						(G)
Exeter C	St Luke's College	02.77	76-77	20	0	0
BAULD Philip (Phil) Spinelli						
Glasgow, 20 September, 1929 Died 1994						(WH)
Plymouth Arg	Clyde	06.53				
Aldershot	Tr	07.54	54	3	-	0
BAURESS Gary Joseph						
Liverpool, 19 January, 1971						(M)
Tranmere Rov	YT	08.89	89	1	0	0
BAVERSTOCK Raymond (Ray)						
Southall, 3 December, 1963						(FB)
Swindon T	App	12.81	82	17	0	0
BAVIN John (Jack)						
Ferriby, 25 May, 1921 Died 2001						(FB)
Tranmere Rov	Leith Ath	04.49	48	2	-	0
BAXTER James (Jimmy) Cunningham						
Dunfermline, 8 November, 1925 Died 1994						(IF)
Barnsley	Dunfermline Ath	08.45	46-51	222	-	54
Preston NE	Tr	07.52	52-58	245	-	65
Barnsley	Tr	07.59	59	26	-	3
BAXTER James (Jim) Curran						
Hill o' Beath, 29 September, 1939 Died 2001 Su23-1/SLge-5/S-34						(M)
Sunderland	Glasgow Rgrs	05.65	65-67	87	0	10
Nottingham F	Tr	12.67	67-68	47	1	3
BAXTER Lawrence (Larry) Raymond						
Leicester, 24 November, 1931						(W)
Northampton T		03.52	52-53	17	-	2
Norwich C	Tr	11.54	54	5	-	0
Gillingham	Tr	10.55	55-57	64	-	7
Torquay U	Tr	09.57	57-61	165	-	22
BAXTER Lee Stuart						
Helsingborg, Sweden, 17 July, 1976						(G)
Sheffield U (L)	Malmo FF (Swe)	12.03	03	1	0	0
BAXTER Michael (Mick) John						
Birmingham, 30 December, 1956 Died 1989						(CD)
Preston NE	App	12.74	74-80	208	1	17
Middlesbrough	Tr	08.81	81-83	122	0	7
BAXTER Paul Albert						
Hackney, 22 April, 1964						(FB)
Crystal Palace	Tottenham H (App)	09.81	81	1	0	0
BAXTER Robert (Bobby) Denholm						
Redcar, 4 February, 1937						(FB)
Darlington	Bo'ness	11.59	59-60	64	-	30
Brighton & Hove A	Tr	06.61	61-66	195	0	6
Torquay U	Tr	07.67	67-68	58	4	6
Darlington	Tr	07.69	69	41	1	0
BAXTER Stuart William						
Wolverhampton, 16 August, 1953 Australia int						(CD)
Preston NE	App	10.71	72-75	35	7	1
Stockport Co	Dundee	12.76	76	4	0	0
BAXTER William (Billy)						
Leven, 21 September, 1924 Died 2002						(WH)
Wolverhampton W	Jnrs	03.45	48-53	43	-	1
Aston Villa	Tr	11.53	53-56	98	-	6
BAXTER William (Bill) Alexander						
Edinburgh, 23 April, 1939						(CD)
Ipswich T	Broxburn Ath	06.60	60-70	409	0	21
Hull C	Tr	03.71	70-71	20	1	0
Watford	L	10.71	71	11	0	0
Northampton T	Tr	06.72	72	41	0	4
BAXTER William (Bill) Amelius						
Nottingham, 6 September, 1917 Died 1992						(CD)
Nottingham F	Berridge Road Inst	12.36	37-46	15	-	0
Notts Co	Tr	10.46	46-53	140	-	0
BAYES Ashley John						
Lincoln, 19 April, 1972 EYth						(G)
Brentford	YT	07.90	89-92	4	0	0
Torquay U	Tr	08.93	93-95	97	0	0
Exeter C	Tr	07.96	96-98	127	0	0
Leyton Orient	Tr	07.99	99-01	68	1	0
BAYLEY Thomas (Tom) Kenneth						
Wednesbury, 25 June, 1921 Died 1996						(G)
Wrexham	Walsall (Am)	08.47	47	6	-	0
BAYLISS David (Dave) Anthony						
Liverpool, 8 June, 1976						(CD)
Rochdale	YT	06.95	94-01	169	17	9
Luton T	Tr	12.01	01-03	28	9	0
Chester C	L	12.04	04	9	0	0
BAYLISS Ronald (Ron)						
Belfast, 20 September, 1944						(FB)
Reading		02.65	64-67	35	2	1
Bradford C	Tr	07.68	68-69	35	4	0
BAYLY Martin Joseph						
Dublin, 14 September, 1966 IRYth/IRu21-1						(M)
Wolverhampton W	App	07.84	83-84	9	1	0
BAYNHAM John (Johnny)						
Rhondda, 21 April, 1918 Died 1995						(W)
Leyton Orient	Brentford (Am)	03.46	46-47	60	-	7
Swindon T	Tr	08.48	48	4	-	1
BAYNHAM Ronald (Ron) Leslie						
Birmingham, 10 June, 1929 EB/FLge-2/E-3						(G)
Luton T	Worcester C	11.51	52-64	388	-	0
BAZELEY Darren Shaun						
Northampton, 5 October, 1972 Eu21-1						(FB)
Watford	YT	05.91	89-98	187	53	21
Wolverhampton W	Tr	07.99	99-00	69	1	4
Walsall	Tr	07.02	02-04	83	6	0
BAZLEY John Alfred						
Runcorn, 4 October, 1936						(W)
Oldham Ath	Bangor Univ	10.56	56-61	130	-	19

BEACH Douglas (Doug) Frederick
Watford, 2 February, 1920 (FB)

League Club	Source	Date Signed	Seasons Played	Apps	Subs	Gls
Luton T	Sheffield Wed (Am)	08.45	46	23	-	0
Southend U	Tr	07.47	47-48	41	-	0

BEACOCK Gary Cedric
Scunthorpe, 22 January, 1960 (M)

League Club	Source	Date Signed	Seasons Played	Apps	Subs	Gls
Grimsby T	(Holland)	05.80	80-82	10	7	0
Hereford U	Tr	08.83	83-85	22	5	4

BEADLE Peter Clifford William James
Lambeth, 13 May, 1972 (F)

League Club	Source	Date Signed	Seasons Played	Apps	Subs	Gls
Gillingham	YT	05.90	88-91	42	25	14
Tottenham H	Tr	06.92				
Bournemouth	L	03.93	92	9	0	2
Southend U	L	03.94	93	8	0	1
Watford	Tr	09.94	94-95	12	11	1
Bristol Rov	Tr	11.95	95-97	98	11	39
Port Vale	Tr	08.98	98	18	5	6
Notts Co	Tr	02.99	98-99	14	8	3
Bristol C	Tr	10.99	99-02	51	31	14
Brentford	Tr	08.03	03	1	0	0

BEADNELL William (Bill)
Fulwell, County Durham, 25 January, 1933 (IF)

League Club	Source	Date Signed	Seasons Played	Apps	Subs	Gls
Chesterfield	Hylton Colliery	06.50				
Middlesbrough	Tr	05.53				
Southport	Tr	05.54	54-55	63	-	19

BEAGRIE Peter Sydney
North Ormesby, 28 November, 1965 Eu21-2/EB-2 (W)

League Club	Source	Date Signed	Seasons Played	Apps	Subs	Gls
Middlesbrough	Jnrs	09.83	84-85	24	9	2
Sheffield U	Tr	08.86	86-87	81	3	11
Stoke C	Tr	06.88	88-89	54	0	7
Everton	Tr	11.89	89-93	88	26	11
Sunderland	L	09.91	91	5	0	1
Manchester C	Tr	03.94	93-96	46	6	3
Bradford C	Tr	07.97	97-00	113	18	20
Everton	L	03.98	97	4	2	0
Wigan Ath	L	02.01	00	7	3	1
Scunthorpe U	Tr	07.01	01-04	132	10	29

BEAL Philip (Phil)
Godstone, 8 January, 1945 EYth (CD)

League Club	Source	Date Signed	Seasons Played	Apps	Subs	Gls
Tottenham H	App	01.62	63-74	330	3	1
Brighton & Hove A	Tr	07.75	75-76	9	1	0
Crewe Alex	Memphis (USA)	08.79	79	4	0	0

BEALE John Michael
Portsmouth, 16 October, 1930 Died 1995 (WH)

League Club	Source	Date Signed	Seasons Played	Apps	Subs	Gls
Portsmouth	Jnrs	08.48	51-52	14	-	1

BEALL Matthew (Billy) John
Enfield, 4 December, 1977 (M)

League Club	Source	Date Signed	Seasons Played	Apps	Subs	Gls
Cambridge U	YT	03.96	95-97	73	9	7
Leyton Orient	Tr	10.98	98-01	62	22	3

BEAMAN Ralph Wesley
Willenhall, 14 January, 1943 (CF)

League Club	Source	Date Signed	Seasons Played	Apps	Subs	Gls
Walsall	Jnrs	12.60	61	1	-	0

BEAMENT Roger John
Croxley, 28 September, 1937 (G)

League Club	Source	Date Signed	Seasons Played	Apps	Subs	Gls
Watford (Am)	Croxley BC	07.56	56	1	-	0

BEAMISH Kenneth (Ken) George
Bebington, 25 August, 1947 (F)

League Club	Source	Date Signed	Seasons Played	Apps	Subs	Gls
Tranmere Rov	Jnrs	07.66	65-71	176	2	49
Brighton & Hove A	Tr	03.72	71-73	86	10	27
Blackburn Rov	Tr	05.74	74-76	86	0	19
Port Vale	Tr	09.76	76-78	84	1	29
Bury	Tr	09.78	78-79	49	0	20
Tranmere Rov	Tr	11.79	79-80	57	2	15
Swindon T	Tr	08.81	81	1	1	0

BEAN Alan
Doncaster, 17 January, 1935 (CD)

League Club	Source	Date Signed	Seasons Played	Apps	Subs	Gls
Blackburn Rov	Jnrs	04.52	52-54	2	-	0

BEAN Alfred (Alf) Samuel
Lincoln, 25 August, 1915 Died 1993 (FB)

League Club	Source	Date Signed	Seasons Played	Apps	Subs	Gls
Lincoln C	Lincoln Corinthians	05.35	34-48	171	-	10

BEAN Marcus Tristam
Hammersmith, 2 November, 1984 (M)

League Club	Source	Date Signed	Seasons Played	Apps	Subs	Gls
Queens Park Rgrs	Sch	07.04	02-04	40	18	2
Swansea C	L	02.05	04	6	2	0

BEAN Ronald (Ron) Eric
Crayford, 10 April, 1926 Died 1992 (G)

League Club	Source	Date Signed	Seasons Played	Apps	Subs	Gls
Gillingham	Gravesend & Northfleet	06.51	51	3	-	0

BEANEY William (Bill) Ronald
Southampton, 29 May, 1954 (CD)

League Club	Source	Date Signed	Seasons Played	Apps	Subs	Gls
Southampton	App	06.72	72-74	2	1	0

BEANLAND Anthony (Tony)
Bradford, 11 January, 1944 (CD)

League Club	Source	Date Signed	Seasons Played	Apps	Subs	Gls
Blackpool	App	01.62				
Southport	Tr	07.62	62-65	143	0	3
Southend U	Tr	03.66	65-66	57	0	3
Wrexham	Tr	07.67	67-68	84	0	5
Bradford PA	Tr	06.69	69	29	2	1

BEARD Malcolm
Cannock, 3 May, 1942 EYth (CD)

League Club	Source	Date Signed	Seasons Played	Apps	Subs	Gls
Birmingham C	Jnrs	05.59	60-70	349	1	26
Aston Villa	Tr	07.71	71-72	5	1	0

BEARD Mark
Roehampton, 8 October, 1974 (FB)

League Club	Source	Date Signed	Seasons Played	Apps	Subs	Gls
Millwall	YT	03.93	93-94	32	13	2
Sheffield U	Tr	08.95	95-97	22	16	0
Southend U	L	10.97	97	6	2	0
Southend U	Tr	07.98	98-99	74	4	1
Southend U	Kingstonian	10.01	01-02	34	16	0

BEARDALL James (Jim) Thomas
Whitefield, 18 October, 1946 (F)

League Club	Source	Date Signed	Seasons Played	Apps	Subs	Gls
Blackburn Rov	Bury (Am)	03.68	67-68	4	2	1
Oldham Ath	Tr	05.69	69	21	1	10

BEARDS Allan
Normanton, 19 October, 1932 (W)

League Club	Source	Date Signed	Seasons Played	Apps	Subs	Gls
Bolton W	Whitewood Jnrs	10.50	50-53	14	-	2
Swindon T	Tr	03.54	53-54	21	-	4
Stockport Co	Tr	07.55	55	5	-	0

BEARDSHAW Ernest Colin
Crawcrook, 26 November, 1912 Died 1977 (CD)

League Club	Source	Date Signed	Seasons Played	Apps	Subs	Gls
Gateshead (Am)	South Hetton CW	02.36	35	12	-	0
Stockport Co	Tr	05.36	37	18	-	0
Bradford C	Tr	07.38	38	42	-	0
Southport	Cork U	10.48	48-50	61	-	0

BEARDSLEY Christopher (Chris) Kelan
Derby, 28 February, 1984 (M)

League Club	Source	Date Signed	Seasons Played	Apps	Subs	Gls
Mansfield T	Sch	07.03	02-03	3	17	1
Doncaster Rov	Tr	08.04	04	1	3	0
Kidderminster Hrs	Tr	12.04	04	15	10	5

BEARDSLEY Donald (Don) Thomas
Alyth, 23 October, 1946 (FB)

League Club	Source	Date Signed	Seasons Played	Apps	Subs	Gls
Hull C	App	11.64	66-72	128	2	0
Doncaster Rov	L	03.72	71	10	0	0
Grimsby T	Tr	08.73	73-74	66	0	0

BEARDSLEY Peter Andrew
Longbenton, 18 January, 1961 FLge/EB/E-59 (F)

League Club	Source	Date Signed	Seasons Played	Apps	Subs	Gls
Carlisle U	Wallsend BC	08.79	79-81	93	11	22
Manchester U	Vancouver (Can)	09.82				
Newcastle U	Vancouver (Can)	09.83	83-86	146	1	61
Liverpool	Tr	07.87	87-90	120	11	46
Everton	Tr	08.91	91-92	81	0	25
Newcastle U	Tr	07.93	93-96	126	3	46
Bolton W	Tr	08.97	97	14	3	2
Manchester C	L	02.98	97	5	1	0
Fulham	Tr	03.98	97-98	19	2	4
Hartlepool U	Tr	12.98	98	22	0	2

BEARDSMORE Russell Peter
Wigan, 28 September, 1968 Eu21-5 (M)

League Club	Source	Date Signed	Seasons Played	Apps	Subs	Gls
Manchester U	App	10.86	88-90	30	26	4
Blackburn Rov	L	12.91	91	1	1	0
Bournemouth	Tr	06.93	93-97	167	11	4

BEARPARK Ian Harper
Dursley, 13 January, 1939 Died 1997 (G)

League Club	Source	Date Signed	Seasons Played	Apps	Subs	Gls
Bristol Rov	Stonehouse	08.60	60	2	-	0

BEARRYMAN Henry (Harry) William
Wandsworth, 26 September, 1924 Died 1976 (WH)

League Club	Source	Date Signed	Seasons Played	Apps	Subs	Gls
Chelsea	Jnrs	09.41				
Colchester U	Tr	07.47	50-53	173	-	3

BEASANT David (Dave) John
Willesden, 20 March, 1959 EB-7/E-2 (G)

League Club	Source	Date Signed	Seasons Played	Apps	Subs	Gls
Wimbledon	Edgware T	08.79	79-87	340	0	0
Newcastle U	Tr	06.88	88	20	0	0
Chelsea	Tr	01.89	88-92	133	0	0
Grimsby T	L	10.92	92	6	0	0
Wolverhampton W	L	01.93	92	4	0	0
Southampton	Tr	11.93	93-96	86	2	0

League Club	Source	Date Signed	Seasons Played	Apps	Subs	Gls
Nottingham F	Tr	08.97	97-00	139	0	0
Portsmouth	Tr	08.01	01	8	0	0
Tottenham H	Tr	11.01				
Portsmouth	Tr	01.02	01	19	0	0
Bradford C	Tr	09.02				
Wigan Ath	Tr	10.02				
Brighton & Hove A	Tr	01.03	02	16	0	0

BEASLEY Albert (Pat) Edward
Stourbridge, 27 July, 1913 Died 1986 E-1 (W)

League Club	Source	Date Signed	Seasons Played	Apps	Subs	Gls
Arsenal	Stourbridge	05.31	31-36	79	-	19
Huddersfield T	Tr	10.36	36-38	108	-	24
Fulham	Tr	12.45	46-49	152	-	13
Bristol C	Tr	08.50	50-51	66	-	5

BEASLEY Andrew (Andy)
Sedgley, 15 February, 1964 (G)

League Club	Source	Date Signed	Seasons Played	Apps	Subs	Gls
Luton T	App	02.82				
Mansfield T	Tr	07.84	84-91	94	0	0
Peterborough U	L	07.86	86	7	0	0
Scarborough	L	03.88	87	4	0	0
Bristol Rov	L	03.93	92	1	0	0
Doncaster Rov	Tr	07.93	93	37	0	0
Chesterfield	Tr	08.94	94-95	31	1	0

BEASON Malcolm Lloyd
Dulwich, 1 December, 1955 (M)

League Club	Source	Date Signed	Seasons Played	Apps	Subs	Gls
Crystal Palace	App	08.73				
Orient	Tr	09.75	75	0	1	0

BEATON William (Bill)
Kincardine, 30 September, 1935 (G)

League Club	Source	Date Signed	Seasons Played	Apps	Subs	Gls
Aston Villa	Dunfermline Ath	10.58	58	1	-	0

BEATTIE Andrew (Andy)
Kintore, 11 August, 1913 Died 1983 SWar-5/S-7 (FB)

League Club	Source	Date Signed	Seasons Played	Apps	Subs	Gls
Preston NE	Inverurie Loco	05.35	34-46	125	-	4

BEATTIE Andrew (Andy) Hugh
Liverpool, 9 February, 1964 (CD)

League Club	Source	Date Signed	Seasons Played	Apps	Subs	Gls
Cambridge U	App	02.82	83-87	94	4	2

BEATTIE Bradley Steven
Torquay, 20 August, 1957 (F)

League Club	Source	Date Signed	Seasons Played	Apps	Subs	Gls
Torquay U	App	●	73-74	2	2	0

BEATTIE George
Aberdeen, 16 June, 1925 (IF)

League Club	Source	Date Signed	Seasons Played	Apps	Subs	Gls
Southampton	Rosslyn Rosemount	08.47	47	1	-	0
Newport Co	Gloucester C	09.50	50-52	113	-	23
Bradford PA	Tr	07.53	53-54	53	-	16

BEATTIE James Scott
Lancaster, 27 February, 1978 Eu21-5/E-5 (F)

League Club	Source	Date Signed	Seasons Played	Apps	Subs	Gls
Blackburn Rov	YT	03.95	96-97	1	3	0
Southampton	Tr	07.98	98-04	161	43	68
Everton	Tr	01.05	04	7	4	1

BEATTIE Thomas **Kevin**
Carlisle, 18 December, 1953 EYth/E-9 (CD)

League Club	Source	Date Signed	Seasons Played	Apps	Subs	Gls
Ipswich T	App	07.71	72-80	225	3	24
Colchester U	Tr	07.82	82	3	1	0
Middlesbrough	Tr	11.82	82	3	1	0

BEATTIE Richard (Dick) Scott
Glasgow, 24 October, 1936 Died 1990 Su23-3/SLge-1 (G)

League Club	Source	Date Signed	Seasons Played	Apps	Subs	Gls
Portsmouth	Glasgow Celtic	08.59	59-61	122	-	0
Peterborough U	Tr	06.62	62	10	-	0

BEATTIE Robert (Bobby)
Stevenston, 24 January, 1916 Died 2002 S-1 (IF)

League Club	Source	Date Signed	Seasons Played	Apps	Subs	Gls
Preston NE	Kilmarnock	09.37	37-53	264	-	57

BEATTIE Stuart Richard
Stevenston, 10 July, 1967 (CD)

League Club	Source	Date Signed	Seasons Played	Apps	Subs	Gls
Doncaster Rov	Glasgow Rgrs	01.87	86-88	26	0	1

BEATTIE Thomas
Stakeford, 12 March, 1921 Died 1988 (IF)

League Club	Source	Date Signed	Seasons Played	Apps	Subs	Gls
Gateshead	Morpeth T	01.47	46-47	18	-	4

BEAUCHAMP Joseph (Joey) Daniel
Oxford, 13 March, 1971 (W)

League Club	Source	Date Signed	Seasons Played	Apps	Subs	Gls
Oxford U	YT	05.89	88-93	117	7	20
Swansea C	L	10.91	91	5	0	2
West Ham U	Tr	06.94				
Swindon T	Tr	08.94	94-95	39	6	3
Oxford U	Tr	10.95	95-01	203	35	43

BEAUMONT Alan
Liverpool, 9 January, 1927 Died 1999 (WH)

League Club	Source	Date Signed	Seasons Played	Apps	Subs	Gls
Chester	South Liverpool	09.48	48	5	-	0

BEAUMONT Christopher (Chris) Paul
Sheffield, 5 December, 1965 (M)

League Club	Source	Date Signed	Seasons Played	Apps	Subs	Gls
Rochdale	Denaby U	07.88	88	31	3	7
Stockport Co	Tr	07.89	89-95	238	20	39
Chesterfield	Tr	07.96	96-00	132	26	6

BEAUMONT David (Dave) Alan
Edinburgh, 10 December, 1963 SYth/Su21-1 (CD)

League Club	Source	Date Signed	Seasons Played	Apps	Subs	Gls
Luton T	Dundee U	01.89	88-91	66	10	0

BEAUMONT Frank
Hoyland, 22 December, 1939 EYth (IF)

League Club	Source	Date Signed	Seasons Played	Apps	Subs	Gls
Barnsley	Jnrs	12.57	57-61	107	-	37
Bury	Tr	09.61	61-63	68	-	12
Stockport Co	Tr	09.64	64-65	52	3	4

BEAUMONT Nigel
Hemsworth, 11 February, 1967 (CD)

League Club	Source	Date Signed	Seasons Played	Apps	Subs	Gls
Bradford C	App	07.85	85	2	0	0
Wrexham	Tr	07.88	88-91	112	3	4

BEAVEN Kenneth (Ken)
Bovingdon, 26 December, 1949 (W)

League Club	Source	Date Signed	Seasons Played	Apps	Subs	Gls
Luton T	App	●	67	1	0	0

BEAVER David
Kirkby-in-Ashfield, 4 April, 1966 (M)

League Club	Source	Date Signed	Seasons Played	Apps	Subs	Gls
Notts Co	App	04.84	84	1	0	0

BEAVERS Paul Mark
Blackpool, 2 October, 1978 (F)

League Club	Source	Date Signed	Seasons Played	Apps	Subs	Gls
Sunderland	YT	04.97				
Shrewsbury T	L	12.98	98	2	0	0
Oldham Ath	Tr	03.99	98-99	10	1	2
Hartlepool U	L	03.00	99	2	5	0
Darlington	Tr	09.00	00	3	4	1

BEAVON Cyril
Barnsley, 27 September, 1937 EYth (FB)

League Club	Source	Date Signed	Seasons Played	Apps	Subs	Gls
Wolverhampton W	Jnrs	12.54				
Oxford U	Tr	01.59	62-68	271	2	7

BEAVON David George
Nottingham, 8 December, 1961 (FB)

League Club	Source	Date Signed	Seasons Played	Apps	Subs	Gls
Notts Co	App	12.79	80	5	0	0
Lincoln C	Tr	11.81	81-82	7	1	0
Northampton T	Tsuen Wan (HK)	03.83	82	2	0	0

BEAVON Michael **Stuart**
Wolverhampton, 30 November, 1958 (M)

League Club	Source	Date Signed	Seasons Played	Apps	Subs	Gls
Tottenham H	App	07.76	78-79	3	1	0
Notts Co	L	12.79	79	6	0	0
Reading	Tr	07.80	80-89	380	16	44
Northampton T	Tr	08.90	90-92	95	3	14

BEBBINGTON Richard **Keith**
Cuddington, 4 August, 1943 (W)

League Club	Source	Date Signed	Seasons Played	Apps	Subs	Gls
Stoke C	Jnrs	08.60	62-65	99	1	17
Oldham Ath	Tr	08.66	66-71	237	0	39
Rochdale	Tr	07.72	72-73	57	3	6

BEBBINGTON Peter Andrew
Oswestry, 13 October, 1946 (FB)

League Club	Source	Date Signed	Seasons Played	Apps	Subs	Gls
Leicester C	Oswestry T	10.65				
Barrow	Tr	11.67	67-68	52	1	3
Stockport Co	Tr	07.69	69	16	1	1

BECK Daniel (Dan) Gordon
Worthing, 14 November, 1983 (M)

League Club	Source	Date Signed	Seasons Played	Apps	Subs	Gls
Brighton & Hove A	Sch	07.03	03	0	1	0

BECK John Alexander
Edmonton, 25 May, 1954 (M)

League Club	Source	Date Signed	Seasons Played	Apps	Subs	Gls
Queens Park Rgrs	App	05.72	72-75	32	8	1
Coventry C	Tr	06.76	76-78	60	9	6
Fulham	Tr	10.78	78-81	113	1	12
Bournemouth	Tr	09.82	82-85	132	5	13
Cambridge U	Tr	07.86	86-89	105	7	11

BECK Mikkel Venge
Aarhus, Denmark, 4 May, 1973 Denmark 19 (F)

League Club	Source	Date Signed	Seasons Played	Apps	Subs	Gls
Middlesbrough	Fortuna Cologne (Ger)	09.96	96-98	66	25	24
Derby Co	Tr	03.99	98-99	11	7	2
Nottingham F	L	11.99	99	5	0	1
Queens Park Rgrs	L	02.00	99	10	1	4

BECKERS Peter
Dundee, 3 October, 1947 Died 1996 (W)

League Club	Source	Date Signed	Seasons Played	Apps	Subs	Gls
Grimsby T	Craigmore Thistle	11.64	64	1	-	0

League Club	Source	Date Signed	Seasons Played	Apps	Subs	Gls
BECKETT Luke John						
Sheffield, 25 November, 1976						(F)
Barnsley	YT	06.95				
Chester C	Tr	06.98	98-99	70	4	25
Chesterfield	Tr	07.00	00-01	58	4	22
Stockport Co	Tr	12.01	01-04	79	5	45
Sheffield U	Tr	11.04	04	1	4	0
Huddersfield T	L	01.05	04	7	0	6
Oldham Ath	L	03.05	04	9	0	6
BECKETT Roy Wilson						
Stoke-on-Trent, 20 March, 1928						(CD)
Stoke C	Jnrs	04.45	50-53	14	-	1
BECKETT William (Billy)						
Kirkdale, 4 July, 1915 Died 1999						(W)
New Brighton	Litherland	11.34	34-35	25	-	4
Tranmere Rov	Tr	07.36				
Blackpool	South Liverpool	04.37				
Bradford C	Tr	07.38	38	5	-	1
Watford	Tr	05.39	46	7	-	1
BECKFORD Darren Richard Lorenzo						
Manchester, 12 May, 1967 ESch/EYth						(F)
Manchester C	App	08.84	84-86	7	4	0
Bury	L	10.85	85	12	0	5
Port Vale	Tr	03.87	86-90	169	9	72
Norwich C	Tr	06.91	91-92	32	6	8
Oldham Ath	Tr	03.93	92-95	31	21	11
Preston NE	Heart of Midlothian	01.97	96	0	2	0
Walsall	Fulham (N/C)	03.97	96	3	5	0
BECKFORD Jason Neil						
Manchester, 14 February, 1970 ESch/EYth						(W)
Manchester C	YT	08.87	87-90	8	12	1
Blackburn Rov	L	03.91	90	3	1	0
Port Vale	L	09.91	91	4	1	1
Birmingham C	Tr	01.92	91-92	5	2	2
Bury	L	03.94	93	3	0	0
Stoke C	Tr	08.94	94	2	2	0
Millwall	Tr	12.94	94	6	3	0
Northampton T	Tr	05.95	95	0	1	0
BECKHAM David Robert Joseph						
Leytonstone, 2 May, 1975 EYth/Eu21-9/E-81						(M)
Manchester U	YT	01.93	94-02	237	28	62
Preston NE	L	02.95	94	4	1	2
BECKWITH Dean Stuart						
Southwark, 18 September, 1983						(CD)
Gillingham	Sch	08.03	04	0	1	0
BECKWITH Robert (Rob)						
London, 12 September, 1984						(G)
Luton T	Sch	07.04	02-03	17	0	0
BEDDOW Ronald (Ronnie) Malcolm						
Walsall, 11 May, 1936						(FB)
Walsall	Jnrs	10.54	54	1	-	0
BEDEAU Anthony (Tony) Charles Osmond						
Hammersmith, 24 March, 1979 Ghana int						(F)
Torquay U	YT	07.97	95-04	207	67	49
Barnsley	L	02.02	01	0	3	0
BEDFORD Noel **Brian**						
Ferndale, 24 December, 1933						(IF)
Reading	Beddau YC	04.54	54	3	-	1
Southampton	Tr	07.55	55	5	-	2
Bournemouth	Tr	08.56	56-58	75	-	32
Queens Park Rgrs	Tr	07.59	59-64	258	-	161
Scunthorpe U	Tr	09.65	65-66	37	0	23
Brentford	Tr	09.66	66	21	0	10
BEDFORD Kevin Edward						
Carshalton, 26 December, 1968						(FB)
Wimbledon	App	11.86	87	4	0	0
Aldershot	L	02.88	87	16	0	0
Colchester U	Tr	07.88	88	24	2	0
BEDROSSIAN Ara						
Nicosia, Cyprus, 2 June, 1967 Cyprus int						(M)
Fulham	AP Limassol (Cyp)	03.93	92-94	34	8	1
BEDSON Raymond (Ray) Arthur						
Newcastle-under-Lyme, 4 February, 1929 Died 1976						(WH)
Crewe Alex		08.52	53	2	-	0
BEE Francis (Frank) Eric						
Nottingham, 23 January, 1927						(IF)
Sunderland	Nottingham F (Am)	06.47	47	5	-	1
Blackburn Rov	Tr	03.49	48	4	-	0
BEEBY Oliver						
Whetstone, Leicestershire, 2 October, 1934 EYth						(FB)
Leicester C	Whitwick Colliery	05.53	55	1	-	0
Notts Co	Tr	06.59	59	13	-	0
BEECH Christopher (Chris)						
Congleton, 5 November, 1975 ESch/EYth						(FB)
Manchester C	YT	11.92				
Cardiff C	Tr	08.97	97	46	0	1
Rotherham U	Tr	06.98	98-02	40	15	1
Doncaster Rov	Tr	12.02	03-04	13	0	0
BEECH Christopher (Chris) Stephen						
Blackpool, 16 September, 1974						(M)
Blackpool	YT	07.93	92-95	53	29	4
Hartlepool U	Tr	07.96	96-98	92	2	23
Huddersfield T	Tr	11.98	98-01	63	8	12
Rochdale	Tr	07.02	02-03	25	7	1
BEECH Cyril						
Tamworth, 12 March, 1925 Died 2001						(W)
Swansea T	Merthyr Tydfil	08.49	49-53	136	-	29
Newport Co	Worcester C	07.55	55-56	40	-	8
BEECH Gilbert						
Tamworth, 9 January, 1922						(FB)
Swansea T	Merthyr Tydfil	11.49	49-57	157	-	3
BEECH Harry William						
Kearsley, 7 January, 1946						(M)
Bolton W	Jnrs	06.64	65-66	14	1	0
Southport	Tr	07.67	67	2	2	0
BEECH Kenneth (Ken)						
Stoke-on-Trent, 18 March, 1958						(M)
Port Vale	App	01.76	74-80	169	6	18
Walsall	Tr	08.81	81-82	78	1	5
Peterborough U	Tr	08.83	83-84	58	2	5
BEECH Thomas (Tom) Philip Edward						
Potton, 2 December, 1985						(F)
Cambridge U	Sch	•	04	0	4	0
BEECHERS Billy Junior						
Oxford, 1 June, 1987						(F)
Oxford U	Sch	•	04	0	3	0
BEEKS Stephen (Steve) John						
Ashford, Middlesex, 10 April, 1971						(M)
Aldershot	YT	07.89	89-90	0	3	0
BEEL William John **Leonard (Lenny)**						
Leominster, 23 August, 1945						(G)
Shrewsbury T	App	07.63	62-63	3	-	0
Birmingham C	Tr	01.65	64	1	-	0
BEENEY Mark Raymond						
Pembury, 30 December, 1967 ESemiPro						(G)
Gillingham	Jnrs	08.85	86	2	0	0
Maidstone U	Tr	01.87	89-90	50	0	0
Aldershot	L	03.90	89	7	0	0
Brighton & Hove A	Tr	03.91	90-92	68	1	0
Leeds U	Tr	04.93	92-97	35	0	0
BEER Alan Desmond						
Swansea, 11 March, 1950 WAmat						(F)
Swansea C	West End (Swansea)	02.71	70-71	10	5	3
Exeter C	Weymouth	11.74	74-77	114	0	52
BEER Colin Edwin						
Exeter, 15 August, 1936						(W)
Exeter C	Exbourne	05.56	56-57	5	-	2
BEESLEY Colin						
Stockton, 6 October, 1951						(W)
Sunderland	App	01.69	68	0	3	0
BEESLEY Mark Anthony						
Burscough, 10 November, 1981						(F)
Preston NE	YT	06.99	99	0	1	0
BEESLEY Michael (Mike) Albert						
High Beech, 10 June, 1942						(M)
West Ham U	Jnrs	10.59	60	2	-	1
Southend U	Tr	08.62	62-64	79	-	34
Peterborough U	Tr	07.65	65-66	23	2	3
Southend U	Tr	08.67	67-70	119	14	11
BEESLEY Paul						
Liverpool, 21 July, 1965						(CD)
Wigan Ath	Marine	09.84	84-89	153	2	3
Leyton Orient	Tr	10.89	89	32	0	1

League Club	Source	Date Signed	Seasons Played	Apps	Subs	Gls
Sheffield U	Tr	07.90	90-94	162	6	7
Leeds U	Tr	08.95	95-96	19	3	0
Manchester C	Tr	02.97	96-97	10	3	0
Port Vale	L	12.97	97	5	0	0
West Bromwich A	L	03.98	97	8	0	0
Port Vale	Tr	08.98	98	33	2	3
Blackpool	Tr	07.99	99	15	3	0

BEESTON Carl Frederick
Stoke-on-Trent, 30 June, 1967 Eu21-1 (M)

League Club	Source	Date Signed	Seasons Played	Apps	Subs	Gls
Stoke C	App	07.85	84-96	224	12	13
Hereford U	L	01.97	96	9	0	2
Southend U	Tr	08.97	97	5	1	0

BEESTON Thomas
Gateshead, 26 April, 1933 (G)

League Club	Source	Date Signed	Seasons Played	Apps	Subs	Gls
Gateshead (Am)		09.56	56	1	-	0

BEETON Alan Matthew
Watford, 4 October, 1978 (FB)

League Club	Source	Date Signed	Seasons Played	Apps	Subs	Gls
Wycombe W	YT	07.97	97-00	39	16	0

BEEVER Anthony (Tony)
Huddersfield, 18 September, 1974 (F)

League Club	Source	Date Signed	Seasons Played	Apps	Subs	Gls
Rochdale	YT	07.93	92	0	1	0

BEEVERS Lee Jonathan
Doncaster, 4 December, 1983 WYth/Wu21-3 (FB)

League Club	Source	Date Signed	Seasons Played	Apps	Subs	Gls
Ipswich T	YT	03.01				
Boston U	Tr	03.03	02-04	71	1	3
Lincoln C	Tr	02.05	04	4	4	0

BEGG James (Jim) Alexander
Dumfries, 14 February, 1930 Died 1987 (G)

League Club	Source	Date Signed	Seasons Played	Apps	Subs	Gls
Liverpool	Auchinleck Talbot	04.52				
Bradford PA	Tr	08.53	53-54	10	-	0

BEGLIN James (Jim) Martin
Waterford, 29 July, 1963 IRu21-4/IRB/IR-15 (FB)

League Club	Source	Date Signed	Seasons Played	Apps	Subs	Gls
Liverpool	Shamrock Rov	05.83	84-86	64	0	2
Leeds U	Tr	07.89	89	18	1	0
Plymouth Arg	L	11.89	89	5	0	0
Blackburn Rov	L	10.90	90	6	0	0

BEHARALL David (Dave) Alexander
Jarrow, 8 March, 1979 (CD)

League Club	Source	Date Signed	Seasons Played	Apps	Subs	Gls
Newcastle U	YT	07.97	98-99	4	2	0
Grimsby T	L	08.01	01	13	1	0
Oldham Ath	Tr	11.01	01-04	58	2	3

BEIGHTON Graham
Sheffield, 1 July, 1939 (G)

League Club	Source	Date Signed	Seasons Played	Apps	Subs	Gls
Sheffield Wed	Firth Brown Tools	03.59				
Stockport Co	Tr	06.61	61-65	137	0	0
Wrexham	Tr	01.66	65	23	0	0

BEINLICH Stefan
Berlin, Germany, 13 January, 1972 (F)

League Club	Source	Date Signed	Seasons Played	Apps	Subs	Gls
Aston Villa	Bergmann Bosnig (Ger)	10.91	91-93	7	9	1

BEIRNE Michael Andrew
Manchester, 21 September, 1973 (F)

League Club	Source	Date Signed	Seasons Played	Apps	Subs	Gls
Doncaster Rov	Droylsden	02.97	96	1	0	0

BEKKER Jan Franciscus
Cardiff, 24 December, 1951 (F)

League Club	Source	Date Signed	Seasons Played	Apps	Subs	Gls
Swansea C	Bridgend T	02.75	74-75	16	6	4

BELCHER James (Jimmy) Alfred
Stepney, 31 October, 1932 (IF)

League Club	Source	Date Signed	Seasons Played	Apps	Subs	Gls
Leyton Orient	Jnrs	03.50				
West Ham U	Snowdown CW	08.52				
Crystal Palace	Tr	06.54	54-57	127	-	22
Ipswich T	Tr	05.58	58-59	27	-	0
Brentford	Tr	07.61	61	30	-	1

BELFIELD Michael (Mike) Robert
Wandsworth, 10 June, 1961 (F)

League Club	Source	Date Signed	Seasons Played	Apps	Subs	Gls
Wimbledon		03.80	79-82	16	8	4

BELFITT Roderick (Rod) Michael
Doncaster, 30 October, 1945 (F)

League Club	Source	Date Signed	Seasons Played	Apps	Subs	Gls
Leeds U	Retford T	07.63	64-71	57	18	17
Ipswich T	Tr	11.71	71-72	40	0	13
Everton	Tr	11.72	72	14	2	2
Sunderland	Tr	10.73	73-74	36	3	4
Fulham	L	11.74	74	6	0	1
Huddersfield T	L	02.75	74	6	0	2
Huddersfield T	Tr	06.75	75	28	0	6

BELFON Frank
Wellingborough, 18 February, 1965 (W)

League Club	Source	Date Signed	Seasons Played	Apps	Subs	Gls
Northampton T	Jnrs	04.82	81-84	64	15	15

BELFORD Dale
Burton-on-Trent, 11 July, 1967 (G)

League Club	Source	Date Signed	Seasons Played	Apps	Subs	Gls
Aston Villa	App	07.85				
Notts Co	Sutton Coldfield T	03.87	87	1	0	0

BELGRAVE Barrington
Bedford, 16 September, 1980 (F)

League Club	Source	Date Signed	Seasons Played	Apps	Subs	Gls
Plymouth Arg	Norwich C (YT)	07.99	99	2	13	0
Southend U	Yeovil T	09.01	01-02	38	17	8

BELL Alexander (Alex) Stewart
Auchinleck, 13 March, 1931 (G)

League Club	Source	Date Signed	Seasons Played	Apps	Subs	Gls
Exeter C	Partick Th	08.54	54-57	40	-	0
Grimsby T	Tr	07.58	58	8	-	0

BELL Andrew (Andy)
Blackburn, 12 February, 1984 EYth (F)

League Club	Source	Date Signed	Seasons Played	Apps	Subs	Gls
Blackburn Rov	YT	02.01				
Wycombe W	Tr	09.03	03	3	8	3
York C	Tr	02.04	03	3	7	1

BELL Andrew (Andy) Donald
Taunton, 6 May, 1956 (F)

League Club	Source	Date Signed	Seasons Played	Apps	Subs	Gls
Exeter C	Taunton T	07.79	79	2	1	0

BELL Anthony (Tony)
North Shields, 27 February, 1955 (G)

League Club	Source	Date Signed	Seasons Played	Apps	Subs	Gls
Newcastle U	App	03.73	74	1	0	0

BELL Arthur
Sedgefield, 5 March, 1931 (WH)

League Club	Source	Date Signed	Seasons Played	Apps	Subs	Gls
Barrow	Hylton Colliery	08.50	50	1	-	0

BELL Barry Russell
Woolwich, 9 April, 1941 (CF)

League Club	Source	Date Signed	Seasons Played	Apps	Subs	Gls
Millwall	Jnrs	10.58	58	1	-	0

BELL Ian Charles (Charlie)
Middlesbrough, 14 November, 1958 (M)

League Club	Source	Date Signed	Seasons Played	Apps	Subs	Gls
Middlesbrough	App	12.76	77-80	10	0	1
Mansfield T	Tr	07.81	81-82	82	2	12

BELL Charles (Charlie) Thomas
Sheffield, 21 March, 1945 (CD)

League Club	Source	Date Signed	Seasons Played	Apps	Subs	Gls
Sheffield U	Jnrs	01.64	66	3	0	1
Chesterfield	Tr	06.68	68-72	148	3	11

BELL Colin
Horsley, Derbyshire, 24 March, 1926 Died 2004 (WH)

League Club	Source	Date Signed	Seasons Played	Apps	Subs	Gls
Derby Co	Holbrook CW	09.46	50-54	77	-	2

BELL Colin
Hesleden, 26 February, 1946 Eu23-2/FLge-4/E-48 (M)

League Club	Source	Date Signed	Seasons Played	Apps	Subs	Gls
Bury	Horden CW	07.63	63-65	82	0	25
Manchester C	Tr	03.66	65-78	393	1	117

BELL David (Dave)
Gorebridge, 24 December, 1909 Died 1986 (FB)

League Club	Source	Date Signed	Seasons Played	Apps	Subs	Gls
Newcastle U	Wallyford Bluebell	05.30	31-33	21	-	1
Derby Co	Tr	06.34	34-38	52	-	0
Ipswich T	Tr	10.38	38-49	171	-	3

BELL David Anthony
Kettering, 21 April, 1984 IRYth/IRu21-2 (M)

League Club	Source	Date Signed	Seasons Played	Apps	Subs	Gls
Rushden & Diamonds	Jnrs	07.01	01-04	96	12	7

BELL David John
Carlisle, 13 September, 1939 (IF)

League Club	Source	Date Signed	Seasons Played	Apps	Subs	Gls
Carlisle U	Jnrs	03.57	58	1	-	1

BELL Derek Martin
Wyberton, 30 October, 1956 (F)

League Club	Source	Date Signed	Seasons Played	Apps	Subs	Gls
Derby Co	App	10.74				
Halifax T	Tr	05.75	75-78	104	8	21
Sheffield Wed	L	03.76	75	5	0	1
Barnsley	Tr	10.78	78-79	45	1	20
Lincoln C	Tr	11.79	79-82	69	14	33
Chesterfield	Tr	08.83	83	15	2	3
Scunthorpe U	Tr	01.84	83-84	22	0	7

BELL Derek Stewart
Fenham, 19 December, 1963 (M)

League Club	Source	Date Signed	Seasons Played	Apps	Subs	Gls
Newcastle U	App	12.81	81-82	3	1	0

BELL Douglas (Doug)
Paisley, 5 September, 1959 Su21-2 (M)

League Club	Source	Date Signed	Seasons Played	Apps	Subs	Gls
Shrewsbury T	Hibernian	12.87	87-89	47	3	6
Hull C	L	03.89	88	4	0	0
Birmingham C	Tr	10.89	89-90	15	1	0

League Club	Source	Date Signed	Seasons Played	Career Record Apps	Subs	Gls
BELL Eric						
Manchester, 27 November, 1929 EB/FLge-1						(WH)
Bolton W	Manchester U (Am)	11.49	50-57	102	-	1
BELL John Eric						
Bedlington, 13 February, 1922 Died 2004 FLge-2						(WH)
Blackburn Rov	Blyth Shipyard	05.45	46-56	323	-	9
BELL Ernest (Ernie)						
Hull, 22 July, 1918 Died 1968						(IF)
Hull C	Blundell Street OB	03.36	36-37	22	-	4
Mansfield T	Tr	05.38	38	28	-	1
Aldershot	Tr	07.39				
Hull C	Tr	08.46	46	5	-	1
BELL Gary						
Stourbridge, 4 April, 1947						(FB)
Cardiff C	Lower Gornal Ath	02.66	66-73	222	1	10
Hereford U	L	03.74	73	8	0	0
Newport Co	Tr	08.74	74-77	126	0	5
BELL George William						
South Shields, 26 March, 1937						(CF)
Doncaster Rov	St Mary's BC	05.55	55	1	-	0
BELL Graham Thomas						
Middleton, 30 March, 1955 EYth						(M)
Oldham Ath	Chadderton	12.73	74-78	166	4	9
Preston NE	Tr	03.79	78-82	140	3	9
Huddersfield T	L	11.81	81	2	0	0
Carlisle U	Tr	08.83	83	11	3	0
Bolton W	Tr	02.84	83-85	86	6	3
Tranmere Rov	Tr	08.86	86	41	1	4
BELL Harold						
Liverpool, 22 November, 1924 Died 1994						(CD)
Tranmere Rov	Jnrs	11.41	46-59	595	-	11
BELL Henry (Harry) Davey						
Sunderland, 14 October, 1924						(WH)
Middlesbrough	Hylton Colliery	09.45	46-54	290	-	9
Darlington	Tr	09.55	55-58	126	-	19
BELL John Albert						
Edinburgh, 25 April, 1936						(WH)
Swindon T	Stirling A	07.60	60-61	29	-	2
BELL John Henry						
Morpeth, 29 August, 1919 Died 1994						(FB)
Gateshead		01.45	46-49	50	-	0
BELL John (Jackie) Russell						
Evenwood, 17 October, 1939 Died 1991						(WH)
Newcastle U	Jnrs	10.56	57-61	111	-	8
Norwich C	Tr	07.62	62-63	48	-	3
Colchester U	Tr	06.65	65	7	0	0
BELL Joseph (Joe)						
Sunderland, 28 July, 1924						(FB)
Chesterfield	Stockton	05.46	47-48	37	-	0
Coventry C	Tr	06.49	49-51	10	-	0
BELL Lee						
Crewe, 26 January, 1983						(M)
Crewe Alex	YT	02.01	02-04	20	17	1
BELL Leon Earl						
Hitchin, 19 December, 1980 ESch						(F)
Barnet	YT	07.99	99-00	7	5	0
BELL Michael (Mickey)						
Newcastle, 15 November, 1971						(FB)
Northampton T	YT	07.90	89-94	133	20	10
Wycombe W	Tr	10.94	94-96	117	1	5
Bristol C	Tr	07.97	97-04	276	16	34
BELL Norman						
Hylton Castle, 16 November, 1955						(F)
Wolverhampton W	App	11.73	75-81	58	22	17
Blackburn Rov	New England (USA)	11.81	81-83	57	4	10
BELL Raymond (Ray) Lloyd						
West Seaham, 6 December, 1930						(G)
Lincoln C	Seaham CW	01.50	50	1	-	0
BELL Robert (Bobby)						
Glasgow, 20 March, 1935 SSch						(IF)
Plymouth Arg	Partick Th	11.55	55	2	-	1
Carlisle U	Partick Th	06.59	59	1	-	0

League Club	Source	Date Signed	Seasons Played	Career Record Apps	Subs	Gls
BELL Robert (Bobby) Charles						
Cambridge, 26 October, 1950						(CD)
Ipswich T	Tottenham H (App)	10.68	68-71	32	0	1
Blackburn Rov	Tr	09.71	71	2	0	0
Crystal Palace	Tr	09.71	71-73	31	0	0
Norwich C	L	02.72	71	3	0	0
York C	(South Africa)	02.77	76	5	0	0
BELL Robert (Bobby) McDicker						
Ayr, 16 September, 1934						(FB)
Watford	Ayr U	05.57	57-64	268	-	2
BELL Stanley (Stan)						
West Ham, 28 October, 1923						(W)
Southend U		07.48	48	3	-	0
BELL Stephen (Steve)						
Middlesbrough, 13 March, 1965 Died 2001 EYth						(W)
Middlesbrough	App	05.82	81-84	79	6	12
Darlington	Whitby T	03.87	86-87	28	12	3
BELL Stuart						
Carlisle, 15 March, 1984						(M)
Carlisle U	YT	07.04	01	3	2	0
BELL Sydney (Syd)						
Stepney, 8 January, 1920						(FB)
Southend U	Monarchs	11.45	46-47	16	-	0
BELL Terence (Terry) John						
Sherwood, 1 August, 1944						(F)
Nottingham F	Burton A	08.64				
Manchester C	Tr	10.64				
Portsmouth	Tr	11.64				
Hartlepools U	Nuneaton Borough	07.66	66-69	111	6	34
Reading	Tr	03.70	69-72	82	5	20
Aldershot	Tr	07.73	73-77	112	12	49
BELL Thomas (Tom)						
Stanley, 14 June, 1924						(CD)
Millwall (Am)	Hammersmith U	03.49	48	1	-	0
BELL Thomas (Tommy) Anthony Peter						
Crompton, 30 December, 1923 Died 1988						(FB)
Oldham Ath	Mossley	12.46	46-51	170	-	0
Stockport Co	Tr	08.52	52	31	-	0
Halifax T	Tr	07.53	53-55	117	-	1
BELL William (Billy)						
Manchester, 16 June, 1953						(M)
Rochdale	Hyde U	05.74	74	5	1	0
BELL William (Willie) John						
Johnstone, 3 September, 1937 SAmat/S-2						(FB)
Leeds U	Queen's Park	07.60	60-67	204	0	15
Leicester C	Tr	09.67	67-68	49	0	0
Brighton & Hove A	Tr	07.69	69	44	0	1
BELLAMY Arthur						
Blackhill, 5 April, 1942						(M)
Burnley	Jnrs	06.59	62-71	204	13	29
Chesterfield	Tr	07.72	72-75	133	0	12
BELLAMY Craig Douglas						
Cardiff, 13 July, 1979 WSch/WYth/Wu21-8/W-33						(F)
Norwich C	YT	01.97	96-00	71	13	32
Coventry C	Tr	08.00	00	33	1	6
Newcastle U	Tr	07.01	01-04	87	6	27
BELLAMY Gary						
Worksop, 4 July, 1962						(CD)
Chesterfield	App	06.80	80-86	181	4	7
Wolverhampton W	Tr	07.87	87-91	133	3	9
Cardiff C	L	03.92	91	9	0	0
Leyton Orient	Tr	09.92	92-95	129	3	6
BELLAS William (Bill) Joseph						
Great Crosby, 21 May, 1925 Died 1994						(CD)
Notts Co	Marine	05.45				
Nottingham F	Tr	05.46				
Southport	Tr	10.48	48-50	88	-	0
Grimsby T	Tr	07.51	51	5	-	0
BELLE Cortez						
Newport, 27 August, 1983						(F)
Chester C	Merthyr Tydfil	07.04	04	17	5	1
BELLETT Walter (Wally) Ronald						
Stratford, 14 November, 1933 EYth						(FB)
Chelsea	Barking	09.54	55-58	35	-	1
Plymouth Arg	Tr	12.58	58-59	41	-	1

League Club	Source	Date Signed	Seasons Played	Career Record Apps	Subs	Gls
Leyton Orient	Chelmsford C	01.61				
Chester	Tr	07.61	61	12	-	1
Wrexham	Tr	07.62	62	2	-	0

BELLION David
Sevres, France, 27 November, 1982 Fru21 (M)

League Club	Source	Date Signed	Seasons Played	Apps	Subs	Gls
Sunderland	AS Cannes (Fr)	08.01	01-02	5	15	1
Manchester U	Tr	07.03	03-04	5	19	3

BELLIS Alfred (Alf)
Ellesmere Port, 8 October, 1920 (W)

League Club	Source	Date Signed	Seasons Played	Apps	Subs	Gls
Port Vale	Burnell's Ironworks	03.38	37-47	82	-	18
Bury	Tr	01.48	47-50	95	-	18
Swansea T	Tr	08.51	51-52	41	-	11
Chesterfield	Tr	08.53	53	13	-	3

BELLIS Thomas **Gilbert (Gib)**
Mold, 21 April, 1919 Died 2000 (WH)

League Club	Source	Date Signed	Seasons Played	Apps	Subs	Gls
Wrexham	Buckley T	05.38	38-48	95	-	1

BELLOTTI Derek Christopher
East Ham, 25 December, 1946 (G)

League Club	Source	Date Signed	Seasons Played	Apps	Subs	Gls
Gillingham	Bedford T	07.66	66-69	35	0	0
Southend U	L	10.70	70	3	0	0
Charlton Ath	Tr	10.70	70-71	14	0	0
Southend U	Tr	12.71	71-73	74	0	0
Swansea C	Tr	05.74	74	19	0	0

BELLOTTI Ross Christopher
Pembury, 15 May, 1978 (G)

League Club	Source	Date Signed	Seasons Played	Apps	Subs	Gls
Exeter C	YT	07.96	94	1	1	0

BELMADI Djemal
Champigny-sur-Marne, France, 27 March, 1976 Algeria int (M)

League Club	Source	Date Signed	Seasons Played	Apps	Subs	Gls
Manchester C (L)	Marseille (Fr)	01.03	02	2	6	0

BELSVIK Petter
Lillehammer, Norway, 2 October, 1967 (F)

League Club	Source	Date Signed	Seasons Played	Apps	Subs	Gls
Southend U (L)	IK Start (Nor)	11.95	95	3	0	1

BEMROSE Frank **Edward (Ted)**
Caistor, 20 October, 1935 Died 2001 (W)

League Club	Source	Date Signed	Seasons Played	Apps	Subs	Gls
Grimsby T (Am)	Caistor	08.58	58-60	2	-	0

BENALI Francis Vincent
Southampton, 30 December, 1968 ESch (FB)

League Club	Source	Date Signed	Seasons Played	Apps	Subs	Gls
Southampton	App	01.87	88-02	271	40	1
Nottingham F	L	01.01	00	15	0	0

BENARBIA Ali
Oran, Algeria, 8 October, 1968 Algeria int (M)

League Club	Source	Date Signed	Seasons Played	Apps	Subs	Gls
Manchester C	Paris St Germain (Fr)	09.01	01-02	59	12	11

BEN ASKAR Aziz
Chateau Gontier, France, 30 March, 1976 (CD)

League Club	Source	Date Signed	Seasons Played	Apps	Subs	Gls
Queens Park Rgrs (L)	Stade Lavallois (Fr)	08.01	01	18	0	0

BENBOW Ian Robert
Hereford, 9 January, 1969 (W)

League Club	Source	Date Signed	Seasons Played	Apps	Subs	Gls
Hereford U	YT	07.87	87-90	60	23	4

BENCE Paul Ian
Littlehampton, 21 December, 1948 (M)

League Club	Source	Date Signed	Seasons Played	Apps	Subs	Gls
Brighton & Hove A	App	05.67	67	0	1	0
Reading	Tr	06.68	68-69	12	2	2
Brentford	Tr	07.70	70-76	238	6	6
Torquay U	L	11.76	76	5	0	0

BENEFIELD James (Jimmy) Patrick
Torquay, 6 May, 1983 (F)

League Club	Source	Date Signed	Seasons Played	Apps	Subs	Gls
Torquay U	YT	07.01	00-03	6	26	0

BEN HAIM Tal
Rishon Le Zion, Israel, 31 March, 1982 Israel 21 (CD)

League Club	Source	Date Signed	Seasons Played	Apps	Subs	Gls
Bolton W	Maccabi Tel Aviv (Isr)	07.04	04	19	2	1

BENJAFIELD Brian James
Barton-on-Sea, 2 August, 1960 (M)

League Club	Source	Date Signed	Seasons Played	Apps	Subs	Gls
Bournemouth	Jnrs	01.79	78	2	0	0

BENJAMIN Christopher (Chris)
Sheffield, 5 December, 1972 (F)

League Club	Source	Date Signed	Seasons Played	Apps	Subs	Gls
Chesterfield	YT	07.91	90-91	5	10	1

BENJAMIN Ian Tracey
Nottingham, 11 December, 1961 EYth (F)

League Club	Source	Date Signed	Seasons Played	Apps	Subs	Gls
Sheffield U	App	07.79	78-79	4	1	3
West Bromwich A	Tr	08.79	80	1	1	0
Notts Co	Tr	02.82				
Peterborough U	Tr	08.82	82-83	77	3	14
Northampton T	Tr	08.84	84-87	147	3	58
Cambridge U	Tr	10.87	87	20	5	2
Chester C	Tr	07.88	88	18	4	2
Exeter C	Tr	02.89	88-89	30	2	4
Southend U	Tr	03.90	89-92	122	0	33
Luton T	Tr	11.92	92-93	7	6	2
Brentford	Tr	09.93	93-94	13	2	2
Wigan Ath	Tr	09.94	94-95	13	7	6

BENJAMIN Trevor Junior
Kettering, 8 February, 1979 Eu21-1/Ja-2 (F)

League Club	Source	Date Signed	Seasons Played	Apps	Subs	Gls
Cambridge U	YT	02.97	95-99	96	27	35
Leicester C	Tr	07.00	00-04	33	48	11
Crystal Palace	L	12.01	01	5	1	1
Norwich C	L	02.02	01	3	3	0
West Bromwich A	L	03.02	01	0	3	1
Gillingham	L	09.03	03	1	3	1
Rushden & Diamonds	L	11.03	03	5	1	1
Brighton & Hove A	L	01.04	03	10	0	5
Northampton T	Tr	12.04	04	5	0	2
Coventry C	Tr	02.05	04	6	6	1

BENJAMIN Tristan
St Kitts, 1 April, 1957 (CD)

League Club	Source	Date Signed	Seasons Played	Apps	Subs	Gls
Notts Co	App	03.75	74-86	296	15	4
Chesterfield	Tr	07.87	87	32	2	0

BENN Alfred (Alf)
Knostrop, 26 January, 1926 (WH)

League Club	Source	Date Signed	Seasons Played	Apps	Subs	Gls
Leeds U	East Leeds	01.47				
Southport	Tr	07.48	48	3	-	0

BENN Wayne
Pontefract, 7 August, 1976 (M)

League Club	Source	Date Signed	Seasons Played	Apps	Subs	Gls
Bradford C	YT	06.94	94	8	2	0

BENNELLICK James (Jim) Arthur
Torquay, 9 September, 1974 (M)

League Club	Source	Date Signed	Seasons Played	Apps	Subs	Gls
Torquay U	YT	•	91	0	1	0

BENNETT Alan
Stoke-on-Trent, 5 November, 1931 EYth (W)

League Club	Source	Date Signed	Seasons Played	Apps	Subs	Gls
Port Vale	Jnrs	05.49	48-56	123	-	8
Crewe Alex	Tr	09.57	57	11	-	0

BENNETT Albert
Chester-le-Street, 16 July, 1944 EYth/Eu23-1 (F)

League Club	Source	Date Signed	Seasons Played	Apps	Subs	Gls
Rotherham U	Chester Moor Jnrs	10.61	61-64	108	-	64
Newcastle U	Tr	07.65	65-68	85	0	22
Norwich C	Tr	02.69	68-70	54	1	15

BENNETT Craig
Doncaster, 29 August, 1973 (F)

League Club	Source	Date Signed	Seasons Played	Apps	Subs	Gls
Doncaster Rov	YT	07.91	90-92	5	3	0

BENNETT Daniel (Dan) Mark
Great Yarmouth, 7 January, 1978 Singapore int (CD)

League Club	Source	Date Signed	Seasons Played	Apps	Subs	Gls
Wrexham	Tanjong Pagar (Mal)	01.02	01	5	1	0
Wrexham	Singapore Armed Fce	08.02	02	14	4	0

BENNETT David (Dave) Anthony
Manchester, 11 July, 1959 FLge (W)

League Club	Source	Date Signed	Seasons Played	Apps	Subs	Gls
Manchester C	Jnrs	08.78	78-80	43	9	9
Cardiff C	Tr	09.81	81-82	75	2	18
Coventry C	Tr	07.83	83-88	157	15	25
Sheffield Wed	Tr	03.89	88-89	20	8	0
Swindon T	Tr	09.90	90	1	0	0
Shrewsbury T	L	11.91	91	2	0	2

BENNETT David (Dave) Michael
Southampton, 5 March, 1939 ESch (W)

League Club	Source	Date Signed	Seasons Played	Apps	Subs	Gls
Arsenal	Jnrs	05.56				
Portsmouth	Tr	06.58				
Bournemouth	Tr	12.60	60-61	12	-	2

BENNETT David (Dave) Paul
Oldham, 26 April, 1960 (W)

League Club	Source	Date Signed	Seasons Played	Apps	Subs	Gls
Norwich C	Manchester C (App)	08.78	78-83	64	7	9

BENNETT Dean Alan
Wolverhampton, 13 December, 1977 ESemiPro-1 (M)

League Club	Source	Date Signed	Seasons Played	Apps	Subs	Gls
West Bromwich A	Aston Villa (Jnrs)	12.96	96	0	1	0
Kidderminster Hrs	Bromsgrove Rov	01.99	00-03	136	18	16
Wrexham	Tr	08.04	04	7	7	0

BENNETT Desmond (Des)
Doncaster, 30 October, 1963 (M)

League Club	Source	Date Signed	Seasons Played	Apps	Subs	Gls
Doncaster Rov	App	06.80	80-81	0	2	0

BENNETT Donald (Don)
Wakefield, 18 December, 1933 EYth (FB)

League Club	Source	Date Signed	Seasons Played	Apps	Subs	Gls
Arsenal	Jnrs	08.51				
Coventry C	Tr	09.59	59-61	73	-	0

League Club	Source	Date Signed	Seasons Played	Apps	Subs	Gls
BENNETT Edgar William						
Stoke-on-Trent, 29 March, 1929						(W)
Luton T	Vauxhall Motors	09.52	53	1	-	0
BENNETT Edward (Ted) Ernest						
Kilburn, 22 August, 1925 EAmat						(G)
Queens Park Rgrs (Am)	Southall	02.49	48	2	-	0
Watford	Southall	12.53	53-55	81	-	0
BENNETT Frank (Frankie)						
Birmingham, 3 January, 1969						(W)
Southampton	Halesowen T	02.93	93-95	5	14	1
Shrewsbury T	L	10.96	96	2	2	3
Bristol Rov	Tr	11.96	96-99	15	29	4
Exeter C	L	02.00	99	8	1	1
BENNETT Gary						
Enfield, 13 November, 1970						(W)
Colchester U	YT	11.88	88-93	65	22	13
BENNETT Gary Ernest						
Manchester, 4 December, 1961						(CD)
Manchester C	Ashton U	09.79				
Cardiff C	Tr	09.81	81-83	85	2	11
Sunderland	Tr	07.84	84-94	362	7	23
Carlisle U	Tr	11.95	95	26	0	5
Scarborough	Tr	08.96	96-97	86	2	18
Darlington	Tr	07.98	98-99	30	4	4
BENNETT Gary Michael						
Kirkby, 20 September, 1962						(F)
Wigan Ath	Kirkby T	10.84	84	10	10	3
Chester C	Tr	08.85	85-88	109	17	36
Southend U	Tr	11.88	88-89	36	6	6
Chester C	Tr	03.90	89-91	71	9	15
Wrexham	Tr	08.92	92-94	120	1	77
Tranmere Rov	Tr	07.95	95	26	3	9
Preston NE	Tr	03.96	95-96	15	9	4
Wrexham	Tr	02.97	96	15	0	5
Chester C	Tr	07.97	97-98	42	6	13
BENNETT George Forest						
South Shields, 16 March, 1938						(FB)
Burnley	Jnrs	04.55				
Barnsley	Tr	01.60	59-60	24	-	0
BENNETT Henry (Harry) Sylvester						
Liverpool, 16 May, 1949						(CD)
Everton	Jnrs	03.67	67	2	0	0
Aldershot	Tr	01.71	70-72	77	12	7
Crewe Alex	Tr	07.73	73	28	2	1
BENNETT Ian Michael						
Worksop, 10 October, 1971						(G)
Newcastle U	Queens Park Rgrs (YT)	03.89				
Peterborough U	Tr	03.91	91-93	72	0	0
Birmingham C	Tr	12.93	93-03	285	2	0
Sheffield U	L	12.04	04	5	0	0
Coventry C	L	02.05	04	6	0	0
BENNETT John						
Rotherham, 15 May, 1949						(W)
Rotherham U	App	•	65	1	0	0
BENNETT John Graham						
Liverpool, 27 March, 1946						(FB)
Liverpool	App	04.63				
Chester	Tr	06.66	66-68	72	4	0
BENNETT Julian Llewellyn						
Nottingham, 17 December, 1984						(CD)
Walsall	Sch	07.04	03-04	30	2	2
BENNETT Kenneth (Ken) Edgar						
Wood Green, 2 October, 1921 Died 1994						(IF)
Tottenham H	Wood Green T	10.40				
Southend U	Tr	06.46	46-47	50	-	10
Bournemouth	Tr	06.48	48	19	-	1
Brighton & Hove A	Guildford C	06.50	50-52	101	-	37
Crystal Palace	Tr	07.53	53	17	-	2
BENNETT Lawson Henry						
Blackburn, 28 August, 1938						(W)
Accrington St	Darwen	05.58	58-60	29	-	2
BENNETT Leslie (Les) Donald						
Wood Green, 10 January, 1918 Died 1999						(IF)
Tottenham H	Jnrs	05.39	46-54	272	-	104
West Ham U	Tr	12.54	54-55	26	-	3

League Club	Source	Date Signed	Seasons Played	Apps	Subs	Gls
BENNETT Martyn						
Birmingham, 4 August, 1961 ESch						(CD)
West Bromwich A	App	08.78	78-89	181	1	9
BENNETT Michael (Mike)						
Bolton, 24 December, 1962 EYth						(FB)
Bolton W	App	01.80	79-82	62	3	1
Wolverhampton W	Tr	06.83	83	6	0	0
Cambridge U	Tr	03.84	83-85	76	0	0
Preston NE	Bradford C (N/C)	09.86	86-89	85	1	1
Carlisle U	Tr	07.90	90-91	21	3	0
BENNETT Michael (Mickey) Richard						
Camberwell, 27 July, 1969 EYth						(W)
Charlton Ath	App	04.87	86-89	24	11	2
Wimbledon	Tr	01.90	89-91	12	6	2
Brentford	Tr	07.92	92-93	40	6	4
Charlton Ath	Tr	03.94	93-94	19	5	1
Millwall	Tr	05.95	95	1	1	0
Cardiff C	Tr	08.96	96	5	9	1
Leyton Orient	Cambridge C	12.97	97	1	1	0
Brighton & Hove A	Tr	08.98	98	37	1	0
BENNETT Neil Robert						
Dewsbury, 29 October, 1980						(G)
Sheffield Wed	YT	10.98				
Rochdale	Drogheda U	03.03	02	1	0	0
BENNETT Paul						
Liverpool, 30 January, 1961						(M)
Port Vale	Everton (App)	09.78	80-81	28	2	1
BENNETT Paul Reginald						
Southampton, 4 February, 1952						(CD)
Southampton	App	11.69	71-75	116	0	1
Reading	Tr	07.76	76-78	105	0	3
Aldershot	Tr	08.79	79-81	112	1	2
BENNETT Peter Christopher						
Plymouth, 29 November, 1939						(CF)
Exeter C	Plymstock	08.59	59-60	6	-	5
BENNETT Peter Leigh						
Hillingdon, 24 June, 1946 ESch						(M)
West Ham U	App	07.63	63-70	38	4	3
Orient	Tr	10.70	70-78	195	4	13
BENNETT Richard John						
Northampton, 16 February, 1945 EYth						(WH)
Peterborough U	Wellingborough T	08.63	63-64	4	-	0
BENNETT Robert (Bobby)						
Harrow, 29 December, 1951						(F)
Southend U	Staines T	06.72	72	1	0	0
Scunthorpe U	L	10.73	73	2	1	0
BENNETT Ronald (Ron)						
Hinckley, 8 May, 1927 Died 1997						(W)
Wolverhampton W		01.45				
Portsmouth	Tr	07.48	49-51	8	-	1
Crystal Palace	Tr	01.52	51-52	27	-	5
Brighton & Hove A	Tr	07.53	53	3	-	0
BENNETT Sean						
Newport, 3 September, 1970						(FB)
Newport Co	YT	•	87	4	1	0
BENNETT Stanley (Stan) Thomas						
Birmingham, 18 September, 1944						(CD)
Walsall	App	09.62	63-74	378	8	12
BENNETT Thomas (Tom) McNeill						
Falkirk, 12 December, 1969						(M)
Aston Villa	YT	12.87				
Wolverhampton W	Tr	07.88	88-94	103	12	2
Stockport Co	Tr	06.95	95-99	105	5	5
Walsall	L	12.99	99	4	0	1
Walsall	Tr	03.00	99-01	75	10	7
Boston U	Tr	08.02	02-04	75	4	1
Kidderminster Hrs	Tr	11.04	04	24	0	0
BENNETT Troy						
Barnsley, 25 December, 1975						(M)
Barnsley	YT	12.93	92	2	0	0
Scarborough	Tr	03.97	96-97	28	11	3
BENNETT Walter						
Mexborough, 15 December, 1918						(CF)
Barnsley	Mexborough Olympia	04.38	46-47	38	-	23
Doncaster Rov	Tr	01.48	47-49	39	-	14
Halifax T	Tr	01.50	49	7	-	1

BENNING Michael (Micky) David
Watford, 3 February, 1938 (W)

League Club	Source	Date Signed	Seasons Played	Apps	Subs	Gls
Watford	Jnrs	09.56	58-61	103	-	14

BENNING Paul Martin
Watford, 7 June, 1963 (FB)

League Club	Source	Date Signed	Seasons Played	Apps	Subs	Gls
Peterborough U	Hayes	12.87	87	2	0	0

BENNION John (Jack) Raymond
Manchester, 2 April, 1934 (WH)

League Club	Source	Date Signed	Seasons Played	Apps	Subs	Gls
Burnley		01.52				
Hull C	Tr	06.57	57-59	35	-	1
Stockport Co	Tr	07.60	60	26	-	1
Barrow	Tr	07.61	61-62	16	-	0

BENNION Stanley (Stan)
Blacon, 9 February, 1938 (W)

League Club	Source	Date Signed	Seasons Played	Apps	Subs	Gls
Wrexham	Jnrs	10.59	59-62	54	-	18
Chester	Tr	06.63	63	20	-	3

BENNYWORTH Ian Robert
Hull, 15 January, 1962 (CD)

League Club	Source	Date Signed	Seasons Played	Apps	Subs	Gls
Hull C	App	01.80	79	1	0	0
Scarborough	Nuneaton Borough	08.86	87-89	88	1	3
Hartlepool U	Tr	12.89	89-91	81	1	3

BENSKIN Denis Walter
Ruddington, 28 May, 1947 (F)

League Club	Source	Date Signed	Seasons Played	Apps	Subs	Gls
Notts Co (Am)	Jnrs	05.65	65	4	0	1

BENSON John Harvey
Arbroath, 23 December, 1942 (CD)

League Club	Source	Date Signed	Seasons Played	Apps	Subs	Gls
Manchester C	Jnrs	07.61	61-63	44	-	0
Torquay U	Tr	06.64	64-70	233	7	7
Bournemouth	Tr	10.70	70-73	85	7	0
Exeter C	L	03.73	72	4	0	0
Norwich C	Tr	12.73	73-74	29	1	1
Bournemouth	Tr	01.75	74-78	56	1	0

BENSON Joseph (Joe) Robert
Misterton, 7 January, 1933 (WH)

League Club	Source	Date Signed	Seasons Played	Apps	Subs	Gls
Scunthorpe U		09.55	55	2	-	0

BENSON Ronald (Ron)
Acomb, 26 March, 1925 Died 1997 (W)

League Club	Source	Date Signed	Seasons Played	Apps	Subs	Gls
York C	Holgates OB	10.47	49	20	-	3

BENSTEAD Graham Mark
Aldershot, 20 August, 1963 EYth (G)

League Club	Source	Date Signed	Seasons Played	Apps	Subs	Gls
Queens Park Rgrs	App	07.81				
Norwich C	Tr	03.85	84-87	16	0	0
Colchester U	L	08.87	87	18	0	0
Sheffield U	Tr	03.88	87-88	47	0	0
Brentford	Tr	07.90	90-93	112	0	0
Brentford	Rushden & Diamonds	07.97	97	1	0	0

BENSTOCK Danny
Hackney, 10 July, 1970 (M)

League Club	Source	Date Signed	Seasons Played	Apps	Subs	Gls
Leyton Orient	Barking	12.92	92-93	17	4	0

BENT Darren Ashley
Wandsworth, 6 February, 1984 EYth/Eu21-12 (F)

League Club	Source	Date Signed	Seasons Played	Apps	Subs	Gls
Ipswich T	YT	07.01	01-04	103	19	49

BENT Geoffrey (Geoff)
Salford, 27 September, 1932 Died 1958 (FB)

League Club	Source	Date Signed	Seasons Played	Apps	Subs	Gls
Manchester U	Jnrs	04.51	54-56	12	-	0

BENT Graham William
Ruabon, 6 October, 1945 Died 2002 WSch (W)

League Club	Source	Date Signed	Seasons Played	Apps	Subs	Gls
Wrexham	Aston Villa (App)	12.63	63-64	10	-	2

BENT Jason
Brampton, Canada, 8 March, 1977 CaYth/Ca-32 (M)

League Club	Source	Date Signed	Seasons Played	Apps	Subs	Gls
Plymouth Arg	Colorado (USA)	09.01	01-03	52	12	5

BENT Junior Antony
Huddersfield, 1 March, 1970 (W)

League Club	Source	Date Signed	Seasons Played	Apps	Subs	Gls
Huddersfield T	YT	12.87	87-89	25	11	6
Burnley	L	11.89	89	7	2	3
Bristol C	Tr	03.90	89-97	142	41	20
Stoke C	L	03.92	91	1	0	0
Shrewsbury T	L	10.96	96	6	0	0
Blackpool	Tr	08.97	97-99	64	39	5

BENT Marcus Nathan
Hammersmith, 19 May, 1978 Eu21-2 (F)

League Club	Source	Date Signed	Seasons Played	Apps	Subs	Gls
Brentford	YT	07.95	95-97	56	14	8
Crystal Palace	Tr	01.98	97-98	13	15	5
Port Vale	Tr	01.99	98-99	17	6	1
Sheffield U	Tr	10.99	99-00	48	0	20
Blackburn Rov	Tr	11.00	00-01	22	15	8
Ipswich T	Tr	11.01	01-03	51	10	21
Leicester C	L	09.03	03	28	5	9
Everton	Tr	07.04	04	31	6	6

BENTALL Charles **Edward**
Helmsley, 28 January, 1922 Died 1947 (CD)

League Club	Source	Date Signed	Seasons Played	Apps	Subs	Gls
York C	English Martyrs	10.45	46	1	-	0

BENTHAM Alan
Wavertree, 12 September, 1940 ESch (FB)

League Club	Source	Date Signed	Seasons Played	Apps	Subs	Gls
Everton	Flint T	11.57				
Southport	Tr	06.60	60-61	25	-	1

BENTHAM Craig Martin
Bingley, 7 March, 1985 (FB)

League Club	Source	Date Signed	Seasons Played	Apps	Subs	Gls
Bradford C	Sch	08.04	04	0	2	0

BENTHAM John James
South Elmsall, 3 March, 1963 (W)

League Club	Source	Date Signed	Seasons Played	Apps	Subs	Gls
York C	App	03.81	81	22	1	0

BENTHAM Stanley (Stan) Joseph
Leigh, 17 March, 1915 Died 2002 (WH)

League Club	Source	Date Signed	Seasons Played	Apps	Subs	Gls
Everton	Wigan Ath	01.34	35-48	110	-	17

BENTLEY Alfred (Alf)
Eythorne, 28 October, 1931 Died 1996 (G)

League Club	Source	Date Signed	Seasons Played	Apps	Subs	Gls
Coventry C	Snowdown CW	10.55	55-56	29	-	0
Gillingham	Margate	08.58	58-61	13	-	0

BENTLEY Anthony (Tony)
Stoke-on-Trent, 20 December, 1939 (FB)

League Club	Source	Date Signed	Seasons Played	Apps	Subs	Gls
Stoke C	Jnrs	12.56	58-60	43	-	15
Southend U	Tr	05.61	61-70	379	2	14

BENTLEY David Alwyn
Edwinstowe, 30 May, 1950 (M)

League Club	Source	Date Signed	Seasons Played	Apps	Subs	Gls
Rotherham U	App	07.67	66-73	241	8	13
Mansfield T	L	09.72	72	1	3	1
Chesterfield	Tr	06.74	74-76	53	2	1
Doncaster Rov	Tr	08.77	77-79	87	2	4

BENTLEY David Michael
Peterborough, 27 August, 1984 EYth/Eu21-3 (F)

League Club	Source	Date Signed	Seasons Played	Apps	Subs	Gls
Arsenal	YT	09.01	03	1	0	0
Norwich C	L	06.04	04	22	4	2

BENTLEY John (Jack)
Liverpool, 17 February, 1942 (W)

League Club	Source	Date Signed	Seasons Played	Apps	Subs	Gls
Everton	Jnrs	11.59	60	1	-	0
Stockport Co	Tr	05.61	61-62	49	-	5

BENTLEY Keith James
Hull, 27 July, 1936 (IF)

League Club	Source	Date Signed	Seasons Played	Apps	Subs	Gls
Hull C		11.57	57	4	-	0

BENTLEY Mark James
Hertford, 7 January, 1978 (M)

League Club	Source	Date Signed	Seasons Played	Apps	Subs	Gls
Southend U	Dagenham & Redbridge	01.04	03-04	50	10	7

BENTLEY Thomas Frank **Roy**
Shirehampton, 17 May, 1924 FLge-3/EB/E-12 (CF)

League Club	Source	Date Signed	Seasons Played	Apps	Subs	Gls
Bristol C	Jnrs	09.41				
Newcastle U	Tr	06.46	46-47	48	-	22
Chelsea	Tr	01.48	47-56	324	-	130
Fulham	Tr	09.56	56-60	142	-	23
Queens Park Rgrs	Tr	06.61	61-62	45	-	0

BENTLEY William (Bill) John
Stoke-on-Trent, 21 October, 1947 ESch/EYth (FB)

League Club	Source	Date Signed	Seasons Played	Apps	Subs	Gls
Stoke C	App	10.64	65-68	44	4	1
Blackpool	Tr	01.69	68-76	289	7	11
Port Vale	Tr	07.77	77-79	92	3	0

BENTON James
Wexford, 9 April, 1975 (M)

League Club	Source	Date Signed	Seasons Played	Apps	Subs	Gls
Northampton T	YT	•	91-92	6	4	1

BERESFORD David
Middleton, 11 November, 1976 ESch/EYth (W)

League Club	Source	Date Signed	Seasons Played	Apps	Subs	Gls
Oldham Ath	YT	07.94	93-96	32	32	2
Swansea C	L	08.95	95	4	2	0
Huddersfield T	Tr	03.97	96-00	24	11	3
Preston NE	L	12.99	99	1	3	0
Port Vale	L	09.00	00	4	0	0
Hull C	Tr	07.01	01	33	8	1
Plymouth Arg	Tr	07.02	02-03	6	11	0
Macclesfield T	L	10.03	03	5	0	0
Tranmere Rov	Tr	11.03	03-04	21	23	3

BERESFORD John
Sheffield, 4 September, 1966 ESch/EYth/EB-2 (FB)

League Club	Source	Date Signed	Seasons Played	Apps	Subs	Gls
Manchester C	App	09.83				
Barnsley	Tr	08.86	86-88	79	9	5
Portsmouth	Tr	03.89	88-91	102	5	8
Newcastle U	Tr	07.92	92-97	176	3	3
Southampton	Tr	02.98	97-99	11	6	0
Birmingham C	L	10.99	99	1	0	0

BERESFORD John Turner
Sunderland, 2 January, 1943 (WH)

League Club	Source	Date Signed	Seasons Played	Apps	Subs	Gls
Hartlepools U (Am)		08.66	66	3	0	0

BERESFORD John William
Sheffield, 25 January, 1946 Died 2003 (WH)

League Club	Source	Date Signed	Seasons Played	Apps	Subs	Gls
Chesterfield	App	01.63	62-64	52	-	10
Notts Co	Tr	05.65	65-66	49	1	13

BERESFORD Marlon
Lincoln, 2 September, 1969 (G)

League Club	Source	Date Signed	Seasons Played	Apps	Subs	Gls
Sheffield Wed	YT	09.87				
Bury	L	08.89	89	1	0	0
Northampton T	L	09.90	90	13	0	0
Crewe Alex	L	02.91	90	3	0	0
Northampton T	L	08.91	91	15	0	0
Burnley	Tr	08.92	92-97	240	0	0
Middlesbrough	Tr	03.98	97-01	8	2	0
Sheffield Wed	L	01.00	00	4	0	0
Burnley	Tr	01.02	01	13	0	0
York C	Tr	08.02	02	6	0	0
Burnley	Tr	10.02	02	33	1	0
Bradford C	Tr	09.03	03	5	0	0
Luton T	Tr	10.03	03	11	0	0
Barnsley	Tr	01.04	03	14	0	0
Luton T	Tr	07.04	04	38	0	0

BERESFORD Philip
Hollingwood, 30 November, 1944 (CF)

League Club	Source	Date Signed	Seasons Played	Apps	Subs	Gls
Chesterfield		01.64	63	7	-	3

BERESFORD Reginald (Reg)
Chesterfield, 29 June, 1924 (CF)

League Club	Source	Date Signed	Seasons Played	Apps	Subs	Gls
Notts Co	Hardwick Colliery	09.45	46	9	-	1

BERESFORD Reginald (Reg) Harold
Walsall, 3 June, 1921 (WH)

League Club	Source	Date Signed	Seasons Played	Apps	Subs	Gls
Aston Villa	Jnrs	10.38				
Birmingham C	Tr	09.46				
Crystal Palace	Tr	08.48	48	7	-	1

BERG Henning
Eidsvell, Norway, 1 September, 1968 NoYth/Nou21-15/No-95 (CD)

League Club	Source	Date Signed	Seasons Played	Apps	Subs	Gls
Blackburn Rov	Lillestrom (Nor)	01.93	92-96	154	5	4
Manchester U	Tr	08.97	97-00	49	17	2
Blackburn Rov	Tr	09.00	00-02	90	1	3

BERGER Patrik
Prague, Czech Rep, 10 November, 1973 CzYth/CzRu21-1/Cz-2/CzR-44 (M)

League Club	Source	Date Signed	Seasons Played	Apps	Subs	Gls
Liverpool	Borussia Dortmund (Ger)	08.96	96-02	106	42	28
Portsmouth	Tr	07.03	03-04	50	2	8

BERGERSEN Kent
Oslo, Norway, 8 February, 1967 (M)

League Club	Source	Date Signed	Seasons Played	Apps	Subs	Gls
Stockport Co	Stromgodset (Nor)	09.99	99-00	18	8	1

BERGKAMP Dennis Nicolaas
Amsterdam, Holland, 18 May, 1969 Hou21/Ho-79 (F)

League Club	Source	Date Signed	Seasons Played	Apps	Subs	Gls
Arsenal	Inter Milan (It)	07.95	95-04	245	46	85

BERGSSON Gudni
Reykjavik, Iceland, 21 July, 1965 IcYth/Icu21-4/Ic-80 (CD)

League Club	Source	Date Signed	Seasons Played	Apps	Subs	Gls
Tottenham H	Valur (Ice)	12.88	88-92	51	20	2
Bolton W	Tr	03.95	94-02	263	7	23

BERHALTER Gregg
Tenafly, New Jersey, USA, 8 January, 1973 USA 29 (CD)

League Club	Source	Date Signed	Seasons Played	Apps	Subs	Gls
Crystal Palace	Cambuur Leeuw (Holl)	02.01	00-01	10	9	1

BERKLEY Austin James
Dartford, 28 January, 1973 (W)

League Club	Source	Date Signed	Seasons Played	Apps	Subs	Gls
Gillingham	YT	05.91	91	0	3	0
Swindon T	Tr	05.92	94	0	1	0
Shrewsbury T	Tr	07.95	95-99	152	20	12
Barnet	Tr	07.00				
Carlisle U	L	08.01	01	2	3	0

BERKOVIC Eyal
Haifa, Israel, 2 April, 1972 IsraelU21/Israel 78 (M)

League Club	Source	Date Signed	Seasons Played	Apps	Subs	Gls
Southampton (L)	Maccabi Haifa (Isr)	10.96	96	26	2	4
West Ham U	Tr	07.97	97-98	62	3	10
Blackburn Rov (L)	Glasgow Celtic	02.01	00	4	7	2
Manchester C	Glasgow Celtic	08.01	01-03	48	8	7
Portsmouth	Tr	01.04	03-04	16	6	2

BERMINGHAM Alan
Liverpool, 11 September, 1944 (FB)

League Club	Source	Date Signed	Seasons Played	Apps	Subs	Gls
Wrexham	Skelmersdale U	06.67	67-70	114	2	2

BERMINGHAM Karl Joseph Kevin
Dublin, 6 October, 1985 IRYth (M)

League Club	Source	Date Signed	Seasons Played	Apps	Subs	Gls
Manchester C	Sch	10.02				
Lincoln C	L	02.05	04	0	2	0

BERNAL Andrew (Andy)
Canberra, Australia, 16 July, 1966 Australia int (FB)

League Club	Source	Date Signed	Seasons Played	Apps	Subs	Gls
Ipswich T	Sporting Gijon (Sp)	09.87	87	4	5	0
Reading	Olympic Sharks (Aus)	07.94	94-99	179	8	2

BERNARD Michael (Mike) Peter
Shrewsbury, 10 January, 1948 EYth/Eu23-3 (M)

League Club	Source	Date Signed	Seasons Played	Apps	Subs	Gls
Stoke C	App	01.65	65-71	124	11	6
Everton	Tr	04.72	72-76	139	8	8
Oldham Ath	Tr	07.77	77-78	6	0	0

BERNARD Narada Michael
Bristol, 30 January, 1981 Jamaica 1 (FB)

League Club	Source	Date Signed	Seasons Played	Apps	Subs	Gls
Arsenal	Tottenham H (YT)	07.99				
Bournemouth	Tr	07.00	00-02	13	16	0
Torquay U	Woking	11.03	03	0	1	0

BERNARD Olivier
Paris, France, 14 October, 1979 (FB)

League Club	Source	Date Signed	Seasons Played	Apps	Subs	Gls
Newcastle U	Lyon (Fr)	10.00	01-04	82	20	6
Darlington	L	03.01	00	9	1	2
Southampton	Tr	01.05	04	12	1	0

BERNARD Paul Robert James
Edinburgh, 30 December, 1972 Su21-15/SB-1/S-2 (M)

League Club	Source	Date Signed	Seasons Played	Apps	Subs	Gls
Oldham Ath	YT	07.91	90-95	105	7	18
Plymouth Arg	Aberdeen	12.02	02	7	3	0

BERNARDEAU Olivier
Bourges, France, 19 August, 1962 (W)

League Club	Source	Date Signed	Seasons Played	Apps	Subs	Gls
Chesterfield	Leeds U (N/C)	08.86	86	5	4	0

BERNTSEN Robin
Tromso, Norway, 10 July, 1970 (F)

League Club	Source	Date Signed	Seasons Played	Apps	Subs	Gls
Port Vale (L)	Tromso (Nor)	11.98	98	1	0	0

BERNTSEN Thomas (Tommy)
Oslo, Norway, 18 December, 1973 (CD)

League Club	Source	Date Signed	Seasons Played	Apps	Subs	Gls
Portsmouth (L)	Lillestrom (Nor)	11.99	99	1	1	0

BERRY David (Dave) Gilbert
Newton-le-Willows, 1 June, 1945 (CD)

League Club	Source	Date Signed	Seasons Played	Apps	Subs	Gls
Blackpool	Jnrs	09.63				
Chester	Tr	07.64	66	0	1	0

BERRY George Frederick
Rostrup, Germany, 19 November, 1957 W-5 (CD)

League Club	Source	Date Signed	Seasons Played	Apps	Subs	Gls
Wolverhampton W	App	11.75	76-81	124	0	4
Stoke C	Tr	08.82	82-89	229	8	27
Doncaster Rov	L	08.84	84	1	0	0
Peterborough U	Tr	07.90	90	28	4	6
Preston NE	Tr	08.91	91	4	0	0

BERRY Gregory (Greg) John
Grays, 5 March, 1971 (W)

League Club	Source	Date Signed	Seasons Played	Apps	Subs	Gls
Leyton Orient	East Thurrock U	07.89	89-91	68	12	14
Wimbledon	Tr	08.92	92-93	6	1	1
Millwall	Tr	03.94	93-96	23	11	1
Brighton & Hove A	L	08.95	95	6	0	2
Leyton Orient	L	03.96	95	4	3	0

BERRY John Andrew
Manchester, 27 August, 1965 (FB)

League Club	Source	Date Signed	Seasons Played	Apps	Subs	Gls
Torquay U		01.84	83	1	0	0

BERRY Reginald John (Johnny)
Aldershot, 1 June, 1926 Died 1994 FLge-1/EB/E-4 (W)

League Club	Source	Date Signed	Seasons Played	Apps	Subs	Gls
Birmingham C	Aldershot YMCA	12.44	47-51	104	-	6
Manchester U	Tr	08.51	51-57	247	-	37

BERRY Leslie (Les) Dennis
Plumstead, 4 May, 1956 (CD)

League Club	Source	Date Signed	Seasons Played	Apps	Subs	Gls
Charlton Ath	App	03.74	75-85	352	6	11
Brighton & Hove A	Tr	08.86	86	22	1	0
Gillingham	Tr	03.87	86-87	26	5	0
Maidstone U	Tr	07.88	89-90	62	1	2

League Club	Source	Date Signed	Seasons Played	Career Record Apps	Subs	Gls
BERRY Michael (Mike) James						
Newbury, 14 February, 1955						(FB)
Southampton	App	02.73	74	2	0	0
BERRY Neil						
Edinburgh, 6 April, 1963 SYth						(CD)
Bolton W	App	03.81	81-84	25	7	0
BERRY Norman						
Bury, 15 August, 1922 Died 2002						(W)
Bury (Am)	Bury Amats	05.46	46-47	23	-	6
BERRY Paul						
Chadwell St Mary, 15 November, 1935						(CD)
Chelsea	Jnrs	04.53	56-57	3	-	0
BERRY Paul Alan						
Oxford, 8 April, 1958						(F)
Oxford U	App	04.76	76-81	98	12	20
BERRY Paul Andrew						
Warrington, 6 December, 1978						(M)
Chester C	Warrington T	08.99	99	0	9	1
BERRY Peter						
Aldershot, 20 September, 1933						(W)
Crystal Palace	Jnrs	08.51	53-57	151	-	27
Ipswich T	Tr	05.58	58-59	38	-	6
BERRY Stephen (Steve) Andrew						
Liverpool, 4 April, 1963						(M)
Portsmouth	App	01.81	81-82	26	2	2
Aldershot	L	03.84	83	5	2	0
Sunderland	Tr	07.84	84-85	32	3	2
Newport Co	Tr	12.85	85-86	60	0	6
Swindon T	Tr	03.87	86-87	4	0	0
Aldershot	Tr	10.87	87-88	48	0	6
Northampton T	Tr	10.88	88-90	95	7	7
BERRY Thomas (Tom)						
Clayton-le-Moors, 31 March, 1922 Died 2003						(CD)
Hull C	Great Harwood	05.47	47-57	275	-	1
BERRY Trevor John						
Haslemere, 1 August, 1974 EYth						(M)
Aston Villa	Bournemouth (YT)	04.92				
Rotherham U	Tr	09.95	95-00	126	47	20
Scunthorpe U	L	02.01	00	6	0	1
BERRY William						
Mansfield, 4 April, 1934						(IF)
Mansfield T	Langwith Colliery	03.56	56	10	-	1
BERRYMAN Stephen (Steve) Christopher						
Blackburn, 26 December, 1966						(G)
Hartlepool U	Leyland Motors	03.90	89	1	0	0
Exeter C	Leyland Motors	08.90				
Cambridge U	Tr	03.91	90	1	0	0
BERSON Mathieu						
Vannes, France, 23 February, 1980 Fru21						(M)
Aston Villa	Nantes (Fr)	08.04	04	7	4	0
BERTHE Mohamed						
Conakry, Guinea, 12 September, 1972						(M)
West Ham U	Gazelac Ajaccio (Aut)	03.98				
Bournemouth	Tr	07.98	98	12	3	2
BERTHE Sekou						
Bamoko, Mali, 7 October, 1977 Mali int						(CD)
West Bromwich A	Troyes (Fr)	09.03	03	2	1	0
BERTHELIN Cedric						
Courrieres, France, 25 December, 1976						(G)
Luton T	ASOR Valence (Fr)	10.02	02	9	0	0
Crystal Palace	Tr	12.02	02-03	26	0	0
BERTI Nicola						
Salsomaggiore Terme, Italy, 14 April, 1967 Italy 39						(M)
Tottenham H	Inter Milan (It)	01.98	97-98	21	0	3
BERTOLINI John (Jack)						
Alloa, 21 March, 1934						(WH)
Workington	Stirling A	01.53	52-57	183	-	36
Brighton & Hove A	Tr	07.58	58-65	258	0	12
BERTOS Leonida (Leo) Christos						
Wellington, New Zealand, 20 December, 1981 NzSch/NzYth/Nzu21/Nz-7						(M)
Barnsley	Wellington Olympic (NZ)	09.00	00-02	4	8	1
Rochdale	Tr	07.03	03-04	73	9	13

League Club	Source	Date Signed	Seasons Played	Career Record Apps	Subs	Gls
BERTRAM James (Jim) Terence						
Whitehaven, 3 February, 1953						(CD)
Workington	Carlisle U (App)	02.72	71	0	1	0
BERTSCHIN Christian (Chris) Frederick						
Kensington, 7 September, 1924 Died 1995						(W)
Reading	Ilford	08.47	47-48	12	-	1
BERTSCHIN Keith Edwin						
Enfield, 25 August, 1956 EYth/Eu21-3						(F)
Ipswich T	Barnet	10.73	75-76	19	13	8
Birmingham C	Tr	07.77	77-80	113	5	29
Norwich C	Tr	08.81	81	35	1	12
Norwich C	Jacksonville (USA)	08.82	82-84	77	1	17
Stoke C	Tr	11.84	84-86	82	6	29
Sunderland	Tr	03.87	86-87	25	11	7
Walsall	Tr	08.88	88-89	40	15	9
Chester C	Tr	11.90	90	14	5	0
BESAGNI Remo (Roy) Giovanni						
Italy, 22 April, 1935						(CF)
Crystal Palace	Jnrs	10.52	52	2	-	0
BEST Andrew (Andy) Keith						
Dorchester, 5 January, 1959						(W)
Torquay U	Teignmouth	11.84	84	15	4	2
BEST Cyril Clyde						
Bermuda, 24 February, 1951						(F)
West Ham U	(Bermuda)	03.69	69-75	178	8	47
BEST David						
Wareham, 6 September, 1943						(G)
Bournemouth	Jnrs	10.60	60-66	230	0	0
Oldham Ath	Tr	09.66	66-68	98	0	0
Ipswich T	Tr	10.68	68-73	168	0	0
Portsmouth	Tr	02.74	73-74	53	0	0
Bournemouth	Tr	07.75	75	2	0	0
BEST George						
Belfast, 22 May, 1946 NI-37						(F)
Manchester U	Jnrs	05.63	63-73	361	0	137
Stockport Co	L	11.75	75	3	0	2
Fulham	Los Angeles (USA)	09.76	76-77	42	0	8
Bournemouth	Glentoran	03.83	82	5	0	0
BEST John Bowers						
Liverpool, 11 July, 1940						(WH)
Liverpool	Jnrs	05.58				
Tranmere Rov	Tr	08.60	60	7	-	0
BEST Leon Julian Brendan						
Nottingham, 19 September, 1986 IRYth						(F)
Southampton	YT	09.04	04	1	2	0
Queens Park Rgrs	L	12.04	04	2	3	0
BEST Thomas (Tommy) Hubert						
Milford Haven, 23 December, 1920						(CF)
Chester	Milford Haven U	07.47	47-48	40	-	14
Cardiff C	Tr	10.48	48-49	28	-	11
Queens Park Rgrs	Tr	12.49	49	13	-	3
BEST William (Billy) James Blaikley						
Gartcosh, 7 September, 1943						(F)
Northampton T	Pollok Jnrs	07.62	63-67	40	0	11
Southend U	Tr	01.68	67-72	225	1	106
Northampton T	Tr	09.73	73-77	201	2	37
BESWETHERICK Jonathan (Jon) Barry						
Liverpool, 15 January, 1978						(FB)
Plymouth Arg	YT	07.96	97-01	133	13	0
Sheffield Wed	Tr	06.02	02-03	9	2	0
Swindon T	L	02.03	02	3	0	0
Macclesfield T	L	01.04	03	3	1	0
Bristol Rov	Tr	07.04				
Kidderminster Hrs	Tr	11.04	04	10	0	0
BESWICK Ivan						
Manchester, 2 January, 1936						(FB)
Manchester U		10.54				
Oldham Ath	Tr	08.58	58-60	47	-	0
BESWICK Keith						
Cardiff, 3 February, 1943						(G)
Millwall	Cardiff Corinthians	01.62	62	12	-	0
Newport Co	Tr	08.64	64-66	56	0	0
BETMEAD Harry						
Grimsby, 11 April, 1912 Died 1984 E-1						(CD)
Grimsby T	Hay Cross	10.30	31-46	296	-	10

BETSY Kevin Eddie Lewis
Seychelles, 20 March, 1978 ESemiPro-1 (F)

League Club	Source	Date Signed	Seasons Played	Apps	Subs	Gls
Fulham	Woking	09.98	98-01	3	12	1
Bournemouth	L	09.99	99	1	4	0
Hull C	L	11.99	99	1	1	0
Barnsley	Tr	02.02	01-03	84	10	15
Hartlepool U	L	08.04	04	3	3	1
Oldham Ath	Tr	09.04	04	34	2	5

BETT Frederick (Fred)
Scunthorpe, 5 December, 1920 Died 2005 (IF)

League Club	Source	Date Signed	Seasons Played	Apps	Subs	Gls
Sunderland	Scunthorpe & Lindsey U	12.37	37-38	3	-	0
Coventry C	Tr	05.46	46-48	27	-	11
Lincoln C	Tr	09.48	48	14	-	2

BETTANY Colin David
Leicester, 15 June, 1932 (FB)

League Club	Source	Date Signed	Seasons Played	Apps	Subs	Gls
Crewe Alex	Leicester C (Am)	08.53	53-54	26	-	6
Birmingham C	Tr	06.55				
Torquay U	Tr	04.57	57-65	335	0	4

BETTANY John William
Laughton, 16 December, 1937 (M)

League Club	Source	Date Signed	Seasons Played	Apps	Subs	Gls
Huddersfield T	Thurcroft CW	09.60	60-64	59	-	6
Barnsley	Tr	03.65	64-69	194	4	25
Rotherham U	Tr	06.70	70	17	0	1

BETTERIDGE Raymond **Michael (Mick)**
Alcester, 11 August, 1924 Died 1999 (IF)

League Club	Source	Date Signed	Seasons Played	Apps	Subs	Gls
West Bromwich A	Warslow Celtic	11.48	49-50	5	-	0
Swindon T	Tr	07.51	51-53	108	-	23
Chester	Tr	03.54	53	8	-	1

BETTNEY Christopher (Chris) John
Chesterfield, 27 October, 1977 (F)

League Club	Source	Date Signed	Seasons Played	Apps	Subs	Gls
Sheffield U	YT	05.96	96	0	1	0
Hull C	L	09.97	97	28	2	1
Chesterfield	Tr	07.99	99	7	6	0
Rochdale	Tr	11.99	99	12	12	0
Macclesfield T	Tr	07.00	00	0	2	0

BETTS Anthony (Tony) Thomas
Derby, 31 October, 1953 EYth (F)

League Club	Source	Date Signed	Seasons Played	Apps	Subs	Gls
Aston Villa	Jnrs	03.72	74	1	3	0
Southport	L	12.74	74	8	0	1
Port Vale	Portland (USA)	10.75	75	1	0	0

BETTS James **Barrie**
Barnsley, 18 September, 1932 (FB)

League Club	Source	Date Signed	Seasons Played	Apps	Subs	Gls
Barnsley	Worsborough Dale St T	11.50	52-56	55	-	0
Stockport Co	Tr	11.57	57-59	112	-	3
Manchester C	Tr	06.60	60-63	101	-	5
Scunthorpe U	Tr	08.64	64	7	-	0

BETTS Eric
Coventry, 27 June, 1925 Died 1990 (W)

League Club	Source	Date Signed	Seasons Played	Apps	Subs	Gls
Mansfield T	Mansfield Villa	02.46	46	19	-	5
Coventry C	Tr	08.47	47	1	-	0
Walsall	Nuneaton Borough	05.49	49	30	-	3
West Ham U	Tr	04.50	50	3	-	1
Rochdale	Nuneaton Borough	10.51	51-52	52	-	8
Crewe Alex	Tr	02.53	52-53	25	-	5
Wrexham	Tr	10.53	53-55	53	-	21
Oldham Ath	Tr	02.56	55-56	26	-	5

BETTS Michael (Mike) James
Barnsley, 21 September, 1956 (CD)

League Club	Source	Date Signed	Seasons Played	Apps	Subs	Gls
Blackpool	App	10.73	75	4	3	0
Bury	Northwich Vic (N/C)	11.80	80	1	0	0

BETTS Robert
Doncaster, 21 December, 1981 (M)

League Club	Source	Date Signed	Seasons Played	Apps	Subs	Gls
Doncaster Rov	YT	●	97	2	1	0
Coventry C	Tr	12.98	99-02	5	8	0
Plymouth Arg	L	02.01	00	3	1	0
Lincoln C	L	10.01	01	1	2	0
Rochdale	Tr	08.03	03	4	1	2
Kidderminster Hrs	Tr	09.03	03	8	1	0

BETTS Simon Richard
Middlesbrough, 3 March, 1973 (M)

League Club	Source	Date Signed	Seasons Played	Apps	Subs	Gls
Ipswich T	YT	07.91				
Colchester U	Scarborough (N/C)	12.92	92-98	182	9	11
Darlington	Yeovil T	07.01	01-02	69	0	1

BETTS Stuart
Barnsley, 21 September, 1956 (F)

League Club	Source	Date Signed	Seasons Played	Apps	Subs	Gls
Blackpool	App	10.73				
Halifax T		09.76				
Crewe Alex	Tr	08.77	77	2	0	0

BEVAN Brian Edward
Bristol, 20 March, 1937 (W)

League Club	Source	Date Signed	Seasons Played	Apps	Subs	Gls
Bristol C	Bridgwater T	02.56	57-59	2	-	0
Carlisle U	Tr	03.60	59-60	27	-	2
Millwall	Tr	02.61	60	3	-	0

BEVAN Paul Philip
Shrewsbury, 20 October, 1952 (CD)

League Club	Source	Date Signed	Seasons Played	Apps	Subs	Gls
Shrewsbury T	App	10.70	70-72	66	7	1
Swansea C	Tr	08.73	73-74	77	3	5
Crewe Alex	Tr	07.75	75-79	170	2	7

BEVAN Scott Anthony
Southampton, 16 September, 1979 (G)

League Club	Source	Date Signed	Seasons Played	Apps	Subs	Gls
Southampton	YT	01.98				
Huddersfield T	L	07.02	02	30	0	0
Wycombe W	L	01.04	03	5	0	0
Wimbledon/MK Dons	Tr	03.04	03-04	17	0	0

BEVANS Stanley (Stan)
Kingsley, 16 April, 1934 (W)

League Club	Source	Date Signed	Seasons Played	Apps	Subs	Gls
Stoke C	Jnrs	04.51	50-54	15	-	1

BEVIS David (Dave) Roger
Southampton, 27 June, 1942 (G)

League Club	Source	Date Signed	Seasons Played	Apps	Subs	Gls
Ipswich T	Jnrs	08.59	63-65	6	0	0

BEVIS William (Billy) Ernest
Warsash, 29 September, 1918 Died 1994 (W)

League Club	Source	Date Signed	Seasons Played	Apps	Subs	Gls
Portsmouth	Jnrs	07.36				
Southampton	Gosport Ath	06.37	37-46	82	-	16

BEWERS Jonathan (Jon) Anthony
Wellingborough, 10 September, 1982 ESch/EYth/Eu20 (FB)

League Club	Source	Date Signed	Seasons Played	Apps	Subs	Gls
Aston Villa	YT	09.99	99	0	1	0
Notts Co	Tr	03.04	03	0	3	0
Walsall	Tr	09.04	04	1	0	0

BEWLEY David (Dave) George
Bournemouth, 22 September, 1920 ESch (FB)

League Club	Source	Date Signed	Seasons Played	Apps	Subs	Gls
Fulham	Gravesend U	05.45	46-48	17	-	1
Reading	Tr	03.50	49-50	11	-	1
Fulham	Tr	11.50				
Watford	Tr	05.53	53-55	113	-	1

BEYNON Edgar Norman
Swansea, 3 May, 1940 (IF)

League Club	Source	Date Signed	Seasons Played	Apps	Subs	Gls
Wrexham	RAF Egypt	07.59	59	1	-	0

BEYNON Edwin (Eddie) Rees
Aberdare, 17 November, 1924 Died 2002 WSch (IF)

League Club	Source	Date Signed	Seasons Played	Apps	Subs	Gls
Wrexham		01.47	46-51	72	-	21
Shrewsbury T	Tr	10.51	51-54	91	-	6

BHUTIA Baichung
Gangtok, Sikkim, 15 June, 1976 India 46 (F)

League Club	Source	Date Signed	Seasons Played	Apps	Subs	Gls
Bury	East Bengal (Ind)	09.99	99-01	20	17	3

BIAGINI Leonardo (Leo) Angel
Arroyo Seco, Argentina, 13 April, 1977 (F)

League Club	Source	Date Signed	Seasons Played	Apps	Subs	Gls
Portsmouth (L)	Real Mallorca (Sp)	02.02	01	6	2	2

BIANCALANI Frederic
Villerupt, France, 21 July, 1974 (FB)

League Club	Source	Date Signed	Seasons Played	Apps	Subs	Gls
Walsall	Nancy (Fr)	08.01	01	13	5	2

BIBBO Salvatore (Sal)
Basingstoke, 24 August, 1974 (G)

League Club	Source	Date Signed	Seasons Played	Apps	Subs	Gls
Sheffield U	Crawley T	08.93				
Chesterfield	L	02.95	94	0	1	0
Reading	Tr	08.96	96-97	7	0	0

[BICA] DI GIUSEPPE Marcos
Sao Paulo, Brazil, 12 March, 1972 (F)

League Club	Source	Date Signed	Seasons Played	Apps	Subs	Gls
Sunderland	Sport Boys Callao (Peru)	09.99				
Walsall	Tr	10.99	99	0	1	0

BICKERSTAFFE John (Jack)
St Helens, 8 November, 1918 Died 1982 (CD)

League Club	Source	Date Signed	Seasons Played	Apps	Subs	Gls
Bury	Peasley Cross	05.39	46-48	27	-	0
Lincoln C	Tr	12.48	48-50	12	-	0
Halifax T	Tr	09.51	51-52	37	-	0

BICKLE Michael (Mike) John
Plymouth, 25 January, 1944 (F)

League Club	Source	Date Signed	Seasons Played	Apps	Subs	Gls
Plymouth Arg	St Austell	12.65	65-71	171	10	71
Gillingham	Tr	11.71	71-72	32	0	7

BICKLES David (Dave)
West Ham, 6 April, 1944 Died 1997 EYth (CD)

League Club	Source	Date Signed	Seasons Played	Apps	Subs	Gls
West Ham U	App	07.61	63-66	24	1	0
Crystal Palace	Tr	10.67				
Colchester U	Tr	09.68	68-69	67	0	3

BICKNELL Charles (Charlie)
Pye Bridge, 6 November, 1905 Died 1994 (FB)

League Club	Source	Date Signed	Seasons Played	Apps	Subs	Gls
Chesterfield	New Tupton Ivanhoe	10.27	28-29	79	-	0
Bradford C	Tr	03.30	30-35	240	-	2
West Ham U	Tr	03.36	35-46	137	-	1

BICKNELL John (Jack)
Edlington, 16 December, 1931 (IF)

League Club	Source	Date Signed	Seasons Played	Apps	Subs	Gls
Walsall	Retford T	02.54	53	3	-	0

BICKNELL Roy
Doncaster, 19 February, 1926 Died 2005 (CD)

League Club	Source	Date Signed	Seasons Played	Apps	Subs	Gls
Wolverhampton W	Jnrs	09.43				
Charlton Ath	Tr	05.47	47-48	7	-	0
Bristol C	Tr	06.49	49-50	21	-	0
Colchester U	Gravesend & Northfleet	06.52	52-53	25	-	0

BICKNELL Stephen (Steve) John
Stockton, Warwickshire, 28 November, 1958 (W)

League Club	Source	Date Signed	Seasons Played	Apps	Subs	Gls
Leicester C	App	12.76	76	6	1	0
Torquay U	Tr	08.78	78	0	3	0

BIDSTRUP Stefan
Helsingoer, Denmark, 24 February, 1975 (CD)

League Club	Source	Date Signed	Seasons Played	Apps	Subs	Gls
Wigan Ath	Lyngby (Den)	11.00	00	10	5	2

BIELBY Paul Anthony
Darlington, 24 November, 1956 EYth (W)

League Club	Source	Date Signed	Seasons Played	Apps	Subs	Gls
Manchester U	App	11.73	73	2	2	0
Hartlepool	Tr	11.75	75-77	74	21	8
Huddersfield T	Tr	08.78	78	29	2	5

BIGGINS Brian
Ellesmere Port, 19 May, 1940 (G)

League Club	Source	Date Signed	Seasons Played	Apps	Subs	Gls
Chester	Jnrs	06.57	57-58	5	-	0

BIGGINS Graham William
Chapeltown, 10 March, 1958 (G)

League Club	Source	Date Signed	Seasons Played	Apps	Subs	Gls
Doncaster Rov	Rotherham U (Am)	07.77	77	2	0	0

BIGGINS Stephen (Steve) James
Lichfield, 20 June, 1954 (F)

League Club	Source	Date Signed	Seasons Played	Apps	Subs	Gls
Shrewsbury T	Hednesford T	12.77	77-81	140	6	41
Oxford U	Tr	07.82	82-84	44	15	22
Derby Co	Tr	10.84	84	8	2	1
Wolverhampton W	L	03.85	84	4	0	0
Port Vale	L	03.86	85	1	3	0
Exeter C	Trelleborg FF (Swe)	10.86	86	14	0	2

BIGGINS Wayne
Sheffield, 20 November, 1961 (F)

League Club	Source	Date Signed	Seasons Played	Apps	Subs	Gls
Lincoln C	App	11.79	80	8	0	1
Burnley	Matlock T	02.84	83-85	78	0	29
Norwich C	Tr	10.85	85-87	66	13	16
Manchester C	Tr	07.88	88	29	3	9
Stoke C	Tr	08.89	89-92	120	2	46
Barnsley	Tr	10.92	92-93	44	3	16
Stoke C	Glasgow Celtic	03.94	93-94	18	9	6
Luton T	L	01.95	94	6	1	1
Oxford U	Tr	07.95	95	8	2	1
Wigan Ath	Tr	11.95	95-96	35	16	5

BIGGS Alfred (Alfie) George
Bristol, 8 February, 1936 (F)

League Club	Source	Date Signed	Seasons Played	Apps	Subs	Gls
Bristol Rov	Jnrs	02.53	53-60	214	-	77
Preston NE	Tr	07.61	61-62	48	-	22
Bristol Rov	Tr	10.62	62-67	210	0	101
Walsall	Tr	03.68	67-68	23	1	9
Swansea T	Tr	11.68	68	16	0	4

BIGGS Anthony (Tony)
Greenford, 17 April, 1936 EAmat (CF)

League Club	Source	Date Signed	Seasons Played	Apps	Subs	Gls
Arsenal	Hounslow T	08.56	57-58	4	-	1
Leyton Orient	Tr	12.58	58-59	4	-	1

BIGNOT Marcus
Birmingham, 22 August, 1974 ESemiPro-1 (FB)

League Club	Source	Date Signed	Seasons Played	Apps	Subs	Gls
Crewe Alex	Kidderminster Hrs	09.97	97-99	93	2	0
Bristol Rov	Tr	08.00	00	26	0	1
Queens Park Rgrs	Tr	03.01	00-01	49	5	1
Rushden & Diamonds	Tr	08.02	02-03	68	0	2
Queens Park Rgrs	Tr	03.04	03-04	47	2	0

BIGNOT Paul Junior
Birmingham, 14 February, 1986 (FB)

League Club	Source	Date Signed	Seasons Played	Apps	Subs	Gls
Crewe Alex	Sch	03.05	04	3	2	0

BILCLIFF Raymond (Ray)
Blaydon, 24 May, 1931 (FB)

League Club	Source	Date Signed	Seasons Played	Apps	Subs	Gls
Middlesbrough	Spennymoor Jnrs	05.49	51-60	182	-	0
Hartlepools U	Tr	01.61	60-63	117	-	0

BILEY Alan Paul
Leighton Buzzard, 26 February, 1957 (F)

League Club	Source	Date Signed	Seasons Played	Apps	Subs	Gls
Cambridge U	Luton T (App)	07.75	75-79	160	5	74
Derby Co	Tr	01.80	79-80	47	0	19
Everton	Tr	07.81	81	16	3	3
Stoke C	L	03.82	81	8	0	1
Portsmouth	Tr	08.82	82-84	101	4	50
Brighton & Hove A	Tr	03.85	84-85	34	1	8
Cambridge U	New York (USA)	11.86	86	0	3	0

BILIC Slaven
Split, Croatia, 11 September, 1968 Croatia 43 (CD)

League Club	Source	Date Signed	Seasons Played	Apps	Subs	Gls
West Ham U	Karlsruhe (Ger)	02.96	95-96	48	0	2
Everton	Tr	07.97	97-98	26	2	0

BILL Roger James
Creswell, 17 May, 1944 (W)

League Club	Source	Date Signed	Seasons Played	Apps	Subs	Gls
Reading	Chelsea (Am)	09.62	62	4	-	0

BILLING Peter Graham
Liverpool, 24 October, 1964 (CD)

League Club	Source	Date Signed	Seasons Played	Apps	Subs	Gls
Everton	South Liverpool	01.86	85	1	0	0
Crewe Alex	Tr	12.86	86-88	83	5	1
Coventry C	Tr	06.89	89-92	51	7	1
Port Vale	Tr	02.93	92-94	23	3	0
Hartlepool U	Tr	08.95	95	35	1	0
Crewe Alex	Tr	08.96	96	9	6	0

BILLINGHAM John (Jack)
Daventry, 3 December, 1914 Died 1981 (CF)

League Club	Source	Date Signed	Seasons Played	Apps	Subs	Gls
Northampton T	Stead & Simpson	09.35	35	3	-	0
Bristol C	Tr	07.37	37	7	-	0
Burnley	Tr	05.38	38-48	93	-	36
Carlisle U	Tr	09.49	49-50	65	-	17
Southport	Tr	03.51	50-54	150	-	37

BILLINGHAM Peter Arnold
Pensnett, 8 October, 1938 (WH)

League Club	Source	Date Signed	Seasons Played	Apps	Subs	Gls
Walsall	Jnrs	10.55	55-59	99	-	11
West Bromwich A	Tr	05.60	60	7	-	0

BILLINGS John
Doncaster, 30 March, 1944 (IF)

League Club	Source	Date Signed	Seasons Played	Apps	Subs	Gls
Doncaster Rov	Jnrs	05.61	62-64	18	-	4

BILLINGTON Brian Keith
Leicester, 28 April, 1951 (F)

League Club	Source	Date Signed	Seasons Played	Apps	Subs	Gls
Notts Co	Leicester C (Am)	10.69	69	4	3	0

BILLINGTON Charles (Charlie) Roy
Chesterfield, 8 November, 1927 Died 1985 (CD)

League Club	Source	Date Signed	Seasons Played	Apps	Subs	Gls
Aldershot	Chesterfield (Am)	12.46	46-55	212	-	11
Norwich C	Tr	01.56	55-56	22	-	0
Watford	Tr	07.57	57	14	-	0
Mansfield T	Tr	06.58	58	1	-	0

BILLINGTON David James
Oxford, 15 October, 1980 (FB)

League Club	Source	Date Signed	Seasons Played	Apps	Subs	Gls
Peterborough U	YT	•	96	2	3	0

BILLINGTON Hugh John Richard
Ampthill, 24 February, 1916 Died 1988 (CF)

League Club	Source	Date Signed	Seasons Played	Apps	Subs	Gls
Luton T	Waterlows	05.38	38-47	86	-	63
Chelsea	Tr	03.48	47-50	82	-	28

BILLINGTON Stanley (Stan)
Wallasey, 23 February, 1937 EYth (FB)

League Club	Source	Date Signed	Seasons Played	Apps	Subs	Gls
Everton	Jnrs	06.55				
Tranmere Rov	Tr	07.60	60-63	93	-	0

BILLINGTON Wilfred (Wilf) Francis
Blackburn, 28 January, 1930 (G)

League Club	Source	Date Signed	Seasons Played	Apps	Subs	Gls
Blackburn Rov		04.48				
Workington	Tr	07.54	54-57	53	-	0

BILLIO Patrizio
Treviso, Italy, 19 April, 1974 (M)

League Club	Source	Date Signed	Seasons Played	Apps	Subs	Gls
Crystal Palace	Monza (It)	03.98	97	1	2	0

BILLY Christopher (Chris) Anthony
Huddersfield, 2 January, 1973 (W)

League Club	Source	Date Signed	Seasons Played	Apps	Subs	Gls
Huddersfield T	YT	07.91	91-94	76	18	4
Plymouth Arg	Tr	08.95	95-97	107	11	9
Notts Co	Tr	07.98	98	3	3	0
Bury	Tr	09.98	98-02	165	13	11
Carlisle U	Tr	08.03	03	39	0	1

BIMPSON James Louis
Rainford, 14 May, 1929 (CF)

League Club	Source	Date Signed	Seasons Played	Apps	Subs	Gls
Liverpool	Burscough	01.53	52-59	94	-	39
Blackburn Rov	Tr	11.59	59-60	22	-	5
Bournemouth	Tr	02.61	60	11	-	1
Rochdale	Tr	08.61	61-62	54	-	16

League Club	Source	Date Signed	Seasons Played	Apps	Subs	Gls
BIMSON Stuart James						
Liverpool, 29 September, 1969						(FB)
Bury	Macclesfield T	02.95	94-96	36	0	0
Lincoln C	Tr	11.96	96-02	157	18	4
Cambridge U	Tr	07.03	03-04	37	6	0
BINCH David						
Nottingham, 10 February, 1956						(F)
Doncaster Rov		02.76	75-76	3	2	0
BINES Henry Melvin						
Cardiff, 17 May, 1930 Died 1979						(WH)
Swindon T		08.50	51-52	6	-	0
BING Douglas (Doug)						
Broadstairs, 27 October, 1928						(WH)
West Ham U	Margate	01.51	51-54	29	-	3
BING Thomas (Tommy) Edward						
Broadstairs, 24 November, 1931						(W)
Tottenham H	Margate	09.54	57	1	-	0
BINGHAM John George						
Ilkeston, 23 September, 1949						(W)
Manchester C	Charlton Ath (App)	10.67				
Oldham Ath	Tr	07.69	69	16	1	3
Mansfield T	Tr	08.70	70-71	18	3	0
Chester	L	03.72	71	7	0	1
Stockport Co	Tr	07.72	72	16	4	3
BINGHAM Michael James						
Leyland, 21 May, 1981 ESch						(G)
Blackburn Rov	YT	07.98				
Mansfield T	Tr	07.01	01	1	1	0
BINGHAM William (Billy) Laurence						
Belfast, 5 August, 1931 IrLge-2/I-7/NI-49						(W)
Sunderland	Glentoran	11.50	50-57	206	-	45
Luton T	Tr	07.58	58-60	87	-	27
Everton	Tr	10.60	60-62	86	-	23
Port Vale	Tr	08.63	63-64	40	-	6
BINGHAM William Peter						
Swindon, 12 July, 1922 Died 1997						(WH)
Swindon T		08.46	46-47	20	-	0
BINGLEY Walter						
Sheffield, 17 April, 1930						(FB)
Bolton W	Eccleshall MW	04.48	49-54	6	-	0
Sheffield Wed	Tr	05.55	55-57	38	-	0
Swindon T	Tr	01.58	57-59	101	-	0
York C	Tr	08.60	60-62	130	-	5
Halifax T	Tr	07.63	63-64	64	-	1
BINKS Martin John						
Romford, 15 September, 1953						(CD)
Colchester U	Leyton Orient (App)	05.72	72	10	0	0
Cambridge U	Tr	01.73	72	1	0	0
BINNEY Frederick (Fred) Edward						
Plymouth, 12 August, 1946						(F)
Torquay U	Launceston	10.66	67-68	5	7	1
Exeter C	Tr	02.69	68	17	0	11
Torquay U	Tr	08.69	69	19	3	10
Exeter C	Tr	03.70	69-73	160	0	79
Brighton & Hove A	Tr	05.74	74-76	68	2	35
Plymouth Arg	St Louis (USA)	10.77	77-79	67	4	39
Hereford U	Tr	01.80	79-81	21	6	6
BINNIE Laurence (Laurie)						
Falkirk, 17 December, 1917						(WH)
Chesterfield	Camelon Jnrs	05.39				
Mansfield T	Tr	11.46	46	20	-	0
BINNS Eric						
Halifax, 13 August, 1924						(CD)
Halifax T	Huddersfield T (Am)	05.46	46	6	-	1
Burnley	Goole T	03.49	52-54	15	-	0
Blackburn Rov	Tr	05.55	55-56	23	-	0
BIRBECK Joseph (Joe)						
Stanley, 15 April, 1932						(WH)
Middlesbrough	Evenwood T	04.53	53-58	38	-	0
Grimsby T	Tr	07.59	59	18	-	0
BIRCH Alan						
West Bromwich, 12 August, 1956						(W)
Walsall	App	08.73	72-78	158	13	23
Chesterfield	Tr	07.79	79-80	90	0	35
Wolverhampton W	Tr	08.81	81	13	2	0
Barnsley	Tr	02.82	81-82	43	1	10
Chesterfield	Tr	08.83	83	30	2	5
Rotherham U	Tr	03.84	83-85	99	2	28
Scunthorpe U	Tr	06.86	86-87	19	4	2
Stockport Co	Tr	10.87	87	18	2	3
BIRCH Brian						
Salford, 18 November, 1931 EYth						(IF)
Manchester U	Jnrs	05.49	49-51	11	-	4
Wolverhampton W	Tr	03.52	51	3	-	1
Lincoln C	Tr	12.52	52-54	56	-	16
Barrow	Boston U	06.56	56-58	60	-	27
Exeter C	Tr	09.58	58-59	19	-	1
Oldham Ath	Tr	01.60	59-60	35	-	11
Rochdale	Tr	03.61	60-61	11	-	0
BIRCH Brian						
Southport, 9 April, 1938 ESch/EYth						(W)
Bolton W	Jnrs	04.55	54-63	165	-	23
Rochdale	Tr	07.64	64-65	60	1	6
BIRCH Clifford (Cliff)						
Crumlin, 1 September, 1928 Died 1990 WLge-2						(W)
Norwich C	Ebbw Vale	12.46	49	5	-	3
Newport Co	Tr	10.50	50-53	143	-	28
Colchester U	Tr	06.54	54	12	-	3
BIRCH Gary Stephen						
Birmingham, 8 October, 1981						(F)
Walsall	YT	10.98	01-04	42	26	7
Exeter C	L	03.01	00	6	3	2
Exeter C	L	08.01	01	5	10	0
Barnsley	L	03.04	03	8	0	2
Kidderminster Hrs	Tr	12.04	04	11	3	4
BIRCH Harold (Harry) Kelvin						
Crieff, 11 January, 1914 Died 1985						(WH)
Barrow	Bangor	09.45	46	26	-	2
BIRCH James (Jim) Victor Tomlinson						
Ashover, 25 October, 1927						(IF)
Huddersfield T	Grenoside	05.45				
Halifax T		08.48	48	3	-	1
BIRCH Jeffrey (Jeff)						
Sheffield, 21 October, 1927						(W)
Sheffield U	Selby T	09.47				
York C	Scarborough	10.49	49	7	-	1
BIRCH Kenneth (Ken) Joseph						
Birkenhead, 31 December, 1933						(WH)
Everton	Jnrs	08.51	55-57	43	-	1
Southampton	Tr	03.58	57-58	34	-	3
BIRCH Mark						
Stoke-on-Trent, 5 January, 1977						(FB)
Stoke C	YT	07.95				
Carlisle U	Northwich Vic	08.00	00-03	109	3	1
BIRCH Paul						
West Bromwich, 20 November, 1962						(M)
Aston Villa	App	07.80	83-90	153	20	16
Wolverhampton W	Tr	02.91	90-95	128	14	15
Preston NE	L	03.96	95	11	0	2
Doncaster Rov	Tr	06.96	96	26	1	2
Exeter C	Tr	03.97	96-97	33	2	5
BIRCH Paul Anthony						
Reading, 3 December, 1968						(F)
Portsmouth	Arsenal (App)	01.87				
Brentford	Tr	12.87	87-88	13	5	2
BIRCH Trevor						
West Bromwich, 20 November, 1933						(WH)
Aston Villa	Accles & Pollock	01.52	54-59	22	-	0
Stockport Co	Tr	11.60	60-61	43	-	0
BIRCH Trevor Nigel						
Ormskirk, 16 February, 1958						(M)
Liverpool	App	12.75				
Shrewsbury T	Tr	03.79	78-79	23	2	4
Chester	Tr	07.80	80	30	1	0
BIRCH James Walter						
Ecclesfield, 5 October, 1917 Died 1991						(CD)
Huddersfield T		05.39				
Rochdale	Tr	03.46	46-52	243	-	10
BIRCH William (Billy)						
Southport, 20 October, 1944						(W)
West Bromwich A	App	10.62				
Crystal Palace	Tr	06.63	63-64	6	-	0

BIRCHALL Adam Stephen
Maidstone, 2 December, 1984 Wu21-9 (F)

League Club	Source	Date Signed	Seasons Played	Apps	Subs	Gls
Arsenal	Sch	07.02				
Wycombe W	L	08.04	04	11	1	4

BIRCHALL Christopher (Chris)
Stafford, 5 May, 1984 Trinidad 4 (F)

League Club	Source	Date Signed	Seasons Played	Apps	Subs	Gls
Port Vale	Sch	05.04	01-04	30	17	6

BIRCHALL Paul William
Norris Green, 3 September, 1957 (M)

League Club	Source	Date Signed	Seasons Played	Apps	Subs	Gls
Southport	Everton (Am)	03.77	76-77	16	3	1

BIRCHAM Bernard
Philadelphia, County Durham, 31 August, 1924 (G)

League Club	Source	Date Signed	Seasons Played	Apps	Subs	Gls
Sunderland	Jnrs	07.43				
Chesterfield	Tr	11.46				
Grimsby T	Tr	06.48	49	8	-	0
Colchester U	Tr	07.50	50	7	-	0

BIRCHAM Walter **Clive**
Herrington, 7 September, 1939 (W)

League Club	Source	Date Signed	Seasons Played	Apps	Subs	Gls
Sunderland	Shiney Row Swifts	09.56	58-59	28	-	2
Hartlepools U	Tr	02.60	59-62	105	-	15

BIRCHAM Marc Stephen John
Wembley, 11 May, 1978 Cau23-1/Ca-17 (M)

League Club	Source	Date Signed	Seasons Played	Apps	Subs	Gls
Millwall	YT	05.96	96-01	86	18	3
Queens Park Rgrs	Tr	07.02	02-04	102	7	5

BIRCHENALL Alan John
East Ham, 22 August, 1945 Eu23-4 (M)

League Club	Source	Date Signed	Seasons Played	Apps	Subs	Gls
Sheffield U	Thorneywood Thistle	06.63	64-67	106	1	31
Chelsea	Tr	11.67	67-69	74	1	20
Crystal Palace	Tr	06.70	70-71	41	0	11
Leicester C	Tr	09.71	71-76	156	7	12
Notts Co	L	03.76	75	5	0	0
Notts Co	San Jose (USA)	09.77	77	28	0	0
Blackburn Rov	Memphis (USA)	07.78	78	17	1	0
Luton T	Tr	03.79	78-79	9	1	0
Hereford U	Tr	10.79	79	11	0	0

BIRCUMSHAW Anthony (Tony)
Mansfield, 8 February, 1945 (FB)

League Club	Source	Date Signed	Seasons Played	Apps	Subs	Gls
Notts Co	App	02.62	60-65	148	0	1
Hartlepools U	Tr	07.66	66-70	182	3	11

BIRCUMSHAW Peter Brian
Mansfield, 29 August, 1938 (W)

League Club	Source	Date Signed	Seasons Played	Apps	Subs	Gls
Notts Co	Jnrs	07.56	56-61	72	-	40
Bradford C	Tr	06.62	62	27	-	7
Stockport Co	Tr	06.63	63	17	-	4

BIRD Adrian Lee
Bristol, 8 July, 1969 (CD)

League Club	Source	Date Signed	Seasons Played	Apps	Subs	Gls
Birmingham C	YT	07.87	86-88	23	4	0

BIRD Anthony (Tony)
Cardiff, 1 September, 1974 WYth/Wu21-8 (F)

League Club	Source	Date Signed	Seasons Played	Apps	Subs	Gls
Cardiff C	YT	08.93	92-95	44	31	13
Swansea C	Barry T	08.97	97-99	51	35	18
Kidderminster Hrs	Tr	07.00	00-01	30	21	3

BIRD David Alan
Gloucester, 26 December, 1984 (M)

League Club	Source	Date Signed	Seasons Played	Apps	Subs	Gls
Cheltenham T	Cinderford T	02.01	02-04	56	16	0

BIRD John Charles
Doncaster, 9 June, 1948 (CD)

League Club	Source	Date Signed	Seasons Played	Apps	Subs	Gls
Doncaster Rov	Doncaster U	03.67	67-70	48	2	3
Preston NE	Tr	03.71	70-75	166	0	9
Newcastle U	Tr	08.75	75-79	84	3	5
Hartlepool U	Tr	07.80	80-84	139	2	16

BIRD Francis **John (Johnny)**
Cardiff, 21 November, 1940 WSch (FB)

League Club	Source	Date Signed	Seasons Played	Apps	Subs	Gls
Newport Co	Jnrs	11.57	57-66	277	0	4
Swansea T	Tr	07.67	67	8	0	0

BIRD Kenneth (Ken) Benjamin
Norwich, 25 September, 1918 Died 1987 ESch (G)

League Club	Source	Date Signed	Seasons Played	Apps	Subs	Gls
Wolverhampton W	Willenhall Rov	05.37				
Bournemouth	Tr	10.38	38-52	249	-	0

BIRD Kevin
Doncaster, 7 August, 1952 (CD)

League Club	Source	Date Signed	Seasons Played	Apps	Subs	Gls
Mansfield T	Doncaster Rov (Am)	07.72	72-82	372	5	55
Huddersfield T	Tr	08.83	83	1	0	0

BIRD Ronald (Ronnie) Philip
Erdington, 27 December, 1941 Died 2005 EYth (W)

League Club	Source	Date Signed	Seasons Played	Apps	Subs	Gls
Birmingham C	Jnrs	01.59				
Bradford PA	Tr	06.61	61-65	129	0	39
Bury	Tr	10.65	65	13	0	3
Cardiff C	Tr	02.66	65-70	97	11	25
Crewe Alex	Tr	07.71	71	19	1	0

BIRKBECK John David
Lincoln, 1 October, 1932 Died 2004 (CF)

League Club	Source	Date Signed	Seasons Played	Apps	Subs	Gls
Lincoln C	Spilsby	01.52	54	2	-	0

BIRKETT Clifford (Cliff)
Haydock, 17 September, 1933 Died 1997 ESch (CF)

League Club	Source	Date Signed	Seasons Played	Apps	Subs	Gls
Manchester U	Jnrs	10.50	50	9	-	2
Southport	Tr	06.56	56	14	-	4

BIRKETT Ronald (Ronnie)
Warrington, 21 July, 1927 Died 1992 (W)

League Club	Source	Date Signed	Seasons Played	Apps	Subs	Gls
Manchester C	Crompton Rec	01.46				
New Brighton	Tr	01.47	46-47	8	-	0
Oldham Ath	Tr	08.48	48	4	-	0
Accrington St	Tr	07.49	49	14	-	2

BIRKETT Wilfred (Wilf)
Haydock, 26 June, 1922 Died 1993 (G)

League Club	Source	Date Signed	Seasons Played	Apps	Subs	Gls
Everton	Haydock C & B	02.44				
Southport	Tr	11.46	46-51	162	-	0
Shrewsbury T	Tr	07.52	52	20	-	0
Southport	Tr	07.53	53	15	-	0

BIRKS Graham
Sheffield, 25 January, 1942 (FB)

League Club	Source	Date Signed	Seasons Played	Apps	Subs	Gls
Sheffield Wed	Jnrs	01.60	62	4	-	0
Peterborough U	Tr	05.64	64-65	34	0	0
Southend U	Tr	01.66	65-69	139	1	1
Chester	Tr	10.69	69-71	71	2	0

BIRMINGHAM Charles Henry
Liverpool, 24 August, 1922 Died 1993 (IF)

League Club	Source	Date Signed	Seasons Played	Apps	Subs	Gls
Tranmere Rov	Everton (Am)	08.46	46	2	-	1

BIRMINGHAM David Paul
Portsmouth, 16 April, 1981 (FB)

League Club	Source	Date Signed	Seasons Played	Apps	Subs	Gls
Portsmouth	Bournemouth (YT)	08.99	99	1	1	0
Bournemouth	Tr	03.01	01	3	1	0

BIRSE Charles (Charlie) Duncan Valentine
Dundee, 26 October, 1916 Died 1995 (WH)

League Club	Source	Date Signed	Seasons Played	Apps	Subs	Gls
Watford	Hibernian	05.46	46	7	-	0

BIRTLES Garry
Nottingham, 27 July, 1956 Eu21-2/EB/E-3 (F)

League Club	Source	Date Signed	Seasons Played	Apps	Subs	Gls
Nottingham F	Long Eaton U	12.76	76-80	87	0	32
Manchester U	Tr	10.80	80-81	57	1	11
Nottingham F	Tr	09.82	82-86	122	3	38
Notts Co	Tr	06.87	87-88	62	1	9
Grimsby T	Tr	07.89	89-91	54	15	9

BISCAN Igor
Zagreb, Croatia, 4 May, 1978 Croatia 15 (M)

League Club	Source	Date Signed	Seasons Played	Apps	Subs	Gls
Liverpool	Dynamo Zagreb (Cro)	12.00	00-04	50	22	2

BISCHOFF Mikkel
Denmark, 3 February, 1982 DeYth/Deu21-4 (CD)

League Club	Source	Date Signed	Seasons Played	Apps	Subs	Gls
Manchester C	AB Copenhagen (Den)	07.02	02	1	0	0
Wolverhampton W	L	09.04	04	7	0	1
Wolverhampton W	L	03.05	04	2	2	0

BISGAARD Morten
Randers, Denmark, 25 June, 1974 DeYth/Deu21-8/De-8 (M)

League Club	Source	Date Signed	Seasons Played	Apps	Subs	Gls
Derby Co	FC Copenhagen (Den)	06.04	04	31	5	4

BISHOP Andrew (Andy) Jamie
Cannock, 19 October, 1982 (F)

League Club	Source	Date Signed	Seasons Played	Apps	Subs	Gls
Walsall	Sch	08.02				
Kidderminster Hrs	L	11.02	02	22	7	5
Kidderminster Hrs	L	08.03	03	8	3	2
Rochdale	L	11.03	03	8	2	1
Yeovil T	L	02.04	03	4	1	2

BISHOP Charles (Charlie) Darren
Nottingham, 16 February, 1968 (CD)

League Club	Source	Date Signed	Seasons Played	Apps	Subs	Gls
Watford	Stoke C (App)	04.86				
Bury	Tr	08.87	87-90	104	10	6
Barnsley	Tr	07.91	91-95	124	6	1
Preston NE	L	01.96	95	4	0	0
Burnley	L	03.96	95	9	0	0
Wigan Ath	Tr	06.96	96-97	27	1	0
Northampton T	Tr	12.97	97-98	11	0	0

BISHOP Edward (Eddie) Michael
Liverpool, 28 November, 1962 (M)

League Club	Source	Date Signed	Seasons Played	Apps	Subs	Gls
Tranmere Rov	Runcorn	03.88	87-90	46	30	19

League Club	Source	Date Signed	Seasons Played	Career Record Apps	Subs	Gls
Chester C	Tr	12.90	90-95	97	18	28
Crewe Alex	L	03.92	91	3	0	0
BISHOP Ian William						
Liverpool, 29 May, 1965 EB-1						(M)
Everton	App	05.83	83	0	1	0
Crewe Alex	L	03.84	83	4	0	0
Carlisle U	Tr	10.84	84-87	131	1	14
Bournemouth	Tr	07.88	88	44	0	2
Manchester C	Tr	08.89	89	18	1	2
West Ham U	Tr	12.89	89-97	240	14	12
Manchester C	Tr	03.98	97-00	53	25	2
Rochdale	Barry T	08.02	02	5	3	0
BISHOP Peter Jason						
Sheffield, 4 January, 1944 EYth						(W)
Sheffield U	Jnrs	04.63				
Chesterfield	Tr	05.65	65-70	78	3	7
BISHOP Raymond (Ray) John						
Hengoed, 24 November, 1955						(F)
Cardiff C	Cheltenham T	01.77	77-80	92	9	26
Newport Co	Tr	02.81	80-81	8	10	2
Torquay U	Tr	08.82	82-83	33	7	8
BISHOP Sidney (Sid) Harold Richard						
Tooting, 8 April, 1934						(CD)
Leyton Orient	Chase of Chertsey	06.52	53-64	296	-	4
BISHTON Dennis Roy						
Windsor, 22 September, 1950						(FB)
Reading	App	09.68	68	2	0	0
BISSELL Steven (Steve) John						
Meriden, 8 October, 1958						(W)
Nottingham F	App	10.76				
Blackpool	Tr	09.78	78	1	0	0
BISSET Thomas (Tommy) Alexander						
Croydon, 21 March, 1932						(FB)
Brighton & Hove A	Redhill	01.53	52-60	115	-	5
BISSETT Nicholas (Nicky)						
Fulham, 5 April, 1964						(CD)
Brighton & Hove A	Barnet	09.88	88-94	94	3	8
BITHELL Brian						
Winsford, 5 October, 1956						(FB)
Stoke C	App	10.73	76	16	1	0
Port Vale	L	09.77	77	2	0	0
Wimbledon	Tr	12.77	77	6	0	0
BJORKLUND Joachim						
Vaxjo, Sweden, 15 March, 1971 Sweden 75						(CD)
Sunderland	Venezia (It)	02.02	01-03	49	8	0
Wolverhampton W	Tr	08.04	04	2	1	0
BJORNEBYE Stig Inge						
Elverum, Norway, 11 December, 1969 NoYth/Nou21/NoB-1/No-76						(FB)
Liverpool	Rosenborg (Nor)	12.92	92-98	132	7	2
Blackburn Rov	Tr	06.00	00-01	53	3	1
BLACK Alan Douglas						
Alexandria, 4 June, 1943						(FB)
Sunderland	Dumbarton	08.64	64-65	4	2	0
Norwich C	Tr	09.66	66-73	172	4	1
BLACK Andrew (Andy)						
Stirling, 23 September, 1917 SLge-2/SWar-4/S-3						(IF)
Manchester C	Heart of Midlothian	06.46	46-49	139	-	47
Stockport Co	Tr	08.50	50-52	94	-	38
BLACK Anthony (Tony) Paul						
Barrow, 15 July, 1969						(W)
Wigan Ath	Bamber Bridge	03.95	94-97	17	14	2
BLACK Christopher (Chris) David						
Ashington, 7 September, 1982						(M)
Sunderland	YT	08.00	02-03	2	1	0
Doncaster Rov	Tr	03.04	03	1	0	0
BLACK Ian Henderson						
Aberdeen, 27 March, 1924 S-1						(G)
Southampton	Aberdeen	12.47	47-49	97	-	0
Fulham	Tr	08.50	50-57	263	-	1
BLACK John						
Blackburn, 4 November, 1945 WSch						(G)
Arsenal	App	02.63				
Swansea T	Tr	12.64	64-65	15	0	0

League Club	Source	Date Signed	Seasons Played	Career Record Apps	Subs	Gls
BLACK John						
Helensburgh, 10 November, 1957						(W)
Wolverhampton W	App	12.75	77-78	5	1	0
Bradford C	Tr	01.80	79-82	50	5	13
Hereford U	Tr	08.83	83	8	1	0
BLACK Kenneth (Kenny) George						
Stenhousemuir, 29 November, 1963 SSch/SYth						(M)
Portsmouth	Heart of Midlothian	07.89	89-90	50	12	3
BLACK Kingsley Terence						
Luton, 22 June, 1968 ESch/NIu21-1/NIB-3/NI-30						(W)
Luton T	Jnrs	07.86	87-91	123	4	26
Nottingham F	Tr	09.91	91-95	80	18	14
Sheffield U	L	03.95	94	8	3	2
Millwall	L	09.95	95	1	2	1
Grimsby T	Tr	07.96	96-00	91	50	8
Lincoln C	L	10.00	00	5	0	0
Lincoln C	Tr	07.01	01-02	30	2	5
BLACK Michael James						
Chigwell, 6 October, 1976 ESch						(M)
Arsenal	YT	07.95				
Millwall	L	10.97	97	13	0	2
Tranmere Rov	Tr	07.99	99	7	15	0
Southend U	Tr	12.00	00	10	5	1
BLACK Neville						
Pegswood, 19 June, 1931						(IF)
Newcastle U	Pegswood	09.49				
Exeter C	Tr	01.53	52	4	-	0
Rochdale	Tr	07.53	53-55	62	-	13
BLACK Russell Palmer						
Dumfries, 29 July, 1960						(F)
Sheffield U	Gretna	08.84	84-85	10	4	0
Halifax T	Dundee	08.86	86-87	63	9	14
BLACK Simon Anthony						
Marston Green, 9 November, 1975						(F)
Birmingham C	YT	06.94	93	2	0	0
BLACK Thomas (Tommy) Robert						
Chigwell, 26 November, 1979						(M)
Arsenal	YT	07.98	99	0	1	0
Carlisle U	L	08.99	99	5	0	1
Bristol C	L	12.99	99	4	0	0
Crystal Palace	Tr	07.00	00-03	67	59	10
Sheffield U	L	09.04	04	3	1	1
BLACKADDER Frederick (Fred)						
Carlisle, 13 January, 1916 Died 1992						(CD)
Carlisle U (Am)	Queens Park	05.37	37-46	3	-	0
BLACKBURN Alan						
Pleasley, 4 August, 1935						(CF)
West Ham U	Jnrs	08.53	54-57	15	-	3
Halifax T	Tr	11.57	57-60	124	-	34
BLACKBURN Christopher (Chris) Raymond						
Crewe, 2 August, 1982						(M)
Chester C	YT	•	99	0	1	0
BLACKBURN Colin						
Thirsk, 16 January, 1961						(W)
Middlesbrough	Jnrs	12.79	80	1	0	0
BLACKBURN Derrick John						
Ryhill, 5 July, 1931						(CD)
Burnley		06.53				
Chesterfield	Tr	06.54				
Swansea T	Ossett T	01.57	57	2	-	0
BLACKBURN Edwin (Eddie) Huitson						
Houghton-le-Spring, 18 April, 1957						(G)
Hull C	App	09.74	74-79	68	0	0
York C	Tr	04.80	80-81	76	0	0
Hartlepool U	Tr	01.83	82-86	161	0	0
BLACKBURN Keith						
Manchester, 17 July, 1940						(IF)
Portsmouth	Bolton W (Am)	07.59	60-63	34	-	8
BLACKBURN Kenneth (Ken) Alan						
Wembley, 13 May, 1951						(F)
Brighton & Hove A	App	05.69	68	1	0	1
BLACKBURN Lee Charles						
Hornchurch, 1 October, 1985						(M)
Cambridge U	YT	•	04	0	3	0

BLACKER James (Jim) Arthur
Leeds, 10 August, 1945 (CD)

League Club	Source	Date Signed	Seasons Played	Apps	Subs	Gls
Bradford C	Middleton Parkside	01.63	63-64	21	-	0

BLACKFORD Gary John
Redhill, 25 September, 1968 (FB)

League Club	Source	Date Signed	Seasons Played	Apps	Subs	Gls
Barnet	Fisher Ath	07.91	91	2	4	0

BLACKHALL Mark Christopher
Barking, 17 November, 1960 (F)

League Club	Source	Date Signed	Seasons Played	Apps	Subs	Gls
Orient	App	11.78	81-82	12	6	1

BLACKHALL Raymond (Ray)
Ashington, 19 February, 1957 (FB)

League Club	Source	Date Signed	Seasons Played	Apps	Subs	Gls
Newcastle U	App	08.74	74-77	25	12	0
Sheffield Wed	Tr	08.78	78-81	115	0	1
Mansfield T	IK Tord (Swe)	11.82	82	15	0	0
Carlisle U	Tr	08.84	84	1	0	0

BLACKHALL Sidney (Sid)
Ashington, 25 September, 1945 (CF)

League Club	Source	Date Signed	Seasons Played	Apps	Subs	Gls
Bradford PA	App	10.62	63	1	-	0

BLACKLAW Adam Smith
Aberdeen, 2 September, 1937 SSch/Su23-2/S-3 (G)

League Club	Source	Date Signed	Seasons Played	Apps	Subs	Gls
Burnley	Jnrs	10.54	56-66	318	0	0
Blackburn Rov	Tr	07.67	67-69	96	0	0
Blackpool	Tr	06.70	70	1	0	0

BLACKLER Martin John
Swindon, 14 March, 1963 (M)

League Club	Source	Date Signed	Seasons Played	Apps	Subs	Gls
Swindon T	App	03.81	82	8	1	0

BLACKLEY Arthur
Carlisle, 31 January, 1939 (W)

League Club	Source	Date Signed	Seasons Played	Apps	Subs	Gls
Chelsea	Jnrs	10.56				
Carlisle U	Tr	11.60	60-61	38	-	7

BLACKLEY John Henderson
West Quarter, 12 May, 1948 Su23-4/SLge-1/S-7 (CD)

League Club	Source	Date Signed	Seasons Played	Apps	Subs	Gls
Newcastle U	Hibernian	10.77	77-78	46	0	0
Preston NE	Tr	07.79	79-81	51	2	2

BLACKMAN Lloyd Jason
Ashford, Middlesex, 24 September, 1983 (F)

League Club	Source	Date Signed	Seasons Played	Apps	Subs	Gls
Brentford	Sch	07.02	02-03	1	3	0

BLACKMAN Ronald (Ronnie) Henry
Portsmouth, 2 April, 1925 (CF)

League Club	Source	Date Signed	Seasons Played	Apps	Subs	Gls
Reading	Gosport Borough	03.47	46-53	228	-	158
Nottingham F	Tr	06.54	54	11	-	3
Ipswich T	Tr	07.55	55-57	27	-	12

BLACKMORE Clayton Graham
Neath, 23 September, 1964 WSch/WYth/Wu21-3/W-39 (FB)

League Club	Source	Date Signed	Seasons Played	Apps	Subs	Gls
Manchester U	App	09.82	83-92	150	36	19
Middlesbrough	Tr	07.94	94-97	45	8	4
Bristol C	L	11.96	96	5	0	1
Barnsley	Tr	02.99	98	4	3	0
Notts Co	Tr	07.99	99	21	0	2

BLACKSHAW William (Bill)
Ashton-under-Lyne, 6 September, 1920 Died 1994 (W)

League Club	Source	Date Signed	Seasons Played	Apps	Subs	Gls
Manchester C	Audenshaw U	05.38	38	3	-	0
Oldham Ath	Tr	07.46	46-48	67	-	22
Crystal Palace	Tr	07.49	49-50	32	-	5

BLACKSTOCK Dexter Anthony
Oxford, 20 May, 1986 EYth (F)

League Club	Source	Date Signed	Seasons Played	Apps	Subs	Gls
Southampton	Sch	05.04	04	8	1	1
Plymouth Arg	L	02.05	04	10	4	4

BLACKSTONE Ian Kenneth
Harrogate, 7 August, 1964 (F)

League Club	Source	Date Signed	Seasons Played	Apps	Subs	Gls
York C	Harrogate T	03.90	90-93	107	22	37
Scarborough	Tr	08.94	94	11	2	0

BLACKWELL Dean Robert
Camden, 5 December, 1969 Eu21-6 (CD)

League Club	Source	Date Signed	Seasons Played	Apps	Subs	Gls
Wimbledon	YT	07.88	89-00	180	25	1
Plymouth Arg	L	03.90	89	5	2	0
Brighton & Hove A	Tr	10.02	02	18	3	2

BLACKWELL Kevin Patrick
Luton, 21 December, 1958 (G)

League Club	Source	Date Signed	Seasons Played	Apps	Subs	Gls
Scarborough	Barnet	11.86	87-89	44	0	0
Notts Co	Tr	11.89				
Torquay U	Tr	01.93	92	18	0	0
Huddersfield T	Tr	08.93	93-94	3	2	0
Plymouth Arg	Tr	08.95	95-96	24	0	0

BLACKWELL Paul
Mancot, 13 January, 1963 (M)

League Club	Source	Date Signed	Seasons Played	Apps	Subs	Gls
Chester	Jnrs	09.81	81-84	89	5	3

BLACKWELL Stephen Geoffrey
Wolverhampton, 8 June, 1967 (F)

League Club	Source	Date Signed	Seasons Played	Apps	Subs	Gls
Wolverhampton W	App	11.84	84	0	1	0

BLACKWELL Wilfred (Wilf)
Maltby, 19 November, 1926 Died 1959 (W)

League Club	Source	Date Signed	Seasons Played	Apps	Subs	Gls
Portsmouth		10.47				
Mansfield T	Tr	08.48				
Aldershot	Tr	06.50	50	1	-	0

BLACKWOOD John Syme Duncan
Cronberry, 25 January, 1935 (IF)

League Club	Source	Date Signed	Seasons Played	Apps	Subs	Gls
Accrington St (Am)	Girvan Jnrs	10.58	58-59	4	-	1

BLACKWOOD Michael Andrew
Birmingham, 30 September, 1979 (F)

League Club	Source	Date Signed	Seasons Played	Apps	Subs	Gls
Aston Villa	YT	04.98				
Chester C	L	09.99	99	9	0	2
Wrexham	Tr	07.00	00-01	24	22	2
Lincoln C	Telford U	07.04	04	5	4	0

BLACKWOOD Robert (Bobby) Rankin
Edinburgh, 20 August, 1934 Died 1997 SLge-1 (M)

League Club	Source	Date Signed	Seasons Played	Apps	Subs	Gls
Ipswich T	Heart of Midlothian	06.62	62-64	62	-	12
Colchester U	Tr	05.65	65-67	104	1	6

BLADES Paul Andrew
Peterborough, 5 January, 1965 EYth (CD)

League Club	Source	Date Signed	Seasons Played	Apps	Subs	Gls
Derby Co	App	12.82	82-89	157	9	1
Norwich C	Tr	07.90	90-91	47	0	0
Wolverhampton W	Tr	08.92	92-94	103	4	2
Rotherham U	Tr	07.95	95-96	43	0	2

BLAGG Edward (Ted) Arthur
Shireoaks, 9 February, 1918 Died 1976 (CD)

League Club	Source	Date Signed	Seasons Played	Apps	Subs	Gls
Nottingham F	Woodend	02.38	46-47	54	-	0
Southport	Tr	11.48	48	11	-	0

BLAIN Colin Anthony
Urmston, 7 March, 1970 (M)

League Club	Source	Date Signed	Seasons Played	Apps	Subs	Gls
Halifax T	YT	06.88	87-88	18	5	0

BLAIN James (Jimmy) Donald
Mossley Hill, 9 April, 1940 (FB)

League Club	Source	Date Signed	Seasons Played	Apps	Subs	Gls
Everton	Jnrs	05.59				
Southport	Tr	02.60	59-62	127	-	40
Rotherham U	Tr	12.62	62-63	23	-	1
Carlisle U	Tr	04.64	64-65	41	0	7
Exeter C	Tr	10.65	65-73	310	10	14

BLAIR Andrew (Andy)
Kirkcaldy, 18 December, 1959 Su21-5 (M)

League Club	Source	Date Signed	Seasons Played	Apps	Subs	Gls
Coventry C	App	10.77	78-80	90	3	6
Aston Villa	Tr	08.81	81-83	24	9	0
Wolverhampton W	L	10.83	83	10	0	0
Sheffield Wed	Tr	08.84	84-85	58	0	3
Aston Villa	Tr	03.86	85-87	19	1	1
Barnsley	L	03.88	87	6	0	0
Northampton T	Tr	10.88	88	1	2	0

BLAIR Douglas (Dougie)
Ecclesfield, 26 June, 1921 Died 1998 (IF)

League Club	Source	Date Signed	Seasons Played	Apps	Subs	Gls
Blackpool		05.39				
Cardiff C	Tr	08.47	47-53	204	-	30

BLAIR James (Jim)
Calderbank, 13 January, 1947 (F)

League Club	Source	Date Signed	Seasons Played	Apps	Subs	Gls
Norwich C	St Mirren	09.72	72-73	3	3	0

BLAIR James (Jimmy) Alfred
Whiteinch, 6 January, 1918 Died 1983 S-1 (IF)

League Club	Source	Date Signed	Seasons Played	Apps	Subs	Gls
Blackpool	Cardiff C (Am)	06.35	37-46	50	-	8
Bournemouth	Tr	10.47	47-49	80	-	8
Leyton Orient	Tr	12.49	49-52	104	-	26

BLAIR Kenneth (Kenny) George
Portadown, 28 September, 1952 (M)

League Club	Source	Date Signed	Seasons Played	Apps	Subs	Gls
Derby Co	Jnrs	06.70				
Halifax T	Tr	10.74	74-75	42	1	4
Stockport Co	L	02.76	75	7	0	0
Southport	Tr	08.76	76	17	0	0

BLAIR Ronald (Ronnie) Victor
Coleraine, 26 September, 1949 NISch/NI-5 (FB)

League Club	Source	Date Signed	Seasons Played	Apps	Subs	Gls
Oldham Ath	Coleraine	10.66	66-69	74	3	1
Rochdale	Tr	03.70	69-71	65	5	3
Oldham Ath	Tr	08.72	72-80	285	10	21
Blackpool	Tr	08.81	81	35	1	3
Rochdale	Tr	08.82	82	3	0	0

BLAKE Anthony (Tony) John
Cofton Hackett, 26 February, 1927 (FB)

League Club	Source	Date Signed	Seasons Played	Apps	Subs	Gls
Birmingham C	Rubery Owen	01.49	49	2	-	0
Gillingham	Tr	07.52	52	10	-	1

BLAKE James (Jimmy) Bernard
Manchester, 5 May, 1966 (FB)

League Club	Source	Date Signed	Seasons Played	Apps	Subs	Gls
Rochdale	Jnrs	09.83	83	2	0	0

BLAKE Mark Antony
Nottingham, 16 December, 1970 ESch/EYth/Eu21-9 (M)

League Club	Source	Date Signed	Seasons Played	Apps	Subs	Gls
Aston Villa	YT	07.89	89-92	26	5	2
Wolverhampton W	L	01.91	90	2	0	0
Portsmouth	Tr	08.93	93	15	0	0
Leicester C	Tr	03.94	93-95	42	7	4
Walsall	Tr	08.96	96-97	51	10	5
Mansfield T	Tr	08.99	99-00	78	6	9
Kidderminster Hrs	Tr	07.01	01	23	1	4

BLAKE Mark Christopher
Portsmouth, 19 December, 1967 EYth (CD)

League Club	Source	Date Signed	Seasons Played	Apps	Subs	Gls
Southampton	App	12.85	85-88	18	0	2
Colchester U	L	09.89	89	4	0	1
Shrewsbury T	L	03.90	89	10	0	0
Shrewsbury T	Tr	07.90	90-93	132	0	3
Fulham	Tr	09.94	94-97	133	7	17

BLAKE Nathan Alexander
Cardiff, 27 January, 1972 WYth/Wu21-5/WB-1/W-29 (F)

League Club	Source	Date Signed	Seasons Played	Apps	Subs	Gls
Cardiff C	Chelsea (YT)	08.90	89-93	113	18	35
Sheffield U	Tr	02.94	93-95	55	14	34
Bolton W	Tr	12.95	95-98	102	5	38
Blackburn Rov	Tr	10.98	98-01	37	17	13
Wolverhampton W	Tr	09.01	01-03	70	5	24
Leicester C	Tr	08.04	04	4	10	0
Leeds U	L	12.04	04	2	0	1

BLAKE Noel Lloyd George
Kingston, Jamaica, 12 January, 1962 (CD)

League Club	Source	Date Signed	Seasons Played	Apps	Subs	Gls
Aston Villa	Sutton Coldfield T	08.79	79-81	4	0	0
Shrewsbury T	L	03.82	81	6	0	0
Birmingham C	Tr	09.82	82-83	76	0	5
Portsmouth	Tr	04.84	84-87	144	0	10
Leeds U	Tr	07.88	88-89	51	0	4
Stoke C	Tr	02.90	89-91	74	1	3
Bradford C	L	02.92	91	6	0	0
Bradford C	Tr	07.92	92-93	38	1	3
Exeter C	Dundee	08.95	95-00	135	12	10

BLAKE Robert (Robbie) James
Middlesbrough, 4 March, 1976 (F)

League Club	Source	Date Signed	Seasons Played	Apps	Subs	Gls
Darlington	YT	07.94	94-96	54	14	21
Bradford C	Tr	03.97	96-01	109	44	40
Nottingham F	L	08.00	00	9	2	1
Burnley	Tr	01.02	01-04	103	17	42
Birmingham C	Tr	01.05	04	2	9	2

BLAKE Russell Timothy
Colchester, 24 July, 1935 (W)

League Club	Source	Date Signed	Seasons Played	Apps	Subs	Gls
Colchester U		04.56	55-60	58	-	8

BLAKEMAN Alan
Oldham, 2 November, 1937 (CF)

League Club	Source	Date Signed	Seasons Played	Apps	Subs	Gls
Rotherham U	Ashton U	05.58	58	2	-	0
Workington	Tr	01.59	58	14	-	7

BLAKEMAN Alec George
Oxford, 11 June, 1918 Died 1994 (IF)

League Club	Source	Date Signed	Seasons Played	Apps	Subs	Gls
Brentford	Oxford C	05.46	46-48	42	-	7
Sheffield U	Tr	11.48	48	5	-	0
Bournemouth	Tr	02.49	48-49	25	-	8

BLAKEY David (Dave)
Newburn, 22 August, 1929 (CD)

League Club	Source	Date Signed	Seasons Played	Apps	Subs	Gls
Chesterfield	Chevington Drift	05.47	48-66	617	0	20

BLAKIE James (Jimmy) Shearlaw
Reston, 9 December, 1926 (W)

League Club	Source	Date Signed	Seasons Played	Apps	Subs	Gls
Barrow		08.50	50	9	-	1

BLAMEY Nathan George
Plymouth, 10 June, 1977 (FB)

League Club	Source	Date Signed	Seasons Played	Apps	Subs	Gls
Southampton	YT	07.95				
Shrewsbury T	Tr	02.97	96-97	15	0	1

BLAMPEY Stuart Leslie
North Ferriby, 13 June, 1951 (CD)

League Club	Source	Date Signed	Seasons Played	Apps	Subs	Gls
Hull C	Jnrs	08.68	69-74	61	11	1

BLANC Laurent Robert
Ales, France, 19 November, 1965 France 97 (CD)

League Club	Source	Date Signed	Seasons Played	Apps	Subs	Gls
Manchester U	Inter Milan (It)	08.01	01-02	44	4	1

BLANCHFLOWER Robert **Dennis (Danny)**
Belfast, 10 February, 1926 Died 1993 IrLge-6/FLge-1/I-9/NI-47 (WH)

League Club	Source	Date Signed	Seasons Played	Apps	Subs	Gls
Barnsley	Glentoran	04.49	48-50	68	-	2
Aston Villa	Tr	03.51	50-54	148	-	10
Tottenham H	Tr	12.54	54-63	337	-	15

BLANCHFLOWER John (Jackie)
Belfast, 7 March, 1933 Died 1998 NISch/NI-12 (IF)

League Club	Source	Date Signed	Seasons Played	Apps	Subs	Gls
Manchester U	Jnrs	03.50	51-57	105	-	26

BLANEY Steven David
Orsett, 24 March, 1977 ESch/Wu21-3 (FB)

League Club	Source	Date Signed	Seasons Played	Apps	Subs	Gls
West Ham U	YT	07.95				
Brentford	Tr	03.98	97	4	1	0

BLANKLEY Barry Steven
Farnborough, 27 October, 1964 (FB)

League Club	Source	Date Signed	Seasons Played	Apps	Subs	Gls
Southampton	App	10.82				
Aldershot	Tr	12.84	84-86	90	0	0

BLANT Colin
Rawtenstall, 7 October, 1946 (CD)

League Club	Source	Date Signed	Seasons Played	Apps	Subs	Gls
Burnley	Rossendale U	08.64	66-69	46	7	7
Portsmouth	Tr	04.70	70-71	64	0	1
Rochdale	Tr	07.72	72-73	51	0	0
Darlington	Tr	01.74	73-75	89	0	0
Grimsby T	Tr	08.76	76	9	0	0
Workington	Tr	11.76	76	21	0	0

BLATCHFORD Patrick (Paddy) John
Plymouth, 28 December, 1925 Died 1981 (W)

League Club	Source	Date Signed	Seasons Played	Apps	Subs	Gls
Plymouth Arg	Saltash U	11.48	48-50	19	-	2
Leyton Orient	Tr	08.51	51-52	60	-	8

BLATHERWICK Steven (Steve) Scott
Hucknall, 20 September, 1973 (CD)

League Club	Source	Date Signed	Seasons Played	Apps	Subs	Gls
Nottingham F	Notts Co (YT)	08.92	93-96	10	0	0
Wycombe W	L	02.94	93	2	0	0
Hereford U	L	09.95	95	10	0	1
Reading	L	03.97	96	6	1	0
Burnley	Tr	07.97	97-98	16	8	0
Chesterfield	L	09.98	98	2	0	0
Chesterfield	Tr	12.98	98-04	184	9	8

BLATSIS Con
Melbourne, Australia, 6 July, 1977 Auu20/Auu23/Au-2 (CD)

League Club	Source	Date Signed	Seasons Played	Apps	Subs	Gls
Derby Co	South Melbourne (Aus)	08.00	00	2	0	0
Sheffield Wed	L	12.00	00	6	0	0
Colchester U	Tr	03.02	01	7	0	0

BLAYNEY Alan
Belfast, 9 October, 1981 NIu21-4/NIu23-1 (G)

League Club	Source	Date Signed	Seasons Played	Apps	Subs	Gls
Southampton	YT	07.01	03-04	3	0	0
Stockport Co	L	10.02	02	2	0	0
Bournemouth	L	12.02	02	2	0	0
Rushden & Diamonds	L	01.05	04	4	0	0
Brighton & Hove A	L	03.05	04	7	0	0

BLEANCH Norman Wesley Swan
Houghton-le-Spring, 19 August, 1940 (CF)

League Club	Source	Date Signed	Seasons Played	Apps	Subs	Gls
West Ham U	Willington	02.60				
Southend U	Tr	07.61	61	3	-	0
Bradford PA	Tr	11.61	61	9	-	3

BLEARS Brian Thomas
Prestatyn, 18 November, 1933 (WH)

League Club	Source	Date Signed	Seasons Played	Apps	Subs	Gls
Chester	Everton (Am)	07.54	54-55	2	-	0

BLEASDALE David George
St Helens, 23 March, 1965 (M)

League Club	Source	Date Signed	Seasons Played	Apps	Subs	Gls
Preston NE	Liverpool (App)	08.83	83	4	1	0

BLEASE Rory
Bebington, 16 August, 1960 (M)

League Club	Source	Date Signed	Seasons Played	Apps	Subs	Gls
Chester C	Pwllheli	12.84	84	4	0	0

BLEIDELIS Imants
Latvia, 16 August, 1975 Latvia 68 (M)

League Club	Source	Date Signed	Seasons Played	Apps	Subs	Gls
Southampton	Skonto Riga (Lat)	02.00	00-01	0	2	0

BLENKINSOPP Thomas (Tommy) William
Blyth, 13 May, 1920 Died 2004 FLge-2 (WH)

League Club	Source	Date Signed	Seasons Played	Apps	Subs	Gls
Grimsby T	West Auckland T	03.39	46-47	74	-	10
Middlesbrough	Tr	05.48	48-52	98	-	0
Barnsley	Tr	11.52	52	8	-	0

BLEWITT Darren Lee
Newham, 3 September, 1985 (CD)

League Club	Source	Date Signed	Seasons Played	Apps	Subs	Gls
West Ham U	Sch	07.04				
Southend U	L	03.05	04	0	1	0

BLICK Michael (Mike) Robert
Berkeley, 20 September, 1948 (CD)

League Club	Source	Date Signed	Seasons Played	Apps	Subs	Gls
Swindon T	App	09.66	67-70	6	0	0

BLINCOW Ernest (Ernie)
Walsall, 9 September, 1921 (W)

League Club	Source	Date Signed	Seasons Played	Apps	Subs	Gls
Walsall	West Bromwich A (Am)	01.47	46	1	-	0

BLINKER Reginald (Regi) Waldie
Surinam, 4 June, 1969 Holland int (W)

League Club	Source	Date Signed	Seasons Played	Apps	Subs	Gls
Sheffield Wed	Feyenoord (Holl)	03.96	95-96	24	18	3

BLINKHORN Matthew David
Blackpool, 2 March, 1985 (F)

League Club	Source	Date Signed	Seasons Played	Apps	Subs	Gls
Blackpool	Sch	06.03	01-04	9	17	3
Luton T	L	07.04	04	0	2	0

BLISSETT Gary Paul
Manchester, 29 June, 1964 (F)

League Club	Source	Date Signed	Seasons Played	Apps	Subs	Gls
Crewe Alex	Altrincham	08.83	83-86	112	10	38
Brentford	Tr	03.87	86-92	220	13	79
Wimbledon	Tr	07.93	93-95	10	21	3
Wycombe W	L	12.95	95	4	0	2
Crewe Alex	L	03.96	95	10	0	1

BLISSETT Luther Loide
Falmouth, Jamaica, 1 February, 1958 Eu21-4/EB/E-14 (F)

League Club	Source	Date Signed	Seasons Played	Apps	Subs	Gls
Watford	Jnrs	07.75	75-82	222	24	95
Watford	AC Milan (It)	08.84	84-88	113	14	44
Bournemouth	Tr	11.88	88-90	121	0	56
Watford	Tr	08.91	91	34	8	9
West Bromwich A	L	10.92	92	3	0	1
Bury	Tr	08.93	93	8	2	1
Mansfield T	L	12.93	93	4	1	1

BLIZZARD Dominic John
High Wycombe, 2 September, 1983 (M)

League Club	Source	Date Signed	Seasons Played	Apps	Subs	Gls
Watford	YT	04.02	03-04	13	6	2

BLIZZARD Leslie (Les) William Benjamin
Acton, 13 March, 1923 Died 1996 (WH)

League Club	Source	Date Signed	Seasons Played	Apps	Subs	Gls
Queens Park Rgrs		07.41	46	5	-	0
Bournemouth	Tr	05.47	47	1	-	0
Leyton Orient	Yeovil T	07.50	50-56	222	-	12

BLOCHEL Jozef (Joe) Edward
Chalfont St Giles, 3 March, 1962 (F)

League Club	Source	Date Signed	Seasons Played	Apps	Subs	Gls
Southampton	App	03.80				
Wimbledon	L	01.82	81	6	0	1

BLOCK Michael (Mike) John
Ipswich, 28 January, 1940 EYth (W)

League Club	Source	Date Signed	Seasons Played	Apps	Subs	Gls
Chelsea	Jnrs	02.57	57-61	37	-	6
Brentford	Tr	01.62	61-65	146	0	30
Watford	Tr	10.66	66	11	2	2

BLOCKLEY Jeffrey (Jeff) Paul
Leicester, 12 September, 1949 Eu23-10/FLge-1/E-1 (CD)

League Club	Source	Date Signed	Seasons Played	Apps	Subs	Gls
Coventry C	App	06.67	68-72	144	2	6
Arsenal	Tr	10.72	72-74	52	0	1
Leicester C	Tr	01.75	74-77	75	1	2
Notts Co	Tr	06.78	78-79	57	2	5

BLOMQVIST Lars **Jesper**
Tavelsjo, Sweden, 5 February, 1974 Sweden 30 (M)

League Club	Source	Date Signed	Seasons Played	Apps	Subs	Gls
Manchester U	Parma (It)	07.98	98	20	5	1
Everton	Tr	11.01	01	10	5	1
Charlton Ath	Tr	08.02	02	0	3	0

BLONDEAU Patrick
Marseille, France, 27 January, 1968 France 2 (FB)

League Club	Source	Date Signed	Seasons Played	Apps	Subs	Gls
Sheffield Wed	AS Monaco (Fr)	07.97	97	5	1	0
Watford	Marseille (Fr)	07.01	01	24	1	0

BLONDEL Frederick (Fred)
Lancaster, 31 October, 1923 Died 1989 (IF)

League Club	Source	Date Signed	Seasons Played	Apps	Subs	Gls
Bury	Morecambe	07.46	46	1	-	0

BLONDEL Jonathan
Belgium, 3 April, 1984 BeYth/Beu21-7/Be-3 (M)

League Club	Source	Date Signed	Seasons Played	Apps	Subs	Gls
Tottenham H	Royal Excelsior M (Bel)	07.02	02-03	0	2	0

BLOOD John (Jack) Foster
Nottingham, 2 October, 1914 Died 1992 (FB)

League Club	Source	Date Signed	Seasons Played	Apps	Subs	Gls
Notts Co	Johnson & Barnes	06.38	38	8	-	0
Exeter C	Tr	05.39	46-47	39	-	1

BLOOMER Brian McGregor
Cleethorpes, 3 May, 1952 (F)

League Club	Source	Date Signed	Seasons Played	Apps	Subs	Gls
Scunthorpe U	Brigg T	08.78	78	3	4	1

BLOOMER James (Jimmy)
Rutherglen, 10 April, 1926 (IF)

League Club	Source	Date Signed	Seasons Played	Apps	Subs	Gls
Hull C	Strathclyde	02.48	47	4	-	2
Grimsby T	Tr	07.49	49-54	109	-	42

BLOOMER James (Jimmy) Moore
Glasgow, 22 August, 1947 (CD)

League Club	Source	Date Signed	Seasons Played	Apps	Subs	Gls
Grimsby T	Jnrs	11.64	65-68	48	4	0

BLOOMER Matthew (Matt) Brian
Grimsby, 3 November, 1978 (CD)

League Club	Source	Date Signed	Seasons Played	Apps	Subs	Gls
Grimsby T	Jnrs	07.97	98-00	3	9	0
Hull C	Tr	07.01	01	0	3	0
Lincoln C	L	03.02	01	4	1	0
Lincoln C	Tr	12.02	02-04	48	29	3

BLOOMER Robert (Bob) Stephen
Sheffield, 21 June, 1966 (M)

League Club	Source	Date Signed	Seasons Played	Apps	Subs	Gls
Chesterfield	Jnrs	08.85	85-89	120	21	15
Bristol Rov	Tr	03.90	90-91	11	11	0
Cheltenham T	Tr	08.92	99-00	6	17	1

BLOOMFIELD Edward (Eddie) William Ashworth
Wisbech, 28 June, 1932 (IF)

League Club	Source	Date Signed	Seasons Played	Apps	Subs	Gls
Carlisle U	Wisbech Con Club	08.53	53-55	5	-	1
Southport	Tr	07.56	56	2	-	0

BLOOMFIELD James (Jimmy) Henry
North Kensington, 15 February, 1934 Died 1983 Eu23-2/FLge-1 (M)

League Club	Source	Date Signed	Seasons Played	Apps	Subs	Gls
Brentford	Walthamstow Ave	10.52	52-53	42	-	5
Arsenal	Tr	07.54	54-60	210	-	54
Birmingham C	Tr	11.60	60-63	123	-	28
Brentford	Tr	06.64	64-65	44	0	4
West Ham U	Tr	10.65	65	9	1	0
Plymouth Arg	Tr	09.66	66-67	25	0	1
Orient	Tr	03.68	67-68	43	2	3

BLOOMFIELD Matthew (Matt)
Ipswich, 8 February, 1984 EYth/Eu20 (M)

League Club	Source	Date Signed	Seasons Played	Apps	Subs	Gls
Ipswich T	YT	07.01				
Wycombe W	Tr	12.03	03-04	30	8	3

BLOOMFIELD Raymond (Ray) George
Kensington, 15 October, 1944 ESch/EYth (WH)

League Club	Source	Date Signed	Seasons Played	Apps	Subs	Gls
Arsenal	Jnrs	11.61				
Aston Villa	Tr	08.64	64-65	3	0	0

BLOOMFIELD William (Billy) George
Kensington, 25 August, 1939 Died 2003 (IF)

League Club	Source	Date Signed	Seasons Played	Apps	Subs	Gls
Brentford	Jnrs	08.56	56-57	2	-	0

BLOOR Alan
Stoke-on-Trent, 16 March, 1943 EYth (CD)

League Club	Source	Date Signed	Seasons Played	Apps	Subs	Gls
Stoke C	Jnrs	03.60	61-77	384	4	17
Port Vale	Tr	06.78	78	5	1	1

BLOOR Michael (Micky) Bennett
Wrexham, 25 March, 1949 (FB)

League Club	Source	Date Signed	Seasons Played	Apps	Subs	Gls
Stoke C	Newport (Shropshire)	04.67				
Lincoln C	Tr	05.71	71-72	71	2	0
Darlington	Tr	08.73	73	7	0	0

BLOOR Robert
Stoke-on-Trent, 8 July, 1932 (WH)

League Club	Source	Date Signed	Seasons Played	Apps	Subs	Gls
Crewe Alex		01.54	53-54	26	-	1

BLORE Reginald (Reg)
Sesswick, 18 March, 1942 Wu23-4 (W)

League Club	Source	Date Signed	Seasons Played	Apps	Subs	Gls
Liverpool	Jnrs	05.59	59	1	-	0
Southport	Tr	07.60	60-63	139	-	55
Blackburn Rov	Tr	11.63	63-65	11	0	0
Oldham Ath	Tr	12.65	65-69	182	5	20

BLOSS Philip (Phil) Kenneth
Colchester, 16 January, 1953 (M)

League Club	Source	Date Signed	Seasons Played	Apps	Subs	Gls
Colchester U	App	01.71	70-72	32	2	2

BLOTT John Paul
Redcar, 26 February, 1965 (G)

League Club	Source	Date Signed	Seasons Played	Apps	Subs	Gls
Manchester C	Jnrs	09.82				
Carlisle U	Scunthorpe U (N/C)	11.84	84	2	0	0
Newport Co	Mansfield T (N/C)	03.87	86	1	0	0

BLOUNT Mark
Derby, 5 January, 1974 (CD)

League Club	Source	Date Signed	Seasons Played	Apps	Subs	Gls
Sheffield U	Gresley Rov	02.94	94-95	11	2	0
Peterborough U	Tr	03.96	95	4	1	0

BLOWMAN Peter
Thornaby, 12 December, 1949 (F)

League Club	Source	Date Signed	Seasons Played	Apps	Subs	Gls
Hartlepools U	Billingham Synthonia	11.67	67-69	57	9	15

League Club	Source	Date Signed	Seasons Played	Career Record Apps	Subs	Gls
BLOXHAM James Alexander (Alec)						
New Houghton, 2 July, 1920 Died 1982						(W)
Hull C	Ollerton Colliery	10.47	47-49	33	-	2
BLUCK David (Dave)						
India, 31 January, 1930						(WH)
Aldershot (Am)		08.51	51	1	-	0
BLUE Archibald (Archie)						
Glasgow, 8 April, 1940						(CF)
Exeter C	Heart of Midlothian	07.61	61	34	-	6
Carlisle U	Tr	07.62	62	2	-	1
BLUNDELL Alan						
Birkenhead, 18 August, 1947						(W)
Tranmere Rov	App	08.65	65-66	3	0	0
BLUNDELL Christopher (Chris) Kenneth						
Billinge, 7 December, 1969						(CD)
Oldham Ath	YT	07.88	87-88	2	1	0
Rochdale	Tr	09.90	90	10	4	0
BLUNDELL Gregg Steven						
Liverpool, 3 October, 1977						(F)
Tranmere Rov	YT	07.96				
Doncaster Rov	Northwich Vic	03.03	03-04	74	11	27
BLUNSTONE Frank						
Crewe, 17 October, 1934 EYth/Eu23-5/FLge-2/E-5						(W)
Crewe Alex	Jnrs	01.52	51-52	47	-	12
Chelsea	Tr	03.53	52-63	317	-	47
BLUNT David						
Goldthorpe, 29 April, 1949						(F)
Bradford PA (Am)		03.68	67	2	0	0
BLUNT Edwin (Eddie)						
Tunstall, 21 May, 1918 Died 1993						(WH)
Northampton T	Lichfield T	05.37	37-48	87	-	2
Accrington St	Tr	07.49	49	9	-	1
BLUNT Jason John						
Penzance, 16 August, 1977						(M)
Leeds U	YT	01.95	95-96	2	2	0
Blackpool	Tr	07.98	98	1	1	0
BLY Terence (Terry) Geoffrey						
Fincham, 22 October, 1935						(CF)
Norwich C	Bury T	08.56	56-59	57	-	31
Peterborough U	Tr	06.60	60-61	88	-	81
Coventry C	Tr	07.62	62	32	-	25
Notts Co	Tr	08.63	63-64	29	-	4
BLY William (Billy)						
Newcastle, 15 May, 1920 Died 1982						(G)
Hull C	Walker Celtic	08.37	38-59	403	-	0
BLYTH James (Jim) Anton						
Perth, 2 February, 1955 S-2						(G)
Preston NE	App	10.72	71	1	0	0
Coventry C	Tr	10.72	75-81	151	0	0
Hereford U	L	03.75	74	7	0	0
Birmingham C	Tr	08.82	82	14	0	0
BLYTH John (Ian) William						
Edinburgh, 26 May, 1947						(M)
Rotherham U	Heart of Midlothian	01.67				
Halifax T	Tr	05.67	66-67	5	0	0
BLYTH Melvyn (Mel) Bernard						
Norwich, 28 July, 1944						(CD)
Scunthorpe U	Yarmouth T	11.67	67	27	0	3
Crystal Palace	Tr	07.68	68-74	213	3	9
Southampton	Tr	09.74	74-76	104	1	6
Crystal Palace	L	11.77	77	6	0	0
Millwall	Margate	11.78	78-80	75	0	0
BLYTHE John David						
Huddersfield, 21 July, 1947						(F)
Hartlepool	Crook T	01.70	69	1	1	0
BLYTHE John Alfred						
Darlington, 31 January, 1924						(CD)
Darlington		06.46	46-48	17	-	0
BOAG James (Jimmy)						
Blairhall, 12 November, 1937						(G)
Exeter C	Bath C	10.62	62	2	-	0
BOAM Stuart William						
Kirkby-in-Ashfield, 28 January, 1948						(CD)
Mansfield T	Kirkby BC	07.66	66-70	175	0	3

League Club	Source	Date Signed	Seasons Played	Career Record Apps	Subs	Gls
Middlesbrough	Tr	06.71	71-78	322	0	14
Newcastle U	Tr	08.79	79-80	69	0	1
Mansfield T	Tr	07.81	81-82	11	4	1
Hartlepool U	Tr	03.83	82	1	0	0
BOA MORTE Luis						
Lisbon, Portugal, 4 August, 1977 PorYth/PorU21-28/Por-21						(F)
Arsenal	Sporting Lisbon (Por)	06.97	97-99	6	19	0
Southampton	Tr	08.99	99	6	8	1
Fulham	Tr	07.00	00-04	122	33	38
BOARDLEY Stuart James						
Ipswich, 14 February, 1985						(M)
Torquay U	Ipswich T (Sch)	09.04	04	2	4	0
BOARDMAN Craig George						
Barnsley, 30 November, 1970						(CD)
Nottingham F	YT	05.89				
Peterborough U	Tr	08.93				
Scarborough	Halifax T	08.95	95	6	3	0
BOARDMAN George						
Glasgow, 14 August, 1943 SAmat						(M)
Shrewsbury T	Queen's Park	06.63	63-68	172	4	48
Barnsley	Tr	06.69	69-72	123	3	14
BOARDMAN Paul						
Tottenham, 6 November, 1967						(F)
Plymouth Arg	Knowsley U	08.92	92-93	2	1	1
BOATENG George						
Nkawkaw, Ghana, 5 September, 1975 Hou21-18/Ho-2						(M)
Coventry C	Feyenoord (Holl)	12.97	97-98	43	4	5
Aston Villa	Tr	07.99	99-01	96	7	4
Middlesbrough	Tr	08.02	02-04	88	0	3
BOBIC Fredi						
Maribor, Slovenia, 30 October, 1971 Germany 19						(F)
Bolton W (L)	Borussia Dortmund (Ger)	01.02	01	14	2	4
BOCANEGRA Carlos						
Alta Loma, California, USA, 25 May, 1979 USA 36						(FB)
Fulham	Chicago (USA)	01.04	03-04	41	2	1
BOCHENSKI Simon						
Worksop, 6 December, 1975						(F)
Barnsley	YT	07.94	95	0	1	0
Scarborough	Tr	08.98	96	5	14	1
BODAK Peter John						
Birmingham, 12 August, 1961						(M)
Coventry C	App	05.79	80-81	30	2	5
Manchester U	Tr	08.82				
Manchester C	Tr	12.82	82	12	2	1
Crewe Alex	Royal Antwerp (Bel)	12.86	86-87	49	4	7
Swansea C	Tr	03.88	87-88	25	6	4
Walsall	Happy Valley (HK)	08.90	90	3	1	1
BODEL Andrew (Andy) Cunningham						
Clydebank, 12 February, 1957						(CD)
Oxford U	App	02.75	75-79	128	0	11
BODELL Norman						
Manchester, 29 January, 1938						(CD)
Rochdale		09.56	58-62	79	-	1
Crewe Alex	Tr	05.63	63-66	108	1	2
Halifax T	Tr	10.66	66-67	36	0	0
BODEN Christopher (Chris) Desmond						
Wolverhampton, 13 October, 1973						(FB)
Aston Villa	YT	12.91	94	0	1	0
Barnsley	L	10.93	93	4	0	0
Derby Co	Tr	03.95	94-95	8	2	0
Shrewsbury T	L	01.96	95	5	0	0
BODEN John (Jackie) Gilbert						
Cleethorpes, 4 October, 1926						(CF)
Lincoln C	Skegness T	04.50	49-50	3	-	2
BODEN Kenneth (Ken)						
Thrybergh, 5 July, 1950						(M)
Doncaster Rov	Bridlington T	03.77	76	1	0	0
BODIN Paul John						
Cardiff, 13 September, 1964 WYth/Wu21-1/W-23						(FB)
Newport Co	Chelsea (Jnrs)	01.82				
Cardiff C	Tr	08.82	82-84	68	7	4
Newport Co	Bath C	01.88	87	6	0	1
Swindon T	Tr	03.88	87-90	87	6	9
Crystal Palace	Tr	03.91	90-91	8	1	0
Newcastle U	L	12.91	91	6	0	0

League Club	Source	Date Signed	Seasons Played	Apps	Subs	Gls
Swindon T	Tr	01.92	91-95	140	6	28
Reading	Tr	06.96	96-97	40	1	1
Wycombe W	L	09.97	97	5	0	0

BODKIN Matthew (Matt) James
Chatham, 23 November, 1983 (F)

League Club	Source	Date Signed	Seasons Played	Apps	Subs	Gls
Nottingham F	Sch	01.03				
Gillingham	Tr	08.04	04	0	2	0

BODLE Harold
Adwick-le-Street, 4 October, 1920 Died 2005 (IF)

League Club	Source	Date Signed	Seasons Played	Apps	Subs	Gls
Rotherham U	Ridgehill Ath	05.38	38	9	-	0
Birmingham	Tr	12.38	38-48	94	-	32
Bury	Tr	03.49	48-51	119	-	40
Stockport Co	Tr	10.52	52	29	-	6
Accrington St	Tr	08.53	53-56	94	-	13

BODLEY Michael (Mick) John
Hayes, 14 September, 1967 (CD)

League Club	Source	Date Signed	Seasons Played	Apps	Subs	Gls
Chelsea	App	09.85	87	6	0	1
Northampton T	Tr	01.89	88	20	0	0
Barnet	Tr	10.89	91-92	69	0	3
Southend U	Tr	07.93	93-95	66	1	2
Gillingham	L	11.94	94	6	1	0
Birmingham C	L	01.95	94	3	0	0
Peterborough U	Tr	08.96	96-98	86	0	1

BOERE Jeroen Willem
Arnhem, Holland, 18 November, 1967 (F)

League Club	Source	Date Signed	Seasons Played	Apps	Subs	Gls
West Ham U	Go Ahead Eagles (Holl)	09.93	93-95	15	10	6
Portsmouth	L	03.94	93	4	1	0
West Bromwich A	L	09.94	94	5	0	0
Crystal Palace	Tr	09.95	95	0	8	1
Southend U	Tr	03.96	95-97	61	12	25

BOERSMA Philip (Phil)
Kirkby, 24 September, 1949 (M)

League Club	Source	Date Signed	Seasons Played	Apps	Subs	Gls
Liverpool	Jnrs	09.68	69-75	73	9	17
Wrexham	L	03.70	69	4	3	0
Middlesbrough	Tr	12.75	75-76	41	6	3
Luton T	Tr	08.77	77-78	35	1	8
Swansea C	Tr	09.78	78	15	3	1

BOERTIEN Paul
Haltwhistle, 21 January, 1979 (FB)

League Club	Source	Date Signed	Seasons Played	Apps	Subs	Gls
Carlisle U	YT	05.97	97-98	16	1	1
Derby Co	Tr	03.99	98-03	82	21	2
Crewe Alex	L	02.00	99	2	0	0
Notts Co	L	01.04	03	5	0	0

BOGAN Thomas (Tommy)
Glasgow, 18 May, 1920 Died 1993 SLge-1/SWar-1 (IF)

League Club	Source	Date Signed	Seasons Played	Apps	Subs	Gls
Preston NE	Glasgow Celtic	10.48	48	11	-	0
Manchester U	Tr	08.49	49-50	29	-	7
Southampton	Aberdeen	12.51	51-52	8	-	2
Blackburn Rov	Tr	08.53	53	1	-	0

BOGARDE Winston
Rotterdam, Holland, 22 October, 1970 Holland 20 (CD)

League Club	Source	Date Signed	Seasons Played	Apps	Subs	Gls
Chelsea	Barcelona (Sp)	09.00	00	2	7	0

BOGIE Ian
Newcastle, 6 December, 1967 ESch (M)

League Club	Source	Date Signed	Seasons Played	Apps	Subs	Gls
Newcastle U	App	12.85	86-88	7	7	0
Preston NE	Tr	02.89	88-90	67	12	12
Millwall	Tr	08.91	91-93	44	7	1
Leyton Orient	Tr	10.93	93-94	62	3	5
Port Vale	Tr	03.95	94-99	133	21	9
Kidderminster Hrs	Tr	08.00	00	14	7	1

BOGIE Malcolm Fisher McKenzie
Edinburgh, 26 December, 1939 SSch (IF)

League Club	Source	Date Signed	Seasons Played	Apps	Subs	Gls
Grimsby T	Hibernian	07.63	63	1	-	0
Aldershot	Tr	07.64	64	2	-	1

BOHINEN Lars
Vadso, Norway, 8 September, 1969 NoYth/Nou21/No-49 (M)

League Club	Source	Date Signed	Seasons Played	Apps	Subs	Gls
Nottingham F	Young Boys Berne (Swi)	11.93	93-95	59	5	7
Blackburn Rov	Tr	10.95	95-97	40	18	7
Derby Co	Tr	03.98	97-00	47	9	1

BOJIC Pedrag (Pedj)
Sydney, Australia, 9 April, 1984 AuYth (CD)

League Club	Source	Date Signed	Seasons Played	Apps	Subs	Gls
Northampton T	Sydney Olympic (Aus)	08.04	04	25	11	0

BOKSIC Alen
Makarska, Hercegovina, 21 January, 1970 Croatia 52 (F)

League Club	Source	Date Signed	Seasons Played	Apps	Subs	Gls
Middlesbrough	SS Lazio (It)	08.00	00-02	59	9	22

BOLAM Thomas (Tom) Edward
Newcastle, 8 July, 1924 (WH)

League Club	Source	Date Signed	Seasons Played	Apps	Subs	Gls
Barrow		08.50	50-51	35	-	0

BOLAND William (Willie) John
Ennis, 6 August, 1975 IRSch/IRYth/IRu21-11/IRB-1 (M)

League Club	Source	Date Signed	Seasons Played	Apps	Subs	Gls
Coventry C	Jnrs	11.92	92-97	43	20	0
Cardiff C	Tr	06.99	99-04	176	18	3

BOLDER Adam Peter
Hull, 25 October, 1980 (M)

League Club	Source	Date Signed	Seasons Played	Apps	Subs	Gls
Hull C	YT	07.99	98-99	18	2	0
Derby Co	Tr	04.00	00-04	75	43	9

BOLDER Christopher (Chris) James
Hull, 19 August, 1982 (M)

League Club	Source	Date Signed	Seasons Played	Apps	Subs	Gls
Grimsby T	Hull C (YT)	07.01	02-03	13	6	0

BOLDER Robert (Bob) John
Dover, 2 October, 1958 (G)

League Club	Source	Date Signed	Seasons Played	Apps	Subs	Gls
Sheffield Wed	Dover	03.77	77-82	196	0	0
Liverpool	Tr	08.83				
Sunderland	Tr	09.85	85	22	0	0
Charlton Ath	Tr	08.86	86-92	249	0	0

BOLESAN Mirko
Genoa, Italy, 6 May, 1975 (CD)

League Club	Source	Date Signed	Seasons Played	Apps	Subs	Gls
Cardiff C	Sestrese (It)	10.95	95	0	1	0

BOLI Roger Zokou
Adjame, Ivory Coast, 29 June, 1965 (F)

League Club	Source	Date Signed	Seasons Played	Apps	Subs	Gls
Walsall	RC Lens (Fr)	08.97	97	41	0	12
Bournemouth	Dundee U	10.98	98	5	1	0

BOLIMA Cedric
Kinshasa, DR Congo, 26 September, 1979 (F)

League Club	Source	Date Signed	Seasons Played	Apps	Subs	Gls
Rotherham U	RC Lens (Fr)	10.00	00	0	1	0

BOLLAND Gordon Edward
Boston, 12 August, 1943 (M)

League Club	Source	Date Signed	Seasons Played	Apps	Subs	Gls
Chelsea	Jnrs	08.60	61	2	-	0
Leyton Orient	Tr	03.62	61-63	63	-	19
Norwich C	Tr	03.64	63-67	104	1	29
Charlton Ath	Tr	11.67	67-68	9	2	2
Millwall	Tr	10.68	68-74	239	5	62

BOLLAND Paul Graham
Bradford, 23 December, 1979 (M)

League Club	Source	Date Signed	Seasons Played	Apps	Subs	Gls
Bradford C	YT	03.98	97-98	4	8	0
Notts Co	Tr	01.99	98-04	153	19	6

BOLLAND Philip (Phil) Christopher
Liverpool, 26 August, 1976 (CD)

League Club	Source	Date Signed	Seasons Played	Apps	Subs	Gls
Oxford U	Southport	07.01	01	20	0	1
Chester C	Tr	03.02	04	42	0	1

BOLLANDS John Frederick
Middlesbrough, 11 July, 1935 (G)

League Club	Source	Date Signed	Seasons Played	Apps	Subs	Gls
Oldham Ath	South Bank	05.53	54-55	23	-	0
Sunderland	Tr	03.56	55-59	61	-	0
Bolton W	Tr	02.60	59	13	-	0
Oldham Ath	Tr	09.61	61-65	131	0	0

BOLT Daniel (Danny) Anthony
Wandsworth, 5 February, 1976 (M)

League Club	Source	Date Signed	Seasons Played	Apps	Subs	Gls
Fulham	YT	07.94	94-95	9	4	2

BOLTON Anthony (Tony) Gordon
Newport, 15 January, 1968 (W)

League Club	Source	Date Signed	Seasons Played	Apps	Subs	Gls
Charlton Ath	Jnrs	01.85				
Newport Co	Tr	08.86	86	6	2	0

BOLTON Ian Robert
Leicester, 13 July, 1953 (CD)

League Club	Source	Date Signed	Seasons Played	Apps	Subs	Gls
Notts Co	Birmingham C (App)	03.72	71-76	61	9	4
Lincoln C	L	08.76	76	1	0	0
Watford	Tr	08.77	77-83	233	1	28
Brentford	Tr	12.83	83	14	0	1

BOLTON John (Jack) McCaig
Lesmahagow, 26 October, 1941 (CD)

League Club	Source	Date Signed	Seasons Played	Apps	Subs	Gls
Ipswich T	Raith Rov	07.63	63-65	69	0	2

BOLTON Joseph (Joe)
Birtley, 2 February, 1955 (FB)

League Club	Source	Date Signed	Seasons Played	Apps	Subs	Gls
Sunderland	App	02.72	71-80	264	9	11
Middlesbrough	Tr	07.81	81-82	59	0	1
Sheffield U	Tr	08.83	83-85	109	0	3

BOLTON Lyall (Laurie)
Gateshead, 11 July, 1932 (WH)

League Club	Source	Date Signed	Seasons Played	Apps	Subs	Gls
Sunderland	Reyrolle Jnrs	08.50	55-56	3	-	0

BOLTON Nigel Alan
Bishop Auckland, 14 January, 1975 (F)

League Club	Source	Date Signed	Seasons Played	Apps	Subs	Gls
Darlington	Shildon	08.94	94	1	1	0

BOLTON Ronald (Danny)
Rotherham, 1 September, 1921 Died 1997 (G)

League Club	Source	Date Signed	Seasons Played	Apps	Subs	Gls
Bolton W		05.39				
Rotherham U	Owen & Dyson	06.48	48-54	151	-	0

BOLTON Ronald (Ronnie)
Golborne, 21 January, 1938 (M)

League Club	Source	Date Signed	Seasons Played	Apps	Subs	Gls
Bournemouth	Crompton Rec	04.58	58-65	199	0	31
Ipswich T	Tr	10.65	65-67	21	1	0
Bournemouth	Tr	09.67	67-68	61	4	17

BONALAIR Thierry
Paris, France, 14 June, 1966 Fru21 (FB)

League Club	Source	Date Signed	Seasons Played	Apps	Subs	Gls
Nottingham F	Neuchatel Xamax (Swi)	07.97	97-99	58	13	5

BOND Anthony (Tony)
Preston, 27 December, 1913 Died 1993 (W)

League Club	Source	Date Signed	Seasons Played	Apps	Subs	Gls
Blackburn Rov	Dick, Kerr's XI	04.32				
Wolverhampton W	Chorley	11.36				
Torquay U	Tr	06.37	37	15	-	0
Southport	Leyland Motors	08.45				
Accrington St	Tr	05.46	46	29	-	4

BOND Dennis Joseph Thomas
Walthamstow, 17 March, 1947 ESch/EYth (M)

League Club	Source	Date Signed	Seasons Played	Apps	Subs	Gls
Watford	App	03.64	64-66	93	0	17
Tottenham H	Tr	03.67	66-70	20	3	1
Charlton Ath	Tr	10.70	70-72	70	5	3
Watford	Tr	02.73	72-77	178	1	21

BOND James **Ernest (Ernie)**
Preston, 4 May, 1929 (W)

League Club	Source	Date Signed	Seasons Played	Apps	Subs	Gls
Manchester U	Leyland Motors	12.50	51-52	20	-	4
Carlisle U	Tr	09.52	52-58	192	-	24

BOND Graham Charles
Torquay, 30 December, 1932 Died 1998 (IF)

League Club	Source	Date Signed	Seasons Played	Apps	Subs	Gls
Torquay U	Hele Spurs	09.51	53-60	128	-	46
Exeter C	Tr	10.60	60	10	-	4
Torquay U	Weymouth	10.61	61	5	-	1

BOND John
Dedham, 17 December, 1932 FLge-2 (FB)

League Club	Source	Date Signed	Seasons Played	Apps	Subs	Gls
West Ham U	Colchester Casuals	03.50	51-64	381	-	32
Torquay U	Tr	01.66	65-68	129	1	12

BOND Kain
Torquay, 19 June, 1985 (F)

League Club	Source	Date Signed	Seasons Played	Apps	Subs	Gls
Torquay U	Sch	07.03	02-04	0	3	0

BOND Kevin John
West Ham, 22 June, 1957 (CD)

League Club	Source	Date Signed	Seasons Played	Apps	Subs	Gls
Norwich C	Bournemouth (App)	07.74	75-80	137	5	12
Manchester C	Seattle (USA)	09.81	81-84	108	2	11
Southampton	Tr	09.84	84-87	139	1	6
Bournemouth	Tr	08.88	88-91	121	5	4
Exeter C	Tr	08.92	92-93	18	1	0

BOND Leonard (Len) Allan
Ilminster, 12 February, 1954 (G)

League Club	Source	Date Signed	Seasons Played	Apps	Subs	Gls
Bristol C	App	09.71	70-76	30	0	0
Exeter C	L	11.74	74	30	0	0
Torquay U	L	10.75	75	3	0	0
Scunthorpe U	L	12.75	75	8	0	0
Colchester U	L	01.76	75	3	0	0
Brentford	Tr	08.77	77-79	122	0	0
Exeter C	St Louis (USA)	10.80	80-83	138	0	0

BOND Richard (Richie)
Blyth, 27 October, 1965 (F)

League Club	Source	Date Signed	Seasons Played	Apps	Subs	Gls
Blackpool	Blyth Spartans	12.91	92	0	1	0

BONDS William (Billy) Arthur
Woolwich, 17 September, 1946 Eu23-2 (CD)

League Club	Source	Date Signed	Seasons Played	Apps	Subs	Gls
Charlton Ath	App	09.64	64-66	95	0	1
West Ham U	Tr	05.67	67-87	655	8	48

BONE James (Jim)
Bridge of Allan, 22 September, 1949 Su23-3/S-2 (F)

League Club	Source	Date Signed	Seasons Played	Apps	Subs	Gls
Norwich C	Partic Thistle	02.72	71-72	39	0	9
Sheffield U	Tr	02.73	72-73	30	1	9

BONE John
Hartlepool, 19 December, 1930 Died 2002 (CD)

League Club	Source	Date Signed	Seasons Played	Apps	Subs	Gls
Sunderland	Wingate	01.51	54-56	11	-	0

BONER David
South Queensferry, 12 October, 1941 SSch (W)

League Club	Source	Date Signed	Seasons Played	Apps	Subs	Gls
Everton	Jnrs	10.58				
Mansfield T	Raith Rov	07.63	63	12	-	1

BONETTI Ivano
Brescia, Italy, 1 August, 1964 Italy int (M)

League Club	Source	Date Signed	Seasons Played	Apps	Subs	Gls
Grimsby T	Torino (It)	09.95	95	19	0	3
Tranmere Rov	Tr	08.96	96	9	4	1
Crystal Palace	Bologna (It)	10.97	97	0	2	0

BONETTI Peter Philip
Putney, 27 September, 1941 Eu23-12/FLge-4/E-7 (G)

League Club	Source	Date Signed	Seasons Played	Apps	Subs	Gls
Chelsea	Jnrs	05.59	59-78	600	0	0

BONNAR Patrick (Paddy)
Ballymena, 27 November, 1920 NIRL-1/IrLge-2/IWar-2 (W)

League Club	Source	Date Signed	Seasons Played	Apps	Subs	Gls
Barnsley	Belfast Celtic	08.49	49	5	-	1
Aldershot	Tr	06.50	50-52	63	-	19

BONNELL Arnold
Barnsley, 23 March, 1921 (FB)

League Club	Source	Date Signed	Seasons Played	Apps	Subs	Gls
Barnsley	Jnrs	04.38	46-47	7	-	0
Rochdale	Tr	07.48	48	5	-	0

BONNER Bernard
Motherwell, 22 July, 1927 (CF)

League Club	Source	Date Signed	Seasons Played	Apps	Subs	Gls
Wrexham	Airdrie	02.52	51	1	-	0

BONNER Mark
Ormskirk, 7 June, 1974 (M)

League Club	Source	Date Signed	Seasons Played	Apps	Subs	Gls
Blackpool	YT	06.92	91-97	156	22	14
Cardiff C	Tr	07.98	98-03	113	30	2
Hull C	L	01.99	98	1	0	1
Oldham Ath	Tr	03.04	03-04	21	5	0

BONNISSEL Jerome
Montpellier, France, 16 April, 1973 (FB)

League Club	Source	Date Signed	Seasons Played	Apps	Subs	Gls
Fulham	Marseille (Fr)	08.03	03	16	0	0

BONNOT Alexandre (Alex)
Paris, France, 31 July, 1973 (M)

League Club	Source	Date Signed	Seasons Played	Apps	Subs	Gls
Watford	SCO Angiers (Fr)	11.98	98-99	8	8	0
Queens Park Rgrs	Tr	08.01	01	17	5	1

BONNYMAN Philip (Phil)
Glasgow, 6 February, 1954 (M)

League Club	Source	Date Signed	Seasons Played	Apps	Subs	Gls
Carlisle U	Hamilton Academical	03.76	75-79	149	3	26
Chesterfield	Tr	03.80	79-81	98	1	25
Grimsby T	Tr	08.82	82-86	146	5	15
Stoke C	L	03.86	85	7	0	0
Darlington	Tr	07.87	87-88	49	1	5

BONSON Joseph (Joe)
Barnsley, 19 June, 1936 Died 1991 (CF)

League Club	Source	Date Signed	Seasons Played	Apps	Subs	Gls
Wolverhampton W	Jnrs	07.53	56	10	-	4
Cardiff C	Tr	11.57	57-59	72	-	36
Scunthorpe U	Tr	06.60	60-61	52	-	11
Doncaster Rov	Tr	02.62	61	14	-	4
Newport Co	Tr	06.62	62-63	83	-	47
Brentford	Tr	06.64	64-65	35	0	13
Lincoln C	Tr	01.66	65-66	46	1	16

BONVIN Pablo Facundo
Concepcion, Argentina, 15 April, 1981 (F)

League Club	Source	Date Signed	Seasons Played	Apps	Subs	Gls
Sheffield Wed (L)	Boca Juniors (Arg)	08.01	01	7	16	4

BOOGERS Marco
Dordrecht, Holland, 12 January, 1967 (F)

League Club	Source	Date Signed	Seasons Played	Apps	Subs	Gls
West Ham U	Sparta Rotterdam (Holl)	07.95	95	0	4	0

BOOK Anthony (Tony) Keith
Bath, 4 September, 1934 (FB)

League Club	Source	Date Signed	Seasons Played	Apps	Subs	Gls
Plymouth Arg	Bath C	08.64	64-65	81	0	3
Manchester C	Tr	07.66	66-73	242	2	4

BOOK Kim Alistair
Bath, 12 February, 1946 (G)

League Club	Source	Date Signed	Seasons Played	Apps	Subs	Gls
Bournemouth	Frome T	07.67	67-68	2	0	0
Northampton T	Tr	10.69	69-71	78	0	0
Mansfield T	L	09.71	71	4	0	0
Doncaster Rov	Tr	12.71	71-73	84	0	0

BOOK Steven (Steve) Kim
Bournemouth, 7 July, 1969 ESemiPro-3 (G)

League Club	Source	Date Signed	Seasons Played	Apps	Subs	Gls
Cheltenham T	Forest Green Rov	07.97	99-03	171	1	0
Swindon T	Tr	08.04	04	1	1	0

BOOKER Kenneth (Ken)
Sheffield, 3 March, 1918 Died 1997 (CD)

League Club	Source	Date Signed	Seasons Played	Apps	Subs	Gls
Chesterfield	Dronfield T	04.36	38-51	183	-	4
Shrewsbury T	Tr	07.52	52	9	-	0

BOOKER Michael (Mike)
Barnsley, 22 October, 1947 ESch (FB)

League Club	Source	Date Signed	Seasons Played	Apps	Subs	Gls
Barnsley	App	10.65	66	0	2	0
Bradford PA	Tr	06.68	68	11	2	0

BOOKER Robert (Bob)
Watford, 25 January, 1958 (M)

League Club	Source	Date Signed	Seasons Played	Apps	Subs	Gls
Brentford	Bedmond Social	10.78	78-88	207	44	42
Sheffield U	Tr	11.88	88-91	91	18	13
Brentford	Tr	11.91	91-92	15	4	2

BOOKER Trevor Christopher
Lambeth, 26 February, 1969 (F)

League Club	Source	Date Signed	Seasons Played	Apps	Subs	Gls
Millwall	Jnrs	07.86	86	1	2	0

BOORN Alan
Folkestone, 11 April, 1953 EYth (M)

League Club	Source	Date Signed	Seasons Played	Apps	Subs	Gls
Brighton & Hove A	Coventry C (Am)	08.71	72	2	0	0

BOOT Edmund (Eddie)
Laughton Common, 13 October, 1915 Died 1999 (WH)

League Club	Source	Date Signed	Seasons Played	Apps	Subs	Gls
Sheffield U	Denaby U	10.35	35-36	41	-	0
Huddersfield T	Tr	03.37	36-51	305	-	5

BOOT Michael (Mickey) Colin
Leicester, 17 December, 1947 ESch (WH)

League Club	Source	Date Signed	Seasons Played	Apps	Subs	Gls
Arsenal	App	12.64	66	3	1	2

BOOTH Andrew (Andy) David
Huddersfield, 6 December, 1973 Eu21-3 (F)

League Club	Source	Date Signed	Seasons Played	Apps	Subs	Gls
Huddersfield T	YT	07.92	91-95	109	14	54
Sheffield Wed	Tr	07.96	96-00	124	9	28
Tottenham H	L	01.01	00	3	1	0
Huddersfield T	Tr	03.01	00-04	131	12	43

BOOTH Anthony (Tony) John
Biggin Hill, 20 June, 1961 (M)

League Club	Source	Date Signed	Seasons Played	Apps	Subs	Gls
Charlton Ath	Jnrs	06.78	78-79	2	6	0

BOOTH Colin
Manchester, 30 December, 1934 Eu23-1 (IF)

League Club	Source	Date Signed	Seasons Played	Apps	Subs	Gls
Wolverhampton W	Jnrs	01.52	54-59	78	-	26
Nottingham F	Tr	10.59	59-61	87	-	39
Doncaster Rov	Tr	08.62	62-63	88	-	57
Oxford U	Tr	07.64	64-65	48	0	23

BOOTH David
Kexborough, 2 October, 1948 (FB)

League Club	Source	Date Signed	Seasons Played	Apps	Subs	Gls
Barnsley	Higham Rov	05.67	68-71	161	3	8
Grimsby T	Tr	06.72	72-77	199	1	7

BOOTH David Christopher
Wilmslow, 25 October, 1962 (M)

League Club	Source	Date Signed	Seasons Played	Apps	Subs	Gls
Stockport Co	Jnrs	04.80	79-80	20	8	4

BOOTH Dennis
Stanley Common, 9 April, 1949 (M)

League Club	Source	Date Signed	Seasons Played	Apps	Subs	Gls
Charlton Ath	App	04.66	66-70	67	10	5
Blackpool	Tr	07.71	71	12	0	0
Southend U	Tr	03.72	71-73	77	1	1
Lincoln C	Tr	02.74	73-77	162	0	9
Watford	Tr	10.77	77-79	97	3	2
Hull C	Tr	05.80	80-84	121	2	2

BOOTH Grenville Vincent
Chester, 2 April, 1925 Died 1991 (WH)

League Club	Source	Date Signed	Seasons Played	Apps	Subs	Gls
Chester	Jnrs	08.48	48	8	-	0

BOOTH Kenneth (Ken) Kershaw
Blackpool, 22 November, 1934 (IF)

League Club	Source	Date Signed	Seasons Played	Apps	Subs	Gls
Blackpool	St Peter's YC	01.52	56	1	-	1
Bradford PA	Tr	05.57	57-58	45	-	14
Workington	Tr	06.59	59	30	-	13
Southport	Tr	07.60	60	26	-	7

BOOTH Paul
Bolton, 7 December, 1965 ESch (CD)

League Club	Source	Date Signed	Seasons Played	Apps	Subs	Gls
Bolton W	App	12.83	84	1	0	0
Crewe Alex	Tr	07.85	85	23	4	0

BOOTH Raymond (Ray)
Wrexham, 5 December, 1949 (W)

League Club	Source	Date Signed	Seasons Played	Apps	Subs	Gls
Wrexham	Jnrs	10.67	66-68	5	0	0

BOOTH Robert (Robbie) Paul
Liverpool, 30 December, 1985 (M)

League Club	Source	Date Signed	Seasons Played	Apps	Subs	Gls
Chester C	Everton (Sch)	05.05	04	7	4	1

BOOTH Samuel (Sam) Stewart
Shotts, 20 April, 1926 (WH)

League Club	Source	Date Signed	Seasons Played	Apps	Subs	Gls
Exeter C	Derry C	08.51	51-53	62	-	0
Bradford C	Tr	07.54	54	15	-	0

BOOTH William **Samuel (Sam)**
Hove, 7 July, 1920 Died 1990 (CD)

League Club	Source	Date Signed	Seasons Played	Apps	Subs	Gls
Port Vale	Brighton & Hove A (Am)	02.39	38	9	-	0
Cardiff C	Tr	05.39				
Brighton & Hove A	Tr	08.47	47-48	28	-	6

BOOTH Thomas (Tommy) Anthony
Middleton, 9 November, 1949 Eu23-4 (CD)

League Club	Source	Date Signed	Seasons Played	Apps	Subs	Gls
Manchester C	Jnrs	08.67	68-81	380	2	25
Preston NE	Tr	10.81	81-84	84	0	2

BOOTH Wilfred (Wilf)
Mapplewell, 26 December, 1918 (CF)

League Club	Source	Date Signed	Seasons Played	Apps	Subs	Gls
Halifax T	Wombwell Ath	12.47	47	6	-	2

BOOTHMAN James (Jerry)
Great Harwood, 2 December, 1920 Died 1980 (FB)

League Club	Source	Date Signed	Seasons Played	Apps	Subs	Gls
Oldham Ath		01.46	46-47	44	-	0

BOOTHROYD Adrian (Adie) Neil
Bradford, 8 February, 1971 (FB)

League Club	Source	Date Signed	Seasons Played	Apps	Subs	Gls
Huddersfield T	YT	07.89	89	9	1	0
Bristol Rov	Tr	06.90	90-91	10	6	0
Mansfield T	Heart of Midlothian	12.93	93-95	99	3	3
Peterborough U	Tr	06.96	96	24	2	1

BOOTHWAY John (Jack)
Manchester, 4 February, 1919 Died 1979 (CF)

League Club	Source	Date Signed	Seasons Played	Apps	Subs	Gls
Manchester C		07.41				
Crewe Alex	Tr	07.44	46	12	-	5
Wrexham	Tr	10.46	46-49	95	-	55

BOOTLE William
Ashton-under-Lyne, 9 January, 1926 (W)

League Club	Source	Date Signed	Seasons Played	Apps	Subs	Gls
Manchester C	Jnrs	06.43	48-49	5	-	0
Crewe Alex	Wigan Ath	03.54	53-54	14	-	4

BOOTY Justin
Colchester, 2 June, 1976 (F)

League Club	Source	Date Signed	Seasons Played	Apps	Subs	Gls
Colchester U	YT	08.94	93	0	1	0

BOOTY Martyn James
Kirby Muxloe, 30 May, 1971 (FB)

League Club	Source	Date Signed	Seasons Played	Apps	Subs	Gls
Coventry C	YT	05.89	91-93	4	1	0
Crewe Alex	Tr	10.93	93-95	95	1	5
Reading	Tr	01.96	95-98	62	2	1
Southend U	Tr	01.99	98-00	78	2	0
Chesterfield	Tr	08.01	01-02	75	3	2
Huddersfield T	Tr	08.03	03	3	1	0

BOPP Eugene
Kiev, Ukraine, 5 September, 1983 (M)

League Club	Source	Date Signed	Seasons Played	Apps	Subs	Gls
Nottingham F	YT	09.00	01-04	37	28	7

BORBOKIS Vassilis
Serres, Greece, 10 February, 1969 Greece 2 (FB)

League Club	Source	Date Signed	Seasons Played	Apps	Subs	Gls
Sheffield U	AEK Athens (Gre)	07.97	97-98	55	0	4
Derby Co	Tr	03.99	98-99	9	7	0

BORG John Carmel Adam
Salford, 22 February, 1980 (M)

League Club	Source	Date Signed	Seasons Played	Apps	Subs	Gls
Doncaster Rov	YT	•	97	1	0	0

BORLAND John Robert
Lancaster, 28 January, 1977 (M)

League Club	Source	Date Signed	Seasons Played	Apps	Subs	Gls
Burnley	YT	07.95	95	1	0	0
Scunthorpe U	Tr	08.96	96	0	2	0

BORLEY David
Newcastle, 14 April, 1983 ESch (M)

League Club	Source	Date Signed	Seasons Played	Apps	Subs	Gls
Bury	YT	07.01	01	16	5	3

BOROTA Petar
Belgrade, Yugoslavia, 5 March, 1952 Yugoslavia int (G)

League Club	Source	Date Signed	Seasons Played	Apps	Subs	Gls
Chelsea	Partizan Belgrade (Yug)	03.79	78-81	107	0	0

BORROWDALE Gary Ian
Sutton, 16 July, 1985 EYth (CD)

League Club	Source	Date Signed	Seasons Played	Apps	Subs	Gls
Crystal Palace	Sch	12.02	02-04	24	19	0

BORROWS Brian
Liverpool, 20 December, 1960 EB-1 (FB)

League Club	Source	Date Signed	Seasons Played	Apps	Subs	Gls
Everton	Jnrs	04.80	81-82	27	0	0
Bolton W	Tr	03.83	82-84	95	0	0
Coventry C	Tr	06.85	85-96	396	13	11
Bristol C	L	09.93	93	6	0	0
Swindon T	Tr	09.97	97-98	80	0	0

BORTHWICK Gary Michael
Slough, 30 November, 1955 (M)

League Club	Source	Date Signed	Seasons Played	Apps	Subs	Gls
Bournemouth	Barnet	03.78	77-79	66	8	4

BORTHWICK John Robert
Hartlepool, 24 March, 1964 (F)

League Club	Source	Date Signed	Seasons Played	Apps	Subs	Gls
Hartlepool U	Owton Manor Soc Club	12.82	82-88	96	21	14

League Club	Source	Date Signed	Seasons Played	Apps	Subs	Gls
Darlington	Tr	08.89	90-91	57	18	15
York C	Tr	07.92	92	28	5	8

BORTHWICK Walter Ross
Edinburgh, 4 April, 1948 (IF)

League Club	Source	Date Signed	Seasons Played	Apps	Subs	Gls
Brighton & Hove A	Morton	05.67	66	1	0	0

BORTOLAZZI Mario
Verona, Italy, 10 January, 1965 (M)

League Club	Source	Date Signed	Seasons Played	Apps	Subs	Gls
West Bromwich A	Genoa (It)	08.98	98	25	10	2

BOS Gijsbert
Spakenburg, Holland, 22 February, 1973 (F)

League Club	Source	Date Signed	Seasons Played	Apps	Subs	Gls
Lincoln C	Ijsselmeervogels (Holl)	03.96	95-96	28	6	6
Rotherham U	Tr	08.97	97-98	7	11	4

BOSANCIC Jovica (Jovo)
Novi Sad, Yugoslavia, 7 August, 1970 Yuu21 (M)

League Club	Source	Date Signed	Seasons Played	Apps	Subs	Gls
Barnsley	Uniao Madeira (Por)	08.96	96-97	30	12	3

BOSHELL Daniel (Danny) Kevin
Bradford, 30 May, 1981 (M)

League Club	Source	Date Signed	Seasons Played	Apps	Subs	Gls
Oldham Ath	YT	07.98	99-04	45	25	2
Bury	L	03.05	04	2	4	0

BOSLEM William (Billy)
Middleton, 11 January, 1958 (CD)

League Club	Source	Date Signed	Seasons Played	Apps	Subs	Gls
Rochdale	Jnrs	11.75	75-77	42	3	1

BOSNICH Mark John
Fairfield, Australia, 13 January, 1972 AuYth/Auu23/Au-17 (G)

League Club	Source	Date Signed	Seasons Played	Apps	Subs	Gls
Manchester U	Sydney Croatia (Aus)	06.89	89-90	3	0	0
Aston Villa	Tr	02.92	91-98	179	0	0
Manchester U	Tr	07.99	99	23	0	0
Chelsea	Tr	01.01	01	5	0	0

BOSSONS Percy Lawrence Powell
Crewe, 10 January, 1924 Died 1950 (WH)

League Club	Source	Date Signed	Seasons Played	Apps	Subs	Gls
Crewe Alex	West Ham U (Am)	06.46	46-48	29	-	2

BOSSU Bertrand (Bert)
Calais, France, 14 October, 1980 (G)

League Club	Source	Date Signed	Seasons Played	Apps	Subs	Gls
Barnet	RC Lens (Fr)	10.99				
Gillingham	Hayes	09.03	03-04	4	2	0
Torquay U	L	08.04	04	2	0	0

BOSSY Fabien
Marseille, France, 1 October, 1977 (M)

League Club	Source	Date Signed	Seasons Played	Apps	Subs	Gls
Darlington	Clyde	08.03	03	4	2	0

BOSTOCK Benjamin (Ben) Roy
Mansfield, 19 April, 1929 Died 1993 (W)

League Club	Source	Date Signed	Seasons Played	Apps	Subs	Gls
Crystal Palace	Jnrs	05.46	48	4	-	0

BOSVELT Paul
Doetinchem, Holland, 26 March, 1970 Holland 24 (F)

League Club	Source	Date Signed	Seasons Played	Apps	Subs	Gls
Manchester C	Feyenoord (Holl)	07.03	03-04	50	3	2

BOSWELL Alan Henry
West Bromwich, 8 August, 1943 (G)

League Club	Source	Date Signed	Seasons Played	Apps	Subs	Gls
Walsall	Jnrs	08.60	61-62	66	-	0
Shrewsbury T	Tr	08.63	63-68	222	0	0
Wolverhampton W	Tr	09.68	68	10	0	0
Bolton W	Tr	10.69	69-70	51	0	0
Port Vale	Tr	08.72	72-73	86	0	0

BOSWELL James (Jimmy)
Chester, 13 March, 1922 (WH)

League Club	Source	Date Signed	Seasons Played	Apps	Subs	Gls
Gillingham	Chester (Am)	07.46	50-57	342	-	6

BOTHAM Ian Terence
Heswall, 24 November, 1955 (CD)

League Club	Source	Date Signed	Seasons Played	Apps	Subs	Gls
Scunthorpe U	Yeovil T	03.80	79-84	7	4	0

BOTHROYD Jay
Islington, 7 May, 1982 ESch/EYth/Eu20/Eu21-1 (F)

League Club	Source	Date Signed	Seasons Played	Apps	Subs	Gls
Arsenal	YT	07.99				
Coventry C	Tr	07.00	00-02	51	21	14
Blackburn Rov (L)	Perugia (It)	09.04	04	6	5	1

BOTTIGLIERI Antonio (Tony)
Chatham, 29 May, 1962 (M)

League Club	Source	Date Signed	Seasons Played	Apps	Subs	Gls
Gillingham	App	04.80	79-81	5	4	0

BOTTOM Arthur Edwin
Sheffield, 28 February, 1930 (IF)

League Club	Source	Date Signed	Seasons Played	Apps	Subs	Gls
Sheffield U	Sheffield YMCA	04.47	48-53	24	-	7
York C	Tr	06.54	54-57	137	-	92
Newcastle U	Tr	01.58	57-58	11	-	10
Chesterfield	Tr	11.58	58-59	33	-	6

BOTTOMLEY Paul
Harrogate, 11 September, 1965 (CD)

League Club	Source	Date Signed	Seasons Played	Apps	Subs	Gls
Doncaster Rov	Bridlington T	08.93	93	10	0	1

BOTTOMS Michael (Mike) Charles
Fulham, 11 January, 1939 (IF)

League Club	Source	Date Signed	Seasons Played	Apps	Subs	Gls
Queens Park Rgrs	Harrow T	07.60	60	2	-	0

BOUANANE Emad
Paris, France, 22 November, 1976 (CD)

League Club	Source	Date Signed	Seasons Played	Apps	Subs	Gls
Wrexham	Avranches (Fr)	08.00	00	13	4	0

BOUAZZA Hameur
Evry, France, 22 February, 1985 (F)

League Club	Source	Date Signed	Seasons Played	Apps	Subs	Gls
Watford	Sch	07.04	03-04	16	21	2

BOUCAUD Andre Christopher
Enfield, 9 October, 1984 Trinidad 6 (M)

League Club	Source	Date Signed	Seasons Played	Apps	Subs	Gls
Reading	YT	03.02				
Peterborough U	L	03.03	02	5	1	0
Peterborough U	L	07.03	03	7	1	1
Peterborough U	Tr	07.04	04	13	9	1

BOUGHEN Dean
Hemsworth, 25 July, 1971 (FB)

League Club	Source	Date Signed	Seasons Played	Apps	Subs	Gls
Newport Co	YT	●	87	1	0	0

BOUGHEN Paul
South Kirkby, 17 September, 1949 (CD)

League Club	Source	Date Signed	Seasons Played	Apps	Subs	Gls
Barnsley	App	10.67	70	3	5	0

BOUGHEY Darren John
Stoke-on-Trent, 30 November, 1970 (W)

League Club	Source	Date Signed	Seasons Played	Apps	Subs	Gls
Stoke C	YT	07.89	89	4	3	0
Wigan Ath	L	01.91	90	2	0	2
Exeter C	L	03.91	90	8	0	1

BOULD Stephen (Steve) Andrew
Stoke-on-Trent, 16 November, 1962 EB-1/E-2 (CD)

League Club	Source	Date Signed	Seasons Played	Apps	Subs	Gls
Stoke C	App	11.80	81-87	179	4	6
Torquay U	L	10.82	82	9	0	0
Arsenal	Tr	06.88	88-98	271	16	5
Sunderland	Tr	07.99	99-00	19	2	0

BOULDING Michael (Mike) Thomas
Sheffield, 8 February, 1976 (F)

League Club	Source	Date Signed	Seasons Played	Apps	Subs	Gls
Mansfield T	Hallam	08.99	99-00	28	38	12
Grimsby T	Tr	08.01	01	24	11	11
Aston Villa	Tr	07.02				
Sheffield U	L	09.02	02	3	3	0
Grimsby T	Tr	01.03	02-03	37	2	16
Barnsley	Tr	02.04	03-04	27	8	10
Cardiff C	L	03.05	04	0	4	0

BOULTER David Arthur
Stepney, 5 October, 1962 (FB)

League Club	Source	Date Signed	Seasons Played	Apps	Subs	Gls
Crystal Palace	App	07.80	81	16	0	0

BOULTON Clinton (Clint) William
Stoke-on-Trent, 6 January, 1948 (CD)

League Club	Source	Date Signed	Seasons Played	Apps	Subs	Gls
Port Vale	App	08.65	64-71	244	0	11
Torquay U	Tr	11.71	71-78	260	2	34

BOULTON Colin Donald
Cheltenham, 12 September, 1945 (G)

League Club	Source	Date Signed	Seasons Played	Apps	Subs	Gls
Derby Co	Cheltenham Police	08.64	64-77	272	0	0
Southampton	L	09.76	76	5	0	0
Lincoln C	Los Angeles (USA)	07.80	80	4	0	0

BOULTON Frank Preece
Chipping Sodbury, 12 August, 1917 Died 1987 (G)

League Club	Source	Date Signed	Seasons Played	Apps	Subs	Gls
Arsenal	Bath C	10.36	36-37	36	-	0
Derby Co	Tr	08.38	38	39	-	0
Swindon T	Tr	08.46	46-49	97	-	0

BOULTON Ralph
Grimsby, 22 July, 1923 Died 1992 (IF)

League Club	Source	Date Signed	Seasons Played	Apps	Subs	Gls
Grimsby T		04.48	47-48	3	-	0

BOUMSONG Jean-Alain Somkong
Douala, Cameroon, 14 December, 1979 France 11 (CD)

League Club	Source	Date Signed	Seasons Played	Apps	Subs	Gls
Newcastle U	Glasgow Rgrs	01.05	04	14	0	0

BOUND Matthew Terence
Melksham, 9 November, 1972 (CD)

League Club	Source	Date Signed	Seasons Played	Apps	Subs	Gls
Southampton	YT	05.91	91-93	2	3	0
Hull C	L	08.93	93	7	0	1
Stockport Co	Tr	10.94	94-96	44	0	5
Lincoln C	L	09.95	95	3	1	0
Swansea C	Tr	11.97	97-01	173	1	9
Oxford U	Tr	12.01	01-03	96	4	2

League Club	Source	Date Signed	Seasons Played	Apps	Subs	Gls
BOURNE Albert						
Golborne, 30 September, 1934						(IF)
Manchester C		08.52				
Oldham Ath	Tr	06.58	58-59	35	-	9
BOURNE George Frederick						
Burslem, 5 March, 1932 Died 2004						(FB)
Stoke C	Burslem A	06.50	52-55	100	-	1
BOURNE Jeffrey (Jeff) Albert						
Linton, Derbyshire, 19 June, 1948						(F)
Derby Co	Burton A	06.69	70-76	35	14	9
Crystal Palace	Tr	03.77	76-77	32	0	10
Sheffield U	Atlanta (USA)	09.79	79	25	1	11
BOURNE Richard Adrian						
Colchester, 9 December, 1954						(CD)
Colchester U	Jnrs	04.73	71-72	3	1	0
Torquay U	Bath C	06.79	79-81	64	4	7
BOUSSATTA Dries						
Amsterdam, Holland, 23 December, 1972 Holland 3						(F)
Sheffield U	Excelsior (Holl)	11.03	03	3	3	0
BOUSTON Bryan John						
Hereford, 3 October, 1960						(FB)
Hereford U	App	10.78	77	4	2	0
BOVINGTON Edward (Eddie) Ernest Perrian						
Edmonton, 23 April, 1941						(M)
West Ham U	Jnrs	05.59	59-67	138	0	1
BOWATER Jason Joseph Barry						
Chesterfield, 5 April, 1978						(M)
Chesterfield	YT	●	96	0	1	0
BOWDEN John (Jack)						
Manchester, 25 August, 1921 Died 1981						(WH)
Oldham Ath	Jnrs	09.45	46-48	72	-	1
BOWDEN Jonathan (Jon) Lee						
Stockport, 21 January, 1963						(M)
Oldham Ath	Jnrs	01.80	81-84	73	9	5
Port Vale	Tr	09.85	85-86	64	6	7
Wrexham	Tr	07.87	87-91	137	10	20
Rochdale	Tr	09.91	91-94	73	33	17
BOWDEN Peter William						
Liverpool, 23 July, 1959						(M)
Doncaster Rov	Jnrs	08.77	76-78	22	6	1
BOWDITCH Benjamin (Ben) Edward						
Bishops Stortford, 19 February, 1984 EYth/Eu20						(CD)
Tottenham H	YT	02.01				
Colchester U	Tr	08.04	04	0	5	0
BOWDITCH Dean Peter						
Bishops Stortford, 15 June, 1986 EYth						(F)
Ipswich T	Sch	07.03	02-04	13	29	7
Burnley	L	03.05	04	8	2	1
BOWEN Daniel (Danny)						
Llanwonno, 16 November, 1921 Died 2000						(W)
Scunthorpe U	Treharris	07.50	50	5	-	0
BOWEN David Lloyd						
Nantyffyllon, 7 June, 1928 Died 1995 W-19						(WH)
Northampton T		07.47	47-48	12	-	0
Arsenal	Tr	07.50	50-58	146	-	2
Northampton T	Tr	07.59	59	22	-	1
BOWEN Jason Peter						
Merthyr Tydfil, 24 August, 1972 WSch/WYth/Wu21-5/WB-1/W-2						(W)
Swansea C	YT	07.90	90-94	93	31	26
Birmingham C	Tr	07.95	95-96	35	13	7
Southampton	L	09.97	97	1	2	0
Reading	Tr	12.97	97-98	12	3	1
Cardiff C	Tr	01.99	98-03	105	29	34
BOWEN Keith Bryn						
Northampton, 26 February, 1958 WSch						(F)
Northampton T	Jnrs	08.76	76-81	61	4	24
Brentford	Tr	09.81	81-82	42	9	9
Colchester U	Tr	03.83	82-85	115	1	38
BOWEN Mark Rosslyn						
Neath, 7 December, 1963 WSch/WYth/Wu21-3/W-41						(FB)
Tottenham H	App	12.81	83-86	14	3	2
Norwich C	Tr	07.87	87-95	315	5	24
West Ham U	Tr	07.96	96	15	2	1
Charlton Ath	Shimizu S Pulse (Jap)	09.97	97-98	36	6	0
Wigan Ath	Tr	08.99	99	7	0	0

League Club	Source	Date Signed	Seasons Played	Apps	Subs	Gls
BOWEN Stewart Anthony						
West Bromwich, 12 December, 1972						(FB)
West Bromwich A	YT	07.91	91	8	0	1
BOWEN Thomas (Tommy) Henry						
West Bromwich, 21 August, 1924						(W)
West Bromwich A	West Bromwich Ath	04.44				
Newport Co	Tr	07.46	46-49	37	-	6
Walsall	Tr	07.50	50-52	94	-	7
BOWER Daniel (Danny) Neil						
Woolwich, 20 November, 1976						(CD)
Fulham	YT	11.95	95	4	0	0
BOWER Kenneth (Ken)						
Huddersfield, 18 March, 1926 Died 2002						(CF)
Darlington		01.47	46-48	75	-	35
Rotherham U	Tr	07.49	49	27	-	10
BOWER Mark James						
Bradford, 23 January, 1980						(CD)
Bradford C	YT	03.98	97-04	103	7	4
York C	L	02.00	99	15	0	1
York C	L	11.00	00	21	0	1
BOWERING Michael (Mike)						
Hull, 15 November, 1936						(W)
Hull C		09.58	58-59	45	-	7
Chesterfield	Tr	06.60	60	16	-	1
BOWERS Ian (Danny)						
Newcastle-under-Lyme, 16 January, 1955						(FB)
Stoke C	Jnrs	06.73	74-77	35	4	2
Shrewsbury T	L	03.78	77	6	0	0
Crewe Alex	Tr	07.79	79-83	170	5	2
BOWERS John (Jack) Anslow						
Leicester, 14 November, 1939						(W)
Derby Co	Derby Corinthians	02.57	59-65	65	0	19
Notts Co	Tr	06.66	66	5	0	0
BOWERY Bertram (Bert) Nathanial						
St Kitts, 29 October, 1954						(F)
Nottingham F	Worksop T	01.75	75	1	0	2
Lincoln C	L	02.76	75	2	2	1
Nottingham F	Boston (USA)	08.76	76	1	0	0
BOWEY Keith Alan						
Newcastle, 9 May, 1960						(M)
Blackpool	App	03.78	78-79	3	0	1
BOWGETT Paul						
Hitchin, 17 June, 1955						(CD)
Tottenham H	Letchworth Garden C	02.78				
Wimbledon	Tr	03.79	78-79	41	0	0
BOWIE James (Jimmy) Duncan						
Aberdeen, 9 August, 1924 Died 2000						(IF)
Chelsea	Park Vale (Aberdeen)	01.44	47-50	76	-	18
Fulham	Tr	01.51	50-51	34	-	7
Brentford	Tr	03.52	51	9	-	0
Watford	Tr	07.52	52-55	125	-	39
BOWIE James (Jim) McAvoy						
Howwood, 11 October, 1941						(M)
Oldham Ath	Arthurlie Jnrs	07.62	62-71	331	2	37
Rochdale	Tr	10.72	72	1	2	0
BOWKER Keith						
West Bromwich, 18 April, 1951						(F)
Birmingham C	App	08.68	70-72	19	2	5
Exeter C	Tr	12.73	73-75	110	0	38
Cambridge U	Tr	05.76	76	12	5	1
Northampton T	L	12.76	76	4	0	0
Exeter C	Tr	08.77	77-79	93	9	28
Torquay U	Tr	08.80	80-81	50	3	9
BOWLER Gerard (Gerry) Columba						
Derry, 8 June, 1919 NIRL-3/I-3						(CD)
Portsmouth	Distillery	08.46	46-48	8	-	0
Hull C	Tr	08.49	49	38	-	0
Millwall	Tr	06.50	50-54	165	-	0
BOWLES John (Jack) Charles						
Cheltenham, 4 August, 1914 Died 1987						(G)
Newport Co	Cheltenham T	05.36	36	4	-	0
Accrington St	Tr	06.37	37	12	-	0
Stockport Co	Tr	07.38	38-52	275	-	0
BOWLES Paul Michael Anthony						
Manchester, 31 May, 1957						(CD)
Crewe Alex	App	05.75	74-79	174	4	20

League Club	Source	Date Signed	Seasons Played	Apps	Subs	Gls
Port Vale	Tr	10.79	79-81	98	0	8
Stockport Co	Tr	06.82	82-84	67	3	0

BOWLES Stanley (Stan)
Manchester, 24 December, 1948 FLge-1/E-5 (M)

League Club	Source	Date Signed	Seasons Played	Apps	Subs	Gls
Manchester C	App	01.67	67-69	15	2	2
Bury	L	07.70	70	5	0	0
Crewe Alex	Tr	09.70	70-71	51	0	18
Carlisle U	Tr	10.71	71-72	33	0	12
Queens Park Rgrs	Tr	09.72	72-79	255	0	71
Nottingham F	Tr	12.79	79	19	0	2
Orient	Tr	07.80	80-81	46	0	7
Brentford	Tr	10.81	81-82	73	0	16
Brentford	Hounslow T	11.83	83	7	1	0

BOWLING Ian
Sheffield, 27 July, 1965 (G)

League Club	Source	Date Signed	Seasons Played	Apps	Subs	Gls
Lincoln C	Gainsborough Trinity	10.88	88-92	59	0	0
Hartlepool U	L	08.89	89	1	0	0
Bradford C	L	03.93	92	7	0	0
Bradford C	Tr	07.93	93-94	29	0	0
Mansfield T	Tr	08.95	95-00	174	0	0

BOWMAN Andrew (Andy)
Pittenweem, 7 March, 1934 SSch (WH)

League Club	Source	Date Signed	Seasons Played	Apps	Subs	Gls
Chelsea	Jnrs	06.51	53	1	-	0
Newport Co	Heart of Midlothian	08.61	61-62	69	-	7

BOWMAN David
Tunbridge Wells, 10 March, 1964 Su21-1/S-6 (M)

League Club	Source	Date Signed	Seasons Played	Apps	Subs	Gls
Coventry C	Heart of Midlothian	12.84	84-85	38	2	2

BOWMAN David Michael
Scarborough, 16 December, 1960 (F)

League Club	Source	Date Signed	Seasons Played	Apps	Subs	Gls
Scarborough	Bridlington T	08.87	87	4	0	2

BOWMAN Richard (Richie) David
Lewisham, 25 September, 1954 (M)

League Club	Source	Date Signed	Seasons Played	Apps	Subs	Gls
Charlton Ath	App	03.73	72-76	93	3	7
Reading	Tr	12.76	76-80	194	1	30
Gillingham	Tr	08.81	81-82	26	0	6

BOWMAN Robert (Rob) Alexander
Durham, 21 November, 1975 EYth (FB)

League Club	Source	Date Signed	Seasons Played	Apps	Subs	Gls
Leeds U	YT	11.92	92-95	4	3	0
Rotherham U	Tr	02.97	96	13	0	0
Carlisle U	Tr	08.97	97-99	42	4	2

BOWMAN Robert (Bob) Craig Caldwell
Motherwell, 21 October, 1920 Died 1991 (FB)

League Club	Source	Date Signed	Seasons Played	Apps	Subs	Gls
New Brighton	Kilmarnock	01.49	48	18	-	0

BOWRON Kenneth (Ken)
Newcastle, 10 April, 1939 (CF)

League Club	Source	Date Signed	Seasons Played	Apps	Subs	Gls
Workington	Berwick Rgrs	12.65	65-66	8	1	2

BOWRY Robert (Bobby) John
Hampstead, 19 May, 1971 St Kitts int (M)

League Club	Source	Date Signed	Seasons Played	Apps	Subs	Gls
Crystal Palace	Carshalton Ath	04.92	92-94	36	14	1
Millwall	Tr	07.95	95-00	125	15	5
Colchester U	Tr	07.01	01-04	85	21	2

BOWSTEAD Peter Edward
Cambridge, 10 May, 1944 (IF)

League Club	Source	Date Signed	Seasons Played	Apps	Subs	Gls
Oxford U	Cambridge U	10.62	62-63	8	-	2

BOWTELL Stephen (Steve) John
Bethnal Green, 2 December, 1950 ESch/EYth (G)

League Club	Source	Date Signed	Seasons Played	Apps	Subs	Gls
Orient	App	01.68	67-71	8	0	0

BOWYER Francis (Frank)
Chesterton, 10 April, 1922 Died 1999 (IF)

League Club	Source	Date Signed	Seasons Played	Apps	Subs	Gls
Stoke C	Jnrs	04.39	47-59	398	-	137

BOWYER Gary David
Manchester, 22 June, 1971 (FB)

League Club	Source	Date Signed	Seasons Played	Apps	Subs	Gls
Hereford U	Westfields	12.89	89	12	2	2
Nottingham F	Tr	09.90				
Rotherham U	Tr	08.95	95-96	33	5	2

BOWYER Ian
Little Sutton, 6 June, 1951 (M)

League Club	Source	Date Signed	Seasons Played	Apps	Subs	Gls
Manchester C	App	08.68	68-70	42	7	13
Orient	Tr	06.71	71-72	75	3	19
Nottingham F	Tr	10.73	73-80	222	17	49
Sunderland	Tr	01.81	80-81	15	0	1
Nottingham F	Tr	01.82	81-86	203	3	19
Hereford U	Tr	07.87	87-89	33	7	1

BOWYER Lee David
Newham, 3 January, 1977 EYth/Eu21-13/E-1 (M)

League Club	Source	Date Signed	Seasons Played	Apps	Subs	Gls
Charlton Ath	YT	04.94	94-95	46	0	8
Leeds U	Tr	07.96	96-02	196	7	38
West Ham U	Tr	01.03	02	10	0	0
Newcastle U	Tr	07.03	03-04	43	8	5

BOXALL Alan Ronald
Woolwich, 11 May, 1953 (CD)

League Club	Source	Date Signed	Seasons Played	Apps	Subs	Gls
Scunthorpe U	Barton T	08.80	80-83	50	4	1
Chesterfield	Tr	11.83	83	4	1	0

BOXALL Daniel (Danny) James
Croydon, 24 August, 1977 IRu21-8 (CD)

League Club	Source	Date Signed	Seasons Played	Apps	Subs	Gls
Crystal Palace	YT	04.95	95-97	5	3	0
Oldham Ath	L	11.97	97	6	0	0
Oldham Ath	L	02.98	97	12	0	0
Brentford	Tr	07.98	98-01	62	6	1
Bristol Rov	Tr	07.02	02-03	58	5	0

BOXLEY John (Jack)
Cradley, 31 May, 1931 (W)

League Club	Source	Date Signed	Seasons Played	Apps	Subs	Gls
Bristol C	Stourbridge	10.50	50-56	193	-	34
Coventry C	Tr	12.56	56-59	92	-	17
Bristol C	Tr	08.60	60	12	-	0

BOXSHALL Daniel (Danny)
Bradford, 2 April, 1920 (W)

League Club	Source	Date Signed	Seasons Played	Apps	Subs	Gls
Queens Park Rgrs	Salem Ath	01.46	46-47	29	-	14
Bristol C	Tr	05.48	48-49	52	-	10
Bournemouth	Tr	07.50	50-51	51	-	8
Rochdale	Tr	07.52	52-53	11	-	3

BOYACK Steven
Edinburgh, 4 September, 1976 Su21-1 (M)

League Club	Source	Date Signed	Seasons Played	Apps	Subs	Gls
Hull C (L)	Glasgow Rgrs	02.98	97	12	0	3
Boston U	Livingston	01.05	04	2	2	0
Blackpool	Tr	03.05	04	0	1	0

BOYCE Emmerson Orlando
Aylesbury, 24 September, 1979 (FB)

League Club	Source	Date Signed	Seasons Played	Apps	Subs	Gls
Luton T	YT	04.98	98-03	171	15	8
Crystal Palace	Tr	07.04	04	26	1	0

BOYCE Robert Alexander
Islington, 7 January, 1974 (M)

League Club	Source	Date Signed	Seasons Played	Apps	Subs	Gls
Colchester U	Enfield	10.95	95	0	2	0

BOYCE Ronald (Ronnie) William
West Ham, 6 January, 1943 ESch/EYth (M)

League Club	Source	Date Signed	Seasons Played	Apps	Subs	Gls
West Ham U	Jnrs	05.60	60-72	275	7	21

BOYD Adam Mark
Hartlepool, 25 May, 1982 (F)

League Club	Source	Date Signed	Seasons Played	Apps	Subs	Gls
Hartlepool U	YT	09.99	99-04	77	46	49
Boston U	L	11.03	03	14	0	4

BOYD Brian George
Carlisle, 4 January, 1938 (IF)

League Club	Source	Date Signed	Seasons Played	Apps	Subs	Gls
Carlisle U	Raffles Rov	08.55	55-58	6	-	0

BOYD Charles (Charlie) Michael
Liverpool, 20 September, 1969 (M)

League Club	Source	Date Signed	Seasons Played	Apps	Subs	Gls
Liverpool	App	05.87				
Chesterfield	Bristol Rov (N/C)	11.90	90	0	1	0

BOYD Gordon
Glasgow, 27 March, 1958 SSch/SYth (M)

League Club	Source	Date Signed	Seasons Played	Apps	Subs	Gls
Fulham	Glasgow Rgrs	05.78	78	1	2	0
Barnsley	Glasgow Rgrs	06.80	80	1	1	0
Scunthorpe U	Tr	03.82	81	10	1	0

BOYD John (Jack)
Consett, 10 April, 1925 (FB)

League Club	Source	Date Signed	Seasons Played	Apps	Subs	Gls
Sunderland	Medomsley Jnrs	05.45				
West Bromwich A	Tr	06.48	48	1	-	0

BOYD John
USA, 10 September, 1926 (W)

League Club	Source	Date Signed	Seasons Played	Apps	Subs	Gls
Bristol C	Gloucester C	12.50	50-51	31	-	6

BOYD John (Jock) Robertson
Bo'ness, 7 March, 1926 (CD)

League Club	Source	Date Signed	Seasons Played	Apps	Subs	Gls
Newport Co	Bo'ness Jnrs	03.47	47	1	-	0

BOYD Leonard (Len) Arthur Miller
Plaistow, 11 November, 1923 EB (WH)

League Club	Source	Date Signed	Seasons Played	Apps	Subs	Gls
Plymouth Arg	Ilford	12.45	46-48	78	-	5
Birmingham C	Tr	01.49	48-55	255	-	14

BOYD Marc Edward
Carlisle, 22 October, 1981 (M)

League Club	Source	Date Signed	Seasons Played	Apps	Subs	Gls
Newcastle U	YT	10.98				
Port Vale	Tr	07.02	02-03	39	3	3
Carlisle U	Tr	03.04	03	9	0	1
Macclesfield T (L)	Gretna	01.05	04	4	1	0

BOYD Stuart
Workington, 22 December, 1954 (FB)

League Club	Source	Date Signed	Seasons Played	Apps	Subs	Gls
Workington (Am)	Jnrs	08.73	72-73	1	4	0

BOYD Thomas (Tommy)
Glasgow, 24 November, 1965 SYth/Su21-5/SB/S-58 (FB)

League Club	Source	Date Signed	Seasons Played	Apps	Subs	Gls
Chelsea	Motherwell	06.91	91	22	1	0

BOYD Walter
Kingston, Jamaica, 1 January, 1972 Jamaica int (F)

League Club	Source	Date Signed	Seasons Played	Apps	Subs	Gls
Swansea C	Arnett Gardens (Jam)	10.99	99-00	35	9	10

BOYD William (Willie)
Bellshill, 18 October, 1958 SYth (G)

League Club	Source	Date Signed	Seasons Played	Apps	Subs	Gls
Hull C	App	10.77				
Doncaster Rov	Tr	02.80	79-83	104	0	0

BOYDEN Joseph (Joe)
Willenhall, 12 February, 1929 (FB)

League Club	Source	Date Signed	Seasons Played	Apps	Subs	Gls
Walsall	Jnrs	12.48	52	4	-	0

BOYER Philip (Phil) John
Nottingham, 25 January, 1949 Eu23-2/E-1 (F)

League Club	Source	Date Signed	Seasons Played	Apps	Subs	Gls
Derby Co	App	11.66				
York C	Tr	07.68	68-70	108	1	27
Bournemouth	Tr	12.70	70-73	139	1	46
Norwich C	Tr	12.74	73-76	115	1	34
Southampton	Tr	08.77	77-80	138	0	49
Manchester C	Tr	11.80	80-82	17	3	3

BOYES Kenneth (Ken)
York, 4 February, 1935 (CD)

League Club	Source	Date Signed	Seasons Played	Apps	Subs	Gls
York C	Scarborough	10.55	57-65	53	0	2

BOYES Walter (Wally) Edward
Killamarsh, 5 January, 1913 Died 1960 FLge-2/E-3 (W)

League Club	Source	Date Signed	Seasons Played	Apps	Subs	Gls
West Bromwich A	Woodhouse Mills U	02.31	31-37	151	-	35
Everton	Tr	02.38	37-48	66	-	11
Notts Co	Tr	08.49	49	3	-	1
Scunthorpe U	Tr	08.50	50	13	-	2

BOYLAN Anthony (Tony)
Hartlepool, 19 February, 1950 (M)

League Club	Source	Date Signed	Seasons Played	Apps	Subs	Gls
Hartlepool (Am)	Bishop Auckland	09.68	69-71	10	1	0

BOYLAN Lee Martin
Witham, 2 September, 1978 IRYth (M)

League Club	Source	Date Signed	Seasons Played	Apps	Subs	Gls
West Ham U	YT	07.97	96	0	1	0
Exeter C	Trelleborgs (Swe)	11.99	99	3	3	1

BOYLE David Walker
North Shields, 24 April, 1929 (IF)

League Club	Source	Date Signed	Seasons Played	Apps	Subs	Gls
Newcastle U		10.47				
Barnsley	Berwick Rgrs	03.51				
Crewe Alex	Tr	06.52	52-53	35	-	3
Chesterfield	Tr	07.54	54-55	42	-	10
Bradford C	Tr	07.56	56-60	92	-	13

BOYLE Henry (Harry)
Possilpark, 22 April, 1924 (FB)

League Club	Source	Date Signed	Seasons Played	Apps	Subs	Gls
Southport	Murton CW	07.47	47-49	88	-	0
Rochdale	Tr	06.50	50	17	-	0
Rochdale	Bangor C	07.52	52-55	158	-	0

BOYLE Ian Richard
Barnsley, 7 December, 1953 (CD)

League Club	Source	Date Signed	Seasons Played	Apps	Subs	Gls
Barnsley	App	12.71	72-73	19	2	0

BOYLE John
Motherwell, 25 December, 1946 (M)

League Club	Source	Date Signed	Seasons Played	Apps	Subs	Gls
Chelsea	Jnrs	08.64	64-73	188	10	10
Brighton & Hove A	L	09.73	73	10	0	0
Orient	Tr	12.73	73-74	18	0	0

BOYLE Lee David
North Shields, 22 January, 1972 (CD)

League Club	Source	Date Signed	Seasons Played	Apps	Subs	Gls
Doncaster Rov	Ipswich T (YT)	07.90	91	2	1	0

BOYLE Terence (Terry) David John
Ammanford, 29 October, 1958 WSch/Wu21-1/W-2 (CD)

League Club	Source	Date Signed	Seasons Played	Apps	Subs	Gls
Tottenham H	App	11.75				
Crystal Palace	Tr	01.78	77-80	24	2	1
Wimbledon	L	09.81	81	5	0	1
Bristol C	Tr	10.81	81-82	36	1	0
Newport Co	Tr	11.82	82-85	165	1	11
Cardiff C	Tr	08.86	86-88	126	2	7
Swansea C	Tr	08.89	89	27	0	1

BOYLE Wesley Samuel
Portadown, 30 March, 1979 NISch/NIYth (M)

League Club	Source	Date Signed	Seasons Played	Apps	Subs	Gls
Leeds U	YT	05.95	96	0	1	0

BOYLEN David
Prestbury, 26 October, 1947 (M)

League Club	Source	Date Signed	Seasons Played	Apps	Subs	Gls
Grimsby T	Ryder Brow BC	07.65	66-77	370	14	34

BOZINOSKI Vlado
Skopje, Macedonia, 30 March, 1964 Australia int (M)

League Club	Source	Date Signed	Seasons Played	Apps	Subs	Gls
Ipswich T	Beira Mar (Por)	12.92	92	3	6	0

BRABIN Gary
Liverpool, 9 December, 1970 ESemiPro-3 (M)

League Club	Source	Date Signed	Seasons Played	Apps	Subs	Gls
Stockport Co	YT	12.89	89-90	1	1	0
Doncaster Rov	Runcorn	07.94	94-95	58	1	11
Bury	Tr	03.96	95	5	0	0
Blackpool	Tr	07.96	96-98	50	13	5
Lincoln C	L	12.98	98	3	1	0
Hull C	Tr	01.99	98-00	89	6	9
Torquay U	Boston U	10.01	01	6	0	0

BRABROOK Peter
Greenwich, 8 November, 1937 EYth/Eu23-9/FLge-3/E-3 (W)

League Club	Source	Date Signed	Seasons Played	Apps	Subs	Gls
Chelsea	Jnrs	03.55	54-61	251	-	47
West Ham U	Tr	10.62	62-67	167	0	33
Orient	Tr	07.68	68-70	70	2	6

BRACE Deryn Paul John
Haverfordwest, 15 March, 1975 WYth/Wu21-8 (FB)

League Club	Source	Date Signed	Seasons Played	Apps	Subs	Gls
Norwich C	YT	07.93				
Wrexham	Tr	04.94	93-99	79	9	2

BRACE Robert (Robbie) Leon
Edmonton, 19 December, 1964 (F)

League Club	Source	Date Signed	Seasons Played	Apps	Subs	Gls
Tottenham H	App	12.82	83	0	1	0

BRACE Stuart Clive
Taunton, 21 September, 1942 (W)

League Club	Source	Date Signed	Seasons Played	Apps	Subs	Gls
Plymouth Arg	Taunton T	11.60	62-65	9	0	0
Watford	Tr	09.65	65	16	0	4
Mansfield T	Tr	07.66	66-67	55	2	25
Peterborough U	Tr	11.67	67-68	22	1	6
Grimsby T	Tr	10.68	68-73	205	1	81
Southend U	Tr	10.73	73-75	106	6	39

BRACEWELL Kenneth (Ken)
Colne, 5 October, 1936 (FB)

League Club	Source	Date Signed	Seasons Played	Apps	Subs	Gls
Burnley	Trawden	04.57				
Tranmere Rov	Tr	05.59	59-60	28	-	1
Lincoln C	(Canada)	11.63	63-64	23	-	1
Bury	Margate	12.66	66	1	0	0
Rochdale	Toronto (Can)	03.68	67	5	0	0

BRACEWELL Paul William
Heswall, 19 July, 1962 Eu21-13/E-3 (M)

League Club	Source	Date Signed	Seasons Played	Apps	Subs	Gls
Stoke C	App	02.80	79-82	123	6	5
Sunderland	Tr	07.83	83	38	0	4
Everton	Tr	05.84	84-88	95	0	7
Sunderland	Tr	08.89	89-91	112	1	2
Newcastle U	Tr	06.92	92-94	64	9	3
Sunderland	Tr	05.95	95-97	76	1	0
Fulham	Tr	10.97	97-98	61	1	1

BRACEY Lee Michael Ian
Barking, 11 September, 1968 (G)

League Club	Source	Date Signed	Seasons Played	Apps	Subs	Gls
West Ham U	YT	07.87				
Swansea C	Tr	08.88	88-91	99	0	0
Halifax T	Tr	10.91	91-92	73	0	0
Bury	Tr	08.93	93-95	65	2	0
Ipswich T	Tr	08.97				
Hull C	Tr	07.99	99-00	19	1	0

BRACK Alistair Holland
Aberdeen, 27 January, 1940 (FB)

League Club	Source	Date Signed	Seasons Played	Apps	Subs	Gls
Cardiff C		09.61	62	1	-	0

BRACKENRIDGE Stephen (Steve) James
Rochdale, 31 July, 1984 (M)

League Club	Source	Date Signed	Seasons Played	Apps	Subs	Gls
Macclesfield T	Sch	07.03	02-03	2	7	2

BRACKSTONE John
Hartlepool, 9 February, 1985 (FB)

League Club	Source	Date Signed	Seasons Played	Apps	Subs	Gls
Hartlepool U	Sch	03.04	03-04	13	2	0

BRACKSTONE Stephen (Steve)
Hartlepool, 19 September, 1982 EYth (M)

League Club	Source	Date Signed	Seasons Played	Apps	Subs	Gls
Middlesbrough	YT	07.00				
York C	Tr	02.02	01-03	32	12	4

BRADBURY Allen
Barnsley, 23 January, 1947 Died 1999 (M)

League Club	Source	Date Signed	Seasons Played	Apps	Subs	Gls
Barnsley	App	01.65	64-69	68	1	9
Hartlepool	Kettering T	01.71	70	7	0	0

BRADBURY Barry
Rochdale, 5 August, 1952 (FB)

League Club	Source	Date Signed	Seasons Played	Apps	Subs	Gls
Rochdale	Matthew Moss	08.72	72-73	12	3	0

BRADBURY Lee Michael
Cowes, 3 July, 1975 Eu21-3 (F)

League Club	Source	Date Signed	Seasons Played	Apps	Subs	Gls
Portsmouth	Cowes	08.95	95-96	41	13	15
Exeter C	L	12.95	95	14	0	5
Manchester C	Tr	08.97	97-98	34	6	10
Crystal Palace	Tr	10.98	98-99	28	4	6
Birmingham C	L	03.99	98	6	1	0
Portsmouth	Tr	10.99	99-02	90	9	28
Sheffield Wed	L	12.02	02	2	1	0
Sheffield Wed	L	03.03	02	8	0	3
Derby Co	L	08.03	03	1	0	0
Derby Co	L	11.03	03	6	0	0
Walsall	Tr	03.04	03	7	1	1
Oxford U	Tr	07.04	04	39	2	4

BRADBURY Shaun
Birmingham, 11 February, 1974 (F)

League Club	Source	Date Signed	Seasons Played	Apps	Subs	Gls
Wolverhampton W	YT	11.92	92	2	0	2

BRADBURY Terence (Terry) Eugene
Paddington, 15 November, 1939 ESch (M)

League Club	Source	Date Signed	Seasons Played	Apps	Subs	Gls
Chelsea	Jnrs	07.57	60-61	29	-	1
Southend U	Tr	09.62	62-65	160	1	19
Leyton Orient	Tr	06.66	66	25	2	0
Wrexham	Tr	06.67	67-68	77	1	3
Chester	Tr	06.69	69-70	90	0	2

BRADBURY William (Bill)
Matlock, 3 April, 1933 Died 1999 (IF)

League Club	Source	Date Signed	Seasons Played	Apps	Subs	Gls
Coventry C	Jnrs	05.50	51-54	24	-	7
Birmingham C	Tr	11.54	54-55	3	-	2
Hull C	Tr	10.55	55-59	178	-	82
Bury	Tr	02.60	59-60	18	-	4
Workington	Tr	11.60	60	23	-	5
Southport	Tr	08.61	61	11	-	2

BRADD Leslie (Les) John
Buxton, 6 November, 1947 (F)

League Club	Source	Date Signed	Seasons Played	Apps	Subs	Gls
Rotherham U	Earl Sterndale	03.66	67	3	0	0
Notts Co	Tr	10.67	67-77	379	16	125
Stockport Co	Tr	08.78	78-80	116	1	31
Wigan Ath	Tr	07.81	81-82	57	6	25
Bristol Rov	L	12.82	82	1	0	1

BRADER Alec
Horncastle, 6 October, 1942 (IF)

League Club	Source	Date Signed	Seasons Played	Apps	Subs	Gls
Grimsby T	Horncastle U	05.60	60	2	-	0

BRADFORD David William
Manchester, 22 February, 1953 (M)

League Club	Source	Date Signed	Seasons Played	Apps	Subs	Gls
Blackburn Rov	App	08.71	71-73	58	6	3
Sheffield U	Tr	07.74	74-76	54	6	2
Peterborough U	L	10.76	76	4	0	0
West Bromwich A	Tr	02.77				
Coventry C	Washington (USA)	10.81	81	6	0	1

BRADFORD Geoffrey (Geoff) Reginald William
Bristol, 18 July, 1927 Died 1994 E-1 (IF)

League Club	Source	Date Signed	Seasons Played	Apps	Subs	Gls
Bristol Rov	Soundwell	05.49	49-63	461	-	242

BRADFORD Lewis (Lew)
Swadlincote, 24 November, 1916 Died 1984 (CD)

League Club	Source	Date Signed	Seasons Played	Apps	Subs	Gls
Preston NE		12.34				
Bradford C	Kilmarnock	10.46	46-48	68	-	1
Newport Co	Tr	11.48	48	24	-	0

BRADLEY Brendan Colin
Derry, 7 June, 1950 (F)

League Club	Source	Date Signed	Seasons Played	Apps	Subs	Gls
Lincoln C	Finn Harps	07.72	72	31	0	12

BRADLEY Charles
York, 15 May, 1922 Died 1984 (IF)

League Club	Source	Date Signed	Seasons Played	Apps	Subs	Gls
York C	York RI	10.41	46	10	-	2

BRADLEY Darren Michael
Birmingham, 24 November, 1965 EYth (CD)

League Club	Source	Date Signed	Seasons Played	Apps	Subs	Gls
Aston Villa	App	12.83	84-85	16	4	0
West Bromwich A	Tr	03.86	85-94	236	18	9
Walsall	Tr	08.95	95-96	66	5	1

BRADLEY David
Salford, 16 January, 1958 ESch (CD)

League Club	Source	Date Signed	Seasons Played	Apps	Subs	Gls
Manchester U	App	01.75				
Wimbledon	L	03.78	77	7	0	0
Doncaster Rov	Tr	08.78	78-79	67	0	5
Bury	Tr	08.80	80	8	0	0

BRADLEY David Hughes
Bolton, 6 December, 1953 (F)

League Club	Source	Date Signed	Seasons Played	Apps	Subs	Gls
Workington	Silcoms	09.75	75	8	0	1

BRADLEY Donald (Don) John
Annesley, 11 September, 1924 Died 1997 (FB)

League Club	Source	Date Signed	Seasons Played	Apps	Subs	Gls
West Bromwich A	Clipstone CW	09.43				
Mansfield T	Tr	08.49	49-61	384	-	6

BRADLEY George Joseph
Maltby, 7 November, 1917 Died 1998 (WH)

League Club	Source	Date Signed	Seasons Played	Apps	Subs	Gls
Rotherham U	Maltby Hall OB	03.37	37-38	28	-	0
Newcastle U	Tr	11.38	38	1	-	0
Millwall	Tr	09.46	46-49	74	-	2

BRADLEY Gordon
Scunthorpe, 20 May, 1925 (G)

League Club	Source	Date Signed	Seasons Played	Apps	Subs	Gls
Leicester C	Scunthorpe U	11.42	46-49	69	-	0
Notts Co	Tr	02.50	50-57	192	-	1

BRADLEY Gordon
Easington, 23 November, 1933 (WH)

League Club	Source	Date Signed	Seasons Played	Apps	Subs	Gls
Bradford PA	Stanley U	01.56	55-56	18	-	1
Carlisle U	Tr	09.57	57-60	133	-	3

BRADLEY James (Jimmy)
Greenock, 21 March, 1927 (IF)

League Club	Source	Date Signed	Seasons Played	Apps	Subs	Gls
Shrewsbury T	Third Lanark	07.52	52	1	-	0

BRADLEY John (Jack)
Hemsworth, 27 November, 1916 Died 2002 (IF)

League Club	Source	Date Signed	Seasons Played	Apps	Subs	Gls
Huddersfield T	South Kirkby Colliery	11.35				
Swindon T	Tr	08.36	36-37	25	-	6
Chelsea	Tr	06.38				
Southampton	Tr	05.39	46-47	49	-	22
Bolton W	Tr	10.47	47-50	92	-	19
Norwich C	Tr	11.50	50-51	6	-	0

BRADLEY Keith
Ellesmere Port, 31 January, 1946 (FB)

League Club	Source	Date Signed	Seasons Played	Apps	Subs	Gls
Aston Villa	App	06.63	64-71	115	7	2
Peterborough U	Tr	11.72	72-75	106	3	0

BRADLEY Lee Herbert
Manchester, 27 May, 1957 (CD)

League Club	Source	Date Signed	Seasons Played	Apps	Subs	Gls
Stockport Co	App	08.75	75	39	1	4
Halifax T	Tr	10.76	76-78	62	10	4

BRADLEY Mark Simon
Dudley, 14 January, 1988 WYth (FB)

League Club	Source	Date Signed	Seasons Played	Apps	Subs	Gls
Walsall	Sch	•	04	1	0	0

BRADLEY Noel Bernard
Manchester, 17 December, 1957 (FB)

League Club	Source	Date Signed	Seasons Played	Apps	Subs	Gls
Manchester C	St Robert's BC	11.78				
Bury	L	03.80	79	9	0	0
Bury	Tr	08.81	81	15	3	1
Chester	Tr	08.82	82	27	1	0

BRADLEY Patrick (Pat)
Sydney, Australia, 27 April, 1972 EYth (FB)

League Club	Source	Date Signed	Seasons Played	Apps	Subs	Gls
Bury	YT	07.90	90	0	1	0

BRADLEY Peter Kenneth
Donnington, 18 March, 1955 (CD)

League Club	Source	Date Signed	Seasons Played	Apps	Subs	Gls
Shrewsbury T	App	07.73	73	3	0	0

BRADLEY Ronald (Ron) John
Ettingshall, 24 April, 1939 EYth (WH)

League Club	Source	Date Signed	Seasons Played	Apps	Subs	Gls
West Bromwich A	Jnrs	06.56	62	13	-	0
Norwich C	Tr	07.64	64-65	4	0	0

BRADLEY Russell
Birmingham, 28 March, 1966 (CD)

League Club	Source	Date Signed	Seasons Played	Apps	Subs	Gls
Nottingham F	Dudley T	05.88				
Hereford U	L	11.88	88	12	0	1
Hereford U	Tr	07.89	89-91	75	2	3
Halifax T	Tr	09.91	91-92	54	2	3
Scunthorpe U	Tr	06.93	93-96	116	3	5
Hartlepool U	L	02.97	96	12	0	1
Hartlepool U	Tr	07.97	97	43	0	1

BRADLEY Shayne
Gloucester, 8 December, 1979 ESch (F)

League Club	Source	Date Signed	Seasons Played	Apps	Subs	Gls
Southampton	YT	01.98	98-99	0	4	0
Swindon T	L	03.99	98	6	1	0
Exeter C	L	09.99	99	6	2	1
Mansfield T	Tr	08.00	00-01	28	14	10
Chesterfield	Tr	12.02	02	1	8	2
Lincoln C	L	03.03	02	3	0	1

BRADLEY Warren
Hyde, 20 June, 1933 EAmat/E-3 (W)

League Club	Source	Date Signed	Seasons Played	Apps	Subs	Gls
Manchester U	Bishop Auckland	11.58	58-61	63	-	20
Bury	Tr	03.62	61-62	13	-	1

BRADLEY William (Willie)
Glasgow, 26 June, 1937 (W)

League Club	Source	Date Signed	Seasons Played	Apps	Subs	Gls
Hartlepools U	Ayr U	07.63	63-65	98	0	15

BRADSHAW Alan
Blackburn, 14 September, 1941 (M)

League Club	Source	Date Signed	Seasons Played	Apps	Subs	Gls
Blackburn Rov	Jnrs	07.63	62-64	11	-	2
Crewe Alex	Tr	05.65	65-72	287	7	51

BRADSHAW Carl
Sheffield, 2 October, 1968 EYth (FB)

League Club	Source	Date Signed	Seasons Played	Apps	Subs	Gls
Sheffield Wed	App	08.86	86-88	16	16	4
Barnsley	L	08.86	86	6	0	1
Manchester C	Tr	09.88	88	1	4	0
Sheffield U	Tr	09.89	89-93	122	25	8
Norwich C	Tr	07.94	94-97	55	10	2
Wigan Ath	Tr	10.97	97-00	109	11	11
Scunthorpe U	Tr	07.01	01	18	3	1

BRADSHAW Darren Shaun
Sheffield, 19 March, 1967 EYth (CD)

League Club	Source	Date Signed	Seasons Played	Apps	Subs	Gls
Chesterfield	Matlock T	08.87	87	18	0	0
York C	Matlock T	11.87	87-88	58	1	3
Newcastle U	Tr	08.89	89-91	32	6	0
Peterborough U	Tr	08.92	92-93	70	3	1
Plymouth Arg	L	08.94	94	5	1	1
Blackpool	Tr	10.94	94-97	61	6	1

BRADSHAW Gary
Beverley, 30 December, 1982 (F)

League Club	Source	Date Signed	Seasons Played	Apps	Subs	Gls
Hull C	YT	07.00	99-02	10	12	1

BRADSHAW George Frederick
Southport, 10 March, 1913 Died 1989 (G)

League Club	Source	Date Signed	Seasons Played	Apps	Subs	Gls
New Brighton	High Park Villa	09.33	32-34	83	-	0
Everton	Tr	11.34	34	2	-	0
Arsenal	Tr	05.35				
Doncaster Rov	Tr	05.36	36-37	53	-	0
Bury	Tr	06.38	38-49	118	-	0
Oldham Ath	Tr	07.50	50	1	-	0

BRADSHAW George Henry
Clay Cross, 24 March, 1920 Died 1994 (CF)

League Club	Source	Date Signed	Seasons Played	Apps	Subs	Gls
Chesterfield	Newstead Colliery	04.46	47	7	-	1

BRADSHAW Mark
Ashton-under-Lyne, 7 June, 1969 ESemiPro-1 (FB)

League Club	Source	Date Signed	Seasons Played	Apps	Subs	Gls
Blackpool	YT	12.87	86-90	34	8	1
York C	L	04.91	90	0	1	0
Halifax T	Macclesfield T	05.95	98-00	73	10	7

BRADSHAW Paul
Sheffield, 2 October, 1953 ESch/EYth (G)

League Club	Source	Date Signed	Seasons Played	Apps	Subs	Gls
Burnley	App	10.70	74-76	11	2	2
Sheffield Wed	Tr	09.76	76-77	62	2	9

BRADSHAW Paul William
Altrincham, 28 April, 1956 EYth/Eu21-4 (G)

League Club	Source	Date Signed	Seasons Played	Apps	Subs	Gls
Blackburn Rov	App	07.73	73-77	78	0	0
Wolverhampton W	Tr	09.77	77-83	200	0	0
West Bromwich A	Vancouver (Can)	04.85	85	8	0	0
Bristol Rov	Walsall (Coach)	03.87	86	5	0	0
Newport Co	Tr	07.87	87	23	0	0
West Bromwich A	Tr	08.88	88-89	6	0	0
Peterborough U	Tr	06.90	90	39	0	0

BRADY Garry
Glasgow, 7 September, 1976 SSch/SYth (M)

League Club	Source	Date Signed	Seasons Played	Apps	Subs	Gls
Tottenham H	YT	09.93	97	0	9	0
Newcastle U	Tr	07.98	98	3	6	0
Norwich C	L	03.00	99	6	0	0
Norwich C	L	09.00	00	2	0	0
Portsmouth	Tr	03.01	00-01	9	5	0

BRADY Jonathan (Jon) Edmund Alexander
Newcastle, Australia, 14 January, 1975 (M)

League Club	Source	Date Signed	Seasons Played	Apps	Subs	Gls
Swansea C	Brentford (YT)	07.93				
Rushden & Diamonds	Hayes	07.98	01	9	13	1

BRADY Kieron
Glasgow, 17 September, 1971 IRu21-3 (M)

League Club	Source	Date Signed	Seasons Played	Apps	Subs	Gls
Sunderland	YT	07.89	89-91	17	16	7
Doncaster Rov	L	10.92	92	4	0	3

BRADY Matthew (Matt) John
Marylebone, 27 October, 1977 (M)

League Club	Source	Date Signed	Seasons Played	Apps	Subs	Gls
Barnet	YT	07.96	94-96	2	8	0
Wycombe W	Boreham Wood	11.99	99-00	6	6	2

BRADY Patrick (Pat) Joseph
Dublin, 11 March, 1936 (FB)

League Club	Source	Date Signed	Seasons Played	Apps	Subs	Gls
Millwall	Home Farm	01.59	58-62	148	-	1
Queens Park Rgrs	Tr	07.63	63-64	62	-	0

BRADY Paul James
Marston Green, 26 March, 1961 (FB)

League Club	Source	Date Signed	Seasons Played	Apps	Subs	Gls
Birmingham C	App	08.78				
Northampton T	Tr	08.81	81-82	49	2	3
Crewe Alex	Tr	02.83	82-83	42	1	1

BRADY Thomas **Raymond (Ray)**
Dublin, 3 June, 1937 IR-6 (CD)

League Club	Source	Date Signed	Seasons Played	Apps	Subs	Gls
Millwall	Transport (Dublin)	07.57	57-62	165	-	4
Queens Park Rgrs	Tr	07.63	63-65	88	0	0

BRADY William (Liam)
Dublin, 13 February, 1956 IR-72 (M)

League Club	Source	Date Signed	Seasons Played	Apps	Subs	Gls
Arsenal	App	08.73	73-79	227	8	43
West Ham U	Ascoli	03.87	86-89	79	10	9

BRAGG Walter (Wally) Leonard
London, 8 July, 1929 (CD)

League Club	Source	Date Signed	Seasons Played	Apps	Subs	Gls
Brentford	Jnrs	01.47	46-56	161	-	6

BRAGSTAD Bjorn Otto
Trondheim, Norway, 15 January, 1971 Norway 15 (CD)

League Club	Source	Date Signed	Seasons Played	Apps	Subs	Gls
Derby Co	Rosenborg (Nor)	08.00	00	10	2	0
Birmingham C	L	09.01	01	3	0	0

BRAHAN Marcel Eric **Louis (Lou)**
Stepney, 3 December, 1926 Died 1995 (CD)

League Club	Source	Date Signed	Seasons Played	Apps	Subs	Gls
Leyton Orient (Am)	Walthamstow Ave	07.55	55	1	-	0

BRAIN Jonathan (Jonny) Robert
Carlisle, 11 February, 1983 (G)

League Club	Source	Date Signed	Seasons Played	Apps	Subs	Gls
Port Vale	Newcastle U (YT)	08.03	03-04	58	1	0

BRAIN Simon Anthony John
Evesham, 31 March, 1966 (F)

League Club	Source	Date Signed	Seasons Played	Apps	Subs	Gls
Hereford U	Cheltenham T	12.90	90-93	81	6	20

BRAITHWAITE Leon Jerome
Hackney, 17 December, 1972 (F)

League Club	Source	Date Signed	Seasons Played	Apps	Subs	Gls
Exeter C	Bishops Stortford	11.95	95-97	40	26	9

BRAITHWAITE Robert (Bobby) Munn
Belfast, 24 February, 1937 NISch/IrLge-8/NI-10 (W)

League Club	Source	Date Signed	Seasons Played	Apps	Subs	Gls
Middlesbrough	Linfield	06.63	63-66	67	1	12

BRAITHWAITE John **Roderick (Rod)**
Isleworth, 19 December, 1965 ESch (F)

League Club	Source	Date Signed	Seasons Played	Apps	Subs	Gls
Fulham	Jnrs	07.84	85-86	7	4	2

BRAMBLE Tesfaye (Tes) Walda Simeon
Ipswich, 20 July, 1980 (F)

League Club	Source	Date Signed	Seasons Played	Apps	Subs	Gls
Southend U	Cambridge C	01.01	00-04	101	38	29
Cambridge U	L	03.05	04	9	0	3

BRAMBLE Titus Malachi
Ipswich, 21 July, 1981 Eu21-10 (CD)

League Club	Source	Date Signed	Seasons Played	Apps	Subs	Gls
Ipswich T	YT	08.98	98-01	41	7	1
Colchester U	L	12.99	99	2	0	0
Newcastle U	Tr	07.02	02-04	58	6	1

BRAMHALL John
Warrington, 20 November, 1956 (CD)

League Club	Source	Date Signed	Seasons Played	Apps	Subs	Gls
Tranmere Rov	Stockton Heath	07.76	76-81	164	6	7
Bury	Tr	03.82	81-85	165	2	17
Chester C	L	11.85	85	4	0	0
Rochdale	Tr	08.86	86-87	86	0	13
Halifax T	Tr	08.88	88-89	62	0	5
Scunthorpe U	Tr	01.90	89-90	32	0	0

BRAMHALL Neil
Blackpool, 16 October, 1965 (F)

League Club	Source	Date Signed	Seasons Played	Apps	Subs	Gls
Blackpool	App	10.83	82	0	3	0

BRAMLEY Arthur
Mansfield, 25 March, 1929 (G)

League Club	Source	Date Signed	Seasons Played	Apps	Subs	Gls
Mansfield T	Bentinck Colliery	10.49	49-52	19	-	0

BRAMLEY Ernest
Mansfield, 29 August, 1920 Died 1993 (FB)

League Club	Source	Date Signed	Seasons Played	Apps	Subs	Gls
Mansfield T	Bolsover Colliery	12.38	38-47	45	-	1

BRAMLEY John **Stewart**
Scunthorpe, 19 April, 1946 (M)

League Club	Source	Date Signed	Seasons Played	Apps	Subs	Gls
Scunthorpe U	App	04.64	64-66	35	0	3

League Club	Source	Date Signed	Seasons Played	Apps	Subs	Gls
BRAMMER David (Dave)						
Bromborough, 28 February, 1975						(M)
Wrexham	YT	07.93	92-98	118	19	12
Port Vale	Tr	03.99	98-00	71	2	3
Crewe Alex	Tr	08.01	01-03	86	1	4
Stoke C	Tr	07.04	04	42	1	1
BRAMWELL John						
Ashton-in-Makerfield, 1 March, 1937						(FB)
Everton	Wigan Ath	04.58	58-59	52	-	0
Luton T	Tr	10.60	60-64	187	-	0
BRAMWELL Steven (Steve)						
Stockport, 9 October, 1970						(M)
Oldham Ath	YT	07.89	88	0	1	0
BRANAGAN James (Jim) Patrick Stephen						
Urmston, 3 July, 1955						(FB)
Oldham Ath	Jnrs	07.73	74-76	24	3	0
Huddersfield T	Cape Town C (SA)	11.77	77-78	37	1	0
Blackburn Rov	Tr	10.79	79-86	290	4	5
Preston NE	Tr	05.87	87	3	0	0
York C	Tr	10.87	87-88	40	2	1
BRANAGAN Keith Graham						
Fulham, 10 July, 1966 IRB/IR-1						(G)
Cambridge U	Jnrs	08.83	83-87	110	0	0
Millwall	Tr	03.88	89-91	46	0	0
Brentford	L	11.89	89	2	0	0
Gillingham	L	10.91	91	1	0	0
Bolton W	Tr	07.92	92-99	214	0	0
Ipswich T	Tr	04.00	00-01	2	1	0
BRANAGAN Kenneth (Ken)						
Salford, 27 July, 1930						(FB)
Manchester C	North Salford BC	11.48	50-59	196	-	3
Oldham Ath	Tr	10.60	60-65	177	0	5
BRANCA Marco						
Grosseto, Italy, 6 January, 1965						(F)
Middlesbrough	Inter Milan (It)	02.98	97-98	11	1	9
BRANCH Graham						
Liverpool, 12 February, 1972						(W)
Tranmere Rov	Heswall Ath	07.91	91-97	55	47	10
Bury	L	11.92	92	3	1	1
Wigan Ath	L	12.97	97	2	1	0
Stockport Co	Tr	07.98	98	10	4	3
Burnley	Tr	12.98	98-04	179	43	15
BRANCH Paul **Michael**						
Liverpool, 18 October, 1978 ESch/EYth/Eu21-1						(F)
Everton	YT	10.95	95-98	16	25	3
Manchester C	L	10.98	98	4	0	0
Wolverhampton W	Tr	11.99	99-01	61	11	10
Reading	L	03.02	01	0	2	0
Hull C	L	10.02	02	6	1	3
Bradford C	Tr	07.03	03	29	4	6
Chester C	Tr	07.04	04	31	2	11
[BRANCO] LEAL VAZ Claudio Ibraim						
Bage, Brazil, 4 April, 1964 Brazil int						(FB)
Middlesbrough	Genoa (It)	03.96	95-96	6	3	0
BRANCO Serge						
Douala, Cameroon, 11 October, 1980 Cameroon int						(M)
Queens Park Rgrs	VfB Stuttgart (Ger)	09.04	04	3	4	0
BRAND Andrew (Drew) Scougal						
Edinburgh, 8 November, 1957						(G)
Everton	App	11.75	75-76	2	0	0
Crewe Alex	L	02.77	76	14	0	0
Crewe Alex	L	08.78	78	1	0	0
Hereford U	Tr	05.80	80-81	54	0	0
Wrexham	L	11.82	82	1	0	0
Blackpool	Witton A	03.84	83	3	0	0
BRAND Kenneth (Ken) Reginald						
Whitechapel, 28 April, 1938						(FB)
Millwall	Eton Manor	09.56	56-57	13	-	0
BRAND Ralph Laidlaw						
Edinburgh, 18 December, 1936 SSch/Su23-1/SLge-5/S-8						(F)
Manchester C	Glasgow Rgrs	08.65	65-66	20	0	2
Sunderland	Tr	08.67	67-68	31	0	7
BRAND Raymond (Ray) Ernest						
Islington, 2 October, 1934						(CD)
Millwall	Hatfield T	10.51	55-60	150	-	8
Southend U	Tr	08.61	61-62	22	-	9

League Club	Source	Date Signed	Seasons Played	Apps	Subs	Gls
BRANDER George Milne						
Aberdeen, 1 November, 1929 Died 1995						(W)
Newcastle U	Raith Rov	03.52	52	5	-	2
BRANDON Christopher (Chris) William						
Bradford, 7 April, 1976						(M)
Torquay U	Bradford PA	08.99	99-01	64	7	8
Chesterfield	Tr	07.02	02-03	74	5	11
Huddersfield T	Tr	07.04	04	42	2	6
BRANDON Kenneth (Ken) Alfred						
Birmingham, 8 February, 1934 Died 1994						(W)
Swindon T (Am)	Kingstanding BC	01.53	52	5	-	0
Chester	Tr	06.53	53-55	39	-	7
Leicester C	Tr	07.56				
Darlington	Tr	06.58	58	16	-	1
BRANFOOT Ian Grant						
Gateshead, 26 January, 1947						(FB)
Sheffield Wed	Gateshead	07.65	65-69	33	3	0
Doncaster Rov	Tr	12.69	69-72	156	0	5
Lincoln C	Tr	07.73	73-77	166	0	11
BRANIFF Kevin Robert						
Belfast, 4 March, 1983 NISch/NIYth/NIu21-10/NIu23-1						(F)
Millwall	YT	04.00	00-04	14	19	1
Rushden & Diamonds	L	08.04	04	11	1	3
BRANNAN Gerard (Ged) Daniel						
Prescot, 15 January, 1972						(M)
Tranmere Rov	YT	07.90	90-96	227	11	20
Manchester C	Tr	03.97	96-97	38	5	4
Norwich C	L	08.98	98	10	1	1
Wigan Ath	Motherwell	02.01	00-02	49	3	0
Rochdale	L	09.03	03	11	0	1
BRANNAN Peter						
Bradford, 7 April, 1947						(M)
Bradford PA		02.69	68-69	38	4	2
BRANNAN Robert						
Bradford, 27 August, 1924 Died 1986						(W)
Bradford C		09.47	47	9	-	2
Bradford C	Scarborough	02.49	48	2	-	0
BRANNIGAN Kenneth (Ken)						
Glasgow, 8 June, 1965						(CD)
Sheffield Wed	Queen's Park	08.86	86	1	0	0
Stockport Co	L	08.86	86	8	0	0
Doncaster Rov	L	12.87	87	15	0	1
BRANSTON Guy Peter Bromley						
Leicester, 9 January, 1979						(CD)
Leicester C	YT	07.97				
Colchester U	L	02.98	97	12	0	1
Colchester U	L	08.98	98	0	1	0
Plymouth Arg	L	11.98	98	7	0	1
Lincoln C	L	08.99	99	4	0	0
Rotherham U	Tr	10.99	99-03	101	3	13
Wycombe W	L	09.03	03	9	0	0
Peterborough U	L	02.04	03	14	0	0
Sheffield Wed	Tr	07.04	04	10	1	0
Peterborough U	L	12.04	04	4	0	1
Oldham Ath	Tr	02.05	04	6	1	1
BRANSTON Terence (Terry) George						
Rugby, 25 July, 1938						(CD)
Northampton T		10.58	60-66	244	2	2
Luton T	Tr	06.67	67-70	100	1	9
Lincoln C	Tr	09.70	70-72	99	1	1
BRASS Christopher (Chris) Paul						
Easington, 24 July, 1975						(CD)
Burnley	YT	07.93	94-99	120	14	1
Torquay U	L	10.94	94	7	0	0
Halifax T	L	09.00	00	6	0	0
York C	Tr	03.01	00-03	128	2	5
BRASS Robert (Bobby) Albert						
Middlesbrough, 9 November, 1943						(WH)
Middlesbrough	Jnrs	06.62				
Hartlepools U	Tr	10.64	64-65	27	1	0
BRASTED Gordon Albert						
Burnham-on-Crouch, 30 June, 1933 Died 2000						(CF)
Arsenal	Burnham Ramblers	12.53				
Gillingham	Tr	07.56	56	5	-	4
BRATLEY Charles **Tony**						
Spalding, 30 April, 1939						(FB)
Grimsby T		08.57	58	2	-	0

League Club	Source	Date Signed	Seasons Played	Apps	Subs	Gls
BRATT Harold						
Salford, 8 October, 1939 ESch						(WH)
Manchester U	Jnrs	11.57				
Doncaster Rov	Tr	05.61	61-62	54	-	0
BRATTAN Gary						
Hull, 1 January, 1960						(M)
Hull C	App	01.78				
Cambridge U	North Ferriby U	08.87	87	7	1	0
BRAVO Raul						
Gandia, Spain, 14 April, 1981 Spain 7						(FB)
Leeds U (L)	Real Madrid (Sp)	02.03	02	5	0	0
BRAY Geoffrey (Geoff) Charles						
Chatham, 30 May, 1951						(F)
Oxford U	Erith & Belvedere	07.71	72-74	22	11	6
Swansea C	Tr	07.75	75-76	43	3	20
Torquay U	Tr	11.76	76	7	0	2
BRAY George						
Oswaldtwistle, 11 November, 1918 Died 2002						(WH)
Burnley	Great Harwood	10.37	38-51	241	-	8
BRAY Ian Michael						
Neath, 6 December, 1962						(FB)
Hereford U	App	12.80	81-84	105	3	4
Huddersfield T	Tr	07.85	85-89	87	2	1
Burnley	Tr	07.90	90-91	15	2	0
BRAY John						
Rishton, 16 March, 1937 Died 1992						(FB)
Blackburn Rov	Jnrs	03.54	59-64	153	-	2
Bury	Tr	04.65	65	32	0	0
BRAY Wayne						
Bristol, 17 November, 1964 ESch						(M)
Bristol C	App	11.81	81-82	28	1	2
BRAYLEY Albert (Berti)						
Basildon, 5 September, 1981						(F)
Queens Park Rgrs	West Ham U (YT)	08.00				
Swindon T	Tr	08.01	01	0	7	0
BRAYSON Paul						
Newcastle, 16 September, 1977 EYth						(F)
Newcastle U	YT	08.95				
Swansea C	L	01.97	96	11	0	5
Reading	Tr	03.98	97-99	15	26	1
Cardiff C	Tr	03.00	99-01	48	36	19
Cheltenham T	Tr	08.02	02-03	34	17	8
BRAYTON Barry James						
Carlisle, 29 September, 1938						(F)
Carlisle U		01.60	59-66	160	1	35
Workington	Tr	02.67	66-67	43	0	8
BRAZIER Colin James						
Solihull, 6 June, 1957 ESemiPro						(CD)
Wolverhampton W	Northfield T	08.75	76-81	69	9	2
Birmingham C	Tr	09.82	82	10	1	1
Lincoln C	AP Leamington	04.83	82	9	0	0
Walsall	Tr	08.83	83-86	114	1	4
BRAZIER Matthew (Matt) Ronald						
Leytonstone, 2 July, 1976						(M)
Queens Park Rgrs	YT	07.94	95-97	36	13	2
Fulham	Tr	03.98	97-98	4	5	1
Cardiff C	L	08.98	98	11	0	2
Cardiff C	Tr	07.99	99-00	43	13	3
Leyton Orient	Tr	01.02	01-03	46	0	2
BRAZIL Alan Bernard						
Glasgow, 15 June, 1959 Su21-8/S-13						(F)
Ipswich T	App	05.77	77	0	2	0
Ipswich T	Detroit (USA)	08.78	78-82	143	9	70
Tottenham H	Tr	03.83	82-83	29	2	9
Manchester U	Tr	06.84	84-85	18	13	8
Coventry C	Tr	01.86	85	15	0	2
Queens Park Rgrs	Tr	06.86	86	1	3	0
BRAZIL Derek Michael						
Dublin, 14 December, 1968 IRSch/IRYth/IRu21-9/IRB						(FB)
Manchester U	Rivermount BC	03.86	88-89	0	2	0
Oldham Ath	L	11.90	90	1	0	0
Swansea C	L	09.91	91	12	0	1
Cardiff C	Tr	08.92	92-95	109	6	1
BRAZIL Gary Nicholas						
Tunbridge Wells, 19 September, 1962						(F)
Sheffield U	Crystal Palace (App)	08.80	80-84	39	23	9

League Club	Source	Date Signed	Seasons Played	Apps	Subs	Gls
Port Vale	L	08.84	84	6	0	3
Preston NE	L	02.85	84	6	0	1
Preston NE	Tr	03.85	84-88	157	3	56
Newcastle U	Tr	02.89	88-89	7	16	2
Fulham	Tr	09.90	90-95	207	7	47
Cambridge U	Tr	08.96	96	1	0	1
Barnet	Tr	09.96	96	15	4	2
BREACKER Timothy (Tim) Sean						
Bicester, 2 July, 1965 Eu21-2						(FB)
Luton T	App	05.83	83-90	204	6	3
West Ham U	Tr	10.90	90-98	229	11	8
Queens Park Rgrs	L	10.98	98	2	0	0
Queens Park Rgrs	Tr	02.99	98-00	39	3	2
BREAKS Edward (Eddie)						
Halifax, 29 December, 1919 Died 2000						(FB)
Halifax T		07.48	48-54	179	-	1
BREARS Paul Arthur						
Oldham, 25 September, 1954						(M)
Rochdale	Oldham Ath (Am)	08.73	73-75	26	1	0
BREBNER Grant Iain						
Edinburgh, 6 December, 1977 SSch/Su21-17						(M)
Manchester U	Hutchison Vale BC	03.95				
Cambridge U	L	01.98	97	6	0	1
Reading	Tr	06.98	98-99	38	3	10
Stockport Co (L)	Hibernian	10.00	00	3	3	0
BRECKIN Ian						
Rotherham, 24 February, 1975						(CD)
Rotherham U	YT	11.93	93-96	130	2	6
Chesterfield	Tr	07.97	97-01	208	4	8
Wigan Ath	Tr	06.02	02-04	92	4	0
BRECKIN John						
Sheffield, 27 July, 1953						(FB)
Rotherham U	App	11.71	71-82	405	4	8
Darlington	L	10.72	72	4	0	0
Bury	Tr	02.83	82	17	0	0
Doncaster Rov	Tr	08.83	83	17	1	0
BREEN Gary Patrick						
Hendon, 12 December, 1973 IRu21-9/IR-62						(CD)
Maidstone U	Charlton Ath (Jnrs)	03.91	91	19	0	0
Gillingham	Tr	07.92	92-93	45	6	0
Peterborough U	Tr	08.94	94-95	68	1	1
Birmingham C	Tr	02.96	95-96	37	3	2
Coventry C	Tr	02.97	96-01	138	8	2
West Ham U	Tr	07.02	02	9	5	0
Sunderland	Tr	08.03	03-04	72	0	6
BREITENFELDER Friedrich Johann						
Vienna, Austria, 16 June, 1980						(M)
Luton T	FCM St Polten (Aut)	08.00	00	2	3	0
BREITKREUTZ Matthias						
Crivitz, Germany, 12 May, 1971						(M)
Aston Villa	Bergmann Borsig (Ger)	10.91	91-93	10	3	0
BREMNER Desmond (Des) George						
Aberchider, 7 September, 1952 Su23-9/SLge-1/S-1						(M)
Aston Villa	Hibernian	09.79	79-84	170	4	9
Birmingham C	Tr	09.84	84-88	167	1	5
Fulham	Tr	08.89	89	7	9	0
Walsall	Tr	03.90	89	2	4	0
BREMNER Kevin Johnston						
Banff, 7 October, 1957						(F)
Colchester U	Keith	10.80	80-82	89	6	31
Birmingham C	L	10.82	82	3	1	1
Wrexham	L	12.82	82	4	0	1
Plymouth Arg	L	01.83	82	5	0	1
Millwall	Tr	02.83	82-84	87	9	32
Reading	Tr	08.85	85-86	60	4	21
Brighton & Hove A	Tr	07.87	87-89	125	3	36
Peterborough U	Tr	07.90	90	13	4	3
Shrewsbury T (L)	Dundee	03.92	91	7	0	2
BREMNER William (Billy) John						
Stirling, 9 December, 1942 Died 1997 SSch/Su23-4/S-54						(M)
Leeds U	Jnrs	12.59	59-76	586	1	90
Hull C	Tr	09.76	76-77	61	0	6
Doncaster Rov	Tr	09.79	79-81	2	3	0
BRENEN Albert (Bert)						
South Shields, 5 October, 1915 Died 1995						(WH)
York C	St John's College	08.38	38-50	204	-	13

League Club	Source	Date Signed	Seasons Played	Apps	Subs	Gls
BRENNAN Bryan						
Halifax, 25 May, 1933 ESch						(CF)
Stockport Co	Jnrs	06.50	50	4	-	0
BRENNAN Dean James Gary						
Dublin, 17 June, 1980						(M)
Sheffield Wed	Stella Maris	11.97				
Luton T	Tr	08.00	00	2	7	0
BRENNAN Francis (Frank)						
Annathill, 23 April, 1924 Died 1997 SWar-2/S-7						(CD)
Newcastle U	Airdrie	05.46	46-55	318	-	3
BRENNAN Harry						
Derby, 17 November, 1930						(IF)
Shrewsbury T	Gresley Rov	12.53	53-54	19	-	3
BRENNAN Ian						
Easington, 25 March, 1953						(FB)
Burnley	App	10.70	73-79	173	2	11
Bolton W	Tr	12.80	80-81	16	1	0
BRENNAN James (Jim)						
Downpatrick, 29 February, 1932						(W)
Birmingham C	Glentoran	06.52				
Swindon T	Tr	06.54	54-55	16	-	1
BRENNAN James (Jim) Gerald						
Toronto, Canada, 8 May, 1977 Cau23-1/Ca-38						(FB)
Bristol C	Sora Lazio (Can)	10.94	96-99	51	4	3
Nottingham F	Tr	10.99	99-02	117	6	1
Huddersfield T	L	03.01	00	0	2	0
Norwich C	Tr	07.03	03-04	13	12	1
BRENNAN Malcolm						
Manchester, 11 November, 1934						(IF)
Crewe Alex		12.52	56	1	-	0
BRENNAN Mark Robert						
Rossendale, 4 October, 1965 EYth/Eu21-5						(M)
Ipswich T	App	04.83	83-87	165	3	19
Middlesbrough	Tr	07.88	88-89	61	4	6
Manchester C	Tr	07.90	90-91	25	4	6
Oldham Ath	Tr	11.92	92-95	82	8	7
BRENNAN Martin Ian						
Leytonstone, 14 September, 1982						(G)
Charlton Ath	Tottenham H (YT)	11.00				
Cambridge U	Tr	08.02	02	1	0	0
BRENNAN Matthew (Matt) Hyland						
Glasgow, 3 January, 1943						(IF)
Luton T	St Roch's	06.62	62	4	-	1
BRENNAN Michael (Mike)						
Salford, 17 May, 1952						(F)
Manchester C	App	12.69	70-72	1	3	0
Stockport Co	L	02.72	71	18	0	3
Rochdale	Tr	10.73	73-74	35	2	4
BRENNAN Patrick (Paddy) Joseph						
Dublin, 1 March, 1924 Died 1991						(WH)
Brighton & Hove A	Shelbourne	08.48	48-50	45	-	0
BRENNAN Raymond (Ray) John						
Blackpool, 13 November, 1944						(IF)
Blackburn Rov	Wolverhampton W (Am)	07.62				
Barrow	Tr	03.64	63-64	46	-	10
BRENNAN Robert (Bobby) Anderson						
Belfast, 14 March, 1925 Died 2002 IrLge-1/I-5						(IF)
Luton T	Distillery	10.47	47-48	69	-	22
Birmingham C	Tr	07.49	49	39	-	7
Fulham	Tr	06.50	50-52	73	-	13
Norwich C	Tr	07.53	53-55	117	-	30
Norwich C	Yarmouth T	03.57	56-59	108	-	14
BRENNAN James **Seamus (Shay)** Anthony						
Manchester, 6 May, 1937 Died 2000 LoI-1/IR-19						(FB)
Manchester U	Jnrs	04.55	57-69	291	1	3
BRENNAN Stephen (Steve) Anthony						
Mile End, 3 September, 1958						(M)
Crystal Palace	App	02.76	76-77	2	1	1
Plymouth Arg	Tr	08.78	78	6	0	0
BRENT Peter						
Staveley, 18 November, 1937 Died 1988						(WH)
Chesterfield	Jnrs	05.55	59	2	-	0

League Club	Source	Date Signed	Seasons Played	Apps	Subs	Gls
BRENTANO Stephen Ronald						
Hull, 9 September, 1961						(FB)
Hull C	North Ferriby U	03.82	84-86	11	1	0
Doncaster Rov	Bridlington T	08.93	93	1	0	0
BRESLAN Geoffrey (Geoff) Francis						
Torquay, 4 June, 1980						(M)
Exeter C	YT	01.99	97-02	61	48	6
BRESSINGTON Graham						
Eton, 8 July, 1966						(M)
Lincoln C	Wycombe W	10.87	88-92	136	5	7
Southend U	Tr	07.93	93-94	46	2	5
BRETHERTON Thomas (Tom) Alexander						
Chorley, 9 April, 1920 Died 1998						(IF)
Accrington St	Leyland Motors	02.47	46	4	-	0
BRETT David Stephen						
Chester, 8 April, 1961						(M)
Chester C	Colwyn Bay	08.83	83-85	52	15	6
BRETT Ronald (Ron) Alexander						
Stanford-le-Hope, 4 September, 1937 Died 1962						(W)
Crystal Palace	Jnrs	09.54	55-58	36	-	12
West Ham U	Tr	06.59	59-60	12	-	4
Crystal Palace	Tr	03.62	61	8	-	1
BRETTELL Raymond (Ray)						
Strood, 22 August, 1935						(W)
Doncaster Rov (Am)		01.61	60	9	-	1
BREVETT Rupis (Rufus) Emanuel						
Derby, 24 September, 1969						(FB)
Doncaster Rov	YT	07.88	87-90	106	3	3
Queens Park Rgrs	Tr	02.91	90-97	141	11	1
Fulham	Tr	01.98	97-02	171	2	1
West Ham U	Tr	01.03	02-04	24	1	1
BREWER Anthony (Tony) Peter						
Edmonton, 20 May, 1932 Died 1989						(G)
Millwall	Jnrs	10.49	50-57	47	-	0
Northampton T	Tr	02.57	58-60	87	-	0
BREWSTER George						
Barlborough, 19 October, 1925						(IF)
Bristol C	Retford T	09.49	49-50	13	-	3
BREWSTER John Robert						
Creswell, 19 August, 1942						(IF)
Sheffield U	Jnrs	04.60				
Torquay U	Tr	08.64	64-65	21	0	2
BREWSTER William (Bill) Clark						
Kinglassie, 4 August, 1933						(G)
Chelsea	Dundonald Bluebell	08.51				
Southend U	Tr	08.55	55	2	-	0
BRICE Gordon Harry Joseph						
Bedford, 4 May, 1924 Died 2003						(CD)
Luton T	Bedford St Clement's	10.44	46	13	-	0
Wolverhampton W	Tr	05.47	47	12	-	0
Reading	Tr	03.48	47-52	198	-	9
Fulham	Tr	12.52	52-55	87	-	1
BRICKLEY Dennis						
Bradford, 9 September, 1929 Died 1983 EYth						(W)
Bradford PA	Huddersfield T (Am)	08.49	50-56	169	-	24
BRIDDON Samuel (Sam)						
Alfreton, 26 July, 1915 Died 1975						(WH)
Brentford	Port Vale (Am)	08.35	38	6	-	0
Swansea T	Tr	07.39	46	18	-	0
BRIDGE Michael **John (Jackie)**						
Great Wakering, 30 May, 1932						(WH)
Southend U	Jnrs	08.50	52-55	53	-	3
BRIDGE Wayne Michael						
Southampton, 5 August, 1980 EYth/Eu21-8/E-20						(FB)
Southampton	YT	01.98	98-02	140	12	2
Chelsea	Tr	07.03	03-04	45	3	1
BRIDGER David (Dave) James						
Hartley Wintney, 8 November, 1941						(FB)
Reading		03.62	62-64	10	-	0
BRIDGES Barry John						
Horsford, 29 April, 1941 ESch/EYth/FLge-1/E-4						(F)
Chelsea	Jnrs	05.58	58-65	174	2	80
Birmingham C	Tr	05.66	66-68	83	0	37

League Club	Source	Date Signed	Seasons Played	Apps	Subs	Gls
Queens Park Rgrs	Tr	08.68	68-70	72	0	31
Millwall	Tr	09.70	70-71	77	0	27
Brighton & Hove A	Tr	09.72	72-73	56	10	14

BRIDGES Benjamin (Ben)
Hull, 3 February, 1937 (IF)

League Club	Source	Date Signed	Seasons Played	Apps	Subs	Gls
Hull C	Jnrs	08.55	57	1	-	0

BRIDGES Bernard
Doncaster, 28 February, 1959 (CD)

League Club	Source	Date Signed	Seasons Played	Apps	Subs	Gls
Scunthorpe U	Jnrs	07.76	76-77	22	1	0

BRIDGES David Stephen
Huntingdon, 22 September, 1982 (M)

League Club	Source	Date Signed	Seasons Played	Apps	Subs	Gls
Cambridge U	YT	03.02	01-03	18	27	5

BRIDGES Harold
Burton-on-Trent, 30 June, 1915 Died 1989 (IF)

League Club	Source	Date Signed	Seasons Played	Apps	Subs	Gls
Manchester C	Burton T	04.37				
Tranmere Rov	Tr	07.39	46-47	33	-	9

BRIDGES Michael
North Shields, 5 August, 1978 ESch/EYth/Eu21-3 (F)

League Club	Source	Date Signed	Seasons Played	Apps	Subs	Gls
Sunderland	YT	11.95	95-98	31	48	16
Leeds U	Tr	07.99	99-03	40	16	19
Newcastle U	L	02.04	03	0	6	0
Bolton W	Tr	07.04				
Sunderland	Tr	09.04	04	5	14	1

BRIDGETT John (Jack)
Walsall, 10 April, 1929 (CD)

League Club	Source	Date Signed	Seasons Played	Apps	Subs	Gls
West Bromwich A	Jnrs	05.46				
Walsall	Tr	08.50	50-54	106	-	18

BRIDGETT Raymond (Ray) Alwyne
Nottingham, 5 April, 1947 Died 1997 (FB)

League Club	Source	Date Signed	Seasons Played	Apps	Subs	Gls
Nottingham F	Jnrs	05.64	67-69	2	2	0

BRIDGE-WILKINSON Marc
Nuneaton, 16 March, 1979 (M)

League Club	Source	Date Signed	Seasons Played	Apps	Subs	Gls
Derby Co	YT	03.97	98	0	1	0
Carlisle U	L	03.99	98	4	3	0
Port Vale	Tr	07.00	00-03	111	13	31
Stockport Co	Tr	08.04	04	19	3	2
Bradford C	Tr	02.05	04	12	0	3

BRIDGWOOD Gerald (Gerry)
Stoke-on-Trent, 17 October, 1944 (M)

League Club	Source	Date Signed	Seasons Played	Apps	Subs	Gls
Stoke C	App	10.61	60-68	90	5	6
Shrewsbury T	Tr	02.69	68-72	113	4	7

BRIEN Anthony (Tony) James
Dublin, 10 February, 1969 IRYth (CD)

League Club	Source	Date Signed	Seasons Played	Apps	Subs	Gls
Leicester C	App	02.87	87-88	12	4	1
Chesterfield	Tr	12.88	88-93	201	3	8
Rotherham U	Tr	10.93	93-94	41	2	2
West Bromwich A	Tr	07.95	95	2	0	0
Mansfield T	L	02.96	95	4	0	0
Chester C	L	03.96	95	8	0	0
Hull C	Tr	07.96	96-97	43	4	1

BRIEN William Roy
Stoke-on-Trent, 11 November, 1930 Died 1987 (WH)

League Club	Source	Date Signed	Seasons Played	Apps	Subs	Gls
Port Vale		05.51	53	1	-	0

BRIER John David
Halifax, 3 April, 1941 (WH)

League Club	Source	Date Signed	Seasons Played	Apps	Subs	Gls
Burnley	Jnrs	06.58				
Halifax T	Tr	08.61	61-65	78	2	0

BRIERLEY Keith
Dewsbury, 14 December, 1951 (F)

League Club	Source	Date Signed	Seasons Played	Apps	Subs	Gls
Halifax T	Jnrs	12.69	69-72	51	4	11

BRIERLEY Kenneth (Ken)
Ashton-under-Lyne, 3 April, 1926 (WH)

League Club	Source	Date Signed	Seasons Played	Apps	Subs	Gls
Oldham Ath	Range Boilers	04.45	46-47	58	-	5
Liverpool	Tr	02.48	47-52	58	-	8
Oldham Ath	Tr	03.53	52-54	67	-	5

BRIGGS Alec Michael
Sheffield, 21 June, 1939 (FB)

League Club	Source	Date Signed	Seasons Played	Apps	Subs	Gls
Bristol C	Jnrs	04.57	57-69	349	2	1

BRIGGS Charles (Charlie) Edward
Newtown, 4 April, 1911 (G)

League Club	Source	Date Signed	Seasons Played	Apps	Subs	Gls
Fulham	Guildford C	12.35				
Crystal Palace	Guildford C	05.36				
Bradford PA	Guildford C	05.37				
Halifax T	Tr	03.38	37-38	53	-	0
Rochdale	Clyde	05.47	46-47	12	-	0

BRIGGS John Cyril
Lower Broughton, 24 November, 1918 Died 1998 ESch (CD)

League Club	Source	Date Signed	Seasons Played	Apps	Subs	Gls
Manchester U	Darwen	10.44				
Accrington St	Tr	08.45	46-49	135	-	1
Southport	Tr	03.50	49	3	-	0

BRIGGS Gary
Leeds, 21 June, 1959 (CD)

League Club	Source	Date Signed	Seasons Played	Apps	Subs	Gls
Middlesbrough	App	05.77				
Oxford U	Tr	01.78	77-88	418	2	18
Blackpool	Tr	06.89	89-94	137	0	4

BRIGGS George
Easington, 27 February, 1923 (CD)

League Club	Source	Date Signed	Seasons Played	Apps	Subs	Gls
Crystal Palace	Shotton Colliery	11.47	48-54	150	-	4

BRIGGS John (Jackie)
Barnsley, 27 October, 1924 Died 1992 (W)

League Club	Source	Date Signed	Seasons Played	Apps	Subs	Gls
Gillingham	Southall	10.46	50-52	52	-	14

BRIGGS Keith
Glossop, 11 December, 1981 (M)

League Club	Source	Date Signed	Seasons Played	Apps	Subs	Gls
Stockport Co	YT	08.99	99-02	47	11	2
Norwich C	Tr	01.03	02-03	2	3	0
Crewe Alex	L	08.04	04	3	0	0
Stockport Co	Tr	01.05	04	14	2	2

BRIGGS Malcolm Douglas
Sunderland, 14 September, 1961 (M)

League Club	Source	Date Signed	Seasons Played	Apps	Subs	Gls
Birmingham C	App	08.79	78	0	1	0

BRIGGS Maxwell (Max) Francis
Bramerton, 9 September, 1948 (M)

League Club	Source	Date Signed	Seasons Played	Apps	Subs	Gls
Norwich C	Jnrs	12.67	68-73	127	8	1
Oxford U	Tr	02.74	73-77	94	3	1

BRIGGS William **Ronald (Ronnie)**
Belfast, 29 March, 1943 NI-2 (G)

League Club	Source	Date Signed	Seasons Played	Apps	Subs	Gls
Manchester U	Jnrs	03.60	60-61	9	-	0
Swansea T	Tr	05.64	64	27	-	0
Bristol Rov	Tr	06.65	65-67	35	0	0

BRIGGS Stephen (Steve)
Leeds, 2 December, 1946 (F)

League Club	Source	Date Signed	Seasons Played	Apps	Subs	Gls
Leeds U	Jnrs	10.65				
Doncaster Rov	Tr	02.69	68-72	114	10	34

BRIGGS Thomas (Tommy) Henry
Chesterfield, 27 November, 1923 Died 1984 EB (CF)

League Club	Source	Date Signed	Seasons Played	Apps	Subs	Gls
Plymouth Arg		03.46				
Grimsby T	Tr	05.47	47-50	116	-	78
Coventry C	Tr	01.51	50-51	11	-	7
Birmingham C	Tr	09.51	51-52	50	-	22
Blackburn Rov	Tr	12.52	52-57	194	-	140
Grimsby T	Tr	03.58	57-58	19	-	9

BRIGGS Thomas (Tom) Raymond
Rotherham, 11 May, 1919 Died 1999 (FB)

League Club	Source	Date Signed	Seasons Played	Apps	Subs	Gls
Huddersfield T		02.46	46-49	45	-	0
Crewe Alex	Tr	12.49	49-55	206	-	2

BRIGGS Walter (Wally)
Middlesbrough, 29 November, 1922 Died 1990 (G)

League Club	Source	Date Signed	Seasons Played	Apps	Subs	Gls
Middlesbrough	Cochranes	05.47	46-47	2	-	0
Southport	Tr	06.48	48	4	-	0
Hartlepools U	Tr	09.49	49-51	44	-	0

BRIGGS Wilson Waite
Gorebridge, 15 May, 1942 Died 2005 (FB)

League Club	Source	Date Signed	Seasons Played	Apps	Subs	Gls
Aston Villa	Arniston Rgrs	08.59	61-62	2	-	0

BRIGHAM Harold (Harry)
Selby, 19 November, 1914 Died 1978 (FB)

League Club	Source	Date Signed	Seasons Played	Apps	Subs	Gls
Stoke C	Frickley Colliery	05.36	36-46	104	-	0
Nottingham F	Tr	11.46	46-47	35	-	2
York C	Tr	07.48	48-49	56	-	5

BRIGHT David
Prudhoe, 24 December, 1946 (FB)

League Club	Source	Date Signed	Seasons Played	Apps	Subs	Gls
Sunderland	West Wylam Jnrs	08.65				
Preston NE	Tr	08.67	68	1	0	0
Oldham Ath	Tr	03.69	68-69	19	0	0

BRIGHT David John
Bath, 5 September, 1972 (F)

League Club	Source	Date Signed	Seasons Played	Apps	Subs	Gls
Stoke C	YT	07.91	90	0	1	0

BRIGHT Gerald (Gerry)
Northampton, 2 December, 1934 (CF)

League Club	Source	Date Signed	Seasons Played	Apps	Subs	Gls
Northampton T		02.57	56-57	4	-	0

BRIGHT Mark Abraham
Stoke-on-Trent, 6 June, 1962 (F)

League Club	Source	Date Signed	Seasons Played	Apps	Subs	Gls
Port Vale	Leek T	10.81	81-83	18	11	10
Leicester C	Tr	07.84	84-86	26	16	6
Crystal Palace	Tr	11.86	86-92	224	3	91
Sheffield Wed	Tr	09.92	92-96	112	21	48
Millwall	L	12.96	96	3	0	1
Charlton Ath	Sion (Swi)	04.97	96-98	18	9	10

BRIGHT Stewart Linden
Colchester, 13 October, 1957 (FB)

League Club	Source	Date Signed	Seasons Played	Apps	Subs	Gls
Colchester U	App	10.75	75-76	23	2	0

BRIGHTON Thomas (Tom) James
Irvine, 28 March, 1984 SYth/Su21-4 (F)

League Club	Source	Date Signed	Seasons Played	Apps	Subs	Gls
Scunthorpe U (L)	Glasgow Rgrs	08.04	04	2	3	0

BRIGHTWELL David John
Lutterworth, 7 January, 1971 (CD)

League Club	Source	Date Signed	Seasons Played	Apps	Subs	Gls
Manchester C	Jnrs	04.88	91-94	35	8	1
Chester C	L	03.91	90	6	0	0
Lincoln C	L	08.95	95	5	0	0
Stoke C	L	09.95	95	0	1	0
Bradford C	Tr	12.95	95-96	23	1	0
Blackpool	L	12.96	96	1	1	0
Northampton T	Tr	07.97	97	34	1	1
Carlisle U	Tr	07.98	98-99	78	0	4
Hull C	Tr	06.00	00	24	3	2
Darlington	Tr	02.01	00-01	34	2	0

BRIGHTWELL Ian Robert
Lutterworth, 9 April, 1968 EYth/Eu21-4 (FB)

League Club	Source	Date Signed	Seasons Played	Apps	Subs	Gls
Manchester C	Congleton T	05.86	86-97	285	36	18
Coventry C	Tr	07.98				
Walsall	Tr	02.00	99-01	77	4	0
Stoke C	Tr	03.02	01	3	1	0
Port Vale	Tr	08.02	02-03	36	1	0
Macclesfield T	Tr	07.04	04	3	3	0

BRIGHTWELL Stuart
Easington, 31 January, 1979 ESch (M)

League Club	Source	Date Signed	Seasons Played	Apps	Subs	Gls
Manchester U	YT	02.96				
Hartlepool U	Tr	07.98	98	8	9	1

BRIGNALL Stephen (Steve) James Charles
Tenterden, 12 June, 1960 (CD)

League Club	Source	Date Signed	Seasons Played	Apps	Subs	Gls
Arsenal	App	05.78	78	0	2	0

BRIGNULL Philip (Phil) Arthur
Stratford, 2 October, 1960 ESch (CD)

League Club	Source	Date Signed	Seasons Played	Apps	Subs	Gls
West Ham U	App	09.78	78	0	1	0
Bournemouth	Tr	08.81	81-84	128	1	11
Wrexham	L	12.85	85	5	0	1
Cardiff C	Tr	02.86	85-86	49	0	0
Newport Co	Tr	08.87	87	3	0	0

BRILEY Leslie (Les)
Lambeth, 2 October, 1956 (M)

League Club	Source	Date Signed	Seasons Played	Apps	Subs	Gls
Chelsea	App	06.74				
Hereford U	Tr	05.76	76-77	60	1	2
Wimbledon	Tr	02.78	77-79	59	2	2
Aldershot	Tr	03.80	79-83	157	0	11
Millwall	Tr	05.84	84-90	225	2	13
Brighton & Hove A	Tr	08.91	91	11	4	0

BRILL Dean Michael
Luton, 2 December, 1985 (G)

League Club	Source	Date Signed	Seasons Played	Apps	Subs	Gls
Luton T	Sch	●	03	4	1	0

BRIMACOMBE Anthony (Tony)
Plymouth, 6 August, 1939 (F)

League Club	Source	Date Signed	Seasons Played	Apps	Subs	Gls
Plymouth Arg (Am)	Barnet	12.65	65-67	15	1	0

BRIMACOMBE John
Plymouth, 25 November, 1968 (FB)

League Club	Source	Date Signed	Seasons Played	Apps	Subs	Gls
Plymouth Arg	Saltash U	08.85	85-89	93	5	3

BRIMS Donald (Don) William
Auchendinny, 8 January, 1936 Died 1987 (WH)

League Club	Source	Date Signed	Seasons Played	Apps	Subs	Gls
Bradford PA	Motherwell	05.58	58-59	76	-	3

BRINDLE John (Jack) James
Blackburn, 12 July, 1917 Died 1975 (IF)

League Club	Source	Date Signed	Seasons Played	Apps	Subs	Gls
Burnley	Blackburn Rov (Am)	03.43				
Rochdale	Howard & Bullough	09.45				
Chelsea	Tr	03.46				
Rochdale	Tr	08.47	47	1	-	0
New Brighton	Tr	03.48	47	9	-	3

BRINDLE William (Billy)
Liverpool, 29 January, 1950 (M)

League Club	Source	Date Signed	Seasons Played	Apps	Subs	Gls
Everton	App	08.67	67	1	0	0
Barnsley	Tr	05.70	70	0	1	0

BRINDLEY Christopher (Chris) Peter
Stoke-on-Trent, 5 July, 1969 (CD)

League Club	Source	Date Signed	Seasons Played	Apps	Subs	Gls
Wolverhampton W	Hednesford T	11.86	86	7	0	0

BRINDLEY John
Ashbourne, 2 May, 1931 (IF)

League Club	Source	Date Signed	Seasons Played	Apps	Subs	Gls
Chesterfield	Buxton	12.53	53	1	-	0

BRINDLEY John (Bill) Charles
Nottingham, 29 January, 1947 ESch/EYth (FB)

League Club	Source	Date Signed	Seasons Played	Apps	Subs	Gls
Nottingham F	Jnrs	02.64	65-69	7	7	1
Notts Co	Tr	05.70	70-75	221	2	0
Gillingham	Tr	07.76	76	19	1	1

BRINE Peter Kenneth
Greenwich, 18 July, 1953 (M)

League Club	Source	Date Signed	Seasons Played	Apps	Subs	Gls
Middlesbrough	App	09.70	72-77	59	20	6

BRINTON Ernest (Ernie) James
Bristol, 26 May, 1908 Died 1981 (WH)

League Club	Source	Date Signed	Seasons Played	Apps	Subs	Gls
Bristol C	Avonmouth T	02.30	29-36	249	-	7
Newport Co	Tr	06.37	37-38	75	-	3
Aldershot	Tr	08.46	46	12	-	0

BRINTON John (Jack) Victor
Avonmouth, 11 July, 1916 Died 1997 (W)

League Club	Source	Date Signed	Seasons Played	Apps	Subs	Gls
Bristol C	Avonmouth T	08.35	35-36	12	-	1
Newport Co	Tr	07.37	37	6	-	0
Derby Co	Tr	01.38	37	8	-	2
Stockport Co	Tr	07.46	46-47	58	-	9
Leyton Orient	Tr	08.48	48	4	-	1

BRISCO Neil Anthony
Wigan, 26 January, 1978 (M)

League Club	Source	Date Signed	Seasons Played	Apps	Subs	Gls
Manchester C	YT	03.97				
Port Vale	Tr	08.98	98-03	105	13	2
Rochdale	Tr	07.04	04	6	5	0

BRISCOE Anthony (Tony) Maurice
Birmingham, 16 August, 1978 (F)

League Club	Source	Date Signed	Seasons Played	Apps	Subs	Gls
Shrewsbury T	YT	●	96	0	1	0

BRISCOE James Edward
Clock Face, 23 April, 1917 Died 1981 (CF)

League Club	Source	Date Signed	Seasons Played	Apps	Subs	Gls
Preston NE	St Helens T	05.34	36	5	-	0
Northampton T	Heart of Midlothian	09.46	46-48	53	-	17

BRISCOE James Patrick
Swinton-on-Dearne, 14 October, 1923 (CF)

League Club	Source	Date Signed	Seasons Played	Apps	Subs	Gls
Sheffield Wed		08.46	46	5	-	3

BRISCOE John
Huddersfield, 31 May, 1947 (F)

League Club	Source	Date Signed	Seasons Played	Apps	Subs	Gls
Barnsley	Jnrs	10.66	66-67	11	0	5

BRISCOE Lee Stephen
Pontefract, 30 September, 1975 Eu21-5 (FB)

League Club	Source	Date Signed	Seasons Played	Apps	Subs	Gls
Sheffield Wed	YT	05.94	93-99	48	30	1
Manchester C	L	02.98	97	5	0	1
Burnley	Tr	07.00	00-02	100	6	7
Preston NE	Tr	07.03	03	2	0	0

BRISCOE Michael James
Northampton, 4 July, 1983 (FB)

League Club	Source	Date Signed	Seasons Played	Apps	Subs	Gls
Coventry C	Harpole	04.03				
Macclesfield T	Tr	07.04	04	12	2	0

BRISCOE Robert Dean
Derby, 4 September, 1969 (FB)

League Club	Source	Date Signed	Seasons Played	Apps	Subs	Gls
Derby Co	YT	09.87	89-90	10	3	1

BRISLEY Terence (Terry) William
Stepney, 4 July, 1950 (M)

League Club	Source	Date Signed	Seasons Played	Apps	Subs	Gls
Orient	App	07.68	70-74	133	9	9
Southend U	L	03.75	74	8	0	0
Millwall	Tr	07.75	75-77	106	1	14
Charlton Ath	Tr	01.78	77-78	44	4	5
Portsmouth	Tr	07.79	79-80	55	0	13

BRISSETT Jason Curtis
Wanstead, 7 September, 1974 (F)

League Club	Source	Date Signed	Seasons Played	Apps	Subs	Gls
Peterborough U	Arsenal (YT)	06.93	93-94	27	8	0
Bournemouth	Tr	12.94	94-97	96	28	8
Walsall	Tr	07.98	98-99	32	10	2
Cheltenham T	L	11.99	99	5	3	0
Leyton Orient	Tr	07.00	00	2	2	0

BRISSETT Trevor Anthony
Stoke-on-Trent, 2 January, 1961 (FB)

League Club	Source	Date Signed	Seasons Played	Apps	Subs	Gls
Stoke C	Jnrs	04.78				
Port Vale	Tr	05.80	80-81	47	8	0
Darlington	Tr	08.82	82	10	2	0

League Club	Source	Date Signed	Seasons Played	Career Record Apps	Subs	Gls
BRISTOW George Andrew						
Chiswick, 25 June, 1933 (WH)						
Brentford	Jnrs	07.50	50-60	245	-	8
BRISTOW Guy Austin						
Kingsbury, 23 October, 1955 (CD)						
Watford	App	07.73	74-76	18	5	0
BRITT Martin Charles						
Leigh-on-Sea, 17 January, 1946 EYth (CF)						
West Ham U	App	01.63	62-65	20	0	6
Blackburn Rov	Tr	03.66	65	8	0	0
BRITTAIN Martin						
Newcastle, 29 December, 1984 (M)						
Newcastle U	Sch	09.03	03	0	1	0
BRITTAN Colin						
Bristol, 2 June, 1927 (WH)						
Tottenham H	Bristol North OB	10.48	50-57	41	-	1
BRITTEN Martyn Edward Walter						
Bristol, 1 May, 1955 (W)						
Bristol Rov	App	05.73	74-76	17	3	2
Reading	Tr	08.77	77-78	6	2	0
BRITTON Gerard (Gerry) Joseph						
Glasgow, 20 October, 1970 (F)						
Reading (L)	Glasgow Celtic	11.91	91	0	2	0
BRITTON Ian						
Dundee, 19 May, 1954 (W)						
Chelsea	App	07.71	72-81	253	10	33
Blackpool	Arbroath	12.83	83-85	100	6	15
Burnley	Tr	08.86	86-88	102	6	10
BRITTON James (Jimmy)						
Salford, 27 May, 1920 (WH)						
Bradford PA	Lowestoft T	01.46	46	1	-	0
Rochdale	Tr	12.47	47-48	20	-	0
BRITTON Leon James						
Merton, 16 September, 1982 EYth (M)						
West Ham U	YT	09.99				
Swansea C	Tr	12.02	02-04	83	14	4
BRKOVIC Ahmet						
Dubrovnik, Croatia, 23 September, 1974 (M)						
Leyton Orient	HNK Dubrovnik (Cro)	10.99	99-00	59	10	8
Luton T	Tr	10.01	01-04	109	22	20
BROAD Joseph (Joe) Reginald						
Bristol, 24 August, 1982 (M)						
Plymouth Arg	YT	02.02	01-02	2	10	0
Torquay U	Tr	09.03	03	4	10	0
Walsall	Tr	08.04	04	5	5	0
BROAD Ronald (Ron)						
Sandbach, 18 August, 1933 (W)						
Crewe Alex (Am)	Congleton T	12.55	55	6	-	0
BROAD Stephen						
Epsom, 10 June, 1980 (CD)						
Chelsea	YT	02.98				
Southend U	Tr	03.01	00-02	57	2	3
BROADBENT Albert Henry						
Dudley, 20 August, 1934 (M)						
Notts Co	Dudley T	03.52	53-54	31	-	11
Sheffield Wed	Tr	07.55	55-57	81	-	17
Rotherham U	Tr	12.57	57-58	48	-	14
Doncaster Rov	Tr	06.59	59-61	100	-	21
Lincoln C	Tr	11.61	61-62	38	-	4
Doncaster Rov	Tr	01.63	62-65	106	0	19
Bradford PA	Tr	10.65	65-66	56	0	11
Hartlepools U	Tr	02.67	66-67	25	0	3
BROADBENT Graham						
Halifax, 20 December, 1958 (F)						
Halifax T	Emley	09.88	88-90	13	19	3
BROADBENT Peter Frank						
Elvington, 15 May, 1933 Eu23-1/EB/FLge-2/E-7 (M)						
Brentford	Dover	05.50	50	16	-	2
Wolverhampton W	Tr	02.51	50-64	452	-	127
Shrewsbury T	Tr	01.65	64-66	69	0	8
Aston Villa	Tr	10.66	66-68	60	4	0
Stockport Co	Tr	10.69	69	31	0	1
BROADFOOT Joseph (Joe) James						
Lewisham, 4 March, 1940 (W)						
Millwall	Jnrs	01.58	58-63	225	-	60
Ipswich T	Tr	10.63	63-65	81	0	17
Northampton T	Tr	11.65	65	17	0	1
Millwall	Tr	07.66	66	26	0	5
Ipswich T	Tr	02.67	66-67	19	1	2
BROADHURST Brian Walter						
Sheffield, 24 November, 1938 (IF)						
Chesterfield	Hallam	10.61	61	7	-	0
BROADHURST Karl Matthew						
Portsmouth, 18 March, 1980 (CD)						
Bournemouth	YT	07.98	99-04	148	10	3
BROADHURST Kevan						
Dewsbury, 3 June, 1959 (CD)						
Birmingham C	App	03.77	76-83	147	6	10
Walsall	L	11.79	79	3	0	0
BROADIS Ivan (Ivor) Arthur						
Poplar, 18 December, 1922 FLge-3/E-14 (IF)						
Carlisle U	Tottenham H (Am)	08.46	46-48	90	-	53
Sunderland	Tr	02.49	48-51	79	-	25
Manchester C	Tr	10.51	51-53	74	-	10
Newcastle U	Tr	10.53	53-54	42	-	15
Carlisle U	Tr	07.55	55-58	157	-	32
BROADLEY Leslie (Les)						
Goole, 10 August, 1930 (CF)						
Scunthorpe U	Goole T	08.52	52	5	-	2
BROADLEY Patrick (Pat) Joseph						
Croy, 13 May, 1926 LoI-3 (WH)						
Oldham Ath	Sligo Rov	06.51	51	4	-	0
BROCK Kevin Stanley						
Middleton Stoney, 9 September, 1962 ESch/Eu21-4/EB (M)						
Oxford U	App	09.79	79-86	229	17	26
Queens Park Rgrs	Tr	08.87	87-88	38	2	2
Newcastle U	Tr	12.88	88-92	135	10	15
Cardiff C	L	02.94	93	14	0	2
BROCK Stuart Alan						
West Bromwich, 26 September, 1976 (G)						
Aston Villa	YT	05.95				
Northampton T	Tr	03.97				
Kidderminster Hrs	Solihull Borough	09.97	00-03	135	0	0
BROCKBANK Andrew (Andy)						
Millom, 23 September, 1961 (FB)						
Blackpool	App	12.79	79-82	32	4	1
BROCKEN Budde (Bud) Jan Peter Maria						
Tilburg, Holland, 12 September, 1957 (M)						
Birmingham C	Willem II Tilburg (Holl)	08.81	81	17	0	0
BROCKIE Vincent (Vince)						
Greenock, 2 February, 1969 (FB)						
Leeds U	YT	07.87	87	2	0	0
Doncaster Rov	Tr	12.88	88-90	43	11	7
BROCKLEHURST John Fletcher						
Horwich, 15 December, 1927 (WH)						
Accrington St	Stalybridge Celtic	05.52	52	34	-	0
Bradford PA	Stalybridge Celtic	08.54	54-55	47	-	1
BRODDLE Julian Raymond						
Laughton, 1 November, 1964 (W)						
Sheffield U	App	11.82	81	1	0	0
Scunthorpe U	Tr	08.83	83-87	126	18	32
Barnsley	Tr	08.87	87-89	63	14	4
Plymouth Arg	Tr	01.90	89	9	0	0
Scunthorpe U (L)	St Mirren	09.92	92	5	0	0
BRODERICK Mortimer						
Cork, 1 September, 1923 LoI-2 (IF)						
Sheffield U	Cork Ath	08.50	50	2	-	0
BRODIE Charles (Chic) Thomas George						
Duntocher, 22 February, 1937 Died 2000 SSch (G)						
Manchester C	Partick Avondale	03.54				
Gillingham	Tr	07.57	57	18	-	0
Aldershot	Tr	07.58	58-60	95	-	0
Wolverhampton W	Tr	02.61	60	1	-	0
Northampton T	Tr	09.61	61-63	87	-	0
Brentford	Tr	11.63	63-70	201	0	0
BRODIE Eric						
Rattray, 8 November, 1940 (M)						
Shrewsbury T	Dundee U	06.63	63-67	181	4	24
Chester	Tr	05.68	68-69	43	1	4
Tranmere Rov	Tr	10.69	69-71	81	3	3

BRODIE John
Bedlington, 8 September, 1947 (FB)

League Club	Source	Date Signed	Seasons Played	Apps	Subs	Gls
Carlisle U	Whitley Bay	12.67	67-68	8	0	0
Bradford PA	Tr	06.69	69	43	0	0
Port Vale	Tr	01.71	70-76	175	4	2

BRODIE Murray
Glasgow, 26 September, 1950 (M)

League Club	Source	Date Signed	Seasons Played	Apps	Subs	Gls
Leicester C	Cumbernauld U	10.69	69	3	0	2
Aldershot	Tr	09.70	70-82	449	11	75

BRODIE Stephen (Steve) Eric
Sunderland, 14 January, 1973 (F)

League Club	Source	Date Signed	Seasons Played	Apps	Subs	Gls
Sunderland	YT	07.91	93-94	1	11	0
Doncaster Rov	L	08.95	95	5	0	1
Scarborough	Tr	12.96	96-98	109	2	27
Swansea C	Tr	11.01	01	21	5	2

BROGAN David (Dave)
Glasgow, 11 January, 1939 (IF)

League Club	Source	Date Signed	Seasons Played	Apps	Subs	Gls
Luton T	St Anthony's	09.60	60	4	-	0

BROGAN Frank Anthony
Stepps, 3 August, 1942 (W)

League Club	Source	Date Signed	Seasons Played	Apps	Subs	Gls
Ipswich T	Glasgow Celtic	06.64	64-69	201	2	58
Halifax T	Morton	11.71	71-72	25	2	6

BROGAN James (Jim) Andrew
Glasgow, 5 June, 1944 SLge-1/S-4 (FB)

League Club	Source	Date Signed	Seasons Played	Apps	Subs	Gls
Coventry C	Glasgow Celtic	08.75	75	28	0	0

BROGDEN Lee Anthony
Leeds, 18 October, 1949 (W)

League Club	Source	Date Signed	Seasons Played	Apps	Subs	Gls
Rotherham U	Ashley Road	12.67	67-71	79	6	17
Rochdale	Tr	03.72	71-73	48	9	7

BROLIN Tomas
Hudiksvall, Sweden, 29 November, 1969 Sweden int (F)

League Club	Source	Date Signed	Seasons Played	Apps	Subs	Gls
Leeds U	Parma (It)	11.95	95	17	2	4
Crystal Palace	Tr	01.98	97	13	0	0

BROLLS Norman
Wigtown, 26 September, 1933 (W)

League Club	Source	Date Signed	Seasons Played	Apps	Subs	Gls
Bradford PA	Third Lanark	06.56	56	11	-	0

BROLLY Michael (Mike) Joseph
Galston, 6 October, 1954 SSch (W)

League Club	Source	Date Signed	Seasons Played	Apps	Subs	Gls
Chelsea	Kilmarnock Star	10.71	72-73	7	1	1
Bristol C	Tr	06.74	74-75	27	3	2
Grimsby T	Tr	09.76	76-81	246	8	27
Derby Co	Tr	08.82	82	41	1	4
Scunthorpe U	Tr	08.83	83-85	92	3	15

BROLLY Richard
York, 5 October, 1969 ESch (W)

League Club	Source	Date Signed	Seasons Played	Apps	Subs	Gls
Wigan Ath	Illinois Univ (USA)	12.92	92	2	0	1

BROLLY Thomas (Tom) Henry
Belfast, 1 June, 1912 Died 1986 NIRL-4/I-4 (WH)

League Club	Source	Date Signed	Seasons Played	Apps	Subs	Gls
Sheffield Wed	Glenavon	05.33	33	2	-	0
Millwall	Tr	07.35	35-49	229	-	8

BROMAGE Russel
Stoke-on-Trent, 9 November, 1959 (FB)

League Club	Source	Date Signed	Seasons Played	Apps	Subs	Gls
Port Vale	App	11.77	77-86	339	8	13
Oldham Ath	L	10.83	83	2	0	0
Bristol C	Tr	08.87	87-89	44	2	1
Brighton & Hove A	Tr	08.90	90	1	0	0
Maidstone U	L	01.91	90	3	0	0

BROMBY Leigh
Dewsbury, 2 June, 1980 ESch (CD)

League Club	Source	Date Signed	Seasons Played	Apps	Subs	Gls
Sheffield Wed	Liversedge	07.98	00-03	98	2	2
Mansfield T	L	12.99	99	10	0	1
Norwich C	L	02.03	02	5	0	0
Sheffield U	Tr	07.04	04	46	0	5

BROMILOW Geoffrey (Geoff)
Farnworth, 14 September, 1945 (F)

League Club	Source	Date Signed	Seasons Played	Apps	Subs	Gls
Bolton W (Am)		10.68	68	3	2	0

BROMILOW George Joseph
Birkdale, 4 December, 1930 EYth/EAmat (CF)

League Club	Source	Date Signed	Seasons Played	Apps	Subs	Gls
Southport (Am)	Northern Nomads	06.55	55-58	84	-	37

BROMLEY Brian
Burnley, 20 March, 1946 EYth (M)

League Club	Source	Date Signed	Seasons Played	Apps	Subs	Gls
Bolton W	App	03.63	62-68	165	1	25
Portsmouth	Tr	11.68	68-71	88	1	3
Brighton & Hove A	Tr	11.71	71-73	47	3	3
Reading	Tr	09.73	73-74	13	1	1
Darlington	L	02.75	74	3	0	0

BROMLEY Thomas (Tom) Charles
West Bromwich, 30 April, 1933 (IF)

League Club	Source	Date Signed	Seasons Played	Apps	Subs	Gls
Walsall (Am)	Swan Village	07.53	53	13	-	1

BROOK Daryl
Holmfirth, 19 November, 1960 (M)

League Club	Source	Date Signed	Seasons Played	Apps	Subs	Gls
Huddersfield T	App	11.78	78	1	0	0

BROOK Gary
Dewsbury, 9 May, 1964 (F)

League Club	Source	Date Signed	Seasons Played	Apps	Subs	Gls
Newport Co	Frickley Ath	12.87	87	14	0	2
Scarborough	Tr	03.88	87-89	59	5	15
Blackpool	Tr	11.89	89-91	27	3	6
Notts Co	L	09.90	90	0	1	0
Scarborough	L	10.90	90	8	0	0

BROOK Harold
Sheffield, 15 October, 1921 Died 1998 (IF)

League Club	Source	Date Signed	Seasons Played	Apps	Subs	Gls
Sheffield U	Hallam	04.43	46-53	229	-	90
Leeds U	Tr	07.54	54-57	103	-	46
Lincoln C	Tr	03.58	57	4	-	1

BROOK Lewis
Northowram, 27 July, 1918 Died 1996 (FB)

League Club	Source	Date Signed	Seasons Played	Apps	Subs	Gls
Huddersfield T	Halifax T (Am)	05.36	37-46	18	-	6
Oldham Ath	Tr	03.48	47-56	189	-	14

BROOKE David
Barnsley, 23 November, 1975 (M)

League Club	Source	Date Signed	Seasons Played	Apps	Subs	Gls
Barnsley	YT	07.93				
Scarborough	Tr	08.96	96	28	6	2

BROOKE Garry James
Bethnal Green, 24 November, 1960 (M)

League Club	Source	Date Signed	Seasons Played	Apps	Subs	Gls
Tottenham H	App	10.78	80-84	49	24	15
Norwich C	Tr	07.85	85-86	8	6	2
Wimbledon	Groningen (Holl)	08.88	88-89	5	7	0
Stoke C	L	03.90	89	6	2	0
Brentford	Tr	08.90	90	8	3	1
Reading	Baldock T	03.91	90	1	3	0

BROOKE Maurice
Thurcroft, 4 June, 1925 (CF)

League Club	Source	Date Signed	Seasons Played	Apps	Subs	Gls
Stockport Co	Buxton	01.51	50	1	-	0

BROOKER Paul
Hammersmith, 25 November, 1976 (F)

League Club	Source	Date Signed	Seasons Played	Apps	Subs	Gls
Fulham	YT	07.95	95-98	13	43	4
Brighton & Hove A	Tr	02.00	99-02	102	32	15
Leicester C	Tr	07.03	03	0	3	0
Reading	L	02.04	03	5	6	0
Reading	Tr	07.04	04	22	9	0

BROOKER Stephen (Steve) Michael Lord
Newport Pagnell, 21 May, 1981 (F)

League Club	Source	Date Signed	Seasons Played	Apps	Subs	Gls
Watford	YT	07.99	99	0	1	0
Port Vale	Tr	01.01	00-04	120	11	35
Bristol C	Tr	09.04	04	33	0	16

BROOKES Colin
Barnsley, 2 January, 1942 ESch (W)

League Club	Source	Date Signed	Seasons Played	Apps	Subs	Gls
Barnsley	Manchester U (Jnrs)	05.59	59-60	47	-	5
West Bromwich A	Tr	06.61				
Peterborough U	Tr	06.62				
Southport	Tr	07.63	63	20	-	2

BROOKES Darren Paul
Sheffield, 7 July, 1978 (CD)

League Club	Source	Date Signed	Seasons Played	Apps	Subs	Gls
Doncaster Rov	Worksop T	07.97	97	9	2	0

BROOKES Eric
Mapplewell, 3 February, 1944 EYth (FB)

League Club	Source	Date Signed	Seasons Played	Apps	Subs	Gls
Barnsley	Jnrs	04.61	60-68	325	1	1
Northampton T	Tr	07.69	69-70	81	0	1
Peterborough U	Tr	06.71	71-72	41	1	1

BROOKES John (Johnny) Vincent
Netherthorpe, 18 October, 1943 (M)

League Club	Source	Date Signed	Seasons Played	Apps	Subs	Gls
Sheffield Wed	Sheffield U (Am)	09.64				
Southport	Tr	07.65	65	14	0	5
York C	Tr	08.66	66	1	0	0
Stockport Co	Sligo Rov	08.70	70	18	3	3

BROOKES Stanley (Stan) Kevin
Doncaster, 2 February, 1953 (CD)

League Club	Source	Date Signed	Seasons Played	Apps	Subs	Gls
Doncaster Rov	App	02.71	71-76	230	6	7

BROOKES William (Billy) Amos
Dudley, 19 April, 1931 (WH)

League Club	Source	Date Signed	Seasons Played	Apps	Subs	Gls
West Bromwich A	Churchfields	05.49	53-56	19	-	0

League Club	Source	Date Signed	Seasons Played	Career Record Apps	Subs	Gls
BROOKFIELD Anthony (Tony) John						
Southport, 11 April, 1959 (F)						
Southport	Jnrs	07.76	76-77	14	5	1
BROOKIN William (Bill) James						
Tilehurst, 14 June, 1919 Died 1976 (G)						
Newport Co	RAF Hereford	08.46	46	2	-	0
BROOKING (Sir) Trevor David						
Barking, 2 October, 1948 ESch/EYth/Eu23-1/FLge-1/E-47 (M)						
West Ham U	App	05.66	67-83	521	7	88
BROOKMAN Nicholas (Nicky) Anthony						
Manchester, 28 October, 1968 (M)						
Bolton W	Wrexham (N/C)	11.86	86-89	47	10	10
Stockport Co	Tr	03.90	89	4	2	0
BROOKS Anthony (Tony)						
Ince, 12 March, 1944 (IF)						
Blackpool	Jnrs	03.62				
Bury		08.63	63	1	-	0
Stockport Co	Tr	06.64	64	2	-	0
BROOKS Christopher (Chris)						
Huthwaite, 6 June, 1972 (F)						
Luton T	Ilkeston T	07.92				
Shrewsbury T	L	02.93	92	1	0	0
BROOKS Harry						
Tibshelf, 2 June, 1915 Died 1994 (CF)						
Doncaster Rov	Heanor T	01.37	36-38	5	-	0
Aldershot	Tr	06.39	46-47	23	-	14
BROOKS Jamie Paul						
Oxford, 12 August, 1983 (F)						
Oxford U	YT	12.00	00-04	27	14	13
BROOKS John (Johnny)						
Reading, 23 December, 1931 E-3 (IF)						
Reading	Mount Pleasant	04.49	49-52	46	-	5
Tottenham H	Tr	02.53	52-59	166	-	46
Chelsea	Tr	12.59	59-60	46	-	6
Brentford	Tr	09.61	61-63	83	-	36
Crystal Palace	Tr	01.64	63	7	-	0
BROOKS John						
Stoke-on-Trent, 8 March, 1927 (WH)						
Stoke C		12.46	50	2	-	0
BROOKS John Terence						
Paddington, 23 August, 1947 (G)						
Queens Park Rgrs	App	08.65				
Ipswich T	Tr	12.66				
Northampton T	Tr	10.67	67	1	0	0
BROOKS Lewis Raymond						
Boston, 4 September, 1987 (M)						
Boston U	Jnrs	●	04	1	1	0
BROOKS Norman Harry						
Reading, 28 May, 1920 Died 1973 (W)						
Reading (Am)	Huntley & Palmers	11.46	46	1	-	0
BROOKS Shaun						
Reading, 9 October, 1962 ESch/EYth (M)						
Crystal Palace	App	10.79	79-83	47	7	4
Orient	Tr	10.83	83-86	140	8	26
Bournemouth	Tr	06.87	87-91	114	14	13
Bournemouth	Dorchester T	10.94	94	1	0	0
Leyton Orient	Tr	11.94	94-95	42	8	2
BROOKS Stephen (Steve) Michael						
Norris Green, 18 June, 1955 (CD)						
Southport	Marine	02.77	76-77	65	0	3
Hartlepool U	Tr	07.78	78-79	62	1	2
Halifax T	Skelmersdale U	03.85	84	16	0	0
BROOKS Thomas (Tommy) William						
Wallsend, 2 February, 1948 (FB)						
Lincoln C	App	02.65	64-70	103	10	1
BROOME Frank Henry						
Berkhamsted, 11 June, 1915 Died 1994 EWar-1/E-7 (W)						
Aston Villa	Berkhamsted T	11.34	34-46	133	-	78
Derby Co	Tr	09.46	46-49	112	-	45
Notts Co	Tr	10.49	49-52	105	-	35
Brentford	Tr	07.53	53	6	-	1
Crewe Alex	Tr	10.53	53-54	36	-	17
BROOMES Marlon Charles						
Birmingham, 28 November, 1977 ESch/EYth/Eu21-2 (CD)						
Blackburn Rov	YT	11.94	97-00	24	7	1

League Club	Source	Date Signed	Seasons Played	Career Record Apps	Subs	Gls
Swindon T	L	01.97	96	12	0	1
Queens Park Rgrs	L	10.00	00	5	0	0
Grimsby T	L	09.01	01	13	2	0
Sheffield Wed	Tr	12.01	01	18	1	0
Preston NE	Tr	08.02	02-04	59	10	0
BROOMFIELD Desmond (Des) Stretton						
Hove, 6 October, 1921 (WH)						
Brighton & Hove A	Jnrs	01.47	46-47	20	-	0
BROOMFIELD Ian Lewis						
Bristol, 17 December, 1950 (F)						
Bristol C	App	08.68	68-72	18	3	2
Stockport Co	Tr	12.72	72-74	22	5	1
Workington	Durban C (SA)	10.75	75	3	0	0
BROOMFIELD John						
Crewe, 6 June, 1934 (CD)						
Crewe Alex (Am)		10.56	56	1	-	0
BROOMHALL Keith Leslie						
Stoke-on-Trent, 21 May, 1951 (FB)						
Port Vale	App	●	68	1	1	0
BROPHY Hugh						
Dublin, 2 September, 1948 NIAmat (F)						
Crystal Palace	Shamrock Rov	07.66	66	0	1	0
BROTHERSTON Noel						
Dundonald, 18 November, 1956 Died 1995 NIu21-1/NI-27 (W)						
Tottenham H	App	04.74	75	1	0	0
Blackburn Rov	Tr	07.77	77-86	307	10	40
Bury	Tr	06.87	87-88	32	6	4
Scarborough	L	10.88	88	5	0	0
BROUGH John Robert						
Ilkeston, 8 January, 1973 (CD)						
Notts Co	YT	07.91				
Shrewsbury T	Tr	07.92	92-93	7	9	1
Hereford U	Telford U	11.94	94-96	70	9	3
Cheltenham T	Tr	07.98	99-04	83	53	6
BROUGH Michael						
Nottingham, 1 August, 1981 WYth/Wu21-3 (M)						
Notts Co	YT	07.99	99-03	67	22	2
BROUGH Neil Keith						
Daventry, 22 December, 1965 (W)						
Northampton T	App	12.83	83-84	6	6	0
BROUGH Paul						
York, 24 January, 1965 (F)						
York C	York RI	08.87	87	0	1	0
BROUGH Scott						
Scunthorpe, 10 February, 1983 (M)						
Scunthorpe U	Jnrs	11.00	00-02	15	31	3
BROUGHTON Drewe Oliver						
Hitchin, 25 October, 1978 (F)						
Norwich C	YT	05.97	96-97	3	6	1
Wigan Ath	L	08.97	97	1	3	0
Brentford	Tr	10.98	98	1	0	0
Peterborough U	Tr	11.98	98-99	19	16	8
Kidderminster Hrs	Tr	01.01	00-02	70	24	19
Southend U	Tr	06.03	03-04	31	13	2
Rushden & Diamonds	L	10.04	04	9	0	4
Wycombe W	L	12.04	04	2	1	0
Rushden & Diamonds	Tr	02.05	04	11	1	2
BROUGHTON Edward (Ted)						
Bradford, 9 February, 1925 (W)						
Bradford C		09.45				
New Brighton	Tr	07.47	47	4	-	0
Crystal Palace	Tr	08.48	48-52	96	-	6
BROWN Aaron Wesley						
Bristol, 14 March, 1980 ESch (M)						
Bristol C	YT	11.97	98-03	135	25	12
Exeter C	L	01.00	99	4	1	1
Queens Park Rgrs	Tr	01.05	04	0	1	0
Torquay U	L	03.05	04	5	0	0
BROWN Adam James						
Sunderland, 17 December, 1987 (F)						
Doncaster Rov	Sch	●	04	0	3	1
BROWN Alan						
Lewes, 11 December, 1937 (CF)						
Brighton & Hove A	Portslade	09.58	61	7	-	2
Exeter C	Tr	01.62	61	11	-	3

League Club	Source	Date Signed	Seasons Played	Career Record Apps	Subs	Gls
BROWN Alan						
Easington, 22 May, 1959						(F)
Sunderland	App	07.76	76-81	87	26	21
Newcastle U	L	11.81	81	5	0	3
Shrewsbury T	Tr	08.82	82-83	65	0	15
Doncaster Rov	Tr	03.84	83-85	15	0	6
BROWN Alan Winston						
Corbridge, 26 August, 1914 Died 1996 FLge-1						(CD)
Huddersfield T	Spen Black & White	03.33	34-38	57	-	0
Burnley	Tr	02.46	46-48	88	-	0
Notts Co	Tr	10.48	48	13	-	0
BROWN Albert (Bert) Edward						
Bristol, 4 March, 1934						(WH)
Crystal Palace	Exeter Univ	08.56	57	3	-	0
BROWN Alexander (Sandy) Dewar						
Grangemouth, 24 March, 1939						(FB)
Everton	Partick Th	09.63	63-70	176	33	9
Shrewsbury T	Tr	05.71	71	21	0	0
Southport	Tr	07.72	72	17	2	0
BROWN Alexander (Alex) Masterson						
Glasgow, 15 August, 1930 Died 2004 SYth						(FB)
Preston NE	Partick Th	06.57				
Carlisle U	Tr	06.58	58-60	102	-	0
BROWN Alexander (Alex) Roy						
Seghill, 21 November, 1914						(W)
Chesterfield	Seghill CW	12.33	34	8	-	1
Darlington	Tr	06.35	35	5	-	0
Gateshead	Shrewsbury T	05.39				
Mansfield T	Tr	11.46	46	5	-	0
BROWN Alistair (Ally)						
Musselburgh, 12 April, 1951						(F)
Leicester C	Jnrs	04.68	68-71	93	8	31
West Bromwich A	Tr	03.72	71-82	254	25	72
Crystal Palace	Tr	03.83	82	11	0	2
Walsall	Tr	08.83	83	37	1	13
Port Vale	Tr	07.84	84-85	62	5	22
BROWN Allan Duncan						
Kennoway, 12 October, 1926 SLge-1/S-14						(IF)
Blackpool	East Fife	12.50	50-56	158	-	68
Luton T	Tr	02.57	56-60	151	-	51
Portsmouth	Tr	03.61	60-62	69	-	8
BROWN Andrew						
Coatbridge, 20 February, 1915 Died 1973						(IF)
Cardiff C	Cumbernauld Thistle	12.36	36-37	2	-	0
Torquay U	Tr	06.38	38-46	34	-	5
BROWN Andrew (Andy)						
Liverpool, 17 August, 1963						(FB)
Tranmere Rov	Jnrs	08.82	82	1	0	0
BROWN Andrew Stewart						
Edinburgh, 11 October, 1976						(F)
Leeds U	St Johnstone (Jnrs)	04.95				
Hull C	Tr	05.96	96-97	7	22	1
BROWN Anthony (Tony) John						
Oldham, 3 October, 1945 FLge-1/E-1						(F)
West Bromwich A	App	10.63	63-79	561	13	218
Torquay U	Jacksonville (USA)	10.81	81-82	38	7	11
BROWN Anthony (Tony) John						
Bradford, 17 September, 1958						(CD)
Leeds U	Thackley	03.83	82-84	24	0	1
Doncaster Rov	L	11.84	84	5	0	0
Doncaster Rov	Tr	03.85	84-86	80	2	2
Scunthorpe U	Tr	07.87	87-88	46	8	2
Rochdale	Tr	08.89	89-92	111	3	0
BROWN Robert **Beresford (Berry)**						
Hartlepool, 6 September, 1927 Died 2001						(G)
Manchester U	Blackhall CW	08.46	47-48	4	-	0
Doncaster Rov	Tr	01.49	48	4	-	0
Hartlepools U	Stockton	08.51	51-55	126	-	0
BROWN Brian David						
Shoreditch, 10 September, 1949						(FB)
Chelsea	App	11.66				
Millwall	Tr	03.68	68-74	186	4	5
BROWN Christopher (Chris) Alan						
Doncaster, 11 December, 1984 EYth						(M)
Sunderland	Sch	08.02	04	13	24	5
Doncaster Rov	L	10.03	03	17	5	10

League Club	Source	Date Signed	Seasons Played	Career Record Apps	Subs	Gls
BROWN Cyril						
Ashington, 25 May, 1918 Died 1990						(IF)
Brentford	Felixstowe	01.39				
Sunderland	Tr	04.45				
Notts Co	Tr	08.46	46	13	-	5
Rochdale	Boston U	08.48	48-50	61	-	11
BROWN Daniel (Danny)						
Bethnal Green, 12 September, 1980						(M)
Leyton Orient	YT	05.98				
Barnet	Tr	05.99	99-00	42	11	3
Oxford U	Tr	07.03	03-04	15	1	0
BROWN David (Dave)						
Wallasey, 21 October, 1963						(FB)
Tranmere Rov		08.82	82	1	0	0
BROWN David Alistair						
Bolton, 2 October, 1978						(F)
Manchester U	YT	10.95				
Hull C	Tr	03.98	97-00	108	23	23
Torquay U	Tr	11.01	01	2	0	0
BROWN David James						
Hartlepool, 28 January, 1957						(G)
Middlesbrough	Horden CW	02.77	77	10	0	0
Plymouth Arg	L	08.79	79	5	0	0
Oxford U	Tr	10.79	79-80	21	0	0
Bury	Tr	09.81	81-84	146	0	0
Preston NE	Tr	06.86	86-88	74	0	0
Scunthorpe U	L	01.89	88	5	0	0
Halifax T	Tr	07.89	89-90	38	0	0
BROWN Dennis John						
Reading, 8 February, 1944						(F)
Chelsea	Jnrs	06.62	63	10	-	1
Swindon T	Tr	11.64	64-66	92	0	38
Northampton T	Tr	02.67	66-68	41	5	10
Aldershot	Tr	07.69	69-74	237	8	55
BROWN William **Dewis**						
Rotherham, 4 June, 1919						(WH)
Stockport Co		08.45	46-49	65	-	15
Rotherham U	Tr	08.50	51	1	-	0
BROWN Douglas (Dougie) Alexander						
Airdrie, 21 March, 1958 Australia int						(F)
Sheffield U	Clydebank	03.79	78-79	17	8	2
BROWN Edward (Eddie) Alfred Cecil Henry						
St Pancras, 4 October, 1927 Died 1996						(CF)
Brentford		02.50				
Aldershot		08.53	53	3	-	0
BROWN Edwin (Eddie)						
Preston, 28 February, 1926						(CF)
Preston NE		08.48	48-50	36	-	16
Southampton	Tr	09.50	50-51	57	-	32
Coventry C	Tr	03.52	51-54	85	-	50
Birmingham C	Tr	10.54	54-58	158	-	74
Leyton Orient	Tr	01.59	58-60	63	-	28
BROWN Ernest (Ernie)						
Stockport, 30 May, 1923 Died 1980						(WH)
Manchester C		04.44				
Aldershot	Tr	06.46	46	12	-	0
Accrington St	Tr	08.49	49	2	-	0
BROWN Ernest (Ernie) Charles						
South Shields, 3 February, 1921 Died 1976						(IF)
Newcastle U	South Shields	12.45				
Southend U	Tr	02.47	46-47	6	-	0
BROWN Frederick (Fred)						
Leyton, 6 December, 1931						(G)
Aldershot	Leytonstone	06.52	52-54	106	-	0
West Bromwich A	Tr	05.55	55-57	11	-	0
Portsmouth	Tr	06.58	58-59	18	-	0
BROWN Gary						
Darwen, 29 October, 1985						(FB)
Rochdale	Sch	•	04	1	0	0
BROWN George						
Sheffield, 18 October, 1934 Died 1995 ESch						(WH)
Liverpool	Jnrs	10.51				
Chesterfield	Tr	05.53	53-54	66	-	5
BROWN George						
Bonnybridge, 12 January, 1932						(G)
Crewe Alex	Stenhousemuir	06.57	57	40	-	0

League Club	Source	Date Signed	Seasons Played	Apps	Subs	Gls
BROWN George Donaldson						
Airdrie, 8 May, 1928						(IF)
Southport	Airdrie	04.51	50	1	-	0
Bradford PA	Clyde	07.56	56	17	-	2
BROWN Gordon						
Dunfermline, 4 February, 1932 Died 1999						(W)
Blackburn Rov	Blairhall Colliery	04.51				
Newport Co	Tr	08.55	55-58	137	-	14
Gillingham	Tr	06.59	59-60	67	-	13
BROWN Gordon						
Ellesmere Port, 30 June, 1933						(IF)
Wolverhampton W	Ellesmere Port T	09.51				
Scunthorpe U	Tr	12.52	52-56	154	-	72
Derby Co	Tr	01.57	56-59	53	-	20
Southampton	Tr	03.60	59-60	8	-	2
Barrow	Tr	07.61	61-63	39	-	16
Southport	Tr	01.64	63	4	-	1
BROWN Gordon Alexander						
East Kilbride, 7 December, 1965						(CD)
Rotherham U	App	12.83	83	1	0	0
BROWN Gordon Steele						
Warsop, 21 March, 1929						(WH)
Nottingham F	Jnrs	12.46	46	1	-	0
York C	Tr	06.50	50-57	322	-	25
BROWN Graham Cummings						
Matlock, 21 March, 1944						(G)
Millwall		12.64				
Mansfield T	Crawley T	08.69	69-73	142	0	0
Doncaster Rov	Tr	07.74	74-75	53	0	0
Swansea C	Portland (USA)	09.76	76	4	0	0
York C	Portland (USA)	08.77	77-79	69	0	0
Rotherham U	Tr	02.80	79-80	31	0	0
Mansfield T	Tr	01.82	81	1	0	0
BROWN Graham Frederick						
Leicester, 5 November, 1950						(F)
Leicester C	App	11.68	69	0	2	0
BROWN Grant Ashley						
Sunderland, 19 November, 1969						(CD)
Leicester C	YT	07.88	87-88	14	0	0
Lincoln C	Tr	08.89	89-01	401	6	15
BROWN Gregory (Greg) Jonathan						
Wythenshawe, 31 July, 1978						(FB)
Chester C	YT	06.96	95-96	1	3	0
Macclesfield T	Tr	12.97	97-99	9	3	0
BROWN Harold (Harry) Thomas						
Kingsbury, 9 April, 1924 Died 1982						(G)
Queens Park Rgrs	Jnrs	04.41				
Notts Co	Tr	04.46	46-48	93	-	0
Derby Co	Tr	10.49	49-50	37	-	0
Queens Park Rgrs	Tr	08.51	51-55	189	-	0
Plymouth Arg	Tr	08.56	56-57	66	-	0
BROWN Henry (Harry) Stanford						
Workington, 23 May, 1918 Died 1963						(CD)
Wolverhampton W	Workington	02.37	38	2	-	0
Hull C	Tr	05.46	46	22	-	0
BROWN Hugh						
Carmyle, 7 December, 1921 Died 1994 SLge-2/S-3						(WH)
Torquay U	Partick Th	11.50	50-51	55	-	0
BROWN Ian O'Neill						
Ipswich, 11 September, 1965						(W)
Birmingham C	App	09.84				
Bristol C	Chelmsford C	05.93	93-94	5	7	1
Colchester U	L	03.94	93	4	0	1
Northampton T	Tr	12.94	94	23	0	4
BROWN Irvin						
Lewes, 20 September, 1935						(CD)
Brighton & Hove A	Jnrs	10.52	57	3	-	0
Bournemouth	Tr	09.58	58-62	65	-	2
BROWN James						
Cumnock, 16 February, 1924 Died 2002						(CF)
Chesterfield	Motherwell	05.48	48	5	-	2
Bradford C	Tr	11.48	48	20	-	11
Carlisle U	Queen of the South	09.50	50-51	15	-	9
BROWN James (Jim)						
Manchester, 5 October, 1935						(W)
Rochdale		04.57	56-60	52	-	4

League Club	Source	Date Signed	Seasons Played	Apps	Subs	Gls
BROWN James Birrell						
Stirling, 7 June, 1939						(WH)
Darlington	Dumbarton	09.60	60-62	14	-	0
BROWN James (Jim) Grady						
Coatbridge, 11 May, 1952 Su23-4/S1						(G)
Chesterfield	Albion Rov	12.72	72-73	47	0	0
Sheffield U	Tr	03.74	73-77	170	0	0
Cardiff C	Chicago (USA)	12.82	82	3	0	0
Chesterfield	Kettering T	07.83	83-88	135	0	1
BROWN James (Jim) Keith						
Musselburgh, 3 October, 1953						(M)
Aston Villa	App	10.70	69-74	73	2	1
Preston NE	Tr	10.75	75-77	64	0	3
Portsmouth	Ethnikos (Gre)	02.80	79	5	0	0
BROWN Jason Roy						
Southwark, 18 May, 1982 WYth/Wu21-7						(G)
Gillingham	Charlton Ath (YT)	03.01	01-04	87	0	0
BROWN Jeremy						
Newport, 13 June, 1961						(F)
Newport Co	App	06.78	78	2	1	0
BROWN Jermaine Anthony Alexander						
Lambeth, 12 January, 1983						(F)
Arsenal	YT	07.01				
Colchester U	Tr	10.03				
Boston U	Tr	02.04	03	3	2	0
BROWN John (Jackie)						
Belfast, 8 November, 1914 IrLge-2/I-10/IR-1						(W)
Wolverhampton W	Belfast Celtic	12.34	34-36	27	-	6
Coventry C	Tr	10.36	36-37	69	-	26
Birmingham	Tr	09.38	38	34	-	6
Ipswich T	Barry T	05.48	48-50	98	-	25
BROWN John (Johnny)						
St Kew, 29 July, 1940						(M)
Plymouth Arg	Wadebridge T	10.60	60-62	9	-	2
Bristol Rov	Tr	07.63	63-67	156	0	32
BROWN John						
Edinburgh, 6 March, 1940						(WH)
Colchester U	Dunbar U	09.61	62	1	-	0
BROWN John Christopher						
Bradford, 30 December, 1947						(G)
Preston NE	App	03.65	66-74	67	0	0
Stockport Co	L	11.70	70	26	0	0
Stockport Co	Tr	07.75	75	15	0	0
Wigan Ath	Tr	07.76	78-81	93	0	0
BROWN John Lewis						
Crook, 23 March, 1921 Died 1989						(FB)
York C	Stanley U	02.48	47-49	22	-	0
BROWN John Michael						
Streatham, 2 February, 1934						(IF)
Shrewsbury T (Am)	Queens Park	05.53	53	5	-	3
BROWN John (Jock) Thomas						
Edinburgh, 2 April, 1935 Died 2000 SSch						(FB)
Tranmere Rov	Third Lanark	01.61	60-61	33	-	0
Hartlepools U	Tr	07.62	62-63	68	-	10
BROWN Jonathan (Jon)						
Barnsley, 8 September, 1966						(FB)
Exeter C	Denaby U	07.90	90-94	149	15	3
Halifax T	Tr	07.95	98	32	8	0
BROWN Joseph (Joe)						
Cramlington, 26 April, 1929						(WH)
Middlesbrough	Jnrs	04.46	49-50	11	-	0
Burnley	Tr	08.52	52	6	-	0
Bournemouth	Tr	06.54	54-59	215	-	5
Aldershot	Tr	07.60	60	5	-	0
BROWN Joseph (Joe) Samuel						
Bebington, 7 May, 1920						(W)
Chester	Port Sunlight	05.47	46-47	15	-	2
BROWN Keith						
Hucknall, 1 January, 1942 ESch						(CF)
Notts Co	Jnrs	01.59	58	8	-	4
BROWN Keith						
Grimsby, 23 September, 1954						(W)
Nottingham F	App	09.72				
Grimsby T	Tr	10.73	73-75	32	7	5

BROWN Keith
Walton, 19 October, 1957 (FB)

League Club	Source	Date Signed	Seasons Played	Apps	Subs	Gls
Southport	East Villa	11.76	76	4	0	0

BROWN Keith Gordon
Coseley, 16 July, 1954 (FB)

League Club	Source	Date Signed	Seasons Played	Apps	Subs	Gls
Walsall	Jnrs	07.73	73-74	8	2	0

BROWN Keith Jack
Bournemouth, 29 January, 1942 (FB)

League Club	Source	Date Signed	Seasons Played	Apps	Subs	Gls
Bournemouth	Pokesdown	09.60	63-64	15	-	0

BROWN John **Keith**
Edinburgh, 24 December, 1979 SYth (CD)

League Club	Source	Date Signed	Seasons Played	Apps	Subs	Gls
Blackburn Rov	YT	01.97				
Barnsley	Tr	09.99	99-00	8	3	0
Oxford U	L	11.00	00	3	0	0

BROWN Keith Timothy
Bristol, 28 September, 1959 (F)

League Club	Source	Date Signed	Seasons Played	Apps	Subs	Gls
Bristol Rov	Bristol St George	10.77	78-80	4	3	0

BROWN Kenneth (Ken)
Forest Gate, 16 February, 1934 E-1 (CD)

League Club	Source	Date Signed	Seasons Played	Apps	Subs	Gls
West Ham U	Neville U	10.51	52-66	386	0	4
Torquay U	Tr	05.67	67-68	40	2	1

BROWN Kenneth (Kenny) Geoffrey
Barnsley, 21 March, 1952 (M)

League Club	Source	Date Signed	Seasons Played	Apps	Subs	Gls
Barnsley	App	04.70	69-77	267	10	24
Bournemouth	Tr	06.78	78-79	29	3	4

BROWN Kenneth (Ken) James
Coventry, 18 October, 1933 (W)

League Club	Source	Date Signed	Seasons Played	Apps	Subs	Gls
Coventry C		01.56				
Nottingham F	Corby T	11.56				
Bournemouth	Tr	07.57	57	6	-	1
Torquay U	Tr	07.58	58	9	-	1

BROWN Kenneth (Kenny) James
Upminster, 11 July, 1967 (FB)

League Club	Source	Date Signed	Seasons Played	Apps	Subs	Gls
Norwich C	Jnrs	07.85	86-87	24	1	0
Plymouth Arg	Tr	08.88	88-90	126	0	4
West Ham U	Tr	08.91	91-95	55	8	5
Huddersfield T	L	09.95	95	5	0	0
Reading	L	10.95	95	12	0	1
Southend U	L	03.96	95	6	0	0
Crystal Palace	L	03.96	95	5	1	2
Reading	L	09.96	96	5	0	0
Birmingham C	Tr	12.96	96	11	0	0
Millwall	Tr	07.97	97	45	0	0
Gillingham	Tr	03.99	98	2	2	0

BROWN Kevan Barry
Andover, 2 January, 1966 (FB)

League Club	Source	Date Signed	Seasons Played	Apps	Subs	Gls
Southampton	Jnrs	07.84				
Brighton & Hove A	Tr	02.87	86-88	52	1	0
Aldershot	Tr	11.88	88-90	108	2	2

BROWN Laurence (Laurie)
Shildon, 22 August, 1937 Died 1998 EAmat (CD)

League Club	Source	Date Signed	Seasons Played	Apps	Subs	Gls
Darlington (Am)	Bishop Auckland	03.59	58	3	-	0
Northampton T	Bishop Auckland	10.60	60	33	-	22
Arsenal	Tr	08.61	61-63	101	-	2
Tottenham H	Tr	04.63	63-65	62	0	3
Norwich C	Tr	09.66	66-68	80	1	2
Bradford PA	Tr	12.68	68-69	36	0	1

BROWN Linton James
Driffield, 12 April, 1968 (F)

League Club	Source	Date Signed	Seasons Played	Apps	Subs	Gls
Halifax T	Guiseley	12.92	92	3	0	0
Hull C	Tr	01.93	92-95	111	10	23
Swansea C	Tr	03.96	95-97	16	11	3
Scarborough	L	08.97	97	4	0	1

BROWN Malcolm
Salford, 13 December, 1956 (FB)

League Club	Source	Date Signed	Seasons Played	Apps	Subs	Gls
Bury	App	12.74	73-76	10	1	0
Huddersfield T	Tr	05.77	77-82	256	0	16
Newcastle U	Tr	08.83	84	39	0	0
Huddersfield T	Tr	06.85	85-88	93	3	1
Rochdale	Tr	02.89	88	11	0	0
Stockport Co	Tr	07.89	89-90	71	0	3
Rochdale	Tr	08.91	91	18	0	1

BROWN Marvin Robert
Bristol, 6 July, 1983 EYth (F)

League Club	Source	Date Signed	Seasons Played	Apps	Subs	Gls
Bristol C	YT	07.00	99-03	2	17	0
Torquay U	L	09.02	02	2	2	0
Cheltenham T	L	01.03	02	11	4	2
Yeovil T	Weymouth	03.05	04	0	2	0

BROWN Michael
Preston, 27 February, 1985 (M)

League Club	Source	Date Signed	Seasons Played	Apps	Subs	Gls
Preston NE	Sch	08.04				
Chester C	L	12.04	04	11	7	0

BROWN Michael (Mike) Antony
Birmingham, 8 February, 1968 (M)

League Club	Source	Date Signed	Seasons Played	Apps	Subs	Gls
Shrewsbury T	App	02.86	86-90	174	16	9
Bolton W	Tr	08.91	91-92	27	6	3
Shrewsbury T	Tr	12.92	92-94	66	1	11
Preston NE	Tr	11.94	95-96	11	5	1
Rochdale	L	09.96	96	5	0	0
Shrewsbury T	Tr	12.96	96-00	111	50	16

BROWN Michael (Mick) John
Walsall, 11 July, 1939 (FB)

League Club	Source	Date Signed	Seasons Played	Apps	Subs	Gls
Hull C	Jnrs	10.58	59-65	8	0	0
Lincoln C	Tr	07.67	67	38	0	0

BROWN Michael (Mick) John
Slough, 11 April, 1944 (W)

League Club	Source	Date Signed	Seasons Played	Apps	Subs	Gls
Fulham	App	09.61	61-62	4	-	0
Millwall	Tr	02.65	64-66	47	5	11
Luton T	Tr	07.67	67-68	9	5	2
Colchester U	Tr	10.68	68-69	47	5	12

BROWN Michael (Mick) John Leslie
Swansea, 27 September, 1951 WSch (CD)

League Club	Source	Date Signed	Seasons Played	Apps	Subs	Gls
Crystal Palace	App	09.69				
Brighton & Hove A	Tr	06.73	73	5	3	1
Brentford	L	09.73	73	3	0	0

BROWN Michael Robert
Hartlepool, 25 January, 1977 Eu21-4 (M)

League Club	Source	Date Signed	Seasons Played	Apps	Subs	Gls
Manchester C	YT	09.94	95-98	67	22	2
Hartlepool U	L	03.97	96	6	0	1
Portsmouth	L	11.99	99	4	0	0
Sheffield U	Tr	12.99	99-03	146	5	27
Tottenham H	Tr	12.03	03-04	37	4	2

BROWN Monty Raymond
Grimsby, 7 September, 1943 (CF)

League Club	Source	Date Signed	Seasons Played	Apps	Subs	Gls
Scunthorpe U	Jnrs	07.63	64-65	19	0	6

BROWN Nathaniel (Nat) Levi
Sheffield, 15 June, 1981 (CD)

League Club	Source	Date Signed	Seasons Played	Apps	Subs	Gls
Huddersfield T	YT	07.99	02-04	56	20	0

BROWN Neil Richard
Sheffield, 16 January, 1966 (FB)

League Club	Source	Date Signed	Seasons Played	Apps	Subs	Gls
Chesterfield	App	11.83	83	5	0	0

BROWN Nicholas (Nicky) James
Northampton, 25 January, 1973 (G)

League Club	Source	Date Signed	Seasons Played	Apps	Subs	Gls
Halifax T	Norwich C (YT)	07.91	91-92	2	0	0

BROWN Nicholas (Nicky) Lee
Hull, 16 October, 1966 (FB)

League Club	Source	Date Signed	Seasons Played	Apps	Subs	Gls
Hull C	App	08.85	85-91	80	6	3

BROWN Owen John
Liverpool, 4 September, 1960 ESch (F)

League Club	Source	Date Signed	Seasons Played	Apps	Subs	Gls
Liverpool	Jnrs	11.78				
Carlisle U	Tr	06.80	80	4	0	2
Tranmere Rov	Tr	08.81	81	29	8	8
Crewe Alex	Tr	08.82	82	1	0	0
Tranmere Rov	Tr	10.82	82-83	47	9	12
Chester C	Tr	08.84	84	9	1	3

BROWN Paul Henry
Liverpool, 10 September, 1984 (F)

League Club	Source	Date Signed	Seasons Played	Apps	Subs	Gls
Tranmere Rov	Sch	06.04	04	1	3	0

BROWN Peter Barry
Andover, 13 July, 1934 (W)

League Club	Source	Date Signed	Seasons Played	Apps	Subs	Gls
Southampton	Jnrs	01.52	53-57	16	-	3
Wrexham	Tr	07.58	58-59	33	-	9

BROWN Peter Ronald
Hemel Hempstead, 1 September, 1961 (FB)

League Club	Source	Date Signed	Seasons Played	Apps	Subs	Gls
Wimbledon	Chelsea (App)	08.80	80-81	53	2	3

BROWN Philip (Phil)
South Shields, 30 May, 1959 (FB)

League Club	Source	Date Signed	Seasons Played	Apps	Subs	Gls
Hartlepool U	St Hilda's Jnrs	07.78	79-84	210	7	8
Halifax T	Tr	07.85	85-87	135	0	19
Bolton W	Tr	06.88	88-93	254	2	14
Blackpool	Tr	07.94	94-95	33	11	5

BROWN Philip (Phil) James
Sheffield, 16 January, 1966 (W)

League Club	Source	Date Signed	Seasons Played	Apps	Subs	Gls
Chesterfield	App	10.83	82-86	82	5	19

League Club	Source	Date Signed	Seasons Played	Apps	Subs	Gls
Stockport Co	Tr	12.86	86	23	0	1
Lincoln C	Tr	08.87	88-89	32	11	3

BROWN Ralph
Ilkeston, 26 February, 1944 (IF)

League Club	Source	Date Signed	Seasons Played	Apps	Subs	Gls
Aston Villa	App	03.61				
Notts Co	Tr	05.62	62	18	-	3

BROWN Raymond (Ray) Moscrop
Carlisle, 11 February, 1928 (W)

League Club	Source	Date Signed	Seasons Played	Apps	Subs	Gls
Notts Co	Queen's Park	08.51	51	7	-	0

BROWN Richard Anthony
Nottingham, 13 January, 1967 (FB)

League Club	Source	Date Signed	Seasons Played	Apps	Subs	Gls
Sheffield Wed	Ilkeston T	01.85				
Blackburn Rov	Kettering T	09.90	91-92	26	2	0
Maidstone U	L	02.91	90	3	0	0
Stockport Co	Tr	03.95	94	1	0	0
Blackpool	Tr	08.95	95	2	1	0

BROWN Richard Colin
Sutton Coldfield, 25 December, 1973 (FB)

League Club	Source	Date Signed	Seasons Played	Apps	Subs	Gls
Walsall	YT	03.92	91	6	3	0

BROWN Robert (Bobby)
Glasgow, 9 August, 1924 (IF)

League Club	Source	Date Signed	Seasons Played	Apps	Subs	Gls
Derby Co	Camerons	10.47				
Southend U	Tr	07.48	48-49	12	-	0
Shrewsbury T	Tr	07.50	50-52	104	-	41
Barnsley	Tr	07.53	53-56	120	-	55
Rotherham U	Tr	09.56	56-57	42	-	12

BROWN Robert (Bob)
Motherwell, 2 December, 1931 (CD)

League Club	Source	Date Signed	Seasons Played	Apps	Subs	Gls
Workington	Motherwell	05.56	56-67	419	1	2

BROWN Robert (Bobby)
Bristol, 14 May, 1949 (M)

League Club	Source	Date Signed	Seasons Played	Apps	Subs	Gls
Bristol Rov	App	06.67	68-71	28	7	4
Newport Co	L	03.70	69	8	1	0

BROWN Robert (Bobby)
Carluke, 23 November, 1955 (FB)

League Club	Source	Date Signed	Seasons Played	Apps	Subs	Gls
Workington	Jnrs	08.74	74-76	44	0	0

BROWN Robert (Sailor) Alan John
Great Yarmouth, 7 November, 1915 EWar-6 (IF)

League Club	Source	Date Signed	Seasons Played	Apps	Subs	Gls
Charlton Ath	Gorleston	08.34	37-38	47	-	21
Nottingham F	Tr	05.46	46-47	45	-	17
Aston Villa	Tr	10.47	47-48	30	-	9

BROWN Robert (Bobby) Christopher
Plymouth, 24 November, 1953 ESch (M)

League Club	Source	Date Signed	Seasons Played	Apps	Subs	Gls
Chelsea	Jnrs	08.72				
Sheffield Wed	Tr	08.74	74-75	17	4	3
Aldershot	L	02.76	75	3	2	0

BROWN Robert (Bobby) Henry
Streatham, 2 May, 1940 EAmat (F)

League Club	Source	Date Signed	Seasons Played	Apps	Subs	Gls
Fulham (Am)	Barnet	09.60	60-61	8	-	4
Watford	Tr	11.61	61-62	28	-	10
Northampton T	Tr	12.63	63-66	50	0	22
Cardiff C	Tr	10.66	66-67	50	0	23

BROWN Roger William
Tamworth, 12 December, 1952 (CD)

League Club	Source	Date Signed	Seasons Played	Apps	Subs	Gls
Bournemouth	AP Leamington	02.78	77-78	63	0	3
Norwich C	Tr	07.79	79	16	0	0
Fulham	Tr	03.80	79-83	141	0	18
Bournemouth	Tr	12.83	83-86	83	1	5

BROWN Ronald (Ron)
Ballymoney, 20 March, 1923 (CF)

League Club	Source	Date Signed	Seasons Played	Apps	Subs	Gls
Plymouth Arg	Linfield	04.45				
Hull C	Tr	03.47	46	7	-	3

BROWN Ronald (Ronnie)
Sunderland, 26 December, 1944 (W)

League Club	Source	Date Signed	Seasons Played	Apps	Subs	Gls
Blackpool	Whitley Bay	11.65	65-70	54	7	13
Plymouth Arg	Tr	02.71	70-72	31	5	3
Bradford C	Tr	09.72	72-74	90	7	11

BROWN Roy
Stockton, 10 June, 1925 (FB)

League Club	Source	Date Signed	Seasons Played	Apps	Subs	Gls
Darlington	Stockton West End	01.47	46-55	158	-	20

BROWN Roy
Retford, 17 June, 1932 (IF)

League Club	Source	Date Signed	Seasons Played	Apps	Subs	Gls
Doncaster Rov	Gainsborough Trinity	05.53	53-56	26	-	6

BROWN Albert **Roy**
Nottingham, 14 August, 1917 (W)

League Club	Source	Date Signed	Seasons Played	Apps	Subs	Gls
Nottingham F	Sneinton	02.36	36-38	51	-	7
Wrexham	Tr	06.39	46	24	-	3
Mansfield T	Tr	07.47	47	17	-	2

BROWN Roy Eric
Shoreham-by-Sea, 5 October, 1945 (G)

League Club	Source	Date Signed	Seasons Played	Apps	Subs	Gls
Tottenham H	App	10.62	66	1	0	0
Reading	Tr	07.68	68-69	63	0	0
Notts Co	Tr	07.70	70-74	113	0	0
Mansfield T	Tr	11.75	75	1	0	0

BROWN Henry **Roy**
Stoke-on-Trent, 20 December, 1923 Died 1989 (CF)

League Club	Source	Date Signed	Seasons Played	Apps	Subs	Gls
Stoke C	Jnrs	08.42	46-52	70	-	14
Watford	Tr	07.53	53-57	142	-	40

BROWN Ryan Anthony
Stoke-on-Trent, 15 March, 1985 (FB)

League Club	Source	Date Signed	Seasons Played	Apps	Subs	Gls
Port Vale	Sch	08.03	02-04	33	5	0

BROWN Scott
Runcorn, 8 May, 1985 EYth (M)

League Club	Source	Date Signed	Seasons Played	Apps	Subs	Gls
Everton	YT	05.02				
Bristol C	Tr	08.04	04	13	6	0

BROWN Simon Alexander
West Bromwich, 18 September, 1983 (M)

League Club	Source	Date Signed	Seasons Played	Apps	Subs	Gls
West Bromwich A	Sch	07.03				
Kidderminster Hrs	L	03.04	03	8	0	2
Kidderminster Hrs	L	07.04	04	11	2	0
Mansfield T	Tr	12.04	04	16	5	2

BROWN Simon James
Chelmsford, 3 December, 1976 (G)

League Club	Source	Date Signed	Seasons Played	Apps	Subs	Gls
Tottenham H	YT	07.95				
Lincoln C	L	12.97	97	1	0	0
Colchester U	Tr	07.99	99-03	141	1	0

BROWN Stanley (Stan)
Lewes, 15 September, 1941 (M)

League Club	Source	Date Signed	Seasons Played	Apps	Subs	Gls
Fulham	Jnrs	05.59	60-72	348	5	16
Brighton & Hove A	L	10.72	72	9	0	0
Colchester U	Tr	12.72	72	23	0	0

BROWN Steven (Steve) Andrew John
Peckham, 13 July, 1952 (W)

League Club	Source	Date Signed	Seasons Played	Apps	Subs	Gls
Millwall	App	06.70	69-74	47	22	5

BROWN Steven (Steve) Byron
Brighton, 13 May, 1972 (FB)

League Club	Source	Date Signed	Seasons Played	Apps	Subs	Gls
Charlton Ath	YT	07.90	91-02	194	48	9
Reading	Tr	12.02	02-03	40	0	1

BROWN Steven (Steve) Ferold
Northampton, 6 July, 1966 (M)

League Club	Source	Date Signed	Seasons Played	Apps	Subs	Gls
Northampton T	Jnrs	08.83	83-84	14	1	3
Northampton T	Irthlingborough Dmnds	07.89	89-93	145	13	19
Wycombe W	Tr	02.94	93-03	332	39	35

BROWN Steven (Steve) Robert
Southend-on-Sea, 6 December, 1973 (F)

League Club	Source	Date Signed	Seasons Played	Apps	Subs	Gls
Southend U	YT	07.92	92	10	0	2
Scunthorpe U	Tr	07.93				
Colchester U	Tr	08.93	93-94	56	6	17
Gillingham	Tr	03.95	94-95	8	1	2
Lincoln C	Tr	10.95	95-97	47	25	8
Macclesfield T	Tr	07.98	98	1	1	0

BROWN Thomas (Tom)
Troon, 26 October, 1919 (G)

League Club	Source	Date Signed	Seasons Played	Apps	Subs	Gls
Ipswich T	Glenafton Ath	10.38	46-50	111	-	0

BROWN Thomas (Tommy)
Galashiels, 7 June, 1929 Died 2000 (IF)

League Club	Source	Date Signed	Seasons Played	Apps	Subs	Gls
Ipswich T	Annbank Jnrs	07.52	52-55	84	-	17
Walsall	Tr	06.56	56-57	38	-	9

BROWN Thomas (Tom)
Leven, 17 November, 1933 (CF)

League Club	Source	Date Signed	Seasons Played	Apps	Subs	Gls
Lincoln C	Newburgh West End	04.56	57	3	-	0

BROWN Thomas (Tom) Emmerson
Throckley, 8 September, 1935 (FB)

League Club	Source	Date Signed	Seasons Played	Apps	Subs	Gls
Middlesbrough	Jnrs	04.53	54-57	44	-	0

BROWN Thomas (Tommy) Graham
Cowdenbeath, 11 August, 1924 (IF)

League Club	Source	Date Signed	Seasons Played	Apps	Subs	Gls
Portsmouth	Worcester C	10.46	47	17	-	1
Watford	Tr	08.49	49-53	108	-	11

BROWN Thomas (Tommy) Hugh
Liverpool, 8 May, 1930 EYth (WH)

League Club	Source	Date Signed	Seasons Played	Apps	Subs	Gls
Doncaster Rov	South Liverpool	02.51	51-53	86	-	1
Swansea T	Tr	12.55	55-58	68	-	0

BROWN Thomas (Tommy) Law
Glenbuck, 17 April, 1921 Died 1966 SLge-1/SWar-3 (WH)

League Club	Source	Date Signed	Seasons Played	Apps	Subs	Gls
Millwall	Heart of Midlothian	01.45	46-48	68	-	7
Charlton Ath	Tr	10.48	48-49	34	-	1
Leyton Orient	Tr	08.50	50-52	99	-	5

BROWN Walter (Wally) Sidney
Oakengates, 8 February, 1921 Died 1989 (W)

League Club	Source	Date Signed	Seasons Played	Apps	Subs	Gls
Walsall	Oakengates T	10.40	46-47	20	-	4

BROWN Wayne Larry
Southampton, 14 January, 1977 (G)

League Club	Source	Date Signed	Seasons Played	Apps	Subs	Gls
Bristol C	YT	07.95	93	1	0	0
Chester C	Weston-super-Mare	09.96	96-04	107	0	0

BROWN Wayne Lawrence
Barking, 20 August, 1977 (CD)

League Club	Source	Date Signed	Seasons Played	Apps	Subs	Gls
Ipswich T	YT	05.96	97-02	28	12	0
Colchester U	L	10.97	97	0	2	0
Queens Park Rgrs	L	03.01	00	2	0	0
Wimbledon	L	09.01	01	17	0	1
Watford	L	01.02	01	10	1	3
Watford	Tr	12.02	02-03	24	1	1
Gillingham	L	09.03	03	4	0	1
Colchester U	Tr	02.04	03-04	54	2	1

BROWN Wesley (Wes) Michael
Manchester, 13 October, 1979 ESch/EYth/Eu21-8/E-8 (CD)

League Club	Source	Date Signed	Seasons Played	Apps	Subs	Gls
Manchester U	YT	11.96	97-04	107	14	1

BROWN William
Dawdon, 27 March, 1928 (WH)

League Club	Source	Date Signed	Seasons Played	Apps	Subs	Gls
Gateshead	Murton CW	09.50	50-57	216	-	7

BROWN William
Kilsyth, 21 February, 1929 Died 1987 (IF)

League Club	Source	Date Signed	Seasons Played	Apps	Subs	Gls
Reading	Bridgeton Waverley	02.50				
Exeter C	Tr	08.51	51	7	-	0

BROWN William (Willie)
Forfar, 17 September, 1928 (CF)

League Club	Source	Date Signed	Seasons Played	Apps	Subs	Gls
Accrington St	Forfar Ath	08.53	53	6	-	2

BROWN William (Willie)
Falkirk, 5 February, 1950 (F)

League Club	Source	Date Signed	Seasons Played	Apps	Subs	Gls
Burnley	Jnrs	02.67	68	0	1	0
Carlisle U	Tr	07.69	69	16	1	8
Barrow	L	09.69	69	6	0	1
Newport Co	Tr	08.70	70-74	166	2	50
Hereford U	L	03.74	73	9	0	6
Brentford	Tr	11.74	74	16	0	9
Torquay U	Tr	03.75	74-77	137	2	47

BROWN William (Bill) Charles
Canning Town, 24 February, 1920 Died 1982 (CF)

League Club	Source	Date Signed	Seasons Played	Apps	Subs	Gls
Leyton Orient	Romford	08.46	46	2	-	1

BROWN William (Bill) Dallas Fyfe
Arbroath, 8 October, 1931 Died 2004 SLge-8/SB/S-28 (G)

League Club	Source	Date Signed	Seasons Played	Apps	Subs	Gls
Tottenham H	Dundee	06.59	59-65	222	0	0
Northampton T	Tr	10.66	66	17	0	0

BROWN William (Willie) Falconer
Larkhall, 20 October, 1922 Died 1978 (FB)

League Club	Source	Date Signed	Seasons Played	Apps	Subs	Gls
Preston NE	Larkhall Thistle	01.42	46-49	40	-	0
Grimsby T	Elgin C	06.51	51-57	265	-	1

BROWN William (Billy) Frederick Thomas
Croydon, 7 February, 1943 (F)

League Club	Source	Date Signed	Seasons Played	Apps	Subs	Gls
Southampton		09.60				
Charlton Ath	Tr	07.61				
Gillingham	Bedford T	02.66	65-67	104	1	33
Portsmouth	Tr	06.68	68	8	0	2
Brentford	Tr	07.69	69	4	0	0

BROWN William (Billy) Hutchinson
Choppington, 11 March, 1909 Died 1996 (WH)

League Club	Source	Date Signed	Seasons Played	Apps	Subs	Gls
Middlesbrough	West Stanley	12.28	31-38	256	-	2
Hartlepools U	Tr	06.46	46-47	80	-	0

BROWN William (Billy) Ian
Silvertown, 6 September, 1910 Died 1993 (WH)

League Club	Source	Date Signed	Seasons Played	Apps	Subs	Gls
Luton T	Silvertown	03.30	30-34	49	-	4
Huddersfield T	Tr	03.35	34-35	20	-	2
Brentford	Tr	03.37	36-46	92	-	2
Leyton Orient	Tr	05.47	46-47	26	-	0

BROWN William (Bill) Inglis
Clydebank, 25 November, 1938 (G)

League Club	Source	Date Signed	Seasons Played	Apps	Subs	Gls
Accrington St	St Mirren	08.59	59	29	-	0
Chester	Tr	06.60	60	41	-	0

BROWNBILL Derek Anthony
Liverpool, 4 February, 1954 (F)

League Club	Source	Date Signed	Seasons Played	Apps	Subs	Gls
Liverpool	Jnrs	02.72	73	1	0	0
Port Vale	Tr	02.75	74-77	84	8	13
Wigan Ath	Tr	09.78	78-79	32	16	8

BROWNE Anthony (Tony)
Sheerness, 12 February, 1977 (FB)

League Club	Source	Date Signed	Seasons Played	Apps	Subs	Gls
Brighton & Hove A	Gravesend & Northfleet	10.98	98	13	0	0

BROWNE Corey Anthony
Enfield, 2 July, 1970 (M)

League Club	Source	Date Signed	Seasons Played	Apps	Subs	Gls
Fulham	Kingsbury T	08.91	91	1	0	0

BROWNE Gary
Dundonald, 17 January, 1983 NIu21-5 (F)

League Club	Source	Date Signed	Seasons Played	Apps	Subs	Gls
Manchester C	YT	07.00				
York C	Whitby T	11.03	03	2	4	0

BROWNE Paul Gerard
Glasgow, 17 February, 1975 (CD)

League Club	Source	Date Signed	Seasons Played	Apps	Subs	Gls
Aston Villa	YT	07.93	95	2	0	0

BROWNE Robert (Bobby) James
Derry, 2 February, 1912 Died 1994 IrLge-1/I-6 (WH)

League Club	Source	Date Signed	Seasons Played	Apps	Subs	Gls
Leeds U	Derry C	10.35	35-46	107	-	0
York C	Tr	08.47	47	5	-	0

BROWNE Stafford Ernest
Cuckfield, 4 January, 1972 (F)

League Club	Source	Date Signed	Seasons Played	Apps	Subs	Gls
Brighton & Hove A	Hastings T	07.98	98	2	1	0

BROWNE Stephen Logan
Hackney, 21 June, 1964 (M)

League Club	Source	Date Signed	Seasons Played	Apps	Subs	Gls
Charlton Ath	App	06.82	81	0	1	0

BROWNING Leonard (Len) James
Doncaster, 30 March, 1928 (CF)

League Club	Source	Date Signed	Seasons Played	Apps	Subs	Gls
Leeds U	Headingley Rgrs	08.46	46-51	97	-	43
Sheffield U	Tr	11.51	51-53	65	-	25

BROWNING Marcus Trevor
Bristol, 22 April, 1971 W-5 (M)

League Club	Source	Date Signed	Seasons Played	Apps	Subs	Gls
Bristol Rov	YT	07.89	89-96	152	22	13
Hereford U	L	09.92	92	7	0	5
Huddersfield T	Tr	02.97	96-98	25	8	0
Gillingham	L	11.98	98	1	0	0
Gillingham	Tr	03.99	98-01	60	17	3
Bournemouth	Tr	08.02	02-04	98	27	1

BROWNLEE Thomas (Tommy) Courtenay
Carnwath, 21 May, 1935 (CF)

League Club	Source	Date Signed	Seasons Played	Apps	Subs	Gls
Walsall	Broxburn	09.56	57-58	30	-	14
York C	Tr	12.58	58	9	-	2
Workington	Tr	06.59	59-60	25	-	2
Bradford C	Netherfield	01.65	64-65	25	0	15

BROWNLIE John Jack
Caldercruix, 11 March, 1952 SLge-1/Su23-5/S-7 (FB)

League Club	Source	Date Signed	Seasons Played	Apps	Subs	Gls
Newcastle U	Hibernian	08.78	78-81	124	0	2
Middlesbrough	Tr	08.82	82	12	0	0
Hartlepool U	Tr	08.84	84	19	0	1

BROWNLOW John (Jackie) Martin
Belfast, 18 June, 1916 Died 1989 (W)

League Club	Source	Date Signed	Seasons Played	Apps	Subs	Gls
Ipswich T	Gravesend U	05.46	46	1	-	0
Hartlepools U	Tr	10.48	48	3	-	0

BROWNRIGG Andrew (Andy) David
Sheffield, 2 August, 1976 SSch (CD)

League Club	Source	Date Signed	Seasons Played	Apps	Subs	Gls
Hereford U	YT	01.95	94	8	0	0

BROWNSWORD Nathan **John (Jack)**
Campsall, 15 May, 1923 (FB)

League Club	Source	Date Signed	Seasons Played	Apps	Subs	Gls
Hull C	Frickley Colliery	09.46	46	10	-	0
Scunthorpe U	Frickley Colliery	07.47	50-64	597	-	50

BRUCE Alexander (Alex) Robert
Dundee, 23 December, 1952 Su23-1 (F)

League Club	Source	Date Signed	Seasons Played	Apps	Subs	Gls
Preston NE	App	05.70	71-73	55	7	22
Newcastle U	Tr	01.74	73-75	16	4	3
Preston NE	Tr	08.75	75-82	288	13	135
Wigan Ath	Tr	08.83	83-84	35	8	7

BRUCE Alexander (Alex) Stephen
Norwich, 28 September, 1984 (CD)

League Club	Source	Date Signed	Seasons Played	Apps	Subs	Gls
Blackburn Rov	Sch	07.02				
Oldham Ath	L	12.04	04	3	3	0

League Club	Source	Date Signed	Seasons Played	Career Record Apps	Subs	Gls
Birmingham C	Tr	01.05				
Oldham Ath	L	01.05	04	5	1	0
Sheffield Wed	L	03.05	04	5	1	0
BRUCE Marcelle Eugene						
Detroit, USA, 15 March, 1971						(FB)
Colchester U	YT	07.89	89	28	1	1
BRUCE Paul Mark						
Lambeth, 18 February, 1978						(FB)
Queens Park Rgrs	YT	07.96	97-01	30	7	3
Cambridge U	L	03.99	98	2	2	0
BRUCE Robert (Bobby)						
Belfast, 14 October, 1928						(W)
Leicester C	Larne T	03.50				
Leyton Orient		11.51	51	1	-	0
BRUCE Stephen (Steve) Roger						
Corbridge, 31 December, 1960 EYth/EB/FLge						(CD)
Gillingham	App	10.78	79-83	203	2	29
Norwich C	Tr	08.84	84-87	141	0	14
Manchester U	Tr	12.87	87-95	309	0	36
Birmingham C	Tr	06.96	96-97	70	2	2
Sheffield U	Tr	07.98	98	10	0	0
BRUCK Dietmar Jurgen						
Danzig, Germany, 19 April, 1944						(FB)
Coventry C	App	05.62	60-70	181	8	7
Charlton Ath	Tr	10.70	70-71	54	2	0
Northampton T	Tr	06.72	72-73	41	0	0
BRUMWELL Philip (Phil)						
Darlington, 8 August, 1975						(M)
Sunderland	YT	06.94				
Darlington	Tr	08.95	95-99	106	50	1
Hull C	Tr	08.00	00	1	3	0
Darlington	Tr	11.00	00-01	35	8	0
BRUNFIELD Peter Stanley						
Treeton, 5 September, 1944						(WH)
Chesterfield		07.64	64	1	-	0
BRUNO Pasquale						
Lecce, Italy, 19 June, 1962						(CD)
Wigan Ath (L)	Heart of Midlothian	02.98	97	1	0	0
BRUNSKILL Joseph (Joe)						
Carlton, County Durham, 22 April, 1932 Died 1989						(CF)
Sunderland	Newcastle U (Am)	04.50				
Oldham Ath	Tr	05.54	54	12	-	2
BRUNT Christopher (Chris)						
Belfast, 14 December, 1984 NIu21-1/NIu23-1/NI-2						(M)
Middlesbrough	Sch	07.02				
Sheffield Wed	Tr	03.04	03-04	35	16	6
BRUNT Geoffrey (Geoff) Reginald						
Nottingham, 24 November, 1926 Died 2000						(WH)
Notts Co	Jnrs	09.49	49-53	29	-	1
BRUNT Malcolm Eric						
Sheffield, 5 December, 1946						(G)
Chesterfield	Sheffield Wed (Am)	07.66	66	7	0	0
BRUSH Paul						
Plaistow, 22 February, 1958						(FB)
West Ham U	App	02.76	77-84	144	7	1
Crystal Palace	Tr	09.85	85-87	50	0	3
Southend U	Tr	01.88	87-89	69	4	1
BRUTON David Edward						
Uley, 31 October, 1952						(CD)
Bristol C	App	07.71	71-72	16	1	0
Swansea C	Tr	08.73	73-78	185	8	19
Newport Co	L	02.77	76	6	0	1
Newport Co	Tr	10.78	78-80	79	3	9
BRUTON Michael (Mike)						
Dursley, 6 May, 1958						(F)
Newport Co	Gloucester C	08.79	79	3	6	1
BRYAN Derek Kirk						
Hammersmith, 11 November, 1974						(F)
Brentford	Hampton	08.97	97-01	16	34	7
BRYAN Ernest (Ernie) Newton						
Hawarden, 6 June, 1926						(FB)
Chester	Jnrs	11.45	48	1	-	0
BRYAN Marvin Lee						
Paddington, 2 August, 1975						(FB)
Queens Park Rgrs	YT	08.92				
Doncaster Rov	L	12.94	94	5	0	1
Blackpool	Tr	08.95	95-99	172	10	4
Bury	Tr	03.00	99	6	3	0
Rotherham U	Tr	07.00	00-02	54	9	0
BRYAN Peter						
Ashbourne, 30 April, 1944 LoI-3						(FB)
Oxford U	Botley Minors	07.61	62-65	18	0	0
BRYAN Peter Anthony						
Birmingham, 22 June, 1943						(FB)
Middlesbrough		08.61	64	4	-	0
Oldham Ath	Tr	07.65	65	5	1	0
BRYANT Eric						
Birmingham, 18 November, 1921 Died 1995						(CF)
Mansfield T		05.46	46-47	35	-	17
Plymouth Arg	Yeovil T	10.49	49-50	11	-	4
Leyton Orient	Tr	07.51	51	12	-	1
BRYANT Jeffrey (Jeff) Stephen						
Redhill, 27 November, 1953 EYth						(FB)
Wimbledon	Walton & Hersham	(N/L)	77-78	70	3	9
Bournemouth	Tr	06.79	79	16	0	2
BRYANT Matthew (Matt)						
Bristol, 21 September, 1970						(CD)
Bristol C	YT	07.89	90-95	201	2	7
Walsall	L	08.90	90	13	0	0
Gillingham	Tr	08.96	96-99	82	21	0
BRYANT Richard John						
Bristol, 20 June, 1963						(CD)
Bristol C	Robinson's DRG	12.85	85	2	0	1
BRYANT Simon Christopher						
Bristol, 22 November, 1982 EYth						(M)
Bristol Rov	YT	01.00	99-03	65	22	2
BRYANT Steven (Steve) Paul						
Islington, 5 September, 1953						(FB)
Birmingham C	App	07.71	74-75	34	2	1
Sheffield Wed	L	08.76	76	2	1	0
Northampton T	Tr	12.76	76-78	95	2	5
Portsmouth	Tr	03.79	78-81	111	0	5
Northampton T	Tr	03.82	81	10	0	0
BRYCELAND Thomas (Tommy)						
Greenock, 1 March, 1939 SSch						(M)
Norwich C	St Mirren	09.62	62-69	253	1	49
Oldham Ath	Tr	03.70	69-71	66	0	10
BRYDON Ian Forrester						
Edinburgh, 22 March, 1927 Died 1973						(CF)
Darlington	Alloa Ath	09.53	53	1	-	0
Accrington St	Tr	11.53	53-54	27	-	19
Bradford PA	Tr	06.55	55	12	-	3
BRYDON Lee						
Stockton, 15 November, 1974 ESch						(CD)
Liverpool	YT	06.92				
Darlington	Tr	08.96	96-97	28	12	0
BRYNGELSSON Fredrik						
Sweden, 10 April, 1975						(FB)
Stockport Co	BK Hacken (Swe)	07.00	00-01	7	1	0
BRYSON James **Ian** Cook						
Kilmarnock, 26 November, 1962						(W)
Sheffield U	Kilmarnock	08.88	88-92	138	17	36
Barnsley	Tr	08.93	93	16	0	3
Preston NE	Tr	11.93	93-96	141	10	19
Rochdale	Tr	07.97	97-98	43	11	1
BUARI Malik						
Accra, Ghana, 21 January, 1984						(M)
Fulham	Sch	07.03	03	1	2	0
BUBB Alvin Ryan						
Paddington, 11 October, 1980						(F)
Queens Park Rgrs	YT	11.98	00	0	1	0
Bristol Rov	Tr	07.01	01	3	10	0
BUBB Byron James						
Harrow, 17 December, 1981						(M)
Millwall	YT	12.98	98-00	3	5	0

League Club	Source	Date Signed	Seasons Played	Apps	Subs	Gls
BUCHAN Alistair Reid						
Aberdeen, 27 May, 1926 Died 2004						(WH)
Rochdale	Huntly	02.51	50-53	107	-	2
BUCHAN George						
Aberdeen, 2 May, 1950						(W)
Manchester U	Aberdeen	05.73	73	0	3	0
Bury	Tr	08.74	74-75	57	8	6
BUCHAN Martin McLean						
Aberdeen, 6 March, 1949 Su23-3/S-34						(CD)
Manchester U	Aberdeen	03.72	71-82	376	0	4
Oldham Ath	Tr	08.83	83-84	28	0	0
BUCHAN Thomas (Tom)						
Edinburgh, 6 December, 1915 Died 1980						(WH)
Blackpool	Woodhall Thistle	05.38	46-47	12	-	0
Carlisle U	Tr	08.49	49	30	-	0
BUCHAN William (Willie) Ralston Murray						
Grangemouth, 17 October, 1914 Died 2003 SLge-2/SWar-1						(IF)
Blackpool	Glasgow Celtic	11.37	37-47	94	-	35
Hull C	Tr	01.48	47-48	40	-	12
Gateshead	Tr	11.49	49-51	89	-	16
BUCHANAN Cameron Campbell						
Holytown, 31 July, 1928						(IF)
Wolverhampton W	Jnrs	09.45				
Bournemouth	Tr	08.49	49-54	83	-	18
Norwich C	Montreal Ukrainia (Can)	10.56	56	3	-	0
BUCHANAN David						
Newcastle, 23 June, 1962 EYth/ESemiPro						(F)
Leicester C	App	06.79	78-82	24	9	7
Northampton T	L	10.82	82	3	2	0
Peterborough U	Tr	08.83	83	13	3	4
Sunderland	Blyth Spartans	08.86	86-87	25	9	8
York C	L	09.87	87	7	0	2
BUCHANAN David Thomas Hugh						
Rochdale, 6 May, 1986 NIYth						(M)
Bury	Sch	●	04	0	3	0
BUCHANAN John (Jock)						
Underwood, Stirlingshire, 9 June, 1928 Died 2000						(IF)
Derby Co	Clyde	02.55	54-56	32	-	12
Bradford PA	Tr	12.57	57-62	164	-	67
BUCHANAN John (Jock)						
Castlecary, 3 January, 1935						(CF)
Newport Co	Raith Rov	08.61	61	31	-	8
BUCHANAN John						
Dingwall, 19 September, 1951						(M)
Northampton T	Ross Co	11.70	70-74	104	10	25
Cardiff C	Tr	10.74	74-81	217	14	54
Northampton T	Tr	09.81	81-82	66	3	6
BUCHANAN Peter Symington						
Glasgow, 13 October, 1915 Died 1977 S-1						(W)
Chelsea	Wishaw Jnrs	11.35	36-38	39	-	6
Fulham	Tr	03.46	46	20	-	1
Brentford	Tr	08.47	47-48	74	-	13
BUCHANAN Wayne Bernard						
Banbridge, 12 January, 1982 NISch/NIYth/NIu21						(CD)
Bolton W	YT	07.01				
Chesterfield	L	03.02	01	3	0	0
BUCHANAN William (Billy) Mack						
Tannochside, 29 July, 1924 Died 1999						(FB)
Carlisle U	Motherwell	07.49	49	9	-	0
Barrow	Tr	10.49	49-55	242	-	0
BUCK Alan Michael						
Colchester, 25 August, 1946						(G)
Colchester U	Jnrs	07.64	64-68	39	0	0
BUCK Anthony (Tony) Rowland						
Clowne, 18 August, 1944						(F)
Oxford U	Eastbourne	08.62	62-67	30	5	6
Newport Co	Tr	12.67	67-68	49	0	16
Rochdale	Tr	02.69	68-72	73	10	29
Bradford C	L	01.72	71	3	0	0
Northampton T	Tr	01.73	72-73	16	1	3
BUCK David Colin						
Colchester, 25 August, 1946 Died 1996						(WH)
Colchester U	Jnrs	05.65	65	0	1	0

League Club	Source	Date Signed	Seasons Played	Apps	Subs	Gls
BUCK George William						
Abingdon, 25 January, 1941						(W)
Reading	Jnrs	01.58	58-60	31	-	4
Stockport Co	Tr	07.62	62	3	-	0
BUCKINGHAM Colin Maurice Ernest						
Plymouth, 12 August, 1943						(WH)
Plymouth Arg	App	08.61	62-65	16	0	0
Exeter C	Tr	09.65	65-66	29	0	0
BUCKINGHAM Victor (Vic) Frederick						
Greenwich, 23 October, 1915 Died 1995 EWar-2						(FB)
Tottenham H	Jnrs	05.35	35-48	204	-	1
BUCKLAND Mark Christopher						
Cheltenham, 18 August, 1961						(M)
Wolverhampton W	AP Leamington	02.84	83-84	44	6	5
BUCKLE Herbert **Edward (Ted)** William						
Southwark, 28 October, 1924 Died 1990						(W)
Manchester U		11.45	46-49	20	-	6
Everton	Tr	11.49	49-54	97	-	31
Exeter C	Tr	07.55	55-56	65	-	12
BUCKLE Paul John						
Hatfield, 16 December, 1970						(M)
Brentford	YT	07.89	87-92	42	15	1
Torquay U	Tr	02.94	93-95	57	2	9
Exeter C	Tr	10.95	95	22	0	2
Colchester U	Wycombe W (N/C)	11.96	96-98	96	9	7
Exeter C	Tr	07.99	99-01	85	8	5
BUCKLEY Adam Christian						
Nottingham, 2 August, 1979						(M)
Grimsby T	West Bromwich A (YT)	08.97	98-99	8	7	0
Lincoln C	Tr	07.01	01-02	19	15	0
BUCKLEY Alan Peter						
Eastwood, 20 April, 1951						(F)
Nottingham F	App	04.68	71-72	16	2	1
Walsall	Tr	08.73	73-78	241	0	125
Birmingham C	Tr	10.78	78	24	4	8
Walsall	Tr	07.79	79-84	161	17	49
BUCKLEY Ambrose (Amby)						
Brinsley, 31 January, 1909 Died 1968						(FB)
Fulham	Sherwood Foresters	03.33	34-38	6	-	0
Doncaster Rov	Tr	05.39				
Stockport Co	Dartford	11.45	46	11	-	0
BUCKLEY Frank Leslie						
Lichfield, 11 May, 1922 Died 1973						(WH)
Notts Co	Jnrs	08.39				
Crystal Palace	Tr	11.46	47-50	69	-	0
BUCKLEY Gary						
Manchester, 3 March, 1961						(M)
Manchester C	App	04.78	80	4	2	0
Preston NE	Tr	10.81	81-82	27	7	0
Bury	Chorley	03.84	83-85	23	8	1
BUCKLEY Glen						
Wigan, 31 August, 1960						(F)
Wigan Ath	Preston NE (N/C)	10.79	79	1	0	0
BUCKLEY Ian						
Oldham, 8 October, 1953 EYth						(FB)
Oldham Ath	App	12.71	71	5	0	0
Rochdale	L	02.74	73	6	0	0
Stockport Co	Tr	08.75	75-76	55	10	2
Cambridge U	Durban C (SA)	11.77	77-80	51	6	2
BUCKLEY John William						
East Kilbride, 18 May, 1962						(W)
Doncaster Rov	Partick Th	07.84	84-85	79	5	11
Leeds U	Tr	06.86	86-87	6	4	1
Leicester C	L	03.87	86	1	4	0
Doncaster Rov	L	10.87	87	6	0	0
Rotherham U	Tr	11.87	87-90	85	20	13
Scunthorpe U	Partick Th	08.91	91-92	39	4	8
Rotherham U	Tr	02.93	92	2	2	0
BUCKLEY Michael (Mick) John						
Manchester, 4 November, 1953 ESch/EYth/Eu23-1						(M)
Everton	App	06.71	71-77	128	7	10
Sunderland	Tr	08.78	78-82	117	4	7
Hartlepool U	Tr	08.83	83	6	0	0
Carlisle U	Tr	09.83	83	24	1	2
Middlesbrough	Tr	06.84	84	27	0	0

League Club	Source	Date Signed	Seasons Played	Apps	Subs	Gls
BUCKLEY Neil Anthony						
Hull, 25 September, 1968 (CD)						
Hull C	App	12.86	86-91	55	5	3
Burnley	L	03.90	89	5	0	0
BUCKLEY Patrick (Pat) McCabe						
Leith, 12 August, 1946 (W)						
Wolverhampton W	Third Lanark	02.64	64-67	28	1	8
Sheffield U	Tr	01.68	67-70	9	6	2
Rotherham U	Tr	06.72	72	1	2	0
BUCKLEY Steven (Steve)						
Eastwood, 16 October, 1953 (FB)						
Luton T	Burton A	04.74	74-77	123	0	9
Derby Co	Tr	01.78	77-85	323	0	21
Lincoln C	Tr	08.86	86	36	0	2
BUDD Kevin John						
Hillingdon, 20 March, 1962 (FB)						
Norwich C	Bournemouth (App)	10.79				
Manchester C	Tr	02.81				
Swansea C	Hillingdon Borough	11.85	85	1	0	0
BUGG Alec Alfred						
Needham Market, 27 November, 1948 (G)						
Ipswich T	Jnrs	06.67	68-69	4	0	0
Bournemouth	L	02.70	69	4	0	0
BUGGIE Lee David						
Bury, 11 February, 1981 (F)						
Bolton W	YT	02.98				
Bury	Tr	05.99	99	0	1	0
Rochdale	L	09.00	00	0	2	0
BUICK Joseph (Joe) Arnot Lorimer						
Broughty Ferry, 1 July, 1933 (WH)						
Lincoln C	Broughty Ath	10.55	55-61	31	-	3
BUIST James (Jimmy) Gibb						
Falkirk, 19 June, 1918 Died 1999 (W)						
New Brighton	Dundee	08.46	46	21	-	6
Plymouth Arg	Tr	06.47	48	1	-	0
BUKOVINA John Frank						
Barnsley, 2 February, 1964 (F)						
Barnsley	App	02.82				
Doncaster Rov	Tr	08.83	83	1	0	0
BUKOWSKI David						
Willington, 2 November, 1952 (CD)						
Northampton T	App	11.70	71-72	10	3	0
BUKRAN Gabor						
Eger, Hungary, 16 November, 1975 HuYth/Huu21/Hu-1 (M)						
Walsall	Xerez CD (Sp)	08.99	99-00	63	10	4
Wigan Ath	Tr	08.01	01	1	0	0
BULCH Robert (Bobby) Stephen						
Washington, 1 January, 1933 (WH)						
Notts Co	Washington	03.53	55-57	27	-	1
Darlington	Tr	06.58	58-59	45	-	1
BULL Gary William						
West Bromwich, 12 June, 1966 (F)						
Southampton	Paget Rgrs	10.86				
Cambridge U	Tr	03.88	87-88	13	6	4
Barnet	Tr	03.89	91-92	83	0	37
Nottingham F	Tr	07.93	93-94	4	8	1
Birmingham C	L	09.94	94	10	0	6
Brighton & Hove A	L	08.95	95	10	0	2
Birmingham C	Tr	12.95	95	3	3	0
York C	Tr	03.96	95-97	66	17	11
Scunthorpe U	Tr	07.98	98-99	7	23	1
BULL Michael (Mickey)						
Twickenham, 3 April, 1930 (W)						
Brentford		09.48	52	3	-	0
Swindon T	Tr	06.53	53-54	69	-	15
BULL Ronald (Ronnie) Rodney						
Hackney, 26 December, 1980 (FB)						
Millwall	YT	05.99	98-02	37	13	0
Yeovil T	L	09.03	03	7	0	0
Brentford	L	01.04	03	20	0	0
Grimsby T	Tr	07.04	04	22	5	2
BULL Stephen (Steve) George						
Tipton, 28 March, 1965 Eu21-5/EB-5/E-13 (F)						
West Bromwich A	Tipton T	08.85	85-86	2	2	2
Wolverhampton W	Tr	11.86	86-98	461	13	250

League Club	Source	Date Signed	Seasons Played	Apps	Subs	Gls
BULL William (Bill)						
Birmingham, 1 April, 1926 (CF)						
Coventry C		03.48	48	1	-	0
BULLARD James (Jimmy) Richard						
Newham, 23 October, 1978 (M)						
West Ham U	Gravesend & Northfleet	02.99				
Peterborough U	Tr	07.01	01-02	62	4	11
Wigan Ath	Tr	01.03	02-04	109	0	6
BULLEN Lee						
Edinburgh, 29 March, 1971 (FB)						
Sheffield Wed	Dunfermline Ath	07.04	04	46	0	7
BULLESS Brian						
Hull, 4 September, 1933 (WH)						
Hull C	Jnrs	10.50	52-63	326	-	30
BULLIMORE Alwyn (Alan) Arthur						
Norwich, 22 October, 1933 Died 2001 (WH)						
Norwich C	Jnrs	10.53	56	1	-	0
BULLIMORE Wayne Alan						
Sutton-in-Ashfield, 12 September, 1970 EYth (M)						
Manchester U	YT	09.88				
Barnsley	Tr	03.91	91-92	27	8	1
Scunthorpe U	Stockport Co (N/C)	11.93	93-95	62	5	11
Bradford C	Tr	12.95	95	1	1	0
Doncaster Rov	L	09.96	96	4	0	0
Peterborough U	Tr	03.97	96-97	10	11	1
Scarborough	Tr	08.98	98	33	2	1
BULLIONS James (Jimmy) Law						
Dennyloanhead, 12 March, 1924 (WH)						
Derby Co	Clowne	10.44	46-47	17	-	0
Leeds U	Tr	11.47	47-49	35	-	0
Shrewsbury T	Tr	09.50	50-53	131	-	2
BULLIVANT Terence (Terry) Paul						
Lambeth, 23 September, 1956 (M)						
Fulham	App	05.74	74-79	94	7	2
Aston Villa	Tr	11.79	79-81	10	2	0
Charlton Ath	Tr	07.82	82	30	0	3
Brentford	Tr	07.83	83-85	36	1	2
BULLOCK Anthony (Tony) Brian						
Warrington, 18 February, 1972 (G)						
Barnsley	Leek T	03.97	98-99	37	1	0
Macclesfield T	Tr	07.00	00	24	0	0
Lincoln C	Tr	03.01	00	2	0	0
BULLOCK Darren John						
Worcester, 12 February, 1969 (M)						
Huddersfield T	Nuneaton Borough	11.93	93-96	127	1	16
Swindon T	Tr	02.97	96-98	55	11	2
Bury	Tr	02.99	98-01	45	8	5
Sheffield U	L	03.01	00	6	0	0
BULLOCK Lee						
Stockton, 22 May, 1981 (M)						
York C	YT	06.99	99-03	156	15	24
Cardiff C	Tr	03.04	03-04	12	20	6
BULLOCK Martin John						
Derby, 5 March, 1975 Eu21-1 (W)						
Barnsley	Eastwood T	09.93	94-00	108	77	4
Port Vale	L	01.00	99	6	0	1
Blackpool	Tr	08.01	01-04	128	25	4
BULLOCK Matthew						
Stoke-on-Trent, 1 November, 1980 EYth (M)						
Stoke C	YT	11.97	99	4	3	0
Macclesfield T	L	10.01	01	2	1	0
BULLOCK Michael (Mickey) Edwin						
Stoke-on-Trent, 2 October, 1946 ESch (F)						
Birmingham C	App	10.63	63-66	27	0	10
Oxford U	Tr	06.67	67-68	58	1	15
Orient	Tr	10.68	68-75	267	10	65
Halifax T	Tr	02.76	75-78	98	8	19
BULLOCK Norman						
Nuneaton, 26 March, 1932 Died 2003 (W)						
Aston Villa	Nuneaton Borough	09.49				
Chester	Tr	07.52	52-59	187	-	41
BULLOCK Peter Leonard						
Stoke-on-Trent, 17 November, 1941 ESch/EYth (F)						
Stoke C	Jnrs	11.58	57-61	44	-	13
Birmingham C	Tr	03.62	61-64	27	-	3
Southend U	Tr	02.65	64-65	12	0	2

League Club	Source	Date Signed	Seasons Played	Apps	Subs	Gls
Colchester U	Tr	10.65	65-67	94	1	33
Exeter C	Tr	07.68	68	14	0	2
Walsall	Tr	12.68	68	7	0	0

BULLOCK Simon John
Stoke-on-Trent, 28 September, 1962 (F)

League Club	Source	Date Signed	Seasons Played	Apps	Subs	Gls
Halifax T	Stoke C (App)	09.80	80-81	15	2	1

BULLOCK Steven (Steve)
Stockport, 5 October, 1966 (FB)

League Club	Source	Date Signed	Seasons Played	Apps	Subs	Gls
Oldham Ath	Jnrs	07.84	83-85	10	8	0
Tranmere Rov	Tr	08.86	86	25	5	1
Stockport Co	Tr	08.87	87-90	106	14	0

BULMAN Dannie
Ashford, Middlesex, 24 January, 1979 (M)

League Club	Source	Date Signed	Seasons Played	Apps	Subs	Gls
Wycombe W	Ashford T	06.98	98-03	160	42	14

BULMER Peter
Liverpool, 31 August, 1965 (FB)

League Club	Source	Date Signed	Seasons Played	Apps	Subs	Gls
Chester	App	08.83	82-84	56	15	2
Preston NE	Rhyl	07.86	86	4	0	0

BULZIS Riccardo
Bedford, 22 November, 1974 (F)

League Club	Source	Date Signed	Seasons Played	Apps	Subs	Gls
Northampton T	YT	•	91	1	3	0

BUMPSTEAD David (Dave) John
Rainham, 6 November, 1935 EAmat (WH)

League Club	Source	Date Signed	Seasons Played	Apps	Subs	Gls
Millwall	Tooting & Mitcham	06.58	57-61	84	-	8
Bristol Rov	Tr	12.61	61-63	40	-	0

BUMSTEAD Charles (Charlie) Henry
Croydon, 8 January, 1922 Died 1974 (G)

League Club	Source	Date Signed	Seasons Played	Apps	Subs	Gls
Millwall		03.43	46-47	12	-	0
Crystal Palace	Tr	08.48	48-51	53	-	0

BUMSTEAD John
Rotherhithe, 27 November, 1958 (M)

League Club	Source	Date Signed	Seasons Played	Apps	Subs	Gls
Chelsea	App	11.76	78-90	314	25	38
Charlton Ath	Tr	07.91	91-92	54	2	3

BUMSTEAD Raymond (Ray) George
Ringwood, 27 January, 1936 (W)

League Club	Source	Date Signed	Seasons Played	Apps	Subs	Gls
Bournemouth	Ringwood T	05.58	58-69	412	3	55

BUNBURY Alexander (Alex)
Plaisance, Guyana, 18 June, 1967 Canada int (F)

League Club	Source	Date Signed	Seasons Played	Apps	Subs	Gls
West Ham U	Supra Montreal (Can)	12.92	92	2	2	0

BUNCE Frederick (Freddie)
Watford, 16 February, 1938 Died 1991 EYth (W)

League Club	Source	Date Signed	Seasons Played	Apps	Subs	Gls
Watford	Jnrs	10.55	55-62	150	-	34

BUNCE Paul Eric
Coalville, 7 January, 1967 (W)

League Club	Source	Date Signed	Seasons Played	Apps	Subs	Gls
Leicester C	App	01.85	86	5	1	0
Northampton T	Tr	03.87	86-87	6	6	2

BUNCLARK Cyril
Rotherham, 27 March, 1931 (W)

League Club	Source	Date Signed	Seasons Played	Apps	Subs	Gls
Rotherham U		11.53	54	2	-	1

BUNJEVCEVIC Goran Petar
Karlovac, Croatia, 17 February, 1973 Yugoslavia 17 (CD)

League Club	Source	Date Signed	Seasons Played	Apps	Subs	Gls
Tottenham H	Red Star Belgrade (Yug)	07.01	01-04	41	10	0

BUNKELL Raymond (Ray) Keith
Edmonton, 18 September, 1949 Died 2000 (M)

League Club	Source	Date Signed	Seasons Played	Apps	Subs	Gls
Tottenham H	App	06.67				
Swindon T	Tr	06.71	71-73	52	4	3
Colchester U	Tr	12.73	73-79	117	12	9

BUNN Frank (Frankie) Stephen
Birmingham, 6 November, 1962 (F)

League Club	Source	Date Signed	Seasons Played	Apps	Subs	Gls
Luton T	App	05.80	80-84	52	7	9
Hull C	Tr	07.85	85-87	89	6	23
Oldham Ath	Tr	12.87	87-89	75	3	26

BUNNER Henry (Harry) Francis
Manchester, 18 September, 1936 (CD)

League Club	Source	Date Signed	Seasons Played	Apps	Subs	Gls
Bury	Bury Amats	04.57	57-64	105	-	0
Stockport Co	Tr	04.65	65	3	0	0

BUNTING Benjamin (Ben)
Rochdale, 14 February, 1923 (FB)

League Club	Source	Date Signed	Seasons Played	Apps	Subs	Gls
Oldham Ath	Rochdale (Am)	08.46	46-47	32	-	0

BURBANKS William **Edwin (Eddie)**
Campsall, 1 April, 1913 Died 1983 (W)

League Club	Source	Date Signed	Seasons Played	Apps	Subs	Gls
Sunderland	Denaby U	02.35	34-47	131	-	25

League Club	Source	Date Signed	Seasons Played	Apps	Subs	Gls
Hull C	Tr	06.48	48-52	143	-	21
Leeds U	Tr	07.53	53	13	-	1

BURBECK Ronald (Ron) Thomas
Leicester, 27 February, 1934 EYth (W)

League Club	Source	Date Signed	Seasons Played	Apps	Subs	Gls
Leicester C	Jnrs	05.52	52-55	3	-	0
Middlesbrough	Tr	10.56	56-62	139	-	24
Darlington	Tr	08.63	63	18	-	1

BURCHILL Mark James
Broxburn, 18 August, 1980 SSch/Su21-15/S-6 (F)

League Club	Source	Date Signed	Seasons Played	Apps	Subs	Gls
Birmingham C (L)	Glasgow Celtic	09.00	00	4	9	4
Ipswich T (L)	Glasgow Celtic	01.01	00	2	5	1
Portsmouth	Glasgow Celtic	08.01	01-02	9	15	8
Wigan Ath	L	08.03	03	1	3	0
Sheffield Wed	L	12.03	03	4	1	0
Rotherham U	L	09.04	04	3	0	1

BURCKITT John (Jack) David
Coventry, 16 December, 1946 Died 1999 EYth (FB)

League Club	Source	Date Signed	Seasons Played	Apps	Subs	Gls
Coventry C	Jnrs	07.64	64	5	-	0
Bradford C	L	03.67	66	9	0	0

BURDEN Brian
West Stockwith, 26 November, 1939 (G)

League Club	Source	Date Signed	Seasons Played	Apps	Subs	Gls
Lincoln C	West Stockwith	03.61	60	1	-	0

BURDEN Ian
Bradford, 27 May, 1944 (CD)

League Club	Source	Date Signed	Seasons Played	Apps	Subs	Gls
York C (Am)	Poppleton Road	10.65	65	3	0	2

BURDEN Thomas (Tommy) David
Andover, 21 February, 1924 Died 2001 (WH)

League Club	Source	Date Signed	Seasons Played	Apps	Subs	Gls
Wolverhampton W	Jnrs	08.41				
Chester	Tr	11.45	46-47	82	-	40
Leeds U	Tr	07.48	48-54	243	-	13
Bristol C	Tr	10.54	54-60	231	-	20

BURDESS John
East Rainton, 10 April, 1946 (IF)

League Club	Source	Date Signed	Seasons Played	Apps	Subs	Gls
Oldham Ath	App	04.64	63-64	3	-	0

BURGESS Andrew (Andy) John
Bozeat, 10 August, 1981 (M)

League Club	Source	Date Signed	Seasons Played	Apps	Subs	Gls
Rushden & Diamonds	Jnrs	07.99	01-04	121	17	10

BURGESS Benjamin (Ben) Keiron
Buxton, 9 November, 1981 IRYth/IRu21-2 (F)

League Club	Source	Date Signed	Seasons Played	Apps	Subs	Gls
Blackburn Rov	YT	11.98	99	1	1	0
Brentford	L	08.01	01	43	0	17
Stockport Co	Tr	08.02	02	17	2	4
Oldham Ath	L	01.03	02	6	1	0
Hull C	Tr	03.03	02-04	51	2	22

BURGESS Albert **Campbell (Cam)**
Birkenhead, 21 September, 1919 Died 1978 (IF)

League Club	Source	Date Signed	Seasons Played	Apps	Subs	Gls
Bolton W	Bromborough	02.38	46-47	5	-	3
Chester	Tr	10.48	48-51	111	-	64
Crystal Palace	Tr	09.51	51-52	47	-	40
York C	Tr	07.53	53	32	-	14

BURGESS Daryl
Marston Green, 24 January, 1971 (CD)

League Club	Source	Date Signed	Seasons Played	Apps	Subs	Gls
West Bromwich A	YT	07.89	89-00	317	15	10
Northampton T	Tr	07.01	01-02	60	1	2
Rochdale	Tr	08.03	03-04	52	4	0

BURGESS David (Dave) John
Liverpool, 20 January, 1960 (FB)

League Club	Source	Date Signed	Seasons Played	Apps	Subs	Gls
Tranmere Rov		08.81	81-85	217	1	1
Grimsby T	Tr	08.86	86-87	66	3	0
Blackpool	Tr	07.88	88-92	101	0	1
Carlisle U	L	02.93	92	6	0	0
Carlisle U	Tr	06.93	93	36	4	1
Hartlepool U	L	09.94	94	11	0	0

BURGESS Eric Robert Charles
Edgware, 27 October, 1944 (FB)

League Club	Source	Date Signed	Seasons Played	Apps	Subs	Gls
Watford	App	07.62	63-64	3	-	0
Torquay U	Tr	07.65	65-67	73	1	0
Plymouth Arg	Tr	07.68	68-69	14	1	0
Colchester U	Plymouth C	12.70	70-71	46	2	9

BURGESS Michael (Mike)
Montreal, Canada, 17 April, 1932 (CF)

League Club	Source	Date Signed	Seasons Played	Apps	Subs	Gls
Bradford PA	Frickley Colliery	08.52				
Leyton Orient	Tr	07.53	53-55	31	-	12
Newport Co	Tr	02.56	55-56	25	-	7
Bournemouth	Tr	06.57	57-60	109	-	34
Halifax T	Tr	07.61	61-62	34	-	3
Gillingham	Tr	03.63	62-65	109	1	2
Aldershot	Tr	11.65	65	6	0	0

League Club	Source	Date Signed	Seasons Played	Career Record Apps	Subs	Gls
BURGESS Oliver (Ollie) David						
Bracknell, 12 October, 1981						(M)
Queens Park Rgrs	YT	07.01	00-02	6	4	1
Northampton T	Tr	07.03	03	3	6	0
BURGESS Richard Daniel						
Bromsgrove, 18 August, 1978						(F)
Aston Villa	YT	07.96				
Stoke C	Tr	05.97				
Port Vale	Bromsgrove Rov	03.01	00-01	1	2	0
BURGESS Robert (Bob) Buchanan Benwood						
Glasgow, 1 April, 1927						(CF)
Walsall (Am)	Third Lanark	09.53	53	2	-	1
BURGESS William Arthur **Ronald (Ron)**						
Cwm, 9 April, 1917 Died 2005 FLge-1/WWar-10/W-32						(WH)
Tottenham H	Cardiff C (Am)	05.36	38-53	297	-	15
Swansea T	Tr	08.54	54-55	46	-	1
BURGESS Walter						
Golborne, 19 June, 1921 Died 1988						(FB)
Halifax T	Coleraine	11.46	46	13	-	2
BURGHER Symon George						
Birmingham, 29 October, 1966						(M)
Exeter C	App	02.85	84	11	3	0
BURGIN Andrew (Andy)						
Sheffield, 6 March, 1947						(FB)
Sheffield Wed	App	03.64	64	1	-	0
Rotherham U	Tr	08.67	67	9	1	0
Halifax T	Detroit (USA)	12.68	68-74	243	0	9
Blackburn Rov	Tr	09.74	74-75	45	0	1
BURGIN Edward (Ted)						
Bradfield, 29 April, 1927 EB						(G)
Sheffield U	Alford T	03.49	49-56	281	-	0
Doncaster Rov	Tr	12.57	57	5	-	0
Leeds U	Tr	03.58	58-60	58	-	0
Rochdale	Tr	01.61	60-65	207	0	0
BURGIN Eric						
Sheffield, 4 January, 1924						(CD)
Sheffield U		12.46				
York C	Tr	05.49	49-50	23	-	0
BURGIN Terence (Terry)						
Nottingham, 9 October, 1938						(CF)
Reading		11.59	60	2	-	0
BURGIN Trevor						
Darfield, 28 August, 1943						(CD)
Bradford PA	Wombwell	07.67	67	12	5	0
BURKE Charles (Charlie)						
Arran, 13 September, 1921 Died 1995						(WH)
Bournemouth	Ardeer Rec	06.39	46	25	-	7
BURKE David Ian						
Liverpool, 6 August, 1960 EYth						(FB)
Bolton W	App	08.77	78-80	65	4	1
Huddersfield T	Tr	06.81	81-87	189	0	3
Crystal Palace	Tr	10.87	87-89	80	1	0
Bolton W	Tr	07.90	90-93	104	2	0
Blackpool	Tr	07.94	94	23	0	0
BURKE John						
Motherwell, 10 August, 1962 SSch						(W)
Sheffield U	Motherwell	07.80				
Exeter C	Tr	03.83	82	3	0	0
Chester C	Tr	08.83	83	3	0	0
BURKE John (Johnny) Joseph						
Dublin, 28 May, 1911 Died 1987						(G)
Chester	Shelbourne	07.31	31-35	91	-	0
Millwall	Tr	06.36	36-46	24	-	0
Gillingham	Tr	09.47	50	5	-	0
BURKE Mark Stephen						
Solihull, 12 February, 1969 ESch/EYth						(W)
Aston Villa	App	02.87	86-87	5	2	0
Middlesbrough	Tr	12.87	87-89	32	25	6
Darlington	L	10.90	90	5	0	1
Wolverhampton W	Tr	03.91	90-93	53	15	11
Luton T	L	03.94	93	2	1	0
Port Vale	Tr	08.94	94	4	11	2
BURKE Marshall						
Glasgow, 26 March, 1959 SSch						(M)
Burnley	App	03.77	77-79	22	2	5
Leeds U	Tr	05.80				
Blackburn Rov	Tr	12.80	80-81	34	5	7
Lincoln C	Tr	10.82	82-83	49	1	7
Cardiff C	L	12.83	83	3	0	0
Tranmere Rov	Scarborough	09.84	84	3	0	0
BURKE Peter						
Rotherham, 26 April, 1957						(CD)
Barnsley	App	04.75	74-76	36	0	1
Halifax T	Tr	03.78	77-79	79	6	9
Rochdale	Tr	07.80	80-81	68	0	2
BURKE Peter Joseph						
Fazakerley, 1 February, 1912 Died 1979						(CD)
Oldham Ath	Prescot Cables	05.33	33-35	93	-	6
Norwich C	Tr	12.35	35-38	114	-	0
Luton T	Tr	06.39				
Southport	Tr	07.46	46	1	-	0
BURKE Richard (Dick)						
Ashton-under-Lyne, 28 October, 1920 Died 2004						(FB)
Blackpool	Droylsden	07.38	38	1	-	0
Newcastle U	Tr	12.46	46	15	-	0
Carlisle U	Tr	08.47	47-48	77	-	8
BURKE Robert Gallee						
Ballymena, 5 November, 1934 IrLge-1						(IF)
Burnley	Albertville U	09.55	55	19	-	5
BURKE Ronald (Ronnie) Stewart						
Marske, 13 August, 1921						(CF)
Manchester U	St Albans C	08.46	46-48	28	-	16
Huddersfield T	Tr	06.49	49-51	27	-	6
Rotherham U	Tr	03.53	52-54	73	-	56
Exeter C	Tr	06.55	55-56	42	-	14
BURKE Steven (Steve) James						
Nottingham, 29 September, 1960 EYth						(W)
Nottingham F	App	03.78				
Queens Park Rgrs	Tr	09.79	79-83	43	24	5
Millwall	L	10.83	83	7	0	1
Notts Co	L	10.84	84	4	1	0
Lincoln C	L	08.85	85	4	1	0
Brentford	L	03.86	85	10	0	1
Doncaster Rov	Tr	08.86	86-87	50	7	8
Stockport Co	L	10.87	87	5	0	0
BURKE Thomas (Tommy)						
Greenock, 18 October, 1939						(IF)
Barnsley	Clyde	02.63	62	1	-	0
BURKETT Jack William						
Edmonton, 21 August, 1942						(FB)
West Ham U	Jnrs	10.59	61-67	141	1	4
Charlton Ath	Tr	06.68	68-69	8	0	0
BURKINSHAW George Allen						
Barnsley, 1 October, 1922 Died 1982						(CD)
Barnsley	Woolley Colliery	03.42				
Carlisle U	Tr	09.46	46	24	-	0
Barnsley	Tr	06.47				
Bradford C	Tr	11.48	48	12	-	0
BURKINSHAW Harry **Keith**						
Darton, 23 June, 1935						(CD)
Liverpool	Denaby U	11.53	54	1	-	0
Workington	Tr	12.57	57-64	295	-	9
Scunthorpe U	Tr	05.65	65-67	107	1	3
BURKITT John (Jack) Orgill						
Wednesbury, 19 January, 1926 Died 2003						(WH)
Nottingham F	Darlaston	05.47	48-61	463	-	14
BURLEIGH Martin Stewart						
Newcastle, 2 February, 1951						(G)
Newcastle U	Willington	12.68	70-73	11	0	0
Darlington	Tr	10.74	74	30	0	0
Carlisle U	Tr	06.75	75-76	26	0	0
Darlington	Tr	08.77	77-78	71	0	0
Hartlepool U	Tr	10.79	79-81	84	0	0
BURLEY Adam Gareth						
Sheffield, 27 November, 1980						(M)
Sheffield U	YT	07.99	99-00	0	3	1
BURLEY Craig William						
Irvine, 24 September, 1971 SSch/SYth/Su21-7/S-46						(M)
Chelsea	YT	09.89	90-96	85	28	7
Derby Co	Glasgow Celtic	12.99	99-02	73	0	10
Preston NE	Dundee	01.04	03	1	3	0
Walsall	Tr	03.04	03	5	0	0

League Club	Source	Date Signed	Seasons Played	Apps	Subs	Gls
BURLEY George Elder						
Cumnock, 3 June, 1956 SSch/SYth/Su21-5/Su23-2/S-11						(FB)
Ipswich T	App	06.73	73-85	394	0	6
Sunderland	Tr	09.85	85-86	54	0	0
Gillingham	Tr	07.88	88	46	0	2
Colchester U	Motherwell	08.94	94	5	2	0
BURLISON Robert (Bob) Lyle						
Newcastle, 29 March, 1920 Died 1987						(W)
Charlton Ath	Horden CW	09.39	46	1	-	0
BURLISON Thomas (Tommy) Henry						
Edmondsley, 23 May, 1936						(WH)
Lincoln C	Jnrs	12.53				
Hartlepools U	Tr	07.57	57-63	148	-	5
Darlington	Tr	08.64	64	26	-	2
BURLURAUX Donald (Don)						
Skelton, 8 June, 1951						(W)
Middlesbrough	Jnrs	07.68	70-71	4	1	0
York C	L	12.71	71	3	0	1
Darlington	Tr	07.72	72-74	105	7	13
BURMAN Anthony (Tony) Paul						
Stockwell, 3 June, 1958						(F)
Charlton Ath	Queens Park Rgrs (App)	08.76	76-77	16	3	3
BURMAN Simon John						
Ipswich, 26 November, 1965						(W)
Colchester U	App	11.83	84-86	28	4	3
BURN Ralph **Gordon**						
Alnwick, 9 November, 1931 Died 1984						(IF)
Northampton T		08.50	50	1	-	0
Crewe Alex	Tr	07.54	54	1	-	0
BURN John Haytor						
South Shields, 21 January, 1930						(G)
Chelsea		10.48				
Chesterfield	Tr	08.50				
Carlisle U		06.55	55	26	-	0
BURNDRED John Nigel						
Stoke-on-Trent, 22 March, 1968						(F)
Port Vale	Knypersley Victoria	02.95	94	1	0	0
BURNELL Joseph (Joe) Michael						
Bristol, 10 October, 1980						(FB)
Bristol C	YT	07.99	99-03	117	14	1
Wycombe W	Tr	07.04	04	23	1	0
BURNETT Alfred (Alf) Price						
Aberdeen, 23 July, 1922 Died 1977						(CF)
Barrow	Dundee	12.46	46-49	87	-	32
Lincoln C	Tr	11.49	49	4	-	1
BURNETT Dennis Henry						
Bermondsey, 27 September, 1944						(CD)
West Ham U	Jnrs	10.62	65-66	48	2	0
Millwall	Tr	08.67	67-73	257	0	3
Hull C	Tr	10.73	73-74	46	0	2
Millwall	L	03.75	74	6	0	2
Brighton & Hove A	St Louis (USA)	09.75	75-76	41	3	1
BURNETT George Gordon						
Liverpool, 11 February, 1920 Died 1985						(G)
Everton	Litherland BC	09.38	46-50	47	-	0
Oldham Ath	Tr	10.51	51-54	100	-	0
BURNETT John						
Market Rasen, 24 June, 1939						(FB)
Grimsby T	Gainsborough Trinity	07.58	58	1	-	0
BURNETT Wayne						
Lambeth, 4 September, 1971 EYth						(M)
Leyton Orient	YT	11.89	89-91	34	6	0
Blackburn Rov	Tr	08.92				
Plymouth Arg	Tr	08.93	93-95	61	9	3
Bolton W	Tr	10.95	95-96	0	2	0
Huddersfield T	Tr	09.96	96-97	44	6	0
Grimsby T	Tr	01.98	97-01	80	26	6
BURNETT William (Billy) John						
Pelaw, 1 March, 1926 Died 1988						(W)
Grimsby T	Wardley CW	07.46	47	10	-	0
Hartlepools U	Tr	11.48	48-53	194	-	17
BURNHAM Jason John						
Mansfield, 8 May, 1973						(FB)
Northampton T	Notts Co (YT)	07.91	91-93	79	9	2
Chester C	Tr	07.94	94-95	62	2	1

League Club	Source	Date Signed	Seasons Played	Apps	Subs	Gls
BURNS Alexander (Alex)						
Bellshill, 4 August, 1973						(F)
Southend U	SC Heracles (Holl)	07.98	98	26	5	5
BURNS Anthony (Tony) John						
Edenbridge, 27 March, 1944						(G)
Arsenal	Tonbridge	03.63	64-65	31	0	0
Brighton & Hove A	Tr	07.66	66-68	54	0	0
Charlton Ath	Tr	03.69	68-69	10	0	0
Crystal Palace	Durban U (SA)	10.73	74-77	90	0	0
Brentford	L	01.77	76	6	0	0
Plymouth Arg	Memphis (USA)	08.78	78	8	0	0
BURNS Barry Ross						
Doncaster, 19 June, 1937						(IF)
Rotherham U	Dunscroft	10.54	57	5	-	4
BURNS Christopher (Chris)						
Manchester, 9 November, 1967						(M)
Portsmouth	Cheltenham T	03.91	91-93	78	12	9
Swansea C	L	12.93	93	4	0	0
Bournemouth	L	03.94	93	13	1	1
Swansea C	Tr	11.94	94	3	2	0
Northampton T	Tr	01.95	94-96	62	4	9
BURNS David						
Ellesmere Port, 12 November, 1958						(FB)
Chester	App	10.76	76-81	66	12	1
BURNS Derek George						
Bournemouth, 23 January, 1950						(CD)
Bournemouth	App	01.68	68	3	1	0
BURNS Eric Owen						
Newton Stewart, 8 March, 1945						(W)
Bradford PA	App	03.62	63-65	26	2	3
Barnsley	Tr	08.66	66	3	0	0
BURNS Francis						
Glenboig, 17 October, 1948 SSch/Su23-1/S-1						(FB)
Manchester U	Jnrs	10.65	67-71	111	10	6
Southampton	Tr	06.72	72	20	1	0
Preston NE	Tr	08.73	73-80	271	2	9
BURNS Francis (Frank) Joseph						
Workington, 11 November, 1924 Died 1987						(WH)
Swansea T	Wolverhampton W (Am)	08.44	46-51	172	-	9
Southend U	Tr	07.52	52-54	89	-	14
Crewe Alex	Tr	11.56	56-57	31	-	7
BURNS Hugh						
Lanark, 13 December, 1965 Su21-2						(FB)
Fulham (L)	Dunfermline Ath	12.89	89	6	0	0
BURNS Jacob Geoffrey						
Sydney, Australia, 21 January, 1978 Auu23-19/Au-2						(M)
Leeds U	Parramatta Power (Aus)	08.00	00-02	5	1	0
Barnsley	Tr	10.03	03-04	49	7	3
BURNS Jamie Daniel						
Blackpool, 6 March, 1984						(M)
Blackpool	Sch	07.03	02-04	26	15	0
BURNS John Christopher						
Dublin, 4 December, 1977 IRYth/IRu21-2						(M)
Nottingham F	Belvedere	12.94	99	3	0	0
Bristol C	Tr	11.99	99	6	5	0
Carlisle U	Tr	08.02	02	4	1	0
BURNS Kenneth (Kenny)						
Glasgow, 23 September, 1953 Su23-2/S-20						(CD)
Birmingham C	App	07.71	71-76	163	7	45
Nottingham F	Tr	07.77	77-81	137	0	13
Leeds U	Tr	10.81	81-83	54	2	2
Derby Co	L	03.83	82	6	1	1
Derby Co	Tr	02.84	83-84	30	1	1
Notts Co	L	02.85	84	2	0	0
Barnsley	Tr	08.85	85	19	3	0
BURNS Kinear (Ken)						
Ramsey, Isle of Man, 24 September, 1923						(IF)
Tranmere Rov	Ramsey	09.46	46	14	-	4
Southport	Runcorn	11.47	47	5	-	0
BURNS Leo Francis						
Manchester, 3 August, 1932						(WH)
Oldham Ath	Manchester C (Am)	09.53	55	4	-	0
BURNS Leslie (Les) George Henry						
Shepherds Bush, 22 June, 1944						(CD)
Charlton Ath	Carshalton Ath	03.67	66-67	8	0	0

League Club	Source	Date Signed	Seasons Played	Career Record Apps	Subs	Gls

BURNS Liam
Belfast, 30 October, 1978 NIYth/NIu21-13 (CD)

League Club	Source	Date Signed	Seasons Played	Apps	Subs	Gls
Port Vale	YT	07.97	97-03	94	24	0
Bristol Rov	Tr	08.04	04	3	0	0
Shrewsbury T	Tr	12.04	04	1	1	0
Kidderminster Hrs	Tr	12.04	04	0	1	0

BURNS Michael (Micky) Edward
Preston, 21 December, 1946 EAmat (F)

League Club	Source	Date Signed	Seasons Played	Apps	Subs	Gls
Blackpool	Skelmersdale U	05.69	69-73	174	7	53
Newcastle U	Tr	07.74	74-77	143	2	39
Cardiff C	Tr	08.78	78	6	0	0
Middlesbrough	Tr	10.78	78-80	58	3	24

BURNS Michael (Mick) Thomas
Leeholme, 7 June, 1908 Died 1982 (G)

League Club	Source	Date Signed	Seasons Played	Apps	Subs	Gls
Newcastle U	Chilton Colliery Rec A	09.27	27-35	104	-	0
Preston NE	Tr	07.36	36-37	12	-	0
Ipswich T	Tr	05.38	38-51	157	-	0

BURNS Neil James
Bellshill, 11 June, 1945 (W)

League Club	Source	Date Signed	Seasons Played	Apps	Subs	Gls
Mansfield T	Bethesda	11.65	65-66	7	3	0

BURNS Oliver (Ollie) Houston
Larkhall, 16 May, 1914 Died 1989 (IF)

League Club	Source	Date Signed	Seasons Played	Apps	Subs	Gls
Burnley	Glenavon	03.39				
Oldham Ath	Tr	10.46	46	25	-	5
Halifax T	Tr	09.47	47	27	-	5

BURNS Peter
Ulverston, 17 April, 1931 Died 2002 (CF)

League Club	Source	Date Signed	Seasons Played	Apps	Subs	Gls
Barrow	Askam U	02.52	51	8	-	2

BURNS Philip (Phil) Martin
Stockport, 18 December, 1966 (G)

League Club	Source	Date Signed	Seasons Played	Apps	Subs	Gls
Reading		03.89	90	12	0	0

BURNS William (Willie)
Motherwell, 10 December, 1969 (FB)

League Club	Source	Date Signed	Seasons Played	Apps	Subs	Gls
Manchester C	YT	01.88				
Rochdale	Tr	07.89	89-90	68	4	2

BURNSIDE David Gort
Kingswood, 10 December, 1939 EYth/Eu23-1 (M)

League Club	Source	Date Signed	Seasons Played	Apps	Subs	Gls
West Bromwich A	Bristol C (Am)	02.57	57-62	127	-	39
Southampton	Tr	10.62	62-64	61	-	22
Crystal Palace	Tr	12.64	64-66	54	4	8
Wolverhampton W	Tr	09.66	66-67	38	2	5
Plymouth Arg	Tr	03.68	67-70	105	0	15
Bristol C	Tr	12.71	71	1	0	0
Colchester U	Tr	03.72	71	13	0	0

BURRELL Gerald (Gerry)
Belfast, 6 September, 1926 (W)

League Club	Source	Date Signed	Seasons Played	Apps	Subs	Gls
Huddersfield T	Dundee	12.53	53-55	59	-	9
Chesterfield	Tr	07.56	56-57	51	-	4

BURRELL Lester (Les) Frank
Brighton, 8 August, 1917 (IF)

League Club	Source	Date Signed	Seasons Played	Apps	Subs	Gls
Crystal Palace	Margate	02.46	46-47	19	-	5

BURRIDGE John
Workington, 3 December, 1951 (G)

League Club	Source	Date Signed	Seasons Played	Apps	Subs	Gls
Workington	App	01.70	68-70	27	0	0
Blackpool	Tr	04.71	70-75	134	0	0
Aston Villa	Tr	09.75	75-76	65	0	0
Southend U	L	01.78	77	6	0	0
Crystal Palace	Tr	03.78	77-79	88	0	0
Queens Park Rgrs	Tr	12.80	80-81	39	0	0
Wolverhampton W	Tr	08.82	82-83	74	0	0
Derby Co	L	09.84	84	6	0	0
Sheffield U	Tr	10.84	84-86	109	0	0
Southampton	Tr	08.87	87-88	62	0	0
Newcastle U	Tr	10.89	89-90	67	0	0
Newcastle U	Hibernian	08.93				
Scarborough	Tr	10.93	93	3	0	0
Lincoln C	Tr	12.93	93	4	0	0
Manchester C	Dumbarton	12.94	94	3	1	0
Notts Co	Tr	08.95				
Darlington	Witton A	11.95	95	3	0	0

BURRIDGE Peter John
Harlow, 30 December, 1933 (IF)

League Club	Source	Date Signed	Seasons Played	Apps	Subs	Gls
Leyton Orient	Barnet	04.58	58-59	6	-	2
Millwall	Tr	08.60	60-61	87	-	58
Crystal Palace	Tr	06.62	62-65	114	0	42
Charlton Ath	Tr	11.65	65-66	42	2	4

BURROWS Adrian Mark
Sutton-in-Ashfield, 16 January, 1959 (CD)

League Club	Source	Date Signed	Seasons Played	Apps	Subs	Gls
Mansfield T		05.79	79-81	77	1	6
Northampton T	Tr	08.82	82-83	88	0	4
Plymouth Arg	Tr	07.84	84-93	272	5	14
Southend U	L	09.87	87	6	0	0

BURROWS Alan
Thorne, 20 October, 1941 (FB)

League Club	Source	Date Signed	Seasons Played	Apps	Subs	Gls
Blackpool	Stockport Co (Am)	05.59	59	1	-	0

BURROWS Arthur
Stockport, 4 December, 1919 Died 2005 (WH)

League Club	Source	Date Signed	Seasons Played	Apps	Subs	Gls
Stockport Co	Jnrs	11.37	38-46	5	-	1
Accrington St	Ashton U	03.48	48	9	-	0

BURROWS David
Dudley, 25 October, 1968 Eu21-7/EB-3/FLge (FB)

League Club	Source	Date Signed	Seasons Played	Apps	Subs	Gls
West Bromwich A	App	11.86	85-88	37	9	1
Liverpool	Tr	10.88	88-93	135	11	3
West Ham U	Tr	09.93	93-94	29	0	1
Everton	Tr	09.94	94	19	0	0
Coventry C	Tr	03.95	94-99	106	5	0
Birmingham C	Tr	07.00	00-01	17	8	0
Sheffield Wed	Tr	03.02	01-02	21	0	0

BURROWS David Williams
Bilsthorpe, 7 April, 1961 (FB)

League Club	Source	Date Signed	Seasons Played	Apps	Subs	Gls
Lincoln C	App	04.79	78	1	0	0

BURROWS Frank
Larkhall, 30 January, 1944 (CD)

League Club	Source	Date Signed	Seasons Played	Apps	Subs	Gls
Scunthorpe U	Raith Rov	06.65	65-67	106	0	4
Swindon T	Tr	07.68	68-76	293	4	9
Mansfield T	L	03.74	73	6	0	0

BURROWS Harold (Harry)
Haydock, 17 March, 1941 Eu23-1 (W)

League Club	Source	Date Signed	Seasons Played	Apps	Subs	Gls
Aston Villa	Jnrs	03.58	59-64	147	-	53
Stoke C	Tr	03.65	64-72	239	6	68
Plymouth Arg	Tr	08.73	73-74	18	1	3

BURROWS Mark
Kettering, 14 August, 1980 (CD)

League Club	Source	Date Signed	Seasons Played	Apps	Subs	Gls
Coventry C	YT	01.98				
Exeter C	Tr	07.00	00-01	27	11	0

BURROWS Paul Samuel
Swansea, 2 October, 1967 WYth (F)

League Club	Source	Date Signed	Seasons Played	Apps	Subs	Gls
Swansea C	App	10.85	85	1	2	0

BURROWS Philip (Phil) Arthur
Stockport, 8 April, 1946 (FB)

League Club	Source	Date Signed	Seasons Played	Apps	Subs	Gls
Manchester C	Jnrs	07.64				
York C	Tr	06.66	66-73	333	4	14
Plymouth Arg	Tr	07.74	74-75	81	0	2
Hereford U	Tr	08.76	76-79	110	0	2
Gillingham	L	10.77	77	5	0	0

BURSELL John Clifford (Cliff)
Hull, 16 January, 1935 Died 1973 (IF)

League Club	Source	Date Signed	Seasons Played	Apps	Subs	Gls
Hull C	Jnrs	11.52	52	2	-	2

BURT James (Jimmy) Hamilton Laird
Harthill, 5 April, 1950 (FB)

League Club	Source	Date Signed	Seasons Played	Apps	Subs	Gls
Leicester C	Whitburn Jnrs	06.67				
Aldershot	Tr	09.70	70-71	22	3	0
Northampton T	Tr	07.72	72	16	5	0
Rochdale	Tr	09.73	73	4	0	0

BURT Jamie Paul
Blyth, 29 September, 1979 ESch (F)

League Club	Source	Date Signed	Seasons Played	Apps	Subs	Gls
Chesterfield	Whitby T	12.01	01-03	29	12	8
Carlisle U	L	12.02	02	4	0	1

BURTENSHAW Charles (Charlie) Edward
Portslade, 16 October, 1922 (W)

League Club	Source	Date Signed	Seasons Played	Apps	Subs	Gls
Luton T	Southwick	01.48	48-49	11	-	1
Gillingham	Tr	10.49	50-51	28	-	4

BURTENSHAW Stephen (Steve)
Portslade, 23 November, 1935 (WH)

League Club	Source	Date Signed	Seasons Played	Apps	Subs	Gls
Brighton & Hove A	Jnrs	11.52	52-66	237	0	3

BURTENSHAW William (Bill) Frederick
Portslade, 13 December, 1925 (IF)

League Club	Source	Date Signed	Seasons Played	Apps	Subs	Gls
Luton T	Southwick	08.48	48	1	-	0
Gillingham	Tr	10.49	50-51	39	-	8

BURTON Alan Richard
Aldershot, 11 January, 1939 (W)

League Club	Source	Date Signed	Seasons Played	Apps	Subs	Gls
Aldershot	Alton T	01.61	60-69	225	5	47

BURTON Alwyn (Ollie) Derek
Chepstow, 11 November, 1941 WSch/Wu23-5/W-9 (CD)

League Club	Source	Date Signed	Seasons Played	Apps	Subs	Gls
Newport Co	Bulwark YC	12.58	58-60	53	-	8
Norwich C	Tr	03.61	60-62	57	-	8
Newcastle U	Tr	06.63	63-71	181	7	6

BURTON Bruce (Brian) Brian
Nottingham, 28 December, 1932 (W)

League Club	Source	Date Signed	Seasons Played	Apps	Subs	Gls
Nottingham F	Basford BC	07.51	54	1	-	0

BURTON Deon John
Reading, 25 October, 1976 Jamaica 49 (F)

League Club	Source	Date Signed	Seasons Played	Apps	Subs	Gls
Portsmouth	YT	02.94	93-96	42	20	10
Cardiff C	L	12.96	96	5	0	2
Derby Co	Tr	08.97	97-02	78	47	25
Barnsley	L	12.98	98	3	0	0
Stoke C	L	02.02	01	11	1	2
Portsmouth	L	08.02	02	6	0	3
Portsmouth	Tr	12.02	02-03	5	5	1
Walsall	L	09.03	03	2	1	0
Swindon T	L	10.03	03	4	0	1
Brentford	Tr	08.04	04	38	2	10

BURTON Ernest (Ernie)
Sheffield, 2 September, 1921 Died 1999 (W)

League Club	Source	Date Signed	Seasons Played	Apps	Subs	Gls
Sheffield Wed	Atlas & Norfolk	11.47				
York C	Tr	08.48	48	3	-	0

BURTON Kenneth (Ken) Owen
Sheffield, 11 February, 1950 (FB)

League Club	Source	Date Signed	Seasons Played	Apps	Subs	Gls
Sheffield Wed	App	05.67	68-71	55	2	2
Peterborough U	L	03.73	72	3	1	0
Chesterfield	Tr	07.73	73-78	234	3	6
Halifax T	Tr	08.80	80	26	1	1

BURTON Mark Anthony
Penistone, 7 May, 1973 (M)

League Club	Source	Date Signed	Seasons Played	Apps	Subs	Gls
Barnsley	YT	06.91	92	5	0	0

BURTON Michael (Micky) James
Tamworth, 5 November, 1969 (M)

League Club	Source	Date Signed	Seasons Played	Apps	Subs	Gls
Birmingham C	YT	07.88	88	0	4	0
Shrewsbury T	Sheffield Wed (N/C)	03.91	90	3	3	0

BURTON Nicholas (Nick) John
Bury St Edmunds, 10 February, 1975 (CD)

League Club	Source	Date Signed	Seasons Played	Apps	Subs	Gls
Torquay U	Portsmouth (Y/T)	08.93	93-94	14	2	2

BURTON Paul David
Enfield, 30 November, 1985 (M)

League Club	Source	Date Signed	Seasons Played	Apps	Subs	Gls
Oxford U	YT	●	04	0	1	0

BURTON Paul Stewart
Hereford, 6 August, 1973 (F)

League Club	Source	Date Signed	Seasons Played	Apps	Subs	Gls
Hereford U	YT	07.91	89-91	1	4	1

BURTON Royston (Roy)
Wokingham, 13 March, 1951 (G)

League Club	Source	Date Signed	Seasons Played	Apps	Subs	Gls
Oxford U	Jnrs	09.70	71-82	397	0	0

BURTON Samuel (Sam)
Swindon, 10 November, 1926 (G)

League Club	Source	Date Signed	Seasons Played	Apps	Subs	Gls
Swindon T	Jnrs	06.45	46-61	463	-	0

BURTON Simon Paul
Farnworth, 29 December, 1973 (M)

League Club	Source	Date Signed	Seasons Played	Apps	Subs	Gls
Preston NE	YT	05.92	92-93	19	5	3

BURTON Steven (Steve) Paul
Doncaster, 9 October, 1983 (F)

League Club	Source	Date Signed	Seasons Played	Apps	Subs	Gls
Ipswich T	Sch	08.02				
Boston U	L	08.02	02	6	2	0
Doncaster Rov	Tr	03.03	03	1	5	0

BURTON Steven (Steve) Peter Graham
Hull, 10 October, 1982 (FB)

League Club	Source	Date Signed	Seasons Played	Apps	Subs	Gls
Hull C	Sch	07.02	02	2	9	0
Kidderminster Hrs	L	10.03	03	6	1	0
Kidderminster Hrs	Tr	03.04	03-04	19	1	0

BURTON-GODWIN Osagyefo (Sagi) Lenin Ernesto
Birmingham, 25 November, 1977 St Kitts int (FB)

League Club	Source	Date Signed	Seasons Played	Apps	Subs	Gls
Crystal Palace	YT	01.96	97-98	19	6	1
Colchester U	Tr	05.99	99	9	0	0
Sheffield U	Tr	11.99				
Port Vale	Tr	01.00	99-01	76	10	2
Crewe Alex	Tr	08.02	02	1	0	0
Peterborough U	Tr	08.02	02-04	71	6	2

BURVILL Glenn
Canning Town, 26 October, 1962 (M)

League Club	Source	Date Signed	Seasons Played	Apps	Subs	Gls
West Ham U	App	09.80				
Aldershot	Tr	08.83	83-84	57	8	15
Reading	Tr	03.85	84-85	24	6	0
Fulham	L	03.86	85	9	0	2
Aldershot	Tr	07.86	86-90	176	19	23

BUSBY David Everett
Paddington, 27 July, 1956 (F)

League Club	Source	Date Signed	Seasons Played	Apps	Subs	Gls
Brighton & Hove A	App	08.74	73-74	1	2	0

BUSBY Hubert George Albert
Kingston, Ontario, Canada, 18 June, 1969 (G)

League Club	Source	Date Signed	Seasons Played	Apps	Subs	Gls
Oxford U	SC Caldas (Por)	08.00	00	0	1	0

BUSBY Martyn George
High Wycombe, 24 March, 1953 EYth (M)

League Club	Source	Date Signed	Seasons Played	Apps	Subs	Gls
Queens Park Rgrs	App	07.70	69-76	72	7	6
Portsmouth	L	02.76	75	6	0	1
Notts Co	Tr	10.76	76-77	37	0	4
Queens Park Rgrs	Tr	09.77	77-79	56	10	11
Burnley	L	02.80	79	4	0	1

BUSBY Vivian (Viv) Dennis
High Wycombe, 19 June, 1949 (F)

League Club	Source	Date Signed	Seasons Played	Apps	Subs	Gls
Luton T	Wycombe W	01.70	69-72	64	13	16
Newcastle U	L	12.71	71	4	0	2
Fulham	Tr	08.73	73-76	114	4	29
Norwich C	Tr	09.76	76-77	22	0	11
Stoke C	Tr	11.77	77-79	33	17	10
Sheffield U	L	01.80	79	3	0	1
Blackburn Rov	Tulsa (USA)	02.81	80	8	0	1
York C	Tulsa (USA)	08.82	82-83	9	10	4

BUSH Bryan
Bristol, 25 April, 1925 (W)

League Club	Source	Date Signed	Seasons Played	Apps	Subs	Gls
Bristol Rov	Soundwell	10.47	47-54	114	-	19

BUSH Terence (Terry) Douglas
Ingoldisthorpe, 29 January, 1943 (F)

League Club	Source	Date Signed	Seasons Played	Apps	Subs	Gls
Bristol C	Jnrs	02.60	60-69	147	15	43

BUSH William Thomas (Tom)
Hodnet, 22 February, 1914 Died 1969 (CD)

League Club	Source	Date Signed	Seasons Played	Apps	Subs	Gls
Liverpool	Shrewsbury T	03.33	33-46	61	-	1

BUSHBY Alan
Stainforth, 15 January, 1932 Died 1967 (WH)

League Club	Source	Date Signed	Seasons Played	Apps	Subs	Gls
Scunthorpe U		08.52	52-58	218	-	10
Rochdale	Tr	07.59	59-60	66	-	0

BUSHBY Dennis Christopher
Poole, 25 December, 1933 (WH)

League Club	Source	Date Signed	Seasons Played	Apps	Subs	Gls
Bournemouth		11.57	57	6	-	0

BUSHBY Thomas (Billy) William
Shildon, 21 August, 1914 Died 1997 (CF)

League Club	Source	Date Signed	Seasons Played	Apps	Subs	Gls
Southend U	Shildon	10.34	34-38	40	-	12
Portsmouth	Tr	06.39				
Southampton	Tr	09.46	46	2	-	0

BUSHELL Alan
Burnley, 4 September, 1932 (W)

League Club	Source	Date Signed	Seasons Played	Apps	Subs	Gls
Accrington St (Am)	Wood Top	05.52	52	8	-	1

BUSHELL Mark John
Northampton, 5 June, 1968 (FB)

League Club	Source	Date Signed	Seasons Played	Apps	Subs	Gls
Northampton T	App	09.85	84	1	0	0

BUSHELL Stephen (Steve) Paul
Manchester, 28 December, 1972 (M)

League Club	Source	Date Signed	Seasons Played	Apps	Subs	Gls
York C	YT	02.91	90-97	156	18	10
Blackpool	Tr	07.98	98-00	64	15	6
Halifax T	Stalybridge Celtic	11.01	01	25	0	1

BUSSCHER Robby
Leischenden, Holland, 23 November, 1982 HoYth (M)

League Club	Source	Date Signed	Seasons Played	Apps	Subs	Gls
Grimsby T	Feyenoord (Holl)	07.01	01	0	1	0

BUSST David (Dave) John
Birmingham, 30 June, 1967 (CD)

League Club	Source	Date Signed	Seasons Played	Apps	Subs	Gls
Coventry C	Moor Green Rov	01.92	92-95	48	2	4

BUTCHER John Melvin
Newcastle, 27 May, 1956 (G)

League Club	Source	Date Signed	Seasons Played	Apps	Subs	Gls
Blackburn Rov		03.76	76-81	104	0	0
Oxford U	Tr	07.82	82	16	0	0
Halifax T	L	09.82	82	5	0	0
Bury	L	12.83	83	11	0	0
Chester C	Tr	08.84	84-86	84	0	0
Bury	L	10.85	85	5	0	0

BUTCHER Reginald (Reg)
Prescot, 13 February, 1916 Died 2000 (FB)

League Club	Source	Date Signed	Seasons Played	Apps	Subs	Gls
Chester	Liverpool (Am)	11.38	38-49	155		1

BUTCHER Richard Tony
Peterborough, 22 January, 1981 (M)

League Club	Source	Date Signed	Seasons Played	Apps	Subs	Gls
Rushden & Diamonds	Northampton T (YT)	11.99				
Lincoln C	Kettering T	11.02	02-04	95	9	11

BUTCHER Terence (Terry) Ian
Singapore, 28 December, 1958 Eu21-7/EB/E-77 (CD)

League Club	Source	Date Signed	Seasons Played	Apps	Subs	Gls
Ipswich T	Jnrs	08.76	77-85	271	0	16
Coventry C	Glasgow Rgrs	11.90	90	6	0	0
Sunderland	(Retired)	07.92	92	37	1	0

BUTLER Andrew (Andy) Peter
Doncaster, 4 November, 1983 (CD)

League Club	Source	Date Signed	Seasons Played	Apps	Subs	Gls
Scunthorpe U	Sch	07.03	03-04	70	2	12

BUTLER Philip **Anthony (Tony)**
Stockport, 28 September, 1972 (CD)

League Club	Source	Date Signed	Seasons Played	Apps	Subs	Gls
Gillingham	YT	05.91	90-95	142	6	5
Blackpool	Tr	07.96	96-98	98	1	0
Port Vale	Tr	03.99	98-99	19	0	0
West Bromwich A	Tr	03.00	99-01	65	5	1
Bristol C	Tr	08.02	02-04	97	1	4
Blackpool	Tr	02.05	04	6	2	0

BUTLER Barry
Stockton, 30 July, 1934 Died 1966 (CD)

League Club	Source	Date Signed	Seasons Played	Apps	Subs	Gls
Sheffield Wed	South Bank	09.52	53-54	26	-	1
Norwich C	Tr	07.57	57-65	303	0	3

BUTLER Barry Geoffrey
Farnworth, 4 June, 1962 (M)

League Club	Source	Date Signed	Seasons Played	Apps	Subs	Gls
Chester C	Atherton Laburnum Rov	12.85	85-92	255	13	15

BUTLER Brian Francis
Salford, 4 July, 1966 (FB)

League Club	Source	Date Signed	Seasons Played	Apps	Subs	Gls
Blackpool	App	07.84	85-87	58	16	5
Stockport Co	Tr	07.88	88	32	0	2
Halifax T	Tr	07.89	89-90	44	12	4

BUTLER David
Thornaby, 23 March, 1945 (FB)

League Club	Source	Date Signed	Seasons Played	Apps	Subs	Gls
Workington	Stockton	11.64	64-70	195	3	8
Watford	Tr	11.70	70-75	168	0	2

BUTLER David (Dave) John
Wolverhampton, 1 September, 1962 (W)

League Club	Source	Date Signed	Seasons Played	Apps	Subs	Gls
Wolverhampton W	App	04.80				
Torquay U	Tr	12.81	81	5	1	0

BUTLER David Joseph
Wednesbury, 30 March, 1953 (W)

League Club	Source	Date Signed	Seasons Played	Apps	Subs	Gls
West Bromwich A	App	04.71				
Shrewsbury T	Tr	06.73	73	5	5	0
Workington	L	03.74	73	10	0	0

BUTLER Dennis Anthony
Macclesfield, 24 April, 1944 (W)

League Club	Source	Date Signed	Seasons Played	Apps	Subs	Gls
Bolton W	Jnrs	06.61	62-67	62	3	11
Rochdale	Tr	02.68	67-72	153	4	36

BUTLER Dennis George
Compton, 4 August, 1952 (M)

League Club	Source	Date Signed	Seasons Played	Apps	Subs	Gls
Reading	App	05.70	69-70	7	3	1

BUTLER Dennis Michael
Parsons Green, 7 March, 1943 (FB)

League Club	Source	Date Signed	Seasons Played	Apps	Subs	Gls
Chelsea	Jnrs	06.60	61-62	18	-	0
Hull C	Tr	06.63	63-69	215	2	0
Reading	Tr	12.69	69-73	169	0	0

BUTLER Ernest (Ernie)
Middlesbrough, 28 August, 1924 (W)

League Club	Source	Date Signed	Seasons Played	Apps	Subs	Gls
Southend U	Stockton	08.48	48-51	36	-	3
Darlington	Tr	06.53	53	6	-	0

BUTLER Ernest (Ernie) Albert Edward
Box, 13 May, 1919 Died 2002 (G)

League Club	Source	Date Signed	Seasons Played	Apps	Subs	Gls
Portsmouth	Bath C	05.38	46-52	222	-	0

BUTLER Geoffrey (Geoff)
Middlesbrough, 26 September, 1946 (FB)

League Club	Source	Date Signed	Seasons Played	Apps	Subs	Gls
Middlesbrough	App	05.64	65-67	54	1	1
Chelsea	Tr	09.67	67	8	1	0
Sunderland	Tr	01.68	67-68	1	2	0
Norwich C	Tr	10.68	68-75	151	2	1
Bournemouth	Tr	03.76	75-80	118	1	1
Peterborough U	Tr	08.81	81	39	0	0

BUTLER Ian
Darton, 1 February, 1944 EYth (W)

League Club	Source	Date Signed	Seasons Played	Apps	Subs	Gls
Rotherham U	App	08.61	60-64	102	-	27
Hull C	Tr	01.65	64-72	300	5	66
York C	Tr	06.73	73-74	43	3	2
Barnsley	L	10.75	75	5	0	1

BUTLER John (Jackie)
Dawley, 16 October, 1920 Died 1984 (FB)

League Club	Source	Date Signed	Seasons Played	Apps	Subs	Gls
Shrewsbury T	Dawley	08.50	50-53	58	-	8

BUTLER John Edward
Liverpool, 7 February, 1962 (FB)

League Club	Source	Date Signed	Seasons Played	Apps	Subs	Gls
Wigan Ath	Prescot Cables	01.82	81-88	238	7	14
Stoke C	Tr	12.88	88-94	258	4	7
Wigan Ath	Tr	06.95	95-96	53	4	1

BUTLER John Herbert
Birmingham, 10 March, 1937 (CD)

League Club	Source	Date Signed	Seasons Played	Apps	Subs	Gls
Notts Co	Bestwood Colliery	10.57	58-61	109	-	0
Chester	Tr	05.62	62-67	220	2	0

BUTLER John Paul
Salford, 7 September, 1964 (M)

League Club	Source	Date Signed	Seasons Played	Apps	Subs	Gls
Blackpool	App	09.82	81-82	4	1	0

BUTLER Joseph (Joe) William
Newcastle, 7 February, 1943 (M)

League Club	Source	Date Signed	Seasons Played	Apps	Subs	Gls
Newcastle U	Jnrs	09.60	63	3	-	0
Swindon T	Tr	08.65	65-75	355	7	18
Aldershot	Tr	08.76	76-77	31	8	0

BUTLER Kenneth (Ken)
Sunderland, 23 August, 1936 (W)

League Club	Source	Date Signed	Seasons Played	Apps	Subs	Gls
Hartlepools U	Whitburn	01.60	59-60	20	-	2

BUTLER Lee Simon
Sheffield, 30 May, 1966 (G)

League Club	Source	Date Signed	Seasons Played	Apps	Subs	Gls
Lincoln C	Harworth CW	08.86	86	30	0	0
Aston Villa	Tr	08.87	88-90	8	0	0
Hull C	L	03.91	90	4	0	0
Barnsley	Tr	07.91	91-95	118	2	0
Scunthorpe U	L	02.96	95	2	0	0
Wigan Ath	Tr	07.96	96-97	63	0	0
Halifax T	Dunfermline Ath	09.99	99-01	92	1	0

BUTLER Malcolm Partridge
Belfast, 6 August, 1913 Died 1987 I-1 (FB)

League Club	Source	Date Signed	Seasons Played	Apps	Subs	Gls
Blackpool	Bangor	01.35	35-38	22	-	0
Accrington St	Tr	07.47	47	32	-	0

BUTLER Martin
Hessle, 3 March, 1966 (F)

League Club	Source	Date Signed	Seasons Played	Apps	Subs	Gls
York C	App	10.84	84-88	40	25	9
Aldershot	L	12.85	85	2	0	1
Exeter C	L	02.87	86	4	0	1
Carlisle U	L	12.88	88	1	0	0
Scunthorpe U	Tr	08.89	89	2	0	0
Scarborough	Macclesfield T	11.89	89	1	5	0

BUTLER Martin Neil
Wordsley, 15 September, 1974 (F)

League Club	Source	Date Signed	Seasons Played	Apps	Subs	Gls
Walsall	YT	05.93	93-96	43	31	8
Cambridge U	Tr	08.97	97-99	100	3	41
Reading	Tr	02.00	99-03	85	18	32
Rotherham U	Tr	09.03	03-04	57	1	21

BUTLER Michael (Mick) Anthony
Worsborough Bridge, 27 January, 1951 (F)

League Club	Source	Date Signed	Seasons Played	Apps	Subs	Gls
Barnsley	Worsborough Bridge	07.73	72-75	118	2	57
Huddersfield T	Tr	03.76	75-77	73	6	22
Bournemouth	Tr	07.78	78-79	68	1	19
Bury	Tr	08.80	80-81	80	2	15

BUTLER Paul John
Stockton, 9 June, 1964 (W)

League Club	Source	Date Signed	Seasons Played	Apps	Subs	Gls
Wolverhampton W	App	06.82	82-84	18	11	2
Hereford U	L	01.84	83	16	0	2
Hereford U	Tr	02.85	84-86	49	15	2
Hartlepool U	Tr	07.87	87	6	3	0

BUTLER Paul John
Manchester, 2 November, 1972 IRB-1/IR-1 (CD)

League Club	Source	Date Signed	Seasons Played	Apps	Subs	Gls
Rochdale	YT	07.91	90-95	151	7	10
Bury	Tr	07.96	96-97	83	1	4
Sunderland	Tr	07.98	98-00	78	1	3
Wolverhampton W	L	11.00	00	5	0	0
Wolverhampton W	Tr	01.01	00-03	118	1	3
Leeds U	Tr	07.04	04	39	0	0

BUTLER Peter James
Halifax, 27 August, 1966 (M)

League Club	Source	Date Signed	Seasons Played	Apps	Subs	Gls
Huddersfield T	App	08.84	84-85	0	5	0
Cambridge U	L	01.86	85	14	0	1
Bury	Tr	07.86	86	9	2	0
Cambridge U	Tr	12.86	86-87	55	0	9
Southend U	Tr	02.88	87-91	135	7	9
Huddersfield T	L	03.92	91	7	0	0
West Ham U	Tr	08.92	92-94	70	0	3
Notts Co	Tr	10.94	94	20	0	0
Grimsby T	L	01.96	95	3	0	0
West Bromwich A	Tr	03.96	95-97	52	8	0
Halifax T	Tr	08.98	98-99	63	0	1

BUTLER Peter Leslie
Nottingham, 3 October, 1942 (G)

League Club	Source	Date Signed	Seasons Played	Apps	Subs	Gls
Notts Co	Jnrs	11.60	61-65	44	0	0
Bradford C	Tr	08.66	66	17	0	0

BUTLER Stanley (Stan)
Stillington, 7 January, 1919 Died 1979 (W)

League Club	Source	Date Signed	Seasons Played	Apps	Subs	Gls
West Bromwich A	Scunthorpe & Lindsey U	05.38	38-46	4	-	0
Southport	Tr	07.47	47	4	-	1

BUTLER Stephen (Steve)
Birmingham, 27 January, 1962 ESemiPro-3 (F)

League Club	Source	Date Signed	Seasons Played	Apps	Subs	Gls
Brentford	Windsor & Eton	12.84	84-85	18	3	3
Maidstone U	Tr	08.86	89-90	76	0	41
Watford	Tr	03.91	90-92	40	22	9
Bournemouth	L	12.92	92	1	0	0
Cambridge U	Tr	12.92	92-95	107	2	51
Gillingham	Tr	12.95	95-98	77	31	20
Peterborough U	Tr	10.98	98	13	1	2
Gillingham	Tr	07.99	99	2	8	2

BUTLER Thomas (Tommy)
Atherton, 28 April, 1918 (W)

League Club	Source	Date Signed	Seasons Played	Apps	Subs	Gls
Bolton W	Astley & Tyldesley	09.36				
Oldham Ath	Macclesfield	02.38	37-38	45	-	9
Middlesbrough	Tr	03.39	38	2	-	0
Oldham Ath	Tr	08.46	46	30	-	3
Accrington St	Tr	07.47	47-52	218	-	26

BUTLER Thomas Anthony
Ballymun, 25 April, 1981 IRYth/IRu21-15/IR-2 (M)

League Club	Source	Date Signed	Seasons Played	Apps	Subs	Gls
Sunderland	YT	06.98	99-03	16	15	0
Darlington	L	10.00	00	8	0	0
Hartlepool U	Dunfermline Ath	03.05	04	5	4	1

BUTLER Walter Garth
Birmingham, 7 February, 1923 Died 1995 (FB)

League Club	Source	Date Signed	Seasons Played	Apps	Subs	Gls
Derby Co		11.45				
Port Vale		06.46	46-50	128	-	0

BUTLIN Barry Desmond
Rosliston, 9 November, 1949 (F)

League Club	Source	Date Signed	Seasons Played	Apps	Subs	Gls
Derby Co	Jnrs	01.67	67-72	4	0	0
Notts Co	L	01.69	68	20	0	8
Notts Co	L	08.69	69	9	1	5
Luton T	Tr	11.72	72-74	56	1	24
Nottingham F	Tr	10.74	74-76	71	3	17
Brighton & Hove A	L	09.75	75	5	0	2
Reading	L	01.77	76	5	0	0
Peterborough U	Tr	08.77	77-78	64	0	12
Sheffield U	Tr	08.79	79-80	50	3	12

BUTT Leonard (Len)
Wilmslow, 26 August, 1910 Died 1994 (IF)

League Club	Source	Date Signed	Seasons Played	Apps	Subs	Gls
Stockport Co	Ashton National	08.28	29-30	8	-	1
Huddersfield T	Macclesfield	05.35	35-36	67	-	11
Blackburn Rov	Tr	01.37	36-46	110	-	44
York C	Tr	01.47	46-47	25	-	2
Mansfield T	Tr	10.47	47	15	-	4

BUTT Nicholas (Nicky)
Manchester, 21 January, 1975 ESch/EYth/Eu21-7/E-39 (M)

League Club	Source	Date Signed	Seasons Played	Apps	Subs	Gls
Manchester U	YT	01.93	92-03	210	60	21
Newcastle U	Tr	07.04	04	16	2	1

BUTT Robert
Chester, 27 March, 1946 (W)

League Club	Source	Date Signed	Seasons Played	Apps	Subs	Gls
Wrexham (Am)	Jnrs	01.65	64	3	-	0

BUTTERFIELD Daniel (Danny) Paul
Boston, 21 November, 1979 EYth (FB)

League Club	Source	Date Signed	Seasons Played	Apps	Subs	Gls
Grimsby T	YT	08.97	97-01	100	24	3
Crystal Palace	Tr	08.02	02-04	98	0	5

BUTTERFIELD John (Jack)
Barnsley, 30 August, 1922 Died 2001 (FB)

League Club	Source	Date Signed	Seasons Played	Apps	Subs	Gls
Burnley	Tamworth	02.46	47	3	-	0

BUTTERS Guy
Hillingdon, 30 October, 1969 Eu21-3 (CD)

League Club	Source	Date Signed	Seasons Played	Apps	Subs	Gls
Tottenham H	YT	08.88	88-89	34	1	1
Southend U	L	01.90	89	16	0	3
Portsmouth	Tr	09.90	90-96	148	6	6
Oxford U	L	11.94	94	3	0	1
Gillingham	Tr	10.96	96-01	155	4	16
Brighton & Hove A	Tr	08.02	02-04	90	0	5

BUTTERWORTH Adam Lawrence
Paignton, 9 August, 1982 (FB)

League Club	Source	Date Signed	Seasons Played	Apps	Subs	Gls
Cambridge U	Torquay U (Jnrs)	07.00	00	0	1	0

BUTTERWORTH Aidan James
Leeds, 7 November, 1961 ESch (F)

League Club	Source	Date Signed	Seasons Played	Apps	Subs	Gls
Leeds U	Jnrs	05.80	80-83	54	10	15
Doncaster Rov	Tr	08.84	84-85	35	15	5

BUTTERWORTH David (Dave) Albert
Bristol, 4 May, 1937 (WH)

League Club	Source	Date Signed	Seasons Played	Apps	Subs	Gls
Exeter C	Guildford C	12.57	57-59	26	-	0

BUTTERWORTH Garry Jeffrey
Whittlesey, 8 September, 1969 (M)

League Club	Source	Date Signed	Seasons Played	Apps	Subs	Gls
Peterborough U	YT	06.88	86-91	101	23	4
Rushden & Diamonds	Dagenham & Redbridge	08.94	01	28	1	1

BUTTERWORTH Ian Stewart
Crewe, 25 January, 1964 Eu21-8 (CD)

League Club	Source	Date Signed	Seasons Played	Apps	Subs	Gls
Coventry C	App	08.81	81-84	80	10	0
Nottingham F	Tr	06.85	85-86	26	1	0
Norwich C	Tr	09.86	86-93	230	5	4

BUTTIGIEG John
Sliema, Malta, 5 October, 1963 Malta int (FB)

League Club	Source	Date Signed	Seasons Played	Apps	Subs	Gls
Brentford	Sliema W (Malta)	11.88	88-89	24	16	0
Swindon T	L	09.90	90	2	1	0

BUTTLE Stephen (Steve) Arthur
Norwich, 1 January, 1953 (M)

League Club	Source	Date Signed	Seasons Played	Apps	Subs	Gls
Ipswich T	App	01.71				
Bournemouth	Tr	08.73	73-76	136	3	12

BUTTRESS Michael (Mike) David
Peterborough, 23 March, 1958 (FB)

League Club	Source	Date Signed	Seasons Played	Apps	Subs	Gls
Aston Villa	App	02.76	76-77	1	2	0
Gillingham	Tr	03.78	77-78	5	2	0

BUXTON Ian Raymond
Cromford, 17 April, 1938 (F)

League Club	Source	Date Signed	Seasons Played	Apps	Subs	Gls
Derby Co	Matlock T	03.59	59-67	144	1	41
Luton T	Tr	09.67	67-68	46	1	14
Notts Co	Tr	07.69	69	4	1	1
Port Vale	Tr	12.69	69	16	2	6

BUXTON Jake Fred
Sutton-in-Ashfield, 4 March, 1985 (FB)

League Club	Source	Date Signed	Seasons Played	Apps	Subs	Gls
Mansfield T	Jnrs	10.02	02-04	41	1	2

BUXTON Lewis Edward
Newport, Isle of Wight, 10 December, 1983 (FB)

League Club	Source	Date Signed	Seasons Played	Apps	Subs	Gls
Portsmouth	YT	04.01	01-02	27	3	0
Exeter C	L	10.02	02	4	0	0
Bournemouth	L	01.03	02	15	2	0
Bournemouth	L	10.03	03	24	2	0
Stoke C	Tr	12.04	04	14	2	0

BUXTON Michael (Mick) James
Corbridge, 29 May, 1943 (FB)

League Club	Source	Date Signed	Seasons Played	Apps	Subs	Gls
Burnley	Jnrs	06.60	62-67	16	2	0
Halifax T	Tr	06.68	68-70	36	0	0

BUXTON Nicholas (Nick) Gareth
Doncaster, 6 September, 1976 (G)

League Club	Source	Date Signed	Seasons Played	Apps	Subs	Gls
Scarborough	Goole T	10.97	97	3	0	0

BUXTON Stephen (Steve) Christopher
Birmingham, 13 March, 1960 (F)

League Club	Source	Date Signed	Seasons Played	Apps	Subs	Gls
Wrexham	Jnrs	07.78	77-83	93	16	21
Stockport Co	Tr	07.84	84	12	6	1
Wrexham	Altrincham	10.85	85-89	86	35	25

BUZSAKY Akos
Hungary, 7 May, 1982 Hungary u21 (M)

League Club	Source	Date Signed	Seasons Played	Apps	Subs	Gls
Plymouth Arg (L)	FC Port (Por)	01.05	04	14	1	1

BYATT Dennis John
Hillingdon, 8 August, 1958 (CD)

League Club	Source	Date Signed	Seasons Played	Apps	Subs	Gls
Fulham	App	05.76				
Peterborough U	Tr	07.78	78	2	1	0
Northampton T	Tr	06.79	79-80	46	1	3

BYCROFT Sydney (Syd)
Lincoln, 19 February, 1912 Died 2004 (CD)

League Club	Source	Date Signed	Seasons Played	Apps	Subs	Gls
Bradford C	Grantham	07.32				
Hull C	Tr	10.32				
Doncaster Rov	Newark T	01.36	35-51	333	-	2

BYERS Richard
Haltwhistle, 19 December, 1951 (F)

League Club	Source	Date Signed	Seasons Played	Apps	Subs	Gls
Workington (Am)	Hadrian Paints	10.71	71	1	0	0

BYFIELD Darren
Sutton Coldfield, 29 September, 1976 Jamaica 7 (F)

League Club	Source	Date Signed	Seasons Played	Apps	Subs	Gls
Aston Villa	YT	02.94	97	1	6	0
Preston NE	L	11.98	98	3	2	1
Northampton T	L	08.99	99	6	0	1
Cambridge U	L	09.99	99	3	1	0
Blackpool	L	03.00	99	3	0	0
Walsall	Tr	06.00	00-01	45	32	13
Rotherham U	Tr	03.02	01-03	53	15	22
Sunderland	Tr	02.04	03	8	9	5
Gillingham	Tr	07.04	04	27	11	6

BYNG David (Dave) Graeme
Walsgrave, 9 July, 1977 (F)

League Club	Source	Date Signed	Seasons Played	Apps	Subs	Gls
Torquay U	YT	07.95	93-95	12	12	3

BYRNE Anthony (Tony) Brendan
Rathdowney, 2 February, 1946 IR-14 (FB)

League Club	Source	Date Signed	Seasons Played	Apps	Subs	Gls
Millwall	Jnrs	08.63	63	1	-	0
Southampton	Tr	08.64	66-73	81	12	3
Hereford U	Tr	08.74	74-76	54	1	0
Newport Co	Tr	03.77	76-78	80	0	1

BYRNE Christopher (Chris) Thomas
Hulme, 9 February, 1975 ESemiPro-1 (M)

League Club	Source	Date Signed	Seasons Played	Apps	Subs	Gls
Crewe Alex	YT	06.93				
Sunderland	Macclesfield T	06.97	97	4	4	0
Stockport Co	Tr	11.97	97-00	43	13	11
Macclesfield T	L	08.99	99	5	0	0
Macclesfield T	Tr	07.01	01-02	28	7	7

BYRNE Clifford (Cliff)
Dublin, 27 April, 1982 IRYth/IRu21-10 (CD)

League Club	Source	Date Signed	Seasons Played	Apps	Subs	Gls
Sunderland	YT	05.99				
Scunthorpe U	L	11.02	02	13	0	0
Scunthorpe U	Tr	07.03	03-04	63	5	2

BYRNE Daniel (Danny) Thomas
Frimley, 30 November, 1984 IRYth (M)

League Club	Source	Date Signed	Seasons Played	Apps	Subs	Gls
Manchester U	Sch	09.03				
Hartlepool U	L	11.03	03	2	0	0

BYRNE David Stuart
Hammersmith, 5 March, 1961 (W)

League Club	Source	Date Signed	Seasons Played	Apps	Subs	Gls
Gillingham	Kingstonian	07.85	85	18	5	3
Millwall	Tr	07.86	86-87	52	11	6
Cambridge U	L	09.88	88	4	0	0
Blackburn Rov	L	02.89	88	4	0	0
Plymouth Arg	Tr	03.89	88-90	52	7	2
Bristol Rov	L	02.90	89	0	2	0
Watford	Tr	11.90	90	16	1	2
Reading	L	08.91	91	7	0	2
Fulham	L	01.92	91	5	0	0
Walsall (L)	Partick Th	02.94	93	5	0	0

BYRNE Desmond (Des)
Dublin, 10 April, 1981 IRYth (FB)

League Club	Source	Date Signed	Seasons Played	Apps	Subs	Gls
Stockport Co	YT	•	98	2	0	0
Wimbledon	St Patrick's Ath	08.00	01	0	1	0
Cambridge U	L	08.01	01	3	1	0
Carlisle U	Tr	10.02	02-03	18	3	0

BYRNE Gerald (Gerry)
Liverpool, 29 August, 1938 Eu23-1/E-2 (FB)

League Club	Source	Date Signed	Seasons Played	Apps	Subs	Gls
Liverpool	Jnrs	08.55	57-68	273	1	2

BYRNE Gerald (Gerry)
Glasgow, 10 April, 1957 (M)

League Club	Source	Date Signed	Seasons Played	Apps	Subs	Gls
Cardiff C	App	04.75	77-78	11	4	0

BYRNE John
Cambuslang, 20 May, 1939 (F)

League Club	Source	Date Signed	Seasons Played	Apps	Subs	Gls
Preston NE	Pollok Jnrs	03.58				
Tranmere Rov	Queen of the South	05.61	61	27	-	4
Barnsley	Hibernian	11.63	63-64	68	-	13
Peterborough U	Tr	07.65	65-67	106	1	28
Northampton T	Tr	12.67	67-68	40	0	4

BYRNE John Frederick
Manchester, 1 February, 1961 IR-23 (F)

League Club	Source	Date Signed	Seasons Played	Apps	Subs	Gls
York C	App	01.79	79-84	167	8	55
Queens Park Rgrs	Tr	10.84	84-87	108	18	30
Brighton & Hove A	Le Havre (Fr)	09.90	90-91	47	4	14
Sunderland	Tr	10.91	91-92	33	0	8
Millwall	Tr	10.92	92-93	12	5	1
Brighton & Hove A	L	03.93	92	5	2	2
Oxford U	Tr	11.93	93-94	52	3	18
Brighton & Hove A	Tr	02.95	94-95	29	10	6

BYRNE John (Johnny) Joseph
West Horsley, 13 May, 1939 Died 1999 EYth/Eu23-7/FLge-4/E-11 (F)

League Club	Source	Date Signed	Seasons Played	Apps	Subs	Gls
Crystal Palace	Guildford C	05.56	56-61	203	-	85
West Ham U	Tr	03.62	61-66	156	0	79
Crystal Palace	Tr	02.67	66-67	36	0	5
Fulham	Tr	03.68	67-68	16	3	2

BYRNE John Joseph Anthony
Wallasey, 24 March, 1949 (W)

League Club	Source	Date Signed	Seasons Played	Apps	Subs	Gls
Tranmere Rov (Am)	Cammell Laird	11.68	68	1	0	0

BYRNE Joseph (Joe)
Workington, 24 April, 1929 Died 1993 (G)

League Club	Source	Date Signed	Seasons Played	Apps	Subs	Gls
Workington (Am)	Frizington	09.52	52	2	-	0

BYRNE Mark John
Billinge, 8 May, 1983 (F)

League Club	Source	Date Signed	Seasons Played	Apps	Subs	Gls
Blackburn Rov	YT	07.01				
Stockport Co	Tr	03.02	01	1	4	0

BYRNE Michael (Mick)
Dublin, 14 January, 1960 (F)

League Club	Source	Date Signed	Seasons Played	Apps	Subs	Gls
Huddersfield T	Shamrock Rov	09.88	88-89	46	10	11

BYRNE Michael Thomas
Huddersfield, 14 May, 1985 (F)

League Club	Source	Date Signed	Seasons Played	Apps	Subs	Gls
Stockport Co	Bolton W (YT)	10.03	03	1	0	1

BYRNE Patrick (Pat) Joseph
Dublin, 15 May, 1956 IR-8 (M)

League Club	Source	Date Signed	Seasons Played	Apps	Subs	Gls
Leicester C	Shelbourne	07.79	79-80	31	5	3

BYRNE Paul
Newcastle, South Africa, 26 November, 1982 (FB)

League Club	Source	Date Signed	Seasons Played	Apps	Subs	Gls
Port Vale	Sch	07.02	00-02	8	3	0

BYRNE Paul Peter
Dublin, 30 June, 1972 IRSch/IRYth/IRu21-1 (W)

League Club	Source	Date Signed	Seasons Played	Apps	Subs	Gls
Oxford U	YT	07.89	89-91	4	2	0
Brighton & Hove A (L)	Glasgow Celtic	03.95	94	8	0	1
Southend U	Glasgow Celtic	08.95	95-97	70	13	6

BYRNE Raymond (Ray)
Newry, 4 July, 1972 (CD)

League Club	Source	Date Signed	Seasons Played	Apps	Subs	Gls
Nottingham F	Newry T	02.91				
Northampton T	Tr	08.94	94	2	0	0

BYRNE Roger William
Manchester, 8 September, 1929 Died 1958 EB/FLge-6/E-33 (FB)

League Club	Source	Date Signed	Seasons Played	Apps	Subs	Gls
Manchester U	Ryder Brow BC	03.49	51-57	245	-	17

BYRNE Shaun Ryan
Chesham, 21 January, 1981 IRYth/IRu21-10 (FB)

League Club	Source	Date Signed	Seasons Played	Apps	Subs	Gls
West Ham U	YT	07.99	99-01	0	2	0
Bristol Rov	L	01.00	99	1	1	0
Swansea C	L	01.04	03	9	0	0

BYRNE Wesley John
Dublin, 9 February, 1977 IRSch/IRYth (FB)

League Club	Source	Date Signed	Seasons Played	Apps	Subs	Gls
Middlesbrough	YT	02.94				
Stoke C	Tr	07.96				
Darlington	Tr	12.96	96	1	1	0

BYRNE William (Billy)
Newcastle-under-Lyme, 22 October, 1918 Died 2001 (W)

League Club	Source	Date Signed	Seasons Played	Apps	Subs	Gls
Port Vale		05.46	46	15	-	2
Crewe Alex	Tr	07.47	47-48	17	-	1

BYROM David John
Padiham, 6 January, 1965 ESch (FB)

League Club	Source	Date Signed	Seasons Played	Apps	Subs	Gls
Blackburn Rov	App	01.83				
Stockport Co	Tr	10.84	84	3	0	0

BYROM John
Blackburn, 28 July, 1944 EYth (F)

League Club	Source	Date Signed	Seasons Played	Apps	Subs	Gls
Blackburn Rov	Jnrs	08.61	61-65	106	2	45
Bolton W	Tr	06.66	66-75	296	8	113
Blackburn Rov	Tr	09.76	76	15	1	5

BYROM Raymond (Ray)
Blackburn, 2 January, 1935 (W)

League Club	Source	Date Signed	Seasons Played	Apps	Subs	Gls
Accrington St	Blackburn Rov (Am)	01.56	57-58	9	-	1
Bradford PA	Tr	12.58	58-60	70	-	14

League Club	Source	Date Signed	Seasons Played	Career Record Apps	Subs	Gls
BYROM Thomas (Tom)						
Upton, 17 March, 1920						(WH)
Tranmere Rov	Heswall	05.39	46	3	-	0
BYROM William (Bill)						
Blackburn, 30 March, 1915 Died 1989						(FB)
Burnley		08.37				
Queens Park Rgrs	Tr	05.39				
Rochdale	Tr	06.46	46-47	30	-	0
BYRON Gordon Frank						
Prescot, 4 September, 1953						(M)
Sheffield Wed	App	07.71				
Lincoln C	Tr	08.74	74	3	3	0
BYRON Paul						
Preston, 9 May, 1965						(CD)
Hartlepool U	Blackburn Rov (N/C)	08.86	86	1	0	0
BYWATER Noel **Leslie (Les)**						
Lichfield, 8 February, 1920 Died 1998						(G)
Huddersfield T		03.45				
Luton T	Tr	09.46	46	19	-	0
Rochdale	Tr	12.47	47-48	34	-	0
BYWATER Stephen (Steve) Michael						
Manchester, 7 June, 1981 EYth/Eu20/Eu21-2						(G)
West Ham U	Rochdale (YT)	08.98	99-04	57	1	0
Wycombe W	L	09.99	99	2	0	0
Hull C	L	11.99	99	4	0	0

League Club	Source	Date Signed	Seasons Played	Career Record Apps	Subs	Gls
CABALLERO Fabian Orlando						
Misiones, Argentina, 31 January, 1978						(F)
Arsenal (L)	Serro Porteno (Por)	10.98	98	0	1	0
CABRIE David McArthur						
Port Glasgow, 3 June, 1918 Died 1985						(WH)
Newport Co	St Mirren	05.46	46	9	-	0
CACERES Adrian Claudio						
Buenos Aires, Argentina, 10 January, 1982						(F)
Southampton	Perth Glory (Aus)	09.00				
Brentford	L	09.01	01	5	0	0
Hull C	Tr	03.02	01	1	3	0
Yeovil T	Perth Glory (Aus)	06.04	04	7	14	3
Wycombe W	Aldershot T	03.05	04	1	2	0
CADAMARTERI Daniel (Danny) Leon						
Cleckheaton, 12 October, 1979 EYth/Eu21-3						(F)
Everton	YT	10.96	96-01	38	55	13
Fulham	L	11.99	99	3	2	1
Bradford C	Tr	02.02	01-03	42	10	5
Leeds U	Tr	07.04				
Sheffield U	Tr	09.04	04	14	7	1
CADDEN Joseph (Joe) Young						
Glasgow, 13 April, 1920 Died 1981						(CD)
Liverpool	Brooklyn W (USA)	07.48	50	4	-	0
Grimsby T	Tr	02.52	52	1	-	0
Accrington St	Tr	06.53	53	17	-	0
CADE David						
Hemsworth, 29 September, 1938 ESch						(W)
Barnsley	Doncaster Rov (Am)	05.57				
Bradford PA	Tr	07.59	59	1	-	0
CADE Jamie William						
Durham, 15 January, 1984 EYth						(F)
Middlesbrough	YT	07.01				
Chesterfield	L	09.03	03	9	1	2
Colchester U	Tr	11.03	03-04	10	14	0
CADETE Santos Reis **Jorge**						
Porto Amelia, Mozambique, 27 August, 1968 Portugal 32						(F)
Bradford C (L)	Benfica (Por)	02.00	99	2	5	0
CADETTE Nathan Daniel						
Cardiff, 6 January, 1980 WYth						(M)
Cardiff C	YT	06.98	97	0	4	0
CADETTE Richard Raymond						
Hammersmith, 21 March, 1965						(F)
Orient	Wembley	08.84	84	19	2	4
Southend U	Tr	08.85	85-86	90	0	49
Sheffield U	Tr	07.87	87	26	2	7
Brentford	Tr	07.88	88-91	67	20	20
Bournemouth	L	03.90	89	4	4	1
Millwall	Falkirk	10.94	94-96	19	5	5
CADIOU Frederic (Freddie)						
Paris, France, 20 April, 1969						(F)
Leyton Orient	Wasquehal (Fr)	10.00	00	0	3	0
CAESAR Gus Cassius						
Tottenham, 5 March, 1966 Eu21-3						(CD)
Arsenal	App	02.84	85-89	27	17	0
Queens Park Rgrs	L	11.90	90	5	0	0
Cambridge U	Tr	07.91				
Bristol C	Tr	09.91	91	9	1	0
Colchester U	Airdrie	08.94	94-95	62	0	3
CAFFREY Henry (Harry)						
Paisley, 15 February, 1966						(W)
Hereford U	Clydebank	07.91	91	12	5	2
CAGIGAO Francisco						
Paddington, 10 November, 1969						(F)
Southend U	Barcelona (Sp)	09.91	92	0	1	0
CAHILL Gary James						
Dronfield, 19 December, 1985 EYth						(CD)
Aston Villa	Sch	12.03				
Burnley	L	11.04	04	27	0	1
CAHILL Oliver (Ollie) Francis						
Clonmel, 29 September, 1975						(W)
Northampton T	Clonmel	09.94	94-95	7	4	1
CAHILL Paul Gerard						
Liverpool, 29 September, 1955 EYth						(CD)
Coventry C	App	01.73				
Portsmouth	Tr	02.75	74-77	95	2	2
Aldershot	L	01.78	77	2	0	0
Tranmere Rov	California (USA)	10.78	78	5	0	0
Stockport Co	Tr	02.79	78	3	0	0
CAHILL Thomas (Tommy)						
Glasgow, 14 June, 1931 Died 2003						(FB)
Newcastle U	Vale of Leven	12.51	52-53	4	-	0
Barrow	Tr	08.55	55-64	285	-	3
CAHILL Timothy (Tim)						
Sydney, Australia, 6 December, 1979 WSamoaYth/Au-4						(M)
Millwall	Sydney U (Aus)	07.97	97-03	212	5	52
Everton	Tr	07.04	04	33	0	11
CAIG Antony (Tony)						
Whitehaven, 11 April, 1974						(G)
Carlisle U	YT	07.92	92-98	223	0	0
Blackpool	Tr	03.99	98-00	49	0	0
Charlton Ath	Tr	11.00	00	0	1	0
Newcastle U	Hibernian	01.03				
Barnsley	L	01.04	03	3	0	0
CAIN James (Jimmy) Patrick						
Fishburn, 29 December, 1933						(WH)
Bristol C	Stockton	05.57				
Hartlepools U	South Shields	08.60	60-61	30	-	0
CAINE Brian						
Nelson, 20 June, 1936						(G)
Blackpool	Accrington St (Am)	02.57	57	1	-	0
Coventry C	Tr	09.59	60	1	-	0
Northampton T	Tr	07.61				
Barrow	Tr	10.61	61-63	109	-	0
CAINE William (Billy) George						
Barrow, 1 July, 1927						(FB)
Barrow	Barrow RFC	07.52	51-54	12	-	0
CAINES Gavin Liam						
Birmingham, 20 September, 1983						(CD)
Walsall	Sch	07.03				
Cheltenham T	Tr	07.04	04	27	2	2
CAIRNEY Charles (Chic)						
Blantyre, 21 September, 1926 Died 1995						(WH)
Leyton Orient	Glasgow Celtic	10.50	50	4	-	0
Bristol Rov	Barry T	07.53	53-54	14	-	1
CAIRNEY James (Jim)						
Glasgow, 13 July, 1931						(CD)
Portsmouth	Shawfield Jnrs	09.49				
York C	Tr	07.56	56-57	53	-	0
CAIRNS Colin						
Alloa, 17 September, 1936						(IF)
Southend U	Heart of Midlothian	02.58	58	2	-	0
CAIRNS John (Jackie) Greenfield						
Newcastle, 13 April, 1922 Died 1988						(IF)
Hartlepools U		03.48	47-49	16	-	2
CAIRNS Kevin William						
Hoole, Lancashire, 29 June, 1937						(FB)
Southport	Dundee U	08.62	62-67	204	2	1
CAIRNS Robert Lynn						
Choppington, 25 December, 1927 Died 1958						(FB)
Gateshead	Sunderland (Am)	09.48	48-56	139	-	0
CAIRNS Robert (Bobby) Seggie						
Glenboig, 27 May, 1929 Died 1998						(WH)
Stoke C	Ayr U	12.53	53-60	175	-	9
CAIRNS Ronald (Ron)						
Chopwell, 4 April, 1934						(IF)
Blackburn Rov	Consett	09.53	55-58	26	-	7
Rochdale	Tr	06.59	59-63	195	-	66
Southport	Tr	07.64	64	34	-	13
CAIRNS William (Billy) Hart						
Newcastle, 7 October, 1914 Died 1988						(CF)
Newcastle U	Stargate Rov	05.33	34-38	87	-	51
Gateshead	Tr	11.44				
Grimsby T	Tr	05.46	46-53	221	-	121

CAIZLEY Kevin
Jarrow, 2 December, 1968 (M)

League Club	Source	Date Signed	Seasons Played	Apps	Subs	Gls
Newcastle U	YT	08.87				
Darlington	Tr	07.88	88	8	4	1

CAKEBREAD Gerald (Gerry)
Acton, 1 April, 1936 EYth (G)

League Club	Source	Date Signed	Seasons Played	Apps	Subs	Gls
Brentford	Jnrs	06.55	54-63	348	-	0

CALDER William (Bill) Carson
Glasgow, 28 September, 1934 (CF)

League Club	Source	Date Signed	Seasons Played	Apps	Subs	Gls
Leicester C	Port Glasgow	08.55	58	3	-	0
Bury	Tr	05.59	59-63	174	-	67
Oxford U	Tr	11.63	63-66	66	1	28
Rochdale	Tr	11.66	66	7	1	1

CALDERBANK George Raymond (Ray)
Manchester, 8 February, 1936 (IF)

League Club	Source	Date Signed	Seasons Played	Apps	Subs	Gls
Rochdale (Am)	Hyde U	08.53	53	1	-	0

CALDERWOOD Colin
Stranraer, 20 January, 1965 SSch/S-36 (CD)

League Club	Source	Date Signed	Seasons Played	Apps	Subs	Gls
Mansfield T	Inverness Caledonian	03.82	81-84	97	3	1
Swindon T	Tr	07.85	85-92	328	2	20
Tottenham H	Tr	07.93	93-98	152	11	6
Aston Villa	Tr	03.99	98-99	23	3	0
Nottingham F	Tr	03.00	99-00	7	1	0
Notts Co	L	03.01	00	5	0	0

CALDERWOOD James (Jimmy)
Glasgow, 28 February, 1955 Su23-1 (FB)

League Club	Source	Date Signed	Seasons Played	Apps	Subs	Gls
Birmingham C	App	07.72	72-79	135	10	4
Cambridge U	L	11.79	79	8	0	0

CALDWELL Anthony (Tony)
Salford, 21 March, 1958 (F)

League Club	Source	Date Signed	Seasons Played	Apps	Subs	Gls
Bolton W	Horwich RMI	06.83	83-86	131	8	58
Bristol C	Tr	07.87	87-88	9	8	3
Chester C	L	01.88	87	4	0	0
Grimsby T	Tr	09.88	88	2	1	0
Stockport Co	Tr	10.88	88-89	23	3	5

CALDWELL David Lees
Clydebank, 7 May, 1932 (FB)

League Club	Source	Date Signed	Seasons Played	Apps	Subs	Gls
Rotherham U	Aberdeen	05.60	60	1	-	0

CALDWELL David (Dave) Wilson
Aberdeen, 31 July, 1960 (F)

League Club	Source	Date Signed	Seasons Played	Apps	Subs	Gls
Mansfield T	Inverness Caledonian	06.79	79-84	145	12	57
Carlisle U	L	12.84	84	4	0	0
Swindon T	L	02.85	84	5	0	0
Chesterfield	Tr	07.85	85-87	64	4	17
Torquay U	Tr	11.87	87	24	0	4
Torquay U (L)	KW Overpelt (Bel)	12.89	89	17	0	6
Chesterfield	KW Overpelt (Bel)	10.90	90-91	27	5	4

CALDWELL Garrett Evan James
Princeton, New Jersey, USA, 6 November, 1973 (G)

League Club	Source	Date Signed	Seasons Played	Apps	Subs	Gls
Colchester U	Princeton Univ (USA)	09.95	96	6	0	0

CALDWELL Gary
Stirling, 12 April, 1982 SSch/SYth/Su21-19/SB-4/S-14 (FB)

League Club	Source	Date Signed	Seasons Played	Apps	Subs	Gls
Newcastle U	YT	04.99				
Darlington	L	11.01	01	4	0	0
Coventry C	L	07.02	02	36	0	0
Derby Co	L	08.03	03	6	3	0

CALDWELL Peter James
Dorchester, Oxfordshire, 5 June, 1972 ESch (G)

League Club	Source	Date Signed	Seasons Played	Apps	Subs	Gls
Queens Park Rgrs	YT	03.90				
Leyton Orient	Tr	07.95	95-96	31	0	0

CALDWELL Stephen (Steve)
Stirling, 12 September, 1980 SYth/Su21-4/SB-3/S-5 (CD)

League Club	Source	Date Signed	Seasons Played	Apps	Subs	Gls
Newcastle U	YT	10.97	00-03	20	8	1
Blackpool	L	10.01	01	6	0	0
Bradford C	L	12.01	01	9	0	0
Leeds U	L	02.04	03	13	0	1
Sunderland	Tr	07.04	04	41	0	4

CALDWELL Terence (Terry)
Sharlston, 5 December, 1938 EYth (FB)

League Club	Source	Date Signed	Seasons Played	Apps	Subs	Gls
Huddersfield T	Jnrs	06.57	59	4	-	0
Leeds U	Tr	12.59	59-60	20	-	0
Carlisle U	Tr	07.61	61-69	339	4	1
Barrow	Tr	07.70	70-71	29	1	0

CALEB Graham Stuart
Oxford, 25 May, 1945 (CD)

League Club	Source	Date Signed	Seasons Played	Apps	Subs	Gls
Luton T	App	05.63	63-64	20	-	0

ALLACHAN Ralph
Edinburgh, 29 April, 1955 (M)

League Club	Source	Date Signed	Seasons Played	Apps	Subs	Gls
Newcastle U	Heart of Midlothian	02.77	77	9	0	0

CALLAGHAN Aaron Joseph
Dublin, 8 October, 1966 IRYth/IRu21-2 (CD)

League Club	Source	Date Signed	Seasons Played	Apps	Subs	Gls
Stoke C	App	10.84	84-86	10	5	0
Crewe Alex	L	11.85	85	8	0	0
Oldham Ath	Tr	10.86	86-87	11	5	2
Crewe Alex	Tr	05.88	88-91	148	10	6
Preston NE	Tr	08.92	92-93	34	2	2

CALLAGHAN Christopher (Chris)
Sandbach, 25 August, 1930 Died 2002 (FB)

League Club	Source	Date Signed	Seasons Played	Apps	Subs	Gls
Crewe Alex	Bideford	12.52	53-56	44	-	0

CALLAGHAN Ernest (Ernie)
Birmingham, 21 January, 1910 Died 1972 (FB)

League Club	Source	Date Signed	Seasons Played	Apps	Subs	Gls
Aston Villa	Atherstone T	09.30	32-46	125	-	0

CALLAGHAN Frederick (Fred) John
Fulham, 19 December, 1944 (FB)

League Club	Source	Date Signed	Seasons Played	Apps	Subs	Gls
Fulham	App	08.62	63-73	291	4	9

CALLAGHAN Henry (Harry) William
Glasgow, 20 March, 1929 (W)

League Club	Source	Date Signed	Seasons Played	Apps	Subs	Gls
Ipswich T	Kirkintilloch Rob Roy	09.54	54	1	-	0

CALLAGHAN Ian Michael
Prescot, 5 August, 1969 (M)

League Club	Source	Date Signed	Seasons Played	Apps	Subs	Gls
Bolton W	YT	07.87	87	1	0	0

CALLAGHAN Ian Robert
Liverpool, 10 April, 1942 Eu23-4/FLge-2/E-4 (W)

League Club	Source	Date Signed	Seasons Played	Apps	Subs	Gls
Liverpool	Jnrs	03.60	59-77	637	3	50
Swansea C	Fort Lauderdale (USA)	09.78	78-79	76	0	1
Crewe Alex	Soudifjord (Nor)	10.81	81	15	0	0

CALLAGHAN Nigel Ian
Singapore, 12 September, 1962 Eu21-9/EB (W)

League Club	Source	Date Signed	Seasons Played	Apps	Subs	Gls
Watford	App	07.80	79-86	209	13	41
Derby Co	Tr	02.87	86-88	76	0	10
Aston Villa	Tr	02.89	88-90	24	2	1
Derby Co	L	09.90	90	12	0	1
Watford	L	03.91	90	6	6	1
Huddersfield T	L	01.92	91	8	0	0

CALLAGHAN Robert (Bobby)
Glasgow, 5 October, 1931 Died 1991 (W)

League Club	Source	Date Signed	Seasons Played	Apps	Subs	Gls
Scunthorpe U	Duntocher Hibernian	08.55	55	19	-	6
Barrow	Tr	10.56	56-57	40	-	10

CALLAGHAN William (Willie)
Glasgow, 7 February, 1930 (IF)

League Club	Source	Date Signed	Seasons Played	Apps	Subs	Gls
Ipswich T	Glasgow Perthshire	07.52	52-54	21	-	7

CALLAGHAN William (Willie) Andrew
Glasgow, 9 December, 1941 (W)

League Club	Source	Date Signed	Seasons Played	Apps	Subs	Gls
Barnsley	Dumbarton	08.64	64	15	-	0

CALLAGHAN William (Bill) Francis
Ebbw Vale, 26 February, 1924 Died 1981 (FB)

League Club	Source	Date Signed	Seasons Played	Apps	Subs	Gls
Aldershot	Frickley Colliery	06.49	49	1	-	0

CALLAGHAN William (Willie) Thomas
Dunfermline, 23 March, 1967 (F)

League Club	Source	Date Signed	Seasons Played	Apps	Subs	Gls
Walsall (L)	Dunfermline Ath	09.88	88	2	0	1

CALLAN Dennis
Merthyr Tydfil, 27 July, 1932 (W)

League Club	Source	Date Signed	Seasons Played	Apps	Subs	Gls
Cardiff C	Troedyrhiw	07.52	55	1	-	0
Exeter C	L	05.54	54	10	-	1

CALLAN Francis Thomas Moore
Belfast, 24 May, 1935 (IF)

League Club	Source	Date Signed	Seasons Played	Apps	Subs	Gls
Doncaster Rov	Dundalk	11.57	57-58	28	-	6

CALLAND Albert
Lanchester, 10 September, 1929 (CF)

League Club	Source	Date Signed	Seasons Played	Apps	Subs	Gls
Torquay U	Langley Park	03.50	51-53	24	-	11

CALLAND Edward (Ted)
Lanchester, 15 June, 1932 Died 1995 (CF)

League Club	Source	Date Signed	Seasons Played	Apps	Subs	Gls
Fulham	Durham C	04.52				
Torquay U	Cornsay Park A	09.52	52-56	47	-	21
Exeter C	Tr	07.57	57-59	105	-	49
Port Vale	Tr	08.60	60	12	-	3
Lincoln C	Tr	07.61	61	7	-	3

CALLAND Ralph
Lanchester, 5 July, 1916 (FB)

League Club	Source	Date Signed	Seasons Played	Apps	Subs	Gls
Charlton Ath		05.37				
Torquay U	Tr	05.39	46-53	207	-	14

CALLENDER John (Jack)
West Wylam, 2 April, 1923 Died 2001 (WH)

League Club	Source	Date Signed	Seasons Played	Apps	Subs	Gls
Gateshead	Spen Black & White	05.45	46-57	471	-	42

CALLENDER Norman
Newburn, 9 June, 1924 Died 1990 (WH)

League Club	Source	Date Signed	Seasons Played	Apps	Subs	Gls
Darlington		06.46	46-48	26	-	1

CALLENDER Thomas (Tom) Sanderson
Bywell, 20 September, 1920 Died 2002 ESch (CD)

League Club	Source	Date Signed	Seasons Played	Apps	Subs	Gls
Lincoln C	Crawcrook A	09.37	38	23	-	0
Gateshead	Tr	11.45	46-56	439	-	58

CALLOWAY Laurence (Laurie) John
Birmingham, 17 June, 1945 (FB)

League Club	Source	Date Signed	Seasons Played	Apps	Subs	Gls
Wolverhampton W	App	10.62				
Rochdale	Tr	07.64	64-67	161	1	4
Blackburn Rov	Tr	03.68	67-69	17	8	1
Southport	Tr	08.70	70	45	0	7
York C	Tr	06.71	71-72	54	1	3
Shrewsbury T	Tr	12.72	72-74	77	5	3

CALOW Charles (Charlie) John Herbert
Belfast, 30 September, 1931 NIAmat (G)

League Club	Source	Date Signed	Seasons Played	Apps	Subs	Gls
Bradford PA	Cliftonville	06.52	52	1	-	0

CALVER Reginald **John**
Mount Florida, 22 September, 1938 (WH)

League Club	Source	Date Signed	Seasons Played	Apps	Subs	Gls
Burnley	Jnrs	09.55				
Southport	Tr	07.61	61	2	-	0

CALVERLEY Alfred (Alf)
Huddersfield, 24 November, 1917 Died 1991 (W)

League Club	Source	Date Signed	Seasons Played	Apps	Subs	Gls
Huddersfield T		11.43				
Mansfield T	Tr	06.46	46	30	-	1
Arsenal	Tr	03.47	46	11	-	0
Preston NE	Tr	07.47	47	13	-	0
Doncaster Rov	Tr	12.47	47-52	142	-	11

CALVERT Clifford (Cliff) Alistair
York, 21 April, 1954 EYth (FB)

League Club	Source	Date Signed	Seasons Played	Apps	Subs	Gls
York C	Jnrs	07.72	72-75	62	5	0
Sheffield U	Tr	09.75	75-78	78	3	5

CALVERT Joseph (Joe) William Herbert
Beighton, 3 February, 1907 Died 1999 (G)

League Club	Source	Date Signed	Seasons Played	Apps	Subs	Gls
Bristol Rov	Frickley Colliery	05.31	31	42	-	0
Leicester C	Tr	05.32	32-47	72	-	0
Watford	Tr	02.48	47	5	-	0

CALVERT Mark Robert
Consett, 11 September, 1970 (M)

League Club	Source	Date Signed	Seasons Played	Apps	Subs	Gls
Hull C	YT	07.89	88-92	24	6	1
Scarborough	Tr	08.93	93-94	68	4	5

CALVERT John **Steven (Steve)**
Barrow, 2 April, 1952 (M)

League Club	Source	Date Signed	Seasons Played	Apps	Subs	Gls
Barrow (Am)	Jnrs	08.70	71	22	0	4

CALVO-GARCIA Alexander (Alex)
Ordizia, Spain, 1 January, 1972 (M)

League Club	Source	Date Signed	Seasons Played	Apps	Subs	Gls
Scunthorpe U	Eibar	10.96	96-03	205	28	32

CAMARA Aboubacar (Titi) Sidiki
Donka, Guinea, 17 November, 1972 Guinea int (F)

League Club	Source	Date Signed	Seasons Played	Apps	Subs	Gls
Liverpool	Marseille (Fr)	06.99	99	22	11	9
West Ham U	Tr	12.00	00-02	5	6	0

CAMARA Ben Ibrahim
Bonn, Germany, 19 June, 1985 (F)

League Club	Source	Date Signed	Seasons Played	Apps	Subs	Gls
Torquay U	Sch	●	02	0	2	0

CAMARA Henri
Dakar, Senegal, 10 May, 1977 Senegal int (F)

League Club	Source	Date Signed	Seasons Played	Apps	Subs	Gls
Wolverhampton W	Sedan (Fr)	08.03	03	29	1	7
Southampton	L	01.05	04	10	3	4

CAMARA Mohamed (Mo)
Conakry, Guinea, 25 June, 1975 (FB)

League Club	Source	Date Signed	Seasons Played	Apps	Subs	Gls
Wolverhampton W	Le Havre (Fr)	08.00	00-01	27	18	0
Burnley	Tr	07.03	03-04	90	0	0

CAMARA Zoumana
Paris, France, 3 April, 1979 FrB-2/Fr-1 (CD)

League Club	Source	Date Signed	Seasons Played	Apps	Subs	Gls
Leeds U (L)	RC Lens (Fr)	08.03	03	13	0	1

CAMDEN Christopher (Chris) Eric
Birkenhead, 28 May, 1963 (F)

League Club	Source	Date Signed	Seasons Played	Apps	Subs	Gls
Chester C	Poulton Victoria	12.83	83	9	0	2
Tranmere Rov	Oswestry T	03.87	86	2	1	1

CAME Mark Raymond
Exeter, 14 September, 1961 (CD)

League Club	Source	Date Signed	Seasons Played	Apps	Subs	Gls
Bolton W	Winsford U	04.84	84-92	188	7	7
Chester C	Tr	12.92	92-93	47	0	1
Exeter C	Tr	07.94	94-95	70	0	5

CAME Shaun Raymond
Crewe, 15 June, 1983 (CD)

League Club	Source	Date Signed	Seasons Played	Apps	Subs	Gls
Macclesfield T	YT	07.00	00-02	5	4	0

CAMERON Alexander (Alex) Ramsey
Leith, 5 October, 1943 (FB)

League Club	Source	Date Signed	Seasons Played	Apps	Subs	Gls
Oldham Ath	Hibernian	05.64	64	15	-	0

CAMERON Colin
Kirkcaldy, 23 October, 1972 S-29 (M)

League Club	Source	Date Signed	Seasons Played	Apps	Subs	Gls
Wolverhampton W	Heart of Midlothian	08.01	01-04	116	25	18

CAMERON Daniel (Danny)
Dundee, 9 November, 1953 (FB)

League Club	Source	Date Signed	Seasons Played	Apps	Subs	Gls
Sheffield Wed	App	07.71	73-75	31	0	1
Colchester U	L	02.75	74	5	0	0
Preston NE	Tr	04.76	75-80	120	2	0

CAMERON Daniel
Dublin, 16 June, 1922 LoI-1 (CD)

League Club	Source	Date Signed	Seasons Played	Apps	Subs	Gls
Everton	Shelbourne	07.48	48	1	-	0

CAMERON David (Davie)
Glasgow, 10 March, 1936 (IF)

League Club	Source	Date Signed	Seasons Played	Apps	Subs	Gls
Bradford C	Rutherglen Glencairn	04.58	58	7	-	2

CAMERON David (Dave) Anthony
Bangor, 24 August, 1975 (F)

League Club	Source	Date Signed	Seasons Played	Apps	Subs	Gls
Brighton & Hove A	British Army	07.99	99	6	11	0
Lincoln C	Worthing	07.00	00-01	33	27	8

CAMERON Duncan George Brown
Uddingston, 1 February, 1936 (W)

League Club	Source	Date Signed	Seasons Played	Apps	Subs	Gls
Swindon T		08.56	56-57	2	-	0

CAMERON Hugh Gibson
Burnbank, 1 February, 1927 (W)

League Club	Source	Date Signed	Seasons Played	Apps	Subs	Gls
Torquay U	Clyde	05.48	48-50	120	-	17
Newcastle U	Tr	04.51	51	2	-	0
Bury	Tr	03.52	51-53	29	-	1
Workington	Tr	11.53	53-55	54	-	5

CAMERON John (Jack)
Dalmuir, 7 March, 1931 (FB)

League Club	Source	Date Signed	Seasons Played	Apps	Subs	Gls
Hartlepools U	Dumbarton	11.53	53-59	175	-	0

CAMERON John (Johnny) Alexander
Greenock, 29 November, 1929 (WH)

League Club	Source	Date Signed	Seasons Played	Apps	Subs	Gls
Bradford PA	Motherwell	07.56	56	3	-	0

CAMERON Martin George William
Dunfermline, 16 August, 1978 (F)

League Club	Source	Date Signed	Seasons Played	Apps	Subs	Gls
Bristol Rov	Alloa Ath	07.00	00-01	16	23	6

CAMERON Robert (Bobby)
Greenock, 23 November, 1932 SSch (IF)

League Club	Source	Date Signed	Seasons Played	Apps	Subs	Gls
Queens Park Rgrs	Port Glasgow	06.50	50-58	256	-	59
Leeds U	Tr	07.59	59-61	58	-	9
Southend U	Gravesend & Northfleet	10.63	63	3	-	0

CAMERON Rodney (Rod) Peter
Newcastle, 11 April, 1939 (FB)

League Club	Source	Date Signed	Seasons Played	Apps	Subs	Gls
Bradford C	Newcastle West End BC	08.57	58	1	-	0

CAMERON Stuart John
Liverpool, 28 November, 1966 (G)

League Club	Source	Date Signed	Seasons Played	Apps	Subs	Gls
Preston NE	App	08.83	83	1	0	0

CAMILIERI-GIOIA Carlo
Brussels, Belgium, 14 May, 1975 (M)

League Club	Source	Date Signed	Seasons Played	Apps	Subs	Gls
Mansfield T	RSC Charleroi (Bel)	09.99	99	0	2	0

CAMM Mark Liam
Mansfield, 1 October, 1981 (FB)

League Club	Source	Date Signed	Seasons Played	Apps	Subs	Gls
Sheffield U	YT	07.99				
Lincoln C	Tr	08.00	00-02	11	21	0

CAMMACK Stephen (Steve) Richard
Sheffield, 20 March, 1954 EYth (F)

League Club	Source	Date Signed	Seasons Played	Apps	Subs	Gls
Sheffield U	App	05.71	71-75	21	15	5
Chesterfield	Tr	01.76	75-78	95	18	21
Scunthorpe U	Tr	09.79	79-80	84	0	27
Lincoln C	Tr	07.81	81	18	0	6
Scunthorpe U	Tr	03.82	81-86	159	2	83
Port Vale	L	12.85	85	1	2	0
Stockport Co	L	01.86	85	3	1	1

CAMP Lee Michael John
Derby, 22 August, 1984 EYth/Eu20/Eu21-2 (G)

League Club	Source	Date Signed	Seasons Played	Apps	Subs	Gls
Derby Co	Sch	07.02	02-04	45	1	0
Queens Park Rgrs	L	03.04	03	12	0	0

CAMP Stephen (Steve)
Manchester, 8 February, 1954 (F)

League Club	Source	Date Signed	Seasons Played	Apps	Subs	Gls
Fulham	Leatherhead U	09.75	75-76	4	1	0
Peterborough U	Tr	08.77	77	6	1	1

CAMPAGNA Samuel (Sam) Patrick Philip
Worcester, 19 November, 1980 (FB)

League Club	Source	Date Signed	Seasons Played	Apps	Subs	Gls
Swindon T	YT	07.99	98-99	1	4	0

CAMPBELL Alan James
Arbroath, 21 January, 1948 SYth/Su23-1 (M)

League Club	Source	Date Signed	Seasons Played	Apps	Subs	Gls
Charlton Ath	Jnrs	02.65	65-70	196	2	28
Birmingham C	Tr	10.70	70-75	169	6	11
Cardiff C	Tr	03.76	75-80	165	2	2
Carlisle U	Tr	11.80	80-81	29	2	2

CAMPBELL Thomas **Alan**
Belfast, 11 September, 1944 IrLge-10 (FB)

League Club	Source	Date Signed	Seasons Played	Apps	Subs	Gls
Grimsby T	Coleraine	10.70	70-72	84	1	0

CAMPBELL Andrew (Andy) Paul
Stockton, 18 April, 1979 EYth/Eu21-4 (F)

League Club	Source	Date Signed	Seasons Played	Apps	Subs	Gls
Middlesbrough	YT	07.96	95-01	28	28	4
Sheffield U	L	12.98	98	5	0	1
Sheffield U	L	03.99	98	6	0	2
Bolton W	L	03.01	00	3	3	0
Cardiff C	Tr	02.02	01-04	30	43	12
Doncaster Rov	L	01.05	04	1	2	0

CAMPBELL Charles
Oban, 27 February, 1928 (WH)

League Club	Source	Date Signed	Seasons Played	Apps	Subs	Gls
Oldham Ath	Rutherglen Glencairn	11.49	49	2	-	0

CAMPBELL Daniel (Danny)
Oldham, 3 February, 1944 (CD)

League Club	Source	Date Signed	Seasons Played	Apps	Subs	Gls
West Bromwich A	Droylsden	11.62	65-67	8	0	0
Stockport Co	Los Angeles (USA)	01.69	68-69	31	0	3
Bradford PA	Tr	03.70	69	10	0	1

CAMPBELL Darren Archibald
Huntingdon, 16 April, 1986 SYth (M)

League Club	Source	Date Signed	Seasons Played	Apps	Subs	Gls
Reading	Sch	04.03	02	0	1	0

CAMPBELL David
Wrexham, 18 February, 1947 (W)

League Club	Source	Date Signed	Seasons Played	Apps	Subs	Gls
Wrexham	Jnrs	07.65	64-66	41	2	7

CAMPBELL David Alistair
Edinburgh, 2 November, 1958 (FB)

League Club	Source	Date Signed	Seasons Played	Apps	Subs	Gls
Charlton Ath	Jnrs	06.77	75-79	71	5	3

CAMPBELL David Anthony
Eglinton, 2 June, 1965 NI-10 (M)

League Club	Source	Date Signed	Seasons Played	Apps	Subs	Gls
Nottingham F	App	06.83	84-87	35	6	3
Notts Co	L	02.87	86	18	0	2
Charlton Ath	Tr	10.87	87-88	26	4	1
Plymouth Arg	L	03.89	88	1	0	0
Bradford C	Tr	03.89	88-89	27	8	4
Rotherham U	Shamrock Rov	11.92	92	0	1	0
Burnley	West Bromwich A (N/C)	03.93	92	7	1	0
Lincoln C	L	02.94	93	2	2	1
Wigan Ath	Tr	08.94	94	7	0	0
Cambridge U	Tr	01.95	94	1	0	0

CAMPBELL David Martin
Dublin, 13 September, 1969 (CD)

League Club	Source	Date Signed	Seasons Played	Apps	Subs	Gls
Huddersfield T	Bohemians	08.90	90-91	4	0	0

CAMPBELL Donald (Don)
Bootle, 19 October, 1932 EYth (FB)

League Club	Source	Date Signed	Seasons Played	Apps	Subs	Gls
Liverpool	Jnrs	11.50	53-57	47	-	2
Crewe Alex	Tr	07.58	58-61	150	-	1
Gillingham	Tr	09.62	62-63	29	-	0

CAMPBELL Dougald
Kirkintilloch, 14 December, 1922 (W)

League Club	Source	Date Signed	Seasons Played	Apps	Subs	Gls
Queens Park Rgrs		03.48				
Crewe Alex	Tr	07.49	49	33	-	0
Barrow	Tr	08.50	50-51	29	-	3
Grimsby T	Tr	10.51	51	6	-	0

CAMPBELL Frank
Dunkeld, 23 December, 1950 (M)

League Club	Source	Date Signed	Seasons Played	Apps	Subs	Gls
Grimsby T	Jnrs	03.68	68	4	0	0

CAMPBELL Gary
Belfast, 4 April, 1966 (M)

League Club	Source	Date Signed	Seasons Played	Apps	Subs	Gls
Arsenal	App	01.84				
Leyton Orient	Leyton-Wingate	01.90	89	4	4	0

CAMPBELL Anthony **Glen**
Leyland, 26 February, 1965 (G)

League Club	Source	Date Signed	Seasons Played	Apps	Subs	Gls
Preston NE	App	02.83	82-84	18	0	0

CAMPBELL Gregory (Greg) Robert
Portsmouth, 13 July, 1965 (F)

League Club	Source	Date Signed	Seasons Played	Apps	Subs	Gls
West Ham U	App	10.82	84-85	3	2	0
Brighton & Hove A	L	02.87	86	0	2	0
Plymouth Arg	Sparta Rotterdam (Holl)	11.88	88-89	21	14	6
Northampton T	Tr	07.90	90-91	32	15	7

CAMPBELL James (Jock)
East Kilbride, 11 November, 1922 Died 1983 (FB)

League Club	Source	Date Signed	Seasons Played	Apps	Subs	Gls
Charlton Ath	RAF Brize Norton	01.45	46-57	255	-	1

CAMPBELL James (Jim)
Glasgow, 25 November, 1918 (W)

League Club	Source	Date Signed	Seasons Played	Apps	Subs	Gls
Leicester C	St Anthony's	10.43				
Walsall	Tr	10.46	46-47	14	-	1

CAMPBELL James (Jimmy) Charles
St Pancras, 11 April, 1937 Died 1994 (W)

League Club	Source	Date Signed	Seasons Played	Apps	Subs	Gls
West Bromwich A	Maidenhead U	10.55	57-58	31	-	9
Portsmouth	Tr	07.59	59-61	50	-	12
Lincoln C	Tr	05.62	62-63	63	-	16

CAMPBELL Jamie
Birmingham, 21 October, 1972 (M)

League Club	Source	Date Signed	Seasons Played	Apps	Subs	Gls
Luton T	YT	07.91	91-93	10	26	1
Mansfield T	L	11.94	94	3	0	1
Cambridge U	L	03.95	94	12	0	0
Barnet	Tr	07.95	95-96	50	17	5
Cambridge U	Tr	08.97	97-98	91	0	6
Brighton & Hove A	Tr	07.99	99	22	1	1
Exeter C	Tr	07.00	00-01	56	2	3

CAMPBELL John
West Wylam, 23 July, 1928 (W)

League Club	Source	Date Signed	Seasons Played	Apps	Subs	Gls
Gateshead		11.49	49-55	181	-	45

CAMPBELL John
Alexandria, 22 September, 1934 (FB)

League Club	Source	Date Signed	Seasons Played	Apps	Subs	Gls
Chesterfield	Motherwell	08.59	59	1	-	0

CAMPBELL John
Liverpool, 17 March, 1922 (WH)

League Club	Source	Date Signed	Seasons Played	Apps	Subs	Gls
Liverpool		04.43				
Blackburn Rov	Tr	12.45	46-55	224	-	19
Oldham Ath	Tr	07.56	56	26	-	5

CAMPBELL John (Johnny) Peter
Belfast, 28 June, 1923 Died 1968 NIRL-1/IrLge-3/I-2 (W)

League Club	Source	Date Signed	Seasons Played	Apps	Subs	Gls
Fulham	Belfast Celtic	03.49	49-52	62	-	4

CAMPBELL Joseph (Joe)
Glasgow, 28 March, 1925 (IF)

League Club	Source	Date Signed	Seasons Played	Apps	Subs	Gls
Leyton Orient	Glasgow Celtic	07.49	49	5	-	1
Gillingham	Tr	09.50	50	12	-	2

CAMPBELL Kevin Joseph
Lambeth, 4 February, 1970 Eu21-4/EB-1 (F)

League Club	Source	Date Signed	Seasons Played	Apps	Subs	Gls
Arsenal	YT	02.88	87-94	124	42	46
Leyton Orient	L	01.89	88	16	0	9
Leicester C	L	11.89	89	11	0	5
Nottingham F	Tr	07.95	95-97	79	1	32
Everton	Trabzonspor (Tu)	03.99	98-04	125	20	45
West Bromwich A	Tr	01.05	04	16	0	3

CAMPBELL Leslie (Les)
Wigan, 26 July, 1935 (W)

League Club	Source	Date Signed	Seasons Played	Apps	Subs	Gls
Preston NE	Wigan Ath	06.53	53-59	64	-	6
Blackpool	Tr	07.60	60	11	-	0
Tranmere Rov	Tr	06.61	61-63	102	-	9

CAMPBELL Michael (Mike)
Oban, 19 November, 1966 (M)

League Club	Source	Date Signed	Seasons Played	Apps	Subs	Gls
Hereford U		08.88	88	1	0	0

CAMPBELL Neil Andrew
Middlesbrough, 26 January, 1977 (F)

League Club	Source	Date Signed	Seasons Played	Apps	Subs	Gls
York C	YT	06.95	96-97	6	6	1
Scarborough	Tr	09.97	97-98	23	22	7
Southend U	Tr	01.99	98-99	15	9	3

CAMPBELL Paul Andrew
Middlesbrough, 29 January, 1980 (M)

League Club	Source	Date Signed	Seasons Played	Apps	Subs	Gls
Darlington	YT	07.98	97-02	35	26	6

CAMPBELL Paul John
Newcastle, 7 October, 1964 (M)

League Club	Source	Date Signed	Seasons Played	Apps	Subs	Gls
Hartlepool U	Gateshead	10.83	83	1	2	0

CAMPBELL Philip (Phil) Anthony
Barnsley, 16 October, 1961 (W)

League Club	Source	Date Signed	Seasons Played	Apps	Subs	Gls
Sheffield Wed	App	10.79	80	0	1	0

CAMPBELL Raymond (Ray) Martin John
Downpatrick, 3 October, 1968 (W)

League Club	Source	Date Signed	Seasons Played	Apps	Subs	Gls
Nottingham F	App	10.86				
Hereford U	L	01.88	87	4	0	0

CAMPBELL Robert (Bobby)
Liverpool, 23 April, 1937 EYth (WH)

League Club	Source	Date Signed	Seasons Played	Apps	Subs	Gls
Liverpool	Jnrs	05.54	58-60	24	-	2
Portsmouth	Wigan Ath	11.61	61-65	60	1	2
Aldershot	Tr	07.66	66	2	3	0

CAMPBELL Robert (Bobby) Inglis
Glasgow, 28 June, 1922 S-5 (W)

League Club	Source	Date Signed	Seasons Played	Apps	Subs	Gls
Chelsea	Falkirk	05.47	47-53	188	-	36
Reading	Tr	08.54	54-57	94	-	12

CAMPBELL Robert (Bobby) McFaul
Belfast, 13 September, 1956 NIYth/NI-2 (F)

League Club	Source	Date Signed	Seasons Played	Apps	Subs	Gls
Aston Villa	App	01.74	73-74	7	3	1
Halifax T	L	02.75	74	14	1	0
Huddersfield T	Tr	04.75	75-76	30	1	9
Sheffield U	Tr	07.77	77	35	2	11
Huddersfield T	Vancouver (Can)	09.78	78	7	0	3
Halifax T	Tr	10.78	78	19	3	3
Bradford C	Brisbane C (Aus)	12.79	79-82	147	1	76
Derby Co	Tr	08.83	83	11	0	4
Bradford C	Tr	11.83	83-86	126	0	45
Wigan Ath	Tr	10.86	86-87	61	8	27

CAMPBELL Roy
Congleton, 19 October, 1934 (WH)

League Club	Source	Date Signed	Seasons Played	Apps	Subs	Gls
Crewe Alex		12.55	55-56	14	-	0

CAMPBELL Sean Martin
Bristol, 31 December, 1974 (W)

League Club	Source	Date Signed	Seasons Played	Apps	Subs	Gls
Colchester U	YT	07.93	93	1	3	0

CAMPBELL Stuart Pearson
Corby, 9 December, 1977 Su21-14 (M)

League Club	Source	Date Signed	Seasons Played	Apps	Subs	Gls
Leicester C	YT	07.96	96-99	12	25	0
Birmingham C	L	03.00	99	0	2	0
Grimsby T	Tr	09.00	00-03	154	1	12
Bristol Rov	Tr	07.04	04	21	4	0

CAMPBELL Sulzeer (Sol) Jeremiah
Newham, 18 September, 1974 EYth/Eu21-11/EB-1/E-65 (CD)

League Club	Source	Date Signed	Seasons Played	Apps	Subs	Gls
Tottenham H	YT	09.92	92-00	246	9	10
Arsenal	Tr	07.01	01-04	113	2	6

CAMPBELL Thomas (Tommy) McMillan
Glasgow, 20 February, 1935 (CF)

League Club	Source	Date Signed	Seasons Played	Apps	Subs	Gls
Tranmere Rov	Dundee U	06.61	61	1	-	0

CAMPBELL William (Billy) Gibson
Belfast, 2 July, 1944 IrLge-3/NI-6 (W)

League Club	Source	Date Signed	Seasons Played	Apps	Subs	Gls
Sunderland	Distillery	09.64	64-65	5	0	0

CAMPBELL Winston Richard
Sheffield, 9 October, 1962 (W)

League Club	Source	Date Signed	Seasons Played	Apps	Subs	Gls
Barnsley	App	10.80	79-86	121	7	9
Doncaster Rov	L	01.83	82	3	0	0
Rotherham U	Tr	09.86	86-87	67	2	9

CAMPBELL-RYCE Jamal Julian
Lambeth, 6 April, 1983 Jau20/Ja-1 (F)

League Club	Source	Date Signed	Seasons Played	Apps	Subs	Gls
Charlton Ath	Sch	07.02	02-03	0	3	0
Leyton Orient	L	08.02	02	16	1	2
Wimbledon	L	02.04	03	3	1	0
Chesterfield	L	08.04	04	14	0	0
Rotherham U	Tr	11.04	04	23	1	0

CAMPO Ramos **Ivan**
San Sebastian, Spain, 21 February, 1974 Spain 4 (CD)

League Club	Source	Date Signed	Seasons Played	Apps	Subs	Gls
Bolton W	Real Madrid (Sp)	08.02	02-04	85	11	6

CANDELA Vincent
Bedarieux, France, 24 October, 1973 France 40 (FB)

League Club	Source	Date Signed	Seasons Played	Apps	Subs	Gls
Bolton W	AS Roma (It)	01.05	04	9	1	0

CANDLIN Maurice Hall
Jarrow, 11 November, 1921 Died 1992 (WH)

League Club	Source	Date Signed	Seasons Played	Apps	Subs	Gls
Northampton T	Stirling A	02.49	49-52	139	-	1
Shrewsbury T	Tr	07.53	53-54	69	-	2

CANERO Peter
Glasgow, 18 January, 1981 Su21-17/SB-3/S-1 (FB)

League Club	Source	Date Signed	Seasons Played	Apps	Subs	Gls
Leicester C	Kilmarnock	01.04	03-04	8	5	0

CANHAM Anthony (Tony)
Leeds, 8 June, 1960 (W)

League Club	Source	Date Signed	Seasons Played	Apps	Subs	Gls
York C	Harrogate RI	01.85	84-94	309	38	57
Hartlepool U	Tr	08.95	95	25	4	1

CANHAM Marc David
Wegburg, Germany, 11 September, 1982 (M)

League Club	Source	Date Signed	Seasons Played	Apps	Subs	Gls
Colchester U	Sch	07.02	01-02	2	2	0

CANHAM Scott Walter
Stratford, 5 November, 1974 (M)

League Club	Source	Date Signed	Seasons Played	Apps	Subs	Gls
West Ham U	YT	07.93				
Torquay U	L	11.95	95	3	0	0
Brentford	L	01.96	95	14	0	0
Brentford	Tr	08.96	96-97	24	11	1
Leyton Orient	Tr	08.98	98-99	3	6	0
Leyton Orient	Chesham U	07.01	01-02	32	8	6

CANN Darren John
Torquay, 17 June, 1968 (CD)

League Club	Source	Date Signed	Seasons Played	Apps	Subs	Gls
Torquay U	App	06.87	86-87	12	1	0

CANN Ralph Graham
Sheffield, 17 November, 1934 (CD)

League Club	Source	Date Signed	Seasons Played	Apps	Subs	Gls
Mansfield T		05.57	57	1	-	0

CANNELL Paul Anthony
Newcastle, 2 September, 1953 ESch (F)

League Club	Source	Date Signed	Seasons Played	Apps	Subs	Gls
Newcastle U	Jnrs	07.72	73-77	48	1	13
Mansfield T	North Shields	01.82	81-82	29	1	4

CANNELL Stuart
Doncaster, 31 December, 1958 (CD)

League Club	Source	Date Signed	Seasons Played	Apps	Subs	Gls
Doncaster Rov	Bentley Victoria	03.78	77-78	22	4	0

CANNING Leslie **Daniel (Danny)**
Pontypridd, 21 February, 1926 (G)

League Club	Source	Date Signed	Seasons Played	Apps	Subs	Gls
Cardiff C	Abercynon	07.45	46-47	80	-	0
Swansea T	Tr	01.49	48-50	47	-	0
Nottingham F	Tr	07.51	51	5	-	0

CANNING Lawrence (Larry)
Cowdenbeath, 1 November, 1925 (WH)

League Club	Source	Date Signed	Seasons Played	Apps	Subs	Gls
Aston Villa	Paget Rgrs	10.47	48-53	39	-	3
Northampton T	Kettering T	06.56	56	2	-	0

CANNON James (Jim)
Coatbridge, 19 March, 1927 (IF)

League Club	Source	Date Signed	Seasons Played	Apps	Subs	Gls
Darlington	Third Lanark	06.56	56	12	-	1

CANNON James (Jim) Anthony
Glasgow, 2 October, 1953 (CD)

League Club	Source	Date Signed	Seasons Played	Apps	Subs	Gls
Crystal Palace	App	05.71	72-87	568	3	30

CANOVILLE Dean
Perivale, 30 November, 1978 (M)

League Club	Source	Date Signed	Seasons Played	Apps	Subs	Gls
Millwall	Jnrs	12.95	96	0	2	0

CANOVILLE Lee
Ealing, 14 March, 1981 ESch/EYth (FB)

League Club	Source	Date Signed	Seasons Played	Apps	Subs	Gls
Arsenal	YT	07.98				
Northampton T	L	01.01	00	2	0	0
Torquay U	Tr	09.01	01-04	107	5	2

CANOVILLE Paul Kenneth
Hillingdon, 4 March, 1962 (W)

League Club	Source	Date Signed	Seasons Played	Apps	Subs	Gls
Chelsea	Hillingdon Borough	12.81	81-85	53	26	11
Reading	Tr	08.86	86-87	16	0	4

CANSDELL-SHERIFF Shane Lewis
Sydney, Australia, 10 November, 1982 (CD)

League Club	Source	Date Signed	Seasons Played	Apps	Subs	Gls
Leeds U	NSW Soccer Acad (Aus)	02.00				
Rochdale	L	11.02	02	3	0	0

CANTELLO Leonard (Len)
Newton Heath, 11 September, 1951 ESch/EYth/Eu23-8 (M)

League Club	Source	Date Signed	Seasons Played	Apps	Subs	Gls
West Bromwich A	App	10.68	68-78	297	4	13
Bolton W	Tr	06.79	79-81	89	1	3
Hereford U	Eastern Ath (HK)	01.83	82	1	0	0
Bury	Tr	02.83	82	8	1	1

CANTONA Eric
Paris, France, 24 May, 1966 France int (F)

League Club	Source	Date Signed	Seasons Played	Apps	Subs	Gls
Leeds U	Nimes (Fr)	02.92	91-92	18	10	9
Manchester U	Tr	11.92	92-96	142	1	64

CANTONA Joel
Paris, France, 26 October, 1967 (M)

League Club	Source	Date Signed	Seasons Played	Apps	Subs	Gls
Stockport Co	Ujpest Dosza (Hun)	03.94	93	0	3	0

CANTWELL Noel Eucharia
Cork, 28 December, 1932 IR-36 (FB)

League Club	Source	Date Signed	Seasons Played	Apps	Subs	Gls
West Ham U	Cork Celtic	09.52	52-60	248	-	11
Manchester U	Tr	11.60	60-66	123	0	6

CANVIN Cyril Edward
Hemel Hempstead, 23 January, 1924 Died 1950 (IF)

League Club	Source	Date Signed	Seasons Played	Apps	Subs	Gls
Leyton Orient	Apsley	03.47	46	3	-	0

CAPALDI Anthony (Tony) Charles
Porsgrunn, Norway, 12 August, 1981 NIYth/NIu21-14/NI-11 (FB)

League Club	Source	Date Signed	Seasons Played	Apps	Subs	Gls
Birmingham C	YT	07.99				
Plymouth Arg	Tr	05.03	02-04	54	15	9

CAPE John (Jackie) Phillips
Carlisle, 16 November, 1911 Died 1994 (W)

League Club	Source	Date Signed	Seasons Played	Apps	Subs	Gls
Carlisle U	Penrith	05.29	29	15	-	2
Newcastle U	Tr	01.30	29-33	51	-	18
Manchester U	Tr	01.34	33-36	59	-	18
Queens Park Rgrs	Tr	06.37	37-38	61	-	12
Carlisle U	Tr	08.39				
Carlisle U	Scarborough	10.46	46	3	-	0

CAPEL Frederick (Fred) John
Manchester, 14 January, 1927 Died 1990 (FB)

League Club	Source	Date Signed	Seasons Played	Apps	Subs	Gls
Chesterfield	Goslings	06.48	49-56	285	-	16

CAPEL John Elwyn
Newport, 31 March, 1937 WSch (W)

League Club	Source	Date Signed	Seasons Played	Apps	Subs	Gls
Newport Co	Jnrs	12.55	55	3	-	0

CAPEL Maurice John
Crewe, 15 February, 1935 (CF)

League Club	Source	Date Signed	Seasons Played	Apps	Subs	Gls
Crewe Alex	Whitchurch Alport	04.56	55-56	6	-	0

CAPEL Thomas (Tommy)
Chorlton, 27 June, 1922 (IF)

League Club	Source	Date Signed	Seasons Played	Apps	Subs	Gls
Manchester C	Droylsden	11.41	46-47	9	-	2
Chesterfield	Tr	10.47	47-48	62	-	27
Birmingham C	Tr	06.49	49	8	-	2
Nottingham F	Tr	11.49	49-53	154	-	69
Coventry C	Tr	06.54	54-55	36	-	19
Halifax T	Tr	10.55	55	7	-	1

CAPEWELL Ronald (Ron)
Sheffield, 26 July, 1929 (G)

League Club	Source	Date Signed	Seasons Played	Apps	Subs	Gls
Sheffield Wed		03.50	52-53	29	-	0
Hull C	Tr	07.54	54	1	-	0

CAPLETON Melvyn (Mel) David
Hackney, 24 October, 1973 (G)

League Club	Source	Date Signed	Seasons Played	Apps	Subs	Gls
Southend U	YT	07.92				
Blackpool	Tr	08.93	94-95	9	2	0
Leyton Orient	Grays Ath	09.98				
Southend U	Tr	10.98	98-00	54	3	0

CAPPER John (Jack)
Wrexham, 23 July, 1931 (CD)

League Club	Source	Date Signed	Seasons Played	Apps	Subs	Gls
Wrexham	Jnrs	11.49	52-54	48	-	0
Lincoln C	Headington U	01.56	55-58	21	-	0
Chester	Tr	09.59	59-60	37	-	0

CAPSTICK Albert Lewin
South Kirkby, 2 January, 1928 (WH)

League Club	Source	Date Signed	Seasons Played	Apps	Subs	Gls
Accrington St	Fleetwood	08.48	48	1	-	0

CARASSO Cedric
Avignon, France, 30 December, 1981 (G)

League Club	Source	Date Signed	Seasons Played	Apps	Subs	Gls
Crystal Palace (L)	Avignon (Fr)	12.01	01	0	1	0

CARBERRY James (Jimmy)
Liverpool, 13 October, 1969 (W)

League Club	Source	Date Signed	Seasons Played	Apps	Subs	Gls
Everton	YT	06.88				
Wigan Ath	Tr	06.89	89-91	30	35	6

CARBERRY Lawrence (Larry) James
Liverpool, 18 January, 1936 (FB)

League Club	Source	Date Signed	Seasons Played	Apps	Subs	Gls
Ipswich T	Bootle	05.56	56-64	257	-	0
Barrow	Tr	07.65	65-66	17	0	0

CARBERRY Robert (Bert)
Glasgow, 16 January, 1931 (CD)

League Club	Source	Date Signed	Seasons Played	Apps	Subs	Gls
Norwich C	Avondale	01.49	53-54	5	-	0
Gillingham	Bedford T	07.56	56	1	-	0
Port Vale	Tr	07.57	57	29	-	0

CARBON Matthew (Matt) Philip
Nottingham, 8 June, 1975 Eu21-4 (CD)

League Club	Source	Date Signed	Seasons Played	Apps	Subs	Gls
Lincoln C	YT	04.93	92-95	66	3	10
Derby Co	Tr	03.96	95-97	11	9	0
West Bromwich A	Tr	01.98	97-00	106	7	5
Walsall	Tr	07.01	01-03	49	6	2
Lincoln C	L	10.03	03	1	0	0
Barnsley	Tr	07.04	04	16	10	0

CARBONARI Horacio Angel
Rosario, Argentina, 2 May, 1973 (CD)

League Club	Source	Date Signed	Seasons Played	Apps	Subs	Gls
Derby Co	Rosario Central (Arg)	07.98	98-02	89	1	9
Coventry C	L	03.02	01	5	0	0

CARBONE Benito
Bagnara Calabra, Italy, 14 August, 1971 Itu21 (F)

League Club	Source	Date Signed	Seasons Played	Apps	Subs	Gls
Sheffield Wed	Inter Milan (It)	10.96	96-99	86	10	25
Aston Villa	Tr	10.99	99	22	2	3
Bradford C	Tr	08.00	00-01	39	3	10
Derby Co	L	10.01	01	13	0	1
Middlesbrough	L	02.02	01	13	0	1

CARDEN Paul Andrew
Liverpool, 29 March, 1979 (M)

League Club	Source	Date Signed	Seasons Played	Apps	Subs	Gls
Blackpool	YT	07.97	96	0	1	0
Rochdale	Tr	03.98	97-99	30	15	0
Chester C	Tr	03.00	99-04	45	6	0

CARDEW Norman
South Shields, 7 November, 1938 (IF)

League Club	Source	Date Signed	Seasons Played	Apps	Subs	Gls
Darlington (Am)	South Shields	07.65	65	5	0	1

CARDWELL Louis
Blackpool, 20 August, 1912 Died 1986 (CD)

League Club	Source	Date Signed	Seasons Played	Apps	Subs	Gls
Blackpool	Whitegate Jnrs	04.30	30-37	132	-	6
Manchester C	Tr	09.38	38-46	39	-	0
Crewe Alex	Netherfield	10.47	47-48	25	-	0

CAREY Alan William
Greenwich, 21 August, 1975 (F)

League Club	Source	Date Signed	Seasons Played	Apps	Subs	Gls
Reading	YT	07.94	93-94	0	3	0

CAREY Brian Patrick
Cork, 31 May, 1968 IRu21-1/IR-3 (CD)

League Club	Source	Date Signed	Seasons Played	Apps	Subs	Gls
Manchester U	Cork C	09.89				
Wrexham	L	01.91	90	3	0	0
Wrexham	L	12.91	91	13	0	1
Leicester C	Tr	07.93	93-95	51	7	1
Wrexham	Tr	07.96	96-04	282	6	15

CAREY John (Johnny) Joseph
Dublin, 23 February, 1919 Died 1995 IWar-2/IR-29/I-7 (FB)

League Club	Source	Date Signed	Seasons Played	Apps	Subs	Gls
Manchester U	St James' Gate	11.36	37-52	304	-	16

CAREY Louis Anthony
Bristol, 20 January, 1977 Su21-1 (FB)

League Club	Source	Date Signed	Seasons Played	Apps	Subs	Gls
Bristol C	YT	07.95	95-03	301	11	5
Coventry C	Tr	07.04	04	23	0	0
Bristol C	Tr	02.05	04	14	0	0

CAREY Peter Richard
Barking, 14 April, 1933 (FB)

League Club	Source	Date Signed	Seasons Played	Apps	Subs	Gls
Leyton Orient	Barking	10.57	56-59	34	-	2
Queens Park Rgrs	Tr	07.60	60	15	-	1
Colchester U	Tr	11.60	60	10	-	0
Aldershot	Tr	08.61	61-62	47	-	0

CAREY Richard (Dick)
Paisley, 19 November, 1927 Died 2004 (WH)

League Club	Source	Date Signed	Seasons Played	Apps	Subs	Gls
Southport	Cowdenbeath	07.49	49	1	-	0

CAREY Shaun Peter
Rushden, 13 May, 1976 IRu21-2 (M)

League Club	Source	Date Signed	Seasons Played	Apps	Subs	Gls
Norwich C	YT	07.94	95-99	50	18	0
Rushden & Diamonds	Tr	08.00	01	7	1	0

CARGILL David Anderson
Arbroath, 21 July, 1936 (W)

League Club	Source	Date Signed	Seasons Played	Apps	Subs	Gls
Burnley	Jnrs	07.53	53-55	5	-	0
Sheffield Wed	Tr	09.56	56-57	10	-	0
Derby Co	Tr	04.58	58-60	56	-	8
Lincoln C	Tr	12.60	60	9	-	0

CARGILL James (Jim) Gordon
Alyth, 22 September, 1945 SSch (G)

League Club	Source	Date Signed	Seasons Played	Apps	Subs	Gls
Nottingham F	Dundee North End	09.62	64-65	2	0	0
Notts Co	Tr	07.66	66	10	0	0

CARLESS Ernest (Ernie) Francis
Barry, 9 September, 1912 Died 1987 (IF)

League Club	Source	Date Signed	Seasons Played	Apps	Subs	Gls
Cardiff C	Wolverhampton W (Am)	10.32	32	1	-	0
Plymouth Arg	Barry T	12.46	46	4	-	0

CARLIN Patrick (Pat)
Dunscroft, 17 December, 1929 (FB)

League Club	Source	Date Signed	Seasons Played	Apps	Subs	Gls
Bradford PA	Dunscroft	07.53	53	6	-	0

CARLIN William (Willie)
Liverpool, 6 October, 1940 ESch/EYth (M)

League Club	Source	Date Signed	Seasons Played	Apps	Subs	Gls
Liverpool	Jnrs	05.58	59	1	-	0
Halifax T	Tr	08.62	62-64	95	-	31
Carlisle U	Tr	10.64	64-67	93	0	20
Sheffield U	Tr	09.67	67-68	36	0	3
Derby Co	Tr	08.68	68-70	89	0	14
Leicester C	Tr	10.70	70-71	31	0	1
Notts Co	Tr	09.71	71-73	57	3	2
Cardiff C	Tr	11.73	73	22	0	1

CARLINE Peter
Chesterfield, 2 March, 1951 Died 2001 (CD)

League Club	Source	Date Signed	Seasons Played	Apps	Subs	Gls
Chesterfield	Jnrs	09.70	70	1	0	0

CARLING Terence (Terry) Patrick
Otley, 26 February, 1939 (G)

League Club	Source	Date Signed	Seasons Played	Apps	Subs	Gls
Leeds U	Dawson's P & E	11.56	60-61	5	-	0
Lincoln C	Tr	07.62	62-63	84	-	0
Walsall	Tr	06.64	64-66	101	0	0
Chester	Tr	12.66	66-70	199	0	0

CARLISLE Clarke James
Preston, 14 October, 1979 Eu21-3 (CD)

League Club	Source	Date Signed	Seasons Played	Apps	Subs	Gls
Blackpool	YT	08.97	97-99	85	8	7
Queens Park Rgrs	Tr	05.00	00-03	93	3	6
Leeds U	Tr	07.04	04	29	6	4

CARLISLE Wayne Thomas
Lisburn, 9 September, 1979 NISch/NIYth/NIu21-9 (M)

League Club	Source	Date Signed	Seasons Played	Apps	Subs	Gls
Crystal Palace	YT	09.96	98-00	29	17	3
Swindon T	L	10.01	01	10	1	2
Bristol Rov	Tr	03.02	01-03	62	9	14
Leyton Orient	Tr	07.04	04	24	4	3

CARLSON George Edward
Liverpool, 27 July, 1925 (CF)

League Club	Source	Date Signed	Seasons Played	Apps	Subs	Gls
Tranmere Rov		09.47	47-48	2	-	0

CARLTON David George
Stepney, 24 November, 1952 (M)

League Club	Source	Date Signed	Seasons Played	Apps	Subs	Gls
Fulham	App	12.69	71-72	5	4	0
Northampton T	Tr	10.73	73-76	99	5	6
Brentford	Tr	10.76	76-79	138	2	7
Northampton T	Tr	09.80	80-81	76	0	1

CARMICHAEL John (Jack)
Newcastle, 11 November, 1948 (CD)

League Club	Source	Date Signed	Seasons Played	Apps	Subs	Gls
Arsenal	Possilpark Jnrs	11.66				
Peterborough U	Tr	01.71	70-79	331	21	5
Swindon T	New England (USA)	09.80				
Peterborough U	Jacksonville (USA)	01.83	82	5	1	0

CARMICHAEL Matthew (Matt)
Singapore, 13 May, 1964 (F)

League Club	Source	Date Signed	Seasons Played	Apps	Subs	Gls
Lincoln C	Basingstoke T	08.89	89-92	113	20	18
Scunthorpe U	Tr	07.93	93-94	51	11	20
Barnet	L	09.94	94	2	1	0
Preston NE	Tr	03.95	94	7	3	3
Mansfield T	Tr	08.95	95	1	0	1
Doncaster Rov	Tr	08.95	95	19	8	4
Darlington	Tr	02.96	95	11	2	2

CARMODY Michael (Mike) Joseph
Huddersfield, 9 February, 1966 (FB)

League Club	Source	Date Signed	Seasons Played	Apps	Subs	Gls
Huddersfield T	Emley	12.84	84	8	0	0
Tranmere Rov	Emley	09.86	86	2	0	0

CARNABY Brian James
Plymouth, 14 December, 1947 (M)

League Club	Source	Date Signed	Seasons Played	Apps	Subs	Gls
Reading	Arcadia Shepherds (SA)	07.72	72-76	136	9	10

CARNEY Leonard (Len) Francis
Liverpool, 30 May, 1915 Died 1996 (IF)

League Club	Source	Date Signed	Seasons Played	Apps	Subs	Gls
Liverpool (Am)	Collegiate OB	07.46	46-47	6	-	1

CARNEY Stephen (Steve)
Wallsend, 22 September, 1957 (CD)

League Club	Source	Date Signed	Seasons Played	Apps	Subs	Gls
Newcastle U	Blyth Spartans	10.79	79-84	125	9	1
Carlisle U	L	03.85	84	6	0	0
Darlington	Tr	08.85	85	10	2	0
Rochdale	L	01.86	85	4	0	0
Hartlepool U	Tr	03.86	85	7	0	0

CAROLAN Joseph (Joe) Francis
Dublin, 8 September, 1937 IR-2 (FB)

League Club	Source	Date Signed	Seasons Played	Apps	Subs	Gls
Manchester U	Home Farm	02.56	58-60	66	-	0
Brighton & Hove A	Tr	12.60	60-61	33	-	0

CAROLE Sebastien
Pontoise, France, 8 September, 1982 (F)

League Club	Source	Date Signed	Seasons Played	Apps	Subs	Gls
West Ham U (L)	AS Monaco (Fr)	01.04	03	0	1	0

CAROLIN Brian
Ashington, 6 December, 1939 (WH)

League Club	Source	Date Signed	Seasons Played	Apps	Subs	Gls
Gateshead		08.57	57-59	17	-	0

CARPENTER Richard
Sheerness, 30 September, 1972 (M)

League Club	Source	Date Signed	Seasons Played	Apps	Subs	Gls
Gillingham	YT	05.91	90-96	107	15	4
Fulham	Tr	09.96	96-97	49	9	7
Cardiff C	Tr	07.98	98-99	69	6	2
Brighton & Hove A	Tr	07.00	00-04	197	8	18

CARPENTER Stephen (Steve)
Torquay, 23 September, 1960 (M)

League Club	Source	Date Signed	Seasons Played	Apps	Subs	Gls
Torquay U	STC	04.86	85	2	0	0

CARPENTER Thomas (Tommy) Albert Edward
Carshalton, 11 March, 1925 (G)

League Club	Source	Date Signed	Seasons Played	Apps	Subs	Gls
Watford	Harrow T	11.50	50	4	-	0

CARR Ashley
Crowland, 15 August, 1968 (M)

League Club	Source	Date Signed	Seasons Played	Apps	Subs	Gls
Peterborough U	Jnrs	08.86	86-88	9	6	0

CARR Christopher (Chris) Paul
Newcastle, 14 December, 1984 (FB)

League Club	Source	Date Signed	Seasons Played	Apps	Subs	Gls
Sheffield Wed	Newcastle U (Sch)	03.04	03	0	2	0

CARR Clifford (Cliff) Paul
Clapton, 19 June, 1964 Eu21-1 (FB)

League Club	Source	Date Signed	Seasons Played	Apps	Subs	Gls
Fulham	App	06.82	82-86	136	9	14
Stoke C	Tr	07.87	87-90	116	8	1
Shrewsbury T	Tr	08.91	91	1	0	1
Mansfield T	Telford U	10.91	91	20	0	0
Chesterfield	Tr	08.92	92-93	62	3	1

CARR Darren John
Bristol, 4 September, 1968 (CD)

League Club	Source	Date Signed	Seasons Played	Apps	Subs	Gls
Bristol Rov	App	08.86	85-87	26	4	0
Newport Co	Tr	10.87	87	9	0	0
Sheffield U	Tr	03.88	87-88	12	1	1
Crewe Alex	Tr	09.90	90-92	96	8	5
Chesterfield	Tr	07.93	93-97	84	2	4
Gillingham	Tr	08.98	98	22	8	2
Brighton & Hove A	Tr	07.99	99-00	18	3	0
Rotherham U	L	11.00	00	1	0	0
Lincoln C	L	01.01	00	3	0	0
Carlisle U	L	02.01	00	10	0	0
Rushden & Diamonds	Tr	01.02	01	1	0	0

CARR David (Dave)
Wheatley Hill, 19 January, 1937 (IF)

League Club	Source	Date Signed	Seasons Played	Apps	Subs	Gls
Darlington	Spennymoor U	05.57	57-61	132	-	50
Workington	Tr	07.62	62-64	108	-	47
Watford	Tr	02.65	64-65	10	0	3

CARR David (Dave)
Aylesham, 31 January, 1957 Died 2005 (CD)

League Club	Source	Date Signed	Seasons Played	Apps	Subs	Gls
Luton T	App	01.75	76-78	39	4	0
Lincoln C	Tr	07.79	79-82	165	3	4
Torquay U	Tr	08.83	83	34	0	0

CARR Derek Henry
Blidworth, 1 September, 1927 (WH)

League Club	Source	Date Signed	Seasons Played	Apps	Subs	Gls
Birmingham C	Lockheed Leamington	02.48	49	3	-	0

CARR Edward (Eddie) Miller
Wheatley Hill, 3 October, 1917 Died 1998 (IF)

League Club	Source	Date Signed	Seasons Played	Apps	Subs	Gls
Arsenal	Wheatley Hill Coll	05.35	37-38	12	-	7
Huddersfield T	Tr	10.45	46	2	-	0
Newport Co	Tr	10.46	46-49	98	-	48
Bradford C	Tr	10.49	49-52	94	-	49
Darlington	Tr	08.53	53	7	-	0

CARR Everton Dale
Antigua, 11 January, 1961 (FB)

League Club	Source	Date Signed	Seasons Played	Apps	Subs	Gls
Leicester C	App	01.79	78-80	11	1	0
Halifax T	Tr	08.81	81-82	49	4	0
Rochdale	Tr	03.83	82	9	0	0

CARR Francis (Frank)
Maltby, 21 April, 1919 (IF)

League Club	Source	Date Signed	Seasons Played	Apps	Subs	Gls
Rotherham U		09.41				
York C	Tr	08.46	46	7	-	3

CARR Franz Alexander
Preston, 24 September, 1966 EYth/Eu21-9 (W)

League Club	Source	Date Signed	Seasons Played	Apps	Subs	Gls
Blackburn Rov	App	07.84				
Nottingham F	Tr	08.84	85-90	122	9	17
Sheffield Wed	L	12.89	89	9	3	0

League Club	Source	Date Signed	Seasons Played	Apps	Subs	Gls
West Ham U	L	03.91	90	1	2	0
Newcastle U	Tr	06.91	91-92	20	5	3
Sheffield U	Tr	01.93	92-93	18	0	4
Leicester C	Tr	09.94	94	12	1	1
Aston Villa	Tr	02.95	94-95	1	2	0
Bolton W	Reggiana (It)	10.97	97	0	5	0
West Bromwich A	Tr	02.98	97	1	3	0

CARR Graeme
Chester-le-Street, 28 October, 1978 (M)

League Club	Source	Date Signed	Seasons Played	Apps	Subs	Gls
Scarborough	YT	09.97	98	5	5	0

CARR Graham Gordon
Darlington, 8 December, 1970 (G)

League Club	Source	Date Signed	Seasons Played	Apps	Subs	Gls
Hartlepool U	YT	08.89	89	1	0	0

CARR William **Graham**
Corbridge, 25 October, 1944 EYth (CD)

League Club	Source	Date Signed	Seasons Played	Apps	Subs	Gls
Northampton T	Jnrs	08.62	62-67	84	1	0
York C	Tr	06.68	68	32	1	1
Bradford PA	Tr	07.69	69	42	0	2

CARR John (Jackie)
Bishopbriggs, 12 January, 1924 (W)

League Club	Source	Date Signed	Seasons Played	Apps	Subs	Gls
Gillingham	Alloa Ath	06.48	50	11	-	2

CARR John William
Durban, South Africa, 10 June, 1926 (W)

League Club	Source	Date Signed	Seasons Played	Apps	Subs	Gls
Huddersfield T	Durban Railway (SA)	10.50	50	1	-	0

CARR Kevin
Morpeth, 6 November, 1958 (G)

League Club	Source	Date Signed	Seasons Played	Apps	Subs	Gls
Newcastle U	Burnley (App)	07.76	77-84	173	0	0
Carlisle U	Tr	08.85	85-86	17	0	0
Darlington	L	11.86	86	3	0	0
Hartlepool U	Middlesbrough (N/C)	07.87	87	31	0	0

CARR Lance Lanyon
Johannesburg, South Africa, 18 February, 1910 Died 1983 (W)

League Club	Source	Date Signed	Seasons Played	Apps	Subs	Gls
Liverpool	Boksburg (SA)	08.33	33-35	31	-	8
Newport Co	Tr	10.36	36	25	-	5
Newport Co	South Liverpool	07.38	38	39	-	9
Bristol Rov	Tr	08.46	46	42	-	8

CARR Michael Andrew
Crewe, 6 December, 1983 (FB)

League Club	Source	Date Signed	Seasons Played	Apps	Subs	Gls
Macclesfield T	Sch	07.03	02-03	11	0	0

CARR Peter
Bishop Middleham, 25 August, 1951 (FB)

League Club	Source	Date Signed	Seasons Played	Apps	Subs	Gls
Darlington	App	08.69	67-72	131	4	1
Carlisle U	Tr	11.72	72-77	202	2	1
Hartlepool U	New England (USA)	10.79	79	22	0	0

CARR Peter
Rawmarsh, 16 November, 1960 (M)

League Club	Source	Date Signed	Seasons Played	Apps	Subs	Gls
Rotherham U	App	11.78	78-81	31	5	3

CARR Stanley (Stan) Rushton
Southport, 1 June, 1926 (FB)

League Club	Source	Date Signed	Seasons Played	Apps	Subs	Gls
Southport	Brockhouse	10.45				
New Brighton	Tr	08.48	48	1	-	0

CARR Stephen (Steve)
Dublin, 29 August, 1976 IRSch/IRYth/IRu21-12/IR-37 (FB)

League Club	Source	Date Signed	Seasons Played	Apps	Subs	Gls
Tottenham H	YT	09.93	93-03	222	4	7
Newcastle U	Tr	08.04	04	26	0	1

CARR William (Willie) McInanny
Glasgow, 6 January, 1950 Su23-4/S-6 (M)

League Club	Source	Date Signed	Seasons Played	Apps	Subs	Gls
Coventry C	App	07.67	67-74	245	7	33
Wolverhampton W	Tr	03.75	74-81	231	6	21
Millwall	Tr	08.82	82	8	0	1

CARRAGHER James (Jamie) Lee Duncan
Bootle, 28 January, 1978 EYth/Eu21-27/EB-2/E-17 (FB)

League Club	Source	Date Signed	Seasons Played	Apps	Subs	Gls
Liverpool	YT	10.96	96-04	242	12	2

CARRAGHER Matthew
Liverpool, 14 January, 1976 (FB)

League Club	Source	Date Signed	Seasons Played	Apps	Subs	Gls
Wigan Ath	YT	11.93	93-96	102	17	0
Port Vale	Tr	07.97	97-02	190	4	1
Macclesfield T	Stafford Rgrs	11.03	03-04	44	5	0

CARRATT Philip (Phil) Edward
Stockport, 22 October, 1981 (F)

League Club	Source	Date Signed	Seasons Played	Apps	Subs	Gls
Stockport Co	YT	09.00	00-01	0	4	0

CARRICK Matthew **David (Dave)**
Evenwood, 5 December, 1946 Died 1989 (W)

League Club	Source	Date Signed	Seasons Played	Apps	Subs	Gls
Wolverhampton W	App	12.64				
Wrexham	Tr	07.66	66-67	20	4	3

League Club	Source	Date Signed	Seasons Played	Apps	Subs	Gls
Port Vale	Altrincham	01.69	68	14	2	1
Preston NE	Witton A	11.73	73	0	2	0
Rochdale	Tr	03.74	73-74	25	1	4

CARRICK Michael
Wallsend, 28 July, 1981 EYth/Eu21-14/E-2 (M)

League Club	Source	Date Signed	Seasons Played	Apps	Subs	Gls
West Ham U	YT	08.98	99-03	128	8	6
Swindon T	L	11.99	99	6	0	2
Birmingham C	L	02.00	99	1	1	0
Tottenham H	Tr	08.04	04	26	3	0

CARRICK William (Willie) Francis
Dublin, 26 September, 1952 (G)

League Club	Source	Date Signed	Seasons Played	Apps	Subs	Gls
Manchester U	App	09.70				
Luton T	Tr	07.72	72	4	0	0

CARRIGAN Brian Eric
Glasgow, 26 September, 1979 Su21-1 (F)

League Club	Source	Date Signed	Seasons Played	Apps	Subs	Gls
Stockport Co	Clyde	08.00	00	3	10	1

CARRINGTON Andrew (Andy)
Grimsby, 14 November, 1936 (CD)

League Club	Source	Date Signed	Seasons Played	Apps	Subs	Gls
Grimsby T	Jnrs	09.55	59-60	4	-	0

CARR-LAWTON Colin
South Shields, 5 September, 1978 (F)

League Club	Source	Date Signed	Seasons Played	Apps	Subs	Gls
Burnley	YT	01.97	97-98	2	3	0

CARRODUS Frank
Manchester, 31 May, 1949 (W)

League Club	Source	Date Signed	Seasons Played	Apps	Subs	Gls
Manchester C	Altrincham	11.69	69-73	33	8	1
Aston Villa	Tr	08.74	74-78	150	0	7
Wrexham	Tr	12.79	79-81	97	0	6
Birmingham C	Tr	08.82	82	7	1	0
Bury	Tr	10.83	83	31	3	1

CARROLL Alfred (Alf)
Bradford, 6 March, 1920 Died 1994 (CD)

League Club	Source	Date Signed	Seasons Played	Apps	Subs	Gls
Bradford C	US Metallic Packing	03.48	48-49	28	-	0

CARROLL David (Dave) Francis
Paisley, 20 September, 1966 ESch (M)

League Club	Source	Date Signed	Seasons Played	Apps	Subs	Gls
Wycombe W	Ruislip Manor	07.88	93-01	277	25	40

CARROLL John (Johnny)
Limerick, 11 May, 1923 (CF)

League Club	Source	Date Signed	Seasons Played	Apps	Subs	Gls
West Ham U	Limerick	05.48	48	5	-	0

CARROLL Joseph (Joe)
Radcliffe, 6 January, 1957 (F)

League Club	Source	Date Signed	Seasons Played	Apps	Subs	Gls
Oldham Ath	Jnrs	07.75	75	3	1	0
Halifax T	Tr	09.76	76-78	76	6	14

CARROLL Michael (Mike)
Aberdeen, 10 September, 1952 SSch (F)

League Club	Source	Date Signed	Seasons Played	Apps	Subs	Gls
Grimsby T	Liverpool (App)	03.71	70	0	1	0

CARROLL Michael (Micky)
Blaydon, 4 October, 1961 (W)

League Club	Source	Date Signed	Seasons Played	Apps	Subs	Gls
Chesterfield	Whickham	09.81	81-82	5	1	1

CARROLL Robert (Robbie)
Greenford, 15 February, 1968 (F)

League Club	Source	Date Signed	Seasons Played	Apps	Subs	Gls
Southampton	App	02.86				
Brentford	Gosport Borough	09.86	86-87	24	10	8

CARROLL Roy Eric
Enniskillen, 30 September, 1977 NIYth/NIu21-11/NI-17 (G)

League Club	Source	Date Signed	Seasons Played	Apps	Subs	Gls
Hull C	YT	09.95	95-96	46	0	0
Wigan Ath	Tr	04.97	97-00	135	0	0
Manchester U	Tr	07.01	01-04	46	3	0

CARROLL Thomas (Tommy) Roger
Dublin, 18 August, 1942 IRAmat/LoI-7/IRu23-1/IR-17 (FB)

League Club	Source	Date Signed	Seasons Played	Apps	Subs	Gls
Ipswich T	Cambridge C	07.66	66-71	115	2	2
Birmingham C	Tr	10.71	71-72	38	0	0

CARRUTHERS Alexander (Alec) Neilson
Loganlea, 12 May, 1915 Died 1977 (W)

League Club	Source	Date Signed	Seasons Played	Apps	Subs	Gls
Bolton W	Falkirk	02.37	36-37	26	-	4
Rochdale	Falkirk	05.46	46	13	-	4

CARRUTHERS Christopher (Chris) Paul
Kettering, 19 August, 1983 EYth/Eu20 (FB)

League Club	Source	Date Signed	Seasons Played	Apps	Subs	Gls
Northampton T	YT	04.02	00-04	52	22	1
Bristol Rov	L	03.05	04	2	3	0

CARRUTHERS Eric
Edinburgh, 2 February, 1953 (F)

League Club	Source	Date Signed	Seasons Played	Apps	Subs	Gls
Derby Co	Heart of Midlothian	01.75	76	0	1	0

CARRUTHERS John Parker
Dumfries, 2 August, 1926 Died 1997 (W)

League Club	Source	Date Signed	Seasons Played	Apps	Subs	Gls
Carlisle U		07.49	49	2	-	0
Workington	Tr	07.51	51	3	-	0

CARRUTHERS Martin George
Nottingham, 7 August, 1972 (F)

League Club	Source	Date Signed	Seasons Played	Apps	Subs	Gls
Aston Villa	YT	07.90	91-92	2	2	0
Hull C	L	10.92	92	13	0	6
Stoke C	Tr	07.93	93-96	60	31	13
Peterborough U	Tr	11.96	96-98	63	4	21
York C	L	01.99	98	3	3	0
Darlington	Tr	03.99	98-99	11	6	2
Southend U	Tr	09.99	99-00	69	1	26
Scunthorpe U	Tr	03.01	00-02	80	6	34
Macclesfield T	Tr	07.03	03	30	9	8
Boston U	Tr	08.04	04	4	2	0
Lincoln C	Tr	09.04	04	7	4	0
Cambridge U	L	01.05	04	5	0	0

CARRUTHERS Matthew (Matt)
Dover, 22 July, 1976 (F)

League Club	Source	Date Signed	Seasons Played	Apps	Subs	Gls
Mansfield T	Dover Ath	02.99	98	0	5	0

CARSLEY Lee Kevin
Birmingham, 28 February, 1974 IRu21-1/IR-29 (M)

League Club	Source	Date Signed	Seasons Played	Apps	Subs	Gls
Derby Co	YT	07.92	94-98	122	16	5
Blackburn Rov	Tr	03.99	98-00	40	6	10
Coventry C	Tr	12.00	00-01	46	1	4
Everton	Tr	02.02	01-04	79	10	10

CARSON Alexander (Alec) McPhee
Clarkston, 12 November, 1942 (WH)

League Club	Source	Date Signed	Seasons Played	Apps	Subs	Gls
Northampton T	Jnrs	11.59	60-61	8	-	0
Aldershot	Tr	05.63	63-64	5	-	0

CARSON Daniel (Danny)
Huyton, 2 February, 1981 (M)

League Club	Source	Date Signed	Seasons Played	Apps	Subs	Gls
Chester C	YT	07.99	98	1	1	0

CARSON Scott Paul
Whitehaven, 3 September, 1985 EYth/Eu21-11 (G)

League Club	Source	Date Signed	Seasons Played	Apps	Subs	Gls
Leeds U	YT	09.02	03	2	1	0
Liverpool	Tr	01.05	04	4	0	0

CARSON Stephen
Ballymoney, 6 October, 1980 NIu21-2 (M)

League Club	Source	Date Signed	Seasons Played	Apps	Subs	Gls
Barnsley	Dundee U	09.03	03	9	2	1
Hartlepool U	Tr	02.04	03	1	2	0

CARSON Thomas (Tom)
Alexandria, 26 March, 1959 (G)

League Club	Source	Date Signed	Seasons Played	Apps	Subs	Gls
Ipswich T (L)	Dundee U	01.88	87	1	0	0

CARSS Anthony (Tony) John
Alnwick, 31 March, 1976 (M)

League Club	Source	Date Signed	Seasons Played	Apps	Subs	Gls
Blackburn Rov	Bradford C (YT)	08.94				
Darlington	Tr	08.95	95-96	33	24	2
Cardiff C	Tr	07.97	97	36	6	1
Chesterfield	Tr	09.98	98-99	26	9	1
Carlisle U	Tr	08.00	00	6	1	0
Oldham Ath	Tr	10.00	00-02	58	17	5
Huddersfield T	Tr	08.03	03-04	58	5	3

CARSTAIRS James (Jim) Wood
St Andrews, 29 January, 1971 (FB)

League Club	Source	Date Signed	Seasons Played	Apps	Subs	Gls
Arsenal	YT	03.89				
Brentford	L	02.91	90	8	0	0
Cambridge U	Tr	07.91				
Stockport Co	Tr	11.91	91-92	33	1	1

CARTER Alfonso (Alfie) Jermaine
Birmingham, 23 August, 1980 (F)

League Club	Source	Date Signed	Seasons Played	Apps	Subs	Gls
Walsall	YT	04.99	98-00	1	2	0

CARTER Brian
Dorchester, 17 November, 1938 (WH)

League Club	Source	Date Signed	Seasons Played	Apps	Subs	Gls
Portsmouth	Weymouth	01.56	57-60	44	-	0
Bristol Rov	Tr	07.61	61	4	-	0

CARTER Daniel (Danny) Stephen
Hackney, 29 June, 1969 (W)

League Club	Source	Date Signed	Seasons Played	Apps	Subs	Gls
Leyton Orient	Billericay T	07.88	88-94	168	20	22
Peterborough U	Tr	06.95	95-96	33	12	1

CARTER Darren Anthony
Solihull, 18 December, 1983 EYth/Eu20 (M)

League Club	Source	Date Signed	Seasons Played	Apps	Subs	Gls
Birmingham C	YT	11.01	01-04	28	17	3
Sunderland	L	09.04	04	8	2	1

CARTER Donald (Don) Frederick
Midsomer Norton, 11 September, 1921 (IF)

League Club	Source	Date Signed	Seasons Played	Apps	Subs	Gls
Bury	Stourbridge	01.39	46-47	56	-	27
Blackburn Rov	Tr	06.48	48	2	-	0
New Brighton	Tr	11.48	48-50	105	-	19

CARTER Geoffrey (Geoff)
Northwich, 14 February, 1943 (W)

League Club	Source	Date Signed	Seasons Played	Apps	Subs	Gls
West Bromwich A	Moulton	02.60	59-64	25	-	3
Bury	Tr	07.66	66	4	0	0
Bradford C	Tr	08.67	67	1	0	0

CARTER Horatio (Raich) Stratton
Sunderland, 21 December, 1913 Died 1994 ESch/FLge-4/LoI-2/EWar-17/E-13 (IF)

League Club	Source	Date Signed	Seasons Played	Apps	Subs	Gls
Sunderland	Esh Winning	11.31	32-38	245	-	118
Derby Co	Tr	12.45	46-47	63	-	34
Hull C	Tr	04.48	47-51	136	-	57

CARTER Ian Noel
Birmingham, 20 September, 1967 Canada int (FB)

League Club	Source	Date Signed	Seasons Played	Apps	Subs	Gls
Peterborough U	Winnipeg (Can)	02.94	93	9	2	0

CARTER James (Jimmy) William Charles
Hammersmith, 9 November, 1965 (W)

League Club	Source	Date Signed	Seasons Played	Apps	Subs	Gls
Crystal Palace	App	11.83				
Queens Park Rgrs	Tr	09.85				
Millwall	Tr	03.87	86-90	99	11	11
Liverpool	Tr	01.91	90	2	3	0
Arsenal	Tr	10.91	91-94	18	7	2
Oxford U	L	03.94	93	5	0	0
Oxford U	L	12.94	94	3	1	0
Portsmouth	Tr	07.95	95-97	60	12	5
Millwall	Tr	07.98	98	16	0	0

CARTER Joseph (Joe)
Bingley, 23 April, 1920 Died 1978 (G)

League Club	Source	Date Signed	Seasons Played	Apps	Subs	Gls
Walsall	Jnrs	11.36				
Notts Co		09.44				
Hull C	Tr	06.46	46	5	-	0

CARTER Lee Richard
Dartford, 22 March, 1970 (FB)

League Club	Source	Date Signed	Seasons Played	Apps	Subs	Gls
Northampton T	YT	07.88	87	0	1	0

CARTER Leslie (Les) Alan
Bromley, 24 October, 1960 ESch (F)

League Club	Source	Date Signed	Seasons Played	Apps	Subs	Gls
Crystal Palace	App	11.77	80	1	1	0
Bristol C	Tr	02.82	81	16	0	0

CARTER Mark Colin
Liverpool, 17 December, 1960 ESemiPro (F)

League Club	Source	Date Signed	Seasons Played	Apps	Subs	Gls
Barnet	Runcorn	02.91	91-93	62	20	30
Bury	Tr	09.93	93-96	113	21	62
Rochdale	Tr	07.97	97	7	4	2

CARTER Michael (Mike)
Warrington, 18 April, 1960 (W)

League Club	Source	Date Signed	Seasons Played	Apps	Subs	Gls
Bolton W	App	07.77	79-81	37	12	8
Mansfield T	L	03.79	78	18	0	4
Swindon T	L	03.82	81	4	1	0
Plymouth Arg	Tr	08.82	82	6	6	1
Hereford U	L	03.83	82	10	0	0
Hereford U	Tr	06.83	84-86	81	6	11
Wrexham	Tr	07.87	87-88	25	9	7

CARTER Michael David
Darlington, 13 November, 1980 (F)

League Club	Source	Date Signed	Seasons Played	Apps	Subs	Gls
Darlington	YT	07.99	98	1	0	1

CARTER Raymond (Ray)
Chester, 1 May, 1951 (M)

League Club	Source	Date Signed	Seasons Played	Apps	Subs	Gls
Chester	Jnrs	09.71	71-73	56	6	0
Crewe Alex	Tr	07.74	74	26	0	3

CARTER Raymond (Ray)
West Hoathly, 1 June, 1933 (IF)

League Club	Source	Date Signed	Seasons Played	Apps	Subs	Gls
Torquay U	Brixham	08.58	58-59	3	-	1
Exeter C	Tr	10.60	60-62	105	-	50

CARTER Robert (Rob) Hector Andrew
Stepney, 23 April, 1982 (M)

League Club	Source	Date Signed	Seasons Played	Apps	Subs	Gls
Leyton Orient	YT	•	99	0	2	0

CARTER Roger Frank
Great Yarmouth, 11 October, 1937 (IF)

League Club	Source	Date Signed	Seasons Played	Apps	Subs	Gls
Aston Villa	Gorleston	12.55				
Torquay U	Tr	07.60	60	5	-	0

CARTER Roy William
Torpoint, 19 February, 1954 (M)

League Club	Source	Date Signed	Seasons Played	Apps	Subs	Gls
Hereford U	Falmouth T	04.75	74-77	64	7	9
Swindon T	Tr	12.77	77-82	193	7	34

League Club	Source	Date Signed	Seasons Played	Apps	Subs	Gls
Torquay U	L	10.82	82	6	0	5
Bristol Rov	L	12.82	82	4	0	1
Torquay U	Tr	02.83	82-83	21	0	3
Newport Co	Tr	09.83	83-86	150	2	22
Exeter C	Tr	06.87	87	37	4	2

CARTER Stanley (Stan) Albert
Exeter, 6 September, 1928 (CD)

League Club	Source	Date Signed	Seasons Played	Apps	Subs	Gls
Exeter C	Heavitree U	11.49	50-51	2	-	0

CARTER Stephen (Steve) Charles
Great Yarmouth, 23 April, 1953 (W)

League Club	Source	Date Signed	Seasons Played	Apps	Subs	Gls
Manchester C	App	08.70	70-71	4	2	2
Notts Co	Tr	02.72	71-78	172	16	21
Derby Co	Tr	08.78	78-79	32	1	1
Bournemouth	Notts Co (N/C)	03.82	81-83	42	4	1
Torquay U	Tr	07.84	84	16	0	1

CARTER Stephen (Steve) George
Sunderland, 13 April, 1972 (W)

League Club	Source	Date Signed	Seasons Played	Apps	Subs	Gls
Scarborough	Manchester U (YT)	07.90	90-91	33	4	3

CARTER Sydney (Syd) Youles
Chesterfield, 28 July, 1916 Died 1978 (CF)

League Club	Source	Date Signed	Seasons Played	Apps	Subs	Gls
Mansfield T	Macclesfield	05.38	38-46	39	-	10

CARTER Timothy (Tim) Douglas
Bristol, 5 October, 1967 EYth (G)

League Club	Source	Date Signed	Seasons Played	Apps	Subs	Gls
Bristol Rov	App	10.85	85-87	47	0	0
Newport Co	L	12.87	87	1	0	0
Sunderland	Tr	12.87	87-92	37	0	0
Carlisle U	L	03.88	87	4	0	0
Bristol C	L	09.88	88	3	0	0
Birmingham C	L	11.91	91	2	0	0
Hartlepool U	Tr	08.92	93	18	0	0
Millwall	Tr	01.94	93-94	4	0	0
Oxford U	Tr	08.95	95	12	0	0
Millwall	Tr	12.95	95-97	62	0	0
Halifax T	Tr	07.98	98	9	1	0

CARTER Wilfred (Wilf)
Wednesbury, 4 October, 1933 (IF)

League Club	Source	Date Signed	Seasons Played	Apps	Subs	Gls
West Bromwich A	Jnrs	01.51	51-56	57	-	12
Plymouth Arg	Tr	03.57	57-63	254	-	134
Exeter C	Tr	05.64	64-65	48	0	6

CARTER William (Billy) Henry John
Woking, 14 September, 1945 (W)

League Club	Source	Date Signed	Seasons Played	Apps	Subs	Gls
Leyton Orient	Jnrs	10.64	65-66	26	3	3

CARTERON Patrice
St Brieuc, France, 30 July, 1970 (FB)

League Club	Source	Date Signed	Seasons Played	Apps	Subs	Gls
Sunderland (L)	St Etienne (Fr)	03.01	00	8	0	1

CARTLEDGE Jonathan (Jon) Robert
Carshalton, 27 November, 1984 (CD)

League Club	Source	Date Signed	Seasons Played	Apps	Subs	Gls
Bury	Sch	08.04	03-04	8	8	1

CARTLIDGE David Thomas
Leicester, 9 April, 1940 (WH)

League Club	Source	Date Signed	Seasons Played	Apps	Subs	Gls
Leicester C	Jnrs	10.57				
Bradford C	Tr	06.61	61	6	-	3
Chester	Tr	11.61	61-62	20	-	0

CARTWRIGHT Ian James
Brierley Hill, 13 November, 1964 (M)

League Club	Source	Date Signed	Seasons Played	Apps	Subs	Gls
Wolverhampton W	App	09.82	82-85	59	2	3

CARTWRIGHT John William
Brixworth, 5 November, 1940 EYth (IF)

League Club	Source	Date Signed	Seasons Played	Apps	Subs	Gls
West Ham U	Jnrs	11.57	59-60	4	-	0
Crystal Palace	Tr	05.61	61-62	11	-	1

CARTWRIGHT Lee
Rawtenstall, 19 September, 1972 (M)

League Club	Source	Date Signed	Seasons Played	Apps	Subs	Gls
Preston NE	YT	07.91	90-03	312	85	22
Stockport Co	Tr	01.04	03-04	32	2	1

CARTWRIGHT Leslie (Les)
Aberdare, 4 April, 1952 Wu23-4/W-7 (M)

League Club	Source	Date Signed	Seasons Played	Apps	Subs	Gls
Coventry C	Jnrs	05.70	73-76	50	18	4
Wrexham	Tr	06.77	77-81	111	4	6
Cambridge U	Tr	03.82	81-84	52	8	1
Southend U	L	09.83	83	2	2	0

CARTWRIGHT Mark Neville
Chester, 13 January, 1973 (G)

League Club	Source	Date Signed	Seasons Played	Apps	Subs	Gls
Stockport Co	York C (YT)	08.91				
Wrexham	Runcorn	03.94	96-98	37	0	0
Brighton & Hove A	Tr	08.00	00	12	1	0

League Club	Source	Date Signed	Seasons Played	Apps	Subs	Gls
Shrewsbury T	Tr	07.01	01	14	0	0
Shrewsbury T	L Wilson College (USA)	02.03	02	13	0	0

CARTWRIGHT Michael (Mick)
Birmingham, 9 October, 1946 (FB)

League Club	Source	Date Signed	Seasons Played	Apps	Subs	Gls
Coventry C		08.65				
Notts Co	Tr	06.67	67-68	15	1	0
Bradford C	L	11.67	67	1	0	0

CARTWRIGHT Neil Andrew
Stourbridge, 20 February, 1971 (M)

League Club	Source	Date Signed	Seasons Played	Apps	Subs	Gls
West Bromwich A	YT	07.89	88-91	5	6	0

CARTWRIGHT Peter
Newcastle, 23 August, 1957 (M)

League Club	Source	Date Signed	Seasons Played	Apps	Subs	Gls
Newcastle U	North Shields	06.79	79-82	57	8	3
Scunthorpe U	L	12.82	82	2	2	1
Darlington	Tr	03.83	82-83	48	2	5

CARTWRIGHT Stephen (Steve) Raymond
Tamworth, 8 January, 1965 (FB)

League Club	Source	Date Signed	Seasons Played	Apps	Subs	Gls
Colchester U	Tamworth	08.88	88	10	0	0

CARTWRIGHT William John
Malpas, 11 June, 1922 Died 1992 (WH)

League Club	Source	Date Signed	Seasons Played	Apps	Subs	Gls
Tranmere Rov		02.41	46-47	9	-	1

CARTY Stephen (Steve) Francis
Dunfermline, 12 January, 1934 (FB)

League Club	Source	Date Signed	Seasons Played	Apps	Subs	Gls
Crewe Alex	Blair Hall	03.57	56-59	37	-	0

CARVALHO Alberto **Ricardo**
Amarante, Portugal, 18 May, 1978 Portugal 16 (CD)

League Club	Source	Date Signed	Seasons Played	Apps	Subs	Gls
Chelsea	FC Porto (Por)	07.04	04	22	3	1

CARVALHO Rogerio
Brazil, 28 May, 1980 (F)

League Club	Source	Date Signed	Seasons Played	Apps	Subs	Gls
York C	Ituano (Br)	08.02	02	0	4	0

CARVER David Francis
Wickersley, 16 April, 1944 (FB)

League Club	Source	Date Signed	Seasons Played	Apps	Subs	Gls
Rotherham U	App	01.62	61-64	82	-	0
Cardiff C	Tr	01.66	65-72	210	0	1
Swansea C	L	12.72	72	3	0	0
Hereford U	Tr	08.73	73	14	0	0
Doncaster Rov	Tr	03.74	73-74	29	1	0

CARVER Gerald (Gerry) Francis
Worcester, 27 June, 1935 (WH)

League Club	Source	Date Signed	Seasons Played	Apps	Subs	Gls
Notts Co	Boldmere St Michael's	08.52	53-65	279	1	10

CARVER John William
Newcastle, 16 January, 1965 (FB)

League Club	Source	Date Signed	Seasons Played	Apps	Subs	Gls
Newcastle U	App	01.83				
Cardiff C	Tr	07.85	85	13	0	0

CARVER Joseph (Joe) Anthony
Illinois, USA, 11 June, 1971 (CD)

League Club	Source	Date Signed	Seasons Played	Apps	Subs	Gls
Chester C	Hampton Rd M's (USA)	09.99	99	1	1	0

CAS Marcel
Breda, Holland, 30 April, 1972 (M)

League Club	Source	Date Signed	Seasons Played	Apps	Subs	Gls
Notts Co	RBC Roosendaal (Holl)	07.01	01-02	49	9	8
Sheffield U	Tr	02.03	02	3	3	0
Grimsby T	Tr	07.03	03	13	7	2

CASCARINO Anthony (Tony) Guy
St Pauls Cray, 1 September, 1962 IR-76 (F)

League Club	Source	Date Signed	Seasons Played	Apps	Subs	Gls
Gillingham	Crockenhill	01.82	81-86	209	10	77
Millwall	Tr	06.87	87-89	105	0	42
Aston Villa	Tr	03.90	89-90	43	3	11
Chelsea	Glasgow Celtic	02.92	91-93	35	5	8

CASE James (Jimmy) Robert
Liverpool, 18 May, 1954 Eu23-1 (M)

League Club	Source	Date Signed	Seasons Played	Apps	Subs	Gls
Liverpool	South Liverpool	05.73	74-80	170	16	23
Brighton & Hove A	Tr	08.81	81-84	124	3	10
Southampton	Tr	03.85	84-90	213	2	10
Bournemouth	Tr	07.91	91	38	2	1
Halifax T	Tr	05.92	92	17	4	2
Wrexham	Tr	02.93	92	1	3	0
Darlington	Wanneroo British (Aus)	10.93	93	1	0	0
Brighton & Hove A	Sittingbourne	12.93	93-95	30	2	0

CASE Norman
Prescot, 1 September, 1925 Died 1973 IrLge-1 (CF)

League Club	Source	Date Signed	Seasons Played	Apps	Subs	Gls
Sunderland	Ards	09.49	49-50	4	-	2
Watford	Tr	12.50	50	10	-	4
Rochdale	Yeovil T	02.52	51	2	-	0

CASEY Gerald (Gerry) Hugh
Birkenhead, 25 August, 1941 (M)

League Club	Source	Date Signed	Seasons Played	Apps	Subs	Gls
Tranmere Rov	Holyhead T	08.67	67-69	49	3	5

CASEY Leonard (Len) John
Hackney, 24 May, 1931 (WH)

League Club	Source	Date Signed	Seasons Played	Apps	Subs	Gls
Chelsea	Leyton	02.54	55-58	34	-	0
Plymouth Arg	Tr	12.58	58-59	44	-	0

CASEY Paul
Rinteln, Germany, 6 October, 1961 (FB)

League Club	Source	Date Signed	Seasons Played	Apps	Subs	Gls
Sheffield U	App	06.79	79-81	23	2	1
Lincoln C	Boston U	03.88	88-90	44	5	4

CASEY Paul
Great Yarmouth, 29 July, 1969 (G)

League Club	Source	Date Signed	Seasons Played	Apps	Subs	Gls
Cambridge U	YT	07.87	87	1	0	0

CASEY Ryan Peter
Coventry, 3 January, 1979 IRYth/IRu21 (W)

League Club	Source	Date Signed	Seasons Played	Apps	Subs	Gls
Swansea C	YT	05.97	96-01	19	43	2

CASEY Terence (Terry) David
Abergwynfi, 5 September, 1943 (WH)

League Club	Source	Date Signed	Seasons Played	Apps	Subs	Gls
Leeds U	Jnrs	10.60	61	3	-	0

CASEY Thomas (Tommy)
Comber, County Down, 11 March, 1930 NI-12 (WH)

League Club	Source	Date Signed	Seasons Played	Apps	Subs	Gls
Leeds U	Bangor	05.49	49	4	-	0
Bournemouth	Tr	08.50	50-51	66	-	1
Newcastle U	Tr	08.52	52-57	116	-	8
Portsmouth	Tr	07.58	58	24	-	1
Bristol C	Tr	03.59	58-62	122	-	9

CASH Brian Dominick
Dublin, 24 November, 1982 IRYth/IRu21-4 (M)

League Club	Source	Date Signed	Seasons Played	Apps	Subs	Gls
Nottingham F	YT	12.99	01-03	0	7	0
Swansea C	L	10.02	02	5	0	0
Rochdale	L	08.04	04	6	0	0
Bristol Rov	Tr	12.04	04	0	1	0

CASH Stuart Paul
Tipton, 5 September, 1965 (FB)

League Club	Source	Date Signed	Seasons Played	Apps	Subs	Gls
Nottingham F	Halesowen T	09.89				
Rotherham U	L	03.90	89	8	0	1
Brentford	L	09.90	90	11	0	0
Shrewsbury T	L	09.91	91	8	0	1
Chesterfield	Tr	08.92	92-93	27	2	0

CASHLEY Alec **Raymond (Ray)**
Bristol, 23 October, 1951 (G)

League Club	Source	Date Signed	Seasons Played	Apps	Subs	Gls
Bristol C	Jnrs	09.70	70-80	227	0	1
Hereford U	L	01.81	80	20	0	0
Bristol Rov	Clevedon T	08.82	83-84	53	0	0
Chester C	Trowbridge T	10.85	85	9	0	0

CASHMORE Norman
Aldershot, 24 March, 1939 (WH)

League Club	Source	Date Signed	Seasons Played	Apps	Subs	Gls
Aldershot	Woking	07.63	64	7	-	0

CASIRAGHI Pierluigi
Monza, Italy, 4 March, 1969 Italy 44 (F)

League Club	Source	Date Signed	Seasons Played	Apps	Subs	Gls
Chelsea	SS Lazio (It)	07.98	98	10	0	1

CASKEY Darren Mark
Basildon, 21 August, 1974 ESch/EYth (M)

League Club	Source	Date Signed	Seasons Played	Apps	Subs	Gls
Tottenham H	YT	03.92	93-95	20	12	4
Watford	L	10.95	95	6	0	1
Reading	Tr	02.96	95-00	180	22	35
Notts Co	Tr	07.01	01-03	101	13	10
Peterborough U	Hornchurch	11.04	04	2	2	0

CASKEY William (Billy) Thomas
Belfast, 12 October, 1953 NI-7 (F)

League Club	Source	Date Signed	Seasons Played	Apps	Subs	Gls
Derby Co	Glentoran	09.78	78-79	26	2	3

CASLEY John (Jack)
Torquay, 27 April, 1926 (G)

League Club	Source	Date Signed	Seasons Played	Apps	Subs	Gls
Torquay U		06.47	47	1	-	0

CASPER Christopher (Chris) Martin
Burnley, 28 April, 1975 EYth/Eu21-1 (CD)

League Club	Source	Date Signed	Seasons Played	Apps	Subs	Gls
Manchester U	YT	02.93	96	0	2	0
Bournemouth	L	01.96	95	16	0	1
Swindon T	L	09.97	97	8	1	1
Reading	Tr	09.98	98-99	46	1	0

CASPER Frank
Barnsley, 9 December, 1944 FLge-1 (F)

League Club	Source	Date Signed	Seasons Played	Apps	Subs	Gls
Rotherham U	App	07.62	62-66	101	1	25
Burnley	Tr	06.67	67-75	230	7	74

CASS David William Royce
Forest Gate, 27 March, 1962 (G)

League Club	Source	Date Signed	Seasons Played	Apps	Subs	Gls
Orient	Billericay T	03.87	86	7	0	0

CASSELL James (Jim)
Prestwich, 23 April, 1947 (M)

League Club	Source	Date Signed	Seasons Played	Apps	Subs	Gls
Bury		07.70	70	2	1	0

CASSELLS Keith Barrington
Islington, 10 July, 1957 (F)

League Club	Source	Date Signed	Seasons Played	Apps	Subs	Gls
Watford	Wembley	11.77	78-80	6	6	0
Peterborough U	L	01.80	79	8	0	0
Oxford U	Tr	11.80	80-81	43	2	13
Southampton	Tr	03.82	81-82	13	6	4
Brentford	Tr	02.83	82-84	80	6	29
Mansfield T	Tr	08.85	85-88	162	1	52

CASSIDY Andrew (Andy) Duncan
Leeds, 1 March, 1959 (G)

League Club	Source	Date Signed	Seasons Played	Apps	Subs	Gls
Stockport Co		02.77	77-78	5	0	0

CASSIDY Francis James Augustine
Watford, 20 August, 1964 (M)

League Club	Source	Date Signed	Seasons Played	Apps	Subs	Gls
Watford	App	08.82				
Plymouth Arg	L	02.84	83	1	0	0
Peterborough U	Tr	08.84	84-85	44	2	9

CASSIDY James (Jimmy) Toner
Falkirk, 1 December, 1943 (FB)

League Club	Source	Date Signed	Seasons Played	Apps	Subs	Gls
Oxford U	Stirling A	07.63	63	5	-	0
Barrow	Tr	03.65	64	5	-	0

CASSIDY Jamie
Liverpool, 21 November, 1977 ESch/EYth (M)

League Club	Source	Date Signed	Seasons Played	Apps	Subs	Gls
Liverpool	YT	03.95				
Cambridge U	Tr	08.99	99	4	4	0

CASSIDY Laurence (Laurie)
Manchester, 10 March, 1923 (IF)

League Club	Source	Date Signed	Seasons Played	Apps	Subs	Gls
Manchester U		02.47	47-51	4	-	0
Oldham Ath	Tr	07.56	56	4	-	1

CASSIDY Nigel
Sudbury, 7 December, 1945 (F)

League Club	Source	Date Signed	Seasons Played	Apps	Subs	Gls
Norwich C	Lowestoft T	07.67	67-68	2	1	0
Scunthorpe U	Tr	12.68	68-70	88	0	35
Oxford U	Tr	11.70	70-73	113	3	33
Cambridge U	Tr	03.74	73-75	52	2	13

CASSIDY Thomas (Tommy)
Belfast, 18 November, 1950 NI-24 (M)

League Club	Source	Date Signed	Seasons Played	Apps	Subs	Gls
Newcastle U	Coleraine	10.70	70-79	170	10	22
Burnley	Tr	07.80	80-82	70	2	4

CASSIDY William (Bill)
Gateshead, 30 June, 1917 (WH)

League Club	Source	Date Signed	Seasons Played	Apps	Subs	Gls
Gateshead	Close Works	01.36	35-52	133	-	6

CASSIDY William (Billy) Pitt
Hamilton, 4 October, 1940 Died 1995 (M)

League Club	Source	Date Signed	Seasons Played	Apps	Subs	Gls
Rotherham U	Glasgow Rgrs	08.61	61-62	25	-	1
Brighton & Hove A	Tr	11.62	62-66	113	5	25
Cambridge U	Detroit (USA)	10.68	70	27	5	6

CASTLE Peter James
Southampton, 12 March, 1987 EYth (CD)

League Club	Source	Date Signed	Seasons Played	Apps	Subs	Gls
Reading	Jnrs	●	02	0	1	0

CASTLE Stephen (Steve) Charles
Barkingside, 17 May, 1966 (M)

League Club	Source	Date Signed	Seasons Played	Apps	Subs	Gls
Orient	App	05.84	84-91	232	11	55
Plymouth Arg	Tr	06.92	92-94	98	3	35
Birmingham C	Tr	07.95	95-96	16	7	1
Gillingham	L	02.96	95	5	1	1
Leyton Orient	L	02.97	96	4	0	1
Peterborough U	Tr	05.97	97-99	96	6	17
Leyton Orient	Tr	07.00	00-01	2	8	0

CASTLEDINE Gary
Dumfries, 27 March, 1970 (M)

League Club	Source	Date Signed	Seasons Played	Apps	Subs	Gls
Mansfield T	Shirebrook Colliery	01.91	91-94	43	23	3

CASTLEDINE Stewart Mark
Wandsworth, 22 January, 1973 (M)

League Club	Source	Date Signed	Seasons Played	Apps	Subs	Gls
Wimbledon	YT	07.91	91-98	18	10	4
Wycombe W	L	08.95	95	7	0	3
Wycombe W	Tr	07.00	00	6	11	0

CASWELL Brian Leonard
Wednesbury, 14 February, 1956 (FB)

League Club	Source	Date Signed	Seasons Played	Apps	Subs	Gls
Walsall	App	09.73	72-84	388	12	17

League Club	Source	Date Signed	Seasons Played	Career Record Apps	Subs	Gls
Doncaster Rov	Tr	08.85	85	15	0	2
Leeds U	Tr	11.85	85-86	9	0	0
Wolverhampton W	L	01.87	86	1	0	0

CASWELL Peter Donald
Leatherhead, 16 January, 1957 (G)

Crystal Palace	App	08.75	76-77	3	0	0
Crewe Alex	Tr	08.78	78	22	0	0

CATER Ronald (Ron)
Fulham, 2 February, 1922 (WH)

West Ham U	Leytonstone	01.44	46-49	63	-	0
Leyton Orient	Tr	06.51	51	13	-	0

CATERER Brian
Hayes, 23 January, 1943 (CD)

Brentford (Am)	Chesham U	05.68	68	1	0	0

CATLEUGH George Charles
Horden, 11 June, 1932 Died 1996 (WH)

Watford	Nuneaton Borough	05.54	54-64	293	-	15

CATLEY John (Jack) William
Grimsby, 16 March, 1945 (W)

Grimsby T	Jnrs	07.62	62	2	-	0

CATLIN Robert (Bob)
Wembley, 22 June, 1965 (G)

Notts Co	Marconi (Aus)	08.92	92-93	3	0	0
Birmingham C	L	03.93	92	8	0	0

CATON Andrew (Andy) James
Oxford, 3 December, 1987 (F)

Swindon T	Sch	●	04	1	7	1

CATON Thomas (Tommy) Stephen
Liverpool, 6 October, 1962 Died 1993 ESch/EYth/Eu21-14 (CD)

Manchester C	App	10.79	79-83	164	1	8
Arsenal	Tr	12.83	83-85	81	0	2
Oxford U	Tr	02.87	86-87	50	3	3
Charlton Ath	Tr	11.88	88-90	56	1	5

CATON William (Bill) Clifford
Stoke-on-Trent, 11 September, 1924 (IF)

Stoke C	Jnrs	09.41	47-49	22	-	2
Carlisle U	Tr	04.50	49-51	61	-	15
Chesterfield	Tr	10.52	52	7	-	0
Crewe Alex	Worcester C	07.54	54	39	-	9

CATTERICK Harry
Darlington, 26 November, 1919 Died 1985 (CF)

Everton	Cheadle Heath	03.37	46-51	59	-	19
Crewe Alex	Tr	12.51	51-52	25	-	11

CATTLIN Christopher (Chris) John
Milnrow, 25 June, 1946 Eu23-1 (FB)

Huddersfield T	Burnley (Am)	08.64	64-67	59	2	1
Coventry C	Tr	03.68	67-75	213	4	0
Brighton & Hove A	Tr	06.76	76-78	95	0	1

CATTRELL Gordon William
Sunderland, 18 December, 1954 ESch (M)

Leeds U	App	01.72				
Darlington	Tr	08.73	73-75	96	6	5

CAU Jean-Michel
Ajaccio, France, 27 October, 1980 (F)

Darlington	Gazelac Ajaccio (Fr)	03.01	00	0	1	0

CAUGHEY Mark
Belfast, 27 August, 1960 IrLge-2/NI-2 (F)

Burnley (L)	Hibernian	02.87	86	8	0	0

CAUGHTER Alan David
Bangor, 19 February, 1946 (FB)

Chester		08.69	69	1	1	0

CAULFIELD Graham William
Leeds, 18 July, 1943 (F)

York C (Am)	Frickley Colliery	02.67	66	9	0	2
Bradford C (Am)	Tr	07.67	67	1	0	0

CAVACO Luis Miguel Pasaro
Almada, Portugal, 1 March, 1972 (W)

Stockport Co	Estoril (Por)	08.96	96-97	19	10	5

CAVANAGH Irvin
Rochdale, 31 July, 1924 (IF)

Bury		05.48	49	1	-	0

CAVANAGH John
Salford, 4 August, 1961 (FB)

Rochdale	Barrow	09.84	84	14	3	0

CAVANAGH Thomas (Tommy) Henry
Liverpool, 29 June, 1928 (IF)

Preston NE		08.49				
Stockport Co	Tr	01.50	49-51	32	-	2
Huddersfield T	Tr	05.52	52-55	93	-	29
Doncaster Rov	Tr	05.56	56-58	119	-	16
Bristol C	Tr	07.59	59	24	-	6
Carlisle U	Tr	06.60	60	33	-	4

CAVE Michael (Micky) John
Weymouth, 28 January, 1949 Died 1985 (M)

Torquay U	Weymouth	07.68	68-70	106	8	17
Bournemouth	Tr	07.71	71-73	91	8	17
Plymouth Arg	L	03.72	71	8	0	4
York C	Tr	08.74	74-76	94	2	13
Bournemouth	Tr	02.77	76-77	42	0	3

CAVEN John
Edinburgh, 6 July, 1934 (W)

Brentford	Kilmarnock	10.57	57-58	7	-	1

CAVEN John (Joe) Brown
Kirkintilloch, 11 October, 1936 (CF)

Brighton & Hove A	Airdrie	03.62	61-62	10	-	0

CAVENER Philip (Phil)
Tynemouth, 2 June, 1961 (M)

Burnley	App	05.79	79-82	55	14	4
Bradford C	L	03.83	82	9	0	2
Gillingham	Tr	10.83	83	4	6	1
Northampton T	Tr	08.84	84-85	41	4	11
Peterborough U	Tr	03.86	85	9	1	0

CAVILL Aaran
Bedford, 5 March, 1984 (M)

Northampton T	YT	●	01	0	1	0

CAWLEY Peter
Walton-on-Thames, 15 September, 1965 (CD)

Wimbledon	Chertsey T	01.87	88	1	0	0
Bristol Rov	L	02.87	86	9	1	0
Fulham	L	12.88	88	3	2	0
Bristol Rov	Tr	07.89	89	1	2	0
Southend U	Tr	07.90	90	6	1	1
Exeter C	Tr	11.90	90	7	0	0
Barnet	Tr	11.91	91	3	0	0
Colchester U	Tr	10.92	92-97	178	2	8

CAWSTON Mervyn William
Diss, 4 February, 1952 ESch (G)

Norwich C	App	07.69	70	4	0	0
Southend U	L	08.74	74	10	0	0
Newport Co	L	01.76	75	4	0	0
Gillingham	Tr	05.76	76	19	0	0
Southend U	Chicago (USA)	08.78	78-83	189	0	0
Stoke C	Tr	03.84				
Southend U	Chelmsford C	11.84	84	9	0	0

CAWTHORN Paul James
Pontefract, 26 May, 1975 (W)

Scarborough	YT	12.93	92-93	8	3	1

CAWTHORNE Graham John
Doncaster, 30 September, 1958 (CD)

Grimsby T	Harworth CW	11.79	79	1	0	0
Doncaster Rov	Tr	03.82	81-82	33	0	1

CECERE Michele (Mike) Joseph
Chester, 4 January, 1968 (F)

Oldham Ath	App	01.86	86-88	35	17	8
Huddersfield T	Tr	11.88	88-89	50	4	8
Stockport Co	L	03.90	89	0	1	0
Walsall	Tr	08.90	90-93	92	20	32
Exeter C	Tr	01.94	93-95	34	9	11
Rochdale	Tr	07.96	96	2	2	1

CECH Petr
Plzen, Czech Republic, 20 May, 1982 CzR-32 (G)

Chelsea	Rennes (Fr)	07.04	04	35	0	0

CEGIELSKI Wayne
Bedwellty, 11 January, 1956 Wu21-2 (CD)

Tottenham H	App	05.73				
Northampton T	L	03.75	74	11	0	0
Wrexham	Schalke 04 (Ger)	09.76	76-81	112	11	0
Port Vale	Tr	08.82	82-84	91	1	5
Blackpool	Tr	03.85	84	5	1	1
Hereford U	Tr	07.85	85-86	46	4	2

League Club	Source	Date Signed	Seasons Played	Career Record Apps	Subs	Gls
CERNY Radek						
Prague, Czech Republic, 18 February, 1974 CzR-3						(G)
Tottenham H (L)	Slavia Prague (Cz)	01.05	04	2	1	0
CHADBOURNE William						
Mansfield, 29 October, 1922						(IF)
Mansfield T	South Normanton	04.47	46-47	9	-	3
CHADWICK Clifton (Cliff)						
Bolton, 26 January, 1914						(W)
Oldham Ath	Fleetwood	10.33	33	18	-	6
Middlesbrough	Tr	02.34	33-38	93	-	27
Hull C	Tr	09.46	46	23	-	7
Darlington	Tr	07.47	47	37	-	5
CHADWICK David (Dave) Edwin						
Ootamund, India, 19 August, 1943						(W)
Southampton	Jnrs	10.60	61-65	25	0	1
Middlesbrough	Tr	07.66	66-69	100	2	3
Halifax T	Tr	01.70	69-71	95	0	15
Bournemouth	Tr	02.72	71-73	29	7	4
Torquay U	L	12.72	72	10	0	0
Gillingham	Tr	09.74	74	35	0	3
CHADWICK Frank Robert						
Blackburn, 9 November, 1927						(WH)
Blackburn Rov	Jnrs	06.46	48-52	11	-	1
CHADWICK Frederick (Fred) William						
Manchester, 8 September, 1913 Died 1987						(CF)
Wolverhampton W	British Dyes	05.35				
Newport Co	Tr	09.36	36-37	40	-	19
Ipswich T	Tr	06.38	38-46	40	-	18
Bristol Rov	Tr	07.47	47	6	-	1
CHADWICK Graham						
Oldham, 8 April, 1942						(WH)
Manchester C	Jnrs	03.62	62-63	12	-	0
Walsall	Tr	08.64	64	9	-	0
Chester	Tr	07.65	65-66	11	1	0
CHADWICK Harold						
Oldham, 25 January, 1919 Died 1987						(W)
Grimsby T		05.45				
Tranmere Rov		03.48	47-48	9	-	0
CHADWICK Keith Michael						
Kidsgrove, 10 March, 1953						(F)
Port Vale	Nantwich T	09.73	73-75	29	12	7
CHADWICK Luke Harry						
Cambridge, 18 November, 1980 EYth/Eu21-13						(M)
Manchester U	YT	02.99	00-02	11	14	2
Reading	L	02.03	02	15	0	1
Burnley	L	07.03	03	23	13	5
West Ham U	Tr	08.04	04	22	10	1
CHADWICK Nicholas (Nick) Gerald						
Market Drayton, 26 October, 1982						(F)
Everton	YT	10.99	01-04	3	11	3
Derby Co	L	02.03	02	4	2	0
Millwall	L	11.03	03	6	0	2
Millwall	L	03.04	03	5	4	2
Plymouth Arg	Tr	02.05	04	11	4	1
CHADWICK Simon Leslie						
Liverpool, 15 March, 1968						(F)
Wrexham	Jnrs	08.85	85	1	1	0
CHALK Martyn Peter Glyn						
Swindon, 30 August, 1969						(W)
Derby Co	Louth U	01.90	91	4	3	1
Stockport Co	Tr	06.94	94-95	29	14	6
Wrexham	Tr	02.96	95-01	136	48	13
CHALK Stephen (Steve) Roger						
Southampton, 15 October, 1957						(G)
Bournemouth	App	10.75	75-77	11	0	0
CHALKIAS Konstantinos						
Larisa, Greece, 30 May, 1974 Greece 5						(G)
Portsmouth	Panathinaikos (Gre)	01.05	04	5	0	0
CHALKLIN Geoffrey (Geoff)						
Swindon, 1 October, 1956 ESch						(CD)
Swindon T	App	10.74	75	3	0	0
CHALLENDER Gregory (Greg) Louis						
Rochdale, 5 February, 1973						(M)
Preston NE	Mossley	05.93	93	5	5	2

League Club	Source	Date Signed	Seasons Played	Career Record Apps	Subs	Gls
CHALLINOR David (Dave) Paul						
Chester, 2 October, 1975 ESch/EYth						(CD)
Tranmere Rov	Bromborough Pool	07.94	96-01	124	16	6
Stockport Co	Tr	01.02	01-03	78	3	1
Bury	L	01.04	03	15	0	0
Bury	Tr	07.04	04	43	0	1
CHALLINOR Paul						
Newcastle-under-Lyme, 6 April, 1976						(CD)
Birmingham C	YT	07.94				
Bury	Telford U	08.99	99	0	1	0
CHALLIS Roger Leonard Alfred						
Rochester, 3 August, 1943 EYth						(FB)
Gillingham	Jnrs	09.60	60-62	10	-	0
Crewe Alex	Tr	08.64	64	3	-	0
CHALLIS Stanley (Stan) Marcel						
Lympstone, 22 April, 1918						(W)
Exeter C	Lympstone	09.45	46	4	-	1
CHALLIS Trevor Michael						
Paddington, 23 October, 1975 EYth/Eu21-2						(FB)
Queens Park Rgrs	YT	07.94	95-96	12	1	0
Bristol Rov	Tr	07.98	98-02	137	8	1
Shrewsbury T	Telford U	03.04	04	38	0	0
CHALMERS Grant						
Guernsey, 12 September, 1969						(M)
Brentford	Northerners	08.92	92	9	2	1
CHALMERS Leonard (Len) Austin						
Geddington, 4 September, 1936						(FB)
Leicester C	Corby T	01.56	57-65	171	0	4
Notts Co	Tr	07.66	66-67	51	0	1
CHALMERS Paul						
Glasgow, 31 October, 1963 SYth						(F)
Bradford C (L)	Glasgow Celtic	01.86	85	2	0	0
Swansea C	St Mirren	11.89	89-91	39	19	13
CHALQI Khalid						
Oujda, Morocco, 28 April, 1971						(M)
Torquay U	Creteil (Fr)	11.00	00	20	1	1
CHAMBERLAIN Alec Francis Roy						
March, 20 June, 1964						(G)
Ipswich T	Ramsey T	07.81				
Colchester U	Tr	08.82	82-86	188	0	0
Everton	Tr	07.87				
Tranmere Rov	L	11.87	87	15	0	0
Luton T	Tr	07.88	88-92	138	0	0
Sunderland	Tr	07.93	93-95	89	1	0
Watford	Tr	07.96	96-04	240	4	0
CHAMBERLAIN Derek Colin						
Nottingham, 6 January, 1933						(FB)
Aston Villa	Parliament St Meth	11.53				
Mansfield T	Tr	11.56	56-57	43	-	0
CHAMBERLAIN Glyn						
Chesterfield, 29 July, 1957						(FB)
Burnley	App	11.74				
Chesterfield	Tr	12.76	76-78	17	1	0
Halifax T	Tr	08.81	81	35	0	0
CHAMBERLAIN Kenneth (Ken) Russell						
Durban, South Africa, 30 June, 1926						(CD)
Charlton Ath	Parkhill	10.51	52-56	42	-	0
CHAMBERLAIN Mark Valentine						
Stoke-on-Trent, 19 November, 1961 ESch/Eu21-4/E-8						(W)
Port Vale	App	05.79	78-81	90	6	18
Stoke C	Tr	08.82	82-85	109	2	17
Sheffield Wed	Tr	09.85	85-87	32	34	8
Portsmouth	Tr	08.88	88-93	143	24	20
Brighton & Hove A	Tr	08.94	94	12	7	2
Exeter C	Tr	08.95	95-96	51	8	4
CHAMBERLAIN Neville Patrick						
Stoke-on-Trent, 22 January, 1960						(F)
Port Vale	App	01.78	77-82	133	8	32
Stoke C	Tr	09.82	82-83	7	0	0
Newport Co	L	11.83	83	6	0	2
Plymouth Arg	L	03.84	83	7	4	3
Newport Co	Tr	06.84	84	39	2	13
Mansfield T	Tr	07.85	85-86	56	5	19
Doncaster Rov	Tr	08.87	87	22	7	4
CHAMBERLAIN Peter Michael						
Liverpool, 30 June, 1935						(CD)
Leicester C		09.56				

League Club	Source	Date Signed	Seasons Played	Career Record Apps	Subs	Gls
Swindon T	Tr	06.57	57-62	80	-	6
Aldershot	Tr	10.62	62-64	46	-	1

CHAMBERLAIN Trevor (Tosh) Charles
Camden Town, 11 July, 1934 ESch/EYth (W)

League Club	Source	Date Signed	Seasons Played	Apps	Subs	Gls
Fulham	Jnrs	07.51	54-64	187	-	59

CHAMBERS Adam Craig
West Bromwich, 20 November, 1980 EYth (FB)

League Club	Source	Date Signed	Seasons Played	Apps	Subs	Gls
West Bromwich A	YT	01.99	00-02	38	18	1
Sheffield Wed	L	02.04	03	8	3	0
Kidderminster Hrs	Tr	03.05	04	2	0	0

CHAMBERS Brian Mark
Newcastle, 31 October, 1949 ESch (M)

League Club	Source	Date Signed	Seasons Played	Apps	Subs	Gls
Sunderland	Jnrs	08.67	70-72	53	10	5
Arsenal	Tr	06.73	73	1	0	0
Luton T	Tr	02.74	74-76	73	3	9
Millwall	Tr	07.77	77-78	54	5	9
Bournemouth	Tr	07.79	79-80	39	3	7
Halifax T	Tr	03.81	80	10	0	1

CHAMBERS David (Dave) Martin
Barnsley, 6 June, 1947 (W)

League Club	Source	Date Signed	Seasons Played	Apps	Subs	Gls
Rotherham U	App	06.65	65-67	23	4	4
Southend U	Cambridge U	10.68	68-70	52	10	5
York C	Tr	03.71	70-71	8	8	1

CHAMBERS James Ashley
West Bromwich, 20 November, 1980 EYth (CD)

League Club	Source	Date Signed	Seasons Played	Apps	Subs	Gls
West Bromwich A	YT	01.99	99-03	54	19	0
Watford	L	08.04	04	40	0	0

CHAMBERS John Frederick
Birmingham, 7 October, 1949 (M)

League Club	Source	Date Signed	Seasons Played	Apps	Subs	Gls
Aston Villa	App	10.66	68	1	1	0
Southend U	Tr	07.69	69	6	1	0

CHAMBERS Leroy Dean
Sheffield, 25 October, 1972 (F)

League Club	Source	Date Signed	Seasons Played	Apps	Subs	Gls
Sheffield Wed	YT	06.91				
Chester C	Tr	08.94	94-95	8	13	1
Macclesfield T	Boston U	12.97	97	17	4	4

CHAMBERS Luke
Kettering, 29 August, 1985 (FB)

League Club	Source	Date Signed	Seasons Played	Apps	Subs	Gls
Northampton T	Sch	11.03	02-04	38	14	0

CHAMBERS Paul Anthony
Wolverhampton, 14 January, 1965 (CD)

League Club	Source	Date Signed	Seasons Played	Apps	Subs	Gls
Plymouth Arg	App	01.83				
Torquay U	Saltash U	10.84	84	1	1	0

CHAMBERS Philip (Phil) Martin
Barnsley, 10 November, 1953 ESch (FB)

League Club	Source	Date Signed	Seasons Played	Apps	Subs	Gls
Barnsley	App	11.71	70-84	441	1	7
Rochdale	Tr	08.85	85	9	1	0
Hartlepool U	Tr	11.85	85	29	0	0

CHAMBERS Stephen (Steve)
Worksop, 20 July, 1968 (FB)

League Club	Source	Date Signed	Seasons Played	Apps	Subs	Gls
Mansfield T	Sheffield Wed (App)	11.86	86-90	42	14	0

CHAMBERS Triston Gregory
Enfield, 25 December, 1982 (F)

League Club	Source	Date Signed	Seasons Played	Apps	Subs	Gls
Colchester U	YT	07.02	01	0	1	0

CHAMPELOVIER Leslie (Les) William
Kensington, 23 April, 1933 EAmat (IF)

League Club	Source	Date Signed	Seasons Played	Apps	Subs	Gls
Brighton & Hove (Am)	Hayes	05.57	57	1	-	0

CHANDLER Dean Andrew Robert
Ilford, 6 May, 1976 (CD)

League Club	Source	Date Signed	Seasons Played	Apps	Subs	Gls
Charlton Ath	YT	04.94	94-95	1	1	1
Torquay U	L	03.97	96	4	0	0

CHANDLER Frederick (Fred) Ernest John
Hythe, Hampshire, 2 August, 1912 (IF)

League Club	Source	Date Signed	Seasons Played	Apps	Subs	Gls
Reading	Newport (IoW)	05.32	32-35	41	-	14
Blackpool	Tr	10.35	35	15	-	2
Swindon T	Tr	05.36	36	21	-	7
Crewe Alex	Tr	05.37	37-46	81	-	21

CHANDLER Ian
Sunderland, 20 March, 1968 ESch (F)

League Club	Source	Date Signed	Seasons Played	Apps	Subs	Gls
Barnsley	Jnrs	08.86	86	8	4	4
Stockport Co	L	08.87	87	4	1	0
Aldershot	Tr	08.88	88	5	4	2

CHANDLER Jeffrey (Jeff) George
Hammersmith, 19 June, 1959 IRu21-1/IR-2 (W)

League Club	Source	Date Signed	Seasons Played	Apps	Subs	Gls
Blackpool	App	08.76	77-78	31	6	6
Leeds U	Tr	09.79	79-80	21	5	2
Bolton W	Tr	10.81	81-84	152	5	36
Derby Co	Tr	07.85	85-86	45	1	9
Mansfield T	L	11.86	86	6	0	0
Bolton W	Tr	07.87	87-89	18	6	4
Cardiff C	Tr	11.89	89-90	21	4	0

CHANDLER Raymond (Ray)
Bath, 14 August, 1931 (G)

League Club	Source	Date Signed	Seasons Played	Apps	Subs	Gls
Bristol Rov	Bristol C (Am)	06.53	53-54	12	-	0
Swindon T	Tr	06.56	56-58	35	-	0

CHANDLER Richard (Ricky) David
Bristol, 26 September, 1961 ESch (F)

League Club	Source	Date Signed	Seasons Played	Apps	Subs	Gls
Bristol C	App	10.78	80-82	57	4	13

CHANDLER Robin Anthony Sydney
Luton, 19 December, 1942 ESch (CF)

League Club	Source	Date Signed	Seasons Played	Apps	Subs	Gls
Luton T	Jnrs	12.61	60-64	13	-	0

CHANNING Justin Andrew
Reading, 19 November, 1968 EYth (FB)

League Club	Source	Date Signed	Seasons Played	Apps	Subs	Gls
Queens Park Rgrs	App	08.86	86-92	42	13	5
Bristol Rov	Tr	10.92	92-95	121	9	10
Leyton Orient	Tr	06.96	96-97	69	5	5

CHANNON Michael (Mike) Roger
Orcheston, 28 November, 1948 Eu23-9/FLge-2/E-46 (F)

League Club	Source	Date Signed	Seasons Played	Apps	Subs	Gls
Southampton	App	12.65	65-76	388	3	157
Manchester C	Tr	07.77	77-79	71	1	24
Southampton	Tr	09.79	79-81	119	0	28
Newcastle U	Carolina Hills (USA)	09.82	82	4	0	1
Bristol Rov	Tr	10.82	82	4	5	0
Norwich C	Tr	12.82	82-84	84	4	16
Portsmouth	Tr	08.85	85	34	0	6

CHAPLOW Richard David
Accrington, 2 February, 1985 EYth/Eu21 (M)

League Club	Source	Date Signed	Seasons Played	Apps	Subs	Gls
Burnley	Sch	09.03	02-04	48	17	7
West Bromwich A	Tr	01.05	04	3	1	0

CHAPMAN Benjamin (Ben)
Scunthorpe, 2 March, 1979 (FB)

League Club	Source	Date Signed	Seasons Played	Apps	Subs	Gls
Grimsby T	YT	07.97	98-01	13	8	0
Boston U	Tr	08.02	02-03	70	4	0

CHAPMAN Campbell
Sutton-in-Ashfield, 28 June, 1963 (M)

League Club	Source	Date Signed	Seasons Played	Apps	Subs	Gls
Peterborough U	App	06.81				
Wolverhampton W	Bilston T	12.84	84-85	47	6	4
Crewe Alex	Preston NE (N/C)	11.86	86	0	1	0

CHAPMAN Cavan
Emsworth, 11 September, 1967 (F)

League Club	Source	Date Signed	Seasons Played	Apps	Subs	Gls
Wolverhampton W	App	07.84	84	1	0	0

CHAPMAN Daniel (Danny) Graham
Peckham, 21 November, 1974 (M)

League Club	Source	Date Signed	Seasons Played	Apps	Subs	Gls
Millwall	YT	03.93	94	4	8	0
Leyton Orient	Tr	07.95	95-96	69	9	4

CHAPMAN Darren Peter
Lincoln, 15 November, 1974 (M)

League Club	Source	Date Signed	Seasons Played	Apps	Subs	Gls
Lincoln C	YT	07.91	91	0	1	0

CHAPMAN Daryl Mark
Kenilworth, 17 September, 1963 (F)

League Club	Source	Date Signed	Seasons Played	Apps	Subs	Gls
Derby Co	Jnrs	07.82				
Crewe Alex	Tr	03.83	82	3	3	2

CHAPMAN Edwin (Eddie)
Blackburn, 2 May, 1919 Died 1976 (CF)

League Club	Source	Date Signed	Seasons Played	Apps	Subs	Gls
Blackburn Rov	Darwen	05.36				
Accrington St	Tr	07.38	38	4	-	1
Oldham Ath	Tr	06.39				
Stockport Co	Tr	08.46	46	9	-	3

CHAPMAN Edwin (Eddie) Maude
East Ham, 3 August, 1923 Died 2002 (IF)

League Club	Source	Date Signed	Seasons Played	Apps	Subs	Gls
West Ham U	Romford	09.42	48	7	-	3

CHAPMAN Gary Anthony
Bradford, 1 May, 1964 (F)

League Club	Source	Date Signed	Seasons Played	Apps	Subs	Gls
Bradford C	Frickley Ath	08.88	88-89	2	3	0
Notts Co	Tr	09.89	89-90	13	12	4
Mansfield T	L	10.90	90	6	0	0
Exeter C	Tr	09.91	91-92	20	4	5
Torquay U	Tr	02.93	92	6	2	0
Darlington	Tr	08.93	93-94	57	17	9

CHAPMAN George
Burton-on-Trent, 8 October, 1920 (IF)

League Club	Source	Date Signed	Seasons Played	Apps	Subs	Gls
West Bromwich A	Donisthorpe	12.38				
Brighton & Hove A	Tr	07.46	46-47	43	-	12

CHAPMAN Harold (Harry)
Liverpool, 4 March, 1921 Died 1990 (WH)

League Club	Source	Date Signed	Seasons Played	Apps	Subs	Gls
Aston Villa	Kidderminster Hrs	02.47	47	6	-	0
Notts Co	Tr	03.49	48-50	53	-	1

CHAPMAN Ian Russell
Brighton, 31 May, 1970 (FB)

League Club	Source	Date Signed	Seasons Played	Apps	Subs	Gls
Brighton & Hove A	App	06.87	86-95	265	16	13
Gillingham	Tr	08.96	96	20	3	1

CHAPMAN John
Sacriston, 24 May, 1945 (FB)

League Club	Source	Date Signed	Seasons Played	Apps	Subs	Gls
Workington	Stockton	02.63	63-65	28	0	1
Reading	Tr	06.66	66-68	102	1	2
Stockport Co	Tr	07.69	69-71	87	2	5

CHAPMAN Kenneth (Ken) Arthur
Coventry, 25 April, 1932 (IF)

League Club	Source	Date Signed	Seasons Played	Apps	Subs	Gls
Blackpool	Jnrs	08.49				
Crewe Alex	Tr	07.53	53	25	-	8
Bradford C	Tr	07.54	54	26	-	4

CHAPMAN Kenneth (Ken) Freeman Raymond
Grimsby, 16 November, 1948 (W)

League Club	Source	Date Signed	Seasons Played	Apps	Subs	Gls
Grimsby T (Am)	Louth U	06.68	69	6	1	0

CHAPMAN Lee Roy
Lincoln, 5 December, 1959 Eu21-1/EB (F)

League Club	Source	Date Signed	Seasons Played	Apps	Subs	Gls
Stoke C	Jnrs	06.78	79-81	95	4	34
Plymouth Arg	L	12.78	78	3	1	0
Arsenal	Tr	08.82	82-83	15	8	4
Sunderland	Tr	12.83	83	14	1	3
Sheffield Wed	Tr	08.84	84-87	147	2	63
Nottingham F	Niort (Fr)	10.88	88-89	48	0	15
Leeds U	Tr	01.90	89-92	133	4	63
Portsmouth	Tr	08.93	93	5	0	2
West Ham U	Tr	09.93	93-94	33	7	7
Southend U	L	01.95	94	1	0	1
Ipswich T	Tr	01.95	94-95	11	11	1
Leeds U	L	01.96	95	2	0	0
Swansea C	Tr	03.96	95	7	0	4

CHAPMAN Leslie (Les)
Oldham, 27 September, 1948 (M)

League Club	Source	Date Signed	Seasons Played	Apps	Subs	Gls
Oldham Ath	Huddersfield T (Am)	01.67	66-69	75	1	9
Huddersfield T	Tr	09.69	69-74	120	14	8
Oldham Ath	Tr	12.74	74-78	186	1	11
Stockport Co	San Jose (USA)	05.79	79	32	0	1
Bradford C	Tr	02.80	79-82	137	2	3
Rochdale	Tr	06.83	83-84	87	1	0
Stockport Co	Tr	07.85	85	38	0	3
Preston NE	Tr	07.86	86-87	50	3	1

CHAPMAN Neville
Cockfield, County Durham, 15 September, 1941 Died 1993 (FB)

League Club	Source	Date Signed	Seasons Played	Apps	Subs	Gls
Middlesbrough	Jnrs	11.58	61-66	51	2	0
Darlington	Tr	09.67	67-68	31	1	0

CHAPMAN Paul Christopher
Cardiff, 28 September, 1951 (CD)

League Club	Source	Date Signed	Seasons Played	Apps	Subs	Gls
Plymouth Arg	App	10.69	69	2	1	0

CHAPMAN Philip (Phil) Edward
Chasetown, 27 January, 1925 (CF)

League Club	Source	Date Signed	Seasons Played	Apps	Subs	Gls
Walsall	Cannock T	09.48	48-50	63	-	36

CHAPMAN Reginald (Reg)
Eccles, 14 June, 1928 (W)

League Club	Source	Date Signed	Seasons Played	Apps	Subs	Gls
Crewe Alex	Hereford U	05.50	50-51	21	-	1

CHAPMAN Reginald (Reg) Frederick James
Shepherds Bush, 7 September, 1921 Died 1992 (CD)

League Club	Source	Date Signed	Seasons Played	Apps	Subs	Gls
Queens Park Rgrs		08.44	46-52	97	-	2

CHAPMAN Robert (Bob) Dennis
Aldridge, 18 August, 1946 (CD)

League Club	Source	Date Signed	Seasons Played	Apps	Subs	Gls
Nottingham F	Jnrs	08.63	63-76	347	12	17
Notts Co	Tr	08.77	77	42	0	0
Shrewsbury T	Tr	07.78	78-79	36	1	6

CHAPMAN Rodger Anthony
Doncaster, 20 November, 1944 (G)

League Club	Source	Date Signed	Seasons Played	Apps	Subs	Gls
Rotherham U		01.65	64	2	-	0
Doncaster Rov	Tr	12.65	65	5	0	0

CHAPMAN Roy Clifford
Birmingham, 18 March, 1934 Died 1983 (F)

League Club	Source	Date Signed	Seasons Played	Apps	Subs	Gls
Aston Villa	Kynoch Works	02.52	53-57	19	-	8
Lincoln C	Tr	11.57	57-61	105	-	45
Mansfield T	Tr	08.61	61-64	136	-	78
Lincoln C	Tr	01.65	64-66	69	1	32
Port Vale	Tr	08.67	67-68	76	0	35
Chester	Tr	06.69	69	9	0	3

CHAPMAN Samuel (Sammy) Edward Campbell
Belfast, 16 February, 1938 NIB (WH)

League Club	Source	Date Signed	Seasons Played	Apps	Subs	Gls
Mansfield T	Shamrock Rov	10.56	56-57	50	-	25
Portsmouth	Tr	02.58	57-61	48	-	10
Mansfield T	Tr	12.61	61-63	105	-	15

CHAPMAN Stuart
Lynemouth, 6 May, 1951 (F)

League Club	Source	Date Signed	Seasons Played	Apps	Subs	Gls
Port Vale	App	07.69	66-69	6	3	0

CHAPMAN Vernon William
Leicester, 9 May, 1921 (W)

League Club	Source	Date Signed	Seasons Played	Apps	Subs	Gls
Leicester C	Bath C	01.42	46	1	-	0
Leyton Orient	Tr	07.47	47-48	31	-	7

CHAPMAN Vincent (Vinny) John
Newcastle, 5 December, 1967 (FB)

League Club	Source	Date Signed	Seasons Played	Apps	Subs	Gls
Huddersfield T	Tow Law T	01.88	87	4	2	0
Rochdale	Tr	07.89	89-90	23	1	1

CHAPPELL Larratt (Lol)
High Green, 19 December, 1930 Died 1988 (CF)

League Club	Source	Date Signed	Seasons Played	Apps	Subs	Gls
Barnsley	Birdwell Rov	05.49	52-58	218	-	94
Doncaster Rov	Tr	08.59	59-60	33	-	5

CHAPPELL Leslie (Les) Alan
Nottingham, 6 February, 1947 (F)

League Club	Source	Date Signed	Seasons Played	Apps	Subs	Gls
Rotherham U	App	02.65	65-67	106	2	37
Blackburn Rov	Tr	05.68	68	7	0	0
Reading	Tr	07.69	69-74	193	8	78
Doncaster Rov	Tr	12.74	74-75	57	1	10
Swansea C	Tr	07.76	76-77	65	2	5

CHAPPLE Philip (Phil) Richard
Norwich, 26 November, 1966 (CD)

League Club	Source	Date Signed	Seasons Played	Apps	Subs	Gls
Norwich C	App	07.85				
Cambridge U	Tr	03.88	87-92	183	4	19
Charlton Ath	Tr	08.93	93-97	128	14	15
Peterborough U	Tr	07.98	98-99	16	1	1

CHAPPLE Shaun Ronald
Swansea, 14 February, 1973 WSch/Wu21-8/WB (M)

League Club	Source	Date Signed	Seasons Played	Apps	Subs	Gls
Swansea C	YT	07.91	91-97	72	35	9

CHAPUIS Cyril Sylvain Thierry
Lyon, France, 21 March, 1979 Fru21 (F)

League Club	Source	Date Signed	Seasons Played	Apps	Subs	Gls
Leeds U (L)	Marseille (Fr)	09.03	03	0	1	0

CHARD Philip (Phil) John
Corby, 16 October, 1960 (FB)

League Club	Source	Date Signed	Seasons Played	Apps	Subs	Gls
Peterborough U	Corby T	01.79	78-84	153	19	18
Northampton T	Tr	08.85	85-87	113	2	27
Wolverhampton W	Tr	03.88	87-89	26	8	5
Northampton T	Tr	10.89	89-93	155	8	19

CHARLERY Kenneth (Ken) Leroy
Stepney, 28 November, 1964 St Lucia 4 (F)

League Club	Source	Date Signed	Seasons Played	Apps	Subs	Gls
Maidstone U	Fisher Ath	03.89	89-90	41	18	11
Peterborough U	Tr	03.91	90-92	45	6	19
Watford	Tr	10.92	92-93	45	3	13
Peterborough U	Tr	12.93	93-94	70	0	24
Birmingham C	Tr	07.95	95	8	9	4
Southend U	L	01.96	95	2	1	0
Peterborough U	Tr	02.96	95-96	55	1	12
Stockport Co	Tr	03.97	96	8	2	0
Barnet	Tr	08.97	97-00	106	18	37

CHARLES Clive Michael
Bow, 3 October, 1951 Died 2003 EYth (FB)

League Club	Source	Date Signed	Seasons Played	Apps	Subs	Gls
West Ham U	App	08.69	71-73	12	2	0
Cardiff C	Tr	03.74	73-76	75	2	5

CHARLES Wesley **Darius** Donald
Ealing, 10 December, 1987 (M)

League Club	Source	Date Signed	Seasons Played	Apps	Subs	Gls
Brentford	Sch	●	04	1	0	0

CHARLES Gary Andrew
Newham, 13 April, 1970 Eu21-4/E-2 (FB)

League Club	Source	Date Signed	Seasons Played	Apps	Subs	Gls
Nottingham F	YT	11.87	88-92	54	2	1
Leicester C	L	03.89	88	5	3	0
Derby Co	Tr	07.93	93-94	61	0	3
Aston Villa	Tr	01.95	94-98	72	7	3
West Ham U	Benfica (Por)	10.99	99-00	2	3	0
Birmingham C	L	09.00	00	3	0	0

CHARLES Jeremy Melvyn
Swansea, 26 September, 1959 Wu21-2/W-19 (F)

League Club	Source	Date Signed	Seasons Played	Apps	Subs	Gls
Swansea C	App	01.77	76-83	224	23	52
Queens Park Rgrs	Tr	11.83	83	10	2	5
Oxford U	Tr	02.85	84-86	41	5	13

CHARLES John William
Canning Town, 20 September, 1944 Died 2002 EYth (FB)

League Club	Source	Date Signed	Seasons Played	Apps	Subs	Gls
West Ham U	App	05.62	62-69	117	1	1

CHARLES William John
Swansea, 27 December, 1931 Died 2004 ItLge-4/W-38 (CD/CF)

League Club	Source	Date Signed	Seasons Played	Apps	Subs	Gls
Leeds U	Jnrs	01.49	48-56	297	-	150
Leeds U	Juventus (It)	08.62	62	11	-	3
Cardiff C	AS Roma (It)	08.63	63-65	68	0	18

CHARLES Julian
Plaistow, 5 February, 1977 St Vincent 2 (F)

League Club	Source	Date Signed	Seasons Played	Apps	Subs	Gls
Brentford	Hampton & R'mond Bor	12.99	99-00	4	8	0

CHARLES Lee Mercury
Hillingdon, 20 August, 1971 (F)

League Club	Source	Date Signed	Seasons Played	Apps	Subs	Gls
Queens Park Rgrs	Chertsey T	08.95	95-96	6	10	1
Barnet	L	09.95	95	2	3	0
Cambridge U	L	02.98	97	7	0	1

CHARLES Melvyn (Mel)
Swansea, 14 May, 1935 Wu23-1/W-31 (WH)

League Club	Source	Date Signed	Seasons Played	Apps	Subs	Gls
Swansea T	Leeds U (Am)	05.52	52-58	233	-	66
Arsenal	Tr	04.59	59-61	60	-	26
Cardiff C	Tr	02.62	61-64	79	-	25
Port Vale	Portmadoc	02.67	66	7	0	0

CHARLES Robert (Bob) John
Bursledon, 26 December, 1941 ESch/EYth (G)

League Club	Source	Date Signed	Seasons Played	Apps	Subs	Gls
Southampton	Jnrs	04.59	59-60	26	-	0

CHARLES Stephen (Steve)
Sheffield, 10 May, 1960 ESch (M)

League Club	Source	Date Signed	Seasons Played	Apps	Subs	Gls
Sheffield U	Sheffield Univ	01.80	79-84	112	11	10
Wrexham	Tr	11.84	84-86	111	2	37
Mansfield T	Tr	08.87	87-92	231	6	38
Scunthorpe U	L	11.92	92	4	0	0
Scarborough	Tr	02.93	92-95	134	0	20

CHARLESWORTH Arnold
Sheffield, 6 July, 1930 (IF)

League Club	Source	Date Signed	Seasons Played	Apps	Subs	Gls
West Bromwich A	Boston U	03.52				
Rotherham U	Tr	08.53				
York C	Tr	04.54	54	1	-	0

CHARLESWORTH Stanley (Stan)
Conisbrough, 8 March, 1920 Died 2003 (CD)

League Club	Source	Date Signed	Seasons Played	Apps	Subs	Gls
Grimsby T	Wath W	12.37	38-46	2	-	0
Barnsley	Tr	12.46	46	7	-	0

CHARLESWORTH Terence (Terry)
Scunthorpe, 13 July, 1933 (G)

League Club	Source	Date Signed	Seasons Played	Apps	Subs	Gls
Scunthorpe U		06.52	52-56	19	-	0

CHARLTON Harold (Harry)
Gateshead, 22 June, 1951 (M)

League Club	Source	Date Signed	Seasons Played	Apps	Subs	Gls
Middlesbrough	App	07.68	70-74	8	2	0
Hartlepool	L	01.76	75	2	1	0
Chesterfield	Tr	03.76	75-76	17	4	0
Darlington	Buxton	08.79	79-81	69	3	4

CHARLTON John (Jack)
Ashington, 8 May, 1935 FLge-6/E-35 (CD)

League Club	Source	Date Signed	Seasons Played	Apps	Subs	Gls
Leeds U	Jnrs	05.52	52-72	629	0	70

CHARLTON John Alfred
Gateshead, 24 March, 1922 Died 1981 (G)

League Club	Source	Date Signed	Seasons Played	Apps	Subs	Gls
Gateshead (Am)		08.49	49	1	-	0

CHARLTON Kevin
Atherstone, 12 September, 1954 ESemiPro (G)

League Club	Source	Date Signed	Seasons Played	Apps	Subs	Gls
Wolverhampton W	App	09.72				
Bournemouth	Tr	12.73	73-74	21	0	0
Hereford U	Tr	06.75	75-77	52	0	0
Scarborough	Telford U	09.88	88	3	0	0

CHARLTON (Sir) Robert (Bobby)
Ashington, 11 October, 1937 ESch/EYth/Eu23-6/FLge-8/E-106 (M)

League Club	Source	Date Signed	Seasons Played	Apps	Subs	Gls
Manchester U	Jnrs	10.54	56-72	604	2	199
Preston NE	Tr	05.74	74	38	0	8

CHARLTON Simon Thomas
Huddersfield, 25 October, 1971 EYth (FB)

League Club	Source	Date Signed	Seasons Played	Apps	Subs	Gls
Huddersfield T	YT	07.89	89-92	121	3	1
Southampton	Tr	06.93	93-97	104	10	2
Birmingham C	Tr	12.97	97-99	69	3	0
Bolton W	Tr	07.00	00-03	108	12	0
Norwich C	Tr	07.04	04	22	2	1

CHARLTON Stanley (Stan)
Exeter, 28 June, 1929 EAmat (FB)

League Club	Source	Date Signed	Seasons Played	Apps	Subs	Gls
Leyton Orient	Bromley	11.52	52-55	151	-	1
Arsenal	Tr	11.55	55-58	99	-	0
Leyton Orient	Tr	12.58	58-64	216	-	1

CHARLTON Wilfred (Wilf) Sydney
Blyth, 12 September, 1933 (WH)

League Club	Source	Date Signed	Seasons Played	Apps	Subs	Gls
Huddersfield T	Portsmouth (Am)	11.50				
Southport	Tr	07.54	54-56	109	-	8
Tranmere Rov	Tr	06.57	57-60	92	-	4

CHARNLEY Derek Lawrence
Doncaster, 7 May, 1954 (F)

League Club	Source	Date Signed	Seasons Played	Apps	Subs	Gls
Scunthorpe U		02.73	72-75	28	10	3

CHARNLEY James (Chic) Callaghan
Glasgow, 11 June, 1963 (M)

League Club	Source	Date Signed	Seasons Played	Apps	Subs	Gls
Bolton W (L)	St Mirren	03.92	91	3	0	0

CHARNLEY Raymond (Ray) Ogden
Lancaster, 29 May, 1935 E-1 (F)

League Club	Source	Date Signed	Seasons Played	Apps	Subs	Gls
Blackpool	Morecambe	05.57	57-67	363	0	193
Preston NE	Tr	12.67	67	23	0	4
Wrexham	Tr	07.68	68	19	1	5
Bradford PA	Tr	01.69	68-69	59	0	15

CHARNOCK Philip (Phil) Anthony
Southport, 14 February, 1975 (M)

League Club	Source	Date Signed	Seasons Played	Apps	Subs	Gls
Liverpool	YT	03.93				
Blackpool	L	02.96	95	0	4	0
Crewe Alex	Tr	09.96	96-01	136	21	8
Port Vale	Tr	08.02	02	14	4	1
Bury	Tr	08.03	03	3	0	0

CHARTER Raymond (Ray)
Ashton-under-Lyne, 10 January, 1950 (FB)

League Club	Source	Date Signed	Seasons Played	Apps	Subs	Gls
Blackburn Rov	App	01.68	69-70	13	5	0
Stockport Co	Tr	07.71	71-73	87	4	2

CHARVET Laurent Jean
Beziers, France, 8 May, 1973 (FB)

League Club	Source	Date Signed	Seasons Played	Apps	Subs	Gls
Chelsea (L)	AS Cannes (Fr)	01.98	97	7	4	2
Newcastle U	AS Cannes (Fr)	07.98	98-00	37	3	1
Manchester C	Tr	10.00	00-01	19	4	0

CHASE Charles (Charlie) Thomas
Steyning, 31 January, 1924 (WH)

League Club	Source	Date Signed	Seasons Played	Apps	Subs	Gls
Watford	Brighton & Hove A (Am)	09.46	46-47	16	-	1
Crystal Palace	Tr	07.48	48-49	55	-	2

CHATHAM Alexander (Alec) Whyte
Glasgow, 7 July, 1936 (CF)

League Club	Source	Date Signed	Seasons Played	Apps	Subs	Gls
Barrow		12.58	58	1	-	0

CHATHAM Raymond (Ray) Harold
Wolverhampton, 20 July, 1924 Died 1999 (CD)

League Club	Source	Date Signed	Seasons Played	Apps	Subs	Gls
Wolverhampton W	Jnrs	06.45	46-53	76	-	0
Notts Co	Tr	01.54	53-58	127	-	4

CHATTERLEY Lawson (Lew) Colin
Birmingham, 15 February, 1945 EYth (M)

League Club	Source	Date Signed	Seasons Played	Apps	Subs	Gls
Aston Villa	App	02.62	62-70	149	4	26
Doncaster Rov	L	03.71	70	9	0	0
Northampton T	Tr	09.71	71	23	0	2
Grimsby T	Tr	02.72	71-73	72	1	16
Southampton	Tr	03.74	73-74	7	2	0
Torquay U	Tr	02.75	74-76	55	2	10

CHATTERTON Nicholas (Nicky) John
Norwood, 18 May, 1954 (M)

League Club	Source	Date Signed	Seasons Played	Apps	Subs	Gls
Crystal Palace	Jnrs	03.72	73-78	142	9	31
Millwall	Tr	11.78	78-85	258	6	56
Colchester U	Tr	09.86	86-88	47	2	8

CHAYTOR Kenneth (Kenny)
Trimdon, 18 November, 1937 (IF)

League Club	Source	Date Signed	Seasons Played	Apps	Subs	Gls
Oldham Ath	Jnrs	11.54	54-59	77	-	20

CHEADLE Thomas (Tom)
Stoke-on-Trent, 8 April, 1919 Died 1993 (CD)

League Club	Source	Date Signed	Seasons Played	Apps	Subs	Gls
Port Vale	Jnrs	05.46	46-56	333	-	14
Crewe Alex	Tr	07.57	57-58	37	-	0

CHEESEBROUGH Albert
Burnley, 17 January, 1935 Eu23-1 (IF)

League Club	Source	Date Signed	Seasons Played	Apps	Subs	Gls
Burnley	Jnrs	01.52	51-58	142	-	35

League Club	Source	Date Signed	Seasons Played	Apps	Subs	Gls
Leicester C	Tr	06.59	59-62	122	-	40
Port Vale	Tr	07.63	63-64	57	-	13
Mansfield T	Tr	07.65	65-66	24	0	0

CHEESEWRIGHT John Anthony
Romford, 12 January, 1973 (G)

League Club	Source	Date Signed	Seasons Played	Apps	Subs	Gls
Southend U	Tottenham H (YT)	03.91				
Birmingham C	Tr	11.91	91	1	0	0
Colchester U	Braintree T	01.94	93-94	40	0	0
Wycombe W	(Hong Kong)	03.96	96	18	0	0

CHEESLEY Paul Martyn
Bristol, 20 October, 1953 (F)

League Club	Source	Date Signed	Seasons Played	Apps	Subs	Gls
Norwich C	App	10.71	72-73	10	3	1
Bristol C	Tr	12.73	73-76	61	3	20

CHEETHAM Hugh David
Manchester, 3 February, 1958 (M)

League Club	Source	Date Signed	Seasons Played	Apps	Subs	Gls
Crewe Alex	App	01.76	75-78	90	6	0
Reading	Tr	07.79	79-80	10	2	0

CHEETHAM Michael (Mike) Martin
Amsterdam, Holland, 30 June, 1967 (M)

League Club	Source	Date Signed	Seasons Played	Apps	Subs	Gls
Ipswich T	Basingstoke T	10.88	88-89	1	3	0
Cambridge U	Tr	10.89	89-93	123	9	22
Chesterfield	Tr	07.94	94	5	0	0
Colchester U	Tr	03.95	94-95	33	4	3

CHEETHAM Roy Alexander John
Eccles, 21 December, 1939 (WH)

League Club	Source	Date Signed	Seasons Played	Apps	Subs	Gls
Manchester C	Jnrs	12.56	57-67	127	4	4
Charlton Ath	Detroit (USA)	10.68				
Chester	Tr	12.68	68-71	122	2	8

CHEETHAM Thomas (Tommy)
Wavertree, 8 December, 1950 Died 2003 (F)

League Club	Source	Date Signed	Seasons Played	Apps	Subs	Gls
Southport	Cambridge Park	12.69	69-70	24	2	4

CHEETHAM Thomas (Tommy) Miles
Byker, 11 October, 1910 Died 1993 (CF)

League Club	Source	Date Signed	Seasons Played	Apps	Subs	Gls
Queens Park Rgrs	Royal Artillery	08.35	35-38	115	-	81
Brentford	Tr	02.39	38	17	-	8
Lincoln C	Tr	10.45	46-47	47	-	29

CHENERY Benjamin (Ben) Roger
Ipswich, 28 January, 1977 (FB)

League Club	Source	Date Signed	Seasons Played	Apps	Subs	Gls
Luton T	YT	03.95	95	2	0	0
Cambridge U	Tr	07.97	97-99	97	1	2

CHENEY Denis
Coalville, 30 June, 1924 (IF)

League Club	Source	Date Signed	Seasons Played	Apps	Subs	Gls
Leicester C	Coalville T	11.41	47-48	2	-	0
Watford	L	02.48	47	18	-	4
Bournemouth	Tr	10.48	48-53	158	-	47
Aldershot	Tr	06.54	54-55	53	-	19

CHENHALL John Colin
Bristol, 23 July, 1927 (FB)

League Club	Source	Date Signed	Seasons Played	Apps	Subs	Gls
Arsenal	Maidenhead U	11.45	51-52	16	-	0
Fulham	Tr	07.53	53-57	91	-	0

CHEREDNIK Alexei
Pamir, Tadzhikistan, 12 December, 1960 USSR int (FB)

League Club	Source	Date Signed	Seasons Played	Apps	Subs	Gls
Southampton	Dnepr (USSR)	02.90	89-90	19	4	0

CHERRY Rex Aubrey
Penistone, 11 November, 1933 (CF)

League Club	Source	Date Signed	Seasons Played	Apps	Subs	Gls
Gillingham		03.53	52-53	10	-	4

CHERRY Steven (Steve) Reginald
Nottingham, 5 August, 1960 EYth (G)

League Club	Source	Date Signed	Seasons Played	Apps	Subs	Gls
Derby Co	App	03.78	79-83	77	0	0
Port Vale	L	11.80	80	4	0	0
Walsall	Tr	08.84	84-85	71	0	0
Plymouth Arg	Tr	10.86	86-88	73	0	0
Chesterfield	L	12.88	88	10	0	0
Notts Co	Tr	02.89	88-94	266	0	0
Watford	Tr	07.95	95	4	0	0
Plymouth Arg	Tr	02.96	95	16	0	0
Rotherham U	Tr	07.96	96	20	0	0
Notts Co	Stalybridge Celtic	03.98				
Mansfield T	Tr	07.98	98	1	0	0

CHERRY Trevor John
Huddersfield, 23 February, 1948 FLge-1/E-27 (CD)

League Club	Source	Date Signed	Seasons Played	Apps	Subs	Gls
Huddersfield T	Jnrs	07.65	66-71	185	3	12
Leeds U	Tr	06.72	72-82	393	6	24
Bradford C	Tr	12.82	82-84	92	0	0

CHESSELL Samuel (Sammy)
Shirebrook, 9 July, 1921 Died 1996 (FB)

League Club	Source	Date Signed	Seasons Played	Apps	Subs	Gls
Mansfield T	Welbeck Colliery	09.45	46-53	256	-	7

CHESTERS Colin Wayne
Crewe, 21 November, 1959 (F)

League Club	Source	Date Signed	Seasons Played	Apps	Subs	Gls
Derby Co	App	11.77	77-78	6	3	1
Crewe Alex	Tr	09.79	79-81	52	9	6

CHETTLE Stephen (Steve)
Nottingham, 27 September, 1968 Eu21-12 (CD)

League Club	Source	Date Signed	Seasons Played	Apps	Subs	Gls
Nottingham F	App	08.86	87-99	398	17	11
Barnsley	Tr	11.99	99-01	91	1	2
Walsall	L	09.01	01	6	0	0
Grimsby T	Tr	08.02	02	18	2	1

CHEUNG Chi Doy
Hong Kong, 30 July, 1941 (IF)

League Club	Source	Date Signed	Seasons Played	Apps	Subs	Gls
Blackpool	Tung Wah (HK)	10.60	60-61	2	-	1

CHEW John (Jackie)
Blackburn, 13 May, 1920 Died 2002 (W)

League Club	Source	Date Signed	Seasons Played	Apps	Subs	Gls
Burnley	Blackburn Rov (Am)	05.45	46-53	225	-	39
Bradford C	Tr	06.54	54	36	-	4

CHEW John (Jack)
Longton, 25 November, 1915 Died 1984 (FB)

League Club	Source	Date Signed	Seasons Played	Apps	Subs	Gls
Luton T		11.42				
Port Vale	Tr	03.46	46	9	-	0

CHEYROU Bruno
Suresnes, France, 10 May, 1978 France 2 (M)

League Club	Source	Date Signed	Seasons Played	Apps	Subs	Gls
Liverpool	OSC Lille (Fr)	07.02	02-03	17	14	2

CHIEDOZIE John Okay
Owerri, Nigeria, 18 April, 1960 Nigeria 9 (W)

League Club	Source	Date Signed	Seasons Played	Apps	Subs	Gls
Orient	App	04.77	76-80	131	14	20
Notts Co	Tr	08.81	81-83	110	1	15
Tottenham H	Tr	08.84	84-86	45	8	12
Derby Co	Tr	08.88	88	2	0	0
Notts Co	Tr	01.90	89	0	1	0
Chesterfield	Tr	03.90	89	5	2	0

CHILCOTT Kenneth (Ken)
Rhondda, 17 March, 1920 Died 2001 (W)

League Club	Source	Date Signed	Seasons Played	Apps	Subs	Gls
Bristol C	Eastville U	10.37	37-48	46	-	6

CHILDS Albert (Bert) Robert
Liverpool, 25 September, 1930 EAmat (FB)

League Club	Source	Date Signed	Seasons Played	Apps	Subs	Gls
Liverpool (Am)	Northern Nomads	09.53	53	2	-	0

CHILDS Gary Paul Colin
Birmingham, 19 April, 1964 EYth (W)

League Club	Source	Date Signed	Seasons Played	Apps	Subs	Gls
West Bromwich A	App	02.82	81-83	2	1	0
Walsall	Tr	10.83	83-86	120	11	17
Birmingham C	Tr	07.87	87-88	39	16	2
Grimsby T	Tr	07.89	89-96	204	29	26

CHILLINGWORTH Daniel (Dan) Thomas
Cambridge, 13 September, 1981 (F)

League Club	Source	Date Signed	Seasons Played	Apps	Subs	Gls
Cambridge U	YT	02.00	99-04	53	34	13
Darlington	L	11.01	01	2	2	1
Leyton Orient	L	12.04	04	8	0	2

CHILTON Allenby
South Hylton, 16 September, 1918 Died 1996 E-2 (CD)

League Club	Source	Date Signed	Seasons Played	Apps	Subs	Gls
Manchester U	Seaham Colliery	11.38	46-54	352	-	3
Grimsby T	Tr	03.55	54-56	63	-	0

CHILTON Anthony (Tony) Julian Thomas
Maryport, 7 September, 1965 (FB)

League Club	Source	Date Signed	Seasons Played	Apps	Subs	Gls
Sunderland	App	09.83				
Burnley	Tr	02.85	84	1	0	0
Hartlepool U	Tr	10.85	85	3	0	0

CHILTON Christopher (Chris) Roy
Sproatley, 25 June, 1943 (F)

League Club	Source	Date Signed	Seasons Played	Apps	Subs	Gls
Hull C	Jnrs	07.60	60-71	415	0	193
Coventry C	Tr	09.71	71	26	1	3

CHILTON Frederick (Fred)
Washington, 10 July, 1935 (FB)

League Club	Source	Date Signed	Seasons Played	Apps	Subs	Gls
Sunderland	Usworth Colliery	05.53	56-57	3	-	0

CHILVERS Geoffrey (Geoff) Thomas
Epsom, 31 January, 1925 Died 1971 ESch (WH)

League Club	Source	Date Signed	Seasons Played	Apps	Subs	Gls
Crystal Palace	Sutton U	03.45	48-53	118	-	1

CHILVERS Gordon Malcolm
Norwich, 15 November, 1933 (G)

League Club	Source	Date Signed	Seasons Played	Apps	Subs	Gls
Walsall	Fordhouses BC	04.52	51-57	123	-	0

CHILVERS Liam Christopher
Chelmsford, 6 November, 1981 (FB)

League Club	Source	Date Signed	Seasons Played	Apps	Subs	Gls
Arsenal	YT	07.00				
Northampton T	L	12.00	00	7	0	0

League Club	Source	Date Signed	Seasons Played	Apps	Subs	Gls
Notts Co	L	11.01	01	9	0	1
Colchester U	L	01.03	02	6	0	0
Colchester U	L	08.03	03	29	3	0
Colchester U	Tr	08.04	04	40	1	1

CHINAGLIA Giorgio
Carrara, Italy, 24 January, 1947 ItLge-1 (CF)

League Club	Source	Date Signed	Seasons Played	Apps	Subs	Gls
Swansea T	App	04.65	64-65	4	1	1

CHINE Athumani Khamiss
Dar es Salaam, Tanzania, 12 March, 1967 (M)

League Club	Source	Date Signed	Seasons Played	Apps	Subs	Gls
Walsall		03.92	91	4	1	0

CHIPPENDALE Brian Albert
Bradford, 29 October, 1964 (W)

League Club	Source	Date Signed	Seasons Played	Apps	Subs	Gls
York C	Bradford C (App)	10.83	83-84	2	6	0
Halifax T	L	11.84	84	1	1	0
Burnley	Tr	08.85	85	6	2	0
Preston NE	Tr	10.85	85	5	1	0

CHIPPO Youssef
Boujaad, Morocco, 10 June, 1973 Morocco 43 (M)

League Club	Source	Date Signed	Seasons Played	Apps	Subs	Gls
Coventry C	FC Porto (Por)	07.99	99-02	100	22	6

CHISHOLM Gordon William
Glasgow, 8 April, 1960 (M)

League Club	Source	Date Signed	Seasons Played	Apps	Subs	Gls
Sunderland	App	04.78	78-85	192	5	10

CHISHOLM John (Jack) Richardson
Edmonton, 9 October, 1924 Died 1977 (CD)

League Club	Source	Date Signed	Seasons Played	Apps	Subs	Gls
Tottenham H	Jnrs	10.42	47	2	-	0
Brentford	Tr	10.47	47-48	49	-	1
Sheffield U	Tr	03.49	48-49	21	-	1
Plymouth Arg	Tr	12.49	49-53	175	-	2

CHISHOLM Kenneth (Ken) McTaggart
Glasgow, 12 April, 1925 Died 1990 SWar-1 (IF)

League Club	Source	Date Signed	Seasons Played	Apps	Subs	Gls
Leeds U	Partick Th	01.48	47-48	40	-	17
Leicester C	Tr	01.49	48-49	42	-	17
Coventry C	Tr	03.50	49-51	68	-	34
Cardiff C	Tr	03.52	51-53	62	-	33
Sunderland	Tr	01.54	53-55	78	-	34
Workington	Tr	08.56	56-57	39	-	14

CHISHOLM Wilfred (Wilf)
Hebburn, 23 May, 1921 (G)

League Club	Source	Date Signed	Seasons Played	Apps	Subs	Gls
Grimsby T	Newcastle U (Am)	09.46	46-50	92	-	0

CHISNALL Joseph **Philip (Phil)**
Manchester, 27 October, 1942 ESch/Eu23-1 (M)

League Club	Source	Date Signed	Seasons Played	Apps	Subs	Gls
Manchester U	Jnrs	11.59	61-63	35	-	8
Liverpool	Tr	04.64	64	6	-	1
Southend U	Tr	08.67	67-70	137	5	28
Stockport Co	Tr	09.71	71	30	0	2

CHISWICK Peter John Henry
Plaistow, 19 September, 1929 Died 1962 (G)

League Club	Source	Date Signed	Seasons Played	Apps	Subs	Gls
West Ham U	Jnrs	07.47	53-54	19	-	0
Gillingham	Tr	07.56	56	14	-	0

CHITTY Wilfred (Wilf) Sidney
Walton-on-Thames, 10 July, 1912 Died 1997 (W)

League Club	Source	Date Signed	Seasons Played	Apps	Subs	Gls
Chelsea	Woking	03.30	31-37	45	-	16
Plymouth Arg	Tr	12.38	38	3	-	1
Reading	Tr	08.39	46-47	23	-	7

CHIVERS Gary Paul Stephen
Stockwell, 15 May, 1960 (FB)

League Club	Source	Date Signed	Seasons Played	Apps	Subs	Gls
Chelsea	App	07.78	78-82	128	5	4
Swansea C	Tr	08.83	83	10	0	0
Queens Park Rgrs	Tr	02.84	84-86	58	2	0
Watford	Tr	09.87	87	14	0	0
Brighton & Hove A	Tr	03.88	87-92	215	2	13
Bournemouth	Lyn Oslo (Nor)	11.93	93-94	29	2	2

CHIVERS Martin Harcourt
Southampton, 27 April, 1945 Eu23-17/FLge-1/E-24 (F)

League Club	Source	Date Signed	Seasons Played	Apps	Subs	Gls
Southampton	Jnrs	09.62	62-67	174	1	97
Tottenham H	Tr	01.68	67-75	268	10	118
Norwich C	Servette (Swi)	07.78	78	11	0	4
Brighton & Hove A	Tr	03.79	78-79	4	1	1

CHMILOWSKY Roman
Bradford, 19 April, 1959 (G)

League Club	Source	Date Signed	Seasons Played	Apps	Subs	Gls
Halifax T (Am)	Jnrs	04.77	76	1	0	0

CHOLERTON William
Derby, 1 January, 1949 (FB)

League Club	Source	Date Signed	Seasons Played	Apps	Subs	Gls
Derby Co	App	12.66	66	1	0	0

CHOPRA Rocky **Michael**
Newcastle, 23 December, 1983 EYth/Eu20/Eu21-1 (F)

League Club	Source	Date Signed	Seasons Played	Apps	Subs	Gls
Newcastle U	YT	01.01	02-04	1	7	0
Watford	L	03.03	02	4	1	5
Nottingham F	L	02.04	03	3	2	0
Barnsley	L	08.04	04	38	1	17

CHORLEY Benjamin (Ben) Francis
Sidcup, 30 September, 1982 (CD)

League Club	Source	Date Signed	Seasons Played	Apps	Subs	Gls
Arsenal	YT	07.01				
Brentford	L	08.02	02	2	0	0
Wimbledon/MK Dons	Tr	03.03	02-04	82	4	4

CHOULES Leonard (Len) George
Orpington, 29 January, 1932 (CD)

League Club	Source	Date Signed	Seasons Played	Apps	Subs	Gls
Crystal Palace	Sutton U	05.51	52-61	258	-	2

CHRISTENSEN Thomas (Tommy) Anton
Aarhus, Denmark, 20 July, 1961 (W)

League Club	Source	Date Signed	Seasons Played	Apps	Subs	Gls
Leicester C	Elche (Sp)	11.85	85	1	1	0
Portsmouth	Tr	11.85	85	3	0	2

CHRISTIANSEN Jesper
Denmark, 18 June, 1980 (F)

League Club	Source	Date Signed	Seasons Played	Apps	Subs	Gls
Kidderminster Hrs	OB Odense (Den)	01.04	03-04	22	16	1

CHRISTIE David
Salford, 26 February, 1973 (W)

League Club	Source	Date Signed	Seasons Played	Apps	Subs	Gls
Preston NE	YT	07.91	91-92	1	3	0
Halifax T	Tr	01.93	92	6	3	0

CHRISTIE Derrick Hugh Michael
Bletchley, 15 March, 1957 (W)

League Club	Source	Date Signed	Seasons Played	Apps	Subs	Gls
Northampton T	App	03.75	73-78	116	22	18
Cambridge U	Tr	11.78	78-83	132	6	19
Reading	Tr	07.84	84	8	6	1
Cardiff C	Tr	10.85	85	18	1	2
Peterborough U	Tr	08.86	86	6	2	0

CHRISTIE Frank
Scone, 17 December, 1927 Died 1996 (WH)

League Club	Source	Date Signed	Seasons Played	Apps	Subs	Gls
Liverpool	Forfar Ath	03.49	49	4	-	0

CHRISTIE Iyseden
Coventry, 14 November, 1976 (F)

League Club	Source	Date Signed	Seasons Played	Apps	Subs	Gls
Coventry C	YT	05.95	95	0	1	0
Bournemouth	L	11.96	96	3	1	0
Mansfield T	L	02.97	96	8	0	0
Mansfield T	Tr	06.97	97-98	44	37	18
Leyton Orient	Tr	07.99	99-01	32	26	12
Mansfield T	Tr	08.02	02-03	53	11	26
Kidderminster Hrs	Tr	08.04	04	1	7	0

CHRISTIE Jeremy John
Whangarei, New Zealand, 22 May, 1983 Nzu17/Nzu20 (M)

League Club	Source	Date Signed	Seasons Played	Apps	Subs	Gls
Barnsley	YT	●	01	0	1	0

CHRISTIE John Alexander
Fraserburgh, 26 September, 1929 (G)

League Club	Source	Date Signed	Seasons Played	Apps	Subs	Gls
Southampton	Ayr U	01.51	50-58	197	-	0
Walsall	Tr	06.59	59-62	102	-	0

CHRISTIE Malcom (Malcolm) Neil
Stamford, 11 April, 1979 Eu21-11 (F)

League Club	Source	Date Signed	Seasons Played	Apps	Subs	Gls
Derby Co	Nuneaton Borough	11.98	98-02	90	26	30
Middlesbrough	Tr	01.03	02-04	20	4	6

CHRISTIE Trevor John
Cresswell, Northumberland, 28 February, 1959 (F)

League Club	Source	Date Signed	Seasons Played	Apps	Subs	Gls
Leicester C	App	12.76	77-78	28	3	8
Notts Co	Tr	06.79	79-83	158	29	64
Nottingham F	Tr	07.84	84	14	0	5
Derby Co	Tr	02.85	84-85	65	0	22
Manchester C	Tr	08.86	86	9	0	3
Walsall	Tr	10.86	86-88	91	8	22
Mansfield T	Tr	03.89	88-90	88	4	24

CHRISTOPHER Paul Anthony
Poole, 19 June, 1954 (F)

League Club	Source	Date Signed	Seasons Played	Apps	Subs	Gls
Bournemouth	App	11.71				
Mansfield T	Tr	07.73	73	7	1	1

CHUNG Cyril (Sammy)
Abingdon, 16 July, 1932 (IF)

League Club	Source	Date Signed	Seasons Played	Apps	Subs	Gls
Reading	Headington U	11.51	53-54	22	-	12
Norwich C	Tr	01.55	54-56	47	-	9
Watford	Tr	06.57	57-64	220	-	22

CHURCH Garry
Pontefract, 20 September, 1944 (WH)

League Club	Source	Date Signed	Seasons Played	Apps	Subs	Gls
Bradford PA	Great Preston Jnrs	07.62	63	4	-	0

CHURCH John
Lowestoft, 17 September, 1919 Died 2004 (W)

League Club	Source	Date Signed	Seasons Played	Apps	Subs	Gls
Norwich C	Lowestoft T	09.36	37-49	110	-	16
Colchester U	Tr	07.50	50-53	118	-	21

CHURCHILL Trevor
Barnsley, 20 November, 1923 (G)

League Club	Source	Date Signed	Seasons Played	Apps	Subs	Gls
Reading	Loughborough Coll	09.46	46	10	-	0
Leicester C	Tr	08.47				
Rochdale	Tr	01.49	48-52	110	-	0
Swindon T	Tr	05.53	53	11	-	0

CHURCHOUSE Gary
Wembley, 1 February, 1957 (M)

League Club	Source	Date Signed	Seasons Played	Apps	Subs	Gls
Charlton Ath	Windsor & Eton	03.79	78-79	13	5	0

CHURMS Dennis John
Rotherham, 8 May, 1931 (IF)

League Club	Source	Date Signed	Seasons Played	Apps	Subs	Gls
Rotherham U	Spurley Hey	04.50	53-55	15	-	0
Coventry C	Tr	06.56	56	10	-	2
Exeter C	Tr	03.57	56-57	44	-	8

CINI Joseph (Joe)
Pieta, Malta, 20 November, 1936 Malta 22 (W)

League Club	Source	Date Signed	Seasons Played	Apps	Subs	Gls
Queens Park Rgrs (Am)	Hibernians (Malta)	08.59	59	7	-	1

CIRCUIT Steven (Steve)
Sheffield, 11 April, 1972 (M)

League Club	Source	Date Signed	Seasons Played	Apps	Subs	Gls
Sheffield U	YT	07.90				
Halifax T	Stafford Rgrs	03.93	92	0	1	0

CISSE Aliou
Zinguinchor, Senegal, 24 March, 1976 Senegal 23 (M)

League Club	Source	Date Signed	Seasons Played	Apps	Subs	Gls
Birmingham C	Montpellier (Fr)	07.02	02-03	26	10	0
Portsmouth	Tr	08.04	04	12	8	0

CISSE Djibril
Arles, France, 12 August, 1981 France 20 (F)

League Club	Source	Date Signed	Seasons Played	Apps	Subs	Gls
Liverpool	Auxerre (Fr)	07.04	04	10	6	4

CISSE Edouard
Pau, France, 30 March, 1978 Fru21 (M)

League Club	Source	Date Signed	Seasons Played	Apps	Subs	Gls
West Ham U (L)	Paris St Germain (Fr)	08.02	02	18	7	0

CITRON Gerald (Gerry) Conrad
Manchester, 8 April, 1935 (W)

League Club	Source	Date Signed	Seasons Played	Apps	Subs	Gls
Chester (Am)	Corinthian Casuals	10.59	59	2	-	0

CLACK Frank Edward
Witney, 30 March, 1912 Died 1995 (G)

League Club	Source	Date Signed	Seasons Played	Apps	Subs	Gls
Birmingham	Witney T	05.33	33-38	60	-	0
Brentford	Tr	07.39				
Bristol C	Tr	05.47	46-48	67	-	0

CLAESEN Nicolas (Nico) Pieter Josef
Leut, Belgium, 1 October, 1962 Belgium int (F)

League Club	Source	Date Signed	Seasons Played	Apps	Subs	Gls
Tottenham H	Standard Liege (Bel)	10.86	86-87	37	13	18

CLAMP Edward (Ted)
Church Gresley, 13 November, 1922 Died 1990 (G)

League Club	Source	Date Signed	Seasons Played	Apps	Subs	Gls
Derby Co	Gresley Rov	11.47	48	1	-	0
Oldham Ath	Tr	07.49	49	3	-	0

CLAMP Harold Edwin (Eddie)
Coalville, 14 September, 1934 Died 1995 ESch/FLge-1/E-4 (WH)

League Club	Source	Date Signed	Seasons Played	Apps	Subs	Gls
Wolverhampton W	Jnrs	04.52	53-61	214	-	23
Arsenal	Tr	11.61	61-62	22	-	1
Stoke C	Tr	09.62	62-63	50	-	2
Peterborough U	Tr	10.64	64	8	-	0

CLAMP Martin
Coventry, 31 January, 1948 (G)

League Club	Source	Date Signed	Seasons Played	Apps	Subs	Gls
Coventry C	Jnrs	01.66				
Plymouth Arg	Tr	07.68	69	8	0	0

CLANCY John Patrick
Perivale, 5 July, 1949 (W)

League Club	Source	Date Signed	Seasons Played	Apps	Subs	Gls
Bristol C	Tottenham H (App)	03.67				
Bradford PA	Tr	07.67	67-68	52	4	2

CLANCY Sean Thomas
Liverpool, 16 September, 1987 (CD)

League Club	Source	Date Signed	Seasons Played	Apps	Subs	Gls
Blackpool	Sch	●	03	1	1	0

CLAPHAM Graham Leslie
Lincoln, 23 September, 1947 (M)

League Club	Source	Date Signed	Seasons Played	Apps	Subs	Gls
Newcastle U	App	09.65				
Shrewsbury T	Tr	08.67	67-71	73	14	5
Chester	Tr	01.72	71-72	37	4	5

CLAPHAM James (Jamie) Richard
Lincoln, 7 December, 1975 (FB)

League Club	Source	Date Signed	Seasons Played	Apps	Subs	Gls
Tottenham H	YT	07.94	96	0	1	0
Leyton Orient	L	01.97	96	6	0	0
Bristol Rov	L	03.97	96	4	1	0
Ipswich T	Tr	01.98	97-02	187	20	10
Birmingham C	Tr	01.03	02-04	56	12	0

CLAPHAM Keith
Fareham, 9 September, 1952 (CD)

League Club	Source	Date Signed	Seasons Played	Apps	Subs	Gls
Bournemouth	App	09.70				
Exeter C	Tr	07.72	72-76	79	12	0

CLAPTON Daniel (Danny) Robert
Stepney, 22 July, 1934 Died 1986 FLge-1/E-1 (W)

League Club	Source	Date Signed	Seasons Played	Apps	Subs	Gls
Arsenal	Leytonstone	08.53	54-61	207	-	25
Luton T	Tr	09.62	62	10	-	0

CLAPTON Dennis Patrick
Hackney, 12 October, 1939 EYth (CF)

League Club	Source	Date Signed	Seasons Played	Apps	Subs	Gls
Arsenal	Bexleyheath	08.58	59-60	4	-	0
Northampton T	Tr	08.61	61	1	-	0

CLARE Daryl Adam
Jersey, 1 August, 1978 IRu21-6/IRB-1 (F)

League Club	Source	Date Signed	Seasons Played	Apps	Subs	Gls
Grimsby T	YT	12.95	95-00	34	45	9
Northampton T	L	11.99	99	9	1	3
Northampton T	L	11.00	00	3	1	0
Cheltenham T	L	12.00	00	4	0	0
Boston U	Tr	07.01	02	7	0	1
Chester C	Tr	11.02	04	3	4	1
Boston U	Tr	11.04	04	14	5	3

CLARE James (Jimmy) Edward
Islington, 6 November, 1959 (F)

League Club	Source	Date Signed	Seasons Played	Apps	Subs	Gls
Chelsea	App	08.78	80	0	1	0

CLARE Robert (Rob)
Belper, 28 February, 1983 Eu20 (CD)

League Club	Source	Date Signed	Seasons Played	Apps	Subs	Gls
Stockport Co	YT	03.00	00-03	107	10	3
Blackpool	Tr	08.04	04	19	4	0

CLARIDGE Stephen (Steve) Edward
Portsmouth, 10 April, 1966 (F)

League Club	Source	Date Signed	Seasons Played	Apps	Subs	Gls
Bournemouth	Fareham T	11.84	84-85	3	4	1
Crystal Palace	Basingstoke T	10.88				
Aldershot	Tr	10.88	88-89	58	4	19
Cambridge U	Tr	02.90	89-91	56	23	28
Luton T	Tr	07.92	92	15	1	2
Cambridge U	Tr	11.92	92-93	53	0	18
Birmingham C	Tr	01.94	93-95	86	2	35
Leicester C	Tr	03.96	95-97	53	10	16
Portsmouth	L	01.98	97	10	0	2
Wolverhampton W	Tr	03.98	97	4	1	0
Portsmouth	Tr	08.98	98-00	94	10	34
Millwall	Tr	03.01	00-02	76	15	29
Brighton & Hove A	Weymouth	11.04	04	5	0	0
Brentford	Tr	12.04	04	3	1	0
Wycombe W	Tr	01.05	04	14	5	4

CLARK Albert Henry
Ashington, 24 July, 1921 Died 1977 (WH)

League Club	Source	Date Signed	Seasons Played	Apps	Subs	Gls
Newcastle U	North Shields	01.48	48	1	-	0

CLARK Alexander (Sandy)
Airdrie, 28 October, 1956 (F)

League Club	Source	Date Signed	Seasons Played	Apps	Subs	Gls
West Ham U	Airdrie	06.82	82	26	0	7

CLARK Anthony Carl
Camden, 5 October, 1984 (M)

League Club	Source	Date Signed	Seasons Played	Apps	Subs	Gls
Southend U	YT	●	01	0	2	0

CLARK Anthony (Tony) John
Lambeth, 7 April, 1977 (F)

League Club	Source	Date Signed	Seasons Played	Apps	Subs	Gls
Wycombe W	Jnrs	07.95	94-95	2	2	0

CLARK Benjamin (Ben)
North Shields, 14 April, 1933 (WH)

League Club	Source	Date Signed	Seasons Played	Apps	Subs	Gls
Sunderland	North Shields	08.50				
Derby Co	Yeovil T	05.54	54-57	16	-	0
Barrow	Tr	02.59	58-63	202	-	7

CLARK Benjamin (Ben)
Consett, 24 January, 1983 ESch/EYth/Eu20 (FB)

League Club	Source	Date Signed	Seasons Played	Apps	Subs	Gls
Sunderland	YT	07.00	02-04	3	5	0
Hartlepool U	Tr	10.04	04	21	4	0

CLARK Brian Donald
Bristol, 13 January, 1943 (F)

League Club	Source	Date Signed	Seasons Played	Apps	Subs	Gls
Bristol C	Jnrs	03.60	60-66	195	0	83
Huddersfield T	Tr	10.66	66-67	28	4	11
Cardiff C	Tr	02.68	67-72	177	5	78

League Club	Source	Date Signed	Seasons Played	Apps	Subs	Gls
Bournemouth	Tr	10.72	72-73	28	2	12
Millwall	Tr	09.73	73-74	66	5	17
Cardiff C	Tr	05.75	75	19	2	1
Newport Co	Tr	08.76	76-78	72	8	18

CLARK Christopher (Chris) James
Shoreham, 9 June, 1984 (F)

League Club	Source	Date Signed	Seasons Played	Apps	Subs	Gls
Portsmouth	Sch	03.03				
Stoke C	L	02.05	04	0	2	0

CLARK Clive
Roundhay, 19 December, 1940 Eu23-1 (W)

League Club	Source	Date Signed	Seasons Played	Apps	Subs	Gls
Leeds U	Ashley Road Meth	01.58				
Queens Park Rgrs	Tr	08.58	58-60	58	-	7
West Bromwich A	Tr	01.61	60-68	300	1	80
Queens Park Rgrs	Tr	06.69	69	7	1	1
Preston NE	Tr	01.70	69-72	71	1	9
Southport	Tr	07.73	73	7	1	1

CLARK David George
Ilford, 19 January, 1938 (CD)

League Club	Source	Date Signed	Seasons Played	Apps	Subs	Gls
Leyton Orient	Leyton	12.61	61-62	4	-	0

CLARK Dean Wayne
Hillingdon, 31 March, 1980 (M)

League Club	Source	Date Signed	Seasons Played	Apps	Subs	Gls
Brentford	YT	10.97	97	0	4	0

CLARK Derek
Newcastle, 10 August, 1931 (W)

League Club	Source	Date Signed	Seasons Played	Apps	Subs	Gls
Lincoln C	Durham C	12.51	51	4	-	1

CLARK Derrick Bryan
Leyburn, 27 December, 1935 Died 1985 (W)

League Club	Source	Date Signed	Seasons Played	Apps	Subs	Gls
Darlington		03.55	54-55	6	-	1

CLARK Frederick **Donald (Don)**
Bristol, 25 October, 1917 (CF)

League Club	Source	Date Signed	Seasons Played	Apps	Subs	Gls
Bristol C	North Bristol OB	05.37	38-50	117	-	67

CLARK Frank Albert
Rowlands Gill, 9 September, 1943 EYth/EAmat/FLge-1 (FB)

League Club	Source	Date Signed	Seasons Played	Apps	Subs	Gls
Newcastle U	Crook T	11.62	63-74	388	1	0
Nottingham F	Tr	07.75	75-78	116	1	1

CLARK Graham John
Aberdeen, 20 January, 1961 SSch (M)

League Club	Source	Date Signed	Seasons Played	Apps	Subs	Gls
Sheffield U	App	10.78				
Darlington	Tr	08.79	79	6	0	0

CLARK Harold (Harry)
Cloughdene, 30 March, 1913 (W)

League Club	Source	Date Signed	Seasons Played	Apps	Subs	Gls
Accrington St	Manchester C (Am)	12.44				
Gateshead	Tr	06.46	46	21	-	1

CLARK Harold (Harry) Maurice
Newcastle, 29 December, 1932 (IF)

League Club	Source	Date Signed	Seasons Played	Apps	Subs	Gls
Darlington	Eastbourne OB	12.50	50-56	141	-	27
Sheffield Wed	Tr	10.57	57	1	-	0
Hartlepools U	Tr	08.58	58-60	118	-	43

CLARK Henry (Harry)
Sunderland, 11 September, 1934 (IF)

League Club	Source	Date Signed	Seasons Played	Apps	Subs	Gls
Sunderland	Sunderland St Benet's	05.56	56	6	-	0

CLARK Howard William
Coventry, 19 September, 1968 (FB)

League Club	Source	Date Signed	Seasons Played	Apps	Subs	Gls
Coventry C	App	09.86	88-90	9	11	1
Darlington	L	09.91	91	5	0	0
Shrewsbury T	Tr	12.91	91-92	51	5	0
Hereford U	Tr	07.93	93-94	52	3	7

CLARK Ian David
Stockton, 23 October, 1974 (M)

League Club	Source	Date Signed	Seasons Played	Apps	Subs	Gls
Doncaster Rov	Stockton	08.95	95-97	23	22	3
Hartlepool U	Tr	10.97	97-01	109	29	17
Darlington	Tr	11.01	01-04	84	35	26

CLARK James (Jim) Donald
Dornoch, 1 May, 1923 Died 1994 (FB)

League Club	Source	Date Signed	Seasons Played	Apps	Subs	Gls
Exeter C	Aberdeen	08.48	48-52	95	-	5
Bradford C	L	09.52	52	6	-	0

CLARK John Brown
Edinburgh, 22 September, 1964 SYth (CD)

League Club	Source	Date Signed	Seasons Played	Apps	Subs	Gls
Stoke C	Dundee U	02.94	93-94	17	0	0

CLARK Jonathan
Swansea, 12 November, 1958 WSch/Wu21-2 (M)

League Club	Source	Date Signed	Seasons Played	Apps	Subs	Gls
Manchester U	App	11.75	76	0	1	0
Derby Co	Tr	09.78	78-80	48	5	3
Preston NE	Tr	08.81	81-86	107	3	10

League Club	Source	Date Signed	Seasons Played	Apps	Subs	Gls
Bury	Tr	12.86	86	13	1	1
Carlisle U	Tr	08.87	87-88	48	1	2

CLARK Joseph (Joe) Thomas Henry
Bermondsey, 2 March, 1920 (FB)

League Club	Source	Date Signed	Seasons Played	Apps	Subs	Gls
Leyton Orient	Gravesend U	02.46	46	18	-	0

CLARK Lee Robert
Wallsend, 27 October, 1972 ESch/EYth/Eu21-11 (M)

League Club	Source	Date Signed	Seasons Played	Apps	Subs	Gls
Newcastle U	YT	12.89	90-96	153	42	23
Sunderland	Tr	06.97	97-98	72	1	16
Fulham	Tr	07.99	99-04	141	8	20

CLARK Martin Alan
Haslingden, 12 September, 1970 (FB)

League Club	Source	Date Signed	Seasons Played	Apps	Subs	Gls
Rotherham U	Southport	06.97	97-98	29	0	0

CLARK Martin John
Uddingston, 13 October, 1968 (M)

League Club	Source	Date Signed	Seasons Played	Apps	Subs	Gls
Nottingham F	Clyde	02.89				
Mansfield T	L	03.90	89	14	0	1
Mansfield T	Tr	08.90	90-91	31	2	0

CLARK Neville
Gateshead, 9 October, 1930 (WH)

League Club	Source	Date Signed	Seasons Played	Apps	Subs	Gls
Grimsby T	Chilton Ath	12.48				
Sunderland		12.49				
Hartlepools U	Tr	08.53	53	2	-	0

CLARK Paul Peterson
Benfleet, 14 September, 1958 ESch/EYth (CD)

League Club	Source	Date Signed	Seasons Played	Apps	Subs	Gls
Southend U	App	07.76	76-77	29	4	1
Brighton & Hove A	Tr	11.77	77-80	69	10	9
Reading	L	10.81	81	2	0	0
Southend U	Tr	08.82	82-90	271	7	3
Gillingham	Tr	07.91	91-93	87	3	1
Cambridge U	Chelmsford C	10.95	95	2	0	0

CLARK Peter James
Romford, 10 December, 1979 (FB)

League Club	Source	Date Signed	Seasons Played	Apps	Subs	Gls
Carlisle U	Arsenal (YT)	08.98	98-99	77	2	1
Stockport Co	Tr	07.00	00-02	66	6	3
Mansfield T	L	09.02	02	2	1	0
Northampton T	Tr	07.03	03	6	0	0

CLARK Joseph **Peter**
Doncaster, 22 January, 1938 (WH)

League Club	Source	Date Signed	Seasons Played	Apps	Subs	Gls
Wolverhampton W	Jnrs	03.55				
Doncaster Rov	Tr	07.59	59	13	-	8
Mansfield T	Tr	06.60	60	2	-	0
Stockport Co	Hereford U	08.65	65	21	0	2
Crewe Alex	Tr	07.66	66	2	0	0

CLARK Ronald (Ronnie)
Clarkston, 21 May, 1932 (W)

League Club	Source	Date Signed	Seasons Played	Apps	Subs	Gls
Gillingham	Kilmarnock	07.56	56-57	33	-	6
Oldham Ath	Tr	06.58	58	4	-	0

CLARK Simon
Boston, 12 March, 1967 (CD)

League Club	Source	Date Signed	Seasons Played	Apps	Subs	Gls
Peterborough U	Stevenage Borough	03.94	93-96	102	5	4
Leyton Orient	Tr	06.97	97-99	98	0	9
Colchester U	Tr	07.00	00-01	52	3	0

CLARK Steven (Steve)
Baldock, 20 September, 1964 (FB)

League Club	Source	Date Signed	Seasons Played	Apps	Subs	Gls
Cambridge U	App	09.82	83-85	63	3	0

CLARK Steven (Steve) Terence
Mile End, 10 February, 1982 (M)

League Club	Source	Date Signed	Seasons Played	Apps	Subs	Gls
West Ham U	YT	07.01				
Southend U	Tr	11.01	01-03	31	20	1
Macclesfield T	L	09.03	03	1	3	0

CLARK Thomas (Tom) Henry
Luton, 5 October, 1924 Died 1981 (IF)

League Club	Source	Date Signed	Seasons Played	Apps	Subs	Gls
Aston Villa	Vauxhall Motors	04.47				
Walsall	Tr	05.48	48	9	-	2

CLARK William (Willie)
Larkhall, 25 February, 1932 (CF)

League Club	Source	Date Signed	Seasons Played	Apps	Subs	Gls
Queens Park Rgrs	Petershill	02.54	53-55	95	-	32

CLARK William (Billy) Raymond
Christchurch, 19 May, 1967 (CD)

League Club	Source	Date Signed	Seasons Played	Apps	Subs	Gls
Bournemouth	YT	09.84	84-87	4	0	0
Bristol Rov	Tr	10.87	87-96	235	13	14
Exeter C	Tr	10.97	97-98	39	2	3

CLARKE Adrian James
Cambridge, 28 September, 1974 ESch/EYth (M)

League Club	Source	Date Signed	Seasons Played	Apps	Subs	Gls
Arsenal	YT	07.93	94-95	4	3	0

League Club	Source	Date Signed	Seasons Played	Apps	Subs	Gls
Rotherham U	L	12.96	96	1	1	0
Southend U	Tr	03.97	96-99	63	16	8
Carlisle U	L	09.99	99	7	0	0
CLARKE Alan						
Houghton Regis, 10 April, 1942 (W)						
Luton T	Jnrs	10.61	61-62	9	-	0
CLARKE Alfred (Alf)						
Hollinwood, 23 August, 1926 Died 1971 (IF)						
Crewe Alex	Stalybridge Celtic	02.48	47-48	22	-	12
Burnley	Tr	12.48	48-51	24	-	6
Oldham Ath	Tr	08.52	52-53	43	-	12
Halifax T	Tr	03.54	53-55	71	-	22
CLARKE Allan John						
Willenhall, 31 July, 1946 Eu23-6/FLge-2/E-19 (F)						
Walsall	App	08.63	63-65	72	0	41
Fulham	Tr	03.66	65-67	85	1	45
Leicester C	Tr	06.68	68	36	0	12
Leeds U	Tr	07.69	69-77	270	3	110
Barnsley	Tr	06.78	78-79	47	0	15
CLARKE Allan (Bobby) Robert						
Liverpool, 13 October, 1941 (IF)						
Chester	Liverpool (Jnrs)	10.61	61-62	30	-	5
CLARKE Allen Frederick						
Crayford, 2 December, 1952 (G)						
Charlton Ath	App	07.71	71	2	0	0
Bristol Rov	L	09.71	71	1	0	0
Exeter C	Tr	02.73	72-73	16	0	0
CLARKE Ambrose						
Walton, 10 September, 1945 (CD)						
Everton	Everton Red Triangle	06.64				
Southport	Tr	01.66	65-70	193	4	4
Barrow	Tr	07.71	71	45	1	0
CLARKE Andrew (Andy) Weston						
Islington, 22 July, 1967 ESemiPro-2 (F)						
Wimbledon	Barnet	02.91	90-97	74	96	17
Port Vale	L	08.98	98	2	4	0
Northampton T	L	01.99	98	2	2	0
Peterborough U	Tr	05.99	99-04	170	60	57
CLARKE Bradie Jason						
Cambridge, 26 May, 1986 (G)						
Oxford U	YT	•	04	3	1	0
CLARKE Brian Roy						
Eastbourne, 10 October, 1968 (CD)						
Gillingham	App	06.87	88-91	42	2	0
CLARKE Christopher (Chris) Edward						
Leeds, 18 December, 1980 (CD)						
Halifax T	Wolverhampton W (YT)	07.99	99-01	50	1	1
Blackpool	Tr	02.02	01-03	33	13	2
Cambridge U	Tr	03.04	03	0	1	0
CLARKE Christopher (Chris) Elliott						
Battersea, 11 December, 1946 (W)						
Millwall	Chelsea (App)	12.63	64-65	19	0	4
Watford	Tr	08.66	66	1	1	0
CLARKE Christopher (Chris) John						
Barnsley, 1 May, 1974 (G)						
Bolton W	YT	07.92				
Rochdale	Tr	07.94	94-95	30	0	0
CLARKE Clive Richard						
Dublin, 14 January, 1980 IRYth/IRu21-11/IR-2 (FB)						
Stoke C	YT	01.97	98-04	205	18	9
CLARKE Colin						
Penilee, 4 April, 1946 (CD)						
Arsenal	Arthurlie Jnrs	10.63				
Oxford U	Tr	07.65	65-77	443	1	23
Plymouth Arg	Los Angeles (USA)	09.78	78	35	0	3
CLARKE Colin John						
Newry, 30 October, 1962 NI-38 (F)						
Ipswich T	App	10.80				
Peterborough U	Tr	07.81	81-83	76	6	18
Gillingham	L	03.84	83	8	0	1
Tranmere Rov	Tr	07.84	84	45	0	22
Bournemouth	Tr	06.85	85	46	0	26
Southampton	Tr	06.86	86-88	82	0	36
Bournemouth	L	12.88	88	3	1	2
Queens Park Rgrs	Tr	03.89	88-89	39	7	11
Portsmouth	Tr	06.90	90-92	68	17	18

League Club	Source	Date Signed	Seasons Played	Apps	Subs	Gls
CLARKE Darrell James						
Mansfield, 16 December, 1977 (M)						
Mansfield T	YT	07.96	95-00	137	24	24
Hartlepool U	Tr	07.01	01-03	92	19	19
Stockport Co	L	01.05	04	1	0	0
CLARKE David Alan						
Nottingham, 3 December, 1964 EYth (FB)						
Notts Co	App	12.82	82-86	113	10	7
Lincoln C	Tr	07.87	88-93	141	6	9
Doncaster Rov	Tr	01.94	93	15	1	0
CLARKE David Arthur						
Long Eaton, 25 September, 1946 (W)						
Nottingham F	Derby Co (Am)	05.64				
Notts Co	Tr	07.66	66	23	1	0
CLARKE David Leslie						
Newcastle, 24 July, 1949 ESemiPro (G)						
Newcastle U	Felham BC	06.67				
Doncaster Rov	Tr	08.69	69	3	0	0
Darlington	L	03.70	69	12	0	0
CLARKE Dean Brian						
Hereford, 28 July, 1977 (FB)						
Hereford U	YT	07.95	93-95	8	3	0
CLARKE Dennis						
Stockton, 18 January, 1948 (CD)						
West Bromwich A	App	02.65	66-68	19	2	0
Huddersfield T	Tr	01.69	68-73	172	0	3
Birmingham C	Tr	09.73	73-74	14	0	0
CLARKE Derek						
Willenhall, 19 February, 1950 (F)						
Walsall	App	12.67	67	6	0	2
Wolverhampton W	Tr	05.68	68-69	2	3	0
Oxford U	Tr	10.70	70-75	172	6	35
Orient	Tr	08.76	76-78	30	6	6
Carlisle U	L	10.78	78	0	1	0
CLARKE Donald (Don) Leslie						
Poole, 29 June, 1931 Died 1993 (IF)						
Cardiff C		08.54				
Brighton & Hove A	Tr	06.55	55	2	-	0
CLARKE Douglas (Doug)						
Bolton, 19 January, 1934 (W)						
Bury	Darwen	02.52	53-55	37	-	15
Hull C	Tr	11.55	55-64	368	-	79
Torquay U	Tr	07.65	65-67	116	3	21
CLARKE Frank James						
Willenhall, 15 July, 1942 (F)						
Shrewsbury T	Willenhall St Giles	11.61	61-67	188	0	77
Queens Park Rgrs	Tr	02.68	67-69	67	0	17
Ipswich T	Tr	03.70	69-72	62	4	15
Carlisle U	Tr	08.73	73-77	121	5	30
CLARKE Frederick (Fred) Jeffrey						
Crewe, 3 January, 1931 Died 2002 (CD)						
Crewe Alex		11.51	53-54	2	-	0
CLARKE Frederick (Fred) Robert George						
Banbridge, 4 November, 1941 IrLge-3/Niu23-4 (FB)						
Arsenal	Glenavon	11.60	61-64	26	-	0
CLARKE Gary						
Boston, 6 November, 1960 (W)						
Bristol Rov	App	11.78	78-79	6	5	0
CLARKE George Edmund						
Ipswich, 27 April, 1921 Died 1981 (CD)						
Ipswich T		11.46	46-52	34	-	1
CLARKE Gerald (Gerry)						
Barrow Hill, 4 January, 1936 (FB)						
Chesterfield	Oaks Fold	03.55	54-67	382	0	21
CLARKE Graham Peter						
Nottingham, 11 August, 1935 EYth (FB)						
Southampton		06.53	57-58	3	-	0
CLARKE Henry (Harry)						
Sunderland, 26 November, 1960 (M)						
Hartlepool U	Middlesbrough (N/C)	08.79	81	5	2	1
CLARKE Henry (Harry) Alfred						
Woodford, 23 February, 1923 Died 2000 EB/E-1 (CD)						
Tottenham H	Lovells Ath	03.49	48-56	295	-	4

CLARKE James **Henry (Harry)**
Darlington, 27 March, 1921 (CF)

League Club	Source	Date Signed	Seasons Played	Apps	Subs	Gls
Darlington	Gateshead (Am)	02.45	46	19	-	17
Leeds U	Tr	02.47	46	14	-	1
Darlington	Tr	11.47	47-48	37	-	24
Hartlepools U	Tr	11.49	49	7	-	1
Darlington	Stockton	09.52	52	14	-	6

CLARKE **Isaac (Ike)**
Tipton, 9 January, 1915 Died 2002 (CF)

League Club	Source	Date Signed	Seasons Played	Apps	Subs	Gls
West Bromwich A	Toll End Wesley	01.37	37-47	108	-	39
Portsmouth	Tr	11.47	47-52	116	-	49

CLARKE **James**
West Bromwich, 7 December, 1923 (FB)

League Club	Source	Date Signed	Seasons Played	Apps	Subs	Gls
Nottingham F		05.47	47-53	18	-	0

CLARKE **James (Jamie)** William
Sunderland, 18 September, 1982 (FB)

League Club	Source	Date Signed	Seasons Played	Apps	Subs	Gls
Mansfield T	Sch	07.02	01-03	29	5	1
Rochdale	Tr	07.04	04	32	9	1

CLARKE **Jeffrey (Jeff)** Derek
Hemsworth, 18 January, 1954 ESch (CD)

League Club	Source	Date Signed	Seasons Played	Apps	Subs	Gls
Manchester C	Jnrs	01.72	74	13	0	0
Sunderland	Tr	06.75	75-81	178	3	6
Newcastle U	Tr	08.82	82-86	124	0	4
Brighton & Hove A	L	08.84	84	4	0	0

CLARKE **John** Leslie
Northampton, 23 October, 1946 EYth (CD)

League Club	Source	Date Signed	Seasons Played	Apps	Subs	Gls
Northampton T	Jnrs	07.65	66-74	228	5	1

CLARKE William **John**
Bargoed, 26 December, 1940 (G)

League Club	Source	Date Signed	Seasons Played	Apps	Subs	Gls
Newport Co	Bargoed YMCA	05.59	59-61	12	-	0

CLARKE **Kelvin** Leslie
Wolverhampton, 16 July, 1957 (FB)

League Club	Source	Date Signed	Seasons Played	Apps	Subs	Gls
Walsall	App	07.75	74-78	4	5	0

CLARKE **Kevin**
Drogheda, 29 April, 1923 Died 2004 (CF)

League Club	Source	Date Signed	Seasons Played	Apps	Subs	Gls
Barrow	Drogheda	12.45	46	12	-	1

CLARKE Patrick **Kevin** Noel
Dublin, 3 December, 1921 LoI-9/IR-2 (WH)

League Club	Source	Date Signed	Seasons Played	Apps	Subs	Gls
Swansea T	Drumcondra	11.48	48-51	10	-	0

CLARKE **Lee**
Peterborough, 28 July, 1983 NIu21-1 (F)

League Club	Source	Date Signed	Seasons Played	Apps	Subs	Gls
Peterborough U	Yaxley	10.01	01-02	0	2	0

CLARKE **Leon** Marvin
Birmingham, 10 February, 1985 (F)

League Club	Source	Date Signed	Seasons Played	Apps	Subs	Gls
Wolverhampton W	Sch	03.04	04	11	17	7
Kidderminster Hrs	L	03.04	03	3	1	0

CLARKE **Malcolm** McQueen
Clydebank, 29 June, 1944 (M)

League Club	Source	Date Signed	Seasons Played	Apps	Subs	Gls
Leicester C	Johnstone Burgh	07.65	65	0	1	0
Cardiff C	Tr	08.67	67-68	44	2	3
Bristol C	Tr	07.69	69	2	1	0
Hartlepool	Tr	07.70	70-71	29	4	0

CLARKE **Matthew (Matt)** John
Sheffield, 3 November, 1973 (G)

League Club	Source	Date Signed	Seasons Played	Apps	Subs	Gls
Rotherham U	YT	07.92	92-95	123	1	0
Sheffield Wed	Tr	07.96	96-97	2	2	0
Bradford C	Tr	07.99	99-00	38	0	0
Bolton W	L	03.01	00	8	0	0
Crystal Palace	Tr	09.01	01-03	38	0	0

CLARKE **Matthew** Paul
Leeds, 18 December, 1980 (CD)

League Club	Source	Date Signed	Seasons Played	Apps	Subs	Gls
Halifax T	Wolverhampton W (YT)	07.99	99-01	42	27	2
Darlington	Tr	07.02	02-04	121	5	10

CLARKE **Michael (Mick)**
Sheffield, 28 November, 1944 (FB)

League Club	Source	Date Signed	Seasons Played	Apps	Subs	Gls
Sheffield U	App	01.62				
Aldershot	Tr	06.64	64	5	-	0
Halifax T	Tr	07.65	65-66	50	1	1

CLARKE **Michael (Micky)** Darren
Marston Green, 22 December, 1967 (W)

League Club	Source	Date Signed	Seasons Played	Apps	Subs	Gls
Barnsley	Birmingham C (App)	11.86	86-88	37	3	3
Scarborough	Tr	08.89	89-90	31	6	1

CLARKE **Nathan**
Halifax, 30 July, 1983 (CD)

League Club	Source	Date Signed	Seasons Played	Apps	Subs	Gls
Huddersfield T	YT	09.01	01-04	100	2	2

CLARKE **Nicholas (Nicky)** John
Walsall, 20 August, 1967 (CD)

League Club	Source	Date Signed	Seasons Played	Apps	Subs	Gls
Wolverhampton W	Jnrs	02.85	85-91	73	8	1
Mansfield T	Tr	12.91	91-93	39	4	5
Chesterfield	L	02.93	92	7	0	0
Doncaster Rov	L	12.93	93	5	0	0

CLARKE **Norman** Frederick Michael
Birmingham, 31 October, 1934 Died 1997 EYth (WH)

League Club	Source	Date Signed	Seasons Played	Apps	Subs	Gls
Aston Villa	Jnrs	07.53	54	1	-	0
Torquay U	Tr	07.56	56-58	54	-	0

CLARKE **Norman** Samson
Ballylougham, 1 April, 1942 NIu23-2/IrLge-2 (W)

League Club	Source	Date Signed	Seasons Played	Apps	Subs	Gls
Sunderland	Ballymena U	02.62	62	4	-	0

CLARKE **Paul** Stewart
Chesterfield, 25 September, 1950 ESch (CD)

League Club	Source	Date Signed	Seasons Played	Apps	Subs	Gls
Liverpool	App	10.67				
Rochdale	Tr	08.69	69-71	11	1	0

CLARKE **Peter** Anthony
Bolton, 6 July, 1949 (G)

League Club	Source	Date Signed	Seasons Played	Apps	Subs	Gls
Bolton W	Jnrs	06.69	70	13	0	0
Stockport Co	Tr	07.71	71-74	49	0	0

CLARKE **Peter** Michael
Southport, 3 January, 1982 ESch/EYth/Eu21-8 (CD)

League Club	Source	Date Signed	Seasons Played	Apps	Subs	Gls
Everton	Jnrs	01.99	00-03	6	3	0
Blackpool	L	08.02	02	16	0	3
Port Vale	L	02.03	02	13	0	1
Coventry C	L	02.04	03	5	0	0
Blackpool	Tr	09.04	04	38	0	5

CLARKE **Raymond (Ray)** Charles
Hackney, 25 September, 1952 EYth (F)

League Club	Source	Date Signed	Seasons Played	Apps	Subs	Gls
Tottenham H	App	10.69	72	0	1	0
Swindon T	Tr	06.73	73	11	3	2
Mansfield T	Tr	08.74	74-75	91	0	52
Brighton & Hove A	FC Bruges (Bel)	10.79	79	30	0	8
Newcastle U	Tr	07.80	80	14	0	2

CLARKE **Richard** James
Enfield, 15 February, 1980 (FB)

League Club	Source	Date Signed	Seasons Played	Apps	Subs	Gls
Luton T	YT	11.98				
Scunthorpe U	Stanway Rov	03.00	99	1	0	0

CLARKE **Royston (Roy)** James
Newport, 1 June, 1925 WWar-1/W-22 (W)

League Club	Source	Date Signed	Seasons Played	Apps	Subs	Gls
Cardiff C	Jnrs	12.42	46	39	-	10
Manchester C	Tr	04.47	46-57	349	-	73
Stockport Co	Tr	09.58	58	25	-	5

CLARKE **Ryan** Anthony
Sutton Coldfield, 22 January, 1984 (CD)

League Club	Source	Date Signed	Seasons Played	Apps	Subs	Gls
Boston U	Notts Co (Sch)	07.03	03	1	3	0

CLARKE **Ryan** James
Bristol, 30 April, 1982 (G)

League Club	Source	Date Signed	Seasons Played	Apps	Subs	Gls
Bristol Rov	YT	07.01	01-04	22	1	0
Southend U	L	10.04	04	1	0	0
Kidderminster Hrs	L	11.04	04	6	0	0

CLARKE **Simon** Nathan
Chelmsford, 23 September, 1971 (M)

League Club	Source	Date Signed	Seasons Played	Apps	Subs	Gls
West Ham U	YT	03.90	90-92	0	3	0

CLARKE **Stephen (Steve)**
Saltcoats, 29 August, 1963 SYth/Su21-8/SB/S-6 (FB)

League Club	Source	Date Signed	Seasons Played	Apps	Subs	Gls
Chelsea	St Mirren	01.87	86-97	321	9	7

CLARKE **Stuart** Anthony
Torquay, 25 January, 1961 (M)

League Club	Source	Date Signed	Seasons Played	Apps	Subs	Gls
Torquay U	Jnrs	02.78	78	4	1	0

CLARKE **Thomas (Tom)**
Ardrossan, 12 April, 1946 (G)

League Club	Source	Date Signed	Seasons Played	Apps	Subs	Gls
Carlisle U	Airdrie	07.70	71-74	23	0	0
Preston NE	Tr	07.75	75	3	0	0

CLARKE **Thomas (Tom)**
Halifax, 21 December, 1987 (FB)

League Club	Source	Date Signed	Seasons Played	Apps	Subs	Gls
Huddersfield T	Sch	01.05	04	12	0	0

CLARKE **Timothy (Tim)** Joseph
Stourbridge, 19 September, 1968 (G)

League Club	Source	Date Signed	Seasons Played	Apps	Subs	Gls
Coventry C	Halesowen T	10.90				
Huddersfield T	Tr	07.91	91-92	70	0	0
Rochdale	L	02.93	92	2	0	0
Shrewsbury T	Altrincham	10.93	94-95	30	1	0
York C	Witton A	06.96	96	17	0	0
Scunthorpe U	Tr	02.97	96-98	78	0	0
Kidderminster Hrs	Tr	10.99	00	25	0	0

CLARKE Wayne
Wolverhampton, 28 February, 1961 ESch/EYth (F)

League Club	Source	Date Signed	Seasons Played	Apps	Subs	Gls
Wolverhampton W	App	03.78	77-83	129	19	30
Birmingham C	Tr	08.84	84-86	92	0	38
Everton	Tr	03.87	86-88	46	11	18
Leicester C	Tr	07.89	89	10	1	1
Manchester C	Tr	01.90	89-91	7	14	2
Shrewsbury T	L	10.90	90	7	0	6
Stoke C	L	03.91	90	9	0	3
Wolverhampton W	L	09.91	91	1	0	0
Walsall	Tr	07.92	92	39	0	21
Shrewsbury T	Tr	08.93	93-94	53	6	22

CLARKE William (Willie) Arthur
Newport, 17 April, 1923 Died 1994 WAmat (W)

League Club	Source	Date Signed	Seasons Played	Apps	Subs	Gls
Ipswich T (Am)		02.47	46	3	-	0

CLARKSON David James
Preston, 1 February, 1968 (M)

League Club	Source	Date Signed	Seasons Played	Apps	Subs	Gls
Brighton & Hove A	Sunshine GC (Aus)	09.91	91	4	9	0

CLARKSON Ian Stewart
Solihull, 4 December, 1970 (FB)

League Club	Source	Date Signed	Seasons Played	Apps	Subs	Gls
Birmingham C	YT	12.88	88-92	125	11	0
Stoke C	Tr	09.93	93-95	72	3	0
Northampton T	Tr	08.96	96-99	91	3	1
Kidderminster Hrs	Tr	11.00	00-01	73	4	0

CLARKSON Philip (Phil) Ian
Hambleton, 13 November, 1968 (M)

League Club	Source	Date Signed	Seasons Played	Apps	Subs	Gls
Crewe Alex	Fleetwood T	10.91	91-95	76	22	27
Scunthorpe U	L	10.95	95	4	0	1
Scunthorpe U	Tr	02.96	95-96	45	3	18
Blackpool	Tr	02.97	96-01	154	17	35
Bury	Tr	03.02	01	4	0	0

CLAXTON Thomas (Tommy)
Rochdale, 17 October, 1944 (W)

League Club	Source	Date Signed	Seasons Played	Apps	Subs	Gls
Bury	Burnley (Am)	03.63	63-68	98	4	3

CLAY John Harfield
Stockport, 22 November, 1946 (F)

League Club	Source	Date Signed	Seasons Played	Apps	Subs	Gls
Manchester C	App	05.64	67	1	1	0

CLAYPOLE Anthony (Tony) William
Weldon, 13 February, 1937 (FB)

League Club	Source	Date Signed	Seasons Played	Apps	Subs	Gls
Northampton T	Jnrs	03.54	56-61	116	-	1

CLAYTON Edward (Eddie)
Bethnal Green, 7 May, 1937 (M)

League Club	Source	Date Signed	Seasons Played	Apps	Subs	Gls
Tottenham H	Eton Manor	12.57	57-67	88	4	20
Southend U	Tr	03.68	67-69	69	2	16

CLAYTON Gary
Sheffield, 2 February, 1963 ESemiPro-1 (M)

League Club	Source	Date Signed	Seasons Played	Apps	Subs	Gls
Doncaster Rov	Burton A	08.86	86	34	1	5
Cambridge U	Tr	07.87	87-93	166	13	14
Peterborough U	L	01.91	90	4	0	0
Huddersfield T	Tr	02.94	93-94	15	4	1
Plymouth Arg	Tr	08.95	95-97	32	6	2
Torquay U	Tr	08.97	97-98	56	0	2

CLAYTON Gordon
Wednesbury, 3 November, 1936 Died 1991 ESch/EYth (G)

League Club	Source	Date Signed	Seasons Played	Apps	Subs	Gls
Manchester U	Jnrs	11.53	56	2	-	0
Tranmere Rov	Tr	11.59	59-60	4	-	0

CLAYTON John
Elgin, 20 August, 1961 (F)

League Club	Source	Date Signed	Seasons Played	Apps	Subs	Gls
Derby Co	App	12.78	78-81	21	3	4
Chesterfield	Bulova (HK)	06.83	83	25	8	5
Tranmere Rov	Tr	07.84	84-85	47	0	35
Plymouth Arg	Tr	08.85	85-87	68	9	22
Burnley	Volendam (Holl)	08.92	92	3	0	1

CLAYTON John (Johnny) Michael
St Asaph, 28 March, 1937 (CF)

League Club	Source	Date Signed	Seasons Played	Apps	Subs	Gls
Everton	Jnrs	06.55				
Southport	Tr	07.59	59-60	32	-	3

CLAYTON Kenneth (Ken)
Preston, 6 April, 1933 (WH)

League Club	Source	Date Signed	Seasons Played	Apps	Subs	Gls
Blackburn Rov	Jnrs	05.50	52-58	72	-	0

CLAYTON Lewis (Lew)
Royston, West Yorkshire, 7 June, 1924 (WH)

League Club	Source	Date Signed	Seasons Played	Apps	Subs	Gls
Barnsley	Monckton Ath	03.42				
Carlisle U	Tr	09.46	46	24	-	0
Barnsley	Tr	06.47	48-49	15	-	0
Queens Park Rgrs	Tr	08.50	50-53	91	-	5
Bournemouth	Tr	05.55	55-56	40	-	1
Swindon T	Tr	06.57	57-58	35	-	2

CLAYTON Paul Spencer
Dunstable, 4 January, 1965 (F)

League Club	Source	Date Signed	Seasons Played	Apps	Subs	Gls
Norwich C	App	01.83	83-85	8	5	0
Darlington	Tr	03.88	87-88	20	2	3
Crewe Alex	Tr	01.89	88-90	51	9	12

CLAYTON Ronald (Ronnie)
Preston, 5 August, 1934 Eu23-6/FLge-10/EB/E-35 (M)

League Club	Source	Date Signed	Seasons Played	Apps	Subs	Gls
Blackburn Rov	Jnrs	08.51	50-68	579	2	15

CLAYTON Ronald (Ronnie)
Hull, 18 January, 1937 (IF)

League Club	Source	Date Signed	Seasons Played	Apps	Subs	Gls
Arsenal	Hereford U	01.58				
Brighton & Hove A	Tr	09.58	58-59	14	-	3

CLAYTON Roy Charles
Dudley, 18 February, 1950 (F)

League Club	Source	Date Signed	Seasons Played	Apps	Subs	Gls
Oxford U	Warley Borough	08.69	69-72	49	4	8

CLEARY George
Bedford, 14 May, 1947 (F)

League Club	Source	Date Signed	Seasons Played	Apps	Subs	Gls
Cambridge U	Dunstable T	12.75	75	5	3	0

CLEARY William (Bill)
Middlesbrough, 20 April, 1931 Died 1991 (WH)

League Club	Source	Date Signed	Seasons Played	Apps	Subs	Gls
Sunderland	South Bank EE Jnrs	05.49				
Norwich C	Tr	05.52	53-55	18	-	0
Port Vale	Wisbech T	11.57	57	8	-	0

CLEAVER Christopher (Chris) William
Hitchin, 24 March, 1979 (F)

League Club	Source	Date Signed	Seasons Played	Apps	Subs	Gls
Peterborough U	YT	03.97	96-98	10	19	3

CLEEVELY Nigel Robert
Cheltenham, 23 December, 1945 (W)

League Club	Source	Date Signed	Seasons Played	Apps	Subs	Gls
Derby Co	Jnrs	07.64	64-66	15	1	3

CLEGG David Lee
Liverpool, 23 October, 1976 (M)

League Club	Source	Date Signed	Seasons Played	Apps	Subs	Gls
Liverpool	YT	05.95				
Hartlepool U	Tr	07.96	96	24	11	2

CLEGG Donald (Don)
Huddersfield, 2 June, 1921 (G)

League Club	Source	Date Signed	Seasons Played	Apps	Subs	Gls
Huddersfield T	ICI	05.40	46-47	3	-	0
Bury	Tr	07.48	48-49	15	-	0
Stoke C	Tr	06.50	50	2	-	0

CLEGG George Gerald
Manchester, 16 November, 1980 (M)

League Club	Source	Date Signed	Seasons Played	Apps	Subs	Gls
Manchester U	YT	07.99				
Wycombe W	L	03.01	00	2	8	0
Bury	Tr	08.01	01-03	57	11	9

CLEGG Malcolm Brook
Leeds, 9 April, 1936 (CF)

League Club	Source	Date Signed	Seasons Played	Apps	Subs	Gls
Bradford PA (Am)	Bradford Rov	01.58	57	6	-	0

CLEGG Michael Jaime
Ashton-under-Lyne, 3 July, 1977 Eu21-2 (FB)

League Club	Source	Date Signed	Seasons Played	Apps	Subs	Gls
Manchester U	YT	07.95	96-99	4	5	0
Ipswich T	L	02.00	99	3	0	0
Wigan Ath	L	03.00	99	6	0	0
Oldham Ath	Tr	02.02	01-03	40	6	0

CLEGG Tony
Keighley, 8 November, 1965 (CD)

League Club	Source	Date Signed	Seasons Played	Apps	Subs	Gls
Bradford C	App	11.83	83-86	41	7	2
York C	Tr	08.87	87-88	38	3	3

CLELAND Alexander (Alex)
Glasgow, 10 December, 1970 SSch/Su21-11/SB-2 (FB)

League Club	Source	Date Signed	Seasons Played	Apps	Subs	Gls
Everton	Glasgow Rgrs	07.98	98-01	21	14	0

CLELAND Peter Melville
Eaglesham, 8 May, 1932 Died 1990 (CF)

League Club	Source	Date Signed	Seasons Played	Apps	Subs	Gls
Norwich C	Cheltenham T	08.58	58	3	-	0

CLELLAND Crawford
New Jersey, USA, 3 December, 1930 (WH)

League Club	Source	Date Signed	Seasons Played	Apps	Subs	Gls
Plymouth Arg	Aberdeen	06.55	55	2	-	0

CLELLAND David (Dave)
Netherburn, 18 March, 1924 (CF)

League Club	Source	Date Signed	Seasons Played	Apps	Subs	Gls
Arsenal		08.46				
Brighton & Hove A	Tr	01.48	47	8	-	1
Crystal Palace	Tr	09.49	49	2	-	0
Scunthorpe U	Weymouth	07.50	50	16	-	8

CLEMENCE Raymond (Ray) Neal
Skegness, 5 August, 1948 Eu23-4/FLge-2/E-61 (G)

League Club	Source	Date Signed	Seasons Played	Apps	Subs	Gls
Scunthorpe U	Notts Co (Am)	08.65	65-66	48	0	0
Liverpool	Tr	06.67	69-80	470	0	0
Tottenham H	Tr	08.81	81-87	240	0	0

CLEMENCE Stephen Neal
Liverpool, 31 March, 1978 ESch/EYth/Eu21-1 (M)

League Club	Source	Date Signed	Seasons Played	Apps	Subs	Gls
Tottenham H	YT	04.95	97-01	68	22	2
Birmingham C	Tr	01.03	02-04	60	12	4

CLEMENT Andrew (Andy) David
Cardiff, 12 November, 1967 WYth (FB)

League Club	Source	Date Signed	Seasons Played	Apps	Subs	Gls
Wimbledon	App	10.85	86-88	14	12	0
Bristol Rov	L	03.87	86	5	1	0
Newport Co	L	12.87	87	5	0	1
Plymouth Arg	Woking	12.90	90-91	28	14	0

CLEMENT David (Dave) Thomas
Battersea, 2 February, 1948 Died 1982 EYth/E-5 (FB)

League Club	Source	Date Signed	Seasons Played	Apps	Subs	Gls
Queens Park Rgrs	Jnrs	07.65	66-78	403	4	21
Bolton W	Tr	06.79	79-80	33	0	0
Fulham	Tr	10.80	80	17	1	0
Wimbledon	Tr	10.81	81	9	0	2

CLEMENT Neil
Reading, 3 October, 1978 ESch/EYth (FB)

League Club	Source	Date Signed	Seasons Played	Apps	Subs	Gls
Chelsea	YT	10.95	96	1	0	0
Reading	L	11.98	98	11	0	1
Preston NE	L	03.99	98	4	0	0
Brentford	L	11.99	99	7	1	0
West Bromwich A	Tr	03.00	99-04	191	13	19

CLEMENT Philippe
Antwerp, Belgium, 22 March, 1974 Belgium 9 (M)

League Club	Source	Date Signed	Seasons Played	Apps	Subs	Gls
Coventry C	KRC Genk (Bel)	07.98	98	6	6	0

CLEMENTS Andrew (Andy) Paul
Swinton, 11 October, 1955 (CD)

League Club	Source	Date Signed	Seasons Played	Apps	Subs	Gls
Bolton W	App	10.73	77	1	0	0
Port Vale	L	02.77	76	2	1	0
York C	Tr	11.77	77-80	146	2	6

CLEMENTS David (Dave)
Larne, 15 September, 1945 NIAmat/NIu23-3/NI-48 (M)

League Club	Source	Date Signed	Seasons Played	Apps	Subs	Gls
Wolverhampton W	Portadown	01.63				
Coventry C	Tr	07.64	64-71	228	2	26
Sheffield Wed	Tr	08.71	71-73	78	0	0
Everton	Tr	09.73	73-75	81	2	6

CLEMENTS Kenneth (Kenny) Henry
Middleton, 9 April, 1955 (CD)

League Club	Source	Date Signed	Seasons Played	Apps	Subs	Gls
Manchester C	Jnrs	07.75	75-78	116	3	0
Oldham Ath	Tr	09.79	79-84	204	2	2
Manchester C	Tr	03.85	84-87	104	2	1
Bury	Tr	03.88	87-89	66	15	1
Shrewsbury T	Limerick	10.90	90	19	1	0

CLEMENTS Matthew (Matt) Carlton
Birmingham, 17 September, 1977 (M)

League Club	Source	Date Signed	Seasons Played	Apps	Subs	Gls
Cambridge U	Mildenhall T	08.01	01	0	1	0

CLEMENTS Paul Robert
Greenwich, 7 November, 1946 EAmat (M)

League Club	Source	Date Signed	Seasons Played	Apps	Subs	Gls
Oldham Ath	Skelmersdale U	06.71	71-72	32	3	0

CLEMENTS Stanley (Stan)
Portsmouth, 25 June, 1923 (CD)

League Club	Source	Date Signed	Seasons Played	Apps	Subs	Gls
Southampton	Gosport Borough	07.44	46-54	116	-	1

CLEMENTS Steven (Steve)
Slough, 26 September, 1972 ESch (M)

League Club	Source	Date Signed	Seasons Played	Apps	Subs	Gls
Arsenal	YT	11.90				
Hereford U	Tr	07.93	93	2	5	0

CLEMPSON Frank
Salford, 27 May, 1930 Died 1970 (WH)

League Club	Source	Date Signed	Seasons Played	Apps	Subs	Gls
Manchester U	Adelphi BC	09.48	49-52	15	-	2
Stockport Co	Tr	02.53	52-58	246	-	35
Chester	Tr	07.59	59-60	67	-	8

CLEVERLEY Benjamin (Ben) Raymond
Bristol, 12 September, 1981 (M)

League Club	Source	Date Signed	Seasons Played	Apps	Subs	Gls
Bristol C	YT	07.01				
Cheltenham T	Tr	08.03	03	2	6	0

CLEWLOW Sidney (Sid) John
Wallasey, 8 November, 1919 Died 1989 (WH)

League Club	Source	Date Signed	Seasons Played	Apps	Subs	Gls
New Brighton	Poulton CYMS	02.39				
Wolverhampton W	Tr	05.39				
New Brighton	Tr	08.46	46	1	-	0

CLEWS Malcolm (Maxie) Derek
Ocker Hill, 12 March, 1931 (W)

League Club	Source	Date Signed	Seasons Played	Apps	Subs	Gls
Wolverhampton W	Jnrs	03.48	51	1	-	0
Lincoln C	Tr	02.54	53-54	7	-	0

CLICHY Gael
Paris, France, 26 February, 1985 Fru21 (FB)

League Club	Source	Date Signed	Seasons Played	Apps	Subs	Gls
Arsenal	AS Cannes (Fr)	08.03	03-04	14	13	0

CLIFF Edward (Eddie)
Liverpool, 30 September, 1951 (FB)

League Club	Source	Date Signed	Seasons Played	Apps	Subs	Gls
Burnley	App	10.68	70-72	21	0	0
Notts Co	Tr	09.73	73	5	0	0
Lincoln C	L	10.74	74	3	0	0
Tranmere Rov	Chicago (USA)	09.76	76-78	44	6	4
Rochdale	Tr	09.79	79-80	25	1	0

CLIFF John George
Middlesbrough, 7 November, 1946 (W)

League Club	Source	Date Signed	Seasons Played	Apps	Subs	Gls
Middlesbrough	App	11.63				
Halifax T	Tr	07.66	66	1	0	0

CLIFF Philip (Phil) Robert
Rotherham, 20 November, 1947 (W)

League Club	Source	Date Signed	Seasons Played	Apps	Subs	Gls
Sheffield U	Jnrs	11.65	66-69	16	6	5
Chesterfield	Tr	02.71	70-72	29	0	2

CLIFFORD Darren Robert
Bristol, 2 November, 1966 (M)

League Club	Source	Date Signed	Seasons Played	Apps	Subs	Gls
Exeter C	App	11.84	84	0	1	0

CLIFFORD Mark Robert
Nottingham, 11 September, 1977 (FB)

League Club	Source	Date Signed	Seasons Played	Apps	Subs	Gls
Mansfield T	YT	07.96	94-96	4	0	0
Boston U	Ilkeston T	02.01	02	5	2	0

CLIFTON Brian
Whitchurch, Hampshire, 15 March, 1934 (WH)

League Club	Source	Date Signed	Seasons Played	Apps	Subs	Gls
Southampton	Whitchurch	02.53	57-62	111	-	35
Grimsby T	Tr	10.62	62-65	104	0	5

CLIFTON Bryan
Bentley, South Yorkshire, 13 February, 1939 (IF)

League Club	Source	Date Signed	Seasons Played	Apps	Subs	Gls
Doncaster Rov		10.58	58	3	-	0

CLIFTON Henry (Harry)
Marley Hill, 28 May, 1914 Died 1998 EWar-1 (IF)

League Club	Source	Date Signed	Seasons Played	Apps	Subs	Gls
West Bromwich A	Lintz Colliery	09.32				
Chesterfield	Scotswood	08.33	33-37	121	-	67
Newcastle U	Tr	06.38	38	29	-	15
Grimsby T	Tr	02.46	46-48	69	-	23

CLINCH Peter John
Coventry, 15 October, 1950 (CD)

League Club	Source	Date Signed	Seasons Played	Apps	Subs	Gls
Oxford U	App	08.69	69	2	0	0

CLINGAN Samuel (Sammy) Gary
Belfast, 13 January, 1984 NISch/NIYth/NIu21-6/NIu23-1 (M)

League Club	Source	Date Signed	Seasons Played	Apps	Subs	Gls
Wolverhampton W	YT	07.01				
Chesterfield	L	10.04	04	15	0	2

CLINTON Thomas (Tommy) Joseph
Dublin, 13 April, 1926 IR-3 (FB)

League Club	Source	Date Signed	Seasons Played	Apps	Subs	Gls
Everton	Dundalk	03.48	48-53	73	-	4
Blackburn Rov	Tr	04.55	55	6	-	0
Tranmere Rov	Tr	06.56	56	9	-	0

CLISH Colin
Hetton-le-Hole, 14 January, 1944 (FB)

League Club	Source	Date Signed	Seasons Played	Apps	Subs	Gls
Newcastle U	Jnrs	01.61	61-63	20	-	0
Rotherham U	Tr	12.63	63-67	128	0	4
Doncaster Rov	Tr	02.68	67-71	99	1	4

CLISH Thomas (Tommy) Partridge
Wheatley Hill, 19 October, 1932 (G)

League Club	Source	Date Signed	Seasons Played	Apps	Subs	Gls
West Ham U	Wheatley Hill	09.53				
Darlington	Tr	07.55	55-57	52	-	0

CLISS David Laurence
Enfield, 15 November, 1939 ESch/EYth (IF)

League Club	Source	Date Signed	Seasons Played	Apps	Subs	Gls
Chelsea	Jnrs	11.56	57-61	24	-	1

CLISS Tony
March, 22 September, 1959 (W)

League Club	Source	Date Signed	Seasons Played	Apps	Subs	Gls
Peterborough U	Jnrs	08.77	77-82	65	20	11
Crewe Alex	Tr	12.82	82-86	109	4	11

CLIST Simon James
Shaftesbury, 13 June, 1981 (M)

League Club	Source	Date Signed	Seasons Played	Apps	Subs	Gls
Bristol C	Tottenham H (YT)	07.99	99-03	54	17	6
Torquay U	L	02.03	02	11	0	2

League Club	Source	Date Signed	Seasons Played	Career Record Apps	Subs	Gls
CLITHEROE Lee John						
Chorley, 18 November, 1978 (W)						
Oldham Ath	YT	07.97	97-98	2	3	0
CLODE Mark James						
Plymouth, 24 February, 1973 (FB)						
Plymouth Arg	YT	03.91				
Swansea C	Tr	07.93	93-98	109	10	3
CLOSE Brian Aidan						
Belfast, 27 January, 1982 NIYth/NIu21-10/NIu23-1 (M)						
Middlesbrough	St Oliver Plunkett BC	10.99				
Chesterfield	L	03.03	02	8	0	1
Darlington	Tr	03.04	03-04	45	5	0
CLOSE Dennis Brian						
Rawdon, 24 January, 1931 EYth (CF)						
Leeds U	Jnrs	02.49				
Arsenal	Tr	08.50				
Bradford C	Tr	10.52	52	6	-	2
CLOSE Shaun Charles						
Islington, 8 September, 1966 (F)						
Tottenham H	App	08.84	86-87	3	6	0
Bournemouth	Tr	01.88	87-88	28	11	8
Swindon T	Tr	09.89	89-92	13	31	1
Barnet	Tr	08.93	93	21	6	2
CLOUGH Brian Howard						
Middlesbrough, 21 March, 1935 Died 2004 Eu23-3/EB/FLge-2/E-2 (CF)						
Middlesbrough	Great Broughton Jnrs	05.53	55-60	213	-	197
Sunderland	Tr	07.61	61-64	61	-	54
CLOUGH James (Jimmy)						
Hazlerigg, 30 August, 1918 Died 1998 (W)						
Southport	Seaton Burn	02.39	38-46	45	-	10
Crystal Palace	Tr	09.47	47-48	67	-	12
Southend U	Tr	05.49	49	34	-	7
Barrow	Tr	07.50	50	18	-	3
CLOUGH Nigel Howard						
Sunderland, 19 March, 1966 Eu21-15/EB/FLge/E-14 (F)						
Nottingham F	Heanor T	09.84	84-92	307	4	101
Liverpool	Tr	06.93	93-95	29	10	7
Manchester C	Tr	01.96	95-96	33	5	4
Nottingham F	L	12.96	96	10	3	1
Sheffield Wed	L	09.97	97	1	0	0
CLOVER William (Bill) Arthur						
Bracknell, 19 February, 1920 Died 1971 (FB)						
Reading	Woodley OB	02.46	46-49	44	-	4
CLOWES John Alan						
Alton, Staffordshire, 5 November, 1929 (CF)						
Stoke C	Crewe Alex (Am)	06.50	50	2	-	2
Shrewsbury T	Tr	06.52	52-53	11	-	2
Stoke C	Wellington T	08.55	55	2	-	0
CLUGSTON James (Jimmy)						
Belfast, 30 October, 1934 Died 2002 NISch (IF)						
Liverpool	Distillery	01.52				
Portsmouth	Glentoran	01.57	56	1	-	0
CLUNIE James (Jim) Robertson						
Kirkcaldy, 4 September, 1933 Died 2003 SLge-1 (CD)						
Bury	St Mirren	07.65	65	10	0	0
CLUROE Malcolm						
Nottingham, 6 February, 1935 (IF)						
Nottingham F		11.54	54	1	-	0
CLUTTON Nigel						
Chester, 12 February, 1954 (F)						
Chester	Blacon	12.77	77	1	0	0
CLYDE Mark Graham						
Limavady, 27 December, 1982 NIu21-5/NI-3 (CD)						
Wolverhampton W	YT	08.01	02-04	38	6	0
Kidderminster Hrs	L	09.02	02	4	0	0
CLYDESDALE William (Bill)						
Fallin, 14 September, 1935 (FB)						
Hartlepools U	Aberdeen	08.60	60	14	-	0
COAD Matthew Paul						
Darlington, 25 September, 1984 (M)						
York C	Sch	•	03	0	3	0
COADY John						
Dublin, 25 August, 1960 LoI-1 (M)						
Chelsea	Shamrock Rov	12.86	86-87	9	7	2
COADY Lewis						
Liverpool, 20 September, 1976 (M)						
Wrexham	YT	07.95	94	2	0	0
Doncaster Rov	Tr	03.97	96	1	0	0
COADY Michael (Mike) Liam						
Dipton, 1 October, 1958 (FB)						
Sunderland	App	07.76	76-79	5	2	0
Carlisle U	Tr	07.80	80-81	48	3	1
Wolverhampton W	Sydney Olympic (Aus)	01.85	84-85	14	1	1
COAK Timothy (Tim) David						
Southampton, 16 January, 1958 (FB)						
Southampton	App	01.76	76-77	4	0	0
COAKLEY Thomas (Tommy)						
Bellshill, 21 May, 1947 (W)						
Arsenal	Motherwell	05.66	66	9	0	1
COATES David Plews						
Newcastle, 11 April, 1935 (IF)						
Hull C	Shiney Row	10.52	56-59	62	-	13
Mansfield T	Tr	03.60	59-63	159	-	17
Notts Co	Tr	07.64	64-66	66	0	1
COATES Frank						
Farington, 16 April, 1922 (W)						
Blackburn Rov	Leyland Motors	01.43				
Accrington St	Leyland Motors	01.48	47	4	-	0
COATES John Albert						
Birkdale, 3 June, 1944 (G)						
Southport	Burscough	02.65	64	5	-	0
Chester	Tr	08.66	66	1	0	0
Southport	Burscough	07.76	76	16	0	0
COATES John Alfred						
Limehouse, 13 May, 1920 (W)						
Crystal Palace (Am)		08.46	46	4	-	0
COATES Jonathan Simon						
Swansea, 27 June, 1975 WYth/Wu21-5/WB-1 (W)						
Swansea C	YT	07.93	93-01	218	32	23
Cheltenham T	Tr	10.02				
Swansea C	Woking	03.03	02-03	16	14	0
COATES Ralph						
Hetton-le-Hole, 26 April, 1946 Eu23-8/FLge-4/E-4 (W)						
Burnley	App	06.63	64-70	214	2	26
Tottenham H	Tr	05.71	71-77	173	15	14
Orient	St Georges (Aus)	10.78	78-80	76	0	12
COATSWORTH Frederick (Fred) William						
Lincoln, 5 July, 1948 (W)						
Scunthorpe U	Jnrs	07.65	65-66	15	0	2
COATSWORTH Gary						
Sunderland, 7 October, 1968 (CD)						
Barnsley		02.87	87	3	3	0
Darlington	Tr	08.89	90-91	15	7	2
Leicester C	Tr	10.91	91-93	27	5	4
COATSWORTH John Robert						
Newcastle, 21 May, 1933 (CF)						
Gateshead	Crook T	03.57	56	16	-	4
COBB Gary Edward						
Luton, 6 August, 1968 (W)						
Luton T	App	08.86	86-87	6	3	0
Northampton T	L	10.88	88	1	0	0
Swansea C	L	08.89	89	5	0	0
Fulham	Tr	08.90	90-91	8	14	0
COBB Paul Mark						
Aveley, 13 December, 1972 (F)						
Leyton Orient	Purfleet	11.90	90-91	3	2	0
COBB Walter William (Billy)						
Newark, 29 September, 1940 (M)						
Nottingham F	Ransome & Marles	05.59	60-62	30	-	5
Plymouth Arg	Tr	10.63	63-64	31	-	0
Brentford	Tr	10.64	64-66	69	2	23
Lincoln C	Tr	11.66	66-67	67	0	10
COBIAN Juan Manuel						
Buenos Aires, Argentina, 11 September, 1975 (CD)						
Sheffield Wed	Boca Juniors (Arg)	08.98	98	7	2	0
Charlton Ath	Tr	08.99				
Swindon T	Aberdeen	07.00	00-01	3	1	0

League Club	Source	Date Signed	Seasons Played	Career Record Apps	Subs	Gls
COCHRAN Albert George						
Ebbw Vale, 26 November, 1939						(G)
Plymouth Arg	Ilford	09.59				
Leyton Orient	Tr	07.60	60	1	-	0
COCHRANE Alan						
Belfast, 16 March, 1956						(W)
Shrewsbury T	App	03.74	73-74	3	0	0
COCHRANE Colin						
Sutton-in-Ashfield, 26 August, 1921 Died 1985						(IF)
Mansfield T		09.47	47	1	-	0
COCHRANE David (Davy) Andrew						
Portadown, 14 August, 1920 Died 2000 NIRL-8/LoI-4/I-12						(W)
Leeds U	Portadown	08.37	37-50	172	-	28
COCHRANE George Napier						
Glasgow, 27 February, 1931						(IF)
New Brighton	Arthurlie	07.50	50	2	-	0
COCHRANE George (Terry) Terence						
Killyleagh, 23 January, 1953 NI-26						(W)
Burnley	Coleraine	10.76	76-78	62	5	13
Middlesbrough	Tr	10.78	78-82	96	15	7
Gillingham	Tr	10.83	83-85	105	2	17
Millwall	Dallas (USA)	11.86	86	1	0	0
Hartlepool U	Tr	01.87	86	2	0	0
COCHRANE Hugh						
Glasgow, 9 February, 1943						(IF)
Barnsley	Dundee U	08.63	63	5	-	0
COCHRANE James						
Kingswinford, 26 October, 1935						(IF)
Birmingham C	Jnrs	10.52	52-53	3	-	1
Walsall	Tr	06.58	58	6	-	1
COCHRANE James (Jimmy) Kyle						
Glasgow, 14 January, 1954						(FB)
Middlesbrough	Drumchapel Amats	05.71	73	3	0	0
Darlington	Tr	02.75	74-79	222	1	5
Torquay U	Tr	08.80	80	16	0	0
COCHRANE John (Ian)						
Bellshill, 27 April, 1959						(F)
Preston NE	App	02.77	76-78	3	2	2
COCHRANE John (Johnny) James						
Belfast, 11 May, 1944						(IF)
Brighton & Hove A	Jnrs	10.61	61-62	14	-	3
Exeter C	Tr	08.63	63	2	-	0
COCHRANE Justin Vincent						
Hackney, 26 January, 1982						(M)
Queens Park Rgrs	YT	07.99	00	0	1	0
Crewe Alex	Hayes	07.03	03-04	58	10	0
COCKBURN Henry						
Ashton-under-Lyne, 14 September, 1921 Died 2004 EB/FLge-1/E-13						(WH)
Manchester U	Goslings	08.44	46-54	243	-	4
Bury	Tr	10.54	54-55	36	-	0
COCKBURN Keith						
Barnsley, 2 September, 1948						(W)
Barnsley	Jnrs	11.66	66	1	0	0
Bradford PA	Tr	07.68	68	16	0	1
Grimsby T	Tr	01.69	68-69	15	4	2
COCKBURN William (Bill) Robb						
Shotton, 3 May, 1937 Died 1995						(FB)
Burnley	Murton Jnrs	08.55				
Gillingham	Tr	06.60	60-61	62	-	1
COCKCROFT Victor (Vic) Herbert						
Harborne, 25 February, 1941 EYth						(FB)
Wolverhampton W	Jnrs	12.59				
Northampton T	Tr	07.62	62-66	46	1	1
Rochdale	Tr	06.67	67	42	0	0
COCKELL David (Dave) John						
Ashford, Middlesex, 1 February, 1939						(WH)
Queens Park Rgrs	Hounslow T	08.60	60-61	9	-	0
COCKER Leslie (Les)						
Stockport, 13 March, 1924 Died 1979						(IF)
Stockport Co		08.47	46-52	173	-	43
Accrington St	Tr	08.53	53-57	122	-	48
COCKER Leslie (Les) James Robert						
Wolverhampton, 18 September, 1939 EYth						(IF)
Wolverhampton W	Jnrs	06.58	60	1	-	0
COCKERILL Glenn						
Grimsby, 25 August, 1959						(M)
Lincoln C	Louth U	11.76	76-79	65	6	10
Swindon T	Tr	12.79	79-80	23	3	1
Lincoln C	Tr	08.81	81-83	114	1	25
Sheffield U	Tr	03.84	83-85	62	0	10
Southampton	Tr	10.85	85-93	272	15	32
Leyton Orient	Tr	12.93	93-95	89	1	7
Fulham	Tr	06.96	96-97	32	8	1
Brentford	Tr	11.97	97	23	0	0
COCKERILL John						
Cleethorpes, 12 July, 1961						(M)
Grimsby T	Stafford Rgrs	08.88	88-91	99	8	19
COCKERILL Ronald (Ron)						
Chapeltown, 28 February, 1935						(CD)
Huddersfield T	High Green Villa	05.52	55-57	40	-	1
Grimsby T	Tr	08.58	58-67	293	1	28
COCKHILL Andrew (Andy) James						
Bowdon, 11 October, 1967						(F)
Stockport Co	Derby Co (App)	08.86	86	3	0	0
COCKRAM Allan Charles						
Kensington, 8 October, 1963						(W)
Tottenham H	App	01.81	83	2	0	0
Bristol Rov	Tr	08.85	85	1	0	0
Brentford	St Albans C	03.88	87-90	66	24	14
Reading	Woking	10.91	91	2	4	1
COCKROFT Hubert						
Barnsley, 21 November, 1918 Died 1979						(WH)
Barnsley		06.38				
Bradford C		05.46	46	27	-	0
Halifax T	Tr	07.47	47	10	-	1
COCKROFT Joseph (Joe)						
Barnsley, 20 June, 1911 Died 1994						(WH)
Rotherham U	Wombwell	02.31	30-31	3	-	1
West Ham U	Gainsborough Trinity	03.33	32-38	251	-	3
Sheffield Wed	Dartford	11.45	46-48	87	-	2
Sheffield U	Tr	11.48	48	12	-	0
COCKS Alan William						
Burscough, 7 May, 1951						(F)
Chelsea	App	04.69				
Brentford	L	01.70	69	11	0	1
Southport	Tr	07.70	70	24	1	7
CODD Ronald (Ronnie) William						
Sheffield, 3 December, 1928						(W)
Bolton W	Meynell YC	03.50	50-53	31	-	5
Sheffield Wed	L	03.53	52	2	-	0
Barrow	Tr	10.54	54-55	45	-	11
CODDINGTON John William						
Worksop, 16 December, 1937						(CD)
Huddersfield T	Worksop BC	01.55	55-66	332	0	17
Blackburn Rov	Tr	06.67	67-69	72	1	3
Stockport Co	Tr	01.70	69-70	52	0	0
CODNER Robert Andrew George						
Walthamstow, 23 January, 1965 ESemiPro						(M)
Leicester C	Tottenham H (Jnrs)	09.83				
Brighton & Hove A	Barnet	09.88	88-94	257	9	39
Reading	Woking	09.95	95	3	1	0
Peterborough U	Tr	03.96	95	1	1	0
Barnet	Tr	03.96	95-96	28	4	1
Southend U	Tr	03.97	96	3	1	0
COE Norman Clive						
Swansea, 6 December, 1940 Died 2001						(G)
Arsenal	Jnrs	08.58				
Northampton T	Tr	07.60	60-65	58	0	0
COEN Lawrence (Laurie)						
Lowestoft, 4 December, 1914 Died 1972 ESch						(FB)
West Bromwich A	Milford Haven	10.32	36	7	-	4
Coventry C	Tr	06.38	38-47	20	-	3
COFFEY Michael (Mike) James Joseph						
Liverpool, 29 September, 1958						(M)
Everton	App	07.76				
Mansfield T	Tr	07.78	78	2	1	0
COFFILL Peter Terence						
Romford, 14 February, 1957						(M)
Watford	App	02.75	75-77	56	7	6
Torquay U	Tr	11.77	77-80	101	21	11
Northampton T	Tr	07.81	81-82	64	5	3

COFFIN Geoffrey (Geoff) William
Chester, 17 August, 1924 (CF)

League Club	Source	Date Signed	Seasons Played	Apps	Subs	Gls
Chester	Heath Rgrs	05.47	47-54	151	-	35

COGAN Barry
Sligo, 4 November, 1984 IRu21-1 (F)

League Club	Source	Date Signed	Seasons Played	Apps	Subs	Gls
Millwall	YT	11.01	03-04	2	8	0

COGGINS Philip (Phil) Reginald
Bristol, 10 July, 1940 (W)

League Club	Source	Date Signed	Seasons Played	Apps	Subs	Gls
Bristol C	Dorset House BC	10.58	59	4	-	0
Bristol Rov	Tr	07.60	60	4	-	0

COGHLAN Michael James
Sunderland, 15 January, 1985 (CD)

League Club	Source	Date Signed	Seasons Played	Apps	Subs	Gls
Darlington	Sch	08.04	03	0	3	0

COGLAN Alan
Barrow, 14 December, 1936 Died 1987 (G)

League Club	Source	Date Signed	Seasons Played	Apps	Subs	Gls
Barrow	Jnrs	04.54	53-61	52	-	0

COHEN Abraham (Avi)
Tel Aviv, Israel, 14 November, 1956 Israel int (FB)

League Club	Source	Date Signed	Seasons Played	Apps	Subs	Gls
Liverpool	Maccabi Tel Aviv (Isr)	07.79	79-80	16	2	1

COHEN Christopher (Chris) David
Norwich, 5 March, 1987 EYth (M)

League Club	Source	Date Signed	Seasons Played	Apps	Subs	Gls
West Ham U	Sch	04.04	03-04	2	16	0

COHEN George Reginald
Kensington, 22 October, 1939 Eu23-8/FLge-4/E-37 (FB)

League Club	Source	Date Signed	Seasons Played	Apps	Subs	Gls
Fulham	Jnrs	10.56	56-68	408	0	6

COHEN Jacob
Tel Aviv, Israel, 25 September, 1956 Israel int (FB)

League Club	Source	Date Signed	Seasons Played	Apps	Subs	Gls
Brighton & Hove A	Maccabi Tel Aviv (Isr)	10.80	80	3	3	0

COID Daniel (Danny) John
Liverpool, 3 October, 1981 (FB)

League Club	Source	Date Signed	Seasons Played	Apps	Subs	Gls
Blackpool	YT	07.00	98-04	176	25	9

COKE Giles Christopher
Westminster, 3 June, 1986 (M)

League Club	Source	Date Signed	Seasons Played	Apps	Subs	Gls
Mansfield T	Kingstonian	03.05	04	7	2	0

COKER Adewunmi (Ade) Olarewaju
Lagos, Nigeria, 19 May, 1954 (F)

League Club	Source	Date Signed	Seasons Played	Apps	Subs	Gls
West Ham U	App	12.71	71-73	9	1	3
Lincoln C	L	12.74	74	6	0	1

COLBOURNE Neil
Swinton, 25 August, 1956 (G)

League Club	Source	Date Signed	Seasons Played	Apps	Subs	Gls
Rochdale	Hyde U	03.80	79	1	0	0

COLBRIDGE Clive
Hull, 27 April, 1934 (W)

League Club	Source	Date Signed	Seasons Played	Apps	Subs	Gls
Leeds U	Hull C (Am)	05.52				
York C	Tr	05.55	55-57	37	-	14
Workington	Tr	09.57	57-58	46	-	8
Crewe Alex	Tr	10.58	58	29	-	8
Manchester C	Tr	05.59	59-61	62	-	12
Wrexham	Tr	02.62	61-64	108	-	33

COLCOMBE Scott
West Bromwich, 15 December, 1971 (W)

League Club	Source	Date Signed	Seasons Played	Apps	Subs	Gls
West Bromwich A	YT	07.90				
Torquay U	Tr	08.91	91-94	78	11	1
Doncaster Rov	Tr	07.95	95-96	30	12	4

COLDICOTT Stacy
Redditch, 29 April, 1974 (M)

League Club	Source	Date Signed	Seasons Played	Apps	Subs	Gls
West Bromwich A	YT	03.92	92-97	64	40	3
Cardiff C	L	08.96	96	6	0	0
Grimsby T	Tr	08.98	98-04	189	32	4

COLDRICK Graham George
Newport, 6 November, 1945 WSch/Wu23-2 (FB)

League Club	Source	Date Signed	Seasons Played	Apps	Subs	Gls
Cardiff C	App	11.62	63-69	91	5	2
Newport Co	Tr	03.70	69-74	156	1	10

COLDWELL George **Cecil (Cec)**
Dungworth, 12 January, 1929 (FB)

League Club	Source	Date Signed	Seasons Played	Apps	Subs	Gls
Sheffield U	Norton Woodseats	09.51	51-66	409	1	2

COLE Andrew (Andy) Alexander
Nottingham, 15 October, 1971 ESch/EYth/Eu21-8/EB-1/E-15 (F)

League Club	Source	Date Signed	Seasons Played	Apps	Subs	Gls
Arsenal	YT	10.89	90	0	1	0
Fulham	L	09.91	91	13	0	3
Bristol C	Tr	03.92	91-92	41	0	20
Newcastle U	Tr	03.93	92-94	69	1	55
Manchester U	Tr	01.95	94-01	161	34	94
Blackburn Rov	Tr	12.01	01-03	74	9	27
Fulham	Tr	07.04	04	29	2	12

COLE Ashley
Stepney, 20 December, 1980 EYth/Eu21-4/E-41 (FB)

League Club	Source	Date Signed	Seasons Played	Apps	Subs	Gls
Arsenal	YT	11.98	99-04	142	3	8
Crystal Palace	L	02.00	99	14	0	1

COLE Carlton Michael
Croydon, 12 November, 1983 EYth/Eu20/Eu21-12 (F)

League Club	Source	Date Signed	Seasons Played	Apps	Subs	Gls
Chelsea	YT	10.00	01-02	4	12	4
Wolverhampton W	L	11.02	02	5	2	1
Charlton Ath	L	08.03	03	8	13	4
Aston Villa	L	07.04	04	18	9	3

COLE David Andrew
Barnsley, 28 September, 1962 (CD)

League Club	Source	Date Signed	Seasons Played	Apps	Subs	Gls
Sunderland		10.83				
Swansea C	Tr	09.84	84	7	1	0
Swindon T	Tr	02.85	84-86	69	0	3
Torquay U	Tr	11.86	86-88	107	3	6
Rochdale	Tr	07.89	89-90	73	11	7
Exeter C	Tr	08.91	91	0	2	0

COLE George **Douglas (Doug)**
Heswall, 2 July, 1916 Died 1959 (FB)

League Club	Source	Date Signed	Seasons Played	Apps	Subs	Gls
Sheffield U	Sheffield Wed (Am)	05.37	37	1	-	0
Chester	Tr	05.39	46-47	20	-	0

COLE James (Jim) Edward
Wrexham, 14 August, 1925 Died 1997 (FB)

League Club	Source	Date Signed	Seasons Played	Apps	Subs	Gls
Bolton W	Wrexham (Am)	05.47				
Chester	Tr	08.49	49	1	-	0

COLE Joseph (Joe) John
Islington, 8 November, 1981 ESch/EYth/Eu21-8/E-23 (M)

League Club	Source	Date Signed	Seasons Played	Apps	Subs	Gls
West Ham U	YT	12.98	98-02	108	18	10
Chelsea	Tr	08.03	03-04	37	26	9

COLE Michael (Mike) Edward
Ilford, 9 June, 1937 (FB)

League Club	Source	Date Signed	Seasons Played	Apps	Subs	Gls
Norwich C	Harwich & P'ston (Am)	08.56	55-57	3	-	0

COLE Michael (Mike) Washington
Stepney, 3 September, 1966 (F)

League Club	Source	Date Signed	Seasons Played	Apps	Subs	Gls
Ipswich T	App	11.83	84-87	24	14	3
Port Vale	L	01.88	87	4	0	1
Fulham	Tr	03.88	87-90	45	3	4

COLE Roy
Barnsley, 8 December, 1953 (CD)

League Club	Source	Date Signed	Seasons Played	Apps	Subs	Gls
Barnsley	App	12.71	71-73	6	0	0

COLEMAN Anthony (Tony) George
Great Crosby, 2 May, 1945 (W)

League Club	Source	Date Signed	Seasons Played	Apps	Subs	Gls
Tranmere Rov	Ellesmere Port T	10.62	62-63	8	-	0
Preston NE	Tr	05.64	64	5	-	1
Doncaster Rov	Bangor C	11.65	65-66	58	0	11
Manchester C	Tr	03.67	66-69	82	1	12
Sheffield Wed	Tr	10.69	69	25	1	2
Blackpool	Tr	08.70	70	17	0	0
Southport	Durban C (SA)	11.73	73	22	1	1
Stockport Co	Tr	06.74	74-75	28	2	3

COLEMAN Christopher (Chris)
Swansea, 10 June, 1970 WSch/WYth/Wu21-3/W-31 (CD)

League Club	Source	Date Signed	Seasons Played	Apps	Subs	Gls
Swansea C	Manchester C (Jnrs)	09.87	87-90	159	1	2
Crystal Palace	Tr	07.91	91-95	143	11	13
Blackburn Rov	Tr	12.95	95-96	27	1	0
Fulham	Tr	12.97	97-00	136	0	8

COLEMAN David Houston
Salisbury, 8 April, 1967 Died 1997 (FB)

League Club	Source	Date Signed	Seasons Played	Apps	Subs	Gls
Bournemouth	Jnrs	09.84	85-90	40	10	2
Colchester U	L	02.88	87	6	0	1

COLEMAN David John
Colchester, 27 March, 1942 (CF)

League Club	Source	Date Signed	Seasons Played	Apps	Subs	Gls
Colchester U	Harwich & Parkeston	11.61	61-62	2	-	1

COLEMAN Dean Samuel
Dudley, 18 September, 1985 (G)

League Club	Source	Date Signed	Seasons Played	Apps	Subs	Gls
Walsall	Jnrs	08.03	04	1	1	0

COLEMAN Edward (Ted)
Middlesbrough, 23 September, 1957 (F)

League Club	Source	Date Signed	Seasons Played	Apps	Subs	Gls
Middlesbrough	App	09.75	75	1	0	0
Workington	L	03.77	76	10	2	1

COLEMAN Geoffrey (Geoff) James
Bedworth, 13 May, 1936 (FB)

League Club	Source	Date Signed	Seasons Played	Apps	Subs	Gls
Northampton T	Bedworth T	05.55	55-58	18	-	0

League Club	Source	Date Signed	Seasons Played	Career Record Apps	Subs	Gls
COLEMAN Gordon Michael						
Nottingham, 11 February, 1954						(M)
Preston NE	Padstow YC	09.73	73-82	248	21	25
Bury	Tr	08.83	83	24	5	0
COLEMAN John Henry						
Hucknall, 3 March, 1946						(FB)
Nottingham F	Jnrs	03.63				
Mansfield T	Tr	08.66	66-67	43	0	1
York C	Tr	07.68	68	8	3	3
COLEMAN Keith						
Washington, 24 May, 1951						(FB)
Sunderland	App	06.68	71-72	49	0	2
West Ham U	Tr	09.73	73-76	96	5	0
Darlington	KV Mechelen (Bel)	07.79	79	25	0	0
COLEMAN Kenneth (Kenny) James						
Cork, 20 September, 1982 IRYth						(FB)
Wolverhampton W	YT	07.00				
Kidderminster Hrs	L	10.02	02	13	2	0
Kidderminster Hrs	Tr	08.03	03	10	0	0
COLEMAN Neville (Tim) James						
Baschurch, 29 January, 1930						(W)
Stoke C	Gorleston	01.55	53-58	114	-	46
Crewe Alex	Tr	02.59	58-60	73	-	17
COLEMAN Nicholas (Nicky)						
Crayford, 6 May, 1966						(FB)
Millwall	App	08.84	84-89	87	1	0
Swindon T	L	09.85	85	13	0	4
COLEMAN Philip (Phil)						
Woolwich, 8 September, 1960						(FB)
Millwall	App	08.78	78-80	23	13	1
Colchester U	Tr	02.81	80-83	82	4	6
Wrexham	L	09.83	83	17	0	2
Exeter C	Chelmsford C	12.84	84	6	0	0
Aldershot	Tr	02.85	84-85	45	0	5
Millwall	Dulwich Hamlet	09.86	86	8	2	0
Colchester U	(Finland)	02.88	88	6	4	0
COLEMAN Simon						
Worksop, 13 March, 1968						(CD)
Mansfield T	Jnrs	07.85	86-89	96	0	7
Middlesbrough	Tr	09.89	89-90	51	4	2
Derby Co	Tr	08.91	91-93	62	8	2
Sheffield Wed	Tr	01.94	93-94	11	5	1
Bolton W	Tr	10.94	94-95	34	0	5
Wolverhampton W	L	09.97	97	3	1	0
Southend U	Tr	02.98	97-99	98	1	9
Rochdale	Tr	07.00	00-01	13	3	1
COLES Arthur						
Crediton, 27 January, 1914 Died 1997						(CD)
Exeter C	Copplestone	06.37	37	2	-	0
Exeter C	Coleraine	08.46	46-48	14	-	0
COLES Daniel (Danny) Richard						
Bristol, 31 October, 1981						(CD)
Bristol C	YT	06.00	99-04	141	7	5
COLES David (Dave) Andrew						
Wandsworth, 15 June, 1964						(G)
Birmingham C	App	04.82				
Mansfield T	Tr	03.83	82	3	0	0
Aldershot	Tr	08.83	83-87	120	0	0
Newport Co	L	01.88	87	14	0	0
Brighton & Hove A	HJK Helsinki (Fin)	02.89	88	1	0	0
Aldershot	Tr	07.89	89-90	30	0	0
COLEY William (Bill) Ernest						
Wolverhampton, 17 September, 1916 Died 1974						(WH)
Wolverhampton W	Jnrs	09.33	36	2	-	0
Bournemouth	Tr	09.37	37	13	-	0
Torquay U	Tr	07.38	38-46	61	-	1
Northampton T	Tr	08.47	47-50	104	-	7
Exeter C	Tr	07.51	51	8	-	0
COLFAR Raymond (Ray) Joseph						
Liverpool, 4 December, 1935						(W)
Crystal Palace	Sutton U	11.58	58-60	41	-	6
Oxford U	Cambridge U	08.62	62-63	18	-	4
COLGAN Nicholas (Nicky) Vincent						
Drogheda, 19 September, 1973 IRSch/IRYth/IRu21-9/IRB-1/IR-8						(G)
Chelsea	YT	10.92	96	1	0	0
Brentford	L	10.97	97	5	0	0
Reading	L	02.98	97	5	0	0
Bournemouth	Tr	07.98				
Stockport Co (L)	Hibernian	08.03	03	14	1	0
Barnsley	Hibernian	07.04	04	12	1	0

League Club	Source	Date Signed	Seasons Played	Career Record Apps	Subs	Gls
COLGAN Walter (Wally)						
Castleford, 3 April, 1937						(FB)
Queens Park Rgrs	Ashley Road	07.54	57-58	3	-	0
COLKIN Lee						
Nuneaton, 15 July, 1974						(FB)
Northampton T	YT	08.92	91-96	74	25	3
Leyton Orient	L	08.97	97	5	6	0
COLL Owen Oliver						
Donegal, 9 April, 1976 IRu21-5						(CD)
Tottenham H	Enfield R	07.94				
Bournemouth	Tr	03.96	95-96	24	0	0
COLL William (Liam) Sean						
Carrickmacross, 16 December, 1929						(W)
Accrington St		08.49	49-50	13	-	0
COLLARD James **Bruce**						
Hetton-le-Hole, 21 August, 1953						(M)
West Bromwich A	App	05.71				
Scunthorpe U	Tr	07.73	73	21	1	0
COLLARD Ian						
Hetton-le-Hole, 31 August, 1947						(M)
West Bromwich A	App	11.64	64-68	63	6	7
Ipswich T	Tr	05.69	69-74	83	9	5
Portsmouth	L	09.75	75	1	0	0
COLLETER Patrick						
Brest, France, 6 November, 1965 FrB						(FB)
Southampton	Brest (Fr)	12.98	98-99	24	0	1
COLLETON Anthony (Tony)						
Manchester, 17 January, 1974						(F)
Rochdale	YT	•	90	0	1	0
COLLETT Andrew (Andy) Alfred						
Stockton, 28 October, 1973						(G)
Middlesbrough	YT	03.92	92	2	0	0
Bristol Rov	L	10.94	94	4	0	0
Bristol Rov	Tr	03.95	95-98	103	0	0
Darlington	Tr	08.99	99-03	125	0	0
COLLETT Ernest (Ernie)						
Sheffield, 17 November, 1914 Died 1980						(WH)
Arsenal	Oughtibridge WMC	04.33	37-46	20	-	0
COLLIER Alan Stanley						
Markyate, 24 March, 1938 ESch/EYth						(G)
Luton T	Jnrs	05.55	58-60	10	-	0
COLLIER Austin						
Dewsbury, 24 July, 1914 Died 1991						(WH)
Mansfield T	Frickley Colliery	05.38	38	21	-	0
York C	Tr	05.39	46	10	-	0
Rochdale	Queen of the South	04.47	46-47	6	-	0
Halifax T	Tr	11.47	47	1	-	0
COLLIER Daniel (Danny) Joseph						
Eccles, 15 January, 1974						(CD)
Wolverhampton W	YT	07.92				
Crewe Alex	Tr	06.94	94-95	5	6	0
COLLIER Darren James						
Stockton, 1 December, 1967						(G)
Blackburn Rov	Middlesbrough (N/C)	12.87	88-90	27	0	0
Darlington	Tr	09.93	93-94	44	0	0
COLLIER David						
Colwyn Bay, 2 October, 1957						(FB)
Shrewsbury T	App	10.75	74-76	20	0	4
Crewe Alex	Tr	08.77	77	24	2	1
COLLIER Gary Bernard						
Bristol, 4 February, 1955						(CD)
Bristol C	App	11.72	72-78	193	0	3
Coventry C	Tr	07.79	79	2	0	0
COLLIER Geoffrey (Geoff) Heywood						
Blackpool, 25 July, 1950						(F)
Notts Co	Macclesfield T	07.73	73	0	3	0
COLLIER Graham Ronald						
Nottingham, 12 September, 1951						(M)
Nottingham F	App	03.69	69-70	13	2	2
Scunthorpe U	Tr	07.72	72-76	155	6	19
Barnsley	Tr	08.77	77	22	2	2
York C	Buxton	09.78	78	5	0	0

League Club	Source	Date Signed	Seasons Played	Apps	Subs	Gls

COLLIER James (Jim) Robert
Stockport, 24 August, 1952 (M)

Stockport Co	App	03.70	68-73	101	6	12

COLLINDRIDGE Colin
Barnsley, 15 November, 1920 (W)

Sheffield U	Barugh Green	01.39	46-49	142	-	52
Nottingham F	Tr	08.50	50-53	151	-	45
Coventry C	Tr	06.54	54-55	34	-	6

COLLINGS Paul Wallace
Liverpool, 30 September, 1968 (G)

Tranmere Rov	Ellesmere Port T	08.88	88-90	4	0	0
Bury	Altrincham	08.93	93	1	0	0

COLLINGWOOD Graham
South Kirkby, 8 December, 1954 (M)

Barnsley	App	12.72	73-74	12	2	0

COLLINS Aidan Arthur
Chelmsford, 18 October, 1986 (M)

Ipswich T	Jnrs	11.03	02	0	1	0

COLLINS Andrew (Andy) Balsillie
Carlisle, 20 October, 1958 (FB)

Carlisle U	Carlisle Spartans	09.77	77-81	47	7	1

COLLINS Anthony (Tony) Norman
Kensington, 19 March, 1926 (W)

Sheffield Wed	Acton U	11.47				
York C	Tr	07.49	49	10	-	1
Watford	Tr	08.50	50-52	90	-	8
Norwich C	Tr	07.53	53-54	29	-	2
Torquay U	Tr	07.55	55-56	85	-	16
Watford	Tr	07.57	57	17	-	1
Crystal Palace	Tr	11.57	57-58	55	-	14
Rochdale	Tr	06.59	59-60	47	-	5

COLLINS Benjamin (Ben) Victor
Kislingbury, 9 March, 1928 (CD)

Northampton T	Jnrs	04.48	48-58	213	-	0

COLLINS Daniel (Danny) Lewis
Buckley, 6 August, 1980 ESemiPro-2/W-1 (CD)

Chester C	Buckley T	12.01	04	12	0	1
Sunderland	Tr	10.04	04	6	8	0

COLLINS Darren
Winchester, 24 May, 1967 (F)

Northampton T	Petersfield U	08.89	88-90	40	11	9

COLLINS David Dennis
Dublin, 30 October, 1971 IRYth/IRu21-6 (CD)

Liverpool	YT	11.88				
Wigan Ath	L	01.92	91	9	0	0
Oxford U	Tr	07.92	92-94	33	9	0

COLLINS Albert **Desmond (Des)**
Chesterfield, 15 April, 1923 (W)

Chesterfield	Jnrs	01.41	46	8	-	0
Halifax T	Tr	11.46	46-47	44	-	10
Carlisle U	Tr	02.48	47-48	19	-	3
Barrow	Tr	12.48	48-49	55	-	7
Bournemouth	Tr	08.50	50	5	-	1
Shrewsbury T	Tr	08.51	51	9	-	2
Accrington St	Tr	07.52	52	17	-	2

COLLINS John **Douglas (Doug)**
Doncaster, 28 August, 1945 (M)

Grimsby T	Rotherham U (App)	06.63	63-68	96	7	9
Burnley	Tr	09.68	68-75	172	15	18
Plymouth Arg	Tr	05.76	76	22	1	2
Sunderland	Tr	03.77	76-77	3	2	0
Rochdale	Tulsa (USA)	01.79	78	6	2	0

COLLINS Eamonn Anthony Stephen
Dublin, 22 October, 1965 IRYth/IRu21-4 (M)

Southampton	App	10.83	84	1	2	0
Portsmouth	Tr	05.86	86	4	1	0
Exeter C	L	11.87	87	8	1	0
Colchester U	Tr	05.89	89	39	0	2
Exeter C	Tr	07.92	92	8	3	0

COLLINS George Cornelius
Hengoed, 6 August, 1935 (CF)

Bristol Rov	Ton Pentre	06.60	60	2	-	1

COLLINS Glyn
Hereford, 18 January, 1946 (G)

Brighton & Hove A (Am)		03.66	65	2	0	0

COLLINS Graham Frank
Bury, 5 February, 1947 (WH)

Rochdale	Jnrs	09.65	66	7	0	0

COLLINS James (Jimmy)
Sorn, 21 December, 1937 (IF)

Tottenham H	Lugar Boswell Thistle	06.56	61	2	-	0
Brighton & Hove A	Tr	10.62	62-66	199	2	44

COLLINS James (Jamie) Ian
Liverpool, 28 May, 1978 (M)

Crewe Alex	YT	07.96	97-00	15	9	1

COLLINS James (Jim) Kenneth
Colne, 7 November, 1923 Died 1996 (IF)

Barrow	Derby Co (Am)	09.47	47-54	295	-	53
Chester	Tr	07.55	55-56	48	-	11

COLLINS James Michael
Newport, 23 August, 1983 WYth/Wu21-8/W-6 (CD)

Cardiff C	YT	04.01	00-04	49	17	3

COLLINS James (Jimmy) Patrick
Urmston, 27 December, 1966 (FB)

Oldham Ath	YT	08.84	83	0	1	0
Bury	Tr	10.86	86-87	10	1	0

COLLINS Jeremy David
Plymouth, 21 December, 1961 (M)

Plymouth Arg	App	01.80	80-81	4	0	0
Torquay U	Falmouth T	08.83	83	6	1	0

COLLINS John Angus Paul
Galashiels, 31 January, 1968 SYth/Su21-8/S-58 (M)

Everton	AS Monaco (Fr)	08.98	98-99	52	3	3
Fulham	Tr	07.00	00-02	54	12	3

COLLINS John Joseph
Manchester, 30 January, 1945 (FB)

Blackburn Rov	Jnrs	02.63				
Stockport Co	Tr	01.64	63-65	84	0	1

COLLINS John Lindsay
Bedwellty, 21 January, 1949 WSch/Wu23-7 (FB)

Tottenham H	App	03.66	65	2	0	0
Portsmouth	Tr	05.71	71-73	71	3	0
Halifax T	Dallas (USA)	08.74	74-75	82	0	1
Sheffield Wed	Tr	07.76	76	7	0	0
Barnsley	Tr	12.76	76-79	129	1	1

COLLINS John William
Chiswick, 10 August, 1942 (F)

Queens Park Rgrs	Jnrs	08.59	59-66	172	0	46
Oldham Ath	Tr	10.66	66	20	1	8
Reading	Tr	08.67	67-68	82	3	27
Luton T	Tr	08.69	69-70	40	2	10
Cambridge U	Tr	02.71	70-72	93	4	16

COLLINS Kenneth (Ken) John
Pontypridd, 11 October, 1933 (FB)

Fulham	Ynysybwl	05.52	55-58	32	-	0

COLLINS Kevin
Birmingham, 21 July, 1964 (FB)

Shrewsbury T	Boldmere St Michael's	01.84	83	1	0	0

COLLINS Lee
Bellshill, 3 February, 1974 (M)

Swindon T	Albion Rov	11.95	95-99	52	11	2
Blackpool	Tr	07.00	00-02	48	18	2

COLLINS Lee David
Birmingham, 10 September, 1977 (CD)

Aston Villa	YT	07.96				
Stoke C	Tr	02.99	98	4	0	0

COLLINS Lyn
Neath, 30 April, 1948 (FB)

Newport Co	Jnrs	06.66	66-67	17	0	0

COLLINS Michael (Mike) Anthony
Johannesburg, South Africa, 27 July, 1953 (F)

Wolverhampton W	Jnrs	08.71				
Swindon T	Chelmsford C	07.73	73	2	4	0

COLLINS Michael Anthony
Halifax, 30 April, 1986 IRYth (M)

Huddersfield T	Sch	05.05	04	7	1	0

COLLINS Michael (Mick) Joseph Anthony
Bermondsey, 1 February, 1938 (CD)

Luton T	Jnrs	03.55	59-61	8	-	0

COLLINS Ronald **Michael (Mike)**
Middlesbrough, 8 June, 1933 (G)

League Club	Source	Date Signed	Seasons Played	Apps	Subs	Gls
Chelsea	Redcar A	11.51	53	1	-	0
Watford	Tr	07.57	57-58	43	-	0

COLLINS Michael Thomas
Belfast, 6 September, 1977 NIYth (M)

League Club	Source	Date Signed	Seasons Played	Apps	Subs	Gls
Darlington	Coleraine	08.96	96	0	1	0

COLLINS Neill William
Irvine, 2 September, 1983 Su21-2 (CD)

League Club	Source	Date Signed	Seasons Played	Apps	Subs	Gls
Sunderland	Dumbarton	08.04	04	8	3	0

COLLINS Patrick Paul
Oman, 4 February, 1985 EYth (CD)

League Club	Source	Date Signed	Seasons Played	Apps	Subs	Gls
Sunderland	YT	03.02				
Sheffield Wed	Tr	07.04	04	25	3	1

COLLINS Paul
West Ham, 11 August, 1966 EYth (M)

League Club	Source	Date Signed	Seasons Played	Apps	Subs	Gls
Gillingham	App	08.84	84-86	30	7	3

COLLINS Peter John
Chelmsford, 29 November, 1948 (CD)

League Club	Source	Date Signed	Seasons Played	Apps	Subs	Gls
Tottenham H	Chelmsford C	01.68	68-72	77	6	4

COLLINS Robert (Bob) Lionel
Winchester, 12 August, 1939 (G)

League Club	Source	Date Signed	Seasons Played	Apps	Subs	Gls
Newport Co	Winchester C	03.63	62	1	-	0

COLLINS Robert (Bobby) Young
Govanhill, 16 February, 1931 SLge-16/S-31 (M)

League Club	Source	Date Signed	Seasons Played	Apps	Subs	Gls
Everton	Glasgow Celtic	09.58	58-61	133	-	42
Leeds U	Tr	03.62	61-66	149	0	24
Bury	Tr	02.67	66-68	74	1	6
Oldham Ath	Sydney C Hakoah (Aus)	10.72	72	6	1	0

COLLINS Roderick (Roddy)
Dublin, 7 August, 1962 (F)

League Club	Source	Date Signed	Seasons Played	Apps	Subs	Gls
Mansfield T	Dundalk	12.85	85-86	11	4	1
Newport Co	Tr	08.87	87	5	2	1

COLLINS Ronald (Sammy) Dudley
Bristol, 13 January, 1923 Died 1998 (IF)

League Club	Source	Date Signed	Seasons Played	Apps	Subs	Gls
Bristol C		11.44	46-47	14	-	2
Torquay U	Tr	06.48	48-57	356	-	204

COLLINS Samuel (Sam) Jason
Pontefract, 5 June, 1977 (CD)

League Club	Source	Date Signed	Seasons Played	Apps	Subs	Gls
Huddersfield T	YT	07.94	96-98	34	3	0
Bury	Tr	07.99	99-01	78	4	2
Port Vale	Tr	07.02	02-04	120	0	11

COLLINS Simon Jonathan
Pontefract, 16 December, 1973 (CD)

League Club	Source	Date Signed	Seasons Played	Apps	Subs	Gls
Huddersfield T	YT	07.92	92-96	31	21	3
Plymouth Arg	Tr	03.97	96-98	81	3	5
Macclesfield T	Tr	07.99	99-00	52	4	3
Shrewsbury T	L	02.01	00	12	0	0

COLLINS Stephen (Steve) Mark
Stamford, 21 March, 1962 (FB)

League Club	Source	Date Signed	Seasons Played	Apps	Subs	Gls
Peterborough U	App	08.79	78-82	92	2	1
Southend U	Tr	08.83	83-84	51	0	0
Lincoln C	Tr	03.85	84-85	24	0	0
Peterborough U	Tr	12.85	85-88	114	8	2

COLLINS Terence (Terry) James
Penrhiwceiber, 8 January, 1943 (M)

League Club	Source	Date Signed	Seasons Played	Apps	Subs	Gls
Swansea T	Ton Pentre	03.67	67	2	0	0

COLLINS Wayne Anthony
Manchester, 4 March, 1969 (M)

League Club	Source	Date Signed	Seasons Played	Apps	Subs	Gls
Crewe Alex	Winsford U	07.93	93-95	102	15	14
Sheffield Wed	Tr	08.96	96-97	16	15	6
Fulham	Tr	01.98	97-00	37	21	4
Crewe Alex	Tr	08.01	01	13	7	0
Stockport Co	Tr	08.03	03	0	2	0

COLLINS William (Bill) Hanna
Belfast, 15 February, 1920 (WH)

League Club	Source	Date Signed	Seasons Played	Apps	Subs	Gls
Luton T	Belfast Celtic	02.48	47-48	7	-	0
Gillingham	Tr	10.49	50	13	-	0

COLLINSON Clifford (Cliff)
Middlesbrough, 3 March, 1920 Died 1990 (G)

League Club	Source	Date Signed	Seasons Played	Apps	Subs	Gls
Manchester U	Urmston BC	09.46	46	7	-	0

COLLINSON Leslie (Les)
Hull, 2 December, 1935 (M)

League Club	Source	Date Signed	Seasons Played	Apps	Subs	Gls
Hull C	Jnrs	09.56	56-66	296	1	14
York C	Tr	02.67	66-67	35	0	2

COLLINSON Roger
Rawmarsh, 5 December, 1940 Died 1989 ESch/EYth (FB)

League Club	Source	Date Signed	Seasons Played	Apps	Subs	Gls
Bristol C	Doncaster Rov (Am)	10.58	59-60	50	-	1
Stockport Co	Tr	07.61	61	2	-	0

COLLIS David (Dave) John
London, 8 November, 1981 (FB)

League Club	Source	Date Signed	Seasons Played	Apps	Subs	Gls
Charlton Ath	YT	05.00				
Barnet	L	03.01	00	1	1	0

COLLIS Stephen (Steve) Philip
Harrow, 18 March, 1981 (G)

League Club	Source	Date Signed	Seasons Played	Apps	Subs	Gls
Barnet	Jnrs	08.99				
Nottingham F	Tr	07.00				
Yeovil T	Tr	08.01	03-04	20	0	0

COLLYMORE Stanley (Stan) Victor
Cannock, 22 January, 1971 E-3 (F)

League Club	Source	Date Signed	Seasons Played	Apps	Subs	Gls
Wolverhampton W	YT	07.89				
Crystal Palace	Stafford Rgrs	01.91	90-92	4	16	1
Southend U	Tr	11.92	92	30	0	15
Nottingham F	Tr	07.93	93-94	64	1	41
Liverpool	Tr	07.95	95-96	55	6	26
Aston Villa	Tr	05.97	97-98	34	11	7
Fulham	L	07.99	99	3	3	0
Leicester C	Tr	02.00	99-00	7	4	5
Bradford C	Tr	10.00	00	5	2	2

COLMAN Edward (Eddie)
Salford, 1 November, 1936 Died 1958 (WH)

League Club	Source	Date Signed	Seasons Played	Apps	Subs	Gls
Manchester U	Jnrs	11.53	55-57	85	-	1

COLOMBO Donald (Don) Simon
Poplar, 26 October, 1928 (W)

League Club	Source	Date Signed	Seasons Played	Apps	Subs	Gls
Portsmouth	Barking	03.53				
Walsall	Tr	12.53	53	20	-	1

COLOSIMO Simon
Melbourne, Australia, 24 August, 1980 Auu20/Au-13 (FB)

League Club	Source	Date Signed	Seasons Played	Apps	Subs	Gls
Manchester C	South Melbourne (Aus)	07.01	01	0	6	0

COLQUHOUN Edmund (Eddie) Peter Skiruing
Prestonpans, 29 March, 1945 S-9 (CD)

League Club	Source	Date Signed	Seasons Played	Apps	Subs	Gls
Bury	Jnrs	03.62	63-66	81	0	2
West Bromwich A	Tr	02.67	66-68	46	0	1
Sheffield U	Tr	10.68	68-77	360	3	21

COLQUHOUN John
Stirling, 3 June, 1940 (W)

League Club	Source	Date Signed	Seasons Played	Apps	Subs	Gls
Oldham Ath	Stirling A	08.61	61-64	163	-	33
Scunthorpe U	Tr	06.65	65-68	149	0	23
Oldham Ath	Tr	11.68	68-69	68	2	6

COLQUHOUN John Mark
Stirling, 14 July, 1963 S-2 (M)

League Club	Source	Date Signed	Seasons Played	Apps	Subs	Gls
Millwall	Heart of Midlothian	08.91	91	27	0	3
Sunderland	Tr	07.92	92	12	8	0

COLRAIN John James
Glasgow, 4 February, 1937 Died 1984 Su23-1 (IF)

League Club	Source	Date Signed	Seasons Played	Apps	Subs	Gls
Ipswich T	Clyde	04.63	63-65	55	1	17

COLUSSO Cristian Daniel
Buenos Aires, Argentina, 2 July, 1977 ArYth (M)

League Club	Source	Date Signed	Seasons Played	Apps	Subs	Gls
Oldham Ath	Rosario Central (Arg)	02.02	01	6	7	2

COLVAN Hugh
Port Glasgow, 24 September, 1925 Died 2002 (IF)

League Club	Source	Date Signed	Seasons Played	Apps	Subs	Gls
Rochdale	Hibernian	02.48	47	1	-	0

COLVILLE Henry (Harry)
Kirkcaldy, 12 February, 1924 Died 1999 (W)

League Club	Source	Date Signed	Seasons Played	Apps	Subs	Gls
Chester	Raith Rov	08.47	47	4	-	1

COLVILLE Robert (Bob) John
Nuneaton, 27 April, 1963 WSemiPro (F)

League Club	Source	Date Signed	Seasons Played	Apps	Subs	Gls
Oldham Ath	Rhos U	02.84	83-86	22	10	4
Bury	Tr	10.86	86-87	5	6	1
Stockport Co	Tr	09.87	87-88	67	4	20
York C	Tr	06.89	89	17	7	0

COLY Ferdinand
Dakar, Senegal, 10 September, 1973 Senegal 22 (FB)

League Club	Source	Date Signed	Seasons Played	Apps	Subs	Gls
Birmingham C (L)	RC Lens (Fr)	01.03	02	1	0	0

COMBE Alan
Edinburgh, 3 April, 1974 (G)

League Club	Source	Date Signed	Seasons Played	Apps	Subs	Gls
Bradford C (L)	Dundee U	02.02	01	16	0	0
Bradford C	Dundee U	07.03	03	21	0	0

League Club	Source	Date Signed	Seasons Played	Apps	Subs	Gls

COMERFORD Patrick (Pat)
Chester-le-Street, 30 November, 1925 Died 2002 (WH)

League Club	Source	Date Signed	Seasons Played	Apps	Subs	Gls
Shrewsbury T	Bedford T	07.52	52	7	-	0

COMFORT Alan
Aldershot, 8 December, 1964 EYth (W)

League Club	Source	Date Signed	Seasons Played	Apps	Subs	Gls
Queens Park Rgrs	App	10.82				
Cambridge U	Tr	09.84	84-85	61	2	5
Orient	Tr	03.86	85-88	145	5	46
Middlesbrough	Tr	07.89	89	15	0	2

COMINELLI Lucas
Buenos Aires, Argentina, 25 December, 1976 (M)

League Club	Source	Date Signed	Seasons Played	Apps	Subs	Gls
Oxford U	Pahang FA (Mal)	01.05	04	11	5	1

COMLEY Leonard (Len) George
Swansea, 25 January, 1922 (IF)

League Club	Source	Date Signed	Seasons Played	Apps	Subs	Gls
Swansea T	Jnrs	10.45	46-47	28	-	7
Newport Co	Milford U	10.48	48-50	76	-	29
Scunthorpe U	Tr	03.51	50	12	-	5

COMMON Alan Robert
Stannington, 16 December, 1954 (FB)

League Club	Source	Date Signed	Seasons Played	Apps	Subs	Gls
West Bromwich A	App	12.72				
Stockport Co	Tr	07.73	73	2	1	0

COMMONS Kristian (Kris) Arran
Mansfield, 30 August, 1983 (M)

League Club	Source	Date Signed	Seasons Played	Apps	Subs	Gls
Stoke C	YT	01.01	02-03	20	21	5
Nottingham F	Tr	07.04	04	19	11	6

COMMONS Michael (Mike)
Adwick-le-Street, 18 April, 1940 (CF)

League Club	Source	Date Signed	Seasons Played	Apps	Subs	Gls
Lincoln C	Wath W	05.58	59-60	2	-	1
Workington	Tr	07.61	61-63	74	-	36
Chesterfield	Tr	07.64	64	10	-	1

COMPTON Denis Charles Scott
Hendon, 23 May, 1918 Died 1997 EWar-12 (W)

League Club	Source	Date Signed	Seasons Played	Apps	Subs	Gls
Arsenal	Jnrs	05.35	36-49	54	-	15

COMPTON John Frederick
Poplar, 27 August, 1937 (FB)

League Club	Source	Date Signed	Seasons Played	Apps	Subs	Gls
Chelsea	Jnrs	02.55	55-59	12	-	0
Ipswich T	Tr	07.60	60-63	111	-	0
Bournemouth	Tr	07.64	64	27	-	1

COMPTON Leslie (Les) Harry
Woodford, 12 September, 1912 Died 1984 FLge-1/EWar-5/E-2 (CD)

League Club	Source	Date Signed	Seasons Played	Apps	Subs	Gls
Arsenal	Hampstead T	02.32	31-51	253	-	5

COMPTON Paul David
Stroud, 6 June, 1961 (CD)

League Club	Source	Date Signed	Seasons Played	Apps	Subs	Gls
Bournemouth	Trowbridge T	10.80	80-82	64	0	0
Aldershot	Tr	12.83	83	13	0	0
Torquay U	Tr	02.84	83-86	95	0	4
Newport Co	Tr	12.86	86	27	0	2
Torquay U	Bashley	08.91	91-92	19	2	0

COMPTON Roy
Lambeth, 8 November, 1954 (F)

League Club	Source	Date Signed	Seasons Played	Apps	Subs	Gls
Swindon T	Millwall (App)	11.72	73	4	0	2

COMPTON Terence (Terry) David
Bristol, 28 November, 1931 Died 1991 (CD)

League Club	Source	Date Signed	Seasons Played	Apps	Subs	Gls
Bristol C	Jnrs	12.48	51-57	44	-	0

COMSTIVE Paul Thomas
Southport, 25 November, 1961 (M)

League Club	Source	Date Signed	Seasons Played	Apps	Subs	Gls
Blackburn Rov	Jnrs	10.79	80-82	3	3	0
Rochdale	L	09.82	82	6	0	2
Rochdale	L	02.83	82	3	0	0
Wigan Ath	Tr	08.83	83-84	35	0	2
Wrexham	Tr	11.84	84-86	95	4	8
Burnley	Tr	07.87	87-88	81	1	17
Bolton W	Tr	09.89	89-90	42	7	3
Chester C	Tr	11.91	91-92	55	2	6

COMYN Andrew (Andy) John
Wakefield, 2 August, 1968 (CD)

League Club	Source	Date Signed	Seasons Played	Apps	Subs	Gls
Aston Villa	Alvechurch	08.89	89-90	12	3	0
Derby Co	Tr	08.91	91-92	59	4	1
Plymouth Arg	Tr	08.93	93-94	76	0	5
West Bromwich A	Tr	03.96	95	3	0	0

COMYN-PLATT Charlie
Manchester, 2 October, 1985 (CD)

League Club	Source	Date Signed	Seasons Played	Apps	Subs	Gls
Bolton W	Sch	09.04				
Wycombe W	L	09.04	04	3	1	0

CONBOY Francis (Frank) Joseph Anthony
Marylebone, 5 September, 1947 (M)

League Club	Source	Date Signed	Seasons Played	Apps	Subs	Gls
Chelsea	App	07.65				
Luton T	Tr	10.66	66	19	0	1

CONDE James (Jim) Patrick
Creswell, 19 July, 1944 (CF)

League Club	Source	Date Signed	Seasons Played	Apps	Subs	Gls
Wolverhampton W	Jnrs	05.62				
Scunthorpe U	Tr	06.63	63	4	-	1

CONDIE James (Jimmy) Collins Armstrong
Hamilton, 24 July, 1926 Died 1999 (W)

League Club	Source	Date Signed	Seasons Played	Apps	Subs	Gls
Walsall	Kilsyth Rgrs	12.47	47-49	49	-	2

CONEY Dean Henry
Dagenham, 18 September, 1963 Eu21-4 (F)

League Club	Source	Date Signed	Seasons Played	Apps	Subs	Gls
Fulham	App	05.81	80-86	209	2	56
Queens Park Rgrs	Tr	06.87	87-88	36	12	7
Norwich C	Tr	03.89	88-89	12	5	1

CONLEY Brian John
Thurnscoe, 21 November, 1948 (CD)

League Club	Source	Date Signed	Seasons Played	Apps	Subs	Gls
Sheffield U	App	01.66				
Bradford PA	Tr	12.68	68-69	11	2	0

CONLEY John (Jack) Joseph
Whitstable, 27 September, 1920 Died 1991 (CF)

League Club	Source	Date Signed	Seasons Played	Apps	Subs	Gls
Torquay U	Charlton Ath (Am)	05.39	46-50	156	-	72

CONLON Barry John
Drogheda, 1 October, 1978 IRu21-7 (F)

League Club	Source	Date Signed	Seasons Played	Apps	Subs	Gls
Manchester C	Queens Park Rgrs (YT)	08.97	97	1	6	0
Plymouth Arg	L	02.98	97	13	0	2
Southend U	Tr	09.98	98	28	6	7
York C	Tr	07.99	99-00	33	15	11
Colchester U	L	11.00	00	23	3	8
Darlington	Tr	07.01	01-03	114	1	39
Barnsley	Tr	07.04	04	17	7	6

CONLON Bryan
Shildon, 14 January, 1943 Died 2000 (F)

League Club	Source	Date Signed	Seasons Played	Apps	Subs	Gls
Newcastle U	Jnrs	05.61				
Darlington	South Shields	08.64	64-67	72	3	27
Millwall	Tr	11.67	67-68	40	1	13
Norwich C	Tr	12.68	68-69	29	0	8
Blackburn Rov	Tr	05.70	70-71	43	2	7
Crewe Alex	L	01.72	71	4	0	1
Cambridge U	Tr	03.72	71-72	17	1	3
Hartlepool	Tr	09.72	72-73	38	3	3

CONLON Paul Robert
Sunderland, 5 January, 1978 (F)

League Club	Source	Date Signed	Seasons Played	Apps	Subs	Gls
Hartlepool U	YT	•	95	11	4	4
Sunderland	Tr	07.96				
Doncaster Rov	Tr	08.97	97	4	10	1

CONMY Oliver (Ollie) Martin
Mulrany, 13 November, 1939 IR-5 (M)

League Club	Source	Date Signed	Seasons Played	Apps	Subs	Gls
Huddersfield T	St Paulinus YC	05.59	60-62	3	-	0
Peterborough U	Tr	05.64	64-71	251	12	34

CONN Alfred (Alfie) James
Edinburgh, 5 April, 1952 Su23-3/S-2 (M)

League Club	Source	Date Signed	Seasons Played	Apps	Subs	Gls
Tottenham H	Glasgow Rgrs	07.74	74-76	35	3	6
Blackpool	Heart of Midlothian	03.81	80	3	0	0

CONNACHAN Edward (Eddie) Devlin
Prestonpans, 27 August, 1935 SLge-4/S-2 (G)

League Club	Source	Date Signed	Seasons Played	Apps	Subs	Gls
Middlesbrough	Dunfermline Ath	08.63	63-65	95	0	0

CONNAUGHTON Patrick **John**
Wigan, 23 September, 1949 EYth (G)

League Club	Source	Date Signed	Seasons Played	Apps	Subs	Gls
Manchester U	App	10.66	71	3	0	0
Halifax T	L	09.69	69	3	0	0
Torquay U	L	10.71	71	22	0	0
Sheffield U	Tr	10.72	73	12	0	0
Port Vale	Tr	06.74	74-79	191	0	0

CONNEALLY Martin
Lichfield, 2 February, 1962 (G)

League Club	Source	Date Signed	Seasons Played	Apps	Subs	Gls
Walsall	App	02.80	80	3	0	0

CONNELL Alan John
Enfield, 15 February, 1983 (F)

League Club	Source	Date Signed	Seasons Played	Apps	Subs	Gls
Bournemouth	Ipswich T (Jnrs)	07.02	02-04	18	36	8

CONNELL Darren Stephen
Liverpool, 3 February, 1982 (M)

League Club	Source	Date Signed	Seasons Played	Apps	Subs	Gls
Blackpool	YT	•	99	1	2	0
Macclesfield T	Tr	09.00	00	0	1	0

CONNELL James (Jim) David
Blackburn, 24 May, 1951 (W)

League Club	Source	Date Signed	Seasons Played	Apps	Subs	Gls
Bury	Blackburn Rov (App)	02.68	69	9	0	2

CONNELL Lee Anthony
Bury, 24 June, 1981 (FB)

League Club	Source	Date Signed	Seasons Played	Apps	Subs	Gls
Bury	YT	07.99	99-03	46	12	9

CONNELL Peter McArthur
East Kilbride, 26 November, 1927 Died 1995 (FB)

League Club	Source	Date Signed	Seasons Played	Apps	Subs	Gls
Northampton T	Morton	05.51	51	13	-	0

CONNELL Roger
Seaford, 8 September, 1946 EAmat (F)

League Club	Source	Date Signed	Seasons Played	Apps	Subs	Gls
Wimbledon	Walton & Hersham	08.74	77-78	30	2	14

CONNELL Thomas (Tom) Eugene
Newry, 25 November, 1957 NI-1 (FB)

League Club	Source	Date Signed	Seasons Played	Apps	Subs	Gls
Manchester U	Coleraine	08.78	78	2	0	0

CONNELLY Dean (Dino)
St Helier, 6 January, 1970 SSch/SYth (M)

League Club	Source	Date Signed	Seasons Played	Apps	Subs	Gls
Arsenal	YT	02.88				
Barnsley	Tr	06.90	90-92	7	6	0
Wigan Ath	L	10.91	91	12	0	2
Carlisle U	L	08.92	92	0	3	0
Wigan Ath	Tr	02.93	92-93	15	5	1

CONNELLY Edward (Eddie) John
Dumbarton, 9 December, 1916 Died 1990 (IF)

League Club	Source	Date Signed	Seasons Played	Apps	Subs	Gls
Newcastle U	Rosslyn	03.35	35-37	25	-	8
Luton T	Tr	03.38	37-38	50	-	16
West Bromwich A	Tr	08.39				
Luton T	Tr	04.46	46-47	38	-	8
Leyton Orient	Tr	06.48	48-49	32	-	5
Brighton & Hove A	Tr	10.49	49	6	-	1

CONNELLY Gordon Paul John
Glasgow, 1 November, 1976 SSch/SYth (W)

League Club	Source	Date Signed	Seasons Played	Apps	Subs	Gls
York C	Airdrie	08.98	98	28	0	4
Southend U	Tr	07.99	99-00	37	5	2
Carlisle U	Tr	11.00	00	21	7	1

CONNELLY John Michael
St Helens, 18 July, 1938 Eu23-1/FLge-8/E-20 (W)

League Club	Source	Date Signed	Seasons Played	Apps	Subs	Gls
Burnley	St Helens T	11.56	56-63	215	-	86
Manchester U	Tr	04.64	64-66	79	1	22
Blackburn Rov	Tr	09.66	66-69	148	1	36
Bury	Tr	06.70	70-72	129	0	37

CONNELLY Michael
Stockport (W)

League Club	Source	Date Signed	Seasons Played	Apps	Subs	Gls
Stockport Co		06.58	59	4	-	0

CONNELLY Sean Patrick
Sheffield, 26 June, 1970 (FB)

League Club	Source	Date Signed	Seasons Played	Apps	Subs	Gls
Stockport Co	Hallam	08.91	92-00	292	10	6
Wolverhampton W	Tr	03.01	00-01	11	3	0
Tranmere Rov	Tr	10.02	02-03	66	4	0
Rushden & Diamonds	Tr	07.04	04	40	2	0

CONNER Richard (Dick) John
Jarrow, 13 August, 1931 Died 1999 (WH)

League Club	Source	Date Signed	Seasons Played	Apps	Subs	Gls
Newcastle U	Jnrs	01.50				
Grimsby T	South Shields	08.52	53-58	186	-	8
Southampton	Tr	07.59	59-60	78	-	2
Tranmere Rov	Tr	07.61	61	4	-	0
Aldershot	Tr	07.62	62	6	-	0

CONNING Terence Peter
Liverpool, 18 October, 1964 ESch (W)

League Club	Source	Date Signed	Seasons Played	Apps	Subs	Gls
Rochdale	Altrincham	08.86	86	40	0	1

CONNOLLY Adam James
Manchester, 10 April, 1986 (M)

League Club	Source	Date Signed	Seasons Played	Apps	Subs	Gls
Cheltenham T	Sch	•	04	1	3	0

CONNOLLY David James
Willesden, 6 June, 1977 IRu21/IR-40 (F)

League Club	Source	Date Signed	Seasons Played	Apps	Subs	Gls
Watford	YT	11.94	94-96	19	7	10
Wolverhampton W (L)	Feyenoord (Holl)	08.98	98	18	14	6
Wimbledon	Feyenoord (Holl)	07.01	01-02	63	0	42
West Ham U	Tr	08.03	03	37	2	10
Leicester C	Tr	07.04	04	43	1	13

CONNOLLY John
Barrhead, 13 June, 1950 Su23-2/S-1 (W)

League Club	Source	Date Signed	Seasons Played	Apps	Subs	Gls
Everton	St Johnstone	03.72	71-75	105	3	16
Birmingham C	Tr	09.76	76-77	49	8	9
Newcastle U	Tr	05.78	78-79	42	7	10

CONNOLLY Karl Andrew
Prescot, 9 February, 1970 (M)

League Club	Source	Date Signed	Seasons Played	Apps	Subs	Gls
Wrexham	Napoli (Liverpool)	05.91	91-99	337	21	88
Queens Park Rgrs	Tr	05.00	00-02	53	19	12
Swansea C	Tr	08.03	03	4	6	1

CONNOLLY Michael (Mike)
Stainforth, 8 September, 1938 (W)

League Club	Source	Date Signed	Seasons Played	Apps	Subs	Gls
Doncaster Rov (Am)	Jnrs	03.57	56	3	-	0
Wolverhampton W	Tr	09.59				
Stockport Co	Tr	11.60	60	2	-	0

CONNOLLY Patrick (Pat) Joseph
Newcastle-under-Lyme, 27 July, 1941 (CF)

League Club	Source	Date Signed	Seasons Played	Apps	Subs	Gls
Crewe Alex		01.61	60-62	9	-	3
Colchester U	Macclesfield T	07.64	64	21	-	6

CONNOLLY Paul
Liverpool, 29 September, 1983 (FB)

League Club	Source	Date Signed	Seasons Played	Apps	Subs	Gls
Plymouth Arg	Sch	07.02	00-04	49	2	0

CONNOR Daniel (Danny) Brian
Dublin, 31 January, 1981 IRYth (G)

League Club	Source	Date Signed	Seasons Played	Apps	Subs	Gls
Peterborough U	YT	04.98	98-02	6	2	0

CONNOR David (Dave) Richard
Wythenshawe, 27 October, 1945 (FB)

League Club	Source	Date Signed	Seasons Played	Apps	Subs	Gls
Manchester C	Jnrs	11.62	64-71	130	11	10
Preston NE	Tr	01.72	71-72	29	0	0

CONNOR Harold (Harry)
Liverpool, 26 December, 1929 (W)

League Club	Source	Date Signed	Seasons Played	Apps	Subs	Gls
Stoke C (Am)	Marine	03.53	52-53	4	-	2

CONNOR James
Sunderland, 28 November, 1938 (W)

League Club	Source	Date Signed	Seasons Played	Apps	Subs	Gls
Darlington (Am)	Stanley U	09.65	65	3	0	0

CONNOR James (Jim) Richard
Twickenham, 22 August, 1974 (M)

League Club	Source	Date Signed	Seasons Played	Apps	Subs	Gls
Millwall	YT	11.92	94-95	8	1	0

CONNOR James Terence
Stockport, 31 January, 1959 (CD)

League Club	Source	Date Signed	Seasons Played	Apps	Subs	Gls
Stockport Co	Jnrs	02.79	78	1	1	0

CONNOR John
Ashton-under-Lyne, 1 February, 1914 Died 1978 (FB)

League Club	Source	Date Signed	Seasons Played	Apps	Subs	Gls
Bolton W	Mossley	10.34	34-38	29	-	0
Tranmere Rov	Tr	06.47	47-48	46	-	3

CONNOR John
Stockport, 15 May, 1965 (G)

League Club	Source	Date Signed	Seasons Played	Apps	Subs	Gls
Stockport Co	Jnrs	08.80	81	1	0	0

CONNOR John (Jack) Ferguson
Maryport, 25 July, 1934 (CD)

League Club	Source	Date Signed	Seasons Played	Apps	Subs	Gls
Huddersfield T	Jnrs	10.52	54-60	85	-	10
Bristol C	Tr	10.60	60-70	354	1	10

CONNOR John (Jack) Thomas
Todmorden, 21 December, 1919 Died 1998 (CF)

League Club	Source	Date Signed	Seasons Played	Apps	Subs	Gls
Ipswich T	Albion Rov	11.44	46	12	-	4
Carlisle U	Tr	12.46	46-47	40	-	12
Rochdale	Ards	12.48	48-50	82	-	42
Bradford C	Tr	04.51	50-51	14	-	7
Stockport Co	Tr	10.51	51-56	206	-	132
Crewe Alex	Tr	09.56	56	27	-	4

CONNOR Kevin Holland
Radcliffe, 12 January, 1945 (FB)

League Club	Source	Date Signed	Seasons Played	Apps	Subs	Gls
Rochdale		01.66	65-66	21	2	1

CONNOR Paul
Bishop Auckland, 12 January, 1979 (F)

League Club	Source	Date Signed	Seasons Played	Apps	Subs	Gls
Middlesbrough	YT	07.96				
Hartlepool U	L	02.98	97	4	1	0
Stoke C	Tr	03.99	98-00	18	18	7
Cambridge U	L	11.00	00	12	1	5
Rochdale	Tr	03.01	00-03	76	18	28
Swansea C	Tr	03.04	03-04	46	6	15

CONNOR Robert
Bradford, 13 October, 1925 (G)

League Club	Source	Date Signed	Seasons Played	Apps	Subs	Gls
Bradford C	Salts	11.49	49-50	28	-	0
Wrexham	Tr	07.51	51-53	77	-	0

CONNOR Terence (Terry) Fitzroy
Leeds, 9 November, 1962 EYth/Eu21-1 (F)

League Club	Source	Date Signed	Seasons Played	Apps	Subs	Gls
Leeds U	App	11.79	79-82	83	13	19
Brighton & Hove A	Tr	03.83	82-86	153	3	51

League Club	Source	Date Signed	Seasons Played	Apps	Subs	Gls
Portsmouth	Tr	06.87	87-89	42	6	12
Swansea C	Tr	08.90	90-91	39	0	6
Bristol C	Tr	09.91	91-92	11	5	1
Swansea C	L	11.92	92	3	0	0

CONNORS John (Jack) Joseph Aloysius
Stockton, 21 August, 1927 (WH)

League Club	Source	Date Signed	Seasons Played	Apps	Subs	Gls
Darlington	Stockton	03.48	47-51	65	-	0

CONROY Gerard (Terry) Anthony Francis
Dublin, 2 October, 1946 IR-26 (F)

League Club	Source	Date Signed	Seasons Played	Apps	Subs	Gls
Stoke C	Glentoran	03.67	67-78	244	27	49
Crewe Alex	Bulova (HK)	01.80	79-80	37	0	5

CONROY Richard **Maurice**
Bradford, 26 April, 1919 (FB)

League Club	Source	Date Signed	Seasons Played	Apps	Subs	Gls
Fulham		05.37				
Accrington St	Tr	07.39	46-48	87	-	1
Scunthorpe U	Tr	09.50	50	1	-	0

CONROY Michael (Mike) George
Johnstone, 31 July, 1957 (M)

League Club	Source	Date Signed	Seasons Played	Apps	Subs	Gls
Blackpool	Hibernian	08.84	84-85	66	0	2
Wrexham	Tr	07.86	86	23	2	2
Leyton Orient	Tr	07.87	87	2	1	0

CONROY Michael (Mike) Kevin
Glasgow, 31 December, 1965 (F)

League Club	Source	Date Signed	Seasons Played	Apps	Subs	Gls
Reading	St Mirren	09.88	88-90	65	15	7
Burnley	Tr	07.91	91-92	76	1	30
Preston NE	Tr	08.93	93-94	50	7	22
Fulham	Tr	08.95	95-97	88	6	32
Blackpool	Tr	03.98	97-98	12	2	0
Chester C	L	12.98	98	10	0	3
Chester C	L	03.99	98	1	4	0

CONROY Richard (Dick)
Bradford, 29 July, 1927 Died 1991 (CD)

League Club	Source	Date Signed	Seasons Played	Apps	Subs	Gls
Bradford C	Swain House	02.48	48-52	158	-	0
Bradford PA	Tr	10.53	53-55	57	-	0

CONROY Robert (Bobby) Bell
Kirkintilloch, 20 June, 1929 Died 1978 (FB)

League Club	Source	Date Signed	Seasons Played	Apps	Subs	Gls
Bury	Glasgow Ashfield	10.51	55-61	216	-	2
Tranmere Rov	Tr	07.62	62-64	103	-	1

CONROY Steven (Steve) Harold
Chesterfield, 19 December, 1956 (G)

League Club	Source	Date Signed	Seasons Played	Apps	Subs	Gls
Sheffield U	App	06.74	77-82	104	0	0
Rotherham U	Tr	02.83	82	5	0	0
Rochdale	Tr	06.83	83-84	49	0	0

CONSTABLE Shaun
Maidstone, 21 March, 1968 (W)

League Club	Source	Date Signed	Seasons Played	Apps	Subs	Gls
Scunthorpe U	Leeds Univ	02.93	92	2	5	0

CONSTANTINE David (Dave)
Dukinfield, 2 February, 1957 ESemiPro (FB)

League Club	Source	Date Signed	Seasons Played	Apps	Subs	Gls
Bury	Hyde U	02.79	78-81	67	3	2

CONSTANTINE James (Jimmy) Joseph
Ashton-under-Lyne, 16 February, 1920 Died 1998 (CF)

League Club	Source	Date Signed	Seasons Played	Apps	Subs	Gls
Rochdale	Ashton National	01.45				
Manchester C	Tr	04.45	46	18	-	12
Bury	Tr	08.47	47	32	-	14
Millwall	Tr	05.48	48-51	141	-	74

CONSTANTINE Leon
Hackney, 24 February, 1978 (F)

League Club	Source	Date Signed	Seasons Played	Apps	Subs	Gls
Millwall	Edgware T	08.00	00	0	1	0
Leyton Orient	L	08.01	01	9	1	3
Brentford	Tr	08.02	02	2	15	0
Southend U	Tr	08.03	03	40	3	21
Peterborough U	Tr	07.04	04	5	6	1
Torquay U	L	10.04	04	4	0	3
Torquay U	Tr	12.04	04	20	3	6

CONSTANTINOU Costakis (Costas) Khriakou
Limassol, Cyprus, 24 September, 1968 Cyprus int (CD)

League Club	Source	Date Signed	Seasons Played	Apps	Subs	Gls
Barnet (L)	Omonia Nicosia (Cyp)	10.96	96	1	0	0

CONTRA Cosmin Marius
Timisoara, Romania, 15 December, 1975 Romania 46 (FB)

League Club	Source	Date Signed	Seasons Played	Apps	Subs	Gls
West Bromwich A (L)	Atletico Madrid (Sp)	08.04	04	5	0	0

CONVERY Mark Peter
Newcastle, 29 May, 1981 (M)

League Club	Source	Date Signed	Seasons Played	Apps	Subs	Gls
Sunderland	YT	03.99				
Darlington	Tr	01.01	00-04	38	38	3

CONVEY Robert (Bobby)
Philadelphia, USA, 27 May, 1983 USA 31 (F)

League Club	Source	Date Signed	Seasons Played	Apps	Subs	Gls
Reading	DC United (USA)	08.04	04	4	14	0

CONWAY Andrew (Andy)
South Shields, 17 February, 1923 Died 1996 (IF)

League Club	Source	Date Signed	Seasons Played	Apps	Subs	Gls
Hull C	North Shields	06.47	47-48	6	-	5

CONWAY Christopher (Chris)
Dundee, 23 July, 1928 (G)

League Club	Source	Date Signed	Seasons Played	Apps	Subs	Gls
Bury	Ayr U	09.54	54-55	44	-	0

CONWAY James (Jimmy)
Motherwell, 27 August, 1940 SSch/IrLge-1 (CF)

League Club	Source	Date Signed	Seasons Played	Apps	Subs	Gls
Norwich C	Glasgow Celtic	05.61	61-63	42	-	13
Southend U	Tr	10.63	63-64	31	-	9

CONWAY James (Jim) Patrick
Dublin, 10 August, 1946 IRAmat/LoI-1/IR-20 (W)

League Club	Source	Date Signed	Seasons Played	Apps	Subs	Gls
Fulham	Bohemians	05.66	66-75	312	4	67
Manchester C	Tr	08.76	76	11	2	1

CONWAY John
Dublin, 11 July, 1951 (W)

League Club	Source	Date Signed	Seasons Played	Apps	Subs	Gls
Fulham	Bohemians	08.71	71-74	30	8	6

CONWAY John George
Gateshead, 24 January, 1931 Died 1981 (IF)

League Club	Source	Date Signed	Seasons Played	Apps	Subs	Gls
Gateshead		05.53	53-54	4	-	0

CONWAY Michael (Mickey) Denis
Sheffield, 11 March, 1956 (W)

League Club	Source	Date Signed	Seasons Played	Apps	Subs	Gls
Brighton & Hove A	App	03.74	72-73	1	1	1
Swansea C	Tr	12.75	75-77	56	5	11

CONWAY Patrick (Pat)
Newcastle, 19 September, 1968 (M)

League Club	Source	Date Signed	Seasons Played	Apps	Subs	Gls
Cambridge U	App	10.85	85-86	2	0	0

CONWAY Paul James
Wandsworth, 17 April, 1970 USA u21 (M)

League Club	Source	Date Signed	Seasons Played	Apps	Subs	Gls
Carlisle U		10.93	93-96	75	14	22
Northampton T	Tr	06.97	97	2	1	0
Scarborough	L	12.97	97	13	0	2

CONWAY Thomas (Tom)
Stoke-on-Trent, 7 November, 1933 (IF)

League Club	Source	Date Signed	Seasons Played	Apps	Subs	Gls
Port Vale	Jnrs	05.51	55	15	-	4

CONWELL Anthony (Tony)
Bradford, 17 January, 1932 (FB)

League Club	Source	Date Signed	Seasons Played	Apps	Subs	Gls
Sheffield Wed	Jnrs	02.49	53-54	44	-	0
Huddersfield T	Tr	07.55	55-58	106	-	2
Derby Co	Tr	06.59	59-61	98	-	1
Doncaster Rov	Tr	07.62	62-63	33	-	0

COOK Aaron
Caerphilly, 6 December, 1979 (FB)

League Club	Source	Date Signed	Seasons Played	Apps	Subs	Gls
Portsmouth	YT	07.98	97	1	0	0

COOK Andrew (Andy) Charles
Romsey, 10 August, 1969 (FB)

League Club	Source	Date Signed	Seasons Played	Apps	Subs	Gls
Southampton	YT	07.87	87-90	11	5	1
Exeter C	Tr	09.91	91-92	70	0	1
Swansea C	Tr	07.93	93-95	54	8	0
Portsmouth	Tr	12.96	96-97	7	2	0
Millwall	Tr	01.98	97-98	4	1	0

COOK Anthony (Tony)
Bristol, 8 October, 1929 Died 1996 (G)

League Club	Source	Date Signed	Seasons Played	Apps	Subs	Gls
Bristol C	Clifton St Vincent's	01.50	52-63	320	-	0

COOK Anthony (Tony)
Hemel Hempstead, 17 September, 1976 (M)

League Club	Source	Date Signed	Seasons Played	Apps	Subs	Gls
Colchester U	YT	•	93	1	1	0

COOK Anthony (Tony)
Crewe, 26 December, 1961 (M)

League Club	Source	Date Signed	Seasons Played	Apps	Subs	Gls
Crewe Alex	Winsford U	05.81	81	2	1	0

COOK Charles (Charlie) Ivor
Cheltenham, 28 January, 1937 (FB)

League Club	Source	Date Signed	Seasons Played	Apps	Subs	Gls
Bristol C	Gloucester C	02.57	56-57	2	-	0

COOK Garry John
Northampton, 31 March, 1978 (M)

League Club	Source	Date Signed	Seasons Played	Apps	Subs	Gls
Hereford U	YT	07.96	96	17	3	0

COOK James (Jamie) Steven
Oxford, 2 August, 1979 (W)

League Club	Source	Date Signed	Seasons Played	Apps	Subs	Gls
Oxford U	YT	07.97	97-00	33	44	7
Boston U	Tr	02.01	02	6	10	2

COOK Jason Peter
Edmonton, 29 December, 1969 (M)

League Club	Source	Date Signed	Seasons Played	Apps	Subs	Gls
Tottenham H	YT	07.88				
Southend U	Tr	07.89	89-90	29	1	1
Colchester U	Tr	09.91	92-93	30	5	1

COOK Jeffrey (Jeff) William
Hartlepool, 14 March, 1953 (F)

League Club	Source	Date Signed	Seasons Played	Apps	Subs	Gls
Stoke C	Hellenic (SA)	10.77	77-81	22	8	5
Bradford C	L	02.79	78	8	0	1
Plymouth Arg	L	12.79	79	4	3	5
Plymouth Arg	Tr	10.81	81-82	54	1	21
Halifax T	Tr	08.83	83-84	49	7	9

COOK John Albert
Iron Acton, 27 June, 1929 (IF)

League Club	Source	Date Signed	Seasons Played	Apps	Subs	Gls
Bristol Rov	Coalpit Heath	09.46	46	2	-	0

COOK Lee
Hammersmith, 3 August, 1982 (M)

League Club	Source	Date Signed	Seasons Played	Apps	Subs	Gls
Watford	Aylesbury U	11.99	00-03	31	28	7
York C	L	10.02	02	7	0	1
Queens Park Rgrs	L	12.02	02	13	0	1
Queens Park Rgrs	Tr	07.04	04	38	4	2

COOK Leslie (Les)
Blackburn, 11 November, 1924 Died 1996 ESch (WH)

League Club	Source	Date Signed	Seasons Played	Apps	Subs	Gls
Blackburn Rov	Jnrs	11.41	46-48	58	-	0
Coventry C	Tr	07.49	49-53	88	-	0

COOK Lewis Leon
High Wycombe, 28 December, 1983 (M)

League Club	Source	Date Signed	Seasons Played	Apps	Subs	Gls
Wycombe W	Sch	01.03	02-03	5	17	0

COOK Malcolm Ian
Glasgow, 24 May, 1943 (WH)

League Club	Source	Date Signed	Seasons Played	Apps	Subs	Gls
Bradford PA	Motherwell	07.63	63-64	45	-	2
Newport Co	Tr	07.65	65	29	2	0

COOK Mark Richard
Boston, 7 August, 1970 (M)

League Club	Source	Date Signed	Seasons Played	Apps	Subs	Gls
Lincoln C	YT	08.88	88-89	7	0	0

COOK Maurice
Berkhamsted, 10 December, 1931 (CF)

League Club	Source	Date Signed	Seasons Played	Apps	Subs	Gls
Watford	Berkhamsted T	05.53	53-57	208	-	68
Fulham	Tr	02.58	57-64	221	-	89
Reading	Tr	05.65	65	12	0	2

COOK Michael (Micky)
Enfield, 9 April, 1951 (FB)

League Club	Source	Date Signed	Seasons Played	Apps	Subs	Gls
Colchester U	Leyton Orient (Am)	07.69	69-83	609	5	21

COOK Michael (Mickey) John
Belmont, Surrey, 25 January, 1950 (F)

League Club	Source	Date Signed	Seasons Played	Apps	Subs	Gls
Crystal Palace	App	02.68	67	1	0	0
Brentford	Tr	08.69	69	16	4	4

COOK Michael (Mike) John
Stroud, 18 October, 1968 (M)

League Club	Source	Date Signed	Seasons Played	Apps	Subs	Gls
Coventry C	App	03.87				
York C	L	08.87	87	6	0	1
Cambridge U	Tr	06.89	89-90	12	5	1
York C	L	11.90	90	3	3	0

COOK Mitchell (Mitch) Christopher
Scarborough, 15 October, 1961 (FB)

League Club	Source	Date Signed	Seasons Played	Apps	Subs	Gls
Darlington	Scarborough	08.84	84-85	34	0	4
Middlesbrough	Tr	09.85	85	3	3	0
Scarborough	Tr	08.86	87-88	61	20	10
Halifax T	Tr	08.89	89-90	52	2	2
Scarborough	L	10.90	90	9	0	1
Darlington	Tr	03.91	90-91	35	1	4
Blackpool	Tr	03.92	91-94	66	2	0
Hartlepool U	Tr	11.94	94	22	2	0
Scarborough	Guiseley	03.96	95	2	0	0

COOK Paul Anthony
Liverpool, 22 June, 1967 (M)

League Club	Source	Date Signed	Seasons Played	Apps	Subs	Gls
Wigan Ath	Marine	07.84	84-87	77	6	14
Norwich C	Tr	05.88	88-89	3	3	0
Wolverhampton W	Tr	11.89	89-93	191	2	19
Coventry C	Tr	08.94	94-95	35	2	3
Tranmere Rov	Tr	02.96	95-97	54	6	4
Stockport Co	Tr	10.97	97-98	48	1	3
Burnley	Tr	03.99	98-02	140	7	12
Wigan Ath	L	11.01	01	6	0	0

COOK Peter Henry
Hull, 1 February, 1927 Died 1960 (WH)

League Club	Source	Date Signed	Seasons Played	Apps	Subs	Gls
Hull C	Kingston Wolves	06.46	46-47	5	-	0

League Club	Source	Date Signed	Seasons Played	Apps	Subs	Gls
Bradford C	Scarborough	05.49	49	1	-	0
Crewe Alex	Tr	08.50	50-52	47	-	6

COOK Reuben (Ben)
Gateshead, 9 March, 1933 (WH)

League Club	Source	Date Signed	Seasons Played	Apps	Subs	Gls
Arsenal	Tow Law T	11.51				
Leyton Orient	Tr	01.56	56	2	-	0

COOK Robert (Bobby) Kenneth
Letchworth, 13 June, 1924 Died 1997 (W)

League Club	Source	Date Signed	Seasons Played	Apps	Subs	Gls
Reading	Letchworth T	03.48				
Tottenham H	Tr	07.49	49	3	-	0
Watford	Tr	08.51	51-52	53	-	8

COOK Trevor
Blidworth, 2 July, 1956 (F)

League Club	Source	Date Signed	Seasons Played	Apps	Subs	Gls
Mansfield T	App	07.74	73	1	0	0

COOKE Alan
Nantwich, 28 December, 1930 Died 1990 (FB)

League Club	Source	Date Signed	Seasons Played	Apps	Subs	Gls
Crewe Alex		08.55	55	8	-	0

COOKE Andrew (Andy) Roy
Shrewsbury, 20 January, 1974 (F)

League Club	Source	Date Signed	Seasons Played	Apps	Subs	Gls
Burnley	Newtown	05.95	95-00	134	37	52
Stoke C	Tr	12.00	00-02	71	17	21
Bradford C	Busan Icons (SK)	01.05	04	20	0	4

COOKE Barry Anthony
Wolverhampton, 22 January, 1938 Died 1998 EYth (WH)

League Club	Source	Date Signed	Seasons Played	Apps	Subs	Gls
West Bromwich A	Erdington	05.55				
Northampton T	Tr	07.59	59-61	58	-	1

COOKE Charles (Charlie)
St Monance, 14 October, 1942 Su23-4/SLge-4/S-16 (W)

League Club	Source	Date Signed	Seasons Played	Apps	Subs	Gls
Chelsea	Dundee	04.66	66-72	204	8	15
Crystal Palace	Tr	10.72	72-73	42	2	0
Chelsea	Tr	01.74	73-77	85	2	7

COOKE David Frederick
Birmingham, 29 November, 1946 (FB)

League Club	Source	Date Signed	Seasons Played	Apps	Subs	Gls
Wolverhampton W	Jnrs	07.65				
Stockport Co	Tr	07.68	68	3	0	0

COOKE Edward John
Barnsley, 18 March, 1942 (G)

League Club	Source	Date Signed	Seasons Played	Apps	Subs	Gls
Port Vale	Jnrs	06.60	60-63	7	-	0

COOKE Gordon
Crewe, 31 May, 1928 (IF)

League Club	Source	Date Signed	Seasons Played	Apps	Subs	Gls
Crewe Alex	Jnrs	05.48	48	3	-	0

COOKE William Henry (Harry)
Oswestry, 7 March, 1919 Died 1992 (FB)

League Club	Source	Date Signed	Seasons Played	Apps	Subs	Gls
Bournemouth		04.38				
Luton T	Tr	01.46	46-52	210	-	4
Shrewsbury T	Tr	07.53	53	4	-	0
Watford	Tr	07.54	54	10	-	0

COOKE Jason Lee
Birmingham, 13 July, 1971 (F)

League Club	Source	Date Signed	Seasons Played	Apps	Subs	Gls
Torquay U	Bilston T	10.95	95	1	0	0

COOKE John
Salford, 25 April, 1962 EYth (M)

League Club	Source	Date Signed	Seasons Played	Apps	Subs	Gls
Sunderland	App	11.79	79-84	42	13	4
Carlisle U	L	11.84	84	5	1	2
Sheffield Wed	Tr	06.85				
Carlisle U	Tr	10.85	85-87	105	1	11
Stockport Co	Tr	07.88	88-89	54	4	7
Chesterfield	Tr	07.90	90-91	48	5	8

COOKE Joseph (Joe)
Dominica, 15 February, 1955 (CD)

League Club	Source	Date Signed	Seasons Played	Apps	Subs	Gls
Bradford C	App	05.72	71-78	184	20	62
Peterborough U	Tr	01.79	78	18	0	5
Oxford U	Tr	08.79	79-80	71	1	13
Exeter C	Tr	06.81	81	17	0	3
Bradford C	Tr	01.82	81-83	61	1	6
Rochdale	Tr	07.84	84-85	75	0	4
Wrexham	Tr	07.86	86-87	49	2	4

COOKE Peter Charles
Northampton, 15 January, 1962 (M)

League Club	Source	Date Signed	Seasons Played	Apps	Subs	Gls
Northampton T	Jnrs	07.80	80	4	1	1

COOKE Richard Edward
Islington, 4 September, 1965 EYth/Eu21-1 (W)

League Club	Source	Date Signed	Seasons Played	Apps	Subs	Gls
Tottenham H	App	05.83	83-85	9	2	2
Birmingham C	L	09.86	86	5	0	0
Bournemouth	Tr	01.87	86-88	63	8	15
Luton T	Tr	03.89	88-89	3	14	1
Bournemouth	Tr	03.91	90-92	38	15	13

COOKE Robert (Robbie) Leslie
Rotherham, 16 February, 1957 (F)

League Club	Source	Date Signed	Seasons Played	Apps	Subs	Gls
Mansfield T	App	02.75	76-77	7	8	1
Peterborough U	Grantham	05.80	80-82	115	0	51
Cambridge U	Tr	02.83	82-84	62	3	14
Brentford	Tr	12.84	84-87	122	2	53
Millwall	Tr	12.87	87	4	0	1

COOKE Stephen Lee
Walsall, 15 February, 1983 EYth (M)

League Club	Source	Date Signed	Seasons Played	Apps	Subs	Gls
Aston Villa	YT	02.00	02	0	3	0
Bournemouth	L	03.02	01	6	1	0
Bournemouth	L	01.04	03	3	0	0
Wycombe W	L	12.04	04	4	2	0

COOKE Terence (Terry) Arthur
Wrexham, 21 February, 1962 (F)

League Club	Source	Date Signed	Seasons Played	Apps	Subs	Gls
Chester	App	02.80	80-82	37	12	11

COOKE Terence (Terry) John
Marston Green, 5 August, 1976 EYth/Eu21-4 (W)

League Club	Source	Date Signed	Seasons Played	Apps	Subs	Gls
Manchester U	YT	07.94	95	1	3	0
Sunderland	L	01.96	95	6	0	0
Birmingham C	L	11.96	96	1	3	0
Wrexham	L	10.98	98	10	0	0
Manchester C	Tr	01.99	98-99	27	7	7
Wigan Ath	L	03.00	99	10	0	1
Sheffield Wed	L	09.00	00	12	1	1
Sheffield Wed	L	12.00	00	4	0	0
Grimsby T	Tr	03.02	01-02	18	10	1
Sheffield Wed	Tr	08.03	03	19	4	2

COOKE Wilfred (Wilf) Hudson
Crewe, 5 October, 1915 Died 1985 (WH)

League Club	Source	Date Signed	Seasons Played	Apps	Subs	Gls
Bradford C	Leeds U (Am)	08.35	36-37	21	-	2
Leeds U	Tr	07.38				
Fulham	Tr	07.39				
Crewe Alex	Tr	02.46	46	9	-	2

COOKSEY Ernest (Ernie) George
Bishops Stortford, 11 June, 1980 (M)

League Club	Source	Date Signed	Seasons Played	Apps	Subs	Gls
Oldham Ath	Crawley T	08.03	03-04	23	14	4
Rochdale	Tr	09.04	04	27	7	5

COOKSEY Scott Andrew
Birmingham, 24 June, 1972 ESemiPro-1 (G)

League Club	Source	Date Signed	Seasons Played	Apps	Subs	Gls
Derby Co	YT	07.90				
Shrewsbury T	Tr	02.91				
Peterborough U	Bromsgrove Rov	12.93	93-94	15	0	0
Shrewsbury T	Hednesford T	10.98	98	2	0	0

COOKSON James (Jimmy)
Ford, Lancashire, 22 August, 1927 Died 1993 (FB)

League Club	Source	Date Signed	Seasons Played	Apps	Subs	Gls
Everton		10.45				
Southport	Tr	08.49	49-51	55	-	1

COOKSON Steven (Steve) John
Wolverhampton, 19 February, 1972 (F)

League Club	Source	Date Signed	Seasons Played	Apps	Subs	Gls
Torquay U	YT	07.90	89-90	7	5	1

COOLE William (Billy)
Manchester, 27 January, 1925 Died 2001 (W)

League Club	Source	Date Signed	Seasons Played	Apps	Subs	Gls
Mansfield T		01.48	47-53	182	-	35
Notts Co	Tr	10.53	53-55	42	-	5
Barrow	Tr	07.56	56-58	56	-	4

COOLING Roy
Barnsley, 9 December, 1921 Died 2003 (IF)

League Club	Source	Date Signed	Seasons Played	Apps	Subs	Gls
Barnsley	Mitchell's Main Welf	03.42	46	6	-	3
Mansfield T	Tr	09.47	47-49	65	-	14

COOMBE Mark Andrew
Torquay, 17 September, 1968 (G)

League Club	Source	Date Signed	Seasons Played	Apps	Subs	Gls
Bristol C	Bournemouth (YT)	08.87				
Colchester U	Carlisle U (N/C)	10.88	88	3	0	0
Torquay U	Tr	12.88	88	8	0	0

COOMBES Jeffrey (Jeff)
Rhondda, 1 April, 1954 WSch (M)

League Club	Source	Date Signed	Seasons Played	Apps	Subs	Gls
Bristol Rov	App	04.72	72-74	10	1	1

COOMBES Lee Edward
Dinnington, 5 July, 1966 (FB)

League Club	Source	Date Signed	Seasons Played	Apps	Subs	Gls
Sheffield Wed	App	07.84				
Scunthorpe U	Tr	08.85				
Chesterfield	Tr	07.86	86	1	2	0

COOMBS Francis (Frank) Henry
East Ham, 24 April, 1925 Died 1998 (G)

League Club	Source	Date Signed	Seasons Played	Apps	Subs	Gls
Bristol C	Dartford	06.49	49	24	-	0
Southend U	Tr	06.50	50	20	-	0
Colchester U	Tr	07.51	51-53	38	-	0

COOMBS Paul Andrew
Bristol, 4 September, 1970 (F)

League Club	Source	Date Signed	Seasons Played	Apps	Subs	Gls
Aldershot	Queens Park Rgrs (YT)	07.89	88-90	9	7	1

COONEY Sean Patrick
Perth, Australia, 31 October, 1983 (FB)

League Club	Source	Date Signed	Seasons Played	Apps	Subs	Gls
Coventry C	Sch	01.03	02	0	1	0

COOP James (Jim) Yates
Horwich, 17 September, 1927 Died 1996 (W)

League Club	Source	Date Signed	Seasons Played	Apps	Subs	Gls
Sheffield U	Brodsworth Main Coll	05.46	47-48	9	-	1
York C	Tr	07.49	49-50	12	-	4

COOP Michael (Mick) Anthony
Grimsby, 10 July, 1948 (FB)

League Club	Source	Date Signed	Seasons Played	Apps	Subs	Gls
Coventry C	App	01.66	66-78	355	12	17
York C	L	11.74	74	4	0	0
Coventry C	Detroit (USA)	09.79	79-80	58	0	1
Derby Co	Tr	07.81	81	17	1	0

COOPER Adrian Stanley John
Reading, 16 January, 1957 ESch (M)

League Club	Source	Date Signed	Seasons Played	Apps	Subs	Gls
Reading	App	01.75	73-75	14	0	2

COOPER Arthur
Etruria, 16 March, 1921 (WH)

League Club	Source	Date Signed	Seasons Played	Apps	Subs	Gls
Port Vale	Shelton St Mark's	08.41	46	4	-	0

COOPER Charles (Charlie)
Farnworth, 14 June, 1941 (FB)

League Club	Source	Date Signed	Seasons Played	Apps	Subs	Gls
Bolton W	Jnrs	05.59	60-68	79	4	0
Barrow	Tr	07.69	69-70	54	1	0

COOPER Colin Terence
Sedgefield, 28 February, 1967 Eu21-8/E-2 (CD)

League Club	Source	Date Signed	Seasons Played	Apps	Subs	Gls
Middlesbrough	Jnrs	07.84	85-90	183	5	6
Millwall	Tr	07.91	91-92	77	0	6
Nottingham F	Tr	06.93	93-97	179	1	20
Middlesbrough	Tr	08.98	98-04	139	18	5
Sunderland	L	03.04	03	0	3	0

COOPER David Andrew
Lambeth, 25 June, 1971 (F)

League Club	Source	Date Signed	Seasons Played	Apps	Subs	Gls
Wimbledon	YT	07.89				
Plymouth Arg	Tr	03.91	90	0	3	0

COOPER David Barry Ernest
Welwyn Garden City, 7 March, 1973 (FB)

League Club	Source	Date Signed	Seasons Played	Apps	Subs	Gls
Exeter C	Luton T (YT)	08.91	91-94	39	9	0

COOPER Douglas (Doug)
Eston, 18 October, 1936 Died 1998 (CF)

League Club	Source	Date Signed	Seasons Played	Apps	Subs	Gls
Middlesbrough	Grangetown BC	10.53	54-56	5	-	0
Rotherham U	Tr	01.59	58	14	-	5
Hartlepools U	Tr	08.60	60	16	-	6

COOPER Frederick (Fred) John
West Ham, 18 November, 1934 Died 1972 ESch (FB)

League Club	Source	Date Signed	Seasons Played	Apps	Subs	Gls
West Ham U	Jnrs	12.51	56-57	4	-	0

COOPER Gary
Hammersmith, 20 November, 1965 ESch/EYth (M)

League Club	Source	Date Signed	Seasons Played	Apps	Subs	Gls
Queens Park Rgrs	App	06.83	84	1	0	0
Brentford	L	09.85	85	9	1	0
Maidstone U	Fisher Ath	03.89	89-90	53	7	7
Peterborough U	Tr	03.91	90-93	83	5	10
Birmingham C	Tr	12.93	93-95	58	4	2

COOPER Gary Smethurst
Horwich, 15 February, 1955 ESch (F)

League Club	Source	Date Signed	Seasons Played	Apps	Subs	Gls
Rochdale	Horwich RMI	12.73	73-76	81	10	14
Southport	Tr	08.77	77	13	7	5

COOPER Geoffrey (Geoff) Victor
Kingston, 27 December, 1960 (FB)

League Club	Source	Date Signed	Seasons Played	Apps	Subs	Gls
Brighton & Hove A	Bognor Regis T	12.87	87-88	2	5	0
Barnet	Tr	07.89	91-92	30	1	1
Barnet	Wycombe W	08.93	93-94	25	12	3

COOPER George
Kingswinford, 1 October, 1932 Died 1994 (IF)

League Club	Source	Date Signed	Seasons Played	Apps	Subs	Gls
Crystal Palace	Brierley Hill Alliance	01.55	54-58	69	-	27
Rochdale	Tr	01.59	58-59	32	-	9

COOPER Graham
Huddersfield, 22 May, 1962 (W)

League Club	Source	Date Signed	Seasons Played	Apps	Subs	Gls
Huddersfield T	Emley	03.84	83-87	61	13	13
Wrexham	Tr	08.88	88-90	50	13	16
York C	L	11.90	90	2	0	0
Halifax T	Northwich Vic	01.91	90-91	32	7	4

COOPER Ian Laurence
Bradford, 21 September, 1946 (FB)

League Club	Source	Date Signed	Seasons Played	Apps	Subs	Gls
Bradford C	Jnrs	08.66	65-76	442	1	4

COOPER James (Jim) Else
Blackpool, 13 January, 1928 (W)

League Club	Source	Date Signed	Seasons Played	Apps	Subs	Gls
Accrington St	Fleetwood	06.52	52	7	-	1

COOPER James (Jimmy) Ernest
Hoole, Cheshire, 19 January, 1942 (W)

League Club	Source	Date Signed	Seasons Played	Apps	Subs	Gls
Chester	Jnrs	09.59	59-61	91	-	17
Southport	Tr	06.62	62	28	-	7
Blackpool	Tr	07.63	63	4	-	0
Mansfield T	Tr	05.64	64	7	-	4
Crewe Alex	Tr	07.65	65	6	0	0

COOPER James (Jim) Thomson
Glasgow, 28 December, 1939 (W)

League Club	Source	Date Signed	Seasons Played	Apps	Subs	Gls
Brighton & Hove A	Airdrie	08.62	62-63	41	-	6
Hartlepools U	Tr	07.65	65	19	0	1

COOPER Joseph (Joe)
Reddish, 16 February, 1918 Died 1992 (FB)

League Club	Source	Date Signed	Seasons Played	Apps	Subs	Gls
Blackpool		01.38				
Crewe Alex	Tr	07.39	46	3	-	0

COOPER Joseph (Joe)
Gateshead, 15 October, 1934 (WH)

League Club	Source	Date Signed	Seasons Played	Apps	Subs	Gls
Newcastle U	Winlaton Mill	09.52	53-57	6	-	0

COOPER Kenny
Baltimore, USA, 21 October, 1984 (F)

League Club	Source	Date Signed	Seasons Played	Apps	Subs	Gls
Manchester U	Dallas Mustangs (USA)	01.04				
Oldham Ath	L	01.05	04	5	2	3

COOPER Kevin Lee
Derby, 8 February, 1975 (W)

League Club	Source	Date Signed	Seasons Played	Apps	Subs	Gls
Derby Co	YT	07.93	94-95	0	2	0
Stockport Co	Tr	03.97	96-00	146	22	21
Wimbledon	Tr	03.01	00-01	50	1	13
Wolverhampton W	Tr	03.02	01-04	32	30	9
Sunderland	L	01.04	03	0	1	0
Norwich C	L	03.04	03	6	4	0

COOPER Leigh Vernon
Reading, 7 May, 1961 (FB)

League Club	Source	Date Signed	Seasons Played	Apps	Subs	Gls
Plymouth Arg	App	05.79	79-89	316	7	15
Aldershot	Tr	09.90	90	33	0	2

COOPER Leonard (Len) Arnold
Lower Gornal, 11 May, 1936 Died 1992 EYth (W)

League Club	Source	Date Signed	Seasons Played	Apps	Subs	Gls
Wolverhampton W	Jnrs	05.53				
Walsall		02.56	55	5	-	2

COOPER Mark David
Watford, 5 April, 1967 (F)

League Club	Source	Date Signed	Seasons Played	Apps	Subs	Gls
Cambridge U	App	10.84	83-86	61	9	17
Tottenham H	Tr	04.87				
Shrewsbury T	L	09.87	87	6	0	2
Gillingham	Tr	10.87	87-88	38	11	11
Leyton Orient	Tr	02.89	88-93	117	33	45
Barnet	Tr	07.94	94-95	58	9	19
Northampton T	Tr	08.96	96	37	4	10

COOPER Mark Nicholas
Wakefield, 18 December, 1968 (M)

League Club	Source	Date Signed	Seasons Played	Apps	Subs	Gls
Bristol C	YT	09.87				
Exeter C	Tr	10.89	89-91	46	4	12
Southend U	L	03.90	89	4	1	0
Birmingham C	Tr	09.91	91-92	30	9	4
Fulham	Tr	11.92	92-93	10	4	0
Huddersfield T	L	03.93	92	10	0	4
Wycombe W	Tr	01.94	93	0	2	1
Exeter C	Tr	02.94	93-95	78	10	20
Hartlepool U	Tr	07.96	96	33	0	9
Macclesfield T	L	09.97	97	8	0	2
Leyton Orient	Tr	12.97	97	0	1	0

COOPER Neale James
Darjeeling, India, 24 November, 1963 SYth/Su21-13 (CD)

League Club	Source	Date Signed	Seasons Played	Apps	Subs	Gls
Aston Villa	Aberdeen	07.86	86-87	19	1	0
Reading	Glasgow Rgrs	07.91	91	6	1	0

COOPER Neil
Aberdeen, 12 August, 1959 SSch/SYth (FB)

League Club	Source	Date Signed	Seasons Played	Apps	Subs	Gls
Barnsley	Aberdeen	01.80	79-81	57	3	6
Grimsby T	Tr	03.82	81-83	47	0	2

COOPER Paul
Darlington, 24 December, 1975 (M)

League Club	Source	Date Signed	Seasons Played	Apps	Subs	Gls
Darlington	YT	07.93	93	1	0	0

COOPER Paul David
Brierley Hill, 21 December, 1953 (G)

League Club	Source	Date Signed	Seasons Played	Apps	Subs	Gls
Birmingham C	App	07.71	71-73	17	0	0
Ipswich T	Tr	03.74	73-86	447	0	0
Leicester C	Tr	06.87	87-88	56	0	0
Manchester C	Tr	03.89	88-89	15	0	0
Stockport Co	Tr	08.90	90	22	0	0

COOPER Paul Terence
Birmingham, 12 July, 1957 (FB)

League Club	Source	Date Signed	Seasons Played	Apps	Subs	Gls
Huddersfield T	App	08.75	76	2	0	0
Grimsby T	Tr	07.77	77	3	0	0

COOPER Richard Anthony
Nottingham, 27 September, 1979 ESch/EYth (M)

League Club	Source	Date Signed	Seasons Played	Apps	Subs	Gls
Nottingham F	YT	10.96	99-00	0	3	0
York C	Tr	03.01	00-03	84	16	4

COOPER Richard David
Wembley, 7 May, 1965 (M)

League Club	Source	Date Signed	Seasons Played	Apps	Subs	Gls
Sheffield U	App	05.83	82-84	2	4	0
Lincoln C	Tr	08.85	85-86	57	4	2
Exeter C	Tr	07.87	87-88	55	7	2

COOPER Robert (Bobby) Charles
Sutton Coldfield, 3 September, 1966 (M)

League Club	Source	Date Signed	Seasons Played	Apps	Subs	Gls
Leicester C	App	05.85				
Preston NE	L	12.85	85	3	2	0

COOPER Ronald (Ron)
Peterborough, 28 August, 1938 (CD)

League Club	Source	Date Signed	Seasons Played	Apps	Subs	Gls
Peterborough U	Jnrs	(N/L)	63-67	132	0	1

COOPER Shaun David
Isle of Wight, 5 October, 1983 (FB)

League Club	Source	Date Signed	Seasons Played	Apps	Subs	Gls
Portsmouth	YT	04.01	01	3	4	0
Leyton Orient	L	10.03	03	9	0	0
Kidderminster Hrs	L	09.04	04	10	0	0

COOPER Stephen (Steve) Brian
Birmingham, 22 June, 1964 Died 2004 (F)

League Club	Source	Date Signed	Seasons Played	Apps	Subs	Gls
Birmingham C	Moor Green Rov	11.83				
Halifax T	L	12.83	83	7	0	1
Newport Co	Tr	09.84	84	38	0	11
Plymouth Arg	Tr	08.85	85-87	58	15	15
Barnsley	Tr	08.88	88-90	62	15	13
Tranmere Rov	Tr	12.90	90-92	16	16	3
Peterborough U	L	03.92	91	2	7	0
Wigan Ath	L	12.92	92	4	0	0
York C	Tr	08.93	93-94	37	1	6

COOPER Steven (Steve) Milne
Stourbridge, 14 December, 1955 EYth (F)

League Club	Source	Date Signed	Seasons Played	Apps	Subs	Gls
Torquay U	Stourbridge	03.78	77-83	219	15	76

COOPER Terence (Terry)
Brotherton, 12 July, 1944 E-20 (FB)

League Club	Source	Date Signed	Seasons Played	Apps	Subs	Gls
Leeds U	App	07.62	63-74	240	10	7
Middlesbrough	Tr	03.75	74-77	105	0	1
Bristol C	Tr	07.78	78	11	0	0
Bristol Rov	Tr	08.79	79-81	53	6	0
Doncaster Rov	Tr	11.81	81	20	0	0
Bristol C	Tr	08.82	82-84	38	22	1

COOPER Terence (Terry)
Croesyceiliog, 11 March, 1950 (CD)

League Club	Source	Date Signed	Seasons Played	Apps	Subs	Gls
Newport Co	Jnrs	07.68	67-69	65	3	1
Notts Co	Tr	07.70	71-72	3	6	0
Lincoln C	L	12.71	71	3	0	0
Lincoln C	Tr	08.72	72-78	265	2	12
Scunthorpe U	L	11.77	77	4	0	0
Bradford C	Tr	06.79	79-80	47	1	2
Rochdale	Tr	08.81	81	35	0	2

COOPER William George Edward
York, 2 November, 1917 Died 1978 (IF)

League Club	Source	Date Signed	Seasons Played	Apps	Subs	Gls
Bradford C	Halifax T (Am)	09.46	46-47	7	-	4

COOTE Adrian
Great Yarmouth, 30 September, 1978 NIu21-14/NIB-1/NI-6 (F)

League Club	Source	Date Signed	Seasons Played	Apps	Subs	Gls
Norwich C	YT	07.97	97-00	20	34	3
Colchester U	Tr	12.01	01-02	12	23	4
Bristol Rov	L	10.02	02	4	1	1

COOTE Kenneth (Ken) Alexander
Paddington, 19 May, 1928 Died 2003 (WH)

League Club	Source	Date Signed	Seasons Played	Apps	Subs	Gls
Brentford	Wembley T	05.49	49-63	514	-	14

COPE Charles (Tony) Anthony
Doncaster, 17 January, 1941 (WH)

League Club	Source	Date Signed	Seasons Played	Apps	Subs	Gls
Doncaster Rov	Jnrs	09.58	58-59	8	-	0

COPE James Andrew
Solihull, 4 October, 1977 (M)

League Club	Source	Date Signed	Seasons Played	Apps	Subs	Gls
Shrewsbury T	YT	07.96	95-96	3	1	0

COPE Ronald (Ron)
Crewe, 5 October, 1934 ESch (CD)

League Club	Source	Date Signed	Seasons Played	Apps	Subs	Gls
Manchester U	Jnrs	10.51	56-60	93	-	2
Luton T	Tr	08.61	61-62	28	-	0

COPELAND Edward (Teddy)
Hetton-le-Hole, 19 May, 1921 Died 2001 (W)

League Club	Source	Date Signed	Seasons Played	Apps	Subs	Gls
Hartlepools U	Easington CW	06.44	46-47	38	-	9

COPELAND Michael (Mike) Wilfred
Newport, 31 December, 1954 (FB)

League Club	Source	Date Signed	Seasons Played	Apps	Subs	Gls
Newport Co	Jnrs	07.73	73	3	1	0

COPELAND William **Philip (Phil)**
Workington, 16 September, 1936 (WH)

League Club	Source	Date Signed	Seasons Played	Apps	Subs	Gls
Workington		02.57	60-62	11	-	0

COPELAND Simon Dean
Sheffield, 10 October, 1968 (FB)

League Club	Source	Date Signed	Seasons Played	Apps	Subs	Gls
Sheffield U	App	06.87				
Rochdale	Tr	07.88	88	27	1	0

COPESTAKE Oliver Francis Reginald
Mansfield, 1 September, 1921 Died 1953 (IF)

League Club	Source	Date Signed	Seasons Played	Apps	Subs	Gls
Mansfield T	Church Warsop	01.46	46	33	-	7

COPLEY Dennis Irwin
Misterton, 21 December, 1921 (IF)

League Club	Source	Date Signed	Seasons Played	Apps	Subs	Gls
Lincoln C	Norwich C (Am)	09.46	46	1	-	0

COPLEY Gary
Rotherham, 30 December, 1960 (G)

League Club	Source	Date Signed	Seasons Played	Apps	Subs	Gls
Barnsley	App	01.79	78	1	0	0

COPP Leonard (Lenny) James Henry
Aberystwyth, 7 October, 1940 Died 2003 (IF)

League Club	Source	Date Signed	Seasons Played	Apps	Subs	Gls
Leeds U	Jnrs	10.57				
Shrewsbury T	Tr	07.58	60	2	-	1

COPPELL Stephen (Steve) James
Liverpool, 9 July, 1955 Eu23-1/FLge/E-42 (W)

League Club	Source	Date Signed	Seasons Played	Apps	Subs	Gls
Tranmere Rov	Liverpool Univ	01.74	73-74	35	3	10
Manchester U	Tr	02.75	74-82	320	2	54

COPPINGER James
Middlesbrough, 10 January, 1981 EYth (F)

League Club	Source	Date Signed	Seasons Played	Apps	Subs	Gls
Newcastle U	Darlington (YT)	03.98	00	0	1	0
Hartlepool U	L	03.00	99	6	4	3
Hartlepool U	L	01.02	01	14	0	2
Exeter C	Tr	08.02	02	35	8	5
Doncaster Rov	Tr	07.04	04	27	4	0

CORAZZIN Giancarlo (Carlo) Michele
New Westminster, Canada, 25 December, 1971 Canada 56 (F)

League Club	Source	Date Signed	Seasons Played	Apps	Subs	Gls
Cambridge U	Vancouver (Can)	12.93	93-95	104	1	39
Plymouth Arg	Tr	03.96	95-97	61	13	22
Northampton T	Tr	07.98	98-99	63	15	30
Oldham Ath	Tr	07.00	00-02	82	28	20

CORBETT Alexander (Alex) McLennan
Saltcoats, 20 April, 1921 Died 1999 (G)

League Club	Source	Date Signed	Seasons Played	Apps	Subs	Gls
New Brighton	Ayr U	07.46	46-47	58	-	0
Hull C	Tr	01.48	47	8	-	0
Hartlepools U	Weymouth	07.53	53	7	-	0

CORBETT Andrew (Andy) John
Worcester, 20 February, 1982 (F)

League Club	Source	Date Signed	Seasons Played	Apps	Subs	Gls
Kidderminster Hrs	Jnrs	07.00	00-01	3	5	0

CORBETT Anthony (Tony)
Bilston, 28 April, 1940 EYth (FB)

League Club	Source	Date Signed	Seasons Played	Apps	Subs	Gls
Wolverhampton W	Jnrs	05.59				
Shrewsbury T	Tr	07.60	60-61	8	-	0

CORBETT Arthur Beech
Birmingham, 17 August, 1928 (IF)

League Club	Source	Date Signed	Seasons Played	Apps	Subs	Gls
Walsall	Sutton T	12.49	49-50	25	-	5

CORBETT David (Dave) Frank
Marshfield, 15 May, 1940 (W)

League Club	Source	Date Signed	Seasons Played	Apps	Subs	Gls
Swindon T	Jnrs	08.58	58-61	68	-	3
Plymouth Arg	Tr	02.62	61-66	84	0	8

CORBETT George
North Walbottle, 11 May, 1925 (W)

League Club	Source	Date Signed	Seasons Played	Apps	Subs	Gls
Sheffield Wed	Shildon	05.45				
West Bromwich A	Spennymoor U	03.51	51	1	-	0
Workington	Tr	07.53	53	9	-	0

CORBETT James (Jimmy) John
Hackney, 6 July, 1980 (M)

League Club	Source	Date Signed	Seasons Played	Apps	Subs	Gls
Gillingham	YT	01.98	97	8	8	2
Blackburn Rov	Tr	05.98				
Darlington	L	02.03	02	9	1	2
Southend U	Tr	07.03	03-04	14	9	2

CORBETT John
Bow, 9 January, 1920 (IF)

League Club	Source	Date Signed	Seasons Played	Apps	Subs	Gls
Hartlepools U		09.43				
Swansea T		08.45				
Crystal Palace		09.46	46	1	-	1

CORBETT Luke John
Worcester, 10 August, 1984 (F)

League Club	Source	Date Signed	Seasons Played	Apps	Subs	Gls
Cheltenham T	Jnrs	01.03	03	0	1	0

CORBETT Norman (Norrie) George
Falkirk, 23 June, 1919 Died 1990 (WH)

League Club	Source	Date Signed	Seasons Played	Apps	Subs	Gls
West Ham U	Heart of Midlothian	04.37	36-49	166	-	3

CORBETT Patrick (Pat) Avalon
Hackney, 12 February, 1963 EYth (CD)

League Club	Source	Date Signed	Seasons Played	Apps	Subs	Gls
Tottenham H	App	10.80	81-82	3	2	1
Orient	Tr	08.83	83-85	77	0	2

CORBETT Peter
Preston, 5 March, 1934 (G)

League Club	Source	Date Signed	Seasons Played	Apps	Subs	Gls
Preston NE		06.56				
Workington	Tr	08.57	57-58	11	-	0
Oldham Ath	Tr	07.59	59	10	-	0

CORBETT Robert (Bobby)
Throckley, 16 March, 1922 Died 1988 (FB)

League Club	Source	Date Signed	Seasons Played	Apps	Subs	Gls
Newcastle U	Throckley Welfare	08.43	46-51	46	-	1
Middlesbrough	Tr	12.51	51-56	92	-	0
Northampton T	Tr	08.57	57	8	-	1

CORBETT William
Wolverhampton, 29 July, 1920 (FB)

League Club	Source	Date Signed	Seasons Played	Apps	Subs	Gls
Doncaster Rov		01.42	46-47	37	-	0
Bristol C	Tr	06.48	48	1	-	0

CORBETT William (Willie)
Falkirk, 31 August, 1922 SWar-1 (CD)

League Club	Source	Date Signed	Seasons Played	Apps	Subs	Gls
Preston NE	Glasgow Celtic	06.48	48	19	-	0
Leicester C	Tr	08.49	49	16	-	0

CORBIN Kirk DeVere
Barbados, 12 March, 1955 (F)

League Club	Source	Date Signed	Seasons Played	Apps	Subs	Gls
Cambridge U	Wokingham T	01.78	78	3	0	0

CORBISHLEY Colin
Stoke-on-Trent, 13 June, 1939 (WH)

League Club	Source	Date Signed	Seasons Played	Apps	Subs	Gls
Port Vale		10.59	60-61	11	-	0
Chester	Tr	08.62	62-64	83	-	11

CORBISIERO Antonio Giovanni
Exeter, 17 November, 1984 (M)

League Club	Source	Date Signed	Seasons Played	Apps	Subs	Gls
Swansea C	Sch	07.04	03	1	4	0

CORBO Mateo Andres
Montevideo, Uruguay, 21 April, 1976 (M)

League Club	Source	Date Signed	Seasons Played	Apps	Subs	Gls
Barnsley	Real Oviedo (Sp)	08.00	00-01	10	8	0
Oxford U	Olimpia Asuncion (Par)	01.05	04	13	0	0

CORDELL John **Graham**
Walsall, 6 December, 1928 Died 1984 (G)

League Club	Source	Date Signed	Seasons Played	Apps	Subs	Gls
Aston Villa	Walsall Star	09.49	51-52	5	-	0
Rochdale	Tr	05.53	53-54	15	-	0

CORDEN Stephen (Steve)
Eston, 9 January, 1967 (M)

League Club	Source	Date Signed	Seasons Played	Apps	Subs	Gls
Middlesbrough	App	06.84	85	1	0	0

CORDEN Simon **Wayne**
Leek, 1 November, 1975 (W)

League Club	Source	Date Signed	Seasons Played	Apps	Subs	Gls
Port Vale	YT	09.94	94-99	30	36	1
Mansfield T	Tr	07.00	00-04	173	19	35
Scunthorpe U	Tr	02.05	04	3	5	0

CORDER Peter Robert
Loughton, 12 December, 1966 (G)

League Club	Source	Date Signed	Seasons Played	Apps	Subs	Gls
Tottenham H	App	10.84				
Peterborough U	L	10.85	85	2	0	0

CORDICE Neil Anthony
Amersham, 7 April, 1960 (F)

League Club	Source	Date Signed	Seasons Played	Apps	Subs	Gls
Northampton T	Tooting & Mitcham	07.78	78	4	4	1

CORDJOHN Barry Ronald
Oxford, 5 September, 1942 (FB)

League Club	Source	Date Signed	Seasons Played	Apps	Subs	Gls
Charlton Ath	Jnrs	06.60				
Aldershot	Tr	07.63				
Portsmouth	Tr	07.64	64	14	-	0

CORDNER Scott
Derby, 3 August, 1972 (M)

League Club	Source	Date Signed	Seasons Played	Apps	Subs	Gls
Chesterfield	YT	•	90	1	3	1

CORDONE Carlos **Daniel**
Buenos Aires, Argentina, 6 November, 1974 Argentina int (F)

League Club	Source	Date Signed	Seasons Played	Apps	Subs	Gls
Newcastle U (L)	Racing Club (Arg)	08.00	00	12	9	2

CORE Frank
Halifax, 5 September, 1932 (WH)

League Club	Source	Date Signed	Seasons Played	Apps	Subs	Gls
Halifax T (Am)		09.53	53	1	-	0

CORE John
Ripponden, 29 March, 1929 (CF)

League Club	Source	Date Signed	Seasons Played	Apps	Subs	Gls
Halifax T (Am)		09.49	49-50	28	-	15

CORFIELD Ernest (Ernie)
Wigan, 18 January, 1931 (IF)

League Club	Source	Date Signed	Seasons Played	Apps	Subs	Gls
Bolton W	Jnrs	04.48	49-51	6	-	0
Stockport Co	Tr	07.53	53	2	-	0

CORICA Stephen (Steve) Christopher
Cairns, Australia, 24 March, 1973 AuYth/Auu20/Auu23/Au-31 (W)

League Club	Source	Date Signed	Seasons Played	Apps	Subs	Gls
Leicester C	Marconi (Aus)	08.95	95	16	0	2
Wolverhampton W	Tr	02.96	95-99	80	20	5
Walsall	San Hiroshima (Jap)	02.02	01-03	63	10	9

CORISH Robert (Bob)
Liverpool, 13 September, 1958 (FB)

League Club	Source	Date Signed	Seasons Played	Apps	Subs	Gls
Derby Co	Jnrs	08.76	77	0	1	0

CORK Alan Graham
Derby, 4 March, 1959 (F)

League Club	Source	Date Signed	Seasons Played	Apps	Subs	Gls
Derby Co	Jnrs	07.77				
Lincoln C	L	09.77	77	5	0	0
Wimbledon	Tr	02.78	77-91	352	78	145
Sheffield U	Tr	03.92	91-93	25	29	7
Fulham	Tr	08.94	94	11	4	3

CORK David
Doncaster, 8 October, 1959 (M)

League Club	Source	Date Signed	Seasons Played	Apps	Subs	Gls
Manchester U	App	10.76				
Doncaster Rov	Tr	08.78	78-79	9	0	1

CORK David
Doncaster, 28 October, 1962 (F)

League Club	Source	Date Signed	Seasons Played	Apps	Subs	Gls
Arsenal	App	06.80	83	5	2	1
Huddersfield T	Tr	07.85	85-87	104	6	25
West Bromwich A	L	09.88	88	1	3	0
Scunthorpe U	Tr	02.89	88	8	7	0
Darlington	Tr	07.89	90-91	53	11	11

CORKAIN Stephen (Steve)
Stockton, 25 February, 1967 (M)

League Club	Source	Date Signed	Seasons Played	Apps	Subs	Gls
Hull C	Jnrs	06.85	86	5	0	1

CORKHILL Robert Douglas
Barrow, 20 November, 1943 (W)

League Club	Source	Date Signed	Seasons Played	Apps	Subs	Gls
Barrow	Holker COB	08.63	63-64	8	-	1

CORKHILL William (Bill) Grant
Belfast, 23 April, 1910 Died 1978 (WH)

League Club	Source	Date Signed	Seasons Played	Apps	Subs	Gls
Notts Co	Marine	05.31	31-37	166	-	9
Cardiff C	Tr	05.38	38	23	-	0
Notts Co	Tr	11.45	46-51	98	-	0

CORMACK Peter Barr
Edinburgh, 17 July, 1946 SAmat/Su23-5/SLge-6/S-9 (M)

League Club	Source	Date Signed	Seasons Played	Apps	Subs	Gls
Nottingham F	Hibernian	03.70	69-71	74	0	15
Liverpool	Tr	07.72	72-75	119	6	21
Bristol C	Tr	11.76	76-79	59	8	15

CORNELLY Christopher (Chris)
Huddersfield, 7 July, 1976 (F)

League Club	Source	Date Signed	Seasons Played	Apps	Subs	Gls
Lincoln C	Ashton U	12.02	02	9	7	0

CORNER Brian
Glasgow, 6 January, 1961 (M)

League Club	Source	Date Signed	Seasons Played	Apps	Subs	Gls
Fulham	App	01.79	80	1	2	0

CORNER David Edward
Sunderland, 15 May, 1966 EYth (CD)

League Club	Source	Date Signed	Seasons Played	Apps	Subs	Gls
Sunderland	App	04.84	84-87	33	0	1
Cardiff C	L	09.85	85	6	0	0
Peterborough U	L	03.88	87	9	0	0
Leyton Orient	Tr	07.88	88	4	0	0
Darlington	Tr	07.89	90	13	2	0

CORNER James **Norman**
Horden, 16 February, 1943 (F)

League Club	Source	Date Signed	Seasons Played	Apps	Subs	Gls
Hull C	Horden Colliery	08.62	63-66	5	0	4
Lincoln C	Tr	10.67	67-68	44	1	12
Bradford C	Tr	01.69	68-71	105	5	16

CORNES James **Stuart**
Usk, 4 March, 1960 (CD)

League Club	Source	Date Signed	Seasons Played	Apps	Subs	Gls
Hereford U	App	01.78	77-81	91	2	3

CORNFIELD Allen Henry
Dudley, 19 December, 1940 (W)

League Club	Source	Date Signed	Seasons Played	Apps	Subs	Gls
Shrewsbury T	Lower Gornal Ath	11.59	59-61	9	-	0

CORNFORTH John Michael
Whitley Bay, 7 October, 1967 W-2 (M)

League Club	Source	Date Signed	Seasons Played	Apps	Subs	Gls
Sunderland	App	10.85	84-90	21	11	2
Doncaster Rov	L	11.86	86	6	1	3
Shrewsbury T	L	11.89	89	3	0	0
Lincoln C	L	01.90	89	9	0	1
Swansea C	Tr	08.91	91-95	147	2	16
Birmingham C	Tr	03.96	95	8	0	0
Wycombe W	Tr	12.96	96-98	35	12	6
Peterborough U	L	02.98	97	3	1	0
Cardiff C	Tr	08.99	99	6	4	1
Scunthorpe U	Tr	11.99	99	2	2	1
Exeter C	Tr	02.00	99-00	23	1	2

CORNISH Ricky George
Newham, 1 December, 1970 (FB)

League Club	Source	Date Signed	Seasons Played	Apps	Subs	Gls
Aldershot	Cornard U	11.90	90	7	2	0

CORNOCK Walter (Wally) Berkeley
Waverley, Australia, 1 January, 1921 (G)

League Club	Source	Date Signed	Seasons Played	Apps	Subs	Gls
Oldham Ath		01.41				
Rochdale	Hereford U	11.47	47	1	-	0

CORNWALL Lucas (Luke) Clarence
Lambeth, 23 July, 1980 (F)

League Club	Source	Date Signed	Seasons Played	Apps	Subs	Gls
Fulham	YT	07.98	98	1	3	1
Grimsby T	L	03.01	00	9	1	4
Lincoln C	L	01.03	02	1	2	0
Bradford C	Tr	07.03	03	2	1	0

CORNWELL Ellis
Coppull, 14 November, 1913 Died 1986 (FB)

League Club	Source	Date Signed	Seasons Played	Apps	Subs	Gls
Accrington St	Chorley	11.45	46	5	-	0

CORNWELL John Anthony
Bethnal Green, 13 October, 1964 (M)

League Club	Source	Date Signed	Seasons Played	Apps	Subs	Gls
Orient	App	10.82	81-86	194	9	35
Newcastle U	Tr	07.87	87-88	28	5	1
Swindon T	Tr	12.88	88-89	7	18	0
Southend U	Tr	08.90	90-92	92	9	5
Cardiff C	L	08.93	93	5	0	2
Brentford	L	09.93	93	4	0	0
Northampton T	L	02.94	93	13	0	1

CORNWELL Kevin John
Birmingham, 10 December, 1941 (CF)

League Club	Source	Date Signed	Seasons Played	Apps	Subs	Gls
Oxford U	Banbury Spencer	07.62	62-63	26	-	10

CORR John Joseph
Glasgow, 18 December, 1946 (W)

League Club	Source	Date Signed	Seasons Played	Apps	Subs	Gls
Arsenal	Possilpark Jnrs	07.65				
Exeter C	Tr	07.67	67-70	75	6	19

CORR Patrick (Pat)
Enniskillen, 31 March, 1927 NIAmat/IrLge-11 (CF)

League Club	Source	Date Signed	Seasons Played	Apps	Subs	Gls
Burnley	Coleraine	10.51	51	1	-	0

CORR Peter Joseph
Dundalk, 22 June, 1923 Died 2001 LoI-2/IR-4 (W)

League Club	Source	Date Signed	Seasons Played	Apps	Subs	Gls
Preston NE	Dundalk	04.47	46	3	-	0
Everton	Tr	08.48	48-49	24	-	2

CORRIGAN Francis (Frank) Joseph
Liverpool, 13 November, 1952 (M)

League Club	Source	Date Signed	Seasons Played	Apps	Subs	Gls
Blackpool	Ormskirk	08.72				
Walsall	Tr	07.73	73	1	0	0
Wigan Ath	Northwich Vic	(N/L)	78-80	113	3	12

CORRIGAN Thomas **Joseph (Joe)**
Sale, 18 November, 1948 Eu2-3/FLge/EB/E-9 (G)

League Club	Source	Date Signed	Seasons Played	Apps	Subs	Gls
Manchester C	Sale	01.67	68-82	476	0	0
Brighton & Hove A	Seattle (USA)	09.83	83	36	0	0
Norwich C	L	09.84	84	3	0	0
Stoke C	L	10.84	84	9	0	0

CORT Carl Edward Richard
Bermondsey, 1 November, 1977 Eu21-12 (F)

League Club	Source	Date Signed	Seasons Played	Apps	Subs	Gls
Wimbledon	YT	06.96	96-99	54	19	16
Lincoln C	L	02.97	96	5	1	1

League Club	Source	Date Signed	Seasons Played	Apps	Subs	Gls
Newcastle U	Tr	07.00	00-02	19	3	7
Wolverhampton W	Tr	01.04	03-04	47	6	20

CORT Leon Terence Anthony
Bermondsey, 11 September, 1979 (CD)

League Club	Source	Date Signed	Seasons Played	Apps	Subs	Gls
Millwall	Dulwich Hamlet	01.98				
Southend U	Tr	07.01	01-03	135	2	11
Hull C	Tr	07.04	04	43	1	6

CORTHINE Peter Alan
Highbury, 19 July, 1937 (IF)

League Club	Source	Date Signed	Seasons Played	Apps	Subs	Gls
Chelsea	Leytonstone	12.57	59	2	-	0
Southend U	Tr	03.60	59-61	73	-	24

COSSLETT Michael (Mike) Paul
Barry, 17 April, 1957 (CD)

League Club	Source	Date Signed	Seasons Played	Apps	Subs	Gls
Newport Co	Barry T	02.78	77-78	2	0	0

COSTA Candido Alves Moreira
Sao Joao da Madeira, Portugal, 30 April, 1981 (M)

League Club	Source	Date Signed	Seasons Played	Apps	Subs	Gls
Derby Co (L)	FC Porto (Por)	08.03	03	23	11	1

COSTA Jorge Paulo
Oporto, Portugal, 14 October, 1971 Portugal 51 (CD)

League Club	Source	Date Signed	Seasons Played	Apps	Subs	Gls
Charlton Ath (L)	FC Porto (Por)	12.01	01	22	2	0

COSTA Ricardo
Lisbon, Portugal, 10 January, 1973 (F)

League Club	Source	Date Signed	Seasons Played	Apps	Subs	Gls
Darlington (L)	Boavista (Por)	01.99	98	0	3	1

COSTELLO John
Prestonpans, 23 March, 1920 (FB)

League Club	Source	Date Signed	Seasons Played	Apps	Subs	Gls
Southend U	Prestonpans	08.52				
Barrow	Tr	07.53	53	6	-	0

COSTELLO Matthew (Matt)
Airdrie, 4 August, 1924 Died 1987 (W)

League Club	Source	Date Signed	Seasons Played	Apps	Subs	Gls
Chesterfield	New Stevenston	05.49	49-51	18	-	2
Chester	Tr	07.52	52	9	-	2

COSTELLO Mortimer (Lou) Daniel
Dagenham, 8 July, 1936 (WH)

League Club	Source	Date Signed	Seasons Played	Apps	Subs	Gls
Aldershot (Am)	Leytonstone	05.56	56	28	-	7
Southend U	Tr	05.57	57-64	251	-	15

COSTELLO Nigel Graham
Catterick, 22 November, 1968 (W)

League Club	Source	Date Signed	Seasons Played	Apps	Subs	Gls
York C	YT	07.87	86-87	2	2	0

COSTELLO Peter
Halifax, 31 October, 1969 (M)

League Club	Source	Date Signed	Seasons Played	Apps	Subs	Gls
Bradford C	YT	07.88	88-89	11	9	2
Rochdale	Tr	07.90	90	31	3	10
Peterborough U	Tr	03.91	90-92	3	5	0
Lincoln C	L	09.91	91	3	0	0
Lincoln C	Tr	09.92	92-93	28	10	7
Boston U	(Hong Kong)	08.99	02	13	5	0

COTHLIFF Harold Thomas
Liverpool, 24 March, 1916 Died 1976 (WH)

League Club	Source	Date Signed	Seasons Played	Apps	Subs	Gls
Manchester C	Prescot Cables	04.36				
Nottingham F	Tr	05.37				
Torquay U	Tr	06.38	38-47	65	-	1

COTON Anthony (Tony) Philip
Tamworth, 19 May, 1961 EB (G)

League Club	Source	Date Signed	Seasons Played	Apps	Subs	Gls
Birmingham C	Mile Oak Rov	10.78	80-84	94	0	0
Watford	Tr	09.84	84-89	233	0	0
Manchester C	Tr	07.90	90-94	162	1	0
Manchester U	Tr	01.96				
Sunderland	Tr	07.96	96	10	0	0

COTON Paul Stanley
Birmingham, 9 February, 1949 (FB)

League Club	Source	Date Signed	Seasons Played	Apps	Subs	Gls
Walsall	App	02.67	66	1	0	0

COTTAM John Edward
Worksop, 5 June, 1950 (CD)

League Club	Source	Date Signed	Seasons Played	Apps	Subs	Gls
Nottingham F	App	04.68	70-75	92	3	4
Mansfield T	L	11.72	72	2	0	1
Lincoln C	L	03.73	72	1	0	0
Chesterfield	Tr	08.76	76-78	120	0	7
Chester	Tr	07.79	79-81	117	3	1

COTTEE Anthony (Tony) Richard
West Ham, 11 July, 1965 EYth/Eu21-8/E-7 (F)

League Club	Source	Date Signed	Seasons Played	Apps	Subs	Gls
West Ham U	App	09.82	82-87	203	9	92
Everton	Tr	08.88	88-94	161	23	72
West Ham U	Tr	09.94	94-96	63	4	23
Leicester C	Selangor (Mal)	08.97	97-00	66	19	27
Birmingham C	L	11.97	97	4	1	1
Norwich C	Tr	09.00	00	5	2	1
Barnet	Tr	10.00	00	16	0	9
Millwall	Tr	03.01	00	0	2	0

COTTERELL Leo Spencer
Cambridge, 2 September, 1974 ESch/EYth (FB)

League Club	Source	Date Signed	Seasons Played	Apps	Subs	Gls
Ipswich T	YT	07.93	94	0	2	0
Bournemouth	Tr	06.96	96	2	7	0

COTTERILL David Rhys George Best
Cardiff, 4 December, 1987 WYth/Wu21-2 (F)

League Club	Source	Date Signed	Seasons Played	Apps	Subs	Gls
Bristol C	Sch	01.05	04	8	4	0

COTTERILL James Michael
Barnsley, 3 August, 1982 (CD)

League Club	Source	Date Signed	Seasons Played	Apps	Subs	Gls
Scunthorpe U	YT	07.01	00-02	19	4	0

COTTERILL Stephen (Steve) John
Cheltenham, 20 July, 1964 (F)

League Club	Source	Date Signed	Seasons Played	Apps	Subs	Gls
Wimbledon	Burton A	02.89	88-92	10	7	6
Brighton & Hove A	L	08.92	92	11	0	4
Bournemouth	Tr	08.93	93-94	44	1	15

COTTEY Philip **Anthony (Tony)**
Swansea, 2 June, 1966 (M)

League Club	Source	Date Signed	Seasons Played	Apps	Subs	Gls
Swansea C	App	06.84	84	2	1	0

COTTINGTON Brian Anthony
Hammersmith, 14 February, 1965 (FB)

League Club	Source	Date Signed	Seasons Played	Apps	Subs	Gls
Fulham	App	02.83	83-86	67	6	1

COTTON Frederick (Fred) Joseph
Halesowen, 12 March, 1932 Died 1994 (IF)

League Club	Source	Date Signed	Seasons Played	Apps	Subs	Gls
Crystal Palace		08.56	56	4	-	0

COTTON John
Stoke-on-Trent, 2 March, 1930 (FB)

League Club	Source	Date Signed	Seasons Played	Apps	Subs	Gls
Stoke C		05.52	53	2	-	0
Crewe Alex	Tr	10.55	55	14	-	0

COTTON Perry
Chislehurst, 11 November, 1965 (M)

League Club	Source	Date Signed	Seasons Played	Apps	Subs	Gls
Scunthorpe U	Nelson U (NZ)	12.88	88-90	24	9	2

COTTON Roy William
Fulham, 14 November, 1955 EYth (W)

League Club	Source	Date Signed	Seasons Played	Apps	Subs	Gls
Brentford (Am)	Jnrs	09.73	73	1	1	0
Orient	Tr	07.74	75	0	3	0
Aldershot	Tr	07.76	77	5	0	0

COTTON Russell Andrew
Wellington, 4 April, 1960 (M)

League Club	Source	Date Signed	Seasons Played	Apps	Subs	Gls
Colchester U	App	04.78	77-81	33	4	1

COTTON Terence (Terry)
Swansea, 25 January, 1946 WAmat (F)

League Club	Source	Date Signed	Seasons Played	Apps	Subs	Gls
Swansea T	Ammanford	06.68	68-70	12	0	1

COUCH Alan
Neath, 15 March, 1953 (F)

League Club	Source	Date Signed	Seasons Played	Apps	Subs	Gls
Cardiff C	Jnrs	08.70	71-72	7	4	0

COUCH Geoffrey (Geoff) Raymond
Crowle, 3 April, 1953 (F)

League Club	Source	Date Signed	Seasons Played	Apps	Subs	Gls
Scunthorpe U	Crowle	03.78	77-79	22	4	5

COUGHLAN Derek James
Cork, 2 January, 1977 (CD)

League Club	Source	Date Signed	Seasons Played	Apps	Subs	Gls
Brighton & Hove A	YT	05.95	95	1	0	0

COUGHLAN Graham
Dublin, 18 November, 1974 (CD)

League Club	Source	Date Signed	Seasons Played	Apps	Subs	Gls
Blackburn Rov	Bray W	10.95				
Swindon T	L	03.97	96	3	0	0
Plymouth Arg	Livingston	06.01	01-04	177	0	25

COUGHLIN Dennis Michael
Houghton-le-Spring, 26 November, 1937 (F)

League Club	Source	Date Signed	Seasons Played	Apps	Subs	Gls
Barnsley	Durham C	10.57				
Bournemouth	Yeovil T	03.63	62-65	86	2	40
Swansea T	Tr	08.66	66-67	39	1	10
Exeter C	L	03.68	67	13	0	2

COUGHLIN James (Jim)
Cheltenham, 26 July, 1953 (F)

League Club	Source	Date Signed	Seasons Played	Apps	Subs	Gls
Hereford U	Albion Rov	03.77	76	1	1	1

COUGHLIN Russell James
Swansea, 15 February, 1960 WSch/WYth (M)

League Club	Source	Date Signed	Seasons Played	Apps	Subs	Gls
Manchester C	App	03.78				
Blackburn Rov	Tr	03.79	78-80	22	2	0

League Club	Source	Date Signed	Seasons Played	Career Record Apps	Subs	Gls
Carlisle U	Tr	10.80	80-83	114	16	13
Plymouth Arg	Tr	07.84	84-87	128	3	18
Blackpool	Tr	12.87	87-89	100	2	8
Shrewsbury T	L	09.90	90	4	1	0
Swansea C	Tr	10.90	90-92	99	2	2
Exeter C	Tr	07.93	93-95	64	4	0
Torquay U	Tr	10.95	95	22	3	0
COULBAULT Regis Arnaud Vincent						
Brignoles, France, 12 August, 1972						(M)
Southend U	Toulon (Fr)	10.97	97	30	4	4
COULL George Thomson						
Dundee, 10 August, 1935						(IF)
Millwall	Dundee Downfield	08.56	56	6	-	1
COULSON Mark David						
Huntingdon, 11 February, 1986						(FB)
Peterborough U	Sch	03.03	04	2	5	0
COULSON William (Willie) John						
North Shields, 14 January, 1950						(W)
Newcastle U	North Shields	09.71				
Southend U	Tr	10.73	73-75	51	1	4
Aldershot	L	02.75	74	3	0	0
Huddersfield T	L	11.75	75	2	0	0
Darlington	L	01.76	75	11	2	1
COUNAGO Pablo						
Pontevedra, Spain, 9 August, 1979 SpYth/Spu21						(F)
Ipswich T	Celta Vigo (Sp)	07.01	01-04	51	49	31
COUPE Joseph (Joe) Norman						
Carlisle, 15 July, 1924 Died 1998						(FB)
Carlisle U	Swift Rov	09.47	48-50	31	-	0
Rochdale	Tr	10.51	51	8	-	0
Workington	Tr	10.52	52	6	-	0
COUPLAND Joseph (Joe)						
Glasgow, 10 April, 1920						(FB)
Bradford C	Ayr U	08.50	50-51	18	-	0
Carlisle U	Tr	07.52	52-53	3	-	0
COURT Colin						
Winchester, 25 March, 1964						(G)
Reading	Andover T	07.81	81	1	0	0
COURT Colin Raymond						
Ebbw Vale, 3 September, 1937 WSch						(W)
Chelsea	Jnrs	09.54				
Torquay U	Tr	05.59	59-60	27	-	5
COURT David John						
Mitcham, 1 March, 1944						(M)
Arsenal	App	01.62	62-69	168	7	17
Luton T	Tr	07.70	70-71	50	2	0
Brentford	Tr	08.72	72	8	4	1
COURT Harold **John (Jack)**						
Tir Phil, 13 June, 1919 Died 1975						(IF)
Cardiff C	Llanbradach	03.39	38	1	-	0
Swindon T	Dundee	06.50	50	16	-	2
COURTOIS Laurent						
Lyon, France, 11 September, 1978						(M)
West Ham U	Toulouse (Fr)	08.01	01	5	2	0
COUSANS William **Eric**						
Doncaster, 10 September, 1929						(W)
Walsall	Goole T	08.54	54	4	-	1
Gillingham	Tr	09.55	55	2	-	0
COUSINS Anthony (Tony) James						
Dublin, 25 August, 1969 IRu21-6						(F)
Liverpool	Dundalk	10.90				
Hereford U	L	11.92	92	3	0	0
COUSINS Harold (Harry)						
Pilsley, 25 September, 1907 Died 1981						(WH)
Chesterfield	North Wingfield	10.26	26-31	86	-	0
Swindon T	Tr	08.32	32-46	272	-	1
COUSINS Jason Michael						
Hayes, 14 October, 1970						(FB)
Brentford	YT	07.89	89-90	20	1	0
Wycombe W	Tr	07.91	93-01	270	26	6
COUSINS Kenneth (Ken) Frank						
Bristol, 6 August, 1922						(G)
Bristol C	Brislington	03.46	46	3	-	0

League Club	Source	Date Signed	Seasons Played	Career Record Apps	Subs	Gls
COUTTS James Ryan						
Weymouth, 15 April, 1987						(M)
Bournemouth	Southampton (Jnrs)	07.04	04	0	1	0
COUTTS Roger Alexander						
Barrow, 18 December, 1944						(W)
Barrow	Walney Rov	08.64	64	2	-	0
COUZENS Andrew (Andy)						
Shipley, 4 June, 1975 Eu21-3						(M)
Leeds U	YT	03.93	94-96	17	11	1
Carlisle U	Tr	07.97	97-98	28	14	2
Blackpool	Tr	03.99	98-99	18	3	0
COVERDALE Andrew (Drew)						
Middlesbrough, 20 September, 1969						(FB)
Middlesbrough	YT	07.88				
Darlington	Tr	07.89	90-91	24	6	3
COWAN Donald (Don)						
Durham, 17 August, 1931						(G)
Darlington		11.52	52-53	17	-	0
COWAN Gavin Patrick						
Hanover, Germany, 24 May, 1981 ESemiPro-2						(CD)
Shrewsbury T	Canvey Island	03.05	04	5	0	0
COWAN Ian						
Falkirk, 27 November, 1944						(W)
Southend U	Dunfermline Ath	07.70	70	3	0	0
COWAN James (Jimmy) Clews						
Paisley, 16 June, 1926 Died 1968 SLge-3/S-25						(G)
Sunderland	Morton	06.53	53	28	-	0
COWAN John						
Belfast, 8 January, 1949 NI-1						(M)
Newcastle U	Crusaders	02.67	69-72	6	3	0
Darlington	Drogheda	08.75	75	10	0	0
COWAN Thomas (Tom)						
Bellshill, 28 August, 1969						(FB)
Sheffield U	Glasgow Rgrs	08.91	91-93	45	0	0
Stoke C	L	10.93	93	14	0	0
Huddersfield T	Tr	03.94	93-98	137	0	8
Burnley	Tr	03.99	98-99	17	3	1
Cambridge U	Tr	02.00	99-01	48	2	3
Peterborough U	L	01.02	01	4	1	1
York C	Tr	07.02	02	31	2	1
Carlisle U	Dundee	11.03	03	20	0	1
COWANS Gordon Sidney						
Cornforth, 27 October, 1958 EYth/Eu21-5/EB/E-10						(M)
Aston Villa	App	09.76	75-84	276	10	42
Aston Villa	Bari	07.88	88-91	114	3	7
Blackburn Rov	Tr	11.91	91-92	49	1	2
Aston Villa	Tr	07.93	93	9	2	0
Derby Co	Tr	02.94	93-94	36	0	0
Wolverhampton W	Tr	12.94	94-95	31	6	0
Sheffield U	Tr	12.95	95	18	2	0
Bradford C	Tr	06.96	96	23	1	0
Stockport Co	Tr	03.97	96	6	1	0
Burnley	Tr	08.97	97	5	1	0
COWDRILL Barry James						
Birmingham, 3 January, 1957						(FB)
West Bromwich A	Sutton Coldfield T	04.79	79-87	127	4	0
Rotherham U	L	10.85	85	2	0	0
Bolton W	Tr	07.88	88-91	117	2	4
Rochdale	Tr	02.92	91	15	0	1
COWE Steven (Steve) Mark						
Gloucester, 29 September, 1974						(F)
Aston Villa	YT	07.93				
Swindon T	Tr	03.96	95-00	59	38	11
COWELL George **Robert (Bobby)**						
Trimdon, 5 December, 1922 Died 1996						(FB)
Newcastle U	Blackhall CW	10.43	46-54	289	-	0
COWEN John Michael						
Lewisham, 1 December, 1944 EYth						(G)
Chelsea	App	10.62				
Watford	Tr	10.64	64-66	17	0	0
COWIE Andrew (Andy) David						
Motherwell, 11 March, 1913 Died 1972 SLge-1						(WH)
Swindon T	Aberdeen	07.48	48-50	89	-	4
COWIE Alexander **George**						
Findochty, 9 May, 1961						(M)
West Ham U	App	08.78	81-82	6	2	0

League Club	Source	Date Signed	Seasons Played	Apps	Subs	Gls
COWLEY Carl						
Stepney, 10 July, 1965						(CD)
Millwall	App	10.82	83	2	1	0
COWLEY Francis						
Stepney, 28 November, 1957						(W)
Derby Co	Sutton U	08.77				
Wimbledon	Tr	02.78	77-78	5	3	0
COWLING Christopher (Chris)						
Scunthorpe, 19 September, 1962						(M)
Scunthorpe U	App	12.79	79-84	117	14	26
COWLING David Roy						
Doncaster, 27 November, 1958						(W)
Mansfield T	App	11.76				
Huddersfield T	Tr	08.77	78-87	331	9	43
Scunthorpe U	L	11.87	87	1	0	0
Reading	Tr	12.87	87	9	1	1
Scunthorpe U	Tr	08.88	88-90	85	4	5
COWLING Jason Paul						
Cambridge, 12 August, 1969						(M)
Cambridge U	Jnrs	07.87	86	0	2	1
COWLING Lee David						
Doncaster, 22 September, 1977						(FB)
Nottingham F	YT	09.94				
Mansfield T	Tr	08.99	99	3	5	0
COWSILL Charles (Charlie) Mills						
Farnworth, 5 May, 1929						(W)
Bury		05.50				
Workington		11.51	51	1	-	0
COX Alan William						
Liverpool, 4 September, 1920 Died 1993						(IF)
Tranmere Rov		03.41	46-47	8	-	2
COX Albert Edward Harrison						
Treeton, 24 June, 1917 Died 2003						(FB)
Sheffield U	Woodhouse Mills U	04.35	35-51	267	-	5
Halifax T	Tr	07.52	52-53	54	-	1
COX Brian Roy						
Sheffield, 7 May, 1961						(G)
Sheffield Wed	App	02.79	78-80	22	0	0
Huddersfield T	Tr	03.82	81-87	213	0	0
Mansfield T	Tr	08.88	88-89	54	0	0
Hartlepool U	Tr	08.90	90	34	0	0
COX David						
Dukinfield, 16 September, 1936						(CF)
Stockport Co	Oldham Ath (Am)	10.55	56-57	7	-	4
COX Frederick (Freddie) James Arthur						
Reading, 1 November, 1920 Died 1973						(W)
Tottenham H	St George's LC	08.38	38-48	99	-	15
Arsenal	Tr	09.49	49-52	79	-	9
West Bromwich A	Tr	07.53	53	4	-	1
COX Geoffrey (Geoff)						
Arley, 30 November, 1934						(IF)
Birmingham C	Jnrs	12.51	52-56	35	-	3
Torquay U	Tr	12.57	57-66	260	1	62
COX Graham Paul						
Willesden, 30 April, 1959						(G)
Brentford	App	04.77	76-77	4	0	0
Aldershot	Wokingham T	01.85	84-85	13	0	0
COX Ian Gary						
Croydon, 25 March, 1971 Trinidad 12						(CD)
Crystal Palace	Carshalton Ath	03.94	94-95	2	13	0
Bournemouth	Tr	03.96	95-99	172	0	16
Burnley	Tr	02.00	99-02	107	8	5
Gillingham	Tr	08.03	03-04	61	3	2
COX James (Jimmy) Darryl						
Gloucester, 11 April, 1980						(F)
Luton T	YT	05.98	98	3	5	0
COX Keith						
Heanor, 26 January, 1936						(WH)
Charlton Ath	Heanor T	04.54	56-58	14	-	0
COX Mark Louis						
Birmingham, 4 October, 1959						(F)
Lincoln C	App	09.77	76-77	3	2	0
Doncaster Rov	Tr	09.78	78	10	5	3

League Club	Source	Date Signed	Seasons Played	Apps	Subs	Gls
COX Maurice						
Torquay, 1 October, 1959 ESch						(F)
Torquay U	Jnrs	01.80	78-81	49	13	13
Huddersfield T	Tr	08.82	82	3	1	1
COX Neil James						
Scunthorpe, 8 October, 1971 Eu21-6						(FB)
Scunthorpe U	YT	03.90	90	17	0	1
Aston Villa	Tr	02.91	91-93	26	16	3
Middlesbrough	Tr	07.94	94-96	103	3	3
Bolton W	Tr	05.97	97-99	77	3	7
Watford	Tr	11.99	99-04	215	4	20
COX Paul Richard						
Nottingham, 6 January, 1972						(CD)
Notts Co	YT	08.89	91-94	39	5	1
Hull C	L	12.94	94	5	0	1
COX Ronald (Ron) Bert						
Foleshill, 2 May, 1919						(CD)
Coventry C	Wyken Pippin	10.45	46-51	29	-	0
COX Samuel (Sam)						
Mexborough, 30 October, 1920 Died 1985						(FB)
West Bromwich A	Denaby U	05.48	48	2	-	0
Accrington St	Tr	07.51	51	43	-	0
Scunthorpe U	Tr	07.52	52	3	-	0
COX Simon Peter						
Clapham, 24 March, 1984 IRYth						(G)
Oxford U	Sch	07.03	03-04	7	1	0
COXHILL David						
Northfields, 10 April, 1952						(M)
Millwall	Jnrs	06.70	70-71	6	2	0
Gillingham	Tr	07.73	73-74	32	2	1
COXON Eric **Gary**						
Liverpool, 31 May, 1946						(FB)
Blackburn Rov	Everton (App)	12.63	66-67	10	0	0
COXON John						
Old Hartley, 7 April, 1922 Died 1998						(FB)
Darlington (Am)	Hartley	05.46	46	1	-	0
COXON William (Billy) George						
Derby, 28 April, 1933						(W)
Derby Co	Jnrs	05.50				
Norwich C	Ilkeston T	05.52	52-57	98	-	24
Lincoln C	Tr	03.58	57-58	11	-	1
Bournemouth	Tr	11.58	58-65	199	1	37
COY Robert (Bobby) Anthony						
Birmingham, 30 November, 1961						(CD)
Wolverhampton W	App	11.79	81-83	40	3	0
Chester C	Tr	03.84	83-85	93	0	2
Northampton T	Tr	08.86	86	15	2	0
COYLE Anthony (Tony) John						
Glasgow, 17 January, 1960						(W)
Stockport Co	Albion Rov	12.79	79-85	215	4	28
Chesterfield	Tr	06.86	86-87	71	5	4
Stockport Co	Tr	08.88	88	23	0	3
Exeter C	Northwich Vic	11.89	89	1	0	0
COYLE Francis (Fay)						
Derry, 1 April, 1924 NIAmat/IrLge-4/NI-4						(CF)
Nottingham F	Coleraine	03.58	57	3	-	0
COYLE Owen Columba						
Paisley, 14 July, 1966 IRu21-2/IRB/IR-1						(F)
Bolton W	Airdrie	06.93	93-95	35	19	12
COYLE Robert (Roy) Irvine						
Belfast, 31 January, 1948 NI-5						(M)
Sheffield Wed	Glentoran	03.72	72-73	38	2	2
Grimsby T	Tr	10.74	74	24	0	1
COYLE Ronald (Ronnie) Paul						
Glasgow, 19 August, 1961						(M)
Middlesbrough	Glasgow Celtic	12.86	86	1	2	0
Rochdale	Tr	08.87	87	23	1	1
COYLE William (Billy)						
Newcastle, 24 October, 1926						(CD)
Darlington	West Auckland	05.49	49	17	-	0
COYNE Brian						
Glasgow, 13 December, 1959						(M)
Shrewsbury T	Glasgow Celtic	06.79	79	1	0	0

League Club	Source	Date Signed	Seasons Played	Apps	Subs	Gls
COYNE Christopher (Chris) John						
Brisbane, Australia, 20 December, 1978 AuYth/Auu23						(CD)
West Ham U	Perth SC	01.96	98	0	1	0
Brentford	L	08.98	98	7	0	0
Southend U	L	03.99	98	0	1	0
Luton T	Dundee	09.01	01-04	150	5	11
COYNE Cyril						
Barnsley, 21 May, 1924 Died 1981						(WH)
Leeds U	Barnsley Main CW	10.44				
Halifax T	Stalybridge Celtic	06.51	51	4	-	0
COYNE Daniel (Danny)						
Prestatyn, 27 August, 1973 WSch/WYth/Wu21-9/WB-1/W-8						(G)
Tranmere Rov	YT	05.92	92-98	110	1	0
Grimsby T	Tr	07.99	99-02	181	0	0
Leicester C	Tr	07.03	03	1	3	0
Burnley	Tr	08.04	04	20	0	0
COYNE Gerard (Gerry) Aloysius						
Hebburn, 9 August, 1948						(CF)
York C	Reyrolles	08.66	66	2	0	0
COYNE John David						
Liverpool, 18 July, 1951						(F)
Tranmere Rov		08.71	71	12	3	3
Hartlepool	Tr	07.72	72-73	47	8	10
Stockport Co	Toronto (Can)	11.75	75	3	1	0
COYNE Peter David						
Hartlepool, 13 November, 1958 ESch						(F)
Manchester U	App	11.75	75	1	1	1
Crewe Alex	Ashton U	08.77	77-80	113	21	47
Swindon T	Hyde U	08.84	84-88	99	11	30
Aldershot	L	08.89	89	3	0	0
COYNE Thomas (Tommy)						
Glasgow, 14 November, 1962 IRB/IR-22						(F)
Tranmere Rov	Glasgow Celtic	03.93	92	9	3	1
COZENS John William						
Hammersmith, 14 May, 1946						(F)
Notts Co	Hillingdon Borough	08.70	70-72	41	3	13
Peterborough U	Tr	11.72	72-77	127	5	41
Cambridge U	Tr	12.77	77-79	52	9	4
COZIC Bertrand Edern						
Quimper, France, 18 May, 1978						(M)
Cheltenham T	Team Bath	08.03	03	7	0	1
Northampton T	Hereford U	08.04	04	8	6	0
Kidderminster Hrs	Tr	02.05	04	13	2	0
CRABBE Stephen Allan **John**						
Weymouth, 20 October, 1954						(M)
Southampton	App	10.72	74-76	8	4	0
Gillingham	Tr	01.76	76-80	181	0	13
Carlisle U	Tr	08.81	81	26	0	4
Hereford U	Tr	08.82	82	15	1	2
Crewe Alex	Tr	08.83	83-85	75	0	7
Torquay U	Tr	09.85	85	27	2	2
CRABTREE Richard Edward						
Exeter, 6 February, 1955						(G)
Bristol Rov	App	02.73	71	7	0	0
Doncaster Rov	L	10.74	74	1	0	0
Torquay U	Dawlish T	08.75	75	1	0	0
Exeter C	Dawlish T	07.83	83	1	0	0
CRADDOCK Darren						
Bishop Auckland, 23 February, 1985						(CD)
Hartlepool U	Sch	07.04	03-04	18	2	0
CRADDOCK Jody Darryl						
Bromsgrove, 25 July, 1975						(CD)
Cambridge U	Christchurch	08.93	93-96	142	3	4
Sunderland	Tr	08.97	97-02	140	6	2
Sheffield U	L	08.99	99	10	0	0
Wolverhampton W	Tr	08.03	03-04	71	3	2
CRADDOCK Leonard **Miller**						
Newent, 21 September, 1926 Died 1960						(CF)
Newport Co	Chelsea (Am)	05.46	46	7	-	0
Aston Villa	Hereford U	09.48	48-50	34	-	10
CRAGGS John Edward						
Flinthill, 21 October, 1948 EYth						(FB)
Newcastle U	App	12.65	66-70	50	2	1
Middlesbrough	Tr	08.71	71-81	408	1	12
Newcastle U	Tr	08.82	82	10	2	0
Darlington	Tr	08.83	83-84	53	1	0

League Club	Source	Date Signed	Seasons Played	Apps	Subs	Gls
CRAIG Albert Hughes						
Glasgow, 3 January, 1962						(W)
Newcastle U	Hamilton Academical	02.87	86-88	6	4	0
Northampton T	L	01.89	88	2	0	1
CRAIG Benjamin (Benny)						
Leadgate, 6 December, 1915 Died 1982						(FB)
Huddersfield T	Eden Colliery	01.34	33-38	98	-	0
Newcastle U	Tr	11.38	38-49	66	-	0
CRAIG David James						
Belfast, 8 June, 1944 NIYth/NIu23-1/NI-25						(FB)
Newcastle U	App	04.62	63-77	346	5	8
CRAIG William **David**						
Liverpool, 27 December, 1921 Died 1994						(W)
Blackpool	Marine	05.46				
Southport	Tr	08.48	48	5	-	2
CRAIG Derek Malcolm						
Ryton-on-Tyne, 28 July, 1952						(CD)
Newcastle U	Jnrs	08.69				
Darlington	San Jose (USA)	09.75	75-79	186	1	10
York C	Tr	05.80	80-81	53	0	1
CRAIG James (Jim) Philip						
Glasgow, 30 April, 1943 S-1						(FB)
Sheffield Wed	Hellenic	12.72	72-73	5	1	0
CRAIG Joseph (Joe)						
Logie, 14 May, 1954 Su23-4/SLge-1/S-1						(F)
Blackburn Rov	Glasgow Celtic	09.78	78-80	44	4	8
CRAIG Robert						
Consett, 16 June, 1928						(FB)
Sunderland	Leadgate Jnrs	11.45	49	1	-	0
CRAIG Robert (Bobby) McAllister						
Airdrie, 8 April, 1935						(IF)
Sheffield Wed	Third Lanark	11.59	59-61	84	-	25
Blackburn Rov	Tr	04.62	61-62	8	-	3
Oldham Ath	St Johnstone	03.64	63-64	18	-	4
CRAIG Thomas (Tommy) Brooks						
Glasgow, 21 November, 1950 SSch/Su21-1/Su23-9/S-1						(M)
Sheffield Wed	Aberdeen	05.69	68-74	210	4	38
Newcastle U	Tr	12.74	74-77	122	2	22
Aston Villa	Tr	01.78	77-78	27	0	2
Swansea C	Tr	07.78	79-80	47	5	9
Carlisle U	Tr	03.82	81-84	92	6	10
CRAIG Tony Andrew						
Greenwich, 20 April, 1985						(FB)
Millwall	Sch	03.03	02-04	19	2	1
Wycombe W	L	10.04	04	14	0	0
CRAIG William James						
Aberdeen, 11 September, 1929						(WH)
Millwall	Dundee	08.56	56-58	21	-	1
CRAINEY Stephen Daniel						
Glasgow, 22 June, 1981 Su21-7/SB-1/S-6						(FB)
Southampton	Glasgow Celtic	01.04	03	5	0	0
Leeds U	Tr	08.04	04	9	0	0
CRAINIE Daniel (Danny)						
Kilsyth, 24 May, 1962 Su21-1						(W)
Wolverhampton W	Glasgow Celtic	12.83	83-85	63	1	4
Blackpool	L	03.85	84	6	0	0
CRAINIE Martin James						
Yeovil, 23 September, 1986 EYth/Eu20						(FB)
Southampton	Sch	09.04	03-04	4	0	0
Bournemouth	L	10.04	04	2	1	0
CRAKER Laurence (Laurie) David						
Aylesbury, 1 March, 1953						(M)
Chelsea	App	08.70				
Watford	Jewish Guild (SA)	11.72	72-76	60	6	4
CRAM Robert (Bobby)						
Hetton-le-Hole, 19 November, 1939						(FB)
West Bromwich A	Jnrs	01.57	59-66	141	0	25
Colchester U	Vancouver (Can)	01.70	69-71	99	1	4
CRAMB Colin						
Lanark, 23 June, 1974						(F)
Southampton	Hamilton Academical	06.93	93	0	1	0
Doncaster Rov	Heart of Midlothian	12.95	95-96	60	2	25
Bristol C	Tr	07.97	97-98	38	15	9
Walsall	L	02.99	98	4	0	4

League Club	Source	Date Signed	Seasons Played	Apps	Subs	Gls
Crewe Alex	Tr	08.99	99-00	43	7	10
Notts Co	L	09.00	00	2	1	0
Bury	L	02.01	00	15	0	5
Bury	Fortuna Sittard (Holl)	01.03	02	17	1	3
Shrewsbury T	Tr	07.03	04	0	2	0
Grimsby T	Tr	09.04	04	7	4	2

CRAMPTON David (Dave) William
Bearpark, 9 June, 1949 (G)

League Club	Source	Date Signed	Seasons Played	Apps	Subs	Gls
Blackburn Rov	Spennymoor U	03.68				
Darlington	Tr	07.69	69	13	0	0

CRAMPTON Paul
Cleethorpes, 28 January, 1953 (FB)

League Club	Source	Date Signed	Seasons Played	Apps	Subs	Gls
Grimsby T	App	•	70	0	1	0

CRANE Andrew (Andy) David
Ipswich, 3 January, 1967 (FB)

League Club	Source	Date Signed	Seasons Played	Apps	Subs	Gls
Ipswich T	App	04.84				
Shrewsbury T	Tr	06.87				
Hereford U	Tr	07.88	88	30	2	0

CRANE Anthony (Tony) Steven
Liverpool, 8 September, 1982 EYth (CD)

League Club	Source	Date Signed	Seasons Played	Apps	Subs	Gls
Sheffield Wed	YT	09.99	00-02	24	25	4
Grimsby T	Tr	07.03	03-04	39	1	3

CRANE Steven (Steve) John
Orsett, 3 June, 1972 (F)

League Club	Source	Date Signed	Seasons Played	Apps	Subs	Gls
Charlton Ath	YT	07.90				
Gillingham	USA	03.93	92-93	3	10	1
Torquay U	(New Zealand)	12.96	96	0	2	0

CRANFIELD Harold (Harry) Richard
Chesterton, Cambridgeshire, 25 December, 1917 Died 1990 (W)

League Club	Source	Date Signed	Seasons Played	Apps	Subs	Gls
Fulham	Cambridge T	12.37	46	1	-	0
Bristol Rov	Tr	06.47	47	24	-	2

CRANGLE James (Jimmy) Patrick
Glasgow, 4 April, 1953 (W)

League Club	Source	Date Signed	Seasons Played	Apps	Subs	Gls
York C	Campsie Black Watch	08.72	72	4	0	0

CRANSON Ian
Easington, 2 July, 1964 Eu21-5 (CD)

League Club	Source	Date Signed	Seasons Played	Apps	Subs	Gls
Ipswich T	App	07.82	83-87	130	1	5
Sheffield Wed	Tr	03.88	87-88	29	1	0
Stoke C	Tr	07.89	89-96	220	3	9

CRANSTON Nicholas (Nick) Geoffrey
Carlisle, 20 October, 1972 (M)

League Club	Source	Date Signed	Seasons Played	Apps	Subs	Gls
Carlisle U	YT	01.92	91	0	2	0

CRANSTON William (Bill)
Kilmarnock, 18 January, 1942 (CD)

League Club	Source	Date Signed	Seasons Played	Apps	Subs	Gls
Blackpool	Saxone YC	08.60	61-64	33	-	0
Preston NE	Tr	12.64	64-69	80	6	1
Oldham Ath	Tr	07.70	70-72	98	2	2

CRAVEN Dean
Shrewsbury, 17 February, 1979 (M)

League Club	Source	Date Signed	Seasons Played	Apps	Subs	Gls
West Bromwich A	YT	07.97				
Shrewsbury T	Tr	03.98	97-98	7	4	0

CRAVEN John Roland
St Annes, 15 May, 1947 Died 1996 (M)

League Club	Source	Date Signed	Seasons Played	Apps	Subs	Gls
Blackpool	App	01.65	65-71	154	11	24
Crystal Palace	Tr	09.71	71-72	56	7	14
Coventry C	Tr	05.73	73-76	86	3	8
Plymouth Arg	Tr	01.77	76-77	45	0	3

CRAVEN Michael (Mike) Anthony
Birkenhead, 20 November, 1957 (G)

League Club	Source	Date Signed	Seasons Played	Apps	Subs	Gls
Chester	Cadbury's	09.75	75-76	4	0	0

CRAVEN Peter
Hanover, Germany, 30 June, 1968 (W)

League Club	Source	Date Signed	Seasons Played	Apps	Subs	Gls
Halifax T	Guiseley	03.93	92	7	0	0

CRAVEN Stephen (Steve) Joseph
Birkenhead, 17 September, 1957 (M)

League Club	Source	Date Signed	Seasons Played	Apps	Subs	Gls
Tranmere Rov		03.78	77-81	106	8	17
Crewe Alex	Tr	08.82	82	26	3	3
Tranmere Rov	Caernarfon T	07.87	87	6	7	0

CRAVEN Terence (Terry)
Barnsley, 27 November, 1944 EYth (WH)

League Club	Source	Date Signed	Seasons Played	Apps	Subs	Gls
Barnsley	Jnrs	06.63	64	3	-	0

CRAWFORD Alan Paterson
Rotherham, 30 October, 1953 (W)

League Club	Source	Date Signed	Seasons Played	Apps	Subs	Gls
Rotherham U	App	10.71	73-78	233	4	49
Mansfield T	L	01.73	72	1	1	0
Chesterfield	Tr	08.79	79-81	88	6	20
Bristol C	Tr	08.82	82-84	85	7	26
Exeter C	Tr	07.85	85	33	0	3

CRAWFORD Andrew (Andy)
Filey, 30 January, 1959 (F)

League Club	Source	Date Signed	Seasons Played	Apps	Subs	Gls
Derby Co	App	01.77	77-79	16	5	4
Blackburn Rov	Tr	10.79	79-81	56	0	21
Bournemouth	Tr	11.81	81-82	31	2	10
Cardiff C	Tr	08.83	83	6	0	1
Middlesbrough	Scarborough	10.83	83	8	1	1
Stockport Co		12.84	84	6	0	2
Torquay U	Tr	02.85	84	3	0	0

CRAWFORD John Robert **Bruce**
Preston, 10 October, 1938 Eu23-1 (WH)

League Club	Source	Date Signed	Seasons Played	Apps	Subs	Gls
Blackpool	Jnrs	05.56	59-64	98	-	11
Tranmere Rov	Tr	09.65	65-66	24	2	5

CRAWFORD Campbell Hackett Rankin
Alexandria, 1 December, 1943 SSch (FB)

League Club	Source	Date Signed	Seasons Played	Apps	Subs	Gls
West Bromwich A	Jnrs	12.60	63-66	10	0	0
Exeter C	Tr	07.67	67-73	224	10	3

CRAWFORD Peter **Graeme**
Falkirk, 7 August, 1947 (G)

League Club	Source	Date Signed	Seasons Played	Apps	Subs	Gls
Sheffield U	East Stirling	09.68	69-70	2	0	0
Mansfield T	L	07.71	71	2	0	0
York C	Tr	10.71	71-76	235	0	0
Scunthorpe U	Tr	08.77	77-79	104	0	0
York C	Tr	01.80	79	17	0	0
Rochdale	Tr	09.80	80-82	70	0	0

CRAWFORD James (Jimmy)
Chicago, USA, 1 May, 1973 IRu21-2 (M)

League Club	Source	Date Signed	Seasons Played	Apps	Subs	Gls
Newcastle U	Bohemians	03.95	96	0	2	0
Rotherham U	L	09.96	96	11	0	0
Reading	Tr	03.98	97-99	17	4	1

CRAWFORD James (Jimmy) Cherrie
Bellshill, 27 September, 1930 (IF)

League Club	Source	Date Signed	Seasons Played	Apps	Subs	Gls
Leicester C	Jnrs	10.47	50-53	10	-	2
Plymouth Arg	Tr	03.54	53-55	25	-	4

CRAWFORD John (Ian)
Edinburgh, 14 July, 1934 Su23-1 (FB)

League Club	Source	Date Signed	Seasons Played	Apps	Subs	Gls
West Ham U	Morton	07.61	61-62	24	-	5
Scunthorpe U	Tr	02.63	62-63	35	-	2
Peterborough U	Tr	07.64	64-68	172	0	6

CRAWFORD John (Ian) Campbell
Falkirk, 27 June, 1922 Died 1996 (IF)

League Club	Source	Date Signed	Seasons Played	Apps	Subs	Gls
Oldham Ath	Ayr U	07.52	52-53	24	-	8
Halifax T	Tr	07.54	54	11	-	2

CRAWFORD Raymond (Ray)
Portsmouth, 13 July, 1936 FLge-3/E-2 (F)

League Club	Source	Date Signed	Seasons Played	Apps	Subs	Gls
Portsmouth	Jnrs	12.54	57-58	19	-	9
Ipswich T	Tr	09.58	58-63	197	-	143
Wolverhampton W	Tr	09.63	63-64	57	-	39
West Bromwich A	Tr	02.65	64-65	14	0	6
Ipswich T	Tr	03.66	65-68	123	0	61
Charlton Ath	Tr	03.69	68-69	21	0	7
Colchester U	Kettering T	06.70	70	45	0	25

CRAWFORD Stephen (Stevie)
Dunfermline, 9 January, 1974 Su21-19/S-25 (F)

League Club	Source	Date Signed	Seasons Played	Apps	Subs	Gls
Millwall	Raith Rov	07.96	96	40	2	11
Plymouth Arg	Dunfermline Ath	07.04	04	19	7	6

CRAWLEY Thomas (Tommy)
Hamilton, 10 November, 1911 Died 1976 (CF)

League Club	Source	Date Signed	Seasons Played	Apps	Subs	Gls
Preston NE	Motherwell	05.35	35	2	-	0
Coventry C	Tr	02.36	35-46	45	-	16

CRAWSHAW Cyril
Barton-on-Irwell, 2 March, 1916 Died 2003 (IF)

League Club	Source	Date Signed	Seasons Played	Apps	Subs	Gls
Rochdale	Rossendale U	11.36	36	2	-	0
Exeter C	Stalybridge Celtic	07.39				
Hull C	Tr	06.46	46	2	-	2

CREAMER Peter Anthony
Hartlepool, 20 September, 1953 ESch (FB)

League Club	Source	Date Signed	Seasons Played	Apps	Subs	Gls
Middlesbrough	App	10.70	72-73	9	0	0
York C	L	11.75	75	4	0	0
Doncaster Rov	Tr	12.75	75-76	31	1	0
Hartlepool	Tr	10.76	76-77	63	0	3
Rochdale	Gateshead	12.78	78	18	2	0

CREANE Gerard (Gerry) Martin
Lincoln, 2 February, 1962 (CD)

League Club	Source	Date Signed	Seasons Played	Apps	Subs	Gls
Lincoln C	App	02.80	78-82	6	1	0

CREANEY Gerard (Gerry) Thomas
Coatbridge, 13 April, 1970 Su21-11/SB-1 (F)

League Club	Source	Date Signed	Seasons Played	Apps	Subs	Gls
Portsmouth	Glasgow Celtic	01.94	93-95	60	0	32
Manchester C	Tr	09.95	95-97	8	13	4
Oldham Ath	L	03.96	95	8	1	2
Ipswich T	L	10.96	96	6	0	1
Burnley	L	09.97	97	9	1	8
Chesterfield	L	01.98	97	3	1	0
Notts Co	St Mirren	02.99	98	13	3	3

CREASER Glyn Robert
Camden, 1 September, 1959 (CD)

League Club	Source	Date Signed	Seasons Played	Apps	Subs	Gls
Wycombe W	Barnet	09.88	93-94	17	2	2

CRELLIN Andrew
Gainsborough, 11 October, 1954 (FB)

League Club	Source	Date Signed	Seasons Played	Apps	Subs	Gls
Doncaster Rov	Ashby Institute	03.74	74	4	0	0

CRERAND Daniel (Danny) Bruno
Eccles, 5 May, 1969 (M)

League Club	Source	Date Signed	Seasons Played	Apps	Subs	Gls
Rochdale	Chapel Villa	02.88	87	3	0	0

CRERAND Patrick (Pat) Timothy
Glasgow, 19 February, 1939 Su23-1/SLge-7/S-16 (M)

League Club	Source	Date Signed	Seasons Played	Apps	Subs	Gls
Manchester U	Glasgow Celtic	02.63	62-70	304	0	10

CRESPO Hernan Jorge
Florida, Argentina, 6 July, 1975 Argentina 46 (F)

League Club	Source	Date Signed	Seasons Played	Apps	Subs	Gls
Chelsea	Inter Milan (It)	08.03	03	13	6	10

CRESSWELL Corbett Eric
Birkenhead, 3 August, 1932 EAmat (CD)

League Club	Source	Date Signed	Seasons Played	Apps	Subs	Gls
Carlisle U	Bishop Auckland	03.58	57-58	14	-	2

CRESSWELL Peter Frank
Linby, 9 November, 1935 (W)

League Club	Source	Date Signed	Seasons Played	Apps	Subs	Gls
Derby Co	Heanor T	04.54	54-56	12	-	2

CRESSWELL Philip
Hucknall, 11 May, 1933 Died 1993 (W)

League Club	Source	Date Signed	Seasons Played	Apps	Subs	Gls
Coventry C	Jnrs	05.50	54	2	-	0

CRESSWELL Richard Paul Wesley
Bridlington, 20 September, 1977 Eu21-4 (F)

League Club	Source	Date Signed	Seasons Played	Apps	Subs	Gls
York C	YT	11.95	95-98	72	23	21
Mansfield T	L	03.97	96	5	0	1
Sheffield Wed	Tr	03.99	98-00	7	24	2
Leicester C	Tr	09.00	00	3	5	0
Preston NE	Tr	03.01	00-04	161	23	49

CRIBLEY Alexander (Alex)
Liverpool, 1 April, 1957 (CD)

League Club	Source	Date Signed	Seasons Played	Apps	Subs	Gls
Liverpool		06.78				
Wigan Ath	Tr	10.80	80-87	268	4	16

CRICHTON George
Leslie, 11 December, 1925 (CD)

League Club	Source	Date Signed	Seasons Played	Apps	Subs	Gls
Workington	Loughborough College	(N/L)	51	4	-	0

CRICHTON Paul Andrew
Pontefract, 3 October, 1968 (G)

League Club	Source	Date Signed	Seasons Played	Apps	Subs	Gls
Nottingham F	Jnrs	05.86				
Notts Co	L	09.86	86	5	0	0
Darlington	L	01.87	86	5	0	0
Peterborough U	L	03.87	86	4	0	0
Darlington	L	09.87	87	3	0	0
Swindon T	L	12.87	87	4	0	0
Rotherham U	L	03.88	87	6	0	0
Torquay U	L	08.88	88	13	0	0
Peterborough U	Tr	11.88	88-89	47	0	0
Doncaster Rov	Tr	08.90	90-92	77	0	0
Grimsby T	Tr	07.93	93-95	133	0	0
West Bromwich A	Tr	09.96	96-97	32	0	0
Burnley	L	08.98	98	1	0	0
Burnley	Tr	11.98	98-00	81	1	0
Norwich C	Tr	06.01	01	5	1	0

CRICKETT Norman
Carlisle, 13 October, 1932 (W)

League Club	Source	Date Signed	Seasons Played	Apps	Subs	Gls
Carlisle U		11.52	55	1	-	0

CRICKMORE Charles (Charlie) Alfred
Hull, 11 February, 1942 (W)

League Club	Source	Date Signed	Seasons Played	Apps	Subs	Gls
Hull C	Jnrs	02.59	59-61	53	-	13
Bournemouth	Tr	07.62	62-65	128	0	17
Gillingham	Tr	06.66	66-67	53	0	13
Rotherham U	Tr	11.67	67	7	1	1
Norwich C	Tr	01.68	67-69	54	2	9
Notts Co	Tr	03.70	69-71	59	0	11

CRICKSON George (Gerry) Edward
Dover, 21 September, 1934 Died 1991 ESch/EYth (WH)

League Club	Source	Date Signed	Seasons Played	Apps	Subs	Gls
Queens Park Rgrs	Dover	09.51	52-55	5	-	0

CRIPPS Henry (Harry) Richard
East Dereham, 29 April, 1941 Died 1995 (FB)

League Club	Source	Date Signed	Seasons Played	Apps	Subs	Gls
West Ham U	Jnrs	09.58				
Millwall	Tr	06.61	61-74	390	10	37
Charlton Ath	Tr	10.74	74-75	17	3	4

CRIPSEY Brian Samuel
Hull, 26 June, 1931 (W)

League Club	Source	Date Signed	Seasons Played	Apps	Subs	Gls
Hull C	Brunswick Institute	11.51	52-58	145	-	19
Wrexham	Tr	09.58	58-59	27	-	3

CRISP Richard Ian
Wordsley, 23 May, 1972 (M)

League Club	Source	Date Signed	Seasons Played	Apps	Subs	Gls
Aston Villa	YT	07.90				
Scunthorpe U	L	03.93	92	6	2	0

CRISP Ronald (Ron) James
Datchet, 24 September, 1938 (WH)

League Club	Source	Date Signed	Seasons Played	Apps	Subs	Gls
Watford	Dulwich Hamlet	01.61	60-64	89	-	14
Brentford	Tr	08.65	65-66	17	1	0

CRISPIN Timothy (Tim)
Leicester, 7 June, 1948 (FB)

League Club	Source	Date Signed	Seasons Played	Apps	Subs	Gls
Notts Co	Jnrs	07.66	66-67	8	0	0

CRITCHLEY Neil
Crewe, 18 October, 1978 (M)

League Club	Source	Date Signed	Seasons Played	Apps	Subs	Gls
Crewe Alex	YT	07.97	99	0	1	0

CRITTENDEN Nicholas (Nicky) James
Bracknell, 11 November, 1978 ESemiPro-1 (FB)

League Club	Source	Date Signed	Seasons Played	Apps	Subs	Gls
Chelsea	YT	07.97	97	0	2	0
Plymouth Arg	L	10.98	98	1	1	0
Yeovil T	Tr	08.00	03	20	9	2

CROCI Laurent
Montbeliard, France, 8 December, 1964 (M)

League Club	Source	Date Signed	Seasons Played	Apps	Subs	Gls
Carlisle U	Bordeaux (Fr)	10.97	97	1	0	0

CROCKER Marcus Alan
Plymouth, 8 October, 1974 (F)

League Club	Source	Date Signed	Seasons Played	Apps	Subs	Gls
Plymouth Arg	YT	06.93	92-94	4	6	0

CROFT Alec Robert
Chester, 17 June, 1937 (W)

League Club	Source	Date Signed	Seasons Played	Apps	Subs	Gls
Chester		08.58	58-60	53	-	3

CROFT Brian Graham Alexander
Chester, 27 September, 1967 (W)

League Club	Source	Date Signed	Seasons Played	Apps	Subs	Gls
Chester C	App	07.86	85-87	36	23	3
Cambridge U	Tr	10.88	88	12	5	2
Chester C	Tr	08.89	89-91	90	24	3
Queens Park Rgrs	Tr	08.92				
Shrewsbury T	L	12.93	93	4	0	0
Blackpool	Tr	07.95				
Torquay U	Tr	08.95	95	0	1	0
Stockport Co	Southport	10.95	95	0	3	0

CROFT Charles (Charlie)
Dewsbury, 26 November, 1918 (WH)

League Club	Source	Date Signed	Seasons Played	Apps	Subs	Gls
Huddersfield T		05.39				
Mansfield T	Tr	05.47	47-49	85	-	5

CROFT Gary
Burton-on-Trent, 17 February, 1974 Eu21-4 (FB)

League Club	Source	Date Signed	Seasons Played	Apps	Subs	Gls
Grimsby T	YT	07.92	90-95	139	10	3
Blackburn Rov	Tr	03.96	96-98	33	7	1
Ipswich T	Tr	09.99	99-00	20	9	1
Wigan Ath	L	01.02	01	7	0	0
Cardiff C	Tr	03.02	01-04	65	12	3

CROFT Lee David
Wigan, 21 June, 1985 EYth/Eu20 (W)

League Club	Source	Date Signed	Seasons Played	Apps	Subs	Gls
Manchester C	Sch	07.02	04	0	7	0
Oldham Ath	L	11.04	04	11	1	0

CROFT Stuart Dunbar
Ashington, 12 April, 1954 (CD)

League Club	Source	Date Signed	Seasons Played	Apps	Subs	Gls
Hull C	App	04.72	72-80	187	3	4
Portsmouth	Tr	03.81	80	6	0	1
York C	Tr	08.81	81	14	0	0

CROFTS Andrew (Andy) Lawrence
Chatham, 29 May, 1984 WYth/Wu21-3 (M)

League Club	Source	Date Signed	Seasons Played	Apps	Subs	Gls
Gillingham	Sch	08.03	00-04	26	10	2

CROKER Edgar (Ted) Alfred
Kingston, 13 February, 1924 Died 1992 (CD)

League Club	Source	Date Signed	Seasons Played	Apps	Subs	Gls
Charlton Ath	Kingstonian	07.48	50	8	-	0

CROKER Peter Harry Lucas
Kingston, 21 December, 1921 (FB)

League Club	Source	Date Signed	Seasons Played	Apps	Subs	Gls
Charlton Ath	Bromley	11.45	46-50	59	-	0
Watford	Tr	06.52	52	23	-	0

CROMACK David (Dave) Charles
Leeds, 22 December, 1948 (G)

League Club	Source	Date Signed	Seasons Played	Apps	Subs	Gls
Doncaster Rov	Hull C (Am)	11.66	66	8	0	0

CROMACK Victor (Vic)
Mansfield, 17 March, 1920 Died 1984 (G)

League Club	Source	Date Signed	Seasons Played	Apps	Subs	Gls
Mansfield T		01.46	46	10	-	0

CROMBIE Dean Malcolm
Lincoln, 9 August, 1957 (CD)

League Club	Source	Date Signed	Seasons Played	Apps	Subs	Gls
Lincoln C	Ruston Bucyrus	02.77	76-77	33	0	0
Grimsby T	Tr	08.78	78-86	316	4	4
Reading	L	11.86	86	4	0	0
Bolton W	Tr	08.87	87-90	90	5	1
Lincoln C	Tr	01.91	90	0	1	0

CROMBIE Thomas (Tom) Ronald
Kirkcaldy, 3 June, 1930 (FB)

League Club	Source	Date Signed	Seasons Played	Apps	Subs	Gls
Blackpool	Jeanfield Swifts	08.51				
Gillingham	Tr	07.55	55-56	17	-	0

CROMPTON Alan
Bolton, 6 March, 1958 (M)

League Club	Source	Date Signed	Seasons Played	Apps	Subs	Gls
Sunderland	App	03.75				
Blackburn Rov	Tr	07.76	76	2	2	0
Wigan Ath	Tr	07.78	78-79	7	7	0

CROMPTON David Gerald
Wigan, 6 March, 1945 (M)

League Club	Source	Date Signed	Seasons Played	Apps	Subs	Gls
Rochdale (Am)		11.66	66-67	15	2	0

CROMPTON Dennis
Bolton, 12 March, 1942 (WH)

League Club	Source	Date Signed	Seasons Played	Apps	Subs	Gls
Bolton W	Wigan Ath	12.59				
Doncaster Rov	Tr	06.63	63	23	-	0

CROMPTON John (Jack)
Chorlton, 18 December, 1921 (G)

League Club	Source	Date Signed	Seasons Played	Apps	Subs	Gls
Manchester U	Goslings	01.45	46-55	191	-	0

CROMPTON Paul **Jonathan**
Orrell, 25 January, 1970 (F)

League Club	Source	Date Signed	Seasons Played	Apps	Subs	Gls
Wigan Ath	YT	07.88	89	1	0	0

CROMPTON Stephen (Steve) Wynn
Wrexham, 3 December, 1958 (F)

League Club	Source	Date Signed	Seasons Played	Apps	Subs	Gls
Hereford U	Wolverhampton W (App)	02.77	76-78	30	4	6

CROMPTON Steven (Steve) Geoffrey
Partington, 20 April, 1968 (G)

League Club	Source	Date Signed	Seasons Played	Apps	Subs	Gls
Manchester C	Jnrs	05.86				
Carlisle U	Tr	07.87	87	10	0	0
Stockport Co	Tr	02.88	87	2	0	0

CRONIN Dennis
Altrincham, 30 October, 1967 (F)

League Club	Source	Date Signed	Seasons Played	Apps	Subs	Gls
Manchester U	App	10.85				
Stockport Co	Tr	08.87	87	11	4	1
Crewe Alex	Tr	08.88	88	12	3	2

CRONIN Glenn
Dublin, 14 September, 1981 IRYth (M)

League Club	Source	Date Signed	Seasons Played	Apps	Subs	Gls
Exeter C	YT	07.00	01-02	52	17	0

CRONIN Lance
Brighton, 11 September, 1985 (G)

League Club	Source	Date Signed	Seasons Played	Apps	Subs	Gls
Crystal Palace	Jnrs	09.02				
Wycombe W	L	03.05	04	1	0	0

CRONIN Thomas (Tommy) Patrick
Richmond, Surrey, 17 December, 1932 (IF)

League Club	Source	Date Signed	Seasons Played	Apps	Subs	Gls
Fulham	East Sheen Ath	09.50	53-54	2	-	0
Reading	Tr	06.56	56-57	30	-	4

CROOK Alfred (Alf) Rowland
Brewood, 13 August, 1923 (FB)

League Club	Source	Date Signed	Seasons Played	Apps	Subs	Gls
Wolverhampton W	Boulton & Paul	05.45	48	1	-	0

CROOK George
Hutton Henry, 30 January, 1935 (IF)

League Club	Source	Date Signed	Seasons Played	Apps	Subs	Gls
Oldham Ath		02.53	53-57	57	-	13

CROOK Ian Stuart
Romford, 18 January, 1963 EB (M)

League Club	Source	Date Signed	Seasons Played	Apps	Subs	Gls
Tottenham H	App	08.80	81-85	10	10	1
Norwich C	Tr	06.86	86-96	314	27	18

CROOK Leslie (Les) Ronald
Manchester, 26 June, 1949 (M)

League Club	Source	Date Signed	Seasons Played	Apps	Subs	Gls
Oxford U	Manchester Amats	10.68	68	1	0	0
Hartlepool	Tr	07.70	70	23	2	3

CROOK Walter
Whittle-le-Woods, 28 April, 1912 Died 1988 EWar-1 (FB)

League Club	Source	Date Signed	Seasons Played	Apps	Subs	Gls
Blackburn Rov	Blackburn Nomads	01.31	31-46	236	-	2
Bolton W	Tr	05.47	47	28	-	0

CROOK William (Billy) Charles
Cannock, 7 June, 1926 (WH)

League Club	Source	Date Signed	Seasons Played	Apps	Subs	Gls
Wolverhampton W	Jnrs	08.45	46-52	196	-	2
Walsall	Tr	10.54	54-55	45	-	2

CROOKES Peter
Liverpool, 7 May, 1982 ESch/EYth (G)

League Club	Source	Date Signed	Seasons Played	Apps	Subs	Gls
Halifax T	Liverpool (YT)	03.01	01	1	0	0

CROOKES Robert (Bobby) Eastland
Retford, 29 February, 1924 (W)

League Club	Source	Date Signed	Seasons Played	Apps	Subs	Gls
Notts Co	Retford T	06.49	49-55	177	-	45

CROOKS Garth Anthony
Stoke-on-Trent, 10 March, 1958 Eu21-4 (F)

League Club	Source	Date Signed	Seasons Played	Apps	Subs	Gls
Stoke C	App	03.76	75-79	141	6	48
Tottenham H	Tr	07.80	80-84	121	4	48
Manchester U	L	11.83	83	6	1	2
West Bromwich A	Tr	08.85	85-86	39	1	16
Charlton Ath	Tr	03.87	86-90	41	15	15

CROOKS Lee Robert
Wakefield, 14 January, 1978 EYth (FB)

League Club	Source	Date Signed	Seasons Played	Apps	Subs	Gls
Manchester C	YT	01.95	96-00	52	24	2
Northampton T	L	12.00	00	3	0	0
Barnsley	Tr	03.01	01-03	50	17	0
Bradford C	Tr	08.04	04	30	2	1

CROOKS Leon Everton George
Greenwich, 21 November, 1985 (CD)

League Club	Source	Date Signed	Seasons Played	Apps	Subs	Gls
MK Dons	Sch	07.04	04	15	2	0

CROOKS Paul
Durham, 12 October, 1966 (F)

League Club	Source	Date Signed	Seasons Played	Apps	Subs	Gls
Stoke C	Caernarfon T	08.86	86	0	1	0

CROOKS Samuel (Sammy) Dickinson
Bearpark, 16 January, 1908 Died 1981 FLge-5/E-26 (W)

League Club	Source	Date Signed	Seasons Played	Apps	Subs	Gls
Durham C	Tow Law T	06.26	26	16	-	4
Derby Co	Tr	04.27	27-46	408	-	101

CROPLEY Alexander (Alex) James
Aldershot, 16 January, 1951 Su23-3/S-2 (M)

League Club	Source	Date Signed	Seasons Played	Apps	Subs	Gls
Arsenal	Hibernian	12.74	74-76	29	1	5
Aston Villa	Tr	09.78	76-79	65	2	7
Newcastle U	L	02.80	79	3	0	0
Portsmouth	Toronto (Can)	09.81	81	8	2	2

CROPLEY John (Jack) Thomas
Edinburgh, 27 September, 1924 (WH)

League Club	Source	Date Signed	Seasons Played	Apps	Subs	Gls
Aldershot	Tranent Jnrs	10.46	47-53	162	-	3

CROPPER Dene James
Chesterfield, 5 January, 1983 (F)

League Club	Source	Date Signed	Seasons Played	Apps	Subs	Gls
Lincoln C	Sheffield Wed (YT)	08.02	02-03	29	21	3
Boston U	Tr	03.04	03	4	1	1

CROSBIE Robert (Bob) Crichton
Glasgow, 2 September, 1925 Died 1994 (CF)

League Club	Source	Date Signed	Seasons Played	Apps	Subs	Gls
Bury		05.47	47-48	9	-	5
Bradford PA	Tr	05.49	49-53	139	-	72
Hull C	Tr	10.53	53-54	61	-	22
Grimsby T	Tr	07.55	55-56	65	-	45

CROSBY Andrew (Andy) Keith
Rotherham, 3 March, 1973 (CD)

League Club	Source	Date Signed	Seasons Played	Apps	Subs	Gls
Doncaster Rov	Leeds U (YT)	07.91	91-92	41	10	0
Darlington	Tr	12.93	93-97	179	2	3
Chester C	Tr	07.98	98	41	0	4
Brighton & Hove A	Tr	07.99	99-01	64	8	5
Oxford U	Tr	12.01	01-03	109	2	12
Scunthorpe U	Tr	08.04	04	43	1	3

CROSBY Gary
Sleaford, 8 May, 1964 (W)

League Club	Source	Date Signed	Seasons Played	Apps	Subs	Gls
Lincoln C	Lincoln U	08.86	86	6	1	0
Nottingham F	Grantham T	12.87	87-93	139	13	12

League Club	Source	Date Signed	Seasons Played	Career Record Apps	Subs	Gls
Grimsby T	L	08.93	93	2	1	0
Huddersfield T	Tr	09.94	94-96	35	9	6

CROSBY Geoffrey (Geoff) John
Stoke-on-Trent, 24 August, 1931 Died 2000 (IF)

League Club	Source	Date Signed	Seasons Played	Apps	Subs	Gls
Stockport Co	Leek T	09.52	52-53	5	-	1

CROSBY Malcolm
South Shields, 4 July, 1954 (M)

League Club	Source	Date Signed	Seasons Played	Apps	Subs	Gls
Aldershot	App	07.72	71-81	272	22	23
York C	Tr	11.81	81-84	99	4	4
Wrexham	L	09.84	84	5	1	0

CROSBY Philip (Phil) Alan
Upton, West Yorkshire, 9 November, 1962 EYth (FB)

League Club	Source	Date Signed	Seasons Played	Apps	Subs	Gls
Grimsby T	App	09.80	79-82	34	5	1
Rotherham U	Tr	08.83	83-88	181	2	2
Peterborough U	Tr	08.89	89-90	85	2	0
York C	Tr	07.91	91	25	0	0

CROSLAND John (Johnny) Ronald
St Annes, 10 November, 1922 EB (CD)

League Club	Source	Date Signed	Seasons Played	Apps	Subs	Gls
Blackpool	Ansdell Rov	05.46	46-53	67	-	0
Bournemouth	Tr	06.54	54-56	106	-	0

CROSS David
Heywood, 8 December, 1950 (F)

League Club	Source	Date Signed	Seasons Played	Apps	Subs	Gls
Rochdale	Jnrs	08.69	69-71	50	6	20
Norwich C	Tr	10.71	71-73	83	1	21
Coventry C	Tr	11.73	73-76	90	1	30
West Bromwich A	Tr	11.76	76-77	38	0	18
West Ham U	Tr	12.77	77-81	178	1	77
Manchester C	Tr	08.82	82	31	0	12
Oldham Ath	Vancouver (Can)	10.83	83	18	4	6
West Bromwich A	Vancouver (Can)	10.84	84	16	0	2
Bolton W	Tr	06.85	85	19	1	8
Bury	L	01.86	85	12	1	0

CROSS David Barron
Bromley, 7 September, 1982 (F)

League Club	Source	Date Signed	Seasons Played	Apps	Subs	Gls
Notts Co	YT	•	99	0	1	0

CROSS Garry Robert
Chelmsford, 7 October, 1980 (FB)

League Club	Source	Date Signed	Seasons Played	Apps	Subs	Gls
Southend U	YT	07.99	99-00	11	5	0

CROSS Graham Frederick
Leicester, 15 November, 1943 (CD)

League Club	Source	Date Signed	Seasons Played	Apps	Subs	Gls
Leicester C	App	11.60	60-75	496	3	29
Chesterfield	L	03.76	75	12	0	0
Brighton & Hove A	Tr	06.76	76	46	0	3
Preston NE	Tr	07.77	77-78	45	0	1
Lincoln C	Enderby T	03.79	78	19	0	0

CROSS James (Jimmy) Keith
Liverpool, 3 December, 1926 Died 1999 (WH)

League Club	Source	Date Signed	Seasons Played	Apps	Subs	Gls
Everton		10.50				
Swindon T	Tr	07.53	53-57	154	-	5

CROSS John (Jack)
Bury, 5 February, 1927 (CF)

League Club	Source	Date Signed	Seasons Played	Apps	Subs	Gls
Bournemouth	Guildford C	06.47	47-53	136	-	64
Northampton T	Tr	10.53	53	10	-	8
Sheffield U	Tr	02.54	53-55	44	-	16
Reading	Tr	10.55	55	15	-	6

CROSS Jonathan (Jon) Neil
Wallasey, 2 March, 1975 (FB)

League Club	Source	Date Signed	Seasons Played	Apps	Subs	Gls
Wrexham	YT	11.92	91-97	92	27	12
Hereford U	L	12.96	96	5	0	1
Chester C	Tr	08.98	98-99	46	6	1

CROSS Mark
Abergavenny, 6 May, 1976 (W)

League Club	Source	Date Signed	Seasons Played	Apps	Subs	Gls
Hereford U	YT	•	92	0	1	0

CROSS Michael (Mike) John
Walkden, 25 April, 1956 (FB)

League Club	Source	Date Signed	Seasons Played	Apps	Subs	Gls
Bolton W	App	04.74				
Stockport Co	Tr	07.75	75	27	0	2

CROSS Nicholas (Nicky) Jeremy Rowland
Birmingham, 7 February, 1961 (F)

League Club	Source	Date Signed	Seasons Played	Apps	Subs	Gls
West Bromwich A	App	02.79	80-84	68	37	15
Walsall	Tr	08.85	85-87	107	2	45
Leicester C	Tr	01.88	87-88	54	4	15
Port Vale	Tr	06.89	89-93	120	24	39
Hereford U	Tr	07.94	94-95	56	9	14

CROSS Paul
Barnsley, 31 October, 1965 (FB)

League Club	Source	Date Signed	Seasons Played	Apps	Subs	Gls
Barnsley	App	10.83	82-91	115	4	0
Preston NE	L	09.91	91	5	0	0
Hartlepool U	Tr	01.92	91-93	73	1	1
Darlington	Tr	11.93	93-94	39	0	2

CROSS Roger George
East Ham, 20 October, 1948 (F)

League Club	Source	Date Signed	Seasons Played	Apps	Subs	Gls
West Ham U	App	07.64	68-69	5	2	1
Orient	L	10.68	68	4	2	2
Brentford	Tr	03.70	69-71	62	0	21
Fulham	Tr	09.71	71-72	39	1	8
Brentford	Tr	12.72	72-76	141	4	52
Millwall	Tr	01.77	76-78	14	4	0

CROSS Roy
Wednesbury, 4 December, 1947 ESch (CD)

League Club	Source	Date Signed	Seasons Played	Apps	Subs	Gls
Walsall	Jnrs	07.66	66-69	11	1	0
Port Vale	Tr	07.70	70-74	136	0	1

CROSS Ryan
Plymouth, 11 October, 1972 (FB)

League Club	Source	Date Signed	Seasons Played	Apps	Subs	Gls
Plymouth Arg	YT	03.91	90-91	18	1	0
Hartlepool U	Tr	06.92	92-93	49	1	2
Bury	Tr	12.93	93-95	40	2	0

CROSS Scott Keith
Northampton, 30 October, 1987 (M)

League Club	Source	Date Signed	Seasons Played	Apps	Subs	Gls
Northampton T	Sch	•	04	0	1	0

CROSS Stephen (Steve) Charles
Wolverhampton, 22 December, 1959 (M)

League Club	Source	Date Signed	Seasons Played	Apps	Subs	Gls
Shrewsbury T	App	12.77	76-85	240	22	33
Derby Co	Tr	06.86	86-91	42	31	3
Bristol Rov	Tr	09.91	91-92	37	6	2

CROSSAN Edward (Eddie)
Derry, 17 November, 1925 I-2/NI-1 (IF)

League Club	Source	Date Signed	Seasons Played	Apps	Subs	Gls
Blackburn Rov	Derry C	11.47	47-56	287	-	73
Tranmere Rov	Tr	08.57	57	39	-	6

CROSSAN Errol Gilmour
Montreal, Canada, 6 October, 1930 (W)

League Club	Source	Date Signed	Seasons Played	Apps	Subs	Gls
Manchester C	Gymnasium (IoM)	01.54				
Gillingham	Tr	07.55	55-56	76	-	16
Southend U	Tr	08.57	57-58	40	-	11
Norwich C	Tr	09.58	58-60	102	-	28
Leyton Orient	Tr	01.61	60	8	-	2

CROSSAN John (Johnny) Andrew
Derry, 29 November, 1938 NI-24 (F)

League Club	Source	Date Signed	Seasons Played	Apps	Subs	Gls
Sunderland	Standard Liege (Bel)	10.62	62-64	82	-	39
Manchester C	Tr	01.65	64-66	94	0	24
Middlesbrough	Tr	08.67	67-69	54	2	7

CROSSLEY James
Belfast, 29 July, 1922 Died 2001 (FB)

League Club	Source	Date Signed	Seasons Played	Apps	Subs	Gls
Portsmouth	Cliftonville	04.45				
Reading	Tr	07.46	46	1	-	0

CROSSLEY Mark Geoffrey
Barnsley, 16 June, 1969 Eu21-3/WB-1/W-8 (G)

League Club	Source	Date Signed	Seasons Played	Apps	Subs	Gls
Nottingham F	YT	07.87	88-99	301	2	0
Millwall	L	02.98	97	13	0	0
Middlesbrough	Tr	07.00	00-01	21	2	0
Stoke C	L	11.02	02	1	0	0
Stoke C	L	03.03	02	11	0	0
Fulham	Tr	08.03	03-04	6	0	0

CROSSLEY Matthew (Matt) John William
Basingstoke, 18 March, 1968 (CD)

League Club	Source	Date Signed	Seasons Played	Apps	Subs	Gls
Wycombe W	Overton U	02.88	93-96	93	3	3

CROSSLEY Paul
Rochdale, 14 July, 1948 Died 1996 (W)

League Club	Source	Date Signed	Seasons Played	Apps	Subs	Gls
Rochdale	St Clement's	09.65	65-66	17	0	2
Preston NE	Tr	11.66	66-67	3	0	0
Southport	L	09.68	68	10	0	2
Tranmere Rov	Tr	06.69	69-75	186	17	37
Chester	Tr	09.75	75-77	93	6	26

CROSSLEY Richard Mark
Huddersfield, 5 September, 1970 (CD)

League Club	Source	Date Signed	Seasons Played	Apps	Subs	Gls
York C	Huddersfield T (YT)	10.89	89-90	6	0	0

CROSSLEY Roy
Hebden Bridge, 16 October, 1923 Died 2003 (CF)

League Club	Source	Date Signed	Seasons Played	Apps	Subs	Gls
Huddersfield T		05.46				
Halifax T		09.48	48-50	41	-	15

CROSSLEY Russell
Hebden Bridge, 25 June, 1927 (G)

League Club	Source	Date Signed	Seasons Played	Apps	Subs	Gls
Liverpool	Jnrs	06.47	50-53	68	-	0
Shrewsbury T	Tr	07.54	54-59	173	-	0

League Club	Source	Date Signed	Seasons Played	Apps	Subs	Gls
CROSSLEY Terence (Terry) Gordon						
Rock Ferry, 24 February, 1936						(W)
Oldham Ath	Bangor Univ	08.57	57	2	-	1
CROSSON David						
Bishop Auckland, 24 November, 1952						(FB)
Newcastle U	Jnrs	11.70	73-74	6	0	0
Darlington	Tr	08.75	75-79	115	13	2
CROTTY Colin						
Aberfan, 12 February, 1951						(F)
Swansea T (Am)	Jnrs	08.68	68	1	1	1
CROUCH Nigel John						
Ardleigh, 24 November, 1958						(FB)
Ipswich T	App	11.76				
Lincoln C	L	08.79	79	7	0	0
Colchester U	Tr	07.80	80	9	1	0
CROUCH Peter James						
Macclesfield, 30 January, 1981 EYth/Eu20/Eu21-6/E-1						(F)
Tottenham H	YT	07.98				
Queens Park Rgrs	Tr	07.00	00	38	4	10
Portsmouth	Tr	07.01	01	37	0	18
Aston Villa	Tr	03.02	01-03	20	17	6
Norwich C	L	09.03	03	14	1	4
Southampton	Tr	07.04	04	18	9	12
CROUDSON Steven (Steve) David						
Grimsby, 14 September, 1979						(G)
Grimsby T	YT	07.98	98-01	5	1	0
Scunthorpe U	L	08.01	01	4	0	0
CROW Daniel (Danny) Stephen						
Great Yarmouth, 26 January, 1986						(CD)
Norwich C	Sch	09.04	04	0	3	0
Northampton T	L	02.05	04	4	6	2
CROWE Alexander (Alec) Allan						
Motherwell, 24 November, 1924 Died 1997						(IF)
Ipswich T	Cowdenbeath	05.53	53-54	50	-	9
CROWE Charles (Charlie) Alfred						
Walker, 30 October, 1924						(WH)
Newcastle U	Heaton & Byker	10.44	46-56	178	-	5
Mansfield T	Tr	02.57	56-57	37	-	0
CROWE Christopher (Chris)						
Newcastle, 11 June, 1939 Died 2003 SSch/EYth/Eu23-4/E-1						(M)
Leeds U	Jnrs	06.56	56-59	95	-	27
Blackburn Rov	Tr	03.60	59-61	51	-	6
Wolverhampton W	Tr	02.62	61-63	83	-	24
Nottingham F	Tr	08.64	64-66	73	0	12
Bristol C	Tr	01.67	66-68	66	1	13
Walsall	Auburn (Aus)	09.69	69	10	3	1
CROWE Dean Anthony						
Stockport, 6 June, 1979						(F)
Stoke C	YT	09.96	97-99	29	31	12
Northampton T	L	02.00	99	3	2	0
Bury	L	03.00	99	4	0	1
Bury	L	08.00	00	1	6	1
Plymouth Arg	L	08.01	01	0	1	0
Luton T	Tr	09.01	01-03	49	20	17
York C	L	09.03	03	2	3	0
Oldham Ath	Tr	03.04	03	2	3	1
CROWE Glen Michael						
Dublin, 25 December, 1977 IRYth/IRu21-2						(F)
Wolverhampton W	YT	07.96	95-97	6	4	1
Exeter C	L	02.97	96	10	0	5
Cardiff C	L	10.97	97	7	1	1
Exeter C	L	08.98	98	3	6	0
Plymouth Arg	Tr	02.99	98	3	8	1
CROWE Jason William Robert						
Sidcup, 30 September, 1978 ESch/EYth						(FB)
Arsenal	YT	05.96				
Crystal Palace	L	11.98	98	8	0	0
Portsmouth	Tr	07.99	99-02	67	19	5
Brentford	L	09.00	00	9	0	0
Grimsby T	Tr	08.03	03-04	64	5	4
CROWE Mark Anthony						
Southwold, 21 January, 1965						(CD)
Norwich C	App	01.83	82	0	1	0
Torquay U	Tr	07.85	85-86	57	0	2
Cambridge U	Tr	12.86	86-87	51	0	0
CROWE Matthew (Matt) Jackson						
Bathgate, 4 July, 1932						(WH)
Bradford PA	Partick Th	07.49	52	1	-	0
Norwich C	Partick Th	05.57	57-61	186	-	14
Brentford	Tr	07.62	62-63	73	-	0
CROWE Michael (Mick)						
Ulverston, 13 August, 1942						(W)
Barrow	Ulverston Ath	08.60	60-62	15	-	1
CROWE Victor (Vic) Herbert						
Abercynon, 31 January, 1932 W-16						(WH)
Aston Villa	West Bromwich A (Am)	06.52	54-63	294	-	10
Peterborough U	Tr	07.64	64-66	56	0	0
CROWELL Matthew (Matty) Thomas						
Bridgend, 3 July, 1984 WYth/Wu21-5						(M)
Southampton	YT	07.01				
Wrexham	Tr	07.03	03-04	31	12	1
CROWN David Ian						
Enfield, 16 February, 1958						(F)
Brentford	Walthamstow Ave	07.80	80-81	44	2	8
Portsmouth	Tr	10.81	81-82	25	3	2
Exeter C	L	03.83	82	6	1	3
Reading	Tr	08.83	83-84	87	1	14
Cambridge U	Tr	07.85	85-87	106	0	45
Southend U	Tr	11.87	87-89	113	0	61
Gillingham	Tr	06.90	90-92	83	3	38
CROWSHAW Allan Alfred						
Bloxwich, 12 December, 1932						(W)
West Bromwich A	Bloxwich Wesleyans	05.50	54-55	11	-	2
Derby Co	Tr	06.56	56-57	18	-	6
Millwall	Tr	05.58	58-59	49	-	10
CROWTHER Kenneth (Ken)						
Halifax, 17 December, 1924 Died 1994						(WH)
Burnley	Halifax T (Am)	09.45				
Bradford PA	Tr	07.48	48	6	-	1
Rochdale	Tr	08.50	50	2	-	0
CROWTHER Stanley (Stan)						
Bilston, 3 September, 1935 Eu23-3						(WH)
Aston Villa	Bilston	08.55	56-57	50	-	4
Manchester U	Tr	02.58	57-58	13	-	0
Chelsea	Tr	12.58	58-59	51	-	0
Brighton & Hove A	Tr	03.61	60	4	-	0
CROWTHER Stephen (Steve) John						
Romiley, 16 January, 1955						(FB)
Stockport Co		01.74	73-74	42	2	4
Hartlepool	Tr	07.75	75	3	0	0
CROY John						
Falkirk, 23 February, 1925 Died 1979						(CD)
Northampton T	Third Lanark	07.50	51-54	25	-	0
CROZIER Joseph (Joe)						
Coatbridge, 2 December, 1914 Died 1985 SWar-3						(G)
Brentford	East Fife	05.37	37-48	200	-	0
CRUDGINGTON Geoffrey (Geoff)						
Wolverhampton, 14 February, 1952 ESch						(G)
Aston Villa	Wolverhampton W (Jnrs)	09.69	70	3	0	0
Bradford C	L	03.71	70	1	0	0
Aston Villa	Toronto (Can)	08.71	71	1	0	0
Crewe Alex	Tr	03.72	71-77	250	0	0
Swansea C	Tr	07.78	78-79	52	0	0
Plymouth Arg	Tr	10.79	79-87	326	0	0
CRUICKSHANK Frank James						
Polmont, 20 November, 1931						(FB)
Notts Co	Nuneaton Borough	01.50	53-59	151	-	5
CRUICKSHANK George Philip						
Malaya, Malaysia, 22 July, 1931						(W)
Carlisle U	Queen of the South	08.57	57	14	-	0
CRUICKSHANK John Paul						
Oldham, 18 January, 1960						(M)
Blackpool	App	08.77				
Bury	Tr	07.79	79-82	65	17	4
CRUMBLEHULME Kevin						
Manchester, 17 June, 1952						(M)
Oldham Ath	App	07.70	71	2	0	0
CRUMPLIN Ian						
Lemington, 12 September, 1954						(F)
Hartlepool U	Blue Star	06.78	78	25	4	5
CRUMPLIN John Leslie						
Bath, 26 May, 1967						(W)
Brighton & Hove A	Bognor Regis T	02.87	86-93	173	34	7

CRUSE Peter Leonard
Camden, 10 January, 1951 EAmat (M)

League Club	Source	Date Signed	Seasons Played	Apps	Subs	Gls
Arsenal	Slough T	04.72				
Luton T	Tr	07.73	73	3	1	0
Shrewsbury T	L	02.74	73	2	0	0

CRUTCHLEY Wilfred **Ronald (Ron)**
Walsall, 20 June, 1922 Died 1987 (WH)

League Club	Source	Date Signed	Seasons Played	Apps	Subs	Gls
Walsall	Hilary Street OB	03.45	46-49	62	-	3
Shrewsbury T	Tr	09.50	50-53	146	-	1

CRUYFF Jordi
Amsterdam, Holland, 9 February, 1974 Holland 9 (F)

League Club	Source	Date Signed	Seasons Played	Apps	Subs	Gls
Manchester U	Barcelona (Sp)	08.96	96-99	15	19	8

CRYAN Colin
Dublin, 23 March, 1981 IRu21-5 (CD)

League Club	Source	Date Signed	Seasons Played	Apps	Subs	Gls
Sheffield U	YT	08.99	00-03	0	5	0

CRYLE George
Aberdeen, 10 April, 1928 (WH)

League Club	Source	Date Signed	Seasons Played	Apps	Subs	Gls
Wolverhampton W	Jnrs	02.46				
Reading	Tr	06.48	48-50	8	-	2
Swindon T	Ayr U	08.52	52	12	-	0

CUBIE Neil George
Cape Town, South Africa, 3 November, 1932 (FB)

League Club	Source	Date Signed	Seasons Played	Apps	Subs	Gls
Bury	Clyde (SA)	10.56				
Hull C	Tr	07.57	57	4	-	0

CUDDIHEY Russell Francis
Rawtenstall, 8 September, 1939 (WH)

League Club	Source	Date Signed	Seasons Played	Apps	Subs	Gls
Accrington St		09.60	60	10	-	0

CUDDY Paul
Kendal, 21 February, 1959 ESemiPro (FB)

League Club	Source	Date Signed	Seasons Played	Apps	Subs	Gls
Rochdale	Jnrs	08.77	77	0	1	0

CUDICINI Carlo
Milan, Italy, 6 September, 1973 ItYth/Itu21 (G)

League Club	Source	Date Signed	Seasons Played	Apps	Subs	Gls
Chelsea	Castel di Sangro (It)	08.99	99-04	116	2	0

CUERVO Philippe
Ris-Orangis, France, 13 August, 1969 (M)

League Club	Source	Date Signed	Seasons Played	Apps	Subs	Gls
Swindon T	St Etienne (Fr)	08.97	97-99	16	19	0

CUFF Patrick (Pat) Joseph
Middlesbrough, 19 March, 1952 ESch (G)

League Club	Source	Date Signed	Seasons Played	Apps	Subs	Gls
Middlesbrough	App	05.69	73-77	31	0	0
Grimsby T	L	09.71	71	2	0	0
Millwall	Tr	08.78	78	42	0	0
Darlington	Tr	06.80	80-82	110	0	0

CUGGY Michael **Steven (Steve)**
Wallsend, 18 March, 1971 (F)

League Club	Source	Date Signed	Seasons Played	Apps	Subs	Gls
Maidstone U	Blyth Spartans	06.91	91	1	12	1

CULKIN Nicholas (Nick) James
York, 6 July, 1978 (G)

League Club	Source	Date Signed	Seasons Played	Apps	Subs	Gls
Manchester U	York C (YT)	09.95	99	0	1	0
Hull C	L	12.99	99	4	0	0
Bristol Rov	L	07.00	00	45	0	0
Queens Park Rgrs	Tr	07.02	02-03	22	0	0

CULLEN Anthony (Tony) Scott
Gateshead, 30 September, 1969 (W)

League Club	Source	Date Signed	Seasons Played	Apps	Subs	Gls
Sunderland	Newcastle U (YT)	09.88	88-91	11	18	0
Carlisle U	L	12.89	89	2	0	1
Rotherham U	L	01.91	90	3	0	1
Bury	L	10.91	91	4	0	0
Swansea C	Tr	08.92	92	20	7	3

CULLEN David **Jonathan (Jon)**
Bishop Auckland, 10 January, 1973 (M)

League Club	Source	Date Signed	Seasons Played	Apps	Subs	Gls
Doncaster Rov	YT	09.91	90-91	8	1	0
Hartlepool U	Morpeth T	03.97	96-97	33	1	12
Sheffield U	Tr	01.98	97-98	0	4	0
Shrewsbury T	L	09.99	99	10	0	1
Halifax T	L	12.99	99	11	0	5
Peterborough U	Tr	03.00	99-01	34	10	5
Carlisle U	L	03.01	00	10	1	0
Darlington	Tr	08.02	02	2	1	0

CULLEN Shane **Jonathan (Jon)** Raymond
Oxford, 9 October, 1962 (FB)

League Club	Source	Date Signed	Seasons Played	Apps	Subs	Gls
Reading	App	10.80	79-81	14	6	0

CULLEN Michael (Mick) Joseph
Glasgow, 3 July, 1931 SB/S-1 (IF)

League Club	Source	Date Signed	Seasons Played	Apps	Subs	Gls
Luton T	Douglasdale Jnrs	08.49	51-57	112	-	17
Grimsby T	Tr	04.58	58-62	178	-	35
Derby Co	Tr	12.62	62-64	24	-	5

CULLEN Patrick (Pat) Joseph
Mexborough, 9 August, 1949 IRAmat (F)

League Club	Source	Date Signed	Seasons Played	Apps	Subs	Gls
Halifax T	Mexborough	05.68	67-73	1	5	0

CULLERTON Michael (Mike) Joseph
Edinburgh, 25 November, 1948 (F)

League Club	Source	Date Signed	Seasons Played	Apps	Subs	Gls
Port Vale		01.66	65-68	95	2	22
Chester	L	03.69	68	5	2	0
Derby Co	Tr	07.69				
Port Vale	Stafford Rgrs	07.75	75-77	67	16	28

CULLING Gary
Braintree, 6 April, 1972 (FB)

League Club	Source	Date Signed	Seasons Played	Apps	Subs	Gls
Colchester U	Braintree T	08.94	94	2	0	0

CULLINGFORD Robert
Bradford, 3 December, 1953 ESch (CD)

League Club	Source	Date Signed	Seasons Played	Apps	Subs	Gls
Bradford C (Am)	Jnrs	10.69	69-71	1	1	0

CULLIP Daniel (Danny)
Bracknell, 17 September, 1976 (CD)

League Club	Source	Date Signed	Seasons Played	Apps	Subs	Gls
Oxford U	YT	07.95				
Fulham	Tr	07.96	96-97	41	9	2
Brentford	Tr	02.98	97-98	15	0	0
Brighton & Hove A	Tr	09.99	99-04	216	1	7
Sheffield U	Tr	12.04	04	11	0	0
Watford	L	03.05	04	4	0	0

CULLIS Stanley (Stan)
Ellesmere Port, 25 October, 1915 Died 2001 FLge-3/EWar-20/E-12 (CD)

League Club	Source	Date Signed	Seasons Played	Apps	Subs	Gls
Wolverhampton W	Ellesmere Port Wed	02.34	34-46	152	-	0

CULLUM Arthur **Richard (Dick)**
Colchester, 28 January, 1931 (CF)

League Club	Source	Date Signed	Seasons Played	Apps	Subs	Gls
Colchester U		01.51	50-53	2	-	1

CULLUM Riley Granville
West Ham, 2 April, 1923 Died 1996 (IF)

League Club	Source	Date Signed	Seasons Played	Apps	Subs	Gls
Charlton Ath	Dartford	10.47	49-52	32	-	6

CULPIN Paul
Kirby Muxloe, 8 February, 1962 ESemiPro (F)

League Club	Source	Date Signed	Seasons Played	Apps	Subs	Gls
Leicester C	Jnrs	05.81				
Coventry C	Nuneaton Borough	06.85	85-86	5	4	2
Northampton T	Tr	10.87	87-89	52	11	23
Peterborough U	Tr	10.89	89-91	30	17	14
Hereford U	Tr	02.92	91	1	1	0

CULVERHOUSE Ian Brett
Bishops Stortford, 22 September, 1964 EYth (FB)

League Club	Source	Date Signed	Seasons Played	Apps	Subs	Gls
Tottenham H	App	09.82	83	1	1	0
Norwich C	Tr	10.85	85-93	295	1	1
Swindon T	Tr	12.94	94-97	95	2	0
Brighton & Hove A	Kingstonian	09.98	98-99	36	0	0

CUMBES James (Jim)
Didsbury, 4 May, 1944 (G)

League Club	Source	Date Signed	Seasons Played	Apps	Subs	Gls
Tranmere Rov	Runcorn	09.65	66-69	136	0	0
West Bromwich A	Tr	08.69	69-71	64	0	0
Aston Villa	Tr	10.71	71-75	157	0	0
Southport	Runcorn	01.78	77	19	0	0

CUMMING David (Dave) Scott
Aberdeen, 6 May, 1910 Died 1993 SWar-1/S-1 (G)

League Club	Source	Date Signed	Seasons Played	Apps	Subs	Gls
Middlesbrough	Arbroath	10.36	36-46	135	-	0

CUMMING Gordon Robert Riddell
Johnstone, 23 January, 1948 (M)

League Club	Source	Date Signed	Seasons Played	Apps	Subs	Gls
Arsenal	Glasgow U	01.65				
Reading	Tr	12.69	69-77	277	18	51

CUMMING Robert (Bobby)
Airdrie, 7 December, 1955 (W)

League Club	Source	Date Signed	Seasons Played	Apps	Subs	Gls
Grimsby T	Baillieston Jnrs	03.74	74-86	338	27	57
Lincoln C	Tr	07.87	88-89	40	1	5

CUMMINGS George Wilfred
Thornbridge, 5 June, 1913 Died 1987 SLge-2/SWar-1/S-9 (FB)

League Club	Source	Date Signed	Seasons Played	Apps	Subs	Gls
Aston Villa	Partick Th	11.35	35-48	210	-	0

CUMMINGS John
Greenock, 5 May, 1944 (CF)

League Club	Source	Date Signed	Seasons Played	Apps	Subs	Gls
Port Vale	Aberdeen	08.65	65	2	1	0

CUMMINGS Robert (Bobby) Douglas
Ashington, 17 November, 1935 (F)

League Club	Source	Date Signed	Seasons Played	Apps	Subs	Gls
Newcastle U	New Hartley Jnrs	05.54				
Newcastle U	Aberdeen	10.63	63-65	43	1	14
Darlington	Tr	10.65	65-67	73	1	43
Hartlepools U	Tr	02.68	67-68	48	4	12

League Club	Source	Date Signed	Seasons Played	Career Record Apps	Subs	Gls
CUMMINGS Thomas (Tommy) Smith						
Castledown, 12 September, 1928 EB/FLge-1						(CD)
Burnley	Stanley U	10.47	48-62	434	-	3
Mansfield T	Tr	03.63	62-63	10	-	0
CUMMINGS Warren						
Aberdeen, 15 October, 1980 Su21-9/S-1						(FB)
Chelsea	YT	07.99				
Bournemouth	L	10.00	00	10	0	1
West Bromwich A	L	03.01	00	1	2	0
West Bromwich A	L	07.01	01	6	8	0
Bournemouth	Tr	02.03	02-04	92	0	4
CUMMINS George Patrick						
Dublin, 12 March, 1931 IR-19						(IF)
Everton	St Patrick's Ath	11.50	51-52	24	-	0
Luton T	Tr	08.53	53-60	184	-	21
Hull C	Cambridge C	11.62	62-63	21	-	2
CUMMINS James (Jimmy) William Heywood						
Hebburn, 15 February, 1925 Died 1981						(CF)
Southport	Horden CW	09.49	49	9	-	1
CUMMINS Michael (Micky) Thomas						
Dublin, 1 June, 1978 IRYth/IRu21-2						(M)
Middlesbrough	YT	07.95	98-99	1	1	0
Port Vale	Tr	03.00	99-04	211	3	21
CUMMINS Stanley (Stan)						
Ferryhill, 6 December, 1958						(F)
Middlesbrough	App	12.76	76-79	39	4	9
Sunderland	Tr	11.79	79-82	132	1	29
Crystal Palace	Tr	08.83	83-84	27	1	7
Sunderland	Tr	10.84	84	13	4	0
CUMNER Reginald **Horace**						
Cwmaman, 31 March, 1918 Died 1999 WWar-10/W-3						(W)
Arsenal	Aberaman Ath	05.36	38	12	-	2
Hull C	L	01.38	37	12	-	4
Notts Co	Tr	08.46	46-47	66	-	11
Watford	Tr	07.48	48-50	62	-	7
Scunthorpe U	Tr	09.50	50-52	102	-	21
CUNDY Jason Victor						
Wandsworth, 12 November, 1969 Eu21-3						(CD)
Chelsea	YT	08.88	90-91	40	1	2
Tottenham H	Tr	03.92	91-95	23	3	1
Crystal Palace	L	12.95	95	4	0	0
Bristol C	L	08.96	96	6	0	1
Ipswich T	Tr	10.96	96-98	54	4	5
Portsmouth	Tr	07.99	99	9	0	0
CUNLIFFE Arthur						
Blackrod, 5 February, 1909 Died 1986 E-2						(W)
Blackburn Rov	Chorley	01.28	29-32	129	-	47
Aston Villa	Tr	05.33	32-35	69	-	11
Middlesbrough	Tr	12.35	35-36	27	-	5
Burnley	Tr	04.37	37	9	-	0
Hull C	Tr	06.38	38	42	-	20
Rochdale	Tr	08.45	46	23	-	5
CUNLIFFE James **Graham**						
Hindley, 16 June, 1936						(WH)
Bolton W		01.55	57-62	25	-	0
Rochdale	Tr	07.64	64	36	-	0
CUNLIFFE James (Jim)						
Adlington, 4 October, 1941						(CF)
Stockport Co (Am)	Horwich RMI	11.60	60	1	-	0
CUNLIFFE James (Jimmy) Nathaniel						
Blackrod, 5 July, 1912 Died 1986 E-1						(IF)
Everton	Adlington	05.30	32-38	174	-	73
Rochdale	Tr	09.46	46	2	-	0
CUNLIFFE John (Jack)						
Wigan, 4 February, 1930 Died 1975						(W)
Port Vale		12.50	50-59	283	-	52
Stoke C	Tr	09.59	59	25	-	3
CUNLIFFE Reginald (Reg)						
Wigan, 4 December, 1920 Died 2000						(FB)
Swansea T	Wigan Ath	06.46	46-47	2	-	0
CUNLIFFE Robert (Bobby)						
Manchester, 17 May, 1945						(IF)
Manchester C	App	08.62	63	3	-	1
York C	Tr	06.65	65	11	1	2
CUNLIFFE Robert (Bobby) Arthur						
Garswood, 27 December, 1928 Died 2000						(W)
Manchester C	Haydock C & B	01.46	49-55	44	-	9

League Club	Source	Date Signed	Seasons Played	Career Record Apps	Subs	Gls
Chesterfield	Tr	06.56	56-57	62	-	19
Southport	Tr	07.58	58	17	-	2
CUNNING Robert (Bobby) Robertson Innes						
Dunfermline, 12 February, 1930						(W)
Sunderland	Port Glasgow Ath	06.50	50	5	-	0
CUNNINGHAM Anthony (Tony) Eugene						
Kingston, Jamaica, 12 November, 1957						(F)
Lincoln C	Stourbridge	05.79	79-82	111	12	32
Barnsley	Tr	09.82	82-83	40	2	11
Sheffield Wed	Tr	11.83	83	26	2	5
Manchester C	Tr	07.84	84	16	2	1
Newcastle U	Tr	02.85	84-86	37	10	4
Blackpool	Tr	07.87	87-88	71	0	17
Bury	Tr	07.89	89-90	55	3	17
Bolton W	Tr	03.91	90	9	0	4
Rotherham U	Tr	08.91	91-92	65	5	24
Doncaster Rov	Tr	07.93	93	19	6	1
Wycombe W	Tr	03.94	93	4	1	0
CUNNINGHAM David (Dave)						
Kirkcaldy, 10 August, 1953						(W)
Southend U	Brechin C	04.73	73-76	55	4	4
Hartlepool	L	03.77	76	10	2	1
Swindon T	Tr	06.77	77-78	18	5	3
Peterborough U	L	11.78	78	4	0	1
Aston Villa	Tr	12.78				
Hereford U	Tr	08.79	79	28	2	2
CUNNINGHAM Edward Milburn						
South Shields, 20 March, 1928						(WH)
Blackburn Rov		09.49				
Chesterfield	North Shields	08.52	52-54	56	-	0
CUNNINGHAM Edwin Burnhope						
Jarrow, 20 September, 1919 Died 1993						(W)
Bristol C		05.39	46	1	-	0
CUNNINGHAM Daniel **Harvey**						
Manchester, 11 September, 1968						(W)
Doncaster Rov	Droylsden	02.97	96-97	43	1	1
CUNNINGHAM Hugh						
Kirkintilloch, 5 April, 1947						(M)
Fulham	Glasgow Celtic	05.66	67	0	1	0
CUNNINGHAM Ian						
Glasgow, 6 September, 1956						(FB)
Bournemouth	App	08.74	74-80	180	8	4
CUNNINGHAM John						
Derry, 30 November, 1966 NIYth						(M)
Mansfield T	Jnrs	08.84	84	3	1	0
CUNNINGHAM Kenneth (Kenny) Edward						
Dublin, 28 June, 1971 IRYth/IRu21-4/IRB-2/IR-68						(FB)
Millwall	Tolka Rov	09.89	89-94	132	4	1
Wimbledon	Tr	11.94	94-01	249	1	0
Birmingham C	Tr	07.02	02-04	103	0	0
CUNNINGHAM Kenneth (Ken) Rankin						
Glasgow, 26 October, 1941						(CF)
Hartlepools U	Falkirk	07.63	63	2	-	0
CUNNINGHAM Laurence (Laurie)						
Consett, 20 October, 1921						(FB)
Barnsley	Consett	11.45	46-47	51	-	1
Bournemouth	Tr	06.48	48-56	273	-	0
CUNNINGHAM Lawrence (Laurie) Paul						
Archway, 8 March, 1956 Died 1989 Eu21-6/E-6						(W)
Orient	App	07.74	74-76	72	3	15
West Bromwich A	Tr	03.77	76-78	81	5	21
Manchester U	Real Madrid (Sp)	03.83	82	3	2	1
Leicester C	Marseille (Fr)	10.85	85	13	2	0
Wimbledon	RSC Charleroi (Bel)	02.88	87	6	0	2
CUNNINGHAM Thomas (Tommy) Edward						
Bethnal Green, 7 December, 1955						(CD)
Chelsea	App	10.73				
Queens Park Rgrs	Tr	05.75	76-78	27	3	2
Wimbledon	Tr	03.79	78-81	99	0	12
Orient	Tr	09.81	81-86	162	0	17
CUNNINGHAM William (Willie) Carruthers						
Hill o' Beath, 22 February, 1925 Died 2000 S-8						(FB)
Preston NE	Airdrie	07.49	49-62	440	-	3
Southport	Tr	03.64	64	12	-	0

CUNNINGHAM William (Willie) Edward
Mallusk, 20 February, 1930 I-2/NI-28 (FB)

League Club	Source	Date Signed	Seasons Played	Apps	Subs	Gls
Leicester C	St Mirren	12.54	54-59	127	-	4

CUNNINGHAM William (Willie) Livingstone
Paisley, 11 July, 1938 (WH)

League Club	Source	Date Signed	Seasons Played	Apps	Subs	Gls
Barnsley	Third Lanark	07.64	64	24	-	0

CUNNINGTON Shaun Gary
Bourne, 4 January, 1966 (M)

League Club	Source	Date Signed	Seasons Played	Apps	Subs	Gls
Wrexham	Bourne T	01.84	82-87	196	3	12
Grimsby T	Tr	02.88	87-91	182	0	13
Sunderland	Tr	07.92	92-94	52	6	8
West Bromwich A	Tr	08.95	95-96	8	5	0
Notts Co	Tr	03.97	96-97	9	8	0

CURBISHLEY Llewellyn (Alan) Charles
Forest Gate, 8 November, 1957 ESch/EYth/Eu21-1 (M)

League Club	Source	Date Signed	Seasons Played	Apps	Subs	Gls
West Ham U	App	08.75	74-78	78	7	5
Birmingham C	Tr	07.79	79-82	128	2	11
Aston Villa	Tr	03.83	82-84	34	2	1
Charlton Ath	Tr	12.84	84-86	62	1	6
Brighton & Hove A	Tr	08.87	87-89	111	5	13
Charlton Ath	Tr	07.90	90-93	22	6	0

CURCIC Sasa
Belgrade, Yugoslavia, 14 February, 1972 Yugoslavia 14 (M)

League Club	Source	Date Signed	Seasons Played	Apps	Subs	Gls
Bolton W	Partizan Belgrade (Yug)	10.95	95	28	0	4
Aston Villa	Tr	08.96	96-97	20	9	0
Crystal Palace	Tr	03.98	97-98	10	13	5

CURETON Jamie
Bristol, 28 August, 1975 EYth (F)

League Club	Source	Date Signed	Seasons Played	Apps	Subs	Gls
Norwich C	YT	02.93	94-95	13	16	6
Bournemouth	L	09.95	95	0	5	0
Bristol Rov	Tr	09.96	96-00	165	9	72
Reading	Tr	08.00	00-02	74	34	50
Queens Park Rgrs	Busan Icons (SK)	02.04	03-04	20	23	6

CURLE Keith
Bristol, 14 November, 1963 EB-4/FLge/E-3 (CD)

League Club	Source	Date Signed	Seasons Played	Apps	Subs	Gls
Bristol Rov	App	11.81	81-82	21	11	4
Torquay U	Tr	11.83	83	16	0	5
Bristol C	Tr	03.84	83-87	113	8	1
Reading	Tr	10.87	87-88	40	0	0
Wimbledon	Tr	10.88	88-90	91	2	3
Manchester C	Tr	08.91	91-95	171	0	11
Wolverhampton W	Tr	08.96	96-99	148	2	9
Sheffield U	Tr	07.00	00-01	53	4	1
Barnsley	Tr	08.02	02	11	0	0
Mansfield T	Tr	12.02	02	11	3	0

CURLE Thomas (Tom) Keith
Bristol, 3 March, 1986 (M)

League Club	Source	Date Signed	Seasons Played	Apps	Subs	Gls
Mansfield T	Sch	•	03	0	1	0

CURLEY Thomas (Tommy)
Glasgow, 11 June, 1945 (W)

League Club	Source	Date Signed	Seasons Played	Apps	Subs	Gls
Brentford	Glasgow Celtic	08.65	65-66	40	0	6
Crewe Alex	Hastings U	08.67	67-68	49	3	7

CURLEY William (Billy)
Trimdon, 20 November, 1945 (FB)

League Club	Source	Date Signed	Seasons Played	Apps	Subs	Gls
Darlington	App	11.63	62-64	28	-	1

CURRAN Christopher (Chris)
Birmingham, 17 September, 1971 (CD)

League Club	Source	Date Signed	Seasons Played	Apps	Subs	Gls
Torquay U	YT	07.90	89-95	144	8	4
Plymouth Arg	Tr	12.95	95-96	26	4	0
Exeter C	Tr	07.97	97-02	146	11	6

CURRAN Christopher (Chris) Patrick
Heywood, 6 January, 1971 (CD)

League Club	Source	Date Signed	Seasons Played	Apps	Subs	Gls
Crewe Alex	YT	09.89	89-90	2	3	0
Scarborough	Tr	03.92	91-92	40	0	4
Carlisle U	Tr	07.93	93	4	2	1

CURRAN Daniel (Danny) Lee James
Brentwood, 13 June, 1981 (F)

League Club	Source	Date Signed	Seasons Played	Apps	Subs	Gls
Leyton Orient	YT	07.99	98	0	1	0

CURRAN Edward (Terry)
Kinsley, 20 March, 1955 (W)

League Club	Source	Date Signed	Seasons Played	Apps	Subs	Gls
Doncaster Rov	Jnrs	07.73	73-75	67	1	11
Nottingham F	Tr	08.75	75-76	46	2	12
Bury	L	10.77	77	2	0	0
Derby Co	Tr	11.77	77	26	0	2
Southampton	Tr	08.78	78	25	1	0
Sheffield Wed	Tr	03.79	78-81	122	3	35
Sheffield U	Tr	08.82	82	31	2	3
Everton	L	12.82	82	7	0	1
Everton	Tr	09.83	83-84	12	4	0
Huddersfield T	Tr	07.85	85	33	1	7
Hull C	Panionios	10.86	86	4	0	0
Sunderland	Tr	11.86	86	9	0	1
Grimsby T	Grantham T	11.87	87	10	2	0
Chesterfield	Tr	03.88	87	0	1	0

CURRAN Frank
Ryton-on-Tyne, 31 May, 1917 Died 1998 (IF)

League Club	Source	Date Signed	Seasons Played	Apps	Subs	Gls
Southport	Washington Colliery	08.35	35-36	16	-	3
Accrington St	Tr	02.37	36-37	34	-	14
Bristol Rov	Tr	06.38	38	27	-	21
Bristol C	Tr	05.39				
Bristol Rov	Tr	05.46	46	10	-	3
Tranmere Rov	Shrewsbury T	06.47	47	17	-	7

CURRAN Hugh Patrick
Glasgow, 25 September, 1943 S-5 (F)

League Club	Source	Date Signed	Seasons Played	Apps	Subs	Gls
Millwall	Corby T	03.64	63-65	57	0	26
Norwich C	Tr	01.66	65-68	112	0	46
Wolverhampton W	Tr	01.69	68-71	77	5	40
Oxford U	Tr	09.72	72-74	69	1	28
Bolton W	Tr	09.74	74-76	40	7	13
Oxford U	Tr	07.77	77-78	30	5	11

CURRAN James (Jimmy)
Macclesfield, 24 September, 1947 (G)

League Club	Source	Date Signed	Seasons Played	Apps	Subs	Gls
Newcastle U	Jnrs	10.64				
Oldham Ath		12.66	66	3	0	0
Crewe Alex	Tr	04.67	68	3	0	0

CURRAN John (Johnny)
Glasgow, 22 June, 1924 Died 1985 (G)

League Club	Source	Date Signed	Seasons Played	Apps	Subs	Gls
Shrewsbury T	East Fife	08.56	56	24	-	0
Watford	Tr	06.57	57	30	-	0

CURRAN Patrick (Pat) Joseph
Sunderland, 13 November, 1917 Died 2003 (IF)

League Club	Source	Date Signed	Seasons Played	Apps	Subs	Gls
Sunderland	Sunderland St Pat's	10.36	37	1	-	0
Ipswich T	Tr	10.38	38	7	-	1
Watford	Tr	06.39				
Bradford C	Tr	06.47	47	5	-	1

CURRAN Terence (Terry) William
Staines, 29 June, 1940 Died 2000 (IF)

League Club	Source	Date Signed	Seasons Played	Apps	Subs	Gls
Brentford	Tottenham H (Am)	09.57	60	5	-	0

CURRIE Anthony (Tony) William
Edgware, 1 January, 1950 EYth/Eu23-13/FLge-3/E-17 (M)

League Club	Source	Date Signed	Seasons Played	Apps	Subs	Gls
Watford	App	05.67	67	17	1	9
Sheffield U	Tr	02.68	67-75	313	0	54
Leeds U	Tr	06.76	76-78	102	0	11
Queens Park Rgrs	Tr	08.79	79-82	79	2	5
Torquay U	Chesham U	02.84	83-84	14	0	1

CURRIE Charles (Charlie)
Belfast, 17 April, 1920 IrLge-6 (WH)

League Club	Source	Date Signed	Seasons Played	Apps	Subs	Gls
Bradford PA	Belfast Celtic	06.49	49-53	118	-	2

CURRIE Darren Paul
Hampstead, 29 November, 1974 (W)

League Club	Source	Date Signed	Seasons Played	Apps	Subs	Gls
West Ham U	YT	07.93				
Shrewsbury T	L	09.94	94	10	2	2
Shrewsbury T	L	02.95	94	5	0	0
Leyton Orient	L	11.95	95	9	1	0
Shrewsbury T	Tr	02.96	95-97	46	20	8
Plymouth Arg	Tr	03.98	97	5	2	0
Barnet	Tr	07.98	98-00	120	7	19
Wycombe W	Tr	07.01	01-03	109	17	14
Brighton & Hove A	Tr	08.04	04	21	1	2
Ipswich T	Tr	12.04	04	19	5	3

CURRIE David Norman
Stockton, 27 November, 1962 (F)

League Club	Source	Date Signed	Seasons Played	Apps	Subs	Gls
Middlesbrough		02.82	81-85	94	19	30
Darlington	Tr	06.86	86-87	76	0	33
Barnsley	Tr	02.88	87-89	80	0	30
Nottingham F	Tr	01.90	89	4	4	1
Oldham Ath	Tr	08.90	90-91	17	14	3
Barnsley	Tr	09.91	91-93	53	22	12
Rotherham U	L	10.92	92	5	0	2
Huddersfield T	L	01.94	93	7	0	1
Carlisle U	Tr	07.94	94-96	84	5	14
Scarborough	Tr	01.97	96	16	0	6

CURRIE James (Jimmy) Adam Campbell
Glasgow, 25 April, 1932 Died 1998 (CF)

League Club	Source	Date Signed	Seasons Played	Apps	Subs	Gls
Exeter C	Falkirk	06.56	56-57	54	-	19
Workington	Tr	10.57	57-59	23	-	8

League Club	Source	Date Signed	Seasons Played	Apps	Subs	Gls

CURRIE James (Jim) Thomson
Bridge of Allan, 6 August, 1948 (M)

League Club	Source	Date Signed	Seasons Played	Apps	Subs	Gls
Scunthorpe U		09.68	68-69	4	2	0

CURRIE John (Jack)
Motherwell, 19 March, 1935 (IF)

League Club	Source	Date Signed	Seasons Played	Apps	Subs	Gls
Accrington St	Cleland Jnrs	11.53	53-54	16	-	3

CURRIE John Edward
Liverpool, 18 March, 1921 Died 1984 (W)

League Club	Source	Date Signed	Seasons Played	Apps	Subs	Gls
Bournemouth (Am)	Stafford Rgrs	10.46	46	7	-	1
Port Vale	Tr	06.47	47	9	-	0

CURRIE John Gemmell
Dumfries, 7 April, 1939 SSch (WH)

League Club	Source	Date Signed	Seasons Played	Apps	Subs	Gls
Leicester C	Jnrs	04.57				
Workington	Tr	07.61	61-62	55	-	2
Chester	Tr	07.63	63	2	-	0

CURRIE Malcolm
Rutherglen, 5 February, 1932 Died 1996 (FB)

League Club	Source	Date Signed	Seasons Played	Apps	Subs	Gls
Bradford C	Rutherglen Glencairn	07.56	56-60	136	-	1

CURRY Robert (Bob)
Gateshead, 2 November, 1918 Died 2001 (IF)

League Club	Source	Date Signed	Seasons Played	Apps	Subs	Gls
Sheffield Wed	Gateshead (Am)	10.37	37	1	-	0
Colchester U	Gainsborough Trinity	(N/L)	50	32	-	13

CURRY Sean Patrick
Liverpool, 13 November, 1966 (F)

League Club	Source	Date Signed	Seasons Played	Apps	Subs	Gls
Liverpool	App	07.84				
Blackburn Rov	Tr	01.87	86-88	25	13	6
Hartlepool U	Tr	08.89	89	0	1	0

CURRY William (Bill) Morton
Walker, 12 October, 1935 Died 1990 Eu23-1 (F)

League Club	Source	Date Signed	Seasons Played	Apps	Subs	Gls
Newcastle U	Jnrs	10.53	54-58	80	-	36
Brighton & Hove A	Tr	07.59	59-60	49	-	26
Derby Co	Tr	10.60	60-64	148	-	67
Mansfield T	Tr	02.65	64-67	102	0	53
Chesterfield	Tr	01.68	67-68	14	0	2

CURTIN Douglas (Doug) James
Cardiff, 15 September, 1947 WSch (W)

League Club	Source	Date Signed	Seasons Played	Apps	Subs	Gls
Mansfield T	Cardiff C (App)	11.65	65	3	0	0

CURTIS Alan Thomas
Ton Pentre, 16 April, 1954 Wu23-1/Wu21-1/W-35 (F)

League Club	Source	Date Signed	Seasons Played	Apps	Subs	Gls
Swansea C	Jnrs	07.72	72-78	244	4	71
Leeds U	Tr	06.79	79-80	28	0	5
Swansea C	Tr	12.80	80-83	82	8	21
Southampton	Tr	11.83	83-85	43	7	5
Stoke C	L	03.86	85	3	0	0
Cardiff C	Tr	07.86	86-89	122	3	10
Swansea C	Tr	10.89	89	21	5	3

CURTIS Andrew (Andy)
Doncaster, 2 December, 1972 (W)

League Club	Source	Date Signed	Seasons Played	Apps	Subs	Gls
York C	YT	07.91	90-91	6	6	0
Peterborough U	Kettering T	09.92	92	8	3	1
York C	(Retired)	07.95	95	0	1	0
Scarborough	Tr	01.96	95	3	2	0

CURTIS Dermot Patrick
Dublin, 26 August, 1932 LoI-2/IR-17 (F)

League Club	Source	Date Signed	Seasons Played	Apps	Subs	Gls
Bristol C	Shelbourne	12.56	56-57	26	-	16
Ipswich T	Tr	09.58	58-62	41	-	17
Exeter C	Tr	08.63	63-65	91	0	23
Torquay U	Tr	08.66	66	12	0	1
Exeter C	Tr	06.67	67-68	64	2	10

CURTIS George Edward
West Thurrock, 3 December, 1919 Died 2004 (IF)

League Club	Source	Date Signed	Seasons Played	Apps	Subs	Gls
Arsenal	Anglo (Purfleet)	04.37	38-46	13	-	0
Southampton	Tr	08.47	47-51	174	-	11

CURTIS George William
Dover, 5 May, 1939 EYth (CD)

League Club	Source	Date Signed	Seasons Played	Apps	Subs	Gls
Coventry C	Snowdown CW	05.56	55-69	483	4	11
Aston Villa	Tr	12.69	69-71	51	0	3

CURTIS John
Poulton-le-Fylde, 2 September, 1954 (FB)

League Club	Source	Date Signed	Seasons Played	Apps	Subs	Gls
Blackpool	App	09.72	73-76	96	6	0
Blackburn Rov	Tr	07.77	77-78	9	1	0
Wigan Ath	Tr	03.79	78-80	32	0	0

CURTIS John Charles Keyworth
Nuneaton, 3 September, 1978 ESch/EYth/Eu21-16/EB-1 (FB)

League Club	Source	Date Signed	Seasons Played	Apps	Subs	Gls
Manchester U	YT	10.95	97-99	4	9	0
Barnsley	L	11.99	99	28	0	2
Blackburn Rov	Tr	06.00	00-02	61	0	0
Sheffield U	L	03.03	02	9	3	0
Leicester C	Tr	08.03	03	14	1	0
Portsmouth	Tr	02.04	03-04	5	2	0
Preston NE	L	09.04	04	12	0	0
Nottingham F	Tr	02.05	04	11	0	0

CURTIS William Norman
Dinnington, 10 September, 1924 (FB)

League Club	Source	Date Signed	Seasons Played	Apps	Subs	Gls
Sheffield Wed	Gainsborough Trinity	01.50	50-59	310	-	21
Doncaster Rov	Tr	08.60	60	40	-	3

CURTIS Paul Anthony Ernest
Woolwich, 1 July, 1963 (FB)

League Club	Source	Date Signed	Seasons Played	Apps	Subs	Gls
Charlton Ath	App	07.81	82-84	69	3	5
Northampton T	Tr	07.85	85	27	0	1
Northampton T	Corby T	08.92	92	22	0	1

CURTIS Robert (Robbie) Anthony
Mansfield, 21 May, 1972 (CD)

League Club	Source	Date Signed	Seasons Played	Apps	Subs	Gls
Northampton T	Boston U	06.94	94	13	0	0

CURTIS Robert (Bob) Dennis
Langwith, 25 January, 1950 (FB)

League Club	Source	Date Signed	Seasons Played	Apps	Subs	Gls
Charlton Ath	App	02.67	66-77	324	13	35
Mansfield T	Tr	02.78	77-79	69	4	7

CURTIS Thomas (Tommy) David
Exeter, 1 March, 1973 (M)

League Club	Source	Date Signed	Seasons Played	Apps	Subs	Gls
Derby Co	Jnrs	07.91				
Chesterfield	Tr	08.93	93-99	235	5	12
Portsmouth	Tr	08.00	00-01	7	6	0
Walsall	L	09.01	01	3	1	0
Tranmere Rov	L	08.02	02	8	0	0
Mansfield T	Tr	12.02	02-04	83	10	0

CURTIS Mark Wayne
Neath, 22 February, 1967 (FB)

League Club	Source	Date Signed	Seasons Played	Apps	Subs	Gls
Cardiff C	Swansea C (Jnrs)	10.84	85	24	3	2

CURWEN Eric
Blackpool, 16 September, 1947 ESch (FB)

League Club	Source	Date Signed	Seasons Played	Apps	Subs	Gls
Everton	App	05.65				
Southport	Tr	12.66	66-68	89	0	0

CURZON Terence (Terry)
Winsford, 26 May, 1936 (W)

League Club	Source	Date Signed	Seasons Played	Apps	Subs	Gls
Crewe Alex	Bolton W (Am)	10.53	53-56	11	-	1

CUSACK David (Dave) Stephen
Thurcroft, 6 June, 1956 (CD)

League Club	Source	Date Signed	Seasons Played	Apps	Subs	Gls
Sheffield Wed	App	06.74	75-77	92	3	1
Southend U	Tr	09.78	78-82	186	0	17
Millwall	Tr	03.83	82-84	98	0	9
Doncaster Rov	Tr	07.85	85-87	100	0	4
Rotherham U	Tr	12.87	87	18	0	0
Doncaster Rov	Boston U	08.89	89	1	0	0

CUSACK Nicholas (Nick) John
Maltby, 24 December, 1965 (M)

League Club	Source	Date Signed	Seasons Played	Apps	Subs	Gls
Leicester C	Alvechurch	06.87	87	5	11	1
Peterborough U	Tr	07.88	88	44	0	10
Darlington	Motherwell	01.92	91	21	0	6
Oxford U	Tr	07.92	92-94	48	13	10
Wycombe W	L	03.94	93	2	2	1
Fulham	Tr	11.94	94-97	109	7	14
Swansea C	Tr	10.97	97-02	184	14	13

CUSH Wilbur
Lurgan, 10 June, 1928 Died 1981 IrLge-32/I-2/NI-24 (WH)

League Club	Source	Date Signed	Seasons Played	Apps	Subs	Gls
Leeds U	Glenavon	11.57	57-59	87	-	9

CUSHIN Edward
Whitehaven, 27 January, 1927 Died 1985 (FB)

League Club	Source	Date Signed	Seasons Played	Apps	Subs	Gls
Workington	Lowca	(N/L)	51-55	119	-	4

CUSHLEY John
Blantyre, 21 January, 1943 (CD)

League Club	Source	Date Signed	Seasons Played	Apps	Subs	Gls
West Ham U	Glasgow Celtic	07.67	67-69	38	0	0

CUSHLOW Richard (Dick)
Shotton, 15 June, 1920 Died 2002 (CD)

League Club	Source	Date Signed	Seasons Played	Apps	Subs	Gls
Chesterfield	Murton CW	05.46	46-47	34	-	0
Sheffield U	Tr	12.47				
Derby Co	Tr	03.48	48-49	2	-	0
Crystal Palace	Tr	02.51	50-51	28	-	0

CUTBUSH William (John) John
Malta, 28 June, 1949 (FB)

League Club	Source	Date Signed	Seasons Played	Apps	Subs	Gls
Tottenham H	App	09.66				
Fulham	Tr	07.72	72-76	131	3	3
Sheffield U	Tr	03.77	76-80	126	3	1

CUTHBERT Ean Richardson
Hurlford, 5 February, 1942 (FB)

League Club	Source	Date Signed	Seasons Played	Apps	Subs	Gls
Blackpool	Alyth U	07.59				
Stockport Co	Tr	07.63	63-65	93	0	0
Crewe Alex	Bangor C	11.66	66	1	0	0

CUTHBERTSON James (Jimmy)
Sunderland, 7 December, 1947 (W)

League Club	Source	Date Signed	Seasons Played	Apps	Subs	Gls
Bradford C	App	07.66	66-67	25	3	7

CUTHBERTSON John
Glasgow, 10 March, 1932 (IF)

League Club	Source	Date Signed	Seasons Played	Apps	Subs	Gls
Mansfield T	App	10.53	53	3	-	0

CUTLER Christopher (Chris) Paul
Manchester, 7 April, 1964 (M)

League Club	Source	Date Signed	Seasons Played	Apps	Subs	Gls
Bury	Jnrs	08.81	81-84	8	15	3
Crewe Alex	Tr	08.85	85-89	116	24	24

CUTLER Neil Anthony
Cannock, 3 September, 1976 ESch/EYth (G)

League Club	Source	Date Signed	Seasons Played	Apps	Subs	Gls
West Bromwich A	YT	09.93				
Chester C	L	03.96	95	1	0	0
Crewe Alex	Tr	07.96				
Chester C	L	08.96	96	5	0	0
Chester C	Tr	07.98	98	23	0	0
Aston Villa	Tr	11.99	99	0	1	0
Oxford U	L	12.00	00	11	0	0
Stoke C	Tr	07.01	01-03	65	4	0
Swansea C	L	02.03	02	13	0	0
Stockport Co	Tr	07.04	04	22	0	0

CUTLER Paul
Welwyn Garden City, 18 June, 1946 (W)

League Club	Source	Date Signed	Seasons Played	Apps	Subs	Gls
Crystal Palace	App	04.64	64-65	10	0	1

CUTLER Reginald (Reg) Victor
Blackheath, Worcestershire, 17 February, 1935 (W)

League Club	Source	Date Signed	Seasons Played	Apps	Subs	Gls
West Bromwich A	Jnrs	02.52	51-54	5	-	0
Bournemouth	Tr	06.56	56-58	96	-	21
Portsmouth	Tr	09.58	58-61	100	-	13
Stockport Co	Tr	07.62	62	34	-	0

CUTTING Noel **Frederick (Fred)** Charles
North Walsham, 4 December, 1921 Died 1997 (IF)

League Club	Source	Date Signed	Seasons Played	Apps	Subs	Gls
Leicester C		01.46				
Norwich C	Tr	09.46				
Colchester U	Tr	12.47	50-51	29	-	12

CUTTING John (Jack) Andrew
Fleetwood, 15 April, 1924 Died 1985 (IF)

League Club	Source	Date Signed	Seasons Played	Apps	Subs	Gls
Oldham Ath		11.46	46	4	-	1
Accrington St	Fleetwood	06.48	48	23	-	5

CUTTING Stanley (Stan) William
St Faiths, 21 September, 1914 Died 2004 (WH)

League Club	Source	Date Signed	Seasons Played	Apps	Subs	Gls
Southampton	Norwich C (Am)	05.37	38	3	-	0
Exeter C	Tr	07.39	46-47	38	-	2

CYGAN Pascal
Lens, France, 19 April, 1974 (CD)

League Club	Source	Date Signed	Seasons Played	Apps	Subs	Gls
Arsenal	OSC Lille (Fr)	08.02	02-04	41	10	1

CYGAN Paul
Doncaster, 4 March, 1972 (M)

League Club	Source	Date Signed	Seasons Played	Apps	Subs	Gls
Doncaster Rov	YT	•	89	0	1	0

CYRUS Andrew (Andy) Daryl
Lambeth, 30 September, 1976 (FB)

League Club	Source	Date Signed	Seasons Played	Apps	Subs	Gls
Crystal Palace	YT	08.95	96	1	0	0
Exeter C	Tr	07.97	97	17	4	0

CZUCZMAN Mychaljo (Mike)
Carlisle, 27 May, 1953 (CD)

League Club	Source	Date Signed	Seasons Played	Apps	Subs	Gls
Grimsby T	Preston NE (App)	08.71	71-75	107	6	6
Scunthorpe U	Tr	08.76	76-78	115	0	1
Stockport Co	Tr	05.79	79	36	0	7
Grimsby T	San Jose (USA)	09.80	80-81	9	0	0
York C	Tr	11.81	81	17	0	0

League Club Source Date Signed Seasons Played Career Record Apps Subs Gls

League Club	Source	Date Signed	Seasons Played	Career Record Apps	Subs	Gls
DABELSTEEN Thomas						
Copenhagen, Denmark, 6 March, 1973						(M)
Scarborough	Kolding (Den)	11.98	98	5	0	1
DABIZAS Nikolaos (Nicos)						
Ptolemaida, Greece, 3 August, 1973 GrYth/Gru21/Gr-69						(CD)
Newcastle U	Olympiakos (Gre)	03.98	97-02	119	11	10
Leicester C	Tr	01.04	03-04	51	0	1
DA COSTA Hugo Alexandre						
Tramagal, Portugal, 4 November, 1973						(CD)
Stoke C	Amadora (Por)	08.96	96	1	1	0
DACOURT Olivier						
Montreuil-sous-Bois, France, 25 September, 1974 Fru21/Fr-9						(M)
Everton	RC Strasbourg (Fr)	06.98	98	28	2	2
Leeds U	RC Lens (Fr)	07.00	00-02	53	4	3
DADASON Rikhardur (Rikki)						
Reykjavik, Iceland, 26 April, 1972 IcYth/Icu21-10/Ic-40						(F)
Stoke C	Viking Stavanger (Nor)	10.00	00-01	19	20	10
DADI Eugene						
Abidjan, Ivory Coast, 20 August, 1973						(F)
Tranmere Rov	Livingston	08.03	03-04	44	25	25
DADLEY Peter Robin						
Farnham, 10 December, 1948						(W)
Aldershot	App	12.66	66	1	0	1
DAGG Henry (Harry) Cable						
Sunderland, 4 March, 1924						(CF)
Lincoln C (Am)	Boston U	12.46	46	1	-	1
DAGGER John Leslie **(Les)**						
Lostock Hall, 25 April, 1933						(W)
Preston NE	West Auckland	05.56	56-60	61	-	8
Carlisle U	Tr	06.61	61-62	74	-	9
Southport	Tr	07.63	63-64	81	-	9
DAGNALL Christopher (Chris)						
Liverpool, 15 April, 1986						(F)
Tranmere Rov	Sch	07.03	03-04	18	15	7
DAGNOGO Moussa Moustapha						
Paris, France, 30 January, 1972						(F)
Bristol Rov	Uniao de Madeira (Por)	09.00	00	0	2	0
DAHLIN Martin						
Udevalla, Sweden, 16 April, 1968 Sweden 60						(F)
Blackburn Rov	AS Roma (It)	07.97	97-98	13	13	4
DAILEY James (Jimmy) Augustine						
Airdrie, 8 September, 1927 Died 2002						(CF)
Sheffield Wed	Third Lanark	10.46	46-48	37	-	24
Birmingham C	Tr	02.49	48-51	41	-	14
Exeter C	Tr	08.52	52-53	45	-	13
Workington	Tr	12.53	53-57	176	-	81
Rochdale	Tr	10.57	57-58	53	-	25
DAILLY Christian Eduard						
Dundee, 23 October, 1973 SSch/SYth/Su21-34/SB-1/S-55						(CD)
Derby Co	Dundee U	08.96	96-98	62	5	4
Blackburn Rov	Tr	08.98	98-00	60	10	4
West Ham U	Tr	01.01	00-04	117	5	2
DAILLY Marcus Graham						
Dundee, 1 October, 1975						(M)
Exeter C	Dundee	08.96	96	8	9	0
DAINES Barry Raymond						
Witham, 30 September, 1951 EYth						(G)
Tottenham H	App	09.69	71-80	146	0	0
Mansfield T	Bulova (HK)	10.83	83	21	0	0
DAINO Daniele (Danny)						
Alessandria, Italy, 8 September, 1979						(FB)
Derby Co (L)	AC Milan (It)	08.01	01	2	0	0
DAINTY Albert						
Lancaster, 4 December, 1923 Died 1979						(W)
Preston NE	Standfast Dyers	10.42	46	1	-	1
Stockport Co	Tr	04.47	46-48	36	-	16
Southport	Tr	02.49	48-50	48	-	11

League Club	Source	Date Signed	Seasons Played	Career Record Apps	Subs	Gls
DAINTY James Anthony (Jim)						
Coleshill, 21 January, 1954						(W)
Walsall	Jnrs	10.71	71-72	4	1	0
DAIR Jason						
Dunfermline, 15 June, 1974 SSch						(M)
Millwall	Raith Rov	07.96	96	21	3	1
DAISH Liam Sean						
Portsmouth, 23 September, 1968 IRu21-5/IRB/IR-5						(CD)
Portsmouth	App	09.86	86	1	0	0
Cambridge U	Tr	07.88	88-93	138	1	4
Birmingham C	Tr	01.94	93-95	72	1	3
Coventry C	Tr	02.96	95-96	31	0	2
DAKIN Simon Mark						
Nottingham, 30 November, 1974						(FB)
Derby Co	YT	07.93				
Hull C	Tr	03.94	93-95	29	7	1
DAKINAH Kofi						
Denmark, 1 February, 1980 DeYth						(CD)
Walsall	Herfolge (Den)	07.04	04	1	0	0
DALE Alan George						
Thorne, 20 September, 1958						(F)
Scunthorpe U	App	09.76	75-76	1	2	0
DALE Carl						
Colwyn Bay, 29 April, 1966						(F)
Chester C	Bangor C	05.88	88-90	106	10	40
Cardiff C	Tr	08.91	91-97	188	25	71
DALE Christopher (Chris)						
York, 16 April, 1950						(W)
York C (Am)	Hull C (Am)	05.68	68	5	0	0
DALE Eric						
Manchester, 6 July, 1924						(W)
Shrewsbury T		03.50	50	1	-	0
DALE Gordon						
Worksop, 20 May, 1928 Died 1996						(W)
Chesterfield	Worksop T	02.48	48-50	92	-	3
Portsmouth	Tr	07.51	51-56	114	-	18
Exeter C	Tr	10.57	57-60	124	-	8
DALE Joseph (Joe)						
Northwich, 3 July, 1921 Died 2000						(W)
Manchester U	Witton A	06.47	47	2	-	0
Port Vale	Tr	04.48	47-48	9	-	1
DALE Leo						
Esh Winning, 11 October, 1933 Died 2003						(W)
Doncaster Rov	Durham C	02.54	54	1	-	0
DALE Robert (Bobby) Jenkins						
Irlam, 31 October, 1931						(WH)
Bury	Altrincham	09.51	52-53	15	-	2
Colchester U	Tr	12.53	53-56	127	-	12
DALE Frederick **William (Billy)**						
Doncaster, 26 October, 1925						(W)
Halifax T	Scunthorpe & Lindsey U	08.49	49-51	70	-	16
Southport	Tr	07.52	52-53	47	-	5
Accrington St	Tr	07.54	54	1	-	0
Crewe Alex	Tr	10.54	54	4	-	3
DALEY Alan James						
Mansfield, 11 October, 1927						(W)
Mansfield T	Pleasley BC	09.46				
Hull C	Tr	07.47	47	7	-	0
Doncaster Rov	Worksop T	03.50	49	1	-	1
Scunthorpe U	Boston U	07.52	52	35	-	8
Mansfield T	Corby T	11.53	53-55	97	-	26
Stockport Co	Tr	02.56	55-57	73	-	17
Crewe Alex	Tr	06.58	58	14	-	1
Coventry C	Tr	11.58	58-60	56	-	10
DALEY Anthony (Tony) Mark						
Birmingham, 18 October, 1967 EYth/EB-1/E-7						(W)
Aston Villa	App	05.85	84-93	189	44	31
Wolverhampton W	Tr	06.94	94-97	16	5	3
Watford	Tr	08.98	98	6	6	1
Walsall	Tr	06.99	99	3	4	0
DALEY Omar						
Jamaica, 25 April, 1981 Jamaica int						(M)
Reading	Portmore U (Jam)	08.03	03	0	6	0
Preston NE	Tr	08.04	04	1	13	0

League Club	Source	Date Signed	Seasons Played	Career Record Apps	Subs	Gls

DALEY Peter John
Liverpool, 14 February, 1970 (M)

Southend U	Knowsley U	09.89	89	0	5	1

DALEY Philip (Phil)
Walton, 12 April, 1967 (F)

Wigan Ath	Newton	10.89	89-93	152	9	39
Lincoln C	Tr	08.94	94-95	25	7	5

DALEY Stephen (Steve)
Barnsley, 15 April, 1953 EYth/EB (M)

Wolverhampton W	App	06.71	71-78	191	21	38
Manchester C	Tr	09.79	79-80	47	1	4
Burnley	Seattle (USA)	11.83	83	20	3	4
Walsall	San Diego (USA)	08.85	85	28	0	1

DALEY Thomas (Tom) Edward
Grimsby, 15 November, 1933 (G)

Grimsby T	Jnrs	08.51	51-56	14	-	0
Huddersfield T	Tr	03.57	56	1	-	0

DALGLISH Kenneth (Kenny) Mathieson
Dalmarnock, 4 March, 1951 Su23-4/S-102 (F)

Liverpool	Glasgow Celtic	08.77	77-89	342	13	118

DALGLISH Paul Kenneth
Glasgow, 18 February, 1977 Su21-7 (F)

Liverpool	Glasgow Celtic	08.96				
Newcastle U	Tr	11.97	98	6	5	1
Bury	L	11.97	97	1	11	0
Norwich C	Tr	03.99	98-00	25	18	2
Wigan Ath	L	03.01	00	5	1	0
Wigan Ath	Tr	08.01	01	17	12	2
Blackpool	Tr	08.02	02	20	7	1
Scunthorpe U	L	03.03	02	5	3	3

DALL David Graham
St Andrews, 10 October, 1957 (CD)

Scunthorpe U	Grantham	10.79	79-81	77	0	2

DALLA BONA Samuele (Sam)
Venice, Italy, 6 February, 1981 ItYth/Itu21 (M)

Chelsea	Atalanta (It)	10.98	99-01	42	13	6

DALLAS William Robert Dempster
Glasgow, 6 March, 1931 (CD)

Luton T	Caledonian Amats	09.52				
Wrexham	St Mirren	07.57	57	8	-	0

DALLI Jean
Enfield, 13 August, 1976 (FB)

Colchester U	Jnrs	08.94	94	1	0	0

DALLING Nigel Aubrey
Swansea, 20 February, 1959 (M)

Swansea C	App	02.77	74-77	2	6	0

DALLMAN William (Bill)
Mansfield, 8 August, 1918 Died 1988 (CD)

Mansfield T	Rufford Colliery	03.47	46-47	5	-	0

DALMAT Stephane
Joue-les-Tours, France, 16 February, 1979 Fru21 (M)

Tottenham H (L)	Inter Milan (It)	09.03	03	12	10	3

DALRYMPLE Malcolm Owen
Bedford, 8 October, 1951 EYth (G)

Luton T	Jnrs	07.70				
Bristol Rov	Margate	10.71	71-72	7	0	0
Watford	Tr	07.73	73	5	0	0

DALTON George
West Moor, 4 September, 1941 (FB)

Newcastle U	Jnrs	11.58	60-66	85	0	2
Brighton & Hove A	Tr	06.67	67	24	0	0

DALTON Paul
Middlesbrough, 25 April, 1967 (W)

Manchester U	Brandon U	05.88				
Hartlepool U	Tr	03.89	88-91	140	11	37
Plymouth Arg	Tr	06.92	92-94	93	5	25
Huddersfield T	Tr	08.95	95-98	79	19	25
Carlisle U	L	12.99	99	3	0	1

DALTON Richard Timothy (Tim)
Waterford, 14 October, 1965 (G)

Coventry C	App	09.83				
Notts Co	Tr	07.84	85	1	0	0
Bradford C	Boston U	09.86				
Tranmere Rov	L	12.86	86	1	0	0

DALY Gerard (Gerry) Anthony
Dublin 30 April, 1954 LoI-1/IRu21-1/IR-47 (M)

Manchester U	Bohemians	04.73	73-76	107	4	23
Derby Co	Tr	03.77	76-79	111	1	30
Coventry C	Tr	08.80	80-83	82	2	19
Leicester C	L	01.83	82	17	0	1
Birmingham C	Tr	08.84	84-85	31	1	1
Shrewsbury T	Tr	10.85	85-86	55	0	8
Stoke C	Tr	03.87	86-87	17	5	1
Doncaster Rov	Tr	07.88	88	37	2	4

DALY Jonathan (Jon) Marvin
Dublin, 8 January, 1983 IRYth/IRu21-9 (F)

Stockport Co	YT	01.00	99-04	65	26	14
Bury	L	01.04	03	7	0	1
Grimsby T	L	10.04	04	3	0	1
Hartlepool U	Tr	02.05	04	4	8	1

DALY Maurice Celsus
Dublin, 28 November, 1955 IRu21-4/IR-2 (FB)

Wolverhampton W	Home Farm	07.73	75-77	28	4	0

DALY Patrick (Pat)
Dublin, 4 December, 1927 LoI-1/IR-1 (FB)

Aston Villa	Shamrock Rov	11.49	49	3	-	0

DALY Patrick (Paddy) John
Withington, 3 January, 1941 (W)

Blackburn Rov	Jnrs	01.58	59-60	3	-	0
Southport	Tr	02.62	61	10	-	0

DALY Ronald (Ron) George
Clerkenwell, 22 July, 1930 Died 1996 (IF)

Watford		10.50	50	3	-	0

DALY Wesley (Wes) James Patrick
Hammersmith, 7 March, 1984 (M)

Queens Park Rgrs	YT	08.04	01-03	4	5	0

DALZIEL Gordon
Motherwell, 16 March, 1962 (F)

Manchester C	Glasgow Rgrs	12.83	83	4	1	0

DALZIEL Ian
South Shields, 24 October, 1962 (FB)

Derby Co	App	10.79	81-82	22	0	4
Hereford U	Tr	05.83	83-87	137	13	8
Carlisle U	Tr	07.88	88-92	90	1	2

DAMERELL Mark Anthony
Plymouth, 31 July, 1965 (W)

Plymouth Arg	St Blazey	11.89	89-91	0	6	0
Exeter C	Tr	12.91	91	1	0	0

DANBY John Robert
Stoke-on-Trent, 20 September, 1983 (G)

Kidderminster Hrs	Jnrs	12.01	01-04	46	2	0

DANCE Trevor
Hetton-le-Hole, 31 July, 1958 (G)

Port Vale	App	07.76	76-80	84	0	0

DANDO Philip (Phil)
Liverpool, 8 June, 1952 (G)

Liverpool	Jnrs	09.69				
Barrow	L	10.70	70	9	0	0

DANGERFIELD Christopher (Chris) George
Coleshill, 9 August, 1955 (F)

Wolverhampton W	App	08.73				
Port Vale	Portland (USA)	09.76	76	0	2	0

DANGERFIELD David Anthony
Tetbury, 27 September, 1951 ESch (M)

Swindon T	App	08.69	68-72	16	4	0

[DANI] CARVALHO DA CRUZ Daniel
Lisbon, Portugal, 2 November, 1976 Portugal u21 (F)

West Ham U (L)	Sporting Lisbon (Por)	02.96	95	3	6	2

[DANI] FERREIRA RODRIGUES Daniel
Madeira, Portugal, 3 March, 1980 Portugal u21 (F)

Bournemouth (L)	Dep Farense (Por)	10.98	98	0	5	0
Southampton	Dep Farense (Por)	03.99	99	0	2	0
Bristol C	L	10.00	00	3	1	0
Bristol C	L	12.01	01	0	4	0
Walsall	Tr	08.02	02	0	1	0
Yeovil T (L)	Ionikos (Gre)	03.04	03	3	1	4
Bournemouth	Tr	07.04	04	10	13	3

DANIEL Alan Winstone
Ashford, Kent, 5 April, 1940 (FB)

League Club	Source	Date Signed	Seasons Played	Apps	Subs	Gls
Luton T	Bexleyheath & Welling	01.58	58-63	50	-	3

DANIEL Melville (Mel) Verdun Reginald John
Llanelli, 26 January, 1916 Died 1997 (IF)

League Club	Source	Date Signed	Seasons Played	Apps	Subs	Gls
Luton T	Ashford T	09.44	46-48	53	-	20
Aldershot	Tr	06.49	49	28	-	1

DANIEL Peter Aylmer
Ripley, 22 December, 1946 (CD)

League Club	Source	Date Signed	Seasons Played	Apps	Subs	Gls
Derby Co	App	12.64	65-78	188	7	7

DANIEL Peter William
Hull, 12 December, 1955 Eu23-3/Eu21-7 (M)

League Club	Source	Date Signed	Seasons Played	Apps	Subs	Gls
Hull C	Jnrs	09.73	74-77	113	0	9
Wolverhampton W	Tr	05.78	78-83	157	0	13
Sunderland	Minnesota (USA)	08.84	84-85	33	1	0
Lincoln C	Tr	11.85	85-86	55	0	2
Burnley	Tr	07.87	87-88	40	1	0

DANIEL Raymond (Ray) Christopher
Luton, 10 December, 1964 (FB)

League Club	Source	Date Signed	Seasons Played	Apps	Subs	Gls
Luton T	App	09.82	82-85	14	8	4
Gillingham	L	09.83	83	5	0	0
Hull C	Tr	06.86	86-88	55	3	3
Cardiff C	Tr	08.89	89-90	56	0	1
Portsmouth	Tr	11.90	90-94	91	9	4
Notts Co	L	10.94	94	5	0	0
Walsall	Tr	08.95	95-96	31	4	0

DANIEL William **Raymond (Ray)**
Swansea, 2 November, 1928 Died 1997 W-21 (CD)

League Club	Source	Date Signed	Seasons Played	Apps	Subs	Gls
Arsenal	Swansea T (Am)	10.46	48-52	87	-	5
Sunderland	Tr	06.53	53-56	136	-	6
Cardiff C	Tr	10.57	57	6	-	0
Swansea T	Tr	03.58	57-59	44	-	7

DANIEL Thomas (Tommy)
Middleton, 14 April, 1923 (WH)

League Club	Source	Date Signed	Seasons Played	Apps	Subs	Gls
Bury	Castleton Gabriels	12.46	47-57	276	-	57

DANIELS Bernard (Barney) Joseph
Salford, 24 November, 1950 (F)

League Club	Source	Date Signed	Seasons Played	Apps	Subs	Gls
Manchester U	Jnrs	04.69				
Manchester C	Ashton U	04.73	73-74	9	4	2
Chester	Tr	07.75	75	8	1	1
Stockport Co	Tr	07.76	76-77	45	2	17

DANIELS David (Dave) William
Bedford, 14 September, 1985 (F)

League Club	Source	Date Signed	Seasons Played	Apps	Subs	Gls
Cambridge U	Sch	●	03	0	1	0

DANIELS Douglas (Doug)
Salford, 21 August, 1924 Died 2004 (G)

League Club	Source	Date Signed	Seasons Played	Apps	Subs	Gls
New Brighton	Manchester C (Am)	08.47	47	25	-	0
Chesterfield	Tr	07.48				
Accrington St	Tr	10.49	49-52	112	-	0

DANIELS Graham David
Farnborough, 9 April, 1962 (W)

League Club	Source	Date Signed	Seasons Played	Apps	Subs	Gls
Cambridge U	Cardiff Corinthians	11.83	83-84	37	2	4

DANIELS Henry (Harry) Augustus George
Kensington, 25 June, 1920 Died 2002 (WH)

League Club	Source	Date Signed	Seasons Played	Apps	Subs	Gls
Queens Park Rgrs	Kensington Sports	10.44	46-47	14	-	0
Brighton & Hove A	Tr	08.48	48-49	32	-	0
York C	Tr	08.50	50	4	-	2

DANIELS John
Sutton, Lancashire, 8 January, 1925 Died 1994 (G)

League Club	Source	Date Signed	Seasons Played	Apps	Subs	Gls
New Brighton	British Cidac	03.48	48	3	-	0

DANIELS John (Jack) Francis
Prestwich, 6 October, 1913 Died 1970 (G)

League Club	Source	Date Signed	Seasons Played	Apps	Subs	Gls
Leeds U	Ashton National	04.34	34	1	-	0
Stockport Co	Tr	06.35	35-37	9	-	0
Accrington St	Tr	07.38	38	10	-	0
Tranmere Rov	Tr	06.39				
Leeds U	Tr	12.40				
Bradford C	Tr	07.45				
Lincoln C	Tr	07.46	46	17	-	0

DANIELS Scott Charles
Benfleet, 22 November, 1969 (CD)

League Club	Source	Date Signed	Seasons Played	Apps	Subs	Gls
Colchester U	YT	06.88	87-89	64	9	0
Exeter C	Tr	08.91	91-94	114	3	7
Northampton T	Tr	01.95	94	5	3	0

DANIELS Stephen Richard
Leeds, 17 December, 1961 (FB)

League Club	Source	Date Signed	Seasons Played	Apps	Subs	Gls
Doncaster Rov	App	10.79	79	0	1	0

DANIELSSON Einar Thor
Reykjavik, Iceland, 19 January, 1970 Iceland 18 (M)

League Club	Source	Date Signed	Seasons Played	Apps	Subs	Gls
Stoke C (L)	KR Reykjavik (Ice)	11.99	99	3	5	1

DANIELSSON Helgi Valur
Reykjavik, Iceland, 13 July, 1981 IcYth/Icu21-16/Ic-1 (M)

League Club	Source	Date Signed	Seasons Played	Apps	Subs	Gls
Peterborough U	Fylkir (Ice)	10.98	00-02	38	17	2

DANILEVICIUS Tomas
Lithuania, 18 July, 1978 Lithuania 8 (F)

League Club	Source	Date Signed	Seasons Played	Apps	Subs	Gls
Arsenal	FC Lausanne (Swi)	12.00	00	0	2	0

DANKS Derek Peter
Cheadle, Staffordshire, 15 February, 1931 (IF)

League Club	Source	Date Signed	Seasons Played	Apps	Subs	Gls
Northampton T		11.53	54	1	-	0

DANKS Mark James
Warley, 8 February, 1984 (F)

League Club	Source	Date Signed	Seasons Played	Apps	Subs	Gls
Bradford C	Wolverhampton W (YT)	11.02	02	0	3	0

DANN Scott
Liverpool, 14 February, 1987 (CD)

League Club	Source	Date Signed	Seasons Played	Apps	Subs	Gls
Walsall	Sch	08.04	04	0	1	0

DANN Terence (Terry) Edward
Shoreditch, 6 July, 1936 (IF)

League Club	Source	Date Signed	Seasons Played	Apps	Subs	Gls
Plymouth Arg	Penzance	07.59	59	8	-	0
Torquay U	Sittingbourne	07.62	62	1	-	0

DANNS Neil Alexander
Liverpool, 23 November, 1982 (M)

League Club	Source	Date Signed	Seasons Played	Apps	Subs	Gls
Blackburn Rov	YT	07.00	02-03	1	2	0
Blackpool	L	08.03	03	12	0	2
Hartlepool U	L	03.04	03	8	1	1
Colchester U	Tr	09.04	04	32	0	11

DANSKIN Jason
Winsford, 28 December, 1967 (M)

League Club	Source	Date Signed	Seasons Played	Apps	Subs	Gls
Everton	App	07.85	84	1	0	0
Mansfield T	Tr	03.87	86	10	0	0
Hartlepool U	L	01.88	87	3	0	0

DANSKIN Robert (Bob)
Scotswood, 28 May, 1908 Died 1985 (CD)

League Club	Source	Date Signed	Seasons Played	Apps	Subs	Gls
Leeds U	Wallsend U	05.29	30-31	5	-	1
Bradford PA	Tr	12.32	32-47	260	-	6

DANZE Anthony
Perth, Australia, 15 March, 1984 AuYth/Auu23-7 (M)

League Club	Source	Date Signed	Seasons Played	Apps	Subs	Gls
Crystal Palace	Perth Glory (Aus)	10.04				
MK Dons	L	12.04	04	2	0	0

DANZEY Michael (Mike) James
Widnes, 8 February, 1971 (F)

League Club	Source	Date Signed	Seasons Played	Apps	Subs	Gls
Nottingham F	YT	05.89				
Chester C	L	02.90	89	0	2	0
Peterborough U		01.91	90	0	1	0
Cambridge U	St Albans C	10.92	92-94	18	9	3
Scunthorpe U	L	02.93	93	3	0	1

DARBY Alan
Sheffield, 3 June, 1942 (G)

League Club	Source	Date Signed	Seasons Played	Apps	Subs	Gls
Doncaster Rov	Goole T	06.59	60	1	-	0

DARBY Brett Thomas
Leicester, 10 November, 1983 (F)

League Club	Source	Date Signed	Seasons Played	Apps	Subs	Gls
Leicester C	YT	12.00				
Southend U	Tr	02.03	02	6	4	0

DARBY Douglas (Doug)
Bolton-on-Dearne, 26 December, 1919 Died 1963 (CF)

League Club	Source	Date Signed	Seasons Played	Apps	Subs	Gls
Wolverhampton W	Wath W	09.41				
Walsall	Tr	05.46	46	15	-	4

DARBY Duane Anthony
Warley, 17 October, 1973 (F)

League Club	Source	Date Signed	Seasons Played	Apps	Subs	Gls
Torquay U	YT	07.92	91-94	60	48	26
Doncaster Rov	Tr	07.95	95	8	9	4
Hull C	Tr	03.96	95-97	75	3	27
Notts Co	Tr	07.98	99	22	6	5
Hull C	L	03.99	98	4	4	0
Rushden & Diamonds	Tr	06.00	01-03	61	18	23
Shrewsbury T	Tr	11.03	04	8	8	1

DARBY Julian Timothy
Farnworth, 3 October, 1967 ESch (M)

League Club	Source	Date Signed	Seasons Played	Apps	Subs	Gls
Bolton W	App	07.86	85-93	258	12	36
Coventry C	Tr	10.93	93-94	52	3	5
West Bromwich A	Tr	11.95	95-96	32	7	1
Preston NE	Tr	06.97	97-99	20	15	1
Rotherham U	L	03.98	97	3	0	0
Carlisle U	Tr	08.00	00	15	3	1

League Club	Source	Date Signed	Seasons Played	Career Record Apps	Subs	Gls
DARBY Lee Alan						
Salford, 20 September, 1969 ESch						(M)
Portsmouth	App	10.86	87	1	0	0
DARBYSHIRE Harold (Harry)						
Leeds, 22 October, 1931						(CF)
Leeds U		02.50				
Halifax T	Tr	07.52	52-56	162	-	32
Bury	Tr	08.57	57-58	29	-	12
Darlington	Tr	06.59	59	15	-	2
DARCHEVILLE Jean-Claude						
Sinnamary, French Guiana, 25 July, 1975						(F)
Nottingham F (L)	Rennes (Fr)	07.98	98	14	2	2
D'ARCY Arnold (Arnie) Joseph						
Blackburn, 13 January, 1933						(W)
Accrington St	St Matthew's	03.52	51-52	38	-	9
Swindon T	Wigan Ath	11.56	56-63	223	-	29
D'ARCY Colin Robert						
Greasby, 5 August, 1954						(G)
Everton		04.73				
Bury	Tr	01.75	74	4	0	0
D'ARCY Francis (Frank) Anthony						
Liverpool, 8 December, 1946						(FB)
Everton	App	08.64	65-70	8	8	0
Tranmere Rov	Tr	07.72	72	7	1	1
D'ARCY Michael Edmund						
Dublin, 8 March, 1933 LoI-10						(G)
Oldham Ath	Dundalk	09.54	54-55	45	-	0
D'ARCY Ross						
Balbriggan, 21 March, 1978 IRu21-6						(CD)
Tottenham H	YT	07.95				
Barnet	Tr	12.99	99-00	1	5	0
D'ARCY Seamus (Jimmy) Donal						
Newry, 14 December, 1921 Died 1985 I-5						(IF)
Charlton Ath	Ballymena U	03.48	47-50	13	-	1
Chelsea	Tr	10.51	51-52	23	-	12
Brentford	Tr	10.52	52	13	-	3
D'ARCY Thomas (Tommy) McDonald						
Edinburgh, 22 June, 1932 Died 1985						(CF)
Bournemouth	Hibernian	09.54				
Southend U	Hibernian	05.56	56-57	4	-	0
DARE Kevin John						
Finchley, 15 November, 1959						(FB)
Crystal Palace	App	02.77	80-81	6	0	0
DARE Reginald (Reg) Arthur						
Blandford Forum, 26 November, 1921 Died 1993						(CF)
Southampton	Windsor & Eton	06.49				
Exeter C	Tr	08.50	50	6	-	0
DARE William (Billy) Thomas Charles						
Willesden, 14 February, 1927 Died 1994						(CF)
Brentford	Hendon	11.48	48-54	208	-	62
West Ham U	Tr	01.55	54-58	111	-	44
DAREY Jeffrey (Jeff) Arthur						
Hammersmith, 26 February, 1934 EAmat						(CF)
Brighton & Hove A	Hendon	03.57	56-60	10	-	2
DARFIELD Stuart Charles						
Leeds, 12 April, 1950						(CD)
Bradford PA	Wolverhampton W App)	07.68	68	15	2	0
DARGIE Ian Charles						
Camberwell, 3 October, 1931						(CD)
Brentford	Tonbridge	02.52	51-62	263	-	2
DARK Trevor Charles						
Morden, 29 January, 1961						(W)
Birmingham C	App	01.79	78	2	3	1
DARKE Peter George						
Exeter, 21 December, 1953						(CD)
Plymouth Arg	App	12.71	71-76	94	5	2
Exeter C	L	10.76	76	5	0	0
Torquay U	Tr	07.77	77-78	58	1	0
DARLING Henry **Leonard (Len)**						
Gillingham, 9 August, 1911 Died 1958						(WH)
Gillingham	Chatham T	05.32	32	14	-	0
Brighton & Hove A	Tr	08.33	33-47	199	-	5

League Club	Source	Date Signed	Seasons Played	Career Record Apps	Subs	Gls
DARLING Malcolm						
Arbroath, 4 July, 1947						(F)
Blackburn Rov	Luncarty Jnrs	10.64	65-69	115	14	30
Norwich C	Tr	05.70	70-71	16	0	5
Rochdale	Tr	10.71	71-73	82	4	16
Bolton W	Tr	09.73	73	6	2	0
Chesterfield	Tr	08.74	74-76	100	4	33
Stockport Co	L	03.77	76	11	0	2
Sheffield Wed	Tr	08.77	77	1	1	0
Hartlepool U	Tr	09.77	77	2	2	0
Bury	Morecambe	03.78	77	1	1	0
DARLINGTON Jermaine Christopher						
Hackney, 11 April, 1974						(FB)
Charlton Ath	YT	06.92	91	1	1	0
Queens Park Rgrs	Aylesbury U	03.99	98-00	70	1	2
Wimbledon	Tr	07.01	01-03	97	8	3
Watford	Tr	08.04	04	25	1	0
DARLOW Kieran Brian						
Bedford, 9 November, 1982						(FB)
York C	YT	●	99-01	1	4	0
DARMODY Aubrey						
Swansea, 17 May, 1921						(FB)
Norwich C	Cardiff Nomads	10.46	46	2	-	0
DARRACOTT Terence (Terry) Michael						
Liverpool, 6 December, 1950						(FB)
Everton	App	07.68	67-78	138	10	0
Wrexham	Tulsa (USA)	06.79	79	22	0	0
DARRAS Frederic Guy Albert						
Calais, France, 19 August, 1966						(FB)
Swindon T	Bastia Fr)	08.96	96-97	42	7	0
DARRELL Michael (Mike) Alan						
Bilston, 14 January, 1947						(M)
Birmingham C	App	01.65	65-69	10	4	2
Newport Co	L	10.70	70	7	0	0
Gillingham	L	12.70	70	19	3	1
Peterborough U	Tr	05.71	71-72	32	10	6
DARTON Scott Richard						
Ipswich, 27 March, 1975						(FB)
West Bromwich A	YT	10.92	92-94	15	0	0
Blackpool	Tr	01.95	94-96	31	11	1
DARVELL Roger Derek						
High Wycombe, 10 February, 1931						(CD)
Charlton Ath	Rickmansworth T	12.53				
Gillingham	Tr	07.57	57	3	-	0
Southport	Tr	07.58	58-64	256	-	1
DARWIN George Hedworth						
Chester-le-Street, 16 May, 1932						(IF)
Huddersfield T	Kimblesworth Jnrs	05.50				
Mansfield T	Tr	11.53	53-56	126	-	63
Derby Co	Tr	05.57	57-60	94	-	32
Rotherham U	Tr	10.60	60	2	-	2
Barrow	Tr	07.61	61-63	92	-	28
DAUBNEY Raymond (Ray)						
Oldham, 7 December, 1946						(W)
Rochdale		12.66	66-67	12	0	2
DAUGHTRY Paul William						
Oldham, 14 February, 1973						(W)
Stockport Co	Winsford U	01.94				
Hartlepool U	Droylsden	11.94	94	14	1	0
D'AURIA David Alan						
Swansea, 26 March, 1970 WYth						(M)
Swansea C	YT	08.88	87-90	27	18	6
Scarborough	Barry T	08.94	94-95	49	3	8
Scunthorpe U	Tr	12.95	95-97	103	4	18
Hull C	Tr	07.98	98-99	52	2	4
Chesterfield	Tr	11.99	99-01	18	7	1
DAVENPORT Calum Raymond Paul						
Bedford, 1 January, 1983 EYth/Eu20/Eu21-7						(CD)
Coventry C	YT	01.00	00-04	64	11	3
Tottenham H	Tr	08.04	04	0	1	0
West Ham U	L	09.04	04	10	0	0
Southampton	L	01.05	04	5	2	0
DAVENPORT Carl						
Farnworth, 30 May, 1944 LoI-2						(CF)
Preston NE	App	05.62				
Stockport Co	Tr	03.63	62-63	16	-	3

League Club	Source	Date Signed	Seasons Played	Apps	Subs	Gls
DAVENPORT Peter						
Birkenhead, 24 March, 1961 EB-1/E-1						(F)
Nottingham F	Cammell Laird	01.82	81-85	114	4	54
Manchester U	Tr	03.86	85-88	73	19	22
Middlesbrough	Tr	11.88	88-89	53	6	7
Sunderland	Tr	07.90	90-92	72	27	15
Stockport Co	St Johnstone	03.95	94	3	3	1
Macclesfield T	Southport	01.97	97-98	2	3	1
DAVEY Frederick (Fred) Albert						
Crediton, 13 April, 1924 Died 2000						(WH)
Exeter C	Crediton T	08.47	47-55	276	-	3
DAVEY Nigel Geoffrey						
Garforth, 20 June, 1946						(FB)
Leeds U	Great Preston Jnrs	02.64	67-70	13	1	0
DAVEY Simon						
Swansea, 1 October, 1970						(M)
Swansea C	YT	07.89	86-91	37	12	4
Carlisle U	Tr	08.92	92-94	105	0	18
Preston NE	Tr	02.95	94-97	97	9	21
Darlington	L	09.97	97	10	1	0
DAVEY Stephen (Steve) Gilbert Richard						
Plymouth, 5 September, 1948 EYth						(M)
Plymouth Arg	App	07.66	66-74	213	11	47
Hereford U	Tr	08.75	75-77	104	3	32
Portsmouth	Tr	06.78	78-80	82	10	8
Exeter C	Tr	08.81	81	15	0	0
DAVEY Stuart						
Haslington, 4 January, 1938						(FB)
Crewe Alex	Jnrs	08.56	56	1	-	0
DAVIDS Neil Graham						
Bingley, 22 September, 1955 EYth						(CD)
Leeds U	App	08.73				
Norwich C	Tr	04.75	75	2	0	0
Northampton T	L	09.75	75	9	0	0
Stockport Co	L	01.76	75	5	0	1
Swansea C	Tr	07.77	77	9	0	0
Wigan Ath	Tr	07.78	78-80	66	2	1
DAVIDSON Adam Richmond						
Invergowrie, 28 November, 1929						(W)
Sheffield Wed	Elmwood	03.48				
Colchester U	Tr	08.51	51	19	-	0
DAVIDSON Alan Edward						
Melbourne, Australia, 1 June, 1960 Australia int						(FB)
Nottingham F	Hellas (Aus)	11.84	84	3	0	0
DAVIDSON Alexander (Alex) Morrison						
Langholm, 6 June, 1920						(IF)
Chelsea	Hibernian	08.46	46	2	-	0
Crystal Palace	Tr	08.48	48	10	-	2
DAVIDSON Andrew (Andy)						
Douglas Water, 13 July, 1932						(FB)
Hull C	Douglas Water Thistle	09.49	52-67	520	0	18
DAVIDSON Angus Gordon						
Forfar, 2 October, 1948						(M)
Grimsby T	Arbroath LC	11.65	65-68	46	5	1
Scunthorpe U	Tr	07.69	69-76	304	15	44
DAVIDSON Brian						
Workington, 23 August, 1951						(W)
Workington (Am)	Jnrs	08.72	72	1	0	0
DAVIDSON Callum Iain						
Stirling, 25 June, 1976 Su21-2/S-17						(FB)
Blackburn Rov	St Johnstone	02.98	97-99	63	2	1
Leicester C	Tr	07.00	00-03	90	11	2
Preston NE	Tr	08.04	04	16	3	1
DAVIDSON David						
Govan Hill, 20 August, 1934						(WH)
Manchester C	Glentyne Thistle	08.51	53	1	-	0
Workington	Tr	07.58	58	3	-	0
DAVIDSON David (Dave) Blyth Logie						
Lanark, 25 March, 1920 Died 1954						(FB)
Bradford PA	Douglas Water Thistle	05.38	46	13	-	0
Leyton Orient	Tr	01.47	46-49	84	-	1
DAVIDSON David Craiglogie						
Douglas Water, 19 March, 1926 Died 1996						(W)
Hull C	Douglas Water Thistle	10.46	46-47	22	-	4

League Club	Source	Date Signed	Seasons Played	Apps	Subs	Gls
DAVIDSON Dennis James						
Aberdeen, 18 May, 1937						(WH)
Portsmouth	Torry Rgrs	05.54	59	1	-	0
DAVIDSON Douglas Bell						
Dundee, 2 December, 1918 Died 1968						(IF)
Blackpool	East Fife	10.48	48-49	14	-	0
Reading	Tr	04.50	49-50	11	-	1
DAVIDSON Duncan						
Elgin, 5 July, 1954						(F)
Manchester C	See Bee (HK)	09.83	83	2	4	1
DAVIDSON Ian						
Pencaitland, 8 September, 1937						(CD)
Preston NE	Kilmarnock	12.62	62-64	67	-	1
Middlesbrough	Tr	02.65	64-66	46	0	0
Darlington	Tr	09.67	67	27	0	0
DAVIDSON Ian						
Goole, 31 January, 1947						(M)
Hull C	Jnrs	02.65	66-67	5	1	1
Scunthorpe U	L	09.68	68	32	3	0
York C	Tr	06.69	69-70	82	4	4
Bournemouth	Tr	07.71	71	7	2	0
Stockport Co	Tr	05.72	72-73	74	4	6
DAVIDSON John (Johnny) Summers						
Stonehouse, Lanarkshire, 6 November, 1931						(IF)
Walsall	Alloa Ath	08.55	55	5	-	0
DAVIDSON Jonathan (Jon) Stewart						
Cheadle, Staffordshire, 1 March, 1970						(FB)
Derby Co	YT	07.88	89-91	7	5	0
Preston NE	Tr	07.92	92	18	3	1
Chesterfield	L	03.93	92	0	1	0
DAVIDSON Peter Edward						
Newcastle, 31 October, 1956						(W)
Queens Park Rgrs	Berwick Rgrs	07.79	79	0	1	0
DAVIDSON Robert (Bobby) Trimming						
Lochgelly, 27 April, 1913 Died 1988 SLge-1						(IF)
Arsenal	St Johnstone	02.35	34-37	57	-	13
Coventry C	Tr	11.37	37-47	47	-	9
DAVIDSON Roger						
Islington, 27 October, 1948 ESch						(M)
Arsenal	App	11.65	67	0	1	0
Portsmouth	Tr	06.69	69	3	0	0
Fulham	Tr	08.70	70	1	0	0
Lincoln C	Tr	10.71	71	6	0	0
Aldershot	L	02.72	71	12	0	2
DAVIDSON Ross James						
Chertsey, 13 November, 1973						(FB)
Sheffield U	Walton & Hersham	06.93	94-95	2	0	0
Chester C	Tr	01.96	95-99	132	0	5
Barnet	Tr	11.99	99	8	1	0
Shrewsbury T	Tr	03.00	99-00	40	3	0
DAVIDSON Victor (Vic) Salvatore Ferla						
Glasgow, 8 November, 1950						(F)
Blackpool	Motherwell	07.78	78	23	2	3
DAVIE Alexander (Sandy) Grimmond						
Dundee, 10 June, 1945						(G)
Luton T	Dundee U	09.68	68-69	58	0	0
Southampton	Tr	05.70	70	1	0	0
DAVIE James (Jim) Graham						
Cambuslang, 7 September, 1922 Died 1984						(WH)
Preston NE	Kilmarnock	06.48	48-49	28	-	0
Northampton T	Tr	07.50	50-52	75	-	1
DAVIE John (Jock)						
Dunfermline, 19 February, 1913 Died 1994						(CF)
Brighton & Hove A	Margate	05.36	36-38	89	-	39
Barnsley	Stockton	12.46	46	6	-	0
DAVIE William (Willie) Clark						
Paisley, 7 January, 1925 Died 1996						(IF)
Luton T	St Mirren	12.50	50-51	42	-	11
Huddersfield T	Tr	12.51	51-56	113	-	16
Walsall	Tr	07.57	57	7	-	0
DAVIES Adam Glen						
Peterborough, 27 March, 1987 WYth						(F)
Cambridge U	Sch	•	04	0	2	0

League Club	Source	Date Signed	Seasons Played	Career Record Apps	Subs	Gls
DAVIES Alan						
Manchester, 5 December, 1961 Died 1992 Wu21-6/W-13 (W)						
Manchester U	App	12.78	81-83	6	1	0
Newcastle U	Tr	08.85	85-86	20	1	1
Charlton Ath	L	03.86	85	1	0	0
Carlisle U	L	11.86	86	4	0	1
Swansea C	Tr	07.87	87-88	84	0	8
Bradford C	Tr	06.89	89	24	2	1
Swansea C	Tr	08.90	90-91	41	2	4
DAVIES Albert John Victor						
Greenwich, 19 April, 1935 (G)						
Millwall		10.56	57	1	-	0
DAVIES Albert Llewellyn						
Pontypridd, 11 March, 1933 (W)						
Newport Co	Merthyr Tydfil	04.51	50	1	-	0
DAVIES Alexander (Alex) John						
Swansea, 2 November, 1982 (G)						
Swansea C	YT	●	00	0	1	0
DAVIES Alexander (Alec) McLean						
Dundonald, 21 May, 1920 Died 1964 (W)						
Sheffield Wed		04.45				
Lincoln C	Tr	07.45	46-48	37	-	9
DAVIES Andrew John						
Stockton, 17 December, 1984 EYth/Eu20/Eu21-1 (CD)						
Middlesbrough	Sch	07.02	02-04	11	3	0
Queens Park Rgrs	L	01.05	04	9	0	0
DAVIES Andrew (Andy) Jonathan						
Wolverhampton, 6 June, 1972 (CD)						
Torquay U	YT	07.88	88-89	9	4	0
Hartlepool U	Tr	06.90	90-91	4	3	0
Torquay U	Tr	08.92	92	1	2	0
DAVIES Arron Rhys						
Cardiff, 22 June, 1984 Wu21-3 (M)						
Southampton	Sch	07.02				
Barnsley	L	02.04	03	1	3	0
Yeovil T	Tr	12.04	04	15	8	8
DAVIES Benjamin (Ben) James						
Birmingham, 27 May, 1981 (M)						
Walsall	Stoke C (YT)	08.99				
Kidderminster Hrs	Tr	03.00	00-01	11	1	0
Chester C	Tr	05.02	04	38	6	2
DAVIES Brian						
Doncaster, 21 August, 1947 (IF)						
Sheffield Wed	App	08.64	65	3	0	1
DAVIES Byron						
Llanelli, 5 February, 1932 (CD)						
Leeds U	Llanelli	05.52	53	1	-	0
DAVIES Cecil Joseph						
Bedwellty, 26 March, 1918 Died 1994 WSch (WH)						
Charlton Ath	Lovells Ath	03.35				
Barrow	Tr	06.38	38-46	75	-	3
Millwall	Tr	07.47	47-48	31	-	0
DAVIES Clint Aaron						
Perth, Australia, 24 April, 1983 (G)						
Birmingham C	Sch	07.02				
Bradford C	Tr	07.03	03	1	1	0
DAVIES Colin Frank						
Shrewsbury, 12 April, 1936 (CD)						
Port Vale		06.59	59-60	13	-	0
DAVIES Craig Martin						
Burton-on-Trent, 9 January, 1986 WYth/Wu21-2 (F)						
Oxford U	Sch	●	04	13	15	6
DAVIES Curtis Eugene						
Waltham Forest, 15 March, 1985 (CD)						
Luton T	Sch	07.04	03-04	48	2	1
DAVIES Cyril						
Swansea, 7 September, 1948 WSch/Wu23-4/W-1 (M)						
Swansea T	App	09.66				
Carlisle U	Tr	06.68	68	1	1	0
Charlton Ath	Yeovil T	05.70	70-72	70	6	5
DAVIES David (Dai) Daniel						
Aberdare, 5 December, 1914 Died 1984 (IF)						
Hull C	Aberaman Ath	08.35	35-46	141	-	30

League Club	Source	Date Signed	Seasons Played	Career Record Apps	Subs	Gls
DAVIES David (Dai) Ivor						
Bridgend, 21 July, 1932 (CF)						
Leyton Orient	Pyle	04.53	53	4	-	0
DAVIES David John						
Neath, 21 May, 1952 (CD)						
Swansea C	Afan Lido	07.73	73-74	27	1	0
DAVIES David Lamb						
Pontypridd, 11 July, 1956 (W)						
Swansea C	App	07.74	72	0	1	0
Crewe Alex	Tr	03.75	74-80	196	13	26
DAVIES William **David (Dai)**						
Ammanford, 1 April, 1948 Wu23-3/W-52 (G)						
Swansea C	Ammanford	08.69	69-70	9	0	0
Everton	Tr	12.70	70-76	82	0	0
Swansea C	L	02.74	73	6	0	0
Wrexham	Tr	09.77	77-80	144	0	0
Swansea C	Tr	07.81	81-82	71	0	0
Tranmere Rov	Tr	06.83	83	42	0	0
DAVIES Dudley						
Shoreham, 27 December, 1924 (W)						
Charlton Ath	Lancing T	01.48				
Leyton Orient	Tr	05.50	50-51	17	-	2
DAVIES Edmund (Eddie)						
Oswestry, 5 June, 1927 (W)						
Arsenal	Liverpool (Am)	08.48				
Queens Park Rgrs	Tr	04.50	50	1	-	1
Crewe Alex	Tr	07.51	51	7	-	0
DAVIES Edward (Eddie)						
Burslem, 3 May, 1923 Died 1995 (CF)						
Port Vale		01.43	46	3	-	0
DAVIES Eric						
Crumpsall, 20 February, 1943 Died 1988 (CF)						
Southport	Southport Trinity	03.62	61-64	3	-	0
DAVIES Frederick (Fred)						
Liverpool, 22 August, 1939 (G)						
Wolverhampton W	Llandudno	04.57	61-67	156	0	0
Cardiff C	Tr	01.68	67-69	98	0	0
Bournemouth	Tr	07.70	70-73	134	0	0
DAVIES Gareth						
Chesterfield, 4 February, 1983 (M)						
Chesterfield	Buxton	08.01	02-04	54	27	2
DAVIES Gareth						
Cardiff, 6 October, 1959 (M)						
Cardiff C	Sully	11.86	86	1	1	0
DAVIES Gareth Melville						
Hereford, 11 December, 1973 Wu21-8 (CD)						
Hereford U	YT	04.92	91-94	91	4	2
Crystal Palace	Tr	07.95	95-97	22	5	2
Cardiff C	L	02.97	96	6	0	2
Reading	Tr	12.97	97-98	18	1	0
Swindon T	Tr	03.99	98-01	23	2	0
DAVIES Geoffrey (Geoff) Peter						
Ellesmere Port, 1 July, 1947 (M)						
Chester	Wigan Ath	08.72	72-73	18	14	5
Wrexham	Tr	10.73	73-75	64	3	15
Port Vale	Chicago (USA)	08.76	76	7	0	0
Hartlepool	L	11.76	76	5	0	1
Wimbledon	San Jose (USA)	08.77	77	23	0	1
DAVIES George						
Rednal, 1 March, 1927 (WH)						
Sheffield Wed	Oswestry T	06.50	50-54	98	-	1
Chester	Tr	07.56	56-57	35	-	4
DAVIES Edward George **Gladstone (Glen)**						
Swansea, 30 June, 1950 (CD)						
Swansea C	Jnrs	07.70	70-75	139	8	13
DAVIES Glen						
Brighton, 20 July, 1976 (CD)						
Burnley	YT	07.94				
Hartlepool U	Tr	06.96	96-97	48	4	1
DAVIES Glyn						
Swansea, 31 May, 1932 (FB)						
Derby Co	Jnrs	07.49	53-61	200	-	5
Swansea T	Tr	07.62	62	18	-	1

League Club	Source	Date Signed	Seasons Played	Career Record Apps	Subs	Gls

DAVIES Gordon
Ardwick, 4 September, 1932 (IF)

League Club	Source	Date Signed	Seasons Played	Apps	Subs	Gls
Manchester C	Ashton U	12.51	51-54	13	-	5
Chester	Tr	06.57	57	22	-	5
Southport	Tr	08.58	58	11	-	1

DAVIES Gordon John
Merthyr Tydfil, 3 August, 1955 WSch/W-18 (F)

League Club	Source	Date Signed	Seasons Played	Apps	Subs	Gls
Fulham	Merthyr Tydfil	03.78	77-84	244	3	114
Chelsea	Tr	11.84	84-85	11	2	6
Manchester C	Tr	10.85	85-86	31	0	9
Fulham	Tr	10.86	86-90	120	27	45
Wrexham	Tr	08.91	91	21	1	4

DAVIES Graham Gilding
Swansea, 3 October, 1921 Died 2003 WSch (G)

League Club	Source	Date Signed	Seasons Played	Apps	Subs	Gls
Swansea T	Jnrs	02.42				
Watford	Tr	06.47	47-48	9	-	0

DAVIES Grant
Barrow, 13 October, 1959 (CD)

League Club	Source	Date Signed	Seasons Played	Apps	Subs	Gls
Preston NE	App	10.77				
Newport Co	Tr	07.78	78-82	147	3	1
Exeter C	L	02.83	82	7	0	0

DAVIES Ian Claude
Bristol, 29 March, 1957 Wu21-1 (FB)

League Club	Source	Date Signed	Seasons Played	Apps	Subs	Gls
Norwich C	App	03.75	73-78	29	3	2
Newcastle U	Tr	06.79	79-81	74	1	3
Manchester C	Tr	08.82	82-83	7	0	0
Bury	L	11.82	82	14	0	0
Brentford	L	11.83	83	2	0	0
Cambridge U	L	02.84	83	5	0	0
Carlisle U	Tr	08.84	84	4	0	0
Exeter C	Tr	12.84	84	5	0	0
Bristol Rov	Diss T	08.85	85	13	1	1
Swansea C	Tr	11.85	85	11	0	0

DAVIES Jamie
Swansea, 12 February, 1980 (F)

League Club	Source	Date Signed	Seasons Played	Apps	Subs	Gls
Swansea C	YT	07.98	98	0	1	0

DAVIES John Gerwyn
Llandyssil, 18 November, 1959 (G)

League Club	Source	Date Signed	Seasons Played	Apps	Subs	Gls
Cardiff C	App	11.77	78-79	7	0	0
Hull C	Tr	07.80	80-82	24	0	0
Notts Co	L	03.86	85	10	0	0

DAVIES John Robert
Portsmouth, 26 September, 1933 (W)

League Club	Source	Date Signed	Seasons Played	Apps	Subs	Gls
Portsmouth	Jnrs	05.52	53-54	2	-	0
Scunthorpe U	Tr	07.55	55-57	67	-	10
Walsall	Tr	01.59	58-60	65	-	17

DAVIES John (Jack) William
Holt, 14 November, 1916 WSch (WH)

League Club	Source	Date Signed	Seasons Played	Apps	Subs	Gls
Chester	Ruthin T	12.34	35-36	18	-	1
Everton	Tr	07.37	46	1	-	0
Plymouth Arg	Tr	02.47	46-47	33	-	0
Bristol C	Tr	05.48	48	30	-	1

DAVIES Joseph (Joe)
Birkenhead, 30 January, 1926 Died 1973 (W)

League Club	Source	Date Signed	Seasons Played	Apps	Subs	Gls
Chester	Bromborough	04.48	47-51	55	-	10

DAVIES Edward Keith
Birkenhead, 19 February, 1934 (IF)

League Club	Source	Date Signed	Seasons Played	Apps	Subs	Gls
Tranmere Rov		07.53	53	1	-	0

DAVIES Kenneth (Ken)
Doncaster, 20 September, 1923 (W)

League Club	Source	Date Signed	Seasons Played	Apps	Subs	Gls
Wolverhampton W		01.44				
Walsall	Tr	06.46	46-47	28	-	5
Brighton & Hove A	Tr	05.48	48-49	36	-	5

DAVIES Kenneth (Kenny) Frank
Stockton, 22 December, 1970 (M)

League Club	Source	Date Signed	Seasons Played	Apps	Subs	Gls
Hartlepool U	YT	07.89	89-90	4	2	0

DAVIES Kevin
Hereford, 1 April, 1963 (M)

League Club	Source	Date Signed	Seasons Played	Apps	Subs	Gls
Hereford U	Westfields	07.85	85	0	1	0

DAVIES Kevin Cyril
Sheffield, 26 March, 1977 EYth/Eu21-3 (F)

League Club	Source	Date Signed	Seasons Played	Apps	Subs	Gls
Chesterfield	YT	04.94	93-96	113	16	22
Southampton	Tr	05.97	97	20	5	9
Blackburn Rov	Tr	06.98	98-99	11	12	1
Southampton	Tr	08.99	99-02	59	23	10
Millwall	L	09.02	02	6	3	3
Bolton W	Tr	07.03	03-04	71	2	17

DAVIES Lawrence
Abergavenny, 3 September, 1977 WYth (F)

League Club	Source	Date Signed	Seasons Played	Apps	Subs	Gls
Leeds U	YT	08.96				
Bradford C	Tr	07.97	97	1	3	0
Darlington	L	12.97	97	2	0	0
Hartlepool U	L	09.98	98	2	1	0
Brighton & Hove A	Tr	02.99	98	2	6	0

DAVIES Leonard (Len)
(G)

League Club	Source	Date Signed	Seasons Played	Apps	Subs	Gls
Southend U		11.45	46	3	-	0

DAVIES David Lyn
Neath, 29 September, 1947 WSch/Wu23-1 (G)

League Club	Source	Date Signed	Seasons Played	Apps	Subs	Gls
Cardiff C	App	10.65	65-66	16	0	0
Swansea C	Llanelli	07.72	72	3	0	0

DAVIES Malcolm
Aberdare, 26 June, 1931 (W)

League Club	Source	Date Signed	Seasons Played	Apps	Subs	Gls
Plymouth Arg	Aberaman Ath	04.49	52-56	84	-	15

DAVIES Mark
Swansea, 9 August, 1972 (FB)

League Club	Source	Date Signed	Seasons Played	Apps	Subs	Gls
Swansea C	YT	07.91	91	1	0	0

DAVIES Martin Lemuel
Swansea, 28 June, 1974 WYth (G)

League Club	Source	Date Signed	Seasons Played	Apps	Subs	Gls
Coventry C	YT	07.92				
Cambridge U	Stafford Rgrs	08.95	95	15	0	0

DAVIES Michael (Mike) John
Stretford, 19 January, 1966 (FB)

League Club	Source	Date Signed	Seasons Played	Apps	Subs	Gls
Blackpool	App	01.84	83-94	276	34	16

DAVIES Paul
Holywell, 10 October, 1952 WSch (F)

League Club	Source	Date Signed	Seasons Played	Apps	Subs	Gls
Arsenal	App	11.69	71	0	1	0
Charlton Ath	Tr	08.72	72-74	51	6	9

DAVIES Paul Andrew
Kidderminster, 9 October, 1960 ESemiPro (F)

League Club	Source	Date Signed	Seasons Played	Apps	Subs	Gls
Cardiff C	Oldswinford	10.78	79-80	1	1	0

DAVIES Peter
Llanelli, 8 March, 1936 WAmat (WH)

League Club	Source	Date Signed	Seasons Played	Apps	Subs	Gls
Arsenal	Llanelli	11.57				
Swansea T	Tr	03.59	58-64	134	-	5
Brighton & Hove A	Tr	07.65	65	6	0	0

DAVIES Peter
Merthyr Tydfil, 1 July, 1942 WAmat (IF)

League Club	Source	Date Signed	Seasons Played	Apps	Subs	Gls
Newport Co	Merthyr Tydfil	05.64	64	1	-	0

DAVIES Leonard Raymond (Ray)
Wallasey, 3 October, 1931 (W)

League Club	Source	Date Signed	Seasons Played	Apps	Subs	Gls
Tranmere Rov		10.49	51-57	120	-	28

DAVIES Ellis Reginald (Reg)
Cymmer, 27 May, 1929 W-6 (IF)

League Club	Source	Date Signed	Seasons Played	Apps	Subs	Gls
Southend U	Southampton (Am)	07.49	49-50	41	-	18
Newcastle U	Tr	04.51	51-58	157	-	49
Swansea T	Tr	10.58	58-61	111	-	29
Carlisle U	Tr	06.62	62-63	65	-	13

DAVIES Reginald (Reg) Walter
Tipton, 10 October, 1933 (G)

League Club	Source	Date Signed	Seasons Played	Apps	Subs	Gls
West Bromwich A	Palethorpes	01.51	53-54	4	-	0
Walsall	Tr	07.55	55-56	53	-	0
Millwall	Tr	05.58	58-62	199	-	0
Leyton Orient	Tr	07.63	63	11	-	0
Port Vale	Tr	07.64	64	13	-	0
Leyton Orient	Tr	03.65	64-65	16	0	0

DAVIES Robert Griffith
Blaenau Ffestiniog, 19 October, 1913 Died 1978 WWar-6 (CD)

League Club	Source	Date Signed	Seasons Played	Apps	Subs	Gls
Nottingham F	Blaenau Ffestiniog	11.36	36-46	55	-	0

DAVIES Roger
Wolverhampton, 25 October, 1950 Eu23-1 (F)

League Club	Source	Date Signed	Seasons Played	Apps	Subs	Gls
Derby Co	Worcester C	09.71	72-75	98	16	31
Preston NE	L	08.72	72	2	0	0
Leicester C	FC Bruges (Bel)	12.77	77-78	22	4	6
Derby Co	Tulsa (USA)	09.79	79	22	0	3
Darlington	Fort Lauderdale Str	11.83	83	10	0	1

DAVIES Ronald (Roy) Alfred
Cape Town, South Africa, 23 August, 1924 Died 1973 South Africa int (W)

League Club	Source	Date Signed	Seasons Played	Apps	Subs	Gls
Luton T	Clyde	05.51	51-56	150	-	24

DAVIES Ronald (Ron) George
Swansea, 13 November, 1935 (WH)

League Club	Source	Date Signed	Seasons Played	Apps	Subs	Gls
Swansea T	Tower U	05.58	58	2	-	0

DAVIES Ronald (Ron) Thomas
Merthyr Tydfil, 21 September, 1932 (FB)

League Club	Source	Date Signed	Seasons Played	Apps	Subs	Gls
Cardiff C	Merthyr Tydfil	10.52	55-57	32	-	3
Southampton	Tr	03.58	57-63	161	-	0
Aldershot	Tr	08.64	64-66	84	1	1

DAVIES Ronald (Ron) Tudor
Holywell, 25 May, 1942 Wu23-3/W-29 (F)

League Club	Source	Date Signed	Seasons Played	Apps	Subs	Gls
Chester	Jnrs	07.59	59-62	94	-	44
Luton T	Tr	10.62	62-63	32	-	21
Norwich C	Tr	09.63	63-65	113	0	58
Southampton	Tr	08.66	66-72	239	1	134
Portsmouth	Tr	04.73	73-74	59	0	18
Manchester U	Tr	11.74	74	0	8	0
Millwall	L	11.75	75	3	0	0

DAVIES Roy
Ealing, 25 October, 1953 (M)

League Club	Source	Date Signed	Seasons Played	Apps	Subs	Gls
Reading	Slough T	09.77	77	37	0	2
Torquay U	Tr	08.78	78-79	65	5	6
Wimbledon	Tr	08.80	80	6	3	0

DAVIES Roy Martin
Cardiff, 19 August, 1971 WYth (FB)

League Club	Source	Date Signed	Seasons Played	Apps	Subs	Gls
Newport Co	YT	•	87	0	2	0

DAVIES Sean Graham
Middlesbrough, 27 February, 1985 (FB)

League Club	Source	Date Signed	Seasons Played	Apps	Subs	Gls
York C	Sch	•	03	6	2	0

DAVIES Simon
Haverfordwest, 23 October, 1979 WYth/Wu21-10/WB-1/W-24 (M)

League Club	Source	Date Signed	Seasons Played	Apps	Subs	Gls
Peterborough U	YT	07.97	97-99	63	2	6
Tottenham H	Tr	01.00	99-04	99	22	13

DAVIES Simon Ithel
Winsford, 23 April, 1974 W-1 (M)

League Club	Source	Date Signed	Seasons Played	Apps	Subs	Gls
Manchester U	YT	07.92	94-95	4	7	0
Exeter C	L	12.93	93	5	1	1
Huddersfield T	L	10.96	96	3	0	0
Luton T	Tr	08.97	97-98	10	12	1
Macclesfield T	Tr	12.98	98-99	39	9	3
Rochdale	Tr	08.00	00	7	5	1

DAVIES Steven (Steve) Easman
Liverpool, 16 July, 1960 (W)

League Club	Source	Date Signed	Seasons Played	Apps	Subs	Gls
Port Vale	Congleton T	12.87	87	1	5	0

DAVIES Wilford Gordon
Swansea, 31 July, 1915 Died 1992 (FB)

League Club	Source	Date Signed	Seasons Played	Apps	Subs	Gls
Swansea T		03.34	34-46	54	-	0

DAVIES William
Troedyrhiw, 22 June, 1910 Died 1995 WWar-1 (W)

League Club	Source	Date Signed	Seasons Played	Apps	Subs	Gls
Watford	New Tredegar	07.30	30-49	283	-	69

DAVIES William (Bill)
Middlesbrough, 16 May, 1930 (CD)

League Club	Source	Date Signed	Seasons Played	Apps	Subs	Gls
Hull C	St Mary's College OB	04.49				
Leeds U	Tr	08.50				
Reading	Scarborough	12.52	54-60	202	-	0

DAVIES William (Will)
Wirksworth, 27 September, 1975 (CD)

League Club	Source	Date Signed	Seasons Played	Apps	Subs	Gls
Derby Co	YT	07.94	94	1	1	0

DAVIES William
(W)

League Club	Source	Date Signed	Seasons Played	Apps	Subs	Gls
Crewe Alex	Droylsden	02.47	46	11	-	3

DAVIES William (Billy) McIntosh
Glasgow, 31 May, 1964 (M)

League Club	Source	Date Signed	Seasons Played	Apps	Subs	Gls
Leicester C	St Mirren	08.90	90	5	1	0

DAVIES Ronald Wyn
Caernarfon, 20 March, 1942 Wu23-4/W-34 (F)

League Club	Source	Date Signed	Seasons Played	Apps	Subs	Gls
Wrexham	Caernarvon T	04.60	60-61	55	-	21
Bolton W	Tr	03.62	61-66	155	0	66
Newcastle U	Tr	10.66	66-70	181	0	40
Manchester C	Tr	08.71	71-72	45	0	8
Manchester U	Tr	09.72	72	15	1	4
Blackpool	Tr	06.73	73-74	34	2	5
Crystal Palace	L	08.74	74	3	0	0
Stockport Co	Tr	08.75	75	28	2	7
Crewe Alex	Arcadia Shepherds (SA)	08.76	76-77	50	5	13

DAVIN Joseph (Joe) James
Dumbarton, 13 February, 1942 SSch (FB)

League Club	Source	Date Signed	Seasons Played	Apps	Subs	Gls
Ipswich T	Hibernian	07.63	63-65	77	0	0

DAVIS Arron Spencer
Wanstead, 11 February, 1972 (FB)

League Club	Source	Date Signed	Seasons Played	Apps	Subs	Gls
Torquay U	YT	08.91	91-92	20	4	0
Colchester U	Dorchester T	08.94	94	4	0	0

DAVIS Claude
Jamaica, 6 March, 1979 Jamaica int (CD)

League Club	Source	Date Signed	Seasons Played	Apps	Subs	Gls
Preston NE	Portmore U (Jam)	08.03	03-04	37	17	1

DAVIS Craig
Rotherham, 12 October, 1977 (G)

League Club	Source	Date Signed	Seasons Played	Apps	Subs	Gls
Rotherham U	YT	06.96				
Doncaster Rov	Denaby U	11.97	97	15	0	0

DAVIS Cyril
Birmingham, 21 July, 1925 Died 1992 (CF)

League Club	Source	Date Signed	Seasons Played	Apps	Subs	Gls
Walsall (Am)	Hednesford T	05.48	48	1	-	0

DAVIS Daniel (Danny) Jonathan Steven
Brighton, 3 October, 1980 (M)

League Club	Source	Date Signed	Seasons Played	Apps	Subs	Gls
Brighton & Hove A	YT	06.99	98	0	1	0

DAVIS Darren John
Sutton-in-Ashfield, 5 February, 1967 EYth (CD)

League Club	Source	Date Signed	Seasons Played	Apps	Subs	Gls
Notts Co	App	02.85	83-87	90	2	1
Lincoln C	Tr	08.88	88-90	97	5	4
Maidstone U	Tr	03.91	90-91	31	0	2
Scarborough	Frickley Ath	08.93	93-94	46	2	3
Lincoln C	Grantham T	07.95	95	3	0	0

DAVIS Derek Edgar Counsell
Colwyn Bay, 19 June, 1922 Died 1985 (G)

League Club	Source	Date Signed	Seasons Played	Apps	Subs	Gls
Norwich C	Plymouth Arg (Am)	10.45	46-47	26	-	0
Torquay U	Tr	08.48	48-50	89	-	0

DAVIS Edward
Brackley, 8 March, 1922 (W)

League Club	Source	Date Signed	Seasons Played	Apps	Subs	Gls
Newport Co	RAF Hereford	10.46	46	3	-	1

DAVIS Eric William Charles
Stonehouse, Devon, 26 February, 1932 (CF)

League Club	Source	Date Signed	Seasons Played	Apps	Subs	Gls
Plymouth Arg	Tavistock T	08.52	52-56	64	-	29
Scunthorpe U	Tr	07.57	57-58	40	-	20
Chester	Tr	02.59	58-59	31	-	11
Oldham Ath	Tr	09.60	60	2	-	1

DAVIS Joseph Frederick (Fred)
Bloxwich, 23 May, 1929 Died 1996 (WH)

League Club	Source	Date Signed	Seasons Played	Apps	Subs	Gls
Reading	Bloxwich Strollers	12.52	53-54	63	-	1
Wrexham	Tr	07.55	55-60	230	-	12

DAVIS Gareth
Bangor, 11 July, 1949 Wu23-4/W-3 (CD)

League Club	Source	Date Signed	Seasons Played	Apps	Subs	Gls
Wrexham	Colwyn Bay	10.67	67-82	482	8	9

DAVIS Gordon
Newcastle, 14 December, 1930 Died 1977 (CD)

League Club	Source	Date Signed	Seasons Played	Apps	Subs	Gls
Gateshead	Everton (Am)	11.49	51-56	87	-	0

DAVIS Ian
Hull, 1 February, 1965 (M)

League Club	Source	Date Signed	Seasons Played	Apps	Subs	Gls
Hull C	App	02.83	81-82	25	3	1

DAVIS James (Jimmy) Roger William
Redditch, 6 February, 1982 Died 2003 ESch/EYth/Eu20 (M)

League Club	Source	Date Signed	Seasons Played	Apps	Subs	Gls
Manchester U	YT	09.99				
Swindon T	L	08.02	02	10	3	2

DAVIS John Leslie
Hackney, 31 March, 1957 (FB)

League Club	Source	Date Signed	Seasons Played	Apps	Subs	Gls
Gillingham	Arsenal (App)	07.75	75	2	1	0
Sheffield Wed	Tr	10.76	76	1	0	0

DAVIS Joseph (Joe)
Glasgow, 22 May, 1941 (FB)

League Club	Source	Date Signed	Seasons Played	Apps	Subs	Gls
Carlisle U	Hibernian	12.69	69-71	75	4	0

DAVIS Joseph (Joe)
Bristol, 24 August, 1938 (CD)

League Club	Source	Date Signed	Seasons Played	Apps	Subs	Gls
Bristol Rov	Soundwell	03.56	60-66	210	1	4
Swansea T	Tr	03.67	66-67	36	0	0

DAVIS Kelvin Geoffrey
Bedford, 29 September, 1976 EYth/Eu21-3 (G)

League Club	Source	Date Signed	Seasons Played	Apps	Subs	Gls
Luton T	YT	07.94	93-98	92	0	0
Torquay U	L	09.94	94	2	0	0
Hartlepool U	L	08.97	97	2	0	0
Wimbledon	Tr	07.99	00-02	131	0	0
Ipswich T	Tr	08.03	03-04	84	0	0

DAVIS Kenneth (Ken) Edward
Romsey, 6 February, 1933 (W)

League Club	Source	Date Signed	Seasons Played	Apps	Subs	Gls
Bristol C	Jnrs	05.52	52	1	-	0

DAVIS Leonard (Len) Philip
Cork, 31 July, 1931 (CF)

League Club	Source	Date Signed	Seasons Played	Apps	Subs	Gls
Arsenal		11.49				
Walsall	Tr	02.54	53-54	25	-	5

DAVIS Mark Ronald
Wallsend, 12 October, 1969 (M)

League Club	Source	Date Signed	Seasons Played	Apps	Subs	Gls
Darlington	App	●	86	0	2	0

DAVIS Michael (Mike) Vernon
Bristol, 19 October, 1974 (F)

League Club	Source	Date Signed	Seasons Played	Apps	Subs	Gls
Bristol Rov	Yate T	04.93	92-95	3	14	1
Hereford U	L	08.94	94	1	0	0

DAVIS Neil Leonard
Bloxwich, 15 August, 1973 (F)

League Club	Source	Date Signed	Seasons Played	Apps	Subs	Gls
Aston Villa	Redditch U	05.91	95	0	2	0
Wycombe W	L	10.96	96	13	0	0
Walsall	Tr	08.98	98	0	1	0

DAVIS Paul Edward
Newham, 31 January, 1968 (FB)

League Club	Source	Date Signed	Seasons Played	Apps	Subs	Gls
Queens Park Rgrs	App	12.85				
Aldershot	Tr	08.87	87	1	0	0

DAVIS Paul Vincent
Dulwich, 9 December, 1961 Eu21-11/EB/FLge (M)

League Club	Source	Date Signed	Seasons Played	Apps	Subs	Gls
Arsenal	App	07.79	79-94	331	20	30
Brentford	Tr	09.95	95	5	0	0

DAVIS Richard (Dickie) Daniel
Birmingham, 22 January, 1922 Died 1999 ESch (CF)

League Club	Source	Date Signed	Seasons Played	Apps	Subs	Gls
Sunderland	Morris Motors	02.39	46-53	144	-	73
Darlington	Tr	05.54	54-56	93	-	32

DAVIS Richard Frederick
Plymouth, 14 November, 1943 (FB)

League Club	Source	Date Signed	Seasons Played	Apps	Subs	Gls
Plymouth Arg	App	11.61	62-63	23	-	0
Southampton	Tr	07.64	64	1	-	0
Bristol C	Tr	07.65	67-68	8	0	0
Barrow	Tr	03.69	68-69	50	0	0

DAVIS Sean
Clapham, 20 September, 1979 Eu21-11 (M)

League Club	Source	Date Signed	Seasons Played	Apps	Subs	Gls
Fulham	YT	07.98	96-03	128	27	14
Tottenham H	Tr	07.04	04	11	4	0

DAVIS Solomon (Sol) Sebastian
Cheltenham, 4 September, 1979 (FB)

League Club	Source	Date Signed	Seasons Played	Apps	Subs	Gls
Swindon T	YT	05.98	97-01	100	17	0
Luton T	Tr	08.02	02-04	113	2	2

DAVIS Stephen (Steve) Mark
Hexham, 30 October, 1968 (CD)

League Club	Source	Date Signed	Seasons Played	Apps	Subs	Gls
Southampton	YT	07.87	89-90	5	1	0
Burnley	L	11.89	89	7	2	0
Notts Co	L	03.91	90	0	2	0
Burnley	Tr	08.91	91-94	162	0	22
Luton T	Tr	07.95	95-98	137	1	21
Burnley	Tr	12.98	98-02	152	4	20
Blackpool	Tr	07.03	03	22	7	1

DAVIS Steven
Ballymena, 1 January, 1985 NISch/NIYth/NIu21-3/NIu23-1/NI-4 (M)

League Club	Source	Date Signed	Seasons Played	Apps	Subs	Gls
Aston Villa	YT	01.02	04	19	9	1

DAVIS Steven (Steve) Peter
Birmingham, 26 July, 1965 EYth (CD)

League Club	Source	Date Signed	Seasons Played	Apps	Subs	Gls
Crewe Alex	Stoke C (App)	08.83	83-87	140	5	1
Burnley	Tr	10.87	87-90	147	0	11
Barnsley	Tr	07.91	91-96	103	4	10
York C	L	09.97	97	2	0	1
Oxford U	Tr	02.98	97-99	38	4	3

DAVISON Aidan John
Sedgefield, 11 May, 1968 NIB-1/NI-3 (G)

League Club	Source	Date Signed	Seasons Played	Apps	Subs	Gls
Notts Co	Billingham Synthonia	03.88	88	1	0	0
Bury	Tr	10.89				
Millwall	Tr	08.91	91-92	34	0	0
Bolton W	Tr	07.93	93-95	35	2	0
Hull C	L	11.96	96	9	0	0
Bradford C	Tr	03.97	96	10	0	0
Grimsby T	Tr	07.97	97-98	77	0	0
Sheffield U	Tr	08.99	99	1	1	0
Bradford C	Tr	01.00	99-02	49	2	0
Grimsby T	Tr	08.03	03	32	0	0
Colchester U	Tr	07.04	04	33	0	0

DAVISON Arthur
Hackney, 21 December, 1915 (FB)

League Club	Source	Date Signed	Seasons Played	Apps	Subs	Gls
Stockport Co		09.45				
Torquay U		11.46	46	1	-	0

DAVISON Daniel (Danny)
Newcastle, 11 November, 1947 (FB)

League Club	Source	Date Signed	Seasons Played	Apps	Subs	Gls
Barrow	Newcastle U (Am)	09.65	66-69	6	1	0

DAVISON Edward (Ted)
Seaham, 15 April, 1933 (CD)

League Club	Source	Date Signed	Seasons Played	Apps	Subs	Gls
Hartlepools U	Seaham Jnrs	08.53	53	1	-	0

DAVISON James (Jimmy) Hawkins
Sunderland, 1 November, 1942 Died 1987 (W)

League Club	Source	Date Signed	Seasons Played	Apps	Subs	Gls
Sunderland	Jnrs	11.59	59-62	62	-	10
Bolton W	Tr	11.63	63	21	-	1

DAVISON Joseph (Joe) Henry
Newcastle, 29 July, 1919 Died 1983 (FB)

League Club	Source	Date Signed	Seasons Played	Apps	Subs	Gls
Darlington	Throckley Welfare	01.47	46-53	240	-	8

DAVISON Robert (Bobby)
South Shields, 17 July, 1959 (F)

League Club	Source	Date Signed	Seasons Played	Apps	Subs	Gls
Huddersfield T	Seaham CW	07.80	80	1	1	0
Halifax T	Tr	08.81	81-82	63	0	29
Derby Co	Tr	12.82	82-87	203	3	83
Leeds U	Tr	11.87	87-91	79	12	31
Derby Co	L	09.91	91	10	0	8
Sheffield U	L	03.92	91	6	5	4
Leicester C	Tr	08.92	92	21	4	6
Sheffield U	Tr	11.93	93	9	3	1
Rotherham U	Tr	10.94	94-95	20	2	4
Hull C	L	11.95	95	11	0	4

DAVOCK Michael (Mike)
St Helens, 27 April, 1935 (W)

League Club	Source	Date Signed	Seasons Played	Apps	Subs	Gls
Stockport Co	St Helens	01.57	56-63	235	-	41

D'AVRAY Jean Michel (Mich)
Johannesburg, South Africa, 19 February, 1962 Eu21-2 (F)

League Club	Source	Date Signed	Seasons Played	Apps	Subs	Gls
Ipswich T	App	05.79	79-89	170	41	37
Leicester C	L	02.87	86	3	0	0

DAVY Stephen (Steve)
Norwich, 9 April, 1955 (CD)

League Club	Source	Date Signed	Seasons Played	Apps	Subs	Gls
Scunthorpe U	West Ham U (N/C)	08.77	77-81	126	8	1

DAWE Simon
Plymouth, 16 March, 1977 (M)

League Club	Source	Date Signed	Seasons Played	Apps	Subs	Gls
Plymouth Arg	YT	07.95	94	3	1	0

DAWES Derek Malcolm
Dawley, 23 June, 1944 (IF)

League Club	Source	Date Signed	Seasons Played	Apps	Subs	Gls
Shrewsbury T	App	06.62	61-62	9	-	0

DAWES Frederick (Fred) William
Frimley Green, 2 May, 1911 Died 1989 (FB)

League Club	Source	Date Signed	Seasons Played	Apps	Subs	Gls
Northampton T	Aldershot	03.30	29-35	162	-	1
Crystal Palace	Tr	02.36	35-49	222	-	2

DAWES Ian Michael
Aldershot, 5 January, 1965 ESch (CD)

League Club	Source	Date Signed	Seasons Played	Apps	Subs	Gls
Newcastle U	Jnrs	06.83				
Northampton T	Tr	06.85	85	3	2	0

DAWES Ian Robert
Croydon, 22 February, 1963 ESch (FB)

League Club	Source	Date Signed	Seasons Played	Apps	Subs	Gls
Queens Park Rgrs	App	12.80	81-87	229	0	3
Millwall	Tr	08.88	88-94	219	6	5

DAWES Malcolm
Trimdon, 3 March, 1944 (CD)

League Club	Source	Date Signed	Seasons Played	Apps	Subs	Gls
Darlington		03.62				
Aldershot	Horden CW	08.65	65-69	160	4	2
Hartlepool	Tr	07.70	70-75	193	2	12
Workington	Tr	11.75	75-76	49	2	1

DAWKINS Derek Anthony
Edmonton, 29 November, 1959 (FB)

League Club	Source	Date Signed	Seasons Played	Apps	Subs	Gls
Leicester C	App	11.77	77	3	0	0
Mansfield T	Tr	12.78	78-80	73	0	0
Bournemouth	Tr	08.81	81-82	4	4	0
Torquay U	Weymouth	02.84	83-88	153	22	7

DAWKINS Trevor Andrew
Rochford, 7 October, 1945 ESch/EYth (M)

League Club	Source	Date Signed	Seasons Played	Apps	Subs	Gls
West Ham U	App	10.62	64-66	5	1	0
Crystal Palace	Tr	10.67	67-70	24	1	3
Brentford	L	09.71	71	3	1	0

DAWS Anthony (Tony)
Sheffield, 10 September, 1966 ESch/EYth (F)

League Club	Source	Date Signed	Seasons Played	Apps	Subs	Gls
Notts Co	App	09.84	84-85	6	2	1
Sheffield U	Tr	08.86	86	7	4	3
Scunthorpe U	Tr	07.87	87-92	166	17	63
Grimsby T	Tr	03.93	92-93	14	2	1
Lincoln C	Tr	02.94	93-95	42	9	13
Scarborough	Tr	08.96	96	4	2	0

DAWS Nicholas (Nick) John
Manchester, 15 March, 1970 (M)

League Club	Source	Date Signed	Seasons Played	Apps	Subs	Gls
Bury	Altrincham	08.92	92-00	356	13	16
Rotherham U	Tr	07.01	01-03	54	18	2
Grimsby T	L	09.03	03	7	0	0
Grimsby T	L	01.04	03	10	0	0

DAWSON Alexander (Alec)
Glasgow, 23 October, 1933 Died 1986 (W)

League Club	Source	Date Signed	Seasons Played	Apps	Subs	Gls
Queens Park Rgrs	Gourock Jnrs	02.57	56-58	59	-	5

DAWSON Alexander (Alex) Downie
Aberdeen, 21 February, 1940 SSch (F)

League Club	Source	Date Signed	Seasons Played	Apps	Subs	Gls
Manchester U	Jnrs	04.57	56-61	80	-	45
Preston NE	Tr	10.61	61-66	199	0	114
Bury	Tr	03.67	66-68	49	1	21
Brighton & Hove A	Tr	12.68	68-70	53	4	26
Brentford	L	09.70	70	10	0	6

DAWSON Alistair (Ally) John
Glasgow, 25 February, 1958 SYth/Su21-8/S-5 (FB)

League Club	Source	Date Signed	Seasons Played	Apps	Subs	Gls
Blackburn Rov	Glasgow Rgrs	08.87	87-89	32	8	0

DAWSON Andrew (Andy)
Northallerton, 20 October, 1978 (FB)

League Club	Source	Date Signed	Seasons Played	Apps	Subs	Gls
Nottingham F	YT	10.95				
Scunthorpe U	Tr	12.98	98-02	192	3	8
Hull C	Tr	07.03	03-04	66	1	3

DAWSON Andrew (Andy) Stephen
York, 8 December, 1979 (FB)

League Club	Source	Date Signed	Seasons Played	Apps	Subs	Gls
York C	YT	07.98	98-99	18	10	1

DAWSON Carl Michael
Dovercourt, 24 June, 1934 Died 1991 (G)

League Club	Source	Date Signed	Seasons Played	Apps	Subs	Gls
Lincoln C (Am)	Jnrs	05.50	50	1	-	0

DAWSON Edward
Chester-le-Street, 16 January, 1913 Died 1970 (G)

League Club	Source	Date Signed	Seasons Played	Apps	Subs	Gls
Manchester C	Blyth Spartans	12.34				
Bristol C	Tr	05.36	36-38	66	-	0
Gateshead	Tr	08.46	46-48	83	-	0

DAWSON George
Glasgow, 13 September, 1930 (WH)

League Club	Source	Date Signed	Seasons Played	Apps	Subs	Gls
Queens Park Rgrs	Motherwell	05.55	55	1	-	0

DAWSON James (Jimmy) Emslie Irvine Bannerman
Stoneyburn, 21 December, 1927 Died 2005 (W)

League Club	Source	Date Signed	Seasons Played	Apps	Subs	Gls
Leicester C	Polkemmet	05.46	46-48	5	-	0
Portsmouth	Tr	06.49	49	1	-	0

DAWSON Jason
Burslem, 9 February, 1971 (F)

League Club	Source	Date Signed	Seasons Played	Apps	Subs	Gls
Rochdale	Port Vale (YT)	07.89	89-90	37	18	7

DAWSON Kevin Edward
Northallerton, 18 June, 1981 (CD)

League Club	Source	Date Signed	Seasons Played	Apps	Subs	Gls
Nottingham F	YT	06.98	99-01	8	3	0
Barnet	L	03.01	00	5	0	0
Chesterfield	Tr	08.02	02-04	49	2	1

DAWSON Michael Richard
Northallerton, 18 November, 1983 EYth/Eu21-7 (CD)

League Club	Source	Date Signed	Seasons Played	Apps	Subs	Gls
Nottingham F	YT	11.00	01-04	82	1	7
Tottenham H	Tr	01.05	04	5	0	0

DAWSON Owen John
Christchurch, 7 March, 1943 EYth (FB)

League Club	Source	Date Signed	Seasons Played	Apps	Subs	Gls
Portsmouth	Jnrs	06.60				
Swindon T	Tr	06.62	62-70	196	6	4

DAWSON Peter
Crewe, 19 January, 1933 (FB)

League Club	Source	Date Signed	Seasons Played	Apps	Subs	Gls
Crewe Alex		01.54	55	2	-	0

DAWSON Joseph **Reginald (Reg)**
Sheffield, 4 October, 1914 Died 1973 (W)

League Club	Source	Date Signed	Seasons Played	Apps	Subs	Gls
Rotherham U		01.39	38-46	32	-	2

DAWSON Richard
Chesterfield, 19 January, 1960 (F)

League Club	Source	Date Signed	Seasons Played	Apps	Subs	Gls
Rotherham U	App	01.78	77-79	21	3	3
Doncaster Rov	Tr	02.81	80-81	39	4	14
Chesterfield	Tr	08.82	82	6	6	0

DAWSON Richard
York, 6 July, 1962 (CD)

League Club	Source	Date Signed	Seasons Played	Apps	Subs	Gls
York C	New Earswick	07.80	81-82	45	0	0

DAWSON Richard
Sheffield, 12 April, 1967 (G)

League Club	Source	Date Signed	Seasons Played	Apps	Subs	Gls
Grimsby T	Stoke C (App)	08.84	84	1	0	0

DAWSON Robert (Bobby)
South Shields, 31 January, 1935 (FB)

League Club	Source	Date Signed	Seasons Played	Apps	Subs	Gls
Leeds U	South Shields	11.53	53	1	-	0
Gateshead	Tr	11.55	55-59	118	-	1

DAWSON Robert Anthony
Bentley, South Yorkshire, 21 June, 1944 (G)

League Club	Source	Date Signed	Seasons Played	Apps	Subs	Gls
Doncaster Rov		12.64	65-66	28	0	0

DAWSON Thomas (Tommy)
Middlesbrough, 6 February, 1915 Died 1972 (IF)

League Club	Source	Date Signed	Seasons Played	Apps	Subs	Gls
Darlington	Whitby U	12.36	36-37	23	-	3
Charlton Ath	Spennymoor U	02.39	38-46	23	-	2
Brentford	Tr	08.47	47	36	-	10
Swindon T	Tr	05.48	48-49	65	-	15

DAWSON William
Glasgow, 5 February, 1931 Died 1991 (CF)

League Club	Source	Date Signed	Seasons Played	Apps	Subs	Gls
Northampton T	Glasgow Ashfield	03.55	54-55	14	-	7

DAWTRY Kevin Austin
Hythe, Hampshire, 15 June, 1958 (M)

League Club	Source	Date Signed	Seasons Played	Apps	Subs	Gls
Southampton	App	06.76	78	0	1	0
Crystal Palace	Tr	05.80				
Bournemouth	Tr	03.81	80-83	58	5	11
Reading	L	09.82	82	4	0	0

DAY Albert
Camberwell, 7 March, 1918 Died 1983 (W)

League Club	Source	Date Signed	Seasons Played	Apps	Subs	Gls
Brighton & Hove A	Hastings & St Leonard	08.38				
Ipswich T	Tr	05.46	46-48	63	-	25
Watford	Tr	08.49	49	4	-	1

DAY Christopher (Chris) Nicholas
Leytonstone, 28 July, 1975 EYth/Eu21-6 (G)

League Club	Source	Date Signed	Seasons Played	Apps	Subs	Gls
Tottenham H	YT	04.93				
Crystal Palace	Tr	08.96	96	24	0	0
Watford	Tr	07.97	99	11	0	0
Lincoln C	L	12.00	00	14	0	0
Queens Park Rgrs	Tr	07.01	01-04	87	0	0
Preston NE	L	02.05	04	6	0	0

DAY Clive Anthony
Orsett, 27 January, 1961 (FB)

League Club	Source	Date Signed	Seasons Played	Apps	Subs	Gls
Fulham	App	08.78	80-81	2	8	0
Mansfield T	L	08.82	82	10	2	1
Aldershot	Tr	08.83	83-84	53	7	0

DAY Eric Charles
Dartford, 6 November, 1921 (W)

League Club	Source	Date Signed	Seasons Played	Apps	Subs	Gls
Southampton	RAF Ford	04.45	46-56	398	-	145

DAY Graham George
Bristol, 22 November, 1953 (CD)

League Club	Source	Date Signed	Seasons Played	Apps	Subs	Gls
Bristol Rov	Bristol St George	05.73	74-78	129	1	1

DAY Burcombe **James (Jimmy)**
Watford, 9 May, 1931 (IF)

League Club	Source	Date Signed	Seasons Played	Apps	Subs	Gls
Watford	Berkhamsted T	12.51	51	3	-	0

DAY James (Jamie) Russell
Bexley, 13 September, 1979 ESch (M)

League Club	Source	Date Signed	Seasons Played	Apps	Subs	Gls
Arsenal	YT	07.97				
Bournemouth	Tr	03.99	98-00	15	5	1

DAY Jamie Robert
High Wycombe, 7 May, 1986 (M)

League Club	Source	Date Signed	Seasons Played	Apps	Subs	Gls
Peterborough U	Sch	08.03	04	0	1	0

DAY John (Jack) Norman
Northfleet, 21 January, 1924 (G)

League Club	Source	Date Signed	Seasons Played	Apps	Subs	Gls
Gillingham	Brighton & Hove A (Am)	07.50	50	1	-	0

DAY Keith David
Grays, 29 November, 1962 (CD)

League Club	Source	Date Signed	Seasons Played	Apps	Subs	Gls
Colchester U	Aveley	08.84	84-86	113	0	12
Leyton Orient	Tr	07.87	87-92	184	8	9

DAY Mervyn Richard
Chelmsford, 26 June, 1955 EYth/Eu23-5 (G)

League Club	Source	Date Signed	Seasons Played	Apps	Subs	Gls
West Ham U	App	03.73	73-78	194	0	0

League Club	Source	Date Signed	Seasons Played	Apps	Subs	Gls
Orient	Tr	07.79	79-82	170	0	0
Aston Villa	Tr	08.83	83-84	30	0	0
Leeds U	Tr	01.85	84-92	227	0	0
Luton T	L	03.92	91	4	0	0
Sheffield U	L	04.92	91	1	0	0
Carlisle U	Tr	07.93	93	16	0	0

DAY Rhys
Bridgend, 31 August, 1982 WYth/Wu21-11 (CD)

League Club	Source	Date Signed	Seasons Played	Apps	Subs	Gls
Manchester C	YT	09.99				
Blackpool	L	12.01	01	4	5	0
Mansfield T	Tr	11.02	02-04	74	8	10

DAY Roger Arthur
Romford, 3 December, 1939 EAmat (IF)

League Club	Source	Date Signed	Seasons Played	Apps	Subs	Gls
Watford (Am)	Enfield	12.61	61	1	-	0

DAY William (Billy)
South Bank, 27 December, 1936 (W)

League Club	Source	Date Signed	Seasons Played	Apps	Subs	Gls
Middlesbrough	South Bank Jnrs	05.55	55-61	120	-	18
Newcastle U	Tr	03.62	61-62	13	-	1
Peterborough U	Tr	04.63	62-63	18	-	2

DAYKIN Reginald **Brian**
Long Eaton, 4 August, 1937 (WH)

League Club	Source	Date Signed	Seasons Played	Apps	Subs	Gls
Derby Co	Long Eaton T	11.55	59-61	4	-	1
Notts Co	Tr	07.62	62	3	-	0

DEACON David Benjamin
Broome, Norfolk,10 March, 1929 Died 1990 (FB)

League Club	Source	Date Signed	Seasons Played	Apps	Subs	Gls
Ipswich T	Bungay T	11.50	50-59	66	-	0

DEACY Eamonn Stephen
Galway, 1 October, 1958 LoI-1/IR-4 (FB)

League Club	Source	Date Signed	Seasons Played	Apps	Subs	Gls
Aston Villa	Galway Rov	03.79	79-83	27	6	1
Derby Co	L	10.83	83	5	0	0

DEACY Michael (Mike)
Cardiff, 29 November, 1943 (CD)

League Club	Source	Date Signed	Seasons Played	Apps	Subs	Gls
Newport Co		08.66	66-69	46	1	2

DEACY Nicholas (Nick) Simon
Cardiff, 19 July, 1953 Wu23-1/Wu21-1/W-12 (F/CD)

League Club	Source	Date Signed	Seasons Played	Apps	Subs	Gls
Hereford U	Merthyr Tydfil	09.74	74	13	4	2
Workington	L	12.74	74	5	0	1
Hull C	Vitesse Arnhem (Holl)	02.80	79-81	80	7	7
Bury	Happy Valley (HK)	10.83	83	30	1	0

DEAKIN Alan Roy
Birmingham, 27 November, 1941 Eu23-6 (M)

League Club	Source	Date Signed	Seasons Played	Apps	Subs	Gls
Aston Villa	Jnrs	12.58	59-69	230	1	9
Walsall	Tr	10.69	69-71	46	4	0

DEAKIN Frederick (Fred) Arthur
Birmingham, 5 February, 1920 Died 2000 (FB)

League Club	Source	Date Signed	Seasons Played	Apps	Subs	Gls
Birmingham		01.38				
Crystal Palace	Tr	09.46	46-47	6	-	0

DEAKIN John
Stocksbridge, 29 September, 1966 (M)

League Club	Source	Date Signed	Seasons Played	Apps	Subs	Gls
Doncaster Rov	Barnsley (App)	08.85	85-86	21	2	0
Birmingham C	Shepshed Charterhouse	09.89	89	3	4	0
Carlisle U	Tr	08.91	91	3	0	0

DEAKIN Michael (Mike) Raymond Frederick
Birmingham, 25 October, 1933 (CF)

League Club	Source	Date Signed	Seasons Played	Apps	Subs	Gls
Crystal Palace	Bromsgrove Rov	11.54	54-59	143	-	56
Northampton T	Tr	10.59	59-60	44	-	31
Aldershot	Tr	01.61	60-61	17	-	5

DEAKIN Peter
Normanton, 25 March, 1938 (M)

League Club	Source	Date Signed	Seasons Played	Apps	Subs	Gls
Bolton W	Jnrs	05.55	57-63	63	-	13
Peterborough U	Tr	06.64	64-66	74	1	34
Bradford PA	Tr	09.66	66-67	36	0	9
Peterborough U	Tr	09.67	67	16	0	1
Brentford	Tr	07.68	68	7	1	2

DEAKIN Raymond (Ray) John
Liverpool, 19 June, 1959 ESch (FB)

League Club	Source	Date Signed	Seasons Played	Apps	Subs	Gls
Everton	App	06.77				
Port Vale	Tr	08.81	81	21	2	6
Bolton W	Tr	08.82	82-84	104	1	2
Burnley	Tr	07.85	85-90	212	1	6

DEAKIN William (Billy) Edward
Maltby, 19 January, 1925 (W)

League Club	Source	Date Signed	Seasons Played	Apps	Subs	Gls
Barnsley	Sunnyside WMC	05.49	49-51	25	-	3
Chester	Tr	07.52	52	27	-	5

DEAN Alan John
Aldershot, 20 January, 1950 (FB)

League Club	Source	Date Signed	Seasons Played	Apps	Subs	Gls
Aldershot	App	01.68	66-67	3	0	0

DEAN Andrew (Andy) Geoffrey
Salford, 27 November, 1966 (FB)

League Club	Source	Date Signed	Seasons Played	Apps	Subs	Gls
Rochdale	Burnley (Jnrs)	10.83	83	1	0	0

DEAN Brian Robert
Stockport, 10 September, 1947 (FB)

League Club	Source	Date Signed	Seasons Played	Apps	Subs	Gls
Blackpool	Jnrs	09.64	67	0	1	0
Barrow	Tr	07.69	69-70	44	3	0

DEAN George Charles
Walsall, 22 February, 1930 (WH)

League Club	Source	Date Signed	Seasons Played	Apps	Subs	Gls
Walsall	Hilary Street OB	05.50	50-53	72	-	13

DEAN Joby
Edwinstowe, 25 November, 1934 (WH)

League Club	Source	Date Signed	Seasons Played	Apps	Subs	Gls
Queens Park Rgrs	Thoresby Colliery	11.52	55-56	16	-	0
Bradford PA	Sutton T	12.57	57-58	53	-	1

DEAN Joseph (Joe)
Manchester, 4 April, 1939 ESch/EYth (G)

League Club	Source	Date Signed	Seasons Played	Apps	Subs	Gls
Bolton W	Jnrs	04.56	55-59	17	-	0
Carlisle U	Tr	07.62	62-69	137	0	0
Barrow	Tr	07.70	70-71	41	0	0

DEAN Mark Christopher
Northwich, 18 November, 1964 (FB)

League Club	Source	Date Signed	Seasons Played	Apps	Subs	Gls
Chester	App	10.82	81-82	23	2	0

DEAN Michael (Mike) James
Weymouth, 9 March, 1978 (M)

League Club	Source	Date Signed	Seasons Played	Apps	Subs	Gls
Bournemouth	YT	07.96	95-98	18	16	0

DEAN Norman
Corby, 13 September, 1944 (F)

League Club	Source	Date Signed	Seasons Played	Apps	Subs	Gls
Southampton	Corby T	04.63	65	18	0	11
Cardiff C	Tr	03.67	66-68	20	1	3
Barnsley	Tr	09.68	68-72	58	2	19

DEAN Raymond (Ray) George
Steventon, 15 December, 1945 (CD)

League Club	Source	Date Signed	Seasons Played	Apps	Subs	Gls
Reading		05.66	66-68	50	4	0
Aldershot	Tr	07.69	69-74	256	0	7

DEANE Brian Christopher
Leeds, 7 February, 1968 EB-3/E-3 (F)

League Club	Source	Date Signed	Seasons Played	Apps	Subs	Gls
Doncaster Rov	Jnrs	12.85	85-87	59	7	12
Sheffield U	Tr	07.88	88-92	197	0	82
Leeds U	Tr	07.93	93-96	131	7	32
Sheffield U	Tr	07.97	97	24	0	11
Middlesbrough	Benfica (Por)	10.98	98-01	72	15	18
Leicester C	Tr	11.01	01-03	44	8	19
West Ham U	Tr	10.03	03	9	17	6
Leeds U	Tr	07.04	04	23	8	6
Sunderland	Tr	03.05	04	0	4	0

DEANS John (Joe) Kelty
Johnstone, 30 July, 1946 S-2 (F)

League Club	Source	Date Signed	Seasons Played	Apps	Subs	Gls
Luton T	Glasgow Celtic	06.76	76	13	1	6
Carlisle U	L	02.77	76	4	0	2

DEANS Raymond (Ray) Alexander
Glasgow, 24 January, 1966 SYth (F)

League Club	Source	Date Signed	Seasons Played	Apps	Subs	Gls
Doncaster Rov	Clyde	02.85	84-85	18	1	5

DEANS Thomas (Tommy) Sneddon
Shieldhill, 7 January, 1922 Died 2000 SLge-1 (FB)

League Club	Source	Date Signed	Seasons Played	Apps	Subs	Gls
Notts Co	Clyde	10.49	49-55	239	-	0

DEAR Brian Charles
Plaistow, 18 September, 1943 ESch (F)

League Club	Source	Date Signed	Seasons Played	Apps	Subs	Gls
West Ham U	App	11.60	62-68	63	2	33
Brighton & Hove A	L	03.67	66	7	0	5
Fulham	Tr	02.69	68	13	0	7
Millwall	Tr	07.69	69	5	1	0
West Ham U	Woodford T	10.70	70	4	0	0

DEAR Gerald (Gerry) Albert
Kensington, 5 January, 1937 (FB)

League Club	Source	Date Signed	Seasons Played	Apps	Subs	Gls
Swindon T		07.56	56	4	-	0

DEARDEN Kevin Charles
Luton, 8 March, 1970 (G)

League Club	Source	Date Signed	Seasons Played	Apps	Subs	Gls
Tottenham H	YT	08.88	92	0	1	0
Cambridge U	L	03.89	88	15	0	0
Hartlepool U	L	08.89	89	10	0	0
Swindon T	L	03.90	89	1	0	0
Peterborough U	L	08.90	90	7	0	0

League Club	Source	Date Signed	Seasons Played	Career Record Apps	Subs	Gls
Hull C	L	01.91	90	3	0	0
Rochdale	L	08.91	91	2	0	0
Birmingham C	L	03.92	91	12	0	0
Brentford	Tr	09.93	93-98	205	0	0
Barnet	L	02.99	98	1	0	0
Wrexham	Tr	06.99	99-00	81	0	0
Torquay U	Tr	08.01	01-04	98	2	0

DEARDEN William (Billy)
Oldham, 11 February, 1944 (F)

League Club	Source	Date Signed	Seasons Played	Apps	Subs	Gls
Oldham Ath	Jnrs	09.63	64-66	32	3	2
Crewe Alex	Tr	12.66	66-67	44	3	5
Chester	Tr	06.68	68-69	85	0	22
Sheffield U	Tr	04.70	70-75	170	5	61
Chester	Tr	02.76	75-76	35	1	7
Chesterfield	Tr	08.77	77-78	18	9	2

DEARSON Donald (Don) John
Ynysybwl, 13 May, 1914 Died 1990 WAmat/WWar-15/W-3 (IF)

League Club	Source	Date Signed	Seasons Played	Apps	Subs	Gls
Birmingham	Barry T	04.34	34-46	131	-	17
Coventry C	Tr	02.47	46-49	84	-	10
Walsall	Tr	03.50	49-50	51	-	12

DEARY John Steele
Ormskirk, 18 October, 1962 (M)

League Club	Source	Date Signed	Seasons Played	Apps	Subs	Gls
Blackpool	App	03.80	80-88	285	18	43
Burnley	Tr	07.89	89-94	209	6	23
Rochdale	Tr	01.95	94-96	90	1	10

DEATH Stephen (Steve) Victor
Elmswell, 19 September, 1949 Died 2003 ESch (G)

League Club	Source	Date Signed	Seasons Played	Apps	Subs	Gls
West Ham U	App	06.67	68	1	0	0
Reading	Tr	11.69	69-81	471	0	0

DEBEC Fabien
Lyon, France, 18 January, 1976 (G)

League Club	Source	Date Signed	Seasons Played	Apps	Subs	Gls
Coventry C	Rennes (Fr)	08.02	02	11	0	0

DEBENHAM Robert (Rob) Karl
Doncaster, 28 November, 1979 (FB)

League Club	Source	Date Signed	Seasons Played	Apps	Subs	Gls
Doncaster Rov	YT	●	97	4	2	0

DEBEVE Michael
Abbeville, France, 1 December, 1970 (M)

League Club	Source	Date Signed	Seasons Played	Apps	Subs	Gls
Middlesbrough	RC Lens (Fr)	02.02	01	1	3	0

DE BILDE Gilles Roger Gerard
Zellik, Belgium, 9 June, 1971 Belgium 25 (F)

League Club	Source	Date Signed	Seasons Played	Apps	Subs	Gls
Sheffield Wed	PSV Eindhoven (Holl)	07.99	99-00	50	9	13
Aston Villa	L	10.00	00	4	0	0

DE BLASIIS Jean-Yves
Bordeaux, France, 25 September, 1973 FrYth (M)

League Club	Source	Date Signed	Seasons Played	Apps	Subs	Gls
Norwich C	Red Star 93 (Fr)	07.99	99-00	28	7	0

DE BOLLA Grant Marcus (Mark)
Camberwell, 1 January, 1983 (F)

League Club	Source	Date Signed	Seasons Played	Apps	Subs	Gls
Aston Villa	YT	04.00				
Charlton Ath	Tr	01.01				
Chesterfield	L	09.03	03	2	1	0
Chesterfield	Tr	03.04	03-04	16	17	4

DE BONT Andrew (Andy) Cornelius
Wolverhampton, 7 February, 1974 (G)

League Club	Source	Date Signed	Seasons Played	Apps	Subs	Gls
Wolverhampton W	YT	07.92				
Hartlepool U	L	10.95	95	1	0	0
Hereford U	L	03.96	95	8	0	0
Hereford U	Tr	08.96	96	27	0	0

DEEGAN Mark
Liverpool, 12 November, 1971 WSemiPro (G)

League Club	Source	Date Signed	Seasons Played	Apps	Subs	Gls
Oxford U	Holywell T	08.94	94	2	0	0

DEEHAN John Matthew
Solihull, 6 August, 1957 EYth/Eu21-7 (F)

League Club	Source	Date Signed	Seasons Played	Apps	Subs	Gls
Aston Villa	App	04.75	75-79	107	3	40
West Bromwich A	Tr	09.79	79-81	44	3	5
Norwich C	Tr	12.81	81-85	158	4	62
Ipswich T	Tr	06.86	86-87	45	4	11
Manchester C	Tr	07.88				
Barnsley	Tr	01.90	90	3	8	2

DEELEY Norman Victor
Wednesbury, 30 November, 1933 ESch/E-2 (W)

League Club	Source	Date Signed	Seasons Played	Apps	Subs	Gls
Wolverhampton W	Jnrs	12.50	51-61	206	-	66
Leyton Orient	Tr	02.62	61-63	73	-	9

DEEN Ahmed Nuru
Sierra Leone, 30 June, 1985 (FB)

League Club	Source	Date Signed	Seasons Played	Apps	Subs	Gls
Peterborough U	Leicester C (Sch)	08.04	04	4	1	0

DEENEY Saul
Derry, 12 March, 1983 IRYth/IRu21-2 (G)

League Club	Source	Date Signed	Seasons Played	Apps	Subs	Gls
Notts Co	YT	09.00	02-04	41	1	0

DEERE Stephen (Steve) Herbert
Burnham Market, 31 March, 1948 (CD)

League Club	Source	Date Signed	Seasons Played	Apps	Subs	Gls
Scunthorpe U	Norwich C (Am)	11.67	67-72	232	4	21
Hull C	Tr	06.73	73-74	65	1	2
Barnsley	L	10.75	75	4	0	0
Stockport Co	L	12.75	75	6	0	0
Scunthorpe U	Scarborough	02.78	77-79	105	0	2

DEFOE Jermain Colin
Beckton, 7 October, 1982 ESch/EYth/Eu21-23/E-12 (F)

League Club	Source	Date Signed	Seasons Played	Apps	Subs	Gls
West Ham U	Charlton Ath (YT)	10.99	00-03	62	31	29
Bournemouth	L	10.00	00	27	2	18
Tottenham H	Tr	02.04	03-04	42	8	20

DE FREITAS Fabian
Paramaribo, Surinam, 28 July, 1972 (F)

League Club	Source	Date Signed	Seasons Played	Apps	Subs	Gls
Bolton W	Volendam (Holl)	08.94	94-95	24	16	7
West Bromwich A	CA Osasuna (Sp)	08.98	98-99	34	27	8

DE GARIS James (Jim) Frederick
Worcester, 9 October, 1952 (M)

League Club	Source	Date Signed	Seasons Played	Apps	Subs	Gls
Arsenal	App	06.70				
Bournemouth	Tr	09.71	71-73	8	4	0
Torquay U	Tr	03.74	73	7	2	0

DEGN Peter
Aarhus, Denmark, 6 April, 1977 Deu21 (M)

League Club	Source	Date Signed	Seasons Played	Apps	Subs	Gls
Everton	Aarhus GF (Den)	02.99	98	0	4	0

DE GOEY Eduard (Ed) Franciscus
Gouda, Holland, 20 December, 1966 Hou21-17/Ho-31 (G)

League Club	Source	Date Signed	Seasons Played	Apps	Subs	Gls
Chelsea	Feyenoord (Holl)	07.97	97-02	123	0	0
Stoke C	Tr	08.03	03-04	54	0	0

DE GOEY Leendert (Len)
Amsterdam, Holland, 29 February, 1952 (M)

League Club	Source	Date Signed	Seasons Played	Apps	Subs	Gls
Sheffield U	Sparta Rotterdam (Holl)	08.79	79	33	0	5

DE GRUCHY Raymond (Ray) Philip
Guernsey, 18 May, 1932 (FB)

League Club	Source	Date Signed	Seasons Played	Apps	Subs	Gls
Nottingham F		08.53				
Grimsby T	Tr	05.54	54-57	74	-	2
Chesterfield	Tr	06.58	58	1	-	0

DEGRYSE Marc
Roeslare, Belgium, 4 September, 1965 Belgium int (M)

League Club	Source	Date Signed	Seasons Played	Apps	Subs	Gls
Sheffield Wed	Anderlecht (Bel)	08.95	95	30	4	8

DE LA CRUZ Bernardo Ulises
Piqulucho, Ecuador, 8 February, 1974 Ecuador 78 (FB)

League Club	Source	Date Signed	Seasons Played	Apps	Subs	Gls
Aston Villa	Hibernian	08.02	02-04	62	20	1

DELANEY Damien
Cork, 20 July, 1981 IRYth/IRu21-1 (CD)

League Club	Source	Date Signed	Seasons Played	Apps	Subs	Gls
Leicester C	Cork C	11.00	00-01	5	3	0
Stockport Co	L	11.01	01	10	2	1
Huddersfield T	L	03.02	01	1	1	0
Mansfield T	L	09.02	02	7	0	0
Hull C	Tr	10.02	02-04	119	0	4

DELANEY James (Jimmy)
Stoneyburn, 3 September, 1914 Died 1989 SLge-6/SWar-5/S-13 (W)

League Club	Source	Date Signed	Seasons Played	Apps	Subs	Gls
Manchester U	Glasgow Celtic	02.46	46-50	164	-	25

DELANEY James (Jim) Christopher
London, 22 July, 1945 (F)

League Club	Source	Date Signed	Seasons Played	Apps	Subs	Gls
Newport Co	Port Talbot	07.69	69	1	0	0

DELANEY John Joseph
Slough, 3 February, 1942 EAmat (CD)

League Club	Source	Date Signed	Seasons Played	Apps	Subs	Gls
Bournemouth	Wycombe W	08.73	73-74	25	0	0

DELANEY Lewis Peter
Bothwell, 28 February, 1921 Died 1968 (FB)

League Club	Source	Date Signed	Seasons Played	Apps	Subs	Gls
Arsenal	Nunhead	05.43				
Crystal Palace	Tr	11.49	49	3	-	0

DELANEY Mark Anthony
Fishguard, 13 May, 1976 W-33 (FB)

League Club	Source	Date Signed	Seasons Played	Apps	Subs	Gls
Cardiff C	Carmarthen	07.98	98	28	0	0
Aston Villa	Tr	03.99	98-04	132	14	1

DELANY Dean
Dublin, 15 September, 1980 IRu21-6 (G)

League Club	Source	Date Signed	Seasons Played	Apps	Subs	Gls
Everton	YT	09.97				
Port Vale	Tr	06.00	00-03	34	2	0

DELAP Rory John
Sutton Coldfield, 6 July, 1976 IRu21-4/IRB-1/IR-11 (M)

League Club	Source	Date Signed	Seasons Played	Apps	Subs	Gls
Carlisle U	YT	07.94	92-97	40	25	7
Derby Co	Tr	02.98	97-00	97	6	11
Southampton	Tr	07.01	01-04	106	10	5

DELAPENHA Lloyd **Lindbergh (Lindy)**
Kingston, Jamaica, 20 May, 1927 (W)

League Club	Source	Date Signed	Seasons Played	Apps	Subs	Gls
Portsmouth	Arsenal (Am)	04.48	48-49	7	-	0
Middlesbrough	Tr	04.50	49-57	260	-	90
Mansfield T	Tr	06.58	58-60	115	-	27

DELF Barrie
Rochford, 5 June, 1961 (G)

League Club	Source	Date Signed	Seasons Played	Apps	Subs	Gls
Southend U	Trinity (Southend)	03.83	82	1	0	0

DELGADO Chala **Agustin**
Ibarra, Ecuador, 23 December, 1974 Ecuador 54 (F)

League Club	Source	Date Signed	Seasons Played	Apps	Subs	Gls
Southampton	Necaxa (Mex)	11.01	01-03	2	9	0

DELGADO Robert (Bob) Allan
Cardiff, 29 January, 1949 (CD)

League Club	Source	Date Signed	Seasons Played	Apps	Subs	Gls
Luton T	Barry T	02.70				
Carlisle U	Tr	07.71	71-73	25	10	3
Workington	L	10.73	73	7	0	0
Rotherham U	Tr	12.73	73-75	69	1	5
Chester	Tr	10.75	75-78	125	3	8
Port Vale	Tr	12.78	78-79	41	0	0

DELL Steven Bradley
Acton, 6 February, 1980 (FB)

League Club	Source	Date Signed	Seasons Played	Apps	Subs	Gls
Wycombe W	Beaconsfield SYCOB	08.03	03	3	1	0

DELLAS Traianos
Salonika, Greece, 31 January, 1976 (CD)

League Club	Source	Date Signed	Seasons Played	Apps	Subs	Gls
Sheffield U	Aris Salonika (Gre)	08.97	97-98	14	12	3

DELLOW Ronald (Ron) William
Crosby, 13 July, 1914 (W)

League Club	Source	Date Signed	Seasons Played	Apps	Subs	Gls
Blackburn Rov	Bootle Celtic	08.33				
Mansfield T	Tr	06.34	34	24	-	10
Manchester C	Tr	01.35	34	10	-	4
Tranmere Rov	Tr	03.36	35-38	105	-	29
Carlisle U	Tr	08.39	46	16	-	5

DELORGE Laurent Jan
Leuven, Belgium, 21 July, 1979 BeYth/Beu21 (M)

League Club	Source	Date Signed	Seasons Played	Apps	Subs	Gls
Coventry C	KAA Gent (Bel)	11.98	01-02	23	7	4

DELOUMEAUX Eric Jean
Montbeliard, France, 12 May, 1973 (M)

League Club	Source	Date Signed	Seasons Played	Apps	Subs	Gls
Coventry C	Aberdeen	01.04	03-04	20	1	1

DEL RIO Walter Jose
Buenos Aires, Argentina, 16 June, 1976 (CD)

League Club	Source	Date Signed	Seasons Played	Apps	Subs	Gls
Crystal Palace (L)	Boca Juniors (Arg)	09.98	98	1	1	0

DE LUCAS Enrique
Llobregat, Spain, 17 August, 1978 Spu21 (M)

League Club	Source	Date Signed	Seasons Played	Apps	Subs	Gls
Chelsea	Espanyol (Sp)	07.02	02	17	8	0

DELVE John Frederick
Ealing, 27 September, 1953 ESch (M)

League Club	Source	Date Signed	Seasons Played	Apps	Subs	Gls
Queens Park Rgrs	App	07.71	72-73	9	6	0
Plymouth Arg	Tr	07.74	74-77	127	5	6
Exeter C	Tr	03.78	77-82	215	0	20
Hereford U	Tr	06.83	83-86	116	2	11
Exeter C	Gloucester C	10.87	87	12	1	1

DEMAINE David (Dave) Jack
Cleveleys, 7 May, 1942 (W)

League Club	Source	Date Signed	Seasons Played	Apps	Subs	Gls
Blackpool	Jnrs	07.60				
Tranmere Rov	Tr	08.61	61	2	-	0
Southport	Tr	07.62	62	5	-	0

DE MANGE Kenneth (Ken) John Philip Petit
Dublin, 3 September, 1964 IRYth/IRu21-5/IR-2 (M)

League Club	Source	Date Signed	Seasons Played	Apps	Subs	Gls
Liverpool	Home Farm	08.83				
Scunthorpe U	L	12.86	86	3	0	2
Leeds U	Tr	09.87	87	14	1	1
Hull C	Tr	03.88	87-90	48	20	1
Cardiff C	L	11.90	90	5	0	0
Cardiff C	L	03.91	90	10	0	0

DE MERIT Jay Michael
Green Bay, USA, 4 December, 1979 (CD)

League Club	Source	Date Signed	Seasons Played	Apps	Subs	Gls
Watford	Northwood	08.04	04	22	2	3

DEMETRIOS Cristakis (Chris)
Dudley, 26 October, 1973 (FB)

League Club	Source	Date Signed	Seasons Played	Apps	Subs	Gls
Walsall	YT	08.92	92	3	4	1

DEMPSEY John
Cumbernauld, 22 June, 1913 (IF)

League Club	Source	Date Signed	Seasons Played	Apps	Subs	Gls
Ipswich T	Queen of the South	06.48	48	22	-	5

DEMPSEY John Thomas
Hampstead, 15 March, 1946 IR-19 (CD)

League Club	Source	Date Signed	Seasons Played	Apps	Subs	Gls
Fulham	App	03.64	64-68	149	0	4
Chelsea	Tr	01.69	68-75	161	4	4

DEMPSEY John William
Birkenhead, 2 April, 1951 (FB)

League Club	Source	Date Signed	Seasons Played	Apps	Subs	Gls
Tranmere Rov	App	04.69	67-71	52	2	1

DEMPSEY Mark Anthony
Dublin, 10 December, 1972 IRYth/IRu21-5 (W)

League Club	Source	Date Signed	Seasons Played	Apps	Subs	Gls
Gillingham	YT	08.90	90-92	27	21	2
Leyton Orient	Tr	07.94	94	43	0	1
Shrewsbury T	Tr	07.95	95-97	62	18	3

DEMPSEY Mark James
Manchester, 14 January, 1964 (M)

League Club	Source	Date Signed	Seasons Played	Apps	Subs	Gls
Manchester U	App	01.82	85	1	0	0
Swindon T	L	01.85	84	5	0	0
Sheffield U	Tr	08.86	86-87	60	3	9
Chesterfield	L	09.88	88	3	0	0
Rotherham U	Tr	10.88	88-90	71	4	7

DEMPSEY Paul
Birkenhead, 3 December, 1981 (FB)

League Club	Source	Date Signed	Seasons Played	Apps	Subs	Gls
Sheffield U	YT	07.00				
Northampton T	Tr	03.01	00-01	18	8	0

DEMPSTER John
Kettering, 1 April, 1983 SYth/Su21 (CD)

League Club	Source	Date Signed	Seasons Played	Apps	Subs	Gls
Rushden & Diamonds	Jnrs	07.01	01-04	31	21	1

DENHAM Charles (Charlie)
Hartlepool, 28 April, 1937 (W)

League Club	Source	Date Signed	Seasons Played	Apps	Subs	Gls
Hartlepools U (Am)	West Amats	11.58	58	5	-	3

DENHAM John William
Middleton, 6 November, 1925 Died 1972 (FB)

League Club	Source	Date Signed	Seasons Played	Apps	Subs	Gls
Hull C	Yorkshire Amats	06.48				
Hartlepools U	Tr	08.49	49	1	-	0

DENIAL Geoffrey (Geoff)
Stocksbridge, 31 January, 1932 (WH)

League Club	Source	Date Signed	Seasons Played	Apps	Subs	Gls
Sheffield U		01.52	52-54	10	-	0
Oxford U	Tr	09.56	62	6	-	0

DENNEHY Jeremiah (Miah)
Cork, 29 March, 1950 IRu23-1/IR-11 (W)

League Club	Source	Date Signed	Seasons Played	Apps	Subs	Gls
Nottingham F	Cork Hibernian	01.73	72-74	37	4	4
Walsall	Tr	07.75	75-77	123	5	22
Bristol Rov	Tr	07.78	78-79	47	5	6

DENNIS Alan George
Colchester, 22 December, 1951 (CD)

League Club	Source	Date Signed	Seasons Played	Apps	Subs	Gls
Colchester U	Jnrs	08.70	69-70	2	3	0

DENNIS John **Anthony (Tony)**
Eton, 1 December, 1963 (W)

League Club	Source	Date Signed	Seasons Played	Apps	Subs	Gls
Plymouth Arg	App	12.81	81-82	7	2	0
Exeter C	Tr	08.83	83	3	1	0
Cambridge U	Slough T	02.89	88-92	89	22	10
Chesterfield	Tr	06.93	93	4	6	0
Colchester U	Tr	08.94	94-95	56	9	5
Lincoln C	Tr	07.96	96	23	5	2

DENNIS Kevin Jason
Islington, 14 December, 1976 (W)

League Club	Source	Date Signed	Seasons Played	Apps	Subs	Gls
Brentford	Arsenal (YT)	07.96	96-97	9	8	0

DENNIS Mark Earl
Streatham, 2 May, 1961 EYth/Eu21-3 (FB)

League Club	Source	Date Signed	Seasons Played	Apps	Subs	Gls
Birmingham C	App	08.78	78-82	130	0	1
Southampton	Tr	11.83	83-86	95	0	2
Queens Park Rgrs	Tr	05.87	87-88	26	2	0
Crystal Palace	Tr	08.89	89-90	8	1	0

DENNISON Robert (Robbie)
Banbridge, 30 April, 1963 NIYth/NIB/NI-17 (W)

League Club	Source	Date Signed	Seasons Played	Apps	Subs	Gls
West Bromwich A	Glenavon	09.85	85-86	9	7	1
Wolverhampton W	Tr	03.87	86-96	264	29	40
Swansea C	L	10.95	95	9	0	0

DENNISON Charles **Robert (Bob)**
Hull, 12 September, 1932 (FB)

League Club	Source	Date Signed	Seasons Played	Apps	Subs	Gls
Hull C	Jnrs	07.54	54-57	24	-	1

League Club	Source	Date Signed	Seasons Played	Career Record Apps	Subs	Gls

DENNISON Robert (Bob) Smith
Amble, 6 March, 1912 Died 1996 (CD)

League Club	Source	Date Signed	Seasons Played	Apps	Subs	Gls
Newcastle U	Radcliffe Welfare U	05.29	32-33	11	-	2
Nottingham F	Tr	05.34	34	15	-	5
Fulham	Tr	06.35	35-38	31	-	0
Northampton T	Tr	09.45	46-47	55	-	0

DENNY Paul Nicholas
Croydon, 5 September, 1957 (M)

League Club	Source	Date Signed	Seasons Played	Apps	Subs	Gls
Southend U	App	09.75	76	8	1	2
Wimbledon	Tr	08.77	77-80	87	16	11

DENTON Edward (Eddie) John
Oxford, 18 September, 1970 (M)

League Club	Source	Date Signed	Seasons Played	Apps	Subs	Gls
Oxford U	YT	07.88	87	0	2	0
Watford	Witney T	02.91	90	0	2	0

DENTON Peter Robert
Gorleston, 1 March, 1946 (W)

League Club	Source	Date Signed	Seasons Played	Apps	Subs	Gls
Coventry C	App	03.64	65-67	10	0	1
Luton T	Tr	01.68	67-68	4	1	0

DENTON Roger William
Stretford, 6 January, 1953 (FB)

League Club	Source	Date Signed	Seasons Played	Apps	Subs	Gls
Bolton W	Jnrs	05.71	71	3	1	0
Bradford C	Tr	07.72	72-73	25	5	0
Rochdale	L	02.74	73	2	0	0

DENYER Albert (Bertie) Thomas Frederick
Swindon, 6 December, 1924 (W)

League Club	Source	Date Signed	Seasons Played	Apps	Subs	Gls
Swindon T		10.45	46	7	-	1

DENYER Peter Russell
Chiddingfold, 26 November, 1957 (M)

League Club	Source	Date Signed	Seasons Played	Apps	Subs	Gls
Portsmouth	App	12.75	75-78	123	8	15
Northampton T	Tr	07.79	79-82	138	9	27

DENYS Ryan Hayden
Brentford, 16 August, 1978 (W)

League Club	Source	Date Signed	Seasons Played	Apps	Subs	Gls
Brentford	YT	07.97	97	12	7	1

DE ORNELAS Fernando
Caracas, Venezuela, 29 July, 1976 Venezuela 13 (M)

League Club	Source	Date Signed	Seasons Played	Apps	Subs	Gls
Crystal Palace	Happy Valley (HK)	09.99	99	5	4	0
Queens Park Rgrs	Celtic	10.01	01	1	1	0

DEPEAR Ernest **Roland (Roly)**
Spalding, 10 December, 1923 Died 2001 (CD)

League Club	Source	Date Signed	Seasons Played	Apps	Subs	Gls
Leeds U	Boston U	05.48	48	4	-	0
Newport Co	Tr	06.49	49	16	-	0
Shrewsbury T	Tr	07.50	50-51	74	-	5

DE PEDRO Javier Francisco
Logrono, Spain, 4 August, 1973 Spain 12 (M)

League Club	Source	Date Signed	Seasons Played	Apps	Subs	Gls
Blackburn Rov	Real Sociedad (Sp)	07.04	04	1	1	0

DE PLACIDO Michael (Mike) Stephen
Scarborough, 9 March, 1954 EYth (W)

League Club	Source	Date Signed	Seasons Played	Apps	Subs	Gls
York C	Jnrs	03.72	71-72	4	7	0

DEPLIDGE William (Bill)
Bradford, 12 November, 1924 (WH)

League Club	Source	Date Signed	Seasons Played	Apps	Subs	Gls
Bradford PA	Jnrs	08.42	46-55	274	-	62

DERBYSHIRE Matthew (Matt) Anthony
Great Harwood, 14 April, 1986 (F)

League Club	Source	Date Signed	Seasons Played	Apps	Subs	Gls
Blackburn Rov	Great Harwood T	11.03	04	0	1	0

DERBYSHIRE Thomas (Tommy)
Manchester, 10 December, 1930 (G)

League Club	Source	Date Signed	Seasons Played	Apps	Subs	Gls
Hartlepools U (Am)	East Yorks Regiment	08.50	50	1	-	0

DERKO Tadeusz **Franciszek (Franco)**
Italy, 22 December, 1946 (WH)

League Club	Source	Date Signed	Seasons Played	Apps	Subs	Gls
Mansfield T	App	01.65	66	1	0	0

DERRETT Stephen (Steve) Clifford
Cardiff, 16 October, 1947 WSch/Wu23-3/W-4 (FB)

League Club	Source	Date Signed	Seasons Played	Apps	Subs	Gls
Cardiff C	App	10.65	66-71	61	6	1
Carlisle U	Tr	04.72	72	13	0	0
Aldershot	L	10.73	73	4	0	0
Rotherham U	Tr	12.73	73-75	79	2	2
Newport Co	Tr	06.76	76-77	61	0	0

DERRICK Albert Edward
Newport, 8 September, 1908 Died 1975 (CF)

League Club	Source	Date Signed	Seasons Played	Apps	Subs	Gls
Newport Co		10.35	35-38	125	-	43
Swindon T	Tr	01.46	46	1	-	0

DERRICK Edward **Albert**
Newport, 6 August, 1939 (F)

League Club	Source	Date Signed	Seasons Played	Apps	Subs	Gls
Newport Co		12.60	60	3	-	1
Newport Co	Hereford U	07.69	69	25	1	8

DERRICK Jantzen Stuart
Bristol, 10 January, 1943 ESch (W)

League Club	Source	Date Signed	Seasons Played	Apps	Subs	Gls
Bristol C	Jnrs	01.60	59-70	253	6	31
Mansfield T	L	03.71	70	2	1	0

DERRY Shaun Peter
Nottingham, 6 December, 1977 (M)

League Club	Source	Date Signed	Seasons Played	Apps	Subs	Gls
Notts Co	YT	04.96	95-97	76	3	4
Sheffield U	Tr	01.98	97-99	62	10	0
Portsmouth	Tr	03.00	99-01	48	1	1
Crystal Palace	Tr	08.02	02-04	62	21	3
Nottingham F	L	12.04	04	7	0	0
Leeds U	Tr	02.05	04	7	0	2

DERVELD Fernando
Vlissingen, Holland, 22 October, 1976 (FB)

League Club	Source	Date Signed	Seasons Played	Apps	Subs	Gls
Norwich C	Haarlem (Holl)	03.00	99-00	20	2	1
West Bromwich A	L	02.01	00	1	1	0

DESAILLY Marcel
Accra, Ghana, 7 September, 1968 Fru21/FrB-1/Fr-116 (CD)

League Club	Source	Date Signed	Seasons Played	Apps	Subs	Gls
Chelsea	AC Milan (It)	07.98	98-03	156	2	6

DESBOROUGH Michael (Mike)
Newham, 28 November, 1969 (G)

League Club	Source	Date Signed	Seasons Played	Apps	Subs	Gls
Colchester U	Chelmsford C	10.93	93	1	0	0

DESCHAMPS Didier
Bayonne, France, 15 October, 1968 France 101 (M)

League Club	Source	Date Signed	Seasons Played	Apps	Subs	Gls
Chelsea	Juventus (It)	06.99	99	24	3	0

DESMEULES Rodney (Rod) Leo
Newbury, 23 September, 1948 (M)

League Club	Source	Date Signed	Seasons Played	Apps	Subs	Gls
Swindon T	App	10.66	66-67	4	0	0

DESMOND Peter
Cork, 23 November, 1926 Died 1990 LoI-2/IR-4 (IF)

League Club	Source	Date Signed	Seasons Played	Apps	Subs	Gls
Middlesbrough	Shelbourne	05.49	49	2	-	0
Southport	Tr	08.50	50	12	-	2
York C	Fleetwood	12.51	51	1	-	0
Hartlepools U	Stockton	08.53	53	1	-	0

DE SOUZA Miguel **Juan**
Newham, 11 February, 1970 (F)

League Club	Source	Date Signed	Seasons Played	Apps	Subs	Gls
Charlton Ath	Clapton	07.89				
Bristol C	Tr	08.90				
Birmingham C	Dagenham & Redbridge	02.94	93-94	5	10	0
Bury	L	11.94	94	2	1	0
Wycombe W	Tr	01.95	94-96	73	10	29
Peterborough U	Tr	03.97	96-98	19	16	5
Southend U	L	08.98	98	2	0	0
Rochdale	L	10.98	98	5	0	0

DEVANEY Martin Thomas
Cheltenham, 1 June, 1980 (M)

League Club	Source	Date Signed	Seasons Played	Apps	Subs	Gls
Coventry C	YT	06.97				
Cheltenham T	Tr	08.99	99-04	154	49	38

DEVANEY Philip (Phil) Charles
Huyton, 12 February, 1969 (F)

League Club	Source	Date Signed	Seasons Played	Apps	Subs	Gls
Burnley	App	02.87	86-87	8	5	1

DEVANNEY Allan
Otley, 5 September, 1941 Died 1992 (CF)

League Club	Source	Date Signed	Seasons Played	Apps	Subs	Gls
Bradford C	Jnrs	02.59	59-61	12	-	4

DEVERALL Harold (Jackie) Reginald
Petersfield, 5 May, 1916 Died 1999 ESch (WH)

League Club	Source	Date Signed	Seasons Played	Apps	Subs	Gls
Reading	Maidenhead U	11.37	38-47	74	-	9
Leyton Orient	Tr	08.48	48-52	115	-	2

DEVEREUX Anthony (Tony) William John
Gibraltar, 6 January, 1940 (FB)

League Club	Source	Date Signed	Seasons Played	Apps	Subs	Gls
Aldershot	Chelsea (Am)	11.58	59-65	132	0	0

DEVEREUX James (Jimmy) Anthony
Fleet, 20 February, 1970 (FB)

League Club	Source	Date Signed	Seasons Played	Apps	Subs	Gls
Aldershot	YT	07.88	88-89	0	2	0

DEVEREUX Robert (Robbie)
Great Cornard, 13 January, 1971 (M)

League Club	Source	Date Signed	Seasons Played	Apps	Subs	Gls
Colchester U	Ipswich T (YT)	05.89	89	1	1	0
Colchester U	Cornard U	08.92	92	3	3	0

DEVEY Raymond (Ray)
Birmingham, 19 December, 1917 Died 2001 (WH)

League Club	Source	Date Signed	Seasons Played	Apps	Subs	Gls
Birmingham C	Shirley Jnrs	08.37	46	1	-	0
Mansfield T	Tr	08.47	47-49	76	-	4

DEVINE John Anthony
Dublin, 11 November, 1958 IRu21-2/IR-12 (FB)

League Club	Source	Date Signed	Seasons Played	Apps	Subs	Gls
Arsenal	App	10.76	77-82	86	3	0

League Club	Source	Date Signed	Seasons Played	Apps	Subs	Gls
Norwich C	Tr	08.83	83-84	51	2	3
Stoke C	Tr	11.85	85	15	0	1
DEVINE John Henry						
Liverpool, 9 July, 1933						(W)
Chester	Rhyl	07.55	55	1	-	0
DEVINE Peter						
Blackburn, 25 May, 1960						(W)
Bristol C	Vancouver (Can)	07.81	81	19	2	1
Blackburn Rov	Tr	09.82	82-83	8	0	2
Burnley	Chorley	06.84	84-85	46	10	4
DEVINE Sean Thomas						
Lewisham, 6 September, 1972 IRB-1						(F)
Millwall	YT	05.91				
Barnet	Famagusta (Cyp)	10.95	95-98	112	14	47
Wycombe W	Tr	03.99	98-02	82	7	41
Exeter C	Tr	01.03	02	21	2	8
DEVINE Stephen (Steve) Bernard						
Strabane, 11 December, 1964 NIYth						(FB)
Wolverhampton W	App	12.82				
Derby Co	Tr	03.83	83-84	10	1	0
Stockport Co	Tr	08.85	85	2	0	0
Hereford U	Tr	10.85	85-92	261	11	4
DEVINE William (Willie)						
Whitletts, 22 August, 1933						(W)
Watford	St Mirren	03.58	57-58	30	-	6
Accrington St	Partick Th	05.60	60	46	-	6
DE VITO Claudio Gaetano						
Peterborough, 21 July, 1978						(F)
Northampton T	YT	07.96				
Barnet	Tr	03.98	97	0	1	0
DEVITT Bernard **Malcolm**						
Bradford, 26 January, 1937						(IF)
Bradford C	Bradford Rov	03.59	58-62	100	-	13
DEVLIN Alan Thomas						
Edinburgh, 10 October, 1953						(F)
Exeter C	Dundee U	11.73	73	1	0	0
DEVLIN Douglas (Doug) Paul Keith						
Glasgow, 17 March, 1953						(M)
Wolverhampton W	App	06.71				
Walsall	Tr	07.72	72	15	3	0
DEVLIN Ernest (Joe)						
Gateshead, 6 March, 1920 Died 1976						(FB)
Gateshead		08.42				
West Ham U	Tr	06.46	46-52	70	-	0
Darlington	Tr	02.54	53-56	115	-	1
DEVLIN John (Johnny)						
Airdrie, 11 December, 1917 Died 2001						(IF)
Walsall	Kilmarnock	12.47	47-51	159	-	51
DEVLIN Joseph (Joe)						
Cleland, 12 March, 1931						(W)
Accrington St	Falkirk	07.53	53-56	114	-	18
Rochdale	Tr	09.56	56-57	38	-	7
Bradford PA	Tr	11.57	57-58	34	-	3
Carlisle U	Tr	07.59	59	3	-	0
DEVLIN Mark Andrew						
Irvine, 18 January, 1973 SYth						(M)
Stoke C	YT	04.91	90-96	39	16	2
Exeter C	Tr	10.97	97	31	2	2
DEVLIN Paul John						
Birmingham, 14 April, 1972 SB-1/S-10						(W)
Notts Co	Stafford Rgrs	02.92	91-95	132	9	25
Birmingham C	Tr	02.96	95-97	61	15	28
Sheffield U	Tr	03.98	97-01	122	25	24
Notts Co	L	10.98	98	5	0	0
Birmingham C	Tr	02.02	01-03	31	16	4
Watford	Tr	09.03	03-04	54	2	4
DEVLIN William						
Glasgow, 30 May, 1931						(W)
Carlisle U	Peterborough U	08.56	56	28	-	6
DE VOGT Wilko						
Breda, Holland, 17 September, 1975						(G)
Sheffield U	NAC Breda (Holl)	07.01	01	5	1	0
DEVONSHIRE Alan Ernest						
Park Royal, 13 April, 1956 E-8						(M)
West Ham U	Southall	10.76	76-89	345	13	29
Watford	Tr	07.90	90-91	23	2	1
DEVONSHIRE Leslie (Les) Ernest						
Acton, 13 June, 1926						(W)
Brentford	Wealdstone	05.48				
Chester	Tr	06.50	50	44	-	4
Crystal Palace	Tr	08.51	51-54	83	-	12
DE VOS Jason Richard						
Appin, Ontario, Canada, 2 January, 1974 CaYth/Cau23-14/Ca-49						(CD)
Darlington	Montreal (Can)	11.96	96-98	43	1	5
Wigan Ath	Dundee U	08.01	01-03	87	3	15
Ipswich T	Tr	06.04	04	45	0	3
DE VRIES Mark						
Paramaribo, Surinam, 24 August, 1975						(F)
Leicester C	Heart of Midlothian	01.05	04	9	7	1
DEVRIES Roger Stuart						
Hull, 25 October, 1950						(FB)
Hull C	Jnrs	09.67	70-79	314	4	0
Blackburn Rov	Tr	07.80	80	13	0	0
Scunthorpe U	Tr	10.81	81	6	0	1
DE-VULGT Leigh Stuart						
Swansea, 17 March, 1981 WYth/Wu21-2						(FB)
Swansea C	YT	07.99	99-02	16	7	0
DE WAARD Raimond						
Rotterdam, Holland, 27 March, 1973						(F)
Norwich C	Cambuur Leeuw'n (Holl)	03.00	99-00	4	6	0
DEWHURST Robert (Rob) Matthew						
Keighley, 10 September, 1971						(CD)
Blackburn Rov	YT	10.90	90	13	0	0
Darlington	L	12.91	91	11	0	1
Huddersfield T	L	10.92	92	7	0	0
Hull C	Tr	11.93	93-98	132	6	13
Exeter C	Tr	08.99	99	21	2	2
DEWICK John Albert						
Rotherham, 28 November, 1919 Died 1997						(G)
Notts Co		10.46	46	1	-	0
DEWIS George Renger						
Burbage, 22 January, 1913 Died 1994						(CF)
Leicester C	Nuneaton T	10.33	33-49	116	-	45
DE WOLF John						
Schiedam, Holland, 10 December, 1962 Holland int						(CD)
Wolverhampton W	Feyenoord (Holl)	12.94	94-95	27	1	5
DEWS George						
Ossett, 5 June, 1921 Died 2003						(IF)
Middlesbrough		08.46	46-47	33	-	8
Plymouth Arg	Tr	10.47	47-54	257	-	76
Walsall	Tr	06.55	55	9	-	1
DEWSBURY John						
Swansea, 16 February, 1932						(FB)
Swansea T	Jnrs	07.50	52	9	-	0
Newport Co	Tr	08.55	55	2	-	0
DEWSNIP George Edward						
Salford, 6 May, 1956						(W)
Southport	Preston NE (App)	06.74	74-76	83	4	11
DEY Geoffrey (Geoff)						
Chesterfield, 11 January, 1964 EYth						(M)
Sheffield U	App	01.82				
Scunthorpe U	Tr	08.83	83-84	17	0	1
DEYNA Kazimierz						
Starograd, Poland, 23 October, 1947 Died 1989 Poland int						(F)
Manchester C	Legia Warsaw (Pol)	11.78	78-80	34	4	12
DE ZEEUW Adrianus (Arjan) Johannes						
Castricum, Holland, 16 April, 1970						(CD)
Barnsley	Telstar (Holl)	11.95	95-98	138	0	7
Wigan Ath	Tr	07.99	99-01	126	0	6
Portsmouth	Tr	07.02	02-04	103	3	5
DIA Aly						
Dakar, Senegal, 20 August, 1965						(F)
Southampton	Blyth Spartans	11.96	96	0	1	0
DIABATE Lassina						
Bouake, Ivory Coast, 16 September, 1974 Iceland int						(M)
Portsmouth	Auxerre (Fr)	10.02	02	16	9	0
DIAF Farid						
Carcassonne, France, 19 April, 1971						(M)
Preston NE	Rennes (Fr)	07.99	99	1	2	0

DIALLO Cherif
Dakar, Senegal, 23 December, 1976 (F)

League Club	Source	Date Signed	Seasons Played	Apps	Subs	Gls
Exeter C	Scarborough	09.01	01	0	2	0

DIALLO Drissa
Nouadhibou, Mauritania, 4 January, 1973 Guinea int (CD)

League Club	Source	Date Signed	Seasons Played	Apps	Subs	Gls
Burnley	KV Mechelen (Bel)	01.03	02	14	0	1
Ipswich T	Tr	06.03	03-04	39	6	0

DIAMOND Anthony (Tony) John
Rochdale, 23 August, 1968 NIu23-1 (F)

League Club	Source	Date Signed	Seasons Played	Apps	Subs	Gls
Blackburn Rov	App	06.86	86-88	9	17	3
Wigan Ath	L	10.88	88	6	0	2
Blackpool	Tr	08.89	89	2	1	1

DIAMOND Barry
Dumbarton, 20 February, 1960 (F)

League Club	Source	Date Signed	Seasons Played	Apps	Subs	Gls
Rochdale	Barrow	07.84	84-85	50	2	16
Stockport Co	L	12.85	85	6	0	0
Halifax T	Tr	02.86	85-86	17	5	3
Wrexham	L	01.87	86	2	2	0

DIAO Salif Alassane
Kedougou, Senegal, 10 February, 1977 Senegal 29 (M)

League Club	Source	Date Signed	Seasons Played	Apps	Subs	Gls
Liverpool	Sedan (Fr)	08.02	02-04	19	18	1
Birmingham C	L	01.05	04	2	0	0

DIAWARA Djibril
Dakar, Senegal, 3 January, 1975 Senegal int (CD)

League Club	Source	Date Signed	Seasons Played	Apps	Subs	Gls
Bolton W (L)	Torino (It)	07.01	01	4	5	0

DIAWARA Kaba
Toulon, France, 16 December, 1975 Fru21 (F)

League Club	Source	Date Signed	Seasons Played	Apps	Subs	Gls
Arsenal	Bordeaux (Fr)	01.99	98	2	10	0
Blackburn Rov (L)	Paris St Germain (Fr)	08.00	00	1	4	0
West Ham U (L)	Paris St Germain (Fr)	09.00	00	6	5	0

DIAZ Ramon **Emilliano**
Naples, Italy, 22 June, 1983 (M)

League Club	Source	Date Signed	Seasons Played	Apps	Subs	Gls
Oxford U	Deportivo Colonia (Ur)	02.05	04	2	5	0

DIAZ Isidro
Valencia, Spain, 15 May, 1972 (W)

League Club	Source	Date Signed	Seasons Played	Apps	Subs	Gls
Wigan Ath	FC Balaguer (Sp)	07.95	95-96	57	19	16
Wolverhampton W	Tr	08.97	97	1	0	0
Wigan Ath	Tr	12.97	97	1	1	0
Rochdale	Tr	08.98	98	12	2	2

DIBBLE Andrew (Andy) Gerald
Cwmbran, 8 May, 1965 WSch/WYth/Wu21-3/W-3 (G)

League Club	Source	Date Signed	Seasons Played	Apps	Subs	Gls
Cardiff C	App	08.82	81-83	62	0	0
Luton T	Tr	07.84	84-87	30	0	0
Sunderland	L	02.86	85	12	0	0
Huddersfield T	L	03.87	86	5	0	0
Manchester C	Tr	07.88	88-96	113	3	0
Middlesbrough	L	02.91	90	19	0	0
Bolton W	L	09.91	91	4	0	0
Bolton W	L	09.91	91	9	0	0
West Bromwich A	L	02.92	91	9	0	0
Luton T	Glasgow Rgrs	09.97	97	1	0	0
Middlesbrough	Tr	01.98	97	2	0	0
Hartlepool U	Altrincham	03.99	99	6	0	0
Carlisle U	L	10.99	99	2	0	0
Stockport Co	Tr	08.00	00-01	22	1	0
Wrexham	Tr	08.02	02-04	83	0	0

DIBBLE Christopher (Chris)
Morden, 10 October, 1960 ESch (M)

League Club	Source	Date Signed	Seasons Played	Apps	Subs	Gls
Millwall	App	11.77	77-81	49	14	5
Wimbledon	Tr	07.82	82-83	7	2	0

DIBDEN William **Keith**
Totton, 17 December, 1933 (IF)

League Club	Source	Date Signed	Seasons Played	Apps	Subs	Gls
Southampton	Jnrs	01.52				
Gillingham	Tr	07.57	57	1	-	0

DI CANIO Paolo
Rome, Italy, 9 July, 1968 (F)

League Club	Source	Date Signed	Seasons Played	Apps	Subs	Gls
Sheffield Wed	Glasgow Celtic	08.97	97-98	39	2	15
West Ham U	Tr	01.99	98-02	114	4	47
Charlton Ath	Tr	08.03	03	23	8	4

DICHIO Daniele (Danny) Salvatore Ernest
Hammersmith, 19 October, 1974 ESch/Eu21-1 (F)

League Club	Source	Date Signed	Seasons Played	Apps	Subs	Gls
Queens Park Rgrs	YT	05.93	94-96	56	19	20
Barnet	L	03.94	93	9	0	2
Sunderland	Sampdoria (It)	01.98	97-00	20	56	11
West Bromwich A	L	08.01	01	3	0	2
West Bromwich A	Tr	11.01	01-03	47	16	12
Derby Co	L	10.03	03	6	0	1
Millwall	Tr	01.04	03-04	42	4	17

DICK Alistair (Ally) John
Stirling, 25 April, 1965 SSch/SYth (W)

League Club	Source	Date Signed	Seasons Played	Apps	Subs	Gls
Tottenham H	App	05.82	81-85	16	1	2

DICK George White
Torphichen, 12 June, 1921 Died 1960 (IF)

League Club	Source	Date Signed	Seasons Played	Apps	Subs	Gls
Blackpool		08.46	46-47	45	-	13
West Ham U	Tr	10.48	48	14	-	1
Carlisle U	Tr	07.49	49-50	52	-	25
Stockport Co	Tr	10.50	50	25	-	12
Workington	Tr	10.51	51-52	56	-	17

DICK John Hart
Glasgow, 19 March, 1930 Died 2000 SB/S-1 (IF)

League Club	Source	Date Signed	Seasons Played	Apps	Subs	Gls
West Ham U	Crittall Ath	06.53	53-62	326	-	153
Brentford	Tr	09.62	62-64	72	-	45

DICK Thomas (Tommy) Woods
Glasgow, 19 July, 1936 (CF)

League Club	Source	Date Signed	Seasons Played	Apps	Subs	Gls
Bradford PA	Third Lanark	06.60	60	4	-	0

DICK Peter **Watt (Wattie)**
Newmains, 20 August, 1927 (WH)

League Club	Source	Date Signed	Seasons Played	Apps	Subs	Gls
Accrington St	Third Lanark	06.55	55-58	125	-	37
Bradford PA	Tr	12.58	58-62	155	-	2

DICKENS Alan William
Plaistow, 3 September, 1964 EYth/Eu21-1 (M)

League Club	Source	Date Signed	Seasons Played	Apps	Subs	Gls
West Ham U	App	08.82	82-88	173	19	23
Chelsea	Tr	08.89	89-91	39	9	1
West Bromwich A	L	12.92	92	3	0	1
Brentford	Tr	02.93	92	13	2	1
Colchester U	Tr	09.93	93	28	4	3

DICKENS Leo
Hemsworth, 16 March, 1927 (FB)

League Club	Source	Date Signed	Seasons Played	Apps	Subs	Gls
Rotherham U	Frickley Colliery	07.50				
Chester	Tr	07.52	52	7	-	0

DICKENSON Kevin James
Hackney, 24 November, 1962 (FB)

League Club	Source	Date Signed	Seasons Played	Apps	Subs	Gls
Charlton Ath	Tottenham H (App)	04.80	79-84	72	3	1
Orient	Tr	07.85	85-91	190	2	3

DICKER Leslie (Les) Raymond
Stockwell, 20 December, 1926 (IF)

League Club	Source	Date Signed	Seasons Played	Apps	Subs	Gls
Tottenham H	Chelmsford C	06.51	52	10	-	2
Southend U	Tr	07.53	53-54	17	-	7

DICKIE Alan Leonard
Charlton, 30 January, 1944 (G)

League Club	Source	Date Signed	Seasons Played	Apps	Subs	Gls
West Ham U	App	02.62	61-65	12	0	0
Coventry C	Tr	03.67	67	2	0	0
Aldershot	Tr	07.68	68	7	0	0

DICKIE Murdoch McFarlane
Dumbarton, 28 December, 1919 (W)

League Club	Source	Date Signed	Seasons Played	Apps	Subs	Gls
Port Vale		05.39				
Port Vale		10.44				
Chelsea	Guildford C	04.45	46	1	-	0
Bournemouth	Tr	02.47	46-47	17	-	1

DICKINS Matthew (Matt) James
Sheffield, 3 September, 1970 (G)

League Club	Source	Date Signed	Seasons Played	Apps	Subs	Gls
Sheffield U	YT	07.89				
Lincoln C	Tr	02.91	90-91	27	0	0
Blackburn Rov	Tr	03.92	91	1	0	0
Blackpool	L	01.93	92	19	0	0
Rochdale	L	10.94	94	4	0	0
Stockport Co	Tr	02.95	94-95	12	1	0

DICKINSON Carl Matthew
Swadlincote, 31 March, 1987 (CD)

League Club	Source	Date Signed	Seasons Played	Apps	Subs	Gls
Stoke C	Sch	●	04	0	1	0

DICKINSON James (Jimmy) Arthur
South Elmsall, 26 September, 1931 Died 2002 (FB)

League Club	Source	Date Signed	Seasons Played	Apps	Subs	Gls
Barrow	Pontefract	08.51	51-57	67	-	0

DICKINSON James (Jimmy) Wiliam
Alton, 24 April, 1925 Died 1982 FLge-11/EB/E-48 (WH)

League Club	Source	Date Signed	Seasons Played	Apps	Subs	Gls
Portsmouth	Jnrs	01.44	46-64	764	-	9

DICKINSON Leonard (Len)
South Elmsall, 6 March, 1942 (IF)

League Club	Source	Date Signed	Seasons Played	Apps	Subs	Gls
Sheffield Wed	Jnrs	02.60				
Oldham Ath	Tr	06.61	61	5	-	2

DICKINSON Martin John
Leeds, 14 March, 1963 (CD)

League Club	Source	Date Signed	Seasons Played	Apps	Subs	Gls
Leeds U	App	05.80	79-85	100	3	2

League Club	Source	Date Signed	Seasons Played	Apps	Subs	Gls
West Bromwich A	Tr	02.86	85-87	46	4	2
Sheffield U	Tr	07.88	88	0	1	0

DICKINSON Michael (Mike) James
Newcastle, 4 May, 1984 (F)

League Club	Source	Date Signed	Seasons Played	Apps	Subs	Gls
Carlisle U	YT	07.02	01	0	1	0

DICKINSON Patrick James
Vancouver, Canada, 6 May, 1978 (M)

League Club	Source	Date Signed	Seasons Played	Apps	Subs	Gls
Hull C	YT	07.97	96-97	2	2	0

DICKINSON Ronald (Ron) Arthur
Coventry, 29 June, 1930 (CD)

League Club	Source	Date Signed	Seasons Played	Apps	Subs	Gls
Shrewsbury T (Am)	Nuneaton Borough	05.53	53	11	-	0

DICKMAN Jonjo
Hexham, 22 September, 1981 (M)

League Club	Source	Date Signed	Seasons Played	Apps	Subs	Gls
Sunderland	Jnrs	11.98	02	0	1	0
York C	L	02.04	03	2	0	0
Darlington	Tr	02.05	04	8	0	1

DICKOV Paul
Livingston, 1 November, 1972 SSch/SYth/Su21-4/S-10 (F)

League Club	Source	Date Signed	Seasons Played	Apps	Subs	Gls
Arsenal	YT	12.90	92-96	6	15	3
Luton T	L	10.93	93	8	7	1
Brighton & Hove A	L	03.94	93	8	0	5
Manchester C	Tr	08.96	96-01	105	51	33
Leicester C	Tr	02.02	01-03	81	8	32
Blackburn Rov	Tr	06.04	04	27	2	9

DICKS Alan Victor
Kennington, 29 August, 1934 (WH)

League Club	Source	Date Signed	Seasons Played	Apps	Subs	Gls
Chelsea	Jnrs	09.51	52-57	33	-	1
Southend U	Tr	11.58	58-61	85	-	2

DICKS Julian Andrew
Bristol, 8 August, 1968 Eu21-4/EB-2 (FB)

League Club	Source	Date Signed	Seasons Played	Apps	Subs	Gls
Birmingham C	App	04.86	85-87	83	6	1
West Ham U	Tr	03.88	87-93	159	0	29
Liverpool	Tr	09.93	93	24	0	3
West Ham U	Tr	10.94	94-98	103	0	21

DICKS Ronald (Ronnie) William
Kennington, 13 April, 1924 Died 2004 (WH)

League Club	Source	Date Signed	Seasons Played	Apps	Subs	Gls
Middlesbrough	Dulwich Hamlet	05.43	47-58	316	-	10

DICKSON Adam
Hamilton, 4 January, 1929 (G)

League Club	Source	Date Signed	Seasons Played	Apps	Subs	Gls
Leicester C	Thorniewood U	06.51	51-54	16	-	0

DICKSON Hugh Robinson
Downpatrick, 28 August, 1981 NIu21 (FB)

League Club	Source	Date Signed	Seasons Played	Apps	Subs	Gls
Wigan Ath	Glentoran	08.00	00	0	1	0

DICKSON Joseph (Joe) James March
Liverpool, 31 January, 1934 Died 1990 EYth (IF)

League Club	Source	Date Signed	Seasons Played	Apps	Subs	Gls
Liverpool	Jnrs	06.52	55	6	-	3

DICKSON Ryan Anthony
Saltash, 14 December, 1986 (M)

League Club	Source	Date Signed	Seasons Played	Apps	Subs	Gls
Plymouth Arg	Sch	•	04	2	1	0

DICKSON William (Bill)
Lurgan, 15 April, 1923 I-9/NI-3 (WH)

League Club	Source	Date Signed	Seasons Played	Apps	Subs	Gls
Notts Co	Glenavon	11.45	46-47	21	-	2
Chelsea	Tr	11.47	47-52	101	-	4
Arsenal	Tr	10.53	53-55	29	-	1
Mansfield T	Tr	07.56	56	19	-	0

DIGBY Derek Francis
Teignmouth, 14 May, 1931 (W)

League Club	Source	Date Signed	Seasons Played	Apps	Subs	Gls
Exeter C	Dawlish T	08.49	51-52	31	-	2
Southampton	Tr	09.53	53-54	15	-	2

DIGBY Fraser Charles
Sheffield, 23 April, 1967 ESch/EYth/Eu21-5 (G)

League Club	Source	Date Signed	Seasons Played	Apps	Subs	Gls
Manchester U	App	04.85				
Swindon T	Tr	09.86	86-97	417	0	0
Crystal Palace	Tr	08.98	98-99	56	0	0
Huddersfield T	Barry T	08.01				
Queens Park Rgrs	Tr	10.01	01-02	20	2	0
Kidderminster Hrs	Tr	01.03	02	11	0	0

DIGHTON Richard (Dick) Anthony
Corby, 26 July, 1951 (G)

League Club	Source	Date Signed	Seasons Played	Apps	Subs	Gls
Peterborough U	Coventry C (App)	11.69	70-71	8	0	0
Stockport Co	L	10.70	70	1	0	0

DIGNAM Joseph (Joe) Colquhoun
Glasgow, 10 January, 1931 Died 1999 (IF)

League Club	Source	Date Signed	Seasons Played	Apps	Subs	Gls
Wrexham	Alloa Ath	07.57	57	8	-	0

DIGWEED Perry Michael
Westminster, 26 October, 1959 (G)

League Club	Source	Date Signed	Seasons Played	Apps	Subs	Gls
Fulham	App	08.77	76-80	15	0	0
Brighton & Hove A	Tr	01.81	80-92	179	0	0
Chelsea	L	02.88	87	3	0	0
Wimbledon	Tr	08.93				
Watford	Tr	12.93	93-94	28	1	0

DIJKSTRA Meindert
Eindhoven, Holland, 28 February, 1967 (FB)

League Club	Source	Date Signed	Seasons Played	Apps	Subs	Gls
Notts Co	Willem II Tilburg (Holl)	08.92	92-93	27	2	1

DIJKSTRA Sieb
Kerkrade, Holland, 20 October, 1966 (G)

League Club	Source	Date Signed	Seasons Played	Apps	Subs	Gls
Queens Park Rgrs	Motherwell	07.94	94	11	0	0
Bristol C	L	09.95	95	8	0	0
Wycombe W	L	03.96	95	13	0	0

DI LELLA Gustavo Martin
Buenos Aires, Argentina, 6 October, 1973 (M)

League Club	Source	Date Signed	Seasons Played	Apps	Subs	Gls
Darlington	Blyth Spartans	12.97	97	0	5	0
Hartlepool U	Blyth Spartans	03.98	97-99	22	9	4

DILLON Andrew (Andy)
Salford, 20 January, 1969 (G)

League Club	Source	Date Signed	Seasons Played	Apps	Subs	Gls
Newport Co	YT	07.87	86-87	15	0	0

DILLON Daniel Martin
Hillingdon, 6 September, 1986 (M)

League Club	Source	Date Signed	Seasons Played	Apps	Subs	Gls
Carlisle U	Sch	•	02	0	1	0

DILLON John
Coatbridge, 9 November, 1942 (W)

League Club	Source	Date Signed	Seasons Played	Apps	Subs	Gls
Sunderland	Jnrs	11.59	60-61	18	-	1
Brighton & Hove A	Tr	07.62	62	21	-	3
Crewe Alex	Tr	07.63	63	5	-	1

DILLON Kevin Paul
Sunderland, 18 December, 1959 EYth/Eu21-1 (M)

League Club	Source	Date Signed	Seasons Played	Apps	Subs	Gls
Birmingham C	App	07.77	77-82	181	5	15
Portsmouth	Tr	03.83	82-88	206	9	45
Newcastle U	Tr	07.89	89-90	62	0	0
Reading	Tr	07.91	91-93	100	1	4

DILLON Michael (Mike) Leslie
Highgate, 29 September, 1952 ESch/EYth (CD)

League Club	Source	Date Signed	Seasons Played	Apps	Subs	Gls
Tottenham H	App	12.69	72-73	21	3	1
Millwall	L	12.74	74	4	0	0
Swindon T	L	03.75	74	7	2	0

DILLON Paul William
Limerick, 22 October, 1978 IRYth/IRu21-1 (CD)

League Club	Source	Date Signed	Seasons Played	Apps	Subs	Gls
Rotherham U	YT	03.97	96-99	65	5	2

DILLON Vincent (Vince)
Manchester, 2 October, 1923 (CF)

League Club	Source	Date Signed	Seasons Played	Apps	Subs	Gls
Bolton W		04.48	47-50	17	-	2
Tranmere Rov	Tr	02.51	50-52	34	-	17

DILLSWORTH Edward (Eddie)
Freetown, Sierra Leone, 16 April, 1946 (CD)

League Club	Source	Date Signed	Seasons Played	Apps	Subs	Gls
Lincoln C (Am)	Wealdstone	03.67	66	2	0	0

DI MATTEO Roberto
Sciaffusa, Switzerland, 29 May, 1970 Italy 34 (M)

League Club	Source	Date Signed	Seasons Played	Apps	Subs	Gls
Chelsea	SS Lazio (It)	07.96	96-00	108	11	15

DIMECH Luke Anthony
Malta, 11 January, 1977 Malta 37 (CD)

League Club	Source	Date Signed	Seasons Played	Apps	Subs	Gls
Mansfield T	Shamrock Rov	08.03	03-04	36	9	1

DIMMER Hyam
Glasgow, 14 March, 1914 Died 1990 (IF)

League Club	Source	Date Signed	Seasons Played	Apps	Subs	Gls
Aldershot	Ayr U	08.46	46	7	-	1
Bristol C	Tr	05.47	47	1	-	0

DIMOND Stuart
Chorlton, 3 January, 1920 Died 2004 (CF)

League Club	Source	Date Signed	Seasons Played	Apps	Subs	Gls
Manchester U		12.42				
Bradford C	Tr	11.45	46	9	-	1

DINE John McQuade
Newton Stewart, 3 May, 1940 (G)

League Club	Source	Date Signed	Seasons Played	Apps	Subs	Gls
Bradford PA	Bulford U	08.62	62-64	32	-	0

DINEEN Jack Anthony
Brighton, 29 September, 1970 (M)

League Club	Source	Date Signed	Seasons Played	Apps	Subs	Gls
Brighton & Hove A	YT	09.87				
Scarborough	Crawley T	01.94	93	1	1	0

League Club	Source	Date Signed	Seasons Played	Apps	Subs	Gls

DINGWALL William Norman
Gateshead, 29 July, 1923 (WH)

League Club	Source	Date Signed	Seasons Played	Apps	Subs	Gls
Sheffield U		03.46				
Halifax T	Tr	07.47	47	9	-	0

DINNING Tony
Wallsend, 12 April, 1975 (M)

League Club	Source	Date Signed	Seasons Played	Apps	Subs	Gls
Newcastle U	YT	10.93				
Stockport Co	Tr	06.94	94-00	159	32	25
Wolverhampton W	Tr	09.00	00-01	35	0	6
Wigan Ath	Tr	09.01	01-03	79	5	12
Stoke C	L	03.02	01	5	0	0
Walsall	L	11.03	03	2	3	0
Blackpool	L	01.04	03	10	0	3
Ipswich T	L	08.04	04	3	4	0
Bristol C	Tr	10.04	04	15	4	0
Port Vale	L	03.05	04	7	0	3

DINSDALE Peter
Bradford, 19 October, 1938 Died 2004 (M)

League Club	Source	Date Signed	Seasons Played	Apps	Subs	Gls
Huddersfield T	Yorkshire Amats	01.56	59-66	213	1	8
Bradford PA	Tr	08.67	67	9	0	0

DIOMEDE Bernard
Saint-Douichard, France, 23 January, 1974 France 8 (M)

League Club	Source	Date Signed	Seasons Played	Apps	Subs	Gls
Liverpool	Auxerre (Fr)	07.00	00	1	1	0

DIOP Pape Bouba
Dakar, Senegal, 28 January, 1978 Senegal int (M)

League Club	Source	Date Signed	Seasons Played	Apps	Subs	Gls
Fulham	RC Lens (Fr)	07.04	04	29	0	6

DIOP Pape Seydou
Dakar, Senegal, 12 January, 1979 Senegal int (FB)

League Club	Source	Date Signed	Seasons Played	Apps	Subs	Gls
Norwich C (L)	RC Lens (Fr)	08.99	99	2	5	0

DIOP Youssouph (Youssou)
Zinguinchor, Senegal, 5 May, 1980 (M)

League Club	Source	Date Signed	Seasons Played	Apps	Subs	Gls
Kidderminster Hrs	Toulouse (Fr)	07.04	04	7	3	0

DIOUF El Hadji Ousseynou
Dakar, Senegal, 15 January, 1981 Senegal 31 (F)

League Club	Source	Date Signed	Seasons Played	Apps	Subs	Gls
Liverpool	RC Lens (Fr)	07.02	02-03	41	14	3
Bolton W	L	08.04	04	23	4	9

DI PIEDI Michele
Palermo, Italy, 4 December, 1980 (F)

League Club	Source	Date Signed	Seasons Played	Apps	Subs	Gls
Sheffield Wed	Perugia (It)	08.00	00-02	9	30	5
Bristol Rov	L	02.03	02	3	2	0

DISLEY Craig Edward
Worksop, 24 August, 1981 (M)

League Club	Source	Date Signed	Seasons Played	Apps	Subs	Gls
Mansfield T	YT	06.99	99-03	106	35	16
Bristol Rov	Tr	07.04	04	18	10	4

DISLEY Martin
Ormskirk, 24 June, 1971 (F)

League Club	Source	Date Signed	Seasons Played	Apps	Subs	Gls
Crewe Alex	YT	09.89	89-91	0	2	0

DISTIN Sylvain
Paris, France, 16 December, 1977 (CD)

League Club	Source	Date Signed	Seasons Played	Apps	Subs	Gls
Newcastle U (L)	Paris St Germain (Fr)	09.01	01	20	8	0
Manchester C	Paris St Germain (Fr)	07.02	02-04	110	0	3

DITCHBURN Edwin (Ted) George
Gillingham, 24 October, 1921 EB/FLge-6/EWar-2/E-6 (G)

League Club	Source	Date Signed	Seasons Played	Apps	Subs	Gls
Tottenham H	Jnrs	05.39	46-58	418	-	0

DIUK Wayne John
Nottingham, 26 May, 1980 (M)

League Club	Source	Date Signed	Seasons Played	Apps	Subs	Gls
Notts Co	YT	07.98	96-97	0	2	0

DIVERS John
Clydebank, 6 August, 1911 Died 1984 S-1 (IF)

League Club	Source	Date Signed	Seasons Played	Apps	Subs	Gls
Oldham Ath	Morton	08.47	47	1	-	0

DIVERS John Rice
Glasgow, 24 November, 1931 (W)

League Club	Source	Date Signed	Seasons Played	Apps	Subs	Gls
Exeter C	Clyde	05.56	56	12	-	1

DIX Richard
South Shields, 17 January, 1924 Died 1990 (W)

League Club	Source	Date Signed	Seasons Played	Apps	Subs	Gls
Bradford PA	North Shields	08.44	46-47	18	-	5
Bradford C	King's Lynn	08.52	52	8	-	1

DIX Ronald (Ronnie) William
Bristol, 5 September, 1912 Died 1998 ESch/FLge-1/E-1 (IF)

League Club	Source	Date Signed	Seasons Played	Apps	Subs	Gls
Bristol Rov	Jnrs	02.28	27-31	100	-	33
Blackburn Rov	Tr	05.32	32	38	-	14
Aston Villa	Tr	05.33	32-36	97	-	30
Derby Co	Tr	02.37	36-38	94	-	35
Tottenham H	Tr	06.39	46-47	36	-	5
Reading	Tr	11.47	47-48	44	-	13

DIXEY Richard
Wigston, 2 September, 1956 (CD)

League Club	Source	Date Signed	Seasons Played	Apps	Subs	Gls
Burnley	Enderby T	12.74	74	3	0	0
Stockport Co	L	02.76	75	14	0	1

DIXON Andrew (Andy)
Louth, 19 April, 1968 (FB)

League Club	Source	Date Signed	Seasons Played	Apps	Subs	Gls
Grimsby T	App	05.86	86-88	35	3	0
Southend U	Tr	08.89	89	24	0	0

DIXON Andrew (Andy) Paul
Hartlepool, 5 August, 1968 (M)

League Club	Source	Date Signed	Seasons Played	Apps	Subs	Gls
Hartlepool U	Seaton Holy Trinity	07.87	86-87	7	7	1
Hartlepool U	RAEC Mons (Bel)	11.95	95	3	0	0

DIXON Arthur
Middleton, 17 November, 1921 (IF)

League Club	Source	Date Signed	Seasons Played	Apps	Subs	Gls
Northampton T	Heart of Midlothian	11.49	49-51	68	-	21
Leicester C	Tr	10.51	51-52	11	-	0

DIXON Benjamin (Ben) Marcus Alexander
Lincoln, 16 September, 1974 (FB)

League Club	Source	Date Signed	Seasons Played	Apps	Subs	Gls
Lincoln C	YT	11.92	91-95	33	10	0
Blackpool	Tr	07.96	96-97	9	9	0

DIXON Cecil Hubert
Trowbridge, 28 March, 1935 (W)

League Club	Source	Date Signed	Seasons Played	Apps	Subs	Gls
Cardiff C	Trowbridge T	07.54	54-56	21	-	1
Newport Co	Tr	07.57	57-60	108	-	16
Northampton T	Tr	08.61	61	15	-	4

DIXON Colin
Newcastle, 24 September, 1963 (CD)

League Club	Source	Date Signed	Seasons Played	Apps	Subs	Gls
Southampton	App	09.81				
Hartlepool U		11.83	83	1	0	0

DIXON John (Johnny) Thomas
Hebburn, 10 December, 1923 (IF)

League Club	Source	Date Signed	Seasons Played	Apps	Subs	Gls
Aston Villa	Reyrolles	01.46	46-60	392	-	132

DIXON John (Johnny) William
Hartlepool, 12 March, 1934 (FB)

League Club	Source	Date Signed	Seasons Played	Apps	Subs	Gls
Hartlepools U	Throston W	10.57	58-60	35	-	2

DIXON Jonathan (Jonny) James
Muria, Spain, 16 January, 1984 (F)

League Club	Source	Date Signed	Seasons Played	Apps	Subs	Gls
Wycombe W	Sch	02.03	02-04	20	26	6

DIXON Joseph (Joe)
Newcastle-under-Lyme, 24 September, 1916 (CF)

League Club	Source	Date Signed	Seasons Played	Apps	Subs	Gls
Northampton T	Audley U	04.45				
Port Vale	Tr	10.46	46	1	-	0

DIXON Kerry Michael
Luton, 24 July, 1961 Eu21-1/E-8 (F)

League Club	Source	Date Signed	Seasons Played	Apps	Subs	Gls
Tottenham H	Chesham U	07.78				
Reading	Dunstable T	07.80	80-82	110	6	51
Chelsea	Tr	08.83	83-91	331	3	147
Southampton	Tr	07.92	92	8	1	2
Luton T	Tr	02.93	92-94	66	9	19
Millwall	Tr	03.95	94-95	24	7	9
Watford	Tr	01.96	95	8	3	0
Doncaster Rov	Tr	08.96	96	13	3	3

DIXON Kevin Lynton
Blackhill, 27 July, 1960 (M)

League Club	Source	Date Signed	Seasons Played	Apps	Subs	Gls
Carlisle U	Tow Law T	08.83	83	5	4	0
Hartlepool U	L	10.83	83	6	0	3
Hartlepool U	Tr	08.84	84-86	103	4	26
Scunthorpe U	L	01.86	85	14	0	2
Scunthorpe U	Tr	08.87	87	37	4	4
Hartlepool U	Tr	06.88	88	14	0	4
York C	Tr	11.88	88-89	33	5	8
Scarborough	L	02.90	89	3	0	0

DIXON Kevin Robert
Easington, 27 June, 1980 EYth (M)

League Club	Source	Date Signed	Seasons Played	Apps	Subs	Gls
Leeds U	YT	07.97				
York C	L	08.99	99	3	0	0

DIXON Lee Michael
Manchester, 17 March, 1964 FLge/EB-4/E-22 (FB)

League Club	Source	Date Signed	Seasons Played	Apps	Subs	Gls
Burnley	Jnrs	07.82	82-83	4	0	0
Chester C	Tr	02.84	83-84	56	1	1
Bury	Tr	07.85	85	45	0	6
Stoke C	Tr	07.86	86-87	71	0	5
Arsenal	Tr	01.88	87-01	439	19	25

DIXON Michael (Mike)
Willesden, 14 March, 1937 (CF)

League Club	Source	Date Signed	Seasons Played	Apps	Subs	Gls
Luton T	Hitchin T	04.57	58-60	3	-	1
Coventry C	Tr	05.61	61	18	-	12

League Club	Source	Date Signed	Seasons Played	Apps	Subs	Gls

DIXON Michael (Mike) George
Reading, 12 October, 1943 Died 1993 ESch (G)

Reading	Jnrs	08.61	62-67	113	0	0
Aldershot	Tr	07.69	69-70	38	0	0

DIXON Milton
Manchester, 30 March, 1925 (W)

Huddersfield T		02.48				
Stockport Co	Tr	10.50	50	21	-	2

DIXON Paul Kenneth
Derry, 22 February, 1960 (CD)

Burnley	App	02.78	79-81	23	1	1

DIXON Raymond (Ray)
Denaby, 31 December, 1930 (CF)

Rotherham U	Denaby U	06.55	55-56	14	-	4

DIXON Robert
Felling, 11 January, 1936 (W)

Arsenal	Crook T	08.57				
Workington	Tr	11.58	58	28	-	5
West Bromwich A	Tr	05.59	59	7	-	1

DIXON Stanley (Stan)
Burnley, 28 August, 1920 Died 1996 (CD)

Plymouth Arg	Hapton U	12.38	46-50	60	-	1

DIXON Thomas (Tommy) Charles
Newcastle, 8 June, 1929 (CF)

West Ham U	Newcastle U (Am)	02.51	52-54	39	-	21
Reading	Tr	03.55	54-58	123	-	63
Brighton & Hove A	Tr	10.58	58-59	35	-	12
Workington	Tr	07.60	60-61	53	-	17
Barrow	Tr	10.61	61-62	62	-	23

DIXON Wilfred (Will) Edward
Wood Green, 20 February, 1950 (FB)

Arsenal	App	02.68				
Reading	Tr	07.69	69-72	150	3	0
Colchester U	Tr	08.73				
Swindon T	Tr	09.73	73-76	134	6	10
Aldershot	Tr	07.77	77-79	114	6	6

D'JAFFO Laurent
Bazas, France, 5 November, 1970 Benin int (F)

Bury	Ayr U	07.98	98	35	2	8
Stockport Co	Tr	08.99	99	20	1	7
Sheffield U	Tr	02.00	99-01	45	24	11
Mansfield T	Aberdeen	03.04	03	4	4	1

DJE Ludovic
Paris, France, 22 July, 1977 (M)

Stockport Co	Francs Borains (Bel)	03.05	04	2	1	0

DJEMBA-DJEMBA Eric Daniel
Douala, Cameroon, 4 May, 1981 Cameroon 26 (M)

Manchester U	Nantes (Fr)	07.03	03-04	13	7	0
Aston Villa	Tr	01.05	04	4	2	0

DJETOU Martin Okelo
Brogohlo, Ivory Coast, 15 December, 1974 Fru21/FrB-2/Fr-6 (M)

Fulham (L)	Parma (It)	07.02	02	22	3	1
Fulham (L)	Parma (It)	07.03	03	19	7	0

DJORDJIC Bojan
Belgrade, Yugoslavia, 6 February, 1982 Swu21-5 (F)

Manchester U	Bromma Pojkarna (Swe)	02.99	00	0	1	0
Sheffield Wed	L	12.01	01	4	1	0

DJORKAEFF Youri
Lyon, France, 9 March, 1968 France 82 (M)

Bolton W	Kaiserslautern (Ger)	02.02	01-03	72	3	19
Blackburn Rov	Tr	09.04	04	3	0	0

DOANE Benjamin (Ben) Nigel David
Sheffield, 22 December, 1979 (FB)

Sheffield U	YT	07.98	99-02	19	4	1
Mansfield T	L	01.03	02	11	0	0

DOBBIE Harold
Bishop Auckland, 20 February, 1923 Died 1988 (CF)

Middlesbrough	South Bank St Peter's	12.46	46-49	23	-	6
Plymouth Arg	Tr	03.50	49-53	30	-	6
Torquay U	Tr	10.53	53-56	113	-	46

DOBBIN James (Jim)
Dunfermline, 17 September, 1963 SYth (M)

Doncaster Rov	Glasgow Celtic	03.84	83-86	56	8	13
Barnsley	Tr	09.86	86-90	116	13	12
Grimsby T	Tr	07.91	91-95	154	10	21
Rotherham U	Tr	08.96	96	17	2	0
Doncaster Rov	Tr	08.97	97	28	3	0
Scarborough	Tr	03.98	97	1	0	0
Grimsby T	Tr	03.98	97-98	1	5	0

DOBBING Robert (Bobby)
Sunderland, 27 June, 1949 (FB)

Coventry C	App	06.67				
Hartlepool	Tr	07.69	69	34	0	1

DOBBINS Lionel Wayne
Bromsgrove, 30 August, 1968 (FB)

West Bromwich A	App	08.86	86-90	30	15	0
Torquay U	Tr	07.91	91	18	3	1

DOBBS Eric
Wymondham, 15 October, 1920 (FB)

Coventry C		08.46	46-47	5	-	0

DOBBS Gerald Francis
Lambeth, 24 January, 1971 (M)

Wimbledon	YT	07.89	91-93	21	12	1
Cardiff C	L	09.95	95	3	0	0

DOBIE Mark Walter Graham
Carlisle, 8 November, 1963 (F)

Carlisle U	Workington	12.86	86	2	4	0
Cambridge U	Gretna	12.90				
Torquay U	Tr	08.91	91	18	2	2
Darlington	Tr	08.92	92	35	1	8

DOBIE Robert Scott
Workington, 10 October, 1978 S-6 (F)

Carlisle U	YT	05.97	96-00	101	35	24
West Bromwich A	Tr	07.01	01-04	57	53	21
Millwall	Tr	11.04	04	15	1	3
Nottingham F	Tr	02.05	04	11	1	1

DOBING Brian George
Sheffield, 29 December, 1937 Died 1995 (G)

Crewe Alex	Knutsford	04.59	58	1	-	0

DOBING Peter Alan
Manchester, 1 December, 1938 Eu23-7/FLge-3 (M)

Blackburn Rov	Jnrs	12.55	56-60	179	-	88
Manchester C	Tr	07.61	61-62	82	-	31
Stoke C	Tr	08.63	63-72	303	4	82

DOBSON Anthony (Tony) John
Coventry, 5 February, 1969 Eu21-4 (CD)

Coventry C	App	07.86	86-90	51	3	1
Blackburn Rov	Tr	01.91	90-92	36	5	0
Portsmouth	Tr	09.93	93-96	48	5	2
Oxford U	L	12.94	94	5	0	0
Peterborough U	L	01.96	95	4	0	0
West Bromwich A	Tr	08.97	97	6	5	0
Gillingham	L	09.98	98	2	0	0
Northampton T	Tr	09.98	98-99	9	3	0

DOBSON Brian Ashley
Colchester, 1 March, 1934 (CD)

Colchester U		01.56	55-59	24	-	0

DOBSON Colin
Eston, 9 May, 1940 Eu23-2 (W)

Sheffield Wed	Jnrs	11.57	61-65	177	0	49
Huddersfield T	Tr	08.66	66-70	149	6	50
Brighton & Hove A	L	01.72	71	2	2	0
Bristol Rov	Tr	07.72	72-75	62	0	4

DOBSON Craig Gregory
Chingford, 23 January, 1984 Jamaica 1 (M)

Cheltenham T	Crystal Palace (Sch)	07.03	03	0	2	0

DOBSON George Richard
Chiswick, 24 August, 1949 (W)

Brentford	App	08.67	66-69	75	11	10

DOBSON Ian
Hull, 3 October, 1957 (CD)

Hull C	App	10.75	75-79	86	6	7
Hereford U	Tr	06.80	80-81	41	0	5

DOBSON John Martin
Rishton, 14 February, 1948 ESch/FLge-1/E-5 (M)

Bolton W	Jnrs	07.66				
Burnley	Tr	08.67	67-74	220	4	43
Everton	Tr	08.74	74-78	190	0	29
Burnley	Tr	08.79	79-83	186	0	20
Bury	Tr	03.84	83-85	60	1	4

DOBSON Michael William
Isleworth, 9 April, 1981 (FB)

League Club	Source	Date Signed	Seasons Played	Apps	Subs	Gls
Brentford	YT	06.99	00-04	161	10	3

DOBSON Paul
Hartlepool, 17 December, 1962 (F)

League Club	Source	Date Signed	Seasons Played	Apps	Subs	Gls
Hartlepool U	Newcastle U (Jnrs)	11.81	81-82	23	8	8
Hartlepool U	Horden CW	12.83	83-85	60	20	24
Torquay U	Tr	07.86	86-87	63	14	38
Doncaster Rov	Tr	08.88	88	22	2	10
Scarborough	Tr	02.89	88-90	54	7	22
Halifax T	L	10.90	90	1	0	1
Hereford U	L	11.90	90	6	0	1
Lincoln C	Tr	01.91	90-91	13	8	5
Darlington	Tr	08.92	92	4	10	2

DOBSON Robert Peter
Frimley, 13 June, 1925 (IF)

League Club	Source	Date Signed	Seasons Played	Apps	Subs	Gls
Ipswich T	Wisbech T	10.49	49-53	30	-	5

DOBSON Ryan Adam
Telford, 24 September, 1978 (FB)

League Club	Source	Date Signed	Seasons Played	Apps	Subs	Gls
Chester C	YT	07.97	97	6	0	0

DOBSON Warren Edward
North Shields, 5 November, 1978 (G)

League Club	Source	Date Signed	Seasons Played	Apps	Subs	Gls
Hartlepool U	Queens Park Rgrs (YT)	08.97	97	1	0	0

DOCHERTY Bernard (Benny)
Bellshill, 11 August, 1941 (IF)

League Club	Source	Date Signed	Seasons Played	Apps	Subs	Gls
Notts Co	Cowdenbeath	08.64	64	25	-	2

DOCHERTY James (Jimmy)
Greenock, 21 April, 1926 Died 2002 (IF)

League Club	Source	Date Signed	Seasons Played	Apps	Subs	Gls
Plymouth Arg	Glasgow Celtic	05.50				
Northampton T	Tr	07.50	50	1	-	0

DOCHERTY James (Jimmy)
Clydebank, 22 April, 1929 (IF)

League Club	Source	Date Signed	Seasons Played	Apps	Subs	Gls
Doncaster Rov	Airdrie	05.51	51	11	-	4
Crewe Alex	Limerick C	02.57	56	2	-	0

DOCHERTY James (Jim)
Broxburn, 8 November, 1956 (F)

League Club	Source	Date Signed	Seasons Played	Apps	Subs	Gls
Chelsea	East Stirling	03.79	78	2	1	0

DOCHERTY John
Glasgow, 29 April, 1940 (W)

League Club	Source	Date Signed	Seasons Played	Apps	Subs	Gls
Brentford	St Roch's	07.59	60	17	-	2
Sheffield U	Tr	03.61	60-65	41	0	9
Brentford	Tr	12.65	65-67	97	0	31
Reading	Tr	02.68	67-69	45	1	8
Brentford	Tr	03.70	69-73	137	4	34

DOCHERTY John
Glasgow, 28 February, 1935 (WH)

League Club	Source	Date Signed	Seasons Played	Apps	Subs	Gls
Colchester U	Heart of Midlothian	06.63	63-64	76	-	2

DOCHERTY Michael (Mike)
Preston, 29 October, 1950 EYth (FB)

League Club	Source	Date Signed	Seasons Played	Apps	Subs	Gls
Burnley	App	11.67	68-75	149	4	0
Manchester C	Tr	04.76	75-76	8	0	0
Sunderland	Tr	12.76	76-78	72	1	6

DOCHERTY Peter
Hebburn, 14 February, 1929 (W)

League Club	Source	Date Signed	Seasons Played	Apps	Subs	Gls
Fulham		09.49				
Darlington	Tr	09.50	50	3	-	1

DOCHERTY Thomas (Tom)
Penshaw, 15 April, 1924 (W)

League Club	Source	Date Signed	Seasons Played	Apps	Subs	Gls
Lincoln C	Murton CW	07.47	47-49	45	-	3
Norwich C	Tr	06.50	50-52	85	-	4
Reading	Tr	07.53	53-54	53	-	2
Newport Co	Tr	06.55	55-57	108	-	1

DOCHERTY Thomas (Tommy) Henderson
Glasgow, 24 August, 1928 SB/S-25 (WH)

League Club	Source	Date Signed	Seasons Played	Apps	Subs	Gls
Preston NE	Glasgow Celtic	11.49	49-57	323	-	5
Arsenal	Tr	08.58	58-60	83	-	1
Chelsea	Tr	09.61	61	4	-	0

DOCKER Ian
Gravesend, 12 September, 1969 ESch (M)

League Club	Source	Date Signed	Seasons Played	Apps	Subs	Gls
Gillingham	YT	09.87	87-90	73	14	3

DOCKER John Barry
Coventry, 25 September, 1947 (W)

League Club	Source	Date Signed	Seasons Played	Apps	Subs	Gls
Coventry C	Jnrs	08.65				
Torquay U	L	07.67	67	4	1	0

DODD Alan
Stoke-on-Trent, 20 September, 1953 Eu23-6/FLge-1 (CD)

League Club	Source	Date Signed	Seasons Played	Apps	Subs	Gls
Stoke C	App	10.70	72-82	349	9	3
Wolverhampton W	Tr	11.82	82-84	88	0	5
Stoke C	Tr	01.85	84	16	0	0
Port Vale	Elfsborg (Swe)	11.86	86	2	0	0

DODD Ashley Michael
Stafford, 7 January, 1982 ESch (M)

League Club	Source	Date Signed	Seasons Played	Apps	Subs	Gls
Manchester U	YT	09.99				
Port Vale	Tr	03.01	00-01	8	4	1

DODD James (Jim) Edward
Wallasey, 12 December, 1933 (CF)

League Club	Source	Date Signed	Seasons Played	Apps	Subs	Gls
Tranmere Rov	Upton	05.56	56-59	63	-	22

DODD Jason Robert
Bath, 2 November, 1970 Eu21-8 (FB)

League Club	Source	Date Signed	Seasons Played	Apps	Subs	Gls
Southampton	Bath C	03.89	89-04	371	27	9
Plymouth Arg	L	03.05	04	4	0	0

DODD William
Bedlington, 30 September, 1936 (CF)

League Club	Source	Date Signed	Seasons Played	Apps	Subs	Gls
Burnley	Whitley Bay	02.56				
Workington	Tr	09.58	58	1	-	0

DODD William (Billy) Dickinson
Chester-le-Street, 25 August, 1933 Died 1982 (FB)

League Club	Source	Date Signed	Seasons Played	Apps	Subs	Gls
Shrewsbury T	Derby Co (Am)	08.50	50-54	28	-	1
Southport	Banbury Spencer	06.57	57-58	70	-	2

DODDS Ephraim (Jock)
Grangemouth, 7 September, 1915 SWar-8 (CF)

League Club	Source	Date Signed	Seasons Played	Apps	Subs	Gls
Huddersfield T	Medomsley Jnrs	02.33				
Lincoln C	Tr	03.33				
Sheffield U	Tr	05.34	34-38	178	-	114
Blackpool	Tr	03.39	38	12	-	10
Everton	Shamrock Rov	11.46	46-48	55	-	36
Lincoln C	Tr	10.48	48-49	60	-	39

DODDS Gerald (Gerry)
Sheffield, 4 January, 1935 (W)

League Club	Source	Date Signed	Seasons Played	Apps	Subs	Gls
Sheffield U	Jnrs	02.52				
Chesterfield	Tr	06.55	55	4	-	0

DODDS Leslie (Les)
Newcastle, 12 October, 1936 ESch (G)

League Club	Source	Date Signed	Seasons Played	Apps	Subs	Gls
Sunderland	Jnrs	10.53	54-55	6	-	0

DODDS Robert
Gateshead, 1 July, 1923 (WH)

League Club	Source	Date Signed	Seasons Played	Apps	Subs	Gls
Darlington		02.47	46-48	35	-	1

DODDS Thomas (Tom) Black
South Shields, 20 December, 1918 Died 1998 (IF)

League Club	Source	Date Signed	Seasons Played	Apps	Subs	Gls
Aston Villa	North Shields	01.39	46	1	-	0
Swansea T	Tr	01.47	46-47	11	-	2

DODDS William (Billy)
New Cumnock, 5 February, 1969 S-26 (F)

League Club	Source	Date Signed	Seasons Played	Apps	Subs	Gls
Chelsea	App	05.86	86-88	0	3	0

DODGE William (Bill) Charles
Hackney, 10 March, 1937 (WH)

League Club	Source	Date Signed	Seasons Played	Apps	Subs	Gls
Tottenham H	Eton Manor	10.57	58-59	6	-	0
Crystal Palace	Tr	07.62	62	3	-	0

DODGIN Norman
Gateshead, 1 November, 1921 Died 2000 (WH)

League Club	Source	Date Signed	Seasons Played	Apps	Subs	Gls
Newcastle U	Whitehall BC	08.40	47-49	84	-	1
Reading	Tr	06.50	50	13	-	1
Northampton T	Tr	09.51	51-52	19	-	1
Exeter C	Tr	08.53	53-54	33	-	1

DODGIN William (Bill)
Wardley, 4 November, 1931 Died 2000 Eu23-1 (CD)

League Club	Source	Date Signed	Seasons Played	Apps	Subs	Gls
Fulham	Southampton (Am)	09.49	51-52	35	-	0
Arsenal	Tr	12.52	52-59	191	-	0
Fulham	Tr	03.61	60-63	69	-	0

DODSON David (Dave) Alfred
Gravesend, 20 January, 1940 EYth (W)

League Club	Source	Date Signed	Seasons Played	Apps	Subs	Gls
Arsenal	Jnrs	11.57				
Swansea T	Tr	07.59	59-61	30	-	11
Portsmouth	Tr	12.61	61-64	53	-	15
Aldershot	Tr	01.65	64-66	59	0	12

DOHERTY Gary Michael Thomas
Carndonagh, 31 January, 1980 EYth/IRu21-7/IR-31 (CD)

League Club	Source	Date Signed	Seasons Played	Apps	Subs	Gls
Luton T	YT	07.97	97-99	46	24	12
Tottenham H	Tr	04.00	99-04	45	19	4
Norwich C	Tr	08.04	04	17	3	2

League Club	Source	Date Signed	Seasons Played	Apps	Subs	Gls

DOHERTY James (Jim) Clarkson
Douglas, 31 January, 1957 (F)

Notts Co	Cumnock Jnrs	07.79	79-80	6	2	0

DOHERTY John Herbert
Manchester, 12 March, 1935 (IF)

Manchester U	Jnrs	03.52	52-57	25	-	7
Leicester C	Tr	10.57	57	12	-	5

DOHERTY John Michael
Stoneleigh, 26 April, 1936 (CF)

Fulham	Chelsea (Am)	09.54	56-61	49	-	7
Aldershot	South Coast U (Aus)	01.65	64-65	18	0	1

DOHERTY Lee Joseph
Camden Town, 6 February, 1980 (CD)

Charlton Ath	Arsenal (YT)	10.98				
Brighton & Hove A	Tr	03.99	98	3	0	0

DOHERTY Michael (Mike)
Liverpool, 8 March, 1961 ESemiPro (F)

Reading	Basingstoke T	10.82	82	23	2	5

DOHERTY Neil
Barrow, 21 February, 1969 (W)

Watford	App	03.87				
Birmingham C	Barrow	02.94	93-95	15	8	2
Northampton T	L	02.96	95	3	6	1

DOHERTY Peter Dermont
Magherafelt, 5 June, 1913 Died 1990 FLge-1/IWar-2/I-16 (IF)

Blackpool	Glentoran	11.33	33-35	83	-	28
Manchester C	Tr	02.36	35-38	119	-	74
Derby Co	Tr	12.45	46	15	-	7
Huddersfield T	Tr	12.46	46-48	83	-	33
Doncaster Rov	Tr	06.49	49-52	103	-	56

DOHERTY Sean Anthony
Basingstoke, 10 May, 1985 EYth/Eu20 (M)

Fulham	YT	02.02				
Blackpool	L	09.03	03	0	1	0

DOHERTY Thomas (Tommy) Edward
Bristol, 17 March, 1979 NI-9 (M)

Bristol C	YT	07.97	97-04	155	33	7

DOIG Christopher (Chris) Ross
Dumfries, 13 February, 1981 SSch/SYth/Su21-13 (CD)

Nottingham F	YT Queen of South	03.98	98-04	62	15	1
Northampton T	L	09.03	03	9	0	0

DOIG Russell
Millport, 17 January, 1964 (W)

Leeds U	East Stirling	07.86	86-87	3	3	0
Peterborough U	L	10.86	86	7	0	0
Hartlepool U	Tr	03.88	87-89	22	11	2

DOLAN Andrew (Andy)
Glasgow, 2 August, 1920 (IF)

Bury	Raith Rov	08.48	48	10	-	2
Accrington St	Tr	09.49	49	19	-	4

DOLAN Eamonn John
Dagenham, 20 September, 1967 IRYth/IRu21-5 (F)

West Ham U	App	03.85	86-89	9	6	3
Bristol C	L	02.89	88	3	0	0
Birmingham C	Tr	12.90	90-91	6	6	1
Exeter C	Tr	09.91	91-92	15	11	4

DOLAN Joseph (Joe) Thomas
Harrow, 27 May, 1980 NIYth/NIu21-6 (CD)

Millwall	Chelsea (Jnrs)	04.98	98-03	47	2	3
Stockport Co	L	01.05	04	11	0	1
Brighton & Hove A	L	03.05	04	3	0	0

DOLAN Patrick (Pat) Daniel
Dagenham, 20 September, 1967 IRYth/IRu21-3 (CD)

Arsenal	App	07.85				
Walsall	Tr	08.86	86	1	0	0

DOLAN Terence (Terry) Peter
Bradford, 11 June, 1950 (M)

Bradford PA	Bradford C (Am)	04.69	68-69	46	2	0
Huddersfield T	Tr	10.70	71-75	157	5	14
Bradford C	Tr	08.76	76-80	191	4	43
Rochdale	Tr	08.81	81	42	1	1

DOLBY Christopher (Chris) John
Dewsbury, 4 September, 1974 (W)

Rotherham U	YT	08.93	93-94	0	3	0

DOLBY Peter
Derby, 18 May, 1940 (CD)

Shrewsbury T	Heanor T	02.60	60-75	303	21	21

DOLBY Tony Christopher
Greenwich, 16 June, 1974 (M)

Millwall	YT	10.91	92-96	38	28	3
Barnet	L	02.94	93	13	3	2

DOLDING Desmond Leonard (Len)
Nundydroog, India, 13 December, 1922 Died 1954 (W)

Chelsea	Wealdstone	07.45	46-47	26	-	2
Norwich C	Tr	07.48	48-49	12	-	1

DOLING Stuart James
Newport, Isle of Wight, 28 October, 1972 EYth (M)

Portsmouth	YT	06.90	91-94	20	17	4
Doncaster Rov	AFC Lymington	10.95	95-96	3	3	0

DOMI Didier
Paris, France, 2 May, 1978 FrYth/Fru21 (FB)

Newcastle U	Paris St Germain (Fr)	01.99	98-00	44	11	3
Leeds U (L)	Paris St Germain (Fr)	08.03	03	9	3	0

DOMINEY Barry William
Edmonton, 21 October, 1955 (CD)

Colchester U	Enfield WMC	01.74	73-76	56	15	3

DOMINGUEZ Jose Manuel Martins
Lisbon, Portugal, 16 February, 1974 PorYth/PorU21/Por-3 (W)

Birmingham C	Benfica (Por)	03.94	93-94	15	20	3
Tottenham H	Sporting Lisbon (Por)	08.97	97-00	12	33	4

DONACHIE Daniel (Danny) James
Manchester, 17 May, 1973 (FB)

Carlisle U	Radcliffe Borough	01.96	95	0	1	0

DONACHIE William (Willie)
Glasgow, 5 October, 1951 Su23-2/S-35 (FB)

Manchester C	Jnrs	12.68	69-79	347	4	2
Norwich C	Portland (USA)	09.81	81	11	0	0
Burnley	Portland (USA)	11.82	82-83	60	0	3
Oldham Ath	Tr	07.84	84-90	158	11	3

DONAGHY Barry
Consett, 21 March, 1956 EYth (W)

West Bromwich A	App	05.73	73-74	4	2	1
Workington	Tr	12.75	75-76	40	4	3

DONAGHY Malachy (Mal) Martin
Belfast, 13 September, 1957 NIu21-1/NI-91 (CD)

Luton T	Larne T	06.78	78-88	410	0	16
Manchester U	Tr	10.88	88-91	76	13	0
Luton T	L	12.89	89	5	0	0
Chelsea	Tr	08.92	92-93	63	5	3

DONALD Alexander (Alex)
Kirkliston, 5 June, 1948 (W)

Port Vale	Jnrs	10.65	65-67	41	2	0

DONALD Ian Richard
Aberdeen, 28 November, 1951 SSch (FB)

Manchester U	Banks o' Dee	07.69	72	4	0	0

DONALD Warren Ramsay
Hillingdon, 7 October, 1964 ESch (M)

West Ham U	App	10.82	83	1	1	0
Northampton T	L	03.85	84	11	0	2
Northampton T	Tr	10.85	85-89	169	8	11
Colchester U	Tr	07.90	92	8	2	0

DONALDSON Andrew (Andy)
Newcastle, 22 March, 1925 Died 1987 (CF)

Newcastle U	Vickers Armstrong	09.43	46-48	19	-	6
Middlesbrough	Tr	01.49	48-50	21	-	7
Exeter C	Peterborough U	09.53	53-54	39	-	16

DONALDSON Brian Leslie
Hove, 3 April, 1936 (W)

Chelsea	Jnrs	07.53				
Swindon T	Tr	10.57	57	1	-	0

DONALDSON Clayton Andrew
Bradford, 7 February, 1984 (F)

Hull C	Sch	02.03	02	0	2	0

DONALDSON David (Dave)
Hillingdon, 28 December, 1941 (CD)

Wimbledon	Walton & Hersham	08.74	77-78	61	0	0

League Club	Source	Date Signed	Seasons Played	Career Record Apps	Subs	Gls
DONALDSON David (Dave) John						
Islington, 12 November, 1954 ESch						(FB)
Arsenal	App	07.72				
Millwall	Tr	06.73	73-79	215	1	1
Cambridge U	Tr	02.80	79-83	130	2	0
DONALDSON Frederick (Fred) Lewis						
Stoke-on-Trent, 7 April, 1937						(FB)
Port Vale	Jnrs	07.54	54-59	47	-	4
Exeter C	Tr	08.60	60	36	-	6
Chester	Tr	07.61	61	21	-	0
DONALDSON James (Jimmy) Dent						
South Shields, 11 June, 1927 Died 1980						(WH)
Chesterfield	South Shields	11.48	49-50	17	-	4
Newport Co	Tr	08.51	51-52	36	-	1
DONALDSON Leslie (Les) Darcy Robert						
Glasgow, 30 July, 1922 Died 1995						(IF)
Wrexham	Rhyl	06.50	50-51	30	-	6
DONALDSON O'Neill McKay						
Birmingham, 24 November, 1969						(F)
Shrewsbury T	Hinckley U	11.91	91-93	15	13	4
Doncaster Rov	Tr	08.94	94	7	2	2
Mansfield T	L	12.94	94	4	0	6
Sheffield Wed	Tr	01.95	94-97	4	10	3
Oxford U	L	01.98	97	6	0	2
Stoke C	Tr	03.98	97	2	0	0
Torquay U	Tr	09.98	98-99	11	16	1
DONALDSON Robert (Bobby) Steve						
South Shields, 26 February, 1921 Died 1990						(WH)
Newcastle U		01.43				
Hartlepools U	Tr	07.47	47-51	131	-	4
DONALDSON William (Willie)						
Wallacetown, 20 January, 1920 Died 1977						(W)
Bradford PA	Leith Ath	05.46	46-50	45	-	6
Mansfield T	Tr	10.50	50-51	52	-	10
DONCEL-VARCARCEL Antonio						
Lugo, Spain, 31 January, 1967						(CD)
Hull C	Ferrol	08.96	96-97	30	8	2
DONE Cyril Charles						
Liverpool, 21 October, 1920 Died 1993						(CF)
Liverpool	Bootle Boys Brigade	01.38	46-51	93	-	32
Tranmere Rov	Tr	05.52	52-54	87	-	61
Port Vale	Tr	12.54	54-56	52	-	34
DONEGAL Glenville (Glen) Paul						
Northampton, 20 June, 1969						(F)
Northampton T	YT	08.87	87-89	7	13	3
Maidstone U	Aylesbury U	08.91	91	9	5	1
DONIS Georgios (George) Yorgos						
Greece, 29 October, 1969 Greece 24						(W)
Blackburn Rov	Panathinaikos (Gre)	07.96	96	11	11	2
Sheffield U	AEK Athens (Gre)	03.99	98	5	2	1
Huddersfield T	Tr	06.99	99	10	10	0
DONN Alan Nigel						
Maidstone, 2 March, 1962						(M)
Gillingham	App	02.80	80-81	2	1	0
Orient	Karpalo (Finland)	08.82	82	22	1	2
DONNELLAN Gary						
Kensington, 3 July, 1962						(W)
Chelsea	App	07.80				
Watford	Tr	11.80				
Reading	Tr	11.81	81-82	33	8	5
DONNELLAN Leo John						
Willesden, 19 January, 1965 IRu21-1						(M)
Chelsea	App	08.82				
Orient	L	12.84	84	6	0	0
Fulham	Tr	08.85	85-89	54	25	4
DONNELLY Andrew (Andy)						
Lanark, 1 May, 1943						(G)
Millwall	Clyde	05.63				
Torquay U	Weymouth	08.67	67-71	160	0	0
DONNELLY Ciaran						
Blackpool, 2 April, 1984 EYth						(M)
Blackburn Rov	YT	07.01				
Blackpool	L	03.04	03	8	1	0
Blackpool	Tr	03.05	04	4	4	0
DONNELLY Darren Charles						
Liverpool, 28 December, 1971						(F)
Blackburn Rov	YT	06.90	90	1	1	0
Chester C	Tr	08.93	93	0	9	0
DONNELLY James (Jim)						
Cork, 6 May, 1919						(IF)
Accrington St	Sligo Rov	08.51	51	4	-	1
DONNELLY John						
Broxburn, 17 December, 1936						(FB)
Preston NE	Glasgow Celtic	04.62	62-66	56	2	1
DONNELLY John						
Glasgow, 8 March, 1961						(M)
Leeds U	Dumbarton	03.83	82-84	36	4	4
DONNELLY Mark Paul						
Leeds, 22 December, 1979						(M)
Doncaster Rov	YT	•	96-97	8	3	1
DONNELLY Paul Anthony						
Liverpool, 23 December, 1971						(W)
Halifax T	YT	03.90	88-90	9	4	0
DONNELLY Paul Michael						
Newcastle-under-Lyme, 16 February, 1981						(CD)
Port Vale	YT	07.99	99-01	5	6	0
DONNELLY Peter						
Hull, 22 September, 1936						(IF)
Doncaster Rov	Jnrs	03.54	53-56	6	-	1
Scunthorpe U	Tr	07.58	58-59	39	-	19
Cardiff C	Tr	06.60	60-61	31	-	8
Swansea T	Tr	10.61	61	16	-	3
Brighton & Hove A	Tr	07.62	62-64	56	-	13
Bradford C	Tr	03.65	64-65	13	0	5
DONNELLY Peter James						
Chester, 11 May, 1965						(M)
Chester C	App	08.83	83	1	0	0
DONNELLY Scott Paul						
Hammersmith, 25 December, 1987						(M)
Queens Park Rgrs	Sch	•	04	0	2	0
DONNELLY Simon Thomas						
Glasgow, 1 December, 1974 Su21-11/S-10						(M)
Sheffield Wed	Glasgow Celtic	07.99	99-02	27	26	8
DONOVAN Daniel (Don) Christopher						
Cork, 23 December, 1929 IR-5						(FB)
Everton	Dalymount Rov	05.49	51-57	179	-	2
Grimsby T	Tr	08.58	58-63	238	-	1
DONOVAN Francis (Frank) James						
Pembroke, 26 February, 1919 Died 2003 WAmat						(W)
Swansea T	Pembroke Borough	05.50	50	15	-	2
DONOVAN Kevin						
Halifax, 17 December, 1971						(M)
Huddersfield T	YT	10.89	89-92	11	9	1
Halifax T	L	02.92	91	6	0	0
West Bromwich A	Tr	10.92	92-96	139	29	19
Grimsby T	Tr	07.97	97-00	150	6	24
Barnsley	Tr	07.01	01-02	48	6	1
Rochdale	Tr	12.03	03	4	3	0
DONOVAN Terence (Terry) Christopher						
Liverpool, 27 February, 1958 ESch/IRu21-1/IR-1						(F)
Grimsby T	Louth U	08.76	76-78	52	12	23
Aston Villa	Tr	09.79	79-81	17	0	6
Oxford U	L	02.83	82	3	0	0
Burnley	Tr	02.83	82-83	13	2	6
Rotherham U	Tr	09.83	83-84	9	4	0
Blackpool	L	10.84	84	2	0	0
DONOWA Brian Louie						
Ipswich, 24 September, 1964 Eu21-3						(W)
Norwich C	App	09.82	82-85	56	6	11
Stoke C	L	12.85	85	4	0	1
Ipswich T	Willem II Tilburg (Holl)	04.89	89	17	6	1
Bristol C	Tr	08.90	90	11	13	3
Birmingham C	Tr	08.91	91-96	78	38	18
Burnley	L	01.93	92	4	0	0
Shrewsbury T	L	01.94	93	4	0	0
Walsall	L	10.96	96	6	0	1
Peterborough U	Tr	12.96	96	16	6	1
Walsall	Tr	08.97	97	5	1	0

League Club	Source	Date Signed	Seasons Played	Career Record Apps	Subs	Gls

DOOLAN John
Liverpool, 10 November, 1968 (M)

Wigan Ath	Knowsley U	03.92	91-95	29	9	1

DOOLAN John
Liverpool, 7 May, 1974 (M)

Everton	YT	06.92				
Mansfield T	Tr	09.94	94-97	128	3	10
Barnet	Tr	01.98	97-00	132	2	7
Doncaster Rov	Tr	03.03	03-04	68	9	2

DOOLEY Derek
Sheffield, 13 December, 1929 (CF)

Lincoln C (Am)	Sheffield YMCA	09.46	46	2	-	2
Sheffield Wed	Tr	06.47	49-52	61	-	62

DOOLEY George
Chesterfield, 29 December, 1922 Died 2004 (IF)

Chesterfield	Parkhouse Colliery	06.45				
Halifax T	Tr	12.46	46	11	-	2

DOONAN Thomas (Tom)
West Calder, 5 October, 1922 Died 1998 (CF)

Bradford C	Albion Rov	06.49	49	13	-	7
Tranmere Rov	Tr	07.50	50	4	-	2

DOONER Gary James
St Helens, 14 September, 1970 (W)

Stockport Co	YT	●	88	1	0	0

DORAN Robert Rennie
Carlisle, 26 December, 1933 (CD)

Carlisle U		10.52	53-61	107	-	0

DORAN Terence (Terry)
Jarrow, 2 April, 1940 (FB)

Gateshead (Am)	St Mary's BC	09.59	59	1	-	0

DORE Leslie **Charles (Charlie)** Albert
Gosport, 22 January, 1931 (G)

Portsmouth	Fleetlands BC	05.50	51-53	18	-	0

DORIGO Anthony (Tony) Robert
Melbourne, Australia, 31 December, 1965 Eu21-11/EB-7/E-15 (FB)

Aston Villa	App	07.83	83-86	106	5	1
Chelsea	Tr	07.87	87-90	146	0	11
Leeds U	Tr	06.91	91-96	168	3	5
Derby Co	Torino (It)	10.98	98-99	37	4	1
Stoke C	Tr	07.00	00	34	2	0

[DORIVA] GHIDONI Dorival
Landeara, Brazil, 28 May, 1972 Brazil 12 (M)

Middlesbrough	Celta Vigo (Sp)	02.03	02-04	37	15	0

DORLING George John
Edmonton, 27 July, 1918 Died 1987 (FB)

Tottenham H	Jnrs	03.46				
Gillingham	Tr	05.47	50	10	-	0

DORMAN Donald (Don)
Hall Green, 18 September, 1922 Died 1997 (IF)

Birmingham C	Shirley Jnrs	05.46	46-51	59	-	4
Coventry C	Tr	09.51	51-54	90	-	29
Walsall	Tr	10.54	54-56	116	-	34

DORNAN Andrew (Andy)
Aberdeen, 19 August, 1961 SSch/SYth (FB)

Walsall	Motherwell	08.86	86-89	117	1	1

DORNAN Peter
Belfast, 30 June, 1953 IrLge-3 (M)

Sheffield U	Linfield	12.76	76	1	2	0
Swindon T	Linfield	02.79	78	0	1	0

DORNER Mario
Baden, Austria, 21 March, 1970 (F)

Darlington	Motherwell	10.97	97-98	34	15	13

DORNEY Alan John
Bermondsey, 18 May, 1947 (CD)

Millwall	Jnrs	05.65	68-76	249	3	1

DORRIAN Christopher (Chris) Stewart
Harlow, 3 April, 1982 (CD)

Leyton Orient	YT	07.00	00-01	4	1	0

DORSETT Richard (Dickie)
Brownhills, 3 December, 1919 Died 1999 (WH)

Wolverhampton W	Jnrs	12.36	37-46	46	-	32
Aston Villa	Tr	09.46	46-52	257	-	32

[DOUDOU] M'BOMBO Aziana Ebele
Kinshasa, DR Congo, 11 September, 1980 (M)

Queens Park Rgrs	AS Monaco (Fr)	08.01	01-02	23	23	3
Oxford U	Farnborough T	12.04	04	0	1	0

DOUGAL Cornelius (Neil)
Falkirk, 7 November, 1921 SWar-1/S-1 (WH)

Burnley	Jnrs	03.40				
Birmingham C	Tr	10.45	46-48	93	-	15
Plymouth Arg	Tr	03.49	48-58	274	-	26

DOUGAL James (Jimmy)
Denny, 3 October, 1913 Died 1999 SWar-1/S-1 (IF)

Preston NE	Falkirk	01.34	33-46	170	-	51
Carlisle U	Tr	10.46	46-48	71	-	13
Halifax T	Tr	10.48	48	21	-	2

DOUGAL John (Jack)
Falkirk, 7 August, 1934 EAmat (FB)

Halifax T (Am)	Pegasus	05.56	55-56	3	-	0

DOUGAL William (Willie)
Falkirk, 30 October, 1923 (WH)

Preston NE	Glasgow Rgrs	12.47	47-48	22	-	2
Barnsley	Tr	08.52	52	21	-	0

DOUGALL Thomas (Tom)
Wishaw, 17 May, 1921 Died 1997 (W)

Coventry C		09.45				
Brentford	Tr	08.47	47	2	-	0
Sunderland	Tr	11.48	48	3	-	0

DOUGAN Alexander **Derek**
Belfast, 20 January, 1938 NISch/NIB/NI-43 (F)

Portsmouth	Distillery	08.57	57-58	33	-	9
Blackburn Rov	Tr	03.59	58-60	59	-	26
Aston Villa	Tr	08.61	61-62	51	-	19
Peterborough U	Tr	06.63	63-64	77	-	38
Leicester C	Tr	05.65	65-66	68	0	35
Wolverhampton W	Tr	03.67	66-74	244	14	95

DOUGAN George
Glasgow, 22 March, 1939 (WH)

Ipswich T	Yiewsley	03.63	62-63	17	-	0

DOUGAN John McKechnie
Glasgow, 12 January, 1931 Died 1995 (IF)

Brighton & Hove A	Bellshill Ath	12.51				
Torquay U	Tr	02.54	53-54	21	-	3

DOUGAN Maxwell (Max) Spalding
Stoneyburn, 23 May, 1938 SAmat (FB)

Leicester C	Queen's Park	09.63	63-66	9	0	0
Luton T	Tr	12.66	66-69	117	1	0

DOUGHERTY Paul
Leamington Spa, 12 May, 1966 (M)

Wolverhampton W	App	05.84	83-86	24	17	3
Torquay U	L	02.85	84	5	0	0

DOUGHERTY Victor (Vic) Robert
Glasgow, 17 January, 1955 (FB)

Bury	App	01.73	72	9	0	0

DOUGHTY Eric
Radstock, 9 April, 1932 (FB)

Arsenal	Peasedown	05.51				
Plymouth Arg	Tr	07.58	58	1	-	0

DOUGHTY Matthew (Matt) Liam
Warrington, 2 November, 1981 (FB)

Chester C	YT	●	99	19	14	1
Rochdale	Tr	07.01	01-03	96	12	1

DOUGLAS Andrew (Andy) Stephen
Penrith, 27 May, 1980 (F)

Carlisle U	YT	07.98	98	0	1	0

DOUGLAS Bryan
Blackburn, 27 May, 1934 Eu23-5/EB/FLge-4/E-36 (W)

Blackburn Rov	Lower Darwen YC	04.52	54-68	438	0	100

DOUGLAS Colin Francis
Hurlford, 9 September, 1962 (FB)

Doncaster Rov	Glasgow Celtic	08.81	81-85	202	10	48
Rotherham U	Tr	07.86	86-87	82	1	4
Doncaster Rov	Tr	08.88	88-92	182	10	5

DOUGLAS James (Jimmy) Stewart
Sunderland, 16 September, 1941 (CF)

Hartlepools U (Am)	Willington	10.62	62	13	-	4

League Club	Source	Date Signed	Seasons Played	Career Record Apps	Subs	Gls

DOUGLAS John
Stockton, 13 March, 1961 (F)

Darlington	Stockton	01.86	85	3	0	0

DOUGLAS John Stewart
West Hartlepool, 1 December, 1917 Died 2001 (WH)

Hartlepools U (Am)	Trimdon Grange	09.38	38	5	-	0
Middlesbrough	Tr	09.45	46	2	-	0
Hartlepools U	Tr	11.48	48-49	27	-	1

DOUGLAS Jonathan
Monaghan, 22 November, 1981 IRYth/IRu21-1/IR-2 (M)

Blackburn Rov	YT	02.00	02-04	14	2	1
Chesterfield	L	03.03	02	7	0	1
Blackpool	L	08.03	03	15	1	3
Gillingham	L	03.05	04	10	0	0

DOUGLAS Patrick (Pat) George
Baschurch, 17 September, 1951 (M)

Shrewsbury T	App	07.69	68	12	1	1

DOUGLAS Stuart Anthony
Enfield, 9 April, 1978 (F)

Luton T	YT	05.96	95-01	104	42	18
Oxford U	L	10.01	01	1	3	0
Rushden & Diamonds	L	01.02	01	4	5	0
Boston U	Tr	08.02	02-03	28	30	8

DOUGLASS Norman
Sunderland, 14 May, 1930 Died 1987 (FB)

Chelsea	Crook T	03.52				
Exeter C	Tr	06.53	53-54	63	-	0

DOUGLIN Troy Alexander
Coventry, 7 May, 1982 (FB)

Torquay U	YT	07.00	00-02	9	5	0

DOUMBE Mathias Kouo
Paris, France, 28 October, 1979 (CD)

Plymouth Arg	Hibernian	06.04	04	24	2	2

DOVE Craig
Hartlepool, 16 August, 1983 EYth/Eu20 (M)

Middlesbrough	YT	07.00				
York C	L	10.03	03	1	0	0
Rushden & Diamonds	Tr	07.04	04	31	5	6

DOVE Henry William
Stepney, 11 March, 1932 (CD)

Arsenal	Essex Company Cadets	08.50				
Millwall	Tr	04.58	58	7	-	0

DOVEY Alan Raymond
Stepney, 18 July, 1952 (G)

Chelsea	App	07.69				
Brighton & Hove A	Tr	03.71	70-72	6	0	0

DOW Andrew (Andy) James
Dundee, 7 February, 1973 Su21-3 (CD)

Chelsea	Dundee	07.93	93-95	14	1	0
Bradford C	L	10.94	94	5	0	0

DOW David
Manchester, 10 June, 1947 (CD)

Rochdale (Am)	Avorton	02.66	66-67	8	0	0

DOWD Henry (Harry) William
Salford, 4 July, 1938 (G)

Manchester C	ICI Blackley	07.60	61-69	181	0	1
Stoke C	L	10.69	69	3	0	0
Oldham Ath	Tr	12.70	70-73	121	0	0

DOWD Hugh Oliver
Lurgan, 19 May, 1951 NI-3 (CD)

Sheffield Wed	Glenavon	07.74	74-78	110	2	0
Doncaster Rov	Tr	08.79	79-82	94	0	3

DOWE Jens
Rostock, Germany, 1 June, 1968 (M)

Wolverhampton W (L)	SV Hamburg (Ger)	10.96	96	5	3	0

DOWE Julian Whytus Lennox
Manchester, 9 September, 1975 (F)

Wigan Ath	YT	09.92				
Rochdale	Colne	08.99	99	1	6	0

DOWELL Wayne Anthony
Easington, 28 December, 1973 (FB)

Burnley	YT	03.93	94-95	6	0	0
Carlisle U	L	03.96	95	2	5	0
Rochdale	Tr	07.96	96	6	1	0
Doncaster Rov	Tr	08.97	97	1	0	0

DOWEY Walter Leslie
Lockton, 12 June, 1923 (FB)

Crewe Alex		04.45	47-48	17	-	0

DOWIE Iain
Hatfield, 9 January, 1965 NIu23-1/NIu21-1/NI-59 (F)

Luton T	Hendon	12.88	88-90	53	13	15
Fulham	L	09.89	89	5	0	1
West Ham U	Tr	03.91	90	12	0	4
Southampton	Tr	09.91	91-94	115	7	30
Crystal Palace	Tr	01.95	94-95	19	0	6
West Ham U	Tr	09.95	95-97	58	10	8
Queens Park Rgrs	Tr	01.98	97-00	16	15	2

DOWIE John
Hamilton, 12 December, 1955 (M)

Fulham	App	05.73	73-76	32	5	2
Doncaster Rov	Glasgow Celtic	07.79	79-80	21	0	0

DOWKER Thomas (Tom)
Liverpool, 7 November, 1922 Died 2001 (W)

Oldham Ath	South Liverpool	07.47	47	1	-	0

DOWLER Michael (Mike)
Caldicot, 12 October, 1957 WSch (G)

Newport Co	Hereford U (App)	10.75	75-80	19	0	0

DOWLING Michael (Mike) Leslie
Bodmin, 3 October, 1952 (FB)

Plymouth Arg	App	10.70	69-73	27	4	0

DOWMAN Stephen (Steve) John
Manor Park, 15 April, 1958 (CD)

Colchester U	App	04.76	76-79	150	4	21
Wrexham	Tr	07.80	80-82	87	0	2
Charlton Ath	Tr	08.83	83-84	60	1	5
Newport Co	Tr	08.85	85	9	0	1
Cambridge U	Tr	10.85	85-86	45	0	3

DOWN David Frederick
Bristol, 7 July, 1948 (F)

Bristol C	App	09.65	66-67	6	1	3
Bradford PA	Tr	10.67	67-68	39	0	7
Oldham Ath	Tr	09.68	68	9	0	1
Swindon T	Tr	08.69	69-70	1	1	0

DOWN William (Billy) Frederick
Bristol, 8 November, 1963 (FB)

Bristol C	App	10.81	81	1	0	0

DOWNER Simon
Romford, 19 October, 1981 (CD)

Leyton Orient	YT	10.99	98-03	64	15	0

DOWNES Aaron Terence
Mudgee, NSW, Australia, 15 May, 1985 AuYth (CD)

Chesterfield	Frickley Ath	07.04	04	7	2	2

DOWNES Christopher (Chris) Bryan
Sheffield, 17 January, 1969 (M)

Sheffield U	App	06.87	88	2	0	0
Scarborough	L	03.88	87	2	0	0
Stockport Co	Tr	08.89	89	10	1	1
Crewe Alex	Tr	08.91	91	1	1	0

DOWNES Eric
Wigan, 25 August, 1926 (CD)

Rochdale	Chester C (Am)	05.49	50-53	54	-	0

DOWNES Robert (Bobby) David
Bloxwich, 18 August, 1949 (W)

West Bromwich A	Jnrs	08.66				
Peterborough U	Tr	09.67	67-68	23	3	3
Rochdale	Tr	08.69	69-73	164	10	10
Watford	Tr	05.74	74-79	192	7	18
Barnsley	Tr	03.80	79-80	43	0	1
Blackpool	Tr	07.82	82-83	27	1	3

DOWNES Stephen
Leeds, 22 November, 1981 (FB)

Grimsby T	Ossett A	09.01				
York C	Tr	07.03	03	4	2	0

DOWNES Steven (Steve) Fleming
Leeds, 2 December, 1949 (F)

Rotherham U	Leeds MDBC	04.67	67-69	54	5	18
Sheffield Wed	Tr	12.69	69-71	26	4	4
Chesterfield	Tr	08.72	72-73	37	4	11
Halifax T	Tr	07.74	74-75	38	12	12
Blackburn Rov	L	03.76	75	6	0	0

League Club	Source	Date Signed	Seasons Played	Apps	Subs	Gls

DOWNES Walter (Wally) John
Hammersmith, 9 June, 1961 (M)

League Club	Source	Date Signed	Seasons Played	Apps	Subs	Gls
Wimbledon	App	01.79	78-86	194	13	15
Newport Co	L	12.87	87	4	0	2
Sheffield U	Tr	02.88	87	6	3	1

DOWNEY Christopher (Chris) Anthony
Warrington, 19 April, 1983 (F)

League Club	Source	Date Signed	Seasons Played	Apps	Subs	Gls
Bolton W	YT	07.01	00	0	1	0

DOWNEY Glen
Sunderland, 20 September, 1978 (CD)

League Club	Source	Date Signed	Seasons Played	Apps	Subs	Gls
Hartlepool U	YT	07.97				
Grimsby T	Scarborough	08.04	04	0	1	0

DOWNIE John (Johnny) Dennis
Lanark, 19 July, 1925 (IF)

League Club	Source	Date Signed	Seasons Played	Apps	Subs	Gls
Bradford PA	Lanark ATC	12.44	46-48	86	-	33
Manchester U	Tr	03.49	48-52	110	-	35
Luton T	Tr	08.53	53	26	-	12
Hull C	Tr	07.54	54	27	-	5
Mansfield T	Wisbech T	10.58	58	18	-	4
Darlington	Tr	05.59	59	15	-	2

DOWNIE Mitchell (Mitch)
Troon, 9 February, 1923 Died 2001 (G)

League Club	Source	Date Signed	Seasons Played	Apps	Subs	Gls
Bradford PA	Airdrie	08.50	50-53	156	-	0
Lincoln C	Tr	05.54	54-58	157	-	0
Bradford C	Goole T	09.59	59-62	134	-	0
Doncaster Rov	Tr	09.63	63	7	-	0

DOWNING David William
Bideford, 6 October, 1969 (W)

League Club	Source	Date Signed	Seasons Played	Apps	Subs	Gls
York C	YT	●	87	1	0	0

DOWNING Derrick Graham
Doncaster, 3 November, 1945 (W)

League Club	Source	Date Signed	Seasons Played	Apps	Subs	Gls
Middlesbrough	Frickley Colliery	02.65	65-71	172	10	39
Orient	Tr	05.72	72-74	100	4	12
York C	Tr	07.75	75-76	44	3	2
Hartlepool U	Tr	07.77	77	40	0	4

DOWNING Keith Gordon
Oldbury, 23 July, 1965 (M)

League Club	Source	Date Signed	Seasons Played	Apps	Subs	Gls
Notts Co	Mile Oak Rov	05.84	84-86	23	0	1
Wolverhampton W	Tr	08.87	87-92	169	22	8
Birmingham C	Tr	07.93	93	1	0	0
Stoke C	Tr	08.94	94	16	0	0
Cardiff C	Tr	08.95	95	3	1	0
Hereford U	Tr	09.95	95-96	45	0	0

DOWNING Stewart
Middlesbrough, 22 July, 1984 EYth/Eu21-7/E-1 (W)

League Club	Source	Date Signed	Seasons Played	Apps	Subs	Gls
Middlesbrough	YT	09.01	01-04	37	23	5
Sunderland	L	10.03	03	7	0	3

DOWNS David
Glasgow, 7 March, 1934 Died 1978 (FB)

League Club	Source	Date Signed	Seasons Played	Apps	Subs	Gls
Plymouth Arg		11.57				
Torquay U	Tr	07.59	59	3	-	0

DOWNS Gregory (Greg)
Carlton, Nottinghamshire, 13 December, 1958 (FB)

League Club	Source	Date Signed	Seasons Played	Apps	Subs	Gls
Norwich C	App	12.76	77-84	162	7	7
Torquay U	L	11.77	77	1	0	1
Coventry C	Tr	07.85	85-89	142	4	4
Birmingham C	Tr	07.90	90	16	1	0
Hereford U	Tr	06.91	91-94	105	3	2

DOWNS Ronald (Ronnie) Henry
Southwark, 27 August, 1932 Died 1994 (W)

League Club	Source	Date Signed	Seasons Played	Apps	Subs	Gls
Crystal Palace	Grove U	12.52	52-53	23	-	2

DOWNSBOROUGH Peter
Halifax, 13 September, 1943 (G)

League Club	Source	Date Signed	Seasons Played	Apps	Subs	Gls
Halifax T	Jnrs	09.60	59-64	148	-	0
Swindon T	Tr	08.65	65-72	274	0	0
Brighton & Hove A	L	08.73	73	3	0	0
Bradford C	Tr	11.73	73-78	225	0	0

DOWSETT Gilbert (Dickie) James
Chelmsford, 3 July, 1931 (IF)

League Club	Source	Date Signed	Seasons Played	Apps	Subs	Gls
Tottenham H	Sudbury T	05.52	54	1	-	1
Southend U	Tr	05.55	55	20	-	4
Southampton	Tr	07.56	56	2	-	0
Bournemouth	Tr	06.57	57-62	169	-	79
Crystal Palace	Tr	11.62	62-64	54	-	22

DOWSON Alan Paul
Gateshead, 17 June, 1970 (FB)

League Club	Source	Date Signed	Seasons Played	Apps	Subs	Gls
Millwall	YT	05.88	90	1	0	0
Fulham	L	01.90	89	4	0	0
Bradford C	Tr	07.91	91	16	2	0
Darlington	Tr	08.92	92	30	2	0

DOWSON John Simpson
Ashington, 18 September, 1926 Died 1989 (W)

League Club	Source	Date Signed	Seasons Played	Apps	Subs	Gls
Manchester C		03.50				
Darlington	Peterborough U	06.52	52-53	65	-	11

DOYLE John Alexander (Ally)
Limavady, 25 October, 1949 (FB)

League Club	Source	Date Signed	Seasons Played	Apps	Subs	Gls
Oldham Ath	Coleraine	10.66	67-68	31	2	0

DOYLE Joseph Brian
Manchester, 15 July, 1930 Died 1992 (FB)

League Club	Source	Date Signed	Seasons Played	Apps	Subs	Gls
Stoke C	Winsford U	03.51	52	17	-	0
Exeter C	Tr	04.54	54-56	100	-	0
Bristol Rov	Tr	08.57	57-59	43	-	1

DOYLE Colin Anthony
Cork, 12 August, 1985 IRYth (G)

League Club	Source	Date Signed	Seasons Played	Apps	Subs	Gls
Birmingham C	Sch	07.04				
Nottingham F	L	12.04	04	2	1	0

DOYLE Daire Michael
Dublin, 18 October, 1980 (M)

League Club	Source	Date Signed	Seasons Played	Apps	Subs	Gls
Coventry C	Cherry Orchard	09.98				
Kidderminster Hrs	Tr	01.01	00-02	14	7	0

DOYLE Ian Patrick
Torquay, 27 February, 1959 (W)

League Club	Source	Date Signed	Seasons Played	Apps	Subs	Gls
Bristol C	Barnstaple T	12.78	79-80	2	1	0

DOYLE Jeffrey (Jeff) Noel
Dublin, 25 February, 1967 (M)

League Club	Source	Date Signed	Seasons Played	Apps	Subs	Gls
Coventry C	App	02.85				
Peterborough U	Tr	08.86	86	13	1	0

DOYLE John Joseph
Oxford, 8 February, 1960 (FB)

League Club	Source	Date Signed	Seasons Played	Apps	Subs	Gls
Oxford U	App	02.78	77-81	66	0	0
Torquay U	Tr	08.82	82	40	1	3

DOYLE Robert Leslie (Les)
Liverpool, 28 June, 1927 Died 1998 (CD)

League Club	Source	Date Signed	Seasons Played	Apps	Subs	Gls
Everton	Jnrs	05.45				
Exeter C	Tr	08.49	49-54	82	-	0

DOYLE Maurice
Ellesmere Port, 17 October, 1969 (M)

League Club	Source	Date Signed	Seasons Played	Apps	Subs	Gls
Crewe Alex	YT	07.88	87-88	6	2	2
Queens Park Rgrs	Tr	04.89	92-93	6	0	0
Crewe Alex	L	01.91	90	6	1	2
Millwall	Tr	05.95	95-97	42	24	1

DOYLE Michael (Mike)
Manchester, 25 November, 1946 Eu23-8/FLge-2/E-5 (CD)

League Club	Source	Date Signed	Seasons Played	Apps	Subs	Gls
Manchester C	App	05.64	64-77	441	7	32
Stoke C	Tr	06.78	78-81	115	0	5
Bolton W	Tr	01.82	81-82	40	0	2
Rochdale	Tr	08.83	83	24	0	1

DOYLE Michael (Micky) Paul
Dublin, 8 July, 1981 IRu21-8/IR-1 (M)

League Club	Source	Date Signed	Seasons Played	Apps	Subs	Gls
Coventry C	Glasgow Celtic	07.03	03-04	81	3	7

DOYLE Nathan Luke Robert
Derby, 12 January, 1987 EYth (M)

League Club	Source	Date Signed	Seasons Played	Apps	Subs	Gls
Derby Co	Sch	01.04	03-04	4	1	0

DOYLE Robert (Bobby)
Dumbarton, 27 December, 1953 (M)

League Club	Source	Date Signed	Seasons Played	Apps	Subs	Gls
Barnsley	Jnrs	12.72	72-75	148	1	16
Peterborough U	Tr	07.76	76-78	130	0	10
Blackpool	Tr	07.79	79-80	47	2	2
Portsmouth	Tr	12.80	80-85	169	8	16
Hull C	Tr	08.85	85-86	43	0	2

DOYLE Stephen (Steve) Charles
Neath, 2 June, 1958 WYth/Wu21-2 (M)

League Club	Source	Date Signed	Seasons Played	Apps	Subs	Gls
Preston NE	App	06.75	74-81	178	19	8
Huddersfield T	Tr	09.82	82-86	158	3	6
Sunderland	Tr	09.86	86-88	99	1	2
Hull C	Tr	08.89	89-90	47	0	2
Rochdale	Tr	11.90	90-94	115	6	1

DOYLEY Lloyd Colin
Whitechapel, 1 December, 1982 (CD)

League Club	Source	Date Signed	Seasons Played	Apps	Subs	Gls
Watford	YT	03.01	01-04	64	16	0

DOZZELL Jason Alvin Winans
Ipswich, 9 December, 1967 EYth/Eu21-9 (M)

League Club	Source	Date Signed	Seasons Played	Apps	Subs	Gls
Ipswich T	App	12.84	83-92	312	20	52

League Club	Source	Date Signed	Seasons Played	Apps	Subs	Gls
Tottenham H	Tr	08.93	93-96	68	16	13
Ipswich T	Tr	10.97	97	8	0	1
Northampton T	Tr	12.97	97	18	3	4
Colchester U	Tr	10.98	98-00	83	7	9
DRAKE Kenneth (Ken) Lawrence						
Skipton, 17 February, 1922						(FB)
Halifax T		01.47	46-51	132	-	0
DRAKE Leonard (Len) George						
Dorchester, 26 July, 1937						(IF)
Bristol Rov	Dorchester T	08.57	58-59	8	-	1
DRAKE Raymond (Ray) Bradwell						
Stockport, 24 October, 1934						(CF)
Stockport Co	Bramhall	03.55	56-57	23	-	19
DRAKE Robert (Bobby) James						
Southgate, 7 September, 1943						(FB)
Fulham	Chelsea (Am)	02.61	63-67	15	0	0
DRAKE Stephen (Steve)						
Goole, 27 August, 1948						(G)
Huddersfield T	Leeds U (Am)	06.66				
Scunthorpe U	Tr	07.67	67-69	23	0	0
DRAPER Craig James Edwin						
Swansea, 4 December, 1982						(M)
Swansea C	YT	07.01	01	0	2	0
DRAPER Derek						
Swansea, 11 May, 1943 Wu23-1						(M)
Swansea T	Jnrs	05.62	62-65	61	0	10
Derby Co	Tr	04.66	66	8	0	1
Bradford PA	Tr	09.67	67-68	60	3	9
Chester	Tr	01.69	68-76	316	6	54
DRAPER Mark Andrew						
Long Eaton, 11 November, 1970 Eu21-3						(M)
Notts Co	YT	12.88	88-93	206	15	40
Leicester C	Tr	07.94	94	39	0	5
Aston Villa	Tr	07.95	95-99	108	12	7
Southampton	Tr	07.00	00-01	17	7	1
DRAPER Richard Walter **William (Bill)**						
Leamington Spa, 26 September, 1932						(CF)
Northampton T	Lockheed Leamington	06.55	55-56	49	-	20
DREWERY Michael (Mike) Stephen						
Snettisham, 16 January, 1949						(G)
Peterborough U	Snettisham	07.67	68-73	209	0	0
DREYER John Brian						
Alnwick, 11 June, 1963						(CD)
Oxford U	Wallingford T	01.85	86-87	57	3	2
Torquay U	L	12.85	85	5	0	0
Fulham	L	03.86	85	12	0	2
Luton T	Tr	06.88	88-93	212	2	13
Stoke C	Tr	07.94	94-96	32	17	3
Bolton W	L	03.95	94	1	1	0
Bradford C	Tr	11.96	96-99	72	8	2
Cambridge U	Tr	07.00	00	40	0	0
DRING Raymond (Ray)						
Lincoln, 13 February, 1924 Died 2003 ESch						(G)
Huddersfield T (Am)		06.47	47	4	-	0
DRINKELL Kevin Smith						
Grimsby, 18 June, 1960						(F)
Grimsby T	App	06.78	76-84	242	30	89
Norwich C	Tr	08.85	85-87	121	0	50
Coventry C	Glasgow Rgrs	10.89	89-91	34	7	5
Birmingham C	L	10.91	91	5	0	2
DRINKWATER Charles (Charlie) John						
Willesden, 25 June, 1914 Died 1998						(W)
Aston Villa	Walthamstow Ave	11.35	35	2	-	1
Charlton Ath	Tr	07.38	38	3	-	0
Watford	Tr	01.45	46	1	-	0
DRINKWATER James (Jimmy) Arthur						
Northwich, 10 February, 1918 Died 1996						(FB)
Torquay U	St Mirren	06.52	52-53	67	-	1
DRINKWATER Raymond (Ray)						
Jarrow, 18 May, 1931						(G)
Portsmouth	Guildford C	11.55	56	8	-	0
Queens Park Rgrs	Tr	02.58	57-62	199	-	0
DRINKWATER Roy						
Altrincham, 25 December, 1954						(M)
Crewe Alex	App	03.71	70	0	1	0

League Club	Source	Date Signed	Seasons Played	Apps	Subs	Gls
DRISCOLL Andrew (Andy)						
Staines, 21 October, 1971						(W)
Brentford	YT	03.90	88-91	10	4	2
DRIVER Allenby						
Blackwell, Derbyshire, 29 December, 1918 Died 1997						(IF)
Sheffield Wed	Mansfield Shoes	04.36	37-38	6	-	3
Luton T	Tr	10.46	46-47	41	-	13
Norwich C	Tr	01.48	47-49	49	-	19
Ipswich T	Tr	01.50	49-51	86	-	25
Walsall	Tr	07.52	52	26	-	2
DRIVER Philip (Phil) Anthony						
Huddersfield, 10 August, 1959						(W)
Wimbledon	Bedford T	12.78	78-80	7	9	3
Chelsea	Tr	09.80	80-82	25	19	4
Wimbledon	Tr	07.83	83-84	2	2	0
DROGBA Didier Yves Tebily						
Abidjan, Ivory Coast, 11 March, 1978 Ivory Coast int						(F)
Chelsea	Marseille (Fr)	07.04	04	18	8	10
DROY Michael (Micky) Robert						
Highbury, 7 May, 1951						(CD)
Chelsea	Slough T	09.70	70-84	263	9	13
Luton T	L	11.84	84	2	0	0
Crystal Palace	Tr	03.85	84-86	49	0	7
Brentford	Tr	11.86	86	19	0	3
DRUCE Mark Andrew						
Oxford, 3 March, 1974						(F)
Oxford U	YT	12.91	91-95	18	34	4
Rotherham U	Tr	09.96	96-97	21	13	4
DRUMMOND Ian Philip						
Brechin, 27 August, 1923						(FB)
Portsmouth	Jeanfield Swifts	05.45				
Bournemouth	Tr	06.49	49-55	265	-	2
DRUMMOND Stewart James						
Preston, 11 December, 1975 ESemiPro-13						(M)
Chester C	Morecambe	06.04	04	44	1	6
DRUMMY Dermot						
Hackney, 16 January, 1961						(M)
Arsenal	App	01.79				
Blackpool	L	03.80	79	4	1	0
DRURY Adam James						
Cottenham, 29 August, 1978						(FB)
Peterborough U	YT	07.96	95-00	138	10	2
Norwich C	Tr	03.01	00-04	159	2	3
DRURY Charles (Chuck) Edward						
Darlaston, 4 July, 1937 EYth						(CD)
West Bromwich A	FH Lloyds	02.55	57-63	146	-	1
Bristol C	Tr	08.64	64-66	51	0	2
Bradford PA	Tr	03.68	67-68	31	0	1
DRURY George Benjamin						
Hucknall, 22 January, 1914 Died 1972						(IF)
Sheffield Wed	Heanor T	09.34	36-37	44	-	9
Arsenal	Tr	03.38	37-46	38	-	3
West Bromwich A	Tr	10.46	46-47	29	-	8
Watford	Tr	07.48	48-49	35	-	3
DRURY James (Jim) Welsh						
Cumnock, 29 May, 1924 Died 2000						(W)
Rochdale	Stirling A	05.51	51	4	-	1
Carlisle U	Tr	08.52	52-53	35	-	5
Southport	Tr	07.54	54	24	-	2
DRYBURGH Thomas (Tom) James Douglas						
Kirkcaldy, 23 April, 1923						(W)
Aldershot	Lochgelly Albert	06.47	47	19	-	2
Rochdale	Tr	07.48	48-49	77	-	17
Leicester C	Tr	09.50	50-53	95	-	29
Hull C	Tr	05.54	54	23	-	3
Oldham Ath	Kings Lynn	08.57	57	1	-	0
Rochdale	Tr	11.57	57	5	-	0
DRYDEN John (Jackie) George						
Sunderland, 16 September, 1919						(W)
Charlton Ath	Washington Chem Wks	03.46				
Swindon T	Hylton Colliery	05.47	47	21	-	3
Leyton Orient	Tr	06.48	48-49	40	-	10
DRYDEN Richard Andrew						
Stroud, 14 June, 1969						(CD)
Bristol Rov	YT	07.87	86-88	12	1	0
Exeter C	Tr	09.88	88-90	92	0	13
Notts Co	Tr	08.91	91-92	30	1	1

League Club	Source	Date Signed	Seasons Played	Career Record Apps	Subs	Gls
Plymouth Arg	L	11.92	92	5	0	0
Birmingham C	Tr	03.93	92-94	48	0	0
Bristol C	Tr	12.94	94-95	32	5	2
Southampton	Tr	08.98	96-99	44	3	1
Stoke C	L	11.99	99	3	0	0
Stoke C	L	03.00	99	8	2	0
Northampton T	L	09.00	00	9	1	0
Swindon T	L	11.00	00	7	0	0
Luton T	Tr	02.01	00-01	22	1	0
DRYHURST Carl David						
Sutton Coldfield, 8 November, 1960						(F)
Halifax T	Sutton Coldfield T	11.79	79	4	4	0
DRYSDALE Brian						
Wingate, 24 February, 1943						(FB)
Lincoln C	Jnrs	09.60	59-64	21	-	0
Hartlepools U	Tr	07.65	65-68	169	1	2
Bristol C	Tr	05.69	69-76	280	2	3
Reading	L	02.77	76	16	0	0
Oxford U	Tr	07.77	77	15	0	0
DRYSDALE Jason						
Bristol, 17 November, 1970 EYth						(FB)
Watford	YT	09.88	89-93	135	10	11
Newcastle U	Tr	08.94				
Swindon T	Tr	03.95	94-97	35	7	0
Northampton T	Tr	03.98	97	1	0	0
DRYSDALE Leon Anthony						
Walsall, 3 February, 1981						(FB)
Shrewsbury T	YT	07.99	98-02	51	14	1
D'SANE Roscoe Niquaye						
Epsom, 16 October, 1980						(M)
Crystal Palace	YT	06.99				
Southend U	Slough T	11.01	01	1	1	0
DUBERRY Michael Wayne						
Enfield, 14 October, 1975 Eu21-5						(CD)
Chelsea	YT	06.93	93-98	77	9	1
Bournemouth	L	09.95	95	7	0	0
Leeds U	Tr	07.99	99-04	54	4	4
Stoke C	L	10.04	04	15	0	0
Stoke C	Tr	03.05	04	10	0	0
DUBLIN Dion						
Leicester, 22 April, 1969 E-4						(F)
Norwich C	Oakham U	03.88				
Cambridge U	Tr	08.88	88-91	133	23	52
Manchester U	Tr	08.92	92-93	4	8	2
Coventry C	Tr	09.94	94-98	144	1	61
Aston Villa	Tr	11.98	98-03	120	35	48
Millwall	L	03.02	01	5	0	2
Leicester C	Tr	07.04	04	34	3	5
DUBLIN Keith Barry Lennox						
High Wycombe, 29 January, 1966 EYth						(CD)
Chelsea	App	01.84	83-86	50	1	0
Brighton & Hove A	Tr	08.87	87-89	132	0	5
Watford	Tr	07.90	90-93	165	3	2
Southend U	Tr	07.94	94-98	175	4	9
Colchester U	L	11.98	98	2	0	0
DUBOIS Joseph (Joe) Martin						
Monkstown, 27 December, 1927 Died 1987 NIAmat						(W)
Doncaster Rov	Brantwood	05.49	49-51	31	-	5
Grimsby T	Bedford T	07.53	53	6	-	1
Halifax T	Tr	07.54	54-56	78	-	10
DUCHART Alexander (Alex)						
Falkirk, 3 May, 1933						(W)
Southend U	Third Lanark	05.56	56	8	-	2
DUCK George Thomas						
Tottenham, 22 February, 1952						(F)
Millwall	App	02.70				
Southend U	Tr	06.71	71	3	0	0
DUCKHOUSE Edward (Ted)						
Walsall, 9 April, 1918 Died 1978						(CD)
Birmingham	Streetly Works	08.38	38-49	119	-	4
Northampton T	Tr	08.50	50-51	68	-	0
DUCROCQ Pierre						
Pontoise, France, 18 December, 1976						(M)
Derby Co (L)	Paris St Germain (Fr)	10.01	01	19	0	0
DUCROS Andrew (Andy) John						
Evesham, 16 September, 1977 ESch/EYth						(W)
Coventry C	YT	09.94	96-97	2	6	0
Kidderminster Hrs	Nuneaton Borough	07.00	00-02	38	12	4

League Club	Source	Date Signed	Seasons Played	Career Record Apps	Subs	Gls
DUDDY John Michael						
Manchester, 8 February, 1956						(M)
Oldham Ath	App	02.74				
Stockport Co	Tr	03.76	75	6	0	0
DUDEK Jerzy						
Rybnik, Poland, 23 March, 1973 Poland 51						(G)
Liverpool	Feyenoord (Holl)	08.01	01-04	119	0	0
DUDFIELD Lawrence (Lawrie) George						
Southwark, 7 May, 1980						(F)
Leicester C	Kettering T	06.97	99	0	2	0
Lincoln C	L	09.00	00	2	1	0
Chesterfield	L	12.00	00	4	10	3
Hull C	Tr	07.01	01-02	39	20	13
Northampton T	Tr	03.03	02-03	20	9	4
Southend U	Tr	02.04	03-04	29	20	9
DUDGEON James Fleming						
Newcastle, 19 March, 1981 SYth						(CD)
Barnsley	YT	07.99				
Lincoln C	L	11.00	00	20	2	3
DUDLEY Craig Bryan						
Ollerton, 12 September, 1979 EYth						(F)
Notts Co	YT	04.97	96-98	11	20	3
Shrewsbury T	L	01.98	97	3	1	0
Hull C	L	11.98	98	4	3	2
Oldham Ath	Tr	03.99	99-01	34	26	10
Chesterfield	L	08.99	99	0	2	0
Scunthorpe U	L	02.02	01	1	3	0
DUDLEY Frank Ernest						
Southend-on-Sea, 9 May, 1925						(CF)
Southend U	Jnrs	10.45	46-48	88	-	32
Leeds U	Tr	08.49	49-50	64	-	23
Southampton	Tr	02.51	50-53	67	-	32
Cardiff C	Tr	09.53	53	5	-	1
Brentford	Tr	12.53	53-56	72	-	32
DUDLEY James (Jimmy) George						
Gartcosh, 24 August, 1928 SB						(WH)
West Bromwich A	Albright YC	05.46	49-59	285	-	9
Walsall	Tr	12.59	59-63	167	-	3
DUDLEY Philip (Phil) William						
Basildon, 17 February, 1959						(FB)
Southend U	App	02.77	77-82	109	3	3
DUDLEY Reginald (Reg) Arthur						
Hemel Hempstead, 3 February, 1915 Died 1994 EAmat						(FB)
Millwall	Apsley	03.35	35-46	42	-	0
Queens Park Rgrs	Tr	12.46	46-49	58	-	0
Watford	Tr	07.50	50	1	-	0
DUERDEN Harold (Harry)						
Barnsley, 5 March, 1948						(WH)
Barnsley	App	09.65	65-66	24	1	1
DUERDEN Ian Christopher						
Burnley, 27 March, 1978						(F)
Burnley	YT	07.96	97	1	0	0
Halifax T	Tr	08.98	98	1	1	0
DUFF Damien Anthony						
Ballyboden, 2 March, 1979 IRSch/IRYth/IRB-1/IR-54						(W)
Blackburn Rov	Lourdes Celtic	03.96	96-02	157	27	27
Chelsea	Tr	07.03	03-04	45	8	11
DUFF Michael James						
Belfast, 11 January, 1978 NI-4						(FB)
Cheltenham T	YT	08.96	99-03	201	0	12
Burnley	Tr	07.04	04	37	5	0
DUFF Shane Joseph						
Wroughton, 2 April, 1982 NIu21-1						(CD)
Cheltenham T	Jnrs	10.00	02-04	73	5	2
DUFF William (Willie)						
Winchburgh, 6 February, 1935 Died 2004 Su23-1/SLge-1						(G)
Charlton Ath	Heart of Midlothian	12.56	56-61	213	-	0
Peterborough U	Tr	05.63	63-66	118	0	0
DUFF William (Billy) Francis Andrew						
Littleborough, 16 December, 1938 Died 2002						(W)
Rochdale	Jnrs	05.56				
Scunthorpe U	Tr	10.58				
Grimsby T	Tr	10.59	59	3	-	1
Accrington St	Toronto (Can)	10.60	60	14	-	3

DUFFETT Edgar
Worcester, 29 August, 1926 (IF)

League Club	Source	Date Signed	Seasons Played	Apps	Subs	Gls
Norwich C	West Bromwich A (Am)	11.47				
Carlisle U	Tr	08.50	50-52	47	-	8

DUFFEY Christopher (Chris) Paul
Kirkby, 8 January, 1952 (W)

League Club	Source	Date Signed	Seasons Played	Apps	Subs	Gls
Bolton W	App	09.69	69-71	8	0	0
Crewe Alex	L	09.72	72	6	0	3
Crewe Alex	Tr	07.73	73-74	54	3	12
Bury	Tr	10.74	74	17	4	8
Shrewsbury T	Tr	05.75	75	4	4	1
Rochdale	L	11.75	75	2	0	0

DUFFIELD Martin John
Park Royal, 28 February, 1964 EYth (M)

League Club	Source	Date Signed	Seasons Played	Apps	Subs	Gls
Queens Park Rgrs	App	01.82	82	0	1	0
Bournemouth	L	09.83	83	6	0	1
Charlton Ath	L	11.84	84	1	0	0

DUFFIELD Peter
Middlesbrough, 4 February, 1969 (F)

League Club	Source	Date Signed	Seasons Played	Apps	Subs	Gls
Middlesbrough	App	11.86				
Sheffield U	Tr	08.87	87-91	34	24	14
Halifax T	L	03.88	87	12	0	6
Rotherham U	L	03.91	90	17	0	4
Blackpool	L	07.92	92	3	2	1
Crewe Alex	L	01.93	92	0	2	0
Stockport Co	L	03.93	92	6	1	4
Darlington	Falkirk	01.99	98-99	31	16	14
York C	Tr	07.00	00-02	41	4	19
Boston U	Tr	01.03	02-03	24	21	9
Carlisle U	Tr	03.04	03	10	0	3

DUFFIN Lionel Joseph
Ulverston, 8 August, 1945 (G)

League Club	Source	Date Signed	Seasons Played	Apps	Subs	Gls
Barrow	Jnrs	07.64	64-67	46	0	0

DUFFY Alan
Stanley, 20 December, 1949 EYth (M)

League Club	Source	Date Signed	Seasons Played	Apps	Subs	Gls
Newcastle U	App	03.67	68-69	2	2	0
Brighton & Hove A	Tr	01.70	69-71	34	16	8
Tranmere Rov	Tr	03.72	71-72	29	4	2
Darlington	Tr	08.73	73	19	5	0

DUFFY Christopher (Chris)
Methil, 21 October, 1918 Died 1978 (W)

League Club	Source	Date Signed	Seasons Played	Apps	Subs	Gls
Charlton Ath	Leith Ath	09.45	46-52	162	-	33

DUFFY Christopher (Chris) John
Eccles, 31 October, 1973 (W)

League Club	Source	Date Signed	Seasons Played	Apps	Subs	Gls
Crewe Alex	YT	06.92				
Wigan Ath	Tr	07.93	93-94	15	16	1

DUFFY Darrell Gerald
Birmingham, 18 January, 1971 ESch/EYth (CD)

League Club	Source	Date Signed	Seasons Played	Apps	Subs	Gls
Aston Villa	YT	07.89	88	1	0	0
Scunthorpe U	Moor Green Rov	02.93	92	4	0	0

DUFFY Gerald (Gerry)
Middlewich, 12 September, 1934 (CF)

League Club	Source	Date Signed	Seasons Played	Apps	Subs	Gls
Oldham Ath	Middlewich	05.56	56-58	58	-	21

DUFFY John
Glasgow, 24 April, 1922 Died 1996 (FB)

League Club	Source	Date Signed	Seasons Played	Apps	Subs	Gls
Norwich C	Raith Rov	03.49	49-53	78	-	0

DUFFY John
Dunfermline, 6 September, 1943 (WH)

League Club	Source	Date Signed	Seasons Played	Apps	Subs	Gls
Darlington	Dunfermline Ath	08.63	63	10	-	1

DUFFY John Gerard
Dundee, 24 August, 1929 Died 2004 (WH)

League Club	Source	Date Signed	Seasons Played	Apps	Subs	Gls
Southend U	Glasgow Celtic	05.54	54-59	114	-	4

DUFFY Lee Alan
Oldham, 24 July, 1982 (FB)

League Club	Source	Date Signed	Seasons Played	Apps	Subs	Gls
Rochdale	YT	09.01	01-02	20	8	0

DUFFY Michael (Mike) Kevin
Leicester, 12 June, 1961 (M)

League Club	Source	Date Signed	Seasons Played	Apps	Subs	Gls
Leicester C	Jnrs	07.78	78-79	7	5	1

DUFFY Richard Michael
Swansea, 30 August, 1985 WYth/Wu21-6 (M)

League Club	Source	Date Signed	Seasons Played	Apps	Subs	Gls
Swansea C	Sch	09.02	03	16	2	1
Portsmouth	Tr	01.04	03	0	1	0
Burnley	L	09.04	04	3	4	1
Coventry C	L	01.05	04	14	0	0

DUFFY Robert James
Swansea, 2 December, 1982 WYth (F)

League Club	Source	Date Signed	Seasons Played	Apps	Subs	Gls
Rushden & Diamonds	Jnrs	07.00	01-04	8	21	1

DUFFY Vincent (Vince) Gerard
Nottingham, 21 September, 1962 (M)

League Club	Source	Date Signed	Seasons Played	Apps	Subs	Gls
Scunthorpe U	Nottingham F (App)	12.80	80-81	3	5	0

DUGARRY Christophe
Bordeaux, France, 24 March, 1972 France 55 (F)

League Club	Source	Date Signed	Seasons Played	Apps	Subs	Gls
Birmingham C	Bordeaux	01.03	02-03	28	2	6

DUGDALE Alan
Liverpool, 11 September, 1952 EYth (CD)

League Club	Source	Date Signed	Seasons Played	Apps	Subs	Gls
Coventry C	App	11.69	72-77	139	3	0
Charlton Ath	Tr	10.77	77-78	34	0	0
Barnsley	L	08.79	79	7	0	0

DUGDALE Gordon
Liverpool, 21 February, 1924 Died 1986 (FB)

League Club	Source	Date Signed	Seasons Played	Apps	Subs	Gls
Everton	Jnrs	06.47	47-49	58	-	0

DUGDALE James (Jimmy) Robert
Liverpool, 15 January, 1932 EB/FLge-1 (CD)

League Club	Source	Date Signed	Seasons Played	Apps	Subs	Gls
West Bromwich A	Harrowby	06.52	52-55	63	-	0
Aston Villa	Tr	01.56	55-61	215	-	3
Queens Park Rgrs	Tr	10.62	62	10	-	0

DUGGAN Andrew (Andy) James
Bradford, 19 September, 1967 (CD)

League Club	Source	Date Signed	Seasons Played	Apps	Subs	Gls
Barnsley	App	07.85	86	1	1	1
Rochdale	L	11.87	87	3	0	0
Huddersfield T	Tr	09.88	88-89	29	0	3
Hartlepool U	L	08.90	90	2	0	0
Rochdale	Tr	03.91	90	1	0	0

DUGGAN Edward (Ted) John
Plaistow, 27 July, 1922 Died 1982 (IF)

League Club	Source	Date Signed	Seasons Played	Apps	Subs	Gls
Luton T	Jnrs	08.39	46-48	48	-	20
Queens Park Rgrs	Tr	02.49	48-50	47	-	5

DUGGAN James (Jim)
Droitwich, 17 November, 1920 Died 1982 (IF)

League Club	Source	Date Signed	Seasons Played	Apps	Subs	Gls
West Bromwich A	Droitwich OB	12.39	46	25	-	8

DUGGINS Eric Edward
Tamworth, 24 November, 1928 Died 1992 (FB)

League Club	Source	Date Signed	Seasons Played	Apps	Subs	Gls
Portsmouth	Atherstone T	08.48				
Southend U	Tr	07.52	52-53	28	-	0

DUGGINS Gordon
Tamworth, 8 December, 1932 (CF)

League Club	Source	Date Signed	Seasons Played	Apps	Subs	Gls
Barnsley	Gresley Rov	11.55	55-57	17	-	6

DUGGINS John Austin
Tamworth, 4 August, 1931 (IF)

League Club	Source	Date Signed	Seasons Played	Apps	Subs	Gls
Portsmouth	Atherstone T	06.50				
Walsall	Tr	08.52	52	16	-	3

DUGNOLLE John (Jack) Henry
Peshawar, India, 24 March, 1914 Died 1977 (WH)

League Club	Source	Date Signed	Seasons Played	Apps	Subs	Gls
Brighton & Hove A	Southwick	10.34	35-37	7	-	0
Plymouth Arg	Tunbridge Wells Rgrs	02.39	38	4	-	0
Brighton & Hove A	Tr	08.46	46-47	59	-	0

DUGUID Karl Anthony
Letchworth, 21 March, 1978 (M)

League Club	Source	Date Signed	Seasons Played	Apps	Subs	Gls
Colchester U	YT	07.96	95-03	212	58	37

DUKE David
Inverness, 7 November, 1978 (M)

League Club	Source	Date Signed	Seasons Played	Apps	Subs	Gls
Sunderland	Redby CA	07.97				
Swindon T	Tr	08.00	00-04	181	23	7

DUKE George Edward
West Hampnett, 6 September, 1920 Died 1988 (G)

League Club	Source	Date Signed	Seasons Played	Apps	Subs	Gls
Luton T	Southwick	01.39	46-48	16	-	0
Bournemouth	Tr	05.49	49	10	-	0

DUKE Matthew (Matt)
Sheffield, 16 June, 1977 (G)

League Club	Source	Date Signed	Seasons Played	Apps	Subs	Gls
Sheffield U	Alfreton T					
Hull C	Burton A	07.04	04	1	1	0

DUKES Harold (Harry) Parkinson
Portsmouth, 31 March, 1912 Died 1988 (G)

League Club	Source	Date Signed	Seasons Played	Apps	Subs	Gls
Norwich C	Ipswich T	08.34	34-38	105	-	0
Norwich C	Bedford T	09.46	46	13	-	0

DULIN Michael (Micky) Charles
Stepney, 25 October, 1935 (W)

League Club	Source	Date Signed	Seasons Played	Apps	Subs	Gls
Tottenham H	Welwyn Garden C	11.52	55-57	10	-	2

DULSON Garry
Nottingham, 21 December, 1953 (FB)

League Club	Source	Date Signed	Seasons Played	Apps	Subs	Gls
Nottingham F	App	10.71				
Port Vale	Tr	10.74	74-77	108	2	3
Crewe Alex	Tr	11.78	78-79	33	5	0

DUMAS Franck
Bayeux, France, 9 January, 1968 (CD)

League Club	Source	Date Signed	Seasons Played	Apps	Subs	Gls
Newcastle U	AS Monaco (Fr)	06.99	99	6	0	0

DUMIGHAN Joseph (Joe)
Langley Park, 25 September, 1938 (CF)

League Club	Source	Date Signed	Seasons Played	Apps	Subs	Gls
Sunderland	Jnrs	11.55				
Darlington	Tr	07.58	58	4	-	1

DUMITRESCU Ilie
Bucharest, Romania, 6 January, 1969 Romania int (F)

League Club	Source	Date Signed	Seasons Played	Apps	Subs	Gls
Tottenham H	Steaua Bucharest (Rom)	08.94	94-95	16	2	4
West Ham U	Tr	03.96	95-96	5	5	0

DUNBAR Ian
Newcastle, 6 June, 1971 ESch (F)

League Club	Source	Date Signed	Seasons Played	Apps	Subs	Gls
Hartlepool U	Jnrs	08.89	89-90	1	2	0

DUNBAVIN Ian Stuart
Huyton, 27 May, 1980 (G)

League Club	Source	Date Signed	Seasons Played	Apps	Subs	Gls
Liverpool	YT	11.98				
Shrewsbury T	Tr	01.00	99-02	91	5	0

DUNCAN Andrew (Andy)
Hexham, 20 October, 1977 ESch (CD)

League Club	Source	Date Signed	Seasons Played	Apps	Subs	Gls
Manchester U	YT	07.96				
Cambridge U	Tr	01.98	97-04	233	9	6

DUNCAN Cameron
Shotts, 4 August, 1965 SYth (G)

League Club	Source	Date Signed	Seasons Played	Apps	Subs	Gls
Sunderland	Shotts	07.84	85	1	0	0

DUNCAN Colin John
Plymstock, 5 August, 1957 (M)

League Club	Source	Date Signed	Seasons Played	Apps	Subs	Gls
Oxford U	App	12.74	74-79	188	1	6
Gillingham	Tr	01.80	79-83	83	2	5
Reading	Tr	09.83	83-84	56	0	3
Aldershot	Tr	08.85	85	15	0	0

DUNCAN David Millar
Markinch, 21 November, 1921 Died 1991 SLge-1/S-3 (W)

League Club	Source	Date Signed	Seasons Played	Apps	Subs	Gls
Crewe Alex	Raith Rov	08.55	55	22	-	0

DUNCAN Derek Henry Junior
Newham, 23 April, 1987 (M)

League Club	Source	Date Signed	Seasons Played	Apps	Subs	Gls
Leyton Orient	Sch	●	03-04	6	10	0

DUNCAN Douglas (Dally)
Aberdeen, 14 October, 1909 Died 1990 S-14 (W)

League Club	Source	Date Signed	Seasons Played	Apps	Subs	Gls
Hull C	Aberdeen Richmond	08.28	28-31	111	-	47
Derby Co	Tr	03.32	31-46	261	-	63
Luton T	Tr	10.46	46-47	32	-	4

DUNCAN George
Glasgow, 16 January, 1937 (W)

League Club	Source	Date Signed	Seasons Played	Apps	Subs	Gls
Southend U	Glasgow Rgrs	06.60	60	6	-	2
Chesterfield	Tr	08.61	61-64	140	-	13

DUNCAN James Robert
Hull, 2 April, 1938 (CF)

League Club	Source	Date Signed	Seasons Played	Apps	Subs	Gls
Hull C	Jnrs	04.55	55-59	26	-	3
Bradford C	Tr	06.60	60	18	-	5

DUNCAN John Gilhespie
Glasgow, 10 December, 1926 (FB)

League Club	Source	Date Signed	Seasons Played	Apps	Subs	Gls
Newcastle U	Ayr U	11.50	51-52	5	-	3

DUNCAN John Pearson
Dundee, 22 February, 1949 SLge-1 (F)

League Club	Source	Date Signed	Seasons Played	Apps	Subs	Gls
Tottenham H	Dundee	10.74	74-78	101	2	53
Derby Co	Tr	09.78	78-80	35	1	12
Scunthorpe U	Tr	06.81	81-82	3	6	0

DUNCAN Joseph (Joe) James
Huyton, 24 February, 1950 (W)

League Club	Source	Date Signed	Seasons Played	Apps	Subs	Gls
Wrexham (Am)	Jnrs	12.68	68	1	0	0

DUNCAN Robert (Bob)
Kirkcaldy, 2 November, 1943 (FB)

League Club	Source	Date Signed	Seasons Played	Apps	Subs	Gls
Southend U	Dunfermline Ath	08.61	61	1	-	0

DUNCAN Thomas (Tommy) Montgomerie
Portsoy, 15 July, 1936 (W)

League Club	Source	Date Signed	Seasons Played	Apps	Subs	Gls
Newport Co (L)	Airdrie	03.58	57	1	-	0

DUNCLIFFE Michael **John (Jack)**
Brighton, 17 September, 1947 (FB)

League Club	Source	Date Signed	Seasons Played	Apps	Subs	Gls
Brighton & Hove A	App	09.65	66-67	22	0	0
Grimsby T	Tr	06.68	68-69	71	1	0
Peterborough U	Tr	07.70	70-72	120	0	0

DUNCUM Samuel (Sam)
Sheffield, 18 February, 1987 (M)

League Club	Source	Date Signed	Seasons Played	Apps	Subs	Gls
Rotherham U	Sch	●	04	1	1	0

DUNDEE Sean William
Durban, South Africa, 7 December, 1972 (F)

League Club	Source	Date Signed	Seasons Played	Apps	Subs	Gls
Liverpool	Karlsruhe (Ger)	06.98	98	0	3	0

DUNDERDALE William **Leonard (Len)**
Willingham-by-Stow, 6 February, 1915 Died 1989 (CF)

League Club	Source	Date Signed	Seasons Played	Apps	Subs	Gls
Walsall	Goole T	03.36	35-37	32	-	19
Watford	Tr	05.38	38	30	-	19
Leeds U	Tr	03.39	38	3	-	0
Watford	Tr	04.46	46-47	44	-	15

DUNFIELD Terence (Terry)
Vancouver, Canada, 20 February, 1982 EYth/CaYth/Cau23-1 (M)

League Club	Source	Date Signed	Seasons Played	Apps	Subs	Gls
Manchester C	YT	05.99	00	0	1	0
Bury	L	08.02	02	15	0	2
Bury	Tr	12.02	02-04	48	11	3

DUNFORD Neil
Rochdale, 18 July, 1967 (G)

League Club	Source	Date Signed	Seasons Played	Apps	Subs	Gls
Rochdale	Castleton Gabriels	09.93	94	2	0	0

DUNGEY James Andrew
Plymouth, 7 February, 1978 ESch/EYth (G)

League Club	Source	Date Signed	Seasons Played	Apps	Subs	Gls
Plymouth Arg	YT	10.95	94-96	9	1	0
Exeter C	Tr	12.97	97	1	0	0
Plymouth Arg	Bodmin T	08.98	98	7	0	0

DUNGWORTH John Henry
Brampton, West Yorkshire, 30 March, 1955 (F)

League Club	Source	Date Signed	Seasons Played	Apps	Subs	Gls
Huddersfield T	App	04.72	72-74	18	5	1
Barnsley	L	10.74	74	2	1	1
Oldham Ath	Tr	03.75	75	2	2	0
Rochdale	L	03.77	76	14	0	3
Aldershot	Tr	09.77	77-79	105	0	58
Shrewsbury T	Tr	11.79	79-81	81	5	17
Hereford U	L	10.81	81	7	0	3
Mansfield T	Tr	08.82	82-83	50	6	16
Rotherham U	Tr	02.84	83-87	177	11	16

DUNKLEY Malcolm
Wolverhampton, 12 July, 1961 (F)

League Club	Source	Date Signed	Seasons Played	Apps	Subs	Gls
Lincoln C	Bromsgrove Rov	02.89	88	9	2	4

DUNKLEY Maurice Edward Frank
Kettering, 19 February, 1914 Died 1989 (W)

League Club	Source	Date Signed	Seasons Played	Apps	Subs	Gls
Northampton T	Kettering T	12.36	36-37	26	-	5
Manchester C	Tr	03.38	37-46	51	-	5
Northampton T	Kettering T	07.49	49	4	-	0

DUNKLEY Robert (Bob)
Stoke-on-Trent, 6 April, 1922 (W)

League Club	Source	Date Signed	Seasons Played	Apps	Subs	Gls
Stoke C		01.41				
Barrow	Tr	08.46	46	11	-	0

DUNLEAVY Christopher (Chris)
Liverpool, 30 December, 1949 (CD)

League Club	Source	Date Signed	Seasons Played	Apps	Subs	Gls
Everton	Jnrs	03.68				
Southport	Tr	07.69	69-72	141	2	9
Southport	Philadelphia (USA)	08.73	73	4	0	0
Chester	Tr	09.73	73-76	74	2	0
Halifax T	Tr	10.76	76-80	181	0	13

DUNLOP Albert
Liverpool, 21 April, 1932 Died 1990 (G)

League Club	Source	Date Signed	Seasons Played	Apps	Subs	Gls
Everton	Jnrs	08.49	56-62	211	-	0
Wrexham	Tr	11.63	63-64	15	-	0

DUNLOP William **Rex**
Dumfries, 21 September, 1927 (WH)

League Club	Source	Date Signed	Seasons Played	Apps	Subs	Gls
Workington	Glasgow Rgrs	11.53	53-55	110	-	19

DUNLOP William (Billy) Lumsden
Airdrie, 20 February, 1926 Died 1994 (IF)

League Club	Source	Date Signed	Seasons Played	Apps	Subs	Gls
Exeter C	Dunfermline Ath	07.50	50	4	-	0
Bristol Rov	Ilfracombe	05.52				
Bradford PA	Tr	05.53	53	36	-	12
Darlington	Tr	10.54	54	18	-	2

DUNMORE David (Dave) Gerald Ivor
Whitehaven, 8 February, 1934 (CF)

League Club	Source	Date Signed	Seasons Played	Apps	Subs	Gls
York C	Cliftonville Minors	05.52	51-53	48	-	25
Tottenham H	Tr	02.54	53-59	75	-	23
West Ham U	Tr	03.60	59-60	36	-	16

League Club	Source	Date Signed	Seasons Played	Apps	Subs	Gls
Leyton Orient	Tr	03.61	60-64	147	-	54
York C	Tr	06.65	65-66	61	2	13

DUNN Barry
Middlesbrough, 17 December, 1939 (W)

League Club	Source	Date Signed	Seasons Played	Apps	Subs	Gls
Doncaster Rov		02.58				
Halifax T	Tr	09.59	59-60	7	-	1

DUNN Barry
Sunderland, 15 February, 1952 (W)

League Club	Source	Date Signed	Seasons Played	Apps	Subs	Gls
Sunderland	Blue Star	09.79	79-80	16	7	2
Preston NE	Tr	10.81	81	8	0	1
Darlington	Tr	08.82	82	16	0	4

DUNN Brian James
Boston, 4 October, 1940 (W)

League Club	Source	Date Signed	Seasons Played	Apps	Subs	Gls
Grimsby T	Jnrs	10.57				
Hartlepools U	Tr	06.58	58-60	27	-	1

DUNN David John Ian
Great Harwood, 27 December, 1979 EYth/Eu21-20/E-1 (M)

League Club	Source	Date Signed	Seasons Played	Apps	Subs	Gls
Blackburn Rov	YT	09.97	98-02	120	16	30
Birmingham C	Tr	07.03	03-04	29	3	4

DUNN Iain George William
Goole, 1 April, 1970 ESch/EYth (W)

League Club	Source	Date Signed	Seasons Played	Apps	Subs	Gls
York C	Jnrs	07.88	88-90	46	31	11
Chesterfield	Tr	08.91	91	8	5	1
Huddersfield T	Goole T	12.92	92-96	62	58	14
Scunthorpe U	L	09.96	96	3	0	0
Chesterfield	Tr	02.97	96-97	10	8	0

DUNN James (Jimmy)
Edinburgh, 25 November, 1923 (IF)

League Club	Source	Date Signed	Seasons Played	Apps	Subs	Gls
Wolverhampton W	Maghull Ath	11.42	46-52	123	-	33
Derby Co	Tr	11.52	52-54	57	-	21

DUNN James (Jimmy)
Rutherglen, 23 October, 1922 Died 2005 (FB)

League Club	Source	Date Signed	Seasons Played	Apps	Subs	Gls
Leeds U	Rutherglen Glencairn	06.47	47-58	422	-	1
Darlington	Tr	07.59	59	27	-	0

DUNN John Alfred
Barking, 21 June, 1944 (G)

League Club	Source	Date Signed	Seasons Played	Apps	Subs	Gls
Chelsea	App	02.62	62-65	13	0	0
Torquay U	Tr	10.66	66-67	44	0	0
Aston Villa	Tr	01.68	67-70	101	0	0
Charlton Ath	Tr	07.71	71-74	104	0	0

DUNN Joseph (Joe)
Glasgow, 20 September, 1925 (CD)

League Club	Source	Date Signed	Seasons Played	Apps	Subs	Gls
Preston NE	Clyde	08.51	51-60	224	-	2

DUNN Richard (Dick)
Easington, 23 December, 1919 Died 1986 (IF)

League Club	Source	Date Signed	Seasons Played	Apps	Subs	Gls
West Ham U	Ferryhill Ath	02.38	46-47	11	-	2
Hartlepools U	Tr	08.49	49	13	-	2

DUNN William (Billy) Charles
Hebburn, 25 March, 1920 Died 1982 (G)

League Club	Source	Date Signed	Seasons Played	Apps	Subs	Gls
Darlington		05.46	46-55	340	-	0

DUNNE Alan James
Dublin, 23 August, 1982 (FB)

League Club	Source	Date Signed	Seasons Played	Apps	Subs	Gls
Millwall	YT	03.00	01-04	22	10	3

DUNNE Anthony (Tony) Peter
Dublin, 24 July, 1941 IR-33 (FB)

League Club	Source	Date Signed	Seasons Played	Apps	Subs	Gls
Manchester U	Shelbourne	04.60	60-72	414	0	2
Bolton W	Tr	08.73	73-78	166	4	0

DUNNE Austin
Limerick, 31 July, 1934 (WH)

League Club	Source	Date Signed	Seasons Played	Apps	Subs	Gls
Colchester U	Limerick	10.53	54	1	-	0

DUNNE James (Jimmy) Christopher
Dublin, 1 December, 1947 IR-1 (CD)

League Club	Source	Date Signed	Seasons Played	Apps	Subs	Gls
Millwall	Shelbourne	02.66				
Torquay U	Tr	07.67	67-69	125	1	13
Fulham	Tr	07.70	70-73	142	1	2
Torquay U	Durban C (SA)	04.76	75-78	119	3	5

DUNNE James (Jimmy) Patrick
Dublin, 16 March, 1935 Died 1985 IR-3 (IF)

League Club	Source	Date Signed	Seasons Played	Apps	Subs	Gls
Leicester C		09.53	54-55	4	-	0
Peterborough U	St Patrick's Ath	07.60	60-61	4	-	0

DUNNE Joseph (Joe) John
Dublin, 25 May, 1973 IRSch/IRYth/IRu21-1 (FB)

League Club	Source	Date Signed	Seasons Played	Apps	Subs	Gls
Gillingham	YT	08.90	90-95	108	7	1
Colchester U	Tr	03.96	95-98	79	22	3
Colchester U	Dover Ath	12.99	99-01	56	6	3

DUNNE Patrick (Pat) Anthony Joseph
Dublin, 9 February, 1943 IRu23-1/IR-5 (G)

League Club	Source	Date Signed	Seasons Played	Apps	Subs	Gls
Everton	Jnrs	05.60				
Manchester U	Shamrock Rov	05.64	64-65	45	0	0
Plymouth Arg	Tr	02.67	66-70	152	0	0

DUNNE Richard Patrick
Dublin, 21 September, 1979 IRSch/IRYth/IRu21-4/IRB-1/IR-23 (CD)

League Club	Source	Date Signed	Seasons Played	Apps	Subs	Gls
Everton	YT	10.96	96-00	53	7	0
Manchester C	Tr	10.00	00-04	152	5	3

DUNNE Seamus (Shay)
Wicklow, 13 April, 1930 IR-15 (FB)

League Club	Source	Date Signed	Seasons Played	Apps	Subs	Gls
Luton T	Shelbourne	07.50	51-60	301	-	0

DUNNE Thomas (Tommy)
Dublin, 19 March, 1927 Died 1988 (WH)

League Club	Source	Date Signed	Seasons Played	Apps	Subs	Gls
Leicester C	Shamrock Rov	11.49	50-53	33	-	0
Exeter C	Tr	07.54	54-55	37	-	1
Shrewsbury T	Tr	08.56	56	3	-	0
Southport	Tr	07.57	57	21	-	0

DUNNE Thomas (Tommy) Joseph
Glasgow, 22 June, 1946 Died 2001 (IF)

League Club	Source	Date Signed	Seasons Played	Apps	Subs	Gls
Leyton Orient	Glasgow Celtic	05.64	64	1	-	0

DUNNIGAN John Young
Dalmuir, 30 November, 1920 (W)

League Club	Source	Date Signed	Seasons Played	Apps	Subs	Gls
Barrow	Bridgeton Waverley	09.45	46	1	-	0

DUNNING Darren
Scarborough, 8 January, 1981 (M)

League Club	Source	Date Signed	Seasons Played	Apps	Subs	Gls
Blackburn Rov	YT	02.99	00	1	0	0
Bristol C	L	08.00	00	9	0	0
Rochdale	L	11.01	01	4	1	0
Blackpool	L	03.02	01	5	0	0
Torquay U	L	11.02	02	4	3	1
Macclesfield T	L	01.03	02	17	0	0
York C	Tr	07.03	03	42	0	3

DUNNING William (Bill) Samuel
Bury, 15 November, 1952 (W)

League Club	Source	Date Signed	Seasons Played	Apps	Subs	Gls
Blackburn Rov	App	11.70	70-71	10	3	2

DUNPHY Eamonn Martin
Dublin, 3 August, 1945 IRu23-1/IR-23 (M)

League Club	Source	Date Signed	Seasons Played	Apps	Subs	Gls
Manchester U	App	08.62				
York C	Tr	08.65	65	22	0	3
Millwall	Tr	01.66	65-73	267	7	24
Charlton Ath	Tr	11.73	73-74	39	3	3
Reading	Tr	07.75	75-76	74	3	3

DUNPHY Nicholas (Nick) Owen
Sutton Coldfield, 3 August, 1974 (CD)

League Club	Source	Date Signed	Seasons Played	Apps	Subs	Gls
Peterborough U	Hednesford T	08.94	94	0	2	0

DUNPHY Sean
Maltby, 5 November, 1970 (CD)

League Club	Source	Date Signed	Seasons Played	Apps	Subs	Gls
Barnsley	YT	06.89	89	5	1	0
Lincoln C	Tr	07.90	91-93	48	5	2
Doncaster Rov	L	10.93	93	1	0	0
Scarborough	L	08.94	94	10	0	0

DUNS Leonard (Len)
Newcastle, 28 September, 1916 Died 1989 (W)

League Club	Source	Date Signed	Seasons Played	Apps	Subs	Gls
Sunderland	Newcastle West End	10.33	35-51	215	-	45

DUNWELL Michael (Mike)
Stockton, 6 January, 1980 (F)

League Club	Source	Date Signed	Seasons Played	Apps	Subs	Gls
Hartlepool U	YT	07.98	98	0	1	0

DUNWELL Peter Matthew
Ecclesfield, 22 November, 1938 (W)

League Club	Source	Date Signed	Seasons Played	Apps	Subs	Gls
Lincoln C	Ecclesfield	09.58	59-60	14	-	1

DUNWELL Richard Kirk
Islington, 17 June, 1971 (F)

League Club	Source	Date Signed	Seasons Played	Apps	Subs	Gls
Aldershot	Millwall (N/C)	11.90	90	0	1	0
Barnet	Collier Row	10.95	95-96	4	10	1

DUQUEMIN Leonard (Len) Stanley
Cobo, Guernsey, 17 July, 1924 Died 2003 (CF)

League Club	Source	Date Signed	Seasons Played	Apps	Subs	Gls
Tottenham H	Vauxbelet	09.46	47-56	274	-	114

DURANDT Clifford (Cliff) Michael
Johannesburg, South Africa, 16 April, 1940 Died 2002 (IF)

League Club	Source	Date Signed	Seasons Played	Apps	Subs	Gls
Wolverhampton W	Marist Bros (SA)	06.57	58-61	43	-	9
Charlton Ath	Tr	03.63	62-64	36	-	4

DURBAN William **Alan**
Bridgend, 7 July, 1941 Wu23-1/W-27 (M)

League Club	Source	Date Signed	Seasons Played	Apps	Subs	Gls
Cardiff C	Jnrs	09.58	59-62	52	-	9

League Club	Source	Date Signed	Seasons Played	Apps	Subs	Gls
Derby Co	Tr	07.63	63-72	336	10	93
Shrewsbury T	Tr	09.73	73-77	150	6	33

DURHAM Raymond **Denis**
East Halton, 26 September, 1923 (WH)

League Club	Source	Date Signed	Seasons Played	Apps	Subs	Gls
Hull C	East Halton U	04.47	46-58	267	-	7

DURHAM Jonathan Simon
Wombwell, 12 June, 1965 (F)

League Club	Source	Date Signed	Seasons Played	Apps	Subs	Gls
Rotherham U	App	06.83	83	3	3	1
Torquay U	Tr	03.85	84-85	20	4	2

DURIE David (Dave) George
Blackpool, 13 August, 1931 (WH)

League Club	Source	Date Signed	Seasons Played	Apps	Subs	Gls
Blackpool	Oxford Amats	05.52	52-63	301	-	84
Chester	Tr	09.64	64-66	87	2	4

DURIE Gordon Scott
Paisley, 6 December, 1965 Su21-4/SB/S-43 (F)

League Club	Source	Date Signed	Seasons Played	Apps	Subs	Gls
Chelsea	Hibernian	04.86	85-90	115	8	51
Tottenham H	Tr	08.91	91-93	58	0	11

DURKAN Kieron John
Chester, 1 December, 1973 IRu21-3 (W)

League Club	Source	Date Signed	Seasons Played	Apps	Subs	Gls
Wrexham	YT	07.92	91-95	43	7	3
Stockport Co	Tr	02.96	95-97	52	12	4
Macclesfield T	Tr	03.98	97-00	92	11	13
York C	L	10.00	00	7	0	0
Rochdale	Tr	07.01	01	16	14	1
Swansea C	Tr	01.03	02-03	15	6	1

DURKIN John
Hill o' Beath, 18 April, 1930 (W)

League Club	Source	Date Signed	Seasons Played	Apps	Subs	Gls
Gillingham	Heart of Midlothian	08.53	53-54	30	-	5

DURKIN William (Billy)
Bradford, 29 September, 1921 Died 2000 (IF)

League Club	Source	Date Signed	Seasons Played	Apps	Subs	Gls
Bradford C		01.47	46-47	28	-	1
Rotherham U	Tr	08.48	48	1	-	0
Aldershot	Tr	08.49	49-53	129	-	17

DURNIN John Paul
Bootle, 18 August, 1965 (F)

League Club	Source	Date Signed	Seasons Played	Apps	Subs	Gls
Liverpool	Waterloo Dock	03.86				
West Bromwich A	L	10.88	88	5	0	2
Oxford U	Tr	02.89	88-92	140	21	44
Portsmouth	Tr	07.93	93-99	118	63	31
Blackpool	L	11.99	99	4	1	1
Carlisle U	Tr	12.99	99	20	2	2
Kidderminster Hrs	Tr	10.00	00	28	3	9
Port Vale	Rhyl	12.01	01-02	43	4	2

DURRANT Frederick (Fred)
Dover, 19 June, 1921 (CF)

League Club	Source	Date Signed	Seasons Played	Apps	Subs	Gls
Brentford	Folkestone	05.39	46	4	-	3
Queens Park Rgrs	Tr	09.46	46-48	51	-	26
Exeter C	Tr	02.49	48-49	17	-	5

DURRANT Iain
Glasgow, 29 October, 1966 SYth/Su21-4/S-11 (M)

League Club	Source	Date Signed	Seasons Played	Apps	Subs	Gls
Everton (L)	Glasgow Rgrs	10.94	94	4	1	0

DURRANT Lee Roger
Great Yarmouth, 18 December, 1973 ESch (M)

League Club	Source	Date Signed	Seasons Played	Apps	Subs	Gls
Ipswich T	YT	07.92	93	3	4	0

DURRANT Paul
East Howden, 21 February, 1943 (W)

League Club	Source	Date Signed	Seasons Played	Apps	Subs	Gls
Wolverhampton W	Sunderland (Am)	07.61				
Bury	Tr	07.62	63-64	21	-	6
Doncaster Rov	Tr	07.65	65-66	13	2	1

DURRELL Joseph (Joe) Timothy
Stepney, 15 March, 1953 (W)

League Club	Source	Date Signed	Seasons Played	Apps	Subs	Gls
West Ham U	App	10.70	71	5	1	0
Bristol C	Tr	07.73	73-74	5	3	0
Cardiff C	L	08.75	75	2	0	0
Gillingham	Tr	11.75	75-76	43	6	9

DURSUN Peter Muhamet Ali
Aarhus, Denmark, 8 January, 1975 (F)

League Club	Source	Date Signed	Seasons Played	Apps	Subs	Gls
Southend U	Aarhus Fremad (Den)	11.96	96	0	1	0

DUTHIE Ian Martin
Forfar, 18 January, 1930 (CF)

League Club	Source	Date Signed	Seasons Played	Apps	Subs	Gls
Huddersfield T	Forfar Celtic	06.49	49-52	7	-	0
Bradford C	Tr	06.54	54-55	28	-	4

DUTHIE James (Jim)
Rescobie, 23 September, 1923 Died 1972 (WH)

League Club	Source	Date Signed	Seasons Played	Apps	Subs	Gls
Grimsby T		09.49	48-50	40	-	0
Hull C	Tr	06.51	51-52	17	-	3
Southend U	Tr	05.53	53-57	160	-	8

DUTHOIT John (Jack)
Leeds, 4 November, 1918 Died 2001 (FB)

League Club	Source	Date Signed	Seasons Played	Apps	Subs	Gls
Leeds U	Carlton U	04.45				
York C	Tr	05.46	46-49	36	-	0

DUTTON Brian
Malton, 12 April, 1985 (F)

League Club	Source	Date Signed	Seasons Played	Apps	Subs	Gls
Cambridge U	Pickering T	11.03	03	0	3	0

DUTTON Charles (Charlie) Alfred
Rugeley, 10 April, 1934 (CF)

League Club	Source	Date Signed	Seasons Played	Apps	Subs	Gls
Coventry C	Derby Co (Am)	10.52	53-55	27	-	8
Northampton T	Tr	03.56	55-56	10	-	2

DUTTON Leonard (Len) Lewis
Cardiff, 17 January, 1922 Died 1998 WSch (WH)

League Club	Source	Date Signed	Seasons Played	Apps	Subs	Gls
Arsenal	Jnrs	05.39				
Norwich C	Tr	08.46	46-52	139	-	11

DUXBURY Lee Edward
Keighley, 7 October, 1969 (M)

League Club	Source	Date Signed	Seasons Played	Apps	Subs	Gls
Bradford C	YT	07.88	88-94	204	5	25
Rochdale	L	01.90	89	9	1	0
Huddersfield T	Tr	12.94	94-95	29	0	2
Bradford C	Tr	11.95	95-96	63	0	7
Oldham Ath	Tr	03.97	96-02	222	26	32
Bury	Tr	08.03	03	36	1	0

DUXBURY Michael (Mike)
Accrington, 1 September, 1959 Eu21-7/E-10 (FB)

League Club	Source	Date Signed	Seasons Played	Apps	Subs	Gls
Manchester U	App	10.76	80-89	274	25	6
Blackburn Rov	Tr	08.90	90-91	25	2	0
Bradford C	Tr	01.92	91-93	64	1	0

DWIGHT Royston (Roy) Edward
Belvedere, 9 January, 1933 Died 2002 (W)

League Club	Source	Date Signed	Seasons Played	Apps	Subs	Gls
Fulham	Hastings U	06.50	54-57	72	-	54
Nottingham F	Tr	07.58	58-59	44	-	21
Coventry C	Gravesend & Northfleet	01.62	61-62	31	-	8
Millwall	Tr	01.64	63-64	7	-	2

DWYER Robert **Alan**
Liverpool, 5 October, 1952 (FB)

League Club	Source	Date Signed	Seasons Played	Apps	Subs	Gls
Wrexham	Halewood YC	10.73	74-80	169	11	2
Stockport Co	Tr	10.81	81	4	0	0

DWYER Noel Michael
Dublin, 30 October, 1934 Died 1993 IRB/IR-14 (G)

League Club	Source	Date Signed	Seasons Played	Apps	Subs	Gls
Wolverhampton W	Ormeau	08.53	57	5	-	0
West Ham U	Tr	12.58	58-59	36	-	0
Swansea T	Tr	08.60	60-64	140	-	0
Plymouth Arg	Tr	01.65	64-65	26	0	0
Charlton Ath	Tr	12.65	65	6	0	0

DWYER Philip (Phil) John
Cardiff, 28 October, 1953 WSch/WYth/Wu23-5/Wu21-1/W-10 (FB)

League Club	Source	Date Signed	Seasons Played	Apps	Subs	Gls
Cardiff C	Jnrs	10.71	72-84	466	5	41
Rochdale	L	03.85	84	15	0	1

DYAS Gordon
Hednesford, 17 May, 1936 (WH)

League Club	Source	Date Signed	Seasons Played	Apps	Subs	Gls
Walsall	Hednesford T	06.55	55	12	-	0

DYCHE Sean Mark
Kettering, 28 June, 1971 (CD)

League Club	Source	Date Signed	Seasons Played	Apps	Subs	Gls
Nottingham F	YT	05.89				
Chesterfield	Tr	02.90	89-96	219	12	8
Bristol C	Tr	07.97	97-98	14	3	0
Luton T	L	01.99	98	14	0	1
Millwall	Tr	07.99	99-01	69	0	3
Watford	Tr	07.02	02-04	68	4	0

DYE Dean Charles
Lincoln, 4 March, 1969 (F)

League Club	Source	Date Signed	Seasons Played	Apps	Subs	Gls
Charlton Ath	Lincoln U	06.91				
Lincoln C	Tr	10.91	91	0	2	0

DYER Alexander (Alex) Constantine
Forest Gate, 14 November, 1965 (W)

League Club	Source	Date Signed	Seasons Played	Apps	Subs	Gls
Blackpool	Watford (App)	10.83	83-86	101	7	19
Hull C	Tr	02.87	86-88	59	1	14
Crystal Palace	Tr	11.88	88-89	16	1	2
Charlton Ath	Tr	11.90	90-92	60	18	13
Oxford U	Tr	07.93	93-94	62	14	6
Lincoln C	Tr	08.95	95	1	0	0
Barnet	Tr	09.95	95	30	5	2
Huddersfield T	FC Maia (Por)	08.97	97	8	4	1
Notts Co	Tr	03.98	97-00	58	20	6

DYER Joseph Alexander (Alec)
Crewe, 13 April, 1913 Died 1984 (W)

League Club	Source	Date Signed	Seasons Played	Apps	Subs	Gls
Crewe Alex		10.33	33-36	51	-	10
Plymouth Arg	Tr	02.37	36-46	53	-	3

DYER Bruce Antonio
Ilford, 13 April, 1975 Eu21-11 (F)

League Club	Source	Date Signed	Seasons Played	Apps	Subs	Gls
Watford	YT	04.93	92-93	29	2	6
Crystal Palace	Tr	03.94	93-98	95	40	37
Barnsley	Tr	10.98	98-02	149	33	59
Watford	Tr	07.03	03-04	39	29	12

DYER Kieron Courtney
Ipswich, 29 December, 1978 EYth/Eu21-11/EB-2/E-28 (M)

League Club	Source	Date Signed	Seasons Played	Apps	Subs	Gls
Ipswich T	YT	01.97	96-98	79	12	9
Newcastle U	Tr	07.99	99-04	145	12	18

DYER Lloyd Richard
Birmingham, 13 September, 1982 (M)

League Club	Source	Date Signed	Seasons Played	Apps	Subs	Gls
West Bromwich A	Aston Villa (Jnrs)	07.01	03-04	2	19	2
Kidderminster Hrs	L	09.03	03	5	2	1
Coventry C	L	03.05	04	6	0	0

DYER Paul David
Leicester, 24 January, 1953 (M)

League Club	Source	Date Signed	Seasons Played	Apps	Subs	Gls
Notts Co		09.72	72-73	1	6	0
Colchester U	Tr	07.75	75-79	124	20	4

DYER Peter Robert Francis
Devonport, 12 October, 1937 (G)

League Club	Source	Date Signed	Seasons Played	Apps	Subs	Gls
Plymouth Arg	Oak Villa	06.55	55-56	8	-	0

DYER Raymond (Ray)
Stockport, 12 May, 1938 (W)

League Club	Source	Date Signed	Seasons Played	Apps	Subs	Gls
Stockport Co	Bolton W (Am)	09.56	56	1	-	0

DYER Stephen (Steve) Paul
Chelmsford, 21 March, 1954 (FB)

League Club	Source	Date Signed	Seasons Played	Apps	Subs	Gls
Southend U	App	03.72	72-76	60	8	0

DYER Wayne
Birmingham, 24 November, 1977 Montserrat int (M)

League Club	Source	Date Signed	Seasons Played	Apps	Subs	Gls
Birmingham C	YT	07.96				
Walsall	Moor Green Rov	08.98	98	0	1	0

DYKE Charles (Charlie)
Caerphilly, 23 September, 1926 (W)

League Club	Source	Date Signed	Seasons Played	Apps	Subs	Gls
Chelsea	Troedyrhiw	11.47	47-50	24	-	2

DYKES Darren Lewis
Aylesbury, 28 April, 1981 (F)

League Club	Source	Date Signed	Seasons Played	Apps	Subs	Gls
Swindon T	Buckingham T	08.02	02	1	1	0
Lincoln C	L	12.02	02	2	1	0

DYKES Donald (Don) William
Ashby-by-Partney, 8 June, 1930 (FB)

League Club	Source	Date Signed	Seasons Played	Apps	Subs	Gls
Lincoln C	M & BDC	06.49	49-58	95	-	4

DYMOND William (Bill) Henry
Dawlish, 13 February, 1920 (W)

League Club	Source	Date Signed	Seasons Played	Apps	Subs	Gls
Bristol C		09.45	46	8	-	1
Exeter C	Tr	06.47	47-48	41	-	7

DYSON John Barry
Oldham, 6 September, 1942 Died 1995 (F)

League Club	Source	Date Signed	Seasons Played	Apps	Subs	Gls
Bury	Jnrs	09.60				
Tranmere Rov	Tr	07.62	62-66	174	0	100
Crystal Palace	Tr	09.66	66-67	33	1	9
Watford	Tr	01.68	67-68	38	0	19
Orient	Tr	12.68	68-72	154	6	28
Colchester U	Tr	07.73	73-74	41	1	6

DYSON Geoffrey (Geoff)
Huddersfield, 16 March, 1923 Died 1989 (IF)

League Club	Source	Date Signed	Seasons Played	Apps	Subs	Gls
Huddersfield T	Jnrs	03.46				
Bradford C	Tr	06.47	47	1	-	0
Accrington St	Tr	01.48	47-48	20	-	1

DYSON Jack
Oldham, 8 July, 1934 Died 2000 Eu23-1 (IF)

League Club	Source	Date Signed	Seasons Played	Apps	Subs	Gls
Manchester C	Nelson	05.52	55-59	63	-	26

DYSON James (Jim)
Ryhope, 16 February, 1935 (G)

League Club	Source	Date Signed	Seasons Played	Apps	Subs	Gls
Hartlepools U	Seaham CW	04.55	54-58	63	-	0

DYSON James Gareth
Wordsley, 20 April, 1979 (CD)

League Club	Source	Date Signed	Seasons Played	Apps	Subs	Gls
Birmingham C	YT	07.97	99	0	2	0

DYSON Jonathan (Jon) Paul
Mirfield, 18 December, 1971 (CD)

League Club	Source	Date Signed	Seasons Played	Apps	Subs	Gls
Huddersfield T	Jnrs	12.90	92-02	184	32	9

DYSON Keith
Blackhill, 10 February, 1950 ESch/Eu23-1 (F)

League Club	Source	Date Signed	Seasons Played	Apps	Subs	Gls
Newcastle U	Jnrs	08.68	68-71	74	2	22
Blackpool	Tr	10.71	71-75	91	3	30

DYSON Paul Ian
Birmingham, 27 December, 1959 Eu21-4 (CD)

League Club	Source	Date Signed	Seasons Played	Apps	Subs	Gls
Coventry C	App	06.77	78-82	140	0	5
Stoke C	Tr	07.83	83-85	106	0	5
West Bromwich A	Tr	03.86	85-88	64	0	5
Darlington	Tr	03.89	88	12	0	3
Crewe Alex	Tr	08.89	89	30	1	2

DYSON Terence (Terry) Kent
Malton, 29 November, 1934 (W)

League Club	Source	Date Signed	Seasons Played	Apps	Subs	Gls
Tottenham H	Scarborough	04.55	54-64	184	-	41
Fulham	Tr	06.65	65-66	21	2	3
Colchester U	Tr	08.68	68-69	53	3	4

DZIADULEWICZ Micczyslaw (Mark)
Wimbledon, 29 January, 1960 (M)

League Club	Source	Date Signed	Seasons Played	Apps	Subs	Gls
Southend U	App	02.78				
Wimbledon	Chelmsford C	02.79	78-79	22	6	1

DZIEKANOWSKI Dariusz (Jackie) Pavel
Warsaw, Poland, 30 September, 1962 Poland int (F)

League Club	Source	Date Signed	Seasons Played	Apps	Subs	Gls
Bristol C	Glasgow Celtic	01.92	91-92	40	3	7

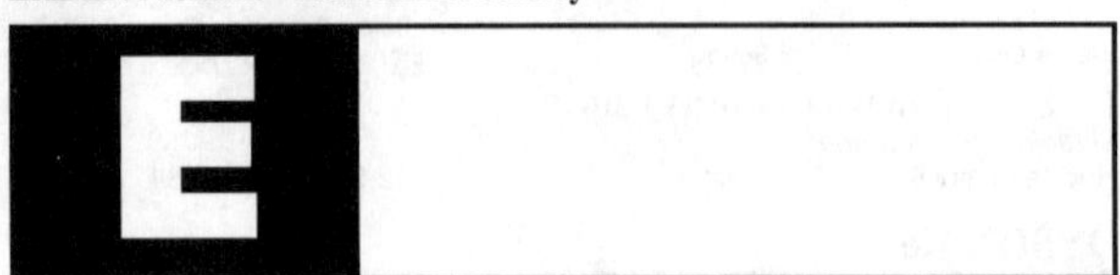

EADEN Nicholas (Nicky) Jeremy
Sheffield, 12 December, 1972 (FB)

League Club	Source	Date Signed	Seasons Played	Apps	Subs	Gls
Barnsley	Jnrs	06.91	92-99	281	12	10
Birmingham C	Tr	07.00	00-01	68	6	3
Wigan Ath	Tr	09.02	02-04	116	6	0

EADES Kevin Michael
Rotherham, 11 March, 1959 (W)

League Club	Source	Date Signed	Seasons Played	Apps	Subs	Gls
Rotherham U	App	03.77	75	1	0	0

EADES Terence (Terry) Gerald
Banbridge, 5 March, 1944 (CD)

League Club	Source	Date Signed	Seasons Played	Apps	Subs	Gls
Cambridge U	Chelmsford C	03.69	70-76	248	0	5
Watford	L	09.76	76	4	0	0

EADIE Darren Malcolm
Chippenham, 10 June, 1975 EYth/Eu21-7 (W)

League Club	Source	Date Signed	Seasons Played	Apps	Subs	Gls
Norwich C	YT	02.93	93-99	153	15	35
Leicester C	Tr	12.99	99-00	31	9	2

EADIE Douglas (Doug)
Edinburgh, 22 September, 1946 (W)

League Club	Source	Date Signed	Seasons Played	Apps	Subs	Gls
West Ham U	Possil YMCA	09.66	66	2	0	0
Orient	L	09.67	67	2	0	0

EADIE Gordon
Glasgow, 17 November, 1950 (W)

League Club	Source	Date Signed	Seasons Played	Apps	Subs	Gls
Bury (Am)	Glasgow U	06.67	67	2	0	0

EADIE James (Jim)
Kirkintilloch, 4 February, 1947 (G)

League Club	Source	Date Signed	Seasons Played	Apps	Subs	Gls
Cardiff C	Dumbarton	09.66	69-71	43	0	0
Chester	L	08.72	72	6	0	0
Bristol Rov	Tr	02.73	72-76	183	0	0

EAGLES Alan James
Edgware, 6 September, 1933 Died 1995 (FB)

League Club	Source	Date Signed	Seasons Played	Apps	Subs	Gls
Leyton Orient	Carshalton Ath	09.57	57-60	75	-	0
Colchester U	Tr	01.61	60	16	-	1
Queens Park Rgrs	Tr	08.61				
Aldershot	Tr	11.61	61-62	15	-	1

EAGLES Christopher (Chris) Mark
Hemel Hempstead, 19 November, 1985 EYth (M)

League Club	Source	Date Signed	Seasons Played	Apps	Subs	Gls
Manchester U	Sch	07.03				
Watford	L	01.05	04	10	3	1

EALING William
Tamworth, 12 March, 1930 (CF)

League Club	Source	Date Signed	Seasons Played	Apps	Subs	Gls
Blackburn Rov		02.50				
Walsall	Tr	07.52	52	1	-	0

EAMES Terence (Terry)
Croydon, 13 October, 1957 (FB)

League Club	Source	Date Signed	Seasons Played	Apps	Subs	Gls
Wimbledon	Crystal Palace (Am)	(N/L)	77-79	46	1	1

EAMES William (Billy) Alan
Malta, 20 September, 1957 (M)

League Club	Source	Date Signed	Seasons Played	Apps	Subs	Gls
Portsmouth	App	09.75	75	9	3	1
Brentford	Tr	08.78	78	2	0	1

EARL Albert (Sam) Thomas
Gateshead, 10 February, 1915 Died 2000 (IF)

League Club	Source	Date Signed	Seasons Played	Apps	Subs	Gls
Bury	Dunston CWS	03.32	33-35	35	-	7
York C	Rhyl Ath	07.37	37-38	58	-	9
Hartlepools U	Tr	07.39				
Stockport Co	Tr	08.46	46-47	42	-	12
Rochdale	Tr	11.47	47	4	-	1
New Brighton	Tr	03.48	47	9	-	1

EARL Stanley (Stan) James William
Alton, 9 July, 1929 (FB)

League Club	Source	Date Signed	Seasons Played	Apps	Subs	Gls
Portsmouth	Alton T	11.49	50-51	8	-	0
Leyton Orient	Tr	07.53	53-55	33	-	0
Swindon T	Tr	11.56	56-57	23	-	0

EARL Steven (Steve)
Scunthorpe, 31 August, 1956 Died 2004 (F)

League Club	Source	Date Signed	Seasons Played	Apps	Subs	Gls
Scunthorpe U (Am)	Appleby Froddingham	09.74	74	7	0	1
Scunthorpe U	Appleby Frodingham	11.78	78-79	30	2	9

EARLAM Donald (Don) Stuart
Altrincham, 25 June, 1931 Died 1988 (WH)

League Club	Source	Date Signed	Seasons Played	Apps	Subs	Gls
Southport (Am)	Broad Heath Central	08.54	54	2	-	0

EARLE Robert (Robbie) Fitzgerald
Newcastle-under-Lyme, 27 January, 1965 Jamaica 11 (M)

League Club	Source	Date Signed	Seasons Played	Apps	Subs	Gls
Port Vale	Jnrs	07.82	82-90	284	10	77
Wimbledon	Tr	07.91	91-99	280	4	59

EARLE Stephen (Steve) John
Feltham, 1 November, 1945 (F)

League Club	Source	Date Signed	Seasons Played	Apps	Subs	Gls
Fulham	App	11.63	63-73	285	6	98
Leicester C	Tr	11.73	73-77	91	8	20
Peterborough U	L	11.77	77	1	0	0

EARLES Patrick (Pat) John Earles
Titchfield, 22 March, 1955 ESch (F)

League Club	Source	Date Signed	Seasons Played	Apps	Subs	Gls
Southampton	App	11.72	74-76	4	8	1
Reading	Tr	01.77	76-82	240	7	68

EARLS Michael (Mike) Patrick Marien
Limerick, 25 March, 1954 (CD)

League Club	Source	Date Signed	Seasons Played	Apps	Subs	Gls
Southampton	App	11.72	73-74	8	0	0
Aldershot	Tr	06.75	75-78	68	5	0

EARLY Michael (Mike)
Dumbarton, 4 April, 1928 Died 1995 (W)

League Club	Source	Date Signed	Seasons Played	Apps	Subs	Gls
Watford	Strathleven	06.46	46	5	-	1

EARNSHAW Robert (Rob)
Zambia, 6 April, 1981 WYth/Wu21-10/W-19 (F)

League Club	Source	Date Signed	Seasons Played	Apps	Subs	Gls
Cardiff C	YT	08.98	97-04	141	37	85
West Bromwich A	Tr	08.04	04	18	13	11

EARNSHAW Robert (Bob) Ian
Rotherham, 15 March, 1943 (W)

League Club	Source	Date Signed	Seasons Played	Apps	Subs	Gls
Barnsley	Jnrs	06.62	62-72	219	6	35

EASDALE John
Dumbarton, 16 January, 1919 (CD)

League Club	Source	Date Signed	Seasons Played	Apps	Subs	Gls
Liverpool		02.37	46	2	-	0
Stockport Co	Tr	09.48	48	6	-	0

EAST Keith Michael George
Southampton, 31 October, 1944 (F)

League Club	Source	Date Signed	Seasons Played	Apps	Subs	Gls
Portsmouth	App	06.63				
Swindon T	Tr	05.64	64-66	43	2	21
Stockport Co	Tr	12.66	66-67	23	2	7
Bournemouth	Tr	11.67	67-69	93	1	34
Northampton T	Tr	07.70	70	26	3	7
Crewe Alex	Tr	07.71	71	32	2	8

EASTER Graham Paul
Epsom, 26 September, 1969 (W)

League Club	Source	Date Signed	Seasons Played	Apps	Subs	Gls
West Bromwich A	YT	07.88				
Huddersfield T	Tr	03.89				
Crewe Alex	Tr	07.89	89	0	3	0
Preston NE	(Finland)	10.90	90	1	0	0

EASTER Jermaine Maurice
Cardiff, 15 January, 1982 WYth (F)

League Club	Source	Date Signed	Seasons Played	Apps	Subs	Gls
Wolverhampton W	YT	07.00				
Hartlepool U	Tr	03.01	00-03	0	27	2
Cambridge U	Tr	02.04	03-04	25	14	8
Boston U	Tr	03.05	04	5	4	3

EASTHAM Brian
Bolton, 26 April, 1937 (FB)

League Club	Source	Date Signed	Seasons Played	Apps	Subs	Gls
Bury	Chorley	09.58	58-66	188	1	3
Rochdale	Toronto (Can)	07.67	67	13	0	0

EASTHAM George Edward
Blackpool, 23 September, 1936 IrLge-3/Eu23-6/FLge-3/E-19 (M)

League Club	Source	Date Signed	Seasons Played	Apps	Subs	Gls
Newcastle U	Ards	05.56	56-59	124	-	29
Arsenal	Tr	10.60	60-65	207	0	41
Stoke C	Tr	08.66	66-73	184	10	4

EASTHAM George Richard
Blackpool, 13 September, 1914 Died 2000 E-1 (IF)

League Club	Source	Date Signed	Seasons Played	Apps	Subs	Gls
Bolton W	South Shore Wed	08.32	32-36	114	-	16
Brentford	Tr	05.37	37-38	49	-	1
Blackpool	Tr	11.38	38-46	44	-	9
Swansea T	Tr	08.47	47	15	-	0
Rochdale	Tr	06.48	48	2	-	0
Lincoln C	Tr	01.49	48-49	27	-	1

EASTHAM Henry (Harry)
Blackpool, 30 June, 1917 Died 1998 (IF)

League Club	Source	Date Signed	Seasons Played	Apps	Subs	Gls
Blackpool	Jnrs	06.34				
Liverpool	Tr	02.36	36-46	63	-	3
Tranmere Rov	Tr	05.48	48-52	154	-	12
Accrington St	Tr	07.53	53	42	-	3

EASTHAM Stanley (Stan)
Bolton, 26 November, 1913 EAmat (WH)

League Club	Source	Date Signed	Seasons Played	Apps	Subs	Gls
Liverpool	Kingstonian	05.38				

League Club	Source	Date Signed	Seasons Played	Apps	Subs	Gls
Exeter C	Tr	04.46				
Stockport Co	Tr	06.46	46	14	-	1

EASTHOPE Joseph (Joe) Donald
Liverpool, 26 September, 1929 Died 1993 (W)

League Club	Source	Date Signed	Seasons Played	Apps	Subs	Gls
Everton		04.50	52	2	-	0
Stockport Co	Tr	06.54	54	9	-	2

EASTMAN Donald (Don) John
Eastry, 9 August, 1923 (FB)

League Club	Source	Date Signed	Seasons Played	Apps	Subs	Gls
Crystal Palace (Am)	Jnrs	08.46	46	1	-	0

EASTOE Peter Robert
Tamworth, 2 August, 1953 EYth (F)

League Club	Source	Date Signed	Seasons Played	Apps	Subs	Gls
Wolverhampton W	App	06.71	71-73	4	2	0
Swindon T	L	11.73	73	11	0	7
Swindon T	Tr	03.74	73-75	80	0	36
Queens Park Rgrs	Tr	03.76	76-78	69	3	15
Everton	Tr	03.79	78-81	88	7	26
West Bromwich A	Tr	08.82	82	30	1	8
Leicester C	L	10.83	83	5	0	1
Huddersfield T	L	03.84	83	8	2	0
Walsall	L	08.84	84	6	0	1
Leicester C	L	10.84	84	6	0	1
Wolverhampton W	L	02.85	84	8	0	0

EASTON Clint Jude
Barking, 1 October, 1977 EYth (M)

League Club	Source	Date Signed	Seasons Played	Apps	Subs	Gls
Watford	YT	07.96	96-00	50	14	1
Norwich C	Tr	06.01	01-03	41	9	5
Wycombe W	Tr	07.04	04	29	4	1

EASTON Henry (Harry) Blair
Shoreham, 12 September, 1938 (IF)

League Club	Source	Date Signed	Seasons Played	Apps	Subs	Gls
Crystal Palace	Jnrs	11.56	59-61	8	-	1

EASTWAY Raymond (Ray) John
Croydon, 12 April, 1929 Died 1989 (FB)

League Club	Source	Date Signed	Seasons Played	Apps	Subs	Gls
Watford	Manchester U (Jnrs)	08.49	51	12	-	0

EASTWOOD Eric
Heywood, 24 March, 1916 Died 1991 (CD)

League Club	Source	Date Signed	Seasons Played	Apps	Subs	Gls
Manchester C	Heywood St James'	04.35	38-46	16	-	0
Port Vale	Tr	03.47	46-48	28	-	1

EASTWOOD Freddy
Epsom, 29 October, 1983 (F)

League Club	Source	Date Signed	Seasons Played	Apps	Subs	Gls
Southend U	Grays Ath	10.04	04	31	2	19

EASTWOOD Philip (Phil) John
Blackburn, 6 April, 1978 (F)

League Club	Source	Date Signed	Seasons Played	Apps	Subs	Gls
Burnley	YT	07.96	97-98	7	9	1

EASTWOOD Raymond (Ray)
Moston, 1 January, 1915 Died 1999 (FB)

League Club	Source	Date Signed	Seasons Played	Apps	Subs	Gls
Oldham Ath	Bacup Borough	05.35				
Aldershot	Altrincham	06.38	38	9	-	0
Accrington St	Tr	07.46	46	3	-	0

EATON Adam Paul
Wigan, 2 May, 1980 (FB)

League Club	Source	Date Signed	Seasons Played	Apps	Subs	Gls
Everton	YT	06.97				
Preston NE	Tr	06.99	00-02	7	7	0
Mansfield T	L	12.02	02	6	0	0
Mansfield T	Tr	02.03	02-04	19	0	0

EATON David Franklin
Liverpool, 30 September, 1981 (F)

League Club	Source	Date Signed	Seasons Played	Apps	Subs	Gls
Everton	YT	07.01				
Macclesfield T	Tr	09.02	02	8	12	5

EATON Jason Cord
Bristol, 29 January, 1969 (F)

League Club	Source	Date Signed	Seasons Played	Apps	Subs	Gls
Bristol Rov	Olveston	06.87	87	0	3	0
Bristol C	Trowbridge T	03.89	88-89	6	7	1

EATON Joseph (Joe) David
Cuckney, 16 May, 1931 (IF)

League Club	Source	Date Signed	Seasons Played	Apps	Subs	Gls
Mansfield T	Langwith BC	08.51	52-53	4	-	1

EATON Stephen (Steve) Paul
Liverpool, 25 December, 1959 (FB)

League Club	Source	Date Signed	Seasons Played	Apps	Subs	Gls
Tranmere Rov	Jnrs	06.77	78	1	0	0

EAVES David Michael Curtis
Blackpool, 13 February, 1973 (M)

League Club	Source	Date Signed	Seasons Played	Apps	Subs	Gls
Preston NE	YT	07.91	90-92	2	5	0

EAVES Ernest (Ernie)
Bryn, 4 January, 1927 (CF)

League Club	Source	Date Signed	Seasons Played	Apps	Subs	Gls
New Brighton	Newton-le-Willows	10.48	48-50	14	-	3

EBANKS Michael Wayne Anthony
Longbridge, 2 October, 1964 (FB)

League Club	Source	Date Signed	Seasons Played	Apps	Subs	Gls
West Bromwich A	App	04.82	83	6	1	0
Stoke C	L	08.84	84	10	0	0
Port Vale	Tr	03.85	84-86	36	3	0
Cambridge U	Tr	08.87	87	3	1	0

EBBRELL John Keith
Bromborough, 1 October, 1969 ESch/EYth/Eu21-14/EB (M)

League Club	Source	Date Signed	Seasons Played	Apps	Subs	Gls
Everton	App	11.86	88-96	207	10	13
Sheffield U	Tr	03.97	96	1	0	0

EBDON Marcus
Pontypool, 17 October, 1970 WYth/Wu21-2 (M)

League Club	Source	Date Signed	Seasons Played	Apps	Subs	Gls
Everton	YT	08.89				
Peterborough U	Tr	07.91	91-96	136	11	15
Chesterfield	Tr	03.97	96-02	180	12	13
Leyton Orient	Tr	08.03	03	10	4	0

EBDON Richard (Dick) George
Ottery St Mary, 3 May, 1913 Died 1987 (IF)

League Club	Source	Date Signed	Seasons Played	Apps	Subs	Gls
Exeter C	Ottery St Mary	12.35	35-47	138	-	50
Torquay U	Tr	07.48	48	5	-	1

E'BEYER Mark Edward
Stevenage, 21 September, 1984 (M)

League Club	Source	Date Signed	Seasons Played	Apps	Subs	Gls
Oxford U	MK Dons (Sch)	07.04	04	6	4	2

EBOUE Emmanuel
Abidjan, Ivory Coast, 4 June, 1983 Ivory Coast int (CD)

League Club	Source	Date Signed	Seasons Played	Apps	Subs	Gls
Arsenal	Beveren (Bel)	01.05	04	0	1	0

ECCLES Peter Edward
Dublin, 24 August, 1962 IR-1 (CD)

League Club	Source	Date Signed	Seasons Played	Apps	Subs	Gls
Leicester C	Dundalk	10.88	88	1	0	0

ECCLES Terence (Terry) Stuart
Leeds, 2 March, 1952 (F)

League Club	Source	Date Signed	Seasons Played	Apps	Subs	Gls
Blackburn Rov	App	08.69	69-72	33	13	6
Mansfield T	Tr	07.73	73-76	115	3	47
Huddersfield T	Tr	01.77	76-77	41	5	6
York C	Ethnikos (Gre)	09.79	79-80	64	0	18

ECCLESHARE Keith
Bolton, 14 December, 1950 EYth (FB)

League Club	Source	Date Signed	Seasons Played	Apps	Subs	Gls
Bury	App	12.68	68-71	79	4	0

ECCLESTON Stuart Ian
Stoke-on-Trent, 4 October, 1961 (CD)

League Club	Source	Date Signed	Seasons Played	Apps	Subs	Gls
Stoke C	App	10.79				
Hull C	Tr	01.81	80-81	22	1	0

ECHANOMI Efe
Nigeria, 27 September, 1986 (F)

League Club	Source	Date Signed	Seasons Played	Apps	Subs	Gls
Leyton Orient	Sch	•	04	4	14	5

ECKERSALL Michael (Mike) William
Bury, 3 February, 1939 (M)

League Club	Source	Date Signed	Seasons Played	Apps	Subs	Gls
Torquay U	Mossley	10.59	60-62	28	-	2
Stockport Co	Tr	07.63	63-65	39	1	2

ECKERSLEY William (Bill)
Southport, 16 July, 1925 Died 1982 FLge-6/EB/E-17 (FB)

League Club	Source	Date Signed	Seasons Played	Apps	Subs	Gls
Blackburn Rov	High Park	03.48	47-60	406	-	20

ECKHARDT Jeffrey (Jeff) Edward
Sheffield, 7 October, 1965 (CD)

League Club	Source	Date Signed	Seasons Played	Apps	Subs	Gls
Sheffield U	Jnrs	08.84	84-87	73	1	2
Fulham	Tr	11.87	87-93	245	4	25
Stockport Co	Tr	07.94	94-95	56	6	7
Cardiff C	Tr	08.96	96-00	129	11	14

ECONOMOU Jon (Joe)
Holloway, 25 October, 1961 (M)

League Club	Source	Date Signed	Seasons Played	Apps	Subs	Gls
Bristol C	App	10.79	81-83	62	3	3

EDDOLLS John Douglas
Bristol, 19 August, 1919 Died 1994 (G)

League Club	Source	Date Signed	Seasons Played	Apps	Subs	Gls
Bristol C	Peasedown	09.45	46	6	-	0

EDDS Ernest (Ernie) Frederick
Plymouth, 19 March, 1926 (W)

League Club	Source	Date Signed	Seasons Played	Apps	Subs	Gls
Plymouth Arg	Portsmouth (Am)	10.46	46-49	59	-	18
Blackburn Rov	Tr	12.49	49-50	18	-	3
Torquay U	Tr	06.51	51-53	84	-	34
Plymouth Arg	Tr	10.53	53-54	26	-	4
Swindon T	Tr	07.55	55	3	-	0

EDDS Gareth James
Sydney, Australia, 3 February, 1981 AuYth/Auu23-2 (FB)

League Club	Source	Date Signed	Seasons Played	Apps	Subs	Gls
Nottingham F	YT	02.98	99-01	11	5	1
Swindon T	Tr	08.02	02	8	6	0

League Club	Source	Date Signed	Seasons Played	Career Record Apps	Subs	Gls
Bradford C	Tr	07.03	03	19	4	0
MK Dons	Tr	07.04	04	37	2	5

EDDY Keith
Barrow, 23 October, 1944 (CD)

League Club	Source	Date Signed	Seasons Played	Apps	Subs	Gls
Barrow	Holker COB	06.62	62-65	127	1	5
Watford	Tr	07.66	66-71	239	1	26
Sheffield U	Tr	08.72	72-75	113	1	16

EDELSTON Maurice
Hull, 27 April, 1918 Died 1976 EAmat/EWar-5 (IF)

League Club	Source	Date Signed	Seasons Played	Apps	Subs	Gls
Fulham (Am)	Jnrs	07.35	35-37	3	-	0
Brentford (Am)	Wimbledon	12.37	37-38	21	-	6
Reading	Corinthians	05.39	46-51	202	-	70
Northampton T	Tr	07.52	52-53	40	-	17

EDEN Alan
Sunderland, 8 October, 1958 (M)

League Club	Source	Date Signed	Seasons Played	Apps	Subs	Gls
Lincoln C	Lambton Star BC	08.77	77-78	5	2	0

EDEN Anthony Frederick
Birmingham, 15 March, 1941 (CD)

League Club	Source	Date Signed	Seasons Played	Apps	Subs	Gls
Aston Villa	Jnrs	04.58				
Walsall	Tr	07.60	60-62	14	-	0

EDESON Matthew (Matt) Kirk
Beverley, 11 August, 1976 (F)

League Club	Source	Date Signed	Seasons Played	Apps	Subs	Gls
Hull C	YT	07.94	92-94	0	5	0

EDEY Cecil (Cec)
Manchester, 12 March, 1965 (FB)

League Club	Source	Date Signed	Seasons Played	Apps	Subs	Gls
Macclesfield T	Witton A	10.95	97	9	4	0

EDGAR Edward (Eddie)
Jarrow, 31 October, 1956 (G)

League Club	Source	Date Signed	Seasons Played	Apps	Subs	Gls
Newcastle U	App	08.74				
Hartlepool	Tr	07.76	76-78	75	0	0

EDGAR John (Johnny)
Worsborough Dale, 9 April, 1936 (IF)

League Club	Source	Date Signed	Seasons Played	Apps	Subs	Gls
Barnsley	Jnrs	05.54	55-57	22	-	6
Gillingham	Tr	06.58	58	45	-	23
York C	Tr	06.59	59-60	47	-	16
Hartlepools U	Tr	06.61	61-62	72	-	31
Exeter C	Tr	07.63	63	6	-	0

EDGAR John David
Aldershot, 1 December, 1930 (IF)

League Club	Source	Date Signed	Seasons Played	Apps	Subs	Gls
Darlington	Ferryhill Ath	12.54	54-55	12	-	0

EDGE Harold **Anthony (Tony)**
Hoylake, 14 March, 1937 (CF)

League Club	Source	Date Signed	Seasons Played	Apps	Subs	Gls
Bristol Rov	Devizes T	08.59	59-60	13	-	4

EDGE Declan John
Malacca, Malaysia, 18 September, 1965 New Zealand int (F)

League Club	Source	Date Signed	Seasons Played	Apps	Subs	Gls
Notts Co	Gisborne C (NZ)	12.85	85	7	3	2

EDGE Derek
Hanley, 14 February, 1942 Died 1991 (W)

League Club	Source	Date Signed	Seasons Played	Apps	Subs	Gls
Port Vale	Stoke C (Am)	09.60	61	2	-	0

EDGE Lewis John Spencer
Lancaster, 12 January, 1987 (G)

League Club	Source	Date Signed	Seasons Played	Apps	Subs	Gls
Blackpool	Sch	●	03	1	0	0

EDGE Roland
Gillingham, 25 November, 1978 (FB)

League Club	Source	Date Signed	Seasons Played	Apps	Subs	Gls
Gillingham	YT	07.97	98-02	93	9	1
Hull C	Hibernian	07.04	04	13	1	0

EDGHILL Richard Arlon
Oldham, 23 September, 1974 Eu21-3/EB-1 (FB)

League Club	Source	Date Signed	Seasons Played	Apps	Subs	Gls
Manchester C	YT	07.92	93-01	178	3	1
Birmingham C	L	11.00	00	3	0	0
Wigan Ath	Tr	10.02				
Sheffield U	Tr	01.03	02	0	1	0
Queens Park Rgrs	Tr	08.03	03-04	28	12	0

EDGLEY Brian Kenneth
Shrewsbury, 26 August, 1937 (CF)

League Club	Source	Date Signed	Seasons Played	Apps	Subs	Gls
Shrewsbury T	Jnrs	02.56	55-59	113	-	12
Cardiff C	Tr	07.60	60	10	-	1
Brentford	Tr	06.61	61-62	31	-	9
Barnsley	Tr	11.62	62	4	-	0

EDINBURGH Justin Charles
Basildon, 18 December, 1969 (FB)

League Club	Source	Date Signed	Seasons Played	Apps	Subs	Gls
Southend U	YT	08.88	88-89	36	1	0
Tottenham H	Tr	07.90	90-99	190	23	1
Portsmouth	Tr	03.00	99-01	34	1	1

[EDINHO] AMARAL Neto Edon
Brazil, 21 February, 1967 (F)

League Club	Source	Date Signed	Seasons Played	Apps	Subs	Gls
Bradford C	Vitoria Guimaraes (Por)	02.97	96-98	50	9	15

EDISBURY William
Tyldesley, 12 November, 1937 (FB)

League Club	Source	Date Signed	Seasons Played	Apps	Subs	Gls
Bolton W	Jnrs	10.56	56-57	2	-	0

EDMAN Erik Kenneth
Huskvarna, Sweden, 11 November, 1978 Sweden 30 (FB)

League Club	Source	Date Signed	Seasons Played	Apps	Subs	Gls
Tottenham H	SC Heerenveen (Holl)	07.04	04	28	0	1

EDMONDS Darren
Watford, 12 April, 1971 (W)

League Club	Source	Date Signed	Seasons Played	Apps	Subs	Gls
Leeds U	YT	05.89				
Ipswich T	Tr	09.91	91	0	2	0
Scarborough	Tr	08.92	92	0	1	0
Halifax T	Mossley	11.92	92	0	2	0

EDMONDS Derek James
Hexham, 9 October, 1950 EYth (G)

League Club	Source	Date Signed	Seasons Played	Apps	Subs	Gls
Leeds U	App	11.67				
Watford	Tr	05.70	70-71	15	0	0
Southport	Cape Town C (SA)	07.74	74	2	0	0

EDMONDS Neil Anthony
Accrington, 18 October, 1968 (M)

League Club	Source	Date Signed	Seasons Played	Apps	Subs	Gls
Oldham Ath	App	06.86	86-87	3	2	0
Rochdale	Tr	09.88	88-89	36	7	8

EDMONDSON Douglas **Barry**
Blowick, 10 February, 1943 (WH)

League Club	Source	Date Signed	Seasons Played	Apps	Subs	Gls
Southport	Blackpool (Am)	12.61	61	1	-	0

EDMONDSON Darren Stephen
Coniston, 4 November, 1971 (FB)

League Club	Source	Date Signed	Seasons Played	Apps	Subs	Gls
Carlisle U	YT	07.90	90-96	205	9	9
Huddersfield T	Tr	03.97	96-99	28	9	0
Plymouth Arg	L	09.98	98	4	0	0
York C	Tr	03.00	99-03	126	5	6
Chester C	Tr	08.04	04	26	1	0

EDMONDSON Stanley (Stan) Glasgow
Bacup, 10 August, 1922 Died 1977 (W)

League Club	Source	Date Signed	Seasons Played	Apps	Subs	Gls
Bradford C (Am)	Bacup Borough	05.46	46	3	-	0

EDMUNDS Paul
Doncaster, 2 December, 1957 (W)

League Club	Source	Date Signed	Seasons Played	Apps	Subs	Gls
Leicester C	Troston Welfare	04.79	79-80	8	0	2
Bournemouth	Tr	07.81	81	13	1	2

EDMUNDS Redvern Esmond
Newport, 10 January, 1943 WSch (W)

League Club	Source	Date Signed	Seasons Played	Apps	Subs	Gls
Portsmouth	Jnrs	06.60	60	5	-	0
Newport Co	Tr	07.61	61	4	-	0

[EDU] GASPAR Eduardo Cesar Daud
Sao Paulo, Brazil, 15 May, 1978 Brazil 15 (M)

League Club	Source	Date Signed	Seasons Played	Apps	Subs	Gls
Arsenal	Corinthians (Br)	01.01	00-04	41	38	7

EDUSEI Akwasi Fobi
London, 12 September, 1986 (M)

League Club	Source	Date Signed	Seasons Played	Apps	Subs	Gls
Gillingham	Sch	●	02	0	2	0

EDWARDS Alistair Martin
Whyalla, Australia, 21 June, 1968 Australia int (F)

League Club	Source	Date Signed	Seasons Played	Apps	Subs	Gls
Brighton & Hove A	Sydney Olympic (Aus)	11.89	89	1	0	0
Millwall	Selangor (Mal)	12.94	94	3	1	0

EDWARDS Andrew (Andy) David
Epping, 17 September, 1971 (CD)

League Club	Source	Date Signed	Seasons Played	Apps	Subs	Gls
Southend U	YT	12.89	88-94	141	6	5
Birmingham C	Tr	07.95	95-96	37	3	1
Peterborough U	Tr	11.96	96-02	266	0	10
Rushden & Diamonds	Tr	03.03	02-03	40	1	4
Southend U	Tr	07.04	04	9	3	1

EDWARDS Andrew (Andy) John
Wrexham, 28 March, 1965 WYth (W)

League Club	Source	Date Signed	Seasons Played	Apps	Subs	Gls
Wrexham	Jnrs	08.83	82-85	89	25	27

EDWARDS Brian Allan
Portsmouth, 6 October, 1930 (FB)

League Club	Source	Date Signed	Seasons Played	Apps	Subs	Gls
Portsmouth	Jnrs	10.48	51	1	-	0

EDWARDS George **Bryan**
Leeds, 27 October, 1930 (WH)

League Club	Source	Date Signed	Seasons Played	Apps	Subs	Gls
Bolton W	Jnrs	10.47	50-64	482	-	8

EDWARDS Akenhaton **Carlos**
Port of Spain, Trinidad, 24 October, 1978 Trinidad 38 (FB)

League Club	Source	Date Signed	Seasons Played	Apps	Subs	Gls
Wrexham	Defence Force (Tr)	08.00	00-04	144	22	23

League Club	Source	Date Signed	Seasons Played	Career Record Apps	Subs	Gls
EDWARDS Christian Nicholas Howells						
Caerphilly, 23 November, 1975 Wu21-7/WB-2/W-1						(CD)
Swansea C	YT	07.94	94-97	113	2	4
Nottingham F	Tr	03.98	98-01	44	10	3
Bristol C	L	12.98	98	3	0	0
Oxford U	L	02.00	99	5	0	1
Crystal Palace	L	11.01	01	9	0	0
Tranmere Rov	L	09.02	02	12	0	0
Oxford U	L	01.03	02	5	1	0
Bristol Rov	Tr	07.03	03-04	79	5	2
EDWARDS Clifford (Cliff)						
Carmarthen, 4 December, 1928						(G)
Swansea T		10.51	52	1	-	0
EDWARDS Clifford (Cliff) Ivor						
Chase Terrace, 8 March, 1921 Died 1989						(WH)
West Bromwich A	Cannock T	10.36	46-47	40	-	1
Bristol C	Tr	06.48	48-49	33	-	3
EDWARDS Emmanuel **Conroy (Roy)**						
Sheffield, 26 November, 1920						(IF)
Lincoln C		06.47	47-48	6	-	0
EDWARDS Craig Alfred						
London, 8 July, 1982						(M)
Southend U	YT	●	00	0	1	0
EDWARDS David Alexander						
Pontesbury, 3 February, 1986 WYth						(M)
Shrewsbury T	Sch	01.04	02-04	16	12	5
EDWARDS David Arthur						
Llangollen, 14 December, 1925 Died 2001						(CF)
Wrexham (Am)		11.49	49	1	-	1
EDWARDS David James						
Treharris, 10 December, 1934						(WH)
Fulham	Treharris	05.52	56-63	38	-	0
EDWARDS David John						
Bridgnorth, 13 January, 1974						(M)
Walsall	YT	01.92	91-92	16	11	1
EDWARDS David (Dai) Samuel						
Bargoed, 11 September, 1916 Died 1990						(W)
Newport Co	Deri	09.37	37	2	-	0
Ipswich T	Gloucester C	06.39				
Swindon T	Tr	06.46	46	3	-	1
EDWARDS Dean Stephen						
Wolverhampton, 25 February, 1962						(F)
Shrewsbury T	App	02.80	79-81	7	6	1
Wolverhampton W	Telford U	10.85	85-86	28	3	9
Exeter C	Tr	03.87	86-87	51	3	17
Torquay U	Tr	08.88	88-91	98	18	26
Exeter C	Tr	12.91	91	4	0	0
Northampton T	Tr	02.92	91	7	0	0
EDWARDS Dennis						
Slough, 19 January, 1937 EAmat						(F)
Charlton Ath	Wycombe W	02.59	58-64	171	-	61
Portsmouth	Tr	01.65	64-67	69	2	14
Brentford	L	09.67	67	11	0	2
Aldershot	Tr	12.67	67	11	3	1
EDWARDS Donald (Don)						
Wrexham, 2 August, 1930 Died 1995						(G)
Norwich C	Wrexham Victoria	09.47	47	2	-	0
EDWARDS Duncan						(WH)
Dudley, 1 October, 1936 Died 1958 ESch/EYth/Eu23-6/EB/FLge-4/E-18						
Manchester U	Jnrs	10.53	52-57	151	-	20
EDWARDS Edward (Ted)						
Seaham, 13 February, 1936						(FB)
Hartlepools U	Dawdon Jnrs	02.57	57	1	-	0
EDWARDS James **Elfyn**						
Aberystwyth, 4 May, 1960						(CD)
Wrexham	Jnrs	07.78				
Tranmere Rov	Tr	07.79	79-80	62	0	1
EDWARDS George						
Treherbert, 2 December, 1920 WAmat/WLge-3/WWar-3/W-12						(W)
Swansea T (Am)	Jnrs	05.38	38	2	-	0
Birmingham C	Coventry C (Am)	07.44	46-48	84	-	9
Cardiff C	Tr	12.48	48-54	195	-	30
EDWARDS George Robert						
Great Yarmouth, 1 April, 1918 Died 1993						(W)
Norwich C	Yarmouth Caledonians	04.36	35-37	9	-	1
Aston Villa	Tr	06.38	38-50	138	-	34

League Club	Source	Date Signed	Seasons Played	Career Record Apps	Subs	Gls
EDWARDS Jeffrey **Gordon**						
Wrexham, 14 October, 1935 WSch						(CD)
Bolton W	Jnrs	10.52	58	3	-	0
EDWARDS Henry (Harry) Patrick						
Whelley, 13 February, 1932 Died 2003						(IF)
Blackpool	Wigan BC	06.51				
Southport	Tr	08.53	54	1	-	0
EDWARDS Howard						
Tipton, 2 June, 1919 Died 1992						(WH)
Derby Co	Stourbridge	01.47				
Crewe Alex	Tr	06.52	52	5	-	0
EDWARDS Robert **Ian**						
Rossett, 30 January, 1955 Wu21-2/W-4						(F)
West Bromwich A	Rhyl Ath	02.73	74-76	13	3	3
Chester	Tr	11.76	76-79	104	0	36
Wrexham	Tr	11.79	79-81	72	4	20
Crystal Palace	Tr	07.82	82	16	2	4
EDWARDS Jake						
Prestwich, 11 May, 1976						(F)
Wrexham	J Maddison Univ (USA)	08.98	98-99	4	7	2
Yeovil T	Telford U	08.03	03	17	10	6
EDWARDS John						
Wrexham, 23 May, 1940						(G)
Wrexham (Am)	Bradley Sports	10.65	65	1	0	0
EDWARDS John (Jack)						
Salford, 23 February, 1924 Died 1979						(IF)
Nottingham F	Long Eaton U	05.44	46-48	77	-	20
Southampton	Tr	06.49	49-51	82	-	16
Notts Co	Kidderminster Hrs	11.52	52-53	25	-	3
EDWARDS John (Jack) Francis						
Wath-on-Dearne, 27 December, 1921						(WH)
Rotherham U	Manvers Main Colliery	09.44	46-53	296	-	9
EDWARDS William **John (Jack)**						
Risca, 6 July, 1929						(FB)
Crystal Palace	Lovells Ath	09.49	49-58	223	-	0
Rochdale	Tr	06.59	59-60	68	-	1
EDWARDS Keith						
Stockton, 16 July, 1957						(F)
Sheffield U	Middlesbrough (Jnrs)	08.75	75-77	64	6	29
Hull C	Tr	08.78	78-81	130	2	57
Sheffield U	Tr	09.81	81-85	183	8	114
Leeds U	Tr	08.86	86-87	28	10	6
Hull C	Aberdeen	03.88	87-89	55	0	29
Stockport Co	Tr	09.89	89	26	1	10
Huddersfield T	L	03.90	89	6	4	4
Huddersfield T	Tr	08.90	90	10	8	4
Plymouth Arg	L	12.90	90	3	0	1
EDWARDS Keith Barry						
Chester, 10 June, 1944						(CF)
Chester (Am)	Buckley W	03.66	65-66	3	0	0
EDWARDS Malcolm **Keith**						
Briton Ferry, 26 September, 1952 WSch						(CD)
Leeds U	App	10.69	71	0	1	0
EDWARDS Leonard (Len) Owen						
Wrexham, 30 May, 1930						(WH)
Sheffield Wed	Wrexham (Am)	01.51	51	2	-	0
Brighton & Hove A	Tr	03.54	54	6	-	0
Crewe Alex	Tr	12.55	55-56	40	-	0
EDWARDS Leslie (Les) Raymond						
Guildford, 12 April, 1924						(FB)
Bristol Rov	Yeovil T	05.48	50-56	47	-	0
EDWARDS Levi Wilfred						
Manchester, 10 September, 1961						(M)
Crewe Alex	Ashton U	08.85	85	10	3	0
Stockport Co	Altrincham	09.86	86-87	40	9	5
EDWARDS Malcolm						
Wrexham, 25 October, 1939 WSch/Wu23-2						(FB)
Bolton W	Jnrs	11.56	56-60	14	-	1
Chester	Tr	02.61	60-61	43	-	5
Tranmere Rov	Tr	07.62	62-63	34	-	2
Barrow	Tr	07.64	64-68	177	0	9
EDWARDS Matthew David						
Hammersmith, 15 June, 1971						(W)
Tottenham H	YT	07.89				
Reading	L	03.91	90	6	2	0

League Club	Source	Date Signed	Seasons Played	Career Record Apps	Subs	Gls
Peterborough U	Tr	03.92				
Brighton & Hove A	Tr	08.92	92-93	49	11	6

EDWARDS Michael (Mike)
Bebington, 10 September, 1974 (M)

League Club	Source	Date Signed	Seasons Played	Apps	Subs	Gls
Tranmere Rov	YT	07.93	94	2	1	0

EDWARDS Michael (Mike)
Hessle, 25 April, 1980 (CD)

League Club	Source	Date Signed	Seasons Played	Apps	Subs	Gls
Hull C	YT	07.98	97-02	165	13	6
Colchester U	Tr	03.03	02	3	2	0
Grimsby T	Tr	08.03	03	32	1	1
Notts Co	Tr	07.04	04	8	1	0

EDWARDS Nathan Mark
Lincoln, 8 April, 1983 (M)

League Club	Source	Date Signed	Seasons Played	Apps	Subs	Gls
Swindon T	Sch	07.02	01-02	2	8	0

EDWARDS Neil Anthony
Rowley Regis, 14 March, 1966 (F)

League Club	Source	Date Signed	Seasons Played	Apps	Subs	Gls
Wolverhampton W	Oldswinford	08.85	85-87	26	3	7

EDWARDS Neil Robert
Liverpool, 2 July, 1967 (F)

League Club	Source	Date Signed	Seasons Played	Apps	Subs	Gls
Burnley	Liverpool (Am)	08.85	85	0	1	0

EDWARDS Neil Ryan
Aberdare, 5 December, 1970 WSch/WYth/Wu21-1 (G)

League Club	Source	Date Signed	Seasons Played	Apps	Subs	Gls
Leeds U	YT	03.89				
Stockport Co	Tr	09.91	91-95	163	1	0
Rochdale	Tr	11.97	97-04	239	0	0

EDWARDS Nigel Steven
Wrexham, 31 December, 1950 Wu23-3 (FB)

League Club	Source	Date Signed	Seasons Played	Apps	Subs	Gls
Chester	Blackburn Rov (Am)	09.68	68-77	281	10	15
Aldershot	Tr	07.78	78-81	137	0	6
Chester	Tr	06.82	82	8	0	1

EDWARDS Patrick Kenneth
Wolverhampton, 9 December, 1939 (W)

League Club	Source	Date Signed	Seasons Played	Apps	Subs	Gls
Walsall	Jnrs	10.57	58	1	-	0

EDWARDS Paul
Liverpool, 22 February, 1965 (G)

League Club	Source	Date Signed	Seasons Played	Apps	Subs	Gls
Crewe Alex	Leek T	08.88	88-91	29	0	0
Shrewsbury T	Tr	08.92	92-00	312	0	0

EDWARDS Paul
Manchester, 1 January, 1980 (W)

League Club	Source	Date Signed	Seasons Played	Apps	Subs	Gls
Doncaster Rov	Ashton U	02.98	97	5	4	0
Swindon T	Altrincham	08.01	01	14	6	0
Wrexham	Tr	07.02	02-03	73	6	4
Blackpool	Tr	07.04	04	22	6	3

EDWARDS Paul
Derby, 10 November, 1982 (F)

League Club	Source	Date Signed	Seasons Played	Apps	Subs	Gls
Crewe Alex	YT	02.01	02-03	2	10	0

EDWARDS Paul Francis
Crompton, 7 October, 1947 Eu23-3/FLge-1 (CD)

League Club	Source	Date Signed	Seasons Played	Apps	Subs	Gls
Manchester U	Jnrs	02.65	69-72	52	2	0
Oldham Ath	Tr	09.72	72-77	108	4	7
Stockport Co	L	01.77	76	2	0	0
Stockport Co	Tr	08.78	78-79	64	3	2

EDWARDS Paul Ronald
Birkenhead, 25 December, 1963 (FB)

League Club	Source	Date Signed	Seasons Played	Apps	Subs	Gls
Crewe Alex	Altrincham	01.88	87-89	82	4	6
Coventry C	Tr	03.90	89-91	32	4	0
Wolverhampton W	Tr	08.92	92-93	43	3	0
West Bromwich A	Tr	01.94	93-95	48	3	0
Bury	L	02.96	95	4	0	0

EDWARDS Reginald (Reg) Charles
Newton-le-Willows, 24 July, 1919 Died 2002 (W)

League Club	Source	Date Signed	Seasons Played	Apps	Subs	Gls
Luton T	Alloa Ath	11.45				
Accrington St	Tr	08.46	46-48	66	-	10

EDWARDS Reginald (Reg) Ernest
Rugeley, 28 January, 1953 (G)

League Club	Source	Date Signed	Seasons Played	Apps	Subs	Gls
Port Vale	Nuneaton Borough	08.72	72-74	8	0	0

EDWARDS Richard (Richie)
Hartlepool, 9 September, 1964 (G)

League Club	Source	Date Signed	Seasons Played	Apps	Subs	Gls
Hartlepool U		08.86	86	1	0	0

EDWARDS Richard (Dick) Leonard
Kingsbury, 5 November, 1943 (FB)

League Club	Source	Date Signed	Seasons Played	Apps	Subs	Gls
Luton T	Admult	06.64	64-65	15	2	1

EDWARDS Richard (Dick) Thomas
Kirkby-in-Ashfield, 20 November, 1942 (CD)

League Club	Source	Date Signed	Seasons Played	Apps	Subs	Gls
Notts Co	East Kirkby Welfare	10.59	59-66	221	0	20
Mansfield T	Tr	03.67	66-67	45	0	1
Aston Villa	Tr	03.68	67-69	68	0	2
Torquay U	Tr	06.70	70-72	99	6	5
Mansfield T	Tr	07.73	73	31	2	1

EDWARDS Robert (Rob)
Manchester, 23 February, 1970 (FB)

League Club	Source	Date Signed	Seasons Played	Apps	Subs	Gls
Crewe Alex	YT	07.88	87-95	110	45	44
Huddersfield T	Tr	03.96	95-99	109	29	14
Chesterfield	Tr	09.00	00-02	89	5	7
Huddersfield T	Tr	08.03	03-04	32	9	3

EDWARDS Robert (Bob) Henry
Guildford, 22 May, 1931 (IF)

League Club	Source	Date Signed	Seasons Played	Apps	Subs	Gls
Chelsea	Woking	11.51	52-54	13	-	2
Swindon T	Tr	07.55	55-59	173	-	65
Norwich C	Tr	12.59	59	1	-	0
Northampton T	Tr	03.61	60-61	23	-	10

EDWARDS Robert (Rob) Owen
Telford, 25 December, 1982 WYth/W-7 (FB)

League Club	Source	Date Signed	Seasons Played	Apps	Subs	Gls
Aston Villa	YT	01.00	02	7	1	0
Crystal Palace	L	11.03	03	6	1	1
Derby Co	L	01.04	03	10	1	1
Wolverhampton W	Tr	07.04	04	15	2	0

EDWARDS Robert (Rob) William
Kendal, 1 July, 1973 WYth/Wu21-17/WB-2/W-4 (FB)

League Club	Source	Date Signed	Seasons Played	Apps	Subs	Gls
Carlisle U	YT	04.90	89-90	48	0	5
Bristol C	Tr	03.91	91-98	188	28	5
Preston NE	Tr	08.99	99-03	156	13	4
Blackpool	Tr	08.04	04	24	2	1

EDWARDS Ronald (Ron)
Liverpool, 11 July, 1927 Died 2001 (W)

League Club	Source	Date Signed	Seasons Played	Apps	Subs	Gls
Chesterfield	South Liverpool	07.53	53	13	-	2

EDWARDS Russell James
Beckenham, 21 December, 1973 (CD)

League Club	Source	Date Signed	Seasons Played	Apps	Subs	Gls
Crystal Palace	Jnrs	06.92				
Barnet	Tr	03.94	93	5	0	1

EDWARDS Stanley (Stan)
West Bromwich, 11 December, 1942 (W)

League Club	Source	Date Signed	Seasons Played	Apps	Subs	Gls
Everton	Jnrs	12.59				
Port Vale	Tr	05.61	61-62	49	-	9

EDWARDS Stanley (Stan) Llewellyn
Dawdon, 17 October, 1926 Died 1989 (CF)

League Club	Source	Date Signed	Seasons Played	Apps	Subs	Gls
Chelsea	Horden CW	10.49				
Colchester U	Tr	06.52	52	16	-	5
Leyton Orient	Tr	06.53	53	2	-	1

EDWARDS Stephen (Steve) Gerald
Birkenhead, 11 January, 1958 (FB)

League Club	Source	Date Signed	Seasons Played	Apps	Subs	Gls
Oldham Ath	App	01.76	77-82	77	3	0
Crewe Alex	Tr	02.83	82-83	57	1	1
Rochdale	Tr	07.84	84	4	0	0
Tranmere Rov	Tr	10.84	84-86	70	0	6

EDWARDS Walter **Thomas (Tommy)**
Llanelli, 11 March, 1923 Died 2000 (W)

League Club	Source	Date Signed	Seasons Played	Apps	Subs	Gls
Fulham	Workington	08.46	47	2	-	0
Southend U	Tr	03.48	47-48	12	-	1
Leicester C	Tr	12.48	48	3	-	1
Walsall	Bath C	05.52	52	12	-	0

EDWARDS Leonard **Trevor**
Rhondda, 24 January, 1937 Wu23-2/W-2 (FB)

League Club	Source	Date Signed	Seasons Played	Apps	Subs	Gls
Charlton Ath	Jnrs	05.55	56-59	64	-	0
Cardiff C	Tr	06.60	60-63	73	-	3

EDWARDS Walter
Mansfield, 26 June, 1924 (W)

League Club	Source	Date Signed	Seasons Played	Apps	Subs	Gls
Mansfield T	Woodhouse	11.47	47-48	25	-	5
Leeds U	Tr	03.49	48	2	-	0

EDWARDS William (Billy)
Paddington, 8 January, 1952 (CD)

League Club	Source	Date Signed	Seasons Played	Apps	Subs	Gls
Wimbledon	Walton & Hersham	08.74	77	21	0	2

EDWARDS William Inman
Bowburn, 10 December, 1933 (CF)

League Club	Source	Date Signed	Seasons Played	Apps	Subs	Gls
Middlesbrough	Bowburn	03.52	52-54	16	-	4

EDWARDSON Barry John
Hindley, 4 November, 1972 (M)

League Club	Source	Date Signed	Seasons Played	Apps	Subs	Gls
Wigan Ath	YT	07.91	91	0	1	0

EDWARDSON John Philemon
Manchester, 9 March, 1944 (W)

League Club	Source	Date Signed	Seasons Played	Apps	Subs	Gls
Crystal Palace	Bethesda	11.66				
Crewe Alex	L	01.68	67	1	0	0

EDWORTHY Marc
Barnstaple, 24 December, 1972 (FB)

League Club	Source	Date Signed	Seasons Played	Apps	Subs	Gls
Plymouth Arg	YT	03.91	91-94	52	17	1
Crystal Palace	Tr	06.95	95-98	120	6	0
Coventry C	Tr	08.98	98-01	62	14	1
Wolverhampton W	Tr	08.02	02	18	4	0
Norwich C	Tr	08.03	03-04	69	2	0

EELES Anthony (Tony) George
Chatham, 15 November, 1970 (M)

League Club	Source	Date Signed	Seasons Played	Apps	Subs	Gls
Gillingham	YT	07.89	88-92	54	19	5

EGAN Christopher (Chris) Anthony
Limerick, 6 August, 1953 (W)

League Club	Source	Date Signed	Seasons Played	Apps	Subs	Gls
Derby Co	Sligo Rov	10.73				
Newport Co	Tr	08.76	76	5	2	0

EGAN John
Kilsyth, 19 August, 1937 (W)

League Club	Source	Date Signed	Seasons Played	Apps	Subs	Gls
Halifax T	Berwick Rgrs	10.59	59	5	-	0
Accrington St	Tr	08.60	60	1	-	0

EGDELL Ernest (Ernie)
Newcastle, 29 May, 1922 Died 1976 (FB)

League Club	Source	Date Signed	Seasons Played	Apps	Subs	Gls
Darlington (Am)	Consett	08.46	46	1	-	0

EGERTON Frank
Atherton, 5 April, 1926 Died 2002 (FB)

League Club	Source	Date Signed	Seasons Played	Apps	Subs	Gls
Blackburn Rov	Atherton Collieries	04.44				
Accrington St	Tr	06.47	47-48	8	-	0

EGGLESTON Thomas (Tommy)
Consett, 21 February, 1920 Died 2004 (FB)

League Club	Source	Date Signed	Seasons Played	Apps	Subs	Gls
Derby Co	Medomsley Jnrs	02.37				
Leicester C	Tr	08.46	46-47	34	-	2
Watford	Tr	02.48	47-52	177	-	6

EGGLESTONE Patrick (Pat)
Penrith, 17 March, 1927 (G)

League Club	Source	Date Signed	Seasons Played	Apps	Subs	Gls
Bradford C	Portsmouth (Am)	05.48	48	2	-	0
Halifax T	Tr	09.49	49	20	-	0
Shrewsbury T	Tr	08.50	50-52	109	-	0
Wrexham	Tr	02.53	52-55	84	-	0

EGLINGTON Thomas (Tommy) Joseph
Dublin, 15 January, 1923 Died 2004 LoI-4/IR-24/I-6 (W)

League Club	Source	Date Signed	Seasons Played	Apps	Subs	Gls
Everton	Shamrock Rov	07.46	46-56	394	-	76
Tranmere Rov	Tr	06.57	57-60	171	-	36

EHIOGU Ugochuku (Ugo)
Hackney, 3 November, 1972 Eu21-15/EB-1/E-4 (CD)

League Club	Source	Date Signed	Seasons Played	Apps	Subs	Gls
West Bromwich A	YT	07.89	90	0	2	0
Aston Villa	Tr	07.91	91-00	223	14	12
Middlesbrough	Tr	10.00	00-04	106	2	7

EINARSSON Gunnar
Reykjavik, Iceland, 7 July, 1976 IcYth/Icu21/Ic-1 (FB)

League Club	Source	Date Signed	Seasons Played	Apps	Subs	Gls
Brentford (L)	Roda JC Kerk (Holl)	01.00	99	1	2	0

EINARSSON Gylfi
Iceland, 27 October, 1978 IcYth/Ic-15 (M)

League Club	Source	Date Signed	Seasons Played	Apps	Subs	Gls
Leeds U	Lillestrom (Nor)	12.04	04	6	2	1

EISENTRAGER Alois (Alec) Bernhard
Hamburg, Germany, 20 July, 1927 (W)

League Club	Source	Date Signed	Seasons Played	Apps	Subs	Gls
Bristol C	Trowbridge T	01.50	49-57	228	-	47

EKELUND Ronald (Ronnie) Michael
Glostrup, Denmark, 21 August, 1972 DeYth/Deu21 (M)

League Club	Source	Date Signed	Seasons Played	Apps	Subs	Gls
Southampton (L)	Barcelona (Sp)	09.94	94	15	2	5
Manchester C (L)	Barcelona (Sp)	12.95	95	2	2	0
Walsall	Toulouse (Fr)	12.00	00	2	7	1

EKNER Daniel (Dan)
Sweden, 5 February, 1927 Died 1975 (CF)

League Club	Source	Date Signed	Seasons Played	Apps	Subs	Gls
Portsmouth (Am)	(Sweden)	11.49	49	5	-	0

EKOKU Efangwu (Efan) Goziem
Manchester, 8 June, 1967 Nigeria 5 (F)

League Club	Source	Date Signed	Seasons Played	Apps	Subs	Gls
Bournemouth	Sutton U	05.90	90-92	43	19	10
Norwich C	Tr	03.93	92-94	26	11	15
Wimbledon	Tr	10.94	94-98	102	21	37
Sheffield Wed	Grasshoppers (Swi)	10.00	00-01	52	7	14

EL-ABD Adam Mohamad
Brighton, 11 September, 1984 (FB)

League Club	Source	Date Signed	Seasons Played	Apps	Subs	Gls
Brighton & Hove A	Sch	12.03	03-04	20	7	0

ELAD Diodene **Efon**
Hillingdon, 5 September, 1970 (M)

League Club	Source	Date Signed	Seasons Played	Apps	Subs	Gls
Northampton T	Fortuna Koln (Ger)	01.94	93	8	2	0
Cambridge U	Tr	08.94	94	2	1	0
Mansfield T	Tr	02.95	94	0	2	0

ELAM Lee Patrick George
Bradford, 24 September, 1976 ESemiPro-4 (W)

League Club	Source	Date Signed	Seasons Played	Apps	Subs	Gls
Yeovil T	Halifax T	10.03	03	6	6	1

ELDER Alexander (Alex) Russell
Lisburn, 25 April, 1941 NISch/NIu23-1/NI-40 (FB)

League Club	Source	Date Signed	Seasons Played	Apps	Subs	Gls
Burnley	Glentoran	01.59	59-66	271	0	15
Stoke C	Tr	08.67	67-72	80	3	1

ELDER Alexander (Alex) Yeoman Pirrie
Perth, 11 September, 1923 (IF)

League Club	Source	Date Signed	Seasons Played	Apps	Subs	Gls
Hartlepools U	Dundee U	08.51	51-52	65	-	20

ELDER James (Jimmy)
Scone, 5 March, 1928 (WH)

League Club	Source	Date Signed	Seasons Played	Apps	Subs	Gls
Portsmouth	Jeanfield Swifts	09.45	49	1	-	0
Colchester U	Tr	07.50	50-54	199	-	15

ELDERSHAW Simon
Stoke-on-Trent, 2 December, 1983 (F)

League Club	Source	Date Signed	Seasons Played	Apps	Subs	Gls
Port Vale	Sch	07.03	02-04	5	10	1

ELDING Anthony Lee
Boston, 16 April, 1982 (F)

League Club	Source	Date Signed	Seasons Played	Apps	Subs	Gls
Boston U	Jnrs	07.01	02	3	5	0

ELEY Kevin
Mexborough, 4 March, 1968 (W)

League Club	Source	Date Signed	Seasons Played	Apps	Subs	Gls
Rotherham U	App	03.86	83-86	3	10	0
Chesterfield	Tr	08.87	87-89	72	9	2

ELGIN Robert Brown
Edinburgh, 23 June, 1949 (M)

League Club	Source	Date Signed	Seasons Played	Apps	Subs	Gls
Stockport Co	Heart of Midlothian	07.69	69-70	30	5	3

ELI Roger
Bradford, 11 September, 1965 (W)

League Club	Source	Date Signed	Seasons Played	Apps	Subs	Gls
Leeds U	App	09.83	84-85	1	1	0
Wolverhampton W	Tr	01.86	85-86	16	2	0
Crewe Alex	Cambridge U (N/C)	09.87	87	20	7	1
York C	Pontefract Colliery	11.88	88	3	1	1
Bury	Tr	12.88	88	0	2	0
Burnley	Northwich Vic	07.89	89-92	70	29	20
Scunthorpe U	(Hong Kong)	02.95	94	0	2	0

EL KARKOURI Talal
Casablanca, Morocco, 8 July, 1976 Morocco int (CD)

League Club	Source	Date Signed	Seasons Played	Apps	Subs	Gls
Sunderland (L)	Paris St Germain (Fr)	01.03	02	8	0	0
Charlton Ath	Paris St Germain (Fr)	07.04	04	28	4	5

EL KHALEJ Tahar
Marrakesh, Morocco, 16 June, 1968 Morocco 69 (CD)

League Club	Source	Date Signed	Seasons Played	Apps	Subs	Gls
Southampton	Benfica (Por)	03.00	99-02	48	10	3
Charlton Ath	Tr	01.03	02	2	1	0

EL KHOLTI Abdelhalim (Abdou)
Annemasse, France, 17 October, 1980 (M)

League Club	Source	Date Signed	Seasons Played	Apps	Subs	Gls
Yeovil T	Raja Casablanca (Mor)	10.02	03	19	4	1
Cambridge U	Tr	07.04	04	13	2	0

ELKINS Gary
Wallingford, 4 May, 1966 EYth (FB)

League Club	Source	Date Signed	Seasons Played	Apps	Subs	Gls
Fulham	App	12.83	84-89	100	4	2
Exeter C	L	12.89	89	5	0	0
Wimbledon	Tr	08.90	90-95	100	10	3
Swindon T	Tr	09.96	96	19	4	1

ELLAM Roy
Hemsworth, 13 January, 1943 (CD)

League Club	Source	Date Signed	Seasons Played	Apps	Subs	Gls
Bradford C	Robin Hood Ath	05.61	61-65	149	0	12
Huddersfield T	Tr	01.66	66-71	206	0	8
Leeds U	Tr	08.72	72-73	9	2	0
Huddersfield T	Tr	07.74	74	18	0	2

ELLAWAY William (Bill) John
Crediton, 12 October, 1932 (IF)

League Club	Source	Date Signed	Seasons Played	Apps	Subs	Gls
Exeter C	Barnstaple T	11.54	53-55	31	-	9
Bournemouth	Tr	06.56	56-57	4	-	0

ELLEGAARD Kevin Stuhr
Copenhagen, Denmark, 23 May, 1983 DeYth/Deu21-9 (G)

League Club	Source	Date Signed	Seasons Played	Apps	Subs	Gls
Manchester C	Farum (Den)	11.01	03	2	2	0
Blackpool	L	12.04	04	2	0	0

League Club	Source	Date Signed	Seasons Played	Career Record Apps	Subs	Gls
ELLENDER Paul						
Scunthorpe, 21 October, 1974 ESemiPro-1						(CD)
Scunthorpe U	YT	04.93				
Boston U	Scarborough	08.01	02-04	106	1	6
ELLERINGTON William (Bill)						
Southampton, 30 June, 1923 ESch/FLge-1/EB/E-2						(FB)
Southampton	Fatfield Colliery	09.40	46-55	227	-	10
ELLINGTON Lee Simon						
Bradford, 3 July, 1980						(F)
Hull C	YT	07.98	96-98	7	8	2
Exeter C	Tr	03.00	99	0	1	0
ELLINGTON Nathan Levi Fontaine						
Bradford, 2 July, 1981						(F)
Bristol Rov	Walton & Hersham	02.99	98-01	76	40	35
Wigan Ath	Tr	03.02	01-04	130	4	59
ELLIOT Robert (Rob)						
Chatham, 30 April, 1986						(G)
Charlton Ath	Sch	01.05				
Notts Co	L	01.05	04	3	1	0
ELLIOTT Andrew (Andy)						
Ashton-under-Lyne, 21 November, 1963						(M)
Manchester C	App	11.81	81	1	0	0
Chester C	Sligo Rov	09.83	83	24	8	3
ELLIOTT Andrew (Andy)						
Newcastle, 2 May, 1974						(M)
Hartlepool U	Spennymoor U	02.97	96-97	2	6	0
ELLIOTT Anthony (Tony) Robert						
Nuneaton, 30 November, 1969 ESch/EYth						(G)
Birmingham C	App	12.86				
Hereford U	Tr	12.88	88-91	75	0	0
Huddersfield T	Tr	07.92	92	15	0	0
Carlisle U	Tr	06.93	93-95	21	1	0
Cardiff C	Tr	07.96	96-97	38	1	0
Scarborough	Tr	02.98	97-98	35	0	0
ELLIOTT Bernard (Bryn) Henry						
Beeston, 3 May, 1925						(WH)
Nottingham F	Beeston BC	10.42	47-48	10	-	0
Southampton	Boston U	10.49	49-57	235	-	2
ELLIOTT Charles (Charlie) Standish						
Bolsover, 24 April, 1912 Died 2004						(FB)
Chesterfield	Bolsover Colliery	11.30				
Coventry C	Tr	08.31	31-47	95	-	2
ELLIOTT David (Dave)						
Tantobie, 10 February, 1945						(M)
Sunderland	App	02.62	63-66	30	1	1
Newcastle U	Tr	12.66	66-70	78	2	4
Southend U	Tr	02.71	70-74	174	4	9
Newport Co	Tr	07.75	75	21	0	0
Newport Co	Bangor C	10.78	78	0	2	0
ELLIOTT Eamonn Gerard						
Belfast, 27 July, 1971						(M)
Carlisle U	YT	07.90	90	3	1	0
ELLIOTT Edward (Ted)						
Carlisle, 24 May, 1919 Died 1984						(G)
Carlisle U		12.37	37-38	11	-	0
Wolverhampton W	Tr	02.39	46-47	7	-	0
Chester	Tr	10.48	48-50	59	-	0
Halifax T	Tr	11.50	50-51	33	-	0
ELLIOTT Frederick (Frank) Francis George						
Lambeth, 23 July, 1929						(G)
Swansea T	Merthyr Tydfil	09.49				
Stoke C	Tr	12.52	52-53	22	-	0
Fulham	Tr	03.54	53-55	25	-	0
Mansfield T	Tr	07.56	56-57	63	-	0
ELLIOTT Harvey						
Middleton, 21 January, 1922 Died 1996						(IF)
Hull C		12.46	46	4	-	0
ELLIOTT Ian						
Barrow, 16 December, 1953						(G)
Barrow	Jnrs	•	69	1	0	0
ELLIOTT John						
Penrith, 6 May, 1938						(IF)
Carlisle U	Jnrs	08.55	55-57	2	-	1
ELLIOTT John Walter						
Warkworth, 23 December, 1946						(W)
Notts Co	Ashington	08.67	67-68	61	3	7
ELLIOTT Kevan						
Chilton, 5 September, 1958						(F)
Hartlepool	App	09.76	75-76	24	3	1
ELLIOTT Lee						
Ormskirk, 5 May, 1970						(F)
Crewe Alex	Everton (YT)	06.88	88	1	0	0
ELLIOTT Richard **Mark**						
Rhondda, 20 March, 1959						(W)
Brighton & Hove A	Merthyr Tydfil	02.77	76	3	0	0
Cardiff C	Tr	09.79	79	6	1	0
Bournemouth	L	01.80	79	4	0	0
Wimbledon	Ton Pentre	02.82	81	7	4	1
ELLIOTT Marvin Conrad						
Wandsworth, 15 September, 1984						(M)
Millwall	YT	02.02	02-04	46	17	1
ELLIOTT Matthew (Matt) Stephen						
Wandsworth, 1 November, 1968 S-18						(CD)
Charlton Ath	Epsom & Ewell	05.88				
Torquay U	Tr	03.89	88-91	123	1	15
Scunthorpe U	Tr	03.92	91-93	61	0	8
Oxford U	Tr	11.93	93-96	148	0	21
Leicester C	Tr	01.97	96-04	239	6	27
Ipswich T	L	03.04	03	10	0	0
ELLIOTT Paul Marcellus						
Lewisham, 18 March, 1964 EYth/Eu21-3/EB						(CD)
Charlton Ath	App	03.81	81-82	61	2	1
Luton T	Tr	03.83	82-85	63	3	4
Aston Villa	Tr	12.85	85-86	56	1	7
Chelsea	Glasgow Celtic	07.91	91-92	42	0	3
ELLIOTT Raymond (Ray) Charles						
Eastleigh, 11 June, 1947						(CF)
Charlton Ath	App	06.65				
Exeter C	Tr	03.66	65-66	28	0	3
ELLIOTT Raymond (Ray) John						
Rhondda, 23 March, 1929						(CF)
Millwall	Woking	11.46	47-48	2	-	0
ELLIOTT Robert (Robbie) James						
Gosforth, 25 December, 1973 EYth/Eu21-2						(FB)
Newcastle U	YT	04.91	90-96	71	8	9
Bolton W	Tr	07.97	97-00	71	15	5
Newcastle U	Tr	07.01	01-04	41	5	2
ELLIOTT Shaun						
Haydon Bridge, 26 January, 1957 EB						(CD)
Sunderland	App	01.75	76-85	316	5	12
Norwich C	Tr	08.86	86-87	29	2	2
Blackpool	Tr	08.88	88-89	66	1	0
ELLIOTT Stephen (Steve) Blair						
Haltwhistle, 15 September, 1958						(F)
Nottingham F	App	09.76	78	4	0	0
Preston NE	Tr	03.79	78-83	202	6	70
Luton T	Tr	07.84	84	12	0	3
Walsall	Tr	12.84	84-85	68	1	21
Bolton W	Tr	07.86	86-88	57	3	10
Bury	Tr	09.88	88	31	0	11
Rochdale	Tr	10.89	89-90	46	6	9
ELLIOTT Stephen William						
Dublin, 6 January, 1984 IRYth/IRu21-10/IR-3						(F)
Manchester C	YT	01.01	03	0	2	0
Sunderland	Tr	08.04	04	29	13	15
ELLIOTT Steven (Steve) William						
Swadlincote, 29 October, 1978 Eu21-2						(CD)
Derby Co	YT	03.97	97-03	58	15	1
Blackpool	Tr	11.03	03	28	0	0
Bristol Rov	Tr	07.04	04	40	1	2
ELLIOTT Stuart						
Belfast, 23 July, 1978 NIu21-3/NIB/NI-27						(M)
Hull C	Motherwell	07.02	02-04	107	7	53
ELLIOTT Stuart Thomas						
Hendon, 27 August, 1977						(CD)
Newcastle U	YT	08.95				
Hull C	L	02.97	96	3	0	0
Swindon T	L	02.98	97	1	1	0
Gillingham	L	10.98	98	4	1	0

League Club	Source	Date Signed	Seasons Played	Apps	Subs	Gls
Hartlepool U	L	01.99	98	5	0	0
Wrexham	L	03.99	98	8	1	0
Bournemouth	L	12.99	99	6	2	0
Stockport Co	L	02.00	99	4	1	0
Darlington	Tr	07.00	00	20	4	0
Plymouth Arg	Tr	03.01	00	11	1	0
Carlisle U	Tr	08.01	01	6	0	0
Exeter C	Tr	02.02	01	0	1	0

ELLIOTT Wade Patrick
Eastleigh, 14 December, 1978 ESch (M)

League Club	Source	Date Signed	Seasons Played	Apps	Subs	Gls
Bournemouth	Bashley	02.00	99-04	178	42	31

ELLIOTT William (Billy)
Poole, 23 October, 1961 (M)

League Club	Source	Date Signed	Seasons Played	Apps	Subs	Gls
Plymouth Arg	App	03.79				
Bournemouth	Tr	05.80	80	6	5	1

ELLIOTT William (Billy) Bethwaite
Harrington, 6 August, 1919 Died 1966 EWar-2 (W)

League Club	Source	Date Signed	Seasons Played	Apps	Subs	Gls
Carlisle U	Jnrs	11.36				
Wolverhampton W	Dudley T	07.37				
Bournemouth	Tr	05.38	38	10	-	1
West Bromwich A	Tr	12.38	38-50	170	-	39

ELLIOTT William (Billy) Henry
Bradford, 20 March, 1925 FLge-4/E-5 (W)

League Club	Source	Date Signed	Seasons Played	Apps	Subs	Gls
Bradford PA	Jnrs	04.42	46-50	176	-	21
Burnley	Tr	09.51	51-52	74	-	14
Sunderland	Tr	06.53	53-58	193	-	23

ELLIS Alan
Alfreton, 17 November, 1951 (M)

League Club	Source	Date Signed	Seasons Played	Apps	Subs	Gls
Charlton Ath	App	11.69	70-72	9	5	0

ELLIS Anthony (Tony) Joseph
Salford, 20 October, 1964 (F)

League Club	Source	Date Signed	Seasons Played	Apps	Subs	Gls
Oldham Ath	Horwich RMI	08.86	86-87	5	3	0
Preston NE	Tr	10.87	87-89	80	6	26
Stoke C	Tr	12.89	89-91	66	11	19
Preston NE	Tr	08.92	92-93	70	2	48
Blackpool	Tr	07.94	94-97	140	6	54
Bury	Tr	12.97	97-98	24	14	8
Stockport Co	Tr	02.99	98-99	17	3	6
Rochdale	Tr	11.99	99-00	55	4	17
Burnley	Tr	07.01	01	0	11	1

ELLIS Clinton (Clint)
Ealing, 7 July, 1977 ESch/EYth (F)

League Club	Source	Date Signed	Seasons Played	Apps	Subs	Gls
Bristol Rov	Willesden Constantine	03.00	00	2	13	1

ELLIS David (Dave)
(W)

League Club	Source	Date Signed	Seasons Played	Apps	Subs	Gls
Bury	Pollok Jnrs	04.47				
Halifax T	Tr	01.48	47	2	-	0
Barrow	Tr	10.48	48	1	-	0

ELLIS Glenn Douglas
Dagenham, 31 October, 1957 ESch (G)

League Club	Source	Date Signed	Seasons Played	Apps	Subs	Gls
Ipswich T	App	10.75				
Colchester U	L	12.76	76	2	0	0

ELLIS Keith Duncan
Sheffield, 6 November, 1935 (CF)

League Club	Source	Date Signed	Seasons Played	Apps	Subs	Gls
Sheffield Wed	Jnrs	04.55	54-63	102	-	52
Scunthorpe U	Tr	03.64	63	10	-	5
Cardiff C	Tr	09.64	64	22	-	9
Lincoln C	Tr	06.65	65	7	0	0

ELLIS Kenneth (Ken)
Buckley, 22 January, 1928 Died 2003 (W)

League Club	Source	Date Signed	Seasons Played	Apps	Subs	Gls
Chester (Am)	Jnrs	05.46	46	1	-	0
Wrexham (Am)		05.49	49	5	-	0

ELLIS Kenneth (Ken)
Sunderland, 29 May, 1948 Died 1992 (F)

League Club	Source	Date Signed	Seasons Played	Apps	Subs	Gls
Hartlepool	Scarborough	07.71	71	32	2	4
Darlington	Verna (Bel)	07.79	79	21	0	0

ELLIS Kevin Edward
Tiptree, 11 May, 1977 (FB)

League Club	Source	Date Signed	Seasons Played	Apps	Subs	Gls
Ipswich T	YT	08.95	94	1	0	0

ELLIS Mark Edward
Bradford, 6 January, 1962 (W)

League Club	Source	Date Signed	Seasons Played	Apps	Subs	Gls
Bradford C	Trinity Ath	08.80	80-89	190	28	30
Halifax T	Tr	10.90	90-91	33	4	4

ELLIS Neil James
Bebington, 30 April, 1969 (W)

League Club	Source	Date Signed	Seasons Played	Apps	Subs	Gls
Chester C	Bangor C	06.90	90	13	8	1
Maidstone U	Tr	07.91	91	22	6	0

ELLIS Peter James
Portsmouth, 20 March, 1956 (FB)

League Club	Source	Date Signed	Seasons Played	Apps	Subs	Gls
Portsmouth	App	03.74	73-83	226	21	1
Southend U	Tr	09.84	84	12	0	1

ELLIS Samuel (Sam)
Ashton-under-Lyne, 12 September, 1946 Eu23-3 (CD)

League Club	Source	Date Signed	Seasons Played	Apps	Subs	Gls
Sheffield Wed	Smiths (Manchester)	09.64	65-70	155	2	1
Mansfield T	Tr	01.72	71-72	64	0	7
Lincoln C	Tr	05.73	73-76	173	0	33
Watford	Tr	08.77	77-78	30	4	4

ELLIS Sydney (Syd) Carey
Charlton, 16 August, 1931 Died 2001 Eu23-1 (FB)

League Club	Source	Date Signed	Seasons Played	Apps	Subs	Gls
Charlton Ath	Crystal Palace (Am)	05.49	53-57	48	-	0
Brighton & Hove A	Tr	11.57	57-58	42	-	0

ELLISON Kevin
Liverpool, 23 February, 1979 (M)

League Club	Source	Date Signed	Seasons Played	Apps	Subs	Gls
Leicester C	Altrincham	02.01	00	0	1	0
Stockport Co	Tr	11.01	01-03	33	15	2
Lincoln C	L	03.04	03	11	0	0
Chester C	Tr	08.04	04	24	0	9
Hull C	Tr	01.05	04	11	5	1

ELLISON Anthony Lee
Bishop Auckland, 13 January, 1973 (F)

League Club	Source	Date Signed	Seasons Played	Apps	Subs	Gls
Darlington	YT	11.90	90-93	54	18	17
Hartlepool U	L	03.93	92	3	1	1
Leicester C	Tr	08.94				
Crewe Alex	Tr	08.95	95-96	3	1	2
Hereford U	Halifax T	10.96	96	0	1	0
Darlington	Bishop Auckland	03.98	97-98	7	21	3

ELLISON Norman
Bebington, 2 November, 1929 Died 1999 (W)

League Club	Source	Date Signed	Seasons Played	Apps	Subs	Gls
Tranmere Rov		10.49	49-50	2	-	0

ELLISON Raymond (Ray)
Newcastle, 31 December, 1950 (FB)

League Club	Source	Date Signed	Seasons Played	Apps	Subs	Gls
Newcastle U	App	10.68	71	5	0	0
Sunderland	Tr	03.73	72	2	0	0
Torquay U	Tr	07.74	74	11	5	0
Workington	Tr	07.75	75-76	57	0	3

ELLISON William Roy
Newbiggin, 5 July, 1948 (M)

League Club	Source	Date Signed	Seasons Played	Apps	Subs	Gls
Newcastle U	App	06.66				
Barrow	Tr	02.68	67-70	76	10	7
Hartlepool	L	10.70	70	5	0	0

ELLISON Samuel Walter
Leadgate, 27 August, 1923 Died 1994 (W)

League Club	Source	Date Signed	Seasons Played	Apps	Subs	Gls
Sunderland	Middlesbrough Crus'rs	10.45	46	3	-	0
Reading	Consett	06.49	49	4	-	0

ELLSON Peter Edward
Audlem, 21 August, 1925 (G)

League Club	Source	Date Signed	Seasons Played	Apps	Subs	Gls
Crewe Alex	Crewe RP	05.49	48-55	219	-	0

ELMES Timothy (Tim)
Croydon, 28 September, 1962 (M)

League Club	Source	Date Signed	Seasons Played	Apps	Subs	Gls
Chelsea	App	07.80	80	2	2	0

ELMS James (Jimmy) Brian
Manchester, 16 September, 1940 EYth (W)

League Club	Source	Date Signed	Seasons Played	Apps	Subs	Gls
Manchester U	Jnrs	04.58				
Crewe Alex	Tr	10.60	60	1	-	0

ELOKOBI George Nganyuo
Cameroon, 31 January, 1986 (FB)

League Club	Source	Date Signed	Seasons Played	Apps	Subs	Gls
Colchester U	Dulwich Hamlet	07.04				
Chester C	L	01.05	04	4	1	0

ELSBY Ian Christopher
Newcastle-under-Lyme, 13 September, 1960 (M)

League Club	Source	Date Signed	Seasons Played	Apps	Subs	Gls
Port Vale	Jnrs	06.78	78-80	32	11	1

ELSBY James (Jim)
Newcastle-under-Lyme, 1 August, 1928 Died 1987 (FB)

League Club	Source	Date Signed	Seasons Played	Apps	Subs	Gls
Port Vale		05.47	48-53	12	-	0

ELSE Frederick (Fred)
Golborne, 31 March, 1933 EB (G)

League Club	Source	Date Signed	Seasons Played	Apps	Subs	Gls
Preston NE	Wigan Ath	08.53	53-60	215	-	0
Blackburn Rov	Tr	08.61	61-65	187	0	0
Barrow	Tr	07.66	66-69	148	0	0

ELSEY Karl William
Swansea, 20 November, 1958 (M)

League Club	Source	Date Signed	Seasons Played	Apps	Subs	Gls
Queens Park Rgrs	Pembroke Borough	01.79	78-79	6	1	0
Newport Co	Tr	07.80	80-83	114	9	15

League Club	Source	Date Signed	Seasons Played	Career Record Apps	Subs	Gls
Cardiff C	Tr	09.83	83-84	59	0	5
Gillingham	Tr	08.85	85-87	126	2	13
Reading	Tr	08.88	88	41	3	3
Maidstone U	Tr	07.89	89-90	70	2	5
Gillingham	Tr	08.91	91	25	2	3

ELSTRUP Lars
Harby, Denmark, 24 March, 1963 Denmark int (F)

League Club	Source	Date Signed	Seasons Played	Apps	Subs	Gls
Luton T	OB Odense (Den)	08.89	89-90	50	10	19

ELSWORTHY John
Nantyderry, 26 July, 1931 (WH)

League Club	Source	Date Signed	Seasons Played	Apps	Subs	Gls
Ipswich T	Newport Co (Am)	05.49	49-64	396	-	44

ELVY Reginald (Reg)
Leeds, 25 November, 1920 Died 1991 (G)

League Club	Source	Date Signed	Seasons Played	Apps	Subs	Gls
Halifax T		03.44	46	22	-	0
Bolton W	Tr	03.47	47-49	31	-	0
Blackburn Rov	Tr	11.51	51-55	192	-	0
Northampton T	Tr	07.56	56-58	67	-	0

ELWELL Terence (Terry) Thomas
Newport, 13 April, 1926 Died 2004 (FB)

League Club	Source	Date Signed	Seasons Played	Apps	Subs	Gls
Swansea T	Barry T	08.48	48-51	62	-	0
Swindon T	Tr	07.52	52-53	61	-	0

ELWISS Michael (Mike) Walter
Doncaster, 2 May, 1954 (F)

League Club	Source	Date Signed	Seasons Played	Apps	Subs	Gls
Doncaster Rov	Jnrs	07.71	71-73	96	1	30
Preston NE	Tr	02.74	73-77	191	1	60
Crystal Palace	Tr	07.78	78	19	1	7
Preston NE	L	03.80	79	8	2	3

ELWOOD Joseph (Joe) Patrick
Belfast, 26 October, 1939 NISch/NIu23-1/NIB (W)

League Club	Source	Date Signed	Seasons Played	Apps	Subs	Gls
Leyton Orient	Glenavon	04.58	58-65	101	2	25

EMANUEL William **John**
Treherbert, 5 April, 1948 WAmat/W-2 (M)

League Club	Source	Date Signed	Seasons Played	Apps	Subs	Gls
Bristol C	Ferndale	05.71	71-75	124	4	10
Swindon T	L	01.76	75	6	0	0
Gillingham	L	02.76	75	4	0	0
Newport Co	Tr	06.76	76-77	79	0	4

EMANUEL David **Leonard (Len)**
Treboreth, 3 September, 1917 WSch (FB)

League Club	Source	Date Signed	Seasons Played	Apps	Subs	Gls
Swansea T		04.36	37-46	49	-	1
Newport Co	Tr	05.47	46-47	33	-	7

EMANUEL Lewis James
Bradford, 14 October, 1983 EYth (FB)

League Club	Source	Date Signed	Seasons Played	Apps	Subs	Gls
Bradford C	YT	07.01	01-04	79	23	2

EMBERSON Carl Wayne
Epsom, 13 July, 1973 (G)

League Club	Source	Date Signed	Seasons Played	Apps	Subs	Gls
Millwall	YT	05.91				
Colchester U	L	12.92	92	13	0	0
Colchester U	Tr	07.94	94-98	178	1	0
Walsall	Tr	06.99	99-00	6	2	0
Luton T	Tr	07.01	01-02	51	2	0
Southend U	Tr	07.03	03	6	0	0

EMBERY Benjamin (Ben) James
Barking, 10 October, 1944 (FB)

League Club	Source	Date Signed	Seasons Played	Apps	Subs	Gls
Tottenham H	App	06.62				
Exeter C	Tr	06.66	66-67	36	3	0

EMBLEN Neil Robert
Bromley, 19 June, 1971 (M)

League Club	Source	Date Signed	Seasons Played	Apps	Subs	Gls
Millwall	Sittingbourne	11.93	93	12	0	0
Wolverhampton W	Tr	07.94	94-96	80	8	9
Crystal Palace	Tr	08.97	97	8	5	0
Wolverhampton W	Tr	03.98	97-00	102	12	7
Norwich C	Tr	07.01	01-02	6	8	0
Walsall	L	01.03	02	2	2	0
Walsall	Tr	05.03	02-04	62	14	7

EMBLEN Paul David
Bromley, 3 April, 1976 (F)

League Club	Source	Date Signed	Seasons Played	Apps	Subs	Gls
Charlton Ath	Tonbridge	05.97	97	0	4	0
Brighton & Hove A	L	11.97	97	15	0	4
Wycombe W	Tr	08.98	98-01	45	18	3

EMBLETON Daniel Charles
Liverpool, 27 March, 1975 (G)

League Club	Source	Date Signed	Seasons Played	Apps	Subs	Gls
Liverpool	YT	04.93				
Walsall	Bury (N/C)	08.94	94	0	1	0

EMBLETON David
Newcastle, 14 September, 1952 (CD)

League Club	Source	Date Signed	Seasons Played	Apps	Subs	Gls
Newcastle U	App	08.71				
Bury	Tr	07.72	72	6	1	0
Hartlepool	Tr	07.73	73-75	24	2	0

EMENALO Michael
Aba, Nigeria, 14 July, 1965 Nigeria int (FB)

League Club	Source	Date Signed	Seasons Played	Apps	Subs	Gls
Notts Co	RWD Molenbeek (Bel)	08.94	94	7	0	0

[EMERSON] COSTA MOISES Emerson
Rio de Janeiro, Brazil, 12 April, 1972 Brazil int (M)

League Club	Source	Date Signed	Seasons Played	Apps	Subs	Gls
Middlesbrough	FC Porto (Por)	06.96	96-97	53	0	9

EMERSON Dean
Salford, 27 December, 1962 (M)

League Club	Source	Date Signed	Seasons Played	Apps	Subs	Gls
Stockport Co	East Manchester	02.82	81-84	156	0	7
Rotherham U	Tr	07.85	85-86	55	0	8
Coventry C	Tr	10.86	86-91	98	16	0
Hartlepool U	Tr	07.92	92-93	44	1	1
Stockport Co	Tr	11.93	93-94	8	3	0
Preston NE	Tr	11.94	94	1	1	0

EMERTON Brett
Sydney, Australia, 22 February, 1979 AuYth/Auu23/Au-40 (M)

League Club	Source	Date Signed	Seasons Played	Apps	Subs	Gls
Blackburn Rov	Feyenoord (Holl)	07.03	03-04	64	10	6

EMERY Anthony (Tony) John
Lincoln, 4 November, 1927 (CD)

League Club	Source	Date Signed	Seasons Played	Apps	Subs	Gls
Lincoln C	Jnrs	08.47	46-58	402	-	1
Mansfield T	Tr	06.59	59-60	26	-	0

EMERY Denis
Sandy, 4 October, 1933 (IF)

League Club	Source	Date Signed	Seasons Played	Apps	Subs	Gls
Tottenham H	Eynesbury Rov	12.51				
Peterborough U	Eynesbury Rov	07.54	60-62	68	-	29

EMERY Donald (Don) Kenneth James
Cardiff, 11 June, 1920 Died 1993 WSch (FB)

League Club	Source	Date Signed	Seasons Played	Apps	Subs	Gls
Swindon T	Cardiff C (Am)	06.37	37-47	69	-	3

EMERY James (Jim)
Lisburn, 2 March, 1940 (CF)

League Club	Source	Date Signed	Seasons Played	Apps	Subs	Gls
Exeter C	Distillery	08.59				
Barrow	Tr	07.60	60	2	-	0

EMERY Stephen (Steve) Roger
Ledbury, 7 February, 1956 (M)

League Club	Source	Date Signed	Seasons Played	Apps	Subs	Gls
Hereford U	App	02.74	73-79	203	1	10
Derby Co	Tr	09.79	79-81	73	2	4
Newport Co	Tr	03.83				
Hereford U	Tr	06.83	83-84	72	3	2
Wrexham	Tr	08.85	85	8	1	0

EMERY Terence (Terry) George
Bristol, 8 September, 1936 (WH)

League Club	Source	Date Signed	Seasons Played	Apps	Subs	Gls
Bristol C		02.57	56-57	11	-	0

EMMANUEL John **Gary**
Swansea, 1 February, 1954 Wu23-1 (M)

League Club	Source	Date Signed	Seasons Played	Apps	Subs	Gls
Birmingham C	App	07.71	74-78	61	10	6
Bristol Rov	Tr	12.78	78-80	59	6	2
Swindon T	Tr	07.81	81-83	109	2	8
Newport Co	Tr	07.84	84	12	0	0
Bristol C	Forest Green Rov	08.85	85	2	0	0
Swansea C	Tr	08.85	85-87	104	7	5

EMMERSON Mark
Cuddington, 7 August, 1965 (M)

League Club	Source	Date Signed	Seasons Played	Apps	Subs	Gls
Wrexham	Jnrs	08.82	82	1	1	0

EMMERSON Morris
Sunniside, 23 October, 1942 ESch (G)

League Club	Source	Date Signed	Seasons Played	Apps	Subs	Gls
Middlesbrough	Jnrs	10.59	62	10	-	0
Peterborough U	Tr	07.63	63	7	-	0

EMMERSON Scott
Durham, 10 October, 1982 (F)

League Club	Source	Date Signed	Seasons Played	Apps	Subs	Gls
York C	YT	●	00-01	3	11	1

EMMERSON Wayne Edward
Ottawa, Canada, 2 November, 1947 (F)

League Club	Source	Date Signed	Seasons Played	Apps	Subs	Gls
Manchester U	Jnrs	09.65				
Crewe Alex	Tr	07.68	68	6	2	1

EMPTAGE Albert Taylor
Grimsby, 26 December, 1917 Died 1997 FLge-1 (WH)

League Club	Source	Date Signed	Seasons Played	Apps	Subs	Gls
Manchester C	Scunthorpe & Lindsey U	02.37	37-50	136	-	1
Stockport Co	Tr	01.51	50-52	36	-	1

EMSON Paul David
Lincoln, 22 October, 1958 (W)

League Club	Source	Date Signed	Seasons Played	Apps	Subs	Gls
Derby Co	Brigg T	09.78	78-82	112	15	13
Grimsby T	Tr	08.83	83-85	90	7	15
Wrexham	Tr	07.86	86-87	42	7	5
Darlington	Tr	08.88	88-90	39	9	5

League Club	Source	Date Signed	Seasons Played	Career Record Apps	Subs	Gls
ENCKELMAN Peter						
Turku, Finland, 10 March, 1977 Fiu21-15/Fi-6						(G)
Aston Villa	TPS Turku (Fin)	02.99	99-02	51	1	0
Blackburn Rov	Tr	11.03	03	2	0	0
ENDEAN Barry						
Chester-le-Street, 22 March, 1946						(F)
Watford	Pelton Fell	09.68	68-70	72	5	28
Charlton Ath	Tr	02.71	70-71	27	0	1
Blackburn Rov	Tr	10.71	71-74	65	14	18
Huddersfield T	Tr	03.75	74-75	8	4	1
Workington	L	10.75	75	8	0	2
Hartlepool	Tr	03.76	75-76	24	1	5
ENDERSBY Scott Ian Glenn						
Lewisham, 20 February, 1962 EYth						(G)
Ipswich T	App	03.79				
Tranmere Rov	Tr	07.81	81-82	79	0	0
Swindon T	Tr	08.83	83-85	85	0	0
Carlisle U	Tr	11.85	85-86	52	0	0
York C	Tr	07.87	87-88	35	0	0
Cardiff C	L	12.87	87	4	0	0
ENES Roberto (Robbie) Manuel						
Sydney, Australia, 22 August, 1975 Australia int						(M)
Portsmouth	Sydney U (Aus)	10.97	97	1	4	0
ENGLAND Frederick (Fred) Watson						
Holmfirth, 11 July, 1923 Died 2002						(IF)
Halifax T	Huddersfield T (Am)	05.46	46-47	18	-	1
ENGLAND Michael (Mike)						
Kingswood, 4 January, 1961						(CD)
Bristol Rov	App	01.79	78	1	0	0
Bristol Rov	Forest Green Rov	09.85	85	17	0	0
ENGLAND Harold **Michael (Mike)**						
Holywell, 2 December, 1941 Wu23-11/W-44						(CD)
Blackburn Rov	Jnrs	04.59	59-65	165	0	21
Tottenham H	Tr	08.66	66-74	300	0	14
Cardiff C	Seattle (USA)	08.75	75	40	0	1
ENGLEFIELD Grahame William Elwyn						
Eltham, 21 September, 1931 Died 2003						(WH)
Charlton Ath	Jnrs	01.49				
Norwich C	Tr	05.54	55-56	22	-	0
ENGLISH Anthony (Tony) Karl						
Luton, 19 October, 1966 EYth						(M)
Colchester U	Coventry C (App)	12.84	84-95	345	6	40
ENGLISH John (Jack)						
South Shields, 19 March, 1923 Died 1985						(W)
Northampton T	Bristol C (Am)	10.46	47-59	302	-	135
ENGLISH Robert (Bobby) Harold						
Stockport, 19 April, 1939						(WH)
Manchester U	Jnrs	03.57				
Southport	Tr	11.61	61-62	20	-	0
ENGLISH Thomas (Tommy) Steven						
Cirencester, 18 October, 1961 EYth						(F)
Coventry C	App	06.79	79-81	62	4	17
Leicester C	Tr	09.82	82-83	29	17	3
Rochdale	Tr	09.84	84	3	0	1
Plymouth Arg	Tr	09.84	84	0	4	1
Colchester U	Canberra C (Aus)	11.85	85-86	34	13	19
Colchester U	Bishops Stortford	10.89	89	12	1	3
ENGONGA Vincente Mate						
Barcelona, Spain, 20 October, 1969 Spain 14						(CD)
Coventry C	Real Oviedo (Sp)	02.03	02	5	3	0
ENGWELL Michael (Micky) Leonard						
Grays, 27 September, 1966						(F)
Southend U	Jnrs	08.84	84-85	7	2	3
Crewe Alex	Tr	10.86	86	0	2	0
ENHUA Zhang						
Dalian, China, 28 April, 1973 China int						(CD)
Grimsby T (L)	Dalian Shide (China)	12.00	00	16	1	3
ENNIS Mark						
Bradford, 6 January, 1962						(FB)
Rochdale	Rochdale Joiners	11.83	83	1	0	0
ENTWISTLE Robert (Bobby) Peter						
Bury, 6 October, 1938 Died 2000						(CF)
Rochdale (Am)	Macclesfield T	03.59	58	1	-	0
Accrington St	Tr	09.60	60	2	-	0
Hartlepools U	Llandudno	10.64	64	14	-	3
ENTWISTLE Wayne Peter						
Bury, 6 August, 1958 EYth						(F)
Bury	App	08.76	76-77	25	6	7
Sunderland	Tr	11.77	77-79	43	2	12
Leeds U	Tr	10.79	79	7	4	2
Blackpool	Tr	11.80	80-81	27	5	6
Crewe Alex	Tr	03.82	81	11	0	0
Wimbledon	Tr	07.82	82	4	5	3
Bury	Grays Ath	08.83	83-84	80	3	32
Carlisle U	Tr	06.85	85	8	1	2
Bolton W	Tr	10.85	85	5	3	0
Burnley	L	08.86	86	6	2	2
Stockport Co	Tr	10.86	86-87	38	11	8
Bury	Tr	08.88	88	0	2	0
Wigan Ath	Tr	10.88	88	24	5	6
Hartlepool U	Altrincham	09.89	89	2	0	0
EPESSE-TITI Steeve						
Bordeaux, France, 5 September, 1979						(CD)
Wolverhampton W	Bordeaux	08.00				
Exeter C	Tr	03.01	00	5	1	0
EPHGRAVE George Arthur						
Reading, 29 April, 1918 Died 2004						(G)
Aston Villa	Northfleet	10.36				
Swindon T	Tr	03.39	38	1	-	0
Southampton	Tr	09.46	46-47	36	-	0
Norwich C	Tr	07.48	48-50	5	-	0
Watford	Tr	08.51	51	4	-	0
ERANIO Stefano						
Genoa, Italy, 29 December, 1966 Italy 20						(M)
Derby Co	AC Milan (It)	07.97	97-00	83	12	7
ERIBENNE Chukwunyeaka (Chukki) Osondu						
Westminster, 2 November, 1980						(F)
Coventry C	YT	01.98				
Bournemouth	Tr	07.00	00-02	12	35	1
ERIKSSON Jan						
Sundsvall, Sweden, 24 August, 1967 Sweden int						(CD)
Sunderland	Helsingborgs (Swe)	01.97	96	1	0	0
ESDAILLE Darren						
Manchester, 4 November, 1974						(FB)
Doncaster Rov	Hyde U	01.97	96-97	37	3	1
ESDAILLE David						
Manchester, 22 July, 1963						(M)
Wrexham	Winsford U	08.92	92	4	0	0
Bury	Tr	01.93	92	1	5	0
Doncaster Rov	Droylsden	08.97	97	10	3	0
ESHELBY Paul						
Sheffield, 29 May, 1970						(W)
Exeter C	Endcliffe U	12.89	89-90	10	9	1
Scarborough	Tr	03.91	90	2	1	0
ESPARTERO Mario						
Frejus, France, 17 January, 1978						(M)
Bolton W (L)	Metz (Fr)	02.02	01	0	3	0
ESSANDOH Roy Kabina						
Belfast, 17 February, 1976 NIYth						(F)
Wycombe W	Rushden & Diamonds	02.01	00	8	5	0
ESSER Edward (David) David						
Altrincham, 20 June, 1957						(M)
Everton	App	05.75				
Rochdale	Tr	07.77	77-81	169	11	24
ESSERS Pierre						
Holland, 20 February, 1959						(F)
Walsall	RSC Charleroi (Bel)	09.91	91	1	0	0
ETHERIDGE Brian George						
Northampton, 4 March, 1944 EYth						(IF)
Northampton T	Jnrs	07.62	61-64	17	-	1
Brentford	Tr	02.66	65-66	22	0	2
ETHERIDGE Richard **Keith**						
Ivybridge, 14 May, 1944						(F)
Plymouth Arg	St Blazey	07.66	66-67	30	1	5
ETHERIDGE Robert (Bobby) James						
Gloucester, 21 March, 1934 Died 1988						(WH)
Bristol C	Gloucester C	09.56	56-63	259	-	42
ETHERINGTON Craig						
Basildon, 16 September, 1979						(M)
West Ham U	YT	07.97				
Halifax T	L	02.99	98	4	0	0
Plymouth Arg	L	03.00	99	4	1	0

ETHERINGTON Matthew
Truro, 14 August, 1981 EYth/Eu21-3 (W)

League Club	Source	Date Signed	Seasons Played	Apps	Subs	Gls
Peterborough U	YT	08.98	96-99	43	8	6
Tottenham H	Tr	01.00	99-02	20	25	1
Bradford C	L	10.01	01	12	1	1
West Ham U	Tr	08.03	03-04	71	3	9

ETUHU Dickson Paul
Kano, Nigeria, 8 June, 1982 (M)

League Club	Source	Date Signed	Seasons Played	Apps	Subs	Gls
Manchester C	YT	12.99	01	11	1	0
Preston NE	Tr	01.02	01-04	94	27	15

EUELL Jason Joseph
Lambeth, 6 February, 1977 EYth/Eu21-6/Ja-1 (F)

League Club	Source	Date Signed	Seasons Played	Apps	Subs	Gls
Wimbledon	YT	06.95	95-00	118	23	41
Charlton Ath	Tr	07.01	01-04	97	32	33

EUSTACE John Mark
Solihull, 3 November, 1979 (M)

League Club	Source	Date Signed	Seasons Played	Apps	Subs	Gls
Coventry C	YT	11.96	99-02	62	24	7
Middlesbrough	L	01.03	02	0	1	0
Stoke C	Tr	08.03	03-04	28	5	5

EUSTACE Peter
Stocksbridge, 31 July, 1944 (M)

League Club	Source	Date Signed	Seasons Played	Apps	Subs	Gls
Sheffield Wed	App	06.62	62-69	189	3	21
West Ham U	Tr	01.70	69-71	41	2	6
Rotherham U	L	03.72	71	6	0	1
Sheffield Wed	Tr	08.72	72-74	48	8	4
Peterborough U	Tr	07.75	75	42	1	5

EUSTACE Scott Douglas
Leicester, 13 June, 1975 (CD)

League Club	Source	Date Signed	Seasons Played	Apps	Subs	Gls
Leicester C	YT	07.93	93	0	1	0
Mansfield T	Tr	06.95	95-97	90	8	6
Chesterfield	Tr	08.98				
Cambridge U	Tr	01.99	98-99	49	3	1
Lincoln C	Tr	07.00	00	0	1	0

EVANS Allan James
Polbeth, 12 October, 1956 S-4 (CD)

League Club	Source	Date Signed	Seasons Played	Apps	Subs	Gls
Aston Villa	Dunfermline Ath	05.77	77-88	374	6	51
Leicester C	Tr	08.89	89	14	0	0
Darlington	Brisbane U (Aus)	03.91	90	0	1	0

EVANS Alun James
Penrycadery, 1 December, 1922 (WH)

League Club	Source	Date Signed	Seasons Played	Apps	Subs	Gls
West Bromwich A	Wilden	01.43	47	18	-	0

EVANS Alun William
Stourport, 30 September, 1949 ESch/EYth/Eu23-4 (F)

League Club	Source	Date Signed	Seasons Played	Apps	Subs	Gls
Wolverhampton W	App	10.66	67-68	20	2	4
Liverpool	Tr	09.68	68-71	77	2	21
Aston Villa	Tr	06.72	72-73	53	7	11
Walsall	Tr	12.75	75-77	78	9	7

EVANS David **Andrew (Andy)**
Aberystwyth, 25 November, 1975 WYth (F)

League Club	Source	Date Signed	Seasons Played	Apps	Subs	Gls
Cardiff C	YT	12.94	93-95	5	10	0
Barnsley	Aberystwyth T	09.99				
Mansfield T	L	03.00	99	4	2	0

EVANS Andrew David Stanley
Swansea, 3 October, 1957 WSch/WYth/Wu21-1 (W)

League Club	Source	Date Signed	Seasons Played	Apps	Subs	Gls
Bristol Rov	App	09.75	75-77	34	8	2

EVANS Anthony (Tony)
Liverpool, 11 January, 1954 (F)

League Club	Source	Date Signed	Seasons Played	Apps	Subs	Gls
Blackpool	Formby	06.73	74	4	2	0
Cardiff C	Tr	06.75	75-78	120	4	47
Birmingham C	Tr	07.79	79-82	62	4	28
Crystal Palace	Tr	08.83	83	19	2	7
Wolverhampton W	Tr	06.84	84	20	3	5
Bolton W	L	02.85	84	4	0	0
Swindon T	Tr	08.85	85	8	2	0

EVANS Anthony (Tony) William
Colchester, 14 March, 1960 (M)

League Club	Source	Date Signed	Seasons Played	Apps	Subs	Gls
Colchester U	App	03.78	77-80	21	9	2

EVANS Arthur
Urmston, 13 May, 1933 ESch/EYth (G)

League Club	Source	Date Signed	Seasons Played	Apps	Subs	Gls
Bury	Jnrs	06.50	50	2	-	0
Stockport Co	Tr	08.52				
Gillingham	Tr	09.53	53-54	14	-	0

EVANS Bernard
Chester, 4 January, 1937 (CF)

League Club	Source	Date Signed	Seasons Played	Apps	Subs	Gls
Wrexham	Saltney Jnrs	08.54	54-60	114	-	47
Queens Park Rgrs	Tr	10.60	60-62	78	-	35
Oxford U	Tr	12.62	62-63	13	-	3
Tranmere Rov	Tr	10.63	63	12	-	5

EVANS Brian Clifford
Brynmawr, 2 December, 1942 Died 2003 Wu23-2/W-7 (W)

League Club	Source	Date Signed	Seasons Played	Apps	Subs	Gls
Swansea T	Abergavenny Thistle	07.63	63-72	340	3	57
Hereford U	Tr	08.73	73-74	44	4	9

EVANS Ceri Lee
Christchurch, New Zealand, 2 October, 1963 New Zealand int (CD)

League Club	Source	Date Signed	Seasons Played	Apps	Subs	Gls
Oxford U	Oxford Univ	02.89	88-92	113	3	3

EVANS Charles (Charlie) James
West Bromwich, 4 February, 1923 Died 1998 (IF)

League Club	Source	Date Signed	Seasons Played	Apps	Subs	Gls
West Bromwich A	Cordley Victoria	08.41	46	1	-	0

EVANS Christopher (Chris) Brian
Rhondda, 13 October, 1962 (FB)

League Club	Source	Date Signed	Seasons Played	Apps	Subs	Gls
Arsenal	App	06.80				
Stoke C	Tr	08.81				
York C	Tr	08.82	82-85	93	3	1
Darlington	Tr	10.85	85-86	58	0	1

EVANS Andrew **Clive**
Heswall, 1 May, 1957 (M)

League Club	Source	Date Signed	Seasons Played	Apps	Subs	Gls
Tranmere Rov	App	05.75	76-80	175	3	26
Wigan Ath	Tr	07.81	81	29	3	2
Crewe Alex	Tr	08.82	82	26	2	7
Stockport Co	Tr	08.83	83-87	158	2	23
Lincoln C	Tr	09.87	88	42	0	2

EVANS Darren
Wolverhampton, 30 September, 1974 (FB)

League Club	Source	Date Signed	Seasons Played	Apps	Subs	Gls
Aston Villa	YT	07.93				
Hereford U	Tr	09.95	95	24	0	0

EVANS David (Dai)
Colwyn Bay, 19 June, 1934 (G)

League Club	Source	Date Signed	Seasons Played	Apps	Subs	Gls
Crewe Alex	Llandudno	03.57	56-59	48	-	0

EVANS David
Chester, 4 April, 1967 (FB)

League Club	Source	Date Signed	Seasons Played	Apps	Subs	Gls
Chester C	App	05.84	83-84	15	1	1

EVANS David (Doug) Douglas
Ystradgynlais, 27 September, 1956 (W)

League Club	Source	Date Signed	Seasons Played	Apps	Subs	Gls
Norwich C	App	08.74	76-79	14	4	1
Cambridge U	Tr	03.80	79-80	11	1	2

EVANS David Gordon
West Bromwich, 20 May, 1958 (CD)

League Club	Source	Date Signed	Seasons Played	Apps	Subs	Gls
Aston Villa	App	02.76	78	2	0	0
Halifax T	Tr	06.79	79-83	218	0	9
Bradford C	Tr	06.84	84-89	222	1	3
Halifax T	Tr	08.90	90-91	68	5	1

EVANS David (Dave) Thom
Peterlee, 6 April, 1959 (F)

League Club	Source	Date Signed	Seasons Played	Apps	Subs	Gls
Hartlepool U		07.78	78-79	2	2	0

EVANS Dennis
Chester, 23 July, 1935 (FB)

League Club	Source	Date Signed	Seasons Played	Apps	Subs	Gls
Wrexham		03.55	55-57	11	-	0
Tranmere Rov	Tr	06.58	58-59	3	-	0

EVANS Dennis Joseph
Old Swan, 18 May, 1930 Died 2000 (FB)

League Club	Source	Date Signed	Seasons Played	Apps	Subs	Gls
Arsenal	Ellesmere Port T	01.51	53-59	189	-	10

EVANS Elfed Ellison
Ferndale, 28 August, 1926 Died 1988 (IF)

League Club	Source	Date Signed	Seasons Played	Apps	Subs	Gls
Cardiff C	Treharris	05.49	49-51	44	-	16
Torquay U	L	03.51	50	12	-	6
West Bromwich A	Tr	06.52	52	17	-	3
Wrexham	Tr	06.55	55-56	34	-	16
Southport	Tr	12.56	56	13	-	0

EVANS Emrys Brian
Tonypandy, 16 September, 1930 (IF)

League Club	Source	Date Signed	Seasons Played	Apps	Subs	Gls
Newport Co	Tottenham H (Am)	08.52	52	18	-	5

EVANS Frederick (Fred) John
Petersfield, 20 May, 1923 (CF)

League Club	Source	Date Signed	Seasons Played	Apps	Subs	Gls
Portsmouth		01.45	46	9	-	2
Notts Co	Tr	07.47	47-50	39	-	14
Crystal Palace	Tr	03.51	50-52	52	-	11
Rochdale	Tr	06.53	53	12	-	0

EVANS Gareth John
Coventry, 14 January, 1967 (F)

League Club	Source	Date Signed	Seasons Played	Apps	Subs	Gls
Coventry C	App	01.85	85-86	5	2	0
Rotherham U	Tr	10.86	86-87	62	1	13
Stoke C (L)	Hibernian	10.90	90	5	0	1
Northampton T (L)	Hibernian	12.90	90	2	0	0

EVANS Gareth Joseph
Leeds, 15 February, 1981 EYth (FB)

League Club	Source	Date Signed	Seasons Played	Apps	Subs	Gls
Leeds U	YT	03.98	00	0	1	0
Huddersfield T	Tr	08.01	01	35	0	0
Blackpool	Tr	08.03	03-04	43	2	0

EVANS Gary Lee
Doncaster, 13 September, 1982 (FB)

League Club	Source	Date Signed	Seasons Played	Apps	Subs	Gls
Bury	YT	03.03	01	1	0	0

EVANS Gary Neil
Doncaster, 20 December, 1968 (F)

League Club	Source	Date Signed	Seasons Played	Apps	Subs	Gls
Chesterfield	Thorne Colliery	08.91	91	1	4	0

EVANS George Albert
Rhostyllen, 6 July, 1935 Died 2000 (CD)

League Club	Source	Date Signed	Seasons Played	Apps	Subs	Gls
Wrexham	Oswestry T	07.57	57-62	175	-	9
Chester	Tr	06.63	63-68	109	4	0

EVANS Gwyn
Ton Pentre, 24 December, 1935 (CD)

League Club	Source	Date Signed	Seasons Played	Apps	Subs	Gls
Crystal Palace	Treorchy	03.55	58-62	80	-	0

EVANS Henry (Harry) Alfred
Lambeth, 17 April, 1919 Died 1962 (IF)

League Club	Source	Date Signed	Seasons Played	Apps	Subs	Gls
Southampton	Woking	10.43	46	1	-	0
Exeter C	Tr	04.47	47-48	41	-	6
Aldershot	Tr	03.49	48-49	16	-	5

EVANS Hubert William Richard
Swansea, 10 August, 1922 (WH)

League Club	Source	Date Signed	Seasons Played	Apps	Subs	Gls
Swansea T	Jnrs	08.39				
Newport Co	Lovells Ath	04.51	50-51	14	-	1

EVANS Gwilym **Hugh**
Ynysybwl, 12 December, 1919 (IF)

League Club	Source	Date Signed	Seasons Played	Apps	Subs	Gls
Birmingham C	Redditch T	12.47	48-49	11	-	0
Bournemouth	Tr	06.50	50	22	-	8
Walsall	Tr	08.51	51	36	-	12
Watford	Tr	08.52	52	7	-	2

EVANS Ian Peter
Egham, 30 January, 1952 Wu23-2/W-13 (CD)

League Club	Source	Date Signed	Seasons Played	Apps	Subs	Gls
Queens Park Rgrs	App	01.70	70-73	39	0	2
Crystal Palace	Tr	09.74	74-77	137	0	14
Barnsley	Tr	12.79	79-82	102	0	3
Exeter C	L	08.83	83	4	0	0
Cambridge U	L	10.83	83	1	0	0

EVANS Ivor James
Cardiff, 25 October, 1933 (IF)

League Club	Source	Date Signed	Seasons Played	Apps	Subs	Gls
Portsmouth	GKN Sankey	09.56	56	1	-	0

EVANS Jason Stuart
Cambridge, 22 January, 1974 (FB)

League Club	Source	Date Signed	Seasons Played	Apps	Subs	Gls
Shrewsbury T	YT	07.92	92	0	1	0

EVANS John
Hetton-le-Hole, 21 October, 1932 (IF)

League Club	Source	Date Signed	Seasons Played	Apps	Subs	Gls
Norwich C	Jnrs	10.49				
Sunderland	Tr	08.54	54	1	-	0

EVANS John Alwyn
Aberystwyth, 22 October, 1922 Died 1956 (FB)

League Club	Source	Date Signed	Seasons Played	Apps	Subs	Gls
Millwall	Aberystwyth	09.43	46-49	73	-	2
Leyton Orient	Tr	06.50	50-53	149	-	0

EVANS John Charles
Torquay, 24 March, 1947 (W)

League Club	Source	Date Signed	Seasons Played	Apps	Subs	Gls
Torquay U	App	04.65	64-66	6	1	1

EVANS John (Johnny) David
Liverpool, 13 March, 1938 Died 2004 (F)

League Club	Source	Date Signed	Seasons Played	Apps	Subs	Gls
Liverpool		05.58				
Bournemouth	Tr	05.59				
Stockport Co		10.62	62-63	52	-	20
Carlisle U	Tr	02.64	63-65	77	0	37
Exeter C	Tr	03.66	65-66	11	1	2
Barnsley	Tr	11.66	66-70	165	5	54

EVANS John David
Chester, 24 March, 1941 (FB)

League Club	Source	Date Signed	Seasons Played	Apps	Subs	Gls
Chester		08.61	61-64	40	-	0

EVANS John (Jack) Joseph
Coventry, 11 March, 1926 (CF)

League Club	Source	Date Signed	Seasons Played	Apps	Subs	Gls
Coventry C	Modern Machine Tools	06.47	48-50	8	-	1

EVANS John Llewellyn
Wattstown, 4 October, 1937 (WH)

League Club	Source	Date Signed	Seasons Played	Apps	Subs	Gls
Gillingham	Lovells Ath	04.56	57	7	-	0

EVANS John William
Tilbury, 28 August, 1929 Died 1999 FLge-1 (IF)

League Club	Source	Date Signed	Seasons Played	Apps	Subs	Gls
Charlton Ath	Tilbury	05.50	50-53	90	-	38
Liverpool	Tr	12.53	53-56	96	-	49
Colchester U	Tr	11.57	57-59	56	-	22

EVANS Keith
Trealaw, 15 September, 1953 (CD)

League Club	Source	Date Signed	Seasons Played	Apps	Subs	Gls
Swansea C	App	08.71	70-72	12	0	0

EVANS Kenneth (Ken) Philip
Swansea, 17 July, 1931 Died 2000 (G)

League Club	Source	Date Signed	Seasons Played	Apps	Subs	Gls
Swansea T	Carmarthen	06.50	54-56	14	-	0
Walsall	Tr	08.57	57	2	-	0

EVANS Kevin
Carmarthen, 16 December, 1980 WYth/Wu21-4 (FB)

League Club	Source	Date Signed	Seasons Played	Apps	Subs	Gls
Leeds U	YT	01.98				
Swansea C	L	01.00	99	1	1	0
Cardiff C	Tr	08.00	00	24	6	3

EVANS Leslie Norman
Kingswinford, 13 October, 1929 (W)

League Club	Source	Date Signed	Seasons Played	Apps	Subs	Gls
Cardiff C	Brierley Hill Alliance	10.50	50-51	3	-	1

EVANS Leslie (Les) Thomas
Rhondda, 26 December, 1924 Died 2002 (CD)

League Club	Source	Date Signed	Seasons Played	Apps	Subs	Gls
Cardiff C		09.45				
Torquay U	L	07.47	47	24	-	0

EVANS Mark
Leeds, 24 August, 1970 (G)

League Club	Source	Date Signed	Seasons Played	Apps	Subs	Gls
Bradford C	YT	07.88	88-91	12	0	0
Scarborough	Tr	08.92	92-93	46	0	0

EVANS Mark Graham
Chester, 16 September, 1982 (F)

League Club	Source	Date Signed	Seasons Played	Apps	Subs	Gls
Wrexham	Sch	07.02	01-02	0	5	0

EVANS Maurice George
Didcot, 22 September, 1936 Died 2000 (WH)

League Club	Source	Date Signed	Seasons Played	Apps	Subs	Gls
Reading	Jnrs	09.53	55-66	407	0	13

EVANS Medwyn John
Brynteg, 8 November, 1964 WSch (M)

League Club	Source	Date Signed	Seasons Played	Apps	Subs	Gls
Wrexham	Jnrs	08.83	82-83	13	4	0

EVANS Michael (Micky)
West Bromwich, 3 August, 1946 (FB)

League Club	Source	Date Signed	Seasons Played	Apps	Subs	Gls
Walsall	Vono Sports	05.64	65-72	229	2	7
Swansea C	Tr	12.72	72-74	92	0	6
Crewe Alex	Tr	07.75	75-76	62	0	4

EVANS Michael
Venlo, Holland, 21 July, 1976 (F)

League Club	Source	Date Signed	Seasons Played	Apps	Subs	Gls
York C	VVV Venlo (Holl)	09.01	01	1	1	0

EVANS Michael (Mickey) Graham
Llanidloes, 4 June, 1947 WSch/Wu23-2 (CD)

League Club	Source	Date Signed	Seasons Played	Apps	Subs	Gls
Wolverhampton W	App	07.64				
Wrexham	Tr	07.66	66-78	368	15	19

EVANS Michael (Mickey) James
Plymouth, 1 January, 1973 IR-1 (F)

League Club	Source	Date Signed	Seasons Played	Apps	Subs	Gls
Plymouth Arg	YT	03.91	90-96	130	33	38
Southampton	Tr	03.97	96-97	14	8	4
West Bromwich A	Tr	10.97	97-99	35	28	6
Bristol Rov	Tr	08.00	00	19	2	4
Plymouth Arg	Tr	03.01	00-04	143	33	30

EVANS Nicholas (Nick)
Trimdon, 23 November, 1925 Died 1992 (W)

League Club	Source	Date Signed	Seasons Played	Apps	Subs	Gls
New Brighton (Am)	Hesleden	03.47	46	1	-	0

EVANS Nicholas (Nicky) Andrew
Carmarthen, 12 May, 1980 (M)

League Club	Source	Date Signed	Seasons Played	Apps	Subs	Gls
Hartlepool U	YT	07.98	98	0	1	0

EVANS Nicholas (Nicky) John
Bedford, 6 July, 1958 (F)

League Club	Source	Date Signed	Seasons Played	Apps	Subs	Gls
Queens Park Rgrs	App	07.76				
Peterborough U	Tr	08.77				
Barnet	Wycombe W	01.91	91-93	16	23	8

EVANS Oswald Vernon
Llanelli, 2 September, 1916 Died 1986 (G)

League Club	Source	Date Signed	Seasons Played	Apps	Subs	Gls
Fulham	Milford Haven	02.46	46	1	-	0

EVANS Paul
Kiveton Park, 24 February, 1949 (G)

League Club	Source	Date Signed	Seasons Played	Apps	Subs	Gls
Sheffield Wed	Jnrs	02.66				
Mansfield T	Boston U	10.75	75	6	0	0

EVANS Paul Alan
Pontypridd, 14 September, 1964 (F)

League Club	Source	Date Signed	Seasons Played	Apps	Subs	Gls
Cardiff C	Jnrs	09.82	83	0	2	0
Newport Co	Brecon Corinthians	07.87	87	9	1	2

EVANS Paul Anthony
Newcastle, South Africa, 28 December, 1973 Sau23-8 (G)

League Club	Source	Date Signed	Seasons Played	Apps	Subs	Gls
Leeds U	Wits Univ	12.95				
Sheffield Wed	Jomo Cosmos (SA)	08.02	02	7	0	0
Rushden & Diamonds	Tr	10.03	03	2	0	0

EVANS Paul Simon
Oswestry, 1 September, 1974 WYth/Wu21-1/W-2 (M)

League Club	Source	Date Signed	Seasons Played	Apps	Subs	Gls
Shrewsbury T	YT	07.93	91-98	178	20	26
Brentford	Tr	03.99	98-01	130	0	31
Bradford C	Tr	08.02	02-03	36	6	5
Blackpool	L	01.03	02	10	0	1
Nottingham F	Tr	03.04	03-04	42	5	4

EVANS Philip (Phil)
Swansea, 14 May, 1957 (CD)

League Club	Source	Date Signed	Seasons Played	Apps	Subs	Gls
Swansea C	Jnrs	08.75	75	10	0	0

EVANS Denzil Ralph
Hungerford, 9 October, 1915 Died 1996 (IF)

League Club	Source	Date Signed	Seasons Played	Apps	Subs	Gls
Bury		07.35				
Halifax T	Yeovil & Petters U	07.36	36	21	-	1
Watford	Tr	07.37	37-47	88	-	30

EVANS Raymond (Ray)
Mansfield, 27 November, 1927 (CF)

League Club	Source	Date Signed	Seasons Played	Apps	Subs	Gls
Coventry C		05.48				
Mansfield T	Stafford Rgrs	11.49	49-52	39	-	12

EVANS Raymond (Ray)
Carlisle, 8 October, 1929 (G)

League Club	Source	Date Signed	Seasons Played	Apps	Subs	Gls
Crewe Alex	Hightown YC	10.48	48-50	20	-	0

EVANS Raymond (Ray)
Preston, 21 June, 1933 (IF)

League Club	Source	Date Signed	Seasons Played	Apps	Subs	Gls
Preston NE	Jnrs	05.51	53-56	33	-	2
Bournemouth	Tr	06.59	59-60	36	-	9

EVANS Raymond (Ray) Leslie
Edmonton, 20 September, 1949 EYth (FB)

League Club	Source	Date Signed	Seasons Played	Apps	Subs	Gls
Tottenham H	App	06.67	68-74	130	4	2
Millwall	Tr	01.75	74-76	74	0	3
Fulham	Tr	03.77	76-78	86	0	6
Stoke C	Tr	08.79	79-81	94	0	1

EVANS Reginald (Reg)
Consett, 18 March, 1939 (W)

League Club	Source	Date Signed	Seasons Played	Apps	Subs	Gls
Newcastle U	Jnrs	03.56	58	4	-	0
Charlton Ath	Tr	03.59	58-59	14	-	2

EVANS Reuben
Dublin, 19 March, 1941 (IF)

League Club	Source	Date Signed	Seasons Played	Apps	Subs	Gls
Bradford PA	Glasgow Rgrs	06.63	63	13	-	5

EVANS Rhys Karl
Swindon, 27 January, 1982 ESch/EYth/Eu20/Eu21-2 (G)

League Club	Source	Date Signed	Seasons Played	Apps	Subs	Gls
Chelsea	YT	02.99				
Bristol Rov	L	02.00	99	4	0	0
Queens Park Rgrs	L	11.01	01	11	0	0
Leyton Orient	L	08.02	02	7	0	0
Swindon T	Tr	07.03	03-04	86	0	0

EVANS Richard Glyn
Cardiff, 19 June, 1983 (M)

League Club	Source	Date Signed	Seasons Played	Apps	Subs	Gls
Birmingham C	Sch	07.02				
Sheffield Wed	Tr	03.03	02-03	8	2	1

EVANS Richard William
Ebbw Vale, 12 April, 1968 (W)

League Club	Source	Date Signed	Seasons Played	Apps	Subs	Gls
Bristol Rov	Weymouth	08.91	91-93	9	6	1
Exeter C	L	10.92	92	5	0	2

EVANS Robert (Bobby)
Glasgow, 16 July, 1927 Died 2001 SLge-25/S-48 (CD)

League Club	Source	Date Signed	Seasons Played	Apps	Subs	Gls
Chelsea	Glasgow Celtic	05.60	60	32	-	0
Newport Co	Tr	06.61	61	31	-	0

EVANS Ronald (Ron)
St Helens, 21 February, 1929 (WH)

League Club	Source	Date Signed	Seasons Played	Apps	Subs	Gls
Stockport Co	Bolton W (Am)	07.50	50-53	6	-	0

EVANS Roy Quintin Echlin
Crosby, 4 October, 1948 ESch (FB)

League Club	Source	Date Signed	Seasons Played	Apps	Subs	Gls
Liverpool	App	10.65	69-73	9	0	0

EVANS Bernard Royden (Roy)
Rotherhithe, 7 October, 1929 (IF)

League Club	Source	Date Signed	Seasons Played	Apps	Subs	Gls
Millwall		03.50				
Watford	Tr	08.51	51	2	-	1

EVANS John Royston
Lampeter, 9 February, 1939 (W)

League Club	Source	Date Signed	Seasons Played	Apps	Subs	Gls
Wolverhampton W	Bangor C	08.56				
Wrexham	Tr	07.57				
Chester	Tr	10.57	57-59	23	-	3
Halifax T	Sankey's	10.60	60	7	-	0

EVANS Royston (Roy) Sidney
Swansea, 5 July, 1943 Died 1969 Wu23-3/W-1 (FB)

League Club	Source	Date Signed	Seasons Played	Apps	Subs	Gls
Swansea T	Jnrs	07.60	62-67	212	2	7

EVANS Stephen (Steve) James
Caerphilly, 25 September, 1980 WYth/Wu21-2 (M)

League Club	Source	Date Signed	Seasons Played	Apps	Subs	Gls
Crystal Palace	YT	10.98	98-00	0	6	0
Swansea C	L	11.01	01	4	0	0
Brentford	Tr	03.02	02-03	34	14	5

EVANS Stewart John
Maltby, 15 November, 1960 (F)

League Club	Source	Date Signed	Seasons Played	Apps	Subs	Gls
Rotherham U	App	11.78				
Sheffield U	Gainsborough Trinity	11.80				
Wimbledon	Tr	03.82	81-85	165	10	50
West Bromwich A	Tr	08.86	86	13	1	1
Plymouth Arg	Tr	03.87	86-88	36	9	10
Rotherham U	Tr	11.88	88-90	45	20	14
Torquay U	L	03.91	90	15	0	5
Crewe Alex	Tr	09.91	91-93	74	9	12

EVANS Terence (Terry)
Pontypridd, 8 January, 1976 Wu21-4 (FB)

League Club	Source	Date Signed	Seasons Played	Apps	Subs	Gls
Cardiff C	YT	07.94	93-95	12	2	0
Swansea C	Barry T	10.01	01-02	41	2	0

EVANS Terence (Terry) William
Hammersmith, 12 April, 1965 (CD)

League Club	Source	Date Signed	Seasons Played	Apps	Subs	Gls
Brentford	Hillingdon Borough	07.85	85-92	228	1	23
Wycombe W	Tr	08.93	93-96	128	8	15

EVANS Thomas (Tom) Raymond
Doncaster, 31 December, 1976 NIYth (G)

League Club	Source	Date Signed	Seasons Played	Apps	Subs	Gls
Sheffield U	YT	07.95				
Crystal Palace	Tr	06.96				
Scunthorpe U	Tr	08.97	97-03	226	1	0

EVANS Duncan Wayne
Abermule, 25 August, 1971 (FB)

League Club	Source	Date Signed	Seasons Played	Apps	Subs	Gls
Walsall	Welshpool	08.93	93-98	173	10	1
Rochdale	Tr	07.99	99-04	259	0	3

EVANS William (Billy) Emmanuel
Birmingham, 5 September, 1921 Died 1960 (IF)

League Club	Source	Date Signed	Seasons Played	Apps	Subs	Gls
Aston Villa	Linread Works	09.46	46-48	7	-	3
Notts Co	Tr	06.49	49-52	96	-	14
Gillingham	Tr	07.53	53-54	89	-	12
Grimsby T	Tr	06.55	55-57	102	-	28

EVANS Wyndham Edgar
Llanelli, 19 March, 1951 (FB)

League Club	Source	Date Signed	Seasons Played	Apps	Subs	Gls
Swansea C	Stoke C (Am)	02.71	70-82	348	4	20
Swansea C	Llanelli	12.83	83-84	35	2	0

EVANSON John Michael
Newcastle-under-Lyme, 10 May, 1947 (M)

League Club	Source	Date Signed	Seasons Played	Apps	Subs	Gls
Oxford U	Towcester	02.65	66-73	144	10	10
Blackpool	Tr	02.74	73-75	63	4	0
Fulham	Miami (USA)	08.76	76-78	84	11	5
Bournemouth	Tr	07.79	79-80	52	1	2

EVATT Ian Ross
Coventry, 19 November, 1981 (CD)

League Club	Source	Date Signed	Seasons Played	Apps	Subs	Gls
Derby Co	YT	12.98	00-02	19	15	0
Northampton T	L	08.01	01	10	1	0
Chesterfield	Tr	08.03	03-04	84	0	9

EVE Angus
Trinidad, 23 February, 1972 Trinidad int (M)

League Club	Source	Date Signed	Seasons Played	Apps	Subs	Gls
Chester C	Joe Public (Tri)	12.99	99	9	5	4

EVELEIGH Gordon
Lymington, 26 July, 1922 (W)

League Club	Source	Date Signed	Seasons Played	Apps	Subs	Gls
Bristol C	Guildford C	05.48	48	2	-	0

EVERALL William (Bill) Frederick
Nantwich, 18 July, 1928 (FB)

League Club	Source	Date Signed	Seasons Played	Apps	Subs	Gls
Crewe Alex		08.53	53	1	-	0

EVERETT Harold
Worksop, 9 June, 1922 Died 2000 (WH)

League Club	Source	Date Signed	Seasons Played	Apps	Subs	Gls
Notts Co	Rufford Colliery	04.43				
Mansfield T	Tr	09.46	46	15	-	0

EVERETT Harry
Worksop, 11 November, 1920 Died 1998 (WH)

League Club	Source	Date Signed	Seasons Played	Apps	Subs	Gls
Mansfield T	Warsop Main	08.45	46	3	-	0

EVERETT Michael (Mike)
Mile End, 21 March, 1958 (F)

League Club	Source	Date Signed	Seasons Played	Apps	Subs	Gls
Orient	Crystal Palace (App)	03.76	75	0	1	0

EVERINGHAM Nicholas (Nick) Peter
Hull, 1 November, 1973 (M)

League Club	Source	Date Signed	Seasons Played	Apps	Subs	Gls
Oldham Ath	YT	07.92				
Halifax T	Tr	02.93	92	2	0	0

EVERITT Michael (Mike) Dennis
Weeley, 16 January, 1941 (FB)

League Club	Source	Date Signed	Seasons Played	Apps	Subs	Gls
Arsenal	Jnrs	02.58	59-60	9	-	1
Northampton T	Tr	02.61	60-66	206	1	15
Plymouth Arg	Tr	03.67	66-67	29	0	0
Brighton & Hove A	Tr	07.68	68-69	24	3	1

EVERITT Richard Ewart
Carlisle, 3 May, 1922 (W)

League Club	Source	Date Signed	Seasons Played	Apps	Subs	Gls
Darlington	Sheffield Wed (Am)	07.45	46	1	-	0

EVERS Sean Anthony
Hitchin, 10 October, 1977 (M)

League Club	Source	Date Signed	Seasons Played	Apps	Subs	Gls
Luton T	YT	05.96	95-98	43	9	6
Reading	Tr	03.99	98-99	8	10	0
Plymouth Arg	Tr	03.01	00-01	5	9	0

EVERSHAM Paul Jonathan
Hereford, 28 January, 1975 (M)

League Club	Source	Date Signed	Seasons Played	Apps	Subs	Gls
Hereford U	YT	07.93	93-94	6	7	1

EVES John Robert
Sunderland, 28 February, 1922 (FB)

League Club	Source	Date Signed	Seasons Played	Apps	Subs	Gls
Sunderland		11.41				
Darlington	Tr	09.46	46-51	176	-	1

EVES Melvyn (Mel) James
Wednesbury, 10 September, 1956 ESch/EB (F)

League Club	Source	Date Signed	Seasons Played	Apps	Subs	Gls
Wolverhampton W	Jnrs	07.75	77-83	169	11	44
Huddersfield T	L	03.84	83	7	0	4
Sheffield U	Tr	12.84	84-85	25	1	10
Gillingham	Tr	08.86	86-87	19	8	9
Mansfield T	L	10.87	87	3	0	0

EVTUSHOK Alexandr (Alex)
Kiev, Ukraine, 11 January, 1970 Ukraine int (FB)

League Club	Source	Date Signed	Seasons Played	Apps	Subs	Gls
Coventry C	Karpaty Lvov (Uk)	02.97	96	3	0	0

EWING David (Dave)
Logierait, 10 May, 1929 Died 1999 (CD)

League Club	Source	Date Signed	Seasons Played	Apps	Subs	Gls
Manchester C	Luncarty Jnrs	06.49	52-61	279	-	1
Crewe Alex	Tr	07.62	62-63	48	-	0

EWING Thomas (Tommy)
Larkhall, 2 May, 1937 SLge-1/S-2 (W)

League Club	Source	Date Signed	Seasons Played	Apps	Subs	Gls
Aston Villa	Paritick Thistle	02.62	61-63	39	-	4

EWING Thomas (Tommy) McCall Halliday
Musselburgh, 8 August, 1934 (WH)

League Club	Source	Date Signed	Seasons Played	Apps	Subs	Gls
Doncaster Rov	Dunfermline Ath	08.51	51-57	39	-	6

EXLEY William
Bradford, 2 May, 1924 Died 1997 (G)

League Club	Source	Date Signed	Seasons Played	Apps	Subs	Gls
Bradford C (Am)		08.52	52	2	-	0

EYDELIE Jean-Jacques
Angouleme, France, 3 February, 1966 (M)

League Club	Source	Date Signed	Seasons Played	Apps	Subs	Gls
Walsall (L)	Sion (Fr)	03.98	97	10	1	0

EYJOLFSSON Sigurdur (Siggi)
Reykjavik, Iceland, 1 December, 1973 IcYth (F)

League Club	Source	Date Signed	Seasons Played	Apps	Subs	Gls
Walsall	IA Akranes (Ice)	01.99	98-99	1	22	2
Chester C	L	01.00	99	9	0	3

EYRE Ernest (Les) Leslie
Ilkeston, 7 January, 1922 Died 1991 (IF)

League Club	Source	Date Signed	Seasons Played	Apps	Subs	Gls
Norwich C	Cardiff C (Am)	07.46	46-51	185	-	58
Bournemouth	Tr	11.51	51-52	38	-	10

EYRE Stanley **Frederick (Fred)**
Manchester, 3 February, 1944 (FB)

League Club	Source	Date Signed	Seasons Played	Apps	Subs	Gls
Manchester C	App	07.61				
Lincoln C	Tr	07.63				
Bradford PA	Rossendale U	12.69	69	1	0	0

EYRE John Robert
Hull, 9 October, 1974 (M)

League Club	Source	Date Signed	Seasons Played	Apps	Subs	Gls
Oldham Ath	YT	07.93	93-94	4	6	1
Scunthorpe U	L	12.94	94	9	0	8
Scunthorpe U	Tr	07.95	95-98	151	13	43
Hull C	Tr	07.99	99-00	43	9	13
Oldham Ath	Tr	07.01	01-04	98	20	14

EYRE Richard Paul
Poynton, 15 September, 1976 (W)

League Club	Source	Date Signed	Seasons Played	Apps	Subs	Gls
Port Vale	YT	06.95	97-00	26	22	1
Macclesfield T	Tr	08.01	01	12	2	0

EYRES David
Liverpool, 26 February, 1964 (W)

League Club	Source	Date Signed	Seasons Played	Apps	Subs	Gls
Blackpool	Rhyl	08.89	89-92	147	11	38
Burnley	Tr	07.93	93-97	171	4	37
Preston NE	Tr	10.97	97-00	85	23	19
Oldham Ath	Tr	10.00	00-04	172	14	32

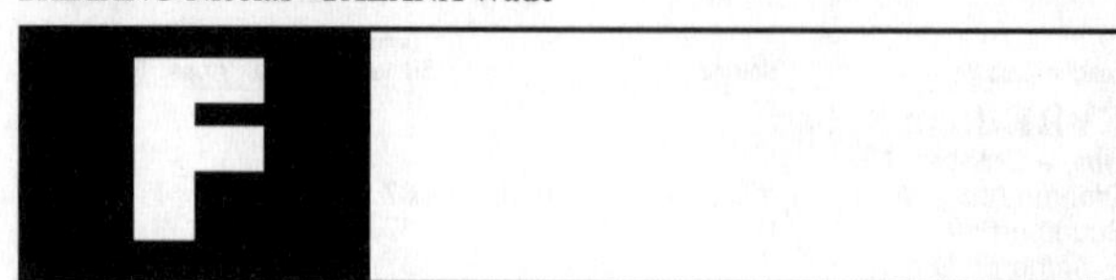

League Club	Source	Date Signed	Seasons Played	Career Record Apps	Subs	Gls

FABIANO Nicolas
Paris, France, 8 February, 1981 FrYth (M)

League Club	Source	Date Signed	Seasons Played	Apps	Subs	Gls
Swansea C (L)	Paris St Germain (Fr)	02.01	00	12	4	1

FABREGAS Francesco (Cesc)
Barcelona, Spain, 4 May, 1987 SpYth/Spu21 (M)

League Club	Source	Date Signed	Seasons Played	Apps	Subs	Gls
Arsenal	YT	09.04	04	24	9	2

FACEY Delroy Michael
Huddersfield, 22 April, 1980 (F)

League Club	Source	Date Signed	Seasons Played	Apps	Subs	Gls
Huddersfield T	YT	05.97	96-01	40	35	15
Bolton W	Tr	07.02	02-03	1	9	1
Bradford C	L	11.02	02	6	0	1
Burnley	L	09.03	03	12	2	5
West Bromwich A	Tr	01.04	03	2	7	0
Hull C	Tr	07.04	04	12	9	4
Huddersfield T	L	02.05	04	4	0	0
Oldham Ath	Tr	03.05	04	1	5	0

FACEY Kenneth (Ken) William
Hackney, 12 October, 1927 (WH)

League Club	Source	Date Signed	Seasons Played	Apps	Subs	Gls
Leyton Orient	Leyton	06.52	52-60	301	-	74

FADIDA Aharon
Israel, 20 September, 1961 (F)

League Club	Source	Date Signed	Seasons Played	Apps	Subs	Gls
Aldershot	Hapoel Haifa (Isr)	12.85	85-86	9	5	6

FADIGA Khalilou
Dakar, Senegal, 30 December, 1974 Senegal int (M)

League Club	Source	Date Signed	Seasons Played	Apps	Subs	Gls
Bolton W	Inter Milan (It)	10.04	04	0	5	0

FAERBER Winston
Surinam, 27 March, 1971 (FB)

League Club	Source	Date Signed	Seasons Played	Apps	Subs	Gls
Cardiff C	ADO Den Haag (Holl)	08.99	99	31	2	1

FAGAN Bernard
Houghton-le-Spring, 29 January, 1949 (W)

League Club	Source	Date Signed	Seasons Played	Apps	Subs	Gls
Sunderland	App	02.66				
Northampton T	Tr	07.69	69	6	0	0

FAGAN Christopher (Kit) James
Manchester, 5 June, 1950 (CD)

League Club	Source	Date Signed	Seasons Played	Apps	Subs	Gls
Liverpool		07.70	70	1	0	0
Tranmere Rov	Tr	07.71	71-74	77	7	2

FAGAN Craig Anthony
Birmingham, 11 December, 1982 (F)

League Club	Source	Date Signed	Seasons Played	Apps	Subs	Gls
Birmingham C	YT	12.01	02	0	1	0
Bristol C	L	01.03	02	5	1	1
Colchester U	Tr	08.03	03-04	55	8	17
Hull C	Tr	02.05	04	11	1	4

FAGAN Fionan (Paddy)
Dublin, 7 June, 1930 IRB/IR-8 (W)

League Club	Source	Date Signed	Seasons Played	Apps	Subs	Gls
Hull C	Transport (Dublin)	03.51	51-53	26	-	2
Manchester C	Tr	12.53	53-59	153	-	34
Derby Co	Tr	03.60	59-60	24	-	6

FAGAN George
Dundee, 27 September, 1934 (WH)

League Club	Source	Date Signed	Seasons Played	Apps	Subs	Gls
Leeds U	Dundee St Joseph	11.53				
Halifax T	Tr	06.58	58-61	67	-	3

FAGAN Joseph (Joe)
Liverpool, 12 March, 1921 Died 2001 (CD)

League Club	Source	Date Signed	Seasons Played	Apps	Subs	Gls
Manchester C	Earlestown Bohemians	10.38	46-50	148	-	2
Bradford PA	Nelson	08.53	53	3	-	0

FAGAN Michael (Mike) Jeffrey
Newcastle, 22 June, 1960 (CD)

League Club	Source	Date Signed	Seasons Played	Apps	Subs	Gls
Hartlepool U	Carlisle U (N/C)	08.79	79-82	36	1	1

FAGAN William (Willie)
Inveresk, 20 February, 1917 Died 1992 SWar-1 (IF)

League Club	Source	Date Signed	Seasons Played	Apps	Subs	Gls
Preston NE	Glasgow Celtic	10.36	36-37	35	-	6
Liverpool	Tr	10.37	37-51	158	-	47

FAHY Alan
Liverpool, 27 January, 1972 (M)

League Club	Source	Date Signed	Seasons Played	Apps	Subs	Gls
Doncaster Rov	Barrow	03.97	96	0	5	0

FAHY John Joseph
Paisley, 13 May, 1943 (CF)

League Club	Source	Date Signed	Seasons Played	Apps	Subs	Gls
Oxford U	Bedford T	01.64	63-65	23	0	14

FAIRBROTHER Barrie Edward
Hackney, 30 December, 1950 (F)

League Club	Source	Date Signed	Seasons Played	Apps	Subs	Gls
Orient	App	01.69	69-74	171	17	41
Millwall	Tr	06.74	75-76	12	3	1

FAIRBROTHER Ian Andrew
Bootle, 2 October, 1966 ESch (M)

League Club	Source	Date Signed	Seasons Played	Apps	Subs	Gls
Liverpool	App	07.84				
Bury	Tr	02.87	86-87	16	10	3
Wrexham	L	10.87	87	7	0	0

FAIRBROTHER John (Jack)
Burton-on-Trent, 16 August, 1917 Died 1999 FLge-1 (G)

League Club	Source	Date Signed	Seasons Played	Apps	Subs	Gls
Preston NE	Burton T	03.37	46	41	-	0
Newcastle U	Tr	07.47	47-51	132	-	0

FAIRBROTHER John
Cricklewood, 12 February, 1941 (F)

League Club	Source	Date Signed	Seasons Played	Apps	Subs	Gls
Watford	Bennetts End	08.59	60-62	40	-	19
Peterborough U	Worcester C	05.65	65-67	69	3	37
Northampton T	Tr	02.68	67-71	135	5	56
Mansfield T	Tr	09.71	71-72	83	2	38
Torquay U	Tr	06.73	73	15	0	3

FAIRCHILD Michael (Mick) Peter
Brixworth, 24 November, 1942 (W)

League Club	Source	Date Signed	Seasons Played	Apps	Subs	Gls
Luton T	Lowestoft T	11.60	60-63	21	-	1
Reading	Tr	07.64	64-65	24	0	6

FAIRCLOUGH Courtney (Chris) Huw
Nottingham, 12 April, 1964 Eu21-7/EB-1 (CD)

League Club	Source	Date Signed	Seasons Played	Apps	Subs	Gls
Nottingham F	App	10.81	82-86	102	5	1
Tottenham H	Tr	07.87	87-88	60	0	5
Leeds U	Tr	03.89	88-94	187	6	21
Bolton W	Tr	07.95	95-97	89	1	8
Notts Co	Tr	07.98	98	16	0	1
York C	Tr	03.99	98-99	36	1	0

FAIRCLOUGH Cyril
Radcliffe, 21 April, 1923 (FB)

League Club	Source	Date Signed	Seasons Played	Apps	Subs	Gls
Bury	Urmston	09.45	46-57	191	-	2

FAIRCLOUGH David
Liverpool, 5 January, 1957 Eu21-1 (F)

League Club	Source	Date Signed	Seasons Played	Apps	Subs	Gls
Liverpool	App	01.74	75-82	64	34	34
Norwich C	Lucerne (Swi)	03.85	84	1	1	0
Oldham Ath	Tr	08.85	85	6	11	1
Tranmere Rov	SK Beveren (Bel)	08.89	89	3	11	1
Wigan Ath	Tr	08.90	90	4	3	1

FAIRCLOUGH Michael (Mick) Joseph
Drogheda, 22 October, 1952 LoI-1/IR-2 (M)

League Club	Source	Date Signed	Seasons Played	Apps	Subs	Gls
Huddersfield T	Drogheda	08.71	71-74	25	10	2

FAIRCLOUGH Wayne Ricks
Nottingham, 27 April, 1968 (CD)

League Club	Source	Date Signed	Seasons Played	Apps	Subs	Gls
Notts Co	App	04.86	85-89	39	32	0
Mansfield T	Tr	03.90	89-93	131	10	12
Chesterfield	Tr	06.94	94-95	12	3	0
Scarborough	L	03.96	95	7	0	0

FAIRFAX Raymond (Ray) John
Smethwick, 13 November, 1941 (FB)

League Club	Source	Date Signed	Seasons Played	Apps	Subs	Gls
West Bromwich A	Jnrs	08.59	62-67	79	2	0
Northampton T	Tr	06.68	68-70	115	0	2

FAIRHURST John
Bentley, South Yorkshire, 15 March, 1944 (WH)

League Club	Source	Date Signed	Seasons Played	Apps	Subs	Gls
Doncaster Rov	App	07.61	61-65	21	0	0

FAIRLEY Thomas (Tom)
Houghton-le-Spring, 12 October, 1932 (G)

League Club	Source	Date Signed	Seasons Played	Apps	Subs	Gls
Sunderland	Bankhead Jnrs	10.51	52	2	-	0
Carlisle U	Tr	05.56	56-58	55	-	0

FAIRWEATHER Carlton
Camberwell, 22 September, 1961 (W)

League Club	Source	Date Signed	Seasons Played	Apps	Subs	Gls
Wimbledon	Tooting & Mitcham	12.84	84-91	118	20	26
Carlisle U	Tr	08.93	93	11	1	1

FAIRWEATHER John Wilson
Dornoch, 12 August, 1924 Died 1989 (WH)

League Club	Source	Date Signed	Seasons Played	Apps	Subs	Gls
Blackburn Rov		04.44				
Carlisle U		11.48	49	1	-	0

FALANA Wade Robert
Westminster, 7 January, 1970 (F)

League Club	Source	Date Signed	Seasons Played	Apps	Subs	Gls
Doncaster Rov	Tooting & Mitcham	10.92	92	2	2	0
Chesterfield	Scarborough (N/C)	03.93	92	4	1	0

FALCO Mark Peter
Hackney, 22 October, 1960 EYth (F)

League Club	Source	Date Signed	Seasons Played	Apps	Subs	Gls
Tottenham H	App	07.78	78-86	162	12	67
Chelsea	L	11.82	82	3	0	0
Watford	Tr	10.86	86	33	0	14
Queens Park Rgrs	Glasgow Rgrs	12.87	87-90	65	22	27
Millwall	Tr	08.91	91	19	2	4

FALCONER Andrew (Andy) Gordon
South Africa, 27 June, 1925 (IF)

League Club	Source	Date Signed	Seasons Played	Apps	Subs	Gls
Blackpool	(South Africa)	09.49	49	4	-	0

FALCONER Henry (Harry)
Newcastle, 22 December, 1954 (FB)

League Club	Source	Date Signed	Seasons Played	Apps	Subs	Gls
Bournemouth	Burnley (App)	07.72	74	4	3	0

FALCONER William (Willie) Henry
Aberdeen, 5 April, 1966 SSch/SYth (M)

League Club	Source	Date Signed	Seasons Played	Apps	Subs	Gls
Watford	Aberdeen	06.88	88-90	85	13	12
Middlesbrough	Tr	08.91	91-92	47	6	10
Sheffield U	Tr	08.93	93	21	2	3
Grimsby T	St Johnstone	03.02	01	1	1	0

FALDER David Edward James
Liverpool, 21 October, 1922 Died 2001 (CD)

League Club	Source	Date Signed	Seasons Played	Apps	Subs	Gls
Everton	Wigan Ath	12.45	49-50	25	-	0

FALLON Henry (Harry)
Paisley, 28 April, 1942 (G)

League Club	Source	Date Signed	Seasons Played	Apps	Subs	Gls
York C	St Johnstone	09.65	65-67	67	0	0

FALLON Kevin Barry
Maltby, 3 December, 1948 (CD)

League Club	Source	Date Signed	Seasons Played	Apps	Subs	Gls
Rotherham U	App	12.65				
Southend U	Sligo Rov	07.70	70	4	0	0

FALLON Peadar (Peter) Domnal
Dublin, 19 October, 1922 (WH)

League Club	Source	Date Signed	Seasons Played	Apps	Subs	Gls
Exeter C		06.47	47-52	110	-	8
Queens Park Rgrs	Tr	08.53	53	1	-	0

FALLON Rory Michael
Gisbourne, New Zealand, 20 March, 1982 EYth (F)

League Club	Source	Date Signed	Seasons Played	Apps	Subs	Gls
Barnsley	YT	03.99	00-03	33	19	11
Shrewsbury T	L	12.01	01	8	3	0
Swindon T	Tr	11.03	03-04	18	32	9
Yeovil T	L	02.05	04	2	4	1

FALLON Shaun
Widnes, 10 September, 1970 (FB)

League Club	Source	Date Signed	Seasons Played	Apps	Subs	Gls
Wigan Ath	YT	07.89	88-89	2	1	0

FALLON Stephen (Steve) Paul
Whittlesey, 3 August, 1956 (CD)

League Club	Source	Date Signed	Seasons Played	Apps	Subs	Gls
Cambridge U	Kettering T	12.74	74-86	405	5	27

FALLON William (Bill) Joseph
Larne, 14 January, 1912 Died 1989 LoI-6/IR-9 (W)

League Club	Source	Date Signed	Seasons Played	Apps	Subs	Gls
Notts Co	Dolphin	02.34	33-37	120	-	20
Sheffield Wed	Tr	03.38	37-38	44	-	12
Notts Co	Dundalk	06.46	46	15	-	3
Exeter C	Tr	06.47	47	8	-	2

FANTHAM John
Sheffield, 6 February, 1939 Eu23-1/FLge-3/E-1 (F)

League Club	Source	Date Signed	Seasons Played	Apps	Subs	Gls
Sheffield Wed	Jnrs	10.56	57-69	381	7	147
Rotherham U	Tr	10.69	69-70	46	5	8

FAREY John Albert
Darlington, 22 July, 1922 Died 1962 (G)

League Club	Source	Date Signed	Seasons Played	Apps	Subs	Gls
Sunderland		02.44				
Carlisle U		11.47	47	2	-	0

FARINA Frank
Queensland, Australia, 5 September, 1964 Australia int (F)

League Club	Source	Date Signed	Seasons Played	Apps	Subs	Gls
Notts Co (L)	Bari (It)	03.92	91	1	2	0

FARLEY Adam John
Liverpool, 12 January, 1980 (FB)

League Club	Source	Date Signed	Seasons Played	Apps	Subs	Gls
Everton	YT	02.98	98	0	1	0

FARLEY Alexander (Alec)
Finchley, 11 May, 1925 (FB)

League Club	Source	Date Signed	Seasons Played	Apps	Subs	Gls
Clapton Orient	Cromwell Ath	11.45	46-47	15	-	0

FARLEY Henry **Brian**
Craven Arms, 1 January, 1927 Died 1962 (CD)

League Club	Source	Date Signed	Seasons Played	Apps	Subs	Gls
Tottenham H	Chelmsford C	07.49	51	1	-	0

FARLEY Craig
Oxford, 17 March, 1981 (CD)

League Club	Source	Date Signed	Seasons Played	Apps	Subs	Gls
Colchester U	Watford (YT)	07.99	99	8	6	0

FARLEY John Denis
Middlesbrough, 21 September, 1951 (W)

League Club	Source	Date Signed	Seasons Played	Apps	Subs	Gls
Watford	Stockton	07.69	70-73	97	8	8
Halifax T	L	09.71	71	6	0	3
Wolverhampton W	Tr	05.74	74-77	35	5	0
Blackpool	L	10.76	76	1	0	0
Hull C	Tr	05.78	78-79	59	1	5
Bury	Tr	08.80	80	17	1	2

FARM George Neil
Slateford, 13 July, 1924 Died 2004 S-10 (G)

League Club	Source	Date Signed	Seasons Played	Apps	Subs	Gls
Blackpool	Hibernian	09.48	48-59	461	-	1

FARMER Frederick **Brian** Webb
Rowley Regis, 29 July, 1933 (FB)

League Club	Source	Date Signed	Seasons Played	Apps	Subs	Gls
Birmingham C	Stourbridge	07.54	56-61	118	-	0
Bournemouth	Tr	01.62	61-64	132	-	0

FARMER James **Edward (Ted)**
Rowley Regis, 21 January, 1940 Eu23-2 (CF)

League Club	Source	Date Signed	Seasons Played	Apps	Subs	Gls
Wolverhampton W	Jnrs	08.57	60-63	57	-	44

FARMER John
Biddulph, 31 August, 1947 Eu23-1 (G)

League Club	Source	Date Signed	Seasons Played	Apps	Subs	Gls
Stoke C	Jnrs	01.65	65-74	163	0	0
Leicester C	L	12.74	74	2	0	0

FARMER Kevin John
Ramsgate, 24 January, 1960 (CD)

League Club	Source	Date Signed	Seasons Played	Apps	Subs	Gls
Leicester C	App	11.77	77	1	0	0
Northampton T	Tr	08.79	79-81	70	7	12

FARMER Michael (Mick) Chester
Leicester, 22 November, 1944 (WH)

League Club	Source	Date Signed	Seasons Played	Apps	Subs	Gls
Birmingham C	App	04.62	63	1	-	1
Lincoln C	Tr	05.65	65	21	1	0

FARMER Ronald (Ron) James
Guernsey, 6 March, 1936 (M)

League Club	Source	Date Signed	Seasons Played	Apps	Subs	Gls
Nottingham F	Jnrs	05.53	57	9	-	0
Coventry C	Tr	11.58	58-67	281	4	47
Notts Co	Tr	10.67	67-68	69	0	5

FARMER Terence (Terry)
Maltby, 11 May, 1931 (CF)

League Club	Source	Date Signed	Seasons Played	Apps	Subs	Gls
Rotherham U	Gainsborough Trinity	07.52	52-57	61	-	24
York C	Tr	01.58	57-59	66	-	28

FARMER William (Bill) Henry
Guernsey, 24 November, 1927 (G)

League Club	Source	Date Signed	Seasons Played	Apps	Subs	Gls
Nottingham F	St Martin's	05.51	53-56	52	-	0
Oldham Ath	Brush Sports	07.57	57	5	-	0

FARNABY Craig
Hartlepool, 8 August, 1967 (M)

League Club	Source	Date Signed	Seasons Played	Apps	Subs	Gls
Hartlepool U	Jnrs	10.84	84	5	0	0
Middlesbrough	Easington Colliery	11.85				
Halifax T	Tr	09.86	86	7	3	1
Stockport Co	Shotton Comrades	09.87	87	17	5	1

FARNEN Austin **Leslie (Les)**
St Helens, 17 September, 1919 Died 1985 (CD)

League Club	Source	Date Signed	Seasons Played	Apps	Subs	Gls
Watford		05.46	46-48	77	-	0
Bradford C	Tr	05.49	49	8	-	0

FARNSWORTH Peter Albert
Barnsley, 17 May, 1946 (WH)

League Club	Source	Date Signed	Seasons Played	Apps	Subs	Gls
Barnsley	App	09.63	64	1	-	0

FARNWORTH Simon
Chorley, 28 October, 1963 ESch (G)

League Club	Source	Date Signed	Seasons Played	Apps	Subs	Gls
Bolton W	App	09.81	83-85	113	0	0
Stockport Co	L	09.86	86	10	0	0
Tranmere Rov	L	01.87	86	7	0	0
Bury	Tr	03.87	86-89	105	0	0
Preston NE	Tr	07.90	90-92	81	0	0
Wigan Ath	Tr	07.93	93-95	126	0	0

FARQUHAR Douglas (Doug) Methven
Buckhaven, 11 June, 1921 (W)

League Club	Source	Date Signed	Seasons Played	Apps	Subs	Gls
Arsenal	St Andrews U	05.44				
Reading	Tr	09.50	50-51	9	-	1

FARR Brian Sydney
Swindon, 19 October, 1930 (WH)

League Club	Source	Date Signed	Seasons Played	Apps	Subs	Gls
Swindon T		04.51	50-51	11	-	0

FARR Craig Jonathan
Newbury, 27 June, 1984 (G)

League Club	Source	Date Signed	Seasons Played	Apps	Subs	Gls
Swindon T	Sch	08.02	02	2	0	0

League Club	Source	Date Signed	Seasons Played	Career Record Apps	Subs	Gls
FARR Ian						
Swindon, 13 February, 1958						(F)
Swindon T	App	●	75	0	1	0
FARR Thomas (Chick) Francis						
Bathgate, 19 February, 1914 Died 1980						(G)
Bradford PA	Broxburn Ath	09.34	34-49	294	-	0
FARRALL Alec						
West Kirby, 3 March, 1936 ESch						(M)
Everton	Jnrs	03.53	52-56	5	-	0
Preston NE	Tr	05.57	57-59	27	-	9
Gillingham	Tr	07.60	60-64	202	-	19
Lincoln C	Tr	06.65	65	20	0	2
Watford	Tr	07.66	66-67	47	1	8
FARRAR John Norman						
St Helens, 6 May, 1928 Died 1988						(WH)
Manchester C		03.48				
Crewe Alex	Tr	01.51	50	2	-	0
FARRELL Andrew (Andy)						
Easington, 21 December, 1983						(F)
Halifax T	YT	●	01	7	2	0
FARRELL Andrew (Andy) James						
Colchester, 7 October, 1965						(M)
Colchester U	App	09.83	83-86	98	7	5
Burnley	Tr	08.87	87-93	237	20	20
Wigan Ath	Tr	09.94	94-95	51	3	1
Rochdale	Tr	07.96	96-98	113	5	6
FARRELL Arthur						
Huddersfield, 1 November, 1920 Died 2000						(FB)
Bradford PA		05.40	46-50	156	-	4
Barnsley	Tr	05.51	51	18	-	0
FARRELL Craig Wayne						
Middlesbrough, 5 December, 1982						(F)
Leeds U	YT	12.99				
Carlisle U	Tr	10.02	02-03	52	11	18
FARRELL David (Dave) William						
Birmingham, 11 November, 1971						(W)
Aston Villa	Redditch U	01.92	92-93	5	1	0
Scunthorpe U	L	01.93	92	4	1	1
Wycombe W	Tr	09.95	95-96	44	16	8
Peterborough U	Tr	07.97	97-04	248	60	36
FARRELL Gerard (Gerry) William						
Liverpool, 19 March, 1952						(FB)
Wolverhampton W	App	03.70				
Blackburn Rov	Tr	10.71	71-72	21	1	1
FARRELL Gregory (Greg) James Philip						
Motherwell, 19 March, 1944						(W)
Birmingham C	App	03.61	62-63	4	-	0
Cardiff C	Tr	03.64	63-66	93	1	8
Bury	Tr	03.67	66-69	83	0	15
FARRELL John (Jackie)						
Clunie, 22 June, 1933						(W)
Accrington St	Perth Celtic	08.54	54	2	-	0
FARRELL Kevin **Michael (Mick)**						
Ilkley, 13 March, 1959						(M)
Scunthorpe U	App	03.77	75-77	5	4	1
FARRELL Paul Anthony						
Liverpool, 1 November, 1958						(F)
Southport	App	●	75	0	2	0
FARRELL Peter Desmond						
Dublin, 16 August, 1922 Died 1999 LoI-7/IR-28/I-7						(WH)
Everton	Shamrock Rov	08.46	46-56	422	-	13
Tranmere Rov	Tr	10.57	57-59	114	-	1
FARRELL Peter John						
Liverpool, 10 January, 1957						(M)
Bury	Ormskirk	09.75	75-78	49	5	9
Port Vale	Tr	11.78	78-81	85	4	10
Rochdale	Tr	08.82	82-84	71	2	17
Crewe Alex	Tr	09.84	84	7	1	1
Crewe Alex	(Iceland)	11.85	85	19	1	1
FARRELL Raymond (Ray) Leo						
Cardiff, 31 May, 1933 Died 1999						(CF)
Crystal Palace	Treharris	05.57	57-58	5	-	0
FARRELL Sean Paul						
Watford, 28 February, 1969						(F)
Luton T	App	03.87	89-91	14	11	1

League Club	Source	Date Signed	Seasons Played	Career Record Apps	Subs	Gls
Colchester U	L	03.88	87	4	5	1
Northampton T	L	09.91	91	4	0	1
Fulham	Tr	12.91	91-93	93	1	31
Peterborough U	Tr	08.94	94-96	49	17	20
Notts Co	Tr	10.96	96-00	58	30	22
FARRELL Stephen (Steve) Edward						
Kilwinning, 8 March, 1973						(M)
Stoke C	YT	07.91	89	0	2	0
FARRELLY Gareth						
Dublin, 28 August, 1975 IRSch/IRYth/IRu21-11/IRB-1/IR-6						(M)
Aston Villa	YT	01.92	95-96	2	6	0
Rotherham U	L	03.95	94	9	1	2
Everton	Tr	07.97	97-98	18	9	1
Bolton W	Tr	11.99	99-02	61	17	5
Rotherham U	L	03.03	02	6	0	0
Burnley	L	09.03	03	9	3	0
Bradford C	L	11.03	03	14	0	0
Wigan Ath	Tr	03.04	03	3	4	0
FARRELLY Michael (Mike)						
Manchester, 1 November, 1962 ESch/ESemiPro						(M)
Preston NE		06.81	81-84	77	5	4
FARRELLY Stephen (Steve)						
Liverpool, 27 March, 1965 ESemiPro						(G)
Rotherham U	Macclesfield T	07.95	96	7	0	0
FARRIMOND Sydney (Syd)						
Hindley, 17 July, 1940 EYth						(FB)
Bolton W	Moss Lane YC	01.58	58-70	364	1	1
Tranmere Rov	Tr	02.71	70-73	132	2	0
FARRINGTON John Robert						
Lynemouth, 19 June, 1947						(W)
Wolverhampton W	App	06.65	66-69	31	3	2
Leicester C	Tr	10.69	69-73	115	3	19
Cardiff C	Tr	11.73	73-74	23	0	6
Northampton T	Tr	10.74	74-79	224	8	29
FARRINGTON Mark Anthony						
Liverpool, 15 June, 1965						(F)
Norwich C	Everton (App)	05.83	83-84	11	3	2
Cambridge U	Tr	03.85	84	10	0	1
Cardiff C	Tr	07.85	85	24	7	3
Brighton & Hove A	Feyenoord (Holl)	08.91	91-93	15	13	4
Hereford U	AIF (Nor)	10.94	94	0	1	0
FARRINGTON Roy Arthur						
Tonbridge, 6 June, 1925						(IF)
Crystal Palace		11.47	47-48	3	-	0
FARROW Desmond (Des) Albert						
Peterborough, 11 February, 1926						(WH)
Stoke C	Leicester C (Am)	10.52	52-53	8	-	0
FARROW George Henry						
Whitburn, 4 October, 1913 Died 1980						(WH)
Stockport Co	Jnrs	10.30	31	6	-	0
Wolverhampton W	Tr	01.32	32	11	-	0
Bournemouth	Tr	07.33	33-35	107	-	12
Blackpool	Tr	06.36	36-47	143	-	15
Sheffield U	Tr	01.48	47	1	-	0
FASCIONE Joseph (Joe) Victor						
Coatbridge, 5 February, 1945						(W)
Chelsea	Kirkintilloch Rob Roy	10.62	65-68	22	7	1
FASHANU John						
Kensington, 18 September, 1962 E-2						(F)
Norwich C	Cambridge U (Jnrs)	10.79	81-82	6	1	1
Crystal Palace	L	08.83	83	1	0	0
Lincoln C	Tr	09.83	83-84	31	5	11
Millwall	Tr	11.84	84-85	50	0	12
Wimbledon	Tr	03.86	85-93	271	5	107
Aston Villa	Tr	08.94	94	11	2	3
FASHANU Justinus (Justin) Soni						
Hackney, 19 February, 1961 Died 1998 EYth/Eu21-11/EB						(F)
Norwich C	App	12.78	78-79	44	6	16
Norwich C	Adelaide C (Aus)	08.80	80	40	0	19
Nottingham F	Adelaide C (Aus)	08.81	81	31	1	3
Southampton	L	08.82	82	9	0	3
Notts Co	Tr	12.82	82-84	63	1	20
Brighton & Hove A	Tr	06.85	85	16	0	2
Manchester C	Edmonton (Can)	10.89	89	0	2	0
West Ham U	Tr	11.89	89	2	0	0
Leyton Orient	Tr	03.90	89	3	2	0
Newcastle U	Southall	10.91				
Torquay U	Toronto (Can)	12.91	91-92	41	0	15

League Club	Source	Date Signed	Seasons Played	Career Record Apps	Subs	Gls
FAULCONBRIDGE Craig Michael						
Nuneaton, 20 April, 1978						(F)
Coventry C	YT	07.96				
Hull C	L	12.98	98	4	6	0
Wrexham	Tr	08.99	99-01	92	19	31
Wycombe W	Tr	07.02	02-04	46	12	8
FAULKES Brian Keith						
Abingdon, 10 April, 1945						(FB)
Reading	Jnrs	09.63	63-66	23	1	0
Northampton T	Tr	07.67	67-68	51	1	2
Torquay U	Tr	07.69	69	6	0	0
FAULKNER David Peter						
Sheffield, 8 October, 1975 ESch/EYth						(CD)
Sheffield Wed	YT	12.92				
Darlington	Tr	08.96	96	2	2	0
FAULKNER John Gilbert						
Orpington, 10 March, 1948						(CD)
Leeds U	Sutton U	03.70	69	2	0	0
Luton T	Tr	03.72	72-77	209	0	6
FAULKNER Kenneth (Ken) Gordon						
Smethwick, 10 September, 1923 Died 2000 ESch						(W)
Birmingham C	Smethwick Highfield	09.44	46	2	-	0
FAULKNER Michael (Mike)						
Conisbrough, 3 January, 1950						(F)
Sheffield U	App	12.67				
Oldham Ath	Tr	07.69	69	1	0	0
FAULKNER Raymond (Ray) Arthur						
Horncastle, 26 May, 1934						(W)
Grimsby T	Horncastle T	10.54	54	5	-	1
FAULKNER Roy Vincent						
Manchester, 28 June, 1935						(IF)
Manchester C	Jnrs	12.52	55	7	-	4
Walsall	Tr	03.58	57-60	100	-	44
FAULKNER Stephen (Steve) Andrew						
Sheffield, 18 December, 1954						(CD)
Sheffield U	App	02.72	72-76	14	1	0
Stockport Co	L	03.78	77	3	1	0
York C	Tr	05.78	78-80	90	0	7
FAWCETT Brian						
Barnburgh, 14 February, 1932 Died 1991						(W)
Scunthorpe U	Bentley Colliery	02.55	54	1	-	0
FAWCETT Roy						
Hunslet, 20 January, 1938						(W)
Blackpool	Jnrs	03.55	55-59	3	-	0
FAWELL Derek Stuart						
Hartlepool, 22 March, 1944						(CF)
Notts Co	Spennymoor U	10.64	64	1	-	0
Lincoln C	Tr	09.65	65	3	0	0
FAWLEY Ronald (Ron)						
Ashton-under-Lyne, 22 April, 1927 Died 1982						(W)
Oldham Ath	Ashton U	08.50	50-57	94	-	9
FAYADH Jassim						
Baghdad, Iraq, 1 July, 1975 Iraq int						(F)
Macclesfield T	Al Jawiya (Iraq)	08.04	04	0	1	0
FAYE Amdy Mustapha						
Dakar, Senegal, 12 March, 1977 Senegal int						(M)
Portsmouth	Auxerre (Fr)	08.03	03-04	44	3	0
Newcastle U	Tr	01.05	04	8	1	0
FAZACKERLEY Derek William						
Preston, 5 November, 1951						(CD)
Blackburn Rov	App	10.69	70-86	593	3	23
Chester C	Tr	01.87	86-87	66	0	0
York C	Tr	07.88	88	16	0	0
Bury	Tr	12.88	88	7	7	0
FAZACKERLEY Michael (Mick) Alexander						
Manchester, 8 April, 1932						(FB)
Bradford PA	Bradford C (Am)	08.55	55	2	-	0
FEALEY Nathan James						
Aldershot, 12 March, 1973						(M)
Reading	YT	07.91	91	1	0	0
FEAR Keith William						
Bristol, 8 May, 1952 ESch						(F)
Bristol C	Jnrs	06.69	70-76	126	25	32

League Club	Source	Date Signed	Seasons Played	Career Record Apps	Subs	Gls
Hereford U	L	09.77	77	6	0	0
Blackburn Rov	L	12.77	77	5	0	2
Plymouth Arg	Tr	02.78	77-79	41	5	9
Brentford	L	11.79	79	7	1	2
Chester	Tr	01.80	79-80	41	3	3
FEAR Peter Stanley						
Sutton, 10 September, 1973 Eu21-3						(M)
Wimbledon	YT	07.92	92-98	51	22	4
Oxford U	Tr	07.99	99-00	27	11	3
FEAR Vivien James						
Bristol, 24 October, 1955						(F)
Hereford U	Bristol C (App)	07.74	74	2	1	0
FEARNLEY Gordon						
Bradford, 25 January, 1950 ESch						(F)
Sheffield Wed	Jnrs	07.68				
Bristol Rov	Tr	07.70	70-76	95	27	21
FEARNLEY Harrison (Harry) Lockhead						
Morley, 27 May, 1923						(G)
Leeds U	Bradford PA (Am)	11.45	46-48	28	-	0
Halifax T	Tr	01.49	48	3	-	0
Newport Co	Tr	07.49	49-52	103	-	0
Rochdale	Selby T	07.55	55	1	-	0
FEARNLEY Henry (Harry)						
Penistone, 16 June, 1935						(G)
Huddersfield T	Jnrs	12.52	55-62	90	-	0
Oxford U	Tr	10.63	63-65	90	0	0
Doncaster Rov	Tr	02.66	65-66	32	0	0
FEARON Ronald (Ron) Thomas						
Romford, 19 November, 1960						(G)
Reading	Dover	02.80	80-82	61	0	0
Ipswich T	Sutton U	09.87	87-88	28	0	0
Brighton & Hove A	L	09.88	88	7	0	0
Walsall	Sutton U	02.93	92	1	0	0
Southend U	Tr	10.93				
Leyton Orient	Barkingside	08.95	95	18	0	0
FEASEY Paul Cedric						
Hull, 4 May, 1933						(CD)
Hull C	York RI	05.50	52-64	271	-	0
FEATHERSTONE James (Jamie) Lee						
Yeadon, 12 November, 1979						(F)
Scunthorpe U	Blackburn Rov (YT)	03.98	97	0	1	0
FEATHERSTONE Keith						
Bradford, 30 August, 1935						(G)
Bradford PA	Wyke Celtic	12.55	55	1	-	0
FEATHERSTONE Lee Paul						
Chesterfield, 20 July, 1983						(M)
Sheffield U	YT	07.01				
Scunthorpe U	Tr	10.02	02-04	17	15	0
FEE Gregory (Greg) Paul						
Halifax, 24 June, 1964						(CD)
Bradford C	App	05.83	82-83	6	1	0
Sheffield Wed	Boston U	08.87	87-89	16	10	0
Preston NE	L	09.90	90	10	0	0
Northampton T	L	11.90	90	1	0	0
Preston NE	L	01.91	90	5	0	0
Leyton Orient	L	03.91	90	4	1	0
Mansfield T	Tr	03.91	90-92	50	4	7
Chesterfield	L	12.92	92	10	0	0
FEEHAN John (Sonny) Ignatius						
Dublin, 17 September, 1926 Died 1995						(G)
Manchester U	Waterford	11.48	49	12	-	0
Northampton T	Tr	08.50	50-51	39	-	0
Brentford	Tr	08.54	54-58	30	-	0
FEELEY Andrew (Andy) James						
Hereford, 30 September, 1961						(FB)
Hereford U	App	08.79	78-79	50	1	3
Leicester C	Trowbridge T	02.84	83-86	74	2	0
Brentford	Tr	08.87	87-88	57	10	0
Bury	Tr	07.89	89-90	46	11	2
FEELY Peter John						
City of London, 3 January, 1950 EYth/EAmat						(F)
Chelsea	Enfield	05.70	70-72	4	1	2
Bournemouth	Tr	02.73	72-73	8	1	2
Fulham	Tr	07.74				
Gillingham	Tr	10.74	74-75	41	0	22
Sheffield Wed	Tr	02.76	75-76	17	2	2
Stockport Co	L	01.77	76	2	0	0

FEENEY James (Jim) McBurney
Belfast, 23 June, 1921 Died 1985 NIRL-3/IWar-2/I-2 (FB)

League Club	Source	Date Signed	Seasons Played	Apps	Subs	Gls
Swansea T	Linfield	12.46	46-49	88	-	0
Ipswich T	Tr	03.50	49-55	214	-	0

FEENEY Joseph (Joe)
Glasgow, 21 July, 1926 Died 1992 (IF)

League Club	Source	Date Signed	Seasons Played	Apps	Subs	Gls
Sunderland	St Theresa's	07.47				
Chester	Rhyl	09.51	51	5	-	0

FEENEY Mark Anthony
Derry, 26 July, 1974 (M)

League Club	Source	Date Signed	Seasons Played	Apps	Subs	Gls
Barnsley	YT	07.93	92	0	2	0

FEENEY Warren James
Belfast, 17 January, 1981 NISch/NIYth/NIu21-8/NI-5 (F)

League Club	Source	Date Signed	Seasons Played	Apps	Subs	Gls
Leeds U	St Andrew's BC	01.98				
Bournemouth	Tr	03.01	00-03	83	25	36
Stockport Co	Tr	07.04	04	31	0	15
Luton T	Tr	03.05	04	1	5	0

FELGATE David Wynne
Blaenau Ffestiniog, 4 March, 1960 WSch/W-1 (G)

League Club	Source	Date Signed	Seasons Played	Apps	Subs	Gls
Bolton W	Blaenau Ffestiniog	08.78				
Rochdale	L	10.78	78	35	0	0
Crewe Alex	L	09.79	79	14	0	0
Rochdale	L	03.80	79	12	0	0
Lincoln C	Tr	09.80	80-84	198	0	0
Cardiff C	L	12.84	84	4	0	0
Grimsby T	L	02.85	84	12	0	0
Grimsby T	Tr	06.85	85-86	24	0	0
Bolton W	L	02.86	85	15	0	0
Bolton W	Tr	02.87	86-91	223	0	0
Bury	Tr	07.93				
Chester C	Wolverhampton W (N/C)	10.93	93-94	71	1	0
Wigan Ath	Tr	07.95	95	3	0	0

FELIX Gary
Manchester, 31 October, 1957 (M)

League Club	Source	Date Signed	Seasons Played	Apps	Subs	Gls
Leeds U	App	11.75				
Chester	Manchester C (N/C)	01.79	78	8	0	0

FELL Geoffrey (Geoff) Mark
Carlisle, 8 May, 1960 (F)

League Club	Source	Date Signed	Seasons Played	Apps	Subs	Gls
Carlisle U	Jnrs	06.77	77-79	0	3	0

FELL Gerald (Gerry) Charles
Newark, 1 March, 1951 (F)

League Club	Source	Date Signed	Seasons Played	Apps	Subs	Gls
Brighton & Hove A	Long Eaton U	11.74	74-77	65	14	19
Southend U	Tr	11.77	77-79	43	2	10
Torquay U	Tr	07.80	80-81	50	0	12
York C	Tr	03.82	81	2	3	0

FELL James (Jimmy) Irving
Cleethorpes, 4 January, 1936 (W)

League Club	Source	Date Signed	Seasons Played	Apps	Subs	Gls
Grimsby T	Waltham	04.54	56-60	166	-	35
Everton	Tr	03.61	60-61	27	-	4
Newcastle U	Tr	03.62	61-62	49	-	16
Walsall	Tr	07.63	63	21	-	4
Lincoln C	Tr	01.64	63-65	64	0	10

FELL Leslie (Les) James
Leyton, 16 December, 1920 (W)

League Club	Source	Date Signed	Seasons Played	Apps	Subs	Gls
Charlton Ath	Gravesend U	12.45	46-51	13	-	2
Crystal Palace	Tr	10.52	52-53	65	-	6

FELLOWES William (Billy) James
Bradford, 15 March, 1910 Died 1987 (WH)

League Club	Source	Date Signed	Seasons Played	Apps	Subs	Gls
Plymouth Arg	Tavistock T	07.27	29-32	5	-	0
Clapton Orient	Tr	07.33	33-34	78	-	1
Luton T	Tr	05.35	35-37	110	-	3
Exeter C	Tr	06.38	38-46	56	-	1

FELLOWS Geoffrey (Geoff) Alan
West Bromwich, 26 July, 1944 (FB)

League Club	Source	Date Signed	Seasons Played	Apps	Subs	Gls
Aston Villa	App	10.61				
Shrewsbury T	Tr	06.65	65-72	276	4	2

FELLOWS Gregory (Greg) Frederick Arthur
Dudley, 10 October, 1953 (F)

League Club	Source	Date Signed	Seasons Played	Apps	Subs	Gls
Aston Villa	App	09.71				
Crewe Alex	L	02.73	72	3	0	1

FELLOWS Stewart
Stockton, 9 October, 1948 (CD)

League Club	Source	Date Signed	Seasons Played	Apps	Subs	Gls
Newcastle U	App	03.66				
York C	Tr	06.67	67	0	2	0

FELTON Graham MacLean
Cambridge, 1 March, 1949 EYth (W)

League Club	Source	Date Signed	Seasons Played	Apps	Subs	Gls
Northampton T	Cambridge U	09.66	66-75	243	10	25
Barnsley	L	02.76	75	12	0	2
Barnsley	Tr	07.76	76	24	0	3

FELTON Kenneth (Ken) Carl
Blackhall, 18 February, 1949 (M)

League Club	Source	Date Signed	Seasons Played	Apps	Subs	Gls
Darlington	Jnrs	04.67	67-69	50	2	7

FELTON Robert Francis Foster
Gateshead, 12 August, 1918 Died 1982 (FB)

League Club	Source	Date Signed	Seasons Played	Apps	Subs	Gls
Everton		08.37				
Port Vale	Tr	06.38	38	10	-	0
Crystal Palace	Tr	09.46	46	1	-	0

FELTON Vivien Edward
Southgate, 13 August, 1929 (CD)

League Club	Source	Date Signed	Seasons Played	Apps	Subs	Gls
Crystal Palace	Barnet	08.54	54-55	2	-	0

FENCOTT Kenneth (Ken) Sydney
Walsall, 27 December, 1943 (W)

League Club	Source	Date Signed	Seasons Played	Apps	Subs	Gls
Aston Villa	App	01.61	61-63	3	-	0
Lincoln C	Tr	06.64	64-66	67	6	13

FENG Li Wei
Jilin, China, 26 January, 1978 China 57 (CD)

League Club	Source	Date Signed	Seasons Played	Apps	Subs	Gls
Everton (L)	Shenzan Ping'an (China)	07.02	02	1	0	0

FENN Neale Michael Charles
Edmonton, 18 January, 1977 IRYth/IRu21-9/IRB-1 (F)

League Club	Source	Date Signed	Seasons Played	Apps	Subs	Gls
Tottenham H	YT	07.95	96-97	0	8	0
Leyton Orient	L	01.98	97	3	0	0
Norwich C	L	03.98	97	6	1	1
Swindon T	L	11.98	98	4	0	0
Lincoln C	L	12.98	98	0	4	0
Peterborough U	Tr	07.01	01-02	33	17	7

FENNEY Stanley (Stan)
Barry, 21 June, 1923 Died 2003 (FB)

League Club	Source	Date Signed	Seasons Played	Apps	Subs	Gls
Barrow	Stranraer	12.45	46	27	-	0

FENOUGHTY Thomas (Tom)
Rotherham, 7 June, 1941 (M)

League Club	Source	Date Signed	Seasons Played	Apps	Subs	Gls
Sheffield U	Sheffield FC	11.63	63-68	47	3	4
Chesterfield	Tr	07.69	69-71	97	3	15

FENSOME Andrew (Andy) Brian
Northampton, 18 February, 1969 (FB)

League Club	Source	Date Signed	Seasons Played	Apps	Subs	Gls
Norwich C	App	02.87				
Cambridge U	Bury T	11.89	89-93	122	4	1
Preston NE	Tr	10.93	93-95	93	0	1
Rochdale	Tr	06.96	96-97	80	2	0

FENTON Anthony (Tony) Brian
Preston, 23 November, 1979 EYth (CD)

League Club	Source	Date Signed	Seasons Played	Apps	Subs	Gls
Manchester C	YT	11.96				
Portsmouth	Tr	03.99	99	0	1	0

FENTON Benjamin (Benny) Robert Vincent
West Ham, 28 October, 1918 Died 2000 (WH)

League Club	Source	Date Signed	Seasons Played	Apps	Subs	Gls
West Ham U	Colchester T	10.35	37-38	21	-	9
Millwall	Tr	03.39	38-46	20	-	7
Charlton Ath	Tr	01.47	46-54	264	-	22
Colchester U	Tr	02.55	54-57	104	-	15

FENTON Alexander Ewan
Dundee, 17 November, 1929 (WH)

League Club	Source	Date Signed	Seasons Played	Apps	Subs	Gls
Blackpool	Dundee North End	11.46	48-58	203	-	20
Wrexham	Tr	05.59	59	24	-	0

FENTON Graham Anthony
Wallsend, 22 May, 1974 Eu21-1 (F)

League Club	Source	Date Signed	Seasons Played	Apps	Subs	Gls
Aston Villa	YT	02.92	93-95	16	16	3
West Bromwich A	L	01.94	93	7	0	3
Blackburn Rov	Tr	11.95	95-96	9	18	7
Leicester C	Tr	08.97	97-99	13	21	3
Walsall	Tr	03.00	99	8	1	1
Stoke C	Tr	08.00	00	2	3	1
Blackpool	St Mirren	08.01	01	6	9	5
Darlington	L	09.02	02	4	2	1

FENTON Michael (Micky)
Stockton, 30 October, 1913 Died 2003 EWar-1/E-1 (CF)

League Club	Source	Date Signed	Seasons Played	Apps	Subs	Gls
Middlesbrough	South Bank East End	03.33	32-49	240	-	147

FENTON Nicholas (Nicky) Leonard
Preston, 23 November, 1979 EYth (CD)

League Club	Source	Date Signed	Seasons Played	Apps	Subs	Gls
Manchester C	YT	11.96	98	15	0	0
Notts Co	L	10.99	99	13	0	1
Bournemouth	L	03.00	99	8	0	0
Bournemouth	L	08.00	00	4	1	0
Notts Co	Tr	09.00	00-03	153	2	9
Doncaster Rov	Tr	07.04	04	37	1	1

FENTON Ronald (Ronnie)
South Shields, 21 September, 1940 (M)

League Club	Source	Date Signed	Seasons Played	Apps	Subs	Gls
Burnley	South Shields	09.57	60-61	11	-	1
West Bromwich A	Tr	11.62	62-64	59	-	16
Birmingham C	Tr	01.65	64-67	28	5	7
Brentford	Tr	01.68	67-69	87	4	19

FENTON Stephen (Steve) James
Hartlepool, 25 February, 1951 EYth (M)

League Club	Source	Date Signed	Seasons Played	Apps	Subs	Gls
Middlesbrough	Jnrs	08.69				
Bradford C	Tr	06.72	72	9	1	1

FENTON William (Billy) Hartes
Hartlepool, 23 June, 1926 Died 1973 (W)

League Club	Source	Date Signed	Seasons Played	Apps	Subs	Gls
Barnsley		11.44				
Blackburn Rov	Horden CW	12.48	48-50	33	-	7
York C	Tr	05.51	51-57	257	-	118

FENWICK Paul Joseph
Camden, 25 August, 1969 Canada int (CD)

League Club	Source	Date Signed	Seasons Played	Apps	Subs	Gls
Birmingham C	Winnipeg (Can)	11.92	92-93	9	10	0

FENWICK Terence (Terry) William
Seaham, 17 November, 1959 EYth/Eu21-11/E-20 (CD)

League Club	Source	Date Signed	Seasons Played	Apps	Subs	Gls
Crystal Palace	App	12.76	77-80	62	8	0
Queens Park Rgrs	Tr	12.80	80-87	256	0	33
Tottenham H	Tr	12.87	87-92	90	3	8
Leicester C	L	10.90	90	8	0	1
Swindon T	Tr	09.93	93-94	25	3	0

FERDINAND Anton Julian
Peckham, 18 February, 1985 EYth/Eu21-3 (CD)

League Club	Source	Date Signed	Seasons Played	Apps	Subs	Gls
West Ham U	Sch	08.02	03-04	33	16	1

FERDINAND Leslie (Les)
Acton, 8 December, 1966 EYth/EB-1/E-17 (F)

League Club	Source	Date Signed	Seasons Played	Apps	Subs	Gls
Queens Park Rgrs	Hayes	03.87	86-94	152	11	80
Brentford	L	03.88	87	3	0	0
Newcastle U	Tr	06.95	95-96	67	1	41
Tottenham H	Tr	08.97	97-02	97	21	33
West Ham U	Tr	01.03	02	12	2	2
Leicester C	Tr	07.03	03	20	9	12
Bolton W	Tr	07.04	04	1	11	1
Reading	Tr	01.05	04	4	8	1

FERDINAND Rio Gavin
Peckham, 7 November, 1978 EYth/Eu21-5/E-38 (CD)

League Club	Source	Date Signed	Seasons Played	Apps	Subs	Gls
West Ham U	YT	11.95	95-00	122	5	2
Bournemouth	L	11.96	96	10	0	0
Leeds U	Tr	11.00	00-01	54	0	2
Manchester U	Tr	07.02	02-04	78	1	0

FEREBEE Stewart Raymond
Carshalton, 6 September, 1960 (F)

League Club	Source	Date Signed	Seasons Played	Apps	Subs	Gls
York C	Harrogate T	07.79	79-80	7	6	0
Darlington	Harrogate T	03.87	86	8	0	0
Halifax T	Tr	07.87	87	6	6	0

FEREDAY Wayne
Warley, 16 June, 1963 Eu21-5/FLge (W)

League Club	Source	Date Signed	Seasons Played	Apps	Subs	Gls
Queens Park Rgrs	App	09.80	80-88	167	29	21
Newcastle U	Tr	06.89	89-90	27	6	0
Bournemouth	Tr	11.90	90-91	20	3	0
West Bromwich A	Tr	12.91	91-93	39	9	3
Cardiff C	Tr	03.94	93-94	43	1	2

FERGUSON Alexander (Alex) Stirling Brown
Lochore, 5 August, 1903 Died 1974 WLge-2 (G)

League Club	Source	Date Signed	Seasons Played	Apps	Subs	Gls
Wigan Bor	Vale of Clyde	11.24	24	1	-	0
Gillingham	Tr	06.25	25-26	67	-	0
Swansea T	Tr	02.27	26-35	280	-	0
Bury	Tr	06.36	36-37	63	-	0
Newport Co	Tr	06.38	38	41	-	0
Bristol C	Tr	05.46	46	32	-	0
Swindon T	Tr	09.47	47	7	-	0

FERGUSON Archibald (Archie)
Lochore, 9 December, 1918 Died 1998 (G)

League Club	Source	Date Signed	Seasons Played	Apps	Subs	Gls
Doncaster Rov	Raith Rov	12.41	46-47	61	-	0
Wrexham	Tr	07.48	48-52	126	-	0

FERGUSON Barry
Dublin, 7 September, 1979 IRu21-6 (CD)

League Club	Source	Date Signed	Seasons Played	Apps	Subs	Gls
Coventry C	Home Farm	09.98				
Colchester U	L	03.00	99	5	1	0
Hartlepool U	L	07.00	00	4	0	0
Northampton T	L	12.00	00	1	2	0

FERGUSON Barry
Glasgow, 2 February, 1978 Su21-12/S-29 (M)

League Club	Source	Date Signed	Seasons Played	Apps	Subs	Gls
Blackburn Rov	Glasgow Rgrs	08.03	03-04	35	1	3

FERGUSON James Brian
Irvine, 14 December, 1960 (M)

League Club	Source	Date Signed	Seasons Played	Apps	Subs	Gls
Newcastle U	Mansfield T (App)	01.79	79	4	1	1
Hull C	Tr	12.80	80-81	24	4	2
Southend U	Goole T	08.83	83-84	31	10	6
Chesterfield	Tr	10.84	84	30	1	0

FERGUSON Charles (Charlie)
Glasgow, 22 April, 1930 (FB)

League Club	Source	Date Signed	Seasons Played	Apps	Subs	Gls
Accrington St	Hamilton Academical	05.54	54	1	-	0
Rochdale	Tr	09.55	55-58	150	-	3
Oldham Ath	Tr	07.59	59-60	57	-	0

FERGUSON Darren
Glasgow, 9 February, 1972 SYth/Su21-5 (M)

League Club	Source	Date Signed	Seasons Played	Apps	Subs	Gls
Manchester U	YT	07.90	90-93	20	7	0
Wolverhampton W	Tr	01.94	93-98	94	23	4
Wrexham	Tr	09.99	99-04	237	1	22

FERGUSON David Dyer
Bonnybridge, 11 March, 1929 (W)

League Club	Source	Date Signed	Seasons Played	Apps	Subs	Gls
Coventry C	Alloa Ath	10.56	56	4	-	0

FERGUSON Derek
Glasgow, 31 July, 1967 SSch/SYth/Su21-5/S-2 (M)

League Club	Source	Date Signed	Seasons Played	Apps	Subs	Gls
Sunderland	Heart of Midlothian	07.93	93-94	64	0	0

FERGUSON Donald (Don)
Toronto, Canada, 2 January, 1963 CaB (G)

League Club	Source	Date Signed	Seasons Played	Apps	Subs	Gls
Wrexham		01.86	85	20	0	0

FERGUSON Duncan Cowan
Stirling, 27 December, 1971 SSch/SYth/Su21-7/SB/S-7 (F)

League Club	Source	Date Signed	Seasons Played	Apps	Subs	Gls
Everton	Glasgow Rgrs	10.94	94-98	110	6	37
Newcastle U	Tr	11.98	98-99	24	6	8
Everton	Tr	08.00	00-04	45	51	22

FERGUSON Edward (Eddie) Brodie
Whitburn, 10 September, 1949 (M)

League Club	Source	Date Signed	Seasons Played	Apps	Subs	Gls
Rotherham U	Dumbarton	02.71	70-73	64	3	5
Grimsby T	L	11.71	71	1	1	0

FERGUSON Hubert
Belfast, 23 May, 1926 Died 1994 (FB)

League Club	Source	Date Signed	Seasons Played	Apps	Subs	Gls
Bradford C	Ballymena U	07.48	48-52	132	-	0
Halifax T	Frickley Colliery	09.54	54-57	95	-	0

FERGUSON Iain John
Newarthill, 4 August, 1962 Su21-4 (F)

League Club	Source	Date Signed	Seasons Played	Apps	Subs	Gls
Charlton Ath (L)	Heart of Midlothian	11.89	89	1	0	0
Bristol C (L)	Heart of Midlothian	03.90	89	8	3	2

FERGUSON James (Jim) Cameron Mars
Glasgow, 20 February, 1935 (G)

League Club	Source	Date Signed	Seasons Played	Apps	Subs	Gls
Oldham Ath	Falkirk	05.59	59	36	-	0
Crewe Alex	Tr	08.60	60-61	27	-	0
Darlington	Tr	07.62	62	32	-	0

FERGUSON John (Jackie)
Maybole, 29 August, 1939 (W)

League Club	Source	Date Signed	Seasons Played	Apps	Subs	Gls
Southend U	Airdrie	06.67	67	13	1	2

FERGUSON John Theodore Hever
Edinburgh, 14 June, 1939 (W)

League Club	Source	Date Signed	Seasons Played	Apps	Subs	Gls
Oldham Ath	St Andrew's U	11.56	56	1	-	0

FERGUSON Mark
Liverpool, 6 November, 1960 (W)

League Club	Source	Date Signed	Seasons Played	Apps	Subs	Gls
Tranmere Rov		08.81	81-84	72	16	13

FERGUSON Martin Murphy
Glasgow, 21 December, 1942 (IF)

League Club	Source	Date Signed	Seasons Played	Apps	Subs	Gls
Barnsley	Morton	08.65	65	40	0	17
Doncaster Rov	Tr	07.66	66	3	0	0

FERGUSON Michael (Mick) John
Newcastle, 3 October, 1954 (F)

League Club	Source	Date Signed	Seasons Played	Apps	Subs	Gls
Coventry C	App	12.71	74-80	121	6	51
Everton	Tr	08.81	81	7	1	4
Birmingham C	L	11.82	82	20	0	8
Birmingham C	Tr	06.83	84	2	0	1
Coventry C	L	03.84	83	7	0	3
Brighton & Hove A	Tr	09.84	84-85	17	0	6
Colchester U	Tr	03.86	85-86	25	1	11

FERGUSON Michael (Mike) Kevin
Burnley, 9 March, 1943 (W)

League Club	Source	Date Signed	Seasons Played	Apps	Subs	Gls
Accrington St	Plymouth Arg (Am)	07.60	60	23	-	1
Blackburn Rov	Tr	03.62	62-67	220	0	29
Aston Villa	Tr	05.68	68-69	38	0	2
Queens Park Rgrs	Tr	11.69	69-72	67	1	2

League Club	Source	Date Signed	Seasons Played	Apps	Subs	Gls
Cambridge U	Tr	07.73	73	39	0	4
Rochdale	Tr	07.74	74-75	68	1	5
Halifax T	IA Akranes (Ice)	12.76	76	2	0	0

FERGUSON Robert (Bob)
Grangetown, 25 July, 1917 (G)

League Club	Source	Date Signed	Seasons Played	Apps	Subs	Gls
Middlesbrough	Hurworth Jnrs	08.35	36-37	10	-	0
York C	Tr	05.39	46	26	-	0

FERGUSON Robert (Bobby)
Kilwinning, 1 March, 1945 Su23-1/SLge-2/S-7 (G)

League Club	Source	Date Signed	Seasons Played	Apps	Subs	Gls
West Ham U	Kilmarnock	06.67	67-79	240	0	0
Sheffield Wed	L	02.74	73	5	0	0

FERGUSON Robert (Bobby) Burnitt
Dudley, Northumberland, 8 January, 1938 (FB)

League Club	Source	Date Signed	Seasons Played	Apps	Subs	Gls
Newcastle U	Dudley Welfare	05.55	55-62	11	-	0
Derby Co	Tr	10.62	62-65	121	0	0
Cardiff C	Tr	12.65	65-68	88	1	0
Newport Co	Barry T	07.69	69-70	71	0	2

FERGUSON Ronald (Ron) Charles
Accrington, 9 February, 1957 (F)

League Club	Source	Date Signed	Seasons Played	Apps	Subs	Gls
Sheffield Wed	App	02.75	74	10	1	1
Scunthorpe U	L	12.75	75	3	0	0
Darlington	Tr	02.76	75-79	101	13	18

FERN Rodney Alan
Measham, 13 December, 1948 (F)

League Club	Source	Date Signed	Seasons Played	Apps	Subs	Gls
Leicester C	Measham Social Welf	12.66	67-71	133	16	31
Luton T	Tr	06.72	72-74	34	5	5
Chesterfield	Tr	06.75	75-78	150	2	54
Rotherham U	Tr	06.79	79-82	98	7	34

FERNANDES Fabrice
Aubervilliers, France, 29 October, 1979 Fru21 (W)

League Club	Source	Date Signed	Seasons Played	Apps	Subs	Gls
Fulham (L)	Rennes (Fr)	08.00	00	23	6	2
Southampton	Rennes (Fr)	12.01	01-04	76	15	5

FERNANDES Tamer Hasan
Paddington, 7 December, 1974 EYth (G)

League Club	Source	Date Signed	Seasons Played	Apps	Subs	Gls
Brentford	YT	07.93	93-96	10	2	0
Colchester U	Tr	01.98	98	8	0	0

FERNEY Martin John
Lambeth, 8 November, 1971 (M)

League Club	Source	Date Signed	Seasons Played	Apps	Subs	Gls
Fulham	YT	07.90	90-94	49	11	1

FERNIE James (Jim)
Kirkcaldy, 31 October, 1936 (IF)

League Club	Source	Date Signed	Seasons Played	Apps	Subs	Gls
Doncaster Rov	Arbroath	10.58	58-60	89	-	31

FERNIE William (Willie)
Kinglassie, 22 November, 1928 SLge-5/SB/S-12 (IF)

League Club	Source	Date Signed	Seasons Played	Apps	Subs	Gls
Middlesbrough	Glasgow Celtic	12.58	58-60	65	-	3

FERNS Philip (Phil)
Liverpool, 14 November, 1937 (CD)

League Club	Source	Date Signed	Seasons Played	Apps	Subs	Gls
Liverpool	Manchester C (Am)	09.57	62-64	27	-	1
Bournemouth	Tr	08.65	65	46	0	0
Mansfield T	Tr	08.66	66-67	55	1	1

FERNS Philip (Phil) David
Liverpool, 12 September, 1961 (FB)

League Club	Source	Date Signed	Seasons Played	Apps	Subs	Gls
Bournemouth	App	02.79	78-80	94	1	6
Charlton Ath	Tr	08.81	81-82	35	3	1
Wimbledon	L	12.82	82	7	0	0
Blackpool	Tr	08.83	83-84	44	3	0
Aldershot	Tr	07.85	85	24	0	2

FERRARI Carlos Eduardo
Londrina, Brazil, 19 February, 1979 (M)

League Club	Source	Date Signed	Seasons Played	Apps	Subs	Gls
Birmingham C (L)	Mirassol (Br)	08.01	01	0	4	0

FERREIRA Renato **Paulo**
Cascais, Portugal, 18 January, 1979 Portugal 22 (FB)

League Club	Source	Date Signed	Seasons Played	Apps	Subs	Gls
Chelsea	FC Porto (Por)	07.04	04	29	0	0

FERRER Albert Llopes
Barcelona, Spain, 6 June, 1970 Spu23/Sp-36 (FB)

League Club	Source	Date Signed	Seasons Played	Apps	Subs	Gls
Chelsea	Barcelona (Sp)	08.98	98-02	71	5	0

FERRETT Christopher (Chris) Andrew
Poole, 10 February, 1977 (M)

League Club	Source	Date Signed	Seasons Played	Apps	Subs	Gls
Bournemouth	YT	●	94	0	1	0

FERRI Jean-Michel
Lyon, France, 7 February, 1969 France 5 (M)

League Club	Source	Date Signed	Seasons Played	Apps	Subs	Gls
Liverpool	Istantbulspor (Tu)	12.98	98	0	2	0

FERRIDAY Leslie (Les)
Manchester, 3 June, 1929 (WH)

League Club	Source	Date Signed	Seasons Played	Apps	Subs	Gls
Walsall	Buxton	05.54	54	32	-	1

FERRIER Henry (Harry)
Ratho, 20 May, 1920 Died 2002 (FB)

League Club	Source	Date Signed	Seasons Played	Apps	Subs	Gls
Barnsley	Ratho Amat	09.37				
Portsmouth	Tr	03.46	46-53	241	-	8

FERRIER John
Edinburgh, 6 October, 1927 (FB)

League Club	Source	Date Signed	Seasons Played	Apps	Subs	Gls
Brighton & Hove A		10.46	46	1	-	1
Exeter C	Clyde	05.56	56	31	-	0

FERRIER Ronald (Ron) Johnson
Cleethorpes, 26 April, 1914 Died 1991 (IF)

League Club	Source	Date Signed	Seasons Played	Apps	Subs	Gls
Grimsby T	Grimsby W	05.33				
Manchester U	Tr	05.35	35-37	18	-	4
Oldham Ath	Tr	03.38	37-46	45	-	25

FERRIS John Owner
Bristol, 4 September, 1939 (G)

League Club	Source	Date Signed	Seasons Played	Apps	Subs	Gls
Torquay U	Minehead	09.58	58	3	-	0

FERRIS Paul James
Lisburn, 10 July, 1965 (W)

League Club	Source	Date Signed	Seasons Played	Apps	Subs	Gls
Newcastle U	App	03.83	81-84	1	10	0

FERRIS Raymond (Ray) Osborn
Newry, 22 September, 1920 Died 1994 I-3 (WH)

League Club	Source	Date Signed	Seasons Played	Apps	Subs	Gls
Crewe Alex	Cambridge T	03.45	46-48	102	-	22
Birmingham C	Tr	03.49	48-52	93	-	3

FERRIS Samuel (Sam)
Motherwell, 14 March, 1951 (F)

League Club	Source	Date Signed	Seasons Played	Apps	Subs	Gls
Chesterfield	Albion Rov	03.72	71-73	25	6	3
Workington	L	02.74	73	2	1	0

FERRY Gordon
Sunderland, 22 December, 1943 (CD)

League Club	Source	Date Signed	Seasons Played	Apps	Subs	Gls
Arsenal	App	01.61	64	11	-	0
Leyton Orient	Tr	05.65	65	42	0	0

FERRY William (Willie)
Sunderland, 21 November, 1966 ESch (F)

League Club	Source	Date Signed	Seasons Played	Apps	Subs	Gls
Scunthorpe U	App	09.84	84-86	2	3	0
Barnsley	Tr	11.86	86	3	1	1

FESTA Gianluca
Cagliari, Italy, 15 March, 1969 (CD)

League Club	Source	Date Signed	Seasons Played	Apps	Subs	Gls
Middlesbrough	Inter Milan (It)	01.97	96-01	132	6	10
Portsmouth	Tr	08.02	02	27	0	1

FETTIS Alan William
Newtownards, 1 February, 1971 NISch/NIYth/NIB3/NI-25 (G)

League Club	Source	Date Signed	Seasons Played	Apps	Subs	Gls
Hull C	Ards	08.91	91-95	131	4	2
West Bromwich A	L	11.95	95	3	0	0
Nottingham F	Tr	01.96	96	4	0	0
Blackburn Rov	Tr	09.97	97-99	9	2	0
York C	Tr	03.00	99-02	125	0	0
Hull C	Tr	01.03	02-03	20	0	0
Sheffield U	L	12.03	03	2	1	0
Grimsby T	L	03.04	03	11	0	0
Macclesfield T	Tr	07.04	04	28	0	0

FEUER Anthony **Ian**
Las Vegas, USA, 20 May, 1971 USA 1 (G)

League Club	Source	Date Signed	Seasons Played	Apps	Subs	Gls
West Ham U	LA Salsa (USA)	03.94				
Peterborough U	L	02.95	94	16	0	0
Luton T	Tr	09.95	95-97	97	0	0
Cardiff C	Colorado (USA)	01.00				
West Ham U	Tr	02.00	99	3	0	0
Wimbledon	Tr	06.00	01	2	2	0
Derby Co	L	10.01	01	2	0	0
Tranmere Rov	Tr	08.02	02	2	0	0

FEWINGS Patrick (Pat) John Henry
Barnstaple, 21 January, 1931 Died 1997 (W)

League Club	Source	Date Signed	Seasons Played	Apps	Subs	Gls
Torquay U	Barnstaple T	11.53	53-54	8	-	0

FEWINGS Paul John
Hull, 18 February, 1978 (F)

League Club	Source	Date Signed	Seasons Played	Apps	Subs	Gls
Hull C	App	08.95	94-97	32	25	2

FICKLING Ashley Spencer
Sheffield, 15 November, 1972 ESch (CD)

League Club	Source	Date Signed	Seasons Played	Apps	Subs	Gls
Sheffield U	Jnrs	07.91				
Darlington	L	11.92	92	14	0	0
Darlington	L	08.93	93	1	0	0
Grimsby T	Tr	03.95	94-96	26	13	2
Darlington	L	03.98	97	8	0	0
Scunthorpe U	Tr	07.98	98-00	55	13	1

FIDLER Denis John
Stockport, 22 June, 1938 (W)

League Club	Source	Date Signed	Seasons Played	Apps	Subs	Gls
Manchester C	Manchester U (Am)	01.57	57-58	5	-	1
Port Vale	Tr	06.60	60-61	38	-	12
Grimsby T	Tr	10.61	61	9	-	3
Halifax T	Tr	04.63	62-66	141	1	40
Darlington	Tr	10.66	66-67	32	2	3

FIDLER Frank
Middleton, 16 August, 1924 (CF)

League Club	Source	Date Signed	Seasons Played	Apps	Subs	Gls
Wrexham	Witton A	05.50	50-51	36	-	15
Leeds U	Tr	10.51	51-52	22	-	8
Bournemouth	Tr	12.52	52-54	61	-	31

FIDLER Richard Michael
Sheffield, 26 October, 1976 ESch (M)

League Club	Source	Date Signed	Seasons Played	Apps	Subs	Gls
Leeds U	Jnrs	07.95				
Hull C	Tr	12.95	95	0	1	0

FIDLER Thomas (Tommy) George
Hounslow, 4 September, 1933 Died 1992 (CF)

League Club	Source	Date Signed	Seasons Played	Apps	Subs	Gls
Queens Park Rgrs	Hounslow	05.54	54	12	-	2

FIELD Anthony (Tony)
Halifax, 6 July, 1946 (F)

League Club	Source	Date Signed	Seasons Played	Apps	Subs	Gls
Halifax T	Illingworth U	07.63	63-65	20	0	3
Barrow	Tr	08.66	66-67	36	2	16
Southport	Tr	03.68	67-71	127	6	41
Blackburn Rov	Tr	10.71	71-73	104	2	45
Sheffield U	Tr	03.74	73-75	63	3	13

FIELD Anthony (Tony) Frederick
Chester, 23 May, 1942 (CF)

League Club	Source	Date Signed	Seasons Played	Apps	Subs	Gls
Chester		08.61	60	2	-	0

FIELD Norman
Durham, 27 August, 1927 Died 1993 (WH)

League Club	Source	Date Signed	Seasons Played	Apps	Subs	Gls
Portsmouth		08.45				
Mansfield T	Tr	06.50	51-52	20	-	0

FIELDER Colin Michael Raynor
Winchester, 5 January, 1964 (M)

League Club	Source	Date Signed	Seasons Played	Apps	Subs	Gls
Aldershot	App	01.82	81-86	56	12	8

FIELDING John (Johnny) Arnold
Speke, 2 September, 1939 (IF)

League Club	Source	Date Signed	Seasons Played	Apps	Subs	Gls
Southport	Wigan Ath	03.61	60-62	76	-	21
Brentford	Tr	03.63	62-65	82	0	18
Grimsby T	Tr	12.65	65-66	29	1	8

FIELDING John Robert
Billingham, 7 April, 1982 (CD)

League Club	Source	Date Signed	Seasons Played	Apps	Subs	Gls
York C	YT	07.01	01	9	0	1

FIELDING Mark John
Bury, 10 November, 1956 (FB)

League Club	Source	Date Signed	Seasons Played	Apps	Subs	Gls
Preston NE	App	11.74	74	9	0	0

FIELDING Michael (Mike) Anthony
Liverpool, 3 December, 1965 (CD)

League Club	Source	Date Signed	Seasons Played	Apps	Subs	Gls
Barnsley	Everton (App)	08.84				
Rochdale	L	10.84	84	6	0	0

FIELDING Paul Anthony
Oldham, 4 December, 1955 (M)

League Club	Source	Date Signed	Seasons Played	Apps	Subs	Gls
Rochdale	App	12.73	72-75	65	7	5

FIELDING Alfred Walter (Wally)
Edmonton, 26 November, 1919 (IF)

League Club	Source	Date Signed	Seasons Played	Apps	Subs	Gls
Everton	Walthamstow Ave	09.45	46-58	380	-	49
Southport	Tr	01.59	58-59	20	-	1

FIELDING William (Bill)
Broadhurst, 17 June, 1915 (G)

League Club	Source	Date Signed	Seasons Played	Apps	Subs	Gls
Cardiff C	Hurst	05.36	36-38	50	-	0
Bolton W	Tr	06.44				
Manchester U	Tr	01.47	46	6	-	0

FIELDS Alfred (Alf) George
Canning Town, 15 November, 1918 (CD)

League Club	Source	Date Signed	Seasons Played	Apps	Subs	Gls
Arsenal	West Ham YC	05.37	38-50	19	-	0

FIELDS Maurice (Mike) John Bernard
Chester, 12 August, 1935 (CF)

League Club	Source	Date Signed	Seasons Played	Apps	Subs	Gls
Chester		08.55	55-57	22	-	1

FIELDWICK Lee Peter
Croydon, 6 September, 1982 (FB)

League Club	Source	Date Signed	Seasons Played	Apps	Subs	Gls
Brentford	YT	07.01	02-03	10	2	0
Swansea C	L	03.04	03	4	1	0

FIFE Adrian
Peterborough, 13 September, 1969 (F)

League Club	Source	Date Signed	Seasons Played	Apps	Subs	Gls
Peterborough U	YT	07.88	86-87	1	1	0

FIFIELD David
Plymouth, 10 December, 1966 (M)

League Club	Source	Date Signed	Seasons Played	Apps	Subs	Gls
Torquay U	App	•	83	0	1	0

FIGGINS Philip (Phil) Eric
Portsmouth, 20 August, 1955 ESch (G)

League Club	Source	Date Signed	Seasons Played	Apps	Subs	Gls
Portsmouth	Waterlooville	07.73	74-77	36	0	0

FIGUEROA Luciano Gabriel
Rosario, Argentina, 19 May, 1981 Aru23-1/Ar-1 (F)

League Club	Source	Date Signed	Seasons Played	Apps	Subs	Gls
Birmingham C	Rosario Central (Arg)	08.03	03	0	1	0

FILAN John Richard
Sydney, Australia, 8 February, 1970 Auu23/Au-2 (G)

League Club	Source	Date Signed	Seasons Played	Apps	Subs	Gls
Cambridge U	Wollongong (Aus)	03.93	92-94	68	0	0
Coventry C	Tr	03.95	94-96	15	1	0
Blackburn Rov	Tr	07.97	97-00	61	1	0
Wigan Ath	Tr	12.01	01-04	162	0	0

FILBY Ian Frederick
Woodford, 9 October, 1954 (W)

League Club	Source	Date Signed	Seasons Played	Apps	Subs	Gls
Orient	App	10.72				
Brentford	L	09.74	74	1	2	0

FILLERY Michael (Mike) Christopher
Mitcham, 17 September, 1960 ESch/EYth (M)

League Club	Source	Date Signed	Seasons Played	Apps	Subs	Gls
Chelsea	App	08.78	78-82	156	5	32
Queens Park Rgrs	Tr	08.83	83-86	95	2	9
Portsmouth	Tr	07.87	87-90	62	5	6
Oldham Ath	Tr	10.90	90	1	1	0
Millwall	L	03.91	90	1	0	0
Torquay U	L	09.91	91	4	0	0

FILSON Robert Martin
St Helens, 25 June, 1968 (CD)

League Club	Source	Date Signed	Seasons Played	Apps	Subs	Gls
Wrexham	Preston NE (N/C)	02.89	88-89	0	2	0

FINAN Robert (Bobby) Joseph
Old Kilpatrick, 1 March, 1912 Died 1983 SWar-1 (CF)

League Club	Source	Date Signed	Seasons Played	Apps	Subs	Gls
Blackpool	Yoker Ath	08.33	33-38	170	-	83
Crewe Alex	Tr	09.47	47-48	62	-	14

FINC Robert (Bobby)
Rochdale, 13 February, 1959 (M)

League Club	Source	Date Signed	Seasons Played	Apps	Subs	Gls
Rochdale	Milton	10.77	77	0	1	0

FINCH Derek
Arley, 29 July, 1940 (FB)

League Club	Source	Date Signed	Seasons Played	Apps	Subs	Gls
West Bromwich A	Jnrs	08.57				
Aldershot	Tr	06.60	60	3	-	0

FINCH Desmond (Des) Richard
Worksop, 26 February, 1950 (G)

League Club	Source	Date Signed	Seasons Played	Apps	Subs	Gls
Mansfield T		03.69	68-70	4	0	0

FINCH John
Lambeth, 5 July, 1966 (CD)

League Club	Source	Date Signed	Seasons Played	Apps	Subs	Gls
Fulham	Dorking	12.90	90-91	6	1	0

FINCH Keith John
Easington, 6 May, 1982 (G)

League Club	Source	Date Signed	Seasons Played	Apps	Subs	Gls
Darlington	YT	07.01	01	11	1	0

FINCH Michael (Mike)
Stockton, 30 June, 1965 (G)

League Club	Source	Date Signed	Seasons Played	Apps	Subs	Gls
Hartlepool U		12.83	83-84	3	0	0

FINCH Robert (Bobby)
Camberwell, 24 August, 1948 Died 1978 (FB)

League Club	Source	Date Signed	Seasons Played	Apps	Subs	Gls
Queens Park Rgrs	App	08.66	67-68	5	0	0

FINCH Roy
Barry Island, 7 April, 1922 (W)

League Club	Source	Date Signed	Seasons Played	Apps	Subs	Gls
Swansea T	Barians	08.39				
West Bromwich A	Tr	06.44	46-48	15	-	1
Lincoln C	Tr	02.49	48-58	275	-	56

FINCHAM Gordon Richard
Peterborough, 8 January, 1935 (CD)

League Club	Source	Date Signed	Seasons Played	Apps	Subs	Gls
Leicester C	Phorpres Sports	11.52	52-57	50	-	0
Plymouth Arg	Tr	07.58	58-62	136	-	4
Luton T	Tr	07.63	63-64	64	-	0

FINDLAY John (Jake) Williamson
Blairgowrie, 13 July, 1954 (G)

League Club	Source	Date Signed	Seasons Played	Apps	Subs	Gls
Aston Villa	App	06.72	73-76	14	0	0
Luton T	Tr	11.78	78-84	167	0	0

League Club	Source	Date Signed	Seasons Played	Apps	Subs	Gls
Barnsley	L	09.83	83	6	0	0
Derby Co	L	01.84	83	1	0	0
Swindon T	Tr	07.85	85	4	0	0

FINDLAY Kenneth (Ken)
Pegswood, 24 March, 1926 (FB)

League Club	Source	Date Signed	Seasons Played	Apps	Subs	Gls
Aldershot	Aberdeen	08.50	50	7	-	0

FINLAY Allan Jackson
Edinburgh, 9 January, 1939 SSch (IF)

League Club	Source	Date Signed	Seasons Played	Apps	Subs	Gls
Newport Co	Barry T	07.61	61	20	-	1

FINLAY Darren Jonathan
Belfast, 19 December, 1973 NIYth/NIB (M)

League Club	Source	Date Signed	Seasons Played	Apps	Subs	Gls
Queens Park Rgrs	YT	05.92				
Doncaster Rov	Tr	08.94	94	6	2	1

FINLAY John
Birtley, 16 February, 1919 Died 1985 (IF)

League Club	Source	Date Signed	Seasons Played	Apps	Subs	Gls
Sunderland	Ouston Jnrs	05.38	46	1	-	0

FINLAY John (Jock)
Glasgow, 1 July, 1925 (W)

League Club	Source	Date Signed	Seasons Played	Apps	Subs	Gls
New Brighton	Clyde	03.51	50	15	-	2
Leeds U	Tr	06.51	51	1	-	0
Walsall	Yeovil T	08.53	53	11	-	0

FINLAY Patrick (Pat)
Birkenhead, 18 March, 1938 (W)

League Club	Source	Date Signed	Seasons Played	Apps	Subs	Gls
Tranmere Rov		08.59	61	3	-	0

FINLAYSON Malcolm John
Bowhill, 14 June, 1930 (G)

League Club	Source	Date Signed	Seasons Played	Apps	Subs	Gls
Millwall	Renfrew Jnrs	02.48	47-55	230	-	0
Wolverhampton W	Tr	08.56	56-63	179	-	0

FINLEY Alan James
Liverpool, 10 December, 1967 (CD)

League Club	Source	Date Signed	Seasons Played	Apps	Subs	Gls
Shrewsbury T	Marine	06.88	88-89	60	3	2
Stockport Co	Tr	08.90	90-93	63	3	5
Carlisle U	L	12.92	92	1	0	0
Rochdale	L	12.93	93	1	0	0

FINLEY Gary
Liverpool, 14 November, 1970 (CD)

League Club	Source	Date Signed	Seasons Played	Apps	Subs	Gls
Doncaster Rov	Netherfield	08.97	97	6	1	0

FINLEY Thomas (Tom)
Frizington, 6 October, 1933 (WH)

League Club	Source	Date Signed	Seasons Played	Apps	Subs	Gls
Workington	Northside Jnrs	01.56	55-59	94	-	2
Southport	Tr	02.60	59	6	-	0

FINN Michael (Mike) Gerard
Liverpool, 1 May, 1954 (G)

League Club	Source	Date Signed	Seasons Played	Apps	Subs	Gls
Burnley	App	12.71	73-74	4	0	0

FINN Neil Edward
Barking, 29 December, 1978 (G)

League Club	Source	Date Signed	Seasons Played	Apps	Subs	Gls
West Ham U	YT	•	95	1	0	0

FINNAN Stephen (Steve) John
Limerick, 20 April, 1976 IRu21-8/IRB-1/IR-36 (FB)

League Club	Source	Date Signed	Seasons Played	Apps	Subs	Gls
Birmingham C	Welling U	06.95	95-96	9	6	1
Notts Co	L	03.96	95	14	3	2
Notts Co	Tr	10.96	96-98	71	9	5
Fulham	Tr	11.98	98-02	171	1	6
Liverpool	Tr	06.03	03-04	48	7	1

FINNEGAN John
Glasgow, 3 July, 1943 (FB)

League Club	Source	Date Signed	Seasons Played	Apps	Subs	Gls
Millwall	Clyde	06.63	63	6	-	0

FINNEY Alan
Langwith, 31 October, 1933 Eu23-3/EB (W)

League Club	Source	Date Signed	Seasons Played	Apps	Subs	Gls
Sheffield Wed	Jnrs	11.50	50-65	455	0	83
Doncaster Rov	Tr	01.66	65-66	30	0	3

FINNEY Richard **Kenneth (Ken)**
St Helens, 10 March, 1929 (W)

League Club	Source	Date Signed	Seasons Played	Apps	Subs	Gls
Stockport Co	St Helens	12.47	47-57	191	-	33
Tranmere Rov	Tr	03.58	57-62	180	-	27

FINNEY Kevin
Newcastle-under-Lyme, 19 October, 1969 (M)

League Club	Source	Date Signed	Seasons Played	Apps	Subs	Gls
Port Vale	App	06.87	87-89	20	17	1
Lincoln C	Tr	07.91	91-92	31	6	2

FINNEY John **Richard**
Rotherham, 14 March, 1956 EYth (W)

League Club	Source	Date Signed	Seasons Played	Apps	Subs	Gls
Rotherham U	Jnrs	07.74	73-80	236	0	67

FINNEY Shaun Barry
Dinnington, 5 October, 1966 (F)

League Club	Source	Date Signed	Seasons Played	Apps	Subs	Gls
Scunthorpe U	Nottingham F (App)	10.84	84	1	1	0

FINNEY Stephen (Steve) Kenneth
Hexham, 31 October, 1973 (F)

League Club	Source	Date Signed	Seasons Played	Apps	Subs	Gls
Preston NE	YT	05.92	91-92	1	5	1
Manchester C	Tr	02.93				
Swindon T	Tr	06.95	95-97	47	26	18
Cambridge U	L	10.97	97	4	3	2
Carlisle U	Tr	07.98	98	22	11	6
Leyton Orient	Tr	03.99	98	2	3	0
Chester C	Barrow	10.99	99	4	9	0

FINNEY (Sir) **Thomas (Tom)**
Preston, 5 April, 1922 FLge-17/E7-6 (W)

League Club	Source	Date Signed	Seasons Played	Apps	Subs	Gls
Preston NE	Jnrs	01.40	46-59	433	-	187

FINNEY Thomas (Tom)
Belfast, 6 November, 1952 NI-14 (M)

League Club	Source	Date Signed	Seasons Played	Apps	Subs	Gls
Luton T	Crusaders	08.73	73	13	1	5
Sunderland	Tr	07.74	74-75	8	7	1
Cambridge U	Tr	08.76	76-83	259	9	56
Brentford	Tr	02.84	83-84	19	1	2
Cambridge U	Tr	12.84	84-85	64	0	5

FINNEY Charles **William (Bill)** Thomas
Stoke-on-Trent, 5 September, 1931 (CF)

League Club	Source	Date Signed	Seasons Played	Apps	Subs	Gls
Stoke C	Crewe Alex (Am)	05.49	52-54	57	-	14
Birmingham C	Tr	11.55	55-56	14	-	0
Queens Park Rgrs	Tr	05.57	57	10	-	1
Crewe Alex	Tr	07.58	58	1	-	0
Rochdale	Tr	09.58	58	31	-	1

FINNIESTON Stephen (Steve) James
Edinburgh, 30 November, 1954 SYth (F)

League Club	Source	Date Signed	Seasons Played	Apps	Subs	Gls
Chelsea	App	12.71	74-77	78	2	34
Cardiff C	L	10.74	74	9	0	2
Sheffield U	Tr	06.78	78	23	0	4

FINNIGAN Anthony (Tony)
Wimbledon, 17 October, 1962 EYth (M)

League Club	Source	Date Signed	Seasons Played	Apps	Subs	Gls
Fulham	App	11.80				
Crystal Palace	(Finland)	02.85	84-87	94	11	10
Blackburn Rov	Tr	07.88	88-89	21	15	0
Hull C	Tr	09.90	90	15	3	1
Swindon T	Tr	03.91	90	2	1	0
Brentford	(Hong Kong)	01.92	91	3	0	0
Barnet	Earnest Borel (HK)	09.93	93	5	1	1
Fulham	Dulwich Hamlet	09.94	94-95	8	5	0

FINNIGAN Denis Vincent
Sheffield, 23 March, 1940 Died 1994 (CD)

League Club	Source	Date Signed	Seasons Played	Apps	Subs	Gls
Sheffield U		04.59	59-66	14	0	0
Chesterfield	Tr	09.68	68-69	27	0	0

FINNIGAN John Francis
Wakefield, 29 March, 1976 (M)

League Club	Source	Date Signed	Seasons Played	Apps	Subs	Gls
Nottingham F	YT	05.93				
Lincoln C	Tr	03.98	97-01	139	4	3
Cheltenham T	Tr	03.02	01-04	109	5	7

FINNIGAN Raymond (Ray) William
Wallsend, 22 January, 1947 (FB)

League Club	Source	Date Signed	Seasons Played	Apps	Subs	Gls
Newcastle U	App	01.65				
Darlington	Tr	07.66	66-67	8	3	0

FINNIGAN Thomas **Trevor**
Bedlington, 14 October, 1952 ESemiPro (F)

League Club	Source	Date Signed	Seasons Played	Apps	Subs	Gls
Everton		05.71				
Blackpool	Runcorn	03.77	76-77	13	4	3
Bournemouth	Tr	01.78	77-78	23	2	5

FINNIS Harold Alexander
Liverpool, 21 October, 1920 Died 1991 (FB)

League Club	Source	Date Signed	Seasons Played	Apps	Subs	Gls
Everton		06.46	46	1	-	0

FIOCCA Paul
Italy, 13 January, 1955 (M)

League Club	Source	Date Signed	Seasons Played	Apps	Subs	Gls
Swindon T	App	01.73	73	1	0	0

FIORE Mark Joseph
Southwark, 18 November, 1969 (W)

League Club	Source	Date Signed	Seasons Played	Apps	Subs	Gls
Wimbledon	YT	07.88	88	1	0	0
Plymouth Arg	Tr	03.90	89-92	74	9	8

FIRM Neil John
Bradford, 23 January, 1958 (CD)

League Club	Source	Date Signed	Seasons Played	Apps	Subs	Gls
Leeds U	App	01.76	79-81	11	1	0
Oldham Ath	L	03.82	81	9	0	0
Peterborough U	Tr	08.82	82-84	71	1	3

League Club	Source	Date Signed	Seasons Played	Career Record Apps	Subs	Gls
FIRMAN Kenneth (Ken)						
Felling, 5 February, 1941 Died 2000						(IF)
Gateshead	Jarrow Mercantile	02.59	58	1	-	0
FIRMANI Edward (Eddie) Ronald						
Cape Town, South Africa, 7 August, 1933						(F)
Charlton Ath	Clyde (SA)	02.50	51-54	100	-	50
Charlton Ath	Genoa (It)	10.63	63-64	55	-	32
Southend U	Tr	06.65	65-66	55	0	24
Charlton Ath	Tr	03.67	66-67	10	0	6
FIRMANI Peter Walter						
Cape Town, South Africa, 14 February, 1936 Died 2004						(FB)
Charlton Ath	Marist Bros (SA)	09.53	55-58	31	-	2
FIRTH Francis (Franny) Martin						
Dewsbury, 27 May, 1956						(W)
Huddersfield T	App	11.73	73-76	26	1	4
Halifax T	Tr	02.78	77-81	157	11	19
Bury	Tr	08.82	82	33	0	4
FISH Mark Anthony						
Cape Town, South Africa, 14 March, 1974 South Africa 62						(CD)
Bolton W	SS Lazio (It)	09.97	97-00	102	1	3
Charlton Ath	Tr	11.00	00-04	101	1	2
FISHENDEN Paul						
Hillingdon, 2 August, 1963						(F)
Wimbledon	App	10.81	81-85	57	18	25
Fulham	L	12.85	85	3	0	0
Millwall	L	09.86	86	3	0	0
Orient	L	10.86	86	4	0	0
Crewe Alex	Tr	02.88	87-89	79	2	25
FISHER Alexander (Alex) James						
Southampton, 30 January, 1973						(FB)
Aldershot	YT	07.91	90	2	0	0
FISHER James **Bernard**						
York, 23 February, 1934						(G)
Hull C	Jnrs	11.55	55-62	126	-	0
Bradford C	Tr	07.63	63-64	60	-	0
FISHER Charles (Charlie) Kitchener						
Pontypridd, 4 January, 1915 Died 1986						(FB)
Swansea T	Lovells Ath	08.39	46-47	65	-	0
FISHER Frederick (Freddie)						
Hetton-le-Hole, 28 November, 1924						(W)
Reading	Slough T	08.44	46-51	139	-	23
Shrewsbury T	Tr	07.52	52-53	64	-	9
Leyton Orient	Tr	07.54	54	2	-	1
FISHER Frederick (Fred) Thomas						
Wednesbury, 12 January, 1920 Died 1993						(FB)
Grimsby T	Fallings Heath	05.37	38-50	166	-	0
Rochdale	Tr	06.51	51	1	-	0
FISHER George Sidney						
Bermondsey, 19 June, 1925						(FB)
Millwall		12.44	46-54	286	-	4
Fulham	Tr	11.54	54	8	-	0
Colchester U	Tr	09.55	55-59	164	-	6
FISHER Hugh Donnelly						
Pollok, 9 January, 1944						(M)
Blackpool	Gowanbank	08.62	63-66	51	3	1
Southampton	Tr	03.67	66-76	297	5	7
Southport	Tr	03.77	76-77	60	0	0
FISHER James (Jimmy)						
Barrow, 12 June, 1934						(IF)
Barrow	Holker COB	10.55	52-57	10	-	1
FISHER John (Jackie) Alfred						
Bermondsey, 19 June, 1925						(FB)
Millwall		05.46	47-48	3	-	0
Bournemouth	Tr	06.49	49-52	52	-	0
FISHER Kenneth (Ken) Douglas Walter						
Bitterne, 30 September, 1921 Died 1989						(WH)
Southampton	Bitterne Nomads	09.46				
Watford	Tr	08.47	47-50	106	-	2
FISHER Leslie (Les) Barry						
Southampton, 8 January, 1948						(FB)
Blackpool		12.67	68	1	0	0
FISHER Neil John						
St Helens, 7 November, 1970						(M)
Bolton W	YT	07.89	91-94	17	7	1
Chester C	Tr	06.95	95-97	91	17	4
Chester C	Bangor C	03.99	98-99	41	8	1
FISHER Paul						
Mansfield, 19 January, 1951						(FB)
Huddersfield T		02.69				
Darlington	Tr	06.70	70	2	1	0
FISHER Peter McArthur						
Edinburgh, 17 February, 1920						(FB)
Northampton T		09.47	47	8	-	0
Shrewsbury T	Tr	08.50	50-51	39	-	0
Wrexham	Tr	10.51	51-53	85	-	0
FISHER Philip (Phil) John						
Ammanford, 10 January, 1958						(W)
Exeter C	Bridgend T	02.81	80-81	9	2	1
Swansea C	Merthyr Tydfil	03.85	84	2	0	0
FISHER Robert (Bobby) Paul						
Wembley, 3 August, 1956						(FB)
Orient	App	08.73	73-82	308	6	4
Cambridge U	Tr	11.82	82-83	42	0	0
Brentford	Tr	02.84	83-84	44	1	0
FISHER Ronald (Ron)						
Sheffield, 9 March, 1923 Died 1987						(FB)
Halifax T		08.50	50	6	-	0
FISHER Stanley (Stan)						
Barnsley, 29 September, 1924 Died 2003						(CF)
Barnsley	Rockingham Colliery	09.44	46	1	-	0
Halifax T	Tr	01.47	46-47	26	-	7
FISHLOCK Murray Edward						
Marlborough, 23 September, 1973						(FB)
Hereford U	Trowbridge T	09.94	94-96	67	4	4
FISKEN Gary Stewart						
Watford, 27 October, 1981						(M)
Watford	YT	02.00	01-03	15	7	1
Swansea C	Tr	07.04	04	1	4	0
FITCH Barry Edward						
Brighton, 19 November, 1943						(FB)
Brighton & Hove A	Jnrs	11.61	63	1	-	0
FITTON John						
Royton, 12 January, 1951						(G)
Oldham Ath	Jnrs	10.68	69	3	0	0
FITZGERALD Alfred (Alf) Malcolm						
Conisbrough, 25 January, 1911 Died 1981						(IF)
Reading	Denaby U	08.34	34-35	6	-	1
Queens Park Rgrs	Tr	05.36	36-38	94	-	43
Aldershot	Tr	11.45	46-47	59	-	1
FITZGERALD Brian Maurice						
Perivale, 23 October, 1983 IRYth						(M)
Queens Park Rgrs	YT	10.00	01	0	1	0
FITZGERALD Gary Michael						
Hampstead, 27 October, 1976						(CD)
Watford	YT	11.94	94	1	0	0
FITZGERALD John Desmond						
Dublin, 10 February, 1984 IRYth/IRu21-11						(CD)
Blackburn Rov	YT	02.01				
Bury	L	01.05	04	14	0	0
FITZGERALD Peter Joseph						
Waterford, 17 June, 1937 LoI-4/IR-5						(CF)
Leeds U	Sparta Rotterdam (Holl)	08.60	60	8	-	0
Chester	Tr	07.61	61-63	80	-	12
FITZGERALD Scott Brian						
Westminster, 13 August, 1969 IRu21-4/IRB-1						(CD)
Wimbledon	YT	07.89	89-95	95	11	1
Sheffield U	L	11.95	95	6	0	0
Millwall	L	10.96	96	7	0	0
Millwall	Tr	07.97	97-00	79	3	1
Colchester U	Tr	10.00	00-03	114	2	0
Brentford	Tr	03.04	03-04	21	0	0
FITZGERALD Scott Peter						
Hillingdon, 18 November, 1979						(F)
Watford	Northwood	03.03	02-04	29	26	11
Swansea C	L	09.04	04	0	3	0
Leyton Orient	L	01.05	04	1	0	0
Brentford	Tr	03.05	04	7	5	4

League Club	Source	Date Signed	Seasons Played	Career Record Apps	Subs	Gls
FITZHENRY Neil						
Billinge, 24 September, 1978						(CD)
Wigan Ath	YT	07.97	97-98	2	2	0
FITZPATRICK Anthony (Tony) Charles						
Glasgow, 3 March, 1956 Su21-5						(M)
Bristol C	St Mirren	08.79	79-80	75	0	1
FITZPATRICK Gary Gerard						
Birmingham, 5 August, 1971 IRYth						(M)
Leicester C	YT	01.90	89	0	1	0
FITZPATRICK Ian Matthew						
Manchester, 22 September, 1980 ESch/EYth						(F)
Manchester U	YT	07.98				
Halifax T	Tr	03.00	99-01	37	12	10
FITZPATRICK John Herbert Norton						
Aberdeen, 18 August, 1946						(M)
Manchester U	Jnrs	09.63	64-72	111	6	8
FITZPATRICK Lee Gareth						
Manchester, 31 October, 1978						(M)
Blackburn Rov	YT	07.96				
Hartlepool U	Tr	09.99	99-00	28	19	6
FITZPATRICK Paul James						
Liverpool, 5 October, 1965						(CD)
Bolton W	Preston NE (N/C)	03.85	84-85	13	1	0
Bristol C	Tr	08.86	86-88	40	4	7
Carlisle U	Tr	10.88	88-90	106	3	4
Preston NE	L	12.88	88	2	0	0
Leicester C	Tr	07.91	91-92	21	6	4
Birmingham C	Tr	01.93	92	7	0	0
Bury	L	03.93	92	8	1	0
Northampton T	Hamilton Academical	02.94	93	1	1	1
FITZPATRICK Peter						
Bebington, 27 April, 1929						(IF)
New Brighton (Am)		01.50	49	1	-	0
FITZPATRICK Trevor Joseph James						
Frimley, 19 February, 1980 IRYth						(F)
Southend U	YT	07.98	97-00	17	36	8
FITZSIMMONS Eric James						
Oldham, 23 October, 1948						(F)
Bradford PA (Am)		02.70	69	1	0	0
FITZSIMONS Arthur Gerard						
Dublin, 16 December, 1929 LoI-2/IR-26						(IF)
Middlesbrough	Shelbourne	05.49	49-58	223	-	49
Lincoln C	Tr	03.59	58	7	-	0
Mansfield T	Tr	08.59	59-60	62	-	23
FJORTOFT Jan Aage						
Aalesund, Norway, 10 January, 1967 Norway 72						(F)
Swindon T	Rapid Vienna (Aut)	07.93	93-94	62	10	28
Middlesbrough	Tr	03.95	94-96	37	4	9
Sheffield U	Tr	01.97	96-97	30	4	19
Barnsley	Tr	01.98	97-98	21	13	9
FLACK Douglas (Doug)						
Staines, 24 October, 1920						(G)
Fulham	Jnrs	12.38	48-52	54	-	0
Walsall	Tr	08.53	53	11	-	0
FLACK William **Leonard (Len)** Wallace						
Cambridge, 1 June, 1916 Died 1995 ESch						(FB)
Norwich C	Cambridge T	07.33	34-46	49	-	0
FLACK Steven (Steve) Richard						
Cambridge, 29 May, 1971						(F)
Cardiff C	Cambridge C	11.95	95-96	6	5	1
Exeter C	Tr	09.96	96-02	213	55	63
FLAHAVAN Aaron Adam						
Southampton, 15 December, 1975 Died 2001						(G)
Portsmouth	YT	02.94	96-00	93	0	0
FLAHAVAN Darryl James						
Southampton, 28 November, 1978						(G)
Southampton	YT	05.96				
Southend U	Chesham U	10.00	00-04	174	2	0
FLAMINI Mathieu						
Marseille, France, 7 March, 1984 Fru21						(M)
Arsenal	Marseille (Fr)	07.04	04	9	12	1
FLANAGAN Alan						
Drogheda, 9 October, 1980 IRYth						(G)
Swindon T	YT	07.99	99	0	1	0

League Club	Source	Date Signed	Seasons Played	Career Record Apps	Subs	Gls
FLANAGAN Daniel Christopher						
Dublin, 24 November, 1924 LoI-1						(CF)
Notts Co (Am)	Dundalk	12.46	46	2	-	2
Manchester C	Shelbourne	02.47				
Bradford C	Tr	12.47	47	13	-	6
FLANAGAN Michael (Mike) Anthony						
Ilford, 9 November, 1952 EYth						(F)
Charlton Ath	Tottenham H (Jnrs)	08.71	71-78	241	13	85
Crystal Palace	Tr	08.79	79-80	56	0	8
Queens Park Rgrs	Tr	12.80	80-83	71	7	20
Charlton Ath	Tr	01.84	83-85	89	4	24
Cambridge U	Tr	09.86	86	7	2	3
FLANAGAN Shaun						
Doncaster, 25 December, 1960						(M)
Doncaster Rov	App	01.79	78-80	41	9	3
FLANNIGAN Raymond (Ray) John						
Margate, 15 March, 1949						(FB)
Reading	Margate	02.70	70-71	36	4	0
FLASH Richard Garfield						
Birmingham, 8 April, 1976						(W)
Manchester U	YT	07.94				
Wolverhampton W	Tr	09.95				
Watford	Tr	07.96	96	0	1	0
Lincoln C	L	10.97	97	2	3	0
Plymouth Arg	Tr	08.98	98	4	1	0
FLATLEY Albert Austin						
Bradford, 5 September, 1919 Died 1987						(IF)
York C	Wolverhampton W (Am)	02.39	38	4	-	0
Port Vale	Tr	06.39				
Bradford PA	Tr	07.44				
Bury	Tr	12.46				
Workington	Alessandria (It)	11.51	51	8	-	0
FLATT Colin Harold						
Blythburgh, 30 January, 1940						(CF)
Leyton Orient	Wisbech T	05.65	65	32	1	8
Southend U	Tr	06.66	66	20	2	8
FLATTS Mark Michael						
Islington, 14 October, 1972 EYth						(W)
Arsenal	YT	12.90	92-94	9	7	0
Cambridge U	L	10.93	93	5	0	1
Brighton & Hove A	L	12.93	93	9	1	1
Bristol C	L	03.95	94	4	2	0
Grimsby T	L	03.96	95	4	1	0
FLAVELL John (Jack) Alfred						
Wall Heath, 15 May, 1929 Died 2004						(FB)
West Bromwich A	Lye T	05.47				
Walsall	Tr	09.53	53	22	-	0
FLAVELL Robert (Bobby) William						
Berwick-on-Tweed, 7 March, 1956						(FB)
Burnley	App	03.73				
Halifax T	Tr	02.76	75-77	91	0	7
Chesterfield	Tr	08.78	78	27	2	2
Barnsley	Tr	07.79	79	25	0	0
Halifax T	Tr	12.80	80	1	0	0
FLAY Stephen (Steve)						
Poole, 2 October, 1954						(FB)
Oxford U	App	10.72	73-74	3	0	0
FLECK Robert William						
Glasgow, 11 August, 1965 SYth/Su21-6/S-4						(F)
Norwich C	Glasgow Rgrs	12.87	87-91	130	13	40
Chelsea	Tr	08.92	92-93	35	5	3
Bolton W	L	12.93	93	6	1	1
Bristol C	L	01.95	94	10	0	1
Norwich C	Tr	08.95	95-97	93	11	16
Reading	Tr	03.98	97-98	5	4	1
FLEET Stephen (Steve)						
Urmston, 2 July, 1937						(G)
Manchester C	Jnrs	02.55	57-60	5	-	0
Wrexham	Tr	06.63	63-65	79	0	0
Stockport Co	Tr	01.66	65-67	36	0	0
FLEETING James (Jim) Taylor						
Glasgow, 8 April, 1955						(CD)
Norwich C	Kilbirnie Ladeside	04.75	76	0	1	0
FLEETWOOD Steven Robert						
Sheffield, 27 February, 1962						(M)
Rotherham U		02.87	86	0	1	0

FLEETWOOD Stuart Keith
Gloucester, 23 April, 1986 WYth/Wu21-2 (F)

League Club	Source	Date Signed	Seasons Played	Apps	Subs	Gls
Cardiff C	Sch	02.04	03-04	1	7	0

FLEMING Bernard James
Middlesbrough, 8 January, 1937 (FB)

League Club	Source	Date Signed	Seasons Played	Apps	Subs	Gls
Grimsby T	RAF Binbrook	04.57	57-60	22	-	0
Workington	Tr	07.61	61	20	-	0
Chester	Tr	05.62	62-63	64	-	0

FLEMING Charles (Charlie)
Culross, 12 July, 1927 Died 1997 S-1 (CF)

League Club	Source	Date Signed	Seasons Played	Apps	Subs	Gls
Sunderland	East Fife	01.55	54-57	107	-	62

FLEMING Craig
Halifax, 6 October, 1971 (CD)

League Club	Source	Date Signed	Seasons Played	Apps	Subs	Gls
Halifax T	YT	03.90	88-90	56	1	0
Oldham Ath	Tr	08.91	91-96	158	6	1
Norwich C	Tr	06.97	97-04	290	7	11

FLEMING Craig Matthew
Stockport, 1 December, 1984 (F)

League Club	Source	Date Signed	Seasons Played	Apps	Subs	Gls
Oldham Ath	Sch	•	03	0	1	0

FLEMING Curtis
Manchester, 8 October, 1968 IRYth/IRu23-2/IRu21-5/IR-10 (FB)

League Club	Source	Date Signed	Seasons Played	Apps	Subs	Gls
Middlesbrough	St Patrick's Ath	08.91	91-01	248	18	3
Birmingham C	L	11.01	01	6	0	0
Crystal Palace	Tr	12.01	01-03	41	4	0
Darlington	Tr	08.04	04	24	3	0

FLEMING Francis (Frank) Joseph
South Shields, 21 December, 1945 (G)

League Club	Source	Date Signed	Seasons Played	Apps	Subs	Gls
Darlington		07.64	64	2	-	0

FLEMING Gary James
Derry, 17 February, 1967 NIYth/NIu23-1/NI-31 (FB)

League Club	Source	Date Signed	Seasons Played	Apps	Subs	Gls
Nottingham F	App	11.84	84-87	71	3	0
Manchester C	Tr	08.89	89	13	1	0
Notts Co	L	03.90	89	3	0	0
Barnsley	Tr	03.90	89-95	236	3	0

FLEMING George Keith
Gourock, 25 February, 1935 Died 1999 (IF)

League Club	Source	Date Signed	Seasons Played	Apps	Subs	Gls
Watford	Morton	06.58	58-59	27	-	10
Carlisle U	Tr	06.60	60	7	-	0
Barrow	Tr	09.60	60	17	-	3

FLEMING Hayden Valentine
Islington, 14 March, 1978 (FB)

League Club	Source	Date Signed	Seasons Played	Apps	Subs	Gls
Cardiff C	YT	07.96	95-96	29	3	0

FLEMING James (Jimmy)
Tannochside, 4 November, 1952 (M)

League Club	Source	Date Signed	Seasons Played	Apps	Subs	Gls
Carlisle U	Manchester U (App)	07.71				
Barrow	L	01.72	71	1	1	0

FLEMING James Freeburn
Glasgow, 7 January, 1929 (FB)

League Club	Source	Date Signed	Seasons Played	Apps	Subs	Gls
Workington	Stirling A	05.54	54-57	88	-	1

FLEMING James (Jim) Paterson
Alloa, 7 January, 1942 (W)

League Club	Source	Date Signed	Seasons Played	Apps	Subs	Gls
Luton T	Partick Th	11.60	60-62	66	-	9

FLEMING John (Ian) Hares
Maybole, 15 January, 1953 (W)

League Club	Source	Date Signed	Seasons Played	Apps	Subs	Gls
Sheffield Wed	Aberdeen	02.79	78-79	13	0	1

FLEMING John Joseph
Nottingham, 1 July, 1953 (M)

League Club	Source	Date Signed	Seasons Played	Apps	Subs	Gls
Oxford U	Jnrs	09.70	71-74	67	8	2
Lincoln C	Tr	07.75	75-78	109	12	17
Port Vale	Tr	03.80	79	3	0	0

FLEMING Mark John
Hammersmith, 11 August, 1969 (FB)

League Club	Source	Date Signed	Seasons Played	Apps	Subs	Gls
Queens Park Rgrs	YT	01.88	87-88	1	2	0
Brentford	Tr	07.89	89-90	33	2	1

FLEMING Michael (Mike) Anthony
India, 23 February, 1928 Died 1994 (IF)

League Club	Source	Date Signed	Seasons Played	Apps	Subs	Gls
Tranmere Rov		09.53	53-57	115	-	8

FLEMING Neil
Felixstowe, 9 January, 1950 (CD)

League Club	Source	Date Signed	Seasons Played	Apps	Subs	Gls
Lincoln C (Am)	Lincoln Claytons	07.73	73	1	0	0

FLEMING Paul
Halifax, 6 September, 1967 (FB)

League Club	Source	Date Signed	Seasons Played	Apps	Subs	Gls
Halifax T	App	09.85	85-90	135	4	1
Mansfield T	Tr	07.91	91-94	65	3	0

FLEMING Terence (Terry) Maurice
Marston Green, 5 January, 1973 (M)

League Club	Source	Date Signed	Seasons Played	Apps	Subs	Gls
Coventry C	YT	07.91	90-92	8	5	0
Northampton T	Tr	08.93	93	26	5	1
Preston NE	Tr	07.94	94-95	25	7	2
Lincoln C	Tr	12.95	95-99	175	8	8
Plymouth Arg	Tr	07.00	00	15	2	0
Cambridge U	Tr	03.01	00-03	96	9	4
Grimsby T	Tr	07.04	04	43	0	2

FLETCHER Alan Frederick
Pendleton, 28 October, 1917 Died 1984 (IF)

League Club	Source	Date Signed	Seasons Played	Apps	Subs	Gls
Blackpool		01.37				
Bournemouth	Tr	06.38	38	12	-	0
Bristol Rov	Tr	06.39				
Crewe Alex	Tr	09.47	47	1	-	0

FLETCHER Andrew (Andy) Michael
Saltburn, 12 August, 1971 (F)

League Club	Source	Date Signed	Seasons Played	Apps	Subs	Gls
Middlesbrough	YT	05.89				
Scarborough	Tr	02.91	90-91	15	12	6

FLETCHER Carl Neil
Camberley, 7 April, 1980 W-8 (M)

League Club	Source	Date Signed	Seasons Played	Apps	Subs	Gls
Bournemouth	YT	07.98	97-04	186	7	19
West Ham U	Tr	08.04	04	26	6	2

FLETCHER Christopher (Chris) Columba
Buncrana, 14 June, 1933 (IF)

League Club	Source	Date Signed	Seasons Played	Apps	Subs	Gls
Brentford	Cheltenham T	12.57	57	3	-	0

FLETCHER Darren Barr
Edinburgh, 1 February, 1984 Su21-2/SB-1/S-15 (M)

League Club	Source	Date Signed	Seasons Played	Apps	Subs	Gls
Manchester U	YT	02.01	03-04	35	5	3

FLETCHER Douglas (Doug)
Sheffield, 17 September, 1930 (CF)

League Club	Source	Date Signed	Seasons Played	Apps	Subs	Gls
Sheffield Wed	Hillsborough BC	01.48	48-49	4	-	0
Bury	Tr	05.51	51-55	67	-	17
Scunthorpe U	Tr	07.56	56-57	64	-	26
Darlington	Tr	07.58	58	43	-	13
Halifax T	Tr	06.59	59	20	-	4

FLETCHER Gavin
Bellshill, 30 October, 1941 (IF)

League Club	Source	Date Signed	Seasons Played	Apps	Subs	Gls
Bradford C	Third Lanark	07.63	63	8	-	1

FLETCHER Hugh Malcolm
Lochgilphead, 8 April, 1933 (FB)

League Club	Source	Date Signed	Seasons Played	Apps	Subs	Gls
Carlisle U	Glasgow Celtic	05.56	56-60	124	-	18

FLETCHER James (Jimmy)
Houghton-le-Spring, 6 November, 1934 (CF)

League Club	Source	Date Signed	Seasons Played	Apps	Subs	Gls
Doncaster Rov	Eppleton CW	01.58	57-59	45	-	15
Stockport Co	Tr	01.60	59-60	61	-	19

FLETCHER James (Jimmy) Alfred
Wouldham, 10 November, 1931 EAmat (IF)

League Club	Source	Date Signed	Seasons Played	Apps	Subs	Gls
Gillingham	Maidstone U	07.57	57	23	-	8

FLETCHER James Robert
Brewood, 23 December, 1926 (W)

League Club	Source	Date Signed	Seasons Played	Apps	Subs	Gls
Birmingham C	Bilston	06.50				
Chester	Tr	07.51	51	23	-	9

FLETCHER John
Sheffield, 22 February, 1943 (FB)

League Club	Source	Date Signed	Seasons Played	Apps	Subs	Gls
Doncaster Rov		06.61	61	1	-	0

FLETCHER Joseph (Joe) Michael
Manchester, 25 September, 1946 (F)

League Club	Source	Date Signed	Seasons Played	Apps	Subs	Gls
Rochdale	Manchester C (Am)	01.67	66-68	55	2	21
Grimsby T	Tr	07.69	69	11	0	1
Barrow	Tr	10.69	69	7	1	1

FLETCHER Kenneth (Ken)
Liverpool, 31 December, 1931 (FB)

League Club	Source	Date Signed	Seasons Played	Apps	Subs	Gls
Everton	Jnrs	08.49				
Chester	Tr	07.53	53-55	34	-	0

FLETCHER Leonard (Len) Gerald George
Hammersmith, 28 April, 1929 (WH)

League Club	Source	Date Signed	Seasons Played	Apps	Subs	Gls
Ipswich T	RAF Didcot	11.49	49-54	20	-	0

FLETCHER Mark Robert John
Barnsley, 1 April, 1965 (FB)

League Club	Source	Date Signed	Seasons Played	Apps	Subs	Gls
Barnsley	App	04.83	83	1	0	0
Bradford C	Tr	06.84	84	4	2	0

FLETCHER Paul John
Bolton, 13 January, 1951 Eu23-4 (F)

League Club	Source	Date Signed	Seasons Played	Apps	Subs	Gls
Bolton W	App	11.68	68-70	33	3	5

League Club	Source	Date Signed	Seasons Played	Apps	Subs	Gls
Burnley	Tr	03.71	70-79	291	2	71
Blackpool	Tr	02.80	79-81	19	1	8

FLETCHER Peter
Manchester, 2 December, 1953 (F)

League Club	Source	Date Signed	Seasons Played	Apps	Subs	Gls
Manchester U	App	12.70	72-73	2	5	0
Hull C	Tr	05.74	74-75	26	10	5
Stockport Co	Tr	05.76	76-77	43	8	13
Huddersfield T	Tr	07.78	78-81	83	16	36

FLETCHER James **Rodney (Rod)**
Preston, 23 September, 1945 (F)

League Club	Source	Date Signed	Seasons Played	Apps	Subs	Gls
Leeds U	Colne	12.62				
Crewe Alex	Madeley College	03.67	66	1	0	0
Lincoln C	Tr	08.67	67-70	86	6	29
Scunthorpe U	Tr	06.71	71-73	97	1	30
Grimsby T	Tr	11.73	73-74	9	3	1

FLETCHER Steven (Steve) Mark
Hartlepool, 26 June, 1972 (F)

League Club	Source	Date Signed	Seasons Played	Apps	Subs	Gls
Hartlepool U	YT	08.90	90-91	19	13	4
Bournemouth	Tr	07.92	92-04	393	32	83

FLEWIN Reginald (Reg)
Portsmouth, 28 November, 1920 EWar-1 (CD)

League Club	Source	Date Signed	Seasons Played	Apps	Subs	Gls
Portsmouth	Ryde Sports	11.37	38-52	150	-	0

FLEXNEY Paul
Glasgow, 18 January, 1965 (CD)

League Club	Source	Date Signed	Seasons Played	Apps	Subs	Gls
Northampton T	Clyde	08.88	88	12	0	0

FLINDERS Scott Liam
Rotherham, 12 June, 1986 EYth (G)

League Club	Source	Date Signed	Seasons Played	Apps	Subs	Gls
Barnsley	Sch	04.05	04	11	0	0

FLINT Kenneth (Ken)
Selston, 12 November, 1923 (W)

League Club	Source	Date Signed	Seasons Played	Apps	Subs	Gls
Tottenham H	Bedford T	07.47	47	5	-	1
Aldershot	Tr	07.50	50-57	324	-	70
Leyton Orient	Tr	06.58	58	4	-	0

FLITCROFT David (Dave) John
Bolton, 14 January, 1974 (M)

League Club	Source	Date Signed	Seasons Played	Apps	Subs	Gls
Preston NE	YT	05.92	92	4	4	2
Lincoln C	L	09.93	93	2	0	0
Chester C	Tr	12.93	93-98	146	21	18
Rochdale	Tr	07.99	99-02	141	19	4
Macclesfield T	Tr	07.03	03	14	1	0
Bury	Tr	01.04	03-04	49	4	3

FLITCROFT Garry William
Bolton, 6 November, 1972 ESch/EYth/Eu21-10 (M)

League Club	Source	Date Signed	Seasons Played	Apps	Subs	Gls
Manchester C	YT	07.91	92-95	109	6	13
Bury	L	03.92	91	12	0	0
Blackburn Rov	Tr	03.96	95-04	230	14	14

FLITNEY Ross Daniel
Hitchin, 1 June, 1984 (G)

League Club	Source	Date Signed	Seasons Played	Apps	Subs	Gls
Fulham	Sch	07.03				
Brighton & Hove A	L	08.03	03	3	0	0

FLO Havard
Volda, Norway, 4 April, 1970 Norway 20 (F)

League Club	Source	Date Signed	Seasons Played	Apps	Subs	Gls
Wolverhampton W	Werder Bremen (Ger)	01.99	98-99	27	11	9

FLO Jostein
Eid, Norway, 3 October, 1964 Norway int (F)

League Club	Source	Date Signed	Seasons Played	Apps	Subs	Gls
Sheffield U	Stryn Sogndal (Nor)	08.93	93-95	74	10	19

FLO Tore Andre
Stryn, Norway, 15 June, 1973 Nou21/No-75 (F)

League Club	Source	Date Signed	Seasons Played	Apps	Subs	Gls
Chelsea	SK Brann Bergen (Nor)	08.97	97-00	59	53	34
Sunderland	Glasgow Rgrs	08.02	02	23	6	4

FLOCKETT Thomas (Tommy) William
Ferryhill, 17 July, 1927 Died 1997 (FB)

League Club	Source	Date Signed	Seasons Played	Apps	Subs	Gls
Chesterfield	Spennymoor U	04.49	49-56	200	-	1
Bradford C	Tr	06.57	57-62	227	-	1

FLOOD Edward (Eddie) David
Liverpool, 19 November, 1952 (FB)

League Club	Source	Date Signed	Seasons Played	Apps	Subs	Gls
Liverpool	App	11.69				
Tranmere Rov	Tr	07.72	72-80	313	2	6
York C	Tr	08.81	81	13	2	0

FLOOD John Ernest
Southampton, 21 October, 1932 ESch (W)

League Club	Source	Date Signed	Seasons Played	Apps	Subs	Gls
Southampton	Jnrs	11.49	52-57	122	-	28
Bournemouth	Tr	06.58	58	17	-	3

FLOOD John Gerard
Glasgow, 25 December, 1960 (W)

League Club	Source	Date Signed	Seasons Played	Apps	Subs	Gls
Sheffield U	App	10.78	78-80	16	3	1

FLOOD Paul Anthony
Dublin, 29 June, 1948 (W)

League Club	Source	Date Signed	Seasons Played	Apps	Subs	Gls
Brighton & Hove A	Bohemians	06.67	67-70	32	3	7

FLOOD William (Willo) Robert
Dublin, 10 April, 1985 IRYth/IRu21-10 (M)

League Club	Source	Date Signed	Seasons Played	Apps	Subs	Gls
Manchester C	YT	04.02	04	4	5	1
Rochdale	L	03.04	03	6	0	0

FLOUNDERS Andrew (Andy) John
Hull, 13 December, 1963 (F)

League Club	Source	Date Signed	Seasons Played	Apps	Subs	Gls
Hull C	App	12.81	80-86	126	33	54
Scunthorpe U	Tr	03.87	86-90	186	10	87
Rochdale	Tr	07.91	91-93	82	3	31
Rotherham U	L	02.93	92	6	0	2
Carlisle U	L	10.93	93	5	0	1
Carlisle U	L	02.94	93	1	2	0
Northampton T	Halifax T	12.94	94	2	0	0

FLOWER Anthony (Tony) John
Carlton, Nottinghamshire, 2 January, 1945 (W)

League Club	Source	Date Signed	Seasons Played	Apps	Subs	Gls
Notts Co	Jnrs	01.62	61-66	127	2	17
Halifax T	Tr	07.67	67-69	78	1	11

FLOWER Johannes (John) Graham
Northampton, 9 December, 1964 (CD)

League Club	Source	Date Signed	Seasons Played	Apps	Subs	Gls
Sheffield U	Corby T	08.89				
Aldershot	Tr	10.90	90	30	2	2

FLOWERS John Edward
Edlington, 26 August, 1944 (M)

League Club	Source	Date Signed	Seasons Played	Apps	Subs	Gls
Stoke C	App	09.61	63-65	8	0	0
Doncaster Rov	Tr	08.66	66-70	162	2	4
Port Vale	Tr	08.71	71	34	0	0

FLOWERS Malcolm Thomas
Mansfield, 9 August, 1938 (CD)

League Club	Source	Date Signed	Seasons Played	Apps	Subs	Gls
Mansfield T	Jnrs	08.56	56	3	-	0

FLOWERS Paul Anthony
Stepney, 7 September, 1974 (CD)

League Club	Source	Date Signed	Seasons Played	Apps	Subs	Gls
Colchester U	YT	08.93	92	2	1	0

FLOWERS Ronald (Ron)
Edlington, 28 July, 1934 Eu23-2/FLge-13/E-49 (CD)

League Club	Source	Date Signed	Seasons Played	Apps	Subs	Gls
Wolverhampton W	Jnrs	08.51	52-66	467	0	33
Northampton T	Tr	09.67	67-68	61	1	4

FLOWERS Timothy (Tim) David
Kenilworth, 3 February, 1967 EYth/Eu21-3/E-11 (G)

League Club	Source	Date Signed	Seasons Played	Apps	Subs	Gls
Wolverhampton W	App	08.84	84-85	63	0	0
Southampton	Tr	06.86	86-93	192	0	0
Swindon T	L	03.87	86	2	0	0
Swindon T	L	11.87	87	5	0	0
Blackburn Rov	Tr	11.93	93-98	175	2	0
Leicester C	Tr	07.99	99-02	54	2	0
Stockport Co	L	10.01	01	4	0	0
Coventry C	L	02.02	01	5	0	0

FLOYD Ronald (Ron) Charles
Coventry, 17 August, 1932 (G)

League Club	Source	Date Signed	Seasons Played	Apps	Subs	Gls
West Bromwich A	Jnrs	11.49				
Crewe Alex	Tr	07.53	53-54	39	-	0

FLYNN Brian
Port Talbot, 12 October, 1955 WSch/Wu23-2/W-66 (M)

League Club	Source	Date Signed	Seasons Played	Apps	Subs	Gls
Burnley	App	10.72	73-77	115	5	8
Leeds U	Tr	11.77	77-82	152	2	11
Burnley	L	03.82	81	2	0	0
Burnley	Tr	11.82	82-84	76	4	10
Cardiff C	Tr	11.84	84-85	32	0	0
Doncaster Rov	Tr	11.85	85	27	0	0
Bury	Tr	07.86	86	19	0	0
Doncaster Rov	Limerick	08.87	87	18	6	1
Wrexham	Tr	02.88	87-92	91	9	5

FLYNN John Edward
Workington, 20 March, 1948 (CD)

League Club	Source	Date Signed	Seasons Played	Apps	Subs	Gls
Workington	Cockermouth	09.67	66-68	35	3	0
Sheffield U	Tr	07.69	69-77	185	5	8
Rotherham U	Tr	07.78	78-79	30	1	1

FLYNN Lee David
Hampstead, 4 September, 1973 (FB)

League Club	Source	Date Signed	Seasons Played	Apps	Subs	Gls
Barnet	Hayes	01.01	00	17	0	0

FLYNN Michael (Mike) Anthony
Oldham, 23 February, 1969 (CD)

League Club	Source	Date Signed	Seasons Played	Apps	Subs	Gls
Oldham Ath	App	02.87	87-88	37	3	1
Norwich C	Tr	12.88				
Preston NE	Tr	12.89	89-92	134	2	7
Stockport Co	Tr	03.93	92-01	386	1	16
Stoke C	L	01.02	01	11	2	0
Barnsley	Tr	03.02	01-02	20	1	0
Blackpool	Tr	01.03	02-04	55	2	1

FLYNN Michael (Mike) John
Newport, 17 October, 1980 WSemiPro (M)

League Club	Source	Date Signed	Seasons Played	Apps	Subs	Gls
Wigan Ath	Barry T	06.02	02-04	5	33	2
Blackpool	L	08.04	04	6	0	0
Gillingham	Tr	02.05	04	16	0	3

FLYNN Peter
Glasgow, 11 October, 1936 (WH)

League Club	Source	Date Signed	Seasons Played	Apps	Subs	Gls
Leeds U	Petershill	10.53	53	1	-	0
Bradford PA	Tr	06.57	58-65	130	1	9

FLYNN Sean Michael
Birmingham, 13 March, 1968 (M)

League Club	Source	Date Signed	Seasons Played	Apps	Subs	Gls
Coventry C	Halesowen T	12.91	91-94	90	7	9
Derby Co	Tr	08.95	95-96	39	20	3
Stoke C	L	03.97	96	5	0	0
West Bromwich A	Tr	08.97	97-99	99	10	8
Tranmere Rov	Tr	07.00	00-01	65	1	6
Kidderminster Hrs	Tr	08.02	02-03	49	2	2

FLYNN William
Kirkmalden, 2 January, 1927 (W)

League Club	Source	Date Signed	Seasons Played	Apps	Subs	Gls
Rotherham U	Maybole Jnrs	07.49	49	6	-	0

FOAN Albert Thomas
Rotherhithe, 30 October, 1923 (IF)

League Club	Source	Date Signed	Seasons Played	Apps	Subs	Gls
Norwich C	BAOR Germany	04.47	47-49	18	-	4
West Ham U	Tr	07.50	50-56	53	-	6

FOE Marc-Vivien
Nkolo, Cameroon, 1 May, 1975 Died 2003 Cameroon 64 (M)

League Club	Source	Date Signed	Seasons Played	Apps	Subs	Gls
West Ham U	RC Lens (Fr)	01.99	98-99	38	0	1
Manchester C (L)	Lyon (Fr)	07.02	02	35	0	9

FOFANA Aboubaka
Paris, France, 4 October, 1982 (F)

League Club	Source	Date Signed	Seasons Played	Apps	Subs	Gls
Millwall	Juventus (It)	08.03	03	9	7	0

FOGARTY Ambrose (Amby) Gerald
Dublin, 11 September, 1933 IR-11 (IF)

League Club	Source	Date Signed	Seasons Played	Apps	Subs	Gls
Sunderland	Glentoran	10.57	57-63	152	-	37
Hartlepools U	Tr	11.63	63-66	127	0	22

FOGARTY Kenneth (Ken) Anthony
Manchester, 25 January, 1955 (CD)

League Club	Source	Date Signed	Seasons Played	Apps	Subs	Gls
Stockport Co	App	11.72	71-79	265	4	6

FOGARTY William (Bill) Francis
Dulwich, 27 June, 1957 (M)

League Club	Source	Date Signed	Seasons Played	Apps	Subs	Gls
Gillingham	App	07.75	74-76	25	4	0

FOGG David
Liverpool, 28 May, 1951 (FB)

League Club	Source	Date Signed	Seasons Played	Apps	Subs	Gls
Wrexham		05.70	70-75	159	2	0
Oxford U	Tr	07.76	76-84	289	4	16

FOGG Ronald (Ron) William James
Tilbury, 3 June, 1938 (CF)

League Club	Source	Date Signed	Seasons Played	Apps	Subs	Gls
Southend U (Am)	Tilbury	08.59	59	2	-	0
Aldershot	Weymouth	07.63	63-64	64	-	28

FOGGO Kenneth (Ken) Taylor
Perth, 7 November, 1943 SSch (W)

League Club	Source	Date Signed	Seasons Played	Apps	Subs	Gls
West Bromwich A	Peebles YMCA	11.60	62-67	128	1	29
Norwich C	Tr	10.67	67-72	181	4	54
Portsmouth	Tr	01.73	72-74	47	13	3
Southend U	Tr	09.75	75	30	0	6

FOGGON Alan
West Pelton, 23 February, 1950 EYth (W)

League Club	Source	Date Signed	Seasons Played	Apps	Subs	Gls
Newcastle U	App	11.67	67-70	54	7	14
Cardiff C	Tr	08.71	71-72	14	3	1
Middlesbrough	Tr	10.72	72-75	105	10	45
Manchester U	Hartford (USA)	07.76	76	0	3	0
Sunderland	Tr	09.76	76	7	1	0
Southend U	Tr	06.77	77	22	0	0
Hartlepool U	L	02.78	77	18	0	2

FOLAN Anthony (Tony) Stephen
Lewisham, 18 September, 1978 IRu21-6 (M)

League Club	Source	Date Signed	Seasons Played	Apps	Subs	Gls
Crystal Palace	YT	09.95	97	0	1	0
Brentford	Tr	09.98	98-00	31	28	7

FOLAN Caleb Colman
Leeds, 26 October, 1982 (F)

League Club	Source	Date Signed	Seasons Played	Apps	Subs	Gls
Leeds U	YT	11.99				
Rushden & Diamonds	L	10.01	01	1	5	0
Hull C	L	11.01	01	0	1	0
Chesterfield	Tr	02.03	02-04	30	22	7

FOLDS Robert (Bobby) James
Bedford, 18 April, 1949 (W)

League Club	Source	Date Signed	Seasons Played	Apps	Subs	Gls
Gillingham	App	04.67	68-70	38	6	1
Northampton T	Tr	08.71	71	29	0	0

FOLETTI Patrick
Sorengo, Switzerland, 27 May, 1974 (G)

League Club	Source	Date Signed	Seasons Played	Apps	Subs	Gls
Derby Co (L)	Lucerne (Swi)	02.02	01	1	1	0

FOLEY Charles
Salford, 7 January, 1952 (M)

League Club	Source	Date Signed	Seasons Played	Apps	Subs	Gls
Stockport Co	App	01.70	69-70	6	0	0

FOLEY David John
South Shields, 12 May, 1987 (F)

League Club	Source	Date Signed	Seasons Played	Apps	Subs	Gls
Hartlepool U	Sch	•	03-04	1	2	0

FOLEY Dominic Joseph
Cork, 7 July, 1976 IRu21-8/IR-6 (F)

League Club	Source	Date Signed	Seasons Played	Apps	Subs	Gls
Wolverhampton W	St James' Gate	08.95	95-98	4	16	3
Watford	L	02.98	97	2	6	1
Notts Co	L	12.98	98	2	0	0
Watford	Tr	06.99	99-02	12	21	5
Queens Park Rgrs	L	10.01	01	1	0	0
Swindon T	L	01.02	01	5	2	1
Queens Park Rgrs	L	03.02	01	2	2	1
Southend U	L	02.03	02	5	0	0
Oxford U	L	03.03	02	4	2	0

FOLEY Kevin Patrick
Luton, 1 November, 1984 IRu21-4 (M)

League Club	Source	Date Signed	Seasons Played	Apps	Subs	Gls
Luton T	Sch	03.04	02-04	70	4	3

FOLEY Peter
Edinburgh, 28 June, 1944 (W)

League Club	Source	Date Signed	Seasons Played	Apps	Subs	Gls
Workington	Preston Ath	02.65	64-66	74	0	15
Scunthorpe U	Tr	07.67	67-68	15	2	3
Chesterfield	Tr	08.69	69	2	0	0

FOLEY Peter
Bicester, 10 September, 1956 IRYth (F)

League Club	Source	Date Signed	Seasons Played	Apps	Subs	Gls
Oxford U	App	09.74	74-82	262	15	71
Gillingham	L	02.83	82	5	0	0
Aldershot	Bulova (HK)	08.84	84	6	3	2
Exeter C		03.87	86	1	0	0

FOLEY Stephen (Steve) Paul
Clacton, 21 June, 1953 (M)

League Club	Source	Date Signed	Seasons Played	Apps	Subs	Gls
Colchester U	App	09.71	71-81	273	10	54

FOLEY Steven (Steve)
Kirkdale, 4 October, 1962 (M)

League Club	Source	Date Signed	Seasons Played	Apps	Subs	Gls
Liverpool	App	09.80				
Fulham	L	12.83	83	2	1	0
Grimsby T	Tr	08.84	84	31	0	2
Sheffield U	Tr	08.85	85-86	56	10	14
Swindon T	Tr	06.87	87-91	142	9	23
Stoke C	Tr	01.92	91-93	106	1	9
Lincoln C	Tr	07.94	94	15	1	0
Bradford C	Tr	08.95	95	0	1	0

FOLEY Terence (Terry)
Portsmouth, 8 February, 1938 (CF)

League Club	Source	Date Signed	Seasons Played	Apps	Subs	Gls
Portsmouth	Ryde	05.59	59	7	-	0
Chesterfield	Tr	07.60	60	28	-	11

FOLEY Theodore (Theo) Cornelius
Dublin, 2 April, 1937 IR-9 (FB)

League Club	Source	Date Signed	Seasons Played	Apps	Subs	Gls
Exeter C	Home Farm	03.55	55-60	155	-	1
Northampton T	Tr	05.61	61-66	204	0	8
Charlton Ath	Tr	08.67	67	6	0	0

FOLEY William (Will)
Bellshill, 25 June, 1960 (F)

League Club	Source	Date Signed	Seasons Played	Apps	Subs	Gls
Swansea C	Frickley Ath	01.86	85	4	1	2
Cardiff C	Tr	03.86	85	5	2	1

FOLLAN Edward (Eddie) Harvey
Greenock, 3 October, 1929 Died 1975 (IF)

League Club	Source	Date Signed	Seasons Played	Apps	Subs	Gls
Aston Villa	Prescot Cables	06.52	54-55	34	-	7

FOLLAND Robert (Bobby)
Hartlepool, 3 December, 1940 (CF)

League Club	Source	Date Signed	Seasons Played	Apps	Subs	Gls
Hartlepools U	Newcastle U (Am)	05.59	59-62	58	-	24

FOLLAND Robert (Rob) William
Swansea, 16 September, 1979 WYth/Wu21-1 (FB)

League Club	Source	Date Signed	Seasons Played	Apps	Subs	Gls
Oxford U	YT	07.98	97-01	18	22	2

FOLLY Yoann
Togo, 6 June, 1985 FrYth (M)

League Club	Source	Date Signed	Seasons Played	Apps	Subs	Gls
Southampton	St Etienne (Fr)	07.03	03-04	10	2	0
Nottingham F	L	01.05	04	0	1	0
Preston NE	L	03.05	04	0	2	0

FONTAINE Liam Vaughan Henry
Beckenham, 7 January, 1986 (CD)

League Club	Source	Date Signed	Seasons Played	Apps	Subs	Gls
Fulham	Sch	03.04	04	0	1	0
Yeovil T	L	08.04	04	15	0	0

FOOT Daniel (Danny) Francis
Edmonton, 6 September, 1975 (FB)

League Club	Source	Date Signed	Seasons Played	Apps	Subs	Gls
Southend U	Tottenham H (YT)	08.94	94	2	1	0

FOOTE Christopher (Chris) Robert Thomas
Bournemouth, 19 November, 1950 (M)

League Club	Source	Date Signed	Seasons Played	Apps	Subs	Gls
Bournemouth	App	08.68	68-69	44	1	2
Cambridge U	Tr	03.71	70-73	76	10	6

FOOTITT Donald (Don)
Grantham, 24 May, 1929 Died 1995 (G)

League Club	Source	Date Signed	Seasons Played	Apps	Subs	Gls
Lincoln C	Grantham St John's	12.46	46	24	-	0
Crewe Alex	Tr	07.49	49	1	-	0

FORAN Mark James
Aldershot, 30 October, 1973 (CD)

League Club	Source	Date Signed	Seasons Played	Apps	Subs	Gls
Millwall	YT	11.90				
Sheffield U	Tr	08.93	94-95	10	1	1
Rotherham U	L	08.94	94	3	0	0
Wycombe W	L	08.95	95	5	0	0
Peterborough U	Tr	02.96	95-97	22	3	1
Lincoln C	L	01.97	96	1	1	0
Oldham Ath	L	03.97	96	0	1	0
Crewe Alex	Tr	12.97	97-99	25	6	1
Bristol Rov	Tr	08.00	00-01	39	4	2

FORAN Richard (Richie)
Dublin, 16 June, 1980 IRu21-2 (F)

League Club	Source	Date Signed	Seasons Played	Apps	Subs	Gls
Carlisle U	Shelbourne	08.01	01-03	84	7	25
Oxford U	L	01.04	03	3	1	0

FORBES Adrian Emmanuel
Greenford, 23 January, 1979 EYth (W)

League Club	Source	Date Signed	Seasons Played	Apps	Subs	Gls
Norwich C	YT	01.97	96-00	66	46	8
Luton T	Tr	07.01	01-03	39	33	14
Swansea C	Tr	07.04	04	36	4	7

FORBES Alexander (Alex) Rooney
Dundee, 21 January, 1925 S-14 (WH)

League Club	Source	Date Signed	Seasons Played	Apps	Subs	Gls
Sheffield U	Dundee North End	12.44	46-47	61	-	6
Arsenal	Tr	02.48	47-55	217	-	20
Leyton Orient	Tr	08.56	56	8	-	0
Fulham	Tr	11.57	57	4	-	0

FORBES Boniek Manuel Gomes
Guinea Bissau, 30 September, 1983 (M)

League Club	Source	Date Signed	Seasons Played	Apps	Subs	Gls
Leyton Orient	Sch	08.03	02-03	0	13	0

FORBES Dudley Douglas
Johannesburg, South Africa, 19 April, 1926 (WH)

League Club	Source	Date Signed	Seasons Played	Apps	Subs	Gls
Charlton Ath	Marist Bros (SA)	12.47	48-50	57	-	1

FORBES Duncan Scott
Edinburgh, 19 June, 1941 (CD)

League Club	Source	Date Signed	Seasons Played	Apps	Subs	Gls
Colchester U	Musselburgh Ath	09.61	61-68	270	0	3
Norwich C	Tr	09.68	68-80	289	6	10
Torquay U	L	10.76	76	7	0	0

FORBES George Parrott
Dukinfield, 21 July, 1914 Died 1964 (CD)

League Club	Source	Date Signed	Seasons Played	Apps	Subs	Gls
Blackburn Rov	Hyde U	01.37	36	2	-	1
Barrow	Tr	06.46	46-50	177	-	3

FORBES Graeme Scott Alexander
Forfar, 29 July, 1958 (CD)

League Club	Source	Date Signed	Seasons Played	Apps	Subs	Gls
Walsall	Motherwell	09.86	86-89	173	0	9

FORBES Richard (Dick) John
Ashford, Kent, 12 March, 1955 (M)

League Club	Source	Date Signed	Seasons Played	Apps	Subs	Gls
Exeter C	Woking	04.78	77-80	55	4	5
Plymouth Arg	Bideford T	08.83	83	3	0	0

FORBES Scott Hugh
Canewdon, 3 December, 1976 (M)

League Club	Source	Date Signed	Seasons Played	Apps	Subs	Gls
Southend U	Saffron Walden T	08.00	00-01	30	17	3

FORBES Steven (Steve) Dudley
Stoke Newington, 24 December, 1975 (M)

League Club	Source	Date Signed	Seasons Played	Apps	Subs	Gls
Millwall	Sittingbourne	07.94	94-95	0	5	0
Colchester U	Tr	03.97	96-99	34	19	4
Peterborough U	L	03.99	98	1	2	0

FORBES Terrell Dishan
Southwark, 17 August, 1981 (FB)

League Club	Source	Date Signed	Seasons Played	Apps	Subs	Gls
West Ham U	YT	07.99				
Bournemouth	L	10.99	99	3	0	0
Queens Park Rgrs	Tr	07.01	01-04	113	1	0
Grimsby T	Tr	09.04	04	33	0	0

FORBES William (Willie)
Glasgow, 25 May, 1922 Died 1999 (WH)

League Club	Source	Date Signed	Seasons Played	Apps	Subs	Gls
Wolverhampton W	Dunfermline Ath	09.46	46-49	71	-	23
Preston NE	Tr	12.49	49-55	191	-	7
Carlisle U	Tr	07.56	56-57	26	-	0

FORD Alan Lenane
Ferndale, 28 October, 1925 Died 1963 (G)

League Club	Source	Date Signed	Seasons Played	Apps	Subs	Gls
Workington (Am)		07.51	51-53	39	-	0

FORD Andrew (Andy) Carl
Minehead, 4 May, 1954 (FB)

League Club	Source	Date Signed	Seasons Played	Apps	Subs	Gls
Bournemouth	Minehead	07.72				
Southend U	Tr	05.73	73-76	135	3	3
Swindon T	Tr	08.77	77-79	92	6	0
Gillingham	Tr	07.80	80-81	62	0	3

FORD Anthony (Tony) Michael
Thornbury, 26 November, 1944 EYth (FB)

League Club	Source	Date Signed	Seasons Played	Apps	Subs	Gls
Bristol C	App	11.61	61-69	170	1	10
Bristol Rov	Tr	12.69	69-70	28	0	1

FORD Clive
Hateley Heath, 10 April, 1945 (F)

League Club	Source	Date Signed	Seasons Played	Apps	Subs	Gls
Wolverhampton W	App	10.62	64	2	-	0
Walsall	Tr	12.64	64-66	11	3	0
Lincoln C	Tr	02.67	66-67	48	1	16

FORD Colin
Lewisham, 18 September, 1960 (FB)

League Club	Source	Date Signed	Seasons Played	Apps	Subs	Gls
Gillingham	App	09.78	79	1	0	0

FORD David
Sheffield, 2 March, 1945 Eu23-2 (F)

League Club	Source	Date Signed	Seasons Played	Apps	Subs	Gls
Sheffield Wed	App	01.63	65-69	117	5	31
Newcastle U	Tr	12.69	69-70	24	2	3
Sheffield U	Tr	01.71	70-72	21	6	2
Halifax T	Tr	08.73	73-75	83	2	6

FORD Francis Martin
Bridgend, 3 February, 1967 (FB)

League Club	Source	Date Signed	Seasons Played	Apps	Subs	Gls
Cardiff C	App	03.85	84	1	1	0

FORD Frederick (Fred) George Luther
Dartford, 10 February, 1916 Died 1981 (WH)

League Club	Source	Date Signed	Seasons Played	Apps	Subs	Gls
Charlton Ath	Erith & Belvedere	03.36	36-37	22	-	0
Millwall	Tr	11.45	46	9	-	0
Carlisle U	Tr	07.47	47	28	-	0

FORD Gary
York, 8 February, 1961 (W)

League Club	Source	Date Signed	Seasons Played	Apps	Subs	Gls
York C	App	02.79	78-86	359	7	52
Leicester C	Tr	07.87	87	15	1	2
Port Vale	Tr	01.88	87-90	66	9	12
Walsall	L	03.90	89	13	0	2
Mansfield T	Tr	03.91	90-92	88	0	6
Hartlepool U	Harstad (Nor)	09.95	95	2	1	0

FORD James Anthony
Portsmouth, 23 October, 1981 (M)

League Club	Source	Date Signed	Seasons Played	Apps	Subs	Gls
Bournemouth	YT	04.00	99-01	5	7	0

FORD Jonathan (Jon) Steven
Stourbridge, 12 April, 1968 (CD)

League Club	Source	Date Signed	Seasons Played	Apps	Subs	Gls
Swansea C	Cradley T	08.91	91-94	145	15	7
Bradford C	Tr	07.95	95	18	1	0
Gillingham	Tr	08.96	96	2	2	0
Barnet	Tr	02.97	96-98	47	0	2

FORD Kenneth (Ken)
Sheffield, 1 December, 1940 (W)

League Club	Source	Date Signed	Seasons Played	Apps	Subs	Gls
Sheffield Wed	Jnrs	03.60				
Oldham Ath	Tr	06.61	61	5	-	1

FORD Liam Anthony
Bradford, 8 September, 1979 (F)

League Club	Source	Date Signed	Seasons Played	Apps	Subs	Gls
Plymouth Arg	YT	07.98	98	0	1	0

League Club	Source	Date Signed	Seasons Played	Apps	Subs	Gls
FORD Mark Stuart						
Pontefract, 10 October, 1975 EYth/Eu21-2 (M)						
Leeds U	YT	03.93	93-96	27	2	1
Burnley	Tr	07.97	97-98	43	5	1
Torquay U	KFC Lommelse (Bel)	07.00	00	28	0	3
Darlington	Tr	02.01	00-02	55	2	9
FORD Michael (Mike) Paul						
Bristol, 9 February, 1966 (FB)						
Leicester C	App	02.84				
Cardiff C	Devizes T	09.84	84-87	144	1	13
Oxford U	Tr	06.88	88-97	273	16	18
Cardiff C	Tr	07.98	98-99	48	3	0
Oxford U	Tr	09.00	00	1	0	0
FORD Peter Leslie						
Hanley, 10 August, 1933 (CD)						
Stoke C	West Bromwich A (Am)	05.53	56-58	14	-	0
Port Vale	Tr	09.59	59-62	104	-	5
FORD Robert (Bobby) John						
Bristol, 22 September, 1974 (M)						
Oxford U	YT	10.92	93-97	104	12	7
Sheffield U	Tr	11.97	97-01	138	17	6
Oxford U	Tr	08.02	02	31	6	1
FORD Robert Milroy						
Rutherglen, 13 August, 1934 (IF)						
Aldershot	Vale of Clyde	07.57	57	2	-	0
FORD Ryan						
Worksop, 3 September, 1978 (M)						
Manchester U	YT	07.97				
Notts Co	Tr	02.00	99	0	1	0
FORD Simon Gary						
Newham, 17 November, 1981 (CD)						
Grimsby T	Charlton Ath (YT)	07.01	01-03	64	14	4
FORD Stephen (Steve) Derek						
Shoreham-by-Sea, 17 February, 1959 ESch (F)						
Stoke C	Lewes	07.81	81	1	1	0
FORD Stuart Trevor						
Sheffield, 20 July, 1971 (G)						
Rotherham U	YT	07.89	89-91	5	0	0
Scarborough	L	03.92	91	6	0	0
Scarborough	Tr	08.92	92	22	0	0
Doncaster Rov	Tr	08.93	93	4	2	0
Scarborough	Tr	07.94	94	6	0	0
FORD Tony						
Grimsby, 14 May, 1959 EB-2 (W)						
Grimsby T	App	05.77	75-85	321	34	55
Sunderland	L	03.86	85	8	1	1
Stoke C	Tr	07.86	86-88	112	0	13
West Bromwich A	Tr	03.89	88-91	114	0	14
Grimsby T	Tr	11.91	91-93	59	9	3
Bradford C	L	09.93	93	5	0	0
Scunthorpe U	Tr	08.94	94-95	73	3	9
Mansfield T	Barrow	10.96	96-98	97	6	7
Rochdale	Tr	07.99	99-01	81	8	6
FORD Trevor						
Swansea, 1 October, 1923 Died 2003 WWar-1/W-38 (CF)						
Swansea T	Tawe U	05.42	46	16	-	9
Aston Villa	Tr	01.47	46-50	120	-	60
Sunderland	Tr	10.50	50-53	108	-	67
Cardiff C	Tr	12.53	53-56	96	-	42
Newport Co	PSV Eindhoven (Holl)	07.60	60	8	-	3
FORDE Clevere						
London, 14 November, 1958 (W)						
Plymouth Arg	Hounslow	12.78	78	4	1	0
FORDE Fabian Wesley						
Harrow, 26 October, 1981 (F)						
Watford	YT	03.01	00	0	1	0
FORDE Stephen (Steve)						
South Kirkby, 29 August, 1914 Died 1992 (FB)						
Sheffield Wed	South Elmsall	01.33				
Rotherham U	Tr	04.33	32-36	116	-	1
West Ham U	Tr	01.37	37-51	170	-	1
FOREMAN Darren						
Southampton, 12 February, 1968 ESch (F)						
Barnsley	Fareham T	08.86	86-89	33	14	8
Crewe Alex	Tr	03.90	89-90	19	4	4
Scarborough	Tr	03.91	90-94	77	20	35

League Club	Source	Date Signed	Seasons Played	Apps	Subs	Gls
FOREMAN Denis Joseph						
Cape Town, South Africa, 1 February, 1933 (IF)						
Brighton & Hove A	Hibernian (SA)	03.52	52-60	211	-	63
FOREMAN Alexander **George**						
Walthamstow, 1 March, 1914 Died 1969 EAmat (CF)						
West Ham U	Walthamstow Ave	03.38	38	6	-	1
Tottenham H	Tr	02.46	46	36	-	14
FOREMAN Matthew (Matt)						
Gateshead, 15 February, 1975 (M)						
Sheffield U	YT	07.93				
Scarborough	Tr	03.96	95	1	3	0
FOREMAN William (Billy) Ernest						
Havant, 3 February, 1958 (M)						
Bristol Rov	Bournemouth (App)	05.76	76-77	0	2	0
FORGAN Thomas (Tommy) Carr						
Middlesbrough, 12 October, 1929 (G)						
Hull C	Sutton Est	05.49	53	10	-	0
York C	Tr	06.54	54-65	388	0	0
FORGE Nicolas						
Roanne, France, 13 May, 1971 (M)						
Leyton Orient	ASOA Valence (Fr)	03.01	00	1	0	0
FORINTON Howard Lee						
Boston, 18 September, 1975 (F)						
Birmingham C	Yeovil T	07.97	97-99	0	5	1
Plymouth Arg	L	12.98	98	8	1	3
Peterborough U	Tr	09.99	99-01	34	16	10
Torquay U	Tr	08.02	02	1	0	0
FORLAN Corazo **Diego**						
Montevideo, Uruguay, 19 May, 1979 Uruguay 27 (F)						
Manchester U	Independiente (Ur)	01.02	01-04	23	40	10
FORMAN Matthew Charles						
Evesham, 8 September, 1967 (M)						
Aston Villa	App	09.85				
Wolverhampton W	Tr	08.86	86	24	1	4
FORMBY Kevin						
Ormskirk, 22 July, 1971 (FB)						
Rochdale	Burscough	03.94	93-96	59	8	1
FORREST Craig Lorne						
Vancouver, Canada, 20 September, 1967 Canada 56 (G)						
Ipswich T	App	08.85	88-96	263	0	0
Colchester U	L	03.88	87	11	0	0
Chelsea	L	03.97	96	2	1	0
West Ham U	Tr	07.97	97-00	26	4	0
FORREST Daniel (Danny) Paul Halafihi						
Keighley, 23 October, 1984 EYth (M)						
Bradford C	Sch	●	02-04	16	34	5
FORREST Ernest (Ernie)						
Sunderland, 19 February, 1919 Died 1987 (WH)						
Bolton W	Usworth Colliery	01.38	38-47	69	-	1
Grimsby T	Tr	05.48	48	33	-	1
Millwall	Tr	06.49	49	37	-	4
FORREST Gerald (Gerry)						
Stockton, 21 January, 1957 (FB)						
Rotherham U	South Bank	02.77	77-85	357	0	7
Southampton	Tr	12.85	85-89	112	3	0
Rotherham U	Tr	08.90	90	32	2	0
FORREST James (Jimmy)						
Dalkeith, 14 November, 1929 Died 1994 (IF)						
Leeds U	Musselburgh Ath	12.50				
Accrington St	Tr	11.51	51	5	-	2
FORREST James (Jim)						
Glasgow, 22 September, 1944 SSch/Su23-2/S-5 (F)						
Preston NE	Glasgow Rgrs	03.67	66-67	24	2	3
FORREST John Anthony						
Tottington, 9 October, 1947 (G)						
Bury	Jnrs	03.66	67-80	430	0	0
FORREST Keith						
Hartlepool, 18 February, 1951 (F)						
Hartlepool (Am)	St James'	07.69	69-70	4	2	0
FORREST Martyn William						
Bury, 2 January, 1979 (M)						
Bury	YT	07.97	98-02	82	24	2

FORREST John Robert (Bob)
Rossington, 13 May, 1931 Died 2005 (IF)

League Club	Source	Date Signed	Seasons Played	Apps	Subs	Gls
Leeds U	Retford T	12.52	52-58	118	-	36
Notts Co	Tr	02.59	58-61	117	-	37

FORREST William
Carriden, 19 January, 1945 (WH)

League Club	Source	Date Signed	Seasons Played	Apps	Subs	Gls
Carlisle U	Heart of Midlothian	07.62	62-63	10	-	0

FORRESTER Anthony (Tony) Charles
Parkstone, 14 January, 1940 (W)

League Club	Source	Date Signed	Seasons Played	Apps	Subs	Gls
West Bromwich A	Jnrs	03.57	58	6	-	3
Southend U	Tr	04.59	59	10	-	1

FORRESTER George Hogg
Edinburgh, 28 August, 1934 Died 2001 (FB)

League Club	Source	Date Signed	Seasons Played	Apps	Subs	Gls
Sunderland	Raith Rov	03.53				
Accrington St	Eyemouth U	02.60	59-60	54	-	0

FORRESTER George Larmouth
Cannock, 8 June, 1927 Died 1981 (WH)

League Club	Source	Date Signed	Seasons Played	Apps	Subs	Gls
Gillingham	West Bromwich A (Am)	08.47	50-54	100	-	3
Reading	Tr	07.55	55	6	-	2

FORRESTER Jamie Mark
Bradford, 1 November, 1974 ESch/EYth (F)

League Club	Source	Date Signed	Seasons Played	Apps	Subs	Gls
Leeds U	Auxerre (Fr)	10.92	92-93	7	2	0
Southend U	L	09.94	94	3	2	0
Grimsby T	L	03.95	94	7	2	1
Grimsby T	Tr	10.95	95-96	27	14	6
Scunthorpe U	Tr	03.97	96-98	99	2	37
Walsall (L)	FC Utrecht (Holl)	12.99	99	2	3	0
Northampton T	FC Utrecht (Holl)	03.00	99-02	109	12	45
Hull C	Tr	01.03	02-03	17	15	7
Bristol Rov	Tr	07.04	04	20	15	7

FORRESTER Mark
Stockton, 15 April, 1981 (F)

League Club	Source	Date Signed	Seasons Played	Apps	Subs	Gls
Torquay U	YT	•	98-99	1	5	0

FORRESTER Paul
Edinburgh, 3 November, 1972 (F)

League Club	Source	Date Signed	Seasons Played	Apps	Subs	Gls
Middlesbrough	Musselburgh Windsor	03.93	93	0	1	0

FORSSELL Mikael Kaj
Steinfurt, Germany, 15 March, 1981 FiYth/Fiu21-8/Fi-32 (F)

League Club	Source	Date Signed	Seasons Played	Apps	Subs	Gls
Chelsea	HJK Helsinki (Fin)	12.98	98-04	6	27	5
Crystal Palace	L	02.00	99	13	0	3
Crystal Palace	L	06.00	00	31	8	13
Birmingham C	L	08.03	03	32	0	17
Birmingham C	L	07.04	04	4	0	0

FORSTER Derek
Newcastle, 19 February, 1949 ESch (G)

League Club	Source	Date Signed	Seasons Played	Apps	Subs	Gls
Sunderland	App	02.66	64-71	18	0	0
Charlton Ath	Tr	07.73	73	9	0	0
Brighton & Hove A	Tr	07.74	74	3	0	0

FORSTER Geoffrey (Geoff) Patrick
Middlesbrough, 3 August, 1954 (F)

League Club	Source	Date Signed	Seasons Played	Apps	Subs	Gls
Rochdale	South Bank	11.78	78	0	1	0
Hartlepool U	Whitby T	05.80	80	10	4	4

FORSTER Leslie James
Byker, 22 July, 1915 Died 1986 (W)

League Club	Source	Date Signed	Seasons Played	Apps	Subs	Gls
Blackpool	Walker Celtic	04.37	38	2	-	0
York C	Tr	09.46	46	10	-	2
Gateshead	Tr	02.47	46-47	14	-	3

FORSTER Mark Erwin
Middlesbrough, 1 November, 1964 (F)

League Club	Source	Date Signed	Seasons Played	Apps	Subs	Gls
Leicester C	Guisborough T	06.83				
Darlington	Tr	03.84	83-85	31	7	13

FORSTER Martyn Gerald
Kettering, 1 February, 1963 ESch (FB)

League Club	Source	Date Signed	Seasons Played	Apps	Subs	Gls
Northampton T	Kettering T	08.83	83	41	1	0

FORSTER Nicholas (Nicky) Michael
Caterham, 8 September, 1973 Eu21-4 (F)

League Club	Source	Date Signed	Seasons Played	Apps	Subs	Gls
Gillingham	Horley T	05.92	92-93	54	13	24
Brentford	Tr	06.94	94-96	108	1	39
Birmingham C	Tr	01.97	96-98	24	44	11
Reading	Tr	06.99	99-04	157	30	60

FORSTER Ronald (Ron)
Stockton, 19 August, 1935 Died 2002 (W)

League Club	Source	Date Signed	Seasons Played	Apps	Subs	Gls
Darlington	Shotton Colliery	05.56	56-59	57	-	4

FORSTER Stanley (Stan) Gerard
Aylesham, 1 November, 1943 (W)

League Club	Source	Date Signed	Seasons Played	Apps	Subs	Gls
Crystal Palace	Margate	11.61	62	2	-	1

FORSYTH Alexander (Alex)
Swinton, Lanarkshire, 5 February, 1952 Su23-1/SLge-1/S-10 (FB)

League Club	Source	Date Signed	Seasons Played	Apps	Subs	Gls
Manchester U	Partick Th	12.72	72-77	99	2	4

FORSYTH Alexander (Alex) Simpson Hutchinson
Falkirk, 29 September, 1928 (W)

League Club	Source	Date Signed	Seasons Played	Apps	Subs	Gls
Darlington	Falkirk	08.52	52	26	-	7

FORSYTH Robert Campbell
Plean, 5 May, 1934 SLge-2/S-4 (G)

League Club	Source	Date Signed	Seasons Played	Apps	Subs	Gls
Southampton	Kilmarnock	12.65	65-67	48	0	0

FORSYTH David
Falkirk, 5 May, 1945 (FB)

League Club	Source	Date Signed	Seasons Played	Apps	Subs	Gls
Leyton Orient	Kirkintilloch Rob Roy	05.64	65-66	32	0	0

FORSYTH John Thomson
Dalmuir, 20 December, 1918 (W)

League Club	Source	Date Signed	Seasons Played	Apps	Subs	Gls
Luton T	Dumbarton	08.42				
New Brighton	Tr	07.46	46-47	64	-	4
Chester	Tr	07.48	48	32	-	1

FORSYTH Michael (Mike) Eric
Liverpool, 20 March, 1966 EYth/Eu21-1/EB-1 (FB)

League Club	Source	Date Signed	Seasons Played	Apps	Subs	Gls
West Bromwich A	App	11.83	83-85	28	1	0
Derby Co	Tr	03.86	86-94	323	2	8
Notts Co	Tr	02.95	94	7	0	0
Hereford U	L	09.96	96	12	0	0
Wycombe W	Tr	12.96	96-98	51	1	2

FORSYTH Richard Michael
Dudley, 3 October, 1970 ESemiPro-3 (M)

League Club	Source	Date Signed	Seasons Played	Apps	Subs	Gls
Birmingham C	Kidderminster Hrs	07.95	95	12	14	2
Stoke C	Tr	07.96	96-98	90	5	17
Blackpool	Tr	07.99	99	10	3	0
Peterborough U	Tr	07.00	00-02	61	9	2
Cheltenham T	Tr	10.02	02-03	28	11	4

FORSYTH William (Bill) Alan
Cardenden, 29 March, 1932 (FB)

League Club	Source	Date Signed	Seasons Played	Apps	Subs	Gls
Blackburn Rov	Bowhill Rov	08.49				
Southport	Tr	07.52	52-56	55	-	5

FORSYTHE Robert Haddon
Belfast, 27 February, 1925 (W)

League Club	Source	Date Signed	Seasons Played	Apps	Subs	Gls
Bradford C	Ballymoney U	07.48	48	1	-	0

FORT Samuel (Sam) Marsh
Bentley, South Yorkshire, 27 April, 1929 (FB)

League Club	Source	Date Signed	Seasons Played	Apps	Subs	Gls
Walsall	Retford T	02.54	53-54	28	-	0

FORTE Jonathan Ronald James
Sheffield, 25 July, 1986 EYth (F)

League Club	Source	Date Signed	Seasons Played	Apps	Subs	Gls
Sheffield U	Sch	07.04	03-04	2	27	1

FORTUNE Clayton Alexander
Forest Gate, 10 November, 1982 (CD)

League Club	Source	Date Signed	Seasons Played	Apps	Subs	Gls
Bristol C	Tottenham H (YT)	03.01	01-04	25	22	0

FORTUNE Jonathan (Jon) Jay
Islington, 23 August, 1980 (CD)

League Club	Source	Date Signed	Seasons Played	Apps	Subs	Gls
Charlton Ath	YT	07.98	01-04	85	19	5
Mansfield T	L	02.00	99	4	0	0
Mansfield T	L	08.00	00	14	0	0

FORTUNE Quinton
Cape Town, South Africa, 21 May, 1977 Sau23-18/Sa-47 (M)

League Club	Source	Date Signed	Seasons Played	Apps	Subs	Gls
Manchester U	Atletico Madrid (Sp)	08.99	99-04	53	23	5

FORTUNE-WEST Leopold (Leo) Paul Osborne
Stratford, 9 April, 1971 (F)

League Club	Source	Date Signed	Seasons Played	Apps	Subs	Gls
Gillingham	Stevenage Borough	07.95	95-97	48	19	18
Leyton Orient	L	03.97	96	1	4	0
Lincoln C	Tr	07.98	98	7	2	1
Rotherham U	L	10.98	98	5	0	4
Brentford	Tr	11.98	98	2	9	0
Rotherham U	Tr	02.99	98-00	59	0	26
Cardiff C	Tr	09.00	00-02	53	39	23
Doncaster Rov	Tr	07.03	03-04	44	19	17

FOSS Sidney Lacy Richard (Dick)
Barking, 28 November, 1912 Died 1995 (IF)

League Club	Source	Date Signed	Seasons Played	Apps	Subs	Gls
Chelsea	Southall	05.36	36-47	41	-	3

FOSTER Adrian Michael
Kidderminster, 19 March, 1971 (F)

League Club	Source	Date Signed	Seasons Played	Apps	Subs	Gls
West Bromwich A	YT	07.89	89-91	13	14	2
Torquay U	Tr	07.92	92-93	55	10	24
Gillingham	Tr	08.94	94-95	28	12	9
Exeter C	L	03.96	95	4	3	0
Hereford U	Tr	08.96	96	42	1	16

League Club	Source	Date Signed	Seasons Played	Apps	Subs	Gls
FOSTER Alan						
South Shields, 20 November, 1934						(CF)
Crewe Alex	Northwich Vic	08.59	59-60	22	-	7
FOSTER Anthony (Tony) Joseph						
Dublin, 13 February, 1949						(M)
Arsenal	Bolton Ath (Dublin)	02.66				
Oldham Ath	Tr	09.66	66-67	8	1	0
FOSTER Barry						
Worksop, 21 September, 1951 EYth						(FB)
Mansfield T	Jnrs	07.70	71-81	282	5	0
FOSTER Benjamin (Ben) Anthony						
Leamington Spa, 3 April, 1983						(G)
Stoke C	Racing Club Warwick	04.01				
Kidderminster Hrs	L	10.04	04	2	0	0
Wrexham	L	01.05	04	17	0	0
FOSTER George **Clifford (Cliff)**						
Shevington, 14 January, 1931 Died 1998						(IF)
Southport (Am)	Burscough	08.51	51-52	10	-	2
FOSTER Colin						
Bulwell, 26 December, 1952						(CD)
Mansfield T	App	12.70	71-78	195	10	17
Peterborough U	Tr	06.79	79-80	71	0	5
FOSTER Colin John						
Chislehurst, 16 July, 1964						(CD)
Orient	App	02.82	81-86	173	1	10
Nottingham F	Tr	03.87	86-89	68	4	5
West Ham U	Tr	09.89	89-93	88	5	5
Notts Co	L	01.94	93	9	0	0
Watford	Tr	03.94	93-95	66	0	8
Cambridge U	Tr	03.97	96-97	33	0	1
FOSTER Craig Andrew						
Melbourne, Australia, 15 April, 1969 AuYth/Au-25						(M)
Portsmouth	Marconi Fairfield (Aus)	09.97	97	13	3	2
Crystal Palace	Tr	10.98	98-99	47	5	3
FOSTER Emanuel (Manny)						
Newcastle-under-Lyme, 4 December, 1921						(G)
Stoke C	Mow Cop	12.43	46	1	-	0
FOSTER George Walter						
Plymouth, 26 September, 1956						(CD)
Plymouth Arg	App	09.74	73-81	201	11	6
Torquay U	L	10.76	76	6	0	3
Exeter C	L	12.81	81	28	0	0
Derby Co	Tr	06.82	82	30	0	0
Mansfield T	Tr	08.83	83-92	373	0	0
FOSTER James **Ian**						
Liverpool, 11 November, 1976 ESch/ESemiPro-1						(F)
Hereford U	Liverpool (Jnrs)	07.96	96	4	15	0
Kidderminster Hrs	Barrow	08.99	00-02	37	35	11
Kidderminster Hrs	Chester C	02.04	03-04	25	13	9
FOSTER John Colin						
Blackley, 19 September, 1973 ESch						(FB)
Manchester C	YT	07.92	93-96	17	2	0
Carlisle U	Tr	03.98	97	7	0	0
Bury	Tr	07.98	98	6	1	0
FOSTER Karl Adolphus						
Birmingham, 15 September, 1965						(F)
Shrewsbury T	App	09.83	82	1	1	0
FOSTER Lee						
Bishop Auckland, 21 October, 1977						(M)
Hartlepool U	YT	•	95	0	1	0
FOSTER Martin						
Sheffield, 29 October, 1977						(M)
Leeds U	YT	06.96				
Blackpool	L	12.97	97	1	0	0
FOSTER Michael (Mike) Sidney						
Leicester, 3 February, 1939						(W)
Leicester C		08.59				
Colchester U	Tr	05.61	61	36	-	8
Norwich C	Tr	09.62				
Millwall	Tr	07.63	63	13	-	2
FOSTER Nigel						
Sutton-in-Ashfield, 23 March, 1968						(FB)
Mansfield T	App	08.85	84	1	0	0

League Club	Source	Date Signed	Seasons Played	Apps	Subs	Gls
FOSTER Robert (Bobby) John						
Sheffield, 19 July, 1929 EB						(IF)
Chesterfield	Jnrs	08.47	48-50	4	-	0
Preston NE	Tr	07.51	51-56	101	-	41
Rotherham U	Tr	05.58	58	1	-	0
FOSTER Ronald (Ronnie) Edmund						
Islington, 22 November, 1938						(M)
Leyton Orient	Clapton	03.57	59-62	72	-	17
Grimsby T	Tr	12.62	62-65	129	0	24
Reading	Tr	07.66	66-67	44	1	4
Brentford	Dallas (USA)	03.69	68	3	1	0
FOSTER Stephen (Steve)						
Mansfield, 3 December, 1974						(CD)
Mansfield T	YT	07.93	93	2	3	0
Bristol Rov	Woking	05.97	97-01	193	4	7
Doncaster Rov	Tr	08.02	03-04	78	0	2
FOSTER Stephen (Steve) Brian						
Portsmouth, 24 September, 1957 Eu21-1/E-3						(CD)
Portsmouth	App	10.75	75-78	101	8	6
Brighton & Hove A	Tr	07.79	79-83	171	1	6
Aston Villa	Tr	03.84	83-84	15	0	3
Luton T	Tr	11.84	84-88	163	0	11
Oxford U	Tr	07.89	89-91	95	0	9
Brighton & Hove A	Tr	08.92	92-95	115	0	7
FOSTER Stephen (Steve) John						
Warrington, 10 September, 1980 ESch						(CD)
Crewe Alex	YT	09.98	98-04	164	15	12
FOSTER Trevor						
Walsall, 11 January, 1941						(W)
Walsall	Jnrs	07.59	59-64	63	-	12
FOSTER Wayne Paul						
Leigh, 11 September, 1963 EYth						(M)
Bolton W	App	08.81	81-84	92	13	13
Preston NE	Tr	06.85	85	25	6	3
Hartlepool U (L)	Heart of Midlothian	10.94	94	4	0	1
FOSTER Winston Arthur						
Birmingham, 1 November, 1941						(CD)
Birmingham C	Jnrs	11.58	60-68	151	1	2
Crewe Alex	L	03.69	68	13	0	0
Plymouth Arg	Tr	06.69	69-70	33	0	0
FOSTERVOLD Knut Anders						
Molde, Norway, 4 October, 1971						(CD)
Grimsby T (L)	Molde FK (Nor)	11.00	00	9	1	0
FOTHERGILL Ashley Grove						
Harrogate, 3 October, 1969						(M)
Rochdale	Middlesbrough (YT)	10.88	88	8	1	0
FOTHERINGHAM James (Jim) Gibb						
Hamilton, 19 December, 1933 Died 1977						(CD)
Arsenal	Jnrs	03.51	54-58	72	-	0
Northampton T	Heart of Midlothian	08.59	59	11	-	0
FOTIADIS Panos **Andrew**						
Hitchin, 6 September, 1977 ESch						(F)
Luton T	Jnrs	07.96	96-02	50	73	18
Peterborough U	Tr	02.03	02-03	6	13	2
FOULDS Albert (Bert)						
Salford, 8 August, 1919						(IF)
Chester	Altrincham	08.48	48	31	-	14
Rochdale	Yeovil T	09.50	50	6	-	1
Rochdale	Scarborough	10.51	51-52	56	-	23
Crystal Palace	Tr	07.53	53	17	-	4
Crewe Alex	Tr	01.54	53	14	-	2
FOULKES Reginald (Reg) Ernest						
Shrewsbury, 23 February, 1923 ESch						(CD)
Walsall	Birmingham C (Am)	08.45	46-49	160	-	6
Norwich C	Tr	05.50	50-55	216	-	8
FOULKES William (Bill) Anthony						
Prescot, 5 January, 1932 Eu23-2/FLge-2/E-1						(CD)
Manchester U	Whiston BC	08.51	52-69	563	3	7
FOULKES William (Billy) Isaiah						
Merthyr Tydfil, 29 May, 1926 Died 1979 W-11						(W)
Cardiff C		02.45				
Chester	Tr	05.48	48-51	118	-	14
Newcastle U	Tr	10.51	51-53	58	-	8
Southampton	Tr	08.54	54	23	-	1
Chester	Winsford U	07.56	56-60	178	-	23

League Club	Source	Date Signed	Seasons Played	Apps	Subs	Gls
FOUNTAIN John (Jack)						
Leeds, 27 May, 1932						(WH)
Sheffield U	Ashley Road	11.49	50-55	31	-	0
Swindon T	Tr	01.57	56-59	81	-	2
York C	Tr	08.60	60-63	130	-	3
FOWLER Derek William						
Torquay, 28 November, 1961						(FB)
Torquay U	STC Paignton	03.84	83-85	65	8	4
FOWLER Jason Kenneth George						
Bristol, 20 August, 1974						(M)
Bristol C	YT	07.93	92-95	16	9	0
Cardiff C	Tr	06.96	96-00	138	7	14
Torquay U	Tr	11.01	01-04	85	12	7
FOWLER John						
Leith, 17 October, 1933						(FB)
Colchester U	Bonnyrigg Rose	06.55	55-67	415	0	5
FOWLER John Anthony						
Preston, 27 October, 1974						(M)
Cambridge U	YT	04.92	92-95	30	11	0
Preston NE	L	02.93	92	5	1	0
FOWLER John (Jack) Berry						
Rotherham, 13 April, 1935						(W)
Sheffield U		07.54				
Halifax T	Tr	06.56	56-58	19	-	3
FOWLER Jordan Michael						
Barking, 1 October, 1984						(M)
Arsenal	Sch	07.02				
Chesterfield	L	01.05	04	4	2	0
FOWLER Lee Anthony						
Cardiff, 10 June, 1983 WYth/Wu21-9						(M)
Coventry C	YT	07.00	01-02	6	8	0
Huddersfield T	Tr	08.03	03-04	35	14	0
FOWLER Lee Edward						
Eastwood, 26 January, 1969						(FB)
Stoke C	YT	07.88	87-91	42	7	1
Preston NE	Tr	07.92	92	29	3	2
Doncaster Rov	Tr	12.93	93	7	4	0
FOWLER Martin						
York, 17 January, 1957						(M)
Huddersfield T	App	01.74	73-77	62	11	2
Blackburn Rov	Tr	07.78	78-79	36	2	0
Hartlepool U	L	03.80	79	6	0	0
Stockport Co	Tr	08.80	80-81	74	1	6
Scunthorpe U	Tr	09.82	82	15	3	0
FOWLER Henry **Norman**						
Stockton, 3 September, 1919 Died 1990 ESch						(FB)
Middlesbrough	South Bank	09.36	37-38	7	-	0
Hull C	Tr	09.46	46-49	52	-	0
Gateshead	Tr	11.49	49-51	64	-	0
FOWLER Robert (Robbie) Bernard						
Liverpool, 9 April, 1975 EYth/Eu21-8/EB-1/E-26						(F)
Liverpool	YT	04.92	93-01	210	26	120
Leeds U	Tr	11.01	01-02	24	6	14
Manchester C	Tr	01.03	02-04	63	13	20
FOWLER Thomas (Tommy)						
Prescot, 16 December, 1924						(W)
Northampton T	Everton (Am)	03.45	46-61	521	-	84
Aldershot	Tr	12.61	61-62	14	-	0
FOWLER Tony						
Birmingham, 3 October, 1962						(G)
Torquay U	Foxhole U	03.85	84-85	9	0	0
FOX Alan						
Holywell, 10 July, 1936 Wu23-1/LoI-1						(CD)
Wrexham	Carmel U	04.54	53-63	350	-	3
Hartlepools U	Tr	06.64	64-65	58	0	0
Bradford C	Tr	10.65	65	33	0	0
FOX Christian						
Auchenbrae, 11 April, 1981						(M)
York C	YT	06.99	99-03	44	26	1
FOX David Lee						
Leek, 13 December, 1983 EYth/Eu20						(M)
Manchester U	YT	12.00				
Shrewsbury T	L	10.04	04	2	2	1

League Club	Source	Date Signed	Seasons Played	Apps	Subs	Gls
FOX Geoffrey (Geoff) Roy						
Bristol, 19 January, 1925 Died 1994						(FB)
Ipswich T	MCW	08.45	46	11	-	1
Bristol Rov	Tr	06.47	47-54	276	-	2
Swindon T	Tr	10.55	55-56	48	-	0
FOX Kevin						
Sheffield, 22 September, 1960						(G)
Lincoln C	Jnrs	03.78	79	4	0	0
FOX Mark Stephen						
Basingstoke, 17 November, 1975						(W)
Brighton & Hove A	YT	07.94	93-96	8	17	1
FOX Matthew Christopher						
Birmingham, 13 July, 1971						(CD)
Birmingham C	YT	07.89	88-90	12	2	0
Northampton T		03.93	92	0	1	0
FOX Michael James Stephen Neil						
Mansfield, 7 September, 1985						(M)
Chesterfield	Sch	●	04	0	1	0
FOX Oscar						
Clowne, 1 January, 1921 Died 1990						(WH)
Sheffield Wed		10.43	46-49	44	-	3
Mansfield T	Tr	06.50	50-56	248	-	30
FOX Peter David						
Scunthorpe, 5 July, 1957						(G)
Sheffield Wed	App	06.75	72-76	49	0	0
Barnsley	L	12.77	77	1	0	0
Stoke C	Tr	03.78	78-92	409	0	0
Exeter C	Tr	07.93	93-96	107	1	0
FOX Raymond (Ray)						
Didsbury, 13 December, 1934						(W)
Oldham Ath (Am)		08.57	57	1	-	0
FOX Raymond (Ray) Victor						
Bristol, 28 January, 1921						(FB)
Bristol C	St Aldhelm's	10.46	46-48	23	-	0
FOX Reginald (Reg) Alan						
Edmonton, 16 October, 1929						(FB)
Fulham	Tufnel Park	12.49				
Brighton & Hove A	Tr	10.52	52-55	20	-	0
FOX Ruel Adrian						
Ipswich, 14 January, 1968 EB-2						(W)
Norwich C	App	01.86	86-93	148	24	22
Newcastle U	Tr	02.94	93-95	56	2	12
Tottenham H	Tr	10.95	95-99	95	11	13
West Bromwich A	Tr	08.00	00-01	38	20	2
FOX Simon Mark						
Basingstoke, 28 August, 1977						(F)
Brighton & Hove A	YT	05.95	93-96	6	15	0
FOX Stephen (Steve) Douglas						
Tamworth, 17 February, 1958						(W)
Birmingham C	App	02.76	76-78	26	3	1
Wrexham	Tr	12.78	78-82	136	6	10
Port Vale	Tr	10.82	82-83	71	3	6
Chester C	Tr	07.84	84-85	29	4	4
FOX Walter						
Bolsover, 10 April, 1921 Died 2000						(FB)
Mansfield T	Creswell Colliery	05.46	46-49	62	-	0
FOXE Hayden						
Canberra, Australia, 23 June, 1977 AuYth/Auu23/Au-11						(CD)
West Ham U	San Hiroshima (Jap)	03.01	00-01	7	4	0
Portsmouth	Tr	06.02	02-03	38	4	2
FOXON David **Neil**						
Nottingham, 10 July, 1948						(W)
Scunthorpe U	Notts Co (Am)	08.65	66-67	20	2	1
FOXTON David **Graham**						
Harrogate, 2 October, 1949						(FB)
Scunthorpe U	App	10.67	67-72	148	6	1
FOXTON John (Jack) Dixon						
Salford, 17 June, 1921						(WH)
Portsmouth	Bolton W (Am)	05.45	46	1	-	0
Swindon T	Tr	09.48	48-50	49	-	0
FOY David Lee						
Coventry, 20 October, 1972						(M)
Birmingham C	YT	07.91	92	3	0	0
Scunthorpe U	Tr	03.93	92	1	2	0

League Club	Source	Date Signed	Seasons Played	Career Record Apps	Subs	Gls
FOY John Joseph						
Huyton, 28 May, 1950						(W)
Southport (Am)	Ormskirk	08.74	74	1	0	0
FOY Keith Patrick						
Crumlin, County Dublin, 30 December, 1981 IRYth/IRu21-7						(FB)
Nottingham F	YT	01.99	00-01	19	3	1
FOY Robert (Robbie) Andrew						
Edinburgh, 29 October, 1985 Su21-5						(F)
Liverpool	Sch	01.03				
Chester C	L	02.05	04	13	0	0
FOYEWA Amos						
Nigeria, 26 December, 1981						(F)
Bournemouth	West Ham U (YT)	07.01	01-02	1	8	0
FOYLE Martin John						
Salisbury, 2 May, 1963						(F)
Southampton	App	08.80	82-83	7	6	1
Aldershot	Tr	08.84	84-86	98	0	35
Oxford U	Tr	03.87	86-90	120	6	36
Port Vale	Tr	06.91	91-99	226	70	83
FRADIN Karim						
St Martin d'Hyeres, France, 2 February, 1972						(M)
Stockport Co	OGC Nice (Fr)	11.99	99-02	72	9	9
FRAIL Stephen Charles						
Glasgow, 10 August, 1969						(FB)
Tranmere Rov	Heart of Midlothian	01.98	97-99	10	4	0
FRAIN David						
Sheffield, 11 October, 1962						(M)
Sheffield U	Norton Woodseats	09.85	85-87	35	9	6
Rochdale	Tr	07.88	88	42	0	12
Stockport Co	Tr	07.89	89-94	176	11	12
Mansfield T	L	09.94	94	4	2	0
FRAIN John William						
Birmingham, 8 October, 1968						(FB)
Birmingham C	App	10.86	85-96	265	9	23
Northampton T	Tr	01.97	96-02	203	4	4
FRAIN Peter John Andrew						
Birmingham, 18 March, 1965						(F)
West Bromwich A	App	03.82				
Mansfield T	L	01.84	83	1	1	0
FRAME William James						
Castle Douglas, 1 August, 1939						(G)
Workington	Dumfries	11.58	58	9	-	0
FRAME William (Billy) Lammie						
Carluke, 7 May, 1912 Died 1992						(FB)
Leicester C	Shawfield Jnrs	10.33	34-49	220	-	0
FRAMPTON Andrew (Andy) James Kerr						
Wimbledon, 3 September, 1979						(FB)
Crystal Palace	YT	05.98	98-02	19	9	0
Brentford	Tr	10.02	02-04	53	13	0
FRANCE Anthony (Tony)						
Sheffield, 11 April, 1939						(IF)
Huddersfield T	Atlas & Norfolk	04.56	57-59	9	-	2
Darlington	Tr	12.61	61-62	47	-	9
Stockport Co	Tr	07.63	63	30	-	8
FRANCE Darren Brian						
Hull, 8 August, 1967						(F)
Hull C	North Ferriby U	11.91	91-92	19	24	7
Doncaster Rov	Tr	08.93	93	0	1	0
FRANCE Gary						
Whitwell, 18 June, 1955						(F)
Sheffield U	App	06.73	73-74	1	1	0
FRANCE Gary Lawton						
Stalybridge, 5 May, 1946						(M)
Burnley	Stalybridge Celtic	04.66	66-67	1	2	0
Bury	Tr	07.68	68	0	1	0
FRANCE John (Jack)						
Stalybridge, 30 November, 1913 Died 1995						(WH)
Swindon T	Stalybridge Celtic	08.37	37	1	-	0
Halifax T	Bath C	06.39	46-47	51	-	1
FRANCE Michael **Paul**						
Holmfirth, 10 September, 1968						(CD)
Huddersfield T	App	06.87	87-88	7	4	0
Bristol C	Tr	07.89				
Burnley	Tr	07.90	90-91	7	1	0
FRANCE Peter						
Huddersfield, 27 March, 1936						(G)
Huddersfield T		09.56				
Bradford PA	Tr	05.57	57	16	-	0
FRANCE Ryan						
Sheffield, 13 December, 1980						(M)
Hull C	Alfreton T	09.03	03-04	29	30	4
FRANCIS Carlos (Carl) Everton						
West Ham, 21 August, 1962						(W)
Birmingham C	App	08.80	82	2	3	0
Hereford U	L	12.83	83	5	0	0
FRANCIS Damien Jerome						
Wandsworth, 27 February, 1979 Jamaica 1						(M)
Wimbledon	YT	03.97	97-02	80	17	15
Norwich C	Tr	07.03	03-04	71	2	14
FRANCIS George Edward						
Acton, 4 February, 1934						(CF)
Brentford	Jnrs	01.53	54-60	228	-	110
Queens Park Rgrs	Tr	05.61	61	2	-	1
Brentford	Tr	10.61	61	32	-	14
Gillingham	Tr	08.62	62-63	51	-	19
FRANCIS Gerald (Gerry)						
Johannesburg, South Africa, 6 December, 1933						(W)
Leeds U	City & Suburban (SA)	07.57	57-61	48	-	9
York C	Tr	10.61	61	16	-	4
FRANCIS Gerald (Gerry) Charles James						
Chiswick, 6 December, 1951 Eu23-6/E-12						(M)
Queens Park Rgrs	App	06.69	68-78	290	5	53
Crystal Palace	Tr	07.79	79-80	59	0	7
Queens Park Rgrs	Tr	02.81	80-81	17	0	4
Coventry C	Tr	02.82	81-82	50	0	2
Exeter C	Tr	08.83	83	28	0	3
Cardiff C	Tr	09.84	84	7	0	0
Swansea C	Tr	10.84	84	3	0	0
Portsmouth	Tr	11.84	84	3	0	0
Bristol Rov	Tr	09.85	85-86	32	0	0
FRANCIS John Andrew						
Dewsbury, 21 November, 1963						(F)
Halifax T	Emley	02.85	84	1	3	0
Sheffield U	Emley	09.88	88-89	14	28	6
Burnley	Tr	01.90	89-91	99	2	26
Cambridge U	Tr	08.92	92	15	14	3
Burnley	Tr	03.93	92-95	44	32	10
Scunthorpe U	Tr	08.96	96	1	4	0
FRANCIS Keith Roy						
Yeovil, 22 July, 1929						(WH)
Leyton Orient	Yeovil T	06.50	50	3	-	0
FRANCIS Kevin Michael Derek						
Moseley, 6 December, 1967 St Kitts int						(F)
Derby Co	Mile Oak Rov	02.89	89-90	0	10	0
Stockport Co	Tr	02.91	90-94	147	5	88
Birmingham C	Tr	01.95	94-97	32	41	13
Oxford U	Tr	02.98	97-99	27	9	8
Stockport Co	Tr	03.00	99	4	0	0
Exeter C	Castleton Gabriels	11.00	00	3	4	1
Hull C	Tr	12.00	00	22	0	5
FRANCIS Lee Charles						
Walthamstow, 24 October, 1969						(FB)
Arsenal	YT	11.87				
Chesterfield	L	03.90	89	2	0	0
Chesterfield	Tr	06.90	90-91	63	5	2
FRANCIS Sean Robert						
Birmingham, 1 August, 1972						(F)
Birmingham C	YT	07.90	90-91	0	6	0
Northampton T	Telford U	08.93	93	0	1	0
FRANCIS Simon Charles						
Nottingham, 16 February, 1985 EYth						(M)
Bradford C	Sch	05.03	02-03	49	6	1
Sheffield U	Tr	03.04	03-04	6	5	0
FRANCIS Stephen (Steve) Stuart						
Billericay, 29 May, 1964 EYth						(G)
Chelsea	App	04.82	81-85	71	0	0
Reading	Tr	02.87	86-92	216	0	0
Huddersfield T	Tr	08.93	93-98	187	0	0
Northampton T	Tr	01.99	98	3	0	0
FRANCIS Terence (Terry)						
Hartlepool, 18 June, 1943						(IF)
Hartlepools U	Billingham Synthonia	12.63	63-64	18	-	4

League Club	Source	Date Signed	Seasons Played	Career Record Apps	Subs	Gls
FRANCIS Thomas (Tom) George						
Bermondsey, 30 October, 1920 Died 1996						(G)
Millwall	Cheltenham T	05.46	46	1	-	0
FRANCIS Trevor John						
Plymouth, 19 April, 1954 EYth/Eu23-5/E-52						(F)
Birmingham C	App	05.71	70-78	278	2	119
Nottingham F	Tr	02.79	78-81	69	1	28
Manchester C	Tr	09.81	81	26	0	12
Queens Park Rgrs	Glasgow Rgrs	03.88	87-89	30	2	12
Sheffield Wed	Tr	02.91	89-93	29	47	5
FRANCIS Willis David						
Nottingham, 26 July, 1985						(M)
Notts Co	Sch	•	02-03	2	11	0
FRANCOMBE Peter						
Cardiff, 4 August, 1963						(FB)
Cardiff C	Crystal Palace (App)	09.81	81	2	1	0
FRANDSEN Per						
Copenhagen, Denmark, 6 February, 1970 DeYth/Deu21/De-23						(M)
Bolton W	FC Copenhagen (Den)	08.96	96-99	129	1	17
Blackburn Rov	Tr	09.99	99	26	5	5
Bolton W	Tr	07.00	00-03	116	19	13
Wigan Ath	Tr	07.04	04	9	0	1
FRANKLAND Anthony (Tony)						
Greeenwich, 11 October, 1972						(W)
Exeter C	YT	07.90	89-90	3	4	0
FRANKLIN Cornelius (Neil)						
Stoke-on-Trent, 24 January, 1922 Died 1996 FLge-5/EWar-10/E-27						(CD)
Stoke C	Jnrs	01.39	46-49	142	-	0
Hull C	Santa Fe (Col)	02.51	50-55	95	-	0
Crewe Alex	Tr	02.56	55-57	66	-	4
Stockport Co	Tr	10.57	57	20	-	0
FRANKLIN Graham Nigel						
Bicester, 25 January, 1957						(F)
Southend U	Lowestoft T	12.77	77-79	1	5	1
FRANKLIN Jeffrey (Jeff) Terence						
Darlington, 8 December, 1973						(W)
Torquay U	YT	•	91	1	1	0
FRANKLIN John						
Stockton, 27 November, 1924						(W)
Middlesbrough		12.43				
Darlington	Bath C	08.47	47	8	-	3
FRANKLIN William **Michael (Mike)**						
Tiverton, 3 March, 1955						(G)
Charlton Ath	App	03.73	72-74	13	0	0
FRANKLIN Neil John						
Lincoln, 10 March, 1969						(FB)
Lincoln C	App	06.87	86	15	0	0
Lincoln C	Nykopings (Swe)	10.88	88	0	1	0
FRANKLIN Paul Leslie						
Hainault, 5 October, 1963						(CD)
Watford	App	08.81	82-86	32	0	0
Shrewsbury T	L	10.86	86	6	0	0
Swindon T	L	11.86	86	5	0	1
Reading	Tr	06.87	87-88	17	3	0
FRANKLIN Stanley (Stan) Thomas						
Shrewsbury, 16 September, 1919						(CD)
Blackpool	Kenwood Jnrs	05.38				
Crewe Alex	Tr	04.46	46-47	29	-	0
FRANKS Albert John						
Boldon, 13 April, 1936						(WH)
Newcastle U	Boldon CW	12.53	56-59	72	-	4
Lincoln C	Glasgow Rgrs	11.61	61-62	58	-	5
FRANKS Colin James						
Willesden, 16 April, 1951						(CD)
Watford	Wealdstone	07.69	69-72	99	13	8
Sheffield U	Tr	07.73	73-78	139	11	7
FRANKS Kenneth (Ken)						
Motherwell, 24 April, 1944						(W)
Brighton & Hove A	Blantyre Vic	06.62	62	1	-	0
FRASER Andrew (Andy) McKnight						
Newtongrange, 29 August, 1940						(CD)
Hartlepools U	Heart of Midlothian	10.61	61-63	82	-	2

League Club	Source	Date Signed	Seasons Played	Career Record Apps	Subs	Gls
FRASER John **Cameron (Cammie)**						
Blackford, 24 May, 1941 Su23-2						(FB)
Aston Villa	Dunfermline Ath	10.62	62-63	33	-	1
Birmingham C	Tr	02.65	64-65	38	1	0
FRASER David McLean						
Newtongrange, 6 June, 1937						(W)
Hull C	Arniston Rgrs	07.54	55-57	11	-	7
Mansfield T	Tr	07.58	58	6	-	1
FRASER Douglas (Doug) Michael						
Busby, 8 December, 1941 S-2						(CD)
West Bromwich A	Aberdeen	09.63	63-70	255	2	8
Nottingham F	Tr	01.71	70-72	85	0	3
Walsall	Tr	07.73	73	26	1	0
FRASER Gordon						
Elgin, 27 November, 1943						(CF)
Cardiff C	Forres Mechanics	01.61	62	4	-	0
Millwall	Tr	09.63	63	5	-	0
Newport Co	Barry T	08.66	66	11	1	2
FRASER James (Jimmy)						
Coatbridge, 17 November, 1932						(FB)
Barrow	Bellshill Ath	03.58	57-58	32	-	0
FRASER John						
White City, 12 July, 1953						(FB)
Fulham	App	06.71	71-75	55	1	1
Brentford	Tr	07.76	76-79	121	2	6
FRASER John Watson						
Belfast, 15 September, 1938						(W)
Sunderland	Glentoran	03.59	58-59	22	-	1
Portsmouth	Tr	06.60	60	1	-	0
Watford	Margate	07.62	62-63	24	-	3
FRASER Robert						
Glasgow, 23 January, 1917 Died 2003						(FB)
Newcastle U	Hibernian	01.47	46-48	26	-	0
FRASER Stuart James						
Cheltenham, 1 August, 1978						(G)
Stoke C	Cheltenham T	07.96	98	0	1	0
Exeter C	Tr	07.00	00-02	15	4	0
FRASER Stuart Thomas						
Edinburgh, 9 January, 1980 Su21-5						(FB)
Luton T	YT	04.98	97-00	36	8	1
FRASER William (Willie) Alexander						
Brighton, Australia, 24 February, 1929 Died 1996 S-2						(G)
Sunderland	Airdrie	03.54	53-58	127	-	0
Nottingham F	Tr	12.58	58	2	-	0
FRASER William Thomas						
Edinburgh, 12 August, 1945						(W)
Huddersfield T	Dunfermline Ath	04.63	63-64	8	-	2
FREAR Brian						
Cleckheaton, 8 July, 1933 Died 1997						(IF)
Huddersfield T	Liversedge	09.50	51-56	37	-	10
Chesterfield	Tr	02.57	56-63	281	-	84
Halifax T	Tr	07.64	64	36	-	7
FRECKLINGTON Lee Craig						
Lincoln, 8 September, 1985						(M)
Lincoln C	Sch	•	04	0	3	0
FREDGAARD Carsten						
Hillesod, Denmark, 20 May, 1976 DeYth/Deu21-9/De-4						(M)
Sunderland	Lyngby (Nor)	07.99	99	0	1	0
West Bromwich A	L	02.00	99	5	0	0
Bolton W	L	11.00	00	1	4	0
FREEBURN William Openshaw						
Hamilton, 7 April, 1930						(FB)
Grimsby T	East Stirling	08.51	51-54	34	-	0
FREEDMAN Douglas (Dougie) Alan						
Glasgow, 21 January, 1974 SSch/Su21-8/SB-1/S-2						(F)
Queens Park Rgrs	YT	05.92				
Barnet	Tr	07.94	94-95	47	0	27
Crystal Palace	Tr	09.95	95-97	72	18	31
Wolverhampton W	Tr	10.97	97	25	4	10
Nottingham F	Tr	08.98	98-00	50	20	18
Crystal Palace	Tr	10.00	00-04	107	43	54
FREEMAN Alfred (Alf)						
Bethnal Green, 2 January, 1920						(IF)
Southampton		11.43	46	7	-	2
Crystal Palace	Tr	04.48	48	2	-	0

League Club	Source	Date Signed	Seasons Played	Career Record Apps	Subs	Gls
FREEMAN Andrew (Andy) James						
Reading, 8 September, 1977						(M)
Reading	YT	07.96	95	0	1	0
FREEMAN Anthony (Tony)						
Melton Mowbray, 29 August, 1928 Died 2004						(W)
Notts Co	Melton T	01.46	46-49	44	-	2
FREEMAN Clive Richard						
Leeds, 12 September, 1962						(M)
Swansea C	Bridlington T	08.90	90-91	10	4	0
Carlisle U	L	01.92	91	4	0	0
Doncaster Rov	Altrincham	08.93	93	23	2	2
FREEMAN Darren Barry Andduet						
Brighton, 22 August, 1973						(F)
Gillingham	Horsham	01.95	94-95	4	8	0
Fulham	Tr	07.96	96-97	32	14	9
Brentford	Tr	07.98	98	16	6	6
Brighton & Hove A	Tr	07.99	99-00	41	13	12
FREEMAN David Barry						
Dublin, 25 November, 1979 IRYth/IRu21-1						(F)
Nottingham F	YT	12.96	99-00	2	6	0
Port Vale	L	09.00	00	2	1	0
Carlisle U	Tr	09.02	02	3	1	0
FREEMAN Donald (Don) Richard						
Dartford, 29 August, 1921						(WH)
Charlton Ath	Dartford	03.46				
Bristol C	Tr	05.49	49	8	-	0
FREEMAN Henry (Harry) George						
Worcester, 4 November, 1918 Died 1997						(FB)
Fulham	Woodstock T	10.37	38-51	179	-	6
Walsall	Tr	10.52	52	20	-	1
FREEMAN Mark Wayne						
Walsall, 27 January, 1970						(CD)
Wolverhampton W	Bilston T	10.87				
Cheltenham T	Gloucester C	03.96	99-00	61	4	2
FREEMAN Neil						
Northampton, 16 February, 1955						(G)
Arsenal	Jnrs	06.72				
Grimsby T	Tr	03.74	73-75	33	0	0
Southend U	Tr	07.76	76-77	69	0	0
Birmingham C	Tr	07.78	78-79	31	0	0
Walsall	L	08.80	80	8	0	0
Huddersfield T	L	01.81	80	18	0	0
Peterborough U	Tr	09.81	81	41	0	0
Northampton T	Tr	08.82	82	22	0	0
FREEMAN Neville Frank						
Brixworth, 25 January, 1925 Died 1984						(G)
Northampton T		10.49	50	1	-	0
FREEMAN Ronald Peter Percy						
Newark, 4 July, 1945						(F)
West Bromwich A	Stourbridge	04.68	69	2	1	0
Lincoln C	Tr	06.70	70-72	76	4	30
Reading	Tr	01.73	72-74	53	7	13
Lincoln C	Tr	01.75	74-76	62	10	34
FREESTONE Christopher (Chris) Mark						
Nottingham, 4 September, 1971						(F)
Middlesbrough	Arnold T	12.94	94-97	2	7	1
Carlisle U	L	03.97	96	3	2	2
Northampton T	Tr	12.97	97-98	40	17	13
Hartlepool U	Tr	03.99	98-99	24	13	7
Cheltenham T	L	02.00	99	5	0	2
Shrewsbury T	Tr	07.00	00-01	19	8	0
FREESTONE Roger						
Caerleon, 19 August, 1968 WSch/WYth/Wu21-1/W-1						(G)
Newport Co	App	04.86	86	11	0	0
Chelsea	Tr	03.87	86-88	42	0	0
Newport Co	L	03.87	86	2	0	0
Swansea C	L	09.89	89	14	0	0
Hereford U	L	03.90	89	8	0	0
Swansea C	Tr	09.91	91-03	549	3	3
FREESTONE Trevor						
Market Bosworth, 16 February, 1954						(F)
Peterborough U	Jnrs	01.73	72	2	1	1
FREIMANIS Edward (Eddie)						
Latvia, 22 February, 1920 Died 1993 Latvia int						(CF)
Northampton T	Peterborough U	05.48	48-49	19	-	4
FRENCH Daniel John						
Peterborough, 25 November, 1979						(M)
Peterborough U	YT	07.98	99-01	2	16	1
FRENCH George Noah						
Colchester, 10 November, 1926						(FB)
Colchester U (Am)		05.52	52-53	3	-	0
FRENCH (LAFITE) Graham Edward						
Wolverhampton, 6 April, 1945 EYth						(W)
Shrewsbury T	App	11.62	61-62	27	-	1
Swindon T	Tr	08.63	63	5	-	0
Watford	Tr	08.64	64	4	-	0
Luton T	Wellington T	10.65	65-72	180	2	21
Reading	L	11.73	73	3	0	0
Southport	Boston (USA)	03.76	75	2	0	0
FRENCH James (Jim) Robert						
Stockton, 27 November, 1926						(IF)
Middlesbrough		08.45				
Northampton T		08.51	51	1	-	0
Darlington	Tr	08.53	53-54	52	-	8
FRENCH John (Jackie) William						
Stockton, 19 January, 1925 Died 2002						(WH)
Middlesbrough		10.43				
Southend U	Tr	02.47	46-52	182	-	19
Nottingham F	Tr	11.52	52-55	80	-	8
Southend U	Tr	07.56	56	5	-	0
FRENCH Jonathan (Jon) Charles						
Bristol, 25 September, 1976						(M)
Bristol Rov	YT	07.95	95-97	8	9	1
Hull C	Tr	07.98	98	9	6	0
FRENCH Michael (Mickey) John						
Eastbourne, 7 May, 1955 EYth						(F)
Queens Park Rgrs	App	05.73				
Brentford	Tr	02.75	74-76	56	9	16
Swindon T	Tr	02.77	76-77	5	5	1
Doncaster Rov	Tr	07.78	78	36	0	5
Aldershot	Tr	05.79	79-81	70	4	16
Rochdale	Tr	08.82	82	35	1	11
FRENCH Nigel Peter						
Swansea, 24 March, 1968						(W)
Swansea C	App	03.86	85-86	13	13	3
FRENCH Raymond (Ray)						
Wigton, 16 December, 1946						(CD)
Workington (Am)	Wigton	11.73	73	2	0	0
FRETWELL David						
Normanton, 18 February, 1952						(CD)
Bradford C	App	07.70	70-77	247	6	5
Wigan Ath	Chicago (USA)	10.78	78-80	111	1	0
FREUND Steffen						
Brandenburg, Germany, 19 January, 1970 GeYth/Geu21/Ge-21						(M)
Tottenham H	Bor Dortmund (Ger)	12.98	98-02	92	10	0
Leicester C (L)	Kaiserslautern (Ger)	01.04	03	13	1	0
FRIAR John Paul						
Glasgow, 6 June, 1963 SYth						(FB)
Leicester C	App	08.80	80-82	56	2	0
Rotherham U	Tr	02.83	82-83	20	0	0
Charlton Ath	Tr	07.84	84-85	36	0	0
Northampton T	L	03.86	85	14	0	0
Aldershot	Tr	08.86	86	29	0	1
FRIARS Emmet Charles						
Derry, 14 September, 1985 NIYth/NIu21-2						(M)
Notts Co	Sch	02.04	04	4	5	0
FRIARS Sean Martin						
Derry, 15 May, 1979 NIu21-14						(F)
Liverpool	Jnrs	05.96				
Ipswich T	Tr	07.98	99	0	1	0
Carlisle U	Newry T	11.01	01	0	1	0
FRIDAY Robin						
Hammersmith, 27 July, 1952 Died 1991						(F)
Reading	Hayes	02.74	73-76	121	0	46
Cardiff C	Tr	12.76	76-77	20	1	6
FRIDAY Terence (Terry) John						
Sittingbourne, 1 May, 1936						(G)
Gillingham (Am)	Sheppey U	03.61	60	2	-	0
FRIDGE Leslie (Les) Francis						
Inverness, 27 August, 1968 SYth/Su21-1						(G)
Chelsea	App	09.85	85	1	0	0

FRIEDEL Bradley (Brad) Howard
Lakewood, USA, 18 May, 1971 USA 82 (G)

League Club	Source	Date Signed	Seasons Played	Apps	Subs	Gls
Liverpool	Columbus Crew (USA)	12.97	97-99	25	0	0
Blackburn Rov	Tr	11.00	00-04	174	0	1

FRIEL Bernard (Benny) James
Glasgow, 16 September, 1941 (IF)

League Club	Source	Date Signed	Seasons Played	Apps	Subs	Gls
Southend U	Dumbarton	05.63	63-64	17	-	8

FRIEL George Patrick
Reading, 11 October, 1970 (W)

League Club	Source	Date Signed	Seasons Played	Apps	Subs	Gls
Reading	YT	06.89	89-90	10	6	1

FRIEL John Patrick
Glasgow, 1 September, 1923 Died 1998 (IF)

League Club	Source	Date Signed	Seasons Played	Apps	Subs	Gls
New Brighton	Third Lanark	06.50	50	3	-	0

FRIEL Peter
Wishaw, 27 March, 1939 (W)

League Club	Source	Date Signed	Seasons Played	Apps	Subs	Gls
Workington	Cambuslang Rgrs	08.61	61	4	-	0

FRIEND Barry Neil
Wandsworth, 13 October, 1951 EAmat (W)

League Club	Source	Date Signed	Seasons Played	Apps	Subs	Gls
Fulham	Leatherhead U	10.73	73	2	1	0

FRIIO David
Thionville, France, 17 February, 1973 (M)

League Club	Source	Date Signed	Seasons Played	Apps	Subs	Gls
Plymouth Arg	ASOA Valence (Fr)	11.00	00-04	158	9	39
Nottingham F	Tr	02.05	04	5	0	0

FRITH David William Malcolm
Liverpool, 17 March, 1929 (FB)

League Club	Source	Date Signed	Seasons Played	Apps	Subs	Gls
Blackpool	Jnrs	05.49	52-56	32	-	0
Tranmere Rov	Tr	08.58	58-62	177	-	0

FRITH William (Billy)
Sheffield, 9 June, 1912 Died 1996 (WH)

League Club	Source	Date Signed	Seasons Played	Apps	Subs	Gls
Chesterfield	Mansfield T	05.31	31	9	-	3
Coventry C	Tr	05.32	32-46	169	-	4

FRIZZELL James (Jimmy) Letson
Greenock, 16 February, 1937 (M)

League Club	Source	Date Signed	Seasons Played	Apps	Subs	Gls
Oldham Ath	Morton	05.60	60-69	308	9	56

FROGGATT John (Jack)
Sheffield, 17 November, 1922 Died 1993 FLge-4/E-13 (W)

League Club	Source	Date Signed	Seasons Played	Apps	Subs	Gls
Portsmouth	Vospers	09.45	46-53	280	-	64
Leicester C	Tr	03.54	53-57	143	-	18

FROGGATT John Lawrence
Stanton Hill, 13 December, 1945 (F)

League Club	Source	Date Signed	Seasons Played	Apps	Subs	Gls
Notts Co	East Kirkby Welfare	06.64	63-64	4	-	0
Colchester U	Boston U	07.74	74-77	155	0	29
Port Vale	Tr	02.78	77-78	12	2	3
Northampton T	Tr	09.78	78	42	0	13

FROGGATT Redfern
Sheffield, 23 August, 1924 Died 2003 FLge-1/EB/E-4 (IF)

League Club	Source	Date Signed	Seasons Played	Apps	Subs	Gls
Sheffield Wed	Sheffield YMCA	08.42	46-59	434	-	140

FROGGATT Stephen (Steve) Junior
Lincoln, 9 March, 1973 Eu21-2 (W)

League Club	Source	Date Signed	Seasons Played	Apps	Subs	Gls
Aston Villa	YT	01.91	91-93	30	5	2
Wolverhampton W	Tr	07.94	94-98	99	7	7
Coventry C	Tr	10.98	98-99	44	5	2

FRONTZECK Michael
Moenchengladbach, Germany, 26 March, 1964 Germany int (FB)

League Club	Source	Date Signed	Seasons Played	Apps	Subs	Gls
Manchester C	Bor M'Gladbach (Ger)	01.96	95-96	19	4	0

FROST Brian Philip
Sheffield, 5 June, 1938 (WH)

League Club	Source	Date Signed	Seasons Played	Apps	Subs	Gls
Chesterfield	Oswestry T	05.59	59-64	103	-	20

FROST Desmond (Des)
Congleton, 3 August, 1926 Died 1993 (CF)

League Club	Source	Date Signed	Seasons Played	Apps	Subs	Gls
Leeds U	Congleton T	04.49	49-50	10	-	2
Halifax T	Tr	01.51	50-53	116	-	54
Rochdale	Tr	11.53	53-54	16	-	6
Crewe Alex	Tr	09.54	54-55	45	-	12

FROST John (Jack)
Wallsend, 13 February, 1920 Died 1988 (G)

League Club	Source	Date Signed	Seasons Played	Apps	Subs	Gls
Grimsby T	North Shields	07.39				
York C	Tr	07.48	48-51	45	-	0

FROST Lee Adrian
Woking, 4 December, 1957 (F)

League Club	Source	Date Signed	Seasons Played	Apps	Subs	Gls
Chelsea	App	07.76	77-79	11	3	5
Brentford	L	10.78	78	5	1	0
Brentford	Tr	12.80	80	15	0	3

FROST Ronald Albert
Stockport, 16 January, 1947 (W)

League Club	Source	Date Signed	Seasons Played	Apps	Subs	Gls
Manchester C	App	05.64	63	2	-	1

FROST Stanley (Stan)
Northampton, 19 October, 1922 (W)

League Club	Source	Date Signed	Seasons Played	Apps	Subs	Gls
Leicester C	Northampton T (Am)	03.41				
Northampton T	Tr	01.47	46	6	-	1

FROWEN John
Trelewis, 11 October, 1931 (FB)

League Club	Source	Date Signed	Seasons Played	Apps	Subs	Gls
Cardiff C	Nelson (Glamorgan)	05.51	52-57	35	-	0
Bristol Rov	Tr	08.58	58-62	84	-	0
Newport Co	Tr	03.63	62-65	67	1	0

FRUDE Roger Gordon
Plymouth, 19 November, 1946 Died 1996 (M)

League Club	Source	Date Signed	Seasons Played	Apps	Subs	Gls
Bristol Rov	App	12.64	63-67	38	3	8
Mansfield T	Tr	09.67	67-68	14	1	0
Brentford	Tr	07.69	69	1	1	0

FRY Adam George
Bedford, 9 February, 1985 (M)

League Club	Source	Date Signed	Seasons Played	Apps	Subs	Gls
Peterborough U	Sch	07.04	04	3	0	0

FRY Barry Francis
Bedford, 7 April, 1945 ESch (W)

League Club	Source	Date Signed	Seasons Played	Apps	Subs	Gls
Manchester U	App	04.62				
Bolton W	Tr	05.64	64	3	-	1
Luton T	Tr	07.65	65	6	0	0
Leyton Orient	Gravesend & Northfleet	12.66	66	2	1	0
Orient	Bedford T	06.67	67	5	5	0

FRY Christopher (Chris) David
Cardiff, 23 October, 1969 WYth (M)

League Club	Source	Date Signed	Seasons Played	Apps	Subs	Gls
Cardiff C	YT	08.88	88-90	22	33	1
Hereford U	Tr	08.91	91-93	76	14	10
Colchester U	Tr	10.93	93-96	102	28	16
Exeter C	Tr	07.97	97-98	43	17	3

FRY David Paul
Bournemouth, 5 January, 1960 (G)

League Club	Source	Date Signed	Seasons Played	Apps	Subs	Gls
Crystal Palace	Weymouth	01.77	77-82	40	0	0
Gillingham	Tr	07.83	83-84	49	0	0
Torquay U	Millwall (N/C)	10.85	85	30	0	0

FRY Keith Frederick
Cardiff, 11 April, 1941 WSch (W)

League Club	Source	Date Signed	Seasons Played	Apps	Subs	Gls
Newport Co	Jnrs	10.58	58-61	57	-	2
Notts Co	Tr	02.62	61-63	73	-	9
Chesterfield	Merthyr Tydfil	01.66	65	2	0	1

FRY Robert (Bob) Philip
Pontypridd, 29 June, 1935 (G)

League Club	Source	Date Signed	Seasons Played	Apps	Subs	Gls
Crystal Palace		04.56	55	6	-	0
Queens Park Rgrs	Bath C	08.57	57	1	-	0

FRY Roger Norman
Southampton, 18 August, 1948 (FB)

League Club	Source	Date Signed	Seasons Played	Apps	Subs	Gls
Southampton	Jnrs	10.67	70-71	23	0	0
Walsall	Tr	07.73	73-76	120	0	1

FRY Russell Harok
Hull, 4 December, 1985 WYth (M)

League Club	Source	Date Signed	Seasons Played	Apps	Subs	Gls
Hull C	Sch	12.02	04	1	0	0

FRYATT James (Jim) Edward
Swaythling, 2 September, 1940 (F)

League Club	Source	Date Signed	Seasons Played	Apps	Subs	Gls
Charlton Ath	Moor End U YC	10.57	59	5	-	3
Southend U	Tr	06.60	60-62	61	-	24
Bradford PA	Tr	06.63	63-65	101	0	38
Southport	Tr	03.66	65-66	39	0	15
Torquay U	Tr	03.67	66-67	27	0	11
Stockport Co	Tr	10.67	67-68	45	0	28
Blackburn Rov	Tr	10.68	68-69	29	8	5
Oldham Ath	Tr	02.70	69-71	76	0	40
Southport	Tr	11.71	71-73	102	2	24
Stockport Co	Philadelphia (USA)	09.74	74	1	0	1
Torquay U	Tr	12.74	74	3	0	0

FRYATT Matthew (Matt) Charles
Nuneaton, 5 March, 1986 EYth (F)

League Club	Source	Date Signed	Seasons Played	Apps	Subs	Gls
Walsall	Sch	04.03	03-04	26	21	16
Carlisle U	L	12.03	03	9	1	1

FRYE John (Johnny) Marr
Ardrossan, 27 July, 1933 Died 2005 (IF)

League Club	Source	Date Signed	Seasons Played	Apps	Subs	Gls
Sheffield Wed	St Mirren	01.61				
Tranmere Rov	Tr	10.61	61	21	-	6

FRYER John (Jack) Hilary
Manchester, 24 June, 1924 (CF)

League Club	Source	Date Signed	Seasons Played	Apps	Subs	Gls
Oldham Ath	Goslings	04.47	47	9	-	3

FUCCILLO Pasquale (Lil)
Bedford, 2 May, 1956 (M)

League Club	Source	Date Signed	Seasons Played	Apps	Subs	Gls
Luton T	App	07.74	74-82	153	7	24
Southend U	Tulsa (USA)	12.83	83-84	40	5	4
Peterborough U	Tr	08.85	85-86	82	0	3
Cambridge U	Valetta (Malta)	01.88	87	18	1	2

FUCHS Uwe
Kaiserslautern, Germany, 23 July, 1966 (F)

League Club	Source	Date Signed	Seasons Played	Apps	Subs	Gls
Middlesbrough (L)	Kaiserslautern (Ger)	01.95	94	13	2	9
Millwall	Kaiserslautern (Ger)	07.95	95	21	11	5

FUDGE Michael (Micky) Henry
Bristol, 5 December, 1945 (W)

League Club	Source	Date Signed	Seasons Played	Apps	Subs	Gls
West Bromwich A	App	12.63	63-64	13	-	5
Exeter C	Wellington T	06.67	67	32	2	6

FUERTES Esteban Oscar
Colonel Dorredo, Argentina, 26 December, 1976 (F)

League Club	Source	Date Signed	Seasons Played	Apps	Subs	Gls
Derby Co	Colon de Santa Fe (Arg)	08.99	99	8	0	1

FUGLESTAD Erik
Randaberg, Norway, 13 August, 1974 Nou21 (FB)

League Club	Source	Date Signed	Seasons Played	Apps	Subs	Gls
Norwich C	Viking Stavanger (Nor)	11.97	97-99	71	3	2

FULBROOK Gary
Bath, 4 May, 1966 (FB)

League Club	Source	Date Signed	Seasons Played	Apps	Subs	Gls
Swindon T	App	09.84	84	0	1	0
Carlisle U	Bath C	09.87	87	6	0	0

FULLAM John (Johnny) Rowan
Dublin, 22 March, 1940 LoI-12/IRB/IR-11 (WH)

League Club	Source	Date Signed	Seasons Played	Apps	Subs	Gls
Preston NE	Home Farm	10.58	59-60	49	-	6

FULLARTON James (Jamie)
Bellshill, 20 July, 1974 Su21-17 (M)

League Club	Source	Date Signed	Seasons Played	Apps	Subs	Gls
Crystal Palace	Bastia (Fr)	08.97	97-00	40	7	1
Bolton W	L	03.99	98	1	0	0
Brentford	Dundee U	08.02	02	22	5	1
Southend U	Tr	07.03	03	7	0	0
Chesterfield	Tr	03.04	03	0	1	0

FULLBROOK John Frederick Albert
Grays, 15 July, 1918 Died 1992 (FB)

League Club	Source	Date Signed	Seasons Played	Apps	Subs	Gls
Leyton Orient	Plymouth Arg (Am)	04.46	46-47	36	-	1

FULLER Ashley John
Bedford, 14 November, 1986 (M)

League Club	Source	Date Signed	Seasons Played	Apps	Subs	Gls
Cambridge U	Sch	●	03-04	0	3	0

FULLER Ricardo Dwayne
Kingston, Jamaica, 31 October, 1979 Jamaica int (F)

League Club	Source	Date Signed	Seasons Played	Apps	Subs	Gls
Crystal Palace	Tivoli Gardens (Jam)	02.01	00	2	6	0
Preston NE	Tr	07.02	02-04	57	1	27
Portsmouth	Tr	08.04	04	13	18	1

FULLER William (Bill) James
Brixton, 6 April, 1944 (FB)

League Club	Source	Date Signed	Seasons Played	Apps	Subs	Gls
Crystal Palace	Jnrs	01.63	62-64	3	-	0

FULLERTON George
Ballymena, 14 June, 1939 (G)

League Club	Source	Date Signed	Seasons Played	Apps	Subs	Gls
Leeds U	Glentoran	05.58				
Barrow	Distillery	07.60	60	12	-	0

FULOP Marton
Budapest, Hungary, 3 May, 1983 Huu21-1/Hu-1 (G)

League Club	Source	Date Signed	Seasons Played	Apps	Subs	Gls
Tottenham H	MTK Hungaria (Hun)	06.04				
Chesterfield	L	03.05	04	7	0	0

FULTON Bryce
Kilwinning, 7 August, 1935 (FB)

League Club	Source	Date Signed	Seasons Played	Apps	Subs	Gls
Manchester U	Jnrs	03.53				
Plymouth Arg	Tr	08.57	57-63	176	-	0
Exeter C	Tr	07.64	64-65	37	0	0

FULTON Raymond (Ray) Hamilton
Hendon, 24 September, 1953 (FB)

League Club	Source	Date Signed	Seasons Played	Apps	Subs	Gls
Orient	West Ham U (App)	08.72	72	1	0	0

FULTON Stephen (Steve)
Greenock, 10 August, 1970 Su21-7 (M)

League Club	Source	Date Signed	Seasons Played	Apps	Subs	Gls
Bolton W	Glasgow Celtic	07.93	93	4	0	0
Peterborough U	L	12.93	93	3	0	0

[FUMACA] ANTUNES Jose Rodriguez Alves
Belem, Brazil, 15 July, 1976 (M)

League Club	Source	Date Signed	Seasons Played	Apps	Subs	Gls
Colchester U	Catuense (Br)	03.99	98	1	0	0
Barnsley	Tr	03.99				
Crystal Palace	Tr	09.99	99	2	1	0
Newcastle U	Tr	09.99	99	1	4	0

FUNNELL Anthony (Tony)
Eastbourne, 20 August, 1957 (F)

League Club	Source	Date Signed	Seasons Played	Apps	Subs	Gls
Southampton	Eastbourne	01.77	77-78	13	4	8
Gillingham	Tr	03.79	78-79	27	6	10
Brentford	Tr	03.80	79-80	29	3	8
Bournemouth	Tr	09.81	81-82	59	5	22

FUNNELL Simon Paul
Shoreham, 8 August, 1974 (F)

League Club	Source	Date Signed	Seasons Played	Apps	Subs	Gls
Brighton & Hove A	YT	07.92	91-94	14	14	2

FURIE John Patrick Christopher
Hammersmith, 13 May, 1948 (FB)

League Club	Source	Date Signed	Seasons Played	Apps	Subs	Gls
Watford	App	05.66	66	0	1	0
Gillingham	Tr	07.67	67	17	0	0

FURLONG Carl David
Liverpool, 18 October, 1976 (F)

League Club	Source	Date Signed	Seasons Played	Apps	Subs	Gls
Wigan Ath	YT	07.95	93-94	1	2	1

FURLONG Paul Anthony
Wood Green, 1 October, 1968 ESemiPro-5 (F)

League Club	Source	Date Signed	Seasons Played	Apps	Subs	Gls
Coventry C	Enfield	07.91	91	27	10	4
Watford	Tr	07.92	92-93	79	0	37
Chelsea	Tr	05.94	94-95	44	20	13
Birmingham C	Tr	07.96	96-01	104	27	50
Queens Park Rgrs	L	08.00	00	3	0	1
Sheffield U	L	02.02	01	4	0	2
Queens Park Rgrs	Tr	08.02	02-04	97	12	47

FURNELL Andrew (Andy) Paul
Peterborough, 13 February, 1977 EYth (F)

League Club	Source	Date Signed	Seasons Played	Apps	Subs	Gls
Peterborough U	YT	12.94	93-95	9	10	1

FURNELL James (Jim)
Clitheroe, 23 November, 1937 (G)

League Club	Source	Date Signed	Seasons Played	Apps	Subs	Gls
Burnley	Jnrs	11.54	59-60	2	-	0
Liverpool	Tr	02.62	61-63	28	-	0
Arsenal	Tr	11.63	63-67	141	0	0
Rotherham U	Tr	09.68	68-69	76	0	0
Plymouth Arg	Tr	12.70	70-75	183	0	0

FURNESS William (Billy) Isaac
New Washington, 8 June, 1909 Died 1980 E-1 (IF)

League Club	Source	Date Signed	Seasons Played	Apps	Subs	Gls
Leeds U	Usworth Colliery	08.28	29-36	243	-	62
Norwich C	Tr	06.37	37-46	93	-	21

FURNISS Frederick (Fred)
Sheffield, 10 July, 1922 (FB)

League Club	Source	Date Signed	Seasons Played	Apps	Subs	Gls
Sheffield U	Hallam	01.43	46-54	279	-	14

FURPHY Keith
Stockton, 30 July, 1958 (W)

League Club	Source	Date Signed	Seasons Played	Apps	Subs	Gls
Queens Park Rgrs	Sheffield U (App)	10.76				
Plymouth Arg	Atlanta (USA)	08.87	87	6	0	1

FURPHY Kenneth (Ken)
Stockton, 28 May, 1931 (FB)

League Club	Source	Date Signed	Seasons Played	Apps	Subs	Gls
Everton		11.50				
Darlington	Runcorn	08.53	53-61	316	-	6
Workington	Tr	07.62	62-64	105	-	3
Watford	Tr	11.64	64-67	95	6	1

FURSDON Alan Harry
Grantham, 16 October, 1947 (FB)

League Club	Source	Date Signed	Seasons Played	Apps	Subs	Gls
Swindon T		09.65				
Oxford U		05.67	68	0	1	0

FURY Paul
Swansea, 16 March, 1955 WSch (FB)

League Club	Source	Date Signed	Seasons Played	Apps	Subs	Gls
Swansea C	App	●	71-72	11	0	0

FUSCHILLO Paul Michael
Islington, 20 October, 1948 ESch/EAmat (CD)

League Club	Source	Date Signed	Seasons Played	Apps	Subs	Gls
Blackpool	Wycombe W	07.71	71-73	8	3	0
Brighton & Hove A	Tr	02.74	73-74	17	0	1

FUTCHER Benjamin (Ben) Paul
Manchester, 20 February, 1981 (CD)

League Club	Source	Date Signed	Seasons Played	Apps	Subs	Gls
Oldham Ath	YT	07.99	99-00	2	8	0
Lincoln C	Doncaster Rov	08.02	02-04	119	2	13

FUTCHER Graham
Chester, 15 June, 1953 (F)

League Club	Source	Date Signed	Seasons Played	Apps	Subs	Gls
Chester	Jnrs	08.71	71-72	5	5	0

League Club	Source	Date Signed	Seasons Played	Career Record Apps	Subs	Gls
FUTCHER Paul						
Chester, 25 September, 1956 Eu21-11						(CD)
Chester	App	01.74	72-73	20	0	0
Luton T	Tr	06.74	74-77	131	0	1
Manchester C	Tr	06.78	78-79	36	1	0
Oldham Ath	Tr	08.80	80-82	98	0	1
Derby Co	Tr	01.83	82-83	35	0	0
Barnsley	Tr	03.84	83-89	229	1	0
Halifax T	Tr	07.90	90	15	0	0
Grimsby T	Tr	01.91	90-94	131	1	0
FUTCHER Ronald (Ron)						
Chester, 25 September, 1956						(F)
Chester	App	01.74	73	4	0	0
Luton T	Tr	06.74	74-77	116	4	40
Manchester C	Tr	08.78	78	10	7	7
Barnsley	NAC Breda (Holl)	12.84	84	18	1	5
Oldham Ath	Tr	07.85	85-86	65	0	30
Bradford C	Tr	03.87	86-87	35	7	18
Port Vale	Tr	08.88	88-89	46	6	20
Burnley	Tr	11.89	89-90	52	5	25
Crewe Alex	Tr	07.91	91	18	3	4
FUTRE Paulo Jorge						
Montijo, Portugal, 28 February, 1966 Portugal int						(F)
West Ham U	AC Milan (It)	06.96	96	4	5	0
FYFE Graham						
Dundee, 7 December, 1982						(M)
Cheltenham T	Glasgow Celtic	08.03	03-04	16	7	0
FYFE Tony						
Carlisle, 23 February, 1962						(F)
Carlisle U	Penrith	09.87	87-89	28	20	12
Scarborough	L	12.89	89	6	0	1
Halifax T	Tr	01.90	89-90	13	3	0
Carlisle U	Tr	10.90	90-91	33	9	8

GAARDSOE Thomas
Randers, Denmark, 23 November, 1979 Deu21-10/De-2 (CD)

League Club	Source	Date Signed	Seasons Played	Apps	Subs	Gls
Ipswich T	AAB Aalborg (Den)	08.01	01-02	40	1	5
West Bromwich A	Tr	08.03	03-04	70	4	4

GABBIADINI Marco
Nottingham, 20 January, 1968 Eu21-2/EB-1/FLge (F)

League Club	Source	Date Signed	Seasons Played	Apps	Subs	Gls
York C	App	09.85	84-87	42	18	14
Sunderland	Tr	09.87	87-91	155	2	74
Crystal Palace	Tr	10.91	91	15	0	5
Derby Co	Tr	01.92	91-96	163	25	50
Birmingham C	L	10.96	96	0	2	0
Oxford U	L	01.97	96	5	0	1
Stoke C	Panionios (Gre)	12.97	97	2	6	0
York C	Tr	02.98	97	5	2	1
Darlington	Tr	07.98	98-99	81	1	47
Northampton T	Tr	06.00	00-02	97	23	25
Hartlepool U	Tr	07.03	03	9	6	5

GABBIADINI Riccardo
Newport, 11 March, 1970 (F)

League Club	Source	Date Signed	Seasons Played	Apps	Subs	Gls
York C	YT	•	87	0	1	0
Sunderland	Tr	06.88	89	0	1	0
Blackpool	L	09.89	89	5	0	3
Grimsby T	Tr	10.89	89	3	0	1
Brighton & Hove A	L	03.90	89	0	1	0
Crewe Alex	L	10.90	90	1	1	0
Hartlepool U	Tr	03.91	90-91	2	12	2
Scarborough	Tr	03.92	91	3	4	1
Carlisle U	Tr	08.92	92	18	6	3

GABBIDON Daniel (Danny) Leon
Cwmbran, 8 August, 1979 WYth/Wu21-17/W-26 (FB)

League Club	Source	Date Signed	Seasons Played	Apps	Subs	Gls
West Bromwich A	YT	07.98	98-99	20	0	0
Cardiff C	Tr	08.00	00-04	194	3	10

GABRIEL James (Jimmy)
Dundee, 16 October, 1940 SSch/Su23-6/S-2 (M)

League Club	Source	Date Signed	Seasons Played	Apps	Subs	Gls
Everton	Dundee	03.60	59-66	255	1	33
Southampton	Tr	07.67	67-71	190	1	25
Bournemouth	Tr	07.72	72-73	53	0	4
Swindon T	L	10.73	73	6	0	0
Brentford	Tr	03.74	73	9	0	0

GABRIELI Emanuele
L'Aquila, Italy, 31 December, 1980 (CD)

League Club	Source	Date Signed	Seasons Played	Apps	Subs	Gls
Sheffield U	Cavese (It)	10.04	04	0	1	0
Boston U	Tr	02.05	04	4	0	0

GADDES Graham **Robert**
Byfleet, 27 September, 1941 EYth (G)

League Club	Source	Date Signed	Seasons Played	Apps	Subs	Gls
Portsmouth	Jnrs	06.60	59	1	-	0

GADSBY Kenneth (Ken) Joseph
Chesterfield, 3 July, 1916 Died 2003 (FB)

League Club	Source	Date Signed	Seasons Played	Apps	Subs	Gls
Leeds U	Scarborough	10.34	36-47	78	-	0

GADSBY Matthew (Matt) John
Sutton Coldfield, 6 September, 1979 (M)

League Club	Source	Date Signed	Seasons Played	Apps	Subs	Gls
Walsall	YT	02.98	97-01	23	14	0
Mansfield T	Tr	11.02	02	13	7	0
Kidderminster Hrs	Tr	07.03	03	23	9	2

GADSBY Michael (Mick) David
Oswestry, 1 August, 1947 (G)

League Club	Source	Date Signed	Seasons Played	Apps	Subs	Gls
Notts Co	Ashbourne	01.68	67	11	0	0
York C	Tr	07.69	69	13	0	0
Grimsby T	L	09.70	70	2	0	0
Bradford C	L	12.70	70	6	0	0
Hartlepool	Tr	07.71	71	21	0	0

GADSTON Joseph (Joe) Edward
Hanwell, 13 September, 1945 (F)

League Club	Source	Date Signed	Seasons Played	Apps	Subs	Gls
Brentford	West Ham U (Am)	08.64				
Bristol Rov	Cheltenham T	05.68	68	10	1	5
Exeter C	Tr	11.69	69-71	85	0	30
Aldershot	Tr	07.72	72	2	2	0
Hartlepool	L	02.73	72	1	0	0

GAFFNEY Terence (Terry)
Hartlepool, 15 February, 1952 (M)

League Club	Source	Date Signed	Seasons Played	Apps	Subs	Gls
Hartlepool U	Billingham Synthonia	07.77	77	10	3	1

GAGE Kevin William
Chiswick, 21 April, 1964 EYth (FB)

League Club	Source	Date Signed	Seasons Played	Apps	Subs	Gls
Wimbledon	App	01.82	80-86	135	33	15
Aston Villa	Tr	07.87	87-90	113	2	8
Sheffield U	Tr	11.91	91-95	107	5	7
Preston NE	Tr	03.96	95-96	20	3	0
Hull C	Tr	09.97	97-98	10	3	0

GAGE Larry Albert
Walthamstow, 10 September, 1922 Died 1996 (G)

League Club	Source	Date Signed	Seasons Played	Apps	Subs	Gls
Fulham	Clapton Orient (Am)	08.44				
Aldershot	Tr	07.46	46-47	38	-	0
Fulham	(Canada)	08.48	48	3	-	0
Gillingham	Tr	06.50	50	40	-	0

GAGE Wakeley Alexander John
Northampton, 5 May, 1958 (CD)

League Club	Source	Date Signed	Seasons Played	Apps	Subs	Gls
Northampton T	Desborough T	10.79	79-84	215	3	17
Chester C	Tr	08.85	85	17	0	1
Peterborough U	Tr	11.85	85-86	73	0	1
Crewe Alex	Tr	06.87	87-88	45	9	1

GAGER Horace Edwin
West Ham, 25 January, 1917 Died 1984 NIRL-2 (CD)

League Club	Source	Date Signed	Seasons Played	Apps	Subs	Gls
Luton T	Vauxhall Motors	11.37	46-47	59	-	2
Nottingham F	Tr	02.48	47-54	258	-	11

GAIA Marcio dos Santos
Sao Mateus, Brazil, 8 September, 1978 BrYth (CD)

League Club	Source	Date Signed	Seasons Played	Apps	Subs	Gls
Exeter C	Agremiacao SA (Br)	07.02	02	33	0	1

GAILLARD Marcel Jean Elie
Charleris, Belgium, 15 January, 1927 Died 1976 (W)

League Club	Source	Date Signed	Seasons Played	Apps	Subs	Gls
Crystal Palace	Tonbridge	02.48	47-49	21	-	3
Portsmouth	Tonbridge	02.51	50-52	58	-	7

GAIN Peter Thomas
Hammersmith, 11 November, 1976 IRYth/IRu21-1 (M)

League Club	Source	Date Signed	Seasons Played	Apps	Subs	Gls
Tottenham H	YT	07.95				
Lincoln C	L	12.98	98	0	3	0
Lincoln C	Tr	03.99	98-04	195	29	21

GALBRAITH David James
Luton, 20 December, 1983 (M)

League Club	Source	Date Signed	Seasons Played	Apps	Subs	Gls
Northampton T	Tottenham H (Sch)	01.04	04	9	16	1

GALBRAITH Walter (Wally) McMurray
Glasgow, 26 May, 1918 Died 1995 (FB)

League Club	Source	Date Signed	Seasons Played	Apps	Subs	Gls
New Brighton	Clyde	09.48	48-50	109	-	1
Grimsby T	Tr	08.51	51-52	77	-	0
Accrington St	Tr	06.53	53	21	-	0

GALE Anthony (Tony) Peter
Westminster, 19 November, 1959 EYth/Eu21-1 (CD)

League Club	Source	Date Signed	Seasons Played	Apps	Subs	Gls
Fulham	App	08.77	77-83	277	0	19
West Ham U	Tr	08.84	84-93	293	7	5
Blackburn Rov	Tr	08.94	94	15	0	0
Crystal Palace	Tr	09.95	95	2	0	0

GALE Colin Maurice
Pontypridd, 31 August, 1932 (CD)

League Club	Source	Date Signed	Seasons Played	Apps	Subs	Gls
Cardiff C	Jnrs	07.50	53-55	13	-	0
Northampton T	Tr	03.56	55-60	211	-	0

GALE Darren
Port Talbot, 25 October, 1963 Wu21-2 (F)

League Club	Source	Date Signed	Seasons Played	Apps	Subs	Gls
Swansea C	App	10.80	81-84	26	11	6
Exeter C	Tr	09.85	85-86	19	1	5

GALE Ian James
Slough, 3 March, 1961 (M)

League Club	Source	Date Signed	Seasons Played	Apps	Subs	Gls
Millwall	App	03.78	78	4	1	0

GALE Shaun Michael
Reading, 8 October, 1969 (FB)

League Club	Source	Date Signed	Seasons Played	Apps	Subs	Gls
Portsmouth	YT	07.88	90	2	1	0
Barnet	Tr	07.94	94-96	109	5	5
Exeter C	Tr	06.97	97-99	81	12	5

GALE Thomas (Tommy)
Washington, 4 November, 1920 Died 1975 (CD)

League Club	Source	Date Signed	Seasons Played	Apps	Subs	Gls
Sheffield Wed	Gateshead (Am)	04.45	46	6	-	0
York C	Tr	08.47	47-48	76	-	0

GALL Benny
Copenhagen, Denmark, 14 March, 1971 (G)

League Club	Source	Date Signed	Seasons Played	Apps	Subs	Gls
Shrewsbury T	De Graafschap (Holl)	08.96	96-97	34	0	0

GALL Kevin Alexander
Merthyr Tydfil, 4 February, 1982 WSch/WYth/Wu21-8 (F)

League Club	Source	Date Signed	Seasons Played	Apps	Subs	Gls
Newcastle U	YT	04.99				
Bristol Rov	Tr	03.01	00-02	28	22	5
Yeovil T	Tr	02.03	03-04	69	17	11

League Club	Source	Date Signed	Seasons Played	Career Record Apps	Subs	Gls
GALL Mark Ian						
Brixton, 14 May, 1963						(F)
Maidstone U	Greenwich Borough	02.88	89-91	69	16	31
Brighton & Hove A	Tr	10.91	91	30	1	13
GALL Norman Albert						
Wallsend, 30 September, 1942						(CD)
Brighton & Hove A	Gateshead	03.62	62-73	427	13	4
GALLACHER Bernard						
Johnstone, 22 March, 1967						(FB)
Aston Villa	App	03.85	86-90	55	2	0
Blackburn Rov	L	11.90	90	4	0	0
Doncaster Rov	Tr	09.91	91	2	0	0
Brighton & Hove A	Tr	10.91	91-92	45	0	1
Northampton T	Tr	01.94	93	5	0	0
GALLACHER Connor (Con)						
Derry, 24 April, 1922						(IF)
Middlesbrough	Lochee Harp	01.47	46	1	-	0
Hull C	Tr	05.47	47	18	-	3
Rochdale	Tr	03.48	47	6	-	1
GALLACHER John Anthony						
Glasgow, 26 January, 1969						(W)
Newcastle U	Falkirk	06.89	89-90	22	7	6
Hartlepool U	Tr	08.92	92-93	18	5	2
GALLACHER Kevin William						
Clydebank, 23 November, 1966 SYth/Su21-7/SB-2/S-53						(F)
Coventry C	Dundee U	01.90	89-92	99	1	28
Blackburn Rov	Tr	03.93	92-99	132	12	46
Newcastle U	Tr	10.99	99-00	27	12	4
Preston NE	Tr	08.01	01	1	4	1
Sheffield Wed	Tr	03.02	01	0	4	0
Huddersfield T	Motherwell	08.02	02	5	2	0
GALLACHER Patrick (Pat)						
Glasgow, 9 January, 1913 Died 1983						(IF)
Millwall	Dunoon	11.33				
Blackburn Rov	Third Lanark	10.36	36-37	11	-	0
Bournemouth	Tr	06.38	38-47	35	-	3
GALLACHER Paul James						
Glasgow, 16 August, 1979 Su21-7/S-8						(G)
Norwich C	Dundee U	06.04				
Gillingham	L	12.04	04	3	0	0
Sheffield Wed	L	03.05	04	8	0	0
GALLAGHER Barry Patrick						
Bradford, 7 April, 1961						(M)
Bradford C	App	04.79	77-82	66	5	22
Mansfield T	L	01.83	82	2	1	0
Halifax T	Tr	03.83	82-85	110	5	27
GALLAGHER Brian						
Oldham, 22 July, 1938						(FB)
Bury	Ashton U	10.56	57-64	131	-	1
Carlisle U	Tr	05.65	65-66	43	2	1
Stockport Co	Tr	07.67	67	13	0	0
GALLAGHER Ian						
Hartlepool, 30 May, 1978						(M)
Hartlepool U	YT	07.96	95	1	0	0
GALLAGHER James (Jimmy)						
Bury, 2 September, 1911 Died 1972						(CD)
Bury		01.36				
Notts Co	Tr	08.37	37-38	23	-	2
Exeter C	Tr	06.39				
Exeter C	Notts Co (Coach)	09.48	48	1	-	0
GALLAGHER John (Jackie) Christopher						
Wisbech, 6 April, 1958						(F)
Lincoln C	March T	02.76	76	1	0	0
Peterborough U	Wisbech T	04.80	79-80	11	2	1
Torquay U	(Hong Kong)	08.82	82	38	4	7
Peterborough U	Wisbech T	08.85	85-86	78	4	20
Wolverhampton W	Tr	06.87	87-88	10	17	4
GALLAGHER Joseph (Joe) Anthony						
Liverpool, 11 January, 1955 EB						(CD)
Birmingham C	App	01.72	73-80	281	5	17
Wolverhampton W	Tr	08.81	81-82	31	0	0
West Ham U	Tr	12.82	82	8	1	0
Burnley	Tr	08.83	83-86	46	1	3
Halifax T	L	10.83	83	4	0	0
GALLAGHER Michael (Mike)						
Cambuslang, 16 January, 1932 Died 1975						(W)
Bolton W	Glasgow Benburb	01.52				
West Bromwich A	Tr	12.52	52	1	-	0
GALLAGHER Nicholas (Nicky)						
Boston, 28 January, 1971 ESch						(W)
Doncaster Rov	Jnrs	05.89	89	0	1	0
GALLAGHER Paul						
Glasgow, 9 August, 1984 Su21-1/SB-1/Su21-4						(F)
Blackburn Rov	Sch	02.03	02-04	17	26	5
GALLAGHER Thomas (Tommy) Duncan						
Nottingham, 25 August, 1974						(FB)
Notts Co	YT	06.92	93-96	42	1	2
GALLANT David						
Middlesbrough, 12 October, 1949						(F)
Leeds U	Jnrs	12.66				
Darlington	L	01.68	67	1	0	0
GALLAS William						
Asnieres, France, 17 August, 1977 FrYth/Fru21/Fr-30						(CD)
Chelsea	Marseille (Fr)	07.01	01-04	114	11	7
GALLEGO Antonio (Tony)						
San Sebastian, Spain, 2 June, 1924						(G)
Norwich C	Cambridge T	03.47	46	1	-	0
GALLEGO Jose Augustin						
San Sebastian, Spain, 8 April, 1923						(W)
Brentford	Abbey U	01.47	46-47	6	-	0
Southampton	Tr	05.48	48	1	-	0
Colchester U	Tr	08.49	50	4	-	0
GALLEN Joseph (Joe) Martin						
Hammersmith, 2 September, 1972 IRu21-6						(F)
Watford	YT	05.91				
Exeter C	L	12.92	92	6	0	0
Shrewsbury T	Tr	07.93	93	4	2	1
GALLEN Kevin Andrew						
Chiswick, 21 September, 1975 ESch/EYth/Eu21-4						(F)
Queens Park Rgrs	YT	09.92	94-99	126	45	36
Huddersfield T	Tr	08.00	00	30	8	10
Barnsley	Tr	07.01	01	8	1	2
Queens Park Rgrs	Tr	11.01	01-04	156	2	47
GALLEY Gordon Walter						
Worksop, 4 February, 1930						(W)
Sheffield Wed	Jnrs	06.47				
Darlington	Tr	10.48	48-51	61	-	12
GALLEY John Edward						
Clowne, 7 May, 1944						(F)
Wolverhampton W	Jnrs	05.61	62-64	5	-	2
Rotherham U	Tr	12.64	64-67	108	0	46
Bristol C	Tr	12.67	67-72	172	0	84
Nottingham F	Tr	12.72	72-74	31	6	6
Peterborough U	L	10.74	74	7	0	1
Hereford U	Tr	12.74	74-76	77	3	10
GALLEY Keith John						
Worksop, 17 October, 1955						(F)
Southport	Morecambe	12.75	75-76	50	10	11
GALLEY Maurice						
Clowne, 10 August, 1934						(WH)
Chesterfield	Jnrs	07.52	54-58	55	-	5
GALLEY Thomas (Tom)						
Hednesford, 4 August, 1915 Died 1999 FLge-1/E-2						(WH)
Wolverhampton W	Notts Co (Am)	04.34	34-47	183	-	41
Grimsby T	Tr	11.47	47-48	32	-	2
GALLI Filippo						
Monza, Italy, 19 May, 1963						(CD)
Watford	Brescia	07.01	01	27	1	1
GALLIER William (Bill) Henry						
Cannock, 24 April, 1932						(FB)
West Bromwich A	Beaudesert Sports	07.53				
Walsall	Tr	06.55	55	10	-	0
GALLIERS Steven (Steve)						
Preston, 21 August, 1957						(M)
Wimbledon	Chorley	06.77	77-81	148	7	10
Crystal Palace	Tr	10.81	81	8	5	0
Wimbledon	Tr	08.82	82-87	145	1	5
Bristol C	L	02.87	86	9	0	0
Bristol C	Tr	09.87	87-88	65	3	6
Maidstone U	Tr	07.89	89	7	1	0
GALLIMORE Anthony (Tony) Mark						
Nantwich, 21 February, 1972						(FB)
Stoke C	YT	07.90	89-91	6	5	0
Carlisle U	L	10.91	91	8	0	0

League Club	Source	Date Signed	Seasons Played	Apps	Subs	Gls
Carlisle U	L	02.92	91	8	0	0
Carlisle U	Tr	03.93	92-95	124	0	9
Grimsby T	Tr	03.96	95-02	263	10	4
Barnsley	Tr	08.03	03	20	0	0
Rochdale	Tr	08.04	04	32	2	0

GALLIMORE Leonard (Len)
Northwich, 14 September, 1912 Died 1978 (FB)

League Club	Source	Date Signed	Seasons Played	Apps	Subs	Gls
Preston NE	Bainton Victoria	01.32	33-36	9	-	0
Watford	Tr	05.37	37-46	64	-	0

GALLOGLY Charles (Charlie)
Banbridge, 16 June, 1925 I-2 (FB)

League Club	Source	Date Signed	Seasons Played	Apps	Subs	Gls
Huddersfield T	Glenavon	12.49	49-51	76	-	0
Watford	Tr	08.52	52-53	47	-	0

GALLON John (Jack) William
Burradon, 12 February, 1914 Died 1993 (IF)

League Club	Source	Date Signed	Seasons Played	Apps	Subs	Gls
Bradford C	Bedlington U	06.36	36-37	20	-	5
Bradford PA	Tr	02.38	37-38	31	-	4
Swansea T	Tr	06.39				
Gateshead	Tr	03.46	46	20	-	2

GALLOWAY John
Bo'ness, 29 October, 1918 (IF)

League Club	Source	Date Signed	Seasons Played	Apps	Subs	Gls
Chelsea	Glasgow Rgrs	08.46	46-47	4	-	0

GALLOWAY Michael (Mick)
Oswestry, 30 May, 1965 SYth/Su21-2/S-1 (CD)

League Club	Source	Date Signed	Seasons Played	Apps	Subs	Gls
Mansfield T	Berwick Rgrs	09.83	83-85	39	15	3
Halifax T	Tr	02.86	85-87	79	0	5
Leicester C (L)	Glasgow Celtic	02.95	94	4	1	0

GALLOWAY Michael (Mick) Anthony
Nottingham, 13 October, 1974 (M)

League Club	Source	Date Signed	Seasons Played	Apps	Subs	Gls
Notts Co	YT	06.93	94-96	17	4	0
Gillingham	Tr	03.97	96-99	58	17	5
Lincoln C	L	09.99	99	5	0	0
Chesterfield	Tr	11.99	99-00	18	2	1
Carlisle U	Tr	11.00	00-02	30	5	1

GALLOWAY Steven (Steve) George
Hanover, Germany, 13 February, 1963 (F)

League Club	Source	Date Signed	Seasons Played	Apps	Subs	Gls
Crystal Palace	Sutton U	10.84	84-85	3	2	1
Cambridge U	L	03.86	85	0	1	0

GALVIN Anthony (Tony)
Huddersfield, 12 July, 1956 ESch/IR-29 (W)

League Club	Source	Date Signed	Seasons Played	Apps	Subs	Gls
Tottenham H	Goole T	01.78	78-86	194	7	20
Sheffield Wed	Tr	08.87	87-88	21	15	1
Swindon T	Tr	08.89	89	6	5	0

GALVIN Christopher (Chris)
Huddersfield, 24 November, 1951 EYth (M)

League Club	Source	Date Signed	Seasons Played	Apps	Subs	Gls
Leeds U	App	11.68	69-72	6	1	0
Hull C	Tr	08.73	73-78	132	11	11
York C	L	12.76	76	22	0	6
Stockport Co	Tr	04.79	78-80	67	1	3

GALVIN David
Denaby, 5 October, 1946 (CD)

League Club	Source	Date Signed	Seasons Played	Apps	Subs	Gls
Wolverhampton W	Jnrs	05.65	68	5	0	0
Gillingham	Tr	10.69	69-76	240	6	17
Wimbledon	Tr	08.77	77-78	73	0	7

GAMBARO Enzo
Genoa, Italy, 23 February, 1966 (M)

League Club	Source	Date Signed	Seasons Played	Apps	Subs	Gls
Bolton W	AC Milan (It)	01.96				
Grimsby T	Tr	03.96	95	0	1	0

GAMBLE Bradley David
Southwark, 4 February, 1975 (F)

League Club	Source	Date Signed	Seasons Played	Apps	Subs	Gls
Leyton Orient	YT	07.93	93	1	0	0

GAMBLE Francis (Frank)
Liverpool, 21 August, 1961 (W)

League Club	Source	Date Signed	Seasons Played	Apps	Subs	Gls
Derby Co	Burscough	05.81	81-82	5	1	2
Rochdale	Barrow	12.84	84-85	41	5	9

GAMBLE Joseph (Joe) Finbar
Cork, 14 January, 1982 IRYth/IRu21-5 (M)

League Club	Source	Date Signed	Seasons Played	Apps	Subs	Gls
Reading	Cork C	08.00	00-01	2	5	0

GAMBLE Simon **William (Willie)**
Cottam, 5 March, 1968 (F)

League Club	Source	Date Signed	Seasons Played	Apps	Subs	Gls
Lincoln C	App	01.86	85-88	44	20	15

GAMBLIN Derek
Havant, 7 April, 1943 EAmat (FB)

League Club	Source	Date Signed	Seasons Played	Apps	Subs	Gls
Portsmouth (Am)	Sutton U	07.65	65	1	0	0

GAMBRILL Brian Daniel
Whitstable, 23 December, 1943 (G)

League Club	Source	Date Signed	Seasons Played	Apps	Subs	Gls
Millwall	Whitstable	12.65	65	1	0	0

GAME Kirk Michael
Rochford, 22 October, 1966 (CD)

League Club	Source	Date Signed	Seasons Played	Apps	Subs	Gls
Colchester U	Southend U (App)	08.85	85-86	28	1	0

GAMMON Stephen (Steve) George
Swansea, 24 September, 1939 Wu23-2 (WH)

League Club	Source	Date Signed	Seasons Played	Apps	Subs	Gls
Cardiff C	Jnrs	04.58	58-64	66	-	1

GANE Alan
Chiswick, 11 June, 1950 ESch (M)

League Club	Source	Date Signed	Seasons Played	Apps	Subs	Gls
Hereford U	Slough T	09.73	73	6	3	1

GANEA Ioan **Viorel (Vio)**
Fagaras, Romania, 10 August, 1973 Romania 44 (F)

League Club	Source	Date Signed	Seasons Played	Apps	Subs	Gls
Wolverhampton W (L)	Bursaspor (Tu)	01.04	03	6	10	3

GANNON Edward (Eddie)
Dublin, 3 January, 1921 Died 1989 LoI-11/IR-14 (WH)

League Club	Source	Date Signed	Seasons Played	Apps	Subs	Gls
Notts Co	Shelbourne	08.46	46-48	107	-	2
Sheffield Wed	Tr	03.49	48-54	204	-	4

GANNON James (Jim) Paul
Southwark, 7 September, 1968 (CD)

League Club	Source	Date Signed	Seasons Played	Apps	Subs	Gls
Sheffield U	Dundalk	04.89				
Halifax T	L	02.90	89	2	0	0
Stockport Co	Tr	03.90	89-99	350	33	52
Notts Co	L	01.94	93	2	0	0
Crewe Alex	Tr	12.00	00	5	2	0

GANNON John Spencer
Wimbledon, 18 December, 1966 (M)

League Club	Source	Date Signed	Seasons Played	Apps	Subs	Gls
Wimbledon	App	12.84	85-87	13	3	2
Crewe Alex	L	12.86	86	14	1	0
Sheffield U	Tr	02.89	88-95	162	12	6
Middlesbrough	L	11.93	93	6	1	0
Oldham Ath	Tr	03.96	95-96	6	0	0

GANNON Michael (Mick) John
Liverpool, 2 February, 1943 (CD)

League Club	Source	Date Signed	Seasons Played	Apps	Subs	Gls
Everton	Jnrs	02.60	61	3	-	0
Scunthorpe U	Tr	05.62	62-63	15	-	0
Crewe Alex	Tr	10.64	64-69	205	3	2

GARBETT William **Edward (Eddie)**
Dawley, 14 September, 1949 (W)

League Club	Source	Date Signed	Seasons Played	Apps	Subs	Gls
Shrewsbury T	App	09.67	67-68	7	4	2
Barrow	Tr	07.69	69-71	119	0	27
Stockport Co	Tr	07.72	72-73	63	7	11

GARBETT Terence (Terry) Graham
Lanchester, 9 September, 1945 (M)

League Club	Source	Date Signed	Seasons Played	Apps	Subs	Gls
Middlesbrough	Stockton	08.63	65	7	0	1
Watford	Tr	08.66	66-71	196	4	46
Blackburn Rov	Tr	09.71	71-73	90	0	6
Sheffield U	Tr	02.74	73-75	26	5	0

GARBUTT Eric John Edward
Scarborough, 27 March, 1920 Died 1997 (G)

League Club	Source	Date Signed	Seasons Played	Apps	Subs	Gls
Newcastle U	Billingham Synthonia	01.39	46-49	52	-	0

GARBUTT Peter
Corbridge, 28 December, 1939 EAmat (CD)

League Club	Source	Date Signed	Seasons Played	Apps	Subs	Gls
Carlisle U	Crook T	08.64	64-70	134	2	13

GARBUTT Raymond (Ray) Hardiman
Middlesbrough, 9 May, 1925 Died 1994 (CF)

League Club	Source	Date Signed	Seasons Played	Apps	Subs	Gls
Manchester C	South Bank	09.47				
Watford	Spennymoor U	05.50	50	22	-	8
Brighton & Hove A	Tr	03.51	50-51	32	-	17
Workington	Tr	10.52	52	8	-	2

GARCIA Anthony (Tony)
Pierre Patte, France, 18 March, 1972 (F)

League Club	Source	Date Signed	Seasons Played	Apps	Subs	Gls
Notts Co	OSC Lille (Fr)	09.98	98	10	9	2

GARCIA Luis Javier
Barcelona, Spain, 24 June, 1978 Spain 2 (M)

League Club	Source	Date Signed	Seasons Played	Apps	Subs	Gls
Liverpool	Barcelona (Sp)	08.04	04	26	3	8

GARCIA Richard
Perth, Australia, 4 September, 1981 AuYth/Auu23 (M)

League Club	Source	Date Signed	Seasons Played	Apps	Subs	Gls
West Ham U	YT	09.98	01-04	4	12	0
Leyton Orient	L	08.00	00	18	0	4
Colchester U	Tr	09.04	04	20	4	4

GARDE Remi
L'Arbresle, France, 3 April, 1966 France 6 (M)

League Club	Source	Date Signed	Seasons Played	Apps	Subs	Gls
Arsenal	Strasbourg (Fr)	08.96	96-98	19	12	0

GARDEN Stuart Robertson
Dundee, 10 February, 1972 (G)

League Club	Source	Date Signed	Seasons Played	Apps	Subs	Gls
Notts Co	Forfar Ath	07.01	01-03	51	1	0

GARDINER Douglas (Doug)
Douglas, 29 March, 1917 (WH)

League Club	Source	Date Signed	Seasons Played	Apps	Subs	Gls
Luton T	Auchinleck Talbot	05.38	46-50	121	-	1

GARDINER John
Chester-le-Street, 5 November, 1914 Died 1997 (IF)

League Club	Source	Date Signed	Seasons Played	Apps	Subs	Gls
Southend U (Am)	Holfords	05.46	46	1	-	0

GARDINER Mark Christopher
Cirencester, 25 December, 1966 (W)

League Club	Source	Date Signed	Seasons Played	Apps	Subs	Gls
Swindon T	App	09.84	83-86	7	3	1
Torquay U	Tr	02.87	86-87	37	12	4
Crewe Alex	Tr	08.88	88-94	179	14	33
Chester C	L	03.95	94	2	1	0
Macclesfield T	Frederikstad (Nor)	10.95	97	7	0	2

GARDINER Matthew (Matt)
Birmingham, 28 March, 1974 (FB)

League Club	Source	Date Signed	Seasons Played	Apps	Subs	Gls
Torquay U	YT	07.92	92	5	2	0

GARDINER William (Willie) Silcock
Larbert, 15 August, 1929 SB (CF)

League Club	Source	Date Signed	Seasons Played	Apps	Subs	Gls
Leicester C	Glasgow Rgrs	08.55	55-57	69	-	48
Reading	Tr	11.58	58-59	8	-	2

GARDNER Anthony
Stone, 19 September, 1980 Eu21-1/E-1 (CD)

League Club	Source	Date Signed	Seasons Played	Apps	Subs	Gls
Port Vale	YT	07.98	98-99	40	1	4
Tottenham H	Tr	01.00	00-04	68	17	1

GARDNER Charles (Charlie) Claridge
Dundee, 17 March, 1925 (WH)

League Club	Source	Date Signed	Seasons Played	Apps	Subs	Gls
Aldershot	St Mirren	08.50	50	6	-	0

GARDNER Charles **Donald (Don)**
Jamaica, 30 August, 1955 (M)

League Club	Source	Date Signed	Seasons Played	Apps	Subs	Gls
Wolverhampton W	App	08.73	74	1	2	0

GARDNER Frederick (Fred) Charles
Bell Green, 4 June, 1922 Died 1979 (W)

League Club	Source	Date Signed	Seasons Played	Apps	Subs	Gls
Birmingham C		09.40				
Coventry C	Tr	05.46	46-48	13	-	3
Newport Co	Tr	05.49	49	4	-	2

GARDNER James (Jimmy) Francis
Dunfermline, 27 September, 1967 (W)

League Club	Source	Date Signed	Seasons Played	Apps	Subs	Gls
Scarborough	St Mirren	08.95	95	5	1	1
Cardiff C	Tr	09.95	95-96	51	12	5
Exeter C	Tr	07.97	97-98	42	8	1

GARDNER Robert **Lee**
Ayr, 11 July, 1970 (M)

League Club	Source	Date Signed	Seasons Played	Apps	Subs	Gls
Oxford U (L)	Aberdeen	03.91	90	2	5	0

GARDNER Paul Anthony
Southport, 22 September, 1957 (FB)

League Club	Source	Date Signed	Seasons Played	Apps	Subs	Gls
Blackpool	App	09.75	76-81	149	3	1
Bury	Tr	08.82	82-83	90	0	0
Swansea C	Tr	10.84	84	4	0	0
Wigan Ath	Preston NE (N/C)	01.85	84	5	0	0

GARDNER Ricardo Wayne
St Andrews, Jamaica, 25 September, 1978 Jamaica 60 (M)

League Club	Source	Date Signed	Seasons Played	Apps	Subs	Gls
Bolton W	Harbour View (Jam)	08.98	98-04	182	27	15

GARDNER Ross
South Shields, 15 December, 1985 EYth (M)

League Club	Source	Date Signed	Seasons Played	Apps	Subs	Gls
Newcastle U	YT	05.02				
Nottingham F	Tr	08.03	03-04	10	6	0

GARDNER Stephen (Steve) David
Hemsworth, 7 October, 1958 ESch (M)

League Club	Source	Date Signed	Seasons Played	Apps	Subs	Gls
Ipswich T	App	10.75				
Oldham Ath	Tr	12.77	77-80	41	12	2

GARDNER Stephen (Steve) George
Middlesbrough, 3 July, 1968 (CD)

League Club	Source	Date Signed	Seasons Played	Apps	Subs	Gls
Manchester U	App	07.86				
Burnley	Tr	07.87	87-89	93	2	0
Bradford C	Glossop	08.91	91	14	0	0
Bury		10.92	92	1	0	0

GARDNER Thomas (Tommy)
Huyton, 28 May, 1910 Died 1970 E-2 (WH)

League Club	Source	Date Signed	Seasons Played	Apps	Subs	Gls
Liverpool	Orrell	04.29	29	5	-	0
Grimsby T	Tr	06.31	31	13	-	0
Hull C	Tr	05.32	32-33	66	-	2
Aston Villa	Tr	02.34	33-37	77	-	1
Burnley	Tr	04.38	38	39	-	3
Wrexham	Tr	12.45	46	33	-	4

GARDNER Thomas
Liverpool, 17 March, 1923 (W)

League Club	Source	Date Signed	Seasons Played	Apps	Subs	Gls
Liverpool	South Liverpool	10.46				
Everton	Tr	06.47	47	1	-	0

GARGAN John
York, 6 June, 1928 (WH)

League Club	Source	Date Signed	Seasons Played	Apps	Subs	Gls
York C	Cliftonville (York)	08.45	46	1	-	0

GARIANI Moshe
Tiberias, Israel, 18 June, 1957 Israel int (M)

League Club	Source	Date Signed	Seasons Played	Apps	Subs	Gls
Brighton & Hove A	Maccabi Netanya (Isr)	06.80	80	0	1	0

GARLAND Christopher (Chris) Stephen
Bristol, 24 April, 1949 Eu23-1 (F)

League Club	Source	Date Signed	Seasons Played	Apps	Subs	Gls
Bristol C	App	05.66	66-71	142	1	31
Chelsea	Tr	09.71	71-74	89	3	22
Leicester C	Tr	02.75	74-76	52	3	15
Bristol C	Tr	12.76	76-82	53	11	11

GARLAND David
Grimsby, 18 June, 1948 (CF)

League Club	Source	Date Signed	Seasons Played	Apps	Subs	Gls
Grimsby T	Jnrs	07.65	65	2	0	0

GARLAND Peter John
Croydon, 20 January, 1971 EYth (M)

League Club	Source	Date Signed	Seasons Played	Apps	Subs	Gls
Tottenham H	YT	07.89	90	0	1	0
Newcastle U	Tr	03.92	91	0	2	0
Charlton Ath	Tr	12.92	92-95	40	13	2
Wycombe W	L	03.95	94	5	0	0
Leyton Orient	Tr	07.96	96	13	8	0

GARLAND Ronald (Ron)
Middlesbrough, 28 July, 1931 Died 1989 (CF)

League Club	Source	Date Signed	Seasons Played	Apps	Subs	Gls
Oldham Ath	South Bank St Peter's	12.51	54-55	9	-	3

GARNER Alan Henry
Lambeth, 2 February, 1951 (CD)

League Club	Source	Date Signed	Seasons Played	Apps	Subs	Gls
Millwall	App	02.69	70	2	0	0
Luton T	Tr	07.71	71-74	88	0	3
Watford	Tr	02.75	74-79	200	0	15
Portsmouth	Tr	02.80	79-81	36	0	2

GARNER Andrew (Andy)
Stonebroom, 8 March, 1966 (F)

League Club	Source	Date Signed	Seasons Played	Apps	Subs	Gls
Derby Co	App	12.83	83-87	48	23	17
Blackpool	Tr	08.88	88-92	151	8	37

GARNER Darren John
Plymouth, 10 December, 1971 (M)

League Club	Source	Date Signed	Seasons Played	Apps	Subs	Gls
Plymouth Arg	YT	03.89	88-92	22	5	1
Rotherham U	Dorchester T	06.95	95-04	248	16	23
Torquay U	L	03.05	04	8	1	0

GARNER Glyn
Pontypool, 9 December, 1976 (G)

League Club	Source	Date Signed	Seasons Played	Apps	Subs	Gls
Bury	Llanelli	07.00	01-04	124	2	0

GARNER Paul
Edlington, 1 December, 1955 EYth (FB)

League Club	Source	Date Signed	Seasons Played	Apps	Subs	Gls
Huddersfield T	App	12.72	72-75	96	0	2
Sheffield U	Tr	11.75	75-83	248	3	7
Gillingham	L	09.83	83	5	0	0
Mansfield T	Tr	09.84	84-88	102	9	8

GARNER Simon
Boston, 23 November, 1959 (F)

League Club	Source	Date Signed	Seasons Played	Apps	Subs	Gls
Blackburn Rov	App	07.78	78-91	455	29	168
West Bromwich A	Tr	08.92	92-93	25	8	8
Wycombe W	Tr	02.94	93-95	53	13	15
Torquay U	L	01.96	95	10	1	1

GARNER Timothy (Tim)
Hitchin, 30 March, 1961 (G)

League Club	Source	Date Signed	Seasons Played	Apps	Subs	Gls
Northampton T	AP Leamington	03.86	85	2	0	0

GARNER William (Willie)
Stirling, 24 July, 1955 (CD)

League Club	Source	Date Signed	Seasons Played	Apps	Subs	Gls
Rochdale (L)	Glasgow Celtic	10.82	82	4	0	0

GARNER William (Bill) David
Leicester, 14 December, 1947 (F)

League Club	Source	Date Signed	Seasons Played	Apps	Subs	Gls
Notts Co	Jnrs	07.66	66	2	0	0
Southend U	Bedford T	11.69	69-72	101	1	41
Chelsea	Tr	09.72	72-78	94	11	31
Cambridge U	Tr	11.78	78-79	17	7	3
Brentford	Bedford T	08.83	83	2	1	1

League Club	Source	Date Signed	Seasons Played	Career Record Apps	Subs	Gls
GARNETT Malcolm John						
Wickersley, 8 September, 1943						(CD)
Doncaster Rov	Jnrs	07.61	61	1	-	0
GARNETT Shaun Maurice						
Wallasey, 22 November, 1969						(CD)
Tranmere Rov	YT	06.88	87-95	110	2	5
Chester C	L	10.92	92	9	0	0
Preston NE	L	12.92	92	10	0	2
Wigan Ath	L	02.93	92	13	0	1
Swansea C	Tr	03.96	95-96	15	0	0
Oldham Ath	Tr	09.96	96-01	165	8	9
GARNEYS Thomas (Tommy) Thurston						
Leyton, 25 August, 1923						(CF)
Notts Co	Leytonstone	08.48				
Brentford	Chingford T	12.49	49-50	12	-	2
Ipswich T	Tr	05.51	51-58	248	-	123
GARNHAM Stuart Edward						
Selby, 30 November, 1955						(G)
Wolverhampton W	App	12.73				
Northampton T	L	09.74	74	1	0	0
Peterborough U	Tr	03.77	76	2	0	0
Northampton T	L	08.77	77	11	0	0
GARRARD Luke Edward						
Barnet, 22 September, 1985						(M)
Swindon T	Tottenham H (Jnrs)	07.02	02-04	8	3	0
GARRATT Geoffrey (Geoff)						
Whitehaven, 2 February, 1930 Died 1999						(IF)
Barrow	Barrow Social	09.51	52	2	-	0
Workington	Tr	08.53	53	2	-	0
GARRATT Martin Blake George						
York, 22 February, 1980						(M)
York C	YT	07.98	98-99	35	10	1
Mansfield T	Tr	03.00	99	4	2	0
Lincoln C	St Patrick's Ath	12.00	00	2	0	0
GARRETT Archibald (Archie) Campbell						
Lesmahagow, 17 June, 1919 Died 1994						(CF)
Preston NE	Heart of Midlothian	12.38	37	2	-	2
Northampton T	Heart of Midlothian	09.46	46-47	51	-	35
Birmingham C	Tr	12.47	47-48	19	-	5
Northampton T	Tr	12.48	48-50	43	-	15
GARRETT James (Jim) Edward						
Dumfries, 15 March, 1939						(W)
Carlisle U	Queen of the South	08.63	63	1	-	0
GARRETT Leonard (Len) George						
Hackney, 14 May, 1936 EYth						(FB)
Arsenal	Eton Manor	05.54				
Ipswich T	Tr	05.58	58	1	-	0
GARRETT Scott						
Gateshead, 9 January, 1974						(FB)
Hartlepool U	YT	05.92	93-94	14	1	0
GARRETT Thomas (Tommy)						
South Shields, 28 February, 1926 FLge-3/E-3						(FB)
Blackpool	Horden CW	10.44	47-60	305	-	3
Millwall	Tr	05.61	61	12	-	0
GARRITY Kenneth (Ken)						
Blackburn, 6 August, 1935						(FB)
Accrington St		02.56	58-59	37	-	5
GARROCHO Carlos Miguel						
Benguela, Angola, 26 January, 1974						(M)
Walsall	Leca (Por)	08.01	01	2	2	0
GARROW Herbert (Bert) Alexander						
Elgin, 24 January, 1942						(G)
Newcastle U	Fochabers	02.60	60-62	4	-	0
GARRY Ryan Felix Mayne						
Hornchurch, 29 September, 1983 EYth/Eu20						(FB)
Arsenal	YT	07.01	02	1	0	0
GARTH James (Jimmy) Russell						
Bridgeton, 1 May, 1922 Died 1968						(IF)
Preston NE	Morton	11.46	46-47	23	-	8
GARTLAND Paul						
Shipley, 8 February, 1959						(FB)
Huddersfield T	App	02.77	76-78	8	0	0

League Club	Source	Date Signed	Seasons Played	Career Record Apps	Subs	Gls
GARTON William (Billy) Francis						
Salford, 15 March, 1965						(CD)
Manchester U	App	03.83	84-88	39	2	0
Birmingham C	L	03.86	85	5	0	0
GARVEY Brian						
Hull, 3 July, 1937						(CD)
Hull C	Jnrs	01.58	57-64	232	-	3
Watford	Tr	07.65	65-69	179	1	2
Colchester U	Tr	06.70	70-71	75	2	1
GARVEY James (Jim)						
Motherwell, 4 June, 1919						(WH)
Northampton T	Stewart & Lloyds	05.39				
Leicester C	Tr	06.46	46-48	15	-	0
GARVEY Stephen (Steve) Hugh						
Stalybridge, 22 November, 1973						(W)
Crewe Alex	YT	10.91	90-97	68	40	8
Chesterfield	L	10.97	97	2	1	0
Blackpool	Tr	07.98	98-99	7	10	1
GARVIE John (Johnny)						
Bellshill, 16 October, 1927 Died 1996						(IF)
Preston NE	Hibernian	08.49	49	5	-	0
Lincoln C	Tr	08.50	50-55	184	-	78
Carlisle U	Tr	05.56	56	25	-	6
GARWOOD Colin Arthur						
Heacham, 29 June, 1949 EYth						(F)
Peterborough U	Jnrs	07.67	67-70	58	8	30
Oldham Ath	Tr	07.71	71-74	84	9	35
Huddersfield T	Tr	12.74	74-75	22	6	8
Colchester U	Tr	02.76	75-77	83	4	25
Portsmouth	Tr	03.78	77-79	62	9	34
Aldershot	Tr	02.80	79-81	79	2	25
GARWOOD Jason						
Birmingham, 23 March, 1969						(W)
Leicester C	App	03.87				
Northampton T	L	09.88	88	5	1	0
GARWOOD Leonard (Len) Frank						
Ranikwet, India, 28 July, 1923 Died 1979						(WH)
Tottenham H	Hitchin T	05.46	48	2	-	0
GASCOIGNE Paul John						
Gateshead, 27 May, 1967 EYth/Eu21-13/EB-4/E-57						(M)
Newcastle U	App	05.85	84-87	83	9	21
Tottenham H	Tr	07.88	88-90	91	1	19
Middlesbrough	Glasgow Rgrs	03.98	97-99	39	2	4
Everton	Tr	07.00	00-01	18	14	1
Burnley	Tr	03.02	01	3	3	0
Boston U	Gansu Tianma (China)	07.04	04	2	2	0
GASKELL Alexander (Alec)						
Leigh, 30 July, 1932						(CF)
Southport	Manchester U (Am)	11.52	51-53	44	-	18
Newcastle U	Tr	10.53	53	1	-	0
Mansfield T	Tr	06.54	54-55	42	-	17
Tranmere Rov	Grantham	06.57	57	6	-	6
GASKELL John **David**						
Wigan, 5 October, 1940 ESch/EYth						(G)
Manchester U	Jnrs	10.57	57-66	96	0	0
Wrexham	Wigan Ath	06.69	69-71	95	0	0
GASKELL Edward (Ted)						
Bredbury, 19 December, 1916						(G)
Brentford		05.38	47-51	34	-	0
GASKELL Ronald (Ronnie)						
Walkden, 1 March, 1926						(WH)
Southport	Walkden Yard	05.50	49-50	2	-	0
GASTON Raymond (Ray)						
Belfast, 22 December, 1946 NIu23-1/NI-1						(F)
Wolverhampton W	Coleraine	05.65				
Oxford U	Coleraine	09.68	68	12	0	2
Lincoln C	L	02.70	69	4	0	1
GATE Kenneth (Ken) Bruce						
Hartlepool, 26 October, 1948						(FB)
Hartlepool (Am)	St Joseph's	08.68	68	1	0	0
GATER Roy						
Chesterton, 22 June, 1940						(CD)
Port Vale	Jnrs	04.60	60-61	5	-	0
Bournemouth	Tr	07.62	62-68	216	0	3
Crewe Alex	Tr	01.69	68-72	156	0	5

GATES Eric Lazenby
Ferryhill, 28 June, 1955 E-2 (F)

League Club	Source	Date Signed	Seasons Played	Apps	Subs	Gls
Ipswich T	App	10.72	73-84	267	29	73
Sunderland	Tr	08.85	85-89	163	18	43
Carlisle U	Tr	06.90	90	33	5	8

GATES William (Bill) Lazenby
Ferryhill, 8 May, 1944 EYth (CD)

League Club	Source	Date Signed	Seasons Played	Apps	Subs	Gls
Middlesbrough	Jnrs	10.61	61-73	277	6	12

GATTING Stephen (Steve) Paul
Park Royal, 29 May, 1959 (CD)

League Club	Source	Date Signed	Seasons Played	Apps	Subs	Gls
Arsenal	App	03.77	78-80	50	8	5
Brighton & Hove A	Tr	09.81	81-90	313	3	19
Charlton Ath	Tr	08.91	91-92	61	3	3

GAUDEN Allan
Ashington, 20 November, 1944 (W)

League Club	Source	Date Signed	Seasons Played	Apps	Subs	Gls
Sunderland	Langley Park Jnrs	03.62	65-67	40	3	6
Darlington	Tr	10.68	68-71	124	3	39
Grimsby T	Tr	02.72	71-72	54	1	12
Hartlepool	Tr	08.73	73-74	63	0	15
Gillingham	Tr	12.74	74-75	41	0	3

GAUDINO Maurizio
Brule, Germany, 12 December, 1966 Germany int (M)

League Club	Source	Date Signed	Seasons Played	Apps	Subs	Gls
Manchester C (L)	Eintracht Frankfurt (Ger)	12.94	94	17	3	3

GAUGHAN Steven (Steve) Edward
Doncaster, 14 April, 1970 (M)

League Club	Source	Date Signed	Seasons Played	Apps	Subs	Gls
Doncaster Rov	Hatfield Main Colliery	01.88	87-89	42	25	3
Sunderland	Tr	07.90				
Darlington	Tr	01.92	91-95	159	12	15
Chesterfield	Tr	08.96	96-97	16	4	0
Darlington	Tr	11.97	97-98	35	12	3
Halifax T	Tr	07.99	99-00	35	12	1

GAULD James (Jimmy)
Aberdeen, 9 May, 1929 Died 2004 LoI-2 (IF)

League Club	Source	Date Signed	Seasons Played	Apps	Subs	Gls
Charlton Ath	Waterford	05.55	55-56	47	-	21
Everton	Tr	10.56	56	23	-	7
Plymouth Arg	Tr	10.57	57-58	64	-	25
Swindon T	Tr	08.59	59	40	-	14
Mansfield T	St Johnstone	11.60	60	4	-	3

GAVAN John Thomas
Walsall, 8 December, 1939 (G)

League Club	Source	Date Signed	Seasons Played	Apps	Subs	Gls
Aston Villa	Walsall Wood	11.62	62-65	9	0	0
Doncaster Rov	Tr	07.67	67-68	21	0	0

GAVILAN Zarate **Diego** Antonio
Ascuncion, Paraguay, 1 March, 1980 Paraguay 23 (M)

League Club	Source	Date Signed	Seasons Played	Apps	Subs	Gls
Newcastle U	Cerro Porteno (Por)	02.00	99-00	2	5	1

GAVIN Jason Joseph
Dublin, 14 March, 1980 IRYth/IRu21-6 (CD)

League Club	Source	Date Signed	Seasons Played	Apps	Subs	Gls
Middlesbrough	YT	03.97	98-01	19	12	0
Grimsby T	L	11.02	02	8	2	0
Huddersfield T	L	03.03	02	10	0	1
Bradford C	Tr	07.03	03-04	38	3	0

GAVIN John (Johnny) Thomas
Limerick, 20 April, 1928 IR-7 (W)

League Club	Source	Date Signed	Seasons Played	Apps	Subs	Gls
Norwich C	Limerick	08.48	48-54	203	-	76
Tottenham H	Tr	10.54	54-55	32	-	15
Norwich C	Tr	11.55	55-57	109	-	46
Watford	Tr	07.58	58	43	-	12
Crystal Palace	Tr	05.59	59-60	66	-	15

GAVIN Mark Wilson
Baillieston, 10 December, 1963 (W)

League Club	Source	Date Signed	Seasons Played	Apps	Subs	Gls
Leeds U	App	12.81	82-84	20	10	3
Hartlepool U	L	03.85	84	7	0	1
Carlisle U	Tr	07.85	85	12	1	1
Bolton W	Tr	03.86	85-86	48	1	3
Rochdale	Tr	08.87	87	23	0	6
Bristol C	Heart of Midlothian	10.88	88-89	62	7	6
Watford	Tr	08.90	90	8	5	0
Bristol C	Tr	12.91	91-93	34	7	2
Exeter C	Tr	02.94	93-95	73	4	4
Scunthorpe U	Tr	08.96	96	10	1	0
Hartlepool U	Tr	09.97	97	0	3	0

GAVIN Patrick (Pat) John
Hammersmith, 5 June, 1967 (F)

League Club	Source	Date Signed	Seasons Played	Apps	Subs	Gls
Gillingham	Hanwell T	03.89	88	13	0	7
Leicester C	Tr	06.89	90	1	2	0
Gillingham	L	09.89	89	18	16	1
Peterborough U	Tr	03.91	90-92	18	5	5
Northampton T	Barnet (N/C)	02.93	92	13	1	4
Wigan Ath	Tr	07.93	93-94	37	5	8

GAVIN Patrick (Paddy) Joseph
Drogheda, 6 June, 1929 IRB/LoI-2 (FB)

League Club	Source	Date Signed	Seasons Played	Apps	Subs	Gls
Doncaster Rov	Dundalk	06.53	53-59	147	-	5

GAWLER Ronald (Ron) Victor
Canterbury, 10 July, 1924 (WH)

League Club	Source	Date Signed	Seasons Played	Apps	Subs	Gls
Southend U	Canterbury C	06.49	49-50	8	-	1

GAY Daniel (Danny) Karl
Norwich, 5 August, 1982 (G)

League Club	Source	Date Signed	Seasons Played	Apps	Subs	Gls
Southend U	Norwich C (YT)	07.01	01-02	10	1	0

GAY Geoffrey (Geoff)
Romford, 4 February, 1957 (M)

League Club	Source	Date Signed	Seasons Played	Apps	Subs	Gls
Bolton W	App	01.75				
Exeter C	L	03.77	76	5	1	0
Southport	Tr	08.77	77	40	0	5
Wigan Ath	Tr	07.78	78	1	0	0

GAYLE Andrew (Andy) Keith
Manchester, 17 September, 1970 (W)

League Club	Source	Date Signed	Seasons Played	Apps	Subs	Gls
Oldham Ath	YT	07.89	88	0	1	0
Crewe Alex	Tr	02.90	89	0	1	0

GAYLE Brian Wilbert
Kingston, 6 March, 1965 (CD)

League Club	Source	Date Signed	Seasons Played	Apps	Subs	Gls
Wimbledon	App	10.84	84-87	76	7	3
Manchester C	Tr	07.88	88-89	55	0	3
Ipswich T	Tr	01.90	89-91	58	0	4
Sheffield U	Tr	09.91	91-95	115	2	9
Exeter C	Tr	08.96	96	10	0	0
Rotherham U	Tr	10.96	96	19	1	0
Bristol Rov	Tr	03.97	96-97	23	0	0
Shrewsbury T	Tr	12.97	97-98	66	0	1

GAYLE Howard Anthony
Liverpool, 18 May, 1958 Eu21-3 (W)

League Club	Source	Date Signed	Seasons Played	Apps	Subs	Gls
Liverpool	Jnrs	11.77	80	3	1	1
Fulham	L	01.80	79	14	0	0
Newcastle U	L	11.82	82	8	0	2
Birmingham C	Tr	01.83	82-83	45	1	9
Sunderland	Tr	08.84	84-85	39	9	4
Stoke C	Dallas (USA)	03.87	86	4	2	2
Blackburn Rov	Tr	07.87	87-91	97	24	29
Halifax T	Tr	08.92	92	2	3	0

GAYLE John
Bromsgrove, 30 July, 1964 (F)

League Club	Source	Date Signed	Seasons Played	Apps	Subs	Gls
Wimbledon	Burton A	03.89	88-90	17	3	2
Birmingham C	Tr	11.90	90-92	39	5	10
Walsall	L	08.93	93	4	0	1
Coventry C	Tr	09.93	93	3	0	0
Burnley	Tr	08.94	94	7	7	3
Stoke C	Tr	01.95	94-96	14	12	4
Gillingham	L	03.96	95	9	0	3
Northampton T	Tr	02.97	96-97	35	13	7
Scunthorpe U	Tr	07.98	98-99	38	11	4
Shrewsbury T	Tr	11.99	99-00	17	2	2
Torquay U	Tr	12.00	00	5	8	1

GAYLE Marcus Anthony
Hammersmith, 27 September, 1970 EYth/Ja-14 (F)

League Club	Source	Date Signed	Seasons Played	Apps	Subs	Gls
Brentford	YT	07.89	88-93	118	38	22
Wimbledon	Tr	03.94	93-00	198	38	37
Watford	Glasgow Rgrs	08.01	01-04	90	12	5
Brentford	Tr	03.05	04	4	2	0

GAYLE Mark Samuel Roye
Bromsgrove, 21 October, 1969 (G)

League Club	Source	Date Signed	Seasons Played	Apps	Subs	Gls
Leicester C	YT	07.88				
Blackpool	Tr	08.89				
Walsall	Worcester C	05.91	91-93	74	1	0
Crewe Alex	Tr	12.93	93-96	82	1	0
Chesterfield	L	10.97	97	5	0	0
Chesterfield	Rushden & Diamonds	08.99	99	29	1	0

GAYNOR James (Jimmy) Michael
Dublin, 22 August, 1928 LoI-1 (W)

League Club	Source	Date Signed	Seasons Played	Apps	Subs	Gls
Ipswich T	Shamrock Rov	03.52	51-52	47	-	3
Aldershot	Tr	09.53	53-57	165	-	39

GAYNOR Leonard (Len) Alfred
Ollerton, 22 September, 1925 (IF)

League Club	Source	Date Signed	Seasons Played	Apps	Subs	Gls
Hull C	Eastwood Colliery	04.48	50	2	-	0
Bournemouth	Tr	06.51	51-53	51	-	12
Southampton	Tr	03.54	53	12	-	1
Aldershot	Tr	02.55	54-56	62	-	9
Oldham Ath	Tr	07.57	57	5	-	0

GAYNOR Thomas (Tommy)
Limerick, 29 January, 1963 (F)

League Club	Source	Date Signed	Seasons Played	Apps	Subs	Gls
Doncaster Rov	Limerick C	12.86	86-87	28	5	7

League Club	Source	Date Signed	Seasons Played	Apps	Subs	Gls
Nottingham F	Tr	10.87	87-91	43	14	10
Newcastle U	L	11.90	90	4	0	1
Millwall	Tr	03.93	92	0	3	0

GAZZARD Gerald (Gerry)
Westbury, 15 March, 1925 (IF)

League Club	Source	Date Signed	Seasons Played	Apps	Subs	Gls
West Ham U	Penzance	05.49	49-53	119	-	29
Brentford	Tr	01.54	53	13	-	6

GEARD Leonard (Len)
Hammersmith, 12 February, 1934 (WH)

League Club	Source	Date Signed	Seasons Played	Apps	Subs	Gls
Fulham	Jnrs	05.51				
Brentford	Tr	03.53	54-55	4	-	0

GEARY Derek Peter
Dublin, 19 June, 1980 (FB)

League Club	Source	Date Signed	Seasons Played	Apps	Subs	Gls
Sheffield Wed	Cherry Orchard	11.97	00-03	95	9	0
Stockport Co	Tr	08.04	04	12	1	0
Sheffield U	Tr	10.04	04	15	4	1

GEBBIE Robert (Bert) Brown Robertson
Cambuslang, 18 November, 1934 (G)

League Club	Source	Date Signed	Seasons Played	Apps	Subs	Gls
Bradford PA	Queen of the South	07.60	60-63	112	-	0

GEDDES Andrew (Andy)
Craigbank, 6 September, 1922 Died 1958 (WH)

League Club	Source	Date Signed	Seasons Played	Apps	Subs	Gls
Bradford C	St Cuthbert's W	06.49	49-50	30	-	4
Mansfield T	Tr	08.51	51	11	-	2
Halifax T	Tr	07.52	52-54	50	-	4

GEDDES Gavin John
Brighton, 7 October, 1972 (W)

League Club	Source	Date Signed	Seasons Played	Apps	Subs	Gls
Brighton & Hove A	Wick	07.93	93	7	5	1

GEDDES James (Jim) George
Burntisland, 25 May, 1942 (WH)

League Club	Source	Date Signed	Seasons Played	Apps	Subs	Gls
Bradford PA	Third Lanark	08.65	65	1	0	0

GEDDES Paul
Paisley, 19 April, 1961 (CD)

League Club	Source	Date Signed	Seasons Played	Apps	Subs	Gls
Leicester C	Kilbirnie Ladeside	04.79				
Wimbledon	Hibernian	11.81	81	2	0	0

GEDDIS David
Carlisle, 12 March, 1958 EYth/EB (F)

League Club	Source	Date Signed	Seasons Played	Apps	Subs	Gls
Ipswich T	App	08.75	76-78	26	17	5
Luton T	L	02.77	76	9	4	4
Aston Villa	Tr	09.79	79-82	43	4	12
Luton T	L	12.82	82	4	0	0
Barnsley	Tr	09.83	83-84	45	0	24
Birmingham C	Tr	12.84	84-86	45	1	18
Brentford	L	11.86	86	4	0	0
Shrewsbury T	Tr	02.87	86-88	36	3	10
Swindon T	Tr	10.88	88	8	2	3
Darlington	Tr	03.90	90	2	11	0

GEDNEY Christopher (Chris)
Boston, 1 September, 1945 (IF)

League Club	Source	Date Signed	Seasons Played	Apps	Subs	Gls
Lincoln C (Am)	Holbeach U	05.62	62-65	9	0	1

GEE Alan
Chesterfield, 16 March, 1932 (W)

League Club	Source	Date Signed	Seasons Played	Apps	Subs	Gls
Rotherham U (Am)		08.52	52	2	-	0

GEE James (Jimmy) Percival
Plymouth, 6 June, 1932 (G)

League Club	Source	Date Signed	Seasons Played	Apps	Subs	Gls
Plymouth Arg (Am)	Launceston T	08.56	56	1	-	0

GEE Philip (Phil) John
Pelsall, 19 December, 1964 (F)

League Club	Source	Date Signed	Seasons Played	Apps	Subs	Gls
Derby Co	Gresley Rov	09.85	85-91	107	17	26
Leicester C	Tr	03.92	91-95	35	18	9
Plymouth Arg	L	01.95	94	6	0	0

GEIDMINTIS Anthony (Tony) Joseph
Stepney, 30 July, 1949 Died 1993 (CD)

League Club	Source	Date Signed	Seasons Played	Apps	Subs	Gls
Workington	App	08.66	64-75	323	5	37
Watford	Tr	07.76	76-77	48	1	0
Northampton T	Tr	02.78	77-78	63	0	1
Halifax T	Tr	07.79	79	10	2	0

GELDARD Albert
Bradford, 11 April, 1914 Died 1989 ESch/FLge-1/E-4 (W)

League Club	Source	Date Signed	Seasons Played	Apps	Subs	Gls
Bradford PA	Jnrs	04.30	29-32	34	-	6
Everton	Tr	11.32	32-37	167	-	31
Bolton W	Tr	06.38	38-46	29	-	1

GELSON Peter William John
Hammersmith, 18 October, 1941 (CD)

League Club	Source	Date Signed	Seasons Played	Apps	Subs	Gls
Brentford	Jnrs	03.60	61-74	468	3	17

GEMMELL Andrew (Andy)
Greenock, 27 July, 1945 (W)

League Club	Source	Date Signed	Seasons Played	Apps	Subs	Gls
Bradford C	Morton	01.67	66	3	0	0

GEMMELL Eric
Manchester, 7 April, 1921 (CF)

League Club	Source	Date Signed	Seasons Played	Apps	Subs	Gls
Manchester C	Manchester U (Am)	03.46				
Oldham Ath	Tr	06.47	47-53	195	-	109
Crewe Alex	Tr	02.54	53-54	14	-	5
Rochdale	Tr	09.54	54-55	65	-	32

GEMMELL James (Jimmy)
Sunderland, 17 November, 1911 Died 1992 (FB)

League Club	Source	Date Signed	Seasons Played	Apps	Subs	Gls
Bury	West Stanley	03.30	30-38	255	-	0
Southport	Tr	08.45	46	25	-	0

GEMMELL Matthew (Matt)
Glasgow, 10 March, 1931 (IF)

League Club	Source	Date Signed	Seasons Played	Apps	Subs	Gls
Portsmouth	Shawfield Jnrs	09.51	53-54	3	-	0
Swindon T	Tr	10.54	54	8	-	2

GEMMELL Thomas (Tommy)
Glasgow, 16 October, 1943 SLge-5/S-18 (FB)

League Club	Source	Date Signed	Seasons Played	Apps	Subs	Gls
Nottingham F	Glasgow Celtic	12.71	71-72	39	0	6

GEMMILL Archibald (Archie)
Paisley, 24 March, 1947 Su23-1/S-43 (M)

League Club	Source	Date Signed	Seasons Played	Apps	Subs	Gls
Preston NE	St Mirren	06.67	67-70	93	8	13
Derby Co	Tr	09.70	70-77	261	0	17
Nottingham F	Tr	09.77	77-78	56	3	4
Birmingham C	Tr	08.79	79-81	97	0	12
Wigan Ath	Jacksonville (USA)	09.82	82	11	0	0
Derby Co	Tr	11.82	82-83	63	0	8

GEMMILL Scot
Paisley, 2 January, 1971 Su21-4/SB-2/S-26 (M)

League Club	Source	Date Signed	Seasons Played	Apps	Subs	Gls
Nottingham F	YT	01.90	90-98	228	17	21
Everton	Tr	03.99	98-02	79	18	5
Preston NE	L	03.04	03	7	0	1
Leicester C	Tr	08.04	04	11	6	0

GENAUX Regis (Reggie) Herve
Charleroi, Belgium, 31 August, 1973 Belgium int (FB)

League Club	Source	Date Signed	Seasons Played	Apps	Subs	Gls
Coventry C	Standard Liege (Bel)	08.96	96	3	1	0

GENDALL Richard (Richie) Martin
Wrexham, 25 September, 1960 (M)

League Club	Source	Date Signed	Seasons Played	Apps	Subs	Gls
Chester	App	09.78	80	4	1	0

GENNOE Terence (Terry) William
Shrewsbury, 16 March, 1953 ESch (G)

League Club	Source	Date Signed	Seasons Played	Apps	Subs	Gls
Bury	Bricklayers Sports	06.73	72-73	3	0	0
Halifax T	Tr	05.75	75-77	78	0	0
Southampton	Tr	02.78	78-79	36	0	0
Crystal Palace	L	01.81	80	3	0	0
Blackburn Rov	Tr	08.81	81-90	289	0	0

GENOVESE Domenico
Peterborough, 2 February, 1961 (F)

League Club	Source	Date Signed	Seasons Played	Apps	Subs	Gls
Peterborough U	Cambridge C	03.88	87-88	8	8	1

GENTLE Justin David
Enfield, 6 June, 1974 (F)

League Club	Source	Date Signed	Seasons Played	Apps	Subs	Gls
Luton T	Boreham Wood	07.93				
Colchester U	L	03.94	93	0	2	0

GEORGE Frederick **Charles (Charlie)**
Islington, 10 October, 1950 Eu23-5/E-1 (F)

League Club	Source	Date Signed	Seasons Played	Apps	Subs	Gls
Arsenal	App	03.68	69-74	113	20	31
Derby Co	Tr	07.75	75-78	106	0	34
Southampton	Minnesota (USA)	12.78	78-80	44	0	11
Nottingham F	L	01.80	79	2	0	0
Bournemouth	Bulova (HK)	03.82	81	2	0	0
Derby Co	Tr	03.82	81	11	0	2

GEORGE Daniel (Danny) Stephen
Lincoln, 22 October, 1978 (CD)

League Club	Source	Date Signed	Seasons Played	Apps	Subs	Gls
Nottingham F	YT	10.95				
Doncaster Rov	Tr	01.98	97	16	2	1

GEORGE Finidi
Port Harcourt, Nigeria, 15 April, 1971 Nigeria int (F)

League Club	Source	Date Signed	Seasons Played	Apps	Subs	Gls
Ipswich T	Real Mallorca (Sp)	08.01	01-02	24	11	7

GEORGE Frank Richard
Stepney, 20 November, 1933 (G)

League Club	Source	Date Signed	Seasons Played	Apps	Subs	Gls
Leyton Orient	Carshalton Ath	07.54	56-62	119	-	0
Watford	Tr	07.63	64	10	-	0

GEORGE Liam Brendan
Luton, 2 February, 1979 IRYth/IRu21-4 (F)

League Club	Source	Date Signed	Seasons Played	Apps	Subs	Gls
Luton T	YT	01.97	97-01	81	21	20
Bury	Stevenage Borough	08.02	02	3	5	1

League Club	Source	Date Signed	Seasons Played	Apps	Subs	Gls
Boston U	Tr	02.03	02	1	2	0
York C	St Patrick's Ath	08.03	03	14	8	3

GEORGE Richard (Ricky) Stuart
Barnet, 28 June, 1946 (W)

League Club	Source	Date Signed	Seasons Played	Apps	Subs	Gls
Tottenham H	App	10.63				
Watford	Tr	08.64	64	4	-	0
Bournemouth	Tr	05.65	65	2	1	0
Oxford U	Tr	07.66	66	6	0	0

GEORGE Ronald (Ron) Anthony
Bristol, 14 August, 1922 Died 1989 (FB)

League Club	Source	Date Signed	Seasons Played	Apps	Subs	Gls
Crystal Palace	BAC	02.47	48-53	122	-	2
Colchester U	Tr	07.54	54	6	-	0

GEORGESON Roderick (Roddie) Bruce
Shubra, Egypt, 31 July, 1948 (CF)

League Club	Source	Date Signed	Seasons Played	Apps	Subs	Gls
Port Vale	Bo'ness U	01.66	65-66	26	1	6

GEORGIADES Georgios
Kavala, Greece, 8 March, 1972 Greece 2 (M)

League Club	Source	Date Signed	Seasons Played	Apps	Subs	Gls
Newcastle U	Panathinaikos (Gre)	08.98	98	7	3	0

GEORGIOU George Jordaris
St Pancras, 19 August, 1972 (F)

League Club	Source	Date Signed	Seasons Played	Apps	Subs	Gls
Fulham	Wembley	08.91	91	1	3	0

GERA Zoltan
Pecs, Hungary, 22 April, 1979 Hungary 30 (F)

League Club	Source	Date Signed	Seasons Played	Apps	Subs	Gls
West Bromwich A	Ferencvaros (Hun)	08.04	04	31	7	6

[GEREMI] N'JITAP FOTSO Geremi Sorele
Cameroon, 20 December, 1978 Cameroon 69 (M)

League Club	Source	Date Signed	Seasons Played	Apps	Subs	Gls
Middlesbrough (L)	Real Madrid	07.02	02	33	0	7
Chelsea	Real Madrid	08.03	03-04	25	13	1

GERHARDI Hugh
South Africa, 5 May, 1933 (IF)

League Club	Source	Date Signed	Seasons Played	Apps	Subs	Gls
Liverpool	Thistle (SA)	08.52	52	6	-	0

GERKEN Dean Jeffery
Southend-on-Sea, 22 May, 1985 (G)

League Club	Source	Date Signed	Seasons Played	Apps	Subs	Gls
Colchester U	Sch	07.04	03-04	14	0	0

GERMAIN Steven (Steve)
Cannes, France, 22 June, 1981 (F)

League Club	Source	Date Signed	Seasons Played	Apps	Subs	Gls
Colchester U	AS Cannes	03.99	98-99	2	7	0

GERMAINE Gary Paul
Birmingham, 2 August, 1976 Su21-1 (G)

League Club	Source	Date Signed	Seasons Played	Apps	Subs	Gls
West Bromwich A	YT	07.94				
Scunthorpe U	L	03.96	95	11	0	0
Shrewsbury T	L	01.98	97	1	0	0

GERMAN David
Sheffield, 16 October, 1973 (FB)

League Club	Source	Date Signed	Seasons Played	Apps	Subs	Gls
Halifax T	YT	07.92	90-92	30	9	2

GERNON Frederick (Irvin) Anthony John
Birmingham, 30 December, 1962 ESch/EYth/Eu21-1 (FB)

League Club	Source	Date Signed	Seasons Played	Apps	Subs	Gls
Ipswich T	App	01.80	81-86	76	0	0
Northampton T	L	11.86	86	9	0	0
Gillingham	Tr	03.87	86-87	33	2	1
Reading	Tr	09.88	88-89	21	4	0
Northampton T	Tr	10.89	89-91	47	1	1

GERRARD Anthony
Liverpool, 6 February, 1986 (CD)

League Club	Source	Date Signed	Seasons Played	Apps	Subs	Gls
Everton	Sch	07.04				
Walsall	L	03.05	04	8	0	0

GERRARD Paul William
Heywood, 22 January, 1973 Eu21-18 (G)

League Club	Source	Date Signed	Seasons Played	Apps	Subs	Gls
Oldham Ath	YT	11.91	92-95	118	1	0
Everton	Tr	07.96	96-02	89	1	0
Oxford U	L	12.98	98	16	0	0
Ipswich T	L	11.02	02	5	0	0
Sheffield U	L	08.03	03	16	0	0
Nottingham F	Tr	03.04	03-04	50	0	0

GERRARD Steven George
Whiston, 30 May, 1980 EYth/Eu21-4/E-34 (M)

League Club	Source	Date Signed	Seasons Played	Apps	Subs	Gls
Liverpool	YT	02.98	98-04	179	21	27

GERRIE Sydney (Syd)
Aberdeen, 14 June, 1927 (CF)

League Club	Source	Date Signed	Seasons Played	Apps	Subs	Gls
Hull C	Dundee	11.50	50-56	146	-	59

GERULA Stanislaw (Stan) Eugeniusz
Dzikow, Poland, 21 February, 1914 Died 1979 Poland Amat (G)

League Club	Source	Date Signed	Seasons Played	Apps	Subs	Gls
Leyton Orient (Am)	Carpathians (Pol)	05.48	48-49	30	-	0

GHAZGHAZI Sufyan Abdel-Ali Benlofti
Honiton, 24 August, 1977 ESch/EYth (F)

League Club	Source	Date Signed	Seasons Played	Apps	Subs	Gls
Exeter C	YT	07.96	96-97	2	13	0

GHENT Matthew Ian
Burton-on-Trent, 5 October, 1980 ESch/EYth (G)

League Club	Source	Date Signed	Seasons Played	Apps	Subs	Gls
Aston Villa	YT	10.97				
Lincoln C	Tr	12.00	00	0	1	0
Barnsley	Forest Green Rov	08.01	01-02	8	0	0

GHRAYIB Naguyan
Nazareth, Israel, 30 January, 1974 Israel 18 (FB)

League Club	Source	Date Signed	Seasons Played	Apps	Subs	Gls
Aston Villa	Hapoel Haifa (Isr)	08.99	99	1	4	0

GIALLANZA Gaetano
Dornach, Switzerland, 6 June, 1974 (F)

League Club	Source	Date Signed	Seasons Played	Apps	Subs	Gls
Bolton W (L)	Nantes (Fr)	03.98	97	0	3	0
Norwich C	Nantes (Fr)	03.00	99-00	7	7	2

GIAMATTEI Aaron Pietro
Reading, 11 October, 1973 (M)

League Club	Source	Date Signed	Seasons Played	Apps	Subs	Gls
Reading	YT	07.92	91	0	2	0

GIANNAKOPOULOS Stylianos (Stelios)
Athens, Greece, 12 July, 1974 Greece 54 (M)

League Club	Source	Date Signed	Seasons Played	Apps	Subs	Gls
Bolton W	Olympiakos (Gre)	07.03	03-04	45	20	9

GIBB Alistair (Ally) Stuart
Salisbury, 17 February, 1976 (FB)

League Club	Source	Date Signed	Seasons Played	Apps	Subs	Gls
Norwich C	YT	07.94				
Northampton T	L	09.95	95	9	0	1
Northampton T	Tr	02.96	95-99	51	71	3
Stockport Co	Tr	02.00	99-03	157	8	1
Bristol Rov	Tr	03.04	03-04	24	7	1

GIBB James Barry
Workington, 21 May, 1940 (WH)

League Club	Source	Date Signed	Seasons Played	Apps	Subs	Gls
Workington	Jnrs	07.60	59-60	6	-	0

GIBB Dean Alan
Newcastle, 26 October, 1966 (M)

League Club	Source	Date Signed	Seasons Played	Apps	Subs	Gls
Hartlepool U	Brandon U	07.86	86-87	32	16	3

GIBB Thomas (Tommy)
Bathgate, 13 December, 1944 Su23-1 (M)

League Club	Source	Date Signed	Seasons Played	Apps	Subs	Gls
Newcastle U	Partick Th	08.68	68-74	190	9	12
Sunderland	Tr	06.75	75-76	7	3	1
Hartlepool U	Tr	07.77	77	40	0	4

GIBBENS Kevin
Southampton, 4 November, 1979 (M)

League Club	Source	Date Signed	Seasons Played	Apps	Subs	Gls
Southampton	YT	01.98	97-00	5	4	0
Stockport Co	L	09.99	99	1	1	0

GIBBINS Edward (Eddie)
Shoreditch, 24 March, 1926 (CD)

League Club	Source	Date Signed	Seasons Played	Apps	Subs	Gls
Tottenham H	Finchley	09.46	52	1	-	0

GIBBINS Roger Graeme
Enfield, 6 September, 1955 ESch (M)

League Club	Source	Date Signed	Seasons Played	Apps	Subs	Gls
Tottenham H	App	12.72				
Oxford U	Tr	08.75	75	16	3	2
Norwich C	Tr	06.76	76-77	47	1	12
Cambridge U	New England (USA)	09.79	79-81	97	3	12
Cardiff C	Tr	08.82	82-85	135	4	18
Swansea C	Tr	10.85	85	35	0	6
Newport Co	Tr	08.86	86-87	79	0	8
Torquay U	Tr	03.88	87-88	32	1	5
Cardiff C	Newport Co	03.89	88-92	132	10	7

GIBBON Arthur Thomas
Greatham, 24 May, 1937 Died 1994 (FB)

League Club	Source	Date Signed	Seasons Played	Apps	Subs	Gls
Hartlepools U		09.58	58	13	-	0

GIBBON Malcolm
North Shields, 24 October, 1950 (W)

League Club	Source	Date Signed	Seasons Played	Apps	Subs	Gls
Port Vale	App	06.66	66-67	4	1	0

GIBBONS Albert (Jackie) Henry
Fulham, 10 April, 1914 EAmat/EWar-1 (CF)

League Club	Source	Date Signed	Seasons Played	Apps	Subs	Gls
Tottenham H (Am)	Kingstonian	07.37	37	27	-	13
Brentford (Am)	Tr	08.38	38	11	-	1
Bradford PA	Tottenham H (Am)	05.46	46	42	-	21
Brentford	Tr	08.47	47-48	56	-	16

GIBBONS David
Belfast, 4 November, 1952 (FB)

League Club	Source	Date Signed	Seasons Played	Apps	Subs	Gls
Manchester C	App	08.70				
Stockport Co	L	02.72	71	1	0	0

League Club	Source	Date Signed	Seasons Played	Apps	Subs	Gls

GIBBONS Ian Kenneth
Stoke-on-Trent, 8 February, 1970 (W)

Stoke C	YT	●	87	0	1	0

GIBBONS John (Johnny) Ronald
Charlton, 8 April, 1925 (CF)

Queens Park Rgrs	Dartford	12.47	48	8	-	2
Ipswich T	Tr	05.49	49	11	-	3

GIBBONS Leonard (Len)
Wirral, 22 November, 1930 (FB)

Wolverhampton W	Jnrs	02.48	51-53	25	-	0

GIBBS Alan Martin
Orpington, 7 February, 1934 (IF)

Cardiff C		10.54				
Swindon T	Tr	05.56	56	16	-	5

GIBBS Brian Richard
Gillingham, Dorset, 6 October, 1936 (F)

Bournemouth	Gosport Borough	10.57	57-62	58	-	15
Gillingham	Tr	10.62	62-68	259	0	101
Colchester U	Tr	09.68	68-71	153	3	38

GIBBS Derek William
Fulham, 22 December, 1934 (IF)

Chelsea	Jnrs	04.55	56-60	23	-	5
Leyton Orient	Tr	11.60	60-62	33	-	4
Queens Park Rgrs	Tr	08.63	63-64	27	-	0

GIBBS Nigel James
St Albans, 20 November, 1965 EYth/Eu21-5 (FB)

Watford	App	11.83	83-01	385	23	5

GIBBS Paul Derek
Gorleston, 26 October, 1972 (FB)

Colchester U	Diss T	03.95	94-96	39	14	3
Torquay U	Tr	07.97	97	40	1	7
Plymouth Arg	Tr	07.98	98-99	30	4	3
Brentford	Tr	07.00	00-01	49	5	3
Barnsley	Tr	03.02	01-03	27	6	1

GIBBS Peter Leslie
Chingola, Zimbabwe, 24 August, 1956 (G)

Watford	Tring T	07.75	75-76	4	0	0

GIBLIN Edward **John**
Stoke-on-Trent, 29 June, 1923 (WH)

Stoke C	Tunstall BC	04.43	47	1	-	0

GIBSON Aidan Michael
Newcastle-under-Lyme, 17 May, 1963 (M)

Derby Co	App	05.81	80-81	0	2	0
Exeter C	Tr	07.82	82	17	1	1

GIBSON Alexander (Alex) Jonathan
Plymouth, 12 August, 1982 (FB)

Port Vale	Stoke C (YT)	07.01	01	1	0	0

GIBSON Alexander (Alex) Pollock Stitt
Kirkconnel, 28 November, 1939 Died 2003 (CD)

Notts Co	Auchinleck Talbot	04.59	59-68	344	3	10

GIBSON Alexander (Alex) Rose
Glasgow, 25 January, 1925 (FB)

Hull C	Clyde	03.50	49-50	21	-	0

GIBSON Alfred (Alf)
Castleford, 9 September, 1919 Died 1988 (CD)

Rotherham U		10.45	46-53	152	-	0

GIBSON Archibald (Archie) Boyle
Dailly, 30 December, 1933 (WH)

Leeds U	Coylton Juv	05.51	54-59	169	-	5
Scunthorpe U	Tr	07.60	60-63	138	-	5

GIBSON Brian
Huddersfield, 22 February, 1928 (FB)

Huddersfield T	Paddock Ath	05.51	51-60	157	-	1

GIBSON Charles
Dumbarton, 12 June, 1961 (M)

Shrewsbury T	St Anthony's	03.81	81	2	4	0

GIBSON Colin Hayward
Normanby, 16 September, 1923 Died 1992 EB/FLge-1 (W)

Cardiff C	Penarth Pontoons	04.44	46-47	71	-	16
Newcastle U	Tr	07.48	48	23	-	5
Aston Villa	Tr	02.49	48-55	158	-	24
Lincoln C	Tr	01.56	55-56	36	-	12

GIBSON Colin John
Bridport, 6 April, 1960 ESch/Eu21-1/EB (FB)

Aston Villa	App	04.78	78-85	181	4	10
Manchester U	Tr	11.85	85-89	74	5	9
Port Vale	L	09.90	90	5	1	2
Leicester C	Tr	12.90	90-93	50	9	4
Blackpool	Tr	08.94	94	1	1	0
Walsall	Tr	09.94	94	31	2	0

GIBSON David
Seaham, 14 February, 1958 (M)

Hull C	App	12.75	75-77	19	5	0
Scunthorpe U	Tr	07.78	78-79	16	6	1

GIBSON David (Dave) James
Runcorn, 18 March, 1931 (W)

Everton	Jnrs	08.50	50-51	3	-	0
Swindon T	Tr	11.54	54-56	70	-	6

GIBSON David Wedderburn
Winchburgh, 23 September, 1938 S-7 (M)

Leicester C	Hibernian	01.62	61-69	274	6	41
Aston Villa	Tr	09.70	70-71	16	3	1
Exeter C	Tr	01.72	71-73	69	2	3

GIBSON Thomas Richard **Donald (Don)**
Manchester, 12 May, 1929 (WH)

Manchester U	Jnrs	08.47	50-54	108	-	0
Sheffield Wed	Tr	06.55	55-59	80	-	2
Leyton Orient	Tr	06.60	60	8	-	0

GIBSON Frank Alec
Croxley Green, 7 June, 1914 (W)

Watford (Am)	Rickmansworth	05.46	46	1	-	0

GIBSON Henry (Harry)
Newcastle, 17 April, 1930 Died 1993 (CD)

Fulham	Spennymoor U	11.52	54	1	-	0
Aldershot	King's Lynn	08.56	56	3	-	0

GIBSON Ian Stewart
Newton Stewart, 30 March, 1943 SSch/Su23-2 (M)

Accrington St (Am)	Jnrs	07.58	58	9	-	3
Bradford PA	Tr	04.60	59-61	88	-	18
Middlesbrough	Tr	03.62	61-65	168	0	44
Coventry C	Tr	07.66	66-69	90	3	13
Cardiff C	Tr	07.70	70-72	89	1	11
Bournemouth	Tr	10.72	72-73	17	3	0

GIBSON James (Jimmy)
Belfast, 4 September, 1940 (WH)

Newcastle U	Linfield	01.59	58-60	2	-	1
Luton T	Cambridge U	02.65	64-65	31	1	0

GIBSON Joseph (Joe)
Banknock, 20 March, 1926 (IF)

Ipswich T	Polkemmet Jnrs	09.47	48	1	-	0

GIBSON Michael (Mike) James
Derby, 15 July, 1939 EYth (G)

Shrewsbury T	Nuneaton Borough	03.60	60-62	76	-	0
Bristol C	Tr	04.63	62-71	331	0	0
Gillingham	Tr	07.72	72-73	80	0	0

GIBSON Neil David
St Asaph, 10 October, 1979 Wu21-3 (M)

Tranmere Rov	YT	11.97	98	0	1	0

GIBSON Paul Richard
Sheffield, 1 November, 1976 (G)

Manchester U	YT	07.95				
Mansfield T	L	10.97	97	13	0	0
Hull C	L	11.98	98	4	0	0
Notts Co	Tr	03.99	98-00	11	0	0
Rochdale	L	02.00	99	5	0	0

GIBSON Reginald (Reg)
Tideswell, 15 May, 1919 Died 1991 (CD)

Manchester U		09.38				
Plymouth Arg	Tr	02.46	46	6	-	0
Exeter C	Tr	06.47	47-48	40	-	0

GIBSON Robert (Bob)
Washington, 29 December, 1916 Died 1995 (IF)

Southend U		06.45	46	2	-	0

GIBSON Robert (Bob) Henry
Ashington, 5 August, 1927 Died 1989 (CF)

Hull C	Aberdeen	10.49	49	12	-	5
Lincoln C	Ashington	05.51	51-54	43	-	20
Gateshead	Peterborough U	03.57	56-58	49	-	22

League Club	Source	Date Signed	Seasons Played	Career Record Apps	Subs	Gls
GIBSON Robin John						
Crewe, 15 November, 1979						(F)
Wrexham	YT	07.98	98-01	49	28	3
GIBSON Simon John						
Nottingham, 10 December, 1964						(CD)
Chelsea	App	12.82				
Swindon T	Tr	11.83	83-84	29	2	3
Preston NE	Tr	12.84	84-85	42	0	5
Rochdale	Tr	08.86	86	3	2	0
GIBSON John Stephen (Steve)						
Huddersfield, 2 May, 1949						(FB)
Bradford PA	Huddersfield T (Am)	12.67	67-68	28	4	0
GIBSON Terence (Terry) Bradley						
Walthamstow, 23 December, 1962 ESch/EYth						(F)
Tottenham H	App	01.80	79-82	16	2	4
Coventry C	Tr	08.83	83-85	97	1	43
Manchester U	Tr	01.86	85-86	14	9	1
Wimbledon	Tr	08.87	87-92	80	6	22
Swindon T	L	03.92	91	8	1	1
Peterborough U	Tr	12.93	93	1	0	0
Barnet	Tr	02.94	93-94	24	8	5
GIBSON William (Billy)						
Lanark, 24 June, 1959						(FB)
Leicester C	Easthouses BC	07.79	80-81	28	0	0
GIBSON William (Bill) James McNab						
Glasgow, 17 September, 1926 Died 1995						(FB)
Brentford	Arsenal (Am)	01.47				
Tranmere Rov	Tr	06.51	51-53	72	-	1
GIDDINGS Stuart James						
Coventry, 27 March, 1986 EYth						(FB)
Coventry C	Sch	06.04	03-04	11	2	0
GIDMAN John						
Liverpool, 10 January, 1954 EYth/Eu23-4/E-1						(FB)
Aston Villa	Liverpool (App)	08.71	72-79	196	1	9
Everton	Tr	10.79	79-80	64	0	2
Manchester U	Tr	08.81	81-85	94	1	4
Manchester C	Tr	10.86	86-87	52	1	1
Stoke C	Tr	08.88	88	7	3	0
Darlington	Tr	02.89	88	13	0	1
GIER Robert (Rob) James						
Bracknell, 6 January, 1980						(CD)
Wimbledon	YT	05.99	00-03	67	4	0
Rushden & Diamonds	Tr	07.04	04	30	2	2
GIGGS Ryan Joseph						
Cardiff, 29 November, 1973 ESch/WYth/Wu21-1/W-51						(W)
Manchester U	YT	12.90	90-04	396	51	91
GIJSBRECHTS David (Davy)						
Heusden, Belgium, 20 September, 1972						(CD)
Sheffield U	KSC Lokeren (Bel)	08.99	99	9	8	0
GILBERG Harold (Harry)						
Tottenham, 27 June, 1923 Died 1994						(IF)
Tottenham H	Jnrs	09.44	46-47	2	-	0
Queens Park Rgrs	Tr	08.51	51-52	66	-	12
Brighton & Hove A	Tr	12.52	52-55	67	-	3
GILBERT Carl Graham						
Folkestone, 20 March, 1948						(F)
Gillingham	Jnrs	10.65	67-69	28	2	11
Bristol Rov	Tr	12.69	69-70	39	5	15
Rotherham U	Tr	03.71	70-73	78	16	37
GILBERT David George						
Smethwick, 5 August, 1940						(W)
Chesterfield	Redditch U	05.60	60	22	-	2
GILBERT David James						
Lincoln, 22 June, 1963						(M)
Lincoln C	App	06.81	80-81	15	15	1
Scunthorpe U	Tr	08.82	82	1	0	0
Northampton T	Boston U	06.86	86-88	120	0	21
Grimsby T	Tr	03.89	88-94	259	0	41
West Bromwich A	Tr	08.95	95-97	46	16	6
York C	L	03.97	96	9	0	1
Grimsby T	L	08.97	97	5	0	0
GILBERT Kenneth (Kenny) Robert						
Aberdeen, 8 March, 1975 SSch/SYth						(M)
Hull C	Aberdeen	01.96	95-96	21	11	1
GILBERT Noel Albert						
North Walsham, 25 December, 1931						(W)
Norwich C	North Walsham	08.55	55	1	-	0

League Club	Source	Date Signed	Seasons Played	Career Record Apps	Subs	Gls
GILBERT Peter						
Newcastle, 31 July, 1983 Wu21-7						(FB)
Birmingham C	Sch	07.02				
Plymouth Arg	Tr	07.03	03-04	78	0	1
GILBERT Philip (Phil) Leonard						
Sandwich, 11 September, 1944						(IF)
Brighton & Hove A	Ramsgate Ath	01.62	61-63	6	-	3
GILBERT Timothy (Tim) Hew						
South Shields, 28 August, 1958 Died 1995						(FB)
Sunderland	App	08.76	76-79	34	2	3
Cardiff C	Tr	02.81	80-81	33	0	1
Darlington	Tr	08.82	82-83	62	3	3
GILBERT William (Billy) Albert						
Lewisham, 10 November, 1959 ESch/EYth/Eu21-11						(CD)
Crystal Palace	App	12.76	77-83	235	2	3
Portsmouth	Tr	06.84	84-88	133	7	0
Colchester U		10.89	89	26	1	0
Maidstone U	Tr	10.90	90	2	2	0
GILBERT William (Billy) Arthur						
Newcastle, 7 November, 1925 Died 1998						(G)
Coventry C	Murton CW	09.48	51-52	14	-	0
Stockport Co	Snowdown CW	07.54	54	33	-	0
[GILBERTO] SILVA Gilberto						
Lagoa da Prata, Brazil, 7 October, 1976 Brazil 31						(M)
Arsenal	Atletico Mineiro (Br)	08.02	02-04	74	6	4
GILCHRIST Alexander (Alex)						
Holytown, 28 September, 1923 Died 1989						(W)
Cardiff C		05.48	48	1	-	0
GILCHRIST John Skidmore						
Wishaw, 5 September, 1939 Died 1991 SSch						(FB)
Millwall	Airdrie	03.61	60-68	279	0	10
Fulham	Tr	07.69	69	20	3	1
Colchester U	Tr	07.70	70-71	41	0	2
GILCHRIST Paul Anthony						
Dartford, 5 January, 1951						(F)
Charlton Ath	App	03.68	69	5	2	0
Doncaster Rov	Tr	07.71	71	22	0	8
Southampton	Tr	03.72	71-76	96	11	17
Portsmouth	Tr	03.77	76-77	38	1	3
Swindon T	Tr	08.78	78-79	10	7	6
Hereford U	Tr	03.80	79	11	0	1
GILCHRIST Philip (Phil) Alexander						
Stockton, 25 August, 1973						(CD)
Nottingham F	YT	12.90				
Middlesbrough	Tr	01.92				
Hartlepool U	Tr	11.92	92-94	77	5	0
Oxford U	Tr	02.95	94-99	173	4	10
Leicester C	Tr	08.99	99-00	23	16	1
West Bromwich A	Tr	03.01	00-03	89	1	0
Rotherham U	Tr	03.04	03-04	31	3	1
GILCHRIST Robert (Bob) Cook						
Bellshill, 17 August, 1932						(FB)
Aldershot	Dunfermline Ath	06.52	52-56	47	-	0
GILDER Carlton (Carl) Eric						
Chelmsford, 25 July, 1957						(F)
Cambridge U	Jnrs	01.75	74-75	0	2	0
GILES Albert Edgar						
Swansea, 4 May, 1924						(WH)
Bristol Rov	Jnrs	05.41	46	1	-	0
GILES Christopher (Chris)						
Milborne Port, 16 April, 1982						(F)
Yeovil T	Sherborne	06.00	03	0	1	0
GILES Christopher (Chris) Joseph						
Dublin, 17 July, 1928 IR-1						(W)
Doncaster Rov	Drumcondra	06.50	50-51	27	-	4
GILES David Charles						
Cardiff, 21 September, 1956 WSch/Wu21-4/W-12						(W)
Cardiff C	App	09.74	74-78	51	8	3
Wrexham	Tr	12.78	78-79	38	0	3
Swansea C	Tr	11.79	79-81	49	5	13
Orient	L	11.81	81	3	0	2
Crystal Palace	Tr	03.82	81-83	83	5	6
Birmingham C	Tr	08.84				
Newport Co	Tr	10.84	84	28	4	1
Cardiff C	Tr	09.85	85-86	50	0	0

GILES James (Jimmy) Archer
Kidlington, 21 April, 1946 (CD)

League Club	Source	Date Signed	Seasons Played	Apps	Subs	Gls
Swindon T	Kidlington	03.65	65-67	12	1	0
Aldershot	Tr	10.68	68-70	81	1	3
Exeter C	Tr	03.71	70-74	183	0	8
Charlton Ath	Tr	06.75	75-77	92	1	6
Exeter C	Tr	12.77	77-80	130	0	5

GILES John Edgar
Bristol, 7 November, 1947 (M)

League Club	Source	Date Signed	Seasons Played	Apps	Subs	Gls
Bristol C	App	06.65	66	3	0	1
Bradford PA	L	03.68	67	9	0	0
Exeter C	Tr	05.69	69-71	55	5	2

GILES Michael John (Johnny)
Dublin 6 January, 1940 IR-60 (M)

League Club	Source	Date Signed	Seasons Played	Apps	Subs	Gls
Manchester U	Home Farm	11.57	59-62	99	-	10
Leeds U	Tr	08.63	63-74	380	3	88
West Bromwich A	Tr	06.75	75-76	74	1	3

GILES Martin William
Shrewsbury, 1 January, 1979 (FB)

League Club	Source	Date Signed	Seasons Played	Apps	Subs	Gls
Chester C	YT	07.97	97	8	2	0

GILES Martyn
Cardiff, 10 April, 1983 WYth (CD)

League Club	Source	Date Signed	Seasons Played	Apps	Subs	Gls
Cardiff C	YT	03.01	00	1	4	0

GILES Paul Anthony
Cardiff, 21 February, 1961 Wu21-3 (W)

League Club	Source	Date Signed	Seasons Played	Apps	Subs	Gls
Cardiff C	Jnrs	06.79	80-82	17	7	1
Exeter C	L	03.82	81	9	0	1
Newport Co	SVV Dordrecht (Holl)	12.84	84	0	1	0
Newport Co	Merthyr Tydfil	03.87	86-87	28	1	2

GILES Philip (Phil) Richard
Walsall, 8 October, 1929 Died 1999 EYth (W)

League Club	Source	Date Signed	Seasons Played	Apps	Subs	Gls
Walsall	Jnrs	05.48	48-52	68	-	14

GILES Terence (Terry)
Halifax, 25 March, 1943 (W)

League Club	Source	Date Signed	Seasons Played	Apps	Subs	Gls
Halifax T (Am)		09.61	61-62	3	-	1

GILFILLAN Robert (Bobby)
Dunfermline, 14 March, 1926 (IF)

League Club	Source	Date Signed	Seasons Played	Apps	Subs	Gls
Blackpool	Jeanfield Swifts	07.47				
Rochdale	Cowdenbeath	06.51	51-53	62	-	11

GILFILLAN Robert (Bob) Inglis
Cowdenbeath, 29 June, 1938 (M)

League Club	Source	Date Signed	Seasons Played	Apps	Subs	Gls
Newcastle U	Cowdenbeath	10.59	59-60	7	-	2
Southend U	Raith Rov	06.63	63-65	65	1	33
Doncaster Rov	Tr	11.65	65-70	178	7	34

GILKES Michael Earl Glenis McDonald
Hackney, 20 July, 1965 Barbados 6 (W)

League Club	Source	Date Signed	Seasons Played	Apps	Subs	Gls
Reading	Leicester C (Jnrs)	07.84	84-96	348	45	43
Chelsea	L	01.92	91	0	1	0
Southampton	L	03.92	91	4	2	0
Wolverhampton W	Tr	03.97	96-98	33	5	1
Millwall	Tr	07.99	99-00	28	4	2

GILKS Matthew (Matty)
Oldham, 4 June, 1982 (G)

League Club	Source	Date Signed	Seasons Played	Apps	Subs	Gls
Rochdale	YT	07.01	00-04	82	2	0

GILL Anthony (Tony) Dean
Bradford, 6 March, 1968 (FB)

League Club	Source	Date Signed	Seasons Played	Apps	Subs	Gls
Manchester U	App	03.86	86-88	5	5	1

GILL Colin John Peter
Swindon, 20 January, 1933 (G)

League Club	Source	Date Signed	Seasons Played	Apps	Subs	Gls
Swindon T		10.55	55	1	-	0

GILL Eric Norman
St Pancras, 3 November, 1930 (G)

League Club	Source	Date Signed	Seasons Played	Apps	Subs	Gls
Charlton Ath	Tonbridge	04.48	51	1	-	0
Brighton & Hove A	Tr	06.52	52-59	280	-	0

GILL Frank
Manchester, 5 December, 1948 (W)

League Club	Source	Date Signed	Seasons Played	Apps	Subs	Gls
Manchester U	App	12.65				
Tranmere Rov	Tr	07.68	68-70	69	4	8

GILL Gary
Middlesbrough, 28 November, 1964 (M)

League Club	Source	Date Signed	Seasons Played	Apps	Subs	Gls
Middlesbrough	App	11.82	83-89	69	8	2
Hull C	L	12.83	83	0	1	0
Darlington	Tr	12.89	90-91	55	1	9
Cardiff C	Tr	03.92	91	3	3	1

GILL Jeremy (Jerry) Morley
Clevedon, 8 September, 1970 ESemiPro-1 (FB)

League Club	Source	Date Signed	Seasons Played	Apps	Subs	Gls
Leyton Orient	Trowbridge T	12.88				
Birmingham C	Yeovil T	07.97	97-01	43	17	0
Northampton T	Tr	08.02	02	41	0	0
Cheltenham T	Tr	02.04	03-04	48	3	0

GILL John (Johnny) Barry Anthony
Wednesbury, 3 February, 1941 (CD)

League Club	Source	Date Signed	Seasons Played	Apps	Subs	Gls
Nottingham F	Jnrs	03.58				
Mansfield T	Tr	07.61	61-65	138	1	0
Hartlepools U	Tr	02.66	65-70	201	3	1

GILL Joseph (Joe)
Sunderland, 10 November, 1945 (G)

League Club	Source	Date Signed	Seasons Played	Apps	Subs	Gls
Hartlepool (Am)	Ashington	01.69	68	4	0	0

GILL Kenneth (Kenny)
Swindon, 5 November, 1955 (W)

League Club	Source	Date Signed	Seasons Played	Apps	Subs	Gls
Newport Co	Forest Green Rov	09.85	85	13	6	1

GILL Matthew James
Cambridge, 8 November, 1980 (M)

League Club	Source	Date Signed	Seasons Played	Apps	Subs	Gls
Peterborough U	YT	03.98	97-03	121	30	5
Notts Co	Tr	06.04	04	38	5	0

GILL Mervyn John
Exeter, 13 April, 1931 (G)

League Club	Source	Date Signed	Seasons Played	Apps	Subs	Gls
Portsmouth (Am)	Bideford	08.53	53	6	-	0
Southampton	Woking	04.56	55	1	-	0
Torquay U	Tr	09.56	56-61	157	-	0

GILL Raymond (Ray)
Manchester, 8 December, 1924 Died 2001 (FB)

League Club	Source	Date Signed	Seasons Played	Apps	Subs	Gls
Manchester C		09.47	48-49	8	-	0
Chester	Tr	06.51	51-61	406	-	3

GILL Robert
Nottingham, 10 February, 1982 (F)

League Club	Source	Date Signed	Seasons Played	Apps	Subs	Gls
Doncaster Rov	Nottingham F (YT)	08.00	03	0	1	0

GILL Wayne John
Chorley, 28 November, 1975 (M)

League Club	Source	Date Signed	Seasons Played	Apps	Subs	Gls
Blackburn Rov	YT	07.94				
Blackpool	Tr	03.00	99	12	0	7
Tranmere Rov	Tr	07.00	00	7	9	2
Oldham Ath	Tr	10.01	01	3	0	0

GILLARD Ian Terry
Kensington, 9 October, 1950 Eu23-5/E-3 (FB)

League Club	Source	Date Signed	Seasons Played	Apps	Subs	Gls
Queens Park Rgrs	App	10.68	68-81	403	5	9
Aldershot	Tr	07.82	82-85	83	0	2

GILLARD Kenneth (Ken) Joseph
Dublin, 30 April, 1972 IRu21-1 (FB)

League Club	Source	Date Signed	Seasons Played	Apps	Subs	Gls
Luton T	YT	05.89				
Northampton T	Tr	03.93	92-93	22	1	0

GILLESPIE Gary Thompson
Bonnybridge, 5 July, 1960 Su21-8/S13 (CD)

League Club	Source	Date Signed	Seasons Played	Apps	Subs	Gls
Coventry C	Falkirk	03.78	78-82	171	1	6
Liverpool	Tr	07.83	84-90	152	4	14
Coventry C	Glasgow Celtic	08.94	94	2	1	0

GILLESPIE Ian Colin
Plymouth, 6 May, 1913 Died 1988 (IF)

League Club	Source	Date Signed	Seasons Played	Apps	Subs	Gls
Crystal Palace	Harwich & Parkeston	02.37	36-38	21	-	4
Ipswich T	Tr	04.46	46	6	-	1

GILLESPIE Keith Robert
Larne, 18 February, 1975 NISch/NIYth/NIu21-1/NI-62 (W)

League Club	Source	Date Signed	Seasons Played	Apps	Subs	Gls
Manchester U	YT	02.93	94	3	6	1
Wigan Ath	L	09.93	93	8	0	4
Newcastle U	Tr	01.95	94-98	94	19	11
Blackburn Rov	Tr	12.98	98-02	67	46	5
Wigan Ath	L	12.00	00	4	1	0
Leicester C	Tr	07.03	03-04	26	16	2

GILLESPIE Norman (Norrie)
Edinburgh, 20 April, 1940 (IF)

League Club	Source	Date Signed	Seasons Played	Apps	Subs	Gls
Wrexham	Falkirk	12.63	63	3	-	0

GILLESPIE Patrick (Pat)
Bellshill, 22 September, 1922 (G)

League Club	Source	Date Signed	Seasons Played	Apps	Subs	Gls
Watford	Partick Th	07.45	46	6	-	0
Northampton T	Tr	08.47	47	1	-	0
Doncaster Rov	Tr	11.47	47-48	8	-	1

GILLESPIE Steven
Liverpool, 4 June, 1984 (F)

League Club	Source	Date Signed	Seasons Played	Apps	Subs	Gls
Bristol C	Liverpool (Sch)	08.04	04	1	7	0
Cheltenham T	L	01.05	04	10	2	5

GILLETT David (Dave) John
Edinburgh, 2 April, 1951 (CD)

League Club	Source	Date Signed	Seasons Played	Apps	Subs	Gls
Crewe Alex	Hibernian	08.72	72-74	64	5	2

GILLIAM Reginald (Reg) Charles
Farnham, 19 February, 1931 (G)

League Club	Source	Date Signed	Seasons Played	Apps	Subs	Gls
Aldershot	Farnham T	02.56	56	1	-	0

GILLIBRAND Ian Victor
Blackburn, 24 November, 1948 (CD)

League Club	Source	Date Signed	Seasons Played	Apps	Subs	Gls
Arsenal	App	12.65				
Wigan Ath	Tr	(N/L)	78	7	0	0

GILLIES Donald (Don) George
Glencoe, 20 June, 1951 Su23-1 (FB)

League Club	Source	Date Signed	Seasons Played	Apps	Subs	Gls
Bristol C	Morton	03.73	72-79	183	17	26
Bristol Rov	Tr	06.80	80-81	56	3	0

GILLIES John Crawford
Glasgow, 22 October, 1918 (W)

League Club	Source	Date Signed	Seasons Played	Apps	Subs	Gls
Brentford	St Mirren	05.46	46	5	-	0

GILLIES Matthew (Matt) Muirhead
Loganlea, 12 August, 1921 Died 1998 (CD)

League Club	Source	Date Signed	Seasons Played	Apps	Subs	Gls
Bolton W	RAF Weeton	10.42	46-51	145	-	1
Leicester C	Tr	01.52	51-54	103	-	0

GILLIGAN Augustus (Gus) Anthony
Abingdon, 19 August, 1959 (F)

League Club	Source	Date Signed	Seasons Played	Apps	Subs	Gls
Swindon T	App	08.77	77	3	1	0
Doncaster Rov	L	09.78	78	1	0	0

GILLIGAN James (Jimmy) Martin
Hammersmith, 24 January, 1964 EYth (F)

League Club	Source	Date Signed	Seasons Played	Apps	Subs	Gls
Watford	App	08.81	81-84	18	9	6
Lincoln C	L	10.82	82	0	3	0
Grimsby T	Tr	08.85	85	19	5	4
Swindon T	Tr	06.86	86	13	4	5
Newport Co	L	02.87	86	4	1	1
Lincoln C	Tr	03.87	86	11	0	1
Cardiff C	Tr	07.87	87-89	99	0	35
Portsmouth	Tr	10.89	89	24	8	5
Swansea C	Tr	08.90	90-91	60	2	23

GILLIGAN John
Abingdon, 2 May, 1957 (M)

League Club	Source	Date Signed	Seasons Played	Apps	Subs	Gls
Swindon T	App	10.75	75-76	2	4	0
Huddersfield T	L	09.76	76	0	1	0
Northampton T	L	01.77	76	5	0	1

GILLIGAN Malcolm
Cardiff, 11 October, 1942 (W)

League Club	Source	Date Signed	Seasons Played	Apps	Subs	Gls
Swansea T		05.62	62	3	-	0

GILLIVER Allan Henry
Swallownest, 3 August, 1944 (F)

League Club	Source	Date Signed	Seasons Played	Apps	Subs	Gls
Huddersfield T	Jnrs	08.61	62-65	45	0	22
Blackburn Rov	Tr	06.66	66-67	32	2	9
Rotherham U	Tr	05.68	68	24	2	2
Brighton & Hove A	Tr	07.69	69-70	54	3	19
Lincoln C	Tr	02.71	70-71	33	4	8
Bradford C	Tr	06.72	72-73	68	2	30
Stockport Co	Tr	06.74	74	22	3	5
Bradford C	Boston U	08.78	78	1	1	0

GILLOTT Peter
Barnsley, 20 July, 1935 EYth (FB)

League Club	Source	Date Signed	Seasons Played	Apps	Subs	Gls
Barnsley	Worsborough C U	05.53	55-58	5	-	0

GILMOUR George Reynolds
Barrhead, 7 May, 1919 Died 1987 (WH)

League Club	Source	Date Signed	Seasons Played	Apps	Subs	Gls
Halifax T	Edinburgh C	09.48	48-49	36	-	2

GILMOUR Ronald (Ron)
Workington, 28 February, 1935 Died 2002 (W)

League Club	Source	Date Signed	Seasons Played	Apps	Subs	Gls
Workington	Jnrs	12.52	53	2	-	0

GILPIN James (Jim)
Edinburgh, 12 June, 1945 (W)

League Club	Source	Date Signed	Seasons Played	Apps	Subs	Gls
Bradford PA	Raith Rov	08.65	65	10	1	1

GILROY David Miles
Yeovil, 23 December, 1982 (F)

League Club	Source	Date Signed	Seasons Played	Apps	Subs	Gls
Bristol Rov	Sch	07.02	01-03	6	13	0

GILROY Joseph (Joe)
Glasgow, 19 October, 1941 (F)

League Club	Source	Date Signed	Seasons Played	Apps	Subs	Gls
Fulham	Clyde	10.67	67-68	23	1	8

GILROY Keith
Sligo, 8 July, 1983 IRYth/IRu21-1 (M)

League Club	Source	Date Signed	Seasons Played	Apps	Subs	Gls
Middlesbrough	Sligo Rov	09.00				
Darlington	Scarborough	02.05	04	1	1	0

GILZEAN Alan John
Coupar Angus, 22 October, 1938 Su23-3/SLge-3/S-22 (F)

League Club	Source	Date Signed	Seasons Played	Apps	Subs	Gls
Tottenham H	Dundee	12.64	64-73	335	8	93

GILZEAN Ian Roger
Enfield, 10 December, 1969 (F)

League Club	Source	Date Signed	Seasons Played	Apps	Subs	Gls
Tottenham H	YT	07.88				
Doncaster Rov (L)	Dundee	02.93	92	3	0	0
Northampton T	Dundee	08.93	93	29	4	10

GINOLA David Desire Marc
Gossin, France, 25 January, 1967 Fru21/FrB-2/Fr-17 (W)

League Club	Source	Date Signed	Seasons Played	Apps	Subs	Gls
Newcastle U	Paris St Germain (Fr)	07.95	95-96	54	4	6
Tottenham H	Tr	07.97	97-99	100	0	12
Aston Villa	Tr	08.00	00-01	14	18	3
Everton	Tr	02.02	01	2	3	0

GINTER Anthony (Tony) Paul
Plymouth, 6 November, 1974 (M)

League Club	Source	Date Signed	Seasons Played	Apps	Subs	Gls
Torquay U	YT	•	92	1	0	0

GINTY Rory Vincent
Galway, 23 January, 1977 (W)

League Club	Source	Date Signed	Seasons Played	Apps	Subs	Gls
Crystal Palace	YT	11.94	97	2	3	0

GIOACCHINI Stefano
Rome, Italy, 25 November, 1976 (F)

League Club	Source	Date Signed	Seasons Played	Apps	Subs	Gls
Coventry C (L)	Venezia (It)	01.99	98	0	3	0

GIPP David Thomas
Forest Gate, 13 July, 1969 (F)

League Club	Source	Date Signed	Seasons Played	Apps	Subs	Gls
Brighton & Hove A	App	07.86	86-87	1	4	0

GIRLING Howard (Dickie) Milton
Birmingham, 24 May, 1922 Died 1992 (W)

League Club	Source	Date Signed	Seasons Played	Apps	Subs	Gls
Crystal Palace		10.43	46	26	-	6
Brentford	Tr	02.47	46-49	86	-	9
Bournemouth	Tr	07.51	51	4	-	0

GISBOURNE Charles (Charlie) Joseph
Bury, 7 October, 1952 (FB)

League Club	Source	Date Signed	Seasons Played	Apps	Subs	Gls
Bury	App	10.70	72-74	13	3	1
Crewe Alex	Tr	10.74	74	5	1	0

GISLASON Sigursteinn (Siggi)
Akranes, Iceland, 25 June, 1968 Iceland 22 (FB)

League Club	Source	Date Signed	Seasons Played	Apps	Subs	Gls
Stoke C (L)	KR Reykjavik (Ice)	11.99	99	4	4	0

GISLASON Valur Fannar
Reykjavik, Iceland, 8 September, 1977 (M)

League Club	Source	Date Signed	Seasons Played	Apps	Subs	Gls
Arsenal	Fram (Ice)	07.96				
Brighton & Hove A	L	10.97	97	7	0	0

GISSING John William
Stapleford, 24 November, 1938 (W)

League Club	Source	Date Signed	Seasons Played	Apps	Subs	Gls
Notts Co	Stapleford BC	07.56	57-60	22	-	1
Chesterfield	Tr	07.61	61	2	-	0

GITSHAM James (Jimmy) William
Hammersmith, 12 May, 1942 (FB)

League Club	Source	Date Signed	Seasons Played	Apps	Subs	Gls
Brentford	Jnrs	07.59	60-62	54	-	0

GITTENS Jonathan (Jon) Antoni
Moseley, 22 January, 1964 (CD)

League Club	Source	Date Signed	Seasons Played	Apps	Subs	Gls
Southampton	Paget Rgrs	10.85	85-86	18	0	0
Swindon T	Tr	07.87	87-90	124	2	6
Southampton	Tr	03.91	90-91	16	3	0
Middlesbrough	L	02.92	91	9	3	1
Middlesbrough	Tr	07.92	92	13	0	0
Portsmouth	Tr	08.93	93-95	81	2	2
Torquay U	Tr	08.96	96-97	78	0	9
Exeter C	Tr	07.98	98-99	82	0	4

GIUMARRA William (Willy) Giorgio
Ontario, Canada, 26 August, 1971 (M)

League Club	Source	Date Signed	Seasons Played	Apps	Subs	Gls
Darlington	Montreal (Can)	08.97	97	0	4	0

GIVEN Seamus (Shay) John James
Lifford, 20 April, 1976 IRYth/IRu21-5/IR-70 (G)

League Club	Source	Date Signed	Seasons Played	Apps	Subs	Gls
Blackburn Rov	Glasgow Celtic (Jnrs)	01.00	96	2	0	0
Swindon T	L	08.95	95	5	0	0
Sunderland	L	01.96	95	17	0	0
Newcastle U	Tr	07.97	97-04	253	0	0

GIVENS Daniel (Don) Joseph
Limerick, 9 August, 1949 IR-56 (F)

League Club	Source	Date Signed	Seasons Played	Apps	Subs	Gls
Manchester U	App	12.66	69	4	4	1
Luton T	Tr	04.70	70-71	80	3	19
Queens Park Rgrs	Tr	07.72	72-77	242	0	77
Birmingham C	Tr	08.78	78-80	49	10	10
Bournemouth	L	03.80	79	5	0	4
Sheffield U	Tr	03.81	80	11	0	3

League Club	Source	Date Signed	Seasons Played	Career Record Apps	Subs	Gls
GLADWIN Robin						
Harlow, 12 August, 1940						(FB)
Norwich C	Chelmsford C	01.66	65-67	16	0	0
Oxford U	Tr	07.68	68-69	44	0	0
GLAISTER George						
Bywell, 18 May, 1918						(W)
Blackburn Rov	North Shields	05.37	46	8	-	1
Stockport Co	Tr	04.47	46-49	92	-	21
Halifax T	Tr	08.50	50	34	-	7
Accrington St	Tr	09.51	51	24	-	1
GLASBY Herbert						
Bradford, 21 September, 1919 Died 1969						(W)
Bradford PA	Aldershot (Am)	05.46	46-48	11	-	1
GLASGOW Byron Fitzgerald						
Tooting, 18 February, 1979						(M)
Reading	YT	08.96	96-98	31	8	1
GLASS James (Jimmy) Robert						
Epsom, 1 August, 1973						(G)
Crystal Palace	YT	07.91				
Portsmouth	L	02.95	94	3	0	0
Bournemouth	Tr	03.96	95-97	94	0	0
Swindon T	Tr	06.98	98-99	11	0	0
Carlisle U	L	04.99	98	3	0	1
Brentford	Cambridge U (N/C)	03.00	99	1	1	0
Oxford U	Tr	08.00	00	1	0	0
GLASS Stephen						
Dundee, 23 May, 1976 SSch/Su21-11/SB-2/S-1						(M)
Newcastle U	Aberdeen	07.98	98-00	24	19	7
Watford	Tr	07.01	01-02	55	9	4
GLAVIN Ronald (Ronnie) Michael						
Glasgow, 27 March, 1951 S-1						(M)
Barnsley	Glasgow Celtic	06.79	79-83	171	5	73
Barnsley	Belenenses (Por)	08.85	85	5	1	0
Stockport Co	Tr	08.86	86	5	5	1
GLAZIER William (Bill) James						
Nottingham, 2 August, 1943 Eu23-3/FLge-1						(G)
Crystal Palace	Torquay U (Am)	10.61	61-64	106	-	0
Coventry C	Tr	10.64	64-74	346	0	0
Brentford	Tr	06.75	75	9	0	0
GLAZZARD James (Jimmy)						
Normanton, 23 April, 1923 Died 1996						(CF)
Huddersfield T	Altofts Colliery	10.43	46-55	299	-	141
Everton	Tr	09.56	56	3	-	0
Mansfield T	Tr	12.56	56-57	21	-	10
GLAZZARD Malcolm						
Eastham, 1 July, 1931						(W)
Liverpool	Jnrs	05.49				
Accrington St	Tr	08.51	51	1	-	0
GLEADALL Dennis						
Sheffield, 15 February, 1934						(CD)
Bury		08.54				
Bradford PA	Tr	07.56	56-57	34	-	0
GLEADALL Edward (Eddie)						
Sheffield, 21 August, 1931 Died 1993						(W)
Bury	Sheffield Wed (Am)	01.52	51-56	74	-	18
Scunthorpe U	Tr	03.57	56-57	6	-	2
GLEASURE Peter Francis						
Luton, 8 October, 1960						(G)
Millwall	App	08.78	80-82	55	0	0
Northampton T	Tr	03.83	82-90	344	0	0
Gillingham	L	03.91	90	3	0	0
GLEAVE Colin						
Stockport, 6 April, 1919						(CD)
Stockport Co		02.38	46-47	57	-	1
GLEDHILL Lee						
Bury, 7 November, 1980						(FB)
Barnet	YT	07.99	98-00	9	7	0
GLEDHILL Samuel (Sammy)						
Castleford, 7 July, 1913 Died 1994						(WH)
York C	Altofts	09.36	36-48	123	-	6
GLEDSTONE Peter Hayward						
Ferndown, 4 May, 1934						(FB)
Bournemouth	Bournemouth Gasworks	11.55	57-63	131	-	2
GLEESON Daniel (Dan) Edward						
Cambridge, 17 February, 1985						(FB)
Cambridge U	Welling U	02.04	03-04	24	13	0
GLEESON Jamie Bradley						
Poole, 15 January, 1985						(F)
Southampton	Sch	07.02				
Kidderminster Hrs	Tr	08.04	04	2	5	0
GLEESON Percy						
Acton, 18 July, 1921						(IF)
Brentford	Hounslow T	03.47	47	9	-	1
GLEGHORN Nigel William						
Seaham, 12 August, 1962						(M)
Ipswich T	Seaham Red Star	08.85	85-87	54	12	11
Manchester C	Tr	08.88	88-89	27	7	7
Birmingham C	Tr	09.89	89-92	142	0	33
Stoke C	Tr	10.92	92-95	162	4	26
Burnley	Tr	07.96	96-97	33	1	4
Brentford	L	11.97	97	11	0	1
Northampton T	L	02.98	97	3	5	1
GLENDINNING Brian						
Newcastle, 26 December, 1934						(W)
Darlington	Felham BC	05.55	55	12	-	2
GLENDINNING Kevin						
Corbridge, 23 January, 1962						(FB)
Darlington	Jnrs	08.80	80	4	0	0
GLENDON Kevin William						
Manchester, 21 June, 1961						(M)
Manchester C	App	06.79				
Crewe Alex	Tr	08.80	80	3	1	0
Burnley	Hyde U	12.83	83	4	0	0
GLENN David Anthony						
Wigan, 30 November, 1962						(FB)
Wigan Ath	App	11.80	80-82	68	4	4
Blackburn Rov	Tr	08.83	83-84	23	1	0
Chester C	Tr	07.85	85-88	70	3	1
GLENNON Christopher (Chris) David						
Manchester, 29 October, 1949						(F)
Manchester C	App	11.67	68-69	3	1	0
Tranmere Rov	L	01.71	70	2	0	0
GLENNON Matthew (Matty) William						
Stockport, 8 October, 1978						(G)
Bolton W	YT	07.97				
Bristol Rov	L	09.00	00	1	0	0
Carlisle U	L	11.00	00	29	0	0
Hull C	Tr	06.01	01-02	35	0	0
Carlisle U	Tr	10.02	02-03	76	0	0
GLIDDEN Gilbert Swinburne						
Sunderland, 15 December, 1915 Died 1988 ESch						(IF)
Sunderland	Jnrs	02.32				
Port Vale	Tr	05.35	35	5	-	1
Reading	Tr	05.36	36-49	111	-	24
Leyton Orient	Tr	11.50	50	1	-	0
GLOSSOP Terence (Terry)						
Sheffield, 10 May, 1940						(W)
Chesterfield		05.59	59	7	-	1
GLOVER Alexander (Alec)						
Glasgow, 28 February, 1922 Died 2000						(W)
Bradford PA	Partick Th	03.48	47-49	48	-	5
Luton T	Tr	09.49	49-50	56	-	6
Blackburn Rov	Tr	09.51	51-53	64	-	4
Barrow	Tr	08.54	54-57	85	-	7
GLOVER Allan Richard						
Laleham, 21 October, 1950						(M)
Queens Park Rgrs	App	03.68	68	5	1	0
West Bromwich A	Tr	06.69	69-76	84	8	9
Southend U	L	01.76	75	0	1	0
Brentford	L	10.76	76	6	0	0
Orient	Tr	03.77	76-77	37	0	5
Brentford	Tr	11.78	78-79	21	2	2
GLOVER Arthur						
Barnsley, 27 March, 1918 Died 1998						(WH)
Barnsley	Regent Street Congs	03.35	37-52	186	-	5
GLOVER Benjamin (Benny) David						
Birmingham, 30 November, 1946						(WH)
Coventry C		10.66	66	0	1	0

GLOVER Bevil (Bev) Arthur
Salford, 25 March, 1926 Died 2000 (CD)

League Club	Source	Date Signed	Seasons Played	Apps	Subs	Gls
Stockport Co	Cheadle	01.48	47-53	137	-	1
Rochdale	Tr	03.54	53-58	169	-	1

GLOVER Dean Victor
West Bromwich, 29 December, 1963 (CD)

League Club	Source	Date Signed	Seasons Played	Apps	Subs	Gls
Aston Villa	App	12.81	84-86	25	3	0
Sheffield U	L	10.86	86	5	0	0
Middlesbrough	Tr	06.87	87-88	44	6	5
Port Vale	Tr	02.89	88-97	354	9	15

GLOVER Edward (Lee) Lee
Kettering, 24 April, 1970 SYth/Su21-3 (F)

League Club	Source	Date Signed	Seasons Played	Apps	Subs	Gls
Nottingham F	App	05.87	87-93	61	15	9
Leicester C	L	09.89	89	3	2	1
Barnsley	L	01.90	89	8	0	0
Luton T	L	09.91	91	1	0	0
Port Vale	Tr	08.94	94-95	38	14	7
Rotherham U	Tr	08.96	96-99	70	15	29
Huddersfield T	L	03.97	96	11	0	0
Macclesfield T	Tr	07.00	00-02	72	13	18
Mansfield T	Tr	09.02	02	0	2	0

GLOVER Gerard (Gerry) John
Liverpool, 27 September, 1946 ESch/EYth (M)

League Club	Source	Date Signed	Seasons Played	Apps	Subs	Gls
Everton	App	08.64	64-65	2	1	0
Mansfield T	Tr	09.67	67	18	1	0

GLOVER John James
Workington, 6 February, 1935 (IF)

League Club	Source	Date Signed	Seasons Played	Apps	Subs	Gls
Workington	Marsh BC	10.54	54	2	-	0

GLOVER Leonard (Len)
Kennington, 31 January, 1944 (W)

League Club	Source	Date Signed	Seasons Played	Apps	Subs	Gls
Charlton Ath	Jnrs	05.62	62-67	177	0	20
Leicester C	Tr	11.67	67-75	245	7	38

GLOVER Peter
Bradford, 16 October, 1936 (WH)

League Club	Source	Date Signed	Seasons Played	Apps	Subs	Gls
Bradford C		11.57	57	1	-	0

GLOZIER Robert (Bob)
East Ham, 20 November, 1948 ESch (FB)

League Club	Source	Date Signed	Seasons Played	Apps	Subs	Gls
West Ham U	App	05.66				
Torquay U	Tr	08.69	69-71	57	0	1

GLYNN Terence (Terry) Robert
Hackney, 17 December, 1958 (F)

League Club	Source	Date Signed	Seasons Played	Apps	Subs	Gls
Orient	App	12.76	76	1	1	0

GNOHERE David **Arthur**
Yamoussoukro, Ivory Coast, 20 November, 1978 (CD)

League Club	Source	Date Signed	Seasons Played	Apps	Subs	Gls
Burnley	SM Caen (Fr)	08.01	01-03	74	7	6
Queens Park Rgrs	L	09.03	03	6	0	0
Queens Park Rgrs	Tr	02.04	03-04	14	1	0

GOAD Alan Michael
Hailsham, 8 August, 1948 (CD)

League Club	Source	Date Signed	Seasons Played	Apps	Subs	Gls
Exeter C	Jnrs	12.65				
Hartlepools U	Tr	07.67	67-77	366	9	11

GOALEN Harold **Keith**
Hindley, 24 May, 1933 (W)

League Club	Source	Date Signed	Seasons Played	Apps	Subs	Gls
Stockport Co	Jnrs	04.53	50-55	18	-	2

GOATER Leonard **Shaun**
Hamilton, Bermuda, 25 February, 1970 BermudaYth/Bermuda 19 (F)

League Club	Source	Date Signed	Seasons Played	Apps	Subs	Gls
Manchester U	North Village (Ber)	05.89				
Rotherham U	Tr	10.89	89-95	169	40	70
Notts Co	L	11.93	93	1	0	0
Bristol C	Tr	07.96	96-97	67	8	40
Manchester C	Tr	03.98	97-02	164	20	84
Reading	Tr	08.03	03-04	32	11	12
Coventry C	L	03.05	04	4	2	0

GOBERN Lewis Thomas
Birmingham, 28 January, 1985 (M)

League Club	Source	Date Signed	Seasons Played	Apps	Subs	Gls
Wolverhampton W	Sch	03.04				
Hartlepool U	L	11.04	04	1	0	0

GOBLE Stephen (Steve) Richard
Erpingham, 5 September, 1960 (W)

League Club	Source	Date Signed	Seasons Played	Apps	Subs	Gls
Norwich C	App	09.78	79-80	30	0	2
Norwich C	Groningen (Holl)	08.84	84	0	1	0
Cambridge U	FC Utrecht (Holl)	02.88	87	1	1	0

GODBOLD Daryl Martin
Ipswich, 5 September, 1964 (FB)

League Club	Source	Date Signed	Seasons Played	Apps	Subs	Gls
Norwich C	App	09.82	83	0	2	0
Colchester U	Tr	08.84	84	4	2	1

GODBOLD Harold (Harry)
Springwell, 31 January, 1939 (W)

League Club	Source	Date Signed	Seasons Played	Apps	Subs	Gls
Sunderland	Usworth Colliery	05.56	57-59	12	-	1
Hartlepools U	Tr	01.61	60-62	65	-	8
Lincoln C	Boston	03.66	65-66	22	1	3

GODDARD Howard John
Over Wallop, 10 May, 1957 (F)

League Club	Source	Date Signed	Seasons Played	Apps	Subs	Gls
Bournemouth	App	07.74	72-75	62	2	18
Swindon T	Tr	06.76	76	10	2	0
Newport Co	Tr	08.77	77-81	101	4	42
Blackpool	L	09.81	81	4	0	2
Bournemouth	Tr	12.81	81	6	3	2
Aldershot	Tr	08.82	82	26	2	9

GODDARD Karl Eric
Leeds, 29 December, 1967 ESch (FB)

League Club	Source	Date Signed	Seasons Played	Apps	Subs	Gls
Manchester U	App	12.85				
Bradford C	Tr	06.86	86-89	67	6	0
Exeter C	L	12.89	89	0	1	0
Colchester U	L	01.90	89	16	0	1
Hereford U	Tr	09.90	90-91	8	1	1

GODDARD Paul
Harlington, 12 October, 1959 Eu21-8/E-1 (F)

League Club	Source	Date Signed	Seasons Played	Apps	Subs	Gls
Queens Park Rgrs	App	07.77	77-79	63	7	23
West Ham U	Tr	08.80	80-86	159	11	54
Newcastle U	Tr	11.86	86-87	61	0	19
Derby Co	Tr	08.88	88-89	49	0	15
Millwall	Tr	12.89	89-90	17	3	1
Ipswich T	Tr	01.91	90-93	59	13	13

GODDARD Raymond (Ray)
Ecclesfield, 17 October, 1920 Died 1974 (CD)

League Club	Source	Date Signed	Seasons Played	Apps	Subs	Gls
Wolverhampton W	Red Rov	09.38	38	4	-	0
Chelsea	Tr	09.46	46-47	14	-	1
Plymouth Arg	Tr	07.48	48-49	43	-	1
Exeter C	Tr	12.49	49-53	130	-	2

GODDARD Raymond (Ray)
Fulham, 13 February, 1949 (G)

League Club	Source	Date Signed	Seasons Played	Apps	Subs	Gls
Leyton Orient	Fulham (App)	02.67	66-73	278	0	0
Millwall	Tr	11.74	75-77	80	0	0
Wimbledon	Tr	02.78	77-80	119	0	1

GODDARD-CRAWLEY Richard Lewis
Burnt Oak, 31 March, 1978 (CD)

League Club	Source	Date Signed	Seasons Played	Apps	Subs	Gls
Brentford	Arsenal (YT)	07.96	96	0	1	0

GODDEN Anthony (Tony) Leonard
Gillingham, 2 August, 1955 (G)

League Club	Source	Date Signed	Seasons Played	Apps	Subs	Gls
West Bromwich A	Ashford T	08.75	76-85	267	0	0
Luton T	L	03.83	82	12	0	0
Walsall	L	10.83	83	19	0	0
Chelsea	Tr	03.86	85-86	34	0	0
Birmingham C	Tr	07.87	87-88	29	0	0
Bury	L	12.88	88	1	0	0
Peterborough U	Tr	07.89	89	24	0	0

GODDERIDGE Alan Edward
Tamworth, 23 May, 1928 (WH)

League Club	Source	Date Signed	Seasons Played	Apps	Subs	Gls
Swansea T	Tamworth	10.50	51	1	-	0
Walsall	Tr	07.52	52	3	-	0

GODDING Earl George
Hawarden, 6 January, 1934 (G)

League Club	Source	Date Signed	Seasons Played	Apps	Subs	Gls
Wrexham	Caergwrle	04.54	52-58	21	-	0
Workington	Tr	08.59	59	10	-	0

GODFREY Anthony (Tony) William
Wokingham, 30 April, 1939 (G)

League Club	Source	Date Signed	Seasons Played	Apps	Subs	Gls
Southampton	Basingstoke T	04.58	58-65	141	0	0
Aldershot	Tr	12.65	65-69	171	0	0
Rochdale	Tr	07.70	70-71	71	0	0
Aldershot	Tr	07.72	72-75	68	0	0

GODFREY Brian Cameron
Flint, 1 May, 1940 Wu23-1/W-3 (F)

League Club	Source	Date Signed	Seasons Played	Apps	Subs	Gls
Everton	Flint Alexandra	05.58	59	1	-	0
Scunthorpe U	Tr	06.60	60-63	87	-	24
Preston NE	Tr	10.63	63-67	126	1	52
Aston Villa	Tr	09.67	67-70	139	4	22
Bristol Rov	Tr	05.71	71-72	79	2	16
Newport Co	Tr	06.73	73-75	117	1	14

GODFREY Elliott James
Toronto, Canada, 22 February, 1983 (F)

League Club	Source	Date Signed	Seasons Played	Apps	Subs	Gls
Watford	YT	03.01	02	0	1	0

GODFREY Kevin
Kennington, 24 February, 1960 (W)

League Club	Source	Date Signed	Seasons Played	Apps	Subs	Gls
Orient	App	03.77	77-87	255	30	62

League Club	Source	Date Signed	Seasons Played	Career Record Apps	Subs	Gls
Plymouth Arg	L	02.86	85	7	0	1
Brentford	Maidenhead U	10.88	88-92	101	39	17

GODFREY Paul
Derby, 27 September, 1972 (M)

League Club	Source	Date Signed	Seasons Played	Apps	Subs	Gls
Chesterfield	YT	•	90	2	0	0

GODFREY Peter Ronald
Woolwich, 15 March, 1938 (W)

League Club	Source	Date Signed	Seasons Played	Apps	Subs	Gls
Charlton Ath	Jnrs	11.55	60	1	-	0
Gillingham	Tr	07.61	61-64	66	-	9
Chesterfield	Tr	07.65	65	27	0	2
Exeter C	Tr	06.66	66	42	0	4

GODFREY Warren Paul Thomas
Liverpool, 31 March, 1973 (M)

League Club	Source	Date Signed	Seasons Played	Apps	Subs	Gls
Liverpool	YT	05.91				
Barnsley	Tr	07.92	92	1	7	0

GODSELL John (Jack) Dryburgh
Lassodie, 13 September, 1924 (FB)

League Club	Source	Date Signed	Seasons Played	Apps	Subs	Gls
Huddersfield T	Forfar Ath	06.46				
Bradford C	Tr	09.48	49	9	-	0
Southport	Tr	08.51	51	3	-	0

GODWIN Donald (Don) John
Aberbargoed, 15 July, 1932 Died 2002 (W)

League Club	Source	Date Signed	Seasons Played	Apps	Subs	Gls
Cardiff C	Bargoed	12.53	56	2	-	0

GODWIN Robert Geoffrey
Wootton Bassett, 3 February, 1928 (IF)

League Club	Source	Date Signed	Seasons Played	Apps	Subs	Gls
Swindon T		09.51	51	2	-	0

GODWIN Thomas (Tommy) Fergus
Dublin, 20 August, 1927 Died 1996 LoI-1/IR-13 (G)

League Club	Source	Date Signed	Seasons Played	Apps	Subs	Gls
Leicester C	Shamrock Rov	10.49	49-51	45	-	0
Bournemouth	Tr	06.52	52-61	357	-	0

GODWIN Verdi
Blackburn, 11 February, 1926 (CF)

League Club	Source	Date Signed	Seasons Played	Apps	Subs	Gls
Blackburn Rov	Jnrs	03.46	46-47	27	-	6
Manchester C	Tr	06.48	48	8	-	3
Stoke C	Tr	06.49	49	22	-	2
Mansfield T	Tr	01.50	49-50	31	-	9
Grimsby T	Tr	01.52	51	1	-	0
Brentford	Tr	03.52	51-52	7	-	1
Southport	Tr	07.54	54	17	-	2
Barrow	Tr	08.55	55	15	-	3
Tranmere Rov	Tr	08.56	56	14	-	2

GOFF Shaun John
Tiverton, 13 April, 1984 (FB)

League Club	Source	Date Signed	Seasons Played	Apps	Subs	Gls
Exeter C	YT	08.02	01	2	0	0

GOFFIN William (Billy) Charles
Tamworth, 12 February, 1920 Died 1987 (W)

League Club	Source	Date Signed	Seasons Played	Apps	Subs	Gls
Aston Villa	Tamworth	12.37	46-53	156	-	36
Walsall	Tr	08.54	54	8	-	1

GOLAC Ivan
Kuprivnica, Yugoslavia, 15 June, 1950 Yugoslavia int (FB)

League Club	Source	Date Signed	Seasons Played	Apps	Subs	Gls
Southampton	Partizan Belgrade (Yug)	11.78	78-81	143	1	4
Bournemouth	Tr	11.82	82	9	0	0
Manchester C	Tr	03.83	82	2	0	0
Southampton	Bjelasica (Yug)	03.84	83-85	24	0	0
Portsmouth	L	01.85	84	8	0	0

GOLBOURNE Scott Julian
Bristol, 29 February, 1988 EYth (FB)

League Club	Source	Date Signed	Seasons Played	Apps	Subs	Gls
Bristol C	Sch	03.05	04	7	2	0

GOLDBAEK Bjarne
Nykobing Falster, Denmark, 6 October, 1968 DeYth/Deu21/DeB-1/De-28 (M)

League Club	Source	Date Signed	Seasons Played	Apps	Subs	Gls
Chelsea	FC Copenhagen (Den)	11.98	98-99	15	14	5
Fulham	Tr	01.00	99-02	73	12	6

GOLDBERG (GAUNT) Leslie (Les)
Leeds, 3 January, 1918 ESch (FB)

League Club	Source	Date Signed	Seasons Played	Apps	Subs	Gls
Leeds U	Jnrs	05.35	37-46	31	-	0
Reading	Tr	03.47	46-49	71	-	0

GOLDER James (Jimmy)
Manchester, 28 March, 1955 Died 2000 (M)

League Club	Source	Date Signed	Seasons Played	Apps	Subs	Gls
Stockport Co	App	•	71	0	1	0

GOLDIE James (Jim)
Denny, 29 June, 1940 (CF)

League Club	Source	Date Signed	Seasons Played	Apps	Subs	Gls
Luton T	Kilsyth Rgrs	04.62	62	7	-	2
York C	Tr	06.63	63	22	-	7

GOLDIE Peter
Dumbarton, 7 June, 1934 (FB)

League Club	Source	Date Signed	Seasons Played	Apps	Subs	Gls
Aldershot	Glasgow Celtic	06.58	58	5	-	0

GOLDING Norman **John** William
Southwark, 23 January, 1937 (W)

League Club	Source	Date Signed	Seasons Played	Apps	Subs	Gls
Queens Park Rgrs	Tonbridge	08.59	59-60	30	-	6

GOLDRING Mark
Brighton, 17 September, 1972 (G)

League Club	Source	Date Signed	Seasons Played	Apps	Subs	Gls
Chesterfield	YT	07.91	91	7	0	0

GOLDSMITH Craig Stephen William
Peterborough, 27 August, 1963 (M)

League Club	Source	Date Signed	Seasons Played	Apps	Subs	Gls
Peterborough U	Mirlees Blackstone	08.88	88-89	39	7	6
Carlisle U	Tr	12.89	89-90	21	9	1

GOLDSMITH Martin Sidney
Carmarthen, 25 May, 1962 (F)

League Club	Source	Date Signed	Seasons Played	Apps	Subs	Gls
Cambridge U	Carmarthen	04.80	80-83	28	7	5
Cardiff C	Tr	01.84	83	3	6	2

GOLDSMITH Martyn
Walsall, 4 November, 1969 (F)

League Club	Source	Date Signed	Seasons Played	Apps	Subs	Gls
Walsall	YT	08.88	88-90	2	5	2

GOLDTHORPE Robert (Bobby) James
Osterley, 6 December, 1950 (CD)

League Club	Source	Date Signed	Seasons Played	Apps	Subs	Gls
Crystal Palace	Jnrs	07.68	71	1	0	0
Charlton Ath	Tr	12.72	72-75	70	9	6
Aldershot	L	02.76	75	16	0	0
Brentford	Tr	07.76	76	19	0	2

GOLDTHORPE Wayne
Staincross, 19 September, 1957 (F)

League Club	Source	Date Signed	Seasons Played	Apps	Subs	Gls
Huddersfield T	App	09.75	75-77	19	7	7
Hartlepool	L	12.76	76	6	1	1
Hartlepool U	Tr	08.78	78-79	43	4	8
Crewe Alex	Tr	10.79	79	0	1	0

GOLLEY Mark Anthony
Beckenham, 28 October, 1962 (CD)

League Club	Source	Date Signed	Seasons Played	Apps	Subs	Gls
Maidstone U	Sutton U	(N/L)	89-90	77	4	3

GOLLOGLY John
Bridlington, 4 July, 1962 (M)

League Club	Source	Date Signed	Seasons Played	Apps	Subs	Gls
Hartlepool U	Whitby T	03.85	84-86	29	2	5

GOMA Alain
Sault, France, 5 October, 1972 FrYth/Fru21/FrB-1/Fr-2 (CD)

League Club	Source	Date Signed	Seasons Played	Apps	Subs	Gls
Newcastle U	Paris St Germain (Fr)	07.99	99-00	32	1	1
Fulham	Tr	03.01	00-04	102	2	0

GOMERSALL Victor (Vic)
Manchester, 17 June, 1942 (FB)

League Club	Source	Date Signed	Seasons Played	Apps	Subs	Gls
Manchester C	Jnrs	07.60	61-65	39	0	0
Swansea T	Tr	08.66	66-70	178	0	6

GOMEZ Fernando Colomer
Valencia, Spain, 11 September, 1965 Spain 1 (M)

League Club	Source	Date Signed	Seasons Played	Apps	Subs	Gls
Wolverhampton W	Valencia (Sp)	08.98	98	17	2	2

GONZAGUE Michael Alexander Granville
Canning Town, 27 March, 1975 (FB)

League Club	Source	Date Signed	Seasons Played	Apps	Subs	Gls
Southend U	YT	07.93				
Hereford U	Tr	08.94	94	2	1	0

GOOCH James (Jimmy) Arthur George
West Ham, 11 July, 1921 Died 2001 (G)

League Club	Source	Date Signed	Seasons Played	Apps	Subs	Gls
Preston NE	Becontree	05.42	46-51	135	-	0
Bradford C	Tr	07.53	53	22	-	0
Watford	Tr	07.54	55-56	43	-	0

GOOD John Russell
Portsmouth, 29 January, 1933 (W)

League Club	Source	Date Signed	Seasons Played	Apps	Subs	Gls
Nottingham F		06.53				
Bury	Tr	06.54				
Tranmere Rov	Buxton	07.55	55	5	-	0

GOODACRE Samuel (Sam) David
Chesterfield, 1 December, 1970 ESch (F)

League Club	Source	Date Signed	Seasons Played	Apps	Subs	Gls
Sheffield Wed	Jnrs	07.89				
Scunthorpe U	Tr	07.91	92-94	24	20	12

GOODALL Alan Jeffrey
Birkenhead, 2 December, 1981 (FB)

League Club	Source	Date Signed	Seasons Played	Apps	Subs	Gls
Rochdale	Bangor C	07.04	04	27	7	2

GOODALL Bernard
Islington, 4 October, 1937 Died 2005 (FB)

League Club	Source	Date Signed	Seasons Played	Apps	Subs	Gls
Reading		07.59	59-61	98	-	0

League Club	Source	Date Signed	Seasons Played	Apps	Subs	Gls
Carlisle U	Tr	07.63	63	1	-	0
Halifax T	Tr	11.64	64	23	-	0

GOODALL David (Dave) George
Madeley, 18 May, 1943 (CD)

League Club	Source	Date Signed	Seasons Played	Apps	Subs	Gls
Shrewsbury T	Jnrs	05.61	61	1	-	0

GOODCHILD Gary Dean
Chelmsford, 27 January, 1958 ESch (F)

League Club	Source	Date Signed	Seasons Played	Apps	Subs	Gls
Arsenal	App	01.75				
Hereford U	Tr	06.76	76	1	3	0
Reading	Tr	09.77	77	0	1	0
Crystal Palace	Kramfors (Swe)	12.79	79-80	0	2	0

GOODCHILD John (Johnny)
Gateshead, 2 January, 1939 (W)

League Club	Source	Date Signed	Seasons Played	Apps	Subs	Gls
Sunderland	Ludworth Jnrs	09.56	57-60	44	-	21
Brighton & Hove A	Tr	05.61	61-65	162	1	44
York C	Tr	06.66	66	29	0	6
Darlington	Tr	07.67	67	2	0	0

GOODE Terence (Terry) Joseph
Islington, 29 October, 1961 (F)

League Club	Source	Date Signed	Seasons Played	Apps	Subs	Gls
Birmingham C	App	09.79	80	0	2	0

GOODEN Ty Michael
Canvey Island, 23 October, 1972 (W)

League Club	Source	Date Signed	Seasons Played	Apps	Subs	Gls
Swindon T	Wycombe W	09.93	93-99	118	28	9
Gillingham	Tr	01.00	99-01	52	7	5

GOODEVE Kenneth (Ken) George Alfred
Manchester, 3 September, 1950 (CD)

League Club	Source	Date Signed	Seasons Played	Apps	Subs	Gls
Manchester U	App	09.67				
Luton T	Tr	04.70	70-72	9	6	0
Brighton & Hove A	Tr	12.73	73	5	1	0
Watford	Tr	06.74	74-75	67	0	4

GOODFELLOW Derrick Ormond
Shilbottle, 26 June, 1914 Died 2001 (G)

League Club	Source	Date Signed	Seasons Played	Apps	Subs	Gls
Gateshead	Jnrs	03.35	34-35	29	-	0
Sheffield Wed	Tr	05.36	36-46	69	-	0
Middlesbrough	Tr	06.47	47	36	-	0

GOODFELLOW James (Jimmy)
Sunderland, 16 September, 1943 (M)

League Club	Source	Date Signed	Seasons Played	Apps	Subs	Gls
Port Vale	Bishop Auckland	06.66	66-68	76	9	10
Workington	Tr	07.69	69-73	199	0	15
Rotherham U	Tr	01.74	73-77	192	0	8
Stockport Co	Tr	08.78	78	2	1	0

GOODFELLOW James (Jimmy) Boyd
Edinburgh, 30 July, 1938 (M)

League Club	Source	Date Signed	Seasons Played	Apps	Subs	Gls
Leicester C	Third Lanark	05.63	63-67	96	2	26
Mansfield T	Tr	03.68	67-70	96	4	14

GOODFELLOW Marc David
Swadlincote, 20 September, 1981 (F)

League Club	Source	Date Signed	Seasons Played	Apps	Subs	Gls
Stoke C	Jnrs	01.99	00-03	17	37	6
Bristol C	Tr	01.04	03-04	8	12	4
Port Vale	L	10.04	04	4	1	0
Swansea C	L	11.04	04	6	0	3
Colchester U	L	03.05	04	4	1	1

GOODFELLOW Sydney (Syd)
Wolstanton, 6 July, 1915 (WH)

League Club	Source	Date Signed	Seasons Played	Apps	Subs	Gls
Port Vale	Hanley	11.36	36	16	-	1
Rochdale	Glentoran	05.38	38	41	-	2
Chesterfield	Tr	04.39	46-47	80	-	0
Doncaster Rov	Tr	05.48	48-49	66	-	2
Oldham Ath	Tr	09.50	50-51	72	-	2
Accrington St	Tr	06.52	52	28	-	3

GOODGAME Anthony (Tony) Alan
Hammersmith, 19 February, 1946 (FB)

League Club	Source	Date Signed	Seasons Played	Apps	Subs	Gls
Fulham	App	02.64				
Leyton Orient	Tr	08.66	66	7	1	0

GOODHIND Warren Ernest
Johannesburg, South Africa, 16 August, 1977 (FB)

League Club	Source	Date Signed	Seasons Played	Apps	Subs	Gls
Barnet	YT	07.96	96-00	73	20	3
Cambridge U	Tr	09.01	01-04	95	8	0

GOODING Michael (Mick) Charles
Newcastle, 12 April, 1959 (M)

League Club	Source	Date Signed	Seasons Played	Apps	Subs	Gls
Rotherham U	Bishop Auckland	07.79	79-82	90	12	9
Chesterfield	Tr	12.82	82	12	0	0
Rotherham U	Tr	09.83	83-86	149	7	32
Peterborough U	Tr	08.87	87-88	47	0	21
Wolverhampton W	Tr	09.88	88-89	43	1	4
Reading	Tr	12.89	89-96	303	11	26
Southend U	Plymouth Arg (coach)	07.98	98-99	19	6	0

GOODING Raymond (Ray)
Hartlepool, 16 February, 1959 (M)

League Club	Source	Date Signed	Seasons Played	Apps	Subs	Gls
Coventry C	App	06.76	76-81	46	3	5
Bristol C	L	03.82	81	3	0	0
Plymouth Arg	Tr	08.82	82	7	0	1

GOODING Scott Osmond
Croydon, 2 January, 1982 (M)

League Club	Source	Date Signed	Seasons Played	Apps	Subs	Gls
Crystal Palace	YT	07.01	01	0	1	0

GOODISON Ian
St James, Jamaica, 21 November, 1972 Jamaica int (FB)

League Club	Source	Date Signed	Seasons Played	Apps	Subs	Gls
Hull C	Olympic Gardens (Jam)	10.99	99-01	67	3	1
Tranmere Rov	Seba U (Jam)	02.04	03-04	55	1	1

GOODISON Christopher Wayne
Wakefield, 23 September, 1964 (FB)

League Club	Source	Date Signed	Seasons Played	Apps	Subs	Gls
Barnsley	App	09.82	82-85	31	5	0
Crewe Alex	Tr	09.86	86-88	90	4	1
Rochdale	Tr	07.89	89-90	78	1	4

GOODLAD Mark
Barnsley, 9 September, 1979 (G)

League Club	Source	Date Signed	Seasons Played	Apps	Subs	Gls
Nottingham F	YT	10.96				
Scarborough	L	02.99	98	3	0	0
Port Vale	Tr	03.00	99-04	139	2	0

GOODLASS Ronald (Ronnie)
Liverpool, 6 September, 1953 ESch (W)

League Club	Source	Date Signed	Seasons Played	Apps	Subs	Gls
Everton	App	07.71	75-77	31	4	2
Fulham	Den Haag (Holl)	09.80	80	21	1	2
Scunthorpe U	Tr	03.82	81	9	0	0
Tranmere Rov	(Hong Kong)	12.83	83-84	19	2	0

GOODMAN Donald (Don) Ralph
Leeds, 9 May, 1966 (F)

League Club	Source	Date Signed	Seasons Played	Apps	Subs	Gls
Bradford C	Collingham	07.84	83-86	65	5	14
West Bromwich A	Tr	03.87	86-91	140	18	60
Sunderland	Tr	12.91	91-94	112	4	40
Wolverhampton W	Tr	12.94	94-97	115	10	33
Barnsley (L)	San Hiroshima (Jap)	12.98	98	5	3	0
Walsall	Motherwell	03.01	00-01	15	10	3
Exeter C	Tr	08.02	02	11	2	1

GOODMAN John
King's Lynn, 8 September, 1935 (G)

League Club	Source	Date Signed	Seasons Played	Apps	Subs	Gls
Crewe Alex		10.58	58	1	-	0

GOODMAN Jonathan (Jon)
Walthamstow, 2 June, 1971 IR-4 (F)

League Club	Source	Date Signed	Seasons Played	Apps	Subs	Gls
Millwall	Bromley	08.90	90-94	97	12	35
Wimbledon	Tr	11.94	94-98	28	32	11

GOODMAN Malcolm John
Solihull, 6 May, 1961 (CD)

League Club	Source	Date Signed	Seasons Played	Apps	Subs	Gls
Halifax T	Bromsgrove Rov	09.79	79-82	70	16	1

GOODRIDGE Gregory (Greg) Ronald St Clair
Barbados, 10 July, 1971 Barbados int (W)

League Club	Source	Date Signed	Seasons Played	Apps	Subs	Gls
Torquay U	Lambada (St V)	03.94	93-94	32	6	4
Queens Park Rgrs	Tr	08.95	95	0	7	1
Bristol C	Tr	08.96	96-01	76	43	14
Cheltenham T	L	02.01	00	10	1	1
Torquay U	Tr	11.01	01	9	8	1

GOODWIN Craig
Wrexham, 12 February, 1974 (CD)

League Club	Source	Date Signed	Seasons Played	Apps	Subs	Gls
Chester C	Aston Villa (YT)	08.92	92	3	2	0

GOODWIN David (Dave)
Nantwich, 15 October, 1954 (F)

League Club	Source	Date Signed	Seasons Played	Apps	Subs	Gls
Stoke C	App	06.72	73-77	22	4	3
Workington	L	10.76	76	7	0	0
Mansfield T	Tr	11.77	77-79	42	4	5
Bury	Tr	09.80	80	2	2	0
Rochdale	Tr	08.81	81	34	5	6
Crewe Alex	Tr	08.82	82	4	3	0

GOODWIN Eric
Chesterfield, 6 March, 1929 (CD)

League Club	Source	Date Signed	Seasons Played	Apps	Subs	Gls
Mansfield T	St Aidan Stags	09.53	53-54	9	-	0

GOODWIN Frederick (Freddie)
Heywood, 28 June, 1933 (WH)

League Club	Source	Date Signed	Seasons Played	Apps	Subs	Gls
Manchester U		10.53	54-59	95	-	7
Leeds U	Tr	03.60	59-63	107	-	2
Scunthorpe U	Tr	12.64	65	5	1	1

GOODWIN Frederick (Freddie) James
Stockport, 4 January, 1944 (M)

League Club	Source	Date Signed	Seasons Played	Apps	Subs	Gls
Wolverhampton W	Jnrs	01.61	61-65	44	1	0

League Club	Source	Date Signed	Seasons Played	Apps	Subs	Gls
Stockport Co	Tr	01.66	65-69	171	5	20
Blackburn Rov	Tr	03.70	69-71	63	1	4
Southport	Tr	10.71	71	10	2	0
Port Vale	Tr	08.72	72	27	0	2
Stockport Co	Macclesfield T	08.74	74	29	0	1
GOODWIN Ian David						
Irlam, 14 November, 1950						(CD)
Coventry C	Oldham Ath (App)	12.68	70	4	0	0
Brighton & Hove A	Tr	10.70	70-73	52	4	0
GOODWIN James (Jim)						
Waterford, 20 November, 1981 IRu21-14/IR-1						(CD)
Stockport Co	Glasgow Celtic	06.02	02-04	81	22	7
GOODWIN John (Jackie) William						
Worcester, 29 September, 1920 Died 1995						(W)
Birmingham C	Worcester C	05.46	46-48	32	-	8
Brentford	Tr	04.49	49-53	131	-	22
GOODWIN Leslie (Les)						
Ardwick, 30 April, 1924 Died 2002						(W)
Oldham Ath	Blackpool (Am)	08.44	46	7	-	0
Southport	Tr	07.47	47-48	16	-	2
GOODWIN Mark Adrian						
Sheffield, 23 February, 1960						(M)
Leicester C	App	11.77	77-80	69	22	8
Notts Co	Tr	03.81	80-86	226	11	24
Walsall	Tr	07.87	87-89	81	11	2
GOODWIN Samuel (Sam) Gourlay						
Tarbolton, 14 March, 1943 Died 2005						(M)
Crystal Palace	Airdrie	09.71	71	18	7	0
GOODWIN Shaun Lee						
Rotherham, 14 June, 1969						(M)
Rotherham U	YT	07.87	87-97	258	22	39
GOODWIN Stephen (Steve) Alan						
Chadderton, 23 February, 1954						(M)
Norwich C	App	02.72	70-74	2	1	0
Scunthorpe U	L	09.73	73	2	0	0
Southend U	Tr	06.75	75-78	68	7	10
GOODWIN Thomas (Tommy) Neil						
Leicester, 8 November, 1979						(CD)
Leicester C	YT	07.98	99	1	0	0
GOODYEAR Clive						
Lincoln, 15 January, 1961						(CD)
Luton T	Lincoln U	10.78	79-83	85	5	4
Plymouth Arg	Tr	08.84	84-86	99	7	5
Wimbledon	Tr	07.87	87-89	25	1	0
Brentford	Tr	03.91	90	10	0	0
GOODYEAR George William						
Luton, 5 July, 1916 Died 2001						(WH)
Luton T	Hitchin T	10.38	46	10	-	0
Southend U	Tr	07.47	47-48	59	-	1
GOPE-FENEPEJ John						
Noumea, New Caledonia, 16 November, 1978						(CD)
Bolton W (L)	Nantes (Fr)	09.00	00	0	2	0
GORAM Andrew (Andy) Lewis						
Bury, 13 April, 1964 Su21-1/S-43						(G)
Oldham Ath	West Bromwich A (App)	08.81	81-87	195	0	0
Notts Co	Glasgow Rgrs	09.98	98	1	0	0
Sheffield U	Tr	09.98	98	7	0	0
Manchester U	Motherwell	03.01	00	2	0	0
Coventry C	Tr	08.01	01	6	1	0
Oldham Ath	Tr	03.02	01	4	0	0
GORAM Lewis Albert						
Edinburgh, 2 July, 1926 Died 1989						(G)
Bury	Third Lanark	06.50	50-56	114	-	0
GORDINE Barry						
Bethnal Green, 1 September, 1948						(G)
Sheffield U	Gravesend & Northfleet	06.68				
Oldham Ath	Tr	12.68	68-70	83	0	0
GORDON Henry **Alexander (Alec)**						
Livingston, 25 July, 1940 Died 1996						(WH)
Bradford PA	Dundee U	08.65	65-66	61	0	2
GORDON Andrew (Andy)						
Bathgate, 6 July, 1944						(F)
Darlington (Am)	West Auckland	08.69	69	2	2	0
GORDON Colin Kenneth						
Stourbridge, 17 January, 1963						(F)
Swindon T	Oldbury U	10.84	84-85	70	2	34
Wimbledon	Tr	06.86	86	2	1	0
Gillingham	L	02.87	86	4	0	2
Reading	Tr	07.87	87-88	23	1	9
Bristol C	L	03.88	87	8	0	4
Fulham	Tr	10.88	88	12	5	2
Birmingham C	Tr	06.89	89-90	17	9	3
Hereford U	L	09.90	90	6	0	0
Walsall	L	12.90	90	6	0	1
Bristol Rov	L	01.91	90	1	3	0
Leicester C	Tr	07.91	91-92	18	6	5
GORDON Dale Andrew						
Caister, 9 January, 1967 ESch/EYth/Eu21-4/EB						(W)
Norwich C	App	01.84	84-91	194	12	31
West Ham U	Glasgow Rgrs	07.93	93-95	8	1	1
Peterborough U	L	03.95	94	6	0	1
Millwall	L	03.96	95	6	0	0
Bournemouth	Tr	08.96	96	14	2	0
GORDON Dean Dwight Joshua						
Thornton Heath, 10 February, 1973 Eu21-13						(FB)
Crystal Palace	YT	07.91	91-97	181	20	20
Middlesbrough	Tr	07.98	98-01	53	10	4
Cardiff C	L	11.01	01	7	0	2
Coventry C	Tr	08.02	02-03	33	2	1
Reading	L	03.04	03	0	3	0
Grimsby T	Tr	08.04	04	20	0	2
GORDON Denis William						
Bilston, 7 June, 1924 Died 1998						(W)
West Bromwich A	Oxford C	09.47	47-51	27	-	2
Brighton & Hove A	Tr	07.52	52-60	277	-	62
GORDON Kenyatta **Gavin**						
Manchester, 24 June, 1979						(F)
Hull C	YT	07.96	95-97	22	16	9
Lincoln C	Tr	11.97	97-00	87	12	28
Cardiff C	Tr	12.00	00-03	26	24	5
Oxford U	L	09.02	02	3	3	1
Notts Co	Tr	07.04	04	23	4	5
GORDON Henry (Harry)						
Glasgow, 10 December, 1931						(WH)
Bury	Stratchclyde	06.51	52-56	21	-	0
GORDON James (Jimmy)						
Fauldhouse, 23 October, 1915 Died 1996						(WH)
Newcastle U	Wishaw Jnrs	04.35	34-38	132	-	2
Middlesbrough	Tr	11.45	46-53	231	-	3
GORDON James (Jimmy) Stephen						
Birmingham, 3 October, 1955 ESch						(G)
Luton T	Blackpool (App)	09.73				
Lincoln C	Tr	07.74	76-77	4	0	0
Scunthorpe U	Reading (N/C)	09.78	79-80	34	0	0
GORDON John (Johnny) Duncan Sinclair						
Portsmouth, 11 September, 1931 Died 2001						(IF)
Portsmouth	Carnoustie Panmure	01.49	51-58	209	-	69
Birmingham C	Tr	09.58	58-60	96	-	32
Portsmouth	Tr	03.61	60-66	234	0	37
GORDON Michael Alexander						
Tooting, 11 October, 1984						(M)
Wimbledon	Arsenal (YT)	03.03	02-03	8	11	0
GORDON Neville Spencer Damian						
Greenwich, 15 November, 1975						(F)
Millwall	YT	05.94				
Reading	Tr	08.95	95	0	1	0
GORDON Peter John						
Northampton, 21 May, 1932 Died 1990						(IF)
Norwich C		12.49	53-57	160	-	34
Watford	Tr	07.58	58-59	43	-	13
Exeter C	Tr	07.60	60-61	67	-	12
Newport Co	Tr	07.62	62	8	-	1
GORDON Robert Baxter						
Ormiston, 5 September, 1923 Died 2001						(IF)
Millwall	Armadale Jnrs	01.45	46-47	5	-	0
GORDON William (Billy) James Woodhouse						
Carlisle, 22 November, 1926 Died 1983						(CF)
Carlisle U		08.48	47-48	16	-	3
Barrow	Tr	07.50	49-57	302	-	145
Workington	Tr	03.58	57-58	33	-	7

GORE Ian George
Prescot, 10 January, 1968 (CD)

League Club	Source	Date Signed	Seasons Played	Apps	Subs	Gls
Birmingham C	App	05.86				
Blackpool	Southport	01.88	88-94	196	4	0
Torquay U	Tr	08.95	95	25	0	2
Doncaster Rov	Tr	03.96	95-97	65	1	1

GORE Shane Stephen
Ashford, Kent, 28 October, 1981 (G)

League Club	Source	Date Signed	Seasons Played	Apps	Subs	Gls
Wimbledon	YT	06.01	01	0	1	0

GORE Shaun Michael
West Ham, 21 September, 1968 (CD)

League Club	Source	Date Signed	Seasons Played	Apps	Subs	Gls
Fulham	App	06.86	85-88	25	1	0
Halifax T	L	02.91	90	15	0	0

GORE Thomas (Tommy) John
Liverpool, 26 November, 1953 (M)

League Club	Source	Date Signed	Seasons Played	Apps	Subs	Gls
Wigan Ath	Tranmere Rov (N/C)	(N/L)	78-80	102	0	14
Bury	Tr	10.80	80-82	118	1	16
Port Vale	Tr	07.83	83	33	3	2

GORIN Edward (Ted) Rosser
Cardiff, 2 March, 1924 (CF)

League Club	Source	Date Signed	Seasons Played	Apps	Subs	Gls
Cardiff C	Grange Ath	10.48	48-49	6	-	2
Scunthorpe U	Tr	07.50	50	26	-	12
Shrewsbury T	Tr	01.51	50-51	18	-	3

GORING Harry (Peter)
Bishop's Cleeve, 2 January, 1927 Died 1994 (WH)

League Club	Source	Date Signed	Seasons Played	Apps	Subs	Gls
Arsenal	Cheltenham T	01.48	49-58	220	-	51

GORMAN Andrew (Andy) David
Cardiff, 13 September, 1974 (FB)

League Club	Source	Date Signed	Seasons Played	Apps	Subs	Gls
Cardiff C	YT	●	91-92	8	4	1

GORMAN John
Winchburgh, 16 August, 1949 (FB)

League Club	Source	Date Signed	Seasons Played	Apps	Subs	Gls
Carlisle U	Glasgow Celtic	09.70	70-76	228	1	5
Tottenham H	Tr	11.76	76-78	30	0	0

GORMAN Keith
Bishop Auckland, 13 October, 1966 (W)

League Club	Source	Date Signed	Seasons Played	Apps	Subs	Gls
Ipswich T	App	01.84				
Colchester U	L	09.86	86	0	1	0
Darlington	Tr	01.87	86	4	3	2

GORMAN Paul Anthony
Dublin, 6 August, 1963 IRYth/IRu21-1 (M)

League Club	Source	Date Signed	Seasons Played	Apps	Subs	Gls
Arsenal	App	10.80	81-83	5	1	0
Birmingham C	Tr	06.84	84	6	0	0
Carlisle U	Tr	03.85	84-89	137	11	7
Shrewsbury T	Tr	11.89	89-91	58	6	1
Carlisle U	Tr	12.91	91	5	0	0

GORMAN Paul Michael
Macclesfield, 18 September, 1968 (F)

League Club	Source	Date Signed	Seasons Played	Apps	Subs	Gls
Doncaster Rov	YT	07.87	87-88	1	15	2
Charlton Ath	Fisher Ath	03.91	90-93	19	21	8

GORMAN William (Bill) Charles
Sligo, 13 July, 1911 Died 1978 IR-13/I-4 (FB)

League Club	Source	Date Signed	Seasons Played	Apps	Subs	Gls
Bury	Shettleston Jnrs	09.34	36-38	52	-	0
Brentford	Tr	12.38	38-49	125	-	0

GORMLEY Edward (Eddie) Joseph
Dublin, 23 October, 1968 IRu21-3 (M)

League Club	Source	Date Signed	Seasons Played	Apps	Subs	Gls
Tottenham H	Bray W	11.87				
Chesterfield	L	11.88	88	4	0	0
Doncaster Rov	Tr	07.90	90-92	110	8	16

GORMLEY Philip (Phil)
Greenock, 13 October, 1924 Died 1988 (CF)

League Club	Source	Date Signed	Seasons Played	Apps	Subs	Gls
Aldershot	Glasgow Celtic	08.50	50-52	65	-	9

GORNALL John (Jack)
Preston, 28 March, 1941 (WH)

League Club	Source	Date Signed	Seasons Played	Apps	Subs	Gls
Preston NE	Jnrs	07.60	61-62	4	-	0

GORRE Dean
Surinam, 10 September, 1970 Hou21 (M)

League Club	Source	Date Signed	Seasons Played	Apps	Subs	Gls
Huddersfield T	Ajax (Holl)	09.99	99-00	49	13	6
Barnsley	Tr	07.01	01-03	48	17	9
Blackpool	Tr	08.04	04	0	1	0

GORRIE David Alexander
Liverpool, 21 January, 1943 (WH)

League Club	Source	Date Signed	Seasons Played	Apps	Subs	Gls
Everton	Jnrs	05.60				
Stockport Co	Tr	07.62	62	18	-	0

GORRY Martin Christopher
Derby, 29 December, 1954 (FB)

League Club	Source	Date Signed	Seasons Played	Apps	Subs	Gls
Barnsley	Jnrs	05.73	75-76	34	0	3
Newcastle U	Tr	10.76	77	0	1	0
Hartlepool U	Tr	07.78	78-79	59	0	0

GORTON Andrew (Andy) William
Salford, 23 September, 1966 (G)

League Club	Source	Date Signed	Seasons Played	Apps	Subs	Gls
Oldham Ath	App	07.84	85-87	26	0	0
Stockport Co	L	12.86	86	14	0	0
Tranmere Rov	L	05.88	87	1	0	0
Stockport Co	Tr	08.88	88	34	0	0
Lincoln C	Tr	08.89	89	20	0	0
Oldham Ath	Glossop	02.91				
Crewe Alex	Tr	03.91	90	3	0	0

GOSLIN Richard William
Bovey Tracey, 31 October, 1956 (F)

League Club	Source	Date Signed	Seasons Played	Apps	Subs	Gls
Torquay U	Nottingham F (App)	04.74	73-75	14	5	2

GOSLING Jamie John
Bath, 21 March, 1982 (M)

League Club	Source	Date Signed	Seasons Played	Apps	Subs	Gls
Yeovil T	Bath C	07.03	03	4	8	1
Torquay U	Team Bath	12.04	04	6	1	1

GOSNEY Andrew (Andy) Robert
Southampton, 8 November, 1963 EYth (G)

League Club	Source	Date Signed	Seasons Played	Apps	Subs	Gls
Portsmouth	App	11.81	81-91	48	0	0
York C	L	10.91	91	5	0	0
Birmingham C	Tr	07.92	92	21	0	0
Exeter C		10.93	93	1	0	0

GOSS Jeremy (Jerry)
Oekolia, Cyprus, 11 May, 1965 ESch/W-9 (M)

League Club	Source	Date Signed	Seasons Played	Apps	Subs	Gls
Norwich C	Jnrs	03.83	83-95	155	33	14

GOTSMANOV Sergei Anaiolyenich
Minsk, Belarus, 17 March, 1959 (F)

League Club	Source	Date Signed	Seasons Played	Apps	Subs	Gls
Brighton & Hove A	Dynamo Minsk (Bs)	02.90	89	14	2	4
Southampton	Dynamo Minsk (Bs)	08.90	90	2	6	0

GOTTS James (Jim) Atkinson
Seaton Delaval, 17 January, 1917 Died 1998 (W)

League Club	Source	Date Signed	Seasons Played	Apps	Subs	Gls
Brentford	Ashington	01.46				
Brighton & Hove A	Tr	07.46	46	2	-	0

GOTTSKALKSSON Olafur (Ole)
Keflavik, Iceland, 12 March, 1968 IcYth/Icu21-7/Ic-9 (G)

League Club	Source	Date Signed	Seasons Played	Apps	Subs	Gls
Brentford	Hibernian	07.00	00-01	73	0	0
Torquay U	Tr	09.04	04	15	0	0

GOUCK Andrew (Andy) Scott
Blackpool, 8 June, 1972 (M)

League Club	Source	Date Signed	Seasons Played	Apps	Subs	Gls
Blackpool	YT	07.90	89-95	121	27	12
Rochdale	Tr	07.96	96-97	58	8	8

GOUGH Alan
Watford, 10 March, 1971 IRYth/IRu21-5 (G)

League Club	Source	Date Signed	Seasons Played	Apps	Subs	Gls
Portsmouth	Shelbourne	07.89				
Fulham	Tr	06.92	92	3	0	0

GOUGH Anthony (Tony) Michael
Bath, 18 March, 1940 (M)

League Club	Source	Date Signed	Seasons Played	Apps	Subs	Gls
Bristol Rov	Bath C	05.58	58	1	-	0
Swindon T	Bath C	07.70	70	25	1	2
Torquay U	Hereford U	07.72	72	2	0	0

GOUGH Charles (Charlie) Storrar
Glasgow, 21 May, 1939 (WH)

League Club	Source	Date Signed	Seasons Played	Apps	Subs	Gls
Charlton Ath	Alton T	06.63	64	4	-	0

GOUGH Keith
Willenhall, 4 February, 1953 ESch (W)

League Club	Source	Date Signed	Seasons Played	Apps	Subs	Gls
Walsall	App	02.71	69-71	11	4	0
Oxford U	Tr	07.72	72-74	32	7	5

GOUGH Matthew **Michael (Mike)**
Beeston, 29 December, 1935 Died 1998 (WH)

League Club	Source	Date Signed	Seasons Played	Apps	Subs	Gls
Aldershot		05.56	56-58	20	-	1

GOUGH Neil
Harlow, 1 September, 1981 (F)

League Club	Source	Date Signed	Seasons Played	Apps	Subs	Gls
Leyton Orient	YT	07.00	99-01	2	13	1

GOUGH Raymond (Ray) John
Belfast, 8 February, 1938 (WH)

League Club	Source	Date Signed	Seasons Played	Apps	Subs	Gls
Exeter C	Linfield	10.63				
Millwall	Tr	10.64	64	13	-	0

GOUGH Charles **Richard**
Stockholm, Sweden, 5 April, 1962 Su21-5/S-61 (CD)

League Club	Source	Date Signed	Seasons Played	Apps	Subs	Gls
Tottenham H	Dundee U	08.86	86-87	49	0	2

League Club	Source	Date Signed	Seasons Played	Apps	Subs	Gls
Nottingham F	San Jose (USA)	03.99	98	7	0	0
Everton	Tr	06.99	99-00	38	0	1

GOUGH Robert (Bobby) George
Ladywood, 20 July, 1949 (F)

League Club	Source	Date Signed	Seasons Played	Apps	Subs	Gls
Walsall	App	07.67	66	1	0	0
Port Vale	Tr	07.68	68-73	189	21	33
Stockport Co	L	02.73	73	6	0	0
Southport	Tr	07.74	74-75	61	0	16
Colchester U	Tr	01.76	75-80	195	1	65

GOULD John Barrie
Ammanford, 18 January, 1944 (CF)

League Club	Source	Date Signed	Seasons Played	Apps	Subs	Gls
Arsenal	App	11.61				
Chelsea	Tr	02.64				
Peterborough U	Tr	07.65	65	18	0	3

GOULD Geoffrey (Geoff)
Blackburn, 7 January, 1945 (W)

League Club	Source	Date Signed	Seasons Played	Apps	Subs	Gls
Bradford PA	App	01.62	62-68	129	2	18
Lincoln C	L	02.68	67	1	0	0
Notts Co	Tr	07.69	69	1	0	0

GOULD Henry (Harry)
Birkenhead, 5 January, 1925 (IF)

League Club	Source	Date Signed	Seasons Played	Apps	Subs	Gls
Tranmere Rov	Liverpool (Am)	09.46	46-48	5	-	2
Southport	Northwich Vic	09.50	50	16	-	2

GOULD James (Jamie) Robert
Kettering, 15 January, 1982 (M)

League Club	Source	Date Signed	Seasons Played	Apps	Subs	Gls
Northampton T	YT	07.00	00	0	1	0
Boston U	Tr	07.01	02	10	10	2

GOULD Jonathan Alan
Paddington, 18 July, 1968 SB-1/S-2 (G)

League Club	Source	Date Signed	Seasons Played	Apps	Subs	Gls
Halifax T	Clevedon T	07.90	90-91	32	0	0
West Bromwich A	Tr	01.92				
Coventry C	Tr	07.92	92-94	25	0	0
Bradford C	Tr	03.96	95-96	18	0	0
Gillingham	L	10.96	96	3	0	0
Preston NE	Glasgow Celtic	01.03	02-04	54	1	0

GOULD Robert (Bobby) Alfred
Coventry, 12 June, 1946 (F)

League Club	Source	Date Signed	Seasons Played	Apps	Subs	Gls
Coventry C	App	06.64	63-67	78	4	40
Arsenal	Tr	02.68	67-69	57	8	16
Wolverhampton W	Tr	06.70	70-71	39	1	18
West Bromwich A	Tr	09.71	71-72	52	0	18
Bristol C	Tr	12.72	72-73	35	0	15
West Ham U	Tr	11.73	73-75	46	5	15
Wolverhampton W	Tr	12.75	75-76	24	10	13
Bristol Rov	Tr	10.77	77-78	35	1	12
Hereford U	Tr	09.78	78-79	42	3	13

GOULD Ronald (Ronnie) Donald
Bethnal Green, 27 September, 1982 (M)

League Club	Source	Date Signed	Seasons Played	Apps	Subs	Gls
Leyton Orient	YT	10.00	99	0	2	0

GOULD Trevor Roy
Coventry, 5 March, 1950 ESch (FB)

League Club	Source	Date Signed	Seasons Played	Apps	Subs	Gls
Coventry C	Jnrs	07.67	69	9	0	0
Northampton T	Tr	10.70	70-72	102	3	6

GOULD Walter (Wally)
Thrybergh, 25 September, 1938 (W)

League Club	Source	Date Signed	Seasons Played	Apps	Subs	Gls
Sheffield U	Rawmarsh Welfare	02.58	58	5	-	1
York C	Tr	02.61	60-63	120	-	25
Brighton & Hove A	Tr	01.64	63-67	166	2	45

GOULDEN Albert Edward
Salford, 5 February, 1945 (FB)

League Club	Source	Date Signed	Seasons Played	Apps	Subs	Gls
Bolton W	Jnrs	02.62	62	1	-	0

GOULDEN Leonard (Len) Arthur
Hackney, 9 July, 1912 Died 1995 ESch/FLge-2/EWar-6/E-14 (IF)

League Club	Source	Date Signed	Seasons Played	Apps	Subs	Gls
West Ham U	Leyton	04.33	32-38	239	-	54
Chelsea	Tr	08.45	46-49	99	-	17

GOULDEN Roy Leonard
Ilford, 22 September, 1937 ESch (IF)

League Club	Source	Date Signed	Seasons Played	Apps	Subs	Gls
Arsenal	Jnrs	09.54	58	1	-	0
Southend U	Tr	05.61	61	9	-	2

GOULDING Eric
Winsford, 22 November, 1924 (WH)

League Club	Source	Date Signed	Seasons Played	Apps	Subs	Gls
Everton	Over Ath	10.45				
Crewe Alex	Tr	10.46	46	1	-	0

GOULDING Stephen (Steve)
Mexborough, 21 January, 1954 Died 1985 (FB)

League Club	Source	Date Signed	Seasons Played	Apps	Subs	Gls
Sheffield U	App	05.71	71-75	28	0	0

GOULET Brent
Tacoma, USA, 19 June, 1964 (F)

League Club	Source	Date Signed	Seasons Played	Apps	Subs	Gls
Bournemouth	Portland (USA)	11.87	87	2	4	0
Crewe Alex	L	01.88	87	2	1	3

GOULOOZE Richard
Alkmaar, Holland, 16 November, 1967 (M)

League Club	Source	Date Signed	Seasons Played	Apps	Subs	Gls
Derby Co	SC Heerenveen (Holl)	09.92	92	7	5	0

GOUNDRY William (Bill)
Middlesbrough, 28 March, 1934 (WH)

League Club	Source	Date Signed	Seasons Played	Apps	Subs	Gls
Brentford	Huddersfield T (Am)	05.55	55-60	141	-	12

GOURLAY Archibald (Archie) Murdoch
Greenock, 29 June, 1969 (M)

League Club	Source	Date Signed	Seasons Played	Apps	Subs	Gls
Newcastle U	Morton	03.88	88-90	2	1	0
Hartlepool U	Motherwell	09.94	94	0	1	0

GOVAN Alexander (Alex)
Glasgow, 16 June, 1929 (W)

League Club	Source	Date Signed	Seasons Played	Apps	Subs	Gls
Plymouth Arg	Bridgeton BC	09.46	46-52	110	-	28
Birmingham C	Tr	06.53	53-57	165	-	53
Portsmouth	Tr	03.58	57-58	11	-	2
Plymouth Arg	Tr	09.58	58-59	32	-	8

GOVAN Charles Pearson
Belfast, 12 January, 1943 NISch (IF)

League Club	Source	Date Signed	Seasons Played	Apps	Subs	Gls
Burnley	Jnrs	01.60				
Mansfield T	Tr	06.63	63-64	11	-	0

GOVIER Stephen (Steve)
Watford, 6 April, 1952 (CD)

League Club	Source	Date Signed	Seasons Played	Apps	Subs	Gls
Norwich C	App	07.69	70-73	22	0	1
Brighton & Hove A	Tr	04.74	74	12	0	1
Grimsby T	Tr	12.74	74-76	23	1	0

GOW Gerald (Gerry)
Glasgow, 29 May, 1952 Su23-1 (M)

League Club	Source	Date Signed	Seasons Played	Apps	Subs	Gls
Bristol C	Jnrs	06.69	69-80	368	7	48
Manchester C	Tr	10.80	80-81	26	0	5
Rotherham U	Tr	01.82	81-82	58	0	4
Burnley	Tr	08.83	83	8	1	0

GOWANS Peter Taylor
Dundee, 25 May, 1944 (W)

League Club	Source	Date Signed	Seasons Played	Apps	Subs	Gls
Crewe Alex	Glasgow Celtic	07.63	63-66	141	0	45
Aldershot	Tr	07.67	67-69	111	2	27
Rochdale	Tr	07.70	70-73	137	8	21
Southport	Tr	07.74	74	3	1	0

GOWER Mark
Edmonton, 5 October, 1978 ESch/EYth/ESemiPro-4 (M)

League Club	Source	Date Signed	Seasons Played	Apps	Subs	Gls
Tottenham H	YT	04.97				
Barnet	Tr	01.01	00	10	4	1
Southend U	Tr	07.03	03-04	72	6	12

GOWLING Alan Edwin
Stockport, 16 March, 1949 ESch/EAmat/Eu23-1 (F)

League Club	Source	Date Signed	Seasons Played	Apps	Subs	Gls
Manchester U	Manchester Univ	04.67	67-71	64	7	18
Huddersfield T	Tr	06.72	72-74	128	0	58
Newcastle U	Tr	08.75	75-77	91	1	30
Bolton W	Tr	03.78	77-81	147	2	28
Preston NE	Tr	09.82	82	37	3	5

GOY Peter John
Beverley, 8 June, 1938 (G)

League Club	Source	Date Signed	Seasons Played	Apps	Subs	Gls
Arsenal	Jnrs	06.55	58	2	-	0
Southend U	Tr	10.60	60-63	118	-	0
Watford	Tr	07.64	64	27	-	0
Huddersfield T	Apollon (SA)	07.65	66	4	0	0

GRABBI Corrado
Turin, Italy, 29 July, 1975 (F)

League Club	Source	Date Signed	Seasons Played	Apps	Subs	Gls
Blackburn Rov	Ternana (It)	07.01	01-03	11	19	2

GRABOVAC Zarko
Ruma, Serbia, 16 March, 1983 (F)

League Club	Source	Date Signed	Seasons Played	Apps	Subs	Gls
Blackpool	Geldrop AEK (Holl)	01.05	04	1	2	0

GRACE Derek George
Chiswick, 29 December, 1944 (IF)

League Club	Source	Date Signed	Seasons Played	Apps	Subs	Gls
Exeter C	Queens Park Rgrs (App)	05.62	62-64	40	-	4
Gillingham	Tr	07.65	65	4	0	0

GRACE John Michael
Dublin, 16 February, 1964 (G)

League Club	Source	Date Signed	Seasons Played	Apps	Subs	Gls
Colchester U	Tolka Rov	07.89	89	19	0	0

GRAFTON Stanley (Stan) Thomas
Heath Town, 2 April, 1923 Died 1953 (WH)

League Club	Source	Date Signed	Seasons Played	Apps	Subs	Gls
Aldershot	Bilston T	08.47	47-48	2	-	0

League Club	Source	Date Signed	Seasons Played	Career Record Apps	Subs	Gls
GRAHAM Allan						
Ryhope, 23 October, 1937						(FB)
Sunderland	Silksworth Jnrs	05.55	57	3	-	0
GRAHAM Arthur						
Glasgow, 26 October, 1952 Su23-3/SLge-1/S-10						(W)
Leeds U	Aberdeen	07.77	77-82	222	1	37
Manchester U	Tr	08.83	83	33	4	5
Bradford C	Tr	06.85	85-86	28	3	2
GRAHAM Benjamin (Ben)						
Pontypool, 23 September, 1975						(FB)
Cardiff C	YT	07.94	93	0	1	0
GRAHAM Daniel (Danny) Anthony William						
Gateshead, 12 August, 1985 EYth						(F)
Middlesbrough	YT	03.04	04	0	11	1
Darlington	L	03.04	03	7	2	2
GRAHAM David						
Edinburgh, 6 October, 1978 Su21-8						(F)
Torquay U	Dunfermline Ath	03.01	00-03	103	17	47
Wigan Ath	Tr	07.04	04	13	17	1
GRAHAM Deiniol William Thomas						
Cannock, 4 October, 1969 WYth/Wu21-1						(F)
Manchester U	YT	10.87	87-89	1	1	0
Barnsley	Tr	08.91	91-93	18	20	2
Preston NE	L	10.92	92	8	0	0
Carlisle U	L	11.93	93	2	0	1
Stockport Co	Tr	06.94	94	5	6	2
Scunthorpe U	Tr	08.95	95	1	2	1
GRAHAM Donald (Don)						
Oldham, 2 April, 1953						(FB)
Bury	Hyde U	10.79	79-80	3	4	0
GRAHAM Douglas (Doug)						
Morpeth, 15 July, 1921 Died 1993						(FB)
Newcastle U	Barrington U	08.40	46-50	71	-	0
Preston NE	Tr	11.50				
Lincoln C	Tr	12.51	51-56	182	-	0
GRAHAM Gareth Lee						
Belfast, 6 December, 1978 NIu21-5						(M)
Crystal Palace	YT	03.97	98	0	1	0
Brentford	Tr	09.99	99-00	5	9	0
GRAHAM George						
Bargeddie, 30 November, 1944 SSch/Su23-2/S-13						(M)
Aston Villa	App	12.61	62-63	8	-	2
Chelsea	Tr	07.64	64-66	72	0	35
Arsenal	Tr	09.66	66-72	219	8	59
Manchester U	Tr	12.72	72-74	41	2	2
Portsmouth	Tr	11.74	74-76	61	0	5
Crystal Palace	Tr	11.76	76-77	43	1	2
GRAHAM Gerald (Gerry) Wilson						
Aspatria, 31 January, 1941						(M)
Blackpool	Jnrs	08.59				
Peterborough U	Tr	07.60	60-63	17	-	1
Mansfield T	Cambridge U	06.64	64	18	-	3
Workington	Worcester C	07.68	68	6	0	0
GRAHAM James (Jimmy)						
Glasgow, 5 November, 1969						(FB)
Bradford C	YT	09.88	88-89	6	1	0
Rochdale	L	11.89	89	11	0	0
Rochdale	Tr	07.90	90-93	120	6	1
Hull C	Tr	08.94	94-95	63	0	1
GRAHAM John						
Leyland, 26 April, 1926						(IF)
Aston Villa	Leyland Motors	11.46	46-48	10	-	3
Wrexham	Tr	06.49	49-51	45	-	7
Rochdale	Wigan Ath	02.53	52	10	-	1
Bradford C	Tr	07.53	53	18	-	1
GRAHAM John (Jackie) Joseph						
Glasgow, 16 July, 1946						(M)
Brentford	Guildford C	07.70	70-79	371	3	38
GRAHAM William George **Leonard (Len)**						
Belfast, 17 October, 1925 I-7/NI-7						(FB)
Doncaster Rov	Brantwood	10.49	49-58	312	-	3
Torquay U	Tr	11.58	58	20	-	0
GRAHAM Leslie (Les)						
Flixton, 14 May, 1924 Died 1998						(IF)
Blackburn Rov	Flixton	04.47	47-52	150	-	42
Newport Co	Tr	02.53	52-54	96	-	39
Watford	Tr	07.55	55-57	90	-	26
Newport Co	Tr	09.57	57-58	64	-	15

League Club	Source	Date Signed	Seasons Played	Career Record Apps	Subs	Gls
GRAHAM Malcolm						
Crigglestone, 26 January, 1934						(IF)
Barnsley	Hall Green	04.53	54-58	109	-	35
Bristol C	Tr	05.59	59	14	-	8
Leyton Orient	Tr	06.60	60-62	75	-	29
Queens Park Rgrs	Tr	07.63	63	21	-	7
Barnsley	Tr	07.64	64	20	-	5
GRAHAM Mark Roland						
Newry, 24 October, 1974 NISch/NIYth/NIB-4						(M)
Queens Park Rgrs	YT	05.93	96	16	2	0
Cambridge U	Tr	08.99	99	0	1	0
GRAHAM Michael (Mike) Anthony						
Lancaster, 24 February, 1959						(FB)
Bolton W	App	02.77	77-80	43	3	0
Swindon T	Tr	07.81	81-84	141	0	1
Mansfield T	Tr	07.85	85-88	132	1	1
Carlisle U	Tr	09.88	88-91	137	1	3
GRAHAM Milton Mackay						
Hackney, 2 November, 1962						(M)
Bournemouth	Jnrs	05.81	81-84	54	19	12
Chester C	Tr	08.85	85-88	123	6	11
Peterborough U	Tr	07.89	89	10	5	2
GRAHAM Peter						
Worsborough Common, 19 April, 1947						(F)
Barnsley	Worsborough Bridge Ath	01.67	66-69	16	3	1
Halifax T	L	03.70	69	6	0	0
Darlington	Tr	06.70	70-73	118	1	44
Lincoln C	Tr	09.73	73-77	142	16	47
Cambridge U	Tr	06.78	78-79	35	3	0
GRAHAM Ralph Cowell						
Belmont, County Durham, 29 December, 1929						(W)
Doncaster Rov	Broadway Ath	05.47	48-49	5	-	0
Southport	Tr	07.50	50-51	29	-	9
GRAHAM Douglas **Richard (Dick)**						
Corby, 6 May, 1922						(G)
Leicester C	Northampton T (Am)	11.44				
Crystal Palace	Tr	12.45	46-50	155	-	0
GRAHAM Richard Ean						
Dewsbury, 28 November, 1974 IRu21-2						(CD)
Oldham Ath	YT	07.93	93-99	139	11	14
GRAHAM Richard Stephen						
Newry, 5 August, 1979 NIYth/NIu21-2						(M)
Queens Park Rgrs	YT	08.96	98	0	2	0
GRAHAM Robert (Bobby)						
Motherwell, 22 November, 1944						(F)
Liverpool	App	11.61	64-71	96	5	31
Coventry C	Tr	03.72	71-72	19	0	3
Tranmere Rov	L	01.73	72	10	0	3
GRAHAM Thomas (Tommy)						
Glasgow, 31 March, 1958						(M)
Aston Villa	Arthurlie	04.78				
Barnsley	Tr	12.78	78-79	36	2	13
Halifax T	Tr	10.80	80-81	68	3	17
Doncaster Rov	Tr	08.82	82	9	2	2
Scunthorpe U	Tr	03.83	82-85	102	7	21
Scarborough	Tr	08.86	87-89	104	7	11
Halifax T	Tr	01.90	89-91	56	2	4
GRAHAM William (Billy) Reynolds						
Carlisle, 8 May, 1929						(W)
Workington		07.51				
Carlisle U	Consett	01.54	53-60	35	-	2
GRAHAM William (Willie) Valentine						
Armagh, 14 February, 1959						(M)
Brentford	Northampton T (App)	08.77	77-80	42	6	3
GRAINGER Colin						
Hemsworth, 10 June, 1933 FLge-3/E-7						(W)
Wrexham	South Elmsall	10.50	50-52	5	-	0
Sheffield U	Tr	07.53	53-56	88	-	26
Sunderland	Tr	02.57	56-59	120	-	14
Leeds U	Tr	07.60	60	33	-	5
Port Vale	Tr	10.61	61-63	39	-	6
Doncaster Rov	Tr	08.64	64-65	40	0	3
GRAINGER Dennis						
Royston, West Yorkshire, 5 March, 1920 Died 1986						(W)
Southport	South Kirkby	10.38				
Leeds U	Tr	10.45	46-47	37	-	5
Wrexham	Tr	12.47	47-50	98	-	12
Oldham Ath	Tr	06.51	51	3	-	0

League Club	Source	Date Signed	Seasons Played	Apps	Subs	Gls
GRAINGER John (Jack)						
Royston, West Yorkshire, 17 July, 1912 Died 1976						(FB)
Barnsley	Royston Ath	08.32	32	1	-	0
Southport	Tr	08.33	33-46	222	-	0
GRAINGER John (Jack)						
Darton, 3 April, 1924 Died 1983 EB						(W)
Rotherham U	Frickley Colliery	11.45	47-56	352	-	112
Lincoln C	Tr	06.57	57-58	42	-	14
GRAINGER Martin Robert						
Enfield, 23 August, 1972						(FB)
Colchester U	YT	07.92	89-93	37	9	7
Brentford	Tr	10.93	93-95	100	1	12
Birmingham C	Tr	03.96	95-03	205	21	25
Coventry C	L	02.04	03	7	0	0
GRAND Simon						
Chorley, 23 February, 1984						(CD)
Rochdale	Sch	07.02	02-03	33	7	2
GRANGER Keith William						
Southampton, 5 October, 1968						(G)
Southampton	App	10.86	85	2	0	0
Darlington	Tr	12.87	87	23	0	0
GRANGER Michael (Mick)						
Leeds, 7 October, 1931						(G)
York C	Cliftonville (York)	12.51	54-61	71	-	0
Hull C	Tr	07.62	62	2	-	0
Halifax T	Tr	07.63	63-64	2	-	0
GRANT Alan James						
Havant, 6 January, 1935						(WH)
Brighton & Hove A	Gosport Borough	04.56	56	1	-	0
Exeter C	Tr	06.60	60	4	-	0
GRANT Alexander (Alick) Frank						
Peasedown St John, 11 August, 1916						(G)
Bury	Sheffield U (Am)	08.37				
Aldershot	Tr	05.38	38	5	-	0
Leicester C	Tr	12.41	46	2	-	0
Derby Co	Tr	11.46	46-47	12	-	0
Newport Co	Tr	11.48	48	20	-	0
Leeds U	Tr	08.49				
York C	Tr	03.50	49	3	-	0
GRANT Anthony (Tony)						
Drogheda, 20 August, 1976 IRSch/IRYth						(F)
Leeds U	YT	08.94				
Preston NE	Tr	11.95	95	0	1	0
GRANT Anthony (Tony) James						
Liverpool, 14 November, 1974 Eu21-1						(M)
Everton	YT	07.93	94-99	43	18	2
Swindon T	L	01.96	95	3	0	1
Tranmere Rov	L	09.99	99	8	1	0
Manchester C	Tr	12.99	99-01	11	10	0
West Bromwich A	L	12.00	00	3	2	0
Burnley	Tr	10.01	01-04	121	20	3
GRANT Anthony Paul Shaun Andrew						
Lambeth, 4 June, 1987						(M)
Chelsea	Sch	●	04	0	1	0
GRANT Bernard						
Airdrie, 23 May, 1920 Died 1984						(IF)
Exeter C	Third Lanark	07.47	48	2	-	0
GRANT Brian Patrick						
Coatbridge, 10 May, 1943						(FB)
Nottingham F	Bellshill Ath	05.60	60-64	18	-	0
Hartlepools U	Tr	01.66	65-66	35	0	0
Cambridge U	Bradford C (N/C)	(N/L)	70	14	0	0
GRANT Cyril						
Wath-on-Dearne, 10 July, 1920 Died 2002						(CF)
Lincoln C	Mexborough	06.39				
Arsenal	Tr	07.46	46	2	-	0
Fulham	Tr	12.46	46-47	14	-	4
Southend U	Tr	03.48	47-54	175	-	63
GRANT David						
Sheffield, 2 June, 1960						(FB)
Sheffield Wed	App	02.78	77-81	132	1	4
Oxford U	Tr	07.82	82-83	24	0	1
Chesterfield	L	09.83	83	7	0	0
Crystal Palace	Tr	01.84				
Cardiff C	Tr	03.84	83-84	25	0	0
Rochdale	Tr	03.85	84-86	97	0	2
GRANT David Bell						
Edinburgh, 31 July, 1943						(W)
Reading	Third Lanark	05.63	63-64	17	-	3
GRANT David John						
Liverpool, 18 December, 1947 ESch						(WH)
Everton	App	12.65				
Wrexham	Tr	09.66	66	6	5	0
GRANT Edward (Eddie) Anthony						
Greenock, 1 October, 1928						(IF)
Sheffield U	Weymouth	05.50	50	4	-	0
Grimsby T	Kilmarnock	07.52	52-53	15	-	5
GRANT Gareth Michael						
Leeds, 6 September, 1980						(F)
Bradford C	YT	04.98	97-01	6	18	1
Halifax T	L	02.99	98	0	3	0
Lincoln C	L	02.01	00	3	0	0
GRANT James (Jim)						
						(W)
Brighton & Hove A (Am)		12.46	46	1	-	0
GRANT James (Jim)						
Chapelhall, 10 June, 1940						(W)
Scunthorpe U	Larkhall Thistle	11.58	58	1	-	0
GRANT John (Jackie) Albert						
High Spen, 8 September, 1924 Died 1999						(WH)
Everton	High Spen Ath	12.42	46-54	121	-	10
Rochdale	Tr	05.56	56-58	102	-	3
Southport	Tr	01.59	58-59	40	-	0
GRANT John Anthony Carlton						
Manchester, 9 August, 1981						(F)
Crewe Alex	YT	07.99	99-01	2	5	0
Shrewsbury T	Telford U	08.04	04	10	9	2
GRANT Kenneth (Ken)						
High Spen, 13 November, 1938						(W)
Gateshead (Am)	Crook T	12.58	58	6	-	0
GRANT Kimberley (Kim) Tyrone						
Sekondi-Takaradi, Ghana, 25 September, 1972 Ghana 7						(F)
Charlton Ath	YT	03.91	90-95	74	49	18
Luton T	Tr	03.96	95-96	18	17	5
Millwall	Tr	08.97	97-98	35	20	11
Notts Co	L	12.98	98	6	0	1
Scunthorpe U	FC Marco (Por)	08.01	01	3	1	1
GRANT Lee Anderson						
Hemel Hempstead, 27 January, 1983 EYth/Eu21-4						(G)
Derby Co	YT	02.01	02-04	63	4	0
GRANT Lee Mark						
York, 31 December, 1985						(M)
York C	Jnrs	●	01	0	1	0
GRANT Peter						
Bellshill, 30 August, 1965 SSch/SYth/Su21-10/SB-2/S-2						(M)
Norwich C	Glasgow Celtic	08.97	97-98	64	4	3
Reading	Tr	08.99	99	27	2	1
Bournemouth	Tr	08.00	00	14	1	0
GRANT Peter John						
Glasgow, 11 April, 1968						(FB)
Stockport Co	Ipswich T (App)	07.86	86	1	0	0
GRANT Robert						
Edinburgh, 25 September, 1940						(IF)
Carlisle U	St Johnstone	07.62	62	2	-	1
GRANT Stephen Hubert						
Birr, 14 April, 1977 IRSch/IRu21-4						(F)
Sunderland	Athlone T	08.95				
Stockport Co	Shamrock Rov	09.97	97-98	10	19	4
GRANT Wilfred (Wilf)						
Ashington, 3 August, 1920 Died 1990 WLge-1/EB						(CF)
Manchester C	Morpeth T	02.43				
Southampton	Tr	10.46	46-49	61	-	12
Cardiff C	Tr	03.50	49-54	154	-	65
Ipswich T	Tr	10.54	54-56	75	-	22
GRANT William Fraser						
Spittalfield, 7 October, 1933						(WH)
Gillingham	Brechin C	08.56	56	1	-	0
GRANVILLE Daniel (Danny) Patrick						
Islington, 19 January, 1975 Eu21-3						(FB)
Cambridge U	YT	05.93	93-96	89	10	7
Chelsea	Tr	03.97	96-97	12	6	0

League Club	Source	Date Signed	Seasons Played	Career Record Apps	Subs	Gls
Leeds U	Tr	07.98	98	7	2	0
Manchester C	Tr	08.99	99-01	56	14	3
Norwich C	L	10.00	00	6	0	0
Crystal Palace	Tr	12.01	01-04	102	5	9
GRANVILLE John Hubert						
Tobago, 6 May, 1956 Trinidad int						(G)
Millwall	Slough T	10.85	85	6	0	0
GRANVILLE Anthony **Ralph**						
Glasgow, 23 April, 1931						(WH)
Nottingham F	Clyde	08.57				
Gateshead	Tr	10.57	57	2	-	0
GRANVILLE Norman **Trevor**						
Newport, 25 November, 1919 Died 1992						(W)
Newport Co	Cliftonville	01.46	46	1	-	0
Exeter C	Tr	10.46	46-47	20	-	1
GRANYCOMBE Neal						
Middlesbrough, 23 October, 1958						(F)
Hartlepool U	South Bank	02.81	80	1	0	0
GRAPES Stephen (Steve) Philip						
Norwich, 25 February, 1953						(M)
Norwich C	App	07.70	70-76	34	7	3
Bournemouth	L	03.76	75	7	0	1
Cardiff C	Tr	10.76	76-81	138	9	6
Torquay U	Tr	08.82	82	31	0	0
GRATRIX Roy						
Salford, 9 February, 1932 Died 2002 EB/FLge-1						(CD)
Blackpool	Taylor Brothers	03.53	53-64	400	-	0
Manchester C	Tr	09.64	64	15	-	0
GRATTAN James (Jimmy)						
Belfast, 30 November, 1958						(F)
Sunderland	App	10.76				
Mansfield T	L	11.78	78	1	0	0
GRATTON Dennis						
Rotherham, 21 April, 1934						(CD)
Sheffield U	Worksop T	10.52	55-58	6	-	0
Lincoln C	Tr	09.59	59-60	45	-	0
GRAVELAINE Xavier						
Tours, France, 5 October, 1968 France 4						(F)
Watford	Paris St Germain (Fr)	11.99	99	7	0	2
GRAVER Andrew (Andy) Martin						
Craghead, 12 September, 1927						(CF)
Newcastle U	Annfield Plain	09.47	49	1	-	0
Lincoln C	Tr	09.50	50-54	170	-	106
Leicester C	Tr	12.54	54	11	-	3
Lincoln C	Tr	07.55	55	15	-	4
Stoke C	Tr	11.55	55-56	37	-	12
Lincoln C	Boston U	10.58	58-60	89	-	33
GRAVES Mark Terence						
Isleworth, 14 December, 1960						(F)
Plymouth Arg	App	09.78	77-80	25	9	3
GRAVES Robert (Bob) Edward						
Marylebone, 7 November, 1942						(G)
Lincoln C	Kirton	04.60	59-64	79	-	0
GRAVES Wayne Alan						
Scunthorpe, 18 September, 1980						(M)
Scunthorpe U	YT	03.99	97-03	97	38	6
GRAVESEN Thomas						
Vejle, Denmark, 11 March, 1976 Deu21-6/De-56						(M)
Everton	SV Hamburg (Ger)	08.00	00-04	131	10	11
GRAVETTE Warren						
Thetford, 13 September, 1968						(M)
Tottenham H	App	08.86				
Brentford	Tr	07.87	87	1	4	0
GRAY Alan Muir						
Carlisle, 2 May, 1974						(FB)
Doncaster Rov	Richmond Univ (USA)	08.96	96	1	0	0
Darlington	Bishop Auckland	08.97	97	6	0	0
Carlisle U	Tr	02.98	97	0	1	0
GRAY Alexander (Alick) David						
Arbroath, 7 November, 1936						(FB)
Burnley	Dundee Violet	06.54				
Cardiff C	Arbroath	03.57	58	2	-	0

League Club	Source	Date Signed	Seasons Played	Career Record Apps	Subs	Gls
GRAY Andrew (Andy)						
Southampton, 25 October, 1973						(F)
Reading	YT	07.92	91-93	8	9	3
Leyton Orient	Tr	07.94	94-95	16	16	3
GRAY Andrew (Andy) Arthur						
Lambeth, 22 February, 1964 Eu21-2/E-1						(M)
Crystal Palace	Dulwich Hamlet	11.84	84-87	91	7	27
Aston Villa	Tr	11.87	87-88	34	3	4
Queens Park Rgrs	Tr	02.89	88	11	0	2
Crystal Palace	Tr	08.89	89-91	87	3	12
Tottenham H	Tr	02.92	91-93	23	10	3
Swindon T	L	12.92	92	3	0	0
Bury	Falkirk	07.97	97	21	0	1
Millwall	Tr	01.98	97	12	0	1
GRAY Andrew (Andy) David						
Harrogate, 15 November, 1977 SYth/SB-3/S-2						(W)
Leeds U	YT	07.95	95-96	13	9	0
Bury	L	12.97	97	4	2	1
Nottingham F	Tr	09.98	98-01	34	30	1
Preston NE	L	02.99	98	5	0	0
Oldham Ath	L	03.99	98	4	0	0
Bradford C	Tr	08.02	02-03	77	0	20
Sheffield U	Tr	02.04	03-04	55	2	24
GRAY Andrew (Andy) Mullen						
Glasgow, 30 November, 1955 Su23-4/S-20						(F)
Aston Villa	Dundee U	10.75	75-78	112	1	54
Wolverhampton W	Tr	09.79	79-83	130	3	38
Everton	Tr	11.83	83-84	44	5	14
Aston Villa	Tr	07.85	85-86	53	1	5
Notts Co	L	08.87	87	3	1	0
West Bromwich A	Tr	09.87	87-88	32	3	10
GRAY David (Davie)						
Coupar Angus, 8 February, 1922						(FB)
Preston NE	Glasgow Rgrs	05.47	47	36	-	0
Blackburn Rov	Tr	08.48	48-52	107	-	5
GRAY David						
Rossendale, 19 January, 1980						(F)
Rochdale	YT	07.98	98	0	3	0
GRAY David Downie						
Clydebank, 13 April, 1923						(WH)
Bradford C	Queensbury	09.48	48-55	242	-	13
GRAY Edward (Eddie)						
Bellshill, 19 October, 1934 SSch						(IF)
Barrow	Yeovil T	12.57	57-58	17	-	4
Accrington St	Tr	07.59	59	6	-	0
GRAY Edwin (Eddie)						
Glasgow, 17 November, 1948 SSch/Su23-2/S-12						(W)
Leeds U	Jnrs	01.65	65-83	441	13	52
GRAY Francis (Frank) Tierney						
Glasgow, 27 October, 1954 SSch/Su23-5/S-32						(FB)
Leeds U	App	11.71	72-78	188	5	17
Nottingham F	Tr	08.79	79-80	81	0	5
Leeds U	Tr	05.81	81-84	139	0	10
Sunderland	Tr	07.85	85-88	118	28	8
Darlington	Tr	07.89	90-91	49	0	7
GRAY Gareth						
Longridge, 24 February, 1970						(G)
Bolton W	Darwen	02.88				
Rochdale	Tr	07.90	91	6	0	0
GRAY George						
Glasgow, 6 October, 1929						(W)
Carlisle U	Vale of Clyde	11.47	47	1	-	1
Scunthorpe U	Sligo Rov	08.51	51	9	-	3
GRAY George James Pope						
Sunderland, 7 July, 1925 Died 1995						(WH)
Grimsby T	Derby Co (Am)	01.47	50	3	-	0
Swindon T	Tr	07.51	51-52	45	-	0
Darlington	Tr	07.53	53	6	-	0
GRAY George Walter						
Canning Town, 30 November, 1922						(CF)
Aldershot	West Ham U (Am)	02.47	46-47	9	-	0
GRAY Harry						
Hemsworth, 26 October, 1918 Died 1989						(IF)
Barnsley	Grimethorpe Rov	02.38	46	7	-	1
Bournemouth	Tr	12.46	46-47	30	-	7
Southend U	Tr	06.48	48-49	19	-	0

GRAY Ian James
Manchester, 25 February, 1975 (G)

League Club	Source	Date Signed	Seasons Played	Apps	Subs	Gls
Oldham Ath	YT	07.93				
Rochdale	L	11.94	94	12	0	0
Rochdale	Tr	07.95	95-96	66	0	0
Stockport Co	Tr	07.97	97-99	14	2	0
Rotherham U	Tr	07.00	00-02	38	2	0
Huddersfield T	Tr	08.03	03-04	29	0	0

GRAY Irvine William
Hoyland, 27 February, 1933 (W)

League Club	Source	Date Signed	Seasons Played	Apps	Subs	Gls
Barnsley		09.52				
Gillingham	Tr	08.56	56	9	-	0

GRAY Julian Raymond
Lewisham, 21 September, 1979 (M)

League Club	Source	Date Signed	Seasons Played	Apps	Subs	Gls
Arsenal	YT	07.98	99	0	1	0
Crystal Palace	Tr	07.00	00-03	100	25	10
Cardiff C	L	10.03	03	5	4	0
Birmingham C	Tr	06.04	04	18	14	2

GRAY Kevin John
Sheffield, 7 January, 1972 (CD)

League Club	Source	Date Signed	Seasons Played	Apps	Subs	Gls
Mansfield T	YT	07.90	88-93	129	12	3
Huddersfield T	Tr	07.94	94-01	214	16	6
Stockport Co	L	08.00	00	1	0	0
Tranmere Rov	Tr	07.02	02-03	11	1	1
Carlisle U	Tr	11.03	03	25	0	3

GRAY Mark Stuart
Tenby, 24 November, 1959 (F)

League Club	Source	Date Signed	Seasons Played	Apps	Subs	Gls
Swansea C	App	09.77	77	1	1	0
Fulham	Tr	01.78				
Orient	Tr	02.79	78	1	1	0

GRAY Martin David
Stockton, 17 August, 1971 (M)

League Club	Source	Date Signed	Seasons Played	Apps	Subs	Gls
Sunderland	YT	02.90	91-95	46	18	1
Aldershot	L	01.91	90	3	2	0
Fulham	L	10.95	95	6	0	0
Oxford U	Tr	03.96	95-98	115	6	4
Darlington	Tr	06.99	99-00	65	1	0

GRAY Matthew (Matt)
Renfrew, 11 July, 1936 (IF)

League Club	Source	Date Signed	Seasons Played	Apps	Subs	Gls
Manchester C	Third Lanark	03.63	62-66	87	4	21

GRAY Michael (Micky)
(IF)

League Club	Source	Date Signed	Seasons Played	Apps	Subs	Gls
Aldershot	Glenavon	09.46	46	7	-	1
Watford	Tr	06.47	47	10	-	3

GRAY Michael
Sunderland, 3 August, 1974 E-3 (FB)

League Club	Source	Date Signed	Seasons Played	Apps	Subs	Gls
Sunderland	YT	07.92	92-03	341	22	16
Blackburn Rov	Tr	01.04	03-04	23	0	0
Leeds U	L	02.05	04	10	0	0

GRAY Nigel Robert
Fulham, 2 November, 1956 (CD)

League Club	Source	Date Signed	Seasons Played	Apps	Subs	Gls
Orient	App	07.74	74-82	233	0	4
Charlton Ath	L	12.82	82	3	0	0
Swindon T	Tr	07.83	83-84	33	0	0
Brentford	L	03.84	83	16	0	1
Aldershot	L	09.84	84	4	0	0

GRAY Robert Paul
Portsmouth, 28 January, 1970 (F)

League Club	Source	Date Signed	Seasons Played	Apps	Subs	Gls
Luton T	YT	06.88	89	2	5	1
Wigan Ath	Tr	05.91	91	2	3	0

GRAY Philip (Phil)
Belfast, 2 October, 1968 NISch/NIYth/NIu21-1/NIu23-1/NI-26 (F)

League Club	Source	Date Signed	Seasons Played	Apps	Subs	Gls
Tottenham H	App	08.86	86-90	4	5	0
Barnsley	L	01.90	89	3	0	0
Fulham	L	11.90	90	3	0	0
Luton T	Tr	08.91	91-92	54	5	22
Sunderland	Tr	07.93	93-95	108	7	34
Luton T	Fortuna Sittard (Holl)	09.97	97-99	74	7	21
Burnley	Tr	07.00	00	5	0	1
Oxford U	Tr	11.00	00-01	35	9	11

GRAY Robert (Bob)
Newcastle, 14 December, 1923 (G)

League Club	Source	Date Signed	Seasons Played	Apps	Subs	Gls
Gateshead	Newcastle U (Am)	03.44	47-58	432	-	0

GRAY Robert (Bobby)
Cambuslang, 18 June, 1927 (W)

League Club	Source	Date Signed	Seasons Played	Apps	Subs	Gls
Lincoln C	Wishaw Jnrs	10.49	49	2	-	0

GRAY Robert
Glasgow, 8 June, 1953 SSch (M)

League Club	Source	Date Signed	Seasons Played	Apps	Subs	Gls
Workington	Nottingham F (App)	08.72	72	0	1	0

GRAY Robert Henry William
Aberdeen, 21 January, 1951 (G)

League Club	Source	Date Signed	Seasons Played	Apps	Subs	Gls
Torquay U (Am)	Inverurie Loca	11.69	69	2	0	0

GRAY Roland (Ron)
North Shields, 25 June, 1920 Died 2002 (WH)

League Club	Source	Date Signed	Seasons Played	Apps	Subs	Gls
Sheffield U	Boldon Colliery	05.38				
Lincoln C	Tr	05.39				
Watford	Tr	08.45	46	16	-	0

GRAY Stewart Alexander
Doncaster, 16 October, 1950 (CD)

League Club	Source	Date Signed	Seasons Played	Apps	Subs	Gls
Doncaster Rov	App	09.68	67-70	53	4	0
Grimsby T	Tr	09.70	70-76	263	1	2
Doncaster Rov	Frickley Ath	03.78	77	6	0	0

GRAY Stuart
Withernsea, 19 April, 1960 (FB)

League Club	Source	Date Signed	Seasons Played	Apps	Subs	Gls
Nottingham F	Withernsea YC	12.80	80-82	48	1	3
Bolton W	L	03.83	82	10	0	0
Barnsley	Tr	08.83	83-87	117	3	23
Aston Villa	Tr	11.87	87-90	102	4	9
Southampton	Tr	09.91	91	10	2	0

GRAY Stuart Edward
Harrogate, 18 December, 1973 Su21-7 (M)

League Club	Source	Date Signed	Seasons Played	Apps	Subs	Gls
Reading	Glasgow Celtic	03.98	97-00	46	6	2
Rushden & Diamonds	Tr	03.01	01-04	116	7	13

GRAY Terence (Terry) Ian
Bradford, 3 June, 1954 ESch/EYth (W)

League Club	Source	Date Signed	Seasons Played	Apps	Subs	Gls
Huddersfield T	Ashley Road	08.72	73-78	146	17	36
Southend U	Tr	07.79	79-81	106	4	28
Bradford C	Tr	08.82	82-84	72	4	15
Preston NE	Tr	10.84	84-85	40	0	1

GRAY Wayne William
Camberwell, 7 November, 1980 (F)

League Club	Source	Date Signed	Seasons Played	Apps	Subs	Gls
Wimbledon	YT	02.99	99-03	33	42	6
Swindon T	L	03.00	99	8	4	2
Port Vale	L	10.00	00	2	1	0
Leyton Orient	L	11.01	01	13	2	5
Brighton & Hove A	L	03.02	01	3	1	1
Southend U	Tr	07.04	04	33	11	11

GRAY William (Billy) Mair
Coventry, 3 December, 1931 (WH)

League Club	Source	Date Signed	Seasons Played	Apps	Subs	Gls
Coventry C	Jnrs	12.48	51	2	-	0

GRAY William (Billy) Patrick
Ashington, 24 May, 1927 EB (W)

League Club	Source	Date Signed	Seasons Played	Apps	Subs	Gls
Leyton Orient	Dinnington Colliery	05.47	47-48	19	-	1
Chelsea	Tr	03.49	48-52	146	-	12
Burnley	Tr	08.53	53-56	120	-	30
Nottingham F	Tr	06.57	57-62	201	-	29
Millwall	Tr	12.63	63-64	20	-	1

GRAYDON Keith
Dublin, 10 February, 1983 (F)

League Club	Source	Date Signed	Seasons Played	Apps	Subs	Gls
Sunderland	YT	02.00				
York C	L	03.03	02	4	3	1

GRAYDON Raymond (Ray) Jack
Bristol, 21 July, 1947 EYth (W)

League Club	Source	Date Signed	Seasons Played	Apps	Subs	Gls
Bristol Rov	App	09.65	65-70	131	2	33
Aston Villa	Tr	06.71	71-76	189	4	68
Coventry C	Tr	07.77	77	17	3	5
Oxford U	Washington (USA)	11.78	78-80	36	6	10

GRAYSON Barry John
Manchester, 12 October, 1944 (IF)

League Club	Source	Date Signed	Seasons Played	Apps	Subs	Gls
Manchester U	App	11.61				
Bury	Tr	01.65	64	1	-	0

GRAYSON Neil
York, 1 November, 1964 ESemiPro-4 (F)

League Club	Source	Date Signed	Seasons Played	Apps	Subs	Gls
Doncaster Rov	Rowntree Mackintosh	03.90	89-90	21	8	6
York C	Tr	03.91	90	0	1	0
Chesterfield	Tr	08.91	91	9	6	0
Northampton T	Boston U	06.94	94-96	103	17	31
Cheltenham T	Hereford U	03.98	99-01	75	33	24

GRAYSON Simon Darrell
Sheffield, 21 October, 1968 (F)

League Club	Source	Date Signed	Seasons Played	Apps	Subs	Gls
Sheffield U	App	10.86				
Chesterfield	L	11.87	87	7	1	0
Hartlepool U	Tr	04.88	87-89	39	5	13

League Club	Source	Date Signed	Seasons Played	Career Record Apps	Subs	Gls
GRAYSON Simon Nicholas						
Ripon, 16 December, 1969						(FB)
Leeds U	YT	06.88	87	2	0	0
Leicester C	Tr	03.92	91-96	175	13	4
Aston Villa	Tr	07.97	97-98	32	16	0
Blackburn Rov	Tr	07.99	99	31	3	0
Sheffield Wed	L	08.00	00	5	0	0
Stockport Co	L	01.01	00	13	0	0
Notts Co	L	09.01	01	10	0	1
Bradford C	L	02.02	01	7	0	0
Blackpool	Tr	08.02	02-04	104	10	6
GRAYSTON Neil James						
Keighley, 25 November, 1975						(FB)
Bradford C	YT	05.94	93-95	7	0	0
GRAZIOLI Giuliano Stefano Luigi						
Marylebone, 23 March, 1975						(F)
Peterborough U	Wembley	10.95	95-98	23	18	16
Swindon T	Tr	07.99	99-01	45	33	18
Bristol Rov	Tr	07.02	02	28	6	11
GREALISH Anthony (Tony) Patrick						
Paddington, 21 September, 1956 IRYth/IR-44						(M)
Orient	App	07.74	74-78	169	2	10
Luton T	Tr	08.79	79-80	78	0	2
Brighton & Hove A	Tr	07.81	81-83	95	5	6
West Bromwich A	Tr	03.84	83-85	55	10	5
Manchester C	Tr	10.86	86	11	0	0
Rotherham U	Tr	08.87	87-89	105	5	6
Walsall	Tr	08.90	90-91	32	4	1
GREATREX Edward **John**						
Nuneaton, 18 November, 1936						(G)
Norwich C	Jnrs	06.54	57	1	-	0
GREAVES Daniel (Danny) Thomas						
Upminster, 31 January, 1963						(F)
Southend U	Tottenham H (Jnrs)	01.81	81-83	30	19	14
Cambridge U	Maldon T	09.84	84	2	2	1
GREAVES Ian Denzil						
Crompton, 26 May, 1932						(FB)
Manchester U	Buxton	05.53	54-59	67	-	0
Lincoln C	Tr	12.60	60	11	-	0
Oldham Ath	Tr	05.61	61-62	22	-	0
GREAVES James (Jimmy) Peter						
East Ham, 20 February, 1940 EYth/Eu23-12/FLge-10/E-57						(F)
Chelsea	Jnrs	05.57	57-60	157	-	124
Tottenham H	AC Milan (It)	12.61	61-69	321	0	220
West Ham U	Tr	03.70	69-70	36	2	13
GREAVES Mark Andrew						
Hull, 22 January, 1975						(CD)
Hull C	Brigg T	06.96	96-02	152	25	10
Boston U	Tr	08.02	02-04	79	6	1
GREAVES Philip (Phil)						
Chesterfield, 5 September, 1961						(W)
Chesterfield	Alfreton T	10.86	86	5	0	0
GREAVES Roy						
Farnworth, 4 April, 1947						(M)
Bolton W	Jnrs	01.65	65-79	487	8	66
Rochdale	Seattle (USA)	11.82	82	19	2	0
GREAVES Steven (Steve) Ronald						
Chelsea, 17 January, 1970						(CD)
Fulham	YT	07.88	87	0	1	0
Preston NE	Tr	08.90	90	2	0	0
Ipswich T	Tr	01.91				
Scunthorpe U	Tr	08.92	92	9	6	0
GREEN Adam						
Hillingdon, 12 January, 1984						(FB)
Fulham	Sch	07.03	03-04	8	0	0
Sheffield Wed	L	01.05	04	3	0	0
Bournemouth	L	03.05	04	3	0	0
GREEN Adrian (Adie)						
Leicester, 22 October, 1957						(M)
Leicester C	App	06.76				
Rochdale	L	12.77	77	7	0	0
Aldershot	Tr	07.78	78-79	7	14	0
GREEN Alan Paul						
Worcester, 1 January, 1954 EYth						(F)
Coventry C	App	01.71	71-78	98	19	30

League Club	Source	Date Signed	Seasons Played	Career Record Apps	Subs	Gls
GREEN Alan Peter Charles						
Fordingbridge, 19 April, 1951						(F)
Bournemouth	Jnrs	07.69				
Mansfield T	Tr	07.72	72	1	0	0
GREEN Allan						
Darfield, 14 December, 1939						(FB)
Barnsley	Dodworth CW	01.59	60-61	19	-	0
GREEN Anthony (Tony)						
Kinning Park, 3 October, 1946 S-6						(M)
Blackpool	Albion Rov	05.67	66-71	121	1	13
Newcastle U	Tr	10.71	71-72	33	0	3
GREEN Arthur						
Liverpool, 28 April, 1928 Died 1992						(FB)
Huddersfield T	Burscough	02.51	51	3	-	0
GREEN Brian Geoffrey						
Droylsden, 5 June, 1935						(CF)
Rochdale	Haggate Lads	08.55	54-58	46	-	8
Southport	Tr	03.59	58-59	20	-	7
Barrow	Colwyn Bay	09.60	60	3	-	0
Exeter C	Altrincham	08.62	62	9	-	1
Chesterfield	Tr	02.63	62	2	-	0
GREEN Clive Peter						
Portsmouth, 6 December, 1959 ESch						(F)
Portsmouth	Jnrs	07.76	76-77	34	6	4
GREEN Colin Robert						
Wrexham, 10 February, 1942 Wu23-7/W-15						(FB)
Everton	Jnrs	02.59	60-61	15	-	1
Birmingham C	Tr	12.62	62-70	183	0	1
Wrexham	L	01.71	70	3	0	0
GREEN Donald (Don)						
Needham Market, 30 November, 1924 Died 1996						(CD)
Ipswich T	Bramford	03.47	46-51	52	-	0
GREEN Donald (Don)						
Blackburn, 13 May, 1932 Died 1992						(FB)
Accrington St (Am)	Blackburn Rov (Am)	05.52	52	12	-	0
GREEN Francis James						
Nottingham, 25 April, 1980						(F)
Peterborough U	Ilkeston T	03.98	97-03	51	57	14
Lincoln C	Tr	09.03	03-04	56	16	15
GREEN Frederick (Freddie) Zeanes						
Sheffield, 9 September, 1916 Died 1998						(FB)
Torquay U	Mosborough Trinity	06.35	35-37	86	-	0
Brighton & Hove A	Tr	06.38	38-47	26	-	0
GREEN George Frederick						
Northowram, 21 December, 1914 Died 1995						(WH)
Bradford PA	Jnrs	05.36	36	2	-	0
Huddersfield T	Tr	10.44	46-47	9	-	1
Reading	Tr	10.47	47-48	44	-	6
GREEN Horace						
Barnsley, 23 April, 1918 Died 2000						(FB)
Halifax T	Worsborough Bridge OB	11.36	37-48	155	-	5
Lincoln C	Tr	02.49	48-54	212	-	14
GREEN Ivan David						
Bexhill, 29 July, 1933						(IF)
Millwall		09.53	54	1	-	0
GREEN John (Johnny)						
Warrington, 22 May, 1939						(CD)
Tranmere Rov	Stockton Heath	02.58	58	17	-	5
Blackpool	Tr	03.59	59-66	135	0	9
Port Vale	Tr	09.67	67-70	92	2	7
GREEN John Richard						
Rotherham, 7 March, 1958						(CD)
Rotherham U	App	03.76	75-83	247	1	8
Scunthorpe U	Tr	09.83	83-85	100	0	4
Darlington	Tr	10.85	85-86	45	0	2
Rotherham U	Tr	12.86	86-88	84	1	3
GREEN Kenneth (Ken)						
Plaistow, 27 April, 1924 Died 2001 EB/FLge-2						(FB)
Birmingham C	Millwall (Am)	11.43	47-58	401	-	3
GREEN Kenneth (Ken)						
Hull, 20 November, 1929						(CF)
Grimsby T	Selby T	04.51	51	1	-	0

GREEN Leonard (Len) Hope
Bishop Auckland, 2 October, 1936 (FB)

League Club	Source	Date Signed	Seasons Played	Apps	Subs	Gls
Darlington		10.55	55-60	50	-	0

GREEN Leslie (Les)
Atherstone, 17 October, 1941 (G)

League Club	Source	Date Signed	Seasons Played	Apps	Subs	Gls
Hull C	Atherstone T	08.60	61	4	-	0
Hartlepools U	Burton A	11.65	65-66	34	0	0
Rochdale	Tr	04.67	67	44	0	0
Derby Co	Tr	05.68	68-70	107	0	0

GREEN Melvyn (Mel)
Hull, 20 October, 1951 (CD)

League Club	Source	Date Signed	Seasons Played	Apps	Subs	Gls
Hull C	App	10.69	71-72	10	0	0
Cambridge U	Tr	07.74	74	3	0	0

GREEN Michael (Mike) Clive
Carlisle, 8 September, 1946 (CD)

League Club	Source	Date Signed	Seasons Played	Apps	Subs	Gls
Carlisle U	App	09.64	65	2	0	0
Gillingham	Tr	07.68	68-70	131	1	24
Bristol Rov	Tr	07.71	71-73	74	3	2
Plymouth Arg	Tr	07.74	74-76	108	0	8
Torquay U	Tr	03.77	76-78	88	0	7

GREEN Michael (Mike) John
Southend-on-Sea, 20 November, 1957 (FB)

League Club	Source	Date Signed	Seasons Played	Apps	Subs	Gls
Exeter C	App	11.75	76	0	1	0

GREEN Paul Jason
Sheffield, 10 April, 1983 (M)

League Club	Source	Date Signed	Seasons Played	Apps	Subs	Gls
Doncaster Rov	YT	08.00	03-04	76	9	15

GREEN Philip (Phil)
Cardiff, 30 October, 1957 (F)

League Club	Source	Date Signed	Seasons Played	Apps	Subs	Gls
Newport Co	Barry T	03.84	83-84	11	5	2

GREEN Richard (Rick)
Scunthorpe, 23 November, 1952 (F)

League Club	Source	Date Signed	Seasons Played	Apps	Subs	Gls
Scunthorpe U	Appleby Frodingham	09.75	75-76	66	0	19
Chesterfield	Tr	02.77	76-77	45	3	13
Notts Co	Tr	06.78	78	6	3	0
Scunthorpe U	Tr	08.79	79-81	66	5	19

GREEN Richard Edward
Wolverhampton, 22 November, 1967 (CD)

League Club	Source	Date Signed	Seasons Played	Apps	Subs	Gls
Shrewsbury T	App	07.86	86-89	120	5	5
Swindon T	Tr	10.90				
Gillingham	Tr	03.92	91-97	206	10	16
Walsall	Tr	08.98	98	22	8	1
Rochdale	L	09.99	99	6	0	0
Northampton T	Tr	01.00	99-00	55	4	2

GREEN Robert Paul
Chertsey, 18 January, 1980 EYth/E-1 (G)

League Club	Source	Date Signed	Seasons Played	Apps	Subs	Gls
Norwich C	YT	07.97	98-04	180	1	0

GREEN Harry **Rodney**
Halifax, 24 June, 1939 (F)

League Club	Source	Date Signed	Seasons Played	Apps	Subs	Gls
Halifax T		08.60	60-61	9	-	2
Bradford PA	Tr	06.62	62	19	-	6
Bradford C	Tr	01.63	62-63	66	-	39
Gillingham	Tr	07.64	64	33	-	17
Grimsby T	Tr	08.65	65-66	65	0	20
Charlton Ath	Tr	02.67	66	3	1	1
Luton T	Tr	08.67	67	9	2	3
Watford	Tr	08.68	68-69	19	11	8

GREEN Roger
Cardiff, 20 September, 1944 (CD)

League Club	Source	Date Signed	Seasons Played	Apps	Subs	Gls
Newport Co	Barry T	01.72	71	1	0	0

GREEN Ronald (Ron) Rex
Birmingham, 3 October, 1956 (G)

League Club	Source	Date Signed	Seasons Played	Apps	Subs	Gls
Walsall	Alvechurch	06.77	77-83	163	0	0
Shrewsbury T	Tr	06.84	84	19	0	0
Bristol Rov	Tr	02.85	84-85	56	0	0
Scunthorpe U	Tr	08.86	86-87	78	0	0
Wimbledon	Tr	08.88	88	4	0	0
Shrewsbury T	L	09.88	88	17	0	0
Walsall	Tr	03.89	88-90	67	0	0
Colchester U	Kidderminster Hrs	11.92	92	4	0	0

GREEN Roy
Loughborough, 8 June, 1931 (IF)

League Club	Source	Date Signed	Seasons Played	Apps	Subs	Gls
Reading	Bloxwich Strollers	12.52	55-56	14	-	3

GREEN Norman **Russell**
Donington, 13 August, 1933 (FB)

League Club	Source	Date Signed	Seasons Played	Apps	Subs	Gls
Lincoln C	Quadring	08.51				
Lincoln C	Corby T	05.57	57-63	125	-	8

GREEN Ryan Michael
Cardiff, 20 October, 1980 WYth/Wu21-16/W-2 (FB)

League Club	Source	Date Signed	Seasons Played	Apps	Subs	Gls
Wolverhampton W	YT	10.97	98-00	6	2	0
Torquay U	L	03.01	00	10	0	0
Millwall	Tr	10.01	01	12	1	0
Cardiff C	Tr	08.02				
Sheffield Wed	Tr	11.02	02	4	0	0

GREEN Scott Paul
Walsall, 15 January, 1970 (FB)

League Club	Source	Date Signed	Seasons Played	Apps	Subs	Gls
Derby Co	YT	07.88				
Bolton W	Tr	03.90	89-96	166	54	25
Wigan Ath	Tr	06.97	97-02	177	22	10
Wrexham	Tr	02.03	02	12	3	3
Wrexham	Telford U	11.04	04	5	7	0

GREEN Stanley (Stan)
West Bromwich, 6 September, 1928 (CD)

League Club	Source	Date Signed	Seasons Played	Apps	Subs	Gls
Bristol Rov	Accles & Pollock	03.52	51	1	-	0

GREEN Stuart
Whitehaven, 15 June, 1981 (M)

League Club	Source	Date Signed	Seasons Played	Apps	Subs	Gls
Newcastle U	YT	07.99				
Carlisle U	L	12.01	01	16	0	3
Hull C	Tr	07.02	02-04	91	8	20
Carlisle U	L	02.03	02	9	1	2

GREEN Thomas (Tommy)
Birkenhead, 18 September, 1926 Died 1952 (WH)

League Club	Source	Date Signed	Seasons Played	Apps	Subs	Gls
Southport	West Lancashire ATC	05.46	46	4	-	0

GREEN William (Bill)
Newcastle, 22 December, 1950 (CD)

League Club	Source	Date Signed	Seasons Played	Apps	Subs	Gls
Hartlepool	Jnrs	06.69	69-72	128	3	9
Carlisle U	Tr	07.73	73-75	119	0	4
West Ham U	Tr	06.76	76-77	35	0	1
Peterborough U	Tr	07.78	78	30	0	0
Chesterfield	Tr	06.79	79-82	160	0	5
Doncaster Rov	Tr	06.83	83	10	1	1

GREEN William (Billy) Charles
Hull, 9 October, 1927 Died 1996 (WH)

League Club	Source	Date Signed	Seasons Played	Apps	Subs	Gls
Wolverhampton W	Jnrs	09.45				
Walsall	Tr	09.49	49-53	180	-	8
Wrexham	Tr	06.54	54-56	60	-	2

GREENACRE Christopher (Chris) Mark
Halifax, 23 December, 1977 (F)

League Club	Source	Date Signed	Seasons Played	Apps	Subs	Gls
Manchester C	YT	07.95	96-98	3	5	1
Cardiff C	L	08.97	97	11	0	2
Blackpool	L	03.98	97	2	2	0
Scarborough	L	12.98	98	10	2	2
Mansfield T	Tr	11.99	99-01	120	1	49
Stoke C	Tr	07.02	02-04	44	31	7

GREENALL Colin Anthony
Billinge, 30 December, 1963 EYth (CD)

League Club	Source	Date Signed	Seasons Played	Apps	Subs	Gls
Blackpool	App	01.81	80-86	179	4	9
Gillingham	Tr	09.86	86-87	62	0	5
Oxford U	Tr	02.88	87-89	67	0	2
Bury	L	01.90	89	3	0	0
Bury	Tr	07.90	90-91	66	2	5
Preston NE	Tr	03.92	91-92	29	0	1
Chester C	Tr	08.93	93	42	0	1
Lincoln C	Tr	07.94	94-95	43	0	3
Wigan Ath	Tr	09.95	95-98	162	0	14

GREENALL George Edward
Liverpool, 5 November, 1937 (CD)

League Club	Source	Date Signed	Seasons Played	Apps	Subs	Gls
Manchester C	Andover	11.58				
Oldham Ath	Tr	09.60	60	25	-	0

GREENAWAY Arthur Robert
Swindon, 5 April, 1928 (IF)

League Club	Source	Date Signed	Seasons Played	Apps	Subs	Gls
Plymouth Arg		08.47				
Exeter C	Tr	05.50	50	1	-	0

GREENAWAY Brian Joseph
Hammersmith, 26 September, 1957 (W)

League Club	Source	Date Signed	Seasons Played	Apps	Subs	Gls
Fulham	App	06.75	76-80	68	17	8

GREENE David Michael
Luton, 26 October, 1973 IRu21-14 (CD)

League Club	Source	Date Signed	Seasons Played	Apps	Subs	Gls
Luton T	Jnrs	09.91	92-94	18	1	0
Colchester U	L	11.95	95	14	0	1
Brentford	L	03.96	95	11	0	0
Colchester U	Tr	06.96	96-99	153	0	15
Cardiff C	Tr	07.00	00	10	0	0
Cambridge U	Tr	03.01	00	1	0	0

GREENER Ronald (Ron)
Easington, 31 January, 1934 (CD)

League Club	Source	Date Signed	Seasons Played	Apps	Subs	Gls
Newcastle U	Easington Colliery	05.51	53	3	-	0
Darlington	Tr	08.55	55-66	439	0	5

GREENHALGH Brian Arthur
Chesterfield, 20 February, 1947 (F)

League Club	Source	Date Signed	Seasons Played	Apps	Subs	Gls
Preston NE	App	02.65	65-67	19	0	9
Aston Villa	Tr	09.67	67-68	37	3	12
Leicester C	Tr	02.69	68	2	2	0
Huddersfield T	Tr	06.69	69-70	15	0	0
Cambridge U	Tr	07.71	71-73	116	0	47
Bournemouth	Tr	02.74	73-74	23	1	7
Torquay U	L	06.74	74	9	0	1
Watford	Tr	03.75	74-75	17	1	1

GREENHALGH James (Jimmy) Radcliffe
Manchester, 25 August, 1923 (WH)

League Club	Source	Date Signed	Seasons Played	Apps	Subs	Gls
Hull C	Newton Heath Loco	08.46	46-50	148	-	5
Bury	Tr	12.50	50-54	122	-	1
Gillingham	Wigan Ath	07.56	56	16	-	1

GREENHALGH Laurence (Laurie) Lee
Salford, 2 April, 1974 (FB)

League Club	Source	Date Signed	Seasons Played	Apps	Subs	Gls
Bury	YT	07.92	92	2	0	0

GREENHALGH Norman
Bolton, 10 August, 1914 Died 1995 FLge-1/EWar-1 (FB)

League Club	Source	Date Signed	Seasons Played	Apps	Subs	Gls
Bolton W		09.33				
New Brighton	Tr	10.35	35-37	77	-	8
Everton	Tr	01.38	37-48	106	-	1

GREENHOFF Brian
Barnsley, 28 April, 1953 Eu23-4/EB/E-18 (CD)

League Club	Source	Date Signed	Seasons Played	Apps	Subs	Gls
Manchester U	App	06.70	73-78	218	3	13
Leeds U	Tr	08.79	79-81	68	4	1
Rochdale	(Hong Kong)	03.83	82-83	15	1	0

GREENHOFF Frank
Barnsley, 3 March, 1924 Died 1999 (W)

League Club	Source	Date Signed	Seasons Played	Apps	Subs	Gls
Barnsley	Manchester C (Am)	09.47				
Bradford C	Tr	10.48	48-51	81	-	11

GREENHOFF James (Jimmy)
Barnsley, 19 June, 1946 Eu23-5/FLge-1 (F)

League Club	Source	Date Signed	Seasons Played	Apps	Subs	Gls
Leeds U	App	08.63	62-68	88	6	21
Birmingham C	Tr	08.68	68	31	0	14
Stoke C	Tr	08.69	69-76	274	0	76
Manchester U	Tr	11.76	76-80	94	3	26
Crewe Alex	Tr	12.80	80	11	0	4
Port Vale	Toronto (Can)	08.81	81-82	44	4	5
Rochdale	Tr	03.83	82-83	16	0	0

GREENING Jonathan
Scarborough, 2 January, 1979 EYth/Eu21-18 (W)

League Club	Source	Date Signed	Seasons Played	Apps	Subs	Gls
York C	YT	12.96	96-97	5	20	2
Manchester U	Tr	03.98	98-00	4	10	0
Middlesbrough	Tr	08.01	01-03	91	8	4
West Bromwich A	Tr	07.04	04	32	2	0

GREENMAN Christopher (Chris)
Bristol, 22 December, 1968 ESch (CD)

League Club	Source	Date Signed	Seasons Played	Apps	Subs	Gls
Coventry C	Jnrs	07.88	91-92	5	1	0
Peterborough U	Tr	03.93	92-93	32	2	0

GREENOUGH Richard (Ricky) Anthony
Mexborough, 30 May, 1961 (CD)

League Club	Source	Date Signed	Seasons Played	Apps	Subs	Gls
Chester C	Alfreton T	01.85	84-87	123	9	16
Scarborough	Tr	07.88				
York C	Tr	11.88	88-89	28	1	1

GREENSMITH Ronald (Ron)
Sheffield, 22 January, 1933 (W)

League Club	Source	Date Signed	Seasons Played	Apps	Subs	Gls
Sheffield Wed	Shiregreen WMC	01.54	54-57	5	-	0
York C	Tr	01.58	57-59	42	-	1

GREENWAY Mark
Halifax, 19 April, 1966 (FB)

League Club	Source	Date Signed	Seasons Played	Apps	Subs	Gls
Halifax T	App	04.84	83-84	15	1	1

GREENWELL Donald (Don)
Chester-le-Street, 4 January, 1924 Died 2002 (WH)

League Club	Source	Date Signed	Seasons Played	Apps	Subs	Gls
York C		12.46	46	1	-	0

GREENWOOD Alexander (Alex) John
Fulham, 17 June, 1933 (FB)

League Club	Source	Date Signed	Seasons Played	Apps	Subs	Gls
Chelsea	Ferryhill Ath	09.53				
Crystal Palace	Tr	05.54	54	2	-	0
Darlington	Scarborough	06.55	55	8	-	0

GREENWOOD John Jones
Manchester, 22 January, 1921 Died 1994 (WH)

League Club	Source	Date Signed	Seasons Played	Apps	Subs	Gls
Manchester C		09.46	48	1	-	0
Exeter C	Tr	06.49	49	31	-	2
Aldershot	Tr	03.51	50	12	-	0

GREENWOOD Nigel Patrick
Preston, 27 November, 1966 (F)

League Club	Source	Date Signed	Seasons Played	Apps	Subs	Gls
Preston NE	App	09.84	84-85	36	9	14
Bury	Tr	08.86	86-89	78	32	25
Preston NE	Tr	02.90	89-91	24	6	4
Halifax T	Tr	07.92	92	21	4	5

GREENWOOD Patrick (Paddy) George
Hull, 17 October, 1946 (CD)

League Club	Source	Date Signed	Seasons Played	Apps	Subs	Gls
Hull C	Jnrs	11.64	65-71	137	12	3
Barnsley	Tr	11.71	71-73	110	1	6
Nottingham F	Boston (USA)	10.74	74	15	0	0

GREENWOOD Peter
Todmorden, 11 September, 1924 (WH)

League Club	Source	Date Signed	Seasons Played	Apps	Subs	Gls
Burnley		10.46				
Chester	Tr	07.48	48-51	62	-	3

GREENWOOD Peter
Rawtenstall, 30 April, 1938 (CF)

League Club	Source	Date Signed	Seasons Played	Apps	Subs	Gls
Bury	Bolton W (Am)	10.56	56	1	-	0

GREENWOOD Ronald (Ron)
Burnley, 11 November, 1921 EB (CD)

League Club	Source	Date Signed	Seasons Played	Apps	Subs	Gls
Chelsea	Belfast Celtic	10.43				
Bradford PA	Tr	12.45	46-47	59	-	0
Brentford	Tr	03.49	48-52	142	-	1
Chelsea	Tr	10.52	52-54	65	-	0
Fulham	Tr	02.55	54-55	42	-	0

GREENWOOD Ross Michael
York, 1 November, 1985 (FB)

League Club	Source	Date Signed	Seasons Played	Apps	Subs	Gls
Sheffield Wed	Sch	●	04	0	2	0

GREENWOOD Roy Thornton
Leeds, 26 September, 1952 (W)

League Club	Source	Date Signed	Seasons Played	Apps	Subs	Gls
Hull C	App	10.70	71-75	118	8	24
Sunderland	Tr	01.76	75-78	45	11	9
Derby Co	Tr	01.79	78-79	26	5	1
Swindon T	Tr	02.80	79-81	49	4	7
Huddersfield T	Tr	08.82	82-83	5	3	0
Tranmere Rov	L	11.83	83	3	0	0

GREENWOOD Roy Tony
Croydon, 22 May, 1931 (FB)

League Club	Source	Date Signed	Seasons Played	Apps	Subs	Gls
Crystal Palace	Beckenham	11.54	54-58	111	-	0

GREER Gordon
Glasgow, 14 December, 1980 (CD)

League Club	Source	Date Signed	Seasons Played	Apps	Subs	Gls
Blackburn Rov	Clyde	05.01				
Stockport Co	L	03.03	02	4	1	1

GREER Ross
Perth, Australia, 23 September, 1967 (F)

League Club	Source	Date Signed	Seasons Played	Apps	Subs	Gls
Chester C	Floreat Athena (Aus)	11.89	89	2	0	0

GREETHAM Harold
Grimsby, 7 March, 1930 (FB)

League Club	Source	Date Signed	Seasons Played	Apps	Subs	Gls
Grimsby T	Jnrs	06.50	50	4	-	0

GREGAN Sean Matthew
Guisborough, 29 March, 1974 (M)

League Club	Source	Date Signed	Seasons Played	Apps	Subs	Gls
Darlington	YT	01.91	91-96	129	7	4
Preston NE	Tr	11.96	96-01	206	6	12
West Bromwich A	Tr	08.02	02-03	76	3	2
Leeds U	Tr	09.04	04	34	1	0

GREGG Frank
Stourbridge, 9 October, 1942 (FB)

League Club	Source	Date Signed	Seasons Played	Apps	Subs	Gls
Walsall	Jnrs	10.59	60-72	389	4	3

GREGG Henry (Harry)
Derry, 25 October, 1932 NISch/NIAmat/IrLge-1/NI-25 (G)

League Club	Source	Date Signed	Seasons Played	Apps	Subs	Gls
Doncaster Rov	Coleraine	10.52	52-57	94	-	0
Manchester U	Tr	12.57	57-66	210	0	0
Stoke C	Tr	12.66	66	2	0	0

GREGG Matthew (Matt) Stephen
Cheltenham, 30 November, 1978 (G)

League Club	Source	Date Signed	Seasons Played	Apps	Subs	Gls
Torquay U	YT	07.97	95-98	32	0	0
Crystal Palace	Tr	10.98	99-00	7	0	0
Swansea C	L	02.99	98	5	0	0
Exeter C	L	09.01	01	2	0	0

League Club	Source	Date Signed	Seasons Played	Career Record Apps	Subs	Gls
GREGOIRE Roland Barry						
Liverpool, 23 November, 1958						(F)
Halifax T	Jnrs	08.76	77	5	0	0
Sunderland	Tr	11.77	77-78	6	3	1
GREGORIO Adolfo						
Turlock, California, USA, 1 October, 1982 UsYth						(M)
Darlington	UCLA (USA)	09.04	04	19	5	2
GREGORY Andrew (Andy)						
Barnsley, 8 October, 1976						(M)
Barnsley	YT	07.95				
Carlisle U	L	09.99	99	6	1	1
GREGORY Anthony (Tony) Charles						
Luton, 16 May, 1937 EYth						(WH)
Luton T	Vauxhall Motors	05.55	55-59	59	-	17
Watford	Tr	03.60	59-63	107	-	14
GREGORY Anthony (Tony) Gerard						
Doncaster, 21 March, 1968 ESch/EYth						(M)
Sheffield Wed	App	01.86	85-88	14	4	1
Halifax T	Tr	08.90	90-91	16	1	1
GREGORY Anthony (Tony) Thomas						
Dawley, 10 March, 1947						(FB)
Shrewsbury T	App	03.65	64-75	286	8	0
GREGORY Brian						
Belfast, 11 January, 1955						(F)
Gillingham	Jnrs	08.74	74	1	1	0
GREGORY David Harry						
Peterborough, 6 October, 1951						(F)
Peterborough U	Chatteris T	08.73	73-76	125	17	32
Stoke C	Tr	06.77	77	22	1	3
Blackburn Rov	Tr	07.78	78	5	0	3
Bury	Tr	09.78	78-79	50	2	13
Portsmouth	Tr	12.79	79-81	64	10	18
Wrexham	Tr	08.82	82-85	145	8	31
Peterborough U	Tr	08.86	86	16	15	8
GREGORY David Peter						
Camden, 19 February, 1960						(FB)
Millwall	Crystal Palace (N/C)	08.78	78-80	52	0	2
GREGORY David Spencer						
Sudbury, 23 January, 1970						(M)
Ipswich T	App	03.87	88-94	16	16	2
Hereford U	L	01.95	94	2	0	0
Peterborough U	Tr	07.95	95	0	3	0
Colchester U	Tr	12.95	95-01	211	14	20
GREGORY Ernest (Ernie)						
Stratford, 10 November, 1921 EB						(G)
West Ham U	Leytonstone	05.39	46-59	382	-	0
GREGORY Charles **Frederick (Fred)**						
Doncaster, 24 October, 1911 Died 1985						(FB)
Doncaster Rov	Brodsworth Colliery	10.28	29	13	-	3
Manchester C	Tr	03.30	31-33	21	-	2
Reading	Tr	03.34	33-37	129	-	6
Crystal Palace	Tr	12.37	37-38	43	-	9
Hartlepools U	Tr	06.46	46	21	-	0
Rotherham U	Tr	02.47	46	1	-	0
GREGORY Gordon **Harold (Harry)**						
Hackney, 24 October, 1943 EYth						(M)
Leyton Orient	Jnrs	10.61	62-65	79	0	12
Charlton Ath	Tr	08.66	66-70	146	3	24
Aston Villa	Tr	10.70	70-71	18	6	2
Hereford U	Tr	08.72	72-74	71	2	6
GREGORY John Charles						
Scunthorpe, 11 May, 1954 E-6						(M)
Northampton T	App	05.72	72-76	187	0	8
Aston Villa	Tr	06.77	77-78	59	6	10
Brighton & Hove A	Tr	07.79	79-80	72	0	7
Queens Park Rgrs	Tr	06.81	81-85	159	2	36
Derby Co	Tr	11.85	85-87	103	0	22
Plymouth Arg	(Retired) Coach	01.90	89	3	0	0
Bolton W	Tr	03.90	89	2	5	0
GREGORY John (Jack) Ernest						
Shoreditch, 24 September, 1926 Died 1995						(IF)
West Ham U	Bromley	06.51	51-52	24	-	6
Scunthorpe U	Tr	06.53	53-56	147	-	63
Aldershot	Tr	06.57	57	6	-	2
GREGORY John Graham						
Hounslow, 16 May, 1977						(G)
Fulham	YT	●	94	0	1	0
GREGORY John (Jack) Leslie						
Southampton, 25 January, 1925						(FB)
Southampton	Woolston	12.44	46-53	66	-	0
Leyton Orient	Tr	07.55	55-58	91	-	0
Bournemouth	Tr	07.59	59	17	-	0
GREGORY Neil Richard						
Ndola, Zambia, 7 October, 1972						(F)
Ipswich T	YT	02.92	94-97	18	27	9
Chesterfield	L	02.94	93	2	1	1
Scunthorpe U	L	03.95	94	10	0	7
Torquay U	L	11.96	96	5	0	0
Peterborough U	L	11.97	97	2	1	1
Colchester U	Tr	01.98	97-98	41	12	11
GREGORY Paul Gordon						
Sheffield, 26 July, 1961						(G)
Chesterfield	App	07.79	80-83	23	0	0
Doncaster Rov	Tr	03.84	84	1	0	0
Scunthorpe U	Tr	10.84	84-86	69	0	0
Halifax T	L	09.86	86	6	0	0
GREGSON Colin						
Newcastle, 19 January, 1958						(M)
West Bromwich A	App	01.76				
Sheffield Wed	Tr	07.77	77	1	1	0
GREGSON John						
Skelmersdale, 17 May, 1939						(W)
Blackpool	Skelmersdale U	05.57	57-58	3	-	1
Chester	Tr	05.62	62	32	-	5
Shrewsbury T	Tr	03.63	62-64	56	-	6
Mansfield T	Tr	11.64	64-66	75	1	5
Lincoln C	Tr	06.67	67	31	5	3
Cambridge U	Tr	07.68	70	32	0	1
GREGSON Peter George						
Blackpool, 12 May, 1953						(G)
Southport	Blackpool (Am)	07.71	71-72	35	0	0
GREIG John **Robert (Bobby)**						
Sunderland, 13 September, 1949						(W)
Leicester C	App	01.67				
Workington	Tr	02.68	67	4	1	0
GRENET Francois						
Bordeaux, France, 8 March, 1975						(FB)
Derby Co	Bordeaux (Fr)	11.01	01-02	14	4	0
GRENFELL Stephen (Steve) John						
Enfield, 27 October, 1966						(FB)
Tottenham H	App	08.84				
Colchester U	Tr	10.86	86-88	67	3	1
GRESKO Vratislav						
Pressburg, Slovakia, 24 July, 1977 Slovakia 24						(FB)
Blackburn Rov	Parma (It)	01.03	02-04	34	3	1
GRESTY Philip (Phil)						
Tarporley, 2 June, 1953						(W)
Crewe Alex (Am)	Jnrs	07.71	74	3	1	0
GREW Mark Stuart						
Bilston, 15 February, 1958						(G)
West Bromwich A	Jnrs	06.76	81-82	33	0	0
Wigan Ath	L	12.78	78	4	0	0
Leicester C	Tr	07.83	83	5	0	0
Oldham Ath	L	10.83	83	5	0	0
Ipswich T	Tr	03.84	84	6	0	0
Fulham	L	09.85	85	4	0	0
West Bromwich A	L	01.86	85	1	0	0
Port Vale	Tr	06.86	86-91	184	0	0
Blackburn Rov	L	10.90	90	13	0	0
Cardiff C	Tr	08.92	92-93	21	0	0
GREWCOCK Neil						
Leicester, 26 April, 1962						(W)
Leicester C	App	07.79	78-80	7	1	1
Gillingham	Tr	03.82	81-82	30	4	4
Burnley	Shepshed Charterhouse	06.84	84-90	180	22	26
GREY William **Brian**						
Swansea, 7 September, 1948						(M)
Swansea T	App	09.66	67-69	27	3	8
GREYGOOSE Dean						
Thetford, 18 December, 1964 EYth						(G)
Cambridge U	App	11.82	83-84	26	0	0
Lincoln C	L	09.85	85	6	0	0
Orient	Tr	12.85	85	1	0	0
Crystal Palace	Tr	08.86				
Crewe Alex	Tr	08.87	87-92	205	0	0

GREYLING Anton
Pretoria, South Africa, 5 November, 1977 Sau23-11 (M)

League Club	Source	Date Signed	Seasons Played	Apps	Subs	Gls
Torquay U	Supersport U (SA)	08.01	01	0	2	0

GRIBBIN Brian Thomas
Newcastle, 2 June, 1954 (FB)

League Club	Source	Date Signed	Seasons Played	Apps	Subs	Gls
Hartlepool	Jnrs	07.73	72	1	0	0

GRICE Michael (Mike) John
Woking, 3 November, 1931 Died 2002 (W)

League Club	Source	Date Signed	Seasons Played	Apps	Subs	Gls
Colchester U	Lowestoft T	06.52	52-55	106	-	15
West Ham U	Tr	03.56	55-60	142	-	18
Coventry C	Tr	08.61	61	37	-	6
Colchester U	Tr	06.62	62-65	138	1	13

GRIDELET Philip (Phil) Raymond
Edgware, 30 April, 1967 ESemiPro (M)

League Club	Source	Date Signed	Seasons Played	Apps	Subs	Gls
Barnsley	Barnet	01.90	90-92	3	3	0
Rotherham U	L	03.93	92	9	0	0
Southend U	Tr	09.93	93-97	149	27	10

GRIEMINK Bart
Groningen, Holland, 29 March, 1972 (G)

League Club	Source	Date Signed	Seasons Played	Apps	Subs	Gls
Birmingham C	WK Emmen (Holl)	11.95	95	20	0	0
Peterborough U	Tr	10.96	96-99	58	0	0
Swindon T	L	02.00	99	4	0	0
Swindon T	Tr	07.00	00-03	118	2	0
Southend U	Tr	07.04	04	19	0	0

GRIERSON Darrell Philip
Blackpool, 13 October, 1968 (G)

League Club	Source	Date Signed	Seasons Played	Apps	Subs	Gls
Tranmere Rov	App	10.86	86	4	0	0

GRIEVE David
Selkirk, 15 February, 1929 (W)

League Club	Source	Date Signed	Seasons Played	Apps	Subs	Gls
Reading	Dalry Thistle	02.52	51-53	19	-	1
Crystal Palace	Tr	04.54	54	22	-	3

GRIEVE Richard Maxwell
Aberdeen, 29 June, 1924 (IF)

League Club	Source	Date Signed	Seasons Played	Apps	Subs	Gls
Rochdale	Montrose	05.50				
Wrexham	Tr	09.50	50	1	-	0

GRIEVES Kenneth (Ken) James
Sydney, Australia, 27 August, 1925 Died 1992 (G)

League Club	Source	Date Signed	Seasons Played	Apps	Subs	Gls
Bury	Wigan Ath	04.47	47-49	59	-	0
Bolton W	Tr	12.51	51-55	49	-	0
Stockport Co	Tr	07.57	57	39	-	0

GRIEVESON Henry (Harry)
Easington, 10 April, 1941 (WH)

League Club	Source	Date Signed	Seasons Played	Apps	Subs	Gls
Sunderland	Jnrs	04.58				
Southend U	Tr	07.61	61	24	-	1

GRIFFIN Adam
Salford, 26 August, 1984 (M)

League Club	Source	Date Signed	Seasons Played	Apps	Subs	Gls
Oldham Ath	Sch	08.03	01-04	58	4	3

GRIFFIN Andrew (Andy)
Billinge, 7 March, 1979 EYth/Eu21-2 (FB)

League Club	Source	Date Signed	Seasons Played	Apps	Subs	Gls
Stoke C	YT	09.96	96-97	52	5	2
Newcastle U	Tr	01.98	97-03	63	13	2
Portsmouth	Tr	07.04	04	18	4	0

GRIFFIN Anthony (Tony) Richard
Bournemouth, 22 March, 1979 (FB)

League Club	Source	Date Signed	Seasons Played	Apps	Subs	Gls
Bournemouth	YT	07.97	98	1	5	0
Cheltenham T	Tr	07.99	99-03	67	29	1

GRIFFIN Charles (Charlie) John
Bath, 25 June, 1979 (F)

League Club	Source	Date Signed	Seasons Played	Apps	Subs	Gls
Swindon T	Chippenham T	01.99	98-00	8	20	2

GRIFFIN Colin Raymond
Dudley, 8 January, 1956 (CD)

League Club	Source	Date Signed	Seasons Played	Apps	Subs	Gls
Derby Co	App	01.74				
Shrewsbury T	Tr	01.76	75-88	402	4	7

GRIFFIN Daniel (Danny) Joseph
Belfast, 19 August, 1977 NIu21-10/NI-29 (CD)

League Club	Source	Date Signed	Seasons Played	Apps	Subs	Gls
Stockport Co	Dundee U	01.04	03-04	31	0	1

GRIFFIN Frank Albert
Pendlebury, 28 March, 1928 (W)

League Club	Source	Date Signed	Seasons Played	Apps	Subs	Gls
Shrewsbury T	St Augustine's	03.51	50	37	-	5
West Bromwich A	Tr	04.51	50-58	240	-	47
Northampton T	Tr	07.59	59	16	-	0

GRIFFIN Kevin Russell
Plymouth, 5 October, 1953 (F)

League Club	Source	Date Signed	Seasons Played	Apps	Subs	Gls
Bristol C	App	09.71	71-74	5	3	0
Mansfield T	L	03.75	74	4	0	2
Cambridge U	L	09.75	75	7	1	1

GRIFFIN William (Billy)
Bircotes, 24 September, 1940 (M)

League Club	Source	Date Signed	Seasons Played	Apps	Subs	Gls
Sheffield Wed	Jnrs	09.57	58-62	35	-	20
Bury	Tr	12.62	62-65	84	4	22
Workington	Tr	02.66	65-68	82	0	18
Rotherham U	Tr	01.69	68-69	14	3	1

GRIFFIT Leandre
Maubeuge, France, 21 May, 1984 (M)

League Club	Source	Date Signed	Seasons Played	Apps	Subs	Gls
Southampton	Amiens (Fr)	07.03	03-04	2	5	2
Leeds U	L	01.05	04	0	1	0
Rotherham U	L	03.05	04	1	1	0

GRIFFITH Cohen
Georgetown, Guyana, 26 December, 1962 Wu21-1 (W)

League Club	Source	Date Signed	Seasons Played	Apps	Subs	Gls
Cardiff C	Kettering T	10.89	89-94	205	29	39

GRIFFITHS Arfon Trevor
Wrexham, 23 August, 1941 Wu23-3/W-17 (M)

League Club	Source	Date Signed	Seasons Played	Apps	Subs	Gls
Wrexham	Jnrs	05.59	59-60	41	-	8
Arsenal	Tr	01.61	60-61	15	-	2
Wrexham	Tr	09.62	62-78	545	6	112

GRIFFITHS Ashley Russell
Barry, 5 January, 1961 WSch/WYth (M)

League Club	Source	Date Signed	Seasons Played	Apps	Subs	Gls
Bristol Rov	App	01.79	79-80	6	1	0

GRIFFITHS Barry
Manchester, 21 November, 1940 Died 1997 (G)

League Club	Source	Date Signed	Seasons Played	Apps	Subs	Gls
Blackburn Rov		07.62	59-62	2	-	0

GRIFFITHS Brian
Penycae, 21 November, 1933 (IF)

League Club	Source	Date Signed	Seasons Played	Apps	Subs	Gls
Wrexham		05.52	51-57	23	-	11
Chester	Tr	07.58	58	2	-	1

GRIFFITHS Bryan
Litherland, 21 November, 1938 (FB)

League Club	Source	Date Signed	Seasons Played	Apps	Subs	Gls
Everton	Jnrs	03.56	58	2	-	0
Southport	Tr	06.60	60-62	117	-	1

GRIFFITHS Bryan Kenneth
Prescot, 26 January, 1965 (W)

League Club	Source	Date Signed	Seasons Played	Apps	Subs	Gls
Wigan Ath	St Helens T	11.88	88-92	176	13	44
Blackpool	Tr	07.93	93-94	54	3	17
Scarborough	L	12.94	94	5	0	1

GRIFFITHS Carl Brian
Welshpool, 15 July, 1971 WYth/Wu21-2/WB-1 (F)

League Club	Source	Date Signed	Seasons Played	Apps	Subs	Gls
Shrewsbury T	YT	09.88	88-93	110	33	54
Manchester C	Tr	10.93	93-94	11	7	4
Portsmouth	Tr	08.95	95	2	12	2
Peterborough U	Tr	03.96	95-96	6	10	2
Leyton Orient	L	10.96	96	5	0	3
Leyton Orient	Tr	03.97	96-98	60	5	29
Wrexham	L	01.99	98	4	0	3
Port Vale	Tr	03.99	98-99	3	5	1
Leyton Orient	Tr	12.99	99-00	46	2	18
Luton T	Tr	07.01	01-02	13	0	8

GRIFFITHS Clive Leslie
Pontypridd, 22 January, 1955 WSch/Wu23-2 (CD)

League Club	Source	Date Signed	Seasons Played	Apps	Subs	Gls
Manchester U	App	01.72	73	7	0	0
Plymouth Arg	L	07.74	74	10	1	0
Tranmere Rov	Tr	11.75	75-76	59	0	0

GRIFFITHS David (Dave)
Woking, 13 December, 1937 (WH)

League Club	Source	Date Signed	Seasons Played	Apps	Subs	Gls
Portsmouth		03.56				
Aldershot	Tr	08.57	58-59	5	-	0

GRIFFITHS David
Newport, 20 May, 1962 (CD)

League Club	Source	Date Signed	Seasons Played	Apps	Subs	Gls
Newport Co	Cwmbran T	03.88	87	0	1	0

GRIFFITHS David Bernard
Liverpool, 25 May, 1951 (FB)

League Club	Source	Date Signed	Seasons Played	Apps	Subs	Gls
Tranmere Rov	Jnrs	02.70	69	6	0	0

GRIFFITHS Dennis
Ruabon, 12 August, 1935 (WH)

League Club	Source	Date Signed	Seasons Played	Apps	Subs	Gls
Wrexham	Jnrs	08.52	53-57	67	-	3

GRIFFITHS Douglas (Doug) James
Birmingham, 23 October, 1948 (CD)

League Club	Source	Date Signed	Seasons Played	Apps	Subs	Gls
Wolverhampton W	App	10.66				
Stockport Co	Tr	07.68	68-69	20	1	0

GRIFFITHS Estyn
Mold, 22 July, 1927 WAmat (WH)

League Club	Source	Date Signed	Seasons Played	Apps	Subs	Gls
Wrexham		04.50	50-51	10	-	0

League Club	Source	Date Signed	Seasons Played	Apps	Subs	Gls
GRIFFITHS Evan Gareth						
Aylesham, 19 April, 1943						(W)
Gillingham		07.61	60	1	-	0
GRIFFITHS Gareth John						
Winsford, 10 April, 1970						(CD)
Port Vale	Rhyl	02.93	93-97	90	4	4
Shrewsbury T	L	10.97	97	6	0	0
Wigan Ath	Tr	07.98	98-00	44	9	2
Rochdale	Tr	07.01	01-04	147	8	12
GRIFFITHS George						
Earlestown, 23 June, 1924 Died 2004						(FB)
Bury	Earlestown	03.42	46-53	239	-	7
Halifax T	Tr	06.54	54-57	166	-	14
GRIFFITHS Gerald (Gerry) Leslie						
Swansea, 15 December, 1934 WSch						(WH)
Swansea T	Jnrs	06.52				
Crewe Alex	Tr	06.56	56	21	-	3
GRIFFITHS James **Henry (Harry)**						
Swansea, 4 January, 1931 Died 1978 WLge-1/W-1						(FB)
Swansea T	Jnrs	06.49	49-63	422	-	72
GRIFFITHS Harry Stanley						
Liverpool, 17 November, 1912 Died 1981						(CD)
Everton		08.32				
Port Vale	Tr	05.35	35-46	103	-	3
GRIFFITHS Ian James						
Birkenhead, 17 April, 1960						(W)
Tranmere Rov	Jnrs	02.79	78-82	110	6	5
Rochdale	Tr	08.83	83-84	40	1	5
Port Vale	Tr	09.84	84	9	3	0
Wigan Ath	Tr	07.85	85-87	73	9	7
Wigan Ath	Mazda Hiroshima (Jap)	08.90	90	6	5	0
Wrexham	Tr	03.91	90-91	14	0	0
GRIFFITHS Ivor						
Port Talbot, 19 June, 1918 Died 1993						(W)
Chester	Tottenham H (Am)	09.46	46	1	-	0
GRIFFITHS James Thomas						
Gowerton, 5 October, 1941						(CF)
Stockport Co		03.63	62	3	-	0
GRIFFITHS Jeffrey (Jeff) Kenneth						
Swansea, 19 March, 1957						(F)
Swansea C		04.76	75-77	7	7	1
GRIFFITHS John						
Oldbury, 16 June, 1951						(M)
Aston Villa	App	11.68	68-69	1	2	0
Stockport Co	Tr	05.70	70-74	167	15	31
GRIFFITHS George **Keith**						
Chester, 30 December, 1927						(G)
Chester	Rhyl	07.55	55-58	54	-	0
GRIFFITHS Kenneth (Kenny) George						
Cardiff, 11 November, 1925 Died 1985						(IF)
Cardiff C	Jnrs	06.43				
Torquay U	L	01.48	47	6	-	1
Torquay U	L	08.48	48	5	-	0
Newport Co	Distillery	09.49	49	14	-	6
GRIFFITHS Kenneth (Ken) James						
Stoke-on-Trent, 2 April, 1930						(IF)
Port Vale	Northwood Mission	03.50	49-57	179	-	52
Mansfield T	Tr	01.58	57-58	42	-	7
GRIFFITHS Leroy						
London, 30 December, 1976						(F)
Queens Park Rgrs	Hampton & Richmond	05.01	01-02	26	10	3
GRIFFITHS William **Malwyn (Mal)**						
Merthyr Tydfil, 8 March, 1919 Died 1969 W-11						(W)
Arsenal	Merthyr Thursday	02.37	37	9	-	5
Leicester C	Tr	09.38	38-55	373	-	66
GRIFFITHS Michael Antony						
Birmingham, 14 March, 1970						(F)
Torquay U	Worcester C	10.99	99	8	14	3
GRIFFITHS Neil						
Newcastle-under-Lyme, 12 October, 1951						(FB)
Chester	St Lukes YC	11.70	70-73	89	1	5
Port Vale	Tr	12.73	73-80	214	4	13
Crewe Alex	Tr	08.81	81	32	2	1

League Club	Source	Date Signed	Seasons Played	Apps	Subs	Gls
GRIFFITHS Neil						
Halifax, 4 September, 1972						(CD)
Halifax T	YT	07.91	90-92	2	2	0
GRIFFITHS Peter						
St Helens, 13 March, 1980						(M)
Macclesfield T	Ashton U	07.98	98	4	0	1
GRIFFITHS Peter James						
Barnstaple, 14 August, 1957						(W)
Stoke C	Bideford T	11.80	80-83	46	14	5
Bradford C	L	03.84	83	2	0	0
Port Vale	Tr	07.84	84-85	32	4	4
GRIFFITHS Raymond (Ray)						
Llanelli, 26 September, 1931						(WH)
Chester	Stockton Heath N	09.55	55-59	18	-	0
GRIFFITHS Richard (Richie) David						
Earls Colne, 21 March, 1942						(FB)
Colchester U	Jnrs	06.61	61-64	48	-	0
GRIFFITHS Robert (Bob) William						
Aldridge, 15 September, 1942						(WH)
Stoke C	Rhyl	09.60				
Chester	Tr	07.62	62	2	-	0
GRIFFITHS Roger David Norman						
Hereford, 20 February, 1945						(FB)
Hereford U	Worcester C	07.70	72	7	2	0
GRIFFITHS James **Stephen (Steve)**						
Stairfoot, 23 February, 1914 Died 1998						(IF)
Chesterfield	Thurnscoe Victoria	10.34				
Halifax T	Tr	07.37	37-38	75	-	14
Portsmouth	Tr	06.39				
Aldershot	Tr	06.46	46	42	-	9
Barnsley	Tr	07.47	47-50	65	-	29
York C	Tr	06.51	51-52	74	-	12
GRIFFITHS Stephen (Steve)						
Billingham, 28 November, 1957						(F)
Hartlepool	App	•	74	0	1	0
GRIFFITHS Vernon						
Birmingham, 14 June, 1936						(WH)
Coventry C	Sheldon T	02.57	57-58	15	-	1
GRIFFITHS William (Bill)						
Earlestown, 13 January, 1921 Died 1964						(FB)
Bury	Earlestown	05.39	46-51	193	-	11
GRIFFITHS William (Billy) Edward						
Warrington, 23 May, 1944						(W)
Torquay U	App	05.62	62	1	-	0
GRIFFITHS Wyn Rhys						
Blaengwynfi, 17 October, 1919						(G)
Cardiff C (Am)	Derby Co (Am)	08.47	47	1	-	0
Newport Co (Am)		01.52	51	3	-	0
GRIGGS Robert (Bobby)						
Petersfield, 12 December, 1952						(M)
Aldershot	App	07.70	68-69	3	1	0
GRIMANDI Gilles						
Gap, France, 11 November, 1970						(CD)
Arsenal	AS Monaco (Fr)	06.97	97-01	85	29	4
GRIMES Augustine **Ashley**						
Dublin, 2 August, 1957 IRu21-6/IR-17						(FB)
Manchester U	Bohemians	03.77	77-82	62	28	10
Coventry C	Tr	08.83	83	29	3	1
Luton T	Tr	08.84	84-88	85	2	3
Stoke C	CA Osasuna (Sp)	01.92	91	4	6	1
GRIMES Vincent (Vince)						
Scunthorpe, 13 May, 1954						(M)
Hull C	App	05.72	73-77	84	5	9
Bradford C	L	12.77	77	7	0	1
Scunthorpe U	Tr	01.78	77-81	143	0	12
GRIMLEY Thomas (Tom) William						
Dinnington, 1 November, 1920 Died 1976						(G)
West Bromwich A	Swallownest	04.39	46-47	30	-	0
New Brighton	Tr	08.48	48-50	94	-	0
GRIMSDITCH Samuel **Walker**						
Great Lever, 10 August, 1920 Died 1996						(G)
Southport	Rossendale U	11.45	46	10	-	0

GRIMSHAW Anthony (Tony)
Manchester, 8 December, 1957 (M)

League Club	Source	Date Signed	Seasons Played	Apps	Subs	Gls
Manchester U	App	12.74	75	0	1	0

GRIMSHAW Christopher (Chris) Anthony
Accrington, 1 October, 1965 (M)

League Club	Source	Date Signed	Seasons Played	Apps	Subs	Gls
Burnley	App	10.83				
Crewe Alex	Tr	03.84	83	1	2	0
Bury	Tr	08.84	84-85	1	2	0

GRIMSHAW Colin George
Betchworth, 16 September, 1925 Died 1995 (WH)

League Club	Source	Date Signed	Seasons Played	Apps	Subs	Gls
Arsenal	Redhill	06.48				
Crystal Palace	Tr	10.52	52	32	-	3

GRINNEY Ian George
Crediton, 8 March, 1936 (W)

League Club	Source	Date Signed	Seasons Played	Apps	Subs	Gls
Exeter C	Crediton	09.54	55	2	-	0

GRIPTON Ernest **William (Billy)**
Tipton, 2 July, 1920 Died 1981 (CD)

League Club	Source	Date Signed	Seasons Played	Apps	Subs	Gls
West Bromwich A	Toll End Wesley	11.37	38-47	13	-	0
Luton T	Tr	06.48	48	3	-	0
Bournemouth	Tr	07.50	50-51	79	-	0

GRITT Stephen (Steve) John
Bournemouth, 31 October, 1957 (M)

League Club	Source	Date Signed	Seasons Played	Apps	Subs	Gls
Bournemouth	App	07.76	76	4	2	3
Charlton Ath	Tr	07.77	77-88	320	27	24
Walsall	Tr	07.89	89	20	0	1
Charlton Ath	Tr	02.90	89-92	15	18	1

GRITTON Martin
Glasgow, 1 June, 1978 (F)

League Club	Source	Date Signed	Seasons Played	Apps	Subs	Gls
Plymouth Arg	Porthleven	08.98	98-01	15	29	7
Torquay U	Tr	08.02	02-04	72	21	23
Grimsby T	Tr	12.04	04	22	1	4

GROBBELAAR Bruce David
Durban, South Africa, 6 October, 1957 FLge/Zimbabwe 20 (G)

League Club	Source	Date Signed	Seasons Played	Apps	Subs	Gls
Crewe Alex	Vancouver (Can)	12.79	79	24	0	1
Liverpool	Vancouver (Can)	03.81	81-93	440	0	0
Stoke C	L	03.93	92	4	0	0
Southampton	Tr	08.94	94-95	32	0	0
Plymouth Arg	Tr	08.96	96	36	0	0
Oldham Ath	Sheffield Wed (N/C)	12.97	97	4	0	0
Bury	Chesham U	09.98	98	1	0	0
Lincoln C	Chesham U	12.98	98	2	0	0

GROCOCK Christopher (Chris) Richard
Grimsby, 30 October, 1968 ESch (W)

League Club	Source	Date Signed	Seasons Played	Apps	Subs	Gls
Grimsby T	Jnrs	06.87	85-88	18	25	1

GRODAS Frode
Sogndal, Norway, 24 October, 1964 Norway int (G)

League Club	Source	Date Signed	Seasons Played	Apps	Subs	Gls
Chelsea	Lillestrom (Nor)	09.96	96	20	1	0

GROENENDIJK Alfons
Leiden, Holland, 17 May, 1964 (M)

League Club	Source	Date Signed	Seasons Played	Apps	Subs	Gls
Manchester C	Ajax	07.93	93	9	0	0

GROGAN John (Johnny)
Paisley, 30 October, 1915 Died 1976 (CD)

League Club	Source	Date Signed	Seasons Played	Apps	Subs	Gls
Leicester C	Shawfield Jnrs	10.33	35-46	46	-	0
Mansfield T	Tr	09.47	47-51	201	-	0

GRONDIN David
Paris, France, 8 May, 1980 FrYth (FB)

League Club	Source	Date Signed	Seasons Played	Apps	Subs	Gls
Arsenal	St Etienne (Fr)	07.98	98	1	0	0

GRONKJAER Jesper
Nuuk, Denmark, 12 August, 1977 Deu21-13/De-55 (M)

League Club	Source	Date Signed	Seasons Played	Apps	Subs	Gls
Chelsea	Ajax (Holl)	12.00	00-03	56	32	7
Birmingham C	Tr	07.04	04	13	3	0

GROOMBRIDGE David (Dave) Henry
Norbury, 13 April, 1930 (G)

League Club	Source	Date Signed	Seasons Played	Apps	Subs	Gls
Leyton Orient	Hayes	06.51	51-59	133	-	0

GROOME Patrick (Pat) Bernard
Nottingham, 16 March, 1934 (FB)

League Club	Source	Date Signed	Seasons Played	Apps	Subs	Gls
Notts Co	Jnrs	11.51	52-57	40	-	0

GROSS Marcus John
Barnstaple, 15 December, 1982 (CD)

League Club	Source	Date Signed	Seasons Played	Apps	Subs	Gls
Exeter C	YT	•	01	1	0	0

GROTIER Peter David
Stratford, 18 October, 1950 (G)

League Club	Source	Date Signed	Seasons Played	Apps	Subs	Gls
West Ham U	App	03.68	68-72	50	0	0
Cardiff C	L	11.73	73	2	0	0
Lincoln C	Tr	08.74	74-79	233	0	0
Cardiff C	Tr	12.79	79-81	38	0	0
Grimsby T	Tr	03.82	82-84	10	0	0

GROVES Alan James
Ainsdale, 24 October, 1948 Died 1978 (W)

League Club	Source	Date Signed	Seasons Played	Apps	Subs	Gls
Southport	Blowick	12.68	68-69	10	4	2
Chester	Tr	07.70	70	21	1	3
Shrewsbury T	Tr	02.71	70-72	76	0	11
Bournemouth	Tr	10.72	72-73	31	5	4
Oldham Ath	Tr	02.74	73-77	136	4	12
Blackpool	Tr	11.77	77	11	4	1

GROVES Edward **Gwynfryn (Gwyn)**
Merthyr Tydfil, 24 July, 1930 Died 1997 WAmat (G)

League Club	Source	Date Signed	Seasons Played	Apps	Subs	Gls
Swansea T	Troedyrhiw	06.52	52-53	34	-	0

GROVES John
Derby, 16 September, 1933 (WH)

League Club	Source	Date Signed	Seasons Played	Apps	Subs	Gls
Luton T	Jnrs	10.50	53-62	218	-	16
Bournemouth	Tr	09.63	63-64	54	-	0

GROVES Kenneth (Ken) Ernest Leonard
Eton, 9 October, 1921 Died 2002 (G)

League Club	Source	Date Signed	Seasons Played	Apps	Subs	Gls
Preston NE	Windsor & Eton	03.39				
Reading	Tr	08.46	46	4	-	0

GROVES Paul
Derby, 28 February, 1966 (M)

League Club	Source	Date Signed	Seasons Played	Apps	Subs	Gls
Leicester C	Burton A	04.88	87-88	7	9	1
Lincoln C	L	08.89	89	8	0	1
Blackpool	Tr	01.90	89-91	106	1	21
Grimsby T	Tr	08.92	92-95	183	1	38
West Bromwich A	Tr	07.96	96	27	2	4
Grimsby T	Tr	07.97	97-03	262	8	33
Scunthorpe U	Tr	02.04	03	13	0	3

GROVES Perry
Bow, 19 April, 1965 (W)

League Club	Source	Date Signed	Seasons Played	Apps	Subs	Gls
Colchester U	App	06.82	81-86	142	14	26
Arsenal	Tr	09.86	86-92	91	65	21
Southampton	Tr	08.92	92	13	2	2

GROVES Victor (Vic) George
Stepney, 5 November, 1932 EYth/EAmat/Eu23-1/EB (WH/CF)

League Club	Source	Date Signed	Seasons Played	Apps	Subs	Gls
Tottenham H (Am)	Leytonstone	06.52	52-53	4	-	3
Leyton Orient	Walthamstow Ave	10.54	54-55	42	-	24
Arsenal	Tr	11.55	55-63	185	-	31

GROZIER William (Bill)
Cumnock, 24 August, 1956 (FB)

League Club	Source	Date Signed	Seasons Played	Apps	Subs	Gls
Mansfield T	App	08.74	73	1	0	0

GRUBB Alan Johnstone
Leven, 5 February, 1928 (W)

League Club	Source	Date Signed	Seasons Played	Apps	Subs	Gls
Tottenham H	Gloucester C	03.52	52	2	-	0
Walsall	Tr	08.53	53	15	-	0

GRUMMETT James (Jimmy)
Birdwell, 3 July, 1918 Died 1996 (WH)

League Club	Source	Date Signed	Seasons Played	Apps	Subs	Gls
Lincoln C	Rustons Sports	09.43	46-51	165	-	12
Accrington St	Tr	09.52	52	40	-	1

GRUMMETT James (Jimmy)
Maltby, 11 July, 1945 EYth (CD)

League Club	Source	Date Signed	Seasons Played	Apps	Subs	Gls
Lincoln C	Ruston Bucyrus	06.63	63-70	246	5	19
Aldershot	Tr	07.71	71-72	81	0	6
Chester	Tr	06.73	73	15	1	0
Rochdale	Tr	12.73	73-74	32	2	2

GRUMMITT Peter Malcolm
Bourne, 19 August, 1942 Eu23-3/FLge-1 (G)

League Club	Source	Date Signed	Seasons Played	Apps	Subs	Gls
Nottingham F	Bourne T	05.60	60-69	313	0	0
Sheffield Wed	Tr	01.70	69-72	121	0	0
Brighton & Hove A	Tr	12.73	73-76	136	0	0

GRUNDY Brian
Atherton, 9 May, 1945 (W)

League Club	Source	Date Signed	Seasons Played	Apps	Subs	Gls
Bury	Wigan Ath	11.67	67-70	92	7	10

GRYBA John **Raymond (Ray)**
Liverpool, 19 August, 1935 Died 1999 (CD)

League Club	Source	Date Signed	Seasons Played	Apps	Subs	Gls
Liverpool	Jnrs	08.52				
Southport	RAOC Feltham	10.55	55-57	72	-	14

GUARD Anthony (Tony) Francis
Swansea, 19 April, 1964 (M)

League Club	Source	Date Signed	Seasons Played	Apps	Subs	Gls
Swansea C	App	04.82	83	1	0	0

GUBBINS Ralph Grayham
Ellesmere Port, 31 January, 1932 (W)

League Club	Source	Date Signed	Seasons Played	Apps	Subs	Gls
Bolton W	Ellesmere Port	10.52	52-59	97	-	15

League Club	Source	Date Signed	Seasons Played	Apps	Subs	Gls
Hull C	Tr	10.59	59-60	45	-	10
Tranmere Rov	Tr	03.61	60-63	107	-	36

GUDJOHNSEN Eidur Smari
Reykjavik, Iceland, 15 September, 1978 IcYth/Icu21-11/Ic-36 (F)

League Club	Source	Date Signed	Seasons Played	Apps	Subs	Gls
Bolton W	KR Reykjavik (Ice)	08.98	98-99	48	7	18
Chelsea	Tr	07.00	00-04	110	50	52

GUDJONSSON Bjarni
Akranes, Iceland, 26 February, 1979 IcYth/Icu21-20/Ic-15 (M)

League Club	Source	Date Signed	Seasons Played	Apps	Subs	Gls
Newcastle U	IA Akranes (Ice)	07.97				
Stoke C	KRC Genk (Bel)	03.00	99-02	119	13	11
Coventry C	VfL Bochum (Ger)	01.04	03-04	20	8	3
Plymouth Arg	Tr	12.04	04	12	3	0

GUDJONSSON Johannes (Joey) Karl
Akranes, Iceland, 25 May, 1980 IcYth/Icu21-10/Ic-23 (M)

League Club	Source	Date Signed	Seasons Played	Apps	Subs	Gls
Aston Villa (L)	Real Betis (Sp)	01.03	02	9	2	2
Wolverhampton W (L)	Real Betis (Sp)	08.03	03	5	6	0
Leicester C	Real Betis (Sp)	08.04	04	26	9	2

GUDJONSSON Thordur
Akranes, Iceland, 14 October, 1973 IcYth/Icu21-10/Ic-58 (M)

League Club	Source	Date Signed	Seasons Played	Apps	Subs	Gls
Derby Co (L)	Las Palmas (Sp)	03.01	00	2	8	1
Preston NE (L)	Las Palmas (Sp)	02.02	01	4	3	0
Stoke C	VfL Bochum (Ger)	01.05	04	0	2	0

GUDMUNDSSON Albert
Reykjavik, Iceland, 5 October, 1923 Died 1994 Iceland int (IF)

League Club	Source	Date Signed	Seasons Played	Apps	Subs	Gls
Arsenal (Am)	Glasgow Rgrs	09.46	46	2	-	0

GUDMUNDSSON Johann Birnir
Reykjavik, Iceland, 5 December, 1977 IcYth/Icu21-11/Ic3 (M)

League Club	Source	Date Signed	Seasons Played	Apps	Subs	Gls
Watford	Keflavik (Ice)	03.98	98-99	7	15	2
Cambridge U	L	11.00	00	3	0	0

GUDMUNDSSON Niklas
Sweden, 29 February, 1972 Sweden int (F)

League Club	Source	Date Signed	Seasons Played	Apps	Subs	Gls
Blackburn Rov	Halmstad (Swe)	12.95	95-96	1	5	0
Ipswich T	L	03.97	96	2	6	2

GUENTCHEV Bontcho Lubomisov
Tchoshevo, Bulgaria, 7 July, 1964 Bugaria int (M)

League Club	Source	Date Signed	Seasons Played	Apps	Subs	Gls
Ipswich T	Sporting Lisbon (Por)	12.92	92-94	39	22	6
Luton T	Tr	08.95	95-96	40	22	10

GUERET Willy July
St Claude, Guadeloupe, 3 August, 1973 (G)

League Club	Source	Date Signed	Seasons Played	Apps	Subs	Gls
Millwall	Le Mans (Fr)	07.00	00-03	13	1	0
Swansea C	Tr	08.04	04	44	0	0

GUERRERO Mario **Ivan**
Comayagua, Honduras, 30 November, 1977 Honduras int (FB)

League Club	Source	Date Signed	Seasons Played	Apps	Subs	Gls
Coventry C	Motagua (Hon)	10.00	00-01	6	1	0

GUEST Brendan John
Barnsley, 19 December, 1958 EYth (FB)

League Club	Source	Date Signed	Seasons Played	Apps	Subs	Gls
Lincoln C	App	12.76	76-79	99	5	2

GUEST Gladstone
Rotherham, 26 June, 1917 Died 1998 (IF)

League Club	Source	Date Signed	Seasons Played	Apps	Subs	Gls
Rotherham U	Rawmarsh CW	12.39	46-55	358	-	130

GUEST William (Billy) Francis
Brierley Hill, 8 February, 1914 Died 1994 (W)

League Club	Source	Date Signed	Seasons Played	Apps	Subs	Gls
Birmingham	Bromley Jnrs	02.32	33-36	76	-	15
Blackburn Rov	Tr	01.37	36-46	88	-	30
Walsall	Tr	08.47	47	5	-	0

GUILD Alan Nicoll
Forfar, 27 March, 1947 SAmat (CD)

League Club	Source	Date Signed	Seasons Played	Apps	Subs	Gls
Luton T	East Fife	07.69	70	1	0	0
Cambridge U	Tr	05.71	71-73	117	10	1

GUILD James (Jimmy)
Glasgow, 10 December, 1928 (WH)

League Club	Source	Date Signed	Seasons Played	Apps	Subs	Gls
New Brighton	Dunoon Ath	09.50	50	2	-	0

GUINAN Stephen (Steve) Anthony
Birmingham, 24 December, 1975 ESemiPro-4 (F)

League Club	Source	Date Signed	Seasons Played	Apps	Subs	Gls
Nottingham F	YT	01.93	95-99	2	5	0
Darlington	L	12.95	95	3	0	1
Burnley	L	03.97	96	0	6	0
Crewe Alex	L	03.98	97	3	0	0
Halifax T	L	10.98	98	12	0	2
Plymouth Arg	L	03.99	98	11	0	7
Scunthorpe U	L	09.99	99	2	1	1
Cambridge U	Tr	12.99	99	4	2	0
Plymouth Arg	Tr	03.00	99-00	15	15	3
Shrewsbury T	Tr	03.02	01	4	1	0
Cheltenham T	Hereford U	05.04	04	35	8	6

GUIVARC'H Stephane
Concameau, France, 6 September, 1970 France 13 (F)

League Club	Source	Date Signed	Seasons Played	Apps	Subs	Gls
Newcastle U	Auxerre (Fr)	07.98	98	2	2	1

GULLAN Stanley (Stan) Knox
Edinburgh, 26 January, 1926 Died 1999 (G)

League Club	Source	Date Signed	Seasons Played	Apps	Subs	Gls
Queens Park Rgrs	Clyde	07.49	50-54	48	-	0

GULLIT Ruud
Surinam, 1 September, 1962 Holland int (M)

League Club	Source	Date Signed	Seasons Played	Apps	Subs	Gls
Chelsea	Sampdoria (It)	07.95	95-97	37	12	4

GULLIVER Joffre (Jeff)
Merthyr Tydfil, 2 August, 1915 Died 1999 (FB)

League Club	Source	Date Signed	Seasons Played	Apps	Subs	Gls
Southend U		08.34				
Leeds U		03.38				
Reading	Tr	06.39	46-50	159	-	0
Swindon T	Tr	08.51	51	11	-	0

GULLIVER Philip (Phil) Stephen
Bishop Auckland, 12 September, 1982 (CD)

League Club	Source	Date Signed	Seasons Played	Apps	Subs	Gls
Middlesbrough	YT	07.00				
Blackpool	L	11.02	02	2	1	0
Carlisle U	L	12.02	02	1	0	0
Bournemouth	L	03.03	02	4	2	0
Bury	L	10.03	03	10	0	0
Scunthorpe U	L	01.04	03	2	0	0
Rushden & Diamonds	Tr	08.04	04	29	3	0

GULLIVER Terence (Terry) Reginald
Salisbury, 30 September, 1944 (FB)

League Club	Source	Date Signed	Seasons Played	Apps	Subs	Gls
Bournemouth	Weymouth	08.66	66-71	162	2	2

GUMMER Jason Craig
Tredegar, 27 October, 1967 WYth (M)

League Club	Source	Date Signed	Seasons Played	Apps	Subs	Gls
Cardiff C	App	07.85	85-89	28	6	5
Torquay U	L	03.89	88	7	0	1

GUNBY Peter
Leeds, 20 November, 1934 (WH)

League Club	Source	Date Signed	Seasons Played	Apps	Subs	Gls
Leeds U		09.55				
Bradford C	Tr	07.56	56	3	-	0

GUNBY Stephen (Steve) Robert
Boston, 14 April, 1984 (M)

League Club	Source	Date Signed	Seasons Played	Apps	Subs	Gls
Bury	Sch	11.02	01-03	1	5	0

GUNN Alfred (Alf) Harman
Germany, 11 July, 1924 (CF)

League Club	Source	Date Signed	Seasons Played	Apps	Subs	Gls
Nottingham F		02.47	46	2	-	0

GUNN Alistair Robert
Broughty Ferry, 2 November, 1924 (W)

League Club	Source	Date Signed	Seasons Played	Apps	Subs	Gls
Huddersfield T	Dundee	01.51	50-53	83	-	11
Bournemouth	Tr	06.54	54	27	-	2

GUNN Andrew (Andy) Charles
Barking, 2 February, 1971 (W)

League Club	Source	Date Signed	Seasons Played	Apps	Subs	Gls
Watford	YT	03.89				
Crewe Alex	Tr	02.90	89-90	2	2	0

GUNN Bryan James
Thurso, 22 December, 1963 SSch/SYth/Su21-9/SB/S-6 (G)

League Club	Source	Date Signed	Seasons Played	Apps	Subs	Gls
Norwich C	Aberdeen	10.86	86-97	390	0	0

GUNN Brynley (Bryn) Charles
Kettering, 21 August, 1958 (FB)

League Club	Source	Date Signed	Seasons Played	Apps	Subs	Gls
Nottingham F	App	08.75	75-84	129	2	1
Shrewsbury T	L	11.85	85	9	0	0
Walsall	L	01.86	85	6	0	0
Mansfield T	L	03.86	85	5	0	0
Peterborough U	Tr	08.86	86-88	130	1	14
Chesterfield	Tr	07.89	89-91	89	2	10

GUNNARSSON Brynjar Bjorn
Reykjavik, Iceland, 16 October, 1975 IcYth/Icu21-8/Ic-50 (M)

League Club	Source	Date Signed	Seasons Played	Apps	Subs	Gls
Stoke C	Orgryte IS (Swe)	01.00	99-02	128	3	16
Nottingham F	Tr	08.03	03	9	4	0
Stoke C	Tr	03.04	03	1	2	0
Watford	Tr	07.04	04	34	2	3

GUNNING Henry (Harry)
Leigh-on-Sea, 8 February, 1932 Died 2005 (W)

League Club	Source	Date Signed	Seasons Played	Apps	Subs	Gls
West Ham U	Gravesend & Northfleet	06.52	52	1	-	0
Crystal Palace	Tr	05.54	54-56	62	-	4
Reading	Tr	05.57	57	12	-	1

GUNNING James (Jimmy) Michael
Helensburgh, 25 June, 1929 Died 1993 (W)

League Club	Source	Date Signed	Seasons Played	Apps	Subs	Gls
Manchester C	Hibernian	11.50	50-52	13	-	0
Barrow	Weymouth	07.54	54	10	-	1

GUNNLAUGSSON Arnar (Arnie) Bergmann
Akranes, Iceland, 6 March, 1973 IcYth/Icu21-6/Ic-30 (F)

League Club	Source	Date Signed	Seasons Played	Apps	Subs	Gls
Bolton W	IA Akranes (Ice)	08.97	97-98	24	18	13
Leicester C	Tr	02.99	98-01	10	20	3
Stoke C	L	03.00	99	10	3	2
Stoke C	Tr	02.02	01	9	0	3

GUNNLAUGSSON Bjarke Bergmann
Akranes, Iceland, 6 March, 1973 IcYth/Icu21-4/Ic-27 (F)

League Club	Source	Date Signed	Seasons Played	Apps	Subs	Gls
Preston NE	KR Reykjavik (Ice)	09.99	99-00	17	28	2

GUNTER David Reginald
Portsmouth, 4 March, 1933 (FB)

League Club	Source	Date Signed	Seasons Played	Apps	Subs	Gls
Southampton	Portsmouth (Am)	05.55	55	7	-	0

GUNTER Philip (Phil) Edward
Portsmouth, 6 January, 1932 Eu23-1/EB (FB)

League Club	Source	Date Signed	Seasons Played	Apps	Subs	Gls
Portsmouth	Jnrs	08.49	51-63	321	-	2
Aldershot	Tr	07.64	64-65	78	0	8

GUNTHORPE Kenneth (Ken)
Sheffield, 14 November, 1938 (CD)

League Club	Source	Date Signed	Seasons Played	Apps	Subs	Gls
Rotherham U		05.58	58	2	-	0

GUPPY Stephen (Steve) Andrew
Winchester, 29 March, 1969 ESemiPro-1/Eu21-1/EB-1/E-1 (W)

League Club	Source	Date Signed	Seasons Played	Apps	Subs	Gls
Wycombe W	Colden Common	09.89	93	41	0	8
Newcastle U	Tr	08.94				
Port Vale	Tr	11.94	94-96	102	3	12
Leicester C	Tr	02.97	96-00	133	13	9
Leicester C	Glasgow Celtic	01.04	03	9	6	0
Leeds U	Tr	08.04	04	1	2	1
Stoke C	Tr	09.04	04	0	4	0
Wycombe W	Tr	11.04	04	12	2	1

GURINOVICH Igor Nikolaivich
Minsk, Belarus, 5 March, 1960 USSR int (F)

League Club	Source	Date Signed	Seasons Played	Apps	Subs	Gls
Brighton & Hove A	Dynamo Minsk (Bs)	11.90	90	3	1	1

GURNEY Andrew (Andy) Robert
Bristol, 25 January, 1974 (FB)

League Club	Source	Date Signed	Seasons Played	Apps	Subs	Gls
Bristol Rov	YT	07.92	93-96	100	8	9
Torquay U	Tr	07.97	97-98	64	0	10
Reading	Tr	01.99	98-00	55	12	3
Swindon T	Tr	07.01	01-04	132	0	20
Swansea C	Tr	09.04	04	25	3	1

GURR Gerald (Gerry) Robert
Brighton, 20 October, 1946 (G)

League Club	Source	Date Signed	Seasons Played	Apps	Subs	Gls
Southampton	Guildford C	03.64	66-69	42	0	0
Aldershot	Tr	03.71	70-71	55	0	0

GUSCOTT Lindon
Lambeth, 29 March, 1972 (F)

League Club	Source	Date Signed	Seasons Played	Apps	Subs	Gls
Gillingham	YT	07.89	88	0	2	0

GUSCOTT Raymond (Ray) Melvin
Newport, 18 November, 1957 WSch (M)

League Club	Source	Date Signed	Seasons Played	Apps	Subs	Gls
Bristol Rov	App	11.75	76	1	0	0
Newport Co	Minehead	10.77	77	12	5	1

GUSTAFSSON (ANTONELIUS) Tomas Emil Rune
Stockholm, Sweden, 7 May, 1973 Sweden 6 (FB)

League Club	Source	Date Signed	Seasons Played	Apps	Subs	Gls
Coventry C	AIK Solna (Swe)	12.99	99-01	10	5	0

GUTHRIE Christopher (Chris) William
Dilston, 7 September, 1953 ESch (F)

League Club	Source	Date Signed	Seasons Played	Apps	Subs	Gls
Newcastle U	App	01.71	71	3	0	0
Southend U	Tr	11.72	72-74	107	1	35
Sheffield U	Tr	05.75	75-76	58	2	15
Swindon T	Tr	07.77	77-78	44	1	12
Fulham	Tr	09.78	78-79	49	1	15
Millwall	Tr	03.80	79	7	0	1

GUTHRIE James (Jimmy) Eric
Luncarty, 13 June, 1913 Died 1981 (WH)

League Club	Source	Date Signed	Seasons Played	Apps	Subs	Gls
Portsmouth	Dundee	08.37	37-38	76	-	1
Crystal Palace	Guildford C	10.46	46	5	-	0

GUTHRIE Peter John
Newcastle, 10 October, 1961 (G)

League Club	Source	Date Signed	Seasons Played	Apps	Subs	Gls
Tottenham H	Weymouth	01.88				
Swansea C	L	02.88	87	14	0	0
Bournemouth	Barnet	08.90	90	10	0	0

GUTHRIE Ralph
West Hartlepool, 13 September, 1932 Died 1996 (G)

League Club	Source	Date Signed	Seasons Played	Apps	Subs	Gls
Arsenal	Tow Law T	05.53	54	2	-	0
Hartlepools U	Tr	07.56	56-57	78	-	0

GUTHRIE Ronald (Ron) George
Burradon, 19 April, 1944 (FB)

League Club	Source	Date Signed	Seasons Played	Apps	Subs	Gls
Newcastle U	Jnrs	07.63	66-72	52	3	2
Sunderland	Tr	01.73	72-74	66	0	1

GUTTRIDGE Luke Horace
Barnstaple, 27 March, 1982 (M)

League Club	Source	Date Signed	Seasons Played	Apps	Subs	Gls
Torquay U	YT	•	99	0	1	0
Cambridge U	Tr	08.00	00-04	127	9	17
Southend U	Tr	03.05	04	3	2	0

GUTTRIDGE Ronald (Ron)
Widnes, 28 April, 1916 (FB)

League Club	Source	Date Signed	Seasons Played	Apps	Subs	Gls
Aston Villa	Prescot Cables	03.37	46-47	15	-	0
Brighton & Hove A	Tr	06.48	48-49	17	-	0

GUTTRIDGE William (Bill) Henry
Darlaston, 4 March, 1931 (FB)

League Club	Source	Date Signed	Seasons Played	Apps	Subs	Gls
Wolverhampton W	Metroshaft Works	03.48	51-53	6	-	0
Walsall	Tr	11.54	54-61	198	-	0

GUTZMORE Leon Johnson Fitzgerald
St Pancras, 30 October, 1976 (F)

League Club	Source	Date Signed	Seasons Played	Apps	Subs	Gls
Cambridge U	YT	09.95	95	0	2	0

GUY Alan
Jarrow, 8 September, 1957 (M)

League Club	Source	Date Signed	Seasons Played	Apps	Subs	Gls
Newcastle U	App	09.75	76-78	3	1	0
Peterborough U	Tr	03.79	78-80	42	11	4

GUY Edward (Eddie) Frederick
Seaham, 6 February, 1956 (G)

League Club	Source	Date Signed	Seasons Played	Apps	Subs	Gls
Hartlepool	App	02.74	74	1	0	0

GUY Harold George
Wolverhampton, 1 January, 1932 (FB)

League Club	Source	Date Signed	Seasons Played	Apps	Subs	Gls
West Bromwich A	Springfield OB	03.50	50	1	-	0

GUY Ivor
Chipping Sodbury, 27 February, 1926 Died 1986 (FB)

League Club	Source	Date Signed	Seasons Played	Apps	Subs	Gls
Bristol C	Hambrook Villa	10.44	46-56	404	-	2

GUY Jamie Lesley
Barking, 1 August, 1987 (F)

League Club	Source	Date Signed	Seasons Played	Apps	Subs	Gls
Colchester U	Sch	•	04	0	2	0

GUY Keith
Seaham, 19 May, 1959 (M)

League Club	Source	Date Signed	Seasons Played	Apps	Subs	Gls
Newcastle U	App	06.77				
Hartlepool U	Tr	06.78	78	7	3	0

GUY Lewis Brett
Penrith, 27 August, 1985 EYth (F)

League Club	Source	Date Signed	Seasons Played	Apps	Subs	Gls
Newcastle U	Sch	08.02				
Doncaster Rov	Tr	03.05	04	4	5	3

GUY Michael (Mike) James
Limavady, 4 February, 1953 (M)

League Club	Source	Date Signed	Seasons Played	Apps	Subs	Gls
Sheffield U	Coleraine	03.78	77-78	12	6	2
Crewe Alex	Tr	09.79	79-80	54	1	7

GUY Richard (Dickie)
Greenwich, 6 January, 1949 (G)

League Club	Source	Date Signed	Seasons Played	Apps	Subs	Gls
Wimbledon	Tooting & Mitcham	01.68	77	13	0	0

GUY Richard (Jimmy) James
Swansea, 29 January, 1921 Died 1990 (CF)

League Club	Source	Date Signed	Seasons Played	Apps	Subs	Gls
Norwich C	RAF St Athan	08.46	46-47	12	-	1

GUY Ronald (Ron)
Salford, 25 April, 1936 (CF)

League Club	Source	Date Signed	Seasons Played	Apps	Subs	Gls
Stockport Co		09.58	58-59	9	-	2

GUYETT Scott Barry
Ascot, Australia, 20 January, 1976 ESemiPro-4 (CD)

League Club	Source	Date Signed	Seasons Played	Apps	Subs	Gls
Oxford U	Southport	07.01	01	20	2	0
Yeovil T	Chester C	07.04	04	13	5	2

GWATKIN Philip (Phil) Arthur
Harrow, 5 August, 1929 (W)

League Club	Source	Date Signed	Seasons Played	Apps	Subs	Gls
Wrexham		10.52	53-55	56	-	8
Tranmere Rov	Tr	06.56	56	21	-	6

GWINNETT Melvyn (Mel) Lawrence
Worcester, 14 May, 1963 (G)

League Club	Source	Date Signed	Seasons Played	Apps	Subs	Gls
Peterborough U	Stourbridge	05.81				
Hereford U	Tr	09.82	82	1	0	0
Bradford C	Gloucester C	06.84				
Exeter C	Tr	08.85	85-88	46	0	0

League Club	Source	Date Signed	Seasons Played	Career Record Apps	Subs	Gls

GWYTHER David (Dave) Jeffrey Andrew
Birmingham, 6 December, 1948 Wu23-2 (F)

League Club	Source	Date Signed	Seasons Played	Apps	Subs	Gls
Swansea T	South Gower	03.66	65-72	212	4	60
Halifax T	Tr	08.73	73-75	104	0	26
Rotherham U	Tr	02.76	75-79	162	0	45
Newport Co	Tr	12.79	79-82	84	21	28
Crewe Alex	L	01.82	81	7	0	1
Newport Co	Port Talbot Ath	03.85	84	1	1	0

GYMER John Paul
Romford, 11 November, 1966 (F)

League Club	Source	Date Signed	Seasons Played	Apps	Subs	Gls
Southend U	App	08.84	83-86	30	25	12
Crewe Alex	Tr	07.87	87	10	5	5

GYNN Michael (Micky)
Peterborough, 19 August, 1961 (M)

League Club	Source	Date Signed	Seasons Played	Apps	Subs	Gls
Peterborough U	App	04.79	78-82	152	4	33
Coventry C	Tr	08.83	83-92	206	35	32
Stoke C	Tr	08.93	93	14	7	0

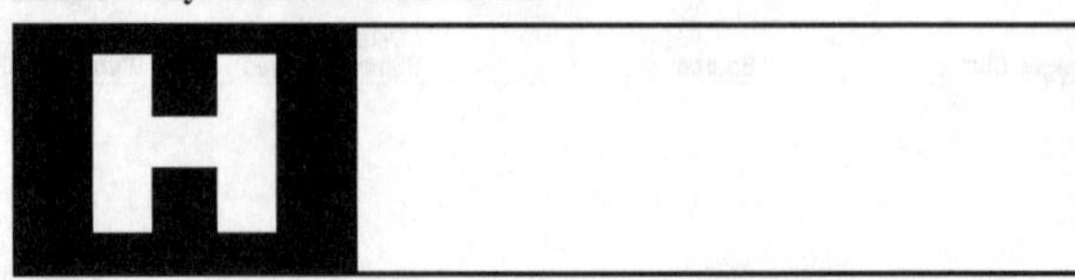

League Club	Source	Date Signed	Seasons Played	Apps	Subs	Gls
HAAG Kelly Jason						
Enfield, 6 October, 1970						(F)
Brentford	YT	07.89	89	1	4	0
Fulham	Tr	08.90	90-92	35	32	9
Barnet	Tr	08.93	93	31	7	8
HAALAND Alf-Inge Rasdal						
Stavanger, Norway, 23 November, 1972 NoYth/Nou21-29/No-34						(FB)
Nottingham F	Bryne (Nor)	01.94	93-96	66	9	7
Leeds U	Tr	07.97	97-99	57	17	8
Manchester C	Tr	06.00	00-01	35	3	3
HAARHOFF James (Jimmy) Phiri						
Lusaka, Zambia, 27 May, 1981						(M)
Birmingham C	YT	06.98	99	0	1	0
HAAS Bernt						
Vienna, Austria, 8 April, 1978 Switzerland 36						(FB)
Sunderland	Grasshoppers (Swi)	08.01	01	27	0	0
West Bromwich A	Tr	08.03	03-04	45	1	1
HAASZ John (Johnny)						
Budapest, Hungary, 7 July, 1937						(IF)
Swansea T		09.60	60	1	-	0
Workington	Tr	07.61	61-62	50	-	13
HABBIN Richard (Dick) Leonard						
Cambridge, 6 January, 1949						(F)
Reading	Cambridge U	03.69	69-74	204	15	42
Rotherham U	Tr	01.75	74-77	79	5	19
Doncaster Rov	Tr	09.77	77-78	57	3	12
HACKETT Bernard Edward Keith						
Ramsbottom, 7 September, 1933						(CF)
Aston Villa		11.53				
Chester	Tr	07.55	55-56	21	-	4
HACKETT Christopher (Chris) James						
Oxford, 1 March, 1983						(M)
Oxford U	YT	04.00	99-04	53	51	7
HACKETT Gary Stuart						
Stourbridge, 11 October, 1962						(W)
Shrewsbury T	Bromsgrove Rov	07.83	83-86	142	8	17
Stoke C	Aberdeen	03.88	87-89	64	9	7
West Bromwich A	Tr	03.90	89-92	26	18	3
Peterborough U	Tr	09.93	93	18	4	1
Chester C	Tr	09.94	94	30	5	5
HACKETT Warren James						
Plaistow, 16 December, 1971 StLucia 7						(FB)
Leyton Orient	Tottenham H (YT)	07.90	90-93	74	2	3
Doncaster Rov	Tr	07.94	94-95	46	0	2
Mansfield T	Tr	10.95	95-98	114	3	5
Barnet	Tr	03.99	98-99	37	4	1
HACKING John (Jack)						
Blackpool, 24 August, 1925						(G)
Accrington St	Blackburn Rov (Am)	09.45	46	8	-	0
Stockport Co	Tr	11.46	46-49	4	-	0
HACKING Robert (Bob) Edward						
Blackburn, 30 March, 1918 Died 2001						(WH)
Luton T	Blackburn Rov (Am)	04.45	46	1	-	0
Brighton & Hove A	Tr	08.47	47	17	-	2
Southport	Tr	08.48	48-53	181	-	6
HACKWORTH Anthony (Tony)						
Durham, 19 May, 1980 EYth						(F)
Leeds U	YT	05.97				
Notts Co	Tr	07.01	01-03	17	37	1
HADDAOUI Riffi						
Copenhagen, Denmark, 24 March, 1971						(M)
Torquay U (L)	Vata	03.96	95	0	2	0
HADDINGTON Harold (Harry)						
Scarborough, 7 August, 1931						(FB)
Bradford PA	Scarborough	02.49	52	2	-	0
West Bromwich A	Tr	05.53				
Walsall	Tr	07.55	55-60	226	-	0
HADDINGTON William **Raymond (Ray)**						
Scarborough, 18 November, 1923 Died 1994						(IF)
Bradford C	Bradford PA (Am)	09.46				
Oldham Ath	Tr	08.47	47-50	117	-	63
Manchester C	Tr	11.50	50	6	-	4
Stockport Co	Tr	12.51	51	11	-	4
Bournemouth	Tr	07.52	52	2	-	0
Rochdale	Tr	10.52	52-53	38	-	12
Halifax T	Tr	11.53	53	8	-	1
HADDOCK Andrew (Andy) Edward Robinson						
Edinburgh, 5 May, 1946						(W)
Chester	Jnrs	08.63	63	12	-	0
Crewe Alex	Tr	08.64	64	4	-	0
Rotherham U	Falkirk	12.66	66	4	0	0
Bradford PA	Chelmsford C	12.67	67	5	0	0
Chester	Tr	03.68	67	10	0	1
HADDOCK Henry (Harry)						
Glasgow, 26 July, 1925 Died 1998 SLge-7/S-6						(FB)
Exeter C (Am)	Renfrew Junrs	05.46	46	1	-	0
HADDOCK Peter Murray						
Newcastle, 9 December, 1961						(CD)
Newcastle U	App	12.79	81-85	53	4	0
Burnley	L	03.86	85	7	0	0
Leeds U	Tr	07.86	86-90	106	12	1
HADDON Henry (Harry) Llewellyn						
Cardiff, 8 April, 1923						(IF)
Cardiff C		04.46				
Newport Co	Bangor C	02.47	46-48	10	-	1
Bristol Rov	Tr	11.48	48	2	-	0
HADDOW Alexander (Alex)						
Aldershot, 8 January, 1982						(M)
Reading	YT	03.00	99-00	1	2	0
Carlisle U	Tr	08.01	01	4	0	0
HADDOW Paul Andrew						
Fleetwood, 11 October, 1978						(M)
Blackpool	YT	07.97	97	0	1	0
HADDRELL Matthew (Matt) Charles						
Stoke-on-Trent, 19 March, 1981						(CD)
Macclesfield T	Vauxhall Motors	03.03	02-03	6	8	1
HADDRICK Robert (Bobby)						
West Ham, 1 May, 1950						(CD)
Southend U	App	•	66	2	0	0
HADFIELD Jordan Michael						
Swinton, 12 August, 1987						(M)
Stockport Co	Sch	•	04	1	0	0
HADJI Mustapha						
Ifrane, Morocco, 16 November, 1971 Morocco 60						(M)
Coventry C	Dep la Coruna (Sp)	08.99	99-00	61	1	12
Aston Villa	Tr	07.01	01-03	24	11	2
HADLAND Philip (Phil) Jonathan						
Warrington, 20 October, 1980						(F)
Reading	YT	06.99				
Rochdale	Tr	08.00	00	12	20	2
Leyton Orient	Tr	07.01	01	0	5	1
Carlisle U	L	11.01	01	4	0	1
Brighton & Hove A	Tr	03.02	01	0	2	0
Darlington	Tr	08.02	02	4	2	0
Colchester U	Tr	08.03	03	0	1	0
HADLEY Anthony (Tony) Paul Frederick						
Upminster, 5 July, 1955						(CD)
Southend U	Basildon U	07.74	74-82	241	21	16
Colchester U	Tr	08.83	83	44	1	0
Southend U	Tr	08.84	84	31	1	3
HADLEY Shaun Leon						
Birmingham, 6 February, 1980						(M)
Torquay U	YT	06.98	98	0	2	0
HADLEY Stewart Anson						
Dudley, 30 December, 1973						(F)
Derby Co	Halesowen T	07.92				
Mansfield T	Tr	02.94	93-97	100	24	31
Kidderminster Hrs	Tr	06.98	00-01	23	20	6
HADLINGTON John (Jack)						
Brierley Hill, 16 August, 1933						(W)
Walsall	Cradley Heath	02.54	53	1	-	0

League Club	Source	Date Signed	Seasons Played	Apps	Subs	Gls
HADZIABDIC Dzemal						
Yugoslavia, 25 July, 1953 Yugoslavia int						(FB)
Swansea C	Velez Mostar (Yug)	08.80	80-82	87	2	1
HAFFEY Francis (Frank)						
Glasgow, 28 November, 1938 S-2						(G)
Swindon T	Glasgow Celtic	10.64	64	4	-	0
HAGAN James (Jimmy)						
Washington, 21 January, 1918 Died 1998 ESch/FLge-3/EWar-16/E-1						(IF)
Derby Co	Liverpool (Am)	01.35	35-38	30	-	7
Sheffield U	Tr	11.38	38-57	361	-	117
HAGAN James (Jim)						
Monkstown, 10 August, 1956						(CD)
Coventry C	Larne T	11.77	78	12	1	0
Torquay U	L	09.79	79	7	0	0
Coventry C	Washington (USA)	07.81	81	3	0	0
Birmingham C	Tr	05.82	82-86	124	13	0
Colchester U	Celta Vigo (Sp)	11.89	89	2	0	0
HAGUE Keith						
Hull, 25 May, 1946						(CD)
York C	Goole T	10.65	65	0	1	0
HAGUE Neil						
Thurcroft, 1 December, 1949 EYth						(CD)
Rotherham U	App	12.66	67-71	135	9	23
Plymouth Arg	Tr	11.71	71-73	98	0	15
Bournemouth	Tr	07.74	74-75	89	0	7
Huddersfield T	Tr	06.76	76	25	0	2
Darlington	Tr	05.77	77-78	80	0	4
HAGUE Paul						
Shotley Bridge, 16 September, 1972						(CD)
Gillingham	YT	05.91	90-93	8	1	0
Leyton Orient	Tr	09.94	94	17	1	1
HAHNEMANN Marcus Stephen						
Seattle, USA, 15 June, 1972 USA 4						(G)
Fulham	Colorado (USA)	07.99	00	2	0	0
Rochdale	L	10.01	01	5	0	0
Reading	L	12.01	01	6	0	0
Reading	Tr	08.02	02-04	123	0	0
HAIG Richard Neil						
Pontypridd, 29 December, 1970						(F)
Cardiff C	YT	07.89	88-89	1	4	0
HAIGH Gordon						
Barnsley, 18 August, 1921						(IF)
Burnley	Ransome & Marles	11.45	46-49	18	-	3
Bournemouth	Tr	04.50	49-50	17	-	3
Watford	Tr	08.51	51	29	-	5
HAIGH Graham						
Huddersfield, 16 September, 1946						(WH)
Halifax T	App	•	64	1	-	0
HAIGH John (Jack)						
Rotherham, 10 September, 1928						(IF)
Liverpool	Gainsborough Trinity	10.49	50-51	11	-	3
Scunthorpe U	Tr	08.52	52-59	329	-	66
Doncaster Rov	Tr	07.60	60-61	72	-	6
HAIGH Paul						
Scarborough, 4 May, 1958 Eu21-1						(CD)
Hull C	App	06.75	74-80	179	1	8
Carlisle U	Tr	11.80	80-86	228	5	4
Hartlepool U	Tr	07.87	87-88	49	1	0
HAILS Julian						
Lincoln, 20 November, 1967						(W)
Fulham	Hemel Hempstead	08.90	91-94	99	10	12
Southend U	Tr	12.94	94-99	143	18	7
HAILS William (Billy)						
Nettlesworth, 19 February, 1935						(W)
Lincoln C	Kimblesworth Jnrs	03.53	53-54	9	-	0
Peterborough U	Tr	(N/L)	60-62	94	-	27
Northampton T	Tr	11.62	62-63	59	-	13
Luton T	Tr	06.64	64	3	-	0
HAILWOOD David (Dave) John						
Blackpool, 17 October, 1954						(W)
Mansfield T		07.73	74	1	0	0
HAINES Donald (Don) Noah						
Ynysybwl, 23 September, 1925						(FB)
Bournemouth		10.48				
Newport Co	Yeovil T	12.51	50-53	77	-	1
HAINES Ivan Gerald						
Chatham, 14 September, 1968						(CD)
Gillingham	App	06.87	87-90	45	6	0
HAINES John (Jack) Thomas William						
Wickhamford, 24 April, 1920 Died 1987 E-1						(IF)
Liverpool	Cheltenham T	11.37				
Swansea T	Tr	06.39	46	29	-	7
Leicester C	Tr	06.47	47	12	-	3
West Bromwich A	Tr	03.48	47-49	59	-	23
Bradford PA	Tr	12.49	49-53	136	-	34
Rochdale	Tr	10.53	53-54	60	-	16
Chester	Tr	07.55	55-56	46	-	8
HAINES Keith Harry						
Wigston, 19 December, 1937 EYth						(CD)
Leeds U	Matlock T	05.59				
Lincoln C	Tr	07.60	60-62	13	-	0
HAINES Mervyn John						
Llanwonno, 2 May, 1923						(W)
Bournemouth	Swansea T (Am)	10.48				
Newport Co	Yeovil T	05.50	50	14	-	2
HAINING William (Will) Wallace						
Glasgow, 2 October, 1982						(CD)
Oldham Ath	YT	10.01	01-04	90	6	9
HAINSWORTH Leonard (Len)						
Rotherham, 25 January, 1918 Died 1990						(FB)
Rotherham U		03.39	38-47	33	-	7
Doncaster Rov	Tr	07.48	48-50	67	-	0
Workington	Tr	07.51	51-52	75	-	0
HAIR George						
Ryton-on-Tyne, 28 April, 1925 Died 1994						(W)
Newcastle U	Spen Jnrs	05.43	46-48	23	-	7
Grimsby T	Tr	02.49	48-50	68	-	8
HAIR Kenneth **Grenville** Arthur						
Burton-on-Trent, 16 November, 1931 Died 1968						(FB)
Leeds U	Newhall U	11.48	50-63	443	-	1
HAIRE Garry						
Sedgefield, 24 July, 1963						(W)
Oxford U	App	07.81				
Bradford C	Whitley Bay	06.83	83-84	43	6	13
Darlington	Tr	02.85	84-85	16	9	2
Rochdale	L	10.85	85	3	0	0
HALBERT Paul John						
St Albans, 28 October, 1973						(F)
Aldershot	YT	•	90	0	3	0
HALDANE Lewis Oliver						
Trowbridge, 13 March, 1985						(F)
Bristol Rov	Sch	10.03	03-04	17	23	5
HALE Alfred (Alfie)						
Waterford, 28 August, 1939 IRAmat/LoI-11/IR-13						(CF)
Aston Villa	Waterford	06.60	60-61	5	-	1
Doncaster Rov	Tr	07.62	62-64	119	-	42
Newport Co	Tr	08.65	65	34	0	21
HALE Denzil (Paddy) William						
Clevedon, 9 April, 1928 Died 2004						(CD)
Bristol Rov	Clevedon T	02.52	53-58	120	-	12
HALE Kenneth (Ken) Oliver						
Blyth, 18 September, 1939						(M)
Newcastle U	Jnrs	10.56	57-62	30	-	15
Coventry C	Tr	12.62	62-65	98	1	27
Oxford U	Tr	03.66	65-67	64	2	13
Darlington	Tr	05.68	68-71	173	0	25
Halifax T	Tr	07.72	72-73	52	0	4
HALE Joseph **Richard (Dixie)**						
Waterford, 29 May, 1935 LoI-3						(M)
Swansea T	Waterford	10.59	59-60	34	-	3
Barrow	Tr	07.61	61-63	118	-	16
Workington	Tr	08.64	64-66	131	0	10
Watford	Tr	07.67	67-69	95	3	7
HALES Derek David						
Lower Halstow, 15 December, 1951						(F)
Luton T	Dartford	03.72	72	5	2	1
Charlton Ath	Tr	10.73	73-76	126	3	73
Derby Co	Tr	12.76	76-77	22	1	4
West Ham U	Tr	09.77	77	23	1	10
Charlton Ath	Tr	07.78	78-84	186	5	76
Gillingham	Tr	03.85	84-85	31	9	9

League Club	Source	Date Signed	Seasons Played	Apps	Subs	Gls
HALES John McKendrick						
Glasgow, 15 May, 1940 (W)						
Brentford	St Roch's	09.58	58-63	62	-	7
HALES Kevin Peter						
Dartford, 13 January, 1961 (M)						
Chelsea	App	01.79	79-82	18	2	2
Orient	Tr	08.83	83-92	285	15	23
HALES Richard Joseph						
Gillingham, 24 August, 1925 (FB)						
Gillingham (Am)	Sittingbourne	08.51	51	5	-	0
HALES William (Bill) Henry						
Gillingham, 6 January, 1920 Died 1984 (CF)						
Gillingham	Sittingbourne (Am)	07.50	50-51	15	-	9
HALEY Grant Richard						
Bristol, 20 September, 1979 (FB)						
Peterborough U	YT	07.98	99	1	0	0
HALEY John						
Sunderland, 24 April, 1932 Died 1956 (WH)						
Gateshead		09.53	53-56	38	-	2
HALFORD Carl						
Ashton-under-Lyne, 27 November, 1958 (M)						
Manchester C	App	08.76				
Stockport Co	Tr	07.77	77-78	65	9	5
Bury	Tr	08.79	79-80	31	0	2
HALFORD Gregory (Greg)						
Chelmsford, 8 December, 1984 EYth (M)						
Colchester U	Sch	08.03	02-04	59	4	8
HALFORD Stephen (Steve) Paul						
Bury, 21 September, 1980 (CD)						
Bury	YT	07.99	99-00	3	2	0
HALL Albert Edwards Benjamin						
Cadoxton, 3 September, 1918 Died 1998 WSch (IF)						
Tottenham H	Jnrs	10.35	35-46	40	-	10
Plymouth Arg	Tr	07.47	47	9	-	0
HALL Alexander (Alec) Frank						
Grimsby, 17 September, 1909 Died 1992 (WH)						
Grimsby T	Cleethorpes T	05.29	29-47	358	-	4
HALL Allan Samuel						
Urmston, 26 May, 1938 EYth (WH)						
Oldham Ath	Manchester U (Am)	11.57	57-60	74	-	5
HALL Almeric (Almer) George						
Hove, 12 November, 1912 Died 1994 (IF)						
Brighton & Hove A	Southwick	02.31				
Tottenham H	Tr	09.33	34-35	16	-	3
Southend U	Tr	05.37	37-38	37	-	10
Bradford C	Tr	06.39				
West Ham U	Tr	12.45	46-48	50	-	11
HALL Anthony (Tony) David						
Billingham, 17 January, 1969 (CD)						
Tranmere Rov	Billingham T	08.87	87	0	1	0
Hartlepool U	Tr	10.87	87	0	1	0
HALL Arthur						
Sheffield, 23 November, 1925 (W)						
Chesterfield	Gainsborough Trinity	07.47	47-48	23	-	4
Scunthorpe U	Goole T	08.51	51	15	-	5
HALL Arthur Brian						
Eynsham, 24 March, 1937 (FB)						
Bristol Rov	Witney T	07.59	60-61	2	-	0
HALL Bernard Roy						
Bath, 8 July, 1942 (G)						
Bristol Rov	Jnrs	09.59	61-66	163	0	0
HALL Brian Samuel						
Burbage, 9 March, 1939 Died 2002 (FB)						
Mansfield T	Belper T	04.59	58-64	72	-	19
Colchester U	Tr	03.65	64-72	324	4	27
HALL Brian William						
Glasgow, 22 January, 1946 (M)						
Liverpool	Manchester Univ	07.68	68-75	140	13	15
Plymouth Arg	Tr	07.76	76-77	49	2	16
Burnley	Tr	11.77	77-79	39	4	3
HALL Christopher (Chris) Michael						
Manchester, 27 November, 1986 (F)						
Oldham Ath	Sch	•	03-04	2	5	0

League Club	Source	Date Signed	Seasons Played	Apps	Subs	Gls
HALL Colin Thomas						
Wolverhampton, 2 February, 1948 EYth (W)						
Nottingham F	Jnrs	03.66	67-69	27	9	2
Bradford C	Tr	06.70	70-71	65	1	7
Bristol C	Tr	07.72	72	0	1	0
Hereford U	L	09.72	72	5	0	0
HALL Daniel (Danny) Andrew						
Ashton-under-Lyne, 14 November, 1983 (FB)						
Oldham Ath	Sch	08.03	02-04	48	6	1
HALL David						
Doncaster, 26 September, 1960 (CD)						
Scunthorpe U	App	09.78	78-79	16	1	0
HALL David Henry						
Sheffield, 16 March, 1954 (M)						
Sheffield Wed	App	03.72				
Bradford C	Tr	07.75	75-76	51	3	3
HALL Kenneth Dennis						
Southwell, 24 December, 1930 Died 2004 (FB)						
Portsmouth	Bilsthorpe	09.48	52-53	10	-	0
Reading	Tr	08.54	54	13	-	0
HALL Derek Robert						
Ashton-under-Lyne, 5 January, 1965 (M)						
Coventry C	App	10.82	82	1	0	0
Torquay U	Tr	03.84	83-84	55	0	6
Swindon T	Tr	07.85	85	9	1	0
Southend U	Tr	08.86	86-88	122	3	15
Halifax T	Tr	07.89	89-90	48	1	4
Hereford U	Tr	07.91	91-93	98	5	18
Rochdale	Tr	08.94	94-95	14	9	2
HALL Fitz						
Leytonstone, 20 December, 1980 (CD)						
Oldham Ath	Chesham U	03.02	01-02	44	0	5
Southampton	Tr	07.03	03	7	4	0
Crystal Palace	Tr	08.04	04	36	0	2
HALL Frederick (Fred)						
Drayton, 20 October, 1914 Died 2003 (G)						
Norwich C	Hellesdon Hospital	09.34	35-46	90	-	0
HALL Frederick (Fred)						
Worksop, 24 November, 1924 (CF)						
Birmingham C	Whitwell OB	03.47	46-48	5	-	2
HALL Frederick (Fred) Wilkinson						
Chester-le-Street, 18 November, 1917 Died 1989 (CD)						
Blackburn Rov	Ouston Jnrs	11.35	36-38	29	-	0
Sunderland	Tr	08.46	46-54	215	-	1
Barrow	Tr	09.55	55	16	-	1
HALL Gareth David						
Croydon, 12 March, 1969 ESch/Wu21-1/W-9 (FB)						
Chelsea	App	04.86	86-95	120	18	4
Sunderland	Tr	12.95	95-97	41	7	0
Brentford	L	10.97	97	6	0	0
Swindon T	Tr	05.98	98-00	80	7	3
HALL Ian						
Egremont, Cumberland, 28 November, 1950 (FB)						
Workington	Egremont T	07.72	71-73	25	11	1
Southport	Tr	07.74	74	0	1	0
HALL Ian William						
Sutton Scarsdale, 27 December, 1939 ESch/EYth (M)						
Derby Co	Wolverhampton W (Am)	09.59	59-61	44	-	13
Mansfield T	Tr	09.62	62-67	145	0	10
HALL James (Jimmy)						
Bootle, 5 October, 1959 (M)						
Blackpool	App	10.77	78	1	0	0
HALL James (Jimmy) Franklin						
Burnage, 7 May, 1945 (FB)						
Oldham Ath	Mather & Platt	07.66	65	2	0	0
HALL James (Jim) Leonard						
Northampton, 21 March, 1945 EYth (F)						
Northampton T	Jnrs	07.63	63-67	54	1	7
Peterborough U	Tr	12.67	67-74	298	4	122
Northampton T	Tr	01.75	74-77	69	0	28
Cambridge U	L	12.76	76	24	0	15
HALL Jeffrey (Jeff) James						
Scunthorpe, 7 September, 1929 Died 1959 FLge-4/EB/E-17 (FB)						
Birmingham C	Bradford PA (Am)	05.50	50-58	227	-	1

HALL John (Jack)
Doncaster, 19 November, 1931 (CF)

League Club	Source	Date Signed	Seasons Played	Apps	Subs	Gls
Doncaster Rov		08.51	51	2	-	0

HALL John Franklin
Bramley, 18 April, 1944 (W)

League Club	Source	Date Signed	Seasons Played	Apps	Subs	Gls
Bradford C	Jnrs	05.62	62-73	417	13	63

HALL Joseph Edgar
Sherburn, 10 April, 1934 (IF)

League Club	Source	Date Signed	Seasons Played	Apps	Subs	Gls
Fulham	Newcastle U (Am)	10.51	55	1	-	0

HALL Lancelot (Lance)
Darlington, 23 January, 1915 Died 1985 (FB)

League Club	Source	Date Signed	Seasons Played	Apps	Subs	Gls
Luton T		01.37				
Barrow	Tr	07.38	38-48	108	-	1

HALL Leigh
Hereford, 10 June, 1975 (M)

League Club	Source	Date Signed	Seasons Played	Apps	Subs	Gls
Hereford U	Ledbury T	03.95	94-95	0	2	0

HALL Leslie (Les) Frederick
St Albans, 1 October, 1921 Died 2001 (CD)

League Club	Source	Date Signed	Seasons Played	Apps	Subs	Gls
Luton T	St Albans C	08.43	47-54	79	-	0

HALL Marcus Thomas Jackson
Coventry, 24 March, 1976 Eu21-8/EB-1 (FB)

League Club	Source	Date Signed	Seasons Played	Apps	Subs	Gls
Coventry C	YT	07.94	94-01	113	19	2
Nottingham F	Tr	08.02	02	1	0	0
Southampton	Tr	08.02				
Stoke C	Tr	12.02	02-04	76	3	1
Coventry C	Tr	02.05	04	10	0	0

HALL Mark
Doncaster, 11 May, 1970 (FB)

League Club	Source	Date Signed	Seasons Played	Apps	Subs	Gls
Doncaster Rov	YT	06.88	87-88	1	1	0

HALL Mark Anthony
Islington, 13 January, 1973 (W)

League Club	Source	Date Signed	Seasons Played	Apps	Subs	Gls
Southend U	Tottenham H (YT)	08.91	91-92	4	8	0
Barnet	L	09.93	93	3	0	0
Torquay U	Tr	07.95	95	22	7	0

HALL Paul Anthony
Manchester, 3 July, 1972 Jamaica 41 (W)

League Club	Source	Date Signed	Seasons Played	Apps	Subs	Gls
Torquay U	YT	07.90	89-92	77	16	1
Portsmouth	Tr	03.93	93-97	148	40	37
Coventry C	Tr	08.98	98-99	2	8	0
Bury	L	02.99	98	7	0	0
Sheffield U	L	12.99	99	1	3	1
West Bromwich A	L	02.00	99	4	0	0
Walsall	Tr	03.00	99-00	46	6	10
Rushden & Diamonds	Tr	10.01	01-03	106	6	26
Tranmere Rov	Tr	03.04	03-04	49	6	13

HALL Peter
Stoke-on-Trent, 29 September, 1939 (W)

League Club	Source	Date Signed	Seasons Played	Apps	Subs	Gls
Port Vale	Stoke C (Am)	05.58	58-60	16	-	4
Bournemouth	Tr	07.61				
Gillingham	Bedford T	11.67	67	9	0	1

HALL Richard Anthony
Ipswich, 14 March, 1972 EYth/Eu21-11 (CD)

League Club	Source	Date Signed	Seasons Played	Apps	Subs	Gls
Scunthorpe U	YT	03.90	89-90	22	0	3
Southampton	Tr	02.91	90-95	119	7	12
West Ham U	Tr	07.96	96	7	0	0

HALL Richard Frank
Weymouth, 3 July, 1945 (M)

League Club	Source	Date Signed	Seasons Played	Apps	Subs	Gls
Bournemouth	Weymouth	06.67	67	8	3	0

HALL Ronald (Ron)
Dudley, 8 February, 1933 (WH)

League Club	Source	Date Signed	Seasons Played	Apps	Subs	Gls
Walsall	Cradley Heath	06.54	54-55	2	-	0

HALL Stanley (Stan) Arthur
Southgate, 18 February, 1917 Died 1999 (G)

League Club	Source	Date Signed	Seasons Played	Apps	Subs	Gls
Clapton Orient	Finchley	03.38	38-46	26	-	0

HALL Wayne
Rotherham, 25 October, 1968 (FB)

League Club	Source	Date Signed	Seasons Played	Apps	Subs	Gls
York C	Hatfield Main Colliery	03.89	88-00	353	20	9

HALL Wilfred (Wilf)
Haydock, 14 October, 1934 (G)

League Club	Source	Date Signed	Seasons Played	Apps	Subs	Gls
Stoke C	Earlestown	10.53	54-59	45	-	0
Ipswich T	Tr	06.60	60-62	16	-	0

HALL William (Billy)
Gosport, 24 August, 1930 (CF)

League Club	Source	Date Signed	Seasons Played	Apps	Subs	Gls
Gillingham	Gosport Borough	09.52	52	9	-	0

HALL William (Willie) Furness
Walton-le-Dale, 6 February, 1926 Died 1986 (G)

League Club	Source	Date Signed	Seasons Played	Apps	Subs	Gls
Preston NE	Jnrs	02.48	47	7	-	0
Blackpool	Tr	07.49	52	3	-	0
Reading	Tr	07.53	53	16	-	0

HALL William (Billy) Wilson
Tuebrook, 3 June, 1917 (W)

League Club	Source	Date Signed	Seasons Played	Apps	Subs	Gls
Liverpool	Thorndale	11.43				
Southport	Tr	06.46	46	16	-	1

HALLAM Anthony (Tony) Kenneth
Chesterfield, 9 October, 1946 (FB)

League Club	Source	Date Signed	Seasons Played	Apps	Subs	Gls
Chesterfield	App	10.64	65-66	5	1	0

HALLAM Norman Henry
Stoke-on-Trent, 23 October, 1920 Died 1997 (WH)

League Club	Source	Date Signed	Seasons Played	Apps	Subs	Gls
Port Vale	Chelsea (Am)	05.46	46-52	63	-	4
Halifax T	Tr	10.53	53	3	-	0

HALLARD William (Billy)
St Helens, 28 August, 1913 Died 1980 (WH)

League Club	Source	Date Signed	Seasons Played	Apps	Subs	Gls
Bury	Runcorn	08.35	35	1	-	0
Bradford PA	Tr	06.37	37-38	69	-	5
Rochdale	Tr	06.46	46	17	-	2
Accrington St	Tr	03.47	46	3	-	0

HALLAS Geoffrey (Geoff)
Oldham, 8 December, 1930 Died 1982 (FB)

League Club	Source	Date Signed	Seasons Played	Apps	Subs	Gls
West Ham U	Warminster	03.54	54	3	-	0

HALLE Gunnar
Larvik, Norway, 11 August, 1965 NoYth/Nou21-23/No-64 (FB)

League Club	Source	Date Signed	Seasons Played	Apps	Subs	Gls
Oldham Ath	Lillestrom (Nor)	02.91	90-96	185	3	17
Leeds U	Tr	12.96	96-98	65	5	4
Bradford C	Tr	06.99	99-01	78	5	1
Wolverhampton W	L	03.02	01	4	1	0

HALLETT Thomas (Tom) Reginald
Glyn Neath, 10 April, 1939 WSch (CD)

League Club	Source	Date Signed	Seasons Played	Apps	Subs	Gls
Leeds U	Jnrs	04.56				
Swindon T	Tr	07.63	63-65	26	0	0
Bradford C	Tr	06.66	66-70	177	2	2

HALLIDAY Brian
Farnworth, 19 January, 1938 (W)

League Club	Source	Date Signed	Seasons Played	Apps	Subs	Gls
Stockport Co	Bolton W (Am)	10.58	58	1	-	0

HALLIDAY Brian Joseph
Liverpool, 30 December, 1944 (W)

League Club	Source	Date Signed	Seasons Played	Apps	Subs	Gls
Liverpool	Jnrs	05.63				
Tranmere Rov	Tr	07.65				
Crewe Alex	Tr	10.65	65	1	0	0

HALLIDAY Bruce
Sunderland, 3 January, 1961 (CD)

League Club	Source	Date Signed	Seasons Played	Apps	Subs	Gls
Newcastle U	App	01.79	80-81	32	0	1
Darlington	L	09.82	82	7	0	0
Bury	Tr	11.82	82	29	0	0
Bristol C	Tr	08.83	83-84	52	1	0
Hereford U	Tr	06.85	85-86	61	1	6

HALLIDAY Gary
Bradford, 9 May, 1951 (F)

League Club	Source	Date Signed	Seasons Played	Apps	Subs	Gls
Bradford PA	Jnrs	08.68	68	0	1	0

HALLIDAY Stephen (Steve) William
Sunderland, 3 May, 1976 (F)

League Club	Source	Date Signed	Seasons Played	Apps	Subs	Gls
Hartlepool U	YT	07.94	93-97	111	19	25
Carlisle U (L)	Motherwell	02.00	99	16	0	7
Carlisle U	Doncaster Rov	10.00	00-01	31	36	8

HALLIDAY Thomas (Tommy)
Ardrossan, 28 April, 1940 (IF)

League Club	Source	Date Signed	Seasons Played	Apps	Subs	Gls
Cardiff C	Dumbarton	10.63	63-64	16	-	2

HALLOWS Paul Charles Richard
Chester, 22 June, 1950 (FB)

League Club	Source	Date Signed	Seasons Played	Apps	Subs	Gls
Bolton W	App	10.67	68-73	44	2	0
Rochdale	Tr	05.74	74-79	197	0	2

HALLS John
Islington, 14 February, 1982 EYth/Eu20 (CD)

League Club	Source	Date Signed	Seasons Played	Apps	Subs	Gls
Arsenal	YT	07.00				
Colchester U	L	01.02	01	6	0	0
Stoke C	Tr	10.03	03-04	54	2	0

HALLWORTH Jonathan (Jon) Geoffrey
Stockport, 26 October, 1965 (G)

League Club	Source	Date Signed	Seasons Played	Apps	Subs	Gls
Ipswich T	App	05.83	85-87	45	0	0
Bristol Rov	L	01.85	84	2	0	0
Oldham Ath	Tr	02.89	88-96	171	3	0
Cardiff C	Tr	08.97	97-99	123	0	0

HALLYBONE James (Jimmy) Michael
Leytonstone, 15 March, 1962 (M)

League Club	Source	Date Signed	Seasons Played	Apps	Subs	Gls
Orient	App	05.80	81	5	3	0
Halifax T	Tr	07.82	82	11	5	0

HALOM Victor (Vic) Lewis
Swadlincote, 3 October, 1948 (F)

League Club	Source	Date Signed	Seasons Played	Apps	Subs	Gls
Charlton Ath	App	01.66	65-67	9	3	0
Orient	Tr	08.67	67-68	53	0	12
Fulham	Tr	11.68	68-71	66	6	22
Luton T	Tr	09.71	71-72	57	2	17
Sunderland	Tr	02.73	72-75	110	3	35
Oldham Ath	Tr	07.76	76-79	121	2	43
Rotherham U	Tr	02.80	79-80	19	1	2

HALPIN John (Johnny) Thomas
Manchester, 5 June, 1927 Died 2001 (FB)

League Club	Source	Date Signed	Seasons Played	Apps	Subs	Gls
Bury		11.48	48	2	-	0
Shrewsbury T	Tr	08.51	51-52	42	-	0

HALPIN John William
Broxburn, 15 November, 1961 SYth (W)

League Club	Source	Date Signed	Seasons Played	Apps	Subs	Gls
Carlisle U	Glasgow Celtic	10.84	84-90	148	5	17
Rochdale	Tr	07.91	91	22	9	1

HALSALL Alan
Menai Bridge, 17 November, 1940 (G)

League Club	Source	Date Signed	Seasons Played	Apps	Subs	Gls
Blackpool	Skelmersdale	04.62	61	2	-	0
Oldham Ath	Tr	07.63	63	2	-	0

HALSALL Michael (Mick)
Bootle, 21 July, 1961 (M)

League Club	Source	Date Signed	Seasons Played	Apps	Subs	Gls
Liverpool	App	05.79				
Birmingham C	Tr	03.83	82-84	35	1	3
Carlisle U	Tr	10.84	84-86	92	0	11
Grimsby T	Tr	02.87	86	12	0	0
Peterborough U	Tr	07.87	87-93	248	1	28

HALSEY Mark Alan
Romford, 1 December, 1959 (M)

League Club	Source	Date Signed	Seasons Played	Apps	Subs	Gls
Norwich C	App	12.77	77-79	3	0	0

HALSTEAD Roy
Whitworth, 26 July, 1931 Died 1997 (IF)

League Club	Source	Date Signed	Seasons Played	Apps	Subs	Gls
Burnley	Jnrs	06.53				
Chester	Tr	06.54	54	21	-	4

HALTON Reginald (Reg) Lloyd
Leek, 11 July, 1916 Died 1988 (WH)

League Club	Source	Date Signed	Seasons Played	Apps	Subs	Gls
Manchester U	Buxton	10.36	36	4	-	1
Notts Co	Tr	06.37	37	6	-	0
Bury	Tr	11.37	37-48	114	-	19
Chesterfield	Tr	12.48	48-50	61	-	10
Leicester C	Tr	09.50	50-51	64	-	3

HAM Michael (Mike) Thomas
Plymouth, 6 December, 1963 (CD)

League Club	Source	Date Signed	Seasons Played	Apps	Subs	Gls
Plymouth Arg	App	12.81	81-84	16	1	0

HAM Robert (Bobby) Stanley
Bradford, 29 March, 1942 (F)

League Club	Source	Date Signed	Seasons Played	Apps	Subs	Gls
Bradford PA	Jnrs	10.61	61-62	25	-	6
Grimsby T	Gainsborough Trinity	02.64	63	2	-	1
Bradford PA	Tr	08.64	64-67	134	0	47
Bradford C	Tr	02.68	67-70	115	0	40
Preston NE	Tr	10.70	70-71	43	0	14
Rotherham U	Tr	10.71	71-72	67	1	24
Bradford C	Tr	07.73	73-74	72	1	24

HAMANN Dietmar
Waldsasson, Germany, 27 August, 1973 GeYth/Geu21/Ge-58 (M)

League Club	Source	Date Signed	Seasons Played	Apps	Subs	Gls
Newcastle U	Bayern Munich (Ger)	08.98	98	22	1	4
Liverpool	Tr	07.99	99-04	161	13	8

HAMER John
Bradford, 5 April, 1944 (FB)

League Club	Source	Date Signed	Seasons Played	Apps	Subs	Gls
Bradford C (Am)		04.64	64	1	-	0

HAMER Kevin John
Merthyr Tydfil, 2 February, 1969 (CD)

League Club	Source	Date Signed	Seasons Played	Apps	Subs	Gls
Newport Co	YT	07.87	85-87	15	2	1

HAMILL Rory
Coleraine, 4 May, 1976 NISch/NIYth (W)

League Club	Source	Date Signed	Seasons Played	Apps	Subs	Gls
Fulham	Portstewart	11.94	94-95	24	24	7

HAMILL Stewart Peter
Glasgow, 22 January, 1960 (W)

League Club	Source	Date Signed	Seasons Played	Apps	Subs	Gls
Leicester C	Pollok Jnrs	09.80	80-81	10	0	2
Scunthorpe U	L	03.82	81	4	0	0
Northampton T	Nuneaton Borough	03.86	85	3	0	1
Scarborough	Altrincham	07.87	87	19	9	3

HAMILTON Alexander (Alex) McGregor
Kirkcolm, 21 November, 1937 (WH)

League Club	Source	Date Signed	Seasons Played	Apps	Subs	Gls
Accrington St	Drumore Jnrs	08.57	58-60	82	-	0
York C	Tr	03.62	61	11	-	0

HAMILTON Bryan
Belfast, 21 December, 1946 NIu23-2/IrLge-3/NI-50 (M)

League Club	Source	Date Signed	Seasons Played	Apps	Subs	Gls
Ipswich T	Linfield	08.71	71-75	142	11	43
Everton	Tr	11.75	75-76	38	3	5
Millwall	Tr	07.77	77-78	48	1	6
Swindon T	Tr	11.78	78-80	19	5	1
Tranmere Rov	Tr	10.80	80-84	95	14	6

HAMILTON Charles McDermott
Glasgow, 16 June, 1933 (W)

League Club	Source	Date Signed	Seasons Played	Apps	Subs	Gls
Plymouth Arg	Jnrs	07.50				
Stockport Co	Tr	11.55	55	7	-	1

HAMILTON David
South Shields, 7 November, 1960 EYth (M)

League Club	Source	Date Signed	Seasons Played	Apps	Subs	Gls
Sunderland	App	09.78				
Blackburn Rov	Tr	01.81	80-85	104	10	7
Cardiff C	L	03.85	84	10	0	0
Wigan Ath	Tr	07.86	86-88	97	6	7
Chester C	Tr	08.89	89	26	4	0
Burnley	Tr	08.90	90-91	11	4	0

HAMILTON David Stewart
Carlisle, 8 February, 1919 (IF)

League Club	Source	Date Signed	Seasons Played	Apps	Subs	Gls
Newcastle U	Shawfield Jnrs	05.39				
Southend U	Tr	05.46	46	4	-	0

HAMILTON Derrick (Des) Vivian
Bradford, 15 August, 1976 Eu21-1 (M)

League Club	Source	Date Signed	Seasons Played	Apps	Subs	Gls
Bradford C	YT	06.94	93-96	67	21	5
Newcastle U	Tr	03.97	97	7	5	0
Sheffield U	L	10.98	98	6	0	0
Huddersfield T	L	02.99	98	10	0	1
Norwich C	L	03.00	99	7	0	0
Tranmere Rov	L	10.00	00	2	0	0
Tranmere Rov	L	01.01	00	3	1	0
Cardiff C	Tr	07.01	01-02	16	9	0
Grimsby T	Tr	07.03	03	20	7	0

HAMILTON Edward (Eddie)
Glasgow, 17 January, 1927 LoI-1 (IF)

League Club	Source	Date Signed	Seasons Played	Apps	Subs	Gls
Barnsley	Dundalk	04.49	49	1	-	0

HAMILTON Gary Ian
Banbridge, 6 October, 1980 NISch/NIYth/NIu21-10 (F)

League Club	Source	Date Signed	Seasons Played	Apps	Subs	Gls
Blackburn Rov	YT	10.97				
Rochdale	L	10.98	00	0	3	0

HAMILTON Gary James
Glasgow, 27 December, 1965 SYth (M)

League Club	Source	Date Signed	Seasons Played	Apps	Subs	Gls
Middlesbrough	App	06.83	82-88	217	12	25
Darlington	L	09.91	91	11	0	2

HAMILTON Hugh (Hughie) Hare
Newton Mearns, 16 June, 1942 (W)

League Club	Source	Date Signed	Seasons Played	Apps	Subs	Gls
Hartlepools U	Falkirk	07.63	63-65	38	1	7

HAMILTON Ian
Thornbury, 12 September, 1940 (F)

League Club	Source	Date Signed	Seasons Played	Apps	Subs	Gls
Bristol Rov	Thornbury T	01.58	58-67	149	0	61
Exeter C	L	10.67	67	4	0	1
Newport Co	Tr	07.68	68	11	2	2

HAMILTON Ian (Chico) Michael
Streatham, 31 October, 1950 EYth (M)

League Club	Source	Date Signed	Seasons Played	Apps	Subs	Gls
Chelsea	App	01.68	66	3	2	2
Southend U	Tr	09.68	68	34	2	11
Aston Villa	Tr	06.69	69-75	189	19	40
Sheffield U	Tr	07.76	76-77	55	5	13

HAMILTON Ian Richard
Stevenage, 14 December, 1967 (M)

League Club	Source	Date Signed	Seasons Played	Apps	Subs	Gls
Southampton	App	12.85				
Cambridge U	Tr	03.88	87-88	23	1	1
Scunthorpe U	Tr	12.88	88-91	139	6	18
West Bromwich A	Tr	06.92	92-97	229	11	23
Sheffield U	Tr	03.98	97-99	38	7	3
Grimsby T	L	11.99	99	6	0	1
Notts Co	Tr	08.00	00-01	29	5	0
Lincoln C	Tr	11.01	01	26	0	0

HAMILTON Ian Walter
South Shields, 21 July, 1956 (M)

League Club	Source	Date Signed	Seasons Played	Apps	Subs	Gls
Darlington	Boldon CW	11.79	79-81	99	4	19

HAMILTON James (Jimmy)
Baillieston, 14 June, 1955 (M)

League Club	Source	Date Signed	Seasons Played	Apps	Subs	Gls
Sunderland	App	06.72	71-73	9	8	2
Plymouth Arg	Tr	11.75	76	6	2	0
Bristol Rov	Tr	12.76	76-77	16	4	1
Carlisle U	Tr	09.77	77-81	150	4	12
Hartlepool U	Gretna	11.82	82	2	1	0

HAMILTON John
Larkhall, 22 January, 1935 Su23-2/SLge-1 (W)

League Club	Source	Date Signed	Seasons Played	Apps	Subs	Gls
Watford	Heart of Midlothian	05.67	67	7	1	2

HAMILTON John Turner
Glasgow, 10 July, 1949 (F)

League Club	Source	Date Signed	Seasons Played	Apps	Subs	Gls
Millwall	Glasgow Rgrs	06.78	78	1	1	0

HAMILTON Lewis Emmanuel
Derby, 21 November, 1984 (FB)

League Club	Source	Date Signed	Seasons Played	Apps	Subs	Gls
Queens Park Rgrs	Derby Co (Sch)	08.04	04	0	1	0

HAMILTON Neville Roy
Leicester, 19 April, 1960 (M)

League Club	Source	Date Signed	Seasons Played	Apps	Subs	Gls
Leicester C	App	11.77	77	4	0	0
Mansfield T	Tr	01.79	78-80	84	5	4
Rochdale	Tr	08.81	81-83	72	2	5

HAMILTON Robert (Bobby) Menzies
Edinburgh, 25 April, 1924 Died 1999 (W)

League Club	Source	Date Signed	Seasons Played	Apps	Subs	Gls
Chester	Heart of Midlothian	11.45	46-47	68	-	10

HAMILTON William (Willie)
Hamilton, 1 September, 1918 (WH)

League Club	Source	Date Signed	Seasons Played	Apps	Subs	Gls
Preston NE	Blantyre Victoria	09.37	46	37	-	0

HAMILTON William (Willie) Murdoch
Chapelhall, 16 February, 1938 Died 1976 SLge-2/S-1 (IF)

League Club	Source	Date Signed	Seasons Played	Apps	Subs	Gls
Sheffield U	Drumpelier Amats	02.56	56-60	79	-	21
Middlesbrough	Tr	02.61	60-61	10	-	1
Aston Villa	Hibernian	08.65	65-66	49	0	9

HAMILTON William (Billy) Robert
Belfast, 9 May, 1957 NIu21-1/NI-41 (F)

League Club	Source	Date Signed	Seasons Played	Apps	Subs	Gls
Queens Park Rgrs	Linfield	04.78	78-79	9	3	2
Burnley	Tr	11.79	79-83	200	0	58
Oxford U	Tr	08.84	84-86	32	0	12

HAMLET Alan Graham
Watford, 30 September, 1977 (FB)

League Club	Source	Date Signed	Seasons Played	Apps	Subs	Gls
Barnet	YT	07.96	94	3	0	0

HAMLETT Thomas Lawrence (Lol)
Stoke-on-Trent, 24 January, 1917 Died 1986 (FB)

League Club	Source	Date Signed	Seasons Played	Apps	Subs	Gls
Bolton W	Congleton T	05.38	46-48	72	-	9
Port Vale	Tr	05.49	49-51	109	-	0

HAMMILL John (Jack)
Irvine, 8 January, 1924 Died 1999 (WH)

League Club	Source	Date Signed	Seasons Played	Apps	Subs	Gls
Newport Co	Arbroath	04.47	46-47	12	-	0

HAMMOND Albert William Arthur
Hanwell, 5 February, 1924 Died 1989 (IF)

League Club	Source	Date Signed	Seasons Played	Apps	Subs	Gls
Brentford	Queens Park Rgrs (Am)	01.46				
Exeter C	Tr	06.46	46	2	-	0

HAMMOND Andrew (Andy) Bendall
Rotherham, 21 November, 1978 (F)

League Club	Source	Date Signed	Seasons Played	Apps	Subs	Gls
Doncaster Rov	YT	●	97	1	0	0

HAMMOND Cyril Samuel
Woolwich, 10 February, 1927 (WH)

League Club	Source	Date Signed	Seasons Played	Apps	Subs	Gls
Charlton Ath	Erith & Belvedere	04.46	50-57	201	-	2
Colchester U	Tr	07.58	58-60	95	-	5

HAMMOND Dean John
Hastings, 7 March, 1983 (M)

League Club	Source	Date Signed	Seasons Played	Apps	Subs	Gls
Brighton & Hove A	YT	06.02	02-04	21	13	4
Leyton Orient	L	10.03	03	6	2	0

HAMMOND Elvis Zark
Accra, Ghana, 6 October, 1980 (F)

League Club	Source	Date Signed	Seasons Played	Apps	Subs	Gls
Fulham	YT	07.99	02-04	3	8	0
Bristol Rov	L	08.01	01	3	4	0
Norwich C	L	08.03	03	0	4	0

HAMMOND Geoffrey (Geoff)
Sudbury, 24 March, 1950 (FB)

League Club	Source	Date Signed	Seasons Played	Apps	Subs	Gls
Ipswich T	Jnrs	07.68	70-73	52	3	2
Manchester C	Tr	09.74	74-75	33	1	2
Charlton Ath	Tr	07.76	76	15	1	0

HAMMOND Nicholas (Nicky) David
Hornchurch, 7 September, 1967 (G)

League Club	Source	Date Signed	Seasons Played	Apps	Subs	Gls
Arsenal	App	07.85				
Bristol Rov	L	08.86	86	3	0	0
Swindon T	Tr	07.87	87-94	65	2	0
Plymouth Arg	Tr	08.95	95	4	0	0
Reading	Tr	02.96	95-98	25	0	0

HAMMOND Paul Anthony
Nottingham, 26 July, 1953 (G)

League Club	Source	Date Signed	Seasons Played	Apps	Subs	Gls
Crystal Palace	App	07.71	72-76	117	0	0

HAMON Christopher (Chris) Anthony
Jersey, 27 April, 1970 (F)

League Club	Source	Date Signed	Seasons Played	Apps	Subs	Gls
Swindon T	St Peter	07.92	92-94	3	5	1

HAMPSHIRE Paul
Guildford, 10 October, 1961 (F)

League Club	Source	Date Signed	Seasons Played	Apps	Subs	Gls
Aldershot	Jnrs	06.79	80-81	4	1	2

HAMPSON Alan
Prescot, 31 December, 1927 (IF)

League Club	Source	Date Signed	Seasons Played	Apps	Subs	Gls
Everton		08.49	50	1	-	0
Halifax T	Tr	11.52	52-55	121	-	32
Bradford C	Tr	07.56	56	6	-	4

HAMPSON Eric
Norton, Staffordshire, 11 November, 1921 (WH)

League Club	Source	Date Signed	Seasons Played	Apps	Subs	Gls
Stoke C	Stafford Rgrs	05.39	48-51	8	-	0

HAMPSON Raymond (Ray) Geoffrey
Manchester, 27 July, 1932 (W)

League Club	Source	Date Signed	Seasons Played	Apps	Subs	Gls
Manchester U	Jnrs	04.51				
Reading	Tr	04.53				
Aldershot	Tr	07.55	55-56	21	-	2
Bournemouth	Tr	07.57	57-58	15	-	2

HAMPTON Derek
Loftus, 25 April, 1952 (W)

League Club	Source	Date Signed	Seasons Played	Apps	Subs	Gls
Hartlepool U	Whitby T	11.79	79-81	66	8	18

HAMPTON Ivan Keith
Kimberley, 15 October, 1942 (FB)

League Club	Source	Date Signed	Seasons Played	Apps	Subs	Gls
Notts Co	Rotherham U (Am)	03.61	60-66	139	2	1
Halifax T	Tr	07.67	67-68	57	2	2
Peterborough U	Tr	07.69	69	3	1	0

HAMPTON Peter John
Oldham, 12 September, 1954 EYth (FB)

League Club	Source	Date Signed	Seasons Played	Apps	Subs	Gls
Leeds U	App	09.71	72-79	63	5	2
Stoke C	Tr	08.80	80-83	134	4	4
Burnley	Tr	08.84	84-86	116	2	2
Rochdale	Tr	08.87	87	19	0	1
Carlisle U	Tr	12.87	87	12	0	0

HAMSHAW Matthew (Matt) Thomas
Rotherham, 1 January, 1982 ESch/EYth/Eu20 (M)

League Club	Source	Date Signed	Seasons Played	Apps	Subs	Gls
Sheffield Wed	YT	01.99	00-04	35	39	2

HAMSHER John James
Lambeth, 14 January, 1978 (FB)

League Club	Source	Date Signed	Seasons Played	Apps	Subs	Gls
Fulham	YT	07.96	95	0	3	0

HAMSON Gary
Sandiacre, 24 August, 1959 (M)

League Club	Source	Date Signed	Seasons Played	Apps	Subs	Gls
Sheffield U	App	11.76	76-78	107	1	8
Leeds U	Tr	07.79	79-85	126	8	3
Bristol C	Tr	07.86	86	12	0	2
Port Vale	Tr	12.86	86-87	36	2	3

HAMSTEAD George William
Rotherham, 24 January, 1946 (W)

League Club	Source	Date Signed	Seasons Played	Apps	Subs	Gls
York C	Rotherham U (Am)	09.64	64-65	32	3	1
Barnsley	Tr	07.66	66-70	147	2	22
Bury	Tr	07.71	71-78	189	7	29
Rochdale	L	01.77	76	3	1	0

HANBY Robert James
Pontefract, 24 December, 1974 (FB)

League Club	Source	Date Signed	Seasons Played	Apps	Subs	Gls
Barnsley	YT	07.93				
Scarborough	Tr	08.96	96	1	3	0

HANCOCK Anthony (Tony) Eric
Manchester, 31 January, 1967 (F)

League Club	Source	Date Signed	Seasons Played	Apps	Subs	Gls
Stockport Co	Stockport Georgians	12.88	88	12	10	5
Burnley	Tr	06.89	89	9	8	0

HANCOCK Barry John
Stoke-on-Trent, 30 December, 1938 (IF)

League Club	Source	Date Signed	Seasons Played	Apps	Subs	Gls
Port Vale		07.57	60-63	21	-	1
Crewe Alex	Tr	08.64	64	3	-	0

HANCOCK Charles Raymond
Stoke-on-Trent, 16 February, 1925 (G)

League Club	Source	Date Signed	Seasons Played	Apps	Subs	Gls
Port Vale	Birches Head	05.48	48-55	50	-	0

HANCOCK David Jeffrey
Exeter, 24 July, 1938 (WH)

League Club	Source	Date Signed	Seasons Played	Apps	Subs	Gls
Plymouth Arg	Jnrs	09.55	56	2	-	0
Torquay U	Tr	01.59	58-63	177	-	11
Exeter C	Tr	03.64	63-64	40	-	3

HANCOCK Glynn Roy
Biddulph, 24 May, 1982 (CD)

League Club	Source	Date Signed	Seasons Played	Apps	Subs	Gls
Stockport Co	YT	08.99	00-01	1	2	0

HANCOCK Kenneth (Ken) Paul
Hanley, 25 November, 1937 (G)

League Club	Source	Date Signed	Seasons Played	Apps	Subs	Gls
Port Vale	Stoke C (Am)	12.58	58-64	241	-	0
Ipswich T	Tr	12.64	64-68	163	0	0
Tottenham H	Tr	03.69	69-70	3	0	0
Bury	Tr	07.71	71-72	35	0	0

HANCOCK Michael (Mike)
Newport, 17 February, 1954 WSch (CD)

League Club	Source	Date Signed	Seasons Played	Apps	Subs	Gls
Newport Co	Cardiff College	08.73	71-75	51	9	1

HANCOCKS John (Johnny)
Oakengates, 30 April, 1919 Died 1994 FLge-2/E-3 (W)

League Club	Source	Date Signed	Seasons Played	Apps	Subs	Gls
Walsall	Oakengates T	08.38	38	30	-	9
Wolverhampton W	Tr	05.46	46-55	343	-	158

HANCOX David Thomas
Conisbrough, 2 October, 1947 (F)

League Club	Source	Date Signed	Seasons Played	Apps	Subs	Gls
Sheffield U	App	09.65				
Chester	Tr	07.67	67	17	2	4

HANCOX Paul Anthony
Manchester, 22 July, 1970 (M)

League Club	Source	Date Signed	Seasons Played	Apps	Subs	Gls
Rochdale	YT	•	87	0	2	0

HANCOX Raymond (Ray)
Mansfield, 1 May, 1929 (IF)

League Club	Source	Date Signed	Seasons Played	Apps	Subs	Gls
Crystal Palace	Sutton U	08.50	50-52	20	-	3

HANCOX Richard James
Wolverhampton, 4 October, 1970 (F)

League Club	Source	Date Signed	Seasons Played	Apps	Subs	Gls
Torquay U	Stourport Swifts	03.93	92-96	56	26	10

HAND Eoin Kevin Joseph Colin
Dublin, 30 March, 1946 LoI-1/IR-20 (CD)

League Club	Source	Date Signed	Seasons Played	Apps	Subs	Gls
Swindon T	Drumcondra	06.64				
Portsmouth	Drumcondra	10.68	68-75	259	1	12
Portsmouth	Shamrock Rov	12.77	77-78	15	2	2

HAND Jamie
Uxbridge, 7 February, 1984 EYth (M)

League Club	Source	Date Signed	Seasons Played	Apps	Subs	Gls
Watford	YT	04.02	01-03	40	15	0
Oxford U	L	08.04	04	11	0	0

HANDFORD Philip (Phil) Michael
Chatham, 18 July, 1964 (M)

League Club	Source	Date Signed	Seasons Played	Apps	Subs	Gls
Gillingham	App	07.82	82-83	29	3	1
Wimbledon	Tr	08.84	84	7	0	0
Crewe Alex	L	01.86	85	9	0	0

HANDLEY Brian
Wakefield, 21 June, 1936 Died 1982 (CF)

League Club	Source	Date Signed	Seasons Played	Apps	Subs	Gls
Aston Villa	Goole T	09.57	59	3	-	0
Torquay U	Tr	09.60	60-63	80	-	32
Rochdale	Bridgwater T	02.66	65	3	0	0

HANDSCOMBE Malcolm (Mal)
Normanton, 29 June, 1934 (CD)

League Club	Source	Date Signed	Seasons Played	Apps	Subs	Gls
Chester (Am)		05.57	57	4	-	0

HANDYSIDE Peter David
Dumfries, 31 July, 1974 Su21-7 (CD)

League Club	Source	Date Signed	Seasons Played	Apps	Subs	Gls
Grimsby T	YT	11.92	92-00	181	9	4
Stoke C	Tr	07.01	01-02	78	0	0
Barnsley	Tr	08.03	03	28	0	0

HANDYSIDES Ian Robert
Jarrow, 14 December, 1962 Died 1990 EYth (W)

League Club	Source	Date Signed	Seasons Played	Apps	Subs	Gls
Birmingham C	App	01.80	80-83	44	18	2
Walsall	Tr	01.84	83-85	58	8	11
Birmingham C	Tr	03.86	85-87	53	3	4
Wolverhampton W	L	09.86	86	11	0	2

HANFORD Harold (Harry)
Blaengwynfi, 9 October, 1907 Died 1995 WSch/WLge-1/W-7 (CD)

League Club	Source	Date Signed	Seasons Played	Apps	Subs	Gls
Swansea T	Blaengwynfi Jnrs	05.26	27-35	201	-	0
Sheffield Wed	Tr	02.36	35-38	85	-	1
Exeter C	Tr	05.46	46	36	-	0

HANKEY Dean Anthony
Sutton-in-Ashfield, 23 August, 1986 (M)

League Club	Source	Date Signed	Seasons Played	Apps	Subs	Gls
Mansfield T	Sch	•	02	0	1	0

HANKEY Albert **Edward (Ted)**
Stoke-on-Trent, 24 May, 1914 Died 1998 (G)

League Club	Source	Date Signed	Seasons Played	Apps	Subs	Gls
Southend U	Charlton Ath (Am)	10.37	37-49	125	-	0

HANKIN Raymond (Ray)
Wallsend, 21 February, 1956 EYth/Eu23-3 (F)

League Club	Source	Date Signed	Seasons Played	Apps	Subs	Gls
Burnley	App	02.73	72-76	110	2	37
Leeds U	Tr	09.76	76-79	82	1	32
Arsenal	Vancouver (Can)	11.81				
Middlesbrough	Vancouver (Can)	09.82	82	19	2	1
Peterborough U	Tr	09.83	83-84	31	2	8
Wolverhampton W	Tr	03.85	84	9	1	1

HANKIN Sean Anthony
Camberley, 28 February, 1981 (M)

League Club	Source	Date Signed	Seasons Played	Apps	Subs	Gls
Crystal Palace	YT	06.99	99	0	1	0
Torquay U	Tr	10.01	01-03	45	2	1

HANKINSON James (Jim)
Preston, 1 July, 1928 (IF)

League Club	Source	Date Signed	Seasons Played	Apps	Subs	Gls
Preston NE		09.47				
Chester	Tr	06.50	50	15	-	1

HANLON John (Johnny) James
Manchester, 12 October, 1917 Died 2002 (CF)

League Club	Source	Date Signed	Seasons Played	Apps	Subs	Gls
Manchester U	St Wilfrid's (Hulme)	11.35	38-48	63	-	20
Bury	Tr	10.48	48-49	31	-	1

HANLON Richard (Richie) Kenneth
Kenton, 26 May, 1978 (M)

League Club	Source	Date Signed	Seasons Played	Apps	Subs	Gls
Southend U	Chelsea (YT)	07.96	96	1	1	0
Peterborough U	Rushden & Diamonds	12.98	98	0	4	1
Peterborough U	Welling U	12.99	99-01	30	13	2
Rushden & Diamonds	Tr	09.01	01-03	51	11	7
Lincoln C	Stevenage Borough	12.04	04	6	6	1

HANLON Stephen (Steve) Henry
Chester, 18 July, 1963 (M)

League Club	Source	Date Signed	Seasons Played	Apps	Subs	Gls
Crewe Alex	App	07.81	80-82	23	4	0

HANLON Walter (Wally) Andrew
Glasgow, 23 September, 1919 Died 1999 (W)

League Club	Source	Date Signed	Seasons Played	Apps	Subs	Gls
Brighton & Hove A	Clyde	08.46	46-47	72	-	4
Bournemouth	Tr	05.48	48	19	-	3
Crystal Palace	Tr	07.48	49-54	126	-	8

HANMER Gareth (Gary) Craig
Shrewsbury, 12 October, 1973 (FB)

League Club	Source	Date Signed	Seasons Played	Apps	Subs	Gls
West Bromwich A	Newtown	06.96				
Shrewsbury T	Tr	07.97	97-00	134	6	1

HANN Matthew
Saffron Walden, 6 September, 1980 (M)

League Club	Source	Date Signed	Seasons Played	Apps	Subs	Gls
Peterborough U	YT	01.99	98	0	4	0

HANN Ralph
Whitburn, 4 July, 1911 Died 1990 (WH)

League Club	Source	Date Signed	Seasons Played	Apps	Subs	Gls
Derby Co	Newcastle Swifts	03.31	32-38	115	-	0
Crystal Palace	Tr	04.47	46	1	-	0

HANNABY Cyril
Doncaster, 11 October, 1923 (G)

League Club	Source	Date Signed	Seasons Played	Apps	Subs	Gls
Wolverhampton W	Wath W	03.44				
Hull C	Tr	08.46	46-47	17	-	0
Halifax T	Tr	02.48	47	2	-	0

HANNAH George
Liverpool, 11 December, 1928 Died 1990 IrLge-1 (IF)

League Club	Source	Date Signed	Seasons Played	Apps	Subs	Gls
Newcastle U	Linfield	09.49	49-56	167	-	41
Lincoln C	Tr	09.57	57-58	38	-	4
Manchester C	Tr	09.58	58-63	114	-	15
Notts Co	Tr	07.64	64-65	25	0	1
Bradford C	Tr	10.65	65	29	1	2

HANNAH John
Wakefield, 25 October, 1962 (F)

League Club	Source	Date Signed	Seasons Played	Apps	Subs	Gls
Darlington	Fryston Colliery	10.83	83-84	15	7	8

HANNAH William (Willie) King
Shotts, 6 August, 1921 Died 1978 (W)

League Club	Source	Date Signed	Seasons Played	Apps	Subs	Gls
Preston NE	Albion Rov	12.47	47-49	15	-	4
Barrow	Tr	02.51	50-53	106	-	16

HANNAM David Vincent
Islington, 10 May, 1944 (W)

League Club	Source	Date Signed	Seasons Played	Apps	Subs	Gls
Brighton & Hove A	Jnrs	06.61	62	5	-	2

HANNAWAY John (Jack)
Bootle, 22 October, 1927 (FB)

League Club	Source	Date Signed	Seasons Played	Apps	Subs	Gls
Manchester C	Seaforth Fellowship	04.50	51-56	64	-	0
Gillingham	Tr	06.57	57-59	126	-	4
Southport	Tr	06.60	60-61	73	-	2

HANNIGAN Al James
Islington, 26 January, 1971 (CD)

League Club	Source	Date Signed	Seasons Played	Apps	Subs	Gls
Arsenal	YT	03.89				
Torquay U	L	03.90	89	5	2	0

HANNIGAN Brendan
Dublin, 3 September, 1943 LoI-2 (IF)

League Club	Source	Date Signed	Seasons Played	Apps	Subs	Gls
Wrexham	Shelbourne	12.65	65	7	0	2

HANNIGAN Ernest (Ernie)
Glasgow, 23 January, 1943 (W)

League Club	Source	Date Signed	Seasons Played	Apps	Subs	Gls
Preston NE	Queen of the South	08.64	64-67	97	0	28
Coventry C	Tr	11.67	67-69	43	4	6
Torquay U	L	12.69	69	2	0	0

HANNIGAN John (Johnny) Leckie
Barrhead, 17 February, 1933 (W)

League Club	Source	Date Signed	Seasons Played	Apps	Subs	Gls
Sunderland	Morton	07.55	55-57	33	-	8
Derby Co	Tr	05.58	58-60	72	-	19
Bradford PA	Tr	06.61	61-63	96	-	26

HANNON Kevin Michael
Whiston, 4 May, 1980 (CD)

League Club	Source	Date Signed	Seasons Played	Apps	Subs	Gls
Wrexham	YT	05.99	99	0	1	0

HANSBURY Roger
Barnsley, 26 January, 1955 (G)

League Club	Source	Date Signed	Seasons Played	Apps	Subs	Gls
Norwich C	App	01.73	74-80	78	0	0
Cambridge U	L	11.77	77	11	0	0
Burnley	Eastern Ath (HK)	08.83	83-84	83	0	0
Cambridge U	Tr	07.85	85	37	0	0
Birmingham C	Tr	03.86	86-89	57	0	0
Sheffield U	L	10.87	87	5	0	0
Wolverhampton W	L	03.89	88	3	0	0
Colchester U	L	08.89	89	4	0	0
Cardiff C	Tr	10.89	89-91	99	0	0

HANSELL Ronald (Ron) Arthur Robert
Norwich, 3 October, 1930 (IF)

League Club	Source	Date Signed	Seasons Played	Apps	Subs	Gls
Norwich C	Norwich St Barnabas	06.50	53-55	29	-	7
Chester	Tr	06.56	56	36	-	9

HANSEN Alan David
Sauchie, 13 June, 1955 Su23-3/S-26 (CD)

League Club	Source	Date Signed	Seasons Played	Apps	Subs	Gls
Liverpool	Partick Th	04.77	77-89	434	0	8

HANSEN Bo
Jutland, Denmark, 16 June, 1972 Denmark 1 (M)

League Club	Source	Date Signed	Seasons Played	Apps	Subs	Gls
Bolton W	Brondby (Den)	02.99	98-01	64	32	15

HANSEN Edwin
Koge, Denmark, 21 January, 1920 (IF)

League Club	Source	Date Signed	Seasons Played	Apps	Subs	Gls
Grimsby T (Am)	Koge KB (Den)	12.46	46	1	-	0

HANSEN John Schnabel
Mannheim, Germany, 14 September, 1973 (M)

League Club	Source	Date Signed	Seasons Played	Apps	Subs	Gls
Cambridge U	Esbjerg (Den)	02.00	99-00	19	9	3

HANSEN Karl
Denmark, 4 July, 1921 Died 1990 (IF)

League Club	Source	Date Signed	Seasons Played	Apps	Subs	Gls
Huddersfield T (Am)		01.49	48	15	-	2

HANSEN Vergard
Drammen, Norway, 8 August, 1969 (FB)

League Club	Source	Date Signed	Seasons Played	Apps	Subs	Gls
Bristol C	Stromgodset (Nor)	11.94	94-95	36	1	0

HANSON Christian
Middlesbrough, 3 August, 1981 ESch/EYth (CD)

League Club	Source	Date Signed	Seasons Played	Apps	Subs	Gls
Middlesbrough	YT	08.98				
Cambridge U	L	03.01	00	8	0	0
Torquay U	L	11.01	01	6	0	0
Port Vale	Spennymoor U	12.04	04	3	2	0

HANSON David (Dave) Paul
Huddersfield, 19 November, 1968 (F)

League Club	Source	Date Signed	Seasons Played	Apps	Subs	Gls
Bury	Farsley Celtic	07.93	93	1	0	0
Leyton Orient	Hednesford T	10.95	95-97	26	22	5
Chesterfield	L	03.97	96	3	0	1
Halifax T	Tr	01.98	98	19	12	2

HANSON Frederick (Fred)
Sheffield, 23 May, 1915 Died 1967 (W)

League Club	Source	Date Signed	Seasons Played	Apps	Subs	Gls
Crystal Palace	Indus Sports	05.35	35	1	-	0
Rotherham U	Tr	03.36	36-46	106	-	29

HANSON John
Bradford, 3 December, 1962 (F)

League Club	Source	Date Signed	Seasons Played	Apps	Subs	Gls
Bradford C	App	12.80	80	1	0	0

HANSON Neil
Blackburn, 16 June, 1964 (F)

League Club	Source	Date Signed	Seasons Played	Apps	Subs	Gls
Preston NE	App	09.81				
Halifax T	Tr	08.83	83	1	1	0

HANSON Stanley (Stan)
Bootle, 27 December, 1915 Died 1987 (G)

League Club	Source	Date Signed	Seasons Played	Apps	Subs	Gls
Bolton W	Litherland	10.35	36-55	384	-	0

HANSSON Mikael
Norrkoping, Sweden, 15 March, 1968 Sweden 1 (FB)

League Club	Source	Date Signed	Seasons Played	Apps	Subs	Gls
Stoke C	Norrkoping (Swe)	12.99	99-00	60	5	2

HANVEY Keith
Manchester, 18 January, 1952 (FB)

League Club	Source	Date Signed	Seasons Played	Apps	Subs	Gls
Manchester C	Jnrs	08.71				
Swansea C	Tr	07.72	72	11	0	0
Rochdale	Tr	07.73	73-76	121	0	10
Grimsby T	Tr	02.77	76-77	54	0	2
Huddersfield T	Tr	07.78	78-83	205	0	14
Rochdale	Tr	07.84	84	15	0	0

HAPGOOD Edris **Anthony (Tony)**
Kettering, 13 June, 1930 (W)

League Club	Source	Date Signed	Seasons Played	Apps	Subs	Gls
Burnley		03.48	51	7	-	2
Watford	Tr	07.53	53	1	-	0

HAPGOOD Leon Duane
Torquay, 7 August, 1979 (M)

League Club	Source	Date Signed	Seasons Played	Apps	Subs	Gls
Torquay U	YT	05.98	96-98	26	14	3

HARBACH Peter Colin
Carlisle, 30 April, 1967 (F)

League Club	Source	Date Signed	Seasons Played	Apps	Subs	Gls
Newcastle U	App	04.85				
Carlisle U	Tr	08.87	87	0	7	0

HARBER William (Billy) Hudson
Hitchin, 3 December, 1944 (W)

League Club	Source	Date Signed	Seasons Played	Apps	Subs	Gls
Swindon T	App	12.61	62	2	-	0
Luton T	Tr	09.64	64-65	28	0	3

HARBERTSON Ronald (Ron)
Redcar, 23 December, 1929 (IF)

League Club	Source	Date Signed	Seasons Played	Apps	Subs	Gls
Newcastle U	North Shields	01.49				
Bradford C	Tr	08.50	50	16	-	1
Brighton & Hove A	Tr	10.51				
Bradford C	Tr	05.52	53	13	-	3
Grimsby T	Tr	07.54	54	26	-	6
Darlington	Ashington	01.57	56-57	49	-	21
Lincoln C	Tr	03.58	57-59	57	-	22
Wrexham	Tr	03.60	59-60	28	-	13
Darlington	Tr	01.61	60	14	-	2
Lincoln C	Tr	07.61	61	29	-	3

HARBEY Graham Keith
Chesterfield, 29 August, 1964 (FB)

League Club	Source	Date Signed	Seasons Played	Apps	Subs	Gls
Derby Co	App	08.82	83-86	35	5	1
Ipswich T	Tr	07.87	87-89	53	6	1
West Bromwich A	Tr	11.89	89-91	97	0	2
Stoke C	Tr	07.92	92-93	18	1	0

HARBOTTLE Mark Stuart
Nottingham, 26 September, 1968 EYth (F)

League Club	Source	Date Signed	Seasons Played	Apps	Subs	Gls
Notts Co	App	09.86	85	1	3	1
Doncaster Rov	L	01.88	87	4	0	0

HARBURN Peter Arthur Patrick
Shoreditch, 18 June, 1931 (CF)

League Club	Source	Date Signed	Seasons Played	Apps	Subs	Gls
Brighton & Hove A	Portsmouth (Am)	02.56	54-57	126	-	61
Everton	Tr	08.58	58	4	-	1
Scunthorpe U	Tr	01.59	58-59	20	-	8
Workington	Tr	10.59	59-60	67	-	23

HARBURN William Nicholson
Stockton, 19 November, 1923 (CF)

League Club	Source	Date Signed	Seasons Played	Apps	Subs	Gls
Darlington (Am)		06.47	47	1	-	0

HARBY Michael (Mick) John
Nottingham, 7 November, 1948 (G)

League Club	Source	Date Signed	Seasons Played	Apps	Subs	Gls
Nottingham F	Jnrs	07.66	67	3	0	0

HARDCASTLE Cyril
Halifax, 22 November, 1919 Died 1982 (CF)

League Club	Source	Date Signed	Seasons Played	Apps	Subs	Gls
Bradford C (Am)		09.48	48	4	-	1

HARDCASTLE Peter David
Leeds, 27 January, 1949 ESch/EAmat (FB)

League Club	Source	Date Signed	Seasons Played	Apps	Subs	Gls
Blackpool	Skelmersdale U	07.71	71-73	29	7	0

League Club	Source	Date Signed	Seasons Played	Career Record Apps	Subs	Gls
Plymouth Arg	Tr	07.74	74-75	12	2	1
Bradford C	Tr	07.76	76-77	62	0	1
HARDEN Leo						
Hartlepool, 7 May, 1923 Died 1999						(W)
Hartlepools U	Railway Ath	05.46	46-55	169	-	47
HARDIE John Clarke						
Edinburgh, 7 February, 1938						(G)
Oldham Ath	Falkirk	07.60	60	17	-	0
Chester	Tr	07.61	61-62	84	-	0
Bradford PA	Tr	12.63	63-69	265	0	0
HARDIKER John David						
Preston, 17 July, 1982						(CD)
Stockport Co	Morecambe	01.02	01-04	94	9	3
HARDING Alan						
Sunderland, 14 May, 1948						(W)
Darlington	Spennymoor U	01.70	69-72	125	4	37
Lincoln C	Tr	03.73	72-78	203	6	38
Hartlepool U	Tr	03.79	78-82	79	5	8
HARDING Benjamin (Ben) Scott						
Carshalton, 6 September, 1984 EYth						(M)
Wimbledon/MK Dons	YT	10.01	03-04	31	10	4
HARDING Daniel (Dan) Andrew						
Gloucester, 23 December, 1983 Eu21-4						(M)
Brighton & Hove A	Sch	07.03	02-04	56	11	1
HARDING David						
Liverpool, 14 August, 1946						(IF)
Wrexham		09.65	65	9	1	0
HARDING Edward (Ted) James						
Croydon, 5 April, 1925						(FB)
Crystal Palace	Coalville	11.44	46-52	151	-	0
HARDING Kevin						
Isleworth, 19 March, 1957						(M)
Brentford	App	●	73-74	8	0	0
HARDING Paul John						
Mitcham, 6 March, 1964						(M)
Notts Co	Barnet	09.90	90-92	45	9	1
Southend U	L	08.93	93	2	3	0
Watford	L	11.93	93	1	1	0
Birmingham C	Tr	12.93	93-94	19	3	0
Cardiff C	Tr	08.95	95	36	0	0
HARDING Stephen (Steve) John						
Bristol, 23 July, 1956						(CD)
Bristol C	App	07.74	75	2	0	0
Southend U	L	01.76	75	2	0	0
Grimsby T	L	09.76	76	8	0	0
Bristol Rov	Tr	06.77	77-79	37	1	1
Brentford	L	01.80	79	3	1	0
HARDING William (Billy)						
Carshalton, 20 January, 1985						(F)
Wycombe W	Sch	●	03	0	2	0
HARDISTY John (Bob) Roderick Elliott						
Chester-le-Street, 1 February, 1921 Died 1986 EAmat						(IF)
Darlington (Am)	Bishop Auckland	12.46	46-48	6	-	0
HARDMAN Colin Arthur						
Altrincham, 13 November, 1955						(W)
Stockport Co		03.76	75-76	6	3	1
HARDMAN John Alan						
Bury, 17 December, 1940 Died 1998						(WH)
Rochdale	Bess's Boys	08.60	60-66	40	0	2
HARDS Neil Andrew						
Portsmouth, 28 January, 1962						(G)
Plymouth Arg	App	01.80	79-82	6	0	0
HARDSTAFF Cecil						
Crewe, 14 November, 1931						(FB)
Crewe Alex	Wolverhampton W (Am)	06.49	49	1	-	0
HARDWICK George Francis Moutry						
Saltburn, 2 February, 1920 Died 2004 FLge-3/EWar-17/E-13						(FB)
Middlesbrough	South Bank East End	04.37	37-50	143	-	5
Oldham Ath	Tr	11.50	50-55	190	-	14
HARDWICK Kenneth (Ken)						
West Auckland, 27 January, 1924 Died 1983						(G)
Doncaster Rov	Rossington Colliery	04.45	47-56	307	-	0
Scunthorpe U	Tr	04.57	56-59	96	-	0
Barrow	Tr	12.59	59	12	-	0

League Club	Source	Date Signed	Seasons Played	Career Record Apps	Subs	Gls
HARDWICK Steven (Steve)						
Mansfield, 6 September, 1956 EYth						(G)
Chesterfield	Jnrs	07.74	74-76	38	0	0
Newcastle U	Tr	12.76	77-82	92	0	0
Oxford U	Tr	02.83	82-87	156	0	0
Crystal Palace	L	03.86	85	3	0	0
Sunderland	L	08.87	87	6	0	0
Huddersfield T	Tr	07.88	88-90	109	0	0
HARDY Edwin Malcolm						
Chesterfield, 16 October, 1953						(G)
Chesterfield	Jnrs	08.71	72	6	0	0
HARDY Gordon (Bob) Douglas						
Kingston, 23 May, 1923 Died 2003						(CD)
Millwall	Brodsworth Colliery	08.45	46	3	-	0
Southport	Tr	07.48	48-49	16	-	0
Bournemouth	Tr	06.50	51-53	76	-	0
HARDY Herbert Thomas						
Barrow, 6 December, 1929						(CF)
Barrow		05.52	51	2	-	1
HARDY Jason Paul						
Burnley, 14 December, 1969						(FB)
Burnley	YT	07.88	86-91	38	5	1
Halifax T	L	01.92	91	0	4	0
Halifax T	Tr	07.92	92	20	2	2
Rochdale	Prestwich Heys	08.95	95	5	2	0
HARDY John (Jack) Henry						
Chesterfield, 15 June, 1910 Died 1978						(WH)
Chesterfield	Unstone	12.34	34-36	48	-	1
Hull C	Tr	07.37	37-38	65	-	0
Lincoln C	Tr	05.39	46	18	-	0
HARDY Lee						
Blackpool, 26 November, 1981						(M)
Blackburn Rov	YT	07.00				
Oldham Ath	Tr	07.01	01	0	1	0
Macclesfield T	Tr	07.02	02	8	8	0
HARDY Neil John Paul						
Bury, 29 December, 1973						(F)
Stockport Co	Radcliffe Borough	06.01	01	4	6	2
HARDY Paul Alan						
Plymouth, 29 August, 1975						(M)
Torquay U	YT	08.93	93	0	1	0
HARDY Philip (Phil)						
Ellesmere Port, 9 April, 1973 IRu21-9						(FB)
Wrexham	YT	11.90	89-00	346	3	1
Port Vale	Tr	07.01	01	8	0	1
HARDY Robin						
Worksop, 18 January, 1941						(CD)
Sheffield Wed	Jnrs	02.58	61-63	30	-	1
Rotherham U	Tr	02.65	64-65	42	0	2
Cambridge U		(N/L)	70	15	1	1
HARDY William						
Whitehaven, 23 August, 1929 Died 2003						(WH)
Workington	Queen of the South	10.51	51-53	55	-	2
HARDYMAN Paul George						
Portsmouth, 11 March, 1964 Eu21-2						(FB)
Portsmouth	Waterlooville	07.83	83-88	113	4	3
Sunderland	Tr	07.89	89-91	101	5	9
Bristol Rov	Tr	08.92	92-94	54	13	5
Wycombe W	Tr	08.95	95	12	3	0
Barnet	Tr	08.96	96	13	3	2
HARE Matthew (Matt)						
Barnstaple, 26 December, 1976						(M)
Exeter C	YT	08.95	95-97	31	14	1
HARE Thomas (Tommy)						
Motherwell, 1 April, 1944						(FB)
Southampton	Fauldhouse U	04.63	65	13	0	0
Luton T	Tr	07.67	67	12	0	0
HAREIDE Aage Fridhjof						
Hareide, Norway, 23 September, 1953 Norway int						(CD)
Manchester C	Molde FK (Nor)	10.81	81-82	17	7	0
Norwich C	Tr	11.82	82-83	38	2	2
HAREWOOD Marlon Anderson						
Hampstead, 25 August, 1979						(F)
Nottingham F	YT	09.96	97-03	124	58	51
Ipswich T	L	01.99	98	5	1	1
West Ham U	Tr	11.03	03-04	73	0	30

HARFIELD Leslie (Les) Philip
Southampton, 22 November, 1952 ESch/EYth (W)

League Club	Source	Date Signed	Seasons Played	Apps	Subs	Gls
Southampton	App	11.69	70	2	0	1
Luton T	Tr	09.72	72	0	1	0

HARFORD Michael (Mick) Gordon
Sunderland, 12 February, 1959 EB/E-2 (F)

League Club	Source	Date Signed	Seasons Played	Apps	Subs	Gls
Lincoln C	Lambton Star BC	07.77	77-80	109	6	41
Newcastle U	Tr	12.80	80	18	1	4
Bristol C	Tr	08.81	81	30	0	11
Birmingham C	Tr	03.82	81-84	92	0	25
Luton T	Tr	12.84	84-89	135	4	58
Derby Co	Tr	01.90	89-91	58	0	15
Luton T	Tr	09.91	91	29	0	12
Chelsea	Tr	08.92	92	27	1	9
Sunderland	Tr	03.93	92	10	1	2
Coventry C	Tr	07.93	93	0	1	1
Wimbledon	Tr	08.94	94-96	37	24	9

HARFORD Paul Raymond Thomas
Chelmsford, 21 October, 1974 (M)

League Club	Source	Date Signed	Seasons Played	Apps	Subs	Gls
Blackburn Rov	Arsenal (YT)	08.93				
Wigan Ath	L	09.94	94	3	0	0
Shrewsbury T	L	12.94	94	3	3	0

HARFORD Raymond (Ray) Thomas
Halifax, 1 June, 1945 Died 2003 (CD)

League Club	Source	Date Signed	Seasons Played	Apps	Subs	Gls
Charlton Ath	Jnrs	05.64	65	3	0	0
Exeter C	Tr	01.66	65-66	55	0	1
Lincoln C	Tr	07.67	67-70	161	0	10
Mansfield T	Tr	06.71	71	7	0	0
Port Vale	Tr	12.71	71-72	20	0	1
Colchester U	Tr	01.73	72-74	107	1	4

HARGREAVES Allan
Dewsbury, 29 March, 1931 (CF)

League Club	Source	Date Signed	Seasons Played	Apps	Subs	Gls
Bradford C		07.54	54-55	4	-	1

HARGREAVES Christian (Chris)
Cleethorpes, 12 May, 1972 (M)

League Club	Source	Date Signed	Seasons Played	Apps	Subs	Gls
Grimsby T	YT	12.89	89-92	15	36	5
Scarborough	L	03.93	92	2	1	0
Hull C	Tr	07.93	93-94	34	15	0
West Bromwich A	Tr	07.95	95	0	1	0
Hereford U	Tr	02.96	95-96	57	4	6
Plymouth Arg	Tr	07.98	98-99	74	2	5
Northampton T	Tr	07.00	00-03	144	7	6
Brentford	Tr	07.04	04	30	0	2

HARGREAVES David
Accrington, 27 August, 1954 (F)

League Club	Source	Date Signed	Seasons Played	Apps	Subs	Gls
Blackburn Rov	Accrington St	12.77	77	2	0	0

HARGREAVES John (Jackie)
Rotherham, 1 May, 1915 Died 1978 (W)

League Club	Source	Date Signed	Seasons Played	Apps	Subs	Gls
Leeds U		08.34	35-38	45	-	10
Bristol C	Tr	08.45	46	26	-	9
Reading	Tr	04.47	46-47	15	-	1

HARGREAVES Joseph (Joe) Albert
Accrington, 30 October, 1915 Died 1992 (CF)

League Club	Source	Date Signed	Seasons Played	Apps	Subs	Gls
Rochdale	Rossendale U	10.45	46-47	35	-	24

HARGREAVES Thomas (Tom)
Blackburn, 29 October, 1917 Died 1997 (CD)

League Club	Source	Date Signed	Seasons Played	Apps	Subs	Gls
Blackburn Rov	Crosshill	10.36	37	4	-	2
Rochdale	Tr	05.46	46	7	-	0

HARGREAVES Wilfred (Wilf) Oscar
Rawmarsh, 15 December, 1921 Died 1993 (WH)

League Club	Source	Date Signed	Seasons Played	Apps	Subs	Gls
Rotherham U	Rawmarsh Welfare	03.45	46-47	3	-	0

HARKER Christopher (Chris) Joseph
Shiremoor, 29 June, 1937 (G)

League Club	Source	Date Signed	Seasons Played	Apps	Subs	Gls
Newcastle U	West Allotment Celtic	03.55	57	1	-	0
Bury	Aberdeen	12.61	61-66	178	0	0
Grimsby T	Tr	06.67	67	10	0	0
Rochdale	Tr	07.68	68-69	92	0	0

HARKES John Andrew
Kearny, New Jersey, USA, 8 March, 1967 USA 70 (M)

League Club	Source	Date Signed	Seasons Played	Apps	Subs	Gls
Sheffield Wed	N Carolina Univ (USA)	10.90	90-92	59	22	7
Derby Co	Tr	08.93	93-95	67	7	2
West Ham U	L	10.95	95	6	5	0
Nottingham F (L)	DCU (USA)	01.99	98	3	0	0

HARKIN James (Jim)
Brinsworth, 8 August, 1913 Died 1988 (WH)

League Club	Source	Date Signed	Seasons Played	Apps	Subs	Gls
Doncaster Rov	Denaby U	08.34	34	1	-	0
Mansfield T	Shrewsbury T	02.39	38-46	23	-	5

HARKIN Maurice (Mo) Presley
Derry, 16 August, 1979 NIYth/NIu21-9 (W)

League Club	Source	Date Signed	Seasons Played	Apps	Subs	Gls
Wycombe W	YT	02.97	96-00	26	47	2
Carlisle U	Tr	08.01	01	2	2	0

HARKIN John Terence (Terry)
Derry, 14 September, 1941 NIu23-1/LoI-2/NI-5 (F)

League Club	Source	Date Signed	Seasons Played	Apps	Subs	Gls
Port Vale	Coleraine	09.62	62-63	27	-	11
Crewe Alex	Tr	06.64	64	42	-	34
Cardiff C	Tr	08.65	65	19	1	10
Notts Co	Tr	09.66	66	27	1	10
Southport	Tr	07.67	67-68	63	1	31
Shrewsbury T	Tr	03.69	68-70	79	0	29

HARKINS Gary
Greenock, 2 January, 1985 (M)

League Club	Source	Date Signed	Seasons Played	Apps	Subs	Gls
Blackburn Rov	Sch	01.04				
Huddersfield T	L	03.04	03	1	2	0
Bury	L	02.05	04	4	1	0

HARKNESS James (Jim)
Edinburgh, 19 May, 1940 (G)

League Club	Source	Date Signed	Seasons Played	Apps	Subs	Gls
Carlisle U	Hamilton Academical	08.61	61-62	16	-	0

HARKNESS Jonathan (Jon)
Antrim, 18 November, 1985 (M)

League Club	Source	Date Signed	Seasons Played	Apps	Subs	Gls
Walsall	Sch	•	04	1	0	0

HARKNESS Steven (Steve)
Carlisle, 27 August, 1971 EYth (FB)

League Club	Source	Date Signed	Seasons Played	Apps	Subs	Gls
Carlisle U	YT	03.89	88	12	1	0
Liverpool	Tr	07.89	91-98	90	12	3
Huddersfield T	L	09.93	93	5	0	0
Southend U	L	02.95	94	6	0	0
Blackburn Rov	Benfica	09.99	99	17	0	0
Sheffield Wed	Tr	02.00	00	28	2	1

HARKNESS William (James) Jardine
Glasgow, 21 July, 1918 Died 1995 (IF)

League Club	Source	Date Signed	Seasons Played	Apps	Subs	Gls
Carlisle U	Stirling A	10.47				
Workington	South Shields	(N/L)	51	7	-	1

HARKOUK Rachid Peter
Chelsea, 19 May, 1956 Algeria int (F)

League Club	Source	Date Signed	Seasons Played	Apps	Subs	Gls
Crystal Palace	Feltham	06.76	76-77	51	3	20
Queens Park Rgrs	Tr	06.78	78-79	15	5	3
Notts Co	Tr	06.80	80-85	124	20	39

HARLAND Stanley (Stan) Clarence
Liverpool, 19 June, 1940 Died 2001 (CD)

League Club	Source	Date Signed	Seasons Played	Apps	Subs	Gls
Everton	New Brighton	02.59				
Bradford C	Tr	07.61	61-63	120	-	20
Carlisle U	Tr	06.64	64-65	77	0	7
Swindon T	Tr	08.66	66-71	237	0	6
Birmingham C	Tr	12.71	71-72	37	1	0

HARLE David
Denaby, 15 August, 1963 EYth (M)

League Club	Source	Date Signed	Seasons Played	Apps	Subs	Gls
Doncaster Rov	App	11.80	79-81	48	13	3
Exeter C	Tr	07.82	82-83	42	1	6
Doncaster Rov	Tr	09.83	83-85	80	3	17
Leeds U	Tr	12.85	85	3	0	0
Bristol C	Tr	03.86	85-86	23	0	2
Scunthorpe U	Tr	11.86	86-88	88	1	10
Peterborough U	Tr	03.89	88-89	21	1	2
Doncaster Rov	Tr	03.90	89-91	39	6	3

HARLE Michael (Mike) James Lee
Lewisham, 31 October, 1972 (FB)

League Club	Source	Date Signed	Seasons Played	Apps	Subs	Gls
Gillingham	YT	•	90	1	1	0
Millwall	Sittingbourne	11.93	96	12	9	1
Bury	L	12.95	95	0	1	0
Barnet	Tr	07.97	97-98	53	1	2

HARLEY Albert George
Chester, 17 April, 1940 Died 1993 (M)

League Club	Source	Date Signed	Seasons Played	Apps	Subs	Gls
Shrewsbury T	Jnrs	04.57	56-64	220	-	14
Swansea T	Tr	09.64	64-65	25	1	0
Crewe Alex	Guildford C	07.66	66	22	0	5
Stockport Co	Tr	02.67	66-68	77	3	11
Chester	Tr	06.69	69	3	0	1

HARLEY Alexander (Alex)
Glasgow, 20 April, 1936 Died 1969 (CF)

League Club	Source	Date Signed	Seasons Played	Apps	Subs	Gls
Manchester C	Third Lanark	08.62	62	40	-	23
Birmingham C	Tr	08.63	63-64	28	-	9

HARLEY James (Jim)
Methil, 2 February, 1917 Died 1989 SWar-2 (FB)

League Club	Source	Date Signed	Seasons Played	Apps	Subs	Gls
Liverpool	Hearts o' Beath	04.34	35-47	114	-	0

League Club	Source	Date Signed	Seasons Played	Apps	Subs	Gls
HARLEY Richard John						
March, 22 April, 1949						(CD)
Reading	Stevenage Ath	09.69	69-72	64	10	6
Aldershot	Tr	07.73	73-74	16	12	0
Hartlepool	Wokingham T	09.76	76	4	0	1
HARLEY Jonathan (Jon)						
Maidstone, 26 September, 1979 EYth/Eu21-3						(FB)
Chelsea	YT	03.97	97-00	22	8	2
Wimbledon	L	10.00	00	6	0	2
Fulham	Tr	08.01	01-03	19	6	1
Sheffield U	L	10.02	02	8	1	1
Sheffield U	L	09.03	03	5	0	0
West Ham U	L	01.04	03	15	0	1
Sheffield U	Tr	08.04	04	44	0	2
HARLEY Lee						
Crewe, 7 July, 1967						(F)
Chester C	App	●	85	0	1	0
HARLEY Leslie (Les)						
Chester, 26 September, 1946						(W)
Chester	Jnrs	09.64	64-66	22	3	3
Blackpool	Tr	07.67				
Rochdale	L	02.68	67	5	0	0
HARLEY Ryan Bernard						
Bristol, 22 January, 1985						(M)
Bristol C	Sch	07.04	04	1	1	0
HARLOCK Desmond (Des) Southern						
Blaenau Ffestiniog, 20 December, 1922 Died 1981						(W)
Tranmere Rov	Liverpool (Am)	03.42	46-53	150	-	17
HARMAN Peter Robert						
Guildford, 11 October, 1950						(F)
Bournemouth	App	08.68	69	1	0	0
Reading	Tr	08.71	71-72	34	2	9
HARMER Thomas (Tommy) Charles						
Hackney, 2 February, 1928 EB						(IF)
Tottenham H	Finchley	08.48	51-59	205	-	47
Watford	Tr	10.60	60-61	63	-	6
Chelsea	Tr	09.62	62-63	8	-	1
HARMON Darren John						
Northampton, 30 January, 1973						(M)
Notts Co	YT	07.91				
Shrewsbury T	Tr	02.92	91-92	1	5	2
Northampton T	Tr	10.92	92-94	76	13	12
HARMSTON Michael (Mick) James						
Sheffield, 7 April, 1950						(FB)
Sheffield U	App	05.67	68	5	0	0
Southend U	L	12.70	70	1	0	0
HARMSWORTH Lee Anthony						
Southwark, 27 October, 1967						(G)
Charlton Ath	App	10.85	84	3	0	0
HARNBY Donald (Don) Reed						
Hurworth, 20 July, 1923						(FB)
Newcastle U	Spennymoor U	05.45				
York C	Tr	08.47	47	1	-	0
Grimsby T	Spennymoor U	09.49	49-51	34	-	0
HARNEY David						
Jarrow, 2 March, 1947						(F)
Grimsby T	Jnrs	11.64				
Scunthorpe U	Tr	07.67	67-68	20	5	1
Brentford	Tr	10.69	69	0	1	0
HARNEY Stephen (Steve) Graham						
Bradford, 18 February, 1951						(FB)
Bradford C (Am)	Drum Rov	07.68	68-70	13	1	0
HARNWELL Jamie						
Perth, Australia, 21 January, 1977						(CD)
Leyton Orient	Perth Glory (Aus)	08.03	03	1	2	0
HAROLD Michael (Mike) Lloyd						
Stockport, 22 September, 1943						(FB)
Stockport Co	Manchester C (Am)	08.64	64	4	-	0
HARPER Alan						
Liverpool, 1 November, 1960 EYth						(FB)
Liverpool	App	04.78				
Everton	Tr	06.83	83-87	103	23	4
Sheffield Wed	Tr	07.88	88-89	32	3	0
Manchester C	Tr	12.89	89-90	46	4	1
Everton	Tr	08.91	91-92	45	6	0
Luton T	Tr	09.93	93	40	1	1
Burnley	Tr	08.94	94-95	30	1	0
Cardiff C	L	11.95	95	5	0	0
HARPER Antony (Tony) Frederick						
Oxford, 26 May, 1925 Died 1982						(WH)
Brentford	Headington U	04.48	48-54	173	-	6
HARPER Colin George						
Ipswich, 25 July, 1946						(FB)
Ipswich T	Jnrs	08.64	65-74	144	4	5
Grimsby T	L	12.76	76	3	0	0
Cambridge U	L	02.77	76	15	0	0
Port Vale	Tr	08.77	77	4	0	0
HARPER David (Dave)						
Peckham, 29 September, 1938 EYth						(M)
Millwall	Jnrs	05.57	57-64	165	-	4
Ipswich T	Tr	03.65	64-66	70	2	2
Swindon T	Tr	07.67	67	4	0	0
Orient	Tr	10.67	67-70	82	3	4
HARPER Dennis						
Tipton, 12 October, 1936						(IF)
Birmingham C	Darlaston	08.56	56	1	-	0
HARPER Donald (Don)						
Blackwell, Derbyshire, 26 October, 1921 Died 1990						(W)
Chesterfield		12.43				
Mansfield T	Tr	07.46	46	21	-	1
HARPER Ian Thomas						
Scunthorpe, 23 November, 1944						(FB)
Scunthorpe U	Jnrs	07.62	63-64	21	-	0
HARPER Ivor Roy						
Watford, 23 June, 1933						(IF)
Watford (Am)	Hemel Hempstead	10.51	51	3	-	0
HARPER James Alan John						
Chelmsford, 9 November, 1980						(M)
Arsenal	YT	07.99				
Cardiff C	L	12.00	00	3	0	0
Reading	Tr	02.01	00-04	136	18	8
HARPER Joseph (Joe) John						
Muirhead, 12 January, 1920 Died 1987						(FB)
Watford	Twechar U	05.37	46-51	159	-	1
HARPER Joseph (Joe) Montgomerie						
Greenock, 11 January, 1948 Su23-2/SLge-1/S-4						(F)
Huddersfield T	Morton	03.67	66-67	26	2	4
Everton	Aberdeen	12.72	72-73	40	3	12
HARPER Kenneth (Ken)						
Worsborough, 15 April, 1917 Died 1994						(FB)
Walsall		03.35	37-38	22	-	2
Bradford C	Tr	01.46	46-48	50	-	0
HARPER Kenneth (Ken)						
Farnworth, 27 April, 1924						(WH)
Blackpool		12.45				
Rochdale		12.47				
Shrewsbury T	Hindsford	08.50	50	1	-	0
HARPER Kevin Patrick						
Oldham, 15 January, 1976 SSch/Su21-7/SB-1						(M)
Derby Co	Hibernian	09.98	98-99	6	26	1
Walsall	L	12.99	99	8	1	1
Portsmouth	Tr	03.00	99-03	85	34	9
Norwich C	L	09.03	03	9	0	0
Leicester C	L	09.04	04	2	0	0
Stoke C	Tr	02.05	04	8	1	0
HARPER Lee Charles Philip						
Chelsea, 30 October, 1971						(G)
Arsenal	Sittingbourne	06.94	96	1	0	0
Queens Park Rgrs	Tr	07.97	97-00	117	1	0
Walsall	Tr	07.01	01	3	0	0
Northampton T	Tr	07.02	02-04	106	0	0
HARPER Lee James						
Bridlington, 24 March, 1975						(FB)
Scarborough	YT	03.94	93	0	2	0
HARPER Robert (Bobby)						
Glasgow, 6 June, 1920 Died 1980						(W)
Huddersfield T	Ayr U	06.46				
Newport Co	Tr	11.46	46-49	114	-	12
Southend U	Tr	07.50	50	6	-	0

League Club	Source	Date Signed	Seasons Played	Career Record Apps	Subs	Gls
HARPER Stephen (Steve) Alan						
Easington, 14 March, 1975						(G)
Newcastle U	Seaham Red Star	07.93	98-04	31	2	0
Bradford C	L	09.95	95	1	0	0
Hartlepool U	L	08.97	97	15	0	0
Huddersfield T	L	12.97	97	24	0	0
HARPER Steven (Steve) James						
Newcastle-under-Lyme, 3 February, 1969						(W)
Port Vale	App	06.87	87-88	16	12	2
Preston NE	Tr	03.89	88-90	57	20	10
Burnley	Tr	07.91	91-92	64	5	8
Doncaster Rov	Tr	08.93	93-95	56	9	11
Mansfield T	Tr	09.95	95-98	157	3	18
Hull C	Tr	07.99	99-00	63	2	4
Darlington	Tr	02.01	00-01	32	8	1
HARRAD Shaun Nicholas						
Nottingham, 11 December, 1984						(M)
Notts Co	Sch	04.04	02-04	4	25	1
HARRIES Paul Graham						
Sydney, Australia, 19 November, 1977						(F)
Portsmouth	NSW Soccer Acad (Aus)	09.97	97	0	1	0
Crystal Palace	Tr	09.98				
Torquay U	L	02.99	98	5	0	0
Carlisle U	Tr	07.99	99	6	14	2
Macclesfield T	Wollongong W's (Aus)	02.01				
Exeter C	Merthyr Tydfil	09.02	02	0	1	0
HARRIGAN Duncan						
Paisley, 26 June, 1921						(CF)
Crewe Alex	St Mirren	08.46	46-47	57	-	23
Aston Villa	Tr	04.48				
Chester	Tr	10.48	48	20	-	4
HARRINGTON Alan Charles						
Cardiff, 17 November, 1933 WLge-1/W-11						(FB)
Cardiff C	Cardiff Nomads	10.51	52-65	348	0	6
HARRINGTON Colin Andrew						
Bicester, 3 April, 1943						(W)
Oxford U	Wolverhampton W (Am)	10.62	62-70	230	4	30
Mansfield T	Tr	06.71	71	7	6	0
HARRINGTON Justin David						
Truro, 18 September, 1975						(M)
Norwich C	YT	07.94				
Leicester C	Tr	08.96				
Bournemouth	Tr	07.97	97	4	4	0
HARRINGTON Paul						
Hartlepool, 26 September, 1964						(M)
Hartlepool U		04.83	83	0	2	0
HARRINGTON Philip (Phil)						
Bangor, 20 November, 1963 WYth						(G)
Chester	App	11.81	81-84	76	0	0
Blackpool	Tr	03.85				
Burnley	L	11.85	85	2	0	0
Preston NE	L	02.86	85	2	0	0
HARRIOTT Marvin Lee						
Dulwich, 20 April, 1974 ESch/EYth						(FB)
Oldham Ath	West Ham U (YT)	04.92				
Barnsley	Tr	04.93				
Leyton Orient	L	10.93	93	8	0	0
Bristol C	Tr	12.93	93-94	36	0	0
HARRIS Albert (Bert) Edward						
Bootle, 21 November, 1931						(G)
Everton	Maghull	01.55	55	5	-	0
Tranmere Rov	Tr	05.57	57-59	33	-	0
Southport	Tr	07.60	60-64	159	-	0
HARRIS Alexander (Sandy)						
Hong Kong, 22 October, 1934						(W)
Blackpool	Scone CB	11.51	52-57	21	-	4
HARRIS Allan John						
Northampton, 28 December, 1942 ESch/EYth						(FB)
Chelsea	Jnrs	06.60	60-64	70	-	0
Coventry C	Tr	11.64	64-65	60	0	0
Chelsea	Tr	05.66	66	12	2	0
Queens Park Rgrs	Tr	07.67	67-70	90	4	0
Plymouth Arg	Tr	03.71	70-72	64	0	0
Cambridge U	Tr	07.73	73	6	0	0
HARRIS Andrew (Andy)						
Birmingham, 17 November, 1970						(M)
Birmingham C	YT	07.89	89	0	1	0
Oxford U	L	10.91	91	1	0	0
Exeter C	Tr	11.91	91-93	32	6	1
HARRIS Andrew (Andy) David Douglas						
Springs, South Africa, 26 February, 1977						(M)
Liverpool	YT	03.94				
Southend U	Tr	07.96	96-98	70	2	0
Leyton Orient	Tr	07.99	99-02	143	6	2
Chester C	Tr	07.03	04	9	10	0
HARRIS Anthony (Tony) Thomas						
Berrington, 20 December, 1945						(CD)
Shrewsbury T	App	07.63	63-66	54	1	4
Bradford PA	Tr	07.68	68	10	0	0
HARRIS Arthur						
Coventry, 28 July, 1914 Died 1973						(WH)
Southend U	Nuneaton T	07.36	36-46	114	-	1
HARRIS Brian						
Bebington, 16 May, 1935 EYth						(CD)
Everton	Port Sunlight	01.54	55-66	310	0	23
Cardiff C	Tr	10.66	66-70	146	3	0
Newport Co	Tr	07.71	71-73	85	0	0
HARRIS Carl Stephen						
Neath, 3 November, 1956 WSch/Wu23-1/W-24						(W)
Leeds U	App	11.73	74-81	123	30	26
Charlton Ath	Tr	07.82	82-84	73	3	8
Bury	Leeds U (N/C)	12.85	85-86	33	5	4
Rochdale	Cardiff C (N/C)	01.88	87-88	24	1	3
Exeter C	Tr	12.88	88	11	5	1
HARRIS Christopher (Chris) Robert						
Hastings, 23 January, 1957						(F)
Millwall	Bexhill U	10.76	76	3	0	0
HARRIS David (Dave)						
Stoke-on-Trent, 19 November, 1953						(CD)
Port Vale		08.73	73-78	175	1	8
Halifax T	Tr	07.79	79-80	69	2	3
HARRIS Frederick (Fred)						
Sparkbrook, 2 July, 1912 Died 1998 FLge-1						(IF)
Birmingham	Osborne Ath	04.33	34-49	280	-	61
HARRIS Gary Wayne						
Birmingham, 31 May, 1959						(W)
Cardiff C	App	05.77	78-79	4	0	0
HARRIS Geoffrey (Geoff) Robert						
Heywood, 1 February, 1956						(F)
Oldham Ath	App	02.74				
Halifax T	Tr	07.75	75-76	10	5	1
HARRIS George						
Stanley, 24 August, 1936						(W)
Preston NE	Craghead	08.57				
Southport	Tr	07.59	59	1	-	0
HARRIS George Alfred						
Lambeth, 10 June, 1940						(W)
Newport Co	Woking	07.61	61	31	-	7
Watford	Tr	04.62	61-65	162	1	55
Reading	Tr	07.66	66-69	134	2	57
Cambridge U	Tr	07.70	70-71	33	2	11
HARRIS Thomas James **George**						
Ogmore, 15 February, 1916 Died 1998						(G)
Charlton Ath		08.39				
Plymouth Arg	Aberaman Ath	05.48	48	3	-	0
HARRIS Gerald (Gerry) William						
Claverley, 8 October, 1935 Eu23-4						(FB)
Wolverhampton W	Bebington	01.54	56-65	235	0	2
Walsall	Tr	04.66	65-67	13	2	0
HARRIS Gordon						
Worksop, 2 June, 1940 Eu23-2/FLge-2/E-1						(M)
Burnley	Firbeck Colliery	01.58	58-67	258	0	69
Sunderland	Tr	01.68	67-71	124	1	16
HARRIS Gordon William						
Campmuir, 19 February, 1943						(FB)
Cardiff C	Forfar Ath	03.65	64	5	-	0
HARRIS Derek **Harold (Harry)**						
Magor, 2 November, 1933 Died 2004						(CD)
Newport Co	Undy U	09.54	54-57	156	-	57
Portsmouth	Tr	07.58	58-70	378	2	48
Newport Co	L	10.70	70	16	0	2
HARRIS James (Jimmy)						
Birkenhead, 18 August, 1933 Eu23-1/FLge-1						(CF)
Everton	Jnrs	09.51	55-60	191	-	65

League Club	Source	Date Signed	Seasons Played	Apps	Subs	Gls
Birmingham C	Tr	12.60	60-63	93	-	37
Oldham Ath	Tr	07.64	64-65	28	1	9

HARRIS James (Jamie) Christopher
Swansea, 28 June, 1979 (F)

League Club	Source	Date Signed	Seasons Played	Apps	Subs	Gls
Swansea C	Mumbles Rgrs	07.97	97	0	6	0

HARRIS Jamie
Exeter, 4 February, 1969 (F)

League Club	Source	Date Signed	Seasons Played	Apps	Subs	Gls
Exeter C	App	08.86	87-88	6	8	1

HARRIS Jason Andre Sebastian
Sutton, 24 November, 1976 (M)

League Club	Source	Date Signed	Seasons Played	Apps	Subs	Gls
Crystal Palace	YT	07.95	96	0	2	0
Bristol Rov	L	11.96	96	5	1	2
Lincoln C	L	08.97	97	0	1	0
Leyton Orient	Tr	09.97	97-98	22	15	7
Preston NE	Tr	08.98	98	9	25	6
Hull C	Tr	07.99	99-00	19	19	4
Shrewsbury T	L	03.01	00	1	3	0
Southend U	Tr	07.01	01	2	3	0

HARRIS Jason Mark
Rochdale, 26 December, 1969 (M)

League Club	Source	Date Signed	Seasons Played	Apps	Subs	Gls
Burnley	YT	07.88	86	4	0	0

HARRIS Jeffrey (Jeff) Bruce
Stepney, 11 June, 1942 EAmat (WH)

League Club	Source	Date Signed	Seasons Played	Apps	Subs	Gls
Leyton Orient	Enfield	05.64	64	14	-	0

HARRIS John
Glasgow, 30 June, 1917 Died 1988 SWar-1 (CD)

League Club	Source	Date Signed	Seasons Played	Apps	Subs	Gls
Swansea T	Swindon T (Am)	08.34	36-38	28	-	4
Tottenham H	Tr	02.39				
Wolverhampton W	Tr	05.39				
Chelsea	Tr	08.45	46-55	326	-	14
Chester	Tr	07.56	56	27	-	1

HARRIS David **John (Johnny)**
Gornal, 3 April, 1939 (FB)

League Club	Source	Date Signed	Seasons Played	Apps	Subs	Gls
Wolverhampton W	Sedgley Rov	05.58	61-62	3	-	0
Walsall	Tr	01.65	64-68	74	0	2

HARRIS John Patrick
Bermondsey, 20 December, 1931 (IF)

League Club	Source	Date Signed	Seasons Played	Apps	Subs	Gls
Millwall (Am)		06.56	56	1	-	0

HARRIS Thomas **John**
Swansea, 18 May, 1934 (CD)

League Club	Source	Date Signed	Seasons Played	Apps	Subs	Gls
Leeds U		11.51				
Halifax T	Tr	10.55	55-56	9	-	0

HARRIS Joseph (Joe)
Belfast, 8 April, 1929 (CF)

League Club	Source	Date Signed	Seasons Played	Apps	Subs	Gls
Blackburn Rov	Larne	01.51	50-51	35	-	15
Oldham Ath	Tr	03.53	52-53	27	-	4

HARRIS Joseph (Joe) Anthony
Liverpool, 20 September, 1926 (W)

League Club	Source	Date Signed	Seasons Played	Apps	Subs	Gls
Everton		07.50	50-52	14	-	4

HARRIS Thomas **Kevin**
Dublin, 20 February, 1918 Died 1984 (IF)

League Club	Source	Date Signed	Seasons Played	Apps	Subs	Gls
Notts Co		09.45				
Brentford		08.48	48	4	-	0

HARRIS Leonard (Len) James
Nuneaton, 29 May, 1949 (FB)

League Club	Source	Date Signed	Seasons Played	Apps	Subs	Gls
Nottingham F	Jnrs	06.66	68-69	2	0	0
Doncaster Rov	L	09.70	70	4	0	0

HARRIS Leslie (Les)
Llanfair, 1 November, 1941 (W)

League Club	Source	Date Signed	Seasons Played	Apps	Subs	Gls
Swansea T	Aberystwyth Univ	08.63	63-64	4	-	0

HARRIS Leslie (Les) Henry
Stocksbridge, 29 May, 1955 (F)

League Club	Source	Date Signed	Seasons Played	Apps	Subs	Gls
Barnsley	Jnrs	05.74	75-76	11	15	2

HARRIS Mark Andrew
Reading, 15 July, 1963 (CD)

League Club	Source	Date Signed	Seasons Played	Apps	Subs	Gls
Crystal Palace	Wokingham T	02.88	88	0	2	0
Burnley	L	08.89	89	4	0	0
Swansea C	Tr	09.89	89-94	228	0	14
Gillingham	Tr	08.95	95-96	63	2	3
Cardiff C	Tr	08.97	97	38	0	1

HARRIS Martin
Doncaster, 22 December, 1955 (W)

League Club	Source	Date Signed	Seasons Played	Apps	Subs	Gls
Workington	Grimsby T (App)	07.74	74-76	97	9	13
Hartlepool U	Tr	12.77	77	0	1	0

HARRIS Neil
Glasgow, 9 February, 1920 (CF)

League Club	Source	Date Signed	Seasons Played	Apps	Subs	Gls
Queens Park Rgrs	Swansea T (Am)	09.46	46	1	-	1

HARRIS Neil
Orsett, 12 July, 1977 (F)

League Club	Source	Date Signed	Seasons Played	Apps	Subs	Gls
Millwall	Cambridge C	03.98	97-04	186	47	93
Cardiff C	L	12.04	04	1	2	1
Nottingham F	Tr	12.04	04	5	8	0

HARRIS Neil John
Manchester, 7 November, 1969 (W)

League Club	Source	Date Signed	Seasons Played	Apps	Subs	Gls
Crewe Alex	YT	07.88	87	3	0	0

HARRIS Paul Edwin
Hackney, 19 May, 1953 (CD)

League Club	Source	Date Signed	Seasons Played	Apps	Subs	Gls
Orient	App	07.70	70-74	96	0	4
Swansea C	Tr	07.75	75-76	47	2	2

HARRIS Peter
Neath, 9 August, 1953 (W)

League Club	Source	Date Signed	Seasons Played	Apps	Subs	Gls
Newport Co	App	08.71	70-72	21	10	1

HARRIS Peter Philip
Portsmouth, 19 December, 1925 Died 2003 FLge-5/E-2 (W)

League Club	Source	Date Signed	Seasons Played	Apps	Subs	Gls
Portsmouth	Gosport Borough	11.44	46-59	479	-	193

HARRIS Philip (Phil)
Swindon, 18 December, 1958 (M)

League Club	Source	Date Signed	Seasons Played	Apps	Subs	Gls
Swindon T	App	•	76	0	1	0

HARRIS Richard Lewis Scott
Croydon, 23 October, 1980 (F)

League Club	Source	Date Signed	Seasons Played	Apps	Subs	Gls
Crystal Palace	YT	12.97	98-00	2	7	0
Mansfield T	L	09.01	01	0	6	0
Wycombe W	Tr	03.02	01-03	13	22	5

HARRIS Ronald (Ron) Edward
Hackney, 13 November, 1944 ESch/EYth/Eu23-4 (CD)

League Club	Source	Date Signed	Seasons Played	Apps	Subs	Gls
Chelsea	Jnrs	11.61	61-79	646	9	13
Brentford	Tr	05.80	80-83	60	1	0

HARRIS Thomas (Tommy) Alfred
Chelsea, 8 November, 1924 Died 2001 (CF)

League Club	Source	Date Signed	Seasons Played	Apps	Subs	Gls
Fulham		09.47				
Leyton Orient	Tr	09.51	51-52	31	-	11
Colchester U	Tr	06.53	53	3	-	0

HARRIS William **Thomas (Tommy)**
Aberbargoed, 30 June, 1913 Died 1997 (FB)

League Club	Source	Date Signed	Seasons Played	Apps	Subs	Gls
Watford	New Tredegar	04.33	35-48	94	-	6

HARRIS Trevor John
Colchester, 6 February, 1936 (WH)

League Club	Source	Date Signed	Seasons Played	Apps	Subs	Gls
Colchester U	Wilson MS	07.54	54-62	99	-	6

HARRIS William (Bill)
Dudley, 1 December, 1918 Died 1996 (G)

League Club	Source	Date Signed	Seasons Played	Apps	Subs	Gls
West Bromwich A	Whiteheath	02.37	37	2	-	0
Oldham Ath	Tr	06.46	46	32	-	0
Accrington St	Tr	08.47	47-49	99	-	0

HARRIS William (Bill) Charles
Swansea, 31 October, 1928 Died 1989 W-6 (WH)

League Club	Source	Date Signed	Seasons Played	Apps	Subs	Gls
Hull C	Llanelli	03.50	49-53	131	-	6
Middlesbrough	Tr	03.54	53-64	360	-	69
Bradford C	Tr	03.65	64-65	9	0	1

HARRISON Andrew (Andy) Frank
Long Eaton, 13 September, 1957 (FB)

League Club	Source	Date Signed	Seasons Played	Apps	Subs	Gls
Scarborough	Kettering T	(N/L)	87	3	1	0

HARRISON Anthony (Tony) Leslie
Gateshead, 9 January, 1954 (G)

League Club	Source	Date Signed	Seasons Played	Apps	Subs	Gls
Southport	Whitley Bay	02.77	76-77	48	0	0
Carlisle U	Tr	06.78	80	8	0	0

HARRISON Bernard (Bernie) Reginald Stanhope
Worcester, 28 September, 1934 (W)

League Club	Source	Date Signed	Seasons Played	Apps	Subs	Gls
Crystal Palace	Portsmouth (Am)	10.55	55-58	92	-	12
Southampton	Tr	08.59	59	3	-	0
Exeter C	Tr	07.60	60	18	-	4

HARRISON Christopher (Chris) Colin
Launceston, 17 October, 1956 (CD)

League Club	Source	Date Signed	Seasons Played	Apps	Subs	Gls
Plymouth Arg	App	10.74	75-84	314	9	7
Swansea C	Tr	09.85	85-87	114	3	14

HARRISON Colin George
Pelsall, 18 March, 1946 (FB)

League Club	Source	Date Signed	Seasons Played	Apps	Subs	Gls
Walsall	Jnrs	11.63	64-81	453	20	33

League Club	Source	Date Signed	Seasons Played	Career Record Apps	Subs	Gls
HARRISON Craig						
Gateshead, 10 November, 1977						(FB)
Middlesbrough	YT	07.96	97-98	19	5	0
Preston NE	L	01.99	98	6	0	0
Crystal Palace	Tr	08.00	00-01	34	4	0
HARRISON Daniel (Danny) Robert						
Liverpool, 4 November, 1982						(M)
Tranmere Rov	YT	05.02	01-04	56	21	2
HARRISON Derek						
Littlethorpe, 9 February, 1950						(CD)
Leicester C	App	02.67				
Torquay U	Tr	01.71	70-74	124	3	4
Colchester U	Tr	06.75	75	5	2	0
HARRISON Eric George						
Mytholmroyd, 5 February, 1938						(CD)
Halifax T	Mytholmroyd	07.57	57-63	199	-	10
Hartlepools U	Tr	08.64	64-65	81	0	4
Barrow	Tr	07.66	66-68	127	3	1
Southport	Tr	06.69	69-70	75	0	0
Barrow	Tr	07.71	71	31	1	1
HARRISON Francis (Frank) John						
Gateshead, 12 November, 1931 Died 1981 EYth						(FB)
Hull C	Ainthorpe Grove YC	05.49	52-59	199	-	0
HARRISON Francis (Frankie) Nicholas						
Eston, 19 September, 1963						(FB)
Middlesbrough	Guisborough T	09.82				
Lincoln C	Carnegie College	11.85	85	0	1	0
Halifax T	Guiseley	03.87	86-89	48	6	0
HARRISON Gary Mark						
Northampton, 12 March, 1975						(M)
Northampton T	Aston Villa (YT)	12.93	93-94	7	0	0
HARRISON Gerald (Gerry) Randall						
Lambeth, 15 April, 1972 ESch						(M)
Watford	YT	12.89	89-90	6	3	0
Bristol C	Tr	07.91	91-93	25	13	1
Cardiff C	L	01.92	91	10	0	1
Hereford U	L	11.93	93	6	0	0
Huddersfield T	Tr	03.94				
Burnley	Tr	08.94	94-97	116	8	3
Sunderland	Tr	07.98				
Luton T	L	12.98	98	14	0	0
Hull C	L	03.99	98	8	0	0
Hull C	L	10.99	99	3	0	0
Halifax T	Tr	08.00	00	7	2	1
HARRISON Harry						
Millfield, County Durham, 26 June, 1917 Died 2000						(FB)
Chesterfield	Hartlepools U (Am)	06.37				
Southport	Tr	07.39	46-50	135	-	1
HARRISON Herbert						
Burnley, 23 January, 1916						(W)
Accrington St (Am)	Morecambe	10.47	47	3	-	0
HARRISON James (Jimmy) Charles						
Leicester, 12 February, 1921 Died 2004						(FB)
Leicester C	Wellington Victoria	12.41	46-48	81	-	1
Aston Villa	Tr	07.49	49	8	-	1
Coventry C	Tr	07.51	51-52	20	-	2
HARRISON James (Jim) Herbert						
Hammersmith, 31 July, 1928						(CF)
Queens Park Rgrs		02.52	52	6	-	1
HARRISON John						
Swansea, 30 September, 1932						(G)
Crewe Alex		08.56	56	2	-	0
HARRISON John Gilbert						
Worksop, 18 May, 1946						(W)
Sheffield U	Worksop T	01.67				
Lincoln C	Tr	07.68	68	4	0	0
HARRISON John James						
York, 7 June, 1961						(FB)
York C	App	06.79	79	8	0	0
HARRISON John Michael						
Stepney, 16 January, 1958						(W)
Charlton Ath	App	01.76	75	5	0	2
HARRISON John Walter						
Leicester, 27 September, 1927						(FB)
Aston Villa		08.48				
Colchester U	Tr	07.50	50-56	237	-	1
HARRISON Kenneth (Ken)						
Stockton, 20 January, 1926						(W)
Hull C	Billingham Synthonia	04.47	46-54	238	-	47
Derby Co	Tr	07.54	54-55	15	-	3
HARRISON Lee David						
Billericay, 12 September, 1971						(G)
Charlton Ath	YT	07.90				
Gillingham	L	03.92	91	2	0	0
Fulham	Tr	12.92	94-95	11	1	0
Barnet	Tr	07.96	96-00	183	0	0
Peterborough U	L	12.02	02	12	0	0
Leyton Orient	Tr	03.03	02-04	59	1	0
HARRISON Mark Simon						
Derby, 11 December, 1960						(G)
Southampton	App	12.78				
Port Vale	Tr	02.80	80-81	70	0	0
Stoke C	Tr	08.82	82	7	0	0
HARRISON Michael (Mike)						
Leicester, 21 December, 1952						(CD)
Birmingham C	App	02.70	70-71	3	0	0
Southend U	Tr	07.72	72	16	0	0
HARRISON Michael (Mike) John						
Ilford, 18 April, 1940 ESch/Eu23-3						(W)
Chelsea	Jnrs	04.57	56-62	61	-	8
Blackburn Rov	Tr	09.62	62-67	160	0	40
Plymouth Arg	Tr	09.67	67	15	0	3
Luton T	Tr	06.68	68-69	28	3	6
HARRISON Peter						
Sleaford, 25 October, 1927						(W)
Leeds U	Peterborough U	01.49	49-51	65	-	9
Bournemouth	Tr	08.52	52-56	173	-	34
Reading	Tr	06.57	57-58	40	-	5
Southport	Tr	07.59	59-61	126	-	22
HARRISON Ralph						
Clayton-le-Moors, 18 December, 1926						(W)
Leeds U	Great Harwood	01.49	49	2	-	0
HARRISON Raymond (Ray) William						
Boston, 21 June, 1921 Died 2000						(CF)
Burnley	Boston U	04.46	46-49	60	-	19
Doncaster Rov	Tr	01.50	49-53	126	-	47
Grimsby T	Tr	07.54	54	38	-	7
HARRISON Reginald (Reg) Frederick						
Derby, 22 May, 1923						(W)
Derby Co	Derby Corinthians	03.44	46-54	254	-	52
HARRISON Robert Alan						
Chatham, 25 December, 1947						(CF)
Gillingham	Jnrs	06.67	66	1	0	0
HARRISON John **Robert**						
Manchester, 23 December, 1930						(W)
Carlisle U		02.53	52-54	67	-	16
HARRISON Ronald (Ron)						
Hebburn, 15 May, 1923						(IF)
Darlington	Gateshead (Am)	08.45	46	8	-	3
Gateshead	Tr	07.47	47	6	-	1
HARRISON Steven (Steve) John						
Blackpool, 26 December, 1952						(FB)
Blackpool	App	12.70	71-77	141	5	0
Watford	Vancouver (Can)	09.78	78-80	82	1	0
Charlton Ath	Tr	07.81	81	3	0	0
HARRISON Terence (Terry) John						
Thornaby, 12 September, 1950						(F)
Newcastle U	Stockton	11.67				
Barrow	Tr	07.70	70	4	0	0
HARRISON Thomas (Tommy) Edward						
Edinburgh, 22 January, 1974 SSch/SYth						(M)
York C	Clyde	01.97	96	0	1	0
Carlisle U	Tr	08.97	97	6	4	0
HARRISON Walter Edward						
Coalville, 16 January, 1923 Died 1979 EB						(WH)
Leicester C	Coalville T	08.45	46-50	125	-	3
Chesterfield	Tr	12.50	50-52	74	-	12
HARRISON Wayne						
Stockport, 15 November, 1967						(F)
Oldham Ath	App	12.84	84	4	1	1
Liverpool	Tr	03.85				

League Club	Source	Date Signed	Seasons Played	Apps	Subs	Gls
Oldham Ath	L	03.85	84	1	0	0
Crewe Alex	L	12.88	88	3	0	1

HARRISON Wayne Moffat
Whitehaven, 16 October, 1957 (M)

League Club	Source	Date Signed	Seasons Played	Apps	Subs	Gls
Workington	Everton (App)	08.75	75	1	3	0
Blackpool	Sheffield Wed (N/C)	09.79	79-81	81	5	6
Carlisle U	Workington	08.87	87	1	1	0

HARRITY Michael (Mick) David
Sheffield, 5 October, 1946 (FB)

League Club	Source	Date Signed	Seasons Played	Apps	Subs	Gls
Rotherham U		10.65	65-68	36	5	0
Doncaster Rov	Tr	09.68	68	2	0	0

HARROLD Mark Anthony
Halifax, 29 January, 1957 (M)

League Club	Source	Date Signed	Seasons Played	Apps	Subs	Gls
Halifax T	Jnrs	08.74	74-75	8	5	1

HARROLD Matthew (Matt) James
Leyton, 25 July, 1984 (F)

League Club	Source	Date Signed	Seasons Played	Apps	Subs	Gls
Brentford	Harlow T	08.03	03-04	11	21	2
Grimsby T	L	03.05	04	6	0	2

HARROP Jack
Manchester, 25 June, 1929 Died 1977 (FB)

League Club	Source	Date Signed	Seasons Played	Apps	Subs	Gls
Swansea T		08.52	52-53	10	-	0
Watford	Tr	07.56	56-59	111	-	0

HARROP Robert (Bobby)
Manchester, 25 August, 1936 (WH)

League Club	Source	Date Signed	Seasons Played	Apps	Subs	Gls
Manchester U	Benchill YC	05.54	57-58	10	-	0
Tranmere Rov	Tr	11.59	59-60	41	-	2

HARROW Andrew (Andy)
Kirkcaldy, 6 November, 1956 (F)

League Club	Source	Date Signed	Seasons Played	Apps	Subs	Gls
Luton T	Raith Rov	09.80	80	3	1	0

HARROWER James (Jimmy)
Alva, 18 August, 1935 Su23-1 (IF)

League Club	Source	Date Signed	Seasons Played	Apps	Subs	Gls
Liverpool	Hibernian	01.58	57-60	96	-	21
Newcastle U	Tr	03.61	60-61	5	-	0

HARROWER James (Jimmy) Swanson
Crossgates, 19 June, 1924 Died 1992 (CD)

League Club	Source	Date Signed	Seasons Played	Apps	Subs	Gls
Accrington St	Third Lanark	12.54	54-60	246	-	2

HARROWER Steven (Steve) Gordon
Exeter, 9 October, 1961 (M)

League Club	Source	Date Signed	Seasons Played	Apps	Subs	Gls
Exeter C	Dawlish T	01.84	83-89	165	22	10

HARROWER William (Bill)
Dunfermline, 13 April, 1922 Died 2003 (WH)

League Club	Source	Date Signed	Seasons Played	Apps	Subs	Gls
Torquay U	Third Lanark	05.46	46-47	16	-	3
Exeter C	Tr	07.48	48-51	85	-	11

HARSLEY Paul
Scunthorpe, 29 May, 1978 (M)

League Club	Source	Date Signed	Seasons Played	Apps	Subs	Gls
Grimsby T	YT	07.96				
Scunthorpe U	Tr	07.97	97-00	110	18	5
Halifax T	Tr	07.01	01	45	0	11
Northampton T	Tr	07.02	02-03	46	13	2
Macclesfield T	Tr	02.04	03-04	60	2	5

HARSTON John (Jack)
Barnsley, 7 October, 1920 (FB)

League Club	Source	Date Signed	Seasons Played	Apps	Subs	Gls
Wolverhampton W	Ardsley Ath	10.37				
Barnsley	Tr	09.38	46-48	20	-	1
Bradford C	Tr	06.49	49	24	-	1

HART Alan Michael
Woolwich, 21 February, 1956 (M)

League Club	Source	Date Signed	Seasons Played	Apps	Subs	Gls
Charlton Ath	App	02.74	74	3	0	2
Millwall	Tr	06.75	75	13	3	0

HART Andrew (Andy)
Great Yarmouth, 14 January, 1963 (FB)

League Club	Source	Date Signed	Seasons Played	Apps	Subs	Gls
Norwich C	App	01.81	81	0	1	0

HART Brian Patrick
Farnworth, 14 July, 1959 (CD)

League Club	Source	Date Signed	Seasons Played	Apps	Subs	Gls
Rochdale	Bolton W (App)	07.77	77-79	73	5	0

HART Gary John
Harlow, 21 September, 1976 (F)

League Club	Source	Date Signed	Seasons Played	Apps	Subs	Gls
Brighton & Hove A	Stansted	06.98	98-04	239	36	41

HART Harold (Harry)
Sheffield, 29 September, 1926 (CF)

League Club	Source	Date Signed	Seasons Played	Apps	Subs	Gls
Rotherham U		12.45	49	10	-	4
Coventry C	Tr	06.50	50-51	10	-	1
Grimsby T	Tr	12.52	52	13	-	3

HART John (Johnny) Paul
Golborne, 8 June, 1928 (IF)

League Club	Source	Date Signed	Seasons Played	Apps	Subs	Gls
Manchester C	Loughton YC	06.45	47-60	169	-	67

HART Charles **Joseph (Joe)** John
Shrewsbury, 19 April, 1987 (G)

League Club	Source	Date Signed	Seasons Played	Apps	Subs	Gls
Shrewsbury T	Sch	08.04	04	6	0	0

HART John **Leslie (Les)**
Ashton-under-Lyne, 28 February, 1917 Died 1996 (CD)

League Club	Source	Date Signed	Seasons Played	Apps	Subs	Gls
Bury	Earlestown White Star	12.36	38-53	280	-	2

HART Nigel
Golborne, 1 October, 1958 (CD)

League Club	Source	Date Signed	Seasons Played	Apps	Subs	Gls
Wigan Ath		08.78	79	1	0	0
Leicester C	Tr	10.79				
Blackpool	Tr	08.81	81-82	36	1	0
Crewe Alex	Tr	11.82	82-86	139	3	10
Bury	Tr	02.87	86-87	33	12	2
Stockport Co	Tr	07.88	88-89	38	1	2
Chesterfield	Tr	08.89	89-90	45	1	2
York C	Tr	02.91	90	1	0	0

HART Paul Anthony
Golborne, 4 May, 1953 (CD)

League Club	Source	Date Signed	Seasons Played	Apps	Subs	Gls
Stockport Co	Jnrs	09.70	70-72	87	0	5
Blackpool	Tr	06.73	73-77	143	0	15
Leeds U	Tr	03.78	77-82	191	0	16
Nottingham F	Tr	05.83	83-84	70	0	1
Sheffield Wed	Tr	08.85	85-86	52	0	2
Birmingham C	Tr	12.86	86	1	0	0
Notts Co	Tr	06.87	87	23	0	0

HART Peter
Wickersley, 6 September, 1949 ESch (FB)

League Club	Source	Date Signed	Seasons Played	Apps	Subs	Gls
Bradford PA	Rotherham U (App)	03.68	67	3	0	0

HART Peter Osborne
Mexborough, 14 August, 1957 (CD)

League Club	Source	Date Signed	Seasons Played	Apps	Subs	Gls
Huddersfield T	App	08.74	73-79	208	2	7
Walsall	Tr	08.80	80-89	389	1	12

HART Roy Ernest
Acton, 30 May, 1933 ESch (CD)

League Club	Source	Date Signed	Seasons Played	Apps	Subs	Gls
Brentford	Jnrs	06.50	54	2	-	0

HART Marvin **Stuart**
Derby, 15 January, 1941 (W)

League Club	Source	Date Signed	Seasons Played	Apps	Subs	Gls
Exeter C	Long Eaton U	08.67	67	20	2	1

HART William (Bill) Robert
North Shields, 1 April, 1923 Died 1990 (WH)

League Club	Source	Date Signed	Seasons Played	Apps	Subs	Gls
Newcastle U		09.40				
Chesterfield	North Shields	03.45	46	1	-	0
Bradford C	Tr	05.47	46-48	25	-	0

HARTBURN John (Johnny)
Houghton-le-Spring, 20 December, 1920 Died 2001 (W)

League Club	Source	Date Signed	Seasons Played	Apps	Subs	Gls
Queens Park Rgrs	Yeovil T	03.47	47-48	58	-	11
Watford	Tr	09.49	49-50	66	-	19
Millwall	Tr	03.51	50-53	104	-	29
Leyton Orient	Tr	06.54	54-57	112	-	36

HARTE Ian Patrick
Drogheda, 31 August, 1977 IRu21-3/IR5-6 (FB)

League Club	Source	Date Signed	Seasons Played	Apps	Subs	Gls
Leeds U	YT	12.95	95-03	199	14	28

HARTENBERGER Uwe
Leuterecken, Germany, 1 February, 1968 (F)

League Club	Source	Date Signed	Seasons Played	Apps	Subs	Gls
Reading	Bayer Uerdingen (Ger)	09.93	93-94	8	16	4

HARTERY John
Waterford, 25 November, 1920 LoI-7 (FB)

League Club	Source	Date Signed	Seasons Played	Apps	Subs	Gls
Plymouth Arg	Limerick	06.48	49	1	-	0

HARTFIELD Charles (Charlie) Joseph
Lambeth, 4 September, 1971 EYth (M)

League Club	Source	Date Signed	Seasons Played	Apps	Subs	Gls
Arsenal	YT	09.89				
Sheffield U	Tr	08.91	91-96	45	11	1
Fulham	L	02.97	96	1	1	0
Swansea C	Tr	11.97	97	22	0	2
Lincoln C	L	09.98	98	3	0	1

HARTFORD Richard **Asa**
Clydebank, 24 October, 1950 Su21-1/Su23-5/S-50 (M)

League Club	Source	Date Signed	Seasons Played	Apps	Subs	Gls
West Bromwich A	Drumchapel Amat	11.67	67-73	206	8	18
Manchester C	Tr	08.74	74-78	184	1	22
Nottingham F	Tr	07.79	79	3	0	0
Everton	Tr	08.79	79-81	81	0	6
Manchester C	Tr	10.81	81-83	75	0	7

League Club	Source	Date Signed	Seasons Played	Career Record Apps	Subs	Gls
Norwich C	Tr	10.84	84	28	0	2
Bolton W	Fort Lauderdale (USA)	07.85	85-86	81	0	8
Stockport Co	Tr	06.87	87-88	42	3	0
Oldham Ath	Tr	03.89	88	3	4	0
Shrewsbury T	Tr	08.89	89-90	22	3	0
HARTLAND Michael (Mick) Leo						
Dunfermline, 7 January, 1944 (M)						
Oxford U	Nuneaton Borough	06.63	63-64	19	-	6
Barrow	Tr	07.65	65-70	168	9	19
Crewe Alex	Tr	12.70	70	3	0	1
Southport	Tr	07.71	71-72	32	5	4
HARTLE Barry						
Salford, 8 August, 1939 (W)						
Watford	Jnrs	08.56	58-59	39	-	7
Sheffield U	Tr	06.60	60-65	101	0	16
Carlisle U	Tr	07.66	66-67	28	1	1
Stockport Co	Tr	09.67	67-69	88	0	1
Oldham Ath	Tr	06.70	70	8	1	2
Southport	Tr	07.71	71	37	4	6
HARTLE Leslie **Roy**						
Catshill, 4 October, 1931 FLge-1 (FB)						
Bolton W	Bromsgrove Rov	02.51	52-65	446	1	11
HARTLEY Edmund (Eddie)						
Burnley, 5 May, 1932 (W)						
Burnley	Jnrs	11.50				
Oldham Ath	Rossendale U	07.56	56	1	-	0
HARTLEY Paul James						
Baillieston, 19 October, 1976 Su21-1 (W)						
Millwall	Hamilton Academical	07.96	96	35	9	4
HARTLEY Thomas (Tom) William						
Gateshead, 7 May, 1917 Died 1984 (IF)						
Gateshead	Birtley BC	02.36	35-36	5	-	1
Bury	Tr	05.38				
Chesterfield	Tr	05.39				
Leicester C	North Shields	01.48				
Watford	Tr	02.48	47	6	-	1
HARTLEY Trevor John						
Doncaster, 16 March, 1947 (W)						
West Ham U	Jnrs	07.64	66-68	4	1	0
Bournemouth	Tr	07.69	69-70	35	8	2
HARTNETT James (Jimmy) Benedict						
Dublin, 21 March, 1927 Died 1988 LoI-1/IR-2 (W)						
Middlesbrough	Dundalk	06.48	48-54	48	-	8
Hartlepools U	Barry T	09.57	57	7	-	1
York C	Tr	08.58	58	2	-	1
HARTSON John						
Swansea, 5 April, 1975 WYth/Wu21-9/W-24 (F)						
Luton T	YT	12.92	93-94	32	22	11
Arsenal	Tr	01.95	94-96	43	10	14
West Ham U	Tr	02.97	96-98	59	1	24
Wimbledon	Tr	01.99	98-00	46	3	19
Coventry C	Tr	02.01	00	12	0	6
HARVEY Alexander (Alex)						
Kirkconnel, 28 August, 1925 (WH)						
Carlisle U	Queen of the South	08.46	46	1	-	0
HARVEY Alexander (Alex)						
Ayr, 28 September, 1928 Died 1998 (IF)						
Chesterfield	Saltcoats Victoria	11.50	50-52	27	-	9
HARVEY Brian						
Liverpool, 12 January, 1947 (WH)						
Chester	Sheffield Wed (Am)	09.64	64	1	-	0
HARVEY Bryan Robert						
Stepney, 26 August, 1938 (G)						
Newcastle U	Wisbech T	09.58	58-60	86	-	0
Blackpool	Cambridge C	02.62	61-63	11	-	0
Northampton T	Tr	10.63	63-67	165	0	0
HARVEY James **Colin**						
Liverpool, 16 November, 1944 Eu23-5/FLge-3/E-1 (M)						
Everton	App	10.62	63-74	317	3	18
Sheffield Wed	Tr	09.74	74-75	45	0	2
HARVEY David						
Leeds, 7 February, 1948 S-16 (G)						
Leeds U	Jnrs	02.65	65-79	277	0	0
Leeds U	Vancouver (Can)	09.82	82-84	73	0	0
Bradford C	Tr	02.85	84	6	0	0
HARVEY David						
Hetton-le-Hole, 15 February, 1954 (W)						
Hartlepool	App	10.69	70	3	2	0
HARVEY Gary						
Colchester, 19 November, 1961 (F)						
Colchester U	App	11.79	79-80	6	0	2
HARVEY James (Jimmy)						
Lurgan, 2 May, 1958 NIu23-1 (M)						
Arsenal	Glenavon	08.77	77-78	2	1	0
Hereford U	Tr	03.80	79-86	276	2	38
Bristol C	Tr	03.87	86-87	2	1	0
Wrexham	L	09.87	87	6	0	0
Tranmere Rov	Tr	10.87	87-91	174	10	18
Crewe Alex	Tr	07.92	92	16	1	0
HARVEY Joseph (Joe)						
Edlington, 11 June, 1918 Died 1989 FLge-3 (WH)						
Bradford PA	Edlington Rgrs	05.36				
Wolverhampton W	Tr	11.36				
Bournemouth	Tr	05.37	37	1	-	0
Bradford C	Tr	07.38				
Newcastle U	Tr	10.45	46-52	224	-	12
HARVEY William **Keith**						
Crediton, 25 December, 1934 (CD)						
Exeter C	Crediton	08.52	52-68	483	0	28
HARVEY Lawrence (Lol)						
Heanor, 25 July, 1934 (FB)						
Coventry C	Jnrs	07.51	51-60	140	-	1
HARVEY Lee Derek						
Harlow, 21 December, 1966 EYth (W)						
Orient	App	12.84	83-92	135	49	23
Nottingham F	Tr	08.93	93	0	2	0
Brentford	Tr	11.93	93-96	87	18	6
HARVEY Leighton						
Neath, 27 August, 1959 (W)						
Swansea C	App	●	75-76	1	1	0
HARVEY Martin						
Belfast, 19 September, 1941 NISch/NIu23-3/NIB/NI-33 (CD)						
Sunderland	Jnrs	09.58	59-71	311	5	5
HARVEY Richard George						
Letchworth, 17 April, 1969 ESch/EYth (FB)						
Luton T	App	01.87	86-97	134	27	4
Blackpool	L	10.92	92	4	1	0
HARVEY William Derek						
Doncaster, 30 September, 1934 (FB)						
Doncaster Rov	Jnrs	11.51	52	2	-	0
HARVEY William James						
Clydebank, 23 November, 1929 (IF)						
Bradford PA	Dunfermline Ath	01.59	58-59	26	-	1
HARWOOD Lee						
Southall, 4 October, 1960 (CD)						
Southampton	App	10.78				
Wimbledon	Tr	01.79	78	1	0	0
Port Vale	Leatherhead	02.80	79-80	19	0	1
HARWOOD Richard Andrew						
Sheffield, 13 September, 1960 (M)						
Sheffield U	App	07.78	78	2	1	0
HASELDEN John James						
Doncaster, 3 August, 1943 (CD)						
Rotherham U	Denaby U	02.62	61-68	98	1	0
Doncaster Rov	Tr	09.68	68-73	168	4	20
Mansfield T	L	02.72	71	4	0	0
HASFORD Jason Miles						
Manchester, 1 April, 1971 (F)						
Rochdale	Manchester C (YT)	07.89	89	0	1	0
HASKINS Anthony John						
Northampton, 26 July, 1935 (FB)						
Northampton T		01.59	59-61	8	-	0
HASLAM Graham						
Doncaster, 29 April, 1956 (G)						
Rotherham U	App	04.74	75	2	0	0
HASLAM Harry						
Manchester, 30 July, 1921 Died 1986 (FB)						
Oldham Ath	Rochdale (Am)	05.46	46	2	-	0

League Club	Source	Date Signed	Seasons Played	Apps	Subs	Gls
Brighton & Hove A	Tr	09.47				
Leyton Orient	Tr	07.48	48	7	-	0

HASLAM Steven (Steve) Robert
Sheffield, 6 September, 1979 ESch/EYth (FB)

League Club	Source	Date Signed	Seasons Played	Apps	Subs	Gls
Sheffield Wed	YT	09.96	98-03	115	29	2
Northampton T	Halifax T	08.04	04	2	1	0

HASLEGRAVE Sean Matthew
Stoke-on-Trent, 7 June, 1951 (M)

League Club	Source	Date Signed	Seasons Played	Apps	Subs	Gls
Stoke C	Jnrs	11.68	70-75	106	7	5
Nottingham F	Tr	07.76	76	5	2	1
Preston NE	Tr	09.77	77-80	111	2	2
Crewe Alex	Tr	08.81	81-82	78	4	1
York C	Tr	07.83	83-86	137	5	0
Torquay U	Tr	08.87	87-88	32	4	1

HASPELL Alan
Northwich, 23 January, 1943 (IF)

League Club	Source	Date Signed	Seasons Played	Apps	Subs	Gls
Burnley	Jnrs	01.60				
Doncaster Rov	Tr	07.63	63	1	-	0

HASSALL Harold William
Tyldesley, 4 March, 1929 FLge-3/E-5 (IF)

League Club	Source	Date Signed	Seasons Played	Apps	Subs	Gls
Huddersfield T	Mossley Common	09.46	48-51	74	-	26
Bolton W	Tr	01.52	51-54	102	-	34

HASSALL Wilfred (Wilf)
Prestwich, 23 September, 1923 Died 1998 (FB)

League Club	Source	Date Signed	Seasons Played	Apps	Subs	Gls
Hull C	RM Alsager	09.46	46-52	141	-	3

HASSELBAINK Jerrel (Jimmy Floyd)
Paramaribo, Surinam, 27 March, 1972 Holland 23 (F)

League Club	Source	Date Signed	Seasons Played	Apps	Subs	Gls
Leeds U	Boavista (Por)	07.97	97-98	66	3	34
Chelsea	Atletico Madrid (Sp)	07.00	00-03	119	17	69
Middlesbrough	Tr	07.04	04	36	0	13

HASSELL Richard (Ricky)
Coatbridge, 12 January, 1951 (M)

League Club	Source	Date Signed	Seasons Played	Apps	Subs	Gls
Carlisle U	Jnrs	01.69	68-69	2	3	0

HASSELL Robert (Bobby) John Francis
Derby, 4 June, 1980 (FB)

League Club	Source	Date Signed	Seasons Played	Apps	Subs	Gls
Mansfield T	YT	07.98	97-03	151	9	3
Barnsley	Tr	07.04	04	37	2	0

HASSELL Thomas (Tommy) William
Stonham, 5 April, 1919 Died 1984 (W)

League Club	Source	Date Signed	Seasons Played	Apps	Subs	Gls
Southampton	Romsey T	02.40				
Aldershot	Tr	05.46	46-49	114	-	16
Brighton & Hove A	Tr	08.50	50	11	-	4

HASTIE John **Kenneth (Ken)** George
Cape Town, South Africa, 6 September, 1928 (CF)

League Club	Source	Date Signed	Seasons Played	Apps	Subs	Gls
Leeds U	Clyde Ath (SA)	08.52	52	4	-	2

HASTY Patrick (Paddy) Joseph
Belfast, 17 March, 1932 Died 2000 NIAmat (CF)

League Club	Source	Date Signed	Seasons Played	Apps	Subs	Gls
Leyton Orient (Am)	Tooting & Mitcham	07.58	58	2	-	2
Queens Park Rgrs (Am)	Tooting & Mitcham	10.59	59	1	-	0
Aldershot	Tooting & Mitcham	03.61	60-62	35	-	14

HATCH Peter Derek
Wargrave, 22 October, 1949 (FB)

League Club	Source	Date Signed	Seasons Played	Apps	Subs	Gls
Oxford U	App	10.66	67-72	15	4	2
Exeter C	Tr	12.73	73-81	343	3	18

HATCHER Clifford (Cliff) Henry
Keynsham, 27 June, 1925 Died 1978 (G)

League Club	Source	Date Signed	Seasons Played	Apps	Subs	Gls
Reading		06.46	47-48	2	-	0

HATCHER Daniel (Danny) Ian
Newport, Isle of Wight, 24 December, 1983 (F)

League Club	Source	Date Signed	Seasons Played	Apps	Subs	Gls
Leyton Orient	YT	•	00-02	3	13	0

HATCHER Douglas (Doug) Terence
Carshalton, 6 March, 1962 (G)

League Club	Source	Date Signed	Seasons Played	Apps	Subs	Gls
Fulham	App	03.80				
Aldershot	Wokingham T	08.83	83	1	0	0

HATELEY Anthony (Tony)
Derby, 13 June, 1941 (F)

League Club	Source	Date Signed	Seasons Played	Apps	Subs	Gls
Notts Co	Jnrs	06.58	58-62	131	-	77
Aston Villa	Tr	08.63	63-66	127	0	68
Chelsea	Tr	10.66	66	26	1	6
Liverpool	Tr	07.67	67-68	42	0	17
Coventry C	Tr	09.68	68	17	0	4
Birmingham C	Tr	08.69	69-70	28	0	6
Notts Co	Tr	11.70	70-71	57	0	32
Oldham Ath	Tr	07.72	73	1	4	1

HATELEY Mark Wayne
Derby, 7 November, 1961 EYth/Eu21-10/E-32 (F)

League Club	Source	Date Signed	Seasons Played	Apps	Subs	Gls
Coventry C	App	12.78	78-82	86	6	25
Portsmouth	Tr	06.83	83	38	0	22
Queens Park Rgrs	Glasgow Rgrs	11.95	95-96	18	9	3
Leeds U	L	08.96	96	5	1	0
Hull C	Glasgow Rgrs	08.97	97-98	12	9	3

HATHAWAY Ian Ashley
Wordsley, 22 August, 1968 (W)

League Club	Source	Date Signed	Seasons Played	Apps	Subs	Gls
Mansfield T	Bedworth U	02.89	88-90	21	23	2
Rotherham U	Tr	03.91	90-91	5	8	1
Torquay U	Tr	07.93	93-96	114	26	14
Colchester U	Tr	06.97	97	5	7	0

HATSELL Dennis
Preston, 9 June, 1930 Died 1998 (CF)

League Club	Source	Date Signed	Seasons Played	Apps	Subs	Gls
Preston NE	Jnrs	06.48	53-59	115	-	54

HATSWELL Wayne Mervin
Swindon, 8 February, 1975 ESemiPro-2 (CD)

League Club	Source	Date Signed	Seasons Played	Apps	Subs	Gls
Oxford U	Forest Green Rov	12.00	00-01	47	1	0
Kidderminster Hrs	Chester C	10.03	03-04	70	2	3

HATTER Stephen (Steve) John
East Ham, 21 October, 1958 (CD)

League Club	Source	Date Signed	Seasons Played	Apps	Subs	Gls
Fulham	App	05.76	77-80	25	1	1
Exeter C	L	09.82	82	11	0	1
Wimbledon	Tr	11.82	82-84	82	2	4
Southend U	Tr	03.85	84-85	61	0	2

HATTON Cyril
Grantham, 14 September, 1918 Died 1987 (IF)

League Club	Source	Date Signed	Seasons Played	Apps	Subs	Gls
Notts Co	Grantham Co-operative	07.36	36-38	62	-	15
Queens Park Rgrs	Tr	04.46	46-52	162	-	64
Chesterfield	Tr	06.53	53	36	-	10

HATTON David (Dave) Howcroft
Farnworth, 30 October, 1943 (CD)

League Club	Source	Date Signed	Seasons Played	Apps	Subs	Gls
Bolton W	Jnrs	11.60	61-69	231	0	8
Blackpool	Tr	09.69	69-75	250	1	7
Bury	Tr	08.76	76-78	96	1	2

HATTON Robert (Bob) James
Hull, 10 April, 1947 (F)

League Club	Source	Date Signed	Seasons Played	Apps	Subs	Gls
Wolverhampton W	Jnrs	11.64	66	10	0	7
Bolton W	Tr	03.67	66-67	23	1	2
Northampton T	Tr	10.68	68	29	4	7
Carlisle U	Tr	07.69	69-71	93	0	38
Birmingham C	Tr	10.71	71-75	170	5	58
Blackpool	Tr	07.76	76-77	75	0	32
Luton T	Tr	07.78	78-79	81	1	29
Sheffield U	Tr	07.80	80-82	92	3	34
Cardiff C	Tr	12.82	82	29	1	9

HAUGHEY Frederick (Fred)
Conisbrough, 12 May, 1921 (FB)

League Club	Source	Date Signed	Seasons Played	Apps	Subs	Gls
Bradford C (Am)	Halifax T (Am)	08.46	46	3	-	0

HAUGHEY William
Glasgow, 20 December, 1932 (IF)

League Club	Source	Date Signed	Seasons Played	Apps	Subs	Gls
Everton	Larkhall Thistle	06.56	56-57	4	-	1

HAUSER Peter Benjamin
Kimberley, South Africa, 20 April, 1934 (WH)

League Club	Source	Date Signed	Seasons Played	Apps	Subs	Gls
Blackpool	(South Africa)	11.55	57-61	83	-	10
Chester	Cheltenham T	08.63	63-66	117	4	3

HAUSER Thomas
Schopfhain, Germany, 10 April, 1965 (F)

League Club	Source	Date Signed	Seasons Played	Apps	Subs	Gls
Sunderland	Basle OB (Swi)	02.89	88-91	22	31	9

HAVENGA William (Willie) Stephanus
Bloemfontein, South Africa, 6 November, 1924 (W)

League Club	Source	Date Signed	Seasons Played	Apps	Subs	Gls
Birmingham C	Bremner OB (SA)	07.48	49	1	-	0
Luton T	Tr	05.50	50-51	18	-	6
Ipswich T	Tr	01.52	51-52	19	-	3

HAVENHAND Keith
Dronfield, 11 September, 1937 EYth (IF)

League Club	Source	Date Signed	Seasons Played	Apps	Subs	Gls
Chesterfield	Jnrs	09.54	53-61	176	-	58
Derby Co	Tr	10.61	61	26	-	14
Oxford U	Tr	12.63	63-64	12	-	3

HAVERSON Paul Timothy
Chigwell, 19 February, 1959 ESch (FB)

League Club	Source	Date Signed	Seasons Played	Apps	Subs	Gls
Queens Park Rgrs	App	08.76				
Wimbledon	Tr	10.78	78-79	27	1	2

HAVERTY Joseph (Joe)
Dublin, 17 February, 1936 IR-32 (W)

League Club	Source	Date Signed	Seasons Played	Apps	Subs	Gls
Arsenal	St Patrick's Ath	07.54	54-60	114	-	25

League Club	Source	Date Signed	Seasons Played	Career Record Apps	Subs	Gls
Blackburn Rov	Tr	08.61	61-62	27	-	1
Millwall	Tr	09.62	62-63	68	-	8
Bristol Rov	Glasgow Celtic	12.64	64	13	-	1
HAW Robert (Rob) Andrew						
York, 10 October, 1986						(F)
York C	Sch	●	03	0	1	0
HAWDEN Kenneth						
Huddersfield, 16 September, 1931						(CF)
Derby Co	Ashenhurst SC	04.53	53	2	-	0
HAWE Steven (Steve) John						
Magherafelt, 23 December, 1980 NISch/NIYth/NIu21-2						(F)
Blackburn Rov	YT	12.97				
Blackpool	L	08.00	00	2	0	0
Halifax T	L	11.00	00	6	2	0
HAWES Steven (Steve) Robert						
High Wycombe, 17 July, 1978						(M)
Sheffield U	YT	03.96	95-96	1	3	0
Doncaster Rov	L	09.97	97	8	3	0
Hull C	Tr	07.98	98	18	1	0
HAWKE Warren Robert						
Durham, 20 September, 1970						(F)
Sunderland	YT	11.88	88-92	7	18	1
Chesterfield	L	09.91	91	7	0	1
Carlisle U	L	10.92	92	8	0	2
Northampton T	L	03.93	92	7	0	1
Scarborough	Raith Rov	12.93	93	0	1	0
HAWKER David						
Hull, 29 November, 1958						(M)
Hull C	App	08.76	77-79	33	2	2
Darlington	Tr	03.80	79-82	84	4	2
Darlington	Bishop Auckland	08.84	84	4	3	0
HAWKER Philip (Phil) Nigel						
Solihull, 7 December, 1962 EYth						(CD)
Birmingham C	App	06.80	80-82	34	1	1
Walsall	Tr	12.82	82-89	159	18	10
West Bromwich A	Tr	09.90	90	1	0	0
HAWKES Barry						
Shotton, County Durham, 21 March, 1938						(W)
Luton T	Shotton CW	11.55	58-59	8	-	0
Darlington	Tr	06.60	60	11	-	3
Hartlepools U	Tr	07.61	61	9	-	0
HAWKES Kenneth (Ken) Kilby						
Easington, County Durham, 6 May, 1933						(FB)
Luton T	Shotton CW	10.51	57-60	90	-	1
Peterborough U	Tr	06.61	61	1	-	0
HAWKINGS Barry						
Birmingham, 7 November, 1931						(CF)
Coventry C	Rugby T	01.49	53-55	34	-	12
Lincoln C	Tr	03.56	55-56	15	-	6
Northampton T	Tr	06.57	57-58	65	-	25
HAWKINS Bertram (Bert) William						
Bristol, 29 September, 1923 Died 2002						(CF)
Bristol Rov	De Veys	08.47				
Bristol C	Tr	05.49	49	8	-	4
West Ham U	Bath C	09.51	51-52	34	-	16
Queens Park Rgrs	Tr	06.53	53	8	-	3
HAWKINS David John						
Kingston, 11 August, 1931						(CF)
Gillingham (Am)	Sheppey U	01.56	55	14	-	8
HAWKINS Dennis Ronald						
Swansea, 22 October, 1947 WSch/Wu23-6						(M)
Leeds U	App	10.64	66-67	2	0	0
Shrewsbury T	Tr	10.68	68-69	50	6	10
Chester	L	09.70	70	6	1	1
Workington	L	03.72	71	6	0	1
Newport Co	Tr	05.72	72	9	0	1
HAWKINS Graham Norman						
Darlaston, 5 March, 1946						(CD)
Wolverhampton W	App	06.63	64-67	28	6	0
Preston NE	Tr	01.68	67-73	241	4	3
Blackburn Rov	Tr	06.74	74-77	108	1	4
Port Vale	Tr	01.78	77-79	61	1	3
HAWKINS George **Harry**						
Middlesbrough, 24 November, 1915 Died 1992						(IF)
Middlesbrough	South Bank East End	02.35	35	1	-	0
Watford	Tr	06.37	37	5	-	0

League Club	Source	Date Signed	Seasons Played	Career Record Apps	Subs	Gls
Southport	Tr	07.38	38-46	79	-	30
Gateshead	Tr	06.47	47	27	-	12
Hartlepools U	Tr	03.48	47-48	30	-	4
HAWKINS Herbert (Bert) Henry						
Lambeth, 15 July, 1923 Died 1982						(CF)
Leyton Orient	Gravesend & Northfleet	06.51	51-52	5	-	0
HAWKINS Nigel Sean						
Bristol, 7 September, 1968						(F)
Bristol C	App	02.87	87-88	8	10	2
Blackpool	Tr	10.89	89	4	3	0
HAWKINS Peter Michael						
Swansea, 18 December, 1951 WSch						(W)
Northampton T	App	12.68	68-73	49	9	10
HAWKINS Peter Steven						
Maidstone, 19 September, 1978						(FB)
Wimbledon	YT	03.97	00-03	113	7	0
York C	L	02.00	99	14	0	0
Rushden & Diamonds	Tr	07.04	04	41	0	1
HAWKSBY John Frederick						
York, 12 June, 1942 EYth						(M)
Leeds U	Jnrs	06.59	60-62	37	-	2
Lincoln C	Tr	08.64	64-65	64	1	4
York C	Tr	03.66	65-67	72	2	7
HAWKSFORD Edward (Eddie)						
Liverpool, 7 November, 1931 Died 1985						(W)
Mansfield T	RAOC Chilwell	03.52	52	1	-	0
HAWKSWORTH Anthony						
Sheffield, 15 January, 1938 ESch/EYth						(G)
Manchester U	Jnrs	04.55	56	1	-	0
HAWKSWORTH Derek Marshall						
Bradford, 16 July, 1927 EB						(W)
Bradford C	Huddersfield T (Am)	10.48	48-50	75	-	20
Sheffield U	Tr	12.50	50-57	255	-	88
Huddersfield T	Tr	05.58	58-59	55	-	14
Lincoln C	Tr	02.60	59-60	36	-	14
Bradford C	Tr	01.61	60-61	44	-	8
HAWLEY Alan James						
Woking, 7 June, 1946						(FB)
Brentford	App	06.63	62-73	315	2	4
HAWLEY John East						
Patrington, 8 May, 1954						(F)
Hull C	Jnrs	04.72	72-77	101	13	22
Leeds U	Tr	04.78	78-79	30	3	16
Sunderland	Tr	10.79	79-80	25	0	11
Arsenal	Tr	09.81	81-82	14	6	3
Orient	L	10.82	82	4	0	1
Hull C	L	12.82	82	3	0	1
Bradford C	Happy Valley (HK)	09.83	83-84	61	6	28
Scunthorpe U	Tr	07.85	85	18	3	7
HAWLEY Karl Leon						
Walsall, 6 December, 1981						(F)
Walsall	YT	01.01	01	0	1	0
HAWORTH Gary						
Bury, 25 April, 1959						(F)
Rochdale	Radcliffe Borough	08.84	84	1	0	0
HAWORTH Herbert						
Accrington, 5 May, 1920 Died 1993						(IF)
Accrington St (Am)	Woodcock Amats	10.46	46	2	-	0
HAWORTH Robert (Rob) John						
Edgware, 21 November, 1975						(F)
Fulham	YT	07.93	93-94	7	14	1
HAWORTH Simon Owen						
Cardiff, 30 March, 1977 WYth/Wu21-12/WB-1/W-5						(F)
Cardiff C	YT	08.95	95-96	27	10	9
Coventry C	Tr	06.97	97-98	5	6	0
Wigan Ath	Tr	10.98	98-01	99	18	44
Tranmere Rov	Tr	02.02	01-04	77	2	31
HAWSON Alexander (Alex)						
Auchencairn, 23 October, 1923						(WH)
Rochdale	Aberdeen	12.48	48	1	-	0
HAWTHORNE Mark						
Sunderland, 21 August, 1979						(CD)
Doncaster Rov	YT	12.96	97	7	1	0

HAWTHORNE Mark David
Glasgow, 31 October, 1973 (M)

League Club	Source	Date Signed	Seasons Played	Apps	Subs	Gls
Crystal Palace	Jnrs	06.92				
Sheffield U	Tr	08.94				
Torquay U	Walsall (N/C)	03.95	94-96	43	15	2

HAWTIN Craig Scott
Buxton, 29 March, 1970 (FB)

League Club	Source	Date Signed	Seasons Played	Apps	Subs	Gls
Chester C	Port Vale (YT)	09.88	87-88	6	1	1

HAY Alan Browning
Dunfermline, 28 November, 1958 (FB)

League Club	Source	Date Signed	Seasons Played	Apps	Subs	Gls
Bolton W	Dundee	03.77				
Bristol C	Tr	07.78	79-81	72	2	1
York C	Tr	08.82	82-85	147	3	3
Tranmere Rov	Tr	08.86	86	27	1	0
York C	Hill o' Beath	12.88	88	1	0	0
Sunderland	Tr	02.89	88	1	0	0
Torquay U	Tr	09.89	89-90	10	0	0

HAY Alexander (Alex) Neil
Birkenhead, 14 October, 1981 (F)

League Club	Source	Date Signed	Seasons Played	Apps	Subs	Gls
Tranmere Rov	YT	03.00	01-03	16	25	3
Rushden & Diamonds	Tr	07.04	04	29	13	3

HAY Christopher (Chris) Drummond
Glasgow, 28 August, 1974 (F)

League Club	Source	Date Signed	Seasons Played	Apps	Subs	Gls
Swindon T	Glasgow Celtic	08.97	97-99	73	21	30
Huddersfield T	Tr	03.00	99-01	21	21	5

HAY Daniel (Danny) John
Auckland, New Zealand, 15 May, 1975 New Zealand 17 (CD)

League Club	Source	Date Signed	Seasons Played	Apps	Subs	Gls
Leeds U	Perth Glory (Aus)	08.99	00	2	2	0
Walsall	Tr	08.02	02-03	40	5	0

HAY Darran Andrew
Hitchin, 17 December, 1969 (F)

League Club	Source	Date Signed	Seasons Played	Apps	Subs	Gls
Cambridge U	Biggleswade T	03.94	93-94	7	22	3
Cambridge U (L)	Woking	10.96	96	0	4	0

HAY David
Paisley, 29 January, 1948 Su23-3/SLge-4/S-27 (CD)

League Club	Source	Date Signed	Seasons Played	Apps	Subs	Gls
Chelsea	Glasgow Celtic	08.74	74-78	107	1	2

HAYCOCK Frederick (Freddie) Joseph
Liverpool, 19 April, 1912 Died 1989 (IF)

League Club	Source	Date Signed	Seasons Played	Apps	Subs	Gls
Aston Villa	Prescot Cables	02.34	36-38	99	-	28
Wrexham	Tr	12.45	46	6	-	1

HAYCOCK Thomas Paul
Sheffield, 8 July, 1962 (F)

League Club	Source	Date Signed	Seasons Played	Apps	Subs	Gls
Rotherham U	Burton A	08.86	86-89	77	20	22

HAYDE Michael (Mick) Patrick
St Helens, 20 June, 1971 (FB)

League Club	Source	Date Signed	Seasons Played	Apps	Subs	Gls
Chester C	Liverpool (YT)	08.89	89	0	1	0

HAYDOCK Frank
Eccles, 29 November, 1940 (CD)

League Club	Source	Date Signed	Seasons Played	Apps	Subs	Gls
Manchester U	Jnrs	12.58	60-62	6	-	0
Charlton Ath	Tr	08.63	63-65	84	0	4
Portsmouth	Tr	12.65	65-68	71	0	1
Southend U	Tr	01.69	68-69	28	3	4

HAYDOCK William (Billy) Edward
Salford, 19 January, 1936 (FB)

League Club	Source	Date Signed	Seasons Played	Apps	Subs	Gls
Manchester C	Buxton	03.59	59-60	3	-	1
Crewe Alex	Tr	03.61	60-64	142	-	31
Grimsby T	Tr	11.64	64	21	-	4
Stockport Co	Tr	08.65	65-70	257	4	4
Southport	Port Elizabeth C (SA)	11.71	71	7	0	0

HAYDON Nicholas (Nicky)
Barking, 10 August, 1978 (FB)

League Club	Source	Date Signed	Seasons Played	Apps	Subs	Gls
Colchester U	YT	08.95	96-98	16	15	2

HAYES Adrian (Adie) Michael
Norwich, 22 May, 1978 (M)

League Club	Source	Date Signed	Seasons Played	Apps	Subs	Gls
Cambridge U	YT	07.96	95-97	25	9	0

HAYES Austin William Patrick
Hammersmith, 15 July, 1958 Died 1986 IRu21-1/IR-1 (W)

League Club	Source	Date Signed	Seasons Played	Apps	Subs	Gls
Southampton	App	07.76	76-79	22	9	5
Millwall	Tr	02.81	80-82	40	7	5
Northampton T	Tr	08.83	83-84	60	4	14

HAYES Hugh
Bangor, County Down, 23 June, 1925 (WH)

League Club	Source	Date Signed	Seasons Played	Apps	Subs	Gls
Ipswich T	Bangor	06.46	48-49	9	-	0

HAYES Joseph (Joe)
Kearsley, 20 January, 1936 Died 1999 Eu23-2 (IF)

League Club	Source	Date Signed	Seasons Played	Apps	Subs	Gls
Manchester C	Jnrs	08.53	53-64	331	-	142
Barnsley	Tr	07.65	65	26	0	3

HAYES Martin
Walthamstow, 21 March, 1966 Eu21-3 (W)

League Club	Source	Date Signed	Seasons Played	Apps	Subs	Gls
Arsenal	App	11.83	85-89	70	32	26
Wimbledon (L)	Glasgow Celtic	02.92	91	1	1	0
Swansea C	Glasgow Celtic	01.93	92-94	44	17	8

HAYES Michael (Mike)
Newport, 11 September, 1954 (CD)

League Club	Source	Date Signed	Seasons Played	Apps	Subs	Gls
Newport Co	Dairy U	01.76	75	4	1	0

HAYES Michael (Mike) Charles
Aberdare, 24 April, 1944 (WH)

League Club	Source	Date Signed	Seasons Played	Apps	Subs	Gls
Swansea T	Jnrs	06.61	62	3	-	0

HAYES Paul Edward
Dagenham, 20 September, 1983 (F)

League Club	Source	Date Signed	Seasons Played	Apps	Subs	Gls
Scunthorpe U	Norwich C (YT)	03.03	02-04	68	31	28

HAYES Philip (Phil) Henry
Chiswick, 23 December, 1935 (W)

League Club	Source	Date Signed	Seasons Played	Apps	Subs	Gls
Millwall	Slough T	12.56	56-58	16	-	1

HAYES Samuel (Sam)
Accrington, 21 June, 1920 Died 1959 (G)

League Club	Source	Date Signed	Seasons Played	Apps	Subs	Gls
Accrington St	Blackburn Rov (Am)	10.46	46	13	-	0

HAYES Stephen (Steve) Charles
Smethwick, 28 January, 1952 (CD)

League Club	Source	Date Signed	Seasons Played	Apps	Subs	Gls
Shrewsbury T	Warley Borough	02.74	74-79	69	3	0
Torquay U	L	09.75	75	1	0	0
Torquay U	Tr	07.80	80	25	0	0

HAYES William (Bill)
Runcorn, 8 June, 1919 Died 2002 (WH)

League Club	Source	Date Signed	Seasons Played	Apps	Subs	Gls
Oldham Ath	Halton Jnrs	01.37	38-50	126	-	3

HAYES William (Billy)
Newcastle-under-Lyme, 2 March, 1918 Died 1996 (CD)

League Club	Source	Date Signed	Seasons Played	Apps	Subs	Gls
Crewe Alex	ROF Radway Green	09.46	46	29	-	0

HAYES William (Bill) Edward
Cork, 7 November, 1915 LoI-2/IR2/I-4 (FB)

League Club	Source	Date Signed	Seasons Played	Apps	Subs	Gls
Huddersfield T	St Vincent's	04.33	34-38	69	-	5
Huddersfield T	Cork U	09.46	46-49	112	-	0
Burnley	Tr	02.50	49-50	12	-	0

HAYES William (Billy) John
Limerick, 30 March, 1928 LoI-1/IRAmat/IR-1 (G)

League Club	Source	Date Signed	Seasons Played	Apps	Subs	Gls
Wrexham	Limerick	07.50	50	14	-	0
Torquay U	Ellesmere Port	08.52	52-55	54	-	0

HAYFIELD Matthew (Matt) Anthony
Bristol, 8 August, 1975 (M)

League Club	Source	Date Signed	Seasons Played	Apps	Subs	Gls
Bristol Rov	YT	07.94	95-97	24	17	0
Shrewsbury T	Tr	08.98	98	1	1	0

HAYHURST Stanley (Stan) Henry
Leyland, 13 May, 1925 Died 1998 (G)

League Club	Source	Date Signed	Seasons Played	Apps	Subs	Gls
Blackburn Rov	Leyland Motors	01.43	46-48	27	-	0
Tottenham H	Tr	10.48				
Barrow	Tr	06.50	50	26	-	0
Grimsby T	Tr	01.51	50-52	62	-	0

HAYLES Barrington (Barry) Edward
Lambeth, 17 May, 1972 ESemiPro-2/Ja-10 (F)

League Club	Source	Date Signed	Seasons Played	Apps	Subs	Gls
Bristol Rov	Stevenage Borough	06.97	97-98	62	0	32
Fulham	Tr	11.98	98-03	116	59	44
Sheffield U	Tr	06.04	04	4	0	0
Millwall	Tr	09.04	04	28	4	12

HAYLOCK Gary Andrew
Bradford, 31 December, 1970 (F)

League Club	Source	Date Signed	Seasons Played	Apps	Subs	Gls
Huddersfield T	YT	07.89	90-91	10	3	4

HAYLOCK Paul
Lowestoft, 24 March, 1963 (FB)

League Club	Source	Date Signed	Seasons Played	Apps	Subs	Gls
Norwich C	App	01.81	81-85	154	1	3
Gillingham	Tr	08.86	86-89	149	3	0
Maidstone U	Tr	03.91	90-91	47	1	1
Shrewsbury T	Tr	09.92	92	16	2	1
Barnet	Woking	10.93	93	18	2	0

HAYMAN James (Jim)
Ramsbottom, 19 February, 1928 (FB)

League Club	Source	Date Signed	Seasons Played	Apps	Subs	Gls
Bury	Radcliffe Borough	11.50	50	5	-	0

League Club	Source	Date Signed	Seasons Played	Apps	Subs	Gls
HAYNES Arthur Edwin Thomas						
Birmingham, 23 May, 1924 Died 1990						(W)
Aston Villa		01.46	46	4	-	0
Walsall	Tr	05.48	48	2	-	0
HAYNES Eric						
Sheffield, 18 June, 1936						(IF)
Rotherham U	Thorncliffe	04.56	55	1	-	0
HAYNES John (Johnny) Norman						
Edmonton, 17 October, 1934 ESch/EYth/Eu23-8/EB/FLge-13/E-56						(M)
Fulham	Jnrs	05.52	52-69	594	0	147
HAYNES Junior Lloyd						
Croydon, 6 April, 1976						(F)
Barnet	Tottenham H (YT)	08.94	94	2	4	0
HAYRETTIN Hakan						
Enfield, 4 February, 1970						(M)
Leyton Orient	YT	07.88				
Barnet	Tr	08.89	91-92	0	6	0
Torquay U	L	01.93	92	3	1	0
Wycombe W	Tr	07.93	93	15	4	1
Cambridge U	Tr	08.94	94	15	2	0
HAYS Christopher **John (Jack)**						
Ashington, 12 December, 1918 Died 1983						(W)
Bradford PA	Ipswich T	08.38	38	17	-	0
Burnley	Tr	05.39	46-50	146	-	12
Bury	Tr	09.51	51-52	27	-	2
HAYTER James Edward						
Sandown, 9 April, 1979						(F)
Bournemouth	YT	07.97	96-04	218	52	64
HAYTON Eric						
Carlisle, 14 January, 1922						(WH)
Carlisle U		08.45	46-50	49	-	5
Rochdale	Tr	05.51	51	12	-	0
Workington	Tr	10.52	52	19	-	0
HAYWARD Andrew (Andy) William						
Barnsley, 21 June, 1970						(M)
Rotherham U	Frickley Ath	08.94	94-97	93	27	15
HAYWARD Carl **Basil**						
Leek, 7 April, 1928 Died 1989						(CD)
Port Vale	Northwood Heath	05.46	46-57	349	-	55
Portsmouth	Tr	07.58	58-59	44	-	4
HAYWARD Douglas (Dougie) Stanworth						
Wellington St Georges, 23 August, 1920						(FB)
Huddersfield T	Jnrs	05.39				
Bristol Rov	Barry T	09.46	46	1	-	0
Newport Co	Tr	11.46	46-55	260	-	11
HAYWARD Lionel **Eric**						
Newcastle-under-Lyme, 2 August, 1917 Died 1976						(CD)
Port Vale	Wardles	08.34	34-36	35	-	0
Blackpool	Tr	07.37	37-51	270	-	0
HAYWARD Keith William						
Hove, 21 November, 1951						(G)
Charlton Ath	App	●	68	1	0	0
HAYWARD Steven (Steve) Lee						
Pelsall, 8 September, 1971 EYth						(M)
Derby Co	Jnrs	09.88	89-94	15	11	1
Carlisle U	Tr	03.95	94-96	88	2	13
Fulham	Tr	06.97	97-00	108	7	7
Barnsley	Tr	01.01	00-03	40	8	2
HAYWOOD Clive						
Ramsgate, 1 November, 1960						(F)
Coventry C	App	08.78	80	1	0	0
HAYWOOD Raymond (Ray)						
Dudley, 12 January, 1949						(F)
Shrewsbury T	Stourbridge	05.74	74-76	75	12	27
Northampton T	Tr	03.77	76-77	14	2	2
HAZAN Alon						
Ashdod, Israel, 14 September, 1967 Israel 64						(M)
Watford	Ironi Ashdod (Isr)	01.98	97-98	15	18	2
HAZARD Michael (Mike)						
Sunderland, 5 February, 1960						(M)
Tottenham H	App	02.78	79-85	73	18	13
Chelsea	Tr	09.85	85-89	78	3	9
Portsmouth	Tr	01.90	89	8	0	1
Swindon T	Tr	09.90	90-93	112	7	17
Tottenham H	Tr	11.93	93-94	15	13	2

League Club	Source	Date Signed	Seasons Played	Apps	Subs	Gls
HAZEL Clifford (Cliff)						
Woolwich, 14 September, 1937						(W)
Gillingham	Hastings U	07.55	57	2	-	0
HAZEL Desmond (Des) St Lloyd						
Bradford, 15 July, 1967 St Kitts int						(W)
Sheffield Wed	App	07.85	87	5	1	0
Grimsby T	L	10.86	86	9	0	2
Rotherham U	Tr	07.88	88-94	204	34	30
Chesterfield	Tr	03.95	95	16	5	0
HAZEL Ian						
Merton, 1 December, 1967						(M)
Wimbledon	App	12.85	87-88	4	3	0
Bristol Rov	L	02.89	88	3	0	0
Bristol Rov	Tr	07.89	89-90	4	10	0
Maidstone U	Tr	03.92	91	6	2	0
HAZEL Julian						
Luton, 25 September, 1973						(F)
Colchester U	YT	08.92	92	2	0	0
HAZELDEN Walter						
Ashton-in-Makerfield, 13 February, 1941 EYth						(IF)
Aston Villa	Jnrs	02.58	57-58	17	-	5
HAZELL Anthony (Tony) Philip						
High Wycombe, 19 September, 1947 EYth						(CD)
Queens Park Rgrs	Jnrs	10.64	64-74	362	7	4
Millwall	Tr	12.74	74-78	153	0	6
Crystal Palace	Tr	11.78	78	5	0	0
Charlton Ath	Tr	09.79	79-80	37	0	0
HAZELL Reuben						
Birmingham, 24 April, 1979						(CD)
Aston Villa	YT	03.97				
Tranmere Rov	Tr	08.99	99-01	38	4	1
Torquay U	Tr	01.02	01-03	77	7	2
HAZELL Robert (Bob) Joseph						
Kingston, Jamaica, 14 June, 1959 EYth/Eu21-1/EB						(CD)
Wolverhampton W	App	05.77	77-78	32	1	1
Queens Park Rgrs	Tr	09.79	79-83	100	6	8
Leicester C	Tr	09.83	83-84	41	0	2
Wolverhampton W	L	09.85	85	1	0	0
Reading	Luton T (N/C)	11.86	86	4	0	1
Port Vale	Tr	12.86	86-88	81	0	1
HAZLEDINE Albert Victor						
Royton, 28 July, 1918						(W)
Halifax T	West Ham U (Am)	11.45	46	10	-	2
HAZLEDINE Donald (Don)						
Arnold, 10 July, 1929						(IF)
Derby Co	Notts Regent	08.51	52-53	26	-	6
Northampton T	Tr	06.54	54	22	-	4
HAZLEDINE Geoffrey (Geoff)						
Arnold, 27 February, 1932 Died 2002						(WH)
Derby Co	Notts Regent	07.52	53	1	-	0
Southport	Boston U	07.57	57	29	-	5
HAZLETT George						
Glasgow, 10 March, 1923						(W)
Bury	Belfast Celtic	08.49	49-51	100	-	10
Cardiff C	Tr	08.52	52	7	-	1
Millwall	Tr	05.53	53-57	131	-	10
HAZZLETON James (Jim)						
Bolton, 29 September, 1930 Died 1991						(IF)
Bury	Atherton Collieries	05.50				
Rochdale	Tr	08.51	51	11	-	1
Accrington St	Tr	07.52	52	4	-	0
HEAD Bertram (Bert) James						
Midsomer Norton, 8 June, 1916 Died 2002						(CD)
Torquay U	Welton Rov	10.36	36-50	222	-	6
Bury	Tr	02.52	51-52	22	-	0
HEAD David George						
Midsomer Norton, 11 August, 1940						(CF)
Swindon T	Jnrs	08.58				
Arsenal	Tr	03.59				
Reading	Tr	07.60	60	12	-	0
HEAD Michael (Mike)						
Hull, 13 April, 1933 Died 1983						(W)
Hull C	Bridlington Central U	12.53	54	3	-	0
HEALD Gregory (Greg) James						
Enfield, 26 September, 1971 ESch/ESemiPro-1						(CD)
Peterborough U	Enfield	07.94	94-96	101	4	6

League Club	Source	Date Signed	Seasons Played	Apps	Subs	Gls
Barnet	Tr	08.97	97-00	141	0	13
Leyton Orient	Tr	03.03	02-03	9	0	1
Rochdale	Tr	03.04	03-04	39	0	3

HEALD Oliver Richard
Vancouver, Canada, 13 March, 1975 (F)

League Club	Source	Date Signed	Seasons Played	Apps	Subs	Gls
Port Vale	Norvan (Can)	10.93				
Scarborough	Tr	08.95	95	1	8	1

HEALD Paul Andrew
Wath-on-Dearne, 20 September, 1968 (G)

League Club	Source	Date Signed	Seasons Played	Apps	Subs	Gls
Sheffield U	App	06.87				
Leyton Orient	Tr	12.88	88-94	176	0	0
Coventry C	L	03.92	91	2	0	0
Swindon T	L	03.94	93	1	1	0
Wimbledon	Tr	07.95	95-03	36	2	0
Sheffield Wed	L	01.02	01	5	0	0

HEALE Gary John
Canvey Island, 15 July, 1958 (F)

League Club	Source	Date Signed	Seasons Played	Apps	Subs	Gls
Luton T	Canvey Island	12.76	77	7	0	1
Exeter C	L	12.77	77	3	1	0
Reading	Tr	08.79	79-81	68	8	20

HEALER Ernest (Ernie)
Birtley, 13 November, 1941 (IF)

League Club	Source	Date Signed	Seasons Played	Apps	Subs	Gls
Darlington		08.61				
Brighton & Hove A	Berwick Rgrs	10.63	63	3	-	1

HEALEY Daniel Kevin
Manchester, 22 October, 1953 (W)

League Club	Source	Date Signed	Seasons Played	Apps	Subs	Gls
Manchester U	App	01.71				
Bolton W	Tr	05.73				
Workington	Tr	07.74	74	13	4	2

HEALEY Jonathan (Jon) Peter
Morecambe, 30 December, 1966 (M)

League Club	Source	Date Signed	Seasons Played	Apps	Subs	Gls
Oldham Ath	App	06.85				
Crewe Alex	Alsager College	12.87	87	7	3	2

HEALEY Ronald (Ron)
Manchester, 30 August, 1952 IR-2 (G)

League Club	Source	Date Signed	Seasons Played	Apps	Subs	Gls
Manchester C	App	10.69	70-73	30	0	0
Coventry C	L	12.71	71	3	0	0
Preston NE	L	12.73	73	6	0	0
Cardiff C	Tr	03.74	73-81	216	0	0

HEALEY William (Bill) Richard Ernest
Liverpool, 22 May, 1926 (WH)

League Club	Source	Date Signed	Seasons Played	Apps	Subs	Gls
Arsenal	Chorley	05.49				
Fulham	Tr	12.52	52	1	-	0
Hartlepools U	Tr	08.55	55	6	-	0

HEALY Brian
Glasgow, 27 December, 1968 ESemiPro-1 (M)

League Club	Source	Date Signed	Seasons Played	Apps	Subs	Gls
Torquay U	Morecambe	12.98	98-01	55	4	11
Darlington	Tr	11.01	01	1	1	1

HEALY Colin
Cork, 14 March, 1980 IRu21-10/IR-13 (M)

League Club	Source	Date Signed	Seasons Played	Apps	Subs	Gls
Coventry C (L)	Glasgow Celtic	01.02	01	17	0	2
Sunderland	Glasgow Celtic	08.03	03	16	4	0

HEALY David Jonathan
Downpatrick, 5 August, 1979 NISch/NIYth/NIu21-8/NIB-1/NI-43 (F)

League Club	Source	Date Signed	Seasons Played	Apps	Subs	Gls
Manchester U	YT	11.97	00	0	1	0
Port Vale	L	02.00	99	15	1	3
Preston NE	Tr	12.00	00-04	104	35	44
Norwich C	L	01.03	02	5	0	1
Norwich C	L	03.03	02	5	3	1
Leeds U	Tr	10.04	04	27	1	7

HEALY Joseph (Joe) Benjamin
Sidcup, 26 December, 1986 (M)

League Club	Source	Date Signed	Seasons Played	Apps	Subs	Gls
Millwall	Jnrs	04.04	04	0	2	0

HEALY Patrick (Felix) Joseph
Derry, 27 September, 1955 IrLge-1/NI-4 (M)

League Club	Source	Date Signed	Seasons Played	Apps	Subs	Gls
Port Vale	Finn Harps	10.78	78-79	40	1	2

HEANEY Anthony (Tony) James
Plymouth, 9 May, 1940 EYth (FB)

League Club	Source	Date Signed	Seasons Played	Apps	Subs	Gls
Southampton	Jnrs	06.58	60	1	-	0

HEANEY Neil Andrew
Middlesbrough, 3 November, 1971 EYth/Eu21-6 (W)

League Club	Source	Date Signed	Seasons Played	Apps	Subs	Gls
Arsenal	YT	11.89	91-93	4	3	0
Hartlepool U	L	01.91	90	2	1	0
Cambridge U	L	01.92	91	9	4	2
Southampton	Tr	03.94	93-96	42	19	5
Manchester C	Tr	11.96	96-97	13	5	1
Charlton Ath	L	03.98	97	4	2	0
Bristol C	L	03.99	98	2	1	0
Darlington	Tr	08.99	99	33	3	5
Plymouth Arg	Dundee U	12.01	01	1	7	0

HEAP Stuart
Nelson, 7 February, 1965 (M)

League Club	Source	Date Signed	Seasons Played	Apps	Subs	Gls
Tranmere Rov	Clitheroe	03.85	84	0	3	0

HEARD Timothy **Patrick**
Hull, 17 March, 1960 EYth (M)

League Club	Source	Date Signed	Seasons Played	Apps	Subs	Gls
Everton	App	03.78	78-79	10	1	0
Aston Villa	Tr	10.79	79-82	20	5	2
Sheffield Wed	Tr	01.83	82-84	22	3	3
Newcastle U	Tr	09.84	84	34	0	2
Middlesbrough	Tr	08.85	85	25	0	2
Hull C	Tr	03.86	85-87	79	1	5
Rotherham U	Tr	07.88	88-89	41	3	7
Cardiff C	Tr	08.90	90-91	45	1	4
Hull C	Hall Road Rgrs	08.92	92	3	1	0

HEARN Charles (Charley) Richard
Ashford, Kent, 5 November, 1983 (M)

League Club	Source	Date Signed	Seasons Played	Apps	Subs	Gls
Millwall	YT	04.01	01-03	9	9	0
Northampton T	L	12.04	04	21	3	1

HEARN Frank Guy
St Pancras, 5 November, 1929 (IF)

League Club	Source	Date Signed	Seasons Played	Apps	Subs	Gls
Torquay U		08.50				
Northampton T	Tr	10.51				
Crystal Palace	Tr	06.54	54	8	-	1

HEARY Thomas Mark
Dublin, 14 February, 1978 IRSch/IRYth/IRu21-4 (FB)

League Club	Source	Date Signed	Seasons Played	Apps	Subs	Gls
Huddersfield T	YT	02.96	96-02	68	24	0

HEASELGRAVE Samuel (Sammy) Ernest
Smethwick, 1 October, 1916 Died 1975 (IF)

League Club	Source	Date Signed	Seasons Played	Apps	Subs	Gls
West Bromwich A	Brierley Hill Alliance	10.34	36-38	49	-	16
Northampton T	Tr	10.45	46-47	42	-	4

HEATH Adrian Paul
Stoke-on-Trent, 11 January, 1961 Eu21-8/EB (F)

League Club	Source	Date Signed	Seasons Played	Apps	Subs	Gls
Stoke C	App	01.79	78-81	94	1	16
Everton	Tr	01.82	81-88	206	20	71
Aston Villa	Espanyol (Sp)	08.89	89	8	1	0
Manchester C	Tr	02.90	89-91	58	17	4
Stoke C	Tr	03.92	91	5	1	0
Burnley	Tr	08.92	92-95	109	6	28
Sheffield U	Tr	12.95	95	0	4	0
Burnley	Tr	03.96	95-96	1	4	0

HEATH Colin
Matlock, 31 December, 1983 (F)

League Club	Source	Date Signed	Seasons Played	Apps	Subs	Gls
Manchester U	YT	01.01				
Cambridge U	L	12.04	04	5	1	0

HEATH Dennis John
Chiswick, 28 September, 1934 (W)

League Club	Source	Date Signed	Seasons Played	Apps	Subs	Gls
Brentford	Jnrs	09.52	54-60	123	-	20

HEATH Donald (Don)
Stockton, 26 December, 1944 (W)

League Club	Source	Date Signed	Seasons Played	Apps	Subs	Gls
Middlesbrough	App	12.62				
Norwich C	Tr	07.64	64-67	79	3	15
Swindon T	Tr	09.67	67-69	82	6	2
Oldham Ath	Tr	07.70	70-71	43	2	1
Peterborough U	Tr	07.72	72	43	1	4
Hartlepool	Tr	07.73	73-74	36	1	2

HEATH Duncan Nigel
Stoke-on-Trent, 23 October, 1961 (FB)

League Club	Source	Date Signed	Seasons Played	Apps	Subs	Gls
Aston Villa	App	07.79				
Crewe Alex	Tr	11.80	81	17	6	0

HEATH Herbert George
Wolverhampton, 29 March, 1970 (CD)

League Club	Source	Date Signed	Seasons Played	Apps	Subs	Gls
Exeter C	Darlaston	02.89	88	3	2	0

HEATH John
Heywood, 5 June, 1936 (G)

League Club	Source	Date Signed	Seasons Played	Apps	Subs	Gls
Bury	Blackburn Rov (Am)	09.56	56-61	8	-	0
Tranmere Rov	Tr	01.62	61-63	58	-	0
Rochdale	Wigan Ath	02.66	65	6	0	0

HEATH Matthew (Matt) Philip
Leicester, 1 November, 1981 (CD)

League Club	Source	Date Signed	Seasons Played	Apps	Subs	Gls
Leicester C	YT	02.01	01-04	42	9	6
Stockport Co	L	10.03	03	8	0	0

HEATH Michael
Hull, 7 February, 1974 (G)

League Club	Source	Date Signed	Seasons Played	Apps	Subs	Gls
Tottenham H	YT	05.92				
Scunthorpe U	Tr	12.93	93	1	1	0

HEATH Michael (Mick)
Hillingdon, 9 January, 1953 (F)

League Club	Source	Date Signed	Seasons Played	Apps	Subs	Gls
Brentford (Am)	Walton & Hersham	04.71	70	1	0	0

HEATH Nicholas (Nick) Alan
Sutton Coldfield, 2 January, 1985 (M)

League Club	Source	Date Signed	Seasons Played	Apps	Subs	Gls
Kidderminster Hrs	Marconi (Coventry)	03.03	02	0	1	0

HEATH Norman Harry
Wolverhampton, 31 January, 1924 Died 1983 (G)

League Club	Source	Date Signed	Seasons Played	Apps	Subs	Gls
West Bromwich A	Henry Meadows BC	10.43	47-53	121	-	0

HEATH Philip (Phil) Adrian
Stoke-on-Trent, 24 November, 1964 (W)

League Club	Source	Date Signed	Seasons Played	Apps	Subs	Gls
Stoke C	App	10.82	82-87	144	12	16
Oxford U	Tr	06.88	88-89	24	13	1
Cardiff C	Tr	03.91	90	11	0	1

HEATH Robert
Newcastle-under-Lyme, 31 August, 1978 (M)

League Club	Source	Date Signed	Seasons Played	Apps	Subs	Gls
Stoke C	YT	07.96	97-99	11	8	0

HEATH Seamus Martin James Paul
Belfast, 6 December, 1961 (M)

League Club	Source	Date Signed	Seasons Played	Apps	Subs	Gls
Luton T	Jnrs	04.79				
Lincoln C	L	08.82	82	6	1	0
Wrexham	Tr	08.83	83	32	0	1
Tranmere Rov	Tr	08.84	84	6	11	0

HEATH Stephen (Steve) Dennis
Hull, 15 November, 1977 EYth (CD)

League Club	Source	Date Signed	Seasons Played	Apps	Subs	Gls
Leeds U	YT	11.94				
Carlisle U	Tr	07.96	96	0	1	0

HEATH Richard **Terence (Terry)**
Leicester, 17 November, 1943 (F)

League Club	Source	Date Signed	Seasons Played	Apps	Subs	Gls
Leicester C	App	11.61	62-63	8	-	2
Hull C	Tr	05.64	64-67	27	6	1
Scunthorpe U	Tr	03.68	67-72	174	2	50
Lincoln C	Tr	02.73	72-73	17	0	1

HEATH William (Bill) Henry Mansell
Bournemouth, 15 April, 1934 (G)

League Club	Source	Date Signed	Seasons Played	Apps	Subs	Gls
Bournemouth	Jnrs	12.51	56-57	34	-	0
Lincoln C	Tr	11.58	58-61	84	-	0

HEATH William (Bill) John
Stepney, 26 June, 1920 Died 1994 (FB)

League Club	Source	Date Signed	Seasons Played	Apps	Subs	Gls
Queens Park Rgrs		09.45	46-52	96	-	3

HEATHCOCK Adrian Neil
Dudley, 26 January, 1975 (W)

League Club	Source	Date Signed	Seasons Played	Apps	Subs	Gls
Hereford U	YT	●	92	1	1	0

HEATHCOTE Jonathan
Frimley, 10 November, 1983 (M)

League Club	Source	Date Signed	Seasons Played	Apps	Subs	Gls
Cambridge U	Sch	04.03	02	2	0	0

HEATHCOTE Michael (Mick)
Kelloe, 10 September, 1965 (CD)

League Club	Source	Date Signed	Seasons Played	Apps	Subs	Gls
Sunderland	Spennymoor U	08.87	87-89	6	3	0
Halifax T	L	12.87	87	7	0	1
York C	L	01.90	89	3	0	0
Shrewsbury T	Tr	07.90	90-91	43	1	6
Cambridge U	Tr	09.91	91-94	123	5	13
Plymouth Arg	Tr	07.95	95-00	195	4	13
Shrewsbury T	Tr	08.01	01-02	39	1	2

HEATHCOTE Peter George Samuel
Leicester, 13 November, 1932 (G)

League Club	Source	Date Signed	Seasons Played	Apps	Subs	Gls
Southend U	Jnrs	11.51	51	2	-	0

HEATHCOTE Wilfred (Wilf)
Hemsworth, 29 June, 1911 Died 1991 (CF)

League Club	Source	Date Signed	Seasons Played	Apps	Subs	Gls
Queens Park Rgrs		10.43	46	5	-	1
Millwall	Tr	12.46	46	8	-	2

HEATHER Leslie **John**
Winchcombe, 25 April, 1933 (IF)

League Club	Source	Date Signed	Seasons Played	Apps	Subs	Gls
Mansfield T	Belper T	08.52	53	1	-	0

HEATON James **Michael (Mick)**
Sheffield, 15 January, 1947 Died 1995 (FB)

League Club	Source	Date Signed	Seasons Played	Apps	Subs	Gls
Sheffield U	App	11.64	66-70	31	3	0
Blackburn Rov	Tr	10.71	71-75	169	2	1

HEATON Paul John
Hyde, 24 January, 1961 (M)

League Club	Source	Date Signed	Seasons Played	Apps	Subs	Gls
Oldham Ath	App	01.79	77-83	124	12	28
Rochdale	Tr	03.84	83-85	85	4	9

HEATON William (Billy) Henry
Leeds, 26 August, 1918 Died 1990 (W)

League Club	Source	Date Signed	Seasons Played	Apps	Subs	Gls
Leeds U	Whitkirk	12.37	46-48	59	-	6
Southampton	Tr	02.49	48	15	-	0
Rochdale	Stalybridge Celtic	11.50	50	5	-	0

HEAVISIDE John
Ferryhill, 7 October, 1943 (FB)

League Club	Source	Date Signed	Seasons Played	Apps	Subs	Gls
Darlington (Am)	Bishops Middleham	08.63	63	2	-	0

HEBBERD Trevor Neal
New Alresford, 19 June, 1958 (M)

League Club	Source	Date Signed	Seasons Played	Apps	Subs	Gls
Southampton	App	06.76	76-81	69	28	7
Bolton W	L	09.81	81	6	0	0
Leicester C	L	11.81	81	4	0	1
Oxford U	Tr	03.82	81-87	260	0	37
Derby Co	Tr	08.88	88-90	70	11	10
Portsmouth	Tr	10.91	91	1	3	0
Chesterfield	Tr	11.91	91-93	67	7	1
Lincoln C	Tr	07.94	94	20	5	0

HEBDITCH Alan
Wigan, 11 October, 1961 (FB)

League Club	Source	Date Signed	Seasons Played	Apps	Subs	Gls
Bradford C	Leeds U (Jnrs)	08.80	80	2	0	0

HEBEL Dirk Josef
Cologne, Germany, 24 November, 1972 (M)

League Club	Source	Date Signed	Seasons Played	Apps	Subs	Gls
Tranmere Rov	Bursaspor (Tu)	09.97				
Brentford	Tr	08.98	98	6	9	0

HECKINGBOTTOM Paul
Barnsley, 17 July, 1977 (FB)

League Club	Source	Date Signed	Seasons Played	Apps	Subs	Gls
Sunderland	Manchester U (YT)	07.95				
Scarborough	L	10.97	97	28	1	0
Hartlepool U	L	09.98	98	5	0	1
Darlington	Tr	03.99	98-01	111	4	5
Norwich C	Tr	07.02	02	7	8	0
Bradford C	Tr	07.03	03	43	0	0
Sheffield Wed	Tr	07.04	04	37	1	4

HECKMAN Ronald (Ron) Ernest
Peckham, 23 November, 1929 Died 1990 EAmat (IF)

League Club	Source	Date Signed	Seasons Played	Apps	Subs	Gls
Leyton Orient	Bromley	07.55	55-57	87	-	38
Millwall	Tr	11.57	57-59	92	-	21
Crystal Palace	Tr	07.60	60-62	84	-	25

HECTOR Kevin James
Leeds, 2 November, 1944 FLge-3/E-2 (F)

League Club	Source	Date Signed	Seasons Played	Apps	Subs	Gls
Bradford PA	Middleton Parkside Jnr	07.62	62-66	176	0	113
Derby Co	Tr	09.66	66-77	426	4	147
Derby Co	Burton A	10.80	80-81	52	4	8

HEDLEY Graeme
Easington, County Durham, 1 March, 1957 (M)

League Club	Source	Date Signed	Seasons Played	Apps	Subs	Gls
Middlesbrough	App	03.75	76-81	36	14	6
Sheffield Wed	L	02.78	77	6	0	1
Darlington	L	03.79	78	14	0	1
York C	L	10.81	81	5	0	1
Hartlepool U	Horden CW	08.84	84	32	0	9

HEDLEY John (Jack) Robert
Willington Quay, 11 December, 1923 Died 1985 (FB)

League Club	Source	Date Signed	Seasons Played	Apps	Subs	Gls
Everton	North Shields	04.45	47-49	54	-	0
Sunderland	Bogota (Col)	08.50	50-58	269	-	0
Gateshead	Tr	07.59	59	11	-	0

HEDMAN Magnus Carl
Stockholm, Sweden, 19 March, 1973 SwYth/Swu21/SwB-1/Sw-49 (G)

League Club	Source	Date Signed	Seasons Played	Apps	Subs	Gls
Coventry C	AIK Solna (Swe)	07.97	97-01	134	0	0

HEDMAN Rudolph (Rudi) Gideon
Lambeth, 16 November, 1964 (CD)

League Club	Source	Date Signed	Seasons Played	Apps	Subs	Gls
Colchester U		02.84	83-88	166	10	10
Crystal Palace	Tr	12.88	88-91	10	11	0
Leyton Orient	L	12.89	89	5	0	0

HEDWORTH Christopher (Chris)
Wallsend, 5 January, 1964 (FB)

League Club	Source	Date Signed	Seasons Played	Apps	Subs	Gls
Newcastle U	App	01.82	82-85	8	1	0
Barnsley	Tr	08.86	86-87	19	6	0
Halifax T	Tr	08.88	88-89	38	0	0
Blackpool	Tr	09.90	90-91	24	0	0

HEELEY David **Mark**
Peterborough, 8 September, 1959 (W)

League Club	Source	Date Signed	Seasons Played	Apps	Subs	Gls
Peterborough U	App	11.76	75-76	12	5	3
Arsenal	Tr	09.77	77-78	9	6	1
Northampton T	Tr	03.80	79-82	84	8	5

League Club	Source	Date Signed	Seasons Played	Apps	Subs	Gls
HEENAN Thomas (Tommy)						
Glasgow, 16 June, 1932						(W)
Bradford PA	Raith Rov	05.58	58	5	-	1
HEEPS James (Jimmy) Andrew						
Luton, 16 May, 1971						(G)
Swansea C	YT	07.89	89	1	0	0
HEEROO Gavin Harry						
Haringey, 2 September, 1984 Mauritius int						(M)
Crystal Palace	Jnrs	09.01	03	0	1	0
HEESOM Darren Lea						
Warrington, 8 May, 1968						(FB)
Burnley	App	12.85	85-86	36	2	1
HEFFER Paul Victor						
West Ham, 21 December, 1947						(CD)
West Ham U	Jnrs	08.65	66-71	11	4	0
HEFFER Robert (Bob) William						
Eriswell, 9 November, 1935						(W)
Norwich C	RAF St Faiths	04.56	56	2	-	1
HEFFERNAN Paul						
Dublin, 29 December, 1981 IRu21-3						(F)
Notts Co	Newtown (Co Wicklow)	10.99	99-03	74	26	36
Bristol C	Tr	07.04	04	10	17	5
HEFFERNAN Thomas (Tom) Patrick						
Dublin, 30 April, 1955						(FB)
Tottenham H	Dunleary Celtic	10.77				
Bournemouth	Tr	05.79	79-82	152	2	21
Sheffield U	Tr	08.83	83-84	82	0	5
Bournemouth	Tr	06.85	85-87	58	5	6
HEFFRON Charles (Charlie) Alphonsus						
Belfast, 13 August, 1927 IrLge-1						(G)
Bradford PA	Belfast Celtic	06.49	51-52	25	-	0
HEGAN Daniel (Danny)						
Coatbridge, 14 June, 1943 NI-7						(M)
Sunderland	Albion Rov	09.61				
Ipswich T	Tr	07.63	63-68	207	0	34
West Bromwich A	Tr	05.69	69	13	1	2
Wolverhampton W	Tr	05.70	70-73	49	4	6
Sunderland	Tr	11.73	73	3	3	0
HEGARTY Kevin Michael						
Edinburgh, 30 July, 1950						(F)
Carlisle U	Heart of Midlothian	09.71	71	1	6	0
HEGARTY Nicholas (Nick) Ian						
Hemsworth, 25 August, 1986						(M)
Grimsby T	Sch	●	04	0	1	0
HEGGARTY James (Jim) Patrick						
Larne, 4 August, 1965						(CD)
Brighton & Hove A	Larne T	09.84				
Burnley	Tr	08.85	85	33	3	1
HEGGEM Vegard						
Trondheim, Norway, 13 July, 1975 Nou21/No-21						(FB)
Liverpool	Rosenborg (Nor)	07.98	98-00	38	16	3
HEGGIE William (Bill) Campbell						
Scone, 7 June, 1927 Died 1977						(CF)
New Brighton	Jeanfield Swifts	02.51	50	10	-	5
Leeds U	Tr	06.51				
Wrexham	Tr	08.52	52-54	33	-	13
Accrington St	Winsford U	02.55	54	1	-	0
HEGGS Carl Sydney						
Leicester, 11 October, 1970						(F)
West Bromwich A	Leicester U	08.91	91-94	13	27	3
Bristol Rov	L	01.95	94	2	3	1
Swansea C	Tr	07.95	95-96	33	13	7
Northampton T	Tr	07.97	97-98	29	17	5
Chester C (L)	Rushden & Diamonds	03.00	99	11	0	2
Carlisle U	Rushden & Diamonds	08.00	00	16	14	5
HEGINBOTHAM Brian						
Hyde, 3 October, 1937						(FB)
Stockport Co	Jnrs	10.54	58-59	11	-	0
HEIDENSTROM Bjorn						
Porsgrunn, Norway, 15 January, 1968 Nou21-10						(M)
Leyton Orient	Odd Grenland (Nor)	12.96	96	3	1	0
HEIGHWAY Stephen (Steve) Derek						
Dublin, 25 November, 1947 ESch/IR-34						(W)
Liverpool	Skelmersdale U	05.70	70-80	312	17	50

League Club	Source	Date Signed	Seasons Played	Apps	Subs	Gls
HEIKKINEN Markus						
Katrineholm, Finland, 13 October, 1978 FiYth/Fiu21/Fi-7						(FB)
Portsmouth (L)	HJK Helsinki (Fin)	01.03	02	0	2	0
HEINEMANN Nicholas (Nicky)						
Bradford, 4 January, 1985						(FB)
Halifax T	YT	●	01	3	0	0
HEINOLA Antti Juhani						
Helsinki, Finland, 20 March, 1973 Fiu21/Fi-8						(FB)
Queens Park Rgrs	Heracles (Holl)	01.98	97-00	23	11	0
HEINZE Gabriel Ivan						
Crespo, Argentina, 19 April, 1978 Argentina 26						(FB)
Manchester U	Paris St Germain (Fr)	07.04	04	26	0	1
HEISELBERG Kim						
Tarm, Denmark, 21 September, 1977 DeYth/Deu21						(FB)
Sunderland	Esbjerg (Den)	03.97				
Swindon T	Midtjyllan (Den)	08.00	00	1	0	0
HELDER Glenn						
Leiden, Holland, 28 October, 1968 Holland int						(F)
Arsenal	Vitesse Arnhem (Holl)	02.95	94-96	27	12	1
[HELDER] RODRIGUEZ Christovao						
Luanda, Angola, 21 March, 1971 Portugal 33						(CD)
Newcastle (L)	Dep la Coruna (Sp)	11.99	99	8	0	1
HELGUSON Heidar						
Akureyri, Iceland, 22 August, 1977 IcYth/Icu21-6/Ic-34						(F)
Watford	Lillestrom (Nor)	01.00	99-04	132	42	55
HELIN Petri Juhani						
Helsinki, Finland, 13 December, 1969 Fi-24						(CD)
Luton T	FC Jokerit (Fin)	11.00	00	23	0	1
Stockport Co	Tr	07.01	01	10	3	0
HELLAWELL John Rodney						
Keighley, 20 December, 1943						(M)
Bradford C	Salts	06.63	62-64	48	-	13
Rotherham U	Tr	01.65	64-65	9	1	3
Darlington	Tr	07.66	66	7	1	1
Bradford PA	Tr	10.68	68	1	0	0
HELLAWELL Michael (Mike) Stephen						
Keighley, 30 June, 1938 E-2						(W)
Queens Park Rgrs	Salts	08.55	55-56	45	-	7
Birmingham C	Tr	05.57	57-64	178	-	30
Sunderland	Tr	01.65	64-66	43	1	2
Huddersfield T	Tr	09.66	66-67	45	1	1
Peterborough U	Tr	12.68	68	9	0	0
HELLEWELL Keith						
Barnsley, 1 April, 1944 Died 2005						(G)
Doncaster Rov	Jnrs	05.61	62-63	12	-	0
HELLIN Anthony (Tony)						
Merthyr Tydfil, 26 September, 1944 WSch						(FB)
Swindon T	App	06.62				
Torquay U	Tr	07.64	64-65	29	0	1
HELLIN Matthew Karl						
Merthyr Tydfil, 12 September, 1966						(CD)
Aston Villa	App	09.84				
Wolverhampton W	Tr	08.86	86	1	0	0
HELLINGS Dennis (Dan) Raymond						
Lincoln, 9 December, 1923 Died 1996						(CF)
Lincoln C	Ransome & Marles	12.45	46	3	-	0
HELLIWELL David						
Blackburn, 28 March, 1948 Died 2003						(W)
Blackburn Rov	App	05.66	66-68	15	0	1
Lincoln C	Tr	05.69	69	11	2	1
Workington	Tr	07.70	70-75	184	14	20
Rochdale	Tr	07.76	76	20	11	3
HELLIWELL Ian						
Rotherham, 7 November, 1962						(F)
York C	Matlock T	10.87	87-90	158	2	40
Scunthorpe U	Tr	08.91	91-92	78	2	22
Rotherham U	Tr	08.93	93-94	47	5	4
Stockport Co	Tr	01.95	94-95	35	4	13
Burnley	Tr	02.96	95	3	1	0
Mansfield T	L	09.96	96	4	1	1
Chester C	L	10.96	96	8	1	1
Doncaster Rov	L	11.97	97	8	0	1
HELMER Thomas						
Herford, Germany, 21 April, 1965 Germany 68						(CD)
Sunderland	Bayern Munich (Ger)	07.99	99	1	1	0

HELVEG Thomas Lund
Odense, Denmark, 24 June, 1971 Deu21-3/De-95 (CD)

League Club	Source	Date Signed	Seasons Played	Apps	Subs	Gls
Norwich C	Inter Milan (It)	08.04	04	16	4	0

HEMMERMAN Jeffrey (Jeff) Lawrence
Hull, 25 February, 1955 (F)

League Club	Source	Date Signed	Seasons Played	Apps	Subs	Gls
Hull C	App	03.73	73-76	45	14	10
Scunthorpe U	L	09.75	75	4	1	1
Port Vale	Tr	06.77	77	13	2	5
Portsmouth	Tr	07.78	78-81	114	9	39
Cardiff C	Tr	07.82	82-83	54	1	22

HEMMING Christopher (Chris) Anthony John
Newcastle-under-Lyme, 13 April, 1966 (CD)

League Club	Source	Date Signed	Seasons Played	Apps	Subs	Gls
Stoke C	Jnrs	04.84	83-88	85	8	2
Wigan Ath	L	01.89	88	4	0	0
Hereford U	Tr	08.89	89-90	39	2	3

HEMMINGS Anthony (Tony) George
Burton-on-Trent, 21 September, 1967 ESemiPro-1 (W)

League Club	Source	Date Signed	Seasons Played	Apps	Subs	Gls
Wycombe W	Northwich Vic	09.93	93-95	28	21	12
Chester C	Ilkeston T	01.00	99	19	0	2
Carlisle U	Tr	08.00	00	16	6	0

HEMSLEY Edward (Ted) John Orton
Stoke-on-Trent, 1 September, 1943 (FB)

League Club	Source	Date Signed	Seasons Played	Apps	Subs	Gls
Shrewsbury T	Jnrs	07.61	60-68	234	1	22
Sheffield U	Tr	08.68	68-76	247	0	7
Doncaster Rov	Tr	07.77	77-78	32	0	1

HEMSTEAD Derek William
Scunthorpe, 22 May, 1943 (FB)

League Club	Source	Date Signed	Seasons Played	Apps	Subs	Gls
Scunthorpe U	Jnrs	05.60	60-68	248	0	2
Carlisle U	Tr	07.69	69-72	97	1	1

HEMSTOCK Brian
Goldthorpe, 9 February, 1949 (M)

League Club	Source	Date Signed	Seasons Played	Apps	Subs	Gls
Barnsley	Jnrs	12.66	66	1	0	0
Bradford PA	Tr	07.68	68	4	0	0

HENCHER Kenneth (Ken) Ernest Edward
Romford, 2 February, 1928 (CD)

League Club	Source	Date Signed	Seasons Played	Apps	Subs	Gls
Millwall		12.49	49-55	48	-	0

HENCHER Nicholas (Nick)
Wrexham, 24 August, 1961 (W)

League Club	Source	Date Signed	Seasons Played	Apps	Subs	Gls
Wrexham	Lex X1	08.85	85-87	26	6	5

HENCHOZ Stephane
Billens, Switzerland, 7 September, 1974 SwitYth/SwitU21/Swit-72 (CD)

League Club	Source	Date Signed	Seasons Played	Apps	Subs	Gls
Blackburn Rov	SV Hamburg (Ger)	07.97	97-98	70	0	0
Liverpool	Tr	07.99	99-03	132	3	0

HENDERSON Anthony (Tony) Joseph
Newcastle, 14 January, 1954 (CD)

League Club	Source	Date Signed	Seasons Played	Apps	Subs	Gls
Rotherham U	App	01.72	73	5	1	0

HENDERSON Brian Charles
Allendale, 12 June, 1930 Died 2001 (FB)

League Club	Source	Date Signed	Seasons Played	Apps	Subs	Gls
Carlisle U		05.50				
Darlington	Tr	07.52	52-63	423	-	3

HENDERSON Damian Michael
Leeds, 12 May, 1973 (F)

League Club	Source	Date Signed	Seasons Played	Apps	Subs	Gls
Leeds U	YT	07.91				
Scarborough	Tr	08.93	93	17	0	5
Scunthorpe U	Tr	12.93	93-94	31	6	4
Hereford U	L	01.95	94	5	0	0
Hartlepool U	Tr	03.95	94-95	45	3	6

HENDERSON Darius Alexis
Sutton, 7 September, 1981 (F)

League Club	Source	Date Signed	Seasons Played	Apps	Subs	Gls
Reading	YT	12.99	99-03	5	66	11
Brighton & Hove A	L	08.03	03	10	0	2
Gillingham	Tr	01.04	03-04	31	5	9
Swindon T	L	08.04	04	6	0	5

HENDERSON George
Hartlepool, 7 March, 1946 Died 1991 (F)

League Club	Source	Date Signed	Seasons Played	Apps	Subs	Gls
Hartlepool (Am)	Bishop Auckland	11.70	70	1	0	0

HENDERSON Ian
Bury St Edmunds, 24 January, 1985 EYth (F)

League Club	Source	Date Signed	Seasons Played	Apps	Subs	Gls
Norwich C	Sch	02.03	02-04	18	24	5

HENDERSON John
Johnshaven, 22 September, 1941 (IF)

League Club	Source	Date Signed	Seasons Played	Apps	Subs	Gls
Charlton Ath	Montrose Victoria	06.59	62	4	-	1
Exeter C	Tr	11.62	62-63	46	-	14
Doncaster Rov	Tr	07.64	64	10	-	0
Chesterfield	Tr	07.65	65	28	0	3

HENDERSON John (Jackie) Gillespie
Bishopbriggs, 17 January, 1932 Died 2005 SB/S-7 (CF)

League Club	Source	Date Signed	Seasons Played	Apps	Subs	Gls
Portsmouth	Kirkintilloch BC	01.49	51-57	217	-	69
Wolverhampton W	Tr	03.58	57-58	9	-	3
Arsenal	Tr	10.58	58-61	103	-	29
Fulham	Tr	01.62	61-63	45	-	7

HENDERSON John (Jock) Swinton Pryde
Glasgow, 13 October, 1923 (IF)

League Club	Source	Date Signed	Seasons Played	Apps	Subs	Gls
Rotherham U	Third Lanark	11.53	53-54	47	-	7
Leeds U	Tr	03.55	54-55	15	-	4

HENDERSON Joseph (Joe)
Cleland, 21 December, 1924 (G)

League Club	Source	Date Signed	Seasons Played	Apps	Subs	Gls
Northampton T	Albion Rov	05.49				
Accrington St	Stenhousemuir	07.53	53	14	-	0

HENDERSON Kevin Malcolm
Ashington, 8 June, 1974 (F)

League Club	Source	Date Signed	Seasons Played	Apps	Subs	Gls
Burnley	Morpeth T	12.97	97-98	0	14	1
Hartlepool U	Tr	07.99	99-03	82	49	29
Carlisle U	Tr	09.03	03	10	9	2

HENDERSON William **Martin** Melville
Kirkcaldy, 3 May, 1956 (F)

League Club	Source	Date Signed	Seasons Played	Apps	Subs	Gls
Leicester C	Airdrie	10.78	78-80	79	12	12
Chesterfield	Tr	09.81	81-83	87	0	23
Port Vale	Tr	10.83	83	27	0	7

HENDERSON Michael (Mick) Robert
Gosforth, 31 March, 1956 (FB)

League Club	Source	Date Signed	Seasons Played	Apps	Subs	Gls
Sunderland	App	03.74	75-78	81	3	2
Watford	Tr	11.79	79-81	50	1	0
Cardiff C	Tr	03.82	81	11	0	0
Sheffield U	Tr	08.82	82-84	65	2	0
Chesterfield	Tr	01.85	84-88	135	1	10

HENDERSON Paul
Sydney, Australia, 22 April, 1976 (G)

League Club	Source	Date Signed	Seasons Played	Apps	Subs	Gls
Bradford C	Northern Spirit (Aus)	08.04	04	40	0	0

HENDERSON Peter
Berwick-on-Tweed, 29 September, 1952 (W)

League Club	Source	Date Signed	Seasons Played	Apps	Subs	Gls
Chester	Witton A	12.78	78-79	59	5	10
Gillingham	Tr	07.80	80	6	1	3
Crewe Alex	L	09.81	81	6	1	0
Chester	Tr	12.81	81	28	0	5

HENDERSON Raymond (Ray)
Wallsend, 31 March, 1937 (M)

League Club	Source	Date Signed	Seasons Played	Apps	Subs	Gls
Middlesbrough	Ashington	05.57	57-60	9	-	5
Hull C	Tr	06.61	61-67	226	3	54
Reading	Tr	10.68	68	5	0	0

HENDERSON Stanley (Stan)
Barrow, 15 October, 1925 Died 1980 (W)

League Club	Source	Date Signed	Seasons Played	Apps	Subs	Gls
Barrow	Holker COB	06.46	46-47	25	-	3

HENDERSON James **Stewart**
Bridge of Allan, 5 June, 1947 SSch (FB)

League Club	Source	Date Signed	Seasons Played	Apps	Subs	Gls
Chelsea	Jnrs	07.64				
Brighton & Hove A	Tr	07.65	65-72	198	0	1
Reading	Tr	06.73	73-82	159	7	6

HENDERSON Thomas (Tom)
Burnley, 1 October, 1927 (W)

League Club	Source	Date Signed	Seasons Played	Apps	Subs	Gls
Burnley	Jnrs	08.45	49	2	-	0

HENDERSON Thomas (Tommy)
Consett, 6 April, 1949 (W)

League Club	Source	Date Signed	Seasons Played	Apps	Subs	Gls
Bradford PA	Tow Law T	02.69	68-69	22	0	3
York C	Tr	10.70	70-71	63	1	7

HENDERSON Thomas (Tommy) Wedlock
Larkhall, 25 July, 1943 (W)

League Club	Source	Date Signed	Seasons Played	Apps	Subs	Gls
Leeds U	St Mirren	11.62	62-64	24	-	2
Bury	Tr	06.65	65	7	0	1
Swindon T	Tr	01.66	65	11	0	3
Stockport Co	Tr	07.66	66	17	2	4

HENDERSON Wayne
Dublin, 16 September, 1983 IRYth/IRu21-10 (G)

League Club	Source	Date Signed	Seasons Played	Apps	Subs	Gls
Aston Villa	YT	09.00				
Wycombe W	L	04.04	03	3	0	0
Notts Co	L	08.04	04	9	0	0
Notts Co	L	12.04	04	2	0	0

HENDERSON William (Willie)
Caldercruix, 24 January, 1944 SSch/Su23-2/SLge-6/S-29 (W)

League Club	Source	Date Signed	Seasons Played	Apps	Subs	Gls
Sheffield Wed	Glasgow Rgrs	07.72	72-73	42	6	5

HENDERSON William (Bill) John
Closeburn, 21 February, 1920 Died 1965 (G)

League Club	Source	Date Signed	Seasons Played	Apps	Subs	Gls
Rochdale	Queen of the South	07.46	46	17	-	0
Southport	Tr	06.47	47	20	-	0

HENDON Ian Michael
Ilford, 5 December, 1971 EYth/Eu21-7 (FB)

League Club	Source	Date Signed	Seasons Played	Apps	Subs	Gls
Tottenham H	YT	12.89	90-91	0	4	0
Portsmouth	L	01.92	91	1	3	0
Leyton Orient	L	03.92	91	5	1	0
Barnsley	L	03.93	92	6	0	0
Leyton Orient	Tr	08.93	93-96	130	1	5
Birmingham C	L	03.95	94	4	0	0
Notts Co	Tr	02.97	96-98	82	0	6
Northampton T	Tr	03.99	98-00	60	0	3
Sheffield Wed	Tr	10.00	00-02	49	0	2
Peterborough U	Tr	01.03	02	7	0	1

HENDRIE John Grattan
Lennoxtown, 24 October, 1963 SYth (W)

League Club	Source	Date Signed	Seasons Played	Apps	Subs	Gls
Coventry C	App	05.81	81-83	15	6	2
Hereford U	L	01.84	83	6	0	0
Bradford C	Tr	07.84	84-87	173	0	46
Newcastle U	Tr	06.88	88	34	0	4
Leeds U	Tr	06.89	89	22	5	5
Middlesbrough	Tr	07.90	90-95	181	11	44
Barnsley	Tr	10.96	96-98	49	16	17

HENDRIE Lee Andrew
Birmingham, 18 May, 1977 EYth/Eu21-13/EB-1/E-1 (M)

League Club	Source	Date Signed	Seasons Played	Apps	Subs	Gls
Aston Villa	YT	05.94	95-04	195	39	26

HENDRIE Paul
Glasgow, 27 March, 1954 (M)

League Club	Source	Date Signed	Seasons Played	Apps	Subs	Gls
Birmingham C	Kirkintilloch Rob Roy	03.72	72-75	19	3	1
Bristol Rov	Tr	09.77	77-78	17	13	1
Halifax T	Tr	07.79	79-83	187	0	11
Stockport Co	Tr	08.84	84-88	114	7	6

HENDRY Edward **Colin** James
Keith, 7 December, 1965 SB-1/S-51 (CD)

League Club	Source	Date Signed	Seasons Played	Apps	Subs	Gls
Blackburn Rov	Dundee	03.87	86-89	99	3	22
Manchester C	Tr	11.89	89-91	57	6	5
Blackburn Rov	Tr	11.91	91-97	229	5	12
Coventry C	Glasgow Rgrs	03.00	99-00	10	1	0
Bolton W	Tr	12.00	00-01	25	0	3
Preston NE	L	02.02	01	2	0	0
Blackpool	L	12.02	02	14	0	0

HENDRY Ian
Glasgow, 19 October, 1959 (M)

League Club	Source	Date Signed	Seasons Played	Apps	Subs	Gls
Aston Villa	App	09.77				
Hereford U	Tr	02.79	78-79	21	0	0

HENDRY John Michael
Glasgow, 6 January, 1970 Su21-1 (F)

League Club	Source	Date Signed	Seasons Played	Apps	Subs	Gls
Tottenham H	Dundee	07.90	90-93	5	12	5
Charlton Ath	L	02.92	91	1	4	1
Swansea C	L	10.94	94	8	0	2

HENLEY Leslie (Les) Donald
Lambeth, 26 September, 1922 Died 1996 ESch (WH)

League Club	Source	Date Signed	Seasons Played	Apps	Subs	Gls
Arsenal	Jnrs	09.40				
Reading	Tr	12.46	46-52	181	-	29

HENNESSEY William **Terence (Terry)**
Llay, 1 September, 1942 WSch/Wu23-6/W-39 (CD)

League Club	Source	Date Signed	Seasons Played	Apps	Subs	Gls
Birmingham C	Jnrs	09.59	60-65	178	0	3
Nottingham F	Tr	11.65	65-69	159	0	5
Derby Co	Tr	02.70	69-72	62	1	4

HENNIGAN Michael (Mike)
Rotherham, 20 December, 1942 (CD)

League Club	Source	Date Signed	Seasons Played	Apps	Subs	Gls
Sheffield Wed	Rotherham U (Am)	03.61				
Southampton	Tr	06.62	63	3	-	0
Brighton & Hove A	Tr	07.64	64	4	-	0

HENNIN Derek
Prescot, 28 December, 1931 Died 1989 EYth (WH)

League Club	Source	Date Signed	Seasons Played	Apps	Subs	Gls
Bolton W	Prescot Cables	06.49	53-60	164	-	8
Chester	Tr	02.61	60-61	54	-	4

HENNINGS Robert Iva
Glyncorrwg, 30 December, 1931 (WH)

League Club	Source	Date Signed	Seasons Played	Apps	Subs	Gls
Swansea T		01.49	55-56	10	-	1

HENRIKSEN Bo
Roskilde, Denmark, 7 February, 1975 (F)

League Club	Source	Date Signed	Seasons Played	Apps	Subs	Gls
Kidderminster Hrs	Herfolge (Den)	11.01	01-03	74	10	30
Bristol Rov	Tr	03.04	03	1	3	0

HENRY Anthony (Tony)
Houghton-le-Spring, 26 November, 1957 (M)

League Club	Source	Date Signed	Seasons Played	Apps	Subs	Gls
Manchester C	App	12.74	76-81	68	11	6
Bolton W	Tr	09.81	81-82	70	0	22
Oldham Ath	Tr	03.83	82-87	185	5	25
Stoke C	Tr	11.87	87-88	59	3	11
Shrewsbury T	Mazda Hiroshima (Jap)	08.91	91	39	1	7

HENRY Anthony Francis
Stepney, 13 September, 1979 (CD)

League Club	Source	Date Signed	Seasons Played	Apps	Subs	Gls
West Ham U	YT	06.97				
Lincoln C	Tr	08.99	99-00	15	3	1

HENRY Charles (Charlie) Anthony
Acton, 13 February, 1962 (M)

League Club	Source	Date Signed	Seasons Played	Apps	Subs	Gls
Swindon T	App	02.80	80-88	200	23	26
Torquay U	L	02.87	86	6	0	1
Northampton T	L	03.87	86	4	0	1
Aldershot	Tr	08.89	89-90	81	0	18

HENRY Gerald (Gerry) Robert
Hemsworth, 5 October, 1920 Died 1979 (IF)

League Club	Source	Date Signed	Seasons Played	Apps	Subs	Gls
Leeds U	Outwood Stormcocks	10.37	38-47	44	-	4
Bradford PA	Tr	11.47	47-49	79	-	31
Sheffield Wed	Tr	02.50	49-51	40	-	7
Halifax T	Tr	12.51	51-52	24	-	3

HENRY Gordon
Troon, 9 October, 1930 (CD)

League Club	Source	Date Signed	Seasons Played	Apps	Subs	Gls
Aldershot	St Mirren	06.56	56-63	175	-	15

HENRY Karl Levi Daniel
Wolverhampton, 26 November, 1982 EYth/Eu20 (M)

League Club	Source	Date Signed	Seasons Played	Apps	Subs	Gls
Stoke C	YT	11.99	01-04	52	44	1
Cheltenham T	L	01.04	03	8	1	1

HENRY Liburd Algernon
Roseau, Dominica, 29 August, 1967 (F)

League Club	Source	Date Signed	Seasons Played	Apps	Subs	Gls
Watford	Leytonstone & Ilford	11.87	88-89	8	2	1
Halifax T	L	09.88	88	1	4	0
Maidstone U	Tr	06.90	90-91	61	6	9
Gillingham	Tr	06.92	92-93	37	5	2
Peterborough U	Tr	08.94	94	22	10	7

HENRY Nicholas (Nick) Ian
Liverpool, 21 February, 1969 (M)

League Club	Source	Date Signed	Seasons Played	Apps	Subs	Gls
Oldham Ath	YT	07.87	87-96	264	9	19
Sheffield U	Tr	02.97	96-98	13	3	0
Walsall	Tr	03.99	98	8	0	0
Tranmere Rov	Tr	07.99	99-01	84	5	2

HENRY Ronald (Ron) Patrick
Shoreditch, 17 August, 1934 E-1 (FB)

League Club	Source	Date Signed	Seasons Played	Apps	Subs	Gls
Tottenham H	Radbourne	03.52	54-65	247	0	1

HENRY Ronnie Stephen
Hemel Hempstead, 2 January, 1984 (FB)

League Club	Source	Date Signed	Seasons Played	Apps	Subs	Gls
Tottenham H	Sch	07.02				
Southend U	L	03.03	02	3	0	0

HENRY Thierry
Paris, France, 17 August, 1977 FrYth/Fr-70 (F)

League Club	Source	Date Signed	Seasons Played	Apps	Subs	Gls
Arsenal	Juventus (It)	08.99	99-04	189	16	137

HENSHAW Gary
Leeds, 18 February, 1965 (W)

League Club	Source	Date Signed	Seasons Played	Apps	Subs	Gls
Grimsby T	App	02.83	83-86	46	4	9
Bolton W	Tr	06.87	87-90	49	21	4
Rochdale	L	03.90	89	8	1	1

HENSON Anthony (Tony) Harold
Dronfield, 15 October, 1960 (M)

League Club	Source	Date Signed	Seasons Played	Apps	Subs	Gls
Chesterfield	Alfreton T	11.81	81-82	26	2	0

HENSON Leonard (Len)
Hull, 6 August, 1921 (WH)

League Club	Source	Date Signed	Seasons Played	Apps	Subs	Gls
Gillingham		05.50	50-51	8	-	0

HENSON Philip (Phil) Michael
Manchester, 30 March, 1953 (M)

League Club	Source	Date Signed	Seasons Played	Apps	Subs	Gls
Manchester C	App	07.70	71-74	12	4	0
Swansea C	L	07.72	72	1	0	0
Sheffield Wed	Tr	02.75	74-76	65	8	9
Stockport Co	Sparta Rotterdam (Holl)	09.78	78-79	65	2	13
Rotherham U	Tr	02.80	79-83	87	5	7

HENWOOD Rodney (Rod) Charles
Portsmouth, 27 November, 1931 (W)

League Club	Source	Date Signed	Seasons Played	Apps	Subs	Gls
Portsmouth	Kingston BC	05.50	53	2	-	0

HEPBURN John
Paisley, 10 March, 1921 (W)

League Club	Source	Date Signed	Seasons Played	Apps	Subs	Gls
Workington	Alloa Ath	08.51	51	1	-	0

League Club	Source	Date Signed	Seasons Played	Apps	Subs	Gls

HEPPELL George
West Hartlepool, 2 September, 1916 Died 1993 (G)

League Club	Source	Date Signed	Seasons Played	Apps	Subs	Gls
Wolverhampton W		09.36				
Port Vale	Tr	05.37	37-51	193	-	0

HEPPLE Gordon
Sunderland, 16 September, 1925 Died 1980 (FB)

League Club	Source	Date Signed	Seasons Played	Apps	Subs	Gls
Middlesbrough	North Sands	07.45	46-53	41	-	0
Norwich C	Tr	06.54	54	5	-	0

HEPPLE John Andrew
Middlesbrough, 12 March, 1970 (F)

League Club	Source	Date Signed	Seasons Played	Apps	Subs	Gls
Sunderland	YT	07.87				
Hartlepool U	L	03.89	88	1	1	0

HEPPLEWHITE George
Edmondsley, 5 September, 1919 Died 1989 (CD)

League Club	Source	Date Signed	Seasons Played	Apps	Subs	Gls
Huddersfield T	Horden CW	05.39	46-50	156	-	3
Preston NE	Tr	03.51				
Bradford C	Tr	07.53	53-54	57	-	2

HEPPLEWHITE Wilson
Washington, 11 June, 1946 Died 2003 (CD)

League Club	Source	Date Signed	Seasons Played	Apps	Subs	Gls
Carlisle U	Crook T	03.65	65	2	0	0
Hartlepools U	Tr	07.67	67-68	50	2	2

HEPPOLETTE Richard (Ricky) Alfred William
Bhusawal, India, 8 April, 1949 (M)

League Club	Source	Date Signed	Seasons Played	Apps	Subs	Gls
Preston NE	App	09.64	67-72	149	5	13
Orient	Tr	12.72	72-76	113	0	10
Crystal Palace	Tr	10.76	76	13	2	0
Chesterfield	Tr	02.77	76-78	46	1	3
Peterborough U	Tr	08.79	79	5	0	0

HEPTON Stanley (Stan)
Leeds, 3 December, 1932 (IF)

League Club	Source	Date Signed	Seasons Played	Apps	Subs	Gls
Blackpool	Ashley Road	03.50	52-56	7	-	3
Huddersfield T	Tr	08.57	57-58	6	-	1
Bury	Tr	06.59	59	15	-	3
Rochdale	Tr	07.60	60-63	149	-	21
Southport	Tr	07.64	64	22	-	2

HEPWORTH Maurice
Hexham, 6 September, 1953 (FB)

League Club	Source	Date Signed	Seasons Played	Apps	Subs	Gls
Sunderland	App	09.70	70	2	0	0
Darlington	L	01.75	74	4	0	0

HEPWORTH Ronald (Ronnie)
Barnsley, 25 January, 1919 (FB)

League Club	Source	Date Signed	Seasons Played	Apps	Subs	Gls
Chesterfield		05.36				
Bradford PA	Tr	05.39	46-50	101	-	0

HERBERT Craig Justin
Coventry, 9 November, 1975 (CD)

League Club	Source	Date Signed	Seasons Played	Apps	Subs	Gls
West Bromwich A		03.94	94	8	0	0
Shrewsbury T	Tr	07.97	97-99	30	4	0

HERBERT David Ronald
Sheffield, 23 January, 1956 (F)

League Club	Source	Date Signed	Seasons Played	Apps	Subs	Gls
Sheffield Wed	App	01.74	74-75	12	5	5

HERBERT Frank
Stocksbridge, 29 June, 1916 Died 1972 (WH)

League Club	Source	Date Signed	Seasons Played	Apps	Subs	Gls
Sheffield Wed	Oughtibridge	05.38				
Bury	Tr	10.45				
Oldham Ath	Tr	06.46	46	4	-	0

HERBERT Rikki Lloyd
Auckland, New Zealand, 10 April, 1961 New Zealand int (CD)

League Club	Source	Date Signed	Seasons Played	Apps	Subs	Gls
Wolverhampton W	Sydney Olympic (Aus)	10.84	84-85	44	1	0

HERBERT Robert (Bobby)
Glasgow, 21 November, 1925 (WH)

League Club	Source	Date Signed	Seasons Played	Apps	Subs	Gls
Doncaster Rov	Blantyre Victoria	06.50	50-55	108	-	15

HERBERT Robert
Durham, 29 August, 1983 (M)

League Club	Source	Date Signed	Seasons Played	Apps	Subs	Gls
Halifax T	YT	10.00	99-01	15	10	0

HERBERT William Stanley **(Stan)**
Whitehaven, 29 August, 1946 (IF)

League Club	Source	Date Signed	Seasons Played	Apps	Subs	Gls
Workington (Am)	Jnrs	09.66	66	1	0	0

HERBERT Trevor Ernest
Reading, 3 June, 1929 (CF)

League Club	Source	Date Signed	Seasons Played	Apps	Subs	Gls
Leyton Orient		08.49				
Crystal Palace	Tr	07.50	50	8	-	2

HERD Alexander (Alex)
Bowhill, 8 November, 1911 Died 1982 SWar-1 (IF)

League Club	Source	Date Signed	Seasons Played	Apps	Subs	Gls
Manchester C	Hamilton Academical	02.33	32-47	257	-	107
Stockport Co	Tr	03.48	47-51	111	-	35

HERD David George
Hamilton, 15 April, 1934 S-5 (F)

League Club	Source	Date Signed	Seasons Played	Apps	Subs	Gls
Stockport Co	Jnrs	04.51	50-53	15	-	6
Arsenal	Tr	08.54	54-60	166	-	97
Manchester U	Tr	07.61	61-67	201	1	114
Stoke C	Tr	07.68	68-69	39	5	11

HERD George
Gartcosh, 6 May, 1936 Su23-2/SLge-3/S-5 (M)

League Club	Source	Date Signed	Seasons Played	Apps	Subs	Gls
Sunderland	Clyde	04.61	60-68	275	2	47
Hartlepool	Tr	06.70	70	10	5	0

HERD Stuart Alexander Laws
Tittensor, 25 February, 1974 (M)

League Club	Source	Date Signed	Seasons Played	Apps	Subs	Gls
Torquay U	Rossington Main	10.92	92	5	2	0

HERITAGE Peter Mark
Bexhill, 8 November, 1960 (F)

League Club	Source	Date Signed	Seasons Played	Apps	Subs	Gls
Gillingham	Hythe T	08.89	89-90	42	15	11
Hereford U	Tr	02.91	90-91	55	2	9
Doncaster Rov	Tr	07.92	92	25	6	2

HERIVELTO Moreira
Tres Rios, Brazil, 23 August, 1975 (M)

League Club	Source	Date Signed	Seasons Played	Apps	Subs	Gls
Walsall	Cruizero (Br)	08.01	01-02	11	17	5
Walsall	Ionikos (Gre)	12.04	04	0	1	0

HERNON James (Jimmy)
Cleland, 6 December, 1924 (IF)

League Club	Source	Date Signed	Seasons Played	Apps	Subs	Gls
Leicester C	Mossvale YMCA	04.42	46-47	31	-	7
Bolton W	Tr	09.48	48-50	43	-	2
Grimsby T	Tr	08.51	51-53	91	-	23
Watford	Tr	07.54	54-55	43	-	10

HEROD Dennis John
Stoke-on-Trent, 27 October, 1923 (G)

League Club	Source	Date Signed	Seasons Played	Apps	Subs	Gls
Stoke C	Trent Vale U	01.41	46-52	191	-	1
Stockport Co	Tr	07.53	53	33	-	0

HERON Brian
Dumbarton, 19 June, 1948 (W)

League Club	Source	Date Signed	Seasons Played	Apps	Subs	Gls
Oxford U	Dumbarton	07.74	74-76	40	3	8
Scunthorpe U	Tr	07.77	77	20	5	1

HERON Daniel (Danny) Craig
Cambridge, 9 October, 1986 (M)

League Club	Source	Date Signed	Seasons Played	Apps	Subs	Gls
Mansfield T	Sch	•	04	1	2	0

HERON Thomas (Tommy) Russell Ferrie
Irvine, 31 March, 1936 (FB)

League Club	Source	Date Signed	Seasons Played	Apps	Subs	Gls
Manchester U	Portadown	03.58	57-60	3	-	0
York C	Tr	05.61	61-65	192	0	6

HERON William Bolton
Washington, 29 March, 1932 (W)

League Club	Source	Date Signed	Seasons Played	Apps	Subs	Gls
Gateshead		02.55	54-56	22	-	1

HERRERA Horacio **Martin**
Rio Puerto, Argentina, 13 September, 1970 (G)

League Club	Source	Date Signed	Seasons Played	Apps	Subs	Gls
Fulham	Dep Alaves (Sp)	07.02	02	1	1	0

HERRERA Roberto (Robbie)
Torquay, 12 June, 1970 (FB)

League Club	Source	Date Signed	Seasons Played	Apps	Subs	Gls
Queens Park Rgrs	YT	03.88	88-90	4	2	0
Torquay U	L	03.92	91	11	0	0
Torquay U	L	10.92	92	5	0	0
Fulham	Tr	10.93	93-97	143	2	1
Torquay U	Tr	08.98	98-01	104	3	1
Leyton Orient	Tr	10.01	01	2	0	0

HERRING David **Harry**
Hartlepool, 4 January, 1939 (W)

League Club	Source	Date Signed	Seasons Played	Apps	Subs	Gls
Hartlepools U	Caledonians	08.58	58	2	-	0

HERRING Ian
Swindon, 14 February, 1984 (M)

League Club	Source	Date Signed	Seasons Played	Apps	Subs	Gls
Swindon T	Sch	07.03	01-03	3	3	0

HERRING Paul John
Hyde, 1 July, 1973 (M)

League Club	Source	Date Signed	Seasons Played	Apps	Subs	Gls
Rochdale	YT	07.91	90	0	1	0

HERRINGTON Eric
Rotherham, 30 October, 1943 (WH)

League Club	Source	Date Signed	Seasons Played	Apps	Subs	Gls
Doncaster Rov	Jnrs	01.61	61	1	-	0

HERRIOT James (Jim)
Airdrie, 20 December, 1939 SLge-2/S-8 (G)

League Club	Source	Date Signed	Seasons Played	Apps	Subs	Gls
Birmingham C	Dunfermline Ath	05.65	65-69	181	0	0
Mansfield T	L	11.70	70	5	0	0

League Club	Source	Date Signed	Seasons Played	Career Record Apps	Subs	Gls
HERRITY Alan Michael						
Newport, 24 October, 1941 WSch						(FB)
Newport Co	Jnrs	12.58	59-61	28	-	0
HERRITY William (Billy) Raymond						
Newport, 2 September, 1938						(IF)
Newport Co	Jnrs	05.57	56-62	62	-	11
HERRON Alan						
Washington, 6 October, 1932						(CD)
Blackburn Rov	Newcastle U (Am)	08.50	55-56	4	-	0
HERRON John						
Widdrington, 2 March, 1938						(WH)
Leeds U		10.56				
Gateshead	Tr	06.57	57-58	8	-	0
HERVE Laurent						
Quimper, France, 19 June, 1976						(M)
MK Dons	Guingamp (Fr)	08.04	04	15	5	0
HERZIG Nico						
Pobneck, Germany, 10 December, 1983						(M)
Wimbledon	Carl Zeiss Jena (Ger)	10.01	03	18	1	0
HESELTINE George Victor						
Wolverhampton, 25 March, 1926						(IF)
Walsall	Hednesford T	02.49	48-49	8	-	0
HESELTINE Wayne Alan						
Bradford, 3 December, 1969						(FB)
Manchester U	YT	12.87				
Oldham Ath	Tr	12.89	89	1	0	0
Bradford C	Tr	08.92	92-93	51	3	1
HESFORD Iain						
Ndola, Zambia, 4 March, 1960 EYth/Eu21-7						(G)
Blackpool	App	08.77	77-82	202	0	0
Sheffield Wed	Tr	08.83				
Fulham	L	01.85	84	3	0	0
Notts Co	L	11.85	85	10	0	0
Sunderland	Tr	08.86	86-88	97	0	0
Hull C	Tr	12.88	88-90	91	0	0
Maidstone U	Tr	08.91	91	42	0	1
HESFORD Robert (Bob) Taylor						
Bolton, 13 April, 1916 Died 1982						(G)
Huddersfield T	South Shore	09.33	34-49	203	-	0
HESKEY Emile William Ivanhoe						
Leicester, 11 January, 1978 EYth/Eu21-16/EB-1/E-43						(F)
Leicester C	YT	10.95	94-99	143	11	40
Liverpool	Tr	03.00	99-03	118	32	39
Birmingham C	Tr	07.04	04	34	0	10
HESLOP Brian						
Carlisle, 4 August, 1947						(FB)
Carlisle U	App	08.65	65-66	4	0	0
Sunderland	Tr	05.67	67-70	57	1	0
Northampton T	Tr	03.71	70-71	49	1	0
Workington	Tr	09.72	72-75	139	1	5
HESLOP George Wilson						
Wallsend, 1 July, 1940						(CD)
Newcastle U	Dudley Welfare	02.59	59-61	27	-	0
Everton	Tr	03.62	62-65	10	0	0
Manchester C	Tr	09.65	65-71	159	3	1
Bury	Tr	08.72	72	37	0	0
HESLOP Norman						
Bolton, 2 August, 1920						(IF)
Southport	Bolton W (Am)	10.46	46-47	30	-	4
HESSENTHALER Andrew (Andy)						
Gravesend, 17 August, 1965 ESemiPro-1						(M)
Watford	Redbridge Forest	09.91	91-95	195	0	12
Gillingham	Tr	08.96	96-04	259	28	19
Hull C	L	01.05	04	6	4	0
HESSEY Sean Peter						
Whiston, 19 September, 1978						(CD)
Leeds U	Liverpool (YT)	09.97				
Wigan Ath	Tr	12.97				
Huddersfield T	Tr	03.98	97-98	7	4	0
Blackpool	Kilmarnock	02.04	03	4	2	0
Chester C	Tr	07.04	04	31	3	1
HETHERINGTON Robert **Brent**						
Carlisle, 6 December, 1961						(F)
Carlisle U	Workington	08.87	87-89	61	27	23
HETHERINGTON Henry (Harry)						
Chester-le-Street, 7 November, 1928 Died 1987						(W)
Sunderland	Shiney Row St O	05.46	47	2	-	0
Gateshead	Tr	01.49	48	2	-	1
HETHERINGTON Thomas (Tom) Burns						
Walker, 22 January, 1911 Died 1968						(G)
Burnley	Walker Celtic	12.33	33-37	67	-	0
Barnsley	Jarrow	02.39				
Gateshead	Tr	10.46	46	1	-	0
HETHERSTON Peter						
Bellshill, 6 November, 1964						(M)
Watford	Falkirk	07.87	87	2	3	0
Sheffield U	Tr	02.88	87	11	0	0
HETZKE Stephen (Steve) Edward Richard						
Marlborough, 3 June, 1955						(CD)
Reading	App	06.73	71-81	254	7	23
Blackpool	Tr	07.82	82-85	140	0	18
Sunderland	Tr	03.86	85-86	31	0	0
Chester C	Tr	06.87	87	14	0	0
Colchester U	Tr	03.88	87-88	27	2	2
HEVICON Ryan						
Manchester, 3 December, 1982						(M)
Blackburn Rov	YT	07.01				
Carlisle U	Tr	08.02	02	0	1	0
HEWARD Brian John						
Lincoln, 17 July, 1935						(CD)
Scunthorpe U	Jnrs	03.54	53-60	137	-	0
Lincoln C	Tr	07.61	61-63	72	-	2
Lincoln C	Bankstown (Aus)	11.64	64-65	25	0	0
HEWARD Graham Keith						
Newcastle, 13 October, 1965						(CD)
Cambridge U	App	10.83	83	1	0	0
HEWIE John Davidson						
Pretoria, South Africa, 13 December, 1927 Su23-1/SB/S-19						(WH)
Charlton Ath	Arcadia Shepherds (SA)	10.49	51-65	495	0	37
HEWITT Daren Peter						
Chichester, 1 September, 1969						(M)
Aldershot	YT	08.88	88	0	2	0
HEWITT Gerald						
Sheffield, 28 January, 1935						(WH)
Sheffield U	Jnrs	07.54	56	2	-	0
HEWITT Harold						
Chesterfield, 24 June, 1919						(W)
Mansfield T	Chesterfield (Am)	11.45	46	1	-	0
HEWITT James (Jamie) Robert						
Chesterfield, 17 May, 1968						(FB)
Chesterfield	App	04.86	85-91	240	9	14
Doncaster Rov	Tr	08.92	92-93	32	1	0
Chesterfield	Tr	10.93	93-01	248	9	12
HEWITT John						
Aberdeen, 9 February, 1963 SSch/SYth/Su21-6						(M)
Middlesbrough (L)	Glasgow Celtic	09.91	91	0	2	0
HEWITT Leonard (Len)						
Wrexham, 20 March, 1920 Died 1979						(CF)
Wrexham		05.46	46	5	-	2
HEWITT Martin (Marty)						
Hartlepool, 24 July, 1965						(F)
Hartlepool U	St James'	08.84	85-86	11	3	2
HEWITT Richard (Dick)						
Moorthorpe, 25 May, 1943						(M)
Huddersfield T	Moorthorpe St J OB	05.61				
Bradford C	Tr	07.64	64	20	-	7
Barnsley	Tr	07.65	65-68	97	2	20
York C	Tr	03.69	68-71	87	4	7
HEWITT Ronald (Ron)						
Chesterfield, 25 January, 1924						(G)
Sheffield U	Youlgreave	11.44				
Lincoln C	Tr	08.46	48	3	-	0
HEWITT Ronald (Ron)						
Flint, 21 June, 1928 Died 2001 W-5						(IF)
Wolverhampton W		07.48				
Walsall	Tr	10.49	49	8	-	2
Darlington	Tr	06.50	50	36	-	3
Wrexham	Tr	07.51	51-56	204	-	83

League Club	Source	Date Signed	Seasons Played	Apps	Subs	Gls
Cardiff C	Tr	06.57	57-58	65	-	27
Wrexham	Tr	07.59	59	27	-	11
Coventry C	Tr	03.60	59-61	59	-	23
Chester	Tr	03.62	61-62	29	-	6

HEWITT Stephen (Steve)
Hull, 17 April, 1973 (G)

League Club	Source	Date Signed	Seasons Played	Apps	Subs	Gls
Scarborough	YT	01.92	91	2	0	0

HEWKINS Kenneth (Ken) John Robert
Pretoria, South Africa, 30 October, 1929 (G)

League Club	Source	Date Signed	Seasons Played	Apps	Subs	Gls
Fulham	Clyde	11.55	55-61	38	-	0

HEWLETT Matthew (Matt) Paul
Bristol, 25 February, 1976 EYth (M)

League Club	Source	Date Signed	Seasons Played	Apps	Subs	Gls
Bristol C	YT	08.93	93-99	111	16	9
Burnley	L	11.98	98	2	0	0
Swindon T	Tr	07.00	00-04	175	4	6

HEWS Chay
Norrkoping, Sweden, 30 September, 1976 (F)

League Club	Source	Date Signed	Seasons Played	Apps	Subs	Gls
Carlisle U	IF Sylvia (Swe)	09.01	01	4	1	2

HEWSON Patrick (Pat) Carroll
Gateshead, 2 June, 1926 (FB)

League Club	Source	Date Signed	Seasons Played	Apps	Subs	Gls
West Bromwich A	Crook T	11.50				
Gateshead	Tr	07.53	53-57	131	-	0

HEY Antoine (Tony)
Berlin, Germany, 19 September, 1970 (M)

League Club	Source	Date Signed	Seasons Played	Apps	Subs	Gls
Birmingham C	Fortuna Cologne (Ger)	06.97	97	8	1	0

HEYDON Cecil
Birkenhead, 24 May, 1919 (WH)

League Club	Source	Date Signed	Seasons Played	Apps	Subs	Gls
New Brighton	Victory Social	02.39	38	1	-	0
Derby Co	Tr	06.39				
Doncaster Rov	Tr	10.45	46-47	6	-	0
Rochdale	Tr	07.48	48	1	-	0

HEYDON John (Jackie)
Birkenhead, 19 October, 1928 (WH)

League Club	Source	Date Signed	Seasons Played	Apps	Subs	Gls
Liverpool	Everton (Am)	01.49	50-52	63	-	0
Millwall	Tr	05.53	53-55	75	-	1
Tranmere Rov	Tr	07.56	56-60	76	-	1

HEYES Darren Lee
Swansea, 11 January, 1967 ESch/EYth (G)

League Club	Source	Date Signed	Seasons Played	Apps	Subs	Gls
Nottingham F	App	01.84				
Wrexham	L	01.87	86	2	0	0
Scunthorpe U	Tr	07.87	87	3	0	0

HEYES George
Bolton, 16 November, 1937 (G)

League Club	Source	Date Signed	Seasons Played	Apps	Subs	Gls
Rochdale	Jnrs	04.56	58-59	24	-	0
Leicester C	Tr	07.60	60-65	25	0	0
Swansea T	Tr	09.65	65-68	99	0	0
Barrow	Tr	07.69	69	26	0	0

HEYES Kenneth (Ken)
Haydock, 4 January, 1936 ESch/EYth (FB)

League Club	Source	Date Signed	Seasons Played	Apps	Subs	Gls
Everton	Jnrs	02.53				
Preston NE	Tr	05.57	59	3	-	0

HEYS Michael (Mike)
Preston, 23 June, 1938 (G)

League Club	Source	Date Signed	Seasons Played	Apps	Subs	Gls
Preston NE	Jnrs	05.57				
Barrow	Tr	03.59	58-61	70	-	0
Workington	Tr	08.62				
Halifax T		11.63	63	1	-	0

HEYWOOD Albert Edwards
Hartlepool, 12 May, 1913 Died 1989 (G)

League Club	Source	Date Signed	Seasons Played	Apps	Subs	Gls
Sunderland	Spennymoor U	03.37	38	4	-	0
Hartlepools U	Tr	05.46	46	39	-	0

HEYWOOD David Ian
Wolverhampton, 25 July, 1967 (FB)

League Club	Source	Date Signed	Seasons Played	Apps	Subs	Gls
Wolverhampton W	App	11.84	84	7	0	0

HEYWOOD Matthew (Matt) Stephen
Chatham, 26 August, 1979 (CD)

League Club	Source	Date Signed	Seasons Played	Apps	Subs	Gls
Burnley	YT	07.98	98	11	2	0
Swindon T	Tr	01.01	00-04	176	7	8

HIBBARD Mark Andrew
Hereford, 12 August, 1977 (FB)

League Club	Source	Date Signed	Seasons Played	Apps	Subs	Gls
Hereford U	YT	07.96	96	5	2	1

HIBBERD Stuart
Sheffield, 11 October, 1961 (W)

League Club	Source	Date Signed	Seasons Played	Apps	Subs	Gls
Lincoln C	App	10.79	80-82	36	6	3

HIBBERT Anthony (Tony) James
Liverpool, 20 February, 1981 (FB)

League Club	Source	Date Signed	Seasons Played	Apps	Subs	Gls
Everton	YT	07.98	00-04	90	8	0

HIBBERT David (Dave) John
Eccleshall, 28 January, 1986 (FB)

League Club	Source	Date Signed	Seasons Played	Apps	Subs	Gls
Port Vale	Sch	●	04	2	7	2

HIBBITT Kenneth (Ken)
Bradford, 3 January, 1951 Eu23-1 (M)

League Club	Source	Date Signed	Seasons Played	Apps	Subs	Gls
Bradford PA	App	11.68	67-68	13	2	0
Wolverhampton W	Seattle Sounders	10.82	82-83	46	8	2
Coventry C	Tr	08.84	84-85	42	5	4
Bristol Rov	Tr	08.86	86-88	51	2	5

HIBBITT Terence (Terry) Arthur
Bradford, 1 December, 1947 Died 1994 (W)

League Club	Source	Date Signed	Seasons Played	Apps	Subs	Gls
Leeds U	Jnrs	12.64	65-70	32	15	9
Newcastle U	Tr	08.71	71-75	138	0	7
Birmingham C	Tr	08.75	75-77	110	0	11
Newcastle U	Tr	05.78	78-80	89	1	5

HIBBS Gary Thomas
Hammersmith, 26 January, 1957 (M)

League Club	Source	Date Signed	Seasons Played	Apps	Subs	Gls
Orient	App	07.74	75	1	0	0
Aldershot	L	02.77	76	4	2	0

HIBBURT James (Jimmy) Anthony
Ashford, 30 October, 1979 ESch (CD)

League Club	Source	Date Signed	Seasons Played	Apps	Subs	Gls
Crystal Palace	YT	11.96	98-99	1	5	0

HICK Leslie (Les) David
York, 23 April, 1927 (W)

League Club	Source	Date Signed	Seasons Played	Apps	Subs	Gls
Bradford C		07.48	48	1	-	0

HICKIE George Noel Ellerton
Hawarden, 25 December, 1922 Died 1994 (FB)

League Club	Source	Date Signed	Seasons Played	Apps	Subs	Gls
Barnsley		05.46				
Carlisle U	Tr	09.46	46	1	-	0

HICKLIN Albert **William (Bill)**
Dudley, 20 September, 1924 (WH)

League Club	Source	Date Signed	Seasons Played	Apps	Subs	Gls
Birmingham C	West Bromwich A (Am)	03.45				
Watford	Tr	06.47	47	21	-	5

HICKMAN Geoffrey (Geoff) Brian
West Bromwich, 7 January, 1950 (G)

League Club	Source	Date Signed	Seasons Played	Apps	Subs	Gls
West Bromwich A	App	01.68				
Bradford PA	Tr	06.69	69	9	0	0

HICKMAN Michael (Mike) Frederick Thomas
Elstead, 2 October, 1946 (F)

League Club	Source	Date Signed	Seasons Played	Apps	Subs	Gls
Brighton & Hove A	Jnrs	06.65	65-67	12	3	0
Grimsby T	Tr	06.68	68-74	247	7	48
Blackburn Rov	Tr	02.75	74-75	23	3	8
Torquay U	Tr	10.75	75-76	17	0	1

HICKS Anthony (Tony) John
Swindon, 20 August, 1945 (G)

League Club	Source	Date Signed	Seasons Played	Apps	Subs	Gls
Swindon T	App	10.62	64-66	51	0	0

HICKS David Christopher
Enfield, 13 November, 1985 (M)

League Club	Source	Date Signed	Seasons Played	Apps	Subs	Gls
Northampton T	Tottenham H (Sch)	02.04	04	1	2	0

HICKS Graham
Oldham, 17 February, 1981 (FB)

League Club	Source	Date Signed	Seasons Played	Apps	Subs	Gls
Rochdale	YT	01.99	98	1	0	0

HICKS James (Jim) Michael
Ipswich, 16 September, 1960 (CD)

League Club	Source	Date Signed	Seasons Played	Apps	Subs	Gls
Exeter C	Warwick Univ	09.83	83	3	0	0
Oxford U	Tr	08.84				
Fulham	Tr	08.85	85-87	39	1	1

HICKS Keith
Oldham, 9 August, 1954 EYth (CD)

League Club	Source	Date Signed	Seasons Played	Apps	Subs	Gls
Oldham Ath	App	08.72	71-79	240	2	11
Hereford U	Tr	09.80	80-84	201	0	2
Rochdale	Tr	07.85	85-86	32	0	1

HICKS Mark
Belfast, 24 July, 1981 (F)

League Club	Source	Date Signed	Seasons Played	Apps	Subs	Gls
Millwall	Jnrs	07.98	98	0	1	0

HICKS Martin
Stratford-on-Avon, 27 February, 1957 (CD)

League Club	Source	Date Signed	Seasons Played	Apps	Subs	Gls
Charlton Ath	Stratford T	02.77				
Reading	Tr	02.78	77-90	499	1	23
Birmingham C	Tr	08.91	91-92	57	3	1

HICKS Stuart Jason
Peterborough, 30 May, 1967 (CD)

League Club	Source	Date Signed	Seasons Played	Apps	Subs	Gls
Peterborough U	App	08.84				
Colchester U	Wisbech T	03.88	87-89	57	7	0
Scunthorpe U	Tr	08.90	90-91	67	0	1
Doncaster Rov	Tr	08.92	92	36	0	0
Huddersfield T	Tr	08.93	93	20	2	1
Preston NE	Tr	03.94	93-94	11	1	0
Scarborough	Tr	02.95	94-96	81	4	2
Leyton Orient	Tr	08.97	97-99	77	1	1
Chester C	Tr	02.00	99	13	0	0
Mansfield T	Tr	07.00	00	25	0	0

HICKSON David (Dave)
Salford, 30 October, 1929 (CF)

League Club	Source	Date Signed	Seasons Played	Apps	Subs	Gls
Everton	Ellesmere Port T	05.48	51-55	139	-	63
Aston Villa	Tr	09.55	55	12	-	1
Huddersfield T	Tr	11.55	55-56	54	-	28
Everton	Tr	08.57	57-59	86	-	32
Liverpool	Tr	11.59	59-60	60	-	37
Bury	Cambridge C	01.62	61	8	-	0
Tranmere Rov	Tr	08.62	62-63	45	-	21

HICKSON George Geoffrey (Geoff)
Crewe, 26 September, 1939 (G)

League Club	Source	Date Signed	Seasons Played	Apps	Subs	Gls
Stoke C	Blackburn Rov (Am)	08.57	59-60	11	-	0
Crewe Alex	Tr	07.62	62-66	104	0	0
Port Vale	L	08.68	68	17	0	0
Southport	Tr	12.68	68	3	0	0

HICKTON John
Brimington, 24 September, 1944 (F)

League Club	Source	Date Signed	Seasons Played	Apps	Subs	Gls
Sheffield Wed	Jnrs	01.62	63-65	52	1	21
Middlesbrough	Tr	09.66	66-77	395	20	159
Hull C	L	01.77	76	6	0	1

HICKTON Roy
Chesterfield, 19 September, 1948 (FB)

League Club	Source	Date Signed	Seasons Played	Apps	Subs	Gls
Chesterfield	App	11.65	68-70	47	2	1

HIDEN Martin
Stainz, Austria, 11 March, 1973 Austria 7 (CD)

League Club	Source	Date Signed	Seasons Played	Apps	Subs	Gls
Leeds U	Rapid Vienna (Aut)	02.98	97-99	25	1	0

HIERRO Fernando Ruiz
Velez, Spain, 23 March, 1968 Spain 89 (CD)

League Club	Source	Date Signed	Seasons Played	Apps	Subs	Gls
Bolton W	Al Rayyan (Qatar)	07.04	04	15	14	1

HIGDON Michael
Liverpool, 2 September, 1983 (M)

League Club	Source	Date Signed	Seasons Played	Apps	Subs	Gls
Crewe Alex	YT	02.01	03-04	8	22	4

HIGGINBOTHAM Daniel (Danny) John
Manchester, 29 December, 1978 (FB)

League Club	Source	Date Signed	Seasons Played	Apps	Subs	Gls
Manchester U	YT	07.97	97-99	2	2	0
Derby Co	Tr	07.00	00-02	82	4	3
Southampton	Tr	01.03	02-04	47	10	1

HIGGINBOTTOM Andrew (Andy) John
Chesterfield, 22 October, 1964 (W)

League Club	Source	Date Signed	Seasons Played	Apps	Subs	Gls
Chesterfield	App	10.82	82	1	2	0
Everton	Tr	07.83				
Cambridge U	Tr	08.84	84	1	0	0
Crystal Palace		09.85	85-86	16	7	2

HIGGINBOTTOM Michael (Mike)
Sheffield, 13 October, 1962 (M)

League Club	Source	Date Signed	Seasons Played	Apps	Subs	Gls
Chesterfield		08.83	83	4	1	0

HIGGINS Alexander (Alex) John
Sheffield, 22 July, 1981 ESch/EYth (M)

League Club	Source	Date Signed	Seasons Played	Apps	Subs	Gls
Sheffield Wed	YT	11.98				
Queens Park Rgrs	Tr	03.01	00	0	1	0
Boston U	Stalybridge Celtic	10.02	02	13	0	0

HIGGINS Andrew (Andy) Martin
Bolsover, 12 February, 1960 (CD)

League Club	Source	Date Signed	Seasons Played	Apps	Subs	Gls
Chesterfield	App	02.78	78	1	0	0
Port Vale	Tr	02.81	80-81	11	3	0
Hartlepool U	King's Lynn	09.82	82	3	1	1
Rochdale	King's Lynn	03.83	82-83	31	2	6
Chester C	Tr	07.84	84	16	3	1

HIGGINS Augustine (Ossie) Robert
Dublin, 19 January, 1931 Died 2000 (CF)

League Club	Source	Date Signed	Seasons Played	Apps	Subs	Gls
Aston Villa	Shamrock Rov	11.49				
Ipswich T	Tr	07.52	52	2	-	0

HIGGINS Charles
Bellshill, 12 May, 1921 (FB)

League Club	Source	Date Signed	Seasons Played	Apps	Subs	Gls
Chester	Arbroath	08.46	46	11	-	0

HIGGINS David (Dave) Anthony
Liverpool, 19 August, 1961 (FB)

League Club	Source	Date Signed	Seasons Played	Apps	Subs	Gls
Tranmere Rov	Eagle	08.83	83-84	27	1	0
Tranmere Rov	Caernarfon T	07.87	87-96	315	4	12

HIGGINS Frederick (Fred) Thomas
Hackney, 21 January, 1930 (CD)

League Club	Source	Date Signed	Seasons Played	Apps	Subs	Gls
Crystal Palace	Wood Green	03.52	52-53	11	-	0

HIGGINS George
Dundee, 16 June, 1925 Died 1993 (FB)

League Club	Source	Date Signed	Seasons Played	Apps	Subs	Gls
Blackburn Rov	Lochee Harp	10.46	46-50	53	-	0
Bolton W	Tr	07.51	51-53	69	-	0
Grimsby T	Tr	05.54	54-56	47	-	0

HIGGINS George
Batley, 12 September, 1932 (FB)

League Club	Source	Date Signed	Seasons Played	Apps	Subs	Gls
Huddersfield T	Jnrs	12.49				
Halifax T	Tr	07.57	57	5	-	0

HIGGINS James (Jimmy)
Dublin, 3 February, 1926 IR-1 (IF)

League Club	Source	Date Signed	Seasons Played	Apps	Subs	Gls
Birmingham C	Dundalk	11.49	49-52	50	-	12

HIGGINS John Oldfield
Bakewell, 15 November, 1932 Died 2005 (CD)

League Club	Source	Date Signed	Seasons Played	Apps	Subs	Gls
Bolton W	Buxton	10.50	52-60	183	-	0

HIGGINS John Wilson
Kilmarnock, 27 January, 1933 (FB)

League Club	Source	Date Signed	Seasons Played	Apps	Subs	Gls
Swindon T	St Mirren	05.59	59-60	28	-	0

HIGGINS Mark Nicholas
Buxton, 29 September, 1958 ESch/EYth (CD)

League Club	Source	Date Signed	Seasons Played	Apps	Subs	Gls
Everton	App	08.76	76-83	150	1	6
Manchester U	(Retired)	12.85	85	6	0	0
Bury	Tr	01.87	86-88	67	1	0
Stoke C	Tr	09.88	88-89	37	2	1

HIGGINS Michael (Mick)
Haslingden, 5 September, 1956 (W)

League Club	Source	Date Signed	Seasons Played	Apps	Subs	Gls
Blackburn Rov	App	12.73				
Workington	Tr	07.76	76	11	4	1

HIGGINS Peter
Blidworth, 1 August, 1944 (CD)

League Club	Source	Date Signed	Seasons Played	Apps	Subs	Gls
Oxford U	Blidworth YC	07.62	62-68	35	5	0
Crewe Alex	Tr	06.69	69-71	56	1	0

HIGGINS Peter Clive
Cardiff, 12 November, 1950 (W)

League Club	Source	Date Signed	Seasons Played	Apps	Subs	Gls
Bristol Rov	App	02.69	68-72	36	0	5
Doncaster Rov	Tr	07.73	73-75	63	5	10
Torquay U	L	03.76	75	3	1	1

HIGGINS Robert (Bob) James
Bolsover, 23 December, 1958 ESch (CD)

League Club	Source	Date Signed	Seasons Played	Apps	Subs	Gls
Burnley	App	07.76	77	3	0	0
Hartlepool U	L	11.79	79	2	0	0
Rochdale	Tr	10.80	80	4	1	0

HIGGINS Ronald (Ronnie) Valentine
Silvertown, 14 February, 1923 (CF)

League Club	Source	Date Signed	Seasons Played	Apps	Subs	Gls
Leyton Orient (Am)	Green & Siley Weir	12.49	49	2	-	0
Brighton & Hove A	Tonbridge	01.52	51	8	-	0
Queens Park Rgrs	Tr	01.53	52	3	-	1

HIGGINS William Charles
Birkenhead, 26 February, 1924 Died 1981 (W)

League Club	Source	Date Signed	Seasons Played	Apps	Subs	Gls
Everton	Tranmere Rov (Am)	03.46	46-49	48	-	8

HIGGINSON Thomas (Tom)
Newtongrange, 6 January, 1937 (M)

League Club	Source	Date Signed	Seasons Played	Apps	Subs	Gls
Brentford	Kilmarnock	06.59	59-69	383	4	15

HIGGS Shane Peter
Oxford, 13 May, 1977 (G)

League Club	Source	Date Signed	Seasons Played	Apps	Subs	Gls
Bristol Rov	YT	07.95	96-97	10	0	0
Cheltenham T	Worcester C	06.99	00-04	98	2	0

HIGH David Henry
Reading, 22 February, 1941 EYth (FB)

League Club	Source	Date Signed	Seasons Played	Apps	Subs	Gls
Reading	Jnrs	02.58	59-63	72	-	2

HIGH Sidney (Sid) William
Waterbeach, 30 September, 1922 (W)

League Club	Source	Date Signed	Seasons Played	Apps	Subs	Gls
Luton T	Abbey U	10.46				
Watford	Tr	08.48	48	7	-	3

HIGHAM John Peter
West Derby, 22 November, 1954 (CD)

League Club	Source	Date Signed	Seasons Played	Apps	Subs	Gls
Liverpool	App	05.74				
Southport	Tr	01.76	75-77	96	0	1

HIGHAM Peter
Wigan, 8 November, 1930 (CF)

League Club	Source	Date Signed	Seasons Played	Apps	Subs	Gls
Portsmouth (Am)	Wigan Ath	11.49	49	1	-	0
Bolton W	Tr	11.50				
Preston NE	Tr	05.52	53-54	15	-	10
Nottingham F	Tr	08.55	55-57	61	-	20
Doncaster Rov	Tr	03.58	57-58	22	-	6

HIGNETT Alan James
Liverpool, 1 November, 1946 ESch (FB)

League Club	Source	Date Signed	Seasons Played	Apps	Subs	Gls
Liverpool	App	11.63	64	1	-	0
Chester	Tr	08.66	66	6	0	0

HIGNETT Craig John
Prescot, 12 January, 1970 (M)

League Club	Source	Date Signed	Seasons Played	Apps	Subs	Gls
Crewe Alex	Liverpool (App)	05.88	88-92	108	13	42
Middlesbrough	Tr	11.92	92-97	126	30	33
Barnsley	Aberdeen	11.98	98-99	62	4	28
Blackburn Rov	Tr	07.00	00-02	20	33	8
Coventry C	L	11.02	02	7	1	2
Leicester C	Tr	07.03	03	3	10	1
Crewe Alex	L	02.04	03	11	4	0
Darlington	Tr	09.04	04	17	2	9

HILAIRE Vince Mark
Forest Hill, 10 October, 1959 EYth/Eu21-9/EB (W)

League Club	Source	Date Signed	Seasons Played	Apps	Subs	Gls
Crystal Palace	App	10.76	76-83	239	16	29
Luton T	Tr	07.84	84	5	1	0
Portsmouth	Tr	11.84	84-87	144	2	25
Leeds U	Tr	07.88	88-89	42	2	6
Stoke C	L	11.89	89	5	0	1
Stoke C	Tr	11.90	90	10	0	2
Exeter C	Tr	09.91	91	24	9	4

HILDERSLEY Ronald (Ronnie)
Kirkcaldy, 6 April, 1965 (M)

League Club	Source	Date Signed	Seasons Played	Apps	Subs	Gls
Manchester C	App	04.83	82	1	0	0
Chester C	L	01.84	83	9	0	0
Chester C	Tr	07.84	84	5	4	0
Rochdale	Tr	08.85	85	12	4	0
Preston NE	Tr	06.86	86-87	54	4	3
Cambridge U	L	02.88	87	9	0	3
Blackburn Rov	Tr	07.88	88-89	25	5	4
Wigan Ath	Tr	08.90	90	4	0	0
Halifax T	Tr	11.91	91-92	21	10	2

HILDITCH Mark
Royton, 20 August, 1960 (F)

League Club	Source	Date Signed	Seasons Played	Apps	Subs	Gls
Rochdale	Heyside	11.78	77-82	184	13	40
Tranmere Rov	Tr	08.83	83-85	47	2	12
Wigan Ath	Altrincham	09.86	86-89	89	14	26
Rochdale	Tr	08.90	90-91	12	4	2

HILEY Scott Patrick
Plymouth, 27 September, 1968 (FB)

League Club	Source	Date Signed	Seasons Played	Apps	Subs	Gls
Exeter C	App	08.86	87-92	205	5	12
Birmingham C	Tr	03.93	92-95	49	0	0
Manchester C	Tr	02.96	95-96	4	5	0
Southampton	Tr	08.98	98-99	30	2	0
Portsmouth	Tr	12.99	99-01	66	9	0
Exeter C	Tr	09.02	02	37	0	0

HILL Alan
Barnsley, 3 November, 1943 (G)

League Club	Source	Date Signed	Seasons Played	Apps	Subs	Gls
Barnsley	Jnrs	04.61	60-65	133	0	0
Rotherham U	Tr	06.66	66-68	81	0	0
Nottingham F	Tr	03.69	68-69	41	0	0

HILL Ernest Alan
Bromborough, 1 July, 1933 (W)

League Club	Source	Date Signed	Seasons Played	Apps	Subs	Gls
Tranmere Rov (Am)	Bebington	11.56	56	6	-	1

HILL Alan George
Chester, 22 June, 1955 (FB)

League Club	Source	Date Signed	Seasons Played	Apps	Subs	Gls
Wrexham	Jnrs	07.73	74-82	173	26	7

HILL Alistair Greenwood
Glasgow, 25 April, 1934 (W)

League Club	Source	Date Signed	Seasons Played	Apps	Subs	Gls
Bristol C	Dundee	11.59	59	3	-	0

HILL Andrew (Andy) Robert
Ilkeston, 10 November, 1960 (F)

League Club	Source	Date Signed	Seasons Played	Apps	Subs	Gls
Derby Co	Kimberley T	06.81	81-83	19	3	2
Carlisle U	Tr	09.83	83-85	73	12	15

HILL Andrew (Andy) Rowland
Maltby, 20 January, 1965 EYth (FB)

League Club	Source	Date Signed	Seasons Played	Apps	Subs	Gls
Manchester U	App	01.83				
Bury	Tr	07.84	84-90	264	0	10
Manchester C	Tr	12.90	90-94	91	7	6
Port Vale	Tr	08.95	95-97	96	4	1

HILL Arthur (Archie)
Chesterfield, 12 November, 1921 Died 1999 (W)

League Club	Source	Date Signed	Seasons Played	Apps	Subs	Gls
Chesterfield		09.46	47	1	-	0

HILL Bert (Bertie)
West Ham, 8 March, 1930 (WH)

League Club	Source	Date Signed	Seasons Played	Apps	Subs	Gls
Chelsea	Jnrs	05.50				
Colchester U	Tr	10.52	52-57	105	-	3

HILL Brian
Sheffield, 6 October, 1937 Died 1968 (FB)

League Club	Source	Date Signed	Seasons Played	Apps	Subs	Gls
Sheffield Wed	Jnrs	04.55	56-65	116	1	1

HILL Brian
Mansfield, 15 December, 1942 (W)

League Club	Source	Date Signed	Seasons Played	Apps	Subs	Gls
Grimsby T	Ollerton Colliery	08.60	60-66	180	0	26
Huddersfield T	Tr	11.66	66-68	85	3	6
Blackburn Rov	Tr	09.69	69-70	34	3	4
Torquay U	Tr	07.71	71	6	1	0

HILL Brian William
Bedworth, 31 July, 1941 (M)

League Club	Source	Date Signed	Seasons Played	Apps	Subs	Gls
Coventry C	Jnrs	08.58	57-70	240	4	7
Bristol C	L	03.71	70	7	0	0
Torquay U	Tr	10.71	71-72	49	0	2

HILL Charles (Charlie) John
Cardiff, 6 September, 1918 Died 1998 (IF)

League Club	Source	Date Signed	Seasons Played	Apps	Subs	Gls
Cardiff C		06.38	38-46	19	-	3
Torquay U	Tr	07.47	47-48	63	-	15
Queens Park Rgrs	Tr	03.49	48-49	21	-	1
Swindon T	Tr	09.50	50	4	-	0

HILL Clinton (Clint) Scott
Knowsley, 19 October, 1978 (CD)

League Club	Source	Date Signed	Seasons Played	Apps	Subs	Gls
Tranmere Rov	YT	07.97	97-01	138	2	16
Oldham Ath	Tr	07.02	02	17	0	1
Stoke C	Tr	07.03	03-04	40	4	1

HILL Colin Frederick
Uxbridge, 12 November, 1963 NI-27 (CD)

League Club	Source	Date Signed	Seasons Played	Apps	Subs	Gls
Arsenal	App	08.81	82-84	46	0	1
Colchester U	CS Maritimo (Por)	10.87	87-88	64	5	0
Sheffield U	Tr	08.89	89-91	77	5	1
Leicester C	Tr	03.92	91-96	140	5	0
Northampton T	Trelleborgs (Swe)	11.97	97-98	49	5	0

HILL Daniel (Danny) Ronald
Enfield, 1 October, 1974 EYth/Eu21-4 (M)

League Club	Source	Date Signed	Seasons Played	Apps	Subs	Gls
Tottenham H	YT	09.92	92-94	4	6	0
Birmingham C	L	11.95	95	5	0	0
Watford	L	02.96	95	1	0	0
Cardiff C	L	02.98	97	7	0	0
Oxford U	Tr	07.98	98	1	8	0
Cardiff C	Tr	11.98	98-00	33	25	4

HILL David
Bradford, 25 May, 1965 (F)

League Club	Source	Date Signed	Seasons Played	Apps	Subs	Gls
Bradford C	YT	08.82	82-83	2	3	1

HILL David
Kettering, 28 September, 1953 (G)

League Club	Source	Date Signed	Seasons Played	Apps	Subs	Gls
Northampton T	App	07.70	70	1	0	0

HILL David Michael
Nottingham, 6 June, 1966 (M)

League Club	Source	Date Signed	Seasons Played	Apps	Subs	Gls
Scunthorpe U	YT	02.85	83-87	139	1	10
Ipswich T	Tr	07.88	88-90	54	7	0
Scunthorpe U	L	03.91	90	8	1	1
Scunthorpe U	Tr	09.91	91-92	55	1	5
Lincoln C	Tr	07.93	93-94	52	6	6
Chesterfield	L	08.94	94	3	0	0

HILL Dennis
Willenhall, 16 August, 1929 (W)

League Club	Source	Date Signed	Seasons Played	Apps	Subs	Gls
Birmingham C	Darlaston	06.51	53-55	4	-	0

HILL Dilwyn
Porth, 1 April, 1937 Died 1963 (IF)

League Club	Source	Date Signed	Seasons Played	Apps	Subs	Gls
Exeter C	Pontypridd	06.55	57-59	14	-	3

HILL Frank Robert
Forfar, 21 May, 1906 Died 1993 SLge-1/S-3 (WH)

League Club	Source	Date Signed	Seasons Played	Apps	Subs	Gls
Arsenal	Aberdeen	05.32	32-35	76	-	4
Blackpool	Tr	06.36	36-37	45	-	8
Southampton	Tr	09.37	37-38	51	-	3
Wrexham	Preston NE (Coach)	08.42				
Crewe Alex	Tr	07.44	46-47	20	-	0

HILL Frederick (Freddie)
Sheffield, 17 January, 1940 Eu23-10/FLge-2/E-2 (M)

League Club	Source	Date Signed	Seasons Played	Apps	Subs	Gls
Bolton W	Jnrs	03.57	57-68	373	2	74

League Club	Source	Date Signed	Seasons Played	Apps	Subs	Gls
Halifax T	Tr	07.69	69	25	0	3
Manchester C	Tr	05.70	70-72	28	7	3
Peterborough U	Tr	08.73	73-74	73	2	7

HILL Geoffrey (Geoff) Raymond
Carlisle, 31 August, 1929 (FB)

League Club	Source	Date Signed	Seasons Played	Apps	Subs	Gls
Carlisle U		10.49	49-57	190	-	0

HILL Gordon Alec
Sunbury, 1 April, 1954 Eu23-1/E-6 (W)

League Club	Source	Date Signed	Seasons Played	Apps	Subs	Gls
Millwall	Southall	01.73	72-75	79	7	20
Manchester U	Tr	11.75	75-77	100	1	39
Derby Co	Tr	04.78	77-79	22	2	5
Queens Park Rgrs	Tr	11.79	79-80	10	4	1

HILL Henry Alec
Lambeth, 19 September, 1947 (M)

League Club	Source	Date Signed	Seasons Played	Apps	Subs	Gls
Ipswich T	(Canada)	03.69				
Gillingham	(South Africa)	07.71	71	1	1	0
Hereford U	(South Africa)	11.78	78	0	1	0

HILL James (Jimmy)
Wishaw, 19 August, 1931 Died 1993 (W)

League Club	Source	Date Signed	Seasons Played	Apps	Subs	Gls
Coventry C	Jnrs	08.48	49-55	67	-	8
Millwall	Tr	07.56	56	1	-	0
Shrewsbury T	Tr	07.57	57	8	-	0

HILL James (Jimmy) William Thomas
Balham, 22 July, 1928 (IF)

League Club	Source	Date Signed	Seasons Played	Apps	Subs	Gls
Brentford	Reading (Am)	05.49	49-51	83	-	10
Fulham	Tr	03.52	51-60	276	-	41

HILL Matthew **James (Jimmy)**
Carrickfergus, 31 October, 1935 NIAmat/IrLge-6/NIB/NI-7 (F)

League Club	Source	Date Signed	Seasons Played	Apps	Subs	Gls
Newcastle U	Linfield	07.57	57	11	-	2
Norwich C	Tr	07.58	58-62	161	-	55
Everton	Tr	08.63	63	7	-	1
Port Vale	Tr	10.65	65-67	63	0	8

HILL John Ernest
Yeovil, 29 November, 1948 (FB)

League Club	Source	Date Signed	Seasons Played	Apps	Subs	Gls
Bournemouth	App	08.66	67	3	1	0

HILL Jonathan (Jon) William
Wigan, 20 August, 1970 (M)

League Club	Source	Date Signed	Seasons Played	Apps	Subs	Gls
Rochdale	Crewe Alex (YT)	07.89	89-90	25	11	1

HILL Keith John
Bolton, 17 May, 1969 (CD)

League Club	Source	Date Signed	Seasons Played	Apps	Subs	Gls
Blackburn Rov	Jnrs	05.87	87-92	89	7	3
Plymouth Arg	Tr	09.92	92-95	117	6	2
Rochdale	Tr	07.96	96-00	171	5	6
Cheltenham T	Tr	06.01	01	2	3	0
Wrexham	L	10.01	01	12	0	1

HILL Kenneth (Ken)
Walsall, 28 April, 1938 (WH)

League Club	Source	Date Signed	Seasons Played	Apps	Subs	Gls
Walsall	Bescot U	11.56	58-62	115	-	1
Norwich C	Tr	07.63	63-65	44	0	0
Walsall	Tr	10.66	66	15	0	0

HILL Kenneth (Kenny) George
Canterbury, 7 March, 1953 ESemiPro (CD)

League Club	Source	Date Signed	Seasons Played	Apps	Subs	Gls
Gillingham	App	03.71	71-76	120	5	7
Lincoln C	L	12.74	74	1	0	0

HILL Kevin
Exeter, 6 March, 1976 (M)

League Club	Source	Date Signed	Seasons Played	Apps	Subs	Gls
Torquay U	Torrington	08.97	97-04	290	36	39

HILL Leonard (Len) Winston
Caerleon, 14 April, 1941 WYth (M)

League Club	Source	Date Signed	Seasons Played	Apps	Subs	Gls
Newport Co	Lovells Ath	11.62	62-69	267	2	51
Swansea C	Tr	07.70	70	12	0	1
Newport Co	Tr	01.72	71-73	93	4	13

HILL Mark Stephen
Perivale, 21 January, 1961 (FB)

League Club	Source	Date Signed	Seasons Played	Apps	Subs	Gls
Queens Park Rgrs	App	07.79				
Brentford	Tr	07.80	80-81	54	2	3

HILL Matthew (Matt) Clayton
Bristol, 26 March, 1981 (CD)

League Club	Source	Date Signed	Seasons Played	Apps	Subs	Gls
Bristol C	YT	02.99	98-04	182	16	6
Preston NE	Tr	01.05	04	11	3	0

HILL Maurice
Halifax, 2 May, 1920 Died 1966 (WH)

League Club	Source	Date Signed	Seasons Played	Apps	Subs	Gls
Everton	Park Side	05.39				
New Brighton	Tr	07.46	46-47	73	-	0

HILL Michael (Mick) Richard
Hereford, 3 December, 1947 W-2 (F)

League Club	Source	Date Signed	Seasons Played	Apps	Subs	Gls
Sheffield U	Bethesda Ath	09.65	66-69	35	2	9
Ipswich T	Tr	10.69	69-72	63	3	18
Crystal Palace	Tr	12.73	73-75	43	2	6

HILL Nicholas (Nicky) Damien
Accrington, 26 February, 1981 (FB)

League Club	Source	Date Signed	Seasons Played	Apps	Subs	Gls
Bury	YT	07.99	99-02	16	6	0

HILL Paul James
Nottingham, 28 January, 1973 (FB)

League Club	Source	Date Signed	Seasons Played	Apps	Subs	Gls
Peterborough U	YT	07.89	90	1	0	0

HILL Peter
Heanor, 8 August, 1931 (IF)

League Club	Source	Date Signed	Seasons Played	Apps	Subs	Gls
Coventry C	Rutland U	08.48	48-61	285	-	74

HILL Raymond (Ray) William
Stourbridge, 15 February, 1936 (IF)

League Club	Source	Date Signed	Seasons Played	Apps	Subs	Gls
Coventry C	Redditch U	11.57	57-58	14	-	5

HILL Richard Wilfred
Hinckley, 20 September, 1963 (W)

League Club	Source	Date Signed	Seasons Played	Apps	Subs	Gls
Leicester C	Jnrs	11.81				
Northampton T	Nuneaton Borough	06.85	85-86	86	0	46
Watford	Tr	05.87	87	2	2	0
Oxford U	Tr	09.87	87-88	48	15	13

HILL Ricky Anthony
Paddington, 5 March, 1959 EYth/E-3 (M)

League Club	Source	Date Signed	Seasons Played	Apps	Subs	Gls
Luton T	App	05.76	75-88	429	7	54
Leicester C	Le Havre (Fr)	08.90	90	19	7	0

HILL Robert (Bobby)
Edinburgh, 9 June, 1938 (IF)

League Club	Source	Date Signed	Seasons Played	Apps	Subs	Gls
Colchester U	Easthouses Lily	06.55	55-64	238	-	21

HILL Stephen Bryan
Prescot, 12 November, 1982 (FB)

League Club	Source	Date Signed	Seasons Played	Apps	Subs	Gls
Rochdale	Sch	07.02	02-03	10	1	0

HILL Stephen (Steve) Thomas
Blackpool, 15 February, 1940 Eu23-4 (W)

League Club	Source	Date Signed	Seasons Played	Apps	Subs	Gls
Blackpool	Jnrs	05.59	59-63	71	-	1
Tranmere Rov	Tr	09.64	64-67	130	1	10

HILL William
Sheffield, 6 January, 1936 (W)

League Club	Source	Date Signed	Seasons Played	Apps	Subs	Gls
York C	Rawmarsh Welfare	02.54	56-59	29	-	3

HILL William Henry
Skegby, 15 March, 1920 Died 1999 (IF)

League Club	Source	Date Signed	Seasons Played	Apps	Subs	Gls
Mansfield T	Skegby MW	11.47	47	2	-	0

HILL William Leslie
Uxbridge, 9 June, 1930 (W)

League Club	Source	Date Signed	Seasons Played	Apps	Subs	Gls
Queens Park Rgrs	Uxbridge T	04.51	51	10	-	1

HILLARD Douglas (Doug) Alfred
Bristol, 10 August, 1935 Died 1997 (FB)

League Club	Source	Date Signed	Seasons Played	Apps	Subs	Gls
Bristol Rov	Bristol Mental Hosp	05.57	58-67	313	5	12

HILLARD John (Jock) Gordon
Aberdeen, 3 September, 1916 Died 2002 (W)

League Club	Source	Date Signed	Seasons Played	Apps	Subs	Gls
Leicester C	Coalville T	11.37				
Grimsby T	Tr	10.38				
Torquay U		09.46	46	6	-	0

HILLEY David (Dave)
Glasgow, 20 December, 1938 Su23-1/SLge-1 (F)

League Club	Source	Date Signed	Seasons Played	Apps	Subs	Gls
Newcastle U	Third Lanark	08.62	62-67	194	0	31
Nottingham F	Tr	12.67	67-70	72	16	14

HILLIER Barry Guy
Redcar, 8 April, 1936 (FB)

League Club	Source	Date Signed	Seasons Played	Apps	Subs	Gls
Southampton	Chester C (Am)	04.53	57-58	9	-	0

HILLIER David
Blackheath, 19 December, 1969 Eu21-1 (M)

League Club	Source	Date Signed	Seasons Played	Apps	Subs	Gls
Arsenal	YT	02.88	90-96	82	22	2
Portsmouth	Tr	11.96	96-98	62	5	4
Bristol Rov	Tr	02.99	98-01	82	1	1

HILLIER Ian Michael
Neath, 26 December, 1979 WSch/WYth/Wu21-5 (FB)

League Club	Source	Date Signed	Seasons Played	Apps	Subs	Gls
Tottenham H	YT	07.98				
Luton T	Tr	08.01	01-03	31	25	1
Chester C	L	12.04	04	7	1	0

HILLIER John (Jack)
Halsall, 10 September, 1933 (G)

League Club	Source	Date Signed	Seasons Played	Apps	Subs	Gls
Chester (Am)	Bootle	11.54	54	6	-	0

HILLMAN Dennis Victor
Southend-on-Sea, 27 November, 1918 Died 1994 (W)

League Club	Source	Date Signed	Seasons Played	Apps	Subs	Gls
Brighton & Hove A		11.44				
Colchester U	Tr	(N/L)	50	4	-	0
Gillingham	Tr	08.51	51	21	-	0

HILLS John David
St Annes, 21 April, 1978 (FB)

League Club	Source	Date Signed	Seasons Played	Apps	Subs	Gls
Blackpool	YT	10.95				
Everton	Tr	11.95	96	1	2	0
Swansea C	L	01.97	96	11	0	0
Swansea C	L	08.97	97	7	0	1
Blackpool	Tr	01.98	97-02	146	16	16
Gillingham	Tr	08.03	03-04	47	5	2

HILLS John (Johnny) Raymond
Northfleet, 24 February, 1934 (FB)

League Club	Source	Date Signed	Seasons Played	Apps	Subs	Gls
Tottenham H	Gravesend & Northfleet	08.53	57-59	29	-	0
Bristol Rov	Tr	07.61	61	7	-	0

HILLYARD Ronald (Ron) William
Brinsworth, 31 March, 1952 (G)

League Club	Source	Date Signed	Seasons Played	Apps	Subs	Gls
York C	Jnrs	12.69	69-73	61	0	0
Hartlepool	L	01.72	71	23	0	0
Gillingham	Tr	07.74	74-90	563	0	0

HILTON Damien Alan
Norwich, 6 September, 1977 (F)

League Club	Source	Date Signed	Seasons Played	Apps	Subs	Gls
Norwich C	YT	07.96				
Brighton & Hove A	Tr	03.98	97	4	1	0

HILTON David
Barnsley, 10 November, 1977 ESch/EYth (FB)

League Club	Source	Date Signed	Seasons Played	Apps	Subs	Gls
Manchester U	YT	12.94				
Darlington	Tr	08.97	97	0	1	0

HILTON Gary
Manchester, 4 March, 1961 (G)

League Club	Source	Date Signed	Seasons Played	Apps	Subs	Gls
Bury	Ramsbottom U	08.83	83	1	0	0

HILTON John (Jack)
Rochdale, 20 February, 1925 (CF)

League Club	Source	Date Signed	Seasons Played	Apps	Subs	Gls
Wrexham	Hyde U	07.50	50	3	-	0

HILTON Joseph (Joe)
Barnborough, 20 July, 1931 Died 1995 (IF)

League Club	Source	Date Signed	Seasons Played	Apps	Subs	Gls
Leeds U	Jnrs	09.48	49	1	-	0
Chester	Tr	08.50	50-53	61	-	9

HILTON Kirk
Flixton, 2 April, 1981 (FB)

League Club	Source	Date Signed	Seasons Played	Apps	Subs	Gls
Manchester U	YT	07.99				
Blackpool	Tr	07.03	03	12	2	1

HILTON Mark Gerard
Middleton, 15 January, 1960 (M)

League Club	Source	Date Signed	Seasons Played	Apps	Subs	Gls
Oldham Ath	App	01.78	77-80	48	2	2
Bury	Tr	08.81	81-82	29	3	3

HILTON Maurice
Stockton, 14 March, 1979 (FB)

League Club	Source	Date Signed	Seasons Played	Apps	Subs	Gls
Doncaster Rov	YT	•	97	9	1	0

HILTON Patrick (Pat) John
Aylesham, 1 May, 1954 (W)

League Club	Source	Date Signed	Seasons Played	Apps	Subs	Gls
Brighton & Hove A	Canterbury C	02.73	72-73	18	2	1
Blackburn Rov	Tr	05.74	74	16	0	2
Gillingham	Tr	09.75	75-76	16	10	1
Aldershot	L	03.77	76	12	1	0
Southport	Tr	07.77	77	22	5	5

HILTON Paul
Oldham, 8 October, 1959 ESch (CD)

League Club	Source	Date Signed	Seasons Played	Apps	Subs	Gls
Bury	Chadderton	07.78	78-83	136	12	39
West Ham U	Tr	02.84	83-88	47	13	7

HILTON Peter Bowes
Tamworth, 20 March, 1929 Died 1968 (FB)

League Club	Source	Date Signed	Seasons Played	Apps	Subs	Gls
West Bromwich A	Tamworth	07.49				
Swindon T	Tr	07.53	53-55	50	-	0

HIMSWORTH Gary Paul
Appleton, North Yorkshire, 19 December, 1969 (M)

League Club	Source	Date Signed	Seasons Played	Apps	Subs	Gls
York C	YT	01.88	87-90	74	14	8
Scarborough	Tr	12.90	90-92	83	9	6
Darlington	Tr	07.93	93-95	86	8	8
York C	Tr	02.96	95-98	60	9	3
Darlington	Tr	03.99	98-00	41	7	1

HINCE Paul Frank
Manchester, 2 March, 1945 (W)

League Club	Source	Date Signed	Seasons Played	Apps	Subs	Gls
Manchester C	Pinnington Celtic	10.66	66-67	7	0	4
Charlton Ath	Tr	02.68	67-68	23	0	2
Bury	Tr	12.68	68-69	39	0	3
Crewe Alex	Tr	07.70	70	23	3	2

HINCH James (Jim) Andrew
Sheffield, 8 November, 1947 (F)

League Club	Source	Date Signed	Seasons Played	Apps	Subs	Gls
Tranmere Rov	Portmadoc	03.70	69-70	36	3	10
Plymouth Arg	Tr	02.71	70-73	102	5	28
Hereford U	Tr	10.73	73	22	5	7
York C	Tr	07.74	74-75	28	11	5
Southport	L	03.75	74	7	0	2
York C	San Fernando (USA)	08.76	76	28	1	7
Sheffield Wed	San Fernando (USA)	10.77	77	0	1	0
Barnsley	Tr	12.77	77	9	3	4

HINCHCLIFFE Alan Arthur
Chesterfield, 8 December, 1936 (G)

League Club	Source	Date Signed	Seasons Played	Apps	Subs	Gls
Sheffield Wed	Jnrs	12.53	56	2	-	0

HINCHCLIFFE Andrew (Andy) George
Manchester, 5 February, 1969 EYth/Eu21-1/E-7 (FB)

League Club	Source	Date Signed	Seasons Played	Apps	Subs	Gls
Manchester C	App	02.86	87-89	107	5	8
Everton	Tr	07.90	90-97	170	12	7
Sheffield Wed	Tr	01.98	97-01	86	0	7

HINCHCLIFFE Thomas (Tom)
Denaby, 6 December, 1913 Died 1978 (IF)

League Club	Source	Date Signed	Seasons Played	Apps	Subs	Gls
Grimsby T	Denaby U	10.33	36-37	27	-	5
Huddersfield T	Tr	02.38	37-38	13	-	4
Derby Co	Tr	11.38	38	6	-	1
Nottingham F	Tr	05.46	46	1	-	0

HINCHLEY Gary
Guisborough, 14 November, 1968 (FB)

League Club	Source	Date Signed	Seasons Played	Apps	Subs	Gls
Darlington	Jnrs	08.86	86-87	13	1	0
Darlington	Guisborough T	02.92	91-92	13	0	1

HINCHLIFFE John (Jackie)
Tillicoultry, 4 June, 1938 SSch (WH)

League Club	Source	Date Signed	Seasons Played	Apps	Subs	Gls
Aston Villa	L Pieter's BC	09.56	57	2	-	0
Workington	Tr	06.58	58-61	116	-	4
Hartlepools U	Tr	10.61	61-63	88	-	8

HINDLE Frank Johnston
Blackburn, 22 June, 1925 (CD)

League Club	Source	Date Signed	Seasons Played	Apps	Subs	Gls
Blackburn Rov		01.43				
Chester	Tr	06.49	49-50	81	-	0
Bradford PA	Tr	04.51	50-56	204	-	0

HINDLE John (Jack)
Preston, 10 November, 1921 Died 1987 (G)

League Club	Source	Date Signed	Seasons Played	Apps	Subs	Gls
Preston NE	Clifton BC	11.46	47	1	-	0
Barrow	Tr	05.48	48-49	84	-	0
Aston Villa	Tr	06.50	50	15	-	0
Barrow	Tr	08.51	51-55	182	-	0

HINDLE Thomas (Tom)
Keighley, 22 February, 1921 (W)

League Club	Source	Date Signed	Seasons Played	Apps	Subs	Gls
Leeds U	Keighley T	09.43	46-48	43	-	2
York C	Tr	02.49	48-49	19	-	3
Halifax T	Tr	09.49	49-51	85	-	17
Rochdale	Tr	03.52	51	6	-	1

HINDLEY Frank Charles
Worksop, 2 November, 1915 Died 2003 (CF)

League Club	Source	Date Signed	Seasons Played	Apps	Subs	Gls
Nottingham F	Netherton U	12.37	38	6	-	3
Brighton & Hove A	Tr	05.39	46	10	-	4

HINDLEY Peter
Worksop, 19 May, 1944 Eu23-1 (FB)

League Club	Source	Date Signed	Seasons Played	Apps	Subs	Gls
Nottingham F	Jnrs	06.61	62-73	366	0	10
Coventry C	Tr	01.74	73-75	33	0	0
Peterborough U	Tr	07.76	76-78	112	0	1

HINDMARCH Robert (Rob)
Stannington, 27 April, 1961 Died 2002 EYth (CD)

League Club	Source	Date Signed	Seasons Played	Apps	Subs	Gls
Sunderland	App	04.78	77-83	114	1	2
Portsmouth	L	12.83	83	2	0	0
Derby Co	Tr	07.84	84-89	164	0	9
Wolverhampton W	Tr	06.90	90	40	0	2

HINDMARSH Edward (Eddie)
Sunderland, 7 September, 1922 Died 1997 (WH)

League Club	Source	Date Signed	Seasons Played	Apps	Subs	Gls
Sunderland		10.43				
Carlisle U	Tr	07.45	46	15	-	0

HINDMARSH John William (Billy)
Crook, 26 December, 1919 Died 1994 (FB)

League Club	Source	Date Signed	Seasons Played	Apps	Subs	Gls
Portsmouth	Willington	04.39	46-50	55	-	0
Swindon T	Tr	07.51	51	11	-	0

HINDS Richard Paul
Sheffield, 22 August, 1980 (CD)

League Club	Source	Date Signed	Seasons Played	Apps	Subs	Gls
Tranmere Rov	Jnrs	07.98	98-02	42	13	0
Hull C	Tr	07.03	03-04	40	5	1
Scunthorpe U	L	03.05	04	6	1	0

HINDSON Gordon
Flint Hill, 8 January, 1950 (W)

League Club	Source	Date Signed	Seasons Played	Apps	Subs	Gls
Newcastle U	Jnrs	08.68	68-71	7	0	1
Luton T	Tr	10.71	71-74	62	6	3
Carlisle U	L	09.75	75	1	2	0
Blackburn Rov	Tr	10.75	75	10	0	0

HINE Mark
Middlesbrough, 18 May, 1964 (M)

League Club	Source	Date Signed	Seasons Played	Apps	Subs	Gls
Grimsby T	Whitby T	10.83	84-85	20	2	1
Darlington	Tr	06.86	86-88	126	2	8
Peterborough U	Tr	01.90	89-90	55	0	8
Scunthorpe U	Tr	03.91	90-91	19	3	2
Doncaster Rov	Tr	06.92	92	18	7	1

HINES Derek Jabez
Woodville, 18 February, 1931 Died 2001 EYth (CF)

League Club	Source	Date Signed	Seasons Played	Apps	Subs	Gls
Leicester C	Moira U	03.48	47-60	299	-	116
Shrewsbury T	Tr	11.61	61-62	16	-	5

HINNIGAN Joseph (Joe) Peter
Liverpool, 3 December, 1955 (FB)

League Club	Source	Date Signed	Seasons Played	Apps	Subs	Gls
Wigan Ath	South Liverpool	(N/L)	78-79	66	0	10
Sunderland	Tr	02.80	79-82	63	0	4
Preston NE	Tr	12.82	82-83	51	1	8
Gillingham	Tr	08.84	84-86	99	4	7
Wrexham	Tr	07.87	87	28	1	1
Chester C	Tr	08.88	88-89	52	2	2

HINSHELWOOD Adam
Oxford, 8 January, 1984 (FB)

League Club	Source	Date Signed	Seasons Played	Apps	Subs	Gls
Brighton & Hove A	Sch	07.03	02-04	57	5	1

HINSHELWOOD Daniel (Danny) Martin
Bromley, 12 December, 1975 EYth (FB)

League Club	Source	Date Signed	Seasons Played	Apps	Subs	Gls
Nottingham F	YT	12.92				
Portsmouth	Tr	02.96	95	5	0	0
Torquay U	L	03.97	96	7	2	0
Brighton & Hove A	Tr	08.98	98	3	1	0

HINSHELWOOD Martin Alan
Reading, 16 June, 1953 (M)

League Club	Source	Date Signed	Seasons Played	Apps	Subs	Gls
Crystal Palace	App	08.70	72-77	66	3	4

HINSHELWOOD Paul Alexander
Bristol, 14 August, 1956 Eu21-2 (FB)

League Club	Source	Date Signed	Seasons Played	Apps	Subs	Gls
Crystal Palace	App	08.73	73-82	271	5	22
Oxford U	Tr	08.83	83-84	45	0	0
Millwall	Tr	01.85	84-86	59	2	2
Colchester U	Tr	09.86	86-87	81	0	6

HINSHELWOOD Walter (Wally) Alexander Alan
Battersea, 27 October, 1929 (W)

League Club	Source	Date Signed	Seasons Played	Apps	Subs	Gls
Fulham	Jnrs	10.46	46-50	17	-	1
Chelsea	Tr	01.51	50	12	-	1
Fulham	Tr	05.51	51	2	-	0
Reading	Tr	12.52	52-55	135	-	31
Bristol C	Tr	02.56	55-59	148	-	16
Millwall	Tr	06.60	60	19	-	1
Newport Co	(Canada)	11.61	61	3	-	0

HINSHELWOOD William (Willie) Douglas
Chapelhall, 11 May, 1935 (WH)

League Club	Source	Date Signed	Seasons Played	Apps	Subs	Gls
Hartlepools U	Tonbridge	07.63	63	17	-	3

HINSLEY George
Sheffield, 19 July, 1914 Died 1989 (WH)

League Club	Source	Date Signed	Seasons Played	Apps	Subs	Gls
Barnsley	Denaby U	09.35	35-38	9	-	0
Bradford C	Tr	10.38	38-48	114	-	17
Halifax T	Tr	07.49	49	32	-	0

HINTON Alan Thomas
Wednesbury, 6 October, 1942 EYth/Eu23-7/E-3 (W)

League Club	Source	Date Signed	Seasons Played	Apps	Subs	Gls
Wolverhampton W	Jnrs	10.59	61-63	75	-	29
Nottingham F	Tr	01.64	63-67	108	4	24
Derby Co	Tr	09.67	67-75	240	13	64

HINTON Craig
Wolverhampton, 26 November, 1977 (CD)

League Club	Source	Date Signed	Seasons Played	Apps	Subs	Gls
Birmingham C	YT	07.96				
Kidderminster Hrs	Tr	08.98	00-03	172	1	3
Bristol Rov	Tr	07.04	04	33	5	0

HINTON Edward (Ted)
Belfast, 20 May, 1922 Died 1988 NIRL-1/I-7 (G)

League Club	Source	Date Signed	Seasons Played	Apps	Subs	Gls
Fulham	Distillery	08.46	46-48	82	-	0
Millwall	Tr	07.49	49-51	91	-	0

HINTON Marvin
Norwood, 2 February, 1940 Eu23-3 (CD)

League Club	Source	Date Signed	Seasons Played	Apps	Subs	Gls
Charlton Ath	Jnrs	04.57	57-63	131	-	2
Chelsea	Tr	08.63	63-74	257	8	3

HINTON Ronald (Ron)
Keighley, 27 November, 1943 Died 1986 (CD)

League Club	Source	Date Signed	Seasons Played	Apps	Subs	Gls
Doncaster Rov	App	07.61				
Chesterfield	Tr	07.63	63	1	-	0

HIPKIN Reginald (Reg) Willmont
Syderstone, 31 December, 1921 (CF)

League Club	Source	Date Signed	Seasons Played	Apps	Subs	Gls
Wolverhampton W	Norwich C (Am)	07.39				
Charlton Ath	Tr	09.46	47	2	-	0
Brighton & Hove A	Tr	02.48	47-48	15	-	1

HIRD Robert **Keith** Bryan
Annfield Plain, 25 November, 1939 Died 1967 (G)

League Club	Source	Date Signed	Seasons Played	Apps	Subs	Gls
Sunderland	Annfield Plain	09.57	60	1	-	0
Darlington	Tr	07.63	63	17	-	0

HIRD Kevin
Colne, 11 February, 1955 (FB)

League Club	Source	Date Signed	Seasons Played	Apps	Subs	Gls
Blackburn Rov	App	02.73	73-78	129	3	20
Leeds U	Tr	03.79	78-83	165	16	19
Burnley	Tr	08.84	84-85	83	0	23

HIRON Raymond (Ray) Michael Charles
Gosport, 22 July, 1943 (F)

League Club	Source	Date Signed	Seasons Played	Apps	Subs	Gls
Portsmouth	Fareham T	05.64	64-74	323	7	110
Reading	Tr	07.75	75-77	88	4	14

HIRONS Paul Terence
Bath, 6 March, 1971 (F)

League Club	Source	Date Signed	Seasons Played	Apps	Subs	Gls
Torquay U	Bristol C (YT)	01.89	88-89	10	11	0

HIRSCHFELD Lars
Edmonton, Canada, 17 October, 1978 Cau23-1/Ca-18 (G)

League Club	Source	Date Signed	Seasons Played	Apps	Subs	Gls
Tottenham H	Calgary Storm (Can)	08.02				
Luton T	L	02.03	02	5	0	0
Gillingham	L	02.04	03	2	0	0
Leicester C	Dundee U	01.05	04	1	0	0

HIRST David Eric
Cudworth, 7 December, 1967 EYth/Eu21-7/EB-3/E-3 (F)

League Club	Source	Date Signed	Seasons Played	Apps	Subs	Gls
Barnsley	App	11.85	85	26	2	9
Sheffield Wed	Tr	08.86	86-97	261	33	106
Southampton	Tr	10.97	97-98	28	2	9

HIRST Keith Richard Halliwell
Bradford, 15 October, 1932 (W)

League Club	Source	Date Signed	Seasons Played	Apps	Subs	Gls
Bradford PA	Low Moor Celtic	01.54	53	1	-	0

HIRST Lee William
Sheffield, 26 January, 1969 (CD)

League Club	Source	Date Signed	Seasons Played	Apps	Subs	Gls
Scarborough	Sheffield Parks	02.90	89-92	107	1	6
Coventry C	Tr	07.93				
Lincoln C	L	12.93	93	7	0	0

HIRST Malcolm William
Cudworth, 28 December, 1937 (CF)

League Club	Source	Date Signed	Seasons Played	Apps	Subs	Gls
Barnsley	Darfield Road Jnrs	05.56	56	1	-	0

HIRST Martyn Paul
Batley, 26 October, 1961 ESch (M)

League Club	Source	Date Signed	Seasons Played	Apps	Subs	Gls
Bristol C	Bath Univ	10.83	83-85	36	5	1
Torquay U	L	09.85	85	4	0	0

HISLOP Terence **Kona**
Hackney, 21 December, 1970 (W)

League Club	Source	Date Signed	Seasons Played	Apps	Subs	Gls
Hartlepool U	Livingston	09.96	96	23	4	0

HISLOP Neil **Shaka**
Hackney, 22 February, 1969 Eu21-1/Trinidad 21 (G)

League Club	Source	Date Signed	Seasons Played	Apps	Subs	Gls
Reading	Howard Univ (USA)	09.92	92-94	104	0	0
Newcastle U	Tr	08.95	95-97	53	0	0
West Ham U	Tr	07.98	98-01	105	0	0
Portsmouth	Tr	07.02	02-04	93	0	0

HITCHCOCK Alan Peter
Bracknell, 5 October, 1949 (FB)

League Club	Source	Date Signed	Seasons Played	Apps	Subs	Gls
Reading	App	10.67	68-69	4	0	0

HITCHCOCK Kevin Joseph
Custom House, 5 October, 1962 (G)

League Club	Source	Date Signed	Seasons Played	Apps	Subs	Gls
Nottingham F	Barking	08.83				
Mansfield T	L	02.84	83	14	0	0
Mansfield T	Tr	06.84	84-87	168	0	0
Chelsea	Tr	03.88	87-98	92	4	0
Northampton T	L	12.90	90	17	0	0

League Club	Source	Date Signed	Seasons Played	Apps	Subs	Gls
HITCHEN Henry (Harry)						
Liverpool, 22 October, 1922 Died 1993						(WH)
New Brighton	Formby	09.46	46-47	70	-	2
Sheffield U	Tr	05.48	48-52	154	-	15
Bury	Tr	05.53	53	2	-	0
HITCHEN Steven (Steve) James						
Salford, 28 November, 1976						(FB)
Blackburn Rov	YT	07.95				
Macclesfield T	Tr	07.97	97-03	143	8	1
HITCHEN Trevor						
Sowerby Bridge, 25 September, 1926						(WH)
Notts Co	Halifax T (Am)	05.45				
Southport	Wellington T	01.49	48-55	242	-	34
Oldham Ath	Tr	08.56	56	3	-	0
Southport	Wigan Ath	08.58	58	5	-	0
HITCHENS Gerald (Gerry) Archibald						
Cannock, 8 October, 1934 Died 1983 Eu23-1/FLge-1/ItLge-2/E-7						(CF)
Cardiff C	Kidderminster Hrs	01.55	54-57	95	-	40
Aston Villa	Tr	12.57	57-60	132	-	78
HITCHON John						
Carlisle, 30 August, 1919 Died 1985						(G)
Carlisle U		04.47	46-49	5	-	0
HITZLSPERGER Thomas						
Munich, Germany, 5 April, 1982 GeYth/Geu21-20/Ge-9						(M)
Aston Villa	Bayern Munich (Ger)	08.00	00-04	74	25	8
Chesterfield	L	10.01	01	5	0	0
HJELDE Jon Olav						
Levanger, Norway, 30 July, 1972						(CD)
Nottingham F	Rosenborg (Nor)	08.97	97-02	136	21	4
Nottingham F	Busan Icons (SK)	08.04	04	13	1	0
HJORTH Jesper						
Denmark, 3 April, 1975						(F)
Darlington	OB Odense (Den)	11.99	99-00	16	29	7
HOADLEY Philip (Phil) Frederick William						
Battersea, 6 January, 1952 EYth						(CD)
Crystal Palace	App	01.69	67-71	62	11	1
Orient	Tr	10.71	71-77	255	0	9
Norwich C	Tr	08.78	78-81	74	3	0
HOBBINS Sydney (Syd) George						
Plumstead, 6 May, 1916 Died 1984						(G)
Charlton Ath	Bromley	05.34	37-46	2	-	0
Millwall	Tr	05.48	48	15	-	0
Leyton Orient	Tr	12.49	49	11	-	0
HOBBIS Harold Henry Frederick						
Dartford, 9 March, 1913 Died 1991 E-2						(W)
Charlton Ath	Bromley	03.31	31-47	248	-	76
HOBBS Jack						
Portsmouth, 18 August, 1988						(FB)
Lincoln C	Sch	●	04	0	1	0
HOBBS John (Jack) Eric						
Swanage, 17 April, 1930						(CF)
Bournemouth	Swanage	10.52	53-54	6	-	1
HOBBS Ronald (Ronnie) George						
Aldershot, 23 August, 1921						(W)
Aldershot	Woking	11.44	46-53	169	-	14
HOBBS Shane Michael						
Bristol, 30 April, 1985						(FB)
Bristol Rov	Sch	●	03	0	2	0
HOBSON Albert						
Glossop, 7 April, 1925						(W)
Blackpool	Glossop	08.45	47-53	62	-	3
Huddersfield T	Tr	07.54	54-55	9	-	0
York C	Tr	03.56	55-56	22	-	1
HOBSON Gary						
North Ferriby, 12 November, 1972						(CD)
Hull C	YT	07.91	90-95	135	7	0
Brighton & Hove A	Tr	03.96	95-99	92	6	1
Chester C	Tr	01.00	99	20	0	0
York C	Tr	07.00	00-02	46	9	0
HOBSON Gordon						
Sheffield, 27 November, 1957						(F)
Lincoln C	Manchester Villa	12.77	77-84	260	12	73
Grimsby T	Tr	06.85	85-86	50	2	18
Southampton	Tr	11.86	86-87	32	1	8
Lincoln C	Tr	09.88	88-89	61	0	23

League Club	Source	Date Signed	Seasons Played	Apps	Subs	Gls
Exeter C	Tr	08.90	90-91	37	1	7
Walsall	Salisbury C	09.91	91	3	0	0
HOBSON John						
Barnsley, 1 June, 1946						(W)
Blackpool	Jnrs	09.63				
Barnsley	Tr	07.65	65-68	30	7	7
Notts Co	Tr	05.69	69-70	46	3	6
HOBSON Norman						
Shrewsbury, 22 August, 1933						(FB)
Shrewsbury T	Oswestry T	10.54	55-60	212	-	5
HOBSON Wilfred (Wilf)						
Consett, 26 January, 1932						(WH)
Oldham Ath	West Stanley	01.53	54-58	170	-	1
Gateshead	Tr	06.59	59	31	-	1
HOCKADAY David						
Sedgefield, 9 November, 1957						(FB)
Blackpool	Billingham Synthonia	06.75	76-82	131	16	24
Swindon T	Tr	08.83	83-90	227	18	7
Hull C	Tr	09.90	90-92	72	0	2
Stoke C	L	03.93	92	7	0	0
Shrewsbury T	Tr	08.93	93-94	46	2	0
HOCKENHULL Darren						
St Helens, 5 September, 1982						(FB)
Blackburn Rov	Sch	07.02				
Rochdale	L	03.03	02	6	1	1
HOCKEY Trevor						
Keighley, 1 May, 1943 Died 1987 W-9						(W)
Bradford C	Jnrs	05.60	59-61	53	-	5
Nottingham F	Tr	11.61	61-63	73	-	6
Newcastle U	Tr	11.63	63-65	52	0	3
Birmingham C	Tr	11.65	65-70	195	1	8
Sheffield U	Tr	01.71	70-72	68	0	4
Norwich C	Tr	02.73	72	13	0	0
Aston Villa	Tr	06.73	73	24	0	1
Bradford C	Tr	06.74	74-75	43	1	1
HOCKING Matthew (Matt) James						
Boston, 30 January, 1978						(CD)
Sheffield U	YT	05.96				
Hull C	Tr	09.97	97-98	55	2	2
York C	Tr	03.99	98-01	83	14	2
Boston U	Tr	08.02	02-03	60	7	1
HOCKLESS Graham						
Hull, 20 October, 1982						(M)
Grimsby T	Hull C (Jnrs)	07.01	02-04	8	12	2
HOCKLEY Matthew (Matt)						
Paignton, 5 June, 1982						(CD)
Torquay U	YT	07.00	00-04	105	32	9
HOCKLEY Wayne						
Torquay, 6 September, 1978						(F)
Torquay U	YT	08.97	96	0	2	0
HOCKTON Daniel (Danny) John						
Barking, 7 February, 1979						(F)
Millwall	YT	03.97	96-98	11	25	4
Leyton Orient	L	09.99	99	1	4	0
HODDER Kenneth (Ken)						
Stockport, 20 August, 1930						(CD)
Stockport Co	Jnrs	03.49	51-63	258	-	1
HODDER Stephen (Steve) John						
Sheffield, 18 October, 1971						(CD)
Nottingham F	YT	07.90				
Notts Co	Tr	03.91				
Doncaster Rov	Tr	07.92	92	1	1	0
HODDLE Carl						
Harlow, 8 March, 1967						(M)
Tottenham H	App	07.84				
Leyton Orient	Bishops Stortford	07.89	89-90	19	9	2
Barnet	Tr	07.91	91-94	80	12	3
HODDLE Glenn						
Hayes, 27 October, 1957 EYth/Eu21-12/EB/E-53						(M)
Tottenham H	App	04.75	75-86	371	7	88
Swindon T	AS Monaco (Fr)	08.91	91-92	63	1	1
Chelsea	Tr	06.93	93-94	19	12	1
HODDY Kevin Raymond						
Romford, 6 January, 1968						(M)
Fulham	App	01.86	86-88	13	9	1

HODGE Eric
Edmonton, 1 June, 1928 Died 1963 (G)

League Club	Source	Date Signed	Seasons Played	Apps	Subs	Gls
Tottenham H		08.48				
Newport Co	Tr	08.49	49	7	-	0

HODGE Eric Richard Carew
Cape Town, South Africa, 3 April, 1933 (CD)

League Club	Source	Date Signed	Seasons Played	Apps	Subs	Gls
Brighton & Hove A	(South Africa)	10.56	57	4	-	0
Aldershot	Tr	07.59	59	17	-	0

HODGE James (Jimmy) Oswald
Perth, 23 October, 1926 (FB)

League Club	Source	Date Signed	Seasons Played	Apps	Subs	Gls
Newport Co	York C (Am)	08.46	46	1	-	0

HODGE John
Ormskirk, 1 April, 1969 (W)

League Club	Source	Date Signed	Seasons Played	Apps	Subs	Gls
Exeter C	Falmouth T	09.91	91-92	57	8	10
Swansea C	Tr	07.93	93-95	87	25	10
Walsall	Tr	09.96	96-97	67	9	12
Gillingham	Tr	07.98	98-99	8	41	1
Northampton T	Tr	03.00	99-01	33	27	2

HODGE Martin John
Southport, 4 February, 1959 (G)

League Club	Source	Date Signed	Seasons Played	Apps	Subs	Gls
Plymouth Arg	App	02.77	77-78	43	0	0
Everton	Tr	07.79	79-80	25	0	0
Preston NE	L	12.81	81	28	0	0
Oldham Ath	L	07.82	82	4	0	0
Gillingham	L	01.83	82	4	0	0
Preston NE	L	02.83	82	16	0	0
Sheffield Wed	Tr	08.83	83-87	197	0	0
Leicester C	Tr	08.88	88-90	75	0	0
Hartlepool U	Tr	08.91	91-92	69	0	0
Rochdale	Tr	07.93	93	42	0	0
Plymouth Arg	Tr	08.94	94	17	0	0

HODGE Robert (Bobby) William
Exeter, 30 April, 1954 (W)

League Club	Source	Date Signed	Seasons Played	Apps	Subs	Gls
Exeter C		07.74	74-78	120	8	18
Colchester U	Tr	09.78	78-80	87	5	14
Torquay U	Tr	08.81	81	3	1	1

HODGE Stephen (Steve) Brian
Nottingham, 25 October, 1962 Eu21-8/EB/E-24 (M)

League Club	Source	Date Signed	Seasons Played	Apps	Subs	Gls
Nottingham F	App	10.80	81-85	122	1	30
Aston Villa	Tr	08.85	85-86	53	0	12
Tottenham H	Tr	12.86	86-87	44	1	7
Nottingham F	Tr	08.88	88-90	79	3	20
Leeds U	Tr	07.91	91-93	28	26	10
Derby Co	L	08.94	94	10	0	2
Queens Park Rgrs	Tr	10.94	94	15	0	0
Watford	Tr	12.95	95	2	0	0
Leyton Orient	(Hong Kong)	08.97	97	1	0	0

HODGES Cyril Leslie
Hackney, 18 September, 1919 Died 1979 (CF)

League Club	Source	Date Signed	Seasons Played	Apps	Subs	Gls
Arsenal	Eton Manor	04.45	46	2	-	0
Brighton & Hove A	Tr	10.46	46	9	-	3

HODGES David
Ross-on-Wye, 17 January, 1970 (M)

League Club	Source	Date Signed	Seasons Played	Apps	Subs	Gls
Mansfield T	Jnrs	08.87	86-90	67	18	7
Torquay U	Tr	01.91	90-91	8	8	0
Shrewsbury T	Bolton W (N/C)	08.92	92	1	0	0

HODGES Glyn Peter
Streatham, 30 April, 1963 WYth/Wu21-5/WB-1/W-18 (W)

League Club	Source	Date Signed	Seasons Played	Apps	Subs	Gls
Wimbledon	App	02.81	80-86	200	32	49
Newcastle U	Tr	07.87	87	7	0	0
Watford	Tr	10.87	87-89	82	4	15
Crystal Palace	Tr	07.90	90	5	2	0
Sheffield U	Tr	01.91	90-95	116	31	19
Derby Co	Tr	02.96	95	1	8	0
Hull C	Sing Tao (HK)	08.97	97	13	5	4
Nottingham F	Tr	02.98	98	3	2	0
Scarborough	Tr	01.99	98	1	0	0

HODGES John Kenneth
Leicester, 22 January, 1980 (G)

League Club	Source	Date Signed	Seasons Played	Apps	Subs	Gls
Leicester C	YT	07.98				
Plymouth Arg	Tr	07.00	00	2	0	0

HODGES Kevin
Bridport, 12 June, 1960 (M)

League Club	Source	Date Signed	Seasons Played	Apps	Subs	Gls
Plymouth Arg	App	03.78	78-92	502	28	81
Torquay U	L	01.92	91	3	0	0
Torquay U	Tr	12.92	92-96	49	19	4

HODGES Lee Leslie
Epping, 4 September, 1973 EYth (F)

League Club	Source	Date Signed	Seasons Played	Apps	Subs	Gls
Tottenham H	YT	02.92	92	0	4	0
Plymouth Arg	L	02.93	92	6	1	2
Wycombe W	L	12.93	93	2	2	0
Barnet	Tr	05.94	94-96	94	11	26
Reading	Tr	07.97	97-00	58	21	10
Plymouth Arg	Tr	08.01	01-04	119	21	11

HODGES Lee Leslie
Plaistow, 2 March, 1978 ESch (W)

League Club	Source	Date Signed	Seasons Played	Apps	Subs	Gls
West Ham U	YT	03.95	97-98	0	3	0
Exeter C	L	09.96	96	16	1	0
Leyton Orient	L	02.97	96	3	0	0
Plymouth Arg	L	11.97	97	9	0	0
Ipswich T	L	11.98	98	0	4	0
Southend U	L	03.99	98	10	0	1
Scunthorpe U	Tr	07.99	99-01	97	16	20
Rochdale	Tr	08.02	02	3	4	0
Bristol Rov	Tr	03.03	02-03	12	9	2

HODGES Leonard (Len) Herbert
Bristol, 17 February, 1920 Died 1959 (IF)

League Club	Source	Date Signed	Seasons Played	Apps	Subs	Gls
Bristol Rov	Soundwell	08.46	46-49	118	-	20
Swansea T	Tr	08.50	50	3	-	0
Reading	Tr	08.51	51-52	6	-	2

HODGES Mark
Sheffield, 24 October, 1971 (CD)

League Club	Source	Date Signed	Seasons Played	Apps	Subs	Gls
Rotherham U	YT	07.90	90	3	1	0

HODGETTS Frank
Dudley, 30 September, 1924 (W)

League Club	Source	Date Signed	Seasons Played	Apps	Subs	Gls
West Bromwich A	Accles & Pollock	10.42	46-48	67	-	11
Millwall	Tr	08.49	49-52	34	-	6

HODGKINS Jeffrey (Jeff)
Portsmouth, 8 October, 1942 (CF)

League Club	Source	Date Signed	Seasons Played	Apps	Subs	Gls
Portsmouth	Jnrs	06.60	60	3	-	0

HODGKINSON Alan
Maltby, 16 August, 1936 Eu23-7/FLge-1/E-5 (G)

League Club	Source	Date Signed	Seasons Played	Apps	Subs	Gls
Sheffield U	Worksop T	08.53	54-70	576	0	0

HODGKINSON Derek John
Weston-super-Mare, 30 April, 1944 (IF)

League Club	Source	Date Signed	Seasons Played	Apps	Subs	Gls
Manchester C	Margate	08.61	63	1	-	1
Stockport Co	Tr	06.64	64-65	46	0	9

HODGKINSON Edwin (Eddie)
Ilkeston, 27 November, 1920 (IF)

League Club	Source	Date Signed	Seasons Played	Apps	Subs	Gls
Leeds U		12.46	46-47	2	-	0
Halifax T	Tr	07.48	48-49	13	-	2

HODGKISS Robert (Bob)
Little Hulton, 22 March, 1918 Died 2003 (FB)

League Club	Source	Date Signed	Seasons Played	Apps	Subs	Gls
Southport	Walkden Methodists	11.38	38	10	-	0
Everton	Tr	08.46				
Southport	Tr	07.47	47-48	20	-	0

HODGKISSON William **Kenneth (Ken)**
West Bromwich, 12 March, 1933 (IF)

League Club	Source	Date Signed	Seasons Played	Apps	Subs	Gls
West Bromwich A	Jnrs	04.50	52-55	21	-	4
Walsall	Tr	01.56	55-65	335	1	59

HODGSON Brian George
Cleethorpes, 29 January, 1936 (CF)

League Club	Source	Date Signed	Seasons Played	Apps	Subs	Gls
Grimsby T	Askern WMC	09.56	56	7	-	1
Workington	Tr	10.59	59	1	-	0

HODGSON David James
Gateshead, 6 August, 1960 Eu21-6 (F)

League Club	Source	Date Signed	Seasons Played	Apps	Subs	Gls
Middlesbrough	Redheugh BC	08.78	78-81	116	9	16
Liverpool	Tr	08.82	82-83	21	7	4
Sunderland	Tr	08.84	84-85	32	8	5
Norwich C	Tr	07.86	86	3	3	1
Middlesbrough	L	02.87	86	2	0	0
Sheffield Wed	Jerez (Sp)	08.88	88	6	5	1
Swansea C	Metz (Fr)	03.92	91	1	2	0

HODGSON Donald (Don)
Liversedge, 22 December, 1922 Died 1995 (IF)

League Club	Source	Date Signed	Seasons Played	Apps	Subs	Gls
Bradford PA	Bradford U	04.48	48-51	41	-	7

HODGSON Douglas (Doug) John
Frankston, Australia, 27 February, 1969 (CD)

League Club	Source	Date Signed	Seasons Played	Apps	Subs	Gls
Sheffield U	Heidelberg Alex (Aus)	07.94	94-96	24	6	0
Plymouth Arg	L	08.95	95	3	2	0
Burnley	L	10.96	96	1	0	0
Oldham Ath	Tr	02.97	96-98	33	8	4
Northampton T	Tr	10.98	98	7	1	1

HODGSON Gordon Henry
Newcastle, 13 October, 1952 Died 1999 ESch/EYth (M)

League Club	Source	Date Signed	Seasons Played	Apps	Subs	Gls
Newcastle U	Jnrs	06.71	71-73	8	1	0
Mansfield T	Tr	05.74	74-78	184	0	23
Oxford U	Tr	09.78	78-79	66	1	3
Peterborough U	Tr	08.80	80-81	82	1	5

HODGSON John Percival
Dawdon, 10 May, 1922 Died 1973 (G)

League Club	Source	Date Signed	Seasons Played	Apps	Subs	Gls
Leeds U	Murton CW	11.43	46-47	20	-	0
Middlesbrough	Tr	03.48	47-54	13	-	0

HODGSON John (Jack) Venner
Seaham Harbour, 30 September, 1913 Died 1970 (FB)

League Club	Source	Date Signed	Seasons Played	Apps	Subs	Gls
Grimsby T	Seaham Colliery	01.32	32-47	212	-	2
Doncaster Rov	Tr	01.48	47-51	95	-	2

HODGSON Kenneth (Ken)
Newcastle, 19 January, 1942 (F)

League Club	Source	Date Signed	Seasons Played	Apps	Subs	Gls
Newcastle U	Montague & N Fenham	05.59	60	6	-	0
Scunthorpe U	Tr	12.61	61-63	88	-	30
Bournemouth	Tr	06.64	64-65	77	1	24
Colchester U	Tr	07.66	66-68	56	1	19

HODGSON Lawrence (Laurie)
Birkenhead, 19 January, 1917 Died 1980 (FB)

League Club	Source	Date Signed	Seasons Played	Apps	Subs	Gls
Tranmere Rov	Silver Green	01.39	46-50	78	-	0

HODGSON Michael (Mike)
Newcastle, 6 July, 1945 (W)

League Club	Source	Date Signed	Seasons Played	Apps	Subs	Gls
Hartlepools U (Am)	Billingham Synthonia	08.64	64	1	-	0

HODGSON Noel
Workington, 25 December, 1938 (W)

League Club	Source	Date Signed	Seasons Played	Apps	Subs	Gls
Workington	Jnrs	08.57	57-62	51	-	12

HODGSON Richard James
Sunderland, 1 October, 1979 (M)

League Club	Source	Date Signed	Seasons Played	Apps	Subs	Gls
Nottingham F	YT	10.96				
Scunthorpe U	Tr	03.00	99	1	0	0
Darlington	Tr	08.00	00-02	66	32	6
Cambridge U	Crawley T	10.04	04	9	1	2

HODGSON Ronald (Ronnie)
Birkenhead, 2 November, 1922 (CD)

League Club	Source	Date Signed	Seasons Played	Apps	Subs	Gls
Tranmere Rov	Jnrs	02.41				
Manchester C	Tr	10.44	46	1	-	0
Southport	Tr	06.47	47-48	42	-	1
Crewe Alex	Tr	02.49	48-49	32	-	0

HODGSON Samuel (Sam)
Seaham Harbour, 21 January, 1919 Died 2000 (WH)

League Club	Source	Date Signed	Seasons Played	Apps	Subs	Gls
Grimsby T	Seaham Colliery	01.36	[illegible]	[illegible]	[illegible]	0
Mansfield T	Tr	07.48	[illegible]	[illegible]	[illegible]	[illegible]

HODGSON William (Billy)
Glasgow, 9 July, 1935

League Club	Source	Date Signed	Seasons Played	Apps	Subs	Gls
Sheffield U	St Johnstone	[illegible]	[illegible]	[illegible]	[illegible]	[illegible]
Leicester C	Tr	[illegible]	[illegible]	[illegible]	[illegible]	[illegible]
Derby Co	Tr	[illegible]	[illegible]	[illegible]	[illegible]	[illegible]
Rotherham U	Tr	[illegible]	[illegible]	[illegible]	[illegible]	[illegible]
York C	Tr	[illegible]	[illegible]	[illegible]	[illegible]	[illegible]

HODKINSON Andrew (Andy) Ja[illegible]
Ashton-under-Lyne, 4 November, 1965 ESc[illegible]

League Club	Source	Date Signed	Seasons Played	Apps	Subs	Gls
Oldham Ath	Bolton W (App)	[illegible]	[illegible]	[illegible]	[illegible]	[illegible]
Stockport Co	Tr	08.[illegible]	[illegible]	[illegible]	[illegible]	[illegible]
Scunthorpe U	Tr	08.88	[illegible]	[illegible]	[illegible]	[illegible]

HODKINSON David
Lancaster, 18 January, 1945

League Club	Source	Date Signed	Seasons Played	Apps	Subs	Gls
Oldham Ath	App	02.63	61	2	-	0

HODOUTO Kwami
Lome, Togo, 31 October, 1974 (FB)

League Club	Source	Date Signed	Seasons Played	Apps	Subs	Gls
Huddersfield T	Auxerre (Fr)	09.99	99	1	1	0

HODSON Simeon Paul
Lincoln, 5 March, 1966 (FB)

League Club	Source	Date Signed	Seasons Played	Apps	Subs	Gls
Notts Co	App	03.84	83-84	27	0	0
Charlton Ath	Tr	03.85	84	5	0	0
Lincoln C	Lincoln U	01.86	85-86	54	2	0
Newport Co	Tr	08.87	87	34	0	1
West Bromwich A	Tr	03.88	87-92	78	5	0
Doncaster Rov	Tr	09.92	92	15	0	0
Mansfield T	Kidderminster Hrs	02.93	92	17	0	0

HODSON Stuart William
Peterborough, 5 November, 1950 (CD)

League Club	Source	Date Signed	Seasons Played	Apps	Subs	Gls
Peterborough U	Ely C	11.74	74-76	24	10	0

HOEKMAN Daniel (Danny)
Nijmegen, Holland, 21 September, 1964 (M)

League Club	Source	Date Signed	Seasons Played	Apps	Subs	Gls
Manchester C	Den Haag (Holl)	10.91	91	0	1	0

HOEKSTRA Peter
Assen, Holland, 4 April, 1973 Hou21/Ho-5 (M)

League Club	Source	Date Signed	Seasons Played	Apps	Subs	Gls
Stoke C	Ajax (Holl)	07.01	01-03	66	12	11

HOGAN Charles (Charlie)
Bury, 23 April, 1926 Died 1992 (W)

League Club	Source	Date Signed	Seasons Played	Apps	Subs	Gls
Bury	Spartan Ath	06.47	47	1	-	0
Accrington St	Tr	08.49	49-50	56	-	4
Southport	Tr	08.51	51	9	-	1
Rochdale	Tr	08.52	52	3	-	0

HOGAN Thomas **Eric**
Cork, 17 December, 1971 (M)

League Club	Source	Date Signed	Seasons Played	Apps	Subs	Gls
Birmingham C	Cobh Ramblers	08.91	91	0	1	0

HOGAN Roy David
Hartlepool, 24 September, 1960 (M)

League Club	Source	Date Signed	Seasons Played	Apps	Subs	Gls
Hartlepool U	App	09.78	77-82	133	10	15
Hartlepool U	Crook T	12.83	83-86	138	3	17

HOGAN John **Terence (Terry)**
Hartlepool, 3 June, 1933 (IF)

League Club	Source	Date Signed	Seasons Played	Apps	Subs	Gls
Hartlepools U		08.57	57	9	-	1

HOGAN William (Billy) James
Salford, 9 January, 1924 (W)

League Club	Source	Date Signed	Seasons Played	Apps	Subs	Gls
Manchester C		05.42	48	3	-	0
Carlisle U	Tr	09.49	49-55	190	-	25

HOGARTH Gordon
Sunderland, 18 November, 1936 (WH)

League Club	Source	Date Signed	Seasons Played	Apps	Subs	Gls
Gateshead	Throckley Welfare	06.57	57-58	12	-	0

HOGG Adam
Airdrie, 26 April, 1934 (FB)

League Club	Source	Date Signed	Seasons Played	Apps	Subs	Gls
Swindon T	Airdrie	06.56	56	1	-	0

HOGG Christopher (Chris) Francis
Middlesbrough, 12 March, 1985 EYth (FB)

League Club	Source	Date Signed	Seasons Played	Apps	Subs	Gls
Ipswich T	Sch	08.02				
Boston U	L	10.03	03	10	0	0

HOGG Derek
Stockton Heath, 4 November, 1930 FLge-1 (W)

League Club	Source	Date Signed	Seasons Played	Apps	Subs	Gls
Leicester C	Chorley	10.52	52-57	161	-	26
West Bromwich A	Tr	04.58	58-60	81	-	11
Cardiff C	Tr	10.60	60-61	41	-	7

HOGG Frederick (Fred) William
Bishop Auckland, 24 April, 1918 (IF)

League Club	Source	Date Signed	Seasons Played	Apps	Subs	Gls
Luton T	West Auckland	12.36	37	4	-	0
Mansfield T	Tr	04.38	46-47	45	-	8
[illegible]alifax T	Tr	10.47	47-49	49	-	3

[illegible] Graeme James
[illegible]n, 17 June, 1964 SYth/Su21-4 (CD)

League Club	Source	Date Signed	Seasons Played	Apps	Subs	Gls
[illegible]ster U	App	06.82	83-87	82	1	1
[illegible]Bromwich A	L	11.87	87	7	0	0
[illegible]mouth	Tr	08.88	88-90	97	3	2
[illegible]s Co	Heart of Midlothian	01.95	94-97	66	0	0
[illegible]entford	Tr	01.98	97	17	0	2

HOGG Graham Stuart
Neath, 15 January, 1922 Died 1999 WAmat (W)

League Club	Source	Date Signed	Seasons Played	Apps	Subs	Gls
Cardiff C	Cardiff Corinthians	06.48	48	1	-	0

HOGG John (Jack)
Blyth, 7 October, 1931 Died 2001 (W)

League Club	Source	Date Signed	Seasons Played	Apps	Subs	Gls
Sunderland		12.49				
Portsmouth	Blyth Spartans	12.54				
Gateshead	Peterborough U	07.57	57-59	80	-	21

HOGG Lewis James
Bristol, 13 September, 1982 (M)

League Club	Source	Date Signed	Seasons Played	Apps	Subs	Gls
Bristol Rov	YT	09.99	00-02	61	13	3

HOGG Anthony **Raymond (Ray)**
Lowick, 11 December, 1929 (FB)

League Club	Source	Date Signed	Seasons Played	Apps	Subs	Gls
Aston Villa	Berwick Rgrs	03.55	54-56	21	-	0
Mansfield T	Tr	07.58	58-59	11	-	0
Peterborough U	Tr	08.60	60	2	-	0

HOGGAN David Matthew
Falkirk, 10 August, 1961 (M)

League Club	Source	Date Signed	Seasons Played	Apps	Subs	Gls
Bolton W	App	08.79	79-82	83	10	11

HOGGART Dennis Joseph
Glasgow, 2 January, 1939 (W)

League Club	Source	Date Signed	Seasons Played	Apps	Subs	Gls
Leeds U	Ferndale Ath	02.57				
York C	Tr	08.60	60-63	45	-	11
Stockport Co	Tr	08.64	64-65	30	0	6

HOGGETH Gary Denis
South Shields, 7 October, 1979 (G)

League Club	Source	Date Signed	Seasons Played	Apps	Subs	Gls
Doncaster Rov	YT	•	97	8	0	0

League Club	Source	Date Signed	Seasons Played	Apps	Subs	Gls
HOGH Jes						
Aalborg, Denmark, 7 May, 1966 Denmark 57						(CD)
Chelsea	Fenerbahce (Tu)	07.99	99	6	3	0
HOLAH Eric Tansley						
Hull, 3 August, 1937						(CF)
Hull C (Am)	Malet Lambert OB	06.60	60	1	-	1
Bradford C	Tr	08.61	61	4	-	2
HOLBROOK Ian Clifford						
Knutsford, 24 November, 1955						(G)
Bolton W	Jnrs	07.74				
Stockport Co	Tr	07.76	76	37	0	0
HOLBROOK Leigh William						
Belper, 6 August, 1979						(CD)
Mansfield T	YT	07.97	96	0	1	0
HOLBROOK Stephen (Steve)						
Richmond, North Yorkshire, 16 September, 1952 ESch						(W)
Hull C	App	09.70	70-71	2	1	0
Darlington	Tr	06.72	72-76	104	12	12
HOLBUTT Barry Lewis						
Birmingham, 11 February, 1943						(CF)
Aston Villa	Jnrs	10.60				
Walsall	Nuneaton Borough	03.65	65	0	1	0
HOLCROFT Peter Ian						
Liverpool, 3 January, 1976						(M)
Everton	YT	07.94				
Swindon T	Tr	11.96	96	2	1	0
Exeter C	L	08.97	97	3	3	0
HOLD John David						
Southampton, 28 March, 1948						(M)
Bournemouth	App	11.64	65-70	80	5	24
Crewe Alex	L	01.69	68	0	2	0
Northampton T	Tr	08.71	71-72	42	2	11
HOLD Oscar						
Carlton, West Yorkshire, 19 October, 1918						(IF)
Barnsley	Denaby U	08.37				
Aldershot	Tr	04.39	46	14	-	4
Norwich C	Tr	03.47	46-48	44	-	18
Notts Co	Tr	10.48	48	19	-	9
Everton	Chelmsford C	02.50	49-50	22	-	5
Queens Park Rgrs	Tr	02.52	51-52	5	-	1
HOLDEN Alan						
Haslingden, 12 October, 1941						(WH)
Blackburn Rov	Jnrs	01.62	63	1	-	0
Stockport Co	Tr	07.66	66	1	0	0
HOLDEN Andrew (Andy) Ian						
Flint, 14 September, 1962 Wu21-1/W-1						(CD)
Chester C	Rhyl	08.83	83-86	100	0	16
Wigan Ath	Tr	10.86	86-88	48	1	4
Oldham Ath	Tr	01.89	88-94	22	0	4
HOLDEN Dean Thomas John						
Salford, 15 September, 1979 EYth						(FB)
Bolton W	YT	12.97	99-00	7	6	1
Oldham Ath	Tr	10.01	01-04	98	10	10
HOLDEN Albert **Douglas (Doug)**						
Manchester, 28 September, 1930 EYth/FLge-1/E-5						(W)
Bolton W	Manchester YMCA	01.50	51-62	419	-	40
Preston NE	Tr	11.62	62-64	90	-	13
HOLDEN Melville (Mel) George						
Dundee, 25 August, 1954 Died 1981						(F)
Preston NE	App	09.72	72-74	69	3	22
Sunderland	Tr	07.75	75-77	66	7	23
Blackpool	Tr	07.78	78	2	1	0
HOLDEN Richard (Rick) William						
Skipton, 9 September, 1964						(W)
Burnley	Carnegie College	03.86	85	0	1	0
Halifax T	Tr	09.86	86-87	66	1	12
Watford	Tr	03.88	87-88	42	0	8
Oldham Ath	Tr	08.89	89-91	125	4	19
Manchester C	Tr	07.92	92-93	49	1	3
Oldham Ath	Tr	10.93	93-94	46	14	9
Blackpool	Tr	09.95	95	19	3	2
HOLDEN Robert (Robbie)						
Sunderland, 28 October, 1965						(F)
Scunthorpe U	Sunderland (App)	09.83	83	6	1	1
HOLDEN Simon John						
Littleborough, 9 March, 1968						(M)
Rochdale	Jnrs	07.85				
Rochdale	Wheatsheaf	01.87	86-87	35	14	4
HOLDEN Stephen (Steve) Anthony						
Luton, 4 September, 1972 ESch/ESemiPro						(CD)
Leicester C	YT	03.91	91	1	0	0
Carlisle U	Tr	10.92	92-93	22	0	1
HOLDEN James **Stewart**						
Grange Moor, 21 April, 1942 Died 2004						(FB)
Huddersfield T	Jnrs	04.59	60-64	28	-	2
Oldham Ath	Tr	07.65	65-66	39	3	5
Rochdale	Tr	01.67	66	21	0	0
HOLDEN William (Bill)						
Bolton, 1 April, 1928 EB						(CF)
Burnley	Everton (Am)	11.49	50-55	187	-	75
Sunderland	Tr	12.55	55	19	-	5
Stockport Co	Tr	10.56	56-58	87	-	37
Bury	Tr	03.59	58-61	100	-	33
Halifax T	Tr	06.62	62	37	-	10
HOLDER Alan Maurice						
Oxford, 10 December, 1931						(IF)
Nottingham F		04.52	54	3	-	0
Lincoln C	Tr	07.55	55	1	-	0
Tranmere Rov	Tr	12.56	56	13	-	1
HOLDER Colin Walter						
Cheltenham, 6 January, 1944						(CF)
Coventry C	App	05.61	60-61	9	-	4
HOLDER David (Dave) James						
Cheltenham, 15 December, 1943 Died 2002						(CD)
Notts Co	Cardiff C (Am)	10.62	63	8	-	0
Barrow	Tr	07.64	64	29	-	0
HOLDER Jorden Andrew						
Oxford, 22 October, 1982						(M)
Oxford U	YT	•	00	0	2	0
HOLDER Philip (Phil)						
Kilburn, 19 January, 1952 EYth						(M)
Tottenham H	App	02.69	71-73	9	4	1
Crystal Palace	Tr	02.75	74-77	93	2	5
Bournemouth	Memphis (USA)	03.79	78-79	58	0	4
HOLDER Stephen (Steve) William						
Nottingham, 21 April, 1952						(W)
Notts Co	App	04.70	69	0	1	0
HOLDING Edwin (Eddie) John						
Wolverhampton, 15 October, 1930						(FB)
Walsall		01.49	50-53	39	-	6
Barrow		07.54	54	5	-	5
HOLDSWORTH Andrew (Andy)						
Pontefract, 29 January, 1984						(M)
Huddersfield T	Sch	12.03	03-04	69	7	0
HOLDSWORTH David Gary						
Walthamstow, 8 November, 1968 EYth/Eu21-1						(CD)
Watford	App	11.86	88-95	249	9	10
Sheffield U	Tr	10.96	96-98	93	0	4
Birmingham C	Tr	03.99	98-01	78	7	7
Walsall	L	01.02	01	9	0	1
HOLDSWORTH Dean Christopher						
Walthamstow, 8 November, 1968 EB-1						(F)
Watford	App	11.86	87-89	2	14	3
Carlisle U	L	02.88	87	4	0	1
Port Vale	L	03.88	87	6	0	2
Swansea C	L	08.88	88	4	1	1
Brentford	L	10.88	88	2	5	1
Brentford	Tr	09.89	89-91	106	4	53
Wimbledon	Tr	07.92	92-97	148	21	58
Bolton W	Tr	10.97	97-02	97	61	39
Coventry C	Tr	11.02	02	13	4	0
Rushden & Diamonds	Tr	03.03	02	4	3	2
Wimbledon	Tr	07.03	03	14	14	3
HOLE Alan Vincent						
Swansea, 26 December, 1930						(CD)
Swansea T		07.53	53	21	-	0
HOLE Barrington (Barry) Gerard						
Swansea, 16 September, 1942 WSch/Wu23-5/W-30						(CD)
Cardiff C	Jnrs	09.59	59-65	208	0	16
Blackburn Rov	Tr	07.66	66-68	79	0	13

League Club	Source	Date Signed	Seasons Played	Apps	Subs	Gls
Aston Villa	Tr	09.68	68-69	47	0	6
Swansea C	Tr	07.70	70-71	78	0	3

HOLE Stuart Mark
Oxford, 17 July, 1985 (CD)

League Club	Source	Date Signed	Seasons Played	Apps	Subs	Gls
Wycombe W	Sch	•	03	0	1	0

HOLGATE Ashan Bayyan Sellasse
Swindon, 9 November, 1986 (F)

League Club	Source	Date Signed	Seasons Played	Apps	Subs	Gls
Swindon T	Sch	•	04	0	2	0

HOLLAND Christopher (Chris) James
Clitheroe, 11 September, 1975 EYth/Eu21-10 (M)

League Club	Source	Date Signed	Seasons Played	Apps	Subs	Gls
Preston NE	YT	•	93	0	1	0
Newcastle U	Tr	01.94	93	2	1	0
Birmingham C	Tr	09.96	96-99	39	31	0
Huddersfield T	Tr	02.00	99-03	113	7	2
Boston U	Tr	03.04	03-04	33	4	0

HOLLAND David William
Chorley, 6 March, 1935 (IF)

League Club	Source	Date Signed	Seasons Played	Apps	Subs	Gls
Stockport Co	Horwich RMI	06.59	59-60	25	-	4

HOLLAND Kenneth (Ken)
Doncaster, 18 April, 1922 Died 1972 (IF)

League Club	Source	Date Signed	Seasons Played	Apps	Subs	Gls
Bury	Wolverhampton W (Am)	09.44				
Bournemouth	Tr	09.48	48	3	-	0

HOLLAND Matthew (Matt) Rhys
Bury, 11 April, 1974 IRB-1/IR-46 (M)

League Club	Source	Date Signed	Seasons Played	Apps	Subs	Gls
West Ham U	YT	07.92				
Bournemouth	Tr	01.95	94-96	97	7	18
Ipswich T	Tr	07.97	97-02	259	0	38
Charlton Ath	Tr	06.03	03-04	69	1	9

HOLLAND Patrick (Pat) George
Poplar, 13 September, 1950 (W)

League Club	Source	Date Signed	Seasons Played	Apps	Subs	Gls
West Ham U	App	04.69	68-80	227	18	23
Bournemouth	L	03.71	70	10	0	0

HOLLAND Paul
Lincoln, 8 July, 1973 ESch/EYth/Eu21-4 (M)

League Club	Source	Date Signed	Seasons Played	Apps	Subs	Gls
Mansfield T	Jnrs	07.91	90-94	149	0	25
Sheffield U	Tr	06.95	95	11	7	1
Chesterfield	Tr	01.96	95-99	108	6	11
Bristol C	Tr	09.99	99-00	27	5	1

HOLLAND Eric **Reginald (Reg)**
Sutton-in-Ashfield, 23 January, 1940 ESch/EYth (FB)

League Club	Source	Date Signed	Seasons Played	Apps	Subs	Gls
Manchester U	Jnrs	05.57				
Wrexham	Tr	03.60	59-65	118	0	0
Chester	Tr	03.66	65-66	5	1	0

HOLLAND Robert James
Willesden, 18 August, 1965 (FB)

League Club	Source	Date Signed	Seasons Played	Apps	Subs	Gls
Crewe Alex	Harrow Borough	09.85	85	7	0	0

HOLLAND Simon Luke David
Sunderland, 26 March, 1973 (F)

League Club	Source	Date Signed	Seasons Played	Apps	Subs	Gls
Doncaster Rov	YT	01.91	90	1	0	0

HOLLETT Ivan Ronald
Pinxton, 22 April, 1940 (F)

League Club	Source	Date Signed	Seasons Played	Apps	Subs	Gls
Mansfield T	Sutton T	08.58	58-64	98	-	40
Chesterfield	Tr	12.64	64-68	157	0	62
Crewe Alex	Tr	11.68	68-70	55	3	19
Cambridge U	Tr	11.70	70-71	37	1	13
Hereford U	Tr	01.72	72	11	0	2

HOLLEY Thomas (Tom)
Sunderland, 15 November, 1913 Died 1992 (CD)

League Club	Source	Date Signed	Seasons Played	Apps	Subs	Gls
Barnsley	Sunderland (Am)	09.32	33-35	72	-	4
Leeds U	Tr	07.36	36-48	162	-	1

HOLLIDAY Edwin (Eddie)
Barnsley, 7 June, 1939 Eu23-5/FLge-1/E-3 (W)

League Club	Source	Date Signed	Seasons Played	Apps	Subs	Gls
Middlesbrough	Jnrs	08.56	57-61	134	-	18
Sheffield Wed	Tr	03.62	61-63	55	-	12
Middlesbrough	Tr	06.65	65	23	0	4
Workington	Hereford U	02.68	67-68	56	0	4
Peterborough U	Tr	07.69	69	12	4	1

HOLLIDAY John Richard
Penrith, 13 March, 1970 (CD)

League Club	Source	Date Signed	Seasons Played	Apps	Subs	Gls
Carlisle U		09.89	90-92	19	0	0

HOLLIDAY Kenneth (Ken) Joseph
Darwen, 19 August, 1925 Died 1999 (FB)

League Club	Source	Date Signed	Seasons Played	Apps	Subs	Gls
Blackburn Rov	Darwen Jnrs	10.46	47-51	29	-	0
Accrington St	Tr	07.52	52-54	96	-	5
Barrow	Tr	09.55	55	5	-	0

HOLLIFIELD Michael (Mike)
Middlesbrough, 2 May, 1961 (FB)

League Club	Source	Date Signed	Seasons Played	Apps	Subs	Gls
Wolverhampton W	App	04.79	80-81	21	0	0
Hull C	Tr	08.83	83-84	45	0	1
Tranmere Rov	Tr	07.85	85	0	1	0

HOLLIGAN Gavin Victor
Lambeth, 13 June, 1980 (F)

League Club	Source	Date Signed	Seasons Played	Apps	Subs	Gls
West Ham U	Kingstonian	03.99	98	0	1	0
Leyton Orient	L	09.99	99	1	0	0
Exeter C	L	10.00	00	3	0	0
Wycombe W	Tr	08.01	01-03	20	23	8

HOLLINS David (Dave) Michael
Bangor, 4 February, 1938 Wu23-2/W-11 (G)

League Club	Source	Date Signed	Seasons Played	Apps	Subs	Gls
Brighton & Hove A	Merrow	11.55	57-60	66	-	0
Newcastle U	Tr	03.61	60-66	112	0	0
Mansfield T	Tr	02.67	66-69	111	0	0
Nottingham F	L	03.70	69	9	0	0
Aldershot	Tr	07.70	70	16	0	0

HOLLINS John William
Guildford, 16 July, 1946 EYth/Eu23-12/EB/FLge-3/E-1 (M)

League Club	Source	Date Signed	Seasons Played	Apps	Subs	Gls
Chelsea	App	07.63	63-74	436	0	47
Queens Park Rgrs	Tr	06.75	75-78	148	3	6
Arsenal	Tr	07.79	79-82	123	4	9
Chelsea	Tr	06.83	83	29	0	1

HOLLINSHEAD Shaun
Sandbach, 21 February, 1961 (M)

League Club	Source	Date Signed	Seasons Played	Apps	Subs	Gls
Crewe Alex	App	•	77	2	3	0

HOLLIS Andrew
Huntingdon, 16 September, 1963 (F)

League Club	Source	Date Signed	Seasons Played	Apps	Subs	Gls
Cambridge U	Ramsey T	04.87	86-87	3	1	0

HOLLIS Harold (Harry)
Shotton, 12 December, 1913 Died 1982 (FB)

League Club	Source	Date Signed	Seasons Played	Apps	Subs	Gls
Wrexham	Connah's Quay	08.46	46	1	-	0

HOLLIS Jermain Phydell
Nottingham, 7 October, 1986 JaYth (CD)

League Club	Source	Date Signed	Seasons Played	Apps	Subs	Gls
Kidderminster Hrs	Eastwood T	11.04	04	0	1	0

HOLLIS Kenneth **Michael (Mick)**
Loughborough, 14 November, 1949 (F)

League Club	Source	Date Signed	Seasons Played	Apps	Subs	Gls
Leicester C	App	11.66				
Barrow	Tr	07.69	69-71	88	3	13
Chester	Tr	07.72	72	34	3	8
Stockport Co	Tr	07.73	73-75	106	6	33
Reading	Tr	03.76	75-76	18	7	6

HOLLIS Roy Walter
Great Yarmouth, 24 December, 1925 Died 1998 (CF)

League Club	Source	Date Signed	Seasons Played	Apps	Subs	Gls
Norwich C	Yarmouth T	05.47	47-51	96	-	52
Tottenham H	Tr	12.52	52	3	-	1
Southend U	Tr	02.54	53-59	240	-	120

HOLLIS Stephen (Steve) John
Liverpool, 22 August, 1972 (FB)

League Club	Source	Date Signed	Seasons Played	Apps	Subs	Gls
Liverpool	YT	05.90				
Wigan Ath	Knowsley U	08.93	93	0	1	0

HOLLOW Michael (Mike) John
Nazeing, 5 September, 1943 Died 2003 (FB)

League Club	Source	Date Signed	Seasons Played	Apps	Subs	Gls
Leyton Orient	Bishops Stortford	08.62	63-64	34	-	0
Peterborough U	Tr	07.65	65	14	0	1

HOLLOWAY Christopher (Chris) David
Swansea, 5 February, 1980 Wu21-2 (M)

League Club	Source	Date Signed	Seasons Played	Apps	Subs	Gls
Exeter C	YT	07.98	97-00	51	17	2

HOLLOWAY Darren
Crook, 3 October, 1977 Eu21-1 (FB)

League Club	Source	Date Signed	Seasons Played	Apps	Subs	Gls
Sunderland	YT	10.95	97-00	46	12	0
Carlisle U	L	08.97	97	5	0	0
Bolton W	L	12.99	99	3	1	0
Wimbledon	Tr	10.00	00-03	84	8	0
Scunthorpe U	L	02.04	03	5	0	1
Bradford C	Tr	08.04	04	33	0	1

HOLLOWAY Ian Scott
Kingswood, 12 March, 1963 (W)

League Club	Source	Date Signed	Seasons Played	Apps	Subs	Gls
Bristol Rov	App	03.81	80-84	104	7	14
Wimbledon	Tr	07.85	85	19	0	2
Brentford	L	03.86	85	13	0	2
Brentford	Tr	07.86	86-87	14	3	0
Torquay U	L	01.87	86	5	0	0
Bristol Rov	Tr	08.87	87-90	179	0	26
Queens Park Rgrs	Tr	08.91	91-95	130	17	4
Bristol Rov	Tr	07.96	96-98	96	11	1

HOLLOWBREAD John Frederick
Enfield, 2 January, 1934 (G)

League Club	Source	Date Signed	Seasons Played	Apps	Subs	Gls
Tottenham H	Enfield	01.52	58-63	67	-	0
Southampton	Tr	05.64	64-65	36	0	0

HOLLUND Martin
Stord, Norway, 11 August, 1974 Nou21 (G)

League Club	Source	Date Signed	Seasons Played	Apps	Subs	Gls
Hartlepool U	SK Brann Bergen (Nor)	11.97	97-01	117	0	0

HOLLYMAN Kenneth (Ken) Charles
Cardiff, 18 November, 1922 WLge-1 (WH)

League Club	Source	Date Signed	Seasons Played	Apps	Subs	Gls
Cardiff C	Cardiff Nomads	04.42	46-53	189	-	8
Newport Co	Tr	11.53	53-59	229	-	4

HOLLYWOOD Denis Fallan
Govan, 3 November, 1944 Su23-1 (FB)

League Club	Source	Date Signed	Seasons Played	Apps	Subs	Gls
Southampton	App	12.61	62-71	234	0	4

HOLMAN Harold (Harry) Western
Exeter, 25 September, 1920 Died 1977 (CF)

League Club	Source	Date Signed	Seasons Played	Apps	Subs	Gls
Exeter C	Budleigh Salterton	12.46	46	4	-	2

HOLMAN Harold (Harry) William
Exeter, 16 November, 1957 ESch (F)

League Club	Source	Date Signed	Seasons Played	Apps	Subs	Gls
Exeter C	Chelsea (App)	07.76	76-78	47	5	9
Peterborough U	Tr	12.78	78	9	0	1

HOLME Philip (Phil) Charles
Briton Ferry, 21 June, 1947 (F)

League Club	Source	Date Signed	Seasons Played	Apps	Subs	Gls
Swansea C	Bridgend Thursday	03.71	70-71	19	4	5
Hull C	Tr	07.72	72-73	29	9	11

HOLMES Albert Valentine
Ecclesfield, 14 February, 1942 (FB)

League Club	Source	Date Signed	Seasons Played	Apps	Subs	Gls
Chesterfield	East Midlands Gas Bd	06.61	61-75	468	3	10

HOLMES Andrew (Andy) John
Stoke-on-Trent, 7 January, 1969 (CD)

League Club	Source	Date Signed	Seasons Played	Apps	Subs	Gls
Stoke C	App	01.87	87-89	6	2	0
Doncaster Rov	Tr	07.90	90	10	1	0

HOLMES Barry
Bradford, 4 October, 1942 (W)

League Club	Source	Date Signed	Seasons Played	Apps	Subs	Gls
Halifax T	Ossett A	09.66	66-72	82	8	8

HOLMES Bert Harold Frank
Norwich, 27 September, 1924 Died 2003 (CD)

League Club	Source	Date Signed	Seasons Played	Apps	Subs	Gls
Norwich C	Gothic	08.47	48-54	58	-	1

HOLMES Albert **Colin**
Winchester, 28 March, 1939 EYth (CD)

League Club	Source	Date Signed	Seasons Played	Apps	Subs	Gls
Southampton	Jnrs	02.57	59	1	-	0

HOLMES Daniel (Danny) Gavin Charles
Clophill, 13 June, 1972 (M)

League Club	Source	Date Signed	Seasons Played	Apps	Subs	Gls
Middlesbrough	YT	01.90				
Bournemouth	Tr	07.91	92	0	1	0

HOLMES David James
Derby, 22 November, 1971 (F)

League Club	Source	Date Signed	Seasons Played	Apps	Subs	Gls
Scarborough	YT	07.91	89-91	4	7	1

HOLMES Derek
Lanark, 18 October, 1978 (F)

League Club	Source	Date Signed	Seasons Played	Apps	Subs	Gls
Bournemouth	Ross Co	09.01	01-04	63	52	16

HOLMES Ian Michael
Wombwell, 8 December, 1950 (M)

League Club	Source	Date Signed	Seasons Played	Apps	Subs	Gls
Sheffield U	Jnrs	01.68	71-72	4	2	0
York C	Tr	07.73	73-77	152	7	30
Huddersfield T	Tr	10.77	77-79	65	8	21

HOLMES James (Jimmy) Paul
Dublin, 11 November, 1953 IR-30 (FB)

League Club	Source	Date Signed	Seasons Played	Apps	Subs	Gls
Coventry C	App	11.70	71-76	122	6	6
Tottenham H	Tr	03.77	76-78	81	0	2
Leicester C	Vancouver (Can)	10.82	82	2	0	0
Brentford	Tr	02.83	82	4	0	0
Torquay U	Tr	03.83	82-83	25	0	3
Peterborough U	Tr	11.83	83-85	48	1	7

HOLMES Joseph
Clay Cross, 10 February, 1926 (WH)

League Club	Source	Date Signed	Seasons Played	Apps	Subs	Gls
Chesterfield	Parkhouse Colliery	09.46	47-51	29	-	3

HOLMES Kyle Jonathon
Abergavenny, 25 September, 1959 (M)

League Club	Source	Date Signed	Seasons Played	Apps	Subs	Gls
Hereford U	App	10.77	77-79	25	3	3

HOLMES Lee Daniel
Mansfield, 2 April, 1987 EYth (M)

League Club	Source	Date Signed	Seasons Played	Apps	Subs	Gls
Derby Co	Sch	05.04	02-04	17	11	2
Swindon T	L	12.04	04	14	1	1

HOLMES Lee John
Aveley, 28 September, 1955 (F)

League Club	Source	Date Signed	Seasons Played	Apps	Subs	Gls
Brentford	Haringey Borough	06.79	79	26	2	6

HOLMES Matthew (Matt) Jason
Luton, 1 August, 1969 (M)

League Club	Source	Date Signed	Seasons Played	Apps	Subs	Gls
Bournemouth	YT	08.88	88-91	105	9	8
Cardiff C	L	03.89	88	0	1	0
West Ham U	Tr	08.92	92-94	63	13	4
Blackburn Rov	Tr	08.95	95	8	1	1
Charlton Ath	Tr	07.97	97	10	6	1

HOLMES Michael (Micky) Arthur
Blackpool, 9 September, 1965 (M)

League Club	Source	Date Signed	Seasons Played	Apps	Subs	Gls
Bradford C	Yeadon Celtic	07.84	84	0	5	0
Wolverhampton W	Burnley (N/C)	11.85	85-87	74	9	13
Huddersfield T	Tr	07.88	88	3	4	0
Cambridge U	Tr	02.89	88	7	4	0
Rochdale	Tr	07.89	89-90	47	7	7
Torquay U	Tr	12.90	90-91	34	6	3
Carlisle U	Tr	02.92	91-92	33	1	4
Northampton T	Tr	03.93	92	6	0	0

HOLMES Nicholas (Nick) Charles
Southampton, 11 November, 1954 (M)

League Club	Source	Date Signed	Seasons Played	Apps	Subs	Gls
Southampton	App	11.72	73-86	437	7	56

HOLMES Paul
Stocksbridge, 18 February, 1968 (FB)

League Club	Source	Date Signed	Seasons Played	Apps	Subs	Gls
Doncaster Rov	App	02.86	85-87	42	5	1
Torquay U	Tr	08.88	88-91	127	12	4
Birmingham C	Tr	06.92	92	12	0	0
Everton	Tr	03.93	92-95	21	0	0
West Bromwich A	Tr	01.96	95-98	102	1	1
Torquay U	Tr	11.99	99-02	82	5	2

HOLMES Peter James
Bishop Auckland, 18 November, 1980 ESch/EYth (M)

League Club	Source	Date Signed	Seasons Played	Apps	Subs	Gls
Sheffield Wed	YT	12.97				
Luton T	Tr	08.00	00-04	48	29	9

HOLMES Richard
Grantham, 7 November, 1980 (CD)

League Club	Source	Date Signed	Seasons Played	Apps	Subs	Gls
Notts Co	YT	03.99	98-02	47	12	0

HOLMES Roger William
Scunthorpe, 9 September, 1942 (M)

League Club	Source	Date Signed	Seasons Played	Apps	Subs	Gls
Lincoln C	Jnrs	09.59	59-71	276	2	36

HOLMES Shaun Paul
Derry, 27 December, 1980 NISch/NIYth/NIu21-13/NI-1 (FB)

League Club	Source	Date Signed	Seasons Played	Apps	Subs	Gls
Manchester C	YT	01.98				
Wrexham	Tr	08.01	01-03	55	28	2

HOLMES Stanley (Stan)
Easington, 27 November, 1920 Died 1994 (FB)

League Club	Source	Date Signed	Seasons Played	Apps	Subs	Gls
Hartlepools U		07.47	49	1	-	0

HOLMES Steven (Steve) Peter
Middlesbrough, 13 January, 1971 (CD)

League Club	Source	Date Signed	Seasons Played	Apps	Subs	Gls
Lincoln C	YT	07.89				
Preston NE	Guisborough T	03.94	94-95	13	0	1
Hartlepool U	L	03.95	94	5	0	2
Lincoln C	L	10.95	95	12	0	1
Lincoln C	Tr	03.96	95-01	185	4	32

HOLMES Thomas (Tommy)
Hemsworth, 14 December, 1934 (IF)

League Club	Source	Date Signed	Seasons Played	Apps	Subs	Gls
Barnsley	Hemsworth YC	03.53	54-58	35	-	7
Halifax T	Tr	07.59	59-60	50	-	16
Chesterfield	Tr	07.61	61	20	-	3

HOLMES William (Bill)
Hunslet, 29 October, 1926 EAmat (IF)

League Club	Source	Date Signed	Seasons Played	Apps	Subs	Gls
Doncaster Rov (Am)	Wolverhampton W (Am)	10.50	50	2	-	0
Blackburn Rov (Am)	Morecambe	01.52	51-52	21	-	16
Bradford C	Morecambe	09.53	53	22	-	5
Southport	Tr	07.54	54-55	56	-	21

HOLMES William (Billy) Gerald
Balham, 4 February, 1951 Died 1988 (F)

League Club	Source	Date Signed	Seasons Played	Apps	Subs	Gls
Millwall	Woking	07.70	70	0	1	0
Luton T	Tr	07.73	73	0	1	0
Wimbledon	Barnet	07.75	77	15	0	5
Hereford U	Tr	11.77	77-78	21	10	5
Brentford	Tr	08.79	79	8	7	2

HOLNESS Dean Thomas
Lewisham, 25 July, 1976 (M)

League Club	Source	Date Signed	Seasons Played	Apps	Subs	Gls
Southend U	Dulwich Hamlet	08.01	01	1	1	0

HOLSGROVE John William
Southwark, 27 September, 1945 EYth (CD)

League Club	Source	Date Signed	Seasons Played	Apps	Subs	Gls
Crystal Palace	Tottenham H (Am)	02.64	64	18	-	2
Wolverhampton W	Tr	05.65	65-70	178	2	7
Sheffield Wed	Tr	06.71	71-74	103	1	5
Stockport Co	Tr	08.75	75	9	0	0

HOLSGROVE Lee
Wendover, 13 December, 1979 (CD)

League Club	Source	Date Signed	Seasons Played	Apps	Subs	Gls
Millwall	Jnrs	07.96				
Wycombe W	Tr	03.98	98-99	5	5	0

HOLSGROVE Paul
Wellington, Shropshire, 26 August, 1969 (M)

League Club	Source	Date Signed	Seasons Played	Apps	Subs	Gls
Aldershot	YT	02.87	87-88	0	3	0
Luton T	Wokingham T	01.91	90-91	1	1	0
Millwall	Heracles (Holl)	08.92	92	3	8	0
Reading	Tr	08.94	94-97	63	7	6
Grimsby T	L	09.97	97	3	7	0
Crewe Alex	Tr	11.97	97	7	1	1
Stoke C	Tr	01.98	97	11	1	1
Brighton & Hove A	Tr	07.98				
Darlington	Hibernian	03.00	99	1	2	0

HOLSTER Marco
Weesp, Holland, 4 December, 1971 (M)

League Club	Source	Date Signed	Seasons Played	Apps	Subs	Gls
Ipswich T	Heracles (Holl)	07.98	98	1	9	0

HOLT Andrew (Andy)
Stockport, 21 May, 1978 (FB)

League Club	Source	Date Signed	Seasons Played	Apps	Subs	Gls
Oldham Ath	YT	07.96	96-00	104	20	10
Hull C	Tr	03.01	00-03	45	26	3
Barnsley	L	08.02	02	4	3	0
Shrewsbury T	L	03.03	02	9	0	0
Wrexham	Tr	08.04	04	45	0	6

HOLT David
Padiham, 26 February, 1952 Died 2003 (CD)

League Club	Source	Date Signed	Seasons Played	Apps	Subs	Gls
Bury	App	10.69	69-74	174	5	9
Oldham Ath	Tr	12.74	74-79	141	1	1
Burnley	Tr	07.80	80-82	84	0	1

HOLT David Arthur
Gorton, 18 November, 1984 (F)

League Club	Source	Date Signed	Seasons Played	Apps	Subs	Gls
Stockport Co	YT	10.02	01	0	1	0

HOLT David Ephraim
Sunniside, 7 January, 1945 (CD)

League Club	Source	Date Signed	Seasons Played	Apps	Subs	Gls
Blackburn Rov	Jnrs	04.63	65-66	10	0	0

HOLT Gary James
Irvine, 9 March, 1973 S-10 (M)

League Club	Source	Date Signed	Seasons Played	Apps	Subs	Gls
Stoke C	Glasgow Celtic (N/C)	10.94				
Norwich C	Kilmarnock	03.01	00-04	161	7	3

HOLT George
Halifax, 28 February, 1927 (IF)

League Club	Source	Date Signed	Seasons Played	Apps	Subs	Gls
Halifax T		07.47	47-53	57	-	12

HOLT Grant
Carlisle, 12 April, 1981 (F)

League Club	Source	Date Signed	Seasons Played	Apps	Subs	Gls
Halifax T	Workington	09.99	99-00	0	6	0
Sheffield Wed	Barrow	03.03	02-03	12	12	3
Rochdale	Tr	01.04	03-04	54	0	21

HOLT Michael Andrew
Burnley, 28 July, 1977 (F)

League Club	Source	Date Signed	Seasons Played	Apps	Subs	Gls
Blackburn Rov	YT	07.95				
Preston NE	Tr	08.96	96-98	12	24	5
Macclesfield T	L	09.98	98	3	1	1
Rochdale	Tr	11.98	98-99	25	13	7

HOLT Raymond (Ray)
Thorne, 29 October, 1939 (CD)

League Club	Source	Date Signed	Seasons Played	Apps	Subs	Gls
Huddersfield T	Moor Ends Ath	08.58	61-63	16	-	0
Oldham Ath	Tr	07.65	65	14	1	0
Halifax T	Tr	07.66	66-67	86	0	0
Scunthorpe U	Tr	07.68	68-69	50	0	0

HOLT William (Billy) Kenneth
Boldon, 31 March, 1926 (CD)

League Club	Source	Date Signed	Seasons Played	Apps	Subs	Gls
Blackburn Rov	Boldon CW	01.49	48-52	78	-	0
Barrow	Weymouth	06.54	54-56	74	-	0

HOLTHAM Dean Mark
Pontypridd, 30 September, 1963 (FB)

League Club	Source	Date Signed	Seasons Played	Apps	Subs	Gls
Cardiff C	App	09.81				
Swansea C	Tr	08.82	83	6	0	0
Newport Co	Ebbw Vale	09.87	87	4	2	0

HOLTON Clifford (Cliff) Charles
Oxford, 29 April, 1929 Died 1996 (F)

League Club	Source	Date Signed	Seasons Played	Apps	Subs	Gls
Arsenal	Oxford C	11.47	50-58	198	-	83
Watford	Tr	10.58	58-61	120	-	84
Northampton T	Tr	09.61	61-62	62	-	50
Crystal Palace	Tr	12.62	62-64	101	-	40
Watford	Tr	05.65	65	24	0	12
Charlton Ath	Tr	02.66	65	18	0	7
Leyton Orient	Tr	07.66	66-67	47	0	17

HOLTON James (Jim) Allan
Lesmahagow, 11 April, 1951 Died 1993 Su23-1/S-15 (CD)

League Club	Source	Date Signed	Seasons Played	Apps	Subs	Gls
West Bromwich A	Jnrs	04.68				
Shrewsbury T	Tr	06.71	71-72	67	0	4
Manchester U	Tr	01.73	72-74	63	0	5
Sunderland	Miami (USA)	09.76	76	15	0	0
Coventry C	Tr	03.77	76-79	91	0	0

HOLTON Patrick (Pat) Carr
Hamilton, 23 December, 1935 (FB)

League Club	Source	Date Signed	Seasons Played	Apps	Subs	Gls
Chelsea	Motherwell	03.59	58	1	-	0
Southend U	Tr	08.60	60	11	-	0

HOLWYN Jermaine Titano Benito
Amsterdam, Holland, 16 April, 1973 (CD)

League Club	Source	Date Signed	Seasons Played	Apps	Subs	Gls
Port Vale	Ajax (Holl)	07.95	96	5	2	0

HOLYOAK Daniel (Danny)
London, 27 November, 1983 (M)

League Club	Source	Date Signed	Seasons Played	Apps	Subs	Gls
Mansfield T	Sch	●	02	0	2	0

HOLYOAK Philip (Phil)
Sunderland, 22 May, 1959 (FB)

League Club	Source	Date Signed	Seasons Played	Apps	Subs	Gls
Tottenham H	App	05.77				
Scunthorpe U	L	02.78	77	1	0	0

HOLZMAN Mark Robin
Bracknell, 22 February, 1973 (FB)

League Club	Source	Date Signed	Seasons Played	Apps	Subs	Gls
Reading	YT	07.91	91-92	23	9	1

HOMER Christopher (Chris)
Stockton, 16 April, 1977 (M)

League Club	Source	Date Signed	Seasons Played	Apps	Subs	Gls
Hartlepool U	YT	07.95	94-96	2	5	0

HONE Mark Joseph
Croydon, 31 March, 1968 ESemiPro (FB)

League Club	Source	Date Signed	Seasons Played	Apps	Subs	Gls
Crystal Palace	Jnrs	11.85	87-88	4	0	0
Southend U	Welling U	08.94	94-95	50	6	0
Lincoln C	Tr	07.96	96-97	48	5	2

HONEYWOOD Brian Roy
Chelmsford, 8 May, 1949 (CD)

League Club	Source	Date Signed	Seasons Played	Apps	Subs	Gls
Ipswich T	App	05.67				
Colchester U	Tr	06.68	68	11	6	0

HONOR Christian (Chris) Robert
Bristol, 5 June, 1968 (FB)

League Club	Source	Date Signed	Seasons Played	Apps	Subs	Gls
Bristol C	App	06.86	85-89	44	16	1
Torquay U	L	11.86	86	3	0	0
Hereford U	L	12.89	89	2	1	0
Swansea C	L	01.91	90	2	0	0
Cardiff C (L)	Airdrie	02.95	94	10	0	0

HONOUR Brian
Horden, 16 February, 1964 (M)

League Club	Source	Date Signed	Seasons Played	Apps	Subs	Gls
Darlington	App	02.82	81-83	59	15	4
Hartlepool U	Peterlee Newtown	02.85	84-94	301	18	26

HONOUR John
Horden, 1 November, 1953 (M)

League Club	Source	Date Signed	Seasons Played	Apps	Subs	Gls
West Bromwich A	App	05.71				
Hartlepool	Tr	07.72	72-75	107	5	6
Workington	Tr	03.76	75-76	38	1	1

HOOD Derek
Washington, 17 December, 1958 (FB)

League Club	Source	Date Signed	Seasons Played	Apps	Subs	Gls
West Bromwich A	App	12.76				
Hull C	Tr	08.77	77-79	20	4	0
York C	Tr	02.80	79-87	287	13	32
Lincoln C	L	03.87	86	9	0	0

HOOD George William
Houghton-le-Spring, 27 November, 1920 Died 1973 (FB)

League Club	Source	Date Signed	Seasons Played	Apps	Subs	Gls
Gateshead		10.47	47-48	30	-	0

HOOD Owen **Glyn**
Pentwyn, 12 March, 1925 Died 2004 (WH)

League Club	Source	Date Signed	Seasons Played	Apps	Subs	Gls
West Bromwich A	Nuffield Works	09.45	46-49	69	-	0

HOOD Henry (Harry) Anthony
Glasgow, 3 October, 1944 Su23-1/SLge-1 (CF)

League Club	Source	Date Signed	Seasons Played	Apps	Subs	Gls
Sunderland	Clyde	11.64	64-66	31	0	9

League Club	Source	Date Signed	Seasons Played	Career Record Apps	Subs	Gls

HOOD John (Jackie) O'Dorman
Glasgow, 8 January, 1938 (IF)

League Club	Source	Date Signed	Seasons Played	Apps	Subs	Gls
Everton	Shettleston	10.56				
Tranmere Rov	Tr	12.59	59	3	-	2

HOOD Melvyn (Mel) Arthur
Reading, 5 October, 1939 (W)

League Club	Source	Date Signed	Seasons Played	Apps	Subs	Gls
Reading	Jnrs	10.56	56-57	10	-	0

HOOD Ronald (Ronnie)
Cowdenbeath, 18 November, 1922 Died 1999 (CF)

League Club	Source	Date Signed	Seasons Played	Apps	Subs	Gls
Aldershot	Hamilton Academical	08.47	47	14	-	8
Rochdale	Tr	11.48	48	9	-	1

HOOKER Allan Thomas
Exeter, 23 June, 1956 (FB)

League Club	Source	Date Signed	Seasons Played	Apps	Subs	Gls
Exeter C	Jnrs	07.74	74-76	46	4	0

HOOKER Jonathan (Jon) William
City of London, 31 March, 1972 (W)

League Club	Source	Date Signed	Seasons Played	Apps	Subs	Gls
Brentford	Hertford T	11.94	94-95	4	1	0

HOOKER Keith William
Fleet, 31 January, 1950 (M)

League Club	Source	Date Signed	Seasons Played	Apps	Subs	Gls
Brentford	App	02.68	66-68	24	8	2

HOOKS Paul
Wallsend, 30 May, 1959 (M)

League Club	Source	Date Signed	Seasons Played	Apps	Subs	Gls
Notts Co	App	06.77	76-82	144	29	30
Derby Co	Tr	03.83	82-84	46	2	4

HOOKS Victor (Vic) Ronald
Belfast, 4 July, 1955 (F)

League Club	Source	Date Signed	Seasons Played	Apps	Subs	Gls
Grimsby T	Manchester U (App)	10.72	72	0	1	0

HOOLE David John
Chesterfield, 16 October, 1970 (FB)

League Club	Source	Date Signed	Seasons Played	Apps	Subs	Gls
Chesterfield	YT	07.89	88-89	6	8	0

HOOLEY Joseph (Joe) Winston
Hoyland, 26 December, 1938 (IF)

League Club	Source	Date Signed	Seasons Played	Apps	Subs	Gls
Barnsley	Jnrs	04.56	56	1	-	0
Sheffield U	Tr	12.57				
Workington	Tr	06.58	58	6	-	2
Bradford PA	Holbeach U	11.59	59-60	13	-	4

HOOLICKIN Garry John
Middleton, 29 October, 1957 (CD)

League Club	Source	Date Signed	Seasons Played	Apps	Subs	Gls
Oldham Ath	App	07.75	76-86	209	2	2

HOOLICKIN Stephen (Steve)
Moston, 13 December, 1951 (FB)

League Club	Source	Date Signed	Seasons Played	Apps	Subs	Gls
Oldham Ath	App	12.69	69-72	8	0	0
Bury	Tr	08.73	73-76	140	0	5
Carlisle U	Tr	10.76	76-80	143	0	2
Hull C	Tr	12.80	80-81	31	0	0

HOOPER Dean Raymond
Harefield, 13 April, 1971 ESemiPro-1 (FB)

League Club	Source	Date Signed	Seasons Played	Apps	Subs	Gls
Swindon T	Hayes	03.95	94	0	4	0
Peterborough U	L	12.95	95	4	0	0
Peterborough U	Kingstonian	08.98	98-01	99	14	2

HOOPER Harry
Pittington, 14 June, 1933 Eu23-2/FLge-5/EB (W)

League Club	Source	Date Signed	Seasons Played	Apps	Subs	Gls
West Ham U	Hylton Colliery	11.50	50-55	119	-	39
Wolverhampton W	Tr	03.56	56	39	-	19
Birmingham C	Tr	12.57	57-60	105	-	34
Sunderland	Tr	09.60	60-62	65	-	16

HOOPER Harry Reed
Burnley, 16 December, 1910 Died 1970 (FB)

League Club	Source	Date Signed	Seasons Played	Apps	Subs	Gls
Nelson	Nelson Trades	11.28	28-29	21	-	0
Sheffield U	Tr	02.30	30-38	269	-	10
Hartlepools U	Tr	07.47	47-49	66	-	4

HOOPER Lyndon
Georgetown, Guyana, 30 May, 1966 Canada int (M)

League Club	Source	Date Signed	Seasons Played	Apps	Subs	Gls
Birmingham C	Toronto (Can)	09.93	93	1	4	0

HOOPER Michael (Mike) Dudley
Bristol, 10 February, 1964 ESch (G)

League Club	Source	Date Signed	Seasons Played	Apps	Subs	Gls
Bristol C	Mangotsfield U	11.83	84	1	0	0
Wrexham	Tr	02.85	84-85	34	0	0
Liverpool	Tr	10.85	86-92	50	1	0
Leicester C	L	09.90	90	14	0	0
Newcastle U	Tr	09.93	93-94	23	2	0

HOOPER Percy William George
Lambeth, 17 December, 1914 Died 1997 (G)

League Club	Source	Date Signed	Seasons Played	Apps	Subs	Gls
Tottenham H	Islington Corinthians	01.35	34-38	97	-	0
Swansea T	Tr	03.47	46-47	12	-	0

HOOPER Peter John
Teignmouth, 2 February, 1933 FLge-1 (W)

League Club	Source	Date Signed	Seasons Played	Apps	Subs	Gls
Bristol Rov	Dawlish T	05.53	53-61	297	-	101
Cardiff C	Tr	07.62	62	40	-	22
Bristol C	Tr	07.63	63-65	54	0	14

HOOPER Stuart Robert John
St Annes, 16 June, 1970 (F)

League Club	Source	Date Signed	Seasons Played	Apps	Subs	Gls
Burnley	Jnrs	07.88	88	0	1	0

HOOPER Wynne
Seven Sisters, Glamorgan, 5 June, 1952 WYth (W)

League Club	Source	Date Signed	Seasons Played	Apps	Subs	Gls
Newport Co	App	06.70	68-76	164	14	21
Swindon T	Tr	12.76	76	4	2	0
Aldershot	Tr	07.77	77-78	21	19	1

HOPE Alexander (Alex) John Henry
Inveresk, 22 June, 1924 (W)

League Club	Source	Date Signed	Seasons Played	Apps	Subs	Gls
Swindon T	Morton	06.54	54	11	-	1

HOPE Christopher (Chris) Jonathan
Sheffield, 14 November, 1972 (CD)

League Club	Source	Date Signed	Seasons Played	Apps	Subs	Gls
Nottingham F	Darlington (Jnrs)	08.90				
Scunthorpe U	Tr	07.93	93-99	278	9	19
Gillingham	Tr	07.00	00-04	210	2	12

HOPE Darren
Stoke-on-Trent, 3 April, 1971 (W)

League Club	Source	Date Signed	Seasons Played	Apps	Subs	Gls
Stoke C	YT	07.89				
Stockport Co	Tr	03.90	89	4	0	0

HOPE Eric
Oakengates, 2 December, 1927 (IF)

League Club	Source	Date Signed	Seasons Played	Apps	Subs	Gls
Manchester C		01.46				
Shrewsbury T	Tr	08.50	50-51	27	-	3
Wrexham	Tr	10.51	51-53	37	-	9

HOPE George
Haltwhistle, 4 April, 1954 (F)

League Club	Source	Date Signed	Seasons Played	Apps	Subs	Gls
Newcastle U	App	04.72	73	6	0	1
Charlton Ath	Tr	06.75	75-76	13	0	2
York C	Tr	11.76	76-77	34	8	8

HOPE James Gibson
Glasgow, 11 September, 1919 (W)

League Club	Source	Date Signed	Seasons Played	Apps	Subs	Gls
Manchester C	Ardeer Rec	02.39	46	7	-	0

HOPE James (Jimmy) Greatrix
East Wemyss, 4 October, 1919 Died 1993 (CD)

League Club	Source	Date Signed	Seasons Played	Apps	Subs	Gls
New Brighton	East Fife	08.47	47-49	43	-	0

HOPE John William March
Shildon, 30 March, 1949 (G)

League Club	Source	Date Signed	Seasons Played	Apps	Subs	Gls
Darlington	App	05.67	64-68	14	0	0
Newcastle U	Tr	03.69	68	1	0	0
Sheffield U	Tr	01.71	70-73	63	0	0
Hartlepool	Tr	07.75	75	23	0	0

HOPE Mark Bryan
Isleworth, 13 June, 1970 (CD)

League Club	Source	Date Signed	Seasons Played	Apps	Subs	Gls
Darlington	Porthleven	01.97	96	1	0	0

HOPE Richard Paul
Stockton, 22 June, 1978 (CD)

League Club	Source	Date Signed	Seasons Played	Apps	Subs	Gls
Blackburn Rov	YT	08.95				
Darlington	Tr	01.97	96-98	62	1	1
Northampton T	Tr	12.98	98-02	113	22	7
York C	Tr	08.03	03	36	0	2
Chester C	Tr	07.04	04	26	2	0

HOPE Robert (Bobby)
Bridge of Allan, 28 September, 1943 SSch/Su23-1/S-2 (M)

League Club	Source	Date Signed	Seasons Played	Apps	Subs	Gls
West Bromwich A	Jnrs	09.60	59-71	331	5	33
Birmingham C	Tr	06.72	72-75	33	1	5
Sheffield Wed	Tr	09.76	76-77	39	3	7

HOPGOOD Ronald (Ron) Frederick
Battersea, 24 November, 1934 Died 1990 (G)

League Club	Source	Date Signed	Seasons Played	Apps	Subs	Gls
Crystal Palace	Spicers Ath	05.57	57-59	14	-	0

HOPKIN David
Greenock, 21 August, 1970 SB-1/S-7 (M)

League Club	Source	Date Signed	Seasons Played	Apps	Subs	Gls
Chelsea	Morton	09.92	92-94	21	19	1
Crystal Palace	Tr	07.95	95-96	79	4	21
Leeds U	Tr	07.97	97-99	64	9	6
Bradford C	Tr	07.00	00	8	3	0
Crystal Palace	Tr	03.01	00-01	21	8	4

HOPKIN Gareth Gersom
Swansea, 12 April, 1923 (W)

League Club	Source	Date Signed	Seasons Played	Apps	Subs	Gls
Swansea T		11.46	47	2	-	0

League Club	Source	Date Signed	Seasons Played	Apps	Subs	Gls
HOPKINS Anthony (Tony)						
Cwmbran, 17 February, 1971						(W)
Newport Co	YT	●	87	2	4	0
Bristol C	Chelsea (YT)	10.89				
Aldershot	Ebbw Vale	02.91	90	9	1	0
HOPKINS Brian						
Derby, 15 March, 1933						(W)
Port Vale (Am)	Keele Univ	08.57	57	2	-	0
HOPKINS Gareth						
Cheltenham, 14 June, 1980						(F)
Cheltenham T	YT	07.98	99-01	1	7	0
HOPKINS Idris (Dai) Morgan						
Merthyr Tydfil, 11 October, 1910 Died 1994 WWar-9/W-12						(W)
Crystal Palace	Ramsgate Press W	05.32	32	4	-	0
Brentford	Tr	11.32	32-46	290	-	77
Bristol C	Tr	05.47	47	24	-	0
HOPKINS Jeffrey (Jeff)						
Swansea, 14 April, 1964 WYth/Wu21-5/W-16						(CD)
Fulham	App	09.81	80-87	213	6	4
Crystal Palace	Tr	08.88	88-89	70	0	2
Plymouth Arg	L	10.91	91	8	0	0
Bristol Rov	Tr	03.92	91	4	2	0
Reading	Tr	07.92	92-96	127	4	3
HOPKINS Kelvin Robert						
Perivale, 26 July, 1953						(G)
Aldershot	App	07.71	70-71	2	0	0
HOPKINS Melvyn (Mel)						
Ystrad Rhondda, 7 November, 1934 Wu23-1/W-34						(FB)
Tottenham H	Ystrad BC	05.52	52-63	219	-	0
Brighton & Hove A	Tr	10.64	64-66	57	1	2
Bradford PA	Canterbury C	01.69	68-69	29	1	0
HOPKINS Oliver (Ollie) Thomas						
South Kirkby, 15 November, 1935						(CD)
Barnsley	Burtonwood	03.54	57-60	50	-	10
Peterborough U	Tr	07.61	61-64	104	-	0
HOPKINS Robert Arthur						
Hall Green, 25 October, 1961						(W)
Aston Villa	App	07.79	79-82	1	2	1
Birmingham C	Tr	03.83	82-86	123	0	21
Manchester C	Tr	08.86	86	7	0	1
West Bromwich A	Tr	10.86	86-88	81	2	11
Birmingham C	Tr	03.89	88-90	43	7	9
Shrewsbury T	Tr	06.91	91	18	9	3
Colchester U	South China (HK)	02.93	92	13	1	1
HOPKINSON Alan						
Chapeltown, 15 April, 1953						(F)
Barnsley	App	04.71	70-73	24	3	5
HOPKINSON Edward (Eddie)						
Wheatley Hill, 29 October, 1935 Died 2004 Eu23-6/FLge-2/E-14						(G)
Oldham Ath	Jnrs	06.51	51	3	-	0
Bolton W	Tr	11.52	56-69	519	0	0
HOPKINSON Gordon						
Sheffield, 19 June, 1933						(FB)
Doncaster Rov	Beighton MW	06.57	57	10	-	0
Bristol C	Tr	07.58	58-60	67	-	1
HOPKINSON Ian John						
Newcastle, 19 October, 1950						(F)
Barrow	Newcastle U (App)	01.69	68-70	17	4	1
Workington	Tr	07.71	71	13	6	7
Darlington	Berwick Rgrs	12.72	72	7	2	1
HOPKINSON Michael (Mick) Edward						
Ambergate, 24 February, 1942						(CD)
Derby Co	West End BC	07.59	60-67	112	3	4
Mansfield T	Tr	07.68	68-69	46	0	1
Port Vale	Tr	07.70	70	12	1	0
HOPKINSON Paul Edward						
Royton, 17 January, 1958						(G)
Stockport Co	Manchester C (App)	10.75	75-76	39	0	0
HOPKINSON Stanley (Stan)						
Kiveton Park, 15 March, 1922 Died 2003						(G)
Watford (Am)	Hemel Hempstead	05.47	46	1	-	0
HOPPER Alan						
Newcastle, 17 July, 1937						(FB)
Newcastle U		10.59				
Barnsley	South Shields	03.61	61-64	135	-	4
Bradford C	Tr	07.65	65	8	0	0

League Club	Source	Date Signed	Seasons Played	Apps	Subs	Gls
HOPPER Tony						
Carlisle, 31 May, 1976						(M)
Carlisle U	YT	07.94	92-99	75	25	1
Carlisle U	Workington	02.01	00-01	24	14	1
HOPPER William (Bill)						
Bishop Auckland, 20 February, 1938						(CF)
Halifax T	West Auckland	12.61	61-62	35	-	9
Workington	Tr	07.63	63-64	46	-	14
Darlington	Tr	07.65	65	6	0	0
HORACE Alain						
Madagascar, 4 December, 1971						(M)
Hartlepool U	Mulhouse (Fr)	10.96	96	0	1	0
HORE Kenneth **John**						
St Austell, 10 February, 1947						(CD)
Plymouth Arg	App	12.64	64-75	393	7	17
Exeter C	Tr	03.76	75-79	193	0	0
HORE John Stephen						
Liverpool, 18 August, 1982						(M)
Carlisle U	YT	06.00	99-01	2	3	0
HORLAVILLE Christophe						
Rouen, France, 1 March, 1969						(F)
Port Vale (L)	Le Havre (Fr)	11.98	98	1	1	0
HORLOCK Kevin						
Erith, 1 November, 1972 NIB-2/NI-32						(M)
West Ham U	YT	07.91				
Swindon T	Tr	08.92	92-96	151	12	22
Manchester C	Tr	01.97	96-02	184	20	37
West Ham U	Tr	08.03	03	23	4	1
Ipswich T	Tr	07.04	04	33	8	0
HORMANTSCHUK Peter Anthony						
Coventry, 11 September, 1962						(FB)
Coventry C	App	09.80	81-83	18	6	1
HORN Graham Roy						
Westminster, 23 August, 1954						(G)
Arsenal	App	04.72				
Portsmouth	L	06.72	72	22	0	0
Luton T	Tr	02.73	72-74	58	0	0
Brentford	L	11.75	75	3	0	0
Charlton Ath	LA Aztecs (USA)	12.76				
Southend U	Kettering T	12.77	77-78	9	0	0
Aldershot	Tr	01.80	79-81	9	0	0
Torquay U	Tr	08.82	82-83	47	0	0
HORN Robert (Bobby) Ian						
Westminster, 15 December, 1961 EYth						(G)
Crystal Palace	App	04.79				
Barnsley	Tr	11.80	81-83	67	0	0
Cambridge U	L	11.83	83	8	0	0
HORN William						
Glasgow, 13 May, 1938						(W)
Brentford	Kilmarnock	10.58	58	1	-	0
HORNBY Eric						
Birkenhead, 31 March, 1923						(FB)
Tranmere Rov	Jnrs	11.44	47-48	32	-	0
Crewe Alex	Tr	08.49	49-50	3	-	0
HORNBY Ronald (Ron)						
Rochdale, 13 April, 1914 Died 1962						(W)
Rochdale	Rochdale St Clem (Am)	02.32	31	2	-	0
Oldham Ath	Tr	07.33				
Burnley	Stalybridge Celtic	05.34	34-47	123	-	16
HORNE Alfred (Alf)						
Brixworth, 6 September, 1926						(W)
Northampton T		09.44	48	1	-	0
HORNE Barry						
St Asaph, 18 May, 1962 W-59						(M)
Wrexham	Rhyl	06.84	84-86	136	0	16
Portsmouth	Tr	07.87	87-88	66	4	7
Southampton	Tr	03.89	88-91	111	1	6
Everton	Tr	07.92	92-95	118	5	3
Birmingham C	Tr	06.96	96	33	0	0
Huddersfield T	Tr	10.97	97-99	55	9	1
Sheffield Wed	Tr	03.00	99	7	0	0
Kidderminster Hrs	Tr	08.00	00	21	6	1
Walsall	Tr	03.01	00	1	2	0
HORNE Brian Simon						
Billericay, 5 October, 1967 EYth/Eu21-5						(G)
Millwall	App	10.85	86-90	163	0	0

League Club	Source	Date Signed	Seasons Played	Apps	Subs	Gls
Middlesbrough	L	08.92	92	3	1	0
Stoke C	L	10.92	92	1	0	0
Portsmouth	Tr	06.93	93	3	0	0
Hartlepool U	Tr	08.94	94-95	73	0	0

HORNE Desmond (Des) Tolton
Johannesburg, South Africa, 12 December, 1939 (W)

League Club	Source	Date Signed	Seasons Played	Apps	Subs	Gls
Wolverhampton W	Jnrs	12.56	58-60	40	-	16
Blackpool	Tr	03.61	60-65	117	1	17

HORNE George
Glasgow, 23 November, 1933 (W)

League Club	Source	Date Signed	Seasons Played	Apps	Subs	Gls
Carlisle U	Maryhill Jnrs	08.57	57	4	-	2

HORNE John Robert
Dudley, 4 November, 1961 (CD)

League Club	Source	Date Signed	Seasons Played	Apps	Subs	Gls
Walsall	App	11.79	79-81	10	6	1

HORNE Kenneth (Ken) William
Burton-on-Trent, 25 June, 1926 (FB)

League Club	Source	Date Signed	Seasons Played	Apps	Subs	Gls
Blackpool	Wolverhampton W (Am)	06.49				
Brentford	Tr	05.50	50-59	223	-	1

HORNE Henry **Leslie (Les)**
Dudley, 2 May, 1923 Died 1986 (CD)

League Club	Source	Date Signed	Seasons Played	Apps	Subs	Gls
West Bromwich A	Netherton W	04.48	49-51	13	-	0
Plymouth Arg	Tr	07.52				
Walsall	Tr	11.52	52-53	52	-	1

HORNE Stanley (Stan) Frederick
Clanfield, 17 December, 1944 (M)

League Club	Source	Date Signed	Seasons Played	Apps	Subs	Gls
Aston Villa	App	12.61	63	6	-	0
Manchester C	Tr	09.65	65-67	48	2	0
Fulham	Tr	02.69	68-72	73	6	0
Chester	Tr	08.73	73	17	1	0
Rochdale	Tr	12.73	73-74	48	0	5

HORNER Philip (Phil) Matthew
Leeds, 10 November, 1966 EYth (CD)

League Club	Source	Date Signed	Seasons Played	Apps	Subs	Gls
Leicester C	App	11.84	86-87	7	3	0
Rotherham U	L	03.86	85	3	1	0
Halifax T	Tr	08.88	88-89	70	2	4
Blackpool	Tr	09.90	90-94	184	3	22

HORNER William (Billy)
Cassop, 7 September, 1942 (CD)

League Club	Source	Date Signed	Seasons Played	Apps	Subs	Gls
Middlesbrough	Jnrs	09.59	60-68	184	3	11
Darlington	Tr	06.69	69-74	211	7	5

HORNSBY Brian Geoffrey
Great Shelford, 10 September, 1954 ESch/EYth (M)

League Club	Source	Date Signed	Seasons Played	Apps	Subs	Gls
Arsenal	App	07.72	72-75	23	3	6
Shrewsbury T	Tr	06.76	76-77	75	0	16
Sheffield Wed	Tr	03.78	77-81	102	4	25
Chester	L	11.81	81	4	0	0
Carlisle U	Edmonton (Can)	08.82	82-83	9	1	1
Chesterfield	L	12.83	83	1	0	0

HORNSBY John
Ferryhill, 3 August, 1945 (W)

League Club	Source	Date Signed	Seasons Played	Apps	Subs	Gls
Colchester U	Evenwood T	10.64	65	11	0	1

HORNUSS Julien
Paris, France, 12 June, 1986 (F)

League Club	Source	Date Signed	Seasons Played	Apps	Subs	Gls
MK Dons	Sedan Ardennes (Fr)	07.04	04	0	3	0

HOROBIN Roy
Brownhills, 10 March, 1935 (IF)

League Club	Source	Date Signed	Seasons Played	Apps	Subs	Gls
West Bromwich A	Walsall Wood	10.52	55-57	54	-	6
Notts Co	Tr	11.58	58-61	123	-	37
Peterborough U	Tr	06.62	62-63	80	-	20
Crystal Palace	Tr	07.64	64	4	-	0

HORREY Rowland George
Bishop Auckland, 7 March, 1943 (W)

League Club	Source	Date Signed	Seasons Played	Apps	Subs	Gls
Blackburn Rov	Ferryhill Ath	12.63	64-65	3	0	0
York C	Tr	07.66	66-67	74	0	9
Cambridge U	Tr	07.68	70-71	37	1	4

HORRIDGE Peter
Manchester, 31 May, 1934 (FB)

League Club	Source	Date Signed	Seasons Played	Apps	Subs	Gls
Manchester C	Newton Heath PCWM	11.52	58	3	-	0

HORRIGAN Darren
Middlesbrough, 2 June, 1983 (G)

League Club	Source	Date Signed	Seasons Played	Apps	Subs	Gls
Lincoln C	YT	10.01	01	0	1	0

HORRIGAN Kenneth (Ken) Peter
Gravesend, 7 December, 1919 (WH)

League Club	Source	Date Signed	Seasons Played	Apps	Subs	Gls
Carlisle U	Imperial Paper Mill	08.46	46	16	-	1

HORRIX Dean Victor
Taplow, 21 November, 1961 Died 1990 (F)

League Club	Source	Date Signed	Seasons Played	Apps	Subs	Gls
Millwall	App	04.79	80-82	65	7	19
Gillingham	Tr	03.83	82	7	7	0
Reading	Tr	08.83	83-87	135	23	35
Cardiff C	L	02.87	86	9	0	3
Millwall	Tr	03.88	87-89	5	6	1
Bristol C	Tr	03.90	89	3	0	0

HORROBIN Thomas (Tom)
Askern, 8 August, 1943 (FB)

League Club	Source	Date Signed	Seasons Played	Apps	Subs	Gls
Sheffield Wed	Jnrs	08.60	62	3	-	0

HORSBURGH John James
Edinburgh, 17 November, 1936 (G)

League Club	Source	Date Signed	Seasons Played	Apps	Subs	Gls
Oldham Ath	Dundee	08.61	61	1	-	0

HORSCROFT Grant
Fletching, 30 July, 1961 (CD)

League Club	Source	Date Signed	Seasons Played	Apps	Subs	Gls
Brighton & Hove A	Lewes	03.87	87	2	0	0

HORSFALL Frank **George**
Perth, Australia, 19 September, 1924 Died 1992 (WH)

League Club	Source	Date Signed	Seasons Played	Apps	Subs	Gls
Southampton	Guildford C	05.47	46	2	-	0
Southend U	Tr	07.49	49	1	-	0

HORSFALL Thomas (Tommy) William
Hamilton, 7 January, 1951 (W)

League Club	Source	Date Signed	Seasons Played	Apps	Subs	Gls
Southend U	Dover	11.72	72-73	11	5	1
Bury	L	11.73	73	0	1	0
Scunthorpe U	L	11.73	73	5	0	2
Cambridge U	Tr	12.74	74-76	79	4	28
Halifax T	Tr	07.77	77	15	1	3

HORSFIELD Alec
Selby, 4 August, 1921 Died 1981 (IF)

League Club	Source	Date Signed	Seasons Played	Apps	Subs	Gls
Arsenal	Selby T	11.46				
Bradford PA	Tr	12.50	50	4	-	2

HORSFIELD Arthur
Newcastle, 5 July, 1946 EYth (F)

League Club	Source	Date Signed	Seasons Played	Apps	Subs	Gls
Middlesbrough	App	07.63	63-68	107	4	51
Newcastle U	Tr	01.69	68	7	2	3
Swindon T	Tr	06.69	69-71	107	1	42
Charlton Ath	Tr	06.72	72-75	139	0	53
Watford	Tr	09.75	75-76	78	0	16

HORSFIELD Geoffrey (Geoff) Malcolm
Barnsley, 1 November, 1973 (F)

League Club	Source	Date Signed	Seasons Played	Apps	Subs	Gls
Scarborough	Jnrs	07.92	92-93	12	0	1
Halifax T	Witton A	05.97	98	10	0	7
Fulham	Tr	10.98	98-99	54	5	22
Birmingham C	Tr	07.00	00-03	75	33	23
Wigan Ath	Tr	09.03	03	16	0	7
West Bromwich A	Tr	12.03	03-04	38	11	10

HORSMAN Leslie (Les)
Burley-in-Wharfedale, 26 May, 1920 Died 1996 (CD)

League Club	Source	Date Signed	Seasons Played	Apps	Subs	Gls
Bradford PA	Guiseley	06.45	46-52	239	-	18
Halifax T	Tr	08.53	53-56	120	-	8

HORSTEAD John **Barry**
Brigg, 8 May, 1935 (CD)

League Club	Source	Date Signed	Seasons Played	Apps	Subs	Gls
Scunthorpe U	Jnrs	05.56	56-67	316	4	3

HORSWILL Michael (Mickey) Frederick
Annfield Plain, 6 March, 1953 (M)

League Club	Source	Date Signed	Seasons Played	Apps	Subs	Gls
Sunderland	App	03.70	71-73	68	1	3
Manchester C	Tr	03.74	73-74	11	3	0
Plymouth Arg	Tr	06.75	75-77	98	4	3
Hull C	Tr	07.78	78-81	82	2	6
Carlisle U	Barrow	08.83	83	1	0	0

HORTON Brian
Hednesford, 4 February, 1949 (M)

League Club	Source	Date Signed	Seasons Played	Apps	Subs	Gls
Port Vale	Hednesford T	07.70	70-75	232	4	33
Brighton & Hove A	Tr	02.76	75-80	217	1	33
Luton T	Tr	08.81	81-83	118	0	8
Hull C	Tr	07.84	84-86	38	0	0

HORTON Duncan
Maidstone, 18 February, 1967 (M)

League Club	Source	Date Signed	Seasons Played	Apps	Subs	Gls
Charlton Ath	App	02.85	84	1	0	0
Barnet	Welling U	03.91	91-92	52	5	3
Wycombe W	Tr	08.93	93	15	0	0

HORTON Henry
Malvern, 18 April, 1923 Died 1998 (WH)

League Club	Source	Date Signed	Seasons Played	Apps	Subs	Gls
Blackburn Rov	Worcester C	01.47	46-50	92	-	5
Southampton	Tr	06.51	51-53	75	-	12
Bradford PA	Tr	05.54	54	26	-	0

HORTON Joseph **Kenneth (Ken)**
Preston, 26 August, 1922 Died 2000 (IF)

League Club	Source	Date Signed	Seasons Played	Apps	Subs	Gls
Preston NE	Jnrs	10.45	46-52	166	-	36
Hull C	Tr	10.52	52-54	76	-	16
Barrow	Tr	08.55	55	22	-	4

HORTON Leonard (Len)
Darlaston, 17 September, 1923 Died 1987 (CD)

League Club	Source	Date Signed	Seasons Played	Apps	Subs	Gls
Walsall		06.47	46	1	-	0

HORTON Leslie (Les)
Salford, 12 July, 1921 (WH)

League Club	Source	Date Signed	Seasons Played	Apps	Subs	Gls
Rochdale	Tydesley U	04.41				
Oldham Ath	Tr	01.43	46-47	79	-	2
Carlisle U	Tr	08.48	48-49	66	-	0
Rochdale	Tr	04.50				
York C	Tr	07.50	50	21	-	0
Halifax T	Tr	03.51	50-51	35	-	1

HORTON William (Billy) George
Aldershot, 27 August, 1942 (IF)

League Club	Source	Date Signed	Seasons Played	Apps	Subs	Gls
Aldershot	Chelsea (Jnrs)	11.61	62-64	9	-	1

HORWOOD Evan David
Billingham, 10 March, 1986 (FB)

League Club	Source	Date Signed	Seasons Played	Apps	Subs	Gls
Sheffield U	Sch	11.04				
Stockport Co	L	03.05	04	10	0	0

HORWOOD Neil Kenneth
Peterhead, 4 August, 1964 (F)

League Club	Source	Date Signed	Seasons Played	Apps	Subs	Gls
Grimsby T	King's Lynn	08.86	86	0	1	0
Halifax T	L	12.86	86	3	0	0
Tranmere Rov	L	03.87	86	4	0	1
Cambridge U	Tr	08.87	87	4	10	2

HOSIE James (Jim) England
Aberdeen, 3 April, 1940 (W)

League Club	Source	Date Signed	Seasons Played	Apps	Subs	Gls
Barnsley	Aberdeen	07.62	62	37	-	0

HOSKER Robert (Bobby) Charles
Cannock, 27 February, 1955 (W)

League Club	Source	Date Signed	Seasons Played	Apps	Subs	Gls
Middlesbrough	App	03.72				
York C	Tr	08.73	75-76	16	9	1

HOSKIN James **Ashley**
Accrington, 27 March, 1968 (W)

League Club	Source	Date Signed	Seasons Played	Apps	Subs	Gls
Burnley	App	12.85	85-88	72	16	11

HOSKIN Michael (Mick) Andrew
Chesterfield, 3 November, 1966 (FB)

League Club	Source	Date Signed	Seasons Played	Apps	Subs	Gls
Chesterfield	YT	08.84	83-84	1	1	0

HOSKINS John Frederick
Southampton, 10 May, 1931 (W)

League Club	Source	Date Signed	Seasons Played	Apps	Subs	Gls
Southampton	Winchester C	07.52	52-58	220	-	64
Swindon T	Tr	07.59	59	10	-	3

HOSKINS William (Will) Richard
Nottingham, 6 May, 1986 EYth (M)

League Club	Source	Date Signed	Seasons Played	Apps	Subs	Gls
Rotherham U	Sch	02.05	03-04	6	20	4

HOTTE Mark Stephen
Bradford, 27 September, 1978 (CD)

League Club	Source	Date Signed	Seasons Played	Apps	Subs	Gls
Oldham Ath	YT	07.97	97-00	59	6	0

HOTTE Timothy (Tim) Alwin
Bradford, 4 October, 1963 (F)

League Club	Source	Date Signed	Seasons Played	Apps	Subs	Gls
Huddersfield T	Arsenal (App)	09.81	81-82	14	2	4
Halifax T	(Finland)	08.85	85	2	2	0
Hull C	North Ferriby U	10.87	87-88	1	4	0
York C	L	09.88	88	1	1	0

HOTTIGER Marc
Lausanne, Switzerland, 7 November, 1967 Switzerland int (FB)

League Club	Source	Date Signed	Seasons Played	Apps	Subs	Gls
Newcastle U	Sion (Fr)	08.94	94-95	38	1	1
Everton	Tr	03.96	95-96	13	4	1

HOUCHEN Keith Morton
Middlesbrough, 25 July, 1960 (F)

League Club	Source	Date Signed	Seasons Played	Apps	Subs	Gls
Hartlepool U	Chesterfield (Jnrs)	02.78	77-81	160	10	65
Orient	Tr	03.82	81-83	74	2	20
York C	Tr	03.84	83-85	56	11	20
Scunthorpe U	Tr	03.86	85	9	0	2
Coventry C	Tr	07.86	86-88	43	11	7
Port Vale	Hibernian	08.91	91-92	44	5	10
Hartlepool U	Tr	08.93	93-96	104	5	27

HOUGH David John
Crewe, 20 February, 1966 WYth (CD)

League Club	Source	Date Signed	Seasons Played	Apps	Subs	Gls
Swansea C	App	02.84	83-91	202	25	9

HOUGH Frederick (Fred) Alan
Stoke-on-Trent, 23 December, 1935 (W)

League Club	Source	Date Signed	Seasons Played	Apps	Subs	Gls
Port Vale		06.55	57	4	-	0

HOUGH Harry
Chapeltown, 26 September, 1924 (G)

League Club	Source	Date Signed	Seasons Played	Apps	Subs	Gls
Barnsley	Thorncliffe Welfare	09.47	47-58	346	-	0
Bradford PA	Tr	06.59	59-60	57	-	0

HOUGH John
Halifax, 9 June, 1954 (G)

League Club	Source	Date Signed	Seasons Played	Apps	Subs	Gls
Halifax T	Irish Dems	09.79	79	1	0	0

HOUGH Thomas (Tommy)
Preston, 17 January, 1922 Died 2001 (IF)

League Club	Source	Date Signed	Seasons Played	Apps	Subs	Gls
Preston NE	Jnrs	05.39				
Barrow	Tr	10.46	46	3	-	0

HOUGHTON Harry **Brian (Bud)**
Madras, India, 1 September, 1936 Died 1994 (CF)

League Club	Source	Date Signed	Seasons Played	Apps	Subs	Gls
Bradford PA	St Wilfred's YC	10.55	55-57	28	-	7
Birmingham C	Tr	10.57	57-58	4	-	1
Southend U	Tr	10.58	58-60	68	-	32
Oxford U	Tr	03.61	62-63	53	-	17
Lincoln C	Tr	10.63	63-64	54	-	22

HOUGHTON William **Eric**
Billingborough, 29 June, 1910 Died 1996 FLge-4/E-7 (W)

League Club	Source	Date Signed	Seasons Played	Apps	Subs	Gls
Aston Villa	Billingborough	08.27	29-46	361	-	160
Notts Co	Tr	12.46	46-48	55	-	10

HOUGHTON Frank Calvert
Preston, 15 February, 1926 Died 1994 (WH)

League Club	Source	Date Signed	Seasons Played	Apps	Subs	Gls
Newcastle U	Ballymena U	12.47	47-50	55	-	10
Exeter C	Tr	08.54	54-56	27	-	10

HOUGHTON Keith
Backworth, 10 March, 1954 ESemiPro (CD)

League Club	Source	Date Signed	Seasons Played	Apps	Subs	Gls
Carlisle U	Blyth Spartans	01.80	79-82	82	5	2
Lincoln C	Tr	08.83	83	26	0	0

HOUGHTON Kenneth (Ken)
Rotherham, 18 October, 1939 (M)

League Club	Source	Date Signed	Seasons Played	Apps	Subs	Gls
Rotherham U	Silverwood Colliery	05.60	60-64	149	-	56
Hull C	Tr	01.65	64-72	253	11	79
Scunthorpe U	Tr	06.73	73	33	0	5

HOUGHTON Peter
Liverpool, 30 November, 1954 (F)

League Club	Source	Date Signed	Seasons Played	Apps	Subs	Gls
Wigan Ath	South Liverpool	(N/L)	78-83	169	16	62
Preston NE	Tr	10.83	83-84	52	4	16
Wrexham	L	11.84	84	5	0	2
Chester C	Tr	08.85	85-87	78	7	13

HOUGHTON Raymond (Ray) James
Glasgow, 9 January, 1962 IR-73 (M)

League Club	Source	Date Signed	Seasons Played	Apps	Subs	Gls
West Ham U	Jnrs	07.79	81	0	1	0
Fulham	Tr	07.82	82-85	129	0	16
Oxford U	Tr	09.85	85-87	83	0	10
Liverpool	Tr	10.87	87-91	147	6	28
Aston Villa	Tr	07.92	92-94	83	12	6
Crystal Palace	Tr	03.95	94-96	69	3	7
Reading	Tr	07.97	97-98	33	10	1

HOUGHTON Scott Aaron
Hitchin, 22 October, 1971 ESch/EYth (W)

League Club	Source	Date Signed	Seasons Played	Apps	Subs	Gls
Tottenham H	YT	08.90	91	0	10	2
Ipswich T	L	03.91	90	7	1	1
Gillingham	L	12.92	92	3	0	0
Charlton Ath	L	02.93	92	6	0	0
Luton T	Tr	08.93	93-94	7	9	1
Walsall	Tr	09.94	94-95	76	2	14
Peterborough U	Tr	07.96	96-98	57	13	13
Southend U	Tr	11.98	98-00	75	4	9
Leyton Orient	Tr	10.00	00-01	27	15	6
Halifax T	Tr	02.02	01	7	0	0

HOUGHTON William (Billy) Gascoigne
Hemsworth, 20 February, 1939 EYth (FB)

League Club	Source	Date Signed	Seasons Played	Apps	Subs	Gls
Barnsley	Jnrs	08.57	57-63	206	-	10
Watford	Tr	07.64	64-65	48	0	2
Ipswich T	Tr	06.66	66-68	107	0	3
Leicester C	Tr	07.69	69	6	2	0
Rotherham U	Tr	01.70	69-73	139	0	1

HOULAHAN Harold (Harry)
Coundon, 14 February, 1930 (IF)

League Club	Source	Date Signed	Seasons Played	Apps	Subs	Gls
Newcastle U	Durham C	02.51				
Oldham Ath	Tr	05.52	52-53	6	-	3
Darlington	Tr	01.54	53-54	23	-	8

HOULT Alan John
Burbage, Leicestershire, 7 October, 1957 ESch (F)

League Club	Source	Date Signed	Seasons Played	Apps	Subs	Gls
Leicester C	Jnrs	09.75				
Hull C	L	01.78	77	3	0	1
Lincoln C	L	03.78	77	2	2	1

HOULT Russell
Ashby-de-la-Zouch, 22 November, 1972 (G)

League Club	Source	Date Signed	Seasons Played	Apps	Subs	Gls
Leicester C	YT	03.91	92	10	0	0
Lincoln C	L	08.91	91	2	0	0
Bolton W	L	11.93	93	3	1	0
Lincoln C	L	08.94	94	15	0	0
Derby Co	Tr	02.95	94-99	121	2	0
Portsmouth	Tr	01.00	99-00	40	0	0
West Bromwich A	Tr	01.01	00-04	175	0	0

HOUNSLEA William (Bill) Hudson
Liverpool, 15 August, 1926 (FB)

League Club	Source	Date Signed	Seasons Played	Apps	Subs	Gls
New Brighton	Unity BC	12.47	47	16	-	0
Chester	Tr	08.48	48	1	-	0

HOUSAM Arthur
Sunderland, 1 October, 1917 Died 1975 (WH)

League Club	Source	Date Signed	Seasons Played	Apps	Subs	Gls
Sunderland	Hylton Colliery	05.37	37-47	55	-	2

HOUSDEN Denis
City of London, 15 March, 1953 (F)

League Club	Source	Date Signed	Seasons Played	Apps	Subs	Gls
Gillingham	App	08.71	71-72	12	4	1

HOUSEMAN Peter
Battersea, 24 December, 1945 Died 1977 (W)

League Club	Source	Date Signed	Seasons Played	Apps	Subs	Gls
Chelsea	App	12.62	63-74	252	17	20
Oxford U	Tr	05.75	75-76	65	0	2

HOUSHAM Steven (Steve) James
Gainsborough, 24 February, 1976 (M)

League Club	Source	Date Signed	Seasons Played	Apps	Subs	Gls
Scunthorpe U	YT	12.93	94-99	90	25	4

HOUSLEY Stuart
Doncaster, 15 September, 1948 (W)

League Club	Source	Date Signed	Seasons Played	Apps	Subs	Gls
Grimsby T	App	07.66	66-68	34	0	3

HOUSTON David
Glasgow, 7 July, 1948 (WH)

League Club	Source	Date Signed	Seasons Played	Apps	Subs	Gls
Cardiff C	Jnrs	07.65	65-66	17	1	0

HOUSTON Graham Robert
Gibraltar, 24 February, 1960 (W)

League Club	Source	Date Signed	Seasons Played	Apps	Subs	Gls
Preston NE	Jnrs	03.78	79-84	90	38	11
Burnley	Tr	09.85				
Wigan Ath	Tr	06.86	86	16	1	4
Carlisle U	Northwich Vic	10.87	87	8	8	1

HOUSTON Joseph (Joe)
Wishaw, 27 February, 1926 (G)

League Club	Source	Date Signed	Seasons Played	Apps	Subs	Gls
Aldershot	Dunfermline Ath	07.51	51-52	47	-	0

HOUSTON Stewart Mackie
Dunoon, 20 August, 1949 Su23-1/S-1 (FB)

League Club	Source	Date Signed	Seasons Played	Apps	Subs	Gls
Chelsea	Port Glasgow Rgrs	08.67	67-69	6	3	0
Brentford	Tr	03.72	71-73	77	0	9
Manchester U	Tr	12.73	73-79	204	1	13
Sheffield U	Tr	07.80	80-82	93	1	1
Colchester U	Tr	08.83	83-85	106	1	5

HOVI Thomas (Tom) Henning
Gjovik, Norway, 15 January, 1972 (CD)

League Club	Source	Date Signed	Seasons Played	Apps	Subs	Gls
Charlton Ath (L)	Hankam (Nor)	01.95	94	0	2	0

HOW Trevor Anthony
Amersham, 8 August, 1957 (FB)

League Club	Source	Date Signed	Seasons Played	Apps	Subs	Gls
Watford	App	03.75	74-79	90	1	2

HOWARD Andrew (Andy) Paul
Southport, 15 March, 1973 (F)

League Club	Source	Date Signed	Seasons Played	Apps	Subs	Gls
Blackpool	Liverpool (YT)	09.91				
Rochdale	Fleetwood T	07.92	92-93	4	16	3

HOWARD Barry Peter
Ashton-under-Lyne, 19 February, 1950 ESemiPro (F)

League Club	Source	Date Signed	Seasons Played	Apps	Subs	Gls
Stockport Co	Runcorn	02.78	77	12	1	1

HOWARD Brian Richard William
Winchester, 23 January, 1983 EYth/Eu20 (M)

League Club	Source	Date Signed	Seasons Played	Apps	Subs	Gls
Southampton	YT	01.00				
Swindon T	Tr	08.03	03-04	49	21	9

HOWARD David Frederick
Hartlepool, 3 June, 1962 (F)

League Club	Source	Date Signed	Seasons Played	Apps	Subs	Gls
Newcastle U	Jnrs	07.79				
Hartlepool U	Tr	03.81	80-81	6	3	4

HOWARD Francis (Frankie) Henry
Acton, 30 January, 1931 (W)

League Club	Source	Date Signed	Seasons Played	Apps	Subs	Gls
Brighton & Hove A	Guildford C	05.50	50-58	200	-	26

HOWARD Jonathan (Jon)
Sheffield, 7 October, 1971 (F)

League Club	Source	Date Signed	Seasons Played	Apps	Subs	Gls
Rotherham U	YT	07.90	90-93	25	11	5
Chesterfield	Buxton	12.94	94-02	152	84	39

HOWARD Lee
Worksop, 6 February, 1967 (W)

League Club	Source	Date Signed	Seasons Played	Apps	Subs	Gls
Mansfield T	App	•	84	0	1	0

HOWARD Mark Edward
King's Lynn, 21 October, 1964 (W)

League Club	Source	Date Signed	Seasons Played	Apps	Subs	Gls
Stockport Co	King's Lynn	04.88	87-89	13	6	2
Cambridge U	L	03.89	88	0	2	0

HOWARD Matthew Jones
Watford, 5 December, 1970 (CD)

League Club	Source	Date Signed	Seasons Played	Apps	Subs	Gls
Brentford	YT	•	87	0	1	0

HOWARD Michael (Mike) Anthony
Birkenhead, 2 December, 1978 (FB)

League Club	Source	Date Signed	Seasons Played	Apps	Subs	Gls
Tranmere Rov	YT	07.97				
Swansea C	Tr	02.98	97-03	221	7	2

HOWARD Patrick (Pat)
Dodworth, 7 October, 1947 (CD)

League Club	Source	Date Signed	Seasons Played	Apps	Subs	Gls
Barnsley	Jnrs	10.65	65-71	176	1	6
Newcastle U	Tr	09.71	71-76	182	2	7
Arsenal	Tr	09.76	76	15	1	0
Birmingham C	Tr	08.77	77-78	40	0	0
Bury	Tr	07.79	79-81	117	1	5

HOWARD Richard James
Birkenhead, 10 June, 1943 (G)

League Club	Source	Date Signed	Seasons Played	Apps	Subs	Gls
Chester	Chester TC	09.65	65	1	0	0

HOWARD Stanley (Stan)
Chorley, 1 July, 1934 Died 2004 (CF)

League Club	Source	Date Signed	Seasons Played	Apps	Subs	Gls
Huddersfield T	Chisnall Rov	07.52	57-59	62	-	13
Bradford C	Tr	06.60	60	18	-	6
Barrow	Tr	01.61	60-63	86	-	22
Halifax T	Tr	07.64	64	21	-	1

HOWARD Steven (Steve) John
Durham, 10 May, 1976 (F)

League Club	Source	Date Signed	Seasons Played	Apps	Subs	Gls
Hartlepool U	Tow Law T	08.95	95-98	117	25	26
Northampton T	Tr	02.99	98-00	67	19	18
Luton T	Tr	03.01	00-04	169	0	81

HOWARD Terence (Terry)
Stepney, 26 February, 1966 EYth (FB)

League Club	Source	Date Signed	Seasons Played	Apps	Subs	Gls
Chelsea	App	03.84	84-86	6	0	0
Crystal Palace	L	01.86	85	4	0	0
Chester C	L	01.87	86	2	0	0
Orient	Tr	03.87	86-94	323	5	31
Wycombe W	Tr	02.95	94-95	56	3	2

HOWARD Timothy (Tim) Matthew
North Brunswick, New Jersey, USA, 6 March, 1979 USA 12 (G)

League Club	Source	Date Signed	Seasons Played	Apps	Subs	Gls
Manchester U	NY/NJ Metro (USA)	07.03	03-04	44	0	0

HOWARD Trevor Edward
King's Lynn, 2 June, 1949 (M)

League Club	Source	Date Signed	Seasons Played	Apps	Subs	Gls
Norwich C	App	07.67	67-73	81	42	13
Bournemouth	Tr	08.74	74-75	86	0	11
Cambridge U	Tr	07.76	76-78	105	0	5

HOWARTH Frank
Budleigh Salterton, 17 November, 1964 (FB)

League Club	Source	Date Signed	Seasons Played	Apps	Subs	Gls
Exeter C	App	11.82	81-84	21	17	1

HOWARTH Jack
Stanley, 27 February, 1945 (F)

League Club	Source	Date Signed	Seasons Played	Apps	Subs	Gls
Chelsea	Stanley U	10.63				
Swindon T	Tr	10.64	64	2	-	0
Aldershot	Tr	07.65	65-71	258	1	114
Rochdale	Tr	01.72	71-72	40	0	12
Aldershot	Tr	11.72	72-76	163	0	59
Bournemouth	Tr	01.77	76-77	39	3	6
Southport	Dorchester T	03.78	77	9	0	1

HOWARTH Lee
Bolton, 3 January, 1968 (CD)

League Club	Source	Date Signed	Seasons Played	Apps	Subs	Gls
Peterborough U	Chorley	08.91	91-93	56	6	0
Mansfield T	Tr	08.94	94-95	56	1	2
Barnet	Tr	01.96	95-97	101	1	5

HOWARTH Neil
Farnworth, 15 November, 1971 ESemiPro-1 (CD)

League Club	Source	Date Signed	Seasons Played	Apps	Subs	Gls
Burnley	YT	07.90	89	0	1	0
Macclesfield T	Tr	09.93	97-98	49	11	3
Cheltenham T	Tr	02.99	99-02	106	14	7

HOWARTH Russell Michael
York, 27 March, 1982 EYth/Eu20 (G)

League Club	Source	Date Signed	Seasons Played	Apps	Subs	Gls
York C	YT	08.99	99-01	6	2	0
Tranmere Rov	Tr	11.02	02-04	10	2	0

HOWARTH Sydney (Syd)
Bristol, 28 June, 1923 Died 2004 (CF)

League Club	Source	Date Signed	Seasons Played	Apps	Subs	Gls
Aston Villa	Merthyr Tydfil	06.48	48-49	8	-	2
Swansea T	Tr	09.50	50-51	40	-	7
Walsall	Tr	09.52	52	6	-	0

HOWAT Ian Stuart
Wrexham, 29 July, 1958 (F)

League Club	Source	Date Signed	Seasons Played	Apps	Subs	Gls
Chester	App	07.76	76-81	48	9	10
Crewe Alex	Tr	02.82	81	16	1	1

HOWCROFT Brian
Farnworth, 20 June, 1938 (FB)

League Club	Source	Date Signed	Seasons Played	Apps	Subs	Gls
Bury	Jnrs	09.56	57-58	20	-	0

HOWDON Stephen (Steve)
Prudhoe, 1 February, 1922 Died 1998 (W)

League Club	Source	Date Signed	Seasons Played	Apps	Subs	Gls
Newcastle U	Hexham Hearts	08.41				
Gateshead	Tr	11.44	46	2	-	1

HOWE Albert (Bert) Richard Henry
Charlton, 16 November, 1938 (FB)

League Club	Source	Date Signed	Seasons Played	Apps	Subs	Gls
Crystal Palace	Faversham T	12.58	58-66	192	1	0
Leyton Orient	Tr	01.67	66-68	91	0	0
Colchester U	Tr	07.69	69	29	0	1

HOWE Anthony (Tony) Valentine
Colchester, 14 February, 1939 (W)

League Club	Source	Date Signed	Seasons Played	Apps	Subs	Gls
Colchester U	Colchester Casuals	03.60	60	10	-	2
Southend U	Haverhill Rov	07.64	64	2	-	0

HOWE Denis Cecil
West Ham, 14 September, 1928 (CD)

League Club	Source	Date Signed	Seasons Played	Apps	Subs	Gls
West Ham U		05.49				
Darlington	Tr	08.51	51-53	88	-	1
Southend U	Tr	08.54	54-57	101	-	0
Aldershot	Tr	07.58	58	33	-	0

HOWE Donald (Don)
Outwood, 26 November, 1917 Died 1978 (WH)

League Club	Source	Date Signed	Seasons Played	Apps	Subs	Gls
Bolton W	Whitehall Printeries	11.34	36-51	266	-	35

HOWE Donald (Don)
Wolverhampton, 12 October, 1935 Eu23-6/EB/FLge-6/E-23 (FB)

League Club	Source	Date Signed	Seasons Played	Apps	Subs	Gls
West Bromwich A	Jnrs	11.52	55-63	342	-	17
Arsenal	Tr	04.64	64-66	70	0	1

HOWE Edward (Eddie) John Frank
Amersham, 29 November, 1977 Eu21-2 (CD)

League Club	Source	Date Signed	Seasons Played	Apps	Subs	Gls
Bournemouth	YT	07.96	95-01	183	17	10
Portsmouth	Tr	03.02	01-02	2	0	0
Bournemouth	Tr	08.04	04	33	2	1

HOWE Ernest (Ernie) James
Chiswick, 15 February, 1953 (CD)

League Club	Source	Date Signed	Seasons Played	Apps	Subs	Gls
Fulham	Hounslow T	10.73	73-77	68	2	10
Queens Park Rgrs	Tr	12.77	77-81	89	0	3
Portsmouth	Tr	08.82	82-83	35	0	4

HOWE Frederick (Fred)
Bredbury, 24 September, 1912 Died 1984 (CF)

League Club	Source	Date Signed	Seasons Played	Apps	Subs	Gls
Stockport Co	Hyde U	09.31	31-32	2	-	0
Liverpool	Hyde U	03.35	34-37	89	-	36
Manchester C	Tr	06.38	38	6	-	5
Grimsby T	Tr	10.38	38	29	-	15
Oldham Ath	Tr	07.46	46	30	-	20

HOWE George
Wakefield, 10 January, 1924 Died 1971 (FB)

League Club	Source	Date Signed	Seasons Played	Apps	Subs	Gls
Huddersfield T	Carlton U	05.42	46-53	40	-	0
York C	Tr	06.54	54-60	307	-	0

HOWE Herbert (Bert) Alexander
Rugby, 1 April, 1916 Died 1972 (FB)

League Club	Source	Date Signed	Seasons Played	Apps	Subs	Gls
Leicester C	Leicester Nomads	02.37	38-46	28	-	0
Notts Co	Tr	07.47	47-48	52	-	0

HOWE Jeremy Raymond
Stancliffe, 5 September, 1973 EYth (M)

League Club	Source	Date Signed	Seasons Played	Apps	Subs	Gls
Bradford C	YT	07.92	91	3	0	0

HOWE John (Jack) Robert
West Hartlepool, 7 October, 1915 Died 1987 E-3 (FB)

League Club	Source	Date Signed	Seasons Played	Apps	Subs	Gls
Hartlepools U	Wingate U	06.34	34-35	24	-	0
Derby Co	Tr	03.36	35-49	223	-	2
Huddersfield T	Tr	10.49	49-50	29	-	1

HOWE Robert (Bobby) John
Chadwell St Mary, 22 December, 1945 (FB)

League Club	Source	Date Signed	Seasons Played	Apps	Subs	Gls
West Ham U	App	01.63	66-71	68	7	4
Bournemouth	Tr	01.72	71-73	100	0	6

HOWE Stephen **Robert (Bobby)**
Annitsford, 6 November, 1973 EYth (M)

League Club	Source	Date Signed	Seasons Played	Apps	Subs	Gls
Nottingham F	YT	12.90	93-96	6	8	2
Ipswich T	L	01.97	96	2	1	0
Swindon T	Tr	01.98	97-01	103	19	6

HOWELL David Christopher
Hammersmith, 10 October, 1958 ESemiPro (CD)

League Club	Source	Date Signed	Seasons Played	Apps	Subs	Gls
Barnet	Enfield	07.90	91-92	57	0	3
Southend U	Tr	07.93	93	6	0	0
Birmingham C	(Retired)	10.94	94	2	0	0

HOWELL Dean George
Burton-on-Trent, 29 November, 1980 (M)

League Club	Source	Date Signed	Seasons Played	Apps	Subs	Gls
Notts Co	YT	07.99	99	0	1	0
Crewe Alex	Tr	07.00	00	0	1	0
Rochdale	L	03.01	00	2	1	0

HOWELL Graham Frank
Urmston, 18 February, 1951 (FB)

League Club	Source	Date Signed	Seasons Played	Apps	Subs	Gls
Manchester C	App	10.68				
Bradford C	Tr	06.71	71-72	45	0	0
Brighton & Hove A	Tr	08.72	72-73	40	4	0
Cambridge U	Tr	07.74	74-75	68	3	3

HOWELL James (Jamie) Alexander
Rustington, 19 February, 1977 ESch/EYth (M)

League Club	Source	Date Signed	Seasons Played	Apps	Subs	Gls
Arsenal	YT	07.95				
Portsmouth	Tr	08.96				
Torquay U	Tr	03.97	96	2	2	0

HOWELL Reginald (Reg) William
Wolverhampton, 12 August, 1938 (G)

League Club	Source	Date Signed	Seasons Played	Apps	Subs	Gls
Plymouth Arg		11.56	56	1	-	0

HOWELL Ronald (Ron) Roger
Tottenham, 22 May, 1949 (M)

League Club	Source	Date Signed	Seasons Played	Apps	Subs	Gls
Millwall	App	03.67	66-69	7	7	0
Cambridge U	Tr	09.70	70	10	2	1
Swindon T	Kettering T	07.72	72	22	3	1
Brighton & Hove A	Tr	07.73	73	26	1	9

HOWELLS David
Guildford, 15 December, 1967 EYth (M)

League Club	Source	Date Signed	Seasons Played	Apps	Subs	Gls
Tottenham H	App	01.85	85-97	238	39	22
Southampton	Tr	07.98	98	8	1	1
Bristol C	L	03.99	98	8	0	1

HOWELLS Gareth Jonathan
Guildford, 13 June, 1970 (G)

League Club	Source	Date Signed	Seasons Played	Apps	Subs	Gls
Tottenham H	YT	07.88				
Torquay U	Tr	08.90	90-91	83	0	0

HOWELLS Jeffrey (Jeff) Denis
Shoreham, 26 September, 1940 (WH)

League Club	Source	Date Signed	Seasons Played	Apps	Subs	Gls
Millwall	Fulham (Am)	10.57	58-60	55	-	3

HOWELLS Lee David
Fremantle, Australia, 14 October, 1968 ESemiPro-2 (M)

League Club	Source	Date Signed	Seasons Played	Apps	Subs	Gls
Bristol Rov	App	10.86				
Cheltenham T	Brisbane Lions (Aus)	12.91	99-03	119	2	6

HOWELLS Peter
Middlesbrough, 23 September, 1932 Died 1993 (W)

League Club	Source	Date Signed	Seasons Played	Apps	Subs	Gls
Sheffield Wed		10.53	54-55	3	-	1
Hartlepools U	Tr	11.56	56	1	-	0

HOWELLS Raymond (Ray)
Rhondda, 27 June, 1926 (W)

League Club	Source	Date Signed	Seasons Played	Apps	Subs	Gls
Crystal Palace	Mid-Rhondda U	06.47	46-49	25	-	5
Exeter C	Tr	07.51	51-52	15	-	3

HOWELLS Roger William
Swansea, 18 September, 1931 (CF)

League Club	Source	Date Signed	Seasons Played	Apps	Subs	Gls
Swansea T	Llanelli	03.50				
Darlington	Tr	02.53	52-53	2	-	0

HOWELLS Ronald (Ron)
Ferndale, 3 August, 1935 (WH)

League Club	Source	Date Signed	Seasons Played	Apps	Subs	Gls
Wolverhampton W	Nuneaton Borough	11.52	55-57	9	-	0
Portsmouth	Tr	03.59	58-60	65	-	2

League Club	Source	Date Signed	Seasons Played	Apps	Subs	Gls
Scunthorpe U	Tr	06.61	61-62	69	-	4
Walsall	Tr	07.63	63	13	-	0

HOWELLS Ronald (Ron) Gilbert
Ponthenry, 12 January, 1927 WLge-1/W-2 (G)

League Club	Source	Date Signed	Seasons Played	Apps	Subs	Gls
Swansea T		04.48	47	9	-	0
Cardiff C	Barry T	07.50	51-56	155	-	0
Chester	Worcester C	09.58	58-59	80	-	0

HOWELLS William (Billy) Mansel
Grimsby, 20 March, 1943 (CD)

League Club	Source	Date Signed	Seasons Played	Apps	Subs	Gls
Grimsby T	Jnrs	10.61	63	6	-	0

HOWES Shaun Colin
Norwich, 7 November, 1977 (FB)

League Club	Source	Date Signed	Seasons Played	Apps	Subs	Gls
Cambridge U	YT	07.96	95	0	1	0
Leyton Orient	Tr	11.96	96	3	2	0

HOWEY Lee Matthew
Sunderland, 1 April, 1969 (CD)

League Club	Source	Date Signed	Seasons Played	Apps	Subs	Gls
Ipswich T	App	10.86				
Sunderland	Bishop Auckland	03.93	92-96	39	30	8
Burnley	Tr	08.97	97-98	24	2	0
Northampton T	Tr	11.98	98-00	47	1	6

HOWEY Peter
Kinsley, 23 January, 1958 (W)

League Club	Source	Date Signed	Seasons Played	Apps	Subs	Gls
Huddersfield T	App	01.76	76-78	20	2	3

HOWEY Stephen (Steve) Norman
Sunderland, 26 October, 1971 E-4 (CD)

League Club	Source	Date Signed	Seasons Played	Apps	Subs	Gls
Newcastle U	YT	12.89	88-99	167	24	6
Manchester C	Tr	08.00	00-02	94	0	11
Leicester C	Tr	07.03	03	13	0	1
Bolton W	Tr	01.04	03	2	1	0
Hartlepool U	New England (USA)	03.05	04	0	1	0

HOWFIELD Robert (Bobby) Michael
Watford, 3 December, 1936 (W)

League Club	Source	Date Signed	Seasons Played	Apps	Subs	Gls
Watford	Bushey U	09.57	57-58	47	-	9
Crewe Alex	Tr	07.59	59	5	-	0
Aldershot	Tr	10.59	59-61	76	-	44
Watford	Tr	07.62	62-63	45	-	13
Fulham	Tr	11.63	63-64	26	-	9
Aldershot	Tr	08.65	65-66	33	1	10

HOWIE Scott
Motherwell, 4 January, 1972 Su21-5 (G)

League Club	Source	Date Signed	Seasons Played	Apps	Subs	Gls
Norwich C	Clyde	08.93	93	1	1	0
Reading	Motherwell	03.98	97-99	84	1	0
Bristol Rov	Tr	08.01	01-02	90	0	0
Shrewsbury T	Tr	08.03	04	40	0	0

HOWITT David John
Birmingham, 4 August, 1952 (FB)

League Club	Source	Date Signed	Seasons Played	Apps	Subs	Gls
Birmingham C	App	08.69	72	2	0	0
Bury	Tr	08.73	73	11	9	4
Workington	Tr	07.74	74	30	5	1
Aldershot	Tr	06.75	75-79	126	11	2

HOWITT Robert (Bobby) Gibb
Glasgow, 15 July, 1929 Died 2005 SLge-1 (IF)

League Club	Source	Date Signed	Seasons Played	Apps	Subs	Gls
Sheffield U	Partick Th	07.55	55-57	89	-	31
Stoke C	Tr	04.58	58-62	133	-	14

HOWLETT Gary Patrick
Dublin, 2 April, 1963 IRYth/IRu21-4/IR-1 (M)

League Club	Source	Date Signed	Seasons Played	Apps	Subs	Gls
Coventry C	Home Farm	11.80				
Brighton & Hove A	Tr	08.82	82-84	30	2	2
Bournemouth	Tr	12.84	84-86	56	4	7
Aldershot	L	08.87	87	1	0	0
Chester C	L	12.87	87	6	0	1
York C	Tr	01.88	87-90	94	7	13

HOWLETT Robert (Bobby) Victor
West Ham, 12 December, 1948 (CD)

League Club	Source	Date Signed	Seasons Played	Apps	Subs	Gls
Chelsea	App	12.65				
Southend U	Tr	09.67	67-68	4	2	0
Colchester U	Tr	07.69	69	10	6	0

HOWSAM Alfred **Dennis**
Sheffield, 21 October, 1922 Died 1981 (CF)

League Club	Source	Date Signed	Seasons Played	Apps	Subs	Gls
Sheffield Wed		11.45				
Chesterfield	Tr	03.47	46-47	12	-	4
Halifax T	Tr	06.48	48	20	-	4

HOWSHALL Gerald (Gerry) Thomas
Stoke-on-Trent, 27 October, 1944 (M)

League Club	Source	Date Signed	Seasons Played	Apps	Subs	Gls
West Bromwich A	App	05.62	63-67	43	2	3
Norwich C	Tr	11.67	67-70	36	4	0

HOWSON Stuart Leigh
Chorley, 30 September, 1981 (CD)

League Club	Source	Date Signed	Seasons Played	Apps	Subs	Gls
Blackburn Rov	YT	07.99				
Chesterfield	Tr	02.02	01-03	51	4	3

HOY Kristian
Doncaster, 27 April, 1976 (F)

League Club	Source	Date Signed	Seasons Played	Apps	Subs	Gls
Doncaster Rov	Jnrs	07.94	94	0	1	0

HOY Robert (Bobby)
Halifax, 10 January, 1950 EYth (W)

League Club	Source	Date Signed	Seasons Played	Apps	Subs	Gls
Huddersfield T	App	11.67	66-74	140	4	18
Blackburn Rov	Tr	03.75	74-75	13	6	0
Halifax T	Tr	06.76	76	30	0	7
York C	Tr	08.77	77	10	4	1
Rochdale	Tr	12.77	77-80	61	5	12

HOY Roger Ernest
Poplar, 6 December, 1946 (M)

League Club	Source	Date Signed	Seasons Played	Apps	Subs	Gls
Tottenham H	Jnrs	05.64	65-67	10	0	0
Crystal Palace	Tr	09.68	68-69	54	0	6
Luton T	Tr	06.70	70	32	0	0
Cardiff C	Tr	08.71	71-72	14	2	0

HOYLAND Jamie William
Sheffield, 23 January, 1966 EYth (M)

League Club	Source	Date Signed	Seasons Played	Apps	Subs	Gls
Manchester C	App	11.83	83-84	2	0	0
Bury	Tr	07.86	86-89	169	3	35
Sheffield U	Tr	07.90	90-94	72	17	6
Bristol C	L	03.94	93	6	0	0
Burnley	Tr	10.94	94-97	77	10	3
Carlisle U	L	11.97	97	5	0	0
Scarborough	Tr	08.98	98	44	0	3

HOYLAND Thomas (Tommy)
Sheffield, 14 June, 1932 (WH)

League Club	Source	Date Signed	Seasons Played	Apps	Subs	Gls
Sheffield U	Jnrs	10.49	49-60	181	-	18
Bradford C	Tr	10.61	61-62	27	-	6

HOYLE Colin Roy
Wirksworth, 15 January, 1972 (CD)

League Club	Source	Date Signed	Seasons Played	Apps	Subs	Gls
Arsenal	YT	01.90				
Chesterfield	L	02.90	89	3	0	0
Barnsley	Tr	07.90				
Bradford C	Tr	08.92	92-93	55	7	1
Notts Co	Tr	08.94	94-95	5	0	0
Mansfield T	L	10.94	94	4	1	0

HOYLE Herbert (Bert)
Baildon, 22 April, 1920 Died 2003 (G)

League Club	Source	Date Signed	Seasons Played	Apps	Subs	Gls
Wolverhampton W		05.46				
Exeter C	Tr	08.46	46-49	82	-	0
Bristol Rov	Tr	05.50	50-52	105	-	0

HOYTE Justin Raymond
Waltham Forest, 20 November, 1984 EYth/Eu20/Eu21-7 (FB)

League Club	Source	Date Signed	Seasons Played	Apps	Subs	Gls
Arsenal	Sch	07.02	02-04	4	3	0

HREIDARSSON Hermann
Reykjavik, Iceland, 11 July, 1974 Icu21-6/Ic-61 (FB)

League Club	Source	Date Signed	Seasons Played	Apps	Subs	Gls
Crystal Palace	IBV (Ice)	08.97	97-98	32	5	2
Brentford	Tr	09.98	98-99	41	0	6
Wimbledon	Tr	10.99	99-00	25	0	1
Ipswich T	Tr	08.00	00-02	101	1	2
Charlton Ath	Tr	03.03	03-04	66	1	3

HRISTOV Georgi
Bitola, Macedonia, 30 January, 1976 MacedoniaU21/Macedonia 30 (F)

League Club	Source	Date Signed	Seasons Played	Apps	Subs	Gls
Barnsley	Partizan Belgrade (Yug)	07.97	97-99	18	26	8

HUBBARD John (Jack)
Wath-on-Dearne, 24 March, 1925 Died 2002 (FB)

League Club	Source	Date Signed	Seasons Played	Apps	Subs	Gls
Notts Co		02.45	46	13	-	2
Scunthorpe U	Scarborough	08.50	50-59	359	-	12

HUBBARD John (Johnny) Gaulton
Pretoria, South Africa, 16 December, 1930 SLge-4 (W)

League Club	Source	Date Signed	Seasons Played	Apps	Subs	Gls
Bury	Glasgow Rgrs	04.59	59-61	109	-	29

HUBBARD Philip (Phil) John
Lincoln, 25 January, 1949 (M)

League Club	Source	Date Signed	Seasons Played	Apps	Subs	Gls
Lincoln C	App	07.66	65-71	150	2	41
Norwich C	Tr	12.71	71-72	6	4	1
Grimsby T	Tr	10.72	72-75	144	2	37
Lincoln C	Tr	08.76	76-79	100	9	11

HUBBARD Terence (Terry) John
Sebastopol, 6 November, 1950 WSch/Wu23-2 (M)

League Club	Source	Date Signed	Seasons Played	Apps	Subs	Gls
Swindon T	App	11.68	70-75	81	1	3

HUBBICK David (Dave)
South Shields, 16 March, 1960 (F)

League Club	Source	Date Signed	Seasons Played	Apps	Subs	Gls
Ipswich T	App	01.78				
Wimbledon	Tr	09.80	80-81	22	4	6
Colchester U	Dagenham	10.83	83-84	4	11	1

HUBBICK Henry (Harry) Edward
Jarrow, 12 November, 1910 Died 1992 (FB)

League Club	Source	Date Signed	Seasons Played	Apps	Subs	Gls
Burnley	Spennymoor U	03.35	35-36	58	-	1
Bolton W	Tr	02.37	36-46	128	-	0
Port Vale	Tr	10.47	47-48	50	-	1
Rochdale	Tr	01.49	48-50	90	-	0

HUCK William (Willie) Roger Fernend
Paris, France, 17 March, 1979 (CD)

League Club	Source	Date Signed	Seasons Played	Apps	Subs	Gls
Arsenal	AS Monaco (Fr)	11.98				
Bournemouth	Tr	03.99	98-01	11	29	0

HUCKER Ian Peter
Hampstead, 28 October, 1959 Eu21-2 (G)

League Club	Source	Date Signed	Seasons Played	Apps	Subs	Gls
Queens Park Rgrs	App	07.77	80-85	160	0	0
Oxford U	Tr	02.87	86-89	66	0	0
West Bromwich A	L	01.88	87	7	0	0
Millwall	Tr	11.89				
Aldershot	Tr	11.90	90	27	0	0

HUCKERBY Darren Carl
Nottingham, 23 April, 1976 Eu21-4/EB-1 (F)

League Club	Source	Date Signed	Seasons Played	Apps	Subs	Gls
Lincoln C	YT	07.93	93-95	20	8	5
Newcastle U	Tr	11.95	95	0	1	0
Millwall	L	09.96	96	6	0	3
Coventry C	Tr	11.96	96-99	85	9	28
Leeds U	Tr	08.99	99-00	11	29	2
Manchester C	Tr	12.00	00-02	44	25	22
Nottingham F	L	02.03	02	9	0	5
Norwich C	Tr	09.03	03-04	72	1	20

HUDD David Clive
Bristol, 9 July, 1944 (IF)

League Club	Source	Date Signed	Seasons Played	Apps	Subs	Gls
Bristol Rov	Old Georgians	07.63	64	5	-	1

HUDDART David (Dave) Joseph
Maryport, 18 November, 1937 (G)

League Club	Source	Date Signed	Seasons Played	Apps	Subs	Gls
Aldershot		06.61				
Gillingham	Tr	07.62	62-64	10	-	0

HUDDLESTONE Edward Thomas
Nottingham, 29 September, 1935 (CF)

League Club	Source	Date Signed	Seasons Played	Apps	Subs	Gls
Nottingham F	Blackpool (Am)	12.56	56	1	-	0

HUDDLESTONE Thomas (Tom) Andrew
Nottingham, 28 December, 1986 EYth/Eu21 (M)

League Club	Source	Date Signed	Seasons Played	Apps	Subs	Gls
Derby Co	Sch	02.04	03-04	84	4	0

HUDGELL Arthur John
Hackney, 28 December, 1920 Died 2000 (FB)

League Club	Source	Date Signed	Seasons Played	Apps	Subs	Gls
Crystal Palace	Eton Manor	12.37	46	25	-	1
Sunderland	Tr	01.47	46-56	260	-	0

HUDSON Alan Anthony
Chelsea, 21 June, 1951 Eu23-10/E-2 (M)

League Club	Source	Date Signed	Seasons Played	Apps	Subs	Gls
Chelsea	App	06.68	68-73	144	1	10
Stoke C	Tr	01.74	73-76	105	0	9
Arsenal	Tr	12.76	76-77	36	0	0
Chelsea	Seattle (USA)	08.83				
Stoke C	Tr	01.84	83-85	38	1	0

HUDSON Albert George
Swansea, 17 June, 1920 Died 2001 WSch (IF)

League Club	Source	Date Signed	Seasons Played	Apps	Subs	Gls
Fulham	Caerau	08.37	46	1	-	0

HUDSON Carl Bernard
Bradford, 10 October, 1966 (CD)

League Club	Source	Date Signed	Seasons Played	Apps	Subs	Gls
Rochdale	Bradford C (App)	08.86	86	13	2	1

HUDSON Charles (Charlie) Arthur
Bytham, 3 April, 1920 (CF)

League Club	Source	Date Signed	Seasons Played	Apps	Subs	Gls
Accrington St (Am)	Guiseley	06.46	46	11	-	3

HUDSON Christopher (Chris) Ben
Rotherham, 13 March, 1951 (FB)

League Club	Source	Date Signed	Seasons Played	Apps	Subs	Gls
Rotherham U	App	03.68	68-71	52	7	1

HUDSON Colin Arthur Richard
Undy, 5 October, 1935 (W)

League Club	Source	Date Signed	Seasons Played	Apps	Subs	Gls
Newport Co	Undy U	04.54	53-56	82	-	20
Cardiff C	Tr	07.57	57-60	60	-	9
Brighton & Hove A	Tr	06.61	61	1	-	0
Newport Co	Tr	02.62	62	30	-	1

HUDSON Daniel (Danny) Robert
Mexborough, 25 June, 1979 (M)

League Club	Source	Date Signed	Seasons Played	Apps	Subs	Gls
Rotherham U	YT	06.97	97-00	29	19	5

HUDSON Gary
West Auckland, 1 November, 1955 (G)

League Club	Source	Date Signed	Seasons Played	Apps	Subs	Gls
Preston NE (Am)		08.73	73	1	0	0

HUDSON Gary Paul
Bradford, 25 February, 1951 (FB)

League Club	Source	Date Signed	Seasons Played	Apps	Subs	Gls
Bradford PA	Jnrs	07.68	67-69	38	1	0

HUDSON Geoffrey (Geoff) Alan
Leeds, 14 October, 1931 (FB)

League Club	Source	Date Signed	Seasons Played	Apps	Subs	Gls
Bradford PA	Jnrs	12.49	50-56	95	-	0
Bradford C	Tr	02.57	56-58	34	-	0
Halifax T	Tr	08.59	59-60	52	-	0
Exeter C	Tr	07.61	61	41	-	0
Crewe Alex	Tr	07.62	62	1	-	0
Gillingham	Tr	07.63	63-64	81	-	1
Lincoln C	Tr	05.65	65	33	0	0

HUDSON George (Garth)
Havant, 26 October, 1923 (CD)

League Club	Source	Date Signed	Seasons Played	Apps	Subs	Gls
Portsmouth		08.45	47	1	-	0
Swindon T	Tr	09.48	48-59	401	-	11

HUDSON George Anthony
Manchester, 14 March, 1937 (F)

League Club	Source	Date Signed	Seasons Played	Apps	Subs	Gls
Blackburn Rov		01.58	58	4	-	1
Accrington St	Tr	07.60	60	44	-	35
Peterborough U	Tr	10.61	61-62	65	-	39
Coventry C	Tr	04.63	62-65	113	0	62
Northampton T	Tr	03.66	65-66	18	0	6
Tranmere Rov	Tr	01.67	66-68	54	1	18

HUDSON John (Jackie)
Blaydon, 5 October, 1921 (CF)

League Club	Source	Date Signed	Seasons Played	Apps	Subs	Gls
Chesterfield	West Stanley	10.46	46-51	169	-	33
Shrewsbury T	Bangor C	09.53	53-54	48	-	20

HUDSON Christopher John
Middleton, 25 November, 1964 (W)

League Club	Source	Date Signed	Seasons Played	Apps	Subs	Gls
Oldham Ath	Manchester C (App)	09.82	82-83	16	4	0
Rochdale	(Sweden)	02.87	86	18	1	1

HUDSON Mark
Bishop Auckland, 24 October, 1980 (M)

League Club	Source	Date Signed	Seasons Played	Apps	Subs	Gls
Middlesbrough	YT	07.99	00-01	0	5	0
Chesterfield	L	08.02	02	15	1	1
Carlisle U	L	12.02	02	14	1	1
Chesterfield	Tr	03.03	02-04	72	5	8

HUDSON Mark Alexander
Guildford, 30 March, 1982 (CD)

League Club	Source	Date Signed	Seasons Played	Apps	Subs	Gls
Fulham	YT	04.99				
Oldham Ath	L	08.03	03	15	0	0
Crystal Palace	Tr	01.04	03-04	21	0	1

HUDSON Morris
Barnsley, 12 September, 1930 (FB)

League Club	Source	Date Signed	Seasons Played	Apps	Subs	Gls
Barnsley	Jnrs	01.49	50-53	36	-	0
Bradford C	Tr	07.55	55	4	-	0

HUDSON Raymond (Ray) James
Slough, 21 November, 1937 (FB)

League Club	Source	Date Signed	Seasons Played	Apps	Subs	Gls
Reading	Jnrs	11.54	55-58	11	-	0

HUDSON Raymond (Ray) Wilfred
Gateshead, 24 March, 1955 (M)

League Club	Source	Date Signed	Seasons Played	Apps	Subs	Gls
Newcastle U	App	03.73	73-77	16	4	1

HUDSON Stanley (Stan) Robert
Fulham, 10 February, 1923 Died 1951 (W)

League Club	Source	Date Signed	Seasons Played	Apps	Subs	Gls
Queens Park Rgrs		09.48	48-49	22	-	7

HUDSON William (Billy) Albert
Swansea, 10 March, 1928 WAmat (W)

League Club	Source	Date Signed	Seasons Played	Apps	Subs	Gls
Leeds U	Pembroke Dock	05.51	51	4	-	0
Sheffield U	Tr	05.52	53	1	-	0
Mansfield T	Tr	05.54	54	8	-	1

HUFFER Philip (Phil)
Bedworth, 23 January, 1932 Died 1995 (CD)

League Club	Source	Date Signed	Seasons Played	Apps	Subs	Gls
Derby Co	Bedworth T	10.53				
Northampton T	Tr	05.54	54	1	-	0

HUGGINS John (Joe) Edward Minden
India, 24 February, 1930 (IF)

League Club	Source	Date Signed	Seasons Played	Apps	Subs	Gls
Aldershot	Alton T	12.55	55	6	-	5

HUGHES Aaron William
Cookstown, 8 November, 1979 NIYth/NIB-2/NI-43 (FB)

League Club	Source	Date Signed	Seasons Played	Apps	Subs	Gls
Newcastle U	YT	03.97	97-04	193	12	4

League Club	Source	Date Signed	Seasons Played	Career Record Apps	Subs	Gls
HUGHES Adrian Francis						
Billinge, 19 December, 1970						(CD)
Preston NE	YT	03.89	87-91	91	9	3
HUGHES Alan						
Wallasey, 5 October, 1948						(F)
Liverpool	Jnrs	09.66				
Chester	L	11.67	67	9	0	2
HUGHES Allan Leslie						
Swansea, 11 March, 1951						(FB)
Swansea T	App	03.69	68	1	0	0
HUGHES Andrew (Andy) John						
Manchester, 2 January, 1978						(M)
Oldham Ath	YT	01.96	95-97	18	15	1
Notts Co	Tr	01.98	97-00	85	25	17
Reading	Tr	07.01	01-04	157	9	18
HUGHES Anthony						
Liverpool, 3 October, 1973 EYth						(CD)
Crewe Alex	YT	06.92	92-93	18	5	1
HUGHES Arthur						
Linlithgow, 23 November, 1927						(IF)
Notts Co	Jeanfield Swifts	07.49				
Nottingham F	Tr	05.51				
Grimsby T	Canterbury C	06.54	54	25	-	11
Gillingham	Tr	05.55	55	5	-	1
HUGHES William **Arthur (Archie)**						
Colwyn Bay, 2 February, 1919 Died 1992 W-5						(G)
Huddersfield T	Newry T	05.39				
Tottenham H	Tr	12.45	46-47	2	-	0
Blackburn Rov	Tr	10.48	48-49	27	-	0
Rochdale	Nelson	09.50	50	9	-	0
Crystal Palace	Tr	02.51	50-51	18	-	0
HUGHES Brian						
Skewen, 22 November, 1937 WSch/Wu23-2						(FB)
Swansea T	Jnrs	07.56	58-66	219	0	7
Swansea T	Merthyr Tydfil	01.69	68	12	0	0
HUGHES Brian David						
Ludgershall, 20 August, 1962						(M)
Swindon T	App	07.80	80-82	67	3	5
Torquay U	Tr	08.83	83	33	5	6
HUGHES Bryan						
Liverpool, 19 June, 1976						(M)
Wrexham	YT	07.94	93-96	71	23	12
Birmingham C	Tr	03.97	96-03	197	51	34
Charlton Ath	Tr	07.04	04	10	7	1
HUGHES Ceri Morgan						
Llwynypia, 26 February, 1971 WYth/WB-2/W-8						(M)
Luton T	YT	07.89	89-96	157	18	17
Wimbledon	Tr	07.97	97-98	21	10	1
Portsmouth	Tr	01.00	99-00	31	3	2
HUGHES Charles (Charlie)						
Manchester, 17 September, 1927						(W)
Manchester U	Jnrs	09.46				
Leeds U	Altrincham	09.50	50-51	21	-	2
HUGHES Charles James						
Blackpool, 7 September, 1939						(G)
Wrexham		10.58	59-60	35	-	0
HUGHES Christopher (Chris)						
Sunderland, 5 March, 1984						(M)
Darlington	Sch	07.03	03-04	29	16	2
HUGHES Daniel (Danny) Paul						
Bangor, 13 February, 1980						(M)
Wolverhampton W	YT	07.98				
Hartlepool U	Tr	03.99	98	6	2	0
HUGHES Darren John						
Prescot, 6 October, 1965						(FB)
Everton	App	10.83	83-84	3	0	0
Shrewsbury T	Tr	06.85	85-86	34	3	1
Brighton & Hove A	Tr	09.86	86	26	0	2
Port Vale	Tr	09.87	87-91	183	1	4
Northampton T	(Retired)	01.95	94-95	19	2	0
Exeter C	Tr	11.95	95-96	58	4	1
HUGHES David James						
Connah's Quay, 27 April, 1943						(W)
Wrexham	Jnrs	05.61				
Tranmere Rov	Tr	07.62	62	2	-	0
HUGHES David John						
Liverpool, 23 September, 1951						(W)
Wrexham (Am)		05.70	70	1	0	0
HUGHES David Robert						
Blackburn, 7 September, 1948						(W)
Preston NE	Blackburn YMCA	09.65	66-71	22	8	0
Southport	Tr	07.72	72	40	0	1
Bury	Tr	08.73	73	12	0	4
Southport	Tr	11.73	73-76	109	4	4
Crewe Alex		08.78	78	12	1	0
HUGHES David Robert						
St Albans, 30 December, 1972 ESch/Wu21-1						(M)
Southampton	Weymouth	07.91	93-98	21	33	3
HUGHES Robert **David**						
Wrexham, 1 February, 1978 WYth/Wu21-13/WB-2						(CD)
Aston Villa	YT	07.96	96	4	3	0
Carlisle U	L	03.98	97	1	0	0
Shrewsbury T	Tr	09.99	99-00	42	4	3
Cardiff C	Tr	02.01	00-01	12	2	0
HUGHES David Thomas						
Birmingham, 19 March, 1958						(M)
Aston Villa	App	02.76	76	3	1	1
Lincoln C	Tr	04.77	77-80	61	1	1
Scunthorpe U	Tr	06.81	81	17	4	0
HUGHES Denis						
Stoke-on-Trent, 9 April, 1931 Died 1990						(W)
Stoke C	Jnrs	09.48	50	1	-	0
HUGHES Derek						
Wrexham, 22 November, 1940						(W)
Wrexham (Am)	Druids U	07.61	61	1	-	0
HUGHES Emlyn Walter						
Barrow, 28 August, 1947 Died 2004 Eu23-8/FLge-9/E-62						(CD)
Blackpool	Jnrs	09.64	65-66	27	1	0
Liverpool	Tr	03.67	66-78	474	0	35
Wolverhampton W	Tr	08.79	79-80	56	2	2
Rotherham U	Tr	09.81	81-82	55	1	6
Hull C	Tr	03.83	82	9	0	0
Swansea C	Mansfield T (N/C)	09.83	83	7	0	0
HUGHES Garry						
Birmingham, 19 November, 1979						(FB)
Northampton T	YT	07.98	99-00	13	5	1
HUGHES Thomas **Glynfor (Glyn)**						
Coedpoeth, 29 November, 1931 Died 1995						(W)
Sheffield Wed		01.51				
Wrexham	Tr	08.52	52-54	92	-	20
Newport Co	Tr	07.55	55	4	-	0
HUGHES Gordon						
Washington, 19 June, 1936						(W)
Newcastle U	Tow Law T	08.56	56-62	133	-	18
Derby Co	Tr	08.63	63-67	184	0	22
Lincoln C	Tr	03.68	67-70	117	0	9
HUGHES Thomas **Gwynfor (Gwyn)**						
Blaenau Ffestiniog, 7 May, 1922 Died 1999						(WH)
Northampton T	Blaenau Ffestiniog	12.45	46-55	225	-	15
HUGHES Harold (Harry) Anthony						
Thurcroft, 12 August, 1937 Died 2001						(FB)
Rotherham U		06.59	59	1	-	0
HUGHES Harold (Harry) James						
Nuneaton, 8 October, 1929						(CD)
Southport	Symingtons	08.50				
Chelsea	Tr	02.51	51	1	-	0
Bournemouth	Tr	06.52	52-57	77	-	2
Gillingham	Tr	07.58	58-62	205	-	14
HUGHES Ian						
Bangor, 2 August, 1974 WYth/Wu21-12						(CD)
Bury	YT	11.91	91-97	137	24	1
Blackpool	Tr	12.97	97-02	139	21	3
Huddersfield T	Tr	08.03	03	12	1	1
HUGHES Ian James						
Sunderland, 24 August, 1961 Wu21-1						(CD)
Sunderland	App	08.79	79	1	0	0
HUGHES Robert **Ian**						
Cefn Mawr, 17 March, 1946						(W)
Wrexham	Oswestry T	02.66	65	9	0	3
Bradford PA	Tr	07.67	67	13	0	0

League Club	Source	Date Signed	Seasons Played	Apps	Subs	Gls
HUGHES Iorwerth (Iorrie)						
Llanddulas, 26 May, 1925 Died 1993 WAmat/W-4						(G)
Luton T	Llandudno	04.49	49-50	36	-	0
Cardiff C	Tr	08.51	51	26	-	0
Newport Co	Worcester C	08.53	53-57	106	-	0
HUGHES James Horace						
Leeds, 28 August, 1918 Died 1979						(WH)
Fulham		09.46	46	1	-	0
HUGHES Jamie Joseph						
Liverpool, 5 April, 1977						(F)
Tranmere Rov	YT	08.95				
Cardiff C	Connah's Quay Nomads	07.99	99	0	2	1
HUGHES John						
West Bromwich, 13 September, 1929						(IF)
Walsall	Golden Lion	05.50	50-52	44	-	10
HUGHES John						
Coatbridge, 3 April, 1943 Su23-4/SLge-6/S-8						(F)
Crystal Palace	Glasgow Celtic	10.71	71-72	20	0	4
Sunderland	Tr	01.73	72	1	0	0
HUGHES John						
Edinburgh, 19 September, 1964						(F)
Swansea C	Berwick Rgrs	11.89	89	16	8	4
HUGHES John Gareth						
Prestatyn, 18 February, 1942						(CF)
Chester	Rhyl	07.62	62	2	-	0
HUGHES John Ifor						
Bangor, 4 May, 1951						(W)
Blackpool	Menai Bridge YC	07.69	69-70	5	3	0
Southport	L	03.71	70	7	1	1
Stockport Co	Altrincham	01.76	75	11	1	3
HUGHES John Michael						
Manchester, 29 November, 1962						(M)
Bury	Winsford U	11.80	81-82	1	1	0
HUGHES John Norman						
Tamworth, 10 July, 1921 Died 2003						(W)
Birmingham C	Tamworth Castle	06.47	47-48	6	-	0
HUGHES Kenneth (Ken) David						
Barmouth, 9 January, 1966						(G)
Crystal Palace	Jnrs	08.85				
Shrewsbury T	Tr	07.86	86-91	74	0	0
Wrexham	Tr	08.92	92	8	0	0
HUGHES Lawrence (Laurie)						
Waterloo, Lancashire, 2 March, 1924 EB/E-3						(CD)
Liverpool	Tranmere Rov (Am)	02.43	46-57	303	-	1
HUGHES Lee						
Smethwick, 22 May, 1976 ESemiPro-4						(F)
West Bromwich A	Kidderminster Hrs	05.97	97-00	137	19	78
Coventry C	Tr	08.01	01-02	38	4	15
West Bromwich A	Tr	08.02	02-03	35	20	11
HUGHES Lyndon James						
Smethwick, 16 September, 1950 ESch/EYth						(M)
West Bromwich A	App	01.68	68-74	89	9	3
Peterborough U	Tr	07.75	75-77	75	2	5
HUGHES Mark						
Port Talbot, 3 February, 1962 WSch						(CD)
Bristol Rov	App	02.80	79-83	73	1	3
Torquay U	L	12.82	82	9	0	1
Swansea C	Tr	07.84	84	12	0	0
Bristol C	Tr	02.85	84-85	21	1	0
Tranmere Rov	Tr	09.85	85-93	258	8	9
Shrewsbury T	Tr	07.94	94-95	20	2	0
HUGHES Mark Anthony						
Dungannon, 16 September, 1983 NISch/NIYth/NIu21-8/NIu23-1						(M)
Tottenham H	YT	07.01				
Northampton T	L	08.04	04	3	0	0
Oldham Ath	Tr	11.04	04	25	2	0
HUGHES Mark Christopher						
Swindon, 17 July, 1967 WYth						(M)
Swindon T	App	•	83	0	1	0
HUGHES Leslie **Mark**						
Wrexham, 1 November, 1963 WSch/WYth/Wu21-5/W-72						(F)
Manchester U	App	11.80	83-85	85	4	37
Manchester U	Barcelona (Sp)	07.88	88-94	251	5	82
Chelsea	Tr	07.95	95-97	88	7	25
Southampton	Tr	07.98	98-99	50	2	2
Everton	Tr	03.00	99-00	15	3	1
Blackburn Rov	Tr	10.00	00-01	25	25	6
HUGHES Michael Eamonn						
Larne, 2 August, 1971 NISch/NIYth/NIu21-1/NIu23-2/NI-71						(W)
Manchester C	YT	08.88	88-91	25	1	1
West Ham U (L)	RC Strasbourg (Fr)	11.94	94	15	2	2
West Ham U (L)	RC Strasbourg (Fr)	10.95	95	28	0	0
West Ham U	RC Strasbourg (Fr)	08.96	96-97	33	5	3
Wimbledon	Tr	09.97	97-01	99	16	13
Birmingham C	L	03.02	01	3	0	0
Crystal Palace	Tr	08.03	03-04	68	2	5
HUGHES Edward **Michael (Mike)**						
Llanidloes, 3 September, 1940						(M)
Cardiff C	Jnrs	12.58	58	1	-	0
Exeter C	Tr	07.61	61-62	36	-	0
Chesterfield	Tr	07.63	63-68	208	2	9
HUGHES Michael (Mike) Richard						
Bridgend, 19 August, 1964 WYth						(G)
Swansea C	App	08.82	83-87	139	0	0
HUGHES Patrick (Pat) Joseph						
Coatbridge, 28 February, 1945						(W)
Darlington	St Mirren	08.65	65	3	0	0
HUGHES Paul						
Denton, 19 December, 1968						(FB)
Bolton W	YT	07.87	87-89	12	1	0
HUGHES John **Paul**						
Hammersmith, 19 April, 1976 ESch						(M)
Chelsea	YT	07.94	96-97	13	8	2
Stockport Co	L	12.98	98	7	0	0
Norwich C	L	03.99	98	2	2	1
Southampton	Tr	03.00				
Luton T	Tr	08.01	01-03	62	17	6
HUGHES Philip (Phil) Anthony						
Belfast, 19 November, 1964 NIYth/NI-3						(G)
Leeds U	Manchester U (App)	01.83	83-84	6	0	0
Bury	Tr	07.85	85-87	80	0	0
Wigan Ath	Tr	11.87	87-90	99	0	0
Scarborough	Rochdale (N/C)	10.91	91	17	0	0
HUGHES Richard (Ricky)						
Barrow, 27 December, 1950						(F)
Barrow (Am)	Jnrs	08.70	71	0	2	0
HUGHES Richard Daniel						
Glasgow, 25 June, 1979 SYth/Su21-9/S-4						(M)
Arsenal	Atalanta (It)	08.97				
Bournemouth	Tr	08.98	98-01	123	8	14
Portsmouth	Tr	06.02	02-04	25	8	0
Grimsby T	L	02.03	02	12	0	1
HUGHES Ronald (Ron)						
Mold, 1 July, 1930						(FB)
Chester	Mold Alexandra	09.50	51-61	399	-	21
HUGHES Ronald (Ron) Hardwick						
Workington, 17 August, 1955						(G)
Workington	RNAD	12.75	75	15	0	0
HUGHES Roy						
Manchester, 13 August, 1949						(M)
Bury	App	09.66	67-71	45	4	2
HUGHES Stephen David						
Motherwell, 14 November, 1982 SYth/Su21-12						(M)
Leicester C	Glasgow Rgrs	01.05	04	13	3	1
HUGHES Stephen (Steve) John						
Warrington, 4 January, 1958						(F)
Crewe Alex	Manchester C (App)	03.76	75	0	2	0
HUGHES Stephen (Billy) John						
Folkestone, 29 July, 1960						(M)
Gillingham	Jnrs	07.77	75-80	110	16	8
Crystal Palace	Tr	07.81	81	3	4	0
Wimbledon	Tr	03.82	81	2	0	0
HUGHES Stephen John						
Reading, 18 September, 1976 ESch/EYth/Eu21-8						(M)
Arsenal	YT	07.95	94-99	22	27	4
Fulham	L	07.99	99	3	0	0
Everton	Tr	03.00	99-00	27	2	1
Watford	Tr	07.01	01	11	4	0
Charlton Ath	Tr	08.03				
Coventry C	Tr	07.04	04	39	1	4

League Club	Source	Date Signed	Seasons Played	Apps	Subs	Gls
HUGHES Stephen Thomas						
High Wycombe, 26 January, 1984						(F)
Brentford	Sch	07.02	02-03	3	9	0
HUGHES Terence (Terry) Philip						
Llanidloes, 10 March, 1953						(F)
Shrewsbury T	App	03.71	69-73	66	5	22
HUGHES Thomas (Tommy) Alexander						
Dalmuir, 11 July, 1947 Su23-2						(G)
Chelsea	Clydebank Jnrs	07.65	66-69	11	0	0
Aston Villa	Tr	06.71	71	16	0	0
Brighton & Hove A	L	02.73	72	3	0	0
Hereford U	Tr	08.73	73-81	240	0	0
HUGHES Walter (Wally) Cyril Joseph						
Dingle, 15 March, 1934						(W)
Liverpool	Winsford U	10.54				
Sheffield U	Winsford U	01.56	55	2	-	0
Bradford PA	Wisbech T	04.57	56-57	20	-	0
Southport	Tr	02.58	57	11	-	0
HUGHES Byron **Wayne**						
Port Talbot, 8 March, 1958 WSch/Wu21-3						(M)
West Bromwich A	App	03.76	76-77	3	3	2
Cardiff C	Tulsa (USA)	10.79	79-81	42	4	1
HUGHES William (Billy)						
Ballymena, 9 May, 1929 Died 2005 I-1						(W)
Bolton W	Larne T	08.48	48-52	47	-	2
Bournemouth	Tr	06.53	53	16	-	1
HUGHES William (Billy)						
Glasgow, 3 March, 1929 Died 2003						(W)
York C	Newcastle U (Am)	05.51	51-61	349	-	55
HUGHES William (Billy)						
Coatbridge, 30 December, 1948 S-1						(F)
Sunderland	Jnrs	02.66	66-76	264	24	74
Derby Co	Tr	08.77	77	17	2	8
Leicester C	Tr	12.77	77-78	36	1	5
Carlisle U	L	09.79	79	5	0	0
HUGHES William (Billy) Henry						
Cardiff, 2 October, 1920 Died 1995 WSch						(CD)
Hartlepools U	Newcastle U (Am)	05.46	46-49	124	-	2
HUGHES William (Billy) Marshall						
Llanelli, 6 March, 1918 Died 1981 WWar-14/W-10						(FB)
Birmingham	Llanelli	05.35	35-46	104	-	0
Luton T	Tr	07.47	47	31	-	0
Chelsea	Tr	03.48	47-50	93	-	0
HUGHES Zacari David						
Bentley, Australia, 6 June, 1971						(CD)
Rochdale	YT	08.89	87	2	0	0
HUGHTON Christopher (Chris) William Gerard						
Stratford, 11 December, 1958 IR-53						(FB)
Tottenham H	Jnrs	06.77	79-89	293	4	12
West Ham U	Tr	11.90	90-91	32	1	0
Brentford	Tr	03.92	91-92	32	0	0
HUGHTON Henry Timothy						
Stratford, 18 November, 1959 IRu21-1						(FB)
Orient	App	12.76	78-81	104	7	2
Crystal Palace	Tr	07.82	82-85	113	5	1
Brentford	Tr	09.86	86	5	3	0
Orient	Tr	12.86	86-87	16	2	0
HUGO Roger Victor						
Woking, 6 September, 1942						(IF)
West Ham U	Jnrs	10.60	63	3	-	2
Watford	Tr	05.65	65	24	1	6
HUKE Shane						
Reading, 2 October, 1985						(FB)
Peterborough U	Sch	10.03	04	6	2	0
HUKIN Arthur						
Sheffield, 22 October, 1937 Died 1983						(CF)
Sheffield Wed	Jnrs	10.54	54	6	-	3
HULBERT Robin James						
Plymouth, 14 March, 1980 ESch/EYth						(M)
Swindon T	YT	09.97	97-99	12	17	0
Bristol C	Tr	03.00	99-02	21	18	0
Shrewsbury T	L	03.03	02	4	3	0
Port Vale	Telford U	07.04	04	23	1	0
HULL Alan Edward						
Rochford, 4 September, 1962						(F)
Leyton Orient	Barking	05.87	87-90	54	25	16

League Club	Source	Date Signed	Seasons Played	Apps	Subs	Gls
HULL Gary						
Sheffield, 21 June, 1956						(FB)
Sheffield Wed	App	06.74	75	6	2	0
HULL Jeffrey (Jeff)						
Rochford, 25 August, 1960						(M)
Southend U	App	08.78	78-80	10	5	1
Colchester U	Basildon U	12.82	82-85	82	1	10
HULLETT William (Bill) Alexander						
Liverpool, 19 November, 1915 Died 1982						(CF)
Everton		12.35				
New Brighton	L	01.37	36	13	-	8
Plymouth Arg	Tr	10.37	37-38	29	-	20
Manchester U	Tr	03.39				
Cardiff C	Merthyr Tydfil	02.48	47-48	27	-	15
Nottingham F	Tr	11.48	48	13	-	2
HULLIGAN Michael (Mick) John						
Liverpool, 28 February, 1923 Died 1978						(W)
Liverpool		12.42				
Port Vale	Tr	07.48	48-54	197	-	22
HULME Eric Martin						
Houghton-le-Spring, 14 January, 1949						(G)
Nottingham F	Spennymoor U	03.70	71	5	0	0
Lincoln C	Tr	09.72	72-73	23	0	0
HULME John						
Mobberley, 6 February, 1945						(CD)
Bolton W	Jnrs	02.62	62-71	186	2	7
Notts Co	L	03.72	71	8	0	0
Reading	Tr	07.72	72-73	86	1	0
Bury	Tr	07.74	74-75	86	0	5
HULME Kevin						
Farnworth, 2 December, 1967						(M)
Bury	Radcliffe Borough	03.89	88-92	82	28	21
Chester C	L	10.89	89	4	0	0
Doncaster Rov	Tr	07.93	93	33	1	8
Bury	Tr	08.94	94-95	24	5	0
Lincoln C	Tr	09.95	95	4	1	0
Halifax T	Macclesfield T	10.96	98-99	32	1	4
York C	Tr	09.99	99-00	34	4	7
HULMES Gary Anthony						
Manchester, 28 February, 1957						(F)
Rochdale	Manchester C (App)	12.74	74-75	4	5	1
HULSE Robert Arthur						
Crewe, 5 November, 1948 EYth						(F)
Stoke C	Nantwich T	04.67	67	2	0	0
HULSE Robert James						
Low Fell, 5 January, 1957						(M)
Darlington	Stade Quimper (Fr)	09.83	83	3	1	0
HULSE Robert (Rob) William						
Crewe, 25 October, 1979						(F)
Crewe Alex	YT	06.98	99-02	97	19	46
West Bromwich A	Tr	08.03	03-04	29	9	10
Leeds U	L	02.05	04	13	0	6
HUMBLE Douglas (Dougie)						
Wolsingham, 16 February, 1920 Died 1989						(CF)
Sunderland	Bishop Auckland	05.45				
Southport	Tr	06.47	47	11	-	4
HUMBLE James **Wilfred (Wilf)**						
Ashington, 10 May, 1936 Died 1985						(FB)
Mansfield T	Ashington	05.59	59-65	198	0	1
HUME Iain						
Brampton, Ontario, Canada, 31 October, 1983 CaYth/Ca-11						(F)
Tranmere Rov	Jnrs	11.00	99-04	95	49	31
HUME Robert William						
Kirkintilloch, 18 March, 1941 Died 1997						(W)
Middlesbrough	Glasgow Rgrs	09.62	62	19	-	5
HUME William Sanderson						
Armadale, 18 December, 1935 Died 1990						(IF)
Birmingham C	Dunfermline Ath	02.58	58-59	10	-	2
HUMES Anthony (Tony)						
Blyth, 19 March, 1966						(CD)
Ipswich T	App	05.83	86-91	107	13	10
Wrexham	Tr	03.92	91-98	191	8	8
HUMES James (Jimmy)						
Carlisle, 6 August, 1942						(W)
Preston NE	Jnrs	09.59	59-61	18	-	1
Bristol Rov	Tr	06.62	62	2	-	0

League Club	Source	Date Signed	Seasons Played	Apps	Subs	Gls
Chester	Tr	07.63	63-66	124	0	31
Barnsley	Tr	07.67	67	7	0	1

HUMPHREY John
Paddington, 31 January, 1961 (FB)

League Club	Source	Date Signed	Seasons Played	Apps	Subs	Gls
Wolverhampton W	App	02.79	79-84	149	0	3
Charlton Ath	Tr	07.85	85-89	194	0	3
Crystal Palace	Tr	08.90	90-94	153	7	2
Reading	L	12.93	93	8	0	0
Charlton Ath	Tr	07.95	95	28	0	0
Gillingham	Tr	06.96	96	9	0	0
Brighton & Hove A	Tr	01.97	96-97	22	0	0

HUMPHREY John Mark
Guildford, 2 July, 1969 (F)

League Club	Source	Date Signed	Seasons Played	Apps	Subs	Gls
Millwall	Leatherhead	02.91				
Exeter C	L	12.91	91	2	0	0

HUMPHREY Thomas (Tommy) Robson
Houghton-le-Spring, 27 October, 1937 (W)

League Club	Source	Date Signed	Seasons Played	Apps	Subs	Gls
Aldershot		03.59	58-60	22	-	3

HUMPHREYS Alan
Chester, 18 October, 1939 (G)

League Club	Source	Date Signed	Seasons Played	Apps	Subs	Gls
Shrewsbury T	Lache YC	10.56	56-59	32	-	0
Leeds U	Tr	02.60	59-61	40	-	0
Mansfield T	Gravesend & Northfleet	01.64	64-67	58	0	0
Chesterfield	Tr	07.68	68-69	51	0	0

HUMPHREYS Derek John Beattie
Belfast, 5 October, 1949 (G)

League Club	Source	Date Signed	Seasons Played	Apps	Subs	Gls
Arsenal	Jnrs	10.66				
Sunderland	Crusaders	11.67				
Hartlepool	L	10.69	69	4	0	0

HUMPHREYS Gerald (Gerry)
Llandudno, 14 January, 1946 WSch/Wu23-5 (W)

League Club	Source	Date Signed	Seasons Played	Apps	Subs	Gls
Everton	App	09.63	65-69	12	0	2
Crystal Palace	Tr	06.70	70	4	7	0
Crewe Alex	Tr	01.72	71-76	184	9	30

HUMPHREYS John Stephen
Farnworth, 18 July, 1964 (F)

League Club	Source	Date Signed	Seasons Played	Apps	Subs	Gls
Oldham Ath	App	07.82	82-83	7	6	0
Rochdale	L	03.84	83	6	0	0

HUMPHREYS John Vaughan
Llandudno, 13 January, 1920 Died 1954 W-1 (CD)

League Club	Source	Date Signed	Seasons Played	Apps	Subs	Gls
Everton	Llandudno T	04.43	46-50	53	-	0

HUMPHREYS Percy Ronald
Bradford, 28 October, 1924 Died 1999 (W)

League Club	Source	Date Signed	Seasons Played	Apps	Subs	Gls
Halifax T	Boothtown	11.43	46	3	-	1

HUMPHREYS Richard (Richie) John
Sheffield, 30 November, 1977 EYth/Eu21-3 (M)

League Club	Source	Date Signed	Seasons Played	Apps	Subs	Gls
Sheffield Wed	YT	02.96	95-00	34	33	4
Scunthorpe U	L	08.99	99	6	0	2
Cardiff C	L	11.99	99	8	1	2
Cambridge U	Tr	02.01	00	7	0	3
Hartlepool U	Tr	07.01	01-04	180	4	22

HUMPHREYS Ronald (Ron)
Tonypandy, 4 April, 1925 (FB)

League Club	Source	Date Signed	Seasons Played	Apps	Subs	Gls
Southend U	Snowdown CW	05.45	46	3	-	0

HUMPHRIES Charles (Charlie) William
Birmingham, 19 March, 1922 Died 1995 (FB)

League Club	Source	Date Signed	Seasons Played	Apps	Subs	Gls
Walsall	Paget Rgrs	09.46	47	6	-	0

HUMPHRIES David (Dave) William
Wolverhampton, 10 August, 1939 (CD)

League Club	Source	Date Signed	Seasons Played	Apps	Subs	Gls
Shrewsbury T		03.60	60	3	-	0

HUMPHRIES Glenn
Hull, 11 August, 1964 EYth (CD)

League Club	Source	Date Signed	Seasons Played	Apps	Subs	Gls
Doncaster Rov	YT	08.82	80-87	174	6	8
Lincoln C	L	03.87	86	9	0	0
Bristol C	Tr	10.87	87-90	81	4	0
Scunthorpe U	Tr	03.91	90-92	71	1	5
Hull C	Golden (HK)	08.95	95	9	3	0

HUMPHRIES Mark
Glasgow, 23 December, 1971 (FB)

League Club	Source	Date Signed	Seasons Played	Apps	Subs	Gls
Leeds U	Aberdeen	06.93				
Bristol C	Tr	10.94	94	4	0	0

HUMPHRIES Robert (Bob)
Hindhead, 4 July, 1933 Died 1988 (WH)

League Club	Source	Date Signed	Seasons Played	Apps	Subs	Gls
Sheffield U	Tottenham H (Am)	12.55				
Brighton & Hove A	Tr	11.56	56	10	-	2
Millwall	Tr	08.57	57-59	47	-	4

HUMPHRIES Stephen (Steve) Rodney
Hull, 29 May, 1961 ESemiPro (G)

League Club	Source	Date Signed	Seasons Played	Apps	Subs	Gls
Leicester C	App	09.78				
Doncaster Rov	Tr	06.81	81	13	0	0
Cardiff C	Tr	08.82	82	1	0	0
Wrexham	Tr	09.82	82	2	0	0

HUMPHRIES William (Willie) McCauley
Belfast, 8 June, 1936 IrLge-12/NI-14 (W)

League Club	Source	Date Signed	Seasons Played	Apps	Subs	Gls
Leeds U	Ards	09.58	58-59	25	-	2
Coventry C	Ards	04.62	61-64	109	-	23
Swansea T	Tr	03.65	64-67	143	0	22

HUMPSTON Ronald (Ron)
Derby, 14 December, 1923 (G)

League Club	Source	Date Signed	Seasons Played	Apps	Subs	Gls
Portsmouth		01.46	47-50	9	-	0
Huddersfield T	Tr	11.51	51	5	-	0

HUNT Andrew (Andy)
Grays, 9 June, 1970 (F)

League Club	Source	Date Signed	Seasons Played	Apps	Subs	Gls
Newcastle U	Kettering T	01.91	90-91	34	9	11
West Bromwich A	Tr	03.93	92-97	201	11	76
Charlton Ath	Tr	07.98	98-00	83	3	35

HUNT David
Leicester, 17 April, 1959 (M)

League Club	Source	Date Signed	Seasons Played	Apps	Subs	Gls
Derby Co	App	04.77	77	5	0	0
Notts Co	Tr	03.78	77-86	331	5	28
Aston Villa	Tr	06.87	87-88	12	1	0
Mansfield T	Tr	06.89	89	21	1	0

HUNT David
Durham, 5 March, 1980 (FB)

League Club	Source	Date Signed	Seasons Played	Apps	Subs	Gls
Darlington	YT	07.98	96	0	1	0

HUNT David
Dulwich, 10 September, 1982 (FB)

League Club	Source	Date Signed	Seasons Played	Apps	Subs	Gls
Crystal Palace	Sch	07.02	02	2	0	0
Leyton Orient	Tr	07.03	03-04	57	8	1
Northampton T	Tr	03.05	04	2	2	0

HUNT Dennis Perrior
Portsmouth, 8 September, 1937 (FB)

League Club	Source	Date Signed	Seasons Played	Apps	Subs	Gls
Gillingham		09.58	58-67	319	2	6
Brentford	Tr	06.68	68	12	0	0

HUNT Douglas (Doug) Arthur
Shipton Bellinger, 19 May, 1914 Died 1989 (CF)

League Club	Source	Date Signed	Seasons Played	Apps	Subs	Gls
Tottenham H	Winchester C	03.34	34-36	17	-	6
Barnsley	Tr	03.37	36-37	36	-	18
Sheffield Wed	Tr	03.38	37-38	42	-	30
Leyton Orient	Tr	04.46	46-47	61	-	16

HUNT George Harold
Bethnal Green, 5 March, 1917 Died 1990 (CD)

League Club	Source	Date Signed	Seasons Played	Apps	Subs	Gls
Charlton Ath	Bexleyheath	05.37				
Barnsley	Tr	05.38				
Watford	Tr	06.46	47-49	35	-	0

HUNT Reginald **George** Albert
Swindon, 27 February, 1922 Died 1987 (FB)

League Club	Source	Date Signed	Seasons Played	Apps	Subs	Gls
Swindon T		01.47	48-57	304	-	0

HUNT George Samuel
Barnsley, 22 February, 1910 Died 1996 E-3 (CF)

League Club	Source	Date Signed	Seasons Played	Apps	Subs	Gls
Chesterfield	Regent Street Congs	09.29	29	14	-	9
Tottenham H	Tr	06.30	30-36	185	-	125
Arsenal	Tr	10.37	37	18	-	3
Bolton W	Tr	02.38	37-46	45	-	24
Sheffield Wed	Tr	11.46	46-47	32	-	8

HUNT James Malcolm
Derby, 17 December, 1976 (M)

League Club	Source	Date Signed	Seasons Played	Apps	Subs	Gls
Notts Co	YT	07.94	95-96	15	4	1
Northampton T	Tr	08.97	97-01	150	22	8
Oxford U	Tr	07.02	02-03	75	5	3
Bristol Rov	Tr	07.04	04	41	0	4

HUNT Jonathan (Jon) Martin
Leeds, 11 September, 1984 (M)

League Club	Source	Date Signed	Seasons Played	Apps	Subs	Gls
Scunthorpe U	Sch	08.04	03	0	1	0

HUNT Jonathan Richard
Camden, 2 November, 1971 (W)

League Club	Source	Date Signed	Seasons Played	Apps	Subs	Gls
Barnet	Jnrs	01.90	91-92	12	21	0
Southend U	Tr	07.93	93-94	41	8	6
Birmingham C	Tr	09.94	94-96	67	10	18
Derby Co	Tr	05.97	97-98	7	18	2
Sheffield U	L	08.98	98	5	1	1
Ipswich T	L	10.98	98	2	4	0
Sheffield U	Tr	03.99	98-99	15	6	1
Cambridge U	L	03.00	99	3	4	1
Wimbledon	Tr	09.00	00	8	4	0

League Club	Source	Date Signed	Seasons Played	Career Record Apps	Subs	Gls
HUNT Lewis James						
Birmingham, 25 August, 1982						(FB)
Derby Co	YT	02.01	02-03	8	3	0
Southend U	Tr	10.03	03-04	50	7	0
HUNT Mark Geoffrey						
Farnworth, 5 October, 1969						(F)
Rochdale	App	•	86-87	1	1	1
HUNT Morgan Marshall						
Bridgend, 5 March, 1931						(WH)
Doncaster Rov	Askern Welfare	02.52	53-57	50	-	2
Norwich C	Tr	07.58	58	7	-	0
Port Vale	Tr	08.59	59	2	-	0
HUNT Nicholas (Nicky) Brett						
Westhoughton, 3 September, 1983 Eu21-7						(FB)
Bolton W	YT	07.01	00-04	57	4	1
HUNT Paul Craig						
Swindon, 8 October, 1970						(F)
Swindon T	YT	07.89	89-92	5	6	0
HUNT Paul Leslie						
Hereford, 7 March, 1959						(CD)
Hereford U	Coventry C (App)	06.77	78-80	41	10	4
HUNT Peter John						
Stepney, 2 July, 1952 EYth						(M)
Southend U	App	09.69	68-71	50	6	1
Charlton Ath	Tr	12.72	72-76	138	20	6
Gillingham	Tr	08.77	77	23	0	0
HUNT Ralph Robert Arthur						
Portsmouth, 14 August, 1933 Died 1964						(CF)
Portsmouth	Gloucester C	08.50	52-53	5	-	0
Bournemouth	Tr	02.54	53-54	33	-	7
Norwich C	Tr	07.55	55-57	124	-	67
Derby Co	Tr	08.58	58	24	-	10
Grimsby T	Tr	08.59	59-60	53	-	39
Swindon T	Tr	07.61	61	21	-	13
Port Vale	Tr	12.61	61	14	-	6
Newport Co	Tr	07.62	62-63	83	-	38
Chesterfield	Tr	07.64	64	17	-	5
HUNT Richard Anthony						
Reading, 5 January, 1971						(CD)
Aldershot	Queens Park Rgrs (YT)	07.89	89	1	1	0
HUNT Robert (Bobby)						
Liverpool, 4 September, 1934						(WH)
Wrexham		07.56				
Chester	Tr	05.58	58-60	84	-	2
HUNT Robert						
Newcastle, 20 September, 1966						(G)
Halifax T	Barnsley (YT)	01.85	84	3	0	0
HUNT Robert (Bobby) Rex						
Colchester, 1 October, 1942						(F)
Colchester U	Jnrs	11.59	59-63	149	-	83
Northampton T	Tr	03.64	63-65	40	0	10
Millwall	Tr	09.66	66-67	43	0	13
Ipswich T	Tr	11.67	67-70	16	10	4
Charlton Ath	Tr	09.70	70-72	34	2	11
Northampton T	L	11.72	72	5	0	3
Reading	Tr	01.73	72-73	15	1	3
HUNT Roger						
Golborne, 20 July, 1938 FLge-5/E-34						(F)
Liverpool	Stockton Heath	05.59	59-69	401	3	245
Bolton W	Tr	12.69	69-71	72	4	24
HUNT Roger (Ernie) Patrick						
Swindon, 17 March, 1943 Eu23-3						(F)
Swindon T	Jnrs	03.60	59-65	214	0	82
Wolverhampton W	Tr	09.65	65-67	74	0	32
Everton	Tr	09.67	67	12	2	3
Coventry C	Tr	03.68	67-73	140	6	45
Doncaster Rov	L	01.73	72	9	0	1
Bristol C	Tr	12.73	73-74	9	3	2
HUNT Ronald (Ron) Geoffrey						
Paddington, 19 December, 1945						(CD)
Queens Park Rgrs	App	03.63	64-72	214	5	1
HUNT Ronald (Ron) Malcolm						
Colchester, 26 September, 1933 Died 1999						(WH)
Colchester U	Jnrs	10.51	51-63	177	-	3
HUNT Simon						
Chester, 17 November, 1962						(M)
Wrexham	Jnrs	08.81	81-83	102	6	18

League Club	Source	Date Signed	Seasons Played	Career Record Apps	Subs	Gls
HUNT Stephen (Steve)						
Port Laoise, 1 August, 1980 IRu21-1						(M)
Crystal Palace	YT	06.99	99	0	3	0
Brentford	Tr	08.01	01-04	126	10	25
HUNT Stephen James						
Southampton, 11 November, 1984						(FB)
Colchester U	Southampton (Sch)	07.04	04	16	4	1
HUNT Stephen (Steve) Kenneth						
Birmingham, 4 August, 1956 E-2						(W)
Aston Villa	App	01.74	74-76	4	3	1
Coventry C	NY Cosmos (USA)	08.78	78-83	178	7	27
West Bromwich A	Tr	03.84	83-85	68	0	15
Aston Villa	Tr	03.86	85-87	61	1	6
HUNT Warren David						
Portsmouth, 2 March, 1984						(M)
Portsmouth	YT	11.01				
Leyton Orient	L	03.04	03	6	0	0
HUNT William (Billy) Edmund						
Colchester, 25 November, 1934						(CD)
Colchester U	Jnrs	08.53	55	1	-	0
HUNT-BROWN Peter Barry						
Halifax, 19 February, 1937						(CF)
Halifax T	Elland U	12.58	58	1	-	0
HUNTER Allan						
Sion Mills, 30 June, 1946 NIAmat/NIu23-1/NI-53						(CD)
Oldham Ath	Coleraine	01.67	66-68	83	0	1
Blackburn Rov	Tr	06.69	69-71	84	0	1
Ipswich T	Tr	09.71	71-80	280	0	8
Colchester U	Tr	05.82	81-82	18	1	0
HUNTER Barry Victor						
Coleraine, 18 November, 1968 NIYth/NIB-2/NI-15						(CD)
Newcastle U	Coleraine	11.87				
Wrexham	Crusaders	08.93	93-95	88	3	4
Reading	Tr	07.96	96-00	76	8	4
Southend U	L	02.99	98	5	0	2
Rushden & Diamonds	Tr	09.01	01-04	106	1	6
HUNTER Christopher (Chris) Paul						
Hong Kong, 18 January, 1964						(F)
Preston NE	App	09.81	82	0	1	0
Preston NE	Chorley	09.84	84	3	3	0
HUNTER Donald (Don)						
Thorne, 10 March, 1927						(WH)
Huddersfield T	Luddenden Foot	03.44	48-50	26	-	1
Halifax T	Tr	08.51	51	11	-	0
Southport	Tr	08.52	52-56	174	-	1
HUNTER Edward (Eddie)						
Tillicoultry, 7 March, 1928 Died 2002						(WH)
Accrington St	Falkirk	08.54	54-58	169	-	4
HUNTER Geoffrey (Geoff)						
Hull, 27 October, 1959						(M)
Manchester U	App	11.76				
Crewe Alex	Tr	08.79	79-80	86	1	8
Port Vale	Tr	08.81	81-86	218	3	15
Wrexham	Tr	08.87	87-90	116	6	14
HUNTER George Irvine						
Troon, 29 August, 1930 Died 1990						(G)
Derby Co	Glasgow Celtic	06.54	54	19	-	0
Exeter C	Tr	08.55	55-58	147	-	0
Darlington	Yiewsley	06.61	61	20	-	0
Lincoln C	Burton A	09.65	65	1	0	0
HUNTER Gordon Greig						
Lyneham, 8 November, 1954						(CD)
York C	Shrewsbury T (Am)	07.73	73-77	70	7	1
HUNTER John Dixon						
Backworth, 20 September, 1934						(G)
Gateshead		08.54	55	4	-	0
HUNTER John Smith						
Coalburn, 26 May, 1934						(W)
Rotherham U	Coltness U	06.56	56	5	-	1
Carlisle U	Tr	07.57	57	1	-	0
Barrow	King's Lynn	07.59	59-60	24	-	0
HUNTER Alvin **Junior**						
Lambeth, 1 February, 1975						(M)
Cambridge U	YT	05.93	93-94	26	14	0

League Club	Source	Date Signed	Seasons Played	Apps	Subs	Gls
HUNTER Lee						
Oldham, 5 October, 1969						(M)
Colchester U	YT	06.88	87-88	5	4	0
HUNTER Leslie (Les)						
Middlesbrough, 15 January, 1958						(CD)
Chesterfield	App	08.75	75-81	156	9	8
Scunthorpe U	Tr	07.82	82-83	61	0	8
Chesterfield	Tr	01.84	83-85	99	0	9
Scunthorpe U	Tr	03.86	85-86	49	0	5
Chesterfield	Lincoln C	12.87	87-88	31	0	3
HUNTER Michael (Mick)						
Hexham, 27 May, 1948						(M)
Blackpool		01.66				
Darlington	Tr	07.67	67	2	1	0
HUNTER Norman						
Eighton Banks, 29 October, 1943 Eu23-3/FLge-6/E-28						(CD)
Leeds U	Jnrs	04.61	62-76	540	0	18
Bristol C	Tr	10.76	76-78	108	0	4
Barnsley	Tr	06.79	79-82	28	3	0
HUNTER Paul						
Kirkcaldy, 30 August, 1968 Su21-3						(F)
Hull C	East Fife	03.90	89-92	37	31	11
HUNTER Philip (Phil)						
Hartlepool, 28 September, 1950						(W)
Hartlepool (Am)	Jnrs	08.69	69	1	0	0
HUNTER Reginald (Reg) John						
Colwyn Bay, 25 October, 1938						(W)
Manchester U	Colwyn Bay	11.56	58	1	-	0
Wrexham	Tr	02.60	59-61	34	-	3
HUNTER Robert (Bob)						
Gateshead, 25 March, 1951						(W)
Hartlepool		02.71	70	1	0	0
HUNTER Robert (Bobby) Russell						
Shotts, 12 March, 1931 Died 2002						(W)
Swindon T	Motherwell	08.54	54	16	-	3
HUNTER Roy Ian						
Saltburn, 29 October, 1973						(M)
West Bromwich A	YT	03.92	91-93	3	6	1
Northampton T	Tr	08.95	95-01	149	28	17
Oxford U	Nuneaton Borough	10.02	02	12	5	1
HUNTER William (Willie) Nibb						
Cambuslang, 7 April, 1942						(IF)
Bradford PA	Glasgow Rgrs	07.64	64	14	-	0
HUNTLEY John						
Great Lumley, 5 November, 1967						(CD)
Darlington	Chester-le-Street	10.85	85	5	1	0
HUNTLEY Keith Stanley Murray						
Swansea, 12 February, 1931 Died 1995 WAmat						(W)
Swansea T		08.50	50	2	-	0
HUNTLEY Richard Bernard						
Sunderland, 5 January, 1949						(CD)
Sunderland	Jnrs	08.67	68	1	0	0
HUNTON Keith						
Wellington, 18 July, 1961						(G)
Carlisle U	Workington	02.87	86	3	0	0
HURDLE Augustus (Gus) Athel						
Kensington, 14 October, 1973 Barbados int						(FB)
Fulham	YT	07.92				
Brentford	Dorchester T	07.94	94-97	63	8	0
HURFORD David George						
Sodbury, 17 January, 1945						(W)
Bristol Rov	App	01.63	62-64	6	-	0
HURLEY Charles (Charlie) John						
Cork, 4 October, 1936 IR-40						(CD)
Millwall	Rainham YC	10.53	53-57	105	-	2
Sunderland	Tr	09.57	57-68	357	1	23
Bolton W	Tr	06.69	69-70	42	1	3
HURLEY Christopher (Chris) Joseph						
Hornchurch, 20 November, 1943						(CF)
Millwall	Rainham T	03.64	63-64	4	-	2
HURLEY William (Billy) Henry						
Leytonstone, 11 December, 1959 ESch						(F)
Orient	App	01.77	76	1	1	0
HURLOCK Terence (Terry) Alan						
Hackney, 22 September, 1958 EB						(M)
Brentford	Leytonstone & Ilford	08.80	80-85	220	0	18
Reading	Tr	02.86	85-86	29	0	0
Millwall	Tr	02.87	86-89	103	1	8
Southampton	Glasgow Rgrs	09.91	91-93	59	2	0
Millwall	Tr	03.94	93	13	0	0
Fulham	Tr	07.94	94	27	0	1
HURLSTONE Gary						
Mexborough, 25 April, 1963						(F)
York C	Hatfield Main Colliery	03.89	88	1	1	0
HURRELL William (Billy)						
Newcastle, 15 September, 1955						(CD)
Northampton T	App	08.72	72	5	0	0
HURRELL William (Willie) Provan						
Dundee, 28 January, 1920 Died 1999						(IF)
Millwall	Raith Rov	01.46	46-52	121	-	32
Queens Park Rgrs	Tr	07.53	53	6	-	1
HURST Charles (Charlie)						
Denton, 25 January, 1919 Died 1999						(WH)
Bristol Rov		09.38				
Oldham Ath		01.43				
Rochdale	Tr	06.46	46	4	-	1
HURST Christopher (Chris) Mark						
Barnsley, 3 October, 1973						(M)
Huddersfield T	Emley	07.97	97	1	2	0
HURST (Sir) **Geoffrey (Geoff)** Charles						
Ashton-under-Lyne, 8 December, 1941 EYth/Eu23-4/FLge-7/E-49						(F)
West Ham U	Jnrs	04.59	59-71	410	1	180
Stoke C	Tr	08.72	72-74	103	5	30
West Bromwich A	Tr	08.75	75	10	0	2
HURST Glynn						
Barnsley, 17 January, 1976						(F)
Barnsley	Tottenham H (YT)	07.94	94-96	0	8	0
Swansea C	L	12.95	95	2	0	1
Mansfield T	L	11.96	96	5	1	0
Stockport Co	Ayr U	02.01	00-01	22	4	4
Chesterfield	Tr	12.01	01-03	77	7	29
Notts Co	Tr	07.04	04	36	5	14
HURST Gordon						
Oldham, 9 October, 1924 Died 1980 FLge-1						(W)
Charlton Ath	Ramsgate Ath	05.46	46-57	369	-	75
HURST Graham John						
Oldham, 23 November, 1967						(M)
Rochdale	App	07.85	84	0	1	0
HURST George **John (Jack)**						
Lever Bridge, 27 October, 1914 Died 2002						(CD)
Bolton W	Lever Bridge Jnrs	05.33	34-46	60	-	2
Oldham Ath	Tr	02.47	46-50	98	-	2
HURST John						
Blackpool, 6 February, 1947 ESch/Eu23-9						(CD)
Everton	App	10.64	65-75	336	11	29
Oldham Ath	Tr	06.76	76-80	169	1	2
HURST Kevan James						
Chesterfield, 27 August, 1985						(M)
Sheffield U	Sch	03.04	04	0	1	0
Boston U	L	03.04	03	3	4	1
Stockport Co	L	02.05	04	14	0	1
HURST Lee Jason						
Nuneaton, 21 September, 1970						(M)
Coventry C	YT	05.89	90-92	46	3	2
HURST Mark Patrick						
Mansfield, 18 February, 1985						(FB)
Mansfield T	Sch	•	02	1	0	0
HURST Paul Michael						
Sheffield, 25 September, 1974						(FB)
Rotherham U	YT	08.93	93-04	335	44	13
HURST Thomas (Tom) William						
Leicester, 23 September, 1987						(CD)
Boston U	Sch	•	04	0	1	0
HURST William (Bill) Robert						
Brierfield, 4 March, 1921						(W)
Burnley	Jnrs	03.38				
Plymouth Arg	Tr	06.39	46	4	-	0
Bury	Nelson	09.47	47	1	-	0
Accrington St	Northwich Vic	10.48	48	1	-	0

League Club	Source	Date Signed	Seasons Played	Career Record Apps	Subs	Gls
HUSBAND James (Jimmy)						
Newcastle, 15 October, 1947 ESch/EYth/Eu23-5						(W)
Everton	App	10.64	64-73	158	7	44
Luton T	Tr	11.73	73-77	138	5	44
HUSBANDS Michael Paul						
Birmingham, 13 November, 1983						(F)
Aston Villa	YT	04.02				
Southend U	Tr	07.03	03-04	3	8	0
HUSSEY Malcolm Frederick						
Darfield, 11 September, 1933						(CD)
Rotherham U	Jnrs	04.52	52-55	24	-	0
Scunthorpe U	Tr	08.56	56-57	23	-	0
Rochdale	Tr	03.59	58	1	-	0
HUTCHINGS Carl Emil						
Hammersmith, 24 September, 1974						(M)
Brentford	YT	07.93	93-97	144	18	7
Bristol C	Tr	06.98	98-99	33	9	3
Brentford	L	02.00	99	7	1	0
Exeter C	L	11.00	00	2	0	0
Southend U	Tr	12.00	00-01	42	1	4
Leyton Orient	Tr	02.02	01-02	30	8	2
HUTCHINGS Christopher (Chris)						
Winchester, 5 July, 1957						(FB)
Chelsea	Harrow Borough	07.80	80-83	83	4	3
Brighton & Hove A	Tr	11.83	83-87	153	0	4
Huddersfield T	Tr	12.87	87-89	110	0	10
Walsall	Tr	08.90	90	40	0	0
Rotherham U	Tr	07.91	91-93	76	2	4
HUTCHINGS Denis George						
Axminster, 1 December, 1924 Died 1990						(W)
Exeter C	Axminster	04.47	46-51	82	-	13
HUTCHINS Donald (Don)						
Middlesbrough, 8 May, 1948						(W)
Leicester C	Stockton	02.66	67-68	4	0	0
Plymouth Arg	Tr	07.69	69-71	94	1	23
Blackburn Rov	Tr	07.72	72-73	37	3	6
Bradford C	Tr	06.74	74-80	252	4	44
HUTCHINSON James **Barry**						
Sheffield, 27 January, 1936 Died 2005						(F)
Chesterfield	Bolton W (Am)	04.53	54-59	154	-	16
Derby Co	Tr	07.60	60-63	107	-	51
Lincoln C	Weymouth	07.65	65	24	0	18
Darlington	Tr	02.66	65-66	28	2	14
Halifax T	Tr	11.66	66	25	0	14
Rochdale	Tr	07.67	67	27	0	3
HUTCHINSON Colin						
Lanchester, 20 October, 1936						(W)
Stoke C	Crook Hall	11.53	54-57	9	-	0
HUTCHINSON David Norman						
Grimsby, 25 September, 1941						(F)
Scunthorpe U	Brigg T	07.71	71	5	4	0
HUTCHINSON Douglas (Doug)						
Gateshead, 3 May, 1922						(W)
Gateshead	Stirling A	08.46	46	3	-	0
HUTCHINSON Edward (Eddie) Stephen						
Kingston, 23 February, 1982						(M)
Brentford	Sutton U	07.00	00-04	78	12	6
HUTCHINSON George Henry						
Allerton Bywater, 31 October, 1929 Died 1996						(W)
Huddersfield T	Jnrs	01.47	47	1	-	0
Sheffield U	Tr	03.48	48-52	73	-	10
Tottenham H	Tr	06.53	53	5	-	1
Leeds U	Guildford C	08.55	55	11	-	5
Halifax T	Tr	07.56	56-57	44	-	11
HUTCHINSON Ian						
Derby, 4 August, 1948 Died 2002 Eu23-2						(F)
Chelsea	Cambridge U	07.68	68-75	112	7	44
HUTCHINSON Ian Nicholas						
Stockton, 7 November, 1972						(FB)
Halifax T	YT	07.92	90-91	7	1	1
Gillingham	Cork C	09.94	94	1	4	0
HUTCHINSON James (Jimmy) Arthur						
Sheffield, 28 December, 1915 Died 1997						(IF)
Sheffield U	Aqueduct (Sheffield)	11.37				
Bournemouth	Tr	06.46	46	8	-	3
Lincoln C	Tr	11.46	46-48	85	-	55
Oldham Ath	Tr	02.49	48-49	14	-	3

League Club	Source	Date Signed	Seasons Played	Career Record Apps	Subs	Gls
HUTCHINSON John (Jack)						
Codnor, 1 June, 1921 Died 2004						(FB)
Nottingham F		08.43	46-58	241	-	0
HUTCHINSON Jonathan (Joey)						
Middlesbrough, 2 April, 1982						(CD)
Birmingham C	YT	07.00	01-02	1	3	0
Darlington	Tr	08.03	03-04	46	1	0
HUTCHINSON Keith Graham						
South Shields, 7 September, 1920 Died 1986						(FB)
Darlington		05.46	46-48	31	-	0
HUTCHINSON Colin **Mark**						
Stoke-on-Trent, 2 November, 1963						(M)
Aston Villa	App	11.81				
Leicester C	Tr	08.83				
Carlisle U	L	08.84	84	6	0	0
Northampton T	Tr	02.85	84	1	1	0
HUTCHINSON Paul						
Eaglescliffe, 20 February, 1953						(FB)
Darlington	Jnrs	09.71	71-72	8	2	0
HUTCHINSON Robert (Bobby)						
Glasgow, 19 June, 1953						(M)
Wigan Ath	Hibernian	07.80	80	34	1	3
Tranmere Rov	Tr	08.81	81-82	32	3	6
Mansfield T	Tr	10.82	82-83	35	0	3
Tranmere Rov	Tr	01.84	83	21	0	4
Bristol C	Tr	07.84	84-86	89	3	10
Walsall	Tr	02.87	86-87	8	8	0
Blackpool	L	09.87	87	3	3	0
Carlisle U	L	01.88	87	12	1	2
HUTCHINSON Robert (Bob) Wayne						
Bolton, 9 May, 1955						(F)
Rochdale	Radcliffe Borough	12.74	74	2	0	1
HUTCHINSON Simon						
Sheffield, 24 September, 1969 ESch						(M)
Manchester U	YT	09.87				
Wycombe W	Eastwood T	09.90	93-94	2	10	0
HUTCHISON Donald (Don)						
Gateshead, 9 May, 1971 SB-2/S-26						(M)
Hartlepool U	YT	03.90	89-90	19	5	2
Liverpool	Tr	11.90	91-93	33	12	7
West Ham U	Tr	08.94	94-95	30	5	11
Sheffield U	Tr	01.96	95-97	70	8	5
Everton	Tr	02.98	97-99	68	7	10
Sunderland	Tr	07.00	00-01	32	2	8
West Ham U	Tr	08.01	01-04	36	27	5
HUTCHISON Thomas (Tommy)						
Cardenden, 22 September, 1947 Su23-1/S-17						(W)
Blackpool	Alloa Ath	02.68	67-72	162	2	10
Coventry C	Tr	10.72	72-80	312	2	24
Manchester C	Tr	10.80	80-81	44	2	4
Burnley	Bulova (HK)	08.83	83-84	92	0	4
Swansea C	Tr	07.85	85-90	163	15	9
HUTH Robert						
Berlin, Germany, 18 August, 1984 GeYth/Geu21-2/Ge-11						(CD)
Chelsea	YT	08.01	01-04	16	13	0
HUTT Geoffrey (Geoff)						
Hazelwood, 28 September, 1949						(FB)
Huddersfield T	App	09.67	68-75	245	0	4
Blackburn Rov	L	09.75	75	10	0	1
York C	Haarlem (Holl)	02.77	76-77	63	0	1
Halifax T	Tr	04.78	78-79	75	1	0
HUTT Stephen (Steve) Graham						
Middlesbrough, 19 February, 1979						(M)
Hartlepool U	YT	07.97	95-98	6	3	0
HUTTON Alexander (Alec) Shaw						
Edinburgh, 10 October, 1941						(FB)
Southend U	Tulliallan Thistle	08.63	64	1	-	0
HUTTON John (Jackie)						
Bellshill, 23 April, 1944						(W)
Scunthorpe U	Hamilton Academical	06.63	63-65	53	1	7
HUTTON Joseph (Joe)						
Dundee, 18 November, 1927 Died 1999						(IF)
Reading	Albion Rov	10.50	49-50	8	-	0
Stoke C	Ayr U	12.53	53-56	34	-	7
Gillingham	Tr	08.57	57	36	-	6
Millwall	Tr	08.58	58-59	24	-	9

HUTTON Rory Neil
Ely, 3 May, 1985 IRYth (FB)

League Club	Source	Date Signed	Seasons Played	Apps	Subs	Gls
Peterborough U	Sch	03.04				
Cambridge U	Tr	08.04	04	0	2	0

HUTTON Thomas (Tom) Osborne
Gateshead, 10 September, 1922 (FB)

League Club	Source	Date Signed	Seasons Played	Apps	Subs	Gls
Accrington St	Red Rose	05.45	46	18	-	0
Carlisle U	Tr	08.47	47-48	44	-	0

HUXFORD Clifford (Cliff) George
Stroud, 8 June, 1937 (CD)

League Club	Source	Date Signed	Seasons Played	Apps	Subs	Gls
Chelsea	Jnrs	02.55	58	6	-	0
Southampton	Tr	05.59	59-66	276	2	4
Exeter C	Tr	06.67	67	40	1	1

HUXFORD Colin John
Stroud, 26 May, 1944 EYth (FB)

League Club	Source	Date Signed	Seasons Played	Apps	Subs	Gls
Chelsea	App	10.61				
Swindon T	Tr	11.62	62	1	-	0

HUXFORD Richard John
Scunthorpe, 25 July, 1969 (FB)

League Club	Source	Date Signed	Seasons Played	Apps	Subs	Gls
Barnet	Kettering T	08.92	92	33	0	1
Millwall	Kettering T	07.93	93-94	25	7	0
Birmingham C	L	02.94	93	5	0	0
Bradford C	Tr	10.94	94-96	55	6	2
Peterborough U	L	10.96	96	7	0	0
Burnley	Tr	01.97	96-97	6	7	0

HYATT John William
Feltham, 20 December, 1932 (CF)

League Club	Source	Date Signed	Seasons Played	Apps	Subs	Gls
Crystal Palace		08.54	54	1	-	0

HYDE Frank Lomas
Wath-on-Dearne, 11 January, 1927 Died 2004 (G)

League Club	Source	Date Signed	Seasons Played	Apps	Subs	Gls
Bradford C	Wath Ath	12.48	48-51	34	-	0

HYDE Gary Stuart
Wolverhampton, 28 December, 1969 (W)

League Club	Source	Date Signed	Seasons Played	Apps	Subs	Gls
Darlington	YT	07.88	87-88	32	7	3
Leicester C	Tr	04.90				
Scunthorpe U	Tr	08.91	91	1	7	0

HYDE Graham
Doncaster, 10 November, 1970 (M)

League Club	Source	Date Signed	Seasons Played	Apps	Subs	Gls
Sheffield Wed	YT	05.88	91-98	126	46	11
Birmingham C	Tr	02.99	98-01	35	17	1
Chesterfield	L	08.01	01	8	1	1
Peterborough U	L	09.02	02	8	1	0
Bristol Rov	Tr	11.02	02-03	54	4	3

HYDE Micah Anthony
Newham, 10 November, 1974 Jamaica 16 (M)

League Club	Source	Date Signed	Seasons Played	Apps	Subs	Gls
Cambridge U	YT	05.93	93-96	89	18	13
Watford	Tr	07.97	97-03	235	18	24
Burnley	Tr	07.04	04	37	1	1

HYDE Paul David
Hayes, 7 April, 1963 (G)

League Club	Source	Date Signed	Seasons Played	Apps	Subs	Gls
Wycombe W	Hillingdon Borough	07.93	93-95	105	0	0
Leicester C	Tr	02.96				
Leyton Orient	Tr	02.97	96	4	0	0
Leicester C	Tr	02.97				
Leyton Orient	Tr	03.97	96-97	37	0	0

HYDE Stephen (Steve) Leslie
High Wycombe, 18 December, 1943 (W)

League Club	Source	Date Signed	Seasons Played	Apps	Subs	Gls
Oxford U	Wycombe W	01.65	64-65	9	0	0

HYDES Arthur
Barnsley, 24 November, 1910 Died 1990 (CF)

League Club	Source	Date Signed	Seasons Played	Apps	Subs	Gls
Leeds U	Ardsley Ath	05.30	30-36	127	-	74
Newport Co	Scunthorpe & Lindsey U	05.38	38	27	-	13
Exeter C	Tr	02.46	46	4	-	0

HYLDGAARD Morten Lauridsen
Herning, Denmark, 26 January, 1978 Deu21 (G)

League Club	Source	Date Signed	Seasons Played	Apps	Subs	Gls
Coventry C	Ikast (Den)	07.99	02	27	0	0
Scunthorpe U	L	01.00	99	5	0	0
Luton T	Hibernian	01.04	03	18	0	0

HYLTON Leon David
Birmingham, 27 January, 1983 EYth/Eu20 (FB)

League Club	Source	Date Signed	Seasons Played	Apps	Subs	Gls
Aston Villa	YT	02.00				
Swansea C	Tr	02.03	02-03	17	2	0

HYMERS Thomas (Tom)
Thorne, 29 April, 1935 Died 1987 (FB)

League Club	Source	Date Signed	Seasons Played	Apps	Subs	Gls
Doncaster Rov	Frickley Colliery	11.58	59-60	23	-	0

HYND John **Roger** Shankly
Falkirk, 2 February, 1942 (CD)

League Club	Source	Date Signed	Seasons Played	Apps	Subs	Gls
Crystal Palace	Glasgow Rgrs	07.69	69	29	1	0
Birmingham C	Tr	07.70	70-75	162	9	4
Oxford U	L	10.75	75	5	0	0
Walsall	Tr	12.75	75-77	89	0	1

HYNES Peter Joseph
Dublin, 28 November, 1983 (F)

League Club	Source	Date Signed	Seasons Played	Apps	Subs	Gls
Aston Villa	YT	11.00				
Doncaster Rov	L	12.03	03	0	5	1
Cheltenham T	L	01.04	03	2	2	0

HYSEN Glenn Ingvar
Gothenburg, Sweden, 30 October, 1959 Sweden int (CD)

League Club	Source	Date Signed	Seasons Played	Apps	Subs	Gls
Liverpool	Fiorentina (It)	07.89	89-91	70	2	2

HYSLOP Christian (Chris) Terence
Watford, 14 June, 1972 (CD)

League Club	Source	Date Signed	Seasons Played	Apps	Subs	Gls
Southend U	YT	04.90	90-92	16	3	0
Northampton T	L	12.93	93	8	0	0
Colchester U	Tr	02.94	93	8	0	0

HYSON Matthew (Matty) Alexander
Stockton, 2 May, 1976 (M)

League Club	Source	Date Signed	Seasons Played	Apps	Subs	Gls
Hartlepool U	YT	07.94	94	1	4	0

HYYPIA Sami
Porvoo, Finland, 7 October, 1973 FiYth/Fiu21-27/Fi-69 (CD)

League Club	Source	Date Signed	Seasons Played	Apps	Subs	Gls
Liverpool	Willem II Tilburg (Holl)	07.99	99-04	216	0	17

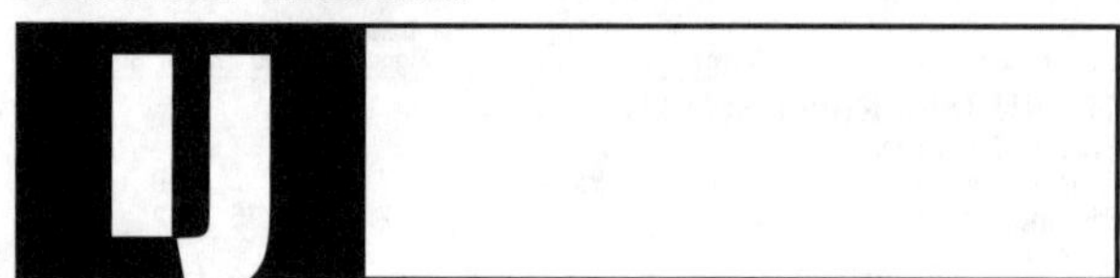

I'ANSON Paul
Shipley, 31 May, 1946 (CD)

League Club	Source	Date Signed	Seasons Played	Apps	Subs	Gls
Bradford PA	App	06.64	63-67	49	1	2

IBBOTSON Daniel (Danny)
Morecambe, 5 October, 1968 (W)

League Club	Source	Date Signed	Seasons Played	Apps	Subs	Gls
Preston NE	App	•	85	1	0	0

IBBOTSON Dennis
Rotherham, 4 December, 1920 Died 2002 ESch (FB)

League Club	Source	Date Signed	Seasons Played	Apps	Subs	Gls
Rotherham U (Am)	Rotherham YMCA	11.46	46	4	-	0

IBBOTSON Wilfred (Wilf)
Sheffield, 1 October, 1926 (IF)

League Club	Source	Date Signed	Seasons Played	Apps	Subs	Gls
Sheffield Wed	Jnrs	04.44	47	1	-	0
Mansfield T	Tr	08.48	48	2	-	0

IBE Okezie (Kezie) Enyeribenyam
Camden Town, 6 December, 1982 (F)

League Club	Source	Date Signed	Seasons Played	Apps	Subs	Gls
Yeovil T	Staines T	08.04	04	0	3	0

IBEHRE Jabo Oshevire
Islington, 28 January, 1983 (F)

League Club	Source	Date Signed	Seasons Played	Apps	Subs	Gls
Leyton Orient	YT	07.01	99-04	60	55	17

ICETON Osborne **Lloyd**
Workington, 30 March, 1920 Died 1994 (W)

League Club	Source	Date Signed	Seasons Played	Apps	Subs	Gls
Preston NE		05.38				
Carlisle U	Tr	10.46	46-49	77	-	18
Tranmere Rov	Tr	06.50	50-54	140	-	18

ICKE David Vaughan
Leicester, 29 May, 1952 (G)

League Club	Source	Date Signed	Seasons Played	Apps	Subs	Gls
Coventry C	App	09.69				
Hereford U	Tr	08.71	72	37	0	0

IDDON Harold (Harry)
Preston, 20 February, 1921 Died 2005 (W)

League Club	Source	Date Signed	Seasons Played	Apps	Subs	Gls
Preston NE	Jnrs	02.43				
Barrow	Tr	10.46	46	25	-	6
Southport	Tr	06.47	47-48	42	-	3

IDE Charlie Joe
Sunbury, 10 May, 1988 (M)

League Club	Source	Date Signed	Seasons Played	Apps	Subs	Gls
Brentford	Sch	•	04	0	1	0

IDIAKEZ Inigo
San Sebastian, Spain, 8 November, 1973 (M)

League Club	Source	Date Signed	Seasons Played	Apps	Subs	Gls
Derby Co	Rayo Vallecano (Sp)	07.04	04	41	0	9

IFEJIAGWA Chukwuemeka (Emeka)
Aba, Nigeria, 30 October, 1977 Nigeria 2 (CD)

League Club	Source	Date Signed	Seasons Played	Apps	Subs	Gls
Charlton Ath	Udaji U (Nig)	08.98				
Brighton & Hove A	L	10.98	98	2	0	1

IFIL Jerel Christopher
Wembley, 27 June, 1982 (CD)

League Club	Source	Date Signed	Seasons Played	Apps	Subs	Gls
Watford	YT	02.00	02-03	10	1	0
Huddersfield T	L	03.02	01	1	1	0
Swindon T	L	01.03	02	5	4	0
Swindon T	L	09.03	03	6	0	0
Swindon T	L	11.03	03	10	0	0
Swindon T	Tr	07.04	04	31	4	0

IFIL Philip Nathan
Willesden, 18 November, 1986 EYth (FB)

League Club	Source	Date Signed	Seasons Played	Apps	Subs	Gls
Tottenham H	Sch	11.04	04	2	0	0

IFILL Paul
Brighton, 20 October, 1979 Barbados int (M)

League Club	Source	Date Signed	Seasons Played	Apps	Subs	Gls
Millwall	YT	06.98	98-04	188	42	40

IGA Andrew Steven
Kampala, Uganda, 9 December, 1977 (G)

League Club	Source	Date Signed	Seasons Played	Apps	Subs	Gls
Millwall	Jnrs	06.95	96	0	1	0

IGGLEDEN Horatio (Ray)
Hull, 17 March, 1925 Died 2003 (IF)

League Club	Source	Date Signed	Seasons Played	Apps	Subs	Gls
Leicester C	Constable Street OB	03.42	46-47	11	-	2
Leeds U	Tr	01.49	48-54	169	-	47
Exeter C	Tr	07.55	55	27	-	8

IGOE Samuel (Sammy) Gary
Staines, 30 September, 1975 (W)

League Club	Source	Date Signed	Seasons Played	Apps	Subs	Gls
Portsmouth	YT	02.94	94-99	100	60	11
Reading	Tr	03.00	99-02	53	34	7
Luton T	L	03.03	02	2	0	0
Swindon T	Tr	07.03	03-04	75	4	9

IKIN David
Stoke-on-Trent, 18 February, 1946 (G)

League Club	Source	Date Signed	Seasons Played	Apps	Subs	Gls
Port Vale		08.65	65	2	0	0

ILES Richard
Bristol, 21 May, 1967 (CD)

League Club	Source	Date Signed	Seasons Played	Apps	Subs	Gls
Bristol Rov	Longwell Green	03.86	85	1	0	0

ILES Robert (Bob) John
Leicester, 2 September, 1955 (G)

League Club	Source	Date Signed	Seasons Played	Apps	Subs	Gls
Bournemouth	App	02.73				
Chelsea	Weymouth	06.78	78-82	14	0	0

ILEY James (Jim)
South Kirkby, 15 December, 1935 Eu23-1/FLge-2 (M)

League Club	Source	Date Signed	Seasons Played	Apps	Subs	Gls
Sheffield U	Pontefract	06.53	54-57	99	-	7
Tottenham H	Tr	08.57	57-58	53	-	1
Nottingham F	Tr	07.59	59-62	93	-	4
Newcastle U	Tr	09.62	62-68	227	5	15
Peterborough U	Tr	01.69	68-72	64	4	4

ILIC Sasa
Melbourne, Australia, 18 July, 1972 Yugoslavia 2 (G)

League Club	Source	Date Signed	Seasons Played	Apps	Subs	Gls
Charlton Ath	St Leonards Stamcroft	10.97	97-00	51	0	0
West Ham U	L	02.00	99	1	0	0
Portsmouth	L	09.01	01	7	0	0
Portsmouth	Zalaegerszegi (Hun)	02.03				
Barnsley	Tr	08.03	03	25	0	0
Sheffield U	Tr	02.04				
Blackpool	Tr	08.04	04	3	0	0

ILLINGWORTH Jeremy Marcus
Huddersfield, 20 May, 1977 (M)

League Club	Source	Date Signed	Seasons Played	Apps	Subs	Gls
Huddersfield T	YT	06.95	96	2	1	0

ILLMAN Neil David
Doncaster, 29 April, 1975 (F)

League Club	Source	Date Signed	Seasons Played	Apps	Subs	Gls
Middlesbrough	YT	03.93	93	0	1	0
Plymouth Arg	Eastwood T	03.96	96-97	13	18	4
Cambridge U	L	03.96	95	1	4	0
Exeter C	Tr	12.97	97	6	2	2

IMLACH Michael (Mike) Thomas
Croydon, 19 September, 1962 (FB)

League Club	Source	Date Signed	Seasons Played	Apps	Subs	Gls
Preston NE	Everton (App)	08.80				
Leeds U	Tr	11.81				
Peterborough U	Tr	08.82	82-83	37	5	1
Tranmere Rov	Tr	08.84	84	4	0	0

IMLACH James John **Stuart**
Lossiemouth, 6 January, 1932 Died 2001 S-4 (W)

League Club	Source	Date Signed	Seasons Played	Apps	Subs	Gls
Bury	Lossiemouth	10.52	52-53	71	-	14
Derby Co	Tr	05.54	54	36	-	2
Nottingham F	Tr	07.55	55-59	184	-	43
Luton T	Tr	06.60	60	8	-	0
Coventry C	Tr	10.60	60-61	73	-	11
Crystal Palace	Tr	07.62	62-64	35	-	2
Crystal Palace	Chelmsford C	02.66	65-66	16	0	1

IMMEL Eike
Marburg Lahn, Germany, 27 November, 1960 W Germany int (G)

League Club	Source	Date Signed	Seasons Played	Apps	Subs	Gls
Manchester C	VfB Stuttgart (Ger)	08.95	95-96	42	0	0

IMPEY Andrew (Andy) Rodney
Hammersmith, 30 September, 1971 Eu21-1 (FB)

League Club	Source	Date Signed	Seasons Played	Apps	Subs	Gls
Queens Park Rgrs	Yeading	06.90	91-96	177	10	13
West Ham U	Tr	09.97	97-98	25	2	0
Leicester C	Tr	11.98	98-03	132	20	1
Nottingham F	Tr	02.04	03-04	33	3	1
Millwall	L	03.05	04	0	5	0

IMPEY John Edward
Exeter, 11 August, 1954 ESch/EYth (CD)

League Club	Source	Date Signed	Seasons Played	Apps	Subs	Gls
Cardiff C	App	08.72	72-74	13	8	0
Bournemouth	Tr	07.75	75-82	280	4	7
Torquay U	Tr	08.83	83-84	72	0	0
Exeter C	Tr	08.85	85	26	0	0
Torquay U	Tr	07.86	86-87	58	0	2

IMRIE Adam Lyle
Annan, 1 October, 1933 (W)

League Club	Source	Date Signed	Seasons Played	Apps	Subs	Gls
Carlisle U	Kilmarnock	05.57	57	10	-	5

INAMOTO Junichi
Kagoshima, Japan, 18 September, 1979 Japan 57 (M)

League Club	Source	Date Signed	Seasons Played	Apps	Subs	Gls
Fulham (L)	Gamba Osaka (Jap)	07.02	02	9	10	2
Fulham (L)	Gamba Osaka (Jap)	07.03	03	15	7	2
West Bromwich A	Gamba Osaka (Jap)	08.04	04	0	3	0
Cardiff C	L	12.04	04	13	1	0

INCE Clayton
Trinidad, 13 July, 1972 Trinidad 34 (G)

League Club	Source	Date Signed	Seasons Played	Apps	Subs	Gls
Crewe Alex	Defence Force (Tr)	09.99	99-04	120	3	0

INCE Paul Emerson Carlyle
Ilford, 21 October, 1967 EYth/Eu21-2/EB-1/E-53 (M)

League Club	Source	Date Signed	Seasons Played	Apps	Subs	Gls
West Ham U	App	07.85	86-89	66	6	7
Manchester U	Tr	09.89	89-94	203	3	25
Liverpool	Inter Milan (It)	07.97	97-98	65	0	14
Middlesbrough	Tr	08.99	99-01	93	0	7
Wolverhampton W	Tr	08.02	02-04	92	5	7

INGEBRIGTSEN Kaare
Rosenborg, Norway, 11 November, 1965 Norway int (M)

League Club	Source	Date Signed	Seasons Played	Apps	Subs	Gls
Manchester C	Rosenborg (Nor)	01.93	92-93	4	11	0

INGER James (Jimmy)
Nottingham, 10 August, 1953 (G)

League Club	Source	Date Signed	Seasons Played	Apps	Subs	Gls
Walsall (Am)	Long Eaton U	03.73	72	2	0	0

INGESSON Klas
Odeshog, Sweden, 20 August, 1968 Sweden int (M)

League Club	Source	Date Signed	Seasons Played	Apps	Subs	Gls
Sheffield Wed	PSV Eindhoven (Holl)	09.94	94-95	12	6	2

INGHAM Anthony (Tony)
Harrogate, 18 February, 1925 (FB)

League Club	Source	Date Signed	Seasons Played	Apps	Subs	Gls
Leeds U	Harrogate T	04.47	47-49	3	-	0
Queens Park Rgrs	Tr	06.50	50-62	514	-	3

INGHAM Frederick (Fred) Roy
Manchester, 3 April, 1954 (F)

League Club	Source	Date Signed	Seasons Played	Apps	Subs	Gls
Stockport Co	App	04.72	71-72	12	7	1
Blackburn Rov	Tr	08.73				
Exeter C	Falmouth T	03.78	77-78	4	4	1

INGHAM Gary
Rotherham, 9 October, 1964 (G)

League Club	Source	Date Signed	Seasons Played	Apps	Subs	Gls
Rotherham U	Bridlington T	03.93				
Doncaster Rov	Tr	03.94	93	1	0	0
Doncaster Rov	Gainsborough Trinity	08.97	97	10	0	0

INGHAM John Robert
Hebburn, 18 October, 1924 (W)

League Club	Source	Date Signed	Seasons Played	Apps	Subs	Gls
Gateshead	Newburn	08.47	47-57	430	-	109

INGHAM Michael Gerard
Preston, 7 September, 1980 NIYth/NIu21-4/NI-1 (G)

League Club	Source	Date Signed	Seasons Played	Apps	Subs	Gls
Sunderland	Cliftonville	07.99	04	1	1	0
Carlisle U	L	10.99	99	7	0	0
Darlington	L	11.02	02	3	0	0
York C	L	01.03	02	17	0	0
Wrexham	L	03.04	03	11	0	0
Doncaster Rov	L	11.04	04	1	0	0

INGHAM William (Billy) Charles
Stakeford, 22 October, 1952 (M)

League Club	Source	Date Signed	Seasons Played	Apps	Subs	Gls
Burnley	App	11.69	71-79	181	30	22
Bradford C	Tr	08.80	80-81	78	0	4

INGIMARSSON Ivar
Reykjavik, Iceland, 20 August, 1977 IcYth/Icu21-14/Ic-16 (M)

League Club	Source	Date Signed	Seasons Played	Apps	Subs	Gls
Torquay U (L)	IBV (Ice)	10.99	99	4	0	1
Brentford	IBV (Ice)	11.99	99-01	109	4	10
Wolverhampton W	Tr	07.02	02	10	3	2
Brighton & Hove A	L	02.03	02	15	0	0
Reading	Tr	10.03	03-04	67	2	4

INGLE Stephen (Steve) Paul
Manningham, 22 October, 1946 (FB)

League Club	Source	Date Signed	Seasons Played	Apps	Subs	Gls
Bradford C	App	08.64	64-66	89	1	15
Southend U	Tr	01.67	66	14	1	3
Wrexham	Tr	07.67	67-71	145	4	5
Stockport Co	Tr	07.72	72	29	0	0
Southport	Tr	07.73	73	2	0	0
Darlington	Tr	10.73	73	8	0	0

INGLEDOW Jamie Graeme
Barnsley, 23 August, 1980 (M)

League Club	Source	Date Signed	Seasons Played	Apps	Subs	Gls
Rotherham U	YT	07.98	98-99	17	8	2
Chesterfield	Tr	07.00	00-01	26	15	3

INGLETHORPE Alexander (Alex) Matthew
Epsom, 14 November, 1971 (F)

League Club	Source	Date Signed	Seasons Played	Apps	Subs	Gls
Watford	Jnrs	07.90	90-93	2	10	2
Barnet	L	03.95	94	5	1	3
Leyton Orient	Tr	05.95	95-99	105	18	32
Exeter C	L	02.00	99	0	1	0
Exeter C	Tr	07.00	00	11	7	2

INGLIS James (Jimmy) McDougal
Glasgow, 14 February, 1924 Died 1999 (CF)

League Club	Source	Date Signed	Seasons Played	Apps	Subs	Gls
Bury	Stirling A	05.50	50	2	-	0

INGLIS John
Gateshead, 5 August, 1933 (G)

League Club	Source	Date Signed	Seasons Played	Apps	Subs	Gls
Gateshead (Am)	Blyth Spartans	06.57	57	2	-	0

INGLIS John
Edinburgh, 16 October, 1966 (CD)

League Club	Source	Date Signed	Seasons Played	Apps	Subs	Gls
Carlisle U	Aberdeen	09.00	00	8	0	0

INGLIS John Francis
Leven, 19 May, 1947 (F)

League Club	Source	Date Signed	Seasons Played	Apps	Subs	Gls
Aston Villa	Glenrothes	09.65	67	1	1	0
Crewe Alex	Tr	07.68	68-69	46	2	10

INGRAM Alexander (Alex) David
Edinburgh, 2 January, 1945 SAmat/SLge-1 (F)

League Club	Source	Date Signed	Seasons Played	Apps	Subs	Gls
Nottingham F	Ayr U	12.69	69-70	28	0	3

INGRAM Christopher (Chris) David
Cardiff, 5 December, 1976 (W)

League Club	Source	Date Signed	Seasons Played	Apps	Subs	Gls
Cardiff C	YT	08.95	95	4	4	1

INGRAM Stuart **Denevan (Denny)**
Sunderland, 27 June, 1976 (FB)

League Club	Source	Date Signed	Seasons Played	Apps	Subs	Gls
Hartlepool U	YT	07.94	93-99	192	7	10

INGRAM Gerald (Gerry)
Woodmansey, 19 August, 1947 (F)

League Club	Source	Date Signed	Seasons Played	Apps	Subs	Gls
Blackpool	Hull Brunswick	03.67	66-67	33	1	17
Preston NE	Tr	09.68	68-71	107	2	40
Bradford C	Tr	03.72	71-76	171	3	60

INGRAM Gerald (Gerry)
Merthyr Tydfil, 28 January, 1951 WSch (M)

League Club	Source	Date Signed	Seasons Played	Apps	Subs	Gls
Swansea C		08.70	70-72	36	2	1

INGRAM Godfrey Patrick
Luton, 26 October, 1959 ESch/EYth (F)

League Club	Source	Date Signed	Seasons Played	Apps	Subs	Gls
Luton T	App	10.77	77-81	22	5	6
Northampton T	L	03.80	79	10	0	4
Cardiff C	San Jose (USA)	09.82	82	7	4	2
Peterborough U	St Louis (USA)	08.92	92	0	1	0

INGRAM Rae
Manchester, 6 December, 1974 (FB)

League Club	Source	Date Signed	Seasons Played	Apps	Subs	Gls
Manchester C	YT	07.93	95-96	18	5	0
Macclesfield T	Tr	03.98	97-00	95	8	1
Port Vale	Tr	07.01	01-02	25	3	0

INMAN Niall Edward
Wakefield, 6 February, 1978 IRYth/IRu21-8 (M)

League Club	Source	Date Signed	Seasons Played	Apps	Subs	Gls
Peterborough U	YT	07.96	95-99	6	6	2

INNES Gary John
Shotley Bridge, 7 October, 1977 ESch/EYth (F)

League Club	Source	Date Signed	Seasons Played	Apps	Subs	Gls
Darlington	Esh Winning	07.96	96	1	14	0

INNES Mark
Bellshill, 27 September, 1978 (M)

League Club	Source	Date Signed	Seasons Played	Apps	Subs	Gls
Oldham Ath	YT	10.95	97-01	52	21	1
Chesterfield	Tr	12.01	01-04	62	14	2
Port Vale	Tr	03.05	04	2	3	0

INSKIP Frederick (Fred) Clive
Cheadle, 20 October, 1924 Died 2000 (W)

League Club	Source	Date Signed	Seasons Played	Apps	Subs	Gls
Nottingham F		12.44				
Crewe Alex	Tr	04.48	47-48	26	-	5

INVINCIBILE Daniel (Danny)
Brisbane, Australia, 31 March, 1979 AuSch/AuYth (M)

League Club	Source	Date Signed	Seasons Played	Apps	Subs	Gls
Swindon T	Marconi Stallions (Aus)	08.00	00-02	109	19	22

INWOOD Gordon Frederick
Kislingbury, 18 June, 1928 (W)

League Club	Source	Date Signed	Seasons Played	Apps	Subs	Gls
West Bromwich A	Rushden T	01.49	49	10	-	0
Hull C	Tr	05.50	50	3	-	0

IORFA Dominic
Lagos, Nigeria, 1 October, 1968 Nigeria 4 (F)

League Club	Source	Date Signed	Seasons Played	Apps	Subs	Gls
Queens Park Rgrs	Royal Antwerp (Bel)	03.90	89-91	1	7	0
Peterborough U	Galatasaray (Tu)	10.92	92-93	27	33	9
Southend U	Tr	08.94	94-95	5	5	1
Southend U	Billericay T	12.98	98	0	2	0

League Club	Source	Date Signed	Seasons Played	Apps	Subs	Gls
IOVAN Stefan						
Bucharest, Romania, 23 August, 1960						(FB)
Brighton & Hove A	Steaua Bucharest (Rom)	03.91	90-91	4	2	0
IPOUA Guy						
Douala, Cameroon, 14 January, 1976						(F)
Bristol Rov	Sevilla (Sp)	08.98	98	15	9	3
Scunthorpe U	Tr	08.99	99-00	50	15	23
Gillingham	Tr	03.01	00-02	42	40	13
Doncaster Rov	Al Shaab (Dubai)	08.04	04	1	8	0
Mansfield T	L	10.04	04	4	1	0
Lincoln C	L	02.05	04	0	6	0
IPPOLITO Mario						
Peterborough, 16 April, 1964						(F)
Peterborough U	Jnrs	04.83	82	8	0	3
IRELAND Craig Robert						
Dundee, 29 November, 1975						(CD)
Notts Co	Dundee	02.01	00-02	77	3	2
Barnsley	Tr	08.03	03	43	0	3
Peterborough U	Tr	08.04	04	22	1	0
Bristol C	L	01.05	04	5	0	0
IRELAND Jeffrey (Jeff) John Charles						
Paddington, 1 December, 1935						(W)
Tottenham H	Finchley	11.57	57-58	3	-	0
Shrewsbury T	Tr	06.59	59	38	-	4
IRELAND Jeremy (Jerry)						
Chester, 14 September, 1938						(IF)
Chester		09.57	57-61	40	-	8
IRELAND Roy Peter						
Exeter, 3 February, 1961						(M)
Exeter C	App	02.79	78-80	17	4	0
IRELAND Simon Piers						
Barnstaple, 23 November, 1971 ESch						(W)
Huddersfield T	Jnrs	07.90	90-92	10	9	0
Wrexham	L	03.92	91	2	3	0
Blackburn Rov	Tr	11.92	92	0	1	0
Mansfield T	Tr	03.94	93-96	89	5	11
Doncaster Rov	L	10.96	96	9	0	1
Doncaster Rov	Tr	01.97	96-97	52	0	1
IRIEKPEN Ezomo (Izzy)						
East London, 14 May, 1982 EYth						(CD)
West Ham U	YT	05.99				
Leyton Orient	L	10.02	02	5	0	1
Cambridge U	L	02.03	02	13	0	1
Swansea C	Tr	08.03	03-04	62	1	3
IROHA Benedict (Ben)						
Aba, Nigeria, 29 November, 1969 Nigeria 33						(M)
Watford	Elche (Sp)	12.98	98	8	2	0
IRONS Kenneth (Kenny)						
Liverpool, 4 November, 1970						(M)
Tranmere Rov	YT	11.89	89-98	313	38	54
Huddersfield T	Tr	06.99	99-02	120	29	11
IRONSIDE Ian						
Sheffield, 8 March, 1964						(G)
Barnsley	Jnrs	09.82				
Scarborough	North Ferriby U	03.88	87-90	88	0	0
Middlesbrough	Tr	08.91	91-92	12	1	0
Scarborough	L	03.92	91	7	0	0
Stockport Co	Tr	09.93	93-94	17	2	0
Scarborough	Tr	03.95	94-96	88	0	0
IRONSIDE Roy						
Sheffield, 28 May, 1935						(G)
Rotherham U	Atlas & Norfolk	07.54	56-64	220	-	0
Barnsley	Tr	07.65	65-68	113	0	0
IRVIN Derek Vincent						
Stockton, 23 August, 1943						(W)
Middlesbrough	Broomhall	09.61				
Watford	Brechin C	06.67	67	0	2	1
IRVINE Alan James						
Broxburn, 20 November, 1962						(F)
Liverpool	Falkirk	11.86	86	0	2	0
Shrewsbury T	Dundee U	02.88	87-88	32	5	6
IRVINE James **Alan**						
Glasgow, 12 July, 1958						(W)
Everton	Queen's Park	05.81	81-83	51	9	4
Crystal Palace	Tr	08.84	84-86	108	1	12
Blackburn Rov	Dundee U	10.89	89-91	40	18	3
IRVINE Archibald (Archie)						
Coatbridge, 25 June, 1946						(M)
Sheffield Wed	Airdrie	09.68	68-69	25	4	1
Doncaster Rov	Tr	12.69	69-74	220	8	16
Scunthorpe U	Tr	07.75	75	22	1	1
IRVINE James (Jimmy)						
Whitburn, 17 August, 1940 SSch						(F)
Middlesbrough	Dundee U	05.64	64-66	90	1	37
Barrow	Heart of Midlothian	07.70	70-71	67	0	17
IRVINE Robert (Bobby) James						
Carrickfergus, 17 January, 1942 NISch/NIu23-1/IrLge-5/NI-8						(G)
Stoke C	Linfield	06.63	63-65	25	0	0
IRVINE Samuel (Sammy)						
Glasgow, 7 January, 1956						(M)
Shrewsbury T	App	01.74	72-77	198	9	18
Stoke C	Tr	06.78	78-79	67	0	10
IRVINE Stuart Christopher						
Hartlepool, 1 March, 1979						(F)
Hartlepool U	YT	07.97	96-98	13	18	2
IRVINE William (Willie) John						
Carrickfergus, 18 June, 1943 NISch/NIu23-3/NI-23						(F)
Burnley	Jnrs	06.60	62-67	124	2	78
Preston NE	Tr	03.68	67-70	77	4	27
Brighton & Hove A	Tr	03.71	70-72	66	3	27
Halifax T	Tr	12.72	72	9	1	1
IRVING David						
Cockermouth, 10 September, 1951 EYth						(F)
Workington	Aspatria	05.70	70-72	57	8	16
Everton	Tr	01.73	73-75	4	2	0
Sheffield U	L	09.75	75	0	2	0
Oldham Ath	Tr	06.76	76-77	18	3	7
IRVING Gerald (Gerry)						
Maryport, 19 September, 1937						(W)
Workington		08.56	56	1	-	0
IRVING Richard James						
Halifax, 10 September, 1975 ESch/EYth						(F)
Manchester U	YT	10.92				
Nottingham F	Tr	07.95	95	0	1	0
Macclesfield T	Tr	10.97	97	6	3	0
IRVING Russell						
Wallsend, 4 January, 1964						(F)
Ipswich T	App	05.81				
Colchester U	Tr	08.84	84-85	36	14	9
IRWIN Cecil (Cec)						
Ellington, 8 April, 1942 EYth						(FB)
Sunderland	Jnrs	04.59	58-71	311	3	1
IRWIN Colin Thomas						
Liverpool, 9 February, 1957						(CD)
Liverpool	Jnrs	12.74	79-80	26	3	3
Swansea C	Tr	08.81	81-83	48	0	0
IRWIN Joseph **Denis**						
Cork, 31 October, 1965 IRSch/IRYth/IRu23-1/IRu21-3/IRB-1/IR-56						(FB)
Leeds U	App	11.83	83-85	72	0	1
Oldham Ath	Tr	05.86	86-89	166	1	4
Manchester U	Tr	06.90	90-01	356	12	22
Wolverhampton W	Tr	07.02	02-03	73	2	2
IRWIN William (Billy)						
Newtownards, 23 July, 1951 NIAmat						(G)
Cardiff C	Bangor	10.71	71-77	180	0	0
ISAAC James (Jimmy)						
Cramlington, 23 October, 1916 Died 1993						(IF)
Huddersfield T	Cramlington	11.34	36-38	33	-	8
Bradford C	Tr	04.45	46	24	-	3
Hartlepools U	Tr	07.47	47-48	56	-	9
ISAAC Robert (Bobby) Charles						
Hackney, 30 November, 1965 EYth						(CD)
Chelsea	App	11.83	84-86	9	0	0
Brighton & Hove A	Tr	02.87	86-88	30	0	0
ISAAC William (Peter) Henry						
Pontypridd, 16 May, 1935						(G)
Stoke C		03.53				
Northampton T	Barry T	07.58	59	8	-	0
ISAACS Anthony (Tony) Brian						
Middlesbrough, 8 April, 1973						(M)
Darlington	YT	07.91	91-93	37	14	2

ISAIAS Marques Soares
Rio de Janeiro, Brazil, 17 November, 1963 (M)

League Club	Source	Date Signed	Seasons Played	Apps	Subs	Gls
Coventry C	Benfica (Por)	08.95	95-96	9	3	2

ISHERWOOD Dennis
Northwich, 9 January, 1924 Died 1974 (W)

League Club	Source	Date Signed	Seasons Played	Apps	Subs	Gls
Wrexham		08.44				
Chester	Tr	04.46	46	3	-	0

ISHERWOOD Dennis
Brierley Hill, 20 January, 1947 (FB)

League Club	Source	Date Signed	Seasons Played	Apps	Subs	Gls
Birmingham C	App	01.64	66	5	0	1

ISHERWOOD Roy Edward
Blackburn, 24 January, 1934 (W)

League Club	Source	Date Signed	Seasons Played	Apps	Subs	Gls
Blackburn Rov	Nelson	10.57	57-61	49	-	9

ISMAEL Valerien
Strasbourg, France, 28 September, 1975 (CD)

League Club	Source	Date Signed	Seasons Played	Apps	Subs	Gls
Crystal Palace	Strasbourg (Fr)	01.98	97	13	0	0

ISSA Pierre
Johannesburg, South Africa, 11 August, 1975 South Africa 45 (CD)

League Club	Source	Date Signed	Seasons Played	Apps	Subs	Gls
Watford	Marseille (Fr)	09.01	01	12	3	1

ISTEAD Steven Brian
South Shields, 23 April, 1986 (M)

League Club	Source	Date Signed	Seasons Played	Apps	Subs	Gls
Hartlepool U	Sch	●	02-04	1	53	1

ITHELL William **James (Jimmy)**
Hawarden, 7 February, 1916 Died 1986 (CD)

League Club	Source	Date Signed	Seasons Played	Apps	Subs	Gls
Bolton W		11.36				
Swindon T	Tr	05.46	46-49	107	-	1

IVERSEN Steffen
Oslo, Norway, 10 November, 1976 NoYth/Nou21-23/No-45 (F)

League Club	Source	Date Signed	Seasons Played	Apps	Subs	Gls
Tottenham H	Rosenborg (Nor)	12.96	96-02	112	31	36
Wolverhampton W	Tr	08.03	03	11	5	4

IVERSON Robert (Bob) Thomas James
Folkestone, 17 October, 1910 Died 1953 (WH)

League Club	Source	Date Signed	Seasons Played	Apps	Subs	Gls
Lincoln C	Ramsgate Press W	09.33	33-34	41	-	13
Wolverhampton W	Tr	02.35	34-36	35	-	7
Aston Villa	Tr	12.36	36-47	135	-	9

IVEY George Harrison
West Stanley, 29 October, 1923 Died 1979 (W)

League Club	Source	Date Signed	Seasons Played	Apps	Subs	Gls
York C	West Stanley U	06.48	48-50	79	-	13

IVEY Paul Henry Winspear
Westminster, 1 April, 1961 (F)

League Club	Source	Date Signed	Seasons Played	Apps	Subs	Gls
Birmingham C	App	01.79	78-80	4	3	0
Chesterfield	Kettering T	12.82	82	0	6	0

IWELUMO Christopher (Chris) Robert
Coatbridge, 1 August, 1978 (F)

League Club	Source	Date Signed	Seasons Played	Apps	Subs	Gls
Stoke C	Aarhus Fremad (Den)	03.00	99-03	40	44	16
York C	L	11.00	00	11	1	2
Cheltenham T	L	02.01	00	2	2	1
Brighton & Hove A	Tr	03.04	03	10	0	4

IZZET Kemal
Whitechapel, 29 September, 1980 (M)

League Club	Source	Date Signed	Seasons Played	Apps	Subs	Gls
Charlton Ath	YT	01.99				
Colchester U	Tr	03.01	00-04	130	9	15

IZZET Mustafa (Muzzy) Kemal
Mile End, 31 October, 1974 Turkey 9 (M)

League Club	Source	Date Signed	Seasons Played	Apps	Subs	Gls
Chelsea	YT	05.93				
Leicester C	Tr	03.96	95-03	265	4	38
Birmingham C	Tr	07.04	04	10	0	1

JAASKELAINEN Jussi
Vaasa, Finland, 19 April, 1975 FiYth/Fiu21-14/Fi-21 (G)

League Club	Source	Date Signed	Seasons Played	Apps	Subs	Gls
Bolton W	VPS Vaasa (Fin)	11.97	98-04	240	1	0

JACK Andrew Mackintosh
Glasgow, 30 June, 1923 (CF)

League Club	Source	Date Signed	Seasons Played	Apps	Subs	Gls
Tranmere Rov	Wishaw Jnrs	06.48	48	3	-	3

JACK Michael Lawrence
Carlisle, 2 October, 1982 (M)

League Club	Source	Date Signed	Seasons Played	Apps	Subs	Gls
Carlisle U	YT	06.01	01-03	19	23	0

JACK Rodney Alphonso
Kingstown, St Vincent, 28 September, 1972 St Vincent int (F)

League Club	Source	Date Signed	Seasons Played	Apps	Subs	Gls
Torquay U	Lambada (St V)	10.95	95-97	82	5	24
Crewe Alex	Tr	08.98	98-02	140	23	33
Rushden & Diamonds	Tr	07.03	03	44	1	12
Oldham Ath	Tr	07.04	04	5	5	2

JACK James **Ross**
Avoch, 21 March, 1959 (F)

League Club	Source	Date Signed	Seasons Played	Apps	Subs	Gls
Everton	App	02.77	78	1	0	1
Norwich C	Tr	12.79	80-82	31	25	10
Lincoln C	Tr	08.83	83-84	52	8	16

JACK Vincent (Vince)
Rosemarkie, 6 August, 1933 (CD)

League Club	Source	Date Signed	Seasons Played	Apps	Subs	Gls
Bury	Inverness Jnrs	04.54	55-56	10	-	0
Swindon T	Tr	10.56	56-58	26	-	0
Accrington St	Tr	07.59	59	22	-	0

JACKETT Frank
Ystalyfera, 5 July, 1927 (WH)

League Club	Source	Date Signed	Seasons Played	Apps	Subs	Gls
Watford	Pontardawe Ath	11.49	49-52	14	-	0
Leyton Orient	Tr	07.53	53	4	-	0

JACKETT Kenneth (Kenny) Francis
Watford, 5 January, 1962 WYth/Wu21-2/W-31 (M)

League Club	Source	Date Signed	Seasons Played	Apps	Subs	Gls
Watford	App	01.80	79-89	328	7	25

JACKMAN Clive Edward James
Farnborough, 21 February, 1936 (G)

League Club	Source	Date Signed	Seasons Played	Apps	Subs	Gls
Aldershot	Jnrs	05.53	52-56	38	-	0
West Bromwich A	Tr	06.57	57-58	21	-	0

JACKMAN Daniel (Danny) James
Worcester, 3 January, 1983 (FB)

League Club	Source	Date Signed	Seasons Played	Apps	Subs	Gls
Aston Villa	YT	04.01				
Cambridge U	L	02.02	01	5	2	1
Stockport Co	Tr	10.03	03-04	51	9	4

JACKMAN Derek Clive
Colchester, 20 August, 1927 (WH)

League Club	Source	Date Signed	Seasons Played	Apps	Subs	Gls
Crystal Palace	Chelmsford C	03.45				
West Ham U	Tr	08.48	48-50	8	-	0

JACKS George Charles
Stepney, 14 March, 1946 (M)

League Club	Source	Date Signed	Seasons Played	Apps	Subs	Gls
Queens Park Rgrs	App	01.64	64	1	-	0
Millwall	Tr	07.65	65-70	144	7	5
Gillingham	Tr	07.72	72-75	159	0	20

JACKSON Alan
Swadlincote, 22 August, 1938 (IF)

League Club	Source	Date Signed	Seasons Played	Apps	Subs	Gls
Wolverhampton W	Jnrs	08.55	57-58	4	-	1
Bury	Tr	06.59	59-62	124	-	43
Brighton & Hove A	Tr	11.62	62-63	21	-	5

JACKSON Alan Edward
Scunthorpe, 14 February, 1938 Died 1996 (W)

League Club	Source	Date Signed	Seasons Played	Apps	Subs	Gls
Lincoln C	Brigg T	11.58	58-60	4	-	0

JACKSON Albert
Manchester, 12 September, 1943 (CF)

League Club	Source	Date Signed	Seasons Played	Apps	Subs	Gls
Oldham Ath	Manchester U (Jnrs)	12.62	63-65	22	0	4

JACKSON Alec
Tipton, 29 May, 1937 FLge-1 (W)

League Club	Source	Date Signed	Seasons Played	Apps	Subs	Gls
West Bromwich A	WG Allen's	09.54	54-63	192	-	50
Birmingham C	Tr	06.64	64-66	78	0	11
Walsall	Tr	02.67	66-67	36	2	7

JACKSON Alexander (Alex) James
Glasgow, 28 November, 1935 (CF)

League Club	Source	Date Signed	Seasons Played	Apps	Subs	Gls
Birmingham C	Heart of Midlothian	04.58	58	6	-	6
Plymouth Arg	Tr	03.60	59-63	67	-	23

JACKSON Alexander (Alec) Wilson
Lesmahagow, 2 October, 1921 (WH)

League Club	Source	Date Signed	Seasons Played	Apps	Subs	Gls
York C	Huddersfield T (Am)	09.46	46-49	50	-	5

JACKSON Arnold
Manchester, 10 November, 1925 (IF)

League Club	Source	Date Signed	Seasons Played	Apps	Subs	Gls
Shrewsbury T		(N/L)	50-53	144	-	39
Stockport Co	Tr	06.54	54-58	153	-	48

JACKSON Charles **Barry**
Askrigg, 2 February, 1938 (CD)

League Club	Source	Date Signed	Seasons Played	Apps	Subs	Gls
York C	Cliftonville (York)	12.56	58-69	481	1	9

JACKSON Benjamin (Ben) Robert
Peterlee, 22 October, 1985 (M)

League Club	Source	Date Signed	Seasons Played	Apps	Subs	Gls
Doncaster Rov	Newcastle U (Sch)	01.04	04	0	1	0

JACKSON Brian
Maltby, 2 February, 1936 Died 1992 (WH)

League Club	Source	Date Signed	Seasons Played	Apps	Subs	Gls
Rotherham U	Maltby Main CW	09.54	55-64	131	-	6
Barnsley	Tr	07.65	65	29	0	0

JACKSON Brian Harvill
Walton-on-Thames, 1 April, 1933 ESch (W)

League Club	Source	Date Signed	Seasons Played	Apps	Subs	Gls
Leyton Orient	Arsenal (Am)	10.50	50-51	38	-	2
Liverpool	Tr	11.51	51-57	124	-	12
Port Vale	Tr	07.58	58-61	159	-	29
Peterborough U	Tr	07.62	62-63	47	-	4
Lincoln C	Tr	05.64	64	10	-	1

JACKSON Christopher (Chris) Dean
Barnsley, 16 January, 1976 ESch/EYth (F)

League Club	Source	Date Signed	Seasons Played	Apps	Subs	Gls
Barnsley	YT	01.93	92-95	16	7	2

JACKSON Clifford (Cliff)
Swindon, 3 September, 1941 ESch (W)

League Club	Source	Date Signed	Seasons Played	Apps	Subs	Gls
Swindon T	Jnrs	09.58	58-62	91	-	30
Plymouth Arg	Tr	06.63	63-66	72	0	19
Crystal Palace	Tr	09.66	66-69	100	6	25
Torquay U	Tr	08.70	70-73	114	13	13

JACKSON Craig
Renishaw, 17 January, 1969 (CD)

League Club	Source	Date Signed	Seasons Played	Apps	Subs	Gls
Notts Co	App	08.86	85-86	3	2	0

JACKSON Darren
Edinburgh, 25 July, 1966 SB-1/S-28 (W)

League Club	Source	Date Signed	Seasons Played	Apps	Subs	Gls
Newcastle U	Meadowbank Th	10.86	86-88	53	16	7
Coventry C (L)	Glasgow Celtic	11.98	98	0	3	0

JACKSON Darren William
Keynsham, 24 September, 1971 (FB)

League Club	Source	Date Signed	Seasons Played	Apps	Subs	Gls
Oxford U	YT	05.90	89-93	11	3	0
Reading	L	02.93	92	5	0	0

JACKSON David
Stoke-on-Trent, 23 January, 1937 (IF)

League Club	Source	Date Signed	Seasons Played	Apps	Subs	Gls
Wrexham (Am)	Jnrs	07.54	54	7	-	1
Bradford C	Marine	03.55	54-60	250	-	61
Tranmere Rov	Tr	07.61	61-62	38	-	5
Halifax T	Tr	07.63	63-64	66	-	2

JACKSON David Kenneth George
Solihull, 22 August, 1978 (FB)

League Club	Source	Date Signed	Seasons Played	Apps	Subs	Gls
Shrewsbury T	YT	●	95	0	1	0

JACKSON David Patrick
Bradford, 16 September, 1958 (F)

League Club	Source	Date Signed	Seasons Played	Apps	Subs	Gls
Manchester U	App	09.75				
Bradford C	Tr	09.78	78	9	3	3

JACKSON Dennis Leonard
Birmingham, 8 March, 1932 (FB)

League Club	Source	Date Signed	Seasons Played	Apps	Subs	Gls
Aston Villa	Hednesford T	10.54	56-58	8	-	0
Millwall	Tr	05.59	59-60	80	-	0

JACKSON Elliot
Swindon, 27 August, 1977 (G)

League Club	Source	Date Signed	Seasons Played	Apps	Subs	Gls
Oxford U	YT	07.96	96-98	7	0	0

JACKSON Ernest
Sheffield, 11 June, 1914 Died 1996 (WH)

League Club	Source	Date Signed	Seasons Played	Apps	Subs	Gls
Sheffield U	Atlas & Norfolk	09.32	32-48	229	-	8

JACKSON Gary Andrew
Swinton, 30 September, 1964 (M)

League Club	Source	Date Signed	Seasons Played	Apps	Subs	Gls
Manchester C	Jnrs	10.81	81	6	2	0
Exeter C	Tr	09.85	85-86	34	1	2

JACKSON George
Liverpool, 14 January, 1911 Died 2002 (FB)

League Club	Source	Date Signed	Seasons Played	Apps	Subs	Gls
Everton	Walton Parish Church	05.32	34-47	75	-	0

JACKSON George
Stretford, 10 February, 1952 (M)

League Club	Source	Date Signed	Seasons Played	Apps	Subs	Gls
Stoke C	App	07.69	71	8	0	0

JACKSON Harold
Halifax, 20 July, 1917 Died 1996 (FB)

League Club	Source	Date Signed	Seasons Played	Apps	Subs	Gls
Halifax T	Sowerby WE	08.36	36-46	83	-	3
Stockport Co	Tr	08.47	47	2	-	0

JACKSON Harry
Blackburn, 30 December, 1918 Died 1984 (CF)

League Club	Source	Date Signed	Seasons Played	Apps	Subs	Gls
Burnley	Darwen	01.42				
Manchester C	Tr	06.46	46-47	8	-	2
Preston NE	Tr	12.47	47-48	18	-	5
Blackburn Rov	Tr	12.48	48	1	-	0
Chester	Tr	07.49	49	21	-	10

JACKSON Harry
Shaw, 12 May, 1934 (CF)

League Club	Source	Date Signed	Seasons Played	Apps	Subs	Gls
Oldham Ath	Jnrs	06.51	51-55	10	-	1
Rochdale	Tr	10.55	55	1	-	1

JACKSON James (Jimmy)
Glasgow, 1 January, 1921 (IF)

League Club	Source	Date Signed	Seasons Played	Apps	Subs	Gls
Bolton W		06.39	47-49	11	-	1
Carlisle U	Tr	07.50	50-54	100	-	23

JACKSON James (Jimmy)
Glasgow, 26 March, 1931 (CF)

League Club	Source	Date Signed	Seasons Played	Apps	Subs	Gls
Notts Co	Mapperley Celtic	03.49	48-57	113	-	47

JACKSON James Potter
Glasgow, 4 August, 1924 (WH)

League Club	Source	Date Signed	Seasons Played	Apps	Subs	Gls
Bury	Third Lanark	05.50	50	1	-	0

JACKSON James (Jimmy) William
Ashington, 30 December, 1933 ESch (FB)

League Club	Source	Date Signed	Seasons Played	Apps	Subs	Gls
Newcastle U	Jnrs	01.51				
Aldershot	Tr	07.55	55-60	197	-	19

JACKSON John
Newcastle-under-Lyme, 7 January, 1923 Died 1992 (CF)

League Club	Source	Date Signed	Seasons Played	Apps	Subs	Gls
Stoke C	Alsager	05.41	46-47	4	-	3

JACKSON John (Johnnie)
Camden, 15 August, 1982 EYth/Eu20 (M)

League Club	Source	Date Signed	Seasons Played	Apps	Subs	Gls
Tottenham H	YT	03.00	03-04	12	7	1
Swindon T	L	09.02	02	12	1	1
Colchester U	L	03.03	02	8	0	0
Coventry C	L	11.03	03	2	3	2
Watford	L	12.04	04	14	1	0

JACKSON John Keith
Hammersmith, 5 September, 1942 EYth/FLge-2 (G)

League Club	Source	Date Signed	Seasons Played	Apps	Subs	Gls
Crystal Palace	Jnrs	03.62	64-73	346	0	0
Orient	Tr	10.73	73-78	226	0	0
Millwall	Tr	08.79	79-80	79	0	0
Ipswich T	Tr	08.81	81	1	0	0
Hereford U	Tr	08.82	82	4	0	0

JACKSON Joseph (Joe) George
Wolverhampton, 22 April, 1966 (M)

League Club	Source	Date Signed	Seasons Played	Apps	Subs	Gls
Wolverhampton W	Jnrs	08.83	83	1	0	0

JACKSON Justin Jonathan
Nottingham, 10 December, 1974 ESemiPro-2 (F)

League Club	Source	Date Signed	Seasons Played	Apps	Subs	Gls
Notts Co	Woking	09.97	97-98	7	18	1
Rotherham U	L	01.99	98	2	0	1
Halifax T	Tr	02.99	98-99	16	1	4
Rushden & Diamonds	Morecambe	06.00	01	5	0	0

JACKSON Kirk Stewart Samuel
Barnsley, 16 October, 1976 ESemiPro-6 (F)

League Club	Source	Date Signed	Seasons Played	Apps	Subs	Gls
Sheffield Wed	YT	05.95				
Scunthorpe U	Tr	07.96	96	0	4	1
Chesterfield	Tr	08.97	97	0	3	0
Darlington	Worksop T	03.01	00-01	6	15	1
Yeovil T	Stevenage Borough	11.02	03	19	11	5

JACKSON Leonard (Len)
Stockport, 10 May, 1923 Died 1968 (FB)

League Club	Source	Date Signed	Seasons Played	Apps	Subs	Gls
Manchester C		01.45				
Rochdale	Tr	09.45	46-47	61	-	0

JACKSON Leonard (Len) Wilfred
Birmingham, 6 September, 1922 Died 1990 (FB)

League Club	Source	Date Signed	Seasons Played	Apps	Subs	Gls
Birmingham C		09.46				
Northampton T	Tr	07.48	48	2	-	0

JACKSON Mark Graham
Barnsley, 30 September, 1977 EYth (CD)

League Club	Source	Date Signed	Seasons Played	Apps	Subs	Gls
Leeds U	YT	07.95	95-97	11	8	0
Huddersfield T	L	10.98	98	5	0	0
Barnsley	L	01.00	99	1	0	0
Scunthorpe U	Tr	03.00	99-04	127	9	4
Kidderminster Hrs	Tr	02.05	04	13	0	0

JACKSON Mark Philip
Preston, 3 February, 1986 (F)

League Club	Source	Date Signed	Seasons Played	Apps	Subs	Gls
Preston NE	Sch	08.04	03-04	0	3	0

JACKSON Matthew (Matt) Alan
Leeds, 19 October, 1971 ESch/Eu21-10 (CD)

League Club	Source	Date Signed	Seasons Played	Apps	Subs	Gls
Luton T	Jnrs	07.90	91	7	2	0
Preston NE	L	03.91	90	3	1	0
Everton	Tr	10.91	91-95	132	6	4
Charlton Ath	L	03.96	95	8	0	0
Queens Park Rgrs	L	08.96	96	7	0	0
Birmingham C	L	10.96	96	10	0	0
Norwich C	Tr	12.96	96-00	158	3	6
Wigan Ath	Tr	10.01	01-04	129	2	3

League Club	Source	Date Signed	Seasons Played	Apps	Subs	Gls
JACKSON Maurice						
Carlton, West Yorkshire, 6 November, 1928 Died 1971						(FB)
Barnsley	Carlton U	09.49	49-55	34	-	0
Barrow	Tr	08.56	56-58	74	-	0
JACKSON Michael Douglas						
Cheltenham, 26 June, 1980						(M)
Cheltenham T	YT	08.97	99-01	2	7	0
Swansea C	Tr	07.02	02	0	1	0
JACKSON Michael James						
Runcorn, 4 December, 1973 EYth						(CD)
Crewe Alex	YT	07.92	91-92	5	0	0
Bury	Tr	08.93	93-96	123	2	9
Preston NE	Tr	03.97	96-03	237	8	17
Tranmere Rov	L	12.02	02	6	0	0
Tranmere Rov	Tr	07.04	04	43	0	5
JACKSON Nigel Anthony						
Pudsey, 27 June, 1950						(FB)
Scunthorpe U	App	07.68	68-72	112	4	5
JACKSON Norman Edward						
Bradford, 6 July, 1925 Died 2003						(FB)
Sheffield Wed	Manningham Mills	10.48	49-52	31	-	0
Bristol C	Tr	06.54	54-55	8	-	0
Oldham Ath	Tr	07.56	56	2	-	0
JACKSON Peter						
Stoke-on-Trent, 23 January, 1937 Died 1991						(WH)
Wrexham (Am)	Jnrs	07.54	54	7	-	1
Bradford C	Marine	03.55	54-60	199	-	15
Tranmere Rov	Tr	07.61	61-64	81	-	3
JACKSON Peter Allan						
Shelf, 6 April, 1961						(CD)
Bradford C	App	04.79	78-86	267	11	24
Newcastle U	Tr	10.86	86-88	60	0	3
Bradford C	Tr	09.88	88-89	55	3	5
Huddersfield T	Tr	09.90	90-93	152	3	3
Chester C	Tr	09.94	94-96	100	0	3
JACKSON Philip (Phil) John						
Manchester, 8 September, 1958						(M)
Stockport Co	Manchester C (App)	08.76	76-77	15	3	1
JACKSON Richard						
Whitby, 18 April, 1980						(FB)
Scarborough	YT	03.98	97-98	21	1	0
Derby Co	Tr	03.99	99-04	75	12	0
JACKSON Richard George						
Rotherham, 13 December, 1932						(G)
Rotherham U	Jnrs	07.51				
York C	Tr	08.54				
Rotherham U		07.56	56	1	-	0
JACKSON Robert (Bob)						
Middleton, 5 June, 1934						(FB)
Oldham Ath	Jnrs	08.51	51-54	29	-	1
Lincoln C	Tr	03.55	55-63	235	-	0
JACKSON Robert (Robbie) Gary						
Altrincham, 9 February, 1973						(F)
Walsall	Manchester C (YT)	03.91	90-91	8	2	2
JACKSON Robert (Bob) Gristwood						
Cornsay, 12 May, 1915 Died 1991						(CD)
Southend U	Stanley U	07.34	35-47	93	-	0
JACKSON Ronald (Ron)						
Crook, 15 October, 1919 Died 1980						(FB)
Wrexham		09.45	46-49	108	-	0
Leicester C	Tr	12.49	49-54	161	-	0
JACKSON Royston (Roy) Leonard						
Swindon, 22 October, 1931						(WH)
Swindon T		11.53	54	2	-	0
JACKSON Simeon Alexander						
Kingston, Jamaica, 28 March, 1987						(F)
Rushden & Diamonds	Sch	•	04	0	2	0
JACKSON Thomas (Tommy)						
Belfast, 3 November, 1946 NIu23-1/NI-35						(M)
Everton	Glentoran	02.68	67-70	30	2	0
Nottingham F	Tr	10.70	70-74	73	8	6
Manchester U	Tr	07.75	75-76	18	1	0
JACKSON Thomas (Tony) Anthony						
Tarleton, 16 August, 1942						(FB)
Southport	Lostock Hall	08.62	62-64	12	-	0

League Club	Source	Date Signed	Seasons Played	Apps	Subs	Gls
JACKSON William (Pat) Patrick						
Liverpool, 8 December, 1924 Died 1974						(WH)
Swindon T		10.47	48-49	4	-	1
Tranmere Rov	Tr	04.51	51-53	14	-	1
JACOBS Francis (Frank) Arthur						
Bristol, 22 April, 1940						(WH)
Bristol C	Jnrs	05.58	59-60	5	-	0
JACOBS Stephen (Steve) Douglas						
West Ham, 5 July, 1961						(CD)
Coventry C	App	11.78	79-83	94	7	0
Brighton & Hove A	Tr	06.84	84-85	47	1	3
Charlton Ath	Tr	08.86				
Gillingham	Tr	12.86	86	6	1	0
JACOBS Trevor Frederick						
Bristol, 28 November, 1946						(FB)
Bristol C	Jnrs	07.65	66-72	130	1	3
Plymouth Arg	L	09.72	72	4	0	0
Bristol Rov	Tr	05.73	73-75	82	0	3
JACOBS Wayne Graham						
Sheffield, 3 February, 1969						(FB)
Sheffield Wed	App	01.87	87	5	1	0
Hull C	Tr	03.88	87-91	127	2	4
Rotherham U	Tr	08.93	93	40	2	2
Bradford C	Tr	08.94	94-04	302	16	12
JACOBSEN Anders						
Oslo, Norway, 18 April, 1968 Norway 4						(CD)
Sheffield U	IK Start (Nor)	12.98	98	8	4	0
Stoke C	Tr	08.99	99	29	4	2
Notts Co	Tr	09.00	00	27	2	2
JACOBSEN Viggo Lund						
Denmark, 11 August, 1953						(M)
Charlton Ath	Kastrup (Den)	11.79	79	9	0	0
JACQUES Anthony (Tony)						
Oddington, 10 October, 1942						(WH)
Oxford U	Jnrs	(N/L)	62	7	-	0
JACQUES Joseph (Joe)						
Consett, 12 September, 1944 Died 1981						(CD)
Preston NE	Jnrs	09.61				
Lincoln C	Tr	05.64	64	22	-	0
Darlington	Tr	07.65	65-69	151	3	5
Southend U	Tr	10.69	69-72	85	2	0
Gillingham	Tr	11.72	72-74	73	0	1
Hartlepool	Dartford	01.76	75	5	0	0
JAGGER George Newman						
Great Houghton, 30 September, 1941						(W)
Barnsley	Houghton Main Coll	06.60	60-62	45	-	2
JAGIELKA Philip (Phil) Nikodem						
Manchester, 17 August, 1982 EYth/Eu20/Eu21-2						(FB)
Sheffield U	YT	05.00	99-04	147	23	6
JAGIELKA Stephen (Steve)						
Manchester, 10 March, 1978						(M)
Stoke C	YT	07.96				
Shrewsbury T	Tr	07.97	97-02	89	76	17
JAGO Gordon Harold						
Poplar, 22 October, 1932 ESch/EYth						(CD)
Charlton Ath	Dulwich Hamlet	05.51	54-61	137	-	1
JAIDI Radhi Ben Abdelmajid						
Tunis, Tunisia, 30 August, 1975 Tunisia int						(CD)
Bolton W	Esp de Tunis (Tun)	07.04	04	20	7	5
JAKEMAN Leslie (Mick)						
Nuneaton, 14 March, 1930						(WH)
Derby Co	Atherstone T	06.47				
Leicester C	Hinckley Ath	05.51	54	1	-	0
JAKOBSSON Andreas						
Lund, Sweden, 6 October, 1972 Sweden 36						(CD)
Southampton	Brondby (Den)	08.04	04	24	3	2
JAKUB Yanek (Joe)						
Falkirk, 7 December, 1956						(M)
Burnley	App	12.73	75-79	42	0	0
Bury	Tr	10.80	80-86	262	3	27
Chester C	AZ67 Alkmaar (Holl)	08.88	88	42	0	1
Burnley	Tr	07.89	89-92	161	2	8
Chester C	Tr	08.93	93	35	1	0
Wigan Ath	Colwyn Bay	09.94	94	16	0	0

JALES Richard (Dick)
Chiswick, 3 April, 1922 (FB)

League Club	Source	Date Signed	Seasons Played	Apps	Subs	Gls
Bradford C		06.45				
Aldershot	Tr	05.46	46-50	78	-	1

JALINK Nicolaas (Nico)
Rotterdam, Holland, 22 June, 1964 (M)

League Club	Source	Date Signed	Seasons Played	Apps	Subs	Gls
Port Vale	RKC Walwijk (Holl)	07.91	91	20	8	1

JAMES Anthony (Tony) Craig
Sheffield, 27 June, 1967 (CD)

League Club	Source	Date Signed	Seasons Played	Apps	Subs	Gls
Lincoln C	Gainsborough Trinity	08.88	88-89	24	5	0
Leicester C	Tr	08.89	89-93	79	30	11
Hereford U	Tr	07.94	94-95	35	0	4
Plymouth Arg	Tr	08.96	96	34	0	1

JAMES Anthony (Tony) Ralph
Swansea, 24 February, 1960 (M)

League Club	Source	Date Signed	Seasons Played	Apps	Subs	Gls
Swansea C	App	12.77	77-79	6	5	1

JAMES Christopher (Chris)
Sheffield, 16 January, 1969 (FB)

League Club	Source	Date Signed	Seasons Played	Apps	Subs	Gls
Scarborough	Worksop T	08.91	91	12	1	0

JAMES Clement Junior
Bracknell, 10 March, 1981 (F)

League Club	Source	Date Signed	Seasons Played	Apps	Subs	Gls
Brentford	YT	06.99	99	0	1	0

JAMES Craig Peter
Middlesbrough, 15 November, 1982 (FB)

League Club	Source	Date Signed	Seasons Played	Apps	Subs	Gls
Sunderland	YT	07.00	03	1	0	0
Darlington	L	11.03	03	10	0	1
Port Vale	Tr	03.04	03-04	31	7	1

JAMES David (Dai)
Swansea, 29 September, 1917 Died 1981 (CF)

League Club	Source	Date Signed	Seasons Played	Apps	Subs	Gls
Leeds U		10.34				
Bradford C	Tr	05.35	36	5	-	0
Chelsea	Mossley	04.38				
Swansea T	Tr	06.47	47	12	-	7

JAMES David
Cambuslang, 12 December, 1942 (W)

League Club	Source	Date Signed	Seasons Played	Apps	Subs	Gls
Brighton & Hove A	Blantyre Victoria	05.62	62	5	-	0

JAMES David Benjamin
Welwyn Garden City, 1 August, 1970 EYth/Eu21-10/EB-1/E-32 (G)

League Club	Source	Date Signed	Seasons Played	Apps	Subs	Gls
Watford	YT	07.88	90-91	89	0	0
Liverpool	Tr	07.92	92-98	213	1	0
Aston Villa	Tr	06.99	99-00	67	0	0
West Ham U	Tr	07.01	01-03	91	0	0
Manchester C	Tr	01.04	03-04	55	0	0

JAMES David John
Southend-on-Sea, 11 March, 1948 (FB)

League Club	Source	Date Signed	Seasons Played	Apps	Subs	Gls
West Ham U	App	03.65				
Torquay U	Tr	05.67	67	8	0	0

JAMES Walter **George**
Swansea, 15 June, 1924 Died 1998 WSch (FB)

League Club	Source	Date Signed	Seasons Played	Apps	Subs	Gls
Swansea T	Tawe U	08.42	49	4	-	0
Newport Co	Tr	07.50	50-51	13	-	5

JAMES Edward **Glyn**
Llangollen, 17 December, 1941 Wu23-2/W-9 (CD)

League Club	Source	Date Signed	Seasons Played	Apps	Subs	Gls
Blackpool	Jnrs	05.59	60-74	395	6	22

JAMES John Brian
Stone, 24 October, 1948 (F)

League Club	Source	Date Signed	Seasons Played	Apps	Subs	Gls
Port Vale	Jnrs	04.66	65-72	202	8	39
Chester	Tr	02.73	72-75	97	1	40
Tranmere Rov	Tr	09.75	75-77	59	14	24

JAMES John Edward
Birmingham, 19 February, 1934 (WH)

League Club	Source	Date Signed	Seasons Played	Apps	Subs	Gls
Birmingham C	Paget Rgrs	03.51	52-53	5	-	2
Torquay U	Tr	06.55	55-60	125	-	11

JAMES Joseph (Joe)
Bootle, 9 September, 1954 (CD)

League Club	Source	Date Signed	Seasons Played	Apps	Subs	Gls
Liverpool	Jnrs	01.74				
Southport	Tr	07.75	75	11	2	0

JAMES Julian Colin
Tring, 22 March, 1970 Eu21-2 (FB)

League Club	Source	Date Signed	Seasons Played	Apps	Subs	Gls
Luton T	YT	07.88	87-97	262	20	13
Preston NE	L	09.91	91	6	0	0

JAMES Keith Andrew
Hillingdon, 18 August, 1961 EYth (FB)

League Club	Source	Date Signed	Seasons Played	Apps	Subs	Gls
Portsmouth	App	07.79	78-79	5	1	0

JAMES Kevin Ernest
Southwark, 3 January, 1980 (F)

League Club	Source	Date Signed	Seasons Played	Apps	Subs	Gls
Charlton Ath	YT	07.98				
Gillingham	Tr	08.00	00-03	18	31	4
Nottingham F	Tr	06.04	04	2	5	0
Boston U	L	12.04	04	6	0	0

JAMES Leighton
Loughor, 16 February, 1953 WSch/Wu23-7/W-54 (W)

League Club	Source	Date Signed	Seasons Played	Apps	Subs	Gls
Burnley	App	02.70	70-75	180	1	44
Derby Co	Tr	10.75	75-77	67	1	15
Queens Park Rgrs	Tr	10.77	77-78	27	1	4
Burnley	Tr	09.78	78-79	76	0	9
Swansea C	Tr	04.80	79-82	88	10	27
Sunderland	Tr	01.83	82-83	50	2	4
Bury	Tr	08.84	84	46	0	5
Newport Co	Tr	08.85	85	21	7	2
Burnley	Tr	08.86	86-88	75	4	13

JAMES Leslie
(W)

League Club	Source	Date Signed	Seasons Played	Apps	Subs	Gls
Darlington (Am)		05.53	53	4	-	0

JAMES Lutel Malik
Manchester, 2 June, 1972 StKitts 3 (F)

League Club	Source	Date Signed	Seasons Played	Apps	Subs	Gls
Scarborough	Yorkshire Amats	02.93	92	0	6	0
Bury	Hyde U	10.98	98-00	34	34	4

JAMES Martin Christopher
Slough, 18 February, 1953 (CD)

League Club	Source	Date Signed	Seasons Played	Apps	Subs	Gls
Reading	Jnrs	08.71	71	21	0	0

JAMES Martin Joseph
Formby, 18 May, 1971 (W)

League Club	Source	Date Signed	Seasons Played	Apps	Subs	Gls
Preston NE	YT	07.89	90-92	92	6	11
Stockport Co	Tr	03.93	92-93	13	19	0
Rotherham U	Tr	08.94	94-96	40	4	0

JAMES Paul John
Cardiff, 11 November, 1963 Canada int (M)

League Club	Source	Date Signed	Seasons Played	Apps	Subs	Gls
Doncaster Rov	Hamilton (Canada)	11.87	87	7	1	0

JAMES Percy George Burge
Rhondda, 9 March, 1917 Died 1993 WAmat (W)

League Club	Source	Date Signed	Seasons Played	Apps	Subs	Gls
Luton T	Oxford C	08.49	49	2	-	1

JAMES Robert (Robbie) Mark
Gorseinon, 23 March, 1957 Died 1998 Wu21-3/W-47 (M)

League Club	Source	Date Signed	Seasons Played	Apps	Subs	Gls
Swansea C	App	04.74	72-82	385	8	102
Stoke C	Tr	07.83	83-84	48	0	6
Queens Park Rgrs	Tr	10.84	84-86	78	9	5
Leicester C	Tr	06.87	87	21	2	0
Swansea C	Tr	01.88	87-89	82	8	16
Bradford C	Tr	08.90	90-91	89	0	6
Cardiff C	Tr	08.92	92-93	51	0	2

JAMES Ronald (Ron)
Birmingham, 16 March, 1922 (WH)

League Club	Source	Date Signed	Seasons Played	Apps	Subs	Gls
Birmingham C		10.47				
Northampton T	Tr	07.48	48	4	-	1

JAMES Royston (Roy) William
Bristol, 19 February, 1941 Died 1990 (CF)

League Club	Source	Date Signed	Seasons Played	Apps	Subs	Gls
Bristol Rov	Old Georgians	07.60	60	1	-	0

JAMES John **Stanley (Stan)**
South Shields, 12 September, 1923 Died 2003 (FB)

League Club	Source	Date Signed	Seasons Played	Apps	Subs	Gls
Bradford PA	South Shields	08.44	49-50	13	-	1

JAMES Steven (Steve) Robert
Coseley, 29 November, 1949 EYth (CD)

League Club	Source	Date Signed	Seasons Played	Apps	Subs	Gls
Manchester U	App	12.66	68-74	129	0	4
York C	Tr	01.76	75-79	105	0	1

JAMES Thomas (Tony) Anthony George
Ynysybwl, 16 September, 1919 (WH)

League Club	Source	Date Signed	Seasons Played	Apps	Subs	Gls
Brighton & Hove A	Folkestone	06.39	46-48	69	-	20
Bristol Rov	Tr	06.49	49-50	21	-	5

JAMES Tyrone Selwyn
Paddington, 19 September, 1956 (FB)

League Club	Source	Date Signed	Seasons Played	Apps	Subs	Gls
Fulham	Jnrs	09.74	75-77	18	2	0
Plymouth Arg	Tr	03.78	77-81	77	4	0
Torquay U	L	03.83	82	13	0	1

JAMES William (Billy) John
Cardiff, 18 October, 1921 Died 1980 WWar-2 (CF)

League Club	Source	Date Signed	Seasons Played	Apps	Subs	Gls
Cardiff C	Cardiff Corinthians	08.39	46	6	-	3

JAMESON John Charles
Belfast, 11 March, 1958 (W)

League Club	Source	Date Signed	Seasons Played	Apps	Subs	Gls
Huddersfield T	Bangor	03.77	77	1	0	0

League Club	Source	Date Signed	Seasons Played	Apps	Subs	Gls
JAMIESON Ian						
Edinburgh, 22 October, 1934						(IF)
Crewe Alex	Third Lanark	08.56	56	4	-	2
JAMIESON John (Iain) Wallace						
Dumbarton, 14 October, 1928						(WH)
Coventry C	Aberdeen	01.49	48-57	181	-	6
JANKOVIC Bozo						
Sarajevo, Bosnia, 22 May, 1951 Died 1993 Yugoslavia int						(F)
Middlesbrough	Zeljeznicar (Yug)	02.79	78-80	42	8	16
JANNEY Mark						
Romford, 2 December, 1977						(F)
Tottenham H	YT	07.96				
Brentford	L	03.97	96	1	1	1
JANSEN Matthew (Matt) Brooke						
Carlisle, 20 October, 1977 EYth/Eu21-6						(F)
Carlisle U	YT	01.96	96-97	26	16	10
Crystal Palace	Tr	02.98	97-98	23	3	10
Blackburn Rov	Tr	01.99	98-04	103	46	44
Coventry C	L	02.03	02	8	1	2
JANSSON Jan						
Kalmar, Sweden, 26 January, 1968 Sweden 7						(M)
Port Vale	IFK Norrkoping (Swe)	11.96	96-98	37	14	6
JANTUNEN Pertti Kalevi						
Lahti, Finland, 25 June, 1952 Finland int						(M)
Bristol C	Eskilstuna (Swe)	03.79	78-79	7	1	1
[JARDEL] RIBEIRO DE ALMEIDA Mario Jardel						
Fortaleza, Brazil, 18 September, 1973 Brazil 7						(F)
Bolton W	Sporting Lisbon (Por)	08.03	03	0	7	0
JARDINE Alexander (Alex)						
Cleland, 12 April, 1926 Died 1978						(FB)
Millwall	Dundee U	08.50	50-57	299	-	25
JARDINE Frederick (Fred)						
Edinburgh, 27 September, 1941						(FB)
Luton T	Dundee	05.61	61-69	218	2	9
Torquay U	Tr	02.71	70-71	11	0	0
JARMAN Harold James						
Bristol, 4 May, 1939						(W)
Bristol Rov	Victoria Ath	08.59	59-72	440	12	127
Newport Co	Tr	05.73	73	34	6	8
JARMAN John Emlyn						
Rhymney, 4 February, 1931						(WH)
Wolverhampton W	Lowhill YC	07.49				
Barnsley	Wellington T	10.50	51-55	45	-	1
Walsall	Tr	06.56	56-57	37	-	2
JARMAN Lee						
Cardiff, 16 December, 1977 WYth/Wu21-9						(FB)
Cardiff C	YT	08.95	95-99	78	16	1
Exeter C	Merthyr Tydfil	03.00	99	7	0	0
Oxford U	Tr	07.00	00	15	6	1
JARMAN Nathan George						
Scunthorpe, 19 September, 1986						(F)
Barnsley	Sch	05.05	04	1	5	0
JARMAN William (Bill) Brynmor						
Pontypridd, 18 July, 1920 Died 1984						(IF)
Bury	Llanbradach	10.46	46	10	-	1
JAROSIK Jiri						
Usti Nad Lebem, Czech Republic, 27 October, 1977 CzR-22						(M)
Chelsea	CSKA Moscow (Rus)	01.05	04	3	11	0
JARRETT Albert Ojumiri						
Sierra Leone, 23 October, 1984						(M)
Wimbledon	Dulwich Hamlet	04.03	03	3	6	0
Brighton & Hove A	Tr	08.04	04	3	9	1
JARRETT Jason Lee Mee						
Bury, 14 September, 1979						(M)
Blackpool	YT	07.98	98	2	0	0
Wrexham	Tr	10.99	99	1	0	0
Bury	Tr	07.00	00-01	45	17	4
Wigan Ath	Tr	03.02	01-04	67	28	1
Stoke C	L	01.05	04	2	0	0
JARRIE Frederick (Fred)						
Hartlepool, 2 August, 1922 Died 2004						(G)
Hartlepools U (Am)		08.47	47	1	-	0
JARVIE Paul						
Aberdeen, 14 June, 1982						(G)
Torquay U	Dundee U	02.05	04	1	0	0
JARVIS Alan Leslie						
Wrexham, 4 August, 1943 W-3						(M)
Everton	Jnrs	07.61				
Hull C	Tr	06.64	65-70	148	11	12
Mansfield T	Tr	03.71	70-72	76	6	0
JARVIS Antony (Tony)						
Radcliffe, 19 March, 1964						(F)
Oldham Ath	Irlam T	03.86				
Crewe Alex	Tr	10.86	86	6	3	1
JARVIS John **Brian**						
Bangor-on-Dee, 26 August, 1933 Died 2004						(WH)
Wrexham		07.52	53-58	64	-	3
Oldham Ath	Tr	07.59	59-62	88	-	2
JARVIS Harry						
Maltby, 8 October, 1928						(WH)
Notts Co	Worksop T	05.51	52-54	29	-	0
JARVIS Joseph						
Farnworth, 27 June, 1929						(FB)
Stockport Co		09.53	54-56	43	-	0
JARVIS Matthew (Matt) Thomas						
Middlesbrough, 22 May, 1986						(M)
Gillingham	Sch	05.04	03-04	14	26	3
JARVIS Mervin John						
Bristol, 20 October, 1924 Died 1994						(W)
Bristol C		05.48	48	4	-	0
JARVIS Nicholas (Nick) Charles						
Mansfield, 19 September, 1955						(FB)
Scunthorpe U	Grantham	07.80	80	21	0	0
JARVIS Nigel Brian						
Totnes, 6 November, 1963						(FB)
Plymouth Arg	App	11.81				
Torquay U	Yeovil T	02.85	84	8	3	0
JARVIS Ryan Robert						
Fakenham, 11 July, 1986 EYth						(F)
Norwich C	Sch	08.03	02-04	3	16	2
Colchester U	L	03.05	04	2	4	0
JASPER Brian						
Plymouth, 25 November, 1933						(FB)
Plymouth Arg	Astor Institute	07.54	56	2	-	0
JASPER Dale William						
Croydon, 14 January, 1964						(M)
Chelsea	App	01.82	83-84	10	0	0
Brighton & Hove A	Tr	05.86	86-87	44	5	6
Crewe Alex	Tr	07.88	88-91	103	8	2
JASZCZUN Antony (Tommy) John						
Kettering, 16 September, 1977						(FB)
Aston Villa	YT	07.96				
Blackpool	Tr	01.00	99-03	107	15	0
Northampton T	Tr	07.04	04	24	8	0
JAVARY Jean-Phillipe						
Montpellier, France, 10 January, 1978 FrYth						(M)
Brentford	Raith Rov	08.00	00	4	2	0
Plymouth Arg	Tr	02.01	00	4	0	0
Sheffield U	Raith Rov	03.02	01-02	8	5	1
JAYES Brian						
Leicester, 13 December, 1932 Died 1978						(WH)
Leicester C	Jnrs	07.54	55	3	-	0
Mansfield T	Tr	07.56	56-59	115	-	1
JAYES Carl Geoffrey						
Leicester, 15 March, 1954 ESch						(G)
Leicester C	Jnrs	06.71	74	5	0	0
Northampton T	Tr	11.77	77-79	68	0	0
JAYES Alfred **Gordon**						
Leicester, 26 November, 1923 Died 1997 ESch						(CF)
Notts Co	Leicester C (Am)	11.46	46-47	27	-	7
JEAN Earl Jude						
St Lucia, 9 October, 1971 St Lucia 4						(F)
Ipswich T	Felguieras (Por)	12.96	96	0	1	0
Rotherham U	Tr	01.97	96	7	11	6
Plymouth Arg	Tr	08.97	97-98	37	28	7

League Club	Source	Date Signed	Seasons Played	Career Record Apps	Subs	Gls
JEANNE Leon Charles						
Cardiff, 17 November, 1980 WYth/Wu21-8						(F)
Queens Park Rgrs	YT	11.97	98-99	8	4	0
Cardiff C	Tr	07.01	01	0	2	0
JEANNIN Alexandre (Alex)						
Troyes, France, 30 December, 1977						(CD)
Darlington	Troyes (Fr)	03.01	00-01	22	0	0
Bristol Rov	Exeter C	05.05	04	1	0	0
JEAVONS Patrick (Pat) William Peter						
Deptford, 5 July, 1946						(G)
Lincoln C	Gravesend & Northfleet	02.66	65	1	0	0
JEFFELS Simon						
Darton, 18 January, 1966 EYth						(CD)
Barnsley	App	01.84	83-87	39	3	0
Preston NE	L	10.87	87	1	0	0
Carlisle U	Tr	07.88	88-91	75	1	5
JEFFERIES Alfred (Alf) James						
Oxford, 9 February, 1922						(G)
Brentford	Oxford C	09.47	49-53	116	-	0
Torquay U	Tr	06.54	54	45	-	0
JEFFERS Francis						
Liverpool, 25 January, 1981 ESch/EYth/Eu21-16/E-1						(F)
Everton	YT	02.98	97-00	37	12	18
Arsenal	Tr	06.01	01-02	4	18	4
Everton	L	09.03	03	5	13	0
Charlton Ath	Tr	08.04	04	9	11	3
JEFFERS John Joseph						
Liverpool, 5 October, 1968 ESch						(W)
Liverpool	App	10.86				
Port Vale	Tr	12.88	88-94	147	33	10
Shrewsbury T	L	01.95	94	3	0	1
Stockport Co	Tr	11.95	95-96	46	11	6
JEFFERSON Arthur						
Goldthorpe, 14 December, 1916 Died 1997						(FB)
Queens Park Rgrs	Peterborough U	02.36	36-49	211	-	1
Aldershot	Tr	03.50	49-54	170	-	0
JEFFERSON Derek						
Morpeth, 5 September, 1948						(CD)
Ipswich T	App	02.66	67-72	163	3	1
Wolverhampton W	Tr	10.72	72-75	41	1	0
Sheffield Wed	L	10.76	76	5	0	0
Hereford U	Tr	11.76	76-77	39	0	0
JEFFERSON Stanley (Stan)						
Goldthorpe, 26 June, 1931 Died 1973						(FB)
Aldershot	Dearne Ath	08.52	52-57	80	-	0
JEFFREY Alick James						
Rawmarsh, 29 January, 1939 Died 2000 ESch/EYth/EAmat/Eu23-2						(F)
Doncaster Rov	Jnrs	02.56	54-56	71	-	34
Doncaster Rov	Auburn (Aus)	12.63	63-68	190	1	93
Lincoln C	Tr	01.69	68-69	19	3	3
JEFFREY Andrew (Andy) Samuel						
Bellshill, 15 January, 1972						(FB)
Leicester C	YT	02.90				
Cambridge U	Cambridge C	07.93	93-95	82	13	2
JEFFREY Michael (Mike) Richard						
Liverpool, 11 August, 1971						(F)
Bolton W	YT	02.89	88-91	9	6	0
Doncaster Rov	Tr	03.92	91-93	48	1	19
Newcastle U	Tr	10.93	93	2	0	0
Rotherham U	Tr	06.95	95	22	0	5
Grimsby T	Kilmarnock	08.00	00-01	19	28	2
Scunthorpe U	L	03.02	01	4	2	1
JEFFREY Robert (Bob)						
Aberdeen, 24 May, 1920 Died 1992						(WH)
Derby Co		12.43				
Exeter C	Montrose	10.47	47	7	-	0
JEFFREY William (Billy) Greenwood						
Clydebank, 25 October, 1956						(M)
Oxford U	App	10.73	73-81	311	3	24
Blackpool	Tr	06.82	82	12	2	1
Northampton T	Tr	03.83	82-83	53	1	6
JEFFRIES Derek						
Longsight, 22 March, 1951						(CD)
Manchester C	App	08.68	69-72	64	9	0
Crystal Palace	Tr	09.73	73-75	107	0	1
Peterborough U	L	10.76	76	7	0	0
Millwall	L	03.77	76	10	1	0
Chester	Tr	07.77	77-80	116	5	2
JEFFRIES Ronald (Ron) James						
Birmingham, 24 March, 1930						(WH)
Aston Villa	Moor Green Rov	12.50	50	2	-	0
Walsall	Tr	11.53	53	3	-	0
JEFFRIES William Arthur						
Acton, 11 March, 1921 Died 1981						(IF)
Mansfield T		03.46	46	2	-	0
JELLEYMAN Gareth Anthony						
Holywell, 14 November, 1980 WYth/Wu21-1						(FB)
Peterborough U	YT	08.98	99-04	80	21	0
Boston U	L	08.04	04	3	0	0
Mansfield T	Tr	01.05	04	14	0	0
JELLY Horace **Edward (Ted)**						
Leicester, 28 August, 1921 Died 2000						(FB)
Leicester C	Belgrave U	05.46	46-50	56	-	1
Plymouth Arg	Tr	08.51	52-53	11	-	0
JEMSON Nigel Bradley						
Preston, 10 August, 1969 Eu21-1						(F)
Preston NE	YT	07.87	85-87	28	4	8
Nottingham F	Tr	03.88	89-91	45	2	13
Bolton W	L	12.88	88	4	1	0
Preston NE	L	03.89	88	6	3	2
Sheffield Wed	Tr	09.91	91-93	26	25	9
Grimsby T	L	09.93	93	6	0	2
Notts Co	Tr	09.94	94-95	7	7	1
Watford	L	01.95	94	3	1	0
Rotherham U	L	02.96	95	16	0	5
Oxford U	Tr	07.96	96-97	68	0	27
Bury	Tr	02.98	97-98	17	12	1
Oxford U	Ayr U	01.00	99	13	5	0
Shrewsbury T	Tr	07.00	00-02	107	2	36
JENAS Jermaine Anthony						
Nottingham, 18 February, 1983 EYth/Eu21-9/E-12						(M)
Nottingham F	YT	02.00	00-01	29	0	4
Newcastle U	Tr	02.02	01-04	83	23	9
JENKIN Kenneth (Ken)						
Grimsby, 27 November, 1931						(W)
Grimsby T	Jnrs	07.50	50-53	23	-	6
JENKINS Brian						
Treherbert, 1 August, 1935						(W)
Cardiff C	Cwmparc	04.56	56-60	29	-	7
Exeter C	Tr	06.61	61-62	73	-	11
Bristol Rov	Tr	07.63	63	7	-	0
JENKINS David John						
Bristol, 2 September, 1946						(F)
Arsenal	App	10.63	67-68	16	1	3
Tottenham H	Tr	10.68	68-69	11	3	2
Brentford	Tr	07.72	72	13	5	1
Hereford U	Tr	03.73	72-73	18	4	3
Newport Co	L	03.74	73	6	0	1
Shrewsbury T	Tr	08.74	74	2	0	1
Workington	Durban C (SA)	10.75	75	6	0	0
JENKINS Iain						
Prescot, 24 November, 1972 NIB-1/NI-6						(FB)
Everton	YT	06.91	90-92	3	2	0
Bradford C	L	12.92	92	6	0	0
Chester C	Tr	08.93	93-97	155	5	1
Shrewsbury T	Dundee U	07.00	00-01	19	2	0
JENKINS Iorweth (Iori) Clifford						
Neath, 11 December, 1959 WSch						(FB)
Chelsea	App	08.78				
Brentford	Tr	11.79	79-80	12	3	1
JENKINS Jamie						
Pontypool, 1 January, 1979						(FB)
Bournemouth	YT	07.97	98	0	1	0
JENKINS Lee David						
Pontypool, 28 June, 1979 WSch/WYth/Wu21-9						(M)
Swansea C	YT	12.96	96-03	125	44	3
Kidderminster Hrs	Tr	12.03	03-04	36	3	0
JENKINS Lee Robert						
West Bromwich, 17 March, 1961 EYth						(M)
Aston Villa	App	01.79	78-79	0	3	0
Port Vale	Tr	11.80	80	1	0	0
Birmingham C	Rovaniemi (Fin)	10.85	85	1	0	0
JENKINS James Lindley						
West Bromwich, 6 April, 1954						(M)
Birmingham C	App	07.71	73	2	0	0
Walsall	Tr	07.74	74	3	0	0

JENKINS Neil
Carshalton, 6 January, 1982 EYth/Eu20 (M)

League Club	Source	Date Signed	Seasons Played	Apps	Subs	Gls
Wimbledon	YT	07.00				
Southend U	Tr	08.02	02-03	36	14	8

JENKINS Peter Leslie
Bow, 7 February, 1947 (FB)

League Club	Source	Date Signed	Seasons Played	Apps	Subs	Gls
Charlton Ath	Chelsea (App)	03.65	65	2	0	0

JENKINS Randolph Joseph
Sligo, 5 September, 1925 (IF)

League Club	Source	Date Signed	Seasons Played	Apps	Subs	Gls
Walsall		01.45				
Northampton T	Tr	06.46	46-47	18	-	6
Fulham	Tr	05.48				
Gillingham	Tr	06.50	50	2	-	0

JENKINS Reginald (Reg)
Millbrook, 7 October, 1938 (F)

League Club	Source	Date Signed	Seasons Played	Apps	Subs	Gls
Plymouth Arg	Truro C	10.57	58-59	16	-	3
Exeter C	Tr	12.60	60	20	-	6
Torquay U	Tr	07.61	61-63	88	-	23
Rochdale	Tr	06.64	64-72	294	11	118

JENKINS Ross Anthony
Kensington, 4 November, 1951 (F)

League Club	Source	Date Signed	Seasons Played	Apps	Subs	Gls
Crystal Palace	App	11.69	71-72	15	0	2
Watford	Tr	11.72	72-82	312	27	118

JENKINS Stephen (Steve) Matthew
Bristol, 2 January, 1980 (FB)

League Club	Source	Date Signed	Seasons Played	Apps	Subs	Gls
Southampton	YT	01.98				
Brentford	L	03.99	98	0	1	0
Brentford	Tr	07.99	99	2	3	0

JENKINS Stephen (Steve) Robert
Merthyr Tydfil, 16 July, 1972 WYth/Wu21-2/W-16 (FB)

League Club	Source	Date Signed	Seasons Played	Apps	Subs	Gls
Swansea C	YT	07.90	90-95	155	10	1
Huddersfield T	Tr	11.95	95-02	257	1	4
Birmingham C	L	12.00	00	3	0	0
Cardiff C	Tr	02.03	02	4	0	0
Notts Co	Tr	08.03	03	17	0	0
Peterborough U	Tr	01.04	03-04	11	3	1
Swindon T	Tr	10.04	04	24	0	0

JENKINS Thomas (Tom) Ernest
Bethnal Green, 2 December, 1947 (W)

League Club	Source	Date Signed	Seasons Played	Apps	Subs	Gls
Leyton Orient		01.66	65	1	0	0
Reading	Margate	07.69	69	21	0	5
Southampton	Tr	12.69	69-72	84	0	4
Swindon T	Tr	11.72	72-75	89	11	4

JENKINS Thomas (Tom) Frederick
Stockton, 5 December, 1925 (IF)

League Club	Source	Date Signed	Seasons Played	Apps	Subs	Gls
Chelsea	Queen of the South	07.49	49	5	-	0

JENKINSON Leigh
Thorne, 9 July, 1969 WB-1 (W)

League Club	Source	Date Signed	Seasons Played	Apps	Subs	Gls
Hull C	App	06.87	87-92	95	35	13
Rotherham U	L	09.90	90	5	2	0
Coventry C	Tr	03.93	92-94	22	10	1
Birmingham C	L	11.93	93	2	1	0
Wigan Ath	St Johnstone	07.98	98	3	4	0

JENNINGS Dennis Bernard
Habberley, 20 July, 1910 Died 1996 (W)

League Club	Source	Date Signed	Seasons Played	Apps	Subs	Gls
Huddersfield T	Kidderminster Hrs	10.30	30-32	33	-	5
Grimsby T	Tr	09.32	32-35	99	-	29
Birmingham	Tr	01.36	35-49	192	-	12

JENNINGS Kentoine (Jedd)
Bermuda, 15 October, 1971 Bermuda int (FB)

League Club	Source	Date Signed	Seasons Played	Apps	Subs	Gls
Hereford U	Pembroke (Ber)	08.91	91-92	11	5	0

JENNINGS Nicholas (Nicky)
Wellington, Somerset, 18 January, 1946 (W)

League Club	Source	Date Signed	Seasons Played	Apps	Subs	Gls
Plymouth Arg	Wellington (Somerset)	08.63	63-66	98	0	11
Portsmouth	Tr	01.67	66-73	199	8	44
Aldershot	L	11.73	73	4	0	1
Exeter C	Tr	05.74	74-77	119	5	15

JENNINGS Patrick (Pat) Anthony
Newry, 12 June, 1945 NIYth/NIu23-1/NI-119 (G)

League Club	Source	Date Signed	Seasons Played	Apps	Subs	Gls
Watford	Newry T	05.63	62-63	48	-	0
Tottenham H	Tr	06.64	64-76	472	0	0
Arsenal	Tr	08.77	77-84	237	0	0

JENNINGS Roy Thomas Edward
Swindon, 31 December, 1931 EYth (CD)

League Club	Source	Date Signed	Seasons Played	Apps	Subs	Gls
Brighton & Hove A	Southampton (Am)	05.52	52-63	276	-	22

JENNINGS Steven (Steve) John
Liverpool, 28 October, 1984 (M)

League Club	Source	Date Signed	Seasons Played	Apps	Subs	Gls
Tranmere Rov	Sch	10.02	03-04	5	10	0

JENNINGS Henry William (Bill)
Norwich, 7 January, 1920 Died 1969 (CF)

League Club	Source	Date Signed	Seasons Played	Apps	Subs	Gls
Northampton T		10.38	38-46	11	-	2
Ipswich T	Tr	05.47	47-50	102	-	41
Rochdale	Tr	06.51	51	3	-	1

JENNINGS William (Billy) John
Hackney, 20 February, 1952 EYth (F)

League Club	Source	Date Signed	Seasons Played	Apps	Subs	Gls
Watford	Jnrs	04.70	70-74	80	13	33
West Ham U	Tr	09.74	74-78	89	10	34
Orient	Tr	08.79	79-81	64	3	21
Luton T	Tr	03.82	81	0	2	1

JENSEN Brian
Copenhagen, Denmark, 8 June, 1975 (G)

League Club	Source	Date Signed	Seasons Played	Apps	Subs	Gls
West Bromwich A	AZ67 Alkmaar (Holl)	03.00	99-01	46	0	0
Burnley	Tr	07.03	03-04	72	1	0

JENSEN Claus William
Nykobing, Denmark, 29 April, 1977 Deu21-17/De-33 (M)

League Club	Source	Date Signed	Seasons Played	Apps	Subs	Gls
Bolton W	Lyngby (Den)	07.98	98-99	85	1	8
Charlton Ath	Tr	07.00	00-03	112	10	16
Fulham	Tr	07.04	04	10	2	0

JENSEN John Faxe
Copenhagen, Denmark, 3 May, 1965 Denmark int (M)

League Club	Source	Date Signed	Seasons Played	Apps	Subs	Gls
Arsenal	Brondby (Den)	08.92	92-95	93	5	1

JENSEN Niclas
Copenhagen, Denmark, 17 August, 1974 Denmark 21 (FB)

League Club	Source	Date Signed	Seasons Played	Apps	Subs	Gls
Manchester C	FC Copenhagen (Den)	01.02	01-02	48	3	2

JENSEN Hans Viggo
Skagen, Denmark, 29 March, 1921 Denmark int (FB)

League Club	Source	Date Signed	Seasons Played	Apps	Subs	Gls
Hull C	Esbjerg (Den)	10.48	48-56	308	-	51

JEPHCOTT Avun Cyd
Coventry, 16 October, 1983 (F)

League Club	Source	Date Signed	Seasons Played	Apps	Subs	Gls
Coventry C	Sch	02.03	02	0	1	0

JEPPSON Hans
Sweden, 10 May, 1925 Sweden int (CF)

League Club	Source	Date Signed	Seasons Played	Apps	Subs	Gls
Charlton Ath (Am)	Djurgaardens (Swe)	01.51	50	11	-	9

JEPSON Arthur
Selston, 12 July, 1915 Died 1997 (G)

League Club	Source	Date Signed	Seasons Played	Apps	Subs	Gls
Mansfield T (Am)	Newark T	11.34	34	2	-	0
Port Vale	Grantham	06.38	38	39	-	0
Stoke C	Tr	09.46	46-47	28	-	0
Lincoln C	Tr	12.48	48-49	58	-	0

JEPSON Charles Barry
Alfreton, 29 December, 1929 Died 2001 (CF)

League Club	Source	Date Signed	Seasons Played	Apps	Subs	Gls
Chesterfield	Alfreton T	11.48				
Mansfield T	Ilkeston T	03.54	53-56	55	-	36
Chester	Tr	01.57	56-59	89	-	42
Southport	Tr	11.59	59	24	-	7

JEPSON Ronald (Ronnie) Francis
Audley, 12 May, 1963 (F)

League Club	Source	Date Signed	Seasons Played	Apps	Subs	Gls
Port Vale	Nantwich T	03.89	88-90	12	10	0
Peterborough U	L	01.90	89	18	0	5
Preston NE	Tr	02.91	90-91	36	2	8
Exeter C	Tr	07.92	92-93	51	3	21
Huddersfield T	Tr	12.93	93-95	95	12	36
Bury	Tr	07.96	96-97	31	16	9
Oldham Ath	Tr	01.98	97	9	0	4
Burnley	Tr	07.98	98-00	4	55	3

JERKAN Nikola
Sinj, Croatia, 8 December, 1964 Croatia int (CD)

League Club	Source	Date Signed	Seasons Played	Apps	Subs	Gls
Nottingham F	Real Oviedo (Sp)	06.96	96	14	0	0

JERMYN Mark Stephen
Germany, 16 April, 1981 (FB)

League Club	Source	Date Signed	Seasons Played	Apps	Subs	Gls
Torquay U	YT	07.99	98	0	1	0

JEROME Cameron Zishan
Huddersfield, 14 August, 1986 (F)

League Club	Source	Date Signed	Seasons Played	Apps	Subs	Gls
Cardiff C		01.04	04	21	8	6

JERVIS David John
Retford, 18 January, 1982 (CD)

League Club	Source	Date Signed	Seasons Played	Apps	Subs	Gls
Mansfield T	YT	07.00	00-02	21	9	0

JERVIS William John
Liverpool, 22 January, 1942 (W)

League Club	Source	Date Signed	Seasons Played	Apps	Subs	Gls
Blackburn Rov	Jnrs	01.59				
Gillingham	Tr	07.61	61	1	-	0

JESS Eoin
Aberdeen, 13 December, 1970 Su21-14/SB-2/S-18 (M)

League Club	Source	Date Signed	Seasons Played	Apps	Subs	Gls
Coventry C	Aberdeen	02.96	95-96	28	11	1
Bradford C	Aberdeen	12.00	00-01	60	2	17
Nottingham F	Tr	08.02	02-04	54	32	7

JESSOP Thomas Stanley (Stan)
Everton, 5 August, 1932 Died 1996 (W)

League Club	Source	Date Signed	Seasons Played	Apps	Subs	Gls
Southport	Kidderminster Hrs	08.53	53	11	-	1

JESSOP William (Willie)
Preston, 2 April, 1922 Died 1994 (W)

League Club	Source	Date Signed	Seasons Played	Apps	Subs	Gls
Preston NE	Jnrs	09.40	46	4	-	0
Stockport Co	Tr	04.47	46-47	17	-	4
Oldham Ath	Tr	02.48	47-50	94	-	16
Wrexham	Tr	06.51	51	14	-	2

JEST Sydney (Syd) Thomas
Ramsgate, 4 June, 1943 (FB)

League Club	Source	Date Signed	Seasons Played	Apps	Subs	Gls
Brighton & Hove A	Ramsgate Ath	12.61	61-62	12	-	0

JEVONS Philip (Phil)
Liverpool, 1 August, 1979 (F)

League Club	Source	Date Signed	Seasons Played	Apps	Subs	Gls
Everton	YT	11.97	98-00	2	6	0
Grimsby T	Tr	07.01	01-03	46	17	18
Hull C	L	09.02	02	13	11	3
Yeovil T	Tr	07.04	04	45	1	27

JEWELL Paul
Liverpool, 28 September, 1964 (F)

League Club	Source	Date Signed	Seasons Played	Apps	Subs	Gls
Liverpool	App	09.82				
Wigan Ath	Tr	12.84	84-87	117	20	35
Bradford C	Tr	07.88	88-95	217	52	56
Grimsby T	L	08.95	95	2	3	1

JEWELL Ronald (Ron) Percival
Plymouth, 6 December, 1920 Died 2000 (W)

League Club	Source	Date Signed	Seasons Played	Apps	Subs	Gls
Torquay U	Plymouth Arg (Am)	09.46	46	1	-	0

JEZZARD Bedford Alfred George
Clerkenwell, 19 October, 1927 Died 2005 FLge-3/EB/E-2 (CF)

League Club	Source	Date Signed	Seasons Played	Apps	Subs	Gls
Fulham	Croxley BC	10.48	48-55	292	-	154

JIHAI Sun
Dalian, China, 30 September, 1977 China 62 (FB)

League Club	Source	Date Signed	Seasons Played	Apps	Subs	Gls
Crystal Palace	Dalian Wanda (China)	09.98	98	22	1	0
Manchester C	Dalian Wanda (China)	02.02	01-04	60	14	3

JINKS James (Jimmy) Thomas
Camberwell, 19 August, 1916 Died 1981 (CF)

League Club	Source	Date Signed	Seasons Played	Apps	Subs	Gls
Millwall	Downham Community	11.38	38-47	45	-	16
Fulham	Tr	08.48	48-49	11	-	3
Luton T	Tr	03.50	49-50	9	-	2
Aldershot	Tr	09.51	51	5	-	0

JOACHIM Julian Kevin
Boston, 20 September, 1974 EYth/Eu21-9 (F)

League Club	Source	Date Signed	Seasons Played	Apps	Subs	Gls
Leicester C	YT	09.92	92-95	77	22	25
Aston Villa	Tr	02.96	95-00	90	51	39
Coventry C	Tr	07.01	01-03	41	15	11
Leeds U	Tr	07.04	04	10	17	2
Walsall	L	03.05	04	8	0	6

JOB Joseph-Desire
Lyon, France, 1 December, 1977 Cameroon 48 (F)

League Club	Source	Date Signed	Seasons Played	Apps	Subs	Gls
Middlesbrough	RC Lens (Fr)	08.00	00-04	62	29	16

JOBLING Keith Allen
Grimsby, 26 March, 1934 (CD)

League Club	Source	Date Signed	Seasons Played	Apps	Subs	Gls
Grimsby T	New Waltham	07.53	53-68	450	0	5

JOBLING Kevin Andrew
Sunderland, 1 January, 1968 (M)

League Club	Source	Date Signed	Seasons Played	Apps	Subs	Gls
Leicester C	App	01.86	86-87	4	5	0
Grimsby T	Tr	02.88	87-97	251	34	10
Shrewsbury T	Tr	07.98	98-99	66	3	3

JOBSON Richard Ian
Holderness, 9 May, 1963 EB-2 (CD)

League Club	Source	Date Signed	Seasons Played	Apps	Subs	Gls
Watford	Burton A	11.82	82-84	26	2	4
Hull C	Tr	02.85	84-90	219	2	17
Oldham Ath	Tr	08.90	90-95	188	1	10
Leeds U	Tr	10.95	95-96	22	0	1
Southend U	L	01.98	97	8	0	1
Manchester C	Tr	03.98	97-99	49	1	4
Watford	L	11.00	00	2	0	0
Tranmere Rov	Tr	12.00	00-01	17	0	0
Rochdale	Tr	09.01	01-02	49	2	3

JOEL Stephen (Steve) Philip
Wavertree, 13 October, 1954 (M)

League Club	Source	Date Signed	Seasons Played	Apps	Subs	Gls
Southport	Portmadoc	11.77	77	0	1	0

JOHANNESON Albert Louis
Johannesburg, South Africa, 12 March, 1940 Died 1995 (W)

League Club	Source	Date Signed	Seasons Played	Apps	Subs	Gls
Leeds U	Germiston Callies (SA)	04.61	60-69	170	2	48
York C	Tr	07.70	70-71	26	0	3

JOHANSEN Martin
Golstrup, Denmark, 22 July, 1972 Denmark int (M)

League Club	Source	Date Signed	Seasons Played	Apps	Subs	Gls
Coventry C	FC Copenhagen (Den)	06.97	97	0	2	0

JOHANSEN Michael Bro
Golstrup, Denmark, 22 July, 1972 Denmark int (W)

League Club	Source	Date Signed	Seasons Played	Apps	Subs	Gls
Bolton W	FC Copenhagen (Den)	08.96	96-99	112	25	16

JOHANSEN Rune Buer
Oslo, Norway, 4 September, 1973 (F)

League Club	Source	Date Signed	Seasons Played	Apps	Subs	Gls
Bristol Rov (L)	Tromso (Nor)	11.00	00	0	2	0

JOHANSEN Stig
Svolvaer, Norway, 13 June, 1972 Norway int (F)

League Club	Source	Date Signed	Seasons Played	Apps	Subs	Gls
Southampton	Bodo Glimpt (Nor)	08.97	97	3	3	0
Bristol C	L	02.98	97	2	1	0

JOHANSSON Andreas
Vanersborg, Sweden, 5 July, 1978 Sweden 12 (M)

League Club	Source	Date Signed	Seasons Played	Apps	Subs	Gls
Wigan Ath	Djurgaardens (Swe)	01.05	04	0	1	0

JOHANSSON Jonatan (JJ) Lillebror
Stockholm, Sweden, 16 August, 1975 Fiu21-7/Fi-64 (F)

League Club	Source	Date Signed	Seasons Played	Apps	Subs	Gls
Charlton Ath	Glasgow Rgrs	08.00	00-04	89	55	27

JOHANSSON Nils-Eric
Stockholm, Sweden, 13 January, 1980 Swu21-21/Sw-3 (CD)

League Club	Source	Date Signed	Seasons Played	Apps	Subs	Gls
Blackburn Rov	Nuremburg (Ger)	10.01	01-04	59	27	0

JOHN Collins
Zwandru, Liberia, 17 October, 1985 HoYth/Hou21 (F)

League Club	Source	Date Signed	Seasons Played	Apps	Subs	Gls
Fulham	Twente Enschede (Holl)	01.04	03-04	16	19	8

JOHN Dennis Carl
Swansea, 27 January, 1935 (FB)

League Club	Source	Date Signed	Seasons Played	Apps	Subs	Gls
Plymouth Arg	Jnrs	02.52	55-56	3	-	0
Swansea T	Tr	08.58	58	4	-	0
Scunthorpe U	Tr	08.59	59-61	88	-	0
Millwall	Tr	06.62	62-65	101	5	6

JOHN Dilwyn
Tonypandy, 3 June, 1944 Wu23-1 (G)

League Club	Source	Date Signed	Seasons Played	Apps	Subs	Gls
Cardiff C	Jnrs	06.61	61-66	88	0	0
Swansea T	Tr	03.67	66-69	80	0	0

JOHN Malcolm
Bridgend, 9 December, 1950 (F)

League Club	Source	Date Signed	Seasons Played	Apps	Subs	Gls
Bristol Rov	Swansea C (Am)	09.71	71-73	4	1	2
Northampton T	Tr	03.74	73-74	34	7	9

JOHN Raymond (Ray) Charles
Swansea, 22 November, 1932 (WH)

League Club	Source	Date Signed	Seasons Played	Apps	Subs	Gls
Barnsley	Tottenham H (Am)	05.53				
Exeter C	Tr	07.54	54-58	144	-	18
Oldham Ath	Tr	12.58	58-59	32	-	5

JOHN Stephen (Steve) Paul
Brentwood, 22 December, 1966 (CD)

League Club	Source	Date Signed	Seasons Played	Apps	Subs	Gls
Orient	App	12.84	85-86	23	0	0

JOHN Stern
Tunapuna, Trinidad, 30 October, 1976 Trinidad 16 (F)

League Club	Source	Date Signed	Seasons Played	Apps	Subs	Gls
Nottingham F	Columbus Crew (USA)	11.99	99-01	49	23	18
Birmingham C	Tr	02.02	01-04	42	35	16
Coventry C	Tr	09.04	04	25	5	11

JOHN-BAPTISTE Alexander (Alex) Aaron
Sutton-in-Ashfield, 31 January, 1986 (CD)

League Club	Source	Date Signed	Seasons Played	Apps	Subs	Gls
Mansfield T	Sch	02.03	02-04	59	3	1

JOHNROSE Leonard (Lenny)
Preston, 29 November, 1969 (M)

League Club	Source	Date Signed	Seasons Played	Apps	Subs	Gls
Blackburn Rov	YT	06.88	87-91	20	22	11
Preston NE	L	01.92	91	1	2	1
Hartlepool U	Tr	02.92	91-93	59	7	11
Bury	Tr	12.93	93-98	181	7	19
Burnley	Tr	02.99	98-02	51	27	4
Bury	Tr	10.02	02	5	1	0
Swansea C	Tr	01.03	02-03	36	4	3
Burnley	Tr	03.04	03	4	3	0

JOHNS Mark
Bristol, 17 May, 1959 (F)

League Club	Source	Date Signed	Seasons Played	Apps	Subs	Gls
Bristol Rov	Bristol Manor Farm	09.86	86	2	0	1

JOHNS Nicholas (Nicky) Paul
Bristol, 8 June, 1957 (G)

League Club	Source	Date Signed	Seasons Played	Apps	Subs	Gls
Millwall	Minehead	02.76	76-77	50	0	0
Sheffield U	Tampa Bay (USA)	09.78	78	1	0	0
Charlton Ath	Tr	12.78	78-87	288	0	0
Queens Park Rgrs	Tr	12.87	87-88	10	0	0
Maidstone U	Tr	10.89	89-90	42	0	0

JOHNS Francis Stanley (Stan)
Liverpool, 28 June, 1924 Died 1986 (IF)

League Club	Source	Date Signed	Seasons Played	Apps	Subs	Gls
West Ham U	South Liverpool	08.50	50	6	-	2

JOHNSEN Erland
Fredrikstad, Norway, 5 April, 1967 Norway int (CD)

League Club	Source	Date Signed	Seasons Played	Apps	Subs	Gls
Chelsea	Bayern Munich (Ger)	12.89	89-96	135	10	1

JOHNSEN Jean Ronny
Sandefjord, Norway, 10 June, 1969 Norway 61 (CD)

League Club	Source	Date Signed	Seasons Played	Apps	Subs	Gls
Manchester U	Besiktas (Tu)	07.96	96-01	85	14	7
Aston Villa	Tr	08.02	02-03	46	3	1
Newcastle U	Tr	09.04	04	3	0	0

JOHNSON Alan
Stoke-on-Trent, 13 March, 1947 (W)

League Club	Source	Date Signed	Seasons Played	Apps	Subs	Gls
Port Vale	Jnrs	09.64	65	2	0	1

JOHNSON Alan Keith
Billinge, 19 February, 1971 (CD)

League Club	Source	Date Signed	Seasons Played	Apps	Subs	Gls
Wigan Ath	YT	04.89	88-93	163	17	13
Lincoln C	Tr	02.94	93-95	57	6	0
Preston NE	L	09.95	95	2	0	0
Rochdale	Tr	08.96	96-98	59	3	4

JOHNSON Albert
Morpeth, 7 September, 1923 Died 1989 (FB)

League Club	Source	Date Signed	Seasons Played	Apps	Subs	Gls
Bradford C	Ashington	05.47	46-49	35	-	0

JOHNSON Albert
Weaverham, 15 July, 1920 (W)

League Club	Source	Date Signed	Seasons Played	Apps	Subs	Gls
Everton	PCI	05.39	46-47	9	-	0
Chesterfield	Tr	09.48	48	19	-	1

JOHNSON Andrew (Andy)
Bedford, 10 February, 1981 EYth/Eu20/E-2 (F)

League Club	Source	Date Signed	Seasons Played	Apps	Subs	Gls
Birmingham C	Jnrs	03.98	98-01	44	39	8
Crystal Palace	Tr	08.02	02-04	104	3	59

JOHNSON Andrew (Andy) James
Bristol, 2 May, 1974 EYth/W-15 (M)

League Club	Source	Date Signed	Seasons Played	Apps	Subs	Gls
Norwich C	YT	03.92	91-96	56	10	13
Nottingham F	Tr	07.97	97-01	102	17	9
West Bromwich A	Tr	09.01	01-04	113	11	7

JOHNSON Arthur
Liverpool, 23 January, 1933 (G)

League Club	Source	Date Signed	Seasons Played	Apps	Subs	Gls
Blackburn Rov	Jnrs	01.50	51	1	-	0
Halifax T	Tr	03.55	54-59	215	-	0
Wrexham	Tr	06.60	60-61	52	-	0
Chester	L	08.62	62	3	-	0

JOHNSON Bradley (Brad) Paul
Hackney, 28 April, 1987 (M)

League Club	Source	Date Signed	Seasons Played	Apps	Subs	Gls
Cambridge U	Jnrs	11.04	04	0	1	0

JOHNSON Brian
Gateshead, 20 March, 1936 (CF)

League Club	Source	Date Signed	Seasons Played	Apps	Subs	Gls
Millwall		10.57	57	7	-	2

JOHNSON Brian
Newcastle, 12 November, 1948 (W)

League Club	Source	Date Signed	Seasons Played	Apps	Subs	Gls
Sunderland	App	11.65				
Luton T	Tr	07.66	66-67	9	1	0

JOHNSON Brian Arthur Bentley
Rudheath, 28 May, 1930 (W)

League Club	Source	Date Signed	Seasons Played	Apps	Subs	Gls
Wrexham		04.50	50-51	14	-	2

JOHNSON Brian Frederick
Isleworth, 21 October, 1955 (W)

League Club	Source	Date Signed	Seasons Played	Apps	Subs	Gls
Plymouth Arg	App	08.73	73-80	186	11	40
Torquay U	L	01.79	78	5	0	2
Torquay U	L	09.81	81	2	0	0

JOHNSON Brian Joseph
Huyton, 29 October, 1948 (F)

League Club	Source	Date Signed	Seasons Played	Apps	Subs	Gls
Tranmere Rov	Jnrs	05.67	68	0	1	0

JOHNSON Christopher (Chris)
Brighton, 25 January, 1979 (M)

League Club	Source	Date Signed	Seasons Played	Apps	Subs	Gls
Watford	YT	02.97	96	1	0	0

JOHNSON Damien Michael
Lisburn, 18 November, 1978 NIYth/NIu21-11/NI-43 (W)

League Club	Source	Date Signed	Seasons Played	Apps	Subs	Gls
Blackburn Rov	YT	02.96	98-01	43	17	3
Nottingham F	L	01.98	97	5	1	0
Birmingham C	Tr	03.02	01-04	104	5	3

JOHNSON David
South Shields, 19 November, 1955 EYth (F)

League Club	Source	Date Signed	Seasons Played	Apps	Subs	Gls
Bristol C	Doncaster Rov (Am)	05.74				
Hartlepool	Tr	02.75	74	1	0	0

JOHNSON David
Blackburn, 17 April, 1950 (G)

League Club	Source	Date Signed	Seasons Played	Apps	Subs	Gls
Tranmere Rov	Atherstone T	07.74	74	3	0	0
Southport	L	01.76	75	6	0	0

JOHNSON David Alan
Dinnington, 29 October, 1970 (F)

League Club	Source	Date Signed	Seasons Played	Apps	Subs	Gls
Sheffield Wed	YT	07.89	91	5	1	0
Hartlepool U	L	10.91	91	7	0	2
Hartlepool U	L	11.92	92	3	0	0
Lincoln C	Tr	08.93	93-95	75	14	13

JOHNSON David Anthony
Kingston, Jamaica, 15 August, 1976 ESch/EB-1/Ja-4 (F)

League Club	Source	Date Signed	Seasons Played	Apps	Subs	Gls
Manchester U	YT	07.94				
Bury	Tr	07.95	95-97	72	25	18
Ipswich T	Tr	11.97	97-00	121	10	55
Nottingham F	Tr	01.01	00-04	110	21	43
Sheffield Wed	L	02.02	01	7	0	2
Burnley	L	03.02	01	8	0	5
Sheffield U	L	03.05	04	0	4	0

JOHNSON David Donald
Northampton, 10 March, 1967 (FB)

League Club	Source	Date Signed	Seasons Played	Apps	Subs	Gls
Northampton T	Irthlingborough Dmnds	07.89	89-91	23	24	0

JOHNSON David Edward
Liverpool, 23 October, 1951 E-8 (F)

League Club	Source	Date Signed	Seasons Played	Apps	Subs	Gls
Everton	App	04.69	70-72	47	2	11
Ipswich T	Tr	11.72	72-75	134	2	35
Liverpool	Tr	08.76	76-81	128	20	55
Everton	Tr	08.82	82-83	32	8	4
Barnsley	L	02.84	83	4	0	1
Manchester C	Tr	03.84	83	4	2	1
Preston NE	Tulsa (USA)	10.84	84	20	4	3

JOHNSON David Nicholas Conrad
Gloucester, 26 December, 1962 (W)

League Club	Source	Date Signed	Seasons Played	Apps	Subs	Gls
Watford	Redhill	03.82	81-83	4	3	0
Peterborough U	Tr	08.84	84-85	28	7	4

JOHNSON Dennis
Sunderland, 20 May, 1934 (IF)

League Club	Source	Date Signed	Seasons Played	Apps	Subs	Gls
Hartlepools U	Seaham CW	02.54	57	2	-	0

JOHNSON Edward (Eddie) William
Chester, 20 September, 1984 EYth/Eu20 (F)

League Club	Source	Date Signed	Seasons Played	Apps	Subs	Gls
Manchester U	YT	10.01				
Coventry C	L	07.04	04	20	6	5

JOHNSON Eric
Moulton, Cheshire, 25 May, 1927 Died 1992 (W)

League Club	Source	Date Signed	Seasons Played	Apps	Subs	Gls
Coventry C	Winsford U	09.52	52-56	90	-	6
Torquay U	Tr	07.57	57-58	49	-	1

JOHNSON Eric
Birkenhead, 16 December, 1944 (WH)

League Club	Source	Date Signed	Seasons Played	Apps	Subs	Gls
Wrexham	Everton (Am)	06.63	63-65	28	0	0

JOHNSON Gary Jack
Peckham, 14 September, 1959 (F)

League Club	Source	Date Signed	Seasons Played	Apps	Subs	Gls
Chelsea	App	09.77	78-80	16	3	9
Brentford	Tr	12.80	80-82	55	5	13
Aldershot	PG Rgrs (SA)	08.85	85-87	73	2	20

JOHNSON Gavin
Stowmarket, 10 October, 1970 (M)

League Club	Source	Date Signed	Seasons Played	Apps	Subs	Gls
Ipswich T	YT	03.89	88-94	114	18	11
Luton T	Tr	07.95	95	4	1	0
Wigan Ath	Tr	12.95	95-97	82	2	8
Colchester U	Dunfermline Ath	11.99	99-04	134	13	13

JOHNSON George
Davyhulme, 27 April, 1936 (IF)

League Club	Source	Date Signed	Seasons Played	Apps	Subs	Gls
Rochdale	Gerrards	12.54	54	1	-	0
Southport	Ashton U	01.63	62	6	-	0

JOHNSON George
Esh, 6 October, 1932 Died 2002 (W)

League Club	Source	Date Signed	Seasons Played	Apps	Subs	Gls
Lincoln C	Langley Park Jnrs	09.51	51	3	-	1

League Club	Source	Date Signed	Seasons Played	Career Record Apps	Subs	Gls
JOHNSON Glen McLeod						
Greenwich, 23 August, 1984 EYth/Eu20/Eu21-12/E-4						(CD)
West Ham U	YT	08.01	02	14	1	0
Millwall	L	10.02	02	7	1	0
Chelsea	Tr	07.03	03-04	30	6	3
JOHNSON Lloyd Glenn						
Vancouver, Canada, 22 April, 1951						(F)
West Bromwich A	Vancouver (Can)	10.69	70-71	2	2	0
JOHNSON Glenn Paul						
Sydney, Australia, 16 July, 1972						(F)
Cardiff C	Blacktown C (Aus)	03.96	95	1	4	0
JOHNSON Glenn William						
Barrow, 7 March, 1952 EYth						(G)
Arsenal	App	07.69				
Doncaster Rov	Tr	06.70	70-72	95	0	0
Walsall	L	12.72	72	3	0	0
Aldershot	Tr	07.73	73-82	424	0	0
JOHNSON Ian Grant						
Dundee, 24 March, 1972 Su21-6						(M)
Huddersfield T	Dundee U	11.97	97-98	64	1	5
JOHNSON William Herbert (Bert)						
Stockton, 4 June, 1916 EWar-2						(WH)
Charlton Ath	Spennymoor U	03.39	46-52	142	-	1
JOHNSON Howard						
Sheffield, 17 July, 1925						(CD)
Sheffield U	Norton Woodseats	03.51	50-56	92	-	0
York C	Tr	08.57	57	28	-	0
JOHNSON Ian						
Oldham, 11 November, 1960						(FB)
Rochdale	Curzon Ashton	09.84	84-86	74	7	1
JOHNSON Ian						
Newcastle, 14 February, 1969						(CD)
Northampton T	Gateshead	11.87	88	2	1	0
Torquay U	Whitley Bay	11.92	92	9	0	1
JOHNSON Ian						
Sunderland, 1 September, 1975						(W)
Middlesbrough	YT	01.94	93	1	1	0
Bradford C	Tr	01.95	94	1	1	0
JOHNSON James (Jim)						
Stockton, 26 March, 1923 Died 1987						(CF)
Grimsby T	York C (Am)	03.45	46-49	6	-	1
Carlisle U	Tr	03.51	50	8	-	0
JOHNSON Jeffrey (Jeff)						
Manchester, 29 October, 1950 ESemiPro						(M)
Stockport Co	Hyde U	09.76	76	6	2	0
JOHNSON Jeffrey (Jeff) David						
Cardiff, 26 November, 1953 WSch						(M)
Manchester C	App	12.70	70-71	4	2	0
Swansea C	L	07.72	72	37	1	5
Crystal Palace	Tr	12.73	73-75	82	5	4
Sheffield Wed	Tr	07.76	76-80	175	5	6
Newport Co	Tr	08.81	81	34	0	2
Gillingham	Tr	09.82	82-84	85	3	4
Port Vale	Tr	07.85	85	10	0	1
JOHNSON Jemal Pierre						
New Jersey, USA, 3 May, 1984						(F)
Blackburn Rov	YT	05.02	04	0	3	0
JOHNSON Jermaine						
Kingston, Jamaica, 25 June, 1980 Jamaica int						(M)
Bolton W	Tivoli Gardens (Jam)	09.01	01-02	4	8	0
Oldham Ath	Tr	11.03	03-04	31	8	9
JOHNSON John (Johnny)						
Hazel Grove, 11 December, 1921 Died 2003						(W)
Stockport Co		01.41				
Millwall	Tr	12.45	46-54	294	-	42
Millwall	Tonbridge	11.55	55-56	15	-	4
JOHNSON John						
South Shields, 4 February, 1929						(IF)
Manchester C		05.49				
Gateshead	North Shields	01.51	50-54	75	-	13
JOHNSON John (Jack) William						
Newcastle, 12 February, 1919 Died 1975						(W)
Huddersfield T	Leicester Nomads	06.36	36-38	18	-	2
Grimsby T	Tr	04.39	46-47	44	-	2
JOHNSON Joseph (Joe)						
South Kirkby, 16 May, 1916						(WH)
Doncaster Rov	Scarborough	12.38				
Southport	Folkestone	12.46	46	5	-	0
JOHNSON Joseph (Joe) Robert						
Greenock, 13 September, 1920						(IF)
Lincoln C	Glasgow Rgrs	11.52	52	11	-	2
Workington	Tr	07.53	53	38	-	5
JOHNSON Kenneth (Ken)						
Hartlepool, 15 February, 1931						(IF)
Hartlepools U	Seaton Holy Trinity	05.49	49-63	384	-	98
JOHNSON Kevin Peter						
Doncaster, 29 August, 1952						(M)
Sheffield Wed	App	07.70	71	0	1	0
Southend U	Tr	09.72	72-73	12	4	1
Gillingham	L	02.74	73	1	0	0
Workington	Tr	07.74	74	15	0	1
Hartlepool	Tr	02.75	74-76	60	1	8
Huddersfield T	Tr	09.76	76-77	80	1	23
Halifax T	Tr	08.78	78-80	51	6	10
Hartlepool U	Tr	01.81	80-83	74	13	3
JOHNSON Lee David						
Newmarket, 7 June, 1981 ESemiPro-5						(M)
Watford	YT	10.98				
Brighton & Hove A	Tr	09.00				
Brentford	Tr	03.01				
Yeovil T	Tr	07.01	03-04	89	0	12
JOHNSON Leon Dean						
Shoreditch, 10 May, 1981						(CD)
Southend U	YT	11.99	00-01	43	5	3
Gillingham	Tr	08.02	02-04	32	14	0
JOHNSON Marvin Anthony						
Wembley, 29 October, 1968						(CD)
Luton T	App	11.86	87-01	352	21	7
JOHNSON Michael (Mick)						
York, 4 October, 1933 Died 2004						(W)
Newcastle U	Jnrs	04.51				
Brighton & Hove A	Blyth Spartans	12.55	56	2	-	0
Fulham	Gloucester C	08.58	58-61	23	-	6
Doncaster Rov	Tr	07.62	62	15	-	2
Barrow	Tr	03.63	62	12	-	2
JOHNSON Michael (Mike) George						
Swansea, 13 October, 1941 Died 1991 Wu23-2/W-1						(WH)
Swansea T	Jnrs	10.58	59-65	165	0	0
JOHNSON Michael (Mike) James						
Oxford, 24 February, 1928						(IF)
Preston NE	Lytham St Annes	09.50				
Accrington St	Tr	06.51	51	3	-	0
JOHNSON Michael Owen						
Nottingham, 4 July, 1973 Jamaica 14						(CD)
Notts Co	YT	07.91	91-94	102	5	0
Birmingham C	Tr	09.95	95-02	227	35	13
Derby Co	Tr	08.03	03-04	74	1	2
JOHNSON Neil Joseph						
Grimsby, 3 December, 1946						(W)
Tottenham H	App	06.64	65-70	27	7	5
Charlton Ath	L	02.71	70	1	0	0
Torquay U	Tr	07.71	71	5	1	1
JOHNSON Nigel Meridon						
Rotherham, 23 June, 1964						(CD)
Rotherham U	App	08.82	82-84	89	0	1
Manchester C	Tr	06.85	85	4	0	0
Rotherham U	Tr	07.87	87-92	172	3	9
JOHNSON Owen Edmund						
Grimsby, 13 November, 1919						(W)
Derby Co		11.37				
Bradford C	Tr	10.46	46	10	-	1
JOHNSON Paul						
Stoke-on-Trent, 25 May, 1959						(FB)
Stoke C	App	05.77	78-80	33	1	0
Shrewsbury T	Tr	05.81	81-86	178	2	3
York C	Tr	07.87	87-88	83	0	1
JOHNSON Paul						
Scunthorpe, 10 May, 1963						(G)
Scunthorpe U	App	05.81	81	2	0	0
Scunthorpe U		01.85	85	12	0	0

League Club	Source	Date Signed	Seasons Played	Career Record Apps	Subs	Gls
JOHNSON Paul Anthony						
Stoke-on-Trent, 19 September, 1955						(M)
Stoke C	App	06.73	76-81	51	5	0
Chester	Tr	08.82	82	18	1	0
JOHNSON Peter						
Rotherham, 31 July, 1931						(FB)
Rotherham U	Rawmarsh Welfare	03.53	53-57	153		23
Sheffield Wed	Tr	12.57	57-64	181	-	6
Peterborough U	Tr	07.65	65-66	42	0	1
JOHNSON Peter Edward						
Harrogate, 5 October, 1958						(FB)
Middlesbrough	App	10.76	77-79	42	1	0
Newcastle U	Tr	10.80	80	16	0	0
Bristol C	L	09.82	82	20	0	0
Doncaster Rov	Tr	03.83	82	12	0	0
Darlington	Tr	08.83	83-84	89	0	2
Crewe Alex	Whitby T	10.85	85	8	0	0
Exeter C	Whitby T	03.86	85	5	0	0
Southend U	Tr	08.86	86-88	126	0	3
Gillingham	Tr	08.89	89-90	67	2	2
Peterborough U	Airdrie	10.91	91	11	0	0
JOHNSON Peter James						
Hackney, 18 February, 1954						(W)
Orient	Tottenham H (Am)	04.72	71-72	1	2	0
Crystal Palace	AEK Athens (Gre)	10.74	74-75	5	2	0
Bournemouth	Tr	06.76	76-78	99	8	11
JOHNSON Victor **Ralph**						
Hethersett, 15 April, 1922						(CF)
Norwich C	Chesterfield (Am)	05.46	46	18	-	8
Leyton Orient	Tr	04.47	47-48	7	-	2
JOHNSON Richard Mark						
Kurri Kurri, Australia, 27 April, 1974 Australia 1						(M)
Watford	YT	05.92	91-02	210	32	20
Northampton T	L	02.03	02	5	1	1
Stoke C	Tr	11.03	03	3	4	0
Queens Park Rgrs	Tr	02.04	03-04	16	1	0
MK Dons	L	10.04	04	2	0	0
JOHNSON Richard (Dickie) Raymond						
Liverpool, 20 February, 1953						(G)
Tranmere Rov	Jnrs	08.72	71-81	355	0	0
JOHNSON Robert (Bob) Emmerson Oliver						
Fencehouses, 25 October, 1911 Died 1982						(CD)
Burnley	Bishop Auckland	09.34	34-48	78	-	0
JOHNSON Robert (Robbie) Nicholas						
Kensington, 30 March, 1962						(FB)
Arsenal	App	02.80				
Brentford	Tr	03.81	80-81	2	0	0
JOHNSON Robert (Rob) Simon						
Bedford, 22 February, 1962						(FB)
Luton T	App	08.79	83-88	91	6	0
Lincoln C	L	08.83	83	4	0	0
Leicester C	Tr	08.89	89-90	19	6	0
Barnet	Tr	08.91	91	2	0	0
JOHNSON Rodney (Rod)						
Leeds, 8 January, 1945 EYth						(M)
Leeds U	Jnrs	03.62	62-67	18	4	4
Doncaster Rov	Tr	03.68	67-70	106	1	23
Rotherham U	Tr	12.70	70-73	108	2	8
Bradford C	Tr	12.73	73-78	190	2	16
JOHNSON Roger						
Ashford, 28 April, 1983						(CD)
Wycombe W	YT	07.01	99-04	101	11	12
JOHNSON Ross Yorke						
Brighton, 2 February, 1976						(CD)
Brighton & Hove A	YT	07.94	93-99	113	19	2
Colchester U	Tr	01.00	99-01	47	5	1
JOHNSON Roy						
Swindon, 18 May, 1933						(CF)
Swindon T		04.52	52-55	31	-	4
JOHNSON Samuel (Sam)						
Barnton, 10 February, 1919 Died 1994						(FB)
Hull C	Northwich Vic	04.47	46-47	10	-	0
JOHNSON Seth Art Maurice						
Birmingham, 12 March, 1979 EYth/Eu21-15/E-1						(M)
Crewe Alex	YT	07.96	96-98	89	4	6
Derby Co	Tr	05.99	99-01	73	0	2
Leeds U	Tr	10.01	01-04	43	11	4

League Club	Source	Date Signed	Seasons Played	Career Record Apps	Subs	Gls
JOHNSON Simon Ainsley						
West Bromwich, 9 March, 1983 EYth/Eu20						(F)
Leeds U	YT	07.00	02-04	3	8	0
Hull C	L	08.02	02	4	8	2
Blackpool	L	12.03	03	3	1	1
Sunderland	L	09.04	04	1	4	0
Doncaster Rov	L	12.04	04	8	3	3
Barnsley	L	02.05	04	10	1	2
JOHNSON Stephen (Steve) Anthony						
Liverpool, 23 June, 1957						(F)
Bury	Altrincham	11.77	77-82	139	15	52
Rochdale	Tr	08.83	83	17	2	7
Wigan Ath	Tr	02.84	83-84	50	1	18
Bristol C	Tr	03.85	84-85	14	7	3
Rochdale	L	12.85	85	3	3	1
Chester C	L	03.86	85	10	0	6
Scunthorpe U	Tr	07.86	86-87	59	13	20
Chester C	Tr	08.88	88	35	3	10
Rochdale	Huskvana (Swe)	10.89	89	20	4	4
JOHNSON Steven (Steve)						
Nottingham, 23 March, 1961						(FB)
Mansfield T	App	03.79	80	1	0	0
JOHNSON Terence (Terry)						
Newcastle, 30 August, 1949						(W)
Newcastle U	Longbenton Jnrs	05.67				
Darlington	L	11.69	69	4	0	1
Southend U	Tr	01.71	70-74	156	2	35
Brentford	Tr	11.74	74-76	98	3	27
JOHNSON Thomas (Tom)						
Ecclesfield, 4 May, 1911 Died 1983						(CD)
Sheffield U	Ecclesfield U	09.28	29-38	183	-	0
Lincoln C	Tr	03.46	46-48	75	-	0
JOHNSON Thomas (Tom)						
Gateshead, 21 September, 1921 Died 1999						(IF)
Gateshead		09.41	46-47	52	-	19
Nottingham F	Tr	08.48	48-51	68	-	27
JOHNSON Thomas (Tom)						
Stockton, 5 March, 1926						(WH)
Middlesbrough		01.45				
Darlington	Tr	08.47	47	6	-	1
Bradford PA	Horden Colliery	08.52	52	1	-	0
JOHNSON Thomas (Tommy)						
Newcastle, 15 January, 1971 Eu21-7						(F)
Notts Co	YT	01.89	88-91	100	18	47
Derby Co	Tr	03.92	91-94	91	7	30
Aston Villa	Tr	01.95	94-96	38	19	13
Everton (L)	Glasgow Celtic	09.99	99	0	3	0
Sheffield Wed	Glasgow Celtic	09.01	01	8	0	3
Gillingham	Kilmarnock	08.02	02-04	20	29	7
Sheffield U	Tr	02.05	04	1	0	0
JOHNSSON Julian Schantz						
Faroe Islands, 24 February, 1975 FaroeIs-43						(M)
Hull C	Sogndal IF (Nor)	06.01	01	38	2	4
JOHNSTON Alan Keith						
Workington, 23 September, 1944						(FB)
Blackpool	Jnrs	10.61				
Workington	Tr	07.62	62-64	65	-	0
JOHNSTON Allan						
Glasgow, 14 December, 1973 Su21-3/SB-2/S-18						(W)
Sunderland	Rennes (Fr)	03.97	96-98	82	4	19
Birmingham C	L	10.99	99	7	2	0
Bolton W	Tr	01.00	99	17	2	3
Middlesbrough	Glasgow Rgrs	09.01	01	13	4	1
Sheffield Wed	L	12.02	02	12	0	2
JOHNSTON Clement (Clem)						
Stoneyburn, 3 September, 1933						(IF)
Walsall	Haddington Ath	08.56	56	7	-	0
JOHNSTON Craig Peter						
Johannesburg, South Africa, 25 June, 1960 Eu21-2						(M)
Middlesbrough	App	02.78	77-80	61	3	16
Liverpool	Tr	04.81	81-87	165	25	30
JOHNSTON David Douglas						
Scothern, 17 September, 1941						(FB)
Leicester C	Bishop Auckland	02.60				
Exeter C	Tr	05.62	62	10	-	0
Stockport Co	Tr	07.63	63	26	-	0

JOHNSTON George
Glasgow, 21 March, 1947 (F)

League Club	Source	Date Signed	Seasons Played	Apps	Subs	Gls
Cardiff C	Maryhill Harp	05.64	64-66	57	2	20
Arsenal	Tr	03.67	67-68	17	4	3
Birmingham C	Tr	05.69	69	6	3	1
Walsall	L	09.70	70	5	0	1
Fulham	Tr	10.70	70-71	33	6	12
Hereford U	Tr	08.72	72	15	3	5
Newport Co	Tr	09.73	73	2	1	0

JOHNSTON Henry (Harry)
Manchester, 26 September, 1919 Died 1973 FLge-4/E-10 (WH)

League Club	Source	Date Signed	Seasons Played	Apps	Subs	Gls
Blackpool	Droylsden Ath	10.36	37-54	387	-	11

JOHNSTON Ian
Workington, 19 September, 1957 (CD)

League Club	Source	Date Signed	Seasons Played	Apps	Subs	Gls
Workington	Jnrs	08.75	74-76	46	2	0

JOHNSTON James (Jimmy) Cruickshank
Aberdeen, 12 April, 1923 (WH)

League Club	Source	Date Signed	Seasons Played	Apps	Subs	Gls
Leicester C	Peterhead	04.47	48-49	35	-	0
Reading	Tr	05.50	50-52	120	-	0
Swindon T	Tr	03.53	52-54	75	-	0

JOHNSTON John (Johnny)
Belfast, 2 May, 1947 NIu23-1 (M)

League Club	Source	Date Signed	Seasons Played	Apps	Subs	Gls
Blackpool	Glentoran	11.68	68-71	19	6	2
Halifax T	L	10.71	71	3	1	1
Bradford C	Tr	07.72	72-73	55	4	4
Southport	Tr	07.74	74-75	82	0	6
Halifax T	Tr	07.76	76-78	67	6	7

JOHNSTON Leslie (Les) Hamilton
Glasgow, 16 August, 1920 Died 2001 S-2 (IF)

League Club	Source	Date Signed	Seasons Played	Apps	Subs	Gls
Stoke C	Glasgow Celtic	10.49	49-52	88	-	22
Shrewsbury T	Tr	07.53	53	16	-	6

JOHNSTON Maurice (Mo) John Giblin
Glasgow, 30 April, 1963 Su21-3/S-38 (F)

League Club	Source	Date Signed	Seasons Played	Apps	Subs	Gls
Watford	Partick Th	11.83	83-84	37	1	23
Everton	Glasgow Rgrs	11.91	91-92	28	6	10

JOHNSTON Christopher Patrick (Pat)
Dublin, 16 July, 1924 Died 1971 LoI-3 (WH)

League Club	Source	Date Signed	Seasons Played	Apps	Subs	Gls
Middlesbrough	Shelbourne	12.47	47-48	3	-	0
Grimsby T	Tr	02.49	48-56	250	-	16

JOHNSTON Raymond (Ray)
Bristol, 5 May, 1981 ESch (G)

League Club	Source	Date Signed	Seasons Played	Apps	Subs	Gls
Bristol Rov	YT	06.99	98	1	0	0

JOHNSTON Robert
Carlisle, 28 January, 1933 (WH)

League Club	Source	Date Signed	Seasons Played	Apps	Subs	Gls
Carlisle U	Jnrs	11.51	51-59	119	-	1

JOHNSTON Ronald (Ron)
Glasgow, 3 April, 1921 Died 1995 (CF)

League Club	Source	Date Signed	Seasons Played	Apps	Subs	Gls
Rochdale	Glasgow Perthshire	11.47	47	17	-	7
Exeter C	Tr	06.48	48	10	-	2
Brighton & Hove A	Headington U	11.50	50	1	-	0

JOHNSTON Stanley (Stan)
Wallsend, 23 February, 1934 (IF)

League Club	Source	Date Signed	Seasons Played	Apps	Subs	Gls
Fulham	Jnrs	08.51				
Gateshead	Durham C	09.54	54	8	-	1

JOHNSTON Thomas (Tommy) Bourhill
Loanhead, 18 August, 1927 (CF)

League Club	Source	Date Signed	Seasons Played	Apps	Subs	Gls
Darlington	Kilmarnock	04.51	51	27	-	9
Oldham Ath	Tr	03.52	51	5	-	3
Norwich C	Tr	06.52	52-54	60	-	28
Newport Co	Tr	10.54	54-55	63	-	46
Leyton Orient	Tr	02.56	55-57	87	-	70
Blackburn Rov	Tr	03.58	57-58	36	-	22
Leyton Orient	Tr	02.59	58-60	93	-	51
Gillingham	Tr	09.61	61	35	-	10

JOHNSTON Thomas (Tom) Deans
Coldstream, 30 December, 1918 Died 1994 (W)

League Club	Source	Date Signed	Seasons Played	Apps	Subs	Gls
Nottingham F	Peterborough U	05.44	46-47	64	-	26
Notts Co	Tr	08.48	48-56	267	-	88

JOHNSTON William (Billy)
(G)

League Club	Source	Date Signed	Seasons Played	Apps	Subs	Gls
Barrow	Morton	04.47	46	1	-	0

JOHNSTON William (Billy) Cecil
Coalisland, 21 May, 1942 IrLge-7/NI-2 (M)

League Club	Source	Date Signed	Seasons Played	Apps	Subs	Gls
Oldham Ath	Glenavon	06.66	66-68	28	1	6

JOHNSTON William (Willie) James
Sunderland, 3 September, 1948 (F)

League Club	Source	Date Signed	Seasons Played	Apps	Subs	Gls
Northampton T	Durham C	07.67	67	0	1	0

JOHNSTON William (Willie) McClure
Glasgow, 19 December, 1946 Su23-2/SLge-2/S-22 (W)

League Club	Source	Date Signed	Seasons Played	Apps	Subs	Gls
West Bromwich A	Glasgow Rgrs	12.72	72-78	203	4	18
Birmingham C	Vancouver (Can)	10.79	79	15	0	0

JOHNSTONE Cyril
Hamilton, 21 December, 1920 (FB)

League Club	Source	Date Signed	Seasons Played	Apps	Subs	Gls
Exeter C	Hamilton Academical	07.47	47-50	134	-	0

JOHNSTONE Derek Joseph
Dundee, 4 November, 1953 Su23-6/SLge-2/S-14 (F)

League Club	Source	Date Signed	Seasons Played	Apps	Subs	Gls
Chelsea	Glasgow Rgrs	09.83	83-84	1	3	0

JOHNSTONE Eric
Newcastle, 22 March, 1943 (W)

League Club	Source	Date Signed	Seasons Played	Apps	Subs	Gls
Carlisle U	Tow Law T	06.63	63-64	15	-	3
Darlington	Tr	07.65	65-66	25	1	9

JOHNSTONE Glenn Paul
Kenya, 5 June, 1967 (G)

League Club	Source	Date Signed	Seasons Played	Apps	Subs	Gls
Preston NE	Lancaster C	01.93	92	10	0	0

JOHNSTONE Ian Donaldson
Galashiels, 2 March, 1939 Died 1993 (IF)

League Club	Source	Date Signed	Seasons Played	Apps	Subs	Gls
Colchester U	Ormiston Primrose	06.58	58-59	2	-	0

JOHNSTONE James (Jimmy) Connolly
Uddingston, 30 September, 1944 Su23-2/SLge-4/S-23 (W)

League Club	Source	Date Signed	Seasons Played	Apps	Subs	Gls
Sheffield U	Glasgow Celtic	11.75	75-76	11	0	2

JOHNSTONE Robert
Cleland, 13 September, 1918 (FB)

League Club	Source	Date Signed	Seasons Played	Apps	Subs	Gls
Tranmere Rov	Raith Rov	09.46	46-47	40	-	0

JOHNSTONE Robert (Bobby)
Selkirk, 7 September, 1929 Died 2001 SLge-6/S-17 (IF)

League Club	Source	Date Signed	Seasons Played	Apps	Subs	Gls
Manchester C	Hibernian	03.55	54-59	124	-	42
Oldham Ath	Hibernian	10.60	60-64	143	-	35

JOHNSTONE Robert (Bobby) Gordon
Edinburgh, 19 November, 1934 (WH)

League Club	Source	Date Signed	Seasons Played	Apps	Subs	Gls
West Ham U	Ormiston Primrose	04.53	56	2	-	0
Ipswich T	Tr	07.57	57-58	35	-	4

JOHNSTONE Stanley (Stan)
Shiremoor, 28 October, 1940 (W)

League Club	Source	Date Signed	Seasons Played	Apps	Subs	Gls
Gateshead	Durham C	12.58	58	5	-	1

JOICEY Brian
Winlaton, 19 December, 1945 (F)

League Club	Source	Date Signed	Seasons Played	Apps	Subs	Gls
Coventry C	North Shields	06.69	69-71	31	8	9
Sheffield Wed	Tr	08.71	71-75	144	1	48
Barnsley	Tr	07.76	76-78	77	16	43

JOKANOVIC Slavisa
Novi Sad, Yugoslavia, 16 August, 1968 Yugoslavia 64 (M)

League Club	Source	Date Signed	Seasons Played	Apps	Subs	Gls
Chelsea	Dep la Coruna (Sp)	10.00	00-01	19	20	0

JOL Maarten (Martin) Cornelius
Den Haag, Holland, 16 January, 1956 (M)

League Club	Source	Date Signed	Seasons Played	Apps	Subs	Gls
West Bromwich A	Twente Enschede (Holl)	10.81	81-83	63	1	4
Coventry C	Tr	07.84	84	15	0	0

JOLLEY Charles (Charlie)
Bebington, 3 March, 1936 EYth (CF)

League Club	Source	Date Signed	Seasons Played	Apps	Subs	Gls
Tranmere Rov	Liverpool (Am)	07.53	53-54	6	-	2
Chester	Tr	05.55	55	7	-	3

JOLLEY Terence (Terry) Arthur
Greenhithe, 13 April, 1959 (F)

League Club	Source	Date Signed	Seasons Played	Apps	Subs	Gls
Gillingham	Jnrs	11.76	76-79	14	7	5

JONES Alan
Abermorddu, 13 January, 1944 (W)

League Club	Source	Date Signed	Seasons Played	Apps	Subs	Gls
Wrexham		07.64	64	2	-	0

JONES Alan
Grimethorpe, 21 January, 1951 (W)

League Club	Source	Date Signed	Seasons Played	Apps	Subs	Gls
Huddersfield T	App	12.68	70-72	30	2	0
Halifax T	Tr	08.73	73-76	109	0	6
Chesterfield	Tr	09.76	76-77	39	0	6
Lincoln C	Tr	11.77	77-78	24	2	4
Bradford C	Columbus (USA)	09.79	79	16	3	1
Rochdale	Tr	08.80	80	40	4	5

JONES Alan Hugh
Wrexham, 22 September, 1949 WSch (CD)

League Club	Source	Date Signed	Seasons Played	Apps	Subs	Gls
Shrewsbury T	App	05.67	68	3	0	0

JONES John Alan
Cefn Mawr, 12 September, 1939 (G)

League Club	Source	Date Signed	Seasons Played	Apps	Subs	Gls
Cardiff C	Druids	06.57	57	1	-	0

League Club	Source	Date Signed	Seasons Played	Apps	Subs	Gls
Exeter C	Tr	07.59	59-61	90	-	0
Norwich C	Tr	07.62	62	9	-	0
Wrexham	Tr	08.63	63	18	-	0
JONES Alan Michael						
Swansea, 6 October, 1945						(CD)
Swansea T	App	10.63	64-67	61	0	6
Hereford U	Tr	07.68	72-73	52	1	2
Southport	Tr	08.74	74-75	49	0	2
JONES Alan William Edward						
Edmonton, 19 November, 1940						(CF)
Fulham	Jnrs	04.58	59	7	-	3
JONES Alexander (Alex)						
Blackburn, 27 November, 1964						(CD)
Oldham Ath	App	12.82	82-84	8	1	0
Stockport Co	L	10.84	84	3	0	0
Preston NE	Tr	06.86	86-89	100	1	3
Carlisle U	Tr	09.89	89-90	62	0	4
Rochdale	Tr	06.91	91	12	1	0
Rochdale	Motherwell	10.92	92-93	31	2	2
JONES Alfred (Alf)						
Liverpool, 2 March, 1937						(FB)
Leeds U	Marine	04.60	60-61	25	-	0
Lincoln C	Tr	06.62	62-66	179	1	3
JONES Allan Powell						
Flint, 6 January, 1940 Died 1993 WSch						(FB)
Liverpool	Jnrs	05.57	59-62	5	-	0
Brentford	Tr	08.63	63-69	244	4	3
JONES Allan Raymond						
Burton-on-Trent, 3 November, 1941						(W)
Aston Villa	Jnrs	11.58	61	1	-	0
JONES Andrew (Andy) Mark						
Wrexham, 9 January, 1963 W-6						(F)
Port Vale	Rhyl	06.85	85-87	87	3	47
Charlton Ath	Tr	09.87	87-90	51	15	15
Port Vale	L	02.89	88	8	9	3
Bristol C	L	11.89	89	2	2	1
Bournemouth	Tr	10.90	90-91	36	4	8
Leyton Orient	Tr	10.91	91-92	44	15	13
JONES Andrew (Andy) Stuart						
Sutton-in-Ashfield, 12 February, 1986						(M)
Mansfield T	Sch	•	02	0	1	0
JONES Anthony (Tony) Peter						
Birmingham, 12 November, 1937 Died 1990						(M)
Oxford U	Birmingham C (Am)	09.59	62-67	226	0	42
Newport Co	Tr	11.67	67-68	53	1	9
JONES Arthur						
Harpurhey, 23 April, 1920 Died 2001						(W)
Rochdale	Goslings	06.45	46	1	-	0
JONES Barrie						
Barnsley, 31 October, 1938						(CF)
Notts Co		09.61	61-63	42	-	15
JONES Barrie Spencer						
Swansea, 10 October, 1941 Wu23-8/W-15						(W)
Swansea T	Jnrs	04.59	59-64	166	-	23
Plymouth Arg	Tr	09.64	64-66	98	0	9
Cardiff C	Tr	03.67	66-69	107	0	19
JONES Barry						
Prescot, 30 June, 1970						(CD)
Liverpool	Prescot Cables	01.89				
Wrexham	Tr	07.92	92-97	184	11	5
York C	Tr	12.97	97-00	130	4	5
JONES Thomas **Benjamin (Benny)**						
Frodsham, 23 March, 1920 Died 1972						(W)
Tranmere Rov	Ellesmere Port T	09.41	46-47	54	-	19
Chelsea	Tr	11.47	47-51	55	-	11
Accrington St	Tr	07.53	53	14	-	0
JONES Bernard						
Stoke-on-Trent, 29 September, 1924 Died 2000						(W)
Port Vale	Longport	10.48	48	6	-	0
JONES Bernard						
Coventry, 10 April, 1934						(IF)
Northampton T		10.52	53-55	43	-	16
Cardiff C	Tr	03.56	55-56	9	-	0
Shrewsbury T	Tr	07.57	57-58	43	-	15

League Club	Source	Date Signed	Seasons Played	Apps	Subs	Gls
JONES Bradley (Brad)						
Armadale, Australia, 19 March, 1982 AuYth/Auu23-4						(G)
Middlesbrough	YT	03.99	03-04	6	0	0
Stockport Co	L	12.02	02	1	0	0
Blackpool	L	11.03	03	5	0	0
Blackpool	L	11.04	04	12	0	0
JONES Brian						
Doncaster, 5 September, 1933						(FB)
Walsall		11.53	53	2	-	0
JONES Brian (Bryn)						
Barnsley, 15 September, 1938						(FB)
Barnsley	Jnrs	05.57	57-58	14	-	0
York C	Tr	05.59	59	1	-	0
JONES Bryn Edward						
Bagillt, 26 May, 1939						(FB)
Watford	Holywell T	01.63	62	2	-	0
Chester	Tr	08.64	64-66	30	0	0
JONES Brynley (Bryn)						
St Asaph, 16 May, 1959						(M)
Chester	App	05.77	76-81	149	13	17
JONES Brynley (Bryn)						
Llandrindod Wells, 8 February, 1948 WSch/Wu23-1						(M)
Cardiff C	App	02.66	66-67	1	2	0
Newport Co	L	02.69	68	13	0	0
Bristol Rov	Tr	06.69	69-74	84	6	7
JONES Brynley (Bryn) Roy						
Swansea, 20 May, 1931 Died 1990						(FB)
Swansea T	Jnrs	09.51	52-57	122	-	4
Newport Co	Tr	06.58	58-59	71	-	12
Bournemouth	Tr	02.60	59-63	118	-	5
Northampton T	Tr	10.63	63	7	-	0
Watford	Tr	11.63	63-66	90	1	1
JONES Brynmor (Bryn)						
Penyard, 14 February, 1912 Died 1985 WWar-8/W-17						(IF)
Wolverhampton W	Aberaman Ath	10.33	33-37	163	-	52
Arsenal	Tr	08.38	38-48	71	-	7
Norwich C	Tr	06.49	49	23	-	1
JONES Charles (Charlie) Wilson						
Pentre Broughton, 29 April, 1914 Died 1986 W-2						(CF)
Wrexham	Brymbo Green	08.32	32-34	7	-	3
Birmingham	Tr	09.34	34-46	135	-	63
Nottingham F	Tr	09.47	47	7	-	5
JONES Christopher (Chris) Harry						
Jersey, 18 April, 1956 Eu21-1						(F)
Tottenham H	App	05.73	74-81	149	15	37
Manchester C	Tr	09.82	82	3	0	0
Crystal Palace	Tr	11.82	82	18	0	3
Charlton Ath	Tr	09.83	83	17	6	2
Orient	Tr	09.84	84-86	106	1	19
JONES Christopher (Chris) Martin Nigel						
Altrincham, 19 November, 1945						(F)
Manchester C	Jnrs	05.64	66-67	6	1	2
Swindon T	Tr	07.68	68-71	49	19	18
Oldham Ath	L	01.72	71	3	0	1
Walsall	L	02.72	71-72	54	5	14
York C	Tr	06.73	73-75	94	1	33
Huddersfield T	Tr	08.76	76	9	5	2
Doncaster Rov	Tr	07.77	77-78	14	6	4
Darlington	L	01.78	77	14	2	3
Rochdale	Tr	12.78	78-79	51	5	19
JONES Clifford (Cliff) William						
Swansea, 7 February, 1935 Wu23-1/FLge-3/W-59						(W)
Swansea T	Jnrs	05.52	52-57	167	-	48
Tottenham H	Tr	02.58	57-68	314	4	135
Fulham	Tr	10.68	68-69	23	2	2
JONES Cobi N'Gai						
Detroit, USA, 16 June, 1970 USA int						(W)
Coventry C	USSF (USA)	09.94	94	16	5	2
JONES George **Colin**						
Chester, 8 September, 1940						(WH)
Chester	Jnrs	03.60	59	3	-	0
JONES Colin Malcolm						
Birmingham, 30 October, 1963						(W)
West Bromwich A	App	10.81				
Mansfield T	Tr	01.85	84	5	0	0

League Club	Source	Date Signed	Seasons Played	Apps	Subs	Gls
JONES Cyril						
Ponciau, 17 July, 1920 Died 1995						(FB)
Wrexham	Johnstown	02.42	46	29	-	0
JONES Darren Lee						
Newport, 28 August, 1983 WSch/WYth						(CD)
Bristol C	YT	09.00	01	1	1	0
Cheltenham T	L	08.03	03	14	0	1
JONES David						
Hodthorpe, 9 April, 1914 Died 1998						(WH)
Bury	Worksop T	08.34	34-49	257	-	12
JONES David						
Blaenau Ffestiniog, 8 September, 1914						(G)
Stoke C	Colwyn Bay	03.37	38	1	-	0
Carlisle U	Tr	05.39	46-47	66	-	0
JONES David (Dave)						
Aberdare, 7 January, 1932						(G)
Brentford	Dover	12.51				
Reading	Tr	07.53	53-60	215	-	0
Aldershot	Tr	07.61	61-65	187	0	0
JONES David (Dai)						
Orpington, 3 March, 1935						(G)
Swansea T		12.55	56-57	3	-	0
JONES David						
Wrexham, 6 May, 1971 WSch						(W)
Aston Villa	YT	06.89				
Wrexham	Tr	01.92	91	0	1	0
JONES David						
Harrow, 3 July, 1964						(F)
Chelsea	(New Zealand)	11.87				
Bury	Barnet	09.88	88	0	1	0
Leyton Orient	Barnet	12.88	88	0	2	0
Burnley	Barnet	02.89	88	4	0	0
Ipswich T	(USA)	10.89				
Doncaster Rov	Tr	11.89	89-90	34	6	14
Bury	Tr	09.91	91	0	9	0
Hull C	Tr	02.93	92	11	1	1
JONES David (Dai) Albert Brynmawr						
Neath, 31 March, 1941 WYth						(F)
Millwall	Ton Pentre	03.64	63-64	12	-	3
Newport Co	Tr	07.65	65-67	81	0	25
Mansfield T	Tr	11.67	67-71	116	14	32
Newport Co	Tr	11.71	71-73	43	4	11
JONES David Edward						
Saltney, 5 March, 1936						(W)
Wrexham	Saltney	04.55	56-58	71	-	11
Crewe Alex	Tr	07.59	59	2	-	0
JONES David Edward						
Gosport, 11 February, 1952 Wu23-4/W-8						(CD)
Bournemouth	App	01.70	70-73	128	6	5
Nottingham F	Tr	08.74	74	36	0	1
Norwich C	Tr	09.75	75-79	120	3	4
JONES David (Davy) Frederick						
Brixham, 18 May, 1950						(M)
Arsenal	App	02.68				
Oxford U	Tr	10.68	68-70	17	4	0
Torquay U	Tr	07.72	72	0	1	0
JONES David Henry						
Tetbury, 4 August, 1937						(WH)
Leeds U	Gloucester C	12.54				
Crewe Alex	Tr	05.60	60-61	16	-	0
JONES David Hilary						
Bradford, 29 December, 1950						(W)
Wolverhampton W		08.68				
York C	Tr	08.70	70	3	0	0
JONES David John						
Ruabon, 16 September, 1952						(F)
Hereford U	Telford U	05.78	78-79	44	3	11
JONES David (Dai) Owen						
Cardiff, 28 October, 1910 Died 1971 W-7						(FB)
Clapton Orient	Ebbw Vale	08.31	31-32	55	-	0
Leicester C	Tr	05.33	33-46	226	-	4
Mansfield T	Tr	10.47	47-48	74	-	0
JONES David Richard						
Onllwyn, 18 January, 1946						(G)
Derby Co		07.65				
Newport Co	Nuneaton Borough	05.68	67-68	3	0	0

League Club	Source	Date Signed	Seasons Played	Apps	Subs	Gls
JONES David (Dave) Ronald						
Liverpool, 17 August, 1956 EYth/Eu21-1						(FB)
Everton	App	05.74	75-78	79	7	1
Coventry C	Tr	06.79	79-80	8	3	0
Preston NE	Seiko (HK)	08.83	83-84	50	0	1
JONES David Wilmott Llewellyn						
Kingsley, Cheshire, 9 April, 1940 EYth						(IF)
Crewe Alex	Jnrs	05.56	56	10	-	1
Birmingham C	Tr	04.57	57-58	9	-	0
Millwall	Tr	12.59	59-63	165	-	71
JONES Denys John						
Aberdare, 19 October, 1930 Died 2003						(W)
Norwich C	Yarmouth T	04.51	51-52	5	-	2
JONES Frederick William **Derek**						
Ellesmere Port, 24 April, 1929						(FB)
Tranmere Rov	Ellesmere Port T	07.53	53-60	155	-	19
JONES Desmond (Des)						
Gelli, 15 March, 1930 Died 1987						(W)
Swansea T	Rhondda	01.48				
Bristol Rov	Tr	06.52	52	6	-	0
Workington	Tr	07.54	54-59	210	-	25
JONES Dilwyn Bowen						
Swansea, 2 January, 1937						(WH)
Leeds U	Jnrs	01.54				
Crewe Alex	Tr	02.58	57	15	-	1
JONES Edward (Eddie) William George						
Finchley, 17 September, 1952 WSch						(FB)
Tottenham H	Jnrs	10.70				
Millwall	Tr	07.73	73-75	58	1	0
JONES Edwin (Eddie) Morris						
Abercynon, 20 April, 1914 Died 1984 WSch						(W)
Bolton W (Am)	Abercynon	04.33	33	1	-	1
Swindon T	Tr	05.36	36-46	124	-	17
JONES Eifion Pritchard						
Caernarfon, 28 September, 1980 WYth						(CD)
Liverpool	YT	10.97				
Blackpool	Tr	03.00	99-00	5	3	0
JONES Eric						
Ulverston, 23 June, 1931						(W)
Preston NE	Notts Co (Am)	01.52	53-54	13	-	0
Nottingham F	Tr	09.55	55-57	18	-	3
Doncaster Rov	Tr	03.58	57-58	15	-	2
Accrington St	Tr	07.59	59	18	-	0
Southport	Tr	07.60	60-61	76	-	18
JONES Eric John						
Dover, 5 March, 1938 Died 1987						(WH)
Coventry C	Snowdown CW	05.55	56-60	14	-	0
JONES Eric Norman						
Stirchley, 5 February, 1915 Died 1985						(W)
Wolverhampton W	Kidderminster Hrs	10.36	36	3	-	0
Portsmouth	Tr	11.37	37	1	-	0
Stoke C	Tr	09.38				
West Bromwich A	Tr	05.39				
Brentford	Tr	12.45				
Crewe Alex	Tr	07.46	46-47	37	-	9
JONES Ernest (Ernie)						
Ruabon, 9 December, 1919						(IF)
Chester	Bangor C	08.49	49-50	6	-	1
JONES Ernest (Ernie)						
Bristol, 12 May, 1919						(WH)
Bristol C	Jnrs	08.39	46-47	27	-	1
JONES William **Ernest (Ernie)** Arthur						
Cwmbwrla, 12 November, 1920 Died 2002 WWar-1/W-4						(W)
Swansea T	Bolton W (Am)	10.43	46	37	-	3
Tottenham H	Tr	06.47	46-48	55	-	14
Southampton	Tr	05.49	49-51	44	-	4
Bristol C	Tr	11.51	51-53	50	-	7
JONES Frank						
Llandudno, 3 October, 1960 Wu21-1						(CD)
Wrexham	Jnrs	07.79	78-80	8	0	0
Wrexham	(Finland)	09.84	84-86	30	1	0
JONES Frederick (Fred) Arthur						
Stoke-on-Trent, 21 October, 1922 Died 1989						(FB)
Port Vale	South Liverpool	06.46	46	12	-	1

JONES Frederick (Freddie) George
Gelligaer, 11 January, 1938 Wu23-2 (W)

League Club	Source	Date Signed	Seasons Played	Apps	Subs	Gls
Arsenal	Hereford U	01.58				
Brighton & Hove A	Tr	09.58	58-60	69	-	14
Swindon T	Tr	12.60	60	18	-	1
Grimsby T	Tr	07.61	61-62	58	-	9
Reading	Tr	07.63	63	30	-	5

JONES Gareth Anthony
Cardiff, 18 June, 1952 (W)

League Club	Source	Date Signed	Seasons Played	Apps	Subs	Gls
Torquay U		10.72	72-73	11	5	0
Bournemouth	Tr	03.74	73-74	1	3	0

JONES Garry Edwin
Wythenshawe, 11 December, 1950 (F)

League Club	Source	Date Signed	Seasons Played	Apps	Subs	Gls
Bolton W	App	01.68	68-78	195	8	41
Sheffield U	L	02.75	74	3	0	1
Blackpool	Tr	11.78	78-79	18	9	5
Hereford U	Tr	08.80	80	21	4	4

JONES Gary
Huddersfield, 6 April, 1969 (F)

League Club	Source	Date Signed	Seasons Played	Apps	Subs	Gls
Doncaster Rov	Rossington Main Coll	01.89	88-89	10	10	2
Southend U	Boston U	06.93	93-95	47	23	16
Lincoln C	L	09.93	93	0	4	2
Notts Co	Tr	03.96	95-98	103	14	38
Scunthorpe U	L	02.97	96	9	2	5
Hartlepool U	Tr	03.99	98-99	42	3	7
Halifax T	L	03.00	99	8	0	1
Halifax T	Tr	06.00	00-01	50	18	9

JONES Gary Kenneth
Whiston, 5 January, 1951 (W)

League Club	Source	Date Signed	Seasons Played	Apps	Subs	Gls
Everton	Jnrs	10.68	70-75	76	6	12
Birmingham C	Tr	07.76	76-77	33	2	1

JONES Gary Roy
Birkenhead, 3 June, 1977 (M)

League Club	Source	Date Signed	Seasons Played	Apps	Subs	Gls
Swansea C	Caernarfon T	07.97	97	3	5	0
Rochdale	Tr	01.98	97-01	123	17	22
Barnsley	Tr	11.01	01-02	56	0	2
Rochdale	Tr	11.03	03-04	65	0	12

JONES Gary Steven
Chester, 10 May, 1975 (M)

League Club	Source	Date Signed	Seasons Played	Apps	Subs	Gls
Tranmere Rov	YT	07.93	93-99	117	61	28
Nottingham F	Tr	07.00	00-01	24	12	2
Tranmere Rov	Tr	08.02	02-04	81	11	16

JONES George
Wrexham, 19 July, 1930 (WH)

League Club	Source	Date Signed	Seasons Played	Apps	Subs	Gls
Wrexham		08.50	50-53	113	-	5

JONES George Alexander
Radcliffe, 21 April, 1945 EYth (F)

League Club	Source	Date Signed	Seasons Played	Apps	Subs	Gls
Bury	App	06.62	61-63	63	-	15
Blackburn Rov	Tr	03.64	63-66	36	3	14
Bury	Tr	11.66	66-72	249	7	101
Oldham Ath	Tr	03.73	72-75	63	8	19
Halifax T	Tr	02.76	75-76	18	1	4
Southport	Tr	01.77	76-77	54	1	11

JONES George Henry
Sheffield, 27 November, 1918 Died 1995 (W)

League Club	Source	Date Signed	Seasons Played	Apps	Subs	Gls
Sheffield U	Woodburn Alliance	08.36	36-50	141	-	36
Barnsley	Tr	02.51	50-51	22	-	6

JONES Gerald (Gerry)
Burslem, 30 December, 1945 (W)

League Club	Source	Date Signed	Seasons Played	Apps	Subs	Gls
Stoke C	App	06.63	64-66	7	0	0

JONES Gerald (Gerry) Kenneth
Newport, 21 April, 1950 (W)

League Club	Source	Date Signed	Seasons Played	Apps	Subs	Gls
Luton T	Barry T	07.72				
Crewe Alex	L	02.73	72	6	1	1

JONES Thomas Gethin
Llanbyther, 8 August, 1981 (FB)

League Club	Source	Date Signed	Seasons Played	Apps	Subs	Gls
Cardiff C	Carmarthen T	08.00	00-01	0	3	0

JONES Glanville (Glan)
Merthyr Tydfil, 27 February, 1921 (W)

League Club	Source	Date Signed	Seasons Played	Apps	Subs	Gls
Hull C	Merthyr Tydfil	06.46	46	7	-	0
Bournemouth	Tr	05.47	48	9	-	3
Crewe Alex	Tr	03.49	48	10	-	1

JONES Glyn
Rotherham, 8 April, 1936 EYth (IF)

League Club	Source	Date Signed	Seasons Played	Apps	Subs	Gls
Sheffield U	Rotherham U (Am)	06.54	55-57	29	-	4
Rotherham U	Tr	12.57	57-58	23	-	6
Mansfield T	Tr	07.59	59-60	45	-	18

JONES Glyn Alan
Newport, 29 March, 1959 (G)

League Club	Source	Date Signed	Seasons Played	Apps	Subs	Gls
Bristol Rov	App	03.77	77-79	9	0	0
Shrewsbury T	Tr	07.80				
Newport Co	Bath C	09.83	83	3	0	0

JONES Gordon Edward
Sedgefield, 6 March, 1943 EYth/Eu23-9 (FB)

League Club	Source	Date Signed	Seasons Played	Apps	Subs	Gls
Middlesbrough	Jnrs	03.60	60-72	457	5	4
Darlington	Tr	02.73	72-74	80	5	5

JONES Graeme Anthony
Gateshead, 13 March, 1970 (F)

League Club	Source	Date Signed	Seasons Played	Apps	Subs	Gls
Doncaster Rov	Bridlington T	08.93	93-95	80	12	26
Wigan Ath	Tr	07.96	96-99	76	20	44
Southend U	St Johnstone	07.02	02	18	3	2
Boston U	Tr	03.03	02-03	33	3	7
Bury	Tr	07.04	04	1	2	1

JONES Graham
Bradford, 5 October, 1957 (FB)

League Club	Source	Date Signed	Seasons Played	Apps	Subs	Gls
Bradford C	Jnrs	06.76	75-77	1	3	0

JONES Graham
Worsley, 2 June, 1959 (FB)

League Club	Source	Date Signed	Seasons Played	Apps	Subs	Gls
Luton T	App	06.76	75-79	31	8	0
Torquay U	Tr	01.80	79-82	114	0	6
Stockport Co	Tr	07.83	83	32	3	2

JONES Graham Osborne
Wrexham, 16 September, 1949 (M)

League Club	Source	Date Signed	Seasons Played	Apps	Subs	Gls
Wrexham	Jnrs	10.67	67	3	0	0

JONES Grenville (Gren) Arthur
Nuneaton, 23 November, 1932 Died 1991 ESch/EYth (W)

League Club	Source	Date Signed	Seasons Played	Apps	Subs	Gls
West Bromwich A	Jnrs	12.49	53	2	-	0
Wrexham	Tr	06.55	55-60	240	-	36

JONES Griffith (Griff) Thomas
Liverpool, 22 June, 1984 (F)

League Club	Source	Date Signed	Seasons Played	Apps	Subs	Gls
Barnsley	Sch	09.03	02	0	2	0

JONES Daniel John Gwilym
Cardigan, 3 April, 1925 Died 1992 (CF)

League Club	Source	Date Signed	Seasons Played	Apps	Subs	Gls
Torquay U	Abergwynfi	09.47	47	6	-	1

JONES Gwyn
Newport, 20 November, 1932 (IF)

League Club	Source	Date Signed	Seasons Played	Apps	Subs	Gls
Leeds U	Llanelli	08.50				
York C	Tr	09.53				
Walsall	Tr	11.53	53	10	-	0

JONES Gwynfor (Gwyn)
Llandwrog, 20 March, 1935 (FB)

League Club	Source	Date Signed	Seasons Played	Apps	Subs	Gls
Wolverhampton W	Caernarfon T	09.55	55-61	21	-	0
Bristol Rov	Tr	08.62	62-65	153	0	0

JONES Harold
Liverpool, 22 May, 1933 Died 2003 (IF)

League Club	Source	Date Signed	Seasons Played	Apps	Subs	Gls
Liverpool	Jnrs	02.52	53	1	-	0

JONES Harvey Cunningham
Rhos, 16 August, 1936 (WH)

League Club	Source	Date Signed	Seasons Played	Apps	Subs	Gls
Wrexham	Liverpool (Am)	11.59	59	13	-	0
Chester	Tr	08.60	60	19	-	0

JONES Haydn
Caernarfon, 8 May, 1946 (FB)

League Club	Source	Date Signed	Seasons Played	Apps	Subs	Gls
Wrexham	Caernarfon T	06.64	64-65	13	1	1

JONES Henry (Jerry)
Hartlepool, 28 September, 1918 (WH)

League Club	Source	Date Signed	Seasons Played	Apps	Subs	Gls
Hartlepools U	Belle Vue Congs	09.46	46-48	75	-	1

JONES Herbert Neville
Mold, 20 January, 1929 (IF)

League Club	Source	Date Signed	Seasons Played	Apps	Subs	Gls
Wrexham	Colwyn Bay	07.51	51	1	-	0

JONES Ian Michael
Germany, 26 August, 1976 WYth (FB)

League Club	Source	Date Signed	Seasons Played	Apps	Subs	Gls
Cardiff C	YT	07.95	93-95	3	0	0

JONES Idwal Gwyn
Ton Pentre, 3 August, 1924 Died 1997 (W)

League Club	Source	Date Signed	Seasons Played	Apps	Subs	Gls
Swansea T	Ton Pentre	10.46	46	4	-	0

JONES Islwyn
Merthyr Tydfil, 8 April, 1935 (WH)

League Club	Source	Date Signed	Seasons Played	Apps	Subs	Gls
Cardiff C	Jnrs	11.52	54-55	26	-	0

League Club	Source	Date Signed	Seasons Played	Career Record Apps	Subs	Gls
JONES John **Ivor**						
Rhondda, 1 April, 1925 Died 1999						(W)
Crystal Palace		06.46	46	1	-	1
JONES James (Jimmy) Alfred						
Birkenhead, 3 August, 1927						(G)
Everton		12.45				
New Brighton	Tr	08.50	50	32	-	0
Lincoln C	Tr	08.51	51-53	76	-	0
Accrington St	Tr	02.54	53-54	46	-	0
Rochdale	Tr	09.55	55-60	177	-	0
JONES Benjamin **James (Jimmy)**						
Rhondda, 16 November, 1919 Died 1976 WAmat						(FB)
Watford	Slough T	09.47	47-53	158	-	0
JONES James Maurice						
Bolton, 23 October, 1925 Died 1994						(IF)
Hull C (Am)		05.47	46	1	-	0
JONES Jason Andrew						
Wrexham, 10 May, 1979 WYth/Wu21-3						(G)
Swansea C	Liverpool (YT)	12.97	97-01	10	0	0
JONES John						
Gourock, 29 January, 1916 Died 1999						(IF)
Bradford C	Third Lanark	09.46	46	2	-	1
JONES John (Jack)						
Wrexham, 9 April, 1921 Died 2001						(IF)
Wrexham		09.46	46-47	20	-	1
Doncaster Rov	Tr	07.48	48	6	-	0
New Brighton	Tr	08.49	49-50	77	-	11
JONES John (Jack) Edward						
Bromborough, 3 July, 1913 Died 1995						(FB)
Everton	Ellesmere Port T	03.32	33-37	98	-	0
Sunderland	Tr	12.45	46	24	-	0
JONES John (Johnny) Morris						
Dafen, 31 October, 1924						(W)
Fulham	Larne	01.47	47	1	-	0
Millwall	Tr	03.50	49-50	27	-	7
JONES John Thomas						
Holywell, 25 November, 1916 Died 1978 WSch						(G)
Port Vale	Flint T	12.36	36	3	-	0
Northampton T	Tr	05.37	38-47	71	-	0
Oldham Ath	Tr	08.48	48	22	-	0
JONES Jonathan (Jon) Berwyn						
Wrexham, 27 October, 1978						(F)
Chester C	YT	03.97	96-99	11	27	2
JONES Joseph (Joey) Patrick						
Llandudno, 4 March, 1955 Wu23-4/W-72						(FB)
Wrexham	Jnrs	01.73	72-74	98	0	2
Liverpool	Tr	07.75	75-77	72	0	3
Wrexham	Tr	10.78	78-82	145	1	6
Chelsea	Tr	10.82	82-84	76	2	2
Huddersfield T	Tr	08.85	85-86	67	1	3
Wrexham	Tr	08.87	87-91	131	1	11
JONES Keith						
Nantyglo, 23 October, 1928 W-1						(G)
Aston Villa	Kidderminster Hrs	05.46	47-56	185	-	0
Port Vale	Tr	07.57	57-58	64	-	0
Crewe Alex	Tr	04.59	58-59	46	-	0
JONES Keith Aubrey						
Dulwich, 14 October, 1964 ESch/EYth						(M)
Chelsea	App	08.83	82-86	43	9	7
Brentford	Tr	09.87	87-91	167	2	13
Southend U	Tr	10.91	91-94	88	2	11
Charlton Ath	Tr	09.94	94-99	142	17	6
Reading	Tr	07.00	00-01	28	11	0
JONES Kenneth (Ken)						
Aberdare, 2 January, 1936 Wu23-1						(G)
Cardiff C	Jnrs	05.53	57-58	24	-	0
Scunthorpe U	Tr	12.58	58-63	168	-	0
Charlton Ath	Tr	09.64	64-65	25	0	0
Exeter C	Tr	06.66	66	17	0	0
JONES Kenneth (Ken)						
Easington, 1 October, 1936 ESch						(FB)
Sunderland	Jnrs	10.53	59	10	-	0
Hartlepools U	Tr	01.61	60-61	33	-	0
JONES Kenneth (Ken)						
Havercroft, 26 June, 1944						(FB)
Bradford PA	Monckton CW	09.61	62-64	100	-	3
Southampton	Tr	06.65	65-69	79	1	0
Cardiff C	Tr	07.71	71	6	0	0
JONES Kenneth (Ken) Boothroyd						
Rhos, 11 May, 1937						(FB)
Wrexham	Jnrs	05.54	57-59	31	-	0
Crystal Palace	Tr	06.60	60	4	-	0
Swindon T	Tr	03.61	60-61	35	-	0
JONES Kenneth (Ken) Brian						
Keighley, 9 February, 1941						(M)
Southend U		10.60	60-63	87	-	34
Millwall	Tr	09.64	64-69	175	3	11
Colchester U	Tr	11.69	69-71	72	5	23
JONES Richard **Kenneth (Ken)**						
Llanelli, 16 April, 1926						(FB)
Coventry C	Llanelli	11.49	51-55	83	-	0
JONES Kenwyne Joel						
Trinidad, 5 October, 1984 TrinidadU21/Trinidad 18						(F)
Southampton	W-Connection (Tr)	05.04	04	1	1	0
Sheffield Wed	L	12.04	04	7	0	7
Stoke C	L	02.05	04	13	0	3
JONES Kevin Richard						
Wrexham, 16 February, 1974						(FB)
Wrexham	YT	08.92	91-93	8	1	0
JONES Lee						
Pontypridd, 9 August, 1970						(G)
Swansea C	AFC Porth	03.94	94-97	6	0	0
Bristol Rov	Tr	03.98	97-99	76	0	0
Stockport Co	Tr	07.00	00-02	72	3	0
Blackpool	Tr	08.03	03-04	50	0	0
JONES Philip **Lee**						
Wrexham, 29 May, 1973 WYth/Wu21-14/WB-1/W-2						(F)
Wrexham	YT	07.91	90-91	24	15	10
Liverpool	Tr	03.92	94-96	0	3	0
Crewe Alex	L	09.93	93	4	4	1
Wrexham	L	01.96	95	20	0	9
Wrexham	L	01.97	96	2	4	0
Tranmere Rov	Tr	03.97	96-99	58	28	16
Barnsley	Tr	07.00	00-01	17	23	5
Wrexham	Tr	03.02	01-03	25	24	14
JONES Leonard (Len)						
Barnsley, 9 June, 1913 Died 1998						(W)
Barnsley	Huddersfield T (Am)	08.33	34-37	57	-	0
Plymouth Arg	Chelmsford C	05.39	46-48	39	-	2
Southend U	Tr	08.49	49	29	-	0
Colchester U	Tr	07.50	50-52	71	-	3
JONES Leslie (Les)						
Ynysybwl, 8 December, 1922 Died 1983 WAmat						(IF)
Millwall	Barry T	12.47	48-51	7	-	1
JONES Leslie (Les) Albert						
Wrexham, 9 November, 1940 WSch						(F)
Bolton W	Jnrs	11.57				
Tranmere Rov	Tr	07.62	62-64	68	-	29
Chester	Tr	04.65	65-68	132	3	35
JONES Leslie (Les) Clifford						
Mountain Ash, 1 January, 1930						(FB)
Luton T	Craig Ath	10.50	50-57	98	-	1
Aston Villa	Tr	01.58	57	5	-	0
JONES Leslie (Les) Jenkin						
Aberdare, 1 July, 1911 Died 1981 WWar-5/W-11						(IF)
Cardiff C	Aberdare & Aberaman	08.29	29-33	142	-	31
Coventry C	Tr	01.34	33-37	139	-	69
Arsenal	Tr	11.37	37-38	46	-	3
Swansea T	Tr	06.46	46	2	-	0
Brighton & Hove A	Barry T	08.48	48	3	-	0
JONES Linden						
New Tredegar, 5 March, 1961 Wu21-3						(FB)
Cardiff C	App	03.79	78-83	142	3	2
Newport Co	Tr	09.83	83-86	141	1	5
Reading	Tr	07.87	87-91	147	5	8
JONES Marcus Lee						
Stone, 24 June, 1974						(M)
Cheltenham T	Scarborough	11.00	00	1	1	0
JONES Mark						
Barnsley, 15 June, 1933 Died 1958 ESch						(CD)
Manchester U	Jnrs	07.50	50-57	103	-	1

JONES Mark
Berinsfield, 26 September, 1961 (W)

League Club	Source	Date Signed	Seasons Played	Apps	Subs	Gls
Oxford U	App	09.79	79-85	101	28	7
Swindon T	Tr	09.86	86	39	1	9
Cardiff C	Tr	08.90	90-91	33	3	2

JONES Mark
Brownhills, 4 January, 1968 (FB)

League Club	Source	Date Signed	Seasons Played	Apps	Subs	Gls
Walsall	App	01.86	87	6	2	0
Exeter C	L	11.88	88	5	0	0
Hereford U	Tr	08.89	89	40	2	8

JONES Mark
Romford, 4 August, 1979 (FB)

League Club	Source	Date Signed	Seasons Played	Apps	Subs	Gls
Southend U	YT	●	96	0	1	0

JONES Mark
Bristol, 2 December, 1965 (M)

League Club	Source	Date Signed	Seasons Played	Apps	Subs	Gls
Bristol C	App	●	82	0	1	0

JONES Mark Alan
Wrexham, 15 August, 1983 Wu21-2 (M)

League Club	Source	Date Signed	Seasons Played	Apps	Subs	Gls
Wrexham	Sch	07.03	02-04	17	23	4

JONES Mark Andrew
Walsall, 7 September, 1979 ESch/EYth (F)

League Club	Source	Date Signed	Seasons Played	Apps	Subs	Gls
Wolverhampton W	YT	09.96	98-99	0	3	0
Cheltenham T	L	10.99	99	3	0	0
Chesterfield	Tr	08.00	00-01	1	8	0

JONES Mark Anthony Waldron
Warley, 22 October, 1961 (FB)

League Club	Source	Date Signed	Seasons Played	Apps	Subs	Gls
Aston Villa	App	07.79	81-83	24	0	0
Brighton & Hove A	Tr	03.84	83-84	9	0	0
Birmingham C	Tr	10.84	84-86	33	1	0
Shrewsbury T	Tr	03.87				
Hereford U	Tr	06.87	87-90	155	1	2

JONES Mark David
Doncaster, 2 October, 1958 (M)

League Club	Source	Date Signed	Seasons Played	Apps	Subs	Gls
Doncaster Rov	App	11.75	75-77	10	3	0

JONES Mark Richard
Mansfield, 21 December, 1965 (CD)

League Club	Source	Date Signed	Seasons Played	Apps	Subs	Gls
Notts Co	App	12.83	83-84	4	2	0

JONES Mark Thomas
Liverpool, 16 September, 1960 (FB)

League Club	Source	Date Signed	Seasons Played	Apps	Subs	Gls
Preston NE	Runcorn	02.84	83-85	76	0	3

JONES Matthew Graham
Llanelli, 1 September, 1980 WYth/Wu21-7/WB-1/W-13 (M)

League Club	Source	Date Signed	Seasons Played	Apps	Subs	Gls
Leeds U	YT	09.97	98-00	11	12	0
Leicester C	Tr	12.00	00-02	19	8	1

JONES Matthew (Matt) Leon
Chiswick, 9 October, 1970 (W)

League Club	Source	Date Signed	Seasons Played	Apps	Subs	Gls
Southend U	YT	05.89	88-89	2	3	0

JONES Matthew Neil
Shrewsbury, 11 October, 1980 (M)

League Club	Source	Date Signed	Seasons Played	Apps	Subs	Gls
Shrewsbury T	YT	07.99	98-00	5	2	0

JONES John Mervyn
Bangor, 30 April, 1931 (W)

League Club	Source	Date Signed	Seasons Played	Apps	Subs	Gls
Liverpool	Bangor C	12.51	51-52	4	-	0
Scunthorpe U	Tr	08.53	53-58	240	-	27
Crewe Alex	Tr	06.59	59-60	84	-	17
Chester	Tr	08.61	61-62	63	-	10
Lincoln C	Tr	10.63	63	1	-	0

JONES Michael
Liverpool, 3 December, 1987 (G)

League Club	Source	Date Signed	Seasons Played	Apps	Subs	Gls
Wrexham	Sch	●	04	0	1	0

JONES Michael (Mick)
Sunderland, 24 March, 1947 (CD)

League Club	Source	Date Signed	Seasons Played	Apps	Subs	Gls
Derby Co	Jnrs	11.64				
Notts Co	Tr	07.69	69-72	82	18	1
Peterborough U	Tr	08.73	73-75	82	6	4

JONES Michael (Mick) Alan
Sutton-in-Ashfield, 4 December, 1942 (FB)

League Club	Source	Date Signed	Seasons Played	Apps	Subs	Gls
Mansfield T	Mansfield CWS	10.60	62-65	91	0	0

JONES Michael (Mick) David
Worksop, 24 April, 1945 Eu23-9/E-3 (F)

League Club	Source	Date Signed	Seasons Played	Apps	Subs	Gls
Sheffield U	App	11.62	62-67	149	0	63
Leeds U	Tr	09.67	67-73	216	4	77

JONES Michael (Mick) Howard
Llangurig, 25 August, 1938 (W)

League Club	Source	Date Signed	Seasons Played	Apps	Subs	Gls
Shrewsbury T		07.59	58-61	22	-	1

JONES Michael (Mick) Keith
Berkhamsted, 8 January, 1945 (FB)

League Club	Source	Date Signed	Seasons Played	Apps	Subs	Gls
Fulham	App	01.63				
Chelsea	Tr	12.64				
Leyton Orient	Tr	02.66	65-71	223	5	16
Charlton Ath	Tr	12.71	71-73	58	1	0

JONES William Morris
Liverpool, 30 November, 1919 Died 1993 (IF)

League Club	Source	Date Signed	Seasons Played	Apps	Subs	Gls
Port Vale	South Liverpool	06.46	46-47	53	-	26
Swindon T	Tr	11.47	47-49	94	-	48
Crystal Palace	Tr	05.50	50	17	-	3
Watford	Tr	03.51	50-51	27	-	7

JONES Murray Lee
Bexley, 7 October, 1964 (F)

League Club	Source	Date Signed	Seasons Played	Apps	Subs	Gls
Southend U	App	08.82				
Crystal Palace	Carshalton Ath	10.89				
Bristol C	Tr	08.90				
Doncaster Rov	L	10.90	90	5	0	0
Exeter C	Tr	01.91	90	16	4	3
Grimsby T	Tr	07.91	91	14	14	3
Brentford	Tr	07.92	92	6	10	0

JONES Nathan Jason
Rhondda, 28 May, 1973 (M)

League Club	Source	Date Signed	Seasons Played	Apps	Subs	Gls
Luton T	Merthyr Tydfil	06.95				
Southend U	Numancia (Sp)	08.97	97-99	82	17	2
Scarborough	L	03.99	98	8	1	0
Brighton & Hove A	Tr	07.00	00-04	109	50	7

JONES Norman Glyn
Rhostyllen, 15 November, 1923 Died 2003 WSch (G)

League Club	Source	Date Signed	Seasons Played	Apps	Subs	Gls
Wrexham	Jnrs	09.41	46	1	-	0

JONES Patrick (Pat) James
Plymouth, 7 September, 1920 Died 1990 (FB)

League Club	Source	Date Signed	Seasons Played	Apps	Subs	Gls
Plymouth Arg	Astor Institute	03.47	46-57	425	-	2

JONES Paul Anthony
Walsall, 6 September, 1965 (M)

League Club	Source	Date Signed	Seasons Played	Apps	Subs	Gls
Walsall	App	09.83	82-89	125	18	15
Wrexham	L	03.89	88	5	0	0
Wolverhampton W	Tr	11.89	89-90	7	7	0

JONES Paul Bernard
Ellesmere Port, 13 May, 1953 (CD)

League Club	Source	Date Signed	Seasons Played	Apps	Subs	Gls
Bolton W	App	06.70	70-82	441	4	38
Huddersfield T	Tr	07.83	83-85	73	0	8
Oldham Ath	Tr	12.85	85-86	32	0	1
Blackpool	Tr	03.87	86-87	31	6	0
Rochdale	Galway C	03.89	88	14	0	2
Stockport Co	Tr	06.89	89	25	0	0

JONES Paul Neil
Liverpool, 3 June, 1978 (CD)

League Club	Source	Date Signed	Seasons Played	Apps	Subs	Gls
Tranmere Rov	YT	12.95				
Oldham Ath	Leigh RMI	11.99	99-00	26	2	3

JONES Paul Philip
Birkenhead, 2 October, 1976 (FB)

League Club	Source	Date Signed	Seasons Played	Apps	Subs	Gls
Wrexham	YT	07.95	96	6	0	0

JONES Paul Stanley
Stockport, 10 September, 1953 (M)

League Club	Source	Date Signed	Seasons Played	Apps	Subs	Gls
Manchester U	App	12.70				
Mansfield T	Tr	06.73	73	15	5	1

JONES Paul Steven
Chirk, 18 April, 1967 W-43 (G)

League Club	Source	Date Signed	Seasons Played	Apps	Subs	Gls
Wolverhampton W	Kidderminster Hrs	07.91	92-95	33	0	0
Stockport Co	Tr	07.96	96	46	0	0
Southampton	Tr	07.97	97-03	192	1	0
Liverpool	L	01.04	03	2	0	0
Wolverhampton W	Tr	01.04	03-04	26	0	0
Watford	L	12.04	04	9	0	0

JONES Paul Timothy
Solihull, 6 February, 1974 (W)

League Club	Source	Date Signed	Seasons Played	Apps	Subs	Gls
Birmingham C	YT	02.92	91	0	1	0

JONES Peter
Caerphilly, 22 September, 1957 (FB)

League Club	Source	Date Signed	Seasons Played	Apps	Subs	Gls
Newport Co	Merthyr Tydfil	08.85	85-86	54	1	1

JONES Peter Alfred
Ellesmere Port, 25 November, 1949 ESch/EYth (FB)

League Club	Source	Date Signed	Seasons Played	Apps	Subs	Gls
Burnley	App	05.67	68-69	2	0	0
Swansea C	Tr	07.71	71-73	80	1	1

League Club	Source	Date Signed	Seasons Played	Apps	Subs	Gls
JONES Ernest Peter						
Manchester, 30 November, 1937 EYth						(FB)
Manchester U	Jnrs	04.55	57	1	-	0
Wrexham	Tr	03.60	59-65	225	1	7
Stockport Co	Tr	07.66	66-67	51	3	1
JONES Philip (Phil) Andrew						
Liverpool, 1 December, 1969						(FB)
Everton	YT	06.88	87	0	1	0
Blackpool	L	03.90	89	6	0	0
Wigan Ath	Tr	01.91	90-92	84	4	2
Bury	Tr	08.93	93	4	0	0
JONES Philip Eric						
Ellesmere Port, 30 March, 1948						(W)
Blackpool	Jnrs	01.66				
Wrexham	Tr	05.67	66	1	0	0
JONES Philip (Phil) Howard						
Mansfield, 12 September, 1961						(M)
Sheffield U	App	06.79	78-80	25	3	1
JONES Ralph						
Maesteg, 19 May, 1921 Died 1997						(CD)
Leicester C		10.44				
Newport Co	Tr	05.46	46-47	19	-	0
Bristol Rov	Tr	12.47	47-49	13	-	1
JONES Raymond (Ray) Michael						
Chester, 4 June, 1944						(FB)
Chester	Jnrs	10.62	62-68	169	1	0
JONES Gordon Richard (Dick)						
Llanrwst, 25 June, 1932						(WH)
Crewe Alex	Holyhead	01.57	56-59	75	-	2
JONES Richard John						
Usk, 26 April, 1969						(M)
Newport Co	YT	07.87	86-87	31	9	1
Hereford U	Tr	08.88	88-92	142	6	9
Swansea C	Tr	07.93	93	6	1	0
JONES Robert						
Coventry, 17 November, 1964 ESch						(F)
Leicester C	Manchester C (App)	09.82	82-85	12	3	3
Walsall	Tr	08.86	86	1	4	0
JONES Robert (Rob) Marc						
Wrexham, 5 November, 1971 WSch/EYth/Eu21-2/E-8						(FB)
Crewe Alex	YT	12.88	87-91	59	16	2
Liverpool	Tr	10.91	91-97	182	1	0
JONES Robert (Bobby) Stanley						
Bristol, 28 October, 1938						(F)
Bristol Rov	Soundwell	05.56	57-66	250	0	64
Northampton T	Tr	09.66	66	17	0	1
Swindon T	Tr	02.67	66	11	0	0
Bristol Rov	Tr	08.67	67-72	159	9	36
JONES Robert Stuart						
Liverpool, 12 November, 1971						(M)
Wrexham	YT	07.90	89-90	5	2	1
JONES Robert (Bobby) William						
Walton, 28 March, 1933 Died 1998						(G)
Southport	4th Southport BB	07.51	51-52	22	-	0
Chester	Tr	08.53	53-57	166	-	0
Blackburn Rov	Tr	03.58	58-65	49	0	0
JONES Robert (Rob) William						
Stockton, 30 November, 1979						(CD)
Stockport Co	Gateshead	04.03	03	14	2	2
Macclesfield T	L	10.03	03	1	0	0
Grimsby T	Tr	07.04	04	18	2	1
JONES Roderick (Rod)						
Rhiwderin, 14 June, 1946						(F)
Newport Co	Lovells Ath	10.69	69-78	271	16	67
JONES Rodney (Rod) Ernest						
Ashton-under-Lyne, 23 September, 1945						(G)
Rotherham U	Ashton U	06.65	65-66	36	0	0
Burnley	Tr	03.67	67-68	9	0	0
Rochdale	Tr	06.71	71-73	19	0	0
JONES Roger						
Upton-on-Severn, 8 November, 1946 Eu23-1						(G)
Portsmouth	App	11.64				
Bournemouth	Tr	05.65	65-69	160	0	0
Blackburn Rov	Tr	01.70	69-75	242	0	0
Newcastle U	Tr	03.76	75	5	0	0
Stoke C	Tr	02.77	76-79	101	0	0
Derby Co	Tr	07.80	80-81	59	0	0
Birmingham C	L	02.82	81	4	0	0
York C	Tr	08.82	82-84	122	0	0
JONES Ronald (Ron)						
Crewe, 9 April, 1918 Died 1987						(W)
Crewe Alex	Heslington Victoria	05.37	36-46	22	-	7
JONES Ronald (Ron) John						
Rhondda, 27 February, 1926 Died 1991						(CF)
Swansea T		07.49				
Scunthorpe U	Tr	08.50	50	3	-	0
JONES Roy						
Stoke-on-Trent, 20 December, 1924						(CD)
Stoke C	Jnrs	10.43	47-49	7	-	0
JONES Roy John						
Clacton, 26 July, 1942						(G)
Swindon T		10.67	67-71	34	0	0
JONES Ryan Anthony						
Sheffield, 23 July, 1973 Wu21-4/WB/W-1						(M)
Sheffield Wed	YT	06.91	92-94	36	5	6
Scunthorpe U	L	01.96	95	11	0	3
JONES Scott						
Sheffield, 1 May, 1975						(CD)
Barnsley	YT	02.94	95-99	76	7	4
Mansfield T	L	08.97	97	6	0	0
Bristol Rov	Tr	08.00	00-01	51	7	3
York C	Tr	03.02	01-02	26	2	1
JONES Thomas Selwyn						
Rhos, 3 April, 1929 Died 1995						(W)
Everton		07.49				
Sheffield Wed		08.51				
Leyton Orient	Tr	07.52	52	6	-	0
JONES Shane Graham						
Tredegar, 8 November, 1972						(M)
Hereford U	YT	08.91	89-91	12	26	1
JONES Sidney (Sid)						
Rothwell, 15 February, 1921 Died 1977						(FB)
Arsenal	Kippax Jnrs	05.39				
Walsall	Tr	07.48	48-51	146	-	1
JONES Eric Sidney (Sid)						
Wrexham, 10 October, 1921 Died 1981						(W)
Bolton W	Jnrs	05.39				
Norwich C	Tr	12.45	46-47	40	-	9
JONES Simon Christopher						
Nettleham, 16 May, 1945						(G)
Rochdale	Gainsborough Trinity	06.63	63-66	47	0	0
Chester	Bangor C	10.67	67	3	0	0
JONES Stanley (Stan)						
						(W)
Crewe Alex		08.47	47	1	-	0
JONES Stanley (Stan) George						
Highley, 16 November, 1938						(CD)
Walsall	Kidderminster Hrs	05.56	57-59	30	-	0
West Bromwich A	Tr	05.60	60-66	239	0	2
Walsall	Tr	03.68	67-72	204	2	7
JONES Stephen Alexander						
Plymouth, 11 March, 1974						(F)
Plymouth Arg	YT	07.92	91	0	1	0
JONES Stephen (Steve) Anthony						
Wrexham, 28 November, 1962						(F)
Wrexham	Jnrs	08.81	80-81	3	2	0
Crewe Alex	Tr	08.82	82	6	4	1
JONES Stephen (Steve) Gary						
Cambridge, 17 March, 1970						(F)
West Ham U	Billericay T	11.92	92-94	8	8	4
Bournemouth	Tr	10.94	94-95	71	3	26
West Ham U	Tr	05.96	96	5	3	0
Charlton Ath	Tr	02.97	96-99	28	24	8
Bournemouth	L	12.97	97	5	0	4
Bristol C	Tr	09.99	99-01	29	8	7
Brentford	L	01.00	99	6	2	0
Southend U	L	03.00	99	9	0	2
Wycombe W	L	07.00	00	5	0	0

League Club	Source	Date Signed	Seasons Played	Career Record Apps	Subs	Gls
JONES Stephen (Steve) Graham						
Derry, 25 October, 1976 NI-16 (F)						
Blackpool	Chadderton	10.95				
Bury	Tr	08.96				
Crewe Alex	Leigh RMI	07.01	01-04	86	32	34
Rochdale	L	02.02	01	6	3	1
JONES Stephen (Steve) Robert						
Bristol, 25 December, 1970 (FB)						
Swansea C	Cheltenham T	11.95	95-00	140	6	4
Cheltenham T	Tr	07.01	01-02	7	3	0
JONES Stephen (Steve) Russell						
Eastbourne, 25 July, 1957 (FB)						
Queens Park Rgrs	App	10.74				
Walsall	Tr	01.79	78	15	0	0
Wimbledon	Tr	07.79	79-82	77	2	1
JONES Samuel Stephen (Steve) Thomas						
Harrogate, 6 September, 1955 (G)						
Bradford C	App	09.73	72	2	0	0
JONES Steven (Steve)						
Stockton, 31 January, 1974 (G)						
Hartlepool U	YT	05.92	91-95	45	3	0
JONES Steven (Steve) Francis						
Liverpool, 18 October, 1960 (M)						
Manchester U	App	10.77				
Port Vale	Tr	05.79	79-80	24	1	3
JONES Steven (Steve) Wynn						
Wrexham, 23 October, 1964 (FB)						
Wrexham	Jnrs	08.83	82-83	9	1	1
JONES Stuart Clive						
Bristol, 24 October, 1977 (G)						
Sheffield Wed	Weston-super-Mare	03.98				
Torquay U	Tr	02.00	99-00	32	0	0
Brighton & Hove A	Weston-super-Mare	02.04	03	2	1	0
Doncaster Rov	Tr	08.04	04	3	1	0
JONES Stuart John						
Aberystwyth, 14 March, 1984 WYth/Wu21-1 (FB)						
Swansea C	Sch	07.03	02-04	23	11	0
JONES Tecwyn						
Holywell, 3 January, 1930 (FB)						
Brentford		03.50	51-52	5	-	0
Wrexham	Tr	07.53	53	4	-	0
JONES Tecwyn Lloyd						
Ruabon, 27 January, 1941 Wu23-1 (WH)						
Wrexham	Jnrs	05.59	61-64	57	-	2
Colchester U	Tr	10.64	64-65	28	0	0
Crewe Alex	Tr	10.65	65	8	0	0
JONES Thomas (Tommy)						
Aldershot, 7 October, 1964 ESemiPro (M)						
Swindon T	Aberdeen	09.88	88-91	162	6	12
Reading	Tr	07.92	92-95	63	16	2
JONES Thomas (Tommy) Edwin						
Liverpool, 11 April, 1930 EYth (CD)						
Everton	Jnrs	01.48	50-61	383	-	14
JONES Thomas (Tommy) George						
Connah's Quay, 12 October, 1917 Died 2004 WSch/WWar-10/W-17 (CD)						
Wrexham	Llanerch Celts	11.34	35	6	-	0
Everton	Tr	03.36	36-49	165	-	4
JONES Thomas (Tommy) William						
Oakengates, 23 March, 1907 Died 1980 (IF)						
West Bromwich A	Oakengates T	07.29				
Burnley	Tr	11.30	30-33	94	-	24
Blackpool	Tr	09.33	33-37	153	-	38
Grimsby T	Tr	07.38	38-46	48	-	8
JONES Trevor						
Aberdare, 27 January, 1923 Died 1983 (W)						
Plymouth Arg	Aberaman	05.48				
Watford	Tr	08.49	49	15	-	2
JONES Vaughan						
Tonyrefail, 2 September, 1959 WYth/Wu21-2 (CD)						
Bristol Rov	App	09.77	76-81	93	8	3
Newport Co	Tr	08.82	82-83	67	1	4
Cardiff C	Tr	07.84	84	11	0	1
Bristol Rov	Tr	12.84	84-92	277	3	9

League Club	Source	Date Signed	Seasons Played	Career Record Apps	Subs	Gls
JONES Vincent (Vinnie) Peter						
Watford, 5 January, 1965 W-9 (M)						
Wimbledon	Wealdstone	11.86	86-88	77	0	9
Leeds U	Tr	06.89	89-90	44	2	5
Sheffield U	Tr	09.90	90-91	35	0	2
Chelsea	Tr	08.91	91-92	42	0	4
Wimbledon	Tr	09.92	92-97	171	6	12
Queens Park Rgrs	Tr	03.98	97-98	8	1	1
JONES Walter						
Lurgan, 4 April, 1925 (WH)						
Blackpool	Linfield	12.47				
Doncaster Rov	Tr	06.50	50-52	69	-	2
York C	Tr	11.54	54	1	-	0
JONES Walter Schofield						
Rochdale, 9 January, 1925 Died 2001 (CF)						
Rochdale	St Chad's	11.46	46	2	-	2
JONES Philip Wayne						
Treorchy, 20 October, 1948 Wu23-6/W-1 (M)						
Bristol Rov	Jnrs	10.66	66-72	218	5	28
JONES William (Billy)						
Shrewsbury, 24 March, 1987 EYth (CD)						
Crewe Alex	Sch	07.04	03-04	43	4	1
JONES William (Bill) Henry						
Macclesfield, 13 May, 1921 FLge-1/EB/E-2 (CD)						
Liverpool	Hayfield St Matthew's	09.38	46-53	257	-	17
JONES William (Willie) John						
Aberbargoed, 5 May, 1925 Died 1999 (W)						
Ipswich T	Bargoed	04.49	49-54	33	-	1
JONES William (Bill) John Beattie						
Liverpool, 6 June, 1924 Died 1995 (CF)						
Manchester C		05.48	48-49	3	-	0
Chester	Tr	06.51	51	29	-	4
JONES William (Billy) Kenneth						
Chatham, 26 March, 1983 (FB)						
Leyton Orient	YT	07.01	00-03	68	4	0
Kidderminster Hrs	Tr	01.05	04	10	2	0
JONK Wim						
Volendam, Holland, 12 October, 1966 Holland 49 (M)						
Sheffield Wed	PSV Eindhoven (Holl)	08.98	98-00	69	1	5
JONSON Mattias						
Orebro, Sweden, 16 January, 1974 Sweden 40 (M)						
Norwich C	Brondby (Den)	08.04	04	19	9	0
JONSSON Sigurdur (Siggi)						
Akranes, Iceland, 27 September, 1966 IcYth/Icu21/Iceland int (M)						
Sheffield Wed	IA Akranes (Ice)	02.85	84-88	59	8	4
Barnsley	L	01.86	85	5	0	0
Arsenal	Tr	07.89	89-90	2	6	1
JOPLING Joseph (Joe)						
South Shields, 21 April, 1951 (CD)						
Aldershot	Horton Westoe	08.69	69-70	35	0	2
Leicester C	Tr	09.70	70-73	2	1	0
Torquay U	L	01.74	73	6	0	0
Aldershot	Tr	03.74	73-83	321	11	11
[JORDAO] BATISTA Adelino Jose Martins						
Malange, Angola, 30 August, 1971 (M)						
West Bromwich A	Sporting Braga (Por)	08.00	00-02	47	16	6
JORDAN Andrew Joseph						
Manchester, 14 December, 1979 Su21-4 (CD)						
Bristol C	YT	12.97	98-00	10	1	0
Cardiff C	Tr	10.00	00	3	2	0
Hartlepool U	Tr	08.03	03	4	1	0
JORDAN Brian Athol						
Bentley, 31 January, 1932 (WH)						
Derby Co		10.51				
Rotherham U	Denaby U	07.53	53-58	38	-	0
Middlesbrough	Tr	11.58	58	5	-	0
York C	Tr	07.60	60	8	-	0
JORDAN Clarence (Clarrie)						
South Kirkby, 20 June, 1922 Died 1992 (CF)						
Doncaster Rov	Upton Colliery	04.40	46-47	60	-	48
Sheffield Wed	Tr	02.48	47-54	92	-	36
JORDAN Colin						
Hemsworth, 2 June, 1934 (FB)						
Bradford PA	Fitzwilliam YC	04.52	53-56	27	-	0

League Club	Source	Date Signed	Seasons Played	Apps	Subs	Gls
JORDAN David Charles						
Gillingham, 26 October, 1971						(F)
Gillingham	YT	06.90	90	0	2	0
JORDAN Gerald (Gerry)						
Seaham, 4 April, 1949						(FB)
Northampton T	Jnrs	06.66	66	1	0	0
JORDAN John (Jack)						
Glasgow, 25 February, 1924						(W)
Reading	Alloa Ath	10.48	48	3	-	0
JORDAN John (Johnny) William						
Romford, 8 November, 1921						(IF)
Tottenham H	Grays Ath	08.47	47	24	-	10
Birmingham C	Juventus (It)	03.49	48-49	24	-	2
Sheffield Wed	Tr	09.50	50	10	-	2
JORDAN Joseph (Joe)						
Carluke, 15 December, 1951 Su23-1/S-52						(F)
Leeds U	Morton	10.70	71-77	139	30	35
Manchester U	Tr	01.78	77-80	109	0	37
Southampton	Verona (It)	08.84	84-86	48	0	12
Bristol C	Tr	02.87	86-89	38	19	8
JORDAN Michael (Mike) John						
Exeter, 8 January, 1956						(W)
Exeter C		07.75	75-76	15	3	3
JORDAN Roy Antony						
Plymouth, 17 April, 1978						(W)
Hereford U	YT	●	96	1	0	0
JORDAN Scott Douglas						
Newcastle, 19 July, 1975						(M)
York C	YT	10.92	92-00	123	44	12
JORDAN Stephen (Steve) Robert						
Warrington, 6 March, 1982						(FB)
Manchester C	YT	03.99	02-04	19	3	0
Cambridge U	L	10.02	02	11	0	0
JORDAN Thomas (Tom) Michael						
Manchester, 24 May, 1981						(FB)
Bristol C	YT	03.01				
Southend U	Tr	08.02	02	0	1	0
JORDAN Timothy (Tim) Edwin						
Littleborough, 12 April, 1960						(F)
Oldham Ath	Jnrs	06.78	78-79	2	3	0
JORGENSEN Claus Beck						
Holstebro, Denmark, 27 April, 1979 FaroeIs-5						(M)
Bournemouth	AC Horsens (Den)	07.99	99-00	77	10	14
Bradford C	Tr	07.01	01-02	41	9	12
Coventry C	Tr	08.03	03-04	15	10	3
Bournemouth	L	01.04	03	16	1	0
JORGENSEN Henrik						
Bogense, Denmark, 12 January, 1979						(FB)
Notts Co	B1909 (Den)	10.00	00-01	3	4	0
[JOSEMI] GONZALEZ Jose Miguel						
Malaga, Spain, 15 November, 1979						(FB)
Liverpool	Malaga (Sp)	07.04	04	13	2	0
JOSEPH David						
Guadeloupe, 22 November, 1976						(F)
Notts Co (L)	Montpellier (Fr)	08.00	00	13	14	4
JOSEPH Francis						
Kilburn, 6 March, 1960						(F)
Wimbledon	Hillingdon Borough	11.80	80-81	42	9	13
Brentford	Tr	07.82	82-86	103	7	43
Wimbledon	L	03.87	86	2	3	1
Reading	Tr	07.87	87	5	6	2
Bristol Rov	L	01.88	87	3	0	0
Aldershot	L	03.88	87	9	1	2
Sheffield U	Tr	07.88	88	5	8	3
Gillingham	Tr	03.89	88-89	12	6	1
Crewe Alex	Tr	12.89	89	9	7	2
Fulham	Tr	08.90	90	2	2	0
Barnet	Racing Ghent (Bel)	10.91	91	1	0	0
JOSEPH Leon						
Stepney, 26 February, 1920 Died 1983 EAmat						(W)
Tottenham H (Am)	Leytonstone (Am)	02.47	46	1	-	0
JOSEPH Marc Ellis						
Leicester, 10 November, 1976						(CD)
Cambridge U	YT	05.95	95-00	136	17	0
Peterborough U	Tr	07.01	01-02	60	1	2
Hull C	Tr	11.02	02-04	79	5	1
JOSEPH Matthew (Matt) Nathaniel Adolphus						
Bethnal Green, 30 September, 1972 EYth/Barbados-2						(FB)
Arsenal	YT	11.90				
Gillingham	Tr	12.92				
Cambridge U	Tr	11.93	93-97	157	2	6
Leyton Orient	Tr	01.98	97-03	219	5	2
JOSEPH Roger Anthony						
Paddington, 24 December, 1965 EB-2						(FB)
Brentford	Southall	10.84	84-87	103	1	2
Wimbledon	Tr	08.88	88-94	155	7	0
Millwall	L	03.95	94	5	0	0
Leyton Orient	Tr	11.96	96	15	0	0
West Bromwich A	Tr	02.97	96	0	2	0
Leyton Orient	Tr	08.97	97-99	26	24	0
JOSLIN Philip (Phil) James						
Kingsteignton, 1 September, 1916 Died 1981						(G)
Torquay U	Plymouth Arg (Am)	01.36	35-47	135	-	0
Cardiff C	Tr	05.48	48-50	108	-	0
JOSLYN Roger Douglas William						
Colchester, 7 May, 1950						(M)
Colchester U	Jnrs	05.68	67-70	92	7	4
Aldershot	Tr	10.70	70-74	186	0	17
Watford	Tr	11.74	74-79	178	4	17
Reading	Tr	11.79	79-81	67	1	1
JOVANOVIC Nikola						
Cetinje, Yugoslavia, 18 September, 1952 Yugoslavia int						(CD)
Manchester U	Red Star Belgrade (Yug)	01.80	79-80	20	1	4
JOWETT Harold (Harry) Uttley						
Halifax, 15 November, 1923						(W)
Halifax T		09.50	50	9	-	1
JOWETT Sylvester **James (Jim)**						
Sheffield, 27 January, 1926						(W)
York C	Sheffield U (Am)	09.46	46	1	-	0
JOWETT Kenneth (Ken) Stuart						
Bradford, 9 March, 1927 Died 1993						(W)
Halifax T	Fryston Colliery	02.47	46-48	29	-	2
JOWSEY James Robert						
Filey, 24 November, 1983						(G)
Manchester U	YT	11.00				
Cambridge U	Scarborough	09.04	04	1	0	0
JOY Bernard						
Fulham, 29 October, 1911 Died 1984 EAmat/EWar-1/E-1						(CD)
Fulham (Am)	Casuals	02.31	33	1	-	0
Arsenal (Am)	Casuals	05.35	35-46	86	-	0
JOY Brian William						
Salford, 26 February, 1951						(FB)
Blackburn Rov	Coventry C (Am)	08.68				
Torquay U	Tr	08.69	69	26	1	0
Tranmere Rov	Tr	06.70	70	21	0	1
Doncaster Rov	Tr	07.72	72	28	6	1
Exeter C	Tr	07.73	73-75	89	1	2
York C	San Diego (USA)	09.76	76	18	0	0
JOY David Frederick						
Barnard Castle, 23 September, 1943 EYth						(FB)
Huddersfield T	Evenwood T	07.62	65	1	0	0
York C	Tr	06.67	67	13	2	0
JOY Harold Cuthbert						
Ebbw Vale, 8 January, 1921 Died 2000						(CF)
Norwich C	Lovells Ath	02.47	46	8	-	4
Newport Co	Tr	01.48	47	2	-	0
JOY Ian Paul						
San Diego, USA, 14 July, 1981 USA u20						(FB)
Tranmere Rov	YT	07.98				
Kidderminster Hrs	Montrose	08.01	01-02	15	7	0
JOYCE Anthony (Tony) John						
Wembley, 24 September, 1971						(FB)
Queens Park Rgrs	YT	03.90				
Aldershot	Tr	05.91	90	3	0	0
JOYCE Christopher (Chris)						
Dumbarton, 19 April, 1933 Died 2002						(IF)
Nottingham F	Vale of Leven	09.56	57	10	-	0
Notts Co	Tr	07.59	59-61	62	-	18

JOYCE Eric
Durham, 3 July, 1924 Died 1977 (WH)

League Club	Source	Date Signed	Seasons Played	Apps	Subs	Gls
Bradford C	Eppleton CW	11.45	46	5	-	0

JOYCE John
Easington, 6 January, 1949 (W)

League Club	Source	Date Signed	Seasons Played	Apps	Subs	Gls
Hartlepools U (Am)	Peterlee Jnrs	03.67	66-68	4	0	0

JOYCE Joseph (Joe) Patrick
Consett, 18 March, 1961 (FB)

League Club	Source	Date Signed	Seasons Played	Apps	Subs	Gls
Barnsley	Jnrs	11.79	79-90	332	2	4
Scunthorpe U	Tr	02.91	90-92	91	0	2
Carlisle U	Tr	08.93	93-94	45	5	0
Darlington	L	09.93	93	4	0	0

JOYCE Nicholas (Nick) John
Leeds, 27 July, 1947 (W)

League Club	Source	Date Signed	Seasons Played	Apps	Subs	Gls
Bradford C (Am)	Ashley Road	11.71	71	5	0	1

JOYCE Sean William
Doncaster, 15 February, 1967 (M)

League Club	Source	Date Signed	Seasons Played	Apps	Subs	Gls
Doncaster Rov	App	09.86	85-87	39	2	2
Exeter C	L	11.86	86	1	0	0
Torquay U	Tr	08.88	88-92	143	15	15

JOYCE Walter
Oldham, 10 September, 1937 Died 1999 (CD)

League Club	Source	Date Signed	Seasons Played	Apps	Subs	Gls
Burnley	Jnrs	10.54	60-63	70	-	3
Blackburn Rov	Tr	02.64	63-67	119	1	4
Oldham Ath	Tr	09.67	67-69	68	3	2

JOYCE Warren Garton
Oldham, 20 January, 1965 (M)

League Club	Source	Date Signed	Seasons Played	Apps	Subs	Gls
Bolton W	Jnrs	06.82	82-87	180	4	17
Preston NE	Tr	10.87	87-91	170	7	35
Plymouth Arg	Tr	05.92	92	28	2	3
Burnley	Tr	07.93	93-95	65	5	9
Hull C	L	01.95	94	9	0	3
Hull C	Tr	07.96	96-99	137	1	12

JOYNES Nathan
Hoyland, 7 August, 1985 (F)

League Club	Source	Date Signed	Seasons Played	Apps	Subs	Gls
Barnsley	Sch	02.05	04	0	1	0

[JUAN] MALDONDO DUARTE Juan
Sao Paulo, Brazil, 6 February, 1982 (FB)

League Club	Source	Date Signed	Seasons Played	Apps	Subs	Gls
Arsenal	Sao Paulo (Br)	07.01				
Millwall	L	08.03	03	2	1	0

[JUANJO] PEREZ Juanjo Carricondo
Barcelona, Spain, 4 May, 1977 (F)

League Club	Source	Date Signed	Seasons Played	Apps	Subs	Gls
Bradford C	Heart of Midlothian	10.01	01-02	7	19	1

JUDD Jeremy Laurence
Bristol, 18 June, 1965 (G)

League Club	Source	Date Signed	Seasons Played	Apps	Subs	Gls
Bournemouth	Jnrs	07.82				
Torquay U	Dorchester T	08.84	84	2	0	0

JUDD Michael (Mike) David
Southampton, 18 June, 1948 (W)

League Club	Source	Date Signed	Seasons Played	Apps	Subs	Gls
Southampton	App	08.65	67-69	14	1	3

JUDD Walter James
Salisbury, 25 October, 1926 Died 1964 (CF)

League Club	Source	Date Signed	Seasons Played	Apps	Subs	Gls
Southampton	Nomansland	08.49	50-52	34	-	13

JUDGE Alan Graham
Kingsbury, 14 May, 1960 (G)

League Club	Source	Date Signed	Seasons Played	Apps	Subs	Gls
Luton T	Jnrs	01.78	79-82	11	0	0
Reading	L	09.82	82	3	0	0
Reading	Tr	11.82	82-84	74	0	0
Oxford U	Tr	12.84	85-90	80	0	0
Lincoln C	L	11.85	85	2	0	0
Cardiff C	L	10.87	87	8	0	0
Hereford U	Tr	07.91	91-93	105	0	0
Swindon T	Banbury U	12.02				
Oxford U	Tr	03.03	02-04	2	0	0

JUDGE Matthew (Matt) Peter
Barking, 18 January, 1985 IRYth (F)

League Club	Source	Date Signed	Seasons Played	Apps	Subs	Gls
Luton T	Sch	●	02-03	0	2	0

JUDGES Barry John
Rainham, Kent, 23 September, 1940 (CD)

League Club	Source	Date Signed	Seasons Played	Apps	Subs	Gls
Gillingham	Jnrs	12.57	57-58	2	-	0

JUKES Norman Geoffrey
Leeds, 14 October, 1932 (FB)

League Club	Source	Date Signed	Seasons Played	Apps	Subs	Gls
Huddersfield T		07.51				
York C	Tr	10.53	53	1	-	0

JULES Mark Anthony
Bradford, 5 September, 1971 (FB)

League Club	Source	Date Signed	Seasons Played	Apps	Subs	Gls
Bradford C	YT	07.90				
Scarborough	Tr	08.91	91-92	57	20	16
Chesterfield	Tr	05.93	93-98	155	31	4
Halifax T	Tr	07.99	99-01	88	9	1

JULIAN Alan John
Ashford, 11 March, 1983 NIYth/NIu21-1 (G)

League Club	Source	Date Signed	Seasons Played	Apps	Subs	Gls
Brentford	YT	07.01	02-03	16	0	0

JULIANS Leonard (Len) Bruce
Tottenham, 19 June, 1933 Died 1993 (CF)

League Club	Source	Date Signed	Seasons Played	Apps	Subs	Gls
Leyton Orient	Walthamstow Ave	06.55	55-58	66	-	35
Arsenal	Tr	12.58	58-59	18	-	7
Nottingham F	Tr	06.60	60-63	58	-	24
Millwall	Tr	01.64	63-66	125	0	58

[JULIO CESAR] SANTOS-CORREIA Julio Cesar
Sao Luis, Brazil, 18 November, 1978 (CD)

League Club	Source	Date Signed	Seasons Played	Apps	Subs	Gls
Bolton W	Real Madrid (Sp)	08.04	04	4	1	0

JULIUSSEN Albert Laurence
Blyth, 20 February, 1920 (CF)

League Club	Source	Date Signed	Seasons Played	Apps	Subs	Gls
Huddersfield T	Dundee North End	10.38				
Portsmouth	Dundee	03.48	47	7	-	4
Everton	Tr	09.48	48	10	-	1

JUMP Stewart Paul
Crumpsall, 27 January, 1952 (CD)

League Club	Source	Date Signed	Seasons Played	Apps	Subs	Gls
Stoke C	App	07.69	70-73	36	8	1
Crystal Palace	Tr	12.73	73-75	67	1	2
Crystal Palace	NY Cosmos (USA)	09.76	76-77	12	1	0
Fulham	L	01.77	76	3	0	0

[JUNINHO] JUNIOR Osvaldo Giroldo
Sao Paulo, Brazil, 22 February, 1973 Brazil 50 (F)

League Club	Source	Date Signed	Seasons Played	Apps	Subs	Gls
Middlesbrough	Sao Paulo (Br)	11.95	95-96	54	2	14
Middlesbrough (L)	Atletico Madrid (Sp)	09.99	99	24	4	4
Middlesbrough	Atletico Madrid (Sp)	08.02	02-03	35	6	11

[JUNIOR] GUIMARAES SANIBIO Jose Luis
Fortaleza, Brazil, 20 July, 1976 (F)

League Club	Source	Date Signed	Seasons Played	Apps	Subs	Gls
Walsall	Treze (Br)	08.02	02	28	8	15
Derby Co	Tr	08.03	03-04	11	19	4
Rotherham U	L	10.04	04	12	0	2

JUPP Duncan Alan
Guildford, 25 January, 1975 Su21-9 (FB)

League Club	Source	Date Signed	Seasons Played	Apps	Subs	Gls
Fulham	YT	07.93	92-95	101	4	2
Wimbledon	Tr	06.96	96-01	23	7	0
Notts Co	Tr	11.02	02	6	2	0
Luton T	Tr	02.03	02	2	3	0
Southend U	Tr	07.03	03-04	67	4	0

JURYEFF Ian Martin
Gosport, 24 November, 1962 (F)

League Club	Source	Date Signed	Seasons Played	Apps	Subs	Gls
Southampton	App	11.80	83	0	2	0
Mansfield T	L	03.84	83	12	0	5
Reading	L	11.84	84	7	0	2
Orient	Tr	02.85	84-88	106	5	44
Ipswich T	L	02.89	88	0	2	0
Halifax T	Tr	08.89	89	15	2	7
Hereford U	Tr	12.89	89-90	25	3	4
Halifax T	Tr	09.90	90-92	72	0	13
Darlington	Tr	08.92	92-93	26	8	6
Scunthorpe U	Tr	08.93	93-94	41	3	13

League Club	Source	Date Signed	Seasons Played	Apps	Subs	Gls
KAAK Anton (Tom) Christian						
Winterswijk, Holland, 31 March, 1978						(M)
Darlington	Heracles (Holl)	07.00	00	7	1	2
KAAMARK Pontus Sven						
Vasteras, Sweden, 5 April, 1969 Sweden 43						(FB)
Leicester C	IFK Gothenburg (Swe)	11.95	95-98	60	5	0
KABBA Stephen (Steve)						
Lambeth, 7 March, 1981						(F)
Crystal Palace	YT	06.99	99-02	2	8	1
Luton T	L	03.02	01	0	3	0
Grimsby T	L	08.02	02	13	0	6
Sheffield U	Tr	11.02	02-04	25	12	9
KABIA James (Jim) Paul						
Mansfield, 11 November, 1954						(F)
Chesterfield	App	11.72	72-73	10	1	1
KABIA Jason Thomas						
Sutton-in-Ashfield, 28 May, 1969						(F)
Lincoln C	Oakham U	01.92	91-92	17	11	4
Doncaster Rov	L	01.93	92	5	0	0
KACHLOUL Hassan						
Agadir, Morocco, 19 February, 1973 Morocco 12						(M)
Southampton	St Etienne (Fr)	10.98	98-00	73	13	14
Aston Villa	Tr	07.01	01	17	5	2
Wolverhampton W	L	09.03	03	0	4	0
KAILE Gordon Walter						
Pimperne, 7 December, 1924 Died 1988						(W)
Nottingham F	RAOC Chilwell	05.45	47-49	65	-	8
Preston NE	Tr	07.51	51-53	7	-	1
Exeter C	Tr	08.54	54	6	-	1
KAISER Rudolph (Rudi) Hendrick						
Amsterdam, Holland, 26 December, 1960						(W)
Coventry C	Royal Antwerp (Bel)	08.81	81	11	5	3
KAKU Blessing						
Ughelli, Nigeria, 5 March, 1978 Nigeria int						(F)
Bolton W	MS Ashdod (Nig)	08.04	04	0	1	0
Derby Co	L	11.04	04	3	1	0
KALAC Zeljko						
Camperdown, Australia, 16 December, 1972 Australia int						(G)
Leicester C	Sydney U (Aus)	10.95	95	1	0	0
KALOGERACOS Vasilios (Vas)						
Perth, Australia, 21 March, 1975						(F)
Birmingham C	Sydney Olympic (Aus)	12.93				
Stockport Co	Perth Glory (Aus)	08.97	97	0	2	0
KAMARA Abdul Salam						
Southampton, 10 February, 1974						(M)
Southampton	Jnrs	08.92				
Bristol C	Tr	03.93	93	0	1	0
KAMARA Alan						
Sheffield, 15 July, 1958						(FB)
York C	Kiveton Park	07.79	79	10	0	0
Darlington	Tr	06.80	80-82	134	0	1
Scarborough	Burton A	11.87	87-90	158	1	2
Halifax T	Tr	08.91	91-92	34	2	0
KAMARA Christopher (Chris)						
Middlesbrough, 25 December, 1957						(M)
Portsmouth	App	12.75	75-76	56	7	7
Swindon T	Tr	08.77	77-80	133	14	21
Portsmouth	Tr	08.81	81	11	0	0
Brentford	Tr	10.81	81-84	150	2	28
Swindon T	Tr	08.85	85-87	86	1	6
Stoke C	Tr	07.88	88-89	60	0	5
Leeds U	Tr	01.90	89-91	15	5	1
Luton T	Tr	11.91	91-92	49	0	0
Sheffield U	L	11.92	92	6	2	0
Middlesbrough	L	02.93	92	3	2	0
Sheffield U	Tr	07.93	93	15	1	0
Bradford C	Tr	07.94	94	22	1	3
KAMARA Diomansy Mehdi						
Paris, France, 8 November, 1980 Senegal int						(F)
Portsmouth	Modena (It)	09.04	04	15	10	4

League Club	Source	Date Signed	Seasons Played	Apps	Subs	Gls
KAMARA Malvin Ginah						
Southwark, 17 November, 1983						(M)
Wimbledon/MK Dons	Sch	07.03	02-04	31	23	3
KAMINSKY Jason Mario George						
Leicester, 5 December, 1973						(F)
Nottingham F	YT	07.91	91	0	1	0
KANCHELSKIS Andrei						
Kirowograd, Ukraine, 23 January, 1969 USSR-17/CIS-6/Russia-36						(W)
Manchester U	Shakhtar Donetsk (Uk)	03.91	90-94	96	27	28
Everton	Tr	08.95	95-96	52	0	20
Manchester C (L)	Glasgow Rgrs	01.01	00	7	3	0
Southampton	Glasgow Rgrs	08.02	02	0	1	0
KANDOL Tresor Osmar						
Banga, DR Congo, 30 August, 1981						(F)
Luton T	YT	09.98	98-00	9	12	3
Cambridge U	Tr	08.01	01	2	2	0
Bournemouth	Tr	10.01	01	3	9	0
KANE Alan						
Falkirk, 20 January, 1957						(M)
Portsmouth	Hibernian	03.75	74-75	6	1	0
KANE John Peter						
Hackney, 15 December, 1960						(CD)
Orient	App	12.78	78	0	1	0
KANE Leonard (Len) Russell						
Belfast, 27 January, 1926 IrLge-3						(FB)
Preston NE	Glentoran	05.47	48-49	5	-	0
KANE Paul James						
Edinburgh, 8 September, 1965 SYth						(M)
Oldham Ath	Hibernian	01.91	90-91	13	8	0
Barnsley (L)	Aberdeen	08.95	95	4	0	0
KANE Peter						
Petershill, 4 April, 1939						(IF)
Northampton T	Queen's Park	10.59	59	28	-	16
Arsenal	Tr	07.60	60	4	-	1
Northampton T	Tr	09.63	63	18	-	8
Crewe Alex	Tr	03.64	63-66	82	1	29
KANE Robert (Bob)						
Cambuslang, 11 May, 1911 Died 1985						(CD)
Leeds U	St Roch's	08.35	35-46	57	-	0
KANOUTE Frederic (Fredi)						
Sainte Foy-les-Lyon, France, 2 September, 1977 Fru21/FrB-1/Mali-5						(F)
West Ham U	Lyon (Fr)	03.00	99-02	79	5	29
Tottenham H	Tr	08.03	03-04	41	18	14
KANU Christopher (Chris)						
Owerri, Nigeria, 4 December, 1979 Nigeria int						(FB)
Peterborough U	TOP Oss (Holl)	08.03	03-04	25	9	0
KANU Nwankwo						
Owerri, Nigeria, 1 August, 1976 NgYth/Ngu23/Ng-39						(F)
Arsenal	Inter Milan (It)	02.99	98-03	63	56	30
West Bromwich A	Tr	07.04	04	21	7	2
KANYUKA Patrick						
Kinshasa, DR Congo, 19 July, 1987						(CD)
Queens Park Rgrs	Jnrs	07.04	04	1	0	0
KAPENGWE Emment						
Zambia, 27 March, 1943						(W)
Aston Villa	Atlanta (USA)	09.69	69	3	0	0
KAPLER Konrad						
Tychy, Poland, 25 February, 1925 Died 1991						(W)
Rochdale	Glasgow Celtic	05.49	49	4	-	0
KAPRIELIAN Mickael						
Marseille, France, 6 October, 1980 FrYth						(F)
Bolton W	Martigues (Fr)	01.00	99	0	1	0
KARAA Roch Di						
Tunisia, 3 April, 1964						(G)
Darlington		03.85	84	1	0	0
KARAM Amine						
Besancon, France, 3 January, 1984						(W)
Oxford U	Sochaux (Fr)	02.04	04	0	2	0
KARBASSIYOON Daniel (Danny)						
Virginia, USA, 10 August, 1984 UsYth						(F)
Arsenal	Roanoke Star (USA)	08.03				
Ipswich T	L	12.04	04	3	2	0

KARELSE John
Kapelle, Holland, 17 May, 1970 HoYth/Hou21 (G)

League Club	Source	Date Signed	Seasons Played	Apps	Subs	Gls
Newcastle U	NAC Breda (Holl)	08.99	99	3	0	0

KAREMBEU Christian Lali
Lifou, New Caledonia, 3 December, 1970 France 51 (M)

League Club	Source	Date Signed	Seasons Played	Apps	Subs	Gls
Middlesbrough	Real Madrid (Sp)	08.00	00	31	2	4

KARIC Amir
Oramovica Ponja, Slovenia, 31 December, 1973 Slovenia 46 (CD)

League Club	Source	Date Signed	Seasons Played	Apps	Subs	Gls
Ipswich T	NK Maribor (Sl)	09.00				
Crystal Palace	L	03.01	00	3	0	0

KARL Steffen
Hohenm-Oelsen, Germany, 3 February, 1970 (W)

League Club	Source	Date Signed	Seasons Played	Apps	Subs	Gls
Manchester C (L)	Bor Dortmund (Ger)	03.94	93	4	2	1

KARLSEN Kent
Oslo, Norway, 17 February, 1973 Nou21 (CD)

League Club	Source	Date Signed	Seasons Played	Apps	Subs	Gls
Luton T	FC Valerenga (Nor)	11.00	00	4	2	0

KARLSSON Par
Gothenburg, Sweden, 29 May, 1978 Swu21 (M)

League Club	Source	Date Signed	Seasons Played	Apps	Subs	Gls
Wimbledon	IFK Gothenburg (Swe)	09.00	00-02	10	16	0

KASULE Victor (Vic) Peter
Glasgow, 28 May, 1965 (W)

League Club	Source	Date Signed	Seasons Played	Apps	Subs	Gls
Shrewsbury T	Meadowbank Th	01.88	87-89	28	12	4

KATALINIC Ivan
Yugoslavia, 17 May, 1951 Yugoslavia int (G)

League Club	Source	Date Signed	Seasons Played	Apps	Subs	Gls
Southampton	Red Star Belgrade (Yug)	02.80	79-81	48	0	0

KATCHOURO Petr
Minsk, Belarus, 2 August, 1972 Belarus 25 (F)

League Club	Source	Date Signed	Seasons Played	Apps	Subs	Gls
Sheffield U	Dynamo Minsk (Bs)	07.96	96-99	50	45	19

KAVANAGH Eamonn Anthony
Manchester, 5 January, 1954 (M)

League Club	Source	Date Signed	Seasons Played	Apps	Subs	Gls
Manchester C	Jnrs	06.71				
Rochdale	Tr	10.73	73	2	2	0
Workington	Bury (N/C)	03.74	73-76	123	6	12
Scunthorpe U	Tr	08.77	77-79	68	8	3

KAVANAGH Edward (Eddie) Mark
Glasgow, 20 July, 1941 (W)

League Club	Source	Date Signed	Seasons Played	Apps	Subs	Gls
Notts Co	Cambuslang Rgrs	05.64	64	25	-	4

KAVANAGH Graham Anthony
Dublin, 2 December, 1973 IRSch/IRYth/IRu21-9/IRB-1/IR-12 (M)

League Club	Source	Date Signed	Seasons Played	Apps	Subs	Gls
Middlesbrough	Home Farm	08.91	92-95	22	13	3
Darlington	L	02.94	93	5	0	0
Stoke C	Tr	09.96	96-00	198	8	35
Cardiff C	Tr	07.01	01-04	140	2	28
Wigan Ath	Tr	03.05	04	11	0	0

KAVANAGH Jason Colin
Meriden, 23 November, 1971 ESch/EYth (FB)

League Club	Source	Date Signed	Seasons Played	Apps	Subs	Gls
Derby Co	YT	12.88	90-95	74	25	1
Wycombe W	Tr	11.96	96-98	84	6	1
Stoke C	Tr	03.99	98	8	0	0
Cambridge U	Tr	12.99	99	19	0	0

KAVANAGH Michael (Micky)
Dublin, 31 December, 1927 (IF)

League Club	Source	Date Signed	Seasons Played	Apps	Subs	Gls
Brighton & Hove A	Bohemians	02.48	48-49	26	-	7

KAVANAGH Peter John
Ilford, 3 November, 1938 (W)

League Club	Source	Date Signed	Seasons Played	Apps	Subs	Gls
Fulham	Dagenham	10.56				
Everton	Ramsgate Ath	02.61	60	6	-	0

KAVELASHVILI Mikhail
Tbilisi, Georgia, 22 July, 1971 Georgia int (F)

League Club	Source	Date Signed	Seasons Played	Apps	Subs	Gls
Manchester C	Spartak Vladik's (Rus)	03.96	95-96	9	19	3

KAVIEDES Ivan
Ecuador, 24 October, 1977 Ecuador 40 (F)

League Club	Source	Date Signed	Seasons Played	Apps	Subs	Gls
Crystal Palace (L)	Barcelona de G (Ec)	08.04	04	1	3	0

KAWAGUCHI Yoshikatsu
Shizuoka, Japan, 15 August, 1975 Japan 52 (G)

League Club	Source	Date Signed	Seasons Played	Apps	Subs	Gls
Portsmouth	Yokohama Mar's (Jap)	10.01	01-02	11	1	0

KAY Anthony (Tony) Herbert
Sheffield, 13 May, 1937 Eu23-7/FLge-4/E-1 (WH)

League Club	Source	Date Signed	Seasons Played	Apps	Subs	Gls
Sheffield Wed	Jnrs	05.54	54-62	179	-	10
Everton	Tr	12.62	62-63	50	-	4

KAY Antony Roland
Barnsley, 21 October, 1982 EYth (F)

League Club	Source	Date Signed	Seasons Played	Apps	Subs	Gls
Barnsley	YT	10.99	00-04	92	14	9

KAY James (Jim)
Preston, 3 May, 1932 Died 1986 (IF)

League Club	Source	Date Signed	Seasons Played	Apps	Subs	Gls
Stockport Co	Leyland Motors	05.53	54-55	9	-	3
Crewe Alex	Tr	12.56	56	6	-	0

KAY John
Great Lumley, 29 January, 1964 (FB)

League Club	Source	Date Signed	Seasons Played	Apps	Subs	Gls
Arsenal	App	08.81	82-83	13	1	0
Wimbledon	Tr	07.84	84-86	63	0	2
Middlesbrough	L	01.85	84	8	0	0
Sunderland	Tr	07.87	87-93	196	3	0
Shrewsbury T	L	03.96	95	7	0	0
Preston NE	Tr	08.96	96	7	0	0
Scarborough	Tr	09.96	96-98	97	1	0

KAY Kenneth (Ken)
Newark, 9 March, 1920 Died 1986 (W)

League Club	Source	Date Signed	Seasons Played	Apps	Subs	Gls
Mansfield T	Ransome & Marles	06.47	47	1	-	0

KAY Robert (Roy)
Edinburgh, 24 October, 1949 (FB)

League Club	Source	Date Signed	Seasons Played	Apps	Subs	Gls
York C	Glasgow Celtic	07.78	78-81	160	0	8

KAYE Arthur
Higham, West Yorkshire, 9 May, 1933 Died 2003 ESch/Eu23-1/FLge1 (W)

League Club	Source	Date Signed	Seasons Played	Apps	Subs	Gls
Barnsley	Jnrs	05.50	50-58	265	-	54
Blackpool	Tr	05.59	59-60	48	-	9
Middlesbrough	Tr	11.60	60-64	164	-	38
Colchester U	Tr	06.65	65-66	48	1	2

KAYE David Nicholas
Huddersfield, 14 November, 1959 (G)

League Club	Source	Date Signed	Seasons Played	Apps	Subs	Gls
Rotherham U	App	11.77				
Chester C	Mexborough T	03.85	84-85	10	0	0

KAYE George **Henry (Harry)**
Liverpool, 19 April, 1919 Died 1992 (WH)

League Club	Source	Date Signed	Seasons Played	Apps	Subs	Gls
Liverpool		04.41	46	1	-	0
Swindon T	Tr	05.47	47-52	170	-	5

KAYE John
Goole, 3 March, 1940 FLge-2 (F)

League Club	Source	Date Signed	Seasons Played	Apps	Subs	Gls
Scunthorpe U	Goole T	09.60	60-62	77	-	25
West Bromwich A	Tr	06.63	63-71	281	3	45
Hull C	Tr	11.71	71-73	71	1	9

KAYE Peter John
Huddersfield, 4 February, 1979 (F)

League Club	Source	Date Signed	Seasons Played	Apps	Subs	Gls
Huddersfield T	YT	09.96	96	0	1	0

KAZIM-RICHARDS Colin
Leyton, 26 August, 1986 (M)

League Club	Source	Date Signed	Seasons Played	Apps	Subs	Gls
Bury	Sch	•	04	10	20	3

KEAN Robert (Rob) Steven
Luton, 3 June, 1978 (M)

League Club	Source	Date Signed	Seasons Played	Apps	Subs	Gls
Luton T	YT	05.96	97	0	1	0

KEAN Stephen (Steve)
Glasgow, 30 September, 1967 (W)

League Club	Source	Date Signed	Seasons Played	Apps	Subs	Gls
Swansea C (L)	Glasgow Celtic	02.87	86	3	1	0

KEANE Keith Francis
Luton, 20 November, 1986 (M)

League Club	Source	Date Signed	Seasons Played	Apps	Subs	Gls
Luton T	Sch	08.04	03-04	25	7	1

KEANE Michael Thomas Joseph
Dublin, 29 December, 1982 IRYth/IRu21-7 (M)

League Club	Source	Date Signed	Seasons Played	Apps	Subs	Gls
Preston NE	YT	08.00	00-03	39	18	3
Grimsby T	L	03.03	02	7	0	2
Hull C	Tr	06.04	04	12	8	3
Rotherham U	Tr	03.05	04	9	1	0

KEANE Robert (Robbie) David
Dublin, 8 July, 1980 IRYth/IRB-1/IR-61 (F)

League Club	Source	Date Signed	Seasons Played	Apps	Subs	Gls
Wolverhampton W	YT	07.97	97-99	66	7	24
Coventry C	Tr	08.99	99	30	1	12
Leeds U	Inter Milan (It)	12.00	00-02	28	18	13
Tottenham H	Tr	08.02	02-04	83	15	38

KEANE Roy Maurice
Cork, 10 August, 1971 IRSch/IRYth/IRu21-4/IR-61 (M)

League Club	Source	Date Signed	Seasons Played	Apps	Subs	Gls
Nottingham F	Cobh Ramblers	06.90	90-92	114	0	22
Manchester U	Tr	07.93	93-04	305	16	33

KEANE Thomas (Tommy) Joseph
Galway, 16 September, 1968 IRYth (M)

League Club	Source	Date Signed	Seasons Played	Apps	Subs	Gls
Bournemouth	App	09.86	85-87	1	2	0
Colchester U	Tr	12.87	87	9	7	0

League Club	Source	Date Signed	Seasons Played	Apps	Subs	Gls
KEANE Thomas (Rory) Roderick						
Limerick, 31 August, 1922 Died 2004 IR-4/I-1						(FB)
Swansea T	Limerick C	06.47	47-54	163	-	0
KEAR Michael (Mike) Philip						
Coleford, 27 May, 1943						(W)
Newport Co	Cinderford T	08.63	63	6	-	0
Nottingham F	Tr	12.63	63-66	26	1	5
Middlesbrough	Tr	09.67	67-69	56	2	7
Barnsley	L	08.70	70	6	0	1
KEARNEY Mark James						
Ormskirk, 12 June, 1962						(M)
Everton	Marine	10.81				
Mansfield T	Tr	03.83	82-90	248	2	29
Bury	L	01.91	90	13	0	1
Bury	Tr	03.91	90-93	96	4	4
KEARNEY Michael (Mike) Joseph						
Glasgow, 18 February, 1953						(F)
Shrewsbury T	Petershill Jnrs	12.72	72-76	143	6	41
Chester	Tr	03.77	76-77	37	1	5
Reading	Tr	01.78	77-79	78	9	24
Chester	Tr	07.80	80	9	0	0
Reading	Tr	10.80	80-82	57	1	12
KEARNEY Noel Michael						
Ipswich, 7 October, 1942						(W)
Ipswich T	Jnrs	10.60				
Colchester U	Tr	09.64	64	3	-	0
KEARNEY Sydney (Syd) Francis						
Liverpool, 28 March, 1917 Died 1982						(WH)
Leicester C	Crowndale	08.36				
Tranmere Rov	Tr	05.37	37-38	9	-	2
Accrington St	Tr	11.38	38-46	30	-	7
Bristol C	Tr	01.47	46-49	65	-	5
KEARNEY Thomas (Tom) James						
Liverpool, 7 October, 1981						(M)
Everton	YT	10.99				
Bradford C	Tr	03.02	01-04	35	4	1
KEARNS Frederick (Freddie) Thomas						
Cork, 8 November, 1927 Died 1987 IR-1						(CF)
West Ham U	Shamrock Rov	05.48	49-53	43	-	14
Norwich C	Tr	06.54	54-55	28	-	11
KEARNS Jamie Adam						
Hammersmith, 28 October, 1971						(FB)
Cambridge U	YT	07.90	90	1	0	0
KEARNS Michael (Mick)						
Banbury, 26 November, 1950 IR-18						(G)
Oxford U	App	07.68	69-71	67	0	0
Plymouth Arg	L	10.72	72	1	0	0
Charlton Ath	L	02.73	72	4	0	0
Walsall	Tr	07.73	73-78	249	0	0
Wolverhampton W	Tr	07.79	79-80	9	0	0
Walsall	Tr	08.82	82-84	26	0	0
KEARNS Michael (Mike) David						
Nuneaton, 10 March, 1938						(FB)
Coventry C	Stockingford Victoria	09.55	57-67	344	0	14
KEARNS Oliver (Ollie) Anthony						
Banbury, 12 June, 1956						(F)
Reading	Banbury U	03.77	76-79	75	11	40
Oxford U	Tr	08.81	81	9	9	4
Walsall	Tr	08.82	82	31	7	11
Hereford U	Tr	06.83	83-87	166	4	58
Wrexham	Tr	12.87	87-89	36	10	14
KEARNS Peter Vincent						
Wellingborough, 26 March, 1937						(F)
Plymouth Arg	Wellingborough T	04.56	56-59	64	-	8
Aldershot	Corby T	12.62	62-67	184	1	64
Lincoln C	Tr	03.68	67-68	45	1	11
KEARTON Jason Brett						
Ipswich, Australia, 9 July, 1969						(G)
Everton	Brisbane Lions (Aus)	10.88	92-94	3	3	0
Stoke C	L	08.91	91	16	0	0
Blackpool	L	01.92	91	14	0	0
Notts Co	L	01.95	94	10	0	0
Crewe Alex	Tr	10.96	96-00	190	1	0
KEATES Dean Scott						
Walsall, 30 June, 1978						(M)
Walsall	YT	08.96	96-01	125	34	9
Hull C	Tr	08.02	02-03	45	5	4
Kidderminster Hrs	Tr	02.04	03-04	48	1	7

League Club	Source	Date Signed	Seasons Played	Apps	Subs	Gls
KEATING Brian Alfred						
Lewisham, 19 March, 1935 Died 2005						(CF)
Crewe Alex (Am)	Barry T	07.56	56-57	8	-	1
KEATING Dennis Joseph						
Cork, 18 October, 1940						(W)
Chester	Saltney Jnrs	06.62	62	1	-	0
KEATING Patrick (Pat) Joseph						
Cork, 17 September, 1930 Died 1981						(W)
Sheffield U	Cork Ath	02.50	50	3	-	0
Bradford PA	Wisbech T	09.53	53	2	-	0
Chesterfield	Tr	10.53	53-56	95	-	21
KEATING Robert						
Oldham, 24 June, 1917 Died 1985						(W)
Oldham Ath		08.41				
Accrington St	Hereford U	12.46	46	5	-	0
KEAVENY Jonathan Mark						
Swansea, 24 May, 1981						(F)
Swansea C	Carmarthen T	07.02	02	4	5	0
KEAY John (Jack) Paul						
Glasgow, 14 June, 1960						(CD)
Shrewsbury T	Glasgow Celtic	07.77	77-81	152	3	20
Wrexham	Tr	09.82	82-85	156	0	9
KEE Paul James						
Derry, 21 February, 1967 NIYth						(F)
Mansfield T	App	01.84	83	0	1	0
KEE Paul Victor						
Belfast, 8 November, 1969 NIYth/NIu21-1/NI-9						(G)
Oxford U	Ards	05.88	89-93	56	0	0
KEEBLE Brian Beverley						
Holbeach, 11 July, 1938						(FB)
Grimsby T	Holbeach U	05.59	59-64	172	-	1
Darlington	Tr	07.65	65-68	154	0	2
KEEBLE Christopher (Chris) Mark						
Colchester, 17 September, 1978						(M)
Ipswich T	YT	06.97	97	0	1	0
Colchester U	Tr	03.00	99-02	12	12	2
KEEBLE Walter **Frederick (Fred)**						
Coventry, 30 August, 1919 Died 1987						(IF)
Grimsby T	Albion Rov	09.46	46	7	-	0
Notts Co	Tr	07.47	47	4	-	1
KEEBLE Matthew						
Chipping Norton, 8 September, 1972						(F)
Oxford U	YT	05.91	92-93	1	1	0
KEEBLE Victor (Vic) Albert William						
Colchester, 25 June, 1930						(CF)
Colchester U	King George YC	(N/L)	50-51	46	-	23
Newcastle U	Tr	02.52	51-57	104	-	56
West Ham U	Tr	10.57	57-59	76	-	45
KEEFE David Edward						
Dagenham, 23 June, 1957						(W)
Southend U	App	07.75	74-75	4	2	1
Torquay U	Tr	08.77	77	2	0	0
KEEGAN Gerard (Ged) Anthony						
Little Horton, 3 October, 1955 Eu21-1						(M)
Manchester C	App	03.73	74-78	32	5	2
Oldham Ath	Tr	02.79	78-82	139	5	5
Mansfield T	Tr	10.83	83	18	0	1
Rochdale	Tr	07.84	84	2	0	0
KEEGAN John Kevin Paul						
Liverpool, 5 August, 1981						(FB)
York C	YT	•	99	2	1	0
KEEGAN Joseph **Kevin**						
Armthorpe, 14 February, 1951 Eu23-5/E-63						(F)
Scunthorpe U	App	12.68	68-70	120	4	18
Liverpool	Tr	05.71	71-76	230	0	68
Southampton	SV Hamburg (Ger)	07.80	80-81	68	0	37
Newcastle U	Tr	08.82	82-83	78	0	48
KEEGAN Michael (Mike) Jerard						
Wallasey, 12 May, 1981						(M)
Swansea C	YT	07.99	99-01	7	3	0
KEEGAN Paul Anthony						
Dublin, 5 July, 1984 IRYth/IRu21-5						(M)
Leeds U	YT	07.01				
Scunthorpe U	L	10.03	03	0	2	0

League Club	Source	Date Signed	Seasons Played	Career Record Apps	Subs	Gls
KEELAN Kevin Damien						
Calcutta, India, 5 January, 1941						(G)
Aston Villa	Carpet Traders	07.58	59-60	5	-	0
Stockport Co	Tr	04.61	60	3	-	0
Wrexham	Kidderminster Hrs	11.61	61-62	68	-	0
Norwich C	Tr	07.63	63-79	571	0	0
KEELER Justin Jack						
Hillingdon, 17 April, 1978						(M)
Bournemouth	Christchurch	01.00	99-00	0	4	0
KEELEY Andrew (Andy) James						
Basildon, 16 September, 1956 EYth						(CD)
Tottenham H	App	01.74	76	5	1	0
Sheffield U	Tr	12.77	77-80	28	0	0
Scunthorpe U	Tr	07.81	81-82	75	2	1
KEELEY Damian						
Salford, 14 February, 1963						(F)
Torquay U		09.81	81	1	2	0
KEELEY Glenn Matthew						
Basildon, 1 September, 1954 EYth						(CD)
Ipswich T	App	08.72	72-73	4	0	0
Newcastle U	Tr	07.74	74-75	43	1	2
Blackburn Rov	Tr	08.76	76-86	365	5	23
Everton	L	10.82	82	1	0	0
Oldham Ath	Tr	08.87	87	10	1	0
Colchester U	L	02.88	87	4	0	0
Bolton W	Tr	09.88	88	20	0	0
KEELEY John Henry						
Plaistow, 27 July, 1961						(G)
Southend U	App	07.79	79-84	63	0	0
Brighton & Hove A	Chelmsford C	08.86	86-89	138	0	0
Oldham Ath	Tr	08.90	91-92	2	0	0
Oxford U	L	11.91	91	6	0	0
Reading	L	02.92	91	6	0	0
Chester C	L	08.92	92	4	0	0
Colchester U	Tr	07.93	93	15	0	0
Stockport Co	Chelmsford C	03.94	93-94	20	0	0
Peterborough U	Tr	01.95	94	3	0	0
KEELEY John (Jackie) James						
Liverpool, 18 October, 1936 ESch/EYth						(IF)
Everton	Jnrs	05.54	57	4	-	1
Accrington St	Tr	07.59	59	10	-	1
Southport	Tr	12.59	59	4	-	0
KEELEY Nolan Bruce						
East Barsham, 24 May, 1951						(M)
Scunthorpe U	Yarmouth T	07.73	72-79	255	4	37
Lincoln C	Tr	01.80	79-80	52	0	3
KEELEY Raymond (Ray)						
Battersea, 25 December, 1946						(W)
Charlton Ath	App	12.64	64	1	-	0
Exeter C	Tr	03.66	65-66	45	1	10
Mansfield T	Crawley T	06.68	68-69	48	4	5
KEELEY Walter						
Manchester, 1 April, 1921 Died 1995						(IF)
Accrington St		12.44	46-47	48	-	21
Bury	Tr	10.47	47	7	-	0
Port Vale	Tr	01.48	47-48	18	-	3
Accrington St	Tr	09.48	48-51	101	-	35
Rochdale	Tr	10.51	51	4	-	0
KEEN Alan						
Barrow, 29 May, 1930						(IF)
Barrow	Barrow Social	05.49	49-53	93	-	14
Chesterfield	Tr	07.54	54-55	54	-	12
Bradford PA	Cheltenham T	02.57	56	11	-	1
Carlisle U	Cheltenham T	09.58	58-59	7	-	0
KEEN Herbert (Bert)						
Barrow, 9 September, 1926 Died 1993						(W)
Barrow	Netherfield	07.53	53	8	-	0
KEEN John (Jack)						
Barrow, 26 January, 1929						(WH)
Barrow	West Bromwich A (Am)	01.48	47-58	275	-	20
Workington	Tr	07.59	59	19	-	0
KEEN Kevin Ian						
Amersham, 25 February, 1967 ESch/EYth						(W)
West Ham U	App	03.84	86-92	187	32	21
Wolverhampton W	Tr	07.93	93-94	37	5	7
Stoke C	Tr	10.94	94-99	147	30	10
Macclesfield T	Tr	09.00	00-01	59	3	2

League Club	Source	Date Signed	Seasons Played	Career Record Apps	Subs	Gls
KEEN Michael (Mike) Andrew Charles						
Wrexham, 12 February, 1953 WSch						(G)
Chester	App	09.81				
Wrexham	Lex X1	06.85	85	5	0	0
KEEN Michael (Mike) Thomas						
High Wycombe, 19 March, 1940						(M)
Queens Park Rgrs	Jnrs	06.58	59-68	393	0	39
Luton T	Tr	01.69	68-71	143	1	11
Watford	Tr	07.72	72-74	124	2	5
KEEN Nigel John						
Barrow, 23 October, 1961						(M)
Manchester U	App	02.79				
Preston NE	Barrow	05.85	85	24	0	0
KEEN Peter Alan						
Middlesbrough, 16 November, 1976						(G)
Newcastle U	YT	03.96				
Carlisle U	Tr	08.99	99-03	60	1	1
Darlington	L	03.01	00	7	0	0
KEENAN Gerald (Gerry) Patrick						
Liverpool, 25 July, 1954						(FB)
Bury	Skelmersdale U	04.75	74-78	69	2	3
Port Vale	Tr	09.78	78-81	105	1	7
Rochdale	Ashton U	11.82	82-83	35	0	1
KEENAN Joseph (Joe) John						
Southampton, 14 October, 1982 EYth/Eu20						(M)
Chelsea	YT	10.99	01-02	0	2	0
KEENAN William George						
Llanelli, 29 December, 1918 Died 1993						(W)
Everton	Hereford U	01.39				
Newport Co	Tr	06.46	46	4	-	1
KEENE Douglas (Doug) Charles						
Hendon, 30 August, 1928 Died 1986						(W)
Brentford	Jnrs	09.47	48-49	13	-	1
Brighton & Hove A	Tr	06.50	50-52	61	-	10
Colchester U	Tr	07.53	53	22	-	1
KEENE James Duncan						
Wells, 26 December, 1985						(F)
Portsmouth	Sch	10.04	04	1	1	0
Kidderminster Hrs	L	10.04	04	5	0	0
KEEP Vernon						
Chester, 23 May, 1963						(M)
Wrexham	Connah's Quay	10.84	84	0	1	0
KEERS James (Jim)						
Stanley, 10 December, 1931						(W)
Darlington	Evenwood T	03.52	51-55	74	-	15
KEERY Stanley (Stan)						
Derby, 9 September, 1931						(WH)
Shrewsbury T	Wilmorton	08.52	52	15	-	2
Newcastle U	Tr	11.52	52-56	19	-	1
Mansfield T	Tr	05.57	57-58	53	-	17
Crewe Alex	Tr	10.58	58-64	252	-	21
KEETCH Robert (Bobby) David						
Tottenham, 25 October, 1941 Died 1996						(CD)
Fulham	West Ham U (Am)	04.59	62-65	106	0	2
Queens Park Rgrs	Tr	11.66	66-68	49	3	0
KEETLEY Ernest **Albert**						
Nottingham, 22 February, 1930						(FB)
Bury	Nottingham F (Am)	03.50	50	4	-	0
Bournemouth	Tr	07.52	53-57	86	-	0
KEETON Albert (Bob)						
Chesterfield, 15 January, 1918 Died 1996						(FB)
Torquay U	Mosborough Trinity	06.37	37-47	77	-	0
KEIGHLEY John **Paul**						
Ribchester, 15 February, 1961						(M)
Bolton W	App	02.79				
Crewe Alex	Tr	08.81	81	25	4	0
KEIR Colin William						
Bournemouth, 14 January, 1938						(W)
Portsmouth	Jnrs	05.55				
Workington	Tr	06.59	59	4	-	0
KEIRS John						
Irvine, 14 August, 1947 Died 1995						(CD)
Charlton Ath	Annbank U	06.65	65-70	73	5	1

KEISTER John Edward Samuel
Manchester, 11 November, 1970 SierraLeone 3 (M)

League Club	Source	Date Signed	Seasons Played	Apps	Subs	Gls
Walsall	Faweh	09.93	93-99	78	28	2
Chester C	Tr	01.00	99	8	2	0
Shrewsbury T	Tr	10.00	00	8	0	0

KEITH Adrian John
Colchester, 16 December, 1962 (CD)

League Club	Source	Date Signed	Seasons Played	Apps	Subs	Gls
West Ham U	App	12.80				
Colchester U		12.82	82	4	0	0

KEITH Joseph (Joey) Richard
Plaistow, 1 October, 1978 (FB)

League Club	Source	Date Signed	Seasons Played	Apps	Subs	Gls
West Ham U	YT	07.97				
Colchester U	Tr	07.99	99-04	178	30	23
Bristol C	L	03.05	04	3	0	0

KEITH Marino
Peterhead, 16 December, 1974 (F)

League Club	Source	Date Signed	Seasons Played	Apps	Subs	Gls
Plymouth Arg	Livingston	11.01	01-04	67	50	30
Colchester U	Tr	03.05	04	12	0	4

KEITH Richard (Dick) Matthewson
Belfast, 15 May, 1933 Died 1967 IrLge-4/NIB/NI-23 (FB)

League Club	Source	Date Signed	Seasons Played	Apps	Subs	Gls
Newcastle U	Linfield	09.56	56-63	208	-	2
Bournemouth	Tr	02.64	63-65	47	0	0

KEIZEWEERD Orpheo **Henk**
Holland, 2 November, 1968 (F)

League Club	Source	Date Signed	Seasons Played	Apps	Subs	Gls
Oldham Ath	Rodez (Fr)	03.93	92	0	1	0

KELL George **Allan**
Spennymoor, 9 April, 1949 (M)

League Club	Source	Date Signed	Seasons Played	Apps	Subs	Gls
Darlington (Am)		08.66	67	0	2	0

KELL Leonard (Len) William
Billingham, 27 May, 1932 (IF)

League Club	Source	Date Signed	Seasons Played	Apps	Subs	Gls
Chelsea	Jnrs	02.52	53	3	-	0
Norwich C	Tr	06.54	54	2	-	0

KELL Richard
Crook, 15 September, 1979 ESch (M)

League Club	Source	Date Signed	Seasons Played	Apps	Subs	Gls
Middlesbrough	YT	07.98				
Torquay U	Tr	02.01	00	15	0	3
Scunthorpe U	Tr	09.01	01-04	80	3	8

KELLARD Robert (Bobby) Sydney William
Edmonton, 1 March, 1943 EYth (M)

League Club	Source	Date Signed	Seasons Played	Apps	Subs	Gls
Southend U	Jnrs	05.60	59-62	106	-	15
Crystal Palace	Tr	09.63	63-65	77	0	6
Ipswich T	Tr	11.65	65	13	0	3
Portsmouth	Tr	03.66	65-67	91	0	8
Bristol C	Tr	07.68	68-69	77	0	6
Leicester C	Tr	08.70	70-71	49	0	8
Crystal Palace	Tr	09.71	71-72	44	2	4
Portsmouth	Tr	12.72	72-74	62	1	6
Hereford U	L	01.75	74	3	0	1
Torquay U	Durban C (SA)	09.75	75	2	0	0

KELLER Francois
Colmar, France, 27 October, 1973 (M)

League Club	Source	Date Signed	Seasons Played	Apps	Subs	Gls
Fulham	Strasbourg (Fr)	12.98	98	0	1	0

KELLER Kasey C
Olympia, USA, 27 November, 1969 USA 81 (G)

League Club	Source	Date Signed	Seasons Played	Apps	Subs	Gls
Millwall	Portland Univ (USA)	02.92	91-95	176	0	0
Leicester C	Tr	08.96	96-98	99	0	0
Tottenham H	Rayo Vallecano (Sp)	08.01	01-03	85	0	0
Southampton	L	11.04	04	4	0	0

KELLER Marc
Colmar, France, 14 January, 1968 France 5 (M)

League Club	Source	Date Signed	Seasons Played	Apps	Subs	Gls
West Ham U	Karlsruhe (Ger)	07.98	98-99	36	8	5
Portsmouth	L	09.00	00	3	0	0
Blackburn Rov	Tr	01.01	00	0	2	0

KELLEY Alan William
Bootle, 24 December, 1952 (FB)

League Club	Source	Date Signed	Seasons Played	Apps	Subs	Gls
Southport	App	12.70	70-71	17	6	2
Crewe Alex	Tr	08.72	72-75	105	2	0

KELLEY Stanley (Stan) Robert
Foleshill, 14 June, 1920 Died 1993 (FB)

League Club	Source	Date Signed	Seasons Played	Apps	Subs	Gls
Coventry C	Herberts Ath	08.39	46	4	-	0

KELLOCK William (Billy)
Glasgow, 7 February, 1954 SSch (M)

League Club	Source	Date Signed	Seasons Played	Apps	Subs	Gls
Cardiff C	Aston Villa (App)	02.72	71-72	33	2	2
Norwich C	Tr	06.73	73	1	2	0
Millwall	Tr	07.74				
Peterborough U	Kettering T	08.79	79-81	134	0	43

League Club	Source	Date Signed	Seasons Played	Apps	Subs	Gls
Luton T	Tr	07.82	82	2	5	0
Wolverhampton W	Tr	03.83	82-83	12	0	3
Southend U	Tr	09.83	83-84	53	0	8
Port Vale	Tr	12.84	84	10	1	4
Halifax T	Tr	07.85	85	41	2	17

KELLOW Tony
Falmouth, 1 May, 1952 (F)

League Club	Source	Date Signed	Seasons Played	Apps	Subs	Gls
Exeter C	Falmouth T	07.76	76-78	107	0	40
Blackpool	Tr	11.78	78-79	57	0	23
Exeter C	Tr	03.80	79-83	140	3	61
Plymouth Arg	Tr	11.83	83	8	2	2
Swansea C	Tr	10.84	84	0	1	0
Newport Co	Tr	11.84	84	17	3	8
Exeter C	Tr	07.85	85-87	51	31	28

KELLY Alan James Alexander
Dublin, 5 July, 1936 LoI-6/IR-47 (G)

League Club	Source	Date Signed	Seasons Played	Apps	Subs	Gls
Preston NE	Drumcondra	04.58	60-73	447	0	0

KELLY Alan Thomas
Preston, 11 August, 1968 IRYth/IRu23-1/IRu21-3/IR-34 (G)

League Club	Source	Date Signed	Seasons Played	Apps	Subs	Gls
Preston NE	App	09.85	85-91	142	0	0
Sheffield U	Tr	07.92	92-98	213	3	0
Blackburn Rov	Tr	07.99	99-02	39	1	0
Stockport Co	L	04.01	00	2	0	0
Birmingham C	L	08.01	01	6	0	0

KELLY Anthony (Tony) Gerald
Prescot, 1 October, 1964 (M)

League Club	Source	Date Signed	Seasons Played	Apps	Subs	Gls
Liverpool	App	09.82				
Wigan Ath	Prescot Cables	01.84	83-85	98	3	15
Stoke C	Tr	04.86	85-86	33	3	4
West Bromwich A	Tr	07.87	87	26	0	1
Chester C	L	09.88	88	5	0	0
Colchester U	L	10.88	88	13	0	2
Shrewsbury T	Tr	01.89	88-90	100	1	15
Bolton W	Tr	08.91	91-94	103	3	5
Port Vale	L	09.94	94	3	1	1
Millwall	Tr	10.94	94	1	1	0
Wigan Ath	Tr	11.94				
Peterborough U	Tr	12.94	94	12	1	2
Wigan Ath	Tr	07.95	95	2	0	0

KELLY Nyrere **Anthony (Tony)** Okpara
Meriden, 14 February, 1966 (W)

League Club	Source	Date Signed	Seasons Played	Apps	Subs	Gls
Bristol C	Jnrs	09.82	82	2	4	1
Stoke C	St Albans C	01.90	89-92	33	25	5
Hull C	L	01.92	91	6	0	1
Cardiff C	L	10.92	92	5	0	1
Bury	Tr	09.93	93-94	53	4	10
Leyton Orient	Tr	07.95	95-96	38	5	4
Colchester U	L	10.96	96	2	1	0

KELLY Arthur
Belfast, 12 March, 1914 Died 1973 (CF)

League Club	Source	Date Signed	Seasons Played	Apps	Subs	Gls
Barrow	Belfast Celtic	09.46	46	8	-	2

KELLY Bernard (Bernie)
Carfin, 21 October, 1932 Died 2004 SB/SLge-1 (IF)

League Club	Source	Date Signed	Seasons Played	Apps	Subs	Gls
Leicester C	Raith Rov	07.58	58	24	-	13
Nottingham F	Tr	04.59	58	2	-	0

KELLY Bernard Alexander
Kensington, 21 August, 1928 (W)

League Club	Source	Date Signed	Seasons Played	Apps	Subs	Gls
Brentford	Bath C	06.50	50	1	-	1

KELLY Brian Leslie
Ilkley, 22 May, 1943 (FB)

League Club	Source	Date Signed	Seasons Played	Apps	Subs	Gls
Bradford C	Jnrs	05.60	61-64	83	-	2
Doncaster Rov	Tr	01.65	64-67	130	1	3
York C	Tr	07.68	68-69	32	1	0

KELLY William **Brian**
Isleworth, 25 September, 1937 (CF)

League Club	Source	Date Signed	Seasons Played	Apps	Subs	Gls
Queens Park Rgrs	Dover	11.58	58	6	-	0

KELLY Christopher (Chris) Miles
Epsom, 14 October, 1948 EAmat (F)

League Club	Source	Date Signed	Seasons Played	Apps	Subs	Gls
Millwall	Leatherhead	01.75	74	9	2	0

KELLY Darren
Derry, 30 June, 1979 (CD)

League Club	Source	Date Signed	Seasons Played	Apps	Subs	Gls
Carlisle U	Derry C	08.02	02-03	39	3	2

KELLY David Thomas
Birmingham, 25 November, 1965 IRu23-1/IRu21-3/IRB-3/IR-26 (F)

League Club	Source	Date Signed	Seasons Played	Apps	Subs	Gls
Walsall	Alvechurch	12.83	83-87	115	32	63
West Ham U	Tr	08.88	88-89	29	12	7
Leicester C	Tr	03.90	89-91	63	3	22
Newcastle U	Tr	12.91	91-92	70	0	35

League Club	Source	Date Signed	Seasons Played	Apps	Subs	Gls
Wolverhampton W	Tr	06.93	93-95	76	7	26
Sunderland	Tr	09.95	95-96	32	2	2
Tranmere Rov	Tr	08.97	97-99	69	19	21
Sheffield U	Tr	07.00	00	21	14	6
Mansfield T	Motherwell	01.02	01	11	6	4

KELLY Desmond (Des) Charles James Jude
Limerick, 1 November, 1950 (G)

League Club	Source	Date Signed	Seasons Played	Apps	Subs	Gls
Norwich C	Limerick	07.70				
Colchester U	Tr	06.72	72	1	0	0

KELLY Donald (Don) Joseph
Market Harborough, 2 July, 1922 (CF)

League Club	Source	Date Signed	Seasons Played	Apps	Subs	Gls
Torquay U	Coventry C (Am)	07.47	46-47	5	-	3

KELLY Douglas (Doug) Cain
Worsborough, 30 May, 1934 (CF)

League Club	Source	Date Signed	Seasons Played	Apps	Subs	Gls
Barnsley	Jnrs	08.51	52-54	18	-	7
Bradford C	Tr	06.55	55-56	43	-	14
Chesterfield	Tr	06.57	57	1	-	1

KELLY Edward (Eddie) Patrick
Glasgow, 7 February, 1951 (M)

League Club	Source	Date Signed	Seasons Played	Apps	Subs	Gls
Arsenal	Possilpark YMCA	02.68	69-75	168	8	13
Queens Park Rgrs	Tr	09.76	76	28	0	1
Leicester C	Tr	07.77	77-79	85	0	4
Notts Co	Tr	07.80	80	26	1	1
Bournemouth	Tr	08.81	81	13	0	0
Leicester C	Tr	12.81	81-82	34	0	0
Torquay U	Melton T	10.84	84-85	35	0	1

KELLY Errington Edison
Sandy Bay, St Vincent, 8 April, 1958 (F)

League Club	Source	Date Signed	Seasons Played	Apps	Subs	Gls
Bristol Rov	Ledbury T	09.81	81-82	12	6	3
Lincoln C	Tr	01.83	82	0	2	0
Bristol C	Tr	02.83	82	4	1	1
Coventry C	Tr	08.83				
Peterborough U	Tr	03.84	83-85	59	13	22
Peterborough U	(Sweden)	12.86	86-87	36	10	6

KELLY Frederick (Fred) Charles
Wednesbury, 11 February, 1921 (FB)

League Club	Source	Date Signed	Seasons Played	Apps	Subs	Gls
Walsall		12.45	46-47	16	-	6

KELLY Gary Alexander
Fulwood, 3 August, 1966 IRu23-1/IRu21-8/IRB-1 (G)

League Club	Source	Date Signed	Seasons Played	Apps	Subs	Gls
Newcastle U	App	06.84	86-89	53	0	0
Blackpool	L	10.88	88	5	0	0
Bury	Tr	10.89	89-95	236	0	0
Oldham Ath	Tr	08.96	96-01	224	1	0
Sheffield U	Northwich Vic	03.03	02	1	0	0

KELLY Gary Oliver
Drogheda, 9 July, 1974 IRSch/IRYth/IRu21-5/IR-52 (FB)

League Club	Source	Date Signed	Seasons Played	Apps	Subs	Gls
Leeds U	Home Farm	09.91	91-04	359	11	2

KELLY Gavin John
Beverley, 29 September, 1968 (G)

League Club	Source	Date Signed	Seasons Played	Apps	Subs	Gls
Hull C	App	05.87	88-89	11	0	0
Bristol Rov	Tr	07.90	90-93	30	0	0
Scarborough	Tr	07.94	94-95	30	0	0

KELLY George Lawson
Aberdeen, 29 June, 1933 (IF)

League Club	Source	Date Signed	Seasons Played	Apps	Subs	Gls
Stoke C	Aberdeen	02.56	55-57	67	-	35
Cardiff C	Tr	05.58	58	8	-	4
Stockport Co	Tr	07.59	59	34	-	4

KELLY Hugh Redmond
Belfast, 17 August, 1919 Died 1977 NIRL-4/IrLge-4/I-4 (G)

League Club	Source	Date Signed	Seasons Played	Apps	Subs	Gls
Fulham	Belfast Celtic	03.49	49	25	-	0
Southampton	Tr	08.50	50	28	-	0
Exeter C	Tr	06.52	52-55	99	-	0

KELLY Hugh Thomas
Valleyfield, 23 July, 1923 SB/S-1 (WH)

League Club	Source	Date Signed	Seasons Played	Apps	Subs	Gls
Blackpool	Jeanfield Swifts	08.44	46-59	429	-	8

KELLY James (Jimmy)
Morpeth, 11 August, 1931 Died 2003 (WH)

League Club	Source	Date Signed	Seasons Played	Apps	Subs	Gls
Watford	Blyth Spartans	03.49	50-54	119	-	4
Blackpool	Tr	10.54	54-60	198	-	9

KELLY James (Jimmy)
Bellshill, 4 June, 1933 (CF)

League Club	Source	Date Signed	Seasons Played	Apps	Subs	Gls
Preston NE	Peterborough U	05.55				
Swindon T	Tr	02.58	57-58	30	-	14
Walsall	Tr	02.59	58	8	-	1

KELLY James
Bradford, 1 July, 1938 (WH)

League Club	Source	Date Signed	Seasons Played	Apps	Subs	Gls
Halifax T	Queensbury U	10.62	63	3	-	0

KELLY James (Jimmy)
Aldergrove, 6 February, 1954 (W)

League Club	Source	Date Signed	Seasons Played	Apps	Subs	Gls
Wolverhampton W	Cliftonville	12.71	73-77	20	2	0
Wrexham	L	09.75	75	4	0	0
Walsall	Tr	08.76	78-79	19	7	3

KELLY James (Jimmy)
Liverpool, 14 February, 1973 (M)

League Club	Source	Date Signed	Seasons Played	Apps	Subs	Gls
Wrexham	YT	07.91	90-91	11	10	0
Wolverhampton W	Tr	02.92	91-93	4	3	0
Walsall	L	03.93	92	7	3	2
Wrexham	L	03.94	93	9	0	0

KELLY James
(FB)

League Club	Source	Date Signed	Seasons Played	Apps	Subs	Gls
Barrow		02.46	46	1	-	0

KELLY James (Jimmy) Edward
Seaham Harbour, 29 December, 1907 Died 1984 (FB)

League Club	Source	Date Signed	Seasons Played	Apps	Subs	Gls
Southport	Murton CW	11.28	28-30	7	-	0
Barrow	Tr	08.31	31-32	55	-	0
Grimsby T	Tr	03.33	32-37	160	-	3
Bradford PA	Tr	05.38	38	2	-	0
York C	Tr	12.38	38	24	-	0
Barrow	Trondheim (Nor)	06.46	46	1	-	0

KELLY James (Jim) Lawrence
Holborn, 14 July, 1926 Died 1996 (W)

League Club	Source	Date Signed	Seasons Played	Apps	Subs	Gls
Gillingham	Dartford	05.51	51	3	-	0

KELLY James Patrick
Drogheda, 16 February, 1925 LoI-2/IrLge-4 (W)

League Club	Source	Date Signed	Seasons Played	Apps	Subs	Gls
Tottenham H	Glenavon	07.49				
Carlisle U	Tr	02.50	49-51	42	-	6

KELLY James (Jimmy) Patrick
Sacriston, 22 November, 1951 (FB)

League Club	Source	Date Signed	Seasons Played	Apps	Subs	Gls
Hartlepool		08.70	71	5	0	0

KELLY James (Jimmy) William
Carlisle, 2 May, 1957 (M)

League Club	Source	Date Signed	Seasons Played	Apps	Subs	Gls
Manchester U	App	05.74	75	0	1	0

KELLY John
Bebington, 20 October, 1960 IRu21-2 (W)

League Club	Source	Date Signed	Seasons Played	Apps	Subs	Gls
Tranmere Rov	Cammell Laird	09.79	79-81	55	9	9
Preston NE	Tr	10.81	81-84	120	10	27
Chester C	Tr	08.85	85-86	85	0	17
Swindon T	Tr	06.87	87	3	4	1
Oldham Ath	Tr	11.87	87-88	51	1	6
Walsall	Tr	08.89	89-90	36	3	1
Huddersfield T	L	03.90	89	9	1	1
Huddersfield T	Tr	02.91	90-91	16	2	0
Chester C	Tr	07.92	92	24	7	1

KELLY John (Johnny) Carmichael
Paisley, 21 February, 1921 Died 2001 SWar-1/S-2 (W)

League Club	Source	Date Signed	Seasons Played	Apps	Subs	Gls
Barnsley	Morton	12.45	46-52	217	-	25
Halifax T	Morton	07.56	56-57	38	-	2

KELLY John Gerald
Glasgow, 14 December, 1935 SSch (WH)

League Club	Source	Date Signed	Seasons Played	Apps	Subs	Gls
Crewe Alex	Third Lanark	08.59	59	20	-	1

KELLY Lawrence (Laurie) John
Wolverhampton, 28 April, 1925 Died 1972 (FB)

League Club	Source	Date Signed	Seasons Played	Apps	Subs	Gls
Wolverhampton W	Jnrs	03.43	47-49	60	-	0
Huddersfield T	Tr	10.50	50-56	225	-	2

KELLY Leon Michael
Coventry, 26 June, 1978 (M)

League Club	Source	Date Signed	Seasons Played	Apps	Subs	Gls
Cambridge U	Atherstone U	08.01	01	1	1	0

KELLY Marcus Philip
Kettering, 16 March, 1986 (FB)

League Club	Source	Date Signed	Seasons Played	Apps	Subs	Gls
Rushden & Diamonds	Jnrs	11.03	03-04	7	12	0

KELLY Mark David
Blackpool, 7 October, 1966 (M)

League Club	Source	Date Signed	Seasons Played	Apps	Subs	Gls
Shrewsbury T		12.85				
Cardiff C	Tr	06.87	87-89	93	12	2
Fulham	Tr	06.90	90-92	55	9	2

KELLY Mark John
Sutton, 27 November, 1969 EYth/IRu23-2/IRu21-3/IR-4 (W)

League Club	Source	Date Signed	Seasons Played	Apps	Subs	Gls
Portsmouth	App	11.86	87-90	24	25	2

KELLY Michael (Mike)
(W)

League Club	Source	Date Signed	Seasons Played	Apps	Subs	Gls
Wolverhampton W		06.39				
Crewe Alex	Tr	11.45	46	15	-	2

League Club	Source	Date Signed	Seasons Played	Apps	Subs	Gls
KELLY Michael (Mike) John						
Northampton, 18 October, 1942 EAmat						(G)
Queens Park Rgrs	Wimbledon	03.66	67-69	54	0	0
Birmingham C	Tr	08.70	70-74	62	0	0
KELLY Michael (Mike) Lawrence						
Belvedere, 22 October, 1954						(M)
Millwall	App	10.72	72-74	16	2	2
Charlton Ath	Tr	12.74	74	10	0	3
KELLY Noel						
Dublin, 28 December, 1921 Died 1991 IrLge-2/IR-1						(IF)
Arsenal	Glentoran	10.47	49	1	-	0
Crystal Palace	Tr	03.50	49-50	42	-	5
Nottingham F	Tr	08.51	51-54	48	-	11
Tranmere Rov	Tr	07.55	55-56	52	-	7
KELLY Norman						
Belfast, 10 October, 1970 NIYth/NIu21-1						(M)
Oldham Ath	YT	07.89	87-88	0	2	0
Wigan Ath	L	10.89	89	0	4	0
KELLY Patrick (Paddy)						
Kirkcaldy, 26 April, 1978 SYth						(CD)
Newcastle U	Glasgow Celtic	08.97				
Reading	L	03.98	97	3	0	0
KELLY Patrick (Pat) Michael						
Johannesburg, South Africa, 9 April, 1918 Died 1985 I-1						(G)
Barnsley	Aberdeen	10.46	46-50	144	-	0
Crewe Alex	Tr	02.52	51-52	38	-	0
KELLY Paul Anthony						
Eccles, 6 March, 1971						(M)
Manchester C	YT	02.90				
Crewe Alex	Tr	02.92	91	0	1	0
KELLY Paul Leon Marvin						
Hillingdon, 24 February, 1974						(M)
Fulham	YT	07.92	91-93	4	2	0
KELLY Paul Michael						
Bexley, 12 October, 1969 ESch/EYth						(M)
West Ham U	YT	06.88	89	0	1	0
KELLY Peter Anthony						
East Kilbride, 6 December, 1956						(FB)
Newcastle U	App	07.74	74-80	31	2	0
KELLY James **Philip (Phil)** Vincent						
Dublin, 10 July, 1939 IR-5						(FB)
Wolverhampton W	Sheldon T	09.57	58-61	16	-	0
Norwich C	Tr	08.62	62-66	114	1	2
KELLY Raymond (Ray)						
Athlone, 29 December, 1976 IRu21-4						(F)
Manchester C	Athlone T	08.94	97	1	0	0
Wrexham	L	10.97	97	5	1	1
Wrexham	L	03.98	97	0	4	0
KELLY Robert (Bob)						
Kirkcaldy, 16 November, 1919 Died 2001						(WH)
Millwall	Raith Rov	06.46	46-47	52	-	1
Bury	Tr	05.48	48	9	-	0
KELLY Robert Anthony						
Birmingham, 21 December, 1964						(M)
Leicester C	App	12.82	83-86	17	7	1
Tranmere Rov	L	12.84	84	5	0	2
Wolverhampton W	Tr	03.87	86-88	13	3	2
KELLY Russell						
Ballymoney, 10 August, 1976 IRSch/IRYth						(M)
Chelsea	YT	07.95				
Leyton Orient	L	03.96	95	5	1	0
Darlington	Tr	09.96	96	13	10	2
KELLY Seamus						
Tullamore, 6 May, 1974						(G)
Cardiff C	UCD (Dublin)	08.98	98-99	12	1	0
KELLY Stephen Michael						
Dublin, 6 September, 1983 IRYth/IRu21-15						(FB)
Tottenham H	YT	09.00	03-04	20	8	2
Southend U	L	01.03	02	10	0	0
Queens Park Rgrs	L	03.03	02	7	0	0
Watford	L	09.03	03	13	0	0
KELLY Terence (Terry) James						
Gateshead, 14 May, 1942						(CF)
Newcastle U	Jnrs	05.60				
Lincoln C	Tr	07.62	62	8	-	2

League Club	Source	Date Signed	Seasons Played	Apps	Subs	Gls
KELLY Terence (Terry) William John						
Luton, 16 January, 1932						(CD)
Luton T	Vauxhall Motors	04.50	54-62	136	-	1
KELLY Thomas (Tom) John						
Bellshill, 28 March, 1964						(FB)
Hartlepool U	Queen of the South	08.85	85	14	1	0
Torquay U	Tr	07.86	86-88	116	4	0
York C	Tr	07.89	89	35	0	2
Exeter C	Tr	03.90	89-92	76	12	9
Torquay U	Tr	01.93	92-95	109	8	8
KELLY Thomas (Tom) William						
Darlington, 22 November, 1919 Died 1970						(CD)
Darlington	Deneside Jnrs	11.37	37-50	157	-	2
KELLY Walter Muir						
Cowdenbeath, 15 April, 1929						(CF)
Bury	Raith Rov	08.52	52-56	159	-	77
Doncaster Rov	Tr	06.57	57	29	-	6
Stockport Co	Tr	03.58	57-59	47	-	12
Chester	Tr	08.59	59-60	56	-	24
KELLY William (Willie) Muir						
Hill o' Beath, 14 August, 1922 Died 1996						(CD)
Blackburn Rov	Airdrie	09.51	51-56	186	-	1
Accrington St	Mossley	09.57	57	24	-	0
KELSALL Charles						
Hawarden, 15 April, 1921						(FB)
Wrexham		08.39	46-51	39	-	0
KELSEY Alfred **John (Jack)**						
Llansamlet, 19 November, 1929 Died 1992 FLge-1/W-41						(G)
Arsenal	Winch Wen	08.49	50-61	327	-	0
KELTIE Clark Stuart						
Newcastle, 31 August, 1983						(M)
Darlington	Walker Central	09.01	01-04	60	23	4
KEMBER Stephen (Steve) Dennis						
Croydon, 8 December, 1948 Eu23-3						(M)
Crystal Palace	App	12.65	65-71	216	2	35
Chelsea	Tr	09.71	71-74	125	5	13
Leicester C	Tr	07.75	75-78	115	2	6
Crystal Palace	Tr	10.78	78-79	39	3	1
KEMP David Michael						
Harrow, 20 February, 1953						(F)
Crystal Palace	Slough T	04.75	74-76	32	3	10
Portsmouth	Tr	11.76	76-77	63	1	30
Carlisle U	Tr	03.78	77-79	60	1	22
Plymouth Arg	Tr	09.79	79-81	82	2	39
Gillingham	L	12.81	81	9	0	2
Brentford	L	03.82	81	3	0	1
KEMP Frederick (Fred) George						
Salerno, Italy, 27 February, 1946						(M)
Wolverhampton W	App	06.63	64	3	-	0
Southampton	Tr	06.65	65-69	58	3	10
Blackpool	Tr	11.70	70-71	19	2	1
Halifax T	Tr	12.71	71-73	106	5	10
Hereford U	Tr	07.74	74	12	1	2
KEMP John						
Clydebank, 11 April, 1934						(W)
Leeds U	Clyde	12.57	58	1	-	0
Barrow	Tr	03.59	58-63	170	-	45
Crewe Alex	Tr	12.63	63-65	47	0	7
KEMP Raymond (Ray) William						
Bristol, 18 January, 1922 Died 1989						(G)
Reading (Am)	Grays Ath	09.49	49	3	-	0
KEMP Robert (Roy) McAlpine						
Falkirk, 15 August, 1941						(W)
Carlisle U	Falkirk	11.60	60	1	-	0
KEMP Samuel (Sam) Patrick						
Stockton, 29 August, 1932 Died 1987						(W)
Sunderland	Whitby T	03.52	52-56	17	-	2
Sheffield U	Tr	02.57	56-57	16	-	1
Mansfield T	Tr	05.58	58	3	-	1
Gateshead	Tr	10.58	58	7	-	1
KEMP Stephen (Steve) Duncan						
Shrewsbury, 2 May, 1955						(CD)
Shrewsbury T	App	07.73	72-73	7	1	0
KENDAL Stephen (Steve) James						
Birtley, 4 August, 1961						(M)
Nottingham F	App	08.79	81	1	0	0

League Club	Source	Date Signed	Seasons Played	Career Record Apps	Subs	Gls
Chesterfield	Tr	12.82	82-86	122	3	14
Torquay U	Tr	10.86	86	4	0	0
KENDALL Harold **Arnold**						
Halifax, 6 April, 1925 Died 2003						(W)
Bradford C	Salts	02.49	48-52	113	-	13
Rochdale	Tr	09.53	53-56	111	-	25
Bradford PA	Tr	09.56	56-58	90	-	12
KENDALL Howard						
Ryton-on-Tyne, 22 May, 1946 ESch/EYth/Eu23-6/FLge-1						(M)
Preston NE	App	05.63	62-66	104	0	13
Everton	Tr	03.67	66-73	227	2	21
Birmingham C	Tr	02.74	73-76	115	0	16
Stoke C	Tr	08.77	77-78	82	0	9
Blackburn Rov	Tr	07.79	79-80	79	0	6
Everton	Tr	08.81	81	4	0	0
KENDALL Ian						
Blackburn, 11 December, 1947						(F)
Blackburn Rov	App	12.65				
Southport	Tr	08.67	67	1	1	0
KENDALL James (Jimmy) Briden						
Birtley, 4 October, 1922						(IF)
Barrow	Gateshead U	05.47	46-48	44	-	16
Gateshead	Tr	11.48	48-51	57	-	20
Barrow	Tr	10.51	51-52	22	-	6
Accrington St	Tr	09.52	52	26	-	8
KENDALL Mark						
Blackwood, Monmouthshire, 20 September, 1958 WSch/WYth/Wu21-1						(G)
Tottenham H	App	07.76	78-80	29	0	0
Chesterfield	L	11.79	79	9	0	0
Newport Co	Tr	09.80	80-86	272	0	0
Wolverhampton W	Tr	12.86	86-89	147	0	0
Swansea C	Tr	07.90	90-91	12	0	0
Burnley	L	12.91	91	2	0	0
KENDALL Mark Ivor						
Nuneaton, 10 December, 1961 EYth						(G)
Aston Villa	App	11.79				
Northampton T	Tr	06.82	82	11	0	0
Birmingham C	Tr	02.84	83	1	0	0
KENDALL Paul Scott						
Halifax, 19 October, 1964						(CD)
Halifax T	App	10.82	81-85	91	15	4
Scarborough	Tr	07.86	87	22	5	1
Halifax T	Tr	03.88	87	9	1	0
KENDRICK Joseph (Joe)						
Dublin, 26 June, 1983 IRYth/IRu21-1						(FB)
Newcastle U	YT	07.00				
Darlington	TSV Munich (Ger)	08.04	04	19	12	1
KENNA Jeffrey (Jeff) Jude						
Dublin, 27 August, 1970 IRSch/IRYth/IRu21-8/IRB-1/IR-27						(FB)
Southampton	YT	04.89	90-94	110	4	4
Blackburn Rov	Tr	03.95	94-00	153	2	1
Tranmere Rov	L	03.01	00	11	0	0
Wigan Ath	L	11.01	01	6	0	1
Birmingham C	Tr	12.01	01-03	71	4	3
Derby Co	Tr	03.04	03-04	49	0	0
KENNEDY Alan Philip						
Sunderland, 31 August, 1954 Eu23-6/E-2						(FB)
Newcastle U	App	08.72	72-77	155	3	9
Liverpool	Tr	08.78	78-85	249	2	15
Sunderland	Tr	09.85	85-86	54	0	2
Hartlepool U	Beerschot (Bel)	10.87	87	4	1	0
Wigan Ath	Grantham T	12.87	87	22	0	0
Wrexham	Colne Dynamoes	03.90	89-90	15	1	0
KENNEDY Andrew (Andy) John						
Stirling, 8 October, 1964 SYth						(F)
Birmingham C	Seiko (HK)	03.85	84-87	51	25	18
Sheffield U	L	03.87	86	8	1	1
Blackburn Rov	Tr	06.88	88-89	49	10	23
Watford	Tr	08.90	90-91	17	8	4
Bolton W	L	10.91	91	1	0	0
Brighton & Hove A	Tr	09.92	92-93	34	8	10
Gillingham	Tr	09.94	94	0	2	0
KENNEDY David (Dave)						
Birkenhead, 14 February, 1949						(W)
Tranmere Rov	Jnrs	05.67	67-69	16	1	0
Chester	Tr	05.70	70-73	79	8	9
Torquay U	Tr	09.73	73-76	144	7	7

League Club	Source	Date Signed	Seasons Played	Career Record Apps	Subs	Gls
KENNEDY David						
Sunderland, 30 November, 1950						(CD)
Leeds U	App	05.68	69	2	0	1
Lincoln C	Tr	07.71	71	6	2	1
KENNEDY Gordon McKay						
Dundee, 15 April, 1924 Died 1999						(FB)
Blackpool		10.43	46-49	8	-	0
Bolton W	Tr	09.50	50	17	-	0
Stockport Co	Tr	08.53	53	20	-	1
KENNEDY Jason Brian						
Stockton, 11 September, 1986						(M)
Middlesbrough	Sch	02.05	04	0	1	0
KENNEDY John (Jack)						
Kilwinning, 26 February, 1941						(IF)
Charlton Ath	Saltcoats Victoria	03.62	61-64	46	-	8
Exeter C	Tr	11.65	65-66	40	1	6
KENNEDY John						
Newtownards, 4 September, 1939 IrLge-3						(G)
Lincoln C	Glentoran	07.67	67-73	251	0	0
KENNEDY John Neil						
Newmarket, 19 August, 1978						(FB)
Ipswich T	YT	06.97	97-98	6	2	0
KENNEDY Jonathan (Jon)						
Rotherham, 30 November, 1980						(G)
Sunderland	Worksop T	05.00				
Blackpool	L	10.00	00	6	0	0
KENNEDY Joseph (Joe) Peter						
Cleator Moor, 15 November, 1925 Died 1986 EB						(CD)
West Bromwich A	Altrincham	12.48	48-60	364	-	3
Chester	Tr	06.61	61	35	-	0
KENNEDY Keith Vernon						
Sunderland, 5 March, 1952						(FB)
Newcastle U	App	07.70	71	1	0	0
Bury	Tr	10.72	72-81	405	0	4
Mansfield T	Tr	08.82	82	32	2	0
KENNEDY Luke Daniel						
Peterborough, 22 May, 1986						(M)
Rushden & Diamonds	Sch	•	04	1	2	0
KENNEDY Malcolm Stephen John						
Swansea, 13 October, 1939						(WH)
Swansea T	Jnrs	05.57	57-60	18	-	0
KENNEDY Mark						
Dublin, 15 May, 1976 IRSch/IRYth/IRu21-7/IR-34						(W)
Millwall	YT	05.92	92-94	37	6	9
Liverpool	Tr	03.95	94-97	5	11	0
Queens Park Rgrs	L	01.98	97	8	0	2
Wimbledon	Tr	03.98	97-98	11	10	0
Manchester C	Tr	07.99	99-00	56	10	8
Wolverhampton W	Tr	07.01	01-04	120	7	10
KENNEDY Michael (Mick) Francis Martin						
Salford, 9 April, 1961 IRu21-4/IR-2						(M)
Halifax T	App	01.79	78-79	74	2	4
Huddersfield T	Tr	08.80	80-81	80	1	9
Middlesbrough	Tr	08.82	82-83	68	0	5
Portsmouth	Tr	06.84	84-87	129	0	4
Bradford C	Tr	01.88	87-88	45	0	2
Leicester C	Tr	03.89	88	9	0	0
Luton T	Tr	08.89	89	30	2	0
Stoke C	Tr	08.90	90-91	51	1	3
Chesterfield	Tr	08.92	92	19	8	1
Wigan Ath	Tr	07.93	93	15	2	1
KENNEDY Patrick (Pat) Antony						
Dublin, 9 October, 1934						(FB)
Manchester U	Johnville	02.53	54	1	-	0
Blackburn Rov	Tr	08.56	57	3	-	0
Southampton	Tr	07.59	59	2	-	0
KENNEDY Peter Henry James						
Lurgan, 10 September, 1973 NIB-1/NI-20						(W)
Notts Co	Portadown	08.96	96	20	2	0
Watford	Tr	07.97	97-00	108	7	18
Wigan Ath	Tr	07.01	01-03	60	5	2
Derby Co	L	10.03	03	5	0	1
Peterborough U	Tr	08.04	04	15	2	2
KENNEDY Raymond (Ray)						
Seaton Delaval, 28 July, 1951 Eu23-6/E-17						(M)
Arsenal	App	11.68	69-73	156	2	53
Liverpool	Tr	07.74	74-81	272	3	51

League Club	Source	Date Signed	Seasons Played	Career Record Apps	Subs	Gls
Swansea C	Tr	01.82	81-83	42	0	2
Hartlepool U	Tr	11.83	83	18	5	3
KENNEDY Richard Joseph						
Waterford, 28 August, 1978						(M)
Crystal Palace	YT	03.97				
Wycombe W	Tr	10.98				
Brentford	Tr	07.99	99-00	5	5	0
KENNEDY Robert (Bobby)						
Motherwell, 23 June, 1937 Su23-1						(M)
Manchester C	Kilmarnock	07.61	61-68	216	3	9
Grimsby T	Tr	03.69	68-70	84	0	1
KENNEDY Stephen (Steve)						
Audenshaw, 22 July, 1965						(FB)
Burnley	App	07.83	83-86	18	0	0
KENNEDY Thomas (Tom) Gordon						
Bury, 24 June, 1985						(M)
Bury	Sch	11.02	03-04	68	5	1
KENNERLEY Kevin Robert						
Chester, 26 April, 1954						(M)
Burnley	Arsenal (App)	05.72	75	6	0	1
Port Vale	Tr	05.76	76-77	16	8	1
Swansea C	L	02.78	77	2	0	0
KENNING Michael (Mike) John						
Erdington, 18 August, 1940						(W)
Aston Villa	Brookhill	10.59	60	3	-	0
Shrewsbury T	Tr	05.61	61-62	62	-	17
Charlton Ath	Tr	11.62	62-66	152	1	43
Norwich C	Tr	12.66	66-67	44	0	9
Wolverhampton W	Tr	01.68	67-68	35	6	5
Charlton Ath	Tr	03.69	68-71	59	7	12
Watford	Tr	12.71	71-72	35	6	2
KENNON Neil **Sandilands (Sandy)**						
Johannesburg, South Africa, 28 November, 1933						(G)
Huddersfield T	Queen's Pk (Bulawayo)	08.56	56-58	78	-	0
Norwich C	Tr	02.59	58-64	213	-	0
Colchester U	Tr	03.65	64-66	76	0	0
KENNY Frederick (Fred)						
Manchester, 14 January, 1923 Died 1985						(FB)
Stockport Co	Manchester C (Am)	12.47	48-56	204	-	0
KENNY Patrick (Paddy) Joseph						
Halifax, 17 May, 1978 IR-5						(G)
Bury	Bradford PA	08.98	99-01	133	0	0
Sheffield U	Tr	07.02	02-04	112	0	0
KENNY Vincent (Vince)						
Sheffield, 29 December, 1924						(FB)
Sheffield Wed	Atlas & Norfolk	11.45	46-54	144	-	0
Carlisle U	Tr	07.55	55-57	112	-	3
KENNY William (Billy) Aidan						
Liverpool, 23 October, 1951 EYth						(M)
Everton	App	07.69	70-74	10	2	0
Tranmere Rov	Tr	03.75	74-76	36	18	5
KENNY William (Billy) Aidan						
Liverpool, 19 September, 1973 Eu23-1						(M)
Everton	YT	06.92	92	16	1	1
Oldham Ath	Tr	08.94	94	4	0	0
KENT Kevin John						
Stoke-on-Trent, 19 March, 1965						(W)
West Bromwich A	App	12.82	83	1	1	0
Newport Co	Tr	07.84	84	23	10	1
Mansfield T	Tr	08.85	85-90	223	5	37
Port Vale	Tr	03.91	90-95	87	28	7
KENT Michael (Mike) John						
North Anston, 12 January, 1951						(M)
Wolverhampton W	Wath W	08.68	69-71	0	2	0
Gillingham	L	03.71	70	11	0	0
Sheffield Wed	Tr	09.73	73	4	0	0
KENT Paul						
Rotherham, 23 February, 1954						(FB)
Norwich C	App	02.72	73	1	2	0
Halifax T	Tr	08.76	76	12	0	0
KENT Terence (Terry) Ian						
Battersea, 21 October, 1939						(W)
Southend U		05.58	58	1	-	0

League Club	Source	Date Signed	Seasons Played	Career Record Apps	Subs	Gls
KENTON Darren Edward						
Wandsworth, 13 September, 1978						(FB)
Norwich C	YT	07.97	97-02	142	16	9
Southampton	Tr	05.03	03-04	12	4	0
Leicester C	L	03.05	04	9	1	0
KENWORTHY Anthony (Tony) David						
Leeds, 30 October, 1958 EYth						(CD)
Sheffield U	App	07.76	75-85	281	5	34
Mansfield T	Tr	03.86	85-89	98	2	0
KENWORTHY Jonathan (Jon) Raymond						
St Asaph, 18 August, 1974 WYth/Wu21-4						(W)
Tranmere Rov	YT	07.93	93-95	14	12	2
Chester C	L	12.95	95	5	2	1
KENWORTHY Stephen (Steve)						
Wrexham, 6 November, 1959 Died 2001						(FB)
Wrexham	Jnrs	11.77	77-80	19	1	0
Bury	Tr	08.81	82	14	0	0
KENYON Frederick (Fred)						
Carlisle, 14 September, 1922 Died 1998						(CD)
Carlisle U		09.43	47-48	4	-	0
KENYON John Francis						
Blackburn, 2 December, 1953						(F)
Blackburn Rov	Great Harwood	12.72	72-75	32	14	7
KENYON Roger Norton						
Blackpool, 4 January, 1949						(CD)
Everton	App	09.66	67-78	254	13	6
Bristol C	Vancouver (Can)	10.79	79	4	0	0
KENYON Roy						
Manchester, 10 March, 1933						(IF)
Leeds U	Bolton W (Am)	12.50				
Southport	Worcester C	09.54	54	1	-	0
KEOGH Andrew (Andy) Declan						
Dublin, 16 May, 1986 IRYth						(F)
Leeds U	Sch	05.03				
Scunthorpe U	L	08.04	04	9	3	2
Bury	L	01.05	04	4	0	2
Scunthorpe U	Tr	02.05	04	4	9	1
KEOUGH Daniel (Danny) Peter						
Rawtenstall, 31 January, 1963						(M)
Manchester U	App	02.80				
Exeter C	Bury (N/C)	10.85	85-86	71	1	0
KEOWN Martin Raymond						
Oxford, 24 July, 1966 EYth/Eu21-8/EB-1/E-43						(CD)
Arsenal	App	02.84	85	22	0	0
Brighton & Hove A	L	02.85	84	16	0	0
Brighton & Hove A	L	08.85	85	5	2	1
Aston Villa	Tr	06.86	86-88	109	3	3
Everton	Tr	08.89	89-92	92	4	0
Arsenal	Tr	02.93	92-03	282	28	4
Leicester C	Tr	07.04	04	16	1	0
Reading	Tr	01.05	04	3	2	0
KERFOOT Eric						
Ashton-under-Lyne, 31 July, 1924 Died 1980						(WH)
Leeds U	Stalybridge Celtic	12.49	49-58	336	-	9
Chesterfield	Tr	07.59	59	9	-	0
KERFOOT Jason John Thomas						
Preston, 17 April, 1973						(M)
Preston NE	YT	07.91	90-91	0	4	0
KERLEY Adam Lewis						
Sutton-in-Ashfield, 25 February, 1985						(F)
Lincoln C	Sch	08.04	04	0	1	0
KERNAGHAN Alan Nigel						
Otley, 25 April, 1967 NISch/IR-22						(CD)
Middlesbrough	App	03.85	84-93	172	40	16
Charlton Ath	L	01.91	90	13	0	0
Manchester C	Tr	09.93	93-97	55	8	1
Bolton W	L	08.94	94	9	2	0
Bradford C	L	02.96	95	5	0	0
KERNAN Anthony (Tony) Paul						
Letterkenny, 31 August, 1963 IRYth						(M)
Wolverhampton W	App	01.81	81	1	0	0
KERNICK Dudley Henry John						
Camelford, 29 August, 1921						(IF)
Torquay U	Tintagel	01.39	46-47	38	-	7

League Club	Source	Date Signed	Seasons Played	Career Record Apps	Subs	Gls
KERR Albert Wigham						
Lanchester, 11 August, 1917 Died 1979						(W)
Aston Villa	Medomsley Jnrs	07.36	36-46	29	-	4
KERR Andrew (Andy)						
Lugar, 29 June, 1931 Died 1997 SB/SLge-2/S-2						(CF)
Manchester C	Partick Th	06.59	59	10	-	0
Sunderland	Kilmarnock	04.63	62-63	18	-	5
KERR Andrew (Andy) Alphonso						
West Bromwich, 7 April, 1966						(FB)
Shrewsbury T	App	04.84	84-85	9	1	0
Cardiff C	Tr	08.86	86	31	0	1
Wycombe W	Telford U	09.88	93	12	2	3
KERR Archibald (Archie)						
Motherwell, 30 August, 1935						(W)
Shrewsbury T	Motherwell	01.57	56	13	-	0
KERR Brian						
Motherwell, 12 October, 1981 SSch/SYth/Su21-14/SB-2/S-3						(M)
Newcastle U	YT	12.98	00-02	4	5	0
Coventry C	L	10.02	02	2	1	0
Coventry C	L	03.04	03	5	4	0
KERR Charles Currie						
Glasgow, 10 December, 1933						(W)
Carlisle U	Morton	08.56	56-57	9	-	3
Barrow	Tonbridge	07.59	59	20	-	3
KERR David						
Govan, 4 December, 1936						(IF)
Liverpool	Bridgeton Waverley	04.56				
Southport	Tr	07.58	58	32	-	4
KERR David William						
Dumfries, 6 September, 1974						(M)
Manchester C	YT	09.91	92-95	4	2	0
Mansfield T	L	09.95	95	4	1	0
Mansfield T	Tr	07.96	96-99	56	24	4
KERR Dylan						
Valetta, Malta, 14 January, 1967						(FB)
Sheffield Wed	Jnrs	09.84				
Leeds U	Arcadia Shepherds (SA)	02.89	88-92	6	7	0
Doncaster Rov	L	08.91	91	7	0	1
Blackpool	L	12.91	91	12	0	1
Reading	Tr	07.93	93-95	84	5	5
Carlisle U	Tr	09.96	96	0	1	0
Kidderminster Hrs	Kilmarnock	09.00	00	0	1	0
Exeter C	Hamilton Academical	08.01	01	5	0	1
KERR George Adams McDonald						
Alexandria, 9 January, 1943						(F)
Barnsley	Renton Select	05.60	61-65	166	0	40
Bury	Tr	03.66	65-66	15	0	2
Oxford U	Tr	09.66	66-67	40	0	5
Scunthorpe U	Tr	02.68	67-72	151	6	31
KERR James (Jimmy)						
Lemington, 3 March, 1932 Died 1994						(W)
Lincoln C	Blyth Spartans	11.52	52-53	15	-	1
Oldham Ath	Tr	06.54	54-55	34	-	4
KERR James (Jimmy) Peter						
Glasgow, 2 September, 1949 SSch						(M)
Bury	Jnrs	09.66	65-69	150	2	38
Blackburn Rov	Tr	05.70	70	11	0	0
KERR John						
Birkenhead, 23 November, 1959						(F)
Tranmere Rov	App	11.77	78-82	145	9	38
Bristol C	Tr	08.83	83	13	1	4
Stockport Co	Tr	01.84	83-84	47	0	16
Bury	Tr	03.85	84-85	21	10	4
KERR John Joseph						
Toronto, Canada, 6 March, 1965 USA int						(F)
Portsmouth	Harrow Borough	08.87	87	2	2	0
Peterborough U	L	12.87	87	10	0	1
Millwall	Chertsey T	02.93	92-94	21	22	8
Walsall	Tr	11.95	95	0	1	0
KERR Paul Andrew						
Portsmouth, 9 June, 1964						(M)
Aston Villa	App	05.82	83-86	16	8	3
Middlesbrough	Tr	01.87	86-90	114	11	13
Millwall	Tr	03.91	90-91	42	2	14
Port Vale	Tr	07.92	92-93	58	5	15
Leicester C	L	03.94	93	4	3	2
Wycombe W	Tr	10.94	94	0	1	1

League Club	Source	Date Signed	Seasons Played	Career Record Apps	Subs	Gls
KERR Peter						
Glasgow, 3 January, 1928 Died 1996						(WH)
Hartlepools U	Maryhill Harp	09.49	49	2	-	0
KERR Peter						
Paisley, 25 September, 1943						(IF)
Reading	Third Lanark	05.63	63-64	41	-	7
KERR Robert						
West Lothian, 10 July, 1942						(CF)
Millwall	Arbroath	08.62	62	1	-	0
KERR Robert (Bobby)						
Alexandria, 16 November, 1947						(M)
Sunderland	Balloch Jnrs	11.64	66-78	355	13	57
Blackpool	Tr	03.79	78-79	18	4	2
Hartlepool U	Tr	07.80	80-81	48	1	2
KERR Robert James						
Coatbridge, 29 November, 1929						(IF)
Darlington	Third Lanark	10.52	52	10	-	2
KERR Scott Anthony						
Leeds, 11 December, 1981						(M)
Bradford C	YT	07.00	00	0	1	0
KERR James **Stewart** Robert						
Bellshill, 13 November, 1974 Su21-10						(G)
Brighton & Hove A (L)	Glasgow Celtic	11.94	94	2	0	0
Wigan Ath	Glasgow Celtic	08.01	01	8	0	0
KERRAY James (Jimmy) Ridley						
Stirling, 2 December, 1935						(IF)
Huddersfield T	Dunfermline Ath	08.60	60-61	54	-	12
Newcastle U	Tr	02.62	61-62	38	-	10
KERRIGAN Daniel (Danny) Anthony						
Basildon, 4 July, 1982						(M)
Southend U	YT	07.00	99-01	6	9	0
KERRIGAN Donald (Don) McDonald						
West Kilbride, 7 May, 1941 Died 1990						(F)
Fulham	Dunfermline Ath	02.68	67-68	4	2	1
Lincoln C	L	03.69	68	12	0	0
KERRIGAN Steven (Steve) John						
Baillieston, 9 October, 1972						(F)
Shrewsbury T	Ayr U	01.98	97-99	63	13	15
Halifax T	Tr	03.00	99-01	70	8	22
KERRINS Patrick (Pat) Michael						
Fulham, 13 September, 1936						(W)
Queens Park Rgrs	Jnrs	12.53	53-59	146	-	30
Crystal Palace	Tr	06.60	60	5	-	0
Southend U	Tr	07.61	61	11	-	0
KERRINS Wayne Michael						
Brentwood, 5 August, 1965						(M)
Fulham	App	08.83	84-88	51	15	1
Port Vale	L	03.85	84	6	2	0
Leyton Orient	L	03.89	88	3	0	0
KERRY Brian Philip						
Maltby, 18 December, 1948						(F)
Grimsby T	App	01.66	65	0	1	0
KERRY Christopher (Chris) Brian						
Chesterfield, 15 April, 1976						(F)
Mansfield T	YT	07.94	93	1	1	0
KERRY David (Dave) Thomas						
Derby, 6 February, 1937 EYth						(CF)
Preston NE	Derby Co (Am)	05.55				
Chesterfield	Tr	07.61	61-62	55	-	23
Rochdale	Tr	07.63	63	12	-	4
KERSHAW Alan Derek						
Southport, 23 April, 1954						(FB)
Preston NE	App	09.72				
Southport	Tr	07.74	74	19	5	0
KERSLAKE David						
Stepney, 19 June, 1966 ESch/EYth/Eu21-1						(FB)
Queens Park Rgrs	App	06.83	84-89	38	20	6
Swindon T	Tr	11.89	89-92	133	2	1
Leeds U	Tr	03.93	92	8	0	0
Tottenham H	Tr	09.93	93-95	34	3	0
Swindon T	L	11.96	96	8	0	0
Ipswich T	Tr	08.97	97	2	5	0
Wycombe W	L	12.97	97	9	1	0
Swindon T	Tr	03.98	97-98	22	2	0

KERSLAKE Michael (Mickey) Leslie
Bethnal Green, 27 February, 1958 EYth (FB)

League Club	Source	Date Signed	Seasons Played	Apps	Subs	Gls
Fulham	App	10.75	75-77	1	2	0

KETSBAIA Temuri
Gali, Georgia, 18 March, 1968 Georgia 51 (F)

League Club	Source	Date Signed	Seasons Played	Apps	Subs	Gls
Newcastle U	AEK Athens (Gre)	07.97	97-99	41	37	8
Wolverhampton W	Tr	08.00	00-01	14	10	3

KETTERIDGE Stephen (Steve) Jack
Stevenage, 7 November, 1959 (M)

League Club	Source	Date Signed	Seasons Played	Apps	Subs	Gls
Wimbledon	Derby Co (App)	04.78	78-84	229	8	33
Crystal Palace	Tr	08.85	85-86	58	1	6
Leyton Orient	Tr	07.87	87-88	26	5	2
Cardiff C	L	10.88	88	6	0	2

KETTLE Albert Henry
Colchester, 3 June, 1922 Died 1999 (FB)

League Club	Source	Date Signed	Seasons Played	Apps	Subs	Gls
Colchester U	Arclight Sports	(N/L)	50-54	23	-	0

KETTLE Brian
Prescot, 22 April, 1956 EYth (FB)

League Club	Source	Date Signed	Seasons Played	Apps	Subs	Gls
Liverpool	App	05.73	75-76	3	0	0
Wigan Ath	Houston (USA)	08.80	80	14	0	1

KETTLEBOROUGH Keith Frank
Rotherham, 29 June, 1935 (M)

League Club	Source	Date Signed	Seasons Played	Apps	Subs	Gls
Rotherham U	Rotherham YMCA	12.55	55-60	118	-	20
Sheffield U	Tr	12.60	60-65	154	0	17
Newcastle U	Tr	12.65	65-66	30	0	0
Doncaster Rov	Tr	12.66	66-67	35	1	0
Chesterfield	Tr	11.67	67-68	66	0	3

KETTLEY Spencer
Rhondda, 22 May, 1921 (IF)

League Club	Source	Date Signed	Seasons Played	Apps	Subs	Gls
Luton T	Newbury T	08.44	46	1	-	0

KEVAN David John
Wigtown, 31 August, 1968 (M)

League Club	Source	Date Signed	Seasons Played	Apps	Subs	Gls
Notts Co	App	08.86	85-89	82	7	3
Cardiff C	L	09.89	89	6	1	0
Stoke C	Tr	01.90	89-93	78	3	2
Maidstone U	L	02.91	90	3	0	0
Bournemouth	L	03.94	93	0	1	0

KEVAN Derek Tennyson
Ripon, 6 March, 1935 Eu23-4/FLge-1/E-14 (F)

League Club	Source	Date Signed	Seasons Played	Apps	Subs	Gls
Bradford PA	Ripon YMCA	10.52	52	15	-	8
West Bromwich A	Tr	07.53	55-62	262	-	157
Chelsea	Tr	03.63	62	7	-	1
Manchester C	Tr	08.63	63-64	67	-	48
Crystal Palace	Tr	07.65	65	21	0	5
Peterborough U	Tr	03.66	65-66	16	1	2
Luton T	Tr	12.66	66	11	0	4
Stockport Co	Tr	03.67	66-67	38	2	10

KEWELL Harold (Harry)
Smithfield, Australia, 22 September, 1978 AuYth/Au-17 (W)

League Club	Source	Date Signed	Seasons Played	Apps	Subs	Gls
Leeds U	NSW Soccer Acad (Aus)	12.95	95-02	169	12	45
Liverpool	Tr	07.03	03-04	51	3	8

KEWLEY John Kevin
Liverpool, 2 March, 1955 (M)

League Club	Source	Date Signed	Seasons Played	Apps	Subs	Gls
Liverpool	App	03.72	77	0	1	0

KEY Daniel (Danny) Charles
Darlington, 2 November, 1977 (M)

League Club	Source	Date Signed	Seasons Played	Apps	Subs	Gls
Darlington	YT	07.96	96	0	3	0

KEY John (Johnny) Peter
Chelsea, 5 November, 1937 (W)

League Club	Source	Date Signed	Seasons Played	Apps	Subs	Gls
Fulham	Jnrs	05.56	58-65	163	0	29
Coventry C	Tr	05.66	66-67	27	1	7
Orient	Tr	03.68	67-68	9	1	0

KEY Lance William
Kettering, 13 May, 1968 (G)

League Club	Source	Date Signed	Seasons Played	Apps	Subs	Gls
Sheffield Wed	Histon	04.90				
Oldham Ath	L	10.93	93	2	0	0
Oxford U	L	01.95	94	6	0	0
Lincoln C	L	08.95	95	5	0	0
Hartlepool U	L	12.95	95	1	0	0
Rochdale	L	03.96	95	14	0	0
Sheffield U	Dundee U	03.97				
Rochdale	Tr	08.97	97	19	0	0

KEY Richard Martin
Coventry, 13 April, 1956 (G)

League Club	Source	Date Signed	Seasons Played	Apps	Subs	Gls
Exeter C	Coventry C (Jnrs)	07.75	75-77	109	0	0
Cambridge U	Tr	08.78	78-82	52	0	0
Northampton T	L	11.82	82	2	0	0
Orient	Tr	08.83	83	42	0	0
Brentford	Tr	08.84	84	1	0	0
Sunderland	Tr	10.84				
Cambridge U	L	03.85	84	13	0	0
Brentford	Swindon T (N/C)	08.85	85	3	0	0

KEYES Anthony (Tony) Joseph
Salford, 29 October, 1953 (M)

League Club	Source	Date Signed	Seasons Played	Apps	Subs	Gls
Stockport Co	Witton A	10.71	71-73	7	1	0

KEYS Paul Andrew
Ipswich, 4 September, 1962 (F)

League Club	Source	Date Signed	Seasons Played	Apps	Subs	Gls
Luton T		07.81				
Halifax T	L	03.82	81	1	1	0

KEYWORTH Kenneth (Ken)
Rotherham, 24 February, 1934 Died 2000 (CF)

League Club	Source	Date Signed	Seasons Played	Apps	Subs	Gls
Rotherham U	Wolverhampton W (Am)	01.52	55-57	85	-	6
Leicester C	Tr	05.58	58-64	177	-	63
Coventry C	Tr	12.64	64	7	-	3
Swindon T	Tr	08.65	65	6	0	0

KEZMAN Mateja
Belgrade, Yugoslavia, 12 April, 1979 Serbia 37 (F)

League Club	Source	Date Signed	Seasons Played	Apps	Subs	Gls
Chelsea	PSV Eindhoven (Holl)	07.04	04	6	19	4

KHARINE Dimitri Victorvitch
Moscow, Russia, 16 August, 1968 Russia 38 (G)

League Club	Source	Date Signed	Seasons Played	Apps	Subs	Gls
Chelsea	CSKA Moscow (Rus)	12.92	92-98	118	0	0

KHELA Inderpaul Singh
Birmingham, 6 October, 1983 (M)

League Club	Source	Date Signed	Seasons Played	Apps	Subs	Gls
Kidderminster Hrs	Bedworth U	08.02	02	0	1	0

KICHENBRAND Donald (Don) Basil
Johannesburg, South Africa, 13 August, 1933 (CF)

League Club	Source	Date Signed	Seasons Played	Apps	Subs	Gls
Sunderland	Glasgow Rgrs	03.58	57-59	53	-	28

KIDD Brian
Manchester, 29 May, 1949 EYth/Eu23-10/FLge-1/E-2 (F)

League Club	Source	Date Signed	Seasons Played	Apps	Subs	Gls
Manchester U	App	06.66	67-73	195	8	52
Arsenal	Tr	08.74	74-75	77	0	30
Manchester C	Tr	07.76	76-78	97	1	44
Everton	Tr	03.79	78-79	40	0	12
Bolton W	Tr	05.80	80-81	40	3	14

KIDD John Oliver
Birkenhead, 15 January, 1936 (IF)

League Club	Source	Date Signed	Seasons Played	Apps	Subs	Gls
Tranmere Rov	Everton (Am)	08.55	55-58	34	-	4

KIDD Ryan Andrew
Heywood, 6 October, 1971 (CD)

League Club	Source	Date Signed	Seasons Played	Apps	Subs	Gls
Port Vale	YT	07.90	91	1	0	0
Preston NE	Tr	07.92	92-01	241	18	9

KIDD William (Billy) Edward
Pegswood, 31 January, 1907 Died 1978 (FB)

League Club	Source	Date Signed	Seasons Played	Apps	Subs	Gls
Chesterfield	Pegswood U	03.32	31-47	316	-	2

KIELY Dean Laurence
Salford, 10 October, 1970 ESch/EYth/IRB-1/IR-8 (G)

League Club	Source	Date Signed	Seasons Played	Apps	Subs	Gls
Coventry C	App	10.87				
York C	Tr	03.90	90-95	210	0	0
Bury	Tr	08.96	96-98	137	0	0
Charlton Ath	Tr	05.99	99-04	219	0	0

KIERAN Leonard (Len) Vincent
Birkenhead, 25 July, 1926 Died 1981 (WH)

League Club	Source	Date Signed	Seasons Played	Apps	Subs	Gls
Tranmere Rov	Jnrs	09.43	47-56	342	-	6

KIERNAN Daniel James
Northampton, 16 December, 1973 (M)

League Club	Source	Date Signed	Seasons Played	Apps	Subs	Gls
Northampton T	YT	09.91	91	6	3	0

KIERNAN Frederick (Fred) William
Dublin, 7 July, 1919 Died 1981 LoI-2/IR-5 (G)

League Club	Source	Date Signed	Seasons Played	Apps	Subs	Gls
Southampton	Shamrock Rov	10.51	51-55	132	-	0

KIERNAN Joseph (Joe)
Coatbridge, 22 October, 1942 (CD)

League Club	Source	Date Signed	Seasons Played	Apps	Subs	Gls
Sunderland	Jnrs	11.59	62	1	-	0
Northampton T	Tr	07.63	63-71	305	3	13

KIERNAN Thomas (Tommy)
Coatbridge, 20 October, 1918 Died 1991 SLge-1 (IF)

League Club	Source	Date Signed	Seasons Played	Apps	Subs	Gls
Stoke C	Glasgow Celtic	09.47	47-48	28	-	6
Luton T	Tr	11.48	48-50	55	-	10

KIERNAN William (Billy) Edward
Penge, 22 May, 1925 EB (W)

League Club	Source	Date Signed	Seasons Played	Apps	Subs	Gls
Charlton Ath	(Hong Kong)	07.49	49-60	378	-	89

KIGHTLY Michael John
Basildon, 24 January, 1986 (M)

League Club	Source	Date Signed	Seasons Played	Apps	Subs	Gls
Southend U	Sch	12.03	02-04	2	11	0

[KIKO] CHARANA BAPTISTA GOMES Manuel Henrique
Cedofeita, Portugal, 24 October, 1976 (M)

League Club	Source	Date Signed	Seasons Played	Apps	Subs	Gls
Stockport Co	Belenenses (Por)	12.96	96	0	3	0

KILBANE Farrell Noel
Preston, 21 October, 1974 (CD)

League Club	Source	Date Signed	Seasons Played	Apps	Subs	Gls
Preston NE	Cambridge U (YT)	07.93	93	0	1	0

KILBANE Kevin Daniel
Preston, 1 February, 1977 IRu21-11/IR-64 (W)

League Club	Source	Date Signed	Seasons Played	Apps	Subs	Gls
Preston NE	YT	07.95	95-96	39	8	3
West Bromwich A	Tr	06.97	97-99	105	1	15
Sunderland	Tr	12.99	99-03	102	11	8
Everton	Tr	09.03	03-04	63	5	4

KILCLINE Brian
Nottingham, 7 May, 1962 Eu21-2 (CD)

League Club	Source	Date Signed	Seasons Played	Apps	Subs	Gls
Notts Co	App	04.80	79-83	156	2	9
Coventry C	Tr	06.84	84-90	173	0	28
Oldham Ath	Tr	08.91	91	8	0	0
Newcastle U	Tr	02.92	91-93	20	12	0
Swindon T	Tr	01.94	93-94	16	1	0
Mansfield T	Tr	12.95	95-96	48	2	3

KILEY Thomas (Tom) James
Swansea, 15 June, 1924 Died 2000 (CD)

League Club	Source	Date Signed	Seasons Played	Apps	Subs	Gls
Swansea T		06.47	49-56	129	-	2

KILFORD Ian Anthony
Bristol, 6 October, 1973 (M)

League Club	Source	Date Signed	Seasons Played	Apps	Subs	Gls
Nottingham F	YT	04.91	93	0	1	0
Wigan Ath	L	12.93	93	7	1	3
Wigan Ath	Tr	07.94	94-01	170	43	29
Bury	Tr	08.02				
Scunthorpe U	Tr	11.02	02-03	38	8	3

KILFORD John Douglas
Derby, 8 November, 1938 (FB)

League Club	Source	Date Signed	Seasons Played	Apps	Subs	Gls
Notts Co	Derby Corinthians	07.57	58	26	-	0
Leeds U	Tr	02.59	58-61	21	-	0

KILGALLON Mark Christopher
Glasgow, 20 December, 1962 (CD)

League Club	Source	Date Signed	Seasons Played	Apps	Subs	Gls
Hull C	Ipswich T (App)	08.80	80	0	1	0

KILGALLON Matthew Shaun
York, 8 January, 1984 EYth/Eu21-4 (CD)

League Club	Source	Date Signed	Seasons Played	Apps	Subs	Gls
Leeds U	YT	01.01	02-04	33	3	2
West Ham U	L	08.03	03	1	2	0

KILGANNON John
Stenhousemuir, 26 June, 1936 Died 1967 (IF)

League Club	Source	Date Signed	Seasons Played	Apps	Subs	Gls
Luton T	Stenhousemuir	04.59	58-59	13	-	1

KILGANNON Sean
Dundee, 8 March, 1981 (M)

League Club	Source	Date Signed	Seasons Played	Apps	Subs	Gls
Middlesbrough	YT	07.99	99	0	1	0

KILHEENEY Ciaran Joseph
Stockport, 9 January, 1984 (F)

League Club	Source	Date Signed	Seasons Played	Apps	Subs	Gls
Manchester C	YT	07.01				
Exeter C	Mossley	03.03	02	0	4	0

KILKELLY Thomas (Tom) Francis
Galway, 22 August, 1955 IRYth (CD)

League Club	Source	Date Signed	Seasons Played	Apps	Subs	Gls
Leicester C	App	07.73				
Northampton T	L	09.74	74	2	2	0

KILKENNY James (Jim)
Stanley, 21 November, 1934 (WH)

League Club	Source	Date Signed	Seasons Played	Apps	Subs	Gls
Doncaster Rov	Annfield Plain	05.52	55-60	132	-	1

KILKENNY Neil Martin
Middlesex, 19 December, 1985 EYth (M)

League Club	Source	Date Signed	Seasons Played	Apps	Subs	Gls
Birmingham C	Arsenal (Sch)	01.04				
Oldham Ath	L	11.04	04	24	3	4

KILLARNEY Arthur
Huddersfield, 26 February, 1921 (WH)

League Club	Source	Date Signed	Seasons Played	Apps	Subs	Gls
Halifax T		05.46	46	2	-	0

KILLEEN Lewis Keith
Peterborough, 23 September, 1982 (F)

League Club	Source	Date Signed	Seasons Played	Apps	Subs	Gls
Sheffield U	YT	07.01	01	0	1	0

KILLEN Christopher (Chris) John
Wellington, New Zealand, 8 October, 1981 NzYth/Nzu20/Nzu23/Nz-16 (F)

League Club	Source	Date Signed	Seasons Played	Apps	Subs	Gls
Manchester C	Miramar Rgrs (NZ)	03.99	01	0	3	0
Wrexham	L	09.00	00	11	1	3
Port Vale	L	09.01	01	8	1	6
Oldham Ath	Tr	07.02	02-04	43	23	15

KILLIN Harold Roy
Toronto, Canada, 18 July, 1929 (FB)

League Club	Source	Date Signed	Seasons Played	Apps	Subs	Gls
Manchester U		04.49				
Lincoln C	Tr	08.52	53	7	-	0

KILLOUGHERY Graham Anthony
London, 22 July, 1984 (M)

League Club	Source	Date Signed	Seasons Played	Apps	Subs	Gls
Torquay U	Sch	07.03	02-03	1	5	0

KILMORE Kevin
Scunthorpe, 11 November, 1959 EYth (M)

League Club	Source	Date Signed	Seasons Played	Apps	Subs	Gls
Scunthorpe U	Jnrs	01.77	76-79	93	9	28
Grimsby T	Tr	09.79	79-82	70	32	27
Rotherham U	Tr	08.83	83-84	82	2	20
Lincoln C	KFC Geel (Bel)	01.86	85-86	40	6	6

KILNER Andrew (Andy) William
Bolton, 11 October, 1966 EYth (W)

League Club	Source	Date Signed	Seasons Played	Apps	Subs	Gls
Burnley	App	07.84	85	2	3	0
Stockport Co	Jonsered (Swe)	12.90	90-91	34	8	14
Rochdale	L	01.92	91	3	0	0
Bury	Tr	08.92	92	4	1	0

KILNER John Ian
Bolton, 3 October, 1959 (G)

League Club	Source	Date Signed	Seasons Played	Apps	Subs	Gls
Preston NE	App	10.77				
Halifax T	Tr	02.79	78-81	114	0	0
Wigan Ath	(South Africa)	07.83	83	4	0	0

KILSHAW Edmund (Eddie) Ainsworth
Prescot, 25 December, 1919 (W)

League Club	Source	Date Signed	Seasons Played	Apps	Subs	Gls
Bury	Prescot Cables	10.37	37-48	147	-	17
Sheffield Wed	Tr	12.48	48	17	-	1

KILSHAW Frederick (Fred)
Wrexham, 24 August, 1916 (IF)

League Club	Source	Date Signed	Seasons Played	Apps	Subs	Gls
Leicester C		01.45				
New Brighton	Tr	07.46	46	8	-	1

KILTY Mark Thomas
Sunderland, 24 June, 1981 (FB)

League Club	Source	Date Signed	Seasons Played	Apps	Subs	Gls
Darlington	YT	07.99	98-01	20	3	1

KIMBERLEY Samuel Kenneth (Ken)
Walsall, 7 August, 1920 Died 1987 (G)

League Club	Source	Date Signed	Seasons Played	Apps	Subs	Gls
Walsall	Cannock Colliery	05.46	46	1	-	0

KIMBLE Alan Frank
Dagenham, 6 August, 1966 (FB)

League Club	Source	Date Signed	Seasons Played	Apps	Subs	Gls
Charlton Ath	Jnrs	08.84	84	6	0	0
Exeter C	L	08.85	85	1	0	0
Cambridge U	Tr	08.86	86-92	295	4	24
Wimbledon	Tr	07.93	93-01	196	19	0
Peterborough U	L	03.02	01	3	0	0
Luton T	Tr	08.02	02	8	4	0

KIMBLE Garry Leslie
Dagenham, 6 August, 1966 (W)

League Club	Source	Date Signed	Seasons Played	Apps	Subs	Gls
Charlton Ath	Jnrs	08.84	84	7	2	1
Exeter C	L	08.85	85	1	0	0
Cambridge U	Tr	08.86	86-87	39	2	2
Doncaster Rov	Tr	10.87	87-88	60	5	1
Fulham	Tr	08.89	89	1	2	0
Maidstone U	Tr	10.89				
Gillingham	St Albans C	02.90	89-90	35	13	1
Peterborough U	Tr	07.91	91	30	0	4

KINDER Vladimir
Bratislava, Slovakia, 9 March, 1969 Cz-1/Slovakia-39 (FB)

League Club	Source	Date Signed	Seasons Played	Apps	Subs	Gls
Middlesbrough	Slovan Bratislava (Slo)	01.97	96-98	29	8	5

KINDON Stephen (Steve) Michael
Warrington, 17 December, 1950 EYth (F)

League Club	Source	Date Signed	Seasons Played	Apps	Subs	Gls
Burnley	App	12.67	68-71	102	7	28
Wolverhampton W	Tr	07.72	72-77	111	17	28
Burnley	Tr	11.77	77-79	73	3	18
Huddersfield T	Tr	12.79	79-81	69	4	35

KINET Christophe
Huy, Belgium, 31 December, 1972 (M)

League Club	Source	Date Signed	Seasons Played	Apps	Subs	Gls
Millwall	RC Strasbourg (Fr)	02.00	99-02	39	28	7

KING Adam
Hillingdon, 4 October, 1969 EYth (M)

League Club	Source	Date Signed	Seasons Played	Apps	Subs	Gls
West Ham U	YT	06.88				
Plymouth Arg	Tr	03.90	89-90	9	7	0

KING Alan
Gateshead, 25 November, 1947 (W)

League Club	Source	Date Signed	Seasons Played	Apps	Subs	Gls
Hartlepools U (Am)	Horden CW	08.67	67	0	1	0

KING Alan John
Birkenhead, 18 January, 1945 (CD)

League Club	Source	Date Signed	Seasons Played	Apps	Subs	Gls
Tranmere Rov	Jnrs	07.63	62-71	341	0	35

KING Andrew (Andy) Edward
Luton, 14 August, 1956 Eu21-2 (M)

League Club	Source	Date Signed	Seasons Played	Apps	Subs	Gls
Luton T	App	07.74	74-75	30	3	9
Everton	Tr	04.76	75-79	150	1	38
Queens Park Rgrs	Tr	09.80	80-81	28	2	9
West Bromwich A	Tr	09.81	81	21	4	4
Everton	Tr	07.82	82-83	43	1	11
Wolverhampton W	SC Cambuur (Holl)	01.85	84-85	28	0	10
Luton T	Tr	12.85	85	3	0	0
Aldershot	Tr	08.86	86	36	0	11

KING Andrew (Andy) John
Thatcham, 30 March, 1970 (F)

League Club	Source	Date Signed	Seasons Played	Apps	Subs	Gls
Reading	YT	06.88	88	0	1	0

KING Barry
Chesterfield, 30 March, 1935 (W)

League Club	Source	Date Signed	Seasons Played	Apps	Subs	Gls
Chelsea	Norton Woodseats	02.58				
Reading	Tr	03.58	57	3	-	0

KING Michael **Bryan**
Bishops Stortford, 18 May, 1947 (G)

League Club	Source	Date Signed	Seasons Played	Apps	Subs	Gls
Millwall	Chelmsford C	06.67	67-74	302	0	0
Coventry C	Tr	08.75	75	23	0	0

KING David (Dave) John
Hull, 24 October, 1940 (IF)

League Club	Source	Date Signed	Seasons Played	Apps	Subs	Gls
Hull C	Jnrs	10.58	59-62	65	-	24

KING David (Dave) Martin
Colchester, 18 September, 1962 (M)

League Club	Source	Date Signed	Seasons Played	Apps	Subs	Gls
Derby Co	App	09.80				
York C	Gresley Rov	03.83	82	0	1	0

KING Dennis
Bearpark, 16 September, 1932 Died 1988 (W)

League Club	Source	Date Signed	Seasons Played	Apps	Subs	Gls
Bradford PA		09.50				
Oldham Ath	Spennymoor U	05.54	54-55	22	-	7

KING Derek Albert
Hackney, 15 August, 1929 Died 2003 (CD)

League Club	Source	Date Signed	Seasons Played	Apps	Subs	Gls
Tottenham H	Jnrs	08.50	51-54	19	-	0
Swansea T	Tr	08.56	56	5	-	0

KING George
Warkworth, 5 January, 1923 Died 2002 (CF)

League Club	Source	Date Signed	Seasons Played	Apps	Subs	Gls
Newcastle U		08.46	46	2	-	0
Hull C	Tr	03.48	47-48	3	-	0
Port Vale	Tr	04.49	48-49	10	-	5
Barrow	Tr	02.50	49-51	86	-	37
Bradford C	Tr	01.52	51-52	23	-	9
Gillingham	Tr	10.52	52	19	-	5

KING Gerald (Gerry) Henry
Radnor, 7 April, 1947 WSch (W)

League Club	Source	Date Signed	Seasons Played	Apps	Subs	Gls
Cardiff C	Jnrs	06.64	64	6	-	0
Torquay U	Tr	06.65	65	18	0	2
Luton T	Tr	06.66	66	21	1	4
Newport Co	Tr	07.67	67-68	49	3	9

KING Jeffrey (Jeff)
Fauldhouse, 9 November, 1953 (M)

League Club	Source	Date Signed	Seasons Played	Apps	Subs	Gls
Derby Co	Albion Rov	04.74	75-77	12	2	0
Notts Co	L	01.76	75	3	0	0
Portsmouth	L	03.76	75	4	0	0
Walsall	Tr	11.77	77-78	50	1	4
Sheffield Wed	Tr	08.79	79-81	54	3	5
Sheffield U	Tr	01.82	81-82	35	2	5
Chesterfield	Tr	10.83	83	1	0	0

KING John
Ferndale, 29 November, 1933 Died 1982 WSch/WLge-3/W-1 (G)

League Club	Source	Date Signed	Seasons Played	Apps	Subs	Gls
Swansea T	Jnrs	02.51	50-63	363	-	0

KING John (Jake)
Glasgow, 29 January, 1955 (FB)

League Club	Source	Date Signed	Seasons Played	Apps	Subs	Gls
Shrewsbury T	App	01.73	72-81	304	2	20
Wrexham	Tr	08.82	82-84	91	1	5
Cardiff C	Tr	11.84	84-85	30	0	0

KING John (Ian) Aitken
Loanhead, 27 May, 1937 SSch (CD)

League Club	Source	Date Signed	Seasons Played	Apps	Subs	Gls
Leicester C	Arniston Rgrs	06.57	57-65	244	0	6
Charlton Ath	Tr	03.66	65-67	63	0	0

KING John (Johnny) Allen
Liverpool, 15 April, 1938 (M)

League Club	Source	Date Signed	Seasons Played	Apps	Subs	Gls
Everton	Jnrs	03.56	57-59	48	-	1
Bournemouth	Tr	07.60	60	21	-	1
Tranmere Rov	Tr	02.61	60-67	240	2	4
Port Vale	Tr	07.68	68-70	99	2	0

KING John (Johnny) Charles
Great Gidding, 5 November, 1926 (WH)

League Club	Source	Date Signed	Seasons Played	Apps	Subs	Gls
Leicester C	Peterborough U	09.44	46-54	197	-	5

KING John (Johnny) William
Wrenbury, 9 August, 1932 (CF)

League Club	Source	Date Signed	Seasons Played	Apps	Subs	Gls
Crewe Alex	Jnrs	10.49	50-53	48	-	17
Stoke C	Tr	09.53	53-60	284	-	106
Cardiff C	Tr	08.61	61	33	-	6
Crewe Alex	Tr	06.62	62-66	178	0	45

KING Ledley Brenton
Stepney, 12 October, 1980 EYth/Eu21-12/E-12 (CD)

League Club	Source	Date Signed	Seasons Played	Apps	Subs	Gls
Tottenham H	YT	07.98	98-04	143	3	4

KING Marlon Francis
Dulwich, 26 April, 1980 Jamaica 11 (F)

League Club	Source	Date Signed	Seasons Played	Apps	Subs	Gls
Barnet	YT	09.98	98-99	36	17	14
Gillingham	Tr	06.00	00-03	82	19	40
Nottingham F	Tr	11.03	03-04	40	10	10
Leeds U	L	03.05	04	4	5	0

KING Martyn Noel Geoffrey
Birmingham, 23 August, 1937 (CF)

League Club	Source	Date Signed	Seasons Played	Apps	Subs	Gls
Colchester U	Pegasus	05.56	56-64	212	-	130
Wrexham	Tr	10.64	64-65	45	0	15

KING Peter
Liverpool, 5 July, 1964 (M)

League Club	Source	Date Signed	Seasons Played	Apps	Subs	Gls
Liverpool	App	07.82				
Crewe Alex	Tr	08.83	83-84	55	9	5

KING Peter Charles
Worcester, 3 April, 1943 (F)

League Club	Source	Date Signed	Seasons Played	Apps	Subs	Gls
Cardiff C	Worcester C	09.60	61-73	351	5	67

KING Philip (Phil) Geoffrey
Bristol, 28 December, 1967 EB-1 (FB)

League Club	Source	Date Signed	Seasons Played	Apps	Subs	Gls
Exeter C	App	01.85	84-85	24	3	0
Torquay U	Tr	07.86	86	24	0	3
Swindon T	Tr	02.87	86-89	112	4	4
Sheffield Wed	Tr	11.89	89-93	124	5	2
Notts Co	L	10.93	93	6	0	0
Aston Villa	Tr	08.94	94	13	3	0
West Bromwich A	L	10.95	95	4	0	0
Swindon T	Tr	03.97	96	5	0	0
Blackpool	L	10.97	97	6	0	0
Brighton & Hove A	Tr	03.99	98	3	0	0

KING Raymond (Ray)
Amble, 15 August, 1924 EB (G)

League Club	Source	Date Signed	Seasons Played	Apps	Subs	Gls
Newcastle U	Amble	04.42				
Leyton Orient	Tr	10.46	46	1	-	0
Port Vale	Ashington	05.49	49-56	252	-	0

KING Robert David
Merthyr Tydfil, 2 September, 1977 WYth (FB)

League Club	Source	Date Signed	Seasons Played	Apps	Subs	Gls
Swansea C	Torquay U (YT)	07.96	96	2	0	0

KING Robert (Bobby) Edward
Edinburgh, 7 September, 1941 (FB)

League Club	Source	Date Signed	Seasons Played	Apps	Subs	Gls
Southend U	Glasgow Rgrs	08.63	63-65	77	2	2

KING Frederick Alfred **Robert (Bobby)**
Northampton, 19 September, 1919 Died 2003 (W)

League Club	Source	Date Signed	Seasons Played	Apps	Subs	Gls
Northampton T		10.37	37-38	42	-	6
Wolverhampton W	Tr	11.39	46	6	-	3
Northampton T	Tr	12.47	47-49	56	-	17

KING Simon
Ebbw Vale, 19 July, 1964 (FB)

League Club	Source	Date Signed	Seasons Played	Apps	Subs	Gls
Newport Co	Cwmbran	10.84	84	1	0	0

KING Simon Daniel Roy
Oxford, 11 April, 1983 (FB)

League Club	Source	Date Signed	Seasons Played	Apps	Subs	Gls
Oxford U	YT	12.00	00-01	3	1	0

KING Thomas (Tommy)
Edinburgh, 18 July, 1933 (G)

League Club	Source	Date Signed	Seasons Played	Apps	Subs	Gls
Watford	Ormiston Primrose	03.54	55	20	-	0

KING Thomas (Tommy) Frederick
Barrow, 2 April, 1934 (WH)

League Club	Source	Date Signed	Seasons Played	Apps	Subs	Gls
Barrow	Holker COB	03.53	52-59	73	-	1

League Club	Source	Date Signed	Seasons Played	Career Record Apps	Subs	Gls

KINGSHOTT Frederick (Freddie) John
St Pancras, 20 June, 1929 (G)

Doncaster Rov	Eastbourne U	02.53	52	2	-	0
Gillingham	Tr	11.55	55-56	45	-	0

KINGSNORTH Thomas (Tom) Henry
Sittingbourne, 16 April, 1917 Died 1992 (CD)

Gillingham	Lloyds Paper Mills	09.46	50	28	-	0

KINGSTON Andrew (Andy) Keith
Oxford, 21 February, 1959 ESch/EYth (CD)

Oxford U	App	10.76	76-81	44	6	0

KINKLADZE Georgiou (Georgi)
Tbilisi, Georgia, 6 November, 1973 Georgia 49 (M)

Manchester C	Mretebi Tibilisi (Geo)	08.95	95-97	105	1	20
Derby Co	Ajax (Holl)	11.99	99-02	60	33	7

KINLOCH Thomas (Tommy) Sutherland
Anderston, 22 February, 1927 Died 1994 (WH)

Carlisle U	Falkirk	05.50	50-55	184	-	15
Workington	Tr	07.56	56-57	70	-	12
Southport	Tr	02.58	57-58	53	-	0

KINNAIRD Paul
Glasgow, 11 November, 1966 SYth (W)

Norwich C	Possilpark YMCA	11.84				
Shrewsbury T (L)	Partick Th	02.93	92	4	0	1
Scarborough	Dunfermline Ath	10.95	95	3	0	0

KINNEAR Joseph (Joe) Patrick
Dublin, 27 December, 1946 IR-25 (CD)

Tottenham H	St Albans C	02.65	65-75	189	7	2
Brighton & Hove A	Tr	08.75	75	15	1	1

KINNELL George
Cowdenbeath, 22 December, 1937 (CD)

Stoke C	Aberdeen	11.63	63-65	89	2	6
Oldham Ath	Tr	08.66	66	12	0	8
Sunderland	Tr	10.66	66-68	67	2	3
Middlesbrough	Tr	10.68	68	12	1	1

KINSELL Thomas **Henry (Harry)**
Cannock, 31 May, 1921 Died 2000 EWar-2 (FB)

West Bromwich A	Jnrs	06.38	46-48	83	-	0
Bolton W	Tr	06.49	49	17	-	0
Reading	Tr	05.50	50	12	-	0
West Ham U	Tr	01.51	50-54	101	-	2

KINSELLA Antony (Tony) Steven
Orsett, 30 October, 1961 IRu21-2 (W)

Millwall	App	11.78	78-80	55	6	1
Ipswich T	Tampa Bay (USA)	04.82	82-83	7	2	0
Millwall	Tr	06.84	84-85	20	2	1
Doncaster Rov	Enfield	02.87	86-87	29	1	4

KINSELLA Leonard (Len)
Alexandria, 14 May, 1946 (M)

Burnley	App	05.63	65-69	7	6	0
Carlisle U	Tr	09.70	70-71	9	4	0
Rochdale	Tr	09.71	71-73	82	3	4

KINSELLA Mark Anthony
Dublin, 12 August, 1972 IRYth/IRu21-8/IRB-1/IR-48 (M)

Colchester U	Home Farm	08.89	89-96	174	6	27
Charlton Ath	Tr	09.96	96-01	200	8	19
Aston Villa	Tr	08.02	02-03	17	4	0
West Bromwich A	Tr	01.04	03	15	3	1
Walsall	Tr	07.04	04	21	1	0

KINSELLA Patrick (Pat) Gerard
Liverpool, 8 November, 1943 (M)

Liverpool	Jnrs	11.60				
Tranmere Rov	Bangor C	08.66	66	1	0	0
Stockport Co	Rhyl	10.68	68	12	1	0

KINSEY Albert John
Liverpool, 19 September, 1945 ESch (F)

Manchester U	App	10.62				
Wrexham	Tr	03.66	65-72	245	8	84
Crewe Alex	Tr	03.73	72-74	30	2	1

KINSEY Brian Robert
Charlton, 4 March, 1938 (FB)

Charlton Ath	Bromley	09.56	56-70	371	6	19

KINSEY Noel
Treorchy, 24 December, 1925 W-7 (IF)

Cardiff C	Jnrs	06.44				
Norwich C	Tr	05.47	47-52	223	-	57
Birmingham C	Tr	05.53	53-57	149	-	48
Port Vale	Tr	02.58	57-60	72	-	6

KINSEY Stephen (Steve)
Manchester, 2 January, 1963 EYth (W)

Manchester C	App	01.80	80-85	87	14	15
Chester	L	09.82	82	3	0	1
Chesterfield	L	11.82	82	3	0	0
Rochdale	Molde FK (Nor)	10.91	91	3	3	1

KIPPAX Dennis Hobson
Sheffield, 7 August, 1926 Died 1970 (W)

Sheffield Wed	Stocksbridge Works	03.46	46	1	-	0

KIPPAX Frederick **Peter**
Burnley, 17 July, 1922 Died 1987 EAmat/FLge-2 (W)

Burnley (Am)	Jnrs	07.46	46-47	32	-	6
Liverpool (Am)	Tr	01.49	48	1	-	0

KIPPE Frode
Oslo, Norway, 17 January, 1978 Nou21-27/NoB-1 (G)

Liverpool	Lillestrom (Nor)	01.99				
Stoke C	L	12.99	99	15	0	1
Stoke C	L	10.00	00	15	4	0

KIRALY Gabor Ferenc
Szombathely, Hungary, 1 April, 1976 Hungary 57 (G)

Crystal Palace	Hertha Berlin (Ger)	08.04	04	32	0	0

KIRBY Alan
Barrow, 19 December, 1926 Died 2003 (G)

Notts Co		05.45				
Barrow		09.47	50-51	21	-	0

KIRBY Denis
Holbeck, 8 November, 1924 (WH)

Leeds U	Jnrs	09.42	47	8	-	0

KIRBY Eric
Sheffield, 12 October, 1926 (WH)

Sheffield Wed		12.49	50	1	-	0
York C	Tr	08.52	52	1	-	0

KIRBY George
Liverpool, 20 December, 1933 Died 2000 (F)

Everton	Jnrs	06.52	55-57	26	-	9
Sheffield Wed	Tr	03.59	59	3	-	0
Plymouth Arg	Tr	01.60	59-62	93	-	38
Southampton	Tr	09.62	62-63	63	-	28
Coventry C	Tr	03.64	63-64	18	-	10
Swansea T	Tr	10.64	64	25	-	8
Walsall	Tr	05.65	65-66	74	1	25
Brentford	New York (USA)	10.68	68	5	0	1

KIRBY Ryan Mark
Chingford, 6 September, 1974 (FB)

Arsenal	YT	07.93				
Doncaster Rov	Tr	07.94	94-95	73	5	0
Wigan Ath	Crewe Alex (N/C)	08.96	96	5	1	0
Northampton T	Tr	09.96	96	0	1	0

KIRK Andrew (Andy) Robert
Belfast, 29 May, 1979 NISch/NIYth/NIu21-9/NI-8 (F)

Boston U	Heart of Midlothian	07.04	04	25	0	19
Northampton T	Tr	03.05	04	8	0	7

KIRK Henry (Harry) Joseph
Saltcoats, 25 August, 1944 (W)

Middlesbrough	Ardeer Rec	05.63	63	1	-	0
Darlington	Dumbarton	06.67	67-69	59	2	7
Hartlepool	Tr	10.69	69-70	42	3	5
Scunthorpe U	Tr	11.70	70-72	112	0	16
Stockport Co	Tr	09.73	73-74	60	8	7

KIRK James (Jimmy)
Tarbolton, 12 November, 1925 (G)

Bury	St Mirren	08.51	51-53	80	-	0
Colchester U	Tr	06.54	54	32	-	0
Torquay U	Tr	08.55	55	39	-	0
Aldershot	Tr	07.56	56	5	-	0

KIRK John Francis
Leicester, 7 February, 1922 (W)

Nottingham F		08.48				
Darlington	Tr	08.51	51	30	-	4

KIRK John McCrae
Winnipeg, Canada, 13 March, 1930 (IF)

Portsmouth	Montrose	01.51				
Accrington St	Tr	03.53	52-53	14	-	1

KIRK Roy
Shuttlewood, 11 June, 1929 Died 1984 (CD)

Leeds U	Bolsover Colliery	10.48	50-51	34	-	1
Coventry C	Tr	03.52	51-59	330	-	6

KIRK Stephen (Steve) David
Kirkcaldy, 3 January, 1963 (FB)

League Club	Source	Date Signed	Seasons Played	Apps	Subs	Gls
Stoke C	East Fife	05.80	81	12	0	0

KIRKALDIE John (Jack)
Coventry, 2 August, 1917 Died 1985 (W)

League Club	Source	Date Signed	Seasons Played	Apps	Subs	Gls
Southend U	Nuneaton T	02.36	36	1	-	0
West Ham U	Tr	02.37	36-38	11	-	1
Doncaster Rov	Tr	04.39	38-47	53	-	17

KIRKBY John
USA, 29 November, 1929 Died 1953 (FB)

League Club	Source	Date Signed	Seasons Played	Apps	Subs	Gls
Stoke C	Banks o' Dee	12.46	48	1	-	0
Wrexham	Tr	08.51	51-52	5	-	0

KIRKHAM John (Jack)
Ellesmere Port, 16 June, 1918 Died 1982 (CF)

League Club	Source	Date Signed	Seasons Played	Apps	Subs	Gls
Wolverhampton W	Ellesmere Port T	03.36	37-38	13	-	5
Bournemouth	Tr	10.38	38-46	48	-	27

KIRKHAM John Kenneth
Wednesbury, 13 May, 1941 EYth/Eu23-2 (M)

League Club	Source	Date Signed	Seasons Played	Apps	Subs	Gls
Wolverhampton W	Ellesmere Port T	05.58	59-64	100	-	12
Peterborough U	Tr	11.65	65-67	46	0	2
Exeter C	Tr	07.68	68	31	1	6

KIRKHAM Paul
Manchester, 5 July, 1969 (F)

League Club	Source	Date Signed	Seasons Played	Apps	Subs	Gls
Huddersfield T	Manchester U (YT)	09.87	87	0	1	0

KIRKHAM Peter Jonathan
Newcastle, 28 October, 1974 (M)

League Club	Source	Date Signed	Seasons Played	Apps	Subs	Gls
Darlington	Newcastle U (YT)	08.93	93-94	5	8	0

KIRKHAM Raymond (Ray) Neville
Thorne, 16 December, 1934 (G)

League Club	Source	Date Signed	Seasons Played	Apps	Subs	Gls
Mansfield T	Thorne T	12.57	57-59	42	-	0

KIRKHAM Reginald (Reg)
Ormskirk, 8 May, 1919 Died 1999 (WH)

League Club	Source	Date Signed	Seasons Played	Apps	Subs	Gls
Wolverhampton W	Ormskirk	03.46				
Burnley	Tr	03.47	48-50	13	-	1

KIRKHAM Royce
Ollerton, 17 October, 1937 (FB)

League Club	Source	Date Signed	Seasons Played	Apps	Subs	Gls
Notts Co	Ollerton Colliery	05.55	56	1	-	0

KIRKLAND Christopher (Chris)
Barwell, 2 May, 1981 EYth/Eu21-8 (G)

League Club	Source	Date Signed	Seasons Played	Apps	Subs	Gls
Coventry C	YT	05.98	00-01	24	0	0
Liverpool	Tr	08.01	01-04	25	0	0

KIRKLAND James (Jim) William
Bedford, 30 October, 1946 (FB)

League Club	Source	Date Signed	Seasons Played	Apps	Subs	Gls
Grimsby T	Aberdeen	07.70	70	12	0	0

KIRKMAN Alan John
Bolton, 21 June, 1936 (F)

League Club	Source	Date Signed	Seasons Played	Apps	Subs	Gls
Manchester C	Bacup Borough	02.56	56-58	7	-	6
Rotherham U	Tr	03.59	58-63	142	-	58
Newcastle U	Tr	09.63	63	5	-	1
Scunthorpe U	Tr	12.63	63-64	32	-	5
Torquay U	Tr	07.65	65-66	59	0	8
Workington	Tr	01.67	66-67	56	0	3

KIRKMAN Kenneth (Ken) Roy
Farnworth, 20 March, 1931 Died 2000 (W)

League Club	Source	Date Signed	Seasons Played	Apps	Subs	Gls
Bournemouth	Lomax's	07.51				
Southport	Tr	08.53	53	1	-	0

KIRKMAN Norman
Bolton, 6 March, 1920 Died 1995 (FB)

League Club	Source	Date Signed	Seasons Played	Apps	Subs	Gls
Burnley		09.39				
Rochdale	Tr	09.46	46-47	53	-	0
Chesterfield	Tr	12.47	47-48	41	-	0
Leicester C	Tr	08.49	49	12	-	0
Southampton	Tr	07.50	50-51	20	-	0
Exeter C	Tr	03.52	51-52	11	-	1

KIRKPATRICK John
Annan, 3 March, 1919 (IF)

League Club	Source	Date Signed	Seasons Played	Apps	Subs	Gls
Carlisle U	Jnrs	11.37	46	33	-	2

KIRKPATRICK Roger Whitworth
Sculcoates, 29 May, 1923 (IF)

League Club	Source	Date Signed	Seasons Played	Apps	Subs	Gls
Chester		08.47	47-52	111	-	26

KIRKUP Brian Alexander
Burnham, 16 April, 1932 (CF)

League Club	Source	Date Signed	Seasons Played	Apps	Subs	Gls
Reading	Bedford T	08.55	55-57	55	-	19
Northampton T	Tr	07.58	58-59	26	-	7
Aldershot	Tr	11.59	59-61	59	-	15

KIRKUP Frank William
Spennymoor, 12 January, 1939 (W)

League Club	Source	Date Signed	Seasons Played	Apps	Subs	Gls
Blackburn Rov	Spennymoor U	02.57				
Workington	Tr	06.59	59-62	140	-	31
Carlisle U	Tr	12.62	62-64	76	-	13
Notts Co	Tr	06.65	65	29	0	3
Workington	Tr	11.66	66	8	0	0

KIRKUP Graeme Stuart
Cramlington, 31 May, 1965 (FB)

League Club	Source	Date Signed	Seasons Played	Apps	Subs	Gls
Exeter C	App	05.83	81-85	103	4	1

KIRKUP Joseph (Joe) Robert
Hexham, 17 December, 1939 EYth/Eu23-3 (FB)

League Club	Source	Date Signed	Seasons Played	Apps	Subs	Gls
West Ham U	Jnrs	05.57	58-65	165	0	6
Chelsea	Tr	03.66	65-67	48	5	2
Southampton	Tr	02.68	67-73	169	0	3

KIRKWOOD Ian
Edinburgh, 29 November, 1932 (IF)

League Club	Source	Date Signed	Seasons Played	Apps	Subs	Gls
Reading	Wokingham T	02.53	52-54	5	-	1

KIRKWOOD John Fleming
Falkirk, 27 February, 1932 (G)

League Club	Source	Date Signed	Seasons Played	Apps	Subs	Gls
Reading	Blairhall Colliery	12.49	52-53	31	-	0

KIRMAN Harold
Hull, 3 December, 1930 (FB)

League Club	Source	Date Signed	Seasons Played	Apps	Subs	Gls
Hull C	Francis Askew YC	12.50				
Gillingham	Tr	07.52	53	8	-	0
Hull C	Tr	01.55	55	2	-	0

KIROVSKI Jovan
Escondido, USA, 18 March, 1976 USA 62 (F)

League Club	Source	Date Signed	Seasons Played	Apps	Subs	Gls
Manchester U	La Jolla Nomads (USA)	07.95				
Crystal Palace	Sporting Lisbon (Por)	08.01	01	25	11	5
Birmingham C	Tr	08.02	02-03	5	18	2

KIRSTEN Kenneth (Ken)
South Africa, 28 October, 1922 (FB)

League Club	Source	Date Signed	Seasons Played	Apps	Subs	Gls
Charlton Ath	Park Villa	03.48				
Aldershot	Tr	08.51	51	5	-	0

KIRTLEY John Harold (Harry)
Washington, 23 May, 1930 (IF)

League Club	Source	Date Signed	Seasons Played	Apps	Subs	Gls
Sunderland	Fatfield Jnrs	05.48	48-54	95	-	18
Cardiff C	Tr	05.55	55	38	-	4
Gateshead	Tr	03.57	56-59	95	-	16

KIRTON John (Jock)
Aberdeen, 4 March, 1916 Died 1996 SWar-1 (WH)

League Club	Source	Date Signed	Seasons Played	Apps	Subs	Gls
Stoke C	Banks o' Dee	11.35	36-52	219	-	2
Bradford C	Tr	07.53	53	8	-	0

KISBY Christopher (Chris) Nigel
Horsforth, 7 November, 1952 (FB)

League Club	Source	Date Signed	Seasons Played	Apps	Subs	Gls
Scunthorpe U	App	10.70	70-72	30	9	2
Workington	Ashby Institute	08.73	73-76	162	2	2
Southport	Tr	08.77	77	42	0	1

KISHISHEV Radostin Prodanov
Burgas, Bulgaria, 30 July, 1974 Bulgaria 57 (FB)

League Club	Source	Date Signed	Seasons Played	Apps	Subs	Gls
Charlton Ath	Liteks Lovech (Bul)	08.00	00-04	109	19	2

KITAMIRIKE Joel Derick
Kampala, Uganda, 5 April, 1984 EYth (CD)

League Club	Source	Date Signed	Seasons Played	Apps	Subs	Gls
Chelsea	YT	04.01				
Brentford	L	09.03	03	21	1	0
Mansfield T	Hornchurch	12.04	04	2	0	0

KITCHEN Benjamin (Ben)
Bolton, 19 August, 1986 (M)

League Club	Source	Date Signed	Seasons Played	Apps	Subs	Gls
Rochdale	Sch	•	04	0	1	0

KITCHEN David (Sam) Edward
Rinteln, Germany, 11 June, 1967 (CD)

League Club	Source	Date Signed	Seasons Played	Apps	Subs	Gls
Leyton Orient	Frickley Ath	08.92	92-93	35	8	1
Doncaster Rov	Tr	02.94	93-94	21	1	1

KITCHEN John (Jack)
Whitehaven, 28 February, 1925 Died 1992 (CD)

League Club	Source	Date Signed	Seasons Played	Apps	Subs	Gls
Barnsley	Kells Ath	10.44	46-51	53	-	0

KITCHEN Michael Peter
Mexborough, 16 February, 1952 (F)

League Club	Source	Date Signed	Seasons Played	Apps	Subs	Gls
Doncaster Rov	App	07.70	70-76	221	7	89
Orient	Tr	07.77	77-78	64	1	28
Fulham	Tr	02.79	78-79	21	3	6
Cardiff C	Tr	08.80	80-81	64	3	21
Orient	Happy Valley (HK)	12.82	82-83	46	3	21
Chester C	Dagenham	03.85	84	3	2	1

League Club	Source	Date Signed	Seasons Played	Career Record Apps	Subs	Gls
KITCHENER Barry Raymond						
Dagenham, 11 December, 1947						(CD)
Millwall	App	08.65	66-81	518	5	25
KITCHENER Raymond (Ray) Alan						
Baldock, 31 October, 1930						(W)
Chelsea	Hitchin T	07.54	55	1	-	0
Norwich C	Tr	09.56	56	18	-	0
KITCHENER William (Bill) Harry						
Arlesey, 3 November, 1946						(FB)
West Ham U	App	11.63	66-67	11	0	0
Torquay U	L	09.66	66	25	0	3
Torquay U	Tr	12.67	67-70	142	0	5
Bournemouth	Tr	07.71	71	36	0	2
KITCHING Phillip (Phil) John						
Lewisham, 30 September, 1967						(M)
York C	Bradford C (N/C)	08.87	87	7	6	0
KITE Philip (Phil) David						
Bristol, 26 October, 1962 ESch/EYth						(G)
Bristol Rov	App	10.80	80-83	96	0	0
Southampton	Tr	08.84	84-85	4	0	0
Middlesbrough	L	03.86	85	2	0	0
Gillingham	Tr	02.87	86-88	70	0	0
Bournemouth	Tr	08.89	89	7	0	0
Sheffield U	Tr	08.90	90-91	11	0	0
Mansfield T	L	11.91	91	11	0	0
Plymouth Arg	L	09.92	92	2	0	0
Rotherham U	L	10.92	92	1	0	0
Crewe Alex	L	11.92	92	5	0	0
Stockport Co	L	03.93	92	5	0	0
Cardiff C	Tr	07.93	93	17	1	0
Bristol C	Tr	08.94	94-95	5	1	0
KITSON David (Dave) Kitson						
Hitchin, 21 January, 1980						(F)
Cambridge U	Arlesey T	03.01	00-03	97	5	40
Reading	Tr	12.03	03-04	47	7	24
KITSON Paul						
Murton, 9 January, 1971 Eu21-7						(F)
Leicester C	YT	12.88	89-91	39	11	6
Derby Co	Tr	03.92	91-94	105	0	36
Newcastle U	Tr	09.94	94-96	26	10	10
West Ham U	Tr	02.97	96-01	46	17	18
Charlton Ath	L	03.00	99	2	4	1
Crystal Palace	L	09.00	00	4	0	0
Brighton & Hove A	Tr	08.02	02	7	3	2
Rushden & Diamonds	Tr	09.03	03	18	10	5
KIWOMYA Andrew (Andy) Derek						
Huddersfield, 1 October, 1967 EYth						(W)
Barnsley	App	07.85	85	1	0	0
Sheffield Wed	Tr	10.86				
Rotherham U	Dundee	10.93	93	4	3	0
Scunthorpe U	Halifax T	03.95	94	9	0	3
Bradford C	Tr	07.95	95-96	27	16	3
Luton T	L	03.97	96	5	0	1
Burnley	L	09.97	97	1	2	0
Notts Co	Tr	12.97	97	0	2	0
KIWOMYA Christopher (Chris) Maurends						
Huddersfield, 2 December, 1969						(F)
Ipswich T	App	03.87	88-94	197	28	51
Arsenal	Tr	01.95	94	5	9	3
Queens Park Rgrs	Selangor (Mal)	08.98	98-00	74	12	25
KJELDBJERG Jakob						
Fredrikstad, Norway, 21 October, 1969 Denmark int						(CD)
Chelsea	Silkeborg (Nor)	08.93	93-94	52	0	2
[KLEBERSON] PEREIRA KLEBERSON Jose						
Urai, Brazil, 19 June, 1979 Brazil 27						(M)
Manchester U	Atlet Paranaense (Br)	08.03	03-04	16	4	2
KLETZENBAUER Carl **Frank**						
Coventry, 21 July, 1936 Died 1996						(FB)
Coventry C	Municipal Sports	03.56	56-63	122	-	3
Walsall	Tr	03.64	63-64	12	-	0
KLINSMANN Jurgen						
Goppingen, Germany, 30 July, 1964 Germany int						(F)
Tottenham H	AS Monaco (Fr)	08.94	94	41	0	20
Tottenham H	Sampdoria (It)	12.97	97	15	0	9
KLONER Hymie						
Johannesburg, South Africa, 23 May, 1929						(WH)
Birmingham C	Marist Bros (SA)	11.50	50	1	-	0

League Club	Source	Date Signed	Seasons Played	Career Record Apps	Subs	Gls
KLUG Bryan Paul						
Coventry, 8 October, 1960 EYth						(M)
Ipswich T	App	11.77				
Wimbledon	L	03.80	79	10	1	0
Chesterfield	Tr	08.83	83	27	7	2
Peterborough U	Tr	08.84	84	39	0	2
KLUIVERT Patrick Stephan						
Amsterdam, Holland, 1 July, 1976 Holland 79						(F)
Newcastle U	Barcelona (Sp)	07.04	04	15	10	6
KNAPP Anthony (Tony)						
Newstead, 13 October, 1936 FLge-1						(CD)
Leicester C	Jnrs	12.53	55-60	86	-	0
Southampton	Tr	08.61	61-66	233	0	2
Coventry C	Tr	08.67	67	11	0	0
Tranmere Rov	LA Wolves (USA)	10.69	69-70	36	0	1
KNIGHT Alan Edward						
Balham, 3 June, 1961 EYth/Eu21-2						(G)
Portsmouth	App	03.79	77-99	683	0	0
KNIGHT Anthony (Tony)						
Romford, 6 March, 1959						(G)
Luton T	App	05.76	76-77	6	0	0
KNIGHT Arnold William						
Guisborough, 30 May, 1919 Died 2003						(IF)
Leeds U	Tottenham H (Am)	10.37				
Plymouth Arg	Tr	07.47	47	7	-	0
Bradford C	Tr	02.48	47-48	7	-	0
KNIGHT Brian James						
Dundee, 28 March, 1949						(M)
Huddersfield T	Dundee	07.69				
Northampton T	Tr	10.69	69	9	3	0
KNIGHT Brian Thomas Arthur						
High Wycombe, 14 November, 1946						(W)
Reading	App	11.64	64-65	4	0	1
KNIGHT Craig						
Wrexham, 24 October, 1973						(CD)
Wrexham	YT	07.92	91	1	0	0
KNIGHT Frank						
Hucknall, 26 October, 1921 Died 1993						(WH)
Nottingham F		05.43	46-49	48	-	1
KNIGHT George Rollinson						
Bolton, 12 May, 1921						(IF)
Burnley	Holdens Temperance	05.38	38-46	9	-	2
KNIGHT Graham John						
Rochester, 5 January, 1952						(FB)
Gillingham	App	01.70	70-78	229	16	10
KNIGHT Ian John						
Hartlepool, 26 October, 1966 Eu21-2						(CD)
Barnsley	App	10.84				
Sheffield Wed	Tr	08.85	85-88	21	0	0
Scunthorpe U	L	08.89	89	2	0	0
Grimsby T	Tr	01.90	89-91	16	5	2
Carlisle U	Tr	08.92	92	1	0	0
KNIGHT Jason George						
Melbourne, Australia, 16 September, 1974						(M)
Doncaster Rov	Hinckley Ath	08.95	95	1	3	0
KNIGHT Jeffrey (Jeff) William						
Sudbury, 10 December, 1926 Died 2002						(IF)
Derby Co		05.46				
Walsall	Tr	08.52	52	4	-	0
KNIGHT John (Jackie)						
Bolton, 12 September, 1922 Died 1996						(IF)
Burnley	Jnrs	08.45	46-48	26	-	5
Preston NE	Tr	12.48	48-49	39	-	7
Chesterfield	Tr	07.51	51	35	-	6
Exeter C	Tr	08.52	52-53	56	-	6
KNIGHT Keith						
Cheltenham, 16 February, 1969 ESch						(W)
Reading	Cheltenham T	09.88	88-90	39	4	8
KNIGHT Leon Leroy						
Hackney, 16 September, 1982 EYth/Eu20						(F)
Chelsea	YT	09.99				
Queens Park Rgrs	L	03.01	00	10	1	0
Huddersfield T	L	10.01	01	31	0	16
Sheffield Wed	L	07.02	02	14	10	3
Brighton & Hove A	Tr	07.03	03-04	76	7	29

League Club	Source	Date Signed	Seasons Played	Career Record Apps	Subs	Gls
KNIGHT Lyndon Alan						
Lydbrook, 3 February, 1961						(G)
Hereford U	App	02.79	78	2	0	0
KNIGHT Peter Richard						
Brighton, 12 November, 1939						(W)
Brighton & Hove A	Lewes	01.64	63-65	9	1	1
KNIGHT Peter Robert						
Ilford, 26 December, 1937						(W)
Southend U		06.58				
Nottingham F	Tr	08.59	59	4	-	0
Oxford U	Tr	07.60	62-64	94	-	12
Reading	Tr	11.64	64-65	26	0	3
KNIGHT Richard						
Burton-on-Trent, 31 August, 1974						(FB)
Walsall	YT	03.92	92-93	27	2	1
KNIGHT Richard						
Burton-on-Trent, 3 August, 1979 EYth						(G)
Derby Co	Burton A	06.97				
Carlisle U	L	03.99	98	6	0	0
Hull C	L	10.99	99	1	0	0
Macclesfield T	L	12.99	99	3	0	0
Oxford U	L	01.00	99	12	1	0
Oxford U	Tr	06.00	00-01	36	0	0
Colchester U	L	03.02	01	1	0	0
KNIGHT Terrie George						
Camden, 1 February, 1932						(G)
Aldershot (Am)	Alton T	10.58	58	4	-	0
KNIGHT Zatyiah (Zat)						
Solihull, 2 May, 1980 Eu21-4/E-2						(CD)
Fulham	Rushall Olympic	02.99	01-04	85	8	1
Peterborough U	L	02.00	99	8	0	0
KNIGHTON Kenneth (Ken)						
Darton, 20 February, 1944						(M)
Wolverhampton W	App	02.61	64-66	13	3	0
Oldham Ath	Tr	11.66	66-67	45	0	4
Preston NE	Tr	11.67	67-68	62	0	4
Blackburn Rov	Tr	06.69	69-70	70	0	11
Hull C	Tr	03.71	70-72	79	1	9
Sheffield Wed	Tr	08.73	73-75	71	5	2
KNIGHTS Anthony (Tony) Frank						
Grimsby, 13 March, 1940 Died 2001						(WH)
Grimsby T	Jnrs	06.58	59-63	75	-	1
Luton T	Tr	08.64	64	2	-	0
Aldershot	Tr	07.65	65	20	0	0
KNIGHTS Darryl James						
Ipswich, 1 May, 1988						(F)
Ipswich T	Sch	05.05	04	0	1	0
KNILL Alan Richard						
Slough, 8 October, 1964 WYth/W-1						(CD)
Southampton	App	10.82				
Halifax T	Tr	07.84	84-86	118	0	6
Swansea C	Tr	08.87	87-88	89	0	3
Bury	Tr	08.89	89-93	141	3	9
Cardiff C	L	09.93	93	4	0	0
Scunthorpe U	Tr	11.93	93-96	131	0	8
Rotherham U	Tr	07.97	97-98	73	1	6
KNOTT Gareth Raymond						
Blackwood, Monmouthshire, 19 January, 1976 WYth/Wu21-1						(M)
Tottenham H	YT	07.94				
Gillingham	L	02.95	94	5	0	0
KNOTT Herbert (Bert)						
Goole, 5 December, 1914 Died 1986						(IF)
Brentford	Arsenal (Am)	09.36				
Walsall	Brierley Hill Alliance	08.37	37	9	-	2
Hull C	Brierley Hill Alliance	10.40				
Hull C		10.46	46	6	-	1
KNOTT William (Billy) Francis						
Leeds, 16 March, 1934 Died 1996 EYth						(IF)
Leeds U	Jnrs	05.51				
Walsall	Tr	02.55	54	1	-	0
KNOWLES James Barry						
Wigan, 25 April, 1959						(FB)
Wigan Ath	Bangor C	10.84	84-87	124	3	3
KNOWLES Cameron						
Ripon, 19 September, 1969						(M)
Chesterfield		08.93	93	1	0	0
KNOWLES Christopher (Chris) James						
Stone, 4 February, 1978						(G)
Chester C	Peterborough U (YT)	08.96	96	2	0	0
KNOWLES Cyril Barry						
Fitzwilliam, 13 September, 1944 Died 1991 Eu23-6/FLge-1/E-4						(FB)
Middlesbrough	Monckton CW	10.62	62-63	37	-	0
Tottenham H	Tr	05.64	64-75	402	1	15
KNOWLES Darren Thomas						
Sheffield, 8 October, 1970						(FB)
Sheffield U	YT	07.89				
Stockport Co	Tr	09.89	89-92	51	12	0
Scarborough	Tr	08.93	93-96	139	5	2
Hartlepool U	Tr	03.97	96-00	164	4	2
KNOWLES John David						
Halifax, 11 April, 1941						(G)
Halifax T	Jnrs	12.58	58-62	72	-	0
Bury	Tr	07.63	64	1	-	0
Bradford C	Tr	08.66	66	21	0	0
KNOWLES Harold (Harry) Frederick						
Hednesford, 6 September, 1932						(W)
Walsall	Excelsior	09.50	50	9	-	1
Cardiff C	Worcester C	02.59	58-59	8	-	0
KNOWLES James (Jimmy)						
Preston, 31 July, 1934						(G)
Preston NE	Jnrs	10.57	57	2	-	0
Barrow	Tr	08.58	58-59	11	-	0
KNOWLES Peter						
Fitzwilliam, 30 September, 1945 EYth/Eu23-4						(F)
Wolverhampton W	App	10.62	63-69	171	3	61
KNOWLES Raymond (Ray)						
Willesden, 30 September, 1952						(F)
Wimbledon	Southall	07.78	78-79	31	8	6
KNOX James (Jimmy) Hay						
Brechin, 26 November, 1935						(IF)
Coventry C	Raith Rov	05.57	57	2	-	0
KNOX Robert (Bobby) Preston						
Ulverston, 26 February, 1946						(M)
Barrow	Jnrs	07.65	64-71	94	14	19
KNOX Thomas (Tommy)						
Glasgow, 5 September, 1939						(W)
Chelsea	East Stirling	06.62	62-64	20	-	0
Newcastle U	Tr	02.65	64-66	24	1	1
Mansfield T	Tr	03.67	66-67	34	0	5
Northampton T	Tr	11.67	67-68	28	2	0
KNOX William (Willie) Jess						
Kilmarnock, 9 September, 1937 SSch						(WH)
Barrow	Third Lanark	07.59	59	1	-	0
KOEJOE Samuel (Sammy)						
Paramaribo, Surinam, 17 August, 1974						(F)
Queens Park Rgrs	Salzburg (Aut)	11.99	99-01	13	21	3
KOENEN Franciscus (Frans) Leonardus Albertus						
Waalwijk, Holland, 4 November, 1958 Hou21						(M)
Newcastle U	NEC Nimegen (Holl)	08.80	80	11	1	1
KOFFMAN Sidney John (Jack)						
Prestwich, 3 August, 1920 Died 1977						(W)
Manchester U	Northwich Vic	08.45				
Hull C	Tr	06.46	46	4	-	0
Oldham Ath	Congleton T	06.47	47	3	-	0
KOLINKO Alexanders (Alex)						
Latvia, 18 June, 1975 Latvia 38						(G)
Crystal Palace	Skonto Riga (Lat)	09.00	00-02	79	3	0
KOLKKA Joonas						
Lahti, Finland, 28 September, 1974 Finland 65						(M)
Crystal Palace	Bor Moencheng'ch (Ger)	07.04	04	20	3	3
KONCHESKY Paul Martyn						
Barking, 15 May, 1981 EYth/Eu21-15/E-1						(FB)
Charlton Ath	YT	05.98	97-04	91	58	5
Tottenham H	L	09.03	03	10	2	0
KONJIC Muhamed (Mo)						
Brijesnica Velika, Bosnia, 14 May, 1970 Bosnia 38						(CD)
Coventry C	AS Monaco (Fr)	02.99	98-03	130	8	4
Derby Co	Tr	05.04	04	13	3	0

League Club	Source	Date Signed	Seasons Played	Career Record Apps	Subs	Gls
KONSTANTINIDIS Kostas						
Greece, 31 August, 1972 Greece 34						(CD)
Bolton W (L)	Hertha Berlin (Ger)	03.02	01	3	0	0
KONSTANTOPOULOS Dimitrios (Dimi)						
Kalamata, Greece, 29 November, 1978 Gru21						(G)
Hartlepool U	Dep Farense (Por)	01.04	04	25	0	0
KONTE Amadou						
Mali, 23 January, 1981 MaliYth						(F)
Cambridge U	Paterno Calcio (It)	10.04	04	6	3	3
KOO-BOOTHE Nathan Djebril						
Westminster, 18 July, 1985						(CD)
Watford	Hayes	02.03				
MK Dons	Tr	07.04	04	1	0	0
KOOGI Anders Bo						
Roskilde, Denmark, 8 September, 1979 DeYth						(M)
Peterborough U	YT	07.97	98-99	0	2	0
KOORDES Rogier						
Haarlem, Holland, 13 June, 1972						(M)
Port Vale	Telstar (Holl)	02.97	96-98	29	9	0
KOPEL Frank						
Falkirk, 28 March, 1949 SSch						(FB)
Manchester U	Jnrs	04.66	67-68	8	2	0
Blackburn Rov	Tr	03.69	68-71	23	2	0
KOPEL Scott Andrew						
Blackburn, 25 February, 1970						(M)
Chesterfield	Dundee U	05.93	92	1	0	0
KORSTEN Willem						
Baxtel, Holland, 21 January, 1975 Hou21						(M)
Leeds U (L)	Vitesse Arnhem (Holl)	01.99	98	4	3	2
Tottenham H	Vitesse Arnhem (Holl)	07.99	99-00	12	11	3
KOSKELA Toni						
Finland, 16 February, 1983 FiYth/Fiu21-5						(M)
Cardiff C	Koo Tee Pee (Fin)	01.05	04	0	2	0
KOSMINA Alexander **John**						
Adelaide, Australia, 17 August, 1956 Australia int						(F)
Arsenal	Adelaide CF (Aus)	03.78	78	0	1	0
KOTTILA Mika						
Helsinki, Finland, 22 September, 1974						(F)
Hereford U (L)	Rovaniemi (Fin)	11.96	96	11	2	1
KOUMANTARAKIS George						
Athens, Greece, 27 March, 1974 Sa-12						(F)
Preston NE	Basle (Swi)	01.03	02-03	11	6	4
KOUMAS Jason						
Wrexham, 25 September, 1979 W-14						(M)
Tranmere Rov	YT	11.97	98-02	96	31	25
West Bromwich A	Tr	08.02	02-04	69	15	14
KOVACEVIC Darko						
Kovin, Yugoslavia, 18 November, 1973 Yugoslavia int						(F)
Sheffield Wed	Red Star Belgrade (Yug)	12.95	95	8	8	4
KOWALSKI Andrew (Andy) Michael						
Warsop, 26 February, 1953						(M)
Chesterfield	Worksop T	02.73	72-82	354	11	30
Doncaster Rov	Tr	07.83	83-84	45	7	1
Peterborough U	Tr	08.85	85	35	0	3
Chesterfield	Burton A	08.86	86	19	9	1
KOWENICKI Ryszard Stefan						
Lodz, Poland, 22 December, 1948						(M)
Oldham Ath	Widzew Lodz (Pol)	12.79	79-80	40	2	5
KOZLUK Robert (Robbie)						
Sutton-in-Ashfield, 5 August, 1977 Eu21-2						(FB)
Derby Co	YT	02.96	97-98	9	7	0
Sheffield U	Tr	03.99	98-04	155	12	2
Huddersfield T	L	09.00	00	14	0	0
Preston NE	L	01.05	04	0	1	0
KOZMA Istvan						
Paszto, Hungary, 3 December, 1964 Hungary int						(M)
Liverpool	Dunfermline Ath	02.92	91-92	3	3	0
KRAAY Hans						
Utrecht, Holland, 22 December, 1959						(CD)
Brighton & Hove A	NAC Breda (Holl)	02.84	83-84	19	4	3
KRISTENSEN Bjorn						
Malling, Denmark, 10 October, 1963 Denmark int						(M)
Newcastle U	Aarhus GF (Den)	03.89	88-91	69	11	4
Bristol C	L	11.92	92	4	0	0
Portsmouth	Tr	03.93	92-94	56	15	1
KRISTINSSON Birkir						
Vestmannaeyjar, Iceland, 15 March, 1964 Iceland 70						(G)
Stoke C	IBV (Ice)	11.00	00	18	0	0
KRIZAN Ales						
Maribor, Slovenia, 25 July, 1971 Slovenia 25						(CD)
Barnsley	Branik Maribor (Sl)	07.97	97-98	13	0	0
KROMHEER Elroy Patrick						
Amsterdam, Holland, 15 January, 1970						(CD)
Reading	FC Zwolle (Holl)	08.98	98	11	0	0
KRUSE Patrick (Pat) Karl						
Arlesey, 30 November, 1953						(CD)
Leicester C	App	02.72	73	2	0	0
Mansfield T	L	09.74	74	6	0	1
Torquay U	Tr	03.75	74-76	79	0	4
Brentford	Tr	03.77	76-81	186	0	12
Northampton T	L	02.82	81	18	0	0
KRUSZYNSKI Zbigniew (Detsi)						
Divschav, Germany, 14 October, 1961						(M)
Wimbledon	FC08 Homburg (Ger)	12.88	88-91	65	6	4
Brentford	L	03.92	91	8	0	0
Brentford	Tr	08.92	92	5	1	0
Coventry C	Saarbrucken (Ger)	09.93	93	1	1	0
Peterborough U	Tr	12.93	93	2	1	0
KRZYWICKI Ryszard (Dick) Lech						
Penley, 2 February, 1947 Wu23-8/W-8						(W)
West Bromwich A	App	02.65	64-69	51	6	9
Huddersfield T	Tr	03.70	69-73	39	8	7
Scunthorpe U	L	02.73	72	2	0	0
Northampton T	L	11.73	73	8	0	3
Lincoln C	Tr	07.74	74-75	55	13	11
KUBICKI Dariusz						
Kozuchow, Poland, 6 June, 1963 Poland 47						(FB)
Aston Villa	Legia Warsaw (Pol)	08.91	91-93	24	1	0
Sunderland	Tr	03.94	93-96	135	1	0
Wolverhampton W	Tr	08.97	97	12	0	0
Tranmere Rov	L	03.98	97	12	0	0
Carlisle U	Tr	07.98	98	7	0	0
Darlington	Tr	10.98	98	2	1	0
KUBICKI Eryk						
Hadjuki, Poland, 18 August, 1925						(W)
York C (Am)	Polish Army	10.46	46	5	-	0
KUDUZOVIC Fahrudin						
Bosnia, 10 October, 1984						(M)
Notts Co	Derby Co (Sch)	09.04	04	0	3	0
KUHL Martin						
Frimley, 10 January, 1965						(M)
Birmingham C	App	01.83	82-86	103	8	5
Sheffield U	Tr	03.87	86-87	38	0	4
Watford	Tr	02.88	87	4	0	0
Portsmouth	Tr	09.88	88-92	146	11	27
Derby Co	Tr	09.92	92-94	68	0	1
Notts Co	L	09.94	94	2	0	0
Bristol C	Tr	12.94	94-96	85	9	7
KUIPERS Michel						
Amsterdam, Holland, 26 June, 1974						(G)
Bristol Rov	SDW Amsterdam (Holl)	01.99	98	1	0	0
Brighton & Hove A	Tr	07.00	00-04	133	1	0
Hull C	L	08.03	03	3	0	0
KULCSAR George						
Budapest, Hungary, 12 August, 1967 Australia 3						(M)
Bradford C	Royal Antwerp (Bel)	03.97	96-97	23	3	1
Queens Park Rgrs	Tr	12.97	97-00	42	14	1
KULKOV Vasili						
Moscow, Russia, 11 June, 1966 Russia int						(M)
Millwall (L)	FC Porto (Por)	01.96	95	6	0	0
KUQI Shefki						
Vuqitern, Albania, 10 November, 1976 Albania-8/Fi3-8						(F)
Stockport Co	FC Jokerit (Fin)	01.01	00-01	32	3	11
Sheffield Wed	Tr	01.02	01-03	58	6	19
Ipswich T	Tr	09.03	03-04	69	10	30

League Club	Source	Date Signed	Seasons Played	Career Record Apps	Subs	Gls

KURILA John
Glasgow, 10 April, 1941 (CD)

League Club	Source	Date Signed	Seasons Played	Apps	Subs	Gls
Northampton T	Glasgow Celtic	08.62	62	40	-	1
Bristol C	Tr	08.63	63	6	-	0
Northampton T	Tr	11.63	63-67	105	3	3
Southend U	Tr	07.68	68-69	87	1	1
Colchester U	Tr	05.70	70-71	53	0	4
Lincoln C	Tr	12.71	71	23	1	0

KURZ Frederick (Fred) John
Grimsby, 3 September, 1918 Died 1978 (CF)

League Club	Source	Date Signed	Seasons Played	Apps	Subs	Gls
Grimsby T	Grimsby YMCA	05.36	38	3	-	0
Crystal Palace	Tr	12.45	46-50	148	-	48

KUSZCZAK Tomasz
Krosno Odrzanskie, Poland, 20 March, 1982 Poland 2 (G)

League Club	Source	Date Signed	Seasons Played	Apps	Subs	Gls
West Bromwich A	Hertha Berlin (Ger)	08.04	04	2	1	0

KVARME Bjorn Tore
Trondheim, Norway, 17 June, 1972 Norway 1 (CD)

League Club	Source	Date Signed	Seasons Played	Apps	Subs	Gls
Liverpool	Rosenborg (Nor)	01.97	96-98	39	6	0

KWIATKOWSKI Richard (Dick)
Peterborough, 7 April, 1948 (M)

League Club	Source	Date Signed	Seasons Played	Apps	Subs	Gls
Peterborough U	Jnrs	07.67	67-71	49	11	0

KYD Michael Robert
Hackney, 21 May, 1977 (F)

League Club	Source	Date Signed	Seasons Played	Apps	Subs	Gls
Cambridge U	YT	05.95	94-99	88	36	23

KYDD David Richard
Penge, 22 December, 1945 (WH)

League Club	Source	Date Signed	Seasons Played	Apps	Subs	Gls
Brighton & Hove A	App	09.63	65	2	0	0

KYLE Kevin Alistair
Stranraer, 7 June, 1981 Su21-12/SB-3/S-9 (F)

League Club	Source	Date Signed	Seasons Played	Apps	Subs	Gls
Sunderland	Ayr Boswell	09.98	00-04	50	26	10
Huddersfield T	L	09.00	00	0	4	0
Darlington	L	11.00	00	5	0	1
Rochdale	L	01.01	00	3	3	0

KYLE Maurice
Darlington, 8 November, 1937 Died 1981 (CD)

League Club	Source	Date Signed	Seasons Played	Apps	Subs	Gls
Wolverhampton W	Jnrs	09.55				
Oxford U	Tr	02.59	62-69	275	0	2
Southend U	L	03.70	69	8	0	0

KYNMAN David John
Hull, 20 May, 1962 (M)

League Club	Source	Date Signed	Seasons Played	Apps	Subs	Gls
Hull C	App	05.80	80-81	11	0	0

KYRATZOGLOU Alexandros (Alex) Bassilios
Armitale, Australia, 27 August, 1974 (F)

League Club	Source	Date Signed	Seasons Played	Apps	Subs	Gls
Oldham Ath	IEK Athens (Gre)	10.97	97	0	1	0

KYZERIDIS Nicos
Salonika, Greece, 20 April, 1971 (M)

League Club	Source	Date Signed	Seasons Played	Apps	Subs	Gls
Portsmouth	Paniliakos (Gre)	07.98	98	2	2	0

League Club Source Date Signed Seasons Played Career Record Apps Subs Gls

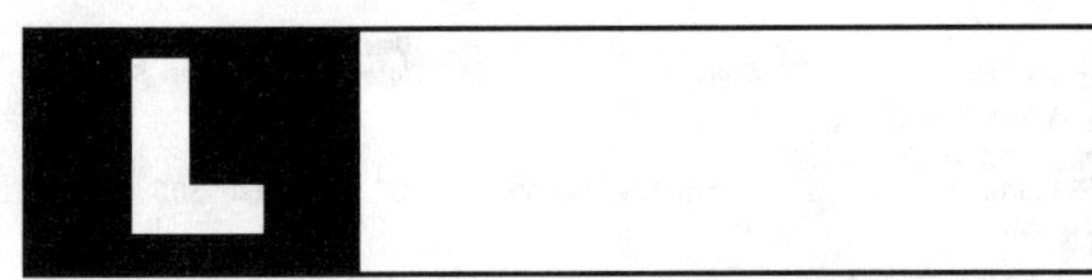

League Club	Source	Date Signed	Seasons Played	Apps	Subs	Gls
LABANT Vladimir						
Zilina, Slovakia, 8 June, 1974 Slovakia 24						(FB)
West Ham U	Sparta Prague (Cz)	01.02	01-02	7	6	0
LABARTHE Albert **Gianfranco** Tome						
Lima, Peru, 20 September, 1984 PeruYth						(M)
Huddersfield T	Sport Boys (Peru)	01.03	02	0	3	0
Derby Co	Tr	08.03	03	0	3	0
LABONE Brian Leslie						
Liverpool, 23 January, 1940 Eu23-7/FLge-5/E-26						(CD)
Everton	Jnrs	07.57	57-71	451	0	2
LACEY Anthony (Tony) John						
Leek, 18 March, 1944						(M)
Stoke C	Leek CSOB	10.65	67-68	2	2	0
Port Vale	Tr	02.70	69-74	194	7	9
Rochdale	Tr	07.75	75-76	83	0	0
LACEY Damien James						
Bridgend, 3 August, 1977						(M)
Swansea C	YT	07.96	96-02	75	29	2
LACEY Desmond (Des)						
Dublin, 3 August, 1925 Died 1974						(W)
Chester (Am)		07.46	46	1	-	0
LACEY William (Bill)						
Tynemouth, 17 November, 1931 Died 1988						(CF)
Middlesbrough		05.52				
Aldershot	Tr	02.53	52-58	210	-	59
Reading	Tr	07.59	59-62	90	-	40
LACK Harry						
Bolsover, 29 November, 1930						(W)
Leeds U		07.51				
Blackburn Rov	Tr	08.52				
Chesterfield	Tr	08.53	53	1	-	0
LACKENBY George						
Newcastle, 22 May, 1931 Died 2004						(FB)
Newcastle U	Jnrs	10.50	51-56	19	-	0
Exeter C	Tr	12.56	56	24	-	4
Carlisle U	Tr	07.57	57-58	46	-	0
Gateshead	Tr	07.59	59	43	-	2
Hartlepools U	Tr	08.60	60-62	86	-	1
LACY John						
Liverpool, 14 August, 1951						(CD)
Fulham	Kingstonian	06.71	72-77	164	4	7
Tottenham H	Tr	07.78	78-82	99	5	2
Crystal Palace	Tr	08.83	83	24	3	0
LADD Ian Martin						
Peterborough, 22 November, 1958						(CD)
Notts Co		09.77	77	1	0	0
LAHTINEN Aki Arimo						
Oulu, Finland, 31 October, 1958 Finland int						(CD)
Notts Co	Oulu Palloseura (Fin)	09.81	81-84	37	8	2
LAIDLAW John						
Aldershot, 5 July, 1936						(FB)
Colchester U	Easthouses Lily	06.57	59-60	41	-	1
LAIDLAW Joseph (Joe) Daniel						
Whickham, 12 July, 1950						(M)
Middlesbrough	App	08.67	67-71	104	5	20
Carlisle U	Tr	07.72	72-75	146	5	44
Doncaster Rov	Tr	06.76	76-78	127	1	27
Portsmouth	Tr	06.79	79-80	60	0	19
Hereford U	Tr	12.80	80-81	61	1	8
Mansfield T	Tr	07.82	82	4	0	0
LAIDLER John (Jackie) Ralph						
Windermere, 5 January, 1919						(W)
Barrow	Windermere	09.36	36-38	40	-	6
Carlisle U	Netherfield	06.46	46	27	-	3
LAIDMAN Frederick (Fred)						
Durham, 20 June, 1913 Died 1987						(IF)
Everton		12.36				
Bristol C	Tr	06.38	38	10	-	1
Darlington	Stockton	07.48	49	2	-	0

League Club	Source	Date Signed	Seasons Played	Apps	Subs	Gls
LAIGHT Ellis Stanley						
Birmingham, 30 June, 1976						(F)
Torquay U	YT	07.95	93-96	18	23	3
LAING David (Davie)						
Strathmiglo, 20 February, 1925 SLge-3						(WH)
Gillingham	Hibernian	08.57	57-58	82	-	5
LAING James **Frederick (Freddie)**						
Glasgow, 25 February, 1920						(IF)
Luton T	Ashfield Jnrs	06.38				
Middlesbrough	Shelbourne	07.47				
Bristol Rov	Tr	07.48	48	2	-	0
LAING Robert (Bobby) Smith						
Glasgow, 1 February, 1925 Died 1985						(W)
Birmingham C	Falkirk	03.46	47-49	19	-	2
Watford	Tr	06.50	50-51	60	-	8
LAIRD Alexander (Alex)						
Newmains, 2 June, 1926						(W)
Chelsea	Stirling A	11.51				
Notts Co	Tr	07.53	53	1	-	0
LAIRD Alexander (Alec) Watson						
Edinburgh, 23 October, 1928						(FB)
Barrow	Dunfermline Ath	11.57	57	22	-	0
LAIRD David Sands						
Rutherglen, 11 February, 1936						(IF)
Aldershot	St Mirren	07.57				
Northampton T	St Mirren	06.60	60	12	-	1
LAIRD David (Davie) Wilson						
Clackmannan, 9 May, 1926 Died 1999						(WH)
Aldershot	Alloa Ath	05.48	48-53	127	-	22
LAIRD Kamu						
Port of Spain, Trinidad, 23 December, 1975 Trinidad 23						(F)
Chester C	Dulwich Hamlet	12.99	99	2	1	1
LAISBY Jonathan (John)						
Ulverston, 27 March, 1957						(G)
Liverpool	App	04.75				
Workington	Barrow	03.77	76	2	0	0
LAITT David John						
Colchester, 1 November, 1946						(FB)
Colchester U	Colchester Casuals	08.65	65	0	1	0
LAKE Huw Gilwyn Taylor						
Swansea, 20 August, 1963 WSch						(M)
Swansea C	App	08.81	82-83	14	5	2
LAKE Leslie (Les) Eric						
Luton, 29 January, 1923 Died 1976						(FB)
Luton T	Holly Rgrs	09.41	46-50	59	-	0
LAKE Michael (Mike) Charles						
Denton, 16 November, 1966 ESemiPro						(M)
Sheffield U	Macclesfield T	10.89	89-92	19	16	4
Wrexham	Tr	11.92	92-94	56	2	6
LAKE Paul Andrew						
Denton, 28 October, 1968 Eu21-5/EB						(M)
Manchester C	YT	05.87	86-92	106	4	7
LAKIN Barry						
Dartford, 19 September, 1973						(M)
Leyton Orient	YT	07.92	92-95	41	13	2
LAKING George Edward						
Harthill, Yorkshire, 17 March, 1913 Died 1997						(FB)
Wolverhampton W	Dinnington	05.34	35-36	27	-	0
Middlesbrough	Tr	10.36	36-46	94	-	1
LAKIS Vassilios						
Thessaloniki, Greece, 10 September, 1976 Greece 34						(M)
Crystal Palace	AEK Athens (Gre)	10.04	04	6	12	0
LALLY Patrick (Pat) Anthony						
Paddington, 11 January, 1952						(M)
Millwall	App	01.70	69	1	0	0
York C	Tr	07.71	71-72	64	7	5
Swansea C	Tr	08.73	73-78	153	8	10
Aldershot	L	10.75	75	3	0	0
Doncaster Rov	Tr	09.78	78-81	118	4	0
LAMA Bernard Pascal						
St Symphorien, France, 7 April, 1963 France int						(G)
West Ham U (L)	Paris St Germain (Fr)	12.97	97	12	0	0

League Club	Source	Date Signed	Seasons Played	Apps	Subs	Gls
LAMB Alan						
Gateshead, 30 January, 1970						(F)
Nottingham F	YT	02.88				
Hereford U	L	03.89	88	9	1	2
Hartlepool U	Tr	09.89	89-90	4	10	0
LAMB Alan David						
Falkirk, 3 July, 1952 Su23-1						(M)
Preston NE	App	05.70	71-76	76	4	2
Port Vale	Tr	03.77	76-77	54	0	3
LAMB Harry Edward						
Bebington, 3 June, 1925 Died 1982						(IF)
Tranmere Rov	Everton (Am)	08.42	47-52	88	-	12
LAMB Thomas **Harold (Harry)**						
Kingswinford, 20 April, 1928						(FB)
Aston Villa	Wordsley	10.49				
Scunthorpe U	Tr	06.54	54-55	36	-	0
LAMB Paul David						
Plumstead, 12 September, 1974						(M)
Northampton T	YT	●	92	2	1	0
LAMB Stephen (Steve) Percy						
Leigh-on-Sea, 2 October, 1955						(M)
Southend U	App	10.73	74-75	6	1	0
LAMBDEN Victor (Vic) David						
Bristol, 24 October, 1925 Died 1996						(CF)
Bristol Rov	Oldland	10.45	46-54	269	-	117
LAMBERT Anton James						
Nottingham, 29 November, 1959						(M)
Scunthorpe U	Long Eaton U	07.80	80-81	35	4	3
LAMBERT Brian						
Sutton-in-Ashfield, 10 July, 1936						(FB)
Mansfield T	Sutton T	10.54	54-59	24	-	0
LAMBERT David						
Ruabon, 7 July, 1939						(FB)
Cardiff C		03.59				
Wrexham	Tr	07.63	63	5	-	0
LAMBERT Eric Victor						
Derby, 4 August, 1920 Died 1979						(CD)
Derby Co	Nottingham F (Am)	10.44				
Hartlepools U	Tr	06.46	46	16	-	0
LAMBERT John **Gilbert (Gil)**						
Preston, 16 March, 1937 Died 1986						(IF)
Preston NE	Jnrs	03.55	58-60	22	-	4
LAMBERT Christopher **James**						
Henley-on-Thames, 14 September, 1973						(W)
Reading	Jnrs	07.92	92-98	77	48	16
Walsall	L	10.98	98	4	2	0
Oxford U	Tr	08.99	99	8	5	2
LAMBERT Kenneth (Ken)						
Sheffield, 7 June, 1928 Died 2002						(IF)
Barnsley	Ecclesfield Colliery R	01.50	50-51	11	-	2
Gillingham	Tr	07.52	52	37	-	10
Swindon T	Tr	07.53	53-54	30	-	5
Bradford C	Tr	11.54	54	19	-	4
LAMBERT Martin Craig						
Southampton, 24 September, 1965 ESch/EYth						(F)
Brighton & Hove A	App	08.83	83	2	1	0
Torquay U	Tr	07.85	85	4	2	2
Brighton & Hove A	Sedan (Fr)	07.89	89	0	1	0
LAMBERT Matthew Roy						
Morecambe, 28 September, 1971						(FB)
Preston NE	YT	07.90	90-91	11	5	2
LAMBERT Michael (Mick) Arnold						
Balsham, 20 May, 1950						(W)
Ipswich T	Newmarket	11.67	68-78	180	30	39
Peterborough U	Tr	07.79	79-80	15	6	2
LAMBERT Raymond (Ray)						
Bagillt, 18 July, 1922 WSch/WWar-4/W-5						(FB)
Liverpool	Jnrs	07.39	46-55	308	-	2
LAMBERT Rickie Lee						
Liverpool, 16 February, 1982						(M)
Blackpool	YT	07.00	99	0	3	0
Macclesfield T	Tr	03.01	00-01	36	8	8
Stockport Co	Tr	04.03	02-04	88	10	18
Rochdale	Tr	02.05	04	15	0	6

League Club	Source	Date Signed	Seasons Played	Apps	Subs	Gls
LAMBERT Roy						
Hoyland, 16 July, 1933						(WH)
Rotherham U	Thorncliffe Welfare	07.54	56-64	307	-	6
Barnsley	Tr	11.65	65	3	0	0
LAMBLE John						
Reading, 10 November, 1948						(W)
Reading	App	11.66	67	3	2	0
LAMBOURDE Bernard						
Pointe-a-Pitre, Guadeloupe, 11 May, 1971						(FB)
Chelsea	Bordeaux (Fr)	07.97	97-00	29	11	2
Portsmouth	L	09.00	00	6	0	0
LAMBOURNE Dennis James						
Swansea, 7 October, 1945						(CF)
Wrexham	Llanelli	07.64	64-65	15	0	4
LAMBTON George **Colin**						
Newcastle, 21 February, 1942						(WH)
Newcastle U	Chester Moor	02.60				
Doncaster Rov	Tr	07.63	63	6	-	0
LAMBTON William (Bill) Ernest						
Nottingham, 2 December, 1914 Died 1976						(G)
Nottingham F	Basford North End	05.35				
Exeter C		04.46				
Doncaster Rov	Tr	10.46	46	3	-	0
LAMBU Goma						
Ghana, 10 November, 1984 EYth						(F)
Millwall	YT	12.01				
Mansfield T	Redbridge	01.05	04	1	0	0
LAMEY Nathan James						
Leeds, 14 October, 1980						(F)
Wolverhampton W	YT	10.97				
Cambridge U	Tr	08.99	99-00	2	4	0
LAMIE Robert (Bob)						
Newarthill, 28 December, 1928 Died 1981						(W)
Cardiff C	Stonehouse Violet	10.49	49-50	6	-	1
Swansea T	Tr	03.51	51	2	-	0
LAMONT David						
Glasgow, 2 April, 1949						(M)
Colchester U	App	04.67	67	0	1	0
LAMONT William (Bill) Turnbull						
Glasgow, 25 December, 1926 Died 1996						(FB)
New Brighton	Kilmarnock	07.50	50	27	-	0
Tranmere Rov	Tr	09.51	51-55	143	-	3
LAMPARD Frank James						
Romford, 20 June, 1978 EYth/Eu21-19/EB-1/E-32						(M)
West Ham U	YT	07.95	95-00	132	16	23
Swansea C	L	10.95	95	8	1	1
Chelsea	Tr	07.01	01-04	147	4	34
LAMPARD Frank Richard George						
East Ham, 20 September, 1948 EYth/Eu23-4/E-2						(FB)
West Ham U	App	09.65	67-84	546	5	18
Southend U	Tr	08.85	85	33	0	1
LAMPE Derek Stanley						
Edmonton, 20 May, 1937 EYth						(CD)
Fulham	Jnrs	05.54	56-62	88	-	0
LAMPKIN Kevin						
Liverpool, 20 December, 1972						(M)
Liverpool	YT	05.91				
Huddersfield T	Tr	07.92	92	13	0	0
Mansfield T	Tr	02.94	93-95	35	7	3
LAMPKIN Stephen (Steve) Charles Arthur						
Silsden, 15 October, 1964						(M)
Bradford C		03.83	82-83	5	2	1
LAMPTEY Nii Odartey						
Accra, Ghana, 10 December, 1974 Ghana int						(F)
Aston Villa	PSV Eindhoven (Holl)	08.94	94	1	5	0
Coventry C	Anderlecht (Bel)	08.95	95	3	3	0
LANCASHIRE Carl Peter						
Blackpool, 17 January, 1969						(M)
Blackpool	App	06.87	87	2	5	0
LANCASHIRE Graham						
Blackpool, 19 October, 1972						(F)
Burnley	YT	07.91	90-94	11	20	8
Halifax T	L	11.92	92	2	0	0

League Club	Source	Date Signed	Seasons Played	Apps	Subs	Gls
Chester C	L	01.94	93	10	1	7
Preston NE	Tr	12.94	94-95	11	12	2
Wigan Ath	L	01.96	95	4	0	3
Wigan Ath	Tr	03.96	95-97	16	10	9
Rochdale	Tr	10.97	97-00	54	29	23

LANCASTER Brian
Bradford, 8 May, 1939 (CD)

League Club	Source	Date Signed	Seasons Played	Apps	Subs	Gls
Torquay U		07.60	61	18	-	0

LANCASTER David (Dave)
Preston, 8 September, 1961 (F)

League Club	Source	Date Signed	Seasons Played	Apps	Subs	Gls
Blackpool	Colne Dynamoes	08.90	90	7	1	1
Chesterfield	L	02.91	90	12	0	4
Chesterfield	Tr	08.91	91-92	66	3	16
Rochdale	Tr	07.93	93	37	3	14
Bury	Halifax T	03.95	94-95	4	6	1
Rochdale	Tr	02.96	95-96	14	6	2

LANCASTER Desmond (Des) Charles
Burnley, 16 July, 1937 Died 2000 (W)

League Club	Source	Date Signed	Seasons Played	Apps	Subs	Gls
Burnley	Jnrs	08.54	56	1	-	0
Darlington	Tr	03.58	57-58	31	-	18
Tranmere Rov	Tr	06.59	59	1	-	0

LANCASTER Joseph (Joe) Gerard
Stockport, 28 April, 1926 (G)

League Club	Source	Date Signed	Seasons Played	Apps	Subs	Gls
Manchester U	Heaton Mersey OB	02.50	49	2	-	0
Accrington St	Tr	11.50	50	1	-	0

LANCASTER Martyn Neil
Wigan, 10 November, 1980 (CD)

League Club	Source	Date Signed	Seasons Played	Apps	Subs	Gls
Chester C	YT	01.99	98-99	22	6	0

LANCASTER Raymond (Ray)
Rotherham, 17 August, 1941 (CD)

League Club	Source	Date Signed	Seasons Played	Apps	Subs	Gls
Rotherham U	Jnrs	11.58	60-64	64	-	2
Grimsby T	Tr	12.64	64-66	16	2	0
Lincoln C	Tr	01.67	66-67	24	0	0

LANCELOTTE Eric Charles
India, 26 February, 1917 (IF)

League Club	Source	Date Signed	Seasons Played	Apps	Subs	Gls
Charlton Ath	Romford	05.35	37-47	40	-	6
Brighton & Hove A	Tr	02.48	47-49	60	-	14

LANDON Richard John
Worthing, 22 March, 1970 (F)

League Club	Source	Date Signed	Seasons Played	Apps	Subs	Gls
Plymouth Arg	Bedworth U	01.94	93-94	21	9	12
Stockport Co	Tr	07.95	95-96	7	6	5
Rotherham U	L	03.97	96	7	1	0
Macclesfield T	Tr	07.97	97-98	16	16	9

LANDSBOROUGH Murray
Thornhill, 30 December, 1915 Died 1987 (FB)

League Club	Source	Date Signed	Seasons Played	Apps	Subs	Gls
Carlisle U	Kilmarnock	08.47	47	1	-	0

LANE Frank (Frankie)
Wallasey, 20 July, 1948 (G)

League Club	Source	Date Signed	Seasons Played	Apps	Subs	Gls
Tranmere Rov	Stanley Arms	08.68	69-71	76	0	0
Liverpool	Tr	09.71	72	1	0	0
Notts Co	Tr	07.75	75	2	0	0

LANE Henry (Harry)
Hednesford, 21 March, 1909 Died 1977 (IF)

League Club	Source	Date Signed	Seasons Played	Apps	Subs	Gls
Birmingham	Bloxwich Strollers	12.29	30	2	-	0
Southend U	Tr	05.33	33-37	155	-	50
Plymouth Arg	Tr	03.38	37-38	47	-	8
Southend U	Tr	05.46	46-48	65	-	14

LANE John (Jackie) George
Birmingham, 10 November, 1931 (CF)

League Club	Source	Date Signed	Seasons Played	Apps	Subs	Gls
Birmingham C	Boldmere St Michael's	09.49	52-55	46	-	14
Notts Co	Tr	07.56	56-58	57	-	19

LANE Kevin John
Willenhall, 11 May, 1957 (F)

League Club	Source	Date Signed	Seasons Played	Apps	Subs	Gls
Torquay U	Walsall (App)	08.75	75-76	17	13	5

LANE Martin John
Altrincham, 12 April, 1961 (FB)

League Club	Source	Date Signed	Seasons Played	Apps	Subs	Gls
Manchester U	Jnrs	05.79				
Chester	Tr	08.82	82-86	175	0	3
Coventry C	Tr	01.87	86-87	0	3	0
Wrexham	L	10.88	88	6	0	0
Chester C	Tr	01.89	88-90	97	2	0
Walsall	Tr	08.91	91	6	4	0

LANE Michael (Mick) Edward
Wellington, Somerset, 6 December, 1966 (F)

League Club	Source	Date Signed	Seasons Played	Apps	Subs	Gls
Exeter C	App	12.84	83	1	0	0

LANE Sean Brendon
Bristol, 16 January, 1964 ESch (M)

League Club	Source	Date Signed	Seasons Played	Apps	Subs	Gls
Hereford U	App	03.81	80-82	39	11	3
Derby Co	Tr	05.83	83	1	0	0

LANG Gavin
Larkhall, 21 March, 1926 Died 1989 (W)

League Club	Source	Date Signed	Seasons Played	Apps	Subs	Gls
Chester	Spalding U	08.56	56	3	-	0

LANG Gavin Thomas
Hereford, 10 November, 1951 (W)

League Club	Source	Date Signed	Seasons Played	Apps	Subs	Gls
Chester	Newcastle U (App)	11.69				
Crewe Alex	Tr	09.70	70	3	0	1

LANG Malcolm Christian
Barnsley, 14 January, 1941 (W)

League Club	Source	Date Signed	Seasons Played	Apps	Subs	Gls
York C	Bridlington T	08.63	63	12	-	2

LANG Thomas (Tommy)
Larkhall, 3 April, 1905 Died 1988 (W)

League Club	Source	Date Signed	Seasons Played	Apps	Subs	Gls
Newcastle U	Larkhall Thistle	10.26	27-34	215	-	53
Huddersfield T	Tr	12.34	34-35	24	-	5
Manchester U	Tr	12.35	35-36	12	-	1
Swansea T	Tr	04.37	37	33	-	1
Ipswich T	Queen of the South	10.46	46	5	-	1

LANGAN David Francis
Dublin, 15 February, 1957 IR-25 (FB)

League Club	Source	Date Signed	Seasons Played	Apps	Subs	Gls
Derby Co	App	02.75	76-79	143	0	1
Birmingham C	Tr	07.80	80-82	92	0	3
Oxford U	Tr	08.84	84-87	112	2	2
Leicester C	L	10.87	87	5	0	0
Bournemouth	Tr	12.87	87	19	1	0
Peterborough U	Tr	08.88	88	18	1	0

LANGAN Kevin
Jersey, 7 April, 1978 (FB)

League Club	Source	Date Signed	Seasons Played	Apps	Subs	Gls
Bristol C	YT	07.96	97-98	1	3	0

LANGE Anthony (Tony) Stephen
West Ham, 10 December, 1964 (G)

League Club	Source	Date Signed	Seasons Played	Apps	Subs	Gls
Charlton Ath	App	12.82	83-85	12	0	0
Aldershot	L	08.85	85	7	0	0
Aldershot	Tr	07.86	86-88	125	0	0
Wolverhampton W	Tr	07.89	89-90	8	0	0
Aldershot	L	11.90	90	2	0	0
Torquay U	L	09.91	91	1	0	0
West Bromwich A	Tr	08.92	92-94	45	3	0
Fulham	Tr	07.95	95-96	59	0	0

LANGFORD Craig Brian
Solihull, 12 March, 1975 (CD)

League Club	Source	Date Signed	Seasons Played	Apps	Subs	Gls
Hereford U	YT	07.93	92-93	4	1	0

LANGFORD John William
Kirkby-in-Ashfield, 4 August, 1937 (W)

League Club	Source	Date Signed	Seasons Played	Apps	Subs	Gls
Nottingham F	Leicester C (Am)	08.55	55	4	-	0
Notts Co	Tr	08.58	58	16	-	0

LANGFORD Timothy (Tim)
Kingswinford, 12 September, 1965 (F)

League Club	Source	Date Signed	Seasons Played	Apps	Subs	Gls
Wycombe W	Telford U	03.93	93-94	19	16	8

LANGLAND John (Johnny)
Easington, 9 November, 1929 (CF)

League Club	Source	Date Signed	Seasons Played	Apps	Subs	Gls
Sunderland		06.48				
Chesterfield	Consett	01.51	52-53	7	-	0
Hartlepools U	Blyth Spartans	07.58	58-59	38	-	11

LANGLEY Geoffrey (Geoff) Ralph
Gateshead, 31 March, 1962 (F)

League Club	Source	Date Signed	Seasons Played	Apps	Subs	Gls
Bolton W	App	03.80	81	3	3	0

LANGLEY Ernest **James (Jimmy)**
Kilburn, 7 February, 1929 FLge-1/EB/E-3 (FB)

League Club	Source	Date Signed	Seasons Played	Apps	Subs	Gls
Leeds U	Guildford C	06.52	52	9	-	3
Brighton & Hove A	Tr	07.53	53-56	166	-	14
Fulham	Tr	02.57	56-64	323	-	31
Queens Park Rgrs	Tr	07.65	65-66	86	1	9

LANGLEY Kevin James
St Helens, 24 May, 1964 (M)

League Club	Source	Date Signed	Seasons Played	Apps	Subs	Gls
Wigan Ath	App	05.82	81-85	156	4	6
Everton	Tr	07.86	86	16	0	2
Manchester C	Tr	03.87	86	9	0	0
Chester C	L	01.88	87	9	0	0
Birmingham C	Tr	03.88	87-89	74	2	2
Wigan Ath	Tr	09.90	90-93	151	6	6

LANGLEY Richard Barrington Michael
Harlesden, 27 December, 1979 EYth/Ja-17 (M)

League Club	Source	Date Signed	Seasons Played	Apps	Subs	Gls
Queens Park Rgrs	YT	12.96	98-03	123	10	18
Cardiff C	Tr	08.03	03-04	63	6	8

LANGLEY Richard John
Lambeth, 20 March, 1965 (FB)

League Club	Source	Date Signed	Seasons Played	Apps	Subs	Gls
Fulham	Corinthian Casuals	11.86	86-90	43	7	0

LANGLEY Thomas (Tommy) William
Lambeth, 8 February, 1958 ESch/EYth/Eu21-1 (F)

League Club	Source	Date Signed	Seasons Played	Apps	Subs	Gls
Chelsea	App	04.75	74-79	129	13	40
Queens Park Rgrs	Tr	08.80	80	24	1	8
Crystal Palace	Tr	03.81	80-82	54	5	9
Coventry C	AEK Athens (Gre)	03.84	83	2	0	0
Wolverhampton W	Tr	07.84	84	22	1	4
Aldershot	L	03.85	84	16	0	4
Aldershot	South China (HK)	08.86	86-87	80	1	21
Exeter C	Tr	07.88	88	14	7	2

LANGMAN Hedley **Neil**
Bere Alston, 21 February, 1932 (CF)

League Club	Source	Date Signed	Seasons Played	Apps	Subs	Gls
Plymouth Arg	Tavistock	09.53	53-57	96	-	49
Colchester U	Tr	11.57	57-60	128	-	50

LANGMAN Peter John Henry
Bere Alston, 1 April, 1928 (CD)

League Club	Source	Date Signed	Seasons Played	Apps	Subs	Gls
Plymouth Arg	Tavistock	06.51	54-57	90	-	0

LANGMEAD Kelvin Steven
Coventry, 23 March, 1985 (F)

League Club	Source	Date Signed	Seasons Played	Apps	Subs	Gls
Preston NE	Sch	02.04	04	0	1	0
Carlisle U	L	02.04	03	3	8	1
Kidderminster Hrs	L	09.04	04	9	1	1
Shrewsbury T	Tr	11.04	04	24	4	3

LANGRIDGE John
Newcastle, 14 November, 1957 (F)

League Club	Source	Date Signed	Seasons Played	Apps	Subs	Gls
Hartlepool U	Easington CW	10.82	82	5	1	0

LANGSTRETH Horace **Lawrence (Lol)**
Blackburn, 19 July, 1931 Died 1990 (WH)

League Club	Source	Date Signed	Seasons Played	Apps	Subs	Gls
Accrington St	Blackburn Rov (Am)	07.53	53	3	-	0
Torquay U	Netherfield	08.56	56	1	-	0

LANGTON Robert (Bobby)
Burscough, 8 September, 1918 Died 1996 EB/FLge-9/NIRL-1/E-11 (W)

League Club	Source	Date Signed	Seasons Played	Apps	Subs	Gls
Blackburn Rov	Burscough Victoria	09.38	38-47	107	-	24
Preston NE	Tr	08.48	48-49	55	-	14
Bolton W	Tr	11.49	49-52	118	-	16
Blackburn Rov	Tr	09.53	53-55	105	-	33

LANSDOWNE William (Billy)
Epping, 28 April, 1959 (F)

League Club	Source	Date Signed	Seasons Played	Apps	Subs	Gls
West Ham U	Jnrs	06.78	78-79	5	4	1
Charlton Ath	Tr	07.81	81-82	28	4	4
Gillingham	Tr	01.83	82	6	0	2

LANSDOWNE William (Bill) Thomas Michael
Shoreditch, 9 November, 1935 (WH)

League Club	Source	Date Signed	Seasons Played	Apps	Subs	Gls
West Ham U	Woodford T	02.56	55-62	57	-	5

LAPHAM Kyle Jonathan
Swindon, 5 January, 1986 (FB)

League Club	Source	Date Signed	Seasons Played	Apps	Subs	Gls
Swindon T	Sch	●	04	2	0	0

LAPOT Stanley (Stan)
Edinburgh, 20 January, 1944 (M)

League Club	Source	Date Signed	Seasons Played	Apps	Subs	Gls
Preston NE	Raith Rov	06.62	62-66	15	3	2

LAPPER Michael (Mike) Steven
California, USA, 28 August, 1970 USA int (CD)

League Club	Source	Date Signed	Seasons Played	Apps	Subs	Gls
Southend U	USSF (USA)	08.95	95-96	46	6	1

LARAMAN Peter Kenneth
Rochester, 24 October, 1940 EYth (IF)

League Club	Source	Date Signed	Seasons Played	Apps	Subs	Gls
Charlton Ath	Jnrs	02.58	58-59	2	-	1
Torquay U	Tr	07.61	61	9	-	5

LARGE Frank
Leeds, 26 January, 1940 Died 2003 (F)

League Club	Source	Date Signed	Seasons Played	Apps	Subs	Gls
Halifax T	BR (Halifax)	06.59	58-61	134	-	50
Queens Park Rgrs	Tr	06.62	62	18	-	5
Northampton T	Tr	03.63	62-63	47	-	30
Swindon T	Tr	03.64	63-64	17	-	4
Carlisle U	Tr	09.64	64-65	50	0	18
Oldham Ath	Tr	12.65	65-66	34	0	18
Northampton T	Tr	12.66	66-67	37	0	15
Leicester C	Tr	11.67	67	26	0	8
Fulham	Tr	06.68	68-69	20	4	3
Northampton T	Tr	08.69	69-72	133	2	42
Chesterfield	Tr	11.72	72-73	46	0	15

LARKIN Anthony (Tony) Gerard
Liverpool, 12 January, 1956 (CD)

League Club	Source	Date Signed	Seasons Played	Apps	Subs	Gls
Wrexham	Jnrs	07.75				
Shrewsbury T	Tr	07.78	78-80	54	1	0
Carlisle U	Tr	07.81	81-82	47	2	2
Hereford U	Tr	03.83	82-84	28	7	2

LARKIN Bernard (Bunny) Patrick
Birmingham, 11 January, 1936 (IF)

League Club	Source	Date Signed	Seasons Played	Apps	Subs	Gls
Birmingham C	Lea Hall YC	07.54	56-59	79	-	23
Norwich C	Tr	03.60	59-61	41	-	12
Doncaster Rov	Tr	09.61	61	25	-	12
Watford	Tr	06.62	62-64	49	-	3
Lincoln C	Tr	11.64	64-65	25	2	3

LARKIN Colin
Dundalk, 27 April, 1982 IRYth (F)

League Club	Source	Date Signed	Seasons Played	Apps	Subs	Gls
Wolverhampton W	YT	05.99	99-00	1	2	0
Kidderminster Hrs	L	09.01	01	31	2	6
Mansfield T	Tr	08.02	02-04	61	31	25

LARKIN Gordon Thomas
Hartlepool, 12 October, 1958 (W)

League Club	Source	Date Signed	Seasons Played	Apps	Subs	Gls
Hartlepool U	Billingham Synthonia	07.77	77-79	5	9	1

LARKIN James (Jim) Thomas
Ontario, Canada, 23 October, 1975 (G)

League Club	Source	Date Signed	Seasons Played	Apps	Subs	Gls
Cambridge U	(Canada)	01.98	97	1	0	0

LARMOUR Albert Andrew James
Belfast, 27 May, 1951 (CD)

League Club	Source	Date Signed	Seasons Played	Apps	Subs	Gls
Cardiff C	Linfield	07.72	72-78	152	2	0
Torquay U	Tr	06.79	79-81	46	4	4

LARMOUR David James
Belfast, 23 August, 1977 NISch/NIYth (F)

League Club	Source	Date Signed	Seasons Played	Apps	Subs	Gls
Doncaster Rov	Liverpool (YT)	08.96	96	3	17	0

LARNACH Ian James
Ferryhill, 10 July, 1951 (F)

League Club	Source	Date Signed	Seasons Played	Apps	Subs	Gls
Darlington	App	07.69	69	1	1	1

LARNACH Michael (Mike)
Lybster, 9 November, 1952 (F)

League Club	Source	Date Signed	Seasons Played	Apps	Subs	Gls
Newcastle U	Clydebank	12.77	77	12	1	0

LA RONDE Everald
East Ham, 24 January, 1963 (FB)

League Club	Source	Date Signed	Seasons Played	Apps	Subs	Gls
West Ham U	App	01.81	81	6	1	0
Bournemouth	Tr	09.83	83-84	24	0	0
Peterborough U	L	01.85	84	8	0	0

LARRIEU Romain
Mont-de-Marsan, France, 31 August, 1976 (G)

League Club	Source	Date Signed	Seasons Played	Apps	Subs	Gls
Plymouth Arg	ASOA Valence (Fr)	11.00	00-04	131	1	0

LARSEN Stig Olav
Bergen, Norway, 26 September, 1973 (F)

League Club	Source	Date Signed	Seasons Played	Apps	Subs	Gls
Hartlepool U	Fana IL (Nor)	12.97	97	0	4	0

LARUSSON Bjarnolfur (Bjarni)
Vestmannaeyjar, Iceland, 11 March, 1976 IcYth/Icu21-10 (M)

League Club	Source	Date Signed	Seasons Played	Apps	Subs	Gls
Walsall	Hibernian	09.98	98-99	45	14	3
Scunthorpe U	Tr	09.00	00	33	0	4

LARYEA Benjamin (Benny) Michael
Ghana, 20 March, 1962 (F)

League Club	Source	Date Signed	Seasons Played	Apps	Subs	Gls
Torquay U	Maidenhead U	03.84	83-84	10	2	3

LASKEY Russell George
Norwich, 17 March, 1937 (IF)

League Club	Source	Date Signed	Seasons Played	Apps	Subs	Gls
Norwich C	Gothic	01.56	56	4	-	2

LASLANDES Lilian
Pauillac, France, 4 September, 1971 France 7 (F)

League Club	Source	Date Signed	Seasons Played	Apps	Subs	Gls
Sunderland	Bordeaux (Fr)	07.01	01	5	7	0

LASLEY Keith William Robert
Glasgow, 21 September, 1979 (M)

League Club	Source	Date Signed	Seasons Played	Apps	Subs	Gls
Plymouth Arg	Motherwell	06.04	04	14	10	0

LATCHAM Leslie (Les) Arnold
Crook, 22 December, 1942 (W)

League Club	Source	Date Signed	Seasons Played	Apps	Subs	Gls
Burnley	Jnrs	01.60	64-70	149	4	10
Plymouth Arg	Tr	07.71	71-72	83	0	13
Bradford C	Tr	07.73	73	15	0	2

LATCHFORD David (Dave) Barry
Birmingham, 9 April, 1949 (G)

League Club	Source	Date Signed	Seasons Played	Apps	Subs	Gls
Birmingham C	App	07.66	68-77	206	0	0
Bury	Motherwell	03.79	78	2	0	0

LATCHFORD Peter William
Birmingham, 27 September, 1952 Eu23-2 (G)

League Club	Source	Date Signed	Seasons Played	Apps	Subs	Gls
West Bromwich A	App	10.69	72-74	81	0	0

LATCHFORD Robert (Bob) Dennis
Birmingham, 18 January, 1951 EYth/Eu23-6/FLge-1/E-12 (F)

League Club	Source	Date Signed	Seasons Played	Apps	Subs	Gls
Birmingham C	App	08.68	68-73	158	2	68
Everton	Tr	02.74	73-80	235	1	106
Swansea C	Brisbane Lions (Aus)	07.81	81-83	87	0	35
Coventry C	NAC Breda (Holl)	07.84	84	11	1	2
Lincoln C	Tr	08.85	85	14	1	2
Newport Co	Tr	01.86	85	20	0	5

LATHAM David Colin
Clayton, 17 October, 1943 (W)

League Club	Source	Date Signed	Seasons Played	Apps	Subs	Gls
Manchester U	App	10.61				
Southport	Tr	07.63	63	22	-	0

LATHAM Harold (Harry)
Sheffield, 9 January, 1921 Died 1983 (CD)

League Club	Source	Date Signed	Seasons Played	Apps	Subs	Gls
Sheffield U	Jnrs	10.38	46-52	190	-	1

LATHAM Leslie (Les)
Coventry, 31 December, 1917 Died 2001 ESch (CD)

League Club	Source	Date Signed	Seasons Played	Apps	Subs	Gls
Aston Villa		10.36				
Coventry C	Tr	10.46	46	1	-	0

LATHAN John George
Sunderland, 12 April, 1952 (M)

League Club	Source	Date Signed	Seasons Played	Apps	Subs	Gls
Sunderland	App	04.69	69-73	41	12	14
Mansfield T	Tr	02.74	73-75	72	2	14
Carlisle U	Tr	02.76	75-77	55	6	8
Barnsley	L	02.77	76	6	1	0
Portsmouth	Tr	03.78	77-79	56	2	4
Mansfield T	Tr	08.79	79	29	0	1

LATIMER Frank Jackson
Sunderland, 3 October, 1923 Died 1994 (WH)

League Club	Source	Date Signed	Seasons Played	Apps	Subs	Gls
Brentford	Snowdown CW	11.45	46-55	171	-	3

LATTE-YEDO Igor
Dabou, Ivory Coast, 14 December, 1978 (CD)

League Club	Source	Date Signed	Seasons Played	Apps	Subs	Gls
Cambridge U	Marseille Endoume (Fr)	08.04	04	5	6	0

LAUDRUP Brian
Vienna, Austria, 22 February, 1969 Denmark 82 (F)

League Club	Source	Date Signed	Seasons Played	Apps	Subs	Gls
Chelsea	Glasgow Rgrs	06.98	98	5	2	0

LAUGHTON Dennis
Dingwall, 22 January, 1948 (CD)

League Club	Source	Date Signed	Seasons Played	Apps	Subs	Gls
Newcastle U	Morton	10.73	73-74	7	0	0

LAUNDERS Brian Terence
Dublin, 8 June, 1976 IRYth/IRu21-9 (M)

League Club	Source	Date Signed	Seasons Played	Apps	Subs	Gls
Crystal Palace	Cherry Orchard	09.93	94-95	1	3	0
Crewe Alex	Tr	08.96	96	6	3	0
Derby Co	BV Veendam (Holl)	09.98	98	0	1	0
Colchester U	Tr	03.99	98-99	7	0	0
Crystal Palace	Tr	10.99	99	1	1	0
Sheffield U	Tr	11.99	99	0	1	0

LAUREL John Albert
Dartford, 11 June, 1935 EYth (CD)

League Club	Source	Date Signed	Seasons Played	Apps	Subs	Gls
Tottenham H	Jnrs	07.52				
Ipswich T	Tr	06.59	60-62	4	-	0

[LAUREN] BISANE-ETAME MAYER Laureano
Lodhji Kribi, Cameroon, 19 January, 1977 Cameroon 25 (FB)

League Club	Source	Date Signed	Seasons Played	Apps	Subs	Gls
Arsenal	Real Mallorca (Sp)	06.00	00-04	130	7	6

LAURENT Pierre
Tulle, France, 13 December, 1970 (F)

League Club	Source	Date Signed	Seasons Played	Apps	Subs	Gls
Leeds U	Bastia (Fr)	03.97	96	2	2	0

LAURSEN Jacob
Vejle, Denmark, 6 October, 1971 Denmark 25 (CD)

League Club	Source	Date Signed	Seasons Played	Apps	Subs	Gls
Derby Co	Silkeborg (Den)	07.96	96-99	135	2	3
Leicester C	FC Copenhagen (Den)	01.02	01	10	0	0

LAURSEN Martin
Silkeborg, Denmark, 26 July, 1977 DeYth/Deu21-14/De-41 (CD)

League Club	Source	Date Signed	Seasons Played	Apps	Subs	Gls
Aston Villa	AC Milan (It)	07.04	04	12	0	1

LAVERICK Michael (Micky) George
Castle Eden, 13 March, 1954 (M)

League Club	Source	Date Signed	Seasons Played	Apps	Subs	Gls
Mansfield T	Jnrs	01.72	72-75	73	16	13
Southend U	Tr	10.76	76-78	108	2	18
Huddersfield T	Tr	07.79	79-81	74	0	9
York C	Tr	01.82	81-82	38	3	6
Huddersfield T	L	01.83	82	2	0	0

LAVERICK Peter Henry
Cleethorpes, 29 January, 1939 (IF)

League Club	Source	Date Signed	Seasons Played	Apps	Subs	Gls
Grimsby T	Jnrs	03.56	57-60	4	-	0

LAVERICK Robert (Bobby)
Castle Eden, 11 June, 1938 EYth (W)

League Club	Source	Date Signed	Seasons Played	Apps	Subs	Gls
Chelsea	Jnrs	06.55	56-57	7	-	0
Everton	Tr	02.59	58-59	22	-	6
Brighton & Hove A	Tr	06.60	60-61	63	-	20
Coventry C	Tr	07.62	62	4	-	0

LAVERTY Patrick (Pat) James
Gorseinon, 24 May, 1934 (IF)

League Club	Source	Date Signed	Seasons Played	Apps	Subs	Gls
Sheffield U	Wellington T	05.56	56-59	7	-	0
Southend U	Tr	07.60	60	21	-	6

LAVERY James (Jim)
Lennoxtown, 13 December, 1948 (G)

League Club	Source	Date Signed	Seasons Played	Apps	Subs	Gls
Scunthorpe U		08.66	67	15	0	0
Scunthorpe U	Brigg T	08.74	74	11	0	0

LAVERY John
Belfast, 24 November, 1919 NISch/LoI-1 (W)

League Club	Source	Date Signed	Seasons Played	Apps	Subs	Gls
Bradford C	Dundalk	08.48	48	5	-	0
Halifax T	Tr	09.48	48	3	-	1

LAVILLE Florent
Valence, France, 7 August, 1973 (CD)

League Club	Source	Date Signed	Seasons Played	Apps	Subs	Gls
Bolton W	Lyon (Fr)	02.03	02-03	15	0	0
Coventry C	L	10.04	04	5	1	0

LAVIN Gerard
Corby, 5 February, 1974 Su21-7 (FB)

League Club	Source	Date Signed	Seasons Played	Apps	Subs	Gls
Watford	YT	05.92	91-95	121	5	3
Millwall	Tr	11.95	95-98	67	7	0
Bristol C	Tr	08.99	99-00	21	1	0
Wycombe W	L	01.01	00	2	0	0
Northampton T	Tr	05.01	01	2	0	0

LAW Brian John
Merthyr Tydfil, 1 January, 1970 WSch/WYth/Wu21-2/W-1 (CD)

League Club	Source	Date Signed	Seasons Played	Apps	Subs	Gls
Queens Park Rgrs	YT	08.87	87-90	19	1	0
Wolverhampton W	(Retired)	12.94	94-96	26	5	1
Millwall	Tr	07.97	97-98	45	0	4

LAW Cecil Richard
Harare, Zimbabwe, 10 March, 1930 (W)

League Club	Source	Date Signed	Seasons Played	Apps	Subs	Gls
Derby Co	Alexandra (Rhodesia)	08.51	52-53	33	-	2
Bury	Tr	05.54	54-55	44	-	5

LAW Denis
Aberdeen, 24 February, 1940 Su23-3/ItLge-2/FLge-2/S-55 (F)

League Club	Source	Date Signed	Seasons Played	Apps	Subs	Gls
Huddersfield T	Jnrs	02.57	56-59	81	-	16
Manchester C	Tr	03.60	59-60	44	-	21
Manchester U	Torino (It)	08.62	62-72	305	4	171
Manchester C	Tr	07.73	73	22	2	9

LAW Gareth Martin
Torquay, 20 August, 1982 (F)

League Club	Source	Date Signed	Seasons Played	Apps	Subs	Gls
Torquay U	YT	11.00	00-01	2	13	1

LAW Graeme
Kirkcaldy, 6 October, 1984 SYth (FB)

League Club	Source	Date Signed	Seasons Played	Apps	Subs	Gls
York C	Sch	•	03	2	2	0

LAW Marcus William
Coventry, 28 September, 1975 (G)

League Club	Source	Date Signed	Seasons Played	Apps	Subs	Gls
Bristol Rov	YT	07.94	94	2	0	0

LAW Nicholas (Nicky)
Greenwich, 8 September, 1961 ESch (CD)

League Club	Source	Date Signed	Seasons Played	Apps	Subs	Gls
Arsenal	App	07.79				
Barnsley	Tr	08.81	81-85	113	1	1
Blackpool	Tr	08.85	85-86	64	2	1
Plymouth Arg	Tr	03.87	86-87	37	1	5
Notts Co	Tr	06.88	88-89	44	3	4
Scarborough	L	11.89	89	12	0	0
Rotherham U	Tr	08.90	90-93	126	2	4
Chesterfield	Tr	10.93	93-96	108	3	11
Hereford U	Tr	10.96	96	14	0	0

LAWFORD Craig Brian
Dewsbury, 25 November, 1972 (FB)

League Club	Source	Date Signed	Seasons Played	Apps	Subs	Gls
Bradford C	YT	07.91	89-93	13	7	1
Hull C	Tr	08.94	94-95	45	17	3

LAWLER Christopher (Chris)
Liverpool, 20 October, 1943 ESch/EYth/Eu23-4/FLge-2/E-4 (FB)

League Club	Source	Date Signed	Seasons Played	Apps	Subs	Gls
Liverpool	Jnrs	10.60	62-74	406	0	41
Portsmouth	Tr	10.75	75-76	35	1	0
Stockport Co	Tr	08.77	77	33	3	3

LAWLER James (Jimmy) Henry
Dublin, 20 November, 1923 (WH)

League Club	Source	Date Signed	Seasons Played	Apps	Subs	Gls
Portsmouth	Glentoran	10.47				
Southend U	Tr	01.49	48-56	269	-	17

LAWLER Joseph (Robin) Frederick
Dublin, 28 August, 1925 Died 1998 IrLge-2/IR-8 (FB)

League Club	Source	Date Signed	Seasons Played	Apps	Subs	Gls
Fulham	Belfast Celtic	03.49	49-61	281	-	0

LAWLESS Arthur **Trevor**
Cottam, 23 March, 1932 (CD)

League Club	Source	Date Signed	Seasons Played	Apps	Subs	Gls
Plymouth Arg	Worcester C	07.55	55	8	-	0
Oldham Ath	Tr	07.56	56	9	-	0
Aldershot	Tr	07.57	57	2	-	0
Southport	Tr	07.58	58	15	-	0

LAWLOR John **Christopher (Kit)**
Dublin, 3 December, 1922 Died 2004 LoI-6/IR-3 (IF)

League Club	Source	Date Signed	Seasons Played	Apps	Subs	Gls
Doncaster Rov	Drumcondra	06.50	50-54	127	-	47

LAWLOR James (Jimmy) Joseph
Dublin 10 May, 1933 IrLge-1 (CD)

League Club	Source	Date Signed	Seasons Played	Apps	Subs	Gls
Doncaster Rov	Drumcondra	08.52	54	10	-	0
Bradford C	Coleraine	03.57	56-61	153	-	5

LAWLOR John (Johnny) Boscoe
Bellshill, 30 January, 1937 SSch (W)

League Club	Source	Date Signed	Seasons Played	Apps	Subs	Gls
Aldershot	Kilmarnock	05.59	59-60	57	-	18

LAWRENCE Cyril
Salford, 12 June, 1920 (W)

League Club	Source	Date Signed	Seasons Played	Apps	Subs	Gls
Blackpool	Jnrs	02.46				
Rochdale	Tr	04.47	46-49	44	-	5
Wrexham	Tr	09.50	50-51	50	-	9

LAWRENCE David
Poole, 12 May, 1933 (FB)

League Club	Source	Date Signed	Seasons Played	Apps	Subs	Gls
Bristol Rov	Poole T	06.55	56	5	-	0
Reading	Tr	06.57	57-58	23	-	0

LAWRENCE David (Dai) William
Swansea, 18 January, 1947 WAmat (FB)

League Club	Source	Date Signed	Seasons Played	Apps	Subs	Gls
Swansea T	Merthyr Tydfil	05.67	67-70	93	4	2

LAWRENCE Denis William
Port of Spain, Trinidad, 1 August, 1974 Trinidad 55 (CD)

League Club	Source	Date Signed	Seasons Played	Apps	Subs	Gls
Wrexham	Defence Force (Tr)	03.01	00-04	149	7	12

LAWRENCE George Randolph
Kensington, 14 September, 1962 (W)

League Club	Source	Date Signed	Seasons Played	Apps	Subs	Gls
Southampton	App	09.80	81-82	7	3	1
Oxford U	L	03.82	81	15	0	4
Oxford U	Tr	11.82	82-84	63	0	21
Southampton	Tr	01.85	84-86	58	12	11
Millwall	Tr	07.87	87-88	26	2	4
Bournemouth	Tr	08.89	89-91	47	28	5
Portsmouth	Weymouth	02.93	92	0	12	0

LAWRENCE James (Jamie) Hubert
Balham, 8 March, 1970 Jamaica 23 (W)

League Club	Source	Date Signed	Seasons Played	Apps	Subs	Gls
Sunderland	Cowes	10.93	93	2	2	0
Doncaster Rov	Tr	03.94	93-94	16	9	3
Leicester C	Tr	01.95	94-96	21	26	1
Bradford C	Tr	06.97	97-02	133	22	12
Walsall	Tr	03.03	02-03	12	10	1
Wigan Ath	L	11.03	03	0	4	0
Grimsby T	Tr	03.04	03	5	0	1
Brentford	Tr	09.04	04	8	6	0

LAWRENCE Keith Derek
Orpington, 25 March, 1954 (CD)

League Club	Source	Date Signed	Seasons Played	Apps	Subs	Gls
Chelsea	App	03.72				
Brentford	Tr	05.74	74-75	78	0	1

LAWRENCE Leslie (Les) Oliver
Rowley Regis, 18 May, 1957 (F)

League Club	Source	Date Signed	Seasons Played	Apps	Subs	Gls
Shrewsbury T	Stourbridge	02.75	75-76	10	4	2
Torquay U	Telford U	07.77	77-81	170	19	46
Port Vale	Tr	08.82	82	5	3	0
Aldershot	Tr	07.83	83	39	0	23
Rochdale	Tr	08.84	84	15	0	4
Burnley	Tr	11.84	84-85	22	9	8
Peterborough U	Tr	07.86	86-87	28	5	8
Cambridge U	Tr	02.88	87	11	2	0

LAWRENCE Liam
Retford, 14 December, 1981 (M)

League Club	Source	Date Signed	Seasons Played	Apps	Subs	Gls
Mansfield T	YT	07.00	99-03	120	16	34
Sunderland	Tr	08.04	04	20	12	7

LAWRENCE Mark
Stockton, 4 December, 1958 (M)

League Club	Source	Date Signed	Seasons Played	Apps	Subs	Gls
Hartlepool U	Nunthorpe Ath	08.77	77-83	155	13	24
Port Vale	L	03.83	82	10	1	0

LAWRENCE Matthew (Matt) James
Northampton, 19 June, 1974 ESch (FB)

League Club	Source	Date Signed	Seasons Played	Apps	Subs	Gls
Wycombe W	Grays Ath	01.96	95-96	13	3	1
Fulham	Tr	02.97	96-98	57	2	0
Wycombe W	Tr	10.98	98-99	63	0	4
Millwall	Tr	03.00	99-04	183	10	0

LAWRENCE Thomas (Tommy) Johnstone
Dailly, 14 May, 1940 Su23-1/S-3 (G)

League Club	Source	Date Signed	Seasons Played	Apps	Subs	Gls
Liverpool	Warrington	10.57	62-70	306	0	0
Tranmere Rov	Tr	09.71	71-73	80	0	0

LAWRENSON Mark Thomas
Preston, 2 June, 1957 IR-38 (CD)

League Club	Source	Date Signed	Seasons Played	Apps	Subs	Gls
Preston NE	Jnrs	08.74	74-76	73	0	2
Brighton & Hove A	Tr	07.77	77-80	152	0	5
Liverpool	Tr	08.81	81-87	233	7	11

LAWRENSON Thomas (Tommy)
Preston, 24 May, 1929 Died 1996 (W)

League Club	Source	Date Signed	Seasons Played	Apps	Subs	Gls
Preston NE	Leyland Motors	04.49	54	1	-	0
Southport	Tr	07.55	55-56	37	-	0

LAWRIE Samuel (Sam)
Glasgow, 15 December, 1934 Died 1979 (W)

League Club	Source	Date Signed	Seasons Played	Apps	Subs	Gls
Middlesbrough	Bedlay Jnrs	02.52	51-56	36	-	5
Charlton Ath	Tr	11.56	56-62	193	-	70
Bradford PA	Tr	10.62	62-65	72	1	16

LAWS Brian
Wallsend, 14 October, 1961 EB/FLge (FB)

League Club	Source	Date Signed	Seasons Played	Apps	Subs	Gls
Burnley	App	10.79	79-82	125	0	12
Huddersfield T	Tr	08.83	83-84	56	0	1
Middlesbrough	Tr	03.85	84-87	103	5	12
Nottingham F	Tr	07.88	88-93	136	11	4
Grimsby T	Tr	12.94	94-96	30	16	2
Darlington	Tr	11.96	96	10	0	0
Scunthorpe U	Tr	01.97	96-97	11	7	0

LAWS Jonathan
Peterborough, 1 September, 1964 (M)

League Club	Source	Date Signed	Seasons Played	Apps	Subs	Gls
Wolverhampton W	App	09.82				
Mansfield T	Tr	03.83	82	0	1	0

LAWSON Allan
Lennoxtown, 13 September, 1941 (CD)

League Club	Source	Date Signed	Seasons Played	Apps	Subs	Gls
Oldham Ath	Glasgow Celtic	06.64	64-69	128	10	1

LAWSON David
Wallsend, 22 December, 1947 (G)

League Club	Source	Date Signed	Seasons Played	Apps	Subs	Gls
Newcastle U	Jnrs	04.66				
Bradford PA	Tr	10.67	67-68	13	0	0
Huddersfield T	Tr	05.69	70-71	51	0	0
Everton	Tr	06.72	72-76	124	0	0
Luton T	Tr	10.78	78	5	0	0
Stockport Co	Tr	03.79	78-80	106	0	0

LAWSON Frederick **Ian** Allison
Ouston, 24 March, 1939 EYth (IF)

League Club	Source	Date Signed	Seasons Played	Apps	Subs	Gls
Burnley	Jnrs	03.56	56-60	23	-	7
Leeds U	Tr	03.62	61-64	44	-	17
Crystal Palace	Tr	06.65	65	15	2	6
Port Vale	Tr	08.66	66	7	1	0

LAWSON Ian James
Huddersfield, 4 November, 1977 (F)

League Club	Source	Date Signed	Seasons Played	Apps	Subs	Gls
Huddersfield T	YT	01.95	96-98	13	29	5
Blackpool	L	11.98	98	5	0	3
Blackpool	L	01.99	98	4	0	0
Bury	Tr	07.99	99	20	5	11
Stockport Co	Tr	02.00	99-00	14	11	4
Bury	Tr	09.01	01-02	15	16	7

LAWSON James (Jimmy) Joseph
Middlesbrough, 11 December, 1947 (W)

League Club	Source	Date Signed	Seasons Played	Apps	Subs	Gls
Middlesbrough	Jnrs	12.64	65-67	25	6	3
Huddersfield T	Tr	08.68	68-75	234	11	42
Halifax T	Tr	06.76	76-78	93	0	9

LAWSON James Peter
Basildon, 21 January, 1987 (F)

League Club	Source	Date Signed	Seasons Played	Apps	Subs	Gls
Southend U	Sch	•	04	0	1	0

LAWSON John Richard
York, 3 February, 1925 Died 1990 (W)

League Club	Source	Date Signed	Seasons Played	Apps	Subs	Gls
York C	Dringhouses	08.44	46	1	-	0

LAWSON Norman
Houghton-le-Spring, 6 April, 1935 (W)

League Club	Source	Date Signed	Seasons Played	Apps	Subs	Gls
Bury	Hednesford T	09.55	55-57	56	-	8
Swansea T	Tr	07.58	58-59	24	-	3

LAWSON William (Willie)
Dundee, 28 November, 1947 (W)

League Club	Source	Date Signed	Seasons Played	Apps	Subs	Gls
Sheffield Wed	Brechin C	10.69	69-70	9	1	0

LAWTHER William **Ian**
Belfast, 20 October, 1939 NIB/NI-4 (F)

League Club	Source	Date Signed	Seasons Played	Apps	Subs	Gls
Sunderland	Crusaders	03.58	59-60	75	-	41
Blackburn Rov	Tr	07.61	61-62	59	-	21
Scunthorpe U	Tr	07.63	63-64	60	-	22
Brentford	Tr	11.64	64-67	138	1	43
Halifax T	Tr	08.68	68-70	87	14	24
Stockport Co	Tr	07.71	71-75	158	6	29

LAWTON Craig Thomas
Mancot, 5 January, 1972 WSch/WYth/Wu21-1/WB (M)

League Club	Source	Date Signed	Seasons Played	Apps	Subs	Gls
Manchester U	YT	07.90				
Port Vale	Tr	08.94	94-95	2	1	0

LAWTON James (Jimmy) Michael
Middlesbrough, 6 July, 1942 (F)

League Club	Source	Date Signed	Seasons Played	Apps	Subs	Gls
Darlington	Middlesbrough (Am)	10.61	61-65	121	0	58
Swindon T	Tr	09.65	65-66	11	0	3
Watford	Tr	03.67	66-67	10	3	1
Darlington	Tr	03.68	67-68	21	0	5

LAWTON John Kenneth
Woore, 6 July, 1936 (CF)

League Club	Source	Date Signed	Seasons Played	Apps	Subs	Gls
Stoke C	Crewe Alex Am)	06.54	55	9	-	3

LAWTON Hubert **Malcolm**
Leeds, 7 November, 1935 (FB)

League Club	Source	Date Signed	Seasons Played	Apps	Subs	Gls
Leeds U	Jnrs	11.52				
Bradford PA	Tr	06.57	57-62	113	-	0

LAWTON Norbert (Nobby)
Manchester, 25 March, 1940 (M)

League Club	Source	Date Signed	Seasons Played	Apps	Subs	Gls
Manchester U	Jnrs	04.58	59-62	36	-	6
Preston NE	Tr	03.63	62-67	144	0	22
Brighton & Hove A	Tr	09.67	67-70	112	0	12
Lincoln C	Tr	02.71	70-71	20	0	0

LAWTON Peter
Barnsley, 25 February, 1944 (FB)

League Club	Source	Date Signed	Seasons Played	Apps	Subs	Gls
Barnsley	Jnrs	05.62	62-63	2	-	0

LAWTON Thomas (Tommy)
Bolton, 6 October, 1919 Died 1996 FLge-3/EWar-23/E-23 (CF)

League Club	Source	Date Signed	Seasons Played	Apps	Subs	Gls
Burnley	Rossendale U	03.36	35-36	25	-	16
Everton	Tr	01.37	36-38	87	-	65
Chelsea	Tr	11.45	46-47	42	-	30
Notts Co	Tr	11.47	47-51	151	-	90
Brentford	Tr	03.52	51-53	50	-	17
Arsenal	Tr	09.53	53-55	35	-	13

LAWTON William (Bill)
Ashton-under-Lyne, 4 June, 1920 (WH)

League Club	Source	Date Signed	Seasons Played	Apps	Subs	Gls
Oldham Ath	Ferranti	02.45	46-48	10	-	0

LAY Peter John
Stratford, 4 December, 1931 (FB)

League Club	Source	Date Signed	Seasons Played	Apps	Subs	Gls
Nottingham F		04.53	54	1	-	0
Queens Park Rgrs	Tr	07.56	56	1	-	0

LAYBOURNE Keith Ernest
Sunderland, 27 January, 1959 (FB)

League Club	Source	Date Signed	Seasons Played	Apps	Subs	Gls
Lincoln C	Lambton Star BC	07.77	77-78	18	0	1

LAYNE David Richard
Sheffield, 29 July, 1939 (F)

League Club	Source	Date Signed	Seasons Played	Apps	Subs	Gls
Rotherham U	Jnrs	07.57	57-58	11	-	4
Swindon T	Tr	06.59	59-60	41	-	28
Bradford C	Tr	12.60	60-61	65	-	44
Sheffield Wed	Tr	02.62	62-63	74	-	52
Sheffield Wed	(Retired)	06.72				
Hereford U	L	12.72	72	4	0	0

LAYTON Alan
Bury, 27 November, 1928 (W)

League Club	Source	Date Signed	Seasons Played	Apps	Subs	Gls
Bolton W		04.49				
Barrow	Tr	10.50	50-55	144	-	19

LAYTON John Henry
Hereford, 29 June, 1951 (CD)

League Club	Source	Date Signed	Seasons Played	Apps	Subs	Gls
Hereford U	Kidderminster Hrs	09.74	74-79	198	2	13
Newport Co	Trowbridge T	01.84	83	1	0	0

LAYTON William (Bill) Herbert
Shirley, 13 January, 1915 Died 1984 (WH)

League Club	Source	Date Signed	Seasons Played	Apps	Subs	Gls
Reading	Shirley T	03.37	37-46	51	-	17
Bradford PA	Tr	01.47	46-48	47	-	5
Colchester U	Tr	08.49	50	7	-	0

LAZARIDIS Stanley (Stan)
Perth, Australia, 16 August, 1972 AuYth/Auu23/Au-56 (W)

League Club	Source	Date Signed	Seasons Played	Apps	Subs	Gls
West Ham U	West Adelaide (Aus)	09.95	95-98	53	16	3
Birmingham C	Tr	07.99	99-04	131	43	8

LAZARUS Mark
Stepney, 5 December, 1938 (W)

League Club	Source	Date Signed	Seasons Played	Apps	Subs	Gls
Leyton Orient	Barking	11.57	58-60	20	-	4
Queens Park Rgrs	Tr	09.60	60-61	37	-	19
Wolverhampton W	Tr	09.61	61	9	-	3
Queens Park Rgrs	Tr	02.62	61-63	81	-	28
Brentford	Tr	01.64	63-65	62	0	20
Queens Park Rgrs	Tr	11.65	65-67	86	2	29
Crystal Palace	Tr	11.67	67-69	63	0	17
Orient	Tr	10.69	69-71	81	1	14

LAZARUS Paul
Stepney, 4 September, 1962 (F)

League Club	Source	Date Signed	Seasons Played	Apps	Subs	Gls
Charlton Ath	App	08.80	80	2	0	1
Wimbledon	TPS Turun (Fin)	10.81	81	17	1	6

LEA Cyril
Moss, 5 August, 1934 WAmat/W-2 (CD)

League Club	Source	Date Signed	Seasons Played	Apps	Subs	Gls
Leyton Orient	Bradley Rgrs	07.57	57-64	205	-	0
Ipswich T	Tr	11.64	64-68	103	4	2

LEA Harold
Wigan, 14 September, 1931 (G)

League Club	Source	Date Signed	Seasons Played	Apps	Subs	Gls
Stockport Co	Horwich RMI	05.58	58-63	117	-	0

LEA Leslie (Les)
Manchester, 5 October, 1942 (W)

League Club	Source	Date Signed	Seasons Played	Apps	Subs	Gls
Blackpool	Jnrs	10.59	60-67	158	2	13
Cardiff C	Tr	11.67	67-69	75	1	6
Barnsley	Tr	08.70	70-75	198	7	32

LEA William (Billy) Thomas
Wigan, 27 May, 1924 (IF)

League Club	Source	Date Signed	Seasons Played	Apps	Subs	Gls
Stockport Co (Am)		11.59	59	1	-	0

LEABURN Carl Winston
Lewisham, 30 March, 1969 EYth (F)

League Club	Source	Date Signed	Seasons Played	Apps	Subs	Gls
Charlton Ath	App	04.87	86-97	276	46	53
Northampton T	L	03.90	89	9	0	0
Wimbledon	Tr	01.98	97-00	36	23	4
Queens Park Rgrs	Tr	12.01	01	0	1	0

LEACH Albert
Bolton, 10 July, 1931 (G)

League Club	Source	Date Signed	Seasons Played	Apps	Subs	Gls
Shrewsbury T		11.51	51	2	-	0

LEACH Brian Ernest
Reading, 20 July, 1932 (WH)

League Club	Source	Date Signed	Seasons Played	Apps	Subs	Gls
Reading		11.50	52-56	108	-	1

LEACH John (Johnny) Norman
Whitehaven, 17 January, 1919 (W)

League Club	Source	Date Signed	Seasons Played	Apps	Subs	Gls
Barrow	Barrow Celtic	09.47	47-49	74	-	12

LEACH Marc Thomas
Hemel Hempstead, 12 July, 1983 (CD)

League Club	Source	Date Signed	Seasons Played	Apps	Subs	Gls
Wycombe W	YT	•	01	1	0	0

LEACH Michael (Mick) John Christopher
Clapton, 16 January, 1947 Died 1992 EYth (M)

League Club	Source	Date Signed	Seasons Played	Apps	Subs	Gls
Queens Park Rgrs	App	02.64	64-77	291	22	61
Cambridge U	Detroit (USA)	09.78	78	18	1	1

LEACOCK Dean Graham
Croydon, 10 June, 1984 EYth/Eu20 (FB)

League Club	Source	Date Signed	Seasons Played	Apps	Subs	Gls
Fulham	Sch	07.02	03	3	1	0
Coventry C	L	09.04	04	12	1	0

LEADBEATER Richard Paul
Dudley, 21 October, 1977 (F)

League Club	Source	Date Signed	Seasons Played	Apps	Subs	Gls
Wolverhampton W	YT	07.96	96	0	1	0

LEADBETTER Albert
Newton-le-Willows, 17 August, 1921 Died 1994 (W)

League Club	Source	Date Signed	Seasons Played	Apps	Subs	Gls
Accrington St (Am)	Earlestown	12.46	46	4	-	0

LEADBETTER James (Jimmy) Hunter
Edinburgh, 15 July, 1928 (W)

League Club	Source	Date Signed	Seasons Played	Apps	Subs	Gls
Chelsea	Edinburgh Thistle	07.49	51	3	-	0
Brighton & Hove A	Tr	08.52	52-54	107	-	29
Ipswich T	Tr	06.55	55-64	344	-	43

LEADBITTER Christopher (Chris) Jonathan
Middlesbrough, 17 October, 1967 (M)

League Club	Source	Date Signed	Seasons Played	Apps	Subs	Gls
Grimsby T	App	09.85				
Hereford U	Tr	08.86	86-87	32	4	1
Cambridge U	Tr	08.88	88-92	144	32	18
Bournemouth	Tr	08.93	93-94	45	9	3

League Club	Source	Date Signed	Seasons Played	Apps	Subs	Gls
Plymouth Arg	Tr	07.95	95-96	46	6	1
Torquay U	Dorchester T	11.97	97-98	58	5	2
Plymouth Arg	Tr	07.99	99-00	37	3	2

LEADBITTER John
Sunderland, 7 May, 1953 (CD)

League Club	Source	Date Signed	Seasons Played	Apps	Subs	Gls
Sunderland	App	05.70				
Darlington	Tr	08.72	72	15	4	0

LEAF Andrew (Andy) Keith
York, 18 January, 1962 (FB)

League Club	Source	Date Signed	Seasons Played	Apps	Subs	Gls
York C	App	01.80	79	1	0	0

LEAH John David
Shrewsbury, 3 August, 1978 (M)

League Club	Source	Date Signed	Seasons Played	Apps	Subs	Gls
Darlington	Newtown	07.98	98	7	0	1

LEAHY Stephen (Steve) David
Battersea, 23 September, 1959 ESch (F)

League Club	Source	Date Signed	Seasons Played	Apps	Subs	Gls
Crystal Palace	App	10.76	80-81	3	1	0

LEAKE Albert George
Stoke-on-Trent, 7 April, 1930 Died 1999 EYth (WH)

League Club	Source	Date Signed	Seasons Played	Apps	Subs	Gls
Port Vale	Stoke C (Am)	02.50	50-59	269	-	34

LEAMON Frederick (Fred) William
Jersey, 11 May, 1919 Died 1981 (CF)

League Club	Source	Date Signed	Seasons Played	Apps	Subs	Gls
Newport Co	Bath C	02.46	46	4	-	3
Bristol Rov	Tr	10.46	46-47	43	-	21
Brighton & Hove A	Tr	07.49	49	11	-	4

LEAN David Reginald
Plymouth, 28 April, 1945 (CD)

League Club	Source	Date Signed	Seasons Played	Apps	Subs	Gls
Plymouth Arg	Embankment	08.69	69-70	44	1	0

LEANING Andrew (Andy) John
Howden, 18 May, 1963 (G)

League Club	Source	Date Signed	Seasons Played	Apps	Subs	Gls
York C	Rowntree Mackintosh	07.85	85-86	69	0	0
Sheffield U	Tr	05.87	87	21	0	0
Bristol C	Tr	09.88	88-92	75	0	0
Lincoln C	Tr	03.94	93-95	36	0	0
Chesterfield	Dundee U	10.96	96-99	22	0	0

LEAR Graham John
Exeter, 18 December, 1930 (G)

League Club	Source	Date Signed	Seasons Played	Apps	Subs	Gls
Exeter C (Am)	Exeter T	06.50	50-51	20	-	0

LEARY Michael Antonio
Ealing, 17 April, 1983 IRYth (M)

League Club	Source	Date Signed	Seasons Played	Apps	Subs	Gls
Luton T	Jnrs	08.01	03-04	9	13	2

LEARY Stuart Edward
Cape Town, South Africa, 30 April, 1933 Died 1988 Eu23-1 (CF)

League Club	Source	Date Signed	Seasons Played	Apps	Subs	Gls
Charlton Ath	Clyde (SA)	02.50	51-61	376	-	153
Queens Park Rgrs	Tr	12.62	62-65	94	0	29

LEATH Terence (Terry) Charles
West Derby, 6 November, 1934 (FB)

League Club	Source	Date Signed	Seasons Played	Apps	Subs	Gls
Southport	Birchfield Rov	03.59	58-59	17	-	0

LEATHER Maurice Peate
Eastleigh, 9 November, 1929 EYth (G)

League Club	Source	Date Signed	Seasons Played	Apps	Subs	Gls
Portsmouth	Southampton (Am)	01.50	50-52	18	-	0

LEAVER Derek
Blackburn, 13 November, 1930 (IF)

League Club	Source	Date Signed	Seasons Played	Apps	Subs	Gls
Blackburn Rov		05.49	50-54	14	-	5
Bournemouth	Tr	07.55	55	29	-	5
Crewe Alex	Tr	03.56	55-56	28	-	5

LEAVY Stephen (Steve) Francis
Longford, Eire, 18 June, 1925 Died 1996 LoI-3 (FB)

League Club	Source	Date Signed	Seasons Played	Apps	Subs	Gls
Swansea T	Sligo Rov	07.50	50-57	37	-	1

LE BIHAN Neil Ernest
Croydon, 14 March, 1976 (M)

League Club	Source	Date Signed	Seasons Played	Apps	Subs	Gls
Peterborough U	Tottenham H (YT)	07.94	94-96	21	10	0

LEBOEUF Frank
Marseille, France, 22 January, 1968 France 40 (CD)

League Club	Source	Date Signed	Seasons Played	Apps	Subs	Gls
Chelsea	RC Strasbourg (Fr)	07.96	96-00	142	2	17

LECK Derek Alan
Deal, 8 February, 1937 (WH)

League Club	Source	Date Signed	Seasons Played	Apps	Subs	Gls
Millwall	Leyton YC	05.55	55-57	7	-	2
Northampton T	Tr	06.58	58-65	246	0	45
Brighton & Hove A	Tr	11.65	65-66	29	1	0

LE CORNU Craig Douglas
Birkenhead, 17 September, 1960 (M)

League Club	Source	Date Signed	Seasons Played	Apps	Subs	Gls
Liverpool	App	09.78				
Tranmere Rov	Tr	12.80	80	3	3	0

LEDGARD Ian
Stockport, 9 February, 1948 (M)

League Club	Source	Date Signed	Seasons Played	Apps	Subs	Gls
Blackburn Rov	Leeds U (Am)	07.67				
Stockport Co	Tr	10.67	67-68	4	4	0

LEDGER Robert (Bob) Hardy
Craghead, 5 October, 1937 (W)

League Club	Source	Date Signed	Seasons Played	Apps	Subs	Gls
Huddersfield T	Jnrs	10.54	55-61	58	-	7
Oldham Ath	Tr	05.62	62-67	221	1	37
Mansfield T	Tr	11.67	67-69	51	6	15
Barrow	Tr	10.69	69	21	1	2

LEDGER Roy
Barnsley, 9 December, 1930 Died 1992 (IF)

League Club	Source	Date Signed	Seasons Played	Apps	Subs	Gls
Barnsley	Smithies U	04.48	50	1	-	0

LEDGERTON Terence (Terry)
Liverpool, 7 October, 1930 (W)

League Club	Source	Date Signed	Seasons Played	Apps	Subs	Gls
Brentford		05.50	51-53	40	-	8
Millwall	Tr	05.54	54	6	-	2

LEDLEY Joseph (Joe) Christopher
Cardiff, 23 January, 1987 WYth/Wu21-3 (M)

League Club	Source	Date Signed	Seasons Played	Apps	Subs	Gls
Cardiff C	Sch	10.04	04	20	8	3

LEE Alan Desmond
Galway, 21 August, 1978 IRu21-5/IR-8 (F)

League Club	Source	Date Signed	Seasons Played	Apps	Subs	Gls
Aston Villa	YT	08.95				
Torquay U	L	11.98	98	6	1	2
Port Vale	L	03.99	98	7	4	2
Burnley	Tr	07.99	99	2	13	0
Rotherham U	Tr	09.00	00-03	105	6	37
Cardiff C	Tr	08.03	03-04	41	20	8

LEE Alan Robert
Wegburg, Germany, 19 June, 1960 (W)

League Club	Source	Date Signed	Seasons Played	Apps	Subs	Gls
Leicester C	Philadelphia (USA)	02.79	78-79	6	0	0

LEE Alfred (Alf)
Farnworth, 11 June, 1927 Died 1991 (WH)

League Club	Source	Date Signed	Seasons Played	Apps	Subs	Gls
Bolton W		10.48				
Oldham Ath	Tr	07.50	50	3	-	1

LEE Andrew (Andy) Gerard
Liverpool, 14 September, 1962 ESch (FB)

League Club	Source	Date Signed	Seasons Played	Apps	Subs	Gls
Tranmere Rov	Stafford Rgrs	07.84	84	14	4	0
Cambridge U	(New Zealand)	08.85	85	8	1	0

LEE Andrew (Andy) Jack
Bradford, 18 August, 1982 (M)

League Club	Source	Date Signed	Seasons Played	Apps	Subs	Gls
Bradford C	YT	07.01	01-02	0	2	0

LEE Anthony (Tony)
Manchester, 4 June, 1937 (W)

League Club	Source	Date Signed	Seasons Played	Apps	Subs	Gls
Southport (Am)	Cheadle Rov	02.58	57-58	10	-	1

LEE John **Anthony (Tony)**
Middlesbrough, 26 November, 1947 (W)

League Club	Source	Date Signed	Seasons Played	Apps	Subs	Gls
Leicester C		10.65				
Bradford C	Tr	07.67	67	6	2	3
Darlington	Stockton	05.68	68	11	3	1

LEE Christian Earl
Aylesbury, 8 October, 1976 (F)

League Club	Source	Date Signed	Seasons Played	Apps	Subs	Gls
Northampton T	Doncaster Rov (YT)	07.95	95-98	25	34	8
Gillingham	Tr	08.99	99	1	2	0
Rochdale	L	10.00	00	2	3	1
Leyton Orient	L	03.01	00	2	1	0
Bristol Rov	Tr	03.01	00	8	1	2
Rushden & Diamonds	Farnborough T	09.01	01	1	0	0

LEE Christopher (Chris)
Batley, 18 June, 1971 (M)

League Club	Source	Date Signed	Seasons Played	Apps	Subs	Gls
Bradford C	YT	07.89				
Rochdale	Tr	06.90	90	24	2	2
Scarborough	Tr	03.91	90-92	75	3	3
Hull C	Tr	07.93	93-95	104	12	5

LEE Colin
Torquay, 12 June, 1956 (F)

League Club	Source	Date Signed	Seasons Played	Apps	Subs	Gls
Bristol C	App	06.74				
Hereford U	L	11.74	74	7	2	0
Torquay U	Tr	01.77	76-77	35	0	14
Tottenham H	Tr	10.77	77-79	57	5	18
Chelsea	Tr	01.80	79-86	167	18	36
Brentford	Tr	07.87	87-88	20	4	1

LEE David John
Kingswood, 26 November, 1969 EYth/Eu21-10 (CD)

League Club	Source	Date Signed	Seasons Played	Apps	Subs	Gls
Chelsea	YT	07.88	88-97	119	32	11
Reading	L	01.92	91	5	0	5
Plymouth Arg	L	03.92	91	9	0	1
Portsmouth	L	08.94	94	4	1	0

League Club	Source	Date Signed	Seasons Played	Apps	Subs	Gls
Sheffield U	L	12.97	97	5	0	0
Bristol Rov	Tr	12.98	98	10	1	1
Crystal Palace	Tr	10.99				
Colchester U	Tr	01.00				
Exeter C	Tr	02.00	99	3	1	0

LEE David John Francis
Basildon, 28 March, 1980 (M)

League Club	Source	Date Signed	Seasons Played	Apps	Subs	Gls
Tottenham H	YT	07.98				
Southend U	Tr	08.00	00	37	5	8
Hull C	Tr	06.01	01	2	9	1
Brighton & Hove A	Tr	01.02	01-03	1	5	0
Bristol Rov	L	10.02	02	5	0	0
Oldham Ath	Thurrock	10.04	04	5	2	0

LEE David Mark
Whitefield, 5 November, 1967 (W)

League Club	Source	Date Signed	Seasons Played	Apps	Subs	Gls
Bury	Jnrs	08.86	85-91	203	5	35
Southampton	Tr	08.91	91-92	11	9	0
Bolton W	Tr	11.92	92-96	124	31	17
Wigan Ath	Tr	07.97	97-99	61	22	11
Blackpool	L	10.99	99	9	0	1
Carlisle U	Tr	08.00	00	1	12	0

LEE Eric George
Chester, 18 October, 1922 EAmat (CD)

League Club	Source	Date Signed	Seasons Played	Apps	Subs	Gls
Chester	Jnrs	05.46	46-56	363	-	10

LEE Francis (Frank)
Chorley, 17 February, 1944 (W)

League Club	Source	Date Signed	Seasons Played	Apps	Subs	Gls
Preston NE	Horwich RMI	11.61	63-70	143	10	22
Southport	Tr	11.70	70-73	115	0	21
Stockport Co	Tr	07.74	74	13	0	1

LEE Francis Henry
Westhoughton, 29 April, 1944 EYth/FLge-1/E-27 (F)

League Club	Source	Date Signed	Seasons Played	Apps	Subs	Gls
Bolton W	Jnrs	05.61	60-67	189	0	92
Manchester C	Tr	10.67	67-73	248	1	112
Derby Co	Tr	08.74	74-75	62	0	24

LEE Garth
Sheffield, 30 September, 1943 EYth (W)

League Club	Source	Date Signed	Seasons Played	Apps	Subs	Gls
Sheffield U	Jnrs	05.61				
Chester	Tr	09.63	63-64	28	-	7

LEE Gary
Doncaster, 30 April, 1966 (CD)

League Club	Source	Date Signed	Seasons Played	Apps	Subs	Gls
Doncaster Rov	YT	07.84	84	1	0	0

LEE George Thomas
York, 4 June, 1919 Died 1991 (W)

League Club	Source	Date Signed	Seasons Played	Apps	Subs	Gls
York C	Scarborough	06.36	36-46	37	-	11
Nottingham F	Tr	08.47	47-48	76	-	20
West Bromwich A	Tr	07.49	49-57	271	-	59

LEE Gordon Francis
Hednesford, 13 July, 1934 (FB)

League Club	Source	Date Signed	Seasons Played	Apps	Subs	Gls
Aston Villa	Hednesford T	10.55	58-64	118	-	2
Shrewsbury T	Tr	07.66	66	2	0	0

LEE Graeme Barry
Middlesbrough, 31 May, 1978 (CD)

League Club	Source	Date Signed	Seasons Played	Apps	Subs	Gls
Hartlepool U	YT	07.96	95-02	208	11	19
Sheffield Wed	Tr	07.03	03-04	49	3	4

LEE Harold (Harry)
Mexborough, 13 January, 1933 (IF)

League Club	Source	Date Signed	Seasons Played	Apps	Subs	Gls
Derby Co	Thomas Hill YC	10.50				
Mansfield T		08.55	55	3	-	2

LEE James (Jimmy)
Rotherham, 26 January, 1926 Died 2001 (FB)

League Club	Source	Date Signed	Seasons Played	Apps	Subs	Gls
Wolverhampton W	Wath W	02.45				
Hull C	Tr	10.48	49	3	-	1
Halifax T	Tr	02.51	50-51	26	-	0
Chelsea	Tr	10.51				
Leyton Orient	Tr	07.54	54-55	67	-	1
Swindon T	Tr	11.56	56-58	35	-	0

LEE Jason Benedict
Forest Gate, 9 May, 1971 (F)

League Club	Source	Date Signed	Seasons Played	Apps	Subs	Gls
Charlton Ath	YT	06.89	89	0	1	0
Stockport Co	L	02.91	90	2	0	0
Lincoln C	Tr	03.91	90-92	86	7	21
Southend U	Tr	08.93	93	18	6	3
Nottingham F	Tr	03.94	93-96	41	35	14
Charlton Ath	L	02.97	96	7	1	3
Grimsby T	L	03.97	96	2	5	2
Watford	Tr	06.97	97-98	36	1	11
Chesterfield	Tr	08.98	98-99	17	11	1
Peterborough U	Tr	01.00	99-02	49	29	17
Boston U	Falkirk	08.04	04	32	7	9

LEE Jeffrey (Jeff) Wreathall
Dewsbury, 3 October, 1945 (FB)

League Club	Source	Date Signed	Seasons Played	Apps	Subs	Gls
Halifax T	Huddersfield T (Am)	01.65	64-72	233	9	3
Peterborough U	Tr	08.73	73-77	170	2	12

LEE John (Jack)
Sileby, 4 November, 1920 Died 1995 E-1 (CF)

League Club	Source	Date Signed	Seasons Played	Apps	Subs	Gls
Leicester C	Quorn Methodists	02.41	46-49	123	-	74
Derby Co	Tr	07.50	50-53	93	-	54
Coventry C	Tr	11.54	54	15	-	8

LEE Martyn James
Guildford, 10 September, 1980 (M)

League Club	Source	Date Signed	Seasons Played	Apps	Subs	Gls
Wycombe W	YT	01.99	98-02	22	19	3
Cheltenham T	L	03.02	01	2	3	0

LEE Michael (Mike) James
Mold, 27 June, 1938 WSch (W)

League Club	Source	Date Signed	Seasons Played	Apps	Subs	Gls
West Bromwich A	Saltney Jnrs	08.56	56	1	-	0
Crewe Alex	Tr	06.58	58	1	-	0

LEE Norman Thomas
Trealaw, 29 May, 1939 (WH)

League Club	Source	Date Signed	Seasons Played	Apps	Subs	Gls
Tottenham H	Jnrs	11.57				
Bournemouth	Tr	09.61				
Southend U	Tr	02.62	61-62	22	-	1

LEE Paul Andrew
Oxford, 30 May, 1952 (F)

League Club	Source	Date Signed	Seasons Played	Apps	Subs	Gls
Hereford U	Oxford C	09.72	73-74	21	7	5

LEE Raymond (Ray) Maurice
Bristol, 19 September, 1970 (W)

League Club	Source	Date Signed	Seasons Played	Apps	Subs	Gls
Arsenal	YT	10.88				
Scarborough	Swindon T (N/C)	02.91	90	2	8	0

LEE Richard (Dick)
Sheffield, 11 September, 1944 (CD)

League Club	Source	Date Signed	Seasons Played	Apps	Subs	Gls
Rotherham U	Jnrs	05.63				
Notts Co	Tr	06.64				
Mansfield T	Tr	08.65	65	3	1	1
Halifax T	Tr	07.66	66-67	14	0	0

LEE Richard Anthony
Oxford, 5 October, 1982 EYth (G)

League Club	Source	Date Signed	Seasons Played	Apps	Subs	Gls
Watford	YT	03.00	02-04	37	0	0

LEE Robert
Newcastle, 23 December, 1957 (M)

League Club	Source	Date Signed	Seasons Played	Apps	Subs	Gls
Doncaster Rov	App	05.74	74	1	0	0
Scunthorpe U	Tr	07.76	76-77	17	2	0

LEE Robert (Bob) Gordon
Melton Mowbray, 2 February, 1953 (F)

League Club	Source	Date Signed	Seasons Played	Apps	Subs	Gls
Leicester C	Blaby BC	02.72	71-76	55	8	17
Doncaster Rov	L	08.74	74	14	0	4
Sunderland	Tr	09.76	76-79	101	6	32
Bristol Rov	Tr	08.80	80	19	4	2
Carlisle U	Tr	08.81	81-82	47	8	12
Darlington	(Hong Kong)	08.83	83	5	0	0

LEE Robert (Rob) Martin
West Ham, 1 February, 1966 Eu21-2/EB-1/E-21 (M)

League Club	Source	Date Signed	Seasons Played	Apps	Subs	Gls
Charlton Ath	Hornchurch	07.83	83-92	274	24	59
Newcastle U	Tr	09.92	92-01	292	11	44
Derby Co	Tr	02.02	01-02	47	1	2
West Ham U	Tr	08.03	03	12	4	0
Oldham Ath	Tr	11.04				
Wycombe W	Tr	03.05	04	6	1	0

LEE Samuel (Sammy)
Liverpool, 7 February, 1959 EYth/Eu21-6/E-14 (M)

League Club	Source	Date Signed	Seasons Played	Apps	Subs	Gls
Liverpool	App	04.76	77-85	190	7	13
Queens Park Rgrs	Tr	08.86	86	29	1	0
Southampton	CA Osasuna (Sp)	01.90	89	0	2	0
Bolton W	Tr	10.90	90	4	0	0

LEE Frederick **Stuart**
Manchester, 11 February, 1953 (F)

League Club	Source	Date Signed	Seasons Played	Apps	Subs	Gls
Bolton W	App	02.71	71-74	77	8	20
Wrexham	Tr	11.75	75-77	46	8	12
Stockport Co	Tr	08.78	78-79	49	0	21
Manchester C	Tr	09.79	79	6	1	2

LEE Terence (Terry) William George
Stepney, 20 September, 1952 Died 1996 (G)

League Club	Source	Date Signed	Seasons Played	Apps	Subs	Gls
Tottenham H	Jnrs	05.70	73	1	0	0
Torquay U	Tr	07.75	75-77	106	0	0
Newport Co	Tr	11.78	78	1	0	0

LEE Thomas (Tommy) Joseph
Horden, 19 December, 1949 (M)

League Club	Source	Date Signed	Seasons Played	Apps	Subs	Gls
Hartlepool	Sunderland College	11.68	69	6	0	0

League Club	Source	Date Signed	Seasons Played	Apps	Subs	Gls
LEE Trevor Carl						
Lewisham, 3 July, 1954						(F)
Millwall	Epsom & Ewell	10.75	75-78	99	9	22
Colchester U	Tr	11.78	78-80	95	1	35
Gillingham	Tr	01.81	80-82	43	4	14
Orient	L	10.82	82	5	0	0
Bournemouth	Tr	11.82	82-83	28	6	9
Cardiff C	Tr	12.83	83	21	0	5
Northampton T	Tr	07.84	84	24	0	0
Fulham	Tr	03.85	84	1	0	0
LEE William (Billy) Richard						
Darwen, 24 October, 1919 Died 1996						(WH)
Blackburn Rov	Pleasington	08.38	38	1	-	0
Barrow	Tr	05.47	46-52	158	-	1
LEEBROOK Peter David						
Saltburn, 18 September, 1968						(FB)
Burnley	App	05.87	86-87	52	0	0
LEECH Frederick (Fred)						
Stalybridge, 5 December, 1923						(CF)
Bradford C	Hurst	12.45	46	7	-	2
LEECH Vincent (Vince) Graham						
Littleborough, 6 December, 1940						(CD)
Blackburn Rov	Burnley (Am)	04.59				
Bury	Tr	07.61	61-67	108	3	0
Rochdale	Tr	07.68	68-70	59	0	1
LEEDER Frederick (Fred)						
New Hartley, 15 September, 1936						(FB)
Everton	New Delaval Jnrs	03.55	57	1	-	0
Darlington	Tr	07.58	58-59	21	-	0
Southport	Tr	07.60	60-61	63	-	0
LEEDHAM John Richard						
Carshalton, 8 November, 1942						(WH)
Millwall	Epsom & Ewell	10.62	62-63	9	-	0
Walsall	Tr	05.64	64	13	-	0
LEEK Kenneth (Ken)						
Ynysybwl, 26 July, 1935 Wu23-1/W-13						(F)
Northampton T	Pontypridd YC	08.52	55-57	71	-	27
Leicester C	Tr	05.58	58-60	93	-	34
Newcastle U	Tr	06.61	61	13	-	6
Birmingham C	Tr	11.61	61-64	104	-	49
Northampton T	Tr	12.64	64-65	16	0	4
Bradford C	Tr	11.65	65-67	99	0	25
LEEMING Clifford (Cliff)						
Turton, 2 February, 1920						(W)
Bury	Bolton W (Am)	10.46	46	1	-	0
Tranmere Rov	Tr	07.47	47	13	-	2
LEES Alfred (Alf)						
Worsley, 28 July, 1923						(CD)
Bolton W		05.47	47	2	-	0
New Brighton	Tr	08.49	49-50	72	-	0
Crewe Alex	Tr	09.51	51-55	186	-	5
LEES Geoffrey (Geoff)						
Rotherham, 1 October, 1933						(WH)
Barnsley	Jnrs	03.51				
Bradford C	Tr	07.55	55	3	-	0
LEES Norman						
Newcastle, 18 November, 1948						(CD)
Hull C	App	11.66	66-70	4	1	0
Hartlepool	L	12.70	70	20	0	1
Darlington	Tr	07.71	71-76	108	12	5
LEES Terence (Terry)						
Stoke-on-Trent, 30 June, 1952						(FB)
Stoke C	App	07.69	70-73	17	7	0
Crewe Alex	L	03.75	74	6	0	0
Port Vale	San Jose (USA)	08.75	75	40	1	2
Birmingham C	JC Roda (Holl)	07.79	79-80	11	1	0
Newport Co	Tr	08.81	81	25	0	0
Scunthorpe U	Altrincham	09.84	84	30	1	0
LEES Walter Joseph						
Glasgow, 2 February, 1947						(CD)
Watford	Kilsyth Rgrs	06.68	68-75	220	6	10
LEESE Lars						
Cologne, Germany, 18 August, 1969						(G)
Barnsley	Bayer Leverkusen (Ger)	07.97	97-98	16	1	0
LEESE William (Billy)						
Stoke-on-Trent, 10 March, 1961						(CD)
Port Vale	App	03.79	79	1	0	0

League Club	Source	Date Signed	Seasons Played	Apps	Subs	Gls
LEESON Donald (Don)						
Askern, 25 August, 1935						(G)
Barnsley	Askern Main Colliery	05.54	56-60	97	-	0
LEET Norman David						
Leicester, 13 March, 1962 ESch						(FB)
Leicester C	Shepshed Charterhouse	06.80	80-82	19	0	0
LE FLEM Richard (Dick) Peter						
Bradford-on-Avon, 12 July, 1942 Eu23-1						(W)
Nottingham F	(Guernsey)	05.60	60-63	132	-	18
Wolverhampton W	Tr	01.64	63-64	19	-	5
Middlesbrough	Tr	02.65	64-65	9	0	1
Leyton Orient	Tr	03.66	65-66	11	0	2
LE FONDRE Adam						
Stockport, 2 December, 1986						(F)
Stockport Co	Sch	02.05	04	11	9	4
LEGATE Roland (Roly) Arthur						
Arlesey, 4 May, 1939						(W)
Luton T	Arlesey T	05.56	56-61	15	-	8
LEGG Andrew (Andy)						
Neath, 28 July, 1966 W-6						(W)
Swansea C	Briton Ferry	08.88	88-92	155	8	29
Notts Co	Tr	07.93	93-95	85	4	9
Birmingham C	Tr	02.96	95-96	31	14	5
Ipswich T	L	11.97	97	6	0	1
Reading	Tr	02.98	97-98	12	0	0
Peterborough U	L	10.98	98	5	0	0
Cardiff C	Tr	12.98	98-02	152	23	12
Peterborough U	Tr	07.03	03-04	76	5	5
LEGG Richard Desmond						
Chippenham, 23 April, 1952						(F)
Swindon T	Chippenham T	08.71	71-73	13	7	3
LEGG William (Billy) Campbell						
Bradford, 17 April, 1948						(FB)
Huddersfield T	App	05.65	64-68	54	2	4
LEGGAT Graham						
Aberdeen, 20 June, 1934 Su23-1/SLge-5/S-18						(W)
Fulham	Aberdeen	08.58	58-66	251	3	127
Birmingham C	Tr	01.67	66-67	13	3	4
Rotherham U	Tr	07.68	68	13	2	7
LEGGETT Peter Robert						
Newton-le-Willows, 16 December, 1943						(W)
Swindon T	Weymouth	05.62	63-64	15	-	1
Brighton & Hove A	Tr	07.65	65	2	1	0
Cambridge U	Tr	01.70	70	21	0	3
LEGWINSKI Sylvain						
Clermont-Ferrand, France, 6 October, 1973 Fru21/FrB-3						(M)
Fulham	Bordeaux (Fr)	08.01	01-04	106	9	8
LEHMANN Dirk Johannes						
Aachen, Germany, 16 August, 1971						(F)
Fulham	Energie Cottbuss (Ger)	08.98	98	16	10	2
Brighton & Hove A	Hibernian	06.01	01	3	4	0
LEHMANN Jens						
Essen, Germany, 10 November, 1969 Germany 25						(G)
Arsenal	Borussia Dortmund (Ger)	08.03	03-04	66	0	0
LEIGERTWOOD Mikele Benjamin						
Enfield, 12 November, 1982						(FB)
Wimbledon	YT	06.01	01-03	55	1	2
Leyton Orient	L	11.01	01	8	0	0
Crystal Palace	Tr	02.04	03-04	23	9	1
LEIGH Dennis						
Barnsley, 26 February, 1949						(FB)
Doncaster Rov	App	03.67	66-67	34	3	1
Rotherham U	Tr	02.68	67-72	153	7	10
Lincoln C	Tr	02.73	72-78	201	4	3
LEIGH Ian Reginald						
Ilfracombe, 11 June, 1962						(G)
Bournemouth	Swaythling	10.79	81-85	123	0	0
Bristol C	L	01.85	84	1	0	0
Torquay U	L	09.85	85	4	0	0
LEIGH Mark Brian						
Manchester, 4 October, 1961						(M)
Stockport Co	Manchester C (App)	11.79	80-83	6	5	1
LEIGH Peter						
Wythenshawe, 4 March, 1939						(FB)
Manchester C	Stamford Lads	08.57	59	2	-	0
Crewe Alex	Tr	06.61	61-71	432	0	3

League Club	Source	Date Signed	Seasons Played	Apps	Subs	Gls
LEIGHTON Anthony (Tony)						
Leeds, 27 November, 1939 Died 1978						(F)
Leeds U	Ashley Road Jnrs	12.56				
Doncaster Rov	Tr	06.59	59-61	84	-	44
Barnsley	Tr	05.62	62-64	107	-	59
Huddersfield T	Tr	01.65	64-67	89	1	40
Bradford C	Tr	03.68	67-69	84	4	23
LEIGHTON James (Jim)						
Johnstone, 24 July, 1958 Su21-1/S-89						(G)
Manchester U	Aberdeen	05.88	88-89	73	0	0
Reading	L	11.91	91	8	0	0
LEIPER John						
Aberdeen, 26 June, 1938						(G)
Plymouth Arg	Aberdeen East End	04.58	60-66	75	0	0
LEISHMAN Graham						
Salford, 6 April, 1968						(F)
Mansfield T	Irlam T	12.88	88-90	8	19	3
LEISHMAN Thomas (Tommy)						
Stenhousemuir, 3 September, 1937						(WH)
Liverpool	St Mirren	11.59	59-62	107	-	6
LEITAO Jorge Manuel Vasconcelos						
Oporto, Portugal, 14 January, 1974						(F)
Walsall	Deportivo Farense (Por)	08.00	00-04	170	37	52
LEITCH Andrew (Andy) Buchanan						
Exeter, 27 March, 1950						(F)
Swansea C	Cadbury Heath	07.75	75	15	2	6
LEITCH Grant						
South Africa, 31 October, 1972						(W)
Blackpool	Jnrs	08.90	91-93	13	12	1
LEITCH Donald **Scott**						
Motherwell, 6 October, 1969						(M)
Swindon T	Heart of Midlothian	03.96	95-99	119	3	1
LEIVERS William (Bill) Ernest						
Bolsover, 29 January, 1932						(FB)
Chesterfield	Jnrs	02.50	51-52	27	-	0
Manchester C	Tr	11.53	54-63	250	-	4
Doncaster Rov	Tr	07.64	64-65	24	0	1
LELLO Cyril Frank						
Ludlow, 24 February, 1920 Died 1997 NIRL-1						(WH)
Everton	Shrewsbury T	09.47	47-56	237	-	9
Rochdale	Tr	11.56	56	11	-	0
LEMAN Dennis						
Newcastle, 1 December, 1954 ESch						(M)
Manchester C	App	12.71	73-75	10	7	1
Sheffield Wed	Tr	12.76	76-81	89	15	9
Wrexham	L	02.82	81	17	0	1
Scunthorpe U	Tr	08.82	82-83	38	0	3
LEMARCHAND Stephane						
Saint-Lo, France, 6 August, 1971						(M)
Carlisle U	SM Caen (Fr)	09.00	00	4	1	1
LEMON Arthur						
Neath, 25 January, 1932						(CF)
Nottingham F		02.51	52-54	24	-	1
LEMON Paul Andrew						
Middlesbrough, 3 June, 1966						(M)
Sunderland	App	05.84	84-88	91	16	15
Carlisle U	L	12.84	84	2	0	0
Walsall	L	11.89	89	2	0	0
Reading	L	12.89	89	3	0	0
Chesterfield	Tr	09.90	90-92	80	5	10
LENAGH Steven (Steve) Michael						
Durham, 21 March, 1979						(CD)
Chesterfield	Sheffield Wed (YT)	11.97	97-98	6	7	1
LENARDUZZI Robert (Bob) Italo						
Vancouver, Canada, 1 May, 1955 Canada int						(FB)
Reading	App	05.73	71-75	63	4	2
LENG Michael (Mike)						
Rotherham, 14 June, 1952						(FB)
Rotherham U	App	07.71	71-75	94	7	2
Workington	Tr	07.76	76	43	0	2
LENIHAN Michael (Micky) Martin						
Swansea, 15 October, 1946						(F)
Swansea C	Swansea GPO	08.72	72-73	9	3	0

League Club	Source	Date Signed	Seasons Played	Apps	Subs	Gls
LENNARD David (Dave)						
Manchester, 31 December, 1944						(M)
Bolton W	Jnrs	12.61	62-68	114	5	3
Halifax T	Tr	07.69	69-71	97	0	16
Blackpool	Tr	10.71	71-72	42	3	9
Cambridge U	Tr	08.73	73-74	39	1	6
Chester	Tr	09.74	74-75	73	2	11
Stockport Co	Tr	07.76	76	39	0	4
Bournemouth	Tr	09.77	77-78	56	3	4
LENNON Aaron Justin						
Leeds, 16 April, 1987 EYth						(M)
Leeds U	Sch	●	03-04	19	19	1
LENNON Alexander (Alex) Vincent						
Glasgow, 25 October, 1925 Died 1992						(IF)
Rotherham U		11.44				
Queens Park Rgrs		01.47	48	1	-	0
Mansfield T	Tr	02.49	48	3	-	0
LENNON Neil Francis						
Lurgan, 25 June, 1971 NIYth/NIu23-1/NIu21-2/NIB-1/NI-39						(M)
Manchester C	YT	08.89	87	1	0	0
Crewe Alex	Tr	08.90	90-95	142	5	15
Leicester C	Tr	02.96	95-00	169	1	6
LENNOX Stephen (Steve) John Martin						
Aberdeen, 14 November, 1964						(M)
Stoke C	App	12.81	82	1	1	0
Torquay U	L	12.83	83	11	0	0
LEONARD Carleton Craig						
Oswestry, 3 February, 1958						(FB)
Shrewsbury T	Jnrs	09.75	75-82	224	3	1
Hereford U	Tr	06.83	83-84	29	1	0
Cardiff C	Tr	07.85	85	4	0	0
LEONARD Christopher (Chris)						
Jarrow, 11 July, 1927						(CD)
Darlington	South Shields	03.52	51-53	26	-	0
LEONARD Gary Alan						
Newcastle, 28 November, 1965						(M)
West Bromwich A	App	11.83				
Shrewsbury T	Tr	07.85	85-87	48	19	1
Hereford U	L	03.88	87	11	0	1
Bury	Tr	07.88	88	4	5	1
Stockport Co	Tr	03.89	88-89	15	2	1
LEONARD Gary Edward						
Northampton, 23 March, 1962						(M)
Northampton T	App	03.80	79-80	2	0	0
LEONARD Henry (Harry)						
Jarrow, 19 May, 1924						(FB)
Bradford PA	Darlington (Am)	05.45	47	1	-	0
Hartlepools U	Tr	11.48	48	2	-	0
LEONARD Keith Andrew						
Birmingham, 10 November, 1950						(F)
Aston Villa	Highgate U	04.72	72-75	36	2	11
Port Vale	L	11.73	73	12	1	1
LEONARD Mark Anthony						
St Helens, 27 September, 1962 ESch						(F)
Everton	Witton A	02.82				
Tranmere Rov	L	03.83	82	6	1	0
Crewe Alex	Tr	06.83	83-84	51	3	15
Stockport Co	Tr	02.85	84-86	73	0	23
Bradford C	Tr	09.86	86-91	120	37	29
Rochdale	Tr	03.92	91	9	0	1
Preston NE	Tr	08.92	92	19	3	1
Chester C	Tr	08.93	93	28	4	8
Wigan Ath	Tr	09.94	94-95	60	4	12
Rochdale	Tr	07.96	96-98	74	6	6
LEONARD Michael (Mick) Christopher						
Carshalton, 9 May, 1959						(G)
Halifax T	Epsom & Ewell	07.76	76-79	69	0	0
Notts Co	Tr	09.79	79-88	204	0	0
Chesterfield	Tr	03.89	88-93	175	1	0
Halifax T	L	11.90	90	3	0	0
LEONARD Patrick (Paddy) Desmond						
Dublin, 25 July, 1929						(IF)
Bristol Rov	Bath C	07.52	52-53	14	-	2
Colchester U	Tr	07.54	54	34	-	5
LEONARD Stanley (Stan)						
Hawarden, 8 October, 1924 Died 1995						(W)
Chester (Am)		01.47	46	1	-	0

League Club	Source	Date Signed	Seasons Played	Career Record Apps	Subs	Gls
LEONHARDSEN Oyvind						
Kristiansund, Norway, 17 August, 1970 NoYth/Nou21-14/No-86						(M)
Wimbledon	Rosenborg (Nor)	11.94	94-96	73	3	13
Liverpool	Tr	06.97	97-98	34	3	7
Tottenham H	Tr	08.99	99-01	46	8	7
Aston Villa	Tr	08.02	02	13	6	3
LEONI Stephane						
Metz, France, 1 September, 1976 Fru21						(FB)
Bristol Rov	Metz (Fr)	08.98	98-99	27	11	0
LE PEN Ulrich						
Auray, France, 21 January, 1974 Fru21						(M)
Ipswich T	Lorient (Fr)	11.01	01	0	1	0
LE ROUX Daniel Leow						
Port Shepstone, South Africa, 25 November, 1933 SAAmat						(W)
Arsenal	Queen's Park (SA)	02.57	57	5	-	0
LE SAUX Graeme Pierre						
Jersey, 17 October, 1968 Eu21-4/EB-2/E-36						(FB)
Chelsea	St Paul's (Jersey)	12.87	88-92	77	13	8
Blackburn Rov	Tr	03.93	92-96	127	2	7
Chelsea	Tr	08.97	97-02	133	7	4
Southampton	Tr	07.03	03-04	43	1	1
LESCOTT Aaron Anthony						
Birmingham, 2 December, 1978 ESch						(M)
Aston Villa	YT	07.96				
Lincoln C	L	03.00	99	3	2	0
Sheffield Wed	Tr	10.00	00-01	19	18	0
Stockport Co	Tr	11.01	01-03	65	7	1
Bristol Rov	Tr	03.04	03-04	32	2	0
LESCOTT Jolean Patrick						
Birmingham, 16 August, 1982 EYth/Eu20/Eu21-2						(CD)
Wolverhampton W	YT	08.99	00-04	160	6	12
LESLIE John Alexander						
Plumstead, 25 October, 1955						(F)
Wimbledon	Dulwich Hamlet	12.75	77-82	242	11	86
Gillingham	Tr	08.83	83-84	60	5	12
Millwall	Tr	08.85	85-86	12	8	2
LESLIE Lawrence (Lawrie) Grant						
Edinburgh, 17 March, 1935 SLge-3/S-5						(G)
West Ham U	Airdrie	06.61	61-62	57	-	0
Stoke C	Tr	10.63	63-65	78	0	0
Millwall	Tr	07.66	66-67	67	0	0
Southend U	Tr	07.68	68	13	0	0
LESLIE Maurice Harrington						
India, 19 August, 1923						(FB)
Swindon T		06.47	46	1	-	0
LESLIE Steven						
Dumfries, 6 February, 1976						(M)
Stoke C	Jnrs	03.93	94	0	1	0
LESLIE Steven (Steve) Robert William						
Hornsey, 4 September, 1952 EYth						(M)
Colchester U	Jnrs	05.71	70-83	411	21	40
LESSLIE Kenneth (Ken) Gordon						
West Ham, 4 January, 1923 Died 1991						(W)
Ipswich T		08.47				
Watford	Tr	07.48	48	7	-	1
LESTER Abraham **Bennett (Benny)**						
Sheffield, 10 February, 1920 Died 1958						(CF)
Hull C	Selby T	09.46	46-47	27	-	17
Lincoln C	Tr	01.48	47-48	37	-	10
Stockport Co	Ransome & Marles	08.49	49	8	-	2
LESTER Jack William						
Sheffield, 8 October, 1975 ESch						(F)
Grimsby T	Jnrs	07.94	94-99	93	40	17
Doncaster Rov	L	09.96	96	5	6	1
Nottingham F	Tr	01.00	99-02	73	26	21
Sheffield U	Tr	08.03	03-04	26	18	12
Nottingham F	Tr	11.04	04	3	0	1
LESTER Leslie (Danny) James						
Cardiff, 17 November, 1923 Died 1991						(WH)
Cardiff C	Cardiff Corinthians	04.44				
Torquay U	Tr	08.48	48-49	31	-	1
Newport Co	Tr	09.50	50	2	-	0
LESTER Michael (Mike) John Anthony						
Manchester, 4 August, 1954						(M)
Oldham Ath	App	08.72	72-73	26	1	2
Manchester C	Tr	11.73	73-76	1	1	0

League Club	Source	Date Signed	Seasons Played	Career Record Apps	Subs	Gls
Stockport Co	L	08.75	75	8	1	1
Grimsby T	Washington (USA)	11.77	77-79	45	3	10
Barnsley	Tr	10.79	79-80	64	0	11
Exeter C	Tr	08.81	81	18	1	6
Bradford C	Tr	02.82	81-82	46	3	2
Scunthorpe U	Tr	03.83	82-85	106	0	9
Hartlepool U	L	01.86	85	11	0	1
Stockport Co	Tr	09.86	86	11	0	0
Blackpool	Ludvik FK (Sweden)	12.87	87	11	0	1
LE TALLEC Anthony						
Hennebont, France, 3 October, 1984 FrYth/Fru21						(M)
Liverpool	Le Havre (Fr)	07.03	03-04	5	12	0
LETHERAN Glanville (Glan)						
Llanelli, 1 May, 1956 Wu23-1/Wu21-2						(G)
Leeds U	App	05.73	74	1	0	0
Scunthorpe U	L	08.76	76	27	0	0
Chesterfield	Tr	12.77	77-79	63	0	0
Swansea C	Tr	09.79	79	21	0	0
LE TISSIER Matthew Paul						
Guernsey, 14 October, 1968 EYth/EB-6/E-8						(F)
Southampton	App	10.86	86-01	377	66	161
LEUTY Leon Harry						
Meole Brace, 23 October, 1920 Died 1955 FLge-2/EB						(CD)
Derby Co	Rolls Royce	05.44	46-49	131	-	1
Bradford PA	Tr	03.50	49-50	19	-	0
Notts Co	Tr	09.50	50-55	188	-	3
LEVER Arthur Richard						
Cardiff, 25 March, 1920 Died 2004 W-1						(FB)
Cardiff C	Cardiff Corinthians	08.43	46-50	155	-	9
Leicester C	Tr	09.50	50-53	119	-	0
Newport Co	Tr	07.54	54-56	72	-	0
LEVER Mark						
Beverley, 29 March, 1970						(CD)
Grimsby T	YT	08.88	87-99	343	18	8
Bristol C	Tr	07.00	00-01	28	3	1
Mansfield T	Tr	08.02	02	15	0	0
LEVERTON Roland (Tot)						
Whitwell, 8 May, 1926 Died 2003						(IF)
Nottingham F	Jnrs	10.43	46-53	103	-	36
Notts Co	Tr	10.53	53-55	45	-	5
Walsall	Tr	07.56	56	17	-	3
LEVY Anthony (Tony) Samuel						
Edmonton, 20 October, 1959						(M)
Plymouth Arg	App	10.77	78	0	1	0
Torquay U	Tr	07.79	79	8	5	1
LEVY Leonard (Len)						
Stepney, 24 December, 1926 Died 2001						(G)
Aldershot	Guildford C	10.50	50	2	-	0
LEWIN Derek James						
Manchester, 18 May, 1930 EAmat						(IF)
Oldham Ath (Am)	St Annes Ath	08.53	53-54	10	-	1
Accrington St (Am)	Bishop Auckland	10.57	57	1	-	0
LEWIN Dennis **Ronald (Ron)**						
Edmonton, 21 June, 1920 Died 1985						(FB)
Bradford C	Enfield	09.43				
Fulham	Tr	06.46	46-48	41	-	0
Gillingham	Tr	06.50	50-54	191	-	1
LEWINGTON Dean Scott						
Kingston, 18 May, 1984						(M)
Wimbledon/MK Dons	Sch	07.03	02-04	71	1	3
LEWINGTON Raymond (Ray)						
Lambeth, 7 September, 1956						(M)
Chelsea	App	02.74	75-78	80	5	4
Wimbledon	Vancouver (Can)	09.79	79	23	0	0
Fulham	Tr	03.80	79-84	172	2	20
Sheffield U	Tr	07.85	85	36	0	0
Fulham	Tr	07.86	86-89	58	2	1
LEWIS Alan Trevor						
Oxford, 19 August, 1954 EYth						(FB)
Derby Co	App	05.72	72	2	0	0
Peterborough U	L	03.74	73	10	0	1
Brighton & Hove A	Tr	01.75	74	3	0	0
Reading	Tr	07.77	77-81	145	4	5
LEWIS Allan						
Pontypridd, 31 May, 1971						(CD)
Cardiff C	YT	07.89	89-91	27	23	0

LEWIS Benjamin (Ben)
Chelmsford, 22 June, 1977 (CD)

League Club	Source	Date Signed	Seasons Played	Apps	Subs	Gls
Colchester U	YT	03.96	95	1	1	0
Southend U	Tr	08.97	97	14	0	1

LEWIS Bernard (Bernie)
Aberfan, 12 March, 1945 Wu23-5 (W)

League Club	Source	Date Signed	Seasons Played	Apps	Subs	Gls
Cardiff C	Jnrs	04.64	63-67	87	1	7
Watford	Tr	12.67	67-69	41	10	9
Southend U	Tr	09.70	70-71	55	3	6

LEWIS Brian
Woking, 26 January, 1943 Died 1998 (M)

League Club	Source	Date Signed	Seasons Played	Apps	Subs	Gls
Crystal Palace	Jnrs	04.60	60-62	32	-	4
Portsmouth	Tr	07.63	63-66	134	0	24
Coventry C	Tr	01.67	66-67	33	2	2
Luton T	Tr	07.68	68-69	45	5	22
Oxford U	Tr	01.70	69-70	12	2	4
Colchester U	Tr	12.70	70-71	46	0	17
Portsmouth	Tr	04.72	71-74	44	16	8

LEWIS Charles Reginald
Liverpool, 11 May, 1921 Died 1999 (W)

League Club	Source	Date Signed	Seasons Played	Apps	Subs	Gls
Halifax T	South Liverpool	10.47	47-48	24	-	4

LEWIS Daniel
Redditch, 18 June, 1982 (G)

League Club	Source	Date Signed	Seasons Played	Apps	Subs	Gls
Kidderminster Hrs	Studley	07.04	04	1	0	0

LEWIS David Sandbrook
Cardigan, 12 February, 1936 (IF)

League Club	Source	Date Signed	Seasons Played	Apps	Subs	Gls
Swansea T		12.57	57-58	19	-	1
Torquay U	Tr	07.60	60	16	-	2

LEWIS Dennis George
Treherbert, 21 April, 1925 Died 1996 (WH)

League Club	Source	Date Signed	Seasons Played	Apps	Subs	Gls
Swansea T		08.46				
Torquay U	Tr	08.47	47-58	442	-	31

LEWIS Derek Ivor Edwin
Edmonton, 10 June, 1929 Died 1953 (IF)

League Club	Source	Date Signed	Seasons Played	Apps	Subs	Gls
Gillingham	Bury T	05.50	50-51	48	-	31
Preston NE	Tr	02.52	51-52	37	-	14

LEWIS Dudley Keith
Swansea, 17 November, 1962 WSch/Wu21-9/W-1 (CD)

League Club	Source	Date Signed	Seasons Played	Apps	Subs	Gls
Swansea C	App	11.79	80-88	228	2	2
Huddersfield T	Tr	07.89	89-90	32	2	0
Halifax T	L	10.91	91	11	0	0
Wrexham	Tr	03.92	91	8	1	0
Halifax T	Tr	08.92	92	10	3	0
Torquay U	Tr	12.92	92	9	0	0

LEWIS Edward (Eddie)
West Bromwich, 21 June, 1926 (G)

League Club	Source	Date Signed	Seasons Played	Apps	Subs	Gls
West Bromwich A	Jnrs	11.44				
Leyton Orient	Tr	03.46	46	5	-	0

LEWIS Edward (Eddie)
Manchester, 3 January, 1935 (FB)

League Club	Source	Date Signed	Seasons Played	Apps	Subs	Gls
Manchester U	Jnrs	01.52	52-55	20	-	9
Preston NE	Tr	12.55	55-56	12	-	2
West Ham U	Tr	11.56	56-57	31	-	12
Leyton Orient	Tr	06.58	58-63	143	-	5

LEWIS Edward (Eddie) James
Cerritos, USA, 17 May, 1974 USA 64 (M)

League Club	Source	Date Signed	Seasons Played	Apps	Subs	Gls
Fulham	San Jose (USA)	03.00	99-01	8	8	0
Preston NE	Tr	09.02	02-04	97	14	15

LEWIS Frederick (Fred) Arthur
Broughton Gifford, 26 July, 1923 Died 1975 (FB)

League Club	Source	Date Signed	Seasons Played	Apps	Subs	Gls
Chelsea	Aylesbury T	03.46	46-52	23	-	0
Colchester U	Tr	07.53	53-54	85	-	0

LEWIS Thomas **George**
Troedyrhiwfuwch, 20 October, 1913 Died 1981 (CF)

League Club	Source	Date Signed	Seasons Played	Apps	Subs	Gls
Watford	New Tredegar	05.34	36-38	25	-	11
Southampton	Tr	07.46	46-47	43	-	12
Brighton & Hove A	Tr	06.48	48	24	-	8

LEWIS Glyndwr (Glyn)
Abertillery, 3 July, 1921 Died 1992 (W)

League Club	Source	Date Signed	Seasons Played	Apps	Subs	Gls
Crystal Palace		05.42	46-47	60	-	4
Bristol C	Tr	07.48	48	18	-	0

LEWIS Graham
Reading, 15 February, 1982 (F)

League Club	Source	Date Signed	Seasons Played	Apps	Subs	Gls
Lincoln C	YT	07.00	99-00	3	4	0

LEWIS Gwynfor (Gwyn)
Bangor, 22 April, 1931 Died 1995 WYth (CF)

League Club	Source	Date Signed	Seasons Played	Apps	Subs	Gls
Everton	Jnrs	05.48	51-55	10	-	6
Rochdale	Tr	06.56	56	27	-	11
Chesterfield	Tr	02.57	56-60	123	-	58

LEWIS Idris
Tonypandy, 26 August, 1915 Died 1996 (W)

League Club	Source	Date Signed	Seasons Played	Apps	Subs	Gls
Swansea T	Gelli Colliery	05.35	35-37	66	-	4
Sheffield Wed	Tr	08.38	38	18	-	7
Swansea T	Tr	03.39				
Bristol Rov	Tr	07.46	46	13	-	2
Newport Co	Tr	10.46	46-47	27	-	4

LEWIS James (Jim) Leonard
Hackney, 26 June, 1927 EAmat (W)

League Club	Source	Date Signed	Seasons Played	Apps	Subs	Gls
Leyton Orient (Am)	Walthamstow Ave	11.50	50	4	-	0
Chelsea (Am)	Walthamstow Ave	09.52	52-57	90	-	38

LEWIS John (Jack)
Walsall, 26 August, 1919 Died 2002 (WH)

League Club	Source	Date Signed	Seasons Played	Apps	Subs	Gls
Crystal Palace	West Bromwich A (Am)	07.38	38-49	124	-	5
Bournemouth	Tr	11.49	49-50	45	-	1
Reading	Tr	07.51	51-52	74	-	17

LEWIS John (Jack)
Tamworth, 1 May, 1920 Died 1988 (G)

League Club	Source	Date Signed	Seasons Played	Apps	Subs	Gls
Walsall	Boldmere St Michael's	12.45	46-52	271	-	0

LEWIS John (Jack)
Walsall, 6 October, 1923 (WH)

League Club	Source	Date Signed	Seasons Played	Apps	Subs	Gls
West Bromwich A	Jnrs	10.45				
Mansfield T	Tr	08.48	48-52	163	-	11

LEWIS John
Tredegar, 15 October, 1955 Wu21-1 (M)

League Club	Source	Date Signed	Seasons Played	Apps	Subs	Gls
Cardiff C	Pontllanfraith	08.78	78-83	135	5	9
Newport Co	Tr	09.83	83-87	153	0	8
Swansea C	Tr	10.87	87	25	0	0

LEWIS Frederick **John (Jack)**
Long Eaton, 22 March, 1948 Wu23-1 (F)

League Club	Source	Date Signed	Seasons Played	Apps	Subs	Gls
Lincoln C	Long Eaton U	03.67	66-69	47	15	9
Grimsby T	Tr	01.70	69-76	231	27	74
Blackburn Rov	Tr	08.77	77	24	4	6
Doncaster Rov	Tr	08.78	78-79	48	16	10

LEWIS John George
Hackney, 9 May, 1954 EYth (M)

League Club	Source	Date Signed	Seasons Played	Apps	Subs	Gls
Orient	Tottenham H (Am)	07.72	72	0	2	0

LEWIS Karl **Junior**
Wembley, 9 October, 1973 (M)

League Club	Source	Date Signed	Seasons Played	Apps	Subs	Gls
Fulham	YT	07.92	92	4	2	0
Gillingham	Hendon	08.99	99-00	47	12	8
Leicester C	Tr	01.01	00-02	24	6	1
Brighton & Hove A	L	02.02	01	14	1	3
Swindon T	L	03.03	02	9	0	0
Swindon T	L	10.03	03	4	0	0
Hull C	Tr	02.04	03-04	44	8	3

LEWIS Kenneth (Ken)
Cardiff, 7 November, 1924 Died 1978 (FB)

League Club	Source	Date Signed	Seasons Played	Apps	Subs	Gls
Torquay U		01.50	50-52	27	-	0

LEWIS Kenneth (Kenny)
Bangor, 12 October, 1929 Died 1990 (IF)

League Club	Source	Date Signed	Seasons Played	Apps	Subs	Gls
Walsall	Bangor C	03.54	53-54	19	-	1
Scunthorpe U	Worcester C	08.56	56	1	-	0

LEWIS Kevin
Ellesmere Port, 19 September, 1940 EYth (W)

League Club	Source	Date Signed	Seasons Played	Apps	Subs	Gls
Sheffield U	Jnrs	10.57	57-59	62	-	23
Liverpool	Tr	06.60	60-62	71	-	39
Huddersfield T	Tr	08.63	63-64	45	-	13

LEWIS Kevin
Hull, 17 October, 1970 (FB)

League Club	Source	Date Signed	Seasons Played	Apps	Subs	Gls
Stoke C	YT	●	87	0	1	0

LEWIS Kevin William
Hull, 25 September, 1952 ESch (FB)

League Club	Source	Date Signed	Seasons Played	Apps	Subs	Gls
Manchester U	App	09.69				
Stoke C	Tr	07.72	72-75	15	0	0
Crewe Alex	Tr	06.79	79-81	117	5	2

LEWIS Matthew (Matt) Thomas
Coventry, 20 March, 1984 (F)

League Club	Source	Date Signed	Seasons Played	Apps	Subs	Gls
Kidderminster Hrs	Marconi (Coventry)	07.01	01-03	1	7	0

League Club	Source	Date Signed	Seasons Played	Career Record Apps	Subs	Gls
LEWIS Michael (Mickey)						
Birmingham, 15 February, 1965 EYth						(M)
West Bromwich A	App	02.82	81-84	22	2	0
Derby Co	Tr	11.84	84-87	37	6	1
Oxford U	Tr	08.88	88-99	279	26	7
LEWIS Morgan Rees						
Bournemouth, 8 September, 1965						(M)
Bournemouth	Jnrs	07.84	83-86	11	1	0
LEWIS Neil Anthony						
Wolverhampton, 28 June, 1974						(FB)
Leicester C	YT	07.92	92-96	53	14	1
Peterborough U	Tr	06.97	97	31	3	0
LEWIS Norman						
Snedshill, 28 May, 1927						(FB)
Shrewsbury T	Oakengates T	08.50	50-52	62	-	0
Newport Co	Gravesend & Northfleet	06.54	54	15	-	0
LEWIS Paul Samuel						
Ystrad Rhondda, 27 September, 1956 WYth						(G)
Bristol Rov	App	10.74	75	1	0	0
LEWIS Reginald (Reg)						
Bilston, 7 March, 1920 Died 1997 EB						(CF)
Arsenal	Dulwich Hamlet	03.37	37-51	154	-	103
LEWIS Roland						
Sandbach, 21 September, 1925 Died 1999						(CF)
Port Vale	Congleton T	03.50	50-53	7	-	0
LEWIS Ronald (Ron)						
Belfast, 10 February, 1932						(IF)
Burnley	Glentoran	06.49				
Barrow	Weymouth	05.54	54	5	-	1
LEWIS Russell						
Blaengwynfi, 15 September, 1956						(CD)
Swindon T	Everwarm (Bridgend)	10.76	76-82	175	6	7
Northampton T	Tr	08.83	83-85	131	1	6
LEWIS Terence (Terry) John						
Newport, 22 October, 1950 WSch						(CD)
Cardiff C	App	10.68	68-69	3	0	0
LEWIS Trevor						
Blackwood, Monmouthshire, 6 January, 1921						(W)
Coventry C	Redditch T	02.48	47-52	11	-	0
Gillingham	Tr	02.53	52-54	26	-	2
LEWIS William (Billy)						
Cardiff, 4 July, 1923						(IF)
Cardiff C	Jnrs	07.41	46-47	10	-	0
Newport Co	Tr	10.47	47-49	49	-	11
LEWIS William (Bill) Albert						
Silvertown, 23 November, 1921 Died 1998 ESch						(FB)
Blackpool	West Ham U (Am)	07.45	46-49	31	-	0
Norwich C	Tr	11.49	49-55	232	-	1
LEWORTHY David (Dave) John						
Portsmouth, 22 October, 1962						(F)
Portsmouth	App	09.80	81	0	1	0
Tottenham H	Fareham T	08.84	84-85	8	3	3
Oxford U	Tr	12.85	85-88	25	12	8
Shrewsbury T	L	10.87	87	6	0	3
Reading	Tr	07.89	89-91	23	21	7
LEY Oliver Albert **George**						
Exminster, 7 April, 1946						(FB)
Exeter C	Hitchin T	09.63	63-66	93	0	7
Portsmouth	Tr	05.67	66-72	183	1	10
Brighton & Hove A	Tr	09.72	72-73	47	0	0
Gillingham	Dallas (USA)	08.74	74-75	87	0	3
LEYDEN Darren Spencer						
Warley, 20 February, 1970						(CD)
Torquay U	YT	07.88	88	7	2	0
LEYFIELD John (Jack) George						
Handbridge, 5 August, 1923						(WH)
Wrexham	Chester (Am)	07.46	46-49	34	-	1
Southport	Tr	08.50	50	26	-	0
LEYLAND Harry Kenneth						
Liverpool, 12 May, 1930						(G)
Everton	Jnrs	08.50	51-55	36	-	0
Blackburn Rov	Tonbridge	08.56	56-60	166	-	0
Tranmere Rov	Tr	03.61	60-65	180	0	0

League Club	Source	Date Signed	Seasons Played	Career Record Apps	Subs	Gls
L'HELGOUALCH Cyrille						
St Nazaire, France, 25 September, 1970						(CD)
Walsall	Angers (Fr)	11.98				
Mansfield T	Tr	12.98	98	3	1	1
LIBBRA Marc						
Toulon, France, 5 August, 1972						(F)
Norwich C	Toulouse (Fr)	08.01	01	17	17	7
LIBURD Richard John						
Nottingham, 26 September, 1973						(FB)
Middlesbrough	Eastwood T	03.93	93	41	0	1
Bradford C	Tr	07.94	94-96	75	3	3
Carlisle U	Tr	02.98	97	9	0	0
Notts Co	Tr	08.98	98-02	127	27	9
Lincoln C	Tr	08.03	03	19	5	0
LIDDELL Andrew (Andy) Mark						
Leeds, 28 June, 1973 Su21-12						(F)
Barnsley	YT	07.91	91-98	142	56	34
Wigan Ath	Tr	10.98	98-03	206	11	70
Sheffield U	Tr	07.04	04	26	7	3
LIDDELL Gary						
Bannockburn, 27 August, 1954						(F)
Leeds U	App	09.71	72-74	2	1	0
Grimsby T	Tr	03.77	76-80	90	15	22
Doncaster Rov	Heart of Midlothian	03.82	81-82	25	12	4
LIDDELL John Cairney						
Stirling, 13 December, 1933 Died 1999						(CF)
Oldham Ath	St Johnstone	09.60	60-61	23	-	10
LIDDELL John Gilbert Hay						
Edinburgh, 17 April, 1915 Died 1986						(IF)
Clapton Orient		03.44				
Bolton W	Tr	09.46				
Brighton & Hove A	Tr	03.47	46	4	-	1
LIDDELL William (Billy) Beveridge						
Townhill, 10 January, 1922 Died 2001 SWar-8/S-28						(W)
Liverpool	Lochgelly Violet	04.39	46-60	494	-	216
LIDDLE Bryan						
Durham, 23 June, 1961						(FB)
Hartlepool U	Brandon U	08.84	84	12	1	0
LIDDLE Craig George						
Chester-le-Street, 21 October, 1971						(CD)
Aston Villa	YT	07.90				
Middlesbrough	Blyth Spartans	07.94	94-97	20	5	0
Darlington	Tr	02.98	97-04	284	1	17
LIDDLE Daniel (Danny) Hamilton Sneddon						
Bo'ness, 19 February, 1912 Died 1982 S-3						(W)
Leicester C	East Fife	05.32	32-38	255	-	64
Mansfield T	Tr	07.46	46	1	-	0
LIDDLE David						
Malta, 21 May, 1957						(M)
Northampton T	App	05.75	77-78	28	3	3
LIDDLE Gavin						
Houghton-le-Spring, 9 May, 1963						(FB)
Darlington	Hartlepool U (App)	08.81	81-82	33	4	0
LIDDLE Kenneth (Ken)						
Gateshead, 6 October, 1928 Died 1998						(IF)
Sunderland		12.49				
Darlington	Tr	06.50	50	1	-	0
LIDDLE Thomas (Tom) Blenkarn						
Middleton, 22 April, 1921 Died 1994						(FB)
Bournemouth	Hartlepools U (Am)	02.47	47	1	-	0
LIEVESLEY Dennis						
Chesterfield, 19 September, 1919 Died 1997						(CD)
Aldershot		08.46	46-48	8	-	0
LIGGITT Norman						
Thornaby, 21 July, 1941						(CD)
Middlesbrough	Jnrs	08.59				
Southend U	Tr	07.62	62	1	-	0
LIGHT Daniel (Danny)						
Chiswick, 10 July, 1948						(F)
Crystal Palace	App	12.65	66-67	18	1	5
Colchester U	Tr	08.68	68-69	65	2	14
LIGHT James (Jimmy) Power						
Oxford, 13 January, 1954						(FB)
Oxford U	App	01.72	72-75	64	0	1

LIGHTBOURNE Kyle Lavince
Bermuda, 29 September, 1968 BermudaYth/Bermuda-22 (F)

League Club	Source	Date Signed	Seasons Played	Apps	Subs	Gls
Scarborough	Pembroke Ham (Ber)	12.92	92	11	8	3
Walsall	Tr	09.93	93-96	158	7	65
Coventry C	Tr	07.97	97	1	6	0
Fulham	L	01.98	97	4	0	2
Stoke C	Tr	02.98	97-00	83	28	21
Swindon T	L	01.01	00	2	0	0
Cardiff C	L	02.01	00	2	1	0
Macclesfield T	Tr	07.01	01-02	61	12	14
Hull C	L	03.02	01	3	1	0

LIGHTBOWN Trevor
Blackburn, 21 November, 1939 (W)

League Club	Source	Date Signed	Seasons Played	Apps	Subs	Gls
Accrington St (Am)	Burnley (Am)	08.59	59	8	-	0
Bradford PA (Am)	Tr	08.60	60	2	-	0

LIGHTENING Arthur Douglas
Durban, South Africa, 1 August, 1936 Died 2001 (G)

League Club	Source	Date Signed	Seasons Played	Apps	Subs	Gls
Nottingham F	Queen's Park (SA)	12.56	57-58	6	-	0
Coventry C	Tr	11.58	58-62	150	-	0
Middlesbrough	Tr	08.62	62	15	-	0

LIGHTFOOT Christopher (Chris) Ian
Penketh, 1 April, 1970 (CD)

League Club	Source	Date Signed	Seasons Played	Apps	Subs	Gls
Chester C	YT	07.88	87-94	263	14	32
Wigan Ath	Tr	07.95	95	11	3	1
Crewe Alex	Tr	03.96	95-99	63	24	4
Oldham Ath	L	09.00	00	3	0	0

LIGHTLY Brian Sydney
Portsmouth, 12 May, 1936 (WH)

League Club	Source	Date Signed	Seasons Played	Apps	Subs	Gls
Exeter C	Portsmouth (Am)	06.57	57	4	-	0

LIGHTOWLER Gerard (Gerry)
Bradford, 5 September, 1940 (FB)

League Club	Source	Date Signed	Seasons Played	Apps	Subs	Gls
Bradford PA	St Bede's	12.58	58-67	207	2	1
Bradford C	Los Angeles (USA)	10.68	68	11	0	0

LILEY Henry (Harry) John Gerald
Trowbridge, 19 August, 1918 Died 2001 (G)

League Club	Source	Date Signed	Seasons Played	Apps	Subs	Gls
Bristol Rov	Dockland Settlement	10.46	46-49	27	-	0

LILL David Arthur
Aldbrough, 17 February, 1947 (M)

League Club	Source	Date Signed	Seasons Played	Apps	Subs	Gls
Hull C	Jnrs	03.65	66-69	16	2	2
Rotherham U	Tr	10.69	69-70	33	5	6
Cambridge U	Tr	07.71	71-75	166	6	22

LILL James Alfred
Barnsley, 4 June, 1933 (W)

League Club	Source	Date Signed	Seasons Played	Apps	Subs	Gls
Mansfield T	Wentworth	03.54	53-55	3	-	0

LILL Michael (Mickey) James
Barking, 3 August, 1936 Died 2004 EYth (W)

League Club	Source	Date Signed	Seasons Played	Apps	Subs	Gls
Wolverhampton W	Storey Ath	06.54	57-59	30	-	15
Everton	Tr	02.60	59-61	31	-	11
Plymouth Arg	Tr	06.62	62	21	-	7
Portsmouth	Tr	03.63	62-64	39	-	5

LILLEY Derek Symon
Paisley, 9 February, 1974 SYth (F)

League Club	Source	Date Signed	Seasons Played	Apps	Subs	Gls
Leeds U	Morton	03.97	96-98	4	17	1
Bury	L	03.99	98	5	0	1
Oxford U	Tr	08.99	99-00	51	12	9

LILLIS Jason Warren
Chatham, 1 October, 1969 (F)

League Club	Source	Date Signed	Seasons Played	Apps	Subs	Gls
Gillingham	YT	10.87	87-88	15	14	3
Maidstone U	Jaro (Fin)	07.89	89-91	57	18	18
Carlisle U	L	02.91	90	4	0	1
Walsall	Sittingbourne	10.93	93-94	14	11	6
Cambridge U	Dover Ath	09.94	94	14	5	4

LILLIS Mark Anthony
Manchester, 17 January, 1960 (F)

League Club	Source	Date Signed	Seasons Played	Apps	Subs	Gls
Huddersfield T	Manchester C (Jnrs)	07.78	78-84	199	7	56
Manchester C	Tr	06.85	85	39	0	11
Derby Co	Tr	08.86	86-87	6	9	1
Aston Villa	Tr	09.87	87-88	30	1	4
Scunthorpe U	Tr	09.89	89-90	62	6	23
Stockport Co	Tr	09.91	91	9	2	2

LILWALL Stephen (Steve)
Solihull, 5 February, 1970 (FB)

League Club	Source	Date Signed	Seasons Played	Apps	Subs	Gls
West Bromwich A	Kidderminster Hrs	06.92	92-94	71	2	0

LILYGREEN Christopher (Chris) Laurence
Bettws, 9 June, 1965 (F)

League Club	Source	Date Signed	Seasons Played	Apps	Subs	Gls
Newport Co	Newport YMCA	08.83	83-84	18	13	4

LIM Harvey Choun
Halesworth, 30 August, 1967 (G)

League Club	Source	Date Signed	Seasons Played	Apps	Subs	Gls
Norwich C	App	07.85				
Gillingham	Ornskoldsvik (Swe)	11.89	89-92	90	0	0

LIMBER Nicholas (Nick)
Doncaster, 23 January, 1974 (FB)

League Club	Source	Date Signed	Seasons Played	Apps	Subs	Gls
Doncaster Rov	YT	01.92	90-91	13	0	1
Manchester C	Tr	01.92				
Peterborough U	L	10.92	92	2	0	0
Doncaster Rov	Tr	03.94	93	3	1	0

LIMBERT Marc
Hawarden, 3 October, 1973 (FB)

League Club	Source	Date Signed	Seasons Played	Apps	Subs	Gls
Chester C	YT	07.92	92	12	2	0

LIMPAR Anders Erik
Solna, Sweden, 24 September, 1965 Sweden int (W)

League Club	Source	Date Signed	Seasons Played	Apps	Subs	Gls
Arsenal	Cremonese (It)	08.90	90-93	76	20	17
Everton	Tr	03.94	93-96	51	15	5
Birmingham C	Tr	01.97	96	3	1	0

LINACRE John Edward
Middlesbrough, 13 December, 1955 (M)

League Club	Source	Date Signed	Seasons Played	Apps	Subs	Gls
Hartlepool U	Whitby T	07.77	77-81	192	4	12
Hartlepool U	Hamrun (Malta)	12.83	83	15	0	0

LINACRE Philip (Phil)
Middlesbrough, 17 May, 1962 (F)

League Club	Source	Date Signed	Seasons Played	Apps	Subs	Gls
Hartlepool U	Coventry C (App)	08.80	80-82	59	4	10
Hartlepool U	Whitby T	01.84	83	19	0	7
Darlington	Blue Star	03.90	90	6	2	3

LINACRE William (Billy)
Chesterfield, 10 August, 1924 (W)

League Club	Source	Date Signed	Seasons Played	Apps	Subs	Gls
Chesterfield	Jnrs	02.44	46-47	22	-	3
Manchester C	Tr	10.47	47-49	75	-	6
Middlesbrough	Tr	09.49	49-51	31	-	2
Hartlepools U	Goole T	08.53	53-55	89	-	10
Mansfield T	Tr	10.55	55	13	-	0

LINAKER John (Johnny) Edward
Southport, 14 January, 1927 (W)

League Club	Source	Date Signed	Seasons Played	Apps	Subs	Gls
Manchester C	Everton (Am)	08.45				
Southport	Tr	11.46	46	15	-	1
Nottingham F	Tr	09.47	48-49	15	-	2
York C	Tr	06.50	50-51	59	-	16
Hull C	Tr	10.51	51-52	26	-	3
York C	Tr	05.53	53-55	39	-	4
Crewe Alex	Scarborough	07.57	57	34	-	3

LINCOLN Greg Dean
Cheshunt, 23 March, 1980 EYth (M)

League Club	Source	Date Signed	Seasons Played	Apps	Subs	Gls
Arsenal	YT	07.98				
Northampton T	Hammarby IF (Swe)	07.02	02-03	9	10	1

LINDEGAARD Andrew (Andy) Rindom
Taunton, 10 September, 1980 (W)

League Club	Source	Date Signed	Seasons Played	Apps	Subs	Gls
Yeovil T	Westlands Sports	06.00	03-04	31	21	3

LINDEROTH Tobias
Marseille, France, 21 April, 1979 Swu21-22/Sw-39 (M)

League Club	Source	Date Signed	Seasons Played	Apps	Subs	Gls
Everton	Stabaek (Nor)	02.02	01-03	29	11	0

LINDLEY Edwin
Epworth, 22 April, 1931 Died 1951 (IF)

League Club	Source	Date Signed	Seasons Played	Apps	Subs	Gls
Nottingham F	Scunthorpe & Lindsey U	10.49	49	1	-	0

LINDLEY James (Jim) Edward
Sutton-in-Ashfield, 23 July, 1981 (G)

League Club	Source	Date Signed	Seasons Played	Apps	Subs	Gls
Notts Co	YT	07.99	99-00	2	1	0

LINDLEY William Maurice
Keighley, 5 December, 1915 Died 1994 (WH)

League Club	Source	Date Signed	Seasons Played	Apps	Subs	Gls
Everton	Keighley T	03.36	47-51	51	-	0

LINDORES William (Billy) Robert Hope
Newcastleton, 3 May, 1933 SSch (FB)

League Club	Source	Date Signed	Seasons Played	Apps	Subs	Gls
Barrow	Heart of Midlothian	07.59	59	4	-	0

LINDSAY Alec
Bury, 27 February, 1948 EYth/E-4 (FB)

League Club	Source	Date Signed	Seasons Played	Apps	Subs	Gls
Bury	App	03.65	64-68	127	0	13
Liverpool	Tr	03.69	69-76	168	2	12
Stoke C	Tr	08.77	77	20	0	3

LINDSAY David (Dave)
Dumbarton, 23 September, 1919 Died 1992 (FB)

League Club	Source	Date Signed	Seasons Played	Apps	Subs	Gls
Luton T	St Mirren	05.48	48	7	-	0
Barnsley	Tr	11.48	48-51	78	-	3

League Club	Source	Date Signed	Seasons Played	Career Record Apps	Subs	Gls
LINDSAY David						
Cambuslang, 29 June, 1922						(FB)
Sunderland	Blantyre Victoria	08.46	46	1	-	0
Southend U	Tr	05.48	48-50	52	-	1
LINDSAY David James						
Romford, 17 May, 1966						(FB)
Crystal Palace	App	05.84	83-85	18	3	0
LINDSAY Hugh Murray						
Ickenham, 23 August, 1938 EAmat						(IF)
Southampton (Am)	Kingstonian	07.60	60	2	-	0
LINDSAY Ian						
Canonbie, 10 February, 1944						(G)
Workington	Hearts of Liddlesdale	11.64	64	9	-	0
LINDSAY James (Jimmy) Young						
Hamilton, 12 July, 1949						(M)
West Ham U	Possilpark YMCA	08.66	68-70	36	3	2
Watford	Tr	08.71	71-73	64	1	12
Colchester U	Tr	07.74	74	45	0	6
Hereford U	Tr	08.75	75-76	79	0	6
Shrewsbury T	Tr	08.77	77-80	80	6	0
LINDSAY John (Jack) McArthur						
Flemington, 11 December, 1921						(CF)
Sheffield Wed	Morton	03.45	46	1	-	1
Bury	Tr	10.46	46	11	-	7
Carlisle U	Tr	08.47	47-50	103	-	46
Southport	Tr	03.51	50-51	50	-	20
Carlisle U	Wigan Ath	01.55	54	13	-	2
LINDSAY John (Jack) Smith						
Auchinleck, 8 August, 1924 Died 1991						(FB)
Everton	Glasgow Rgrs	03.51	50-53	105	-	2
Bury	Worcester C	05.56	56	7	-	0
LINDSAY Laurence (Laurie)						
Dumbarton, 7 October, 1921						(CD)
Crewe Alex	Dundee	01.48	47-49	40	-	0
LINDSAY Malcolm (Mal)						
Ashington, 26 September, 1940						(F)
Cambridge U	King's Lynn	02.70	70	6	0	1
LINDSAY Mark Edward						
Lambeth, 6 March, 1955						(M)
Crystal Palace	App	03.73	73-74	27	3	0
LINDSEY Barry						
Scunthorpe, 17 April, 1944						(CD)
Scunthorpe U	App	05.61	61-70	210	6	13
LINDSEY Keith						
Scunthorpe, 25 November, 1946 Died 2003						(FB)
Scunthorpe U	App	12.64	65	15	0	0
Doncaster Rov	Tr	07.66	66	16	2	1
Southend U	Cambridge U	01.69	68-71	89	2	4
Port Vale	Tr	12.71	71-72	24	0	0
Gillingham	Tr	12.72	72-74	73	0	5
LINDSEY Scott						
Walsall, 4 May, 1972						(M)
Gillingham	Bridlington T	07.94	94	11	1	0
LINEKER Gary Winston						
Leicester, 30 November, 1960 EB/E-80						(F)
Leicester C	App	11.79	78-84	187	7	95
Everton	Tr	07.85	85	41	0	30
Tottenham H	Barcelona (Sp)	07.89	89-91	105	0	67
LINES Barry						
Northampton, 16 May, 1942						(W)
Northampton T	Bletchley T	09.60	60-69	260	6	48
LINEY Patrick (Pat)						
Paisley, 14 July, 1936						(G)
Bradford PA	St Mirren	06.66	66	11	0	0
Bradford C	Tr	09.67	67-71	147	0	0
LINFORD John Russell						
Norwich, 6 December, 1957						(F)
Ipswich T	Gorleston	08.81				
Colchester U	L	01.83	82	7	0	0
Southend U	L	03.83	82	6	0	3
Birmingham C (L)	DS79 (Holl)	11.84	84	1	1	0
LING Martin						
West Ham, 15 July, 1966						(M)
Exeter C	App	01.84	82-85	109	8	14
Swindon T	Tr	07.86	86	2	0	0
Southend U	Tr	10.86	86-90	124	12	30
Mansfield T	L	01.91	90	3	0	0
Swindon T	Tr	03.91	90-95	132	18	10
Leyton Orient	Tr	07.96	96-99	143	5	8
Brighton & Hove A	Tr	03.00	99	2	6	1
LINGER Paul Hayden						
Stepney, 20 December, 1974						(M)
Charlton Ath	YT	07.93	92-95	5	18	1
Leyton Orient	Tr	09.97	97	1	2	0
Brighton & Hove A	Tr	12.97	97	17	2	0
LINIGHAN Andrew (Andy)						
Hartlepool, 18 June, 1962 EB-4						(CD)
Hartlepool U	Henry Smith's BC	09.80	80-83	110	0	4
Leeds U	Tr	05.84	84-85	66	0	3
Oldham Ath	Tr	01.86	85-87	87	0	6
Norwich C	Tr	03.88	87-89	86	0	8
Arsenal	Tr	07.90	90-96	101	17	5
Crystal Palace	Tr	01.97	96-00	108	3	4
Queens Park Rgrs	L	03.99	98	4	3	0
Oxford U	Tr	10.00	00	12	1	0
LINIGHAN Brian						
Hartlepool, 2 November, 1973						(CD)
Sheffield Wed	YT	07.92	93	1	0	0
Bury	Tr	07.97	99	2	1	0
LINIGHAN William **Brian**						
Hartlepool, 17 May, 1936						(CD)
Lincoln C		12.53				
Darlington	L	10.58	58	1	-	1
LINIGHAN David						
Hartlepool, 9 January, 1965 FLge						(CD)
Hartlepool U	Jnrs	03.82	81-85	84	7	5
Derby Co	Tr	08.86				
Shrewsbury T	Tr	12.86	86-87	65	0	2
Ipswich T	Tr	06.88	88-95	275	2	12
Blackpool	Tr	11.95	95-97	97	3	5
Mansfield T	Dunfermline Ath	03.99	98-99	38	0	0
LINK Thomas (Tom) Henry						
Halifax, 15 December, 1918 Died 1990						(W)
Bradford C		05.48	47-48	6	-	0
LINNECOR Albert (Bert) Roy						
Nechells, 30 November, 1933						(WH)
Birmingham C	Brookhill Jnrs	05.52	55-56	17	-	0
Lincoln C	Tr	04.57	56-63	264	-	52
LINNELL John Lovell Leonard						
Holcot, 2 January, 1944						(CD)
Northampton T	Jnrs	09.63				
Peterborough U	Tr	07.67	67	24	2	1
LINNEY David William						
Birmingham, 5 September, 1961						(FB)
Birmingham C	App	09.79	81	0	1	0
Oxford U	Tr	08.82	82	26	0	0
LINSTREM Kenneth (Ken) Richard						
Salford, 12 October, 1928 Died 1996						(WH)
Crewe Alex	Stockport (Am)	06.50	50-51	13	-	1
LINTERN Melvin (Mel)						
Seaton Delaval, 17 May, 1950						(IF)
Port Vale	Jnrs	03.68	66	0	1	0
LINTON Desmond (Des) Martin						
Birmingham, 5 September, 1971						(FB)
Leicester C	YT	01.90	89-91	6	5	0
Luton T	Tr	10.91	91-96	65	18	1
Peterborough U	Tr	03.97	96-98	41	5	0
Swindon T	L	03.99	98	7	1	0
LINTON Ivor						
West Bromwich, 20 November, 1959						(M)
Aston Villa	App	09.77	76-81	16	11	0
Peterborough U	Tr	08.82	82-83	24	3	3
Birmingham C	Tr	12.83	83	3	1	0
LINTON James (Jimmy) Alfred						
Glasgow, 2 December, 1930						(G)
Notts Co	Kirkintilloch Rob Roy	11.52	52-58	114	-	0
Watford	Tr	07.59	59-62	71	-	0
LINTON Malcolm Wilton						
Southend-on-Sea, 13 February, 1952						(CD)
Orient	Southend U (Am)	08.72	72-74	14	5	0

LINTON Thomas (Tommy) Neilson Goodwin
Falkirk, 15 October, 1920 Died 2002 (FB)

League Club	Source	Date Signed	Seasons Played	Apps	Subs	Gls
Southend U		05.45	46-48	67	-	0

LINWOOD Alexander (Alex) Bryce
Glasgow, 13 March, 1920 Died 2003 SLge-1/SWar-1/S-1 (CF)

League Club	Source	Date Signed	Seasons Played	Apps	Subs	Gls
Middlesbrough	St Mirren	06.46	46	14	-	3

LINWOOD Paul Anthony
Birkenhead, 24 October, 1983 (CD)

League Club	Source	Date Signed	Seasons Played	Apps	Subs	Gls
Tranmere Rov	YT	04.02	03-04	22	8	0

LIPA Andreas
Vienna, Austria, 26 April, 1971 Austria 1 (M)

League Club	Source	Date Signed	Seasons Played	Apps	Subs	Gls
Port Vale	Xanthi (Gre)	07.03	03-04	27	5	2

LIPTROTT David (Dave)
Stockport, 26 February, 1965 (F)

League Club	Source	Date Signed	Seasons Played	Apps	Subs	Gls
Stockport Co	Jnrs	09.82	82	0	1	0

LISBIE Kevin Anthony
Hackney, 17 October, 1978 EYth/Ja-9 (F)

League Club	Source	Date Signed	Seasons Played	Apps	Subs	Gls
Charlton Ath	YT	05.96	96-04	61	80	16
Gillingham	L	03.99	98	4	3	4
Reading	L	11.99	99	1	1	0
Queens Park Rgrs	L	12.00	00	1	1	0

LISHMAN Douglas (Doug) John
Birmingham, 14 September, 1923 Died 1994 EB/FLge-1 (IF)

League Club	Source	Date Signed	Seasons Played	Apps	Subs	Gls
Walsall	Paget Rgrs	08.46	46-47	59	-	26
Arsenal	Tr	07.48	48-55	226	-	125
Nottingham F	Tr	03.56	55-56	38	-	22

LISTER Alexander (Sandy) Duncan
Glasgow, 20 January, 1924 (IF)

League Club	Source	Date Signed	Seasons Played	Apps	Subs	Gls
Rochdale	Alloa Ath	05.52	52	2	-	0

LISTER Eric
Willenhall, 13 August, 1933 (W)

League Club	Source	Date Signed	Seasons Played	Apps	Subs	Gls
Notts Co	Wolverhampton W (Am)	09.51	54-56	8	-	0

LISTER Herbert (Bert) Francis
Manchester, 4 October, 1939 (F)

League Club	Source	Date Signed	Seasons Played	Apps	Subs	Gls
Manchester C	Jnrs	11.57	58	2	-	0
Oldham Ath	Tr	10.60	60-64	135	-	76
Rochdale	Tr	01.65	64-66	56	0	16
Stockport Co	Tr	01.67	66	16	0	11

LISTER Stephen (Steve) Haley
Doncaster, 17 November, 1961 (CD)

League Club	Source	Date Signed	Seasons Played	Apps	Subs	Gls
Doncaster Rov	App	05.79	78-84	228	9	30
Scunthorpe U	Tr	07.85	85-91	176	6	30
York C	L	03.91	90	4	0	1

LITA Leroy Halirou
DR Congo, 28 December, 1984 Eu21-1 (F)

League Club	Source	Date Signed	Seasons Played	Apps	Subs	Gls
Bristol C	Sch	03.03	02-04	44	41	31

LITCHFIELD Peter
Manchester, 27 July, 1956 (G)

League Club	Source	Date Signed	Seasons Played	Apps	Subs	Gls
Preston NE	Droylsden	01.79	80-84	107	0	0
Bradford C	Tr	07.85	85-88	88	0	0
Oldham Ath	L	10.88	88	3	0	0
Scunthorpe U	Tr	07.89	89-90	25	0	0

LITHGO Gordon
Hartlepool, 14 August, 1942 (W)

League Club	Source	Date Signed	Seasons Played	Apps	Subs	Gls
Hartlepools U	Seaton Holy Trinity	08.59	60-63	37	-	8

LITMANEN Jari Olaui
Lahti, Finland, 20 February, 1971 Finland 76 (F)

League Club	Source	Date Signed	Seasons Played	Apps	Subs	Gls
Liverpool	Barcelona (Sp)	01.01	00-01	12	14	5

LITT Stephen (Steve) Eric
Carlisle, 21 May, 1954 (CD)

League Club	Source	Date Signed	Seasons Played	Apps	Subs	Gls
Luton T	Blackpool (App)	06.72	73-75	15	0	0
Northampton T	Minnesota (USA)	09.77	77	19	1	0

LITTLE Alan
Horden, 5 February, 1955 (M)

League Club	Source	Date Signed	Seasons Played	Apps	Subs	Gls
Aston Villa	App	01.73	74	2	1	0
Southend U	Tr	12.74	74-76	102	1	12
Barnsley	Tr	08.77	77-79	91	0	14
Doncaster Rov	Tr	12.79	79-82	84	1	11
Torquay U	Tr	10.82	82-83	51	0	4
Halifax T	Tr	11.83	83-84	68	0	6
Hartlepool U	Tr	07.85	85	12	0	1

LITTLE Barry Brian
Greenwich, 25 August, 1964 Died 1994 EYth (M)

League Club	Source	Date Signed	Seasons Played	Apps	Subs	Gls
Charlton Ath	App	07.82	82	2	0	1

LITTLE Brian
Horden, 25 November, 1953 E-1 (F)

League Club	Source	Date Signed	Seasons Played	Apps	Subs	Gls
Aston Villa	App	03.71	71-79	242	5	60

LITTLE Colin Campbell
Wythenshawe, 4 November, 1972 (M)

League Club	Source	Date Signed	Seasons Played	Apps	Subs	Gls
Crewe Alex	Hyde U	02.96	95-02	135	58	33
Mansfield T	L	10.02	02	5	0	0
Macclesfield T	L	12.02	02	1	0	0
Macclesfield T	Tr	03.03	02-03	21	8	6

LITTLE George
Newcastle, 1 December, 1915 Died 2002 (W)

League Club	Source	Date Signed	Seasons Played	Apps	Subs	Gls
Doncaster Rov	Throckley Welfare	08.36	36-47	49	-	11
York C	Tr	12.47	47	15	-	2

LITTLE Glen Matthew
Wimbledon, 15 October, 1975 (W)

League Club	Source	Date Signed	Seasons Played	Apps	Subs	Gls
Crystal Palace	YT	07.94				
Burnley	Glentoran	11.96	96-03	211	35	32
Reading	L	03.03	02	6	0	1
Bolton W	L	09.03	03	0	4	0
Reading	Tr	05.04	04	29	6	0

LITTLE John (Jackie)
Gateshead, 17 May, 1912 (W)

League Club	Source	Date Signed	Seasons Played	Apps	Subs	Gls
Ipswich T	Needham Market	11.37	38-49	146	-	20

LITTLE Ronald (Ronnie)
Carlisle, 24 January, 1934 Died 2002 (W)

League Club	Source	Date Signed	Seasons Played	Apps	Subs	Gls
Carlisle U (Am)	Longsowerby Hearts	05.55	55	5	-	0

LITTLE Roy
Manchester, 1 June, 1931 (FB)

League Club	Source	Date Signed	Seasons Played	Apps	Subs	Gls
Manchester C	Greenwood Victoria	08.49	52-58	168	-	2
Brighton & Hove A	Tr	10.58	58-60	83	-	0
Crystal Palace	Tr	05.61	61-62	38	-	1

LITTLEJOHN Adrian Sylvester
Wolverhampton, 26 September, 1970 EYth (F)

League Club	Source	Date Signed	Seasons Played	Apps	Subs	Gls
Walsall	West Bromwich A (YT)	05.89	89-90	26	18	1
Sheffield U	Tr	08.91	91-94	44	25	12
Plymouth Arg	Tr	09.95	95-97	100	10	29
Oldham Ath	Tr	03.98	97-98	16	5	5
Bury	Tr	11.98	98-00	69	30	14
Sheffield U	Tr	10.01	01	1	2	0
Port Vale	(USA)	02.03	02-03	36	13	10
Lincoln C	Tr	08.04	04	1	7	0
Rushden & Diamonds	Tr	01.05	04	8	7	0

LITTLEJOHN Roy Derek
Bournemouth, 2 June, 1933 EAmat (W)

League Club	Source	Date Signed	Seasons Played	Apps	Subs	Gls
Bournemouth (Am)	Jnrs	05.52	52	9	-	0
Bournemouth (Am)	Oxford C	06.55	55	13	-	2

LITTLEJOHNS Colin
Liverpool, 8 September, 1968 (M)

League Club	Source	Date Signed	Seasons Played	Apps	Subs	Gls
Cambridge U	YT	10.85	85-86	10	2	0

LITTLER Joseph **Eric**
St Helens, 14 April, 1929 (CF)

League Club	Source	Date Signed	Seasons Played	Apps	Subs	Gls
Leicester C	Stubshaw Cross	05.51	51-54	5	-	2
Lincoln C	Tr	12.54	54	6	-	2
Wrexham	Tr	06.55	55	12	-	1
Crewe Alex	Tr	12.55	55	10	-	2

LITTLER Thomas (Tom)
Stockport, 6 March, 1936 (W)

League Club	Source	Date Signed	Seasons Played	Apps	Subs	Gls
Stockport Co		04.55	55	1	-	0

LIVERMORE David
Edmonton, 20 May, 1980 (M)

League Club	Source	Date Signed	Seasons Played	Apps	Subs	Gls
Arsenal	YT	07.98				
Millwall	Tr	07.99	99-04	228	4	10

LIVERMORE Douglas (Doug) Ernest
Prescot, 27 December, 1947 (M)

League Club	Source	Date Signed	Seasons Played	Apps	Subs	Gls
Liverpool	Jnrs	11.65	67-70	13	3	0
Norwich C	Tr	11.70	70-74	113	1	4
Bournemouth	L	03.75	74	10	0	0
Cardiff C	Tr	08.75	75-77	84	4	5
Chester	Tr	10.77	77-78	71	0	6

LIVERSIDGE Ronnie
Huddersfield, 12 September, 1934 Died 1997 (CF)

League Club	Source	Date Signed	Seasons Played	Apps	Subs	Gls
Bradford C	Ossett T	10.56	56-58	48	-	27

LIVESEY Charles (Charlie) Edward
West Ham, 6 February, 1938 Died 2005 (F)

League Club	Source	Date Signed	Seasons Played	Apps	Subs	Gls
Southampton	Custom House	03.56	58	25	-	14
Chelsea	Tr	05.59	59-60	39	-	17
Gillingham	Tr	08.61	61-62	47	-	17

League Club	Source	Date Signed	Seasons Played	Apps	Subs	Gls
Watford	Tr	10.62	62-63	64	-	26
Northampton T	Tr	08.64	64-65	28	0	4
Brighton & Hove A	Tr	09.65	65-68	124	2	28

LIVESEY Daniel (Danny) Richard
Salford, 31 December, 1984 (CD)

League Club	Source	Date Signed	Seasons Played	Apps	Subs	Gls
Bolton W	Sch	08.02	02	0	2	0
Notts Co	L	09.03	03	9	2	0
Rochdale	L	02.04	03	11	2	0
Blackpool	L	08.04	04	1	0	0

LIVESEY John (Jack)
Preston, 8 March, 1924 Died 1988 (IF)

League Club	Source	Date Signed	Seasons Played	Apps	Subs	Gls
Preston NE	Jnrs	04.44				
Bury	Tr	05.46	46	7	-	1
Doncaster Rov	Tr	01.47	47	3	-	0
Rochdale	Tr	04.48	47-50	113	-	36
Southport	Tr	07.51	51	31	-	9

LIVETT Simon Robert
East Ham, 8 January, 1969 (M)

League Club	Source	Date Signed	Seasons Played	Apps	Subs	Gls
West Ham U	App	01.87	90	1	0	0
Leyton Orient	Tr	08.92	92-93	16	8	0
Cambridge U	Tr	10.93	93-94	12	0	0
Southend U	Grays Ath	07.98	98	19	4	1

LIVIE Gordon
Billingham, 10 June, 1932 (CD)

League Club	Source	Date Signed	Seasons Played	Apps	Subs	Gls
Leicester C	Jnrs	12.49				
Mansfield T	Tr	07.52	52-53	21	-	0

LIVINGSTONE Archibald (Archie)
Pencaitland, 15 November, 1915 Died 1961 (IF)

League Club	Source	Date Signed	Seasons Played	Apps	Subs	Gls
Newcastle U	Dundee	05.35	35-37	33	-	5
Bury	Tr	06.38	38	24	-	8
Everton	Peterborough U	05.46	46	4	-	2
Southport	Tr	06.47	47	23	-	2

LIVINGSTONE Glen
Birmingham, 13 October, 1972 ESch/EYth (G)

League Club	Source	Date Signed	Seasons Played	Apps	Subs	Gls
Aston Villa	YT	01.91				
Walsall	York C (N/C)	03.94	93	2	1	0

LIVINGSTONE Joseph (Joe)
Middlesbrough, 18 June, 1942 (CF)

League Club	Source	Date Signed	Seasons Played	Apps	Subs	Gls
Middlesbrough	Jnrs	01.60	60-62	20	-	7
Carlisle U	Tr	11.62	62-65	81	1	42
Hartlepools U	Tr	05.66	65-66	15	0	5

LIVINGSTONE Stephen (Steve) Carl
Middlesbrough, 8 September, 1968 (F)

League Club	Source	Date Signed	Seasons Played	Apps	Subs	Gls
Coventry C	App	07.86	86-90	17	14	5
Blackburn Rov	Tr	01.91	90-92	25	5	10
Chelsea	Tr	03.93	92	0	1	0
Port Vale	L	09.93	93	4	1	0
Grimsby T	Tr	10.93	93-02	226	63	43
Carlisle U	Tr	08.03	03	6	0	0

LIVINGSTONE Wilfred (Wilf) Egerton
Barrow, 22 October, 1919 Died 2002 (CF)

League Club	Source	Date Signed	Seasons Played	Apps	Subs	Gls
Barrow	Holker COB	09.47	47-48	4	-	0

LIVINGSTONE William (Billy)
Coventry, 13 August, 1964 SYth (F)

League Club	Source	Date Signed	Seasons Played	Apps	Subs	Gls
Wolverhampton W	App	08.82	82-83	21	3	4

LIVINGSTONE William (Billy) Rennison
Greenock, 8 February, 1929 (CD)

League Club	Source	Date Signed	Seasons Played	Apps	Subs	Gls
Reading	Ardeer Rec	04.49	49-54	49	-	2
Chelsea	Tr	06.55	56-57	20	-	0
Brentford	Tr	07.59	59	19	-	0

LIVSEY Gordon William
Keighley, 24 January, 1947 (G)

League Club	Source	Date Signed	Seasons Played	Apps	Subs	Gls
Wrexham	Kettering T	01.67	67-70	79	0	0
Chester	Tr	08.71	71	44	0	0
Hartlepool U	Workington	12.77	77	6	0	0

LJUNGBERG Karl **Fredrik (Freddie)**
Halmstad, Sweden, 16 April, 1977 SwYth/Swu21-12/Sw-52 (M)

League Club	Source	Date Signed	Seasons Played	Apps	Subs	Gls
Arsenal	BK Halmstad (Swe)	09.98	98-04	151	22	45

LLEWELLYN Andrew (Andy) David
Bristol, 26 February, 1966 EYth (FB)

League Club	Source	Date Signed	Seasons Played	Apps	Subs	Gls
Bristol C	App	02.84	82-93	296	12	3
Exeter C	L	03.94	93	15	0	0
Hereford U	Tr	10.94	94	3	1	0

LLEWELLYN Christopher (Chris) Mark
Merthyr Tydfil, 29 August, 1979 WYth/Wu21-14/WB-1/W-4 (F)

League Club	Source	Date Signed	Seasons Played	Apps	Subs	Gls
Norwich C	YT	01.97	97-02	103	39	17
Bristol Rov	L	02.03	02	14	0	3
Wrexham	Tr	08.03	03-04	91	0	15

LLEWELLYN David John
Cardiff, 9 August, 1949 Wu23-1 (W)

League Club	Source	Date Signed	Seasons Played	Apps	Subs	Gls
West Ham U	Jnrs	08.66	69-71	2	4	0
Peterborough U	Tr	08.73	73-74	11	2	3
Mansfield T	L	08.74	74	6	2	0

LLEWELLYN Herbert (Bert) Arthur
Golborne, 5 February, 1939 EYth (CF)

League Club	Source	Date Signed	Seasons Played	Apps	Subs	Gls
Everton	Jnrs	05.56	56-57	11	-	2
Crewe Alex	Tr	07.58	58-60	96	-	49
Port Vale	Tr	11.60	60-62	88	-	42
Northampton T	Tr	02.63	62	1	-	0
Walsall	Tr	02.64	63-64	17	-	6

LLOYD Anthony Francis
Taunton, 14 March, 1984 (FB)

League Club	Source	Date Signed	Seasons Played	Apps	Subs	Gls
Huddersfield T	Sch	08.03	03-04	40	2	3

LLOYD Barry David
Hillingdon, 19 February, 1949 EYth (M)

League Club	Source	Date Signed	Seasons Played	Apps	Subs	Gls
Chelsea	App	02.66	66-68	8	2	0
Fulham	Tr	12.68	68-75	249	8	29
Hereford U	Tr	10.76	76	12	2	0
Brentford	Tr	06.77	77	26	5	4

LLOYD Brian William
St Asaph, 18 March, 1948 Wu23-2/W-3 (G)

League Club	Source	Date Signed	Seasons Played	Apps	Subs	Gls
Stockport Co	Rhyl	03.67	67-68	32	0	0
Southend U	Tr	09.69	69-70	46	0	0
Wrexham	Tr	08.71	71-77	266	0	0
Chester	Tr	09.77	77-79	94	0	0
Port Vale	L	02.81	80	16	0	0
Stockport Co	Tr	08.81	81-82	91	0	1

LLOYD Callum
Nottingham, 1 January, 1986 (M)

League Club	Source	Date Signed	Seasons Played	Apps	Subs	Gls
Mansfield T	Sch	05.05	04	7	3	4

LLOYD Clifford (Cliff)
Frodsham, 14 November, 1916 Died 2000 (FB)

League Club	Source	Date Signed	Seasons Played	Apps	Subs	Gls
Liverpool		11.37				
Fulham		12.43	46	2	-	0

LLOYD Robert **Clive**
Merthyr Tydfil, 4 September, 1945 (IF)

League Club	Source	Date Signed	Seasons Played	Apps	Subs	Gls
Norwich C	App	09.62				
Cardiff C	Tr	08.64	64	2	-	0

LLOYD David
Gateshead, 1 June, 1928 Died 2000 (CF)

League Club	Source	Date Signed	Seasons Played	Apps	Subs	Gls
Sheffield U	North Fenhem	09.49				
York C	Tr	03.51	50	1	-	0

LLOYD Frank
Mapplewell, 16 January, 1928 (WH)

League Club	Source	Date Signed	Seasons Played	Apps	Subs	Gls
Bradford C	Barnsley (Am)	07.51	51-53	24	-	0

LLOYD Robert **Geoffrey (Geoff)**
Wrexham, 18 August, 1942 (F)

League Club	Source	Date Signed	Seasons Played	Apps	Subs	Gls
Wrexham	Llangollen	10.66	66	13	1	5
Bradford PA	Tr	07.67	67	32	0	10

LLOYD Grahame
Liverpool, 10 January, 1951 (G)

League Club	Source	Date Signed	Seasons Played	Apps	Subs	Gls
Liverpool	App	01.68				
Portsmouth	Motherwell	07.75	75-76	73	0	0

LLOYD Harold Demane
Flint, 12 March, 1920 Died 1984 (G)

League Club	Source	Date Signed	Seasons Played	Apps	Subs	Gls
Tranmere Rov	Flint T	10.45	46-56	188	-	0

LLOYD John David
Hitchin, 10 December, 1944 (FB)

League Club	Source	Date Signed	Seasons Played	Apps	Subs	Gls
Swindon T	App	01.62				
Oxford U	Tr	10.64	65-68	68	4	0
Aldershot	Tr	02.69	68-69	11	2	0

LLOYD John Walter
Rossett, 15 February, 1948 (W)

League Club	Source	Date Signed	Seasons Played	Apps	Subs	Gls
Wrexham (Am)	Jnrs	08.65	65-66	2	0	0

LLOYD Joseph (Joe) Millington
Shotton, 30 September, 1910 Died 1996 (WH)

League Club	Source	Date Signed	Seasons Played	Apps	Subs	Gls
Everton	Connah's Q & Shotton	02.31				
Swansea T	Tr	08.32	33-38	211	-	1
Wrexham	Tr	07.46	46	20	-	0

LLOYD Kevin Gareth
Llanidloes, 26 September, 1970 (FB)

League Club	Source	Date Signed	Seasons Played	Apps	Subs	Gls
Hereford U	Caersws	11.94	94-95	49	2	3
Cardiff C	Tr	08.96	96-97	27	6	1

LLOYD Kevin John James
Wolverhampton, 12 June, 1958 (F)

League Club	Source	Date Signed	Seasons Played	Apps	Subs	Gls
Cardiff C	Darlaston	05.79	79	0	1	0
Gillingham	Tr	07.80	80	0	1	0

LLOYD Laurence (Larry) Valentine
Bristol, 6 October, 1948 EYth/Eu23-8/E-4 (CD)

League Club	Source	Date Signed	Seasons Played	Apps	Subs	Gls
Bristol Rov	Jnrs	07.67	68	43	0	1
Liverpool	Tr	04.69	69-73	150	0	4
Coventry C	Tr	08.74	74-76	50	0	5
Nottingham F	Tr	10.76	76-80	148	0	6
Wigan Ath	Tr	03.81	80-82	52	0	2

LLOYD Norman Philip
Neath, 8 March, 1930 (WH)

League Club	Source	Date Signed	Seasons Played	Apps	Subs	Gls
Cardiff C		03.48				
Torquay U	Tr	09.49	52-56	29	-	1

LLOYD Norman (Norrie) William McLean
Torrance, 6 September, 1949 (M)

League Club	Source	Date Signed	Seasons Played	Apps	Subs	Gls
Preston NE	Twechar YC	09.66	68-70	17	2	6
Stockport Co	L	01.71	70	10	0	0
Southport	Tr	07.71	71-73	93	10	13
Stockport Co	Tr	07.74	74	36	2	2

LLOYD Peter John
Pattingham, 26 April, 1933 (W)

League Club	Source	Date Signed	Seasons Played	Apps	Subs	Gls
Walsall	Pattingham	03.51	53	5	-	0

LLOYD Philip (Phil) Rowan
Hemsworth, 26 December, 1964 (CD)

League Club	Source	Date Signed	Seasons Played	Apps	Subs	Gls
Middlesbrough	App	12.82				
Barnsley	Tr	09.83				
Darlington	Tr	03.84	83-86	127	0	3
Torquay U	Tr	08.87	87-91	169	1	7

LLOYD William **Stanley (Stan)**
West Auckland, 1 October, 1924 ESch (W)

League Club	Source	Date Signed	Seasons Played	Apps	Subs	Gls
Sunderland	Silksworth Jnrs	12.41	46-47	24	-	5
Grimsby T	Tr	08.48	48-52	148	-	23
Scunthorpe U	Worksop T	07.54	54	1	-	0

LLOYD William (Bill) Frederick
Poplar, 10 July, 1934 (G)

League Club	Source	Date Signed	Seasons Played	Apps	Subs	Gls
Millwall	Bromley	08.56	56-57	74	-	0

LLOYD William (Billy) Lorraine
Rhondda, 22 May, 1915 Died 1978 (FB)

League Club	Source	Date Signed	Seasons Played	Apps	Subs	Gls
Swindon T	Milford Haven	08.39	46-50	107	-	2

LOADWICK Derek
Middlesbrough, 4 October, 1956 (FB)

League Club	Source	Date Signed	Seasons Played	Apps	Subs	Gls
Leeds U	App	10.73				
Stockport Co	Tr	07.76	76-78	84	0	0
Hartlepool U	Tr	10.78	78-79	49	2	1

LOASBY Alan Arthur
Wellingborough, 19 March, 1937 (W)

League Club	Source	Date Signed	Seasons Played	Apps	Subs	Gls
Luton T	Jnrs	04.54				
Northampton T	Tr	07.58	58	2	-	0

LOBBETT Patrick Sidney **John**
Exeter, 8 January, 1938 (G)

League Club	Source	Date Signed	Seasons Played	Apps	Subs	Gls
Exeter C	Barnstaple	03.56	58-60	44	-	0

LOCHERTY Joseph (Joe)
Dundee, 5 September, 1925 (WH)

League Club	Source	Date Signed	Seasons Played	Apps	Subs	Gls
Sheffield Wed	Dundee Jnrs	09.47	48-49	10	-	0
Colchester U	Tr	07.50	50	10	-	1

LOCHHEAD Andrew (Andy) Lorimar
Lenzie, 9 March, 1941 Su23-1 (F)

League Club	Source	Date Signed	Seasons Played	Apps	Subs	Gls
Burnley	Renfrew Jnrs	12.58	60-68	225	1	101
Leicester C	Tr	10.68	68-69	40	4	12
Aston Villa	Tr	02.70	69-72	127	4	34
Oldham Ath	Tr	08.73	73-74	44	1	10

LOCK Anthony (Tony) Charles
Harlow, 3 September, 1976 (F)

League Club	Source	Date Signed	Seasons Played	Apps	Subs	Gls
Colchester U	YT	04.95	94-00	44	58	13

LOCK Frank William
Whitechapel, 12 March, 1922 Died 1985 (FB)

League Club	Source	Date Signed	Seasons Played	Apps	Subs	Gls
Charlton Ath	Finchley	12.45	46-53	222	-	8
Liverpool	Tr	12.53	53-54	41	-	0
Watford	Tr	06.55	55-56	42	-	1

LOCK Kevin Joseph
Plaistow, 27 December, 1953 EYth/Eu23-4 (CD)

League Club	Source	Date Signed	Seasons Played	Apps	Subs	Gls
West Ham U	App	12.71	71-77	122	10	2
Fulham	Tr	05.78	78-84	210	1	27
Southend U	Tr	08.85	85	10	0	0

LOCK Matthew John
Barnstaple, 10 March, 1984 (FB)

League Club	Source	Date Signed	Seasons Played	Apps	Subs	Gls
Exeter C	Sch	08.02	02	1	2	0

LOCKE Adam Spencer
Croydon, 20 August, 1970 (M)

League Club	Source	Date Signed	Seasons Played	Apps	Subs	Gls
Crystal Palace	YT	06.88				
Southend U	Tr	08.90	90-93	56	17	4
Colchester U	L	10.93	93	4	0	0
Colchester U	Tr	09.94	94-96	64	15	8
Bristol C	Tr	07.97	97-98	61	4	4
Luton T	Tr	08.99	99-01	45	17	5

LOCKE Gary
Edinburgh, 16 June, 1975 Su21-10 (M)

League Club	Source	Date Signed	Seasons Played	Apps	Subs	Gls
Bradford C	Heart of Midlothian	01.01	00-01	32	6	2

LOCKE Gary Robert
Kingsbury, 12 July, 1954 EYth (FB)

League Club	Source	Date Signed	Seasons Played	Apps	Subs	Gls
Chelsea	App	07.71	72-82	270	2	3
Crystal Palace	Tr	01.83	82-85	84	0	1

LOCKE Leslie (Les) Cameron
Perth, 24 January, 1934 SAmat (IF)

League Club	Source	Date Signed	Seasons Played	Apps	Subs	Gls
Queens Park Rgrs	Bromley	05.58	56-59	76	-	24

LOCKER Stephen (Steve)
Ashington, 5 November, 1970 (CD)

League Club	Source	Date Signed	Seasons Played	Apps	Subs	Gls
Hartlepool U	Nottingham F (YT)	09.88	88	0	1	0

LOCKETT Philip (Phil) Barry
Stockport, 6 September, 1972 (M)

League Club	Source	Date Signed	Seasons Played	Apps	Subs	Gls
Rochdale	YT	07.91	89-90	1	2	0

LOCKETT Ryan David Carl William
Cambridge, 11 November, 1986 (F)

League Club	Source	Date Signed	Seasons Played	Apps	Subs	Gls
Cambridge U	Sch	•	03	1	1	0

LOCKHART Crichton (Jock)
Perth, 6 March, 1930 (W)

League Club	Source	Date Signed	Seasons Played	Apps	Subs	Gls
Southend U	Chertsey	08.50	50-56	45	-	11
Rochdale	Tr	06.57	57	40	-	11

LOCKHART Keith Samuel
Wallsend, 19 July, 1964 (W)

League Club	Source	Date Signed	Seasons Played	Apps	Subs	Gls
Cambridge U	App	07.82	81-85	55	3	8
Wolverhampton W	Tr	03.86	85-86	24	1	4
Hartlepool U	Tr	12.86	86	2	0	0

LOCKHART Norman
Belfast, 4 March, 1924 I-4/NI-4 (W)

League Club	Source	Date Signed	Seasons Played	Apps	Subs	Gls
Swansea T	Linfield	10.46	46-47	47	-	13
Coventry C	Tr	10.47	47-52	182	-	41
Aston Villa	Tr	09.52	52-55	74	-	10
Bury	Tr	11.56	56-57	41	-	6

LOCKIE Alexander (Alex) James
South Shields, 11 April, 1915 (CD)

League Club	Source	Date Signed	Seasons Played	Apps	Subs	Gls
Sunderland	South Shields St A	09.35	36-38	40	-	1
Notts Co	Tr	09.46	46	23	-	0

LOCKIER Maurice Reginald
Bristol, 27 November, 1924 Died 2001 (W)

League Club	Source	Date Signed	Seasons Played	Apps	Subs	Gls
Bristol Rov		07.47	49	2	-	0

LOCKWOOD Adam Brian
Wakefield, 26 October, 1981 ESemiPro-2 (FB)

League Club	Source	Date Signed	Seasons Played	Apps	Subs	Gls
Reading	YT	03.99				
Yeovil T	Tr	10.01	03-04	49	4	4

LOCKWOOD Edward
Goldthorpe, 4 August, 1925 (FB)

League Club	Source	Date Signed	Seasons Played	Apps	Subs	Gls
Scunthorpe U	Denaby U	06.51	51-52	9	-	0

LOCKWOOD Matthew (Matt) Dominic
Rochford, 17 October, 1976 (FB)

League Club	Source	Date Signed	Seasons Played	Apps	Subs	Gls
Queens Park Rgrs	Southend U (YT)	05.95				
Bristol Rov	Tr	07.96	96-97	58	5	1
Leyton Orient	Tr	08.98	98-04	236	9	31

LOCKWOOD Roy
Barnsley, 20 June, 1933 EYth (FB)

League Club	Source	Date Signed	Seasons Played	Apps	Subs	Gls
Sheffield Wed	Jnrs	04.51				
Norwich C	Tr	09.55	55-57	36	-	0

LODGE Andrew (Andy) Robert
Peterborough, 17 July, 1978 (FB)

League Club	Source	Date Signed	Seasons Played	Apps	Subs	Gls
Boston U	Stamford AFC	01.00	02	1	1	0

LODGE Frank
Oldham, 28 November, 1919 Died 1973 (CF)

League Club	Source	Date Signed	Seasons Played	Apps	Subs	Gls
Stockport Co (Am)	Ward Street OB	03.47	46	1	-	0

League Club	Source	Date Signed	Seasons Played	Apps	Subs	Gls
LODGE George Raymond						
Wallsend, 27 January, 1943						(W)
Workington		12.61				
Newcastle U	Tr	07.62				
Barrow	Tr	07.63	63	6	-	0
LODGE Joe Thomas						
Skelmanthorpe, 16 April, 1921						(WH)
Huddersfield T	Jnrs	08.39	46-47	2	-	0
LODGE Paul						
Liverpool, 13 February, 1961 ESch						(M)
Everton	App	02.79	80-81	20	4	0
Wigan Ath	L	08.82	82	5	0	1
Rotherham U	L	01.83	82	4	0	0
Preston NE	Tr	02.83	82-83	36	2	0
Bolton W	Tr	07.84	84	4	0	0
Port Vale	L	11.84	84	3	0	0
Stockport Co	Tr	03.85	84-85	10	3	2
LODGE Robert (Bobby) William						
Retford, 1 July, 1941						(W)
Sheffield Wed		05.59	60	3	-	2
Doncaster Rov	Tr	05.61	61	23	-	4
LOFTHOUSE Nathaniel (Nat)						
Bolton, 27 August, 1925 EB/FLge-15/E-33						(CF)
Bolton W	Jnrs	08.42	46-60	452	-	255
LOFTUS Robert (Bob)						
Liverpool, 15 December, 1931						(IF)
Bradford PA	Llanelli	12.55	55	3	-	0
LOFTY James (Jim) Kenneth						
Farnham, 5 December, 1945						(W)
Reading	Jnrs	05.63	63	2	-	0
LOGAN Carlos Sean						
Wythenshawe, 7 November, 1985						(M)
Manchester C	Sch	07.04				
Chesterfield	L	03.05	04	6	3	1
LOGAN David						
Middlesbrough, 5 December, 1963						(FB)
Mansfield T	Whitby T	06.84	84-86	67	0	1
Northampton T	Tr	02.87	86-87	39	2	1
Halifax T	Tr	08.88	88	3	0	0
Stockport Co	Tr	10.88	88-89	60	0	4
Scarborough	Tr	08.90	90-91	54	1	1
LOGAN Douglas (Doug)						
Aberdeen, 30 August, 1933 Died 1984						(WH)
Southampton	RAF Lamport	01.54	55-57	21	-	0
LOGAN Gordon Taylor						
Kirkliston, 3 October, 1949 SYth						(FB)
Port Vale	Tynecastle Ath	03.67	66-69	33	2	1
LOGAN John William						
Horden, 16 August, 1912 Died 1980						(WH)
Charlton Ath	Horden CW	07.34				
Darlington	Tr	05.35	35-36	65	-	5
Barnsley	Tr	03.37	36-46	99	-	5
Sheffield Wed	Tr	01.47	46	4	-	0
LOGAN Richard Adam						
Washington, 18 February, 1988						(F)
Darlington	Sch	●	04	0	1	0
LOGAN Richard Anthony						
Barnsley, 24 May, 1969						(CD)
Huddersfield T	Gainsborough Trinity	11.93	93-95	35	10	1
Plymouth Arg	Tr	10.95	95-97	67	19	12
Scunthorpe U	Tr	07.98	98-99	77	3	7
Lincoln C	Tr	07.00	00-02	14	3	1
LOGAN Richard James						
Bury St Edmunds, 4 January, 1982 ESch/EYth						(F)
Ipswich T	YT	01.99	98-99	0	3	0
Cambridge U	L	01.01	00	5	0	1
Torquay U	L	12.01	01	16	0	4
Boston U	Tr	11.02	02-03	30	5	10
Peterborough U	Tr	09.03	03-04	27	28	11
Shrewsbury T	L	09.04	04	5	0	1
LOGGIE David McKie						
Newbiggin, 31 May, 1957						(F)
Burnley	App	06.74	75-77	6	1	0
York C	Tr	06.78	78-79	47	3	11
LOGIE James (Jimmy) Tullis						
Edinburgh, 23 November, 1919 Died 1984 S-1						(IF)
Arsenal	Lochore Welfare	06.39	46-54	296	-	68
LOGUE Samuel (Sam) Walker						
Glasgow, 9 April, 1934 Died 2004						(IF)
Accrington St	Clyde	06.60	60	2	-	0
LOHMAN Johannes (Jan) Hermanus Petrus						
Dussen, Holland, 18 February, 1959 Hou21						(M)
Watford	Lokeren (Bel)	10.81	81-85	51	12	6
LOMAS Albert (Bert)						
Tyldesley, 14 October, 1924						(G)
Leeds U	Bolton W (Am)	09.48	48	1	-	0
Rochdale	Mossley	05.50	50	9	-	0
Chesterfield	Tr	07.51	51	29	-	0
LOMAS Andrew (Andy) James						
Hartlepool, 26 April, 1965						(G)
Cambridge U (L)	Stevenage Borough	03.95	94	2	0	0
LOMAS Clive Ian						
Ealing, 18 January, 1947						(WH)
Watford	App	01.65	65	6	1	0
LOMAS James (Jamie) Duncan						
Chesterfield, 18 October, 1977						(M)
Chesterfield	YT	09.96	96-99	17	13	0
Mansfield T	Tr	08.00	00	4	2	0
LOMAS Peter						
Royton, 9 May, 1933						(FB)
Southport	Royton Amats	04.52	51-56	18	-	0
LOMAS Stephen (Steve) Martin						
Hanover, Germany, 18 January, 1974 NISch/NIYth/NIB-1/NI-45						(M)
Manchester C	YT	01.91	93-96	102	9	8
West Ham U	Tr	03.97	96-04	179	8	10
LOMAX Geoffrey (Geoff) William						
Droylsden, 6 July, 1964						(FB)
Manchester C	Jnrs	07.81	82-84	23	2	1
Wolverhampton W	L	10.85	85	5	0	0
Carlisle U	Tr	12.85	85-86	37	0	0
Rochdale	Tr	07.87	87-88	70	1	0
LOMAX Kelvin						
Bury, 12 November, 1986						(FB)
Oldham Ath	Sch	●	03-04	7	3	0
LOMAX Michael (Mike) John						
Withington, 7 December, 1979						(FB)
Macclesfield T	Blackburn Rov (YT)	07.98	98	0	1	0
LOMBARDO Attilio						
St Maria la Fossa, Italy, 6 January, 1966 Italy 18						(M)
Crystal Palace	Juventus (It)	08.97	97-98	40	3	8
LONERGAN Andrew (Andy)						
Preston, 19 October, 1983 IRYth/EYth/Eu20						(G)
Preston NE	YT	10.00	00-04	32	0	1
Darlington	L	12.02	02	2	0	0
LONERGAN Darren						
Cork, 28 January, 1974						(CD)
Oldham Ath	Waterford	09.94	95	1	1	0
LONG Christopher (Chris)						
Hatfield, 7 February, 1948						(W)
Luton T	Hatfield T	02.66	65	1	0	0
LONG John William						
Southampton, 8 May, 1921						(FB)
Exeter C	Chester (Am)	04.46	46	1	-	0
LONG Nigel						
Doncaster, 31 March, 1955						(M)
Doncaster Rov		05.74	74	1	0	0
LONG Herbert **Raymond (Ray)**						
Stickney, 4 October, 1936						(CD)
Lincoln C	Louth U	12.58	59	1	-	0
LONG Terence (Terry) Anthony						
Tylers Green, 17 November, 1934						(CD)
Crystal Palace	Wycombe W	05.55	55-68	432	10	16
LONG Trevor George						
Smethwick, 1 July, 1931						(W)
Wolverhampton W	Mitchell & Butlers	12.50				
Gillingham	Tr	07.52	52-54	67	-	15
Reading	Tr	07.55	55	12	-	5
LONG Wilfred (Wilf) Roy						
Wallasey, 28 December, 1922 Died 1993						(W)
New Brighton	Everton (Am)	07.46	46	2	-	0

LONGBOTTOM (LANGLEY) Arthur
Leeds, 30 January, 1933 (IF)

League Club	Source	Date Signed	Seasons Played	Apps	Subs	Gls
Queens Park Rgrs	Methley U	03.54	54-60	201	-	62
Port Vale	Tr	05.61	61-62	52	-	18
Millwall	Tr	01.63	62	10	-	1
Oxford U	Tr	08.63	63-64	34	-	14
Colchester U	Tr	10.64	64	33	-	12

LONGDEN Colin
Rotherham, 21 July, 1933 ESch (W)

League Club	Source	Date Signed	Seasons Played	Apps	Subs	Gls
Rotherham U	Jnrs	08.50	52	3	-	0
York C	Tr	08.55	57	2	-	0

LONGDEN David Paul
East Ardsley, 28 September, 1962 (FB)

League Club	Source	Date Signed	Seasons Played	Apps	Subs	Gls
Barnsley	App	09.80	81-82	5	0	0
Scunthorpe U	Tr	08.83	83-92	364	4	0

LONGDON Charles (Charlie) William
Mansfield, 6 May, 1917 Died 1986 (CF)

League Club	Source	Date Signed	Seasons Played	Apps	Subs	Gls
Brighton & Hove A	Folkestone T	05.39				
Bournemouth	Tr	05.46	46	9	-	1
Rochdale	Tr	07.47	47	2	-	0

LONGHORN Dennis
Hythe, Hampshire, 12 September, 1950 (M)

League Club	Source	Date Signed	Seasons Played	Apps	Subs	Gls
Bournemouth	App	08.68	67-71	23	7	1
Mansfield T	Tr	12.71	71-73	93	3	5
Sunderland	Tr	02.74	73-76	35	5	3
Sheffield U	Tr	10.76	76-77	34	2	1
Aldershot	Tr	02.78	77-79	46	7	3
Colchester U	Tr	05.80	80-82	62	9	0

LONGHURST David John
Northampton, 15 January, 1965 Died 1990 (F)

League Club	Source	Date Signed	Seasons Played	Apps	Subs	Gls
Nottingham F	App	01.83				
Halifax T	Tr	07.85	85-86	85	0	24
Northampton T	Tr	06.87	87-88	34	3	7
Peterborough U	Tr	10.88	88-89	51	7	7
York C	Tr	01.90	89-90	6	0	2

LONGLAND John (Johnny)
Southampton, 24 September, 1932 (WH)

League Club	Source	Date Signed	Seasons Played	Apps	Subs	Gls
Brighton & Hove A		04.54	54	3	-	0

LONGLEY Nicholas (Nick)
Mexborough, 21 May, 1961 (G)

League Club	Source	Date Signed	Seasons Played	Apps	Subs	Gls
Crewe Alex		05.81	81-85	23	0	0

LONGLEY Scott Edward
Wakefield, 16 July, 1973 (M)

League Club	Source	Date Signed	Seasons Played	Apps	Subs	Gls
Halifax T	YT	07.92	91	1	0	0

LONGRIDGE George Paterson
Glasgow, 23 August, 1931 (G)

League Club	Source	Date Signed	Seasons Played	Apps	Subs	Gls
Leyton Orient	Denistoun Waverley	07.50				
Darlington	Tr	09.51	51	2	-	0

LONGWORTH Steven (Steve) Paul
Leyland, 6 February, 1980 (F)

League Club	Source	Date Signed	Seasons Played	Apps	Subs	Gls
Blackpool	YT	07.98	97	0	2	0

LONSDALE Joseph Stanley (Stan)
Washington, 13 April, 1931 Died 2003 (FB)

League Club	Source	Date Signed	Seasons Played	Apps	Subs	Gls
Huddersfield T	Seaham Jnrs	12.48				
Halifax T	Tr	03.55	54-59	202	-	21
Hartlepools U	Tr	11.60	60	9	-	0

LOPES Osvaldo
Frejus, France, 6 April, 1980 (M)

League Club	Source	Date Signed	Seasons Played	Apps	Subs	Gls
Plymouth Arg	Draguignan (Fr)	08.02	02	4	5	0
Torquay U	Cork C	01.05	04	1	0	0

LOPES Richard (Richie)
Waterford, 10 August, 1981 (M)

League Club	Source	Date Signed	Seasons Played	Apps	Subs	Gls
Sheffield U	YT	07.00				
Northampton T	Tr	03.01	00	3	3	0

LOPEZ Carlos
Mexico City, Mexico, 18 April, 1970 (FB)

League Club	Source	Date Signed	Seasons Played	Apps	Subs	Gls
Wycombe W	Chester C	01.02	01	1	0	0

LOPEZ Rik Alexander
Northwick Park, 25 October, 1979 (FB)

League Club	Source	Date Signed	Seasons Played	Apps	Subs	Gls
Queens Park Rgrs	YT	04.97				
Bristol Rov	Uniao Leiria (Por)	08.01	01	5	2	0

LORAM Mark Julian
Paignton, 13 August, 1967 (F)

League Club	Source	Date Signed	Seasons Played	Apps	Subs	Gls
Torquay U	Brixham Villa	01.85	84-85	50	2	8
Queens Park Rgrs	Tr	05.86				
Torquay U	Tr	03.87	86-91	188	21	40
Stockport Co	L	03.92	91	1	3	0
Exeter C	L	09.92	92	2	1	0
Torquay U	Minehead	08.93	93	0	1	0

LORAN Tyrone
Amsterdam, Holland, 29 June, 1981 Hou21 (CD)

League Club	Source	Date Signed	Seasons Played	Apps	Subs	Gls
Manchester C	Volendam (Holl)	07.02				
Tranmere Rov	Tr	12.02	02-04	42	5	0
Port Vale	L	12.04	04	6	0	0

LORD Albert Ernest
Farnworth, 10 September, 1944 (G)

League Club	Source	Date Signed	Seasons Played	Apps	Subs	Gls
Bolton W	Jnrs	01.63				
Southport	Tr	03.66	65	16	0	0

LORD Barry
Goole, 17 November, 1937 (G)

League Club	Source	Date Signed	Seasons Played	Apps	Subs	Gls
Hull C	Goole Buchanan	04.56	58-60	5	-	0

LORD Frank
Chadderton, 13 March, 1936 Died 2005 (F)

League Club	Source	Date Signed	Seasons Played	Apps	Subs	Gls
Rochdale	Royton Amats	10.53	53-60	122	-	54
Crewe Alex	Tr	07.61	61-63	108	-	68
Plymouth Arg	Tr	11.63	63-65	69	0	23
Stockport Co	Tr	02.66	65-66	27	0	18
Blackburn Rov	Tr	12.66	66	10	0	1
Chesterfield	Tr	06.67	67	12	0	6
Plymouth Arg	Tr	10.67	68	6	0	2

LORD William Graham
Rawtenstall, 9 July, 1936 (FB)

League Club	Source	Date Signed	Seasons Played	Apps	Subs	Gls
Accrington St	Rossendale U	07.57	58-60	67	-	0

LORD Malcolm
Driffield, 25 October, 1946 ESch (M)

League Club	Source	Date Signed	Seasons Played	Apps	Subs	Gls
Hull C	Jnrs	08.65	66-78	271	27	24

LORD Walter
Grimsby, 1 November, 1933 (IF)

League Club	Source	Date Signed	Seasons Played	Apps	Subs	Gls
Grimsby T	Jnrs	08.51	52-53	7	-	1
Lincoln C	Tr	05.56	56	1	-	0

LORENSON Roy Vincent
Liverpool, 8 April, 1932 (WH)

League Club	Source	Date Signed	Seasons Played	Apps	Subs	Gls
Halifax T	St Elizabeth's	02.52	51-60	217	-	7
Tranmere Rov	Tr	10.60	60-61	14	-	0

LORENZO Nestor Gabriel
Buenos Aires, Argentina, 28 February, 1966 Argentina int (CD)

League Club	Source	Date Signed	Seasons Played	Apps	Subs	Gls
Swindon T	Bari (It)	10.90	90-91	20	4	2

LORIMER Peter Patrick
Dundee, 14 December, 1946 SSch/SYth/Su23-2/S-21 (F)

League Club	Source	Date Signed	Seasons Played	Apps	Subs	Gls
Leeds U	Jnrs	12.63	62-78	429	20	151
York C	Toronto (Can)	09.79	79	29	0	8
Leeds U	Toronto (Can)	03.84	83-85	74	2	17

LORMOR Anthony (Tony)
Ashington, 29 October, 1970 (F)

League Club	Source	Date Signed	Seasons Played	Apps	Subs	Gls
Newcastle U	YT	02.88	87-88	6	2	3
Lincoln C	Tr	01.90	89-93	90	10	30
Peterborough U	Tr	07.94	94	2	3	0
Chesterfield	Tr	12.94	94-97	97	16	35
Preston NE	Tr	11.97	97	9	3	3
Notts Co	L	02.98	97	2	5	0
Mansfield T	Tr	07.98	98-99	68	6	20
Hartlepool U	Tr	08.00	00-01	26	22	9
Shrewsbury T	L	02.02	01	7	0	2

LORNIE John (Jackie)
Aberdeen, 2 March, 1939 SSch (CF)

League Club	Source	Date Signed	Seasons Played	Apps	Subs	Gls
Leicester C	Banks o' Dee	03.58	58-60	8	-	3
Luton T	Tr	06.61	61-62	19	-	6
Carlisle U	Tr	06.63	63	4	-	0
Tranmere Rov	Tr	06.64	64-65	33	2	6

LOSKA Anthony (Tony) Stephen Patrick
Chesterton, 11 February, 1950 (FB)

League Club	Source	Date Signed	Seasons Played	Apps	Subs	Gls
Shrewsbury T	App	03.68	68-70	12	0	0
Port Vale	Tr	07.71	71-73	74	6	5
Chester	Tr	12.73	73-76	103	7	5
Halifax T	Tr	10.76	76-78	101	1	0

LOSS Colin Paul
Brentwood, 15 August, 1973 (M)

League Club	Source	Date Signed	Seasons Played	Apps	Subs	Gls
Derby Co	Norwich C (YT)	11.91				
Bristol C	Gresley Rov	03.94	94	3	2	0

LOUGH John Douglas
Gateshead, 31 October, 1922 Died 1987 (W)

League Club	Source	Date Signed	Seasons Played	Apps	Subs	Gls
Gateshead (Am)		09.46	46	1	-	0

LOUGHLAN Antony (Tony) John
Croydon, 19 January, 1970 (W)

League Club	Source	Date Signed	Seasons Played	Apps	Subs	Gls
Nottingham F	Leicester U	08.89	90	2	0	1
Lincoln C	Kettering T	10.93	93	4	8	2

LOUGHLAN John
Coatbridge, 12 June, 1943 (FB)

League Club	Source	Date Signed	Seasons Played	Apps	Subs	Gls
Leicester C		08.61				
Crystal Palace	Morton	09.68	68-71	58	2	0
Wrexham	L	03.72	71	5	0	0

LOUGHNANE John **Brian**
Manchester, 16 August, 1930 (W)

League Club	Source	Date Signed	Seasons Played	Apps	Subs	Gls
Leeds U	Witton A	08.52				
Shrewsbury T	Tr	07.53	53-55	42	-	7
Bournemouth	Tr	07.56	56-58	43	-	5

LOUGHNANE Peter Brian
Bournemouth, 18 March, 1958 (W)

League Club	Source	Date Signed	Seasons Played	Apps	Subs	Gls
Manchester U	App	03.75				
Shrewsbury T	Tr	02.77	76-78	24	7	4

LOUGHRAN Joseph (Joe) Lane
Consett, 12 August, 1915 Died 1994 (FB)

League Club	Source	Date Signed	Seasons Played	Apps	Subs	Gls
Birmingham	Dudley College	08.33	35-36	31	-	2
Luton T	Tr	05.37	37-38	25	-	0
Burnley	Tr	07.39	46-49	65	-	0
Southend U	Tr	09.49	49-52	147	-	1

LOUGHTON Michael (Mick) George
Colchester, 8 December, 1942 (CD)

League Club	Source	Date Signed	Seasons Played	Apps	Subs	Gls
Colchester U	Jnrs	08.61	64-67	121	1	7

LOUIS Jefferson Lee
Harrow, 22 February, 1979 (F)

League Club	Source	Date Signed	Seasons Played	Apps	Subs	Gls
Oxford U	Thame U	03.02	01-04	18	38	8
Bristol Rov	Woking	05.05	04	1	0	0

LOUIS-JEAN Mathieu
Mont St Aignan, France, 22 February, 1976 FrYth/Fru21 (FB)

League Club	Source	Date Signed	Seasons Played	Apps	Subs	Gls
Nottingham F	Le Havre (Fr)	09.98	98-04	188	10	3

LOUKES Gordon
Sheffield, 15 June, 1928 (W)

League Club	Source	Date Signed	Seasons Played	Apps	Subs	Gls
Sheffield U		04.49	50	1	-	0
Southend U	Tr	07.51	51	2	-	0

[LOURENCO] DA SILVA Louis Carlos Lourenco
Luanda, Angola, 5 June, 1983 PortugalYth (F)

League Club	Source	Date Signed	Seasons Played	Apps	Subs	Gls
Bristol C (L)	Sporting Lisbon (Por)	03.01	00	1	2	1
Oldham Ath (L)	Sporting Lisbon (Por)	07.02	02	1	6	1

LOVATT John (Jack)
Burton-on-Trent, 23 August, 1941 (CF)

League Club	Source	Date Signed	Seasons Played	Apps	Subs	Gls
West Bromwich A	Jnrs	12.58	60-62	18	-	5

LOVATT John
Middlesbrough, 21 January, 1962 (FB)

League Club	Source	Date Signed	Seasons Played	Apps	Subs	Gls
Derby Co	App	01.80	81	2	2	0

LOVE Alistair James
Edinburgh, 9 May, 1955 (M)

League Club	Source	Date Signed	Seasons Played	Apps	Subs	Gls
West Bromwich A	Melbourne Thistle	03.73				
Southend U	Tr	05.74	74	6	5	0
Newport Co	Tr	07.75	75	41	1	2

LOVE Andrew (Andy) Mark
Grimsby, 28 March, 1979 (G)

League Club	Source	Date Signed	Seasons Played	Apps	Subs	Gls
Grimsby T	YT	07.96	96-98	12	0	0

LOVE Ian James
Cardiff, 1 March, 1958 (F)

League Club	Source	Date Signed	Seasons Played	Apps	Subs	Gls
Swansea C	Eastern Ath (HK)	08.86	86-88	33	8	9
Torquay U	Tr	03.89	88	8	1	0
Cardiff C	Tr	09.89	89	1	1	0

LOVE John (Johnny)
Eynsham, 11 March, 1937 (W)

League Club	Source	Date Signed	Seasons Played	Apps	Subs	Gls
Oxford U	Wolverhampton W (Am)	03.55	62-63	25	-	5

LOVE John Ernest
Hillingdon, 22 April, 1951 (CD)

League Club	Source	Date Signed	Seasons Played	Apps	Subs	Gls
Crystal Palace	Staines T	01.75	74	1	0	0

LOVE John (Jack) Thomson
Edinburgh, 18 March, 1924 (IF)

League Club	Source	Date Signed	Seasons Played	Apps	Subs	Gls
Nottingham F	Albion Rov	02.49	48-51	59	-	21
Walsall	Llanelli	03.55	54-55	40	-	10

LOVE Michael (Mickey) John
Stockport, 27 November, 1973 (M)

League Club	Source	Date Signed	Seasons Played	Apps	Subs	Gls
Wigan Ath	Hinckley Ath	01.96	96	0	3	0

LOVELL Alan John
Swansea, 17 May, 1940 (W)

League Club	Source	Date Signed	Seasons Played	Apps	Subs	Gls
Swansea T	Jnrs	06.57				
Stockport Co	Tr	07.60	60	1	-	0

LOVELL Frederick (Fred)
Crewe, 18 June, 1929 (IF)

League Club	Source	Date Signed	Seasons Played	Apps	Subs	Gls
Notts Co	Loughborough Coll (Am)	04.53	52-53	7	-	2

LOVELL Mark
Bromley, 16 July, 1983 (FB)

League Club	Source	Date Signed	Seasons Played	Apps	Subs	Gls
Gillingham	YT	04.01	00	0	1	0

LOVELL Mark Anthony
Kensington, 20 January, 1961 (M)

League Club	Source	Date Signed	Seasons Played	Apps	Subs	Gls
Fulham	App	08.78	77-78	4	2	0

LOVELL Michael (Mike) Graham
Doncaster, 28 October, 1946 (FB)

League Club	Source	Date Signed	Seasons Played	Apps	Subs	Gls
Doncaster Rov	App	10.64	65	2	0	0

LOVELL Stephen (Steve) John
Swansea, 16 July, 1960 WSch/W-6 (F)

League Club	Source	Date Signed	Seasons Played	Apps	Subs	Gls
Crystal Palace	App	08.77	80-82	68	6	3
Stockport Co	L	10.79	79	12	0	0
Millwall	Tr	03.83	82-85	143	3	43
Swansea C	L	02.87	86	2	0	1
Gillingham	Tr	02.87	86-92	222	11	94
Bournemouth	Tr	11.92	92	3	0	0

LOVELL Stephen (Steve) William Henry
Amersham, 6 December, 1980 (F)

League Club	Source	Date Signed	Seasons Played	Apps	Subs	Gls
Bournemouth	YT	07.99	98-99	1	7	0
Portsmouth	Tr	08.99	99-01	13	19	3
Exeter C	L	03.00	99	4	1	1
Sheffield U	L	03.02	01	3	2	1

LOVELL Stuart Andrew
Sydney, Australia, 9 January, 1972 (F)

League Club	Source	Date Signed	Seasons Played	Apps	Subs	Gls
Reading	YT	07.90	90-97	177	50	58

LOVELL Trevor
Halifax, 19 January, 1940 (W)

League Club	Source	Date Signed	Seasons Played	Apps	Subs	Gls
Halifax T (Am)	Jnrs	08.60	60-62	8	-	0

LOVEMAN Robert (Bobby) Leith
Greenock, 30 September, 1921 Died 1986 (G)

League Club	Source	Date Signed	Seasons Played	Apps	Subs	Gls
Newport Co	Baillieston Jnrs	03.48	47-48	20	-	0

LOVERIDGE James (Jimmy) Charles
Swansea, 19 October, 1962 WSch/Wu21-3 (M)

League Club	Source	Date Signed	Seasons Played	Apps	Subs	Gls
Swansea C	App	11.79	79-84	39	8	4
Charlton Ath	Tr	06.85	85	5	1	0

LOVERIDGE John
Wolverhampton, 28 February, 1959 (M)

League Club	Source	Date Signed	Seasons Played	Apps	Subs	Gls
West Bromwich A	App	03.77				
Walsall	Tr	08.81	81	23	3	2

LOVERING John (Jack)
Nuneaton, 10 December, 1922 (WH)

League Club	Source	Date Signed	Seasons Played	Apps	Subs	Gls
Coventry C	Holbrooks OB	06.46	46-47	6	-	0

LOVESEY William Samuel
Marylebone, 8 December, 1922 Died 1994 (WH)

League Club	Source	Date Signed	Seasons Played	Apps	Subs	Gls
Swindon T	Wolverhampton W (Am)	05.45	46	4	-	0

LOVETT Eric
Radcliffe, 20 August, 1925 Died 1998 (CD)

League Club	Source	Date Signed	Seasons Played	Apps	Subs	Gls
Accrington St		11.49	49-50	41	-	1

LOVETT Graham John
Sheldon, 5 August, 1947 (M)

League Club	Source	Date Signed	Seasons Played	Apps	Subs	Gls
West Bromwich A	App	11.64	64-70	106	8	8
Southampton	L	11.71	71	3	0	0

LOVETT Jay
Brighton, 22 January, 1978 (FB)

League Club	Source	Date Signed	Seasons Played	Apps	Subs	Gls
Brentford	Crawley T	02.00	00-02	24	4	0

LOVETT John Ernest
Portsmouth, 31 October, 1940 (W)

League Club	Source	Date Signed	Seasons Played	Apps	Subs	Gls
Portsmouth		09.58				
Millwall	Tr	03.60	59	6	-	2

LOVETT Percival (Percy) Reginald
Bayston, 1 August, 1921 Died 1982 (G)

League Club	Source	Date Signed	Seasons Played	Apps	Subs	Gls
Everton	Kenwood Jnrs	08.38				
Wrexham	Tr	02.47	46	13	-	0

LOVIE James (Jim) Theirs Harrison
Peterhead, 19 September, 1932 (W)

League Club	Source	Date Signed	Seasons Played	Apps	Subs	Gls
Bury	Peterhead	01.57	57-59	51	-	10
Bournemouth	Tr	07.60	60	9	-	0
Chesterfield	Tr	07.61	61-63	95	-	7

LOW Gordon Alexander
Aberdeen, 11 July, 1940 (CD)

League Club	Source	Date Signed	Seasons Played	Apps	Subs	Gls
Huddersfield T	Jnrs	07.57	57-60	67	-	6
Bristol C	Tr	03.61	60-67	203	2	12
Stockport Co	Tr	07.68	68-69	63	1	7
Crewe Alex	Tr	08.70	70	5	0	0

LOW Joshua (Josh) David
Bristol, 15 February, 1979 WYth/Wu21-4 (W)

League Club	Source	Date Signed	Seasons Played	Apps	Subs	Gls
Bristol Rov	YT	08.96	95-98	11	11	0
Leyton Orient	Tr	05.99	99	2	3	1
Cardiff C	Tr	11.99	99-01	54	21	6
Oldham Ath	Tr	08.02	02	19	2	3
Northampton T	Tr	08.03	03-04	61	6	10

LOW Norman Harvey
Aberdeen, 23 March, 1914 Died 1994 (CD)

League Club	Source	Date Signed	Seasons Played	Apps	Subs	Gls
Liverpool	Rosehill Villa	10.33	34-36	13	-	0
Newport Co	Tr	11.36	36-46	112	-	0
Norwich C	Tr	10.46	46-49	150	-	0

LOW Anthony **Roy**
Watford, 8 July, 1944 ESch (W)

League Club	Source	Date Signed	Seasons Played	Apps	Subs	Gls
Tottenham H	Jnrs	07.61	64-66	6	2	1
Watford	Tr	02.67	66-68	25	1	4

LOWDEN George
Isleworth, 2 March, 1933 (FB)

League Club	Source	Date Signed	Seasons Played	Apps	Subs	Gls
Brentford	Jnrs	05.51	53-56	29	-	0

LOWDER Thomas (Tommy)
Worksop, 17 October, 1924 Died 1999 (W)

League Club	Source	Date Signed	Seasons Played	Apps	Subs	Gls
Rotherham U	Worksop T	08.47	48	8	-	5
Southampton	Boston U	10.49	49-52	39	-	2
Southend U	Tr	05.53	53	21	-	3

LOWE Daniel (Danny) James
Barnsley, 12 January, 1984 (M)

League Club	Source	Date Signed	Seasons Played	Apps	Subs	Gls
Northampton T	YT	●	00	0	4	0

LOWE David Anthony
Liverpool, 30 August, 1965 EYth/Eu21-2 (F)

League Club	Source	Date Signed	Seasons Played	Apps	Subs	Gls
Wigan Ath	App	06.83	82-86	179	9	40
Ipswich T	Tr	06.87	87-91	121	13	37
Port Vale	L	03.92	91	8	1	2
Leicester C	Tr	07.92	92-95	68	26	22
Port Vale	L	02.94	93	18	1	5
Wigan Ath	Tr	03.96	95-98	85	23	26
Wrexham	Tr	07.99	99	4	6	1

LOWE Edward (Eddie)
Halesowen, 11 July, 1925 E-3 (WH)

League Club	Source	Date Signed	Seasons Played	Apps	Subs	Gls
Aston Villa	Kynoch Works	05.45	46-49	104	-	3
Fulham	Tr	05.50	50-62	473	-	8
Notts Co	Tr	09.63	63-64	9	-	0

LOWE Garry
Prescot, 21 February, 1967 (CD)

League Club	Source	Date Signed	Seasons Played	Apps	Subs	Gls
Bury	YT	06.86	85	3	1	0

LOWE Gary Walter
Manchester, 25 September, 1959 (M)

League Club	Source	Date Signed	Seasons Played	Apps	Subs	Gls
Crystal Palace	App	10.76				
Manchester C	Tr	12.79				
Hereford U	Tr	06.80	80	9	0	0

LOWE Keith Stephen
Wolverhampton, 13 September, 1985 (FB)

League Club	Source	Date Signed	Seasons Played	Apps	Subs	Gls
Wolverhampton W	Sch	●	04	11	0	0

LOWE Kenneth (Kenny)
Sedgefield, 6 November, 1961 ESemiPro (M)

League Club	Source	Date Signed	Seasons Played	Apps	Subs	Gls
Hartlepool U	App	11.78	81-83	50	4	3
Scarborough	Barrow	01.88	87	4	0	0
Barnet	Barrow	03.91	91-92	55	17	5
Stoke C	Tr	08.93	93	3	6	0
Birmingham C	Tr	12.93	93-95	14	7	3
Carlisle U	L	09.94	94	1	1	0
Hartlepool U	L	08.95	95	13	0	3
Darlington	Gateshead	03.97	96-97	10	4	0

LOWE Matthew Ian
Birmingham, 25 February, 1974 (G)

League Club	Source	Date Signed	Seasons Played	Apps	Subs	Gls
Torquay U	YT	07.92	91-93	30	0	0

LOWE Nicholas (Nick) Paul
Oxford, 28 October, 1952 (CD)

League Club	Source	Date Signed	Seasons Played	Apps	Subs	Gls
Oxford U	App	07.70	72-76	71	0	3
Halifax T	L	08.74	74	9	0	0

LOWE Onandi
Kingston, Jamaica, 2 December, 1973 Jamaica int (F)

League Club	Source	Date Signed	Seasons Played	Apps	Subs	Gls
Port Vale (L)	Rochester (USA)	02.01	00	4	1	1
Rushden & Diamonds	Kansas C (USA)	11.01	01-03	87	3	49
Coventry C	Tr	03.04	03	1	1	1

LOWE Reginald (Reg)
Halesowen, 15 December, 1926 (FB)

League Club	Source	Date Signed	Seasons Played	Apps	Subs	Gls
Aston Villa	Finchley	08.44				
Fulham	Tr	05.50	50-52	66	-	0

LOWE Ryan Thomas
Liverpool, 18 September, 1978 (F)

League Club	Source	Date Signed	Seasons Played	Apps	Subs	Gls
Shrewsbury T	Burscough	07.00	00-04	81	56	23
Chester C	Tr	03.05	04	8	0	4

LOWE Simon John
Westminster, 26 December, 1962 (F)

League Club	Source	Date Signed	Seasons Played	Apps	Subs	Gls
Barnsley	Ossett T	12.83	83	2	0	0
Halifax T	Tr	07.84	84-85	74	3	19
Hartlepool U	Tr	08.86	86	12	2	1
Colchester U	Tr	12.86	86-87	32	4	8
Scarborough	Tr	11.87	87	14	2	3

LOWE Terence (Terry) John
Cheadle, 27 May, 1943 (FB)

League Club	Source	Date Signed	Seasons Played	Apps	Subs	Gls
Port Vale	Stoke C (Am)	06.60	61-65	55	0	0

LOWELL Eric James
Cheadle, 8 March, 1935 (IF)

League Club	Source	Date Signed	Seasons Played	Apps	Subs	Gls
Derby Co	Jnrs	03.52	53	1	-	1
Stoke C	Tr	05.55	55	7	-	3

LOWERY Anthony (Tony) William
Wallsend, 6 July, 1961 (M)

League Club	Source	Date Signed	Seasons Played	Apps	Subs	Gls
West Bromwich A	Ashington	03.81	81	1	0	0
Walsall	L	02.82	81	4	2	1
Mansfield T	Tr	04.83	82-90	249	3	19
Walsall	L	10.90	90	6	0	0
Carlisle U	Tr	10.91	91	6	1	0

LOWERY Harry
Moor Row, 26 February, 1918 (WH)

League Club	Source	Date Signed	Seasons Played	Apps	Subs	Gls
West Bromwich A	Cleator Moor Celtic	05.35	37	17	-	0
Northampton T	Tr	11.45	46-48	76	-	2

LOWERY Jeremiah (Jerry)
Newcastle, 19 October, 1924 (G)

League Club	Source	Date Signed	Seasons Played	Apps	Subs	Gls
Newcastle U	CA Parsons Ath	06.47	49-51	6	-	0
Lincoln C	Tr	03.52	52-53	51	-	0
Barrow	Peterborough U	06.56	56-57	86	-	0
Crewe Alex	Tr	07.58	58	4	-	0

LOWERY Stewart
Thornaby, 21 February, 1951 (F)

League Club	Source	Date Signed	Seasons Played	Apps	Subs	Gls
Watford	Bishop Auckland	10.70				
Walsall	L	11.70	70	0	2	0

LOWES Arnold Richardson
Sunderland, 27 February, 1919 Died 1994 (WH)

League Club	Source	Date Signed	Seasons Played	Apps	Subs	Gls
Sheffield Wed	Washington Chemicals	10.37	38-47	42	-	8
Doncaster Rov	Tr	02.48	47-50	72	-	3

LOWES Barry Thomas
Barrow, 16 March, 1939 (W)

League Club	Source	Date Signed	Seasons Played	Apps	Subs	Gls
Barrow	Holker COB	01.60	59-61	55	-	15
Blackpool	Tr	11.61				
Workington	Tr	08.62	62-65	121	0	34
Bury	Tr	02.66	65-66	33	0	6
Coventry C	Tr	03.67	66	3	0	0
Swindon T	Tr	08.67	67	2	0	0

LOWEY John Anthony
Manchester, 7 March, 1958 (M)

League Club	Source	Date Signed	Seasons Played	Apps	Subs	Gls
Manchester U	App	03.75				
Blackburn Rov	Chicago (USA)	07.77				
Port Vale	Tr	12.77				
Sheffield Wed	California (USA)	10.78	78-79	35	7	4
Blackburn Rov	Tr	11.80	80-85	136	5	14
Wigan Ath	Tr	07.86	86	1	2	0
Chesterfield	L	11.86	86	2	0	0
York C	L	03.87	86	3	3	0
Preston NE	Tr	08.87	87	4	0	1
Chester C	Tr	03.88	87	9	0	0

LOWIS Paul Noble
Shap, 17 October, 1937 (WH)

League Club	Source	Date Signed	Seasons Played	Apps	Subs	Gls
Blackpool	BABC	05.57				
Stockport Co	Tr	06.59	59	9	-	0

LOWNDES Nathan Peter
Salford, 2 June, 1977 (F)

League Club	Source	Date Signed	Seasons Played	Apps	Subs	Gls
Leeds U	YT	04.95				
Watford	Tr	10.95	96-97	1	6	0
Rotherham U (L)	Livingstone	03.02	01	2	0	0
Plymouth Arg	Livingstone	07.02	02-04	25	28	10
Port Vale	Tr	11.04	04	7	5	1

LOWNDES Stephen (Steve) Robert
Cwmbran, 17 June, 1960 Wu21-4/W-10 (W)

League Club	Source	Date Signed	Seasons Played	Apps	Subs	Gls
Newport Co	Jnrs	10.77	77-82	200	8	39
Millwall	Tr	08.83	83-85	95	1	16
Barnsley	Tr	08.86	86-89	108	8	20
Hereford U	Tr	10.90	90-91	45	4	4

LOWNDS Mark Usher
Sunderland, 28 November, 1940 (WH)

League Club	Source	Date Signed	Seasons Played	Apps	Subs	Gls
Luton T	Ryhope Colliery	01.60	61-64	59	-	3

LOWREY Patrick (Pat)
Newcastle, 11 October, 1950 ESch (F)

League Club	Source	Date Signed	Seasons Played	Apps	Subs	Gls
Sunderland	Newcastle U (App)	11.67	68-71	13	2	3
Darlington	RU Bruges (Bel)	08.75	75	14	6	2
Workington	Tr	07.76	76	15	0	3

LOWRIE George
Tonypandy, 19 December, 1919 Died 1989 WWar-9/W-4 (IF)

League Club	Source	Date Signed	Seasons Played	Apps	Subs	Gls
Swansea T	Tonypandy	01.37	36-37	19	-	3
Preston NE	Tr	12.37	37	5	-	0
Coventry C	Tr	06.39	46-47	56	-	44
Newcastle U	Tr	03.48	47-49	12	-	5
Bristol C	Tr	09.49	49-51	48	-	21
Coventry C	Tr	02.52	51-52	27	-	12

LOWRIE Thomas (Tommy)
Glasgow, 14 January, 1928 (WH)

League Club	Source	Date Signed	Seasons Played	Apps	Subs	Gls
Manchester U	Troon Ath	08.47	47-49	13	-	0
Oldham Ath	Aberdeen	08.52	52-54	79	-	5

LOWRY Brian Thomas
Manchester, 12 December, 1936 (W)

League Club	Source	Date Signed	Seasons Played	Apps	Subs	Gls
Grimsby T	Manchester U (Am)	08.54	54-55	12	-	1

LOWRY Thomas (Tommy)
Liverpool, 26 August, 1945 (FB)

League Club	Source	Date Signed	Seasons Played	Apps	Subs	Gls
Liverpool	App	04.63	64	1	-	0
Crewe Alex	Tr	07.66	66-77	435	1	2

LOWTHER Shaun
North Shields, 24 January, 1962 (FB)

League Club	Source	Date Signed	Seasons Played	Apps	Subs	Gls
Peterborough U	Middlesbrough (N/C)	01.85	84	1	0	0

LOWTHORPE Adam
Hull, 7 August, 1975 (FB)

League Club	Source	Date Signed	Seasons Played	Apps	Subs	Gls
Hull C	YT	07.93	93-97	70	11	3

LOXLEY Anthony (Tony) Dale
Nottingham, 14 December, 1959 (CD)

League Club	Source	Date Signed	Seasons Played	Apps	Subs	Gls
Lincoln C	App	12.77	78	1	0	0

LOXLEY Herbert (Bert)
Matlock, 3 February, 1934 (CD)

League Club	Source	Date Signed	Seasons Played	Apps	Subs	Gls
Notts Co	Bonsall	03.52	54-63	245	-	9
Mansfield T	Tr	07.64				
Lincoln C	Lockheed Leamington	10.66	66	7	0	0

LOYDEN Edward (Eddie)
Liverpool, 22 December, 1945 (F)

League Club	Source	Date Signed	Seasons Played	Apps	Subs	Gls
Blackpool	Jnrs	12.63	64	2	-	0
Carlisle U	Tr	06.66				
Chester	Tr	07.67	67	37	0	22
Shrewsbury T	Tr	05.68	68	11	1	2
Barnsley	Tr	12.68	68-70	64	1	23
Chester	Tr	11.70	70-71	62	0	26
Tranmere Rov	Tr	06.72	72-73	61	0	22

LUA LUA Lumana Tresor
Kinshasa, DR Congo, 28 December, 1980 Congo 4 (F)

League Club	Source	Date Signed	Seasons Played	Apps	Subs	Gls
Colchester U	Leyton College	09.98	98-00	37	24	15
Newcastle U	Tr	09.00	00-03	14	45	5
Portsmouth	Tr	02.04	03-04	30	10	10

LUCAS Alec Leroy
Wrexham, 1 December, 1945 Wu23-1 (FB)

League Club	Source	Date Signed	Seasons Played	Apps	Subs	Gls
Wrexham	Bexley U	08.65	65-66	51	4	0

LUCAS Brian Andrew
Farnborough, 31 January, 1961 (M)

League Club	Source	Date Signed	Seasons Played	Apps	Subs	Gls
Aldershot	Jnrs	07.78	79-83	112	13	19

LUCAS David Anthony
Preston, 23 November, 1977 EYth (G)

League Club	Source	Date Signed	Seasons Played	Apps	Subs	Gls
Preston NE	YT	12.94	95-03	117	5	0
Darlington	L	12.95	95	6	0	0
Darlington	L	10.96	96	7	0	0
Scunthorpe U	L	12.96	96	6	0	0
Sheffield Wed	L	10.03	03	17	0	0
Sheffield Wed	Tr	06.04	04	34	0	0

LUCAS Frederick (Fred) Charles
Slade Green, 29 September, 1933 (WH)

League Club	Source	Date Signed	Seasons Played	Apps	Subs	Gls
Charlton Ath	Jnrs	01.52	55-63	185	-	29
Crystal Palace	Tr	10.63	63-64	16	-	0

LUCAS Peter **Malcolm (Mal)**
Wrexham, 7 October, 1938 Wu23-1/W-4 (M)

League Club	Source	Date Signed	Seasons Played	Apps	Subs	Gls
Leyton Orient	Bradley Rgrs	09.58	58-64	157	-	6
Norwich C	Tr	09.64	64-69	180	3	8
Torquay U	Tr	03.70	69-73	118	4	3

LUCAS Oliver Henry
Paisley, 14 January, 1923 (FB)

League Club	Source	Date Signed	Seasons Played	Apps	Subs	Gls
Leyton Orient	St Mirren	07.48	48-49	2	-	0

LUCAS Paul
Coseley, 27 April, 1936 Died 1992 (W)

League Club	Source	Date Signed	Seasons Played	Apps	Subs	Gls
Aston Villa	Jnrs	04.54				
Gillingham	Tr	08.56	56-57	44	-	7

LUCAS Richard
Chapeltown, 22 September, 1970 (FB)

League Club	Source	Date Signed	Seasons Played	Apps	Subs	Gls
Sheffield U	YT	07.89	90-91	8	2	0
Preston NE	Tr	12.92	92-93	47	3	0
Lincoln C	L	10.94	94	4	0	0
Scarborough	Tr	07.95	95-96	63	9	0
Hartlepool U	Tr	03.97	96-97	49	0	2
Halifax T	Tr	08.98	98-99	39	9	0

LUCAS Richard (Dick) John
Witney, 22 January, 1948 (FB)

League Club	Source	Date Signed	Seasons Played	Apps	Subs	Gls
Oxford U	Jnrs	07.65	67-74	190	1	2

LUCAS Robert (Bob) Walter
Bethnal Green, 6 January, 1925 (G)

League Club	Source	Date Signed	Seasons Played	Apps	Subs	Gls
Crystal Palace	Hendon	06.46	46	4	-	0

LUCAS William (Billy) Henry
Newport, 15 January, 1918 Died 1998 WLge-3/WWar-8/W-7 (IF)

League Club	Source	Date Signed	Seasons Played	Apps	Subs	Gls
Wolverhampton W	Treharris	05.36				
Swindon T	Tr	05.37	37-47	141	-	32
Swansea T	Tr	03.48	47-53	205	-	35
Newport Co	Tr	12.53	53-57	93	-	6

LUCIC Teddy
Biskopsgaard, Sweden, 15 April, 1973 Sweden 52 (CD)

League Club	Source	Date Signed	Seasons Played	Apps	Subs	Gls
Leeds U (L)	AIK Solna (Swe)	08.02	02	16	1	1

LUCKETT Paul
Coventry, 12 January, 1957 (FB)

League Club	Source	Date Signed	Seasons Played	Apps	Subs	Gls
Halifax T	Coventry C (App)	08.74	74-75	26	1	0
Hartlepool	Tr	03.76	75-76	19	0	0

LUCKETTI Christopher (Chris) James
Littleborough, 28 September, 1971 (CD)

League Club	Source	Date Signed	Seasons Played	Apps	Subs	Gls
Rochdale	YT	•	88	1	0	0
Stockport Co	Tr	08.90				
Halifax T	Tr	07.91	91-92	73	5	2
Bury	Tr	10.93	93-98	235	0	8
Huddersfield T	Tr	06.99	99-01	68	0	1
Preston NE	Tr	08.01	01-04	161	0	9

LUDDEN Dominic James
Basildon, 30 March, 1974 ESch (FB)

League Club	Source	Date Signed	Seasons Played	Apps	Subs	Gls
Leyton Orient	Billericay T	07.92	92-93	50	8	1
Watford	Tr	08.94	94-96	28	5	0
Preston NE	Tr	07.98	98-00	29	8	0
Halifax T	Tr	07.01	01	2	0	0

LUDFORD George Albert
Barnet, 22 March, 1915 Died 2001 (WH)

League Club	Source	Date Signed	Seasons Played	Apps	Subs	Gls
Tottenham H	Jnrs	05.36	36-49	75	-	7

LUDLAM Craig
Sheffield, 8 November, 1976 (FB)

League Club	Source	Date Signed	Seasons Played	Apps	Subs	Gls
Sheffield Wed	YT	05.95				
Notts Co	L	10.96	96	1	0	0

LUDLAM Steven (Steve) John
Chesterfield, 18 October, 1955 (M)

League Club	Source	Date Signed	Seasons Played	Apps	Subs	Gls
Sheffield U	App	01.73	75-76	26	1	1
Carlisle U	Tr	05.77	77-79	90	6	11
Chester	Tr	07.80	80-82	100	2	12

LUFF Neil John
Bletchley, 9 April, 1969 (M)

League Club	Source	Date Signed	Seasons Played	Apps	Subs	Gls
Gillingham	Jnrs	06.87	87	0	1	0

LUGG Raymond (Ray)
Jarrow, 18 July, 1948 (M)

League Club	Source	Date Signed	Seasons Played	Apps	Subs	Gls
Middlesbrough	Jnrs	07.65	66-69	34	3	3
Watford	Tr	11.69	69-71	51	8	3
Plymouth Arg	Tr	07.72	72	22	2	1
Crewe Alex	Tr	07.73	73-77	183	2	10
Bury	Tr	07.78	78-79	68	3	2

LUKE George
Hetton-le-Hole, 9 November, 1948 ESch (WH)

League Club	Source	Date Signed	Seasons Played	Apps	Subs	Gls
Newcastle U	App	03.66				
Chelsea	Tr	03.67	66	1	0	0

LUKE George Baron
Lanchester, 20 October, 1932 Died 2001 (CF)

League Club	Source	Date Signed	Seasons Played	Apps	Subs	Gls
Sheffield U	Esh Winning	01.52	53-54	7	-	0
Scunthorpe U	Tr	05.56	56	18	-	6

LUKE George Thomas
Newcastle, 17 December, 1933 (W)

League Club	Source	Date Signed	Seasons Played	Apps	Subs	Gls
Newcastle U	Jnrs	12.50				
Hartlepools U	Tr	10.53	53-59	186	-	60
Newcastle U	Tr	10.59	59-60	27	-	4
Darlington	Tr	01.61	60-62	68	-	11

LUKE Noel Emmanuel
Birmingham, 28 December, 1964 (W)

League Club	Source	Date Signed	Seasons Played	Apps	Subs	Gls
West Bromwich A	App	04.82	82-83	8	1	1
Mansfield T	Tr	07.84	84-85	41	7	9
Peterborough U	Tr	08.86	86-92	270	7	27
Rochdale	Tr	03.93	92	2	1	0

LUKE William (Billy)
Aberdeen, 19 April, 1932 (IF)

League Club	Source	Date Signed	Seasons Played	Apps	Subs	Gls
Crewe Alex	East Fife	10.55	55	1	-	0

LUKIC Jovan (John)
Chesterfield, 11 December, 1960 EYth/Eu21-7/EB (G)

League Club	Source	Date Signed	Seasons Played	Apps	Subs	Gls
Leeds U	App	12.78	79-82	146	0	0
Arsenal	Tr	07.83	83-89	223	0	0
Leeds U	Tr	06.90	90-95	209	0	0
Arsenal	Tr	07.96	96-00	18	0	0

LUMBY James (Jim) Anthony
Grimsby, 2 October, 1954 (CD)

League Club	Source	Date Signed	Seasons Played	Apps	Subs	Gls
Grimsby T	Jnrs	10.72	73-74	28	3	12
Scunthorpe U	Brigg T	03.77	76-77	55	0	28
Carlisle U	Tr	04.78	77-78	24	3	7
Tranmere Rov	Tr	07.79	79-80	43	3	21
Mansfield T	Tr	01.81	80-81	49	2	18

LUMLEY Robert (Bobby)
Leadgate, 6 January, 1933 (IF)

League Club	Source	Date Signed	Seasons Played	Apps	Subs	Gls
Charlton Ath	Jnrs	01.50	53-54	6	-	0
Hartlepools U	Tr	02.55	54-57	107	-	19
Chesterfield	Tr	12.57	57-58	25	-	2
Gateshead	Tr	06.59	59	40	-	6
Hartlepools U	Tr	07.60	60	38	-	6

LUMLEY Ilderton Thomas (Tommy)
Leadgate, 9 December, 1924 (IF)

League Club	Source	Date Signed	Seasons Played	Apps	Subs	Gls
Charlton Ath	Consett	12.48	48-51	37	-	10
Barnsley	Tr	03.52	51-55	146	-	36
Darlington	Tr	08.56	56	15	-	3

LUMSDEN Alexander (Alex)
Falkirk, 24 May, 1946 (IF)

League Club	Source	Date Signed	Seasons Played	Apps	Subs	Gls
Southend U	Camelon Jnrs	02.66	65-66	2	0	0

LUMSDEN James (Jimmy) Murdoch
Glasgow, 7 November, 1947 (M)

League Club	Source	Date Signed	Seasons Played	Apps	Subs	Gls
Leeds U	Jnrs	11.66	66-69	3	1	0
Southend U	Tr	09.70	70	12	0	0

LUMSDEN John David
Newcastle-under-Lyme, 30 July, 1956 (FB)

League Club	Source	Date Signed	Seasons Played	Apps	Subs	Gls
Stoke C	App	08.73	75-77	26	2	0
Port Vale	L	03.78	77	5	0	0

LUMSDEN John Ivor
Heanor, 1 July, 1942 (FB)

League Club	Source	Date Signed	Seasons Played	Apps	Subs	Gls
Aston Villa	Jnrs	07.59				
Workington	Tr	02.62	61-67	251	2	6
Chesterfield	Tr	03.68	67-70	94	0	0

LUMSDEN John Watson
Edinburgh, 15 December, 1960 (M)

League Club	Source	Date Signed	Seasons Played	Apps	Subs	Gls
Stoke C	East Fife	02.80	79-81	2	4	0

LUMSDON Christopher (Chris)
Newcastle, 15 December, 1979 (M)

League Club	Source	Date Signed	Seasons Played	Apps	Subs	Gls
Sunderland	YT	07.97	97-99	2	0	0
Blackpool	L	02.00	99	6	0	1
Crewe Alex	L	09.00	00	14	2	0
Barnsley	Tr	10.01	01-03	70	15	13

LUNAN Daniel (Danny) Dean
Bromley, 14 March, 1984 (FB)

League Club	Source	Date Signed	Seasons Played	Apps	Subs	Gls
Southend U	YT	•	01	0	1	0

LUND Andreas
Kristiansand, Norway, 7 May, 1975 Norway 8 (F)

League Club	Source	Date Signed	Seasons Played	Apps	Subs	Gls
Wimbledon	Molde FK (Nor)	02.00	99	10	2	2

LUND Gary James
Grimsby, 13 September, 1964 ESch/Eu21-3 (F)

League Club	Source	Date Signed	Seasons Played	Apps	Subs	Gls
Grimsby T	Jnrs	07.83	83-85	47	13	24
Lincoln C	Tr	08.86	86	41	3	13
Notts Co	Tr	06.87	87-94	223	25	62
Hull C	L	08.92	92	5	0	2
Hull C	L	01.93	92	6	0	1
Hull C	L	03.95	94	11	0	3
Chesterfield	Tr	12.95	95-96	13	5	1

LUNDEKVAM Claus
Austevoll, Norway, 22 February, 1973 Nou21-16/No-37 (CD)

League Club	Source	Date Signed	Seasons Played	Apps	Subs	Gls
Southampton	SK Brann Bergen (Nor)	09.96	96-04	283	7	1

LUNDIN Paul Michael
Osby, Sweden, 21 November, 1964 (G)

League Club	Source	Date Signed	Seasons Played	Apps	Subs	Gls
Oxford U	Osters IF (Swe)	03.99	98-99	28	1	0

LUNDON Sean
Liverpool, 7 March, 1969 (M)

League Club	Source	Date Signed	Seasons Played	Apps	Subs	Gls
Chester C	YT	12.86	86-90	48	8	4

LUNDSTRUM Colin Francis
Colchester, 9 October, 1938 (W)

League Club	Source	Date Signed	Seasons Played	Apps	Subs	Gls
Ipswich T	West Ham U (Am)	11.56	57-59	13	-	1
Colchester U	Tr	08.61	61	1	-	0

LUNN Dennis
Barnsley, 20 November, 1938 (CD)

League Club	Source	Date Signed	Seasons Played	Apps	Subs	Gls
Doncaster Rov	Wombwell	10.58	59-61	85	-	0

LUNN George
Bolton-on-Dearne, 28 June, 1915 Died 2000 (CD)

League Club	Source	Date Signed	Seasons Played	Apps	Subs	Gls
Aston Villa	Frickley Colliery	05.38				
Birmingham C	Tr	09.46				
Watford	Tr	10.47	47	5	-	0

LUNN Grant
Guildford, 26 August, 1967 (G)

League Club	Source	Date Signed	Seasons Played	Apps	Subs	Gls
Aldershot	Farnborough T	08.85	85	9	0	0

LUNN Henry (Harry)
Lurgan, 20 March, 1925 Died 1980 (W)

League Club	Source	Date Signed	Seasons Played	Apps	Subs	Gls
Notts Co	Glenavon	07.46	46	24	-	5
Portsmouth	Tr	07.47	47	1	-	0
Swindon T	Tr	05.48	48-53	196	-	30

LUNN Jack (Jackie)
Smithies, 14 October, 1937 Died 1988 (W)

League Club	Source	Date Signed	Seasons Played	Apps	Subs	Gls
Barnsley	Jnrs	05.56	56-60	56	-	19
Chesterfield	Tr	07.61	61	40	-	13

LUNN William (Billy) John
Lurgan, 8 May, 1923 Died 2000 NISch (IF)

League Club	Source	Date Signed	Seasons Played	Apps	Subs	Gls
West Bromwich A	Hereford U	02.46	46-47	10	-	5
Bournemouth	Tr	02.48	47-49	47	-	19
Newport Co	Tr	07.50	50-51	6	-	1

LUNNISS Roy Evan
Islington, 4 November, 1939 (FB)

League Club	Source	Date Signed	Seasons Played	Apps	Subs	Gls
Crystal Palace	Carshalton Ath	04.60	59-62	25	-	1
Portsmouth	Tr	06.63	63-65	69	0	1
Luton T	Addington (SA)	12.66	66	1	0	0

LUNT Kenneth (Kenny) Vincent
Runcorn, 20 November, 1979 ESch/EYth (M)

League Club	Source	Date Signed	Seasons Played	Apps	Subs	Gls
Crewe Alex	YT	06.97	97-04	300	30	31

LUNT Robert John
Widnes, 11 December, 1973 (W)

League Club	Source	Date Signed	Seasons Played	Apps	Subs	Gls
Wrexham	YT	●	90-91	1	8	0

LUNTALA Tresor
Dreux, France, 31 May, 1982 (M)

League Club	Source	Date Signed	Seasons Played	Apps	Subs	Gls
Birmingham C	Rennes (Fr)	08.99	01	9	6	0

LUSCOMBE Lee James
Guernsey, 16 July, 1971 (W)

League Club	Source	Date Signed	Seasons Played	Apps	Subs	Gls
Southampton	YT	04.89				
Brentford	Tr	10.91	91-92	29	13	6
Millwall	Tr	06.93	93	0	2	0
Doncaster Rov	Tr	02.94	93	5	3	0

LUSTED Leslie (Les) Reginald
Reading, 20 September, 1931 (IF)

League Club	Source	Date Signed	Seasons Played	Apps	Subs	Gls
Leyton Orient	Harwich & Parkeston	12.52	52-53	23	-	6
Aldershot	Tr	07.54	54-55	10	-	1

LUTTON Robert (Bertie) John
Banbridge, 13 July, 1950 NI-6 (W)

League Club	Source	Date Signed	Seasons Played	Apps	Subs	Gls
Wolverhampton W	Jnrs	09.67	68-70	16	5	1
Brighton & Hove A	Tr	09.71	71-72	18	11	4
West Ham U	Tr	01.73	72-73	8	4	1

LUZHNY Oleg
Kiev, Ukraine, 5 August, 1968 USSR-8/Ukraine-52 (FB)

League Club	Source	Date Signed	Seasons Played	Apps	Subs	Gls
Arsenal	Dynamo Kiev (Uk)	07.99	99-02	58	17	0
Wolverhampton W	Tr	07.03	03	4	2	0

LUZI BERNARDI Patrice
Ajaccio, France, 8 July, 1980 (G)

League Club	Source	Date Signed	Seasons Played	Apps	Subs	Gls
Liverpool	AS Monaco (Fr)	08.02	03	0	1	0

LYALL George
Wick, 4 May, 1947 (M)

League Club	Source	Date Signed	Seasons Played	Apps	Subs	Gls
Preston NE	Raith Rov	03.66	65-71	91	14	16
Nottingham F	Tr	05.72	72-75	108	8	24
Hull C	Tr	12.75	75-76	42	0	5

LYALL John Angus
Ilford, 24 February, 1940 EYth (FB)

League Club	Source	Date Signed	Seasons Played	Apps	Subs	Gls
West Ham U	Jnrs	05.57	59-62	31	-	0

LYDERSEN Pal
Odense, Denmark, 10 September, 1965 Norway int (FB)

League Club	Source	Date Signed	Seasons Played	Apps	Subs	Gls
Arsenal	IK Start (Nor)	11.91	91-92	12	3	0

LYDIATE Jason Lee
Manchester, 29 October, 1971 (CD)

League Club	Source	Date Signed	Seasons Played	Apps	Subs	Gls
Manchester U	YT	07.90				
Bolton W	Tr	03.92	91-94	29	1	0
Blackpool	Tr	03.95	94-97	81	5	2
Scarborough	Tr	08.98	98	26	1	1
Rochdale	L	02.99	98	14	0	1

LYDON George Michael (Micky)
Sunderland, 25 November, 1933 ESch (IF)

League Club	Source	Date Signed	Seasons Played	Apps	Subs	Gls
Sunderland	Hylton Colliery Jnrs	12.50				
Leeds U	Tr	06.54	54	4	-	1
Gateshead	Tr	11.55	55-58	106	-	24

LYMAN Colin Charles
Northampton, 9 March, 1914 Died 1986 (W)

League Club	Source	Date Signed	Seasons Played	Apps	Subs	Gls
Southend U	Rushden T	03.34	33	1	-	0
Northampton T	Tr	11.34	34-37	86	-	29
Tottenham H	Tr	10.37	37-38	46	-	10
Port Vale	Tr	05.46	46	11	-	1
Nottingham F	Tr	10.46	46	23	-	9
Notts Co	Tr	08.47	47	21	-	5

LYNAM Christopher (Chris) Anthony
Manchester, 22 January, 1962 (W)

League Club	Source	Date Signed	Seasons Played	Apps	Subs	Gls
Manchester U	App	01.80				
Carlisle U	Ryoden (HK)	08.86	86	1	1	0

LYNCH Anthony (Tony) Junior
Paddington, 20 January, 1966 (W)

League Club	Source	Date Signed	Seasons Played	Apps	Subs	Gls
Brentford	Maidstone U	01.84	83-85	35	10	6
Barnet	Wealdstone	10.90	91-93	18	18	4

LYNCH Barry John
Birmingham, 8 June, 1951 (FB)

League Club	Source	Date Signed	Seasons Played	Apps	Subs	Gls
Aston Villa	App	01.69	68-69	2	0	0
Grimsby T	Atlanta (USA)	09.72	72	10	4	0
Scunthorpe U	Tr	07.73	73-74	62	2	0
Torquay U	Portland (USA)	09.75	75-76	67	3	2

LYNCH Christopher (Chris) John
Middlesbrough, 18 November, 1974 (M)

League Club	Source	Date Signed	Seasons Played	Apps	Subs	Gls
Hartlepool U	Halifax T (YT)	08.93	92-95	38	12	2

LYNCH Gavin
Chester, 7 September, 1985 (F)

League Club	Source	Date Signed	Seasons Played	Apps	Subs	Gls
Chester C	YT	●	04	0	1	0

LYNCH John
Uddingston, 22 September, 1917 (G)

League Club	Source	Date Signed	Seasons Played	Apps	Subs	Gls
Workington	Dunfermline Ath	10.52	52	2	-	0

LYNCH Mark John
Manchester, 2 September, 1981 (FB)

League Club	Source	Date Signed	Seasons Played	Apps	Subs	Gls
Manchester U	YT	07.01				
Sunderland	Tr	07.04	04	5	6	0

LYNCH Patrick (Pat)
Belfast, 22 January, 1950 (CD)

League Club	Source	Date Signed	Seasons Played	Apps	Subs	Gls
Middlesbrough	Cliftonville	06.70	71	0	1	0

LYNCH Simon George
Montreal, Canada, 19 May, 1982 Su21-13/SB-2 (F)

League Club	Source	Date Signed	Seasons Played	Apps	Subs	Gls
Preston NE	Glasgow Celtic	01.03	02-04	14	31	2
Stockport Co	L	12.03	03	9	0	3
Blackpool	L	12.04	04	5	2	0

LYNCH Terence (Terry) John
Newport, 17 May, 1952 (G)

League Club	Source	Date Signed	Seasons Played	Apps	Subs	Gls
Newport Co	Jnrs	11.69	69-71	56	0	0

LYNCH Thomas (Tommy) Michael
Limerick, 10 October, 1964 (FB)

League Club	Source	Date Signed	Seasons Played	Apps	Subs	Gls
Sunderland	Limerick	08.88	88	4	0	0
Shrewsbury T	Tr	01.90	89-95	220	14	14

LYNE Neil George Francis
Leicester, 4 April, 1970 (W)

League Club	Source	Date Signed	Seasons Played	Apps	Subs	Gls
Nottingham F	Leicester U	08.89				
Walsall	L	03.90	89	6	1	0
Shrewsbury T	L	03.91	90	16	0	6
Shrewsbury T	Tr	07.91	91-92	61	3	11
Cambridge U	Tr	01.93	92-93	5	12	0
Chesterfield	L	09.93	93	5	1	1
Hereford U	Tr	07.94	94-95	49	14	2
Northampton T	Tr	08.96	96	1	0	0

LYNEX Steven (Steve) Charles
West Bromwich, 23 January, 1958 (W)

League Club	Source	Date Signed	Seasons Played	Apps	Subs	Gls
West Bromwich A	App	01.76				
Birmingham C	Shamrock Rov	04.79	78-80	28	18	10
Leicester C	Tr	02.81	80-86	200	13	57
Birmingham C	L	10.86	86	10	0	2
West Bromwich A	Tr	03.87	86-87	26	3	3
Cardiff C	Tr	07.88	88-89	56	6	2

LYNG Ciaran
Wexford, 24 July, 1985 IRYth (M)

League Club	Source	Date Signed	Seasons Played	Apps	Subs	Gls
Preston NE	Sch	09.03				
Shrewsbury T	Tr	12.04	04	0	4	0

LYNN Francis (Frank)
Consett, 29 May, 1929 (W)

League Club	Source	Date Signed	Seasons Played	Apps	Subs	Gls
Grimsby T	Blackhall CW	12.47	48	2	-	0

LYNN Joseph (Joe)
Seaton Sluice, 31 January, 1925 Died 1992 (WH)

League Club	Source	Date Signed	Seasons Played	Apps	Subs	Gls
Huddersfield T	Cramlington	05.47	49	5	-	0
Exeter C	Tr	06.50	50	29	-	2
Rochdale	Tr	07.51	51-55	193	-	23

LYNN Samuel (Sammy)
St Helens, 25 December, 1920 Died 1995 (WH)

League Club	Source	Date Signed	Seasons Played	Apps	Subs	Gls
Manchester U	Jnrs	01.38	47-49	13	-	0
Bradford PA	Tr	02.51	50-52	73	-	0

LYNN Stanley (Stan)
Bolton, 18 June, 1928 Died 2002 (FB)

League Club	Source	Date Signed	Seasons Played	Apps	Subs	Gls
Accrington St	Whitworths	07.47	46-49	35	-	2
Aston Villa	Tr	03.50	50-61	281	-	36
Birmingham C	Tr	10.61	61-65	131	0	26

LYNN William
Newcastle, 20 January, 1947 (W)

League Club	Source	Date Signed	Seasons Played	Apps	Subs	Gls
Huddersfield T		07.65	65-66	4	0	0

LYNNE Michael (Mike) George Anthony
Kettering, 20 March, 1938 (G)

League Club	Source	Date Signed	Seasons Played	Apps	Subs	Gls
Preston NE	Jnrs	03.56	58	2	-	0
Bournemouth	Tr	06.59	59-60	17	-	0

LYON David Edward
Oldham, 21 November, 1948 (M)

League Club	Source	Date Signed	Seasons Played	Apps	Subs	Gls
Bolton W	App	11.66				
Southport	Sacramento (USA)	09.76	76	11	2	1

League Club	Source	Date Signed	Seasons Played	Career Record Apps	Subs	Gls
LYON David George						
Bowden, 18 January, 1951						(CD)
Bury	App	01.69	68-71	65	6	0
Huddersfield T	Tr	09.71	71-73	24	1	0
Mansfield T	L	11.73	73	2	0	0
Cambridge U	Tr	07.74	74-76	84	1	11
Northampton T	Tr	10.77	77	6	0	0
LYON Thomas (Tom) King						
Clydebank, 17 March, 1915						(IF)
Blackpool	Albion Rov	03.37	36-37	6	-	0
Chesterfield	Tr	09.38	38-47	41	-	22
New Brighton	Tr	07.48	48	36	-	7
LYONS Andrew (Andy)						
Blackpool, 19 October, 1966						(W)
Crewe Alex	Fleetwood T	10.92	92-93	7	4	2
Wigan Ath	Tr	10.93	93-95	79	8	27
LYONS Barry						
Shirebrook, 14 March, 1945						(W)
Rotherham U	Jnrs	09.62	63-66	125	0	23
Nottingham F	Tr	11.66	66-72	201	2	28
York C	Tr	09.73	73-75	80	5	11
Darlington	Tr	07.76	76-78	97	0	10
LYONS Brian						
Darfield, 3 December, 1948						(CD)
Bradford PA (Am)	Houghton Main Colliery	03.68	67	3	0	0
LYONS Darren Peter						
Manchester, 9 November, 1966						(W)
Bury	Ashton U	03.92	91-92	23	13	7
LYONS Albert **Edward (Eddie)**						
Rochdale, 20 May, 1920 Died 1996						(FB)
Bury		04.45	47-48	2	-	0
Millwall	Tr	03.50	49-51	6	-	0
Crewe Alex	Tr	07.52	52-53	23	-	0
Rochdale	Tr	12.53	53-54	19	-	1
LYONS George William						
Rochdale, 1 May, 1935						(W)
Rochdale		12.53	53-56	29	-	4
LYONS John Patrick						
Buckley, 8 November, 1956 Died 1982						(F)
Wrexham	Jnrs	06.75	74-78	63	23	23
Millwall	Tr	07.79	79-80	55	0	20
Cambridge U	Tr	10.80	80-81	20	1	6
Colchester U	Tr	02.82	81-82	31	2	9
LYONS Michael (Mike)						
Liverpool, 8 December, 1951 Eu23-5/EB						(CD)
Everton	App	07.69	70-81	364	25	48
Sheffield Wed	Tr	08.82	82-85	129	0	12
Grimsby T	Tr	11.85	85-86	50	0	4
LYONS Michael (Mike) Charles						
Iron Acton, 31 January, 1932						(FB)
Bristol C	Jnrs	06.50	50-51	2	-	0
Bristol Rov	Tr	07.53	53	2	-	0
Bournemouth	Tr	07.56	56-58	105	-	0
Swindon T	Tr	11.59	59	2	-	0
LYONS Paul						
Leigh, 24 June, 1977						(FB)
Rochdale	Manchester U (YT)	09.95	95	1	2	0
LYONS Simon Ronald						
Watchet, 2 December, 1982						(CD)
Torquay U	YT	07.01	00	0	9	1
LYONS Terence (Terry)						
Bradford, 14 April, 1929 Died 1986						(W)
Burnley		10.49	50	12	-	3
Bradford PA	Tr	09.51	51-52	38	-	6
LYSKE James (Jimmy) Herbert Alexander						
Lurgan, 7 October, 1932						(FB)
Sunderland	Glenavon	11.57				
Darlington	Tr	02.58	57-58	16	-	0
LYTHGOE Arnold						
Bolton, 7 March, 1922						(WH)
Accrington St	Linfield	09.45	46	10	-	0
LYTHGOE Derrick						
Bolton, 5 May, 1933						(IF)
Blackpool	Jnrs	05.50	55-57	4	-	1
Norwich C	Tr	03.58	57-61	62	-	22
Bristol C	Tr	08.62	62-63	13	-	2
LYTHGOE Philip (Phil)						
Norwich, 18 December, 1959						(M)
Norwich C	App	12.77	77-79	9	3	1
Bristol Rov	L	09.78	78	6	0	0
Oxford U	Tr	08.80	80-81	23	5	3
LYTTLE Desmond (Des)						
Wolverhampton, 24 September, 1971						(W)
Leicester C	YT	09.90				
Swansea C	Worcester C	07.92	92	46	0	1
Nottingham F	Tr	07.93	93-98	177	8	3
Port Vale	L	11.98	98	7	0	0
Watford	Tr	07.99	99	11	0	0
West Bromwich A	Tr	03.00	99-02	61	15	1
Northampton T	Stourport Swifts	11.03	03	23	4	0

League Club	Source	Date Signed	Seasons Played	Career Record Apps	Subs	Gls
MABBUTT Gary Vincent						
Bristol, 23 August, 1961 EYth/Eu21-7/EB/E-16						(CD)
Bristol Rov	App	01.79	78-81	122	9	10
Tottenham H	Tr	08.82	82-97	458	19	27
MABBUTT Kevin Richard						
Bristol, 5 December, 1958 ESch						(F)
Bristol C	App	01.76	77-81	112	17	29
Crystal Palace	Tr	10.81	81-84	67	8	22
MABBUTT Raymond (Ray) William						
Aylesbury, 13 March, 1936						(M)
Bristol Rov	Yorkshire Amats	08.56	57-68	392	2	27
Newport Co	Tr	09.69	69-70	39	6	14
MABEE Gary Lee						
Oxford, 1 February, 1955						(F)
Tottenham H	App	02.72				
Northampton T	Tr	08.74	74-75	29	4	13
MABIZELA Oldjohn **Mbulelo**						
Pietermaritzburg, South Africa, 16 September, 1980 South Africa 37						(CD)
Tottenham H	Orlando Pirates (SA)	08.03	03-04	1	6	1
McADAM David Frederick						
Hereford, 3 April, 1923						(WH)
Leeds U	Stapenhill WMC	05.48	48-49	24	-	0
Wrexham	Tr	05.50	50	10	-	0
McADAM Neil Bernard						
East Kilbride, 30 July, 1957						(G)
Port Vale	Northwich Vic	08.82	82	2	0	0
McADAM Steven (Steve)						
Portadown, 2 April, 1960						(FB)
Burnley	Portadown	05.78	79	5	0	0
Wigan Ath	Barnsley (N/C)	11.80	80-81	26	0	0
McADAM Thomas (Tom) Ian						
Glasgow, 9 April, 1954 SLge-1						(CD)
Stockport Co	Glasgow Celtic	08.86	86	5	0	1
McADAMS William (Billy) John						
Belfast, 20 January, 1934 Died 2002 NI-15						(F)
Manchester C	Distillery	12.53	53-59	127	-	62
Bolton W	Tr	09.60	60-61	44	-	26
Leeds U	Tr	12.61	61	11	-	3
Brentford	Tr	07.62	62-64	75	-	36
Queens Park Rgrs	Tr	09.64	64-65	33	0	11
Barrow	Tr	07.66	66-67	53	0	9
McALEA Robert Joseph						
Belfast, 13 September, 1920						(IF)
Bradford C	Ballymoney U	07.48	48	4	-	0
McALEER Francis (Frank)						
Glasgow, 16 October, 1945						(M)
Shrewsbury T	Morton	03.70				
Barrow	Tr	08.70	70	9	1	0
McALINDEN James (Jimmy)						
Belfast, 31 December, 1917 Died 1993 IrLge-5/NIRL-8/LoI-1/IR-2/I-4						(IF)
Portsmouth	Belfast Celtic	12.38	38-47	53	-	9
Stoke C	Tr	09.47	47-48	33	-	2
Southend U	Tr	10.48	48-53	217	-	12
McALINDEN Robert (Bobby)						
Salford, 22 May, 1946						(W)
Manchester C	Aston Villa (App)	05.64	63	1	-	0
Port Vale	Toronto (Can)	09.65				
Bournemouth	Los Angeles (USA)	09.76	76	1	0	0
McALINDON Gareth Edward						
Hexham, 6 April, 1977						(F)
Carlisle U	Newcastle U (YT)	07.95	95-98	22	37	5
McALINDON John (Johnny)						
Carlisle, 25 December, 1930 Died 2002						(CF)
Shrewsbury T	Glasgow Celtic	05.57	57	12	-	3
McALISKEY John James						
Huddersfield, 2 September, 1984 IRu21-1						(F)
Huddersfield T	Sch	05.04	03-04	12	14	6

League Club	Source	Date Signed	Seasons Played	Career Record Apps	Subs	Gls
McALISTER Thomas (Tom) Gerald						
Clydebank, 10 December, 1952						(G)
Sheffield U	App	05.70	71-75	63	0	0
Rotherham U	Tr	01.76	75-78	159	0	0
Blackpool	Tr	07.79	79	16	0	0
Swindon T	Tr	05.80	80	1	0	0
Bristol Rov	L	02.81	80	13	0	0
West Ham U	Tr	05.81	81-88	85	0	0
Colchester U	L	02.89	88	20	0	0
McALLE John Edward						
Liverpool, 31 January, 1950						(CD)
Wolverhampton W	App	02.67	67-80	394	12	0
Sheffield U	Tr	08.81	81	18	0	0
Derby Co	Tr	04.82	81-83	51	7	1
McALLISTER Brian						
Glasgow, 30 November, 1970 S-3						(CD)
Wimbledon	YT	03.89	89-97	74	11	0
Plymouth Arg	L	12.90	90	7	1	0
Crewe Alex	L	03.96	95	13	0	1
McALLISTER Donald (Don)						
Radcliffe, 26 May, 1953						(FB)
Bolton W	App	06.70	69-74	155	1	2
Tottenham H	Tr	02.75	74-80	168	4	9
Charlton Ath	Tr	08.81	81-82	55	0	6
Rochdale	Tampa Bay (USA)	11.84	84	3	0	0
McALLISTER Gary						
Motherwell, 25 December, 1964 Su21-1/SB-2/S-57						(M)
Leicester C	Motherwell	08.85	85-89	199	2	46
Leeds U	Tr	07.90	90-95	230	1	31
Coventry C	Tr	07.96	96-99	119	0	20
Liverpool	Tr	07.00	00-01	35	20	5
Coventry C	Tr	07.02	02-03	55	0	10
McALLISTER James (Jimmy)						
Barrhead, 30 October, 1931 Died 2001						(IF)
Millwall	Neilston Jnrs	06.54	54-55	20	-	6
Bradford PA	Morton	05.59	59-60	43	-	14
McALLISTER Kevin						
Falkirk, 8 November, 1962						(W)
Chelsea	Falkirk	05.85	85-90	78	28	7
McALONE Robert (Bob)						
Whitehaven, 16 February, 1928						(CD)
Workington	Kells	(N/L)	51-53	68	-	3
McALOON Gerald (Gerry) Padua						
Gorbals, 13 September, 1916 Died 1987						(IF)
Brentford	St Francis Jnrs	06.34	37-38	21	-	8
Wolverhampton W	Tr	03.39	38	2	-	1
Brentford	Tr	12.45	46	7	-	4
McANDREW Anthony (Tony)						
Glasgow, 11 April, 1956						(CD)
Middlesbrough	App	08.73	73-81	245	2	13
Chelsea	Tr	09.82	82-83	20	0	4
Middlesbrough	Tr	09.84	84-85	66	0	2
Darlington	Willington	11.88	88	11	0	0
Hartlepool U	Tr	03.89	88	4	0	0
MacANDREW Robert (Bob)						
Derby, 6 April, 1943						(FB)
Derby Co	Jnrs	06.61	63	1	-	0
McANEARNEY James (Jim)						
Dundee, 20 March, 1935						(M)
Sheffield Wed	St Stephen's (Dundee)	03.52	53-58	38	-	10
Plymouth Arg	Tr	01.60	59-63	135	-	34
Watford	Tr	11.63	63-66	84	2	19
Bradford C	Tr	09.66	66-67	41	4	5
McANEARNEY Thomas (Tom)						
Dundee, 6 January, 1933						(M)
Sheffield Wed	Dundee North End	10.51	52-64	352	-	19
Peterborough U	Tr	11.65	65	12	0	0
Aldershot	Tr	03.66	65-68	106	0	3
McANESPIE Kieran Liam						
Gosport, 11 September, 1979 SYth/Su21-4						(F)
Fulham	St Johnstone	08.00				
Bournemouth	L	02.02	01	3	4	1
Plymouth Arg	Tr	03.03	02	2	2	0
McANESPIE Stephen (Steve)						
Kilmarnock, 1 February, 1972 SYth						(FB)
Bolton W	Raith Rov	09.95	95-97	19	5	0
Fulham	Tr	11.97	97-98	3	4	0
Bradford C	L	03.98	97	7	0	0
Cambridge U	Tr	08.00	00-01	20	4	0

McANUFF Joel (Jobi) Joshua Frederick
Edmonton, 9 November, 1981 Jamaica 1 (M)

League Club	Source	Date Signed	Seasons Played	Apps	Subs	Gls
Wimbledon	YT	07.00	01-03	76	20	13
West Ham U	Tr	02.04	03-04	4	9	1
Cardiff C	Tr	08.04	04	42	1	2

McAREAVEY Paul
Belfast, 3 December, 1980 NIYth/NIu21-7 (M)

League Club	Source	Date Signed	Seasons Played	Apps	Subs	Gls
Swindon T	YT	07.99	97-01	10	14	1

McAREE Rodney (Rod) Joseph
Dungannon, 19 August, 1974 NISch/NIYth (M)

League Club	Source	Date Signed	Seasons Played	Apps	Subs	Gls
Liverpool	YT	08.91				
Bristol C	Tr	07.94	94	4	2	0
Fulham	Dungannon Swifts	12.95	95-97	22	6	3

MACARI Luigi (Lou)
Edinburgh, 7 June, 1949 Su23-2/S-24 (M)

League Club	Source	Date Signed	Seasons Played	Apps	Subs	Gls
Manchester U	Glasgow Celtic	01.73	72-83	311	18	78
Swindon T	Tr	07.84	84-85	33	3	3

MACARI Michael
Kilwinning, 4 February, 1973 (F)

League Club	Source	Date Signed	Seasons Played	Apps	Subs	Gls
Stoke C	West Ham U (YT)	07.91	96	15	15	3

MACARI Paul
Manchester, 23 August, 1976 (F)

League Club	Source	Date Signed	Seasons Played	Apps	Subs	Gls
Stoke C	Jnrs	08.93	97	0	3	0
Sheffield U	Tr	12.98				
Huddersfield T	Tr	07.00	01-02	0	11	0

McARTHUR Barry
Nottingham, 4 May, 1947 (F)

League Club	Source	Date Signed	Seasons Played	Apps	Subs	Gls
Nottingham F	Jnrs	05.65	65	7	1	4
Barrow	Tr	07.69	69	6	2	0
York C	Tr	12.69	69	1	0	0

McARTHUR Duncan Edward
Brighton, 6 May, 1981 (M)

League Club	Source	Date Signed	Seasons Played	Apps	Subs	Gls
Brighton & Hove A	YT	●	98	3	0	0

McARTHUR Thomas (Tom)
Neilston, 23 April, 1925 Died 1994 (CD)

League Club	Source	Date Signed	Seasons Played	Apps	Subs	Gls
Leicester C	Neilston Victoria	01.47	46-53	97	-	0
Plymouth Arg	Tr	01.54	53	2	-	0

McARTHUR Walter (Wally)
Denaby, 21 March, 1912 Died 1980 (WH)

League Club	Source	Date Signed	Seasons Played	Apps	Subs	Gls
Bristol Rov	Goldthorpe U	01.33	32-49	261	-	14

McATEER Andrew (Andy) William
Preston, 24 April, 1961 (FB)

League Club	Source	Date Signed	Seasons Played	Apps	Subs	Gls
Preston NE	App	04.79	79-86	236	2	8
Blackpool	Tr	12.86	86-87	37	4	0
Preston NE	Tr	05.88	88	11	2	1

McATEER Jason Wynn
Birkenhead, 18 June, 1971 IRB-1/IR-52 (M)

League Club	Source	Date Signed	Seasons Played	Apps	Subs	Gls
Bolton W	Marine	01.92	92-95	109	5	8
Liverpool	Tr	09.95	95-98	84	16	3
Blackburn Rov	Tr	01.99	98-01	58	14	4
Sunderland	Tr	10.01	01-03	53	0	5
Tranmere Rov	Tr	07.04	04	32	2	4

McAUGHTRIE Craig James
Burton-on-Trent, 3 March, 1981 (CD)

League Club	Source	Date Signed	Seasons Played	Apps	Subs	Gls
Sheffield U	YT	07.99				
Carlisle U	Tr	08.00	00-01	2	8	1

McAUGHTRIE David
Cumnock, 30 January, 1963 (CD)

League Club	Source	Date Signed	Seasons Played	Apps	Subs	Gls
Stoke C	App	01.81	80-83	48	3	2
Carlisle U	Tr	07.84	84	28	0	1
York C	Tr	06.85	85-86	64	0	1
Darlington	Tr	07.87	87-88	36	3	0

MACAULAY Archibald (Archie) Renwick
Falkirk, 30 July, 1915 Died 1993 SWar-5/S-7 (WH)

League Club	Source	Date Signed	Seasons Played	Apps	Subs	Gls
West Ham U	Glasgow Rgrs	06.37	37-46	83	-	29
Brentford	Tr	10.46	46	26	-	2
Arsenal	Tr	07.47	47-49	103	-	1
Fulham	Tr	06.50	50-52	49	-	4

McAULEY Gareth
Larne, 5 December, 1979 NISch/NIB-1/NI-1 (CD)

League Club	Source	Date Signed	Seasons Played	Apps	Subs	Gls
Lincoln C	Coleraine	08.04	04	32	5	3

McAULEY Hugh Albert
Bootle, 8 January, 1953 (W)

League Club	Source	Date Signed	Seasons Played	Apps	Subs	Gls
Liverpool	App	01.70				
Tranmere Rov	L	08.73	73	13	0	1
Plymouth Arg	Tr	10.74	74-76	76	1	7
Charlton Ath	Tr	12.76	76-77	55	0	9
Tranmere Rov	Tr	08.78	78	41	2	0
Carlisle U	Tr	07.79	79-80	14	3	1

McAULEY Hugh Francis
Plymouth, 13 May, 1976 (M)

League Club	Source	Date Signed	Seasons Played	Apps	Subs	Gls
Cheltenham T	Leek T	07.99	99-02	70	30	9
Kidderminster Hrs	Tr	03.03	02	0	4	0

MACAULEY James (Jimmy) Austin Russell
Edinburgh, 19 October, 1922 (WH)

League Club	Source	Date Signed	Seasons Played	Apps	Subs	Gls
Chelsea	Edinburgh Thistle	10.46	46-49	86	-	5
Aldershot	Tr	08.51	51	31	-	3

McAULEY Patrick (Pat) Comerford
Barrhead, 31 July, 1921 Died 1970 SLge-1 (WH)

League Club	Source	Date Signed	Seasons Played	Apps	Subs	Gls
Luton T	Glasgow Celtic	12.50	50	8	-	1

McAULEY Sean
Sheffield, 23 June, 1972 SYth/Su21-1 (FB)

League Club	Source	Date Signed	Seasons Played	Apps	Subs	Gls
Manchester U	YT	07.90				
Chesterfield (L)	St Johnstone	11.94	94	1	0	1
Hartlepool U	St Johnstone	07.95	95-96	84	0	1
Scunthorpe U	Tr	03.97	96-99	63	6	1
Scarborough	L	03.99	98	6	1	0
Rochdale	Tr	02.00	99-01	34	3	0

MACAULEY Stephen (Steve) Roy
Lytham, 4 March, 1969 (CD)

League Club	Source	Date Signed	Seasons Played	Apps	Subs	Gls
Manchester C	YT	11.87				
Crewe Alex	Fleetwood T	03.92	91-01	247	14	26
Macclesfield T	L	12.01	01	4	0	0
Macclesfield T	L	02.02	01	8	0	0
Rochdale	Tr	07.02	02	6	0	0
Macclesfield T	L	11.02	02	3	0	1
Macclesfield T	Tr	01.03	02-03	33	0	0

McAVENNIE Frank
Glasgow, 22 November, 1959 SYth/Su21-5/S-5 (F)

League Club	Source	Date Signed	Seasons Played	Apps	Subs	Gls
West Ham U	St Mirren	06.85	85-87	85	0	33
West Ham U	Glasgow Celtic	03.89	88-91	49	19	16
Aston Villa	Tr	08.92	92	0	3	0
Swindon T (L)	Glasgow Celtic	02.94	93	3	4	0

McAVOY Alan Joseph
Wigton, 4 October, 1963 Died 2001 (M)

League Club	Source	Date Signed	Seasons Played	Apps	Subs	Gls
Blackpool		02.81	81	6	0	0

McAVOY Andrew (Andy) David
Middlesbrough, 28 August, 1979 (M)

League Club	Source	Date Signed	Seasons Played	Apps	Subs	Gls
Blackburn Rov	YT	07.97				
Hartlepool U	Tr	11.99	99-00	7	14	0
Macclesfield T	Tr	08.01	01	4	6	0

McAVOY Douglas (Doug) Haig
Kilmarnock, 29 November, 1918 (IF)

League Club	Source	Date Signed	Seasons Played	Apps	Subs	Gls
Liverpool	Kilmarnock	12.47	47-48	2	-	0

McAVOY Lawrence (Larry) David
Lambeth, 7 September, 1979 (FB)

League Club	Source	Date Signed	Seasons Played	Apps	Subs	Gls
Cambridge U	YT	05.98	98	1	0	0

McBAIN Alan
Aberdeen, 10 February, 1940 (FB)

League Club	Source	Date Signed	Seasons Played	Apps	Subs	Gls
Swansea T	Aberdeen East End	01.59				
Carlisle U	Tr	06.60	60-62	70	-	0
Luton T	Tr	06.63	63-64	60	-	0

McBAIN Gordon Archibald
Glasgow, 4 December, 1934 (W)

League Club	Source	Date Signed	Seasons Played	Apps	Subs	Gls
Rochdale	Kilmarnock	05.58	58	10	-	1

McBAIN Neil
Campbeltown, 15 November 1895 Died 1974 S-3 (CD)

League Club	Source	Date Signed	Seasons Played	Apps	Subs	Gls
Manchester U	Third Lanark	11.21	21-22	42	-	2
Everton	Tr	01.23	22-25	97	-	1
Liverpool	St Johnstone	03.28	27-28	12	-	0
Watford	Tr	11.28	28-30	85	-	5
New Brighton	(Team Manager)	03.47	46	1	-	0

MacBENNETT James (Seamus) Congall
Newcastle, County Down, 16 November, 1925 Died 1995 (W)

League Club	Source	Date Signed	Seasons Played	Apps	Subs	Gls
Cardiff C	Belfast Celtic	09.47	47	4	-	2
Tranmere Rov	Tr	11.48	48-49	12	-	1

McBETH George
Belfast, 4 September, 1954 (W)

League Club	Source	Date Signed	Seasons Played	Apps	Subs	Gls
Manchester C	App	10.71				
Stockport Co	Tr	07.76	76-77	51	5	3

League Club	Source	Date Signed	Seasons Played	Apps	Subs	Gls
McBLAIN Andrew						
Bo'ness, 11 August, 1926						(WH)
Newport Co	Forth W	02.47	46-48	36	-	1
McBRIDE Andrew (Andy) David						
Kenya, 15 March, 1954						(CD)
Crystal Palace	App	10.71	73	1	0	0
McBRIDE Brian Robert						
Arlington Heights, USA, 19 June, 1972 USA 88						(F)
Preston NE (L)	Columbus (USA)	09.00	00	8	1	1
Everton (L)	Columbus (USA)	02.03	02	7	1	4
Fulham	Columbus (USA)	01.04	03-04	20	27	10
McBRIDE John						
Kilsyth, 31 December, 1923						(G)
Reading	Third Lanark	03.48	47-52	100	-	0
Shrewsbury T	Tr	12.52	52-55	78	-	0
McBRIDE Joseph (Joe)						
Kilmarnock, 10 June, 1938 SLge-4/S-2						(CF)
Wolverhampton W	Kilmarnock	12.59				
Luton T	Tr	02.60	59-60	25	-	9
McBRIDE Joseph (Joe)						
Glasgow, 17 August, 1960 SSch/Su21-1						(W)
Everton	App	08.78	79-81	51	6	9
Rotherham U	Tr	08.82	82-83	45	0	12
Oldham Ath	Tr	09.83	83-84	28	8	5
McBRIDE Peter Patrick						
Motherwell, 22 December, 1946						(M)
Manchester U	North Motherwell BC	12.63				
Southport	Tr	07.66	66	1	2	0
Bradford PA	Tr	07.67	67	5	2	0
McBRIDE Vincent (Vince)						
Manchester, 21 January, 1934						(G)
Walsall	Ashton U	05.54	54	11	-	0
Aston Villa	Tr	03.56				
Mansfield T	Tr	07.58	58	10	-	0
McBRIDE William (Bill)						
Brampton, Cumberland, 8 November, 1913 Died 1985						(FB)
Carlisle U		02.46	46	14	-	1
McBURNEY Michael (Mike) Leslie						
Wrexham, 12 September, 1953 WSch						(F)
Wrexham	Jnrs	07.71	70-72	20	4	4
Bolton W	Tr	05.73	73	1	0	0
Hartlepool	L	11.74	74	5	1	1
Tranmere Rov	L	03.75	74	4	1	0
MacCABE Andrew (Andy) Bruce						
Glasgow, 22 February, 1935 Died 1963						(W)
Chesterfield	Corby T	11.54	55-58	53	-	7
McCABE James (Jim) Joseph						
Draperstown, 17 September, 1918 Died 1989 I-5/NI-1						(WH)
Middlesbrough	South Bank East End	05.37	46-47	34	-	0
Leeds U	Tr	03.48	47-53	152	-	0
McCAFFERTY James (Jim)						
Motherwell, 10 July, 1957						(W)
Hereford U	Bristol C (App)	04.75	75	0	3	0
McCAFFERTY Neil						
Derry, 19 July, 1984						(M)
Charlton Ath	YT	08.01				
Cambridge U	L	12.03	03	5	1	0
Rushden & Diamonds	L	01.05	04	16	0	0
McCAFFERY Aidan						
Jarrow, 30 August, 1957 EYth						(CD)
Newcastle U	App	01.74	74-77	57	2	4
Derby Co	Tr	08.78	78-79	31	6	4
Bristol Rov	Tr	08.80	80-84	183	1	11
Bristol C	Tr	02.82	81	6	0	1
Torquay U	L	03.85	84	6	0	0
Exeter C	Tr	07.85	85-86	55	3	0
Hartlepool U	Tr	02.87	86	6	0	1
Carlisle U	Whitley Bay	01.88	87	14	0	0
McCAFFREY James (Jim)						
Luton, 12 October, 1951 EYth						(W)
Nottingham F	App	03.69	69	2	6	1
Mansfield T	Tr	07.72	72-76	170	8	21
Huddersfield T	Tr	01.77	76-77	23	4	0
Portsmouth	Tr	02.78	77-78	11	1	1
Northampton T	Tr	12.78	78-79	56	1	6

League Club	Source	Date Signed	Seasons Played	Apps	Subs	Gls
McCAIG Robert (Bobby) Alexander Marshall						
Lockerbie, 15 August, 1923 Died 1986						(W)
Carlisle U	Queen of the South	08.48	48	5	-	0
Blackburn Rov	Tr	12.48	48-50	30	-	2
Stockport Co	Tr	08.51	51	15	-	2
Halifax T	Tr	01.52	51	17	-	2
Crewe Alex	Tr	08.52	52-53	19	-	1
McCALDON Ian						
Liverpool, 14 September, 1974						(G)
Oxford U	Livingston	08.01	01	28	0	0
McCALL Alexander (Alex) Noteman						
Annan, 26 March, 1939						(WH)
Carlisle U		09.58	59	1	-	0
McCALL Andrew (Andy)						
Hamilton, 15 March, 1925						(IF)
Blackpool	Blantyre Celtic	07.47	47-50	87	-	15
West Bromwich A	Tr	01.51	50-51	31	-	3
Leeds U	Tr	08.52	52-54	62	-	8
Halifax T	Lovells Ath	07.56	56-59	139	-	15
McCALL Anthony (Tony) Edward						
Thatcham, 15 January, 1936						(W)
Reading	Jnrs	05.53	55-56	8	-	1
McCALL David						
Carlisle, 24 January, 1948						(W)
Workington	Jnrs	01.66	66	1	0	0
McCALL Ian Holland						
Dumfries, 13 September, 1964						(M)
Bradford C	Glasgow Rgrs	01.90	89	11	1	1
McCALL John (Johnny)						
Glasgow, 29 September, 1918 Died 1992						(IF)
Bradford PA	Workington	09.37	37-47	41	-	5
McCALL Peter						
West Ham, 11 September, 1936						(WH)
Bristol C	King's Lynn	04.55	57-61	78	-	1
Oldham Ath	Tr	05.62	62-64	108	-	5
McCALL Robert (Bob) Henry						
Worksop, 29 December, 1915 Died 1992						(FB)
Nottingham F	Worksop T	02.35	35-51	162	-	1
McCALL Stephen (Steve) Harold						
Carlisle, 15 October, 1960 EYth/Eu21-6/EB-1						(M)
Ipswich T	App	10.78	79-86	249	8	7
Sheffield Wed	Tr	06.87	87-90	21	8	2
Carlisle U	L	02.90	89	6	0	0
Plymouth Arg	Tr	03.92	91-95	97	3	5
Torquay U	Tr	07.96	96-97	43	8	2
Plymouth Arg	Tr	08.98	98-99	28	5	1
McCALL Andrew **Stuart** Murray						
Leeds, 10 June, 1964 EYth/Su21-2/S-40						(M)
Bradford C	App	06.82	82-87	235	3	37
Everton	Tr	06.88	88-90	99	4	6
Bradford C	Glasgow Rgrs	06.98	98-01	154	3	8
Sheffield U	Tr	07.02	02-03	69	2	2
McCALL William (Willie)						
Glasgow, 14 November, 1920						(W)
Newcastle U	Aberdeen	01.48	47-48	16	-	4
McCALLIOG James (Jim)						
Glasgow, 23 September, 1946 SSch/Su23-2/S-5						(M)
Chelsea	Leeds (Am)	09.63	64-65	7	0	2
Sheffield Wed	Tr	10.65	65-68	150	0	19
Wolverhampton W	Tr	08.69	69-73	158	5	34
Manchester U	Tr	03.74	73-74	31	0	7
Southampton	Tr	02.75	74-76	70	2	8
Lincoln C	Lyn Oslo (Nor)	09.78	78	9	0	0
McCALLUM Stewart						
Bearsden, 9 May, 1927						(WH)
Wrexham	Rhyl	06.50	50-52	67	-	0
Workington	Kettering T	06.54	54-55	10	-	1
Coventry C	Tr	02.56				
Hartlepools U	Tr	07.56	56	2	-	0
Southport	Tr	08.57	57	9	-	0
McCALMAN Donald (Don) Stuart						
Greenock, 18 October, 1935						(CD)
Bradford PA	Hibernian	06.59	59-65	297	0	5
Barrow	Tr	07.66	66	13	0	0
McCAMBRIDGE David (Dave) Thomas						
Larne, 26 July, 1921 Died 1982						(CD)
Barrow	Larne T	09.46	46-49	16	-	1

McCAMMON Mark Jason
Barnet, 7 August, 1978 (F)

League Club	Source	Date Signed	Seasons Played	Apps	Subs	Gls
Cambridge U	Cambridge C	12.96	97-98	1	3	0
Charlton Ath	Tr	03.99	99	1	3	0
Swindon T	L	01.00	99	4	0	0
Brentford	Tr	07.00	00-02	46	29	10
Millwall	Tr	03.03	02-04	15	7	2
Brighton & Hove A	Tr	12.04	04	16	2	3

McCANCE Daren
Consett, 13 September, 1973 (CD)

League Club	Source	Date Signed	Seasons Played	Apps	Subs	Gls
Reading	YT	07.92	92	1	0	0

McCANN Albert
Maidenhead, 1 November, 1941 (M)

League Club	Source	Date Signed	Seasons Played	Apps	Subs	Gls
Luton T	Jnrs	04.59	59-60	6	-	0
Coventry C	Tr	08.61	61	22	-	3
Portsmouth	Tr	08.62	62-73	331	7	83

McCANN Henry Austin
Alexandria, 21 January, 1980 (CD)

League Club	Source	Date Signed	Seasons Played	Apps	Subs	Gls
Boston U	Clyde	08.04	04	45	0	1

McCANN Gavin Peter
Blackpool, 10 January, 1978 E-1 (M)

League Club	Source	Date Signed	Seasons Played	Apps	Subs	Gls
Everton	YT	07.95	97	5	6	0
Sunderland	Tr	11.98	98-02	106	10	8
Aston Villa	Tr	07.03	03-04	48	0	1

McCANN Grant Samuel
Belfast, 14 April, 1980 NIu21-11/NI-9 (M)

League Club	Source	Date Signed	Seasons Played	Apps	Subs	Gls
West Ham U	YT	07.98	00-01	0	4	0
Notts Co	L	08.00	00	2	0	0
Cheltenham T	L	10.00	00	27	3	3
Cheltenham T	L	10.02	02	8	0	0
Cheltenham T	Tr	01.03	02-04	101	0	18

McCANN James (Jim)
Dundee, 20 May, 1954 (F)

League Club	Source	Date Signed	Seasons Played	Apps	Subs	Gls
Nottingham F	App	05.72	74-75	2	4	1
Stockport Co	L	10.75	75	4	1	0
Halifax T	L	10.76	76	2	0	1

McCANN John (Johnny)
Govan, 27 July, 1934 SB (W)

League Club	Source	Date Signed	Seasons Played	Apps	Subs	Gls
Barnsley	Bridgeton Waverley	12.55	55-58	118	-	17
Bristol C	Tr	05.59	59-60	30	-	0
Huddersfield T	Tr	10.60	60-62	20	-	1
Derby Co	Tr	09.62	62-63	55	-	2
Darlington	Tr	08.64	64	4	-	0
Chesterfield	Tr	10.64	64-65	41	0	9

McCANN Neil Doherty
Greenock, 11 August, 1974 Su21-9/SB-2/S-23 (W)

League Club	Source	Date Signed	Seasons Played	Apps	Subs	Gls
Southampton	Glasgow Rgrs	08.03	03-04	14	15	0

McCANN Ryan Patrick
Coatbridge, 21 September, 1981 (M)

League Club	Source	Date Signed	Seasons Played	Apps	Subs	Gls
Hartlepool U	Glasgow Celtic	08.03	03	0	4	0

MACCARONE Massimo
Galliate, Italy, 9 September, 1979 Itu21/It-2 (F)

League Club	Source	Date Signed	Seasons Played	Apps	Subs	Gls
Middlesbrough	Empoli (It)	07.02	02-03	39	18	15

McCARRICK Mark Bernard
Liverpool, 4 February, 1962 (FB)

League Club	Source	Date Signed	Seasons Played	Apps	Subs	Gls
Birmingham C	Witton A	05.83	83	12	3	0
Lincoln C	Tr	07.84	84-85	42	2	0
Crewe Alex	Tr	02.86	85	10	1	0
Tranmere Rov	Runcorn	08.87	87-90	125	0	14

McCARRISON Dugald
Lanark, 22 December, 1969 (F)

League Club	Source	Date Signed	Seasons Played	Apps	Subs	Gls
Darlington (L)	Glasgow Celtic	10.91	91	5	0	2

McCARRON Francis (Frank) Paul
Kinning Park, 1 October, 1943 (CD)

League Club	Source	Date Signed	Seasons Played	Apps	Subs	Gls
Carlisle U	Glasgow Celtic	07.67	67	7	2	1

McCARTER James (Jim) Joseph
Glasgow, 19 March, 1923 Died 2002 (W)

League Club	Source	Date Signed	Seasons Played	Apps	Subs	Gls
Sheffield Wed	Vale of Clyde	01.46	46	6	-	0
Mansfield T	Tr	08.48	48-49	67	-	10

McCARTHY Alan James
Wandsworth, 11 January, 1972 EYth/Wu21-3/WB (CD)

League Club	Source	Date Signed	Seasons Played	Apps	Subs	Gls
Queens Park Rgrs	YT	12.89	90-94	8	3	0
Watford	L	11.93	93	8	1	0
Plymouth Arg	L	02.94	93	1	1	0
Leyton Orient	Tr	08.95	95-96	43	4	0

McCARTHY Anthony (Tony) Paul
Dublin, 9 November, 1969 IRYth/IRu21-5 (CD)

League Club	Source	Date Signed	Seasons Played	Apps	Subs	Gls
Millwall	Shelbourne	06.92	92-94	20	1	1
Crewe Alex	L	12.94	94	2	0	0
Colchester U	Tr	03.95	94-96	88	1	1

McCARTHY Daniel (Danny) John Anthony
Abergavenny, 26 September, 1942 (W)

League Club	Source	Date Signed	Seasons Played	Apps	Subs	Gls
Cardiff C	Abergavenny Thistle	07.60	61	7	-	0

McCARTHY Gerard (Gerry)
Limerick, 30 March, 1934 LoI-1 (CD)

League Club	Source	Date Signed	Seasons Played	Apps	Subs	Gls
Charlton Ath	Limerick	07.56	56	4	-	0

McCARTHY Ian
Porth, 4 September, 1960 (F)

League Club	Source	Date Signed	Seasons Played	Apps	Subs	Gls
Swansea C	Coventry C (App)	03.78	77	0	1	0

McCARTHY John
Dunmanway, 22 January, 1922 LoI-4 (CF)

League Club	Source	Date Signed	Seasons Played	Apps	Subs	Gls
Bristol C	Cork U	07.49	49	3	-	0

McCARTHY Jonathan (Jon) David
Middlesbrough, 18 August, 1970 NIB-2/NI-18 (W)

League Club	Source	Date Signed	Seasons Played	Apps	Subs	Gls
Hartlepool U	Jnrs	11.87	87	0	1	0
York C	Shepshed Charterhouse	03.90	90-94	198	1	31
Port Vale	Tr	08.95	95-97	93	1	11
Birmingham C	Tr	09.97	97-01	107	17	8
Sheffield Wed	L	03.02	01	4	0	0
Port Vale	Tr	08.02	02	5	3	0
York C	Doncaster Rov	11.02	02	1	0	0
Carlisle U	Tr	11.02	02	19	2	1

McCARTHY Kevin John
Bethnal Green, 24 December, 1957 (M)

League Club	Source	Date Signed	Seasons Played	Apps	Subs	Gls
Watford	App	01.76	75-77	35	1	1

McCARTHY Michael (Mick) Joseph
Barnsley, 7 February, 1959 IRu23-1/IR-57 (CD)

League Club	Source	Date Signed	Seasons Played	Apps	Subs	Gls
Barnsley	App	07.77	77-83	272	0	7
Manchester C	Tr	12.83	83-86	140	0	2
Millwall	Lyon (Fr)	03.90	89-91	31	4	2

McCARTHY Patrick (Paddy)
Dublin, 31 May, 1983 IRYth/IRu21-7 (CD)

League Club	Source	Date Signed	Seasons Played	Apps	Subs	Gls
Manchester C	YT	06.00				
Boston U	L	11.02	02	11	1	0
Notts Co	L	03.03	02	6	0	0
Leicester C	Tr	03.05	04	12	0	0

McCARTHY Paul Jason
Cork, 4 August, 1971 IRSch/IRYth/IRu21-10 (CD)

League Club	Source	Date Signed	Seasons Played	Apps	Subs	Gls
Brighton & Hove A	YT	04.89	89-95	180	1	6
Wycombe W	Tr	07.96	96-02	199	13	9
Oxford U	Tr	03.03	02-03	34	1	3

McCARTHY Philip (Phil)
Liverpool, 19 February, 1943 Died 1996 (W)

League Club	Source	Date Signed	Seasons Played	Apps	Subs	Gls
Oldham Ath	Skelmersdale U	07.65	65	2	1	0
Halifax T	Tr	01.66	65-70	179	1	18

McCARTHY Robert (Bob) Zepp
Lyndhurst, 2 November, 1948 (FB)

League Club	Source	Date Signed	Seasons Played	Apps	Subs	Gls
Southampton	App	11.65	67-74	112	0	2

McCARTHY Roydon (Roy) Stuart
Barugh Green, 17 January, 1945 (W)

League Club	Source	Date Signed	Seasons Played	Apps	Subs	Gls
Barnsley	Barugh Green Sports	05.62	61-62	3	-	0
Barrow	Tr	07.64	64-68	189	0	41
Southport	Tr	06.69	69	33	1	4

McCARTHY Sean Casey
Bridgend, 12 September, 1967 WB-1 (F)

League Club	Source	Date Signed	Seasons Played	Apps	Subs	Gls
Swansea C	Bridgend T	10.85	85-87	76	15	25
Plymouth Arg	Tr	08.88	88-89	67	3	19
Bradford C	Tr	07.90	90-93	127	4	60
Oldham Ath	Tr	12.93	93-97	117	23	42
Bristol C	L	03.98	97	7	0	1
Plymouth Arg	Tr	08.98	98-00	66	16	19
Exeter C	Tr	07.01	01	18	8	6

McCARTHY William (Bill) Edward
Bootle, 25 November, 1941 ESch (CD)

League Club	Source	Date Signed	Seasons Played	Apps	Subs	Gls
Liverpool	Jnrs	12.58				
Southport	Tr	10.60	60-62	27	-	1

McCARTNEY George
Belfast, 29 April, 1981 NISch/NIYth/NIu21-5/NI-19 (CD)

League Club	Source	Date Signed	Seasons Played	Apps	Subs	Gls
Sunderland	YT	05.98	00-04	104	17	0

League Club	Source	Date Signed	Seasons Played	Apps	Subs	Gls
McCARTNEY Michael (Mike)						
Musselburgh, 28 September, 1954 SSch						(FB)
West Bromwich A	App	12.71				
Carlisle U	Tr	05.73	73-79	148	8	17
Southampton	Tr	07.80	80	22	0	1
Plymouth Arg	Tr	08.81	81-82	49	0	5
Carlisle U	Tr	03.83	82-86	130	1	7
McCARTNEY William (Willie) Raymond						
Newcraighall, 1 August, 1947						(CF)
Port Vale	Glasgow Rgrs	06.66	66	14	1	1
McCAVANA William **Terence (Terry)**						
Belfast, 24 January, 1921 NIAmat/IrLge-6/NI-3						(FB)
Notts Co (Am)	Coleraine	08.48	48	3	-	0
MACCIOCHI David Andrew						
Harlow, 14 January, 1972						(W)
Queens Park Rgrs	YT	01.90				
Brighton & Hove A	Tr	09.92	92	0	2	0
McCLAIR Brian John						
Airdrie, 8 December, 1963 SYth/Su21-8/SB/S-30						(F)
Manchester U	Glasgow Celtic	07.87	87-97	296	59	88
McCLARE Sean Patrick						
Rotherham, 12 January, 1978 IRYth/IRu21-3						(M)
Barnsley	YT	07.96	98-00	29	21	6
Rochdale	L	03.00	99	5	4	0
Port Vale	Tr	10.01	01-02	28	12	1
Rochdale	Tr	07.03	03	33	5	0
McCLAREN Christopher (Chris)						
Bristol, 14 March, 1963						(M)
Darlington	Walton & Hersham	03.87	86	1	2	0
McCLAREN Stephen (Steve)						
Fulford, 3 May, 1961						(M)
Hull C	App	04.79	79-84	171	7	16
Derby Co	Tr	08.85	85-87	23	2	0
Lincoln C	L	02.87	86	8	0	0
Bristol C	Tr	02.88	87-88	60	1	2
Oxford U	Tr	08.89	89-91	27	6	0
McCLATCHEY Derek Heywood						
Whiston, 29 April, 1956						(F)
Liverpool	App	05.73				
Southport	L	02.76	75	2	1	0
McCLEAN Christian Alphonso						
Colchester, 17 October, 1963						(F)
Bristol Rov	Clacton T	03.88	87-90	28	23	6
Swansea C	Tr	07.91	91	4	0	0
Northampton T	Tr	11.91	91	19	0	3
McCLELLAN Sidney (Sid) Benjamin						
Bromley, 11 June, 1925 Died 2000						(W)
Tottenham H	Chelmsford C	08.49	50-55	68	-	29
Portsmouth	Tr	11.56	56-57	37	-	9
Leyton Orient	Tr	07.58	58	12	-	4
McCLELLAND Charles (Charlie)						
Lochgelly, 8 January, 1924						(W)
Blackburn Rov	Hyde U	12.46	46-48	13	-	2
Exeter C	Tr	07.49	49-54	183	-	60
McCLELLAND David						
Newcastle, 25 December, 1941						(W)
Port Vale	Bishop Auckland	08.67	67	2	2	0
McCLELLAND John						
Belfast, 7 December, 1955 FLge/NI-53						(CD)
Cardiff C	Portadown	02.74	74	1	3	1
Mansfield T	Bangor C	05.78	78-80	122	3	8
Watford	Glasgow Rgrs	11.84	84-88	184	0	3
Leeds U	Tr	06.89	89-91	22	2	0
Watford	L	01.90	89	1	0	0
Notts Co	L	03.92	91	6	0	0
Darlington	(Coach)	10.96	96	1	0	0
McCLELLAND John (Jack)						
Lurgan, 19 May, 1940 Died 1976 IrLge-2/NI-6						(G)
Arsenal	Glenavon	10.60	60-63	46	-	0
Fulham	Tr	12.64	65-68	51	0	0
Lincoln C	L	12.68	68	12	0	0
McCLELLAND John Bonar						
Bradford, 5 March, 1935						(W)
Manchester C	Manchester YMCA	03.53	56-58	8	-	2
Lincoln C	Tr	09.58	58-61	121	-	32
Queens Park Rgrs	Tr	09.61	61-62	71	-	22
Portsmouth	Tr	05.63	62-67	136	1	35
Newport Co	Tr	07.68	68	36	0	10
McCLELLAND John (Johnny) William						
Colchester, 11 August, 1930						(IF)
Colchester U		09.51				
Stoke C	Tr	06.52	52	4	-	0
Swindon T	Tr	06.54	54	14	-	1
Rochdale	Tr	06.55	55	24	-	5
McCLELLAND Joseph (Joe)						
Edinburgh, 12 October, 1935 Died 1999						(FB)
Wrexham	Hibernian	06.64	64	32	-	0
McCLEN James (Jamie) David						
Newcastle, 13 May, 1979						(M)
Newcastle U	YT	07.97	98-02	7	7	0
McCLENAGHAN Albert (Bert)						
Derry, 7 July, 1954						(CD)
Watford	Larne T	12.77	77	2	0	0
McCLENAHAN Trent James						
Australia, 4 February, 1985 AuYth						(FB)
West Ham U	Sch	01.05	04	0	2	0
MK Dons	L	03.05	04	7	1	0
McCLURE Douglas (Doug) Hugh						
Islington, 6 September, 1964 ESch/EYth						(FB)
Queens Park Rgrs	App	08.82				
Exeter C	Tr	11.84	84	0	1	0
Torquay U	Tr	12.84	84	3	1	0
Wimbledon	Tr	01.85	84	2	0	0
Peterborough U	(Finland)	10.85	85	4	0	0
Crewe Alex	Tr	01.86	85	3	0	0
McCLURE William (Willie)						
Shotts, 16 May, 1921 Died 1992						(W)
Preston NE	Albion Rov	12.47	47	12	-	2
New Brighton	Tr	07.48	48-49	45	-	7
Carlisle U	Tr	10.49	49	8	-	0
Hartlepools U	Morton	08.50	50-52	118	-	24
McCLUSKEY Andrew (Andy)						
Manchester, 29 March, 1951						(M)
Hartlepool	St Joseph's	09.69	69	4	2	0
McCLUSKEY George McKinlay Cassidy						
Hamilton, 19 September, 1957 Su21-6						(F)
Leeds U	Glasgow Celtic	08.83	83-85	57	16	16
McCLUSKEY Ronald (Ronnie)						
Johnstone, 3 November, 1936						(G)
Accrington St	East Fife	11.60	60	4	-	0
McCLUSKIE James (Jim) Alexander Joseph						
Rawtenstall, 29 September, 1966						(F)
Rochdale	Jnrs	07.84	83-85	14	5	0
McCOIST Alistair (Ally) Murdoch						
Bellshill, 24 September, 1962 SYth/Su21-1/S-59						(F)
Sunderland	St Johnstone	08.81	81-82	38	18	8
McCOLE John						
Glasgow, 18 September, 1936						(CF)
Bradford C	Falkirk	09.58	58-59	42	-	32
Leeds U	Tr	09.59	59-61	78	-	45
Bradford C	Tr	10.61	61-62	46	-	15
Rotherham U	Tr	12.62	62	14	-	5
Newport Co	Shelbourne	10.64	64	6	-	2
McCOLL Duncan John						
Glasgow, 28 December, 1945						(IF)
Barnsley	Partick Th	01.66	65	5	0	0
McCOLL Thomas (Tommy) Gunn						
Glasgow, 19 September, 1945						(IF)
Colchester U	Denistoun Waverley	06.63	63-64	11	-	2
McCOMBE Jamie Paul						
Scunthorpe, 1 January, 1983						(CD)
Scunthorpe U	YT	11.01	01-03	42	21	1
Lincoln C	Tr	03.04	03-04	45	4	3
McCOMBE John Paul						
Pontefract, 7 May, 1985						(M)
Huddersfield T	Sch	07.04	02-04	4	2	0
McCONNELL Barry						
Exeter, 1 January, 1977						(FB)
Exeter C	YT	08.95	95-02	108	54	15

League Club	Source	Date Signed	Seasons Played	Apps	Subs	Gls
McCONNELL Peter						
Reddish, 3 March, 1937						(M)
Leeds U	Jnrs	03.54	58-61	48	-	4
Carlisle U	Tr	08.62	62-68	271	1	26
Bradford C	Tr	07.69	69-70	76	3	0
McCONVILLE Ian John						
Doncaster, 1 May, 1959						(W)
Doncaster Rov	App	04.77	75-77	9	2	1
McCORD Brian John						
Derby, 24 August, 1968						(M)
Derby Co	App	06.87	87-89	3	2	0
Barnsley	L	11.89	89	5	0	0
Barnsley	Tr	03.90	89-91	35	3	2
Mansfield T	L	08.92	92	11	0	1
Stockport Co	Tr	12.92	92	4	4	0
McCORKINDALE John						
Campbeltown, 10 August, 1934 Died 2004						(W)
Gillingham	Tonbridge	10.57	57	8	-	0
McCORMACK Alan						
Dublin, 10 January, 1984 IRSch/IRYth						(M)
Preston NE	Stella Maris BC	08.02	03-04	2	6	0
Leyton Orient	L	08.03	03	8	2	0
Southend U	L	03.05	04	5	2	2
McCORMACK John **Cecil (Cec)**						
Chester-le-Street, 15 February, 1922 Died 1995						(CF)
Gateshead		09.41	46	29	-	19
Middlesbrough	Tr	04.47	46-48	37	-	15
Barnsley	Chelmsford C	07.50	50-51	50	-	42
Notts Co	Tr	11.51	51-55	82	-	35
McCORMACK Francis (Frank) Adamson						
Glasgow, 25 September, 1924						(CD)
Oldham Ath	Clyde	11.49	49	14	-	0
McCORMACK Murdoch						
Glasgow, 7 October, 1920 Died 1951						(W)
Manchester C	Glasgow Rgrs	04.47	46	1	-	0
Blackpool	Tr	07.47	47	12	-	3
Crewe Alex	Tr	07.48	48	31	-	3
McCORMICK David						
Halifax, 3 November, 1920						(G)
Halifax T		10.47	47-54	118	-	0
McCORMICK David						
Southwark, 29 December, 1951						(F)
Peterborough U	Biggleswade T	08.75	75	1	0	0
McCORMICK Henry (Harry)						
Coleraine, 10 January, 1924 IrLge-1						(W)
Derby Co	Coleraine	10.46	46-47	7	-	0
Everton	Tr	07.48	48	4	-	0
McCORMICK James (Jimmy)						
Rotherham, 26 September, 1912 Died 1968						(W)
Rotherham U	Rotherham YMCA	03.31	30-31	19	-	2
Chesterfield	Scarborough	08.32	32	15	-	2
Tottenham H	Tr	03.33	32-38	137	-	26
Fulham	Tr	04.46	46	9	-	2
Lincoln C	Tr	08.47	47-48	64	-	6
Crystal Palace	Tr	02.49	48	13	-	2
McCORMICK James						
Rotherham, 1 April, 1937						(W)
Sheffield U		10.56	56	1	-	0
McCORMICK John						
Glasgow, 18 July, 1936						(CD)
Crystal Palace	Aberdeen	05.66	66-72	194	0	6
McCORMICK Joseph (Joe) Michael						
Holywell, 15 July, 1916						(WH)
Bolton W		10.37				
Rochdale		05.46	46-47	66	-	0
Scunthorpe U	Boston U	(N/L)	50	7	-	0
McCORMICK Luke Martin						
Coventry, 15 August, 1983						(G)
Plymouth Arg	Sch	07.02	00-04	66	1	0
Boston U	L	10.04	04	2	0	0
McCORMICK Stephen (Steve)						
Dumbarton, 14 August, 1969						(F)
Leyton Orient (L)	Dundee	09.98	98	1	3	0

League Club	Source	Date Signed	Seasons Played	Apps	Subs	Gls
McCOURT Francis (Frank) Joseph						
Portadown, 9 December, 1925 I-6						(WH)
Bristol Rov	Shamrock Rov	11.45				
Bristol Rov	Shamrock Rov	03.49	49	32	-	1
Manchester C	Tr	12.50	50-53	61	-	4
Colchester U	Tr	06.54	54	12	-	0
McCOURT Patrick (Paddy) James						
Derry, 16 December, 1983 NIu21-8/NI-1						(M)
Rochdale	YT	02.02	01-04	31	48	8
McCOY Michael (Mick) Paul						
Sunderland, 29 January, 1934 Died 2002						(IF)
Burnley	Silksworth CW	10.53				
Southport	Tr	07.57	57	5	-	1
McCOY Peter Joseph						
Wingate, 31 July, 1923 Died 1986						(FB)
Newcastle U	Shotton Jnrs	09.46				
Norwich C	Tr	02.49	48	6	-	0
McCOY Wilfred (Wilf)						
Birmingham, 4 March, 1921 Died 2005						(CD)
Portsmouth		08.46	46-47	18	-	0
Northampton T	Tr	12.48	48-49	60	-	0
Brighton & Hove A	Tr	01.51	50-53	112	-	0
McCRAE Alexander (Alex)						
Stoneyburn, 2 January, 1920 Died 2000 IrLge-1						(IF)
Charlton Ath	Heart of Midlothian	05.47	47-48	43	-	8
Middlesbrough	Tr	11.48	48-52	122	-	47
McCRAE Ian						
West Ham, 1 October, 1935						(FB)
Accrington St		07.57	59-60	14	-	0
McCREADIE Edward (Eddie) Graham						
Glasgow, 15 April, 1940 S-23						(FB)
Chelsea	East Stirling	04.62	62-73	327	4	4
McCREADIE Edward (Eddie) James						
Alexandria, 23 February, 1924						(W)
Walsall	Elgin C	09.53	53	4	-	0
McCREADIE William **Harvey**						
Glenluce, 1 October, 1942						(CF)
Accrington St	Stranraer	10.59	58-59	28	-	10
Luton T	Tr	01.60	59	1	-	0
Wrexham	Tr	11.60	60	10	-	2
McCREADY Bernard Thomas						
Dumbarton, 23 April, 1937						(G)
Rochdale	Glasgow Celtic	05.57	57-58	29	-	0
Oldham Ath	Tr	03.59	58	7	-	0
McCREADY Christopher (Chris) James						
Ellesmere Port, 5 September, 1981 ESch						(CD)
Crewe Alex	YT	05.00	01-04	40	11	0
McCREADY Thomas (Tommy)						
Port Glasgow, 28 September, 1923 Died 2004						(IF)
Hartlepools U	Cowdenbeath	08.49	49	34	-	3
Lincoln C	Tr	08.50	50	11	-	1
McCREADY Thomas (Tommy)						
Johnstone, 19 October, 1943 SSch						(FB)
Watford	Hibernian	07.63	63	1	-	0
McCREDIE Norman (Norrie) James						
Glasgow, 17 May, 1928						(FB)
Accrington St	Partick Th	05.55	55-56	51	-	3
Southport	Tr	08.57	57	33	-	2
Barrow	Tr	08.58	58	23	-	0
McCREERY David						
Belfast, 16 September, 1957 NISch/NIYth/NIu21-1/NI-67						(M)
Manchester U	App	10.74	74-78	48	39	7
Queens Park Rgrs	Tr	08.79	79-80	56	1	4
Newcastle U	Tulsa (USA)	10.82	82-88	237	6	2
Hartlepool U	Heart of Midlothian	08.91	91	27	3	0
Carlisle U	Coleraine	10.92	92-93	25	10	0
Hartlepool U		10.94	94	7	2	0
McCREESH Andrew (Andy)						
Billingham, 8 September, 1962						(FB)
Middlesbrough	App	09.80	81	2	0	0
McCRINDLE William (Willie)						
Kilmarnock, 28 June, 1923 Died 1982						(FB)
Newport Co	Pollok Jnrs	12.48	48-49	5	-	0

McCROHAN Roy
Reading, 22 September, 1930 (WH)

League Club	Source	Date Signed	Seasons Played	Apps	Subs	Gls
Reading	Jnrs	01.49	49-50	4	-	1
Norwich C	Tr	08.51	51-61	385	-	20
Colchester U	Tr	09.62	62-63	75	-	4
Bristol Rov	Tr	08.64	64	10	-	1

McCRORY Samuel (Sammy) McKee
Belfast, 11 October, 1924 NIRL-1/NIB/NI-1 (IF)

League Club	Source	Date Signed	Seasons Played	Apps	Subs	Gls
Swansea T	Linfield	10.46	46-49	105	-	47
Ipswich T	Tr	03.50	49-51	97	-	39
Plymouth Arg	Tr	08.52	52-54	50	-	11
Southend U	Tr	06.55	55-59	205	-	91

McCRYSTAL Dennis
Welwyn Garden City, 13 January, 1932 (G)

League Club	Source	Date Signed	Seasons Played	Apps	Subs	Gls
Watford	Kingsway YC	03.50	50	1	-	0

McCUBBIN Robert (Bert)
Kilmarnock, 13 February, 1943 (W)

League Club	Source	Date Signed	Seasons Played	Apps	Subs	Gls
Hartlepools U	Ayr U	06.63	63	2	-	0

McCUE Alexander (Alec) Brian
Greenock, 25 November, 1927 Died 1989 (W)

League Club	Source	Date Signed	Seasons Played	Apps	Subs	Gls
Carlisle U	Falkirk	10.50	50	32	-	11
Grimsby T	Tr	07.51	51-52	37	-	15
Shrewsbury T	Tr	05.53	53-55	91	-	28

McCUE John William
Stoke-on-Trent, 22 August, 1922 Died 1999 (FB)

League Club	Source	Date Signed	Seasons Played	Apps	Subs	Gls
Stoke C	Jnrs	04.40	46-59	502	-	2
Oldham Ath	Tr	09.60	60-61	56	-	0

McCULLAGH Paul Andrew
Brigg, 6 February, 1974 (CD)

League Club	Source	Date Signed	Seasons Played	Apps	Subs	Gls
Scunthorpe U	YT	07.92	92	5	0	1

McCULLOCH Adam Andrew Ball Ross
Crossford, 4 June, 1920 (CF)

League Club	Source	Date Signed	Seasons Played	Apps	Subs	Gls
Northampton T	Third Lanark	06.49	49-51	89	-	37
Shrewsbury T	Tr	01.52	51-52	46	-	18
Aldershot	Tr	02.53	52-54	79	-	32

McCULLOCH Andrew (Andy)
Northampton, 3 January, 1950 (F)

League Club	Source	Date Signed	Seasons Played	Apps	Subs	Gls
Queens Park Rgrs	Walton & Hersham	10.70	70-72	30	12	10
Cardiff C	Tr	10.72	72-73	58	0	24
Oxford U	Tr	07.74	74-75	41	0	9
Brentford	Tr	03.76	75-78	115	2	48
Sheffield Wed	Tr	06.79	79-82	122	3	44
Crystal Palace	Tr	08.83	83	25	0	3
Aldershot	Tr	11.84	84	16	0	2

McCULLOCH David (Dave)
Hamilton, 5 October, 1911 Died 1979 SLge-1/SWar-1/S-7 (CF)

League Club	Source	Date Signed	Seasons Played	Apps	Subs	Gls
Brentford	Heart of Midlothian	11.35	35-38	117	-	85
Derby Co	Tr	10.38	38	31	-	16
Leicester C	Tr	08.46	46	4	-	2

McCULLOCH John (Iain) Balfour
Kilmarnock, 28 December, 1954 Su21-2 (W)

League Club	Source	Date Signed	Seasons Played	Apps	Subs	Gls
Notts Co	Kilmarnock	04.78	78-83	212	3	51

McCULLOCH Lee Henry
Bellshill, 14 May, 1978 SYth/SB-1/Su21-14/S-4 (F)

League Club	Source	Date Signed	Seasons Played	Apps	Subs	Gls
Wigan Ath	Motherwell	03.01	00-04	140	25	35

McCULLOCH Scott Anderson James
Cumnock, 29 November, 1975 SSch (CD)

League Club	Source	Date Signed	Seasons Played	Apps	Subs	Gls
Cardiff C	Dundee U	09.00	00	9	12	1

McCULLOCH Thomas (Tommy)
Glasgow, 25 December, 1921 (W)

League Club	Source	Date Signed	Seasons Played	Apps	Subs	Gls
Northampton T	Queen of the South	12.49	49	2	-	0
Bradford C	Tr	01.51	50-53	109	-	9
Crewe Alex	Tr	07.54	54	28	-	5

McCULLOCH William (Billy) Duncan
Edinburgh, 25 June, 1922 Died 1961 (WH)

League Club	Source	Date Signed	Seasons Played	Apps	Subs	Gls
Stockport Co		03.44	46-53	309	-	4
Rochdale	Tr	07.54	54-57	140	-	2

McCULLOUGH Paul James
Birmingham, 26 October, 1959 (G)

League Club	Source	Date Signed	Seasons Played	Apps	Subs	Gls
Reading	Brixham	09.78				
Brentford	Dawlish T	07.80	80	7	0	0

McCULLOUGH William (Billy) James
Carrickfergus, 27 July, 1935 IrLge-1/NI-10 (FB)

League Club	Source	Date Signed	Seasons Played	Apps	Subs	Gls
Arsenal	Portadown	09.58	58-65	253	0	4
Millwall	Tr	08.66	66	17	2	0

McCUNNELL Barry
Hull, 20 September, 1948 (W)

League Club	Source	Date Signed	Seasons Played	Apps	Subs	Gls
Hull C	Endike Jnrs	10.66	69	0	1	0

McCURDY Colin Charles
Belfast, 18 July, 1954 IrLge-1/NI-1 (F)

League Club	Source	Date Signed	Seasons Played	Apps	Subs	Gls
Fulham	Larne T	11.77	77	1	0	0

McCURLEY Kevin
Consett, 2 April, 1926 Died 2000 (CF)

League Club	Source	Date Signed	Seasons Played	Apps	Subs	Gls
Brighton & Hove A		09.48	48-50	21	-	9
Liverpool	Tr	06.51				
Colchester U	Tr	03.52	51-59	224	-	92
Oldham Ath	Tr	06.60	60	1	-	0

McCUSKER James (Jim)
Maghera, 27 December, 1939 (G)

League Club	Source	Date Signed	Seasons Played	Apps	Subs	Gls
Bradford C	Jnrs	02.57	58	7	-	0
Stockport Co	Tr	08.59	59	2	-	0

McDERMENT William (Billy) Stirling
Paisley, 5 January, 1943 (CD)

League Club	Source	Date Signed	Seasons Played	Apps	Subs	Gls
Leicester C	Johnstone Burgh	05.61	62-66	20	3	1
Luton T	Tr	07.67	67-68	28	12	1
Notts Co	Tr	05.69	69	2	1	0

McDERMOTT Andrew (Andy)
Sydney, Australia, 24 March, 1977 Auu23 (FB)

League Club	Source	Date Signed	Seasons Played	Apps	Subs	Gls
Queens Park Rgrs	Inst of Sport (Aus)	08.95	96	6	0	2
West Bromwich A	Tr	03.97	96-99	49	3	1
Notts Co	Tr	08.00	00	20	5	0

McDERMOTT Brian James
Slough, 8 April, 1961 EYth (W)

League Club	Source	Date Signed	Seasons Played	Apps	Subs	Gls
Arsenal	App	02.79	78-83	38	23	12
Fulham	L	03.83	82	0	3	0
Oxford U	Tr	12.84	84-86	16	8	2
Huddersfield T	L	10.86	86	4	0	1
Cardiff C	Tr	08.87	87-88	49	2	8
Exeter C	Tr	02.89	88-90	65	3	4

McDERMOTT James (Jimmy) Lawrence
Earlestown, 25 May, 1932 (W)

League Club	Source	Date Signed	Seasons Played	Apps	Subs	Gls
Southport	Crompton Rec	07.55	55-58	157	-	30

McDERMOTT John
Middlesbrough, 3 February, 1969 (FB)

League Club	Source	Date Signed	Seasons Played	Apps	Subs	Gls
Grimsby T	App	06.87	86-04	574	18	10

McDERMOTT John Charles
Manchester, 14 October, 1959 (M)

League Club	Source	Date Signed	Seasons Played	Apps	Subs	Gls
Manchester U	App	10.76				
Rochdale	Wigan Ath (N/C)	09.79	79	5	3	1

McDERMOTT Maurice Patrick
Pelton Fell, 21 February, 1923 Died 1988 (FB)

League Club	Source	Date Signed	Seasons Played	Apps	Subs	Gls
Sunderland	Consett	11.45				
York C	Consett	07.47	47	7	-	0

McDERMOTT Steven (Steve)
Gateshead, 30 December, 1964 (F)

League Club	Source	Date Signed	Seasons Played	Apps	Subs	Gls
Darlington	Sunderland (App)	02.83	82	0	2	0

McDERMOTT Terence (Terry)
Kirkby, 8 December, 1951 Eu23-1/EB/E-25 (M)

League Club	Source	Date Signed	Seasons Played	Apps	Subs	Gls
Bury	App	10.69	69-72	83	7	8
Newcastle U	Tr	02.73	72-74	55	1	6
Liverpool	Tr	11.74	74-82	221	11	54
Newcastle U	Tr	09.82	82-83	74	0	12

McDEVITT Kenneth (Kenny) Richard
Liverpool, 4 March, 1929 (W)

League Club	Source	Date Signed	Seasons Played	Apps	Subs	Gls
Tranmere Rov	Unity BC	01.50	51-59	237	-	40

McDONAGH James (Seamus) Martin
Rotherham, 6 October, 1952 EYth/IR-24 (G)

League Club	Source	Date Signed	Seasons Played	Apps	Subs	Gls
Rotherham U	App	10.70	70-75	121	0	0
Bolton W	Tr	08.76	76-79	161	0	0
Everton	Tr	07.80	80	40	0	0
Bolton W	Tr	08.81	81-82	81	0	1
Notts Co	Tr	07.83	83-84	35	0	0
Birmingham C	L	09.84	84	1	0	0
Gillingham	L	03.85	84	10	0	0
Sunderland	L	08.85	85	7	0	0
Scarborough	Wichita (USA)	11.87	87	9	0	0
Huddersfield T	L	01.88	87	6	0	0

McDONAGH William (Willie)
Dublin, 14 March, 1983 (M)

League Club	Source	Date Signed	Seasons Played	Apps	Subs	Gls
Carlisle U	Bohemians	10.01	01-03	40	23	4

League Club	Source	Date Signed	Seasons Played	Career Record Apps	Subs	Gls
McDONALD Alan						
Belfast, 12 October, 1963 NISch//NIYth/NI-52						(CD)
Queens Park Rgrs	App	08.81	83-96	395	7	13
Charlton Ath	L	03.83	82	9	0	0
Swindon T	Tr	07.97	97	30	3	1
MacDONALD Charles (Charlie) Lea						
Southwark, 13 February, 1981						(F)
Charlton Ath	YT	11.98	99-01	1	7	1
Cheltenham T	L	03.01	00	7	1	2
Torquay U	L	02.02	01	5	0	0
Colchester U	L	03.02	01	2	2	1
McDONALD Christopher (Chris) William						
Edinburgh, 14 October, 1975 SSch						(M)
Arsenal	YT	12.93				
Stoke C	Tr	08.95				
Hartlepool U	Tr	08.96	96-98	18	2	0
McDONALD Colin						
Edinburgh, 10 April, 1974 SSch/Su21-5						(F)
Swansea C	Falkirk	03.96	95-96	6	12	0
McDONALD Colin Agnew						
Ramsbottom, 15 October, 1930 FLge-3/E-8						(G)
Burnley	Hawkshaw St Mary's	10.48	53-58	186	-	0
McDONALD Colin Barry						
Norwich, 15 May, 1950						(W)
Norwich C	App	07.67	67	4	0	0
Scunthorpe U	Tr	07.70	70-72	77	8	11
McDONALD David Anderson						
Dundee, 9 May, 1931						(G)
Crystal Palace	Dundee Violet	03.51	52-54	30	-	0
McDONALD David Hugh						
Dublin, 2 January, 1971 IRSch/IRYth/IRu21-3/IRB						(FB)
Tottenham H	YT	08.88	92	2	0	0
Gillingham	L	09.90	90	10	0	0
Bradford C	L	08.92	92	7	0	0
Reading	L	03.93	92	11	0	0
Peterborough U	Tr	08.93	93	28	1	0
Barnet	Tr	03.94	93-97	86	10	0
MacDONALD Garry						
Middlesbrough, 26 March, 1962						(F)
Middlesbrough	App	03.80	80-83	40	13	5
Carlisle U	Tr	07.84	84	7	2	0
Darlington	Tr	10.84	84-88	153	9	35
Stockport Co	Tr	07.89	89	1	0	0
Hartlepool U	Tr	12.89	89-90	10	8	1
McDONALD Gary						
Sunderland, 20 November, 1969						(F)
Mansfield T	Ipswich T (YT)	08.89	89	1	1	0
MACDONALD Gary						
Iselone, Germany, 25 October, 1979						(CD)
Portsmouth	YT	07.98				
Peterborough U	Havant & Waterlooville	02.01	00-02	13	4	1
McDONALD Gavin James						
Salford, 6 October, 1970						(F)
Chesterfield	YT	•	88	5	7	1
McDONALD Gerard (Gerry)						
Milnthorpe, 3 December, 1952						(M)
Blackburn Rov	App	12.70	71	19	2	2
Halifax T	Tr	08.73	73	10	3	0
McDONALD Gordon						
Hampstead, 7 February, 1932 Died 1995						(FB)
Crystal Palace	Eastbourne	12.54	54-56	13	-	0
Swindon T	Tr	07.57	57	10	-	0
McDONALD Harry						
Salford, 11 September, 1926						(FB)
Crystal Palace	Ashton U	09.50	50-54	140	-	1
McDONALD Ian						
Inverness, 5 February, 1951						(M)
Wolverhampton W	Jnrs	08.68				
Darlington	Tr	09.70	70	21	4	3
MacDONALD Ian Campbell Aitken						
Rinteln, Germany, 30 August, 1953						(CD)
Carlisle U	St Johnstone	05.76	76-80	186	1	7
McDONALD Ian Clifford						
Barrow, 10 May, 1953						(M)
Barrow	App	05.71	70-71	31	5	2
Workington	Tr	02.73	72-73	42	0	4
Liverpool	Tr	01.74				

League Club	Source	Date Signed	Seasons Played	Career Record Apps	Subs	Gls
Colchester U	L	02.75	74	5	0	2
Mansfield T	Tr	07.75	75-76	47	9	4
York C	Tr	11.77	77-81	175	0	29
Aldershot	Tr	11.81	81-88	340	0	50
McDONALD James						
Greenock, 18 April, 1932						(W)
Gillingham	Dumbarton	08.56	56	1	-	0
MacDONALD Jack						
Liverpool, 1 September, 1921 Died 1999						(FB)
Liverpool		08.44				
Tranmere Rov	Tr	06.49	49-51	89	-	0
MacDONALD John						
Glasgow, 15 April, 1961 SSch/SYth/Su21-8						(F)
Charlton Ath	(Hong Kong)	09.86	86	2	0	0
Barnsley	Tr	11.86	86-89	87	7	20
Scarborough	Tr	11.89	89-90	39	1	6
McDONALD John (Jack) Christopher						
Maltby, 27 August, 1921						(W)
Wolverhampton W	Jnrs	09.38	38	2	-	0
Bournemouth	Tr	05.39	46-47	80	-	36
Fulham	Tr	06.48	48-51	75	-	19
Southampton	Tr	08.52	52	16	-	4
Southend U	Tr	05.53	53-54	28	-	6
MacDONALD John Sutherland						
Edinburgh, 23 September, 1922						(FB)
Notts Co	Carshalton Ath	08.48	48	1	-	0
McDONALD Joseph (Joe)						
Blantyre, 10 February, 1929 Died 2003 S-2						(FB)
Sunderland	Falkirk	03.54	53-57	137	-	1
Nottingham F	Tr	07.58	58-60	109	-	0
MacDONALD Kevin Duncan						
Inverness, 22 November, 1960						(M)
Leicester C	Inverness Caledonian	05.80	80-84	133	5	8
Liverpool	Tr	11.84	84-88	29	11	1
Leicester C	L	12.87	87	3	0	0
Coventry C	Tr	07.89	89-90	26	5	0
Cardiff C	L	03.91	90	8	0	0
Walsall	Tr	07.91	91-92	48	5	6
MacDONALD Leslie (Les)						
Newcastle, 2 April, 1934						(FB)
Portsmouth		05.55				
Exeter C	Tr	06.57	57-65	294	0	0
McDONALD Malcolm						
Glasgow, 26 October, 1913 Died 1999 SLge-1/SWar-3						(FB)
Brentford	Kilmarnock	10.46	46-48	87	-	1
MACDONALD Malcolm Ian						
Fulham, 7 January, 1950 Eu23-4/FLge-1/E-14						(F)
Fulham	Tonbridge	08.68	68	10	3	5
Luton T	Tr	07.69	69-70	88	0	49
Newcastle U	Tr	05.71	71-75	187	0	95
Arsenal	Tr	08.76	76-78	84	0	42
MacDONALD Martin						
Kilsyth, 5 September, 1931						(WH)
Portsmouth	Jnrs	11.48				
Bournemouth	Tr	11.51	52-55	51	-	1
McDONALD Martin Joseph						
Irvine, 4 December, 1973 ESemiPro-1						(M)
Stockport Co	Bramhall	08.92				
Doncaster Rov	Southport	08.96	96-97	48	0	4
Macclesfield T	Tr	12.97	97-98	45	0	3
McDONALD Michael (Mike) Flynn						
Glasgow, 8 November, 1950						(G)
Stoke C	Clydebank	10.72	72-73	5	0	0
McDONALD Neil						
Barrow, 27 May, 1954						(W)
Workington	Barrow	03.77	76	5	1	0
McDONALD Neil Raymond						
Willington Quay, 2 November, 1965 ESch/EYth/Eu21-5						(FB)
Newcastle U	App	02.83	82-87	163	17	24
Everton	Tr	08.88	88-91	76	14	4
Oldham Ath	Tr	10.91	91-93	19	5	1
Bolton W	Tr	07.94	94	4	0	0
Preston NE	Tr	11.95	95-96	20	13	0
McDONALD Paul Thomas						
Motherwell, 20 April, 1968						(W)
Southampton	Hamilton Academical	06.93	94-95	0	3	0
Burnley	L	09.95	95	8	1	1
Brighton & Hove A	Tr	02.96	95-97	52	9	5

McDONALD Richard (Rikki) Robertson
Paisley, 18 December, 1933 Died 2004 (CF)

League Club	Source	Date Signed	Seasons Played	Apps	Subs	Gls
Barnsley	Saltcoats Victoria	12.57	58	1	-	0

MacDONALD Robert (Bob)
Kilpatrick, 26 October, 1935 (FB)

League Club	Source	Date Signed	Seasons Played	Apps	Subs	Gls
Manchester C	Vale of Leven	09.56	61	5	-	0
Bournemouth	Tr	09.63	63	1	-	0

McDONALD Robert (Rob) Roderick
Hull, 22 January, 1959 (F)

League Club	Source	Date Signed	Seasons Played	Apps	Subs	Gls
Hull C	App	01.77	76-79	17	8	2
Newcastle U	PSV Eindhoven (Holl)	11.88	88	6	4	1

McDONALD Robert (Bobby) Wood
Aberdeen, 13 April, 1955 (FB)

League Club	Source	Date Signed	Seasons Played	Apps	Subs	Gls
Aston Villa	App	09.72	72-75	33	6	3
Coventry C	Tr	08.76	76-80	161	0	14
Manchester C	Tr	10.80	80-82	96	0	11
Oxford U	Tr	09.83	83-86	93	1	14
Leeds U	Tr	02.87	86-87	18	0	1
Wolverhampton W	L	02.88	87	6	0	0

McDONALD Rodney (Rod)
Westminster, 20 March, 1967 (F)

League Club	Source	Date Signed	Seasons Played	Apps	Subs	Gls
Walsall	Colne Dynamoes	08.90	90-93	142	7	41
Chester C	Southport	11.96	96-97	43	10	11

McDONALD Roger Brown
Glasgow, 2 February, 1933 Died 1996 (FB)

League Club	Source	Date Signed	Seasons Played	Apps	Subs	Gls
Mansfield T	St Mirren	03.55	54-55	13	-	0

McDONALD Scott
Dandenong, Australia, 21 August, 1983 AuYth/Auu23-2 (F)

League Club	Source	Date Signed	Seasons Played	Apps	Subs	Gls
Southampton	Eastern Pride (Aus)	08.00	01	0	2	0
Huddersfield T	L	07.02	02	7	6	1
Bournemouth	Tr	03.03	02	3	4	1
Wimbledon	Tr	08.03	03	0	2	0

McDONALD Terence (Terry)
Belfast, 5 February, 1947 (FB)

League Club	Source	Date Signed	Seasons Played	Apps	Subs	Gls
Middlesbrough	Jnrs	02.64				
Southport	Tr	07.65	65-66	33	0	1
Barrow	Tr	07.67	67-68	34	1	0

McDONALD Terence (Terry) James
Limehouse, 12 November, 1938 EYth (W)

League Club	Source	Date Signed	Seasons Played	Apps	Subs	Gls
West Ham U	Jnrs	04.56				
Leyton Orient	Tr	07.59	59-64	152	-	23
Reading	Tr	05.65	65	13	0	2

McDONALD Thomas (Tommy)
Hill o' Beath, 24 May, 1930 Died 2004 SB-1 (W)

League Club	Source	Date Signed	Seasons Played	Apps	Subs	Gls
Wolverhampton W	Hibernian	04.54	54-55	5	-	1
Leicester C	Tr	07.56	56-59	113	-	27

McDONALD Thomas (Tom)
Walthamstow, 15 September, 1980 (CD)

League Club	Source	Date Signed	Seasons Played	Apps	Subs	Gls
Southend U	YT	08.99	99-00	1	3	0

McDONALD William Love
Longriggend, 30 August, 1918 Died 1997 (WH)

League Club	Source	Date Signed	Seasons Played	Apps	Subs	Gls
Carlisle U	Airdrie	08.46	46	3	-	0

McDONNELL Charles (Charlie)
Birkenhead, 15 July, 1936 (IF)

League Club	Source	Date Signed	Seasons Played	Apps	Subs	Gls
Tranmere Rov	Stork	09.57	57-60	68	-	26
Stockport Co	Tr	06.61	61-63	84	-	32
Tranmere Rov	Tr	10.63	63-64	45	-	25
Southport	Tr	07.65	65	10	0	1

McDONNELL Martin Henry
Newton-le-Willows, 27 April, 1924 Died 1988 (CD)

League Club	Source	Date Signed	Seasons Played	Apps	Subs	Gls
Everton	Haydock C & B	08.42				
Southport	Earlestown	08.46	46	38	-	0
Birmingham C	Tr	05.47	47-49	32	-	0
Coventry C	Tr	10.49	49-54	232	-	0
Derby Co	Tr	07.55	55-57	93	-	0
Crewe Alex	Tr	07.58	58	17	-	0

McDONNELL Peter Anthony
Kendal, 11 June, 1953 (G)

League Club	Source	Date Signed	Seasons Played	Apps	Subs	Gls
Bury	Netherfield	10.73	73	1	0	0
Liverpool	Tr	08.74				
Oldham Ath	Tr	08.78	78-81	137	0	0

McDONOUGH Darron Karl
Antwerp, Belgium, 7 November, 1962 (M)

League Club	Source	Date Signed	Seasons Played	Apps	Subs	Gls
Oldham Ath	App	01.80	80-86	178	5	14
Luton T	Tr	09.86	86-91	88	17	5
Newcastle U	Tr	03.92	91	2	1	0

McDONOUGH Roy
Solihull, 16 October, 1958 (F)

League Club	Source	Date Signed	Seasons Played	Apps	Subs	Gls
Birmingham C	App	10.76	76	2	0	1
Walsall	Tr	09.78	78-80	76	6	15
Chelsea	Tr	10.80				
Colchester U	Tr	02.81	80-82	89	4	24
Southend U	Tr	08.83	83	22	0	4
Exeter C	Tr	01.84	83-84	19	1	1
Cambridge U	Tr	10.84	84	30	2	5
Southend U	Tr	08.85	85-89	163	23	30
Colchester U	Tr	10.90	92-93	57	6	16

McDOUGALD David Eugene **Junior**
Big Spring, Texas, USA, 12 January, 1975 EYth (F)

League Club	Source	Date Signed	Seasons Played	Apps	Subs	Gls
Tottenham H	YT	07.93				
Brighton & Hove A	Tr	05.94	94-95	71	7	14
Chesterfield	L	03.96	95	9	0	3
Rotherham U	Tr	07.96	96	14	4	2
Millwall	Cambridge C	07.98	98	0	1	0
Leyton Orient	Tr	10.98	98	3	5	0

MacDOUGALL Edward (Ted) John
Inverness, 8 January, 1947 S-7 (F)

League Club	Source	Date Signed	Seasons Played	Apps	Subs	Gls
Liverpool	ICI Recs	01.66				
York C	Tr	07.67	67-68	84	0	34
Bournemouth	Tr	07.69	69-72	146	0	103
Manchester U	Tr	09.72	72	18	0	5
West Ham U	Tr	03.73	72-73	24	0	5
Norwich C	Tr	12.73	73-76	112	0	51
Southampton	Tr	09.76	76-78	86	0	42
Bournemouth	Tr	11.78	78-79	51	1	16
Blackpool	Tr	03.80	79-80	11	2	0

McDOUGALL Laybourne
Tynemouth, 12 May, 1917 Died 1994 (FB)

League Club	Source	Date Signed	Seasons Played	Apps	Subs	Gls
Carlisle U		06.37	37	3	-	0
Preston NE	Tr	03.38				
Blackpool	Tr	05.39				
Gateshead	Tr	10.46	46-48	60	-	0

McDOWALL Daniel (Danny)
Kirkintilloch, 22 May, 1929 Died 2000 (IF)

League Club	Source	Date Signed	Seasons Played	Apps	Subs	Gls
Middlesbrough	Kirkintilloch Rob Roy	02.47				
Workington	Glasgow Celtic	08.51	51-52	82	-	23
Lincoln C	Tr	07.53	53	17	-	4
Millwall	Tr	06.54	54-55	10	-	1

MacDOWALL Duncan John
Paddington, 18 December, 1963 (F)

League Club	Source	Date Signed	Seasons Played	Apps	Subs	Gls
Birmingham C	App	08.81	81	2	0	0

McDOWALL James (Jim) Cowan
Glasgow, 25 October, 1940 (G)

League Club	Source	Date Signed	Seasons Played	Apps	Subs	Gls
Notts Co	Baillieston Jnrs	09.59				
Scunthorpe U	Boston U	12.61	61	1	-	0

McDOWALL Kenneth (Ken) Francis
Manchester, 6 May, 1938 (W)

League Club	Source	Date Signed	Seasons Played	Apps	Subs	Gls
Manchester U	Rhyl	09.59				
Rochdale	Tr	10.60	60	6	-	0

McDOWALL Leslie (Les) John
Gunga Pur, India, 25 October, 1912 Died 1991 (CD)

League Club	Source	Date Signed	Seasons Played	Apps	Subs	Gls
Sunderland	Glentyne Thistle	12.32	34-37	13	-	0
Manchester C	Tr	03.38	37-48	117	-	8
Wrexham	Tr	11.49	49	3	-	0

McDOWELL John Alfred
East Ham, 7 September, 1951 EYth/Eu23-13 (FB)

League Club	Source	Date Signed	Seasons Played	Apps	Subs	Gls
West Ham U	App	08.69	70-78	243	6	8
Norwich C	Tr	08.79	79-80	40	1	1

MACEDO Elio (Tony)
Gibraltar, 22 February, 1938 Eu23-10 (G)

League Club	Source	Date Signed	Seasons Played	Apps	Subs	Gls
Fulham	Jnrs	10.55	57-67	346	0	0
Colchester U	Tr	09.68	68	38	0	0

McELHATTON Michael (Mike) Terrence
Killarney, 16 April, 1975 IRSch (M)

League Club	Source	Date Signed	Seasons Played	Apps	Subs	Gls
Bournemouth	YT	07.93	92-95	21	21	2
Scarborough	Tr	09.96	96-97	64	6	7
Rushden & Diamonds	Tr	07.98	01	4	3	1

McELHINNEY Gerard (Gerry)
Derry, 19 September, 1956 NI-6 (CD)

League Club	Source	Date Signed	Seasons Played	Apps	Subs	Gls
Bolton W	Distillery	09.80	80-84	107	2	2
Rochdale	L	11.82	82	20	0	1
Plymouth Arg	Tr	01.85	84-87	90	1	2
Peterborough U	Tr	08.88	88-90	87	0	1

McELHOLM Brendan Anthony
Omagh, 7 July, 1982 NIYth (CD)

League Club	Source	Date Signed	Seasons Played	Apps	Subs	Gls
Leyton Orient	YT	07.00	99-01	6	11	0

League Club	Source	Date Signed	Seasons Played	Career Record Apps	Subs	Gls
McELVANEY David Anthony						
Chesterfield, 3 November, 1954						(M)
Chesterfield		10.75	75	4	0	1
McEVELEY James (Jay) Michael						
Liverpool, 11 February, 1985 Eu21-1						(FB)
Blackburn Rov	Sch	07.02	02-04	14	0	0
Burnley	L	12.03	03	0	4	0
Gillingham	L	03.05	04	10	0	1
McEVILLY Lee Richard						
Liverpool, 15 April, 1982 NIu21-9/NIu23-1/NI-1						(F)
Rochdale	Burscough	12.01	01-03	55	30	25
McEVOY Matthew **Andrew (Andy)**						
Dublin, 15 July, 1938 Died 1994 LoI-4/IR-17						(IF)
Blackburn Rov	Bray W	10.56	58-66	183	0	89
McEVOY Donald (Don) William						
Golcar, 3 December, 1928 Died 2004						(CD)
Huddersfield T	Bradley U	09.47	49-54	148	-	3
Sheffield Wed	Tr	12.54	54-57	105	-	1
Lincoln C	Tr	01.59	58-59	23	-	0
Barrow	Tr	07.60	60-61	74	-	1
McEVOY Richard (Ricky) Patrick						
Gibraltar, 6 August, 1967 IRYth						(M)
Luton T	App	08.85	86	0	1	0
Cambridge U	L	02.87	86	10	1	1
MacEWAN James (Jimmy)						
Dundee, 22 March, 1929						(W)
Aston Villa	Raith Rov	07.59	59-65	143	0	28
Walsall	Tr	08.66	66	10	0	1
MacEWAN Malcolm **Peter**						
Roodepoort, South Africa, 23 May, 1933						(CF)
Luton T	Germiston Callies (SA)	02.54	53-55	26	-	11
McEWAN Stanley (Stan)						
Cambuskenneth, 8 June, 1957						(CD)
Blackpool	App	07.74	74-81	204	10	24
Exeter C	Tr	07.82	82-83	65	0	15
Hull C	Tr	03.84	83-87	113	0	25
Wigan Ath	Tr	12.87	87-88	26	3	4
Hartlepool U	Tr	08.89	89	14	0	2
McEWAN Stephen (Steve)						
Bowhill, 28 March, 1930						(IF)
Liverpool		07.50				
Accrington St	Tr	08.51	51	2	-	1
McEWAN William (Billy)						
Glasgow, 29 August, 1914 Died 1991						(W)
Queens Park Rgrs	Petershill	06.38	38-49	96	-	17
Leyton Orient	Tr	02.50	49-50	21	-	3
McEWAN William (Billy) Johnston McGowan						
Cleland, 20 June, 1951						(M)
Blackpool	Hibernian	05.73	73	4	0	0
Brighton & Hove A	Tr	02.74	73-74	27	0	3
Chesterfield	Tr	11.74	74-76	79	1	7
Mansfield T	Tr	01.77	76-77	32	0	3
Peterborough U	Tr	11.77	77-78	62	1	3
Rotherham U	Tr	07.79	79-83	86	9	10
McEWEN David (Dave)						
Westminster, 2 November, 1977						(F)
Tottenham H	Dulwich Hamlet	01.00	99-00	0	4	0
Queens Park Rgrs	Tr	07.01	01	2	3	0
McEWEN Francis (Frank) Kevin						
Dublin, 15 February, 1948 IRu23-1/LoI-1						(M)
Manchester U	App	05.65				
Rochdale	Tr	11.66	66-67	17	0	2
MACEY John Robert Thornbury						
Bristol, 13 November, 1947 ESch						(G)
Bristol C	App	05.65				
Grimsby T	Tr	07.68	68-69	36	1	0
Newport Co	Tr	07.70	70-75	194	0	0
McFADDEN Anthony (Tony)						
Hexham, 18 May, 1957						(F)
Darlington	Reyrolles	08.81	81-82	44	3	10
McFADDEN James						
Glasgow, 14 April, 1983 Su21-7/SB-1/S-21						(W)
Everton	Motherwell	09.03	03-04	18	28	1

League Club	Source	Date Signed	Seasons Played	Career Record Apps	Subs	Gls
McFADZEAN Clive Stuart						
Kilmarnock, 11 March, 1958						(F)
Bradford C	App	03.76	75-76	3	1	2
McFADZEAN John Paul						
Sheffield, 2 April, 1966						(F)
Rotherham U	App	●	83	0	1	0
McFALL David (Dave) Patrick						
Ballymena, 14 March, 1935						(IF)
Aldershot	Sittingbourne	10.58	58	3	-	0
McFARLAND Roy Leslie						
Liverpool, 5 April, 1948 Eu23-5/FLge-6/E-28						(CD)
Tranmere Rov	Edge Hill BC	07.66	66-67	35	0	0
Derby Co	Tr	08.67	67-80	434	0	44
Bradford C	Tr	06.81	81-82	40	0	1
Derby Co	Tr	08.83	83	3	5	0
McFARLANE Andrew (Andy) Antonie						
Wolverhampton, 30 November, 1966						(F)
Portsmouth	Cradley T	11.90	91	0	2	0
Swansea C	Tr	08.92	92-94	33	22	8
Scunthorpe U	Tr	08.95	95-96	48	12	19
Torquay U	Tr	01.97	96-98	42	14	11
McFARLANE Ian						
Lanark, 26 January, 1933						(FB)
Chelsea	Aberdeen	08.56	56-57	40	-	0
Leicester C	Tr	05.58	58	1	-	0
McFARLANE William **Noel**						
Bray, 20 December, 1934						(W)
Manchester U	Jnrs	04.52	53	1	-	0
McFARLANE Robert (Bobby) Robertson						
Bo'ness, 12 October, 1913 Died 1971						(WH)
Arsenal		03.36				
Doncaster Rov	Tr	05.37	37-47	131	-	4
McFAUL Shane						
Dublin, 23 May, 1986 IRYth						(M)
Notts Co	Sch	02.04	03-04	19	11	0
McFAUL William (Iam) Stewart						
Coleraine, 1 October, 1943 NIAmat/NI-6						(G)
Newcastle U	Linfield	11.66	66-74	290	0	0
McFEAT Archibald (Archie)						
Kincardine, 23 January, 1924 Died 1996						(G)
Torquay U	Dumbarton	05.48	48	9	-	0
McFLYNN Terence (Terry) Martin						
Magherafelt, 27 March, 1981 NISch/NIYth/NIu21-7						(M)
Queens Park Rgrs	YT	05.98	00	1	1	0
McGAIRY Thomas (Tom)						
Glasgow, 25 November, 1927						(IF)
Walsall	Dumbarton	08.54	54	7	-	1
McGANN William Thomas Arden						
Wilmslow, 12 July, 1923 Died 1986						(FB)
Stockport Co		05.48	49-50	14	-	0
McGARRIGLE Dennis						
Luton, 4 November, 1936						(G)
Bristol C	Gourock Jnrs	02.60				
Crewe Alex	Tr	06.60	60-61	12	-	0
McGARRIGLE Kevin						
Newcastle, 9 April, 1977						(CD)
Brighton & Hove A	YT	07.94	93-96	34	11	1
McGARRITY Thomas (Tom) Welsh						
Scotstoun, 24 November, 1922 Died 1999						(W)
Southampton	Morton	11.52	52	5	-	1
McGARRY Ronald (Ron) James						
Whitehaven, 5 December, 1937						(F)
Workington	Whitehaven	10.58	58-61	93	-	26
Bolton W	Tr	02.62	61-62	27	-	7
Newcastle U	Tr	12.62	62-66	118	3	41
Barrow	Tr	03.67	66-67	30	0	4
Barrow	Balgownie (Aus)	09.70	70	14	3	4
McGARRY William (Bill) Harry						
Stoke-on-Trent, 10 June, 1927 Died 2005 FLge-1/EB/E-4						(WH)
Port Vale	Northwood Mission	06.45	46-50	146	-	5
Huddersfield T	Tr	03.51	50-60	363	-	25
Bournemouth	Tr	03.61	60-62	78	-	2

McGARVEY Scott Thomas
Glasgow, 22 April, 1963 Su21-4 (F)

League Club	Source	Date Signed	Seasons Played	Apps	Subs	Gls
Manchester U	App	04.80	80-82	13	12	3
Wolverhampton W	L	03.84	83	13	0	2
Portsmouth	Tr	07.84	84-85	17	6	6
Carlisle U	L	01.86	85	10	0	3
Carlisle U	Tr	07.86	86	25	0	8
Grimsby T	Tr	03.87	86-87	49	1	7
Bristol C	Tr	09.88	88	20	6	9
Oldham Ath	Tr	05.89	89	2	2	1
Wigan Ath	L	09.89	89	3	0	0

McGAVIN Steven (Steve) James
North Walsham, 24 January, 1969 (F)

League Club	Source	Date Signed	Seasons Played	Apps	Subs	Gls
Ipswich T	App	01.87				
Colchester U	Sudbury T	07.92	92-93	55	3	17
Birmingham C	Tr	01.94	93-94	16	7	2
Wycombe W	Tr	03.95	94-98	103	17	14
Southend U	Tr	02.99	98	4	7	0
Northampton T	Tr	07.99				
Colchester U	Tr	10.99	99-00	49	26	18

McGEACHIE George
Calder, 26 October, 1916 (WH)

League Club	Source	Date Signed	Seasons Played	Apps	Subs	Gls
New Brighton	St Johnstone	07.46	46-47	63	-	4
Leyton Orient	Tr	07.48				
Rochdale	Tr	12.48	48-50	90	-	6
Crystal Palace	Tr	06.51	51	46	-	5

McGEACHIE George
Falkirk, 9 September, 1939 (W)

League Club	Source	Date Signed	Seasons Played	Apps	Subs	Gls
Darlington	Dundee	01.64	63-66	119	0	9

McGEACHY Joseph (Joe)
Glasgow, 21 April, 1920 Died 1985 (W)

League Club	Source	Date Signed	Seasons Played	Apps	Subs	Gls
Leyton Orient	Third Lanark	05.48	48-50	74	-	4
Workington	Hereford U	09.52	52	2	-	1

McGEADY John Thomas
Glasgow, 17 April, 1958 (W)

League Club	Source	Date Signed	Seasons Played	Apps	Subs	Gls
Sheffield U	Third Lanark	01.76	75-76	13	3	0
Newport Co	California (USA)	10.78	78	2	0	0

McGEE Owen Edward
Middlesbrough, 29 April, 1970 (FB)

League Club	Source	Date Signed	Seasons Played	Apps	Subs	Gls
Middlesbrough	YT	07.88	89-90	18	3	1
Scarborough	Leicester C (N/C)	03.92	91-92	21	3	0

McGEE Paul
Dublin, 17 May, 1968 IRu21-4 (W)

League Club	Source	Date Signed	Seasons Played	Apps	Subs	Gls
Colchester U	Bohemians	02.89	88	3	0	0
Wimbledon	Tr	03.89	88-92	54	6	9
Peterborough U	L	03.94	93	5	1	0

McGEE Paul Gerard
Sligo, 19 June, 1954 IRu21-2/IR-15 (F)

League Club	Source	Date Signed	Seasons Played	Apps	Subs	Gls
Queens Park Rgrs	Sligo Rov	11.77	77-78	31	8	7
Preston NE	Tr	10.79	79-81	62	4	13
Burnley	Tr	11.81	81-82	33	1	9
Preston NE	Dundalk	11.84	84	2	0	0

McGEENEY Patrick (Paddy) Michael
Sheffield, 31 October, 1966 (M)

League Club	Source	Date Signed	Seasons Played	Apps	Subs	Gls
Sheffield U	App	10.84	84-85	15	1	0
Rochdale	L	11.86	86	3	0	0
Chesterfield	Tr	08.87	87-88	45	4	1

McGEORGE James (Jimmy) Lumley
Sunderland, 8 June, 1945 (W)

League Club	Source	Date Signed	Seasons Played	Apps	Subs	Gls
Leyton Orient	Spennymoor U	03.64	64-65	16	0	0
Mansfield T	Tr	07.66	66	5	4	0

McGEOUGH James (Jimmy)
Belfast, 14 July, 1946 IrLge-2/LoI-5 (M)

League Club	Source	Date Signed	Seasons Played	Apps	Subs	Gls
Lincoln C	Waterford	06.72	72-74	61	4	0
Hartlepool	L	03.73	72	1	1	0

McGETTIGAN John Anthony
Motherwell, 28 November, 1945 (W)

League Club	Source	Date Signed	Seasons Played	Apps	Subs	Gls
Workington	Meadow Thistle	03.68	67-68	13	1	0

McGETTIGAN Lawrence (Larry)
Hackney, 25 December, 1952 Died 1994 (W)

League Club	Source	Date Signed	Seasons Played	Apps	Subs	Gls
Watford	App	11.70	71-74	40	10	3

McGHEE David Christopher
Worthing, 19 June, 1976 (CD)

League Club	Source	Date Signed	Seasons Played	Apps	Subs	Gls
Brentford	YT	07.94	94-97	95	22	8
Leyton Orient	Stevenage Borough	11.99	99-03	108	7	7

McGHEE James (Jim) William
Motherwell, 21 August, 1930 (W)

League Club	Source	Date Signed	Seasons Played	Apps	Subs	Gls
Darlington	Kilmarnock	07.52	52	15	-	4
Newport Co	Barry T	05.54	54	11	-	1

McGHEE Mark Edward
Glasgow, 20 May, 1957 Su21-1/S-4 (F)

League Club	Source	Date Signed	Seasons Played	Apps	Subs	Gls
Newcastle U	Morton	12.77	77-78	21	7	5
Newcastle U	Glasgow Celtic	08.89	89-90	63	4	24
Reading	IK Braga (Swe)	05.91	91-92	32	13	7

McGHEE Thomas (Tommy) Edward
Manchester, 10 May, 1929 EAmat/EB (FB)

League Club	Source	Date Signed	Seasons Played	Apps	Subs	Gls
Portsmouth	Wealdstone	05.54	54-58	136	-	0
Reading	Tr	07.59	59	8	-	0

McGHIE William (Billy) Lambert
Lanark, 19 January, 1958 SYth (M)

League Club	Source	Date Signed	Seasons Played	Apps	Subs	Gls
Leeds U	App	01.76	76	2	0	1
York C	Tr	12.79	79-81	39	4	1

McGIBBON Douglas (Doug)
Netley, 24 February, 1919 Died 2002 (CF)

League Club	Source	Date Signed	Seasons Played	Apps	Subs	Gls
Southampton	Hamble AST	12.38	38-46	13	-	9
Fulham	Tr	01.47	46-47	42	-	18
Bournemouth	Tr	09.48	48-50	103	-	65

McGIBBON Patrick (Pat) Colm
Lurgan, 6 September, 1973 NISch/NIu21-1/NIB-5/NI-7 (CD)

League Club	Source	Date Signed	Seasons Played	Apps	Subs	Gls
Manchester U	Portadown	08.92				
Swansea C	L	09.96	96	1	0	0
Wigan Ath	Tr	03.97	96-01	163	10	11
Scunthorpe U	L	02.02	01	6	0	0
Tranmere Rov	Tr	08.02	02	4	0	0

McGIFFORD Grahame Leslie
Carshalton, 1 May, 1955 (FB)

League Club	Source	Date Signed	Seasons Played	Apps	Subs	Gls
Huddersfield T	App	07.72	72-75	41	1	0
Hull C	Tr	05.76	76	1	0	0
Port Vale	Tr	06.77	77	20	0	0

McGILL Andrew
Glasgow, 11 July, 1924 Died 1988 (WH)

League Club	Source	Date Signed	Seasons Played	Apps	Subs	Gls
Bradford C	Clyde	11.47	47-51	164	-	24
Scunthorpe U	Tr	07.52	52-56	183	-	15

McGILL Austin Michael
Dumfries, 29 January, 1935 (CF)

League Club	Source	Date Signed	Seasons Played	Apps	Subs	Gls
Carlisle U	Queen of the South	08.59	59	29	-	12

McGILL Brendan
Dublin, 22 March, 1981 IRYth (M)

League Club	Source	Date Signed	Seasons Played	Apps	Subs	Gls
Sunderland	River Valley Rgrs	07.98				
Carlisle U	L	09.01	01	27	1	2
Carlisle U	Tr	08.02	02-03	64	14	10

McGILL Derek
Lanark, 14 October, 1975 (F)

League Club	Source	Date Signed	Seasons Played	Apps	Subs	Gls
Port Vale	Queen's Park	10.98	98	0	3	0

McGILL James (Jimmy)
Kilsyth, 10 March, 1926 (IF)

League Club	Source	Date Signed	Seasons Played	Apps	Subs	Gls
Bury	Maryhill Harp	12.45	46	1	-	0
Derby Co	Tr	03.47	46-47	8	-	0

McGILL James (Jimmy) Hopkins
Bellshill, 2 October, 1939 (FB)

League Club	Source	Date Signed	Seasons Played	Apps	Subs	Gls
Oldham Ath	Partick Th	05.59	59	38	-	2
Crewe Alex	Tr	08.60	60-62	81	-	2
Chester	Tr	10.62	62-63	32	-	0
Wrexham	Tr	10.63	63	17	-	0

McGILL James (Jimmy) Morrison
Glasgow, 27 November, 1946 (M)

League Club	Source	Date Signed	Seasons Played	Apps	Subs	Gls
Arsenal	Possilpark YMCA	07.65	65-66	6	4	0
Huddersfield T	Tr	09.67	67-71	161	3	8
Hull C	Tr	10.71	71-75	141	6	2
Halifax T	Tr	02.76	75-76	31	1	0

McGILLIVRAY Findlay
Newtongrange, 19 March, 1940 (FB)

League Club	Source	Date Signed	Seasons Played	Apps	Subs	Gls
Bradford PA	Glasgow Rgrs	05.66	66	38	1	0

McGINLAY John
Inverness, 8 April, 1964 SB-2/S-13 (F)

League Club	Source	Date Signed	Seasons Played	Apps	Subs	Gls
Shrewsbury T	Elgin C	02.89	88-89	58	2	27
Bury	Tr	07.90	90	16	9	9
Millwall	Tr	01.91	90-92	27	7	10
Bolton W	Tr	09.92	92-97	180	12	87
Bradford C	Tr	11.97	97	12	5	3
Oldham Ath	Tr	10.98	98	4	3	1

League Club	Source	Date Signed	Seasons Played	Career Record Apps	Subs	Gls

McGINLAY Patrick (Pat) David
Glasgow, 30 May, 1967 (M)

League Club	Source	Date Signed	Seasons Played	Apps	Subs	Gls
Blackpool		05.85	86	2	10	1

McGINLEY John
Rowlands Gill, 11 June, 1959 (W)

League Club	Source	Date Signed	Seasons Played	Apps	Subs	Gls
Sunderland	Gateshead	01.82	81	3	0	0
Lincoln C	Nairn County	09.84	84-86	69	2	11
Rotherham U	Tr	09.86	86	1	2	0
Hartlepool U	L	01.87	86	2	0	0
Lincoln C	Tr	01.87	86-88	36	5	7
Doncaster Rov	Tr	06.89	89	4	6	0

McGINLEY William (Billy) David
Dumfries, 12 November, 1954 SSch (W)

League Club	Source	Date Signed	Seasons Played	Apps	Subs	Gls
Leeds U	App	01.72	72	0	1	0
Huddersfield T	Tr	09.74	74	11	4	1
Bradford C	Tr	06.75	75-76	52	8	11
Crewe Alex	Tr	08.77	77	36	2	2

McGINN Francis (Frank)
Cambuslang, 2 March, 1919 Died 1995 (W)

League Club	Source	Date Signed	Seasons Played	Apps	Subs	Gls
Wrexham		04.47	46	2	-	0
Ipswich T	Tr	08.48	48	8	-	2

McGINN William (Billy) Bell
Ardrossan, 2 February, 1943 (FB)

League Club	Source	Date Signed	Seasons Played	Apps	Subs	Gls
Oldham Ath	Ardrossan Winton Rov	11.63	63-65	37	1	0

McGINTY Brian
East Kilbride, 10 December, 1976 (M)

League Club	Source	Date Signed	Seasons Played	Apps	Subs	Gls
Hull C	Glasgow Rgrs	11.97	97-98	43	10	6

McGIVEN Michael (Mick)
Newcastle, 7 February, 1951 (CD)

League Club	Source	Date Signed	Seasons Played	Apps	Subs	Gls
Sunderland	Jnrs	07.68	69-73	107	6	9
West Ham U	Tr	11.73	73-77	46	2	0

McGIVERN Leighton Terence
Liverpool, 2 June, 1984 (F)

League Club	Source	Date Signed	Seasons Played	Apps	Subs	Gls
Rochdale	Vauxhall Motors	07.04	04	2	23	1

McGLASHAN John
Dundee, 3 June, 1967 SYth (M)

League Club	Source	Date Signed	Seasons Played	Apps	Subs	Gls
Millwall	Montrose	08.90	90-91	9	7	0
Fulham	L	12.92	92	5	0	1
Cambridge U	L	01.93	92	0	1	0
Peterborough U	Tr	01.93	92-93	44	2	3
Rotherham U	Tr	11.94	94-96	68	6	5

McGLEISH John Joseph
Airdrie, 9 November, 1951 (W)

League Club	Source	Date Signed	Seasons Played	Apps	Subs	Gls
Northampton T	Jnrs	11.68	70-72	7	1	0

McGLEISH Scott
Barnet, 10 February, 1974 (F)

League Club	Source	Date Signed	Seasons Played	Apps	Subs	Gls
Charlton Ath	Edgware T	05.94	94	0	6	0
Leyton Orient	L	03.95	94	4	2	1
Peterborough U	Tr	07.95	95-96	3	10	0
Colchester U	L	02.96	95	1	5	2
Colchester U	L	03.96	95	9	0	4
Cambridge U	L	09.96	96	10	0	7
Leyton Orient	Tr	11.96	96-97	36	0	7
Barnet	Tr	10.97	97-00	106	28	36
Colchester U	Tr	01.01	00-03	118	26	38
Northampton T	Tr	05.04	04	43	1	13

McGLEN William (Bill)
Bedlington, 27 April, 1921 Died 1999 (WH)

League Club	Source	Date Signed	Seasons Played	Apps	Subs	Gls
Manchester U	Blyth Spartans	05.46	46-51	110	-	2
Lincoln C	Tr	07.52	52	13	-	0
Oldham Ath	Tr	02.53	52-55	68	-	3

McGLENNON Thomas (Tom)
Bearpark, 20 October, 1933 (WH)

League Club	Source	Date Signed	Seasons Played	Apps	Subs	Gls
Blackpool	Jnrs	11.50				
Rochdale	Tr	05.57	57-58	61	-	2
Barrow	Burton A	11.59	59-60	61	-	6

McGLINCHEY Brian Kevin
Derry, 26 October, 1977 NIYth/NIu21-14/NIB-1 (FB)

League Club	Source	Date Signed	Seasons Played	Apps	Subs	Gls
Manchester C	YT	12.95				
Port Vale	Tr	07.98	98	10	5	1
Gillingham	Tr	08.99	99-00	7	7	1
Plymouth Arg	Tr	12.00	00-02	54	14	2
Torquay U	Tr	09.03	03-04	66	1	0

McGOLDRICK David
Nottingham, 29 November, 1987 (F)

League Club	Source	Date Signed	Seasons Played	Apps	Subs	Gls
Notts Co	Jnrs	●	03	2	2	0

McGOLDRICK Edward (Eddie) John Paul
Islington, 30 April, 1965 IRB/IR-15 (W)

League Club	Source	Date Signed	Seasons Played	Apps	Subs	Gls
Northampton T	Nuneaton Borough	08.86	86-88	97	10	9
Crystal Palace	Tr	01.89	88-92	139	8	11
Arsenal	Tr	06.93	93-95	32	6	0
Manchester C	Tr	09.96	96-97	39	1	0
Stockport Co	L	03.98	97	2	0	0

McGOLDRICK John
Coatbridge, 23 September, 1963 (FB)

League Club	Source	Date Signed	Seasons Played	Apps	Subs	Gls
Leeds U	Glasgow Celtic	06.83	83	7	0	0

McGOLDRICK Thomas (Tom) Joseph
Doncaster, 20 September, 1929 (CF)

League Club	Source	Date Signed	Seasons Played	Apps	Subs	Gls
Rotherham U	Maltby Main	11.49	51	5	-	2
Chesterfield	Tr	05.53	53-54	36	-	16

McGONIGAL Robert (Bert) Edwin
Cookstown, 2 May, 1942 NISch/IrLge-2 (G)

League Club	Source	Date Signed	Seasons Played	Apps	Subs	Gls
Brighton & Hove A	Glentoran	02.62	62-65	57	0	0

McGORRIGHAN Francis (Frank) Owen
Easington, 20 November, 1921 Died 1998 (IF)

League Club	Source	Date Signed	Seasons Played	Apps	Subs	Gls
Middlesbrough	Eppleton Colliery	04.44				
Carlisle U	Tr	10.45				
Hull C	Tr	08.46	46	20	-	1
Blackburn Rov	Tr	02.47	46-47	5	-	0
Hull C	Tr	09.47	47	6	-	0
Southport	Tr	08.48	48	4	-	0

McGORRY Brian Paul
Liverpool, 16 April, 1970 (M)

League Club	Source	Date Signed	Seasons Played	Apps	Subs	Gls
Bournemouth	Weymouth	08.91	91-93	56	5	11
Peterborough U	Tr	02.94	93-94	44	8	6
Wycombe W	Tr	08.95	95	0	4	0
Cardiff C	L	03.96	95	7	0	0
Hereford U	Tr	03.97	96	7	0	1
Torquay U	Tr	07.98	98	31	3	1

McGOVERN Brendan
Camborne, 9 February, 1980 (M)

League Club	Source	Date Signed	Seasons Played	Apps	Subs	Gls
Plymouth Arg	YT	07.98	98	0	2	0

McGOVERN Brian
Dublin, 28 April, 1980 IRYth/IRu21-2 (CD)

League Club	Source	Date Signed	Seasons Played	Apps	Subs	Gls
Arsenal	Cherry Orchard	09.97	99	0	1	0
Queens Park Rgrs	L	12.99	99	3	2	0
Norwich C	Tr	07.00	00-01	8	13	1
Peterborough U	Tr	11.02	02	1	0	0

McGOVERN John Prescott
Montrose, 28 October, 1949 Su23-2 (M)

League Club	Source	Date Signed	Seasons Played	Apps	Subs	Gls
Hartlepools U	App	05.67	65-68	69	3	5
Derby Co	Tr	09.68	68-73	186	4	16
Leeds U	Tr	08.74	74	4	0	0
Nottingham F	Tr	02.75	74-81	249	4	6
Bolton W	Tr	06.82	82-83	16	0	0

McGOVERN Jon-Paul
Glasgow, 3 October, 1980 (M)

League Club	Source	Date Signed	Seasons Played	Apps	Subs	Gls
Sheffield U (L)	Glasgow Celtic	08.02	02	11	4	1
Sheffield Wed	Livingston	06.04	04	46	0	6

McGOVERN Michael (Mick) John
Hayes, 15 February, 1951 (M)

League Club	Source	Date Signed	Seasons Played	Apps	Subs	Gls
Queens Park Rgrs	App	11.68	67-71	10	2	0
Watford	L	08.72	72	4	0	0
Swindon T	Tr	02.73	72-74	28	4	2
Aldershot	L	03.75	74	6	0	1

McGOVERN Patrick (Paddy) Munro
Edinburgh, 14 May, 1948 (M)

League Club	Source	Date Signed	Seasons Played	Apps	Subs	Gls
Notts Co	Royston BC	07.67	67	1	2	0

McGOVERN Simon
Bradford, 25 February, 1965 (M)

League Club	Source	Date Signed	Seasons Played	Apps	Subs	Gls
Bradford C	Jnrs	08.82	82	1	0	0

McGOWAN Aloysius (Ally)
Whiterigg, 22 January, 1930 Died 2005 (FB)

League Club	Source	Date Signed	Seasons Played	Apps	Subs	Gls
Wrexham	St Johnstone	05.53	53-64	408	-	2

McGOWAN Andrew (Andy)
Corby, 17 July, 1956 Died 1999 EYth (M)

League Club	Source	Date Signed	Seasons Played	Apps	Subs	Gls
Northampton T	Corby T	06.75	75-77	93	12	15

McGOWAN Daniel (Danny)
Dublin, 8 November, 1924 Died 1994 IR-3 (IF)

League Club	Source	Date Signed	Seasons Played	Apps	Subs	Gls
West Ham U	Shelbourne	05.48	48-53	81	-	8

McGOWAN Gavin Gregory
Blackheath, 16 January, 1976 ESch/EYth (FB)

League Club	Source	Date Signed	Seasons Played	Apps	Subs	Gls
Arsenal	YT	07.94	92-97	3	3	0
Luton T	L	03.97	96	2	0	0
Luton T	L	07.97	97	6	2	0
Luton T	Tr	07.98	98-00	42	8	0

McGOWAN George
Carluke, 30 November, 1943 (CF)

League Club	Source	Date Signed	Seasons Played	Apps	Subs	Gls
Preston NE	Wishaw Jnrs	08.62				
Chester	Tr	03.63	62-63	18	-	3
Stockport Co	Tr	09.64	64	5	-	0

McGOWAN Gerard (Gerry) James
Kilwinning, 4 August, 1944 (W)

League Club	Source	Date Signed	Seasons Played	Apps	Subs	Gls
Oldham Ath	Ardeer Rec	11.63	65	5	0	1

McGOWAN James (Jimmy)
Cambuslang, 12 January, 1924 Died 1984 (IF)

League Club	Source	Date Signed	Seasons Played	Apps	Subs	Gls
Grimsby T	Dumbarton	07.46	46-48	34	-	4
Southampton	Tr	03.50	49-57	78	-	9

McGOWAN James (Jimmy)
Glasgow, 31 July, 1939 (W)

League Club	Source	Date Signed	Seasons Played	Apps	Subs	Gls
Mansfield T	St Johnstone	06.61	61	3	-	0

McGOWAN Kenneth (Ken)
Wolverhampton, 13 May, 1920 (CF)

League Club	Source	Date Signed	Seasons Played	Apps	Subs	Gls
Walsall		10.47	47-48	11	-	4

McGOWAN Neil William
Glasgow, 15 April, 1977 (FB)

League Club	Source	Date Signed	Seasons Played	Apps	Subs	Gls
Oxford U	Albion Rov	08.99	99-00	26	5	0

McGRATH Roland Christopher (Chris)
Belfast, 29 November, 1954 NI-21 (W)

League Club	Source	Date Signed	Seasons Played	Apps	Subs	Gls
Tottenham H	App	01.72	73-75	30	8	5
Millwall	L	02.76	75	15	0	3
Manchester U	Tr	10.76	76-80	12	16	1

McGRATH Derek Brendan Joseph
Dublin, 21 January, 1972 IRu21-9 (M)

League Club	Source	Date Signed	Seasons Played	Apps	Subs	Gls
Brighton & Hove A	YT	12.89	89-90	2	4	0

McGRATH James
Belfast, 15 November, 1921 Died 2000 (WH)

League Club	Source	Date Signed	Seasons Played	Apps	Subs	Gls
Barrow		08.45	46	3	-	0

McGRATH John
Tidworth, 21 March, 1932 (IF)

League Club	Source	Date Signed	Seasons Played	Apps	Subs	Gls
Notts Co	Aldershot (Am)	08.53	55-57	54	-	5
Darlington	Tr	05.58	58	25	-	6

McGRATH John Matthew
Limerick, 27 March, 1980 IRu21-5 (M)

League Club	Source	Date Signed	Seasons Played	Apps	Subs	Gls
Aston Villa	Belvedere	09.99	00	0	3	0
Doncaster Rov	Tr	07.03	03	4	7	0
Shrewsbury T	L	08.04	04	7	1	0
Kidderminster Hrs	Tr	01.05	04	18	1	0

McGRATH John Thomas
Manchester, 23 August, 1938 Died 1998 Eu23-1/FLge-1 (CD)

League Club	Source	Date Signed	Seasons Played	Apps	Subs	Gls
Bury	Miles Platting Swifts	10.55	56-60	148	-	2
Newcastle U	Tr	02.61	60-67	169	1	2
Southampton	Tr	02.68	67-73	167	1	1
Brighton & Hove A	L	12.72	72	3	0	0

McGRATH Lloyd Anthony
Birmingham, 24 February, 1965 EYth/Eu21-1 (M)

League Club	Source	Date Signed	Seasons Played	Apps	Subs	Gls
Coventry C	App	12.82	83-93	200	14	4
Portsmouth	Sing Tao (HK)	10.94	94	15	3	0

McGRATH Martin Lawrence
Hendon, 15 October, 1960 ESch (M)

League Club	Source	Date Signed	Seasons Played	Apps	Subs	Gls
Southampton	App	10.78	79	0	1	0
Bournemouth	Tr	06.80	80	17	5	0

McGRATH Michael (Mick)
Dublin, 7 April, 1936 IRB/FLge-1/IR-22 (WH)

League Club	Source	Date Signed	Seasons Played	Apps	Subs	Gls
Blackburn Rov	Home Farm	08.54	55-65	268	0	8
Bradford PA	Tr	03.66	65-66	50	0	2

McGRATH Paul
Greenford, 4 December, 1959 FLge/IR-83 (CD)

League Club	Source	Date Signed	Seasons Played	Apps	Subs	Gls
Manchester U	St Patrick's Ath	04.82	82-88	159	4	12
Aston Villa	Tr	08.89	89-95	248	5	9
Derby Co	Tr	10.96	96	23	1	0
Sheffield U	Tr	08.97	97	12	0	0

McGRAW John (Ian)
Glasgow, 30 August, 1926 (G)

League Club	Source	Date Signed	Seasons Played	Apps	Subs	Gls
Leicester C	Arbroath	12.48	48-50	13	-	0

McGREAL John
Birkenhead, 2 June, 1972 (CD)

League Club	Source	Date Signed	Seasons Played	Apps	Subs	Gls
Tranmere Rov	YT	07.90	91-98	193	2	1
Ipswich T	Tr	08.99	99-03	120	3	4
Burnley	Tr	08.04	04	38	1	1

McGREEVEY Brian Edmund
Prestwich, 29 September, 1935 (W)

League Club	Source	Date Signed	Seasons Played	Apps	Subs	Gls
Arsenal	Preston NE (Am)	03.54				
Stockport Co	Tr	03.57	56	1	-	0

McGREGOR Alexander (Alex) George Penman
Glasgow, 12 November, 1950 (W)

League Club	Source	Date Signed	Seasons Played	Apps	Subs	Gls
Shrewsbury T	Hibernian	01.75	74-75	46	3	7
Aldershot	Tr	09.76	76-81	168	9	17

MacGREGOR Colin
Bradford, 13 November, 1940 (W)

League Club	Source	Date Signed	Seasons Played	Apps	Subs	Gls
Bradford PA	Bradford C (Am)	03.58	58-59	3	-	0

McGREGOR John Reid
Airdrie, 5 January, 1963 (CD)

League Club	Source	Date Signed	Seasons Played	Apps	Subs	Gls
Liverpool	Queen's Park	06.82				
Leeds U	L	10.85	85	5	0	0

McGREGOR Mark Dale Thomas
Chester, 16 February, 1977 (FB)

League Club	Source	Date Signed	Seasons Played	Apps	Subs	Gls
Wrexham	YT	07.95	94-00	237	7	11
Burnley	Tr	07.01	01-03	46	8	2
Blackpool	Tr	07.04	04	36	2	0

McGREGOR Paul Anthony
Liverpool, 17 December, 1974 (F)

League Club	Source	Date Signed	Seasons Played	Apps	Subs	Gls
Nottingham F	YT	12.91	94-96	7	23	3
Carlisle U	L	09.98	98	9	1	3
Preston NE	Tr	03.99	98	1	3	0
Plymouth Arg	Tr	07.99	99-00	75	2	19
Northampton T	Tr	07.01	01-02	54	8	5

MacGREGOR James Peter
Hartlepool, 22 December, 1931 Died 1994 (IF)

League Club	Source	Date Signed	Seasons Played	Apps	Subs	Gls
Hartlepools U	Elwick Road OB	02.50	53-56	6	-	0

MacGREGOR Terence (Terry) James
Hartlepool, 24 May, 1938 (WH)

League Club	Source	Date Signed	Seasons Played	Apps	Subs	Gls
Hartlepools U	Jnrs	12.56	58-62	43	-	2

McGREGOR William (Willie)
Paisley, 1 December, 1923 (FB)

League Club	Source	Date Signed	Seasons Played	Apps	Subs	Gls
Leicester C	Mossdale YMCA	04.47	47-51	9	-	0
Mansfield T	Tr	09.53	53-55	119	-	0

McGRELLIS Francis (Frank)
Falkirk, 5 October, 1958 (F)

League Club	Source	Date Signed	Seasons Played	Apps	Subs	Gls
Coventry C	App	10.76				
Huddersfield T	L	08.78	78	4	1	0
Hereford U	Tr	03.79	78-81	80	5	24

McGROARTY James (Jim) Martin
Derry, 30 August, 1957 (W)

League Club	Source	Date Signed	Seasons Played	Apps	Subs	Gls
Stoke C	Finn Harps	09.77	77-78	6	1	2

McGROGAN Hugh
Dumbarton, 1 March, 1957 Died 1998 (W)

League Club	Source	Date Signed	Seasons Played	Apps	Subs	Gls
Oxford U	App	03.75	74-79	101	25	13
Carlisle U	Tr	05.80	80	1	1	0

McGRORY Shaun Patrick
Coventry, 29 February, 1968 (FB)

League Club	Source	Date Signed	Seasons Played	Apps	Subs	Gls
Coventry C	App	07.86				
Burnley	Tr	07.87	87-89	34	12	2

McGROTTY William (Willie)
Glasgow, 12 August, 1952 (W)

League Club	Source	Date Signed	Seasons Played	Apps	Subs	Gls
Blackpool	Yoker Ath	06.70	70-72	2	2	1

McGUCKIN George Kay Whyte
Dundee, 11 August, 1938 (WH)

League Club	Source	Date Signed	Seasons Played	Apps	Subs	Gls
Cardiff C	Dundee Shamrock	12.55	57	4	-	0

McGUCKIN Thomas Ian
Middlesbrough, 24 April, 1973 (CD)

League Club	Source	Date Signed	Seasons Played	Apps	Subs	Gls
Hartlepool U	YT	06.91	91-96	147	5	8
Fulham	Tr	06.97				
Hartlepool U	L	12.98	98	8	0	0
Oxford U	Tr	07.00	00	6	1	0

McGUFFIE Alwyn Scott
Drummore, 13 April, 1937 (WH)

League Club	Source	Date Signed	Seasons Played	Apps	Subs	Gls
Luton T	Queen of the South	09.54	55-63	79	-	10

League Club	Source	Date Signed	Seasons Played	Apps	Subs	Gls
McGUGAN John (Jackie) Hannah						
Airdrie, 12 June, 1939						(CD)
Leeds U	St Mirren	08.60	60	1	-	0
Tranmere Rov	Tr	02.61	60-61	35	-	0
McGUGAN Paul Joseph						
Glasgow, 17 July, 1964						(CD)
Barnsley	Glasgow Celtic	10.87	87-88	47	2	2
Chesterfield	Tr	01.91	90-93	74	3	6
McGUIGAN James (Jimmy)						
Addiewell, 1 March, 1924 Died 1988						(W)
Sunderland	Hamilton Academical	06.47	47-48	3	-	1
Stockport Co	Tr	06.49	49-50	43	-	9
Crewe Alex	Tr	08.50	50-55	209	-	32
Rochdale	Tr	08.56	56-58	70	-	2
McGUIGAN John (Johnny) Joseph						
Motherwell, 29 October, 1932						(W)
Southend U	St Mirren	05.55	55-57	125	-	34
Newcastle U	Tr	07.58	58-61	50	-	15
Scunthorpe U	Tr	01.62	61-62	57	-	17
Southampton	Tr	08.63	63-64	33	-	8
Swansea T	Tr	03.65	64-65	28	0	4
McGUIGAN Thomas (Tommy)						
Whitburn, 22 November, 1922 Died 1997						(IF)
Hartlepools U	Ayr U	08.50	50-57	325	-	75
McGUINESS Hendry (Harry) Alistair Johnstone						
Saltcoats, 17 February, 1928 Died 1997						(CD)
Torquay U		08.50	49-54	81	-	0
McGUINNESS Paul						
Manchester, 2 March, 1966						(M)
Manchester U	Jnrs	07.84				
Crewe Alex	Tr	08.86	86	11	2	0
Manchester U		07.89				
Chester C	Bury (N/C)	07.91	91	3	4	0
McGUINNESS Robert (Bobby) Francis						
Motherwell, 29 January, 1954						(F)
Portsmouth	Motherwell	07.75	75-76	27	4	3
McGUINNESS Wilfred (Wilf)						
Manchester, 25 October, 1937 ESch/EYth/Eu23-4/FLge-1/E-2						(WH)
Manchester U	Jnrs	11.54	55-59	81	-	2
McGUIRE Bernard Patrick						
Liverpool, 23 November, 1932						(W)
Shrewsbury T		07.53	53	2	-	0
McGUIRE Douglas (Dougie) John						
Bathgate, 6 September, 1967 SYth						(W)
Sunderland (L)	Glasgow Celtic	03.88	87	1	0	0
Coventry C	Glasgow Celtic	08.88	89	1	3	0
McGUIRE James Gary						
Campsall, 30 September, 1938						(G)
Torquay U	Hakoah (Aus)	02.66	65-66	32	0	0
McGUIRE Leslie (Les) George Robert						
Bethnal Green, 31 January, 1929						(IF)
Gillingham		(N/L)	50-51	6	-	2
McGUIRE Michael (Mick) James						
Blackpool, 4 September, 1952 EYth						(M)
Coventry C	Jnrs	11.69	71-74	60	12	1
Norwich C	Tr	01.75	74-77	54	3	4
Norwich C	Tampa Bay (USA)	08.78	78-82	118	7	7
Barnsley	Tr	03.83	82-84	44	3	6
Oldham Ath	Tr	01.85	84-86	65	4	3
McGUIRE Reginald (Reg)						
Birkenhead, 24 August, 1959						(F)
Tranmere Rov	Cammell Laird	08.82	82	0	4	0
McGURK David Michael						
Middlesbrough, 30 September, 1982						(FB)
Darlington	Sch	08.02	01-04	44	9	6
McHALE Christopher (Chris) Mark						
Birmingham, 4 November, 1984						(M)
Kidderminster Hrs	Jnrs	03.04	03-04	11	4	0
McHALE John (Sam)						
Oldham, 7 May, 1954						(CD)
Reading (Am)	Alton T	01.75	74	1	0	0
McHALE John (Kevin) Kevin						
Darfield, 1 October, 1939 ESch/EYth						(W)
Huddersfield T	Jnrs	10.56	56-67	345	0	60

League Club	Source	Date Signed	Seasons Played	Apps	Subs	Gls
Crewe Alex	Tr	01.68	67-70	116	0	22
Chester	Tr	10.70	70-71	61	3	4
McHALE Raymond (Ray)						
Sheffield, 12 August, 1950						(M)
Chesterfield	Hillsborough BC	08.70	71-74	123	1	27
Halifax T	Tr	10.74	74-76	86	0	21
Swindon T	Tr	09.76	76-79	171	2	33
Brighton & Hove A	Tr	05.80	80	9	2	0
Barnsley	Tr	03.81	80-81	52	1	1
Sheffield U	Tr	08.82	82-84	66	1	2
Bury	L	02.83	82	6	0	0
Swansea C	Tr	01.85	84-85	45	2	1
Rochdale	Scarborough	08.86	86	6	1	0
Scarborough	Tr	12.86	87	25	0	3
McHALE Thomas (Tom) Anthony						
Liverpool, 3 September, 1951						(FB)
Bradford C	Prescot Cables	09.71	71-72	34	2	0
McHALE William						
Kelty, 9 August, 1929 Died 2002						(IF)
Carlisle U	Dunfermline Ath	08.53	53	1	-	0
Halifax T		03.55	54	3	-	0
McHARD Archibald (Archie)						
Dumbarton, 10 June, 1934						(W)
Bradford PA	Clyde	05.59	59-60	27	-	3
MACHENT Stanley (Stan) Charles						
Chesterfield, 23 March, 1921						(WH)
Sheffield U		10.38	46-47	22	-	2
Chesterfield	Tr	11.47	47-48	21	-	7
MACHIN Alec Harold						
Hampstead, 6 July, 1920 Died 2005						(WH)
Chelsea	Royal Hampshire Rgmt	10.44	46-47	53	-	8
Plymouth Arg	Tr	06.48	48-50	26	-	1
MACHIN Ernest (Ernie)						
Walkden, 26 April, 1944						(M)
Coventry C	Nelson	03.62	62-72	255	2	33
Plymouth Arg	Tr	12.72	72-73	57	0	6
Brighton & Hove A	Tr	08.74	74-75	64	0	2
MACHIN Melvyn (Mel)						
Newcastle-under-Lyme, 16 April, 1945						(M)
Port Vale	Jnrs	07.62	62-65	29	1	6
Gillingham	Tr	07.66	66-70	155	1	11
Bournemouth	Tr	12.70	70-73	110	0	7
Norwich C	Tr	12.73	73-77	93	3	4
MACHO Jurgen						
Vienna, Austria, 24 August, 1977 Austria u21						(G)
Sunderland	First Vienna (Aut)	07.00	00-02	20	2	0
McHUGH Frazer Joseph						
Nottingham, 14 July, 1981						(M)
Swindon T	YT	08.99	98-00	13	6	0
Bradford C	Halesowen T	03.03	02-03	5	0	0
Notts Co	Tr	01.04	03	9	4	0
McHUGH Michael Bernard						
Donegal, 3 April, 1971						(F)
Bradford C	Jnrs	12.89	90-93	18	13	4
Scarborough	Tr	03.94	93	1	2	0
McILHARGEY Stephen (Steve)						
Glasgow, 23 August, 1964						(G)
Walsall	Blantyre Celtic	07.87				
Blackpool	Tr	08.89	89-93	100	1	0
Chester C	L	09.93	93	1	0	0
McILHATTON John						
Ardeer, 3 January, 1921 Died 1954						(W)
Everton	Albion Rov	04.46	46-48	55	-	1
McILMOYLE Hugh						
Cambuslang, 29 January, 1940						(F)
Leicester C	Port Glasgow Ath	08.59	60-61	20	-	5
Rotherham U	Tr	07.62	62	12	-	4
Carlisle U	Tr	03.63	62-64	77	-	47
Wolverhampton W	Tr	10.64	64-66	90	0	35
Bristol C	Tr	03.67	66-67	20	0	4
Carlisle U	Tr	09.67	67-69	79	0	30
Middlesbrough	Tr	09.69	69-70	69	1	19
Preston NE	Tr	07.71	71-72	59	1	10
Carlisle U	Morton	07.74	74	15	3	2
McILROY James (Jimmy)						
Lambeg, 25 October, 1931 FLge-2/I-6/NI-49						(M)
Burnley	Glentoran	03.50	50-62	439	-	116

League Club	Source	Date Signed	Seasons Played	Apps	Subs	Gls
Stoke C	Tr	03.63	62-65	96	2	16
Oldham Ath	Tr	03.66	65-67	35	4	1

McILROY Samuel (Sammy) Baxter
Belfast, 2 August, 1954 NI-88 (M)

League Club	Source	Date Signed	Seasons Played	Apps	Subs	Gls
Manchester U	App	08.71	71-81	320	22	57
Stoke C	Tr	02.82	81-84	132	1	14
Manchester C	Tr	08.85	85	12	0	1
Manchester C	Orgryte IS (Swe)	11.86	86	1	0	0
Bury	Tr	03.87	86-87	43	0	6
Bury	VFB Modling (Aut)	08.88	88-89	52	5	2
Preston NE	Tr	02.90	89	20	0	0

McILVENNY Edward (Ed) Joseph
Greenock, 21 October, 1924 Died 1989 LoI-3/USA (W)

League Club	Source	Date Signed	Seasons Played	Apps	Subs	Gls
Wrexham	Morton	03.47	46-47	7	-	1
Manchester U	Philadelphia Nat (USA)	08.50	50	2	-	0

McILVENNY Harold (Harry)
Bradford, 5 October, 1922 EAmat (CF)

League Club	Source	Date Signed	Seasons Played	Apps	Subs	Gls
Bradford PA (Am)	Yorkshire Amats	08.46	46-49	43	-	17

McILVENNY John Anthony
Barnstaple, 2 March, 1930 (W)

League Club	Source	Date Signed	Seasons Played	Apps	Subs	Gls
West Bromwich A	Stafford Rgrs	10.49				
Bristol Rov	Cheltenham T	07.52	52-58	80	-	11
Reading	Tr	06.59	59-60	77	-	4

McILVENNY Patrick (Paddy) Dennis
Belfast, 11 September, 1924 (WH)

League Club	Source	Date Signed	Seasons Played	Apps	Subs	Gls
Cardiff C	Merthyr Tydfil	05.50				
Brighton & Hove A	Tr	07.51	51-54	60	-	5
Aldershot	Tr	12.55	55-56	16	-	0

McILVENNY Robert (Bobby)
Belfast, 7 July, 1926 (IF)

League Club	Source	Date Signed	Seasons Played	Apps	Subs	Gls
Oldham Ath	Merthyr Tydfil	03.50	49-53	139	-	36
Bury	Tr	08.54	54	12	-	1
Southport	Tr	08.55	55-56	77	-	16
Barrow	Tr	07.57	57-58	43	-	11

McILWAINE Matthew (Matt)
Glasgow, 20 September, 1920 Died 1997 (WH)

League Club	Source	Date Signed	Seasons Played	Apps	Subs	Gls
Bolton W	Dundee U	08.51	52	2	-	0

McILWRAITH James (Jimmy) McLean
Troon, 17 April, 1954 (M)

League Club	Source	Date Signed	Seasons Played	Apps	Subs	Gls
Bury	Motherwell	09.75	75-77	80	9	21
Portsmouth	Tr	07.78	78	16	3	0
Bury	Tr	07.79	79	28	1	3
Halifax T	Tr	10.80	80-81	33	3	6

McINALLY Alan Bruce
Ayr, 10 February, 1963 S-8 (F)

League Club	Source	Date Signed	Seasons Played	Apps	Subs	Gls
Aston Villa	Glasgow Celtic	07.87	87-88	50	9	18

McINALLY Charles (Charlie)
Glasgow, 1 February, 1939 (WH)

League Club	Source	Date Signed	Seasons Played	Apps	Subs	Gls
Brentford	St Roch's	09.58	59	1	-	0

McINALLY James (Jim) Edward
Glasgow, 19 February, 1964 SYth/Su21-1/S-10 (FB)

League Club	Source	Date Signed	Seasons Played	Apps	Subs	Gls
Nottingham F	Glasgow Celtic	06.84	84-85	36	0	0
Coventry C	Tr	01.86	85	5	0	0

McINALLY John Stewart
Gatehouse of Fleet, 26 September, 1951 SSch (G)

League Club	Source	Date Signed	Seasons Played	Apps	Subs	Gls
Manchester U	Jnrs	03.69				
Lincoln C	Tr	08.70	70-71	22	0	0
Colchester U	Tr	11.72	72	27	0	0

McINCH James (Jim) Reid
Glasgow, 27 June, 1953 (F)

League Club	Source	Date Signed	Seasons Played	Apps	Subs	Gls
Cardiff C	Jnrs	08.70	72-74	11	2	0

McINDEWAR Archibald (Archie)
Glasgow, 26 July, 1921 (G)

League Club	Source	Date Signed	Seasons Played	Apps	Subs	Gls
Workington	Stirling A	08.51	51	20	-	0

McINDOE Michael
Edinburgh, 2 December, 1979 SB-1 (M)

League Club	Source	Date Signed	Seasons Played	Apps	Subs	Gls
Luton T	YT	04.98	98-99	19	20	0
Doncaster Rov	Yeovil T	08.03	03-04	88	1	20

McINERNEY Ian
Limerick, 1 September, 1972 (F)

League Club	Source	Date Signed	Seasons Played	Apps	Subs	Gls
Peterborough U	YT	07.91	91	3	7	1

McINERNEY Ian Dominic
Liverpool, 26 January, 1964 (W)

League Club	Source	Date Signed	Seasons Played	Apps	Subs	Gls
Huddersfield T	Blue Star	08.88	88	5	5	1
Stockport Co	Tr	07.89	89-90	37	5	8
Rochdale	L	02.91	90	4	0	1

McINNES Derek John
Paisley, 5 July, 1971 S-21 (M)

League Club	Source	Date Signed	Seasons Played	Apps	Subs	Gls
Stockport Co (L)	Glasgow Rgrs	11.98	98	13	0	0
West Bromwich A	Toulouse (Fr)	08.00	00-02	87	1	6

McINNES Graham James
Aberdeen, 7 April, 1938 (IF)

League Club	Source	Date Signed	Seasons Played	Apps	Subs	Gls
Bury	Aberdeen	06.59	60	1	-	0

McINNES Ian
Hamilton, 22 March, 1967 (W)

League Club	Source	Date Signed	Seasons Played	Apps	Subs	Gls
Rotherham U	App	09.84	83-84	6	3	0
Lincoln C	Tr	01.86	85-86	38	5	4

McINNES John
Ayr, 29 March, 1923 (IF)

League Club	Source	Date Signed	Seasons Played	Apps	Subs	Gls
Bradford C	Raith Rov	05.49	49-50	21	-	6

McINNES John Smith
Glasgow, 11 August, 1927 Died 1973 (W)

League Club	Source	Date Signed	Seasons Played	Apps	Subs	Gls
Chelsea	Morton	05.47	46-49	37	-	7

McINNES Joseph (Joe) Clarke
Glasgow, 9 December, 1932 (W)

League Club	Source	Date Signed	Seasons Played	Apps	Subs	Gls
Accrington St	Partick Th	03.56	55	14	-	2

McINNES William (Willie)
Douglas West, 20 May, 1931 (G)

League Club	Source	Date Signed	Seasons Played	Apps	Subs	Gls
Accrington St	Lesmahagow	10.55	55-60	153	-	0
Southport	Tr	07.61	61-62	26	-	0

McINTOSH Alan
Llandudno, 29 July, 1939 WAmat (W)

League Club	Source	Date Signed	Seasons Played	Apps	Subs	Gls
Cardiff C	Llandudno	02.62	61-63	64	-	11

McINTOSH Albert
Dundee, 6 April, 1930 (CF)

League Club	Source	Date Signed	Seasons Played	Apps	Subs	Gls
Swansea T		03.54	53-57	15	-	3

McINTOSH Alexander (Alex)
Dunfermline, 14 April, 1916 (IF)

League Club	Source	Date Signed	Seasons Played	Apps	Subs	Gls
Wolverhampton W	Folkestone	10.37	37-46	44	-	7
Birmingham C	Tr	01.47	46-47	23	-	4
Coventry C	Tr	02.48	47-48	20	-	3

McINTOSH Alexander (Alex) James
Inverurie, 19 October, 1923 Died 1998 (FB)

League Club	Source	Date Signed	Seasons Played	Apps	Subs	Gls
Barrow	Dundee	04.47	46-49	89	-	1
Carlisle U	Tr	10.49	49-54	227	-	4

McINTOSH Austin James
Newham, 5 November, 1987 (F)

League Club	Source	Date Signed	Seasons Played	Apps	Subs	Gls
Mansfield T	Sch	●	04	1	0	0

McINTOSH David (Dave)
Girvan, 4 May, 1925 Died 1995 (G)

League Club	Source	Date Signed	Seasons Played	Apps	Subs	Gls
Sheffield Wed	Girvan Ath	10.47	47-57	293	-	0
Doncaster Rov	Tr	01.58	57-58	15	-	0

McINTOSH James (Jimmy) McLauchlan
Dumfries, 5 April, 1918 Died 2000 IrLge-1 (CF)

League Club	Source	Date Signed	Seasons Played	Apps	Subs	Gls
Blackpool	Droylsden	09.35	35-37	5	-	0
Preston NE	Tr	11.37	37-38	27	-	3
Blackpool	Tr	05.46	46-48	66	-	22
Everton	Tr	03.49	48-50	58	-	19

McINTOSH James (Jim) William
Forfar, 19 August, 1950 (W)

League Club	Source	Date Signed	Seasons Played	Apps	Subs	Gls
Nottingham F	Montrose	10.70	70-75	45	7	2
Chesterfield	L	01.76	75	3	0	0
Hull C	Tr	03.76	75-76	20	0	1

McINTOSH John (Ian) McGregor
Glasgow, 14 September, 1933 (IF)

League Club	Source	Date Signed	Seasons Played	Apps	Subs	Gls
Bury	Partick Th	12.57	57-58	29	-	14

McINTOSH Malcolm Patrick
Oxford, 6 July, 1959 (FB)

League Club	Source	Date Signed	Seasons Played	Apps	Subs	Gls
Oxford U	App	07.77	78-80	53	3	0
Oxford U	Kettering T	08.82	82	2	0	0

McINTOSH Martin Wyllie
East Kilbride, 19 March, 1971 SSch/SB-2 (CD)

League Club	Source	Date Signed	Seasons Played	Apps	Subs	Gls
Stockport Co	Hamilton Academical	08.97	97-99	96	3	5
Rotherham U	Hibernian	08.01	01-04	122	0	16

McINTOSH William (Willie) Dowling
Glasgow, 7 December, 1919 Died 1990 (CF)

League Club	Source	Date Signed	Seasons Played	Apps	Subs	Gls
Preston NE	St Johnstone	05.46	46-48	91	-	46
Blackpool	Tr	01.49	48-51	51	-	15
Stoke C	Tr	09.51	51-52	26	-	5
Walsall	Tr	11.52	52	22	-	9

League Club	Source	Date Signed	Seasons Played	Apps	Subs	Gls
McINTYRE James (Jim)						
Motherwell, 22 March, 1933						(G)
Accrington St	Albion Rov	03.57	56	4	-	0
McINTYRE James (Jimmy)						
Alexandria, 24 May, 1972 SB						(W)
Bristol C	Duntocher BC	10.91	91	1	0	0
Exeter C	L	02.93	92	12	3	3
Reading	Kilmarnock	03.98	97-00	68	29	14
McINTYRE Joseph (Joe) Gerald						
Manchester, 19 June, 1971						(FB)
Rochdale	YT	10.88	88	2	2	0
McINTYRE Kevin						
Liverpool, 23 December, 1977						(CD)
Tranmere Rov	YT	11.96	97	0	2	0
Chester C	Doncaster Rov	05.02	04	9	1	0
Macclesfield T	Tr	12.04	04	21	2	0
McINTYRE Patrick Finucane						
Aylesham, 14 March, 1943						(FB)
Gillingham	Jnrs	07.61	60-62	10	-	0
McINTYRE Stephen (Steve)						
Ayr, 15 May, 1966						(FB)
Hereford U	Ayr U	07.91	91	12	0	0
McIVER Frederick (Fred)						
Birtley, 14 February, 1952						(M)
Sunderland	App	04.69	71	1	0	0
Sheffield Wed	Racing Jet (Bel)	07.74	74-75	34	3	0
MacIVOR Ronald (Ron) William						
Edinburgh, 23 March, 1951						(FB)
Wigan Ath	East Fife	10.79	79	3	0	1
McJANNET William **Leslie (Les)**						
Cumnock, 2 August, 1961						(FB)
Mansfield T	Jnrs	08.79	79-81	73	1	0
Scarborough	Matlock T	08.87	87-88	29	5	0
Darlington	Tr	12.88	88-91	83	2	5
McJARROW Hugh						
Motherwell, 29 January, 1928 Died 1987						(CF)
Chesterfield	Newarthill Hearts	03.46	46-49	33	-	11
Sheffield Wed	Tr	03.50	49-51	46	-	21
Luton T	Tr	02.52	51-53	15	-	10
Plymouth Arg	Tr	12.53	53-55	30	-	3
MACKAY Angus MacDougall						
Glasgow, 24 April, 1925 Died 2000						(IF)
Ipswich T	Hamilton Academical	05.46	46	5	-	0
Exeter C	Tr	09.47	47-54	257	-	79
Millwall	Tr	06.55	55	17	-	4
MACKAY David						
Rutherglen, 2 May, 1981						(FB)
Oxford U	Dundee	07.04	04	44	0	0
MACKAY David (Dave) Craig						
Musselburgh, 14 November, 1934 SSch/Su23-4/SLge-3/FLge-2/S-22						(WH)
Tottenham H	Heart of Midlothian	03.59	58-67	268	0	42
Derby Co	Tr	07.68	68-70	122	0	5
Swindon T	Tr	05.71	71	25	1	1
McKAY Derek						
Banff, 13 December, 1949						(W)
Barrow	Aberdeen	09.71	71	18	0	0
MACKAY Donald (Don) Scrimgeour						
Glasgow, 19 March, 1940						(G)
Southend U	Dundee U	07.72	72-73	13	0	0
McKAY James (Jim)						
Stirling, 11 June, 1918						(CF)
Tranmere Rov	Cowdenbeath	08.49	49	12	-	1
McKAY Joffre						
Conon Bridge, 21 January, 1937						(G)
Bury	Ross Co	12.58				
Rochdale	Tr	07.60	60	9	-	0
McKAY John (Johnny)						
Port Glasgow, 27 June, 1927						(W)
Queens Park Rgrs	Irvine Meadow	03.49	49-51	17	-	1
MACKAY Malcolm (Malky) George						
Bellshill, 19 February, 1972 S-5						(CD)
Norwich C	Glasgow Celtic	09.98	98-03	198	14	15
West Ham U	Tr	09.04	04	17	1	2

League Club	Source	Date Signed	Seasons Played	Apps	Subs	Gls
McKAY Mark Brian						
Edinburgh, 12 November, 1967						(W)
Doncaster Rov	Dalkeith Jnrs	01.90	89	0	1	0
McKAY Matthew (Matt) Paul						
Warrington, 21 January, 1981						(M)
Chester C	YT	•	97	3	2	0
McKAY Paul Wilson						
Banbury, 28 January, 1971						(FB)
Burnley	YT	11.89	89	8	4	0
McKAY Peter Walker						
Newburgh, 23 February, 1925 Died 2000						(CF)
Burnley	Dundee U	05.54	54-56	60	-	36
MACKAY Robert (Bobby)						
Harthill, 6 May, 1948						(M)
Leicester C	Harthill Jnrs	05.65	68	6	1	1
McKAY William (Billy)						
Rothesay, 10 March, 1927						(W)
Queens Park Rgrs	Deal T	07.55	55	6	-	0
McKEARNEY David Jonathan						
Crosby, 20 June, 1968						(FB)
Bolton W	Prescot Cables	11.87				
Crewe Alex	Northwich Vic	10.89	89-92	95	13	12
Wigan Ath	Tr	07.93	93-94	45	4	9
McKECHNIE Ian Hector						
Bellshill, 4 October, 1941						(G)
Arsenal	Lenzie	05.59	61-63	23	-	0
Southend U	Tr	05.64	64-65	62	0	0
Hull C	Tr	08.66	66-73	255	0	0
McKECHNIE Thomas (Tommy) Sharp						
Milngavie, 9 February, 1940						(F)
Luton T	Kirkintilloch Rob Roy	05.61	61-65	129	2	31
Bournemouth	Tr	07.66	66	14	0	2
Colchester U	Tr	09.67	67	22	1	5
McKEE Colin						
Glasgow, 22 August, 1973						(F)
Manchester U	YT	06.91	93	1	0	0
Bury	L	01.93	92	2	0	0
McKEE Francis (Frank) Joseph						
Cowdenbeath, 25 January, 1923 Died 1988						(WH)
Birmingham C	Dundee U	02.48	48-50	22	-	0
Gillingham	Tr	07.52	52-54	53	-	0
McKEE Raymond (Ray) Trevor						
Plaistow, 16 June, 1926						(G)
Northampton T	Finchley T	03.47	46	5	-	0
McKEE Stephen (Steve)						
Belfast, 15 April, 1956						(W)
Sheffield U	Linfield	12.76	76	4	3	0
McKEE William (Bill) Andrew						
Burtonwood, 6 June, 1928 Died 1999						(WH)
Blackburn Rov	Earlestown	11.49	50	1	-	0
McKEENAN Alexander **Peter**						
Port Glasgow, 26 February, 1924						(IF)
Leyton Orient	Port Glasgow	06.46	46	1	-	0
McKEEVER Mark Anthony						
Derry, 16 November, 1978 NIYth/IRu21-4						(W)
Peterborough U	YT	•	96	2	1	0
Sheffield Wed	Tr	04.97	98-99	2	3	0
Bristol Rov	L	12.98	98	5	2	0
Reading	L	03.99	98	6	1	2
Bristol Rov	Tr	02.01	00-02	20	16	0
McKELLAR David						
Ardrossan, 22 May, 1956						(G)
Ipswich T	App	03.74				
Derby Co	Ardrossan Winton Rov	04.78	78-79	41	0	0
Brentford	Tr	09.80	80-81	84	0	0
Carlisle U	(Hong Kong)	08.83	83-84	82	0	0
Newcastle U (L)	Hibernian	02.86	85	10	0	0
Hartlepool U (L)	Dunfermline Ath	08.88	88	5	0	0
Carlisle U	Dunfermline Ath	10.88	88-89	69	0	0
MACKEN Anthony (Tony)						
Dublin, 30 July, 1950 IRu23-1/LoI-1/IR-1						(FB)
Derby Co	Waterford	08.74	75-77	20	3	1
Portsmouth	L	11.75	75	5	0	0
Portsmouth	L	02.76	75	5	0	1
Walsall	Tr	10.77	77-81	190	0	1

League Club	Source	Date Signed	Seasons Played	Career Record Apps	Subs	Gls
MACKEN Jonathan (Jon) Paul						
Manchester, 7 September, 1977 EYth/IR-1						(F)
Manchester U	YT	07.96				
Preston NE	Tr	07.97	97-01	155	29	63
Manchester C	Tr	03.02	01-04	27	24	7
McKENNA Alan Millar						
Edinburgh, 4 August, 1961						(F)
Millwall	App	10.78	78-81	23	7	4
McKENNA Brian Francis						
Dublin, 30 January, 1972 IRu21-4						(G)
Brighton & Hove A	Home Farm	07.89	90	1	0	0
McKENNA Francis (Frank)						
Blaydon, 8 January, 1933 EAmat						(W)
Leeds U	Bishop Auckland	07.56	56	6	-	4
Carlisle U	Tr	02.58	57-58	46	-	11
Hartlepools U	Tr	07.59	59	32	-	5
McKENNA John (Johnny)						
Belfast, 6 June, 1926 Died 1980 IrLge-3/IWar-2/I-7						(W)
Huddersfield T	Linfield	09.48	48-52	134	-	8
Blackpool	Tr	07.54	54-56	24	-	2
Southport	Tr	07.57	57	15	-	1
McKENNA Kenneth (Kenny) Michael						
Birkenhead, 2 July, 1960						(F)
Tranmere Rov	Poulton Victoria	08.82	82	2	2	0
Tranmere Rov	Telford U	08.87	87-88	13	3	3
McKENNA Michael (Mike) Joseph						
Darkley, 3 November, 1916 Died 1974						(WH)
Northampton T	Bromsgrove Rov	07.46	46	4	-	0
McKENNA Patrick (Pat)						
Glasgow, 26 April, 1920 Died 1995						(FB)
Plymouth Arg	Aberdeen	08.52	52	1	-	0
McKENNA Paul Stephen						
Chorley, 20 October, 1977						(M)
Preston NE	YT	02.96	96-04	251	20	24
McKENNA Thomas (Tom)						
Paisley, 11 November, 1919						(WH)
Reading	St Mirren	06.46	46-47	28	-	1
Grimsby T	Tr	06.48	48-49	50	-	2
McKENNAN Peter Stewart						
Airdrie, 16 July, 1918 Died 1991 SLge-2/NIRL-2						(IF)
West Bromwich A	Partick Th	10.47	47	11	-	4
Leicester C	Tr	03.48	47-48	18	-	7
Brentford	Tr	09.48	48	24	-	6
Middlesbrough	Tr	05.49	49-50	40	-	18
Oldham Ath	Tr	07.51	51-53	78	-	28
MacKENZIE Aiden						
Athlone, 15 July, 1959						(F)
Lincoln C	Galway Rov	12.78	79	4	2	0
MACKENZIE Christopher (Chris) Neil						
Northampton, 14 May, 1972						(G)
Hereford U	Corby T	07.94	94-95	59	1	1
Leyton Orient	Farnborough T	10.97	97-98	30	0	0
Chester C	Telford U	07.04	04	23	1	0
MacKENZIE Donald (Don) Alexander						
Liverpool, 30 January, 1942						(W)
Everton		01.63				
Rochdale	Tr	10.63	63-64	41	-	7
McKENZIE Donald (Don) Cameron						
Glasgow, 9 June, 1927						(IF)
Grimsby T	Glasgow Rgrs	08.51	51	4	-	0
McKENZIE Duncan						
Grimsby, 10 June, 1950						(F)
Nottingham F	Old Clee	07.68	69-73	105	6	41
Mansfield T	L	03.70	69	7	3	3
Mansfield T	L	02.73	72	6	0	7
Leeds U	Tr	08.74	74-75	64	2	27
Everton	Anderlecht (Bel)	12.76	76-77	48	0	14
Chelsea	Tr	09.78	78	15	0	4
Blackburn Rov	Tr	03.79	78-80	74	0	16
MacKENZIE Hamish James Todd						
Denny, 11 March, 1945						(FB)
Liverpool	App	03.62				
Brentford	Dunfermline Ath	08.64	65-66	19	0	0

League Club	Source	Date Signed	Seasons Played	Career Record Apps	Subs	Gls
McKENZIE Ian Edward						
Wallsend, 22 August, 1966						(FB)
Barnsley	Newcastle U (App)	08.85	85	1	0	0
Stockport Co	Tr	09.86	86-88	51	8	0
MacKENZIE Ian Stanley						
Rotherham, 27 September, 1950						(CD)
Sheffield U	Jnrs	06.68	69-74	43	2	1
Southend U	L	03.75	74	5	1	0
Mansfield T	Tr	07.75	75-77	69	1	1
MACKENZIE John (Johnny) Archibald						
Glasgow, 4 September, 1925 SLge-2/S-9						(W)
Bournemouth	Partick Th	08.47	47	38	-	9
MacKENZIE Matthew **Laurence**						
Old Kilpatrick, 7 July, 1924						(WH)
Sheffield Wed	Clydebank Ath	12.45	46-47	6	-	0
Grimsby T	Tr	07.49	49-50	58	-	11
McKENZIE Leon Mark						
Croydon, 17 May, 1978						(F)
Crystal Palace	YT	10.95	95-00	44	41	7
Fulham	L	10.97	97	1	2	0
Peterborough U	L	08.98	98	4	0	3
Peterborough U	L	11.98	98	10	0	5
Peterborough U	Tr	10.00	00-03	83	7	45
Norwich C	Tr	12.03	03-04	36	19	16
McKENZIE Malcolm James						
Edinburgh, 1 May, 1950						(W)
Port Vale	Jnrs	05.67	65-67	7	1	1
MacKENZIE Neil David						
Birmingham, 15 April, 1976						(M)
Stoke C	West Bromwich A (YT)	11.95	96-99	15	27	1
Cambridge U	L	03.99	98	3	1	1
Cambridge U	Tr	10.99	99-00	20	8	0
Kidderminster Hrs	Tr	11.00	00	20	3	3
Blackpool	Tr	07.01	01	6	8	1
Mansfield T	Tr	08.02	02-04	50	21	4
Macclesfield T	Tr	11.04	04	16	2	0
McKENZIE Paul						
Aberdeen, 4 October, 1969						(M)
Sunderland	YT	07.87				
Burnley	Peterhead	02.92	91	1	3	0
McKENZIE Robert Alexander						
Hexham, 22 March, 1979						(M)
Rotherham U	YT	06.97	96	6	5	0
McKENZIE Roger Mark						
Sheffield, 27 January, 1973						(F)
Doncaster Rov	YT	07.91	91	7	10	1
Scarborough	Tr	08.92	92	0	1	0
MACKENZIE Stephen (Steve)						
Romford, 23 November, 1961 EYth/Eu21-3/EB						(M)
Crystal Palace	App	07.79				
Manchester C	Tr	07.79	79-80	56	2	8
West Bromwich A	Tr	08.81	81-86	153	3	23
Charlton Ath	Tr	06.87	87-90	92	8	7
Sheffield Wed	Tr	02.91	90-91	5	10	2
Shrewsbury T	Tr	12.91	91-93	19	5	1
McKENZIE Stuart Ronald						
Hull, 19 September, 1967						(FB)
York C	App	12.85	85-87	30	2	0
McKEOWN Gary Joseph						
Oxford, 19 October, 1970 ESch/EYth						(M)
Arsenal	YT	11.88				
Shrewsbury T	L	03.92	91	8	0	1
Exeter C (L)	Dundee	12.96	96	3	0	0
McKEOWN Joseph (Joe) Francis						
Bannockburn, 9 April, 1924						(IF)
Hartlepools U	Stirling A	08.50	50	46	-	7
McKEOWN Isaac **Lindsay**						
Belfast, 11 July, 1957 IrLge-2						(M)
Manchester U	App	07.74				
Sheffield Wed	Tr	07.76	76-77	6	5	0
McKEOWN Thomas (Tom)						
Cleland, 2 October, 1930						(W)
Accrington St	Queen of the South	05.54	54	12	-	2
McKERNON Craig Andrew						
Gloucester, 23 February, 1968						(FB)
Mansfield T	App	02.86	84-89	79	14	0

League Club	Source	Date Signed	Seasons Played	Career Record Apps	Subs	Gls
MACKEY Benjamin (Ben) Michael						
Leamington Spa, 27 October, 1986						(M)
Coventry C	Jnrs	•	02	0	3	0
MACKIE James (Jamie) Charles						
Dorking, 22 September, 1985						(F)
Wimbledon/MK Dons	Leatherhead	01.04	03-04	8	8	0
MACKIE John George						
Whitechapel, 5 July, 1976						(CD)
Reading	Sutton U	11.99	00-03	61	10	3
Leyton Orient	Tr	01.04	03-04	46	1	5
MACKIE Thomas (Tom) Forbes						
Burntisland, 30 March, 1918 Died 1989						(FB)
New Brighton	St Johnstone	05.47	47	2	-	0
Chester	Tr	08.48	48	5	-	0
McKIM John (Johnny)						
Greenock, 22 January, 1926 Died 2000						(IF)
Chelsea	Port Glasgow	06.47				
Colchester U	Tr	08.50	50-54	129	-	44
MACKIN John						
Glasgow, 18 November, 1943						(FB)
Northampton T		11.63	65-68	94	7	11
Lincoln C	Tr	07.69	69	3	0	0
York C	Tr	09.69	69-72	157	3	7
Darlington	L	03.73	72	2	0	0
MACKIN Levi Alan						
Chester, 4 April, 1986						(M)
Wrexham	Sch	•	03-04	6	5	0
McKINLAY Ian Joseph						
Huyton, 21 June, 1949						(W)
Southport	Wrexham (Am)	09.66	66-67	11	1	1
McKINLAY Robert (Bobby)						
Lochgelly, 10 October, 1932 Died 2002						(CD)
Nottingham F	Bowhill Rov	10.49	51-69	611	3	9
McKINLAY Thomas (Tosh) Valley						
Glasgow, 3 December, 1964 SYth/Su21-6/SB/S-22						(FB)
Stoke C (L)	Glasgow Celtic	01.98	97	3	0	0
McKINLAY William (Billy) James Alexander						
Glasgow, 22 April, 1969 SSch/SYth/Su21-6/SB-1/S-29						(M)
Blackburn Rov	Dundee U	10.95	95-98	76	14	3
Bradford C	Tr	11.00	00	10	1	0
Preston NE	Tr	09.01				
Leicester C	Clydebank	08.02	02-03	44	9	1
Fulham	Tr	07.04	04	1	1	0
McKINNEY Richard						
Ballymoney, 18 May, 1979						(G)
Manchester C	Ballymena U	08.99				
Swindon T	Tr	07.01	01	1	0	0
Colchester U	Tr	08.02	02-03	25	1	0
Walsall	Tr	07.04	04	3	0	0
McKINNEY William (Bill)						
Newcastle, 20 July, 1936						(FB)
Newcastle U	Wallsend St Luke's	05.56	57-64	85	-	6
Bournemouth	Tr	08.65	65	17	0	0
Mansfield T	Tr	07.66	66-67	51	1	2
McKINNON Paul John						
Frimley, 1 August, 1958						(F)
Blackburn Rov	Sutton U	12.86	86	5	0	0
McKINNON Raymond (Ray)						
Dundee, 5 August, 1970 SSch/Su21-6						(M)
Nottingham F	Dundee U	07.92	92	5	1	1
Luton T	Dundee U	08.98	98-99	29	4	2
McKINNON Robert (Rob)						
Glasgow, 31 July, 1966 SB-2/S-3						(FB)
Newcastle U	Rutherglen Glencairn	11.84	85	1	0	0
Hartlepool U	Tr	08.86	86-91	246	1	7
Hartlepool U (L)	Heart of Midlothian	02.99	98	7	0	0
Carlisle U (L)	Heart of Midlothian	02.00	99	8	0	0
McKINVEN John James						
Campbeltown, 1 May, 1941						(W)
Southend U	Raith Rov	05.60	60-69	284	2	62
Cambridge U	Tr	12.69	70	18	0	2
MACKLEWORTH Colin						
Bow, 24 March, 1947						(G)
West Ham U	App	04.64	66	3	0	0
Leicester C	Tr	11.67	67-70	6	0	0

League Club	Source	Date Signed	Seasons Played	Career Record Apps	Subs	Gls
McKNIGHT Allen Darrell						
Antrim, 27 January, 1964 NIu23-1/NI-10						(G)
West Ham U	Glasgow Celtic	07.88	88	23	0	0
Rotherham U	Airdrie	10.91	91	3	0	0
Walsall	Tr	11.91	91	8	0	0
Exeter C	South China (HK)	03.94	93	9	1	0
McKNIGHT George						
Newtownards, 17 November, 1923 Died 1996						(IF)
Blackpool	Coleraine	06.46	46-53	40	-	9
Chesterfield	Northwich Vic	07.55	55	5	-	1
Southport	Tr	09.57	57	1	-	0
McKNIGHT Philip (Phil)						
Camlachie, 15 June, 1924						(WH)
Chelsea	Alloa Ath	01.47	47-53	33	-	1
Leyton Orient	Tr	07.54	54-58	161	-	2
McKOP Henry George						
Bulawayo, Zimbabwe, 8 July, 1967 Zimbabwe int						(CD)
Bristol C	Bonner SC (Zim)	02.94	93-94	2	3	0
McKOY Nicholas (Nick) Paul						
Newham, 3 September, 1986						(M)
Wimbledon	Sch	•	03	1	2	0
MACKRETH Stephen (Steve) Francis						
Rossett, 1 July, 1950						(FB)
Wrexham	Jnrs	10.67	68	1	1	0
McLACHLAN Dugald						
Falkirk, 10 September, 1953						(F)
Preston NE	App	11.71				
Halifax T	L	10.72	72	1	1	0
Peterborough U	Tr	07.73	73	1	0	0
McLACHLAN Fraser Malcolm						
Knutsford, 9 November, 1982						(M)
Stockport Co	YT	07.01	01-03	43	10	4
Mansfield T	Tr	11.04	04	16	5	0
McLACHLAN Stephen (Steve)						
Kirkcudbright, 19 September, 1918 Died 1990						(WH)
Derby Co	Dalbeattie Star	03.38	38-52	58	-	1
McLAFFERTY Maurice						
Lanark, 7 August, 1922 Died 1999						(FB)
Sheffield U	St Mirren	08.51	51	18	-	0
Brighton & Hove A	Tr	07.52	52	21	-	0
McLAIN Thomas (Tommy)						
Morpeth, 19 January, 1922 Died 1995						(WH)
Sunderland	Ashington	08.46	46-51	67	-	1
Northampton T	Tr	07.52	52-55	96	-	11
McLAREN Andrew (Andy)						
Larkhall, 24 January, 1922 Died 1996 S-4						(IF)
Preston NE	Larkhall Thistle	02.39	46-48	69	-	29
Burnley	Tr	12.48	48	3	-	1
Sheffield U	Tr	03.49	48-50	31	-	4
Barrow	Tr	02.51	50-54	155	-	52
Bradford PA	Tr	10.54	54	18	-	7
Southport	Tr	06.55	55	4	-	1
Rochdale	Tr	11.55	55-56	44	-	12
McLAREN Andrew (Andy)						
Glasgow, 5 June, 1973 SSch/Su21-4/S-1						(M)
Reading	Dundee U	03.99	98-99	9	0	1
MacLAREN David (Dave)						
Auchterarder, 12 June, 1934						(G)
Leicester C	Dundee	01.57	56-59	85	-	0
Plymouth Arg	Tr	06.60	60-64	131	-	0
Wolverhampton W	Tr	01.65	64-66	44	0	0
Southampton	Tr	09.66	66	22	0	0
McLAREN Edward (Eddie)						
Dundee, 8 September, 1929						(FB)
Blackpool	Dunkeld Jnrs	06.48				
Reading	Tr	10.52	53-58	184	-	2
McLAREN Hugh						
Hamilton, 24 June, 1926 Died 1988						(W)
Derby Co	Kilmarnock	10.49	49-53	119	-	53
Nottingham F	Tr	01.54	53-54	33	-	15
Walsall	Tr	07.55	55	31	-	8
McLAREN James Danks						
Birkenhead, 29 July, 1936						(W)
Chesterfield	Wigan Ath	06.58	59	11	-	2

League Club	Source	Date Signed	Seasons Played	Career Record Apps	Subs	Gls
MacLAREN James (Jimmy) Scott						
Crieff, 26 November, 1921 Died 2004						(G)
Chester	Berwick Rgrs	01.47	46-48	30	-	0
Carlisle U	Tr	12.48	48-54	262	-	0
McLAREN Paul Andrew						
High Wycombe, 17 November, 1976						(M)
Luton T	YT	01.94	93-00	137	30	4
Sheffield Wed	Tr	06.01	01-03	83	13	8
Rotherham U	Tr	08.04	04	32	1	1
McLAREN Robert (Bobby)						
Chryston, 5 August, 1929						(IF)
Cardiff C	Barry T	02.50	49	1	-	0
Scunthorpe U	Barry T	08.51	51	6	-	0
MacLAREN Ross						
Edinburgh, 14 April, 1962						(CD)
Shrewsbury T	Glasgow Rgrs	08.80	80-84	158	3	18
Derby Co	Tr	07.85	85-87	113	9	4
Swindon T	Tr	08.88	88-94	195	2	9
MacLAREN John James **Roy**						
Auchterarder, 12 February, 1930						(G)
Bury	St Johnstone	12.55	55-58	86	-	0
Sheffield Wed	Tr	10.58	58-63	31	-	0
McLAREN Thomas (Tommy)						
Livingston, 1 June, 1949 Died 1978						(M)
Port Vale	Berwick Rgrs	11.67	67-76	301	32	28
McLARTY Jesse Jones						
Ayr, 3 March, 1920 Died 2001						(IF)
Wrexham	Chester (Am)	09.45	46-47	24	-	9
McLAUGHLAN Alexander (Sandy) Donaldson						
Kilwinning, 17 July, 1936 SLge-1						(G)
Sunderland	Kilmarnock	09.64	64-65	43	0	0
McLAUGHLIN Brian						
Bellshill, 14 May, 1974 Su21-8						(M)
Wigan Ath	Dundee U	07.99	00	13	5	0
McLAUGHLIN Hugh						
Glasgow, 2 September, 1943						(WH)
Brentford	St Roch's	09.61	63-65	4	1	0
McLAUGHLIN James						
Paisley, 11 February, 1926						(IF)
Walsall	Glenavon	06.48	48-49	14	-	0
McLAUGHLIN James (Jimmy) Charles						
Stirling, 10 December, 1926						(W)
Hartlepools U	Alloa Ath	07.53	53	13	-	2
McLAUGHLIN James (Jimmy) Christopher						
Derry, 22 December, 1940 NIu23-2/NI-12						(W)
Birmingham C	Derry C	06.58				
Shrewsbury T	Tr	07.60	60-62	124	-	56
Swansea T	Tr	05.63	63-66	133	3	45
Peterborough U	Tr	03.67	66	8	0	2
Shrewsbury T	Tr	09.67	67-72	159	14	21
Swansea C	Tr	11.72	72-73	20	7	2
McLAUGHLIN John						
Lennoxtown, 13 November, 1936						(IF)
Millwall	Morton	07.63	63	21	-	5
McLAUGHLIN John						
Edmonton, 29 October, 1954 EYth						(FB)
Colchester U	App	05.72	71-73	66	0	2
Swindon T	Tr	12.73	73-78	199	3	8
Portsmouth	Tr	07.79	79-83	172	0	1
McLAUGHLIN John Ian						
Stirling, 3 January, 1948						(FB)
Everton	Falkirk	10.71	71-75	59	2	1
McLAUGHLIN John Montgomery Lamont						
Clarkston, 12 April, 1936						(G)
Shrewsbury T (L)	Third Lanark	09.63	63	5	-	0
McLAUGHLIN John Thomas						
Liverpool, 25 February, 1952						(M)
Liverpool	App	02.69	69-73	38	2	2
Portsmouth	L	10.75	75	5	0	0
McLAUGHLIN Joseph (Joe)						
Greenock, 2 June, 1960 Su21-10						(CD)
Chelsea	Morton	06.83	83-88	220	0	5
Charlton Ath	Tr	08.89	89	31	0	0
Watford	Tr	08.90	90-91	46	0	2

League Club	Source	Date Signed	Seasons Played	Career Record Apps	Subs	Gls
McLAUGHLIN Michael (Mick) Anthony						
Newport, 5 January, 1943						(CD)
Newport Co	Nash U	11.61				
Newport Co	Lovells Ath	08.68	68-69	90	0	3
Hereford U	Tr	08.70	72-74	84	0	1
Newport Co	Cheltenham T	03.78	77	7	0	0
McLAUGHLIN Robert (Bobby)						
Belfast, 6 December, 1925 Died 2003 IrLge-1						(WH)
Wrexham	Distillery	01.50	49	17	-	0
Cardiff C	Tr	04.50	50-53	48	-	3
Southampton	Tr	10.53	53-58	169	-	5
McLAUGHLIN William James						
USA, 31 January, 1918 Died 1972						(WH)
Crewe Alex		10.46	46	1	-	0
McLEAN Aaron						
Hammersmith, 25 May, 1983						(F)
Leyton Orient	YT	07.01	99-02	5	35	2
McLEAN Angus (Gus)						
Queensferry, 20 September, 1925 Died 1979						(FB)
Wolverhampton W	Aberystwyth	11.42	46-50	144	-	2
Bury	Bromsgrove Rov	05.53	53	12	-	0
Crewe Alex	Tr	06.54	54	44	-	10
McLEAN Colin						
Cambusbarron, 16 May, 1928 Died 2000						(IF)
Southport	Forfar Ath	06.52	52-53	59	-	18
Crewe Alex	Tr	07.54	54	11	-	1
McLEAN David John						
Newcastle, 24 November, 1957 ESch						(M)
Newcastle U	App	11.75	75-77	7	2	0
Carlisle U	Tr	03.78	77-78	9	6	0
Darlington	Tr	08.79	79-85	289	5	46
Scunthorpe U	Tr	07.86	86-87	23	1	3
Hartlepool U	L	03.87	86	6	0	0
McLEAN John **Derek**						
Brotton, 21 December, 1932						(IF)
Middlesbrough		10.52	55-61	119	-	30
Hartlepools U	Tr	10.61	61-63	89	-	16
McLEAN George Roy						
Paisley, 16 September, 1937						(F)
Norwich C	Glasgow Rgrs	03.62				
Grimsby T	Tr	09.62	62-64	91	-	41
Exeter C	Tr	06.65	65-66	47	0	12
Workington	Tr	01.67	66-67	53	0	15
Barrow	Tr	06.68	68	26	1	9
MacLEAN Hugh						
Stornoway, 20 January, 1952						(W)
West Bromwich A	Tantallon U	02.69	71-72	4	2	0
Swindon T	Tr	07.74	74	17	2	0
McLEAN Ian						
Paisley, 13 August, 1966 Canada int						(CD)
Bristol Rov	Metroford (Can)	09.93	93-95	21	14	2
Cardiff C	L	09.94	94	4	0	0
Rotherham U	L	01.96	95	9	0	0
McLEAN Ian James						
Leeds, 13 September, 1978						(FB)
Bradford C	YT	01.97				
Oldham Ath	Tr	10.98	98-99	6	0	0
McLEAN James						
Alloa, 3 April, 1934 Died 1995						(IF)
Port Vale	Alva Albion Rov	03.58	57	3	-	0
McLEAN Peter Young						
Lochgelly, 27 November, 1923						(WH)
Reading	Lochgelly Violet	01.49	49-52	70	-	6
Exeter C	Tr	08.53	53	15	-	0
MacLEAN Steven (Steve)						
Edinburgh, 23 August, 1982 Su21-4						(F)
Scunthorpe U (L)	Glasgow Rgrs	08.03	03	37	5	23
Sheffield Wed	Glasgow Rgrs	07.04	04	36	0	18
McLEAN Stewart Duff						
Barrhead, 30 August, 1923						(IF)
Rotherham U	Partick Th	05.46	46-47	35	-	20
McLEAN William (Willie)						
Scotland						(W)
New Brighton	Queen of the South	06.47	47	12	-	2

League Club	Source	Date Signed	Seasons Played	Career Record Apps	Subs	Gls
McLEAN William (Billy)						
Liverpool, 14 August, 1931						(W)
Blackburn Rov	Burscough	02.53	53	12	-	0
McLEAN William Graham						
Dumbarton, 14 October, 1933 Died 1996						(IF)
Walsall		02.54	53	2	-	0
McLEARY Alan Terry						
Lambeth, 6 October, 1964 EYth/Eu21-1/EB						(CD)
Millwall	App	10.81	82-92	289	18	5
Sheffield U	L	07.92	92	3	0	0
Wimbledon	L	10.92	92	4	0	0
Charlton Ath	Tr	05.93	93-94	66	0	3
Bristol C	Tr	07.95	95-96	31	3	0
Millwall	Tr	02.97	96-98	36	0	0
McLEISH Hugh						
Shotts, 10 June, 1948						(F)
Sunderland	Dundee U	08.67				
Luton T	Tr	11.67	67	1	1	0
McLELLAN Alistair Alexander Angus						
Glasgow, 16 April, 1922						(IF)
New Brighton	Albion Rov	08.46	46-47	34	-	7
Tranmere Rov	Tr	05.48	48	2	-	0
MacLEOD Alexander (Alisdair) Hector McMillan						
Glasgow, 1 January, 1951						(F)
Southampton	St Mirren	05.73	73	2	1	0
Huddersfield T	L	10.74	74	3	1	1
MacLEOD Alistair (Ally) Reid						
Glasgow, 26 February, 1931 Died 2004						(W)
Blackburn Rov	St Mirren	06.56	56-60	193	-	47
McLEOD George James						
Inverness, 30 November, 1932						(W)
Luton T	Clachnacuddin	01.55	55-58	51	-	6
Brentford	Tr	10.58	58-63	207	-	20
Queens Park Rgrs	Tr	01.64	63-64	41	-	4
McLEOD Izale Michael						
Perry Barr, 15 October, 1984						(F)
Derby Co	Sch	02.03	02-03	24	15	4
Sheffield U	L	03.04	03	1	6	0
MK Dons	Tr	08.04	04	39	4	16
McLEOD John Murdoch						
Edinburgh, 23 November, 1938 Su23-1/SLge-1/S-4						(W)
Arsenal	Hibernian	07.61	61-64	101	-	23
Aston Villa	Tr	09.64	64-67	123	2	16
McLEOD Kevin Andrew						
Liverpool, 12 September, 1980						(M)
Everton	YT	09.98	00	0	5	0
Queens Park Rgrs	L	03.03	02	8	0	2
Queens Park Rgrs	Tr	08.03	03-04	30	29	4
Swansea C	Tr	02.05	04	7	4	0
McLEOD Norman Andrew						
Manchester, 29 July, 1930						(FB)
Crewe Alex	Hyde U	08.57	57-58	25	-	1
McLEOD Robert (Bobby) Alexander						
Inverness, 24 February, 1947						(CD)
Hartlepools U	Sunderland College	11.65	65-68	23	5	0
McLEOD Robert (Bob) Boyd						
Fraserburgh, 22 January, 1919 Died 2000						(IF)
Brighton & Hove A		11.47	47	1	-	0
McLEOD Samuel (Sammy) Mark						
Glasgow, 4 January, 1934						(IF)
Colchester U	Easthouses Lily	06.55	55-62	152	-	23
McLEOD Thomas (Tommy)						
Musselburgh, 26 December, 1920 Died 1999						(WH)
Liverpool	BAOR Germany	10.45	46-48	7	-	0
Chesterfield	Tr	07.51	51	25	-	3
McLINTOCK Francis (Frank)						
Glasgow, 28 December, 1939 Su23-1/S-9						(M/CD)
Leicester C	Shawfield Jnrs	01.57	59-64	168	-	25
Arsenal	Tr	10.64	64-72	312	2	26
Queens Park Rgrs	Tr	06.73	73-76	126	1	5
McLOUGHLIN Alan Francis						
Manchester, 20 April, 1967 IRB-3/IR-42						(M)
Manchester U	App	04.85				
Swindon T	Tr	08.86	86-90	101	5	19
Torquay U	L	03.87	86	16	0	1
Torquay U	L	08.87	87	5	3	3
Southampton	Tr	12.90	90-91	22	2	1
Portsmouth	Tr	02.92	91-99	297	12	54
Wigan Ath	Tr	12.99	99-01	12	10	1
Rochdale	Tr	12.01	01	15	3	1
McLOUGHLIN Anthony (Tony) Joseph						
Liverpool, 24 September, 1946						(W)
Everton	Jnrs	02.64				
Wrexham	Tr	07.66	66-67	27	2	9
Chester	Tr	10.67	67	2	2	0
McLOUGHLIN Paul Brendan						
Bristol, 23 December, 1963						(F)
Cardiff C	Gisborne C (NZ)	12.84	84-85	40	9	4
Bristol C	Oster Vaxjo (Swe)	01.87				
Hereford U	Tr	06.87	87-88	72	2	14
Wolverhampton W	Tr	07.89	89-91	12	16	4
Walsall	L	09.91	91	9	0	4
York C	L	01.92	91	1	0	0
Mansfield T	Tr	01.92	91-93	49	12	9
MacLUCKIE George Robertson						
Falkirk, 19 September, 1931						(W)
Blackburn Rov	Lochore Welfare	08.52	52	20	-	2
Ipswich T	Tr	05.53	53-57	141	-	24
Reading	Tr	06.58	58-60	85	-	8
McLUCKIE Robert (Sandy) John						
Doncaster, 5 October, 1955						(M)
Doncaster Rov	App	10.73	72-73	2	3	0
McMAHON Anthony						
Bishop Auckland, 24 March, 1986 EYth						(FB)
Middlesbrough	Sch	02.05	04	12	1	0
McMAHON Daryl						
Dublin, 10 October, 1983 IRYth						(M)
West Ham U	YT	10.00				
Torquay U	L	03.04	03	0	1	0
Port Vale	Tr	09.04	04	1	4	0
Leyton Orient	Tr	11.04	04	22	2	3
McMAHON David						
Dublin, 17 January, 1981 IRYth						(F)
Newcastle U	YT	02.98				
Darlington	L	12.00	00	5	3	1
McMAHON Desmond (Des)						
Reading, 22 March, 1956						(F)
Reading	Hungerford T	08.82	82	0	2	0
McMAHON Francis (Frank) Gerard						
Belfast, 4 January, 1950						(M)
Coventry C	Distillery	10.69				
Lincoln C	Waterford	07.71	71-72	54	2	2
Darlington	Tr	03.73	72-73	19	4	1
Hartlepool	L	10.73	73	7	0	0
McMAHON Gerard (Gerry) Joseph						
Belfast, 29 December, 1973 NISch/NIYth/NIu21-1/NIB/NI-17						(W)
Tottenham H	Glenavon	07.92	94-95	9	7	0
Barnet	L	10.94	94	10	0	2
Stoke C	Tr	09.96	96-97	38	14	3
McMAHON Hugh (Hughie)						
Grangetown, 24 September, 1909 Died 1986						(W)
Reading	Mexborough T	09.32	32	1	-	0
Southend U	Tr	05.33	33	10	-	3
Reading	Tr	06.34	34-35	10	-	2
Queens Park Rgrs	Tr	05.36	36-37	41	-	3
Sunderland	Tr	11.37	37-38	8	-	1
Hartlepools U	Tr	06.45	46-47	28	-	7
Rotherham U	Tr	09.47	47-48	59	-	8
McMAHON Ian						
Wells, 7 October, 1964						(M)
Oldham Ath	App	10.82	82	2	0	0
Rochdale	Tr	01.84	83-85	89	2	8
McMAHON John						
Manchester, 7 December, 1949						(FB)
Preston NE	App	12.67	70-78	256	1	7
Southend U	L	09.70	70	4	0	0
Chesterfield	L	09.79	79	1	0	0
Crewe Alex	Tr	10.79	79-80	67	0	2
Wigan Ath	Tr	08.81	81-82	71	0	5
Tranmere Rov	Tr	08.83	83	39	1	0
McMAHON John Albert						
Middlesbrough, 25 October, 1965						(F)
Middlesbrough	App	10.83				
Darlington	Tr	03.85	84	0	4	0

League Club	Source	Date Signed	Seasons Played	Career Record Apps	Subs	Gls

McMAHON Kevin
Tantobie, 1 March, 1946 (F)

League Club	Source	Date Signed	Seasons Played	Apps	Subs	Gls
Newcastle U	Consett	08.67				
York C	Tr	05.69	69-71	85	8	31
Bolton W	L	03.72	71	4	2	1
Barnsley	Tr	07.72	72	4	1	0
Hartlepool	Tr	07.73	73-75	104	3	29

McMAHON Lewis James
Doncaster, 2 May, 1985 (M)

League Club	Source	Date Signed	Seasons Played	Apps	Subs	Gls
Sheffield Wed	Sch	07.04	03-04	22	3	2

McMAHON Patrick (Pat)
Kilsyth, 19 September, 1945 (M)

League Club	Source	Date Signed	Seasons Played	Apps	Subs	Gls
Aston Villa	Glasgow Celtic	06.69	69-74	121	9	25

McMAHON Peter John
Marylebone, 30 April, 1934 (WH)

League Club	Source	Date Signed	Seasons Played	Apps	Subs	Gls
Leyton Orient	Chase of Chertsey	05.51	51-57	66	-	1
Aldershot	Tr	10.58	58-59	39	-	0

McMAHON Samuel (Sam) Keiron
Newark, 10 February, 1976 (M)

League Club	Source	Date Signed	Seasons Played	Apps	Subs	Gls
Leicester C	YT	07.94	94-97	1	4	1
Cambridge U	Tr	03.99	98	1	2	0

McMAHON Stephen (Steve)
Liverpool, 20 August, 1961 Eu21-6/EB/FLge/E-17 (M)

League Club	Source	Date Signed	Seasons Played	Apps	Subs	Gls
Everton	App	08.79	80-82	99	1	11
Aston Villa	Tr	05.83	83-85	74	1	7
Liverpool	Tr	09.85	85-91	202	2	29
Manchester C	Tr	12.91	91-94	83	4	1
Swindon T	Tr	12.94	94-97	38	4	0

McMAHON Stephen Joseph
Southport, 31 July, 1984 (M)

League Club	Source	Date Signed	Seasons Played	Apps	Subs	Gls
Blackpool	Sch	07.03	02-03	10	8	0
Kidderminster Hrs	L	09.04	04	3	2	0

McMAHON Steven (Steve)
Glasgow, 22 April, 1970 (F)

League Club	Source	Date Signed	Seasons Played	Apps	Subs	Gls
Swansea C	Ferguslie	08.91	92	2	0	0
Carlisle U	Tr	07.93	93	2	0	0
Darlington	Partick Th	01.96	95	6	4	1

McMANAMAN Steven (Steve)
Bootle, 11 February, 1972 EYth/Eu21-7/E-37 (M)

League Club	Source	Date Signed	Seasons Played	Apps	Subs	Gls
Liverpool	YT	02.90	90-98	258	14	46
Manchester C	Real Madrid (Sp)	08.03	03-04	25	10	0

McMANUS Brendan
Kilkeel, 2 December, 1923 (G)

League Club	Source	Date Signed	Seasons Played	Apps	Subs	Gls
Huddersfield T	Newry T	10.45	46	1	-	0
Oldham Ath	Tr	07.47	47	35	-	0
Bradford C	Tr	10.48	48-52	125	-	0

McMANUS Edward (Eddie) James
Ramsgate, 8 August, 1937 (W)

League Club	Source	Date Signed	Seasons Played	Apps	Subs	Gls
Bournemouth	Dover	08.54	58-59	4	-	0
Gillingham	Tr	08.60	60	3	-	0

McMANUS Charles **Eric**
Limavady, 14 November, 1950 NIAmat (G)

League Club	Source	Date Signed	Seasons Played	Apps	Subs	Gls
Coventry C	Coleraine	08.68	69-71	6	0	0
Notts Co	Tr	05.72	72-78	229	0	0
Stoke C	Tr	10.79	81	4	0	0
Lincoln C	L	12.79	79	21	0	0
Bradford C	Tr	08.82	82-84	113	0	0
Middlesbrough	L	01.86	85	2	0	0
Peterborough U	L	03.86	85	18	0	0
Tranmere Rov	Tr	08.86	86	3	0	0

McMANUS Stanley (Stan)
Carlisle, 31 October, 1932 (W)

League Club	Source	Date Signed	Seasons Played	Apps	Subs	Gls
Bury	Canterbury C	01.56				
Southport	Tr	07.57	57	5	-	0

McMANUS Steven
Nottingham, 8 March, 1975 (M)

League Club	Source	Date Signed	Seasons Played	Apps	Subs	Gls
Walsall	YT	05.93	92	0	1	0

McMANUS Stuart Joseph
Falkirk, 19 March, 1965 (F)

League Club	Source	Date Signed	Seasons Played	Apps	Subs	Gls
Southampton	Jnrs	07.84	85	2	0	1
Newport Co	L	08.85	85	4	1	0

McMANUS Thomas (Tom) Kelly
Glasgow, 28 February, 1981 Su21-14 (F)

League Club	Source	Date Signed	Seasons Played	Apps	Subs	Gls
Boston U (L)	Hibernian	08.04	04	5	3	0

McMASTER Christopher (Chris)
Darlington, 16 June, 1959 (F)

League Club	Source	Date Signed	Seasons Played	Apps	Subs	Gls
Hartlepool	App	07.77	76-77	3	1	0

McMASTER Jamie
Sydney, Australia, 29 November, 1982 EYth/Eu20 (F)

League Club	Source	Date Signed	Seasons Played	Apps	Subs	Gls
Leeds U	YT	11.99	02-04	0	11	0
Coventry C	L	11.02	02	2	0	0
Chesterfield	L	01.04	03	4	2	2
Swindon T	L	09.04	04	2	2	1
Peterborough U	L	01.05	04	3	0	0
Chesterfield	Tr	03.05	04	6	2	0

McMENAMIN Christopher (Chris)
Donegal, 27 December, 1973 (FB)

League Club	Source	Date Signed	Seasons Played	Apps	Subs	Gls
Coventry C	Hitchin T	09.96				
Peterborough U	Tr	08.97	97-98	29	4	0

McMENEMY Paul Christopher
Farnborough, 5 November, 1966 (F)

League Club	Source	Date Signed	Seasons Played	Apps	Subs	Gls
West Ham U	App	11.84				
Aldershot	L	03.86	85	10	0	5
Northampton T	L	01.87	86	4	0	2

McMICHAEL Alfred (Alf)
Belfast, 1 October, 1927 IrLge-8/I-12/NI-28 (FB)

League Club	Source	Date Signed	Seasons Played	Apps	Subs	Gls
Newcastle U	Linfield	09.49	49-62	402	-	1

McMILLAN Lyndon **Andre (Andy)**
Bloemfontein, South Africa, 22 June, 1968 (FB)

League Club	Source	Date Signed	Seasons Played	Apps	Subs	Gls
York C	Northwood & St Peter's	10.87	87-98	409	12	5

McMILLAN Duncan
Glasgow, 18 January, 1922 Died 1992 (CD)

League Club	Source	Date Signed	Seasons Played	Apps	Subs	Gls
Grimsby T	Glasgow Celtic	03.49	48-54	188	-	2

McMILLAN Eric
Beverley, 2 November, 1936 (WH)

League Club	Source	Date Signed	Seasons Played	Apps	Subs	Gls
Chelsea		04.58	59	5	-	0
Hull C	Tr	07.60	60-63	150	-	3
Halifax T	Tr	07.65	65-66	49	1	8

McMILLAN George Sneddon
Motherwell, 15 March, 1930 (W)

League Club	Source	Date Signed	Seasons Played	Apps	Subs	Gls
Wrexham	Aberdeen	05.52	52	1	-	0

McMILLAN George Sorbie
Stonehouse, Lanarkshire, 10 August, 1929 (G)

League Club	Source	Date Signed	Seasons Played	Apps	Subs	Gls
Ipswich T	Newarthill Hearts	02.53	54-57	53	-	0

McMILLAN John Shaw
Renton, 14 April, 1937 (W)

League Club	Source	Date Signed	Seasons Played	Apps	Subs	Gls
Cardiff C	Dumbarton	02.58	60	2	-	0
Exeter C	Tr	10.61	61-62	20	-	1

McMILLAN Paul Anthony
Lennoxtown, 13 July, 1950 (F)

League Club	Source	Date Signed	Seasons Played	Apps	Subs	Gls
Chelsea	Jnrs	08.67	67	1	0	0

McMILLAN Samuel (Sammy) Thomas
Belfast, 29 September, 1941 NIu23-1/NI-2 (F)

League Club	Source	Date Signed	Seasons Played	Apps	Subs	Gls
Manchester U	Boyland BC	11.59	61-62	15	-	6
Wrexham	Tr	12.63	63-67	149	0	52
Southend U	Tr	09.67	67-69	76	4	5
Chester	Tr	12.69	69	16	2	0
Stockport Co	Tr	07.70	70-71	74	0	29

McMILLAN Stephen (Steve) Thomas
Edinburgh, 19 January, 1976 Su21-4 (FB)

League Club	Source	Date Signed	Seasons Played	Apps	Subs	Gls
Wigan Ath	Motherwell	03.01	00-04	81	9	0

McMILLAN Thomas (Tommy)
Glasgow, 12 February, 1931 Died 1999 (W)

League Club	Source	Date Signed	Seasons Played	Apps	Subs	Gls
Norwich C	Glasgow Celtic	07.54	54	19	-	2
Workington	Tr	09.55	55	1	-	0

McMILLAN Thomas (Tommy) Pearson
Auchinleck, 16 January, 1936 (IF)

League Club	Source	Date Signed	Seasons Played	Apps	Subs	Gls
Watford	Maybole Jnrs	09.56	56-57	33	-	13
Carlisle U	Tr	07.58	58-60	89	-	7

McMILLEN Walter
Belfast, 24 November, 1913 Died 1987 IAmat/IrLge-1/NIRL-4/I-7 (CD)

League Club	Source	Date Signed	Seasons Played	Apps	Subs	Gls
Manchester U	Cliftonville	08.33	33-34	27	-	2
Chesterfield	Tr	12.36	36-38	85	-	17
Millwall	Tr	05.39	46-49	91	-	0

McMINN Kevin (Ted) Clifton
Castle Douglas, 28 September, 1962 (W)

League Club	Source	Date Signed	Seasons Played	Apps	Subs	Gls
Derby Co	Sevilla (Sp)	02.88	87-92	108	15	9
Birmingham C	Tr	07.93	93	19	3	0
Burnley	Tr	04.94	93-95	38	8	3

McMINN Robert (Bob) William
Doncaster, 9 October, 1946 (FB)

League Club	Source	Date Signed	Seasons Played	Apps	Subs	Gls
Doncaster Rov	App	10.64	63-65	4	1	0

McMORDIE Alexander (Eric)
Belfast, 12 August, 1946 NIu23-1/NI-21 (M)

League Club	Source	Date Signed	Seasons Played	Apps	Subs	Gls
Middlesbrough	Dundela	09.64	65-73	231	10	22
Sheffield Wed	L	10.74	74	9	0	6
York C	Tr	05.75	75-76	42	0	2
Hartlepool	Tr	12.76	76-77	46	1	2

McMORRAN Edward (Eddie) James
Larne, 2 September, 1923 Died 1984 NISch/IrLge-3/NI-15 (IF)

League Club	Source	Date Signed	Seasons Played	Apps	Subs	Gls
Manchester C	Belfast Celtic	08.47	47-48	33	-	12
Leeds U	Tr	01.49	48-49	38	-	6
Barnsley	Tr	07.50	50-52	104	-	32
Doncaster Rov	Tr	02.53	52-57	128	-	32
Crewe Alex	Tr	11.57	57	26	-	6

McMORRAN James (Jimmy) Wilson
Muirkirk, 29 October, 1942 SSch (M)

League Club	Source	Date Signed	Seasons Played	Apps	Subs	Gls
Aston Villa	Jnrs	10.59	60-61	11	-	1
Walsall	Third Lanark	11.64	64-67	93	1	9
Swansea T	Tr	06.68	68	14	0	1
Walsall	Tr	11.68	68	9	1	1
Notts Co	Tr	07.69	69	6	0	0

McMORRAN John
Forth, 11 May, 1934 Died 2001 (IF)

League Club	Source	Date Signed	Seasons Played	Apps	Subs	Gls
Bradford C	Forth W	12.54	54	1	-	0

McMORRAN Robert
Forth, 12 March, 1926 Died 1990 (W)

League Club	Source	Date Signed	Seasons Played	Apps	Subs	Gls
Manchester U	Glasgow Rgrs	02.47				
Walsall	Tr	02.50	49	8	-	1

McMULLEN David
Harrington, 6 January, 1936 Died 1999 (WH)

League Club	Source	Date Signed	Seasons Played	Apps	Subs	Gls
Workington		08.59	59	1	-	0

McMULLEN David
Denny, 13 June, 1960 (M)

League Club	Source	Date Signed	Seasons Played	Apps	Subs	Gls
Wigan Ath	Cumbernauld U	02.80	79-80	20	7	1

McMULLEN Ian
Hoylake, 17 November, 1965 (M)

League Club	Source	Date Signed	Seasons Played	Apps	Subs	Gls
Tranmere Rov		09.84	84	2	0	0

McMURRAY John Daniel
Billingham, 5 October, 1931 Died 1982 (WH)

League Club	Source	Date Signed	Seasons Played	Apps	Subs	Gls
Middlesbrough	Billingham Synthonia	05.49	53-54	3	-	0

McNAB Alexander (Sandy)
Glasgow, 27 December, 1911 Died 1962 S-2 (WH)

League Club	Source	Date Signed	Seasons Played	Apps	Subs	Gls
Sunderland	Pollok Jnrs	05.32	32-37	97	-	6
West Bromwich A	Tr	03.38	37-38	49	-	2
Newport Co	Tr	04.46	46	3	-	0

McNAB Alexander (Alex) Duncan
Birmingham, 6 April, 1932 SSch (WH)

League Club	Source	Date Signed	Seasons Played	Apps	Subs	Gls
Shrewsbury T		12.54	54-56	4	-	0

McNAB James (Jimmy)
Denny, 13 April, 1940 SSch (CD)

League Club	Source	Date Signed	Seasons Played	Apps	Subs	Gls
Sunderland	Kilsyth Rgrs	06.57	58-66	284	1	13
Preston NE	Tr	03.67	66-73	222	2	6
Stockport Co	Tr	07.74	74-75	30	0	1

McNAB Neil
Greenock, 4 June, 1957 SSch/Su21-1 (M)

League Club	Source	Date Signed	Seasons Played	Apps	Subs	Gls
Tottenham H	Morton	02.74	73-78	63	9	3
Bolton W	Tr	11.78	78-79	33	2	4
Brighton & Hove A	Tr	02.80	79-82	100	3	4
Leeds U	L	12.82	82	5	0	0
Manchester C	Tr	07.83	83-89	216	5	16
Tranmere Rov	Tr	01.90	89-92	94	11	6
Huddersfield T	L	01.92	91	11	0	0
Darlington	Ayr U	09.93	93	4	0	0

McNAB Robert (Bob)
Huddersfield, 20 July, 1943 FLge-1/E-4 (FB)

League Club	Source	Date Signed	Seasons Played	Apps	Subs	Gls
Huddersfield T	Moldgreen Civic YC	04.62	63-66	68	0	0
Arsenal	Tr	10.66	66-74	277	1	4
Wolverhampton W	Tr	07.75	75	13	0	0

McNAB Samuel (Sam)
Glasgow, 20 October, 1926 Died 1995 (IF)

League Club	Source	Date Signed	Seasons Played	Apps	Subs	Gls
Sheffield U	Dalry Thistle	01.52	52-53	11	-	4
York C	Tr	05.54	54	19	-	3

McNAB Thomas (Tom) Copeland
Glasgow, 15 July, 1933 (WH)

League Club	Source	Date Signed	Seasons Played	Apps	Subs	Gls
Nottingham F	Partick Th	03.54				
Wrexham	Partick Th	03.57	56-58	43	-	5
Barrow	Tr	03.59	58-60	43	-	4

McNALLY Bernard Anthony
Shrewsbury, 17 February, 1963 NI-5 (M)

League Club	Source	Date Signed	Seasons Played	Apps	Subs	Gls
Shrewsbury T	App	02.81	80-88	278	4	23
West Bromwich A	Tr	07.89	89-94	137	19	10

McNALLY John **Brendan**
Dublin, 22 January, 1935 IRB/IR-3 (FB)

League Club	Source	Date Signed	Seasons Played	Apps	Subs	Gls
Luton T	Shelbourne	05.56	56-62	134	-	3

McNALLY Errol Alexander
Lurgan, 27 August, 1943 (G)

League Club	Source	Date Signed	Seasons Played	Apps	Subs	Gls
Chelsea	Portadown	12.61	61-63	9	-	0

McNALLY Mark
Bellshill, 10 March, 1971 Su21-2 (CD)

League Club	Source	Date Signed	Seasons Played	Apps	Subs	Gls
Southend U	Glasgow Celtic	12.95	95-96	52	2	2
Stoke C	Tr	03.97	96-97	6	1	0

McNALLY Paul Anthony
Consett, 19 December, 1949 (M)

League Club	Source	Date Signed	Seasons Played	Apps	Subs	Gls
Bradford C	Consett Jnrs	07.67	68	1	2	0

McNALLY Ross Jonathan
Dublin, 6 September, 1978 (CD)

League Club	Source	Date Signed	Seasons Played	Apps	Subs	Gls
Brighton & Hove A	YT	07.97	97	1	1	0

McNAMARA Anthony (Tony)
Liverpool, 3 October, 1929 (W)

League Club	Source	Date Signed	Seasons Played	Apps	Subs	Gls
Everton		05.50	51-57	111	-	22
Liverpool	Tr	12.57	57	10	-	3
Crewe Alex	Tr	07.58	58	9	-	2
Bury	Tr	09.58	58	14	-	0

McNAMARA Brett Robert James
Newark, 8 July, 1972 (F)

League Club	Source	Date Signed	Seasons Played	Apps	Subs	Gls
Northampton T	Stamford T	08.94	94	0	1	0

McNAMARA Anthony **Dennis**
Liverpool, 8 March, 1935 (W)

League Club	Source	Date Signed	Seasons Played	Apps	Subs	Gls
Tranmere Rov		11.54	54	1	-	0

McNAMARA Niall Anthony
Limerick, 26 January, 1982 IRYth (F)

League Club	Source	Date Signed	Seasons Played	Apps	Subs	Gls
Nottingham F	YT	02.99				
Notts Co	Tr	07.01	01	0	4	0
Lincoln C	Belper T	08.03	03-04	2	9	0

McNAMEE Anthony
Kensington, 13 July, 1984 EYth/Eu20 (F)

League Club	Source	Date Signed	Seasons Played	Apps	Subs	Gls
Watford	YT	04.02	01-04	4	42	1

McNAMEE Gerard (Ged)
Consett, 16 August, 1960 (W)

League Club	Source	Date Signed	Seasons Played	Apps	Subs	Gls
Hartlepool U		11.79	79-82	2	2	1

McNAMEE John
Coatbridge, 11 June, 1941 (CD)

League Club	Source	Date Signed	Seasons Played	Apps	Subs	Gls
Newcastle U	Hibernian	12.66	66-71	115	2	8
Blackburn Rov	Tr	11.71	71-72	56	0	9
Hartlepool	Morton	12.73	73	2	0	0
Workington	Lancaster C	08.75	75	2	0	0

MacNAMEE John James
Edinburgh, 31 July, 1942 (W)

League Club	Source	Date Signed	Seasons Played	Apps	Subs	Gls
Reading	Montrose	12.64				
Tranmere Rov	Corby T	08.67	67-69	67	5	12

McNAMEE Peter
Glasgow, 20 March, 1935 (W)

League Club	Source	Date Signed	Seasons Played	Apps	Subs	Gls
Peterborough U	Lanark Ath	(N/L)	60-65	192	0	60
Notts Co	King's Lynn	01.66	65	3	0	0

McNAUGHT John
Glasgow, 19 June, 1964 Died 1996 (M)

League Club	Source	Date Signed	Seasons Played	Apps	Subs	Gls
Chelsea	Hamilton Academical	04.86	85-87	9	1	2

McNAUGHT Kenneth (Ken)
Kirkcaldy, 11 January, 1955 (CD)

League Club	Source	Date Signed	Seasons Played	Apps	Subs	Gls
Everton	App	05.72	74-76	64	2	3
Aston Villa	Tr	08.77	77-82	207	0	8
West Bromwich A	Tr	08.83	83	42	0	1
Manchester C	L	12.84	84	7	0	0
Sheffield U	Tr	07.85	85	34	0	5

McNAUGHTON Michael Ian
Blackpool, 29 January, 1980 (CD)

League Club	Source	Date Signed	Seasons Played	Apps	Subs	Gls
Scarborough	YT	07.98	98	22	9	1

McNEE Terence (Terry) Allan
Birkenhead, 5 June, 1925 Died 1999 (G)

League Club	Source	Date Signed	Seasons Played	Apps	Subs	Gls
Wrexham	Park Villa	12.46	46	11	-	0

McNEICE Vincent (Vince)
Cricklewood, 25 October, 1938 (CD)

League Club	Source	Date Signed	Seasons Played	Apps	Subs	Gls
Watford	Jnrs	03.57	57-63	231	-	0

McNEIL David (Dave)
Chester, 14 May, 1921 Died 1993 (FB)

League Club	Source	Date Signed	Seasons Played	Apps	Subs	Gls
Chester	Hoole Alexandra	05.42	46-50	114	-	1

McNEIL Hamish Grant
Alva, 16 November, 1934 (IF)

League Club	Source	Date Signed	Seasons Played	Apps	Subs	Gls
Colchester U	Bonnyrigg Rose	08.57	57	2	-	1

McNEIL Mark John
Bethnal Green, 3 December, 1962 (M)

League Club	Source	Date Signed	Seasons Played	Apps	Subs	Gls
Orient	App	12.79	81-84	76	13	13
Aldershot	Tr	12.84	84-85	20	5	2

McNEIL Martin James
Rutherglen, 28 September, 1980 (CD)

League Club	Source	Date Signed	Seasons Played	Apps	Subs	Gls
Cambridge U	YT	12.98	98-00	38	3	0
Torquay U	Tr	08.01	01	16	0	0

McNEIL Matthew (Matt) Alexander
Glasgow, 28 July, 1927 Died 1977 (CD)

League Club	Source	Date Signed	Seasons Played	Apps	Subs	Gls
Newcastle U	Hibernian	12.49	50	9	-	0
Barnsley	Tr	08.51	51-52	68	-	1
Brighton & Hove A	Tr	07.53	53-55	53	-	0
Norwich C	Tr	03.56	55-56	44	-	2

McNEIL Michael (Mick)
Middlesbrough, 7 February, 1940 Eu23-9/FLge-1/E-9 (FB)

League Club	Source	Date Signed	Seasons Played	Apps	Subs	Gls
Middlesbrough	Jnrs	06.57	58-63	178	-	3
Ipswich T	Tr	07.64	64-71	141	5	4

McNEIL Richard (Dixie)
Melton Mowbray, 16 January, 1947 (F)

League Club	Source	Date Signed	Seasons Played	Apps	Subs	Gls
Leicester C	Holwell Works	11.64				
Exeter C	Tr	06.66	66	31	0	11
Northampton T	Corby T	05.69	69-71	85	1	33
Lincoln C	Tr	01.72	71-73	96	1	53
Hereford U	Tr	08.74	74-77	128	1	85
Wrexham	Tr	09.77	77-82	166	1	54
Hereford U	Tr	10.82	82	12	0	3

McNEIL Robert (Bobby) Muirhead
Hamilton, 1 November, 1962 (FB)

League Club	Source	Date Signed	Seasons Played	Apps	Subs	Gls
Hull C	App	11.80	80-84	135	3	3
Lincoln C	Blackpool (N/C)	10.85	85	4	0	0
Preston NE	Tr	12.85	85-86	43	0	0
Carlisle U	Tr	08.87	87	18	1	0

McNEILL Alexander (Alan)
Belfast, 16 August, 1945 NIAmat (M)

League Club	Source	Date Signed	Seasons Played	Apps	Subs	Gls
Middlesbrough	Crusaders	08.67	67-68	3	0	0
Huddersfield T	Tr	11.68	68	1	1	0
Oldham Ath	Tr	10.69	69-74	154	16	19
Stockport Co	Tr	07.75	75-76	69	2	1

McNEILL Brian
Newcastle, 1 April, 1956 (FB)

League Club	Source	Date Signed	Seasons Played	Apps	Subs	Gls
Bristol C	App	04.74	75-76	0	3	0
Plymouth Arg	Tr	12.78	78-80	47	0	0

McNEILL Edward (Ted) Vincent
Warrenpoint, 26 March, 1929 (G)

League Club	Source	Date Signed	Seasons Played	Apps	Subs	Gls
Sunderland	Portadown	12.51	53	7	-	0

McNEILL John (Ian) McKeand
Baillieston, 24 February, 1932 (IF)

League Club	Source	Date Signed	Seasons Played	Apps	Subs	Gls
Leicester C	Aberdeen	03.56	55-58	72	-	26
Brighton & Hove A	Tr	03.59	58-61	116	-	12
Southend U	Tr	07.62	62-63	41	-	3

McNEISH Samuel (Sam)
Bo'ness, 4 August, 1930 (IF)

League Club	Source	Date Signed	Seasons Played	Apps	Subs	Gls
Leeds U	Linlithgow Rose	02.51	50	1	-	0

McNICHOL Alexander (Alex) Hogarth
Baillieston, 10 October, 1919 (IF)

League Club	Source	Date Signed	Seasons Played	Apps	Subs	Gls
Aldershot	Dunfermline Ath	08.47	47-50	110	-	20
Rochdale	Tr	01.51	50	17	-	3

McNICHOL James (Jim) Anthony
Glasgow, 9 June, 1958 Su21-7 (CD)

League Club	Source	Date Signed	Seasons Played	Apps	Subs	Gls
Luton T	Ipswich T (App)	07.76	76-78	13	2	0
Brentford	Tr	10.78	78-83	151	4	22
Exeter C	Tr	07.84	84-85	87	0	10
Torquay U	Tr	07.86	86-88	124	0	13
Exeter C	Tr	08.89	89-90	42	0	8
Torquay U	Tr	07.91	91	2	0	0

McNICHOL John (Johnny)
Kilmarnock, 20 August, 1925 (IF)

League Club	Source	Date Signed	Seasons Played	Apps	Subs	Gls
Newcastle U	Hurlford Jnrs	08.46				
Brighton & Hove A	Tr	08.48	48-51	158	-	37
Chelsea	Tr	08.52	52-57	181	-	59
Crystal Palace	Tr	03.58	57-62	189	-	15

McNICHOL Robert (Bob) Hugh
Dumbarton, 13 February, 1933 Died 1980 (FB)

League Club	Source	Date Signed	Seasons Played	Apps	Subs	Gls
Accrington St	Stirling A	05.56	56-58	134	-	5
Brighton & Hove A	Tr	06.59	59-61	93	-	0
Carlisle U	Gravesend & Northfleet	10.63	63	1	-	0

McNICHOLAS John
Preston, 30 October, 1949 (M)

League Club	Source	Date Signed	Seasons Played	Apps	Subs	Gls
Blackpool		10.68	70	0	1	0

McNIVEN David Jonathan
Leeds, 27 May, 1978 (F)

League Club	Source	Date Signed	Seasons Played	Apps	Subs	Gls
Oldham Ath	YT	10.95	96-99	8	18	2
York C	Tr	08.00	00	25	16	8

McNIVEN David Scott
Stonehouse, Lanarkshire, 9 September, 1955 Su21-3 (F)

League Club	Source	Date Signed	Seasons Played	Apps	Subs	Gls
Leeds U	App	09.72	75-77	15	5	6
Bradford C	Tr	02.78	77-82	202	10	64
Blackpool	Tr	02.83	82-83	45	4	11
Halifax T	Pittsburgh (USA)	03.85	84	12	0	4

McNIVEN Scott Andrew
Leeds, 27 May, 1978 SYth/Su21-1 (FB)

League Club	Source	Date Signed	Seasons Played	Apps	Subs	Gls
Oldham Ath	YT	10.95	94-01	204	18	3
Oxford U	Tr	07.02	02-03	85	0	1
Mansfield T	Tr	07.04	04	24	1	0

McNULTY Joseph (Joe)
Dundalk, 17 July, 1923 Died 1986 (G)

League Club	Source	Date Signed	Seasons Played	Apps	Subs	Gls
Burnley	Ards	05.49	50-51	8	-	0

McNULTY Thomas (Tom)
Salford, 30 December, 1929 Died 1979 (FB)

League Club	Source	Date Signed	Seasons Played	Apps	Subs	Gls
Manchester U	Jnrs	06.47	49-53	57	-	0
Liverpool	Tr	02.54	53-57	36	-	0

McNULTY William George
Edinburgh, 9 February, 1949 (G)

League Club	Source	Date Signed	Seasons Played	Apps	Subs	Gls
Port Vale	Jnrs	04.66	66	1	0	0
Chesterfield	Tr	07.68	68	6	0	0

MACOWAT Ian Stuart
Oxford, 19 November, 1965 ESch/EYth (FB)

League Club	Source	Date Signed	Seasons Played	Apps	Subs	Gls
Everton	App	11.83				
Gillingham	Tr	01.85	84-85	4	1	0
Crewe Alex	Tr	07.86	86-88	64	8	1

McPARLAND Ian John
Edinburgh, 4 October, 1961 (F)

League Club	Source	Date Signed	Seasons Played	Apps	Subs	Gls
Notts Co	Ormiston Primrose	12.80	80-88	190	31	69
Hull C	Tr	03.89	88-90	31	16	7
Walsall	Tr	03.91	90	11	0	6
Lincoln C	Falkirk	08.92	92	3	1	0
Northampton T	Sliema W (Malta)	10.92	92	11	0	3

McPARLAND Peter James
Newry, 25 April, 1934 FLge-1/NI-34 (W)

League Club	Source	Date Signed	Seasons Played	Apps	Subs	Gls
Aston Villa	Dundalk	09.52	52-61	294	-	97
Wolverhampton W	Tr	01.62	61-62	24	-	10
Plymouth Arg	Tr	01.63	62-63	38	-	14

McPARTLAND Desmond (Des)
Middlesbrough, 5 October, 1947 EYth (G)

League Club	Source	Date Signed	Seasons Played	Apps	Subs	Gls
Middlesbrough	App	10.64	65-67	35	0	0
Carlisle U	Tr	12.67	67	5	0	0
Northampton T	Tr	07.69	69	6	0	0
Hartlepool	Tr	03.70	69-70	56	0	0

McPEAKE Matthew (Matt)
Ballymena, 19 June, 1919 (WH)

League Club	Source	Date Signed	Seasons Played	Apps	Subs	Gls
Everton	Ballymena U	07.46				
Grimsby T	Tr	06.47				
New Brighton	Tr	07.48	48-49	50	-	2

MacPHAIL John
Dundee, 7 December, 1955 (CD)

League Club	Source	Date Signed	Seasons Played	Apps	Subs	Gls
Sheffield U	Dundee	01.79	78-82	135	0	7
York C	Tr	02.83	82-85	141	1	24
Bristol C	Tr	07.86	86	26	0	1
Sunderland	Tr	07.87	87-90	130	0	22
Hartlepool U	Tr	09.90	90-94	159	4	4

McPHAIL Stephen John Paul
Westminster, 9 December, 1979 IRYth/IRu21-7/IR-10 (M)

League Club	Source	Date Signed	Seasons Played	Apps	Subs	Gls
Leeds U	YT	12.96	97-03	52	26	3
Millwall	L	03.02	01	3	0	0
Nottingham F	L	08.03	03	13	1	0
Barnsley	Tr	07.04	04	36	0	2

McPHEAT William (Willie)
Caldercruix, 4 September, 1942 (IF)

League Club	Source	Date Signed	Seasons Played	Apps	Subs	Gls
Sunderland	Calder Jnrs	09.59	60-62	58	-	19
Hartlepools U	Tr	09.65	65	13	2	2

McPHEE Christopher (Chris) Simon
Eastbourne, 20 March, 1983 (F)

League Club	Source	Date Signed	Seasons Played	Apps	Subs	Gls
Brighton & Hove A	YT	06.02	99-04	25	28	4

McPHEE John
Motherwell, 21 November, 1937 (CD)

League Club	Source	Date Signed	Seasons Played	Apps	Subs	Gls
Blackpool	Motherwell	07.62	62-69	249	10	15
Barnsley	Tr	06.70	70	26	0	3
Southport	Tr	07.71	71-72	85	0	1

MacPHEE Magnus (Tony) George
Edinburgh, 30 April, 1914 Died 1960 (CF)

League Club	Source	Date Signed	Seasons Played	Apps	Subs	Gls
Bradford PA	Workington	10.36	36	30	-	18
Coventry C	Tr	06.37	37	12	-	6
Reading	Tr	05.38	38-48	132	-	90

McPHEE Stephen (Steve)
Glasgow, 5 June, 1981 Su21-1 (F)

League Club	Source	Date Signed	Seasons Played	Apps	Subs	Gls
Coventry C	YT	11.98				
Port Vale	Tr	07.01	01-03	125	5	39

McPHEE Stewart Douglas
Middlesbrough, 5 January, 1965 (M)

League Club	Source	Date Signed	Seasons Played	Apps	Subs	Gls
Darlington	Whitby T	09.86	86	7	2	1

McPHERSON Albert
Salford, 8 July, 1927 (CD)

League Club	Source	Date Signed	Seasons Played	Apps	Subs	Gls
Bury		06.49				
Walsall	Stalybridge Celtic	05.54	54-63	351	-	8

MacPHERSON Angus Ian
Glasgow, 11 October, 1968 (FB)

League Club	Source	Date Signed	Seasons Played	Apps	Subs	Gls
Exeter C (L)	Glasgow Rgrs	03.90	89	11	0	1

McPHERSON Ian Buchanan
Glasgow, 26 July, 1920 Died 1983 (W)

League Club	Source	Date Signed	Seasons Played	Apps	Subs	Gls
Notts Co	Glasgow Rgrs	08.45				
Arsenal	Tr	08.46	46-50	152	-	19
Notts Co	Tr	08.51	51-52	50	-	7
Brentford	Tr	07.53	53	4	-	0

McPHERSON Keith Anthony
Greenwich, 11 September, 1963 (CD)

League Club	Source	Date Signed	Seasons Played	Apps	Subs	Gls
West Ham U	App	09.81	84	1	0	0
Cambridge U	L	09.85	85	11	0	1
Northampton T	Tr	01.86	85-89	182	0	8
Reading	Tr	08.90	90-98	264	7	8
Brighton & Hove A	Tr	03.99	98-99	33	2	1

McPHERSON Kenneth (Ken)
Hartlepool, 25 March, 1927 (CF)

League Club	Source	Date Signed	Seasons Played	Apps	Subs	Gls
Notts Co	Horden CW	08.50	50-52	26	-	10
Middlesbrough	Tr	08.53	53-55	33	-	15
Coventry C	Tr	11.55	55-57	88	-	38
Newport Co	Tr	06.58	58-60	128	-	51
Swindon T	New York Am's (USA)	08.61	61-64	107	-	3

McPHERSON Malcolm
Glasgow, 19 December, 1974 (F)

League Club	Source	Date Signed	Seasons Played	Apps	Subs	Gls
West Ham U	Yeovil T	01.94				
Brentford	Tr	06.96	96-97	9	3	0

McPHILLIPS Terence (Terry) Peter
Manchester, 1 October, 1968 (F)

League Club	Source	Date Signed	Seasons Played	Apps	Subs	Gls
Halifax T	Liverpool (App)	09.87	87-90	61	32	28
Northampton T	L	11.89	89	0	1	0
Crewe Alex	Tr	08.91	91	5	1	0

McQUADE James (Jim)
Barrhead, 14 October, 1933 IrLge-2 (IF)

League Club	Source	Date Signed	Seasons Played	Apps	Subs	Gls
Halifax T	Dumbarton	08.57	57	9	-	2

McQUADE John
Glasgow, 8 July, 1970 (F)

League Club	Source	Date Signed	Seasons Played	Apps	Subs	Gls
Port Vale	Hamilton Academical	07.98	98	0	3	0

McQUADE Terence (Terry) James
Hackney, 24 February, 1941 (W)

League Club	Source	Date Signed	Seasons Played	Apps	Subs	Gls
Millwall	Enfield	10.61	61-62	34	-	7
Queens Park Rgrs	Tr	07.63	63	20	-	2
Millwall	Dover	11.65	65	3	0	1

McQUAID Thomas (Tom) Joseph
Dublin, 1 February, 1936 (WH)

League Club	Source	Date Signed	Seasons Played	Apps	Subs	Gls
Bradford C	Thackley	11.57	58-59	23	-	2

McQUARRIE Andrew (Andy)
Glasgow, 2 October, 1939 (IF)

League Club	Source	Date Signed	Seasons Played	Apps	Subs	Gls
Chesterfield	Albion Rov	11.62	62-63	38	-	12
Brighton & Hove A	Tr	07.64	64	2	-	1

McQUEEN Gordon
Kilbirnie, 26 June, 1952 S-30 (CD)

League Club	Source	Date Signed	Seasons Played	Apps	Subs	Gls
Leeds U	St Mirren	09.72	72-77	140	0	15
Manchester U	Tr	02.78	77-84	184	0	20

McQUEEN Ian David
Manchester, 4 February, 1946 Died 1985 (CF)

League Club	Source	Date Signed	Seasons Played	Apps	Subs	Gls
Rochdale		01.66	65-66	14	2	4

McQUEEN Thomas (Tommy)
West Calder, 21 February, 1929 (G)

League Club	Source	Date Signed	Seasons Played	Apps	Subs	Gls
Accrington St	Queen of the South	06.54	54-56	80	-	0

McQUEEN Thomas (Tommy) Feeney
Bellshill, 1 April, 1963 (FB)

League Club	Source	Date Signed	Seasons Played	Apps	Subs	Gls
West Ham U	Aberdeen	03.87	86-89	24	6	0

McQUILLAN Dennis
Derby, 16 March, 1934 (W)

League Club	Source	Date Signed	Seasons Played	Apps	Subs	Gls
Derby Co	Jnrs	03.51	52-55	18	-	1

McQUILLAN Patrick (Pat) Gerard
Belfast, 27 June, 1961 (FB)

League Club	Source	Date Signed	Seasons Played	Apps	Subs	Gls
Swansea C	Pembroke Borough	08.79				
Swansea C	Pembroke Borough	12.83	83-84	25	1	1

MacRAE Keith Alexander
Glasgow, 5 February, 1951 Su23-2/SLge-1 (G)

League Club	Source	Date Signed	Seasons Played	Apps	Subs	Gls
Manchester C	Motherwell	10.73	73-80	56	0	0

MACREADY Brian Leslie
Leicester, 25 March, 1942 (IF)

League Club	Source	Date Signed	Seasons Played	Apps	Subs	Gls
West Bromwich A	Hull C (Am)	02.60	60-63	14	-	1
Mansfield T	Tr	07.64	64-65	49	1	11

McROBERT Lee Peter
Bromley, 4 October, 1972 (M)

League Club	Source	Date Signed	Seasons Played	Apps	Subs	Gls
Millwall	Sittingbourne	02.95	94-97	12	11	1

MACROW Geoffrey (Geoff) Cyril
East Harling, 26 September, 1932 Died 1987 (W)

League Club	Source	Date Signed	Seasons Played	Apps	Subs	Gls
Ipswich T	Thetford T	08.55	55-56	2	-	0

McSEVENEY John Haddon
Shotts, 8 February, 1931 (W)

League Club	Source	Date Signed	Seasons Played	Apps	Subs	Gls
Sunderland	Hamilton Academical	10.51	51-54	35	-	3
Cardiff C	Tr	05.55	55-56	75	-	19
Newport Co	Tr	07.57	57-60	172	-	53
Hull C	Tr	07.61	61-64	161	-	60

McSHANE Anthony (Tony)
Belfast, 28 February, 1927 (WH)

League Club	Source	Date Signed	Seasons Played	Apps	Subs	Gls
Plymouth Arg	Brantwood	12.48	49-54	85	-	2
Swindon T	Tr	06.55	55-56	41	-	0

McSHANE Henry (Harry)
Holytown, 8 April, 1920 (W)

League Club	Source	Date Signed	Seasons Played	Apps	Subs	Gls
Blackburn Rov		04.37	37	2	-	0
Huddersfield T	Tr	09.46	46	15	-	1
Bolton W	Tr	07.47	47-50	93	-	6
Manchester U	Tr	09.50	50-53	56	-	8
Oldham Ath	Tr	02.54	53-54	41	-	5

McSHANE Paul David
Wicklow, 6 January, 1986 IRu21-1/IRYth (CD)

League Club	Source	Date Signed	Seasons Played	Apps	Subs	Gls
Manchester U	Sch	01.03				
Walsall	L	12.04	04	3	1	1

McSHEFFREY Gary
Coventry, 13 August, 1982 EYth/Eu20 (F)

League Club	Source	Date Signed	Seasons Played	Apps	Subs	Gls
Coventry C	YT	08.99	98-04	62	35	28
Stockport Co	L	11.01	01	3	2	1
Luton T	L	08.03	03	18	0	9
Luton T	L	09.04	04	1	4	1

McSPORRAN Jermaine
Manchester, 1 January, 1977 (F)

League Club	Source	Date Signed	Seasons Played	Apps	Subs	Gls
Wycombe W	Oxford C	11.98	98-03	117	41	30
Walsall	Tr	03.04	03	2	4	0
Doncaster Rov	Tr	06.04	04	15	11	1

McSTAY James (Jimmy) Gerald
Newry, 4 August, 1922 LoI-1 (W)

League Club	Source	Date Signed	Seasons Played	Apps	Subs	Gls
Grimsby T	Dundalk	08.48	48-50	61	-	2

McSTAY Raymond (Ray) James
Hamilton, 16 May, 1970 SSch (M)

League Club	Source	Date Signed	Seasons Played	Apps	Subs	Gls
Cardiff C	Hamilton Academical	12.96	96	1	0	0

McSTAY William (Willie) John
Hamilton, 26 November, 1961 (FB)

League Club	Source	Date Signed	Seasons Played	Apps	Subs	Gls
Huddersfield T	Glasgow Celtic	03.87	86-87	4	5	0
Notts Co	Tr	02.88	87-89	33	12	1
Hartlepool U	L	11.89	89	3	0	0

McSWEENEY David (Dave)
Basildon, 28 December, 1981 (FB)

League Club	Source	Date Signed	Seasons Played	Apps	Subs	Gls
Southend U	YT	04.01	00-03	54	16	1

McSWEGAN Gary John
Glasgow, 24 September, 1970 SSch/SYth/S-2 (F)

League Club	Source	Date Signed	Seasons Played	Apps	Subs	Gls
Notts Co	Glasgow Rgrs	07.93	93-95	47	15	21
Barnsley (L)	Heart of Midlothian	12.01	01	1	4	0
Luton T (L)	Heart of Midlothian	02.02	01	2	1	0

McTAFF Stephen (Steve)
Tanfield, 11 March, 1922 Died 1983 (WH)

League Club	Source	Date Signed	Seasons Played	Apps	Subs	Gls
Bradford PA	Eden Colliery	05.45	46-47	29	-	0
New Brighton	Tr	07.48	48-50	100	-	3

McTAVISH John Robert
Glasgow, 2 February, 1932 (CD)

League Club	Source	Date Signed	Seasons Played	Apps	Subs	Gls
Manchester C	Dalry Thistle	06.52	53-59	93	-	0

McTURK John
Lugar, 11 July, 1936 (FB)

League Club	Source	Date Signed	Seasons Played	Apps	Subs	Gls
Wrexham	St Mirren	07.57	57	2	-	0

McVAY David Reid
Workington, 5 March, 1955 ESch (FB)

League Club	Source	Date Signed	Seasons Played	Apps	Subs	Gls
Notts Co	Ilkeston T	07.73	73-78	101	12	2
Torquay U	L	09.77	77	8	0	0
Peterborough U	Tr	07.79	79-80	47	2	1
Lincoln C	Tr	08.81	81	13	0	0

McVEIGH James (Jim)
Bamford, 2 July, 1949 (FB)

League Club	Source	Date Signed	Seasons Played	Apps	Subs	Gls
Wolverhampton W		05.68	68	2	0	0
Gillingham	Tr	10.70	70-71	48	0	1

McVEIGH Paul Francis
Belfast, 6 December, 1977 NISch/NIYth/NIu21-11/NI-20 (F)

League Club	Source	Date Signed	Seasons Played	Apps	Subs	Gls
Tottenham H	YT	07.96	96	2	1	1
Norwich C	Tr	03.00	99-04	120	39	29

McVICAR Donald (Don) Frederick
Perth, 6 November, 1962 (CD)

League Club	Source	Date Signed	Seasons Played	Apps	Subs	Gls
Tranmere Rov	St Johnstone	08.85	85	7	0	0

MacVINISH Thomas (Tommy)
Inverness, 1 January, 1921 (W)

League Club	Source	Date Signed	Seasons Played	Apps	Subs	Gls
Preston NE	Hamilton Academical	08.48				
Darlington	Tr	08.50	50	1	-	0

McVITIE George James
Carlisle, 7 September, 1948 ESch (W)

League Club	Source	Date Signed	Seasons Played	Apps	Subs	Gls
Carlisle U	App	12.65	65-70	124	3	21
West Bromwich A	Tr	08.70	70-71	42	0	5
Oldham Ath	Tr	08.72	72-75	108	5	19
Carlisle U	Tr	12.75	75-80	191	7	20

McWHINNIE Archibald (Archie)
Glasgow, 17 July, 1926 (WH)

League Club	Source	Date Signed	Seasons Played	Apps	Subs	Gls
Wrexham	Rutherglen Glencairn	05.51	51	2	-	0

MADAR Mickael Raymond
Paris, France, 8 May, 1968 France 3 (F)

League Club	Source	Date Signed	Seasons Played	Apps	Subs	Gls
Everton	Deportivo la Coruna (Sp)	12.97	97-98	17	2	6

MADDEN Craig Anthony
Manchester, 25 September, 1958 (F)

League Club	Source	Date Signed	Seasons Played	Apps	Subs	Gls
Bury	Northern Nomads	03.78	77-85	278	19	128
West Bromwich A	Tr	03.86	85-86	10	2	3
Blackpool	Tr	02.87	86-89	73	18	24
Wrexham	L	01.90	89	6	2	0
York C	Tr	03.90	89	3	1	0

MADDEN David John
Stepney, 6 January, 1963 (M)

League Club	Source	Date Signed	Seasons Played	Apps	Subs	Gls
Southampton	App	01.81				
Bournemouth	L	01.83	82	5	0	0
Arsenal	Tr	08.83	83	2	0	0
Charlton Ath	Tr	06.84	84	19	1	1
Reading	Los Angeles (USA)	11.87	87	7	2	1
Crystal Palace	Tr	08.88	88-89	19	8	5
Birmingham C	L	01.90	89	5	0	1
Maidstone U	Tr	06.90	90	10	0	0

MADDEN Lawrence (Lawrie) David
Hackney, 28 September, 1955 (CD)

League Club	Source	Date Signed	Seasons Played	Apps	Subs	Gls
Mansfield T	Manchester Univ	03.75	74-75	9	1	0
Charlton Ath	Boston U	03.78	77-81	109	4	7
Millwall	Tr	03.82	81-82	44	3	1
Sheffield Wed	Tr	08.83	83-90	200	12	2
Leicester C	L	01.91	90	3	0	0
Wolverhampton W	Tr	08.91	91-92	62	5	1
Darlington	Tr	09.93	93	5	0	0
Chesterfield	Tr	10.93	93-95	37	0	1

MADDEN Neil
Luton, 6 February, 1962 (M)

League Club	Source	Date Signed	Seasons Played	Apps	Subs	Gls
Luton T	App	12.79	79	1	0	0

MADDEN Peter
Bradford, 31 October, 1934 (CD)

League Club	Source	Date Signed	Seasons Played	Apps	Subs	Gls
Rotherham U	Thornton	10.55	55-65	309	2	7
Bradford PA	Tr	07.66	66	25	3	1
Aldershot	Tr	07.67	67	26	1	1

MADDICK Kevin Andrew
Newcastle, 18 September, 1974 (F)

League Club	Source	Date Signed	Seasons Played	Apps	Subs	Gls
Darlington	Middlesbrough (YT)	09.92	92-93	1	2	0

MADDISON Donald (Don)
Washington, 15 February, 1927 (G)

League Club	Source	Date Signed	Seasons Played	Apps	Subs	Gls
Bradford PA	Sunderland (Am)	06.46				
Blackpool	Tr	02.48				
Darlington	Tr	08.50	50	1	-	0

MADDISON Frank
Worksop, 6 May, 1934 Died 1993 (FB)

League Club	Source	Date Signed	Seasons Played	Apps	Subs	Gls
Notts Co		08.53	56-57	15	-	0

MADDISON George
Sculcoates, 6 October, 1930 Died 1987 (G)

League Club	Source	Date Signed	Seasons Played	Apps	Subs	Gls
Aldershot		08.48	48	2	-	0
York C	Tr	09.52	53	11	-	0

MADDISON William Hartley
Sunderland, 6 April, 1954 (W)

League Club	Source	Date Signed	Seasons Played	Apps	Subs	Gls
Hartlepool (Am)		08.73	73-74	3	1	0

MADDISON James (Jimmy)
South Shields, 9 November, 1924 Died 1992 (W)

League Club	Source	Date Signed	Seasons Played	Apps	Subs	Gls
Middlesbrough	Jnrs	12.45	46	1	-	0
Darlington	Tr	08.49	49	41	-	7
Grimsby T	Tr	06.50	50-58	272	-	40
Chesterfield	Tr	03.59	58-60	98	-	16

MADDISON John (Jack) Anthony
Barrow, 1 October, 1940 (W)

League Club	Source	Date Signed	Seasons Played	Apps	Subs	Gls
Barrow	Holker COB	07.60	61-64	88	-	18

MADDISON Lee Robert
Bristol, 5 October, 1972 (FB)

League Club	Source	Date Signed	Seasons Played	Apps	Subs	Gls
Bristol Rov	YT	07.91	91-94	68	5	0
Northampton T	Tr	09.95	95-96	55	0	0
Carlisle U	Dundee	10.00	00-03	59	5	1
Oxford U	L	02.02	01	11	0	0

MADDISON Neil Stanley
Darlington, 2 October, 1969 (M)

League Club	Source	Date Signed	Seasons Played	Apps	Subs	Gls
Southampton	YT	04.88	88-97	149	20	19
Middlesbrough	Tr	10.97	97-99	32	24	4
Barnsley	L	11.00	00	3	0	0
Bristol C	L	03.01	00	4	3	1
Darlington	Tr	07.01	01-04	100	14	4

MADDISON Ralph
Bentley, South Yorkshire, 28 August, 1918 Died 1994 (W)

League Club	Source	Date Signed	Seasons Played	Apps	Subs	Gls
Doncaster Rov	Bentley Colliery	01.46	46-47	61	-	19
Stockport Co	Tr	05.48	48	5	-	0
Southport	Tr	02.49	48-49	34	-	4

MADDIX Daniel (Danny) Shawn
Ashford, 11 October, 1967 Jamaica 2 (CD)

League Club	Source	Date Signed	Seasons Played	Apps	Subs	Gls
Tottenham H	App	07.85				
Southend U	L	11.86	86	2	0	0
Queens Park Rgrs	Tr	07.87	87-00	259	35	13
Sheffield Wed	Tr	07.01	01-02	55	4	2

MADDREN William (Willie) Dixon
Billingham, 11 January, 1951 Died 2000 Eu23-5 (CD)

League Club	Source	Date Signed	Seasons Played	Apps	Subs	Gls
Middlesbrough	App	06.68	68-77	293	3	19

League Club	Source	Date Signed	Seasons Played	Career Record Apps	Subs	Gls
MADDY Paul Michael						
Cwmcarn, 17 August, 1962 Wu21-1						(M)
Cardiff C	App	08.80	80-82	35	8	3
Hereford U	L	03.83	82	9	0	1
Swansea C	Tr	08.83	83	18	2	3
Hereford U	Tr	03.84	83-85	75	2	16
Brentford	Tr	07.86	86	29	2	5
Chester C	Tr	07.87	87	17	1	1
Hereford U	Tr	03.88	87-88	27	8	1
MADELEY Paul Edward						
Beeston, West Yorkshire, 20 September, 1944 EYth/FLge-1/E-24						(CD)
Leeds U	Farsley Celtic	05.62	63-80	528	8	25
MADRICK Carl James						
Bolton, 20 September, 1968						(F)
Huddersfield T	App	06.87	87	3	5	1
Peterborough U	Tr	09.88	88	3	5	0
MAFFEY Denis						
Sunderland, 22 February, 1922 Died 1995						(CF)
Ipswich T	Walton U	07.47	47	5	-	1
MAGEE Eric						
Lurgan, 24 August, 1947 NIAmat/IrLge-2						(W)
Oldham Ath	Glenavon	06.67	67-68	41	4	9
Port Vale	Tr	07.69	69	11	7	1
MAGEE Kevin						
Bangour, 10 April, 1971						(W)
Preston NE	Partick Th	05.93	93-95	23	3	1
Plymouth Arg	Tr	09.95	95	0	4	0
Scarborough	Tr	12.95	95	26	2	1
MAGENNIS Mark Arthur						
Newtownards, 15 March, 1983 NIYth						(M)
Coventry C	YT	04.01				
Carlisle U	Linfield	10.02	02	6	0	1
MAGGIORE Anthony (Tony)						
Sunderland, 28 October, 1957						(FB)
Hartlepool	Sunderland (App)	11.75	75-76	24	4	0
MAGILL Edward **James (Jimmy)**						
Lurgan, 17 May, 1939 NIu23-1/NI-26						(FB)
Arsenal	Portadown	05.59	59-64	116	-	0
Brighton & Hove A	Tr	10.65	65-67	50	0	1
MAGILTON James (Jim)						
Belfast, 6 May, 1969 NISch/NIYth/NIu23-2/NIu21-1/NI-52/FLge						(M)
Liverpool	App	05.86				
Oxford U	Tr	10.90	90-93	150	0	34
Southampton	Tr	02.94	93-97	124	6	13
Sheffield Wed	Tr	09.97	97-98	14	13	1
Ipswich T	Tr	01.99	98-04	218	21	15
MAGUIRE James **Edward (Teddy)**						
Meadowfield, 23 July, 1917 Died 2000						(W)
Wolverhampton W	Willington	11.35	36-38	79	-	7
Swindon T	Tr	05.47	47	28	-	4
Halifax T	Tr	10.48	48-49	55	-	7
MAGUIRE Gavin Terence						
Hammersmith, 24 November, 1967 WB/W-7						(CD)
Queens Park Rgrs	App	10.85	86-88	33	7	0
Portsmouth	Tr	01.89	88-92	87	4	0
Newcastle U	L	10.91	91	3	0	0
Millwall	Tr	03.93	92-93	12	0	0
Scarborough	L	03.94	93	2	0	0
MAGUIRE James (Jim) Smith						
Eaglesham, 3 February, 1932						(W)
Rochdale	Queen of the South	08.58	58	15	-	0
MAGUIRE Paul Bernard						
Glasgow, 21 August, 1956						(W)
Shrewsbury T	Kilbirnie Ladeside	08.76	76-79	143	8	35
Stoke C	Tr	09.80	80-83	93	14	24
Port Vale	Tacoma (USA)	07.85	85-87	101	14	22
MAGUIRE Peter Jason						
Holmfirth, 11 September, 1969						(F)
Leeds U	YT	06.88	87	2	0	0
Huddersfield T	Tr	09.89	89-90	1	6	1
Stockport Co	L	09.90	90	0	2	0
MAGUIRE Thomas (Tommy)						
Dublin, 22 July, 1955						(M)
Liverpool	App	11.72				
Crewe Alex	Tr	02.74	73-75	23	4	1
MAHER Aiden						
Liverpool, 1 December, 1946 ESch						(W)
Everton	App	12.64	67	1	0	0
Plymouth Arg	Tr	10.68	68-70	64	0	3
Tranmere Rov	Tr	06.71	71	2	5	1
MAHER John (Johnny)						
Manchester, 6 November, 1933						(IF)
Walsall	Manchester C (Am)	05.54	54	1	-	0
Gillingham	Tr	07.55	55	2	-	1
MAHER Kevin Andrew						
Ilford, 17 October, 1976 IRu21-4						(M)
Tottenham H	YT	07.95				
Southend U	Tr	01.98	97-04	272	7	16
MAHER Shaun Patrick						
Dublin, 20 June, 1978						(CD)
Fulham	Bohemians	12.97				
Bournemouth	Bohemians	08.01	01-04	87	17	5
MAHON Alan Joseph						
Dublin, 4 April, 1978 IRSch/IRYth/IRu21-18/IR-1						(W)
Tranmere Rov	YT	04.95	95-99	84	36	13
Blackburn Rov	Sporting Lisbon (Por)	12.00	00-03	25	11	1
Cardiff C	L	01.03	02	13	2	2
Ipswich T	L	09.03	03	7	4	1
Wigan Ath	Tr	02.04	03-04	34	7	8
MAHON Gavin Andrew						
Birmingham, 2 January, 1977						(M)
Wolverhampton W	YT	07.95				
Hereford U	Tr	07.96	96	10	1	1
Brentford	Tr	11.98	98-01	140	1	8
Watford	Tr	03.02	01-04	93	5	2
MAHON Michael (Mick) John						
Manchester, 17 September, 1944 EAmat						(W)
Port Vale	North Shields	04.67	66-68	91	0	21
York C	Tr	07.69	69	27	2	10
Colchester U	Tr	05.70	70-73	131	5	26
MAHONEY Anthony (Tony) Joseph						
Barking, 29 September, 1959 EYth						(F)
Fulham	App	08.77	76-80	53	6	10
Northampton T	L	10.81	81	6	0	0
Brentford	Tr	07.82	82-83	33	8	12
Crystal Palace	Tr	06.84	84	17	1	4
MAHONEY Brian						
Tantobie, 12 May, 1952						(F)
Huddersfield T	App	11.69	70-71	18	2	2
Barnsley	Tr	03.72	71-74	82	8	16
MAHONEY John Francis						
Cardiff, 20 September, 1946 Wu23-3/W-51						(M)
Crewe Alex	Ashton U	03.66	65-66	16	2	5
Stoke C	Tr	03.67	66-76	270	12	25
Middlesbrough	Tr	08.77	77-78	77	0	1
Swansea C	Tr	07.79	79-82	106	4	1
MAHONEY Michael (Mike) James						
Bristol, 25 October, 1950						(G)
Bristol C	App	08.68	67-69	4	0	0
Torquay U	Tr	08.70	70-74	157	0	0
Newcastle U	Tr	03.75	74-78	108	0	0
MAHONEY-JOHNSON Michael Anthony						
Paddington, 6 November, 1976						(F)
Queens Park Rgrs	YT	04.95	96-97	0	3	0
Wycombe W	L	08.96	96	2	2	2
Brighton & Hove A	L	02.98	97	3	1	0
MAHORN Paul Gladstone						
Leytonstone, 13 August, 1973						(F)
Tottenham H	YT	01.92	93-97	3	0	0
Fulham	L	09.93	93	1	2	0
Burnley	L	03.96	95	3	5	1
Port Vale	Tr	03.98	97	0	1	0
MAHY Barry						
Doncaster, 21 January, 1942						(IF)
Scunthorpe U	(Jersey)	05.63	63-66	21	1	2
MAIDENS Michael Douglas						
Middlesbrough, 7 May, 1987						(M)
Hartlepool U	Sch	●	04	0	1	0
MAIDMENT Ian Michael						
Newbury, 9 August, 1947						(W)
Reading	App	08.65	65	7	0	0

MAIL David
Bristol, 12 September, 1962 (CD)

League Club	Source	Date Signed	Seasons Played	Apps	Subs	Gls
Aston Villa	App	07.80				
Blackburn Rov	Tr	01.82	82-89	200	6	4
Hull C	Tr	07.90	90-94	140	10	2

MAILER Ronald (Ron) George
Auchterarder, 18 May, 1932 (W)

League Club	Source	Date Signed	Seasons Played	Apps	Subs	Gls
Darlington	Dunfermline Ath	03.54	54	11	-	2

MAILEY William (Willie)
Duntocher, 13 June, 1943 Died 1992 SSch (G)

League Club	Source	Date Signed	Seasons Played	Apps	Subs	Gls
Everton	Jnrs	06.60				
Crewe Alex	Tr	03.63	63-69	216	0	0

MAIN Ian Roy
Weston-super-Mare, 31 October, 1959 Died 1998 ESch (G)

League Club	Source	Date Signed	Seasons Played	Apps	Subs	Gls
Exeter C	Gloucester C	09.78	78-81	78	0	0

MAINWARING Carl Andrew
Swansea, 15 March, 1980 (F)

League Club	Source	Date Signed	Seasons Played	Apps	Subs	Gls
Swansea C	YT	07.98	97	2	1	0

MAIORANA Giuliano
Cambridge, 18 April, 1969 (W)

League Club	Source	Date Signed	Seasons Played	Apps	Subs	Gls
Manchester U	Histon	11.88	88-89	2	5	0

MAIR Gordon
Bothwell, 18 December, 1958 SSch (W)

League Club	Source	Date Signed	Seasons Played	Apps	Subs	Gls
Notts Co	App	12.76	76-83	123	8	15
Lincoln C	Tr	08.84	84-85	57	0	3

MAIR Lee
Aberdeen, 9 December, 1980 (CD)

League Club	Source	Date Signed	Seasons Played	Apps	Subs	Gls
Stockport Co	Dundee	06.04	04	9	5	0

MAITLAND Lloyd Curtis
Coleshill, 21 March, 1957 (W)

League Club	Source	Date Signed	Seasons Played	Apps	Subs	Gls
Huddersfield T	App	03.74	74-76	31	8	2
Darlington	Tr	03.77	76-78	58	13	6

MAJOR John (Jack) Leonard
Islington, 12 March, 1929 Died 1986 EAmat (W)

League Club	Source	Date Signed	Seasons Played	Apps	Subs	Gls
Hull C (Am)	Hull Amats	04.47	46	3	-	0
Hull C	Bishop Auckland	06.55	55-56	10	-	0

MAJOR Leslie (Les) Dennis
Yeovil, 25 January, 1926 Died 2001 (G)

League Club	Source	Date Signed	Seasons Played	Apps	Subs	Gls
Leicester C	Brush Sports	06.43	47-48	26	-	0
Plymouth Arg	Tr	05.49	49-55	75	-	0

MAKEL Lee Robert
Sunderland, 11 January, 1973 (M)

League Club	Source	Date Signed	Seasons Played	Apps	Subs	Gls
Newcastle U	YT	02.91	90-91	6	6	1
Blackburn Rov	Tr	07.92	92-95	1	5	0
Huddersfield T	Tr	10.95	95-97	62	3	5
Bradford C	Heart of Midlothian	08.01	01	2	11	0
Plymouth Arg	Livingston	06.04	04	13	6	0

MAKELELE Claude
Kinshasa, DR Congo, 18 February, 1973 Fru21/FrB-4/Fr-35 (M)

League Club	Source	Date Signed	Seasons Played	Apps	Subs	Gls
Chelsea	Real Madrid (Sp)	09.03	03-04	62	4	1

MAKEPEACE Brian
Rossington, 6 October, 1931 (FB)

League Club	Source	Date Signed	Seasons Played	Apps	Subs	Gls
Doncaster Rov	Rossington Colliery	03.49	50-60	353	-	0

MAKIN Christopher (Chris) Gregory
Manchester, 8 May, 1973 ESch/EYth/Eu21-5 (FB)

League Club	Source	Date Signed	Seasons Played	Apps	Subs	Gls
Oldham Ath	YT	11.91	93-95	93	1	4
Wigan Ath	L	08.92	92	14	1	2
Sunderland	Marseille (Fr)	08.97	97-00	115	5	1
Ipswich T	Tr	03.01	00-03	78	0	0
Leicester C	Tr	08.04	04	21	0	0
Derby Co	Tr	02.05	04	13	0	0

MAKIN Joseph (Joe)
Manchester, 21 September, 1950 (FB)

League Club	Source	Date Signed	Seasons Played	Apps	Subs	Gls
Oldham Ath	App	10.67	66-67	6	0	0

MAKIN Samuel (Sammy) Hansbrew
Radcliffe, 14 November, 1925 Died 1981 (W)

League Club	Source	Date Signed	Seasons Played	Apps	Subs	Gls
Rochdale	Moss Rov	05.44	46	5	-	1

MAKOFO Serge
Kinshasa, DR Congo, 22 October, 1986 (F)

League Club	Source	Date Signed	Seasons Played	Apps	Subs	Gls
MK Dons	Sch	•	04	0	1	0

MALAM Albert
Liverpool, 20 January, 1913 Died 1992 (IF)

League Club	Source	Date Signed	Seasons Played	Apps	Subs	Gls
Chesterfield	Colwyn Bay U	11.32	32-34	58	-	25
Huddersfield T	Tr	09.34	34	21	-	11
Doncaster Rov	Tr	09.36	36-38	95	-	26
Wrexham	Tr	02.46	46	6	-	1

MALAN Norman Frederick
Johannesburg, South Africa, 23 November, 1923 (G)

League Club	Source	Date Signed	Seasons Played	Apps	Subs	Gls
Middlesbrough	Defos (SA)	10.45	46	2	-	0
Darlington	Tr	08.48				
Scunthorpe U	Tr	06.50	50-55	136	-	0
Bradford PA	Tr	07.56	56	24	-	0

MALBRANQUE Steed
Mouscron, Belgium, 6 January, 1980 Fru21 (M)

League Club	Source	Date Signed	Seasons Played	Apps	Subs	Gls
Fulham	Lyon (Fr)	08.01	01-04	128	10	26

MALCOLM Alexander (Alex) Anderson
Hamilton, 13 February, 1956 (FB)

League Club	Source	Date Signed	Seasons Played	Apps	Subs	Gls
Luton T	App	07.73				
Northampton T	Tr	08.76	76	2	0	0

MALCOLM Alexander (Alex) Mitchell
Alloa, 15 December, 1921 Died 1987 (W)

League Club	Source	Date Signed	Seasons Played	Apps	Subs	Gls
Barnsley	Alloa Ath	06.46	46-47	5	-	0

MALCOLM Andrew (Andy)
West Ham, 4 May, 1933 ESch/EYth/FLge-1 (WH)

League Club	Source	Date Signed	Seasons Played	Apps	Subs	Gls
West Ham U	Jnrs	07.50	53-61	283	-	4
Chelsea	Tr	11.61	61	27	-	1
Queens Park Rgrs	Tr	10.62	62-64	84	-	5

MALCOLM Walter **Grant** Lees
Musselburgh, 25 October, 1940 SSch (W)

League Club	Source	Date Signed	Seasons Played	Apps	Subs	Gls
Newcastle U	Dalkeith Thistle	11.57	59	1	-	0

MALCOLM John Moore
Clackmannan, 20 May, 1917 (WH)

League Club	Source	Date Signed	Seasons Played	Apps	Subs	Gls
Accrington St		10.44	46	25	-	0
Tranmere Rov	Tr	07.47	47	22	-	0

MALCOLM Kenneth (Ken) Campbell
Aberdeen, 25 July, 1926 (FB)

League Club	Source	Date Signed	Seasons Played	Apps	Subs	Gls
Ipswich T	Arbroath	05.54	54-62	274	-	2

MALCOLM Paul Anthony
Felling, 11 December, 1964 (G)

League Club	Source	Date Signed	Seasons Played	Apps	Subs	Gls
Newcastle U	App	12.82				
Rochdale	Durham C	09.84	84	24	0	0
Shrewsbury T	Tr	07.85				
Barnsley	Tr	08.86	86	3	0	0
Doncaster Rov	Tr	07.88	88	34	0	0

MALCOLM Stuart Ross
Edinburgh, 2 August, 1979 (CD)

League Club	Source	Date Signed	Seasons Played	Apps	Subs	Gls
Plymouth Arg	St Johnstone	08.02	02	3	0	0

MALE Charles **George**
Plaistow, 8 May, 1910 Died 1998 FLge-2/E-19 (FB)

League Club	Source	Date Signed	Seasons Played	Apps	Subs	Gls
Arsenal	Clapton	05.30	30-47	285	-	0

MALE Norman Alfred
West Bromwich, 27 May, 1917 Died 1992 (FB)

League Club	Source	Date Signed	Seasons Played	Apps	Subs	Gls
West Bromwich A	Bush Rov	10.34	37	3	-	1
Walsall	Tr	03.38	38-48	70	-	2

MALESSA Antony (Tony) George
Ascot, 13 November, 1980 (G)

League Club	Source	Date Signed	Seasons Played	Apps	Subs	Gls
Bristol C	Southampton (YT)	02.99	00	0	1	0

MALEY Mark
Newcastle, 26 January, 1981 ESch/EYth (FB)

League Club	Source	Date Signed	Seasons Played	Apps	Subs	Gls
Sunderland	YT	01.98				
Blackpool	L	10.00	00	2	0	0
Northampton T	L	11.00	00	2	0	0
York C	L	09.01	01	11	2	0

MALKIN Christopher (Chris) Gregory
Hoylake, 4 June, 1967 (F)

League Club	Source	Date Signed	Seasons Played	Apps	Subs	Gls
Tranmere Rov	Stork	07.87	87-94	184	48	59
Millwall	Tr	07.95	95-96	46	6	14
Blackpool	Tr	10.96	96-98	45	19	6

MALKIN John (Jack)
Normacot, 9 November, 1925 Died 1994 (W)

League Club	Source	Date Signed	Seasons Played	Apps	Subs	Gls
Stoke C		07.47	47-55	175	-	24

MALLENDER Gary
Barnsley, 12 March, 1959 (M)

League Club	Source	Date Signed	Seasons Played	Apps	Subs	Gls
Barnsley	App	03.77	76-78	0	2	0

MALLENDER Kenneth (Ken)
Thrybergh, 10 December, 1943 (CD)

League Club	Source	Date Signed	Seasons Played	Apps	Subs	Gls
Sheffield U	App	02.61	61-68	141	2	2
Norwich C	Tr	10.68	68-70	46	0	1
Hereford U	Tr	07.71	72-73	71	1	1

League Club	Source	Date Signed	Seasons Played	Apps	Subs	Gls
MALLENDER Paul Richard						
Norwich, 30 November, 1969						(CD)
Hereford U	App	09.86	87	0	1	0
MALLETT Joseph (Joe)						
Gateshead, 8 January, 1916 Died 2004						(WH)
Charlton Ath	Dunston CWS	11.35				
Queens Park Rgrs	Tr	10.37	37	29	-	4
Charlton Ath	Tr	07.38	38	2	-	0
Queens Park Rgrs	Tr	02.39	38-46	41	-	7
Southampton	Tr	02.47	46-52	215	-	3
Leyton Orient	Tr	07.53	53-54	27	-	1
MALLEY Philip (Phil)						
Felling, 1 November, 1965						(M)
Hartlepool U	Sunderland (App)	11.83	83	0	1	0
Burnley	Berwick Rgrs	02.84	83-87	91	4	5
Stockport Co	L	11.84	84	3	0	0
MALLINSON David John						
Sheffield, 7 July, 1946						(WH)
Mansfield T	Jnrs	03.65	65	10	1	1
MALLINSON Trevor						
Huddersfield, 25 April, 1945						(FB)
Hallifax T (Am)	Huddersfield T (App)	12.64	64	3	-	0
MALLON James (Jim) Gillan						
Glasgow, 28 August, 1938						(FB)
Oldham Ath	Stirling A	03.59	58-59	31	-	8
Barrow	Morton	10.65	65-68	149	1	3
MALLON Ryan						
Sheffield, 22 March, 1983						(F)
Sheffield U	Jnrs	07.01	01	0	1	0
MALLORY Richard (Dick) James Leroy						
Bermuda, 10 August, 1942						(W)
Cardiff C	(Bermuda)	05.63	63	3	-	0
MALLOY Daniel (Danny)						
Dennyloanhead, 6 November, 1930 SB/SLge-1						(CD)
Cardiff C	Dundee	10.55	55-60	226	-	1
Doncaster Rov	Tr	08.61	61	42	-	0
MALONE Richard (Dick) Philip						
Carfin, 22 August, 1947 Su23-1						(FB)
Sunderland	Ayr U	10.70	70-76	235	1	2
Hartlepool U	Tr	07.77	77-78	36	0	2
Blackpool	Tr	11.78	78-79	48	0	1
MALONEY Derek Thomas						
Newton-le-Willows, 27 March, 1936						(WH)
Crewe Alex	St Helens T	02.58	57	15	-	0
MALONEY Jonathan (Jon) Duncan						
Leeds, 3 March, 1985						(F)
Doncaster Rov	Sch	07.03	03-04	1	2	0
MALONEY Joseph (Joe) John						
Liverpool, 26 January, 1934						(CD)
Liverpool	Jnrs	01.51	52-53	12	-	0
Shrewsbury T	Tr	07.54	54-59	237	-	1
Port Vale	Tr	07.61	61	1	-	0
Crewe Alex	Tr	08.61	61-62	26	-	0
MALONEY Paul John						
Rossington, 13 January, 1952						(W)
Huddersfield T	App	11.69				
York C	Tr	02.70	69-71	3	5	0
MALONEY Sean						
Hyde, 4 October, 1962						(F)
Stockport Co	Jnrs	08.79	79	0	1	0
MALOY Kenneth (Ken) Frederick						
Edmonton, 16 September, 1940						(W)
Plymouth Arg	Ilford	09.59	60-63	62	-	11
Peterborough U	Tr	07.64	64	6	-	1
Aldershot	Tr	07.65	65-66	51	1	11
MALOY Kevin William						
Aldershot, 12 November, 1966						(G)
Exeter C	Taunton T	07.91	91	4	0	0
MALPASS Frank Love						
Consett, 16 October, 1932						(G)
Gateshead	Jnrs	10.49	49	3	-	0
MALPASS Samuel (Sam) Thomas						
Consett, 12 September, 1918 Died 1983						(FB)
Huddersfield T		10.36				
Fulham	Tr	05.39	46	2	-	0
Watford	Tr	01.47	46-48	41	-	0
MALT Robert						
Ryhope, 4 November, 1951						(F)
Leeds U	App	11.68				
Darlington	Tr	06.70	70	2	2	0
MALTBY John (Jack)						
Leadgate, 31 July, 1939						(IF)
Sunderland	Crookhall Jnrs	08.57	56-60	22	-	4
Darlington	Tr	06.61	61-64	114	-	32
Bury	Tr	07.65	65-66	56	1	8
MALZ Stefan						
Ludwigshafen, Germany, 15 June, 1972						(M)
Arsenal	TSV Munich (Ger)	07.99	99-00	2	4	1
MAMOUN Blaise Noel Emmanuel						
Bamenda, Cameroon, 25 December, 1979 CmYth						(F)
Scunthorpe U	St Etienne (Fr)	08.00	00	0	1	0
MANANGU Eric Mavambu						
DR Congo, 9 September, 1985						(F)
Rushden & Diamonds	Sch	●	03	0	1	0
MANCINI Michael (Mike)						
Hammersmith, 8 June, 1956						(F)
Orient	Hendon	03.84	83	2	0	0
MANCINI Roberto						
Jesi, Italy, 27 November, 1964 Italy 36						(M)
Leicester C (L)	SS Lazio (It)	01.01	00	3	1	0
MANCINI Terence (Terry) John						
St Pancras, 4 October, 1942 IR-5						(CD)
Watford	Jnrs	07.61	61-65	66	1	0
Orient	Port Elizabeth C (SA)	11.67	67-71	167	0	16
Queens Park Rgrs	Tr	10.71	71-74	94	0	3
Arsenal	Tr	10.74	74-75	52	0	1
Aldershot	Tr	09.76	76	21	0	0
MANDERS Ronald (Ron) Ernest						
Shrewsbury, 13 November, 1931 Died 1980						(WH)
Shrewsbury T	Jnrs	12.54	54-56	6	-	0
MANDERSON David Anthony						
Glasgow, 18 October, 1973						(M)
Scarborough	YT	08.92	91	0	1	0
[MANEL] MARTINEZ FERNANDEZ Manuel						
Barcelona, Spain, 3 November, 1973						(F)
Derby Co	Espanyol (Sp)	01.04	03	12	4	3
MANGAN Andrew Francis						
Liverpool, 30 August, 1986						(F)
Blackpool	Sch	●	03	0	2	0
MANKELOW Jamie Anthony						
Clapton, 4 September, 1964						(F)
Orient	App	09.82	82	1	1	0
MANKTELOW Brian						
Farnham, 29 March, 1951						(F)
Aldershot	App	●	68	1	0	0
MANLEY Malcolm Richardson						
Johnstone, 1 December, 1949 SSch						(CD)
Leicester C	Johnstone Burgh	01.67	67-72	107	10	5
Portsmouth	Tr	12.73	73-74	11	0	0
MANLEY Thomas (Tom) Ronald						
Northwich, 7 October, 1912 Died 1988						(WH)
Manchester U	Northwich Vic	05.31	31-38	188	-	40
Brentford	Tr	07.39	46-50	116	-	7
MANN Adrian Gary						
Northampton, 12 July, 1967						(M)
Northampton T	App	05.85	83-87	71	11	5
Torquay U	L	03.87	86	6	2	0
Newport Co	Tr	11.87	87	17	0	1
MANN Arthur Fraser						
Burntisland, 23 January, 1948 Died 1999						(M)
Manchester C	Heart of Midlothian	11.68	68-70	32	3	0
Blackpool	L	11.71	71	3	0	0
Notts Co	Tr	07.72	72-78	243	10	21
Shrewsbury T	Tr	06.79	79	8	0	1
Mansfield T	Tr	10.79	79-81	114	2	3

League Club	Source	Date Signed	Seasons Played	Career Record Apps	Subs	Gls
MANN James (Jimmy) Arthur						
Goole, 15 December, 1952						(M)
Leeds U	App	12.69	71-72	2	0	0
Bristol C	Tr	05.74	74-81	205	26	31
Barnsley	Tr	02.82	81-82	14	1	0
Scunthorpe U	Tr	01.83	82	2	0	0
Doncaster Rov	Tr	02.83	82	13	0	0
MANN Neil						
Nottingham, 9 November, 1972						(M)
Grimsby T	Notts Co (Jnrs)	09.90				
Hull C	Grantham T	07.93	93-00	138	37	10
MANN Ronald (Ron) Harold						
Nottingham, 8 October, 1932						(FB)
Notts Co	Meadow BC	12.50	50	1	-	0
Aldershot	Tr	07.56	56-57	24	-	4
MANNERS Peter John						
Sunderland, 31 July, 1959						(M)
Newcastle U	App	07.77	78	2	0	0
MANNERS Wingrove						
West Indies, 7 March, 1955						(F)
Bradford C	App	●	71	1	0	0
MANNING John Joseph						
Liverpool, 11 December, 1940						(F)
Tranmere Rov	Liverpool (Am)	05.62	62-66	130	0	70
Shrewsbury T	Tr	10.66	66-67	39	0	18
Norwich C	Tr	09.67	67-68	60	0	21
Bolton W	Tr	03.69	68-70	27	2	7
Walsall	Tr	07.71	71	13	1	6
Tranmere Rov	Tr	03.72	71	5	0	1
Crewe Alex	Tr	08.72	72	37	1	6
Barnsley	Tr	09.73	73-74	41	4	7
Crewe Alex	Tr	11.75	75	7	0	5
MANNING Paul James						
Lewisham, 21 January, 1974						(FB)
Millwall	YT	10.91	92	1	0	0
MANNINGER Alexander (Alex)						
Salzburg, Austria, 4 June, 1977 AustriaYth/AustriaU21/Austria-7						(G)
Arsenal	Sturm Graz (Aut)	06.97	97-00	38	1	0
MANNINI Moreno						
Imola, Italy, 15 August, 1962 Italy 10						(CD)
Nottingham F	Sampdoria (It)	08.99	99	7	1	0
MANNION Gerard (Gerry) Patrick						
Burtonwood, 21 December, 1939 Died 1994 EYth/Eu23-2						(W)
Wolverhampton W	Jnrs	11.57	59-60	17	-	7
Norwich C	Tr	09.61	61-67	100	0	17
Chester	Tr	01.68	67	6	0	0
MANNION Sean						
Dublin, 3 March, 1980						(M)
Stockport Co	Stella Maris	02.98	98	0	1	0
MANNION Wilfred (Wilf) James						
South Bank, 16 May, 1918 Died 2000 EB/FLge-8/EWar-4/E-26						(IF)
Middlesbrough	South Bank St Peter's	09.36	36-53	341	-	100
Hull C	Tr	12.54	54	16	-	1
MANNS Paul Henry						
Great Haywood, 15 April, 1961						(M)
Notts Co	Cardiff C (N/C)	08.79	79-80	5	2	1
Chester	Tr	03.83	82-83	28	0	3
MANSARAM Darren Timothy						
Doncaster, 25 June, 1984						(F)
Grimsby T	Sch	09.02	02-04	35	38	6
MANSELL Ronald **Barrington (Barry)**						
Petersfield, 8 March, 1932						(FB)
Portsmouth	Hillside YC	08.49	51-53	16	-	0
Reading	Tr	02.54	53-55	84	-	0
MANSELL George William						
Doncaster, 19 January, 1943						(CF)
Doncaster Rov		09.62	62	1	-	0
MANSELL John (Jack)						
Salford, 22 August, 1927 EB/WLge-1/FLge-2						(FB)
Brighton & Hove A	Manchester U (Am)	03.49	48-52	116	-	10
Cardiff C	Tr	10.52	52-53	25	-	0
Portsmouth	Tr	11.53	53-57	134	-	7
MANSELL Lee Richard Samuel						
Gloucester, 28 October, 1982						(M)
Luton T	YT	05.01	00-04	35	12	8
MANSFIELD Frederick (Fred) Charles Adam						
Cambridge, 9 March, 1915 Died 1992						(FB)
Brentford	Cambridge T	04.39				
Norwich C	Tr	02.47	46-47	34	-	0
MANSFIELD John Vincent						
Colchester, 13 September, 1946						(M)
Colchester U	Jnrs	08.64	64-68	28	6	3
MANSFIELD Ronald (Ron) William						
Romford, 31 December, 1923 Died 1997						(W)
Millwall	Ilford	04.41	46-52	97	-	25
Southend U	Tr	11.52	52	8	-	3
MANSLEY Allan						
Liverpool, 31 August, 1946 Died 2001						(W)
Blackpool	Skelmersdale U	06.67				
Brentford	Tr	01.68	67-70	94	1	24
Fulham	Tr	12.70	70	1	0	0
Notts Co	L	03.71	71	11	0	2
Lincoln C	L	12.71	71	3	0	0
MANSLEY Chad Andrew						
Newcastle, Australia, 13 November, 1980 AuSch						(M)
Leyton Orient	Newcastle Break's (Aus)	11.00	00	0	1	0
MANSLEY Vincent **Clifford (Cliff)**						
Skipton, 5 April, 1921						(WH)
Preston NE		09.40				
Barnsley	Tr	11.45	46-47	30	-	0
Chester	Tr	06.48	48	22	-	0
Leyton Orient	Yeovil T	07.52	52	10	-	0
MANSOURI Yazid						
Revin, Algeria, 25 February, 1978 Algeria int						(M)
Coventry C (L)	Le Havre (Fr)	08.03	03	9	5	0
MANUEL William (Billy) Albert James						
Hackney, 28 June, 1969						(M)
Tottenham H	YT	07.87				
Gillingham	Tr	02.89	88-90	74	13	5
Brentford	Tr	06.91	91-93	83	11	1
Cambridge U	Stevenage Borough	10.94	94	10	0	0
Peterborough U	Tr	02.95	94-95	27	0	2
Gillingham	Tr	01.96	95-96	9	12	0
Barnet	Tr	07.97	97-98	13	16	1
MAPES Charles (Charlie) Edward						
St Pancras, 4 July, 1982						(M)
Cardiff C	Tottenham H (YT)	09.00				
Wycombe W	Berkhamsted T	07.03	03	10	5	3
MAPSON John (Johnny)						
Birkenhead, 2 May, 1917 Died 1999 EWar-1						(G)
Reading	Swindon T (Am)	04.35	35	2	-	0
Sunderland	Tr	03.36	35-52	346	-	0
MARANGONI Claudio Oscar						
Rosario, Argentina, 17 November, 1954 Argentina int						(M)
Sunderland	San Lorenzo (Arg)	12.79	79-80	19	1	3
MARCELINO Elena						
Santander, Spain, 26 September, 1971 Spain 5						(CD)
Newcastle U	Real Mallorca (Sp)	07.99	99-00	15	2	0
MARCELLE Clinton (Clint) Sherwin						
Port of Spain, Trinidad, 9 November, 1968 Trinidad 9						(M)
Barnsley	Felgueiras (Por)	08.96	96-98	37	32	8
Scunthorpe U	L	10.99	99	8	2	0
Hull C	Goole AFC	09.00	00	16	7	2
Darlington	Tr	02.01	00-01	8	7	0
Grimsby T	Scarborough	08.04	04	0	3	0
[MARCELO] CIPRIANO DOS SANTOS Marcelo						
Niteroi, Brazil, 11 October, 1969						(F)
Sheffield U	Dep Alaves (Sp)	10.97	97-99	47	19	24
Birmingham C	Tr	10.99	99-01	47	30	24
Walsall	Tr	02.02	01	9	0	1
MARCH John Edmund						
Norwich, 12 May, 1940						(FB)
Norwich C	Jnrs	05.57				
Bradford PA	Tr	06.61	61-62	62	-	1
MARCH Stanley (Stan)						
Manchester, 26 December, 1938						(IF)
Port Vale	Altrincham	08.59	59	1	-	0
MARCH William (Billy)						
Chester-le-Street, 28 February, 1925 Died 1974						(FB)
Barnsley	Ferryhill Ath	11.47	51	2	-	0
Gateshead	Tr	07.52	52-56	134	-	0

MARCHANT Marwood Godfrey
Milford Haven, 18 June, 1922 Died 1972 (IF)

League Club	Source	Date Signed	Seasons Played	Apps	Subs	Gls
Cardiff C	Milford U	01.51	50	12	-	3
Torquay U	Tr	11.51	51-52	40	-	19

MARCHI Anthony (Tony) Vittorio
Edmonton, 21 January, 1933 ESch/EYth/EB (WH)

League Club	Source	Date Signed	Seasons Played	Apps	Subs	Gls
Tottenham H	Jnrs	06.50	49-56	131	-	2
Tottenham H	Torino (It)	07.59	59-64	101	-	5

MARCOLIN Dario
Brescia, Italy, 28 October, 1971 (M)

League Club	Source	Date Signed	Seasons Played	Apps	Subs	Gls
Blackburn Rov (L)	SS Lazio (It)	10.98	98	5	5	1

MARDEN Reuben (Ben) John
Fulham, 10 February, 1927 Died 2000 (W)

League Club	Source	Date Signed	Seasons Played	Apps	Subs	Gls
Arsenal	Chelmsford C	02.50	50-54	42	-	11
Watford	Tr	06.55	55-56	41	-	11

MARDENBOROUGH Stephen (Steve) Alexander
Selly Oak, 11 September, 1964 (W)

League Club	Source	Date Signed	Seasons Played	Apps	Subs	Gls
Coventry C	App	08.82				
Wolverhampton W	Tr	09.83	83	9	0	1
Cambridge U	L	02.84	83	6	0	0
Swansea C	Tr	07.84	84	32	4	7
Newport Co	Tr	07.85	85-86	50	14	11
Cardiff C	Tr	03.87	86-87	18	14	1
Hereford U	Tr	07.88	88	20	7	0
Darlington	Cheltenham T	07.90	90-92	79	27	18
Lincoln C	Tr	07.93	93	14	7	2
Scarborough	Tr	02.95	94	0	1	0
Colchester U	Stafford Rgrs	08.95	95	4	8	2
Swansea C	Tr	12.95	95	1	0	0

MARDON Paul Jonathan
Bristol, 14 September, 1969 WB-1/W-1 (CD)

League Club	Source	Date Signed	Seasons Played	Apps	Subs	Gls
Bristol C	YT	01.88	87-90	29	13	0
Doncaster Rov	L	09.90	90	3	0	0
Birmingham C	Tr	08.91	91-93	54	10	1
West Bromwich A	Tr	11.93	93-98	125	14	3
Oldham Ath	L	01.99	98	12	0	3
Plymouth Arg	L	09.00	00	3	0	1
Wrexham	L	10.00	00	6	1	0

MARESCA Enzo
Pontecagnano, Italy, 10 February, 1980 ItYth (M)

League Club	Source	Date Signed	Seasons Played	Apps	Subs	Gls
West Bromwich A	Cagliari (It)	08.98	98-99	28	19	5

MARGAS Javier
Santiago, Chile, 10 May, 1969 Chile 62 (CD)

League Club	Source	Date Signed	Seasons Played	Apps	Subs	Gls
West Ham U	Univ Catolica (Chile)	08.98	98-00	21	3	1

MARGERISON Lee
Bradford, 10 September, 1973 (M)

League Club	Source	Date Signed	Seasons Played	Apps	Subs	Gls
Bradford C	YT	07.92	92	1	2	0

MARGERRISON John William
Bushey, 20 October, 1955 (M)

League Club	Source	Date Signed	Seasons Played	Apps	Subs	Gls
Tottenham H	App	12.72				
Fulham	Tr	07.75	75-78	63	8	9
Orient	Tr	07.79	79-81	77	3	6

MARGETSON Martyn Walter
Neath, 8 September, 1971 WSch/WYth/Wu21-7/WB-1/W-1 (G)

League Club	Source	Date Signed	Seasons Played	Apps	Subs	Gls
Manchester C	YT	07.90	90-97	51	0	0
Bristol Rov	L	12.93	93	2	1	0
Southend U	Tr	08.98	98	32	0	0
Huddersfield T	Tr	08.99	00-01	47	1	0
Cardiff C	Tr	08.02	02-04	31	1	0

MARGINSON Karl Kevin
Manchester, 11 November, 1970 (W)

League Club	Source	Date Signed	Seasons Played	Apps	Subs	Gls
Rotherham U	Ashton U	03.93	92-94	11	4	1

MARIC Silvio
Zagreb, Croatia, 20 March, 1975 Croatia 16 (M)

League Club	Source	Date Signed	Seasons Played	Apps	Subs	Gls
Newcastle U	Croatia Zagreb (Cro)	02.99	98-99	12	11	0

MARINELLI Carlos Ariel
Buenos Aires, Argentina, 14 March, 1982 ArYth (M)

League Club	Source	Date Signed	Seasons Played	Apps	Subs	Gls
Middlesbrough	Boca Juniors (Arg)	10.99	99-03	18	25	3

MARINELLO Peter
Edinburgh, 20 February, 1950 Su23-2/SLge-1 (W)

League Club	Source	Date Signed	Seasons Played	Apps	Subs	Gls
Arsenal	Hibernian	01.70	69-72	32	6	3
Portsmouth	Tr	07.73	73-75	92	3	7
Fulham	Motherwell	12.78	78-79	25	2	1

MARINER Paul
Bolton, 22 May, 1953 E-35 (F)

League Club	Source	Date Signed	Seasons Played	Apps	Subs	Gls
Plymouth Arg	Chorley	07.73	73-76	134	1	56
Ipswich T	Tr	09.76	76-83	260	0	96
Arsenal	Tr	02.84	83-85	52	8	14
Portsmouth	Tr	07.86	86-87	49	7	9

MARINKOV Alexandre (Alex)
Grenoble, France, 2 December, 1967 (CD)

League Club	Source	Date Signed	Seasons Played	Apps	Subs	Gls
Scarborough	Raon L'Etape (Fr)	08.98	98	22	0	4

MARKER Nicholas (Nicky) Robert
Budleigh Salterton, 3 May, 1965 (CD)

League Club	Source	Date Signed	Seasons Played	Apps	Subs	Gls
Exeter C	App	05.83	81-87	196	6	3
Plymouth Arg	Tr	10.87	87-92	201	1	13
Blackburn Rov	Tr	09.92	92-96	41	13	1
Sheffield U	Tr	07.97	97-98	60	1	5
Plymouth Arg	L	02.99	98	4	0	0

MARKHAM Colin
Clowne, 2 March, 1916 Died 1967 (WH)

League Club	Source	Date Signed	Seasons Played	Apps	Subs	Gls
Torquay U		07.37	37-46	25	-	1

MARKHAM Leo Sargent
High Wycombe, 22 March, 1953 (CD)

League Club	Source	Date Signed	Seasons Played	Apps	Subs	Gls
Watford	Marlow	08.72	72-74	22	11	3

MARKHAM Peter
Scunthorpe, 18 March, 1954 (FB)

League Club	Source	Date Signed	Seasons Played	Apps	Subs	Gls
Scunthorpe U	App	03.72	71-76	121	1	1

MARKIE John
Bo'ness, 16 December, 1944 SSch (WH)

League Club	Source	Date Signed	Seasons Played	Apps	Subs	Gls
Newcastle U	App	04.62	63	2	-	0

MARKLEW Roger Kelsey
Sheffield, 30 January, 1940 (W)

League Club	Source	Date Signed	Seasons Played	Apps	Subs	Gls
Sheffield Wed	Sheffield U (Am)	05.58				
Accrington St	Tr	05.59				
Grimsby T	Tr	08.60	60	6	-	1

MARKMAN Damien Liam
Ascot, 7 January, 1978 (F)

League Club	Source	Date Signed	Seasons Played	Apps	Subs	Gls
Wycombe W	Slough T	11.95	95-96	0	4	0

MARKS Charles (Charlie) William Alfred
Eccles, Kent, 21 December, 1919 Died 2005 (FB)

League Club	Source	Date Signed	Seasons Played	Apps	Subs	Gls
Gillingham	Tooting & Mitcham	(N/L)	50-56	265	-	8

MARKS William **George**
Amesbury, 9 April, 1915 Died 1998 EWar-8 (G)

League Club	Source	Date Signed	Seasons Played	Apps	Subs	Gls
Arsenal	Salisbury Corinthians	03.36	38	2	-	0
Blackburn Rov	Tr	08.46	46-47	67	-	0
Bristol C	Tr	08.48	48	9	-	0
Reading	Tr	10.48	48-52	118	-	0

MARKS Jamie
Belfast, 18 March, 1977 NISch/NIYth (M)

League Club	Source	Date Signed	Seasons Played	Apps	Subs	Gls
Leeds U	YT	04.95				
Hull C	Tr	02.96	95-96	11	4	0

MARKS Michael (Mike) David
Lambeth, 23 March, 1968 (F)

League Club	Source	Date Signed	Seasons Played	Apps	Subs	Gls
Millwall	App	07.86	86	36	0	10
Mansfield T	L	01.88	87	0	1	0
Leyton Orient	Tr	02.88	87	3	0	0

MARKSTEDT Peter
Vasteras, Sweden, 11 January, 1972 (CD)

League Club	Source	Date Signed	Seasons Played	Apps	Subs	Gls
Barnsley	Vasteras SK (Swe)	11.97	97-98	8	1	0

MARLET Steve
Pithiviers, France, 10 January, 1974 FrB-1/Fr-23 (F)

League Club	Source	Date Signed	Seasons Played	Apps	Subs	Gls
Fulham	Lyon (Fr)	09.01	01-03	50	5	11

MARLEY Allan
Durham, 29 February, 1956 (FB)

League Club	Source	Date Signed	Seasons Played	Apps	Subs	Gls
Grimsby T	App	11.73	74-75	39	1	2

MARLEY George
Gateshead, 22 April, 1921 Died 1992 (IF)

League Club	Source	Date Signed	Seasons Played	Apps	Subs	Gls
Gateshead		09.47	47-49	22	-	2

MARLOW Frederick (Fred)
Sheffield, 9 November, 1928 (WH)

League Club	Source	Date Signed	Seasons Played	Apps	Subs	Gls
Arsenal	Hillsborough BC	09.47				
Sheffield Wed	Tr	09.50				
Grimsby T	Buxton	08.51	51	12	-	6
York C	Boston U	10.53	53-54	24	-	0

MARLOW Geoffrey (Geoff) Arthur
Worksop, 13 December, 1914 Died 1978 (W)

League Club	Source	Date Signed	Seasons Played	Apps	Subs	Gls
Lincoln C	Dinnington Ath	05.37	37-38	16	-	5
Lincoln C	Newark T	11.40	46-48	64	-	21

League Club	Source	Date Signed	Seasons Played	Career Record Apps	Subs	Gls
MARLOWE (MARKOWSKI) Richard (Ricky) Ronald						
Edinburgh, 10 August, 1950						(F)
Derby Co	Bonnyrigg Rose	06.69				
Shrewsbury T	Tr	12.73	73	31	0	4
Brighton & Hove A	Tr	07.74	74	24	1	5
Aldershot	L	01.76	75	2	0	0
MARMON Neale Gordon						
Bournemouth, 21 April, 1961						(CD)
Torquay U		03.80	79	4	0	0
Colchester U	Hanover 96 (Ger)	01.90	89	22	0	4
MARNEY Daniel (Danny) Gary						
Sidcup, 2 October, 1981						(F)
Brighton & Hove A	YT	08.01	02-03	6	9	0
Southend U	L	12.02	02	13	4	0
MARNEY Dean Edward						
Barking, 31 January, 1984 Eu21-1						(M)
Tottenham H	Sch	07.02	03-04	4	4	2
Swindon T	L	12.02	02	8	1	0
Queens Park Rgrs	L	01.04	03	1	1	0
Gillingham	L	11.04	04	3	0	0
MARPLES Christopher (Chris)						
Chesterfield, 3 August, 1964						(G)
Chesterfield	Goole T	03.84	84-86	84	0	0
Stockport Co	Tr	03.87	86-87	57	0	0
York C	Tr	07.88	88-92	138	0	0
Scunthorpe U	L	02.92	91	1	0	0
Chesterfield	Tr	12.92	92-94	57	0	0
MARPLES Simon James						
Sheffield, 30 July, 1975 ESemiPro-2						(FB)
Doncaster Rov	Stocksbridge Pk Steels	09.99	03-04	28	0	0
MARQUIS Paul Raymond						
Enfield, 29 August, 1972						(CD)
West Ham U	YT	07.91	93	0	1	0
Doncaster Rov	Tr	03.94	93-96	28	1	1
MARRIOTT Alan						
Bedford, 3 September, 1978						(G)
Tottenham H	YT	07.97				
Lincoln C	Tr	08.99	99-04	228	0	0
MARRIOTT Andrew (Andy)						
Sutton-in-Ashfield, 11 October, 1970 ESch/EYth/Eu21-1/W-5						(G)
Arsenal	YT	10.88				
Nottingham F	Tr	06.89	91-92	11	0	0
West Bromwich A	L	09.89	89	3	0	0
Blackburn Rov	L	12.89	89	2	0	0
Colchester U	L	03.90	89	10	0	0
Burnley	L	08.91	91	15	0	0
Wrexham	Tr	10.93	93-97	213	0	0
Sunderland	Tr	08.98	98-99	2	0	0
Barnsley	Tr	03.01	01-02	53	1	0
Birmingham C	Tr	03.03	02	1	0	0
Coventry C	Beira Mar (Por)	08.04				
Colchester U	Tr	10.04				
Bury	Tr	11.04	04	19	0	0
Torquay U	Tr	03.05	04	11	0	0
MARRIOTT Ernest (Ernie)						
Sutton-in-Ashfield, 25 January, 1913 Died 1989						(FB)
Brighton & Hove A	Sutton Junction	01.34	34-47	163	-	1
MARRIOTT Jack (Jackie)						
Hollins End, 16 July, 1915 Died 1989						(IF)
Doncaster Rov	Normanton Sports	02.45	46-47	6	-	0
Southport	Tr	12.47	47-48	23	-	5
MARRIOTT John (Jack) Leonard						
Scunthorpe, 1 April, 1928						(W)
Sheffield Wed	Scunthorpe & Lindsey U	02.47	46-54	153	-	19
Huddersfield T	Tr	07.55	55-56	38	-	4
Scunthorpe U	Tr	06.57	57-63	212	-	26
MARRIOTT Paul William						
Liverpool, 26 September, 1973						(F)
Cardiff C	YT	●	91	0	1	0
MARRIOTT Stanley (Stan)						
Rochdale, 21 July, 1929 Died 2002						(CF)
Rochdale (Am)	Rochdale YMCA	12.52	52	6	-	2
MARRON Christopher (Chris)						
Jarrow, 7 February, 1925 Died 1986						(CF)
Chesterfield	South Shields	10.47	47-51	108	-	44
Mansfield T	Tr	07.52	52-53	53	-	25
Bradford PA	Tr	07.54	54	2	-	1

League Club	Source	Date Signed	Seasons Played	Career Record Apps	Subs	Gls
MARSDEN Anthony (Tony) Joseph						
Bolton, 11 September, 1948						(F)
Blackpool	App	07.66	67-68	4	1	0
Doncaster Rov	Tr	07.69	69-70	14	3	2
Grimsby T	L	11.69	69	2	0	0
MARSDEN Christopher (Chris)						
Sheffield, 3 January, 1969						(M)
Sheffield U	App	01.87	87	13	3	1
Huddersfield T	Tr	07.88	88-93	113	8	9
Coventry C	L	11.93	93	5	2	0
Wolverhampton W	Tr	01.94	93	8	0	0
Notts Co	Tr	11.94	94-95	10	0	0
Stockport Co	Tr	01.96	95-97	63	2	3
Birmingham C	Tr	10.97	97-98	51	1	3
Southampton	Tr	02.99	98-03	118	11	6
Sheffield Wed	Busan Icons (SK)	06.04	04	15	0	0
MARSDEN Eric						
Bolsover, 3 January, 1930						(CF)
Crystal Palace	Winchester C	04.50	50-52	34	-	11
Southend U	Tr	10.52	52	14	-	6
Shrewsbury T	Tr	03.53	52-53	11	-	0
MARSDEN Frederick (Fred)						
Blackburn, 6 September, 1911 Died 1989						(FB)
Accrington St	Manchester Central	10.34	34	5	-	0
Wolverhampton W	Tr	01.35	35	1	-	0
Bournemouth	Tr	05.36	36-48	194	-	1
MARSDEN Jack						
Leeds, 17 December, 1931						(CD)
Leeds U	Osmondthorpe YMCA	08.50	52-58	71	-	0
Barrow	Tr	03.59	58-59	47	-	0
Carlisle U	Tr	09.60	60-63	89	-	0
Doncaster Rov	Tr	07.64	64	2	-	0
MARSDEN James Richard						
Rotherham, 10 April, 1928						(IF)
Rotherham U	Parkgate Welfare	08.52	52-54	11	-	2
MARSDEN Keith						
Darley Dale, 10 April, 1934 Died 1986						(CF)
Chesterfield	Youlgreave BC	06.52	53-54	22	-	15
Manchester C	Tr	07.55	55-57	14	-	1
MARSDEN Liddle						
Fatfield, 13 May, 1936						(WH)
Workington	South Shields	11.56	56	2	-	0
MARSH Adam						
Sheffield, 20 February, 1982						(F)
Darlington	Worksop T	11.00	00-01	2	6	0
MARSH Arthur						
Rowley Regis, 4 May, 1947						(CD)
Bolton W	App	05.65	66-70	71	2	0
Rochdale	Tr	12.71	71-73	89	1	0
Darlington	Tr	07.74	74	23	0	1
MARSH Christopher (Chris) Jonathan						
Sedgley, 14 January, 1970						(M)
Walsall	YT	07.88	87-00	355	37	23
Wycombe W	Tr	03.01	00-01	11	1	0
Northampton T	Tr	09.01	01-02	41	0	0
MARSH Clifford (Cliff)						
Atherton, 29 December, 1920 Died 1990						(IF)
Leeds U	Winsford U	09.48	48	4	-	1
Bournemouth	Tr	05.49	49-51	39	-	2
MARSH Wilson **Edmund (Eddie)**						
Dundee, 14 December, 1927						(G)
Charlton Ath	Erith & Belvedere	12.45	50-56	26	-	0
Luton T	Tr	06.57	57-58	2	-	0
Torquay U	Tr	07.59	59-61	61	-	0
MARSH Frank Kitchener						
Bolton, 7 June, 1916 Died 1978						(WH)
Bolton W		05.38	38	3	-	0
Chester	Tr	05.39	46-47	69	-	2
MARSH Ian James						
Swansea, 27 October, 1969						(FB)
Swansea C	YT	07.88	87	1	0	0
MARSH John (Jackie) Henry						
Stoke-on-Trent, 31 May, 1948						(FB)
Stoke C	App	06.65	67-78	346	9	2

MARSH John (Jack) Kirk
Mansfield, 8 October, 1922 Died 1997 (IF)

League Club	Source	Date Signed	Seasons Played	Apps	Subs	Gls
Notts Co	Mansfield BC	08.42	46-48	42	-	18
Coventry C	Tr	09.48	48-49	20	-	7
Leicester C	Tr	03.50	49-50	14	-	4
Chesterfield	Tr	09.50	50	26	-	4

MARSH John Stanley
Farnworth, 31 August, 1940 (IF)

League Club	Source	Date Signed	Seasons Played	Apps	Subs	Gls
Oldham Ath	Little Hulton	10.57	59	2	-	0

MARSH John (Jack) William
Leeds, 17 December, 1947 (G)

League Club	Source	Date Signed	Seasons Played	Apps	Subs	Gls
Bradford C	New Farnley Jnrs	05.66	66-67	12	0	0

MARSH Kevin William
Walton, 27 July, 1949 (F)

League Club	Source	Date Signed	Seasons Played	Apps	Subs	Gls
Liverpool	App	03.66				
Southport	Tr	05.70	70	35	2	8

MARSH Michael (Mike) Andrew
Liverpool, 21 July, 1969 (M)

League Club	Source	Date Signed	Seasons Played	Apps	Subs	Gls
Liverpool	Kirkby T	08.87	88-93	42	27	2
West Ham U	Tr	09.93	93-94	46	3	1
Coventry C	Tr	12.94	94	15	0	2
Southend U	Galatasaray (Tu)	09.95	95-97	84	0	11

MARSH Rodney William
Hatfield, 11 October, 1944 Eu23-2/E-9 (F)

League Club	Source	Date Signed	Seasons Played	Apps	Subs	Gls
Fulham	App	10.62	62-65	63	0	22
Queens Park Rgrs	Tr	03.66	65-71	211	0	106
Manchester C	Tr	03.72	71-75	116	2	36
Fulham	Tampa Bay (USA)	08.76	76	16	0	5

MARSH Simon Thomas Peter
Ealing, 29 January, 1977 Eu21-1 (FB)

League Club	Source	Date Signed	Seasons Played	Apps	Subs	Gls
Oxford U	YT	11.94	94-98	49	7	3
Birmingham C	Tr	12.98	98	6	1	0
Brentford	L	09.00	00	3	1	0

MARSHALL Alexander (Alex) Stewart
Alloa, 27 November, 1935 (IF)

League Club	Source	Date Signed	Seasons Played	Apps	Subs	Gls
Accrington St	Stirling A	10.60	60	8	-	2

MARSHALL Alfred (Alf) George
Dagenham, 21 May, 1933 (FB)

League Club	Source	Date Signed	Seasons Played	Apps	Subs	Gls
Colchester U	Dagenham	10.57	58-60	30	-	0

MARSHALL Andrew (Andy) John
Bury St Edmunds, 14 April, 1975 EYth/Eu21-4 (G)

League Club	Source	Date Signed	Seasons Played	Apps	Subs	Gls
Norwich C	YT	07.93	94-00	194	1	0
Bournemouth	L	09.96	96	11	0	0
Gillingham	L	11.96	96	5	0	0
Ipswich T	Tr	07.01	01-02	53	0	0
Millwall	Tr	01.04	03-04	37	1	0

MARSHALL Brian
Bolton-on-Dearne, 20 September, 1954 (CD)

League Club	Source	Date Signed	Seasons Played	Apps	Subs	Gls
Huddersfield T	App	12.71	72-74	30	2	0
Scunthorpe U	L	10.74	74	3	0	0

MARSHALL Clifford (Cliff)
Liverpool, 4 November, 1955 ESch (W)

League Club	Source	Date Signed	Seasons Played	Apps	Subs	Gls
Everton	App	11.73	74-75	6	1	0
Southport	Miami (USA)	09.76	76	11	2	0

MARSHALL Colin
Glasgow, 1 November, 1969 (F)

League Club	Source	Date Signed	Seasons Played	Apps	Subs	Gls
Barnsley	YT	04.88	88-90	0	4	0
Wrexham	L	09.91	91	3	0	0
Scarborough	L	03.92	91	4	0	1

MARSHALL Daniel (Danny) John
Newark, 18 December, 1975 (M)

League Club	Source	Date Signed	Seasons Played	Apps	Subs	Gls
Chesterfield	Notts Co (YT)	08.94	94	0	1	0

MARSHALL David Howard
Manchester, 12 November, 1955 (M)

League Club	Source	Date Signed	Seasons Played	Apps	Subs	Gls
Workington	Headley Colliery	11.76	76	2	0	0

MARSHALL Dwight Wayne
St Lucia, 3 October, 1965 (F)

League Club	Source	Date Signed	Seasons Played	Apps	Subs	Gls
Plymouth Arg	Grays Ath	08.91	91-93	93	6	27
Middlesbrough	L	03.93	92	0	3	0
Luton T	Tr	07.94	94-98	90	38	28
Plymouth Arg	Tr	10.98	98	25	3	12

MARSHALL Ernest (Ernie)
Dinnington, 23 May, 1918 Died 1983 (WH)

League Club	Source	Date Signed	Seasons Played	Apps	Subs	Gls
Sheffield U	Dinnington Ath	05.35	36-37	13	-	0
Cardiff C	Tr	05.39	46	1	-	0

MARSHALL Frank
Sheffield, 26 January, 1929 (WH)

League Club	Source	Date Signed	Seasons Played	Apps	Subs	Gls
Rotherham U	Scarborough	05.51	51-56	117	-	5
Scunthorpe U	Tr	07.57	57-58	80	-	0
Doncaster Rov	Tr	10.59	59-61	35	-	0

MARSHALL Gary
Bristol, 20 April, 1964 (W)

League Club	Source	Date Signed	Seasons Played	Apps	Subs	Gls
Bristol C	Shepton Mallet	07.83	83-87	48	20	7
Torquay U	L	12.84	84	7	0	1
Carlisle U	Tr	07.88	88	18	3	2
Scunthorpe U	Tr	07.89	89-90	38	3	3
Exeter C	Tr	10.90	90-91	48	12	6

MARSHALL Gordon
Farnham, 2 July, 1939 Eu23-1 (G)

League Club	Source	Date Signed	Seasons Played	Apps	Subs	Gls
Newcastle U	Heart of Midlothian	06.63	63-67	177	0	0
Nottingham F	Tr	10.68	68	7	0	0

MARSHALL Gordon George Banks
Edinburgh, 19 April, 1964 S-1 (G)

League Club	Source	Date Signed	Seasons Played	Apps	Subs	Gls
Stoke C (L)	Glasgow Celtic	12.93	93	10	0	0

MARSHALL Ian Paul
Liverpool, 20 March, 1966 (CD)

League Club	Source	Date Signed	Seasons Played	Apps	Subs	Gls
Everton	App	03.84	85-87	9	6	1
Oldham Ath	Tr	03.88	87-92	165	5	36
Ipswich T	Tr	08.93	93-96	79	5	32
Leicester C	Tr	08.96	96-99	49	34	18
Bolton W	Tr	08.00	00-01	13	25	6
Blackpool	Tr	11.01	01	21	0	1

MARSHALL John
Rawtenstall, 1 November, 1938 (G)

League Club	Source	Date Signed	Seasons Played	Apps	Subs	Gls
Accrington St		05.57	57-58	7	-	0

MARSHALL John (Jack) Gilmore
Turton, 29 May, 1917 Died 1998 (FB)

League Club	Source	Date Signed	Seasons Played	Apps	Subs	Gls
Burnley	Jnrs	11.36	38-46	26	-	0

MARSHALL John James
Glasgow, 12 February, 1949 (W)

League Club	Source	Date Signed	Seasons Played	Apps	Subs	Gls
Preston NE		02.67				
Rotherham U	Ross Co	09.68	68	4	0	0

MARSHALL John Philip
Balham, 18 August, 1964 (M)

League Club	Source	Date Signed	Seasons Played	Apps	Subs	Gls
Fulham	App	08.82	83-95	393	18	28

MARSHALL Julian Paul
Swansea, 6 July, 1957 (CD)

League Club	Source	Date Signed	Seasons Played	Apps	Subs	Gls
Hereford U	Merthyr Tydfil	08.75	76-79	91	1	4
Bristol C	Tr	08.80	80-81	29	0	0
Walsall	Tr	08.82	82	10	0	0

MARSHALL Lee Alan
Nottingham, 1 August, 1975 (M)

League Club	Source	Date Signed	Seasons Played	Apps	Subs	Gls
Nottingham F	YT	08.92				
Stockport Co	Tr	03.95	94	1	0	0
Scunthorpe U	Eastwood T	06.97	97-99	18	27	2

MARSHALL Lee Keith
Islington, 21 January, 1979 Eu21-1 (M)

League Club	Source	Date Signed	Seasons Played	Apps	Subs	Gls
Norwich C	Enfield	03.97	97-00	95	22	11
Leicester C	Tr	03.01	00-02	37	8	0
West Bromwich A	Tr	08.02	02	4	5	1
Hull C	L	01.04	03	10	1	0

MARSHALL Peter
Barrow, 2 October, 1947 Died 1996 (W)

League Club	Source	Date Signed	Seasons Played	Apps	Subs	Gls
Barrow	Holker COB	01.66	65-66	4	0	1

MARSHALL Peter William
Worksop, 5 December, 1934 (G)

League Club	Source	Date Signed	Seasons Played	Apps	Subs	Gls
Scunthorpe U	Worksop T	09.54	54-56	64	-	0

MARSHALL Ralph
Baillieston, 30 January, 1944 Died 2003 (FB)

League Club	Source	Date Signed	Seasons Played	Apps	Subs	Gls
Crewe Alex	Glasgow Rgrs	09.64	64-66	72	1	0

MARSHALL Richard (Dickie)
Burbage, 23 November, 1945 Died 1992 (W)

League Club	Source	Date Signed	Seasons Played	Apps	Subs	Gls
Leicester C	App	08.63				
Southport	Tr	07.65	65-66	29	2	7

MARSHALL Roy Cyril
Fulham, 22 May, 1932 Died 2002 (G)

League Club	Source	Date Signed	Seasons Played	Apps	Subs	Gls
Brighton & Hove A	Jnrs	06.50				
Aldershot	Tr	08.57	57-60	34	-	0

League Club	Source	Date Signed	Seasons Played	Career Record Apps	Subs	Gls
MARSHALL Scott Roderick						
Edinburgh, 1 May, 1973 SYth/Su21-5 (CD)						
Arsenal	YT	03.91	92-97	19	5	1
Rotherham U	L	12.93	93	10	0	1
Sheffield U	L	08.94	94	17	0	0
Southampton	Tr	08.98	98	2	0	0
Brentford	Tr	10.99	99-02	73	2	3
Wycombe W	Tr	11.03	03	8	0	0
MARSHALL Shaun Andrew						
Fakenham, 3 October, 1978 (G)						
Cambridge U	YT	02.97	96-04	150	5	0
MARSHALL Stanley (Stan) Kenneth						
Goole, 20 April, 1946 (F)						
Middlesbrough	Goole T	08.63	65	2	0	0
Notts Co	Tr	06.66	66-67	43	6	17
MARSHALL Terence (Terry) William James						
Whitechapel, 26 December, 1935 (W)						
Newcastle U	Wisbech T	12.58	58-60	5	-	1
MARSHALL William (Billy)						
Belfast, 11 July, 1936 NIB (FB)						
Burnley	Distillery	10.53	59-60	6	-	0
Oldham Ath	Tr	08.62	62-63	57	-	0
Hartlepools U	Tr	08.64	64-65	57	0	0
MARSHALL William (Willie) Forsyth						
Rutherglen, 9 May, 1933 (CF)						
Bradford C	Rutherglen Glencairn	01.57	56-58	33	-	16
Swindon T	Tr	02.59	58-59	30	-	12
MARSLAND Gordon						
Blackpool, 20 March, 1945 (CD)						
Blackpool	App	05.62				
Carlisle U	Tr	06.65	65-68	63	2	4
Bristol Rov	Tr	06.69	69	16	0	1
Crewe Alex	L	09.70	70	5	0	0
Oldham Ath	L	03.71	70	1	3	0
MARSTON James (Joe) Edward						
Sydney, Australia, 7 January, 1926 FLge-1 (CD)						
Preston NE	Leichhardt (Aus)	02.50	50-54	185	-	0
MARSTON Maurice						
Trimdon, 24 March, 1929 Died 2002 (FB)						
Sunderland	Silksworth Jnrs	06.49	51-52	9	-	0
Northampton T	Tr	07.53	53-56	149	-	2
MARTEINSSON Petur						
Reykjavik, Iceland, 14 July, 1973 IcYth/Icu21-19/Ic-27 (M)						
Stoke C	Stabaek IF (Nor)	01.02	01-03	12	6	2
MARTIN John **Alan**						
Smallthorne, 23 November, 1923 Died 2004 (IF)						
Port Vale	Nettlebank Villa	12.42	46-51	169	-	28
Stoke C	Tr	09.51	51-54	104	-	6
Port Vale	Bangor C	07.57	57-58	19	-	0
MARTIN Alvin Edward						
Bootle, 29 July, 1958 EYth/EB/E-17 (CD)						
West Ham U	App	07.76	77-95	462	7	27
Leyton Orient	Tr	06.96	96	16	1	0
MARTIN Andrew (Andy) Peter						
Cardiff, 28 February, 1980 WYth/Wu21-1 (F)						
Crystal Palace	YT	02.97	98-99	12	10	2
Torquay U	Tr	03.02	01	5	0	0
MARTIN Barrie						
Birmingham, 29 September, 1935 (FB)						
Blackpool	Highfield YC	12.53	57-63	189	-	1
Oldham Ath	Tr	08.64	64	42	-	4
Tranmere Rov	Tr	06.65	65-67	99	4	0
MARTIN Cornelius (Con) Joseph						
Dublin, 20 March, 1923 IR-30/I-6 (CD/G)						
Leeds U	Glentoran	01.47	46-48	47	-	1
Aston Villa	Tr	10.48	48-55	194	-	1
MARTIN David (Dave)						
East Ham, 25 April, 1963 EYth (M)						
Millwall	App	05.80	79-84	131	9	6
Wimbledon	Tr	09.84	84-85	30	6	3
Southend U	Tr	08.86	86-92	212	9	20
Bristol C	Tr	07.93	93-94	36	2	1
Northampton T	L	02.95	94	7	0	1
Gillingham	Tr	08.95	95	27	4	1
Leyton Orient	Tr	07.96	96	8	0	0
Northampton T	Tr	11.96	96	10	2	0
Brighton & Hove A	L	03.97	96	1	0	0

League Club	Source	Date Signed	Seasons Played	Career Record Apps	Subs	Gls
MARTIN David Edward						
Romford, 22 January, 1986 EYth (G)						
Wimbledon/MK Dons	Sch	01.04	03-04	17	0	0
MARTIN Dean Edward						
Islington, 31 August, 1972 (W)						
West Ham U	Fisher Ath	06.91	91	1	1	0
Colchester U	L	12.92	92	8	0	2
Brentford	(Iceland)	10.95	95	14	5	1
MARTIN Dean Stacey						
Halifax, 9 September, 1967 (M)						
Halifax T	App	09.85	86-90	149	4	7
Scunthorpe U	Tr	07.91	91-94	100	6	7
Rochdale	Tr	01.95	94-96	45	8	0
MARTIN Dennis Victor						
Eastleigh, 8 November, 1928 (WH)						
Bournemouth	Jnrs	08.47	48-53	23	-	0
MARTIN Dennis William						
Edinburgh, 27 October, 1947 (W)						
West Bromwich A	Kettering T	07.67	67-69	14	2	1
Carlisle U	Tr	07.70	70-77	271	4	48
Newcastle U	Tr	10.77	77	9	2	2
Mansfield T	Tr	03.78	77-78	46	0	3
MARTIN Donald (Don)						
Corby, 15 February, 1944 EYth (F)						
Northampton T	Jnrs	07.62	62-67	136	0	52
Blackburn Rov	Tr	02.68	67-75	218	6	57
Northampton T	Tr	11.75	75-77	77	15	17
MARTIN Edward (Eddie)						
Baillieston, 31 March, 1921 (IF)						
Accrington St	Alloa Ath	08.50	50	2	-	0
MARTIN Eliot James						
Plumstead, 27 September, 1972 (FB)						
Gillingham	YT	05.91	91-93	52	1	1
Gillingham	Chelmsford C	03.95	94	7	0	0
MARTIN Eric						
Perth, 31 March, 1946 (G)						
Southampton	Dunfermline Ath	03.67	66-74	248	0	0
MARTIN Frederick (Fred)						
Nottingham, 13 December, 1925 (CF)						
Nottingham F		10.44	47-48	5	-	0
MARTIN Frederick (Fred) John						
Nottingham, 14 April, 1925 (WH)						
Blackburn Rov	Sutton T	12.49				
Accrington St	Tr	07.50	50-51	64	-	0
MARTIN Geoffrey (Geoff)						
New Tupton, 9 March, 1940 (W)						
Chesterfield	Parkhouse Colliery	10.58	58	2	-	0
Leeds U	Tr	05.60				
Darlington	Tr	07.61	61	20	-	6
Carlisle U	Tr	05.62	61-62	15	-	2
Workington	Tr	12.62	62-66	144	0	24
Grimsby T	Tr	11.66	66-67	71	0	5
Chesterfield	Tr	07.68	68-69	43	0	2
MARTIN Harold John						
Blackburn, 15 March, 1955 (CD)						
Bolton W		11.73				
Rochdale	Tr	07.74	74	11	2	0
MARTIN Jae Andrew						
Hampstead, 5 February, 1976 (W)						
Southend U	YT	05.93	93-94	1	7	0
Leyton Orient	L	09.94	94	1	3	0
Birmingham C	Tr	07.95	95	1	6	0
Lincoln C	Tr	08.96	96-97	29	12	5
Peterborough U	Tr	07.98	98-99	7	12	1
MARTIN James						
Glasgow, 3 March, 1937 (W)						
Nottingham F	Baillieston Jnrs	06.58	58	1	-	0
MARTIN James (Jimmy) Caird						
Dundee, 27 May, 1938 (CF)						
Blackpool	Evenwood T	12.61				
Reading	Tr	06.62	62-63	22	-	6
MARTIN John (Johnny)						
Ashington, 4 December, 1946 (W)						
Aston Villa	App	07.64	64	1	-	0
Colchester U	Tr	05.66	66-68	77	1	11
Workington	Chelmsford C	07.69	69-73	206	2	32
Southport	Tr	08.74	74-75	54	9	7

League Club	Source	Date Signed	Seasons Played	Career Record Apps	Subs	Gls
MARTIN John (Johnny)						
Bethnal Green, 15 July, 1981						(M)
Leyton Orient	YT	08.98	97-02	74	18	5
MARTIN John Grieve						
Dundee, 20 August, 1935						(FB)
Sheffield Wed	Dundee North End	02.54	54-60	63	-	0
Rochdale	Tr	06.62	62-63	24	-	1
MARTIN John (Jackie) Rowland						
Hamstead, 5 August, 1914 Died 1996 EWar-2						(IF)
Aston Villa	Hednesford T	01.36	36-48	81	-	22
MARTIN Kevin						
Bromsgrove, 22 June, 1976						(G)
Scarborough	YT	07.95	94-97	23	0	0
MARTIN Lee Andrew						
Hyde, 5 February, 1968 Eu21-2						(FB)
Manchester U	App	05.86	87-93	56	17	1
Bristol Rov	Glasgow Celtic	08.96	96	25	0	0
Huddersfield T	L	09.97	97	2	1	0
MARTIN Lee Brendan						
Huddersfield, 9 September, 1968 ESch						(G)
Huddersfield T	YT	07.87	87-91	54	0	0
Blackpool	Tr	07.92	92-94	98	0	0
Halifax T	Rochdale (N/C)	08.97	98	37	0	0
Macclesfield T	Tr	07.99	99-02	52	1	0
MARTIN Lilian						
Valreas, France, 28 May, 1971						(FB)
Derby Co	Marseille (Fr)	11.00	00	7	2	0
MARTIN Lionel John						
Ludlow, 15 May, 1947						(M)
Aston Villa	App	07.64	66-71	36	11	4
Doncaster Rov	L	03.71	70	2	0	0
MARTIN Michael (Mick) Paul						
Dublin, 9 July, 1951 IRAmat/IRu23-1/LoI-1/IR-51						(M)
Manchester U	Bohemians	01.73	72-74	33	7	2
West Bromwich A	Tr	10.75	75-78	85	4	11
Newcastle U	Tr	12.78	78-82	139	8	5
Cardiff C	Willington Ath	11.84	84	7	0	0
Peterborough U	Tr	01.85	84	13	0	0
Rotherham U	Tr	08.85	85	5	0	0
Preston NE	Tr	09.85	85	35	0	0
MARTIN Neil						
Tranent, 20 October, 1940 Su23-1/SLge-2/S-3						(F)
Sunderland	Hibernian	10.65	65-67	86	0	38
Coventry C	Tr	02.68	67-70	106	0	40
Nottingham F	Tr	02.71	70-74	116	3	28
Brighton & Hove A	Tr	07.75	75	13	4	8
Crystal Palace	Tr	03.76	75	8	1	1
MARTIN Peter						
South Shields, 29 December, 1950						(W)
Middlesbrough	Chilton BC	06.69				
Darlington	Tr	07.71	71	3	0	0
Barnsley	Tr	10.71	71-72	18	8	6
MARTIN Raymond (Ray) Barry						
Coseley, 23 January, 1945						(FB)
Birmingham C	Aston Villa (Am)	05.62	63-75	325	8	1
MARTIN Roy						
Kilbirnie, 16 May, 1929						(FB)
Birmingham C	Kilwinning Rgrs	03.50	50-55	69	-	0
Derby Co	Tr	03.56	55-59	81	-	0
MARTIN Russell Kenneth Alexander						
Brighton, 4 January, 1986						(M)
Wycombe W	Lewes	08.04	04	1	6	0
MARTIN Thomas (Tommy)						
Glasgow, 21 December, 1924						(IF)
Doncaster Rov	Stirling A	07.50	50-52	71	-	9
Nottingham F	Tr	11.52	52-54	48	-	4
Hull C	Tr	06.55	55-56	32	-	2
MARTIN Wayne Lawrence						
Basildon, 16 December, 1965						(FB)
Crystal Palace	App	07.82	83	1	0	0
MARTINDALE David (Dave)						
Liverpool, 9 April, 1964						(M)
Tranmere Rov	Caernarfon T	07.87	87-93	128	38	9
MARTINDALE Gary						
Liverpool, 24 June, 1971						(F)
Bolton W	Burscough	03.94				
Peterborough U	Tr	07.95	95	26	5	15
Notts Co	Tr	03.96	95-97	34	32	13
Mansfield T	L	02.97	96	5	0	2
Rotherham U	Tr	03.98	97-99	17	10	6
MARTINDALE Leonard (Len)						
Bolton, 30 June, 1920 Died 1971						(WH)
Burnley	Jnrs	07.37	37-50	69	-	2
Accrington St	Tr	12.51	51	16	-	0
MARTINEZ Eugene						
Chelmsford, 6 July, 1957						(W)
Bradford C	Harrogate RI	07.77	77-79	38	14	5
Rochdale	Tr	07.80	80-82	110	6	16
Newport Co	Tr	08.83	83	18	2	1
Northampton T	L	02.84	83	12	0	2
MARTINEZ Jairo Manfredo						
Yoro, Honduras, 14 May, 1978 Honduras int						(F)
Coventry C	CD Montagua (Hon)	10.00	01	5	6	3
MARTINEZ Roberto						
Balaguer Lerida, Spain, 13 July, 1973						(M)
Wigan Ath	Vipla Balaguer (Sp)	07.95	95-00	148	39	17
Walsall	Motherwell	08.02	02	1	5	0
Swansea C	Tr	01.03	02-04	77	6	2
MARTYN Antony **Nigel**						
Bethel, Cornwall, 11 August, 1966 Eu21-11/EB-6/E-23						(G)
Bristol Rov	St Blazey	08.87	87-89	101	0	0
Crystal Palace	Tr	11.89	89-95	272	0	0
Leeds U	Tr	07.96	96-01	207	0	0
Everton	Tr	09.03	03-04	65	1	0
MARUSTIK Christopher (Chris)						
Swansea, 10 August, 1961 WSch/Wu21-7/W-6						(M)
Swansea C	App	08.78	78-85	143	9	11
Cardiff C	Tr	10.85	85-86	43	5	1
MARVIN Walter						
Derby, 6 July, 1920 Died 1997						(CF)
Accrington St	Newport Co (Am)	12.46	46-47	9	-	3
MARWOOD Brian						
Seaham, 5 February, 1960 E-1						(W)
Hull C	App	02.78	79-83	154	4	51
Sheffield Wed	Tr	08.84	84-87	125	3	27
Arsenal	Tr	03.88	87-89	52	0	16
Sheffield U	Tr	09.90	90-91	14	8	3
Middlesbrough	L	10.91	91	3	0	0
Swindon T	N/C	03.93	92	6	5	1
Barnet	Tr	08.93	93	18	5	0
MASEFIELD Keith Leonard						
Birmingham, 26 February, 1957						(FB)
Aston Villa	App	10.74	74-76	1	3	0
MASEFIELD Paul Darren						
Lichfield, 21 October, 1970						(FB)
Birmingham C	YT	07.89				
Exeter C	Cheltenham T	02.92	91	1	0	0
Stockport Co	Bromsgrove Rov	08.92	92	7	0	0
Doncaster Rov	Tr	02.93	92	8	1	0
Preston NE	Tr	08.93	93	6	0	0
MASIELLO Luciano						
Italy, 2 January, 1951						(W)
Charlton Ath	App	01.69	69-70	6	0	0
MASINGA Philomen (Phil) Raul						
Johannesburg, South Africa, 28 June, 1969 S Africa int						(F)
Leeds U	Mamelodi Sund's (SA)	08.94	94-95	20	11	5
MASKELL Craig Dell						
Aldershot, 10 April, 1968						(F)
Southampton	App	04.86	85-86	2	4	1
Huddersfield T	Tr	05.88	88-89	86	1	43
Reading	Tr	08.90	90-91	60	12	26
Swindon T	Tr	07.92	92-93	40	7	22
Southampton	Tr	02.94	93-95	8	9	1
Bristol C	L	12.95	95	5	0	1
Brighton & Hove A	Tr	03.96	95-97	68	1	20
Leyton Orient	Happy Valley (HK)	03.98	97-98	15	8	2
MASKELL Dennis						
Mountain Ash, 16 April, 1931						(W)
Watford		09.51	51	5	-	0

League Club	Source	Date Signed	Seasons Played	Career Record Apps	Subs	Gls
MASKELL Michael (Mike) Richard						
Eynsham, 25 January, 1952						(FB)
Chelsea	App	02.69				
Brentford	Tr	07.70	70	1	0	0
MASKERY Christopher (Chris) Paul						
Stoke-on-Trent, 25 September, 1964						(M)
Stoke C	App	09.82	82-86	82	10	3
MASON Andrew (Andy)						
Stretford, 26 October, 1966						(M)
Crewe Alex	YT	08.84	84	1	1	0
MASON Andrew (Andy) John						
Bolton, 22 November, 1974						(F)
Bolton W	YT	05.93				
Hull C	Tr	06.95	95-96	14	12	3
Chesterfield	Tr	03.97	96	1	1	0
Macclesfield T	Tr	08.97	97	7	5	0
MASON Christopher (Chris) Joseph						
Newton Aycliffe, 26 June, 1986						(FB)
Darlington	Sch	●	03	0	1	0
MASON Clifford (Cliff) Ernest						
York, 27 November, 1929						(FB)
Sunderland		01.50				
Darlington	Tr	07.52	52-54	107	-	0
Sheffield U	Tr	08.55	55-61	97	-	2
Leeds U	Tr	03.62	61-62	31	-	0
Scunthorpe U	Tr	02.64	63	12	-	1
Chesterfield	Tr	07.64	64	5	-	0
MASON Gary Ronald						
Edinburgh, 15 October, 1979 SSch/Su21-1						(M)
Manchester C	YT	10.96	98	18	1	0
Hartlepool U	L	11.99	99	5	1	0
MASON George William						
Birmingham, 5 September, 1913 Died 1993 ESch/EWar-2						(CD)
Coventry C	Redhill Amats	11.31	31-51	330	-	6
MASON James (Jimmy)						
Glasgow, 17 April, 1933						(W)
Accrington St	Dundee	06.55	55-56	14	-	1
Chester	Tr	06.57	57-58	64	-	7
MASON John Francis						
Birmingham, 23 January, 1943 EAmat						(F)
Peterborough U	Alvechurch	05.66	66-67	37	0	18
MASON Keith Michael						
Leicester, 19 July, 1958						(G)
Huddersfield T	Leicester C (N/C)	07.82	82-85	30	0	0
MASON Maurice						
Sedgefield, 25 June, 1927						(WH)
Huddersfield T		01.48				
Darlington	Blackhall CW	07.52	52	3	-	0
MASON Michael (Mike) Barry						
Bloxwich, 20 October, 1944						(IF)
Walsall	App	09.62	63	4	-	0
MASON Paul David						
Liverpool, 3 September, 1963						(M)
Ipswich T	Aberdeen	06.93	93-97	103	10	25
MASON Richard (Dick) James						
Arley, 2 April, 1918 Died 1992						(FB)
Coventry C	Nuneaton Borough	05.46	46-53	253	-	2
MASON Robert (Bobby) Henry						
Tipton, 22 March, 1936						(IF)
Wolverhampton W	Jnrs	05.53	55-61	143	-	44
Leyton Orient	Chelmsford C	03.63	62-63	23	-	0
MASON Stuart James						
Whitchurch, 2 June, 1948 EYth						(FB)
Wrexham	Jnrs	07.66	65-66	28	0	0
Liverpool	Tr	10.66				
Doncaster Rov	L	11.67	67	1	0	0
Wrexham	Tr	06.68	68-72	144	13	3
Chester	Tr	06.73	73-77	132	5	7
Rochdale	L	12.76	76	2	0	0
Crewe Alex	L	10.77	77	4	0	1
MASON Thomas (Tommy) Herbert Andrew						
Buxton, 20 February, 1953						(M)
Derby Co	App	07.72				
Brighton & Hove A	Tr	09.74	74	23	2	2

League Club	Source	Date Signed	Seasons Played	Career Record Apps	Subs	Gls
MASON Thomas (Tom) Joseph Robert						
Fulham, 19 June, 1960						(FB)
Fulham	App	01.78	77-79	6	0	0
MASON Thomas (Tom) William						
Hartlepool, 21 April, 1925						(WH)
Hartlepools U	Railway Ath	05.46	46	5	-	0
MASSART David (Dave) Louis						
Birmingham, 2 November, 1919						(CF)
Birmingham C	Bells Ath	02.39	46	3	-	0
Walsall	Tr	06.47	47	27	-	23
Bury	Tr	03.48	47-50	85	-	44
Chesterfield	Tr	02.51	50	11	-	5
MASSEY Andrew (Andy) Thomas						
New Cross, 20 October, 1961 IRYth						(M)
Millwall	Jnrs	03.79	80-83	73	15	8
Port Vale	L	03.84	83	4	0	1
Aldershot	Tr	05.84	84-85	65	6	3
MASSEY Bernard Kendrick Woolley						
Ripley, 5 November, 1920						(IF)
Halifax T	Peterborough U	09.38	38-50	82	-	7
MASSEY Eric						
Derby, 11 September, 1923						(FB)
Bury	Spartan Ath	09.46	46-56	201	-	6
MASSEY Kevin James						
Gainsborough, 30 November, 1965						(M)
Cambridge U	App	12.83	83-85	9	7	1
MASSEY Richard						
Selsdon, 11 October, 1968						(CD)
Exeter C	App	07.86	85-87	22	6	1
MASSEY Robert (Bob) William						
Marylebone, 6 April, 1940						(FB)
Bournemouth	Jnrs	05.58	59-60	5	-	0
MASSEY Roy						
Mexborough, 10 September, 1943 EYth						(F)
Rotherham U		07.64	64-66	15	1	6
Orient	Tr	09.67	67-68	58	5	13
Colchester U	Tr	07.69	69-70	30	4	11
MASSEY Stephen (Steve)						
Denton, 28 March, 1958						(F)
Stockport Co	App	07.75	74-77	87	14	20
Bournemouth	Tr	07.78	78-80	85	12	19
Peterborough U	Tr	08.81	81	13	5	3
Northampton T	Tr	02.82	81-82	60	0	26
Hull C	Tr	07.83	83-84	34	8	9
Cambridge U	Tr	08.85	85	28	3	11
Wrexham	Tr	07.86	86-87	38	5	10
MASSEY Stuart Anthony						
Crawley, 17 November, 1964						(M)
Crystal Palace	Sutton U	07.92	92-93	1	1	0
Oxford U	Tr	07.94	94-97	82	21	8
MASSIE Leslie (Les)						
Aberdeen, 20 July, 1935						(F)
Huddersfield T	Banks o' Dee	08.53	56-66	334	1	100
Darlington	Tr	10.66	66	20	0	2
Halifax T	Tr	06.67	67-68	89	0	40
Bradford PA	Tr	08.69	69	14	0	2
Workington	Tr	12.69	69-70	62	0	15
MASSIMO Franco						
Horsham, 23 September, 1968						(F)
Brighton & Hove A	App	09.86	85	0	1	0
MASSON Donald (Don) Sanderson						
Banchory, 26 August, 1946 S-17						(M)
Middlesbrough	Jnrs	09.63	64-67	50	3	6
Notts Co	Tr	09.68	68-74	273	0	81
Queens Park Rgrs	Tr	12.74	74-77	116	0	18
Derby Co	Tr	10.77	77	23	0	1
Notts Co	Tr	08.78	78-81	129	0	11
MASTERS Graham						
Bristol, 13 August, 1931						(W)
Bristol C	Jnrs	08.48	51	9	-	1
MASTERS Neil Bradley						
Lisburn, 25 May, 1972 NIYth						(FB)
Bournemouth	YT	08.90	92-93	37	1	2
Wolverhampton W	Tr	12.93	93-95	10	2	0
Gillingham	Tr	04.97	97	11	0	0

MATERAZZI Marco
Perugia, Italy, 19 August, 1973 Italy int (CD)

League Club	Source	Date Signed	Seasons Played	Apps	Subs	Gls
Everton	Perugia (It)	07.98	98	26	1	1

MATEU Jose-Luis
Castellon, Spain, 15 January, 1966 (F)

League Club	Source	Date Signed	Seasons Played	Apps	Subs	Gls
Torquay U	Castellon (Sp)	10.95	95	5	5	1

MATHER Harold (Harry)
Bolton, 24 January, 1921 Died 1999 (FB)

League Club	Source	Date Signed	Seasons Played	Apps	Subs	Gls
Burnley	Jnrs	05.38	46-54	301	-	0

MATHER Shaun
Hereford, 9 September, 1965 (M)

League Club	Source	Date Signed	Seasons Played	Apps	Subs	Gls
Newport Co	Presteigne	08.83	83	0	1	0

MATHIAS Raymond (Ray)
Liverpool, 13 December, 1946 (FB)

League Club	Source	Date Signed	Seasons Played	Apps	Subs	Gls
Tranmere Rov	App	12.64	67-84	557	10	6

MATHIE Alexander (Alex)
Bathgate, 20 December, 1968 SYth (F)

League Club	Source	Date Signed	Seasons Played	Apps	Subs	Gls
Port Vale (L)	Morton	03.93	92	0	3	0
Newcastle U	Morton	07.93	93-94	3	22	4
Ipswich T	Tr	02.95	94-98	90	19	38
Preston NE (L)	Dundee U	09.99	99	5	7	2
York C	Dundee U	09.00	00-02	26	26	3

MATHIE David
Motherwell, 15 August, 1919 Died 1954 (CF)

League Club	Source	Date Signed	Seasons Played	Apps	Subs	Gls
Workington	Kilmarnock	10.53	53	2	-	0

MATIAS Pedro Manuel Miguel
Madrid, Spain, 11 October, 1973 Spu21 (M)

League Club	Source	Date Signed	Seasons Played	Apps	Subs	Gls
Macclesfield T	CD Logrones (Sp)	12.98	98	21	1	2
Tranmere Rov	Tr	08.99	99	1	3	0
Walsall	Tr	10.99	99-03	105	36	24
Blackpool	L	03.04	03	7	0	1
Kidderminster Hrs	Tr	11.04	04	4	1	1

MATIER Gerald (Gerry)
Lisburn, 1 December, 1912 Died 1984 LoI-7 (G)

League Club	Source	Date Signed	Seasons Played	Apps	Subs	Gls
Blackburn Rov	Coleraine	07.37	37-38	20	-	0
Bradford C	Glentoran	08.39				
Plymouth Arg	Tr	09.46				
Torquay U	Tr	11.46	46	17	-	0

MATRECANO Salvatore
Naples, Italy, 5 October, 1970 Itu21 (CD)

League Club	Source	Date Signed	Seasons Played	Apps	Subs	Gls
Nottingham F	Perugia (It)	08.99	99	11	0	0

MATTEO Dominic
Dumfries, 28 April, 1974 EYth/Eu21-4/EB-1/S-6 (CD)

League Club	Source	Date Signed	Seasons Played	Apps	Subs	Gls
Liverpool	YT	05.92	93-99	112	15	1
Sunderland	L	03.95	94	1	0	0
Leeds U	Tr	08.00	00-03	115	0	2
Blackburn Rov	Tr	06.04	04	25	3	0

MATTHEW Damian
Islington, 23 September, 1970 Eu21-9 (M)

League Club	Source	Date Signed	Seasons Played	Apps	Subs	Gls
Chelsea	YT	06.89	89-92	13	8	0
Luton T	L	09.92	92	3	2	0
Crystal Palace	Tr	02.94	93-95	17	7	1
Bristol Rov	L	01.96	95	8	0	0
Burnley	Tr	07.96	96-97	50	9	7
Northampton T	Tr	07.98	98-99	1	1	0

MATTHEWS John Barry
Sheffield, 18 January, 1926 Died 1995 (W)

League Club	Source	Date Signed	Seasons Played	Apps	Subs	Gls
Lincoln C (Am)	Sheffield U (Am)	10.49	49	2	-	0

MATTHEWS David
Hackney, 20 November, 1965 (F)

League Club	Source	Date Signed	Seasons Played	Apps	Subs	Gls
West Ham U	App	11.82				
Walsall	Basildon U	11.87				
Southend U	Tr	03.88	88	1	5	0

MATTHEWS David (Dai) Ivor
Pontygwaith, 24 September, 1921 Died 1986 (G)

League Club	Source	Date Signed	Seasons Played	Apps	Subs	Gls
Cardiff C		09.47				
Newport Co	Tr	04.48	48	6	-	0

MATTHEWS Francis (Frank) John
London, 7 January, 1948 (FB)

League Club	Source	Date Signed	Seasons Played	Apps	Subs	Gls
Southend U	App	01.66	65-67	20	6	0
Torquay U	Tr	06.68	68	6	1	0

MATTHEWS Graham
Newcastle-under-Lyme, 2 November, 1942 (F)

League Club	Source	Date Signed	Seasons Played	Apps	Subs	Gls
Stoke C	Jnrs	11.59	60-62	16	-	3
Walsall	Tr	08.63	63-64	67	-	21
Crewe Alex	Tr	08.65	65-67	56	2	19

MATTHEWS Jason Lee
Paulton, 13 March, 1975 (G)

League Club	Source	Date Signed	Seasons Played	Apps	Subs	Gls
Exeter C	Taunton T	08.99	99	11	1	0

MATTHEWS John Melvin
Camden, 1 November, 1955 (M)

League Club	Source	Date Signed	Seasons Played	Apps	Subs	Gls
Arsenal	App	08.73	74-77	38	7	2
Sheffield U	Tr	08.78	78-81	98	5	14
Mansfield T	Tr	08.82	82-83	70	2	6
Chesterfield	Tr	08.84	84	38	0	1
Plymouth Arg	Tr	08.85	85-88	131	4	4
Torquay U	Tr	07.89	89	22	3	0

MATTHEWS John **Keith**
Wrexham, 7 March, 1934 (W)

League Club	Source	Date Signed	Seasons Played	Apps	Subs	Gls
Wrexham		12.52	52-54	9	-	0

MATTHEWS Lee Joseph
Middlesbrough, 16 January, 1979 EYth (F)

League Club	Source	Date Signed	Seasons Played	Apps	Subs	Gls
Leeds U	YT	02.96	97	0	3	0
Notts Co	L	09.98	98	4	1	0
Gillingham	L	03.00	99	2	3	0
Bristol C	Tr	03.01	00-03	14	29	9
Darlington	L	12.03	03	6	0	1
Bristol Rov	L	01.04	03	9	0	0
Yeovil T	L	03.04	03	2	2	0
Port Vale	Tr	07.04	04	21	10	10

MATTHEWS Mark
Reading, 17 September, 1961 (M)

League Club	Source	Date Signed	Seasons Played	Apps	Subs	Gls
Reading		07.81	81-83	5	3	1

MATTHEWS Michael (Mike)
Hull, 25 September, 1960 (M)

League Club	Source	Date Signed	Seasons Played	Apps	Subs	Gls
Wolverhampton W	App	10.78	80-83	72	4	7
Scunthorpe U	Tr	02.84	83-85	56	2	5
Halifax T	North Ferriby U	09.86	86-88	98	1	8
Scarborough	Tr	12.88	88	7	0	1
Stockport Co	Tr	02.89	88-89	35	0	3
Scarborough	Tr	12.89	89-90	64	2	3
Hull C	Tr	08.91	91	10	6	2
Halifax T	Tr	08.92	92	23	0	2

MATTHEWS Neil
Grimsby, 19 September, 1966 (F)

League Club	Source	Date Signed	Seasons Played	Apps	Subs	Gls
Grimsby T	App	09.84	84-86	9	2	1
Scunthorpe U	L	11.85	85	1	0	0
Halifax T	L	10.86	86	9	0	2
Bolton W	L	03.87	86	1	0	0
Halifax T	Tr	08.87	87-89	99	6	29
Stockport Co	Tr	06.90	90-92	27	16	15
Halifax T	L	09.91	91	3	0	0
Lincoln C	Tr	12.92	92-94	69	14	20
Bury	L	12.94	94	2	0	1

MATTHEWS Neil Peter
Manchester, 3 December, 1967 NIYth/NIu21-1/NIB (FB)

League Club	Source	Date Signed	Seasons Played	Apps	Subs	Gls
Blackpool	App	12.85	85-89	67	9	1
Cardiff C	Tr	08.90	90-92	60	6	2
Rochdale	Tr	07.93	93-94	15	4	0

MATTHEWS Paul William
Leicester, 30 September, 1946 (M)

League Club	Source	Date Signed	Seasons Played	Apps	Subs	Gls
Leicester C	App	08.64	64-70	56	5	5
Southend U	L	09.72	72	1	0	0
Mansfield T	Tr	12.72	72-77	121	3	6
Rotherham U	Tr	10.77	77	8	0	0
Northampton T	L	03.79	78	13	1	0

MATTHEWS Reginald (Reg) Derrick
Coventry, 20 December, 1932 Died 2001 Eu23-4/EB/FLge-2/E-5 (G)

League Club	Source	Date Signed	Seasons Played	Apps	Subs	Gls
Coventry C	Jnrs	05.50	52-56	111	-	0
Chelsea	Tr	11.56	56-60	135	-	0
Derby Co	Tr	10.61	61-67	225	0	0

MATTHEWS Robert (Rob) David
Slough, 14 October, 1970 ESch (W)

League Club	Source	Date Signed	Seasons Played	Apps	Subs	Gls
Notts Co	Loughborough Univ	03.92	91-94	23	20	11
Luton T	Tr	03.95	94	6	5	0
York C	Tr	09.95	95	14	3	1
Bury	Tr	01.96	95-98	54	20	11
Stockport Co	Tr	11.98	98-00	29	9	4
Blackpool	L	12.99	99	5	1	2
Halifax T	L	02.01	00	8	0	2
Hull C	Tr	03.01	00-01	17	6	3

MATTHEWS Roy Henderson
Slough, 29 March, 1940 (IF)

League Club	Source	Date Signed	Seasons Played	Apps	Subs	Gls
Charlton Ath	Arbroath Victoria	04.57	59-66	160	0	46

League Club	Source	Date Signed	Seasons Played	Apps	Subs	Gls
MATTHEWS (Sir) **Stanley**						
Hanley, 1 February, 1915 Died 2000 ESch/FLge-14/EWar-29/E-54						(W)
Stoke C	Jnrs	02.32	31-46	259	-	51
Blackpool	Tr	05.47	47-61	380	-	17
Stoke C	Tr	10.61	61-64	59	-	3
MATTHEWS George **Terence (Terry)** Leonard						
Leyton, 25 February, 1936						(IF)
West Ham U	Jnrs	02.53	55	9	-	1
Aldershot	Tr	07.57	57-61	62	-	20
Gillingham	Tr	08.62	62	10	-	1
MATTHEWS Wayne John						
Cardiff, 11 September, 1964						(M)
Cardiff C	Jnrs	01.83	83	4	10	0
MATTHEWSON Reginald (Reg)						
Sheffield, 6 August, 1939						(CD)
Sheffield U	Campsie Black Watch	06.58	61-67	146	3	3
Fulham	Tr	02.68	67-72	156	2	1
Chester	Tr	01.73	72-75	86	1	1
MATTHEWSON Robert (Bob)						
Newcastle, 13 April, 1930 Died 2000						(CD)
Bolton W	Byker YC	03.48	50-52	3	-	0
MATTHEWSON Trevor						
Sheffield, 12 February, 1963						(CD)
Sheffield Wed	App	02.81	80-82	3	0	0
Newport Co	Tr	10.83	83-84	73	2	0
Stockport Co	Tr	09.85	85-86	79	1	0
Lincoln C	Tr	08.87	88	43	0	2
Birmingham C	Tr	08.89	89-92	167	1	12
Preston NE	Tr	08.93	93	12	0	1
Bury	Tr	09.94	94-95	34	0	0
Hereford U	Witton A	10.96	96	35	0	2
MATTHIAS Terence (Terry)						
Wrexham, 10 November, 1949 WSch						(CD)
Shrewsbury T	App	05.67	65-73	96	2	0
MATTINSON Harry						
Ireby, 20 July, 1925 Died 2001						(CD)
Middlesbrough	Sunderland (Am)	11.45	46	3	-	0
Preston NE	Tr	03.49	48-58	124	-	0
MATTIS Dwayne Antony						
Huddersfield, 31 July, 1981 IRYth/IRu21-2						(M)
Huddersfield T	YT	07.99	98-03	50	19	2
Bury	Tr	07.04	04	39	0	5
MATTISON Paul Andrew						
Wakefield, 24 April, 1973						(M)
Darlington	Ferrybridge Ams	08.94	94-95	5	12	0
MATTSON Jesper Bo						
Visby, Sweden, 18 April, 1968 Sweden 1						(CD)
Nottingham F	Halmstad (Swe)	12.98	98	5	1	0
MAUCHLEN Alistair (Ally) Henry						
Kilwinning, 29 June, 1960						(M)
Leicester C	Motherwell	08.85	85-91	228	11	11
MAUGE Ronald (Ronnie) Carlton						
Islington, 10 March, 1969 Trinidad 8						(M)
Charlton Ath	YT	07.87				
Fulham	Tr	09.88	88-89	47	3	2
Bury	Tr	07.90	90-94	92	16	10
Plymouth Arg	Tr	07.95	95-98	119	16	14
Bristol Rov	Tr	07.99	99-01	50	3	0
MAUGHAN Wesley (Wes) James						
Southampton, 17 February, 1939						(CF)
Southampton	Cowes	05.57	58-61	6	-	1
Reading	Tr	03.62	61-62	16	-	3
MAUND John (Jack) Henry						
Hednesford, 5 January, 1916 Died 1994						(W)
Aston Villa	Hednesford T	10.34	35-37	47	-	8
Nottingham F	Tr	05.39				
Walsall	Tr	10.46	46-47	32	-	7
MAUTONE Stefano (Steve)						
Myrtleford, Australia, 10 August, 1970 Auu23						(G)
West Ham U	Canberra Cosmos (Aus)	03.96	96	1	0	0
Crewe Alex	L	09.96	96	3	0	0
Reading	Tr	02.97	96-97	29	0	0
Wolverhampton W	Tr	08.99				
Crystal Palace	Tr	11.99	99	2	0	0
Gillingham	Tr	03.00	99	1	0	0

League Club	Source	Date Signed	Seasons Played	Apps	Subs	Gls
MAVRAK Darko						
Mostar, Bosnia, 19 January, 1969						(M)
Walsall	Falkenberg FF (Swe)	01.99	98-99	13	4	2
MAW John Rex						
Scunthorpe, 22 December, 1934						(FB)
Scunthorpe U		06.57	57	1	-	0
MAWENE Youl						
Caen, France, 16 July, 1979						(CD)
Derby Co	RC Lens (Fr)	08.00	00-03	54	1	1
Preston NE	Tr	08.04	04	46	0	2
MAWER Shaun Kerry						
Ulceby, 6 August, 1959						(FB)
Grimsby T	App	08.77	77-79	57	3	0
MAWSON Craig John						
Skipton, 16 May, 1979						(G)
Burnley	YT	07.97				
Halifax T	Tr	02.01	00	9	0	0
Oldham Ath	Morecambe	08.04	04	3	1	0
MAWSON Joseph (Joe)						
Workington, 7 January, 1934						(W)
Workington (Am)		06.55	55	1	-	0
MAWSON Ronald (Ron)						
Bishop Auckland, 16 September, 1914 Died 1981						(G)
Crewe Alex	RAF Tern Hill	06.45	46-47	23	-	0
Wrexham	Tr	09.48	48	6	-	0
MAXFIELD John (Jack)						
Carlisle, 17 June, 1919 Died 2004						(W)
Carlisle U		08.39	46-50	26	-	4
Workington	Tr	07.51	51	13	-	4
MAXFIELD Scott						
Doncaster, 13 July, 1976						(FB)
Doncaster Rov	YT	07.94	94-95	22	7	1
Hull C	Tr	03.96	95-97	23	12	0
MAXWELL Alistair (Ally) Elspie						
Hamilton, 16 February, 1965						(G)
Bolton W (L)	Motherwell	03.92	91	3	0	0
MAXWELL Hugh						
Rigghead, 14 May, 1938						(IF)
Bradford PA	Stirling A	04.62	61-62	12	-	5
MAXWELL Jason Dean						
Scunthorpe, 1 September, 1972						(F)
Scunthorpe U	Appleby Frodingham	01.93	92	0	2	0
MAXWELL Kenneth (Ken)						
Glasgow, 11 February, 1928						(FB)
Northampton T	Kilmarnock	06.49	50	2	-	0
Bradford PA	East Stirling	11.57	57	2	-	0
MAXWELL Leyton Jonathan						
Rhyl, 3 October, 1979 WYth/Wu21-14						(M)
Liverpool	YT	07.97				
Stockport Co	L	07.00	00	8	12	2
Cardiff C	Tr	08.01	01-03	10	24	1
Swansea C	Tr	03.04	03	1	2	0
Mansfield T	Newport Co	12.04	04	1	0	0
MAXWELL Patrick (Pat)						
Ayr, 10 January, 1929 Died 2000						(W)
Chesterfield	Saltcoats Victoria	08.51	51-52	18	-	3
MAY Andrew (Andy) Michael Peter						
Bury, 26 February, 1964 ESch/Eu21-1						(M)
Manchester C	App	01.82	80-86	141	9	8
Huddersfield T	Tr	07.87	87-89	112	2	5
Bolton W	L	03.88	87	9	1	2
Bristol C	Tr	08.90	90-91	88	2	4
Millwall	Tr	06.92	92-94	49	5	1
MAY Benjamin (Ben) Steven						
Gravesend, 10 March, 1984						(F)
Millwall	YT	05.01	02-04	8	10	2
Colchester U	L	03.03	02	4	2	0
Brentford	L	08.03	03	38	3	7
Colchester U	L	08.04	04	5	9	1
Brentford	L	12.04	04	7	3	1
MAY Christopher (Chris) John						
Wakefield, 2 September, 1985						(G)
Brighton & Hove A	Sch	•	04	0	1	0

League Club	Source	Date Signed	Seasons Played	Career Record Apps	Subs	Gls
MAY David						
Oldham, 24 June, 1970						(CD)
Blackburn Rov	YT	06.88	88-93	123	0	3
Manchester U	Tr	07.94	94-02	68	17	6
Huddersfield T	L	12.99	99	1	0	0
Burnley	Tr	08.03	03	34	1	4
MAY Donald (Don) Ivor						
Broseley, 31 May, 1931						(WH)
Bury	Broseley	03.51	51-61	134	-	11
MAY Edward (Eddie) Skillion						
Edinburgh, 30 August, 1967 SYth/Su21-2						(M)
Brentford	Hibernian	07.89	89-90	46	1	10
MAY Edwin (Eddie) Charles						
Epping, 19 May, 1943						(CD)
Southend U	Dagenham	01.65	64-67	106	4	3
Wrexham	Tr	06.68	68-75	330	4	35
Swansea C	Tr	08.76	76-77	90	0	8
MAY Gary Colin						
Darlington, 7 May, 1967						(M)
Darlington		11.86	86	1	1	0
MAY Harry						
Glasgow, 15 October, 1928						(FB)
Cardiff C	Thorniewood U	08.48	49	1	-	0
Swindon T	Tr	06.50	50-51	78	-	1
Barnsley	Tr	05.52	52-54	105	-	0
Southend U	Tr	09.55	55	19	-	1
MAY Jonathan (John)						
Crosby, 28 January, 1960 ESch						(CD)
Blackpool	App	11.78	78	4	0	0
MAY Lawrence (Larry) Charles						
Sutton Coldfield, 26 December, 1958						(CD)
Leicester C	App	12.76	76-82	180	7	12
Barnsley	Tr	09.83	83-86	122	0	3
Sheffield Wed	Tr	02.87	86-87	30	1	1
Brighton & Hove A	Tr	09.88	88	24	0	3
MAY Leroy Armstrong						
Wolverhampton, 12 August, 1969						(F)
Walsall	Tividale	01.92	91	1	3	0
Hereford U	Tividale	01.93	92-93	16	5	3
MAY Rory Joseph						
Birmingham, 25 November, 1984						(F)
Lincoln C	Coventry C (Sch)	08.03	03	1	4	0
MAY Warren Derek						
Rochford, 31 December, 1964						(CD)
Southend U	App	01.83	82-85	77	12	4
MAYBANK Edward (Teddy) Glen						
Lambeth, 11 October, 1956						(F)
Chelsea	App	02.74	74-76	28	0	6
Fulham	Tr	11.76	76-77	27	0	14
Brighton & Hove A	Tr	11.77	77-79	62	2	16
Fulham	Tr	12.79	79	19	0	3
MAYBURY Alan						
Dublin, 8 August, 1978 IRYth/IRu21-8/IRB-1/IR-10						(FB)
Leeds U	St Kevin's BC	08.95	95-01	10	4	0
Reading	L	03.99	98	8	0	0
Crewe Alex	L	10.00	00	6	0	0
Leicester C	Heart of Midlothian	01.05	04	17	0	2
MAYE Daniel (Danny) Peter Christopher						
Leicester, 14 July, 1982						(M)
Port Vale	YT	09.01	01	0	2	0
Southend U	Tr	07.02	02	0	2	0
MAYERS Alan						
Delamere, 20 April, 1937						(W)
Chester	Jnrs	05.55	55	1	-	0
MAYERS Derek						
Liverpool, 24 January, 1935						(W)
Everton	Jnrs	08.52	52-56	18	-	7
Preston NE	Tr	05.57	57-60	118	-	26
Leeds U	Tr	06.61	61	20	-	5
Bury	Tr	07.62	62-63	32	-	6
Wrexham	Tr	10.63	63	21	-	2
MAYES Alan Kenneth						
Edmonton, 11 December, 1953						(F)
Queens Park Rgrs	App	07.71				
Watford	Tr	11.74	74-78	110	23	31
Northampton T	L	01.76	75	10	0	4
Swindon T	Tr	02.79	78-80	89	0	38
Chelsea	Tr	12.80	80-82	61	5	18
Swindon T	Tr	07.83	83-84	52	10	27
Carlisle U	Tr	07.85	85	8	2	2
Newport Co	L	02.86	85	3	0	1
Blackpool	Tr	09.86	86	12	1	6
MAYFIELD Leslie (Les)						
Mansfield, 19 January, 1926						(FB)
Mansfield T	Ilkeston	09.48	49-52	34	-	0
MAYLE John **Robert (Bobby)**						
Llandyssil, 18 December, 1938						(CF)
Shrewsbury T	Sentinel Jnrs	05.57	57	8	-	0
MAYLETT Bradley (Brad)						
Manchester, 24 December, 1980						(W)
Burnley	YT	02.99	98-02	3	42	0
Swansea C	L	03.03	02	6	0	0
Swansea C	Tr	06.03	03-04	30	19	5
Boston U	Tr	03.05	04	8	1	3
MAYMAN Paul Francis						
Crewe, 29 May, 1958 ESemiPro						(M)
Crewe Alex	Jnrs	07.76	75-76	42	1	3
MAYNARD Michael (Mike) Clements						
Guyana, 7 January, 1947						(FB)
Crystal Palace	Hounslow T	03.66				
Peterborough U	Tr	07.67	67	2	1	0
MAYO Joseph (Joe)						
Tipton, 25 May, 1952						(F)
Walsall	Dudley T	09.72	72	2	5	1
West Bromwich A	Tr	02.73	73-76	67	5	16
Orient	Tr	03.77	76-81	150	5	36
Cambridge U	Tr	09.81	81-82	35	1	14
Blackpool	L	10.82	82	5	0	1
MAYO Kerry						
Cuckfield, 21 September, 1977						(FB)
Brighton & Hove A	YT	07.96	96-04	277	26	11
MAYO Paul						
Lincoln, 13 October, 1981						(FB)
Lincoln C	YT	04.00	99-03	92	14	6
Watford	Tr	03.04	03-04	25	0	0
MAYRLEB Christian						
Leonding, Austria, 8 June, 1972						(F)
Sheffield Wed	FC Tyrol (Aut)	01.98	97	0	3	0
MAYS Albert Edward						
Ynyshir, 18 April, 1929 Died 1973						(WH)
Derby Co	Jnrs	05.46	49-59	272	-	21
Chesterfield	Tr	07.60	60	37	-	5
MAZZARELLI Giuseppe						
Uster, Switzerland, 14 August, 1972 Switzerland int						(M)
Manchester C (L)	FC Zurich (Swi)	03.96	95	0	2	0
MAZZINA Jorge **Nicolas**						
Buenos Aires, Argentina, 31 January, 1979 ArYth/Aru21						(M)
Swansea C	AC Kimberley (Arg)	08.01	01	3	0	0
York C	Tr	09.02	02	0	3	0
MAZZON Giorgio						
Waltham Cross, 4 September, 1960						(CD)
Tottenham H	Hertford T	04.79	80-82	3	1	0
Aldershot	Tr	08.83	83-88	184	11	6
MBOMA Patrick						
Douala, Cameroon, 15 November, 1970 Cameroon 53						(F)
Sunderland (L)	Parma (It)	02.02	01	5	4	1
MBOME Herve **Kingsley**						
Yaounde, Cameroon, 21 November, 1981 CmYth						(M)
Sheffield U	St Etienne (Fr)	04.00				
Cambridge U	GAP (Fr)	09.04	04	12	1	1
MEACHAM Jeffrey (Jeff)						
Bristol, 6 February, 1962						(F)
Bristol Rov	Trowbridge T	03.87	86-87	19	7	9
MEACHIN Paul						
Bebington, 17 July, 1956						(F)
Southport (Am)	Ashville	10.74	74	3	0	0
MEACOCK Kevin Michael						
Bristol, 16 September, 1963						(F)
Cardiff C	Devizes T	12.84	84-85	20	5	3

MEAD Peter Sidney
Luton, 9 September, 1956 (FB)

League Club	Source	Date Signed	Seasons Played	Apps	Subs	Gls
Luton T	App	07.74				
Northampton T	Tr	08.77	77-78	75	1	4

MEADE Raphael Joseph
Islington, 22 November, 1962 (F)

League Club	Source	Date Signed	Seasons Played	Apps	Subs	Gls
Arsenal	App	06.80	81-84	25	16	14
Luton T	Dundee U	03.89	88	2	2	0
Ipswich T	BK Odense (Den)	01.90	89	0	1	0
Plymouth Arg	BK Odense (Den)	01.91	90	2	3	0
Brighton & Hove A	Tr	08.91	91	35	5	9
Brighton & Hove A	(Hong Kong)	08.94	94	0	3	0

MEADOWS Frank
Maltby, 27 June, 1933 Died 2001 (WH)

League Club	Source	Date Signed	Seasons Played	Apps	Subs	Gls
Rotherham U		04.52	53-55	8	-	0
Coventry C	Tr	06.56	56	8	-	0

MEADOWS James (Jimmy)
Breightmet, 21 July, 1931 Died 1994 FLge-1/E-1 (W)

League Club	Source	Date Signed	Seasons Played	Apps	Subs	Gls
Southport	Bolton YMCA	03.49	48-50	60	-	6
Manchester C	Tr	03.51	50-54	130	-	30

MEADOWS John (Johnny) Alfred
Hoxton, 13 November, 1930 (WH)

League Club	Source	Date Signed	Seasons Played	Apps	Subs	Gls
Watford	St Albans C	06.51	51-59	222	-	42

MEADOWS Robert
Melton Mowbray, 25 April, 1938 (FB)

League Club	Source	Date Signed	Seasons Played	Apps	Subs	Gls
Stoke C	Jnrs	05.55				
Doncaster Rov	Northwich Vic	12.62	62-63	43	-	0

MEADOWS John **Ronald (Ron)**
Lancaster, 4 December, 1920 (G)

League Club	Source	Date Signed	Seasons Played	Apps	Subs	Gls
Burnley	Glasson Dock	09.46				
Bournemouth	Tr	04.50	50-51	16	-	0
Accrington St	Tr	07.52	52	18	-	0

MEAGAN John George
Shap, 11 November, 1935 (CD)

League Club	Source	Date Signed	Seasons Played	Apps	Subs	Gls
Workington	Jnrs	12.52	54	1	-	0

MEAGAN Michael (Mick) Kevin
Dublin, 29 May, 1934 IRSch/LoI-2/IRB/IR-17 (CD)

League Club	Source	Date Signed	Seasons Played	Apps	Subs	Gls
Everton	Johnville Jnrs	09.52	57-63	165	-	1
Huddersfield T	Tr	07.64	64-67	118	1	1
Halifax T	Tr	07.68	68	23	0	0

MEAGAN Thomas (Tom) Patrick
Liverpool, 14 November, 1959 (M)

League Club	Source	Date Signed	Seasons Played	Apps	Subs	Gls
Doncaster Rov	App	11.77	77-78	32	5	1
Doncaster Rov		09.82	82	2	0	0

MEAKER Michael John
Greenford, 18 August, 1971 Wu21-2/WB-1 (W)

League Club	Source	Date Signed	Seasons Played	Apps	Subs	Gls
Queens Park Rgrs	YT	02.90	90-94	21	13	1
Plymouth Arg	L	11.91	91	4	0	0
Reading	Tr	07.95	95-97	46	21	2
Bristol Rov	Tr	08.98	98-00	19	8	2
Swindon T	L	03.00	99	6	0	0
Plymouth Arg	Tr	02.01	00	5	6	1

MEAKIN Harry
Stoke-on-Trent, 8 September, 1919 Died 1986 (FB)

League Club	Source	Date Signed	Seasons Played	Apps	Subs	Gls
Stoke C	Summerbank	11.45	46-49	35	-	0

MEALAND Kenneth **Barry**
Carshalton, 24 January, 1943 (FB)

League Club	Source	Date Signed	Seasons Played	Apps	Subs	Gls
Fulham	Jnrs	10.61	61-67	28	1	0
Rotherham U	Tr	08.68	68-69	44	1	0

MEAN Scott James
Crawley, 13 December, 1973 (M)

League Club	Source	Date Signed	Seasons Played	Apps	Subs	Gls
Bournemouth	YT	08.92	92-95	52	22	8
West Ham U	Tr	11.96	97	0	3	0
Port Vale	L	08.98	98	1	0	0
Bournemouth	Tr	07.99	99	26	6	4

MEANEY John Francis
Stoke-on-Trent, 19 November, 1919 Died 2000 (WH)

League Club	Source	Date Signed	Seasons Played	Apps	Subs	Gls
Crewe Alex	Ravensdale	03.47	46-53	284	-	37

MEANEY Terence (Terry)
Stoke-on-Trent, 25 May, 1922 Died 1999 (CF)

League Club	Source	Date Signed	Seasons Played	Apps	Subs	Gls
Bury	Ravensdale	05.44	46	4	-	2
Crewe Alex	Tr	07.47	47	4	-	3

MEARA James (Jim) Stephen
Hammersmith, 7 October, 1972 (M)

League Club	Source	Date Signed	Seasons Played	Apps	Subs	Gls
Watford	YT	04.91	92	1	1	0
Doncaster Rov	Tr	07.94	94-95	14	2	1

MEARS Tyrone
Stockport, 18 February, 1983 (FB)

League Club	Source	Date Signed	Seasons Played	Apps	Subs	Gls
Manchester C	Jnrs	07.00	01	0	1	0
Preston NE	Tr	07.02	02-04	23	15	2

MEASHAM Ian
Barnsley, 14 December, 1964 (FB)

League Club	Source	Date Signed	Seasons Played	Apps	Subs	Gls
Huddersfield T	App	12.82	84	17	0	0
Lincoln C	L	10.85	85	6	0	0
Rochdale	L	03.86	85	12	0	0
Cambridge U	Tr	08.86	86	46	0	0
Burnley	Barnet	11.88	88-93	181	1	2
Doncaster Rov	Tr	09.93	93-95	29	3	0

MEASURES George Allan
Walthamstow, 17 December, 1958 (F)

League Club	Source	Date Signed	Seasons Played	Apps	Subs	Gls
Cambridge U	Bowers U	11.83	83	4	0	0

MEATH Trevor John
Wednesbury, 20 March, 1944 (M)

League Club	Source	Date Signed	Seasons Played	Apps	Subs	Gls
Walsall	Darlaston	05.64	64-69	59	7	16
Lincoln C	Tr	10.69	69-71	42	1	5

MEDD Gordon Ernest
Birmingham, 17 August, 1925 Died 1996 (W)

League Club	Source	Date Signed	Seasons Played	Apps	Subs	Gls
Birmingham C	Worcester C	10.46				
Walsall	Worcester C	06.49	49	22	-	2
Rochdale	Tr	07.50	50	5	-	1
York C	Tr	01.51	50	1	-	0

MEDHURST Henry (Harry) Edward Pafford
Byfleet, 5 February, 1916 Died 1984 (G)

League Club	Source	Date Signed	Seasons Played	Apps	Subs	Gls
West Ham U	Woking	11.36	38-46	24	-	0
Chelsea	Tr	01.47	46-51	143	-	0
Brighton & Hove A	Tr	11.52	52	12	-	0

MEDLEY Leslie (Les) Dennis
Edmonton, 3 September, 1920 Died 2001 ESch/FLge-1/E-6 (W)

League Club	Source	Date Signed	Seasons Played	Apps	Subs	Gls
Tottenham H	Jnrs	09.36	46-52	150	-	45

MEDLIN Nicholas (Nicky) Ryan Maxwell
Camborne, 23 November, 1976 (M)

League Club	Source	Date Signed	Seasons Played	Apps	Subs	Gls
Exeter C	YT	08.95	95-97	20	17	1

MEDLOCK Owen Wilfred
Whittlesey, 8 March, 1938 (G)

League Club	Source	Date Signed	Seasons Played	Apps	Subs	Gls
Chelsea	Jnrs	05.55				
Swindon T	Tr	02.59	59	3	-	0
Oxford U	Tr	12.59	62	19	-	0

MEDOU-OTYE Andre **Parfait**
Ekoundendi, Cameroon, 29 November, 1976 FrYth (FB)

League Club	Source	Date Signed	Seasons Played	Apps	Subs	Gls
Kidderminster Hrs	Morton	11.00	00-01	18	1	0

MEDWIN Terence (Terry) Cameron
Swansea, 25 September, 1932 WSch/WLge-1/W-30 (W)

League Club	Source	Date Signed	Seasons Played	Apps	Subs	Gls
Swansea T	Jnrs	11.49	51-55	147	-	57
Tottenham H	Tr	04.56	56-62	197	-	65

MEE George Edwin
Blackpool, 20 May, 1923 Died 1974 (CF)

League Club	Source	Date Signed	Seasons Played	Apps	Subs	Gls
Nottingham F	Jnrs	05.40	46	9	-	1

MEECHAN Alexander (Alex) Thomas
Plymouth, 29 January, 1980 (F)

League Club	Source	Date Signed	Seasons Played	Apps	Subs	Gls
Swindon T	YT	•	97	0	1	0
Bristol C	Tr	07.98	98-99	5	8	4

MEECHAN David Anderson
Loganlea, 10 November, 1943 (CF)

League Club	Source	Date Signed	Seasons Played	Apps	Subs	Gls
Sheffield Wed	Burnley (Am)	12.60				
Scunthorpe U	Tr	06.61				
York C	Tr	06.63	63	6	-	0

MEEK George
Glasgow, 15 February, 1934 (W)

League Club	Source	Date Signed	Seasons Played	Apps	Subs	Gls
Leeds U	Hamilton Academical	08.52	52-59	195	-	19
Walsall	L	01.54	53	18	-	2
Walsall	L	08.54	54	26	-	4
Leicester C	Tr	08.60	60	13	-	0
Walsall	Tr	07.61	61-64	128	-	22

MEENS Harold
Doncaster, 15 October, 1919 Died 1987 (CD)

League Club	Source	Date Signed	Seasons Played	Apps	Subs	Gls
Hull C	Shepherd's Road Club	10.38	38-51	146	-	0

MEESON David (Dave) John
Oxford, 6 July, 1934 Died 1991 (G)

League Club	Source	Date Signed	Seasons Played	Apps	Subs	Gls
Wolverhampton W	Oxford C	02.52				
Reading	Tr	08.54	54-62	156	-	0
Coventry C	Tr	09.62	62-64	24	-	0

League Club	Source	Date Signed	Seasons Played	Career Record Apps	Subs	Gls
MEGSON Donald (Don) Harry						
Sale, 12 June, 1936 FLge-1						(FB)
Sheffield Wed	Mossley	06.53	59-69	386	0	6
Bristol Rov	Tr	03.70	69-70	31	0	1
MEGSON Gary John						
Manchester, 2 May, 1959						(M)
Plymouth Arg	App	05.77	77-79	78	0	10
Everton	Tr	12.79	79-80	20	2	2
Sheffield Wed	Tr	08.81	81-83	123	0	13
Nottingham F	Tr	08.84				
Newcastle U	Tr	11.84	84-85	21	3	1
Sheffield Wed	Tr	12.85	85-88	107	3	12
Manchester C	Tr	01.89	88-91	78	4	2
Norwich C	Tr	07.92	92-94	42	4	1
Lincoln C	Tr	07.95	95	2	0	0
Shrewsbury T	Tr	09.95	95	2	0	0
MEGSON Kevin Craig						
Halifax, 1 July, 1971						(FB)
Bradford C	YT	07.89	89-90	24	3	0
Halifax T	Tr	03.91	90-92	37	4	1
MEHEW David Stephen						
Camberley, 29 October, 1967						(M)
Bristol Rov	Leeds U (YT)	07.85	85-92	195	27	63
Exeter C	L	03.94	93	5	2	0
Walsall	Tr	07.94	94	6	7	0
MEHMET David Nedjate						
Camberwell, 2 December, 1960						(M)
Millwall	App	12.77	76-80	97	17	15
Charlton Ath	Tampa Bay (USA)	01.82	81-82	29	0	2
Gillingham	Tr	03.83	82-85	128	4	39
Millwall	Tr	07.86	86-87	17	1	1
MEIJER Erik						
Meersen, Holland, 2 August, 1969 Hou21/Ho-2						(F)
Liverpool	Bayer Leverkusen (Ger)	07.99	99-00	7	17	0
Preston NE	L	10.00	00	9	0	0
MEIJER Geert						
Amsterdam, Holland, 15 March, 1951 Holland int						(W)
Bristol C	Ajax (Holl)	03.79	78-79	12	3	2
MEIRELLES Bruno						
Leiria, Portugal, 23 February, 1982						(M)
Torquay U	Amadora (Por)	08.04	04	5	4	0
MELAUGH Gavin Mark John						
Derry, 9 July, 1981 NIu21-8						(M)
Aston Villa	YT	07.98				
Rochdale	Tr	11.02	02	17	2	1
MELCHIOT Mario						
Amsterdam, Holland, 4 November, 1976 HoYth/Hou21-13/Ho-13						(FB)
Chelsea	Ajax (Holl)	07.99	99-03	117	13	4
Birmingham C	Tr	07.04	04	33	1	1
MELDRUM Colin						
Glasgow, 26 November, 1941						(FB)
Arsenal	Jnrs	12.58				
Watford	Tr	12.60	60-62	32	-	0
Reading	Tr	04.63	62-69	265	1	8
Cambridge U	Tr	10.69	70	36	1	4
Workington	Hillingdon Borough	12.74	74	0	2	0
MELIA James (Jimmy)						
Liverpool, 1 November, 1937 ESch/EYth/FLge-1/E-2						(M)
Liverpool	Jnrs	11.54	55-63	269	-	76
Wolverhampton W	Tr	03.64	63-64	24	-	4
Southampton	Tr	11.64	64-68	139	0	11
Aldershot	Tr	11.68	68-71	135	0	14
Crewe Alex	Tr	02.72	71	2	2	0
MELL Stewart Albert						
Doncaster, 15 October, 1957 ESemiPro						(F)
Doncaster Rov	Appleby Frodingham	02.80	79-82	62	14	14
Halifax T	Tr	07.83	83	22	8	8
Scarborough	Burton A	07.86	87-88	30	9	8
MELLANBY Daniel (Danny)						
Bishop Auckland, 17 July, 1979						(F)
Darlington	Bishop Auckland	07.01	01-03	33	11	8
MELLBERG Erik **Olof**						
Gullspang, Sweden, 3 September, 1977 Sweden 56						(CD)
Aston Villa	Racing Santander (Sp)	07.01	01-04	133	0	5
MELLEDEW Stephen (Steve) Thomas						
Rochdale, 28 November, 1945						(F)
Rochdale	Whipp & Bourne	12.66	66-69	88	9	23
Everton	Tr	09.69				
Aldershot	Tr	07.71	71-73	90	2	27
Bury	Tr	11.73	73-74	14	6	2
Crewe Alex	Tr	10.74	74-75	49	7	2
Rochdale	Tr	07.76	76-77	76	2	12
MELLIGAN John James						
Dublin, 11 February, 1982 IRYth/IRu21-1						(M)
Wolverhampton W	YT	07.00	02	0	2	0
Bournemouth	L	11.01	01	7	1	0
Kidderminster Hrs	L	09.02	02	10	0	5
Kidderminster Hrs	L	12.02	02	18	1	5
Kidderminster Hrs	L	10.03	03	5	0	1
Doncaster Rov	L	11.03	03	21	0	2
Cheltenham T	Tr	07.04	04	23	6	2
MELLING Terence (Terry)						
Haverton Hill, 24 January, 1940						(F)
Newcastle U	Tow Law	12.65				
Watford	Tr	05.66	65-66	23	1	5
Newport Co	Tr	02.67	66-67	34	0	14
Mansfield T	Tr	11.67	67-68	33	0	7
Rochdale	Tr	09.68	68	20	0	8
Darlington	Tr	03.69	68-69	20	0	6
MELLISH Stuart Michael						
Hyde, 19 November, 1969						(M)
Rochdale	YT	07.88	87-88	24	3	1
MELLON Michael (Mickey) Joseph						
Paisley, 18 March, 1972						(M)
Bristol C	YT	12.89	89-92	26	9	1
West Bromwich A	Tr	02.93	92-94	38	7	6
Blackpool	Tr	11.94	94-97	123	1	14
Tranmere Rov	Tr	10.97	97-98	45	12	3
Burnley	Tr	01.99	98-00	72	12	5
Tranmere Rov	Tr	03.01	00-03	102	15	3
Kidderminster Hrs	Tr	08.04	04	5	2	0
MELLOR John Allan						
Droylsden, 16 October, 1921 Died 1997						(WH)
Hull C	Ashton U	05.47	47-51	104	-	4
MELLOR Robert **Brett**						
Huddersfield, 4 February, 1960						(CD)
Huddersfield T	App	02.78	77	1	0	0
MELLOR Ian						
Sale, 19 February, 1950						(W)
Manchester C	Wythenshawe Amats	12.69	70-72	36	4	7
Norwich C	Tr	03.73	72-73	28	1	2
Brighton & Hove A	Tr	04.74	74-77	116	6	31
Chester	Tr	02.78	77-78	38	2	11
Sheffield Wed	Tr	06.79	79-81	54	16	11
Bradford C	Tr	06.82	82-83	27	9	4
MELLOR Kenneth (Ken) Edward						
Leicester, 22 August, 1934						(CD)
Leicester C		07.55				
Mansfield T	Tr	07.57	57-58	66	-	0
Swindon T	Tr	07.59	59-60	32	-	4
MELLOR Neil Andrew						
Sheffield, 4 November, 1982						(F)
Liverpool	YT	02.02	02-04	7	5	2
West Ham U	L	08.03	03	8	8	2
MELLOR Peter Joseph						
Prestbury, 20 November, 1947 EYth						(G)
Burnley	Witton A	04.69	69-71	69	0	0
Chesterfield	L	01.72	71	4	0	0
Fulham	Tr	02.72	71-76	190	0	0
Hereford U	Tr	09.77	77	32	0	0
Portsmouth	Tr	07.78	78-80	129	0	0
MELLOR William (Bill)						
Manchester, 29 June, 1925						(FB)
Accrington St	Droylsden	06.50	50-53	138	-	2
MELLOWS Michael (Mick) Anthony						
Epsom, 14 November, 1947 ESch/EYth/EAmat						(M)
Reading (Am)	Sutton U	09.70	70	14	2	2
Portsmouth	Wycombe W	09.73	73-77	174	8	16
MELROSE James (Jim) Millsopp						
Glasgow, 7 October, 1958 SSch/Su21-8/SLge-1						(F)
Leicester C	Partick Th	07.80	80-82	57	15	21
Coventry C	Tr	09.82	82	21	3	8
Wolverhampton W (L)	Glasgow Celtic	09.84	84	6	1	2
Manchester C	Glasgow Celtic	11.84	84-85	27	7	8
Charlton Ath	Tr	03.86	85-87	44	4	19
Leeds U	Tr	09.87	87	3	1	0
Shrewsbury T	Tr	02.88	87-89	27	22	3

MELTON Stephen (Steve)
Lincoln, 3 October, 1978 (M)

League Club	Source	Date Signed	Seasons Played	Apps	Subs	Gls
Nottingham F	YT	10.95	98-99	2	1	0
Stoke C	Tr	02.00	99	0	5	0
Brighton & Hove A	Tr	08.00	00-02	21	25	3
Hull C	Tr	12.02	02-03	19	11	0
Boston U	Tr	03.04	03-04	14	4	2

MELVANG Lars Mandrup
Seattle, USA, 3 April, 1969 (FB)

League Club	Source	Date Signed	Seasons Played	Apps	Subs	Gls
Watford	Silkeborg (Den)	08.97	97	4	0	1

MELVILLE Alan Allistair
Hartlepool, 13 March, 1941 (CD)

League Club	Source	Date Signed	Seasons Played	Apps	Subs	Gls
Hartlepools U	St Joseph's	09.60	60-61	5	-	0

MELVILLE Andrew (Andy) Roger
Swansea, 29 November, 1968 Wu21-2/WB-1/W-64 (CD)

League Club	Source	Date Signed	Seasons Played	Apps	Subs	Gls
Swansea C	App	07.86	85-89	165	10	22
Oxford U	Tr	07.90	90-92	135	0	13
Sunderland	Tr	08.93	93-98	204	0	14
Bradford C	L	02.98	97	6	0	1
Fulham	Tr	07.99	99-03	150	3	4
West Ham U	Tr	01.04	03-04	14	3	0
Nottingham F	L	02.05	04	13	0	0

MELVILLE Leslie (Les)
Ormskirk, 29 November, 1930 EYth (WH)

League Club	Source	Date Signed	Seasons Played	Apps	Subs	Gls
Everton	Jnrs	04.50				
Bournemouth	Tr	07.56	56-57	25	-	0
Oldham Ath	Tr	03.58	57	2	-	0

MENDES Albert **Junior** Hillyard Andrew
Balham, 15 September, 1976 Montserrat int (M)

League Club	Source	Date Signed	Seasons Played	Apps	Subs	Gls
Chelsea	YT	07.95				
Carlisle U (L)	St Mirren	11.98	98	5	1	1
Mansfield T	St Mirren	01.03	02-03	54	3	12
Huddersfield T	Tr	07.04	04	13	12	5

MENDES Miguel **Pedro**
Guimaraes, Portugal, 26 February, 1979 Portugal 2 (M)

League Club	Source	Date Signed	Seasons Played	Apps	Subs	Gls
Tottenham H	FC Porto (Por)	07.04	04	22	2	1

MENDEZ Gabriel
Buenos Aires, Argentina, 12 March, 1973 Australia int (M)

League Club	Source	Date Signed	Seasons Played	Apps	Subs	Gls
Notts Co (L)	Parrametta (Aus)	03.97	96	2	1	0

MENDEZ RODRIGUEZ Alberto
Nuremburg, Germany, 24 October, 1974 (F)

League Club	Source	Date Signed	Seasons Played	Apps	Subs	Gls
Arsenal	FC Feucht (Ger)	07.97	97-98	1	3	0

MENDHAM Peter Stanley
King's Lynn, 9 April, 1960 (M)

League Club	Source	Date Signed	Seasons Played	Apps	Subs	Gls
Norwich C	App	04.78	78-86	200	11	23

MENDIETA Gaizka
Bilbao, Spain, 27 March, 1974 Spain 40 (M)

League Club	Source	Date Signed	Seasons Played	Apps	Subs	Gls
Middlesbrough (L)	SS Lazio (It)	08.03	03	30	1	2
Middlesbrough (L)	SS Lazio (It)	07.04	04	7	0	0

MENDONCA Clive Paul
Islington, 9 September, 1968 (F)

League Club	Source	Date Signed	Seasons Played	Apps	Subs	Gls
Sheffield U	App	09.86	86-87	8	5	4
Doncaster Rov	L	02.88	87	2	0	0
Rotherham U	Tr	03.88	87-90	71	13	27
Sheffield U	Tr	08.91	91	4	6	1
Grimsby T	L	01.92	91	10	0	3
Grimsby T	Tr	06.92	92-96	151	5	58
Charlton Ath	Tr	05.97	97-99	78	6	40

MENDY Bernard
Evreux, France, 20 August, 1981 FrYth/Fru21 (FB)

League Club	Source	Date Signed	Seasons Played	Apps	Subs	Gls
Bolton W (L)	Paris St Germain (Fr)	07.02	02	20	1	0

MENDY Jules
Pikine, Senegal, 4 September, 1973 (M)

League Club	Source	Date Signed	Seasons Played	Apps	Subs	Gls
Torquay U	Racing Club (Fr)	08.00	00	7	14	2

MENETRIER Mickael
Reims, France, 23 September, 1978 (G)

League Club	Source	Date Signed	Seasons Played	Apps	Subs	Gls
Bournemouth	Metz (Fr)	08.00	00-01	12	1	0

MENMUIR William Fraser
Glasgow, 3 February, 1952 (M)

League Club	Source	Date Signed	Seasons Played	Apps	Subs	Gls
Bristol C	Sandyhills	06.69	69-70	1	1	0

MENZIES Norman
Washington, 20 June, 1926 (IF)

League Club	Source	Date Signed	Seasons Played	Apps	Subs	Gls
Barnsley	Hexham Hearts	10.49				
Aldershot	Tr	05.50	50-57	221	-	91

MENZIES Adam **Ross**
Rutherglen, 31 October, 1934 SSch (WH)

League Club	Source	Date Signed	Seasons Played	Apps	Subs	Gls
Cardiff C	Glasgow Rgrs	08.57	57	1	-	0

MEOLA Antonio (Tony) Michael
Belleville, USA, 21 February, 1969 USA int (G)

League Club	Source	Date Signed	Seasons Played	Apps	Subs	Gls
Brighton & Hove A	Missouri Ath (USA)	08.90	90	1	0	0

MERCER Arthur **David**
Hull, 14 February, 1918 Died 1986 (W)

League Club	Source	Date Signed	Seasons Played	Apps	Subs	Gls
Torquay U		02.46	46-48	66	-	8

MERCER James (Jimmy) Robertson
Dunfermline, 17 March, 1935 (W)

League Club	Source	Date Signed	Seasons Played	Apps	Subs	Gls
Bury	Rosyth Rec	06.57	57-58	18	-	1
Crewe Alex	Tr	06.59	59	3	-	0

MERCER Joseph (Joe)
Ellesmere Port, 9 August, 1914 Died 1990 FLge-2/EWar-27/E-5 (WH)

League Club	Source	Date Signed	Seasons Played	Apps	Subs	Gls
Everton	Ellesmere Port T	09.32	32-46	170	-	1
Arsenal	Tr	12.46	46-53	247	-	2

MERCER Keith
Lewisham, 14 October, 1956 (F)

League Club	Source	Date Signed	Seasons Played	Apps	Subs	Gls
Watford	App	09.74	72-79	109	25	46
Southend U	Tr	02.80	79-82	131	0	35
Blackpool	Tr	08.83	83	31	0	9

MERCER Stanley (Stan)
Birkenhead, 11 September, 1919 Died 2003 (CF)

League Club	Source	Date Signed	Seasons Played	Apps	Subs	Gls
Leicester C	Blackpool (Am)	11.44	46	1	-	0
Accrington St	Tr	01.47	46-48	68	-	36
Mansfield T	Tr	10.48	48	12	-	6

MERCER Stephen (Steve) Jack
Barking, 1 May, 1965 (FB)

League Club	Source	Date Signed	Seasons Played	Apps	Subs	Gls
Peterborough U	Cambridge U (N/C)	09.82	82	3	0	0

MERCER William (Billy)
Liverpool, 22 May, 1969 (G)

League Club	Source	Date Signed	Seasons Played	Apps	Subs	Gls
Liverpool	YT	08.87				
Rotherham U	Tr	02.89	89-94	104	0	0
Sheffield U	Tr	10.94	94-95	4	0	0
Chesterfield	Tr	09.95	95-98	149	0	0
Bristol C	Tr	10.99	99	25	0	0

MEREDITH John Frederick
Hatfield, South Yorkshire, 23 September, 1940 (W)

League Club	Source	Date Signed	Seasons Played	Apps	Subs	Gls
Doncaster Rov	Jnrs	01.58	58-60	59	-	8
Sheffield Wed	Tr	02.61	60	1	-	0
Chesterfield	Tr	07.62	62-63	81	-	6
Gillingham	Tr	03.64	63-68	227	1	7
Bournemouth	Tr	08.69	69-70	51	0	1

MEREDITH Robert Garfield
Swansea, 3 September, 1917 Died 1994 WSch (W)

League Club	Source	Date Signed	Seasons Played	Apps	Subs	Gls
Carlisle U		01.47	46	1	-	0

MEREDITH Thomas (Tom) James Anthony
Enfield, 27 October, 1977 (FB)

League Club	Source	Date Signed	Seasons Played	Apps	Subs	Gls
Peterborough U	YT	07.96	95	1	1	0

MEREDITH Trevor George
Bridgnorth, 25 December, 1936 (W)

League Club	Source	Date Signed	Seasons Played	Apps	Subs	Gls
Burnley	Kidderminster Hrs	11.57	59-63	37	-	8
Shrewsbury T	Tr	04.64	64-71	229	6	41

MERINO Carlos Alberto
Bilbao, Spain, 15 March, 1980 (M)

League Club	Source	Date Signed	Seasons Played	Apps	Subs	Gls
Nottingham F	Urdaneta (Sp)	09.97	99	3	6	0

MERRICK Alan Ronald
Birmingham, 20 June, 1950 EYth (CD)

League Club	Source	Date Signed	Seasons Played	Apps	Subs	Gls
West Bromwich A	App	08.67	68-75	131	8	5
Peterborough U	L	09.75	75	5	0	0

MERRICK Geoffrey (Geoff)
Bristol, 29 April, 1951 ESch (CD)

League Club	Source	Date Signed	Seasons Played	Apps	Subs	Gls
Bristol C	App	08.68	67-81	361	6	10

MERRICK Gilbert (Gil) Harold
Birmingham, 26 January, 1922 FLge-11/E-23 (G)

League Club	Source	Date Signed	Seasons Played	Apps	Subs	Gls
Birmingham C	Solihull T	08.39	46-59	485	-	0

MERRICK Neil Gilbert
Birmingham, 6 April, 1952 ESemiPro (CD)

League Club	Source	Date Signed	Seasons Played	Apps	Subs	Gls
Bournemouth	Worcester C	09.74	74	13	2	0

MERRIFIELD Royston (Roy) Gordon
Mile End, 11 October, 1931 (W)

League Club	Source	Date Signed	Seasons Played	Apps	Subs	Gls
Chelsea	Rainham T	02.54				
Millwall	Tr	06.56	56	2	-	0

MERRINGTON David (Dave) Robert
Newcastle, 26 January, 1945 (CD)

League Club	Source	Date Signed	Seasons Played	Apps	Subs	Gls
Burnley	App	02.62	64-70	96	2	1

MERRIS David (Dave) Andrew
Rotherham, 13 October, 1980 (FB)

League Club	Source	Date Signed	Seasons Played	Apps	Subs	Gls
York C	Harrogate T	08.03	03	42	2	0

MERRITT Harold George
Ormskirk, 22 September, 1920 (IF)

League Club	Source	Date Signed	Seasons Played	Apps	Subs	Gls
Everton	Jnrs	12.37				
Clapton Orient	Tr	09.46	46	1	-	0

MERSON Paul Charles
Harlesden, 20 March, 1968 EYth/Eu21-4/EB-4/E-21 (F)

League Club	Source	Date Signed	Seasons Played	Apps	Subs	Gls
Arsenal	App	12.85	86-96	289	38	78
Brentford	L	01.87	86	6	1	0
Middlesbrough	Tr	07.97	97-98	48	0	11
Aston Villa	Tr	09.98	98-01	101	16	18
Portsmouth	Tr	08.02	02	44	1	12
Walsall	Tr	08.03	03-04	62	8	6

MESSER Gary Michael
Consett, 22 September, 1979 (F)

League Club	Source	Date Signed	Seasons Played	Apps	Subs	Gls
Doncaster Rov	YT	09.98	96-97	4	10	1

METCALF Colin Christopher Anthony
Norwich, 3 March, 1939 (CD)

League Club	Source	Date Signed	Seasons Played	Apps	Subs	Gls
Norwich C	Norman YC	07.60	62-63	12	-	1
Southend U	Tr	09.64	64	3	-	0

METCALF Mark Peter
Norwich, 25 September, 1965 ESch (M)

League Club	Source	Date Signed	Seasons Played	Apps	Subs	Gls
Norwich C	App	09.83	82	0	1	0

METCALF Matthew Adam
Norwich, 28 July, 1969 (F)

League Club	Source	Date Signed	Seasons Played	Apps	Subs	Gls
Brentford	Braintree T	09.93	93	3	4	0

METCALF Michael (Mickey)
Liverpool, 24 May, 1939 (F)

League Club	Source	Date Signed	Seasons Played	Apps	Subs	Gls
Wrexham	Everton (Am)	05.57	57-63	121	-	58
Chester	Tr	12.63	63-68	221	0	68

METCALFE John
Birmingham, 2 June, 1935 Died 1996 (W)

League Club	Source	Date Signed	Seasons Played	Apps	Subs	Gls
Birmingham C	Jnrs	10.52	52	2	-	0
York C	Tr	06.57	57	3	-	2
Walsall	Tr	07.58	58	2	-	0

METCALFE Ronald
South Shields, 8 December, 1947 (W)

League Club	Source	Date Signed	Seasons Played	Apps	Subs	Gls
Derby Co	Marsden CW Jnrs	01.65	66	1	0	0

METCALFE Stuart Michael
Blackburn, 6 October, 1950 EYth (M)

League Club	Source	Date Signed	Seasons Played	Apps	Subs	Gls
Blackburn Rov	App	01.68	67-79	375	11	21
Carlisle U	Tr	07.80	80	23	2	3
Blackburn Rov	Carolina (USA)	10.82				
Crewe Alex	Tr	01.83	82	3	0	0
Blackburn Rov	Tr	02.83	82	1	0	0

METCALFE Victor (Vic)
Barrow, 3 February, 1922 Died 2003 FLge-2/E-2 (W)

League Club	Source	Date Signed	Seasons Played	Apps	Subs	Gls
Huddersfield T	Ravensthorpe A	01.40	46-57	434	-	87
Hull C	Tr	06.58	58-59	6	-	3

METCHICK David (Dave) John
Bakewell, 14 August, 1943 EYth (M)

League Club	Source	Date Signed	Seasons Played	Apps	Subs	Gls
Fulham	Jnrs	08.61	61-64	47	-	9
Leyton Orient	Tr	12.64	64-66	75	0	15
Peterborough U	Tr	03.67	66-67	38	0	6
Queens Park Rgrs	Tr	08.68	68-69	0	3	1
Arsenal	Tr	09.70				
Brentford	Atlanta (USA)	09.73	73-74	57	4	4

METGOD Johannes (Johnny) Anthonius Bernardus
Amsterdam, Holland, 27 February, 1958 Holland int (M)

League Club	Source	Date Signed	Seasons Played	Apps	Subs	Gls
Nottingham F	Real Madrid (Sp)	08.84	84-86	113	3	15
Tottenham H	Tr	07.87	87	5	7	0

METHLEY Irvin
Worsborough, 22 September, 1925 Died 2004 (FB)

League Club	Source	Date Signed	Seasons Played	Apps	Subs	Gls
Wolverhampton W	Jnrs	10.42				
Walsall	Tr	03.46	46-50	113	-	1

METHVEN Colin John
India, 10 December, 1955 (CD)

League Club	Source	Date Signed	Seasons Played	Apps	Subs	Gls
Wigan Ath	East Fife	10.79	79-85	295	1	21
Blackpool	Tr	07.86	86-89	166	7	11
Carlisle U	L	09.90	90	12	0	0
Walsall	Tr	11.90	90-92	97	0	3

METTIOUI Ahmed
Tangier, Morocco, 3 November, 1965 (W)

League Club	Source	Date Signed	Seasons Played	Apps	Subs	Gls
Crewe Alex	Fath Union SC (Mor)	07.92	92	1	2	0

METTOMO Lucien
Douala, Cameroon, 19 April, 1977 Cameroon 30 (CD)

League Club	Source	Date Signed	Seasons Played	Apps	Subs	Gls
Manchester C	St Etienne (Fr)	10.01	01-02	20	7	1

MEYER Adrian Michael
Yate, 22 September, 1970 (CD)

League Club	Source	Date Signed	Seasons Played	Apps	Subs	Gls
Scarborough	YT	06.89	89-94	114	0	9

MEYER Barrie John
Bournemouth, 21 August, 1932 (IF)

League Club	Source	Date Signed	Seasons Played	Apps	Subs	Gls
Bristol Rov	Sneyd Park	11.49	50-57	139	-	60
Plymouth Arg	Tr	08.58	58	8	-	5
Newport Co	Tr	02.59	58-60	70	-	27
Bristol C	Tr	09.61	61-62	11	-	8

MEZAGUE Valery
Marseille, France, 8 December, 1983 (M)

League Club	Source	Date Signed	Seasons Played	Apps	Subs	Gls
Portsmouth (L)	Montpellier (Fr)	09.04	04	3	8	0

MICALLEF Constantinous (Tarki)
Cardiff, 24 January, 1961 WSch/Wu21-3 (M)

League Club	Source	Date Signed	Seasons Played	Apps	Subs	Gls
Cardiff C	App	01.79	78-82	67	14	11
Newport Co	Tr	09.83	83	22	2	2
Gillingham	N/C	08.84	84	2	0	1
Cardiff C	Tr	09.84	84-85	26	14	1
Bristol Rov	Tr	08.86	86	15	3	1

MICHAEL James (Jamie) David
Pontypridd, 28 October, 1978 WYth (W)

League Club	Source	Date Signed	Seasons Played	Apps	Subs	Gls
Cardiff C	YT	•	96	0	1	0

MICHOPOULOS Nikolaos (Nik)
Karditsa, Greece, 20 February, 1970 Greece 13 (G)

League Club	Source	Date Signed	Seasons Played	Apps	Subs	Gls
Burnley	PAOK Salonika	08.00	00-02	85	0	0
Crystal Palace	L	09.02	02	5	0	0

MICKLEWHITE Gary
Southwark, 21 March, 1961 (W)

League Club	Source	Date Signed	Seasons Played	Apps	Subs	Gls
Manchester U	App	03.78				
Queens Park Rgrs	Tr	07.79	80-84	97	9	11
Derby Co	Tr	02.85	84-92	223	17	31
Gillingham	Tr	07.93	93-95	78	17	3

MICKLEWRIGHT Andrew (Andy) Alfred Joseph
Birmingham, 31 January, 1931 (IF)

League Club	Source	Date Signed	Seasons Played	Apps	Subs	Gls
Bristol Rov	Smethwick Highfield	01.52	51-52	8	-	1
Bristol C	Tr	05.53	53-54	39	-	17
Swindon T	Tr	09.55	55-58	114	-	31
Exeter C	Tr	07.59	59	38	-	11

MICKLEWRIGHT John Leslie **(Les)**
Stoke-on-Trent, 13 October, 1915 Died 1991 (WH)

League Club	Source	Date Signed	Seasons Played	Apps	Subs	Gls
Crewe Alex	Stafford Rgrs	09.46	46-49	71	-	0

MIDDLEBROUGH Alan
Wardle, 4 December, 1925 (CF)

League Club	Source	Date Signed	Seasons Played	Apps	Subs	Gls
Bolton W		07.46	46-47	5	-	1
Bradford C	Tr	08.48	48	4	-	0
Rochdale	Tr	10.48	48-51	47	-	25

MIDDLEMASS Clive
Leeds, 25 August, 1944 (CD)

League Club	Source	Date Signed	Seasons Played	Apps	Subs	Gls
Leeds U	Jnrs	08.62				
Workington	Tr	11.63	63-69	168	1	6

MIDDLEMISS Ernest (Ernie)
Newcastle, 30 August, 1920 Died 1999 (CF)

League Club	Source	Date Signed	Seasons Played	Apps	Subs	Gls
Lincoln C	South Shields	06.48	48	2	-	0

MIDDLETON Craig Dean
Nuneaton, 10 September, 1970 (M)

League Club	Source	Date Signed	Seasons Played	Apps	Subs	Gls
Coventry C	YT	05.89	89-92	2	1	0
Cambridge U	Tr	07.93	93-95	55	4	10
Cardiff C	Tr	08.96	96-99	95	24	8
Plymouth Arg	L	01.00	99	6	0	2
Halifax T	Tr	03.00	99-01	66	10	8

MIDDLETON Derek
Ashby-de-la-Zouch, 30 May, 1934 (WH)

League Club	Source	Date Signed	Seasons Played	Apps	Subs	Gls
York C	Burton A	11.58	58	1	-	0

MIDDLETON Frederick (Fred) Thomas
West Hartlepool, 2 August, 1930 (WH)

League Club	Source	Date Signed	Seasons Played	Apps	Subs	Gls
Newcastle U	Jnrs	04.48				
Lincoln C	Tr	05.54	54-62	300	-	16

MIDDLETON Henry (Harry)
Birmingham, 18 March, 1937 EYth (F)

League Club	Source	Date Signed	Seasons Played	Apps	Subs	Gls
Wolverhampton W	Jnrs	08.54	55	1	-	0
Scunthorpe U	Tr	09.59	59-60	29	-	11
Portsmouth	Tr	06.61	61	17	-	5
Shrewsbury T	Tr	02.62	61-64	85	-	36
Mansfield T	Tr	11.64	64-65	45	1	24
Walsall	Tr	03.66	65-67	56	2	27

MIDDLETON James
Blackridge, 25 April, 1922 (WH)

League Club	Source	Date Signed	Seasons Played	Apps	Subs	Gls
Bradford C	Third Lanark	05.49	49	8	-	0

MIDDLETON John
Rawmarsh, 11 July, 1955 (CD)

League Club	Source	Date Signed	Seasons Played	Apps	Subs	Gls
Bradford C	App	07.73	72-78	188	4	5

MIDDLETON John
Skegness, 24 December, 1956 EYth/Eu21-3 (G)

League Club	Source	Date Signed	Seasons Played	Apps	Subs	Gls
Nottingham F	App	11.74	74-77	90	0	0
Derby Co	Tr	09.77	77-79	73	0	0

MIDDLETON Lee John
Nuneaton, 10 September, 1970 (FB)

League Club	Source	Date Signed	Seasons Played	Apps	Subs	Gls
Coventry C	YT	05.89	89	0	2	0
Swindon T	Tr	07.92				
Cambridge U	Tr	11.95	95	1	2	0

MIDDLETON Matthew (Matt) Young
Boldon Colliery, 24 October, 1907 Died 1979 (G)

League Club	Source	Date Signed	Seasons Played	Apps	Subs	Gls
Southport	Boldon CW	02.31	31-32	63	-	0
Sunderland	Tr	08.33	33-38	56	-	0
Plymouth Arg	Tr	05.39				
Bradford C	Horden CW	08.46	46-48	94	-	0
York C	Tr	02.49	48-49	55	-	0

MIDDLETON Peter Watson
Rawmarsh, 13 September, 1948 Died 1977 (M)

League Club	Source	Date Signed	Seasons Played	Apps	Subs	Gls
Sheffield Wed	App	09.65				
Bradford C	Tr	06.68	68-72	127	4	25
Plymouth Arg	Tr	09.72	72	1	0	1

MIDDLETON Raymond (Ray)
Boldon, 6 September, 1919 Died 1977 EB (G)

League Club	Source	Date Signed	Seasons Played	Apps	Subs	Gls
Chesterfield	North Shields	10.37	38-50	250	-	0
Derby Co	Tr	06.51	51-53	116	-	0

MIDDLETON Robert (Ray) Rex
Retford, 8 December, 1933 (IF)

League Club	Source	Date Signed	Seasons Played	Apps	Subs	Gls
Southend U	Bulford U	11.57	57	5	-	1
Workington	Tr	10.58	58	2	-	0
Swindon T	Tr	12.58	58	5	-	0
Aldershot	Tr	07.59	59	5	-	0

MIDDLETON Stephen (Steve) Roy
Portsmouth, 28 March, 1953 (G)

League Club	Source	Date Signed	Seasons Played	Apps	Subs	Gls
Southampton	App	07.70	73-76	24	0	0
Torquay U	L	03.75	74	10	0	0
Portsmouth	Tr	07.77	77	26	0	0

MIDGLEY Craig Steven
Bradford, 24 May, 1976 (F)

League Club	Source	Date Signed	Seasons Played	Apps	Subs	Gls
Bradford C	YT	07.95	94-97	0	11	1
Scarborough	L	12.95	95	14	2	1
Scarborough	L	03.97	96	6	0	2
Darlington	L	12.97	97	1	0	0
Hartlepool U	Tr	03.98	97-00	61	35	18
Halifax T	Tr	07.01	01	12	12	3

MIDGLEY Neil Alan
Cambridge, 21 October, 1978 (F)

League Club	Source	Date Signed	Seasons Played	Apps	Subs	Gls
Ipswich T	YT	06.97	99	1	3	1
Luton T	L	09.99	99	8	2	3
Barnet	Tr	03.01	00	3	1	0

[MIDO] HOSSAM Ahmed Abdel Hamid
Cairo, Egypt, 23 February, 1983 Egypt int (F)

League Club	Source	Date Signed	Seasons Played	Apps	Subs	Gls
Tottenham H (L)	AS Roma (It)	01.05	04	4	5	2

MIDWOOD Michael Adrian
Burnley, 19 April, 1976 (F)

League Club	Source	Date Signed	Seasons Played	Apps	Subs	Gls
Huddersfield T	YT	07.94				
Huddersfield T	Halifax T	08.97	97	0	1	0

MIELCZAREK Raymond (Ray)
Caernarfon, 10 February, 1946 Wu23-2/W-1 (CD)

League Club	Source	Date Signed	Seasons Played	Apps	Subs	Gls
Wrexham	Jnrs	05.64	64-67	76	0	0
Huddersfield T	Tr	09.67	67-70	25	1	1
Rotherham U	Tr	01.71	70-73	114	1	7

MIGLIORANZI Stefani
Pocos de Caldas, Brazil, 20 September, 1977 (M)

League Club	Source	Date Signed	Seasons Played	Apps	Subs	Gls
Portsmouth	St John's Univ (USA)	03.99	98-01	25	10	2
Swindon T	Tr	08.02	02-04	89	8	7

MIHAILOV Borislav (Bobby) Biserov
Sofia, Bulgaria, 12 February, 1963 Bulgaria int (G)

League Club	Source	Date Signed	Seasons Played	Apps	Subs	Gls
Reading	Botev Plovdiv (Bul)	09.95	95-96	24	0	0

MIHALY Ronald (Ron) Raymond
Chesterfield, 14 October, 1952 ESch (CD)

League Club	Source	Date Signed	Seasons Played	Apps	Subs	Gls
Chesterfield	App	08.71	71	4	0	0

MIKE Adrian (Adie) Roosevelt
Manchester, 16 November, 1973 ESch/EYth (F)

League Club	Source	Date Signed	Seasons Played	Apps	Subs	Gls
Manchester C	YT	07.92	91-94	5	11	2
Bury	L	03.93	92	5	2	1
Stockport Co	Tr	08.95	95-96	4	5	0
Hartlepool U	L	10.96	96	7	0	1
Doncaster Rov	L	02.97	96	5	0	1
Doncaster Rov	Tr	08.97	97	42	0	4
Lincoln C	Stalybridge Celtic	08.02	02	5	12	2

MIKE Leon Jonathan
Manchester, 4 September, 1981 ESch/EYth (F)

League Club	Source	Date Signed	Seasons Played	Apps	Subs	Gls
Manchester C	YT	09.98	01	1	1	0
Oxford U	L	09.00	00	1	2	0
Halifax T	L	02.01	00	2	5	0

MIKLOSKO Ludek
Ostrava, Czech Republic, 9 December, 1961 Czu23/CzB-1/Cz-44 (G)

League Club	Source	Date Signed	Seasons Played	Apps	Subs	Gls
West Ham U	Banik Ostrava (Cz)	02.90	89-97	315	0	0
Queens Park Rgrs	Tr	10.98	98-00	57	0	0

MILBOURNE Ian
Hexham, 21 January, 1979 (F)

League Club	Source	Date Signed	Seasons Played	Apps	Subs	Gls
Newcastle U	YT	07.97				
Scarborough	Tr	08.98	98	2	14	0

MILBURN George William
Ashington, 24 June, 1910 Died 1980 (FB)

League Club	Source	Date Signed	Seasons Played	Apps	Subs	Gls
Leeds U	Ashington CW	03.28	28-36	157	-	1
Chesterfield	Tr	05.37	37-47	105	-	16

MILBURN James (Jim)
Ashington, 21 June, 1919 Died 1985 (FB)

League Club	Source	Date Signed	Seasons Played	Apps	Subs	Gls
Leeds U	Ashington	10.36	46-51	207	-	15
Bradford PA	Tr	06.52	52-54	90	-	10

MILBURN John (Jack)
Ashington, 18 March, 1908 Died 1979 (FB)

League Club	Source	Date Signed	Seasons Played	Apps	Subs	Gls
Leeds U	Spen Black & White	11.27	29-38	386	-	28
Norwich C	Tr	02.39	38	15	-	0
Bradford C	Tr	10.46	46	14	-	3

MILBURN John (Jackie) Edward Thompson
Ashington, 11 May, 1924 Died 1988 FLge-3/IrLge-4/E-13 (CF)

League Club	Source	Date Signed	Seasons Played	Apps	Subs	Gls
Newcastle U	Ashington ATC	08.43	46-56	353	-	177

MILBURN Stanley (Stan)
Ashington, 27 October, 1926 EB/FLge-2 (FB)

League Club	Source	Date Signed	Seasons Played	Apps	Subs	Gls
Chesterfield	Ashington	01.47	46-51	179	-	0
Leicester C	Tr	03.52	51-57	173	-	1
Rochdale	Tr	01.59	58-64	238	-	26

MILBURN William Renton Wakenshaw
Sunniside, 25 January, 1932 (WH)

League Club	Source	Date Signed	Seasons Played	Apps	Subs	Gls
Gateshead		04.55	56	2	-	0

MILD Hakan
Trollhattan, Sweden, 14 June, 1971 Sweden 74 (M)

League Club	Source	Date Signed	Seasons Played	Apps	Subs	Gls
Wimbledon	IFK Gothenburg (Swe)	11.01	01	8	1	0

MILDENHALL Stephen (Steve) James
Swindon, 13 May, 1978 (G)

League Club	Source	Date Signed	Seasons Played	Apps	Subs	Gls
Swindon T	YT	07.96	96-00	29	4	0
Notts Co	Tr	07.01	01-04	75	1	0
Oldham Ath	Tr	12.04	04	6	0	0

MILES Andrew (Andy)
Tredegar, 25 May, 1961 (W)

League Club	Source	Date Signed	Seasons Played	Apps	Subs	Gls
Newport Co	Ebbw Vale	08.85	85	3	1	2

MILES Denis
Normanton, 6 August, 1936 (W)

League Club	Source	Date Signed	Seasons Played	Apps	Subs	Gls
Bradford PA	Snydale Ath	09.53	53-54	24	-	1
Southport	Tr	06.55	55-56	51	-	12

MILES Jeffrey (Jeff)
Caldicot, 17 January, 1949 (G)

League Club	Source	Date Signed	Seasons Played	Apps	Subs	Gls
Newport Co	Cheltenham T	04.68	67-68	4	0	0

League Club	Source	Date Signed	Seasons Played	Apps	Subs	Gls
MILES John Francis						
Fazakerley, 28 September, 1981						(F)
Liverpool	YT	04.99				
Stoke C	Tr	03.02	01	0	1	0
Crewe Alex	Tr	08.02	02	0	5	1
Macclesfield T	Tr	03.03	02-04	44	23	13
MILES Sidney (Sid) George						
Bournemouth, 16 May, 1934						(CD)
Bournemouth		12.56	57	1	-	0
MILES Terence (Terry)						
Stoke-on-Trent, 7 May, 1937						(CD)
Port Vale	Milton YC	06.55	56-67	358	7	17
MILKINS Albert John						
Dagenham, 3 January, 1944 EYth						(G)
Portsmouth	Jnrs	05.61	60-73	344	0	0
Oxford U	Tr	08.74	74-78	53	0	0
MILLAR Alexander (Ally)						
Glasgow, 15 January, 1952						(M)
Barnsley	Glasgow Benburb	02.71	70-79	273	16	17
York C	Tr	07.80	80	11	1	0
MILLAR Albert James						
Falkirk, 21 December, 1927 Died 1997						(FB)
Crewe Alex	Deal T	08.58	58-59	56	-	2
MILLAR John						
Coatbridge, 8 December, 1966						(FB)
Chelsea	Jnrs	08.84	85-86	11	0	0
Northampton T	L	01.87	86	1	0	0
Blackburn Rov	Tr	07.87	87-90	122	4	1
MILLAR John						
Auchterderran, 31 December, 1927 Died 1991						(IF)
Bradford C	Queen of the South	10.48	49-51	44	-	7
Grimsby T	Tr	05.52	52	5	-	2
MILLAR John Ross						
Armadale, 25 October, 1923 Died 1986						(CF)
Bradford C	Albion Rov	06.49	49	3	-	1
MILLAR William Paul						
Belfast, 16 November, 1966 NIu23-1						(M)
Port Vale	Portadown	12.88	89-90	19	21	5
Hereford U	L	10.90	90	5	0	2
Cardiff C	Tr	08.91	91-94	91	29	17
MILLAR Thomas (Tommy) Thomson						
Edinburgh, 3 December, 1938 Died 2001						(FB)
Colchester U	Bo'ness U	06.59	59-61	44	-	4
MILLAR William (Willie)						
Irvine, 24 July, 1924 Died 1995						(W)
Swindon T	Stirling A	08.50	50-52	75	-	18
Gillingham	Tr	07.53	53-55	91	-	35
Accrington St	Tr	07.56	56	26	-	11
MILLAR William (Billy)						
Mansfield, 7 February, 1952						(G)
Doncaster Rov (Am)	Folkhouse OB	02.75	74	1	0	0
MILLARD Lance Julian						
Bristol, 24 June, 1938						(G)
Aldershot		03.61	60	12	-	0
Barrow	Tr	07.64	64-65	52	0	0
MILLARD Leonard (Len)						
Coseley, 7 March, 1919 Died 1997						(FB)
West Bromwich A	Sunbeam	05.37	46-57	436	-	7
MILLARD Robert (Ray)						
South Shields, 2 June, 1927						(IF)
Middlesbrough		12.45				
Reading	Blyth Spartans	06.49	49	2	-	0
Walsall	Tr	06.50	50	10	-	1
MILLBANK Joseph (Joe) Henry						
Edmonton, 30 September, 1919 Died 1999						(CD)
Wolverhampton W		07.38				
Crystal Palace	Tr	08.39	46-47	38	-	1
Queens Park Rgrs	Tr	07.48	48	1	-	0
MILLEN Keith Derek						
Croydon, 26 September, 1966						(CD)
Brentford	Jnrs	08.84	84-92	301	4	17
Watford	Tr	03.94	93-98	163	2	5
Bristol C	Tr	11.99	99-02	59	1	4

League Club	Source	Date Signed	Seasons Played	Apps	Subs	Gls
MILLER Adam Edward						
Hemel Hempstead, 19 February, 1982						(M)
Queens Park Rgrs	Aldershot T	11.04	04	9	5	0
MILLER Alan John						
Epping, 29 March, 1970 ESch/EYth/Eu21-4						(G)
Arsenal	YT	05.88	92-93	6	2	0
Plymouth Arg	L	11.88	88	13	0	0
West Bromwich A	L	08.91	91	3	0	0
Birmingham C	L	12.91	91	15	0	0
Middlesbrough	Tr	08.94	94-96	57	0	0
Grimsby T	L	01.97	96	3	0	0
West Bromwich A	Tr	02.97	96-99	98	0	0
Blackburn Rov	Tr	02.00	99	1	0	0
Bristol C	L	08.00	00	4	0	0
Coventry C	L	11.00	00	0	1	0
MILLER Alan John						
Preston, 13 September, 1970						(W)
Torquay U	Bury (YT)	08.89	89	3	1	0
MILLER Alfred (Alf) George Abraham						
Portsmouth, 5 March, 1917 Died 1999						(WH)
Portsmouth	Jnrs	11.35				
Bristol Rov	Margate	07.37				
Southport	Tr	10.37	37-38	32	-	2
Plymouth Arg	Tr	07.39	46-47	9	-	0
MILLER James Alistair Williamson						
Glasgow, 24 January, 1936						(W)
Brighton & Hove A	St Mirren	04.62	61	1	-	0
Norwich C	Tr	05.62	62-63	23	-	2
MILLER Anthony (Tony) William						
Chelmsford, 26 October, 1937						(IF)
Colchester U	Jnrs	05.58	59-63	3	-	0
MILLER Archibald (Archie)						
Larkhall, 5 September, 1913 SLge-1/SWar-1/S-1						(WH)
Blackburn Rov	Heart of Midlothian	11.47	47	6	-	0
Carlisle U	Kilmarnock	09.50	50	1	-	0
Workington	Heart of Midlothian	02.52	51	1	-	0
MILLER Barry Steven						
Greenford, 29 March, 1976						(CD)
Gillingham	Farnborough T	08.99	99	1	3	0
MILLER Brian George						
Hapton, 19 January, 1937 Eu23-3/FLge-2/E-1						(WH)
Burnley	Jnrs	02.54	55-66	379	0	29
MILLER Charles (Charlie)						
Glasgow, 18 March, 1976 SSch/Su21-8/S-1						(M)
Leicester C (L)	Glasgow Rgrs	03.99	98	1	3	0
Watford	Glasgow Rgrs	10.99	99	9	5	0
MILLER Colin Fyfe						
Lanark, 4 October, 1964 Canada int						(M)
Doncaster Rov	Glasgow Rgrs	12.86	86-87	61	0	3
MILLER David (Dave)						
Middlesbrough, 21 January, 1921 Died 1989						(WH)
Middlesbrough	Jnrs	09.38				
Wolverhampton W	Tr	08.45	46	2	-	0
Derby Co	Tr	04.47	47	1	-	0
Doncaster Rov	Tr	01.48	47-52	140	-	3
Aldershot	Tr	03.54	53	11	-	0
MILLER David (Dave) Brian						
Burnley, 8 January, 1964						(CD)
Burnley	App	01.82	82-84	27	5	3
Crewe Alex	L	03.83	82	3	0	0
Tranmere Rov	Tr	07.85	85	25	4	1
Preston NE	Colne Dynamoes	12.86	86-89	50	8	2
Burnley	L	02.89	88	4	0	0
Carlisle U	Tr	09.89	89-91	108	1	7
Stockport Co	Tr	03.92	91-94	72	9	1
Wigan Ath	Tr	10.94	94-95	35	3	3
MILLER Edward (Eddie)						
Ulverston, 21 June, 1920 Died 2002						(IF)
Barrow	Ulverston	05.46	46-50	124	-	30
MILLER George						
Larkhall, 20 May, 1939 SLge-1						(WH)
Wolverhampton W	Dunfermline Ath	10.64	64-65	37	0	3
MILLER Ernest George						
South Africa, 17 October, 1927						(IF)
Leeds U	Arcadia Shepherds (SA)	11.50	50-51	13	-	1
Workington	Tr	03.52	51	11	-	0

MILLER Graham Joseph Patrick
South Africa, 25 August, 1927 (CF)

League Club	Source	Date Signed	Seasons Played	Apps	Subs	Gls
Workington		12.52	52	10	-	1

MILLER Ian
Perth, 13 May, 1955 (W)

League Club	Source	Date Signed	Seasons Played	Apps	Subs	Gls
Bury	Jeanfield Swifts	08.73	73	9	6	0
Nottingham F	Tr	08.74				
Doncaster Rov	Tr	08.75	75-77	124	0	14
Swindon T	Tr	07.78	78-80	123	4	9
Blackburn Rov	Tr	08.81	81-88	252	16	16
Port Vale	Tr	07.89	89	14	7	1
Scunthorpe U	Tr	08.90	90	8	4	0

MILLER John (Johnny) Tony
Ipswich, 21 September, 1950 (W)

League Club	Source	Date Signed	Seasons Played	Apps	Subs	Gls
Ipswich T	Jnrs	07.68	68-73	38	13	2
Norwich C	Tr	10.74	74-75	22	1	3
Mansfield T	Tr	07.76	76-79	109	4	14
Port Vale	Tr	09.80	80	22	4	4

MILLER Joseph McSpirits
Glasgow, 2 October, 1934 (W)

League Club	Source	Date Signed	Seasons Played	Apps	Subs	Gls
Swindon T	Hamilton Academical	06.56	56	12	-	0

MILLER Justin James
Johannesburg, South Africa, 16 December, 1980 (CD)

League Club	Source	Date Signed	Seasons Played	Apps	Subs	Gls
Ipswich T	Jnrs	11.99				
Leyton Orient	L	09.02	02	13	0	0
Leyton Orient	Tr	01.03	02-04	76	7	2

MILLER Keith Raymond
Lewisham, 26 January, 1948 (FB)

League Club	Source	Date Signed	Seasons Played	Apps	Subs	Gls
West Ham U	Walthamstow Ave	09.65	68-69	1	2	0
Bournemouth	Tr	07.70	70-79	381	2	19

MILLER Kenneth (Kenny)
Edinburgh, 23 December, 1979 Su21-7/SB-1/S-19 (F)

League Club	Source	Date Signed	Seasons Played	Apps	Subs	Gls
Wolverhampton W (L)	Glasgow Rgrs	09.01	01	3	2	2
Wolverhampton W	Glasgow Rgrs	12.01	01-04	95	32	40

MILLER Kevin
Falmouth, 15 March, 1969 (G)

League Club	Source	Date Signed	Seasons Played	Apps	Subs	Gls
Exeter C	Newquay	03.89	88-92	163	0	0
Birmingham C	Tr	05.93	93	24	0	0
Watford	Tr	08.94	94-96	128	0	0
Crystal Palace	Tr	07.97	97-98	66	0	0
Barnsley	Tr	08.99	99-01	115	0	0
Exeter C	Tr	08.02	02	46	0	0
Bristol Rov	Tr	07.03	03-04	72	0	0

MILLER Lee Adamson
Lanark, 18 May, 1983 (F)

League Club	Source	Date Signed	Seasons Played	Apps	Subs	Gls
Bristol C	Falkirk	07.03	03-04	34	15	8

MILLER Liam William Peter
Cork, 13 February, 1981 IRu21-15/IR-9 (M)

League Club	Source	Date Signed	Seasons Played	Apps	Subs	Gls
Manchester U	Glasgow Celtic	07.04	04	3	5	0

MILLER Mark John
Tynemouth, 22 September, 1962 (W)

League Club	Source	Date Signed	Seasons Played	Apps	Subs	Gls
Gillingham	Whitley Bay	10.81	81-82	5	4	1
Doncaster Rov	Whitley Bay	08.83	83	21	9	4
Darlington	Tr	08.84	84	4	3	1

MILLER Paul Anthony
Bisley, 31 January, 1968 (M)

League Club	Source	Date Signed	Seasons Played	Apps	Subs	Gls
Wimbledon	Yeovil T	08.87	87-92	65	15	10
Newport Co	L	10.87	87	6	0	2
Bristol C	L	01.90	89	0	3	0
Bristol Rov	Tr	08.94	94-96	100	5	22
Lincoln C	Tr	08.97	97-00	93	22	11

MILLER Joseph **Paul**
Wolverhampton, 9 December, 1940 Died 1963 (G)

League Club	Source	Date Signed	Seasons Played	Apps	Subs	Gls
Shrewsbury T	St Nicholas BC	07.59	59-62	77	-	0

MILLER Paul Richard
Stepney, 11 October, 1959 (CD)

League Club	Source	Date Signed	Seasons Played	Apps	Subs	Gls
Tottenham H	App	05.77	78-86	206	2	7
Charlton Ath	Tr	02.87	86-88	40	2	2
Watford	Tr	10.88	88	20	0	1
Bournemouth	Tr	08.89	89-90	43	4	1
Brentford	L	11.89	89	3	0	0
Swansea C	Tr	01.91	90	8	4	0

MILLER Peter Derek
Hoyland, 4 December, 1929 (CF)

League Club	Source	Date Signed	Seasons Played	Apps	Subs	Gls
Bradford C		08.52	52-55	18	-	2

MILLER Ralph Ernest
Slough, 22 June, 1941 (FB)

League Club	Source	Date Signed	Seasons Played	Apps	Subs	Gls
Charlton Ath	Slough T	09.63	64	8	-	0
Gillingham	Tr	05.65	65-67	103	0	4
Bournemouth	Tr	07.68	68-70	71	1	1

MILLER Robert (Robbie)
Bedford, 28 March, 1980 (M)

League Club	Source	Date Signed	Seasons Played	Apps	Subs	Gls
Coventry C	West Ham U (YT)	08.98				
Cambridge U	Tr	08.99	99	0	1	0

MILLER Robert James
Manchester, 3 November, 1972 (FB)

League Club	Source	Date Signed	Seasons Played	Apps	Subs	Gls
Oldham Ath	YT	07.91				
Hull C	Tr	10.92	92-93	22	6	0

MILLER Lumley **Robert (Bob)**
Blaydon, 3 August, 1938 (W)

League Club	Source	Date Signed	Seasons Played	Apps	Subs	Gls
Sheffield U		07.62				
Hartlepools U	Tr	11.62	62	9	-	2

MILLER Roger Lucas
Rushden, 18 August, 1938 (IF)

League Club	Source	Date Signed	Seasons Played	Apps	Subs	Gls
Northampton T	Jnrs	11.56	56-58	4	-	1

MILLER Thomas (Tommy) William
Easington, 8 January, 1979 (M)

League Club	Source	Date Signed	Seasons Played	Apps	Subs	Gls
Hartlepool U	YT	07.97	97-00	130	7	35
Ipswich T	Tr	07.01	01-04	101	16	30

MILLER Walter
Cornforth, 11 August, 1930 (WH)

League Club	Source	Date Signed	Seasons Played	Apps	Subs	Gls
Hartlepools U		09.48	49	1	-	0

MILLER William (Willie) Nesbit
Edinburgh, 1 November, 1969 (FB)

League Club	Source	Date Signed	Seasons Played	Apps	Subs	Gls
Wrexham (L)	Dundee	09.01	01	5	0	0

MILLETT Glynne Alexander
Crickhowell, 13 October, 1968 (M)

League Club	Source	Date Signed	Seasons Played	Apps	Subs	Gls
Newport Co	YT	07.87	86-87	23	13	2

MILLETT Michael Paul
Wigan, 22 September, 1977 Died 1995 ESch/EYth (CD)

League Club	Source	Date Signed	Seasons Played	Apps	Subs	Gls
Wigan Ath	YT	10.94	94	1	2	0

MILLIGAN Charles (Chic) Campbell
Ardrossan, 26 July, 1930 (CD)

League Club	Source	Date Signed	Seasons Played	Apps	Subs	Gls
Colchester U	Ardrossan Winton Rov	05.56	56-60	185	-	3

MILLIGAN Dudley
Johannesburg, South Africa, 7 November, 1916 I-1 (CF)

League Club	Source	Date Signed	Seasons Played	Apps	Subs	Gls
Chesterfield	Clyde (SA)	11.38	38-46	47	-	18
Bournemouth	Tr	08.47	47-48	45	-	25
Walsall	Tr	10.48	48	5	-	1

MILLIGAN Jamie
Blackpool, 3 January, 1980 EYth (M)

League Club	Source	Date Signed	Seasons Played	Apps	Subs	Gls
Everton	YT	06.97	98-99	0	4	0
Blackpool	Tr	03.01	00-02	10	20	1

MILLIGAN Laurence (Laurie) Courtney
Liverpool, 20 April, 1958 (FB)

League Club	Source	Date Signed	Seasons Played	Apps	Subs	Gls
Blackpool	App	04.76	76-78	19	0	0
Portsmouth	L	03.79	78	7	0	0
Rochdale	Aldershot (N/C)	10.79	79	8	1	0

MILLIGAN Michael (Mike) Joseph
Manchester, 20 February, 1967 IRu23-1/IRu21-1/IRB-2/IR-1 (M)

League Club	Source	Date Signed	Seasons Played	Apps	Subs	Gls
Oldham Ath	App	03.85	85-89	161	1	17
Everton	Tr	08.90	90	16	1	1
Oldham Ath	Tr	07.91	91-93	117	0	6
Norwich C	Tr	06.94	94-99	113	11	5
Blackpool	Tr	07.00	00-01	25	3	1

MILLIGAN Ross
Dumfries, 2 June, 1978 (FB)

League Club	Source	Date Signed	Seasons Played	Apps	Subs	Gls
Carlisle U	Glasgow Rgrs	07.97	97	2	5	0

MILLIGAN Stephen (Steve) Jonathan Francis
Hyde, 13 June, 1973 (FB)

League Club	Source	Date Signed	Seasons Played	Apps	Subs	Gls
Rochdale	YT	●	89	5	0	1

MILLIGAN Terence (Terry) John
Manchester, 10 January, 1966 (M)

League Club	Source	Date Signed	Seasons Played	Apps	Subs	Gls
Manchester C	App	11.83				
Oldham Ath	(New Zealand)	02.86				
Crewe Alex	Tr	07.86	86-87	71	6	5

MILLIN Alfred (Alf)
Rotherham, 18 December, 1933 (W)

League Club	Source	Date Signed	Seasons Played	Apps	Subs	Gls
Derby Co	Jnrs	08.51	55	1	-	0

MILLINGTON Anthony (Tony) Horace
Hawarden, 5 June, 1943 Wu23-4/W-21 (G)

League Club	Source	Date Signed	Seasons Played	Apps	Subs	Gls
West Bromwich A	Sutton T	07.60	61-62	40	-	0
Crystal Palace	Tr	10.64	64-65	16	0	0
Peterborough U	Tr	03.66	66-68	118	0	0
Swansea C	Tr	07.69	69-73	178	0	0

MILLINGTON Grenville (Gren) Rodney
Queensferry, 10 December, 1951 WAmat (G)

League Club	Source	Date Signed	Seasons Played	Apps	Subs	Gls
Chester (Am)	Rhyl	07.68	68	1	0	0
Chester	Witton A	09.73	73-82	289	0	0
Wrexham	Oswestry T	12.83	83	13	0	0

MILLINGTON John Henry
Coseley, 21 February, 1930 (WH)

League Club	Source	Date Signed	Seasons Played	Apps	Subs	Gls
Aston Villa	Jnrs	09.48				
Walsall	Tr	07.51	51-52	23	-	0

MILLINGTON Ralph Victor
Neston, 18 June, 1930 Died 1999 (CD)

League Club	Source	Date Signed	Seasons Played	Apps	Subs	Gls
Tranmere Rov	Neston	01.50	50-60	357	-	3

MILLION Esmond
Ashington, 15 March, 1938 (G)

League Club	Source	Date Signed	Seasons Played	Apps	Subs	Gls
Middlesbrough	Amble Jnrs	05.56	56-61	52	-	0
Bristol Rov	Tr	06.62	62	38	-	0

MILLS Brian
Stone, 26 December, 1971 EYth (F)

League Club	Source	Date Signed	Seasons Played	Apps	Subs	Gls
Port Vale	YT	04.90	90-91	14	9	4

MILLS Daniel (Danny) John
Norwich, 18 May, 1977 EYth/Eu21-14/E-19 (FB)

League Club	Source	Date Signed	Seasons Played	Apps	Subs	Gls
Norwich C	YT	11.94	95-97	46	20	0
Charlton Ath	Tr	03.98	97-98	45	0	3
Leeds U	Tr	07.99	99-02	96	5	3
Middlesbrough	L	08.03	03	28	0	0
Manchester C	Tr	07.04	04	29	3	0

MILLS Daniel (Danny) Raymond
Sidcup, 13 February, 1975 (W)

League Club	Source	Date Signed	Seasons Played	Apps	Subs	Gls
Charlton Ath	YT	07.93				
Barnet	Tr	09.95	95-97	10	17	0
Brighton & Hove A	Tr	07.98	98	1	1	0

MILLS David John
Robin Hood's Bay, 6 December, 1951 Eu23-8/EB (F)

League Club	Source	Date Signed	Seasons Played	Apps	Subs	Gls
Middlesbrough	App	12.68	68-78	278	18	76
West Bromwich A	Tr	01.79	78-82	44	15	6
Newcastle U	L	01.82	81	23	0	4
Sheffield Wed	Tr	01.83	82	15	0	3
Newcastle U	Tr	08.83	83	10	6	5
Middlesbrough	Tr	06.84	84	31	1	14
Darlington	Whitby T	08.86	86	12	5	2

MILLS Donald (Don)
Maltby, 17 August, 1926 Died 1994 (IF)

League Club	Source	Date Signed	Seasons Played	Apps	Subs	Gls
Queens Park Rgrs		08.46	46-50	76	-	9
Torquay U	L	03.49	48	12	-	4
Torquay U	L	08.49	49	22	-	9
Cardiff C	Tr	02.51	50	1	-	0
Leeds U	Tr	09.51	51-52	34	-	9
Torquay U	Tr	12.52	52-61	308	-	68

MILLS Garry Leonard
Faversham, 20 May, 1981 (M)

League Club	Source	Date Signed	Seasons Played	Apps	Subs	Gls
Rushden & Diamonds	Jnrs	07.99	01-04	58	18	2

MILLS Gary Roland
Northampton, 11 November, 1961 ESch/EYth/Eu21-2 (M)

League Club	Source	Date Signed	Seasons Played	Apps	Subs	Gls
Nottingham F	App	11.78	78-81	50	8	8
Derby Co	Seattle (USA)	10.82	82	18	0	2
Nottingham F	Seattle (USA)	03.83	83-86	63	15	4
Notts Co	Tr	08.87	87-88	75	0	8
Leicester C	Tr	03.89	88-94	195	5	15
Notts Co	Tr	09.94	94-95	44	3	0

MILLS Henry (Harry)
Bishop Auckland, 23 July, 1922 (IF)

League Club	Source	Date Signed	Seasons Played	Apps	Subs	Gls
Sheffield U	Consett	06.46	46	3	-	2
Rotherham U	Tr	03.48	47	6	-	3
Rochdale	Tunbridge Wells	04.51	50	1	-	0

MILLS Henry (Harry) Owen
Blyth, 23 August, 1922 Died 1990 (G)

League Club	Source	Date Signed	Seasons Played	Apps	Subs	Gls
Huddersfield T	Blyth Spartans	03.48	47-55	157	-	0
Halifax T	Tr	12.55	55-56	27	-	0

MILLS James
Dalton Brook, 30 September, 1915 Died 1994 (WH)

League Club	Source	Date Signed	Seasons Played	Apps	Subs	Gls
Rotherham U	Dinnington Ath	08.37	37-38	54	-	4
Hull C	Tr	10.46	46-47	42	-	1
Halifax T	Tr	12.47	47	19	-	0

MILLS Jamie Mark
Swindon, 31 August, 1981 (M)

League Club	Source	Date Signed	Seasons Played	Apps	Subs	Gls
Swindon T	YT	07.99	00	0	2	0

MILLS John
Bagillt, 19 December, 1920 Died 1982 (FB)

League Club	Source	Date Signed	Seasons Played	Apps	Subs	Gls
Chester		05.46	46	3	-	0

MILLS Keith
Newcastle, 30 December, 1963 (M)

League Club	Source	Date Signed	Seasons Played	Apps	Subs	Gls
Carlisle U	North Shields	02.88	87	0	1	0

MILLS Keith David
Egham, 29 December, 1942 (WH)

League Club	Source	Date Signed	Seasons Played	Apps	Subs	Gls
Grimsby T	Jnrs	01.60	60	2	-	0

MILLS Rowan Lee
Mexborough, 10 July, 1970 (F)

League Club	Source	Date Signed	Seasons Played	Apps	Subs	Gls
Wolverhampton W	Stocksbridge Pk Steels	12.92	93-94	12	13	2
Derby Co	Tr	02.95	94	16	0	7
Port Vale	Tr	08.95	95-97	81	28	35
Bradford C	Tr	08.98	98-99	63	2	28
Manchester C	L	03.00	99	1	2	0
Portsmouth	Tr	08.00	00-01	24	2	4
Coventry C	Tr	11.01	01-02	30	8	7
Stoke C	Tr	01.03	02	7	4	2

MILLS Matthew Claude
Swindon, 14 July, 1986 EYth (CD)

League Club	Source	Date Signed	Seasons Played	Apps	Subs	Gls
Southampton	Sch	07.04				
Coventry C	L	09.04	04	4	0	0
Bournemouth	L	02.05	04	12	0	3

MILLS Michael (Mick) Denis
Godalming, 4 January, 1949 EYth/Eu23-5/FLge-2/E-42 (FB)

League Club	Source	Date Signed	Seasons Played	Apps	Subs	Gls
Ipswich T	Portsmouth (App)	02.66	65-82	588	3	22
Southampton	Tr	11.82	82-84	103	0	3
Stoke C	Tr	07.85	85-87	38	0	0

MILLS Neil
Littleborough, 27 October, 1963 (F)

League Club	Source	Date Signed	Seasons Played	Apps	Subs	Gls
Rochdale	Tim Bobbin	08.86	86	4	6	0
Stockport Co	Tr	08.87	87	5	2	0

MILLS Pablo Simeon
Birmingham, 27 May, 1984 EYth (CD)

League Club	Source	Date Signed	Seasons Played	Apps	Subs	Gls
Derby Co	Sch	07.02	02-04	40	17	0

MILLS Robert (Bobby) Brian
Edmonton, 16 March, 1955 (M)

League Club	Source	Date Signed	Seasons Played	Apps	Subs	Gls
Colchester U	App	12.72	71-73	20	6	0

MILLS Roland (Roly) Walter George
Daventry, 22 June, 1933 EYth (WH)

League Club	Source	Date Signed	Seasons Played	Apps	Subs	Gls
Northampton T	Jnrs	05.51	54-63	305	-	30

MILLS Sean Douglas
Ebbw Vale, 1 June, 1968 (M)

League Club	Source	Date Signed	Seasons Played	Apps	Subs	Gls
Newport Co	Sunderland (Am)	08.86	86	5	2	0

MILLS Simon Ashley
Sheffield, 16 August, 1964 EYth (FB)

League Club	Source	Date Signed	Seasons Played	Apps	Subs	Gls
Sheffield Wed	App	08.82	82-84	1	4	0
York C	Tr	06.85	85-87	97	2	5
Port Vale	Tr	12.87	87-92	180	4	8

MILLS Stephen (Steve) John
Portsmouth, 9 December, 1953 Died 1988 Eu23-1 (FB)

League Club	Source	Date Signed	Seasons Played	Apps	Subs	Gls
Southampton	App	07.71	72-76	57	4	0

MILLWARD Horace Douglas (Doug)
Sheffield, 10 August, 1931 (IF)

League Club	Source	Date Signed	Seasons Played	Apps	Subs	Gls
Southampton	Doncaster Rov (Am)	02.52				
Ipswich T	Tr	07.55	55-62	143	-	35

MILNE Alexander (Alec) Soutar
Dundee, 4 June, 1937 Su23-1 (FB)

League Club	Source	Date Signed	Seasons Played	Apps	Subs	Gls
Cardiff C	Arbroath	03.57	57-64	172	-	1

MILNE Gordon
Preston, 29 March, 1937 FLge-2/E-14 (M)

League Club	Source	Date Signed	Seasons Played	Apps	Subs	Gls
Preston NE	Morecambe	01.56	56-60	81	-	3
Liverpool	Tr	09.60	60-66	234	2	18
Blackpool	Tr	05.67	67-69	60	4	4

MILNE John (Johnny) Buchanan
Rosehearty, 27 April, 1911 Died 1994 (FB)

League Club	Source	Date Signed	Seasons Played	Apps	Subs	Gls
Plymouth Arg	Fraserburgh	05.33	34-36	3	-	0
Southend U	Tr	06.37	37-38	66	-	1
Barrow	Tr	08.46	46	32	-	0
Oldham Ath	Tr	08.47	47	13	-	0

MILNE Maurice
Dundee, 21 October, 1932 Died 1998 (W)

League Club	Source	Date Signed	Seasons Played	Apps	Subs	Gls
Norwich C	Dundee U	05.57	57	5	-	0

MILNE Michael (Mike)
Aberdeen, 17 August, 1959 (FB)

League Club	Source	Date Signed	Seasons Played	Apps	Subs	Gls
Sunderland	App	05.77				
Rochdale		02.79	78	1	1	0

MILNE Ralph
Dundee, 13 May, 1961 SYth/Su21-3 (W)

League Club	Source	Date Signed	Seasons Played	Apps	Subs	Gls
Charlton Ath	Dundee U	01.87	86-87	19	3	0
Bristol C	Tr	01.88	87-88	29	1	6
Manchester U	Tr	11.88	88-89	19	4	3

MILNE Steven Craig
Forfar, 5 May, 1980 (F)

League Club	Source	Date Signed	Seasons Played	Apps	Subs	Gls
Plymouth Arg	Dundee	07.04	04	0	12	0

MILNER Alfred (Alf) John George
Harrogate, 6 February, 1919 Died 2002 (W)

League Club	Source	Date Signed	Seasons Played	Apps	Subs	Gls
Aldershot		08.46	46	7	-	1
Darlington		03.48	47-48	28	-	5

MILNER Andrew (Andy) John
Kendal, 10 February, 1967 (F)

League Club	Source	Date Signed	Seasons Played	Apps	Subs	Gls
Manchester C	Netherfield	01.89				
Rochdale	Tr	01.90	89-93	103	24	25
Chester C	Tr	08.94	94-97	106	19	24

MILNER James (Jimmy) Edward
Newcastle, 3 February, 1933 (IF)

League Club	Source	Date Signed	Seasons Played	Apps	Subs	Gls
Burnley	Blyth Spartans	12.52	53	1	-	0
Darlington	Tr	12.57	57-60	149	-	27
Accrington St	Tr	09.61				
Tranmere Rov	Tr	06.62	62	18	-	3

MILNER James Philip
Leeds, 4 January, 1986 ESch/EYth/Eu20/Eu21-10 (M)

League Club	Source	Date Signed	Seasons Played	Apps	Subs	Gls
Leeds U	Sch	02.03	02-03	28	20	5
Swindon T	L	09.03	03	6	0	2
Newcastle U	Tr	07.04	04	13	12	1

MILNER John
Huddersfield, 14 May, 1942 (WH)

League Club	Source	Date Signed	Seasons Played	Apps	Subs	Gls
Huddersfield T	Jnrs	05.59	60-62	17	-	0
Lincoln C	Tr	10.63	63-66	109	0	6
Bradford PA	Tr	02.67	66	6	2	0

MILNER Jonathan Robert
Mansfield, 30 March, 1981 (F)

League Club	Source	Date Signed	Seasons Played	Apps	Subs	Gls
Mansfield T	YT	●	97	1	6	0

MILNER Michael (Mike)
Hull, 21 September, 1939 (CD)

League Club	Source	Date Signed	Seasons Played	Apps	Subs	Gls
Hull C	Jnrs	07.57	58-67	160	0	0
Stockport Co	Tr	07.68	68	41	0	0
Barrow	Tr	09.69	69	11	0	0
Bradford C	Tr	12.69	69	0	1	0

MILOSAVLJEVIC Goran
Kraljevo, Yugoslavia, 11 April, 1967 (M)

League Club	Source	Date Signed	Seasons Played	Apps	Subs	Gls
Chester C	US Montelimar (Fr)	09.99	99	11	1	0

MILOSEVIC Dejan (Danny)
Carlton, Australia, 26 June, 1978 AuYth/Auu23 (G)

League Club	Source	Date Signed	Seasons Played	Apps	Subs	Gls
Leeds U	Perth Glory (Aus)	01.00				
Plymouth Arg	L	11.02	02	1	0	0
Crewe Alex	L	01.03	02	1	0	0

MILOSEVIC Savo
Bijeljina, Bosnia, 2 September, 1973 Yugoslavia int (F)

League Club	Source	Date Signed	Seasons Played	Apps	Subs	Gls
Aston Villa	Partizan Belgrade (Yug)	07.95	95-97	84	6	28

MILSOM Paul Jason
Bristol, 5 October, 1974 (F)

League Club	Source	Date Signed	Seasons Played	Apps	Subs	Gls
Bristol C	YT	07.93	93	1	2	0
Cardiff C	Tr	03.95	94	1	2	0

MILTON Clement Arthur
Bristol, 10 March, 1928 E-1 (W)

League Club	Source	Date Signed	Seasons Played	Apps	Subs	Gls
Arsenal	Jnrs	07.46	50-54	75	-	18
Bristol C	Tr	02.55	54	14	-	3

MILTON Roy
Brixham, 27 November, 1934 (G)

League Club	Source	Date Signed	Seasons Played	Apps	Subs	Gls
Bury	Jnrs	10.52				
Torquay U	Tr	08.56	56	1	-	0

MILTON Russell Maurice
Folkestone, 12 January, 1969 ESemiPro-2 (M)

League Club	Source	Date Signed	Seasons Played	Apps	Subs	Gls
Arsenal	App	02.87				
Cheltenham T	Dover Ath	08.97	99-02	108	9	14

MILTON Simon Charles
Fulham, 23 August, 1963 (M)

League Club	Source	Date Signed	Seasons Played	Apps	Subs	Gls
Ipswich T	Bury T	07.87	87-97	217	64	48
Exeter C	L	11.87	87	2	0	3
Torquay U	L	03.88	87	4	0	1

MILTON Stephen (Steve)
Fulham, 13 April, 1963 (F)

League Club	Source	Date Signed	Seasons Played	Apps	Subs	Gls
West Ham U	App	04.81				
Fulham	Whyteleafe	10.89	89-91	39	19	9

MIMMS Robert (Bobby) Andrew
York, 12 October, 1963 Eu21-3 (G)

League Club	Source	Date Signed	Seasons Played	Apps	Subs	Gls
Halifax T	App	08.81				
Rotherham U	Tr	11.81	81-84	83	0	0
Everton	Tr	05.85	85-87	29	0	0
Notts Co	L	03.86	85	2	0	0
Sunderland	L	12.86	86	4	0	0
Blackburn Rov	L	01.87	86	6	0	0
Manchester C	L	09.87	87	3	0	0
Tottenham H	Tr	02.88	87-89	37	0	0
Blackburn Rov	Tr	12.90	90-95	126	2	0
Crystal Palace	Tr	08.96	96	1	0	0
Preston NE	Tr	09.96	96	27	0	0
Rotherham U	Tr	08.97	97	43	0	0
York C	Tr	08.98	98-99	63	0	0
Mansfield T	Tr	03.00	99-00	45	0	0

MINETT Jason Keith
Peterborough, 12 August, 1971 (FB)

League Club	Source	Date Signed	Seasons Played	Apps	Subs	Gls
Norwich C	YT	07.89	90-92	0	3	0
Exeter C	Tr	03.93	92-94	83	5	3
Lincoln C	Tr	07.95	95-96	41	5	5
Exeter C	Tr	01.97	96-97	19	0	0

MINNOCK John Joseph
Tullamore, 12 November, 1949 IRu23-2/LoI-2 (W)

League Club	Source	Date Signed	Seasons Played	Apps	Subs	Gls
Charlton Ath	St Patrick's Ath	02.69	69	0	1	0

MINSHULL Raymond (Ray)
Bolton, 15 July, 1920 Died 2005 (G)

League Club	Source	Date Signed	Seasons Played	Apps	Subs	Gls
Liverpool	Southport (Am)	09.46	46-49	28	-	0
Southport	Tr	07.51	51-57	217	-	0
Bradford PA	Tr	12.57	57-58	28	-	0

MINTO Scott Christopher
Bromborough, 6 August, 1971 EYth/Eu21-6 (FB)

League Club	Source	Date Signed	Seasons Played	Apps	Subs	Gls
Charlton Ath	YT	02.89	88-93	171	9	7
Chelsea	Tr	05.94	94-96	53	1	4
West Ham U	Benfica (Por)	01.99	98-02	44	7	0
Rotherham U	Tr	08.03	03-04	41	5	0

MINTON Albert Edward
Walsall, 22 September, 1937 EYth (CF)

League Club	Source	Date Signed	Seasons Played	Apps	Subs	Gls
Blackpool	Derby Co (Am)	10.54				
Scunthorpe U	Tr	07.57	57-58	5	-	2
Doncaster Rov	Tr	12.58	58	11	-	2

MINTON Jeffrey (Jeff) Simon Thompson
Hackney, 28 December, 1973 (M)

League Club	Source	Date Signed	Seasons Played	Apps	Subs	Gls
Tottenham H	YT	01.92	91	2	0	1
Brighton & Hove A	Tr	07.94	94-98	167	7	31
Port Vale	Tr	07.99	99-00	34	2	4
Rotherham U	Tr	03.01	00	5	4	2
Leyton Orient	Tr	07.01	01	32	1	5

MINTON Roger Christopher
Birmingham, 4 June, 1951 (FB)

League Club	Source	Date Signed	Seasons Played	Apps	Subs	Gls
West Bromwich A	App	06.69	70-74	24	2	1

MIOTTO Simon Jonathan
Tasmania, Australia, 5 September, 1969 (G)

League Club	Source	Date Signed	Seasons Played	Apps	Subs	Gls
Hartlepool U	Riverside Olympic (Aus)	07.98	98	5	0	0

MIRANDA Jose Silvio Lima Gomes
Lisbon, Portugal, 2 April, 1974 (M)

League Club	Source	Date Signed	Seasons Played	Apps	Subs	Gls
Rotherham U	FC Felgueiras (Por)	08.01	01	2	0	0

[MIRANDINHA] DA SILVA Francisco Ernandi Lima
Fortaleza, Brazil, 2 July, 1959 Brazil int (F)

League Club	Source	Date Signed	Seasons Played	Apps	Subs	Gls
Newcastle U	Palmeiras (Br)	08.87	87-88	47	7	20

MIRFIN David Matthew
Sheffield, 18 April, 1985 (M)

League Club	Source	Date Signed	Seasons Played	Apps	Subs	Gls
Huddersfield T	Sch	12.03	02-04	53	10	6

MIROCEVIC Anton (Ante)
Titograd, Yugoslavia, 6 August, 1952 Yugoslavia int (M)

League Club	Source	Date Signed	Seasons Played	Apps	Subs	Gls
Sheffield Wed	FC Budocnost (Yug)	10.80	80-82	58	3	6

MIRZA Nicolas
Paris, France, 21 July, 1985 (M)

League Club	Source	Date Signed	Seasons Played	Apps	Subs	Gls
Yeovil T	Paris St Germain (Fr)	07.04	04	0	3	0

League Club	Source	Date Signed	Seasons Played	Career Record Apps	Subs	Gls

MISKELLY David Thomas
Newtownards, 3 September, 1979 NIYth/NIu21-11 (G)

League Club	Source	Date Signed	Seasons Played	Apps	Subs	Gls
Oldham Ath	YT	07.97	98-02	17	3	0

MISON Michael
Southwark, 8 November, 1975 (M)

League Club	Source	Date Signed	Seasons Played	Apps	Subs	Gls
Fulham	YT	07.94	93-96	35	20	5

MISSE-MISSE Jean-Jacques
Yaounde, Cameroon, 7 August, 1968 Cameroon int (F)

League Club	Source	Date Signed	Seasons Played	Apps	Subs	Gls
Chesterfield	Dundee U	03.98	97	1	0	0

MITCHELL Albert (Bert) James
Cobridge, 22 January, 1922 Died 1997 EB (W)

League Club	Source	Date Signed	Seasons Played	Apps	Subs	Gls
Stoke C	Burslem A	05.41	46-47	10	-	2
Blackburn Rov	Tr	02.48	47	3	-	0
Northampton T	Kettering T	05.49	49-50	81	-	21
Luton T	Tr	07.51	51-54	106	-	41
Middlesbrough	Tr	09.54	54-55	50	-	6
Southport	Tr	08.56	56	16	-	3

MITCHELL Alexander (Alec) Russell
Greenock, 24 May, 1918 Died 1990 (FB)

League Club	Source	Date Signed	Seasons Played	Apps	Subs	Gls
Ipswich T	Bute Ath	08.46	47-49	42	-	2

MITCHELL Andrew (Andy) Barry
Rotherham, 12 September, 1976 (FB)

League Club	Source	Date Signed	Seasons Played	Apps	Subs	Gls
Aston Villa	YT	09.93				
Chesterfield	Tr	09.96	96	1	1	0

MITCHELL Anthony (Tony) John
Redruth, 7 September, 1956 (FB)

League Club	Source	Date Signed	Seasons Played	Apps	Subs	Gls
Exeter C	Leatherhead	07.77	78-81	60	0	0

MITCHELL Arnold
Rotherham, 1 December, 1929 (WH)

League Club	Source	Date Signed	Seasons Played	Apps	Subs	Gls
Derby Co	Sheffield Wed (Am)	02.48				
Nottingham F	Tr	03.50				
Notts Co	Tr	05.51	51	1	-	0
Exeter C	Tr	07.52	52-65	495	0	44

MITCHELL Barrie
Aberdeen, 15 March, 1947 (F)

League Club	Source	Date Signed	Seasons Played	Apps	Subs	Gls
Tranmere Rov	Aberdeen	02.74	73-75	77	6	10
Preston NE	Vancouver (Can)	07.76	76	7	4	2
York C	Tr	09.77	77	1	2	0

MITCHELL Charles **Brian**
Stonehaven, 16 July, 1963 SSch (FB)

League Club	Source	Date Signed	Seasons Played	Apps	Subs	Gls
Bradford C	Aberdeen	02.87	86-91	170	8	9
Bristol C	Tr	07.92	92	15	1	0
Hull C	Tr	08.93	93	9	0	0

MITCHELL Craig Richard
Mansfield, 6 May, 1985 (F)

League Club	Source	Date Signed	Seasons Played	Apps	Subs	Gls
Mansfield T	Sch	07.03	02-03	3	13	1

MITCHELL David (Dave) John
Stoke-on-Trent, 24 August, 1945 (CF)

League Club	Source	Date Signed	Seasons Played	Apps	Subs	Gls
Port Vale	Jnrs	03.64	64-65	21	0	4
Ipswich T	Tr	08.66	66	0	2	0

MITCHELL David Stewart
Glasgow, 13 June, 1962 Australia int (F)

League Club	Source	Date Signed	Seasons Played	Apps	Subs	Gls
Chelsea	Feyenoord (Holl)	01.89	88-90	7	0	0
Newcastle U	L	01.91	90	2	0	1
Swindon T	Tr	07.91	91-92	61	7	16
Millwall	Altay Izmir (Tu)	10.93	93-94	49	6	15

MITCHELL Frank Rollason
Goulburn, Australia, 3 June, 1922 Died 1984 (WH)

League Club	Source	Date Signed	Seasons Played	Apps	Subs	Gls
Birmingham C	Coventry C (Am)	09.43	46-48	93	-	6
Chelsea	Tr	01.49	48-51	75	-	1
Watford	Tr	08.52	52-56	193	-	0

MITCHELL Graham Lee
Shipley, 16 February, 1968 (CD)

League Club	Source	Date Signed	Seasons Played	Apps	Subs	Gls
Huddersfield T	App	06.86	86-94	235	9	2
Bournemouth	L	12.93	93	4	0	0
Bradford C	Tr	12.94	94-96	64	1	1
Cardiff C	Raith Rov	08.98	98	46	0	0
Halifax T	Tr	07.99	99-01	128	2	3

MITCHELL Ian David
Tredegar, 1 October, 1971 (F)

League Club	Source	Date Signed	Seasons Played	Apps	Subs	Gls
Hereford U	Merthyr Tydfil	10.90	90	0	3	0

MITCHELL James (Jamie)
Glasgow, 6 November, 1976 (F)

League Club	Source	Date Signed	Seasons Played	Apps	Subs	Gls
Norwich C	YT	07.95				
Scarborough	Tr	08.96	96-97	31	47	10

MITCHELL James Donald
Heanor, 1 July, 1937 (G)

League Club	Source	Date Signed	Seasons Played	Apps	Subs	Gls
Derby Co	Ilkeston T	10.58	58-59	6	-	0

MITCHELL James (Jimmy) Robert
Liverpool, 13 June, 1967 (FB)

League Club	Source	Date Signed	Seasons Played	Apps	Subs	Gls
Wigan Ath	App	06.85	84	2	0	0

MITCHELL John (Ian)
Falkirk, 9 May, 1946 Died 1996 SSch/Su23-2 (W)

League Club	Source	Date Signed	Seasons Played	Apps	Subs	Gls
Newcastle U	Dundee U	07.70	70	2	1	0

MITCHELL John
St Albans, 12 March, 1952 (F)

League Club	Source	Date Signed	Seasons Played	Apps	Subs	Gls
Fulham	St Albans C	02.72	72-77	158	12	57
Millwall	Tr	06.78	78-80	78	3	18

MITCHELL John Desmond
Titchfield, 19 November, 1928 Died 2000 (W)

League Club	Source	Date Signed	Seasons Played	Apps	Subs	Gls
Southampton	Gosport Borough	03.49	50	7	-	0

MITCHELL John George
Gateshead, 1 August, 1919 Died 1977 (CF)

League Club	Source	Date Signed	Seasons Played	Apps	Subs	Gls
Hartlepools U	Billingham Synthonia	11.46	46	3	-	2

MITCHELL Kenneth (Kenny)
Sunderland, 26 May, 1957 (FB)

League Club	Source	Date Signed	Seasons Played	Apps	Subs	Gls
Newcastle U	App	04.75	76-80	61	5	2
Darlington	Tr	08.81	81	12	1	1

MITCHELL Kenneth (Ken) Samuel
Wearhead, 26 December, 1933 (CF)

League Club	Source	Date Signed	Seasons Played	Apps	Subs	Gls
Plymouth Arg	Whitby Rov	03.56	55-56	8	-	4

MITCHELL Neil Nicholas
Lytham, 7 November, 1974 ESch (F)

League Club	Source	Date Signed	Seasons Played	Apps	Subs	Gls
Blackpool	YT	11.92	91-94	39	28	8
Rochdale	L	12.95	95	3	1	0
Macclesfield T	Tr	07.96	97	2	4	0

MITCHELL Norman
Sunderland, 7 November, 1931 (W)

League Club	Source	Date Signed	Seasons Played	Apps	Subs	Gls
Chesterfield	West Stanley	10.51	51-52	66	-	7
Workington	West Stanley	11.53	53-57	140	-	23
Hartlepools U	Tr	03.58	57-58	23	-	6

MITCHELL Paul Alexander
Stalybridge, 26 August, 1981 (CD)

League Club	Source	Date Signed	Seasons Played	Apps	Subs	Gls
Wigan Ath	YT	07.00	00-04	30	34	0
Halifax T	L	03.01	00	11	0	0
Swindon T	L	09.04	04	7	0	0
MK Dons	L	12.04	04	13	0	0

MITCHELL Paul Robert
Bournemouth, 20 October, 1971 ESch/EYth (M)

League Club	Source	Date Signed	Seasons Played	Apps	Subs	Gls
Bournemouth	YT	08.89	90-92	6	6	0
West Ham U	Tr	08.93	93	0	1	0
Bournemouth	Tr	03.96	95	2	2	0
Torquay U	Tr	08.96	96-97	33	5	1

MITCHELL Paul Robert
Nottingham, 8 November, 1978 (CD)

League Club	Source	Date Signed	Seasons Played	Apps	Subs	Gls
Notts Co	YT	07.97	96-97	1	1	0

MITCHELL Peter
Oldham, 5 August, 1946 (FB)

League Club	Source	Date Signed	Seasons Played	Apps	Subs	Gls
Oldham Ath	St Patrick's (Oldham)	07.66	65	0	1	0

MITCHELL Robert (Bobby)
Petersfield, 17 December, 1948 (F)

League Club	Source	Date Signed	Seasons Played	Apps	Subs	Gls
Aldershot	Alton T	09.69	69-70	6	7	1

MITCHELL Robert (Bobby)
South Shields, 4 January, 1955 (M)

League Club	Source	Date Signed	Seasons Played	Apps	Subs	Gls
Sunderland	App	01.72	73-75	1	2	0
Blackburn Rov	Tr	07.76	76-77	17	12	6
Grimsby T	Tr	06.78	78-81	142	0	6
Carlisle U	Tr	08.82	82	2	0	0
Rotherham U	Tr	03.83	82-84	86	9	2
Lincoln C	Hamrun (Malta)	01.86	85-86	41	3	2

MITCHELL Robert (Bobby) Barr
Campbeltown, 17 January, 1927 Died 2002 (CF)

League Club	Source	Date Signed	Seasons Played	Apps	Subs	Gls
Exeter C	Third Lanark	07.51	51	3	-	0

MITCHELL Robert (Bobby) Carmichael
Glasgow, 16 August, 1924 Died 1993 SLge-2/S-2 (W)

League Club	Source	Date Signed	Seasons Played	Apps	Subs	Gls
Newcastle U	Third Lanark	02.49	48-60	367	-	95

MITCHELL Ronald (Ron) Gilbert
Morecambe, 13 February, 1935 (FB)

League Club	Source	Date Signed	Seasons Played	Apps	Subs	Gls
Leeds U	Morecambe	11.58	58	4	-	0

MITCHELL Ronald (Ron) James
Barrhead, 27 May, 1925 (W)

League Club	Source	Date Signed	Seasons Played	Apps	Subs	Gls
Exeter C	Glasgow Celtic	08.49	49	2	-	0

MITCHELL Roy
Liverpool, 10 March, 1964 (M)

League Club	Source	Date Signed	Seasons Played	Apps	Subs	Gls
Stockport Co		10.86	86	2	1	0

MITCHELL Scott Andrew
Ely, 2 September, 1985 (FB)

League Club	Source	Date Signed	Seasons Played	Apps	Subs	Gls
Ipswich T	Sch	03.04	03	0	2	0

MITCHELL Stewart Anderson
Glasgow, 3 March, 1933 (G)

League Club	Source	Date Signed	Seasons Played	Apps	Subs	Gls
Newcastle U	Glasgow Benburb	09.53	54-62	45	-	0

MITCHELSON Kenneth (Ken)
Edmonton, 16 May, 1928 (FB)

League Club	Source	Date Signed	Seasons Played	Apps	Subs	Gls
Charlton Ath	Tottenham H (Am)	09.47				
Bristol C	Tr	05.49	49-52	28	-	0

MITCHESON Francis (Frank) John
Stalybridge, 10 March, 1924 Died 1981 (IF)

League Club	Source	Date Signed	Seasons Played	Apps	Subs	Gls
Doncaster Rov	Droylsden	05.44	46-48	22	-	5
Crewe Alex	Tr	11.48	48-53	180	-	34
Rochdale	Tr	06.54	54-55	50	-	8

MITCHINSON Thomas (Tommy) William
Sunderland, 24 February, 1943 (M)

League Club	Source	Date Signed	Seasons Played	Apps	Subs	Gls
Sunderland	Jnrs	12.60	62-65	16	3	2
Mansfield T	Tr	01.66	65-67	76	0	15
Aston Villa	Tr	08.67	67-68	49	0	9
Torquay U	Tr	05.69	68-71	108	0	9
Bournemouth	Tr	12.71	71-72	31	1	1

MITTEN Charles (Charlie)
Rangoon, Burma, 17 January, 1921 Died 2002 (W)

League Club	Source	Date Signed	Seasons Played	Apps	Subs	Gls
Manchester U	Strathallan Hawthorn	01.38	46-49	142	-	50
Fulham	Bogota (Col)	01.52	51-55	154	-	32
Mansfield T	Tr	02.56	55-57	100	-	25

MITTEN Charles (Charlie)
Altrincham, 14 December, 1943 (IF)

League Club	Source	Date Signed	Seasons Played	Apps	Subs	Gls
Mansfield T	Newcastle U (App)	11.61				
Halifax T	Altrincham	10.65	65	1	0	0

MITTEN John
Davyhulme, 30 March, 1941 ESch/EYth (W)

League Club	Source	Date Signed	Seasons Played	Apps	Subs	Gls
Mansfield T	Jnrs	01.58	57	3	-	0
Newcastle U	Tr	09.58	58-60	9	-	3
Leicester C	Tr	09.61	61	12	-	0
Coventry C	Tr	08.63	63-66	34	2	5
Plymouth Arg	Tr	01.67	66-67	43	0	8
Exeter C	Tr	07.68	68-70	96	4	17

MITTON Gilbert **Keith**
Leyland, 30 December, 1928 Died 1995 (G)

League Club	Source	Date Signed	Seasons Played	Apps	Subs	Gls
Preston NE	Leyland Motors	05.50	53	2	-	0
Carlisle U	Tr	06.54	54-56	47	-	0

MOBLEY David Leslie
Oxford, 24 August, 1948 (FB)

League Club	Source	Date Signed	Seasons Played	Apps	Subs	Gls
Sheffield Wed	Jnrs	09.65				
Grimsby T	Tr	07.69	69	26	1	0

MOBLEY Victor (Vic) John
Oxford, 11 October, 1943 Eu23-13/FLge-1 (CD)

League Club	Source	Date Signed	Seasons Played	Apps	Subs	Gls
Sheffield Wed	Oxford C	09.61	63-69	187	0	8
Queens Park Rgrs	Tr	10.69	69-70	24	1	0

MOCHAN Dennis
Falkirk, 12 December, 1935 (FB)

League Club	Source	Date Signed	Seasons Played	Apps	Subs	Gls
Nottingham F	Raith Rov	06.62	62-65	108	0	1
Colchester U	Tr	09.66	66-69	113	3	2

MOCHAN Neil
Larbert, 6 April, 1927 Died 1994 SB/S-3 (CF)

League Club	Source	Date Signed	Seasons Played	Apps	Subs	Gls
Middlesbrough	Morton	05.51	51-52	38	-	14

MOCKLER Andrew James
Stockton, 18 November, 1970 (M)

League Club	Source	Date Signed	Seasons Played	Apps	Subs	Gls
Arsenal	YT	11.88				
Scarborough	Tr	07.90	90-93	66	8	10

MOFFAT Adam
Lochgelly, 1 April, 1941 (IF)

League Club	Source	Date Signed	Seasons Played	Apps	Subs	Gls
Newport Co	East Fife	10.61	61	17	-	5

MOFFATT Gregory (Greg) Thomas
Liverpool, 8 January, 1964 (FB)

League Club	Source	Date Signed	Seasons Played	Apps	Subs	Gls
Chester	App	01.82	82	6	1	0

MOFFATT John (Johnny) Black
Greenock, 22 December, 1929 (W)

League Club	Source	Date Signed	Seasons Played	Apps	Subs	Gls
Brighton & Hove A	Bellshill Ath	12.51	52	2	-	0

MOFFATT Robert (Bob) Wallace
Portsmouth, 7 October, 1945 (M)

League Club	Source	Date Signed	Seasons Played	Apps	Subs	Gls
Portsmouth	App	10.63				
Gillingham	Tr	05.65	65-67	24	1	1

MOFFITT Kenneth (Ken)
Newcastle, 2 February, 1933 (FB)

League Club	Source	Date Signed	Seasons Played	Apps	Subs	Gls
Brentford	Berwick Rgrs	08.53				
Gateshead	Berwick Rgrs	09.57	57-59	76	-	2

MOGFORD Reginald (Reg) William James
Newport, 12 June, 1919 Died 1992 (CF)

League Club	Source	Date Signed	Seasons Played	Apps	Subs	Gls
Newport Co	Jnrs	06.38	38-47	20	-	9

MOHAN Nicholas (Nicky)
Middlesbrough, 6 October, 1970 (CD)

League Club	Source	Date Signed	Seasons Played	Apps	Subs	Gls
Middlesbrough	Jnrs	11.87	88-93	93	6	4
Hull C	L	09.92	92	5	0	1
Leicester C	Tr	07.94	94	23	0	0
Bradford C	Tr	07.95	95-96	83	0	4
Wycombe W	Tr	08.97	97-98	58	0	2
Stoke C	Tr	03.99	98-00	92	0	6
Hull C	Tr	07.01	01	26	1	1

MOILANEN Teuvo (Tepi) Johannes
Oulu, Finland, 12 December, 1973 FiYth/Fiu21/Fi-3 (G)

League Club	Source	Date Signed	Seasons Played	Apps	Subs	Gls
Preston NE	FF Jaro (Fin)	12.95	95-02	155	3	0
Scarborough	L	12.96	96	4	0	0
Darlington	L	01.97	96	16	0	0

MOIR Ian
Aberdeen, 30 June, 1943 (W)

League Club	Source	Date Signed	Seasons Played	Apps	Subs	Gls
Manchester U	Jnrs	07.60	60-64	45	-	5
Blackpool	Tr	02.65	64-66	61	0	12
Chester	Tr	05.67	67	25	0	3
Wrexham	Tr	01.68	67-71	144	6	20
Shrewsbury T	Tr	03.72	71-72	22	3	2
Wrexham	Tr	07.73	73-74	11	4	0

MOIR James (Jim)
Newcastle, 23 March, 1918 (CF)

League Club	Source	Date Signed	Seasons Played	Apps	Subs	Gls
Accrington St	Newcastle West End	10.37	37-38	20	-	9
Carlisle U	Tr	08.46	46-47	42	-	20

MOIR Richard (Ricky) John
Glasgow, 22 October, 1945 (M)

League Club	Source	Date Signed	Seasons Played	Apps	Subs	Gls
Shrewsbury T	Cumnock Jnrs	03.69	69-73	159	6	27
Halifax T	Tr	07.74	74	16	3	5

MOIR William (Willie)
Bucksburn, 19 April, 1922 Died 1988 SB/S-1 (IF)

League Club	Source	Date Signed	Seasons Played	Apps	Subs	Gls
Bolton W	RAF Kirkham	04.43	46-55	325	-	118
Stockport Co	Tr	09.55	55-57	70	-	26

MOKOENA Aaron Teboho
Johannesburg, South Africa, 25 November, 1980 South Africa 50 (CD)

League Club	Source	Date Signed	Seasons Played	Apps	Subs	Gls
Blackburn Rov	KRC Genk (Bel)	01.05	04	16	0	0

MOKONE Stephen (Steve) Madi
Pretoria, South Africa, 23 March, 1932 South Africa int (W)

League Club	Source	Date Signed	Seasons Played	Apps	Subs	Gls
Coventry C	Pretoria HS (SA)	10.56	56	4	-	1
Cardiff C	PSV Eindhoven (Holl)	06.59	59	3	-	1

MOLANGO Maheta
St Imier, Switzerland, 24 July, 1982 (F)

League Club	Source	Date Signed	Seasons Played	Apps	Subs	Gls
Brighton & Hove A	SV Wacker Burg (Aut)	07.04	04	4	1	1

MOLBY Jan
Kolding, Denmark, 4 July, 1963 Denmark int (M)

League Club	Source	Date Signed	Seasons Played	Apps	Subs	Gls
Liverpool	Ajax (Holl)	08.84	84-94	195	23	44
Barnsley	L	09.95	95	5	0	0
Norwich C	L	12.95	95	3	0	0
Swansea C	Tr	02.96	95-97	39	2	8

MOLDOVAN Viorel Dinu
Bistrita, Romania, 8 July, 1972 Romania int (F)

League Club	Source	Date Signed	Seasons Played	Apps	Subs	Gls
Coventry C	Grasshoppers (Swi)	01.98	97	5	5	1

MOLENAAR Robert
Zaandam, Holland, 27 February, 1969 (CD)

League Club	Source	Date Signed	Seasons Played	Apps	Subs	Gls
Leeds U	FC Volendam (Holl)	01.97	96-98	47	4	5
Bradford C	Tr	12.00	00-02	70	1	2

MOLESKI George Kyriakos
Hillingdon, 24 July, 1987 (CD)

League Club	Source	Date Signed	Seasons Played	Apps	Subs	Gls
Brentford	Sch	●	04	0	1	0

MOLLATT Ronald (Ron) Vincent
Edwinstowe, 24 February, 1932 Died 2001 (WH)

League Club	Source	Date Signed	Seasons Played	Apps	Subs	Gls
Leeds U	Thoresby Colliery	02.50	51-54	17	-	0
York C	Tr	07.55	55-59	124	-	1
Bradford C	Tr	07.60	60-62	88	-	0

MOLLER Jan Borje
Malmo, Sweden, 17 September, 1953 Sweden int (G)

League Club	Source	Date Signed	Seasons Played	Apps	Subs	Gls
Bristol C	FF Malmo (Swe)	12.80	80-81	48	0	0

MOLLER Peter Nielsen
Gistrup, Denmark, 23 March, 1972 Denmark 17 (F)

League Club	Source	Date Signed	Seasons Played	Apps	Subs	Gls
Fulham (L)	Real Oviedo (Sp)	01.01	00	2	3	1

MOLLOY David Anthony
Newcastle, 29 August, 1986 (W)

League Club	Source	Date Signed	Seasons Played	Apps	Subs	Gls
Carlisle U	Sch	•	03	3	4	0

MOLLOY Gerard (Gerry)
Rochdale, 13 March, 1936 (WH)

League Club	Source	Date Signed	Seasons Played	Apps	Subs	Gls
Rochdale	Jnrs	11.55	55-56	6	-	0

MOLLOY Peter
Athlone, 1921 Died 1973 LoI-2/IrLge-4 (CH)

League Club	Source	Date Signed	Seasons Played	Apps	Subs	Gls
Notts Co	Distillery	04.48	47	1	-	0

MOLLOY Trevor
Dublin, 14 April, 1977 (F)

League Club	Source	Date Signed	Seasons Played	Apps	Subs	Gls
Carlisle U	Shelbourne	08.02	02	7	0	1

MOLLOY George **William (Billy)**
Coventry, 28 August, 1929 (W)

League Club	Source	Date Signed	Seasons Played	Apps	Subs	Gls
Southampton		10.49	49	1	-	0
Newport Co	Lockheed Leamington	11.50	50	3	-	0

MOLYNEAUX Lee Alexander
Portsmouth, 16 January, 1983 (CD)

League Club	Source	Date Signed	Seasons Played	Apps	Subs	Gls
Portsmouth	YT	12.01				
Oxford U	Weymouth	07.04	04	6	10	0

MOLYNEUX Bernard
Prescot, 17 September, 1933 (W)

League Club	Source	Date Signed	Seasons Played	Apps	Subs	Gls
Everton	Jnrs	12.51				
Tranmere Rov	Tr	05.56	56	11	-	3

MOLYNEUX Frederick (Fred) George
Wallasey, 25 July, 1944 (CD)

League Club	Source	Date Signed	Seasons Played	Apps	Subs	Gls
Liverpool	Jnrs	06.62				
Southport	Tr	08.65	65-68	123	0	1
Plymouth Arg	Tr	08.68	68-70	79	0	5
Exeter C	L	02.71	70	2	0	0
Tranmere Rov	Tr	02.71	70-72	71	1	0
Southport	Tr	07.73	73	32	1	1

MOLYNEUX Geoffrey (Geoff) Barry
Warrington, 23 January, 1943 (W)

League Club	Source	Date Signed	Seasons Played	Apps	Subs	Gls
Chester (Am)	Rylands YC	05.62	62	1	-	0

MOLYNEUX John Allan
Warrington, 3 February, 1931 EYth (FB)

League Club	Source	Date Signed	Seasons Played	Apps	Subs	Gls
Chester	Orford YC	02.49	49-54	178	-	1
Liverpool	Tr	06.55	55-61	229	-	2
Chester	Tr	08.62	62-64	67	-	0

MOLYNEUX Raymond (Ray)
Kearsley, 13 June, 1930 EYth (W)

League Club	Source	Date Signed	Seasons Played	Apps	Subs	Gls
Bradford C		12.48	48	2	-	1

MOLYNEUX William (Billy) Stanley
Liverpool, 10 January, 1944 (G)

League Club	Source	Date Signed	Seasons Played	Apps	Subs	Gls
Liverpool	Earle	11.63	64	1	-	0
Oldham Ath	Tr	06.67	68	8	0	0

MONAGHAN Derek James
Bromsgrove, 20 January, 1959 EYth (F)

League Club	Source	Date Signed	Seasons Played	Apps	Subs	Gls
West Bromwich A	App	01.77	79-83	14	5	2
Port Vale	Tr	07.84	84	4	3	0

MONCRIEFF James Conradi
Todmorden, 14 June, 1922 Died 1975 (CF)

League Club	Source	Date Signed	Seasons Played	Apps	Subs	Gls
Halifax T (Am)	Pegasus	06.46	46-54	42	-	13

MONCRIEFFE Prince
Jamaica, 27 February, 1977 (F)

League Club	Source	Date Signed	Seasons Played	Apps	Subs	Gls
Doncaster Rov	Hyde U	07.97	97	30	8	8

MONCUR John Frederick
Stepney, 22 September, 1966 (M)

League Club	Source	Date Signed	Seasons Played	Apps	Subs	Gls
Tottenham H	App	08.84	86-90	10	11	1
Doncaster Rov	L	09.86	86	4	0	0
Cambridge U	L	03.87	86	3	1	0
Portsmouth	L	03.89	88	7	0	0
Brentford	L	10.89	89	5	0	1
Ipswich T	L	10.91	91	5	1	0
Swindon T	Tr	03.92	91-93	53	5	5
West Ham U	Tr	06.94	94-02	131	44	6

MONCUR Robert (Bobby)
Perth, 19 January, 1945 SSch/Su23-1/S-16 (CD)

League Club	Source	Date Signed	Seasons Played	Apps	Subs	Gls
Newcastle U	App	04.62	62-73	293	3	3
Sunderland	Tr	06.74	74-76	86	0	2
Carlisle U	Tr	11.76	76	11	0	0

MONEY Richard
Lowestoft, 13 October, 1955 EB (CD)

League Club	Source	Date Signed	Seasons Played	Apps	Subs	Gls
Scunthorpe U	Lowestoft T	07.73	73-77	165	8	4
Fulham	Tr	12.77	77-79	106	0	3
Liverpool	Tr	04.80	80	12	2	0
Derby Co	L	12.81	81	5	0	0
Luton T	Tr	03.82	81-82	44	0	1
Portsmouth	Tr	08.83	83-85	17	0	0
Scunthorpe U	Tr	10.85	85-89	105	1	0

MONINGTON Mark David
Bilsthorpe, 21 October, 1970 (CD)

League Club	Source	Date Signed	Seasons Played	Apps	Subs	Gls
Burnley	Jnrs	03.89	88-93	65	19	5
Rotherham U	Tr	11.94	94-97	75	4	3
Rochdale	Tr	07.98	98-00	90	5	12
Boston U	Tr	07.01	02	1	0	0

MONK Brian
Leeds, 15 May, 1937 (IF)

League Club	Source	Date Signed	Seasons Played	Apps	Subs	Gls
Leeds U	Jnrs	02.55				
Crewe Alex	Tr	05.58	58	5	-	0

MONK Frederick (Fred) John
Brighton, 9 October, 1920 Died 1987 ESch (FB)

League Club	Source	Date Signed	Seasons Played	Apps	Subs	Gls
Brentford	Guildford C	03.48	47-53	206	-	47
Aldershot	Tr	07.54	54-55	49	-	0

MONK Garry Alan
Bedford, 6 March, 1979 (CD)

League Club	Source	Date Signed	Seasons Played	Apps	Subs	Gls
Torquay U	YT	•	95	4	1	0
Southampton	Tr	05.97	98-02	9	2	0
Torquay U	L	09.98	98	6	0	0
Stockport Co	L	09.99	99	2	0	0
Oxford U	L	01.01	00	5	0	0
Sheffield Wed	L	12.02	02	15	0	0
Barnsley	Tr	11.03	03	14	3	0
Swansea C	Tr	07.04	04	34	0	0

MONKHOUSE Alan Thompson William
Stockton, 23 October, 1930 Died 1982 (CF)

League Club	Source	Date Signed	Seasons Played	Apps	Subs	Gls
Millwall	Thornaby	08.50	49-53	65	-	20
Newcastle U	Tr	10.53	53-55	21	-	9
York C	Tr	06.56	56	12	-	1

MONKHOUSE Andrew (Andy) William
Leeds, 23 October, 1980 (W)

League Club	Source	Date Signed	Seasons Played	Apps	Subs	Gls
Rotherham U	YT	11.98	98-04	61	55	8

MONKHOUSE Graham
Carlisle, 26 April, 1954 (G)

League Club	Source	Date Signed	Seasons Played	Apps	Subs	Gls
Workington	Penrith	08.76	76	4	0	0

MONKOU Kenneth (Ken) John
Surinam, 29 November, 1964 Hou21 (CD)

League Club	Source	Date Signed	Seasons Played	Apps	Subs	Gls
Chelsea	Feyenoord (Holl)	03.89	88-91	92	2	2
Southampton	Tr	08.92	92-98	190	8	10
Huddersfield T	Tr	08.99	99-00	21	0	1

MONKS John
Stockport, 3 June, 1921 Died 1983 (FB)

League Club	Source	Date Signed	Seasons Played	Apps	Subs	Gls
Stockport Co		04.47	46-52	91	-	0

MONOGHAN William
Glasgow, 2 September, 1919 (FB)

League Club	Source	Date Signed	Seasons Played	Apps	Subs	Gls
Bury	Alloa Ath	08.46				
Carlisle U	Ayr U	08.47	47-49	19	-	0

MONTGOMERY Alec Webster
Tamworth, 16 September, 1926 (FB)

League Club	Source	Date Signed	Seasons Played	Apps	Subs	Gls
Walsall	Baddesley	08.49	51-52	29	-	0

MONTGOMERY Derek
Houghton-le-Spring, 5 May, 1950 (M)

League Club	Source	Date Signed	Seasons Played	Apps	Subs	Gls
Leeds U	App	12.67				
Bradford C	Tr	08.68	68	4	0	0

MONTGOMERY Gary Stephen
Leamington Spa, 8 October, 1982 (G)

League Club	Source	Date Signed	Seasons Played	Apps	Subs	Gls
Coventry C	YT	01.01	02	8	0	0
Kidderminster Hrs	L	03.02	01	2	0	0
Rotherham U	Tr	07.03	03-04	4	1	0

MONTGOMERY James (Jim)
Sunderland, 9 October, 1943 EYth/Eu23-6 (G)

League Club	Source	Date Signed	Seasons Played	Apps	Subs	Gls
Sunderland	Jnrs	10.60	61-76	537	0	0
Southampton	L	10.76	76	5	0	0
Birmingham C	Tr	02.77	76-78	66	0	0

MONTGOMERY Nicholas (Nick) Anthony
Leeds, 28 October, 1981 Su21-2 (M)

League Club	Source	Date Signed	Seasons Played	Apps	Subs	Gls
Sheffield U	YT	07.00	00-04	91	51	6

MONTGOMERY Stanley (Stan) William
West Ham, 7 July, 1920 Died 2000 WLge-1 (CD)

League Club	Source	Date Signed	Seasons Played	Apps	Subs	Gls
Hull C	Romford	09.44	46	5	-	0
Southend U	Tr	09.46	46-48	96	-	7
Cardiff C	Tr	12.48	48-54	230	-	4
Newport Co	Worcester C	11.55	55	9	-	0

MOODY Adrian James Harkin
Birkenhead, 29 September, 1982 (CD)

League Club	Source	Date Signed	Seasons Played	Apps	Subs	Gls
Wrexham	YT	•	00-01	2	2	0

MOODY Alan
Middlesbrough, 18 January, 1951 ESch (CD)

League Club	Source	Date Signed	Seasons Played	Apps	Subs	Gls
Middlesbrough	App	01.68	68-72	44	2	0
Southend U	Tr	10.72	72-83	444	2	41

MOODY Kenneth (Ken) George
Grimsby, 12 November, 1924 Died 1990 (FB)

League Club	Source	Date Signed	Seasons Played	Apps	Subs	Gls
Grimsby T	Humber U	10.42	47-50	114	-	0

MOODY Paul
Portsmouth, 13 June, 1967 (F)

League Club	Source	Date Signed	Seasons Played	Apps	Subs	Gls
Southampton	Waterlooville	07.91	91-93	7	5	0
Reading	L	12.92	92	5	0	1
Oxford U	Tr	02.94	93-96	98	38	49
Fulham	Tr	07.97	97-98	29	11	19
Millwall	Tr	07.99	99-01	45	15	24
Oxford U	Tr	09.01	01	29	6	13

MOODY Vincent Roy
Worksop, 12 March, 1923 (W)

League Club	Source	Date Signed	Seasons Played	Apps	Subs	Gls
Lincoln C	Worksop T	11.46	46	1	-	0

MOONEY Brian John
Dublin, 2 February, 1966 IRYth/IRu23-2/IRu21-4 (W)

League Club	Source	Date Signed	Seasons Played	Apps	Subs	Gls
Liverpool	Home Farm	08.83				
Wrexham	L	12.85	85	9	0	2
Preston NE	Tr	10.87	87-90	125	3	20
Sunderland	Tr	02.91	90-92	21	6	1
Burnley	L	09.92	92	6	0	0

MOONEY Dean Francis
Paddington, 24 July, 1956 (F)

League Club	Source	Date Signed	Seasons Played	Apps	Subs	Gls
Orient	App	07.74	74-75	16	6	3
Bournemouth	GAIS Gothenburg (Swe)	12.80	80-81	27	0	10
Torquay U	RS Southampton	08.84	84	15	0	2

MOONEY Francis (Frank)
Fauldhouse, 1 January, 1932 (W)

League Club	Source	Date Signed	Seasons Played	Apps	Subs	Gls
Manchester U	Bathgate St Mary's	05.49				
Blackburn Rov	Tr	02.54	53-55	58	-	19
Carlisle U	Tr	05.56	56-59	124	-	24

MOONEY John (Johnny)
Fauldhouse, 21 February, 1926 Died 2000 (W)

League Club	Source	Date Signed	Seasons Played	Apps	Subs	Gls
Doncaster Rov	Hamilton Academical	05.53	53-58	168	-	32

MOONEY Kevin William
Liverpool, 23 August, 1959 (CD)

League Club	Source	Date Signed	Seasons Played	Apps	Subs	Gls
Bury	Bangor C	03.80	80	1	0	0
Tranmere Rov	Telford U	08.82	82	21	1	0

MOONEY Thomas (Tom)
Newry, 14 December, 1973 (M)

League Club	Source	Date Signed	Seasons Played	Apps	Subs	Gls
Huddersfield T	YT	06.92	92	1	0	0

MOONEY Thomas (Tommy) John
Billingham, 11 August, 1971 (F)

League Club	Source	Date Signed	Seasons Played	Apps	Subs	Gls
Aston Villa	YT	11.89				
Scarborough	Tr	08.90	90-92	96	11	30
Southend U	Tr	07.93	93	9	5	5
Watford	Tr	03.94	93-00	221	29	60
Birmingham C	Tr	07.01	01-02	29	5	13
Stoke C	L	09.02	02	11	1	3
Sheffield U	L	01.03	02	2	1	0
Derby Co	L	03.03	02	7	1	0
Swindon T	Tr	07.03	03	41	4	19
Oxford U	Tr	07.04	04	42	0	15

MOOR Anthony (Tony) John
Scarborough, 18 January, 1940 (G)

League Club	Source	Date Signed	Seasons Played	Apps	Subs	Gls
York C	Scarborough	05.62	62-64	57	-	0
Darlington	Tr	07.65	65-71	239	0	0

MOOR Reinier Sean
Den Haag, Holland, 12 June, 1983 IRYth (F)

League Club	Source	Date Signed	Seasons Played	Apps	Subs	Gls
Exeter C	Sch	08.02	01-02	2	17	3

MOORCROFT David (Dave) Stanley
Liverpool, 16 March, 1947 (CD)

League Club	Source	Date Signed	Seasons Played	Apps	Subs	Gls
Tranmere Rov	Skelmersdale U	12.68	68-71	107	1	1

MOORCROFT Maurice
Chesterfield, 4 November, 1929 EYth (G)

League Club	Source	Date Signed	Seasons Played	Apps	Subs	Gls
Sheffield U	Jnrs	07.48				
Gillingham	Tr	07.52	52	8	-	0

MOORE Alan
Hebburn, 7 March, 1927 (W)

League Club	Source	Date Signed	Seasons Played	Apps	Subs	Gls
Sunderland		05.46				
Chesterfield	Spennymoor U	12.48	48-50	67	-	2
Hull C	Tr	07.51	51	13	-	4
Nottingham F	Tr	01.52	51-54	102	-	38
Coventry C	Tr	12.54	54-56	57	-	13
Swindon T	Tr	07.57	57-58	19	-	3
Rochdale	Tr	11.58	58	11	-	2

MOORE Alan
Dublin, 25 November, 1974 IRSch/IRYth/IRu21-4/IR-8 (W)

League Club	Source	Date Signed	Seasons Played	Apps	Subs	Gls
Middlesbrough	YT	12.91	92-98	98	20	14
Barnsley	L	10.98	98	4	1	0
Burnley	Tr	07.01	01-03	42	27	4

MOORE Andrew (Andy)
Wantage, 2 October, 1964 (M)

League Club	Source	Date Signed	Seasons Played	Apps	Subs	Gls
Reading	App	•	81	0	1	0

MOORE Andrew (Andy) Roy
Cleethorpes, 14 November, 1965 (CD)

League Club	Source	Date Signed	Seasons Played	Apps	Subs	Gls
Grimsby T	App	11.83	83-86	62	2	1

MOORE Anthony (Tony) Paul
York, 7 February, 1943 (CF)

League Club	Source	Date Signed	Seasons Played	Apps	Subs	Gls
York C (Am)	Heworth	05.62	62	2	-	0

MOORE Anthony (Tony) Peter
Scarborough, 4 September, 1947 (W)

League Club	Source	Date Signed	Seasons Played	Apps	Subs	Gls
Chesterfield	App	01.65	64-70	148	7	13
Grimsby T	L	03.71	70	2	1	0
Chester	Tr	08.71	71	9	4	3

MOORE Anthony (Tony) Peter
Wolverhampton, 19 September, 1957 (FB)

League Club	Source	Date Signed	Seasons Played	Apps	Subs	Gls
Sheffield U	Burton A	07.79	79-81	29	0	0
Crewe Alex	Tr	08.82	82	17	0	2
Rochdale	Goole T	10.84	84	1	2	0

MOORE John Frederick Beriah
Cardiff, 25 December, 1919 (W)

League Club	Source	Date Signed	Seasons Played	Apps	Subs	Gls
Cardiff C	Cardiff Corinthians	09.41	47-48	6	-	4
Newport Co	Bangor C	07.50	50-52	121	-	45

MOORE Bernard John
Brighton, 18 December, 1923 (CF)

League Club	Source	Date Signed	Seasons Played	Apps	Subs	Gls
Brighton & Hove A	Jnrs	09.45	47	8	-	2
Luton T	Hastings U	01.51	50-53	74	-	31
Brighton & Hove A	Tr	03.54	53-54	29	-	10

MOORE Brian
Hemsworth, 24 December, 1938 (W)

League Club	Source	Date Signed	Seasons Played	Apps	Subs	Gls
Mansfield T	Loughborough Coll (Am)	09.60	60	4	-	0
Notts Co	Tr	12.61	61-62	27	-	3
Doncaster Rov	Tr	07.63	63	1	-	0

MOORE Brian McGowan
Belfast, 29 December, 1933 IrLge-1 (IF)

League Club	Source	Date Signed	Seasons Played	Apps	Subs	Gls
West Ham U	Glentoran	02.55	54-55	9	-	1

MOORE Christian (Chris)
Derby, 4 November, 1972 (F)

League Club	Source	Date Signed	Seasons Played	Apps	Subs	Gls
Stockport Co	Leicester C (YT)	08.91	91	0	1	0

MOORE Craig Andrew
Canterbury, Australia, 12 December, 1975 Australia 7 (CD)

League Club	Source	Date Signed	Seasons Played	Apps	Subs	Gls
Crystal Palace	Glasgow Rgrs	10.98	98	23	0	3

MOORE Darren Mark
Birmingham, 22 April, 1974 Jamaica 3 (CD)

League Club	Source	Date Signed	Seasons Played	Apps	Subs	Gls
Torquay U	YT	11.92	91-94	102	1	8
Doncaster Rov	Tr	07.95	95-96	76	0	7
Bradford C	Tr	06.97	97-98	62	0	3
Portsmouth	Tr	11.99	99-01	58	1	2
West Bromwich A	Tr	09.01	01-04	90	9	6

League Club	Source	Date Signed	Seasons Played	Career Record Apps	Subs	Gls
MOORE David						
Grimsby, 17 December, 1959						(FB)
Grimsby T	App	12.77	78-82	136	0	2
Carlisle U	Tr	08.83	83	13	0	1
Blackpool	Tr	12.83	83-86	114	1	1
Grimsby T	Tr	12.86	86-87	3	1	0
Darlington	Tr	08.88	88	25	5	1
MOORE David Leon						
Worsley, 4 April, 1985						(F)
Wigan Ath	Sch	07.04				
Bury	L	01.05	04	0	3	0
MOORE Eric						
St Helens, 16 July, 1926 Died 2004						(FB)
Everton		02.49	49-56	171	-	0
Chesterfield	Tr	01.57	56	6	-	0
Tranmere Rov	Tr	07.57	57	36	-	0
MOORE Gary						
Sedgefield, 4 November, 1945						(F)
Sunderland	Jnrs	11.62	64-66	13	0	2
Grimsby T	Tr	02.67	66-68	52	1	15
Southend U	Tr	11.68	68-73	156	8	46
Colchester U	L	03.74	73	11	0	7
Chester	Tr	08.74	74-75	29	14	4
Swansea C	Tr	07.76	76-77	30	4	9
MOORE Gary						
Greenwich, 29 December, 1968						(F)
Maidstone U	Alma Swanley	03.91	90	0	5	1
MOORE Gordon Alexander						
Greenock, 27 June, 1968						(W)
Bristol C	Jnrs	06.86	85	0	1	0
MOORE Graham						
Hengoed, 7 March, 1941 Wu23-9/FLge-1/W-21						(M)
Cardiff C	Jnrs	05.58	58-61	85	-	23
Chelsea	Tr	12.61	61-63	68	-	13
Manchester U	Tr	11.63	63	18	-	4
Northampton T	Tr	12.65	65-66	53	0	10
Charlton Ath	Tr	06.67	67-70	110	0	8
Doncaster Rov	Tr	09.71	71-73	67	2	3
MOORE Howard						
Canterbury, 5 March, 1947						(W)
Coventry C	Ashford T	03.66				
Gillingham	Tr	07.67	67	17	0	0
Southend U	Tr	01.68	67-68	6	1	0
MOORE Ian Ronald						
Birkenhead, 26 August, 1976 EYth/Eu21-7						(F)
Tranmere Rov	YT	07.94	94-96	41	17	12
Bradford C	L	09.96	96	6	0	0
Nottingham F	Tr	03.97	96-97	3	12	1
West Ham U	L	09.97	97	0	1	0
Stockport Co	Tr	07.98	98-00	83	10	20
Burnley	Tr	11.00	00-04	170	22	37
Leeds U	Tr	03.05	04	4	2	0
MOORE Joe-Max						
Tulsa, USA, 23 February, 1971 Usu21/USA-100						(F)
Everton	New England (USA)	12.99	99-01	22	30	8
MOORE John						
Harthill, 21 December, 1943						(CD)
Luton T	Motherwell	05.65	65-72	264	9	13
Brighton & Hove A	L	10.72	72	5	0	0
Northampton T	Tr	08.74	74	14	0	0
MOORE John						
Liverpool, 9 September, 1945						(CD)
Stoke C	Everton (App)	07.63	67	12	1	0
Shrewsbury T	Tr	08.68	68-72	147	0	1
Swansea C	Tr	01.73	72-73	31	0	0
MOORE John						
Consett, 1 October, 1966						(F)
Sunderland	App	10.84	84-87	4	12	1
Newport Co	L	12.85	85	2	0	0
Darlington	L	11.86	86	2	0	1
Mansfield T	L	03.87	86	5	0	1
Rochdale	L	01.88	87	10	0	2
Hull C	Tr	06.88	88	11	3	1
Sheffield U	L	03.89	88	4	1	0
Shrewsbury T	FC Utrecht (Holl)	07.90	90	7	1	1
Crewe Alex	Tr	01.91	90	0	1	0
Scarborough	FC Utrecht (Holl)	08.91	91	3	4	1
MOORE John Michael						
Carlton, Nottinghamshire, 1 February, 1943						(W)
Lincoln C	Arnold St Mary's	11.61	61-64	30	-	5

League Club	Source	Date Signed	Seasons Played	Career Record Apps	Subs	Gls
MOORE John William Michael						
Chiswick, 25 September, 1923						(WH)
Brentford		09.46	46-47	4	-	0
Colchester U	Tr	07.49	51	2	-	0
MOORE Jonathan (Jon)						
Cardiff, 17 November, 1955 WSch/WYth						(FB)
Bristol Rov	App	11.73				
Millwall	Tr	12.74	74-78	119	0	5
Bournemouth	Tr	05.79	79-80	36	0	2
MOORE Kenneth (Ken)						
Bradford, 13 September, 1921						(FB)
Halifax T		11.47	47-49	32	-	2
MOORE Kevin						
Loughborough, 20 October, 1957						(M)
Shrewsbury T	App	10.75	74-77	15	3	1
MOORE Kevin John						
Blackpool, 30 January, 1956						(W)
Blackpool	App	10.73	74-76	33	6	3
Bury	L	12.76	76	4	0	0
Swansea C	Tr	07.77	77-78	51	4	6
Newport Co	Tr	02.79	78-82	140	8	13
Swindon T	L	03.83	82	1	0	0
MOORE Kevin Thomas						
Grimsby, 29 April, 1958 ESch						(CD)
Grimsby T	Jnrs	07.76	76-86	397	3	28
Oldham Ath	Tr	02.87	86	13	0	1
Southampton	Tr	08.87	87-93	144	4	10
Bristol Rov	L	01.92	91	7	0	0
Bristol Rov	L	10.92	92	4	0	1
Fulham	Tr	07.94	94-95	48	3	4
MOORE John Leslie						
Sheffield, 7 July, 1933 Died 1992						(CD)
Derby Co	Worksop T	11.57	57-63	144	-	3
Lincoln C	Boston	10.65	65-66	59	0	0
MOORE Luke Isaac						
Birmingham, 13 February, 1986 EYth						(F)
Aston Villa	Sch	02.03	03-04	5	27	1
Wycombe W	L	12.03	03	6	0	4
MOORE Malcolm						
Silksworth, 18 December, 1948						(F)
Sunderland	App	12.65	67-68	10	2	3
Crewe Alex	L	03.70	69	8	0	0
Tranmere Rov	Tr	07.70	70-72	83	10	21
Hartlepool	Tr	08.73	73-75	127	2	34
Workington	Tr	08.76	76	22	0	2
MOORE Mark Steven						
Bradford, 9 July, 1972						(M)
Cambridge U	N Hampshire Coll (USA)	03.98	97	0	1	0
MOORE Martin Terence						
Middlesbrough, 10 January, 1966						(W)
Peterborough U	Stockton	01.90	89	6	1	0
MOORE Michael (Micky)						
Chorley, 20 July, 1952						(F)
Preston NE	Blackburn Rov (Am)	06.70				
Southport	Tr	07.71	71-73	62	21	11
Port Vale	Wigan Ath	03.78	77	13	0	0
Wigan Ath	Tr	08.78	78-79	57	7	12
MOORE Michael Thomas						
Birmingham, 7 October, 1973						(F)
Derby Co	YT	06.92				
Swansea C	Tr	06.93	93	0	1	0
MOORE Neil						
Liverpool, 21 September, 1972						(CD)
Everton	YT	06.91	92-93	4	1	0
Blackpool	L	09.94	94	7	0	0
Oldham Ath	L	02.95	94	5	0	0
Carlisle U	L	08.95	95	13	0	0
Rotherham U	L	03.96	95	10	1	0
Norwich C	Tr	01.97	96	2	0	0
Burnley	Tr	08.97	97-98	48	4	3
Macclesfield T	Tr	12.99	99	12	3	2
Mansfield T	Telford U	07.02	02	18	0	0
MOORE Norman Woodliffe						
Grimsby, 15 October, 1919						(CF)
Grimsby T	Jnrs	03.39	46	7	-	1
Hull C	Tr	04.47	46-49	81	-	46
Blackburn Rov	Tr	03.50	49-50	7	-	1
Bury	Tr	08.51	51	2	-	0

MOORE Raymond (Ray)
Workington, 2 November, 1956 (W)

League Club	Source	Date Signed	Seasons Played	Apps	Subs	Gls
Workington	Sekers	11.75	75	3	0	0

MOORE Robert
Campsall, 14 December, 1932 (IF)

League Club	Source	Date Signed	Seasons Played	Apps	Subs	Gls
Rotherham U	Worksop T	05.55	55-56	19	-	2
Chesterfield	Tr	10.56	56-58	19	-	3

MOORE Robert (Bobby) Frederick Chelsea
Barking, 12 April, 1941 Died 1993 EYth/Eu23-8/FLge-12/E-108 (CD)

League Club	Source	Date Signed	Seasons Played	Apps	Subs	Gls
West Ham U	Jnrs	06.58	58-73	543	1	24
Fulham	Tr	03.74	73-76	124	0	1

MOORE Ronald (Ronnie) David
Liverpool, 29 January, 1953 (F)

League Club	Source	Date Signed	Seasons Played	Apps	Subs	Gls
Tranmere Rov	Jnrs	05.71	71-78	248	1	72
Cardiff C	Tr	02.79	78-79	54	2	6
Rotherham U	Tr	08.80	80-83	124	1	52
Charlton Ath	Tr	09.83	83-84	60	2	13
Rochdale	Tr	07.85	85	43	0	9
Tranmere Rov	Tr	07.86	86-88	75	0	6

MOORE Thomas **Roy**
Grimsby, 18 December, 1923 Died 1991 (CD)

League Club	Source	Date Signed	Seasons Played	Apps	Subs	Gls
Grimsby T		06.47	48-49	3	-	0

MOORE Samuel (Sammy) Christopher
Birmingham, 6 September, 1934 Died 1994 (W)

League Club	Source	Date Signed	Seasons Played	Apps	Subs	Gls
Wolverhampton W	Aldershot (Am)	11.54				
Walsall	Tr	05.55	55-57	64	-	10
Gillingham	Tr	06.58	58-59	33	-	9

MOORE Stefan
Birmingham, 28 September, 1983 EYth (F)

League Club	Source	Date Signed	Seasons Played	Apps	Subs	Gls
Aston Villa	YT	10.00	02-04	9	13	2
Chesterfield	L	10.01	01	1	1	0
Millwall	L	08.04	04	3	3	0
Leicester C	L	03.05	04	2	5	0

MOORE Stephen (Steve) John
Chester, 17 December, 1969 (F)

League Club	Source	Date Signed	Seasons Played	Apps	Subs	Gls
Chester C	YT	•	87	0	1	0

MOORE Thomas (Tom) Lynch
Trimdon, 25 July, 1936 (G)

League Club	Source	Date Signed	Seasons Played	Apps	Subs	Gls
Darlington (Am)	Trimdon	08.56	56	1	-	0

MOORE Watson (Wattie) Evans
Hartlepool, 30 August, 1925 Died 1967 (CD)

League Club	Source	Date Signed	Seasons Played	Apps	Subs	Gls
Hartlepools U	Oxford Street OB	05.48	48-59	447	-	3

MOORES James **Craig**
Macclesfield, 1 February, 1961 (F)

League Club	Source	Date Signed	Seasons Played	Apps	Subs	Gls
Bolton W	App	02.79	80	0	1	0
Swindon T	Tr	07.81	81	1	1	0

MOORES Ian Richard
Chesterton, 5 October, 1954 Died 1998 Eu23-2 (F)

League Club	Source	Date Signed	Seasons Played	Apps	Subs	Gls
Stoke C	App	06.72	73-75	40	10	15
Tottenham H	Tr	08.76	76-78	25	4	6
Orient	Tr	10.78	78-81	110	7	26
Bolton W	Tr	07.82	82	23	3	3
Barnsley	L	02.83	82	3	0	0

MOORHOUSE Alan
Wardle, 12 October, 1925 (W)

League Club	Source	Date Signed	Seasons Played	Apps	Subs	Gls
Rochdale	Blackburn Rov (Am)	03.47	46-47	17	-	3

MOORS Christopher (Chris) Anthony
Yeovil, 18 August, 1976 (F)

League Club	Source	Date Signed	Seasons Played	Apps	Subs	Gls
Torquay U	West Ham U (YT)	11.95	95	0	1	0

MORAH Olisa (Ollie) Henry
Islington, 3 September, 1972 ESch/EYth (F)

League Club	Source	Date Signed	Seasons Played	Apps	Subs	Gls
Tottenham H	YT	07.91				
Hereford U	L	11.91	91	0	2	0
Swindon T	Tr	11.92				
Cambridge U	Sutton U	06.94	94	8	6	2
Torquay U	L	03.95	94	2	0	0

MORAIS Nuno Miguel Barbosa
Penafiel, Portugal, 29 January, 1984 Portugal u21 (CD)

League Club	Source	Date Signed	Seasons Played	Apps	Subs	Gls
Chelsea	Penafiel (Por)	08.04	04	0	2	0

MORALEE Jamie David
Wandsworth, 2 December, 1971 (F)

League Club	Source	Date Signed	Seasons Played	Apps	Subs	Gls
Crystal Palace	YT	07.90	91	2	4	0
Millwall	Tr	09.92	92-93	56	11	19
Watford	Tr	07.94	94-95	40	9	7
Crewe Alex	Tr	08.96	96-97	10	6	0
Brighton & Hove A	Tr	08.98	98	22	9	3
Colchester U	Tr	07.99	99	20	7	1

MORAN Brian Joseph
Hemsworth, 3 June, 1947 (W)

League Club	Source	Date Signed	Seasons Played	Apps	Subs	Gls
Barnsley	Jnrs	01.67	66	1	0	0

MORAN Douglas (Doug) Walter
Musselburgh, 29 July, 1934 (IF)

League Club	Source	Date Signed	Seasons Played	Apps	Subs	Gls
Ipswich T	Falkirk	07.61	61-63	104	-	31

MORAN Edward (Eddie)
Cleland, 20 July, 1930 (IF)

League Club	Source	Date Signed	Seasons Played	Apps	Subs	Gls
Leicester C	Cleland Jnrs	09.47	48-50	8	-	1
Stockport Co	Tr	10.51	51-56	110	-	44
Rochdale	Tr	02.57	56-58	43	-	13
Crewe Alex	Tr	09.58	58	23	-	7

MORAN James (Jimmy)
Cleland, 6 March, 1935 (IF)

League Club	Source	Date Signed	Seasons Played	Apps	Subs	Gls
Leicester C	Wishaw Jnrs	12.55	56	3	-	1
Norwich C	Tr	11.57	57-59	36	-	17
Northampton T	Tr	01.61	60-61	24	-	6
Darlington	Tr	08.62	62	26	-	6
Workington	Tr	07.63	63-65	100	0	21

MORAN John
Cleland, 9 March, 1933 (IF)

League Club	Source	Date Signed	Seasons Played	Apps	Subs	Gls
Derby Co	Coltness U	11.54	54	2	-	0

MORAN Kevin Bernard
Dublin, 29 April, 1956 IR-70 (CD)

League Club	Source	Date Signed	Seasons Played	Apps	Subs	Gls
Manchester U	Pegasus (Dublin)	02.78	78-87	228	3	21
Blackburn Rov	Sporting Gijon (Sp)	01.90	89-93	143	4	10

MORAN Lister Ferguson
Ryton-on-Tyne, 24 June, 1930 (WH)

League Club	Source	Date Signed	Seasons Played	Apps	Subs	Gls
Gateshead	Wearmouth Colliery	10.50	53-56	19	-	0

MORAN Michael (Mike) Edward
Leek, 26 December, 1935 (IF)

League Club	Source	Date Signed	Seasons Played	Apps	Subs	Gls
Port Vale		07.54				
Crewe Alex	Tr	07.57	57	13	-	3

MORAN Paul
Enfield, 22 May, 1968 (W)

League Club	Source	Date Signed	Seasons Played	Apps	Subs	Gls
Tottenham H	App	07.85	86-93	14	22	2
Portsmouth	L	01.89	88	3	0	0
Leicester C	L	11.89	89	10	0	1
Newcastle U	L	02.91	90	1	0	0
Southend U	L	03.91	90	1	0	0
Peterborough U	Tr	07.94	94	5	2	0

MORAN Richard (Richie)
Hammersmith, 9 September, 1963 (F)

League Club	Source	Date Signed	Seasons Played	Apps	Subs	Gls
Birmingham C	Fujita Tokyo (Jap)	08.90	90	2	6	1

MORAN Ronald (Ronnie)
Liverpool, 28 February, 1934 FLge-2 (FB)

League Club	Source	Date Signed	Seasons Played	Apps	Subs	Gls
Liverpool	Jnrs	01.52	52-64	343	-	14

MORAN Stephen (Steve) James
Croydon, 10 January, 1961 ESch/Eu21-2 (F)

League Club	Source	Date Signed	Seasons Played	Apps	Subs	Gls
Southampton	Jnrs	08.79	79-85	173	7	78
Leicester C	Tr	09.86	86-87	35	8	14
Reading	Tr	11.87	87-90	91	25	30
Exeter C	Tr	08.91	91-92	50	7	27
Hull C	Tr	08.93	93	11	6	5

MORAN Thomas (Tommy)
Glasgow, 31 May, 1924 (WH)

League Club	Source	Date Signed	Seasons Played	Apps	Subs	Gls
Accrington St	Ayr U	08.53	53	7	-	0

MORAN Thomas (Tom)
Edinburgh, 5 February, 1930 (W)

League Club	Source	Date Signed	Seasons Played	Apps	Subs	Gls
Carlisle U	Cowdenbeath	05.54	54-55	35	-	4
Darlington	Tr	05.56	56-57	70	-	13

MORDUE James (Jimmy)
Seaton Delaval, 18 February, 1924 (WH)

League Club	Source	Date Signed	Seasons Played	Apps	Subs	Gls
Bradford PA	North Shields	09.46	48	2	-	0

MORDUE William (Billy)
Sacriston, 23 February, 1937 (CD)

League Club	Source	Date Signed	Seasons Played	Apps	Subs	Gls
Doncaster Rov	Bentley Colliery	03.58	57-60	78	-	0

MOREAU Fabrice
Paris, France, 7 October, 1967 (M)

League Club	Source	Date Signed	Seasons Played	Apps	Subs	Gls
Notts Co	Airdrie	03.01	00	2	3	0

MOREFIELD William **John** Thomas
Gloucester, 26 October, 1922 Died 1997 (FB)

League Club	Source	Date Signed	Seasons Played	Apps	Subs	Gls
Halifax T		05.46	46-48	65	-	0

League Club	Source	Date Signed	Seasons Played	Apps	Subs	Gls

MOREIRA Fabio da Silva
Rio de Janeiro, Brazil, 14 March, 1972 (M)

Middlesbrough	Chaves (Por)	02.97	97	1	0	0

MOREIRA Joao Manuel Silva
Angola, 30 June, 1970 (FB)

Swansea C	Benfica (Por)	06.96	96-97	15	0	0

MORELAND Victor (Vic)
Belfast, 15 June, 1957 NIu21-1/NI-6 (M)

Derby Co	Glentoran	09.78	78-79	38	4	1

MORELINE David (Dave) John
Stepney, 2 December, 1950 (FB)

Fulham	App	01.68	68-73	63	7	0
Reading	Tr	06.74	74-80	166	0	0

MOREMONT Ralph
Sheffield, 24 September, 1924 Died 1982 (WH)

Sheffield U	Hampton's Sports	09.46	49	2	-	0
Chester	Tr	05.50	50-52	121	-	19
Rochdale		08.55	55	1	-	0

MORENO Jaime Morales
Santa Cruz, Bolivia, 19 January, 1974 Bolivia int (M)

Middlesbrough	Blooming (Bol)	09.94	94-95	8	13	1
Middlesbrough (L)	DC United (USA)	12.97	97	1	4	1

MORENO Valera **Javier (Javi)**
Silla, Spain, 10 September, 1974 Spain 5 (F)

Bolton W (L)	Atletico Madrid (Sp)	01.04	03	1	7	0

MORGAN Alan
Swansea, 2 January, 1936 (CD)

Leeds U		01.54				
Crewe Alex	Tr	09.56	56	5	-	0

MORGAN Alan Meredith
Aberystwyth, 2 November, 1973 WSch/WYth/Wu21-2 (M)

Tranmere Rov	YT	05.92	95-01	42	23	1

MORGAN Alan William
Edinburgh, 27 November, 1983 SYth (M)

Blackburn Rov	YT	12.00				
Darlington	L	10.03	03	4	1	1
Cheltenham T	L	03.05	04	8	0	0

MORGAN Arthur Robert
Ogmore Vale, 13 September, 1930 Died 2000 (FB)

Swansea T		12.48	50-52	12	-	0
Plymouth Arg	Tr	11.53	53-56	36	-	4

MORGAN David **Bari** Rees
Carmarthen, 13 August, 1980 (M)

Swansea C	YT	07.99	00	0	5	0

MORGAN Christopher (Chris) Paul
Barnsley, 9 November, 1977 (CD)

Barnsley	YT	07.96	97-02	182	3	7
Sheffield U	Tr	08.03	03-04	72	1	3

MORGAN Clifford (Cliff) Ivor
Bristol, 26 September, 1913 Died 1975 (WH)

Bristol C	Bristol Boys Brigade	06.30	31-48	245	-	11

MORGAN Craig
St Asaph, 18 June, 1985 WYth/Wu21-6 (FB)

Wrexham	Sch	07.03	01-04	33	19	1

MORGAN Daniel (Danny) Frederick
Stepney, 4 November, 1984 (F)

Oxford U	Wimbledon (Sch)	07.04	04	0	3	0

MORGAN Darren Joseph
Camberwell, 5 November, 1967 WYth (M)

Millwall	App	11.85	86-90	35	8	2
Bradford C	L	03.90	89	2	0	0
Peterborough U	L	03.91	90	5	0	0
Bradford C	Tr	08.91	91	9	2	0

MORGAN Dean Lance
Enfield, 3 October, 1983 (F)

Colchester U	YT	08.01	00-02	23	48	6
Reading	Tr	11.03	03-04	13	18	3

MORGAN Denley James
Llanelli, 13 February, 1951 (FB)

Swansea T	Jnrs	02.71	68-71	14	0	0

MORGAN Richard **Dennis**
Seven Sisters, Glamorgan, 22 September, 1925 Died 1980 (FB)

Cardiff C	Briton Ferry	04.44				
Norwich C	Tr	10.46	46-55	225	-	3

MORGAN Donald (Don)
Huddersfield, 8 June, 1925 Died 1976 (WH)

Accrington St	Huddersfield T (Am)	06.47	46-47	8	-	1

MORGAN Ernest (Ernie)
Barnsley, 13 January, 1927 (IF)

Lincoln C	Rawmarsh	09.49	52	3	-	0
Gillingham	Tr	08.53	53-56	155	-	73

MORGAN Gary
Consett, 1 April, 1961 (FB)

Darlington	Berwick Rgrs	07.85	85-88	146	0	3

MORGAN George William
Cardiff, 28 March, 1923 Died 1989 (W)

Norwich C	Cardiff C (Am)	01.47	46-49	65	-	15

MORGAN Gerald (Gerry)
Llanidloes, 23 February, 1950 (G)

Walsall (Am)		03.74	73	1	0	0

MORGAN Huw
Neath, 20 August, 1964 (M)

Swansea C	App	08.82	83	5	2	0

MORGAN Ian Arthur
Walthamstow, 14 November, 1946 (W)

Queens Park Rgrs	App	09.64	64-72	161	12	26
Watford	Tr	10.73	73	15	1	1

MORGAN James (Jamie) Alexander
Plymouth, 1 October, 1975 (M)

Plymouth Arg	YT	06.94	92-94	9	2	0
Exeter C	Tr	08.95	95	2	4	0

MORGAN William **James (Jimmy)**
Bristol, 19 June, 1922 Died 1976 (IF)

Bristol Rov	Univ Settlement	04.46	46-51	104	-	24

MORGAN Jonathan (Jon) Peter
Cardiff, 10 July, 1970 WYth (M)

Cardiff C	YT	07.88	88-90	43	12	3

MORGAN Keith
Trowbridge, 19 February, 1940 (WH)

Swindon T	Westbury U	08.58	58-66	325	0	6

MORGAN Kenneth (Ken) Sidney
Swansea, 28 July, 1932 (W)

Fulham	Rickmansworth	09.50				
Watford	Tr	09.52				
Northampton T		09.54				
Crystal Palace	Tr	10.55	55	1	-	0

MORGAN Laurence (Lol)
Rotherham, 5 May, 1931 (FB)

Huddersfield T	Sheffield U (Am)	03.49	49-50	7	-	0
Rotherham U	Tr	08.54	54-63	291	-	0
Darlington	Tr	07.64	64-65	30	1	0

MORGAN Lewis (Lew)
Cowdenbeath, 30 April, 1911 Died 1988 SLge-1 (FB)

Portsmouth	Dundee	08.35	35-38	123	-	0
Watford	Tr	07.46	46-47	50	-	0

MORGAN Lionel Anthony
Tottenham, 17 February, 1983 EYth/Eu20 (W)

Wimbledon	YT	08.00	00-03	13	17	2

MORGAN Nicholas (Nicky)
East Ham, 30 October, 1959 (F)

West Ham U	App	11.77	78-82	14	7	2
Portsmouth	Tr	03.83	82-86	79	16	32
Stoke C	Tr	11.86	86-89	73	15	20
Bristol C	Tr	03.90	89-92	75	5	23
Bournemouth	L	10.92	92	6	0	1
Exeter C	Tr	02.94	93	12	0	4

MORGAN Mark **Paul** Thomas
Belfast, 23 October, 1978 NIu21-1 (CD)

Preston NE	YT	05.97				
Lincoln C	Tr	07.01	01-04	157	2	1

MORGAN Peter William
Cardiff, 28 October, 1951 (CD)

Cardiff C	Jnrs	11.69	72	16	0	0
Hereford U	Tr	08.74	74	16	0	0
Newport Co	Tr	03.76	75-76	22	2	1

MORGAN Philip (Phil) Jonathan
Stoke-on-Trent, 18 December, 1974 ESch/EYth (G)

Ipswich T	YT	07.93	94	1	0	0

League Club	Source	Date Signed	Seasons Played	Apps	Subs	Gls
Stoke C	Tr	07.95				
Chesterfield	L	10.96	96	2	0	0

MORGAN Richard (Richie) Leslie
Cardiff, 3 October, 1946 WSch/Wu23-1 (CD)

League Club	Source	Date Signed	Seasons Played	Apps	Subs	Gls
Cardiff C	Cardiff Corinthians	02.66	67-76	68	0	0

MORGAN Roger Ernest
Walthamstow, 14 November, 1946 EYth/Eu23-1 (W)

League Club	Source	Date Signed	Seasons Played	Apps	Subs	Gls
Queens Park Rgrs	App	09.64	64-68	180	0	39
Tottenham H	Tr	02.69	68-71	66	2	8

MORGAN Ronald (Ron)
Twynrodyn, 6 September, 1915 Died 1990 (CF)

League Club	Source	Date Signed	Seasons Played	Apps	Subs	Gls
Bournemouth	Wolverhampton T (Am)	06.35	35	2	-	1
Doncaster Rov	Northfleet	05.37	37-38	6	-	1
Accrington St	Tr	06.39	46	4	-	0

MORGAN Ryan Stephen
Bristol, 12 July, 1978 (M)

League Club	Source	Date Signed	Seasons Played	Apps	Subs	Gls
Bristol Rov	YT	03.97	96	1	0	0

MORGAN Samuel (Sammy) John
Belfast, 3 December, 1946 NI-18 (F)

League Club	Source	Date Signed	Seasons Played	Apps	Subs	Gls
Port Vale	Gorleston	07.70	69-72	109	5	25
Aston Villa	Tr	08.73	73-75	35	5	9
Brighton & Hove A	Tr	12.75	75-76	19	16	8
Cambridge U	Tr	08.77	77	34	3	4

MORGAN Scott
Colchester, 22 March, 1975 (CD)

League Club	Source	Date Signed	Seasons Played	Apps	Subs	Gls
Brentford	Bournemouth (YT)	08.93	93	1	0	0

MORGAN Sidney Samuel
Bristol, 1 August, 1926 (G)

League Club	Source	Date Signed	Seasons Played	Apps	Subs	Gls
Bristol C	AG Farmers	12.47	48-53	71	-	0
Millwall	Tr	03.58	57-58	16	-	0

MORGAN Simon Charles
Birmingham, 5 September, 1966 Eu21-2 (CD)

League Club	Source	Date Signed	Seasons Played	Apps	Subs	Gls
Leicester C	App	11.84	85-89	147	15	4
Fulham	Tr	10.90	90-00	343	10	48
Brighton & Hove A	Tr	07.01	01	42	0	1

MORGAN Simon Dean
Merthyr Tydfil, 3 September, 1970 (M)

League Club	Source	Date Signed	Seasons Played	Apps	Subs	Gls
Newport Co	YT	•	87	0	2	0

MORGAN Alfred Stanley (Stan)
Abergwynfi, 10 October, 1920 Died 1971 (IF)

League Club	Source	Date Signed	Seasons Played	Apps	Subs	Gls
Arsenal	Gwynfi Welfare	12.41	46	2	-	0
Walsall	Tr	06.48	48	10	-	1
Millwall	Tr	12.48	48-52	156	-	41
Leyton Orient	Tr	05.53	53-55	96	-	24

MORGAN Stephen (Steve) Alphonso
Oldham, 19 September, 1968 EYth (FB)

League Club	Source	Date Signed	Seasons Played	Apps	Subs	Gls
Blackpool	App	08.86	85-89	135	9	10
Plymouth Arg	Tr	07.90	90-92	120	1	6
Coventry C	Tr	07.93	93-94	65	3	2
Bristol Rov	L	03.96	95	5	0	0
Wigan Ath	Tr	07.96	96-97	31	5	2
Bury	L	09.97	97	5	0	0
Burnley	Tr	08.98	98	17	0	0
Hull C	Tr	07.99	99	17	2	1
Halifax T	Tr	09.00	00	1	0	0

MORGAN Stephen (Steve) James
Wrexham, 28 December, 1970 WYth (W)

League Club	Source	Date Signed	Seasons Played	Apps	Subs	Gls
Oldham Ath	YT	07.89	87-88	1	1	0
Wrexham	L	03.90	89	7	0	1
Rochdale	Tr	03.91	90-91	12	11	3

MORGAN Stuart Edward
Swansea, 23 September, 1949 (CD)

League Club	Source	Date Signed	Seasons Played	Apps	Subs	Gls
West Ham U	Jnrs	03.67				
Torquay U	L	02.69	68	14	0	0
Reading	Tr	11.69	69-71	42	4	1
Colchester U	Tr	08.72	72-74	79	2	10
Bournemouth	Tr	03.75	74-76	80	1	5

MORGAN Trevor James
Forest Gate, 30 September, 1956 (F)

League Club	Source	Date Signed	Seasons Played	Apps	Subs	Gls
Bournemouth	Leytonstone & Ilford	09.80	80-81	53	0	13
Mansfield T	Tr	11.81	81	12	0	6
Bournemouth	Tr	03.82	81-83	88	0	33
Bristol C	Tr	03.84	83-84	32	0	8
Exeter C	Tr	11.84	84-85	30	0	9
Bristol Rov	Tr	09.85	85-86	54	1	24
Bristol C	Tr	01.87	86	19	0	7
Bolton W	Tr	06.87	87-88	65	12	17
Colchester U	Tr	10.89	89	31	1	12

League Club	Source	Date Signed	Seasons Played	Apps	Subs	Gls
Exeter C	Happy Valley (HK)	11.90	90	14	3	3
Birmingham C	Sun Valley (HK)	10.93	93	0	1	0
Exeter C	(Retired)	09.94	94	4	5	1

MORGAN Wendell
Gorseinon, 22 April, 1935 (W)

League Club	Source	Date Signed	Seasons Played	Apps	Subs	Gls
Cardiff C	Grovesend	05.52				
Brentford	Tr	06.54	55-57	47	-	6
Gillingham	Tr	09.57	57	34	-	3
Swansea T	Tr	07.58	58	7	-	0
Newport Co	Tr	06.59	59	26	-	3
Carlisle U	Tr	06.60	60	36	-	2

MORGAN Westley (Wes) Nathan
Nottingham, 21 January, 1984 (FB)

League Club	Source	Date Signed	Seasons Played	Apps	Subs	Gls
Nottingham F	Dunkirk (Nottingham)	07.02	03-04	72	3	3
Kidderminster Hrs	L	02.03	02	5	0	1

MORGAN William (Willie)
Glasgow, 2 October, 1944 Su23-1/S-21 (W)

League Club	Source	Date Signed	Seasons Played	Apps	Subs	Gls
Burnley	Fishcross	10.61	62-67	183	0	19
Manchester U	Tr	08.68	68-74	236	2	25
Burnley	Tr	06.75	75	12	1	0
Bolton W	Tr	03.76	75-79	154	1	10
Blackpool	Tr	09.80	80-81	41	1	4

MORGAN William (Bill) Alfred
Rotherham, 26 September, 1926 (WH)

League Club	Source	Date Signed	Seasons Played	Apps	Subs	Gls
Wolverhampton W	Jnrs	11.43				
Sheffield U	Tr	09.46				
Halifax T	Tr	08.48	48-52	110	-	3
Rochdale	Tr	07.53	53-54	28	-	0

MORGAN Wynffrwd (Gwyn)
Abergwynfi, 7 August, 1925 (W)

League Club	Source	Date Signed	Seasons Played	Apps	Subs	Gls
Bristol Rov (Am)	Coventry C (Am)	12.46	46	2	-	0

MORGANS Morgan Gwyn
Blaenau Ffestiniog, 20 April, 1932 (WH)

League Club	Source	Date Signed	Seasons Played	Apps	Subs	Gls
Northampton T	Blaenau Ffestiniog	08.55				
Wrexham	Tr	07.56	56-57	28	-	2
Southport	Tr	07.58	58	14	-	0

MORGANS Jeffrey (Jeff)
Farnborough, 12 August, 1942 Died 1995 (IF)

League Club	Source	Date Signed	Seasons Played	Apps	Subs	Gls
Crewe Alex	Jnrs	09.59	60-61	9	-	2

MORGANS Kenneth (Ken) Godfrey
Swansea, 16 March, 1939 Wu23-2 (W)

League Club	Source	Date Signed	Seasons Played	Apps	Subs	Gls
Manchester U	Jnrs	04.56	57-60	17	-	0
Swansea T	Tr	03.61	60-63	54	-	8
Newport Co	Tr	06.64	64-66	125	0	44

MORIENTES Fernando
Caceres, Spain, 5 April, 1976 Spain 24 (F)

League Club	Source	Date Signed	Seasons Played	Apps	Subs	Gls
Liverpool	Real Madrid (Sp)	01.05	04	12	1	3

MORINI Emanuele
Rome, Italy, 31 January, 1982 (F)

League Club	Source	Date Signed	Seasons Played	Apps	Subs	Gls
Bolton W	AS Roma (It)	09.00	00	1	1	0

MORISON Steven (Steve) William
Enfield, 29 August, 1983 (F)

League Club	Source	Date Signed	Seasons Played	Apps	Subs	Gls
Northampton T	Sch	07.03	01-04	7	16	3

MORLEY William Anthony (Tony)
Ormskirk, 26 August, 1954 EYth/Eu23-1/EB/E-6 (W)

League Club	Source	Date Signed	Seasons Played	Apps	Subs	Gls
Preston NE	App	08.72	72-75	78	6	15
Burnley	Tr	02.76	75-78	78	13	5
Aston Villa	Tr	06.79	79-83	128	9	25
West Bromwich A	Tr	12.83	83-84	33	0	4
Birmingham C	L	11.84	84	4	0	3
West Bromwich A	Den Haag (Holl)	08.87	87	27	1	7
Burnley	L	10.88	88	5	0	0

MORLEY Benjamin (Ben)
Hull, 20 December, 1980 (FB)

League Club	Source	Date Signed	Seasons Played	Apps	Subs	Gls
Hull C	YT	12.98	97-01	7	19	0
Boston U	Tr	08.02	02	1	1	0

MORLEY Brian James
Fleetwood, 4 October, 1960 (FB)

League Club	Source	Date Signed	Seasons Played	Apps	Subs	Gls
Blackburn Rov	App	10.78	78-79	20	0	0
Tranmere Rov	Tr	08.81	81	10	6	2

MORLEY David Thomas
St Helens, 25 September, 1977 (CD)

League Club	Source	Date Signed	Seasons Played	Apps	Subs	Gls
Manchester C	YT	01.96	97	1	2	1
Southend U	Tr	08.98	98-00	63	13	0
Carlisle U	Tr	01.01	00-01	37	4	1
Oxford U	Tr	12.01	01	16	2	3
Doncaster Rov	Tr	07.02	03-04	24	6	1
Macclesfield T	Tr	01.05	04	19	0	2

League Club	Source	Date Signed	Seasons Played	Apps	Subs	Gls
MORLEY Trevor William						
Nottingham, 20 March, 1961 ESemiPro						(F)
Northampton T	Nuneaton Borough	06.85	85-87	107	0	39
Manchester C	Tr	01.88	87-89	69	3	18
West Ham U	Tr	12.89	89-94	159	19	57
Reading	Brann Bergen (Nor)	08.95	95-97	67	10	31
MORLEY William (Bill)						
Nottingham, 30 July, 1925 Died 1978						(WH)
Nottingham F	Mapperley Celtic	08.45	46-58	282	-	10
MORNAR Ivica						
Split, Croatia, 12 January, 1974 Croatia 20						(F)
Portsmouth	Anderlecht (Holl)	01.04	03	3	5	1
MORONEY Thomas (Tommy)						
Cork, 10 November, 1923 Died 1980 LoI-7/IR-12						(WH)
West Ham U	Cork U	08.47	47-52	148	-	8
MORRAD Frank						
Brentford, 28 February, 1920						(FB)
Notts Co	Southall	08.44	46	1	-	0
Leyton Orient	Tr	11.46	46	25	-	11
Fulham	Tr	08.47				
Brighton & Hove A	Tr	02.48	47-50	43	-	3
Brentford	Tr	08.51	51-52	6	-	2
MORRALL Alfred (Alf) Douglas						
Duddeston, 1 July, 1916 Died 1998						(WH)
Northampton T	Redditch T	10.44	46-47	34	-	11
Newport Co	Tr	07.48	48	28	-	0
MORRALL Stephen (Steve) Asbury						
Torquay, 25 September, 1952						(W)
Torquay U	Jnrs	08.72	72-76	133	32	12
MORRALL Terence (Terry) Stephen						
Smethwick, 24 November, 1938						(CD)
Aston Villa	Jnrs	11.55	59-60	8	-	0
Shrewsbury T	Tr	05.61	60-62	31	-	0
Wrexham	Tr	07.63	63-64	42	-	0
Southport	Tr	07.65	65	1	0	0
MORRELL Andrew (Andy) Jonathan						
Doncaster, 28 September, 1974						(F)
Wrexham	Newcastle Blue Star	12.98	98-02	76	34	40
Coventry C	Tr	07.03	03-04	43	21	15
MORRELL Paul David						
Poole, 23 March, 1961						(FB)
Bournemouth	Weymouth	06.83	83-92	337	6	21
MORRELL Robert (Bobby) Ian						
Hesleden, 4 June, 1944						(WH)
Hartlepools U	Blackhall Colliery	03.64	63-64	34	-	0
MORREY Bernard Joseph						
Liverpool, 8 April, 1927						(W)
Tranmere Rov	Jnrs	08.44				
Newport Co	Llandudno	10.52	52-53	22	-	2
Chester	Tr	12.53	53-54	30	-	6
MORRIN Anthony (Tony) John						
Swinton, 31 July, 1946						(M)
Bury	App	10.63	63-64	3	-	0
Burnley	Tr	07.65				
Stockport Co	Tr	10.66	66-68	26	5	2
Barrow	Tr	03.69	68-70	97	0	6
Exeter C	Tr	07.71	71-76	180	2	15
Stockport Co	Tr	03.77	76	13	0	1
Rochdale	Tr	08.77	77-78	29	1	0
MORRIS Alan						
Swansea, 6 February, 1941						(W)
Swansea T	Jnrs	06.58	57-62	12	-	1
Reading	Tr	08.63	63	12	-	0
MORRIS Alan Geoffrey						
Chester, 15 July, 1954 Died 1998						(FB)
Chester C	Bangor C	06.84	84	0	1	0
MORRIS Alfred (Alf)						
Cadishead						(WH)
Accrington St	Rochdale (Am)	10.45	46-47	15	-	0
MORRIS Andrew (Andy) Dean						
Sheffield, 17 November, 1967						(F)
Rotherham U	Jnrs	07.85	84-86	0	7	0
Chesterfield	Tr	01.88	87-98	225	41	56
Exeter C	L	03.92	91	4	3	2
Rochdale	Tr	12.98	98-99	26	6	7

League Club	Source	Date Signed	Seasons Played	Apps	Subs	Gls
MORRIS Christopher (Chris) Barry						
Newquay, 24 December, 1963 ESch/IR-35						(FB)
Sheffield Wed	Jnrs	10.82	83-86	61	13	1
Middlesbrough	Glasgow Celtic	08.92	92-96	75	7	3
MORRIS Christopher (Chris) Joseph						
Spilsby, 12 October, 1939 Died 1997						(W)
Hull C	Jnrs	10.57	58-60	17	-	4
MORRIS Colin						
Blyth, 22 August, 1953						(W)
Burnley	App	08.71	74-75	9	1	0
Southend U	Tr	01.77	76-79	133	0	25
Blackpool	Tr	12.79	79-81	87	0	26
Sheffield U	Tr	02.82	81-87	235	5	67
Scarborough	Tr	07.88	88-89	20	4	3
MORRIS David						
Swansea, 20 September, 1957						(F)
Manchester U	App	10.74				
York C	L	03.77	76	1	6	0
MORRIS David Kenneth						
Plumstead, 19 November, 1971						(CD)
Bournemouth	YT	07.90	90	0	1	0
Hereford U	Tr	02.93	92-93	33	7	1
MORRIS Douglas (Doug)						
Durham, 29 July, 1925						(W)
Hartlepools U	Ushaw Moor	01.46	46-50	19	-	3
MORRIS John **Edward (Ed)**						
Crewe, 27 November, 1937						(WH)
Crewe Alex	Jnrs	12.54	54	2	-	0
MORRIS Edwin (Ted) Keith						
Pontypool, 6 May, 1921 Died 2000						(G)
Cardiff C	Barry T	05.48	48-50	8	-	0
MORRIS Elfed						
Colwyn Bay, 9 June, 1942						(W)
Wrexham		05.60	60-61	9	-	6
Chester	Tr	06.62	62-67	164	3	69
Halifax T	Tr	03.68	67-68	9	0	2
MORRIS Edward **Eric**						
Mold, 15 April, 1940						(FB)
Chester		06.60	60	1	-	0
MORRIS Ernest						
Stocksbridge, 11 May, 1921						(CF)
Nottingham F		08.47	47	4	-	1
York C	Tr	06.48				
Halifax T	Grantham	11.50	50	1	-	0
MORRIS Frank						
Penge, 28 March, 1932 Died 2002						(W)
Crystal Palace		03.56	56	8	-	0
MORRIS Frederick (Freddie) Alfred						
Sheffield, 11 March, 1920 Died 1973						(IF)
Barnsley		09.46	46-48	23	-	9
Southend U	Tr	01.49	48-49	34	-	16
MORRIS Frederick (Fred) William						
Oswestry, 15 June, 1929 Died 1997						(W)
Walsall	Oswestry T	05.50	50-56	213	-	44
Mansfield T	Tr	03.57	56-57	56	-	17
Liverpool	Tr	05.58	58-59	47	-	14
Crewe Alex	Tr	06.60	60	8	-	1
Gillingham	Tr	01.61	60	11	-	1
Chester	Tr	07.61	61	29	-	3
MORRIS Geoffrey (Geoff)						
Birmingham, 8 February, 1949						(W)
Walsall	App	02.66	65-72	172	5	35
Shrewsbury T	Tr	01.73	72-74	71	4	9
Port Vale	Tr	08.75	75	10	5	1
MORRIS George Edward						
Crewe, 22 November, 1929						(FB)
Crewe Alex	Crewe Cadets	08.48	48-53	28	-	0
MORRIS Glenn James						
Woolwich, 20 December, 1983						(G)
Leyton Orient	Sch	03.03	01-04	63	1	0
MORRIS Gordon John						
Wrottesley, 27 June, 1926						(IF)
West Bromwich A	East Park	11.44				
Walsall	Tr	07.49	49	6	-	2

League Club	Source	Date Signed	Seasons Played	Career Record Apps	Subs	Gls
MORRIS Ian Gwynfor						
Manchester, 10 June, 1948						(W)
Stockport Co	Bolton W (Am)	03.68	67	1	1	0
MORRIS James Henry						
St Helens, 16 November, 1915						(CD)
Stockport Co	St Helens T	08.39	46-48	61	-	3
MORRIS Jody Steven						
Hammersmith, 22 December, 1978 ESch/EYth/Eu21-7						(M)
Chelsea	YT	01.96	95-02	82	42	5
Leeds U	Tr	07.03	03	11	1	0
Rotherham U	Tr	03.04	03	9	1	1
Millwall	Tr	07.04	04	35	2	5
MORRIS John (Johnny)						
Radcliffe, 27 September, 1923 EB/FLge-5/E-3						(IF)
Manchester U	Jnrs	03.41	46-48	83	-	32
Derby Co	Tr	03.49	48-52	130	-	44
Leicester C	Tr	10.52	52-57	206	-	33
MORRIS Joseph (Joe) Richard						
Canning Town, 13 April, 1934						(IF)
Crewe Alex		08.54	54	3	-	0
MORRIS Kevin George						
Much Wenlock, 22 September, 1953						(FB)
Shrewsbury T	App	07.71	70-71	9	0	0
MORRIS Lee						
Blackpool, 30 April, 1980 EYth/Eu21-1						(F)
Sheffield U	YT	12.97	97-99	14	12	6
Derby Co	Tr	10.99	99-03	62	29	17
Huddersfield T	L	03.01	00	5	0	1
Leicester C	Tr	02.04	04	2	8	0
MORRIS Maldwyn Jones Gravell						
Swansea, 3 August, 1932 Died 2000						(CF)
Swansea T	Pembroke Borough	10.56	56-57	14	-	5
MORRIS Mark						
Chester, 1 August, 1968						(G)
Wrexham	YT	08.87	85-93	101	0	0
MORRIS Mark John						
Morden, 26 September, 1962						(CD)
Wimbledon	App	09.80	81-86	167	1	9
Aldershot	L	09.85	85	14	0	0
Watford	Tr	07.87	87-88	41	0	1
Sheffield U	Tr	07.89	89-90	53	3	3
Bournemouth	Tr	07.91	91-96	190	4	8
Gillingham	L	09.96	96	6	0	0
Brighton & Hove A	Tr	10.96	96-97	30	1	2
MORRIS Michael (Mike) John						
Plaistow, 20 January, 1943						(W)
Oxford U	Faversham	07.64	64-66	89	1	15
Port Vale	Tr	08.67	67-71	176	8	24
MORRIS Neil Anthony						
Sheffield, 3 May, 1970						(F)
York C	Doncaster Rov (YT)	09.88	88	3	1	0
Doncaster Rov	Worksop T	02.92	91	0	1	0
MORRIS Paul Ian						
Bolton, 6 February, 1975						(CD)
Bury	YT	●	92	0	1	0
MORRIS Paul Whittington						
Glasfryn, 8 January, 1957						(F)
Hereford U	Llanelli	02.80	79-80	2	2	1
MORRIS Peter Andrew						
Farnworth, 23 November, 1958						(W)
Preston NE	App	10.76				
Blackburn Rov	Tr	07.78	78	2	2	0
MORRIS Peter John						
New Houghton, 8 November, 1943						(M)
Mansfield T	Jnrs	11.60	60-67	286	1	50
Ipswich T	Tr	03.68	67-73	213	7	13
Norwich C	Tr	06.74	74-75	66	0	1
Mansfield T	Tr	07.76	76-77	41	0	3
Peterborough U	Newcastle U (Coach)	08.79	79	1	0	0
MORRIS Ronald (Ronnie)						
Birmingham, 25 September, 1970 ESch						(W)
Birmingham C	YT	09.88	87-88	3	8	0
MORRIS Samuel (Sam)						
Warrington, 12 February, 1930						(WH)
Chester	Stockton Heath	12.51	51-56	90	-	0
MORRIS Stephen (Steve)						
Liverpool, 13 May, 1976						(F)
Wrexham	Liverpool (YT)	09.94	94-96	24	18	9
MORRIS Stephen (Steve) Albert						
Bristol, 6 July, 1949						(FB)
Bristol C	App	06.67				
Exeter C	Tr	06.69	69-71	61	11	2
MORRIS Steven (Steve) Granville						
Swansea, 8 October, 1958						(FB)
Swansea C	App	06.76	75-78	33	6	1
MORRIS William (Billy)						
Llanddulas, 30 July, 1918 Died 2002 WWar-1/W-5						(IF)
Burnley	Llandudno T	01.39	38-52	211	-	47
MORRIS William (Billy)						
Radcliffe, 1 April, 1931						(W)
Bury	Jnrs	05.48				
Derby Co	Tr	10.51				
Rochdale	Tr	11.52	52	4	-	1
MORRIS William (Billy) Henry						
Swansea, 28 September, 1920 Died 1994						(W)
Swansea T		05.46	47-48	16	-	1
Brighton & Hove A	Tr	09.49	49-50	28	-	4
MORRIS William (Billy) Walker						
Handsworth, 26 March, 1913 Died 1995 E-3						(FB)
Wolverhampton W	Halesowen T	05.33	33-46	175	-	2
MORRISON Andrew (Andy) Charles						
Inverness, 30 July, 1970						(CD)
Plymouth Arg	YT	07.88	87-92	105	8	6
Blackburn Rov	Tr	08.93	93	1	4	0
Blackpool	Tr	12.94	94-95	47	0	3
Huddersfield T	Tr	07.96	96-98	43	2	2
Manchester C	Tr	10.98	98-00	36	1	4
Blackpool	L	09.00	00	6	0	1
Crystal Palace	L	10.00	00	5	0	0
Sheffield U	L	03.01	00	3	1	0
MORRISON Angus Cameron						
Dingwall, 26 April, 1924 Died 2002 SB						(W)
Derby Co	Ross Co	10.44	46-47	52	-	21
Preston NE	Tr	11.48	48-56	261	-	69
Millwall	Tr	10.57	57	15	-	4
MORRISON Charles						
Newton Aycliffe, 12 January, 1953						(CD)
Chelsea	App	08.70				
Doncaster Rov	Tr	07.72	72	5	1	0
MORRISON Clinton Hubert						
Tooting, 14 May, 1979 IRu21-2/IR-30						(F)
Crystal Palace	YT	03.97	97-01	141	16	62
Birmingham C	Tr	08.02	02-04	56	30	14
MORRISON David (Dave) Ellis						
Walthamstow, 30 November, 1974						(W)
Peterborough U	Chelmsford C	05.94	94-96	59	18	12
Leyton Orient	Tr	03.97	96-99	21	25	3
MORRISON George Charles						
Ayr, 27 November, 1924						(CD)
Hartlepools U	St Johnstone	08.51	51	2	-	0
MORRISON James Clark						
Darlington, 25 May, 1986 EYth						(W)
Middlesbrough	Sch	07.03	03-04	4	11	0
MORRISON John						
Greenock, 4 August, 1929						(IF)
Torquay U	Morton	07.51	51	2	-	0
MORRISON John						
Kettering, 27 July, 1970						(M)
Torquay U	YT	07.88	88-89	24	8	0
MORRISON Murdoch (Murdo)						
Glasgow, 9 October, 1924 Died 1975						(G)
Luton T	Bellhaven Star	09.45	46	1	-	0
Leyton Orient	Tr	08.47	47	10	-	0
MORRISON John Owen						
Derry, 8 December, 1981 NISch/NIYth/NIu21-7						(F)
Sheffield Wed	YT	01.99	98-02	31	25	8
Hull C	L	08.02	02	1	1	0
Sheffield U	Tr	02.03	02	3	5	0
Stockport Co	Tr	08.03	03-04	11	12	1
Bradford C	Tr	12.04	04	17	5	2

MORRISON Peter Anthony
Manchester, 29 June, 1980 (M)

League Club	Source	Date Signed	Seasons Played	Apps	Subs	Gls
Bolton W	YT	07.98				
Scunthorpe U	Tr	05.00	00	8	10	0

MORRISON Robert Crosson
Chapelhall, 16 February, 1933 Died 1999 IrLge-1 (IF)

League Club	Source	Date Signed	Seasons Played	Apps	Subs	Gls
Nottingham F	Glasgow Rgrs	07.58	58	1	-	0
Workington	Tr	07.59	59-60	53	-	20

MORRISON Thomas (Tommy)
Croy, 6 March, 1943 (IF)

League Club	Source	Date Signed	Seasons Played	Apps	Subs	Gls
Port Vale	Aberdeen	08.65	65	5	0	1

MORRISON William (Willie)
Edinburgh, 31 March, 1934 Died 2001 (WH)

League Club	Source	Date Signed	Seasons Played	Apps	Subs	Gls
Sunderland	Merchiston Thistle	05.51	54-56	19	-	0
Southend U	Tr	01.58	57-59	60	-	4

MORRISON William (Willie)
Croy, 10 October, 1939 (FB)

League Club	Source	Date Signed	Seasons Played	Apps	Subs	Gls
Portsmouth	Croy Guilds	05.58	58	3	-	0

MORRISON-HILL Jamie Steven
Plymouth, 8 June, 1981 (M)

League Club	Source	Date Signed	Seasons Played	Apps	Subs	Gls
Plymouth Arg	YT	07.99	99	0	1	0

MORRISSEY John (Johnny) Joseph
Liverpool, 18 April, 1940 ESch/FLge-1 (W)

League Club	Source	Date Signed	Seasons Played	Apps	Subs	Gls
Liverpool	Jnrs	05.57	57-60	36	-	6
Everton	Tr	09.62	62-71	257	2	43
Oldham Ath	Tr	05.72	72	6	0	1

MORRISSEY John Joseph
Liverpool, 8 March, 1965 EYth (W)

League Club	Source	Date Signed	Seasons Played	Apps	Subs	Gls
Everton	App	03.83	84	1	0	0
Wolverhampton W	Tr	08.85	85	5	5	1
Tranmere Rov	Tr	10.85	85-98	396	74	50

MORRISSEY Patrick (Pat) Joseph
Enniscorthy, 23 February, 1948 Died 2005 IRu23-1 (F)

League Club	Source	Date Signed	Seasons Played	Apps	Subs	Gls
Coventry C	App	07.65	66-67	6	4	0
Torquay U	Tr	07.68	68	19	2	0
Crewe Alex	Tr	07.69	69-71	95	1	28
Chester	Tr	10.71	71	9	0	1
Watford	Tr	12.71	71-74	101	6	27
Aldershot	Tr	11.74	74-76	109	0	27
Swansea C	L	10.77	77	3	1	0

MORRITT Gordon Raymond
Rotherham, 8 February, 1942 (G)

League Club	Source	Date Signed	Seasons Played	Apps	Subs	Gls
Rotherham U	Steel Peach & Tozer	06.61	61-65	77	0	0
Doncaster Rov	Durban C (SA)	09.67	67-68	40	0	0
Northampton T	Tr	08.68	68-69	42	0	0
York C	Tr	10.69	69-71	41	0	0
Rochdale	Tr	08.72	72	31	0	0
Darlington	Tr	08.73	73	34	0	0

MORROW Andrew (Andy) Gareth
Bangor, County Down, 5 October, 1980 NISch/NIYth/NIu21-1 (F)

League Club	Source	Date Signed	Seasons Played	Apps	Subs	Gls
Northampton T	YT	12.98	99-00	2	6	0

MORROW Grant Ralph
Glasgow, 4 October, 1970 (F)

League Club	Source	Date Signed	Seasons Played	Apps	Subs	Gls
Doncaster Rov	Rowntree Mackintosh	07.89	89-92	46	18	7
Colchester U	Tr	08.93	93	0	1	0

MORROW Hugh (Hughie)
Larne, 9 July, 1930 (W)

League Club	Source	Date Signed	Seasons Played	Apps	Subs	Gls
West Bromwich A	Nuneaton Borough	08.47	48	5	-	2
Northampton T	Lockheed Leamington	06.56	56	30	-	3

MORROW John James
Belfast, 20 November, 1971 NIYth/NIB (W)

League Club	Source	Date Signed	Seasons Played	Apps	Subs	Gls
Oldham Ath	Glasgow Rgrs	08.96	96	1	1	0

MORROW Samuel (Sam)
Derry, 3 March, 1985 NIYth (F)

League Club	Source	Date Signed	Seasons Played	Apps	Subs	Gls
Ipswich T	Sch	08.02				
Boston U	L	12.03	03	0	2	0

MORROW Stephen (Steve) Joseph
Bangor, County Down, 2 July, 1970 NISch/NIYth/NIu23-2/NIB-1/NI-39 (FB)

League Club	Source	Date Signed	Seasons Played	Apps	Subs	Gls
Arsenal	YT	05.88	91-96	39	23	1
Reading	L	01.91	90	10	0	0
Watford	L	08.91	91	7	1	0
Reading	L	10.91	91	3	0	0
Barnet	L	03.92	91	1	0	0
Queens Park Rgrs	Tr	03.97	96-00	84	7	2
Peterborough U	L	03.01	00	11	0	0

MORSE Richard Anthony
Newport, 17 December, 1966 (CD)

League Club	Source	Date Signed	Seasons Played	Apps	Subs	Gls
Newport Co	Jnrs	08.83	83	0	1	0

MORTENSEN Henrik
Odder, Denmark, 12 February, 1968 (F)

League Club	Source	Date Signed	Seasons Played	Apps	Subs	Gls
Norwich C	Aarhus GF (Den)	10.89	89-90	12	6	0

MORTENSEN Stanley (Stan) Harding (CF)
South Shields, 26 May, 1921 Died 1991 FLge-5/WWar-1/EWar-3/E-25

League Club	Source	Date Signed	Seasons Played	Apps	Subs	Gls
Blackpool	South Shields	05.38	46-55	319	-	197
Hull C	Tr	11.55	55-56	42	-	18
Southport	Tr	02.57	56-57	36	-	10

MORTIMER Alexander (Alex) Barry
Manchester, 28 November, 1982 (M)

League Club	Source	Date Signed	Seasons Played	Apps	Subs	Gls
Leicester C	YT	01.00				
Shrewsbury T	Tr	10.02	02	0	1	0

MORTIMER Dennis George
Liverpool, 5 April, 1952 EYth/Eu23-6/EB (M)

League Club	Source	Date Signed	Seasons Played	Apps	Subs	Gls
Coventry C	App	09.69	69-75	179	14	10
Aston Villa	Tr	12.75	75-84	316	1	31
Sheffield U	L	12.84	84	7	0	0
Brighton & Hove A	Tr	08.85	85	40	0	2
Birmingham C	Tr	08.86	86	33	0	4

MORTIMER John (Johnny) McCormick
Birkenhead, 5 December, 1923 (FB)

League Club	Source	Date Signed	Seasons Played	Apps	Subs	Gls
Wrexham		01.47	46-48	23	-	0
New Brighton	Tr	10.49	49-50	5	-	0

MORTIMER Paul Henry
Kensington, 8 May, 1968 Eu21-2 (M)

League Club	Source	Date Signed	Seasons Played	Apps	Subs	Gls
Charlton Ath	Farnborough T	09.87	87-90	108	5	17
Aston Villa	Tr	07.91	91	10	2	1
Crystal Palace	Tr	10.91	91-92	18	4	2
Brentford	L	01.93	92	6	0	0
Charlton Ath	Tr	07.94	94-98	67	19	15
Bristol C	Tr	08.99	99	22	1	0

MORTIMORE Charles (Charlie) Thomas Reginald
Gosport, 12 April, 1928 EAmat (CF)

League Club	Source	Date Signed	Seasons Played	Apps	Subs	Gls
Aldershot (Am)	Woking	08.49	49-52	66	-	28
Portsmouth (Am)	Woking	10.53	53	1	-	0
Aldershot (Am)	Woking	12.55	55	2	-	0

MORTIMORE John Henry
Farnborough, 23 September, 1934 EAmat/EYth (CD)

League Club	Source	Date Signed	Seasons Played	Apps	Subs	Gls
Chelsea	Woking	04.56	55-64	249	-	8
Queens Park Rgrs	Tr	09.65	65	10	0	0

MORTON Alan
Peterborough, 6 March, 1942 (IF)

League Club	Source	Date Signed	Seasons Played	Apps	Subs	Gls
Arsenal	Peterborough U	04.59				
Peterborough U	Tr	10.61	61-62	7	-	2
Lincoln C	Wisbech T	07.63	63-64	58	-	20
Chesterfield	Tr	07.65	65	28	1	6

MORTON Alan
Erith, 13 April, 1950 (F)

League Club	Source	Date Signed	Seasons Played	Apps	Subs	Gls
Crystal Palace	Woking	11.67				
Stockport Co	L	08.69	69	12	2	2
Fulham	Nuneaton Borough	08.70	70	1	0	1

MORTON Albert
Newcastle, 27 July, 1919 Died 1991 (G)

League Club	Source	Date Signed	Seasons Played	Apps	Subs	Gls
Sheffield Wed	St Peter's A	03.38	47-50	41	-	0
Rochdale	Tr	07.53	53-56	89	-	0

MORTON Geoffrey (Geoff) Dalgleish
Acton, 27 July, 1924 Died 2000 (G)

League Club	Source	Date Signed	Seasons Played	Apps	Subs	Gls
Watford	Chelmsford C	10.48	48-51	107	-	0
Southend U	Tr	02.52	51-52	25	-	0
Exeter C	Tr	09.54	54	6	-	0

MORTON George Edmund
Liverpool, 30 September, 1943 (IF)

League Club	Source	Date Signed	Seasons Played	Apps	Subs	Gls
Everton	Jnrs	10.60				
Rochdale	Tr	07.62	62-65	146	1	51

MORTON Gerald (Gerry) William
Newcastle, 17 March, 1944 (CD)

League Club	Source	Date Signed	Seasons Played	Apps	Subs	Gls
Newcastle U	North Shields	08.62				
Workington	Tr	04.63	62-63	3	-	0

MORTON Keith
Consett, 11 August, 1934 (W)

League Club	Source	Date Signed	Seasons Played	Apps	Subs	Gls
Crystal Palace (Am)		08.53	53	5	-	3
Sunderland	Tr	07.54				
Darlington	Tr	05.55	55-60	171	-	49

League Club	Source	Date Signed	Seasons Played	Apps	Subs	Gls
MORTON Kenneth (Ken)						
Chorley, 19 May, 1947 ESch (W)						
Manchester U	App	05.64				
York C	Tr	05.65	65	9	1	2
Blackpool	Tr	08.66				
Darlington	Fleetwood	07.68	68	4	1	0
MORTON Neil						
Congleton, 21 December, 1968 (W)						
Crewe Alex	YT	09.87	86-88	18	13	1
Chester C	Northwich Vic	10.90	90-92	63	32	13
Wigan Ath	Tr	07.93	93-94	41	7	5
MORTON Norman						
Barnsley, 22 May, 1925 Died 1977 (CF)						
Leeds U	Woolley Colliery	12.47	47	1	-	0
MORTON Robert (Bob) Hendy						
Aston Clinton, 25 September, 1927 Died 2002 EB (WH)						
Luton T	Waterlows	02.46	48-63	495	-	48
MORTON Roy Steven						
Birmingham, 29 October, 1955 ESch/EYth (M)						
Manchester U	App	11.72				
Birmingham C	Tr	09.73	74	3	0	0
MORTON William (Mick)						
Grangemouth, 2 April, 1928 (CD)						
Millwall		10.45	46-50	11	-	0
MOSBY Harold (Harry)						
Kippax, 25 June, 1926 (W)						
Rotherham U	Huddersfield T (Am)	01.47	47-49	26	-	9
Scunthorpe U	Tr	07.50	50-54	149	-	21
Crewe Alex	Worksop T	08.56	56	38	-	4
MOSELEY Graham						
Manchester, 16 November, 1953 EYth (G)						
Blackburn Rov	App	09.71				
Derby Co	Tr	09.71	72-76	32	0	0
Aston Villa	L	08.74	74	3	0	0
Walsall	L	10.77	77	3	0	0
Brighton & Hove A	Tr	11.77	77-85	189	0	0
Cardiff C	Tr	08.86	86-87	38	0	0
MOSES Adrian (Adie) Paul						
Doncaster, 4 May, 1975 Eu21-2 (CD)						
Barnsley	Jnrs	07.93	94-00	137	14	3
Huddersfield T	Tr	12.00	00-02	63	6	1
Crewe Alex	Tr	07.03	03-04	34	8	0
MOSES George						
High Spen, 11 September, 1920 Died 1987 (IF)						
Newcastle U		10.39				
Hartlepools U	Tr	08.46	46	19	-	4
MOSES Remi Mark						
Manchester, 14 November, 1960 Eu21-8 (M)						
West Bromwich A	App	11.78	79-81	63	0	5
Manchester U	Tr	09.81	81-87	143	7	7
MOSS Amos						
Birmingham, 28 August, 1921 Died 2004 (WH)						
Aston Villa	Jnrs	05.39	46-55	102	-	5
MOSS Craig Anthony						
Birmingham, 11 March, 1961 (W)						
Wolverhampton W	App	03.79	78-81	4	0	0
MOSS Darren Michael						
Wrexham, 24 May, 1981 WYth/Wu21-4 (FB)						
Chester C	YT	07.99	98-99	33	9	0
Shrewsbury T	Tr	07.01	01-04	84	13	10
Crewe Alex	Tr	03.05	04	6	0	0
MOSS David Albert						
Doncaster, 15 November, 1968 (M)						
Doncaster Rov	Boston U	03.93	92-93	18	0	5
Chesterfield	Tr	10.93	93-95	59	12	16
Scunthorpe U	Tr	07.96	96	4	0	0
Swansea C	Falkirk	08.02	02	3	6	2
MOSS David John						
Witney, 18 March, 1952 (W)						
Swindon T	Witney T	07.69	71-77	217	13	60
Luton T	Tr	05.78	78-84	218	3	88
Swindon T	Tr	07.85	85	4	0	0
MOSS Donald (Don) Richard						
Tamworth, 27 June, 1925 Died 1999 (WH)						
Cardiff C	Boldmere St Michael's	05.51				
Crystal Palace	Tr	05.53	53-56	56	-	2
MOSS Edward (Eddie)						
Skelmersdale, 27 October, 1939 (IF)						
Liverpool	Skelmersdale U	10.58				
Southport	Tr	07.59	59-60	51	-	15
MOSS Ernest (Ernie)						
Chesterfield, 19 October, 1949 (F)						
Chesterfield	Chesterfield Tube Wks	10.68	68-75	271	0	95
Peterborough U	Tr	01.76	75-76	34	1	9
Mansfield T	Tr	12.76	76-78	56	1	21
Chesterfield	Tr	01.79	78-80	105	2	33
Port Vale	Tr	06.81	81-82	74	0	23
Lincoln C	Tr	03.83	82	10	1	2
Doncaster Rov	Tr	06.83	83	41	3	15
Chesterfield	Tr	07.84	84-86	90	1	34
Stockport Co	Tr	12.86	86	26	0	7
Scarborough	Tr	08.87	87	22	1	4
Rochdale	L	03.88	87	10	0	2
MOSS Frank						
Aston, 16 September, 1917 Died 1997 (CD)						
Sheffield Wed	Worcester C	11.35	36-37	22	-	0
Aston Villa	Tr	05.38	38-54	296	-	3
MOSS Jack (Jackie)						
Blackrod, 1 September, 1923 Died 1975 (IF)						
Bury	Horwich Central	12.43	46	7	-	2
Rochdale	Tr	01.47	46-48	58	-	17
Leeds U	Tr	01.49	48-50	23	-	2
Halifax T	Tr	01.51	50-53	124	-	11
MOSS Neil Graham						
New Milton, 10 May, 1975 (G)						
Bournemouth	YT	01.93	92-95	21	1	0
Southampton	Tr	12.95	96-01	22	2	0
Gillingham	L	08.97	97	10	0	0
Bournemouth	Tr	09.02	02-04	125	0	0
MOSS Paul Michael						
Birmingham, 2 August, 1957 (M)						
Wolverhampton W	Northfield Jnrs	07.76				
Hull C	Tr	09.79	79-80	53	1	7
Scunthorpe U	Tr	09.81	81	42	0	7
MOSS Robert (Bobby)						
Chigwell, 13 February, 1952 (F)						
Orient	App	02.70	70	2	3	1
Colchester U	Tr	05.72	72	16	1	3
MOSS Robert (Bob) Stephen						
Kenton, 15 February, 1949 (W)						
Fulham	App	02.66	67	8	1	3
Peterborough U	Tr	07.69	69-72	86	18	17
MOSS Roy Graham						
Maldon, 5 September, 1941 ESch (IF)						
Tottenham H	Jnrs	01.60				
Gillingham	Tr	09.62	62-63	14	-	3
MOSS Ryan James						
Dorchester, 14 November, 1986 (F)						
Bournemouth	Sch	•	04	0	1	0
MOSS Terence (Terry) John						
Bristol, 2 January, 1932 (W)						
Swindon T (Am)		03.56	55	7	-	0
MOSSMAN David John						
Sheffield, 27 July, 1964 ESch (W)						
Sheffield Wed	Jnrs	08.82				
Bradford C	L	03.85	84	0	3	1
Stockport Co	L	10.85	85	9	0	4
Rochdale	Tr	01.86	85	8	0	0
Stockport Co	Tr	03.86	85-86	28	2	1
MOSSOP Graham						
Wellington, 11 January, 1958 (F)						
Workington	Liverpool (App)	11.75	75	1	0	0
Carlisle U		07.79	80	2	0	0
MOSTYN Roger						
Wrexham, 31 August, 1953 (F)						
Wrexham	Jnrs	11.71	71-73	16	3	4
MOTTERSHEAD Brian Leslie						
Rochdale, 13 July, 1935 Died 1985 (IF)						
Notts Co	Hamer YC	09.52				
Rochdale	Tr	08.53	53	1	-	0
MOTTERSHEAD Keith Anthony						
Stafford, 12 December, 1944 (W)						
Doncaster Rov	Stafford Rgrs	10.66	66-67	34	6	0

MOUGHTON Colin Edward
Harrow, 30 December, 1947 (CD)

League Club	Source	Date Signed	Seasons Played	Apps	Subs	Gls
Queens Park Rgrs	App	12.65	65-66	6	0	0
Colchester U	Tr	07.68	68	4	0	0

MOULD William (Billy)
Great Chell, 6 October, 1919 Died 1999 (FB)

League Club	Source	Date Signed	Seasons Played	Apps	Subs	Gls
Stoke C	Summerbank	07.36	37-51	177	-	0
Crewe Alex	Tr	07.52	52-53	66	-	1

MOULDEN Anthony (Tony)
Farnworth, 28 August, 1942 (IF)

League Club	Source	Date Signed	Seasons Played	Apps	Subs	Gls
Bury	Blackburn Rov (Am)	05.60	60-61	4	-	0
Rochdale	Tr	06.62	62	5	-	1
Peterborough U	Tr	11.62	62-64	62	-	9
Notts Co	Tr	05.65	65	23	0	1
Rochdale	Tr	09.66	66	1	0	0

MOULDEN Paul Anthony Joseph
Farnworth, 6 September, 1967 ESch/EYth (F)

League Club	Source	Date Signed	Seasons Played	Apps	Subs	Gls
Manchester C	App	09.84	85-88	48	16	18
Bournemouth	Tr	08.89	89	32	0	0
Oldham Ath	Tr	03.90	89-92	17	21	4
Brighton & Hove A	L	08.92	92	11	0	5
Birmingham C	Tr	03.93	92-93	18	2	5
Huddersfield T	Tr	03.95	94	0	2	0
Rochdale	Tr	08.95	95	6	10	1

MOULSON George Bernard
Clogheen, 6 August, 1914 Died 1994 IR-3 (G)

League Club	Source	Date Signed	Seasons Played	Apps	Subs	Gls
Grimsby T		07.36	46	1	-	0
Lincoln C	Tr	06.47	47-48	60	-	0

MOUNCER Frank Edmund
Grimsby, 22 November, 1920 Died 1977 ESch (FB)

League Club	Source	Date Signed	Seasons Played	Apps	Subs	Gls
Grimsby T	Humber U	09.38	46-48	22	-	0

MOUNTAIN Patrick (Pat) Douglas
Pontypridd, 1 August, 1976 WYth/Wu21-2 (G)

League Club	Source	Date Signed	Seasons Played	Apps	Subs	Gls
Cardiff C	Barry T	07.95	96	5	0	0

MOUNTAIN Robert (Bob) Brian
Wombwell, 11 September, 1956 (F)

League Club	Source	Date Signed	Seasons Played	Apps	Subs	Gls
Huddersfield T	App	11.73	73	1	0	0

MOUNTFIELD Derek Neal
Liverpool, 2 November, 1962 Eu21-1/EB-1 (CD)

League Club	Source	Date Signed	Seasons Played	Apps	Subs	Gls
Tranmere Rov	App	11.80	80-81	26	0	1
Everton	Tr	06.82	82-87	100	1	19
Aston Villa	Tr	06.88	88-91	88	2	9
Wolverhampton W	Tr	11.91	91-93	79	4	4
Carlisle U	Tr	08.94	94	30	1	3
Northampton T	Tr	10.95	95	4	0	0
Walsall	Tr	11.95	95-97	96	1	2
Scarborough	Bromsgrove Rov	01.99	98	5	1	0

MOUNTFORD David
Hanley, 9 January, 1931 Died 1985 (W)

League Club	Source	Date Signed	Seasons Played	Apps	Subs	Gls
Crewe Alex	Jnrs	11.48	48-51	36	-	5
West Bromwich A	Tr	12.51	52	4	-	0
Crewe Alex	Tr	10.53	53-56	27	-	7

MOUNTFORD Derek
Stoke-on-Trent, 24 March, 1934 Died 1994 (WH)

League Club	Source	Date Signed	Seasons Played	Apps	Subs	Gls
Port Vale	Jnrs	05.51	54-56	26	-	0
Crewe Alex	Tr	07.57	57	13	-	0

MOUNTFORD Frank
Campsall, 30 March, 1923 (WH)

League Club	Source	Date Signed	Seasons Played	Apps	Subs	Gls
Stoke C	Jnrs	04.40	46-57	391	-	21

MOUNTFORD George Frederick
Stoke-on-Trent, 30 March, 1921 Died 1973 (W)

League Club	Source	Date Signed	Seasons Played	Apps	Subs	Gls
Stoke C	Kidderminster Hrs	09.38	46-49	123	-	25
Stoke C	Independiente (Col)	09.51	51-52	25	-	0
Queens Park Rgrs	Tr	10.52	52-53	35	-	2

MOUNTFORD Peter
Stoke-on-Trent, 13 September, 1960 (M)

League Club	Source	Date Signed	Seasons Played	Apps	Subs	Gls
Norwich C	App	09.78	81-82	1	3	0
Charlton Ath	Tr	09.83	83	10	1	1
Orient	Tr	01.85	84-86	27	6	2

MOUNTFORD Raymond (Ray)
Mexborough, 28 April, 1958 (G)

League Club	Source	Date Signed	Seasons Played	Apps	Subs	Gls
Manchester U	App	04.75				
Rotherham U	Tr	07.78	78-82	123	0	0
Bury	L	11.83	83	4	0	0

MOUNTFORD Robert (Bob) William
Stoke-on-Trent, 23 February, 1952 (F)

League Club	Source	Date Signed	Seasons Played	Apps	Subs	Gls
Port Vale	App	02.70	68-74	64	17	9
Scunthorpe U	L	10.74	74	1	2	0
Crewe Alex	L	12.74	74	5	0	0
Rochdale	Tr	01.75	74-77	97	1	37
Huddersfield T	Tr	10.77	77	12	2	4
Halifax T	Tr	03.78	77-79	56	6	11
Crewe Alex	Tr	08.80	80	3	0	0
Stockport Co	Tr	11.80	80	6	1	3

MOUSSADDIK Choukri (Chuck)
Meknes, Morocco, 23 February, 1970 Morocco int (G)

League Club	Source	Date Signed	Seasons Played	Apps	Subs	Gls
Wycombe W	Wimbledon (Jnrs)	08.90	95	1	0	0

MOVERLEY Robert (Rob)
Batley, 18 January, 1969 (G)

League Club	Source	Date Signed	Seasons Played	Apps	Subs	Gls
Bradford C	App	06.87				
Hartlepool U	Tr	12.88	88-89	29	0	0

MOWBRAY Anthony (Tony) Mark
Saltburn, 22 November, 1963 EB-2 (CD)

League Club	Source	Date Signed	Seasons Played	Apps	Subs	Gls
Middlesbrough	App	11.81	82-91	345	3	26
Ipswich T	Glasgow Celtic	10.95	95-99	125	3	5

MOWBRAY Darren Karl
Middlesbrough, 24 January, 1978 (CD)

League Club	Source	Date Signed	Seasons Played	Apps	Subs	Gls
Scarborough	Middlesbrough (YT)	08.96	96	2	1	0

MOWBRAY Henry (Harry)
Hamilton, 1 May, 1947 (FB)

League Club	Source	Date Signed	Seasons Played	Apps	Subs	Gls
Blackpool	Cowdenbeath	05.67	67-70	88	3	0
Bolton W	Tr	06.71	71-72	31	0	0

MOWER Kenneth (Ken) Matthew
Bloxwich, 1 December, 1960 (FB)

League Club	Source	Date Signed	Seasons Played	Apps	Subs	Gls
Walsall	App	11.78	78-90	410	5	8

MOWL Joseph William
Bulwell, 23 June, 1922 (G)

League Club	Source	Date Signed	Seasons Played	Apps	Subs	Gls
Notts Co		10.44	48	3	-	0

MOXHAM Graham
Exeter, 3 January, 1949 (W)

League Club	Source	Date Signed	Seasons Played	Apps	Subs	Gls
Bournemouth	Preston NE (App)	07.66				
Exeter C	Bideford T	07.75	75	4	2	0

MOXHAM Robert (Bob)
Barrow, 5 July, 1922 Died 1990 (CF)

League Club	Source	Date Signed	Seasons Played	Apps	Subs	Gls
Barrow	Holker COB	09.48	48	5	-	1

MOYES David William
Blythswood, 25 April, 1963 SSch/SYth (CD)

League Club	Source	Date Signed	Seasons Played	Apps	Subs	Gls
Cambridge U	Glasgow Celtic	10.83	83-85	79	0	1
Bristol C	Tr	10.85	85-87	83	0	6
Shrewsbury T	Tr	10.87	87-89	91	5	11
Preston NE	Hamilton Academical	09.93	93-97	142	1	15

MOYES John David
Heage, 17 July, 1951 (CD)

League Club	Source	Date Signed	Seasons Played	Apps	Subs	Gls
Chesterfield	App	07.69	68-71	13	0	0

MOYLON Craig
Munster, Germany, 16 October, 1972 (FB)

League Club	Source	Date Signed	Seasons Played	Apps	Subs	Gls
Preston NE	Jnrs	07.91	92	0	1	0

MOYSE Alexander (Alec) Rodney
Mitcham, 5 August, 1935 Died 1994 (CF)

League Club	Source	Date Signed	Seasons Played	Apps	Subs	Gls
Crystal Palace	Chatham	02.56	55-56	4	-	1
Swindon T	Tr	08.58	58	4	-	0
Millwall	Tr	09.58	58-59	22	-	3

MOYSE Ronald (Ron)
Portsmouth, 2 April, 1920 Died 1992 (FB)

League Club	Source	Date Signed	Seasons Played	Apps	Subs	Gls
Reading		10.46	46-52	189	-	0

MOYSES Christopher (Chris) Raymond
Lincoln, 1 November, 1965 (CD)

League Club	Source	Date Signed	Seasons Played	Apps	Subs	Gls
Lincoln C	App	11.83	83	2	2	0
Halifax T	Tr	07.84	84	21	4	0

MOZLEY Bertram (Bert)
Derby, 23 September, 1923 FLge-1/E-3 (FB)

League Club	Source	Date Signed	Seasons Played	Apps	Subs	Gls
Derby Co	Nottingham F (Am)	06.46	46-54	297	-	2

MUDD Paul Andrew
Hull, 13 November, 1970 ESch (FB)

League Club	Source	Date Signed	Seasons Played	Apps	Subs	Gls
Hull C	YT	07.89	88	1	0	0
Scarborough	Tr	07.90	90-92	95	3	2
Scunthorpe U	Tr	07.93	93-94	66	2	4
Lincoln C	Tr	07.95	95	2	2	0

MUDGE James (Jamie) Robert Mark
Exeter, 25 March, 1983 (F)

League Club	Source	Date Signed	Seasons Played	Apps	Subs	Gls
Exeter C	YT	●	00	0	3	0

MUDIE John (Jackie) Knight
Dundee, 10 April, 1930 Died 1992 S-17 (IF)

League Club	Source	Date Signed	Seasons Played	Apps	Subs	Gls
Blackpool	Lochee Harp	05.47	49-60	323	-	144
Stoke C	Tr	03.61	60-63	88	-	32
Port Vale	Tr	11.63	63-66	54	0	9

MUGGLETON Carl David
Leicester, 13 September, 1968 Eu21-1 (G)

League Club	Source	Date Signed	Seasons Played	Apps	Subs	Gls
Leicester C	App	09.86	88-92	46	0	0
Chesterfield	L	09.87	87	17	0	0
Blackpool	L	02.88	87	2	0	0
Hartlepool U	L	10.88	88	8	0	0
Stockport Co	L	03.90	89	4	0	0
Stoke C	L	08.93	93	6	0	0
Stoke C	Glasgow Celtic	07.94	94-00	148	1	0
Rotherham U	L	11.95	95	6	0	0
Sheffield U	L	03.96	95	0	1	0
Mansfield T	L	09.99	99	9	0	0
Chesterfield	L	12.99	99	5	0	0
Cardiff C	L	03.01	00	6	0	0
Cheltenham T	Tr	07.01	01	7	0	0
Bradford C	L	12.01	01	4	0	0
Chesterfield	Tr	07.02	02-04	109	0	0

MUHREN Arnold Johannes Hyacinthus
Volendam, Holland, 2 June, 1951 Holland int (M)

League Club	Source	Date Signed	Seasons Played	Apps	Subs	Gls
Ipswich T	Twente Enschede (Holl)	08.78	78-81	161	0	21
Manchester U	Tr	08.82	82-84	65	5	13

MUIR Alexander (Alex) Johnston
Inverkeithing, 10 December, 1923 Died 1995 (W)

League Club	Source	Date Signed	Seasons Played	Apps	Subs	Gls
Liverpool	Lochgelly Violet	07.47	47	4	-	0

MUIR Ian Baker
Motherwell, 16 June, 1929 (CD)

League Club	Source	Date Signed	Seasons Played	Apps	Subs	Gls
Bristol Rov	Motherwell	05.53	53-56	26	-	0
Oldham Ath	Tr	06.57	57	35	-	0

MUIR Ian James
Coventry, 5 May, 1963 ESch/EYth (F)

League Club	Source	Date Signed	Seasons Played	Apps	Subs	Gls
Queens Park Rgrs	App	09.80	80	2	0	2
Burnley	L	10.82	82	1	1	1
Birmingham C	Tr	08.83	83	1	0	0
Brighton & Hove A	Tr	02.84	83-84	3	1	0
Swindon T	L	01.85	84	2	0	0
Tranmere Rov	Tr	07.85	85-94	283	31	140
Birmingham C	Tr	06.95	95	1	0	0
Darlington	L	09.95	95	4	0	1

MUIR John George
Sedgley, 26 April, 1963 (F)

League Club	Source	Date Signed	Seasons Played	Apps	Subs	Gls
Doncaster Rov	Dudley T	02.90	89-91	64	11	18
Stockport Co	Tr	02.92	91-92	10	3	3
Torquay U	L	02.93	92	7	5	0

MUIR Maurice Moyston
Wimbledon, 19 March, 1963 ESch (M)

League Club	Source	Date Signed	Seasons Played	Apps	Subs	Gls
Northampton T	App	02.82	79-83	15	13	0

MUIR William (Billy) Miller
Ayr, 27 August, 1925 Died 2005 (W)

League Club	Source	Date Signed	Seasons Played	Apps	Subs	Gls
Queens Park Rgrs	Irvine Meadow	02.49	48-52	17	-	4
Torquay U	Tr	10.52	52	9	-	0

MUIR William (Willie) Nelson
Port Glasgow, 14 August, 1934 Died 2000 (CF)

League Club	Source	Date Signed	Seasons Played	Apps	Subs	Gls
Aldershot	St Mirren	05.56	56	8	-	4

MUIRHEAD Benjamin (Ben) Robinson
Doncaster, 5 January, 1983 EYth (W)

League Club	Source	Date Signed	Seasons Played	Apps	Subs	Gls
Manchester U	YT	01.00				
Bradford C	Tr	03.03	02-04	43	33	3

MULDOON John Patrick Joseph
Bebington, 21 November, 1964 (W)

League Club	Source	Date Signed	Seasons Played	Apps	Subs	Gls
Wrexham	Jnrs	12.82	82-85	64	19	11

MULDOON Terence (Terry)
Ashington, 10 August, 1951 Died 1971 (W)

League Club	Source	Date Signed	Seasons Played	Apps	Subs	Gls
Scunthorpe U (Am)		05.70	70	2	0	0

MULGREW Thomas (Tommy)
Motherwell, 13 April, 1929 (IF)

League Club	Source	Date Signed	Seasons Played	Apps	Subs	Gls
Northampton T	Morton	07.49	50-52	8	-	1
Newcastle U	Tr	10.52	52-53	14	-	1
Southampton	Tr	07.54	54-61	293	-	90
Aldershot	Tr	08.62	62-64	112	-	2

MULGROVE Keith Arnold
Haltwhistle, 21 August, 1959 (CD)

League Club	Source	Date Signed	Seasons Played	Apps	Subs	Gls
Newcastle U	App	07.77	78	0	1	0

MULHALL George
Falkirk, 8 May, 1936 SLge-3/S-3 (W)

League Club	Source	Date Signed	Seasons Played	Apps	Subs	Gls
Sunderland	Aberdeen	09.62	62-68	249	4	55

MULHEARN Kenneth (Ken) John
Liverpool, 16 October, 1945 (G)

League Club	Source	Date Signed	Seasons Played	Apps	Subs	Gls
Everton	App	07.63				
Stockport Co	Tr	08.64	64-67	100	0	0
Manchester C	Tr	09.67	67-69	50	0	0
Shrewsbury T	Tr	03.71	70-79	370	0	0
Crewe Alex	Tr	08.80	80-81	88	0	0

MULHERON Peter
Glasgow, 21 June, 1921 (IF)

League Club	Source	Date Signed	Seasons Played	Apps	Subs	Gls
Crystal Palace	Tonbridge	10.48	48-49	38	-	2

MULHOLLAND Francis (Frank) Gerard
Belfast, 28 October, 1927 IrLge-3 (WH)

League Club	Source	Date Signed	Seasons Played	Apps	Subs	Gls
Middlesbrough	Glentoran	10.51	51-57	46	-	0

MULHOLLAND George Rush
Paisley, 4 August, 1928 Died 2001 (FB)

League Club	Source	Date Signed	Seasons Played	Apps	Subs	Gls
Stoke C		07.50	50	3	-	0
Bradford C	Tr	07.53	53-59	277	-	0
Darlington	Tr	07.60	60-62	106	-	0

MULHOLLAND James (Jimmy)
Knightswood, 10 April, 1938 (F)

League Club	Source	Date Signed	Seasons Played	Apps	Subs	Gls
Chelsea	East Stirling	10.62	62-63	11	-	2
Barrow	Morton	08.65	65-68	132	2	46
Stockport Co	Tr	10.68	68-69	28	4	5
Crewe Alex	Tr	08.70	70	0	1	0

MULHOLLAND John Anthony
Dumbarton, 20 January, 1932 Died 2000 (CF)

League Club	Source	Date Signed	Seasons Played	Apps	Subs	Gls
Southampton	Condorrat Thistle	12.51				
Chester	Tr	07.56	56	8	-	1
Halifax T	Tr	06.57	57	8	-	1

MULHOLLAND John Ross
Dumbarton, 7 December, 1928 (W)

League Club	Source	Date Signed	Seasons Played	Apps	Subs	Gls
Plymouth Arg	Renton BG	10.46				
Grimsby T	Tr	08.49	49-50	2	-	0
Scunthorpe U	Tr	10.50	50	6	-	1

MULHOLLAND Scott Rene
Bexleyheath, 7 September, 1986 (M)

League Club	Source	Date Signed	Seasons Played	Apps	Subs	Gls
Queens Park Rgrs	Sch	●	04	0	1	0

MULKERRIN James (Jimmy)
Dumbarton, 25 December, 1931 SB (IF)

League Club	Source	Date Signed	Seasons Played	Apps	Subs	Gls
Accrington St	Hibernian	03.57	56-58	70	-	36
Tranmere Rov	Tr	08.59	59-60	38	-	8

MULLAN Brendan Gerald Joseph
Coleraine, 2 January, 1950 NIu23-1/IrLge-2 (F)

League Club	Source	Date Signed	Seasons Played	Apps	Subs	Gls
Fulham	Coleraine	02.68	67-68	2	2	0

MULLARD Albert Thomas
Walsall, 22 November, 1920 Died 1984 (IF)

League Club	Source	Date Signed	Seasons Played	Apps	Subs	Gls
Walsall	Hinckley Ath	11.45	46-48	61	-	12
Crewe Alex	Tr	06.49	49-50	44	-	15
Stoke C	Tr	08.50	50-51	21	-	3
Port Vale	Tr	09.51	51-55	163	-	22

MULLEN Andrew (Andy)
Newcastle, 28 July, 1928 (W)

League Club	Source	Date Signed	Seasons Played	Apps	Subs	Gls
Aston Villa		07.48				
Workington	Annfield Plain	08.51	51-52	66	-	5
Scunthorpe U	South Shields	08.55	55-56	10	-	1

MULLEN James (Jimmy)
Newcastle, 6 January, 1923 Died 1987 ESch/EB/FLge-1/EWar-3/E-12 (W)

League Club	Source	Date Signed	Seasons Played	Apps	Subs	Gls
Wolverhampton W	Jnrs	01.40	38-58	445	-	98

MULLEN James (Jimmy)
Oxford, 16 March, 1947 (W)

League Club	Source	Date Signed	Seasons Played	Apps	Subs	Gls
Reading	Oxford C	11.66	66-67	8	0	1
Charlton Ath	Tr	11.67	67-68	7	0	0
Rotherham U	Tr	02.69	68-73	174	3	24
Blackburn Rov	Tr	08.74	74-75	6	4	0
Bury	Tr	06.76	76	2	2	0
Rochdale	L	03.77	76	6	2	1

MULLEN James (Jimmy)
Jarrow, 8 November, 1952 (CD)

League Club	Source	Date Signed	Seasons Played	Apps	Subs	Gls
Sheffield Wed	App	10.70	70-79	222	7	10
Rotherham U	Tr	08.80	80-81	49	0	1
Preston NE	L	11.81	81	1	0	0
Cardiff C	Tr	03.82	81-85	128	5	12
Newport Co	Tr	06.86	86	19	0	0

MULLEN James Welsh
Larne, 10 January, 1921 Died 2002 (IF)

League Club	Source	Date Signed	Seasons Played	Apps	Subs	Gls
Barrow	Belfast Celtic	02.46	46-47	55	-	9
Crystal Palace	Tr	07.48	48	11	-	0
Bristol C	Tr	02.49	48-49	17	-	2
Barrow	Tr	09.50	50	9	-	0

MULLEN Roger Colin
Cowbridge, 2 March, 1966 WYth (FB)

League Club	Source	Date Signed	Seasons Played	Apps	Subs	Gls
Swansea C	App	03.84	83-84	2	1	0

MULLEN Stephen (Steve) Anthony
Glasgow, 8 September, 1959 (W)

League Club	Source	Date Signed	Seasons Played	Apps	Subs	Gls
Bury	Darwen	02.79	78-81	76	16	5

MULLER Adam Philip
Leeds, 17 April, 1982 (F)

League Club	Source	Date Signed	Seasons Played	Apps	Subs	Gls
Sheffield Wed	Ossett T	05.00	00	1	4	0

MULLERY Alan Patrick
Notting Hill, 23 November, 1941 Eu23-3/FLge-2/E-35 (M)

League Club	Source	Date Signed	Seasons Played	Apps	Subs	Gls
Fulham	Jnrs	12.58	58-63	199	-	13
Tottenham H	Tr	03.64	63-71	312	0	25
Fulham	L	03.72	71	6	0	1
Fulham	Tr	07.72	72-75	158	1	23

MULLETT Joseph (Joe)
Rowley Regis, 2 October, 1936 Died 1995 (FB)

League Club	Source	Date Signed	Seasons Played	Apps	Subs	Gls
Birmingham C	Malt Hill U	02.55	57	3	-	0
Norwich C	Tr	02.59	58-67	211	2	2

MULLIGAN David (Dave) James
Fazakerley, 24 March, 1982 Nzu20/Nz-6 (M)

League Club	Source	Date Signed	Seasons Played	Apps	Subs	Gls
Barnsley	YT	10.00	01-03	59	6	1
Doncaster Rov	Tr	02.04	03-04	41	4	2

MULLIGAN Gary
Dublin, 23 April, 1985 (M)

League Club	Source	Date Signed	Seasons Played	Apps	Subs	Gls
Wolverhampton W	Sch	07.02	04	0	1	0
Rushden & Diamonds	L	10.04	04	12	1	3

MULLIGAN James (Jimmy)
Dublin, 21 April, 1974 (F)

League Club	Source	Date Signed	Seasons Played	Apps	Subs	Gls
Stoke C	YT	07.92				
Bury	L	11.93	93	2	1	1
Bury	Tr	07.94	94-95	9	8	2

MULLIGAN Lance Martin
Sutton-in-Ashfield, 21 October, 1985 (F)

League Club	Source	Date Signed	Seasons Played	Apps	Subs	Gls
Mansfield T	Sch	•	03	0	1	0

MULLIGAN Patrick (Paddy) Martin
Dublin, 17 March, 1945 IRu23-1/LoI-5/IR-50 (FB)

League Club	Source	Date Signed	Seasons Played	Apps	Subs	Gls
Chelsea	Shamrock Rov	10.69	69-72	55	3	2
Crystal Palace	Tr	09.72	72-74	57	0	2
West Bromwich A	Tr	09.75	75-77	109	0	1

MULLIGAN Peter Granville
Carlton, West Yorkshire, 17 July, 1942 (W)

League Club	Source	Date Signed	Seasons Played	Apps	Subs	Gls
Barnsley	Jnrs	07.63	59-63	9	-	0

MULLIN John Michael
Bury, 11 August, 1975 (M)

League Club	Source	Date Signed	Seasons Played	Apps	Subs	Gls
Burnley	YT	08.92	93-94	7	11	2
Sunderland	Tr	08.95	95-98	23	12	4
Preston NE	L	02.98	97	4	3	0
Burnley	L	03.98	97	6	0	0
Burnley	Tr	07.99	99-01	38	39	8
Rotherham U	Tr	10.01	01-04	119	18	10

MULLINEUX Ian Joseph
Salford, 10 November, 1968 (W)

League Club	Source	Date Signed	Seasons Played	Apps	Subs	Gls
Bolton W	App	•	86	1	1	0

MULLINGTON Philip (Phil) Thomas
Oldham, 25 September, 1956 (M)

League Club	Source	Date Signed	Seasons Played	Apps	Subs	Gls
Oldham Ath	App	07.75				
Rochdale	Tr	01.76	75-76	59	7	6
Crewe Alex	Northwich Vic	01.78	77	1	0	0
Rochdale	Winsford U	08.78	78	8	1	0

MULLINS Hayden Ian
Reading, 27 March, 1979 Eu21-3 (CD)

League Club	Source	Date Signed	Seasons Played	Apps	Subs	Gls
Crystal Palace	YT	02.97	98-03	219	3	18
West Ham U	Tr	10.03	03-04	59	5	1

MULLINS John (Johnny) Christopher
Hampstead, 6 November, 1985 (CD)

League Club	Source	Date Signed	Seasons Played	Apps	Subs	Gls
Reading	Sch	12.04				
Kidderminster Hrs	L	12.04	04	21	0	2

MULRAIN Steven (Steve)
Lambeth, 23 October, 1972 ESch (F)

League Club	Source	Date Signed	Seasons Played	Apps	Subs	Gls
Leeds U	YT	07.91				
Rochdale	Charlton Ath (N/C)	12.92	92-93	3	5	2

MULRANEY Ambrose (Jock) Aloysius
Wishaw, 18 May, 1916 Died 2001 (W)

League Club	Source	Date Signed	Seasons Played	Apps	Subs	Gls
Ipswich T	Dartford	11.36	38	28	-	8
Birmingham C	Tr	10.45	46	27	-	8
Aston Villa	Kidderminster Hrs	09.48	48	12	-	2

MULRYNE Philip (Phil) Patrick
Belfast, 1 January, 1978 NIYth/NIu21-3/NIB-1/NI-26 (M)

League Club	Source	Date Signed	Seasons Played	Apps	Subs	Gls
Manchester U	YT	03.95	97	1	0	0
Norwich C	Tr	03.99	98-04	132	29	18

MULVANEY James (Jimmy)
Airdrie, 27 April, 1921 Died 1993 (WH)

League Club	Source	Date Signed	Seasons Played	Apps	Subs	Gls
Luton T	Dumbarton	06.48	48-49	8	-	2
Brighton & Hove A	Tr	08.50	50	8	-	0
Bradford C	Tr	10.51	51	19	-	0
Halifax T	Bath C	11.52	52	1	-	0

MULVANEY James (Jimmy)
Sunderland, 13 May, 1941 Died 1982 (F)

League Club	Source	Date Signed	Seasons Played	Apps	Subs	Gls
Hartlepools U	Whitby T	08.65	65-67	67	2	31
Barrow	Tr	11.67	67-69	71	8	34
Stockport Co	Tr	07.70	70-71	38	2	8

MULVANEY Richard (Dick)
Sunderland, 5 August, 1942 (CD)

League Club	Source	Date Signed	Seasons Played	Apps	Subs	Gls
Blackburn Rov	Murton CW	02.64	64-70	135	6	4
Oldham Ath	Tr	08.71	71-74	88	4	2
Rochdale	Tr	10.74	74-76	72	1	4

MULVEY Edward **Patrick (Paddy)** Noel
Dublin, 29 December, 1934 (IF)

League Club	Source	Date Signed	Seasons Played	Apps	Subs	Gls
Stockport Co	Glentoran	11.57	57-59	26	-	5

MULVOY Terence (Terry) John
Manchester, 2 December, 1938 (IF)

League Club	Source	Date Signed	Seasons Played	Apps	Subs	Gls
Rochdale		02.56	56	2	-	0

MUMBY Peter
Bradford, 22 February, 1969 (W)

League Club	Source	Date Signed	Seasons Played	Apps	Subs	Gls
Leeds U	YT	07.87	87-88	3	3	0
Burnley	Tr	07.89	89-91	36	10	9

MUMFORD Andrew Owen
Neath, 18 June, 1981 WSch/WYth/Wu21-4 (M)

League Club	Source	Date Signed	Seasons Played	Apps	Subs	Gls
Swansea C	Llanelli	06.00	00-02	47	15	6

MUMFORD Wayne Ernest
Rhymney, 3 November, 1964 (FB)

League Club	Source	Date Signed	Seasons Played	Apps	Subs	Gls
Birmingham C	Manchester C (App)	09.82	82-83	5	2	0

MUNCIE William (Bill) Paul
Carluke, 28 August, 1911 Died 1992 (W)

League Club	Source	Date Signed	Seasons Played	Apps	Subs	Gls
Leicester C	Shettleston Jnrs	08.34	34-37	42	-	11
Southend U	Tr	05.38	38	14	-	2
Crewe Alex	Hinckley U	10.46	46	1	-	0

MUNDAY Stuart Clifford
Newham, 28 September, 1972 (FB)

League Club	Source	Date Signed	Seasons Played	Apps	Subs	Gls
Brighton & Hove A	YT	07.90	91-95	78	17	4

MUNDEE Brian George
Hammersmith, 12 January, 1964 (FB)

League Club	Source	Date Signed	Seasons Played	Apps	Subs	Gls
Bournemouth	Hungerford T	01.82	82	3	1	0
Northampton T	Tr	10.83	83-85	96	4	3
Cambridge U	Tr	03.86	85-86	16	0	1

MUNDEE Dennis (Denny) William John
Swindon, 10 October, 1968 (M)

League Club	Source	Date Signed	Seasons Played	Apps	Subs	Gls
Swindon T	Queens Park Rgrs (App)	08.86				
Bournemouth	Salisbury	03.88	88-92	76	24	6
Torquay U	L	09.89	89	9	0	0
Brentford	Tr	08.93	93-95	64	20	16
Brighton & Hove A	Tr	10.95	95-96	58	3	7

MUNDY Albert Edward
Gosport, 12 May, 1926 Died 2002 (IF)

League Club	Source	Date Signed	Seasons Played	Apps	Subs	Gls
Portsmouth	Gosport Borough	01.51	50-53	51	-	12
Brighton & Hove A	Tr	11.53	53-57	165	-	87
Aldershot	Tr	02.58	57-60	130	-	12

MUNDY Harold **James (Jimmy)**
Wythenshawe, 2 September, 1948 (M)

League Club	Source	Date Signed	Seasons Played	Apps	Subs	Gls
Manchester C	Ashland Rov	08.66	68-69	2	1	0
Oldham Ath	L	09.70	70	3	5	2

MUNGALL Steven (Steve) Henry
Bellshill, 22 May, 1958 (FB)

League Club	Source	Date Signed	Seasons Played	Apps	Subs	Gls
Tranmere Rov	Motherwell	07.79	79-95	479	34	14

MUNKS David
Sheffield, 29 April, 1947 EYth (CD)

League Club	Source	Date Signed	Seasons Played	Apps	Subs	Gls
Sheffield U	App	08.64	65-68	108	4	1
Portsmouth	Tr	05.69	69-73	132	5	2
Swindon T	Tr	12.73	73-74	21	0	0
Exeter C	Tr	12.74	74-75	20	0	0

MUNRO Alexander (Alex)
Glasgow, 3 October, 1944 (FB)

League Club	Source	Date Signed	Seasons Played	Apps	Subs	Gls
Bristol Rov	Drumchapel Amats	10.62	62-70	159	9	11

MUNRO Alexander (Alex) Dewar
Corridon, 6 April, 1912 Died 1986 S-3 (W)

League Club	Source	Date Signed	Seasons Played	Apps	Subs	Gls
Blackpool	Heart of Midlothian	03.37	36-48	144	-	17

MUNRO Francis (Frank) Michael
Broughty Ferry, 25 October, 1947 Su23-4/S-9 (CD)

League Club	Source	Date Signed	Seasons Played	Apps	Subs	Gls
Wolverhampton W	Aberdeen	01.68	67-76	290	6	14

MUNRO Alexander **Iain** Fordyce
Uddingston, 24 August, 1951 SLge-1/S-7 (FB)

League Club	Source	Date Signed	Seasons Played	Apps	Subs	Gls
Stoke C	St Mirren	10.80	80	32	0	1
Sunderland	Tr	08.81	81-83	80	0	0

MUNRO James (Jimmy) Ferguson
Garmouth, 25 March, 1926 Died 1997 (W)

League Club	Source	Date Signed	Seasons Played	Apps	Subs	Gls
Manchester C	Waterford	11.47	47-49	25	-	4
Oldham Ath	Tr	03.50	49-52	119	-	20
Lincoln C	Tr	02.53	52-57	161	-	24
Bury	Tr	01.58	57-58	41	-	7

MUNRO Malcolm George
Melton Mowbray, 21 May, 1953 ESch/EYth (CD)

League Club	Source	Date Signed	Seasons Played	Apps	Subs	Gls
Leicester C	App	05.70	71-74	69	1	1

MUNRO Roderick (Roddie) Alexander
Inverness, 27 July, 1920 Died 1976 (FB)

League Club	Source	Date Signed	Seasons Played	Apps	Subs	Gls
Brentford		05.46	46-52	199	-	0

MUNRO Stuart David
Falkirk, 15 September, 1962 SB (FB)

League Club	Source	Date Signed	Seasons Played	Apps	Subs	Gls
Blackburn Rov	Glasgow Rgrs	08.91	91	1	0	0
Bristol C	Tr	02.93	92-95	91	3	0

MUNRO William (Bill) Davidson
Glasgow, 21 June, 1934 (IF)

League Club	Source	Date Signed	Seasons Played	Apps	Subs	Gls
Barrow	Kilmarnock	06.59	59-60	15	-	2

MUNROE Karl Augustus
Manchester, 23 September, 1979 (M)

League Club	Source	Date Signed	Seasons Played	Apps	Subs	Gls
Swansea C	YT	07.98	97	0	1	0
Macclesfield T	Tr	10.99	99-03	94	25	1

MUNROE William (Liam) James
Dublin, 28 November, 1933 IR-1 (IF)

League Club	Source	Date Signed	Seasons Played	Apps	Subs	Gls
Bristol C	Ards	12.57	57	1	-	0

MUNSON Nathan Wayne
Colchester, 10 November, 1974 (G)

League Club	Source	Date Signed	Seasons Played	Apps	Subs	Gls
Colchester U	YT	06.93	92-93	3	1	0

MURCHISON Ronald (Ron) Angus
Kilmarnock, 12 February, 1927 (WH)

League Club	Source	Date Signed	Seasons Played	Apps	Subs	Gls
Ipswich T	Auchterarder Primrose	06.50	50-54	42	-	2

MURCOTT Stephen (Steve)
Streetly, 17 January, 1961 (G)

League Club	Source	Date Signed	Seasons Played	Apps	Subs	Gls
Coventry C	App	11.78	79	1	0	0

MURDOCH Robert (Bobby) White
Bothwell, 17 August, 1944 Died 2001 Su23-1/SLge-5/S-12 (M)

League Club	Source	Date Signed	Seasons Played	Apps	Subs	Gls
Middlesbrough	Glasgow Celtic	09.73	73-75	93	2	6

MURDOCH William (Bobby) Robert
Garston, 25 January, 1936 (IF)

League Club	Source	Date Signed	Seasons Played	Apps	Subs	Gls
Liverpool	South Liverpool	05.57	57-58	17	-	5
Barrow	Tr	05.59	59	41	-	17
Stockport Co	Tr	08.60	60-61	58	-	17
Carlisle U	Tr	01.62	61	10	-	2
Southport	Tr	07.62	62	33	-	10

MURDOCK Colin James
Ballymena, 2 July, 1975 NISch/NIYth/NIB-3/NI-28 (CD)

League Club	Source	Date Signed	Seasons Played	Apps	Subs	Gls
Manchester U	YT	07.92				
Preston NE	Tr	05.97	97-02	163	14	6
Crewe Alex	Hibernian	01.05	04	15	1	0

MURFIN Andrew John
Doncaster, 26 November, 1976 (FB)

League Club	Source	Date Signed	Seasons Played	Apps	Subs	Gls
Scunthorpe U	Jnrs	09.95	95	1	0	0

MURPHY Aidan
Manchester, 17 September, 1967 ESch/EYth (M)

League Club	Source	Date Signed	Seasons Played	Apps	Subs	Gls
Manchester U	App	09.84				
Lincoln C	L	10.86	86	2	0	0
Crewe Alex	Tr	05.87	87-91	94	19	13
Scarborough	Tr	08.92	92	7	1	0

MURPHY Andrew (Andy) Colin
Preston, 18 October, 1966 (M)

League Club	Source	Date Signed	Seasons Played	Apps	Subs	Gls
Preston NE	App	07.84	83-84	9	1	0

MURPHY Laurence **Barry**
Consett, 10 February, 1940 (FB)

League Club	Source	Date Signed	Seasons Played	Apps	Subs	Gls
Barnsley	South Shields	07.62	62-77	509	5	3

MURPHY Bernard (Ben) Anthony Paul
Dublin, 19 November, 1947 (IF)

League Club	Source	Date Signed	Seasons Played	Apps	Subs	Gls
Torquay U	App	11.65	64-66	6	0	0

MURPHY Brian
Waterford, 7 May, 1983 IRYth/IRu21-3 (G)

League Club	Source	Date Signed	Seasons Played	Apps	Subs	Gls
Manchester C	YT	05.00				
Peterborough U	L	05.03	02	1	0	0
Swansea C	Waterford	08.03	03-04	13	0	0

MURPHY Christopher (Chris) Patrick
Leamington Spa, 8 March, 1983 (F)

League Club	Source	Date Signed	Seasons Played	Apps	Subs	Gls
Shrewsbury T	Sch	07.02	00-02	0	8	0
Cheltenham T	Telford U	07.04	04	0	4	0

MURPHY Daniel (Danny)
Burtonwood, 10 May, 1922 Died 2001 (WH)

League Club	Source	Date Signed	Seasons Played	Apps	Subs	Gls
Bolton W	Burtonwood Ath	02.43	46-50	66	-	1
Crewe Alex	Tr	01.52	51-53	107	-	1
Rochdale	Tr	07.54	54-56	109	-	0

MURPHY Daniel (Danny) Benjamin
Chester, 18 March, 1977 ESch/EYth/Eu21-5/E-9 (M)

League Club	Source	Date Signed	Seasons Played	Apps	Subs	Gls
Crewe Alex	YT	03.94	93-96	110	24	27
Liverpool	Tr	07.97	97-03	114	56	25
Crewe Alex	L	02.99	98	16	0	1
Charlton Ath	Tr	08.04	04	37	1	3

MURPHY Daniel (Danny) Thomas
Southwark, 4 December, 1982 IRYth (FB)

League Club	Source	Date Signed	Seasons Played	Apps	Subs	Gls
Queens Park Rgrs	YT	12.99	01-02	14	9	0

MURPHY David Paul
Hartlepool, 1 March, 1984 EYth (FB)

League Club	Source	Date Signed	Seasons Played	Apps	Subs	Gls
Middlesbrough	YT	07.01	01-02	4	9	0
Barnsley	L	03.04	03	10	0	2

MURPHY Donal Patrick
Dublin, 23 February, 1955 (W)

League Club	Source	Date Signed	Seasons Played	Apps	Subs	Gls
Coventry C	App	08.72	75-77	33	10	10
Millwall	L	10.77	77	3	0	0
Torquay U	Tr	05.78	78-79	81	4	20
Plymouth Arg	Tr	06.80	80-81	44	4	9
Torquay U	L	12.81	81	2	1	0
Blackburn Rov	Tr	02.82	81	1	2	0

MURPHY Edward (Eddie)
Hamilton, 13 May, 1924 (IF)

League Club	Source	Date Signed	Seasons Played	Apps	Subs	Gls
Northampton T	Morton	06.49	49-50	71	-	15
Barnsley	Tr	03.51	50-51	18	-	2
Exeter C	Tr	06.52	52-55	94	-	13

MURPHY Edward (Eddie) Cullinane
Glasgow, 1 June, 1934 (CD)

League Club	Source	Date Signed	Seasons Played	Apps	Subs	Gls
Oldham Ath	Clyde	05.56	56-58	72	-	0

MURPHY Thomas **Edwin (Eddie)**
South Bank, 25 March, 1921 Died 2003 (IF)

League Club	Source	Date Signed	Seasons Played	Apps	Subs	Gls
Middlesbrough	South Bank St Peter's	05.39	46-47	9	-	1
Blackburn Rov	Tr	12.47	47-48	31	-	6
Halifax T	Tr	03.49	48-53	217	-	29

MURPHY Francis (Frank)
Glasgow, 1 June, 1959 (F)

League Club	Source	Date Signed	Seasons Played	Apps	Subs	Gls
Barnet	Kettering T	08.88	91	3	12	5

MURPHY George
Cwmfelinfach, 22 July, 1915 Died 1983 WWar-2 (IF)

League Club	Source	Date Signed	Seasons Played	Apps	Subs	Gls
Bradford C	Cwmfelinfach Colts	11.34	34-47	180	-	43
Hull C	Tr	12.47	47	15	-	9

MURPHY James (Jamie)
Islington, 17 November, 1971 (M)

League Club	Source	Date Signed	Seasons Played	Apps	Subs	Gls
Aldershot	Leyton Orient (YT)	07.90	90	1	2	0

League Club	Source	Date Signed	Seasons Played	Career Record Apps	Subs	Gls

MURPHY James (Jamie) Anthony
Manchester, 25 February, 1973 (CD)

League Club	Source	Date Signed	Seasons Played	Apps	Subs	Gls
Blackpool	Jnrs	08.90	92-94	48	7	1
Doncaster Rov	Tr	09.95	95-96	47	7	0
Halifax T	Tr	03.97	98	21	2	1

MURPHY James (Jim) Baird
Glasgow, 29 November, 1942 (M)

League Club	Source	Date Signed	Seasons Played	Apps	Subs	Gls
Notts Co	Raith Rov	02.68	67-68	33	0	7

MURPHY Jeremiah (Jerry) Michael
Stepney, 23 September, 1959 ESch/IR-3 (M)

League Club	Source	Date Signed	Seasons Played	Apps	Subs	Gls
Crystal Palace	App	10.76	76-84	214	15	20
Chelsea	Tr	08.85	85-87	34	0	3

MURPHY Francis **John**
Edinburgh, 16 August, 1949 (M)

League Club	Source	Date Signed	Seasons Played	Apps	Subs	Gls
Notts Co	Edina Hearts	08.67	67-68	17	2	2

MURPHY John James
Whiston, 18 October, 1976 (F)

League Club	Source	Date Signed	Seasons Played	Apps	Subs	Gls
Chester C	YT	07.95	94-98	65	38	20
Blackpool	Tr	08.99	99-04	201	17	75

MURPHY Joseph (Joe)
Dublin, 21 August, 1981 IRYth/IRu21-14/IR-1 (G)

League Club	Source	Date Signed	Seasons Played	Apps	Subs	Gls
Tranmere Rov	YT	07.99	99-01	61	2	0
West Bromwich A	Tr	07.02	02-03	3	2	0
Walsall	L	10.04	04	25	0	0

MURPHY Joseph Patrick
Waterford, 30 March, 1924 (FB)

League Club	Source	Date Signed	Seasons Played	Apps	Subs	Gls
Brighton & Hove A		02.48				
Crystal Palace	Shelbourne	02.49	48-50	37	-	0

MURPHY Marcus Montagu
Tavistock, 16 November, 1914 (IF)

League Club	Source	Date Signed	Seasons Played	Apps	Subs	Gls
Plymouth Arg	Plymouth U	08.46	46-47	15	-	1

MURPHY Matthew (Matt) Simon
Northampton, 20 August, 1971 (M)

League Club	Source	Date Signed	Seasons Played	Apps	Subs	Gls
Oxford U	Corby T	02.93	92-00	168	78	38
Scunthorpe U	L	12.97	97	1	2	0
Bury	Tr	08.01	01	5	4	0
Swansea C	Tr	07.02	02	9	3	2

MURPHY Michael (Mike)
Reading, 15 April, 1939 (G)

League Club	Source	Date Signed	Seasons Played	Apps	Subs	Gls
Reading (Am)	Thorneycroft Ath	04.58	57	1	-	0

MURPHY Michael (Mick) John
Slough, 5 May, 1977 (F)

League Club	Source	Date Signed	Seasons Played	Apps	Subs	Gls
Reading	Jnrs	10.94	94	0	1	0

MURPHY Neil Anthony
Liverpool, 19 May, 1980 EYth (FB)

League Club	Source	Date Signed	Seasons Played	Apps	Subs	Gls
Liverpool	YT	10.97				
Blackpool	Tr	07.00	00-01	4	3	0

MURPHY Nicholas (Nick) Michael
West Bromwich, 25 December, 1946 (M)

League Club	Source	Date Signed	Seasons Played	Apps	Subs	Gls
Manchester U	Jnrs	02.66				
Reading	Tr	07.70	70	3	1	0

MURPHY Patrick (Pat)
Merthyr Tydfil, 19 December, 1947 (WH)

League Club	Source	Date Signed	Seasons Played	Apps	Subs	Gls
Cardiff C	App	12.65	65	0	1	0

MURPHY Paul
Ashington, 16 March, 1954 (F)

League Club	Source	Date Signed	Seasons Played	Apps	Subs	Gls
Rotherham U	Ashington	02.72	73	1	0	0
Workington	L	08.73	73	10	2	1

MURPHY Peter
Hartlepool, 7 March, 1922 Died 1975 (IF)

League Club	Source	Date Signed	Seasons Played	Apps	Subs	Gls
Coventry C	Dunlop	05.46	46-49	115	-	37
Tottenham H	Tr	06.50	50-51	38	-	14
Birmingham C	Tr	01.52	51-59	245	-	107

MURPHY Peter
Dublin, 27 October, 1980 IRYth/IRu21 (FB)

League Club	Source	Date Signed	Seasons Played	Apps	Subs	Gls
Blackburn Rov	YT	07.98				
Halifax T	L	10.00	00	18	3	1
Carlisle U	Tr	08.01	01-03	110	5	3

MURPHY Philip (Phil)
Liverpool, 21 November, 1960 (F)

League Club	Source	Date Signed	Seasons Played	Apps	Subs	Gls
Blackpool	CD Nacional (Por)	09.84	84	1	7	0
Burnley	Witton A	11.86	86	12	3	5

MURPHY Shaun Peter
Sydney, Australia, 5 November, 1970 AuYth/Auu23/Au20 (CD)

League Club	Source	Date Signed	Seasons Played	Apps	Subs	Gls
Notts Co	Perth Italia (Aus)	09.92	92-96	100	9	5
West Bromwich A	Tr	12.96	96-98	60	11	7
Sheffield U	Tr	07.99	99-02	157	1	10
Crystal Palace	L	02.02	01	11	0	0

MURPHY Stephen
Dublin, 5 April, 1978 IRYth (M)

League Club	Source	Date Signed	Seasons Played	Apps	Subs	Gls
Huddersfield T	Belvedere	05.95				
Halifax T	Tr	08.98	98-99	20	7	1

MURPHY Terence (Terry)
Liverpool, 14 January, 1940 (WH)

League Club	Source	Date Signed	Seasons Played	Apps	Subs	Gls
Crewe Alex	Northwch Victoria	09.61	61	1	-	0

MURPHY John **William (Bill)**
Birstall, 21 November, 1921 (WH)

League Club	Source	Date Signed	Seasons Played	Apps	Subs	Gls
Bradford C	Liverpool (Am)	09.46	46-51	144	-	9

MURPHY William (Billy) Robinson
Barrhead, 22 March, 1928 (W)

League Club	Source	Date Signed	Seasons Played	Apps	Subs	Gls
Exeter C	Stirling A	11.49	49	2	-	0
Bristol Rov	Tr	07.50	50	3	-	0

MURRAY Adam David
Birmingham, 30 September, 1981 EYth/Eu20 (M)

League Club	Source	Date Signed	Seasons Played	Apps	Subs	Gls
Derby Co	YT	10.98	98-02	25	31	0
Mansfield T	L	02.02	01	13	0	7
Kidderminster Hrs	L	08.03	03	3	0	0
Notts Co	Burton A	11.03	03	1	2	0
Kidderminster Hrs	Tr	01.04	03	16	3	3
Mansfield T	Tr	07.04	04	27	5	5

MURRAY Alan
Newcastle, 5 November, 1949 (M)

League Club	Source	Date Signed	Seasons Played	Apps	Subs	Gls
Middlesbrough	Jnrs	09.67	69-70	6	4	1
York C	L	01.72	71	4	0	0
Brentford	Tr	06.72	72	42	3	7
Doncaster Rov	Tr	07.73	73-76	133	13	21

MURRAY Alastair (Ally)
Longtown, 22 December, 1943 (IF)

League Club	Source	Date Signed	Seasons Played	Apps	Subs	Gls
Sunderland	Jnrs	01.61				
Barnsley	Tr	07.63	63	21	-	1

MURRAY Albert (Bert) George
Hoxton, 22 September, 1942 ESch/EYth/Eu23-6 (W)

League Club	Source	Date Signed	Seasons Played	Apps	Subs	Gls
Chelsea	Jnrs	05.61	61-65	156	4	39
Birmingham C	Tr	08.66	66-70	126	6	22
Brighton & Hove A	Tr	02.71	70-73	99	3	25
Peterborough U	Tr	09.73	73-75	123	0	10

MURRAY Antonio James
Cambridge, 15 September, 1984 (M)

League Club	Source	Date Signed	Seasons Played	Apps	Subs	Gls
Ipswich T	Sch	07.03	02	0	1	0

MURRAY Bruce Edward
Washington, USA, 25 January, 1966 USA int (F)

League Club	Source	Date Signed	Seasons Played	Apps	Subs	Gls
Millwall	USSF (USA)	08.93	93	7	6	2
Stockport Co	L	03.94	93	2	1	0

MURRAY Daniel (Dan)
Cambridge, 16 May, 1982 (CD)

League Club	Source	Date Signed	Seasons Played	Apps	Subs	Gls
Peterborough U	YT	03.00	99-00	3	2	0

MURRAY Ian **David**
Otterburn, 11 July, 1949 (F)

League Club	Source	Date Signed	Seasons Played	Apps	Subs	Gls
Workington	Corbridge U	03.74	73-75	79	3	22

MURRAY David Robert
Chorley, 30 September, 1967 (F)

League Club	Source	Date Signed	Seasons Played	Apps	Subs	Gls
Chester C	Wigan Ath (Jnrs)	09.85	85	3	3	1

MURRAY Dennis Patrick
Stoke-on-Trent, 11 June, 1932 (G)

League Club	Source	Date Signed	Seasons Played	Apps	Subs	Gls
Crewe Alex	Jnrs	10.50	51	2	-	0

MURRAY Donald (Don) James
Duffus, 18 January, 1946 Su23-1 (CD)

League Club	Source	Date Signed	Seasons Played	Apps	Subs	Gls
Cardiff C	Burghead Thistle	01.63	62-74	406	0	6
Swansea C	L	10.74	74	5	0	0
Newport Co	Heart of Midlothian	10.76	76	16	2	0

MURRAY Edward (Eddie) James
Crosby, 10 July, 1962 (W)

League Club	Source	Date Signed	Seasons Played	Apps	Subs	Gls
Tranmere Rov	Stork	08.87	87-88	11	16	1

MURRAY Edwin (Eddie) John
Ilford, 31 August, 1973 (FB)

League Club	Source	Date Signed	Seasons Played	Apps	Subs	Gls
Swindon T	YT	07.91	90-95	7	5	1

League Club	Source	Date Signed	Seasons Played	Career Record Apps	Subs	Gls
MURRAY Frederick (Fred) Anthony						
Clonmel, 22 May, 1982 IRYth						(FB)
Blackburn Rov	YT	05.99				
Cambridge U	Tr	12.01	01-03	80	8	0
Northampton T	Tr	07.04	04	38	0	0
MURRAY Hugh						
Drybridge, 3 August, 1936						(W)
Manchester C	Dalry Thistle	04.55	55	1	-	0
MURRAY Ivan Hugh						
Ballymoney, 29 May, 1944 IrLge-2						(CD)
Fulham	Coleraine	02.68	67-68	4	1	0
MURRAY Jade (Jay) Alan						
Islington, 23 September, 1981						(F)
Leyton Orient	YT	07.00	99	0	2	0
MURRAY James						
Motherwell, 13 July, 1922 Died 1998						(FB)
Exeter C	Shawfield Jnrs	08.45	46	1	-	0
MURRAY James (Jimmy)						
Edinburgh, 4 February, 1933						(IF)
Reading	Heart of Midlothian	02.54	53-54	7	-	3
MURRAY Alexander James (Jimmy)						
Thornton, Lancashire, 4 February, 1945						(W)
Southport	Burscough	07.65	64	3	-	0
MURRAY James (Jamie) Gerald						
Ayr, 27 December, 1958						(FB)
Cambridge U	Rivet Sports	09.76	76-83	213	16	3
Sunderland	L	03.84	83	1	0	0
Brentford	Tr	07.84	84-87	134	0	3
Cambridge U	Tr	09.87	87	13	0	0
MURRAY James (Jimmy) Robert						
Elvington, 11 October, 1935 Eu23-2/FLge-1						(F)
Wolverhampton W	Jnrs	11.53	55-63	273	-	155
Manchester C	Tr	11.63	63-66	70	0	43
Walsall	Tr	05.67	66-68	53	4	13
MURRAY James (Jimmy) William						
Lambeth, 16 March, 1935 Died 2002						(IF)
Crystal Palace	Jnrs	07.55	55-57	37	-	13
Walsall	Tr	01.58	57-58	14	-	2
MURRAY John						
Newcastle, 2 March, 1948						(W)
Burnley	Jnrs	03.65	66-69	20	2	6
Blackpool	Tr	03.70	69-70	6	3	1
Bury	Tr	02.71	70-73	117	9	37
Reading	Tr	08.74	74-77	123	8	44
Brentford	Tr	02.78	77	2	3	1
MURRAY John Anthony						
Saltcoats, 5 February, 1949						(FB)
Cambridge U	Morton	07.71	71	3	0	0
MURRAY John George						
Lambeth, 15 July, 1927						(FB)
Leyton Orient	Chelmsford C	08.49				
Gillingham	Sittingbourne	06.51	51	4	-	0
MURRAY John McCann						
Glasgow, 9 March, 1945 Died 1997						(FB)
Lincoln C	Stirling A	11.66	66	4	0	0
MURRAY Joseph (Joey) Ernest						
Liverpool, 5 November, 1971 ESch						(M)
Wrexham	Marine	03.91	90	11	0	0
MURRAY Karl Anthony						
Islington, 24 June, 1982						(M)
Shrewsbury T	YT	02.00	99-02	77	32	5
MURRAY Kenneth (Ken)						
Darlington, 2 April, 1928 Died 1993						(IF)
Darlington	Bishop Auckland	07.50	50-52	70	-	19
Mansfield T	Tr	07.53	53-56	140	-	60
Oldham Ath	Tr	03.57	56-57	35	-	14
Wrexham	Tr	02.58	57-58	32	-	10
Gateshead	Yeovil T	08.59	59	18	-	6
MURRAY Leslie (Les)						
Kinghorn, 29 September, 1928 Died 1993						(IF)
Rochdale	Arbroath	05.52	52	16	-	3
MURRAY Malcolm						
Buckie, 26 July, 1964						(FB)
Hull C	Heart of Midlothian	03.89	88-89	9	2	0
Mansfield T	Tr	12.89	89-91	56	3	0
MURRAY Mark						
Manchester, 13 June, 1973						(FB)
Blackpool	Jnrs	10.90	91-92	3	0	0
MURRAY Matthew (Matt)						
Paisley, 25 December, 1929						(W)
Barrow	St Mirren	08.58	58	33	-	2
Carlisle U	Tr	07.59	59	28	-	4
MURRAY Matthew (Matt) William						
Solihull, 2 May, 1981 EYth/Eu21-5						(G)
Wolverhampton W	YT	05.98	02-04	42	0	0
MURRAY Maxwell (Max)						
Falkirk, 7 November, 1935 SAmat/Su23-2						(CF)
West Bromwich A	Glasgow Rgrs	11.62	62	3	-	0
MURRAY Neil Andrew						
Bellshill, 21 February, 1973 SSch/Su21-16						(M)
Grimsby T (L)	FSV Mainz 05 (Ger)	11.00	00	1	1	0
MURRAY Paul						
Carlisle, 31 August, 1976 EYth/Eu21-4/EB-1						(M)
Carlisle U	YT	06.94	93-95	27	14	1
Queens Park Rgrs	Tr	03.96	95-00	115	25	7
Southampton	Tr	08.01	01	0	1	0
Oldham Ath	Tr	12.01	01-03	93	2	15
MURRAY Robert (Rob) James						
Hammersmith, 21 October, 1974 Su21-1						(M)
Bournemouth	YT	01.93	92-97	88	59	12
MURRAY Robert (Bob) Law						
Kemnay, 24 April, 1932						(WH)
Stockport Co	Inverurie Loco	11.51	52-62	465	-	32
MURRAY Scott George						
Aberdeen, 26 May, 1974 SB-2						(M)
Aston Villa	Fraserburgh	03.94	95-96	4	0	0
Bristol C	Tr	12.97	97-02	193	31	46
Reading	Tr	07.03	03	25	9	5
Bristol C	Tr	03.04	03-04	35	13	8
MURRAY Shaun						
Newcastle, 7 February, 1970 ESch/EYth						(M)
Tottenham H	YT	12.87				
Portsmouth	Tr	06.89	90-92	21	13	1
Scarborough	Tr	11.93	93	29	0	5
Bradford C	Tr	08.94	94-97	105	25	8
Notts Co	Tr	08.98	98-00	43	12	3
MURRAY Steven						
Kilmarnock, 1 December, 1967 SYth						(M)
Nottingham F	App	04.85				
York C	L	09.86	86	2	1	0
MURRAY Terence (Terry)						
Dublin, 22 May, 1928 LoI-6/IR-1						(IF)
Hull C	Dundalk	10.51	51-53	32	-	6
Bournemouth	Tr	03.54	53-54	13	-	1
MURRAY Thomas (Tommy)						
Airdrie, 5 February, 1933						(IF)
Darlington	Headington U	06.56	56	3	-	0
MURRAY Thomas (Tommy)						
Bellshill, 14 January, 1933						(W)
Leeds U	Queen of the South	08.60	60	7	-	2
Tranmere Rov	Tr	03.61	60-61	10	-	1
MURRAY Thomas (Tommy)						
Caldercruix, 1 June, 1943						(F)
Carlisle U	Airdrie	03.67	66-70	123	11	38
MURRAY Thomas (Tom) Alec						
Barrow, 16 October, 1944						(FB)
Barrow	Jnrs	07.64	63-64	8	-	0
MURRAY William (Billy) Joseph						
Burnley, 26 January, 1922 Died 1992						(WH)
Manchester C	Arbroath	01.47	46-49	20	-	1
MURTY Graeme Stuart						
Saltburn, 13 November, 1974 SB-1/S-1						(FB)
York C	YT	03.93	93-97	106	11	7
Reading	Tr	07.98	98-04	204	11	1
MURTY Joseph (Joe) Dougan						
Glasgow, 6 November, 1957						(W)
Rochdale	App	11.75	74-75	15	5	2
Bury	Tr	08.76	77	0	1	0

League Club	Source	Date Signed	Seasons Played	Career Record Apps	Subs	Gls
MUSAMPA Kizito (Kiki)						
Kinshasa, DR Congo, 20 July, 1977 Hou21-22						(M)
Manchester C (L)	Atletico Madrid (Sp)	01.05	04	14	0	3
MUSCAT Kevin Vincent						
Crawley, 7 August, 1973 AuYth/Auu23/Au-45						(CD)
Crystal Palace	South Melbourne (Aus)	08.96	96-97	51	2	2
Wolverhampton W	Tr	10.97	97-01	178	2	14
Millwall	Glasgow Rgrs	08.03	03-04	52	1	0
MUSGRAVE David (Dave)						
South Shields, 20 April, 1928						(W)
Manchester U	Hordens (SA)	12.47				
New Brighton	Fleetwood	08.50	50	35	-	2
Southport	Tr	10.51	51-52	52	-	7
Accrington St	Tr	09.53	53	30	-	7
MUSGROVE Malcolm						
Lynemouth, 8 July, 1933						(W)
West Ham U	Lynemouth Colliery	12.53	53-62	283	-	84
Leyton Orient	Tr	12.62	62-65	83	0	14
MUSGROVE Martin						
Wanstead, 21 November, 1961						(M)
Torquay U	Heavitree U	03.82	81	1	1	0
MUSIAL Adam						
Wielicza, Poland, 18 December, 1948 Poland int						(CD)
Hereford U	Arkagdynia (Pol)	08.80	80-82	44	2	0
MUSKER Russell						
Liverpool, 10 July, 1962						(M)
Bristol C	App	08.79	80-83	44	2	1
Exeter C	L	10.83	83	6	0	0
Gillingham	Tr	11.83	83-85	54	10	7
Torquay U	Tr	08.86	86-87	36	9	0
Torquay U	Dawlish T	07.90	90	20	1	1
Walsall	Tr	08.91	91	3	0	0
MUSSELWHITE Paul Stephen						
Portsmouth, 22 December, 1968						(G)
Portsmouth	App	12.86				
Scunthorpe U	Tr	03.88	88-91	132	0	0
Port Vale	Tr	07.92	92-99	312	0	0
Hull C	Tr	09.00	00-03	94	1	0
Scunthorpe U	Tr	08.04	04	46	0	0
MUSSON Ian Samuel						
Lincoln, 13 December, 1953						(W)
Sheffield Wed	App	02.71				
Lincoln C	Tr	07.73	73	11	0	0
MUSSON Walter (Chick) Urban						
Kilburn, Derbyshire, 8 October, 1920 Died 1955 FLge-1						(WH)
Derby Co	Holbrook St Michael's	10.37	46-53	246	-	0
MUSTAFA Tarkan						
Islington, 28 August, 1973 ESemiPro-2						(FB)
Barnet	Kettering T	08.97	97	2	9	0
Rushden & Diamonds	Kingstonian	06.00	01-02	31	3	1
MUSTARD William (Bill)						
South Shields, 28 November, 1920 Died 1976						(W)
Exeter C	Bath C	05.46	46	14	-	0
MUSTOE Neil John						
Gloucester, 5 November, 1976						(M)
Manchester U	YT	07.95				
Wigan Ath	Tr	01.98				
Cambridge U	Tr	07.98	98-01	71	28	4
MUSTOE Robin (Robbie)						
Witney, 28 August, 1968						(M)
Oxford U	Jnrs	07.86	86-89	78	13	10
Middlesbrough	Tr	07.90	90-01	327	38	25
Charlton Ath	Tr	08.02	02	6	0	0
Sheffield Wed	Tr	08.03	03	22	3	1
MUTCH Andrew (Andy) Todd						
Liverpool, 28 December, 1963 Eu21-1/EB						(F)
Wolverhampton W	Southport	02.86	85-92	277	12	96
Swindon T	Tr	08.93	93-94	34	16	6
Wigan Ath	L	08.95	95	7	0	1
Stockport Co	Tr	03.96	95-97	28	36	10
MUTCH George						
Ferryhill, Aberdeenshire, 21 September, 1912 Died 2001 SSch/S1						(IF)
Manchester U	Arbroath	05.34	34-37	112	-	46
Preston NE	Tr	09.37	37-46	80	-	24

League Club	Source	Date Signed	Seasons Played	Career Record Apps	Subs	Gls
Bury	Tr	10.46	46	21	-	8
Southport	Tr	10.47	47	14	-	2
MUTCHELL Robert (Rob) David						
Solihull, 3 January, 1974						(FB)
Oxford U	YT	07.92				
Barnet	Tr	12.93	93-94	21	1	0
MUTRIE Leslie (Les) Alan						
Newcastle, 1 April, 1952 ESemiPro						(F)
Carlisle U	Gateshead	06.77	77	4	1	0
Hull C	Blyth Spartans	12.80	80-83	114	1	49
Doncaster Rov	L	12.83	83	6	0	1
Colchester U	Tr	01.84	83	10	4	2
Hartlepool U	Tr	08.84	84	18	0	4
MUTTOCK Jonathan (Jon) Lee						
Oxford, 23 December, 1961						(CD)
Oxford U	YT	05.90	89	1	0	0
MUTTON Thomas (Tommy) James						
Huddersfield, 17 January, 1978						(F)
Swansea C	Bangor C	09.99	99-00	4	3	0
MUTU Adrian						
Calinesti, Romania, 8 January, 1979 RoYth/Rou21/Ro-39						(F)
Chelsea	Parma (It)	08.03	03-04	21	6	6
MUXWORTHY Graham John						
Bristol, 11 October, 1938						(W)
Crystal Palace	Exeter U	09.57	57	2	-	0
Bristol Rov	Chippenham T	06.60	62	8	-	0
MUZINIC Drazen						
Yugoslavia, 25 January, 1953 Yugoslavia int						(FB)
Norwich C	Hajduk Split (Yug)	09.80	80-81	15	4	0
MWILA Frederick (Freddie)						
Kasama, Zambia, 6 July, 1946						(M)
Aston Villa	Atlanta (USA)	06.69	69	1	0	0
MYALL Stuart Thomas						
Eastbourne, 12 November, 1974						(FB)
Brighton & Hove A	YT	07.93	92-95	69	11	4
Brentford	Tr	06.96	97	2	0	0
MYCOCK Albert						
Manchester, 31 January, 1923 Died 2003						(W)
Manchester U		05.44				
Crystal Palace	Tr	06.46	46-47	59	-	9
Barrow	Tr	07.48	48-49	42	-	4
MYCOCK David						
Sunderland, 30 August, 1921 Died 1990						(CD)
Halifax T	Sunderland (Am)	05.46	46-51	169	-	17
MYCOCK David Christopher						
Todmorden, 18 September, 1969						(FB)
Rochdale	YT	07.88	87-88	19	3	0
MYCOCK John (Jack)						
Manchester, 11 February, 1936						(W)
Shrewsbury T (Am)	Congleton T	12.58	58	6	-	1
MYCOCK Thomas (Tommy)						
Ryhope, 22 August, 1923 Died 1988 IrLge-1						(IF)
Southport	Silksworth CW	10.46	46	19	-	3
Aldershot	Tr	04.47	46-47	16	-	2
Brentford	Distillery	12.50				
Tranmere Rov	Tr	05.52	52-53	45	-	2
Bradford C	Tr	02.54	53-54	22	-	3
MYERS Alan William						
Newcastle, 12 February, 1928						(G)
Gateshead		03.52	51	1	-	0
MYERS Andrew (Andy) John						
Hounslow, 3 November, 1973 EYth/Eu21-4						(CD)
Chelsea	YT	07.91	90-98	74	10	2
Bradford C	Tr	07.99	99-02	74	15	3
Portsmouth	L	03.00	99	4	4	0
Colchester U	Tr	07.03	03	21	0	0
Brentford	Tr	07.04	04	6	4	0
MYERS Christopher (Chris)						
Yeovil, 1 April, 1969						(M)
Torquay U	App	06.87	86	8	1	0
Torquay U	Barnstaple T	08.90	90-92	88	8	7
Torquay U (L)	Dundee U	12.93	93	6	0	0
Scarborough	Dundee U	01.96	95	8	1	0
Exeter C	Tr	03.96	95-96	38	3	2

MYERS Clifford (Cliff) William
Southwark, 23 September, 1946 (M)

League Club	Source	Date Signed	Seasons Played	Apps	Subs	Gls
Charlton Ath	App	09.64	65-66	16	2	2
Brentford	Tr	06.67	67	7	3	0
Torquay U	Yeovil T	07.73	73-75	80	6	12

MYERS Peter William
Dronfield, 15 September, 1982 (M)

League Club	Source	Date Signed	Seasons Played	Apps	Subs	Gls
Halifax T	YT	●	00	0	1	0

MYERS John **Rodney (Rod)**
Sheffield, 16 February, 1939 (FB)

League Club	Source	Date Signed	Seasons Played	Apps	Subs	Gls
Doncaster Rov		01.63	63	20	-	0

MYERSCOUGH William (Billy) Henry
Bolton, 22 June, 1930 Died 1977 (IF)

League Club	Source	Date Signed	Seasons Played	Apps	Subs	Gls
Walsall	Ashfield	06.54	54	26	-	6
Aston Villa	Tr	07.55	56-58	64	-	15
Rotherham U	Tr	07.59	59	38	-	11
Coventry C	Tr	07.60	60-61	58	-	16
Chester	Tr	03.62	61-62	36	-	10
Wrexham	Tr	07.63	63	35	-	5

MYHILL Glyn (Boaz) Oliver
California, USA, 9 November, 1982 EYth/Eu20 (G)

League Club	Source	Date Signed	Seasons Played	Apps	Subs	Gls
Aston Villa	YT	11.00				
Bradford C	L	11.02	02	2	0	0
Macclesfield T	L	08.03	03	15	0	0
Stockport Co	L	11.03	03	2	0	0
Hull C	Tr	12.03	03-04	68	0	0

MYHRE Thomas
Sarpsborg, Norway, 16 October, 1973 NoYth/Nou21-27/No-40 (G)

League Club	Source	Date Signed	Seasons Played	Apps	Subs	Gls
Everton	Viking Stavanger (Nor)	11.97	97-00	70	0	0
Birmingham C	L	03.00	99	7	0	0
Tranmere Rov	L	11.00	00	3	0	0
Sunderland	Besiktas (Tu)	07.02	02-04	35	2	0
Crystal Palace	L	10.03	03	15	0	0

MYLES Neil Thomson
Falkirk, 17 June, 1927 Died 1993 (WH)

League Club	Source	Date Signed	Seasons Played	Apps	Subs	Gls
Ipswich T	Third Lanark	08.49	49-59	223	-	15

MYNARD Leslie (Les) Daniel
Bewdley, 19 December, 1925 (W)

League Club	Source	Date Signed	Seasons Played	Apps	Subs	Gls
Wolverhampton W	Bewdley	05.45	47	3	-	0
Derby Co	Tr	07.49	49-50	14	-	2
Scunthorpe U	Tr	08.52	52	18	-	3

MYTON Brian
Strensall, 26 September, 1950 (FB)

League Club	Source	Date Signed	Seasons Played	Apps	Subs	Gls
Middlesbrough	App	09.67	68-70	10	0	0
Southend U	L	11.71	71	0	1	0

League Club Source Date Signed Seasons Played Career Record Apps Subs Gls

FNACCA Francesco (Franco)
Venezuela, 9 November, 1982 (M)

League Club	Source	Date Signed	Seasons Played	Apps	Subs	Gls
Cambridge U	YT	04.01	02-03	11	15	0

NAFTI Mehdi
Toulouse, France, 28 November, 1978 Tunisia int (M)

League Club	Source	Date Signed	Seasons Played	Apps	Subs	Gls
Birmingham C (L)	Racing Santander (Sp)	01.05	04	7	3	0

NAGY Niklos (Mick)
Hungary, 1 May, 1929 (IF)

League Club	Source	Date Signed	Seasons Played	Apps	Subs	Gls
Scunthorpe U		01.51				
Swindon T	Tr	08.51	51	2	-	0

NAIL Desmond **Roy**
St Columb, 28 December, 1924 Died 1983 (CF)

League Club	Source	Date Signed	Seasons Played	Apps	Subs	Gls
Plymouth Arg	St Blazey	10.47	47	1	-	0

NAINBY Lewis **John**
Seaton Delaval, 2 January, 1940 (IF)

League Club	Source	Date Signed	Seasons Played	Apps	Subs	Gls
Sheffield Wed		02.58				
Darlington	Tr	07.59	59	3	-	1

NAISBETT Philip (Phil)
Seaham, 2 January, 1979 (G)

League Club	Source	Date Signed	Seasons Played	Apps	Subs	Gls
Sunderland	YT	04.97				
Scarborough	Gateshead	01.99	98	2	0	0

NAISBITT Daniel (Danny) John
Bishop Auckland, 25 November, 1978 (G)

League Club	Source	Date Signed	Seasons Played	Apps	Subs	Gls
Walsall	YT	07.97				
Barnet	Tr	08.99	99-00	19	4	0
Carlisle U	L	08.02	02	1	0	0

NALIS Lilian Bernard Pierre
Nogent-sur-Marne, France, 29 September, 1971 (M)

League Club	Source	Date Signed	Seasons Played	Apps	Subs	Gls
Leicester C	Chievo (It)	07.03	03-04	43	16	6

NANCEKIVELL Kevin William
Barnstaple, 22 October, 1971 (F)

League Club	Source	Date Signed	Seasons Played	Apps	Subs	Gls
Plymouth Arg	Tiverton T	08.00	00	0	6	1

NAPIER Alexander (Alex) Stevenson
Kirkcaldy, 8 August, 1935 (CF)

League Club	Source	Date Signed	Seasons Played	Apps	Subs	Gls
Darlington	Raith Rov	05.55	55	1	-	0

NAPIER Christopher (Kit) Robin Anthony
Dunblane, 26 September, 1943 (F)

League Club	Source	Date Signed	Seasons Played	Apps	Subs	Gls
Blackpool	Jnrs	11.60	62	2	-	0
Preston NE	Tr	06.63	63	1	-	0
Workington	Tr	07.64	64-65	58	0	26
Newcastle U	Tr	11.65	65	8	0	0
Brighton & Hove A	Tr	09.66	66-72	249	7	84
Blackburn Rov	Tr	08.72	72-73	53	1	10

NAPIER Robert **John**
Lurgan, 23 September, 1946 NIu23-2/NI-1 (CD)

League Club	Source	Date Signed	Seasons Played	Apps	Subs	Gls
Bolton W	Jnrs	09.63	64-66	69	0	2
Brighton & Hove A	Tr	08.67	67-72	218	1	5
Bradford C	Tr	10.72	72-74	106	0	3
Bradford C	San Diego (USA)	08.76	76	0	1	0

NARBETT Jonathan (Jon) Vellenzer
Birmingham, 21 November, 1968 (M)

League Club	Source	Date Signed	Seasons Played	Apps	Subs	Gls
Shrewsbury T	App	09.86	86-87	20	6	3
Hereford U	Tr	10.88	88-91	148	1	31
Oxford U	Tr	07.92	92-93	13	2	0
Chesterfield	Merthyr Tydfil	12.94	94-95	13	7	1

NARDIELLO Daniel (Danny) Antony
Coventry, 22 October, 1982 ESch/EYth (F)

League Club	Source	Date Signed	Seasons Played	Apps	Subs	Gls
Manchester U	YT	11.99				
Swansea C	L	10.03	03	3	1	0
Barnsley	L	01.04	03	14	2	7
Barnsley	L	07.04	04	11	17	7

NARDIELLO Donato (Don)
Cardigan, 9 April, 1957 Wu21-1/W-2 (W)

League Club	Source	Date Signed	Seasons Played	Apps	Subs	Gls
Coventry C	App	04.74	77-79	32	1	1

NARDIELLO Gerardo (Gerry)
Warley, 5 May, 1966 EYth (F)

League Club	Source	Date Signed	Seasons Played	Apps	Subs	Gls
Shrewsbury T	App	05.84	82-85	32	6	11
Cardiff C	L	03.86	85	7	0	4
Torquay U	Tr	07.86	86-87	28	9	11

NASH Carlo James
Bolton, 13 September, 1973 (G)

League Club	Source	Date Signed	Seasons Played	Apps	Subs	Gls
Crystal Palace	Clitheroe	07.96	96	21	0	0
Stockport Co	Tr	06.98	98-00	89	0	0
Manchester C	Tr	01.01	00-02	37	1	0
Middlesbrough	Tr	08.03	03-04	3	0	0
Preston NE	Tr	03.05	04	7	0	0

NASH Frank (Paddy) Cooper
South Bank, 30 June, 1918 Died 1989 (G)

League Club	Source	Date Signed	Seasons Played	Apps	Subs	Gls
Middlesbrough	South Bank East End	09.37	37-47	19	-	0
Southend U	Tr	12.47	47-50	57	-	0

NASH Gerard Thomas
Dublin, 11 July, 1986 IRYth (FB)

League Club	Source	Date Signed	Seasons Played	Apps	Subs	Gls
Ipswich T	Sch	07.03	03	0	1	0

NASH Marc
Newcastle, 13 May, 1978 (F)

League Club	Source	Date Signed	Seasons Played	Apps	Subs	Gls
Hartlepool U	Benfield Park	09.97	97	0	1	0

NASH Martin John
Regina, Canada, 27 December, 1975 Cau23-11/Ca-26 (W)

League Club	Source	Date Signed	Seasons Played	Apps	Subs	Gls
Stockport Co	Regina (Can)	11.96	96-97	0	11	0
Chester C	Vancouver (Can)	09.99	99	12	4	0
Macclesfield T	Rochester (USA)	01.03	02	1	4	0

NASH Robert (Bobby) Graham
Hammersmith, 8 February, 1946 Died 1998 (FB)

League Club	Source	Date Signed	Seasons Played	Apps	Subs	Gls
Queens Park Rgrs	Jnrs	02.64	64	17	-	0
Exeter C	Tr	06.66	66	1	0	0

NASSARI Derek James
Salford, 20 October, 1971 (M)

League Club	Source	Date Signed	Seasons Played	Apps	Subs	Gls
Chester C	YT	07.88	89	0	1	0

NASTRI Carlo Luciano Raffaele
Finchley, 22 October, 1935 (W)

League Club	Source	Date Signed	Seasons Played	Apps	Subs	Gls
Crystal Palace	Kingstonian	07.58	58	2	-	0

NATTRASS Irving
Fishburn, 12 December, 1952 Eu23-1 (FB)

League Club	Source	Date Signed	Seasons Played	Apps	Subs	Gls
Newcastle U	App	07.70	70-78	226	12	16
Middlesbrough	Tr	08.79	79-85	186	5	2

NATTRESS Clive
Durham, 24 May, 1951 (FB)

League Club	Source	Date Signed	Seasons Played	Apps	Subs	Gls
Blackpool	Consett	08.70				
Darlington	Tr	08.72	72-79	297	5	15
Halifax T	Tr	06.80	80	37	0	5
Darlington	Bishop Auckland	08.85	85	1	0	0

NAUGHTON William (Willie) Balloch Stirling
Catrine, 20 March, 1962 (W)

League Club	Source	Date Signed	Seasons Played	Apps	Subs	Gls
Preston NE	App	03.80	79-84	148	14	10
Walsall	Tr	03.85	84-88	139	12	16
Shrewsbury T	Tr	08.89	89-90	43	6	4
Walsall	Tr	01.91	90	15	1	1

NAVARRO Alan Edward
Liverpool, 31 May, 1981 (M)

League Club	Source	Date Signed	Seasons Played	Apps	Subs	Gls
Liverpool	YT	04.99				
Crewe Alex	L	03.01	00	5	3	1
Crewe Alex	L	08.01	01	7	0	0
Tranmere Rov	Tr	11.01	01-03	35	10	1
Chester C	L	08.04	04	3	0	0
Macclesfield T	L	12.04	04	11	0	1

NAYBET Noureddine
Casablanca, Morocco, 10 February, 1970 Morocco 105 (CD)

League Club	Source	Date Signed	Seasons Played	Apps	Subs	Gls
Tottenham H	Deportivo la Coruna (Sp)	08.04	04	27	0	1

NAYIM Mohamed Amar Ali
Ceuta, Morocco, 5 November, 1968 Spu21 (M)

League Club	Source	Date Signed	Seasons Played	Apps	Subs	Gls
Tottenham H	Barcelona (Sp)	11.88	88-92	95	17	11

NAYLOR Anthony (Tony) Joseph
Manchester, 29 March, 1967 (F)

League Club	Source	Date Signed	Seasons Played	Apps	Subs	Gls
Crewe Alex	Droylsden	03.90	89-93	104	18	45
Port Vale	Tr	07.94	94-00	207	46	71
Cheltenham T	Tr	08.01	01-02	62	12	18

NAYLOR Dominic John
Watford, 12 August, 1970 (FB)

League Club	Source	Date Signed	Seasons Played	Apps	Subs	Gls
Watford	YT	09.88				
Halifax T	Tr	12.89	89	5	1	1
Barnet	(Hong Kong)	08.91	91-92	50	1	0
Plymouth Arg	Tr	07.93	93-94	84	1	0
Gillingham	Tr	08.95	95	30	1	1
Leyton Orient	Tr	08.96	96-97	87	0	4

League Club	Source	Date Signed	Seasons Played	Career Record Apps	Subs	Gls
NAYLOR Edward Arnold						
Bradford, 24 December, 1921 Died 2000						(WH)
Bradford PA		05.45				
Halifax T	Tr	09.48	48	7	-	0
NAYLOR Geoffrey (Geoff)						
Goole, 28 December, 1949						(M)
Scunthorpe U	App	09.67	67	9	1	0
NAYLOR Glenn						
Howden, 11 August, 1972						(F)
York C	YT	03.90	89-96	78	33	30
Darlington	L	10.95	95	3	1	1
Darlington	Tr	09.96	96-02	157	52	46
NAYLOR Harold Francis						
Leeds, 6 June, 1928						(CF)
Oldham Ath (Am)		04.51	50	1	-	0
NAYLOR Lee Martyn						
Bloxwich, 19 March, 1980 EYth/Eu21-3						(CD)
Wolverhampton W	YT	10.97	97-04	229	21	6
NAYLOR Martyn Paul						
Walsall, 2 August, 1977						(FB)
Shrewsbury T	Telford U	07.97	97	2	0	0
NAYLOR Richard Alan						
Leeds, 28 February, 1977						(F)
Ipswich T	YT	07.95	96-04	143	84	34
Millwall	L	01.02	01	2	1	0
Barnsley	L	03.02	01	7	1	0
NAYLOR Stuart William						
Wetherby, 6 December, 1962 EYth/EB-3						(G)
Lincoln C	Yorkshire Amats	06.80	81-85	49	0	0
Peterborough U	L	02.83	82	8	0	0
Crewe Alex	L	10.83	83	38	0	0
Crewe Alex	L	08.84	84	17	0	0
West Bromwich A	Tr	02.86	85-95	354	1	0
Bristol C	Tr	08.96	96-97	37	0	0
Mansfield T	L	12.98	98	6	0	0
Walsall	Tr	03.99				
Exeter C	Tr	08.99	99	30	0	0
NAYLOR Terence (Terry) Michael Patrick						
Islington, 5 December, 1948						(FB)
Tottenham H	Smithfield Market	07.69	69-79	237	6	0
Charlton Ath	Tr	11.80	80-83	69	4	0
NAYLOR Thomas (Tommy) Vincent						
Blackburn, 1 April, 1946						(CD)
Bournemouth	App	10.63	64-70	139	4	3
Hereford U	Tr	08.72	72-74	73	2	4
NAYLOR Thomas **William (Bill)**						
Leeds, 7 December, 1924						(FB)
Huddersfield T	Outwood Stormcocks	02.43				
Oldham Ath	Tr	03.48	47-58	224	-	0
NAYSMITH Gary Andrew						
Edinburgh, 16 November, 1978 SSch/Su21-22/SB-1/S-28						(FB)
Everton	Heart of Midlothian	10.00	00-04	96	16	5
NDAH George Ehialimolisa						
Dulwich, 23 December, 1974 EYth						(F)
Crystal Palace	YT	08.92	92-97	33	45	8
Bournemouth	L	10.95	95	12	0	2
Gillingham	L	08.97	97	4	0	0
Swindon T	Tr	11.97	97-99	66	1	14
Wolverhampton W	Tr	10.99	99-02	44	29	14
NDAH Jamie Jidefor Ogoegbunan						
Camberwell, 5 August, 1971						(F)
Torquay U	Kingstonian	08.95	95-96	25	3	4
Barnet	Tr	02.97	96	12	2	4
N'DIAYE Sada						
Dakar, Senegal, 27 March, 1975						(F)
Southend U	Troyes (Fr)	10.97	97	15	2	2
N'DIAYE Seyni						
Dakar, Senegal, 1 June, 1973						(F)
Tranmere Rov	SM Caen (Fr)	03.01	00-01	11	8	4
NDIWA-LORD Kangana						
Maquela do Zambo, Angola, 28 February, 1984 SwYth/Congo int						(CD)
Bolton W	Djurgaarden (Swe)	07.03				
Oldham Ath	L	08.03	03	3	1	0
Rochdale	L	02.04	03	0	1	0
NDLOVU Peter						
Bulawayo, Zimbabwe, 25 February, 1973 Zimbabwe int						(W)
Coventry C	Highlanders (Zim)	08.91	91-96	141	36	37
Birmingham C	Tr	07.97	97-00	78	29	22
Huddersfield T	L	12.00	00	6	0	4
Sheffield U	Tr	02.01	00-03	114	21	25
N'DOUR Alassane						
Dakar, Senegal, 12 December, 1981 Senegal int						(FB)
West Bromwich A (L)	St Etienne (Fr)	09.03	03	2	0	0
N'DUMBU-NSUNGU Guylain						
Kinshasa, DR Congo, 26 December, 1982						(F)
Sheffield Wed	Amiens (Fr)	09.03	03-04	24	11	10
Preston NE	L	09.04	04	4	2	0
Colchester U	Tr	01.05	04	2	6	1
NEAL Ashley James						
Northampton, 16 December, 1974						(FB)
Liverpool	YT	04.93				
Brighton & Hove A	L	09.96	96	8	0	0
Huddersfield T	Tr	12.96				
Peterborough U	Tr	03.97	96-97	6	2	0
NEAL Christopher (Chris)						
Kirkby-in-Ashfield, 27 June, 1947						(W)
Darlington (Am)	Crook T	06.67	67	5	0	0
NEAL Christopher (Chris) Michael						
St Albans, 23 October, 1985						(G)
Preston NE	Sch	12.04	04	0	1	0
NEAL Dean John						
Edmonton, 5 January, 1961						(F)
Queens Park Rgrs	App	01.79	79-80	20	2	8
Millwall	Tulsa (USA)	10.81	81-84	101	19	42
Southend U	Tr	01.86	85-87	35	5	6
Cambridge U	L	12.87	87	4	0	0
NEAL George Charles						
Wellingborough, 29 December, 1919 Died 1997						(WH)
Northampton T	Kettering T	01.45	46	3	-	0
NEAL John						
Seaham, 3 April, 1932						(FB)
Hull C	Silksworth Colliery	08.49	49-55	60	-	1
Swindon T	King's Lynn	07.57	57-58	91	-	2
Aston Villa	Tr	07.59	59-62	96	-	0
Southend U	Tr	11.62	62-65	100	0	1
NEAL John James						
Hornsey, 11 March, 1966 ESch						(F)
Millwall	App	03.83	83	3	3	1
NEAL Lewis Ryan						
Leicester, 14 July, 1981						(M)
Stoke C	YT	07.98	00-04	29	41	2
NEAL Philip (Phil) George						
Irchester, 20 February, 1951 E-50						(FB)
Northampton T	App	12.68	68-74	182	2	29
Liverpool	Tr	10.74	74-85	453	2	41
Bolton W	Tr	12.85	85-88	56	8	3
NEAL Richard (Dick) Marshall						
Dinnington, 1 October, 1933 Eu23-4						(WH)
Wolverhampton W	Jnrs	03.51				
Lincoln C	Tr	07.54	54-56	115	-	11
Birmingham C	Tr	04.57	56-61	165	-	15
Middlesbrough	Tr	10.61	61-62	33	-	4
Lincoln C	Tr	08.63	63-64	41	-	4
NEALE Duncan Frederick						
Portslade, 1 October, 1939						(M)
Newcastle U	Ilford	06.59	60-62	88	-	8
Plymouth Arg	Tr	08.63	63-69	141	5	8
NEALE John William						
Barnstaple, 15 January, 1949						(W)
Exeter C	Barnstaple T	03.72	71-74	51	14	5
NEALE Keith Ian						
Birmingham, 19 January, 1935						(CF)
Birmingham C		02.54	56-57	5	-	1
Lincoln C	Tr	11.57	57-58	8	-	1
NEALE Peter						
Bolsover, 9 April, 1934						(CD)
Oldham Ath	Chesterfield (Jnrs)	01.53	55-58	117	-	28
Scunthorpe U	Tr	10.58	58-66	221	5	7
Chesterfield	Tr	10.66	66-67	69	0	4

NEALE Philip (Phil) Anthony
Scunthorpe, 5 June, 1954 (FB)

League Club	Source	Date Signed	Seasons Played	Apps	Subs	Gls
Lincoln C	Scunthorpe U (Am)	10.74	74-84	327	8	22

NEALE William (Billy) Elwood
Wallsend, 20 May, 1933 Died 2001 (WH)

League Club	Source	Date Signed	Seasons Played	Apps	Subs	Gls
Sunderland	Jnrs	06.50				
Darlington	North Shields	05.57	57	15	-	0

NEARY Harold **Frank**
Aldershot, 6 March, 1921 Died 2003 (CF)

League Club	Source	Date Signed	Seasons Played	Apps	Subs	Gls
Queens Park Rgrs	Finchley	07.45	46	9	-	6
West Ham U	Tr	01.47	46-47	17	-	15
Leyton Orient	Tr	11.47	47-49	78	-	44
Queens Park Rgrs	Tr	10.49	49	18	-	5
Millwall	Tr	08.50	50-53	123	-	50

NEATE Derek George Stanbridge
Uxbridge, 1 October, 1927 (W)

League Club	Source	Date Signed	Seasons Played	Apps	Subs	Gls
Brighton & Hove A	Hayes	04.56	55-56	24	-	6

NEATE Gordon
Reading, 14 March, 1941 (FB)

League Club	Source	Date Signed	Seasons Played	Apps	Subs	Gls
Reading	Jnrs	03.58	58-65	99	0	2

NEAVE Ian James **Gordon**
Glasgow, 10 October, 1924 Died 2003 (WH)

League Club	Source	Date Signed	Seasons Played	Apps	Subs	Gls
Portsmouth	Pollok Jnrs	03.47				
Bournemouth	Tr	06.49	50-53	85	-	0
Aldershot	Tr	07.55	55-57	79	-	2

NEBBELING Gavin Mark
Johannesburg, South Africa, 15 May, 1963 (CD)

League Club	Source	Date Signed	Seasons Played	Apps	Subs	Gls
Crystal Palace	Arcadia Shepherds (SA)	08.81	81-88	145	6	8
Northampton T	L	10.85	85	11	0	0
Fulham	Tr	07.89	89-92	85	3	2
Hereford U	L	12.91	91	3	0	0
Preston NE	Tr	07.93	93	22	0	4

NEDERGAARD Steen
Aalborg, Denmark, 25 February, 1970 (FB)

League Club	Source	Date Signed	Seasons Played	Apps	Subs	Gls
Norwich C	OB Odense (Den)	07.00	00-02	81	9	5

NEEDHAM Andrew (Andy) Paul
Oldham, 13 September, 1955 (F)

League Club	Source	Date Signed	Seasons Played	Apps	Subs	Gls
Birmingham C	App	08.73	75	2	1	1
Blackburn Rov	Tr	07.76	76	4	1	0
Aldershot	Tr	03.77	76-79	92	3	29

NEEDHAM Anthony (Tony)
Scunthorpe, 4 January, 1941 (FB)

League Club	Source	Date Signed	Seasons Played	Apps	Subs	Gls
Scunthorpe U	Jnrs	07.59	59-64	33	-	0

NEEDHAM David (Dave) William
Leicester, 21 May, 1949 (CD)

League Club	Source	Date Signed	Seasons Played	Apps	Subs	Gls
Notts Co	App	07.66	65-76	429	1	32
Queens Park Rgrs	Tr	06.77	77	18	0	3
Nottingham F	Tr	12.77	77-81	81	5	9

NEEDHAM Andrew **Paul**
Buxton, 15 June, 1961 (FB)

League Club	Source	Date Signed	Seasons Played	Apps	Subs	Gls
Chester	App	06.79	80-82	55	2	1

NEENAN Joseph (Joe) Patrick
Manchester, 17 March, 1959 (G)

League Club	Source	Date Signed	Seasons Played	Apps	Subs	Gls
York C	App	03.77	76-79	56	0	0
Scunthorpe U	Tr	01.80	79-84	191	0	0
Burnley	L	01.85	84	9	0	0
Burnley	Tr	07.85	85-86	81	0	0
Peterborough U	Tr	07.87	87-88	55	0	0
Scarborough	L	01.88	87	6	0	0

NEGOUAI Christian
Fort de France, Martinique, 20 January, 1975 (M)

League Club	Source	Date Signed	Seasons Played	Apps	Subs	Gls
Manchester C	RSC Charleroi (Bel)	11.01	01-04	2	4	1
Coventry C	L	01.05	04	1	0	0

NEIGHBOUR James (Jimmy) Edward
Chingford, 15 November, 1950 (W)

League Club	Source	Date Signed	Seasons Played	Apps	Subs	Gls
Tottenham H	App	11.68	70-76	104	15	8
Norwich C	Tr	09.76	76-79	104	2	5
West Ham U	Tr	09.79	79-82	66	7	5
Bournemouth	L	01.83	82	6	0	0

NEIL Alexander (Alex)
Bellshill, 9 June, 1981 (M)

League Club	Source	Date Signed	Seasons Played	Apps	Subs	Gls
Barnsley	Airdrie	07.00	00-03	83	38	4
Mansfield T	Tr	07.04	04	40	1	1

NEIL Gary Derek Campbell
Glasgow, 16 August, 1978 (F)

League Club	Source	Date Signed	Seasons Played	Apps	Subs	Gls
Leicester C	YT	07.97				
Torquay U	Tr	03.99	98-00	19	8	1

NEIL Hugh Moorhead
Cumnock, 2 October, 1936 Died 1978 SSch (FB)

League Club	Source	Date Signed	Seasons Played	Apps	Subs	Gls
Carlisle U	St Johnstone	06.61	61-68	247	2	2

NEIL James (Jimmy) Darren
Bury St Edmunds, 28 February, 1976 (FB)

League Club	Source	Date Signed	Seasons Played	Apps	Subs	Gls
Grimsby T	YT	07.94	95-96	1	1	0
Scunthorpe U	Tr	08.97	97	6	1	0

NEIL Patrick (Pat) Thomas
Portsmouth, 24 October, 1937 ESch/EAmat (W)

League Club	Source	Date Signed	Seasons Played	Apps	Subs	Gls
Portsmouth (Am)	Jnrs	06.55	55	9	-	3
Wolverhampton W (Am)	Tr	08.56	56	4	-	1
Portsmouth	Corinthian Casuals	05.62	62	1	-	0

NEIL William (Billy) Marshbanks
Lanark, 20 April, 1924 (IF)

League Club	Source	Date Signed	Seasons Played	Apps	Subs	Gls
Bradford PA	Morton	12.47	47	3	-	0

NEIL William (Billy) Waugh
Roslin, 10 November, 1944 (W)

League Club	Source	Date Signed	Seasons Played	Apps	Subs	Gls
Millwall	Bonnyrigg Rose	04.64	64-71	178	8	26

NEILL Lucas Edward
Sydney, Australia, 9 March, 1978 AuYth/Auu23-12/Au-13 (FB)

League Club	Source	Date Signed	Seasons Played	Apps	Subs	Gls
Millwall	NSW Soccer Acad (Aus)	11.95	95-01	124	28	13
Blackburn Rov	Tr	09.01	01-04	129	4	4

NEILL William John **Terence (Terry)**
Belfast, 8 May, 1942 NISch/NIu23-4/NI-59 (CD)

League Club	Source	Date Signed	Seasons Played	Apps	Subs	Gls
Arsenal	Bangor	12.59	60-69	240	1	8
Hull C	Tr	07.70	70-72	103	0	4

NEILL Thomas (Tommy) Kerr
Methil, 3 October, 1930 Died 1996 (WH)

League Club	Source	Date Signed	Seasons Played	Apps	Subs	Gls
Bolton W	RAF Wharton	09.50	52-56	40	-	2
Bury	Tr	12.56	56-59	89	-	8
Tranmere Rov	Tr	10.60	60-62	79	-	2

NEILL Warren Anthony
Acton, 21 November, 1962 ESch (FB)

League Club	Source	Date Signed	Seasons Played	Apps	Subs	Gls
Queens Park Rgrs	App	09.80	80-87	177	4	3
Portsmouth	Tr	07.88	88-94	216	2	3
Watford	Tr	01.96	95	1	0	0

NEILSON Alan Bruce
Wegburg, Germany, 26 September, 1972 Wu21-7/WB-2/W-5 (CD)

League Club	Source	Date Signed	Seasons Played	Apps	Subs	Gls
Newcastle U	YT	02.91	90-94	35	7	1
Southampton	Tr	06.95	95-97	42	13	0
Fulham	Tr	11.97	97-00	24	5	2
Grimsby T	Tr	10.01	01	8	2	0
Luton T	Tr	02.02	01-04	46	11	1

NEILSON Gordon
Glasgow, 28 May, 1947 (W)

League Club	Source	Date Signed	Seasons Played	Apps	Subs	Gls
Arsenal	Glasgow U	06.64	65-66	14	0	2
Brentford	Tr	10.68	68-71	80	12	15

NEILSON John Crane
Hamilton, 2 August, 1921 Died 1988 (CF)

League Club	Source	Date Signed	Seasons Played	Apps	Subs	Gls
Bradford C	Clyde	10.47	47-48	29	-	11

NEILSON Norman Frederick
Johannesburg, South Africa, 6 November, 1928 Died 2002 (CD)

League Club	Source	Date Signed	Seasons Played	Apps	Subs	Gls
Charlton Ath	Arcadia Pretoria (SA)	07.49	49	1	-	0
Derby Co	Tr	09.51	51-53	57	-	8
Bury	Tr	05.54	54-56	100	-	5
Hull C	Tr	04.57	56-57	25	-	0

NEILSON Stephen (Steve) Bruce
Newtongrange, 25 April, 1931 (WH)

League Club	Source	Date Signed	Seasons Played	Apps	Subs	Gls
Rotherham U	Heart of Midlothian	07.55	56	9	-	0

NEILSON Thomas (Tom)
Armadale, 28 July, 1922 (WH)

League Club	Source	Date Signed	Seasons Played	Apps	Subs	Gls
Ipswich T	Heart of Midlothian	05.48	48	1	-	0

NEKREWS Thomas (Tommy) John
Chatham, 20 March, 1933 (CD)

League Club	Source	Date Signed	Seasons Played	Apps	Subs	Gls
Gillingham	Chelsea (Am)	09.53	53-57	42	-	0

NELMES Alan Victor
Hackney, 20 October, 1948 (CD)

League Club	Source	Date Signed	Seasons Played	Apps	Subs	Gls
Chelsea	Jnrs	10.65				
Brentford	Tr	07.67	67-75	311	5	2

NELSEN Ryan
Christchurch, New Zealand, 18 October, 1977 New Zealand int (M)

League Club	Source	Date Signed	Seasons Played	Apps	Subs	Gls
Blackburn Rov	DC United (USA)	01.05	04	15	0	0

League Club	Source	Date Signed	Seasons Played	Apps	Subs	Gls
NELSON Andrew (Andy) Nesbitt						
Custom House, 5 July, 1935						(CD)
West Ham U	Jnrs	12.53	57-58	15	-	1
Ipswich T	Tr	06.59	59-64	193	-	0
Leyton Orient	Tr	09.64	64-65	43	0	0
Plymouth Arg	Tr	10.65	65-67	94	0	1
NELSON Anthony (Tony) James						
Cardiff, 12 April, 1930 WAmat						(CD)
Newport Co		06.52	51-53	19	-	6
Bristol C	Tr	05.54				
Bournemouth	Tr	06.56	56-64	194	-	1
NELSON Colin Armstrong						
Boldon, 13 March, 1938						(FB)
Sunderland	Usworth Colliery	03.58	58-64	146	-	2
Mansfield T	Tr	03.65	64-65	38	0	0
NELSON David (Dave)						
Douglas Water, 3 February, 1918 Died 1988						(WH)
Arsenal	St Bernard's	05.36	36-46	27	-	4
Fulham	Tr	12.46	46	23	-	3
Brentford	Tr	08.47	47-49	106	-	5
Queens Park Rgrs	Tr	02.50	49-50	31	-	0
Crystal Palace	Tr	03.52	51-52	12	-	0
NELSON Dennis Nicolson						
Edinburgh, 25 February, 1950						(F)
Crewe Alex	Dunfermline Ath	07.74	74-75	65	6	18
Reading	Tr	03.76	75-77	53	6	6
Crewe Alex	Tr	07.78	78-80	97	10	15
NELSON Fernando de Jesus						
Lisbon, Portugal, 5 November, 1971 Portugal int						(FB)
Aston Villa	Sporting Lisbon (Por)	06.96	96-97	54	5	0
NELSON Garry Paul						
Braintree, 16 January, 1961						(W)
Southend U	Jnrs	07.79	79-82	106	23	17
Swindon T	Tr	08.83	83-84	78	1	7
Plymouth Arg	Tr	07.85	85-86	71	3	20
Brighton & Hove A	Tr	07.87	87-90	132	12	47
Notts Co	L	11.90	90	0	2	0
Charlton Ath	Tr	08.91	91-95	147	38	37
Torquay U	Tr	08.96	96	30	4	8
NELSON George						
Mexborough, 5 February, 1925						(WH)
Sheffield U	Denaby Rov	08.43				
Lincoln C	Tr	09.46	46	1	-	0
NELSON James (Jimmy) Frederick						
Newcastle, 4 November, 1943						(FB)
Sunderland		08.62				
Ipswich T	Tr	07.63				
Barrow	Tr	01.65	64-65	15	0	0
NELSON Michael John						
Gateshead, 28 March, 1980						(CD)
Bury	Bishop Auckland	03.01	00-02	68	4	8
Hartlepool U	Tr	07.03	03-04	80	3	4
NELSON Samuel (Sammy)						
Belfast, 1 April, 1949 NIu23-1/NI-51						(FB)
Arsenal	Jnrs	04.66	69-80	245	10	10
Brighton & Hove A	Tr	09.81	81-82	40	0	1
NELSON Samuel (Sammy) Edward						
Belfast, 26 May, 1924 NISch/IrLge-1						(W)
Blackpool	Linfield Swifts	10.46	46-47	13	-	0
Luton T	Tr	01.48	47-48	4	-	1
NELSON Stuart James						
Stroud, 17 September, 1981						(G)
Millwall	Cirencester T	10.00				
Brentford	Hucknall T	02.04	03-04	52	0	0
NELSON William (Bill) Edward						
Silvertown, 20 September, 1929						(FB)
West Ham U		10.50	54	2	-	0
Queens Park Rgrs	Tr	07.55	55	9	-	0
NELTHORPE Craig Robert						
Doncaster, 10 June, 1987						(FB)
Doncaster Rov	Sch	●	04	0	1	0
NEMETH Szilard						
Komarno, Slovakia, 8 August, 1977 SlovakiaU21/Slovakia-52						(F)
Middlesbrough	Inter Bratislava (Slo)	07.01	01-04	61	51	23
NESBIT Anthony (Tony)						
Sunderland, 26 January, 1968 ESch						(M)
Newcastle U	App	01.86	86	1	2	0
NESBITT Edward (Eddie)						
Boldon, 12 October, 1951						(G)
Hartlepool (Am)	Longbenton Jnrs	08.71	71	1	0	0
NESBITT John						
Washington, 24 September, 1933						(CD)
Newcastle U	South Shields	12.55	57	3	-	0
NESBITT Mark Thomas						
Doncaster, 11 January, 1972						(FB)
Middlesbrough	YT	01.90				
Hartlepool U	Tr	03.91	90-91	2	0	0
NESBITT Michael (Mike) David						
Doncaster, 8 January, 1969 EYth						(F)
Doncaster Rov	App	01.86	85-87	6	5	1
NESS Hugh Preston						
Dunfermline, 30 April, 1940						(W)
Accrington St	Raith Rov	07.59	59	14	-	1
NETHERCOTT Kenneth (Ken) Walter Samuel						
Bristol, 22 July, 1925 EB						(G)
Norwich C	Bristol C (Am)	04.47	47-58	378	-	0
NETHERCOTT Stuart David						
Ilford, 21 March, 1973 Eu21-8						(CD)
Tottenham H	YT	08.91	92-96	31	23	0
Maidstone U	L	09.91	91	13	0	1
Barnet	L	02.92	91	3	0	0
Millwall	Tr	01.98	97-03	206	9	10
Wycombe W	Tr	01.04	03-04	49	2	1
NETTLESHIP Reginald (Reg)						
Warsop, 23 February, 1925 Died 2001						(IF)
Sheffield U	Welbeck Colliery	06.43				
Mansfield T	Tr	07.46	46	1	-	0
NETTLETON Ernest (Ernie)						
Sheffield, 7 January, 1918						(W)
York C		07.46	46	7	-	2
NEVES Rui Santos Cordeiro						
Vinhais, Portugal, 10 March, 1965						(F)
Darlington	Famalicao Por)	08.95	95	3	2	0
NEVILLE Christopher (Chris) William						
Downham Market, 22 October, 1970						(G)
Ipswich T	YT	05.89	89	1	0	0
NEVILLE David (Dave) Raymond						
Birmingham, 8 January, 1929 Died 1991						(FB)
Bournemouth	Paget Rgrs	04.49				
Chelsea	Tr	07.50				
Rochdale	Burton A	08.55	55	1	-	0
NEVILLE Gary Alexander						
Bury, 18 February, 1975 EYth/E-76						(FB)
Manchester U	YT	01.93	93-04	301	14	5
NEVILLE Philip (Phil) John						
Bury, 21 January, 1977 ESch/EYth/Eu21-7/E-52						(FB)
Manchester U	YT	06.94	94-04	210	53	5
NEVILLE Steven (Steve) Francis						
Walthamstow, 18 September, 1957						(W)
Southampton	App	09.75	77	5	0	1
Exeter C	Tr	09.78	78-80	90	3	22
Sheffield U	Tr	10.80	80-81	40	9	6
Exeter C	Tr	10.82	82-84	89	3	27
Bristol C	Tr	11.84	84-87	128	6	40
Exeter C	Tr	07.88	88-90	115	5	39
NEVILLE William (Billy)						
Cork, 15 May, 1935 IRB						(CF)
West Ham U	Wembley T	11.56	57	3	-	0
NEVIN Patrick (Pat) Kevin Francis Michael						
Glasgow, 6 September, 1963 SYth/Su21-5/SB/S-28						(W)
Chelsea	Clyde	07.83	83-87	190	3	36
Everton	Tr	07.88	88-91	81	28	16
Tranmere Rov	L	03.92	91	8	0	0
Tranmere Rov	Tr	08.92	92-96	181	12	30
NEVIN Paul Richard						
Lewisham, 23 June, 1969						(F)
Carlisle U	Evansville (USA)	09.91	91	2	6	0
NEVIN Ridley Walter						
Corbridge, 28 July, 1956						(M)
Everton	App	05.74				
Workington	Tr	08.75	75	3	1	0

League Club	Source	Date Signed	Seasons Played	Career Record Apps	Subs	Gls
NEVINS Laurence (Laurie)						
Gateshead, 2 July, 1920 Died 1972						(W)
Newcastle U		09.40				
Brighton & Hove A	Tr	05.47	47	5	-	0
Hartlepools U	Tr	03.48	47-48	18	-	8
NEVLAND Erik						
Stavanger, Norway, 10 November, 1977 Norway 3						(F)
Manchester U	Viking Stavanger (Nor)	07.97	97	0	1	0
NEW Martin Peter						
Swindon, 11 May, 1959 ESch						(G)
Arsenal	App	03.77				
Mansfield T	Tr	06.78	78-79	21	0	0
Barnsley	Tr	06.80	80	24	0	0
NEWALL James **Donald (Danny)**						
Newport, 5 June, 1921 Died 1997						(WH)
Newport Co	Melrose Stars	06.38	38-54	236	-	4
NEWBERY Peter John						
Derby, 4 March, 1938						(CF)
Derby Co	Jnrs	03.55	58-60	5	-	2
NEWBOLD Alfred (Alf)						
Hartlepool, 7 August, 1921 Died 2001						(FB)
Huddersfield T	Ouston W	12.45	46	2	-	0
Newport Co	Tr	10.46	46	22	-	0
NEWBY Thomas **Geoffrey (Geoff)**						
Barrow, 9 October, 1949						(CD)
Barrow (Am)	Jnrs	11.68	68	1	0	0
NEWBY Jonathan (Jon) Philip Robert						
Warrington, 28 November, 1978						(F)
Liverpool	Jnrs	05.97	99	0	1	0
Crewe Alex	L	03.00	99	5	1	0
Sheffield U	L	08.00	00	3	10	0
Bury	Tr	02.01	00-02	109	0	21
Huddersfield T	Tr	08.03	03	10	4	0
York C	L	03.04	03	6	1	0
Bury	Tr	08.04	04	17	19	4
NEWCOMBE Bernard (Len) John						
Swansea, 28 February, 1931 Died 1996						(W)
Fulham	Jnrs	05.48	51-54	23	-	3
Brentford	Tr	04.56	55-58	85	-	8
NEWCOMBE Giles Alan						
Doncaster, 9 July, 1968						(G)
Rotherham U	App	06.87	86	6	0	0
NEWELL Edgar						
Swansea, 17 April, 1920						(FB)
Swansea T		08.46	47-50	22	-	0
NEWELL George						
Rochdale, 17 March, 1936						(CD)
Rochdale		04.57	57	1	-	0
NEWELL Justin James						
Germany, 8 February, 1980						(F)
Torquay U	YT	06.98	97	0	1	0
NEWELL Michael (Mike) Colin						
Liverpool, 27 January, 1965 Eu21-4/EB-2						(F)
Crewe Alex	Liverpool (Jnrs)	09.83	83	3	0	0
Wigan Ath	Tr	10.83	83-85	64	8	25
Luton T	Tr	01.86	85-87	62	1	18
Leicester C	Tr	09.87	87-88	81	0	21
Everton	Tr	07.89	89-91	48	20	15
Blackburn Rov	Tr	11.91	91-95	113	17	28
Birmingham C	Tr	07.96	96	11	4	1
West Ham U	L	12.96	96	6	1	0
Bradford C	L	03.97	96	7	0	0
Crewe Alex	Aberdeen	03.99	98	1	3	0
Blackpool	Doncaster Rov	02.00	99-00	16	2	2
NEWELL Paul Clayton						
Woolwich, 23 February, 1969						(G)
Southend U	App	06.87	87-88	15	0	0
Leyton Orient	Tr	08.90	90-93	61	0	0
Colchester U	L	08.92	92	14	0	0
Barnet	Tr	07.94	94-95	16	0	0
Darlington	Tr	01.96	95-96	41	0	0
NEWEY Thomas (Tom) William						
Huddersfield, 31 October, 1982						(FB)
Leeds U	YT	08.00				
Cambridge U	L	02.03	02	6	0	0
Darlington	L	03.03	02	7	0	1
Leyton Orient	Tr	08.03	03-04	34	20	3
Cambridge U	Tr	01.05	04	15	1	0

League Club	Source	Date Signed	Seasons Played	Career Record Apps	Subs	Gls
NEWHOUSE Aidan Robert						
Wallasey, 23 May, 1972 EYth						(F)
Chester C	YT	07.89	87-89	29	15	6
Wimbledon	Tr	02.90	89-92	7	16	3
Port Vale	L	01.94	93	0	2	0
Portsmouth	L	12.94	94	6	0	1
Torquay U	L	12.95	95	4	0	2
Fulham	Tr	06.97	97	7	1	1
Swansea C	Tr	10.97	97-98	8	6	0
Brighton & Hove A	Tr	08.99	99	1	11	2
NEWLAND Raymond (Ray) James						
Liverpool, 19 July, 1971						(G)
Plymouth Arg	St Helens T	07.92	92-93	25	1	0
Chester C	Tr	07.94	94	9	1	0
Torquay U	Tr	01.96	95-96	28	0	0
NEWLANDS Douglas (Doug) Haigh						
Edinburgh, 29 October, 1931						(W)
Burnley	Aberdeen	03.55	54-58	98	-	21
Stoke C	Tr	07.59	59	32	-	8
NEWLANDS Malcolm (Monty)						
Wishaw, 28 March, 1925 Died 1996						(G)
Preston NE	St Mirren	07.48	48-52	80	-	0
Workington	Tr	11.52	52-59	250	-	0
NEWLOVE Peter						
Bradford, 27 December, 1947						(WH)
Bradford C	App	01.66	64-66	2	1	0
NEWMAN Albert Dorcin						
Lichfield, 1 March, 1915 Died 1981						(WH)
Walsall	Brierley Hill Alliance	11.39	46-49	135	-	2
NEWMAN Darren Lewis						
Brighton, 14 August, 1968						(CD)
Brighton & Hove A	App	08.86	85	1	0	0
NEWMAN Eric Ivan Alfred						
Romford, 24 November, 1924 Died 1971						(G)
Arsenal	Romford	10.46				
Ipswich T	Tr	09.50	52	18	-	0
NEWMAN Harry (Mick) Maurice						
London, Canada, 2 April, 1932						(IF)
West Ham U	Dagenham	02.57	56-57	7	-	2
NEWMAN John Henry George						
Hereford, 13 December, 1933						(CD)
Birmingham C	Jnrs	03.51	51-57	60	-	0
Leicester C	Tr	11.57	57-59	61	-	2
Plymouth Arg	Tr	01.60	59-67	298	0	9
Exeter C	Tr	11.67	67-71	91	1	1
NEWMAN Keith						
Farnham, 20 November, 1949 ESch						(CD)
Aldershot	App	11.66	66-69	19	4	0
York C	Tr	07.70	70	3	1	0
NEWMAN Richard (Ricky) Adrian						
Guildford, 5 August, 1970						(FB)
Crystal Palace	Jnrs	01.88	92-94	43	5	3
Maidstone U	L	02.92	91	9	1	1
Millwall	Tr	07.95	95-99	144	6	5
Reading	Tr	03.00	99-04	98	23	1
NEWMAN Robert (Rob) Nigel						
Bradford-on-Avon, 13 December, 1963						(CD)
Bristol C	App	10.81	81-90	382	12	52
Norwich C	Tr	07.91	91-97	181	19	14
Wigan Ath	L	03.98	97	8	0	0
Southend U	Tr	07.98	98-01	63	9	11
NEWMAN Ronald (Ron)						
Pontypridd, 1 May, 1933						(IF)
Northampton T	Ynysybwl	10.53	54-55	18	-	5
Coventry C	Tr	03.56	55-56	13	-	2
Torquay U	Tr	07.57	57	4	-	0
NEWMAN Ronald (Ron) Vernon						
Fareham, 19 January, 1934						(W)
Portsmouth	Woking	01.55	54-60	109	-	21
Leyton Orient	Tr	01.61	60-61	14	-	1
Crystal Palace	Tr	10.62	62	6	-	0
Gillingham	Tr	09.63	63-65	90	3	20
NEWSHAM Marc Anthony						
Hatfield, Yorkshire, 24 March, 1987						(F)
Rotherham U	Sch	●	04	0	4	0

NEWSHAM Stanley (Stan)
Farnworth, 24 March, 1931 Died 2001 (IF)

League Club	Source	Date Signed	Seasons Played	Apps	Subs	Gls
Bournemouth		06.52	52-56	142	-	74
Notts Co	Tr	08.57	57-61	99	-	44

NEWSOME Jonathan (Jon)
Sheffield, 6 September, 1970 (CD)

League Club	Source	Date Signed	Seasons Played	Apps	Subs	Gls
Sheffield Wed	YT	07.89	89-90	6	1	0
Leeds U	Tr	06.91	91-93	62	14	3
Norwich C	Tr	06.94	94-95	61	1	7
Sheffield Wed	Tr	03.96	95-99	50	4	4
Bolton W	L	11.98	98	6	0	0

NEWSOME Robinson (Robin)
Hebden Bridge, 25 September, 1919 Died 1999 (IF)

League Club	Source	Date Signed	Seasons Played	Apps	Subs	Gls
West Bromwich A	Congleton T	03.39				
Coventry C	Tr	06.47	47	7	-	2

NEWSON Mark Joseph
Stepney, 7 December, 1960 ESemiPro (CD)

League Club	Source	Date Signed	Seasons Played	Apps	Subs	Gls
Charlton Ath	App	12.78				
Bournemouth	Maidstone U	05.85	85-89	172	5	23
Fulham	Tr	02.90	89-92	98	4	4
Barnet	Tr	08.93	93-94	58	1	4

NEWTON Adam Lee
Grays, 4 December, 1980 Eu21-1/StKitts int (M)

League Club	Source	Date Signed	Seasons Played	Apps	Subs	Gls
West Ham U	YT	07.99	99	0	2	0
Portsmouth	L	07.99	99	1	2	0
Notts Co	L	11.00	00	13	7	1
Leyton Orient	L	03.02	01	10	0	1
Peterborough U	Tr	07.02	02-04	86	17	4

NEWTON Benjamin (Ben)
Grimsby, 10 October, 1934 (IF)

League Club	Source	Date Signed	Seasons Played	Apps	Subs	Gls
Grimsby T	Jnrs	07.53	53	3	-	0

NEWTON Christopher (Chris) John
Leeds, 15 November, 1979 (F)

League Club	Source	Date Signed	Seasons Played	Apps	Subs	Gls
Halifax T	YT	07.98	98-99	12	10	1

NEWTON Stanley **Douglas**
Newcastle, 16 January, 1959 (M)

League Club	Source	Date Signed	Seasons Played	Apps	Subs	Gls
Scarborough	Boston U	03.88	87	4	1	0

NEWTON Edward (Eddie) John Ikem
Hammersmith, 13 December, 1971 Eu21-2 (M)

League Club	Source	Date Signed	Seasons Played	Apps	Subs	Gls
Chelsea	YT	05.90	91-98	139	26	8
Cardiff C	L	01.92	91	18	0	4
Birmingham C	Tr	07.99	99	2	2	0
Oxford U	Tr	03.00	99	7	0	0
Barnet	Tr	08.00	00	2	2	0

NEWTON Eric David
Sheffield, 21 June, 1932 (IF)

League Club	Source	Date Signed	Seasons Played	Apps	Subs	Gls
Halifax T	Norton Woodseats	12.54	54	10	-	3

NEWTON Graham Wilfred
Bilston, 22 December, 1942 (M)

League Club	Source	Date Signed	Seasons Played	Apps	Subs	Gls
Blackpool	Wolverhampton W (Am)	08.61				
Walsall	Tr	02.62	62-63	30	-	10
Coventry C	Tr	01.64	63	8	-	3
Bournemouth	Tr	12.64	64-66	27	1	3
Port Vale	Atlanta (USA)	11.68	68	4	0	1

NEWTON Henry Albert
Nottingham, 18 February, 1944 Eu23-4/FLge-1 (M)

League Club	Source	Date Signed	Seasons Played	Apps	Subs	Gls
Nottingham F	Jnrs	06.61	63-70	282	0	17
Everton	Tr	10.70	70-73	76	0	5
Derby Co	Tr	09.73	73-76	111	6	5
Walsall	Tr	07.77	77	16	0	0

NEWTON John
Edinburgh, 19 January, 1940 (WH)

League Club	Source	Date Signed	Seasons Played	Apps	Subs	Gls
Notts Co	Craiglea Thistle	10.57	58-60	5	-	0

NEWTON John (Jackie) Laws
Bishop Auckland, 25 May, 1925 (WH)

League Club	Source	Date Signed	Seasons Played	Apps	Subs	Gls
Newcastle U		05.44				
Hartlepools U	Tr	05.46	46-57	332	-	15

NEWTON Keith Robert
Manchester, 23 June, 1941 Died 1998 Eu23-4/FLge-5/E-27 (FB)

League Club	Source	Date Signed	Seasons Played	Apps	Subs	Gls
Blackburn Rov	Jnrs	10.58	60-69	306	0	9
Everton	Tr	12.69	69-71	48	1	1
Burnley	Tr	06.72	72-77	209	0	5

NEWTON Reginald (Reg) William
Limehouse, 30 June, 1926 (G)

League Club	Source	Date Signed	Seasons Played	Apps	Subs	Gls
Leyton Orient	Dagenham Works	04.48	48	23	-	0
Brentford	Tr	07.49	49-56	87	-	0

NEWTON Robert (Bob)
Chesterfield, 23 November, 1956 (F)

League Club	Source	Date Signed	Seasons Played	Apps	Subs	Gls
Huddersfield T	App	11.73	73-76	37	5	7
Hartlepool U	Tr	08.77	77-82	150	0	48
Port Vale	Tr	09.82	82-83	48	0	22
Chesterfield	Tr	10.83	83-84	78	0	29
Hartlepool U	New England (USA)	07.85	85	8	3	2
Stockport Co	L	03.86	85	6	0	1
Bristol Rov	Chesterfield (N/C)	02.87	86	7	1	0

NEWTON Robert (Bob) Arthur
Earl Shilton, 19 January, 1946 (W)

League Club	Source	Date Signed	Seasons Played	Apps	Subs	Gls
Leicester C	App	08.63	64	2	-	0
Bradford C	Tr	05.65	65	19	1	4

NEWTON Shaun O'Neill
Camberwell, 20 August, 1975 Eu21-3 (M)

League Club	Source	Date Signed	Seasons Played	Apps	Subs	Gls
Charlton Ath	YT	07.93	92-00	189	51	20
Wolverhampton W	Tr	08.01	01-04	115	15	12
West Ham U	Tr	03.05	04	11	0	0

NGATA Heremaia (Herry)
Wanganui, New Zealand, 24 August, 1971 (F)

League Club	Source	Date Signed	Seasons Played	Apps	Subs	Gls
Hull C	Jnrs	07.89	89-91	8	17	0

NGONGE Felix **Michel**
Huy, Belgium, 10 January, 1967 Congo 6 (F)

League Club	Source	Date Signed	Seasons Played	Apps	Subs	Gls
Watford	Samsunspor (Tu)	07.98	98-00	29	18	9
Huddersfield T	L	03.00	99	0	4	0
Queens Park Rgrs	Tr	12.00	00	7	6	3

N'GOTTY Bruno
Lyon, France, 10 June, 1971 FrB-10/Fr-6 (CD)

League Club	Source	Date Signed	Seasons Played	Apps	Subs	Gls
Bolton W	Marseille (Fr)	09.01	01-04	116	3	4

NIBLETT Victor (Vic)
Frimley, 9 December, 1924 Died 2004 (CD)

League Club	Source	Date Signed	Seasons Played	Apps	Subs	Gls
Reading	Jnrs	08.44	46-49	6	-	0
West Ham U	Tr	06.50				
Gillingham	Tr	08.51	51-55	154	-	0

NIBLOE John Allister
Sheffield, 1 June, 1939 Died 1964 (IF)

League Club	Source	Date Signed	Seasons Played	Apps	Subs	Gls
Sheffield U		08.58	58-60	25	-	4
Stoke C	Tr	10.61	61-62	20	-	4
Doncaster Rov	Tr	10.62	62-63	36	-	7
Stockport Co	Tr	07.64	64	22	-	4

NIBLOE Joseph (Joe)
Glasgow, 10 December, 1926 (W)

League Club	Source	Date Signed	Seasons Played	Apps	Subs	Gls
Cardiff C	Clydebank Jnrs	03.48	48	1	-	0

NICHOL George Wallace
Bannockburn, 20 July, 1923 (G)

League Club	Source	Date Signed	Seasons Played	Apps	Subs	Gls
Aldershot	Falkirk	08.51	51	19	-	0

NICHOL Robert Wishart
Carlisle, 19 January, 1941 (WH)

League Club	Source	Date Signed	Seasons Played	Apps	Subs	Gls
Carlisle U (Am)	Jnrs	06.58	58-59	3	-	1

NICHOLAS Andrew Peter
Liverpool, 10 October, 1983 (FB)

League Club	Source	Date Signed	Seasons Played	Apps	Subs	Gls
Swindon T	Liverpool (Sch)	07.03	03-04	36	11	1
Chester C	L	03.05	04	5	0	0

NICHOLAS Anthony (Tony) Wallace Long
West Ham, 16 April, 1938 EYth (IF)

League Club	Source	Date Signed	Seasons Played	Apps	Subs	Gls
Chelsea	Jnrs	05.55	56-59	59	-	18
Brighton & Hove A	Tr	11.60	60-61	65	-	22
Leyton Orient	Chelmsford C	06.65	65	8	1	2

NICHOLAS Charles **Brian**
Aberdare, 20 April, 1933 ESch (WH)

League Club	Source	Date Signed	Seasons Played	Apps	Subs	Gls
Queens Park Rgrs	Jnrs	05.50	48-54	113	-	2
Chelsea	Tr	07.55	55-57	26	-	1
Coventry C	Tr	02.58	57-61	113	-	0

NICHOLAS Charles (Charlie)
Glasgow, 30 December, 1961 SYth/Su21-6/S-20 (F)

League Club	Source	Date Signed	Seasons Played	Apps	Subs	Gls
Arsenal	Glasgow Celtic	07.83	83-87	145	6	34

NICHOLAS Glyn
Dartmouth, 2 December, 1946 (CF)

League Club	Source	Date Signed	Seasons Played	Apps	Subs	Gls
Plymouth Arg	App	09.64	64-65	2	0	0
Crewe Alex	L	03.66	65	2	0	1

NICHOLAS John (Jack) Thomas
Derby, 26 November, 1910 Died 1977 WSch (WH)

League Club	Source	Date Signed	Seasons Played	Apps	Subs	Gls
Derby Co	Jnrs	12.27	28-46	347	-	14

NICHOLAS Kenneth (Ken) William
Northampton, 3 February, 1938 ESch/EYth (FB)

League Club	Source	Date Signed	Seasons Played	Apps	Subs	Gls
Arsenal	Jnrs	05.55				
Watford	Tr	05.59	59-64	198	-	4

NICHOLAS Peter
Newport, 10 November, 1959 WSch/Wu21-3/W-73 (M)

League Club	Source	Date Signed	Seasons Played	Apps	Subs	Gls
Crystal Palace	App	12.76	77-80	127	0	7
Arsenal	Tr	03.81	80-82	57	3	1
Crystal Palace	Tr	10.83	83-84	47	0	7
Luton T	Tr	01.85	84-86	102	0	1
Chelsea	Aberdeen	08.88	88-90	79	1	2
Watford	Tr	03.91	90-91	40	0	1

NICHOLL Christopher (Chris) John
Wilmslow, 12 October, 1946 NI-51 (CD)

League Club	Source	Date Signed	Seasons Played	Apps	Subs	Gls
Burnley	Jnrs	04.65				
Halifax T	Witton A	06.68	68-69	42	0	3
Luton T	Tr	08.69	69-71	97	0	6
Aston Villa	Tr	03.72	71-76	210	0	11
Southampton	Tr	06.77	77-82	228	0	8
Grimsby T	Tr	08.83	83-84	70	0	0

NICHOLL James (Jimmy) Michael
Hamilton, Canada, 28 December, 1956 NISch/NIu21-1/NI-73 (FB)

League Club	Source	Date Signed	Seasons Played	Apps	Subs	Gls
Manchester U	App	02.74	74-81	188	9	3
Sunderland	L	12.81	81	3	0	0
Sunderland	Toronto (Can)	09.82	82	29	0	0
West Bromwich A	Glasgow Rgrs	11.84	84-85	56	0	0

NICHOLL Terence (Terry) John
Wilmslow, 16 September, 1952 (M)

League Club	Source	Date Signed	Seasons Played	Apps	Subs	Gls
Crewe Alex		02.72	71-72	46	0	7
Sheffield U	Tr	03.73	73-74	12	10	1
Southend U	Tr	05.75	75-76	50	0	3
Gillingham	Tr	10.76	76-80	184	0	11

NICHOLLS Alan
Plymouth, 10 February, 1963 (CD)

League Club	Source	Date Signed	Seasons Played	Apps	Subs	Gls
Bristol C	App	02.80	80-82	70	0	5

NICHOLLS Alan
Sutton Coldfield, 28 August, 1973 Died 1995 Eu21-1 (G)

League Club	Source	Date Signed	Seasons Played	Apps	Subs	Gls
Plymouth Arg	Cheltenham T	08.93	93-94	64	1	0

NICHOLLS Ashley Joseph
Ipswich, 30 October, 1981 ESch (M)

League Club	Source	Date Signed	Seasons Played	Apps	Subs	Gls
Ipswich T	Ipswich W	07.00				
Darlington	Tr	08.02	02-03	65	2	6
Cambridge U	Tr	02.04	03-04	40	4	1

NICHOLLS David
Bradford, 3 November, 1956 ESch (M)

League Club	Source	Date Signed	Seasons Played	Apps	Subs	Gls
Huddersfield T	App	11.73				
Bradford C	Tr	08.75	75	0	4	0

NICHOLLS James (Jim) Henry
Coseley, 27 November, 1919 Died 2002 (G)

League Club	Source	Date Signed	Seasons Played	Apps	Subs	Gls
Bradford PA		05.46	46-49	36	-	0
Rochdale	Tr	08.51	51-52	50	-	0

NICHOLLS John (Johnny)
Wolverhampton, 3 April, 1931 Died 1995 Eu23-1/E-2 (IF)

League Club	Source	Date Signed	Seasons Played	Apps	Subs	Gls
West Bromwich A	Heath Town U	08.51	51-56	131	-	58
Cardiff C	Tr	05.57	57	8	-	2
Exeter C	Tr	11.57	57-58	55	-	23

NICHOLLS Kevin John Richard
Newham, 2 January, 1979 EYth (M)

League Club	Source	Date Signed	Seasons Played	Apps	Subs	Gls
Charlton Ath	YT	01.96	96-97	4	8	1
Brighton & Hove A	L	02.99	98	4	0	1
Wigan Ath	Tr	06.99	99-00	19	9	0
Luton T	Tr	08.01	01-04	142	1	26

NICHOLLS Mark
Hillingdon, 30 May, 1977 (M)

League Club	Source	Date Signed	Seasons Played	Apps	Subs	Gls
Chelsea	YT	07.95	96-98	11	25	3
Reading	L	12.99	99	4	1	1
Grimsby T	L	02.00	99	6	0	0
Colchester U	L	10.00	00	3	1	0
Torquay U	Tr	09.01	01	4	5	1

NICHOLLS Philip (Phil) Roy
Bilston, 22 June, 1952 (CD)

League Club	Source	Date Signed	Seasons Played	Apps	Subs	Gls
Wolverhampton W	App	07.70				
Crewe Alex	Tr	09.72	72-76	155	8	8
Bradford C	Tr	03.77	76-77	19	2	2
Crewe Alex	Tr	08.78	78	10	3	0

NICHOLLS Raymond (Ray) Ian
Peterborough, 7 April, 1965 (M)

League Club	Source	Date Signed	Seasons Played	Apps	Subs	Gls
Cambridge U	App	08.82	81-83	18	5	1

NICHOLLS Ronald (Ron) Bernard
Sharpness, 4 December, 1933 Died 1994 (G)

League Club	Source	Date Signed	Seasons Played	Apps	Subs	Gls
Bristol Rov	Cheltenham T	11.54	55-57	71	-	0
Cardiff C	Tr	08.58	58-60	51	-	0
Bristol C	Tr	07.61	61-63	39	-	0

NICHOLLS Ronald (Ron) Henry
Cannock, 18 October, 1935 (WH)

League Club	Source	Date Signed	Seasons Played	Apps	Subs	Gls
West Bromwich A	Jnrs	11.52				
Walsall	Tr	08.53	53	2	-	0

NICHOLLS Ryan Rhys
Cardiff, 10 May, 1973 WSch (W)

League Club	Source	Date Signed	Seasons Played	Apps	Subs	Gls
Leeds U	YT	07.91				
Cardiff C	Tr	01.95	94	6	6	1

NICHOLLS Wayne Keith
Wolverhampton, 21 October, 1952 (F)

League Club	Source	Date Signed	Seasons Played	Apps	Subs	Gls
Leicester C	Wolverhampton W (App)	11.70				
Workington	Tr	08.71	71-72	21	12	1

NICHOLS Adam Anthony
Ilford, 14 September, 1962 (CD)

League Club	Source	Date Signed	Seasons Played	Apps	Subs	Gls
Ipswich T	App	10.79				
Colchester U	(South Africa)	09.83	83	4	2	1

NICHOLS Brian Albert
Dagenham, 30 May, 1945 (FB)

League Club	Source	Date Signed	Seasons Played	Apps	Subs	Gls
Fulham	App	07.63	65-67	50	1	1
Millwall	Tr	07.68	68-69	9	1	0

NICHOLS Jonathan (Jon) Anthony
Plymouth, 10 September, 1980 (FB)

League Club	Source	Date Signed	Seasons Played	Apps	Subs	Gls
Torquay U	YT	07.99	98-99	6	1	0

NICHOLSON Derek
Harrow, 8 April, 1936 (W)

League Club	Source	Date Signed	Seasons Played	Apps	Subs	Gls
Leyton Orient	Chase of Chertsey	11.53	57	6	-	0

NICHOLSON Gary Anthony
Hexham, 4 November, 1960 (W)

League Club	Source	Date Signed	Seasons Played	Apps	Subs	Gls
Newcastle U	App	11.78	78-80	7	5	0
Mansfield T	Tr	08.81	81-83	112	6	21
York C	Tr	07.84	84	23	1	4
Halifax T	Tr	07.85	85-86	54	5	4

NICHOLSON George (Harry) Henry
Wetheral, 25 January, 1932 (G)

League Club	Source	Date Signed	Seasons Played	Apps	Subs	Gls
Grimsby T	Carlisle U (Am)	08.52	53	17	-	0
Nottingham F	Tr	07.55	55-56	72	-	0
Accrington St	Tr	03.58	58	1	-	0
Leyton Orient	Tr	03.59	59	4	-	0
Bristol C	Tr	07.60	60	1	-	0

NICHOLSON James (Jimmy) Joseph
Belfast, 27 February, 1943 NISch/NIu23-4/NIB/NI-41 (M)

League Club	Source	Date Signed	Seasons Played	Apps	Subs	Gls
Manchester U	Jnrs	02.60	60-62	58	-	5
Huddersfield T	Tr	12.64	64-73	280	1	25
Bury	Tr	12.73	73-75	79	4	0

NICHOLSON John Purcel
Liverpool, 2 September, 1936 Died 1966 (CD)

League Club	Source	Date Signed	Seasons Played	Apps	Subs	Gls
Liverpool		01.57	59	1	-	0
Port Vale	Tr	08.61	61-65	184	0	1
Doncaster Rov	Tr	09.65	65-66	41	0	0

NICHOLSON John Reay
Harrington, 23 November, 1928 Died 1993 (W)

League Club	Source	Date Signed	Seasons Played	Apps	Subs	Gls
Barrow	Frizington	05.49	49	4	-	1

NICHOLSON Kevin John
Derby, 2 October, 1980 ESch/EYth (FB)

League Club	Source	Date Signed	Seasons Played	Apps	Subs	Gls
Sheffield Wed	YT	10.97	00	0	1	0
Northampton T	Tr	01.01	00	6	1	0
Notts Co	Tr	03.01	00-03	74	21	3

NICHOLSON Maximillian (Max)
Leeds, 3 October, 1971 (W)

League Club	Source	Date Signed	Seasons Played	Apps	Subs	Gls
Doncaster Rov	YT	06.90	89-91	23	4	2
Hereford U	Tr	05.92	92-93	52	11	7
Torquay U	Tr	09.94	94	1	0	0
Scunthorpe U	Tr	11.94	94-95	27	24	5

NICHOLSON Peter
Cleator Moor, 12 January, 1951 (FB)

League Club	Source	Date Signed	Seasons Played	Apps	Subs	Gls
Blackpool	Carlisle U (App)	08.69	70	3	3	0
Bolton W	Tr	06.71	71-81	303	15	12
Rochdale	Lytham St Annes	11.82	82	7	0	0
Carlisle U	Lytham St Annes	03.83	82-83	1	2	0

NICHOLSON Peter William
Hull, 11 December, 1936 (CF)

League Club	Source	Date Signed	Seasons Played	Apps	Subs	Gls
Hull C (Am)	Kingburn Ath	06.60	60	1	-	0

NICHOLSON Reece
Bircotes, 4 April, 1936 (IF)

League Club	Source	Date Signed	Seasons Played	Apps	Subs	Gls
Doncaster Rov	Jnrs	09.53	54-57	28	-	8

NICHOLSON Shane Michael
Newark, 3 June, 1970 (FB)

League Club	Source	Date Signed	Seasons Played	Apps	Subs	Gls
Lincoln C	YT	07.88	86-91	122	11	7
Derby Co	Tr	04.92	92-95	73	1	1
West Bromwich A	Tr	02.96	95-97	50	2	0
Chesterfield	Tr	08.98	98	23	1	0
Stockport Co	Tr	06.99	99-00	73	4	3
Sheffield U	Tr	07.01	01	21	4	3
Tranmere Rov	Tr	07.02	02-03	45	9	6
Chesterfield	Tr	07.04	04	42	1	7

NICHOLSON Stanley (Stan)
Middlesbrough, 20 August, 1931 (IF)

League Club	Source	Date Signed	Seasons Played	Apps	Subs	Gls
Middlesbrough	South Bank	05.49				
Leeds U	Tr	08.51				
Hartlepools U	Horden CW	07.58	58	7	-	1

NICHOLSON William (Bill) Edward
Scarborough, 26 January, 1919 Died 2004 EB/FLge-1/E-1 (WH)

League Club	Source	Date Signed	Seasons Played	Apps	Subs	Gls
Tottenham H	Scarborough Y Libs	08.38	38-54	314	-	6

NICKALLS James (Jim) Horatio
Amble, 29 May, 1934 (CD)

League Club	Source	Date Signed	Seasons Played	Apps	Subs	Gls
Sunderland		04.53				
Darlington	Tr	05.54	54	18	-	0

NICKEAS Mark
Southport, 20 October, 1956 (FB)

League Club	Source	Date Signed	Seasons Played	Apps	Subs	Gls
Plymouth Arg	App	07.74				
Chester	Tr	08.75	75-78	58	2	1

NICKLAS Charles (Charlie)
Sunderland, 26 April, 1930 (CF)

League Club	Source	Date Signed	Seasons Played	Apps	Subs	Gls
Hull C	Silksworth Colliery	12.50	51	6	-	1
Darlington	Tr	05.53	53	17	-	6

NICOL Bennett
Glasgow, 10 March, 1921 Died 2000 (IF)

League Club	Source	Date Signed	Seasons Played	Apps	Subs	Gls
Bolton W		11.46				
Rochdale	Winsford U	07.49	49	5	-	1

NICOL Paul John
Scunthorpe, 31 October, 1967 (CD)

League Club	Source	Date Signed	Seasons Played	Apps	Subs	Gls
Scunthorpe U	App	07.86	86-89	68	7	2

NICOL Robert (Bobby) Benjamin Mathieson
Edinburgh, 11 May, 1936 SSch/Su23-2 (WH)

League Club	Source	Date Signed	Seasons Played	Apps	Subs	Gls
Barnsley	Hibernian	08.62	62-63	37	-	1

NICOL Stephen (Steve)
Irvine, 11 December, 1961 Su21-14/S-27 (M)

League Club	Source	Date Signed	Seasons Played	Apps	Subs	Gls
Liverpool	Ayr U	10.81	82-94	328	14	37
Notts Co	Tr	01.95	94-95	32	0	2
Sheffield Wed	Tr	11.95	95-97	41	8	0
West Bromwich A	L	03.98	97	9	0	0

NICOLAS Alexis Peter
Westminster, 13 February, 1983 Cyprus u21 (M)

League Club	Source	Date Signed	Seasons Played	Apps	Subs	Gls
Aston Villa	YT	04.01				
Chelsea	Tr	12.01	03	1	1	0
Brighton & Hove A	Tr	08.04	04	29	4	0

NICOLAU Nicky George
St Pancras, 12 October, 1983 (FB)

League Club	Source	Date Signed	Seasons Played	Apps	Subs	Gls
Arsenal	Sch	07.02				
Southend U	Tr	03.04	03-04	24	7	1

NICOLL Paul
Ellesmere Port, 10 November, 1966 (M)

League Club	Source	Date Signed	Seasons Played	Apps	Subs	Gls
Wrexham	Jnrs	07.84	84	0	1	0

NIEDZWIECKI Andrej **Edward (Eddie)**
Bangor, 3 May, 1959 WSch/W-2 (G)

League Club	Source	Date Signed	Seasons Played	Apps	Subs	Gls
Wrexham	Jnrs	07.76	77-82	111	0	0
Chelsea	Tr	06.83	83-87	136	0	0

NIELSEN Allan
Esbjerg, Denmark, 13 March, 1971 Deu21/De-45 (M)

League Club	Source	Date Signed	Seasons Played	Apps	Subs	Gls
Tottenham H	Brondby (Den)	09.96	96-99	78	19	12
Wolverhampton W	L	03.00	99	7	0	2
Watford	Tr	08.00	00-02	95	6	19

NIELSEN David
Sonderberg, Denmark, 1 December, 1976 (F)

League Club	Source	Date Signed	Seasons Played	Apps	Subs	Gls
Grimsby T (L)	FC Copenhagen (Den)	10.00	00	16	1	5
Wimbledon	FC Copenhagen (Den)	03.01	00-01	15	8	4
Norwich C	Tr	12.01	01-03	35	23	14

NIELSEN John Schmidt
Aarhus, Denmark, 7 April, 1972 (M)

League Club	Source	Date Signed	Seasons Played	Apps	Subs	Gls
Southend U	Ikast (Den)	09.96	96-97	18	11	3

NIELSEN Kent
Frederiksberg, Denmark, 28 December, 1961 Denmark int (CD)

League Club	Source	Date Signed	Seasons Played	Apps	Subs	Gls
Aston Villa	Brondby (Den)	06.89	89-91	74	5	4

NIELSEN Martin Ulrich
Aarhus, Denmark, 24 March, 1973 (M)

League Club	Source	Date Signed	Seasons Played	Apps	Subs	Gls
Huddersfield T	FC Copenhagen (Den)	03.98	97	0	3	0

NIELSEN Thomas
Aarhus, Denmark, 25 March, 1972 (FB)

League Club	Source	Date Signed	Seasons Played	Apps	Subs	Gls
Shrewsbury T	AG Fremad (Den)	08.96	96	19	3	1

NIEMI Antti
Oulu, Finland, 31 May, 1972 FiYth/Fiu21-17/Fi-66 (G)

League Club	Source	Date Signed	Seasons Played	Apps	Subs	Gls
Southampton	Heart of Midlothian	08.02	02-04	81	0	0

NIESTROJ Robert Waldemar
Oppeln, Poland, 2 December, 1974 (M)

League Club	Source	Date Signed	Seasons Played	Apps	Subs	Gls
Wolverhampton W	Fortuna Dusseldorf (Ger)	11.98	98-99	2	4	0

NIEUWENHUYS Berry
Boksburg, South Africa, 5 November, 1911 Died 1984 (W)

League Club	Source	Date Signed	Seasons Played	Apps	Subs	Gls
Liverpool	Germiston Callies (SA)	09.33	33-46	236	-	74

NIGHTINGALE Albert
Thrybergh, 10 November, 1923 (IF)

League Club	Source	Date Signed	Seasons Played	Apps	Subs	Gls
Sheffield U	Thurcroft	06.41	46-47	62	-	15
Huddersfield T	Tr	03.48	47-51	119	-	20
Blackburn Rov	Tr	10.51	51-52	35	-	5
Leeds U	Tr	10.52	52-56	130	-	48

NIGHTINGALE David Reginald
Liverpool, 15 August, 1927 (FB)

League Club	Source	Date Signed	Seasons Played	Apps	Subs	Gls
Tranmere Rov		09.46	46	3	-	0

NIGHTINGALE Luke Raymond
Portsmouth, 22 December, 1980 (F)

League Club	Source	Date Signed	Seasons Played	Apps	Subs	Gls
Portsmouth	YT	11.98	98-00	14	31	4
Swindon T	L	12.02	02	2	1	0
Southend U	Tr	08.03	03	0	4	0

NIGHTINGALE Mark Barry Douglas
Salisbury, 1 February, 1957 EYth (FB)

League Club	Source	Date Signed	Seasons Played	Apps	Subs	Gls
Bournemouth	App	07.74	74-75	44	5	4
Crystal Palace	Tr	06.76				
Norwich C	Tr	07.77	77-81	28	7	0
Bournemouth	Bulova (HK)	11.82	82-85	144	6	4
Peterborough U	Tr	07.86	86-87	71	7	3

NIGHTINGALE Ronald (Ron)
Darwen, 27 January, 1937 (WH)

League Club	Source	Date Signed	Seasons Played	Apps	Subs	Gls
Accrington St		07.57	58-60	14	-	0

NIJHOLT Luc
Zaandam, Holland, 29 July, 1961 (CD)

League Club	Source	Date Signed	Seasons Played	Apps	Subs	Gls
Swindon T	Motherwell	07.93	93-94	66	1	1

NIKOLIC Dusan
Belgrade, Yugoslavia, 23 January, 1953 Yugoslavia int (W)

League Club	Source	Date Signed	Seasons Played	Apps	Subs	Gls
Bolton W	Red Star Belgrade (Yug)	10.80	80-81	22	0	2

NILIS Luc
Hasselt, Belgium, 25 May, 1967 Belgium 56 (F)

League Club	Source	Date Signed	Seasons Played	Apps	Subs	Gls
Aston Villa	PSV Eindhoven (Holl)	07.00	00	3	0	1

NILSEN Roger
Tromso, Norway, 8 August, 1969 Norway 21 (FB)

League Club	Source	Date Signed	Seasons Played	Apps	Subs	Gls
Sheffield U	Viking Stavanger (Nor)	11.93	93-98	157	9	0
Tottenham H	Tr	03.99	98	3	0	0

NILSSON Mikael
Kristianstad, Sweden, 24 June, 1978 Sweden 25 (M)

League Club	Source	Date Signed	Seasons Played	Apps	Subs	Gls
Southampton	Halmstads (Swe)	07.04	04	12	4	0

NILSSON Nils Lennart **Roland**
Helsingborg, Sweden, 27 November, 1963 Sweden 116 (FB)

League Club	Source	Date Signed	Seasons Played	Apps	Subs	Gls
Sheffield Wed	IFK Gothenburg (Swe)	11.89	89-93	151	0	2
Coventry C	Helsingborg (Swe)	07.97	97-98	60	0	0
Coventry C	Helsingborg (Swe)	07.01	01	9	0	0

NIMMO Ian Wallace
Boston, 23 January, 1958 (F)

League Club	Source	Date Signed	Seasons Played	Apps	Subs	Gls
Sheffield Wed	App	01.76	75-78	26	19	10
Peterborough U	L	01.77	76	4	0	1
Doncaster Rov	Tr	06.79	79-81	77	9	29

NIMMO Liam Wallace
Boston, 28 December, 1984 (F)

League Club	Source	Date Signed	Seasons Played	Apps	Subs	Gls
Grimsby T	Sch	•	03	0	2	0

NIMMO William (Willie) Brown
Forth, 11 January, 1934 Died 1991 (G)

League Club	Source	Date Signed	Seasons Played	Apps	Subs	Gls
Leeds U	Alloa Ath	02.56	57	1	-	0
Doncaster Rov	Tr	03.58	57-61	182	-	0

NIMNI Avi
Tel Aviv, Israel, 26 April, 1972 Israel 47 (M)

League Club	Source	Date Signed	Seasons Played	Apps	Subs	Gls
Derby Co	Maccabi Tel Aviv (Isr)	11.99	99	2	2	1

NISBET Gordon James Mackay
Wallsend, 18 September, 1951 Eu23-1 (FB)

League Club	Source	Date Signed	Seasons Played	Apps	Subs	Gls
West Bromwich A	Willington BC	09.68	69-75	136	0	0
Hull C	Tr	09.76	76-80	190	3	1
Plymouth Arg	Tr	12.80	80-86	281	0	14
Exeter C	Tr	06.87	87	12	0	0

NISH David John
Burton-on-Trent, 26 September, 1947 ESch/EYth/Eu23-10/FLge-5/E-5 (FB)

League Club	Source	Date Signed	Seasons Played	Apps	Subs	Gls
Leicester C	Measham Social Welf	07.66	66-72	228	0	25
Derby Co	Tr	08.72	72-78	184	4	10

NIVEN Derek
Falkirk, 12 December, 1983 (M)

League Club	Source	Date Signed	Seasons Played	Apps	Subs	Gls
Bolton W	Raith Rov	11.01				
Chesterfield	Tr	12.03	03-04	60	0	2

NIVEN Stuart Thomas
Glasgow, 24 December, 1978 SYth (M)

League Club	Source	Date Signed	Seasons Played	Apps	Subs	Gls
Ipswich T	YT	09.96	96	2	0	0
Barnet	Tr	09.00	00	20	4	2

NIX Peter
Rotherham, 25 January, 1958 (W)

League Club	Source	Date Signed	Seasons Played	Apps	Subs	Gls
Rotherham U	Jnrs	08.76	77-79	22	0	2

NIXON Eric Walter
Manchester, 4 October, 1962 (G)

League Club	Source	Date Signed	Seasons Played	Apps	Subs	Gls
Manchester C	Curzon Ashton	12.83	85-87	58	0	0
Wolverhampton W	L	08.86	86	16	0	0
Bradford C	L	11.86	86	3	0	0
Southampton	L	12.86	86	4	0	0
Carlisle U	L	01.87	86	16	0	0
Tranmere Rov	L	03.88	87	8	0	0
Tranmere Rov	Tr	07.88	88-96	333	0	0
Blackpool	L	02.96	95	20	0	0
Bradford C	L	09.96	96	12	0	0
Stockport Co	Tr	08.97	97	43	0	0
Wigan Ath	L	08.98	98	1	0	0
Wigan Ath	Tr	03.99	98	2	0	0
Tranmere Rov	Tr	07.99	99-02	1	4	0
Kidderminster Hrs	L	10.01	01	2	0	0
Sheffield Wed	Tr	09.03	03	0	1	0

NIXON Jonathan (Jon) Charles
Ilkeston, 20 January, 1948 (W)

League Club	Source	Date Signed	Seasons Played	Apps	Subs	Gls
Derby Co	Jnrs	09.65				
Notts Co	Ilkeston T	01.70	69-74	167	12	32
Peterborough U	Tr	09.74	74-76	104	6	16
Shrewsbury T	Tr	08.77	77	21	2	3
Barnsley	Tr	03.78	77	6	4	0
Halifax T	Tr	06.78	78	12	7	1

NIXON Marc Steven
Hexham, 29 January, 1984 (F)

League Club	Source	Date Signed	Seasons Played	Apps	Subs	Gls
Carlisle U	Sch	07.02	02	3	4	0

NIXON Paul
Seaham, 23 September, 1963 New Zealand int (F)

League Club	Source	Date Signed	Seasons Played	Apps	Subs	Gls
Bristol Rov	Seaham Red Star	01.89	88-90	31	13	6

NIXON Thomas (Tom) James
Backworth, 25 March, 1931 Died 2003 (WH)

League Club	Source	Date Signed	Seasons Played	Apps	Subs	Gls
Darlington	Newcastle U (Am)	05.51	51	1	-	0

NIXON William (Billy) John
Ballynahinch, 28 September, 1941 NISch (IF)

League Club	Source	Date Signed	Seasons Played	Apps	Subs	Gls
Norwich C	Distillery	03.61	61	1	-	0
Shrewsbury T	Tr	03.62	61-64	17	-	1

NOAKE David John
Yeovil, 9 June, 1940 (W)

League Club	Source	Date Signed	Seasons Played	Apps	Subs	Gls
Luton T	Dorchester T	11.59	59-60	17	-	0
Bristol C	Tr	06.61	61	11	-	3

NOAKES Alfred (Alfie) George Edward
Stratford, 14 August, 1933 (FB)

League Club	Source	Date Signed	Seasons Played	Apps	Subs	Gls
West Ham U	Jnrs	08.50				
Crystal Palace	Sittingbourne	06.55	55-61	195	-	14
Portsmouth	Tr	07.62	62-63	13	-	0

NOBBS Alan Keith
Bishop Auckland, 18 September, 1961 (FB)

League Club	Source	Date Signed	Seasons Played	Apps	Subs	Gls
Middlesbrough	App	09.79	80	1	0	0
Halifax T	Tr	08.82	82-83	87	0	1
Hartlepool U	Bishop Auckland	08.85	85-92	274	6	1

NOBLE Alfred (Alf) William Thomas
Hackney, 18 September, 1924 Died 1999 EAmat (IF)

League Club	Source	Date Signed	Seasons Played	Apps	Subs	Gls
Colchester U (Am)	Briggs Sports	09.55	55	1	-	0

NOBLE Barry
Stockton, 5 June, 1951 (G)

League Club	Source	Date Signed	Seasons Played	Apps	Subs	Gls
Hartlepool	Jnrs	08.70	71	1	0	0

NOBLE Daniel (Danny) William
Hull, 2 September, 1970 (G)

League Club	Source	Date Signed	Seasons Played	Apps	Subs	Gls
Stoke C	YT	07.89	89-90	3	0	0
Crewe Alex	Tr	06.91	91	7	0	0

NOBLE David James
Hitchin, 2 February, 1982 EYth/Eu20/Su21-2/SB-1 (M)

League Club	Source	Date Signed	Seasons Played	Apps	Subs	Gls
Arsenal	YT	03.01				
Watford	L	07.01	01	5	10	1
West Ham U	Tr	01.03	03	0	3	0
Boston U	Tr	02.04	03-04	44	2	5

NOBLE Frank
Sheffield, 26 October, 1945 (FB)

League Club	Source	Date Signed	Seasons Played	Apps	Subs	Gls
Sheffield Wed	Jnrs	05.63	63-65	2	0	0
Peterborough U	Tr	07.67	67-71	205	2	1

NOBLE John
Manchester, 20 May, 1919 Died 1996 (W)

League Club	Source	Date Signed	Seasons Played	Apps	Subs	Gls
Stockport Co	Warte Villa	03.39	46	1	-	0

NOBLE Mark James
West Ham, 8 May, 1987 (M)

League Club	Source	Date Signed	Seasons Played	Apps	Subs	Gls
West Ham U	Sch	07.04	04	10	3	0

NOBLE Norman
Barnsley, 8 August, 1923 Died 1973 (CD)

League Club	Source	Date Signed	Seasons Played	Apps	Subs	Gls
Huddersfield T		06.43				
Bradford C	Tr	10.45				
Rotherham U	Ransome & Marles	05.48	48-57	326	-	21

NOBLE Peter
Newcastle, 19 August, 1944 (F)

League Club	Source	Date Signed	Seasons Played	Apps	Subs	Gls
Newcastle U	Consett	11.64	65-67	22	3	7
Swindon T	Tr	01.68	67-72	212	4	62
Burnley	Tr	06.73	73-79	241	2	63
Blackpool	Tr	01.80	79-82	92	5	14

NOBLE Robert (Bobby)
Manchester, 18 December, 1945 EYth (FB)

League Club	Source	Date Signed	Seasons Played	Apps	Subs	Gls
Manchester U	App	12.62	65-66	31	0	0

NOBLE Robert (Bobby)
South Gosforth, 25 May, 1949 Died 2005 (CD)

League Club	Source	Date Signed	Seasons Played	Apps	Subs	Gls
Newcastle U	App	04.67				
Barrow	L	08.69	69	19	0	3
Bury	Tr	08.70	70	6	0	0
Barrow	Tr	10.70	70-71	72	1	5
Colchester U	Tr	08.72	72	25	2	0
Southport	Tr	03.73	72-74	61	2	6
Darlington	Tr	08.75	75-76	54	0	3

NOBLE Stuart William
Edinburgh, 14 October, 1983 (F)

League Club	Source	Date Signed	Seasons Played	Apps	Subs	Gls
Fulham	Sch	08.03				
Torquay U	L	08.04	04	2	1	0
Northampton T	L	02.05	04	0	4	0

NOBLE Wayne Ian
Bristol, 11 June, 1967 (M)

League Club	Source	Date Signed	Seasons Played	Apps	Subs	Gls
Bristol Rov	App	03.85	85-86	16	6	1

NOEL-WILLIAMS Gifton Ruben Elisha
Islington, 21 January, 1980 EYth (F)

League Club	Source	Date Signed	Seasons Played	Apps	Subs	Gls
Watford	YT	02.97	96-02	107	62	33
Stoke C	Tr	05.03	03-04	81	7	23

NOGAN Kurt
Cardiff, 9 September, 1970 Wu21-2/WB-1 (F)

League Club	Source	Date Signed	Seasons Played	Apps	Subs	Gls
Luton T	YT	07.89	89-91	17	16	3
Peterborough U	Tr	09.92				
Brighton & Hove A	Tr	10.92	92-94	97	0	49
Burnley	Tr	04.95	94-96	87	5	33
Preston NE	Tr	03.97	96-99	74	19	27
Cardiff C	Tr	03.00	99-00	4	14	1

NOGAN Lee Martin
Cardiff, 21 May, 1969 Wu21-1/WB-1/W-2 (F)

League Club	Source	Date Signed	Seasons Played	Apps	Subs	Gls
Oxford U	App	03.87	87-91	57	7	10
Brentford	L	03.87	86	10	1	2
Southend U	L	09.87	87	6	0	1
Watford	Tr	12.91	91-94	97	8	26
Southend U	L	03.94	93	4	1	0
Reading	Tr	01.95	94-96	71	20	26
Notts Co	L	02.97	96	6	0	0
Grimsby T	Tr	07.97	97-98	63	11	10
Darlington	Tr	07.99	99-00	37	12	6
Luton T	L	11.00	00	7	0	1
York C	Tr	02.01	00-03	133	10	32

NOLAN David Joseph
Liverpool, 24 February, 1968 (M)

League Club	Source	Date Signed	Seasons Played	Apps	Subs	Gls
Chester C	Bromborough Pool	01.92	91	1	0	0

NOLAN George
Liverpool, 9 December, 1925 (WH)

League Club	Source	Date Signed	Seasons Played	Apps	Subs	Gls
Southport	A1 Control	06.46	46	3	-	0

NOLAN Ian Robert
Liverpool, 9 July, 1970 NI-18 (FB)

League Club	Source	Date Signed	Seasons Played	Apps	Subs	Gls
Tranmere Rov	Marine	08.91	91-93	87	1	1
Sheffield Wed	Tr	08.94	94-99	164	1	4
Bradford C	Tr	07.00	00	17	4	0
Wigan Ath	Tr	08.01	01	5	3	0

NOLAN Kevin Anthony Jance
Liverpool, 24 June, 1982 EYth/Eu20/Eu21 (M)

League Club	Source	Date Signed	Seasons Played	Apps	Subs	Gls
Bolton W	YT	01.00	99-04	138	38	23

NOLAN Matthew (Matt) Lee
Hitchin, 25 February, 1982 (F)

League Club	Source	Date Signed	Seasons Played	Apps	Subs	Gls
Peterborough U	Hitchin T	09.03	03	0	1	0

NOLAN Michael (Mike) William
Dublin, 8 July, 1950 (FB)

League Club	Source	Date Signed	Seasons Played	Apps	Subs	Gls
Oldham Ath	App	08.67	66-67	2	0	0

NOLAN Philip (Phil)
Edmonton, 29 December, 1923 (CD)

League Club	Source	Date Signed	Seasons Played	Apps	Subs	Gls
Watford	Hayes	10.47	47-54	91	-	8

NOLAN Terence (Terry) Stephen
Whiston, 16 March, 1956 (F)

League Club	Source	Date Signed	Seasons Played	Apps	Subs	Gls
Southport	Prescot T	02.78	77	0	1	0

NOON Harry
Sutton-in-Ashfield, 6 October, 1937 Died 1996 (FB)

League Club	Source	Date Signed	Seasons Played	Apps	Subs	Gls
Notts Co	Bentinck Methodists	05.55	57-61	122	-	0
Bradford C	Tr	07.62	62	1	-	0

NOON Mark Richard
Leamington Spa, 23 September, 1983 (M)

League Club	Source	Date Signed	Seasons Played	Apps	Subs	Gls
Coventry C	YT	08.01	02	0	2	0

NORBURY Michael (Mick) Shaun
Hemsworth, 22 January, 1969 (F)

League Club	Source	Date Signed	Seasons Played	Apps	Subs	Gls
Scarborough	Ossett T	12.89				
Cambridge U	Bridlington T	02.92	91-92	11	15	3
Preston NE	Tr	12.92	92-93	32	10	13
Doncaster Rov	Tr	11.94	94-95	19	8	5

NORCROSS William (Bill)
Preston, 29 December, 1937 (W)

League Club	Source	Date Signed	Seasons Played	Apps	Subs	Gls
Southport (Am)	Chorley	07.59	59	1	-	0

NORFOLK Lee Richard
Dunedin, New Zealand, 17 October, 1975 (M)

League Club	Source	Date Signed	Seasons Played	Apps	Subs	Gls
Ipswich T	YT	07.94	94	1	2	0

NORMAN Anthony (Tony) Joseph
Mancot, 24 February, 1958 WB/W-5 (G)

League Club	Source	Date Signed	Seasons Played	Apps	Subs	Gls
Burnley	Jnrs	08.76				
Hull C	Tr	02.80	79-88	372	0	0
Sunderland	Tr	12.88	88-94	198	0	0
Huddersfield T	Tr	07.95	95-96	6	0	0

NORMAN Derek Antony
Birmingham, 11 February, 1946 EYth (WH)

League Club	Source	Date Signed	Seasons Played	Apps	Subs	Gls
Southampton	Alvechurch	01.64				
Aldershot	Tr	05.65	65	22	1	0

NORMAN Albert Griffith (Griff)
Cardiff, 20 February, 1926 (WH)

League Club	Source	Date Signed	Seasons Played	Apps	Subs	Gls
Cardiff C		04.50	51	1	-	0
Torquay U	Tr	10.52	52-57	216	-	6

NORMAN John
Birkenhead, 26 June, 1971 (F)

League Club	Source	Date Signed	Seasons Played	Apps	Subs	Gls
Tranmere Rov	YT	02.90				
Bury	Heswall	08.92	92	1	1	0

NORMAN Malcolm Allen
Cardiff, 24 October, 1934 (G)

League Club	Source	Date Signed	Seasons Played	Apps	Subs	Gls
Bristol Rov	Cardiff Corinthians	05.58	58-61	69	-	0

NORMAN Maurice
Mulbarton, 8 May, 1934 Eu23-3/FLge-1/E-23 (CD)

League Club	Source	Date Signed	Seasons Played	Apps	Subs	Gls
Norwich C	Wymondham OB	09.52	54-55	35	-	0
Tottenham H	Tr	11.55	55-65	357	0	16

NORMAN Richard (Richie)
Newcastle, 5 September, 1935 (FB)

League Club	Source	Date Signed	Seasons Played	Apps	Subs	Gls
Leicester C	Horden CW	11.58	59-67	303	0	2
Peterborough U	Tr	07.68	68	9	1	0

NORMAN Sean
Lowestoft, 27 November, 1966 (M)

League Club	Source	Date Signed	Seasons Played	Apps	Subs	Gls
Colchester U	Lowestoft T	07.85	86-87	18	3	1

NORMANN Runar
Harstad, Norway, 1 March, 1978 NoYth/Nou21-3 (M)

League Club	Source	Date Signed	Seasons Played	Apps	Subs	Gls
Coventry C	Lillestrom (Nor)	08.99	99-02	3	10	1

NORMANTON Graham Stephen
Hartlepool, 13 November, 1959 (FB)

League Club	Source	Date Signed	Seasons Played	Apps	Subs	Gls
Hartlepool U	Middlesbrough (App)	07.78	79-80	17	1	0

NORMANTON Sidney (Sid) Albert
Barnsley, 20 August, 1926 Died 1995 (WH)

League Club	Source	Date Signed	Seasons Played	Apps	Subs	Gls
Barnsley	Barnsley Main CW	09.45	47-53	123	-	2
Halifax T	Tr	07.54	54	13	-	0

NORRIE Craig Thomas
Hull, 22 July, 1960 (F)

League Club	Source	Date Signed	Seasons Played	Apps	Subs	Gls
Hull C	App	08.78	78-81	22	9	4

NORRIS David Martin
Stamford, 22 February, 1981 (M)

League Club	Source	Date Signed	Seasons Played	Apps	Subs	Gls
Bolton W	Boston U	02.00				
Hull C	L	03.02	01	3	3	1
Plymouth Arg	Tr	10.02	02-04	104	9	14

NORRIS Derek
Beighton, 19 June, 1935 Died 1997 (WH)

League Club	Source	Date Signed	Seasons Played	Apps	Subs	Gls
Peterborough U	Gainsborough Trinity	(N/L)	60	5	-	0

NORRIS George Albert
Aldershot, 19 September, 1935 (CF)

League Club	Source	Date Signed	Seasons Played	Apps	Subs	Gls
Aldershot	Farnborough T	12.58	58-63	106	-	59

NORRIS Graham John
Hampton, 8 February, 1954 (W)

League Club	Source	Date Signed	Seasons Played	Apps	Subs	Gls
Crystal Palace	App	02.72				
Southend U	L	03.73	72	1	0	0

NORRIS Michael (Mike)
Mansfield, 27 February, 1957 (G)

League Club	Source	Date Signed	Seasons Played	Apps	Subs	Gls
Scunthorpe U	App	02.75	73-75	25	0	0

NORRIS Oliver (Ollie)
Derry, 1 April, 1929 (CF)

League Club	Source	Date Signed	Seasons Played	Apps	Subs	Gls
Middlesbrough	Jnrs	07.48	51-53	12	-	2
Bournemouth	Worcester C	07.55	55-58	96	-	34
Northampton T	Tr	09.58	58	14	-	1
Rochdale	Ashford T	01.61	60	2	-	1

NORRIS Raymond (Ray) George
Bristol, 15 July, 1922 Died 1972 (CD)

League Club	Source	Date Signed	Seasons Played	Apps	Subs	Gls
Bristol C	Bedminster	05.47	47	3	-	0

NORRIS Robert (Rob) Paul
Radcliffe-on-Trent, 12 October, 1987 (W)

League Club	Source	Date Signed	Seasons Played	Apps	Subs	Gls
Boston U	Sch	•	04	1	1	0

NORRIS Russell
Hoo, 1 February, 1971 (FB)

League Club	Source	Date Signed	Seasons Played	Apps	Subs	Gls
Gillingham	YT	07.89	89	2	3	0

NORRIS Stephen (Steve) Mark
Coventry, 22 September, 1961 ESemiPro (F)

League Club	Source	Date Signed	Seasons Played	Apps	Subs	Gls
Scarborough	Telford U	07.88	88-89	35	10	13
Notts Co	L	11.89	89	0	1	0
Carlisle U	Tr	12.89	89-90	21	8	5
Halifax T	Tr	10.90	90-91	56	0	35
Chesterfield	Tr	01.92	91-94	84	13	43
Scarborough	L	01.95	94	8	0	4

League Club	Source	Date Signed	Seasons Played	Career Record Apps	Subs	Gls
NORTH Daniel (Danny) Jamie						
Grimsby, 7 September, 1987						(F)
Grimsby T	Sch	●	04	0	1	0
NORTH Eric						
Halifax, 6 October, 1923 Died 1992						(W)
Halifax T (Am)	Lee Mount	08.48	48	1	-	0
NORTH Marc Victor						
Ware, 29 May, 1966 Died 2001						(F)
Luton T	App	03.84	85-86	11	7	3
Lincoln C	L	03.85	84	4	0	0
Scunthorpe U	L	01.87	86	4	1	2
Birmingham C	L	03.87	86	4	1	1
Grimsby T	Tr	08.87	87-88	64	3	17
Leicester C	Tr	03.89	88-90	51	20	9
Grimsby T	Luton T (N/C)	08.91	91	0	1	0
NORTH Stacey Stewart						
Luton, 25 November, 1964 EYth						(CD)
Luton T	App	08.82	83-87	24	1	0
Wolverhampton W	L	11.85	85	3	0	0
West Bromwich A	Tr	12.87	87-89	96	2	0
Fulham	Tr	10.90	90	38	0	0
NORTH Thomas (Tom) Williamson						
Barrow-on-Soar, 31 October, 1919 Died 1996						(IF)
Nottingham F	Banbury Spencer	01.45	46	1	-	0
NORTHCOTT George Edward						
Torquay, 7 May, 1935						(CD)
Torquay U	Jnrs	10.52	54-61	163	-	2
Exeter C	Cheltenham T	08.63	63	1	-	0
NORTHCOTT Thomas (Tommy) Theodore						
Torquay, 5 December, 1931 EYth						(CF)
Torquay U	Hele Spurs	12.48	48-52	60	-	10
Cardiff C	Tr	10.52	52-54	76	-	13
Lincoln C	Tr	07.55	55-57	94	-	34
Torquay U	Tr	11.57	57-65	348	2	126
NORTHMORE Ryan						
Plymouth, 5 September, 1980						(G)
Torquay U	YT	07.99	99-00	26	2	0
NORTHOVER Stanley (Stan) Oswald						
Weymouth, 3 July, 1926 Died 1990						(IF)
Luton T (Am)	Weymouth	02.50	49	1	-	0
NORTON David (Dave) John						
Gateshead, 24 January, 1957						(CD)
Hartlepool U	Whickham	12.78	78-79	14	3	2
NORTON David Wayne						
Cannock, 3 March, 1965 EYth						(FB)
Aston Villa	App	03.83	84-87	42	2	2
Notts Co	Tr	08.88	88-90	22	5	1
Rochdale	L	10.90	90	9	0	0
Hull C	L	01.91	90	15	0	0
Hull C	Tr	08.91	91-93	134	0	5
Northampton T	Tr	08.94	94-95	78	4	0
Hereford U	Tr	08.96	96	45	0	0
NORTON Paul						
Mexborough, 17 September, 1969						(G)
Hartlepool U	Sheffield U (YT)	08.88	88	5	0	0
NORTON Peter						
Manchester, 11 November, 1947						(FB)
Bournemouth	Jnrs	11.66	66-67	18	1	1
NORTON Ralph						
Aylesham, 11 October, 1942						(M)
Reading	Jnrs	10.59	60-65	99	1	9
Bournemouth	Tr	07.66	66-67	44	3	4
NORVILLE Jason						
Trinidad, 9 September, 1983						(F)
Watford	YT	04.02	01-02	6	8	1
NOSWORTHY Nyron Paul Henry						
Brixton, 11 October, 1980						(FB)
Gillingham	YT	12.98	98-04	151	23	5
NOTEMAN Kevin Simon						
Preston, 15 October, 1969						(W)
Leeds U	YT	06.88	87	0	1	0
Doncaster Rov	Tr	11.89	89-91	105	1	20
Mansfield T	Tr	03.92	91-94	77	18	15
Doncaster Rov	Tr	08.95	95	4	0	1
Chester C	Tr	09.95	95-96	57	11	18

League Club	Source	Date Signed	Seasons Played	Career Record Apps	Subs	Gls
NOTMAN Alexander (Alex) McKeachie						
Edinburgh, 10 December, 1979 SSch/SYth/Su21-11						(F)
Manchester U	YT	12.96				
Sheffield U	L	01.00	99	7	3	3
Norwich C	Tr	11.00	00-03	18	36	1
NOTTINGHAM Steven (Steve) Edward						
Peterborough, 21 June, 1980						(CD)
Scunthorpe U	YT	07.98	97	1	0	0
NOVACKI Jan						
Manchester, 4 December, 1958 EYth						(W)
Bolton W	App	12.76				
York C	L	12.77	77	24	1	3
NOWAK Tadeusz						
Trzcinsko, Poland, 28 November, 1948 Poland int						(W)
Bolton W	Legia Warsaw (Pol)	03.79	78-80	22	2	1
NOWLAND Adam Christopher						
Preston, 6 July, 1981						(F)
Blackpool	YT	01.99	97-00	18	51	5
Wimbledon	Tr	06.01	01-03	35	21	5
West Ham U	Tr	01.04	03-04	5	10	1
Gillingham	L	09.04	04	3	0	1
Nottingham F	Tr	11.04	04	5	0	0
NTAMARK Charles (Charlie) Batmbog						
Paddington, 22 July, 1964 Cameroon int						(M)
Walsall	Boreham Wood	08.90	90-96	256	20	12
NTIMBAN-ZEH Harry Dave						
Paris, France, 26 September, 1973						(CD)
Wimbledon/MK Dons	Sporting Espinho (Por)	03.04	03-04	20	1	0
N'TOYA-ZOA Tcham						
Kinshasa, DR Congo, 3 November, 1983						(F)
Chesterfield	Troyes (Fr)	03.04	03-04	21	23	8
NUGENT Arthur						
Glasgow, 30 May, 1926 Died 1995						(FB)
Darlington	Canterbury C	06.56	56	5	-	0
NUGENT William **Clifford (Cliff)**						
Islington, 3 March, 1929						(W)
Cardiff C	Headington U	01.51	51-58	113	-	19
Mansfield T	Tr	11.58	58-59	52	-	7
NUGENT David James						
Liverpool, 2 May, 1985 EYth						(F)
Bury	Sch	03.03	01-04	58	30	18
Preston NE	Tr	01.05	04	13	5	8
NUGENT Kevin Patrick						
Edmonton, 10 April, 1969 IRYth						(F)
Leyton Orient	YT	07.87	87-91	86	8	20
Plymouth Arg	Tr	03.92	91-95	124	7	32
Bristol C	Tr	09.95	95-96	48	22	14
Cardiff C	Tr	08.97	97-01	94	5	29
Leyton Orient	Tr	01.02	01-02	17	11	4
Swansea C	Tr	01.03	02-04	53	20	16
NUGENT Richard Joseph						
Birmingham, 20 March, 1964						(CD)
Barnet	St Albans C	10.88	91	2	0	0
NUGENT Stephen (Steve)						
Orrell, 7 May, 1973						(F)
Wigan Ath	YT	08.91	89-92	7	6	0
NULTY Geoffrey (Geoff) Owen						
Prescot, 13 February, 1949						(M)
Stoke C	St Helens T	07.67				
Burnley	Tr	07.68	69-74	123	7	20
Newcastle U	Tr	12.74	74-77	101	0	11
Everton	Tr	07.78	78-79	22	5	2
NUNDY Jeffrey (Jeff) William						
Hull, 29 November, 1935						(CD)
Huddersfield T		12.53				
Bradford C	Tr	07.57	57-59	32	-	0
NUNEZ Antonio						
Madrid, Spain, 15 January, 1979						(M)
Liverpool	Real Madrid (Sp)	08.04	04	8	10	0
NUNEZ Garcia **Milton** Omar						
Honduras, 30 October, 1972 Honduras 31						(F)
Sunderland	PAOK Salonika (Gre)	03.00	99	0	1	0

League Club	Source	Date Signed	Seasons Played	Apps	Subs	Gls
NUNN Walter						
Deptford, 16 January, 1920 Died 1965						(WH)
Charlton Ath	Bexleyheath & Welling	05.39				
Swindon T	Tr	06.47	47	4	-	0
NURSE Melvyn (Mel) Tudor George						
Swansea, 11 October, 1937 WSch/Wu23-2/W-12						(CD)
Swansea T	Jnrs	06.55	55-62	159	-	9
Middlesbrough	Tr	10.62	62-65	113	0	8
Swindon T	Tr	09.65	65-67	122	1	10
Swansea T	Tr	06.68	68-70	97	1	3
NUTE Stephen (Steve) Leslie Rodney						
Plymouth, 18 April, 1962						(G)
Exeter C	App	04.80	80	5	0	0
NUTLEY Robert (Bobby)						
Paisley, 10 September, 1916 Died 1996 SLge-1						(W)
Portsmouth	Hibernian	08.46	46	9	-	1
NUTT Gordon Edward						
South Yardley, 8 November, 1932						(W)
Coventry C	Sheldon T	11.49	51-54	76	-	11
Cardiff C	Tr	12.54	54-55	17	-	4
Arsenal	Tr	09.55	55-59	49	-	10
Southend U	Tr	10.60	60	16	-	2
NUTT Philip (Phil) James						
Westminster, 18 May, 1958						(F)
Queens Park Rgrs	App	07.75	75-76	0	4	1
NUTTALL James (Jimmy)						
Garston, 14 October, 1929						(CF)
Southport	Skelmersdale U	05.50	50-52	67	-	29
NUTTALL Martin						
Oldham, 12 September, 1961						(F)
Oldham Ath	App	09.79	80-81	8	5	1
Halifax T	Tr	08.82	82-83	39	11	10
NUTTALL William (Billy)						
Preston, 7 December, 1920						(FB)
Preston NE		07.46	46	2	-	0
Barrow	Tr	08.48	48-50	65	-	0
NUTTELL Michael (Mike) John						
Boston, 22 November, 1968						(F)
Peterborough U	YT	08.87	85-87	12	9	0
Crewe Alex	L	12.87	87	2	1	1
Carlisle U	L	11.88	88	1	2	0
NUTTER John Robert William						
Taplow, 13 June, 1982						(CD)
Wycombe W	YT	•	00	1	0	0
NUTTON Michael (Mickey) William						
St Johns Wood, 3 October, 1959						(CD)
Chelsea	App	10.77	78-82	77	2	0
Reading	L	02.83	82	6	0	0
Millwall	Tr	03.83	82-85	81	1	4
NWADIKE Chukwuemeka (Emeka) Ibezimife						
Camberwell, 9 August, 1978						(CD)
Wolverhampton W	YT	07.96				
Shrewsbury T	Tr	12.96	96-97	2	1	0
NWAJIOBI Chukwuemeka (Emeka)						
Nibo Awka, Nigeria, 25 May, 1959 ESch						(F)
Luton T	Dulwich Hamlet	12.83	83-87	59	13	17
NYAMAH Kofi						
Islington, 20 June, 1975						(W)
Cambridge U	YT	05.93	93-94	9	14	2
Stoke C	Kettering T	12.96	96-97	9	8	0
Luton T	Tr	08.98				
Exeter C	Kingstonian	08.99	99	23	12	1
NYARKO Alex						
Accra, Ghana, 15 October, 1973 Ghana int						(M)
Everton	RC Lens (Fr)	08.00	00-03	26	7	1
NZAMBA Guy Roger						
Port Gentil, Gabon, 13 July, 1970						(F)
Southend U	Trieste (It)	09.97	97	0	1	0
N'ZOGBIA Charles						
France, 28 May, 1986						(W)
Newcastle U	Le Havre (Fr)	09.04	04	8	6	0

League Club Source Date Signed Seasons Played Career Record Apps Subs Gls

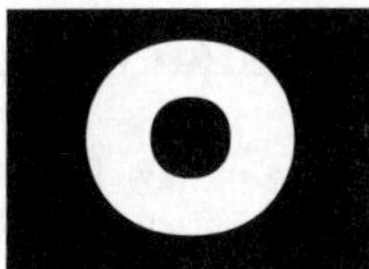

OAKES Alan Arthur
Winsford, 7 September, 1942 FLge-1 (M)

League Club	Source	Date Signed	Seasons Played	Apps	Subs	Gls
Manchester C	Jnrs	09.59	59-75	561	3	26
Chester	Tr	07.76	76-81	211	0	15
Port Vale	(Coach)	10.83	83	1	0	0

OAKES Andrew (Andy) Mark
Northwich, 11 January, 1977 (G)

League Club	Source	Date Signed	Seasons Played	Apps	Subs	Gls
Hull C	Winsford U	12.98	98	19	0	0
Derby Co	Tr	06.99	00-03	43	0	0
Bolton W	L	08.04	04	1	0	0
Walsall	Tr	03.05	04	9	0	0

OAKES Dennis Raymond
Bedworth, 10 April, 1946 (CD)

League Club	Source	Date Signed	Seasons Played	Apps	Subs	Gls
Coventry C	App	08.64				
Notts Co	Tr	06.67	67-70	107	12	0
Peterborough U	Tr	05.71	71-72	84	1	5

OAKES Donald (Don) Joseph
St Asaph, 8 October, 1928 Died 1977 (WH)

League Club	Source	Date Signed	Seasons Played	Apps	Subs	Gls
Arsenal	Downend ATC OB	07.46	52-54	11	-	1

OAKES George
Orrell, 18 October, 1918 Died 1990 (W)

League Club	Source	Date Signed	Seasons Played	Apps	Subs	Gls
Southport	Astley & Tyldesley	08.45	46	7	-	0

OAKES John (Jack)
Winsford, 13 September, 1905 Died 1992 EWar-1 (CD)

League Club	Source	Date Signed	Seasons Played	Apps	Subs	Gls
Nottingham F	Cargo Fleet	08.28	29	2	-	0
Southend U	Crook T	05.31	31	2	-	0
Aldershot	Spennymoor U	08.34	34-35	61	-	19
Charlton Ath	Tr	03.36	35-46	130	-	3
Plymouth Arg	Tr	07.47	47	36	-	0

OAKES John (Jackie)
Hamilton, 6 December, 1919 (W)

League Club	Source	Date Signed	Seasons Played	Apps	Subs	Gls
Huddersfield T	Queen of the South	11.43				
Blackburn Rov	Queen of the South	02.47	46-47	35	-	9
Manchester C	Tr	06.48	48-50	77	-	9

OAKES John Francis
Hamilton, 16 January, 1921 Died 1987 (W)

League Club	Source	Date Signed	Seasons Played	Apps	Subs	Gls
Rochdale	Queen of the South	02.47	46	1	-	0

OAKES Keith Brian
Bedworth, 3 July, 1956 (CD)

League Club	Source	Date Signed	Seasons Played	Apps	Subs	Gls
Peterborough U	App	07.73	72-77	48	13	2
Newport Co	Tr	09.78	78-83	232	0	27
Gillingham	Tr	08.84	84-86	84	2	7
Fulham	Tr	09.86	86-87	76	0	3
Peterborough U	Tr	08.88	88-90	95	2	9

OAKES Michael (Mike) Christian
Northwich, 30 October, 1973 Eu21-6 (G)

League Club	Source	Date Signed	Seasons Played	Apps	Subs	Gls
Aston Villa	Jnrs	07.91	96-98	49	2	0
Scarborough	L	11.93	93	1	0	0
Wolverhampton W	Tr	10.99	99-04	182	0	0

OAKES Scott John
Leicester, 5 August, 1972 Eu21-1 (W)

League Club	Source	Date Signed	Seasons Played	Apps	Subs	Gls
Leicester C	YT	05.90	89-91	1	1	0
Luton T	Tr	10.91	91-95	136	37	27
Sheffield Wed	Tr	08.96	96-98	7	17	1
Cambridge U	Tr	08.00	00	7	11	0
Leyton Orient	Tr	07.01	01	11	0	0

OAKES Stefan Trevor
Leicester, 6 September, 1978 (M)

League Club	Source	Date Signed	Seasons Played	Apps	Subs	Gls
Leicester C	YT	07.97	98-02	39	25	2
Crewe Alex	L	03.03	02	3	4	0
Walsall	Tr	07.03	03	1	4	0
Notts Co	Tr	02.04	03-04	42	3	5

OAKES Thomas
Manchester, 6 February, 1922 Died 1993 (W)

League Club	Source	Date Signed	Seasons Played	Apps	Subs	Gls
Manchester C	Manchester U (Am)	04.47	46	1	-	0

OAKEY Graham
Droitwich, 5 October, 1954 (FB)

League Club	Source	Date Signed	Seasons Played	Apps	Subs	Gls
Coventry C	App	10.72	74-77	87	1	0

OAKLEY Kenneth (Ken)
Rhymney, 9 May, 1929 (CF)

League Club	Source	Date Signed	Seasons Played	Apps	Subs	Gls
Cardiff C	Ebbw Vale	03.50	50-53	7	-	1
Northampton T	Tr	07.54	54	13	-	6

OAKLEY Matthew
Peterborough, 17 August, 1977 Eu21-4 (M)

League Club	Source	Date Signed	Seasons Played	Apps	Subs	Gls
Southampton	YT	07.95	94-04	209	23	12

OAKLEY Norman
Stockton, 4 June, 1939 (G)

League Club	Source	Date Signed	Seasons Played	Apps	Subs	Gls
Doncaster Rov	Jnrs	04.57				
Hartlepools U	Tr	09.58	58-63	182	-	0
Swindon T	Tr	03.64	63-64	21	-	0
Grimsby T	Tr	09.66	66	15	0	0

OAKLEY Royston (Roy) James
Tipton, 5 January, 1928 (FB)

League Club	Source	Date Signed	Seasons Played	Apps	Subs	Gls
Southampton	Guernsey	11.50	53-55	6	-	0

OATES Graham
Scunthorpe, 4 December, 1943 (W)

League Club	Source	Date Signed	Seasons Played	Apps	Subs	Gls
Blackpool	App	05.61	61-68	119	3	26
Grimsby T	Tr	10.68	68-70	80	1	9

OATES Graham
Bradford, 14 March, 1949 (M)

League Club	Source	Date Signed	Seasons Played	Apps	Subs	Gls
Bradford C	Manningham Mills	02.70	69-73	158	3	19
Blackburn Rov	Tr	06.74	74-75	76	0	10
Newcastle U	Tr	03.76	75-77	26	9	3

OATES Robert (Bob) Anthony
Leeds, 26 July, 1956 EYth (CD)

League Club	Source	Date Signed	Seasons Played	Apps	Subs	Gls
Scunthorpe U	Ashley Road	08.74	74-82	306	9	17
Rochdale	Tr	08.83	83	42	0	1

OATWAY Anthony (Charlie) Philip David Terry Frank Donald Stanley Gerry Gordon Stephen James
Hammersmith, 28 November, 1973 (M)

League Club	Source	Date Signed	Seasons Played	Apps	Subs	Gls
Cardiff C	Yeading	08.94	94-95	29	3	0
Torquay U	Tr	12.95	95-97	65	2	1
Brentford	Tr	08.97	97-98	37	20	0
Lincoln C	L	10.98	98	3	0	0
Brighton & Hove A	Tr	07.99	99-04	183	23	8

OBEBO Godfrey
Lagos, Nigeria, 16 April, 1966 (F)

League Club	Source	Date Signed	Seasons Played	Apps	Subs	Gls
Halifax T	Collier Row	03.93	92	0	3	0

OBENEY Henry (Harry) Richard
Bethnal Green, 9 March, 1938 (WH)

League Club	Source	Date Signed	Seasons Played	Apps	Subs	Gls
West Ham U	Briggs Sports	05.56	56-60	25	-	12
Millwall	Tr	06.61	61-63	76	-	10

O'BERG Paul John
Hull, 8 May, 1958 (M)

League Club	Source	Date Signed	Seasons Played	Apps	Subs	Gls
Scunthorpe U	Bridlington T	07.79	79-83	117	13	23
Wimbledon	Tr	08.84	84	2	1	0
Stockport Co	L	11.84	84	2	0	0
Chester C	L	12.84	84	5	0	1
Scunthorpe U	L	03.85	84	0	2	0

OBI Anthony (Tony) Lloyd
Birmingham, 15 September, 1965 EYth (W)

League Club	Source	Date Signed	Seasons Played	Apps	Subs	Gls
Aston Villa	App	09.83				
Walsall	L	12.84	84	1	1	0
Plymouth Arg	L	02.85	84	5	0	0
Bristol Rov	Tr	08.85	85	1	0	0
Oxford U	Tr	10.85	86	0	1	0
Brentford	L	08.86	86	10	0	0

O'BRIEN Andrew (Andy) James
Harrogate, 29 June, 1979 EYth/Eu21-1/IRu21-8/IR-21 (CD)

League Club	Source	Date Signed	Seasons Played	Apps	Subs	Gls
Bradford C	YT	10.96	96-00	113	20	3
Newcastle U	Tr	03.01	00-04	114	6	6

O'BRIEN Anthony (Tony)
Norris Green, 4 September, 1956 (FB)

League Club	Source	Date Signed	Seasons Played	Apps	Subs	Gls
Southport	St Theresa's	08.74	74-76	17	3	1

O'BRIEN Colin
Dunfermline, 19 April, 1956 (W)

League Club	Source	Date Signed	Seasons Played	Apps	Subs	Gls
Bristol C	Swaythling	11.77				
Hereford U	L	12.78	78	1	1	0

O'BRIEN George
Dunfermline, 22 November, 1935 (F)

League Club	Source	Date Signed	Seasons Played	Apps	Subs	Gls
Leeds U	Dunfermline Ath	03.57	56-58	44	-	6
Southampton	Tr	07.59	59-65	244	0	154
Leyton Orient	Tr	03.66	65-66	17	0	3
Aldershot	Tr	12.66	66-67	38	3	8

O'BRIEN George
Toxteth Park, 21 October, 1939 Died 1995 (IF)

League Club	Source	Date Signed	Seasons Played	Apps	Subs	Gls
Everton	Jnrs	02.59				
Southport	Tr	07.60	60	3	-	1

O'BRIEN Gerald (Gerry)
Glasgow, 10 November, 1949 (W)

League Club	Source	Date Signed	Seasons Played	Apps	Subs	Gls
Southampton	Clydebank	03.70	69-75	66	12	2
Bristol Rov	L	03.74	73	3	0	0
Swindon T	Tr	03.76	75-76	24	3	0

O'BRIEN Jonathan (Jon) Mark
Rochford, 2 November, 1961 (G)

League Club	Source	Date Signed	Seasons Played	Apps	Subs	Gls
Southend U	Tilbury	01.85	84	11	0	0

O'BRIEN Joseph (Joe)
Dublin, 9 May, 1924 (W)

League Club	Source	Date Signed	Seasons Played	Apps	Subs	Gls
Luton T	Dundalk	11.47	47-48	11	-	3
Ipswich T	Tr	06.49	49-50	50	-	12

O'BRIEN Joseph (Joey) Martin
Dublin, 17 February, 1986 IRYth/IRu21-3 (M)

League Club	Source	Date Signed	Seasons Played	Apps	Subs	Gls
Bolton W	Sch	11.04	04	0	1	0
Sheffield Wed	L	12.04	04	14	1	2

O'BRIEN Michael (Mick) George
Liverpool, 25 September, 1979 ESch (M)

League Club	Source	Date Signed	Seasons Played	Apps	Subs	Gls
Everton	YT	10.97				
Torquay U	Tr	07.99	99-01	32	20	5

O'BRIEN Noel William
Islington, 18 December, 1956 (M)

League Club	Source	Date Signed	Seasons Played	Apps	Subs	Gls
Arsenal	App	01.74				
Mansfield T	Tr	06.75	75	7	0	0

O'BRIEN Raymond (Ray) Christopher
Dublin, 21 May, 1951 IRu23-2/LoI-1/IR-4 (FB)

League Club	Source	Date Signed	Seasons Played	Apps	Subs	Gls
Manchester U	Shelbourne	05.73				
Notts Co	Tr	03.74	73-82	323	0	33
Derby Co	L	09.83	83	4	0	0

O'BRIEN Robert (Rob) Louis
Leeds, 28 November, 1983 (M)

League Club	Source	Date Signed	Seasons Played	Apps	Subs	Gls
Doncaster Rov	Leeds U (Jnrs)	01.03	03	1	0	0

O'BRIEN Roy Joseph
Cork, 27 November, 1974 IRSch/IRYth (CD)

League Club	Source	Date Signed	Seasons Played	Apps	Subs	Gls
Arsenal	YT	07.93				
Bournemouth	Tr	08.96	96	1	0	0
Yeovil T	Dorchester T	08.00	03-04	23	4	0

O'BRIEN William (Willie)
Middlesbrough, 26 January, 1929 (CD)

League Club	Source	Date Signed	Seasons Played	Apps	Subs	Gls
Darlington		02.50	50	2	-	0

O'BRIEN William (Liam) Francis
Dublin, 5 September, 1964 IRSch/IRYth/IRu23-1/IR-16 (M)

League Club	Source	Date Signed	Seasons Played	Apps	Subs	Gls
Manchester U	Shamrock Rov	10.86	86-88	16	15	2
Newcastle U	Tr	11.88	88-93	131	20	19
Tranmere Rov	Tr	01.94	93-98	169	12	12

O'CALLAGHAN Brendan Richard
Bradford, 23 July, 1955 IRSch/IRYth/IRu21-1/IR-6 (F)

League Club	Source	Date Signed	Seasons Played	Apps	Subs	Gls
Doncaster Rov	Jnrs	07.73	73-77	184	3	65
Stoke C	Tr	03.78	77-84	255	10	44
Oldham Ath	Tr	02.85	84-85	10	0	0

O'CALLAGHAN Brian Patrick
Limerick, 24 February, 1981 IRYth/IRu21-4 (FB)

League Club	Source	Date Signed	Seasons Played	Apps	Subs	Gls
Barnsley	Pike Rov	07.98	00-03	58	17	1

O'CALLAGHAN George
Cork, 5 September, 1979 IRYth (M)

League Club	Source	Date Signed	Seasons Played	Apps	Subs	Gls
Port Vale	YT	07.98	98-01	22	12	4

O'CALLAGHAN Kevin
Dagenham, 19 October, 1961 IRYth/IRu21-1/IR-20 (W)

League Club	Source	Date Signed	Seasons Played	Apps	Subs	Gls
Millwall	App	11.78	78-79	15	5	3
Ipswich T	Tr	01.80	79-84	72	43	4
Portsmouth	Tr	01.85	84-86	84	3	16
Millwall	Tr	06.87	87-90	65	11	14
Southend U	Tr	07.91	91-92	10	11	1

O'CONNELL Brendan John
Lambeth, 12 November, 1966 (M)

League Club	Source	Date Signed	Seasons Played	Apps	Subs	Gls
Portsmouth	App	07.85				
Exeter C	Tr	08.86	86-87	73	8	19
Burnley	Tr	07.88	88-89	62	2	17
Huddersfield T	L	11.89	89	11	0	1
Barnsley	Tr	03.90	89-95	212	28	35
Charlton Ath	Tr	07.96	96	33	5	2
Wigan Ath	Tr	08.97	97	17	0	5

O'CONNELL Brian (Pat) Edward
Kensington, 13 September, 1937 (W)

League Club	Source	Date Signed	Seasons Played	Apps	Subs	Gls
Fulham	Jnrs	03.56	58-65	152	0	26
Crystal Palace	Tr	07.66	66	20	1	2

O'CONNELL Iain Andrew
Rochford, 9 October, 1970 (W)

League Club	Source	Date Signed	Seasons Played	Apps	Subs	Gls
Southend U	YT	07.89	89	0	4	0

O'CONNELL Seamus
Carlisle, 1 January, 1930 EAmat (IF)

League Club	Source	Date Signed	Seasons Played	Apps	Subs	Gls
Middlesbrough (Am)	Queen's Park	05.53	53	3	-	2
Chelsea (Am)	Bishop Auckland	08.54	54-55	16	-	11
Carlisle U (Am)	Crook T	02.58	57	4	-	2

O'CONNOR Aaron Derek
Nottingham, 9 August, 1983 (F)

League Club	Source	Date Signed	Seasons Played	Apps	Subs	Gls
Scunthorpe U	Ilkeston T	12.02	02	0	3	0

O'CONNOR Derek Peter Luke
Dublin, 9 March, 1978 IRSch/IRYth/IRu21-3 (G)

League Club	Source	Date Signed	Seasons Played	Apps	Subs	Gls
Huddersfield T	YT	05.95	97	1	0	0

O'CONNOR Douglas (Doug)
Barnsley, 29 April, 1954 (F)

League Club	Source	Date Signed	Seasons Played	Apps	Subs	Gls
Barnsley	App	04.72	70-73	27	9	7
Mansfield T	Tr	07.74	74	11	6	2
Scunthorpe U	Tr	07.75	75-76	28	3	9

O'CONNOR Garreth
Dublin, 10 November, 1978 (F)

League Club	Source	Date Signed	Seasons Played	Apps	Subs	Gls
Bournemouth	Bohemians	06.00	00-04	109	59	24

O'CONNOR Gary
Newtongrange, 7 April, 1974 SSch/SYth (G)

League Club	Source	Date Signed	Seasons Played	Apps	Subs	Gls
Doncaster Rov	Heart of Midlothian	01.96	95-96	26	0	0

O'CONNOR James Francis Edward
Birmingham, 20 November, 1984 (FB)

League Club	Source	Date Signed	Seasons Played	Apps	Subs	Gls
Aston Villa	Sch	04.04				
Port Vale	L	09.04	04	13	0	0
Bournemouth	Tr	02.05	04	6	0	0

O'CONNOR James (Jimmy) Kelly
Lanark, 27 June, 1951 (W)

League Club	Source	Date Signed	Seasons Played	Apps	Subs	Gls
Bury	Kirkstyles Amat	07.70	70	7	0	2

O'CONNOR James Kevin
Dublin, 1 September, 1979 IRYth/IRu21-9 (M)

League Club	Source	Date Signed	Seasons Played	Apps	Subs	Gls
Stoke C	YT	09.96	98-02	176	0	16
West Bromwich A	Tr	08.03	03	27	3	0
Burnley	L	10.04	04	12	1	0
Burnley	Tr	03.05	04	8	0	2

O'CONNOR Vincent **John (Jackie)**
Durham, 12 March, 1929 (W)

League Club	Source	Date Signed	Seasons Played	Apps	Subs	Gls
Hartlepools U	Middlesbrough (Am)	12.47	48	2	-	0

O'CONNOR Jonathan (Jon)
Darlington, 29 October, 1976 EYth/Eu21-3 (FB)

League Club	Source	Date Signed	Seasons Played	Apps	Subs	Gls
Everton	YT	10.93	95-97	3	2	0
Sheffield U	Tr	02.98	97-98	2	2	0
Blackpool	Tr	10.00	00	10	1	0

O'CONNOR Kevin Patrick
Blackburn, 24 February, 1982 IRu21-6 (M)

League Club	Source	Date Signed	Seasons Played	Apps	Subs	Gls
Brentford	YT	03.00	99-04	136	31	9

O'CONNOR Malcolm Joseph
Ashton-under-Lyne, 25 April, 1965 (F)

League Club	Source	Date Signed	Seasons Played	Apps	Subs	Gls
Rochdale	Curzon Ashton	03.83	82-83	12	4	3

O'CONNOR Mark Andrew
Rochford, 10 March, 1963 IRu21-1 (M)

League Club	Source	Date Signed	Seasons Played	Apps	Subs	Gls
Queens Park Rgrs	App	06.80	81-82	2	1	0
Exeter C	L	10.83	83	38	0	1
Bristol Rov	Tr	08.84	84-85	79	1	10
Bournemouth	Tr	03.86	85-89	115	13	12
Gillingham	Tr	12.89	89-92	107	9	8
Bournemouth	Tr	07.93	93-94	56	2	3
Gillingham	Tr	08.95	95-96	36	4	1

O'CONNOR Martin John
Walsall, 10 December, 1967 CaymanIs-2 (M)

League Club	Source	Date Signed	Seasons Played	Apps	Subs	Gls
Crystal Palace	Bromsgrove Rov	06.92	93	2	0	0
Walsall	L	03.93	92	10	0	1
Walsall	Tr	02.94	93-95	94	0	21
Peterborough U	Tr	07.96	96	18	0	3
Birmingham C	Tr	11.96	96-01	181	6	16
Walsall	Tr	02.02	01-02	45	3	2
Shrewsbury T	Tr	08.03	04	13	8	0

League Club	Source	Date Signed	Seasons Played	Apps	Subs	Gls
O'CONNOR Michael (Mike)						
Romford, 11 January, 1952						(W)
Southend U	App	●	69	1	0	0
O'CONNOR Patrick (Pat)						
Wishaw, 1 May, 1934						(WH)
Barrow	Bellshill Ath	06.58	58-59	20	-	4
O'CONNOR Paul Daniel						
Easington, 17 August, 1971						(G)
Leicester C	YT	03.89				
Hartlepool U	Blyth Spartans	04.96	95-96	31	0	0
O'CONNOR Philip (Phil) Kelvin						
Romford, 10 October, 1953 Died 1985 Auu21						(W)
Luton T	Bexley U	12.72	72	1	1	0
Lincoln C	L	01.75	74	4	0	1
O'CONNOR Robert Thomas						
Gateshead, 9 August, 1940						(W)
Gateshead (Am)	Jnrs	05.58	58	2	-	0
O'CONNOR Timothy (Tim) Daniel						
Neath, 3 October, 1967 WYth						(M)
Cardiff C	Afan Lido	01.85	85	1	1	0
O'CONNOR Turlough Luac						
Athlone, 22 July, 1946 IRAmat/LoI-3/IR-7						(F)
Fulham	Bohemians	05.66	67	1	0	0
ODEJAYI Olukayode (Kay)						
Ibadon, Nigeria, 21 February, 1982						(F)
Bristol C	YT	07.00	99-00	0	6	0
Cheltenham T	Forest Green Rov	06.03	03-04	24	38	6
O'DELL Andrew (Andy)						
Hull, 2 January, 1963						(M)
Grimsby T	App	01.81	81-82	18	2	0
Rotherham U	Tr	08.83	83-84	16	2	0
Torquay U	Tr	03.85	84	12	2	2
Darlington	North Ferriby U	09.87	87	1	2	0
O'DELL Robert (Bobby) Edward						
Isle of Wight, 10 December, 1934						(CD)
Reading	Jnrs	07.52	53	2	-	0
O'DOHERTY Kenneth (Ken) Brendan						
Dublin, 30 March, 1963 IRu21-1						(CD)
Crystal Palace	UCD	02.85	85-87	41	1	0
Huddersfield T	Tr	06.88	88-91	63	2	1
Exeter C	L	08.91	91	2	0	0
O'DONNELL Brian Francis						
Port Glasgow, 8 August, 1957						(M)
Bristol Rov	Bournemouth (App)	05.76				
Bournemouth	Blacktown C (Aus)	01.82	81-82	9	5	0
Torquay U	Tr	10.82	82	19	0	0
O'DONNELL Christopher (Chris)						
Newcastle, 26 May, 1968						(CD)
Ipswich T	App	06.85	86-88	10	4	0
Northampton T	L	01.88	87	1	0	0
Leeds U	Tr	07.89	89	0	1	0
Exeter C	Tr	08.91	91	2	0	0
O'DONNELL Daniel (Danny)						
Dumbarton, 27 February, 1939						(IF)
Brentford	Kirkintilloch Rob Roy	02.60	60-61	11	-	0
O'DONNELL Edward (Eddie)						
Barrow, 5 February, 1921 Died 1994						(FB)
Barrow		09.46	46-52	34	-	0
O'DONNELL Francis (Frank) Joseph						
Buckhaven, 31 August, 1911 Died 1952 S-6						(CF)
Preston NE	Glasgow Celtic	05.35	35-37	92	-	36
Blackpool	Tr	11.37	37-38	30	-	17
Aston Villa	Tr	11.38	38	29	-	14
Nottingham F	Tr	01.46	46	11	-	5
O'DONNELL Hugh						
Buckhaven, 15 February, 1913 Died 1965						(W)
Preston NE	Glasgow Celtic	05.35	35-38	132	-	29
Blackpool	Tr	03.39	38-46	11	-	2
Rochdale	Tr	03.47	46-47	40	-	14
Halifax T	Tr	03.48	47-48	13	-	1
O'DONNELL James (Jimmy)						
Methil, 18 April, 1934						(IF)
Blackburn Rov	Wellesley Jnrs	05.52				
Oldham Ath	Tr	10.53	54-55	15	-	3
O'DONNELL Jonathan (Jon) David						
Leeds, 21 March, 1954 Died 1997						(FB)
Leeds U	App	03.71				
Cambridge U	Tr	07.73	73-75	79	0	8
Colchester U	L	08.75	75	1	0	0
Hartlepool	Tr	07.76	76	30	1	1
Scunthorpe U	Tr	07.77	77-79	60	0	0
O'DONNELL Neil						
Glasgow, 21 December, 1949						(M)
Norwich C	Jnrs	12.66	67-73	31	19	2
Gillingham	Tr	08.74	74-75	18	6	0
Sheffield Wed	Tr	10.75	75-76	40	0	1
O'DONNELL Philip (Phil)						
Motherwell, 25 March, 1972 Su21-8/S-1						(M)
Sheffield Wed	Glasgow Celtic	07.99	99-01	13	7	0
O'DONNELL Ralph						
Cudworth, 17 October, 1931						(WH)
Sheffield Wed	Upton Colliery	05.49	51-61	170	-	3
O'DONNELL Stephen James						
Bellshill, 10 July, 1983						(M)
Boston U	Dundee U	01.05	04	2	2	0
O'DONNELL William (Willie)						
Clydebank, 9 August, 1924						(IF)
Northampton T	Partick Th	06.51	51-53	105	-	44
Shrewsbury T	Tr	07.54	54-57	130	-	45
O'DONOGHUE Michael (Mike) Gerard						
Islington, 13 September, 1956						(F)
Southampton	Wembley	01.79				
Northampton T	L	11.79	79	4	0	1
O'DOWD Adrian Gregory						
Solihull, 16 September, 1959						(F)
Aston Villa	App	08.77				
Oxford U	Tr	02.80	79-80	8	2	1
O'DOWD Gregory (Greg) Henry						
Dublin, 16 March, 1973						(CD)
Brighton & Hove A	YT	11.90	91	0	1	0
O'DRISCOLL John (Jack) Francis						
Cork, 20 September, 1921 Died 1988 LoI-1/IR-3/I-3						(W)
Swansea T	Cork U	05.47	47-51	118	-	24
O'DRISCOLL Sean Michael						
Wolverhampton, 1 July, 1957 IRu21-3/IR-3						(M)
Fulham	Alvechurch	11.79	79-83	141	7	14
Bournemouth	Tr	02.84	83-94	409	12	19
ODUBADE Yemi						
Lagos, Nigeria, 4 July, 1984						(F)
Yeovil T	Eastbourne U	07.04	04	0	4	0
ODUNSI Saheed **Adeleke (Leke)**						
Walworth, 5 December, 1980						(M)
Millwall	YT	02.99	98-01	5	12	0
Colchester U	L	08.02	02	3	3	0
Southend U	Carshalton Ath	07.03	03	12	0	1
OELOFSE Roelof (Ralph) Johannes Gysbertus						
Johannesburg, South Africa, 12 November, 1926						(FB)
Chelsea	Berea Park (SA)	10.51	51-52	8	-	0
Watford	Tr	07.53	53	15	-	0
O'FARRELL Francis (Frank)						
Cork, 9 October, 1927 IR-9						(WH)
West Ham U	Cork U	01.48	50-56	197	-	6
Preston NE	Tr	11.56	56-60	118	-	2
OFFIONG Richard						
South Shields, 17 December, 1983 EYth/Eu20						(F)
Newcastle U	YT	09.01				
Darlington	L	11.02	02	7	0	2
York C	L	03.04	03	2	2	0
O'FLANAGAN (Dr) **Kevin** Patrick						
Dublin, 10 June, 1919 NIAmat/LoI-8/IWar-2/IR-10						(W)
Arsenal (Am)	Bohemians	10.45	46	14	-	3
Brentford (Am)	Barnet	11.49	49	6	-	0
OFODILE Adolphus						
Fungu, Nigeria, 15 December, 1979 Ngu21						(F)
Walsall	FC Magdeburg (Ger)	07.01	01	0	1	0
OGBURN Michael (Mike) George						
Portsmouth, 19 February, 1948						(FB)
Brentford	Portsmouth (App)	05.65	66	12	0	0

League Club	Source	Date Signed	Seasons Played	Apps	Subs	Gls
OGDEN Alan						
Thrybergh, 15 April, 1954						(FB)
Sheffield U	App	05.71	71-73	6	6	0
York C	Tr	09.74	74	7	0	0
OGDEN Christopher (Chris) John						
Oldham, 3 February, 1953						(G)
Oldham Ath	Jnrs	07.71	71-77	128	0	0
Swindon T	Tr	08.78	78-79	24	0	0
Rotherham U	Tr	11.79	79	3	0	0
OGDEN Frederick (Fred)						
Oldham, 3 April, 1925						(G)
Oldham Ath	Edge Lane BC	12.47	47-54	151	-	0
Chesterfield	Tr	06.55				
Oldham Ath	Tr	03.56	55	5	-	0
OGDEN Neil						
Billinge, 29 November, 1975						(FB)
Wigan Ath	YT	03.94	92-95	11	4	0
OGDEN Paul						
Leek, 18 December, 1946						(W)
Port Vale (Am)	Leek Castle	11.65	65	2	0	0
OGDEN Paul						
Salford, 16 October, 1969						(M)
Hartlepool U	Oldham Ath (YT)	08.88	88-89	9	3	0
OGDEN Trevor						
Culcheth, 12 June, 1945						(CF)
Manchester C		09.64	64	9	-	3
Doncaster Rov	Tr	06.65	65-66	39	0	14
OGHANI George William						
Manchester, 2 September, 1960						(F)
Bury	Sheffield U (Jnrs)	02.78				
Bolton W	Hyde U	10.83	83-86	86	13	27
Wrexham	L	03.87	86	6	1	0
Burnley	Tr	06.87	87-88	73	1	21
Stockport Co	Tr	06.89	89	5	3	2
Hereford U	Tr	10.89	89	7	1	2
Scarborough	Hyde U	02.90	89-90	43	7	18
Carlisle U	Evagoras (Cyp)	08.92	92-93	45	8	15
OGILVIE Gary Francis						
Dundee, 16 November, 1967						(FB)
Sunderland	Dundee	03.88	88	0	1	0
OGILVIE John Forest						
Motherwell, 28 October, 1928						(FB)
Leicester C	Hibernian	09.55	55-58	82	-	2
Mansfield T	Tr	01.60	59-60	24	-	1
OGILVIE John Leofric						
Workington, 20 December, 1943						(FB)
Workington	Blackpool (Am)	04.63	62-74	386	4	15
OGLEY Alan						
Darton, 4 February, 1946 ESch						(G)
Barnsley	App	03.63	62	9	-	0
Manchester C	Tr	07.63	63-67	51	0	0
Stockport Co	Tr	09.67	67-74	240	0	0
Darlington	Tr	08.75	75-76	80	0	0
OGLEY Mark Alan						
Barnsley, 10 March, 1967						(CD)
Barnsley	App	03.85	85-86	19	0	0
Aldershot	L	12.87	87	6	2	0
Carlisle U	Tr	03.88	87-89	33	0	1
Aldershot	Tr	11.89	89-90	58	4	0
O'GORMAN David John						
Chester, 20 June, 1972						(F)
Wrexham	YT	07.90	90	8	9	0
Swansea C	Barry T	08.97	97-98	13	26	5
O'GRADY Christopher (Chris) James						
Nottingham, 25 January, 1986 EYth						(M)
Leicester C	Sch	08.04	02	0	1	0
Notts Co	L	09.04	04	3	6	0
O'GRADY Michael (Mike)						
Leeds, 11 October, 1942 Eu23-3/FLge-3/E-2						(W)
Huddersfield T	Jnrs	10.59	59-65	160	0	26
Leeds U	Tr	10.65	65-69	90	1	12
Wolverhampton W	Tr	09.69	69-72	28	5	5
Birmingham C	L	02.72	71	2	1	0
Rotherham U	Tr	11.72	72-73	24	0	2
OGRIZOVIC Steven (Steve)						
Mansfield, 12 September, 1957 FLge						(G)
Chesterfield	ONRYC Mansfield	07.77	77	16	0	0
Liverpool	Tr	11.77	77-80	4	0	0
Shrewsbury T	Tr	08.82	82-83	84	0	0
Coventry C	Tr	06.84	84-99	507	0	1
OGSTON John Kessack						
Aberdeen, 15 January, 1939 Su23-3						(G)
Liverpool	Aberdeen	08.65	66	1	0	0
Doncaster Rov	Tr	08.68	68-70	70	0	0
O'HAGAN Daniel (Danny) Alexander Nicholas						
Padstow, 24 April, 1976						(F)
Plymouth Arg	YT	06.94	94-95	1	8	1
Plymouth Arg	Weston-super-Mare	11.97	97	5	4	0
O'HAGAN Patrick (Pat) John						
Llanbadoc, 15 March, 1971						(G)
Newport Co	YT	●	87	3	0	0
O'HALLORAN Keith James						
Dublin, 10 November, 1975 IRSch/IRYth/IRu21-3						(FB)
Middlesbrough	Cherry Orchard	09.94	94-95	3	1	0
Scunthorpe U	L	03.96	95	6	1	0
Cardiff C	L	11.96	96	8	0	0
Swindon T	St Johnstone	07.00	00-01	46	0	7
O'HALLORAN Matthew (Matt) Vincent						
Nottingham, 18 November, 1982						(M)
Derby Co	Sch	07.02				
Oldham Ath	Tr	08.03	03	2	11	1
Chesterfield	Tr	12.03	03	1	2	0
Boston U	Tr	08.04	04	5	3	1
O'HALLORAN Neil						
Cardiff, 21 June, 1933 Died 1995						(W)
Cardiff C		08.54	55-56	10	-	4
Newport Co	Tr	07.57	57	14	-	2
OHANDJANIAN Demis Armen						
Manchester, 1 May, 1978						(F)
Doncaster Rov	Curzon Ashton	02.97	96	0	1	0
O'HANLON Kelham Gerard						
Saltburn, 16 May, 1962 IRu21-2/IR-1						(G)
Middlesbrough	App	05.80	82-84	87	0	0
Rotherham U	Tr	08.85	85-90	248	0	0
Carlisle U	Tr	08.91	91-92	83	0	0
Preston NE	Tr	07.93	93	23	0	0
Preston NE	Dundee U	09.96	96-00	13	1	0
O'HANLON Sean Philip						
Southport, 2 January, 1983 EYth/Eu20						(CD)
Everton	YT	02.00				
Swindon T	Tr	01.04	03-04	57	2	5
O'HARA Daniel (Dan)						
Airdrie, 28 September, 1937						(IF)
Mansfield T	Glasgow Celtic	06.61	61	3	-	1
O'HARA Albert **Edward (Eddie)**						
Glasgow, 28 October, 1935 SSch/Su23-3						(W)
Everton	Falkirk	06.58	58-59	29	-	2
Rotherham U	Tr	02.60	59-60	20	-	3
Barnsley	Morton	07.62	62-64	127	-	36
O'HARA Edward Patrick						
Dublin, 22 February, 1927 Died 1987						(W)
Birmingham C	Dundalk	11.49	49-50	6	-	0
O'HARA Gerald (Gerry) John						
Wolverhampton, 3 December, 1956						(M)
Wolverhampton W	App	12.74	75-76	7	2	0
Hereford U	Tr	08.78	78	1	0	0
O'HARA Michael (Mike) John						
Coventry, 30 August, 1944						(G)
Luton T	App	11.61	60	2	-	0
Swindon T	Tr	11.61	61-62	30	-	0
O'HARA Stephen (Steve)						
Lanark, 21 February, 1971						(FB)
Walsall	YT	07.89	89-93	104	18	4
O'HARE Alan Patrick James						
Drogheda, 31 July, 1982						(CD)
Bolton W	YT	11.01				
Chesterfield	L	01.02	01	19	0	0
Chesterfield	Tr	10.02	02-04	72	11	1

O'HARE John
Renton, 24 September, 1946 Su23-3/S-13 (F)

League Club	Source	Date Signed	Seasons Played	Apps	Subs	Gls
Sunderland	Drumchapel Amat	10.63	64-66	51	0	14
Derby Co	Tr	08.67	67-73	247	1	65
Leeds U	Tr	08.74	74	6	0	1
Nottingham F	Tr	02.75	74-79	94	7	14

OKAFOR Samuel Amaechi
Xtiam, Nigeria, 17 March, 1982 (M)

League Club	Source	Date Signed	Seasons Played	Apps	Subs	Gls
Colchester U	YT	•	98	0	1	0

OKAI Stephen Patrick
Ghana, 3 December, 1973 (W)

League Club	Source	Date Signed	Seasons Played	Apps	Subs	Gls
Leyton Orient	Jnrs	07.92	91-93	11	14	4

O'KAMBACK Joseph (Joe)
Tottenham, 13 March, 1915 Died 1981 (WH)

League Club	Source	Date Signed	Seasons Played	Apps	Subs	Gls
Millwall		04.46	46	1	-	0

O'KANE Aiden
Belfast, 24 November, 1979 (M)

League Club	Source	Date Signed	Seasons Played	Apps	Subs	Gls
York C	Cliftonville	08.01	01	11	1	0

O'KANE John Andrew
Nottingham, 15 November, 1974 (M)

League Club	Source	Date Signed	Seasons Played	Apps	Subs	Gls
Manchester U	YT	01.93	95-96	1	1	0
Bury	L	10.96	96	2	2	2
Bury	L	01.97	96	9	0	1
Bradford C	L	10.97	97	7	0	0
Everton	Tr	01.98	97-98	14	0	0
Burnley	L	10.98	98	8	0	0
Bolton W	Tr	11.99	99-00	32	6	2
Blackpool	Tr	07.01	01-02	42	10	4

O'KANE Vincent (Vince)
Stepney, 20 November, 1952 (M)

League Club	Source	Date Signed	Seasons Played	Apps	Subs	Gls
Charlton Ath	App	12.70	70-72	29	3	1

O'KANE William (Liam) James
Derry, 17 June, 1948 NI-20 (CD)

League Club	Source	Date Signed	Seasons Played	Apps	Subs	Gls
Nottingham F	Derry C	12.68	68-75	186	3	0

O'KEEFE Eamon Gerard
Manchester, 13 October, 1953 ESemiPro/IRu21-4/IR-5 (F)

League Club	Source	Date Signed	Seasons Played	Apps	Subs	Gls
Plymouth Arg	Stalybridge Celtic	02.74				
Everton	Mossley	07.79	79-81	26	14	6
Wigan Ath	Tr	01.82	81-82	56	2	25
Port Vale	Tr	07.83	83-84	50	9	17
Blackpool	Tr	03.85	84-86	33	3	23
Chester C	St Patrick's Ath	03.89	88-89	12	5	4

O'KEEFE Patrick John
Peterborough, 17 July, 1967 (M)

League Club	Source	Date Signed	Seasons Played	Apps	Subs	Gls
Peterborough U	App	07.85	84	0	1	0

O'KEEFE James **Vincent (Vince)**
Birmingham, 2 April, 1957 (G)

League Club	Source	Date Signed	Seasons Played	Apps	Subs	Gls
Birmingham C	Paget Rgrs	07.75				
Walsall	Tr	07.76				
Exeter C	AP Leamington	06.78	78-79	53	0	0
Torquay U	Tr	02.80	79-81	108	0	0
Blackburn Rov	Tr	08.82	82-88	68	0	0
Bury	L	10.83	83	2	0	0
Blackpool	L	12.86	86	1	0	0
Blackpool	L	02.89	88	6	0	0
Wrexham	Tr	07.89	89-91	83	0	0
Exeter C	Tr	08.92	92	2	0	0

O'KELLY Richard Florence
West Bromwich, 8 January, 1957 (F)

League Club	Source	Date Signed	Seasons Played	Apps	Subs	Gls
Walsall	Alvechurch	10.79	80-85	189	15	56
Port Vale	Tr	07.86	86-87	26	2	4
Walsall	Tr	01.88	87	7	5	1
Grimsby T	Tr	07.88	88	38	1	10

OKENLA Folorunso (Foley)
Nigeria, 9 October, 1967 (W)

League Club	Source	Date Signed	Seasons Played	Apps	Subs	Gls
Birmingham C	Burnley (N/C)	08.91	91	2	5	1

OKOCHA Augustine (Jay Jay) Azuka
Enugu, Nigeria, 14 August, 1973 Nigeria 65 (M)

League Club	Source	Date Signed	Seasons Played	Apps	Subs	Gls
Bolton W	Paris St Germain (Fr)	08.02	02-04	88	9	13

OKOLI James Chuks
Nigeria, 11 January, 1976 (FB)

League Club	Source	Date Signed	Seasons Played	Apps	Subs	Gls
York C	Motherwell	08.02	02	1	2	0

OKON Paul Michael
Sydney, Australia, 5 April, 1972 AuYth/Auu23/Au-35 (M)

League Club	Source	Date Signed	Seasons Played	Apps	Subs	Gls
Middlesbrough	Fiorentina (It)	08.00	00-01	24	4	0
Watford	Tr	01.02	01	14	1	0
Leeds U	Tr	08.02	02	15	0	0

OKORIE Chima Ephraim
Izomber, Nigeria, 8 October, 1968 Nigeria int (F)

League Club	Source	Date Signed	Seasons Played	Apps	Subs	Gls
Grimsby T	Peterborough U (N/C)	09.93	93	0	5	0
Torquay U	Tr	03.94	93-94	32	4	6

OKORONKWO Isaac
Nbene, Nigeria, 1 May, 1978 Nigeria 12 (CD)

League Club	Source	Date Signed	Seasons Played	Apps	Subs	Gls
Wolverhampton W	Shakhtar Donetsk (Uk)	07.03	03	7	0	0

OKUONGHAE Magnus
Nigeria, 16 February, 1986 (F)

League Club	Source	Date Signed	Seasons Played	Apps	Subs	Gls
Rushden & Diamonds	Sch	•	03	0	1	0

OLAH Bela Josef
Oyd, Hungary, 8 June, 1938 (W)

League Club	Source	Date Signed	Seasons Played	Apps	Subs	Gls
Northampton T	Bedford T	12.58	58-60	42	-	8

OLAOYE Dolapo (Del)
Lagos, Nigeria, 17 October, 1982 (M)

League Club	Source	Date Signed	Seasons Played	Apps	Subs	Gls
Port Vale	YT	•	00	0	1	0

OLDBURY Marcus John
Bournemouth, 29 March, 1976 (M)

League Club	Source	Date Signed	Seasons Played	Apps	Subs	Gls
Norwich C	YT	07.94				
Bournemouth	Tr	07.95	95	2	11	0

OLDFIELD Craig
Warley, 24 November, 1963 (F)

League Club	Source	Date Signed	Seasons Played	Apps	Subs	Gls
Colchester U		03.83	83	0	3	0

OLDFIELD David Charles
Perth, Australia, 30 May, 1968 Eu21-1 (M)

League Club	Source	Date Signed	Seasons Played	Apps	Subs	Gls
Luton T	App	05.86	87-88	21	8	4
Manchester C	Tr	03.89	88-89	18	8	6
Leicester C	Tr	01.90	89-94	163	25	26
Millwall	L	02.95	94	16	1	6
Luton T	Tr	07.95	95-97	99	18	18
Stoke C	Tr	07.98	98-99	50	15	7
Peterborough U	Tr	03.00	99-01	68	10	4
Oxford U	Tr	08.02	02-03	20	11	2

OLDFIELD John Edward
Helsby, 13 July, 1918 (WH)

League Club	Source	Date Signed	Seasons Played	Apps	Subs	Gls
Port Vale	Helsby	03.46	46	1	-	0

OLDFIELD John Stephen
Lindrick, 19 August, 1943 Died 2002 (G)

League Club	Source	Date Signed	Seasons Played	Apps	Subs	Gls
Huddersfield T	Jnrs	08.61	63-68	152	0	0
Wolverhampton W	Tr	12.69	69-70	19	0	0
Crewe Alex	L	11.71	71	5	0	0
Bradford C	Tr	12.71	71-72	31	0	0

OLDFIELD Terence (Terry) James
Bristol, 1 April, 1939 (WH)

League Club	Source	Date Signed	Seasons Played	Apps	Subs	Gls
Bristol Rov	Clifton St Vincent's	02.58	60-65	131	1	11
Wrexham	Tr	07.66	66	39	1	6

OLDHAM Eric
Newcastle, 27 June, 1933 Died 1994 (FB)

League Club	Source	Date Signed	Seasons Played	Apps	Subs	Gls
Bolton W	Seaton Delaval	10.53				
Gateshead	Tr	07.56	56-57	53	-	0
Hartlepools U	Kidderminster Hrs	06.59	59	12	-	0

OLDHAM George
Tintwistle, 20 April, 1920 Died 1993 (FB)

League Club	Source	Date Signed	Seasons Played	Apps	Subs	Gls
Stoke C	Mottram Central	10.37	38	2	-	0
Newport Co	Tr	09.46	46-47	63	-	0

OLDHAM John (Jack)
Oswaldtwistle, 30 January, 1926 (CD)

League Club	Source	Date Signed	Seasons Played	Apps	Subs	Gls
Accrington St	Oswaldtwistle Imm	08.50	50-52	10	-	0

OLDHAM John
Nottingham, 24 October, 1949 (CF)

League Club	Source	Date Signed	Seasons Played	Apps	Subs	Gls
Mansfield T	Nuthall BC	02.67	66	0	1	0

OLDRIDGE Andrew **Robert (Bob)**
Barton-on-Humber, 17 November, 1957 (F)

League Club	Source	Date Signed	Seasons Played	Apps	Subs	Gls
Grimsby T		01.76	75-76	9	6	1

OLDROYD Darren Robert
Ormskirk, 1 November, 1966 (FB)

League Club	Source	Date Signed	Seasons Played	Apps	Subs	Gls
Everton	App	11.84	84	0	1	0
Wolverhampton W	Tr	08.86	86	10	0	0

O'LEARY Daniel
Cork, 11 January, 1951 (F)

League Club	Source	Date Signed	Seasons Played	Apps	Subs	Gls
Millwall	App	05.68				
Fulham	Tr	07.69	69	0	1	0

League Club	Source	Date Signed	Seasons Played	Career Record Apps	Subs	Gls
O'LEARY David Anthony						
Stoke Newington, 2 May, 1958 IR-66 (CD)						
Arsenal	App	07.75	75-92	523	35	11
Leeds U	Tr	06.93	93	10	0	0
O'LEARY Donal Patrick						
Limehouse, 24 June, 1936 (W)						
Blackburn Rov		10.54	55	6	-	1
O'LEARY Kristian (Kris) Denis						
Port Talbot, 30 August, 1977 WYth (CD)						
Swansea C	YT	07.96	95-04	202	33	8
O'LEARY Stephen Michael						
Barnet, 12 February, 1985 IRYth (M)						
Luton T	Sch	08.04	03-04	15	7	2
OLEKSEWYCZ Stephen (Steve) Michael						
Sowerby Bridge, 24 February, 1983 (F)						
Halifax T	Jnrs	08.00	00-01	0	5	0
OLEMBE Saloman						
Yaounde, Cameroon, 8 December, 1980 Cameroon 54 (M)						
Leeds U (L)	Marseille (Fr)	08.03	03	8	4	0
OLI Dennis Chiedozie						
Newham, 28 January, 1984 (F)						
Queens Park Rgrs	YT	10.01	01-03	8	15	0
Swansea C	Tr	08.04	04	0	1	0
Cambridge U	Tr	09.04	04	4	0	1
O'LINN (OLINSKY) Sydney (Syd)						
Oudtschoorn, South Africa, 5 May, 1927 (IF)						
Charlton Ath	Green Point (SA)	12.47	47-56	187	-	32
OLINYK Peter						
Bolton, 4 October, 1953 (M)						
Bolton W	App	06.71	73-74	7	3	0
Stockport Co	Tr	11.74	74	4	0	0
OLIPHANT David						
Carlisle, 29 January, 1942 Died 2004 (WH)						
Wolverhampton W	Jnrs	06.59				
Carlisle U	Tr	12.60	60-64	109	-	11
OLIVE Robert **Leslie (Les)**						
Salford, 27 April, 1928 (G)						
Manchester U (Am)	Jnrs	01.53	52	2	-	0
OLIVEIRA Filipe Vilaca						
Braga, Portugal, 27 May, 1984 PortugalYth/Portugal u21 (F)						
Chelsea	FC Porto (Por)	09.01	02-04	0	5	0
Preston NE	L	12.04	04	1	4	0
OLIVEIRA Raul Miguel Silva						
Lisbon, Portugal, 26 August, 1972 PortugalU21 (CD)						
Bradford C (L)	Deportivo Farense (Por)	03.97	96	2	0	0
OLIVER Adam						
West Bromwich, 25 October, 1980 EYth (M)						
West Bromwich A	YT	08.98	98-00	2	21	1
OLIVER Joseph **Allen**						
Blyth, 8 September, 1924 (W)						
Derby Co	Crofton CW	10.46	47-49	16	-	2
Stockport Co	Tr	08.50	50-53	139	-	29
Gateshead	Tr	07.54	54-57	146	-	37
OLIVER Antony (Tony) John						
Portsmouth, 22 September, 1967 (G)						
Brentford	Portsmouth (N/C)	08.87	87	11	0	0
OLIVER Brian Charles						
Liverpool, 6 March, 1957 (G)						
Rochdale	Bury (App)	03.75	75	3	0	0
Southport	L	12.75	75	2	0	0
OLIVER Darren						
Liverpool, 1 November, 1971 (FB)						
Bolton W	YT	05.90	92	3	0	0
Rochdale	Tr	10.93	93-94	22	6	0
OLIVER Howard **Derek**						
Sunderland, 16 April, 1950 (W)						
Sheffield Wed	Jnrs	04.67				
Hartlepool	Tr	08.68	68	0	1	0
OLIVER Edmund (Ted) Alan						
Manchester, 17 March, 1961 (M)						
Rochdale	App	03.79	77-79	19	3	1

League Club	Source	Date Signed	Seasons Played	Career Record Apps	Subs	Gls
OLIVER Eric						
Spennymoor, 8 July, 1940 (G)						
Darlington (Am)	West Auckland	12.63	63	2	-	0
OLIVER Gavin Ronald						
Felling, 6 September, 1962 (CD)						
Sheffield Wed	App	08.80	80-84	14	6	0
Tranmere Rov	L	01.83	82	17	0	1
Brighton & Hove A	L	08.85	85	15	1	0
Bradford C	Tr	11.85	85-94	308	5	9
OLIVER George						
Houghton-le-Spring, 22 January, 1919 Died 1981 (W)						
Halifax T		10.45				
Gateshead	Tr	10.46	46	13	-	1
OLIVER Henry (Harry) Spoors						
Sunderland, 16 February, 1921 Died 1994 ESch (CD)						
Hartlepools U	Houghton CW	03.38	37	9	-	0
Brentford	Tr	05.38	46-47	18	-	0
Watford	Tr	05.48	48-51	122	-	2
OLIVER James (Jim)						
Uxbridge, 28 August, 1949 (FB)						
Crystal Palace	App	03.67	67-69	3	0	0
OLIVER James (Jim)						
Fearn, 13 January, 1958 (M)						
Wigan Ath	Montrose	08.80	80	1	1	0
OLIVER James (Jim) Robert						
Falkirk, 3 December, 1941 SSch (F)						
Norwich C	Falkirk	08.62	62-64	40	-	14
Brighton & Hove A	Tr	03.65	64-67	37	6	6
Colchester U	Tr	02.68	67-69	65	10	10
OLIVER John						
Red Row, 6 October, 1920 (IF)						
Chesterfield	Amble	10.46	46-47	24	-	5
OLIVER John (Jack)						
Bradford, 21 September, 1946 (FB)						
Bradford PA	Jnrs	09.66	65	1	0	0
OLIVER Keith						
South Shields, 15 January, 1976 (M)						
Hartlepool U	YT	07.94	93-95	25	7	0
OLIVER Kenneth (Ken)						
Pelton, 26 November, 1938 (IF)						
Sunderland	Birtley ROF	05.58				
Barnsley	South Shields	02.60	59-62	94	-	38
Watford	Tr	07.63	63-64	58	-	26
Workington	Tr	02.65	64-66	84	0	18
Bournemouth	Tr	01.67	66	14	0	4
OLIVER James Henry **Kenneth (Ken)**						
Loughborough, 10 August, 1924 Died 1994 (CD)						
Sunderland	Brush Sports	08.46	47-48	8	-	1
Derby Co	Tr	09.49	49-57	184	-	1
Exeter C	Tr	01.58	57-59	92	-	0
OLIVER Luke John						
Acton, 1 May, 1984 (CD)						
Wycombe W	Brook House	07.02	02-03	0	4	0
OLIVER Michael						
Middlesbrough, 2 August, 1975 (M)						
Middlesbrough	YT	08.92				
Stockport Co	Tr	07.94	94-95	17	5	1
Darlington	Tr	07.96	96-99	135	16	14
Rochdale	Tr	07.00	00-02	87	16	9
OLIVER Neil						
Berwick-on-Tweed, 11 April, 1967 (FB)						
Blackburn Rov	Berwick Rgrs	08.89	89-90	5	1	0
OLIVER Peter Francis Raeside						
Dunfermline, 14 August, 1948 (FB)						
York C	Heart of Midlothian	07.74	74-75	41	0	0
Huddersfield T	Tr	05.76	76	41	0	1
OLIVER Ralph John						
Tredegar, 30 March, 1934 (WH)						
Shrewsbury T	Hereford U	08.55	55-57	7	-	0
OLLERENSHAW John						
Stockport, 3 April, 1925 (FB)						
Arsenal	Manchester C (Am)	09.46				
Hartlepools U	Tr	06.50	50	2	-	0

OLLERENSHAW Scott
Sydney, Australia, 9 February, 1968 Australia int (F)

League Club	Source	Date Signed	Seasons Played	Apps	Subs	Gls
Walsall	Leichhardt (Aus)	08.92	92	8	12	4

OLNEY Ian Douglas
Luton, 17 December, 1969 Eu21-10 (F)

League Club	Source	Date Signed	Seasons Played	Apps	Subs	Gls
Aston Villa	YT	07.88	88-91	62	26	16
Oldham Ath	Tr	07.92	92-95	43	2	13

OLNEY Kevin John
Doncaster, 12 February, 1959 (CD)

League Club	Source	Date Signed	Seasons Played	Apps	Subs	Gls
Doncaster Rov	Jnrs	08.76	76-78	65	1	1

OLOFINJANA Seyi
Lagos, Nigeria, 30 June, 1980 Nigeria int (M)

League Club	Source	Date Signed	Seasons Played	Apps	Subs	Gls
Wolverhampton W	SK Brann Bergen (Nor)	08.04	04	41	1	5

O'LOUGHLIN Nigel
Rochdale, 19 January, 1954 (M)

League Club	Source	Date Signed	Seasons Played	Apps	Subs	Gls
Shrewsbury T	Rhyl	08.72	72-75	23	10	7
Rochdale	Tr	08.76	76-81	242	3	17

O'LOUGHLIN William (Billy) James
Bolton, 18 January, 1937 (W)

League Club	Source	Date Signed	Seasons Played	Apps	Subs	Gls
Oldham Ath	Rossendale U	02.60	59-60	27	-	0

OLSEN Benjamin (Ben) Robert
Harrisburg, USA, 15 March, 1977 USA 19 (M)

League Club	Source	Date Signed	Seasons Played	Apps	Subs	Gls
Nottingham F (L)	DC United (USA)	10.00	00	14	4	2

OLSEN James Paul
Bootle, 23 October, 1981 (FB)

League Club	Source	Date Signed	Seasons Played	Apps	Subs	Gls
Tranmere Rov	Liverpool (YT)	03.01	00-02	1	3	0
Macclesfield T	Tr	03.04	03	0	2	0

OLSEN Jesper
Fakse, Denmark, 20 March, 1961 Denmark int (W)

League Club	Source	Date Signed	Seasons Played	Apps	Subs	Gls
Manchester U	Ajax (Holl)	07.84	84-88	119	20	21

OLSEN Kim Plougman
Herning, Denmark, 11 February, 1979 (F)

League Club	Source	Date Signed	Seasons Played	Apps	Subs	Gls
Sheffield Wed	Midtjylland (Den)	02.04	03	6	4	0

OLSSON Paul
Hull, 24 December, 1965 (M)

League Club	Source	Date Signed	Seasons Played	Apps	Subs	Gls
Hull C	App	01.84				
Exeter C	Tr	03.87	86-87	38	5	2
Scarborough	Tr	08.88	88-89	34	14	5
Hartlepool U	Tr	12.89	89-93	162	9	13
Darlington	Tr	07.94	94-95	76	0	8

OLSZAR Sebastian
Poland, 10 December, 1981 Poland u21 (F)

League Club	Source	Date Signed	Seasons Played	Apps	Subs	Gls
Portsmouth	Admira Modling (Aut)	01.04				
Coventry C	L	03.04	03	1	4	0

OLUGBODI Jide Michael
Lagos, Nigeria, 20 November, 1977 (M)

League Club	Source	Date Signed	Seasons Played	Apps	Subs	Gls
Brentford	Austria Lustenau (Aut)	10.03	03	0	2	0

O'MAHONEY Francis (Frank) Kevin
Aldershot, 5 April, 1935 (CF)

League Club	Source	Date Signed	Seasons Played	Apps	Subs	Gls
Swindon T		04.57	56-57	8	-	5

O'MAHONY Matthew (Matt) Augustine
Mullinavat, 19 January, 1913 Died 1992 IR-6/I-1 (CD)

League Club	Source	Date Signed	Seasons Played	Apps	Subs	Gls
Southport	Hoylake	04.35	34	12	-	0
Wolverhampton W	Tr	05.35				
Newport Co	Tr	03.36	35	8	-	0
Bristol Rov	Tr	05.36	36-38	101	-	6
Ipswich T	Tr	07.39	46-48	58	-	4

OMAN Alan John
Newcastle, 6 October, 1952 (FB)

League Club	Source	Date Signed	Seasons Played	Apps	Subs	Gls
Northampton T	App	10.70	70-74	83	5	3

O'MARA John
Farnworth, 19 March, 1947 (F)

League Club	Source	Date Signed	Seasons Played	Apps	Subs	Gls
Gillingham	Margate	10.65				
Brentford	Wimbledon	03.71	70-72	53	0	28
Blackburn Rov	Tr	09.72	72-73	30	5	10
Bradford C	Chelmsford C	12.74	74	3	0	1

O'MEARA Alan Michael
Grantham, 15 December, 1958 (G)

League Club	Source	Date Signed	Seasons Played	Apps	Subs	Gls
Scunthorpe U	App	07.76	75-76	41	0	0

OMIGIE Joseph (Joe) Eghodalo
Hammersmith, 13 June, 1972 (F)

League Club	Source	Date Signed	Seasons Played	Apps	Subs	Gls
Brentford	Donna	08.94	95-97	10	14	1

OMMEL Sergio
Den Haag, Holland, 2 September, 1977 (F)

League Club	Source	Date Signed	Seasons Played	Apps	Subs	Gls
Bristol Rov	KR Reykjavik (Ice)	11.01	01	18	5	8

OMOYINMI Emmanuel (Manny)
Nigeria, 28 December, 1977 ESch (F)

League Club	Source	Date Signed	Seasons Played	Apps	Subs	Gls
West Ham U	YT	05.95	96-98	1	8	2
Bournemouth	L	09.96	96	5	2	0
Leyton Orient	L	03.99	98	3	1	1
Gillingham	L	09.99	99	7	2	3
Scunthorpe U	L	12.99	99	6	0	1
Barnet	L	02.00	99	1	5	0
Oxford U	Tr	07.00	00-03	32	35	9

ONE Armand
Paris, France, 15 March, 1983 (F)

League Club	Source	Date Signed	Seasons Played	Apps	Subs	Gls
Cambridge U	Nantes (Fr)	09.01	01	18	14	4
Northampton T	L	09.02	02	6	0	1
Wrexham	Tr	09.03	03	2	1	0

O'NEIL Brian
Bedlington, 4 January, 1944 Eu23-1/FLge-2 (M)

League Club	Source	Date Signed	Seasons Played	Apps	Subs	Gls
Burnley	Jnrs	01.61	62-69	231	4	22
Southampton	Tr	05.71	70-74	148	1	16
Huddersfield T	Tr	10.74	74-75	60	1	3

O'NEIL Brian
Paisley, 6 September, 1972 SSch/SYth/Su21-7/S-6 (M)

League Club	Source	Date Signed	Seasons Played	Apps	Subs	Gls
Nottingham F (L)	Glasgow Celtic	03.97	96	4	1	0
Derby Co	VfL Wolfsburg (Ger)	11.00	00-02	14	3	0
Preston NE	Tr	01.03	02-04	79	8	4

O'NEIL Gary Paul
Bromley, 18 May, 1983 EYth/Eu20/Eu21-6 (M)

League Club	Source	Date Signed	Seasons Played	Apps	Subs	Gls
Portsmouth	YT	06.00	99-04	69	33	9
Walsall	L	09.03	03	7	0	0
Cardiff C	L	09.04	04	8	1	1

O'NEIL Joseph (Joe)
Glasgow, 15 August, 1931 Died 2005 (WH)

League Club	Source	Date Signed	Seasons Played	Apps	Subs	Gls
Southend U (L)	Aberdeen	11.52	52-53	24	-	11
Leicester C	Aberdeen	03.56	57	5	-	2
Northampton T	Tr	10.57	57-58	28	-	4

O'NEIL Thomas (Tommy) Henry
Spennymoor, 5 January, 1925 Died 1978 (FB)

League Club	Source	Date Signed	Seasons Played	Apps	Subs	Gls
Newcastle U	Spennymoor U	09.42				
Newport Co	Tr	04.48	48	9	-	0

O'NEIL Thomas (Tommy) Patrick
St Helens, 25 October, 1952 ESch (M)

League Club	Source	Date Signed	Seasons Played	Apps	Subs	Gls
Manchester U	App	11.69	70-72	54	0	0
Blackpool	L	01.73	72	7	0	0
Southport	Tr	08.73	73-77	192	6	20
Tranmere Rov	Tr	06.78	78-79	74	0	10
Halifax T	Tr	08.80	80-81	39	1	2

O'NEILL Alan
Cork, 27 August, 1973 (F)

League Club	Source	Date Signed	Seasons Played	Apps	Subs	Gls
Birmingham C	Cobh Ramblers	02.92	91	2	2	0

O'NEILL (HOPE) Alan
Leadgate, 13 November, 1937 (IF)

League Club	Source	Date Signed	Seasons Played	Apps	Subs	Gls
Sunderland	Jnrs	02.55	56-60	74	-	27
Aston Villa	Tr	10.60	60-62	23	-	6
Plymouth Arg	Tr	11.62	62-63	40	-	14
Bournemouth	Tr	02.64	63-65	37	0	8

O'NEILL Frank Simon
Dublin, 13 April, 1940 LoI-15/IR-20 (W)

League Club	Source	Date Signed	Seasons Played	Apps	Subs	Gls
Arsenal	Home Farm	04.59	60	2	-	0

O'NEILL George
Port Glasgow, 26 July, 1942 (CD)

League Club	Source	Date Signed	Seasons Played	Apps	Subs	Gls
Barrow	Coleraine	10.64	64	7	-	0

O'NEILL George Patrick
Liverpool, 21 July, 1923 Died 2003 (IF)

League Club	Source	Date Signed	Seasons Played	Apps	Subs	Gls
Port Vale (Am)	Ellemere Port	11.48	48	5	-	0

O'NEILL James (Jimmy)
Larne, 24 November, 1941 NISch/NIu23-1/NI-1 (F)

League Club	Source	Date Signed	Seasons Played	Apps	Subs	Gls
Sunderland	Jnrs	11.58	61	7	-	6
Walsall	Tr	12.62	62-64	38	-	13
Darlington	Hakoah (Aus)	10.67	67	21	3	4

O'NEILL James (Jimmy) Anthony
Dublin, 13 October, 1931 IR-17 (G)

League Club	Source	Date Signed	Seasons Played	Apps	Subs	Gls
Everton	Bulfin U	05.49	50-59	201	-	0
Stoke C	Tr	07.60	60-63	130	-	0
Darlington	Tr	03.64	63-64	32	-	0
Port Vale	Tr	02.65	64-65	42	0	0

O'NEILL James (Sean) Joseph
Belfast, 24 February, 1952 (FB)

League Club	Source	Date Signed	Seasons Played	Apps	Subs	Gls
Leeds U	App	05.69				
Chesterfield	Tr	07.74	74-85	437	5	6

O'NEILL John
Dublin, 9 September, 1935 IR-1 (FB)

League Club	Source	Date Signed	Seasons Played	Apps	Subs	Gls
Preston NE	Drumcondra	04.58	58-62	50	-	0
Barrow	Tr	07.63	63	35	-	3

O'NEILL John (Jon) Joseph
Glasgow, 3 January, 1974 (F)

League Club	Source	Date Signed	Seasons Played	Apps	Subs	Gls
Bournemouth	Glasgow Celtic	03.96	95-00	79	45	10

O'NEILL John Patrick
Derry, 11 March, 1958 NI-39 (CD)

League Club	Source	Date Signed	Seasons Played	Apps	Subs	Gls
Leicester C	Derry ABC	03.76	78-86	313	0	10
Queens Park Rgrs	Tr	07.87	87	2	0	0
Norwich C	Tr	12.87	87	1	0	0

O'NEILL Joseph (Joe)
Blackburn, 28 October, 1982 (F)

League Club	Source	Date Signed	Seasons Played	Apps	Subs	Gls
Preston NE	Sch	07.02	04	0	2	0
Bury	L	07.03	03	10	13	3
Mansfield T	L	08.04	04	3	12	0
Chester C	L	01.05	04	5	6	1

O'NEILL Keith Padre Gerard
Dublin, 16 February, 1976 IRSch/IRYth/IRu21-1/IR-13 (W)

League Club	Source	Date Signed	Seasons Played	Apps	Subs	Gls
Norwich C	YT	07.94	94-98	54	19	9
Middlesbrough	Tr	03.99	98-00	32	5	0
Coventry C	Tr	08.01	01-03	7	5	0

O'NEILL Leslie (Les) Arthur
Blyth, 4 December, 1943 (M)

League Club	Source	Date Signed	Seasons Played	Apps	Subs	Gls
Newcastle U	Blyth Spartans	11.61	63	1	-	0
Darlington	Tr	01.65	64-69	178	2	35
Bradford C	Tr	03.70	69-71	95	2	17
Carlisle U	Tr	05.72	72-76	148	7	20

O'NEILL Martin Hugh Michael
Kilrea, 1 March, 1952 NI-64 (M)

League Club	Source	Date Signed	Seasons Played	Apps	Subs	Gls
Nottingham F	Distillery	10.71	71-80	264	21	48
Norwich C	Tr	02.81	80	11	0	1
Manchester C	Tr	06.81	81	12	1	0
Norwich C	Tr	01.82	81-82	54	1	11
Notts Co	Tr	08.83	83-84	63	1	5

O'NEILL Matthew (Matt) Paul
Accrington, 25 June, 1984 (M)

League Club	Source	Date Signed	Seasons Played	Apps	Subs	Gls
Burnley	Sch	07.03	02-04	2	11	0

O'NEILL Michael Andrew Martin
Portadown, 5 July, 1969 NISch/NIYth/NIu23-1/NIu21-1/NIB-2/NI-31 (M)

League Club	Source	Date Signed	Seasons Played	Apps	Subs	Gls
Newcastle U	Coleraine	10.87	87-88	36	12	15
Coventry C	Hibernian	07.96	96-97	3	2	0
Reading	L	03.98	97	9	0	1
Wigan Ath	Tr	09.98	98-99	65	1	2

O'NEILL Paul Dennis
Farnworth, 17 June, 1982 (CD)

League Club	Source	Date Signed	Seasons Played	Apps	Subs	Gls
Macclesfield T	YT	07.00	99-02	23	13	0

O'NEILL Thomas (Tommy)
Kirkintilloch, 2 February, 1958 (M)

League Club	Source	Date Signed	Seasons Played	Apps	Subs	Gls
Cambridge U	Ipswich T (App)	07.76	76-82	96	20	8
Northampton T	Tr	06.83	83	43	0	6

O'NEILL William (Billy)
Glasgow, 30 December, 1940 SLge-1 (CD)

League Club	Source	Date Signed	Seasons Played	Apps	Subs	Gls
Carlisle U	Glasgow Celtic	05.69	69	15	0	0

O'NEILL William (Billy) Anthony
Cork, 29 December, 1919 LoI-2/NIRL-2/IrLge-1 (IF)

League Club	Source	Date Signed	Seasons Played	Apps	Subs	Gls
Burnley	Chelmsford C	06.49	50	1	-	1
Walsall	Tr	01.51	50-51	51	-	16

ONIBUJE Folawiyo (Fola)
Lagos, Nigeria, 25 September, 1984 (M)

League Club	Source	Date Signed	Seasons Played	Apps	Subs	Gls
Preston NE	Charlton Ath (Jnrs)	11.02				
Huddersfield T	L	11.03	03	0	2	0
Barnsley	Tr	07.04	04	0	3	0
Peterborough U	Tr	03.05	04	0	2	0

ONSLOW Leslie (Les) Gordon
Swindon, 29 August, 1926 (WH)

League Club	Source	Date Signed	Seasons Played	Apps	Subs	Gls
Swindon T		10.45	46-48	4	-	0

ONSLOW Roy
Swindon, 12 September, 1928 (IF)

League Club	Source	Date Signed	Seasons Played	Apps	Subs	Gls
Swindon T		11.47	47-55	140	-	23

ONUOHA Chinedum (Nedum)
Warri, Nigeria, 12 November, 1986 EYth (CD)

League Club	Source	Date Signed	Seasons Played	Apps	Subs	Gls
Manchester C	Sch	11.04	04	11	6	0

ONUORA Ifem (Iffy)
Glasgow, 28 July, 1967 (F)

League Club	Source	Date Signed	Seasons Played	Apps	Subs	Gls
Huddersfield T	Bradford Univ	07.89	89-93	115	50	30
Mansfield T	Tr	07.94	94-95	17	11	8
Gillingham	Tr	08.96	96-97	53	9	23
Swindon T	Tr	03.98	97-99	64	9	25
Gillingham	Tr	01.00	99-01	69	17	26
Sheffield U	Tr	07.02	02	7	0	1
Wycombe W	L	08.03	03	6	0	0
Grimsby T	Tr	09.03	03	18	1	3
Tranmere Rov	Tr	02.04	03	1	2	0
Huddersfield T	Tr	03.04	03	0	3	0

ONWERE Udo Alozie
Hammersmith, 9 November, 1971 (M)

League Club	Source	Date Signed	Seasons Played	Apps	Subs	Gls
Fulham	YT	07.90	90-93	66	19	7
Lincoln C	Tr	08.94	94-95	40	3	4
Blackpool	Dover Ath	09.96	96	5	4	0
Barnet	Tr	08.97	97-98	25	11	2

ONYEALI Elkanah Bollington
Port Harcourt, Nigeria, 7 June, 1939 (CF)

League Club	Source	Date Signed	Seasons Played	Apps	Subs	Gls
Tranmere Rov	(Nigeria)	08.60	60	13	-	8

OOSTHUIZEN Ronald (Ron)
South Africa, 16 March, 1936 (W)

League Club	Source	Date Signed	Seasons Played	Apps	Subs	Gls
Charlton Ath	Marist Bros (SA)	09.53	55	1	-	0
Carlisle U	Yeovil T	09.59	59	1	-	0

OPARA Kelechi Chrysantus
Oweri Imo State, Nigeria, 21 December, 1981 (F)

League Club	Source	Date Signed	Seasons Played	Apps	Subs	Gls
Colchester U	YT	•	98-00	2	17	0
Leyton Orient	Tr	12.00	00	3	3	0

OPARA Junior **Lloyd**
Edmonton, 6 January, 1984 (F)

League Club	Source	Date Signed	Seasons Played	Apps	Subs	Gls
Colchester U	YT	•	01-02	0	6	0
Cambridge U	Tr	04.03	02-03	1	9	1

OPINEL Sacha Fernand Henry
Bourg-Saint-Maurice, France, 9 April, 1977 (FB)

League Club	Source	Date Signed	Seasons Played	Apps	Subs	Gls
Plymouth Arg	Raith Rov	12.00				
Leyton Orient	Tr	02.01	00	9	2	1

ORAM Dennis Graham
Bristol, 14 January, 1920 (FB)

League Club	Source	Date Signed	Seasons Played	Apps	Subs	Gls
Bristol C (Am)	St Pancras BC	08.46	46	3	-	0

ORD Brian Rigby
Dunston-on-Tyne, 21 June, 1939 (FB)

League Club	Source	Date Signed	Seasons Played	Apps	Subs	Gls
Charlton Ath	Bleach Green	11.57	61-62	13	-	1

ORD Kenneth (Ken)
South Shields, 21 September, 1939 Died 1992 (WH)

League Club	Source	Date Signed	Seasons Played	Apps	Subs	Gls
Sunderland	Cleadon Colliery	11.57				
Chesterfield	Tr	06.61	61	3	-	0

ORD Richard John
Murton, 3 March, 1970 Eu21-3 (CD)

League Club	Source	Date Signed	Seasons Played	Apps	Subs	Gls
Sunderland	YT	07.87	87-97	223	20	7
York C	L	02.90	89	3	0	0

ORD Thomas (Tommy)
Woolwich, 15 October, 1952 (F)

League Club	Source	Date Signed	Seasons Played	Apps	Subs	Gls
Chelsea	Erith & Belvedere	12.72	72	3	0	1

O'REGAN Kieran Michael
Cork, 9 November, 1963 IRYth/IRu21-1/IR-4 (M)

League Club	Source	Date Signed	Seasons Played	Apps	Subs	Gls
Brighton & Hove A	Tramore Ath	04.83	82-86	69	17	2
Swindon T	Tr	08.87	87	23	3	1
Huddersfield T	Tr	08.88	88-92	187	12	25
West Bromwich A	Tr	07.93	93-94	36	9	2
Halifax T	Tr	08.95	98	15	4	2

O'REILLY Alexander (Alex)
Loughton, 15 September, 1979 (G)

League Club	Source	Date Signed	Seasons Played	Apps	Subs	Gls
West Ham U	YT	08.98				
Northampton T	L	08.99	99	7	0	0

O'REILLY Gary Miles
Isleworth, 21 March, 1961 ESch/IRYth (CD)

League Club	Source	Date Signed	Seasons Played	Apps	Subs	Gls
Tottenham H	Grays Ath	09.79	80-83	39	6	0
Brighton & Hove A	Tr	08.84	84-86	78	1	3
Crystal Palace	Tr	01.87	86-89	65	5	2
Birmingham C	L	03.91	90	1	0	0
Brighton & Hove A	Tr	07.91	91	28	0	3

League Club	Source	Date Signed	Seasons Played	Career Record Apps	Subs	Gls

ORGILL Harold (Harry)
Hucknall, 1 October, 1920 Died 1979 (G)

League Club	Source	Date Signed	Seasons Played	Apps	Subs	Gls
Nottingham F		04.47	46	7	-	0
Notts Co	Tr	06.47	47	2	-	0

ORHAN Remzi Yilmaz
Nicosia, Cyprus, 13 March, 1955 (F)

League Club	Source	Date Signed	Seasons Played	Apps	Subs	Gls
West Ham U	Aveley	10.72	75-76	6	2	0

O'RILEY Paul John
Prescot, 17 October, 1950 (F)

League Club	Source	Date Signed	Seasons Played	Apps	Subs	Gls
Hull C	App	10.68	68-73	19	11	2
Scunthorpe U	L	03.71	70	11	0	4
Barnsley	Tr	07.74	74	11	3	2
Southport	Goole T	03.75	74-76	19	11	4

O'RIORDAN Donald (Don) Joseph
Dublin, 14 May, 1957 IRYth/IRu21-1 (CD)

League Club	Source	Date Signed	Seasons Played	Apps	Subs	Gls
Derby Co	App	05.75	76-77	2	4	1
Doncaster Rov	L	01.78	77	2	0	0
Preston NE	Tulsa (USA)	10.78	78-82	153	5	8
Carlisle U	Tr	08.83	83-84	84	0	18
Middlesbrough	Tr	08.85	85	41	0	2
Grimsby T	Tr	08.86	86-87	86	0	14
Notts Co	Tr	07.88	88-92	102	7	5
Mansfield T	L	09.89	89	6	0	0
Torquay U	Tr	02.93	92-95	76	3	3
Scarborough	Tr	12.95	95	1	0	0

ORLYGSSON Thorvaldur (Toddi)
Odense, Denmark, 2 August, 1966 Iceland 41 (M)

League Club	Source	Date Signed	Seasons Played	Apps	Subs	Gls
Nottingham F	KA Akureyri (Ice)	12.89	89-92	31	6	2
Stoke C	Tr	08.93	93-95	86	4	16
Oldham Ath	Tr	12.95	95-98	65	11	1

ORMANDY John (Jack)
Knotty Ash, 25 January, 1912 Died 1997 (W)

League Club	Source	Date Signed	Seasons Played	Apps	Subs	Gls
Bradford C	Prescot Cables	06.32	32-35	63	-	9
Bury	Tr	06.36	36-38	87	-	18
Southend U	Tr	06.39				
Oldham Ath	Tr	07.46	46	30	-	5
Halifax T	Tr	07.47	47	7	-	0

ORMEROD Anthony
Middlesbrough, 31 March, 1979 EYth (W)

League Club	Source	Date Signed	Seasons Played	Apps	Subs	Gls
Middlesbrough	YT	05.96	97-99	8	11	3
Carlisle U	L	01.99	98	5	0	0
York C	L	09.99	99	9	3	0
Hartlepool U	L	09.01	01	2	0	0

ORMEROD Brett Ryan
Blackburn, 18 October, 1976 (F)

League Club	Source	Date Signed	Seasons Played	Apps	Subs	Gls
Blackpool	Accrington St	03.97	96-01	105	23	45
Southampton	Tr	12.01	01-04	49	31	11
Leeds U	L	09.04	04	6	0	0
Wigan Ath	L	03.05	04	3	3	2

ORMEROD Mark Ian
Bournemouth, 5 February, 1976 (G)

League Club	Source	Date Signed	Seasons Played	Apps	Subs	Gls
Brighton & Hove A	YT	07.94	96-99	85	0	0

ORMOND John (Ian) Lambie
Harthill, 10 August, 1947 New Zealand int (W)

League Club	Source	Date Signed	Seasons Played	Apps	Subs	Gls
Barnsley	(New Zealand)	12.67	68	1	0	1

ORMOND William (Bill)
Greenock, 26 August, 1926 Died 1992 (W)

League Club	Source	Date Signed	Seasons Played	Apps	Subs	Gls
Blackpool	Partick Th	10.47				
Oldham Ath	Tr	12.49	49-53	122	-	25
Barrow	Tr	02.54	53-57	140	-	20
Scunthorpe U	Tr	08.58	58	3	-	0

ORMONDROYD Ian
Bradford, 22 September, 1964 (F)

League Club	Source	Date Signed	Seasons Played	Apps	Subs	Gls
Bradford C	Thackley	09.85	85-88	72	15	20
Oldham Ath	L	03.87	86	8	2	1
Aston Villa	Tr	02.89	88-91	41	15	6
Derby Co	Tr	09.91	91	25	0	8
Leicester C	Tr	03.92	91-94	67	10	7
Hull C	L	01.95	94	10	0	6
Bradford C	Tr	07.95	95-96	28	10	6
Oldham Ath	Tr	09.96	96-97	26	5	8
Scunthorpe U	Tr	09.97	97	7	13	0

ORMROD Leslie (Les)
Stockport, 8 October, 1952 ESch (FB)

League Club	Source	Date Signed	Seasons Played	Apps	Subs	Gls
Stockport Co	Everton (App)	03.70	69-73	103	5	0

ORMSBY Brendan Thomas Christopher
Birmingham, 1 October, 1960 ESch/EYth (CD)

League Club	Source	Date Signed	Seasons Played	Apps	Subs	Gls
Aston Villa	App	10.78	78-85	115	2	4
Leeds U	Tr	02.86	85-88	46	0	5
Shrewsbury T	L	01.90	89	1	0	0
Doncaster Rov	Tr	07.90	90-91	78	0	8
Scarborough	Tr	08.92	92	15	1	1
Wigan Ath	Waterford U	08.94	94	2	0	0

ORMSTON Alexander (Alec)
Stoke-on-Trent, 10 February, 1919 Died 1975 FLge-3 (W)

League Club	Source	Date Signed	Seasons Played	Apps	Subs	Gls
Stoke C	Summerbank	07.36	37-51	172	-	29

O'ROURKE James
Glasgow, 17 October, 1948 (FB)

League Club	Source	Date Signed	Seasons Played	Apps	Subs	Gls
Arsenal	Possilpark Jnrs	10.65				
Carlisle U	Tr	10.67	67	0	1	0

O'ROURKE John
Northampton, 11 February, 1945 ESch/EYth/Eu23-1 (F)

League Club	Source	Date Signed	Seasons Played	Apps	Subs	Gls
Chelsea	Arsenal (Jnrs)	04.62				
Luton T	Tr	12.63	63-65	84	0	64
Middlesbrough	Tr	07.66	66-67	63	1	38
Ipswich T	Tr	02.68	67-69	69	0	30
Coventry C	Tr	11.69	69-71	52	2	17
Queens Park Rgrs	Tr	10.71	71-72	33	1	12
Bournemouth	Tr	01.74	73-74	21	1	4

O'ROURKE Kenneth (Ken)
Lambeth, 8 December, 1949 (F)

League Club	Source	Date Signed	Seasons Played	Apps	Subs	Gls
Arsenal	Leyton Orient (App)	02.67				
Colchester U	Tr	10.68	68	1	0	0

O'ROURKE William (Billy) James
Nottingham, 2 April, 1960 Died 2002 (G)

League Club	Source	Date Signed	Seasons Played	Apps	Subs	Gls
Burnley	App	02.78	79-82	14	0	0
Blackpool	L	08.83	83	6	0	0
Chester C	Tr	03.84	83	5	0	0
Blackpool	Tr	06.84	84-85	92	0	0
Tranmere Rov	L	09.86	86	15	0	0
Tranmere Rov	Tr	02.87	86-87	38	0	0

ORPHAN Leslie (Les) James
Newport, 17 April, 1923 Died 1995 WAmat (IF)

League Club	Source	Date Signed	Seasons Played	Apps	Subs	Gls
Newport Co	Girlings (Cwmbran)	02.49	48	1	-	0

ORR Anderson (Alan)
Glasgow, 19 December, 1923 (WH)

League Club	Source	Date Signed	Seasons Played	Apps	Subs	Gls
Nottingham F	Third Lanark	08.51	51-54	46	-	0

ORR Bradley James
Liverpool, 1 November, 1982 (M)

League Club	Source	Date Signed	Seasons Played	Apps	Subs	Gls
Newcastle U	YT	07.01				
Burnley	L	01.04	03	1	3	0
Bristol C	Tr	07.04	04	23	14	0

ORR Douglas (Doug) McDonald
Glasgow, 8 November, 1937 SAmat (W)

League Club	Source	Date Signed	Seasons Played	Apps	Subs	Gls
Queens Park Rgrs (Am)	Hendon	06.57	57	5	-	0

ORR Henry (Harry)
Lisburn, 31 October, 1936 (WH)

League Club	Source	Date Signed	Seasons Played	Apps	Subs	Gls
Sheffield U	Distillery	11.58	58-63	10	-	1
Peterborough U	Tr	07.64	64-66	47	1	0

ORR Neil Ian
Greenock, 13 May, 1959 Su21-7/SLge-1 (CD)

League Club	Source	Date Signed	Seasons Played	Apps	Subs	Gls
West Ham U	Morton	01.82	81-87	133	13	4

ORRITT Bryan
Cwm-y-Glo, 22 February, 1937 Wu23-3 (IF)

League Club	Source	Date Signed	Seasons Played	Apps	Subs	Gls
Birmingham C	Bangor C	01.56	56-61	99	-	23
Middlesbrough	Tr	03.62	61-65	115	3	22

OSBORN Kenneth (Ken) George
Hampstead, 23 November, 1948 (W)

League Club	Source	Date Signed	Seasons Played	Apps	Subs	Gls
Gillingham	Queens Park Rgrs (App)	06.66	68-69	2	0	0

OSBORN Mark
Bletchley, 18 June, 1981 (G)

League Club	Source	Date Signed	Seasons Played	Apps	Subs	Gls
Wycombe W	YT	03.99	99	1	0	0

OSBORN Simon Edward
New Addington, 19 January, 1972 (M)

League Club	Source	Date Signed	Seasons Played	Apps	Subs	Gls
Crystal Palace	YT	01.90	90-93	47	8	5
Reading	Tr	08.94	94	31	1	5
Queens Park Rgrs	Tr	07.95	95	6	3	1
Wolverhampton W	Tr	12.95	95-00	151	11	11
Tranmere Rov	Tr	03.01	00	9	0	1
Port Vale	Tr	09.01	01	7	0	0
Gillingham	Tr	10.01	01-02	38	8	5
Walsall	Tr	07.03	03-04	71	10	3

OSBORNE Glyn
Crewe, 23 August, 1954 (F)

League Club	Source	Date Signed	Seasons Played	Apps	Subs	Gls
Crewe Alex	App	•	70-71	2	5	0

League Club	Source	Date Signed	Seasons Played	Apps	Subs	Gls
OSBORNE Ian Leonard						
Leicester, 28 October, 1952						(FB)
Birmingham C	App	10.70	75	10	0	0
Port Vale	Tr	06.76	76	14	1	0
OSBORNE John (Johnny)						
Renfrew, 14 October, 1919 Died 1981						(IF)
Leicester C	Linwood Thistle	09.38				
Watford	Tr	02.48	47-48	34	-	12
OSBORNE John						
Barlborough, 1 December, 1940 Died 1998 ESch						(G)
Chesterfield	Bolton W (Am)	09.60	60-66	110	0	0
West Bromwich A	Tr	01.67	66-76	250	0	0
Walsall	L	02.73	72	3	0	0
OSBORNE Junior						
Watford, 12 February, 1988						(FB)
Watford	Sch	•	04	0	1	0
OSBORNE Karleigh Anthony Jonathan						
Southall, 19 March, 1988						(FB)
Brentford	Sch	•	04	1	0	0
OSBORNE Lawrence (Lawrie) William						
Stratford, 20 October, 1967						(M)
Arsenal	App	07.85				
Newport Co	Tr	11.87	87	15	0	0
Maidstone U	Redbridge Forest	07.90	90-91	49	4	8
Gillingham	Tr	12.91	91-92	5	1	1
OSBORNE Roger Charles						
Otley, Suffolk, 9 March, 1950						(M)
Ipswich T	Grundisburgh	03.71	73-80	109	15	9
Colchester U	Tr	02.81	80-85	196	10	11
OSBORNE Steven (Steve) Colin						
Middlesbrough, 3 March, 1969						(F)
Peterborough U	South Bank	03.89	88-90	18	42	7
York C	Tr	08.91	91	6	3	0
OSBORNE Wayne						
Stockton, 14 January, 1977						(FB)
York C	YT	06.95	95	5	1	0
OSBOURNE Calbert **Gary** James						
Wolverhampton, 22 October, 1969						(FB)
Shrewsbury T	YT	07.88	88	3	4	0
OSBOURNE Isaac Samuel						
Birmingham, 22 June, 1986						(M)
Coventry C	Sch	07.03	02-04	9	2	0
OSCROFT Harry						
Mansfield, 10 March, 1926						(W)
Mansfield T	Mansfield Colliery	04.47	46-49	113	-	41
Stoke C	Tr	01.50	49-58	326	-	103
Port Vale	Tr	09.59	59-60	47	-	12
OSEI-KUFFOUR Jonathan (Jo)						
Edmonton, 17 November, 1981						(F)
Arsenal	YT	07.00				
Swindon T	L	08.01	01	4	7	2
Torquay U	Tr	10.02	02-04	77	28	21
OSGOOD Keith						
Isleworth, 8 May, 1955 ESch/EYth						(CD)
Tottenham H	App	05.72	73-77	112	1	13
Coventry C	Tr	01.78	77-78	24	0	1
Derby Co	Tr	10.79	79-81	61	8	10
Orient	Tr	12.81	81-83	36	0	0
Cambridge U	HJK Helsinki (Fin)	11.84	84-85	34	1	1
OSGOOD Peter Leslie						
Windsor, 20 February, 1947 EYth/Eu23-6/FLge-3/E-4						(F)
Chelsea	Jnrs	09.64	65-73	276	3	103
Southampton	Tr	03.74	73-77	122	4	28
Norwich C	L	11.76	76	3	0	0
Chelsea	Philadelphia (USA)	12.78	78-79	10	0	2
OSGOOD Stephen (Steve)						
Bracknell, 20 January, 1962						(G)
Aldershot	Newbury T	02.89	88	1	0	0
O'SHAUGHNESSY Brian						
Wednesbury, 8 September, 1932 Died 1986						(IF)
Walsall		03.54	53	1	-	0
O'SHAUGHNESSY Michael (Mike) John						
Poplar, 15 April, 1955						(G)
Orient	App	08.73	73	1	0	0
O'SHAUGHNESSY Paul Joseph						
Bury, 3 October, 1981						(M)
Bury	YT	07.01	01-03	27	18	1
O'SHAUGHNESSY Stephen (Steve)						
Wrexham, 13 October, 1967 WYth						(M)
Leeds U	App	10.85				
Bradford C	Tr	11.85	87	0	1	0
Rochdale	Tr	08.88	88-90	101	8	16
Exeter C	Tr	07.91	91	1	2	0
Darlington	Tr	01.92	91-93	88	0	2
O'SHEA Daniel (Danny) Edward						
Kennington, 26 March, 1963						(CD)
Arsenal	App	12.80	82	6	0	0
Charlton Ath	L	02.84	83	9	0	0
Exeter C	Tr	08.84	84	45	0	2
Southend U	Tr	08.85	85-88	117	2	12
Cambridge U	Tr	08.89	89-94	186	17	1
Northampton T	Tr	03.95	94-96	73	7	1
O'SHEA John Francis						
Waterford, 30 April, 1981 IRYth/IRu21-13/IR-24						(FB)
Manchester U	Waterford	09.98	01-04	78	19	4
Bournemouth	L	01.00	99	10	0	1
O'SHEA Timothy (Tim) James						
Pimlico, 12 November, 1966 IRYth/IRu21-2						(FB)
Tottenham H	App	08.84	86-87	1	2	0
Newport Co	L	10.86	86	10	0	0
Leyton Orient	Tr	07.88	88	7	2	1
Gillingham	Tr	02.89	88-91	102	10	2
OSMAN Harold (Harry) James						
Bentworth, 29 January, 1911						(W)
Plymouth Arg	Poole T	12.35	35-36	5	-	0
Southampton	Tr	06.37	37-38	70	-	31
Millwall	Tr	03.39	38-47	34	-	3
Bristol C	Tr	10.47	47	18	-	1
OSMAN Leon						
Billinge, 17 May, 1981 ESch/EYth						(W)
Everton	YT	08.98	02-04	27	8	7
Carlisle U	L	10.02	02	10	2	1
Derby Co	L	01.04	03	17	0	3
OSMAN Rex Charles Herbert						
Derby, 4 April, 1932 Died 2005 EYth						(WH)
Derby Co	Jnrs	07.49	53-54	2	-	0
OSMAN Russell Charles						
Repton, 14 February, 1959 EYth/Eu21-7/EB/E-11						(CD)
Ipswich T	App	03.76	77-84	294	0	17
Leicester C	Tr	07.85	85-87	108	0	8
Southampton	Tr	06.88	88-91	92	4	6
Bristol C	Tr	10.91	91-93	67	3	3
Plymouth Arg	Sudbury T	03.95				
Brighton & Hove A	Tr	09.95	95	11	1	0
Cardiff C	Tr	02.96	95	14	1	0
OSMOND Avery Noel						
Huddersfield, 25 December, 1924						(IF)
Southend U	Peterborough U	05.48	48	2	-	0
OSMOND Colin Albert Eric						
Whitchurch, Hampshire, 15 May, 1937 EYth						(CD)
Portsmouth	Jnrs	05.54	57	1	-	0
OSTENSTAD Egil						
Haugesund, Norway, 2 January, 1972 NoYth/Nou21-27/No-18						(F)
Southampton	Viking Stavanger (Nor)	10.96	96-99	80	16	28
Blackburn Rov	Tr	08.99	99-02	38	24	12
Manchester C	L	02.01	00	1	3	0
OSTER John Morgan						
Boston, 8 December, 1978 WYth/Wu21-9/WB-1/W-13						(W)
Grimsby T	YT	07.96	96	21	3	3
Everton	Tr	07.97	97-98	22	18	1
Sunderland	Tr	08.99	99-04	48	20	5
Barnsley	L	10.01	01	2	0	0
Grimsby T	L	11.02	02	10	0	5
Grimsby T	L	02.03	02	7	0	1
Leeds U	L	11.04	04	8	0	1
Burnley	Tr	01.05	04	12	3	1
OSTERGAARD John (Johnny) Brian						
Denmark, 6 February, 1955						(F)
Charlton Ath	Ikast (Den)	11.79	79-80	8	4	1
O'SULLIVAN Cyril John						
Lewisham, 22 February, 1920 Died 2003						(G)
Reading	Crown Villa	09.46	46-47	36	-	0

O'SULLIVAN John
Cork, 30 May, 1922 (W)

League Club	Source	Date Signed	Seasons Played	Apps	Subs	Gls
Swansea T	Waterford	01.48	47	2	-	0

O'SULLIVAN Peter Anthony
Conway, 4 March, 1951 WSch/Wu23-6/W-3 (W)

League Club	Source	Date Signed	Seasons Played	Apps	Subs	Gls
Manchester U	App	03.68				
Brighton & Hove A	Tr	04.70	70-80	432	3	39
Fulham	Tr	06.81	81-82	45	1	1
Charlton Ath	L	10.82	82	5	0	0
Reading	L	11.82	82	9	0	0
Aldershot	(Hong Kong)	07.83	83	13	1	0

O'SULLIVAN Wayne St John
Akrotiri, Cyprus, 25 February, 1974 IRu21-2 (M)

League Club	Source	Date Signed	Seasons Played	Apps	Subs	Gls
Swindon T	YT	05.93	94-96	65	24	3
Cardiff C	Tr	08.97	97-98	78	7	4
Plymouth Arg	Tr	07.99	99-00	83	2	3

O'SULLIVAN William (Willie) Finbar
Lambeth, 5 October, 1959 IRYth (W)

League Club	Source	Date Signed	Seasons Played	Apps	Subs	Gls
Charlton Ath	App	10.77	76-77	1	1	0

OSVOLD Kjetil
Aalesund, Norway, 5 June, 1961 Norway 37 (W)

League Club	Source	Date Signed	Seasons Played	Apps	Subs	Gls
Nottingham F	Lillestrom (Nor)	03.87	86-87	5	2	0
Leicester C	L	12.87	87	3	1	0

O'TOOLE Gavin Francis
Dublin, 19 September, 1975 IRSch/IRYth/IRu21-2 (M)

League Club	Source	Date Signed	Seasons Played	Apps	Subs	Gls
Coventry C	YT	07.93				
Hereford U	L	11.96	96	1	0	0

O'TOOLE Christopher **Patrick (Pat)**
Dublin, 2 January, 1965 (M)

League Club	Source	Date Signed	Seasons Played	Apps	Subs	Gls
Leicester C	Shelbourne	02.90				
Exeter C	L	12.90	90	6	0	0
Shrewsbury T	Tr	03.91	90-92	26	20	1
Torquay U	Cobh Ramblers	08.93	93	3	0	0

OTSEMOBOR John
Liverpool, 23 March, 1983 EYth/Eu20 (FB)

League Club	Source	Date Signed	Seasons Played	Apps	Subs	Gls
Liverpool	YT	03.00	03	4	0	0
Hull C	L	03.03	02	8	1	3
Bolton W	L	02.04	03	1	0	0
Crewe Alex	L	09.04	04	14	0	1

OTTA Walter Nicolas
Cordoba, Argentina, 20 December, 1973 (M)

League Club	Source	Date Signed	Seasons Played	Apps	Subs	Gls
Walsall	Deportes Temuco (Chile)	11.98	98	6	2	3

OTTEWELL Sidney (Sid)
Horsley, Derbyshire, 23 October, 1919 (IF)

League Club	Source	Date Signed	Seasons Played	Apps	Subs	Gls
Chesterfield	Holbrook CW	11.36	36-46	42	-	12
Birmingham C	Tr	06.47	47	5	-	2
Luton T	Tr	12.47	47	15	-	4
Nottingham F	Tr	07.48	48-49	32	-	3
Mansfield T	Tr	01.50	49-51	67	-	21
Scunthorpe U	Tr	03.52	51-52	30	-	12

OTTO Hendrikus (Heine) Matheus
Amsterdam, Holland, 24 August, 1954 Holland int (M)

League Club	Source	Date Signed	Seasons Played	Apps	Subs	Gls
Middlesbrough	Twente Enschede (Holl)	08.81	81-84	163	3	24

OTTO Ricky
Hackney, 9 November, 1967 (W)

League Club	Source	Date Signed	Seasons Played	Apps	Subs	Gls
Leyton Orient	Dartford	11.90	90-92	41	15	13
Southend U	Tr	07.93	93-94	63	1	17
Birmingham C	Tr	12.94	94-96	25	21	6
Charlton Ath	L	09.96	96	5	2	0
Peterborough U	L	02.97	96	15	0	4
Notts Co	L	09.97	97	4	0	0

OTTOSSON Ulf Peter
Degefors, Sweden, 2 July, 1968 (F)

League Club	Source	Date Signed	Seasons Played	Apps	Subs	Gls
Norwich C (L)	Norrkoping (Swe)	01.97	96	4	3	1

OTULAKOWSKI Anton
Dewsbury, 29 January, 1956 (M)

League Club	Source	Date Signed	Seasons Played	Apps	Subs	Gls
Barnsley	Ossett T	03.75	74-76	42	0	2
West Ham U	Tr	10.76	76-77	10	7	0
Southend U	Tr	03.79	78-82	161	2	8
Millwall	Tr	03.83	82-85	114	0	14
Crystal Palace	Tr	08.86	86	12	0	1

OUADDOU Abdeslam
Ksar-Askour, Morocco, 1 November, 1978 Morocco int (FB)

League Club	Source	Date Signed	Seasons Played	Apps	Subs	Gls
Fulham	Nancy (Fr)	08.01	01-02	13	8	0

OULARE Souleymane
Conakry, Guinea, 16 October, 1972 Guinea int (F)

League Club	Source	Date Signed	Seasons Played	Apps	Subs	Gls
Stoke C	Fenerbahce (Tu)	12.01	01	0	1	0

OUTHART Anthony (Tony)
Scarborough, 17 September, 1963 (F)

League Club	Source	Date Signed	Seasons Played	Apps	Subs	Gls
Scarborough	Bridlington T	11.87	87-88	3	3	1

OUTHWAITE George
Ferryhill, 19 May, 1928 (G)

League Club	Source	Date Signed	Seasons Played	Apps	Subs	Gls
Oldham Ath (Am)	Chilton Ath	03.56	55	4	-	0

OUTTERSIDE Mark Jeremy
Hexham, 13 January, 1967 (FB)

League Club	Source	Date Signed	Seasons Played	Apps	Subs	Gls
Sunderland	App	01.85	86	1	0	0
Darlington	Tr	07.87	87	37	1	0

OVARD Frank Colin
Evesham, 16 December, 1955 ESemiPro (F)

League Club	Source	Date Signed	Seasons Played	Apps	Subs	Gls
Gillingham	Maidstone U	12.81	81	4	2	0

OVENDALE Mark John
Leicester, 22 November, 1973 (G)

League Club	Source	Date Signed	Seasons Played	Apps	Subs	Gls
Northampton T	Wisbech T	08.94	94	6	0	0
Bournemouth	Barry T	05.98	98-99	89	0	0
Luton T	Tr	08.00	00-02	44	1	0
York C	Tr	08.03	03	41	0	0

OVER Eric
Sheffield, 5 July, 1933 (W)

League Club	Source	Date Signed	Seasons Played	Apps	Subs	Gls
Sheffield U	Sheffield FC	11.54	54	2	-	0
Barrow	Tr	01.56	55-57	19	-	1
Oldham Ath	Tr	12.57	57	21	-	2

OVERFIELD Jack
Leeds, 14 May, 1932 (W)

League Club	Source	Date Signed	Seasons Played	Apps	Subs	Gls
Leeds U	Yorkshire Amats	05.53	55-59	159	-	20
Sunderland	Tr	08.60	60-62	65	-	5
Peterborough U	Tr	02.63	62	1	-	0
Bradford C	Tr	07.64	64	11	-	0

OVERMARS Marc
Emst, Holland, 29 March, 1973 Ho60 (W)

League Club	Source	Date Signed	Seasons Played	Apps	Subs	Gls
Arsenal	Ajax (Holl)	07.97	97-99	91	9	25

OVERSON Richard John
Kettering, 3 June, 1959 (CD)

League Club	Source	Date Signed	Seasons Played	Apps	Subs	Gls
Burnley	App	06.77	77-79	5	1	0
Hereford U	Tr	05.80	80-81	6	5	1

OVERSON Vincent (Vince) David
Kettering, 15 May, 1962 EYth (CD)

League Club	Source	Date Signed	Seasons Played	Apps	Subs	Gls
Burnley	App	11.79	79-85	207	4	6
Birmingham C	Tr	06.86	86-90	179	3	3
Stoke C	Tr	08.91	91-95	167	3	6
Burnley	Tr	08.96	96	6	2	0
Shrewsbury T	L	09.97	97	2	0	0

OVERTON John
Rotherham, 2 May, 1956 (CD)

League Club	Source	Date Signed	Seasons Played	Apps	Subs	Gls
Aston Villa	App	01.74	75	2	1	0
Halifax T	L	03.76	75	14	0	2
Gillingham	Tr	06.76	76-80	177	1	10

OVERTON Paul Henry
Soham, 18 April, 1961 (G)

League Club	Source	Date Signed	Seasons Played	Apps	Subs	Gls
Ipswich T	App	07.78	77	1	0	0

OWEN Aled Watkin
Brynteg, 7 January, 1934 (W)

League Club	Source	Date Signed	Seasons Played	Apps	Subs	Gls
Tottenham H	Bangor C	09.53	53	1	-	0
Ipswich T	Tr	07.58	58-61	30	-	3
Wrexham	Tr	07.63	63	3	-	0

OWEN Brian Ernest
Harefield, 2 November, 1944 (W)

League Club	Source	Date Signed	Seasons Played	Apps	Subs	Gls
Watford	App	07.62	62-69	148	5	17
Colchester U	Tr	05.70	70-71	11	1	2
Wolverhampton W	Tr	01.72	72	4	0	0

OWEN Brian Gordon
Bath, 7 July, 1942 (F)

League Club	Source	Date Signed	Seasons Played	Apps	Subs	Gls
Hereford U	Bath C	07.70	72-73	46	11	13

OWEN Bryn
Rochdale, 25 April, 1939 (FB)

League Club	Source	Date Signed	Seasons Played	Apps	Subs	Gls
Rochdale	Turf Hill	08.60	60-61	6	-	0

OWEN Ronald **Derek**
Ellesmere Port, 25 September, 1938 (G)

League Club	Source	Date Signed	Seasons Played	Apps	Subs	Gls
Chester (Am)	Ellesmere Port	05.58	58-60	7	-	0

OWEN Derek William
Shrewsbury, 11 March, 1938 (W)

League Club	Source	Date Signed	Seasons Played	Apps	Subs	Gls
Shrewsbury T	Coton Rov	01.57	56-57	13	-	3

OWEN Gareth
Chester, 21 October, 1971 Wu21-8/WB-1 (M)

League Club	Source	Date Signed	Seasons Played	Apps	Subs	Gls
Wrexham	YT	07.90	89-00	298	52	36

OWEN Gareth David
Pontypridd, 21 September, 1982 WYth (CD)

League Club	Source	Date Signed	Seasons Played	Apps	Subs	Gls
Stoke C	YT	07.01	03-04	1	4	0
Oldham Ath	L	01.04	03	15	0	1
Torquay U	L	07.04	04	2	3	0
Oldham Ath	L	03.05	04	9	0	0

OWEN Gary Alfred
St Helens, 7 July, 1958 EYth/Eu21-22/EB (M)

League Club	Source	Date Signed	Seasons Played	Apps	Subs	Gls
Manchester C	App	08.75	75-78	101	2	19
West Bromwich A	Tr	06.79	79-85	185	2	21
Sheffield Wed	Panionios (Gre)	08.87	87	12	5	0

OWEN Gordon
Barnsley, 14 June, 1959 (W)

League Club	Source	Date Signed	Seasons Played	Apps	Subs	Gls
Sheffield Wed	Jnrs	11.76	77-82	32	15	5
Rotherham U	L	03.80	79	9	0	0
Doncaster Rov	L	11.82	82	9	0	0
Chesterfield	L	03.83	82	6	0	2
Cardiff C	Tr	08.83	83	38	1	14
Barnsley	Tr	08.84	84-85	68	0	25
Bristol C	Tr	08.86	86-87	51	2	11
Hull C	L	12.87	87	3	0	0
Mansfield T	Tr	01.88	87-88	54	4	8
Blackpool	Tr	07.89	89-90	21	8	4
Carlisle U	L	10.90	90	4	1	0
Exeter C	L	12.90	90	4	0	0

OWEN John **Leslie (Les)**
Hawarden, 11 April, 1933 (FB)

League Club	Source	Date Signed	Seasons Played	Apps	Subs	Gls
Chester		07.54	56	1	-	0

OWEN Maurice
Abingdon, 4 July, 1924 Died 2000 (CF)

League Club	Source	Date Signed	Seasons Played	Apps	Subs	Gls
Swindon T	Abingdon	12.46	46-62	555	-	150

OWEN Michael James
Chester, 14 December, 1979 ESch/EYth/Eu21-1/E-70 (F)

League Club	Source	Date Signed	Seasons Played	Apps	Subs	Gls
Liverpool	Jnrs	12.96	96-03	193	23	118

OWEN Neil
Bury, 14 October, 1959 (M)

League Club	Source	Date Signed	Seasons Played	Apps	Subs	Gls
Sheffield Wed	App	•	76	1	0	0

OWEN Robert (Bobby)
Farnworth, 17 October, 1947 (F)

League Club	Source	Date Signed	Seasons Played	Apps	Subs	Gls
Bury	App	08.65	64-67	81	3	36
Manchester C	Tr	07.68	68-69	18	4	3
Swansea C	L	03.70	69	5	1	1
Carlisle U	Tr	06.70	70-76	185	19	51
Northampton T	L	10.76	76	5	0	0
Workington	L	12.76	76	8	0	2
Bury	L	02.77	76	4	0	1
Doncaster Rov	Tr	07.77	77-78	74	3	22

OWEN Robert (Bobby) Gibson
Sunderland, 5 May, 1924 Died 1999 (WH)

League Club	Source	Date Signed	Seasons Played	Apps	Subs	Gls
Huddersfield T	Murton CW	04.45				
Lincoln C	Murton CW	01.47	46-54	246	-	5

OWEN Sydney (Syd) William
Small Heath, 28 February, 1922 Died 1998 FLge-2/E-3 (CD)

League Club	Source	Date Signed	Seasons Played	Apps	Subs	Gls
Birmingham C		10.45	46	5	-	0
Luton T	Tr	06.47	47-58	388	-	3

OWEN Leslie **Terence (Terry)**
Liverpool, 11 September, 1949 (F)

League Club	Source	Date Signed	Seasons Played	Apps	Subs	Gls
Everton	App	12.66	67	2	0	0
Bradford C	Tr	06.70	70-71	41	11	6
Chester	Tr	06.72	72-76	161	15	41
Cambridge U	Tr	08.77	77	1	0	0
Rochdale	Tr	09.77	77-78	80	2	21
Port Vale	Tr	07.79	79	14	4	3

OWEN Trefor
Flint, 20 February, 1933 Died 2001 WAmat (CD)

League Club	Source	Date Signed	Seasons Played	Apps	Subs	Gls
Leyton Orient	Tooting & Mitcham	01.58	58-60	15	-	0

OWEN William (Billy)
Llanfairfechan, 30 June, 1914 Died 1976 (WH)

League Club	Source	Date Signed	Seasons Played	Apps	Subs	Gls
Manchester C	Northwich Vic	06.34	35	9	-	3
Tranmere Rov	Tr	03.36	35	6	-	4
Newport Co	Tr	06.36	36-46	69	-	5
Exeter C	Tr	10.46	46	20	-	9

OWENS John Gilbert
Ynysybwl, 25 March, 1932 (WH)

League Club	Source	Date Signed	Seasons Played	Apps	Subs	Gls
Exeter C	Pontypridd	10.53	53-54	14	-	0

OWENS Thomas **Leslie (Les)**
Monkwearmouth, 17 October, 1919 Died 1974 (CF)

League Club	Source	Date Signed	Seasons Played	Apps	Subs	Gls
Charlton Ath	Washington Chem Wks	09.37	37-38	12	-	5
Doncaster Rov	Tr	02.39	38-47	21	-	11
Southport	Tr	12.47	47-48	53	-	11
Hartlepools U	Tr	07.49	49	28	-	12
Norwich C	Tr	03.50	49-50	20	-	8
Reading	Tr	07.51	51	8	-	4
Brighton & Hove A	Tr	06.52	52	15	-	4

OWER John (Ian) Campion Taylor
Glasgow, 2 January, 1939 (G)

League Club	Source	Date Signed	Seasons Played	Apps	Subs	Gls
Workington	St Johnstone	02.63	62-67	200	0	0

OWERS Adrian Richard
Danbury, 26 February, 1965 (M)

League Club	Source	Date Signed	Seasons Played	Apps	Subs	Gls
Southend U	App	02.83	82-84	19	9	0
Brighton & Hove A	Chelmsford C	12.87	87-90	32	8	4
Gillingham	L	03.91	90	9	1	0
Maidstone U	Tr	10.91	91	1	0	0

OWERS Gary
Newcastle, 3 October, 1968 FLge (M)

League Club	Source	Date Signed	Seasons Played	Apps	Subs	Gls
Sunderland	App	10.86	87-94	259	9	25
Bristol C	Tr	12.94	94-97	121	5	9
Notts Co	Tr	07.98	98-01	147	7	12

OWERS Philip (Phil)
Bishop Auckland, 28 April, 1955 (G)

League Club	Source	Date Signed	Seasons Played	Apps	Subs	Gls
Darlington	Jnrs	06.73	72-74	45	0	0
Gillingham	Tr	07.75	75	2	0	0
Darlington	Tr	07.76	76-79	69	0	0
Hartlepool U	Brandon U	08.87	87	2	0	0

OWUSU Ansah Ossei
Hackney, 22 November, 1979 (M)

League Club	Source	Date Signed	Seasons Played	Apps	Subs	Gls
Wimbledon	YT	06.98	00	1	3	0
Bristol Rov	L	02.01	00	11	6	0

OWUSU Lloyd Magnus
Slough, 12 December, 1976 (F)

League Club	Source	Date Signed	Seasons Played	Apps	Subs	Gls
Brentford	Slough T	07.98	98-01	148	16	64
Sheffield Wed	Tr	07.02	02-03	24	28	9
Reading	Tr	12.03	03-04	25	16	10

OWUSU-ABEYIE Quincy Jamie
Amsterdam, Holland, 15 April, 1986 HoYth (F)

League Club	Source	Date Signed	Seasons Played	Apps	Subs	Gls
Arsenal	Sch	07.04	04	1	0	0

OXBROW Darren William
Ipswich, 1 September, 1969 (CD)

League Club	Source	Date Signed	Seasons Played	Apps	Subs	Gls
Ipswich T	YT	06.88				
Maidstone U	Tr	08.89	89-91	84	1	2
Colchester U	Tr	08.92	92	12	4	4
Barnet	Tr	12.92	92	1	0	0

OXFORD Kenneth (Ken)
Oldham, 14 November, 1929 Died 1993 EYth (G)

League Club	Source	Date Signed	Seasons Played	Apps	Subs	Gls
Manchester C	Ardwick LC	10.47	47	1	-	0
Chesterfield		06.50				
Norwich C	Tr	07.51	53-57	128	-	0
Derby Co	Tr	12.57	57-62	151	-	0
Doncaster Rov	Tr	07.64	64	16	-	0

OXLEY Albert
Gateshead, 21 October, 1915 Died 1994 (IF)

League Club	Source	Date Signed	Seasons Played	Apps	Subs	Gls
Gateshead	Windy Nook	01.35	34-46	120	-	25

OXLEY Scott
Sheffield, 22 November, 1976 (M)

League Club	Source	Date Signed	Seasons Played	Apps	Subs	Gls
York C	YT	07.95	95	1	1	0

OXTOBY Richard (Dick)
Chesterfield, 5 September, 1939 (CD)

League Club	Source	Date Signed	Seasons Played	Apps	Subs	Gls
Bolton W	Jnrs	01.57	59	3	-	0
Tranmere Rov	Tr	07.63	63	5	-	0

OYEDELE Ade Shola
Kano, Nigeria, 14 September, 1984 (FB)

League Club	Source	Date Signed	Seasons Played	Apps	Subs	Gls
Wimbledon/MK Dons	Sch	08.04	03-04	27	7	0

OYEN Davy
Bilzen, Belgium, 17 July, 1975 Belgium 3 (FB)

League Club	Source	Date Signed	Seasons Played	Apps	Subs	Gls
Nottingham F	Anderlecht (Bel)	01.03	02-03	4	4	0

League Club	Source	Date Signed	Seasons Played	Career Record Apps	Subs	Gls
PAATELAINEN Mika (Mixu) Matti Petteri						
Helsinki, Finland, 3 February, 1967 Finland int						(F)
Bolton W	Aberdeen	07.94	94-96	58	11	15
Wolverhampton W	Tr	08.97	97	10	13	0
PACE Derek John						
Bloxwich, 11 March, 1932 Died 1989						(CF)
Aston Villa	Bloxwich Strollers	09.49	50-57	98	-	40
Sheffield U	Tr	12.57	57-64	253	-	140
Notts Co	Tr	12.64	64-65	29	0	15
Walsall	Tr	07.66	66	4	1	1
PACEY David (Dave)						
Luton, 2 October, 1936 Eu23-1						(WH)
Luton T	Hitchin T	08.56	57-64	246	-	16
PACEY Denis Frank						
Feltham, 27 September, 1928						(CF)
Leyton Orient	Walton & Hersham	12.51	51-54	120	-	46
Millwall	Tr	10.54	54-58	133	-	37
Aldershot	Tr	09.58	58-59	32	-	13
PACK Leonard (Lenny) John						
Salisbury, 27 September, 1976						(M)
Cambridge U	YT	07.95	94-96	5	10	0
PACK Roy James						
Stoke Newington, 20 September, 1946						(FB)
Arsenal	App	11.63	65	1	0	0
Portsmouth	Tr	07.66	66-68	91	0	0
PACKARD Edgar						
Mansfield, 7 March, 1919 Died 1996						(CD)
Sheffield Wed	Clipstone CW	12.36	46-51	124	-	1
Halifax T	Tr	08.52	52-53	85	-	0
PACKER Leslie (Les) John						
Sunderland, 8 April, 1959						(F)
Doncaster Rov		09.78	78-79	5	2	2
PACKER Michael (Mike) David						
Willesden, 20 April, 1950						(FB)
Watford	App	04.68	68-72	57	11	2
Crewe Alex	L	03.72	71	12	0	0
Colchester U	Tr	07.73	73-82	337	7	20
PACKER Norman James						
Ynysybwl, 14 June, 1931						(WH)
Exeter C	Pontypridd	07.55	55-60	18	-	0
PACKHAM William (Will) Joseph						
Brighton, 13 January, 1981						(G)
Brighton & Hove A	YT	06.99	00-01	1	1	0
PACQUETTE Richard Francis						
Kilburn, 28 January, 1983						(F)
Queens Park Rgrs	YT	02.00	00-03	13	18	6
Mansfield T	L	02.04	03	3	2	1
MK Dons	Tr	09.04	04	1	4	0
Brentford	Fisher Ath	11.04	04	1	0	0
PADDON Graham Charles						
Manchester, 24 August, 1950 Eu23-1						(M)
Coventry C	App	05.68	68-69	3	2	1
Norwich C	Tr	10.69	69-73	162	0	19
West Ham U	Tr	12.73	73-76	115	0	11
Norwich C	Tr	11.76	76-81	126	2	6
Millwall	L	12.81	81	5	0	1
PADOVANO Michele						
Turin, Italy, 28 August, 1966 Italy 1						(F)
Crystal Palace	Juventus (It)	11.97	97-98	8	4	1
PADULA Diego **Gino** Mauro						
Buenos Aires, Argentina, 11 July, 1976						(FB)
Walsall	Xerez (Sp)	11.99	99	23	2	0
Wigan Ath	Tr	07.00	00	2	2	0
Queens Park Rgrs	Tr	07.02	02-04	81	9	4
PAGAL Jean-Claude						
Cameroon, 15 September, 1964 Cameroon int						(M)
Carlisle U	St Etienne (Fr)	02.98	97	1	0	0

League Club	Source	Date Signed	Seasons Played	Career Record Apps	Subs	Gls
PAGE Donald (Don) Richard						
Manchester, 18 January, 1964						(F)
Wigan Ath	Runcorn	03.89	88-90	62	12	15
Rotherham U	Tr	08.91	91-92	40	15	13
Rochdale	L	02.93	92	3	1	1
Doncaster Rov	Tr	11.93	93	18	4	4
Chester C	Tr	07.94	94	22	8	5
Scarborough	Tr	08.95	95	26	11	5
PAGE John						
Frimley, 21 October, 1934						(CD)
Southampton	Jnrs	10.51	52-60	190	-	24
PAGE Malcolm Edward						
Knucklas, 5 February, 1947 WSch/Wu23-6/W-28						(FB)
Birmingham C	App	09.64	64-80	328	8	8
Oxford U	Tr	02.81	80-81	14	0	1
PAGE Raymond (Ray) Michael						
Swindon, 26 September, 1930						(FB)
Swindon T		04.51	50-54	32	-	0
PAGE Robert John						
Llwynypia, 3 September, 1974 WSch/WYth/Wu21-6/WB-1/W-38						(CD)
Watford	YT	04.93	93-00	209	7	2
Sheffield U	Tr	08.01	01-03	106	1	1
Cardiff C	Tr	07.04	04	8	1	0
Coventry C	Tr	02.05	04	9	0	0
PAHARS Marian						
Latvia, 5 August, 1976 Latvia 63						(F)
Southampton	Skonto Riga (Lat)	03.99	98-03	105	24	42
PAINE Terence (Terry) Lionel						
Winchester, 23 March, 1939 Eu23-4/FLge-5/E-19						(W)
Southampton	Winchester C	02.57	56-73	709	4	160
Hereford U	Tr	08.74	74-76	106	5	8
PAINTER Edward (Eddie) George						
Swindon, 23 June, 1921 Died 2001						(WH)
Swindon T		10.38	46-50	77	-	0
PAINTER Ian John						
Wombourne, 28 December, 1964 EYth/Eu21-1						(F)
Stoke C	App	12.82	82-85	105	8	20
Coventry C	Tr	07.86	86	0	3	0
PAINTER Peter Robert **(Robbie)**						
Ince, 26 January, 1971						(F)
Chester C	YT	07.88	87-90	58	26	8
Maidstone U	Tr	08.91	91	27	3	5
Burnley	Tr	03.92	91-92	16	10	2
Darlington	Tr	09.93	93-96	104	11	28
Rochdale	Tr	10.96	96-98	101	11	30
Halifax T	Tr	07.99	99-00	46	12	8
PAINTER Trevor Alfred						
Norwich, 2 July, 1949						(CD)
Norwich C	App	07.67	67	2	0	0
Colchester U	Tr	05.70	70	1	0	0
PAISLEY Robert (Bob)						
Hetton-le-Hole, 23 January, 1919 Died 1996						(WH)
Liverpool	Bishop Auckland	05.39	46-53	253	-	10
PALADINO Giuseppe (Joe)						
Whiston, 21 August, 1965						(G)
Wigan Ath	St Helens T	12.90	90	7	0	0
PALETHORPE Christopher (Chris) Glynne						
Maidenhead, 6 November, 1942						(W)
Reading	Jnrs	11.59	60-62	55	-	10
Aldershot	Tr	06.63	63-64	56	-	4
PALFREYMAN George Barry						
Sheffield, 13 March, 1933						(G)
Halifax T (Am)	Sheffield FC	01.54	53	1	-	0
PALGRAVE Brian Uriel						
Birmingham, 12 July, 1966						(F)
Walsall	Alvechurch	07.84	84-87	5	3	1
PALIN Grenville						
Armthorpe, 13 February, 1940						(FB)
Wolverhampton W	Jnrs	03.57				
Walsall	Tr	07.60	60-63	130	-	10
PALIN Leigh Grenville						
Worcester, 12 September, 1965 EYth						(M)
Aston Villa	App	09.83				
Shrewsbury T	L	12.84	84	2	0	0
Nottingham F	Tr	11.85				

League Club	Source	Date Signed	Seasons Played	Apps	Subs	Gls
Bradford C	Tr	10.86	86-88	65	6	10
Stoke C	Tr	09.89	89	17	2	3
Hull C	Tr	03.90	89-91	57	0	7
Rochdale	L	10.91	91	3	0	0
Burnley	Tr	10.92	92	1	0	0

PALIOS Markos (Mark)
Birkenhead, 9 November, 1952 (M)

League Club	Source	Date Signed	Seasons Played	Apps	Subs	Gls
Tranmere Rov		07.73	73-79	177	13	25
Crewe Alex	Tr	01.80	79-82	114	4	23
Tranmere Rov	Tr	03.83	82-84	55	4	7

PALLISTER Gary Andrew
Ramsgate, 30 June, 1965 EB-9/FLge/E-22 (CD)

League Club	Source	Date Signed	Seasons Played	Apps	Subs	Gls
Middlesbrough	Billingham T	11.84	85-89	156	0	5
Darlington	L	10.85	85	7	0	0
Manchester U	Tr	08.89	89-97	314	3	12
Middlesbrough	Tr	07.98	98-00	55	0	1

PALLISTER Gordon
Howden-le-Wear, 2 April, 1917 Died 1999 FLge-1 (FB)

League Club	Source	Date Signed	Seasons Played	Apps	Subs	Gls
Bradford C	Willington Jnrs	05.34	37-38	28	-	0
Barnsley	Tr	10.38	38-51	220	-	3

PALMER Aiden Witting
Enfield, 2 January, 1987 (FB)

League Club	Source	Date Signed	Seasons Played	Apps	Subs	Gls
Leyton Orient	Sch	●	04	3	2	0

PALMER Calvin Ian
Skegness, 21 October, 1940 (M)

League Club	Source	Date Signed	Seasons Played	Apps	Subs	Gls
Nottingham F	Skegness T	03.58	58-63	91	-	14
Stoke C	Tr	09.63	63-67	165	0	24
Sunderland	Tr	02.68	67-69	35	5	5
Crewe Alex	Cape Town C (SA)	10.71	71	2	0	0

PALMER Carlton Lloyd
Rowley Regis, 5 December, 1965 Eu21-4/EB-5/E-18 (M)

League Club	Source	Date Signed	Seasons Played	Apps	Subs	Gls
West Bromwich A	App	12.84	85-88	114	7	4
Sheffield Wed	Tr	02.89	88-93	204	1	14
Leeds U	Tr	06.94	94-96	100	2	5
Southampton	Tr	09.97	97-98	44	1	3
Nottingham F	Tr	01.99	98-99	14	2	1
Coventry C	Tr	09.99	99-00	27	3	1
Watford	L	12.00	00	5	0	0
Sheffield Wed	L	02.01	00	12	0	0
Sheffield Wed	L	09.01	01	10	0	0
Stockport Co	Tr	11.01	01-02	42	1	4

PALMER Charles (Charlie) Anthony
Aylesbury, 10 July, 1963 (FB)

League Club	Source	Date Signed	Seasons Played	Apps	Subs	Gls
Watford	App	07.81	83	10	0	1
Derby Co	Tr	07.84	84-85	51	0	2
Hull C	Tr	02.87	86-88	69	1	1
Notts Co	Tr	02.89	88-93	178	4	7
Walsall	Tr	07.94	94-95	54	0	2

PALMER Christopher (Chris) Louis
Derby, 16 October, 1983 (FB)

League Club	Source	Date Signed	Seasons Played	Apps	Subs	Gls
Derby Co	Sch	07.03				
Notts Co	Tr	07.04	04	23	2	4

PALMER David John
Bristol, 10 April, 1961 (FB)

League Club	Source	Date Signed	Seasons Played	Apps	Subs	Gls
Bristol Rov	App	01.79	78	1	0	0

PALMER Desmond (Des) Frederick
Swansea, 23 September, 1931 W-3 (CF)

League Club	Source	Date Signed	Seasons Played	Apps	Subs	Gls
Swansea T	Jnrs	04.50	52-58	84	-	38
Liverpool	Tr	03.59				
Derby Co	Durban C (SA)	06.61	61	18	-	6

PALMER Frank
Sunderland, 29 October, 1923 (W)

League Club	Source	Date Signed	Seasons Played	Apps	Subs	Gls
Gateshead (Am)	Bishop Auckland	02.51	50	2	-	1

PALMER Geoffrey (Geoff)
Barnsley, 12 November, 1940 (FB)

League Club	Source	Date Signed	Seasons Played	Apps	Subs	Gls
Bristol C	Doncaster Rov (Am)	08.58	61	1	-	0

PALMER Geoffrey (Geoff)
Cannock, 11 July, 1954 Eu23-12 (FB)

League Club	Source	Date Signed	Seasons Played	Apps	Subs	Gls
Wolverhampton W	App	07.72	73-84	389	5	13
Burnley	Tr	11.84	84-85	34	0	0
Wolverhampton W	Tr	12.85	85-86	21	1	0

PALMER Jermaine Ashley Clifton
Derby, 28 August, 1986 (F)

League Club	Source	Date Signed	Seasons Played	Apps	Subs	Gls
Stoke C	Sch	01.05	03-04	0	4	0

PALMER John Neville
Bristol, 1 July, 1958 (M)

League Club	Source	Date Signed	Seasons Played	Apps	Subs	Gls
Bristol C	Weston-super-Mare	03.83	82	2	6	0

PALMER Lee James
Gillingham, 19 September, 1970 (FB)

League Club	Source	Date Signed	Seasons Played	Apps	Subs	Gls
Gillingham	YT	07.89	87-94	109	11	5
Cambridge U	Tr	08.95	95-96	30	1	1

PALMER Leslie
Barrow, 16 December, 1923 Died 2002 (WH)

League Club	Source	Date Signed	Seasons Played	Apps	Subs	Gls
Barrow	Holker COB	10.49	49	1	-	0

PALMER Leslie (Les) James
Birmingham, 5 September, 1971 (F)

League Club	Source	Date Signed	Seasons Played	Apps	Subs	Gls
West Bromwich A	YT	07.90	90-91	5	3	1

PALMER Roger Neil
Manchester, 30 January, 1959 (F)

League Club	Source	Date Signed	Seasons Played	Apps	Subs	Gls
Manchester C	App	01.77	77-80	22	9	9
Oldham Ath	Tr	11.80	80-93	419	47	141

PALMER Ryan Warren John
Dulwich, 2 February, 1980 (FB)

League Club	Source	Date Signed	Seasons Played	Apps	Subs	Gls
Fulham	YT	07.98				
Brighton & Hove A	Tr	07.99	99	1	0	0

PALMER Stephen (Steve) Leonard
Brighton, 31 March, 1968 ESch (CD)

League Club	Source	Date Signed	Seasons Played	Apps	Subs	Gls
Ipswich T	Cambridge Univ	08.89	89-95	87	24	2
Watford	Tr	09.95	95-00	222	13	8
Queens Park Rgrs	Tr	07.01	01-03	116	11	9
MK Dons	Tr	07.04	04	27	5	1

PAMAROT Louis **Noe**
Paris, France, 14 April, 1979 (FB)

League Club	Source	Date Signed	Seasons Played	Apps	Subs	Gls
Portsmouth (L)	OGC Nice (Fr)	09.99	99	1	1	0
Tottenham H	OGC Nice (Fr)	08.04	04	23	0	1

PAMMENT Michael (Mike)
Huddersfield, 12 May, 1945 EYth (CF)

League Club	Source	Date Signed	Seasons Played	Apps	Subs	Gls
Bradford C (Am)	Kirkburton YC	07.64	64	1	-	0

PAMPHLETT Tony John
Westminster, 13 April, 1960 (CD)

League Club	Source	Date Signed	Seasons Played	Apps	Subs	Gls
Maidstone U	Dartford	07.86	89	7	0	0

PANAYI Sofroni **James (Jimmy)**
Hammersmith, 24 January, 1980 (CD)

League Club	Source	Date Signed	Seasons Played	Apps	Subs	Gls
Watford	YT	07.98	99-01	10	3	0

PANDIANI Walter Gerardo
Montevideo, Uruguay, 27 April, 1976 Uruguay 3 (F)

League Club	Source	Date Signed	Seasons Played	Apps	Subs	Gls
Birmingham C (L)	Dep la Coruna (Sp)	02.05	04	13	1	4

PANES Simon Michael
Almondsbury, 22 February, 1960 (F)

League Club	Source	Date Signed	Seasons Played	Apps	Subs	Gls
Bristol C	Melksham T	08.82	82	2	2	0

PANOPOULOS Mikael (Mike)
Melbourne, Australia, 9 October, 1976 AuYth (M)

League Club	Source	Date Signed	Seasons Played	Apps	Subs	Gls
Portsmouth	Aris Salonika (Gre)	09.99	99-01	45	9	7

PANTER Derek
Blackpool, 22 November, 1943 (IF)

League Club	Source	Date Signed	Seasons Played	Apps	Subs	Gls
Manchester C	West Bromwich A Am)	08.62	63	1	-	0
Torquay U	Tr	05.64	64	5	-	1

PANUCCI Christian
Savona, Italy, 12 April, 1973 Itu21/It-17 (FB)

League Club	Source	Date Signed	Seasons Played	Apps	Subs	Gls
Chelsea (L)	Inter Milan (It)	08.00	00	7	1	0

PAPACONSTANTINOU Loukas
Toronto, Canada, 10 May, 1974 (G)

League Club	Source	Date Signed	Seasons Played	Apps	Subs	Gls
Darlington	Alabama Saints (USA)	07.97	97	1	0	0

PAPADOPOULOS Dimitrios
Kazakhstan, 20 September, 1981 Gru21/Gr-1 (F)

League Club	Source	Date Signed	Seasons Played	Apps	Subs	Gls
Burnley	Akratitos (Gre)	07.01	01-02	7	33	3

PAPAVASILIOU Nicodemos (Nicky)
Limassol, Cyprus, 31 August, 1970 Cyprus int (W)

League Club	Source	Date Signed	Seasons Played	Apps	Subs	Gls
Newcastle U	OF Iraklion (Crete)	07.93	93	7	0	0

PAPE Andrew (Andy) Maurice
Hammersmith, 22 March, 1962 ESemiPro (G)

League Club	Source	Date Signed	Seasons Played	Apps	Subs	Gls
Queens Park Rgrs	Feltham	07.80	79	1	0	0
Barnet	Enfield	08.91	91-93	40	0	0

PARDEW Alan Scott
Wimbledon, 18 July, 1961 (M)

League Club	Source	Date Signed	Seasons Played	Apps	Subs	Gls
Crystal Palace	Yeovil T	03.87	87-91	111	17	8
Charlton Ath	Tr	11.91	91-94	98	6	24
Barnet	Tr	07.95	95-96	64	3	0

League Club	Source	Date Signed	Seasons Played	Career Record Apps	Subs	Gls
PARDOE Glyn						
Winsford, 1 June, 1946 ESch/Eu23-4						(FB)
Manchester C	App	06.63	61-74	303	2	17
PARFITT Henry (Harry) Edward						
Cardiff, 26 September, 1929						(FB)
Cardiff C		05.49	53	1	-	0
Torquay U	L	10.52	52	28	-	0
Torquay U	L	08.53	53	30	-	0
PARIS Alan David						
Slough, 15 August, 1964						(FB)
Watford	Slough T	11.82				
Peterborough U	Tr	08.85	85-87	135	2	2
Leicester C	Tr	07.88	88-90	80	8	3
Notts Co	Tr	01.91	90-91	39	3	1
PARK Colin Sidney John						
Swansea, 8 February, 1945						(G)
Swansea T	Jnrs	09.63	63	1	-	0
PARK Robert (Bobby)						
Douglas, Lanarkshire, 7 April, 1930						(G)
Crewe Alex	Airdrie	08.55	55-56	61	-	0
PARK Robert (Bobby)						
Coatbridge, 5 January, 1952						(M)
Sunderland	Jnrs	01.69	69-71	50	14	4
PARK Robert (Bobby) Clydesdale						
Edinburgh, 3 July, 1946						(M)
Aston Villa	App	07.63	64-68	60	14	7
Wrexham	Tr	05.69	69-71	98	4	8
Peterborough U	Tr	06.72	72	15	3	1
Northampton T	Tr	02.73	72-73	21	3	0
Hartlepool	Tr	07.74	74	14	3	0
PARK Terence (Terry) Charles						
Liverpool, 7 February, 1957						(M)
Wolverhampton W	Jnrs	03.74				
Stockport Co	Blackpool (N/C)	07.76	76-79	87	3	8
Stockport Co	Minnesota Kicks	03.81	80-82	72	0	7
Manchester C	L	01.83	82	0	2	0
Bury	Tr	07.83	83	18	3	1
PARK William						
Gateshead, 23 February, 1919 Died 1999						(CD)
Blackpool	Felling Red Star	05.38	38	2	-	0
York C	Tr	09.46	46	22	-	1
PARKE John						
Belfast, 6 August, 1937 IrLge-5/NI-14						(CD)
Sunderland	Hibernian	11.64	64-67	83	2	0
PARKER Albert Edward						
Liverpool, 13 September, 1927						(FB)
Crewe Alex	South Liverpool	12.48	48-51	113	-	0
Wrexham	Tr	11.51	51-58	216	-	1
PARKER Alexander (Alex) Hershaw						
Irvine, 2 August, 1935 Su23-6/SLge-9/S-15						(FB)
Everton	Falkirk	06.58	58-64	198	-	5
Southport	Tr	09.65	65-67	76	0	0
PARKER Brian Thomas						
Chorley, 4 August, 1955 ESemiPro						(G)
Crewe Alex	Jnrs	08.72	73	26	0	0
PARKER Carl						
Burnley, 25 March, 1971						(M)
Rochdale	Rossendale U	02.92	91-92	9	7	1
PARKER Henry **Clifford (Cliff)**						
Denaby, 6 September, 1913 Died 1983						(W)
Doncaster Rov	Denaby U	08.31	31-33	52	-	11
Portsmouth	Tr	12.33	33-50	242	-	57
PARKER Derek						
Wivenhoe, 23 June, 1926						(WH)
West Ham U	Grays Ath	10.44	46-56	199	-	9
Colchester U	Tr	03.57	56-60	130	-	1
PARKER Derrick						
Wallsend, 7 February, 1957						(F)
Burnley	App	02.74	74-75	5	1	2
Southend U	Tr	02.77	76-79	129	3	43
Barnsley	Tr	02.80	79-82	104	3	32
Oldham Ath	Tr	08.83	83-84	54	3	11
Doncaster Rov	L	12.84	84	5	0	1
Burnley	Tr	10.85	85-86	43	0	10
Rochdale	Haka Valkeakoski (Fin)	10.87	87	6	1	1
PARKER Garry Stuart						
Oxford, 7 September, 1965 EYth/Eu21-6/EB-1						(M)
Luton T	App	05.83	82-85	31	11	3
Hull C	Tr	02.86	85-87	82	2	8
Nottingham F	Tr	03.88	87-91	99	4	17
Aston Villa	Tr	11.91	91-94	91	4	13
Leicester C	Tr	02.95	94-98	89	25	10
PARKER Graham Sydney						
Coventry, 23 May, 1946 ESch						(M)
Aston Villa	App	05.63	63-67	16	1	1
Rotherham U	Tr	12.67	67	3	0	0
Lincoln C	Tr	07.68	68	4	1	0
Exeter C	Tr	03.69	68-73	180	1	12
Torquay U	Tr	05.74	74-75	41	2	3
PARKER Harold (Harry)						
Blackburn, 8 February, 1933						(W)
Blackburn Rov	Lower Darwen YC	08.51	51	3	-	0
PARKER Jeffrey (Jeff) Samuel						
Liverpool, 23 January, 1969						(M)
Crewe Alex	YT	07.87	87	7	3	0
PARKER John William						
Birkenhead, 5 July, 1925 Died 1988						(IF)
Everton	St Lawrence CYMS	12.48	50-55	167	-	82
Bury	Tr	05.56	56-58	82	-	43
PARKER Keigan						
Livingston, 8 June, 1982 Su21-1						(F)
Blackpool	St Johnstone	07.04	04	26	9	9
PARKER Kevin James						
Plymouth, 20 September, 1979						(F)
Norwich C	YT	06.99				
Torquay U	Tr	08.00	00-01	8	9	2
PARKER Martin Thomas						
Exeter, 18 October, 1970						(M)
Exeter C	YT	●	88	0	1	0
PARKER Neil						
Blackburn, 19 October, 1957						(FB)
Leeds U	App	10.75	77	0	1	0
PARKER Patrick (Pat) John						
Bow, Devon, 15 July, 1929						(CD)
Southampton	Newton Abbot	08.51	51-58	132	-	0
PARKER Paul Andrew						
West Ham, 4 April, 1964 EYth/Eu21-8/EB/E-19						(FB)
Fulham	App	04.82	80-86	140	13	2
Queens Park Rgrs	Tr	06.87	87-90	121	4	1
Manchester U	Tr	08.91	91-95	100	5	1
Derby Co	Tr	08.96	96	4	0	0
Sheffield U	Tr	11.96	96	7	3	0
Fulham	Tr	01.97	96	3	0	0
Chelsea	Tr	03.97	96	1	3	0
PARKER Raymond (Ray) Dennis						
Doncaster, 27 January, 1925						(FB)
Chesterfield	Thurcroft	02.45	47	14	-	0
Sheffield Wed	Tr	04.48	48	1	-	0
Bradford C	Buxton	06.51	51-52	41	-	1
PARKER Reginald (Reg) Ernest Arundel						
Pontyclun, 10 June, 1921 Died 1997 WLge-2						(CF)
Cardiff C		11.46	47	2	-	0
Newport Co	Tr	08.48	48-53	201	-	99
PARKER Richard John						
Wolverhampton, 6 July, 1973						(F)
Walsall	Cradley T	09.92	92	0	1	0
PARKER Robert (Bobby)						
Coventry, 11 November, 1952 EYth						(CD)
Coventry C	App	05.70	69-73	77	3	0
Carlisle U	Tr	06.74	74-83	373	2	6
PARKER Robert (Bob) William						
Seaham, 26 November, 1935						(FB)
Huddersfield T	Murton CW	06.54	59-64	65	-	0
Barnsley	Tr	07.65	65-68	108	0	0
PARKER Samuel (Sam)						
Liverpool, 5 April, 1924						(FB)
Accrington St	Marine	07.48	48	13	-	6
Barnsley	Tr	12.48				
Accrington St	Tr	09.49	49-50	36	-	6
Crewe Alex	Tr	11.50	50-51	41	-	5

PARKER Scott Matthew
Lambeth, 13 October, 1980 ESch/EYth/Eu21-12/E-2 (M)

League Club	Source	Date Signed	Seasons Played	Apps	Subs	Gls
Charlton Ath	YT	10.97	97-03	104	24	9
Norwich C	L	10.00	00	6	0	1
Chelsea	Tr	01.04	03-04	8	7	1

PARKER Sean
Newcastle, 23 August, 1973 (M)

League Club	Source	Date Signed	Seasons Played	Apps	Subs	Gls
Northampton T	YT	07.91	91-92	9	1	0

PARKER Sonny
Middlesbrough, 28 February, 1983 EYth (FB)

League Club	Source	Date Signed	Seasons Played	Apps	Subs	Gls
Birmingham C	YT	04.99				
Bristol Rov	Tr	12.02	02-03	26	4	1

PARKER Stanley (Stan) Frederick
Worksop, 31 July, 1920 Died 1994 (IF)

League Club	Source	Date Signed	Seasons Played	Apps	Subs	Gls
Ipswich T	Worksop Life Brig OB	05.46	46-50	126	-	43

PARKER Stuart John
Preston, 16 February, 1954 (F)

League Club	Source	Date Signed	Seasons Played	Apps	Subs	Gls
Blackpool	App	04.72	72-74	10	6	2
Southend U	Tr	07.75	75-76	62	2	23
Chesterfield	Tr	02.77	76-77	30	4	8
Blackburn Rov	Sparta Rotterdam (Holl)	07.79	79	5	4	1
Bury	Frecheville Comm (N/C)	09.82	82	26	8	9
Chester C	KV Mechelen (Bel)	09.83	83	9	0	5
Stockport Co	Drogheda	02.84	83	0	1	0

PARKER Stuart Kevin
Nantwich, 13 April, 1963 (G)

League Club	Source	Date Signed	Seasons Played	Apps	Subs	Gls
Wrexham	Jnrs	08.81	82-84	31	0	0

PARKER Terence (Terry) James
Southampton, 20 December, 1983 (M)

League Club	Source	Date Signed	Seasons Played	Apps	Subs	Gls
Portsmouth	Sch	03.03				
Oxford U	Tr	07.04	04	6	2	0

PARKER Thomas (Tommy) Robertson
Hartlepool, 13 February, 1924 Died 1996 (WH)

League Club	Source	Date Signed	Seasons Played	Apps	Subs	Gls
Ipswich T		08.46	46-56	428	-	86

PARKER Walter
Doncaster, 28 June, 1929 (FB)

League Club	Source	Date Signed	Seasons Played	Apps	Subs	Gls
Hull C	Jnrs	08.47				
Crewe Alex	Tr	08.51	51-55	59	-	0

PARKER Wesley (Wes) Jaye
Boston, 7 December, 1983 (FB)

League Club	Source	Date Signed	Seasons Played	Apps	Subs	Gls
Grimsby T	Sch	●	02-03	1	8	0

PARKER William (Bill)
Liverpool, 15 August, 1925 (IF)

League Club	Source	Date Signed	Seasons Played	Apps	Subs	Gls
Reading	Runcorn	06.50	50-52	32	-	6
Swindon T	Tr	02.53	52	10	-	0
Exeter C	Tr	07.53	53	18	-	2

PARKER William (Bill) Frederick
Clubmoor, 29 March, 1932 (CD)

League Club	Source	Date Signed	Seasons Played	Apps	Subs	Gls
Liverpool	Burscough	04.53				
Southport	Shelbourne	07.59	59	9	-	0

PARKER William Thomas
Bolsover, 6 October, 1920 Died 1953 (G)

League Club	Source	Date Signed	Seasons Played	Apps	Subs	Gls
Crewe Alex		07.47	47-48	18	-	0

PARKES Alan
Hartlepool, 12 January, 1929 (CF)

League Club	Source	Date Signed	Seasons Played	Apps	Subs	Gls
Charlton Ath	Murton CW	10.49				
Darlington	Tonbridge	03.55	54	1	-	0

PARKES Barry Joseph
Hartlepool, 21 January, 1940 (IF)

League Club	Source	Date Signed	Seasons Played	Apps	Subs	Gls
Hartlepools U	Easington CW	11.60	60-62	29	-	7

PARKES Henry (Harry) Arthur
Birmingham, 4 January, 1920 (FB)

League Club	Source	Date Signed	Seasons Played	Apps	Subs	Gls
Aston Villa	Boldmere St Michael's	04.39	46-54	320	-	3

PARKES Philip (Phil)
West Bromwich, 14 July, 1947 (G)

League Club	Source	Date Signed	Seasons Played	Apps	Subs	Gls
Wolverhampton W	Jnrs	09.64	66-77	303	0	0

PARKES Philip (Phil) Benjamin Neil Frederick
Sedgley, 8 August, 1950 Eu23-6/Eu21-1/EB/E-1 (G)

League Club	Source	Date Signed	Seasons Played	Apps	Subs	Gls
Walsall	Brierley Hill Alliance	01.68	68-69	52	0	0
Queens Park Rgrs	Tr	06.70	70-78	344	0	0
West Ham U	Tr	02.79	78-89	344	0	0
Ipswich T	Tr	08.90	90	3	0	0

PARKES Sidney (Sid)
Hartlepool, 20 September, 1919 Died 1989 (G)

League Club	Source	Date Signed	Seasons Played	Apps	Subs	Gls
Hartlepools U	Hetton U	08.46	46-47	6	-	0

PARKES Tony
Sheffield, 5 May, 1949 (M)

League Club	Source	Date Signed	Seasons Played	Apps	Subs	Gls
Blackburn Rov	Buxton	05.70	70-80	345	5	38

PARKHILL James Archibald
Belfast, 27 July, 1934 (G)

League Club	Source	Date Signed	Seasons Played	Apps	Subs	Gls
Exeter C	Cliftonville	09.63	63	1	-	0

PARKHOUSE Richard McDonald
Calne, 30 August, 1914 Died 1992 (FB)

League Club	Source	Date Signed	Seasons Played	Apps	Subs	Gls
Swindon T	Calne T	10.35	35-46	27	-	0

PARKIN Albert Geoffrey
Mansfield, 11 April, 1928 (CF)

League Club	Source	Date Signed	Seasons Played	Apps	Subs	Gls
Derby Co	Jnrs	05.46	49	9	-	0

PARKIN Brian
Birkenhead, 12 October, 1965 (G)

League Club	Source	Date Signed	Seasons Played	Apps	Subs	Gls
Oldham Ath	Jnrs	03.83	83-84	6	0	0
Crewe Alex	Tr	11.84	84-87	98	0	0
Crystal Palace	Tr	07.88	88-89	20	0	0
Bristol Rov	Tr	11.89	89-95	241	0	0
Wycombe W	Tr	07.96	96-97	25	0	0
Notts Co	Tr	10.98	98	1	0	0
Bristol Rov	Yeovil T	10.99	99-00	2	3	0

PARKIN Derek
Newcastle, 2 January, 1948 Eu23-5/FLge-1 (FB)

League Club	Source	Date Signed	Seasons Played	Apps	Subs	Gls
Huddersfield T	Jnrs	05.65	64-67	60	1	1
Wolverhampton W	Tr	02.68	67-81	500	1	6
Stoke C	Tr	03.82	81-82	40	0	0

PARKIN Herbert Buttery
Sheffield, 10 April, 1920 Died 1992 (FB)

League Club	Source	Date Signed	Seasons Played	Apps	Subs	Gls
Sheffield U	Atlas & Norfolk	04.42	47-50	35	-	0
Chesterfield	Tr	08.51	51-52	55	-	0

PARKIN Jonathan (Jon)
Barnsley, 30 December, 1981 (F)

League Club	Source	Date Signed	Seasons Played	Apps	Subs	Gls
Barnsley	YT	01.99	98-01	8	2	0
Hartlepool U	L	12.01	01	0	1	0
York C	Tr	02.02	01-03	64	10	14
Macclesfield T	Tr	02.04	03-04	54	0	23

PARKIN Maurice
Sheffield, 8 September, 1949 (FB)

League Club	Source	Date Signed	Seasons Played	Apps	Subs	Gls
Leeds U	App	10.67				
Shrewsbury T	Tr	07.68	68	4	1	0

PARKIN Samuel (Sam)
Roehampton, 14 March, 1981 ESch/SB-1 (F)

League Club	Source	Date Signed	Seasons Played	Apps	Subs	Gls
Chelsea	Jnrs	08.98				
Millwall	L	09.00	00	5	2	4
Wycombe W	L	11.00	00	5	3	1
Oldham Ath	L	03.01	00	3	4	3
Northampton T	L	07.01	01	31	9	4
Swindon T	Tr	08.02	02-04	120	4	67

PARKIN Stephen (Steve) John
Mansfield, 7 November, 1965 ESch/EYth/Eu21-5 (M)

League Club	Source	Date Signed	Seasons Played	Apps	Subs	Gls
Stoke C	App	11.83	82-88	104	9	5
West Bromwich A	Tr	06.89	89-91	44	4	2
Mansfield T	Tr	07.92	92-95	84	3	3

PARKIN Thomas (Tommy) Aitchison
Gateshead, 1 February, 1956 (M)

League Club	Source	Date Signed	Seasons Played	Apps	Subs	Gls
Ipswich T	App	12.73	77-86	52	18	0
Grimsby T	L	03.76	75	6	0	0
Peterborough U	L	07.76	76	3	0	0

PARKIN Timothy (Tim) John
Penrith, 31 December, 1957 (CD)

League Club	Source	Date Signed	Seasons Played	Apps	Subs	Gls
Blackburn Rov	App	03.76	76-78	13	0	0
Bristol Rov	Almondsbury Greenway	08.81	81-85	205	1	12
Swindon T	Tr	07.86	86-89	109	1	6
Port Vale	Tr	12.89	89-91	41	7	1
Shrewsbury T	L	09.91	91	5	0	0
Darlington	Tr	08.92	92	40	0	2

PARKINSON Alan
Normanton, 5 May, 1932 Died 2002 (CF)

League Club	Source	Date Signed	Seasons Played	Apps	Subs	Gls
Bradford PA	Jnrs	10.50	51-54	13	-	4

PARKINSON Alan
Dagenham, 12 April, 1945 (G)

League Club	Source	Date Signed	Seasons Played	Apps	Subs	Gls
Leyton Orient (Am)	Aveley	03.67	66	1	0	0

PARKINSON Alfred (Alf)
Camden Town, 30 April, 1922 Died 2003 (WH)

League Club	Source	Date Signed	Seasons Played	Apps	Subs	Gls
Queens Park Rgrs		09.43	46-50	76	-	5

PARKINSON Allan Arnold
Longton, Lancashire, 19 July, 1933 (FB)

League Club	Source	Date Signed	Seasons Played	Apps	Subs	Gls
Southport	Leyland Motors	08.53	53-58	106	-	0

PARKINSON Andrew (Andy) James
Johannesburg, South Africa, 5 May, 1959 (F)

League Club	Source	Date Signed	Seasons Played	Apps	Subs	Gls
Newcastle U	Highlands Park (SA)	03.78	77-78	0	3	0
Peterborough U	Tr	08.79	79	12	1	5

PARKINSON Andrew (Andy) John
Liverpool, 27 May, 1979 (W)

League Club	Source	Date Signed	Seasons Played	Apps	Subs	Gls
Tranmere Rov	Liverpool (YT)	04.97	97-02	102	62	18
Sheffield U	Tr	07.03	03	3	4	0
Notts Co	L	01.04	03	5	0	3
Notts Co	L	03.04	03	5	4	0
Grimsby T	Tr	07.04	04	43	2	8

PARKINSON Eric
Longridge, 14 December, 1930 (WH)

League Club	Source	Date Signed	Seasons Played	Apps	Subs	Gls
Preston NE	Longridge U	02.51				
Southport	Tr	06.56	57	4	-	0

PARKINSON Gary Anthony
Thornaby, 10 January, 1968 (FB)

League Club	Source	Date Signed	Seasons Played	Apps	Subs	Gls
Middlesbrough	Everton (Jnrs)	01.86	86-92	194	8	5
Southend U	L	10.92	92	6	0	0
Bolton W	Tr	03.93	92-93	1	2	0
Burnley	Tr	01.94	93-96	134	1	4
Preston NE	Tr	05.97	97-00	82	2	6
Blackpool	Tr	03.01	00-01	22	2	0

PARKINSON John
Trimdon, 2 June, 1953 (M)

League Club	Source	Date Signed	Seasons Played	Apps	Subs	Gls
Hartlepool U (Am)	Trimdon Village	09.71	71	1	0	0

PARKINSON Joseph (Joe) Simon
Eccles, 11 June, 1971 (M)

League Club	Source	Date Signed	Seasons Played	Apps	Subs	Gls
Wigan Ath	YT	04.89	88-92	115	4	6
Bournemouth	Tr	07.93	93	30	0	1
Everton	Tr	03.94	94-96	88	2	3

PARKINSON Keith James
Preston, 28 January, 1956 (CD)

League Club	Source	Date Signed	Seasons Played	Apps	Subs	Gls
Leeds U	App	02.73	75-80	25	6	0
Hull C	L	11.81	81	0	1	0
Doncaster Rov	Tr	01.82	81	5	0	0

PARKINSON Noel David
Hull, 16 November, 1959 EYth (M)

League Club	Source	Date Signed	Seasons Played	Apps	Subs	Gls
Ipswich T	App	12.76				
Bristol Rov	L	11.79	79	5	0	1
Brentford	L	02.80	79	9	1	0
Mansfield T	Tr	07.80	80-81	66	4	13
Scunthorpe U	Tr	08.82	82-83	39	2	7
Colchester U	Tr	08.84	84-85	79	0	13

PARKINSON Philip (Phil) John
Chorley, 1 December, 1967 (M)

League Club	Source	Date Signed	Seasons Played	Apps	Subs	Gls
Southampton	App	12.85				
Bury	Tr	03.88	87-91	133	12	5
Reading	Tr	07.92	92-02	332	30	20

PARKINSON Stephen (Steve)
Lincoln, 27 August, 1974 (M)

League Club	Source	Date Signed	Seasons Played	Apps	Subs	Gls
Lincoln C	YT	05.93	92-93	1	4	0

PARKINSON Stuart George
Fleetwood, 18 February, 1976 (M)

League Club	Source	Date Signed	Seasons Played	Apps	Subs	Gls
Blackpool	Preston NE (YT)	03.94	94	0	1	0

PARKS Albert
Lurgan, 9 February, 1926 (W)

League Club	Source	Date Signed	Seasons Played	Apps	Subs	Gls
Notts Co	Glenavon	11.45	46-47	30	-	4

PARKS Anthony (Tony)
Hackney, 28 January, 1963 (G)

League Club	Source	Date Signed	Seasons Played	Apps	Subs	Gls
Tottenham H	App	09.80	81-87	37	0	0
Oxford U	L	10.86	86	5	0	0
Gillingham	L	09.87	87	2	0	0
Brentford	Tr	08.88	88-90	71	0	0
Fulham	Tr	02.91	90	2	0	0
West Ham U	Tr	08.91	91	6	0	0
Stoke C	Tr	08.92	92	2	0	0
Blackpool	Falkirk	09.96				
Burnley	Tr	08.97				
Doncaster Rov	L	02.98	97	6	0	0
Scarborough	Barrow	02.99	98	15	0	0
Halifax T	Tr	07.99	99-00	5	1	0

PARKS John Alfred
Wath-on-Dearne, 14 September, 1943 (F)

League Club	Source	Date Signed	Seasons Played	Apps	Subs	Gls
Sheffield U	App	11.60	63	1	-	0
Halifax T	Tr	09.66	66-67	41	0	14

PARLANE Derek James
Helensburgh, 5 May, 1953 Su23-5/Su21-1/SLge-2/S-12 (F)

League Club	Source	Date Signed	Seasons Played	Apps	Subs	Gls
Leeds U	Glasgow Rgrs	03.80	79-82	45	5	10
Manchester C	Bulova (HK)	08.83	83-84	47	1	20
Swansea C	Tr	01.85	84	21	0	3
Rochdale	Racing Jet (Bel)	12.86	86-87	42	0	10

PARLOUR Raymond (Ray)
Romford, 7 March, 1973 Eu21-12/EB-1/E-10 (M)

League Club	Source	Date Signed	Seasons Played	Apps	Subs	Gls
Arsenal	YT	03.91	91-03	282	57	22
Middlesbrough	Tr	07.04	04	32	1	0

PARMENTER Steven (Steve) James
Chelmsford, 22 January, 1977 (W)

League Club	Source	Date Signed	Seasons Played	Apps	Subs	Gls
Queens Park Rgrs	Southend U (YT)	05.95				
Bristol Rov	Tr	07.96	96-97	11	7	2

PARMENTER Terence (Terry) Leslie
Romford, 21 October, 1947 (W)

League Club	Source	Date Signed	Seasons Played	Apps	Subs	Gls
Fulham	App	11.64	64-68	18	0	1
Orient	Tr	02.69	68-70	34	3	3
Gillingham	Tr	08.71	71-72	48	1	0

PARNABY Stuart
Bishop Auckland, 19 July, 1982 ESch/EYth/Eu20/Eu21-4 (FB)

League Club	Source	Date Signed	Seasons Played	Apps	Subs	Gls
Middlesbrough	YT	07.99	02-04	45	8	0
Halifax T	L	10.00	00	6	0	0

PARNABY Thomas (Tom) William
South Shields, 6 January, 1922 (IF)

League Club	Source	Date Signed	Seasons Played	Apps	Subs	Gls
Plymouth Arg		07.39				
Oldham Ath	Tr	02.47	47	7	-	1

PARNELL Denis Russell
Farnborough, 17 January, 1940 EYth (W)

League Club	Source	Date Signed	Seasons Played	Apps	Subs	Gls
Aldershot	West Bromwich A (Am)	08.58	58-60	66	-	11
Norwich C	Tr	07.61	61	2	-	0

PARNELL Francis (Frank) William
Birkenhead, 4 November, 1935 (CF)

League Club	Source	Date Signed	Seasons Played	Apps	Subs	Gls
Tranmere Rov		01.56	55-56	4	-	3

PARNELL Roy
Birkenhead, 8 October, 1943 (W)

League Club	Source	Date Signed	Seasons Played	Apps	Subs	Gls
Everton	Jnrs	10.60	60-63	3	-	0
Tranmere Rov	Tr	08.64	64-66	105	0	2
Bury	Tr	02.67	66-69	97	0	2

PARODI Leslie (Les) Vincent
Lambeth, 1 April, 1954 (FB)

League Club	Source	Date Signed	Seasons Played	Apps	Subs	Gls
Bournemouth	Slough T	09.72	73-74	45	4	2

PARR Gordon John
Bristol, 6 December, 1938 (CD)

League Club	Source	Date Signed	Seasons Played	Apps	Subs	Gls
Bristol C	Jnrs	02.57	57-71	281	6	4

PARR Henry (Harry)
Newark, 23 October, 1915 EAmat (IF)

League Club	Source	Date Signed	Seasons Played	Apps	Subs	Gls
Lincoln C (Am)	Ransome & Marles	08.46	46-50	112	-	13

PARR Jack (Jackie)
Derby, 21 November, 1920 Died 1985 (FB)

League Club	Source	Date Signed	Seasons Played	Apps	Subs	Gls
Derby Co	Holbrook St Michael's	03.38	46-52	112	-	0
Shrewsbury T	Tr	07.53	53-55	112	-	0

PARR John Barry
Weston-super-Mare, 23 November, 1942 (G)

League Club	Source	Date Signed	Seasons Played	Apps	Subs	Gls
Nottingham F	Ransome & Marles	11.62	63	1	-	0

PARR Stephen (Steve) Valentine
Bamber Bridge, 22 December, 1926 (FB)

League Club	Source	Date Signed	Seasons Played	Apps	Subs	Gls
Liverpool	Farington Villa	05.48	51-52	20	-	0
Exeter C	Tr	05.55	55-56	8	-	0
Rochdale	Tr	12.56	56-57	16	-	1

PARR Trevor William
Bradford, 21 December, 1961 (F)

League Club	Source	Date Signed	Seasons Played	Apps	Subs	Gls
Birmingham C	App	12.79				
Bradford C	Tr	07.80				
Huddersfield T	Tr	11.80				
Peterborough U	Boston U	11.84	84	0	1	0

PARRIS George Michael
Ilford, 11 September, 1964 ESch (M)

League Club	Source	Date Signed	Seasons Played	Apps	Subs	Gls
West Ham U	App	09.82	84-92	211	28	12
Birmingham C	Tr	03.93	92-94	36	3	1
Brentford	L	08.94	94	5	0	0
Bristol C	L	12.94	94	6	0	0
Brighton & Hove A	L	02.95	94	18	0	2
Brighton & Hove A	Norrkoping (Swe)	09.95	95-96	55	1	3
Southend U	Tr	08.97	97	1	0	0

League Club	Source	Date Signed	Seasons Played	Career Record Apps	Subs	Gls
PARRISH Donald (Don) Arthur						
Bilston, 22 November, 1944						(IF)
Wrexham	Jnrs	06.63	62-65	4	0	0
PARRISH Sean						
Wrexham, 14 March, 1972						(M)
Shrewsbury T	YT	07.90	89-90	1	2	0
Doncaster Rov	Telford U	05.94	94-95	64	2	8
Northampton T	Tr	08.96	96-99	103	6	13
Chesterfield	Tr	07.00	00-01	44	11	11
Kidderminster Hrs	Tr	07.02	02-03	37	19	8
PARROTT John Frank						
Scunthorpe, 5 June, 1934						(IF)
Scunthorpe U		12.55	55	1	-	0
PARRY Anthony (Tony) John						
Burton-on-Trent, 8 September, 1945						(CD)
Hartlepools U	Burton A	11.65	65-71	181	8	5
Derby Co	Tr	01.72	72	4	2	0
Mansfield T	L	01.74	73	0	1	0
PARRY Colin						
Stockport, 16 February, 1941						(CD)
Stockport Co	Vernon Park	07.62	62-67	132	1	0
Bradford C	L	09.65	65	5	0	0
Rochdale	Tr	07.68	68-71	155	2	1
PARRY Cyril						
Derby, 13 December, 1937 ESch						(W)
Notts Co	Derby Co (Am)	05.55	57-58	12	-	2
PARRY David (Dave) Edward						
Southport, 11 February, 1948						(W)
Blackpool	App	12.65				
Tranmere Rov	Tr	07.67	67	3	0	0
Halifax T	Tr	09.68	68	2	0	0
PARRY John (Jack)						
Derby, 29 July, 1931						(IF)
Derby Co	Jnrs	07.48	48-65	482	1	105
PARRY Brinley **John (Jack)**						
Pontardawe, 11 January, 1924 W-1						(G)
Swansea T	Clydach	09.46	46-50	96	-	0
Ipswich T	Tr	08.51	51-54	138	-	0
PARRY John Ernan						
Holywell, 4 September, 1939						(FB)
Liverpool	Jnrs	09.56				
Doncaster Rov	Tr	09.61	61	14	-	0
PARRY Leslie (Les) Irvine						
Wallasey, 13 November, 1953						(CD)
Tranmere Rov	Jnrs	09.72	72-83	254	4	4
PARRY Mark						
Wrexham, 21 May, 1970						(W)
Chester C	YT	●	87	4	1	1
PARRY Oswald (Ossie)						
Dowlais, 16 August, 1908 Died 1991						(FB)
Crystal Palace	Wimbledon	05.31	31-35	141	-	0
Ipswich T	Tr	06.36	38-48	104	-	0
PARRY Paul Ian						
Chepstow, 19 August, 1980 W-4						(M)
Cardiff C	Hereford U	01.04	03-04	26	15	5
PARRY Raymond (Ray) Alan						
Derby, 19 January, 1936 Died 2003 ESch/EYth/Eu23-4/FLge-2/E-2						(M)
Bolton W	Jnrs	01.53	51-60	270	-	68
Blackpool	Tr	10.60	60-64	128	-	27
Bury	Tr	10.64	64-71	137	10	17
PARRY Stephen (Steve)						
Upton, West Yorkshire, 11 December, 1956						(G)
Barnsley	App	12.74	73-74	5	0	0
PARRY William (Bill)						
Blaenau Ffestiniog, 18 February, 1933						(FB)
Tottenham H	Portmadoc	09.53				
Gillingham	Tr	07.55	55-60	200	-	4
PARSELLE Norman John						
Newport, 8 January, 1970						(M)
Newport Co	YT	●	87	4	6	0
PARSLEY Neil Robert						
Liverpool, 25 April, 1966						(FB)
Leeds U	Witton A	11.88				
Chester C	L	12.89	89	6	0	0
Huddersfield T	Tr	07.90	90-92	55	2	0

League Club	Source	Date Signed	Seasons Played	Career Record Apps	Subs	Gls
Doncaster Rov	L	02.91	90	2	1	0
West Bromwich A	Tr	09.93	93-94	38	5	0
Exeter C	Tr	08.95	95	29	3	0
PARSLEY Wilfred **Norman**						
Shildon, 28 November, 1923 Died 1993						(WH)
Darlington	Shildon	10.45	46-52	161	-	14
PARSONS David (Dave)						
Greenwich, 25 February, 1982						(M)
Leyton Orient	YT	07.00	99	1	0	0
PARSONS Dennis Ronald						
Birmingham, 29 May, 1925 Died 1980						(G)
Wolverhampton W	BSA Cycles	11.44	48-51	23	-	0
Aston Villa	Hereford U	09.52	52-54	36	-	0
PARSONS Derek John						
Hammersmith, 24 October, 1929						(WH)
Queens Park Rgrs		02.50	52	2	-	1
PARSONS Edward (Ted) John						
Bristol, 22 March, 1928 Died 1996						(CF)
Bristol Rov	Frome T	08.49	49	5	-	2
PARSONS Eric George						
Worthing, 9 November, 1923 EB						(W)
West Ham U	Jnrs	10.43	46-50	145	-	34
Chelsea	Tr	12.50	50-56	158	-	37
Brentford	Tr	11.56	56-60	118	-	18
PARSONS Frank Ronald						
Amersham, 29 October, 1947						(G)
Crystal Palace	Jnrs	07.65	66	4	0	0
Cardiff C	Tr	08.70	70-72	17	0	0
Reading	Tr	09.74	74	1	0	0
PARSONS Geoffrey (Geoff) Roy						
Belper, 2 August, 1931 Died 1996						(W)
Mansfield T	Jnrs	05.51				
Chesterfield	Tr	07.52	52	1	-	0
PARSONS John Stuart						
Cardiff, 10 December, 1950 WSch						(F)
Cardiff C	App	12.68	70-72	7	8	6
Bournemouth	Tr	02.73	72-74	6	1	1
Newport Co	Tr	03.75	74-76	57	3	22
PARSONS Lindsay William						
Bristol, 20 March, 1946						(FB)
Bristol Rov	App	04.64	63-76	354	5	0
Torquay U	Tr	08.77	77-78	56	0	0
PARSONS Mark Christopher						
Luton, 24 February, 1975						(FB)
Northampton T	YT	07.93	91-93	51	0	0
PARSONS Stephen (Steve) Paul James						
Hammersmith, 7 October, 1957						(M)
Wimbledon	Walton & Hersham	12.77	77-79	91	3	19
Orient	Tr	03.80	79-80	36	0	6
PARSONS Stuart						
Staveley, 24 May, 1948						(IF)
Chesterfield	Jnrs	08.67	66	1	0	0
PARTNER Andrew (Andy) Neil						
Colchester, 21 October, 1974						(CD)
Colchester U	YT	06.93	92-94	0	2	0
PARTON Andrew (Andy)						
Doncaster, 29 September, 1983						(M)
Scunthorpe U	Sch	07.03	01-04	1	12	0
PARTON Jeffrey (Jeff) John						
Swansea, 24 February, 1953 WSch/Wu23-3						(G)
Burnley	App	03.70	71-73	3	0	0
Northampton T	Tr	07.75	75-77	25	0	0
PARTRIDGE Brendan (Don) David						
Manchester, 17 September, 1941						(W)
Stockport Co		11.60	60-61	31	-	6
Darlington	Tr	07.62	62	3	-	0
PARTRIDGE Cyril						
York, 12 October, 1931						(W)
Queens Park Rgrs		08.54				
Rotherham U		08.57	57	7	-	2
PARTRIDGE David William						
Westminster, 26 November, 1978 W-2						(FB)
West Ham U	YT	07.97				
Leyton Orient (L)	Dundee U	01.02	01	6	1	0

PARTRIDGE Donald (Don)
Bolton, 22 October, 1925 Died 2003 (WH)

League Club	Source	Date Signed	Seasons Played	Apps	Subs	Gls
Rochdale	Farnworth	10.45	46-55	103	-	2

PARTRIDGE John Thomas
Chesterfield, 14 September, 1962 (FB)

League Club	Source	Date Signed	Seasons Played	Apps	Subs	Gls
Chesterfield	App	09.80	81-82	34	4	0
Mansfield T	L	09.83	83	1	0	0

PARTRIDGE Malcolm
Calow, 28 August, 1950 ESch (F)

League Club	Source	Date Signed	Seasons Played	Apps	Subs	Gls
Mansfield T	App	09.68	67-70	65	2	20
Leicester C	Tr	09.70	70-73	24	12	4
Charlton Ath	L	01.72	71	1	1	0
Grimsby T	Tr	03.75	74-78	134	4	25
Scunthorpe U	Tr	07.79	79-81	91	6	21

PARTRIDGE Maurice Edward
Birmingham, 20 February, 1941 (FB)

League Club	Source	Date Signed	Seasons Played	Apps	Subs	Gls
Birmingham C	Jnrs	03.58				
Walsall	Tr	07.61	61-62	3	-	0

PARTRIDGE Richard (Richie) Joseph
Dublin, 12 September, 1980 IRYth/IRu21-8 (W)

League Club	Source	Date Signed	Seasons Played	Apps	Subs	Gls
Liverpool	YT	09.97				
Bristol Rov	L	03.01	00	4	2	1
Coventry C	L	09.02	02	23	4	4

PARTRIDGE Scott Malcolm
Leicester, 13 October, 1974 (F)

League Club	Source	Date Signed	Seasons Played	Apps	Subs	Gls
Bradford C	YT	07.92	92-93	0	5	0
Bristol C	Tr	02.94	93-96	24	33	7
Torquay U	L	10.95	95	5	0	2
Plymouth Arg	L	01.96	95	6	1	2
Scarborough	L	03.96	95	5	2	0
Cardiff C	Tr	02.97	96-97	29	8	2
Torquay U	Tr	03.98	97-98	33	1	12
Brentford	Tr	02.99	98-01	79	13	21
Rushden & Diamonds	Tr	09.01	01-02	28	16	5
Exeter C	L	12.02	02	2	2	2
Shrewsbury T	Tr	03.03	02	2	2	0

PASANEN Petri Mikael
Lahti, Finland, 24 September, 1980 FIYth/Fiu21-6/Fi-20 (FB)

League Club	Source	Date Signed	Seasons Played	Apps	Subs	Gls
Portsmouth (L)	Ajax (Holl)	01.04	03	11	1	0

PASCOE Colin James
Port Talbot, 9 April, 1965 WSch/WYth/Wu21-4/W-10 (W)

League Club	Source	Date Signed	Seasons Played	Apps	Subs	Gls
Swansea C	App	04.83	82-87	167	7	39
Sunderland	Tr	03.88	87-91	116	10	22
Swansea C	L	07.92	92	15	0	4
Swansea C	Tr	08.93	93-95	72	9	11
Blackpool	Tr	03.96	95	0	1	0

PASCOE Jason
Jarrow, 15 February, 1970 (FB)

League Club	Source	Date Signed	Seasons Played	Apps	Subs	Gls
Northampton T	Clipstone CW	06.94	94	11	4	0

PASCOLO Marco
Sion, Switzerland, 9 May, 1966 Switzerland int (G)

League Club	Source	Date Signed	Seasons Played	Apps	Subs	Gls
Nottingham F	Cagliari (It)	06.97	97	5	0	0

PASHLEY Robert Wilminson
Sheffield, 9 September, 1937 (W)

League Club	Source	Date Signed	Seasons Played	Apps	Subs	Gls
Sheffield U	Sheffield Wed (Am)	01.56				
Scunthorpe U	Gainsborough Trinity	05.59	59	3	-	1
Barrow	Tr	06.60	60	26	-	2

PASHLEY Terence (Terry)
Chesterfield, 11 October, 1956 ESch (FB)

League Club	Source	Date Signed	Seasons Played	Apps	Subs	Gls
Burnley	App	10.73	75-77	16	2	0
Blackpool	Tr	08.78	78-82	201	0	7
Bury	Tr	08.83	83-88	205	12	5

PASKIN William **John**
Cape Town, South Africa, 1 February, 1962 (F)

League Club	Source	Date Signed	Seasons Played	Apps	Subs	Gls
West Bromwich A	Seiko (HK)	08.88	88	14	11	5
Wolverhampton W	Tr	06.89	89-91	21	13	3
Stockport Co	L	09.91	91	3	2	1
Birmingham C	L	11.91	91	8	2	3
Shrewsbury T	L	02.92	91	1	0	0
Wrexham	Tr	02.92	91-93	28	23	11
Bury	Tr	07.94	94-95	15	23	8

PASSEY Peter Thord John
Birmingham, 13 July, 1952 EYth (FB)

League Club	Source	Date Signed	Seasons Played	Apps	Subs	Gls
Birmingham C	App	07.69				
Newport Co	Tr	01.72	71-75	136	0	2

PASSI Franck
Bergerac, France, 28 March, 1966 Fru21 (M)

League Club	Source	Date Signed	Seasons Played	Apps	Subs	Gls
Bolton W	Compostella (Sp)	11.99	99-00	21	17	0

PASSMOOR Thomas (Tom)
Chester-le-Street, 12 February, 1937 Died 1991 (CD)

League Club	Source	Date Signed	Seasons Played	Apps	Subs	Gls
Sunderland	Jnrs	05.54				
Scunthorpe U	South Shields	05.59	59-63	27	-	0
Carlisle U	Tr	12.63	63-69	241	2	0

PASSMORE Edward (Ernie)
Hetton-le-Hole, 28 April, 1922 Died 1988 (CF)

League Club	Source	Date Signed	Seasons Played	Apps	Subs	Gls
Swansea T	Portsmouth (Am)	02.44	46	6	-	2
Gateshead	Tr	04.47	46-49	41	-	26

PASTON Mark
Hastings, New Zealand, 13 December, 1976 New Zealand 7 (G)

League Club	Source	Date Signed	Seasons Played	Apps	Subs	Gls
Bradford C	Napier C Rgrs (NZ)	08.03	03	13	0	0
Walsall	Tr	06.04	04	8	1	0

PATCHING Martin
Rotherham, 1 November, 1958 ESch/EYth (M)

League Club	Source	Date Signed	Seasons Played	Apps	Subs	Gls
Wolverhampton W	App	03.76	75-79	78	12	10
Watford	Tr	12.79	79-83	24	1	3
Northampton T	L	01.83	82	6	0	1

PATE Alexander (Sandy) Montgomerie
Lennoxtown, 15 August, 1944 (FB)

League Club	Source	Date Signed	Seasons Played	Apps	Subs	Gls
Watford	Renfrew Jnrs	03.65	64-66	14	1	0
Mansfield T	Tr	10.67	67-77	412	1	2

PATERSON Alexander (Alex)
Hardgate, 18 March, 1922 Died 1992 (WH)

League Club	Source	Date Signed	Seasons Played	Apps	Subs	Gls
New Brighton	Alloa Ath	07.46	46-47	67	-	10
Stockport Co	Tr	03.48	47-52	160	-	7

PATERSON George Denholm
Denny, 26 September, 1914 Died 1985 SLge-2/SWar-3/S-1 (WH)

League Club	Source	Date Signed	Seasons Played	Apps	Subs	Gls
Brentford	Glasgow Celtic	10.46	46-49	62	-	0

PATERSON George Longmore
Aberdeen, 19 December, 1916 Died 1996 (IF)

League Club	Source	Date Signed	Seasons Played	Apps	Subs	Gls
Liverpool	Hall, Russell & Co	05.37	38	2	-	0
Swindon T	Tr	10.46	46-49	53	-	6

PATERSON Jamie Ryan
Dumfries, 26 April, 1973 (W)

League Club	Source	Date Signed	Seasons Played	Apps	Subs	Gls
Halifax T	YT	07.91	90-92	34	10	5
Scunthorpe U	Falkirk	10.95	95-96	34	21	2
Halifax T	Tr	07.97	98-99	56	8	17
Doncaster Rov	Tr	07.00	03	7	1	1

PATERSON Martin Andrew
Tunstall, 13 May, 1987 (F)

League Club	Source	Date Signed	Seasons Played	Apps	Subs	Gls
Stoke C	Sch	•	04	0	3	0

PATERSON Scott Thomas
Aberdeen, 13 May, 1972 (CD)

League Club	Source	Date Signed	Seasons Played	Apps	Subs	Gls
Liverpool	Cove Rgrs	03.92				
Bristol C	Tr	07.94	94-97	40	10	1
Cardiff C	L	11.97	97	5	0	0
Carlisle U	Tr	07.98	98	18	1	1
Cambridge U	Tr	09.99	99	6	0	0
Plymouth Arg	Tr	03.00	99	5	0	0

PATERSON Sean Patrick
Greenock, 26 March, 1987 (F)

League Club	Source	Date Signed	Seasons Played	Apps	Subs	Gls
Blackpool	Sch	•	04	0	2	0

PATERSON Steven (Steve) William
Elgin, 8 April, 1958 (CD)

League Club	Source	Date Signed	Seasons Played	Apps	Subs	Gls
Manchester U	Nairn County	07.75	76-79	3	3	0

PATERSON Thomas (Tommy)
Lochore, 3 April, 1927 (IF)

League Club	Source	Date Signed	Seasons Played	Apps	Subs	Gls
Leicester C	Lochgelly Albert	03.48	48-49	17	-	4
Newcastle U	Tr	06.50	50-51	2	-	0
Watford	Tr	07.52	52-54	45	-	7

PATERSON Thomas (Tommy)
Ashington, 30 March, 1954 (F)

League Club	Source	Date Signed	Seasons Played	Apps	Subs	Gls
Middlesbrough	Leicester C (Am)	09.74	74	1	0	0
Bournemouth	Tr	04.76	76-77	45	12	10
Darlington	Tr	06.78	78	6	1	2

PATERSON Toby Lee
Dumfries, 15 May, 1971 (CD)

League Club	Source	Date Signed	Seasons Played	Apps	Subs	Gls
Halifax T	YT	•	88	0	1	0

PATERSON William (Billy)
Bellshill, 6 October, 1927 (CF)

League Club	Source	Date Signed	Seasons Played	Apps	Subs	Gls
Accrington St	Morton	08.49	49	1	-	0

PATERSON William (Bill) Alexander Kennedy
Kinlochleven, 25 February, 1930 Died 2002 SB (CD)

League Club	Source	Date Signed	Seasons Played	Apps	Subs	Gls
Doncaster Rov	Ransome & Marles	03.50	50-54	113	-	0
Newcastle U	Tr	10.54	54-57	22	-	1

PATES Colin George
Carshalton, 10 August, 1961 EYth (CD)

League Club	Source	Date Signed	Seasons Played	Apps	Subs	Gls
Chelsea	App	07.79	79-88	280	1	10
Charlton Ath	Tr	10.88	88-89	37	1	0
Arsenal	Tr	01.90	89-92	12	9	0
Brighton & Hove A	L	03.91	90	17	0	0
Brighton & Hove A	Tr	08.93	93-94	49	1	0

PATMORE Warren James
Kingsbury, 14 August, 1971 ESemiPro-7 (F)

League Club	Source	Date Signed	Seasons Played	Apps	Subs	Gls
Cambridge U	Northwood	03.92	92	1	0	0
Millwall	Bashley	08.93	93	0	1	0
Northampton T	Tr	12.93	93-94	12	9	2
Rushden & Diamonds	Yeovil T	06.01	01	4	0	1

PATON David (Dave) Samuel Craig
Saltcoats, 13 December, 1943 (CD)

League Club	Source	Date Signed	Seasons Played	Apps	Subs	Gls
Southampton	St Mirren	07.63	63-67	13	0	0
Aldershot	Tr	11.69	69-70	30	0	0

PATON John (Johnny) Aloysius
Glasgow, 2 April, 1923 (W)

League Club	Source	Date Signed	Seasons Played	Apps	Subs	Gls
Chelsea	Glasgow Celtic	11.46	46	18	-	3
Brentford	Glasgow Celtic	09.49	49-51	90	-	14
Watford	Tr	07.52	52-54	84	-	17

PATON Robert (Danny) Simpson Reid
West Calder, 27 January, 1936 (IF)

League Club	Source	Date Signed	Seasons Played	Apps	Subs	Gls
Oxford U	Heart of Midlothian	07.64	64	2	-	1

PATON Thomas (Tommy) Gracie
Saltcoats, 22 December, 1918 Died 1991 (WH)

League Club	Source	Date Signed	Seasons Played	Apps	Subs	Gls
Wolverhampton W	Ardeer Thistle	06.37				
Swansea T	Tr	10.38	38	6	-	0
Bournemouth	Tr	02.39	38-47	46	-	8
Watford	Tr	01.48	47-51	141	-	1

PATRICK Alfred (Alf)
York, 25 September, 1921 (CF)

League Club	Source	Date Signed	Seasons Played	Apps	Subs	Gls
York C	Cooks	09.46	46-52	228	-	109

PATRICK Bert (Bertie)
Kilsyth, 26 April, 1946 (FB)

League Club	Source	Date Signed	Seasons Played	Apps	Subs	Gls
Preston NE	Stirling A	08.63	64-69	50	0	1
Barrow	Tr	07.71	71	34	0	1

PATRICK Matthew (Matt)
Slamannan, 13 June, 1919 Died 2005 (W)

League Club	Source	Date Signed	Seasons Played	Apps	Subs	Gls
York C	Cowdenbeath	09.40	46-53	248	-	47

PATRICK Roy
Overseal, 4 December, 1935 Died 1998 (FB)

League Club	Source	Date Signed	Seasons Played	Apps	Subs	Gls
Derby Co	Jnrs	02.52	52-55	49	-	0
Nottingham F	Tr	05.59	59-60	57	-	0
Southampton	Tr	06.61	61-62	31	-	0
Exeter C	Tr	03.63	62-64	50	-	0

PATRICK William (Bill) Cecil Gibson
Lochgelly, 12 March, 1932 Died 2003 (FB)

League Club	Source	Date Signed	Seasons Played	Apps	Subs	Gls
Coventry C	Snowdown CW	11.54	55-57	44	-	6
Gillingham	Tr	06.58	58-59	47	-	14

PATTERSON Darren James
Belfast, 15 October, 1969 NIYth/NIu21-1/NIB-3/NI-17 (CD)

League Club	Source	Date Signed	Seasons Played	Apps	Subs	Gls
West Bromwich A	YT	07.88				
Wigan Ath	Tr	04.89	89-91	69	28	6
Crystal Palace	Tr	07.92	94	22	0	1
Luton T	Tr	08.95	95-97	52	4	0
Preston NE	L	10.96	96	2	0	0
York C	Dundee U	12.00	00	4	2	0
Oxford U	Tr	02.01	00-01	20	0	1

PATTERSON Gary
Newcastle, 27 November, 1972 (M)

League Club	Source	Date Signed	Seasons Played	Apps	Subs	Gls
Notts Co	YT	07.91				
Shrewsbury T	Tr	07.93	93-94	52	5	2
Wycombe W	Tr	12.94	94-96	46	13	2
Barnet	L	01.97	96	3	0	0
Chesterfield	L	02.97	96	7	2	0

PATTERSON George Thomas
Castleton, North Yorkshire, 15 September, 1934 (WH)

League Club	Source	Date Signed	Seasons Played	Apps	Subs	Gls
Hull C	Silksworth Jnrs	10.52	54-55	7	-	1
York C	South Shields	05.57	57-59	57	-	4
Hartlepools U	Tr	06.60	60	18	-	1

PATTERSON Ian Daniel
Chatham, 4 April, 1973 (CD)

League Club	Source	Date Signed	Seasons Played	Apps	Subs	Gls
Sunderland	YT	03.92				
Burnley	Tr	08.93	93	0	1	0
Wigan Ath	Tr	03.94	93	2	2	0

PATTERSON John (Jack) George
Cramlington, 6 July, 1922 Died 2002 (G)

League Club	Source	Date Signed	Seasons Played	Apps	Subs	Gls
Blackburn Rov	North Shields	04.45	48-56	107	-	0

PATTERSON Mark
Leeds, 13 September, 1968 (FB)

League Club	Source	Date Signed	Seasons Played	Apps	Subs	Gls
Carlisle U	App	08.86	86-87	19	3	0
Derby Co	Tr	11.87	88-92	41	10	3
Plymouth Arg	Tr	07.93	93-96	131	3	3
Gillingham	Tr	10.97	97-02	118	6	2

PATTERSON Mark Andrew
Darwen, 24 May, 1965 (M)

League Club	Source	Date Signed	Seasons Played	Apps	Subs	Gls
Blackburn Rov	App	05.83	83-87	89	12	20
Preston NE	Tr	06.88	88-89	54	1	19
Bury	Tr	02.90	89-90	42	0	10
Bolton W	Tr	01.91	90-95	158	11	11
Sheffield U	Tr	12.95	95-97	72	2	4
Southend U	L	03.97	96	4	0	0
Bury	Tr	12.97	97-98	27	4	2
Blackpool	L	12.98	98	7	0	0
Southend U	Tr	03.99	98	5	0	0

PATTERSON Robert Alexander
Newcastle, 12 March, 1935 (G)

League Club	Source	Date Signed	Seasons Played	Apps	Subs	Gls
Gateshead	Stanley U	03.59	58-59	26	-	0

PATTERSON Ronald (Ron) Lindsay
Seaham, 30 October, 1929 (FB)

League Club	Source	Date Signed	Seasons Played	Apps	Subs	Gls
Middlesbrough	Whitehall Jnrs	06.49	51	1	-	0
Northampton T	Tr	06.52	52-61	300	-	5

PATTERSON Rory Christopher
Derry, 16 July, 1984 (M)

League Club	Source	Date Signed	Seasons Played	Apps	Subs	Gls
Rochdale	Sch	●	02-03	5	10	0

PATTERSON Simon George
Northwick Park, 4 September, 1982 (F)

League Club	Source	Date Signed	Seasons Played	Apps	Subs	Gls
Watford	Wembley	09.00				
Wycombe W	L	07.03	03	3	1	2

PATTIMORE Michael Richard
Newport, 15 March, 1979 WYth (M)

League Club	Source	Date Signed	Seasons Played	Apps	Subs	Gls
Swindon T	YT	07.97	96-97	0	3	0

PATTISON Frank McKay
Barrhead, 23 December, 1930 (W)

League Club	Source	Date Signed	Seasons Played	Apps	Subs	Gls
Barnsley	Alloa Ath	12.51	51-54	29	-	5

PATTISON John (Johnny) Morris
Glasgow, 19 December, 1918 (W)

League Club	Source	Date Signed	Seasons Played	Apps	Subs	Gls
Queens Park Rgrs	Motherwell	05.37	37-49	92	-	26
Leyton Orient	Tr	02.50	49-50	43	-	10

PATTISON John William Philip
Portsmouth, 23 February, 1925 Died 1993 (WH)

League Club	Source	Date Signed	Seasons Played	Apps	Subs	Gls
Reading	Portsmouth CS	07.45	46	2	-	0

PATTON Aaron Anthony
Westminster, 27 February, 1979 (FB)

League Club	Source	Date Signed	Seasons Played	Apps	Subs	Gls
Wycombe W	YT	07.97	97	0	1	0

PAUL Anthony (Tony) George
Islington, 6 April, 1961 (M)

League Club	Source	Date Signed	Seasons Played	Apps	Subs	Gls
Crystal Palace	App	04.78	80	0	1	0

PAUL David Dryburgh
Kirkcaldy, 19 February, 1936 SSch (G)

League Club	Source	Date Signed	Seasons Played	Apps	Subs	Gls
Derby Co	Jnrs	02.53	53-55	2	-	0

PAUL Ian Kevin
Wolverhampton, 23 January, 1961 (M)

League Club	Source	Date Signed	Seasons Played	Apps	Subs	Gls
Walsall	App	08.78	77-80	68	2	9

PAUL Martyn Leighton
Whalley, 2 February, 1975 (F)

League Club	Source	Date Signed	Seasons Played	Apps	Subs	Gls
Bristol Rov	YT	07.93	93-95	11	11	1

PAUL Roy
Ton Pentre, 18 April, 1920 Died 2002 W-33 (WH)

League Club	Source	Date Signed	Seasons Played	Apps	Subs	Gls
Swansea T	Ton Pentre	10.38	46-49	159	-	13
Manchester C	Tr	07.50	50-56	270	-	9

PAUL Thomas (Tom)
Grimsby, 14 May, 1933 (W)

League Club	Source	Date Signed	Seasons Played	Apps	Subs	Gls
Grimsby T		05.55	58	1	-	0

PAULO Pedro Saraiva Antonio
Angola, 21 November, 1973 Died 2000 (W)

League Club	Source	Date Signed	Seasons Played	Apps	Subs	Gls
Darlington	Sporting Lisbon (Por)	08.95	95	4	2	0

League Club	Source	Date Signed	Seasons Played	Career Record Apps	Subs	Gls
PAVITT William (Bill) Ernest						
West Ham, 30 June, 1920 Died 1989						(CD)
Fulham	RAF Debden	08.46	49-52	50	-	1
Southend U	Tr	05.53	53-54	79	-	0
PAWSON Henry **Anthony (Tony)**						
Chertsey, 22 August, 1921 EAmat						(W)
Charlton Ath (Am)	Pegasus	12.51	51-52	2	-	1
PAXTON John William						
Wolverhampton, 24 March, 1928						(FB)
Wolverhampton W	Jnrs	04.45				
Notts Co	Tr	05.50	50	2	-	0
PAYE Michael (Mike) Charles						
Orpington, 30 July, 1966						(FB)
Charlton Ath	App	●	83	2	0	0
PAYNE Albert Charles						
Liverpool, 11 November, 1923						(WH)
Tranmere Rov		08.46	46-48	10	-	0
PAYNE Brian						
Altrincham, 4 November, 1937						(W)
Huddersfield T	Jnrs	10.55				
Gillingham	Tr	07.57	57-59	36	-	3
PAYNE Clive Edward						
Aylsham, 2 March, 1950						(FB)
Norwich C	App	03.68	68-73	122	3	0
Bournemouth	Tr	12.73	73-75	101	0	3
PAYNE David Ronald						
Thornton Heath, 25 April, 1947 Eu23-1						(FB)
Crystal Palace	App	11.64	64-72	281	3	9
Orient	Tr	08.73	73-77	88	5	0
PAYNE Derek Richard						
Edgware, 26 April, 1967						(M)
Barnet	Hayes	07.91	91-92	50	1	6
Southend U	Tr	07.93	93	32	3	0
Watford	Tr	07.94	94-95	33	3	1
Peterborough U	Tr	08.96	96-98	79	3	4
PAYNE Donald (Don)						
Swansea, 18 November, 1950						(G)
Swansea C	Jnrs	12.70	71	11	0	0
Torquay U	Tr	06.72				
Newport Co	Tr	08.73	73-74	32	0	0
PAYNE Frank Ernest						
Ipswich, 18 March, 1926 Died 2001						(G)
Derby Co	Ollerton Colliery	10.47				
Hull C	Tr	08.48				
Lincoln C	Tr	08.49	49	5	-	0
PAYNE George Henry						
Liverpool, 22 August, 1921 Died 1987						(G)
Tranmere Rov		04.47	46-60	439	-	0
PAYNE Ian Neil						
Crawley, 19 January, 1977 WYth						(FB)
Plymouth Arg	YT	07.95	94	1	0	0
PAYNE Irving (Joe) Ernest Henry						
Briton Ferry, 29 June, 1921 Died 2001						(IF)
Swansea T	Jnrs	07.38	46-48	52	-	12
Newport Co	Tr	10.49	49	12	-	1
Scunthorpe U	Tr	07.50	50	40	-	2
Northampton T	Tr	08.51	51	32	-	6
PAYNE James (Jim)						
West Bromwich, 25 May, 1936						(CF)
Walsall		08.55	55	1	-	0
PAYNE James (Jimmy) Bolcherson						
Liverpool, 10 March, 1926 EB						(W)
Liverpool	Bootle ATC	11.44	48-55	224	-	37
Everton	Tr	04.56	55-56	5	-	2
PAYNE Jeremy (Jess)						
Dartford, 7 March, 1958						(CD)
Leicester C	Jnrs	07.76				
Torquay U	Tr	12.77	77-78	25	0	1
PAYNE Joseph (Joe)						
Brinnington Common, 17 January, 1914 Died 1975 E-1						(CF)
Luton T	Biggleswade T	06.34	34-37	72	-	82
Chelsea	Tr	03.38	37-38	36	-	21
West Ham U	Tr	12.46	46	10	-	6

League Club	Source	Date Signed	Seasons Played	Career Record Apps	Subs	Gls
PAYNE Lee John						
Luton, 12 December, 1966						(W)
Newcastle U	Barnet	09.88	88	6	1	0
Reading	Tr	03.89	88-89	25	2	3
PAYNE Mark Ian						
Swindon, 2 September, 1966						(W)
Swindon T	App	09.84	84	0	3	0
PAYNE Mark Richard Crawford						
Cheltenham, 3 August, 1960						(M)
Stockport Co	SC Cambuur (Holl)	08.88	88-90	77	10	16
Rochdale	Tr	05.91	91-92	58	4	8
PAYNE Russell						
Wigan, 8 July, 1970						(W)
Liverpool	Skelmersdale U	03.90				
Crewe Alex	L	10.91	91	3	3	0
PAYNE Stephen (Steve) John						
Pontefract, 1 August, 1975 ESemiPro-1						(CD)
Huddersfield T	YT	07.93				
Macclesfield T	Tr	12.94	97-98	71	6	2
Chesterfield	Tr	07.99	99-03	146	5	8
Macclesfield T	Tr	03.04	03	13	0	0
PAYNTER William (Billy) Paul						
Liverpool, 13 July, 1984						(F)
Port Vale	Sch	07.02	00-04	103	25	28
PAYTON Andrew (Andy) Paul						
Padiham, 23 October, 1967						(F)
Hull C	App	07.85	86-91	116	27	55
Middlesbrough	Tr	11.91	91	8	11	3
Barnsley	Glasgow Celtic	11.93	93-95	100	8	41
Huddersfield T	Tr	07.96	96-97	42	1	17
Burnley	Tr	01.98	97-02	115	41	68
Blackpool	L	12.01	01	4	0	1
PAYTON Clifford (Cliff) Charles						
Brighton, 16 October, 1935						(IF)
Accrington St	Wisbech T	07.56				
Gillingham	Tonbridge	03.59	58-59	24	-	5
PAZ Charquero **Adrian**						
Montevideo, Uruguay, 9 September, 1968 Uruguay int						(F)
Ipswich T	Penarol (Ur)	09.94	94	13	4	1
PEACH David Sidney						
Bedford, 21 January, 1951 Eu21-6						(FB)
Gillingham	App	01.69	69-73	186	1	30
Southampton	Tr	01.74	73-79	221	3	34
Swindon T	Tr	03.80	79-81	52	1	2
Orient	Tr	03.82	81-82	47	0	6
PEACH Geoffrey (Geoff) Leonard						
Torpoint, 11 October, 1932 Died 2003						(IF)
Plymouth Arg	Millwall (Am)	07.56	56	1	-	0
PEACH John (Jack)						
Barnsley, 4 April, 1923						(IF)
Barnsley	York C (Am)	11.45				
Hull C	Selby T	10.46	46-47	19	-	2
PEACHEY John Michael						
Cambridge, 21 July, 1952						(F)
York C	Hillingdon Borough	08.73	73-74	6	2	3
Barnsley	Tr	11.74	74-78	116	11	31
Darlington	L	12.75	75	5	1	3
Darlington	Tr	03.79	78-79	16	4	6
Plymouth Arg	Tr	07.80	80	1	2	0
PEACOCK Alan						
Middlesbrough, 29 October, 1937 EYth/E-6						(F)
Middlesbrough	Jnrs	11.54	55-63	218	-	125
Leeds U	Tr	02.64	63-66	54	0	27
Plymouth Arg	Tr	10.67	67	11	0	1
PEACOCK Darren						
Bristol, 3 February, 1968						(CD)
Newport Co	App	02.86	85-87	24	4	0
Hereford U	Tr	03.89	88-90	56	3	4
Queens Park Rgrs	Tr	12.90	90-93	123	3	6
Newcastle U	Tr	03.94	93-97	131	2	2
Blackburn Rov	Tr	07.98	98-99	42	5	1
Wolverhampton W	L	10.00	00	2	2	0
PEACOCK Dennis						
Lincoln, 19 April, 1953						(G)
Nottingham F	App	04.71	72-74	22	0	0
Walsall	L	03.73	72	10	0	0

League Club	Source	Date Signed	Seasons Played	Apps	Subs	Gls
Doncaster Rov	Tr	07.75	75-79	199	0	0
Bolton W	Tr	03.80	80-81	16	0	0
Doncaster Rov	Tr	08.82	82-85	130	0	0
Burnley	L	09.85	85	8	0	0

PEACOCK Ernest (Ernie) Anderson
Renfrew, 10 August, 1942 (WH)

League Club	Source	Date Signed	Seasons Played	Apps	Subs	Gls
Workington	St Mirren	01.64	63	1	-	0

PEACOCK Ernest (Ernie) Gilbert
Bristol, 11 December, 1924 Died 1966 (WH)

League Club	Source	Date Signed	Seasons Played	Apps	Subs	Gls
Notts Co	Syston	03.45				
Bristol C	Tr	10.46	46-58	343	-	7

PEACOCK Frank Edwin
Bolton, 17 May, 1945 (WH)

League Club	Source	Date Signed	Seasons Played	Apps	Subs	Gls
Stockport Co	Blackburn Rov (Am)	11.64	64	5	-	0

PEACOCK Gavin Keith
Welling, 18 November, 1967 ESch/EYth (M)

League Club	Source	Date Signed	Seasons Played	Apps	Subs	Gls
Queens Park Rgrs	App	11.84	86-87	7	10	1
Gillingham	Tr	10.87	87-88	69	1	11
Bournemouth	Tr	08.89	89-90	56	0	8
Newcastle U	Tr	11.90	90-92	102	3	35
Chelsea	Tr	08.93	93-95	92	11	17
Queens Park Rgrs	Tr	11.96	96-01	182	8	35
Charlton Ath	L	08.01	01	1	4	0

PEACOCK George
Pontypool, 10 February, 1924 Died 1984 (FB)

League Club	Source	Date Signed	Seasons Played	Apps	Subs	Gls
Bristol Rov	Pentwyn	05.46	46	7	-	0

PEACOCK John Charles
Leeds, 27 March, 1956 (FB)

League Club	Source	Date Signed	Seasons Played	Apps	Subs	Gls
Scunthorpe U	Jnrs	08.74	74-79	185	5	1

PEACOCK Keith
Barnehurst, 2 May, 1945 (M)

League Club	Source	Date Signed	Seasons Played	Apps	Subs	Gls
Charlton Ath	Jnrs	07.62	62-78	513	21	92

PEACOCK Lee Anthony
Paisley, 9 October, 1976 SYth/Su21-1 (F)

League Club	Source	Date Signed	Seasons Played	Apps	Subs	Gls
Carlisle U	YT	03.95	93-97	52	24	11
Mansfield T	Tr	10.97	97-99	79	10	29
Manchester C	Tr	11.99	99	4	4	0
Bristol C	Tr	08.00	00-03	131	13	54
Sheffield Wed	Tr	07.04	04	18	11	4

PEACOCK Michael (Mike) Richards
Fishburn, 28 September, 1940 (G)

League Club	Source	Date Signed	Seasons Played	Apps	Subs	Gls
Darlington	Shildon	08.60	60-62	46	-	0

PEACOCK Richard John
Sheffield, 29 October, 1972 (W)

League Club	Source	Date Signed	Seasons Played	Apps	Subs	Gls
Hull C	Sheffield FC	10.93	93-98	144	30	21
Lincoln C	Tr	01.99	98-00	41	27	6

PEACOCK Robert John
Rushden, 8 December, 1937 (WH)

League Club	Source	Date Signed	Seasons Played	Apps	Subs	Gls
Northampton T	Rushden T	02.57	57	2	-	0

PEACOCK Terence (Terry) McGhee
Hull, 18 April, 1935 (CF)

League Club	Source	Date Signed	Seasons Played	Apps	Subs	Gls
Hull C	Jnrs	12.52	55	2	-	0
Queens Park Rgrs	Tr	08.56	56-57	16	-	4

PEAD Craig George
Bromsgrove, 15 September, 1981 EYth/Eu20 (M)

League Club	Source	Date Signed	Seasons Played	Apps	Subs	Gls
Coventry C	YT	09.98	01-03	24	18	3
Notts Co	L	09.04	04	4	1	0
Walsall	L	03.05	04	8	0	0

PEAKE Andrew (Andy) Michael
Market Harborough, 1 November, 1961 EYth/Eu21-1 (M)

League Club	Source	Date Signed	Seasons Played	Apps	Subs	Gls
Leicester C	App	01.79	78-84	141	6	13
Grimsby T	Tr	08.85	85-86	39	0	4
Charlton Ath	Tr	09.86	86-91	174	3	5
Middlesbrough	Tr	11.91	91-93	83	3	1

PEAKE Dudley John
Swansea, 26 October, 1934 (CD)

League Club	Source	Date Signed	Seasons Played	Apps	Subs	Gls
Swansea T	Tawe U	04.56	55-57	57	-	2
Newport Co	Tr	06.58	58-62	129	-	0

PEAKE Jason William
Coalville, 29 September, 1971 ESch/EYth (M)

League Club	Source	Date Signed	Seasons Played	Apps	Subs	Gls
Leicester C	YT	01.90	90	4	4	1
Hartlepool U	L	02.92	91	5	1	1
Halifax T	Tr	08.92	92	32	1	1
Rochdale	Tr	03.94	93-95	91	4	6
Brighton & Hove A	Tr	07.96	96	27	3	1
Bury	Tr	10.97	97	3	3	0
Rochdale	Tr	07.98	98-99	74	7	11
Plymouth Arg	Tr	07.00	00	7	3	2

PEAKE Trevor
Nuneaton, 10 February, 1957 ESemiPro (CD)

League Club	Source	Date Signed	Seasons Played	Apps	Subs	Gls
Lincoln C	Nuneaton Borough	06.79	79-82	171	0	7
Coventry C	Tr	07.83	83-91	276	1	6
Luton T	Tr	08.91	91-97	175	4	0

PEAPELL Frederick Dennis
Swindon, 16 November, 1945 (WH)

League Club	Source	Date Signed	Seasons Played	Apps	Subs	Gls
Swindon T	App	11.63	64	2	-	0
Exeter C	Tr	07.65	65	23	1	1

PEARCE Alan James
Middlesbrough, 25 October, 1965 (W)

League Club	Source	Date Signed	Seasons Played	Apps	Subs	Gls
York C	Jnrs	10.83	83-86	76	2	9
Torquay U	Tr	08.87	87	20	7	2

PEARCE Allan David
Wellington, New Zealand, 7 April, 1983 NzYth/Nzu20/Nzu23 (F)

League Club	Source	Date Signed	Seasons Played	Apps	Subs	Gls
Lincoln C	Barnsley (YT)	10.02	02-03	9	10	1

PEARCE Andrew (Andy) John
Bradford-on-Avon, 20 April, 1966 (CD)

League Club	Source	Date Signed	Seasons Played	Apps	Subs	Gls
Coventry C	Halesowen T	05.90	90-92	68	3	4
Sheffield Wed	Tr	06.93	93-95	66	3	3
Wimbledon	Tr	11.95	95	6	1	0

PEARCE Christopher (Chris) Leslie
Newport, 7 August, 1961 WSch/WYth (G)

League Club	Source	Date Signed	Seasons Played	Apps	Subs	Gls
Blackburn Rov	Wolverhampton W (App)	10.79				
Rochdale	L	08.80	80	5	0	0
Rochdale	Tr	08.82	82	36	0	0
Port Vale	Tr	06.83	83-85	48	0	0
Wrexham	Tr	07.86	86	25	0	0
Burnley	Tr	07.87	87-91	181	0	0
Bradford C	Tr	07.92	92	9	0	0

PEARCE David
Northolt, 7 December, 1959 ESemiPro (F)

League Club	Source	Date Signed	Seasons Played	Apps	Subs	Gls
Millwall		02.78	77	1	0	0

PEARCE David Gordon
Scunthorpe, 19 December, 1934 Died 1999 (WH)

League Club	Source	Date Signed	Seasons Played	Apps	Subs	Gls
Scunthorpe U		07.56	58	2	-	0

PEARCE Dennis Anthony
Wolverhampton, 10 September, 1974 (FB)

League Club	Source	Date Signed	Seasons Played	Apps	Subs	Gls
Aston Villa	YT	06.93				
Wolverhampton W	Tr	07.95	95-96	7	2	0
Notts Co	Tr	07.97	97-00	108	10	3
Peterborough U	Tr	05.01	01-03	11	3	0

PEARCE Graham Charles
Hammersmith, 8 July, 1959 (FB)

League Club	Source	Date Signed	Seasons Played	Apps	Subs	Gls
Brighton & Hove A	Barnet	01.82	82-85	87	1	2
Gillingham	Tr	07.86	86-87	65	0	0
Brentford	Tr	09.88	88	11	7	0
Maidstone U	Tr	07.89	89	24	3	0

PEARCE Alexander Gregory (Greg)
Bolton, 26 May, 1980 (M)

League Club	Source	Date Signed	Seasons Played	Apps	Subs	Gls
Chesterfield	YT	03.98	98-01	14	5	0

PEARCE Ian Anthony
Bury St Edmunds, 7 May, 1974 EYth/Eu21-3 (CD)

League Club	Source	Date Signed	Seasons Played	Apps	Subs	Gls
Chelsea	Jnrs	08.91	90-92	0	4	0
Blackburn Rov	Tr	10.93	93-97	43	19	2
West Ham U	Tr	09.97	97-03	135	7	9
Fulham	Tr	01.04	03-04	23	1	0

PEARCE James (Jimmy) William
Tottenham, 27 November, 1947 ESch (W)

League Club	Source	Date Signed	Seasons Played	Apps	Subs	Gls
Tottenham H	App	05.65	68-72	108	33	21

PEARCE John
Watford, 12 December, 1950 (FB)

League Club	Source	Date Signed	Seasons Played	Apps	Subs	Gls
Watford	Jnrs	07.69	70	0	1	0

PEARCE John Arthur
Grimsby, 29 February, 1940 (WH)

League Club	Source	Date Signed	Seasons Played	Apps	Subs	Gls
Grimsby T	Jnrs	12.58	58-61	48	-	0

PEARCE Reginald (Reg) Stanley
Liverpool, 12 January, 1930 FLge-2 (WH)

League Club	Source	Date Signed	Seasons Played	Apps	Subs	Gls
Luton T	Winsford U	11.54	54-57	75	-	5
Sunderland	Tr	02.58	57-60	61	-	4
Peterborough U	Cambridge C	08.63	63	28	-	2

League Club	Source	Date Signed	Seasons Played	Apps	Subs	Gls
PEARCE Stuart						
Shepherds Bush, 24 April, 1962 Eu21-1/E-78						(FB)
Coventry C	Wealdstone	10.83	83-84	52	0	4
Nottingham F	Tr	06.85	85-96	401	0	63
Newcastle U	Tr	07.97	97-98	37	0	0
West Ham U	Tr	08.99	99-00	42	0	2
Manchester C	Tr	07.01	01	38	0	3
PEARCE Trevor George						
Canterbury, 30 May, 1949						(W)
Arsenal	Folkestone T	02.70				
Aldershot	Tr	05.71	71-72	19	6	2
PEARCEY Jason Kevin						
Leamington Spa, 23 July, 1971						(G)
Mansfield T	YT	07.89	88-94	77	0	0
Grimsby T	Tr	11.94	94-97	49	0	0
Brentford	Tr	07.98	98-99	23	0	0
PEARS Jeffrey (Jeff)						
York, 14 June, 1920 Died 2003						(G)
York C	Terry's	09.47	47-48	3	-	0
PEARS Richard James						
Exeter, 16 July, 1976						(F)
Exeter C	YT	07.94	93-96	43	17	8
PEARS Stephen (Steve)						
Brandon, 22 January, 1962						(G)
Manchester U	App	01.79	84	4	0	0
Middlesbrough	L	11.83	83	12	0	0
Middlesbrough	Tr	07.85	85-94	327	0	0
Liverpool	Tr	08.95				
Hartlepool U	Tr	08.96	96	16	0	0
PEARSON Andrew (Andy) John						
Newmarket, 19 November, 1960						(F)
Luton T	App	11.78	79	1	1	0
PEARSON Aubrey **David (Dave)** John						
Shotton, 13 October, 1947 WSch/Wu23-1						(FB)
Everton	App	10.65				
Southport	Tr	08.67	67-69	91	2	0
Rochdale	Tr	09.70	70	3	0	0
PEARSON David (Dave) Thomson						
Dunfermline, 9 November, 1932						(IF)
Blackburn Rov	Jnrs	11.49				
Ipswich T	Tr	05.54				
Oldham Ath	Darwen	08.56	56	25	-	12
Rochdale	Tr	03.57	56-57	32	-	17
Crewe Alex	Tr	05.58	58	9	-	2
PEARSON Donald (Don) James						
Swansea, 14 March, 1930						(WH)
Swansea T		06.50	52-57	52	-	1
Aldershot	Tr	07.58	58	31	-	2
PEARSON Gary						
Houghton-le-Spring, 7 December, 1976						(CD)
Sheffield U	YT	07.95				
Darlington	Durham C	08.01	01-03	39	9	3
PEARSON Gregory (Greg) Edward						
Birmingham, 3 April, 1985						(F)
West Ham U	Sch	05.04				
Lincoln C	L	08.04	04	1	2	0
PEARSON Ian Trevor						
Leeds, 18 September, 1950						(F)
Plymouth Arg	Goole T	07.74	74-75	6	6	0
Millwall	Wycombe W	08.77	77-78	41	3	9
Exeter C	Tr	11.78	78-80	67	2	10
Plymouth Arg	Bideford	08.83	83	5	3	1
PEARSON James (Jim) Findlay						
Falkirk, 24 March, 1953 Su23-6						(F)
Everton	St Johnstone	07.74	74-77	76	17	15
Newcastle U	Tr	08.78	78-79	11	0	3
PEARSON John						
Wigan, 18 October, 1946 ESch						(W)
Manchester U	App	11.63				
York C	Tr	07.65	65	14	1	4
PEARSON John						
Ferryhill, 8 March, 1945						(F)
Hartlepool (Am)	Ferryhill Ath	01.69	68	1	0	0
PEARSON John Arthur						
Isleworth, 23 April, 1935						(IF)
Brentford	Jnrs	11.52	55-56	5	-	0
Queens Park Rgrs	Tr	06.58	58-59	21	-	9

League Club	Source	Date Signed	Seasons Played	Apps	Subs	Gls
PEARSON John George						
Gateshead, 10 April, 1931 Died 1996						(FB)
Hartlepools U	Reyrolles	04.53	52	1	-	0
PEARSON John Stuart						
Sheffield, 1 September, 1963 EYth						(F)
Sheffield Wed	App	05.81	80-84	64	41	24
Charlton Ath	Tr	05.85	85-86	52	9	15
Leeds U	Tr	01.87	86-90	51	48	12
Rotherham U	L	03.91	90	11	0	5
Barnsley	Tr	07.91	91-92	29	3	4
Hull C	L	01.92	91	15	0	0
Carlisle U	Tr	08.93	93-94	5	3	0
Mansfield T	Tr	11.94	94	0	2	0
Cardiff C	Tr	01.95	94	12	0	0
PEARSON Lawrence (Lawrie)						
Wallsend, 2 July, 1965						(FB)
Hull C	Gateshead	06.84	84-86	58	1	0
Bristol C	Tr	06.87				
Port Vale	Tr	08.87	87	3	0	0
Darlington	Barrow	08.93	93	26	2	4
Chesterfield	Tr	03.94	93	0	1	0
PEARSON Mark						
Sheffield, 28 October, 1939 ESch/EYth						(M)
Manchester U	Jnrs	05.57	57-62	68	-	12
Sheffield Wed	Tr	10.63	63-64	39	-	9
Fulham	Tr	05.65	65-67	53	5	7
Halifax T	Tr	03.68	68	2	3	1
PEARSON Michael (Mike)						
Bilston, 5 December, 1942						(IF)
Manchester C	Jnrs	12.59				
Walsall	Tr	05.62	62	3	-	1
PEARSON Nigel Graham						
Nottingham, 21 August, 1963						(CD)
Shrewsbury T	Heanor T	11.81	82-87	153	0	5
Sheffield Wed	Tr	10.87	87-93	176	9	14
Middlesbrough	Tr	07.94	94-97	115	1	5
PEARSON Richard (Ricky)						
Ulcombe, 18 October, 1970						(CD)
Gillingham	YT	07.89	88-89	7	2	0
PEARSON Richard (Dick) John						
Portsmouth, 14 June, 1931						(WH)
Portsmouth	Gosport Borough	05.49	53	4	-	1
PEARSON Stanley (Stan) Clare						
Salford, 11 January, 1919 Died 1997 FLge-1/E-8						(IF)
Manchester U	Adelphi LC	05.36	37-53	312	-	127
Bury	Tr	02.54	53-57	121	-	56
Chester	Tr	10.57	57-58	57	-	16
PEARSON James **Stuart**						
Hull, 21 June, 1949 Eu23-1/E-15						(F)
Hull C	Jnrs	07.68	69-73	126	3	44
Manchester U	Tr	05.74	74-77	138	1	55
West Ham U	Tr	08.79	79-81	28	6	6
PEARSON Thomas (Tommy) Usher						
Edinburgh, 6 March, 1913 Died 1999 FLge-1/SLge-1/EWar-1/S-2						(W)
Newcastle U	Murrayfield Amats	03.33	33-47	212	-	46
PEARSON Trevor						
Sheffield, 4 April, 1952						(G)
Sheffield Wed (Am)	Woodseats WMC	03.72	71	4	0	0
PEARSON Walter (Wally)						
Ottershaw, 13 November, 1928						(G)
Aldershot (Am)	Tooting & Mitcham	03.61	60	1	-	0
PEARSON William (Billy) George Arthur						
Clonmel, 23 October, 1921						(W)
Grimsby T		09.43	46-48	35	-	9
Chester	Tr	06.49	49	12	-	3
PEART Robert (Bob) Charles						
Swindon, 17 December, 1926 Died 1966						(CF)
Swindon T	Burnley (Am)	04.48	49-51	13	-	5
PEART Ronald (Ron)						
Brandon, 8 March, 1920 Died 1999						(CD)
Hartlepools U	Langley Moor	09.38	38	8	-	0
Derby Co	Tr	05.39	46	1	-	0
York C	Tr	06.48	48	5	-	0
PEAT William **Arthur**						
Walton, 1 September, 1940						(M)
Everton	Jnrs	04.59				

League Club	Source	Date Signed	Seasons Played	Career Record Apps	Subs	Gls
Southport	Tr	07.61	61-71	401	0	27
Crewe Alex	Tr	07.72	72-73	82	0	5
PEAT James Leslie						
Birmingham, 29 May, 1951						(W)
Workington	Cadbury's	08.73	73	0	1	0
PEAT John (Jack)						
						(W)
Workington	Kilmarnock	10.53	53	1	-	0
PEAT Nathan Neil Martin						
Hull, 19 September, 1982						(FB)
Hull C	Sch	07.02	02-03	0	2	0
Cambridge U	L	12.03	03	3	3	0
Lincoln C	L	07.04	04	6	4	0
PEATTIE Donald (Don) Simpson						
York, 5 April, 1963						(F)
Sheffield U	Gretna	08.84	84	3	2	0
Doncaster Rov	L	01.86	85	3	1	0
PECK Dennis **Trevor**						
Llanelli, 25 May, 1938						(FB)
Cardiff C	Llanelli	02.58	59-64	42	-	0
PECKETT Andrew (Andy) Richard						
Sheffield, 19 September, 1969						(M)
Doncaster Rov	YT	06.88	87-88	2	7	0
PEDDELTY John						
Bishop Auckland, 2 April, 1955 EYth						(CD)
Ipswich T	App	01.73	72-76	44	0	5
Plymouth Arg	Tr	10.76	76-77	30	3	1
PEDDELTY John **Maurice**						
Carlisle, 23 May, 1950						(M)
Carlisle U	App	12.67	68-69	9	4	1
Darlington	Tr	07.70	70-71	51	5	1
PEDEN George Wright Watson						
Rosewell, 12 April, 1943						(FB)
Lincoln C	Heart of Midlothian	04.67	66-73	223	2	15
PEDERSEN Henrik						
Copenhagen, Denmark, 10 June, 1975 Denmark 3						(F)
Bolton W	Silkeborg (Nor)	07.01	01-04	68	36	20
PEDERSEN Jan Ove						
Oslo, Norway, 12 November, 1968 Norway int						(M)
Hartlepool U (L)	SK Brann Bergen (Nor)	10.97	97	17	0	1
PEDERSEN Morten Gamst						
Vadso, Norway, 8 September, 1981 Norway 15						(M)
Blackburn Rov	Tromso (Nor)	08.04	04	19	0	4
PEDERSEN Per Werner						
Aalborg, Denmark, 30 March, 1969 Denmark int						(F)
Blackburn Rov	Odense (Den)	02.97	96	6	5	1
PEDERSEN Tore						
Fredrikstad, Norway, 29 September, 1969 Norway 46						(CD)
Oldham Ath	SK Brann Bergen (Nor)	10.93	93	7	3	0
Blackburn Rov	St Pauli (Ger)	09.97	97	3	2	0
Wimbledon	Eintracht Frankfurt (Ger)	06.99	99	6	0	0
PEEBLES Richard (Dick) Winter						
Glasgow, 30 August, 1923 Died 2004						(IF)
Swindon T	St Johnstone	05.50	50	12	-	1
PEEK James (Jim)						
Hartlepool, 7 July, 1933						(FB)
Hartlepools U (Am)	West View A	12.59	59	7	-	0
PEEL Kenneth (Ken)						
Manchester, 8 November, 1922 Died 2002						(IF)
Crewe Alex	Rusholme	09.46	46	1	-	0
PEEL Nathan James						
Blackburn, 17 May, 1972						(F)
Preston NE	YT	07.90	90	1	9	1
Sheffield U	Tr	08.91	91	0	1	0
Halifax T	L	02.93	92	3	0	0
Burnley	Tr	09.93	93-94	4	12	2
Rotherham U	L	03.95	94	9	0	4
Mansfield T	L	10.95	95	2	0	0
Doncaster Rov	L	02.96	95	2	0	0
Rotherham U	Tr	07.96				
Macclesfield T	Tr	01.97	97	10	4	3

League Club	Source	Date Signed	Seasons Played	Career Record Apps	Subs	Gls
PEEL Trevor						
Huddersfield, 25 October, 1945						(FB)
Bradford PA	Huddersfield T (Am)	04.67	66-67	11	0	0
PEER Dean						
Dudley, 8 August, 1969						(M)
Birmingham C	YT	07.87	86-92	106	14	8
Mansfield T	L	12.92	92	10	0	0
Walsall	Tr	11.93	93-94	41	4	8
Northampton T	Tr	08.95	95-99	97	31	6
Shrewsbury T	Tr	01.00	99-00	53	3	0
PEETERS Bob						
Lier, Belgium, 10 January, 1974 Belgium 2						(F)
Millwall	Vitesse Arnhem (Holl)	08.03	03-04	16	7	3
PEGG David						
Doncaster, 20 September, 1935 Died 1958 ESch/Eu23-3/EB/E-1						(W)
Manchester U	Jnrs	09.52	52-57	127	-	24
PEGG James (Jimmy) Kenneth						
Salford, 4 January, 1926 Died 1999						(G)
Manchester U	Jnrs	11.47	47	2	-	0
Torquay U	Tr	08.49	49	2	-	0
York C	Tr	08.50	50	1	-	0
PEHRSSON Magnus Karl						
Malmo, Sweden, 25 May, 1976 Sweden u21						(M)
Bradford C (L)	Djurgaarden (Swe)	10.96	96	1	0	0
PEJIC Melvyn (Mel)						
Chesterton, 27 April, 1959						(CD)
Stoke C	Jnrs	01.77	79	1	0	0
Hereford U	Tr	06.80	80-91	404	8	14
Wrexham	Tr	01.92	91-94	103	3	3
PEJIC Michael (Mike)						
Chesterton, 25 January, 1950 Eu23-8/E-4						(FB)
Stoke C	App	01.68	68-76	274	0	6
Everton	Tr	02.77	76-78	76	0	2
Aston Villa	Tr	09.79	79	10	0	0
PEJIC Shaun Melvyn						
Hereford, 16 November, 1982 WYth/Wu21-6						(FB)
Wrexham	Sch	08.02	00-04	85	11	0
PELL Dennis						
Normanton, 19 April, 1929 Died 2003						(W)
Rotherham U	Methley	05.52	52-55	11	-	3
Grimsby T	Tr	10.55	55-56	3	-	1
PELL Robert Anthony						
Leeds, 5 February, 1979						(F)
Rotherham U	YT	06.97	96	2	0	0
Doncaster Rov	L	11.97	97	6	4	1
PELLEGRINO Mauricio Andres						
Leones, Argentina, 5 October, 1971 Argentina 3						(CD)
Liverpool (L)	Valencia (Sp)	01.05	04	11	1	0
PEMBERTON James (Jim) Henry Arthur						
Wolverhampton, 30 April, 1916 Died 1996						(FB)
West Bromwich A	Brownhills A	08.38	46-50	162	-	0
PEMBERTON James (Jim) Thomas						
Kingswinford, 14 November, 1925						(WH)
West Bromwich A	Round Oak	05.45				
Luton T	Stourbridge	11.47	50-56	92	-	8
PEMBERTON John Matthew						
Oldham, 18 November, 1964						(FB)
Rochdale	Chadderton	09.84	84	1	0	0
Crewe Alex	Chadderton	03.85	84-87	116	5	1
Crystal Palace	Tr	03.88	87-89	76	2	2
Sheffield U	Tr	07.90	90-93	67	1	0
Leeds U	Tr	11.93	93-95	44	9	0
Crewe Alex	Tr	08.97	97	1	0	0
PEMBERTON Martin Calvin						
Bradford, 1 February, 1976						(FB)
Oldham Ath	YT	07.94	95-96	0	5	0
Doncaster Rov	Tr	03.97	96-97	33	2	2
Scunthorpe U	Tr	03.98	97	3	3	0
Hartlepool U	Tr	07.98	98	0	4	0
Mansfield T	Bradford PA	08.00	00-01	49	7	5
Stockport Co	Tr	04.02	02-03	20	6	0
Rochdale	L	01.04	03	1	0	0
PEMBERTON Selwyn Robert						
Cardiff, 13 October, 1928						(FB)
Newport Co		03.52	52	1	-	0

PEMBERY Gordon Dennis
Cardiff, 10 October, 1926 (WH)

League Club	Source	Date Signed	Seasons Played	Apps	Subs	Gls
Norwich C	Cardiff Nomads	01.47	46	1	-	0
Cardiff C	Tr	08.48	49	1	-	0
Torquay U	Tr	06.50	50-51	51	-	7
Charlton Ath	Tr	01.52	51-55	18	-	1
Swindon T	Tr	06.56	56	37	-	2

PEMBRIDGE Mark Anthony
Merthyr Tydfil, 29 November, 1970 WSch/Wu21-1/WB-2/W-54 (M)

League Club	Source	Date Signed	Seasons Played	Apps	Subs	Gls
Luton T	YT	07.89	90-91	60	0	6
Derby Co	Tr	06.92	92-94	108	2	28
Sheffield Wed	Tr	07.95	95-97	88	5	11
Everton	Benfica (Por)	08.99	99-03	82	9	4
Fulham	Tr	09.03	03-04	35	5	1

PENDER John Patrick
Luton, 19 November, 1963 IRYth/IRu21-5 (CD)

League Club	Source	Date Signed	Seasons Played	Apps	Subs	Gls
Wolverhampton W	App	11.81	81-84	115	2	3
Charlton Ath	Tr	07.85	85-87	41	0	0
Bristol C	Tr	10.87	87-89	83	0	3
Burnley	Tr	10.90	90-95	171	0	8
Wigan Ath	Tr	08.95	95-96	67	3	1
Rochdale	Tr	07.97	97	14	0	0

PENDERGAST William (Bill) James
Pen-y-groes, 13 April, 1915 Died 2001 (CF)

League Club	Source	Date Signed	Seasons Played	Apps	Subs	Gls
Manchester U	Wrexham (Am)	12.35				
Wolverhampton W	Tr	01.36				
Bristol Rov	Tr	05.36	36-37	7	-	3
Chester	Colchester U	07.38	38	34	-	26
New Brighton	Tr	08.46	46-47	69	-	26

PENDLEBURY Ian David
Bolton, 3 September, 1983 (FB)

League Club	Source	Date Signed	Seasons Played	Apps	Subs	Gls
Wigan Ath	YT	08.01	01	4	0	0

PENDLEBURY Derek **Keith**
Stockport, 22 January, 1934 (WH)

League Club	Source	Date Signed	Seasons Played	Apps	Subs	Gls
Stockport Co	Jnrs	03.51	53	2	-	0

PENDREY Gary James Sidney
Birmingham, 9 February, 1949 (FB)

League Club	Source	Date Signed	Seasons Played	Apps	Subs	Gls
Birmingham C	App	10.66	68-78	287	19	4
West Bromwich A	Tr	08.79	79	18	0	0
Torquay U	Tr	08.81	81	12	0	0
Bristol Rov	Tr	12.81	81	1	0	0
Walsall	Tr	08.82	82	8	0	1

PENFOLD Mark
Woolwich, 10 December, 1956 (FB)

League Club	Source	Date Signed	Seasons Played	Apps	Subs	Gls
Charlton Ath	App	04.74	73-78	65	5	0
Orient	Tr	07.79	79	3	0	1

PENFORD Dennis Henry
Reading, 31 August, 1931 (FB)

League Club	Source	Date Signed	Seasons Played	Apps	Subs	Gls
Reading		05.52	53-58	101	-	6
Torquay U	Tr	06.59	59-61	77	-	0

PENFORD Thomas (Tom) James
Leeds, 5 January, 1985 (M)

League Club	Source	Date Signed	Seasons Played	Apps	Subs	Gls
Bradford C	Sch	●	02-04	3	7	0

PENGELLY Richard **Norman**
Looe, 6 October, 1919 (CD)

League Club	Source	Date Signed	Seasons Played	Apps	Subs	Gls
Plymouth Arg	Looe	05.47	47-49	9	-	0

PENHALIGON Gary
St Austell, 13 May, 1970 (G)

League Club	Source	Date Signed	Seasons Played	Apps	Subs	Gls
Plymouth Arg	YT	07.88	88	1	0	0

PENK Henry (Harry)
Wigan, 19 July, 1934 (W)

League Club	Source	Date Signed	Seasons Played	Apps	Subs	Gls
Portsmouth	Wigan Ath	09.55	55-56	9	-	2
Plymouth Arg	Tr	06.57	57-59	104	-	14
Southampton	Tr	07.60	60-63	52	-	6

PENMAN Christopher (Chris)
Houghton-le-Spring, 12 September, 1945 (G)

League Club	Source	Date Signed	Seasons Played	Apps	Subs	Gls
Darlington	Preston NE (App)	12.62	62-63	30	-	0

PENMAN William (Willie) Salmond Thomson
Wemyss, 7 August, 1939 (M)

League Club	Source	Date Signed	Seasons Played	Apps	Subs	Gls
Newcastle U	Glasgow Rgrs	04.63	62-65	62	1	18
Swindon T	Tr	09.66	66-69	87	11	18
Walsall	Tr	08.70	70-72	118	5	6

PENN Donald (Don) John
Smethwick, 15 March, 1960 (F)

League Club	Source	Date Signed	Seasons Played	Apps	Subs	Gls
Walsall	Warley Borough	01.78	77-82	132	9	54

PENN Frank Reginald
Edmonton, 15 April, 1927 Died 2001 (W)

League Club	Source	Date Signed	Seasons Played	Apps	Subs	Gls
Crystal Palace	Guildford C	09.49	49	1	-	0

PENNANT Jermaine
Nottingham, 15 January, 1983 ESch/EYth/Eu21-24 (W)

League Club	Source	Date Signed	Seasons Played	Apps	Subs	Gls
Arsenal	Notts Co (Jnrs)	03.00	02-04	2	10	3
Watford	L	01.02	01	9	0	2
Watford	L	11.02	02	12	0	0
Leeds U	L	08.03	03	34	2	2
Birmingham C	Tr	01.05	04	12	0	0

PENNEY David Mark
Wakefield, 17 August, 1964 (M)

League Club	Source	Date Signed	Seasons Played	Apps	Subs	Gls
Derby Co	Pontefract Collieries	09.85	86-88	6	13	0
Oxford U	Tr	06.89	89-93	76	34	15
Swansea C	L	03.91	90	12	0	3
Swansea C	Tr	03.94	93-96	112	7	20
Cardiff C	Tr	07.97	97-98	33	2	5

PENNEY Steven (Steve) Alexander
Ballymena, 6 January, 1964 NI-17 (W)

League Club	Source	Date Signed	Seasons Played	Apps	Subs	Gls
Brighton & Hove A	Ballymena U	11.83	83-88	125	13	15
Burnley	Heart of Midlothian	07.92	92	10	1	3

PENNICK Raymond (Ray)
Ferryhill, 30 November, 1946 (F)

League Club	Source	Date Signed	Seasons Played	Apps	Subs	Gls
York C (Am)	Willington	03.69	68	0	1	0

PENNINGTON Jack
Tadcaster, 12 September, 1928 Died 1987 (W)

League Club	Source	Date Signed	Seasons Played	Apps	Subs	Gls
Halifax T	Marsden	11.53	53-54	7	-	2

PENNINGTON James (Jimmy)
Burtonwood, 13 November, 1928 Died 1976 (IF)

League Club	Source	Date Signed	Seasons Played	Apps	Subs	Gls
Huddersfield T	Burtonwood OB	08.49				
Southport	Tr	07.51	51-53	55	-	11

PENNINGTON James (Jim)
Golborne, 26 April, 1939 (W)

League Club	Source	Date Signed	Seasons Played	Apps	Subs	Gls
Manchester C	Jnrs	08.56	58	1	-	0
Crewe Alex	Tr	03.61	60-62	34	-	3
Grimsby T	Tr	04.63	62-64	89	-	8
Oldham Ath	Tr	07.65	65	23	0	0
Rochdale	Tr	07.66	66	14	0	0

PENNOCK Adrian Barry
Ipswich, 27 March, 1971 (CD)

League Club	Source	Date Signed	Seasons Played	Apps	Subs	Gls
Norwich C	YT	07.89	89	1	0	0
Bournemouth	Tr	08.92	92-95	130	1	9
Gillingham	Tr	10.96	96-02	164	4	2

PENNOCK Anthony (Tony)
Swansea, 10 April, 1971 (G)

League Club	Source	Date Signed	Seasons Played	Apps	Subs	Gls
Stockport Co	Clydach U	08.90				
Wigan Ath	L	12.90	90	2	0	0
Wigan Ath	Tr	06.91	92	8	0	0
Hereford U	Tr	07.94	94	13	2	0
Rushden & Diamonds	Yeovil T	06.01	01	3	2	0

PENNY Christian (Chris) Vincent
Rochford, 16 February, 1973 (FB)

League Club	Source	Date Signed	Seasons Played	Apps	Subs	Gls
Doncaster Rov	Brigg T	02.92	91	1	0	0

PENNY John
Plymouth, 19 August, 1938 (W)

League Club	Source	Date Signed	Seasons Played	Apps	Subs	Gls
Plymouth Arg	Jnrs	11.55	57-59	7	-	0

PENNY Shaun
Bristol, 24 September, 1957 ESch (F)

League Club	Source	Date Signed	Seasons Played	Apps	Subs	Gls
Bristol C	App	09.74				
Bristol Rov	Tr	08.79	79-81	57	3	13

PENNYFATHER Glenn Julian
Billericay, 11 February, 1963 (M)

League Club	Source	Date Signed	Seasons Played	Apps	Subs	Gls
Southend U	App	02.81	80-87	232	6	36
Crystal Palace	Tr	11.87	87-88	31	3	1
Ipswich T	Tr	10.89	89-92	11	4	1
Bristol C	Tr	02.93	92-93	21	5	1

PENRHYN Norman Andrew
Lambeth, 28 February, 1950 (F)

League Club	Source	Date Signed	Seasons Played	Apps	Subs	Gls
Plymouth Arg	App	●	67	0	1	0

PENRICE Gary Kenneth
Bristol, 23 March, 1964 (F)

League Club	Source	Date Signed	Seasons Played	Apps	Subs	Gls
Bristol Rov	Mangotsfield U	11.84	84-89	186	2	54
Watford	Tr	11.89	89-90	41	2	17
Aston Villa	Tr	03.91	90-91	14	6	1
Queens Park Rgrs	Tr	10.91	91-95	55	27	20
Watford	Tr	11.95	95-96	26	13	2
Bristol Rov	Tr	07.97	97-99	48	21	6

League Club	Source	Date Signed	Seasons Played	Career Record Apps	Subs	Gls
PENROSE Colin Richard						
Bradford, 1 November, 1949						(F)
Bradford PA (Am)	Sedbergh YC	09.68	68	6	0	1
PENROSE Norman						
Consett, 10 March, 1922 Died 2000 ESch						(WH)
Grimsby T	Medomsley	05.39	46-47	9	-	0
PENSEE-BILONG Michel						
Cameroon, 16 June, 1973 Cameroon int						(CD)
MK Dons	San Hiroshima (Jap)	01.05	04	18	0	1
PENTECOST Michael (Mike) Eric						
Hounslow, 13 April, 1948						(FB)
Fulham	Sutton U	08.66	66-72	81	6	0
PEPLOW Ronald (Ron) Rupert						
Willesden, 4 May, 1935						(WH)
Brentford	Southall	08.55	55-60	61	-	5
PEPLOW Stephen (Steve) Thomas						
Liverpool, 8 January, 1949						(W)
Liverpool	App	01.66	69	2	0	0
Swindon T	Tr	05.70	70-72	37	3	11
Nottingham F	Tr	07.73	73	3	0	0
Mansfield T	L	12.73	73	4	0	3
Tranmere Rov	Tr	01.74	73-80	232	16	44
PEPPER Carl						
Darlington, 26 July, 1980						(FB)
Darlington	YT	07.98	98	5	1	0
PEPPER Colin **Nigel**						
Rotherham, 25 April, 1968						(M)
Rotherham U	App	04.86	85-89	35	10	1
York C	Tr	07.90	90-96	223	12	39
Bradford C	Tr	02.97	96-98	47	5	11
Southend U (L)	Aberdeen	12.99	99	9	3	2
Scunthorpe U	Aberdeen	07.00	00-01	2	1	0
PEPPITT Sydney (Syd)						
Stoke-on-Trent, 8 September, 1919 Died 1992 ESch						(IF)
Stoke C	Jnrs	09.36	36-49	94	-	29
Port Vale	Tr	05.50	50	11	-	3
PERALTA Sixto Raimundo						
Comodoro Rivadavia, Argentina, 16 April, 1979 ArYth						(M)
Ipswich T (L)	Inter Milan (It)	08.01	01	16	6	3
PERCH James Robert						
Mansfield, 29 September, 1985						(FB)
Nottingham F	Sch	11.02	04	17	5	0
PERCIVAL Jason Charles						
Nuneaton, 20 September, 1973						(F)
Stoke C	YT	09.90				
Exeter C	Tr	07.93	93	0	4	0
PERCIVAL John (Jack)						
Pittington, 16 May, 1913 Died 1979						(WH)
Manchester C	Durham C	10.32	33-46	161	-	8
Bournemouth	Tr	05.47	47-48	52	-	1
PERCIVAL Ronald Frederick **John (Jack)**						
Norwood, 19 April, 1924						(CD)
Huddersfield T	Tunbridge Wells	02.48	47-49	8	-	0
Chesterfield	Tr	05.50	50	6	-	0
PERDOMO Jose						
Montevideo, Uruguay, 6 January, 1965 Uruguay int						(M)
Coventry C	Genoa (It)	08.90	90	4	0	0
PEREZ Lionel						
Bagnols Ceze, France, 24 April, 1967						(G)
Sunderland	Bordeaux (Fr)	08.96	96-97	74	1	0
Newcastle U	Tr	07.98				
Scunthorpe U	L	10.99	99	13	0	0
Cambridge U	Tr	03.00	99-01	87	1	0
PEREZ Sebastien						
Saint-Chamond, France, 24 November, 1973						(FB)
Blackburn Rov	Bastia (Fr)	07.98	98	4	1	1
PERICARD Vincent de Paul						
Efok, Cameroon, 3 October, 1982						(F)
Portsmouth	Juventus (It)	07.02	02-03	18	20	9
PERIFIMOU Christopher (Chris) James						
Enfield, 27 November, 1975						(W)
Leyton Orient	YT	●	94	3	1	0

League Club	Source	Date Signed	Seasons Played	Career Record Apps	Subs	Gls
PERKINS Christopher (Chris) Paul						
Stepney, 1 March, 1980						(CD)
Southend U	YT	07.98	97	3	2	0
PERKINS Christopher (Chris) Peter						
Nottingham, 9 January, 1974						(FB)
Mansfield T	YT	11.92	92-93	3	5	0
Chesterfield	Tr	07.94	94-98	136	11	3
Hartlepool U	Tr	07.99	99	7	1	0
Chesterfield	Tr	10.99	99-00	37	2	0
Lincoln C	Tr	01.01	00	11	1	0
PERKINS Declan Oliver						
Ilford, 17 October, 1975 IRu21-4						(W)
Southend U	YT	05.94	94	1	5	0
Cambridge U	L	09.95	95	1	1	1
PERKINS Eric						
West Bromwich, 19 August, 1934						(FB)
West Bromwich A	Hill Top F	06.52	55	2	-	0
Walsall	Tr	06.56	56-58	67	-	1
PERKINS Glen Stewart						
Little Billing, 12 October, 1960						(M)
Northampton T	App	10.78	78	0	1	0
PERKINS Stephen (Steve) Arthur						
Stepney, 3 October, 1954						(FB)
Chelsea	App	11.71				
Queens Park Rgrs	Tr	06.77	77	2	0	0
Wimbledon	Tr	10.78	78-80	52	0	0
PERKINS Steven (Steve) William						
St Helens, 5 November, 1975						(M)
Plymouth Arg	Crediton U	02.97	96	1	3	0
PERKS Stephen (Steve) John						
Bridgnorth, 19 April, 1963						(G)
Shrewsbury T	App	04.81	84-91	243	0	0
PERON Jean-Francois (Jeff)						
St Omer, France, 11 October, 1965						(M)
Walsall	Caen (Fr)	08.97	97	38	0	1
Portsmouth	Tr	09.98	98-99	46	2	3
Wigan Ath	Tr	11.99	99	19	4	0
PERPETUINI David Peter						
Hitchin, 26 September, 1979						(M)
Watford	YT	07.97	98-00	17	2	1
Gillingham	Tr	08.01	01-04	55	31	5
Wycombe W	Tr	01.05	04	1	1	0
Walsall	Tr	03.05	04	7	0	0
PERRETT Darren John						
Cardiff, 29 December, 1969						(W)
Swansea C	Cheltenham T	07.93	93-95	13	17	1
PERRETT George Richard						
Kennington, 2 May, 1915 Died 1952						(WH)
Ipswich T	Fulham (Am)	06.36	38-49	131	-	4
PERRETT Russell (Russ)						
Barton-on-Sea, 18 June, 1973						(CD)
Portsmouth	AFC Lymington	09.95	95-98	66	6	2
Cardiff C	Tr	07.99	99-00	28	1	1
Luton T	Tr	08.01	01-04	72	6	8
PERRIN Steven (Steve) Charles						
Paddington, 13 February, 1952 ESch						(F)
Crystal Palace	Wycombe W	03.76	76-77	45	3	13
Plymouth Arg	Tr	03.78	77-79	33	1	6
Portsmouth	Tr	11.79	79-80	18	10	3
Northampton T	Hillingdon Borough	12.81	81-82	22	0	5
PERRY Andrew (Andy)						
Dulwich, 28 December, 1962						(M)
Portsmouth	Dulwich Hamlet	11.86	87	1	3	0
Gillingham	Tr	08.88	88	8	5	0
PERRY Arthur						
Doncaster, 15 October, 1932						(FB)
Hull C		12.50				
Bradford PA	Tr	07.56	56-57	60	-	0
Rotherham U	Tr	07.58	58	2	-	0
PERRY Christopher (Chris) John						
Carshalton, 26 April, 1973						(CD)
Wimbledon	YT	07.91	93-98	158	9	2
Tottenham H	Tr	07.99	99-02	111	9	3
Charlton Ath	Tr	09.03	03-04	42	6	2

PERRY David
Sheffield, 17 May, 1967 (FB)

League Club	Source	Date Signed	Seasons Played	Apps	Subs	Gls
Chesterfield	Jnrs	07.87	85-87	12	5	0

PERRY Frederick (Fred) Noel
Cheltenham, 30 October, 1933 (FB)

League Club	Source	Date Signed	Seasons Played	Apps	Subs	Gls
Liverpool	Worthing	07.54	55	1	-	0

PERRY Jason
Caerphilly, 2 April, 1970 WSch/WYth/Wu21-3/WB-2/W-1 (CD)

League Club	Source	Date Signed	Seasons Played	Apps	Subs	Gls
Cardiff C	Jnrs	08.87	86-96	278	3	5
Bristol Rov	Tr	07.97	97	24	1	0
Lincoln C	Tr	07.98	98	10	2	0
Hull C	Tr	12.98	98-00	14	1	0

PERRY Leonard (Len)
Walsall, 14 May, 1930 Died 2004 (FB)

League Club	Source	Date Signed	Seasons Played	Apps	Subs	Gls
Walsall	Jnrs	10.50	53	3	-	0

PERRY Mark James
Perivale, 19 October, 1978 ESch/EYth (FB)

League Club	Source	Date Signed	Seasons Played	Apps	Subs	Gls
Queens Park Rgrs	YT	10.95	96-01	54	12	1

PERRY Michael (Micky) Alexander
Wimbledon, 4 April, 1964 (F)

League Club	Source	Date Signed	Seasons Played	Apps	Subs	Gls
West Bromwich A	App	02.82	82-83	14	6	5
Torquay U	L	10.84	84	5	0	2
Northampton T	L	12.84	84	4	0	0
Torquay U	Tr	03.85	84-85	18	0	0

PERRY Peter
Rotherham, 11 April, 1936 (FB)

League Club	Source	Date Signed	Seasons Played	Apps	Subs	Gls
Rotherham U	Treeton RR	07.56	57-61	99	-	12
York C	Tr	07.62	62	23	-	0

PERRY William (Bill)
Johannesburg, South Africa, 10 September, 1930 EB/FLge-1/E-3 (W)

League Club	Source	Date Signed	Seasons Played	Apps	Subs	Gls
Blackpool	Johannesburg Rgrs (SA)	11.49	49-61	394	-	119
Southport	Tr	06.62	62	26	-	0

PERRYMAN Gerald (Gerry)
West Haddon, 3 October, 1947 (FB)

League Club	Source	Date Signed	Seasons Played	Apps	Subs	Gls
Northampton T	Jnrs	09.66	66	1	0	0
Colchester U	Tr	07.68	68	1	1	0

PERRYMAN Stephen (Steve) John
Ealing, 21 December, 1951 ESch/EYth/Eu23-17/E-1 (CD)

League Club	Source	Date Signed	Seasons Played	Apps	Subs	Gls
Tottenham H	App	01.69	69-85	653	2	31
Oxford U	Tr	03.86	85-86	17	0	0
Brentford	Tr	11.86	86-89	44	9	0

PESCHISOLIDO Paolo (Paul) Pasquale
Scarborough, Ontario, Canada, 25 May, 1971 CaYth/Cau23-11/Ca-53 (F)

League Club	Source	Date Signed	Seasons Played	Apps	Subs	Gls
Birmingham C	Toronto (Can)	11.92	92-93	37	6	16
Stoke C	Tr	08.94	94-95	59	7	19
Birmingham C	Tr	03.96	95	7	2	1
West Bromwich A	Tr	07.96	96-97	36	9	18
Fulham	Tr	10.97	97-99	69	26	24
Queens Park Rgrs	L	11.00	00	5	0	1
Sheffield U	L	01.01	00	4	1	2
Norwich C	L	03.01	00	3	2	0
Sheffield U	Tr	07.01	01-03	35	44	17
Derby Co	Tr	03.04	03-04	21	22	12

PETCHEY George
Whitechapel, 24 June, 1931 (WH)

League Club	Source	Date Signed	Seasons Played	Apps	Subs	Gls
West Ham U	Jnrs	08.48	52	2	-	0
Queens Park Rgrs	Tr	07.53	53-59	255	-	22
Crystal Palace	Tr	06.60	60-63	143	-	12

PETERS Alan Gerard
Newport, 14 October, 1958 (M)

League Club	Source	Date Signed	Seasons Played	Apps	Subs	Gls
Hereford U	Aston Villa (App)	06.76	76	1	0	0

PETERS Gary David
Carshalton, 3 August, 1954 (FB)

League Club	Source	Date Signed	Seasons Played	Apps	Subs	Gls
Reading	Guildford C	05.75	75-78	150	6	7
Fulham	Tr	08.79	79-81	57	7	2
Wimbledon	Tr	07.82	82-83	83	0	7
Aldershot	Tr	07.84	84	17	0	1
Reading	Tr	02.85	84-87	93	7	4
Fulham	Tr	08.88	88-89	7	4	2

PETERS Jeffrey (Jeff)
Wideopen, 7 March, 1961 (FB)

League Club	Source	Date Signed	Seasons Played	Apps	Subs	Gls
Middlesbrough	App	03.79	79	6	0	0

PETERS Mark
Flint, 6 July, 1972 WYth/Wu21-3/WB (F)

League Club	Source	Date Signed	Seasons Played	Apps	Subs	Gls
Manchester C	YT	07.90				
Norwich C	Tr	09.92				
Peterborough U	Tr	08.93	93	17	2	0
Mansfield T	Tr	09.94	94-98	107	1	9
Rushden & Diamonds	Tr	07.99	01-02	65	2	1
Leyton Orient	Tr	09.03	03-04	39	2	2

PETERS Mark William
Frimley, 4 October, 1983 (F)

League Club	Source	Date Signed	Seasons Played	Apps	Subs	Gls
Southampton	YT	10.00				
Brentford	Tr	02.02	02-03	5	15	1

PETERS Martin Stanford
Plaistow, 8 November, 1943 ESch/EYth/Eu23-5/FLge-6/E-67 (M)

League Club	Source	Date Signed	Seasons Played	Apps	Subs	Gls
West Ham U	App	11.60	61-69	302	0	81
Tottenham H	Tr	03.70	69-74	189	0	46
Norwich C	Tr	03.75	74-79	206	1	44
Sheffield U	Tr	08.80	80	23	1	4

PETERS Robert (Rob) Anthony Angus
Kensington, 18 May, 1971 (M)

League Club	Source	Date Signed	Seasons Played	Apps	Subs	Gls
Brentford	YT	07.89	89-93	16	14	1
Carlisle U	Tr	11.94	94	5	3	0

PETERS Roger (Lou) Douglas
Cheltenham, 5 March, 1944 EYth (W)

League Club	Source	Date Signed	Seasons Played	Apps	Subs	Gls
Bristol C	App	03.61	60-67	158	0	25
Bournemouth	Tr	06.68	68-69	35	2	3

PETERS Ryan Vincent
Wandsworth, 21 August, 1987 (F)

League Club	Source	Date Signed	Seasons Played	Apps	Subs	Gls
Brentford	Sch	•	04	1	8	1

PETERS Thomas (Tom)
Droylsden, 22 December, 1920 (IF)

League Club	Source	Date Signed	Seasons Played	Apps	Subs	Gls
Doncaster Rov		05.44				
Bury	Tr	12.46	47	10	-	1
Leeds U	Tr	08.48				
Mansfield T	Tr	03.49	48	6	-	2
Accrington St	Droylsden	10.49	49	4	-	2

PETERSON Eric **Brian**
Durban, South Africa, 28 October, 1936 (IF)

League Club	Source	Date Signed	Seasons Played	Apps	Subs	Gls
Blackpool	Berea Park (SA)	10.56	56-61	103	-	16

PETERSON Frank Arthur
Croydon, 3 April, 1951 (F)

League Club	Source	Date Signed	Seasons Played	Apps	Subs	Gls
Millwall	App	02.69	68	3	0	0

PETERSON Paul Wayne
Hitchin, 22 December, 1949 (FB)

League Club	Source	Date Signed	Seasons Played	Apps	Subs	Gls
Leeds U	App	12.66	69	3	1	0
Swindon T	Tr	06.71	71	1	0	0

PETHARD Frederick (Freddie) James
Glasgow, 7 October, 1950 SSch (FB)

League Club	Source	Date Signed	Seasons Played	Apps	Subs	Gls
Cardiff C	Glasgow Celtic	08.69	71-78	161	10	0
Torquay U	Tr	08.79	79-81	104	1	0

PETHERBRIDGE George
Devonport, 19 May, 1927 (W)

League Club	Source	Date Signed	Seasons Played	Apps	Subs	Gls
Bristol Rov	Colston Sports	10.45	46-61	452	-	85

PETHICK Robert (Robbie) John
Tavistock, 8 September, 1970 (FB)

League Club	Source	Date Signed	Seasons Played	Apps	Subs	Gls
Portsmouth	Weymouth	10.93	93-98	157	32	3
Bristol Rov	Tr	02.99	98-00	60	3	2
Brighton & Hove A	Tr	07.01	01-03	44	20	0

PETIT Emmanuel
Dieppe, France, 22 September, 1970 France 63 (M)

League Club	Source	Date Signed	Seasons Played	Apps	Subs	Gls
Arsenal	AS Monaco (Fr)	06.97	97-99	82	3	9
Chelsea	Barcelona (Sp)	07.01	01-03	52	3	2

PETRACHI Gianluca
Lecce, Italy, 14 January, 1969 (M)

League Club	Source	Date Signed	Seasons Played	Apps	Subs	Gls
Nottingham F	Perugia (It)	08.99	99	10	3	0

PETRESCU Daniel (Dan) Vasile
Bucharest, Romania, 22 December, 1967 Rou21/Ro-95 (FB)

League Club	Source	Date Signed	Seasons Played	Apps	Subs	Gls
Sheffield Wed	Genoa (It)	08.94	94-95	28	9	3
Chelsea	Tr	11.95	95-99	134	16	18
Bradford C	Tr	08.00	00	16	1	1
Southampton	Tr	01.01	00-01	8	3	2

PETRESCU Tomi Christian
Jyvaskyla, Finland, 24 July, 1986 FiYth (M)

League Club	Source	Date Signed	Seasons Played	Apps	Subs	Gls
Leicester C	Sch	08.03	02	0	1	0

PETRIC Gordan
Belgrade, Yugoslavia, 30 July, 1969 Yugoslavia 4 (FB)

League Club	Source	Date Signed	Seasons Played	Apps	Subs	Gls
Crystal Palace	Glasgow Rgrs	11.98	98	18	0	1

PETROVIC Vladimir
Belgrade, Yugoslavia, 1 July, 1955 Yugoslavia int (M)

League Club	Source	Date Signed	Seasons Played	Apps	Subs	Gls
Arsenal	Red Star Belgrade (Yug)	12.82	82	10	3	2

PETTA Robert (Bobby) Alfred Manuel
Rotterdam, Holland, 6 August, 1974 (W)

League Club	Source	Date Signed	Seasons Played	Apps	Subs	Gls
Ipswich T	Feyenoord (Holl)	06.96	96-98	55	15	9
Fulham (L)	Glasgow Celtic	01.04	03	3	6	0
Darlington	Glasgow Celtic	01.05	04	12	0	1

PETTEFER Carl James
Taplow, 22 March, 1981 (M)

League Club	Source	Date Signed	Seasons Played	Apps	Subs	Gls
Portsmouth	YT	11.98	00-01	1	2	0
Exeter C	L	10.02	02	30	1	1
Southend U	Tr	02.04	03-04	57	0	0

PETTERSON Andrew (Andy) Keith
Fremantle, Australia, 29 September, 1969 (G)

League Club	Source	Date Signed	Seasons Played	Apps	Subs	Gls
Luton T	East Freemantle (Aus)	12.88	92-93	16	3	0
Ipswich T	L	03.93	92	1	0	0
Charlton Ath	Tr	07.94	94-98	68	4	0
Bradford C	L	12.94	94	3	0	0
Ipswich T	L	09.95	95	1	0	0
Plymouth Arg	L	01.96	95	6	0	0
Colchester U	L	03.96	95	5	0	0
Portsmouth	L	11.98	98	13	0	0
Portsmouth	Tr	07.99	99-00	19	0	0
Torquay U	L	03.01	00	6	0	0
West Bromwich A	Tr	03.02				
Brighton & Hove A	Tr	08.02	02	6	1	0
Bournemouth	Tr	12.02				
Southend U	Derry C	09.03	03	1	0	0
Walsall	Derry C	01.04	03	3	0	0

PETTINGER Andrew (Andy) Richard
Scunthorpe, 21 April, 1984 (G)

League Club	Source	Date Signed	Seasons Played	Apps	Subs	Gls
Everton	YT	05.01				
Grimsby T	Tr	12.02	03	3	0	0

PETTINGER Paul Allen
Barnsley, 1 October, 1975 ESch/EYth (G)

League Club	Source	Date Signed	Seasons Played	Apps	Subs	Gls
Leeds U	YT	10.92				
Torquay U	L	12.94	94	3	0	0
Rotherham U	L	08.95	95	0	1	0
Gillingham	Tr	03.96				
Carlisle U	Tr	08.96				
Rotherham U	Tr	08.97	97-00	16	0	0
Lincoln C	Tr	07.01	01	3	0	0

PETTIT Raymond (Ray) John
Hull, 11 December, 1946 (CD)

League Club	Source	Date Signed	Seasons Played	Apps	Subs	Gls
Hull C	App	12.64	66-71	78	1	0
Barnsley	Tr	09.72	72-73	49	2	1

PETTS John William Frederick James
Edmonton, 2 October, 1938 EYth (M)

League Club	Source	Date Signed	Seasons Played	Apps	Subs	Gls
Arsenal	Jnrs	05.56	57-61	32	-	0
Reading	Tr	10.62	62-64	34	-	0
Bristol Rov	Tr	07.65	65-69	88	4	3

PETTS Paul Andrew
Hackney, 27 September, 1961 EYth (W)

League Club	Source	Date Signed	Seasons Played	Apps	Subs	Gls
Bristol Rov	App	06.79	78-79	12	1	0
Shrewsbury T	Tr	08.80	80-84	138	11	16

PETTY Benjamin (Ben) James
Solihull, 22 March, 1977 (M)

League Club	Source	Date Signed	Seasons Played	Apps	Subs	Gls
Aston Villa	YT	05.95				
Stoke C	Tr	11.98	98-00	26	20	0
Hull C	Tr	07.01	01-02	24	5	0

PEVERELL John Richard
Richmond, North Yorkshire, 17 September, 1941 (FB)

League Club	Source	Date Signed	Seasons Played	Apps	Subs	Gls
Darlington	Ferryhill Ath	09.59	61-71	418	1	13

PEVERELL Nicholas (Nicky) John
Middlesbrough, 28 April, 1973 (F)

League Club	Source	Date Signed	Seasons Played	Apps	Subs	Gls
Middlesbrough	YT	07.91				
Hartlepool U	Tr	11.92	92-93	14	21	3
Hartlepool U	Kuitan Sports (HK)	12.94	94	0	1	0
York C	Tr	02.95	94-95	13	16	2

PEYTON Gerald (Gerry) Joseph
Birmingham, 20 May, 1956 IRu21-2/IR-33 (G)

League Club	Source	Date Signed	Seasons Played	Apps	Subs	Gls
Burnley	Atherstone T	05.75	75-76	30	0	0
Fulham	Tr	12.76	76-85	345	0	0
Southend U	L	09.83	83	10	0	0
Bournemouth	Tr	07.86	86-90	202	0	0
Everton	Tr	07.91				
Bolton W	L	02.92	91	1	0	0
Brentford	L	09.92	92	14	0	0
Chelsea	L	01.93	92	0	1	0
Brentford	Tr	03.93	92	5	0	0

PEYTON Noel
Dublin, 4 December, 1935 LoI-5/IRB/IR-6 (IF)

League Club	Source	Date Signed	Seasons Played	Apps	Subs	Gls
Leeds U	Shamrock Rov	01.58	57-62	105	-	17
York C	Tr	07.63	63-64	37	-	4

PEYTON Robert Andrew
Birmingham, 1 May, 1954 (M)

League Club	Source	Date Signed	Seasons Played	Apps	Subs	Gls
Port Vale	Chelmsley T	01.72	71	1	1	0

PEYTON Warren
Manchester, 13 December, 1979 (M)

League Club	Source	Date Signed	Seasons Played	Apps	Subs	Gls
Rochdale	Bolton W (N/C)	10.99	99	1	0	0
Bury	Tr	09.00	00	0	1	0

PHELAN Albert
Sheffield, 27 April, 1945 (CD)

League Club	Source	Date Signed	Seasons Played	Apps	Subs	Gls
Chesterfield	Charlton U	07.64	64-74	386	5	14
Halifax T	Tr	10.74	74-76	118	0	4

PHELAN Leeyon
Hammersmith, 6 October, 1982 (F)

League Club	Source	Date Signed	Seasons Played	Apps	Subs	Gls
Wycombe W	YT	07.01	00-01	0	3	0

PHELAN Michael (Mike) Christopher
Nelson, 24 September, 1962 EYth/E-1 (M)

League Club	Source	Date Signed	Seasons Played	Apps	Subs	Gls
Burnley	App	07.80	80-84	166	2	9
Norwich C	Tr	07.85	85-88	155	1	9
Manchester U	Tr	07.89	89-93	88	14	2
West Bromwich A	Tr	07.94	94-95	18	3	0

PHELAN Terence (Terry) Michael
Manchester, 16 March, 1967 IRYth/IRu23-1/IRu21-1/IRB-1/IR-42 (FB)

League Club	Source	Date Signed	Seasons Played	Apps	Subs	Gls
Leeds U	App	08.84	85	12	2	0
Swansea C	Tr	07.86	86	45	0	0
Wimbledon	Tr	07.87	87-91	155	4	1
Manchester C	Tr	08.92	92-95	102	1	1
Chelsea	Tr	11.95	95-96	13	2	0
Everton	Tr	01.97	96-99	23	2	0
Crystal Palace	L	10.99	99	14	0	0
Fulham	Tr	02.00	99-00	18	1	2
Sheffield U	Tr	08.01	01	8	0	0

PHENIX William (Bill) Brian
Tyldesley, 10 December, 1937 Died 1997 (W)

League Club	Source	Date Signed	Seasons Played	Apps	Subs	Gls
Southport	Boothstown Holy Family	12.57	57-58	15	-	3

PHILLIBEN John
Stirling, 14 March, 1964 SYth (CD)

League Club	Source	Date Signed	Seasons Played	Apps	Subs	Gls
Doncaster Rov	Stirling A	03.84	83-86	66	5	1
Cambridge U	L	12.85	85	6	0	0

PHILLIP Iain Frederick
Dundee, 14 February, 1951 SSch/Su23-1/SLge-1 (M)

League Club	Source	Date Signed	Seasons Played	Apps	Subs	Gls
Crystal Palace	Dundee	09.72	72-73	35	0	1

PHILLIPS Benjamin (Ben)
Hazel Grove, 9 June, 1960 (FB)

League Club	Source	Date Signed	Seasons Played	Apps	Subs	Gls
Bury	Macclesfield T	09.80	80	14	0	0

PHILLIPS Brendon Ulysses
St Catherine, Jamaica, 16 July, 1954 ESemiPro (M)

League Club	Source	Date Signed	Seasons Played	Apps	Subs	Gls
Leicester C	App	07.72				
Peterborough U	Tr	08.73	73	1	0	0
Mansfield T	Boston U	08.80	80	17	0	0

PHILLIPS John **Brian**
Cadishead, 9 November, 1931 (CD)

League Club	Source	Date Signed	Seasons Played	Apps	Subs	Gls
Middlesbrough	Altrincham	06.54	54-59	121	-	2
Mansfield T	Tr	06.60	60-62	103	-	3

PHILLIPS Cornelius (Con) Patrick
Liverpool, 10 May, 1938 (CF)

League Club	Source	Date Signed	Seasons Played	Apps	Subs	Gls
Liverpool	Jnrs	06.55				
Southport	Tr	07.57	57	19	-	6

PHILLIPS David Owen
Wegburg, Germany, 29 July, 1963 WYth/Wu21-4/W-62 (M)

League Club	Source	Date Signed	Seasons Played	Apps	Subs	Gls
Plymouth Arg	App	08.81	81-83	65	8	15
Manchester C	Tr	08.84	84-85	81	0	13
Coventry C	Tr	06.86	86-88	93	7	8
Norwich C	Tr	07.89	89-92	152	0	18
Nottingham F	Tr	08.93	93-96	116	10	5
Huddersfield T	Tr	11.97	97-98	44	8	3
Lincoln C	Tr	03.99	98-99	15	2	0

PHILLIPS Donald (Don)
Llanelli, 3 March, 1933 (IF)

League Club	Source	Date Signed	Seasons Played	Apps	Subs	Gls
Swansea T	Llanelli	12.56	56-57	3	-	0

League Club	Source	Date Signed	Seasons Played	Apps	Subs	Gls
PHILLIPS Edward (Ted) John						
Leiston, 21 August, 1933						(IF)
Ipswich T	Leiston	12.53	53-63	269	-	161
Leyton Orient	Tr	03.64	63-64	36	-	17
Luton T	Tr	02.65	64	12	-	8
Colchester U	Tr	09.65	65	32	0	13
PHILLIPS Ernest (Ernie)						
North Shields, 29 November, 1923 Died 2004						(FB)
Manchester C	South Shields	01.47	48-51	80	-	0
Hull C	Tr	11.51	51-53	42	-	0
York C	Tr	06.54	54-57	164	-	2
PHILLIPS Gareth Russell						
Porth, 19 August, 1979 WSch/WYth/Wu21-3						(M)
Swansea C	YT	07.98	96-02	59	29	2
PHILLIPS Gary Christopher						
St Albans, 20 September, 1961 ESemiPro						(G)
West Bromwich A	Brighton & Hove A (App)	06.79				
Brentford	Barnet	12.84	84-87	143	0	0
Reading	Tr	08.88	88	24	0	0
Hereford U	L	09.89	89	6	0	0
Barnet	Tr	12.89	91-94	117	0	0
PHILLIPS Gordon David						
Uxbridge, 17 November, 1946						(G)
Brentford	Hayes	11.63	64-72	206	0	0
PHILLIPS Ian Alexander						
Cumnock, 23 April, 1959						(FB)
Mansfield T	Ipswich T (App)	08.77	77-78	18	5	0
Peterborough U	Tr	08.79	79-81	97	0	3
Northampton T	Tr	08.82	82	42	0	1
Colchester U	Tr	09.83	83-86	150	0	10
Aldershot	Tr	08.87	87-89	106	0	2
Colchester U	Kettering T	07.91	92	0	1	0
PHILLIPS James (Jimmy) Neil						
Bolton, 8 February, 1966						(FB)
Bolton W	App	08.83	83-86	103	5	2
Oxford U	Glasgow Rgrs	08.88	88-89	79	0	7
Middlesbrough	Tr	03.90	89-92	139	0	6
Bolton W	Tr	07.93	93-99	210	11	3
PHILLIPS John Edgar						
Portsmouth, 4 March, 1937						(WH)
Portsmouth	Jnrs	05.55	55-59	77	-	0
PHILLIPS Thomas John Seymour						
Shrewsbury, 7 July, 1951 Wu23-4/W-4						(G)
Shrewsbury T	App	11.68	68-69	51	0	0
Aston Villa	Tr	10.69	69	15	0	0
Chelsea	Tr	08.70	70-78	125	0	0
Crewe Alex	L	08.79	79	6	0	0
Brighton & Hove A	Tr	03.80	80	1	0	0
Charlton Ath	Tr	07.81	81	2	0	0
PHILLIPS Joseph (Joe) Roy						
Cardiff, 8 July, 1923 Died 1992						(FB)
Cardiff C	Cardiff Corinthians	04.42	46	2	-	0
PHILLIPS Justin Lee						
Derby, 17 December, 1971 EYth						(CD)
Derby Co	YT	07.90	90	3	0	1
PHILLIPS Kevin Mark						
Hitchin, 25 July, 1973 EB-1/E-8						(F)
Watford	Baldock T	12.94	94-96	54	5	24
Sunderland	Tr	07.97	97-02	207	1	113
Southampton	Tr	08.03	03-04	49	15	22
PHILLIPS Lee						
Aberdare, 18 March, 1979 WYth						(FB)
Cardiff C	YT	07.97	96-99	11	5	0
PHILLIPS Lee Paul						
Penzance, 16 September, 1980						(F)
Plymouth Arg	YT	07.98	96-00	18	32	1
PHILLIPS Leighton						
Briton Ferry, 25 September, 1949 WSch/Wu23-4/Wu21-1/W-58						(CD)
Cardiff C	App	04.67	66-74	169	13	11
Aston Villa	Tr	09.74	74-78	134	6	4
Swansea C	Tr	11.78	78-80	97	0	0
Charlton Ath	Tr	08.81	81-82	45	0	1
Exeter C	Tr	03.83	82	10	0	0
PHILLIPS Horace Leonard (Len)						
Shoreditch, 11 September, 1922 FLge-2/E-3						(IF)
Portsmouth	Hillside YC	01.46	46-54	245	-	48

League Club	Source	Date Signed	Seasons Played	Apps	Subs	Gls
PHILLIPS Leslie (Les) Michael						
Lambeth, 7 January, 1963						(M)
Birmingham C	App	08.80	81-83	36	8	3
Oxford U	Tr	03.84	83-92	165	14	10
Northampton T	Tr	07.93	93	26	0	0
PHILLIPS Lionel Arthur Raymond						
Much Dewchurch, 13 December, 1929						(IF)
Portsmouth	Yeovil T	02.53	53	4	-	1
PHILLIPS Marcus Stuart						
Bradford-on-Avon, 17 October, 1973						(W)
Swindon T	YT	05.93				
Oxford U	Witney T	02.97	96	0	1	0
PHILLIPS Mark Ian						
Lambeth, 27 January, 1982						(CD)
Millwall	YT	05.00	01-04	33	0	1
PHILLIPS Martin John						
Exeter, 13 March, 1976						(W)
Exeter C	YT	07.94	92-95	36	16	5
Manchester C	Tr	11.95	95-96	3	12	0
Scunthorpe U	L	01.98	97	2	1	0
Exeter C	L	03.98	97	7	1	0
Portsmouth	Tr	08.98	98-99	4	20	1
Bristol Rov	L	02.99	98	2	0	0
Plymouth Arg	Tr	08.00	00-03	90	24	10
Torquay U	Tr	07.04	04	19	11	2
PHILLIPS Michael Edward						
Dulwich, 22 January, 1983						(M)
Gillingham	YT	04.01	00	0	1	0
PHILLIPS Michael (Mike) Shirkie						
Cumnock, 18 January, 1933						(CF)
Grimsby T	Cumnock Jnrs	01.55	54	6	-	1
PHILLIPS Nicholas (Nicky)						
West Ham, 29 November, 1960						(M)
Coventry C	App	08.78	79	4	1	0
PHILLIPS Peter Stuart						
Wellingborough, 29 June, 1946 EAmat						(F)
Luton T	Bishops Stortford	06.69	69	2	3	0
Torquay U	L	01.71	70	2	0	1
Cambridge U	Tr	03.71	70-72	40	13	13
PHILLIPS Ralph						
Hetton-le-Hole, 9 August, 1933						(FB)
Middlesbrough		05.54				
Northampton T	Tr	08.58	58-60	83	-	1
Darlington	Tr	06.61	61-62	29	-	2
PHILLIPS Reginald (Reg) Roydon						
Llanelli, 9 March, 1921 Died 1972						(CF)
Crewe Alex	Shrewsbury T	05.49	49-51	63	-	35
PHILLIPS Ronald (Ron) Daniel						
Worsley, 30 March, 1947 Died 2002						(W)
Bolton W	Jnrs	10.65	66-74	135	10	17
Chesterfield	L	01.75	74	5	0	0
Bury	Tr	06.75	75-76	68	4	5
Chester	Tr	09.77	77-80	128	2	21
PHILLIPS Russell George Thomas						
Exeter, 22 June, 1916 Died 2000						(W)
Millwall		01.45				
Torquay U	Tr	01.46	46	30	-	3
PHILLIPS Stephen (Steve) Edward						
Edmonton, 4 August, 1954 EYth						(F)
Birmingham C	App	08.71	71-75	15	5	1
Torquay U	L	12.74	74	6	0	0
Northampton T	Tr	10.75	75-76	50	1	8
Brentford	Tr	02.77	76-79	156	1	65
Northampton T	Tr	08.80	80-81	75	0	29
Southend U	Tr	03.82	81-85	157	1	66
Torquay U	Tr	01.86	85-86	32	0	11
Peterborough U	Tr	11.86	86-87	46	2	16
Exeter C	L	09.87	87	5	1	1
Chesterfield	L	01.88	87	9	0	2
PHILLIPS Steven (Steve) John						
Bath, 6 May, 1978						(G)
Bristol C	Paulton Rov	11.96	98-04	237	1	0
PHILLIPS Stewart Gavin						
Halifax, 30 December, 1961						(F)
Hereford U	App	11.79	77-87	285	8	84
West Bromwich A	Tr	03.88	87-88	15	0	4

League Club	Source	Date Signed	Seasons Played	Apps	Subs	Gls
Swansea C	Tr	01.89	88-89	10	10	1
Hereford U	Tr	08.90	90	31	6	10
Wrexham	Tr	08.91	91	1	1	1

PHILLIPS Trevor
Rotherham, 18 September, 1952 EYth (F)

League Club	Source	Date Signed	Seasons Played	Apps	Subs	Gls
Rotherham U	App	03.70	69-78	289	32	80
Hull C	Tr	06.79	79	22	0	3
Chester	Tr	03.80	79-81	57	7	11
Stockport Co	Tr	03.82	81-82	49	2	13
Chester C	Tr	08.83	83	9	1	2

PHILLIPS Waynne
Bangor, 15 December, 1970 WB-1 (M)

League Club	Source	Date Signed	Seasons Played	Apps	Subs	Gls
Wrexham	YT	08.89	89-97	184	23	16
Stockport Co	Tr	02.98	97-98	14	8	0
Wrexham	Tr	07.99	99-02	35	3	2

PHILLIPSON William (Bill) Ernest
Barrow, 4 April, 1917 Died 1974 (G)

League Club	Source	Date Signed	Seasons Played	Apps	Subs	Gls
Barrow	Holker COB	10.38	46-47	14	-	0

PHILLIPSON-MASTERS Forbes Ernest
Bournemouth, 14 November, 1955 (CD)

League Club	Source	Date Signed	Seasons Played	Apps	Subs	Gls
Southampton	App	11.73	76-77	9	0	0
Exeter C	L	09.76	76	6	0	0
Bournemouth	L	09.77	77	7	0	2
Luton T	L	03.79	78	10	0	0
Plymouth Arg	Tr	08.79	79-82	119	0	0
Bristol C	Tr	11.82	82-84	94	0	4
Exeter C	L	03.85	84	5	2	1

PHILLISKIRK Anthony (Tony)
Sunderland, 10 February, 1965 ESch (F)

League Club	Source	Date Signed	Seasons Played	Apps	Subs	Gls
Sheffield U	Jnrs	08.83	83-87	62	18	20
Rotherham U	L	10.86	86	6	0	1
Oldham Ath	Tr	07.88	88	3	7	1
Preston NE	Tr	02.89	88	13	1	6
Bolton W	Tr	06.89	89-92	139	2	51
Peterborough U	Tr	10.92	92-93	37	6	15
Burnley	Tr	01.94	93-95	33	7	9
Carlisle U	L	10.95	95	3	0	1
Cardiff C	Tr	12.95	95-96	55	6	5
Macclesfield T	L	02.98	97	1	9	1

PHILO Mark William
Bracknell, 5 October, 1984 (M)

League Club	Source	Date Signed	Seasons Played	Apps	Subs	Gls
Wycombe W	Sch	07.03	03-04	6	11	0

PHILP David
Fowey, 8 July, 1960 (G)

League Club	Source	Date Signed	Seasons Played	Apps	Subs	Gls
Plymouth Arg	Newquay	07.84	84	7	0	0

PHILPOTT Alan
Stoke-on-Trent, 8 November, 1942 (M)

League Club	Source	Date Signed	Seasons Played	Apps	Subs	Gls
Stoke C	Jnrs	11.59	60-67	41	4	1
Oldham Ath	Tr	11.67	67-68	28	3	1

PHILPOTT Lee
Barnet, 21 February, 1970 (W)

League Club	Source	Date Signed	Seasons Played	Apps	Subs	Gls
Peterborough U	App	07.86	87-88	1	3	0
Cambridge U	Tr	05.89	89-92	118	16	17
Leicester C	Tr	11.92	92-95	57	18	3
Blackpool	Tr	03.96	95-97	51	20	5
Lincoln C	Tr	07.98	98-99	33	14	3
Hull C	Tr	08.00	00-02	45	9	2

PHILPOTTS David (Dave) Ronald
Bromborough, 31 March, 1954 (CD)

League Club	Source	Date Signed	Seasons Played	Apps	Subs	Gls
Coventry C	App	10.71	73	3	0	0
Southport	L	01.74	73	8	0	0
Tranmere Rov	Tr	09.74	74-77	174	1	5
Tranmere Rov	Carolina (USA)	10.83	83-84	36	0	6

PHIPPS Harold James
Dartford, 15 January, 1916 Died 2000 (CD)

League Club	Source	Date Signed	Seasons Played	Apps	Subs	Gls
Charlton Ath	Middlesex Regiment	10.43	46-50	185	-	2
Watford	Tr	06.52	52-53	47	-	0

PHOENIX William **Eric**
Manchester, 20 January, 1932 (IF)

League Club	Source	Date Signed	Seasons Played	Apps	Subs	Gls
Gillingham	Hastings U	07.54	54-55	17	-	2
Exeter C	Tr	07.56	56	5	-	0

PHOENIX Peter Patrick
Urmston, 31 December, 1936 (W)

League Club	Source	Date Signed	Seasons Played	Apps	Subs	Gls
Oldham Ath	Tamworth	02.58	57-62	161	-	26
Rochdale	Tr	10.62	62-63	36	-	4
Exeter C	Tr	10.63	63	15	-	1
Southport	Tr	01.64	63	10	-	0
Stockport Co	Tr	07.64	64	19	-	1

PHOENIX Ronald (Ron) James
Stretford, 30 June, 1929 (WH)

League Club	Source	Date Signed	Seasons Played	Apps	Subs	Gls
Manchester C	Humphrey Park	03.50	51-59	53	-	2
Rochdale	Tr	02.60	60-61	64	-	0

PHYTHIAN Ernest (Ernie) Rixon
Farnworth, 16 July, 1942 EYth (CD)

League Club	Source	Date Signed	Seasons Played	Apps	Subs	Gls
Bolton W	Jnrs	07.59	59-61	10	-	3
Wrexham	Tr	03.62	61-64	134	-	44
Hartlepools U	Tr	06.65	65-67	124	0	51

PICK Gary Mark
Leicester, 9 July, 1971 (M)

League Club	Source	Date Signed	Seasons Played	Apps	Subs	Gls
Stoke C	Leicester U	08.92				
Hereford U	Tr	06.94	94-95	33	10	2
Cambridge U	Tr	03.96	95	2	2	0

PICKARD Leonard (Len) James
Barnstaple, 29 November, 1924 (CF)

League Club	Source	Date Signed	Seasons Played	Apps	Subs	Gls
Bristol Rov	Barnstaple T	01.51	51	4	-	1
Bristol C	Tr	05.53				
Bradford PA	Tr	10.53	53-55	76	-	31

PICKARD Owen Anthony
Barnstaple, 18 November, 1969 (F)

League Club	Source	Date Signed	Seasons Played	Apps	Subs	Gls
Plymouth Arg	YT	07.88	88-91	6	10	1
Hereford U	Tr	07.92	92-93	66	7	14

PICKERING Albert (Ally) Gary
Manchester, 22 June, 1967 (FB)

League Club	Source	Date Signed	Seasons Played	Apps	Subs	Gls
Rotherham U	Buxton	02.90	89-93	87	1	2
Coventry C	Tr	10.93	93-95	54	11	0
Stoke C	Tr	08.96	96-98	81	2	1
Burnley	Tr	12.98	98	21	0	1
Cambridge U	Altrincham	12.99				
Chester C	Tr	01.00	99	7	0	1

PICKERING Frederick (Fred)
Blackburn, 19 January, 1941 Eu23-3/FLge-1/E-3 (F)

League Club	Source	Date Signed	Seasons Played	Apps	Subs	Gls
Blackburn Rov	Jnrs	01.58	59-63	123	-	59
Everton	Tr	03.64	63-66	97	0	56
Birmingham C	Tr	08.67	67-68	74	0	27
Blackpool	Tr	06.69	69-70	49	1	24
Blackburn Rov	Tr	03.71	70	11	0	2

PICKERING John (Jack)
Chapeltown, 18 December, 1908 Died 1977 FLge-1/E-1 (IF)

League Club	Source	Date Signed	Seasons Played	Apps	Subs	Gls
Sheffield U	Mortomley St Sav	12.25	26-47	344	-	103

PICKERING John
Stockton, 7 November, 1944 Died 2001 (CD)

League Club	Source	Date Signed	Seasons Played	Apps	Subs	Gls
Newcastle U	Stockton	07.63				
Halifax T	Tr	09.65	65-73	364	3	5
Barnsley	Tr	07.74	74	42	1	2

PICKERING Michael (Mike) John
Mirfield, 29 September, 1956 (CD)

League Club	Source	Date Signed	Seasons Played	Apps	Subs	Gls
Barnsley	Jnrs	10.74	74-76	100	0	1
Southampton	Tr	06.77	77-78	44	0	0
Sheffield Wed	Tr	10.78	78-82	106	4	1
Norwich C	L	09.83	83	0	1	0
Bradford C	L	11.83	83	4	0	0
Barnsley	L	12.83	83	3	0	0
Rotherham U	Tr	01.84	83-85	102	0	1
York C	Tr	07.86	86	31	1	1
Stockport Co	Tr	07.87	87-88	15	1	0

PICKERING Nicholas (Nick)
Newcastle, 4 August, 1963 EYth/Eu21-15/E-1 (M)

League Club	Source	Date Signed	Seasons Played	Apps	Subs	Gls
Sunderland	App	08.81	81-85	177	2	18
Coventry C	Tr	01.86	85-87	76	2	9
Derby Co	Tr	08.88	88-91	35	10	3
Darlington	Tr	10.91	91-92	57	0	7
Burnley	Tr	03.93	92	4	0	0

PICKERING Peter Barlow
New Earswick, 24 March, 1926 (G)

League Club	Source	Date Signed	Seasons Played	Apps	Subs	Gls
York C	Earswick	04.44	46-47	49	-	0
Chelsea	Tr	05.48	48-50	27	-	0
Northampton T	Kettering T	07.55	55-57	86	-	0

PICKERING William (Bill) Henry
Sheffield, 10 December, 1919 Died 1983 EAmat (FB)

League Club	Source	Date Signed	Seasons Played	Apps	Subs	Gls
Sheffield Wed	Jnrs	10.37	38	3	-	0
Oldham Ath	Tr	07.48	48-49	78	-	0

PICKETT Reginald (Reg) Arthur
India, 6 January, 1927 (WH)

League Club	Source	Date Signed	Seasons Played	Apps	Subs	Gls
Portsmouth	Weymouth	03.49	49-56	123	-	3
Ipswich T	Tr	07.57	57-62	140	-	3

PICKRELL Anthony (Tony) David
Neath, 3 November, 1942 (W)

League Club	Source	Date Signed	Seasons Played	Apps	Subs	Gls
Cardiff C	Jnrs	09.60	60-61	18	-	4

PICKUP John **Antony (Tony)**
Wakefield, 3 December, 1931 (IF)

League Club	Source	Date Signed	Seasons Played	Apps	Subs	Gls
Bradford PA	Frickley Colliery	09.55	55	2	-	0

PICKUP Reginald (Reg) John
Stoke-on-Trent, 6 September, 1929 (IF)

League Club	Source	Date Signed	Seasons Played	Apps	Subs	Gls
Stoke C	Jnrs	08.49	49	1	-	0

PICKWICK Donald (Don) Henry John
Pen-y-graig, 7 February, 1925 Died 2004 (WH)

League Club	Source	Date Signed	Seasons Played	Apps	Subs	Gls
Norwich C	Bristol C (Am)	08.47	47-55	224	-	9

PIDCOCK Frederick (Fred) Charles
Canada, 29 June, 1933 Died 1999 (G)

League Club	Source	Date Signed	Seasons Played	Apps	Subs	Gls
Walsall (Am)	Moor Green	09.53	53	1	-	0

PIDGELEY Leonard (Lenny) James
Twickenham, 7 February, 1984 EYth/Eu20 (G)

League Club	Source	Date Signed	Seasons Played	Apps	Subs	Gls
Chelsea	Sch	07.03	04	0	1	0
Watford	L	09.03	03	26	1	0

PIEARCE Stephen (Steve)
Sutton Coldfield, 27 September, 1974 (F)

League Club	Source	Date Signed	Seasons Played	Apps	Subs	Gls
Wolverhampton W	YT	07.93				
Doncaster Rov	Tr	07.96	96	8	11	1

PIECHNIK Torben
Copenhagen, Denmark, 21 May, 1963 Denmark int (CD)

League Club	Source	Date Signed	Seasons Played	Apps	Subs	Gls
Liverpool	FC Copenhagen (Den)	09.92	92-93	16	1	0

PIEKALNIETIS John Andrew
Penrith, 23 September, 1951 EYth (CD)

League Club	Source	Date Signed	Seasons Played	Apps	Subs	Gls
Nottingham F	Jnrs	03.69				
Southend U	Tr	04.71	70	1	0	0

PIERCE John **Barry**
Liverpool, 13 August, 1934 (IF)

League Club	Source	Date Signed	Seasons Played	Apps	Subs	Gls
Crystal Palace	Truro C	08.55	55-58	85	-	23
Millwall	Tr	05.59	59-60	46	-	17
York C	Tr	07.61	61	12	-	5
Exeter C	Tr	07.62	62	28	-	4

PIERCE David Edward
Manchester, 4 October, 1975 (G)

League Club	Source	Date Signed	Seasons Played	Apps	Subs	Gls
Rotherham U	Manchester U (YT)	08.94				
Chesterfield	Tr	08.95	95	1	0	0

PIERCE Gary
Bury, 2 March, 1951 (G)

League Club	Source	Date Signed	Seasons Played	Apps	Subs	Gls
Huddersfield T	Mossley	02.71	71-72	23	0	0
Wolverhampton W	Tr	08.73	73-78	98	0	0
Barnsley	Tr	07.79	79-82	81	0	0
Blackpool	Tr	08.83	83	27	0	0

PIERCY John William
Forest Gate, 18 September, 1979 EYth (M)

League Club	Source	Date Signed	Seasons Played	Apps	Subs	Gls
Tottenham H	YT	07.98	99-00	1	7	0
Brighton & Hove A	Tr	09.02	02-04	10	20	4

PIERRE Nigel Nigus
Port of Spain, Trinidad, 2 June, 1979 TrinidadU23/Trinidad-4 (F)

League Club	Source	Date Signed	Seasons Played	Apps	Subs	Gls
Bristol Rov	Joe Public (Tr)	02.00	99	1	2	0

PIGGOTT Gary David
Warley, 1 April, 1969 (F)

League Club	Source	Date Signed	Seasons Played	Apps	Subs	Gls
West Bromwich A	Dudley T	03.91	91	3	2	0
Shrewsbury T	Tr	03.93	92	3	1	0

PIKE Christopher (Chris)
Cardiff, 19 October, 1961 (F)

League Club	Source	Date Signed	Seasons Played	Apps	Subs	Gls
Fulham	Barry T	03.85	85-87	32	10	4
Cardiff C	L	12.86	86	6	0	2
Cardiff C	Tr	07.89	89-92	134	14	65
Hereford U	Tr	07.93	93-94	36	2	18
Gillingham	Tr	09.94	94	26	1	13

PIKE Geoffrey (Geoff) Alan
Clapton, 28 September, 1956 (M)

League Club	Source	Date Signed	Seasons Played	Apps	Subs	Gls
West Ham U	App	09.74	75-86	275	16	32
Notts Co	Tr	07.87	87-88	80	2	17
Leyton Orient	Tr	09.89	89-90	36	8	1

PIKE Martin Russell
South Shields, 21 October, 1964 (FB)

League Club	Source	Date Signed	Seasons Played	Apps	Subs	Gls
West Bromwich A	App	10.82				
Peterborough U	Tr	08.83	83-85	119	7	8
Sheffield U	Tr	08.86	86-89	127	2	5
Tranmere Rov	L	11.89	89	2	0	0
Bolton W	L	12.89	89	5	0	1
Fulham	Tr	02.90	89-93	187	3	14
Rotherham U	Tr	08.94	94-95	7	2	0

PILGRIM John **Alan**
Billingborough, 20 July, 1947 (CD)

League Club	Source	Date Signed	Seasons Played	Apps	Subs	Gls
Lincoln C	Billingborough	05.65	65-71	20	3	1

PILKINGTON Brian
Leyland, 12 February, 1933 EB/FLge-2/E-1 (W)

League Club	Source	Date Signed	Seasons Played	Apps	Subs	Gls
Burnley	Leyland Motors	04.51	52-60	300	-	67
Bolton W	Tr	03.61	60-63	82	-	11
Bury	Tr	02.64	63-64	20	-	0
Barrow	Tr	02.65	64-66	86	1	9

PILKINGTON George
Hemsworth, 3 June, 1926 (WH)

League Club	Source	Date Signed	Seasons Played	Apps	Subs	Gls
Rotherham U	Great Houghton	11.48	49	1	-	0
Chester	Tr	07.52	52	16	-	0
Stockport Co	Tr	05.53	53-55	77	-	4

PILKINGTON George Edward
Rugeley, 7 November, 1981 EYth (CD)

League Club	Source	Date Signed	Seasons Played	Apps	Subs	Gls
Everton	YT	11.98				
Exeter C	L	11.02	02	7	0	0
Port Vale	Tr	07.03	03-04	86	1	1

PILKINGTON Joel Thomas
Accrington, 1 August, 1984 (M)

League Club	Source	Date Signed	Seasons Played	Apps	Subs	Gls
Burnley	Sch	07.03	03-04	0	2	0

PILKINGTON Kevin William
Hitchin, 8 March, 1974 ESch (G)

League Club	Source	Date Signed	Seasons Played	Apps	Subs	Gls
Manchester U	YT	07.92	94-97	4	2	0
Rochdale	L	02.96	95	6	0	0
Rotherham U	L	01.97	96	17	0	0
Port Vale	Tr	07.98	98-99	23	0	0
Mansfield T	Aberystwyth T	09.00	00-04	167	0	0

PILKINGTON Leslie (Les)
Darwen, 23 June, 1925 Died 1995 (W)

League Club	Source	Date Signed	Seasons Played	Apps	Subs	Gls
Arsenal	Darwen Corinthians	03.48				
Watford	Tr	03.50	49-50	5	-	0

PILLING Andrew (Andy) James
Wigan, 30 June, 1969 (M)

League Club	Source	Date Signed	Seasons Played	Apps	Subs	Gls
Preston NE	App	•	85	1	0	0
Wigan Ath	Tr	07.87	87-92	131	25	20

PILLING John (Jack) James
Peasley Cross, 4 June, 1913 Died 1997 (WH)

League Club	Source	Date Signed	Seasons Played	Apps	Subs	Gls
Liverpool	Burscough	09.42				
Southport	Tr	02.46	46	9	-	0

PILLING Anthony **Stuart**
Sheffield, 26 March, 1951 (FB)

League Club	Source	Date Signed	Seasons Played	Apps	Subs	Gls
Preston NE	Jnrs	07.69				
Hull C	Tr	07.70				
Scunthorpe U	Tr	05.73	73-81	246	16	26

PILLING Vincent (Vince)
Bolton, 8 January, 1932 (W)

League Club	Source	Date Signed	Seasons Played	Apps	Subs	Gls
Bolton W	Lomax's	10.52	52-54	7	-	0
Bradford PA	Tr	08.55	55	9	-	1

PILVI Tero
Vihti, Finland, 21 February, 1976 (M)

League Club	Source	Date Signed	Seasons Played	Apps	Subs	Gls
Cambridge U	Airdrie	03.01	00	3	2	0

PIMBLETT Francis (Frank) Roy
Liverpool, 12 March, 1957 ESch (M)

League Club	Source	Date Signed	Seasons Played	Apps	Subs	Gls
Aston Villa	App	10.74	74-75	9	0	0
Newport Co	L	03.76	75	7	0	0
Stockport Co	Tr	07.76	76	0	1	0
Hartlepool U	Brisbane C (Aus)	03.80	79	3	0	0

PIMBLEY Douglas (Doug) William
King's Norton, 19 June, 1917 Died 1988 (WH)

League Club	Source	Date Signed	Seasons Played	Apps	Subs	Gls
Birmingham C	Stourbridge	07.46	46	2	-	0
Notts Co	Tr	03.48	47-49	23	-	1

PIMLOTT John Gordon
Radcliffe, 21 January, 1939 Died 1992 (IF)

League Club	Source	Date Signed	Seasons Played	Apps	Subs	Gls
Bury		12.57				
Chester	Tr	08.59	59-60	41	-	11

PINAMONTE Lorenzo
Foggia, Italy, 9 May, 1978 (F)

League Club	Source	Date Signed	Seasons Played	Apps	Subs	Gls
Bristol C	Foggia (It)	09.98	98-99	3	4	1
Brighton & Hove A	L	12.99	99	8	1	2
Brentford	Tr	02.00	99-00	8	15	2
Leyton Orient	L	02.01	00	5	6	2

PINAULT Thomas
Grasse, France, 4 December, 1981 (M)

League Club	Source	Date Signed	Seasons Played	Apps	Subs	Gls
Colchester U	AS Cannes (Fr)	07.99	99-03	104	29	5
Grimsby T	Tr	07.04	04	32	11	7

PINCHBECK Clifford (Cliff) Brian
Cleethorpes, 20 January, 1925 Died 1996 (CF)

League Club	Source	Date Signed	Seasons Played	Apps	Subs	Gls
Everton	Scunthorpe & Lindsey U	12.47	47	3	-	0
Brighton & Hove A	Tr	08.49	49	14	-	5
Port Vale	Tr	11.49	49-51	69	-	34
Northampton T	Tr	12.51	51	3	-	3

PINCOTT Frederick (Fred)
Bristol, 19 March, 1913 Died 2000 (CD)

League Club	Source	Date Signed	Seasons Played	Apps	Subs	Gls
Wolverhampton W	Bristol Royal Victoria	11.31	32	2	-	0
Bournemouth	Tr	05.34	34-38	196	-	0
Newport Co	Gravesend U	07.47	47	14	-	0

PINDER John (Jack) James
Acomb, 1 December, 1912 Died 2004 ESch (FB)

League Club	Source	Date Signed	Seasons Played	Apps	Subs	Gls
York C	Jnrs	02.30	32-47	199	-	4

PINGEL Frank Mortensen
Resskov, Denmark, 9 May, 1964 Denmark int (F)

League Club	Source	Date Signed	Seasons Played	Apps	Subs	Gls
Newcastle U	AGF Aarhus (Den)	01.89	88	13	1	1

PINKNEY Alan John
Battersea, 1 January, 1947 ESch (M)

League Club	Source	Date Signed	Seasons Played	Apps	Subs	Gls
Exeter C	St Lukes College	02.68	67-68	7	0	1
Crystal Palace	Tr	07.69	69-73	19	5	0
Fulham	L	01.73	72	11	1	0

PINNER Michael (Mike) John
Boston, 16 February, 1934 EAmat (G)

League Club	Source	Date Signed	Seasons Played	Apps	Subs	Gls
Aston Villa (Am)	Pegasus	05.54	54-56	4	-	0
Sheffield Wed (Am)	Corinthian Casuals	12.57	57-58	7	-	0
Queens Park Rgrs (Am)	Tr	07.59	59	19	-	0
Manchester U (Am)	Tr	02.61	60	4	-	0
Chelsea (Am)	Tr	10.61	61	1	-	0
Swansea T (Am)	Tr	05.62	61	1	-	0
Leyton Orient	Hendon	10.62	62-64	77	-	0

PINNOCK James Edward
Dartford, 1 August, 1978 (F)

League Club	Source	Date Signed	Seasons Played	Apps	Subs	Gls
Gillingham	YT	07.97	96-99	0	9	0

PINTO Sergio Paulo Viera
Escudos, Portugal, 8 January, 1973 (W)

League Club	Source	Date Signed	Seasons Played	Apps	Subs	Gls
Bradford C	Boavista (Por)	10.96	96	7	11	0

PIPE David Ronald
Caerphilly, 5 November, 1983 WYth/Wu21-12/W-1 (M)

League Club	Source	Date Signed	Seasons Played	Apps	Subs	Gls
Coventry C	YT	11.00	02	11	10	1
Notts Co	Tr	01.04	03-04	56	3	2

PIPER Gilbert Harold
Northfleet, 21 June, 1921 Died 1987 (CD)

League Club	Source	Date Signed	Seasons Played	Apps	Subs	Gls
Tottenham H		01.40				
Gillingham	Tr	08.46	50	4	-	0

PIPER Leonard (Lenny) Henry
Camberwell, 8 August, 1977 EYth (M)

League Club	Source	Date Signed	Seasons Played	Apps	Subs	Gls
Wimbledon	YT	06.95				
Gillingham	Tr	07.96	96-97	4	16	1

PIPER Matthew (Matt) James
Leicester, 29 September, 1981 (W)

League Club	Source	Date Signed	Seasons Played	Apps	Subs	Gls
Leicester C	YT	08.99	01	14	2	1
Mansfield T	L	11.01	01	8	0	1
Sunderland	Tr	08.02	02-04	13	11	0

PIPER Norman John
North Tawton, 8 January, 1948 EYth/Eu23-4 (M)

League Club	Source	Date Signed	Seasons Played	Apps	Subs	Gls
Plymouth Arg	App	02.65	64-69	215	0	35
Portsmouth	Tr	05.70	70-77	309	4	51

PIPER Ronald (Ron) David
Cresswell, Northumberland, 16 March, 1943 (IF)

League Club	Source	Date Signed	Seasons Played	Apps	Subs	Gls
Tottenham H	Arsenal (Am)	10.60	62	1	-	0

PIPER Stephen (Steve) Paul
Brighton, 2 November, 1953 (CD)

League Club	Source	Date Signed	Seasons Played	Apps	Subs	Gls
Brighton & Hove A	Jnrs	09.72	72-77	160	2	9
Portsmouth	Tr	02.78	77-78	27	2	2

PIRES Robert
Reims, France, 29 October, 1973 France 79 (M)

League Club	Source	Date Signed	Seasons Played	Apps	Subs	Gls
Arsenal	Marseille (Fr)	07.00	00-04	136	20	55

[PIRI] MORI COSTA Francisco Javier
Canea de Onis, Spain, 10 November, 1970 (M)

League Club	Source	Date Signed	Seasons Played	Apps	Subs	Gls
Barnsley (L)	Merida (Sp)	03.99	98	2	0	0

PIRIE Frederick (Fred) William
Coupar Angus, 19 January, 1934 (FB)

League Club	Source	Date Signed	Seasons Played	Apps	Subs	Gls
Accrington St	Coupar Angus	01.54	54-59	17	-	0

PISANTI David
Israel, 27 May, 1962 (M)

League Club	Source	Date Signed	Seasons Played	Apps	Subs	Gls
Queens Park Rgrs	FC Cologne (Ger)	09.87	87-88	16	5	0

PISTONE Alessandro (Sandro)
Milan, Italy, 27 July, 1975 Itu21 (FB)

League Club	Source	Date Signed	Seasons Played	Apps	Subs	Gls
Newcastle U	Inter Milan (It)	07.97	97-99	45	1	1
Everton	Tr	07.00	00-04	92	9	1

PITCHER Darren Edward James
Stepney, 12 October, 1969 EYth (FB)

League Club	Source	Date Signed	Seasons Played	Apps	Subs	Gls
Charlton Ath	YT	01.88	90-93	170	3	8
Crystal Palace	Tr	07.94	94-96	60	4	0
Leyton Orient	L	01.98	97	1	0	0

PITCHER Geoffrey (Geoff)
Sutton, 15 August, 1975 (M)

League Club	Source	Date Signed	Seasons Played	Apps	Subs	Gls
Millwall	YT	03.93				
Watford	Tr	07.94	94-95	4	9	2
Colchester U	Kingstonian	02.97	96	0	1	0
Brighton & Hove A	Kingstonian	06.01	01	2	8	0

PITMAN Jamie Roy
Warminster, 6 January, 1976 (M)

League Club	Source	Date Signed	Seasons Played	Apps	Subs	Gls
Swindon T	YT	07.94	94	2	1	0
Hereford U	Tr	02.96	95-96	16	5	0

PITT Courtney Leon
Westminster, 17 December, 1981 (FB)

League Club	Source	Date Signed	Seasons Played	Apps	Subs	Gls
Chelsea	YT	07.00				
Portsmouth	Tr	07.01	01	29	10	3
Luton T	L	08.03	03	11	1	0
Coventry C	L	12.03	03	1	0	0
Oxford U	Tr	03.04	03	5	3	0
Boston U	Tr	08.04	04	20	12	4

PITT John (Jackie) Henry
Willenhall, 20 May, 1920 Died 2004 (WH)

League Club	Source	Date Signed	Seasons Played	Apps	Subs	Gls
Bristol Rov	Aberavon	05.46	46-57	467	-	16

PITT Richard (Richie) Ernest
Ryhope, 22 October, 1951 ESch (CD)

League Club	Source	Date Signed	Seasons Played	Apps	Subs	Gls
Sunderland	Jnrs	11.68	68-73	126	0	7

PITT Stephen (Steve) William
Willesden, 1 August, 1948 (W)

League Club	Source	Date Signed	Seasons Played	Apps	Subs	Gls
Tottenham H	App	08.65	65	1	0	0
Colchester U	Tr	06.69	69	4	2	0

PITTMAN Stephen (Steve) Lee
North Carolina, USA, 18 July, 1967 (FB)

League Club	Source	Date Signed	Seasons Played	Apps	Subs	Gls
Shrewsbury T	East Fife	03.89	88-89	31	1	2

PITTS Matthew
Middlesbrough, 25 December, 1979 (FB)

League Club	Source	Date Signed	Seasons Played	Apps	Subs	Gls
Sunderland	YT	06.98				
Carlisle U	Tr	07.99	99-00	21	13	1

PLACE Brendan Anthony
Dublin, 13 December, 1965 (CD)

League Club	Source	Date Signed	Seasons Played	Apps	Subs	Gls
Gillingham	Athlone T	10.89	89	3	1	0

PLACE Charles (Charlie) Arthur
Ilkeston, 26 November, 1937 (W)

League Club	Source	Date Signed	Seasons Played	Apps	Subs	Gls
Derby Co	Jnrs	11.54	55	2	-	0

PLACE Mark Gerald
Mansfield, 16 November, 1969 (FB)

League Club	Source	Date Signed	Seasons Played	Apps	Subs	Gls
Mansfield T	YT	07.88	88-89	12	3	0
Doncaster Rov	Tr	08.90	90	1	0	0

PLANT Kenneth (Ken) George
Nuneaton, 15 August, 1925 (CF)

League Club	Source	Date Signed	Seasons Played	Apps	Subs	Gls
Bury	Nuneaton Borough	02.50	49-53	119	-	54
Colchester U	Tr	01.54	53-58	189	-	82

PLASKETT Stephen (Steve) Colin
Newcastle, 24 April, 1971 (FB)

League Club	Source	Date Signed	Seasons Played	Apps	Subs	Gls
Hartlepool U	YT	07.89	88-89	19	1	0

PLATNAUER Nicholas (Nicky) Robert
Leicester, 10 June, 1961 (FB)

League Club	Source	Date Signed	Seasons Played	Apps	Subs	Gls
Bristol Rov	Bedford T	08.82	82	21	3	7
Coventry C	Tr	08.83	83-84	38	6	6
Birmingham C	Tr	12.84	84-85	23	5	2
Reading	L	01.86	85	7	0	0
Cardiff C	Tr	09.86	86-88	110	5	6

League Club	Source	Date Signed	Seasons Played	Apps	Subs	Gls
Notts Co	Tr	08.89	89-90	57	0	1
Port Vale	L	01.91	90	14	0	0
Leicester C	Tr	07.91	91-92	32	3	0
Scunthorpe U	Tr	03.93	92	14	0	2
Mansfield T	Kettering T	08.93	93	25	0	0
Lincoln C	Tr	02.94	93-95	26	1	0

PLATT Clive Linton
Wolverhampton, 27 October, 1977 (F)

League Club	Source	Date Signed	Seasons Played	Apps	Subs	Gls
Walsall	YT	07.96	95-98	18	14	4
Rochdale	Tr	08.99	99-02	151	18	30
Notts Co	Tr	08.03	03	19	0	3
Peterborough U	Tr	01.04	03-04	35	2	6
MK Dons	Tr	01.05	04	20	0	3

PLATT David Andrew
Chadderton, 10 June, 1966 Eu21-3/EB-3/E-62 (M)

League Club	Source	Date Signed	Seasons Played	Apps	Subs	Gls
Manchester U	Chadderton	07.84				
Crewe Alex	Tr	01.85	84-87	134	0	55
Aston Villa	Tr	02.88	87-90	121	0	50
Arsenal	Sampdoria (It)	07.95	95-97	65	23	13
Nottingham F	(Retired)	08.99	99-00	3	2	1

PLATT Edward (Ted) Hewitt
Wolstanton, 26 March, 1921 Died 1996 (G)

League Club	Source	Date Signed	Seasons Played	Apps	Subs	Gls
Arsenal	Colchester U	01.39	46-52	53	-	0
Portsmouth	Tr	09.53	53-54	31	-	0
Aldershot	Tr	08.55	55	16	-	0

PLATT James (Jim) Archibald
Ballymoney, 26 January, 1952 NIAmat/NI-23 (G)

League Club	Source	Date Signed	Seasons Played	Apps	Subs	Gls
Middlesbrough	Ballymena U	05.70	71-82	401	0	0
Hartlepool U	L	08.78	78	13	0	0
Cardiff C	L	11.78	78	4	0	0

PLATT John Roger
Ashton-under-Lyne, 22 August, 1954 (G)

League Club	Source	Date Signed	Seasons Played	Apps	Subs	Gls
Oldham Ath	Ashton U	06.72	75-80	109	0	0
Bury	Tr	08.81	81-82	20	0	0
Bolton W	Tr	07.83	83	10	0	0
Tranmere Rov	L	11.84	84	8	0	0
Preston NE	Tr	02.85	84-85	38	0	0

PLATT John Stephen
Bermondsey, 29 January, 1942 (W)

League Club	Source	Date Signed	Seasons Played	Apps	Subs	Gls
Charlton Ath	Brookhill BC	06.61	61	2	-	0

PLATT Matthew
Crewe, 15 October, 1983 (F)

League Club	Source	Date Signed	Seasons Played	Apps	Subs	Gls
Crewe Alex	Sch	07.02	04	0	1	0

PLATTS Lawrence (Laurie)
Worksop, 31 October, 1921 (G)

League Club	Source	Date Signed	Seasons Played	Apps	Subs	Gls
Nottingham F	Jnrs	10.43	46-49	6	-	0
Chesterfield	Tr	07.51	51	11	-	0
Stockport Co	Buxton	02.53	52-53	28	-	0

PLATTS Mark Anthony
Sheffield, 23 May, 1979 ESch/EYth (W)

League Club	Source	Date Signed	Seasons Played	Apps	Subs	Gls
Sheffield Wed	YT	10.96	95	0	2	0
Torquay U	Tr	03.99	98-00	16	18	1

PLATTS Peter
Dinnington, 14 January, 1928 (CF)

League Club	Source	Date Signed	Seasons Played	Apps	Subs	Gls
Scunthorpe U (Am)		07.51	51	2	-	2

PLAYER Percival **Roy** Ivan
Portsmouth, 10 May, 1928 Died 1992 (CD)

League Club	Source	Date Signed	Seasons Played	Apps	Subs	Gls
Grimsby T	Portsmouth (Am)	08.52	52-58	57	-	0
Oldham Ath	Tr	05.59	59	2	-	0

PLEAT David John
Nottingham, 15 January, 1945 ESch/EYth (W)

League Club	Source	Date Signed	Seasons Played	Apps	Subs	Gls
Nottingham F	Jnrs	03.62	61-63	6	-	1
Luton T	Tr	08.64	64-66	67	3	9
Shrewsbury T	Tr	07.67	67	10	2	1
Exeter C	Tr	07.68	68-69	66	2	13
Peterborough U	Tr	07.70	70	28	1	2

PLENDERLEITH John (Jackie) Boyd
Bellshill, 6 October, 1937 SSch/Su23-5/S-1 (CD)

League Club	Source	Date Signed	Seasons Played	Apps	Subs	Gls
Manchester C	Hibernian	07.60	60-62	41	-	0

PLLU Charles (Charlie) Lamont
Saltcoats, 28 February, 1934 (G)

League Club	Source	Date Signed	Seasons Played	Apps	Subs	Gls
Sheffield Wed	Scarborough	12.56	56-57	19	-	0

PLUCK (MILES) Colin Ian
Edmonton, 6 September, 1978 (CD)

League Club	Source	Date Signed	Seasons Played	Apps	Subs	Gls
Watford	YT	02.97	97	1	0	0
Yeovil T	Dover Ath	07.01	03-04	56	1	4

PLUCK Lee Kenneth
Enfield, 27 February, 1982 (FB)

League Club	Source	Date Signed	Seasons Played	Apps	Subs	Gls
Barnet	YT	07.00	00	0	1	0

PLUCKROSE Alan
Southwater, 3 July, 1963 (FB)

League Club	Source	Date Signed	Seasons Played	Apps	Subs	Gls
Torquay U	Falmouth T	03.83	82	3	0	0

PLUMB Richard (Dick) Kevin
Swindon, 24 September, 1946 (F)

League Club	Source	Date Signed	Seasons Played	Apps	Subs	Gls
Swindon T	App	12.63				
Bristol Rov	Tr	04.65	65-68	39	0	8
Charlton Ath	Yeovil T	09.70	70-71	32	11	10
Exeter C	Tr	08.72	72-73	59	0	17

PLUME Richard (Dickie) William
Tottenham, 10 June, 1949 (M)

League Club	Source	Date Signed	Seasons Played	Apps	Subs	Gls
Millwall	App	03.67	66-68	12	4	0
Orient	Tr	05.69	69-70	12	6	1

PLUMLEY Gary Edward
Birmingham, 24 March, 1956 (G)

League Club	Source	Date Signed	Seasons Played	Apps	Subs	Gls
Leicester C	App	03.74				
Newport Co	Tr	06.76	76-80	182	0	0
Hereford U	Happy Valley (HK)	09.82	82	13	0	0
Newport Co	Tr	12.82	82	2	0	0
Cardiff C	Happy Valley (HK)	08.83	83-84	25	0	0
Newport Co	L	08.84	84	2	0	0
Newport Co	Ebbw Vale	03.87	86	1	0	0

PLUMMER Calvin Anthony
Nottingham, 14 February, 1963 (W)

League Club	Source	Date Signed	Seasons Played	Apps	Subs	Gls
Nottingham F	App	02.81	81-82	10	2	2
Chesterfield	Tr	12.82	82	28	0	7
Derby Co	Tr	08.83	83	23	4	3
Barnsley	Tr	03.84	83-86	41	13	7
Nottingham F	Tr	12.86				
Nottingham F	Lahden Reipas (Fin)	10.87	87	8	0	2
Plymouth Arg	Tr	09.88	88	17	6	1
Chesterfield	Tr	07.89	89-90	67	4	12

PLUMMER Christopher (Chris) Scott
Isleworth, 12 October, 1976 EYth/Eu21-5 (CD)

League Club	Source	Date Signed	Seasons Played	Apps	Subs	Gls
Queens Park Rgrs	YT	07.94	95-02	54	8	2
Bristol Rov	L	11.02	02	2	0	0
Peterborough U	Barnet	09.04	04	21	0	0

PLUMMER Dwayne Jermaine
Bristol, 12 May, 1978 (W)

League Club	Source	Date Signed	Seasons Played	Apps	Subs	Gls
Bristol C	YT	09.95	95-97	1	13	0
Bristol Rov	Chesham U	09.00	00-01	29	6	1

PLUMMER Norman Leonard
Leicester, 12 January, 1924 Died 1999 (CD)

League Club	Source	Date Signed	Seasons Played	Apps	Subs	Gls
Leicester C	Leicester ATC	11.42	47-51	66	-	1
Mansfield T	Tr	07.52	52-55	166	-	5

PLUNKETT Sidney (Sid) Ernest
Norwich, 2 October, 1920 Died 1986 (W)

League Club	Source	Date Signed	Seasons Played	Apps	Subs	Gls
Norwich C	Norwich YMCA	04.38	38	3	-	0
Wolverhampton W	Tr	04.39				
Norwich C	Tr	02.46	46	28	-	7

POBORSKY Karel
Jindrichuv-Hradec, Czech Rep, 30 March, 1972 Czech Rep int (W)

League Club	Source	Date Signed	Seasons Played	Apps	Subs	Gls
Manchester U	Slavia Prague (Cz)	06.96	96-97	18	14	5

PODD Cyril (Cec) Casey Marcel
St Kitts, 7 August, 1952 (FB)

League Club	Source	Date Signed	Seasons Played	Apps	Subs	Gls
Bradford C	Jnrs	08.70	70-83	494	8	3
Halifax T	Tr	08.84	84-85	52	5	0
Scarborough	Tr	07.86	87	3	0	0

PODMORE Edgar
Fenton, 21 April, 1918 (G)

League Club	Source	Date Signed	Seasons Played	Apps	Subs	Gls
Stoke C		08.43				
Crewe Alex	Tr	08.47	47	1	-	0

POGLIACOMI Leslie (Les) Amado
Perth, Australia, 3 May, 1976 AuYth/Auu20 (G)

League Club	Source	Date Signed	Seasons Played	Apps	Subs	Gls
Oldham Ath	Parramatta Power (Aus)	07.02	02-04	120	0	0

POINTER Keith Cecil
Norwich, 16 February, 1951 (M)

League Club	Source	Date Signed	Seasons Played	Apps	Subs	Gls
West Ham U	Norwich C (Am)	06.68				
Cambridge U	Tr	03.72	71-72	6	2	2

POINTER Raymond (Ray)
Cramlington, 10 October, 1936 Eu23-5/FLge-2/E-3 (F)

League Club	Source	Date Signed	Seasons Played	Apps	Subs	Gls
Burnley	Dudley Welfare	08.57	57-64	223	-	118
Bury	Tr	08.65	65	19	0	17
Coventry C	Tr	12.65	65-66	26	0	13
Portsmouth	Tr	01.67	66-72	148	4	31

POINTER Reginald (Reg) Ernest
Norwich, 28 January, 1935 (CD)

League Club	Source	Date Signed	Seasons Played	Apps	Subs	Gls
Norwich C	CNSOBU	06.56	56	11	-	0

POINTON Neil Geoffrey
Church Warsop, 28 November, 1964 (FB)

League Club	Source	Date Signed	Seasons Played	Apps	Subs	Gls
Scunthorpe U	App	08.82	81-85	159	0	2
Everton	Tr	11.85	85-89	95	6	5
Manchester C	Tr	07.90	90-91	74	0	2
Oldham Ath	Tr	07.92	92-95	92	3	3
Walsall	Heart of Midlothian	07.98	98-99	61	0	0
Chesterfield	Tr	01.00	99	9	1	0

POINTON Raymond (Ray) Evison
Birkenhead, 6 November, 1947 (FB)

League Club	Source	Date Signed	Seasons Played	Apps	Subs	Gls
Tranmere Rov	App	11.65	67-70	41	6	0

POINTON William (Bill) James
Hanley, 25 November, 1920 (CF)

League Club	Source	Date Signed	Seasons Played	Apps	Subs	Gls
Port Vale		07.40	46-48	74	-	26
Queens Park Rgrs	Tr	01.49	48-49	26	-	6
Brentford	Tr	02.50	49-50	16	-	2

POLAND George
Penarth, 21 September, 1913 Died 1988 WWar-4/W-2 (G)

League Club	Source	Date Signed	Seasons Played	Apps	Subs	Gls
Cardiff C	Swindon T (Am)	11.35	35-36	24	-	0
Wrexham		07.38	38	39	-	0
Liverpool	Tr	07.39				
Cardiff C	Tr	08.46	46	2	-	0

POLE Harold **Edward (Ted)** William
Kessingland, 25 March, 1922 (CF)

League Club	Source	Date Signed	Seasons Played	Apps	Subs	Gls
Ipswich T		10.46	46-50	39	-	13
Leyton Orient	Tr	07.51	51-52	12	-	0

POLK Stanley (Stan)
Liverpool, 28 October, 1921 (IF)

League Club	Source	Date Signed	Seasons Played	Apps	Subs	Gls
Liverpool	South Liverpool	03.40	46-47	13	-	0
Port Vale	Tr	07.48	48-51	159	-	14

POLLARD Brian Edward
York, 22 May, 1954 EYth (W)

League Club	Source	Date Signed	Seasons Played	Apps	Subs	Gls
York C	Jnrs	03.72	71-77	151	11	34
Watford	Tr	11.77	77-79	68	3	8
Mansfield T	Tr	01.80	79-80	45	9	5
Blackpool	Tr	08.81	81	0	1	0
York C	Tr	09.81	81-83	98	4	26
Chesterfield	Scarborough (N/C)	09.84	84	0	1	0
Hartlepool U	Scarborough (N/C)	01.85	84	2	0	0

POLLARD Gary
Staveley, 30 December, 1959 (CD)

League Club	Source	Date Signed	Seasons Played	Apps	Subs	Gls
Chesterfield	Jnrs	07.77	77-82	83	4	1
Port Vale	Tr	06.83	83	17	1	0
Mansfield T	Tr	07.84	84-86	66	1	1
Peterborough U	Tr	08.87	87-88	20	0	0

POLLARD James
Liverpool, 4 June, 1926 (W)

League Club	Source	Date Signed	Seasons Played	Apps	Subs	Gls
Newport Co	Tredomen	05.46				
Tranmere Rov		11.47	47-48	24	-	1

POLLARD Kelly **John**
Chelmsford, 17 November, 1971 (CD)

League Club	Source	Date Signed	Seasons Played	Apps	Subs	Gls
Colchester U	YT	•	88-89	1	8	1

POLLET Ludovic (Ludo)
Vieux-Conde, France, 18 June, 1970 (CD)

League Club	Source	Date Signed	Seasons Played	Apps	Subs	Gls
Wolverhampton W	Le Havre (Fr)	09.99	99-02	74	4	7
Walsall	L	11.02	02	5	0	0

POLLITT John (Jack)
Farnworth, 29 March, 1937 (CF)

League Club	Source	Date Signed	Seasons Played	Apps	Subs	Gls
Bolton W	Jnrs	12.54				
Bury	Tr	08.58	58	4	-	0
Accrington St	Tr	03.60	59	3	-	1
Rochdale	Tr	08.60	60	6	-	1

POLLITT Michael (Mike) Francis
Farnworth, 29 February, 1972 (G)

League Club	Source	Date Signed	Seasons Played	Apps	Subs	Gls
Manchester U	YT	07.90				
Bury	Tr	07.91				
Lincoln C	L	09.92	92	5	0	0
Lincoln C	Tr	12.92	92-93	52	0	0
Darlington	Tr	08.94	94-95	55	0	0
Notts Co	Tr	11.95	96-97	10	0	0
Oldham Ath	L	08.97	97	16	0	0
Gillingham	L	12.97	97	6	0	0
Brentford	L	01.98	97	5	0	0
Sunderland	Tr	02.98				
Rotherham U	Tr	07.98	98-99	92	0	0
Chesterfield	Tr	06.00	00	46	0	0
Rotherham U	Tr	05.01	01-04	175	0	0

POLLOCK Jamie
Stockton, 16 February, 1974 EYth/Eu21-3 (M)

League Club	Source	Date Signed	Seasons Played	Apps	Subs	Gls
Middlesbrough	YT	12.91	90-95	144	11	17
Bolton W	CA Osasuna (Sp)	11.96	96-97	43	3	5
Manchester C	Tr	03.98	97-99	49	9	5
Crystal Palace	Tr	08.00	00	29	2	4
Birmingham C	L	03.01	00	4	1	0

POLLOCK Maitland (Matt) Alexander Inglis
Dumfries, 31 October, 1952 SSch (W)

League Club	Source	Date Signed	Seasons Played	Apps	Subs	Gls
Nottingham F	App	10.70				
Walsall	Tr	07.73	73	1	1	0
Luton T	Burton A	03.74	75	3	3	0
Portsmouth	Tr	07.76	76-77	50	4	10

POLLOCK Stewart
Bellshill, 25 September, 1933 Died 2003 (IF)

League Club	Source	Date Signed	Seasons Played	Apps	Subs	Gls
Gillingham	Motherwell	07.56	56	10	-	0

POLLOCK William (Bill)
Barrhead, 7 June, 1920 (WH)

League Club	Source	Date Signed	Seasons Played	Apps	Subs	Gls
Oldham Ath	Manchester U (Am)	07.47	47	4	-	0

POLSTON Andrew (Andy) Alfred
Walthamstow, 26 July, 1970 (FB)

League Club	Source	Date Signed	Seasons Played	Apps	Subs	Gls
Tottenham H	YT	07.88	89	0	1	0
Cambridge U	L	10.89	89	3	0	0
Gillingham	L	11.91	91	1	1	0

POLSTON John David
Walthamstow, 10 June, 1968 EYth (CD)

League Club	Source	Date Signed	Seasons Played	Apps	Subs	Gls
Tottenham H	App	07.85	86-89	17	7	1
Norwich C	Tr	07.90	90-97	200	15	8
Reading	Tr	07.98	98-99	16	2	1

POLYCARPOU Andrew (Andy)
Islington, 15 August, 1958 (M)

League Club	Source	Date Signed	Seasons Played	Apps	Subs	Gls
Southend U		09.76	76-80	41	20	10
Cambridge U	Tr	08.81	81	1	4	0
Cardiff C	Tr	04.82	81	7	0	0

POMPHREY Edric (Syd) Alfred
Stretford, 31 May, 1916 Died 1987 (FB)

League Club	Source	Date Signed	Seasons Played	Apps	Subs	Gls
Notts Co	Hyde U	09.44				
Rochdale	Tr	10.45	46	9	-	0

PONTE Raimondo
Naples, Italy, 4 April, 1954 Switzerland int (M)

League Club	Source	Date Signed	Seasons Played	Apps	Subs	Gls
Nottingham F	Grasshoppers (Swi)	08.80	80	17	4	3

PONTIN Keith
Pontyclun, 14 June, 1956 Wu21-1/W-2 (CD)

League Club	Source	Date Signed	Seasons Played	Apps	Subs	Gls
Cardiff C	App	05.74	76-82	193	0	5

POOK David Charles
Plymouth, 16 January, 1955 (W)

League Club	Source	Date Signed	Seasons Played	Apps	Subs	Gls
Torquay U	App	01.73	71-72	13	3	1

POOK Michael David
Swindon, 22 October, 1985 (M)

League Club	Source	Date Signed	Seasons Played	Apps	Subs	Gls
Swindon T	Sch	•	04	3	2	0

POOLE Andrew (Andy) John
Chesterfield, 6 July, 1960 (G)

League Club	Source	Date Signed	Seasons Played	Apps	Subs	Gls
Northampton T	Mansfield T (App)	07.78	78-81	141	0	0
Wolverhampton W	Tr	08.82				
Port Vale	Tr	03.83	82	2	0	0

POOLE Cyril John
Mansfield, 13 March, 1921 Died 1996 (FB)

League Club	Source	Date Signed	Seasons Played	Apps	Subs	Gls
Mansfield T (Am)	Annesley CW	02.37	36	1	-	0
Mansfield T	Gillingham	02.44	49-50	16	-	1

POOLE Gary John
Stratford, 11 September, 1967 (FB)

League Club	Source	Date Signed	Seasons Played	Apps	Subs	Gls
Tottenham H	Arsenal (Jnrs)	07.85				
Cambridge U	Tr	08.87	87-88	42	1	0
Barnet	Tr	03.89	91	39	1	2
Plymouth Arg	Tr	06.92	92	39	0	5
Southend U	Tr	07.93	93-94	43	1	2
Birmingham C	Tr	09.94	94-96	70	2	0
Charlton Ath	Tr	11.96	96	14	2	1

POOLE Henry (Harry)
Stoke-on-Trent, 31 January, 1935 (M)

League Club	Source	Date Signed	Seasons Played	Apps	Subs	Gls
Port Vale	Oxford C	04.56	55-67	450	1	73

POOLE John Arthur Frederick
Stoke-on-Trent, 12 December, 1932 (G)

League Club	Source	Date Signed	Seasons Played	Apps	Subs	Gls
Port Vale	Stoke C (Am)	09.53	55-60	33	-	0

POOLE Joseph
Huddersfield, 25 May, 1923 (W)

League Club	Source	Date Signed	Seasons Played	Apps	Subs	Gls
Huddersfield T	David Brown's Works	06.41	46	2	-	0
Bradford C	Tr	02.47	46-48	56	-	5

POOLE Kenneth (Ken) James
Thurgarton, 27 April, 1934 (WH)

League Club	Source	Date Signed	Seasons Played	Apps	Subs	Gls
Swansea T	Jnrs	11.53				
Northampton T	Tr	06.56	56	4	-	0

POOLE Kevin
Bromsgrove, 21 July, 1963 (G)

League Club	Source	Date Signed	Seasons Played	Apps	Subs	Gls
Aston Villa	App	06.81	84-86	28	0	0
Northampton T	L	11.84	84	3	0	0
Middlesbrough	Tr	08.87	87-89	34	0	0
Hartlepool U	L	03.91	90	12	0	0
Leicester C	Tr	07.91	91-96	163	0	0
Birmingham C	Tr	08.97	97-00	56	0	0
Bolton W	Tr	10.01	01-04	4	1	0

POOLE Michael (Mike) David
Morley, 23 April, 1955 (G)

League Club	Source	Date Signed	Seasons Played	Apps	Subs	Gls
Rochdale	Coventry C (App)	09.73	73-77	192	0	0
Rochdale	Portland (USA)	08.81	81	27	0	0

POOLE Richard John
Heston, 3 July, 1957 (F)

League Club	Source	Date Signed	Seasons Played	Apps	Subs	Gls
Brentford	App	07.75	73-75	12	9	1
Watford	Tr	07.76	76	3	4	1

POOLE Roy
Sheffield, 2 December, 1939 (CF)

League Club	Source	Date Signed	Seasons Played	Apps	Subs	Gls
Wolverhampton W	Jnrs	01.57				
Rotherham U	Tr	07.58				
Chesterfield	Tr	07.61	61-63	50	-	14

POOLE Terence (Terry)
Sheffield, 8 December, 1937 (WH)

League Club	Source	Date Signed	Seasons Played	Apps	Subs	Gls
Sheffield Wed	Jnrs	04.55				
Darlington	Tr	07.59	59-60	41	-	3

POOLE Terence (Terry)
Chesterfield, 16 December, 1949 (G)

League Club	Source	Date Signed	Seasons Played	Apps	Subs	Gls
Manchester U	Jnrs	02.67				
Huddersfield T	Tr	08.68	68-76	207	0	0
Bolton W	Tr	01.77	80	29	0	0
Sheffield U	L	03.80	79	7	0	0

POOM Mart
Tallinn, Estonia, 3 February, 1972 Estonia 101 (G)

League Club	Source	Date Signed	Seasons Played	Apps	Subs	Gls
Portsmouth	FC Wil (Swi)	08.94	95	4	0	0
Derby Co	Flora Tallinn (Est)	03.97	96-02	143	3	0
Sunderland	Tr	11.02	02-04	58	0	1

POPE David William
St Pancras, 8 January, 1936 (WH)

League Club	Source	Date Signed	Seasons Played	Apps	Subs	Gls
Crystal Palace	Jnrs	09.53				
Swansea T		09.56	57	2	-	0

POPE Neil Lester
Cambridge, 9 October, 1972 (M)

League Club	Source	Date Signed	Seasons Played	Apps	Subs	Gls
Peterborough U	Cambridge U (YT)	03.91	90	1	1	0

POPE Steven (Steve) Anthony
Mow Cop, 8 September, 1976 (CD)

League Club	Source	Date Signed	Seasons Played	Apps	Subs	Gls
Crewe Alex	YT	06.95	97	2	4	0

POPE Terence (Terry) John
Newport, 27 January, 1926 Died 2003 (G)

League Club	Source	Date Signed	Seasons Played	Apps	Subs	Gls
Newport Co	Bargoed U	07.50	50-54	83	-	0

POPELY Peter Charles Francis
York, 7 April, 1943 (FB)

League Club	Source	Date Signed	Seasons Played	Apps	Subs	Gls
York C	Cliftonville (York)	08.62	62-66	24	1	0

POPESCU Gheorghe (Gica)
Calafat, Romania, 9 October, 1967 Romania int (M)

League Club	Source	Date Signed	Seasons Played	Apps	Subs	Gls
Tottenham H	PSV Eindhoven (Holl)	09.94	94	23	0	3

POPOVIC Anthony (Tony)
Sydney, Australia, 4 July, 1973 AuYth/Auu23/Au-49 (CD)

League Club	Source	Date Signed	Seasons Played	Apps	Subs	Gls
Crystal Palace	San Hiroshima (Jap)	08.01	01-04	111	2	6

POPPITT John (Johnny)
West Sleekburn, 20 January, 1923 (FB)

League Club	Source	Date Signed	Seasons Played	Apps	Subs	Gls
Derby Co	West Sleekburn	05.45	46-49	16	-	0
Queens Park Rgrs	Tr	09.50	50-53	106	-	0

POPPLETON David John
Doncaster, 19 December, 1979 (M)

League Club	Source	Date Signed	Seasons Played	Apps	Subs	Gls
Everton	YT	07.97				
Lincoln C	Tr	08.99	99	4	1	0

POPPY Arthur
Yeovil, 6 January, 1961 (CD)

League Club	Source	Date Signed	Seasons Played	Apps	Subs	Gls
Northampton T	App	●	77	1	0	0

PORFIRIO Hugo Cardosa
Lisbon, Portugal, 29 September, 1973 Portugal 3 (M)

League Club	Source	Date Signed	Seasons Played	Apps	Subs	Gls
West Ham U (L)	Sporting Lisbon (Por)	09.96	96	15	8	2
Nottingham F (L)	Benfica (Por)	01.99	98	3	6	1

PORIC Adem
Kensington, 22 April, 1973 Australia int (M)

League Club	Source	Date Signed	Seasons Played	Apps	Subs	Gls
Sheffield Wed	Budapest St Geo (Aus)	10.93	93-97	3	11	0
Southend U	L	02.97	96	7	0	0
Rotherham U	Tr	02.98	97	4	0	0
Notts Co	Tr	03.98	97	3	1	0

PORRITT Walter
Heckmondwike, 19 July, 1914 Died 1993 (W)

League Club	Source	Date Signed	Seasons Played	Apps	Subs	Gls
Huddersfield T		05.35				
York C	Tr	08.36	36-46	40	-	5

PORT Bernard Harry
Burton-on-Trent, 14 December, 1925 (G)

League Club	Source	Date Signed	Seasons Played	Apps	Subs	Gls
Hull C	Newhall	09.50				
Chester	Tr	08.51	51-52	9	-	0

PORTEOUS John (Jack) Robert
India, 12 January, 1933 (IF)

League Club	Source	Date Signed	Seasons Played	Apps	Subs	Gls
Aldershot	Alton T	02.56	55	1	-	0

PORTEOUS John (Johnny) Robertson
Motherwell, 5 December, 1921 (WH)

League Club	Source	Date Signed	Seasons Played	Apps	Subs	Gls
Plymouth Arg	Alloa Ath	07.49	49-55	215	-	13
Exeter C	Tr	03.56	55-56	40	-	0

PORTEOUS Trevor
Hull, 9 October, 1933 Died 1997 (WH)

League Club	Source	Date Signed	Seasons Played	Apps	Subs	Gls
Hull C	Jnrs	10.50	51-55	61	-	1
Stockport Co	Tr	06.56	56-64	337	-	9

PORTER Andrew (Andy)
Stewarton, 21 January, 1937 (WH)

League Club	Source	Date Signed	Seasons Played	Apps	Subs	Gls
Watford	Darvel Jnrs	06.59	59-62	72	-	4

PORTER Andrew (Andy) Michael
Holmes Chapel, 17 September, 1968 (M)

League Club	Source	Date Signed	Seasons Played	Apps	Subs	Gls
Port Vale	App	06.87	86-97	313	44	22
Wigan Ath	Tr	07.98	98-99	8	13	1
Mansfield T	L	10.99	99	5	0	0
Chester C	L	02.00	99	16	0	0
Port Vale	(retirement)	11.04	04	0	2	0

PORTER Christopher (Chris)
Wigan, 12 December, 1983 (F)

League Club	Source	Date Signed	Seasons Played	Apps	Subs	Gls
Bury	QEGS OB	03.03	02-04	48	23	18

PORTER Christopher (Chris) Ian
Sunderland, 10 November, 1979 (G)

League Club	Source	Date Signed	Seasons Played	Apps	Subs	Gls
Sunderland	YT	08.98				
Darlington	Leiftur (Ice)	03.02	01-02	9	1	0
York C	Tr	07.03	03	5	0	0

PORTER Christopher (Chris) John
North Petherton, 30 April, 1949 (W)

League Club	Source	Date Signed	Seasons Played	Apps	Subs	Gls
Swindon T	Bridgwater T	11.69	70-73	33	2	4

PORTER Derek
Ulverston, 22 June, 1936 (W)

League Club	Source	Date Signed	Seasons Played	Apps	Subs	Gls
Barrow	Dalton T	05.57	57-58	15	-	1

PORTER Gary Michael
Sunderland, 6 March, 1966 EYth/Eu21-12 (M)

League Club	Source	Date Signed	Seasons Played	Apps	Subs	Gls
Watford	App	03.84	83-96	362	38	47
Walsall	Tr	06.97	97-98	39	5	1
Scarborough	Tr	02.99	98	11	2	0

PORTER George
Chirk, 5 February, 1935 (W)

League Club	Source	Date Signed	Seasons Played	Apps	Subs	Gls
Wrexham (Am)	Chirk AAA	05.59	59	1	-	0

PORTER Joel William
Adelaide, Australia, 25 December, 1978 Australia 4 (F)

League Club	Source	Date Signed	Seasons Played	Apps	Subs	Gls
Hartlepool U	Olympic Sharks (Aus)	11.03	03-04	54	12	17

PORTER Leslie (Les)
Gateshead, 5 May, 1923 Died 2002 (WH)

League Club	Source	Date Signed	Seasons Played	Apps	Subs	Gls
Newcastle U	Redheugh Steelworks	09.44				
York C	Tr	03.49	48-53	38	-	1

PORTER Michael (Mike) Robert
Stoke-on-Trent, 19 May, 1945 (IF)

League Club	Source	Date Signed	Seasons Played	Apps	Subs	Gls
Port Vale	Jnrs	07.62	63-64	13	-	2

PORTER Trevor James
Guildford, 16 October, 1956 (G)

League Club	Source	Date Signed	Seasons Played	Apps	Subs	Gls
Fulham	App	05.74				
Brentford	Slough T	08.78	78-79	15	0	0

PORTER William (Bill)
Durham, 23 November, 1923 Died 1975 (FB)

League Club	Source	Date Signed	Seasons Played	Apps	Subs	Gls
Hartlepools U	Horden CW	09.43	46	2	-	0

PORTERFIELD John (Ian)
Dunfermline, 11 February, 1946 (M)

League Club	Source	Date Signed	Seasons Played	Apps	Subs	Gls
Sunderland	Raith Rov	12.67	67-75	217	12	17
Reading	L	11.76	76	5	0	0
Sheffield Wed	Tr	07.77	77-79	103	3	3

PORTEUS Joseph (Joe)
Shildon, 20 April, 1925 Died 1995 (WH)

League Club	Source	Date Signed	Seasons Played	Apps	Subs	Gls
York C	Chesterfield (Am)	08.46	46	23	-	0

PORTWOOD Clifford (Cliff)
Salford, 17 October, 1937 (F)

League Club	Source	Date Signed	Seasons Played	Apps	Subs	Gls
Preston NE	Manchester Ath	02.55				
Port Vale	Tr	08.59	59-60	61	-	33
Grimsby T	Tr	07.61	61-63	92	-	35
Portsmouth	Tr	05.64	64-68	95	4	28

POSKETT Malcolm
Middlesbrough, 19 July, 1953 (F)

League Club	Source	Date Signed	Seasons Played	Apps	Subs	Gls
Middlesbrough	South Bank	04.73	73	0	1	0
Hartlepool	Tr	07.74				
Hartlepool	Whitby T	11.76	76-77	50	1	20
Brighton & Hove A	Tr	02.78	77-79	33	12	17
Watford	Tr	01.80	79-81	57	6	17
Carlisle U	Tr	08.82	82-84	108	2	40
Darlington	Tr	07.85	85	18	3	4
Stockport Co	Tr	01.86	85	8	0	1
Hartlepool U	L	03.86	85	4	1	0
Carlisle U	Tr	08.86	86-87	67	9	20

POSKETT Thomas (Tom) William
Esh Winning, 26 December, 1909 Died 1972 (G)

League Club	Source	Date Signed	Seasons Played	Apps	Subs	Gls
Grimsby T	Crook T	12.28	28-30	2	-	0
Lincoln C	Tr	05.32	33	10	-	0
Notts Co	Tr	05.34	34	10	-	0
Tranmere Rov	Tr	08.35	35-36	22	-	0
Crewe Alex	Tr	07.37	37-46	99	-	0

POSSEE Derek James
Southwark, 14 February, 1946 (W)

League Club	Source	Date Signed	Seasons Played	Apps	Subs	Gls
Tottenham H	App	03.63	63-65	19	0	4
Millwall	Tr	08.67	67-72	222	1	79
Crystal Palace	Tr	01.73	72-73	51	2	13
Orient	Tr	07.74	74-76	77	3	11

POSTIGA Manuel **Helder** Marques
Povoa de Varzim, Portugal, 2 August, 1982 Portugal 9 (F)

League Club	Source	Date Signed	Seasons Played	Apps	Subs	Gls
Tottenham H	FC Porto (Por)	07.03	03	9	10	1

POSTLEWHITE Dennis John
Birkenhead, 13 October, 1957 (CD)

League Club	Source	Date Signed	Seasons Played	Apps	Subs	Gls
Tranmere Rov	App	07.76	76-78	31	2	1

POSTMA Stefan
Utrecht, Holland, 10 June, 1976 (G)

League Club	Source	Date Signed	Seasons Played	Apps	Subs	Gls
Aston Villa	De Graafschap (Holl)	05.02	02-04	7	4	0

POTRAC Anthony (Tony) Joseph
Victoria, Australia, 21 January, 1953 (F)

League Club	Source	Date Signed	Seasons Played	Apps	Subs	Gls
Chelsea	App	08.70	71	1	0	0

POTTER Daniel (Danny) Raymond John
Ipswich, 18 March, 1979 (G)

League Club	Source	Date Signed	Seasons Played	Apps	Subs	Gls
Colchester U	Chelsea (YT)	10.97				
Exeter C	Tr	08.98	98-99	10	0	0

POTTER Darren Michael
Liverpool, 21 December, 1984 IRYth/IRu21-9 (M)

League Club	Source	Date Signed	Seasons Played	Apps	Subs	Gls
Liverpool	YT	04.02	04	0	2	0

POTTER Frederick (Fred)
Cradley Heath, 29 November, 1940 (G)

League Club	Source	Date Signed	Seasons Played	Apps	Subs	Gls
Aston Villa	Cradley Heath	07.59	60	3	-	0
Doncaster Rov	Tr	07.62	62-65	123	0	0
Hereford U	Burton A	07.70	72-73	10	0	0

POTTER Gary Charles
Chester, 6 August, 1952 (CD)

League Club	Source	Date Signed	Seasons Played	Apps	Subs	Gls
Chester		07.73	73-74	11	0	0

POTTER George Ross
Arbroath, 7 October, 1946 (FB)

League Club	Source	Date Signed	Seasons Played	Apps	Subs	Gls
Luton T	Forfar Ath	03.68	67-68	3	5	0
Torquay U	Tr	07.69	69-70	32	4	0
Hartlepool	Tr	07.71	71-76	211	2	4

POTTER Graham Stephen
Solihull, 20 May, 1975 EYth/Eu21-1 (FB)

League Club	Source	Date Signed	Seasons Played	Apps	Subs	Gls
Birmingham C	YT	07.92	92-93	23	2	2
Wycombe W	L	09.93	93	2	1	0
Stoke C	Tr	12.93	93-95	41	4	1
Southampton	Tr	07.96	96	2	6	0
West Bromwich A	Tr	02.97	96-99	31	12	0
Northampton T	L	10.97	97	4	0	0
Reading	L	12.99	99	4	0	0
York C	Tr	07.00	00-02	108	6	5
Boston U	Tr	07.03	03	11	1	0
Macclesfield T	Tr	02.04	03-04	55	2	8

POTTER Harold (Harry)
Tyldesley, 20 May, 1923 Died 1992 (FB)

League Club	Source	Date Signed	Seasons Played	Apps	Subs	Gls
Shrewsbury T	Winsford U	(N/L)	50-51	67	-	0
Rochdale	Tr	06.52	52-53	52	-	0

POTTER James
Belfast, 20 November, 1941 (WH)

League Club	Source	Date Signed	Seasons Played	Apps	Subs	Gls
Sunderland	Jnrs	11.58				
Darlington	Tr	09.63	63	19	-	1

POTTER Lee
Salford, 3 September, 1978 (F)

League Club	Source	Date Signed	Seasons Played	Apps	Subs	Gls
Bolton W	YT	07.97				
Halifax T	Tr	12.99	99-00	13	9	2

POTTER Raymond (Ray) John
Beckenham, 7 May, 1936 (G)

League Club	Source	Date Signed	Seasons Played	Apps	Subs	Gls
Crystal Palace	Jnrs	05.53	53-57	44	-	0
West Bromwich A	Tr	06.58	58-66	217	0	0
Portsmouth	Tr	05.67	67-69	3	0	0

POTTER Ronald (Ron) Charles
Wolverhampton, 5 December, 1948 (CD)

League Club	Source	Date Signed	Seasons Played	Apps	Subs	Gls
West Bromwich A	App	12.66	68-69	8	1	0
Swindon T	Tr	11.70	70-74	84	2	0

POTTER Stephen (Steve) Derek
Belper, 1 October, 1955 (G)

League Club	Source	Date Signed	Seasons Played	Apps	Subs	Gls
Manchester C	App	10.73				
Swansea C	Tr	08.74	74-77	118	0	0

POTTS Brian
Sunderland, 3 September, 1948 (FB)

League Club	Source	Date Signed	Seasons Played	Apps	Subs	Gls
Leicester C	App	09.65	67-68	9	1	0
Peterborough U	Tr	07.69	69-70	49	1	0

POTTS Craig
Carlisle, 25 February, 1974 (W)

League Club	Source	Date Signed	Seasons Played	Apps	Subs	Gls
Carlisle U	YT	09.92	91-92	9	5	0

POTTS Eric Thomas
Liverpool, 16 March, 1950 (W)

League Club	Source	Date Signed	Seasons Played	Apps	Subs	Gls
Sheffield Wed	Oswestry T	12.69	70-76	142	17	21
Brighton & Hove A	Tr	06.77	77	19	14	5
Preston NE	Tr	08.78	78-80	50	7	5
Burnley	Tr	09.80	80-81	48	8	5
Bury	Tr	10.82	82-83	46	5	7

POTTS Harry
Hetton-le-Hole, 22 October, 1920 Died 1996 (IF)

League Club	Source	Date Signed	Seasons Played	Apps	Subs	Gls
Burnley	Jnrs	11.37	46-50	165	-	47
Everton	Tr	10.50	50-55	59	-	15

POTTS Henry James
Carlisle, 23 January, 1925 EAmat (W)

League Club	Source	Date Signed	Seasons Played	Apps	Subs	Gls
Northampton T (Am)	Pegasus	08.50	50	10	-	0

POTTS Reginald (Reg)
Stoke-on-Trent, 31 July, 1927 Died 1996 (FB)

League Club	Source	Date Signed	Seasons Played	Apps	Subs	Gls
Port Vale	Northwood Mission	08.45	48-56	277	-	3

POTTS Steven (Steve) John
Hartford, USA, 7 May, 1967 EYth (CD)

League Club	Source	Date Signed	Seasons Played	Apps	Subs	Gls
West Ham U	App	05.84	84-00	362	37	1

POTTS Victor (Vic) Ernest
Birmingham, 20 August, 1915 Died 1996 (FB)

League Club	Source	Date Signed	Seasons Played	Apps	Subs	Gls
Tottenham H	Metro Welfare	08.34				
Doncaster Rov	Tr	08.38	37-38	27	-	0
Aston Villa	Tr	08.45	46-47	62	-	0

POULTON George Henry
Holborn, 23 April, 1929 (W)

League Club	Source	Date Signed	Seasons Played	Apps	Subs	Gls
Gillingham		08.49	51	5	-	1
Leyton Orient	Tr	07.52	52-54	61	-	24

POUND John Henry **Kenneth (Ken)**
Portsmouth, 24 August, 1944 (W)

League Club	Source	Date Signed	Seasons Played	Apps	Subs	Gls
Swansea T	Yeovil T	07.64	64-65	25	1	4
Bournemouth	Tr	08.66	66-68	102	0	24
Gillingham	Tr	07.69	69-70	62	11	11

POUNDER Albert William
Charlton, 27 July, 1931 (W)

League Club	Source	Date Signed	Seasons Played	Apps	Subs	Gls
Charlton Ath	Harvey Sports	02.50	52	1	-	0
Queens Park Rgrs	Tr	02.54	53-55	53	-	6

POUNDER John **Anthony (Tony)**
Sheffield, 16 March, 1935 (W)

League Club	Source	Date Signed	Seasons Played	Apps	Subs	Gls
Luton T	Atlas Sports	12.55	55-56	3	-	0
Coventry C	Tr	06.57	57	6	-	1
Crewe Alex	Yeovil T	12.57	57-58	29	-	5

POUNDER Anthony (Tony) Mark
Yeovil, 11 March, 1966 (W)

League Club	Source	Date Signed	Seasons Played	Apps	Subs	Gls
Bristol Rov	Weymouth	07.90	90-93	102	11	10
Hereford U	Weymouth	09.94	94-95	54	8	4

POUNEWATCHY Stephane Zeusnagapa
Paris, France, 10 February, 1968 (CD)

League Club	Source	Date Signed	Seasons Played	Apps	Subs	Gls
Carlisle U	Gueugnon (Fr)	08.96	96-97	81	0	3
Port Vale	Dundee	08.98	98	2	0	0
Colchester U	Tr	02.99	98	15	0	1

POUNTNEY Craig Frank
Bromsgrove, 23 November, 1979 (F)

League Club	Source	Date Signed	Seasons Played	Apps	Subs	Gls
Shrewsbury T	YT	04.98	97	0	1	0

POUNTNEY David (Dave) Harold
Baschurch, 12 October, 1939 (CD)

League Club	Source	Date Signed	Seasons Played	Apps	Subs	Gls
Shrewsbury T	Myddle	09.57	57-63	175	-	11
Aston Villa	Tr	10.63	63-67	109	4	7
Shrewsbury T	Tr	02.68	67-69	54	4	1
Chester	Tr	06.70	70-72	135	0	1

POUNTNEY Ronald (Ron) Alan
Bilston, 19 March, 1955 (M)

League Club	Source	Date Signed	Seasons Played	Apps	Subs	Gls
Walsall	Jnrs	07.73	72	1	0	0
Port Vale	Tr	10.73				
Southend U	Bilston	01.75	74-84	327	22	26

POUTCH Neil Anthony
Dublin, 27 November, 1969 IRu21-8 (FB)

League Club	Source	Date Signed	Seasons Played	Apps	Subs	Gls
Luton T	YT	11.87	89	0	1	0

POUTON Alan
Newcastle, 1 February, 1977 (M)

League Club	Source	Date Signed	Seasons Played	Apps	Subs	Gls
Oxford U	Newcastle (U (YT)	11.95				
York C	Tr	12.95	96-98	79	11	7
Grimsby T	Tr	08.99	99-03	100	21	12
Gillingham	Tr	01.04	03-04	22	9	0
Hartlepool U	L	09.04	04	5	0	0

POVEY Neil Andrew
Birmingham, 26 June, 1977 (M)

League Club	Source	Date Signed	Seasons Played	Apps	Subs	Gls
Torquay U	YT	07.95	94-95	8	3	0

POVEY Victor (Vic) Richard
Wolverhampton, 16 March, 1944 (W)

League Club	Source	Date Signed	Seasons Played	Apps	Subs	Gls
Wolverhampton W	Jnrs	07.61				
Notts Co	Tr	08.63	63-64	35	-	3

POVEY William
Billingham, 11 January, 1943 (W)

League Club	Source	Date Signed	Seasons Played	Apps	Subs	Gls
Middlesbrough	Jnrs	05.60	62	6	-	0
York C	Tr	03.64	64	3	-	0

POWELL Andrew (Andy)
Plymouth, 27 June, 1955 (G)

League Club	Source	Date Signed	Seasons Played	Apps	Subs	Gls
Hereford U		10.82	82	4	0	0

POWELL Anthony (Tony)
Severn Beach, 11 February, 1947 (CD)

League Club	Source	Date Signed	Seasons Played	Apps	Subs	Gls
Bournemouth	Bath C	04.68	68-73	214	5	10
Norwich C	Tr	08.74	74-80	235	2	3

POWELL Aubrey
Cwmtwrch, 19 April, 1918 WWar-4/W-8 (IF)

League Club	Source	Date Signed	Seasons Played	Apps	Subs	Gls
Leeds U	Swansea T (Am)	11.35	36-47	112	-	25
Everton	Tr	07.48	48-49	35	-	5
Birmingham C	Tr	08.50	50	15	-	1

POWELL Baden
Hebburn, 17 June, 1931 (W)

League Club	Source	Date Signed	Seasons Played	Apps	Subs	Gls
Darlington	South Shields	10.50	50-53	9	-	0

POWELL Barry Ivor
Kenilworth, 29 January, 1954 Eu23-4 (M)

League Club	Source	Date Signed	Seasons Played	Apps	Subs	Gls
Wolverhampton W	App	01.72	72-74	58	6	7
Coventry C	Portland (USA)	09.75	75-79	162	2	27
Derby Co	Tr	10.79	79-81	86	0	7
Burnley	Bulova (HK)	07.84	84	9	2	0
Swansea C	Tr	02.85	84	8	0	0
Wolverhampton W	South China (HK)	11.86	86-87	10	4	0

POWELL Christopher (Chris) George Robin
Lambeth, 8 September, 1969 E-5 (FB)

League Club	Source	Date Signed	Seasons Played	Apps	Subs	Gls
Crystal Palace	YT	12.87	88	2	1	0
Aldershot	L	01.90	89	11	0	0
Southend U	Tr	08.90	90-95	246	2	3
Derby Co	Tr	01.96	95-97	89	2	1
Charlton Ath	Tr	07.98	98-03	190	10	1
West Ham U	Tr	09.04	04	35	1	0

POWELL Clifford (Cliff) George
Watford, 21 February, 1968 (FB)

League Club	Source	Date Signed	Seasons Played	Apps	Subs	Gls
Watford	App	02.86				
Hereford U	L	12.87	87	7	0	0
Sheffield U	Tr	03.88	87-88	7	3	0
Doncaster Rov	L	03.89	88	4	0	0
Cardiff C	L	11.89	89	0	1	0

POWELL Colin David
Hendon, 7 July, 1948 (W)

League Club	Source	Date Signed	Seasons Played	Apps	Subs	Gls
Charlton Ath	Barnet	01.73	72-80	301	20	30
Gillingham	Tr	08.81	81-82	54	1	1

POWELL Darren David
Hammersmith, 10 March, 1976 (CD)

League Club	Source	Date Signed	Seasons Played	Apps	Subs	Gls
Brentford	Hampton	07.98	98-01	128	0	6
Crystal Palace	Tr	08.02	02-04	53	2	2
West Ham U	L	11.04	04	5	0	1

POWELL Darryl Anthony
Lambeth, 15 January, 1971 Jamaica 17 (M)

League Club	Source	Date Signed	Seasons Played	Apps	Subs	Gls
Portsmouth	YT	12.88	88-94	83	49	16
Derby Co	Tr	07.95	95-01	187	20	10
Birmingham C	Tr	09.02	02	3	8	0
Sheffield Wed	Tr	01.03	02	8	0	0
Nottingham F	Colorado (USA)	02.05	04	11	0	0

POWELL David
Dolgarrog, 15 October, 1944 Wu23-4/W-11 (CD)

League Club	Source	Date Signed	Seasons Played	Apps	Subs	Gls
Wrexham	Gwydyr Rov	05.63	62-68	132	2	4
Sheffield U	Tr	09.68	68-70	89	0	2
Cardiff C	Tr	09.72	72-74	36	0	1

POWELL David (Dai) Morgan
Swansea, 19 January, 1935 (FB)

League Club	Source	Date Signed	Seasons Played	Apps	Subs	Gls
Blackpool		12.52				
Rochdale	Tr	07.58	58-60	76	-	1

POWELL David Robert
Cannock, 24 September, 1967 (G)

League Club	Source	Date Signed	Seasons Played	Apps	Subs	Gls
West Bromwich A	Cherry Valley	04.86	87	2	0	0
Wrexham	L	02.87	86	2	0	0

POWELL Francis (Franny) Michael
Burnley, 17 June, 1977 (W)

League Club	Source	Date Signed	Seasons Played	Apps	Subs	Gls
Rochdale	Burnley (YT)	09.95	95	0	2	0

POWELL Gary
Hoylake, 2 April, 1969 (F)

League Club	Source	Date Signed	Seasons Played	Apps	Subs	Gls
Everton	YT	07.87				
Lincoln C	L	09.90	90	11	0	0
Scunthorpe U	L	11.90	90	3	1	1
Wigan Ath	L	03.91	90	13	1	4
Wigan Ath	Tr	08.91	91-92	44	26	13
Bury	Tr	08.93	93	4	1	0

POWELL George Reginald
Fulham, 11 October, 1924 Died 1989 (FB)

League Club	Source	Date Signed	Seasons Played	Apps	Subs	Gls
Queens Park Rgrs	Fulham (Am)	12.46	47-52	145	-	0

POWELL Ivor Verdun
Gilfach, 5 July, 1916 WWar-4/W-8 (WH)

League Club	Source	Date Signed	Seasons Played	Apps	Subs	Gls
Queens Park Rgrs	Barnet	09.37	38-48	110	-	2
Aston Villa	Tr	12.48	48-50	79	-	5
Port Vale	Tr	08.51	51	6	-	0
Bradford C	Barry T	06.52	52-54	83	-	9

POWELL Brian **John** Edward
York, 10 March, 1936 (W)

League Club	Source	Date Signed	Seasons Played	Apps	Subs	Gls
York C	Cliftonville (York)	09.56	56-59	27	-	5

POWELL Kenneth (Kenny)
Mansfield, 2 March, 1920 Died 1976 (W)

League Club	Source	Date Signed	Seasons Played	Apps	Subs	Gls
Derby Co	Mansfield CWS	05.39	46	13	-	0
Southport	Tr	06.47	47-50	90	-	18

League Club	Source	Date Signed	Seasons Played	Career Record Apps	Subs	Gls

POWELL Kenneth (Ken) Leigh
Chester, 25 September, 1924 Died 2005 (WH)

League Club	Source	Date Signed	Seasons Played	Apps	Subs	Gls
Cardiff C	Chester C (Am)	09.47				
Exeter C	Tr	06.48	48-49	22	-	1
Bristol Rov	Tr	07.51	51	4	-	0

POWELL Lee
Caerleon, 2 June, 1973 Wu21-4 (W)

League Club	Source	Date Signed	Seasons Played	Apps	Subs	Gls
Southampton	YT	05.91	91-93	2	5	0

POWELL Michael (Mike)
Newport, 26 April, 1951 (FB)

League Club	Source	Date Signed	Seasons Played	Apps	Subs	Gls
Newport Co	Newport YMCA	01.76	75-77	7	2	0

POWELL Michael (Mike) Philip
Slough, 18 April, 1933 (CD)

League Club	Source	Date Signed	Seasons Played	Apps	Subs	Gls
Queens Park Rgrs	Jnrs	01.51	52-58	105	-	0

POWELL Neville David
Flint, 2 September, 1963 (W)

League Club	Source	Date Signed	Seasons Played	Apps	Subs	Gls
Tranmere Rov	App	08.81	80-84	76	10	4

POWELL Paul
Wallingford, 30 June, 1978 (FB)

League Club	Source	Date Signed	Seasons Played	Apps	Subs	Gls
Oxford U	YT	07.96	95-02	143	35	17

POWELL Raymond (Ray)
Swansea, 5 August, 1924 (CF)

League Club	Source	Date Signed	Seasons Played	Apps	Subs	Gls
Swansea T	Haverfordwest	05.47	47-50	18	-	5
Scunthorpe U	Tr	08.51	51	31	-	14

POWELL Richard
Chesterfield, 3 September, 1969 (G)

League Club	Source	Date Signed	Seasons Played	Apps	Subs	Gls
Blackpool	YT	06.88	86-87	14	0	0

POWELL Ronald (Ronnie) William Herbert
Knighton, 2 December, 1929 Died 1992 (G)

League Club	Source	Date Signed	Seasons Played	Apps	Subs	Gls
Manchester C	Knighton T	11.48	49	12	-	0
Chesterfield	Tr	06.52	52-64	471	-	0

POWELL Stephen (Steve)
Derby, 20 September, 1955 ESch/EYth/Eu23-1 (M)

League Club	Source	Date Signed	Seasons Played	Apps	Subs	Gls
Derby Co	App	11.72	71-84	342	10	20

POWELL Thomas (Tommy) Ernest
Derby, 12 April, 1925 Died 1998 (W)

League Club	Source	Date Signed	Seasons Played	Apps	Subs	Gls
Derby Co	Derby Corinthians	04.42	48-61	380	-	57

POWELL Wayne
Caerphilly, 25 October, 1956 WYth (F)

League Club	Source	Date Signed	Seasons Played	Apps	Subs	Gls
Bristol Rov	App	10.74	75-77	25	7	10
Halifax T	L	10.77	77	4	0	1
Hereford U	Tr	06.78	78	6	0	2

POWER Graeme Richard
Northwick Park, 7 March, 1977 ESch/EYth (FB)

League Club	Source	Date Signed	Seasons Played	Apps	Subs	Gls
Queens Park Rgrs	YT	04.95				
Bristol Rov	Tr	07.96	96-97	25	1	0
Exeter C	Tr	08.98	98-02	165	6	2

POWER John
Chelsea, 10 December, 1959 (G)

League Club	Source	Date Signed	Seasons Played	Apps	Subs	Gls
Brentford	Kingstonian	03.87	86	2	0	0

POWER Lee Michael
Lewisham, 30 June, 1972 IRYth/IRu21-13/IRB (F)

League Club	Source	Date Signed	Seasons Played	Apps	Subs	Gls
Norwich C	YT	07.90	89-93	28	16	10
Charlton Ath	L	12.92	92	5	0	0
Sunderland	L	08.93	93	1	2	0
Portsmouth	L	10.93	93	1	1	0
Bradford C	Tr	03.94	93-94	14	16	5
Peterborough U	Tr	07.95	95	25	13	6
Plymouth Arg	Hibernian	08.98	98	7	9	0
Halifax T	Tr	12.98	98-99	17	8	5

POWER Michael (Mike) David
Stockport, 3 October, 1961 (F)

League Club	Source	Date Signed	Seasons Played	Apps	Subs	Gls
Stockport Co	Jnrs	08.80	80-85	67	4	16

POWER Paul Christopher
Manchester, 30 October, 1953 EB (M)

League Club	Source	Date Signed	Seasons Played	Apps	Subs	Gls
Manchester C	Leeds Polytechnic	09.73	75-85	358	7	26
Everton	Tr	06.86	86-87	52	0	6

POWER Philip (Phil) Damian
Salford, 25 July, 1966 (F)

League Club	Source	Date Signed	Seasons Played	Apps	Subs	Gls
Crewe Alex	Northwich Vic	08.85	85-86	18	9	3
Macclesfield T	Barrow	10.93	97	21	17	7

POWLING Richard (Richie) Frederick
Barking, 21 May, 1956 EYth (CD)

League Club	Source	Date Signed	Seasons Played	Apps	Subs	Gls
Arsenal	App	07.73	73-77	50	5	3

POWNER Robert (Bob) James
Newcastle-under-Lyme, 2 July, 1967 (G)

League Club	Source	Date Signed	Seasons Played	Apps	Subs	Gls
Crewe Alex	KJnrs	06.86	85-86	6	0	0

POWNEY Brian William
Seaford, 7 October, 1944 (G)

League Club	Source	Date Signed	Seasons Played	Apps	Subs	Gls
Brighton & Hove A	App	11.61	61-73	351	0	0

POWTON Brian
Newcastle, 29 August, 1929 Died 1985 (G)

League Club	Source	Date Signed	Seasons Played	Apps	Subs	Gls
Newcastle U		10.50				
Preston NE	Tr	08.51				
Hartlepools U	Tr	07.52	52	4	-	0

POYET Gustavo Augusto
Montevideo, Uruguay, 15 November, 1967 UruguayYth/Uruguay-31 (M)

League Club	Source	Date Signed	Seasons Played	Apps	Subs	Gls
Chelsea	Real Zaragoza (Sp)	07.97	97-00	79	26	36
Tottenham H	Tr	07.01	01-03	66	16	18

POYNER Robert (Bobby) Christopher
Maesglas, 25 December, 1932 Died 1977 WSch/WYth (CD)

League Club	Source	Date Signed	Seasons Played	Apps	Subs	Gls
Newport Co	Jnrs	01.51	50-51	2	-	0

POYNTON William (Bill)
Shiremoor, 30 June, 1944 (FB)

League Club	Source	Date Signed	Seasons Played	Apps	Subs	Gls
Burnley	Jnrs	07.61				
Mansfield T	Tr	07.64	64-65	20	0	0
Lincoln C	Lockheed Leamington	10.66	66	0	1	0

POYSER George Henry
Stanton Hill, 6 February, 1910 Died 1995 (FB)

League Club	Source	Date Signed	Seasons Played	Apps	Subs	Gls
Wolverhampton W	Stanton Hill	05.28				
Port Vale	Mansfield T	05.31	31-33	72	-	0
Brentford	Tr	06.34	34-38	149	-	0
Plymouth Arg	Tr	04.46	46	3	-	0

PRAGG Michael (Mickey) Kenneth
Shrewsbury, 8 October, 1941 EAmat (IF)

League Club	Source	Date Signed	Seasons Played	Apps	Subs	Gls
Shrewsbury T (Am)	Jnrs	05.59	60-62	5	-	1

PRANGLEY Samuel (Sam)
Newport, 30 September, 1924 (WH)

League Club	Source	Date Signed	Seasons Played	Apps	Subs	Gls
Newport Co	Lovells Ath	11.46	46	7	-	0

PRASKI Josef
France, 22 January, 1926 Died 1998 (W)

League Club	Source	Date Signed	Seasons Played	Apps	Subs	Gls
Notts Co	Jeanfield Swifts	03.49	48	3	-	0

PRATLEY Darren Antony
Barking, 22 April, 1985 (M)

League Club	Source	Date Signed	Seasons Played	Apps	Subs	Gls
Fulham	YT	04.02	03	0	1	0
Brentford	L	02.05	04	11	3	1

PRATLEY Richard (Dick) George
Banbury, 12 January, 1963 (CD)

League Club	Source	Date Signed	Seasons Played	Apps	Subs	Gls
Derby Co	Banbury U	07.83	83-86	29	2	1
Scunthorpe U	L	03.84	83	10	0	0
Shrewsbury T	Tr	02.88	87-89	44	2	1

PRATT John Arthur
Hackney, 26 June, 1948 (M)

League Club	Source	Date Signed	Seasons Played	Apps	Subs	Gls
Tottenham H	Jnrs	11.65	68-79	307	24	39

PRATT John Leslie
Atherstone, 1 March, 1943 (G)

League Club	Source	Date Signed	Seasons Played	Apps	Subs	Gls
Reading	Wycombe W	07.69	69-71	29	0	0

PRATT Lee Stuart
Cleethorpes, 31 March, 1970 (G)

League Club	Source	Date Signed	Seasons Played	Apps	Subs	Gls
Grimsby T	YT	06.88	86	1	0	0

PRATT Michael (Mick) Wayne
Newport, 15 January, 1966 WYth (F)

League Club	Source	Date Signed	Seasons Played	Apps	Subs	Gls
Newport Co	Jnrs	08.83	83-84	4	5	2

PRATT Raymond (Ray) Ernest
Burry Port, 11 November, 1955 WYth (F)

League Club	Source	Date Signed	Seasons Played	Apps	Subs	Gls
Exeter C	Merthyr Tydfil	03.80	79-85	127	46	61

PRATT Wayne
Southampton, 1 March, 1960 (M)

League Club	Source	Date Signed	Seasons Played	Apps	Subs	Gls
Southampton	App	03.78	80	1	0	0

PRECIOUS Derek
Crewe, 2 June, 1931 (IF)

League Club	Source	Date Signed	Seasons Played	Apps	Subs	Gls
Crewe Alex		09.55	55-56	18	-	3

PREECE Andrew (Andy) Paul
Evesham, 27 March, 1967 (F)

League Club	Source	Date Signed	Seasons Played	Apps	Subs	Gls
Northampton T	Evesham U	08.88	88	0	1	0
Wrexham	Worcester C	03.90	89-91	44	7	7
Stockport Co	Tr	12.91	91-93	89	8	42

League Club	Source	Date Signed	Seasons Played	Apps	Subs	Gls
Crystal Palace	Tr	06.94	94	17	3	4
Blackpool	Tr	07.95	95-97	114	12	35
Bury	Tr	07.98	98-03	87	81	27
Carlisle U	Tr	12.03	03	23	2	3
PREECE Brian James						
Hereford, 16 February, 1958 Died 1992 (W)						
Hereford U	App	02.76	74-76	5	1	0
Newport Co	Tr	03.77	76-77	38	6	12
PREECE David Douglas						
Sunderland, 26 August, 1976 (G)						
Sunderland	YT	06.94				
Darlington	Tr	07.97	97-98	91	0	0
PREECE David William						
Much Wenlock, 28 May, 1963 EB-3 (M)						
Walsall	App	07.80	80-84	107	4	5
Luton T	Tr	12.84	84-94	328	8	21
Derby Co	Tr	08.95	95	10	3	1
Birmingham C	L	11.95	95	6	0	0
Swindon T	L	03.96	95	7	0	1
Cambridge U	Tr	09.96	96-00	40	35	2
Torquay U	Tr	10.01	01	4	2	0
PREECE John (Jack) Causer						
Wolverhampton, 30 April, 1914 Died 2003 (FB)						
Wolverhampton W	Sunbeam Motors	05.31	33	2	-	0
Bristol Rov	Tr	05.35	35-37	79	-	0
Bradford C	Tr	07.38	38	3	-	0
Southport	Tr	05.39	46	36	-	0
Swindon T	Tr	06.47	47	7	-	0
PREECE Paul William						
Penarth, 16 May, 1957 (M)						
Newport Co	App	06.75	74-75	17	6	0
PREECE Roger						
Much Wenlock, 9 June, 1969 (M)						
Wrexham	Coventry C (Jnrs)	08.86	86-89	89	21	12
Chester C	Tr	08.90	90-95	165	5	4
Shrewsbury T	Telford U	07.97	97-99	46	6	3
PREECE Ryan						
Briton Ferry, 10 January, 1969 (M)						
Newport Co	YT	10.87	87	7	3	2
PREEDY Philip (Phil)						
Hereford, 20 November, 1975 (M)						
Hereford U	YT	07.94	93-96	31	20	4
[PREKI] RADOSAVLJEVIC Predrag						
Belgrade, Yugoslavia, 24 June, 1963 USA int (W)						
Everton	St Louis (USA)	08.92	92-93	22	24	4
Portsmouth	Tr	07.94	94	30	10	5
PRENDERGAST Michael (Mick) John						
Denaby, 24 November, 1950 (F)						
Sheffield Wed	App	11.67	68-77	170	13	53
Barnsley	Tr	05.78	77-78	12	8	2
Halifax T	L	10.78	78	4	0	1
PRENDERGAST Rory						
Pontefract, 6 April, 1978 (W)						
Barnsley	YT	04.97				
York C	Tr	08.98	98	1	2	0
PRENDERVILLE Barry						
Dublin, 16 October, 1976 (CD)						
Coventry C	Cherry Orchard	08.94				
Oldham Ath	St Patrick's Ath	09.00	00-01	16	5	0
PRENTIS John						
Liverpool, 22 March, 1939 (FB)						
Blackpool		10.62	64-65	6	0	0
Stockport Co	Tr	10.66	66-67	16	3	0
PRESCOTT Francis (Frank) Stephen						
Birkenhead, 12 August, 1922 Died 1969 (CF)						
Tranmere Rov	St Annes	10.46	46	2	-	0
PRESCOTT James (Jimmy) Lawrence						
Lowton, 2 November, 1930 (IF)						
Southport	Leeds U (Am)	03.54	53-54	53	-	9
York C	Tr	06.55	55	18	-	5
Southport	Tr	10.56	56	17	-	1
PRESLAND Edward (Eddie) Robert						
Loughton, 27 March, 1943 (FB)						
West Ham U	Jnrs	10.60	64-65	6	0	1
Crystal Palace	Tr	01.67	66-68	61	0	0
Colchester U	L	10.69	69	5	0	0

League Club	Source	Date Signed	Seasons Played	Apps	Subs	Gls
PRESLEY Charles **Derek**						
Warminster, 8 March, 1930 (WH)						
Bristol C	Warminster T	03.50	50-51	9	-	0
PRESSDEE James (Jim) Stuart						
Swansea, 19 June, 1933 WSch (FB)						
Swansea T	Jnrs	08.51	53-55	8	-	0
PRESSLEY Steven John						
Elgin, 11 October, 1973 Su21-20 (CD)						
Coventry C	Glasgow Rgrs	10.94	94	18	1	1
PRESSMAN Kevin Paul						
Fareham, 6 November, 1967 ESch/EYth/Eu21-1/EB-3 (G)						
Sheffield Wed	App	11.85	87-03	400	4	0
Stoke C	L	03.92	91	4	0	0
Leicester C	Tr	07.04	04	13	0	0
PRESTON Michael John						
Plymouth, 22 November, 1977 (W)						
Torquay U	YT	07.96	95-96	4	6	0
PRESTON Richard Frank						
Nottingham, 10 June, 1967 (F)						
Scarborough	Stanton T	03.88	87	1	3	0
PRESTON Richard John						
Basildon, 7 April, 1976 (FB)						
Northampton T	YT	08.94	93	1	0	0
PRICE Albert Edward						
Langwith, 4 April, 1926 Died 1983 (G)						
Crewe Alex	Creswell Colliery	12.46	46	5	-	0
PRICE Allen Douglas						
Gelligaer, 24 March, 1968 WYth (FB)						
Cardiff C	Newport Co (Jnrs)	08.85	85	2	0	0
PRICE Arthur						
Rowlands Gill, 12 January, 1921 Died 1995 (WH)						
Newcastle U	Spen Black & White	08.40				
Leeds U	Consett	05.46	46	6	-	0
PRICE Brynley (Bryn)						
Treorchy, 15 January, 1936 (WH)						
Barnsley	Treorchy BC	05.55	56-57	2	-	0
PRICE Cecil						
Cardiff, 2 December, 1919 (W)						
Cardiff C		09.48	48	1	-	0
Bradford C	Tr	06.49	49	7	-	0
PRICE Christopher (Chris) John						
Hereford, 30 March, 1960 EYth (FB)						
Hereford U	App	01.78	76-85	327	3	27
Blackburn Rov	Tr	07.86	86-87	83	0	11
Aston Villa	Tr	05.88	88-91	109	2	2
Blackburn Rov	Tr	02.92	91-92	13	6	3
Portsmouth	Tr	01.93	92-93	14	4	0
PRICE David James						
Caterham, 23 June, 1955 ESch/EYth (M)						
Arsenal	App	08.72	72-80	116	10	16
Peterborough U	L	01.75	74	6	0	1
Crystal Palace	Tr	03.81	80-81	25	2	2
Orient		03.83	82	10	0	0
PRICE Derrick						
Wellington, 14 February, 1932 (W)						
Shrewsbury T	Donnington	02.53	53-57	125	-	28
Aldershot	Tr	07.58	58-59	4	-	1
PRICE Thomas **Dudley (Duggie)**						
Swansea, 17 November, 1931 (IF)						
Swansea T	Jnrs	04.50	53-57	34	-	9
Southend U	Tr	01.58	57-60	91	-	41
Hull C	Tr	09.60	60-62	76	-	26
Bradford C	Tr	07.63	63-64	62	-	21
PRICE Ernest (Ernie)						
Easington, 12 May, 1926 (WH)						
Sunderland		01.45				
Darlington		12.48	48-50	69	-	0
Crystal Palace	Tr	07.51	51-52	34	-	5
PRICE Gareth Michael						
Swindon, 21 February, 1970 Died 1998 (M)						
Mansfield T	YT	07.88				
Bury	Tr	07.89	89-90	1	3	0
PRICE George						
Crewe, 2 December, 1929 (W)						
Crewe Alex		02.54	53	4	-	0

League Club	Source	Date Signed	Seasons Played	Apps	Subs	Gls
PRICE James (Jamie) Benjamin						
Normanton, 27 October, 1981						(FB)
Doncaster Rov	YT	08.99	03-04	22	3	0
PRICE James (Jamie) Richard						
Preston, 1 February, 1978						(FB)
Rochdale	YT	07.96	95	3	0	0
PRICE Jason Jeffrey						
Pontypridd, 12 April, 1977 Wu21-7						(M)
Swansea C	Aberaman Ath	07.95	96-00	133	11	17
Brentford	Tr	08.01	01	15	0	1
Tranmere Rov	Tr	11.01	01-02	34	15	11
Hull C	Tr	07.03	03-04	35	25	11
PRICE John (Jack)						
Shotton, 29 August, 1918						(IF)
Hartlepools U	Wolverhampton W (Am)	06.38	38-48	89	-	12
York C	Tr	12.48	48	2	-	2
PRICE John (Johnny)						
Easington, 25 October, 1943 Died 1995						(W)
Burnley	Horden CW	11.60	63-64	21	-	2
Stockport Co	Tr	05.65	65-71	241	5	23
Blackburn Rov	Tr	09.71	71-73	63	13	12
Stockport Co	Tr	03.74	73-75	51	15	1
PRICE John (Johnny)						
Leadgate, 14 April, 1947						(W)
Leeds U	App	05.65				
Southport	Tr	07.66	66	16	2	2
PRICE John						
Middlewich, 28 April, 1960						(M)
Rochdale	Middlewich A	01.78	77-78	10	2	0
PRICE John (Jack) David						
Camden, 31 December, 1932						(CD)
Tottenham H	Eastbourne U	09.54				
Aldershot	Tr	01.57	56-58	86	-	1
Watford	Tr	06.59	59	22	-	0
PRICE John Geraint						
Aberystwyth, 22 November, 1936						(FB)
Liverpool	Fordhouse YC	10.54	55	1	-	0
Aston Villa	Tr	03.57				
Walsall	Tr	07.57				
Shrewsbury T	Tr	07.58	58-59	9	-	0
PRICE Kenneth (Ken) Edward						
Ellesmere Port, 25 March, 1939						(CF)
Aston Villa	West Bromborough	08.59				
Tranmere Rov	Tr	12.60	60	3	-	2
Hartlepools U	Tr	07.61	61	8	-	3
PRICE Kenneth (Ken) Gordon						
Dudley, 26 February, 1954						(F)
Southend U	Dudley T	05.76	76	1	0	0
Gillingham	Tr	12.76	76-82	247	8	78
Reading	Tr	01.83	82-84	40	3	6
PRICE Leslie Eugene						
Consett, 26 August, 1930						(W)
Sunderland		08.50				
Gateshead	Tr	07.52	52-53	39	-	13
PRICE Lewis Peter						
Bournemouth, 19 July, 1984 WYth/Wu21-6						(G)
Ipswich T	Southampton (Jnrs)	08.02	03-04	8	1	0
Cambridge U	L	11.04	04	6	0	0
PRICE Mark Anthony						
Keighley, 15 October, 1973						(M)
Scarborough	YT	•	91	2	1	1
PRICE Michael (Mike)						
Ashington, 3 April, 1983						(G)
Leicester C	YT	02.01				
Darlington	Tr	08.03	03	36	0	0
PRICE Michael (Mike) David						
Wrexham, 29 April, 1982 Wu21-11						(FB)
Everton	YT	01.00				
Hull C	Tr	07.01	01-02	1	3	0
PRICE Neil						
Hemel Hempstead, 15 February, 1964						(FB)
Watford	App	02.82	83	7	1	0
Plymouth Arg	L	02.84	83	1	0	0
Blackpool	L	03.85	84	13	0	0
Swansea C	Tr	07.85	85	0	2	0
PRICE Paul Terence						
St Albans, 23 May, 1954 Wu21-1/W-25						(CD)
Luton T	Welwyn Garden U	07.71	72-80	206	1	8
Tottenham H	Tr	06.81	81-83	35	4	0
Swansea C	Minnesota (USA)	01.85	84-85	62	0	1
Peterborough U	Saltash U	08.86	86-87	86	0	0
PRICE Peter						
Tarbolton, 26 February, 1932						(IF)
Darlington	Gloucester C	01.54	53-54	3	-	0
PRICE Peter William						
Wrexham, 17 August, 1949 Wu23-4						(F)
Liverpool	App	08.66				
Peterborough U	Tr	07.68	68-71	114	5	62
Portsmouth	Tr	06.72	72-73	13	1	2
Peterborough U	L	07.74	74	2	0	0
Barnsley	Tr	11.74	74-77	72	7	28
PRICE Raymond (Ray)						
Hetton-le-Hole, 18 May, 1944 Died 1990						(FB)
Norwich C	Jnrs	07.63	63	1	-	0
Colchester U	Tr	07.64	64-66	15	2	0
PRICE Raymond (Ray) John						
Northampton, 30 November, 1948						(F)
Northampton T	App	12.66	66-67	7	0	0
PRICE Ryan						
Wolverhampton, 13 March, 1970 ESemiPro-6						(G)
Birmingham C	Stafford Rgrs	08.94				
Macclesfield T	Tr	11.95	97-99	99	1	0
PRICE Terence (Terry) Edmund						
Colchester, 11 October, 1945						(W)
Leyton Orient	App	08.63	64-67	86	1	18
Colchester U	Tr	09.67	67-68	55	2	5
PRICE Trevor Henry Richard						
Ellesmere Port, 27 December, 1944						(W)
Workington		06.64	64	2	-	1
PRICE Walter Booth						
Neston, 14 February, 1921 Died 1984						(CD)
Tranmere Rov		03.41	46	2	-	0
Rochdale	Tr	08.48	48	1	-	0
PRICE Albert James **William (Billy)**						
Hadley, 10 April, 1917 Died 1995						(CF)
Huddersfield T	Wrockwardine Wood	10.37	37-47	51	-	23
Reading	Tr	10.47	47-48	15	-	2
Hull C	Tr	01.49	48	8	-	5
Bradford C	Tr	11.49	49-51	54	-	28
PRIDAY Marcus Albert						
Knighton, 16 October, 1971 WYth						(G)
Hereford U	YT	08.90	89	3	0	0
PRIDAY Robert (Bob) Herbert						
Cape Town, South Africa, 29 March, 1925 Died 1998						(W)
Liverpool	Cape Town C (SA)	12.45	46-48	34	-	6
Blackburn Rov	Tr	03.49	48-50	44	-	11
Accrington St	Northwich Vic	12.52	52	5	-	0
Rochdale	Tr	08.53	53	5	-	1
PRIDDLE Sean Patrick						
Hammersmith, 14 December, 1965						(M)
Wimbledon	App	12.83				
Crewe Alex	Tr	02.85	84	6	5	0
Exeter C	Wimbledon (N/C)	07.86	86	18	0	1
Brentford	Tr	07.87	87	5	1	0
PRIDDY Paul Joseph						
Isleworth, 11 July, 1953						(G)
Brentford	Walton & Hersham	10.72	72-76	121	0	0
Wimbledon	Tooting & Mitcham	10.78	78	1	0	0
Brentford	Hayes	08.81	81	1	0	0
PRIEST Christopher (Chris)						
Leigh, 18 October, 1973						(M)
Everton	YT	06.92				
Chester C	L	09.94	94	11	0	1
Chester C	Tr	01.95	94-98	151	5	25
Macclesfield T	Tr	07.99	99-03	140	10	13
PRIEST Harry						
Clay Cross, 26 October, 1935						(IF)
Sheffield U	Clay Cross Works	02.54	56	2	-	1
Halifax T	Tr	01.58	57-58	30	-	12

PRIEST Philip (Phil)
Warley, 9 September, 1966 ESch/EYth (M)

League Club	Source	Date Signed	Seasons Played	Apps	Subs	Gls
Chelsea	App	09.83				
Blackpool	L	12.86	86	1	0	0
Brentford	L	03.87	86	3	2	1
Shrewsbury T	Tr	07.87	87-89	54	6	3

PRIESTLEY Derek
Queensbury, 22 December, 1926 Died 1999 (W)

League Club	Source	Date Signed	Seasons Played	Apps	Subs	Gls
Halifax T		10.50	51-55	145	-	19

PRIESTLEY Gerald (Gerry)
Halifax, 2 March, 1931 (W)

League Club	Source	Date Signed	Seasons Played	Apps	Subs	Gls
Nottingham F		12.50				
Exeter C	Tr	06.53	53-54	42	-	6
Grimsby T	Tr	06.55	55-58	110	-	11
Crystal Palace	Tr	11.58	58-59	28	-	2
Halifax T	Tr	07.60	60-62	105	-	23

PRIESTLEY Jason Aaron
Leeds, 25 October, 1970 (G)

League Club	Source	Date Signed	Seasons Played	Apps	Subs	Gls
Carlisle U	YT	07.89	90	22	0	0
Hartlepool U	L	12.89	89	16	0	0
Scarborough	L	08.91	91	9	0	0

PRIESTLEY Maurice
Bradford, 27 October, 1922 Died 1986 (CF)

League Club	Source	Date Signed	Seasons Played	Apps	Subs	Gls
Bradford PA		09.46				
Halifax T	Tr	01.48	47-48	24	-	8

PRIESTLEY Philip (Phil) Alan
Wigan, 30 March, 1976 (G)

League Club	Source	Date Signed	Seasons Played	Apps	Subs	Gls
Rochdale	Atherton Laburnum Rov	09.98	98-99	2	1	0

PRIESTLEY Royston (Roy) Maurice
Barnsley, 26 November, 1948 (F)

League Club	Source	Date Signed	Seasons Played	Apps	Subs	Gls
Barnsley (Am)	Jnrs	08.67	67	1	0	0

PRIET Nicolas
Lyon, France, 31 January, 1983 (FB)

League Club	Source	Date Signed	Seasons Played	Apps	Subs	Gls
Leicester C	Lyon (Fr)	07.03				
Doncaster Rov	Tr	07.04	04	7	0	0

PRIMUS Linvoy Stephen
Forest Gate, 14 September, 1973 (CD)

League Club	Source	Date Signed	Seasons Played	Apps	Subs	Gls
Charlton Ath	YT	08.92	92	4	0	0
Barnet	Tr	07.94	94-96	127	0	7
Reading	Tr	07.97	97-99	94	1	1
Portsmouth	Tr	08.00	00-04	133	8	3

PRINCE Eric
Ipstones, 11 December, 1924 Died 2003 (IF)

League Club	Source	Date Signed	Seasons Played	Apps	Subs	Gls
Port Vale	Ipstones	09.44	46	14	-	2

PRINCE Francis (Frankie) Anthony
Penarth, 1 December, 1949 Wu23-4 (M)

League Club	Source	Date Signed	Seasons Played	Apps	Subs	Gls
Bristol Rov	App	12.67	67-79	360	2	23
Exeter C	Tr	07.80	80-81	27	4	2

PRINCE Harold
Stoke-on-Trent, 4 December, 1921 (G)

League Club	Source	Date Signed	Seasons Played	Apps	Subs	Gls
Port Vale	Bucknall	08.44	47-48	5	-	0

PRINCE Neil Michael
Liverpool, 17 March, 1983 EYth (M)

League Club	Source	Date Signed	Seasons Played	Apps	Subs	Gls
Torquay U	Liverpool (YT)	08.02	02	3	4	0

PRINDIVILLE Steven (Steve) Alan
Harlow, 26 December, 1968 (FB)

League Club	Source	Date Signed	Seasons Played	Apps	Subs	Gls
Leicester C	App	12.86	87	0	1	0
Chesterfield	Tr	06.88	88	43	0	1
Mansfield T	Tr	06.89	89-90	26	2	0
Doncaster Rov	Hinckley Ath	02.92	91-93	58	1	2

PRING Dennis Frederick
Newport, 8 November, 1940 (IF)

League Club	Source	Date Signed	Seasons Played	Apps	Subs	Gls
Southampton	Newport YMCA	02.59	58	4	-	0

PRING Keith David
Newport, 11 March, 1943 W-3 (W)

League Club	Source	Date Signed	Seasons Played	Apps	Subs	Gls
Newport Co	Nash U	11.61	61-64	62	-	3
Rotherham U	Tr	10.64	64-67	81	0	6
Notts Co	Tr	12.67	67-68	41	3	2
Southport	Tr	07.69	69-70	48	0	4

PRINGLE Brian
Chathill, 12 March, 1949 (M)

League Club	Source	Date Signed	Seasons Played	Apps	Subs	Gls
Hartlepool (Am)	Alnwick T	04.73	72	1	0	0

PRINGLE Ulf **Martin**
Gothenburg, Sweden, 18 November, 1970 SwB-1/Sw-2 (F)

League Club	Source	Date Signed	Seasons Played	Apps	Subs	Gls
Charlton Ath	Benfica (Por)	01.99	98-00	28	30	8
Grimsby T	L	02.02	01	2	0	0

PRINGLE William Alexander
Liverpool, 24 February, 1932 (IF)

League Club	Source	Date Signed	Seasons Played	Apps	Subs	Gls
Leeds U	Jnrs	08.49				
Grimsby T	Tr	05.54	54	2	-	0

PRINS Jason
Wisbech, 1 November, 1974 (F)

League Club	Source	Date Signed	Seasons Played	Apps	Subs	Gls
Carlisle U	YT	08.93	91-93	7	11	0

PRIOR Kenneth (Ken) George
Ashington, 13 October, 1932 (W)

League Club	Source	Date Signed	Seasons Played	Apps	Subs	Gls
Newcastle U	Sunderland (Am)	03.52	51-52	8	-	3
Millwall	Tr	05.54	54-55	61	-	16
Newcastle U	Tr	07.56	56	2	-	0

PRIOR Spencer Justin
Rochford, 22 April, 1971 (CD)

League Club	Source	Date Signed	Seasons Played	Apps	Subs	Gls
Southend U	YT	05.89	88-92	135	0	3
Norwich C	Tr	06.93	93-95	67	7	1
Leicester C	Tr	08.96	96-97	61	3	0
Derby Co	Tr	08.98	98-99	48	6	1
Manchester C	Tr	03.00	99-00	27	3	4
Cardiff C	Tr	07.01	01-03	72	9	2
Southend U	Tr	08.04	04	41	0	2

PRISCOTT Anthony (Tony) John
Eastleigh, 19 March, 1941 (W)

League Club	Source	Date Signed	Seasons Played	Apps	Subs	Gls
Portsmouth	Jnrs	07.59	59-61	35	-	6
Aldershot	Tr	08.62	62-65	141	0	44
Bournemouth	Tr	01.66	65-66	60	1	7
Aldershot	Tr	08.67	67-70	126	10	27

PRITCHARD Alan Stewart
Chester, 24 August, 1943 (IF)

League Club	Source	Date Signed	Seasons Played	Apps	Subs	Gls
Chester	Jnrs	10.60	60-63	19	-	6

PRITCHARD Alfred (Alf) Vincent
Chester, 31 August, 1920 Died 1995 (CF)

League Club	Source	Date Signed	Seasons Played	Apps	Subs	Gls
Millwall	Chester (Am)	07.37				
Wrexham	Dumbarton	08.46	46-49	36	-	8

PRITCHARD David Michael
Wolverhampton, 27 May, 1972 WB-1 (FB)

League Club	Source	Date Signed	Seasons Played	Apps	Subs	Gls
West Bromwich A	YT	07.90	91	1	4	0
Bristol Rov	Telford U	02.94	93-01	157	6	1

PRITCHARD Howard Keith
Cardiff, 18 October, 1958 WYth/W-1 (W)

League Club	Source	Date Signed	Seasons Played	Apps	Subs	Gls
Bristol C	App	08.76	78-80	31	7	2
Swindon T	Tr	08.81	81-82	59	6	11
Bristol C	Tr	08.83	83-85	117	2	22
Gillingham	Tr	08.86	86-87	84	4	20
Walsall	Tr	07.88	88-89	40	5	7
Maidstone U	Tr	10.89	89-90	29	4	6

PRITCHARD Harvey **John (Jack)**
Meriden, 30 January, 1918 Died 2000 (W)

League Club	Source	Date Signed	Seasons Played	Apps	Subs	Gls
Coventry C	Exhall Colliery	10.35	36	5	-	2
Crystal Palace	Tr	06.37	37	30	-	6
Manchester C	Tr	03.38	37-38	22	-	5
Southend U	Tr	02.47	46-51	71	-	8

PRITCHARD Joseph (Joe) Henry
Birkenhead, 4 September, 1943 (M)

League Club	Source	Date Signed	Seasons Played	Apps	Subs	Gls
Tranmere Rov	Liverpool (Am)	09.62	62-69	176	2	29

PRITCHARD Keith
Wallasey, 20 October, 1919 Died 1998 (IF)

League Club	Source	Date Signed	Seasons Played	Apps	Subs	Gls
New Brighton (Am)	New Brighton Baptists	07.46	46-47	25	-	8

PRITCHARD Mark Owen
Tredegar, 23 November, 1985 (F)

League Club	Source	Date Signed	Seasons Played	Apps	Subs	Gls
Swansea C	Sch	•	03	1	3	0

PRITCHARD Philip (Phil) John
Wordsley, 9 January, 1965 (G)

League Club	Source	Date Signed	Seasons Played	Apps	Subs	Gls
Stoke C	App	01.82				
Southend U	L	03.84	83	9	0	0

PRITCHARD Raymond (Ray)
Everton, 23 June, 1954 ESch (FB)

League Club	Source	Date Signed	Seasons Played	Apps	Subs	Gls
Tranmere Rov	Everton (App)	02.73	72-73	13	1	0
Southport	L	01.74	73	3	0	0

PRITCHARD Roy Thomas
Dawley, 9 May, 1925 Died 1993 (FB)

League Club	Source	Date Signed	Seasons Played	Apps	Subs	Gls
Wolverhampton W	Jnrs	05.42	46-54	202	-	0
Aston Villa	Tr	02.55	55-57	3	-	0
Notts Co	Tr	11.57	57	18	-	0
Port Vale	Tr	08.58	58-59	24	-	0

PRITCHETT Darrol
Bentley, 22 March, 1933 (FB)

League Club	Source	Date Signed	Seasons Played	Apps	Subs	Gls
Hull C	Jnrs	01.51				
Walsall	Tr	05.54	54	1	-	0

PRITCHETT Keith Bernard
Glasgow, 8 November, 1953 (FB)

League Club	Source	Date Signed	Seasons Played	Apps	Subs	Gls
Wolverhampton W		04.72				
Doncaster Rov	Tr	07.73	73	6	0	0
Queens Park Rgrs	Tr	03.74	74	4	0	0
Brentford	Tr	07.76	76	11	0	1
Watford	Tr	11.76	76-81	133	7	9
Blackpool	Tr	11.82	82-83	36	1	1

PRITTY George Joseph
Birmingham, 4 March, 1915 Died 1996 (WH)

League Club	Source	Date Signed	Seasons Played	Apps	Subs	Gls
Aston Villa	HB Metro	05.33	36-37	3	-	0
Nottingham F	Tr	12.38	38-47	49	-	1

PROBERT Eric William
South Kirkby, 17 February, 1952 Died 2004 EYth (M)

League Club	Source	Date Signed	Seasons Played	Apps	Subs	Gls
Burnley	App	02.69	68-72	62	5	11
Notts Co	Tr	07.73	73-76	122	0	14
Darlington	Tr	07.78	78-79	20	1	0

PROBETS Ashley
Bexleyheath, 13 December, 1984 (FB)

League Club	Source	Date Signed	Seasons Played	Apps	Subs	Gls
Arsenal	Sch	07.03				
Rochdale	Tr	07.04	04	4	5	0

PROCTOR David
Belfast, 10 October, 1929 (WH)

League Club	Source	Date Signed	Seasons Played	Apps	Subs	Gls
Blackpool	Portadown	08.49				
Norwich C	Tr	01.53	52-53	17	-	0
Barrow	Northwich Vic	10.54	54-58	160	-	2
Wrexham	Tr	08.59	59	2	-	0

PROCTOR Michael Henry (Harry)
Ushaw Moor, 10 July, 1912 Died 1984 (WH)

League Club	Source	Date Signed	Seasons Played	Apps	Subs	Gls
Hartlepools U	Washington Colliery	07.32	32-33	61	-	14
Norwich C	Tr	05.34	34-46	108	-	3

PROCTOR James Anthony
Doncaster, 25 October, 1976 (W)

League Club	Source	Date Signed	Seasons Played	Apps	Subs	Gls
Rochdale	Bradford C (YT)	10.95	95	1	2	0

PROCTOR Mark Gerard
Middlesbrough, 30 January, 1961 EYth/Eu21-4 (M)

League Club	Source	Date Signed	Seasons Played	Apps	Subs	Gls
Middlesbrough	App	09.78	78-80	107	2	12
Nottingham F	Tr	08.81	81-82	60	4	5
Sunderland	L	03.83	82	5	0	0
Sunderland	Tr	08.83	83-87	110	2	19
Sheffield Wed	Tr	09.87	87-88	59	0	4
Middlesbrough	Tr	03.89	88-92	101	19	6
Tranmere Rov	Tr	03.93	92-93	31	0	1
Hartlepool U	South Shields	03.97	96	6	0	0

PROCTOR Michael Anthony
Sunderland, 3 October, 1980 (F)

League Club	Source	Date Signed	Seasons Played	Apps	Subs	Gls
Sunderland	YT	10.97	02-03	15	23	3
Halifax T	L	03.01	00	11	1	4
York C	L	08.01	01	40	1	14
Bradford C	L	08.02	02	10	2	4
Rotherham U	Tr	02.04	03-04	32	13	7
Swindon T	L	02.05	04	4	0	2

PROKAS Richard
Penrith, 22 January, 1976 (M)

League Club	Source	Date Signed	Seasons Played	Apps	Subs	Gls
Carlisle U	Yt	07.94	94-00	184	20	3
Cambridge U	Tr	03.01	00-01	9	3	1

PROLZE Brian Joseph
Altrincham, 11 April, 1932 Died 1996 (CF)

League Club	Source	Date Signed	Seasons Played	Apps	Subs	Gls
Crewe Alex (Am)	Altrincham	02.54	53	1	-	0

PROPHETT Colin George
Crewe, 8 March, 1947 (CD)

League Club	Source	Date Signed	Seasons Played	Apps	Subs	Gls
Sheffield Wed	Crewe YC	06.68	69-72	111	8	7
Norwich C	Tr	06.73	73	34	1	0
Swindon T	Tr	09.74	74-77	158	2	10
Chesterfield	Tr	09.78	78-79	35	2	1
Crewe Alex	Tr	10.79	79-80	79	0	1

PROSINECKI Robert
Schwerninger, Germany, 12 January, 1969 Yu-15/Cro-49 (M)

League Club	Source	Date Signed	Seasons Played	Apps	Subs	Gls
Portsmouth	Standard Liege (Bel)	08.01	01	30	3	9

PROSSER Neil Albert
Edmonton, 8 March, 1957 (F)

League Club	Source	Date Signed	Seasons Played	Apps	Subs	Gls
Bournemouth	Harlow T	07.80	80	1	1	0
Tranmere Rov		09.82	82	1	1	0

PROUDLER Arthur
Kingswinford, 3 October, 1929 Died 2000 (WH)

League Club	Source	Date Signed	Seasons Played	Apps	Subs	Gls
Aston Villa	Halesowen T	12.47	54	1	-	0
Crystal Palace	Tr	06.56	56-58	26	-	2

PROUDLOCK Adam David
Telford, 9 May, 1981 EYth (F)

League Club	Source	Date Signed	Seasons Played	Apps	Subs	Gls
Wolverhampton W	YT	07.99	00-02	42	29	13
Nottingham F	L	03.02	01	3	0	0
Tranmere Rov	L	10.02	02	5	0	0
Sheffield Wed	L	12.02	02	3	2	2
Sheffield Wed	Tr	09.03	03-04	37	7	9

PROUDLOCK George Thomas
Morpeth, 19 September, 1919 (IF)

League Club	Source	Date Signed	Seasons Played	Apps	Subs	Gls
West Ham U	Amble Jnrs	11.37	38-47	18	-	5

PROUDLOCK Paul
Hartlepool, 25 October, 1965 (W)

League Club	Source	Date Signed	Seasons Played	Apps	Subs	Gls
Hartlepool U		09.84	84-85	8	7	0
Middlesbrough	Tr	11.86	86-88	2	3	1
Carlisle U	Tr	03.89	88-92	137	18	20
Hartlepool U	L	09.92	92	3	3	0

PROUDLOVE Andrew (Andy) George
Buxton, 15 January, 1955 (W)

League Club	Source	Date Signed	Seasons Played	Apps	Subs	Gls
Reading	App	●	71	4	1	0
Sheffield Wed	Buxton	09.75	75	10	5	0
Norwich C	Tr	02.76	76	0	1	0
Hereford U	Tr	05.77	77	6	5	0
Port Vale	Tr	11.78	78	5	0	0

PROUTON Ralph Oliver
Southampton, 1 March, 1926 (WH)

League Club	Source	Date Signed	Seasons Played	Apps	Subs	Gls
Arsenal	Romsey T	08.49				
Swindon T	Romsey T	08.52	52	13	-	0

PROVAN Andrew (Andy) McKelvie Hughes
Greenock, 1 January, 1944 (W)

League Club	Source	Date Signed	Seasons Played	Apps	Subs	Gls
Barnsley	St Mirren	05.63	63	3	-	0
York C	Tr	08.64	64-68	159	1	49
Chester	Tr	08.68	68-69	78	4	18
Wrexham	Tr	04.70	70-71	48	2	10
Southport	Tr	07.72	72-73	82	1	28
Torquay U	Philadelphia (USA)	08.74	74-76	83	8	14

PROVAN David
Falkirk, 11 March, 1941 Su23-1/SLge-1/S-5 (FB)

League Club	Source	Date Signed	Seasons Played	Apps	Subs	Gls
Crystal Palace	Glasgow Rgrs	06.70	70	1	0	0
Plymouth Arg	Tr	03.71	70-74	128	1	10

PROVERBS Roy John
Wednesbury, 8 July, 1932 (FB)

League Club	Source	Date Signed	Seasons Played	Apps	Subs	Gls
Coventry C	Stratford T	05.56	56	10	-	0
Bournemouth	Tr	07.57				
Gillingham	Tr	02.58	57-61	143	-	2

PROVETT Robert James (Jim)
Stockton, 22 December, 1982 (G)

League Club	Source	Date Signed	Seasons Played	Apps	Subs	Gls
Hartlepool U	YT	04.02	03-04	66	0	0

PRUDHAM Charles Edward (Eddie)
Felling, 12 April, 1952 (F)

League Club	Source	Date Signed	Seasons Played	Apps	Subs	Gls
Sheffield Wed	Jnrs	07.69	70-74	14	5	2
Carlisle U	Tr	11.74	74-76	15	2	2
Hartlepool	L	09.76	76	3	0	0
Workington	L	02.77	76	15	0	6
Stockport Co	Tr	07.77	77-79	80	7	22
Bournemouth	Tr	05.80	80	2	2	0

PRUDHOE Mark
Washington, 8 November, 1963 (G)

League Club	Source	Date Signed	Seasons Played	Apps	Subs	Gls
Sunderland	App	09.81	82	7	0	0
Hartlepool U	L	11.83	83	3	0	0
Birmingham C	Tr	09.84	84	1	0	0
Walsall	Tr	02.86	85-86	26	0	0
Doncaster Rov	L	12.86	86	5	0	0
Grimsby T	L	03.87	86	8	0	0
Hartlepool U	L	08.87	87	13	0	0
Bristol C	L	11.87	87	3	0	0
Carlisle U	Tr	12.87	87-88	34	0	0
Darlington	Tr	03.89	88-92	146	0	0
Stoke C	Tr	06.93	93-96	82	0	0
Peterborough U	L	09.94	94	6	0	0
York C	L	02.97	96	2	0	0
Bradford C	Tr	07.97	97	8	0	0
Southend U	Tr	11.99	99	6	0	0

PRUNIER William
Montreuil, France, 14 August, 1967 France int (CD)

League Club	Source	Date Signed	Seasons Played	Apps	Subs	Gls
Manchester U (L)	Bordeaux (Fr)	12.94	95	2	0	0

League Club	Source	Date Signed	Seasons Played	Career Record Apps	Subs	Gls
PRUTTON David Thomas						
Hull, 12 September, 1981 EYth/Eu21-25						(M)
Nottingham F	YT	10.98	99-02	141	2	7
Southampton	Tr	01.03	02-04	50	12	2
PRYCE Idris						
Wrexham, 24 February, 1941						(W)
Wrexham	Jnrs	09.59	59	3	-	0
PRYDE David (Dave)						
Newtongrange, 10 November, 1913 Died 1987						(WH)
Arsenal		05.35	38	4	-	0
Torquay U	Tr	10.46	46-49	64	-	0
PRYDE Robert (Bob) Ireland						
Methil, 25 April, 1913 Died 1998 FLge-2						(CD)
Blackburn Rov	St Johnstone	05.33	33-48	320	-	11
PRYDE William (Bill)						
Polmont, 20 May, 1919						(WH)
Southend U	Bo'ness	07.47	47-48	17	-	0
PRYER Terence (Terry)						
London, 4 December, 1967						(CD)
Southend U	Yt	10.85	85	2	0	0
PUCKETT David Charles						
Southampton, 29 October, 1960						(F)
Southampton	App	10.78	80-85	51	43	14
Bournemouth	Tr	07.86	86-88	29	6	14
Stoke C	L	03.88	87	7	0	0
Swansea C	L	11.88	88	7	1	3
Aldershot	Tr	01.89	88-90	113	0	50
Bournemouth	Tr	03.92	91	1	3	0
PUGH Daniel (Danny) Adam						
Manchester, 19 October, 1982						(M)
Manchester U	YT	07.00	02	0	1	0
Leeds U	Tr	07.04	04	33	5	5
PUGH Daral James						
Crynant, 5 June, 1961 Wu21-2						(W)
Doncaster Rov	App	12.78	78-82	136	18	15
Huddersfield T	Tr	09.82	82-84	52	33	7
Rotherham U	Tr	07.85	85-87	106	6	6
Cambridge U	L	12.87	87	6	0	1
Torquay U	Tr	08.88	88-89	29	3	0
PUGH David						
Liverpool, 19 September, 1964						(W)
Chester C	Runcorn	07.89	89-93	168	11	23
Bury	Tr	08.94	94-97	101	2	28
PUGH David						
Markham, 22 January, 1947 WSch/Wu23-2						(M)
Newport Co	Jnrs	04.64	64-67	73	5	9
Chesterfield	Tr	12.67	67-72	212	1	12
Halifax T	Tr	08.73	73-75	91	5	3
Rotherham U	Tr	07.76	76-78	57	1	0
York C	Tr	11.78	78-80	73	4	2
PUGH Gary						
Wrexham, 10 January, 1967						(W)
Wrexham	Jnrs	07.84	84	1	0	0
PUGH Gary Kevin						
Ramsgate, 11 February, 1961						(M)
West Ham U	Jnrs	02.78				
Bournemouth	Dover	01.81	80	0	3	1
Torquay U	Thanet U	11.84	84	4	0	0
PUGH John **Graham**						
Hoole, 12 February, 1948 Eu23-1						(M)
Sheffield Wed	App	02.65	65-71	136	6	7
Huddersfield T	Tr	05.72	72-74	80	0	1
Chester	Tr	02.75	74-76	67	2	3
Barnsley	Tr	10.76	76-79	128	2	8
Scunthorpe U	Tr	01.80	79-80	54	1	0
PUGH Kevin John						
Corbridge, 11 October, 1960						(M)
Newcastle U	App	10.78	81	0	1	0
Darlington	Gateshead	09.83	83	0	2	0
PUGH Stephen						
Bangor, 27 November, 1973 WYth/Wu21-2						(F)
Wrexham	YT	07.92	92-94	3	8	0
PUGH Stephen (Steve) John						
Wolverhampton, 1 February, 1965						(FB)
Wolverhampton W	App	12.82				
Torquay U	Tr	10.83	83-85	115	5	4
Exeter C	Tr	08.86	86	23	1	1

League Club	Source	Date Signed	Seasons Played	Career Record Apps	Subs	Gls
PUGSLEY David George						
Merthyr Tydfil, 15 August, 1931						(G)
Newport Co (Am)	Gloucester C	03.53	52	1	-	0
PULIS Anthony James						
Bristol, 21 July, 1984						(M)
Portsmouth	Sch	03.03				
Stoke C	Tr	12.04				
Torquay U	L	12.04	04	1	2	0
PULIS Anthony (Tony) Richard						
Newport, 16 January, 1958						(CD)
Bristol Rov	App	09.75	75-80	78	7	3
Bristol Rov	Happy Valley (HK)	06.82	82-83	44	1	2
Newport Co	Tr	07.84	84-85	75	2	0
Bournemouth	Tr	08.86	86-88	68	6	3
Gillingham	Tr	08.89	89	16	0	0
Bournemouth	Tr	08.90	90-91	12	4	1
PULIS Raymond (Ray)						
Newport, 21 November, 1964						(F)
Newport Co	App	11.82	82	0	1	0
PULLAN Christopher (Chris) John						
Durham, 11 December, 1967						(M)
Watford	Jnrs	07.86	86-90	5	7	0
Halifax T	L	02.89	88	5	0	1
Maidstone U	Tr	03.91	90	0	1	0
PULLAR David (Dave) Harry						
Durham, 13 February, 1959						(W)
Portsmouth	App	02.77	75-78	84	9	4
Exeter C	Tr	07.79	79-82	124	6	22
Crewe Alex	Tr	07.83	83-86	120	12	7
PULLEN James Daniel						
Chelmsford, 18 March, 1982						(G)
Ipswich T	Heybridge Swifts	10.99	02	1	0	0
Blackpool	L	08.01	01	16	0	0
Peterborough U	Tr	11.03	03	3	0	0
PULLEN Walter (Wally) Ernest						
Ripley, Surrey, 2 August, 1919 Died 1977						(IF)
Leyton Orient	Fulham (Am)	01.46	46-50	117	-	37
PULLEY Gordon Albert						
Stourbridge, 18 September, 1936						(W)
Millwall	Oswestry T	09.56	56-57	60	-	9
Gillingham	Tr	05.58	58-65	204	0	46
Peterborough U	Tr	11.65	65-66	16	1	4
PUNCHEON Jason David Ian						
Croydon, 26 June, 1986						(FB)
Wimbledon/MK Dons	Sch	10.04	03-04	14	19	1
PUNTER Brian						
Bromsgrove, 16 August, 1935 EYth						(CF)
Wolverhampton W	Jnrs	09.53				
Leicester C	Bromsgrove Rov	05.58				
Lincoln C	Tr	11.59	59-63	75	-	21
PUNTON William (Bill)						
Morpeth, 18 December, 1957						(G)
Bradford C	Gainsborough Trinity	08.75	75-76	7	0	0
PUNTON William (Bill) Hamilton						
Glenkinchie, 4 May, 1934						(W)
Newcastle U	Portadown	02.54	53-57	23	-	1
Southend U	Tr	07.58	58	38	-	6
Norwich C	Tr	07.59	59-66	219	0	24
Sheffield U	Tr	11.66	66-67	16	0	1
Scunthorpe U	Tr	01.68	67-68	45	1	2
PURCELL Brian Patrick John						
Swansea, 23 November, 1938 Died 1969						(CD)
Swansea T	Tower U	01.58	59-67	164	1	1
PURCELL Daniel						
Chesterfield, 15 September, 1948						(F)
Chesterfield (Am)	Jnrs	05.65	65	0	1	0
PURCHES Stephen (Steve) Richard						
Ilford, 14 January, 1980						(M)
West Ham U	YT	07.98				
Bournemouth	Tr	07.00	00-04	161	14	9
PURDIE Bernard Charles						
Wrexham, 20 April, 1949						(F)
Wrexham	Jnrs	10.67	68-69	7	3	3
Chester	Tr	07.71	71-72	54	9	14
Crewe Alex	Tr	07.73	73-79	203	10	44
Huddersfield T	Tr	10.79	79-81	37	9	1
Crewe Alex	Tr	08.82	82	14	2	0

League Club	Source	Date Signed	Seasons Played	Career Record Apps	Subs	Gls
PURDIE Ian						
Bellshill, 7 March, 1953 Su23-1						(W)
Wigan Ath	Motherwell	07.78	78-79	54	1	12
Portsmouth	Tr	11.79	79	4	1	1
PURDIE James **John (Jock)**						
Berwick-on-Tweed, 24 May, 1918 Died 1988						(G)
Millwall	Airdrie	02.46	46-47	50	-	0
Southport	Kilmarnock	02.49	48	6	-	0
Aldershot	Tonbridge	10.50	50	16	-	0
PURDIE Jonathan (Jon)						
Corby, 22 February, 1967 ESch						(W)
Arsenal	App	01.85				
Wolverhampton W	Tr	07.85	85-87	82	7	12
Cambridge U	L	10.87	87	7	0	2
Oxford U	Tr	07.88	88	5	6	0
Brentford	Tr	03.89	88	5	1	0
Shrewsbury T	Tr	06.89	89	9	3	1
PURDON Edward (Ted) John						
Johannesburg, South Africa, 1 March, 1930						(CF)
Birmingham C	Marist Bros (SA)	08.50	51-53	64	-	27
Sunderland	Tr	01.54	53-56	90	-	40
Workington	Tr	03.57	56-57	33	-	9
Barrow	Tr	03.58	57-58	37	-	12
Bristol Rov	Bath C	08.60	60	4	-	1
PURNELL Philip (Phil)						
Bristol, 16 September, 1964						(W)
Bristol Rov	Mangotsfield U	09.85	85-91	130	23	22
Swansea C	L	12.91	91	5	0	1
PURSE Darren John						
Stepney, 14 February, 1977 Eu21-2						(CD)
Leyton Orient	YT	02.94	93-95	48	7	3
Oxford U	Tr	07.96	96-97	52	7	5
Birmingham C	Tr	02.98	97-03	143	25	9
West Bromwich A	Tr	06.04	04	22	0	0
PURSELL Robert William						
Glasgow, 28 September, 1919						(FB)
Port Vale	Chesterton	12.39	46-47	39	-	0
PURSER Wayne Montague						
Basildon, 13 April, 1980						(F)
Queens Park Rgrs	YT	04.97				
Barnet	Tr	08.00	00	4	14	3
Leyton Orient	Tr	03.03	02-04	36	14	9
Peterborough U	Hornchurch	11.04	04	15	11	6
PURVES Charles (Charlie) Reuben						
High Spen, 17 February, 1921						(IF)
Charlton Ath	Spennymoor U	10.46	46-49	46	-	4
Southampton	Tr	06.51	51-53	30	-	2
PURVIS Bartholomew (Bart)						
Gateshead, 15 October, 1921 Died 2001						(FB)
Everton	North Shields	01.46				
Gateshead	Tr	10.46	46	1	-	0
Plymouth Arg	Tr	06.47				
Notts Co	Tr	05.48	48-50	25	-	0
Carlisle U	Tr	08.51	51	4	-	0
PURVIS William (Willie) Youngson Rule						
Berwick-on-Tweed, 14 December, 1938						(CF)
Grimsby T	Berwick Rgrs	08.61	61-62	7	-	2
Doncaster Rov	Tr	12.62	62	2	-	0
PUTNEY Trevor Anthony						
Harold Hill, 9 April, 1960						(M)
Ipswich T	Brentwood & Warley	09.80	82-85	94	9	8
Norwich C	Tr	06.86	86-88	76	6	9
Middlesbrough	Tr	07.89	89-90	45	3	1
Watford	Tr	08.91	91-92	42	10	2
Leyton Orient	Tr	07.93	93	20	2	2
Colchester U	L	08.94	94	7	0	0
Colchester U	Tr	10.94	94	21	0	2
PUTTNAM David Paul						
Leicester, 3 February, 1967						(W)
Leicester C	Leicester U	02.89	88-89	4	3	0
Lincoln C	Tr	01.90	89-95	160	17	21
Gillingham	Tr	10.95	95-96	15	25	2
Swansea C	Tr	08.97	97	4	0	0
PYATT John Henry						
Barnet, 26 September, 1948						(M)
Liverpool	Chesham U	07.67				
Peterborough U	Tr	07.68	68	15	1	1
PYE Frederick (Fred)						
Stockport, 11 March, 1928						(IF)
Accrington St	Stalybridge Celtic	04.48	47-48	4	-	0
PYE Jesse						
Treeton, 22 December, 1919 Died 1984 EB/FLge-1/EWar-1/E-1						(CF)
Sheffield U	Treeton Rov	12.38				
Notts Co		08.45				
Wolverhampton W	Tr	05.46	46-51	188	-	90
Luton T	Tr	07.52	52-54	61	-	32
Derby Co	Tr	10.54	54-56	61	-	24
PYE William (Billy)						
Rainford, 8 November, 1930						(IF)
Stockport Co		08.49				
Chester	Tr	07.52	53-55	28	-	11
PYGALL David Allen						
Watford, 23 January, 1939						(IF)
Watford	Jnrs	01.56	55-60	20	-	2
PYKE Malcolm						
Eltham, 6 March, 1938						(WH)
West Ham U	Jnrs	03.55	56-57	17	-	0
Crystal Palace	Tr	06.59	59	2	-	0
PYLE Walter **David**						
Trowbridge, 12 December, 1936 Died 2002						(CD)
Bristol Rov	Trowbridge T	07.55	56-61	139	-	0
Bristol C	Tr	07.62	62	8	-	0
PYLE Elijah St Quentin						
Chester-le-Street, 22 September, 1918						(IF)
York C	West Stanley	11.47	47-48	10	-	3
PYLE Stephen (Steve)						
North Shields, 28 September, 1963						(W)
Cambridge U	App	07.81	80-85	56	13	8
Torquay U	Tr	12.85	85-86	27	6	5
PYM Ernest (Ernie) Frederick						
Torquay, 23 March, 1935 Died 2004						(W)
Torquay U	St Marychurch	09.57	57-64	284	-	83
QUAILEY Brian Sullivan						
Leicester, 21 March, 1978						(F)
West Bromwich A	Nuneaton Borough	09.97	97-98	1	6	0
Exeter C	L	12.98	98	8	4	2
Blackpool	L	12.99	99	1	0	0
Scunthorpe U	Tr	02.00	99-01	39	32	16
QUAIRNEY John (Jock)						
Girvan, 7 January, 1927						(G)
Rotherham U	Girvan Jnrs	07.48	48-59	260	-	0
QUAMINA Mark Ezzard						
Guyana, 25 November, 1969						(M)
Wimbledon	YT	07.88	88	1	0	0
Plymouth Arg	Tr	07.91	91	4	1	0
QUARTERMAIN Patrick (Pat) George						
Oxford, 16 April, 1937						(FB)
Oxford U	Jnrs	09.55	62-66	184	1	0
QUASHIE Nigel Francis						
Nunhead, 20 July, 1978 EYth/Eu21-4/EB-1/S-7						(M)
Queens Park Rgrs	YT	08.95	95-97	50	7	3
Nottingham F	Tr	08.98	98-99	37	7	2
Portsmouth	Tr	08.00	00-04	140	8	13
Southampton	Tr	01.05	04	13	0	1
QUAYLE Mark Leslie						
Liverpool, 2 October, 1978						(F)
Everton	YT	10.95				
Notts Co	Tr	06.98	98	2	3	0
QUEEN Gerald (Gerry)						
Glasgow, 15 January, 1945						(F)
Crystal Palace	Kilmarnock	07.69	69-72	101	7	25
Orient	Tr	09.72	72-76	149	7	34
QUESTED Wilfred **Leonard (Len)**						
Folkestone, 9 January, 1925 EB						(WH)
Fulham	Folkestone	08.46	46-51	175	-	6
Huddersfield T	Tr	11.51	51-56	220	-	8
QUEUDRUE Franck						
Paris, France, 27 August, 1978 FrB						(FB)
Middlesbrough	RC Lens (Fr)	10.01	01-04	119	2	8

League Club	Source	Date Signed	Seasons Played	Career Record Apps	Subs	Gls
QUIGLEY Edward (Eddie)						
Bury, 13 July, 1921 Died 1997 EB						(IF)
Bury	Jnrs	09.41	46-47	42	-	18
Sheffield Wed	Tr	10.47	47-49	74	-	49
Preston NE	Tr	12.49	49-51	52	-	17
Blackburn Rov	Tr	11.51	51-55	159	-	92
Bury	Tr	08.56	56	10	-	3
QUIGLEY Gilbert						
Ulverston, 17 February, 1921						(WH)
Barrow	Vickers Sports	12.45	46-48	27	-	0
QUIGLEY John (Johnny)						
Glasgow, 28 June, 1935 Died 2004						(M)
Nottingham F	Glasgow Celtic	07.57	57-64	236	-	51
Huddersfield T	Tr	02.65	64-66	66	1	4
Bristol C	Tr	10.66	66-67	66	0	7
Mansfield T	Tr	07.68	68-70	105	0	2
QUIGLEY Mark						
Dublin, 27 October, 1985 IRYth/IRu21-1						(M)
Millwall	Sch	11.02	03-04	4	5	0
QUIGLEY Michael (Mike) Anthony Joseph						
Manchester, 2 October, 1970						(M)
Manchester C	YT	07.89	91-93	3	9	0
Wrexham	L	02.95	94	4	0	0
Hull C	Tr	07.95	95-97	36	15	3
Hull C	Altrincham	01.00	99	0	3	0
QUIGLEY Thomas (Tommy) Cook						
East Calder, 26 March, 1932						(CF)
Portsmouth	Barry T	12.55				
Queens Park Rgrs	Tr	06.56	56	16	-	7
QUINLAN Maurice **Edward (Eddie)**						
Finsbury Park, 15 August, 1931						(W)
Tottenham H	Yarmouth T	03.52				
Reading	Tr	06.53	53-55	51	-	11
QUINLAN Michael (Mike)						
Barnsley, 4 December, 1941						(CD)
Bristol C	Doncaster Rov (Am)	03.59	60	2	-	0
QUINLAN Philip (Phil) Edward						
Southport, 17 April, 1971 EYth						(F)
Everton	YT	07.89				
Huddersfield T	L	03.91	90	7	1	2
Doncaster Rov	Tr	08.92	92	2	7	0
QUINN Alan						
Dublin, 13 June, 1979 IRYth/IRu21-8/IR-6						(M)
Sheffield Wed	Cherry Orchard	12.97	97-03	147	10	16
Sunderland	L	10.03	03	5	1	0
Sheffield U	Tr	07.04	04	38	5	7
QUINN Albert						
Lanchester, 18 April, 1920						(IF)
Sunderland	Esh Winning Jnrs	11.46	47	6	-	2
Darlington	Tr	05.48	48-50	86	-	42
QUINN Anthony (Tony) Michael						
Liverpool, 24 July, 1959						(F)
Wigan Ath	Everton (N/C)	01.79	79-80	36	7	14
QUINN Barry Scott						
Dublin, 9 May, 1979 IRYth/IRu21-17/IR-4						(M)
Coventry C	YT	11.96	98-02	67	16	0
Rushden & Diamonds	L	01.04	03	4	0	0
Oxford U	Tr	03.04	03-04	39	3	0
QUINN Desmond (Des)						
Tullyverry, 21 March, 1926 Died 1980						(FB)
Blackburn Rov		08.47	47	1	-	0
Millwall	Tr	06.49	49-54	43	-	0
QUINN Gordon Patrick						
Hammersmith, 11 May, 1932						(IF)
Queens Park Rgrs	Eastcote BC	08.52	52-56	22	-	1
Plymouth Arg	Tr	09.56	56-57	14	-	2
QUINN James (Jimmy)						
Croy, 23 November, 1947 Died 2002						(FB)
Sheffield Wed	Glasgow Celtic	01.75	74-75	46	0	1
QUINN James (Jimmy) Martin						
Belfast, 18 November, 1959 NIB-1/NI-48						(F)
Swindon T	Oswestry T	12.81	81-83	34	15	10
Blackburn Rov	Tr	08.84	84-86	58	13	17
Swindon T	Tr	12.86	86-87	61	3	30
Leicester C	Tr	06.88	88	13	18	6
Bradford C	Tr	03.89	88-89	35	0	14
West Ham U	Tr	12.89	89-90	34	13	18
Bournemouth	Tr	08.91	91	43	0	19
Reading	Tr	07.92	92-96	149	33	71
Peterborough U	Tr	07.97	97-98	47	2	25
Swindon T	Tr	11.98	99	1	6	0
QUINN Stephen **James**						
Coventry, 15 December, 1974 NIYth/NIu21-1/NIB-2/NI-37						(F)
Birmingham C	YT	●	92	1	3	0
Blackpool	Tr	07.93	93-97	128	23	37
Stockport Co	L	03.94	93	0	1	0
West Bromwich A	Tr	02.98	97-01	85	29	9
Notts Co	L	11.01	01	6	0	3
Bristol Rov	L	03.02	01	6	0	1
Sheffield Wed	Willem II Tilburg (Holl)	01.05	04	10	5	2
QUINN John David						
Widnes, 30 May, 1938						(M)
Sheffield Wed	Prescot Cables	05.59	59-67	166	7	20
Rotherham U	Tr	11.67	67-71	114	0	7
Halifax T	Tr	07.72	72-74	88	4	1
QUINN Michael (Mick)						
Liverpool, 2 May, 1962						(F)
Wigan Ath	Derby Co (App)	09.79	79-81	56	13	19
Stockport Co	Tr	07.82	82-83	62	1	39
Oldham Ath	Tr	01.84	83-85	78	2	34
Portsmouth	Tr	03.86	85-88	115	6	54
Newcastle U	Tr	07.89	89-92	110	5	59
Coventry C	Tr	11.92	92-94	57	7	25
Plymouth Arg	L	11.94	94	3	0	0
Watford	L	03.95	94	4	1	0
QUINN Niall John						
Dublin, 6 October, 1966 IRSch/IRYth/IRu23-1/IRu21-6/IRB-1/IR-91						(F)
Arsenal	Jnrs	11.83	85-89	59	8	14
Manchester C	Tr	03.90	89-95	183	20	66
Sunderland	Tr	08.96	96-02	168	35	61
QUINN Noel Peter Anthony						
Dublin, 2 November, 1949						(W)
Oldham Ath	Blackburn Rov (Am)	01.67	67	4	0	0
QUINN Patrick (Pat)						
Glasgow, 26 April, 1936 SLge-6/S-4						(IF)
Blackpool	Motherwell	11.62	62-63	34	-	9
QUINN Patrick (Pat) Anthony						
Croy, 18 June, 1918 Died 1979						(IF)
Halifax T	Glasgow Ashfield	07.46	46	25	-	6
QUINN Robert (Rob) John						
Sidcup, 8 November, 1976 IRu21-5/IRB-1						(M)
Crystal Palace	YT	03.95	95-97	18	5	1
Brentford	Tr	07.98	98-00	98	11	2
Oxford U	Tr	01.01	00-01	23	6	2
Bristol Rov	Tr	07.02	02-03	67	12	3
QUINN Wayne Richard						
Hayle, 19 November, 1976 EYth/Eu21-2/EB-1						(FB)
Sheffield U	YT	12.94	97-00	131	8	6
Newcastle U	Tr	01.01	00	14	1	0
Sheffield U	L	01.03	02	6	0	0
West Ham U	Tr	09.03	03	22	0	0
QUINNEY Henry **Jesse**						
Rugby, 15 October, 1922 Died 2002						(FB)
Northampton T	Wolverhampton W (Am)	01.43	46	3	-	0
QUINNEY John						
Rugby, 2 October, 1932 Died 1986						(FB)
Coventry C	Jnrs	11.49	52	3	-	0
QUINTON Darren John						
Romford, 28 April, 1986						(M)
Cambridge U	Sch	02.05	03-04	14	18	0
QUINTON Walter (Wally)						
Anston, 13 December, 1917 Died 1996						(FB)
Rotherham U	Dinnington	07.38	38	32	-	0
Birmingham C	Tr	07.39	47	8	-	0
Brentford	Tr	04.49	48-50	42	-	0
Shrewsbury T	Tr	10.52	52	3	-	0
QUIRKE David						
Ballina, 11 January, 1947						(CD)
Gillingham	Bedford T	07.66	67-73	221	9	0
QUITONGO Jose Manuel						
Luanda, Angola, 18 November, 1974						(W)
Darlington	Norrkoping (Swe)	09.95	95	1	0	0

League Club	Source	Date Signed	Seasons Played	Career Record Apps	Subs	Gls

QUIXALL Albert
Sheffield, 9 August, 1933 ESch/Eu23-1/EB/FLge-4/E-5 (IF)

League Club	Source	Date Signed	Seasons Played	Apps	Subs	Gls
Sheffield Wed	Jnrs	08.50	50-58	241	-	64
Manchester U	Tr	09.58	58-63	165	-	50
Oldham Ath	Tr	09.64	64-65	36	0	11
Stockport Co	Tr	07.66	66	13	0	0

QUOW Trevor
Peterborough, 28 September, 1960 (M)

League Club	Source	Date Signed	Seasons Played	Apps	Subs	Gls
Peterborough U	App	09.78	78-85	191	12	17
Gillingham	Tr	08.86	86-88	64	15	3
Northampton T	Tr	01.89	88-89	42	6	2
Northampton T	Kettering T	02.91	90-91	36	4	0

RABJOHN Christopher (Chris)
Sheffield, 10 March, 1945 (M)

League Club	Source	Date Signed	Seasons Played	Apps	Subs	Gls
Rotherham U	Jnrs	07.63	65-67	76	2	5
Doncaster Rov	Tr	02.68	67-72	137	12	8

RACHEL Adam
Birmingham, 10 December, 1976 (G)

League Club	Source	Date Signed	Seasons Played	Apps	Subs	Gls
Aston Villa	YT	05.95	98	0	1	0
Blackpool	Tr	09.99	99	1	0	0

RACHUBKA Paul Stephen
San Luis Obispo, California, USA, 21 May, 1981 EYth (G)

League Club	Source	Date Signed	Seasons Played	Apps	Subs	Gls
Manchester U	YT	07.99	00	1	0	0
Oldham Ath	L	11.01	01	16	0	0
Charlton Ath	Tr	05.02				
Huddersfield T	L	03.04	03	13	0	0
MK Dons	L	08.04	04	4	0	0
Northampton T	L	09.04	04	10	0	0
Huddersfield T	Tr	11.04	04	29	0	0

RACKHAM Derrick Richard
Norwich, 14 June, 1928 Died 1996 (W)

League Club	Source	Date Signed	Seasons Played	Apps	Subs	Gls
Norwich C	Norman YC	11.49	51	8	-	2

RACKLEY Robert (Bob) William
Teignmouth, 15 March, 1940 (W)

League Club	Source	Date Signed	Seasons Played	Apps	Subs	Gls
Exeter C	Newton Abbot Spurs	03.58				
Bristol Rov	Tr	07.60				
Oldham Ath	Tr	10.60	60	19	-	5

RACKSTRAW Charles (Charlie)
Sheffield, 23 April, 1938 (F)

League Club	Source	Date Signed	Seasons Played	Apps	Subs	Gls
Chesterfield		03.58	58-63	172	-	48
Gillingham	Tr	05.64	64-66	93	1	25
Bradford C	Tr	01.67	66-69	94	10	27

RADCLIFFE Mark
Hyde, 26 October, 1919 (G)

League Club	Source	Date Signed	Seasons Played	Apps	Subs	Gls
Oldham Ath		12.42				
Fulham	Tr	08.46	46-47	11	-	0
Rochdale	Witton A	11.52	52	1	-	0

RADCLIFFE Vincent (Vince)
Manchester, 9 June, 1945 (FB)

League Club	Source	Date Signed	Seasons Played	Apps	Subs	Gls
Portsmouth	App	06.63	64-66	10	0	0
Peterborough U	Tr	07.67	67	2	0	0
Rochdale	Tr	07.68	68	26	0	1

RADEBE Lucas Valeriu
Johannesburg, South Africa, 12 April, 1969 South Africa 70 (CD)

League Club	Source	Date Signed	Seasons Played	Apps	Subs	Gls
Leeds U	Kaiser Chiefs (SA)	09.94	94-04	180	20	0

RADFORD Arthur
Rotherham, 7 October, 1925 Died 1981 (FB)

League Club	Source	Date Signed	Seasons Played	Apps	Subs	Gls
Huddersfield T		10.44				
Rotherham U		05.47	47-49	44	-	0
Rochdale	Tr	06.51	51	27	-	0
Swindon T	Tr	08.52	52	16	-	0

RADFORD William **Howard**
Abercynon, 8 September, 1930 (G)

League Club	Source	Date Signed	Seasons Played	Apps	Subs	Gls
Bristol Rov	Penrhiwceiber	08.51	51-61	244	-	0

RADFORD John
Hemsworth, 22 February, 1947 Eu23-4/FLge-2/E-2 (F)

League Club	Source	Date Signed	Seasons Played	Apps	Subs	Gls
Arsenal	App	03.64	63-76	375	4	111
West Ham U	Tr	12.76	76-77	28	0	0
Blackburn Rov	Tr	02.78	77-78	36	0	10

RADFORD Mark
Leicester, 20 December, 1968 (M)

League Club	Source	Date Signed	Seasons Played	Apps	Subs	Gls
Colchester U	Jnrs	05.87	87-89	47	17	5

RADFORD Ronald (Ronnie)
South Elmsall, 12 July, 1943 (M)

League Club	Source	Date Signed	Seasons Played	Apps	Subs	Gls
Leeds U	Sheffield Wed (Am)	10.61				
Newport Co	Cheltenham T	07.69	69-70	63	3	7
Hereford U	Tr	07.71	72-73	61	0	6

RADIGAN Neil Thomas
Middlesbrough, 4 July, 1980 (M)

League Club	Source	Date Signed	Seasons Played	Apps	Subs	Gls
Scarborough	YT	07.98	98	4	5	0

RADUCIOIU Florin
Bucharest, Romania, 17 March, 1970 Romania int (F)

League Club	Source	Date Signed	Seasons Played	Apps	Subs	Gls
West Ham U	Espanyol (Sp)	06.96	96	6	5	2

RADZINSKI Tomasz
Poznan, Poland, 14 December, 1973 Cau23-3/Ca-27 (F)

League Club	Source	Date Signed	Seasons Played	Apps	Subs	Gls
Everton	Anderlecht (Bel)	08.01	01-03	78	13	25
Fulham	Tr	08.04	04	25	10	6

RAE Alexander (Alex) McFarlane
Glasgow, 23 August, 1946 (M)

League Club	Source	Date Signed	Seasons Played	Apps	Subs	Gls
Bury	East Fife	05.69	69	10	1	0

RAE Alexander (Alex) Scott
Glasgow, 30 September, 1969 Su21-8/SB-4 (M)

League Club	Source	Date Signed	Seasons Played	Apps	Subs	Gls
Millwall	Falkirk	08.90	90-95	205	13	63
Sunderland	Tr	06.96	96-01	90	24	12
Wolverhampton W	Tr	09.01	01-03	88	19	15

RAE Ian Johnstone
Grangemouth, 19 January, 1933 Died 2005 Su23-1/SB (FB)

League Club	Source	Date Signed	Seasons Played	Apps	Subs	Gls
Bristol C	Falkirk	10.57	57	12	-	0

RAE Joseph (Joe)
Glasgow, 6 March, 1925 Died 1987 (CF)

League Club	Source	Date Signed	Seasons Played	Apps	Subs	Gls
Torquay U	Glasgow Celtic	07.48	48	20	-	4

RAFFELL Stephen (Steve) Christopher
Blyth, 27 April, 1970 (CD)

League Club	Source	Date Signed	Seasons Played	Apps	Subs	Gls
Doncaster Rov	YT	06.88	87-89	45	9	0

RAFFERTY Bernard
Manchester, 9 July, 1948 (M)

League Club	Source	Date Signed	Seasons Played	Apps	Subs	Gls
Bradford PA		10.69	69	8	5	1

RAFFERTY James (Jim)
Manchester, 7 November, 1930 Died 1999 (WH)

League Club	Source	Date Signed	Seasons Played	Apps	Subs	Gls
Manchester C		12.48				
Bradford PA	Tr	06.52	52	2	-	0

RAFFERTY Kevin Brian
Kenya, 9 November, 1960 (G)

League Club	Source	Date Signed	Seasons Played	Apps	Subs	Gls
Crewe Alex	App	11.78	78-79	22	0	0

RAFFERTY Ronald (Ron)
South Shields, 6 May, 1934 (F)

League Club	Source	Date Signed	Seasons Played	Apps	Subs	Gls
Portsmouth	Wycombe W	07.54	54-56	23	-	5
Grimsby T	Tr	12.56	56-62	264	-	145
Hull C	Tr	07.63	63-64	16	-	6
Aldershot	Tr	07.66	66-68	79	2	10

RAFFERTY William (Billy) Henry
Port Glasgow, 30 December, 1950 (F)

League Club	Source	Date Signed	Seasons Played	Apps	Subs	Gls
Coventry C	Port Glasgow Rgrs	07.68	69-72	27	0	3
Blackpool	Tr	10.72	72-73	35	1	9
Plymouth Arg	Tr	03.74	73-75	89	1	35
Carlisle U	Tr	05.76	76-77	72	0	27
Wolverhampton W	Tr	03.78	77-79	41	3	6
Newcastle U	Tr	10.79	79-80	34	5	6
Portsmouth	Tr	12.80	80-82	98	4	40
Bournemouth	Tr	02.84	83-84	58	0	18

RAFTER Sean
Rochford, 20 May, 1957 (G)

League Club	Source	Date Signed	Seasons Played	Apps	Subs	Gls
Southend U	App	06.75	75-77	23	0	0
Leicester C	Tr	01.78				
Orient	Tr	07.79	80	2	0	0

RAFTERY Patrick Thomas
Stoke-on-Trent, 28 November, 1925 (IF)

League Club	Source	Date Signed	Seasons Played	Apps	Subs	Gls
Port Vale	Ravensdale	01.49	48-49	5	-	0

RAGGETT Brian Charles
Staincross, 11 January, 1949 (CD)

League Club	Source	Date Signed	Seasons Played	Apps	Subs	Gls
Barnsley	App	01.67	66-71	56	8	0

RAHIM Brent Dominic
Diego Martin, Trinidad, 8 August, 1978 Trinidad int (M)

League Club	Source	Date Signed	Seasons Played	Apps	Subs	Gls
Northampton T (L)	Levski Sofia (Bul)	01.03	02	6	0	1

RAHMBERG Marino
Orebro, Sweden, 7 August, 1974 Sweden int (F)

League Club	Source	Date Signed	Seasons Played	Apps	Subs	Gls
Derby Co	Degerfors (Swe)	01.97	96	0	1	0

RAINE David
Darlington, 28 March, 1937 (FB)

League Club	Source	Date Signed	Seasons Played	Apps	Subs	Gls
Port Vale		05.57	56-61	144	-	0
Doncaster Rov	Tr	07.62	62-64	107	-	2
Colchester U	Tr	06.65	65-66	44	4	0

RAINE Robert (Bob) Reginald
Chesterfield, 17 November, 1927 (CF)

League Club	Source	Date Signed	Seasons Played	Apps	Subs	Gls
Chesterfield	Newbold Colliery	02.49	49	1	-	0
Aldershot	Kidderminster Hrs	02.51	50-53	47	-	21

RAINEY Hugh
Dumbarton, 7 January, 1935 (WH)

League Club	Source	Date Signed	Seasons Played	Apps	Subs	Gls
Portsmouth	Renton Guild	06.53				
Queens Park Rgrs	Tr	06.55				
Aldershot	Tr	07.57	57	8	-	0

RAINFORD David John
Stepney, 21 April, 1979 (M)

League Club	Source	Date Signed	Seasons Played	Apps	Subs	Gls
Colchester U	YT	07.97	98	0	1	0
Scarborough	L	12.98	98	0	2	0

RAINFORD John (Johnny) William
Camden Town, 11 December, 1930 Died 2001 (IF)

League Club	Source	Date Signed	Seasons Played	Apps	Subs	Gls
Crystal Palace	Jnrs	03.49	48-52	64	-	8
Cardiff C	Tr	05.53	53	3	-	1
Brentford	Tr	10.53	53-61	299	-	42

RAINFORD Kenneth (Ken) Sydney
Saughall Massie, 4 November, 1926 Died 1997 (CF)

League Club	Source	Date Signed	Seasons Played	Apps	Subs	Gls
New Brighton	New Brighton Baptists	02.48	47	3	-	1

RAJKOVIC Ante
Sarajevo, Bosnia, 17 August, 1952 Yugoslavia int (CD)

League Club	Source	Date Signed	Seasons Played	Apps	Subs	Gls
Swansea C	Sarajevo (Yug)	03.81	80-84	79	1	2

RALSTON Peter
Fauldhouse, 31 January, 1929 (CD)

League Club	Source	Date Signed	Seasons Played	Apps	Subs	Gls
Accrington St	Falkirk	08.57	57-58	6	-	0

RALSTON Walter (Wally)
Glasgow, 3 October, 1935 (FB)

League Club	Source	Date Signed	Seasons Played	Apps	Subs	Gls
Aldershot (L)	Partick Th	06.58	58	3	-	0

RAMAGE Alan
Guisborough, 29 November, 1957 (CD)

League Club	Source	Date Signed	Seasons Played	Apps	Subs	Gls
Middlesbrough	App	12.75	75-79	65	4	2
Derby Co	Tr	07.80	80-81	32	1	2

RAMAGE Andrew (Andy) William
Barking, 3 October, 1974 (M)

League Club	Source	Date Signed	Seasons Played	Apps	Subs	Gls
Gillingham	Dagenham & Redbridge	07.94	94	8	5	1

RAMAGE Craig Darren
Derby, 30 March, 1970 Eu21-3 (M)

League Club	Source	Date Signed	Seasons Played	Apps	Subs	Gls
Derby Co	YT	07.88	89-93	33	9	4
Wigan Ath	L	02.89	88	10	0	2
Watford	Tr	02.94	93-96	99	5	27
Peterborough U	L	02.97	96	7	0	0
Bradford C	Tr	06.97	97-98	24	11	1
Notts Co	Tr	08.99	99-00	50	5	7

RAMAGE George McIntosh
Dalkeith, 29 January, 1937 (G)

League Club	Source	Date Signed	Seasons Played	Apps	Subs	Gls
Colchester U	Third Lanark	08.61	62-63	38	-	0
Leyton Orient	Tr	07.64	64	4	-	0
Luton T	Tr	11.65	65	7	0	0

RAMAGE Peter Iain
Whitley Bay, 22 November, 1983 (CD)

League Club	Source	Date Signed	Seasons Played	Apps	Subs	Gls
Newcastle U	Sch	07.03	04	2	2	0

RAMASUT Mahan William **Thomas (Tom)**
Cardiff, 30 August, 1977 WYth/Wu21-4/WB (W)

League Club	Source	Date Signed	Seasons Played	Apps	Subs	Gls
Norwich C		07.95				
Bristol Rov	Tr	09.96	96-97	30	12	6

RAMMELL Andrew (Andy) Victor
Nuneaton, 10 February, 1967 (F)

League Club	Source	Date Signed	Seasons Played	Apps	Subs	Gls
Manchester U	Atherstone U	09.89				
Barnsley	Tr	09.90	90-95	149	36	44
Southend U	Tr	02.96	95-97	50	19	13
Walsall	Tr	07.98	98-99	60	9	23
Wycombe W	Tr	09.00	00-02	69	5	25
Bristol Rov	Tr	03.03	02-03	8	4	6

RAMPLING Dennis
Gainsborough, 25 November, 1923 (W)

League Club	Source	Date Signed	Seasons Played	Apps	Subs	Gls
Fulham		11.42	47	2	-	0
Bournemouth	Tr	07.48	48	24	-	4
Brentford	Tr	05.49	49	1	-	0

RAMPLING Edward (Eddie)
Wigan, 17 February, 1948 (W)

League Club	Source	Date Signed	Seasons Played	Apps	Subs	Gls
Chester	Newton-le-Willows YC	03.67	67	2	1	0

RAMSAY Craig James
Dunfermline, 19 September, 1962 (F)

League Club	Source	Date Signed	Seasons Played	Apps	Subs	Gls
Lincoln C	App	09.80	79-80	3	2	2

RAMSAY George Albert
Sunderland, 24 April, 1923 Died 1996 (W)

League Club	Source	Date Signed	Seasons Played	Apps	Subs	Gls
Gateshead	Raith Rov	11.46	46	9	-	1

RAMSAY John William
Sunderland, 25 January, 1979 (M)

League Club	Source	Date Signed	Seasons Played	Apps	Subs	Gls
Doncaster Rov	N/C	10.97	97	2	8	0

RAMSAY Scott Alan
Hastings, 16 October, 1980 (F)

League Club	Source	Date Signed	Seasons Played	Apps	Subs	Gls
Brighton & Hove A	YT	06.99	99-00	10	25	2

RAMSBOTTOM Neil
Blackburn, 25 February, 1946 (G)

League Club	Source	Date Signed	Seasons Played	Apps	Subs	Gls
Bury	Jnrs	07.64	65-70	174	0	0
Blackpool	Tr	02.71	70-71	12	0	0
Crewe Alex	L	01.72	71	3	0	0
Coventry C	Tr	03.72	72-74	51	0	0
Sheffield Wed	Tr	08.75	75	18	0	0
Plymouth Arg	Tr	07.76	76	39	0	0
Blackburn Rov	Tr	01.78	78	10	0	0
Sheffield U	Miami (USA)	10.79	79	2	0	0
Bradford C	Tr	08.80	80-82	73	0	0
Bournemouth	Tr	08.83	83	4	0	0

RAMSCAR Frederick (Fred) Thomas
Salford, 24 January, 1919 Died 2003 NIRL-1 (IF)

League Club	Source	Date Signed	Seasons Played	Apps	Subs	Gls
Wolverhampton W	Stockport Co (Am)	09.45	46	16	-	1
Queens Park Rgrs	Tr	10.47	47-49	51	-	4
Preston NE	Tr	11.49	49-50	19	-	4
Northampton T	Tr	07.51	51-54	139	-	55
Millwall	Tr	09.54	54	30	-	5

RAMSDEN Bernard (Barney)
Sheffield, 8 November, 1917 Died 1976 (FB)

League Club	Source	Date Signed	Seasons Played	Apps	Subs	Gls
Liverpool	Sheffield Victoria	03.35	37-47	57	-	0
Sunderland	Tr	03.48	47-48	12	-	0
Hartlepools U	Tr	01.50	49	13	-	0

RAMSDEN Simon Paul
Bishop Auckland, 17 December, 1981 (FB)

League Club	Source	Date Signed	Seasons Played	Apps	Subs	Gls
Sunderland	YT	08.00				
Notts Co	L	08.02	02	21	11	0
Grimsby T	Tr	08.04	04	23	2	0

RAMSEY (Sir) **Alfred (Alf)** Ernest
Dagenham, 22 January, 1920 Died 1999 FLge-6/E-32 (FB)

League Club	Source	Date Signed	Seasons Played	Apps	Subs	Gls
Southampton	Portsmouth (Am)	04.44	46-48	90	-	8
Tottenham H	Tr	05.49	49-54	226	-	24

RAMSEY Christopher (Chris) Leroy
Birmingham, 28 April, 1962 (FB)

League Club	Source	Date Signed	Seasons Played	Apps	Subs	Gls
Brighton & Hove A	Bristol C (App)	08.80	80-83	30	0	0
Swindon T	Tr	08.84	84-86	99	1	5
Southend U	Tr	08.87	87	8	5	0

RAMSEY Donald (Don)
Manchester, 27 September, 1928 (W)

League Club	Source	Date Signed	Seasons Played	Apps	Subs	Gls
Oldham Ath		11.46	49	2	-	0

RAMSEY Paul Christopher
Derry, 3 September, 1962 NISch/NI-14 (M)

League Club	Source	Date Signed	Seasons Played	Apps	Subs	Gls
Leicester C	App	04.80	80-90	278	12	13
Cardiff C	Tr	08.91	91-92	69	0	7
Cardiff C (L)	St Johnstone	11.94	94	11	0	0
Torquay U	Telford U	11.95	95	18	0	0

RAMSEY Robert (Bob)
Sunderland, 24 February, 1935 (FB)

League Club	Source	Date Signed	Seasons Played	Apps	Subs	Gls
Huddersfield T	Jnrs	01.53				
York C	Tr	05.58	58-60	75	-	0

RANDALL Adrian John
Amesbury, 10 November, 1968 EYth (M)

League Club	Source	Date Signed	Seasons Played	Apps	Subs	Gls
Bournemouth	App	09.86	85-87	3	0	0
Aldershot	Tr	09.88	88-90	102	5	12
Burnley	Tr	12.91	91-95	105	20	8
York C	Tr	12.95	95-96	26	6	2
Bury	Tr	12.96	96-97	16	17	3

RANDALL Ernest (Ernie) Albert Walter
Bognor Regis, 13 January, 1926 (CF)

League Club	Source	Date Signed	Seasons Played	Apps	Subs	Gls
Chelsea	Bognor Regis T	12.50	51	3	-	1
Crystal Palace	Tr	06.53	53-54	22	-	11

RANDALL Kevin
Ashton-under-Lyne, 20 August, 1945 (F)

League Club	Source	Date Signed	Seasons Played	Apps	Subs	Gls
Bury	Droylsden	10.65	65	4	0	0
Chesterfield	Tr	07.66	66-71	258	0	96
Notts Co	Tr	08.72	72-75	119	2	38
Mansfield T	Tr	11.75	75-77	62	4	20
York C	Tr	10.77	77-80	96	11	27

RANDALL Maurice
Manchester, 4 August, 1919 Died 1976 (FB)

League Club	Source	Date Signed	Seasons Played	Apps	Subs	Gls
Crewe Alex	Droylsden	02.47	46-48	41	-	0

RANDALL Paul
Liverpool, 16 February, 1958 (F)

League Club	Source	Date Signed	Seasons Played	Apps	Subs	Gls
Bristol Rov	Frome T	08.77	77-78	49	3	33
Stoke C	Tr	12.78	78-80	38	8	7
Bristol Rov	Tr	01.81	80-85	169	15	61

RANDELL Colin William
Skewen, 12 December, 1952 WSch/Wu23-1 (M)

League Club	Source	Date Signed	Seasons Played	Apps	Subs	Gls
Coventry C	App	05.70				
Plymouth Arg	Tr	09.73	73-76	137	2	9
Exeter C	Tr	09.77	77-78	78	0	4
Plymouth Arg	Tr	07.79	79-81	110	0	8
Blackburn Rov	Tr	08.82	82-84	72	1	7
Newport Co	L	03.84	83	15	0	0
Swansea C	Tr	07.85	85-86	20	2	1

RANDLES Thomas (Tommy)
Blackpool, 13 October, 1940 (IF)

League Club	Source	Date Signed	Seasons Played	Apps	Subs	Gls
Stoke C	Ellesmere Port	02.60	61	2	-	0

RANKIN Andrew (Andy) George
Bootle, 11 May, 1944 Eu23-1 (G)

League Club	Source	Date Signed	Seasons Played	Apps	Subs	Gls
Everton	Jnrs	10.61	63-70	85	0	0
Watford	Tr	11.71	71-79	299	0	0
Huddersfield T	Tr	12.79	79-81	71	0	0

RANKIN George
Walton, 29 January, 1930 Died 1989 EYth (FB)

League Club	Source	Date Signed	Seasons Played	Apps	Subs	Gls
Everton	Jnrs	08.48	50-55	36	-	0
Southport	Tr	07.56	56-59	144	-	0

RANKIN Isaiah
Edmonton, 22 May, 1978 (F)

League Club	Source	Date Signed	Seasons Played	Apps	Subs	Gls
Arsenal	YT	09.95	97	0	1	0
Colchester U	L	09.97	97	10	1	5
Bradford C	Tr	08.98	98-00	15	22	4
Birmingham C	L	01.00	99	11	2	4
Bolton W	L	08.00	00	9	7	2
Barnsley	Tr	01.01	00-03	18	29	8
Grimsby T	Tr	02.04	03	12	0	4
Brentford	Tr	07.04	04	33	8	8

RANKIN James
Gateshead, 8 September, 1927 Died 1985 (W)

League Club	Source	Date Signed	Seasons Played	Apps	Subs	Gls
Newcastle U	Jnrs	09.44				
Brighton & Hove A		08.49				
Grimsby T	Tr	01.50	49-50	5	-	1

RANKINE Simon **Mark**
Doncaster, 30 September, 1969 (M)

League Club	Source	Date Signed	Seasons Played	Apps	Subs	Gls
Doncaster Rov	YT	07.88	87-91	160	4	20
Wolverhampton W	Tr	01.92	91-95	112	20	1
Preston NE	Tr	09.96	96-02	217	16	12
Sheffield U	Tr	03.03	02-03	11	8	0
Tranmere Rov	Tr	07.04	04	41	0	0

RANKINE Michael Lee
Doncaster, 15 January, 1985 (F)

League Club	Source	Date Signed	Seasons Played	Apps	Subs	Gls
Scunthorpe U	Barrow	09.04	04	1	20	1

RANKMORE Frank Edward John
Cardiff, 21 July, 1939 Wu23-2/W-1 (CD)

League Club	Source	Date Signed	Seasons Played	Apps	Subs	Gls
Cardiff C	Cardiff Corinthians	12.57	61-62	67	-	0
Peterborough U	Tr	08.63	63-67	201	0	7
Northampton T	Tr	08.68	68-70	103	0	15

RANSHAW Jack William
Nettleham, 19 December, 1916 Died 2003 (W)

League Club	Source	Date Signed	Seasons Played	Apps	Subs	Gls
Lincoln C	Grantham	03.46	46	3	-	0

RANSHAW Richard (Rick) William Graham
Sleaford, 17 April, 1970 (F)

League Club	Source	Date Signed	Seasons Played	Apps	Subs	Gls
Lincoln C	YT	08.88	88	0	1	0

RANSON Raymond (Ray)
St Helens, 12 June, 1960 ESch/EYth/Eu21-10 (FB)

League Club	Source	Date Signed	Seasons Played	Apps	Subs	Gls
Manchester C	App	06.77	78-83	181	3	1
Birmingham C	Tr	11.84	84-88	136	1	0
Newcastle U	Tr	12.88	88-92	78	5	1
Manchester C	Tr	01.93	92	17	0	0
Reading	Tr	07.93	93	22	2	0

RANTANEN Jari Juhani
Helsinki, Finland, 31 December, 1961 Finland int (F)

League Club	Source	Date Signed	Seasons Played	Apps	Subs	Gls
Leicester C	IFK Gothenburg (Swe)	09.87	87	10	3	3

RAPER Kenneth (Kenny)
Stanley, 15 May, 1956 (M)

League Club	Source	Date Signed	Seasons Played	Apps	Subs	Gls
Stoke C	App	06.73				
Torquay U	Tr	07.77	77-78	51	1	8

RAPLEY Kevin John
Reading, 21 September, 1977 (F)

League Club	Source	Date Signed	Seasons Played	Apps	Subs	Gls
Brentford	YT	07.96	96-98	27	24	12
Southend U	L	11.98	98	9	0	4
Notts Co	Tr	02.99	98-00	21	31	4
Exeter C	L	11.00	00	6	1	0
Scunthorpe U	L	03.01	00	1	4	0
Colchester U	Tr	08.01	01-02	40	16	11
Chester C	Tr	07.03	04	12	9	2

RAPLEY Peter David
Portsmouth, 24 October, 1936 (W)

League Club	Source	Date Signed	Seasons Played	Apps	Subs	Gls
Exeter C	Portsmouth (Am)	06.57	57-59	10	-	4

RAPONI Juan Pablo
Santa Fe, Argentina, 7 May, 1980 (M)

League Club	Source	Date Signed	Seasons Played	Apps	Subs	Gls
Oxford U	Olimpo (Arg)	02.05	04	5	5	0

RASIAK Grzegorz
Szczecin, Poland, 12 January, 1979 Poland 18 (F)

League Club	Source	Date Signed	Seasons Played	Apps	Subs	Gls
Derby Co	Groclin Dyskobolia (Pol)	09.04	04	35	0	16

RASMUSSEN Mark Alan
Newcastle, 28 November, 1983 (M)

League Club	Source	Date Signed	Seasons Played	Apps	Subs	Gls
Burnley	New Hartley	07.01	02	0	2	0

RATCLIFFE James **Barrie**
Blackburn, 21 September, 1941 (W)

League Club	Source	Date Signed	Seasons Played	Apps	Subs	Gls
Blackburn Rov	Jnrs	09.58	59-63	36	-	4
Scunthorpe U	Tr	05.64	64	26	-	7
Rochdale	Tr	07.65	65	12	0	1

RATCLIFFE Beaumont (Bill)
Barnburgh, 24 April, 1909 Died 2003 (CD)

League Club	Source	Date Signed	Seasons Played	Apps	Subs	Gls
New Brighton	Bradford PA (Am)	10.31	31-34	131	-	4
Oldham Ath	Le Havre (Fr)	06.35	35-38	156	-	1
Reading	Tr	05.46	46-47	32	-	0
Watford	Tr	05.48	48	24	-	0

RATCLIFFE David
Dewsbury, 9 March, 1957 (CD)

League Club	Source	Date Signed	Seasons Played	Apps	Subs	Gls
Bradford C	App	03.75	74-77	17	11	1

RATCLIFFE Donald (Don)
Newcastle-under-Lyme, 13 November, 1934 (W)

League Club	Source	Date Signed	Seasons Played	Apps	Subs	Gls
Stoke C		05.53	54-63	238	-	16
Middlesbrough	Tr	09.63	63-65	65	0	3
Darlington	Tr	02.66	65-67	85	1	12
Crewe Alex	Tr	01.68	67-68	45	2	2

RATCLIFFE Kevin
Mancot, 12 November, 1960 WSch/WYth/Wu21-2/W-59 (CD)

League Club	Source	Date Signed	Seasons Played	Apps	Subs	Gls
Everton	App	11.78	79-91	356	3	2
Everton	Dundee	10.92				
Cardiff C	Tr	01.93	92-93	25	0	1
Derby Co	Nottingham F (N/C)	01.94	93	6	0	0
Chester C	Tr	07.94	94	23	0	0

RATCLIFFE Patrick (Paddy) Christopher
Dublin, 31 December, 1919 (FB)

League Club	Source	Date Signed	Seasons Played	Apps	Subs	Gls
Notts Co	Bohemians	11.45				
Wolverhampton W	Tr	06.46	46	2	-	0
Plymouth Arg	Tr	06.47	47-55	236	-	10

RATCLIFFE Raymond (Ray)
St Helens, 3 November, 1929 (WH)

League Club	Source	Date Signed	Seasons Played	Apps	Subs	Gls
Stockport Co		03.49	48	1	-	0

RATCLIFFE Simon
Davyhulme, 8 February, 1967 ESch/EYth (CD)

League Club	Source	Date Signed	Seasons Played	Apps	Subs	Gls
Manchester U	App	02.85				
Norwich C	Tr	06.87	87	6	3	0
Brentford	Tr	01.89	88-94	197	17	14
Gillingham	Tr	08.95	95-97	100	5	10

RATHBONE Graham Charles
Newport, 22 August, 1942 (CD)

League Club	Source	Date Signed	Seasons Played	Apps	Subs	Gls
Newport Co	Merthyr Tydfil	03.61	60-66	191	0	6
Grimsby T	Tr	11.66	66-72	232	1	11
Cambridge U	Tr	02.73	72-73	35	1	0

RATHBONE Michael (Mike) John
Birmingham, 6 November, 1958 EYth (FB)

League Club	Source	Date Signed	Seasons Played	Apps	Subs	Gls
Birmingham C	App	11.76	76-78	17	3	0
Blackburn Rov	Tr	03.79	78-86	270	3	2
Preston NE	Tr	07.87	87-90	82	9	4

League Club	Source	Date Signed	Seasons Played	Career Record Apps	Subs	Gls
RATTLE Jonathan (Jon) Paul						
Melton, Suffolk, 22 July, 1976						(M)
Cambridge U	YT	05.94	94	6	0	0
Cambridge U	Stevenage Borough	09.95	95	7	2	0
RATTRAY Kevin Winston						
Tottenham, 6 October, 1968						(M)
Gillingham	Woking	06.95	95	18	8	3
Barnet	Tr	09.96	96	9	0	0
RATTRAY Peter Kerr						
Bannockburn, 7 November, 1925 Died 2004						(IF)
Plymouth Arg	Dundee	09.50	50-51	54	-	22
Norwich C	Tr	06.52	52-53	24	-	5
RAVANELLI Fabrizio						
Perugia, Italy, 11 December, 1968 Italy 21						(F)
Middlesbrough	Juventus (It)	08.96	96-97	35	0	17
Derby Co	SS Lazio (It)	08.01	01-02	46	4	14
RAVEN David Haydn						
Birkenhead, 10 March, 1985 EYth						(FB)
Liverpool	YT	05.02	04	0	1	0
RAVEN Paul Duncan						
Salisbury, 28 July, 1970 ESch/EYth						(CD)
Doncaster Rov	Jnrs	06.88	87-88	52	0	4
West Bromwich A	Tr	03.89	88-99	249	10	15
Doncaster Rov	L	11.91	91	7	0	0
Rotherham U	L	10.98	98	11	0	2
Grimsby T	Tr	07.00	00-02	21	10	0
Carlisle U	Tr	02.03	02-03	24	0	1
RAVENHILL Richard (Ricky) John						
Doncaster, 16 January, 1981						(M)
Barnsley	YT	06.99				
Doncaster Rov	Tr	01.02	03-04	35	36	6
RAVENSCROFT Craig Anthony						
Hammersmith, 20 December, 1974						(F)
Brentford	YT	07.93	93-95	6	3	1
RAWCLIFFE Frank						
Blackburn, 16 December, 1921 Died 1986						(CF)
Wolverhampton W	Tranmere Rov (Am)	01.39				
Notts Co	Colchester U	02.43				
Newport Co	Tr	06.46	46	37	-	14
Swansea T	Tr	05.47	47	25	-	16
Aldershot	Tr	07.48	48	35	-	14
RAWCLIFFE Peter						
Cleethorpes, 8 December, 1963						(F)
Grimsby T	Louth U	09.86	86-87	9	13	2
Lincoln C	Holbeach U	08.90	90	0	1	0
RAWES Herbert						
Frizington, 23 November, 1932						(CF)
Carlisle U		09.53	53-54	10	-	1
RAWLE Mark Anthony						
Leicester, 27 April, 1979						(F)
Southend U	Boston U	02.01	00-02	69	9	15
Oxford U	Tr	07.03	03-04	10	27	8
Kidderminster Hrs	Tr	02.05	04	5	6	3
RAWLINGS Charles (Charlie) John						
Coleshill, 4 November, 1932						(WH)
West Bromwich A	Erdington A	03.50				
Walsall	Tr	06.56	56-62	200	-	5
Port Vale	Tr	07.63	63-64	31	-	2
RAWLINGS James **Sydney (Syd)** Dean						
Wombwell, 5 May, 1913 Died 1956						(W)
Preston NE	Dick, Kerr's XI	03.32	33	12	-	0
Huddersfield T	Tr	03.34	33-34	11	-	2
West Bromwich A	Tr	03.35	34-35	10	-	1
Northampton T	Tr	06.36	36-37	48	-	18
Millwall	Tr	12.37	37-38	53	-	27
Everton	Tr	11.45				
Plymouth Arg	Tr	05.46	46-47	56	-	20
RAWLINGSON John Anderson						
Wallsend, 7 April, 1944						(CD)
Bury	Corinthian Jnrs	07.62	64	2	-	0
Barrow	Tr	07.65	65	19	0	2
RAWLINS David						
Llay, 12 December, 1943						(W)
Wrexham (Am)		11.65	65	1	0	0

League Club	Source	Date Signed	Seasons Played	Career Record Apps	Subs	Gls
RAWLINSON Mark David						
Bolton, 9 June, 1975						(M)
Manchester U	YT	07.93				
Bournemouth	Tr	07.95	95-99	48	31	2
Exeter C	Tr	07.00	00	18	7	2
RAWSON Colin						
Shirebrook, 12 November, 1926						(WH)
Nottingham F	Welbeck Colliery	09.44	46	1	-	0
Rotherham U	Peterborough U	07.48	49-52	113	-	12
Sheffield U	Tr	03.53	53-55	70	-	1
Millwall	Tr	10.55	55-58	159	-	5
Torquay U	Tr	07.59	59-61	86	-	2
RAWSON Kenneth (Ken)						
Nottingham, 31 March, 1921						(CD)
Nottingham F		12.46	47-49	6	-	0
RAWSON Kenneth (Ken)						
Ripley, 18 September, 1931 Died 1986						(CD)
Notts Co	Ripley	05.53	54-60	34	-	0
RAY Cecil Holmes						
West Grinstead, 25 October, 1911 Died 1995						(CF)
Aldershot	Lewes U	01.36	35-46	89	-	39
RAY John (Johnny) Dennis						
Wolverhampton, 7 November, 1946						(WH)
Shrewsbury T		01.65	65	7	0	0
RAY John Walter						
Newmarket, 21 November, 1968						(CD)
Colchester U	YT	10.87	87	0	1	0
RAY Philip (Phil)						
Wallsend, 21 November, 1964						(FB)
Burnley	App	11.82	82	1	0	0
Hartlepool U	L	10.83	83	5	0	1
RAYBOULD Eric						
Manchester, 8 December, 1940						(WH)
Chester		07.60	60-61	10	-	0
RAYBOULD Philip (Phil) Edward						
Caerphilly, 26 May, 1948 WSch/WAmat						(M)
Swansea T	Bridgend T	07.67	67-68	9	1	4
Newport Co	Tr	09.69	69	5	1	1
RAYMENT Joseph (Joe) Watson						
Hartlepool, 25 September, 1934						(W)
Middlesbrough	Jnrs	10.51	52-54	24	-	4
Hartlepools U	Tr	07.55	55-57	63	-	17
Darlington	Tr	07.58	58-64	173	-	31
RAYMENT Patrick (Pat) John						
Peterborough, 11 April, 1965						(FB)
Peterborough U	App	04.83	81-84	24	6	3
Cambridge U	Tr	10.84	84-86	42	6	2
RAYNER Edward (Ted)						
Hemsworth, 28 September, 1916 Died 1988						(G)
Halifax T	Scarborough	10.40	46-50	137	-	0
RAYNER Albert **Edward**						
Salford, 13 August, 1932						(WH)
Stoke C	Northwich Vic	05.55	56-59	4	-	0
RAYNER James (Jim) Patrick						
Cornsay, 31 March, 1935						(WH)
Grimsby T	Langley Park Jnrs	05.52	52-53	12	-	3
Bury	Tr	05.54				
Hartlepools U	Tr	11.54				
Bury	Tr	06.55				
Barrow	Tr	09.55	55	11	-	1
Peterborough U	Grantham	07.58	60-62	119	-	12
Notts Co	Grantham	09.64	64	32	-	13
RAYNER Simon Christopher						
Vancouver, Canada, 8 July, 1983						(G)
Lincoln C	Port Talbot T	08.04	04	1	0	0
RAYNER Warren Anthony						
Bradford, 24 April, 1957						(W)
Bradford C	App	04.75	74-76	13	4	0
RAYNES John						
Sheffield, 4 November, 1928 Died 1995						(W)
Sheffield U	Jnrs	11.45				
Rotherham U		03.49	49	5	-	1

RAYNES Michael Bernard
Wythenshawe, 15 October, 1987 (FB)

League Club	Source	Date Signed	Seasons Played	Apps	Subs	Gls
Stockport Co	Sch	03.05	04	15	4	0

RAYNES William (Willie) Arnold
Sheffield, 30 October, 1964 (W)

League Club	Source	Date Signed	Seasons Played	Apps	Subs	Gls
Rotherham U	Heanor T	09.83	83-84	17	3	2
Stockport Co	L	01.85	84	2	0	0
Wolverhampton W	Tr	12.85	85	6	1	0

RAYNOR Paul Edward
Chester, 3 September, 1957 (FB)

League Club	Source	Date Signed	Seasons Played	Apps	Subs	Gls
Chester	App	09.75	76-81	196	1	9
Chester C	Oswestry T	08.83	83	3	0	0

RAYNOR Paul James
Nottingham, 29 April, 1966 (M)

League Club	Source	Date Signed	Seasons Played	Apps	Subs	Gls
Nottingham F	App	04.84	84	3	0	0
Bristol Rov	L	03.85	84	7	1	0
Huddersfield T	Tr	08.85	85-86	38	12	9
Swansea C	Tr	03.87	86-91	170	21	27
Wrexham	L	10.88	88	6	0	0
Cambridge U	Tr	03.92	91-92	46	3	2
Preston NE	Tr	07.93	93-95	72	8	9
Cambridge U	Tr	09.95	95-96	78	1	7
Leyton Orient	Guang Deong (China)	02.98	97-98	6	9	0

RAYNOR Robert
Nottingham, 30 August, 1940 (G)

League Club	Source	Date Signed	Seasons Played	Apps	Subs	Gls
Nottingham F		05.64				
Halifax T	Tr	08.65	65-66	17	0	0

REA Kenneth (Ken) Wilfred
Liverpool, 17 February, 1935 (WH)

League Club	Source	Date Signed	Seasons Played	Apps	Subs	Gls
Everton	Jnrs	06.52	56-58	46	-	0

REA Simon
Kenilworth, 20 September, 1976 (CD)

League Club	Source	Date Signed	Seasons Played	Apps	Subs	Gls
Birmingham C	YT	01.95	95	0	1	0
Peterborough U	Tr	08.99	99-04	146	13	8
Cambridge U	L	01.05	04	4	0	0

REA Wallis
Uddingston, 21 August, 1935 Died 1998 (W)

League Club	Source	Date Signed	Seasons Played	Apps	Subs	Gls
Bradford C	Motherwell	07.59	59	11	-	2

READ John **Anthony (Tony)**
St Helens, 5 July, 1942 (G/F)

League Club	Source	Date Signed	Seasons Played	Apps	Subs	Gls
Sheffield Wed	Wolverhampton W (Am)	01.60				
Peterborough U	Tr	05.64	64	2	-	0
Luton T	Tr	03.65	65-71	195	4	12

READ David (Dave) Peter
Stafford, 15 January, 1941 (W)

League Club	Source	Date Signed	Seasons Played	Apps	Subs	Gls
Wolverhampton W	Jnrs	10.58				
Chester	Tr	10.62	62-66	68	4	6

READ Paul Colin
Harlow, 25 September, 1973 ESch (F)

League Club	Source	Date Signed	Seasons Played	Apps	Subs	Gls
Arsenal	YT	10.91				
Leyton Orient	L	03.95	94	11	0	0
Southend U	L	10.95	95	3	1	1
Wycombe W	Tr	01.97	96-98	32	25	9
Luton T	OFK Ostersund (Swe)	12.99				
Exeter C	OFK Ostersund (Swe)	11.00	00-01	13	13	1

READER Peter Edward
East Ham, 8 March, 1941 EYth (G)

League Club	Source	Date Signed	Seasons Played	Apps	Subs	Gls
West Ham U	Jnrs	06.59				
Millwall	Tr	06.61	61	1	-	0

READFERN Thomas **Edward**
Crook, 9 July, 1944 (CF)

League Club	Source	Date Signed	Seasons Played	Apps	Subs	Gls
West Bromwich A	Langley Park Jnrs	08.61	63	4	-	0

READY Karl
Neath, 14 August, 1972 WSch/Wu21-5/WB-2/W-5 (CD)

League Club	Source	Date Signed	Seasons Played	Apps	Subs	Gls
Queens Park Rgrs	YT	08.90	91-00	206	20	10

REAGAN Charles **Martin**
Scotswood, 12 May, 1924 (W)

League Club	Source	Date Signed	Seasons Played	Apps	Subs	Gls
York C	Jnrs	09.46	46	1	-	0
Hull C	Tr	04.47	46-47	18	-	1
Middlesbrough	Tr	02.48	47-50	24	-	4
Shrewsbury T	Tr	08.51	51-52	58	-	9
Portsmouth	Tr	01.53	52	5	-	0
Norwich C	Tr	06.54	54-55	34	-	4

REANEY Paul
Fulham, 22 October, 1944 Eu23-5/FLge-3/E-3 (FB)

League Club	Source	Date Signed	Seasons Played	Apps	Subs	Gls
Leeds U	Jnrs	10.61	62-77	549	7	6
Bradford C	Tr	06.78	78-79	37	1	0

REAY Edwin (Ted) Peel
Tynemouth, 5 August, 1914 (FB)

League Club	Source	Date Signed	Seasons Played	Apps	Subs	Gls
Sheffield U	North Shields	03.37				
Queens Park Rgrs	Tr	06.37	37-49	34	-	0

REBROV Sergei
Gorlovka, Ukraine, 3 June, 1974 Ukraine 65 (F)

League Club	Source	Date Signed	Seasons Played	Apps	Subs	Gls
Tottenham H	Dynamo Kiev (Ukr)	06.00	00-01	37	22	10
West Ham U	Tr	08.04	04	12	14	1

RECK Sean Mark
Oxford, 5 May, 1967 (M)

League Club	Source	Date Signed	Seasons Played	Apps	Subs	Gls
Oxford U	App	04.85	86-88	11	3	0
Newport Co	L	08.85	85	15	0	0
Reading	L	03.86	85	1	0	0
Wrexham	Tr	07.89	89-90	41	4	2

REDDIE Thomas (Tom) McGregor
Grangemouth, 5 October, 1926 (CD)

League Club	Source	Date Signed	Seasons Played	Apps	Subs	Gls
Aldershot	Falkirk	07.51	51-56	96	-	1

REDDING Thomas (Tom) Richard
Grimsby, 17 March, 1932 (CD)

League Club	Source	Date Signed	Seasons Played	Apps	Subs	Gls
Grimsby T	Brigg T	07.54	54-56	4	-	0

REDDINGTON Stuart
Lincoln, 21 February, 1978 (CD)

League Club	Source	Date Signed	Seasons Played	Apps	Subs	Gls
Chelsea	Lincoln U	08.99				
Mansfield T	Tr	03.01	00-02	48	6	1

REDDISH Shane
Bolsover, 5 May, 1971 (M)

League Club	Source	Date Signed	Seasons Played	Apps	Subs	Gls
Mansfield T	YT	07.89				
Doncaster Rov	Tr	02.90	89-92	51	9	3
Carlisle U	Tr	07.93	93-94	35	2	1
Chesterfield	L	09.94	94	2	1	0
Hartlepool U	Tr	11.94	94-95	41	2	0

REDDY Michael
Kilkenny City, 24 March, 1980 IRYth/IRu21-8 (F)

League Club	Source	Date Signed	Seasons Played	Apps	Subs	Gls
Sunderland	Kilkenny C	08.99	99-00	0	10	1
Swindon T	L	01.01	00	17	1	4
Hull C	L	09.01	01	1	4	4
York C	L	11.02	02	10	1	2
Sheffield Wed	L	01.03	02	13	2	3
Sheffield Wed	L	10.03	03	9	3	1
Grimsby T	Tr	08.04	04	24	16	9

REDFEARN Brian
Bradford, 20 February, 1935 (W)

League Club	Source	Date Signed	Seasons Played	Apps	Subs	Gls
Bradford PA	Jnrs	08.52	52-57	130	-	32
Blackburn Rov	Tr	12.57				
Darlington	Tr	06.59	59-60	48	-	16
Halifax T	Tr	06.61	61-62	67	-	9
Bradford C	Tr	07.63	63	7	-	2

REDFEARN Neil David
Dewsbury, 20 June, 1965 (M)

League Club	Source	Date Signed	Seasons Played	Apps	Subs	Gls
Bolton W	Nottingham F (Jnrs)	06.82	82-83	35	0	1
Lincoln C	Tr	03.84	83-85	96	4	13
Doncaster Rov	Tr	08.86	86	46	0	14
Crystal Palace	Tr	07.87	87-88	57	0	10
Watford	Tr	11.88	88-89	22	2	3
Oldham Ath	Tr	01.90	89-90	56	6	16
Barnsley	Tr	09.91	91-97	289	3	71
Charlton Ath	Tr	07.98	98	29	1	3
Bradford C	Tr	08.99	99	14	3	1
Wigan Ath	Tr	03.00	99-00	18	4	7
Halifax T	Tr	03.01	00-01	39	3	6
Boston U	Tr	08.02	02-03	46	8	12
Rochdale	Tr	03.04	03	9	0	0

REDFERN David
Sheffield, 8 November, 1962 (G)

League Club	Source	Date Signed	Seasons Played	Apps	Subs	Gls
Sheffield Wed	Jnrs	06.81				
Rochdale	Tr	03.85	84-86	87	0	0
Wigan Ath	L	10.87	87	3	0	0
Stockport Co	Gainsborough Trinity	07.89	89-92	48	0	0

REDFERN Edward (Ted)
Liverpool, 24 June, 1924 Died 1994 (W)

League Club	Source	Date Signed	Seasons Played	Apps	Subs	Gls
New Brighton	Unity BC	01.48	47-49	22	-	0

REDFERN Frederick (Fred)
Hyde, 28 September, 1914 Died 1989 (FB)

League Club	Source	Date Signed	Seasons Played	Apps	Subs	Gls
Stockport Co	Hyde U	08.45	46-47	36	-	0

REDFERN James (Jimmy)
Kirkby, 1 August, 1952 (W)

League Club	Source	Date Signed	Seasons Played	Apps	Subs	Gls
Bolton W	App	08.69	69-72	19	5	2
Chester	Tr	08.73	73-76	98	8	15

League Club	Source	Date Signed	Seasons Played	Career Record Apps	Subs	Gls
REDFERN Robert (Bob)						
Crook, 3 March, 1918 Died 2002						(W)
Wolverhampton W	Tow Law T	05.36				
Bournemouth	Cradley Heath	02.37	36-46	89	-	4
Brighton & Hove A	Tr	08.47	47	5	-	1
REDFORD Ian Petrie						
Perth, 5 April, 1960 SYth/Su21-6						(M)
Ipswich T	Dundee U	11.88	88-90	59	9	8
REDHEAD William (Bill) Sylvester						
Newcastle, 10 October, 1935 Died 2000						(WH)
Newcastle U	George Angus	08.54	56	1	-	0
Gateshead	Tr	08.59	59	20	-	0
REDKNAPP Henry (Harry) James						
Poplar, 2 March, 1947 EYth						(W)
West Ham U	App	03.64	65-71	146	3	7
Bournemouth	Tr	08.72	72-75	96	5	5
Brentford	Tr	09.76	76	1	0	0
Bournemouth	(Team Coach)	09.82	82	1	0	0
REDKNAPP Jamie Frank						
Barton-on-Sea, 25 June, 1973 ESch/EYth/Eu21-19/EB-1/E-17						(M)
Bournemouth	YT	06.90	89-90	6	7	0
Liverpool	Tr	01.91	91-01	207	30	30
Tottenham H	Tr	04.02	02-04	37	11	4
Southampton	Tr	01.05	04	16	0	0
REDMAN William (Bill)						
Manchester, 29 January, 1928 Died 1994						(FB)
Manchester U	Jnrs	11.46	50-53	36	-	0
Bury	Tr	06.54	54-55	37	-	1
REDMILE Matthew (Matt) Ian						
Nottingham, 12 November, 1976						(CD)
Notts Co	YT	07.95	96-00	140	7	7
Shrewsbury T	Tr	11.00	00-02	107	0	6
REDMOND Harold (Harry)						
Manchester, 24 March, 1933 Died 1985						(FB)
Crystal Palace	Tavistock	04.57	57	2	-	0
Millwall	Tr	05.58	58-60	54	-	0
REDMOND Stephen (Steve)						
Liverpool, 2 November, 1967 EYth/Eu21-14						(CD)
Manchester C	App	12.84	85-91	231	4	7
Oldham Ath	Tr	07.92	92-97	195	10	4
Bury	Tr	07.98	98-02	145	6	6
REDROBE William **Eric**						
Wigan, 23 August, 1944 EYth						(F)
Bolton W	Jnrs	02.62	63-65	4	0	1
Southport	Tr	08.66	66-72	186	6	55
Hereford U	Tr	10.72	72-75	75	11	17
Hereford U	Bath C	01.78	77	0	1	0
REDSHAW Raymond (Ray)						
Salford, 23 December, 1958						(F)
Wigan Ath	Horwich RMI	07.84	84	2	2	0
REDWOOD Barry Keith						
Torquay, 11 September, 1946						(CF)
Exeter C	App	09.64	64	1	-	0
REDWOOD Toby Richard Barry						
Newton Abbot, 7 October, 1973						(FB)
Exeter C	YT	06.92	91-93	15	5	0
REECE Andrew (Andy) John						
Shrewsbury, 5 September, 1962						(M)
Bristol Rov	Dudley T	08.87	87-92	230	9	17
Walsall	L	11.92	92	9	0	1
Walsall	L	08.93	93	6	0	0
Hereford U	Tr	11.93	93-95	69	2	5
REECE Gilbert (Gil) Ivor						
Cardiff, 2 July, 1942 Died 2003 WSch/W-29						(W)
Cardiff C	Pembroke Borough	05.61				
Newport Co	Pembroke Borough	06.63	63-64	32	-	9
Sheffield U	Tr	04.65	65-72	197	14	59
Cardiff C	Tr	09.72	72-75	94	6	23
Swansea C	Tr	07.76	76	0	2	0
REECE Paul John						
Nottingham, 16 July, 1968						(G)
Stoke C	App	07.86	86	2	0	0
Grimsby T	Kettering T	07.88	88-91	54	0	0
Doncaster Rov	Kettering T	09.92	92	1	0	0
Oxford U	Tr	10.92	92-93	39	0	0
Notts Co	Tr	08.94	94	11	0	0
West Bromwich A	Tr	08.95	95	1	0	0

League Club	Source	Date Signed	Seasons Played	Career Record Apps	Subs	Gls
REECE Thomas (Tom) Samuel						
Wolverhampton, 17 May, 1919 Died 1990						(WH)
Wolverhampton W		07.37				
Crystal Palace	Tr	09.38	38-47	76	-	5
REED Adam Maurice						
Bishop Auckland, 18 February, 1975						(CD)
Darlington	YT	07.93	91-94	45	7	1
Blackburn Rov	Tr	08.95				
Darlington	L	02.97	96	14	0	0
Rochdale	L	12.97	97	10	0	0
Darlington	Tr	07.98	98-02	80	14	2
REED Barry Reginald Frank						
Peterborough, 24 November, 1937						(FB)
Leicester C	St Neots	03.55				
Luton T	Tr	05.61	61	1	-	0
REED Frank Nicholas						
Seaham, 12 October, 1933 Died 1975						(G)
Charlton Ath	Murton CW	08.54	55-62	29	-	0
REED George						
Normanton, 16 July, 1938						(CD)
Halifax T	Swillington	08.61	62	2	-	0
REED Graham						
Doncaster, 24 June, 1961						(FB)
Barnsley	App	06.79	78-79	3	0	0
Northampton T	Frickley Ath	06.85	85-88	105	7	2
REED Graham Albert William						
King's Lynn, 6 February, 1938						(WH)
Sunderland	King's Lynn	02.55	57	5	-	0
REED Hugh Dennett						
Dumbarton, 23 August, 1950 Died 1992						(W)
West Bromwich A	Jnrs	08.67	68-70	5	3	2
Plymouth Arg	Tr	11.71	71-73	44	12	9
Brentford	L	10.73	73	3	1	0
Crewe Alex	Tr	07.74	74-75	38	9	9
Hartlepool	Huddersfield T (N/C)	10.76	76	6	0	1
REED Ian Paul						
Lichfield, 4 September, 1975						(M)
Shrewsbury T	YT	07.94	94-96	10	8	2
REED John Paul						
Rotherham, 27 August, 1972						(W)
Sheffield U	YT	07.90	91-95	11	4	2
Scarborough	L	01.91	90	14	0	5
Scarborough	L	09.91	91	5	1	0
Darlington	L	03.93	92	8	2	2
Mansfield T	L	09.93	93	12	1	2
Blackpool	Tr	07.97	97	0	3	0
REED Kevin David						
Leicester, 22 September, 1960						(W)
Leicester C	App	05.78	78	0	1	0
REED Martin John						
Scarborough, 10 January, 1978						(CD)
York C	YT	07.96	96-00	39	7	0
REED Thomas **Roland (Ron)**						
Haltwhistle, 4 October, 1934 Died 1998						(WH)
Newport Co	Newport Barracks	01.54	53-54	2	-	0
REED Stephen (Steve) Eric						
Doncaster, 6 January, 1956						(FB)
Doncaster Rov	App	01.74	72-78	137	3	2
REED Steven (Steve)						
Barnstaple, 18 June, 1985						(CD)
Yeovil T	Jnrs	09.02	03-04	4	4	0
REED William (Billy) George						
Rhondda, 25 January, 1928 Died 2003 WSch/WAmat/W-2						(W)
Cardiff C	Rhondda Transport	07.47				
Brighton & Hove A	Tr	08.48	48-52	129	-	36
Ipswich T	Tr	07.53	53-57	155	-	43
Swansea T	Tr	02.58	57	8	-	0
REES Anthony (Tony) Andrew						
Merthyr Tydfil, 1 August, 1964 WSch/WYth/Wu21-1/WB/W-1						(F)
Aston Villa	App	08.82				
Birmingham C	Tr	07.83	83-87	75	20	12
Peterborough U	L	10.85	85	5	0	2
Shrewsbury T	L	03.86	85	1	1	0
Barnsley	Tr	03.88	87-88	27	4	3
Grimsby T	Tr	08.89	89-93	124	17	33
West Bromwich A	Tr	11.94	94-95	11	12	2

League Club	Source	Date Signed	Seasons Played	Career Record Apps	Subs	Gls

REES Barrie Gwyn
Rhyl, 4 February, 1944 Died 1965 (WH)

League Club	Source	Date Signed	Seasons Played	Apps	Subs	Gls
Everton	Jnrs	09.61	63-64	4	-	2
Brighton & Hove A	Tr	01.65	64	12	-	1

REES Robert **Clive**
Nantymoel, 7 September, 1937 Died 1997 (G)

League Club	Source	Date Signed	Seasons Played	Apps	Subs	Gls
Newport Co (Am)	Caerau	03.63	62	4	-	0

REES William **Derrick**
Swansea, 18 February, 1934 Died 1998 (IF)

League Club	Source	Date Signed	Seasons Played	Apps	Subs	Gls
Portsmouth		05.54	54-56	46	-	15
Ipswich T	Tr	05.57	57-60	90	-	29

REES Douglas (Doug) Charles
Slyne, 12 February, 1923 Died 2000 WAmat (CD)

League Club	Source	Date Signed	Seasons Played	Apps	Subs	Gls
Ipswich T	Troedyrhiw	02.49	48-58	356	-	1

REES John **Graham**
Pontypridd, 28 August, 1937 (W)

League Club	Source	Date Signed	Seasons Played	Apps	Subs	Gls
Exeter C	Pontypridd YC	09.54	54-65	345	0	85

REES David **Ian**
Cross Hands, 21 September, 1943 (M)

League Club	Source	Date Signed	Seasons Played	Apps	Subs	Gls
Swansea T	Ammanford	12.61	64	1	-	0
Swansea T		08.68	68	1	1	0

REES Jason Mark
Aberdare, 22 December, 1969 WSch/WYth/Wu21-3/WB-1/W-1 (M)

League Club	Source	Date Signed	Seasons Played	Apps	Subs	Gls
Luton T	YT	07.88	89-93	59	23	0
Mansfield T	L	12.93	93	15	0	1
Portsmouth	Tr	07.94	94-96	30	13	3
Exeter C	L	01.97	96	7	0	0
Cambridge U	Tr	08.97	97	17	3	0
Exeter C	Tr	07.98	98-99	86	1	5
Torquay U	Tiverton T	12.00	00-01	51	7	2

REES John Frederick
Bedlinog, 3 February, 1933 WYth/WAmat (CF)

League Club	Source	Date Signed	Seasons Played	Apps	Subs	Gls
Newport Co (Am)	Troedyrhiw	08.52	52	2	-	0

REES Maldwyn (Mal) James Francis
Neath, 21 April, 1924 (IF)

League Club	Source	Date Signed	Seasons Played	Apps	Subs	Gls
Norwich C	Swansea T (Am)	05.47				
Brighton & Hove A	Tr	09.49	49	2	-	0
Scunthorpe U	Barry T	07.50	50	18	-	1

REES Mark
Smethwick, 13 October, 1961 ESch (W)

League Club	Source	Date Signed	Seasons Played	Apps	Subs	Gls
Walsall	App	08.79	78-89	188	49	37
Rochdale	L	10.86	86	2	1	0

REES Matthew (Matt) Richard
Swansea, 2 September, 1982 Wu21-4 (CD)

League Club	Source	Date Signed	Seasons Played	Apps	Subs	Gls
Millwall	YT	04.00				
Swansea C	L	03.04	03	3	0	1

REES Melvyn (Mel) John
Cardiff, 25 January, 1967 Died 1993 WYth (G)

League Club	Source	Date Signed	Seasons Played	Apps	Subs	Gls
Cardiff C	App	09.84	84-86	31	0	0
Watford	Tr	07.87	87	3	0	0
Crewe Alex	L	08.89	89	6	0	0
Leyton Orient	L	01.90	89	9	0	0
West Bromwich A	Tr	09.90	90	18	0	0
Sheffield U	Tr	03.92	91	8	0	0

REES Nigel Richard
Bridgend, 11 July, 1953 (W)

League Club	Source	Date Signed	Seasons Played	Apps	Subs	Gls
Cardiff C	Jnrs	08.70	70-72	21	6	1

REES Peter Noel
Machynlleth, 5 May, 1932 (W)

League Club	Source	Date Signed	Seasons Played	Apps	Subs	Gls
Tranmere Rov (Am)	Llandidloes	10.56	56	9	-	4

REES Ronald (Ronnie) Raymond
Ystradgynlais, 4 April, 1944 Wu23-7/W-39 (W)

League Club	Source	Date Signed	Seasons Played	Apps	Subs	Gls
Coventry C	App	05.62	62-67	230	0	42
West Bromwich A	Tr	03.68	67-68	34	1	9
Nottingham F	Tr	02.69	68-71	76	9	12
Swansea C	Tr	01.72	71-74	88	1	5

REES William (Billy)
Blaengarw, 10 March, 1924 Died 1996 WWar-1/W-4 (IF)

League Club	Source	Date Signed	Seasons Played	Apps	Subs	Gls
Cardiff C	Caernarvon Rov	02.44	46-48	101	-	34
Tottenham H	Tr	06.49	49	11	-	3
Leyton Orient	Tr	07.50	50-55	184	-	58

REES William
Swansea, 30 September, 1937 (W)

League Club	Source	Date Signed	Seasons Played	Apps	Subs	Gls
Swansea T	Jnrs	10.54	54-57	6	-	0
Crystal Palace	Peterborough U	05.59	59	17	-	1

REESON Maurice **Anthony (Tony)**
Rotherham, 24 September, 1933 Died 1990 (IF)

League Club	Source	Date Signed	Seasons Played	Apps	Subs	Gls
Rotherham U	Jnrs	11.53	54	4	-	1
Grimsby T	Tr	06.55	55-57	76	-	20
Doncaster Rov	Tr	02.58	57-58	21	-	6
Southport	Tr	06.59	59	42	-	9

REEVE Edward (Eddie) Gordon
Islington, 3 December, 1947 (M)

League Club	Source	Date Signed	Seasons Played	Apps	Subs	Gls
Brentford	App	12.65	65-67	20	4	0

REEVE Frederick (Fred) William
Clapton, 1 May, 1918 Died 1994 (WH)

League Club	Source	Date Signed	Seasons Played	Apps	Subs	Gls
Crystal Palace	Ashford T	05.35	36	1	-	0
Tottenham H	Tr	05.37				
Rochdale	Tr	07.38	38	27	-	3
Grimsby T	Tr	07.39	46-47	46	-	0
Reading	Tr	06.48	48-49	34	-	1

REEVE James (Jamie) Michael
Weymouth, 26 November, 1975 (F)

League Club	Source	Date Signed	Seasons Played	Apps	Subs	Gls
Bournemouth	YT	07.94	94	2	5	0
Hereford U	Tr	03.95	94	0	5	0

REEVE Kenneth (Ken) Eric
Grimsby, 13 January, 1921 (IF)

League Club	Source	Date Signed	Seasons Played	Apps	Subs	Gls
Grimsby T	Humber U	02.38	46-47	24	-	5
Doncaster Rov	Tr	07.48	48	30	-	12
Mansfield T	Tr	07.49	49-53	139	-	62

REEVES Alan
Birkenhead, 19 November, 1967 (CD)

League Club	Source	Date Signed	Seasons Played	Apps	Subs	Gls
Norwich C	Heswall	09.88				
Gillingham	L	02.89	88	18	0	0
Chester C	Tr	08.89	89-90	31	9	2
Rochdale	Tr	07.91	91-94	119	2	9
Wimbledon	Tr	09.94	94-96	52	5	4
Swindon T	Tr	06.98	98-04	190	17	12

REEVES Thomas **Brian**
Skelmersdale, 18 February, 1939 (G)

League Club	Source	Date Signed	Seasons Played	Apps	Subs	Gls
Blackburn Rov	Burscough	08.60	60-61	12	-	0
Scunthorpe U	Tr	04.62	62-64	38	-	0
Southport	Tr	07.65	65-68	143	0	0

REEVES David Edward
Birkenhead, 19 November, 1967 (F)

League Club	Source	Date Signed	Seasons Played	Apps	Subs	Gls
Sheffield Wed	Heswall	08.86	88	8	9	2
Scunthorpe U	L	12.86	86	3	1	2
Scunthorpe U	L	10.87	87	6	0	4
Burnley	L	11.87	87	16	0	8
Bolton W	Tr	08.89	89-92	111	23	29
Notts Co	Tr	03.93	92-93	9	4	2
Carlisle U	Tr	10.93	93-96	127	0	48
Preston NE	Tr	10.96	96-97	45	2	12
Chesterfield	Tr	11.97	97-01	160	8	46
Oldham Ath	Tr	12.01	01	11	2	3
Chesterfield	Tr	08.02	02-03	54	17	12

REEVES Dennis John Richardson
Lochmaben, 1 December, 1944 (G)

League Club	Source	Date Signed	Seasons Played	Apps	Subs	Gls
Chester		09.63	63-66	139	0	0
Wrexham	Tr	10.67	67-68	15	0	0

REEVES Derek Brian
Poole, 27 August, 1934 Died 1995 (CF)

League Club	Source	Date Signed	Seasons Played	Apps	Subs	Gls
Southampton	Bournemouth Gasworks	12.54	54-62	273	-	145
Bournemouth	Tr	11.62	62-64	35	-	8

REEVES Frank
Peckham, 11 July, 1921 Died 1993 (WH)

League Club	Source	Date Signed	Seasons Played	Apps	Subs	Gls
Millwall	Sidcup	02.47	47-54	179	-	1

REEVES John Charles
Hackney, 8 July, 1963 (M)

League Club	Source	Date Signed	Seasons Played	Apps	Subs	Gls
Fulham	App	06.81	81-84	9	5	0
Colchester U	Tr	08.85	85-87	58	3	7

REEVES Kevin Philip
Burley, 20 October, 1957 EYth/Eu21-10/EB/E-2 (F)

League Club	Source	Date Signed	Seasons Played	Apps	Subs	Gls
Bournemouth	App	07.75	74-76	60	3	20
Norwich C	Tr	01.77	76-79	118	1	37
Manchester C	Tr	03.80	79-82	129	1	34
Burnley	Tr	07.83	83	20	1	12

REEVES Martin Lee
Birmingham, 7 September, 1981 (M)

League Club	Source	Date Signed	Seasons Played	Apps	Subs	Gls
Leicester C	YT	11.00	01-02	1	7	0
Hull C	L	03.03	02	5	3	1
Northampton T	Tr	06.03	03-04	9	6	0

REEVES Michael (Mike) Randall
Saltash, 13 January, 1943 (FB)

League Club	Source	Date Signed	Seasons Played	Apps	Subs	Gls
Plymouth Arg	Saltash U	06.61	62-69	107	3	0

REEVES Peter John
Eltham, 7 February, 1949 EYth (CD)

League Club	Source	Date Signed	Seasons Played	Apps	Subs	Gls
Charlton Ath	App	02.66	65-73	263	5	2

REEVES Peter Philip
Swansea, 20 January, 1959 (M)

League Club	Source	Date Signed	Seasons Played	Apps	Subs	Gls
Coventry C	App	12.76				
Swansea C	Tr	07.78	78	2	2	0

REEVES Raymond (Ray) Henry Ernest
Reading, 12 August, 1931 EYth (FB)

League Club	Source	Date Signed	Seasons Played	Apps	Subs	Gls
Reading		05.49	52-60	284	-	29
Brentford	Tr	07.61	61	5	-	0

REEVES-JONES Adrian Kenneth
Stoke-on-Trent, 18 October, 1966 (W)

League Club	Source	Date Signed	Seasons Played	Apps	Subs	Gls
Port Vale	App	10.84	84	2	1	0

REGAN Carl Anthony
Liverpool, 14 January, 1980 EYth (FB)

League Club	Source	Date Signed	Seasons Played	Apps	Subs	Gls
Everton	YT	01.98				
Barnsley	Tr	06.00	00-01	31	6	0
Hull C	Tr	08.02	02	33	5	0
Chester C	Droylsden	03.05	04	4	2	0

REGAN Douglas (Duggie)
Stoke-under-Ham, 3 June, 1922 (W)

League Club	Source	Date Signed	Seasons Played	Apps	Subs	Gls
Exeter C		03.45	46-52	206	-	63
Bristol C	Tr	12.52	52-55	39	-	11

REGAN James (Jim)
Hemsworth, 7 December, 1927 Died 1977 (WH)

League Club	Source	Date Signed	Seasons Played	Apps	Subs	Gls
Rotherham U	Moorthorpe Colliery	08.49	51-52	12	-	0
Bristol C	Tr	06.53	53-55	51	-	1
Coventry C	Tr	03.56	55-56	26	-	0

REGAN John Henry
Dalton-in-Furness, 8 June, 1925 (W)

League Club	Source	Date Signed	Seasons Played	Apps	Subs	Gls
Barrow	Swarthmoor	01.48	48-50	9	-	1

REGAN Matthew **John**
Worcester, 18 June, 1944 (F)

League Club	Source	Date Signed	Seasons Played	Apps	Subs	Gls
Birmingham C	Claines	09.61	62-63	5	-	2
Shrewsbury T	Tr	10.64	64-65	21	0	6
Brentford	Tr	03.66	65-66	14	0	5
Crewe Alex	Tr	11.66	66-68	47	3	18
Doncaster Rov	Tr	09.68	68-70	91	3	25

REGAN Terence (Terry)
Bradford, 26 June, 1926 (W)

League Club	Source	Date Signed	Seasons Played	Apps	Subs	Gls
Bradford C (Am)	Salts (Am)	10.48	48	1	-	0

REGIS Cyrille
Mariapousoula, French Guiana, 9 February, 1958 Eu21-6/EB/E-5 (F)

League Club	Source	Date Signed	Seasons Played	Apps	Subs	Gls
West Bromwich A	Hayes	05.77	77-84	233	4	82
Coventry C	Tr	10.84	84-90	231	6	47
Aston Villa	Tr	07.91	91-92	46	6	12
Wolverhampton W	Tr	08.93	93	8	11	2
Wycombe W	Tr	08.94	94	30	5	9
Chester C	Tr	08.95	95	29	0	7

REGIS David (Dave)
Paddington, 3 March, 1964 (F)

League Club	Source	Date Signed	Seasons Played	Apps	Subs	Gls
Notts Co	Barnet	09.80	90-91	31	15	15
Plymouth Arg	Tr	11.91	91-92	28	3	4
Bournemouth	L	08.92	92	6	0	2
Stoke C	Tr	10.92	92-93	49	14	15
Birmingham C	Tr	08.94	94	4	2	2
Southend U	Tr	09.94	94-95	34	4	9
Barnsley	Tr	02.96	95-96	4	12	1
Peterborough U	L	09.96	96	4	3	1
Notts Co	L	02.97	96	7	3	2
Scunthorpe U	L	08.97	97	5	0	0
Leyton Orient	Tr	10.97	97	4	0	0
Lincoln C	Tr	12.97	97	0	1	0
Scunthorpe U	Wivenhoe T	02.98	97	4	0	2

REGIS Robert
Huddersfield, 24 January, 1967 (F)

League Club	Source	Date Signed	Seasons Played	Apps	Subs	Gls
Burnley	Huddersfield T (Jnrs)	08.86	86	3	1	1

REGTOP Erik
Emmen, Holland, 16 February, 1968 (F)

League Club	Source	Date Signed	Seasons Played	Apps	Subs	Gls
Bradford C	SC Heerenveen (Holl)	07.96	96	5	3	1

REHMAN Zeshan (Zesh)
Birmingham, 14 October, 1983 EYth (M)

League Club	Source	Date Signed	Seasons Played	Apps	Subs	Gls
Fulham	YT	06.01	03-04	15	3	0
Brighton & Hove A	L	09.03	03	9	2	2

REHN Jan Stefan
Stockholm, Sweden, 22 September, 1966 Sweden int (M)

League Club	Source	Date Signed	Seasons Played	Apps	Subs	Gls
Everton	Djurgaarden (Swe)	06.89	89	1	3	0

REICH Marco
Meisenheim, Germany, 30 December, 1977 Germany 1 (M)

League Club	Source	Date Signed	Seasons Played	Apps	Subs	Gls
Derby Co	Werder Bremen (Ger)	01.04	03-04	36	14	7

REID Dennis **Alexander (Alex)**
Glasgow, 2 March, 1947 (M)

League Club	Source	Date Signed	Seasons Played	Apps	Subs	Gls
Newcastle U	Dundee U	10.71	71-72	15	8	0

REID Andrew (Andy) Matthew
Dublin, 29 July, 1982 IRYth/IRu21-15/IR-16 (M)

League Club	Source	Date Signed	Seasons Played	Apps	Subs	Gls
Nottingham F	YT	08.99	00-04	121	23	21
Tottenham H	Tr	01.05	04	13	0	1

REID Andrew (Andy) Merrick
Urmston, 4 July, 1962 ESemiPro (CD)

League Club	Source	Date Signed	Seasons Played	Apps	Subs	Gls
Bury	Altrincham	08.92	92-93	27	6	1

REID Anthony (Tony) James
Nottingham, 9 May, 1963 (M)

League Club	Source	Date Signed	Seasons Played	Apps	Subs	Gls
Derby Co	App	05.80	80-82	27	3	1
Scunthorpe U	L	02.83	82	6	0	0
Newport Co	Tr	03.83	82-84	74	2	12
Chesterfield	Tr	07.85	85-87	63	4	7

REID Brian Robertson
Paisley, 15 June, 1970 Su21-4 (CD)

League Club	Source	Date Signed	Seasons Played	Apps	Subs	Gls
Burnley	Morton	09.98	98	30	1	3
Blackpool	Dunfermline Ath	10.00	00-01	55	0	2

REID David Alexander
Glasgow, 3 January, 1923 (WH)

League Club	Source	Date Signed	Seasons Played	Apps	Subs	Gls
Rochdale	Glasgow Perthshire	01.48	47-50	36	-	2
Bradford PA	Tr	09.50	50-51	13	-	0
Workington	Tr	07.53	53	8	-	1
Crewe Alex	Tr	08.54	54	3	-	0

REID John **Douglas (Duggie)** Jamieson
Mauchline, 3 October, 1917 Died 2002 (IF)

League Club	Source	Date Signed	Seasons Played	Apps	Subs	Gls
Stockport Co	Heaton Chapel	08.35	36-38	84	-	23
Portsmouth	Tr	03.46	46-55	308	-	129

REID Ernest (Ernie) James
Pentrebach, 25 March, 1914 (FB)

League Club	Source	Date Signed	Seasons Played	Apps	Subs	Gls
Swansea T	Plymouth U	07.32	32	1	-	0
Chelsea	Tr	09.37	38	1	-	0
Norwich C	Tr	07.39	46	5	-	0

REID Francis (Frank)
Mauchline, 16 June, 1920 Died 1970 (W)

League Club	Source	Date Signed	Seasons Played	Apps	Subs	Gls
Huddersfield T	Cumnock Jnrs	08.46	46-48	7	-	0
Stockport Co	Tr	06.49	49-50	23	-	0

REID James Provan
Dundee, 14 December, 1935 (IF)

League Club	Source	Date Signed	Seasons Played	Apps	Subs	Gls
Bury	Dundee U	01.57	56-58	21	-	9
Stockport Co	Tr	03.59	58	11	-	2

REID John
Edinburgh, 23 July, 1935 (W)

League Club	Source	Date Signed	Seasons Played	Apps	Subs	Gls
Watford	Airdrie	12.56	56	1	-	1
Norwich C	Airdrie	06.58				
Barrow	Tr	07.59	59	20	-	4

REID John
Newmains, 20 August, 1932 (M)

League Club	Source	Date Signed	Seasons Played	Apps	Subs	Gls
Bradford C	Hamilton Academical	12.57	57-61	147	-	32
Northampton T	Tr	11.61	61-63	85	-	14
Luton T	Tr	11.63	63-65	111	0	7
Torquay U	Tr	06.66	66	21	2	1
Rochdale	Tr	07.67	67	37	2	3

REID John Herkess
Edinburgh, 4 May, 1925 (CF)

League Club	Source	Date Signed	Seasons Played	Apps	Subs	Gls
Torquay U	Hibernian	05.49	49-51	51	-	10

REID Levi Stanley Junior
Stafford, 19 January, 1983 (M)

League Club	Source	Date Signed	Seasons Played	Apps	Subs	Gls
Port Vale	Sch	07.03	02-04	28	14	0

REID Mark
Kilwinning, 15 September, 1961 SYth/Su21-2 (FB)

League Club	Source	Date Signed	Seasons Played	Apps	Subs	Gls
Charlton Ath	Glasgow Celtic	05.85	85-90	209	2	15

REID Michael (Micky) James
Wolverhampton, 7 August, 1927 Died 1975 (CF)

League Club	Source	Date Signed	Seasons Played	Apps	Subs	Gls
Wolverhampton W		02.48				
Bournemouth	Tr	02.49	48	5	-	2
Portsmouth	Tr	07.50	50	5	-	1
Watford	Tr	12.52	52	19	-	8

League Club	Source	Date Signed	Seasons Played	Apps	Subs	Gls
REID Nicholas (Nicky) Scott						
Urmston, 30 October, 1960 Eu21-6						(CD)
Manchester C	App	11.78	78-86	211	5	2
Blackburn Rov	Tr	07.87	87-91	160	14	9
Bristol C	L	09.92	92	3	1	0
West Bromwich A	Tr	11.92	92-93	13	7	0
Wycombe W	Tr	03.94	93-94	6	2	0
Bury	Witton A	12.95	95-96	19	6	0
REID Paul James						
Sydney, Australia, 6 July, 1979 Auu20						(M)
Bradford C	Wollongong W's (Aus)	09.02	02	7	1	2
Brighton & Hove A	Tr	03.04	03-04	37	2	2
REID Paul Mark						
Carlisle, 18 February, 1982 EYth/Eu20						(CD)
Carlisle U	YT	02.99	99	17	2	0
Preston NE (L)	Glasgow Rgrs	01.02	01	0	1	1
Northampton T (L)	Glasgow Rgrs	12.02	02	19	0	0
Northampton T	Glasgow Rgrs	06.03	03	33	0	2
Barnsley	Tr	07.04	04	38	3	3
REID Paul Robert						
Oldbury, 19 January, 1968						(W)
Leicester C	App	01.86	86-91	140	22	21
Bradford C	L	03.92	91	7	0	0
Bradford C	Tr	07.92	92-93	80	2	15
Huddersfield T	Tr	05.94	94-96	70	7	6
Oldham Ath	Tr	03.97	96-98	93	0	6
Bury	Tr	07.99	99-01	102	8	9
Swansea C	Tr	07.02	02	18	2	1
REID Peter						
Huyton, 20 June, 1956 Eu21-6/E-13						(M)
Bolton W	App	05.74	74-82	222	3	23
Everton	Tr	12.82	82-88	155	4	8
Queens Park Rgrs	Tr	02.89	88-89	29	0	1
Manchester C	Tr	12.89	89-93	90	13	1
Southampton	Tr	09.93	93	7	0	0
Notts Co	Tr	02.94	93	5	0	0
Bury	Tr	07.94	94	1	0	0
REID Robert (Bobby)						
Hamilton, 19 February, 1911 Died 1987 SLge-2/S-2						(W)
Brentford	Hamilton Academical	01.36	35-38	103	-	33
Sheffield U	Tr	02.39	38-46	14	-	4
Bury	Tr	11.46	46	17	-	1
REID Robert Bell Alexander						
Dundee, 18 November, 1936 Died 2000						(G)
Swansea T	Downfield Jnrs	09.57	57-59	17	-	0
REID Ronald (Ron) Eric						
Liversedge, 9 November, 1944						(W)
Chesterfield	Retford T	07.67	67	6	1	1
REID Shaun						
Huyton, 13 October, 1965						(M)
Rochdale	App	09.83	83-88	126	7	4
Preston NE	L	12.85	85	3	0	0
York C	Tr	12.88	88-91	104	2	7
Rochdale	Tr	08.92	92-94	106	1	10
Bury	Tr	07.95	95	20	1	0
Chester C	Tr	11.96	96-99	53	9	2
REID Steven John						
Kingston, 10 March, 1981 EYth/IRu21-3/IR-13						(W)
Millwall	YT	05.98	97-02	115	24	18
Blackburn Rov	Tr	07.03	03-04	32	12	2
REID Wesley Andrew						
Lewisham, 10 September, 1968						(M)
Arsenal	App	07.86				
Millwall	Tr	06.87	88-89	5	1	0
Bradford C	Tr	01.91	90-91	31	4	3
REID William Dunlop						
Ayr, 13 January, 1920						(WH)
Newport Co	Cumnock Jnrs	05.48	49	9	-	0
REILLY Alan						
Dublin, 22 August, 1980						(M)
Manchester C	YT	09.98				
Halifax T	Tr	12.99	99-01	30	15	2
REILLY Andrew (Andy) Daniel						
Luton, 26 October, 1985 SYth/Su21-1						(FB)
Wycombe W	Sch	04.04	03	5	0	0
REILLY Daniel (Danny)						
Peterborough, 17 November, 1966						(M)
Peterborough U	App	08.84	84	0	1	0
REILLY David John						
Chester, 24 November, 1966						(M)
Wrexham	Jnrs	07.84	84	0	1	0
REILLY Felix McCairney						
Wallyford, 12 September, 1933						(IF)
Bradford PA	East Fife	03.60	59-61	31	-	12
Crewe Alex	Tr	12.61	61	6	-	1
REILLY George Gerard						
Bellshill, 14 September, 1957						(F)
Northampton T	Corby T	06.76	76-79	124	3	46
Cambridge U	Tr	11.79	79-82	136	2	36
Watford	Tr	08.83	83-84	46	2	14
Newcastle U	Tr	02.85	84-85	31	0	10
West Bromwich A	Tr	12.85	85-87	42	1	9
Cambridge U	Tr	07.88	88	20	0	7
REILLY Leonard (Len) Harold						
Rotherhithe, 31 January, 1917 Died 1998						(CD)
Norwich C	Diss T	02.36	37-46	30	-	0
REILLY Mark Francis						
Bellshill, 30 March, 1969 SB-1						(M)
Reading	Kilmarnock	07.98	98	4	2	0
REILLY Terence (Terry)						
High Valleyfield, 1 July, 1924						(FB)
Chesterfield	Bo'ness U	03.49				
Southport	Tr	08.50	50-54	191	-	2
Bradford PA	Tr	06.55	55	14	-	0
REINA Enrique (Ricky) Iglesia						
Folkestone, 2 October, 1971						(F)
Brentford	Dover Ath	09.97	97	2	4	1
REINELT Robert (Robbie) Squire						
Loughton, 11 March, 1974						(F)
Aldershot	YT	●	90	3	2	0
Gillingham	Wivenhoe T	03.93	93-94	34	18	5
Colchester U	Tr	03.95	94-96	22	26	10
Brighton & Hove A	Tr	02.97	96-97	32	12	7
Leyton Orient	Tr	08.98	98	2	5	0
REIZIGER Michael John						
Amsterdam, Holland, 3 May, 1973 Holland 72						(FB)
Middlesbrough	Barcelona (Sp)	07.04	04	15	3	1
RELISH John Derek						
Huyton, 5 October, 1953						(FB)
Chester	App	10.71	72-73	10	1	1
Newport Co	Tr	06.74	74-86	319	19	9
REMY Christophe Philippe						
Besancon, France, 6 August, 1971						(FB)
Oxford U	Auxerre (Fr)	07.97	97-98	23	5	1
REMY Ellis Nathan						
City of London, 13 February, 1984						(F)
Wimbledon	Jnrs	06.01				
Lincoln C	Hastings T	08.03	03	0	1	0
RENNIE David						
Edinburgh, 29 August, 1964 SYth						(CD)
Leicester C	App	05.82	83-85	21	0	1
Leeds U	Tr	01.86	85-88	95	6	5
Bristol C	Tr	07.89	89-91	101	3	8
Birmingham C	Tr	02.92	91-92	32	3	4
Coventry C	Tr	03.93	92-95	80	2	3
Northampton T	Tr	08.96	96-97	45	3	3
Peterborough U	Tr	12.97	97-98	27	0	0
RENNIE Paul Andrew						
Nantwich, 26 October, 1971						(FB)
Crewe Alex	YT	●	89	1	1	0
Stoke C	Tr	05.90	90-91	4	0	0
Wigan Ath	Tr	08.93	93-94	36	4	3
RENNISON Graham Lee						
Northallerton, 2 October, 1978						(CD)
York C	YT	07.98	97	1	0	0
RENNISON Shaun						
Northallerton, 23 November, 1980						(CD)
Scarborough	YT	02.99	98	15	0	1
RENSHAW Derrick						
Gateshead, 18 September, 1924 Died 1998						(FB)
Sunderland		12.47				
Barrow	Tr	06.50	50-54	150	-	0

League Club	Source	Date Signed	Seasons Played	Apps	Subs	Gls
RENSHAW Ian Francis						
Chelmsford, 14 April, 1978						(FB)
Scarborough	Basildon U	11.98	98	0	1	0
RENTON William (Billy)						
Cardenden, 4 February, 1942						(M)
Southport	Dunfermline Ath	11.70				
Barrow	Tr	01.71	70-71	23	1	2
RENWICK Craig						
Lanark, 22 September, 1958						(CD)
Sheffield U	East Stirling	04.78	78-79	8	1	0
RENWICK Richard (Dick)						
Gilsland, 27 November, 1942						(FB)
Grimsby T	Jnrs	12.59				
Aldershot	Tr	07.63	63-68	203	2	4
Brentford	Tr	02.69	68-70	96	0	5
Stockport Co	Tr	10.71	71	30	0	1
Rochdale	Tr	07.72	72-73	48	1	0
Darlington	L	01.74	73	19	0	0
REO-COKER Nigel Shola Andre						
Thornton Heath, 14 May, 1984 EYth/Eu21-6						(M)
Wimbledon	Sch	07.02	01-03	57	1	6
West Ham U	Tr	01.04	03-04	47	7	5
REPKA Tomas						
Slavicin Zlin, Czech Republic, 2 January, 1974 Cz-1/CzR-46						(CD)
West Ham U	Fiorentina (It)	09.01	01-04	145	0	0
RESCH Franz						
Vienna, Austria, 4 May, 1969 Austria int						(FB)
Darlington	Motherwell	10.97	97	15	2	1
RESTARICK Stephen (Steve) Leonard James						
Barking, 28 November, 1971						(F)
Colchester U	YT	•	89	0	1	0
RETALLICK Graham						
Cambridge, 8 February, 1970						(M)
Peterborough U	Histon	08.92	92	2	3	0
REUSER Martijn Franciscus						
Amsterdam, Holland, 1 February, 1975 Hou21-12/Ho-1						(M)
Ipswich T	Vitesse Arnhem (Holl)	03.00	99-03	42	49	14
REVEL Gordon Harold						
Mansfield, 19 September, 1927						(CD)
Mansfield T	Westfield FH	08.50	52	1	-	0
REVELL Alexander (Alex) David						
Cambridge, 7 July, 1983						(F)
Cambridge U	YT	04.01	00-03	19	38	5
REVELL Charles (Charlie)						
Belvedere, 5 June, 1919 Died 1999						(WH)
Charlton Ath	Northfleet	05.39	46-50	104	-	15
Derby Co	Tr	03.51	50-51	22	-	2
REVIE Donald (Don) George						
Middlesbrough, 10 July, 1927 Died 1989 FLge-2/EB/E-6						(IF)
Leicester C	Middlesbrough Swifts	08.44	46-49	96	-	25
Hull C	Tr	11.49	49-51	76	-	12
Manchester C	Tr	10.51	51-56	162	-	37
Sunderland	Tr	11.56	56-58	64	-	15
Leeds U	Tr	12.58	58-61	76	-	11
REW Roy Edward						
Belfast, 26 May, 1924						(CF)
Exeter C	Seamills	02.49	48-49	4	-	1
REWBURY Jamie Richard						
Wattstown, 15 February, 1986 WYth						(FB)
Swansea C	Sch	•	03	1	1	0
REYES Jose Antonio						
Utrera, Spain, 1 September, 1983 Spain 12						(F)
Arsenal	Sevilla (Sp)	01.04	03-04	32	11	11
REYNA Claudio						
Livingston, New Jersey, USA, 20 July, 1973 USA 106						(M)
Sunderland	Glasgow Rgrs	12.01	01-02	28	0	3
Manchester C	Tr	08.03	03-04	35	5	3
REYNOLDS Arthur **Brayley**						
Blackwood, Monmouthshire, 30 May, 1935						(CF)
Cardiff C	Lovells Ath	05.56	56-58	55	-	14
Swansea T	Tr	05.59	59-64	150	-	58
REYNOLDS Graham Edward Arthur						
Newport, 23 January, 1937 WAmat						(CF)
Newport Co (Am)	Caerleon	10.56	56	4	-	1
Newport Co	Brecon Corries	07.63	63-66	42	1	11
REYNOLDS Hugh						
Wishaw, 19 September, 1926						(WH)
Torquay U	Morton	05.48	48	3	-	0
REYNOLDS James (Jim) Andrew						
Swindon, 27 October, 1967 EYth						(M)
Swindon T	App	09.85	84-86	0	2	0
REYNOLDS Joseph (Joe) John						
Cleland, 13 February, 1939 Died 1998						(CD)
Crewe Alex		08.60	60	5	-	0
REYNOLDS Mark David						
Glapwell, 1 January, 1966						(FB)
Mansfield T	App	•	82	4	0	0
REYNOLDS Richard (Dick) John						
Looe, 15 February, 1948 EYth						(M)
Plymouth Arg	App	02.65	64-70	123	8	24
Portsmouth	Tr	07.71	71-75	134	7	24
REYNOLDS Ronald (Ron) Sidney Maurice						
Haslemere, 2 June, 1928 Died 1999						(G)
Aldershot	Jnrs	12.45	46-49	114	-	0
Tottenham H	Tr	07.50	53-57	86	-	0
Southampton	Tr	03.60	59-63	90	-	0
REYNOLDS Thomas (Tommy)						
Felling, 2 October, 1922 Died 1998						(W)
Sunderland	Felling Jnrs	07.46	46-52	167	-	18
Darlington	King's Lynn	12.54	54-55	43	-	6
REZAI Carl						
Manchester, 16 October, 1982						(FB)
Halifax T	YT	10.00	00	8	3	1
RHOADES-BROWN Peter						
Hampton, 2 January, 1962						(W)
Chelsea	App	07.79	79-83	86	10	4
Oxford U	Tr	01.84	83-88	87	25	13
RHODES Alan						
Bradford, 5 January, 1946						(WH)
Bradford C (Am)	Salts	07.64	64-65	7	0	0
RHODES Albert						
Anston, 29 April, 1936						(FB)
Queens Park Rgrs	Worksop T	12.54	55-56	5	-	0
RHODES Alexander (Alex) Graham						
Cambridge, 23 January, 1982						(F)
Brentford	Newmarket T	11.03	03-04	4	21	4
RHODES Andrew (Andy) Charles						
Askern, 23 August, 1964						(G)
Barnsley	App	08.82	83-84	36	0	0
Doncaster Rov	Tr	10.85	85-87	106	0	0
Oldham Ath	Tr	03.88	87-89	69	0	0
Scarborough (L)	Airdrie	11.97	97	11	0	0
RHODES John Anthony **(Tony)**						
Dover, 17 September, 1946						(CD)
Derby Co	Jnrs	10.63	64-70	5	0	0
Halifax T	Tr	11.70	70-75	233	0	9
Southport	Tr	08.76	76	7	2	0
RHODES Benjamin (Ben) Peter						
York, 2 May, 1983						(M)
York C	YT	•	01	0	1	0
RHODES Brian William						
Marylebone, 23 October, 1937 Died 1993						(G)
West Ham U	Jnrs	01.55	57-62	61	-	0
Southend U	Tr	09.63	63	11	-	0
RHODES Christopher (Chris) Kyle						
Mansfield, 9 January, 1987						(M)
Notts Co	Sch	•	03	0	1	0
RHODES Mark Nigel						
Sheffield, 26 August, 1957						(M)
Rotherham U	App	08.75	75-84	235	11	13
Darlington	L	10.82	82	14	0	0
Mansfield T	L	03.83	82	4	0	0
Burnley	Tr	03.85	84-85	12	1	0

RHODES Stanley (Stan)
Sheffield, 19 April, 1929 (IF)

League Club	Source	Date Signed	Seasons Played	Apps	Subs	Gls
Leeds U		05.48				
Sheffield U	Worksop T	11.51	51	1	-	0

RHODES Trevor Charles
Southend-on-Sea, 9 August, 1948 (M)

League Club	Source	Date Signed	Seasons Played	Apps	Subs	Gls
Arsenal	App	09.65				
Millwall	Tr	09.66	66	4	0	0
Bristol Rov	Tr	07.68	68	2	0	0

RIBEIRO Bruno Miguel Fernandes
Setubal, Portugal, 22 October, 1975 (M)

League Club	Source	Date Signed	Seasons Played	Apps	Subs	Gls
Leeds U	Vitoria Setubal (Por)	07.97	97-98	35	7	4
Sheffield U	Tr	10.99	99-00	12	13	1

RICARD Cuesta **Hamilton**
Choco, Colombia, 12 January, 1974 ColombiaU21/Colombia-29 (F)

League Club	Source	Date Signed	Seasons Played	Apps	Subs	Gls
Middlesbrough	Deportivo Cali (Col)	03.98	97-01	92	23	33

[RICARDO] LOPEZ Ricardo Felipe
Madrid, Spain, 30 December, 1971 Spain 1 (G)

League Club	Source	Date Signed	Seasons Played	Apps	Subs	Gls
Manchester U	Real Valladolid (Sp)	08.02	02	0	1	0

RICE Brian
Bellshill, 11 October, 1963 SYth/Su21-1 (W)

League Club	Source	Date Signed	Seasons Played	Apps	Subs	Gls
Nottingham F	Hibernian	08.85	85-90	86	5	9
Grimsby T	L	10.86	86	4	0	0
West Bromwich A	L	01.89	88	2	1	0
Stoke C	L	02.91	90	18	0	0

RICE Gary James
Zambia, 25 September, 1975 (FB)

League Club	Source	Date Signed	Seasons Played	Apps	Subs	Gls
Exeter C	YT	07.94	94-96	31	13	0

RICE Patrick (Pat) James
Belfast, 17 March, 1949 NIu23-2/NI-49 (FB)

League Club	Source	Date Signed	Seasons Played	Apps	Subs	Gls
Arsenal	Jnrs	03.66	67-80	391	6	12
Watford	Tr	11.80	80-83	112	0	1

RICE Ronald (Ron) Henry
Birkenhead, 13 April, 1923 (IF)

League Club	Source	Date Signed	Seasons Played	Apps	Subs	Gls
Bradford C	Huddersfield T (Am)	09.46	46	1	-	0
Tranmere Rov	Tr	10.46	46	5	-	1

RICHARD Fabrice
Saintes, France, 16 August, 1973 (FB)

League Club	Source	Date Signed	Seasons Played	Apps	Subs	Gls
Colchester U	AS Cannes (Fr)	03.99	98-99	23	1	0

RICHARDS Anthony (Tony) Willis
Smethwick, 6 March, 1934 (CF)

League Club	Source	Date Signed	Seasons Played	Apps	Subs	Gls
Birmingham C	Hopes' Works	12.51				
Walsall	Tr	09.54	54-62	334	-	183
Port Vale	Tr	03.63	62-65	59	4	30

RICHARDS Carroll (Carl) Lloyd
St Mary's, Jamaica, 12 January, 1960 ESemiPro (F)

League Club	Source	Date Signed	Seasons Played	Apps	Subs	Gls
Bournemouth	Enfield	07.86	86-88	57	14	16
Birmingham C	Tr	10.88	88	18	1	2
Peterborough U	Tr	07.89	89	16	4	5
Blackpool	Tr	01.90	89-91	32	9	8
Maidstone U	L	10.91	91	4	0	2

RICHARDS Craig Alan
Neath, 10 October, 1959 (M)

League Club	Source	Date Signed	Seasons Played	Apps	Subs	Gls
Queens Park Rgrs	App	07.77				
Wimbledon	Tr	06.79	79	2	0	0

RICHARDS Dean Ivor
Bradford, 9 June, 1974 Eu21-4 (CD)

League Club	Source	Date Signed	Seasons Played	Apps	Subs	Gls
Bradford C	YT	07.92	91-94	82	4	4
Wolverhampton W	Tr	03.95	94-98	118	4	7
Southampton	Tr	07.99	99-01	67	0	3
Tottenham H	Tr	09.01	01-03	73	0	4

RICHARDS Gary Vivian
Swansea, 2 August, 1963 (FB)

League Club	Source	Date Signed	Seasons Played	Apps	Subs	Gls
Swansea C	App	08.81	81-84	63	3	1
Lincoln C	(Sweden)	11.85	85	2	5	0
Cambridge U	Tr	03.86	85	8	0	0
Torquay U	Tr	07.86	86	24	1	1

RICHARDS Geoffrey (Geoff) Mottram
Bilston, 24 April, 1929 (IF)

League Club	Source	Date Signed	Seasons Played	Apps	Subs	Gls
West Bromwich A	Albion Works	08.46	46-47	3	-	1

RICHARDS Gordon
Rhos, 23 October, 1933 Died 1993 (W)

League Club	Source	Date Signed	Seasons Played	Apps	Subs	Gls
Wrexham	Ruabon	05.52	52-57	96	-	24
Chester	Tr	01.58	57-60	74	-	16

RICHARDS Ian
Barnsley, 5 October, 1979 (M)

League Club	Source	Date Signed	Seasons Played	Apps	Subs	Gls
Blackburn Rov	YT	07.97				
Halifax T	Tr	07.99	99-00	13	11	0

RICHARDS John Barrington
West Bromwich, 14 June, 1931 Died 2001 (IF)

League Club	Source	Date Signed	Seasons Played	Apps	Subs	Gls
Swindon T		11.55	55-59	105	-	36
Norwich C	Tr	12.59	59	5	-	2
Aldershot	Tr	10.60	60	19	-	8

RICHARDS John Peter
Warrington, 9 November, 1950 ESch/Eu23-6/Eu21-1/FLge-1/E-1 (F)

League Club	Source	Date Signed	Seasons Played	Apps	Subs	Gls
Wolverhampton W	Jnrs	07.69	69-82	365	20	144
Derby Co	L	11.82	82	10	0	2

RICHARDS Justin
West Bromwich, 16 October, 1980 (F)

League Club	Source	Date Signed	Seasons Played	Apps	Subs	Gls
West Bromwich A	YT	01.99	98	0	1	0
Bristol Rov	Tr	01.01	00-02	3	13	0
Colchester U	L	10.02	02	0	2	0

RICHARDS Lloyd George
Jamaica, 11 February, 1958 (M)

League Club	Source	Date Signed	Seasons Played	Apps	Subs	Gls
Notts Co	App	02.76	75-77	7	2	0
York C	Tr	06.80	80	17	1	1

RICHARDS Marc John
Wolverhampton, 8 July, 1982 EYth/Eu20 (F)

League Club	Source	Date Signed	Seasons Played	Apps	Subs	Gls
Blackburn Rov	YT	07.99				
Crewe Alex	L	08.01	01	1	3	0
Oldham Ath	L	10.01	01	3	2	0
Halifax T	L	02.02	01	5	0	0
Swansea C	L	11.02	02	14	3	7
Northampton T	Tr	07.03	03-04	35	18	10
Rochdale	L	03.05	04	4	1	2

RICHARDS Matthew (Matt) Lee
Harlow, 26 December, 1984 Eu21-1 (FB)

League Club	Source	Date Signed	Seasons Played	Apps	Subs	Gls
Ipswich T	YT	01.02	02-04	66	15	2

RICHARDS Michael (Mike) James
Codsall, 26 May, 1939 (G)

League Club	Source	Date Signed	Seasons Played	Apps	Subs	Gls
Oxford U	Wellington T	07.62	62-63	30	-	0

RICHARDS Peter (Pedro)
Edmonton, 11 November, 1956 Died 2001 (FB)

League Club	Source	Date Signed	Seasons Played	Apps	Subs	Gls
Notts Co	App	11.74	74-85	397	2	5

RICHARDS Stanley (Stan) Verdun
Cardiff, 21 January, 1917 Died 1987 W-1 (CF)

League Club	Source	Date Signed	Seasons Played	Apps	Subs	Gls
Cardiff C	Cardiff Corinthians	01.46	46-47	57	-	39
Swansea T	Tr	06.48	48-50	62	-	35

RICHARDS Stephen (Steve)
Dundee, 24 October, 1961 (CD)

League Club	Source	Date Signed	Seasons Played	Apps	Subs	Gls
Hull C	App	10.79	79-82	55	3	2
York C	Gainsborough Trinity	12.84	84	6	1	0
Lincoln C	Tr	08.85	85	21	0	0
Cambridge U	Tr	03.86	85	4	0	2
Scarborough	Tr	08.86	87-90	164	0	13
Halifax T	Tr	08.91	91	24	1	0
Doncaster Rov	Tr	05.92	92	36	2	3

RICHARDS Tony
New Houghton, 9 June, 1944 (WH)

League Club	Source	Date Signed	Seasons Played	Apps	Subs	Gls
Mansfield T	App	06.62	61-63	3	-	0

RICHARDS Tony Spencer
Newham, 17 September, 1973 (F)

League Club	Source	Date Signed	Seasons Played	Apps	Subs	Gls
West Ham U	YT	08.92				
Cambridge U	Sudbury T	08.95	95-96	29	13	5
Leyton Orient	Tr	10.97	97-99	47	16	11
Barnet	Tr	08.00	00	27	6	8
Southend U	Tr	07.01	01	9	8	2

RICHARDS Wayne
Scunthorpe, 10 May, 1961 (FB)

League Club	Source	Date Signed	Seasons Played	Apps	Subs	Gls
Derby Co	App	05.79	79-81	16	3	0

RICHARDSON Anthony (Tony) Frederick
Alford, 5 November, 1943 (CF)

League Club	Source	Date Signed	Seasons Played	Apps	Subs	Gls
Nottingham F	Jnrs	11.60				
Bradford C (Am)	Cheltenham T	05.62	62	2	-	1

RICHARDSON Anthony (Tony) Joseph
Southwark, 7 January, 1932 (FB)

League Club	Source	Date Signed	Seasons Played	Apps	Subs	Gls
Queens Park Rgrs	Slough Sport Club	04.51	51	2	-	0

RICHARDSON Barry
Willington Quay, 5 August, 1969 (G)

League Club	Source	Date Signed	Seasons Played	Apps	Subs	Gls
Sunderland	YT	05.88				
Scunthorpe U	Tr	03.89				

League Club	Source	Date Signed	Seasons Played	Apps	Subs	Gls
Scarborough	Seaham Red Star	08.89	89-90	30	0	0
Northampton T	Stockport Co (N/C)	09.91	91-93	96	0	0
Preston NE	Tr	07.94	94-95	20	0	0
Lincoln C	Tr	10.95	95-99	131	0	0
Mansfield T	L	08.99	99	6	0	0
Halifax T	Doncaster Rov	12.01	01	24	0	0

RICHARDSON Brian
Sheffield, 5 October, 1934 (WH)

League Club	Source	Date Signed	Seasons Played	Apps	Subs	Gls
Sheffield U		12.54	55-64	291	-	9
Swindon T	Tr	01.66	65	11	0	0
Rochdale	Tr	07.66	66	19	0	1

RICHARDSON Craig Thomas
Newham, 8 October, 1979 (FB)

League Club	Source	Date Signed	Seasons Played	Apps	Subs	Gls
Leyton Orient	YT	●	97	1	0	0

RICHARDSON Damien John
Dublin, 2 August, 1947 LoI-1/IR-3 (F)

League Club	Source	Date Signed	Seasons Played	Apps	Subs	Gls
Gillingham	Shamrock Rov	10.72	72-80	314	9	94

RICHARDSON David (Dave)
Billingham, 11 March, 1932 (FB)

League Club	Source	Date Signed	Seasons Played	Apps	Subs	Gls
Leicester C	Jnrs	11.49	54	2	-	0
Grimsby T	Tr	06.55	55-59	175	-	1
Swindon T	Tr	06.60				
Barrow	Tr	07.61	61-62	31	-	0

RICHARDSON Derek
Hackney, 13 July, 1956 EYth/ESemiPro (G)

League Club	Source	Date Signed	Seasons Played	Apps	Subs	Gls
Chelsea	App	02.74				
Queens Park Rgrs	Tr	04.76	76-78	31	0	0
Sheffield U	Tr	12.79	79-80	42	0	0

RICHARDSON Frazer
Rotherham, 29 October, 1982 EYth/Eu20 (FB)

League Club	Source	Date Signed	Seasons Played	Apps	Subs	Gls
Leeds U	YT	11.99	03-04	30	12	1
Stoke C	L	01.03	02	6	1	0
Stoke C	L	11.03	03	6	0	1

RICHARDSON Frederick (Fred)
Spennymoor, 18 August, 1925 (CF)

League Club	Source	Date Signed	Seasons Played	Apps	Subs	Gls
Chelsea	Bishop Auckland	09.46	46	2	-	0
Hartlepools U	Tr	10.47	47-48	43	-	16
Barnsley	Tr	10.48	48-49	41	-	12
West Bromwich A	Tr	06.50	50-51	29	-	8
Chester	Tr	02.52	51-52	23	-	6
Hartlepools U	Tr	11.52	52-55	106	-	19

RICHARDSON Garbutt
Newcastle, 24 October, 1938 (CD)

League Club	Source	Date Signed	Seasons Played	Apps	Subs	Gls
Huddersfield T	Jnrs	10.55				
Preston NE	Tr	07.57	59-60	15	-	1
Accrington St	Tr	07.61				
Halifax T	Tr	11.62	62-63	20	-	1
Barrow	Tr	07.64	64	30	-	5

RICHARDSON George
Worksop, 12 December, 1912 Died 1968 (IF)

League Club	Source	Date Signed	Seasons Played	Apps	Subs	Gls
Huddersfield T	Manton Colliery	04.33	33	1	-	0
Sheffield U	Tr	05.34	35-38	32	-	9
Hull C	Tr	11.38	38-47	36	-	15

RICHARDSON Graham Charles
Sedgefield, 20 March, 1958 (G)

League Club	Source	Date Signed	Seasons Played	Apps	Subs	Gls
Hartlepool	Darlington (Am)	08.75	75-80	89	0	0

RICHARDSON Ian George
Barking, 22 October, 1970 ESemiPro-1 (CD)

League Club	Source	Date Signed	Seasons Played	Apps	Subs	Gls
Birmingham C	Dagenham & Redbridge	08.95	95	3	4	0
Notts Co	L	01.96	95	4	0	0
Notts Co	Tr	03.96	95-04	233	16	21

RICHARDSON Ian Paul
Ely, 9 May, 1964 (F)

League Club	Source	Date Signed	Seasons Played	Apps	Subs	Gls
Watford	App	05.82	83-84	5	3	2
Blackpool	L	12.82	82	4	1	2
Rotherham U	L	02.85	84	5	0	2
Chester C	Tr	11.85	85-86	31	4	10
Scunthorpe U	Tr	10.86	86-88	11	7	4

RICHARDSON James (Jimmy) Robert
Ashington, 8 February, 1911 Died 1964 ESch/FLge-1/E-2 (IF)

League Club	Source	Date Signed	Seasons Played	Apps	Subs	Gls
Newcastle U	Blyth Spartans	04.28	29-34	136	-	42
Huddersfield T	Tr	10.34	34-37	120	-	32
Newcastle U	Tr	10.37	37	14	-	4
Millwall	Tr	03.38	37-38	52	-	16
Leyton Orient	Tr	01.48	47	15	-	0

RICHARDSON Jay Grant
Bromley, 14 November, 1979 (M)

League Club	Source	Date Signed	Seasons Played	Apps	Subs	Gls
Chelsea	YT	02.98				
Exeter C	Tr	07.01	01	5	13	0

RICHARDSON John (Jack)
Rock Ferry, 24 May, 1933 (G)

League Club	Source	Date Signed	Seasons Played	Apps	Subs	Gls
Southport	Canterbury C	07.56	56-59	103	-	0

RICHARDSON John
Worksop, 20 April, 1945 (FB)

League Club	Source	Date Signed	Seasons Played	Apps	Subs	Gls
Derby Co	App	04.62	62-70	118	0	4
Notts Co	Tr	07.71	71	0	2	0

RICHARDSON John
Durham, 28 July, 1966 (F)

League Club	Source	Date Signed	Seasons Played	Apps	Subs	Gls
Colchester U	Chesham U	09.93	93	1	7	0

RICHARDSON John Pattinson
Stannington, 5 February, 1949 Died 1984 (CD)

League Club	Source	Date Signed	Seasons Played	Apps	Subs	Gls
Millwall	App	12.64	65	1	0	0
Brentford	Tr	08.66	66-69	83	2	7
Fulham	Tr	08.69	69-72	61	10	6
Aldershot	Tr	07.73	73-76	120	1	6

RICHARDSON Jonathan (Jon) Derek
Nottingham, 29 August, 1975 (CD)

League Club	Source	Date Signed	Seasons Played	Apps	Subs	Gls
Exeter C	YT	07.94	93-99	242	5	8
Oxford U	Tr	08.00	00-01	57	2	2

RICHARDSON Joseph (Joe) Arthur Searles
Sheffield, 17 March, 1942 Died 1966 (IF)

League Club	Source	Date Signed	Seasons Played	Apps	Subs	Gls
Birmingham C	Winsford U	09.59				
Sheffield U	Tr	01.60				
Rochdale	Tr	10.60	60-64	115	-	31

RICHARDSON Kevin
Newcastle, 4 December, 1962 E-1 (M)

League Club	Source	Date Signed	Seasons Played	Apps	Subs	Gls
Everton	App	12.80	81-86	95	15	16
Watford	Tr	09.86	86	39	0	2
Arsenal	Tr	08.87	87-89	88	8	5
Aston Villa	Real Sociedad (Sp)	08.91	91-94	142	1	13
Coventry C	Tr	02.95	94-97	75	3	0
Southampton	Tr	09.97	97	25	3	0
Barnsley	Tr	07.98	98-99	28	2	0
Blackpool	L	01.00	99	20	0	1

RICHARDSON Kieran Edward
Greenwich, 21 October, 1984 Eu21-3/E-2 (W)

League Club	Source	Date Signed	Seasons Played	Apps	Subs	Gls
Manchester U	Sch	08.03	02-04	0	4	0
West Bromwich A	L	01.05	04	11	1	3

RICHARDSON Leam Nathan
Leeds, 19 November, 1979 (FB)

League Club	Source	Date Signed	Seasons Played	Apps	Subs	Gls
Blackburn Rov	YT	12.97				
Bolton W	Tr	07.00	00-01	5	8	0
Notts Co	L	11.01	01	20	1	0
Blackpool	L	12.02	02	20	0	0
Blackpool	Tr	07.03	03-04	44	7	0

RICHARDSON Lee James
Halifax, 12 March, 1969 (M)

League Club	Source	Date Signed	Seasons Played	Apps	Subs	Gls
Halifax T	YT	07.87	86-88	43	13	2
Watford	Tr	02.89	88-89	40	1	1
Blackburn Rov	Tr	08.90	90-91	50	12	3
Oldham Ath	Aberdeen	08.94	94-96	82	6	21
Stockport Co	L	08.97	97	4	2	0
Huddersfield T	Tr	10.97	97-98	29	7	3
Bury	L	08.99	99	5	0	1
Chesterfield	Livingston	08.00	00-01	43	1	1

RICHARDSON Lloyd Matthew
Dewsbury, 7 October, 1977 EYth (M)

League Club	Source	Date Signed	Seasons Played	Apps	Subs	Gls
Oldham Ath	YT	10.94	96	0	1	0

RICHARDSON Marcus Glenroy
Reading, 31 August, 1977 (F)

League Club	Source	Date Signed	Seasons Played	Apps	Subs	Gls
Cambridge U	Harrow Borough	03.01	00-01	7	9	2
Torquay U	Tr	09.01	01-02	21	18	8
Hartlepool U	Tr	10.02	02-03	23	4	5
Lincoln C	L	08.03	03	9	3	4
Lincoln C	Tr	12.03	03-04	32	8	10
Rochdale	L	02.05	04	1	1	0
Yeovil T	Tr	03.05	04	2	2	0

RICHARDSON Neil Thomas
Sunderland, 3 March, 1968 (CD)

League Club	Source	Date Signed	Seasons Played	Apps	Subs	Gls
Rotherham U	Brandon U	08.89	89-98	168	16	9
Exeter C	L	11.96	96	14	0	0
Mansfield T	Tr	08.99	99	31	0	0

RICHARDSON Nicholas (Nick) John
Halifax, 11 April, 1967 (M)

League Club	Source	Date Signed	Seasons Played	Apps	Subs	Gls
Halifax T	Emley	11.88	88-91	89	12	17
Cardiff C	Tr	08.92	92-94	106	5	13
Wrexham	L	10.94	94	4	0	2
Chester C	L	12.94	94	6	0	1

League Club	Source	Date Signed	Seasons Played	Apps	Subs	Gls
Bury	Tr	08.95	95	3	2	0
Chester C	Tr	09.95	95-99	158	11	11
York C	Tr	02.01	00-01	33	6	1

RICHARDSON Norman
Hamsterley, 15 April, 1915 Died 1991 (FB)

League Club	Source	Date Signed	Seasons Played	Apps	Subs	Gls
Bolton W	Medomsley Jnrs	05.33				
New Brighton	Tr	02.36	35-50	213	-	0

RICHARDSON Paul
Selston, 25 October, 1949 EYth (M)

League Club	Source	Date Signed	Seasons Played	Apps	Subs	Gls
Nottingham F	App	08.67	67-76	199	23	18
Chester	Tr	10.76	76	28	0	2
Stoke C	Tr	06.77	77-80	124	3	10
Sheffield U	Tr	08.81	81-82	35	1	2
Blackpool	L	01.83	82	4	0	0
Swindon T	Tr	07.83	83	7	0	0
Swansea C	Tr	09.84	84	12	0	0

RICHARDSON Paul Andrew
Hucknall, 7 November, 1962 ESemiPro (M)

League Club	Source	Date Signed	Seasons Played	Apps	Subs	Gls
Derby Co	Nuneaton Borough	08.84	84	7	7	0

RICHARDSON Roderick (Rod) Keith
Hunstanton, 1 October, 1942 (IF)

League Club	Source	Date Signed	Seasons Played	Apps	Subs	Gls
Torquay U	Norwich C (Am)	07.62	62-63	7	-	1

RICHARDSON Russell Lee
Sheffield, 21 October, 1964 ESch (FB)

League Club	Source	Date Signed	Seasons Played	Apps	Subs	Gls
Scunthorpe U	YT	08.83	83	2	0	0

RICHARDSON Stanley (Stan)
Harrington, 28 April, 1924 (W)

League Club	Source	Date Signed	Seasons Played	Apps	Subs	Gls
Workington	Frizington	08.51	51	9	-	1

RICHARDSON Steven (Steve) Earl
Slough, 11 February, 1962 (FB)

League Club	Source	Date Signed	Seasons Played	Apps	Subs	Gls
Southampton	App	02.80				
Reading	Tr	07.82	82-92	373	7	3

RICHARDSON Stuart
Leeds, 12 June, 1938 (WH)

League Club	Source	Date Signed	Seasons Played	Apps	Subs	Gls
Queens Park Rgrs	Methley U	11.56	58	1	-	0
Oldham Ath	Tr	07.59	59	22	-	0

RICHARDSON Thomas (Tommy)
Reading, 1 February, 1931 Died 1976 (IF)

League Club	Source	Date Signed	Seasons Played	Apps	Subs	Gls
Middlesbrough		09.52				
Southport	Tr	05.54				
Aldershot	Tr	07.55	55-57	41	-	9

RICHARDSON William (Bill)
Bedlington, 25 October, 1943 (FB)

League Club	Source	Date Signed	Seasons Played	Apps	Subs	Gls
Sunderland	Jnrs	10.60				
Mansfield T	Tr	10.65	65-67	61	2	0
York C	Tr	06.68	68	24	0	0

RICHES Steven (Steve) Alexander
Sydney, Australia, 6 August, 1976 (W)

League Club	Source	Date Signed	Seasons Played	Apps	Subs	Gls
Leyton Orient	Warringah Dolph's (Aus)	09.96	96	2	3	0

RICHLEY Lionel (Len)
Gateshead, 2 July, 1924 Died 1980 (WH)

League Club	Source	Date Signed	Seasons Played	Apps	Subs	Gls
Hartlepools U	Tonbridge	06.51	51-53	72	-	0

RICHMOND Andrew (Andy) John
Nottingham, 9 January, 1983 (G)

League Club	Source	Date Signed	Seasons Played	Apps	Subs	Gls
Chesterfield	Sch	07.02	02-04	7	1	0

RICHMOND John Frederick
Derby, 17 September, 1938 (WH)

League Club	Source	Date Signed	Seasons Played	Apps	Subs	Gls
Derby Co	Derby Corinthians	01.56	57-62	6	-	0

RICKABY Stanley (Stan)
Stockton, 12 March, 1924 FLge-1/E-1 (FB)

League Club	Source	Date Signed	Seasons Played	Apps	Subs	Gls
Middlesbrough	South Bank	07.46	47-49	10	-	0
West Bromwich A	Tr	02.50	49-54	189	-	2

RICKARD Derek Bryan Philip
Plymouth, 1 October, 1947 (F)

League Club	Source	Date Signed	Seasons Played	Apps	Subs	Gls
Plymouth Arg	St Austell	12.69	69-73	101	9	41
Bournemouth	Tr	07.74	74-75	22	10	6

RICKARDS Kenneth (Ken)
Middlesbrough, 22 March, 1929 (CF)

League Club	Source	Date Signed	Seasons Played	Apps	Subs	Gls
Hull C	Middlesbrough A	05.47				
Darlington	Tr	01.50	49	8	-	0

RICKARDS Scott
Sutton Coldfield, 3 November, 1981 (F)

League Club	Source	Date Signed	Seasons Played	Apps	Subs	Gls
Kidderminster Hrs	Tamworth	12.03	03-04	5	12	1

RICKERS Paul Steven
Pontefract, 9 May, 1975 (M)

League Club	Source	Date Signed	Seasons Played	Apps	Subs	Gls
Oldham Ath	YT	07.93	94-01	242	19	20
Northampton T	Tr	07.02	02	8	3	0

RICKETT Horace Francis John
Orsett, 3 January, 1912 Died 1989 (G)

League Club	Source	Date Signed	Seasons Played	Apps	Subs	Gls
Reading	Chelmsford C	06.46	46-47	22	-	0

RICKETT Walter
Sheffield, 20 March, 1917 Died 1991 EB (W)

League Club	Source	Date Signed	Seasons Played	Apps	Subs	Gls
Sheffield U	Aqueduct (Sheffield)	05.39	46-47	57	-	16
Blackpool	Tr	01.48	47-49	42	-	7
Sheffield Wed	Tr	10.49	49-52	95	-	13
Rotherham U	Tr	09.52	52	28	-	4
Halifax T	Tr	08.53	53	31	-	2

RICKETTS Alan
Crawley, 30 October, 1962 (F)

League Club	Source	Date Signed	Seasons Played	Apps	Subs	Gls
Crewe Alex	Wrexham (N/C)	08.81	81	14	3	2

RICKETTS Donovan Damon
Kingston, Jamaica, 7 June, 1977 Jamaica int (G)

League Club	Source	Date Signed	Seasons Played	Apps	Subs	Gls
Bradford C	Village U (Jam)	08.04	04	4	0	0

RICKETTS Graham Anthony
Oxford, 30 July, 1939 EYth (M)

League Club	Source	Date Signed	Seasons Played	Apps	Subs	Gls
Bristol Rov	Jnrs	08.56	56-60	32	-	0
Stockport Co	Tr	07.61	61-63	119	-	6
Doncaster Rov	Tr	07.64	64-67	143	7	16
Peterborough U	Tr	03.68	67-68	46	3	1

RICKETTS Michael Barrington
Birmingham, 4 December, 1978 E-1 (F)

League Club	Source	Date Signed	Seasons Played	Apps	Subs	Gls
Walsall	YT	09.96	95-99	31	45	14
Bolton W	Tr	07.00	00-02	63	35	37
Middlesbrough	Tr	01.03	02-03	12	20	3
Leeds U	Tr	07.04	04	9	12	0
Stoke C	L	02.05	04	1	10	0

RICKETTS Rohan Anthony
Clapham, 22 December, 1982 EYth/Eu20 (M)

League Club	Source	Date Signed	Seasons Played	Apps	Subs	Gls
Arsenal	YT	09.01				
Tottenham H	Tr	07.02	03-04	17	13	1
Coventry C	L	10.04	04	5	1	0
Wolverhampton W	L	03.05	04	3	4	1

RICKETTS Samuel (Sam) Derek
Aylesbury, 11 October, 1981 ESemiPro-4/W-3 (FB)

League Club	Source	Date Signed	Seasons Played	Apps	Subs	Gls
Oxford U	YT	04.00	00-02	32	13	1
Swansea C	Telford U	06.04	04	42	0	0

RICKIS Victor (Vic) Allen Fyfe Mann
Edinburgh, 26 November, 1940 (W)

League Club	Source	Date Signed	Seasons Played	Apps	Subs	Gls
Millwall	Dalkeith Thistle	12.59	60	3	-	1

RIDDICK Gordon George
Langleybury, 6 November, 1943 (M)

League Club	Source	Date Signed	Seasons Played	Apps	Subs	Gls
Luton T	Jnrs	04.61	62-66	101	1	16
Gillingham	Tr	03.67	66-69	114	0	24
Charlton Ath	Tr	11.69	69-70	26	3	5
Orient	Tr	10.70	70-72	13	8	3
Northampton T	Tr	12.72	72-73	28	0	3
Brentford	Tr	10.73	73-76	106	4	5

RIDEOUT Brian James
Bristol, 15 September, 1940 (FB)

League Club	Source	Date Signed	Seasons Played	Apps	Subs	Gls
Bristol Rov	Jnrs	02.59	60	1	-	0

RIDEOUT Paul David
Bournemouth, 14 August, 1964 ESch/EYth/Eu21-5 (F)

League Club	Source	Date Signed	Seasons Played	Apps	Subs	Gls
Swindon T	App	08.81	80-82	90	5	38
Aston Villa	Tr	06.83	83-84	50	4	19
Southampton	Bari (It)	07.88	88-91	68	7	19
Swindon T	L	03.91	90	9	0	1
Notts Co	Tr	09.91	91	9	2	3
Everton	Glasgow Rgrs	08.92	92-96	86	26	29
Tranmere Rov	Shengzhen (China)	07.00	00-01	42	4	6

RIDGE Roy
Sheffield, 21 October, 1934 (FB)

League Club	Source	Date Signed	Seasons Played	Apps	Subs	Gls
Sheffield U	Ecclesfield	11.51	53-60	11	-	0
Rochdale	Tr	08.64	64-65	85	0	0

RIDGEWELL Liam Matthew
Bexleyheath, 21 July, 1984 EYth/Eu21-5 (CD)

League Club	Source	Date Signed	Seasons Played	Apps	Subs	Gls
Aston Villa	YT	07.01	03-04	17	9	0
Bournemouth	L	10.02	02	2	3	0

RIDGWAY Ian David
Reading, 28 December, 1975 (M)

League Club	Source	Date Signed	Seasons Played	Apps	Subs	Gls
Notts Co	YT	07.94	94-96	3	4	0

League Club	Source	Date Signed	Seasons Played	Career Record Apps	Subs	Gls
RIDING Alan						
Preston, 14 March, 1945						(CF)
Exeter C	Colchester U (Am)	07.64	65	1	0	0
RIDINGS David (Dave)						
Farnworth, 27 February, 1970						(M)
Halifax T	Curzon Ashton	01.93	92	21	0	4
Lincoln C	Tr	02.94	93	10	0	0
Crewe Alex	Ashton U	07.95	95	1	0	0
RIDLER David (Dave) George						
Liverpool, 12 March, 1976						(CD)
Wrexham	Rocky's	07.96	96-00	104	12	1
Macclesfield T	Tr	07.01	01-02	53	3	0
Shrewsbury T	Tr	07.03	04	6	3	0
RIDLEY David (Dave) George Henry						
Pontypridd, 16 December, 1916 Died 1998						(CF)
Millwall	Bedford T	01.45				
Brighton & Hove A	Tr	07.46	46	5	-	0
RIDLEY John						
Consett, 27 April, 1952						(CD)
Port Vale	Sheffield Univ	08.73	73-78	149	7	3
Leicester C	Tr	10.78	78	17	7	0
Chesterfield	Tr	08.79	79-81	121	3	8
Port Vale	Tr	08.82	82-84	105	9	5
RIDLEY Lee						
Scunthorpe, 5 December, 1981						(FB)
Scunthorpe U	YT	07.01	00-04	70	9	1
RIDLEY Robert (Bob) Michael						
Reading, 30 May, 1942						(W)
Portsmouth	Jnrs	06.60				
Gillingham	Tr	07.61	61-66	71	2	8
RIDYARD Alfred (Alf)						
Cudworth, 5 March, 1908 Died 1981						(CD)
Barnsley	Shafton	08.28	30-31	21	-	3
West Bromwich A	Tr	06.32	32-36	31	-	0
Queens Park Rgrs	Tr	03.38	37-47	28	-	0
RIEDLE Karl-Heinz						
Weiler, Germany, 16 September, 1965 GeYth/Geu21/Ge-42						(F)
Liverpool	Bor Dortmund (Ger)	08.97	97-99	34	26	11
Fulham	Tr	09.99	99-00	16	19	6
RIEPER Marc Jensen						
Rodoure, Denmark, 5 June, 1968 Denmark int						(CD)
West Ham U	Brondby (Den)	12.94	94-97	83	7	5
RIGBY Anthony (Tony) Angelo						
Ormskirk, 10 August, 1972						(M)
Crewe Alex	YT	05.90				
Bury	Barrow	01.93	92-98	120	46	19
Scarborough	L	02.97	96	5	0	1
Shrewsbury T	Tr	09.99	99	4	4	1
RIGBY Edward (Eddie)						
Atherton, 20 April, 1925						(WH)
Manchester C		02.48				
Barrow	Tr	07.49	49	19	-	0
RIGBY Ernest (Ernie)						
Kirkham, 8 April, 1928 Died 1999						(FB)
Accrington St	Blackpool (Am)	02.51	50-51	10	-	0
RIGBY Jack						
Golborne, 29 July, 1924 Died 1997						(CD)
Manchester C	Bryn Boys Brigade	12.46	46-52	100	-	0
RIGBY Jonathan (Jon) Kendall						
Bury St Edmunds, 31 January, 1965						(F)
Norwich C	App	08.82	83-84	7	3	0
Aldershot	Tr	03.86	85	1	0	0
Cambridge U	Tr	10.86	86-87	28	3	5
RIGBY Norman						
Warsop, 23 May, 1923 Died 2001						(CD)
Notts Co	Ransome & Marles	09.44	47-50	46	-	0
Peterborough U	Tr	07.51	60-61	55	-	0
RIGBY William (Bill)						
Chester, 9 June, 1921						(G)
Chester	Jnrs	08.46	46	1	-	0
RIGG Thomas (Tommy)						
Bedlington, 20 February, 1920 Died 1995						(G)
Middlesbrough	Ashington	02.39				
Watford	Ashington	06.46	46-48	80	-	0
Gillingham	Consett	08.51	51-55	192	-	0

League Club	Source	Date Signed	Seasons Played	Career Record Apps	Subs	Gls
RIGGOTT Christopher (Chris)						
Derby, 1 September, 1980 EYth/Eu21-9						(CD)
Derby Co	YT	10.98	99-02	87	4	5
Middlesbrough	Tr	01.03	02-04	38	5	4
RIGGS Leslie (Les) John						
Portsmouth, 30 May, 1935						(WH)
Gillingham	Jnrs	06.52	53-57	152	-	3
Newport Co	Tr	06.58	58-60	110	-	3
Bury	Tr	06.61	61	6	-	0
Crewe Alex	Tr	02.63	62-63	67	-	6
Gillingham	Tr	09.64	64-65	17	1	1
RIGOGLIOSO Adriano						
Liverpool, 28 May, 1979 ESemiPro-1						(M)
Doncaster Rov	Morecambe	11.03	03-04	7	22	0
RIIHILAHTI Aki						
Helsinki, Finland, 9 September, 1976 FiYth/Fiu21-2/Fi-59						(M)
Crystal Palace	Valerenga (Nor)	03.01	00-04	121	21	11
RIISE John Arne						
Molde, Norway, 24 September, 1980 NoYth/Nou21-17/No-45						(FB)
Liverpool	AS Monaco (Fr)	07.01	01-04	121	19	19
RILEY Brian Francis						
Bolton, 14 September, 1937						(W)
Bolton W	Jnrs	12.54	56-58	8	-	1
RILEY Christopher (Chris) John						
Rhyl, 19 January, 1939 Died 1983						(IF)
Crewe Alex	Rhyl	03.58	57-63	139	-	46
RILEY David Sydney						
Northampton, 8 December, 1960						(F)
Nottingham F	Keyworth U	01.84	83-86	7	5	2
Darlington	L	02.87	86	6	0	2
Peterborough U	L	07.87	87	12	0	2
Port Vale	Tr	10.87	87-89	75	1	11
Peterborough U	Tr	03.90	89-91	73	11	21
RILEY Glyn						
Barnsley, 24 July, 1958						(F)
Barnsley	App	07.76	74-81	103	28	16
Doncaster Rov	L	12.79	79	7	1	2
Bristol C	Tr	08.82	82-86	184	15	61
Torquay U	L	09.87	87	6	0	1
Aldershot	Tr	10.87	87-88	48	10	5
RILEY Howard						
Wigston, 18 August, 1938 EYth/Eu23-2						(W)
Leicester C	Jnrs	08.55	55-64	193	-	38
Walsall	Tr	01.66	65	24	0	3
Barrow	Atlanta (USA)	07.68	68	21	3	6
RILEY Hughen William						
Accrington, 12 June, 1947						(M)
Rochdale		12.66	67-71	81	8	12
Crewe Alex	Tr	12.71	71-74	116	5	9
Bury	Tr	12.74	74-75	47	4	3
Bournemouth	Tr	04.76	76-77	69	3	7
RILEY Ian Michael						
Tollesbury, 8 February, 1947						(FB)
Southend U	Maldon T	11.67	67-68	3	1	0
RILEY Joseph (Joe)						
Stockton						(IF)
Darlington (Am)	Stockton	08.49	49	8	-	2
RILEY Paul Anthony						
Eastwood, 29 September, 1982						(FB)
Notts Co	YT	12.01	01-03	18	10	3
RIMMER Gilbert (Gil) Henry						
Southport, 14 July, 1932						(W)
Southport (Am)	Leyland Road	07.55	55	2	-	0
RIMMER John James **(Jimmy)**						
Southport, 10 February, 1948 E-1						(G)
Manchester U	App	05.65	67-72	34	0	0
Swansea C	L	10.73	73	17	0	0
Arsenal	Tr	02.74	73-76	124	0	0
Aston Villa	Tr	08.77	77-82	229	0	0
Swansea C	Tr	08.83	83-85	66	0	0
RIMMER Neill						
Liverpool, 13 November, 1967 ESch/EYth						(M)
Everton	App	04.84	84	0	1	0
Ipswich T	Tr	08.85	85-87	19	3	3
Wigan Ath	Tr	07.88	88-95	184	6	10

RIMMER Raymond (Ray)
Southport, 6 August, 1938 (W)

League Club	Source	Date Signed	Seasons Played	Apps	Subs	Gls
Southport (Am)	Formby Dons	08.55	55-57	8	-	0

RIMMER Stephen (Steve) Anthony
Liverpool, 23 May, 1979 (CD)

League Club	Source	Date Signed	Seasons Played	Apps	Subs	Gls
Manchester C	YT	05.96				
Port Vale	Tr	07.99	99	0	2	0

RIMMER Stuart Alan
Southport, 12 October, 1964 EYth (F)

League Club	Source	Date Signed	Seasons Played	Apps	Subs	Gls
Everton	App	10.82	81-83	3	0	0
Chester C	Tr	01.85	84-87	110	4	67
Watford	Tr	03.88	87-88	10	0	1
Notts Co	Tr	11.88	88	3	1	2
Walsall	Tr	02.89	88-90	85	3	31
Barnsley	Tr	03.91	90	10	5	1
Chester C	Tr	08.91	91-97	213	33	67
Rochdale	L	09.94	94	3	0	0
Preston NE	L	12.94	94	0	2	0

RIMMER Warwick Robert
Birkenhead, 1 March, 1941 ESch (CD)

League Club	Source	Date Signed	Seasons Played	Apps	Subs	Gls
Bolton W	Jnrs	03.58	60-74	462	7	17
Crewe Alex	Tr	03.75	74-78	114	14	0

RIMMINGTON Norman
Staincross, 29 November, 1923 (G)

League Club	Source	Date Signed	Seasons Played	Apps	Subs	Gls
Barnsley	Mapplewell T	02.45	46	27	-	0
Hartlepools U	Tr	12.47	47-51	124	-	0

RING Michael (Mike) Paul
Brighton, 13 February, 1961 (W)

League Club	Source	Date Signed	Seasons Played	Apps	Subs	Gls
Brighton & Hove A	App	02.79	81-83	1	4	0
Hull C	Ballymena U	07.84	84-85	17	7	2
Bolton W	L	03.86	85	1	2	0
Aldershot	Tr	07.86	86-88	53	26	16

RING Thomas (Tommy)
Glasgow, 8 August, 1930 Died 1997 SLge-8/S-12 (W)

League Club	Source	Date Signed	Seasons Played	Apps	Subs	Gls
Everton	Clyde	01.60	59-60	27	-	6
Barnsley	Tr	11.61	61-62	21	-	1

RINGER Walter Albert
Stanley, West Yorkshire, 7 October, 1941 (W)

League Club	Source	Date Signed	Seasons Played	Apps	Subs	Gls
Halifax T		12.59	59-60	6	-	0

RINGSTEAD Alfred (Alf)
Dublin, 14 October, 1927 Died 2000 IR-20 (W)

League Club	Source	Date Signed	Seasons Played	Apps	Subs	Gls
Sheffield U	Northwich Vic	11.50	50-58	247	-	101
Mansfield T	Tr	07.59	59	27	-	3

RINTANEN Mauno Olavi
Helsinki, Finland, 28 April, 1925 (G)

League Club	Source	Date Signed	Seasons Played	Apps	Subs	Gls
Hull C (Am)	HJK Helsinki (Fin)	09.56	56	4	-	0

RIOCH Bruce David
Aldershot, 6 September, 1947 S-24 (M)

League Club	Source	Date Signed	Seasons Played	Apps	Subs	Gls
Luton T	App	09.64	64-68	148	1	47
Aston Villa	Tr	07.69	69-73	149	5	34
Derby Co	Tr	02.74	73-76	106	0	34
Everton	Tr	12.76	76-77	30	0	3
Derby Co	Tr	11.77	77-79	40	1	4
Birmingham C	L	12.78	78	3	0	0
Sheffield U	L	03.79	78	8	0	1
Torquay U	Seattle (USA)	10.80	80-83	64	7	6

RIOCH Daniel (Neil) Gordon
Paddington, 13 April, 1951 EYth (CD)

League Club	Source	Date Signed	Seasons Played	Apps	Subs	Gls
Luton T	App	07.68				
Aston Villa	Tr	09.69	69-74	17	5	3
York C	L	02.72	71	0	1	0
Northampton T	L	03.72	71	14	0	4
Plymouth Arg	Tr	05.75	75	3	2	0

RIOCH Gregor (Greg) James
Sutton Coldfield, 24 June, 1975 (FB)

League Club	Source	Date Signed	Seasons Played	Apps	Subs	Gls
Luton T	YT	07.93				
Barnet	L	09.93	93	3	0	0
Peterborough U	Tr	08.95	95	13	5	0
Hull C	Tr	07.96	96-98	86	5	6
Macclesfield T	Tr	07.99	99-00	58	1	6
Shrewsbury T	Tr	03.01	00-01	46	0	2

RIPLEY Andrew (Andy) Ian
Middlesbrough, 10 December, 1975 (W)

League Club	Source	Date Signed	Seasons Played	Apps	Subs	Gls
Darlington	YT	11.93	93	0	2	0

RIPLEY Keith Anthony
Normanton, 10 October, 1954 (FB)

League Club	Source	Date Signed	Seasons Played	Apps	Subs	Gls
Huddersfield T	Gainsborough Trinity	08.78	78	2	3	0
Doncaster Rov	Tr	08.79	79	5	0	0

RIPLEY Stanley Keith
Normanton, 29 March, 1935 (WH)

League Club	Source	Date Signed	Seasons Played	Apps	Subs	Gls
Leeds U	Altofts YMCA	04.52	54-57	67	-	15
Norwich C	Tr	08.58	58	12	-	6
Mansfield T	Tr	11.58	58-59	31	-	5
Peterborough U	Tr	07.60	60-61	82	-	12
Doncaster Rov	Tr	08.62	62-65	123	5	7

RIPLEY Stuart Edward
Middlesbrough, 20 November, 1967 EYth/Eu21-8/E-2 (W)

League Club	Source	Date Signed	Seasons Played	Apps	Subs	Gls
Middlesbrough	App	12.85	84-91	210	39	26
Bolton W	L	02.86	85	5	0	1
Blackburn Rov	Tr	07.92	92-97	172	15	13
Southampton	Tr	07.98	98-01	36	17	1
Barnsley	L	11.00	00	8	2	1
Sheffield Wed	L	03.01	00	5	1	1

RISBRIDGER Gareth John
High Wycombe, 31 October, 1981 (M)

League Club	Source	Date Signed	Seasons Played	Apps	Subs	Gls
Southend U	Yeovil T	07.01	01	0	1	0

RISDON Stanley (Stan) William
Exeter, 13 August, 1913 Died 1979 (WH)

League Club	Source	Date Signed	Seasons Played	Apps	Subs	Gls
Exeter C	St Mary's Majors	10.33	33-35	35	-	1
Brighton & Hove A	Tr	08.36	36-46	23	-	0

RISEBOROUGH Cyril
Doncaster, 22 February, 1933 (W)

League Club	Source	Date Signed	Seasons Played	Apps	Subs	Gls
Swindon T		02.55	54-56	26	-	1

RISETH Vidar
Levanger, Norway, 21 April, 1972 Norway int (F)

League Club	Source	Date Signed	Seasons Played	Apps	Subs	Gls
Luton T	Kongsvinger (Nor)	10.95	95	6	5	0

RISHWORTH Stephen (Steve) Peter
Chester, 8 June, 1980 (M)

League Club	Source	Date Signed	Seasons Played	Apps	Subs	Gls
Wrexham	Jnrs	08.98	98	0	4	0

RISOM Henrik
Vildbjerg, Denmark, 24 July, 1968 Denmark 9 (M)

League Club	Source	Date Signed	Seasons Played	Apps	Subs	Gls
Stoke C	Vejle BK (Den)	08.00	00	9	16	0

RIST Frank Henry
Leyton, 30 March, 1914 Died 2001 (CD)

League Club	Source	Date Signed	Seasons Played	Apps	Subs	Gls
Clapton Orient	Grays Ath	08.32				
Charlton Ath	Tr	06.33	34-46	47	-	1

RITCHIE Andrew (Andy) Timothy
Manchester, 28 November, 1960 ESch/EYth/Eu21-1 (F)

League Club	Source	Date Signed	Seasons Played	Apps	Subs	Gls
Manchester U	App	12.77	77-80	26	7	13
Brighton & Hove A	Tr	10.80	80-82	82	7	23
Leeds U	Tr	03.83	82-86	127	9	40
Oldham Ath	Tr	08.87	87-94	187	30	82
Scarborough	Tr	08.95	95-96	59	9	17
Oldham Ath	Tr	02.97	96-98	14	12	2

RITCHIE David Mark
Stoke-on-Trent, 20 January, 1971 (F)

League Club	Source	Date Signed	Seasons Played	Apps	Subs	Gls
Stoke C	YT	07.89				
Stockport Co	Tr	03.90	89	0	1	0

RITCHIE John (Jack)
Blairhall, 31 March, 1927 (WH)

League Club	Source	Date Signed	Seasons Played	Apps	Subs	Gls
Accrington St	Crossgates Primrose	06.49	49	13	-	0

RITCHIE John
Ashington, 10 April, 1944 EAmat (FB)

League Club	Source	Date Signed	Seasons Played	Apps	Subs	Gls
Port Vale	Whitley Bay	12.65	65-66	50	0	3
Preston NE	Tr	04.67	66-71	94	0	5
Bradford C	Tr	03.72	71-72	20	0	0

RITCHIE John
Paddington, 28 February, 1951 EAmat (F)

League Club	Source	Date Signed	Seasons Played	Apps	Subs	Gls
Arsenal	Slough T	04.72				
Hereford U	Tr	03.74	73-74	19	3	4

RITCHIE John Brough
Auchterderran, 12 June, 1947 (G)

League Club	Source	Date Signed	Seasons Played	Apps	Subs	Gls
Bradford C	Brechin C	07.71	71-73	64	0	0

RITCHIE John Henry
Kettering, 12 July, 1941 FLge-1 (F)

League Club	Source	Date Signed	Seasons Played	Apps	Subs	Gls
Stoke C	Kettering T	06.62	62-66	110	0	64
Sheffield Wed	Tr	11.66	66-68	88	1	34
Stoke C	Tr	07.69	69-74	151	8	71

RITCHIE Paul Michael
St Andrews, 25 January, 1969 (F)

League Club	Source	Date Signed	Seasons Played	Apps	Subs	Gls
Gillingham (L)	Dundee	02.93	92	6	0	3
Gillingham (L)	Dundee	09.94	94	5	0	1

League Club	Source	Date Signed	Seasons Played	Apps	Subs	Gls
RITCHIE Paul Simon						
Kirkcaldy, 21 August, 1975 SSch/Su21-7/SB/S-7						(FB)
Bolton W	Heart of Midlothian	12.99	99	13	1	0
Manchester C	Glasgow Rgrs	08.00	00-01	11	9	0
Portsmouth	L	09.02	02	8	4	0
Derby Co	L	03.03	02	7	0	0
Walsall	Tr	08.03	03	33	0	1
RITCHIE Robert (Bob)						
Glasgow, 1 February, 1920						(IF)
Watford	Rickmansworth	02.48	48	1	-	0
RITCHIE Stephen (Steve) Kilcar						
Glasgow, 17 February, 1954 SSch						(FB)
Bristol C	App	09.71	72	1	0	0
Hereford U	Morton	06.75	75-77	102	0	3
Torquay U	Aberdeen	03.79	78-79	58	0	2
RITCHIE Stuart Arthur						
Southampton, 20 May, 1968						(M)
Aston Villa	App	05.86	86	0	1	0
Crewe Alex	Tr	06.87	87	13	5	0
RITCHIE Thomas (Tommy)						
Bangor, County Down, 10 July, 1930						(IF)
Manchester U	Bangor	12.50				
Reading	Tr	02.53	52-54	18	-	5
Grimsby T	Dartford	08.58	58	1	-	0
Barrow	Tr	12.58	58	16	-	6
RITCHIE Thomas (Tom) Gibb						
Edinburgh, 2 January, 1952						(F)
Bristol C	Bridgend Thistle	07.69	72-80	308	13	77
Sunderland	Tr	01.81	80-81	32	3	8
Carlisle U	L	03.82	81	14	1	0
Bristol C	Tr	06.82	82-84	92	1	25
RITCHIE William (Bill) Saunders						
Dundee, 13 November, 1932						(IF)
Bury	Stirling A	06.57	57-58	13	-	7
Stockport Co	Tr	03.59	58-60	52	-	12
RITSON John Albert						
Liverpool, 6 September, 1949						(FB)
Bolton W	App	09.66	67-77	321	3	9
Bury	Tr	09.78	78-79	41	0	2
RITSON Ledger						
Gateshead, 28 April, 1921 Died 1977						(FB)
Leyton Orient		03.46	46-48	84	-	0
RIVERS Alan Desmond						
Portsmouth, 27 January, 1946						(CD)
Luton T	App	01.64	65-66	25	5	1
Watford	Tr	09.67	67	0	2	0
RIVERS Mark Alan						
Crewe, 26 November, 1975						(W)
Crewe Alex	YT	05.94	95-00	177	26	43
Norwich C	Tr	06.01	01-03	54	20	10
Crewe Alex	Tr	07.04	04	26	8	7
RIX Benjamin (Ben)						
Wolverhampton, 11 December, 1982						(M)
Crewe Alex	YT	02.01	01-03	41	29	2
RIX Graham						
Askern, 23 October, 1957 Eu21-7/EB/E-17						(W)
Arsenal	App	01.75	76-87	338	13	41
Brentford	L	12.87	87	6	0	0
Chelsea	Dundee	05.94	94	0	1	0
RIZA Omer Kerime						
Enfield, 8 November, 1979 Tuu21						(F)
Arsenal	YT	07.98				
West Ham U	Tr	12.99				
Barnet	L	10.00	00	7	3	4
Cambridge U	L	03.01	00	10	2	3
Cambridge U	Tr	08.02	02	43	3	11
RIZZO Nicholas (Nicky) Anthony						
Sydney, Australia, 9 June, 1979 Auu23-8/Au-1						(M)
Liverpool	Sydney Olympic (Aus)	09.96				
Crystal Palace	Tr	07.98	98-99	15	21	1
MK Dons	AC Prato (It)	11.04	04	13	5	2
ROACH Neville						
Reading, 29 September, 1978						(F)
Reading	YT	05.97	96-98	5	11	1
Southend U	Tr	02.99	98-99	13	3	2
Oldham Ath	Eastern Pride (Aus)	03.01	00	0	1	0
Torquay U	Tr	08.01	01	5	7	1
ROAST Jesse						
Barking, 16 March, 1964						(FB)
Maidstone U	Barking	01.87	89-90	31	1	0
ROBB David Thomson						
Broughty Ferry, 15 December, 1947 Su23-3/SLge-3/S-5						(F)
Norwich C	Tampa Bay (USA)	09.78	78	4	1	1
ROBB George						
Finsbury Park, 1 June, 1926 EAmat/FLge-1/EB/E-1						(W)
Tottenham H	Finchley	12.51	51-58	182	-	53
ROBB Ian Alexander						
Doncaster, 1 June, 1955						(CD)
York C	Jnrs	02.73	73-74	4	0	0
ROBB William (Willie) Lawson						
Cambuslang, 23 December, 1927 Died 2002						(WH)
Leyton Orient	Aberdeen	05.50	50	5	-	0
Bradford C	Albion Rov	10.54	54-57	127	-	4
ROBBEN Arjan						
Groningen, Holland, 23 January, 1984 Holland 14						(W)
Chelsea	PSC Eindhoven (Holl)	07.04	04	14	4	7
ROBBINS Gordon						
Barnsley, 7 February, 1936						(WH)
Rotherham U	Wombwell	05.53				
Crewe Alex	Goole T	12.58	58	4	-	0
ROBBINS Robert (Robbie)						
Newton Abbot, 20 September, 1953						(G)
Torquay U	Newton Abbot	08.76	76	19	0	0
ROBBINS Terence (Terry) John						
Southwark, 14 January, 1965 ESemiPro						(F)
Barnet	Welling U	07.95	95	9	6	1
ROBER Hans **Jurgen**						
Gernrode, Germany, 25 December, 1953						(M)
Nottingham F	Chicago (USA)	12.81	81	21	1	3
ROBERT Laurent						
Saint-Benoit, Reunion, 21 May, 1975 FrYth/FrB-4/Fr-9						(M)
Newcastle U	Paris St Germain (Fr)	08.01	01-04	110	19	22
ROBERTS Alan						
Bury, 23 April, 1946						(FB)
Bradford PA	Mossley	11.69	69	15	0	0
ROBERTS Alan						
Newcastle, 8 December, 1964						(W)
Middlesbrough	App	12.82	82-85	28	10	2
Darlington	Tr	09.85	85-87	116	3	19
Sheffield U	Tr	07.88	88-89	31	5	2
Lincoln C	Tr	10.89	89	10	0	0
ROBERTS Albert (Arthur)						
Goldthorpe, 27 January, 1907 Died 1957						(FB)
Southampton	Ardsley Ath	08.29	30-37	156	-	0
Swansea T	Tr	08.38	38	16	-	0
York C	Tr	07.46	46	1	-	0
ROBERTS Andrew (Andy) James						
Dartford, 20 March, 1974 Eu21-5						(M)
Millwall	YT	10.91	91-94	132	6	5
Crystal Palace	Tr	07.95	95-97	106	2	2
Wimbledon	Tr	03.98	97-01	92	9	6
Norwich C	L	01.02	01	4	1	0
Millwall	Tr	08.02	02-03	60	6	3
ROBERTS Anthony (Tony) Mark						
Holyhead, 4 August, 1969 WYth/Wu21-2/WB-2/W-2						(G)
Queens Park Rgrs	YT	07.87	87-97	122	0	0
Millwall	Tr	08.98	98	8	0	0
ROBERTS Benjamin (Ben) James						
Bishop Auckland, 22 June, 1975 Eu21-1						(G)
Middlesbrough	YT	03.93	96-97	15	1	0
Hartlepool U	L	10.95	95	4	0	0
Wycombe W	L	12.95	95	15	0	0
Bradford C	L	08.96	96	2	0	0
Millwall	L	02.99	98	11	0	0
Luton T	L	02.00	99	14	0	0
Charlton Ath	Tr	07.00	02	0	1	0
Reading	L	01.02	01	6	0	0
Luton T	L	08.02	02	5	0	0
Brighton & Hove A	L	01.03	02	3	0	0
Brighton & Hove A	Tr	07.03	03	32	0	0
ROBERTS Brian James						
Windsor, 3 February, 1967						(F)
Reading	App	07.85	84-85	0	5	0

League Club	Source	Date Signed	Seasons Played	Career Record Apps	Subs	Gls

ROBERTS Brian Leslie Ford
Manchester, 6 November, 1955 (FB)

League Club	Source	Date Signed	Seasons Played	Apps	Subs	Gls
Coventry C	App	11.73	75-83	209	6	1
Hereford U	L	02.75	74	5	0	0
Birmingham C	Tr	03.84	83-89	182	5	0
Wolverhampton W	Tr	06.90	90	17	4	0

ROBERTS Christian (Chris) John
Cardiff, 22 October, 1979 WYth/Wu21-1 (F)

League Club	Source	Date Signed	Seasons Played	Apps	Subs	Gls
Cardiff C	YT	10.97	97-99	6	17	3
Exeter C	Tr	07.00	00-01	67	12	18
Bristol C	Tr	03.02	01-04	65	29	20
Swindon T	Tr	10.04	04	18	3	3

ROBERTS Cledwyn
Colwyn Bay, 12 August, 1947 (WH)

League Club	Source	Date Signed	Seasons Played	Apps	Subs	Gls
Wrexham	Glan Conwy	08.65	65	1	0	0

ROBERTS Colin
Castleford, 16 September, 1933 (WH)

League Club	Source	Date Signed	Seasons Played	Apps	Subs	Gls
Bradford PA	Altofts Welfare	05.51	53-55	75	-	0
Bradford C	Frickley Colliery	06.59	59-60	57	-	0

ROBERTS James **Dale**
Newcastle, 8 October, 1956 Died 2003 EYth (CD)

League Club	Source	Date Signed	Seasons Played	Apps	Subs	Gls
Ipswich T	App	09.74	74-77	17	1	0
Hull C	Tr	02.80	79-84	149	4	6

ROBERTS Darren Anthony
Birmingham, 12 October, 1969 (F)

League Club	Source	Date Signed	Seasons Played	Apps	Subs	Gls
Wolverhampton W	Burton A	04.92	92	12	9	5
Hereford U	L	03.94	93	5	1	5
Chesterfield	Tr	07.94	94-95	10	15	1
Darlington	Tr	07.96	96-98	76	20	33
Peterborough U	L	02.98	97	2	1	0
Scarborough	Tr	02.99	98	18	0	3
Exeter C	Tr	07.00	00	3	5	1

ROBERTS David (Dave)
Birmingham, 21 December, 1946 (W)

League Club	Source	Date Signed	Seasons Played	Apps	Subs	Gls
Aston Villa	Jnrs	12.63	65-67	15	1	1
Shrewsbury T	Tr	03.68	67-73	224	6	20
Swansea C	Tr	05.74	74	31	5	1

ROBERTS David Frazer
Southampton, 26 November, 1949 Wu23-4/W-17 (CD)

League Club	Source	Date Signed	Seasons Played	Apps	Subs	Gls
Fulham	App	09.67	68-70	21	1	0
Oxford U	Tr	02.71	70-74	160	1	7
Hull C	Tr	02.75	74-77	86	0	4
Cardiff C	Tr	08.78	78-80	40	1	2

ROBERTS David Gordon
Plymouth, 8 May, 1944 (FB)

League Club	Source	Date Signed	Seasons Played	Apps	Subs	Gls
Plymouth Arg	App	12.61	61-63	11	-	0

ROBERTS Dean
Mexborough, 12 January, 1967 (F)

League Club	Source	Date Signed	Seasons Played	Apps	Subs	Gls
Bolton W	App	01.85				
Exeter C	Tr	07.86	86	23	2	7

ROBERTS Dennis
West Bretton, 5 February, 1918 Died 2001 (CD)

League Club	Source	Date Signed	Seasons Played	Apps	Subs	Gls
Notts Co		08.37				
Bristol C	Tr	05.38	38-53	303	-	2

ROBERTS John **Dilwyn**
Pentre Broughton, 22 July, 1928 Died 2000 (W)

League Club	Source	Date Signed	Seasons Played	Apps	Subs	Gls
Wrexham (Am)	Brymbo Steel Works	04.51	50	1	-	0

ROBERTS Donald (Don) Campbell
Arlecdon, 3 February, 1933 (WH)

League Club	Source	Date Signed	Seasons Played	Apps	Subs	Gls
Workington	Whitehaven	07.52	52-53	21	-	0
Barrow		10.57	57-58	22	-	3

ROBERTS Dudley Edward
Derby, 16 October, 1945 (F)

League Club	Source	Date Signed	Seasons Played	Apps	Subs	Gls
Coventry C	Jnrs	11.63	65-67	11	1	6
Mansfield T	Tr	03.68	67-73	194	6	66
Doncaster Rov	L	02.73	72	7	0	0
Scunthorpe U	Tr	02.74	73-75	56	3	17

ROBERTS Edward (Ted)
Chesterfield, 2 November, 1916 Died 1970 (CF)

League Club	Source	Date Signed	Seasons Played	Apps	Subs	Gls
Derby Co	Glapwell Colliery	04.34	35	4	-	0
Coventry C	Tr	03.37	36-51	211	-	85

ROBERTS Edward (Eddie) John
Liverpool, 16 November, 1947 (G)

League Club	Source	Date Signed	Seasons Played	Apps	Subs	Gls
Tranmere Rov	Harrowby Jnrs	05.67	68-69	8	0	0

ROBERTS Eric
Batley, 16 January, 1921 Died 1985 (W)

League Club	Source	Date Signed	Seasons Played	Apps	Subs	Gls
Halifax T	Altofts Colliery	08.47	47	5	-	1

ROBERTS Frederick (Fred)
Rhyl, 7 May, 1916 Died 1985 (W)

League Club	Source	Date Signed	Seasons Played	Apps	Subs	Gls
Bury	Rhyl	04.38	38-46	12	-	5
Leyton Orient	Tr	11.46	46	18	-	2

ROBERTS Gareth William
Hull, 15 November, 1960 Wu21-1 (W)

League Club	Source	Date Signed	Seasons Played	Apps	Subs	Gls
Hull C	App	11.78	78-90	409	5	47

ROBERTS Gareth Wyn
Wrexham, 6 February, 1978 Wu21-10/WB-1/W-8 (FB)

League Club	Source	Date Signed	Seasons Played	Apps	Subs	Gls
Liverpool	YT	05.96				
Tranmere Rov	Panionios (Gre)	08.99	99-04	232	5	11

ROBERTS Gary Paul Michael
Rhyl, 5 April, 1960 (F)

League Club	Source	Date Signed	Seasons Played	Apps	Subs	Gls
Brentford	Wembley	10.80	80-85	180	7	45

ROBERTS Gary Steven
Chester, 4 February, 1987 EYth (M)

League Club	Source	Date Signed	Seasons Played	Apps	Subs	Gls
Crewe Alex	Sch	07.04	03-04	2	2	0

ROBERTS Geoffrey (Geoff) Michael
Liverpool, 29 December, 1949 (FB)

League Club	Source	Date Signed	Seasons Played	Apps	Subs	Gls
Bolton W	App	01.67	67-69	5	0	0

ROBERTS Glyn Shane
Ipswich, 19 October, 1974 (M)

League Club	Source	Date Signed	Seasons Played	Apps	Subs	Gls
Rotherham U	Norwich C (YT)	07.93	93-94	11	5	1

ROBERTS Douglas **Gordon**
Foleshill, 30 May, 1925 Died 1991 (W)

League Club	Source	Date Signed	Seasons Played	Apps	Subs	Gls
Wolverhampton W	Jnrs	09.42				
Northampton T	Tr	09.45	46-48	57	-	7
Brighton & Hove A	Tr	03.49	48-49	17	-	3
Accrington St	Tr	07.51	51	39	-	11

ROBERTS Gordon Richard
Cardiff, 30 December, 1946 WSch (W)

League Club	Source	Date Signed	Seasons Played	Apps	Subs	Gls
Wolverhampton W	App	01.64				
Bury	Tr	09.65	65	2	0	0

ROBERTS Graham Paul
Southampton, 3 July, 1959 EB/E-6 (CD)

League Club	Source	Date Signed	Seasons Played	Apps	Subs	Gls
Portsmouth	Sholing Sports	03.77				
Tottenham H	Weymouth	05.80	80-86	200	9	23
Chelsea	Glasgow Rgrs	08.88	88-89	70	0	18
West Bromwich A	Tr	11.90	90-91	39	0	6

ROBERTS Griffith Orthin
Blaenau Ffestiniog, 2 October, 1920 (G)

League Club	Source	Date Signed	Seasons Played	Apps	Subs	Gls
Nottingham F	Blaenau Ffestiniog	05.46	46	9	-	0

ROBERTS Harold
Liverpool, 12 January, 1920 (W)

League Club	Source	Date Signed	Seasons Played	Apps	Subs	Gls
Chesterfield	Harrowby Jnrs	08.39	46-48	92	-	9
Birmingham C	Tr	11.48	48-50	34	-	2
Shrewsbury T	Tr	06.51	51-52	70	-	16
Scunthorpe U	Tr	07.53	53-54	17	-	1

ROBERTS Ian Mark
Colwyn Bay, 28 February, 1961 (M)

League Club	Source	Date Signed	Seasons Played	Apps	Subs	Gls
Wrexham	Jnrs	07.79	78-79	2	4	0

ROBERTS Ian Patterson
Glasgow, 28 September, 1955 (FB)

League Club	Source	Date Signed	Seasons Played	Apps	Subs	Gls
Shrewsbury T	App	09.72	71-75	93	3	0
Crewe Alex	Tr	07.76	76-78	89	4	0

ROBERTS Iwan Wyn
Bangor, 26 June, 1968 WSch/WYth/WB-1/W-15 (F)

League Club	Source	Date Signed	Seasons Played	Apps	Subs	Gls
Watford	YT	07.86	85-89	40	23	9
Huddersfield T	Tr	08.90	90-93	141	1	50
Leicester C	Tr	11.93	93-95	92	8	41
Wolverhampton W	Tr	07.96	96	24	9	12
Norwich C	Tr	07.97	97-03	232	46	84
Gillingham	Tr	07.04	04	11	9	3
Cambridge U	L	03.05	04	11	0	3

ROBERTS James (Jimmy) Nicoll
Falkirk, 12 June, 1923 (W)

League Club	Source	Date Signed	Seasons Played	Apps	Subs	Gls
Ipswich T	Dundee	09.49	49-51	73	-	15
Barrow	Tr	07.52	52	11	-	2

ROBERTS Jamie Steven
Doncaster, 11 April, 1974 (M)

League Club	Source	Date Signed	Seasons Played	Apps	Subs	Gls
Doncaster Rov	YT	07.92	92	1	1	0

ROBERTS Jason Andre Davis
Park Royal, 25 January, 1978 Grenada 6 (F)

League Club	Source	Date Signed	Seasons Played	Apps	Subs	Gls
Wolverhampton W	Hayes	09.97				
Torquay U	L	12.97	97	13	1	6
Bristol C	L	03.98	97	1	2	1

League Club	Source	Date Signed	Seasons Played	Apps	Subs	Gls
Bristol Rov	Tr	08.98	98-99	73	5	38
West Bromwich A	Tr	07.00	00-02	75	14	24
Portsmouth	L	09.03	03	4	6	1
Wigan Ath	Tr	01.04	03-04	59	0	29

ROBERTS Jeremy
Middlesbrough, 24 November, 1966 EYth (G)

League Club	Source	Date Signed	Seasons Played	Apps	Subs	Gls
Hartlepool U	Jnrs	12.83	83	1	0	0
Leicester C	Tr	07.84	85	3	0	0
Darlington	Tr	03.87	86-87	29	0	0
Brentford	Tr	09.88	88	5	0	0

ROBERTS John Griffith
Abercynon, 11 September, 1946 Wu23-5/Wu21-1/W-22 (CD)

League Club	Source	Date Signed	Seasons Played	Apps	Subs	Gls
Swansea T	Abercynon Ath	07.64	65-67	36	1	16
Northampton T	Tr	11.67	67-68	62	0	11
Arsenal	Tr	05.69	69-72	56	3	4
Birmingham C	Tr	10.72	72-75	61	5	1
Wrexham	Tr	08.76	76-79	145	0	5
Hull C	Tr	08.80	80	26	0	1

ROBERTS Hopkin **John (Jackie)**
Swansea, 30 June, 1918 Died 2001 WSch/W-1 (FB)

League Club	Source	Date Signed	Seasons Played	Apps	Subs	Gls
Bolton W	Cwmbwrla Jnrs	04.36	37-50	162	-	19
Swansea T	Tr	09.50	50	16	-	1

ROBERTS John Thomas
Cessnock, Australia, 24 March, 1944 Australia int (G)

League Club	Source	Date Signed	Seasons Played	Apps	Subs	Gls
Blackburn Rov	APIA Leichhardt (Aus)	04.66	65	3	0	0
Chesterfield	L	08.67	67	46	0	0
Bradford C	Tr	08.68	68-70	44	0	0
Southend U	Tr	01.71	70-71	47	0	0
Northampton T	Tr	07.72	72	13	0	0

ROBERTS Jonathan (Jon) Wesley
Llwynypia, 30 December, 1968 WYth (G)

League Club	Source	Date Signed	Seasons Played	Apps	Subs	Gls
Cardiff C	YT	11.87	87-88	9	0	0

ROBERTS Kenneth (Ken)
Crewe, 10 March, 1931 (W)

League Club	Source	Date Signed	Seasons Played	Apps	Subs	Gls
Aston Villa	Crewe Villa	08.51	51-53	42	-	7

ROBERTS Kenneth (Ken) Owen
Cefn Mawr, 27 March, 1936 (W)

League Club	Source	Date Signed	Seasons Played	Apps	Subs	Gls
Wrexham (Am)	Jnrs	05.51	51	1	-	0
Aston Villa	Tr	05.53	53-57	38	-	3

ROBERTS Kevin John
Bristol, 25 July, 1955 (G)

League Club	Source	Date Signed	Seasons Played	Apps	Subs	Gls
Swindon T	Welton Rov	03.77	77	1	0	0

ROBERTS Lee John
Market Drayton, 23 March, 1957 (CD)

League Club	Source	Date Signed	Seasons Played	Apps	Subs	Gls
Shrewsbury T	App	01.75	73-77	9	6	1
Exeter C	L	03.77	76	5	2	0
Exeter C	Tr	09.77	77-82	135	9	12

ROBERTS Mark Alan
Northwich, 16 October, 1983 (FB)

League Club	Source	Date Signed	Seasons Played	Apps	Subs	Gls
Crewe Alex	Sch	07.03	04	3	3	0

ROBERTS Maurice Ernest Stanley
Bristol, 5 July, 1922 Died 1993 (W)

League Club	Source	Date Signed	Seasons Played	Apps	Subs	Gls
Brentford		08.46	46	10	-	0

ROBERTS Michael (Mike) John
Birmingham, 21 May, 1960 (M)

League Club	Source	Date Signed	Seasons Played	Apps	Subs	Gls
Shrewsbury T		07.78	78	0	1	0

ROBERTS Neil Wyn
Wrexham, 7 April, 1978 WYth/Wu21-2/WB-1/W-3 (F)

League Club	Source	Date Signed	Seasons Played	Apps	Subs	Gls
Wrexham	YT	07.96	97-99	58	17	17
Wigan Ath	Tr	02.00	99-03	64	61	19
Hull C	L	01.02	01	3	3	0
Bradford C	L	09.04	04	3	0	1
Doncaster Rov	Tr	10.04	04	30	1	6

ROBERTS Owen John
Maerdy, 16 February, 1919 Died 2000 (G)

League Club	Source	Date Signed	Seasons Played	Apps	Subs	Gls
Plymouth Arg		02.38				
Swansea T	Aberaman Ath	10.45	46-47	24	-	0
Newport Co	Tr	08.48	48	7	-	0

ROBERTS Paul
West Ham, 27 April, 1962 (FB)

League Club	Source	Date Signed	Seasons Played	Apps	Subs	Gls
Millwall	App	04.79	78-82	142	4	0
Brentford	Tr	09.83	83-84	61	1	0
Swindon T	(Finland)	09.85	85	25	2	0
Southend U	Tr	07.86	86	38	0	0
Aldershot	Tr	08.87	87	36	3	0
Exeter C	Leytonstone & Ilford	12.88	88	3	0	0
Southend U	Tr	01.89	88-89	53	1	0
Colchester U	Fisher Ath	09.91	92-93	63	0	1

ROBERTS Paul
Bangor, 29 July, 1977 Wu21-1 (F)

League Club	Source	Date Signed	Seasons Played	Apps	Subs	Gls
Wrexham	Porthmadog	12.96	96	0	1	0

ROBERTS Peter
Chesterfield, 21 July, 1955 (W)

League Club	Source	Date Signed	Seasons Played	Apps	Subs	Gls
Chesterfield	Chesterfield Tube (N/C)	09.73	74-75	2	0	0

ROBERTS Peter Lorenga
Sherburn, 16 July, 1925 (CF)

League Club	Source	Date Signed	Seasons Played	Apps	Subs	Gls
Leeds U	Newcastle U (Am)	09.46				
New Brighton	Tr	07.48	48	3	-	0

ROBERTS Philip (Phil) Stanley
Cardiff, 24 February, 1950 Wu23-6/W-4 (FB)

League Club	Source	Date Signed	Seasons Played	Apps	Subs	Gls
Bristol Rov	App	11.68	69-72	174	1	6
Portsmouth	Tr	05.73	73-77	152	1	1
Hereford U	Tr	07.78	78	3	0	0
Exeter C	Tr	02.79	78-81	103	2	0

ROBERTS Robert (Bobby)
Edinburgh, 2 September, 1940 Su23-1/SLge-1 (M)

League Club	Source	Date Signed	Seasons Played	Apps	Subs	Gls
Leicester C	Motherwell	09.63	63-69	225	5	25
Mansfield T	Tr	09.70	70-71	76	4	4
Colchester U	Coventry C (Coach)	07.73	72	0	2	0

ROBERTS Ronald (Ronnie)
Llay, 14 September, 1942 Wu23-2 (W)

League Club	Source	Date Signed	Seasons Played	Apps	Subs	Gls
Wrexham	Jnrs	04.60	59-62	67	-	4
Tranmere Rov	Tr	03.63	62-63	56	-	2

ROBERTS Sean Joseph
Johannesburg, South Africa, 2 January, 1983 (G)

League Club	Source	Date Signed	Seasons Played	Apps	Subs	Gls
Sheffield Wed	Southern Gauteng (SA)	10.01	01	0	1	0

ROBERTS Stanley (Stan)
Wrexham, 10 April, 1921 Died 1995 (CF)

League Club	Source	Date Signed	Seasons Played	Apps	Subs	Gls
Wrexham	Cross Street	09.46	46-47	27	-	10
New Brighton	Tr	07.48	48-50	103	-	25

ROBERTS Stephen (Steve) Wyn
Wrexham, 24 February, 1980 WYth/Wu21-4/W-1 (CD)

League Club	Source	Date Signed	Seasons Played	Apps	Subs	Gls
Wrexham	YT	01.98	99-04	143	7	6

ROBERTS Stuart Ian
Carmarthen, 22 July, 1980 Wu21-13 (W)

League Club	Source	Date Signed	Seasons Played	Apps	Subs	Gls
Swansea C	YT	07.98	98-01	58	34	14
Wycombe W	Tr	10.01	01-03	37	33	4
Swansea C	Tr	02.04	03	8	4	1
Kidderminster Hrs	Tr	08.04	04	4	1	1

ROBERTS Stuart William
Chirk, 25 March, 1967 WYth (G)

League Club	Source	Date Signed	Seasons Played	Apps	Subs	Gls
Stoke C	App	03.85	84	3	0	0

ROBERTS Thomas (Tommy)
Liverpool, 28 July, 1927 Died 2001 (FB)

League Club	Source	Date Signed	Seasons Played	Apps	Subs	Gls
Blackburn Rov	Skelmersdale U	12.51	51-53	6	-	0
Watford	Tr	12.54	54	1	-	0
Chester	Tr	02.56	55	5	-	0

ROBERTS Thomas (Tommy)
Kirkdale, 27 December, 1945 (W)

League Club	Source	Date Signed	Seasons Played	Apps	Subs	Gls
Everton	App	11.63				
Stockport Co	Tr	03.65	64-65	20	0	0
Southport	Tr	07.66	66	4	0	1

ROBERTS Thomas (Tom) Walter George
Reading, 11 June, 1932 (IF)

League Club	Source	Date Signed	Seasons Played	Apps	Subs	Gls
Birmingham C		05.53				
Barrow	Tr	10.55	55-56	40	-	14

ROBERTS Trevor Edwin
Caernarfon, 25 February, 1942 Died 1972 WAmat (G)

League Club	Source	Date Signed	Seasons Played	Apps	Subs	Gls
Liverpool	Liverpool Univ	06.63				
Southend U	Tr	01.66	65-69	171	0	0
Cambridge U	Tr	08.70	70-71	36	0	0

ROBERTS Trevor Lee
Southampton, 9 May, 1961 (CD)

League Club	Source	Date Signed	Seasons Played	Apps	Subs	Gls
Portsmouth	Southampton (App)	02.79	78-79	1	2	0

ROBERTS Walter (Wally)
Wrexham, 23 November, 1917 (CD)

League Club	Source	Date Signed	Seasons Played	Apps	Subs	Gls
Wrexham		08.38	38-47	60	-	1
Bournemouth	Tr	07.48	48-49	15	-	0

ROBERTS William (Bill) Ernest
Flint, 22 October, 1918 Died 1994 (G)

League Club	Source	Date Signed	Seasons Played	Apps	Subs	Gls
Rochdale		04.46	46-48	43	-	0

ROBERTS William (Billy) John
Bradford, 9 April, 1963 (F)

League Club	Source	Date Signed	Seasons Played	Apps	Subs	Gls
Rochdale	Farsley Celtic	11.88	88	1	0	0

ROBERTS Winston
Hartlepool, 5 July, 1939 (IF)

League Club	Source	Date Signed	Seasons Played	Apps	Subs	Gls
Hartlepools U	Caledonians	09.58	58	3	-	0

ROBERTSON Alexander (Sandy)
Edinburgh, 26 April, 1971 Su21-1 (M)

League Club	Source	Date Signed	Seasons Played	Apps	Subs	Gls
Coventry C	Glasgow Rgrs	01.94	93-94	0	4	0

ROBERTSON Alistair (Ally) Peter
Philpstoun, 9 September, 1952 SSch (CD)

League Club	Source	Date Signed	Seasons Played	Apps	Subs	Gls
West Bromwich A	App	09.69	69-85	504	2	8
Wolverhampton W	Tr	09.86	86-89	107	0	0

ROBERTSON David (Dave)
Baillieston, 12 January, 1945 (W)

League Club	Source	Date Signed	Seasons Played	Apps	Subs	Gls
Crewe Alex	Motherwell	07.63	63	11	-	2

ROBERTSON David Alexander
Aberdeen, 17 October, 1968 Su21-7/SB/S-3 (FB)

League Club	Source	Date Signed	Seasons Played	Apps	Subs	Gls
Leeds U	Glasgow Rgrs	06.97	97	24	2	0

ROBERTSON Edward (Eddie) Harold Yeoman
Edinburgh, 19 December, 1935 Died 1981 (FB)

League Club	Source	Date Signed	Seasons Played	Apps	Subs	Gls
Bury	Linlithgow Rose	07.54	56-62	196	-	7
Wrexham	Tr	10.63	63	24	-	0
Tranmere Rov	Tr	07.64	64-68	143	4	1

ROBERTSON George Jenkins
Falkirk, 20 April, 1930 Died 2003 (FB)

League Club	Source	Date Signed	Seasons Played	Apps	Subs	Gls
Plymouth Arg	Gairdoch Jnrs	01.50	50-63	358	-	2

ROBERTSON Graham Stuart
Edinburgh, 2 November, 1976 (F)

League Club	Source	Date Signed	Seasons Played	Apps	Subs	Gls
Millwall	Raith Rov	08.96	96-97	0	2	0

ROBERTSON Gregor Aedan
Edinburgh, 19 January, 1984 Su21-10 (FB)

League Club	Source	Date Signed	Seasons Played	Apps	Subs	Gls
Nottingham F	Heart of Midlothian (Jnrs)	02.01	03-04	25	11	0

ROBERTSON Hugh Scott
Aberdeen, 19 March, 1975 Su21-2 (M)

League Club	Source	Date Signed	Seasons Played	Apps	Subs	Gls
Hartlepool U	Ross Co	01.04	03-04	35	3	6

ROBERTSON James (Jimmy)
Leith, 7 July, 1940 (IF)

League Club	Source	Date Signed	Seasons Played	Apps	Subs	Gls
Newport Co	Aberdeen	07.61	61	29	-	5

ROBERTSON James (Jim)
Gateshead, 24 November, 1969 (FB)

League Club	Source	Date Signed	Seasons Played	Apps	Subs	Gls
Carlisle U	YT	07.88	87-89	10	2	0

ROBERTSON James (Jimmy) Gillen
Cardonald, 17 December, 1944 Su23-4/S-1 (W)

League Club	Source	Date Signed	Seasons Played	Apps	Subs	Gls
Tottenham H	St Mirren	03.64	63-68	153	4	25
Arsenal	Tr	10.68	68-69	45	1	7
Ipswich T	Tr	03.70	69-71	87	0	10
Stoke C	Tr	06.72	72-76	99	15	12
Walsall	Seattle (USA)	09.77	77	16	0	0
Crewe Alex	Tr	09.78	78	32	1	0

ROBERTSON James (Jimmy) Wright
Falkirk, 20 February, 1929 (W)

League Club	Source	Date Signed	Seasons Played	Apps	Subs	Gls
Arsenal	Dunipace Thistle	06.48	51	1	-	0
Brentford	Tr	09.53	53-55	84	-	14

ROBERTSON John Alexander
Irvine, 28 March, 1976 (FB)

League Club	Source	Date Signed	Seasons Played	Apps	Subs	Gls
Oxford U	Ayr U	07.00	00	37	3	0

ROBERTSON John (Jackie) Craig
Aberdeen, 15 July, 1928 (IF)

League Club	Source	Date Signed	Seasons Played	Apps	Subs	Gls
Portsmouth	Ayr U	08.55	55	12	-	4
York C	Tr	06.57	57	17	-	5
Barrow	Tr	08.58	58-61	156	-	47

ROBERTSON John Grant
Edinburgh, 2 October, 1964 Su21-2/SB/S-16 (F)

League Club	Source	Date Signed	Seasons Played	Apps	Subs	Gls
Newcastle U	Heart of Midlothian	04.88	88	7	5	0

ROBERTSON John Neilson
Uddingston, 20 January, 1953 SSch/SYth/S-28 (W)

League Club	Source	Date Signed	Seasons Played	Apps	Subs	Gls
Nottingham F	App	05.70	70-82	374	13	61
Derby Co	Tr	06.83	83-84	72	0	3
Nottingham F	Tr	08.85	85	10	1	0

ROBERTSON John Nicholas
Liverpool, 8 January, 1974 (CD)

League Club	Source	Date Signed	Seasons Played	Apps	Subs	Gls
Wigan Ath	YT	07.92	92-95	108	4	4
Lincoln C	Tr	12.95	95-97	38	2	1

ROBERTSON Archibald Lamond (Lammie)
Paisley, 27 September, 1947 (M)

League Club	Source	Date Signed	Seasons Played	Apps	Subs	Gls
Burnley	Glasgow Benburb	09.66				
Bury	Tr	06.68	68	3	2	0
Halifax T	Tr	02.69	68-72	142	8	20
Brighton & Hove A	Tr	12.72	72-73	42	4	9
Exeter C	Tr	06.74	74-77	132	1	25
Leicester C	Tr	09.77	77	6	1	0
Peterborough U	Tr	08.78	78	12	3	1
Bradford C	Tr	01.79	78-80	41	2	3

ROBERTSON Leonard (Len) Verdun
Middlesbrough, 1 March, 1916 Died 1979 (IF)

League Club	Source	Date Signed	Seasons Played	Apps	Subs	Gls
Watford	Stockton	06.46	46	6	-	2
Hull C	Tr	04.47	46-47	9	-	2
Accrington St	Tr	07.48	48	3	-	0

ROBERTSON Mark William
Sydney, Australia, 6 April, 1977 AuYth/Auu23-5/Au-1 (M)

League Club	Source	Date Signed	Seasons Played	Apps	Subs	Gls
Burnley	Marconi Stallions (Aus)	10.97	97-99	27	9	1
Swindon T	L	08.00	00	4	6	1
Stockport Co	Dundee	01.04	03-04	27	5	1

ROBERTSON Paul
Stockport, 5 February, 1972 (FB)

League Club	Source	Date Signed	Seasons Played	Apps	Subs	Gls
Stockport Co	York C (YT)	08.89	89-90	7	3	0
Bury	Tr	07.91	91-92	8	0	0
Doncaster Rov	Runcorn	10.95	95-96	15	5	0

ROBERTSON Stuart
Glasgow, 29 September, 1959 (W)

League Club	Source	Date Signed	Seasons Played	Apps	Subs	Gls
Burnley	App	07.77	78-81	30	2	0
Exeter C	Tr	03.82	81	5	1	0
Doncaster Rov	Newcastle KBU	10.82	82	25	0	0

ROBERTSON Stuart John
Nottingham, 16 December, 1946 (CD)

League Club	Source	Date Signed	Seasons Played	Apps	Subs	Gls
Nottingham F	Jnrs	08.64				
Doncaster Rov	Tr	07.66	66-71	224	2	8
Northampton T	Tr	05.72	72-78	254	0	24

ROBERTSON Thomas (Tom) Smith
Coventry, 28 September, 1944 (W)

League Club	Source	Date Signed	Seasons Played	Apps	Subs	Gls
Crystal Palace	St Mirren	10.66	66	5	0	0

ROBERTSON William George
Glasgow, 4 November, 1936 (W)

League Club	Source	Date Signed	Seasons Played	Apps	Subs	Gls
Middlesbrough	L Pieter's BC	11.53	54	5	-	2

ROBERTSON William (Bill) Gibb
Glasgow, 13 November, 1928 Died 1973 (G)

League Club	Source	Date Signed	Seasons Played	Apps	Subs	Gls
Chelsea	Arthurlie	07.46	50-59	199	-	0
Leyton Orient	Tr	09.60	60-62	47	-	0

ROBERTSON William (Bill) Harold
Crowthorne, 25 March, 1923 Died 2003 (G)

League Club	Source	Date Signed	Seasons Played	Apps	Subs	Gls
Chelsea	RAF Lossiemouth	10.45	46-47	37	-	0
Birmingham C	Tr	12.48	48-51	2	-	0
Stoke C	Tr	06.52	52-59	238	-	0

ROBERTSON William (Willie) James Tavendale
Montrose, 9 November, 1923 (WH)

League Club	Source	Date Signed	Seasons Played	Apps	Subs	Gls
Preston NE	Montrose Roselea	03.42	46-52	52	-	0
Southport	Tr	07.55	55	28	-	0

ROBINS Ian
Bury, 22 February, 1952 (F)

League Club	Source	Date Signed	Seasons Played	Apps	Subs	Gls
Oldham Ath	App	02.70	69-76	202	18	40
Bury	Tr	07.77	77-78	49	0	5
Huddersfield T	Tr	08.78	78-81	145	11	59

ROBINS Mark Gordon
Ashton-under-Lyne, 22 December, 1969 Eu21-6 (F)

League Club	Source	Date Signed	Seasons Played	Apps	Subs	Gls
Manchester U	App	12.86	88-91	19	29	11
Norwich C	Tr	08.92	92-94	57	10	20
Leicester C	Tr	01.95	94-96	40	16	12
Reading	L	08.97	97	5	0	0
Manchester C	Panionios (Gre)	03.99	98	0	2	0
Walsall	Tr	08.99	99	30	10	6
Rotherham U	Tr	07.00	00-03	84	24	44
Bristol C	L	02.03	02	6	0	4
Sheffield Wed	Tr	12.03	03	14	1	3

ROBINSON Alan
Grantham, 2 December, 1955 (F)

League Club	Source	Date Signed	Seasons Played	Apps	Subs	Gls
Sheffield Wed	App	12.73				
Scunthorpe U	Tr	08.75	75	1	0	0

ROBINSON Albert
Chester, 1 June, 1948 Died 1995 (M)

League Club	Source	Date Signed	Seasons Played	Apps	Subs	Gls
Chester	Jnrs	07.68	67-68	4	1	0

League Club	Source	Date Signed	Seasons Played	Career Record Apps	Subs	Gls
ROBINSON Andrew (Andy) Craig						
Oldham, 10 March, 1966 ESch						(M)
Manchester U	App	03.84				
Burnley	L	10.85	85	5	0	1
Bury	Tr	01.86	85-86	12	7	0
Carlisle U	Tr	03.87	86-87	43	3	3
ROBINSON Andrew (Andy) Mark						
Birkenhead, 3 November, 1979						(M)
Tranmere Rov	Cammell Laird	11.02				
Swansea C	Tr	08.03	03-04	63	11	16
ROBINSON Anthony (Tony)						
Hebburn, 5 November, 1958						(W)
Hartlepool U	Blue Star	09.86	86	1	1	0
ROBINSON Bernard Cecil						
Cambridge, 5 December, 1911 Died 2004						(WH)
Norwich C	King's Lynn	12.31	31-48	360	-	13
ROBINSON Brian Thomas Arthur						
Paddington, 2 April, 1946						(G)
Peterborough U	App	04.64	64-65	8	0	0
ROBINSON Carl Philip						
Llandrindod Wells, 13 October, 1976 WYth/Wu21-6/WB-2/W-21						(M)
Wolverhampton W	YT	07.95	96-01	129	35	19
Shrewsbury T	L	03.96	95	2	2	0
Portsmouth	Tr	07.02	02-03	11	5	0
Sheffield Wed	L	01.03	02	4	0	1
Walsall	L	02.03	02	10	1	1
Rotherham U	L	09.03	03	14	0	0
Sheffield U	L	01.04	03	4	1	0
Sunderland	Tr	03.04	03-04	46	1	5
ROBINSON Colin Roy						
Birmingham, 15 May, 1960						(F)
Shrewsbury T	Mile Oak Rov	11.82	82-87	176	18	41
Birmingham C	Tr	01.88	87-88	34	3	6
Hereford U	Tr	08.89	89-90	41	23	6
ROBINSON Cyril						
Nottingham, 4 March, 1929						(WH)
Blackpool	Mansfield T (Am)	09.49	51-54	22	-	2
Bradford PA	Northwich Vic	06.56	56-58	89	-	3
Southport	Tr	07.59	59	37	-	0
ROBINSON David (Dave)						
Birmingham, 14 July, 1948						(CD)
Birmingham C	App	07.66	68-71	110	2	2
Walsall	Tr	02.73	72-76	164	1	3
ROBINSON David Alan						
Haverton Hill, 14 January, 1965						(CD)
Hartlepool U	Billingham T	08.83	83-85	64	2	1
Halifax T	Tr	08.86	86-88	72	0	1
Peterborough U	Tr	07.89	89-92	95	0	9
Notts Co	Tr	09.92	92-93	3	0	1
ROBINSON David John						
Newcastle, 27 November, 1969						(F)
Newcastle U	YT	06.88	88-91	0	8	0
Peterborough U	L	02.91	90	7	0	3
Reading	Tr	03.92	91	8	0	0
Blackpool	Tr	07.92	92-93	21	5	4
Cambridge U	Bishop Auckland	12.95	95	4	13	1
ROBINSON David Stanley						
Exeter, 6 January, 1937						(W)
Exeter C	Whipton	12.54	57-58	16	-	4
ROBINSON David (Dave) William						
Manchester, 25 November, 1921						(WH)
Shrewsbury T	Manchester U Am)	08.49	50	10	-	0
ROBINSON Edward						
Bywell, 15 January, 1922 Died 1987						(FB)
Gateshead		11.45	46-52	91	-	7
ROBINSON Eric Michael						
Manchester, 1 July, 1935						(IF)
West Bromwich A	Altrincham	03.57	57	1	-	0
Rotherham U	Tr	01.59	58-59	13	-	1
ROBINSON Frederick (Fred) James						
Rotherham, 29 December, 1954						(FB)
Rotherham U	App	01.73	73	4	0	0
Doncaster Rov	Tr	10.75	75-78	111	8	3
Huddersfield T	Tr	08.79	79-80	72	0	2
ROBINSON George Dennis						
Old Swan, 28 May, 1937						(W)
Southport	Unit Construction	02.59	58	2	-	0

League Club	Source	Date Signed	Seasons Played	Career Record Apps	Subs	Gls
ROBINSON George Frederick						
Melton Mowbray, 17 June, 1925 Died 2000						(FB)
Notts Co	Holwell Works	08.44	46	29	-	0
ROBINSON George Henry						
Marlpool, 11 January, 1908 Died 1963						(IF)
Sunderland	Ilkeston U	04.27	27-30	31	-	8
Charlton Ath	Tr	06.31	31-32	40	-	5
Charlton Ath	Burton T	08.34	34-46	198	-	37
ROBINSON Henry (Harry)						
Southport, 14 September, 1947						(W)
Blackpool	App	01.65				
Southport	Tr	02.66				
Burnley	Tr	09.66				
Newport Co	Tr	11.67	67-68	38	1	3
ROBINSON Herbert						
Padiham, 30 April, 1922						(CF)
Accrington St	Barnoldswick T	12.46	46	5	-	4
ROBINSON Ian Brendan						
Nottingham, 25 August, 1978						(M)
Mansfield T	YT	07.96	95-96	7	10	1
ROBINSON Jake David						
Brighton, 23 October, 1986						(M)
Brighton & Hove A	Sch	12.03	03-04	2	17	1
ROBINSON James Gilbert						
Whiston, 18 September, 1982						(M)
Crewe Alex	YT	11.01	02-03	1	9	1
ROBINSON Jamie						
Liverpool, 26 February, 1972						(CD)
Liverpool	YT	06.90				
Barnsley	Tr	07.92	92-93	8	1	0
Carlisle U	Tr	01.94	93-96	46	11	4
Torquay U	Tr	07.97	97-98	75	0	1
Exeter C	Tr	09.99	99	11	1	0
Chester C	Tr	01.00	99	9	0	0
ROBINSON John						
Lurgan, 2 April, 1920 Died 1981						(WH)
Wolverhampton W	Glenavon	01.42				
Walsall	Tr	03.47	46-47	5	-	0
ROBINSON John (Johnny)						
Chorley, 18 April, 1936						(W)
Bury	Leyland Motors	09.54	54-59	120	-	21
Oldham Ath	Tr	07.61	61	3	-	0
ROBINSON John						
Middlesbrough, 10 February, 1934						(WH)
Middlesbrough	Jnrs	10.51	53-54	3	-	0
Hartlepools U	Horden CW	06.59	59	9	-	0
ROBINSON John (Jackie) Allan						
Shiremoor, 10 August, 1917 Died 1972 FLge-1/E-4						(IF)
Sheffield Wed	Shiremoor	10.34	34-46	108	-	34
Sunderland	Tr	10.46	46-48	82	-	32
Lincoln C	Tr	10.49	49	8	-	5
ROBINSON John (Jack) James						
Oswaldtwistle, 23 April, 1918 Died 1993						(G)
Accrington St	Sacred Heart	05.35	35-36	16	-	0
Manchester C	Tr	04.37	38-46	2	-	0
Bury	Tr	11.46	46	12	-	0
Southend U	Tr	08.47	47	6	-	0
ROBINSON John Robert Campbell						
Bulawayo, Zimbabwe, 29 August, 1971 Wu21-5/W-30						(W)
Brighton & Hove A	YT	04.89	89-92	57	5	6
Charlton Ath	Tr	09.92	92-02	296	36	35
Cardiff C	Tr	07.03	03-04	39	3	3
Gillingham	Tr	10.04	04	2	2	0
ROBINSON Joseph (Joe)						
Morpeth, 4 March, 1919 Died 1991						(G)
Hartlepools U	Hexham Hearts	05.38	38	11	-	0
Blackpool	Tr	07.46	47-48	25	-	0
Hull C	Tr	02.49	48-52	70	-	0
ROBINSON Joseph (Joe)						
Lanchester, 14 November, 1918 Died 1988						(WH)
Norwich C	Ouston U	11.37	46	2	-	0
ROBINSON Keith						
Bolton, 30 December, 1937						(IF)
Oldham Ath		09.58	58-60	40	-	4

ROBINSON Leonard (Len) James
Nottingham, 1 October, 1946 (FB)

League Club	Source	Date Signed	Seasons Played	Apps	Subs	Gls
Notts Co	Nottingham F (Am)	03.64	63-64	4	-	0

ROBINSON Leslie (Les)
Shirebrook, 1 March, 1967 (FB)

League Club	Source	Date Signed	Seasons Played	Apps	Subs	Gls
Mansfield T	Nottingham F (Jnrs)	10.84	84-86	11	4	0
Stockport Co	Tr	11.86	86-87	67	0	3
Doncaster Rov	Tr	03.88	87-89	82	0	12
Oxford U	Tr	03.90	89-99	379	5	3
Mansfield T	Tr	07.00	00-01	80	0	0

ROBINSON Spencer Liam
Bradford, 29 December, 1965 (F)

League Club	Source	Date Signed	Seasons Played	Apps	Subs	Gls
Huddersfield T	Nottingham F (Jnrs)	01.84	83-85	17	4	2
Tranmere Rov	L	12.85	85	4	0	3
Bury	Tr	07.86	86-92	248	14	89
Bristol C	Tr	07.93	93	31	10	4
Burnley	Tr	07.94	94-96	43	20	9
Scarborough	Tr	08.97	97-98	45	20	7

ROBINSON Mark
Guisborough, 24 July, 1981 (FB)

League Club	Source	Date Signed	Seasons Played	Apps	Subs	Gls
Hartlepool U	YT	07.99	00-03	80	5	0

ROBINSON Mark James
Rochdale, 21 November, 1968 (FB)

League Club	Source	Date Signed	Seasons Played	Apps	Subs	Gls
West Bromwich A	App	01.87	85-86	2	0	0
Barnsley	Tr	06.87	87-92	117	20	6
Newcastle U	Tr	03.93	92-93	14	11	0
Swindon T	Tr	07.94	94-01	255	14	4

ROBINSON Mark Jeffrey
Nottingham, 26 November, 1960 (F)

League Club	Source	Date Signed	Seasons Played	Apps	Subs	Gls
Notts Co	Ilkeston T	01.85	84-85	12	14	1

ROBINSON Mark William
Middlesbrough, 22 October, 1961 (M)

League Club	Source	Date Signed	Seasons Played	Apps	Subs	Gls
Middlesbrough	App	10.79				
Hartlepool U	Guisborough T	01.83	82-83	34	1	4

ROBINSON Martin John
Ilford, 17 July, 1957 (F)

League Club	Source	Date Signed	Seasons Played	Apps	Subs	Gls
Tottenham H	App	05.75	75-77	5	1	2
Charlton Ath	Tr	02.78	77-84	218	10	58
Reading	L	09.82	82	6	0	2
Gillingham	Tr	10.84	84-86	91	5	23
Southend U	Tr	07.87	87-88	43	13	14
Cambridge U	Tr	08.89	89	7	9	1

ROBINSON Marvin Leon St Clair
Crewe, 11 April, 1980 ESch (F)

League Club	Source	Date Signed	Seasons Played	Apps	Subs	Gls
Derby Co	YT	07.98	98-02	3	9	1
Stoke C	L	09.00	00	3	0	1
Tranmere Rov	L	11.02	02	1	5	1
Chesterfield	Tr	09.03	03	17	15	6
Notts Co	Tr	09.04	04	1	1	0
Rushden & Diamonds	Tr	11.04	04	0	2	0
Walsall	Tr	12.04	04	4	6	4
Stockport Co	Tr	03.05	04	3	0	0

ROBINSON Matthew (Matt) Adam
Newmarket, 22 March, 1984 (F)

League Club	Source	Date Signed	Seasons Played	Apps	Subs	Gls
Bournemouth	Ipswich T (Sch)	10.03				
Cambridge U	Tr	02.04	03-04	1	6	0

ROBINSON Matthew (Matt) Richard
Exeter, 23 December, 1974 (FB)

League Club	Source	Date Signed	Seasons Played	Apps	Subs	Gls
Southampton	YT	07.93	94-97	3	11	0
Portsmouth	Tr	02.98	97-99	65	4	1
Reading	Tr	01.00	99-01	62	3	0
Oxford U	Tr	07.02	02-04	127	0	4

ROBINSON Maurice
Newark, 9 November, 1929 (W)

League Club	Source	Date Signed	Seasons Played	Apps	Subs	Gls
Leeds U		04.49				
Doncaster Rov	Gainsborough Trinity	12.52	52-53	19	-	7
Northampton T	Kettering T	06.57	57	11	-	2

ROBINSON Michael (Mike) Anthony
Sunderland, 30 October, 1968 (FB)

League Club	Source	Date Signed	Seasons Played	Apps	Subs	Gls
Newcastle U	YT	08.87				
Darlington	Tr	07.88	88	0	1	0

ROBINSON Michael John
Leicester, 12 July, 1958 IR-23 (F)

League Club	Source	Date Signed	Seasons Played	Apps	Subs	Gls
Preston NE	App	07.76	75-78	45	3	15
Manchester C	Tr	07.79	79	29	1	8
Brighton & Hove A	Tr	07.80	80-82	111	2	37
Liverpool	Tr	08.83	83-84	26	4	6
Queens Park Rgrs	Tr	12.84	84-86	41	7	5

ROBINSON Neil
Liverpool, 20 April, 1957 (FB)

League Club	Source	Date Signed	Seasons Played	Apps	Subs	Gls
Everton	App	05.74	75-78	13	3	1
Swansea C	Tr	10.79	79-84	114	9	7
Grimsby T	Tr	09.84	84-87	109	0	6
Darlington	Tr	07.88	88	35	2	1

ROBINSON Neil David
Liverpool, 18 November, 1979 (F)

League Club	Source	Date Signed	Seasons Played	Apps	Subs	Gls
Macclesfield T	Prescot Cables	07.02	02-03	2	9	0

ROBINSON Joseph Norman
Middlesbrough, 5 January, 1921 Died 1990 (CD)

League Club	Source	Date Signed	Seasons Played	Apps	Subs	Gls
Middlesbrough	South Bank St Peter's	01.46	46-47	16	-	0
Grimsby T	Tr	06.48	48	5	-	0

ROBINSON Paul
Hampstead, 5 January, 1963 ESch/EYth (FB)

League Club	Source	Date Signed	Seasons Played	Apps	Subs	Gls
Millwall	App	01.80	79-83	56	3	2

ROBINSON Paul
Scarborough, 2 January, 1974 (G)

League Club	Source	Date Signed	Seasons Played	Apps	Subs	Gls
Sheffield Wed	YT	07.92				
Scarborough	Tr	08.93	93	3	1	0

ROBINSON Paul
Seaton Delaval, 25 May, 1983 (F)

League Club	Source	Date Signed	Seasons Played	Apps	Subs	Gls
Tranmere Rov	YT	05.02				
Grimsby T	L	09.04	04	1	1	0

ROBINSON Paul Derrick
Sunderland, 20 November, 1978 (F)

League Club	Source	Date Signed	Seasons Played	Apps	Subs	Gls
Darlington	YT	07.97	95-97	7	19	3
Newcastle U	Tr	03.98	99	2	9	0
Wimbledon	Tr	08.00	00-01	0	4	0
Burnley	L	10.00	00	0	4	0
Grimsby T	L	03.02	01	1	4	0
Grimsby T	L	08.02	02	5	7	1
Carlisle U	L	11.02	02	1	4	1
Blackpool	Tr	03.03	02	5	2	1
Hartlepool U	Tr	07.03	03	19	12	7

ROBINSON Paul James
Nottingham, 21 February, 1971 (F)

League Club	Source	Date Signed	Seasons Played	Apps	Subs	Gls
Scarborough	Bury (YT)	05.89	89	13	7	3
Plymouth Arg	Tr	05.90	90	7	4	3
Hereford U	Tr	06.91	91	7	4	0

ROBINSON Paul Mark James
Barnet, 7 January, 1982 (CD)

League Club	Source	Date Signed	Seasons Played	Apps	Subs	Gls
Millwall	YT	10.00	02-04	26	4	1
Torquay U	L	12.04	04	12	0	0

ROBINSON Paul Peter
Watford, 14 December, 1978 Eu21-3 (FB)

League Club	Source	Date Signed	Seasons Played	Apps	Subs	Gls
Watford	YT	02.97	96-03	201	18	8
West Bromwich A	Tr	10.03	03-04	58	3	1

ROBINSON Paul William
Beverley, 15 October, 1979 Eu21-11/E-12 (G)

League Club	Source	Date Signed	Seasons Played	Apps	Subs	Gls
Leeds U	YT	05.97	98-03	93	2	0
Tottenham H	Tr	05.04	04	36	0	0

ROBINSON Peter
Manchester, 29 January, 1922 Died 2000 (WH)

League Club	Source	Date Signed	Seasons Played	Apps	Subs	Gls
Manchester C	Jnrs	05.40	46	1	-	0
Chesterfield	Tr	10.47	47-48	60	-	0
Notts Co	Buxton	02.50	49-52	82	-	1

ROBINSON Peter
Newbiggin, 4 September, 1957 ESemiPro (CD)

League Club	Source	Date Signed	Seasons Played	Apps	Subs	Gls
Burnley	Jnrs	06.76	76-79	48	7	3
Rochdale	Blyth Spartans	03.85	84	9	3	0
Darlington	Tr	08.85	85-87	110	2	5
Halifax T	L	12.85	85	3	2	0

ROBINSON Peter John
St Ives, 11 April, 1949 (CD)

League Club	Source	Date Signed	Seasons Played	Apps	Subs	Gls
Southend U	Cambridge U	03.69	68-69	1	3	0

ROBINSON Philip (Phil) Brian
Doncaster, 21 November, 1942 Died 1989 (W)

League Club	Source	Date Signed	Seasons Played	Apps	Subs	Gls
Huddersfield T	Montrose Victoria	04.60				
Doncaster Rov	Tr	08.61	61-65	157	0	19
Bradford PA	Tr	07.66	66-68	108	8	8
Darlington	Tr	07.69	69	26	1	4

ROBINSON Philip (Phil) Daniel
Manchester, 28 September, 1980 (CD)

League Club	Source	Date Signed	Seasons Played	Apps	Subs	Gls
Blackpool	YT	01.99	98-99	6	5	0

ROBINSON Philip (Phil) John
Stafford, 6 January, 1967 (CD)

League Club	Source	Date Signed	Seasons Played	Apps	Subs	Gls
Aston Villa	App	01.85	86	2	1	1
Wolverhampton W	Tr	07.87	87-88	63	8	8
Notts Co	Tr	08.89	89-91	65	1	5
Birmingham C	L	03.91	90	9	0	0
Huddersfield T	Tr	09.92	92-93	74	1	5
Northampton T	L	09.94	94	14	0	0
Chesterfield	Tr	12.94	94-95	60	1	17
Notts Co	Tr	08.96	96-97	63	14	5
Stoke C	Tr	06.98	98-99	53	9	2

ROBINSON Raymond (Ray)
Durham, 2 December, 1950 (F)

League Club	Source	Date Signed	Seasons Played	Apps	Subs	Gls
Preston NE	App	12.68	68	2	0	0

ROBINSON Richard (Dicky)
Whitburn, 19 January, 1927 FLge-5 (FB)

League Club	Source	Date Signed	Seasons Played	Apps	Subs	Gls
Middlesbrough	Marsden CW Jnrs	04.45	46-58	390	-	1
Barrow	Tr	06.59	59-62	139	-	0

ROBINSON Robert (Bobby)
Ashington, 23 June, 1921 Died 1975 (G)

League Club	Source	Date Signed	Seasons Played	Apps	Subs	Gls
Sunderland	Newbiggin	02.47	47-51	31	-	0
Newcastle U	Tr	08.52	52	5	-	0

ROBINSON Ronald (Ronnie)
Sunderland, 22 October, 1966 (FB)

League Club	Source	Date Signed	Seasons Played	Apps	Subs	Gls
Ipswich T	SC Vaux	11.84				
Leeds U	Vaux Breweries	11.85	85-86	27	0	0
Doncaster Rov	Tr	02.87	86-88	76	2	5
West Bromwich A	Tr	03.89	88	1	0	0
Rotherham U	Tr	08.89	89-91	86	0	2
Peterborough U	Tr	12.91	91-92	44	3	0
Exeter C	Tr	07.93	93-94	37	2	1
Huddersfield T	L	01.94	93	2	0	0
Scarborough	Tr	08.95	95	1	0	0

ROBINSON Ryan
Kendal, 13 October, 1982 (G)

League Club	Source	Date Signed	Seasons Played	Apps	Subs	Gls
Blackburn Rov	YT	01.02				
Southend U	Tr	07.03	03	2	0	0

ROBINSON Simon William
West Bromwich, 6 April, 1965 (M)

League Club	Source	Date Signed	Seasons Played	Apps	Subs	Gls
Blackpool	Alvechurch	12.90				
Walsall	Alvechurch	12.91	91	0	1	0

ROBINSON Stephen (Steve)
Lisburn, 10 December, 1974 NISch/NIYth/NIu21-1/NIB-4/NI-5 (M)

League Club	Source	Date Signed	Seasons Played	Apps	Subs	Gls
Tottenham H	YT	01.93	93	1	1	0
Bournemouth	Tr	10.94	94-99	227	13	51
Preston NE	Tr	05.00	00-01	6	18	1
Bristol C	L	03.02	01	6	0	1
Luton T	Tr	06.02	02-04	83	11	7

ROBINSON Steven (Steve) Eli
Nottingham, 17 January, 1975 (M)

League Club	Source	Date Signed	Seasons Played	Apps	Subs	Gls
Birmingham C	YT	06.93	94-00	53	28	0
Peterborough U	L	03.96	95	5	0	0
Swindon T	Tr	02.01	00-04	128	14	5

ROBINSON Steven Martin
Sheffield, 14 June, 1964 (M)

League Club	Source	Date Signed	Seasons Played	Apps	Subs	Gls
Chesterfield	App	06.82	81-82	8	1	0

ROBINSON Stuart Alan
Middlesbrough, 16 January, 1959 (W)

League Club	Source	Date Signed	Seasons Played	Apps	Subs	Gls
Newcastle U	App	07.77	77-78	11	1	2
Aldershot	Tr	07.80	80-82	71	6	10

ROBINSON Terence (Terry)
Woodhams, 8 November, 1929 EAmat (CD)

League Club	Source	Date Signed	Seasons Played	Apps	Subs	Gls
Brentford (Am)	Loughborough Coll (Am)	09.54	54-56	35	-	1
Northampton T (Am)	Sutton U	07.57	57	13	-	0

ROBINSON Terence (Terry) Allan Charles
Stewkley, 24 March, 1954 (F)

League Club	Source	Date Signed	Seasons Played	Apps	Subs	Gls
Luton T	App	03.72				
Cambridge U	L	09.72	72	6	0	1
Crewe Alex	Tr	12.72	72-73	7	4	1

ROBINSON Trevor Kymar
Jamaica, 20 September, 1984 (M)

League Club	Source	Date Signed	Seasons Played	Apps	Subs	Gls
Millwall	Sch	01.04	03-04	1	2	0

ROBINSON William (Bill)
Whitburn, 4 April, 1919 Died 1992 (CF)

League Club	Source	Date Signed	Seasons Played	Apps	Subs	Gls
Sunderland	Hylton Colliery Jnrs	04.36	37-38	24	-	14
Charlton Ath	Tr	05.46	46-48	52	-	16
West Ham U	Tr	01.49	48-51	101	-	60

ROBINSON William (Billy)
Manchester, 17 November, 1925 Died 1953 (WH)

League Club	Source	Date Signed	Seasons Played	Apps	Subs	Gls
Stockport Co		08.49	49	9	-	2
Accrington St	Tr	12.50	50-52	96	-	2

ROBINSON Joseph **William (Billy)**
Chester-le-Street, 13 April, 1932 (W)

League Club	Source	Date Signed	Seasons Played	Apps	Subs	Gls
Newcastle U	Jnrs	09.51				
Hartlepools U	West Stanley	07.54	55-57	43	-	11
Gateshead	Tr	08.58	58	22	-	5

ROBLEDO Edward (Ted) Oliver
Iquique, Chile, 26 July, 1928 Died 1970 (WH)

League Club	Source	Date Signed	Seasons Played	Apps	Subs	Gls
Barnsley	Jnrs	04.46	47-48	5	-	0
Newcastle U	Tr	02.49	49-52	37	-	0
Notts Co	Colo Colo (Chile)	09.57	57	2	-	0

ROBLEDO George Oliver
Iquique, Chile, 14 April, 1926 Died 1989 Chile int (CF)

League Club	Source	Date Signed	Seasons Played	Apps	Subs	Gls
Barnsley	Huddersfield T (Am)	04.43	46-48	105	-	45
Newcastle U	Tr	01.49	48-52	146	-	82

ROBLEY Keith
Cockermouth, 3 June, 1944 (W)

League Club	Source	Date Signed	Seasons Played	Apps	Subs	Gls
Workington (Am)	Flimby	08.65	65	2	0	0

ROBSHAW Henry (Harry) William
Edmonton, 10 May, 1927 Died 1990 (WH)

League Club	Source	Date Signed	Seasons Played	Apps	Subs	Gls
Tottenham H	Golders Green	11.48	51	1	-	0
Reading	Tr	02.53	52-53	20	-	1

ROBSON Albert (Bert) Proud
Crook, 14 November, 1916 Died 1990 (CF)

League Club	Source	Date Signed	Seasons Played	Apps	Subs	Gls
Crystal Palace	Godalming	12.34	36-47	85	-	22

ROBSON Benjamin (Benny) Thomas
Gateshead, 3 January, 1922 Died 1999 (FB)

League Club	Source	Date Signed	Seasons Played	Apps	Subs	Gls
Southport	Aberdeen	08.49	49	2	-	0

ROBSON Bryan
Witton Gilbert, 11 January, 1957 EYth/Eu21-7/EB/FLge/E-90 (M)

League Club	Source	Date Signed	Seasons Played	Apps	Subs	Gls
West Bromwich A	App	08.74	74-81	194	4	40
Manchester U	Tr	10.81	81-93	326	19	74
Middlesbrough	Tr	05.94	94-96	23	2	1

ROBSON Bryan (Pop) Stanley
Sunderland, 11 November, 1945 Eu23-2/FLge-1 (F)

League Club	Source	Date Signed	Seasons Played	Apps	Subs	Gls
Newcastle U	Jnrs	11.62	64-70	205	1	82
West Ham U	Tr	02.71	70-73	120	0	47
Sunderland	Tr	07.74	74-76	90	0	34
West Ham U	Tr	10.76	76-78	107	0	47
Sunderland	Tr	06.79	79-80	49	3	23
Carlisle U	Tr	03.81	80-81	48	0	21
Chelsea	Tr	08.82	82	11	4	3
Carlisle U	L	03.83	82	11	0	4
Sunderland	Tr	08.83	83	7	5	3
Carlisle U	Tr	07.84	84-85	10	3	1

ROBSON David Mark
Castle Eden, 5 October, 1966 (M)

League Club	Source	Date Signed	Seasons Played	Apps	Subs	Gls
Hartlepool U		11.86	86	1	0	0

ROBSON James **Donald (Don)**
Winlaton, 5 February, 1934 (CF)

League Club	Source	Date Signed	Seasons Played	Apps	Subs	Gls
Doncaster Rov		07.51				
Gateshead	Tr	09.53	53-56	34	-	11

ROBSON Gary
Chester-le-Street, 6 July, 1965 (M)

League Club	Source	Date Signed	Seasons Played	Apps	Subs	Gls
West Bromwich A	App	05.83	82-92	184	34	28
Bradford C	Tr	07.93	93-95	72	3	3

ROBSON Glenn Alan
Sunderland, 25 September, 1977 (F)

League Club	Source	Date Signed	Seasons Played	Apps	Subs	Gls
Rochdale	Murton	11.96	96-97	0	10	0
Darlington	Durham C	08.03	03	3	3	0

ROBSON James (Jimmy)
Pelton, 23 January, 1939 Eu23-1 (F)

League Club	Source	Date Signed	Seasons Played	Apps	Subs	Gls
Burnley	Jnrs	01.56	56-64	202	-	79
Blackpool	Tr	03.65	64-67	60	4	14
Barnsley	Tr	01.68	67-69	87	0	15
Bury	Tr	08.70	70-72	100	3	3

ROBSON John Dixon
Consett, 15 July, 1950 Died 2004 Eu23-7/FLge-1 (FB)

League Club	Source	Date Signed	Seasons Played	Apps	Subs	Gls
Derby Co	Birtley YC	10.67	67-72	170	1	3
Aston Villa	Tr	10.72	72-77	141	3	1

ROBSON John Douglas
Washington, 20 July, 1942 (CD)

League Club	Source	Date Signed	Seasons Played	Apps	Subs	Gls
Darlington		10.62	62-64	34	-	0

ROBSON Keith
Hetton-le-Hole, 15 November, 1953 (F)

League Club	Source	Date Signed	Seasons Played	Apps	Subs	Gls
Newcastle U	Jnrs	05.71	72-73	14	0	3
West Ham U	Tr	09.74	74-76	65	3	13
Cardiff C	Tr	08.77	77	21	0	5
Norwich C	Tr	02.78	77-80	61	4	13
Leicester C	Tr	09.81	81-82	8	1	0
Carlisle U	L	03.83	82	10	1	4

ROBSON Lancelot (Lance)
Newcastle, 27 December, 1939 Died 1987 (F)

League Club	Source	Date Signed	Seasons Played	Apps	Subs	Gls
Newcastle U	Stannington	10.58				
Darlington	Tr	07.60	60-63	144	-	47
Darlington	Gateshead	07.68	68-69	69	0	18
Hartlepool	Tr	02.70	69	8	0	2

ROBSON Charles Leslie (Les)
South Shields, 1 November, 1931 (W)

League Club	Source	Date Signed	Seasons Played	Apps	Subs	Gls
Hull C	North Hull Jnrs	05.50	51	3	-	1
Darlington	Tr	05.53	53-54	66	-	19
Liverpool	Tr	07.55				
Crewe Alex	Tr	01.56	55	14	-	2

ROBSON Mark Andrew
Newham, 22 May, 1969 (W)

League Club	Source	Date Signed	Seasons Played	Apps	Subs	Gls
Exeter C	App	12.86	86	26	0	7
Tottenham H	Tr	07.87	88-89	3	5	0
Reading	L	03.88	87	5	2	0
Watford	L	10.89	89	1	0	0
Plymouth Arg	L	12.89	89	7	0	0
Exeter C	L	01.92	91	7	1	1
West Ham U	Tr	08.92	92-93	42	5	8
Charlton Ath	Tr	11.93	93-96	79	26	9
Notts Co	Tr	06.97	97-99	26	6	4
Wycombe W	L	10.98	98	1	3	0

ROBSON Matthew (Matt)
Easington, 29 December, 1954 (CD)

League Club	Source	Date Signed	Seasons Played	Apps	Subs	Gls
Sunderland	App	01.72				
Darlington	L	03.75	74	1	0	0

ROBSON Matthew (Matty) James
Spennymoor, 23 January, 1985 (M)

League Club	Source	Date Signed	Seasons Played	Apps	Subs	Gls
Hartlepool U	Sch	03.04	03-04	39	11	3

ROBSON Thomas Raymond (Ray)
Newcastle, 11 August, 1928 (FB)

League Club	Source	Date Signed	Seasons Played	Apps	Subs	Gls
Cardiff C		02.49				
Bradford C	Tr	07.50	50-51	10	-	0
Grimsby T	Tr	06.52	52-54	58	-	2

ROBSON (Sir) Robert (Bobby) William
Sacriston, 18 February, 1933 Eu23-1/FLge-5/E-20 (IF)

League Club	Source	Date Signed	Seasons Played	Apps	Subs	Gls
Fulham	Middlesbrough (Am)	05.50	50-55	152	-	68
West Bromwich A	Tr	03.56	55-61	239	-	56
Fulham	Tr	08.62	62-66	192	0	9

ROBSON Ronald (Ron)
Sunderland, 12 September, 1932 Died 1993 (FB)

League Club	Source	Date Signed	Seasons Played	Apps	Subs	Gls
Gateshead	Albion Sports Club	06.57	57-58	7	-	0

ROBSON Stewart Ian
Billericay, 6 November, 1964 EYth/Eu21-8 (M)

League Club	Source	Date Signed	Seasons Played	Apps	Subs	Gls
Arsenal	App	11.81	81-86	150	1	16
West Ham U	Tr	01.87	86-90	68	1	4
Coventry C	Tr	03.91	90-93	55	2	3

ROBSON Thomas (Tom)
Sunderland, 1 February, 1936 (CD)

League Club	Source	Date Signed	Seasons Played	Apps	Subs	Gls
Sunderland	Jnrs	09.57	58-59	5	-	0
Darlington	Tr	08.60	60	1	-	0

ROBSON Thomas (Tommy) Henry
Gateshead, 31 July, 1944 EYth (W)

League Club	Source	Date Signed	Seasons Played	Apps	Subs	Gls
Northampton T	App	08.61	61-65	73	1	20
Chelsea	Tr	12.65	65	6	1	0
Newcastle U	Tr	12.66	66-68	46	2	11
Peterborough U	Tr	11.68	68-80	440	42	111

ROBSON Trevor
Stoke-on-Trent, 4 January, 1959 (F)

League Club	Source	Date Signed	Seasons Played	Apps	Subs	Gls
Port Vale	App	01.77	75	0	1	0

ROBSON William Henderson
Whitehaven, 13 October, 1931 (IF)

League Club	Source	Date Signed	Seasons Played	Apps	Subs	Gls
Workington	Kells	08.51	51-59	128	-	55
Carlisle U	Tr	11.59	59	12	-	1

ROBY Donald (Don)
Wigan, 15 November, 1933 (W)

League Club	Source	Date Signed	Seasons Played	Apps	Subs	Gls
Notts Co	Orrell Bisphan Meth	02.51	50-60	226	-	37
Derby Co	Tr	08.61	61-62	70	-	6

ROCA Carlos Jose
Manchester, 4 September, 1984 (M)

League Club	Source	Date Signed	Seasons Played	Apps	Subs	Gls
Oldham Ath	Sch	●	03	0	7	0

ROCASTLE Craig Aaron
Lewisham, 17 August, 1981 (M)

League Club	Source	Date Signed	Seasons Played	Apps	Subs	Gls
Chelsea	Slough T	09.03				
Barnsley	L	02.04	03	4	1	0
Lincoln C	L	03.04	03	0	2	0
Sheffield Wed	Tr	02.05	04	9	2	1

ROCASTLE David Carlyle
Lewisham, 2 May, 1967 Died 2001 Eu21-14/EB/E-14 (M)

League Club	Source	Date Signed	Seasons Played	Apps	Subs	Gls
Arsenal	App	12.84	85-91	204	14	24
Leeds U	Tr	08.92	92-93	17	8	2
Manchester C	Tr	12.93	93	21	0	2
Chelsea	Tr	08.94	94-95	27	2	0
Norwich C	L	01.97	96	11	0	0
Hull C	L	10.97	97	10	0	1

ROCCA Jonathan (Jon) Christian
Sheffield, 4 November, 1972 (FB)

League Club	Source	Date Signed	Seasons Played	Apps	Subs	Gls
Scarborough	YT	06.91	91	3	0	0

ROCHA Carlos
Lisbon, Portugal, 4 December, 1974 (F)

League Club	Source	Date Signed	Seasons Played	Apps	Subs	Gls
Bury	Boston (USA)	08.99	99	0	3	0

ROCHE Barry Christopher
Dublin, 6 April, 1982 IRYth (G)

League Club	Source	Date Signed	Seasons Played	Apps	Subs	Gls
Nottingham F	YT	06.99	00-04	10	3	0

ROCHE David
Wallsend, 13 December, 1970 (M)

League Club	Source	Date Signed	Seasons Played	Apps	Subs	Gls
Newcastle U	YT	08.88	88-91	23	13	0
Peterborough U	L	01.93	92	4	0	0
Doncaster Rov	Tr	10.93	93-94	49	1	8
Southend U	Tr	03.95	94	0	4	0

ROCHE John (Johnny) Anthony
Poplar, 18 May, 1932 Died 1988 (CF)

League Club	Source	Date Signed	Seasons Played	Apps	Subs	Gls
Millwall	Margate	06.57	57-58	25	-	14
Crystal Palace	Tr	05.59	59	36	-	11

ROCHE Lee Paul
Bolton, 28 October, 1980 EYth/Eu21-1 (FB)

League Club	Source	Date Signed	Seasons Played	Apps	Subs	Gls
Manchester U	YT	02.99	02	0	1	0
Wrexham	L	07.00	00	41	0	0
Burnley	Tr	07.03	03-04	38	16	2

ROCHE Patrick (Paddy) Joseph Christopher
Dublin, 4 January, 1951 IRu23-1/IR-7 (G)

League Club	Source	Date Signed	Seasons Played	Apps	Subs	Gls
Manchester U	Shelbourne	10.73	74-81	46	0	0
Brentford	Tr	08.82	82-83	71	0	0
Halifax T	Tr	07.84	84-88	184	0	0

ROCHE Stephen Michael
Dublin, 2 October, 1978 IRSch/IRYth (FB)

League Club	Source	Date Signed	Seasons Played	Apps	Subs	Gls
Millwall	Belvedere	10.94	96-98	7	4	0

ROCHFORD William (Bill)
Esh Winning, 23 May, 1913 Died 1984 FLge-1 (FB)

League Club	Source	Date Signed	Seasons Played	Apps	Subs	Gls
Portsmouth	Esh Winning Jnrs	08.31	32-38	137	-	1
Southampton	Tr	07.46	46-49	128	-	0
Colchester U	Tr	07.50	50	2	-	0

ROCKETT Jason
London, 26 September, 1969 (CD)

League Club	Source	Date Signed	Seasons Played	Apps	Subs	Gls
Rotherham U	British Universities	03.92				
Scarborough	Tr	08.93	93-97	171	1	11

ROCKETT Trevor Dennis
Finchampstead, 8 October, 1951 (G)

League Club	Source	Date Signed	Seasons Played	Apps	Subs	Gls
Aldershot	Fleet	07.76	76-77	5	0	0

RODAWAY William (Billy) Vincent
Liverpool, 26 September, 1954 ESch (CD)

League Club	Source	Date Signed	Seasons Played	Apps	Subs	Gls
Burnley	App	09.71	71-80	201	2	1
Peterborough U	Tr	07.81	81-82	80	1	0
Blackpool	Tr	08.83	83	41	0	0
Tranmere Rov	Tr	07.84	84-85	55	3	5
Burnley	Tr	08.86	86	44	0	2

RODDIE Andrew (Andy) Robert
Glasgow, 4 November, 1971 (M)

League Club	Source	Date Signed	Seasons Played	Apps	Subs	Gls
Notts Co	Motherwell	01.97				
Carlisle U	Happy Valley (HK)	08.99	99	1	1	0

RODDOM Joseph (Joe) Norman
Spennymoor, 16 May, 1924 Died 1998 (WH)

League Club	Source	Date Signed	Seasons Played	Apps	Subs	Gls
Chesterfield	Blyth Spartans	01.48				
Darlington	Tr	06.50	50	6	-	0

League Club	Source	Date Signed	Seasons Played	Apps	Subs	Gls
RODGER Graham						
Glasgow, 1 April, 1967 Eu21-4						(CD)
Wolverhampton W	App	•	83	1	0	0
Coventry C	Tr	02.85	85-88	31	5	2
Luton T	Tr	08.89	89-91	27	1	2
Grimsby T	Tr	01.92	91-97	134	12	11
RODGER James (Jim) McPhail						
Cleland, 15 September, 1933						(IF)
Newport Co (L)	St Mirren	02.57	56-57	5	-	1
RODGER Richard John						
Hemsworth, 1 July, 1936						(W)
Halifax T	Jnrs	09.54	54-56	15	-	3
RODGER Simon Lee						
Shoreham, 3 October, 1971						(M)
Crystal Palace	Bognor Regis T	07.90	91-01	242	34	11
Manchester C	L	10.96	96	8	0	1
Stoke C	L	02.97	96	5	0	0
Brighton & Hove A	Woking	10.02	02-03	34	2	2
RODGER William (Willie)						
Dalkeith, 24 June, 1947						(W)
Bradford PA	Newtongrange Star	04.65	65-66	6	2	0
RODGERS Alwyn						
Chesterfield, 29 May, 1938						(FB)
Doncaster Rov		11.56	58	1	-	0
RODGERS Arnold William						
Wickersley, 5 December, 1923 Died 1993						(CF)
Huddersfield T	Wickersley	03.42	46-49	28	-	17
Bristol C	Tr	10.49	49-55	195	-	106
Shrewsbury T	Tr	06.56	56	13	-	3
RODGERS Clifford (Cliff) Frederick						
Rotherham, 3 October, 1921 Died 1990						(FB)
York C	RAF Pocklington	11.45	46	26	-	0
RODGERS David Michael						
Bristol, 28 February, 1952 ESch						(CD)
Bristol C	Jnrs	07.69	70-81	190	2	15
Torquay U	Tr	02.82	81	5	0	1
Lincoln C	Tr	03.82	81	3	0	0
RODGERS Luke John						
Birmingham, 1 January, 1982 ESemiPro-2						(F)
Shrewsbury T	YT	07.00	99-04	122	20	52
RODGERS Mark						
Broxburn, 20 September, 1967						(M)
Preston NE	YT	09.85	85	1	0	0
RODGERSON Alan Ralph						
Easington, 19 March, 1939 ESch						(IF)
Middlesbrough	Jnrs	05.56	58-60	13	-	3
RODGERSON Ian						
Hereford, 9 April, 1966						(FB)
Hereford U	Pegasus Jnrs	07.85	85-87	95	5	6
Cardiff C	Tr	08.88	88-90	98	1	4
Birmingham C	Tr	12.90	90-92	87	8	13
Sunderland	Tr	07.93	93-94	5	5	0
Cardiff C	Tr	07.95	95-96	43	12	1
RODI Joseph (Joe)						
Glasgow, 23 July, 1913 Died 1965						(W)
Grimsby T		04.45				
Rochdale	Boston U	04.46	46	9	-	3
RODIC Alexsander						
Serbia, 26 December, 1979 Slovenia 4						(F)
Portsmouth	NK Gorica (Sl)	01.05	04	1	3	0
RODON Christopher (Chris) Peter						
Swansea, 9 June, 1963						(F)
Brighton & Hove A	Pontardawe	01.83	82	0	1	0
Cardiff C	L	08.83	83	4	0	0
RODON Peter Clive						
Morriston, 5 February, 1945 Died 2000						(CF)
Swansea T	Jnrs	11.62				
Bradford C	Tr	07.64	64-66	60	4	15
RODOSTHENOUS Michael						
Islington, 25 August, 1976						(F)
West Bromwich A	YT	07.95	96	0	1	0
Cambridge U	Tr	10.97	97	0	2	0
[RODRIGO] DE ALMEIDA Juliano Rodrigo						
Santos, Brazil, 7 August, 1976						(F)
Everton (L)	Botafogo (Br)	07.02	02	0	4	0
RODRIGUES Hugo Miguel						
Santa Maria do Feira, Portugal, 22 November, 1979						(CD)
Yeovil T	Pedras Rubras (Por)	08.03	03	23	11	1
RODRIGUES Peter Joseph						
Cardiff, 21 January, 1944 WSch/Wu23-5/W-40						(FB)
Cardiff C	Jnrs	05.61	63-65	85	0	2
Leicester C	Tr	01.66	65-70	138	0	6
Sheffield Wed	Tr	10.70	70-74	162	0	2
Southampton	Tr	07.75	75-76	59	0	3
RODRIGUEZ Bruno						
Bastia, France, 25 November, 1972						(F)
Bradford C (L)	Paris St Germain (Fr)	09.99	99	0	2	0
RODWELL Anthony (Tony)						
Southport, 26 August, 1962						(W)
Blackpool	Colne Dynamoes	08.90	90-94	137	5	17
Scarborough	Tr	12.94	94	6	2	1
Wigan Ath	L	01.95	94	5	0	1
RODWELL James (Jimmy) Richard						
Lincoln, 20 November, 1970						(CD)
Darlington	YT	01.89	88	1	0	0
Rushden & Diamonds	Halesowen T	08.96	01	8	1	0
Boston U	Tr	02.02	02	2	1	0
RODWELL Joseph (Joe)						
Southport, 13 October, 1928						(W)
Accrington St (Am)	Birkdale Ath	09.48	48	2	-	0
ROE John						
Broxburn, 7 January, 1938 Died 1996						(FB)
Colchester U	West Calder	07.58	59	2	-	0
ROE Maurice (Len) Leonard						
Hayes, 11 January, 1932						(WH)
Brentford	Ruislip Manor	05.51	54-56	7	-	0
ROEDER Glenn Victor						
Woodford, 13 December, 1955 EB						(CD)
Orient	App	12.73	74-77	107	8	4
Queens Park Rgrs	Tr	08.78	78-83	157	0	17
Notts Co	L	11.83	83	4	0	0
Newcastle U	Tr	12.83	83-88	193	0	8
Watford	Tr	07.89	89-90	74	4	2
Leyton Orient	Tr	01.92	91	6	2	0
Gillingham	Purfleet	11.92	92	6	0	0
ROFE Dennis						
Epping, 1 June, 1950 Eu23-1						(FB)
Orient	App	02.68	67-72	170	1	6
Leicester C	Tr	08.72	72-79	290	0	5
Chelsea	Tr	02.80	79-81	58	1	0
Southampton	Tr	07.82	82-83	18	1	0
ROFFEY William (Bill) Robert						
Stepney, 6 February, 1954						(FB)
Crystal Palace	App	05.71	72-73	24	0	0
Orient	Tr	10.73	73-83	324	4	8
Brentford	L	03.84	83	13	0	1
Millwall	Tr	08.84	84-85	36	1	2
ROFFI Guido (George) Tomaso Angelo						
Matthewstown, 6 March, 1924 Died 1973						(WH)
Newport Co	Tynte Rov	02.47	46-50	112	-	27
ROGAN Anthony (Anton) Gerard Patrick						
Belfast, 25 March, 1966 NI-18						(FB)
Sunderland	Glasgow Celtic	10.91	91-92	45	1	1
Oxford U	Tr	08.93	93-94	56	2	3
Millwall	Tr	08.95	95-96	30	6	8
Blackpool	Tr	07.97	97-98	10	5	0
ROGAN Leslie (Mike) Michael						
Fleetwood, 29 May, 1948						(G)
Workington	App	08.66	66-76	390	0	0
Stockport Co	Tr	06.77	77-80	73	0	0
Crewe Alex	L	03.79	78	3	0	0
ROGERS Alan						
Liverpool, 3 January, 1977 Eu21-3						(FB)
Tranmere Rov	YT	07.95	95-96	53	4	2
Nottingham F	Tr	07.97	97-01	135	2	17
Leicester C	Tr	11.01	01-03	57	5	0
Wigan Ath	L	12.03	03	5	0	0
Nottingham F	Tr	02.04	03-04	44	1	0
ROGERS Alan James						
Plymouth, 6 July, 1954						(W)
Plymouth Arg	App	07.72	73-78	107	10	5
Portsmouth	Tr	07.79	79-83	154	7	14

League Club	Source	Date Signed	Seasons Played	Apps	Subs	Gls
Southend U	Tr	03.84	83-85	84	3	4
Cardiff C	Tr	08.86	86	25	2	1

ROGERS Alfred (Alf)
Ecclesall, 10 April, 1921 Died 1992 (IF)

League Club	Source	Date Signed	Seasons Played	Apps	Subs	Gls
Sheffield Wed	Birley Carr	06.42	46-49	30	-	8

ROGERS Alfred (Alf) Harper
Willenhall, 17 January, 1920 Died 1981 (FB)

League Club	Source	Date Signed	Seasons Played	Apps	Subs	Gls
Aldershot	West Bromwich A (Am)	05.46	46-53	317	-	5

ROGERS Andrew (Andy)
Chatteris, 1 December, 1956 ESch (W)

League Club	Source	Date Signed	Seasons Played	Apps	Subs	Gls
Peterborough U	Chatteris T	07.76	75-77	25	4	1
Southampton	Hampton	02.80	79-81	0	5	0
Plymouth Arg	Tr	09.81	81-84	159	4	15
Reading	Tr	07.85	85-86	44	0	5
Southend U	Tr	10.86	86-87	40	5	2

ROGERS Darren John
Birmingham, 9 April, 1970 (FB)

League Club	Source	Date Signed	Seasons Played	Apps	Subs	Gls
West Bromwich A	YT	07.88	90-91	7	7	1
Birmingham C	Tr	07.92	92-93	15	3	0
Wycombe W	L	11.93	93	0	1	0
Walsall	Tr	07.94	94-97	48	10	0

ROGERS David (Dave) Raymond
Liverpool, 25 August, 1975 (CD)

League Club	Source	Date Signed	Seasons Played	Apps	Subs	Gls
Tranmere Rov	YT	07.94				
Chester C	Tr	08.95	95-96	18	7	1
Peterborough U (L)	Ayr U	10.00	00	1	2	0
Scunthorpe U	Ayr U	03.01	00	1	0	0
Carlisle U	Portadown	09.01	01	26	1	1

ROGERS Dennis
Chorley, 28 March, 1936 (G)

League Club	Source	Date Signed	Seasons Played	Apps	Subs	Gls
Accrington St	Netherfield	03.59	58	3	-	0

ROGERS Donald (Don) Edward
Paulton, 25 October, 1945 EYth/Eu23-2/FLge-1 (W)

League Club	Source	Date Signed	Seasons Played	Apps	Subs	Gls
Swindon T	App	10.62	62-72	400	0	146
Crystal Palace	Tr	11.72	72-74	69	1	28
Queens Park Rgrs	Tr	09.74	74	13	5	5
Swindon T	Tr	03.76	75-76	11	1	2

ROGERS Edward **Eamonn**
Dublin, 16 April, 1947 IRu23-1/IR-19 (M)

League Club	Source	Date Signed	Seasons Played	Apps	Subs	Gls
Blackburn Rov	App	05.65	65-71	158	6	30
Charlton Ath	Tr	10.71	71-72	37	2	3
Northampton T	L	11.72	72	4	0	1

ROGERS Ehud (Tim)
Chirk, 15 October, 1909 Died 1996 WAmat/WWar2 (W)

League Club	Source	Date Signed	Seasons Played	Apps	Subs	Gls
Wrexham	Oswestry T	05.34	34	11	-	2
Arsenal	Tr	01.35	34-35	16	-	5
Newcastle U	Tr	06.36	36-38	56	-	10
Swansea T	Tr	05.39				
Wrexham	Tr	12.45	46	1	-	0

ROGERS Graham Reginald
Newport, 5 September, 1955 (CD)

League Club	Source	Date Signed	Seasons Played	Apps	Subs	Gls
Newport Co	App	09.73	74	0	4	0
Newport Co	Barry T	08.85	85	6	1	0

ROGERS James (Jimmy) Richard
Wednesbury, 31 December, 1929 Died 1996 (W)

League Club	Source	Date Signed	Seasons Played	Apps	Subs	Gls
Wolverhampton W	Rubery Owen	05.48				
Bristol C	Tr	05.50	50-56	155	-	74
Coventry C	Tr	12.56	56-58	77	-	27
Bristol C	Tr	12.58	58-61	115	-	28

ROGERS John Charles
Liverpool, 16 September, 1950 ESemiPro (F)

League Club	Source	Date Signed	Seasons Played	Apps	Subs	Gls
Port Vale	Wigan Ath	10.76	76	25	1	6
Wigan Ath	Altrincham	08.82	82	4	2	2

ROGERS Kenneth (Kenny) John
Chatham, 21 November, 1954 (W)

League Club	Source	Date Signed	Seasons Played	Apps	Subs	Gls
Gillingham	App	11.72	72-73	11	2	1

ROGERS Kevin Perry
Merthyr Tydfil, 23 September, 1963 WSch/WYth (M)

League Club	Source	Date Signed	Seasons Played	Apps	Subs	Gls
Aston Villa	App	09.81				
Birmingham C	Tr	04.83	83	8	1	1
Wrexham	Tr	07.84	84	30	4	3

ROGERS Kristian Raleigh John
Chester, 2 October, 1980 ESch (G)

League Club	Source	Date Signed	Seasons Played	Apps	Subs	Gls
Wrexham	Chester C (Jnrs)	08.98	99-02	39	1	0

ROGERS Lee Julian
Doncaster, 21 October, 1966 (FB)

League Club	Source	Date Signed	Seasons Played	Apps	Subs	Gls
Doncaster Rov	YT	07.84				
Chesterfield	Tr	08.86	86-97	310	24	1

ROGERS Lee Martyn
Bristol, 8 April, 1967 (CD)

League Club	Source	Date Signed	Seasons Played	Apps	Subs	Gls
Bristol C	App	12.84	84-86	30	0	0
Hereford U	L	03.87	86	13	0	0
York C	L	12.87	87	5	2	0
Exeter C	Tr	06.88	88-90	74	4	0

ROGERS Mark Alvin
Guelph, Ontario, Canada, 3 November, 1975 Canada 7 (CD)

League Club	Source	Date Signed	Seasons Played	Apps	Subs	Gls
Wycombe W	Burnaby Can's (Can)	12.98	99-03	123	16	4

ROGERS Martyn
Nottingham, 26 January, 1960 Died 1992 ESch (FB)

League Club	Source	Date Signed	Seasons Played	Apps	Subs	Gls
Manchester U	App	01.77	77	1	0	0
Queens Park Rgrs	Tr	07.79	79	2	0	0

ROGERS Martyn
Bristol, 7 March, 1955 EYth (FB)

League Club	Source	Date Signed	Seasons Played	Apps	Subs	Gls
Bristol C	App	03.73				
Exeter C	Bath C	07.79	79-84	129	3	5

ROGERS Paul Anthony
Portsmouth, 21 March, 1965 ESemiPro-6 (M)

League Club	Source	Date Signed	Seasons Played	Apps	Subs	Gls
Sheffield U	Sutton U	01.92	91-95	120	5	10
Notts Co	Tr	12.95	95-96	21	1	2
Wigan Ath	L	12.96	96	7	2	3
Wigan Ath	Tr	03.97	96-98	85	6	2
Brighton & Hove A	Tr	07.99	99-02	105	14	15

ROGERS Peter Philip
Bristol, 22 April, 1953 (F)

League Club	Source	Date Signed	Seasons Played	Apps	Subs	Gls
Exeter C	Bath C	02.79	78-83	194	11	39

ROGERS William (Billy)
Ulverston, 3 July, 1919 Died 1974 (WH)

League Club	Source	Date Signed	Seasons Played	Apps	Subs	Gls
Preston NE		08.37				
Blackburn Rov	Tr	06.38	38-47	73	-	24
Barrow	Tr	10.47	47-52	196	-	14

ROGERSON Lee Antony
Darwen, 21 March, 1967 (M)

League Club	Source	Date Signed	Seasons Played	Apps	Subs	Gls
Wigan Ath	Clitheroe	01.90	89-90	1	3	0

ROGET Leo Thomas Earl
Ilford, 1 August, 1977 (CD)

League Club	Source	Date Signed	Seasons Played	Apps	Subs	Gls
Southend U	YT	07.95	95-00	105	15	7
Stockport Co	Tr	03.01	00-01	28	3	1
Reading	L	02.02	01	1	0	0
Brentford	Tr	08.02	02-03	29	0	0
Rushden & Diamonds	Tr	01.04	03	16	1	0
Oxford U	Tr	07.04	04	35	0	2

ROLES Albert (Albie)
Southampton, 29 September, 1921 (FB)

League Club	Source	Date Signed	Seasons Played	Apps	Subs	Gls
Southampton	Jnrs	08.42	48	1	-	0

ROLFE James (Jimmy)
Liverpool, 8 February, 1932 (W)

League Club	Source	Date Signed	Seasons Played	Apps	Subs	Gls
Liverpool	Jnrs	07.52				
Chester	Tr	07.53	53-54	50	-	4
Crewe Alex	Tr	08.55	55-57	101	-	11
Barrow	Tr	07.58	58	12	-	3

ROLLING Franck Jacques
Colmar, France, 23 August, 1968 (CD)

League Club	Source	Date Signed	Seasons Played	Apps	Subs	Gls
Leicester C	Ayr U	09.95	95-96	18	0	0
Bournemouth	Tr	08.97	97	26	4	4
Gillingham	Tr	09.98	98	1	0	0

ROLLINGS Andrew (Andy) Nicholas
Portishead, 14 December, 1954 (CD)

League Club	Source	Date Signed	Seasons Played	Apps	Subs	Gls
Norwich C	App	12.72	73	4	0	0
Brighton & Hove A	Tr	04.74	74-79	168	0	11
Swindon T	Tr	05.80	80	11	1	1
Portsmouth	Tr	05.81	81-82	29	0	1
Torquay U	Tr	08.83	83	2	0	0
Brentford	Tr	11.83	83	1	0	0

ROLLINS Kevin
Halifax, 2 January, 1947 (FB)

League Club	Source	Date Signed	Seasons Played	Apps	Subs	Gls
Halifax T	App	•	64	1	-	0

ROLLO Alexander (Alex)
Dumbarton, 18 September, 1926 Died 2004 SLge-1 (FB)

League Club	Source	Date Signed	Seasons Played	Apps	Subs	Gls
Workington	Dumbarton	06.57	57-59	126	-	3

League Club	Source	Date Signed	Seasons Played	Career Record Apps	Subs	Gls
ROLLO James (Jimmy) Shepherd						
Kildonan, 16 November, 1937						(G)
Oldham Ath	Poole T	05.60	60-62	59	-	0
Southport	Tr	07.63	63	38	-	0
Bradford C	Tr	07.64	64-65	37	0	0
ROLLO James (Jimmy) Stuart						
Wisbech, 22 May, 1976						(FB)
Walsall	YT	05.95				
Cardiff C	Bath C	03.97	96-97	6	9	0
ROLPH Andrew (Andy) John Peter						
Meriden, 28 October, 1969						(W)
Chesterfield	Mile Oak Rov	01.89	88-90	14	22	1
ROLPH Darren Gregory						
Romford, 19 November, 1968 ESch						(FB)
Barnsley	King's Lynn	08.87	87	1	1	0
ROLPH Gary Leslie						
Stepney, 24 February, 1960						(F)
Brentford	App	02.78	76-78	8	4	1
ROMA Dominic Mark						
Sheffield, 29 November, 1985 EYth						(FB)
Sheffield U	Sch	07.04				
Boston U	L	02.05	04	2	0	0
ROMANO Serge						
Metz, France, 25 May, 1964						(FB)
Wolverhampton W	Martigues (Fr)	08.96	96	1	3	0
ROMMEDAHL Dennis						
Copenhagen, Denmark, 22 July, 1978 DeYth/Deu21-15/De-53						(M)
Charlton Ath	PSV Eindhoven (Holl)	07.04	04	19	7	2
ROMO David						
Nimes, France, 7 August, 1978 FrYth						(M)
Swansea C	Guingamp (Fr)	10.00	00-01	31	12	1
[RONALDO] AVEIRO DOS SANTOS Cristiano Ronaldo						
Madeira, Portugal, 5 February, 1985 PorYth/PorU21-15/Por-21						(W)
Manchester U	Sporting Lisbon (Por)	08.03	03-04	40	22	9
RONALDSON Kenneth (Ken)						
Leith, 27 September, 1945						(M)
Bristol Rov	Aberdeen	07.65	65-68	72	4	15
Gillingham	Tr	11.69	69-70	6	0	0
RONSON Brian						
Durham, 7 August, 1935 Died 2003						(G)
Fulham	Willington	03.53	53	2	-	0
Southend U	Tr	08.56	56-58	30	-	0
Norwich C	Tr	08.59	59	1	-	0
Peterborough U	Tr	07.61	61-62	50	-	0
RONSON William (Billy)						
Fleetwood, 22 January, 1957						(M)
Blackpool	App	02.74	74-78	124	4	12
Cardiff C	Tr	07.79	79-81	90	0	4
Wrexham	Tr	10.81	81	31	1	1
Barnsley	Tr	08.82	82-85	111	2	3
Birmingham C	L	11.85	85	2	0	0
Blackpool	Tr	01.86	85	3	0	0
ROOKE Rodney						
Orsett, 7 April, 1970						(FB)
Colchester U	YT	06.88	89	4	0	0
ROOKE Ronald (Ron)						
Carlisle, 12 December, 1926						(W)
Carlisle U (Am)	Carlisle Young Libs	09.49	49	1	-	0
ROOKE Ronald (Ronnie) Leslie						
Guildford, 7 December, 1911 Died 1985 EWar-1						(CF)
Crystal Palace	Woking	03.33	33-36	18	-	6
Fulham	Tr	10.36	36-46	105	-	70
Arsenal	Tr	12.46	46-48	88	-	68
Crystal Palace	Tr	06.49	49-50	45	-	26
ROOKE Steven (Steve) Alan						
Carlisle, 21 September, 1982						(FB)
Carlisle U	YT	06.01	01	0	1	0
ROOKES Philip (Phil) William						
Dulverton, 23 April, 1919 Died 2003						(FB)
Bradford C	Worksop T	10.36	37	11	-	0
Portsmouth	Tr	01.38	38-50	114	-	0
Colchester U	Tr	07.51	51-52	68	-	0
ROOKS Richard (Dickie)						
Sunderland, 29 May, 1940						(CD)
Sunderland	Jnrs	06.57	60-64	34	-	2
Middlesbrough	Tr	08.65	65-68	136	0	14
Bristol C	Tr	06.69	69-71	96	0	4
ROONEY James (Jimmy)						
Dundee, 10 December, 1945						(W)
Peterborough U	Lochee Harp	07.65	65-66	7	0	2
ROONEY Robert (Bob)						
Glasgow, 26 October, 1920 Died 1992 SSch						(CD)
Leyton Orient	Falkirk	05.48	48-50	66	-	2
Workington	Tr	06.51	51	27	-	0
ROONEY Robert (Bobby)						
Cowie, 8 July, 1938						(IF)
Sheffield U	Clydebank	06.58	58-59	15	-	3
Doncaster Rov	Tr	10.62	62	5	-	1
Lincoln C	Tr	01.63	62-63	28	-	3
ROONEY Simon Anthony						
Manchester, 10 July, 1970						(W)
Blackpool	YT	07.88	87-88	4	5	0
ROONEY Thomas (Tommy) Anthony						
Liverpool, 30 December, 1984						(F)
Macclesfield T	Tranmere Rov (Sch)	06.04	04	0	1	0
ROONEY Wayne Mark						
Liverpool, 24 October, 1985 EYth/E-23						(F)
Everton	Sch	02.03	02-03	40	27	15
Manchester U	Tr	08.04	04	24	5	11
ROOST William (Bill) Charles						
Bristol, 22 March, 1924						(IF)
Bristol Rov	Stonehouse	09.48	48-56	177	-	49
Swindon T	Tr	05.57	57-58	18	-	3
ROPER Alan John						
Tipton, 21 May, 1939						(FB)
Walsall		05.59	62-64	53	-	2
ROPER David						
Ilkley, 26 September, 1944 EYth						(G)
Bradford C (Am)	Salts	09.62	62	13	-	0
ROPER Donald (Don) George Beaumont						
Botley, 14 December, 1922 Died 2001 EB/FLge-1						(W)
Southampton	Bitterne Nomads	06.40	46	40	-	8
Arsenal	Tr	08.47	47-56	297	-	88
Southampton	Tr	01.57	56-58	80	-	32
ROPER Ian Robert						
Nuneaton, 20 June, 1977						(CD)
Walsall	YT	05.95	95-04	228	26	2
ROQUE JUNIOR Jose Victor						
Santa Rita do Spaucai, Brazil, 31 August, 1976 Brazil 33						(CD)
Leeds U (L)	AC Milan (It)	09.03	03	5	0	0
ROSARIO Robert Michael						
Hammersmith, 4 March, 1966 EYth/Eu21-4						(F)
Norwich C	Hillingdon Borough	12.83	83-90	115	11	18
Wolverhampton W	L	12.85	85	2	0	1
Coventry C	Tr	03.91	90-92	54	5	8
Nottingham F	Tr	03.93	92-94	25	2	3
ROSCOE Andrew (Andy) Ronald						
Liverpool, 4 June, 1973						(W)
Bolton W	Liverpool (YT)	07.91	93	2	1	0
Rotherham U	Tr	10.94	94-98	184	18	18
Mansfield T	Tr	08.99	99	29	10	2
Exeter C	Tr	07.00	00-02	91	23	11
ROSCOE Philip (Phil)						
Barnsley, 3 March, 1934						(FB)
Barnsley	Jnrs	08.51				
Halifax T	Tr	07.56	56-63	258	-	5
ROSE Andrew Mark						
Ascot, 9 August, 1978						(CD)
Oxford U	YT	07.97	97-98	1	4	0
ROSE Colin James						
Winsford, 22 January, 1972 ESemiPro						(M)
Crewe Alex	YT	04.90	90-91	17	5	1
Macclesfield T	Witton A	08.97	97	15	4	0
ROSE Frederick (Freddy)						
Stannington, 27 March, 1955						(W)
Huddersfield T	App	04.72				
Workington	Tr	07.74	74	0	2	0

ROSE Gordon
Sheffield, 22 March, 1935 (W)

League Club	Source	Date Signed	Seasons Played	Apps	Subs	Gls
Sheffield U		10.56				
Halifax T	Scarborough	07.58	58	8	-	1

ROSE Jack
Sheffield, 26 October, 1921 (FB)

League Club	Source	Date Signed	Seasons Played	Apps	Subs	Gls
Queens Park Rgrs	Peterborough U	03.45	46-47	17	-	0

ROSE James (Jim)
Clayton-le-Moors, 4 March, 1918 Died 1989 (G)

League Club	Source	Date Signed	Seasons Played	Apps	Subs	Gls
Accrington St	Clayton Villa	02.39	38-46	20	-	0

ROSE John
Woolwich, 12 August, 1920 (W)

League Club	Source	Date Signed	Seasons Played	Apps	Subs	Gls
Bournemouth	Salisbury	02.46	46	1	-	0

ROSE Karl Barrie
Barnsley, 12 October, 1978 (F)

League Club	Source	Date Signed	Seasons Played	Apps	Subs	Gls
Barnsley	Jnrs	11.95	98	2	2	0
Mansfield T	L	03.99	98	0	1	0

ROSE Kenneth (Ken)
Eckington, 18 March, 1930 Died 1996 (CF)

League Club	Source	Date Signed	Seasons Played	Apps	Subs	Gls
Chesterfield		11.50				
Exeter C	Tr	06.52	52	11	-	3
Rochdale	Tr	07.53	53	11	-	0
Workington	Tr	06.54	54	6	-	2

ROSE Kevin Philip
Evesham, 23 November, 1960 (G)

League Club	Source	Date Signed	Seasons Played	Apps	Subs	Gls
Lincoln C	Ledbury T	08.79				
Hereford U	Ledbury T	03.83	82-88	268	0	0
Bolton W	Tr	07.89	89-91	10	0	0
Carlisle U	L	03.90	89	11	0	0
Rochdale	L	02.91	90	3	0	0
Rochdale	Tr	11.91	91-92	68	0	0

ROSE Matthew David
Dartford, 24 September, 1975 Eu21-2 (FB)

League Club	Source	Date Signed	Seasons Played	Apps	Subs	Gls
Arsenal	YT	07.94	95-96	2	3	0
Queens Park Rgrs	Tr	05.97	97-04	195	21	8

ROSE Michael Charles
Salford, 28 July, 1982 (FB)

League Club	Source	Date Signed	Seasons Played	Apps	Subs	Gls
Manchester U	YT	09.99				
Yeovil T	Hereford U	05.04	04	37	3	1

ROSE Michael (Mick) John
New Barnet, 22 July, 1943 (G)

League Club	Source	Date Signed	Seasons Played	Apps	Subs	Gls
Charlton Ath	St Albans C	07.63	63-66	75	0	0
Notts Co	Tr	03.67	66-69	109	0	0
Mansfield T	L	08.70	70	3	0	0

ROSE Richard Alan
Pembury, 8 September, 1982 (FB)

League Club	Source	Date Signed	Seasons Played	Apps	Subs	Gls
Gillingham	YT	04.01	00-04	31	13	0
Bristol Rov	L	12.02	02	9	0	0

ROSENIOR Leroy De Graft
Clapton, 24 August, 1964 ESch/EYth/Eu21 (F)

League Club	Source	Date Signed	Seasons Played	Apps	Subs	Gls
Fulham	Jnrs	08.82	82-84	53	1	15
Queens Park Rgrs	Tr	08.85	85-86	27	11	8
Fulham	Tr	06.87	87	34	0	20
West Ham U	Tr	03.88	87-91	44	9	15
Fulham	L	09.90	90	11	0	3
Charlton Ath	L	11.91	91	3	0	0
Bristol C	Tr	03.92	91-93	35	16	12

ROSENIOR Liam James
Wandsworth, 9 July, 1984 EYth/Eu21-2 (FB)

League Club	Source	Date Signed	Seasons Played	Apps	Subs	Gls
Bristol C	YT	08.01	01-02	2	20	2
Fulham	Tr	11.03	04	16	1	0
Torquay U	L	03.04	03	9	1	0

ROSENTHAL Abram (Abe) Wallace
Liverpool, 12 October, 1921 Died 1986 (IF)

League Club	Source	Date Signed	Seasons Played	Apps	Subs	Gls
Tranmere Rov	Liverpool (Am)	01.39	38-46	27	-	8
Bradford C	Tr	04.47	46-48	44	-	11
Tranmere Rov	Tr	08.49	49-51	69	-	24
Bradford C	Tr	01.52	52-53	63	-	32
Tranmere Rov	Tr	07.54	54	21	-	3
Bradford C	Tr	07.55	55	1	-	0

ROSENTHAL Ronny
Haifa, Israel, 11 October, 1963 Israel 60 (F)

League Club	Source	Date Signed	Seasons Played	Apps	Subs	Gls
Liverpool	Standard Liege (Bel)	03.90	89-93	32	42	21
Tottenham H	Tr	01.94	93-96	55	33	4
Watford	Tr	08.97	97-98	25	5	8

ROSLER Uwe
Attenburg, Germany, 15 November, 1968 EGermany 5 (F)

League Club	Source	Date Signed	Seasons Played	Apps	Subs	Gls
Manchester C	FC Nurnberg (Ger)	03.94	93-97	141	11	50
Southampton	Tennis Borussia (Ger)	07.00	00-01	9	15	0
West Bromwich A	L	10.01	01	5	0	1

ROSS Alan
Ellesmere Port, 7 February, 1933 (G)

League Club	Source	Date Signed	Seasons Played	Apps	Subs	Gls
Oldham Ath (Am)	Bishop Auckland	09.56	56	3	-	0
Accrington St	Oldham Ath (Am)	03.59	58	1	-	0

ROSS James **Alan**
Glasgow, 26 May, 1942 Died 1999 (G)

League Club	Source	Date Signed	Seasons Played	Apps	Subs	Gls
Luton T	Hamilton Academical	04.62				
Carlisle U	Tr	06.63	63-78	465	1	0

ROSS Alexander (Alex) Malcolm Cameron
Glasgow, 17 December, 1923 (WH)

League Club	Source	Date Signed	Seasons Played	Apps	Subs	Gls
West Bromwich A	Shawfield Jnrs	10.47				
Crystal Palace	Tr	08.48	48-50	34	-	0

ROSS William **Bernard**
Swansea, 8 November, 1924 Died 1999 (IF)

League Club	Source	Date Signed	Seasons Played	Apps	Subs	Gls
Cardiff C	Towey U	03.43	46-47	8	-	2
Sheffield U	Tr	05.48	48	3	-	1
Southport	Tr	08.49	49-50	47	-	13

ROSS Bryce Thomas
Edinburgh, 4 December, 1927 Died 1969 (IF)

League Club	Source	Date Signed	Seasons Played	Apps	Subs	Gls
Newcastle U	Jnrs	12.43				
Carlisle U		11.46	46-47	3	-	0

ROSS Colin
Dailly, 29 August, 1962 (M)

League Club	Source	Date Signed	Seasons Played	Apps	Subs	Gls
Middlesbrough	App	09.80	80-82	37	1	0
Chesterfield	L	03.83	82	6	0	0
Darlington	Tr	08.83	83-84	14	0	0

ROSS William **Eric**
Belfast, 19 September, 1944 NIu23-1/IrLge-1/NI-1 (M)

League Club	Source	Date Signed	Seasons Played	Apps	Subs	Gls
Newcastle U	Glentoran	08.67	67-68	2	0	0
Northampton T	Tr	08.69	69-71	51	4	5
Hartlepool	L	11.71	71	2	0	0

ROSS George
Inverness, 15 April, 1943 (FB)

League Club	Source	Date Signed	Seasons Played	Apps	Subs	Gls
Preston NE	Hilton Ath	04.60	60-72	384	2	3
Southport	L	11.72	72	4	0	0
Southport	Tr	07.73	73	27	0	0

ROSS George Alfred
Deptford, 1 November, 1920 (WH)

League Club	Source	Date Signed	Seasons Played	Apps	Subs	Gls
Millwall	Metro Gas	01.46				
Carlisle U	Tr	05.47	47	9	-	0

ROSS Ian
Glasgow, 26 January, 1947 (CD)

League Club	Source	Date Signed	Seasons Played	Apps	Subs	Gls
Liverpool	Possilpark YMCA	08.65	66-71	42	6	2
Aston Villa	Tr	02.72	71-75	175	0	3
Notts Co	L	10.76	76	4	0	1
Northampton T	L	11.76	76	2	0	0
Peterborough U	Tr	12.76	76-78	112	0	1
Wolverhampton W	Santa Barbara (USA)	08.79				
Hereford U	(Team Coach)	10.82	82	15	0	0

ROSS John (Jack) James
Falkirk, 5 June, 1976 (FB)

League Club	Source	Date Signed	Seasons Played	Apps	Subs	Gls
Hartlepool U	Clyde	07.04	04	21	3	0

ROSS Louis Alexander Purdie
Dublin, 19 September, 1920 Died 1990 (FB)

League Club	Source	Date Signed	Seasons Played	Apps	Subs	Gls
Walsall	Queen of the South	08.48	48	8	-	0

ROSS Michael (Micky) Patrick
Southampton, 2 September, 1971 ESch (F)

League Club	Source	Date Signed	Seasons Played	Apps	Subs	Gls
Portsmouth	YT	12.88	88-91	0	4	0
Exeter C	Tr	08.93	93-94	27	1	9
Plymouth Arg	Tr	11.94	94	11	6	0
Exeter C	L	11.95	95	7	0	2

ROSS Neil James
West Bromwich, 10 August, 1982 (F)

League Club	Source	Date Signed	Seasons Played	Apps	Subs	Gls
Leeds U	YT	08.99				
Stockport Co	Tr	01.00	99-02	3	6	2
Bristol Rov	L	10.01	01	2	3	0
Macclesfield T	Tr	01.03	02-03	7	7	0

ROSS Robert (Bobby)
Glasgow, 2 February, 1917 Died 1994 (WH)

League Club	Source	Date Signed	Seasons Played	Apps	Subs	Gls
Watford	Dumbarton	07.46	46	33	-	6

ROSS Robert (Bobby) Alexander
Wishaw, 25 May, 1927 Died 1992 (FB)

League Club	Source	Date Signed	Seasons Played	Apps	Subs	Gls
Leeds U	Workington	08.50	51	5	-	0
Stockport Co	Tr	06.54	54	9	-	0

ROSS Robert (Bobby) Cochrane
Edinburgh, 9 September, 1941 (M)

League Club	Source	Date Signed	Seasons Played	Apps	Subs	Gls
Grimsby T	St Mirren	06.65	65-70	208	4	18

ROSS Robert (Bobby) Herdman
Edinburgh, 18 May, 1942 (M)

League Club	Source	Date Signed	Seasons Played	Apps	Subs	Gls
Shrewsbury T	Heart of Midlothian	06.63	63-65	99	0	29
Brentford	Tr	03.66	65-72	288	4	58
Cambridge U	Tr	10.72	72-73	57	8	14

ROSS Robert Russell
Cowdenbeath, 13 December, 1925 Died 1984 (CD)

League Club	Source	Date Signed	Seasons Played	Apps	Subs	Gls
Millwall	Dundee U	08.52	52	1	-	0

ROSS Stewart
Woking, 11 September, 1945 (M)

League Club	Source	Date Signed	Seasons Played	Apps	Subs	Gls
Wolverhampton W		11.65	67-68	1	2	0

ROSS Thomas (Tommy)
Tain, 27 February, 1947 (M)

League Club	Source	Date Signed	Seasons Played	Apps	Subs	Gls
Peterborough U	Lochee Harp	07.65	65-66	5	2	2
York C	Tr	06.67	67-68	56	5	20

ROSS Trevor William
Ashton-under-Lyne, 16 January, 1957 ESch/Su21-1 (M)

League Club	Source	Date Signed	Seasons Played	Apps	Subs	Gls
Arsenal	App	06.74	74-77	57	1	5
Everton	Tr	11.77	77-82	120	4	16
Portsmouth	L	10.82	82	5	0	0
Sheffield U	L	12.82	82	4	0	0
Sheffield U	AEK Athens (Gre)	01.84	83	4	0	0
Bury	Tr	08.84	84-86	96	2	11

ROSS William
Glasgow, 2 May, 1919 Died 1990 (CF)

League Club	Source	Date Signed	Seasons Played	Apps	Subs	Gls
Bradford C	Arbroath	07.50	50	4	-	2

ROSSER Douglas (Doug) Richard
Swansea, 8 September, 1948 (CD)

League Club	Source	Date Signed	Seasons Played	Apps	Subs	Gls
Swansea T	JNrs	05.67	68-70	28	1	1
Crewe Alex	Barry T	08.71	71	28	1	0

ROSSI Generoso
Naples, Italy, 3 January, 1979 (G)

League Club	Source	Date Signed	Seasons Played	Apps	Subs	Gls
Queens Park Rgrs	Palermo (It)	01.05	04	3	0	0

ROSSITER Donald (Don) Paul
Strood, 8 June, 1935 EYth (IF)

League Club	Source	Date Signed	Seasons Played	Apps	Subs	Gls
Arsenal	Jnrs	06.52				
Leyton Orient	Tr	03.56	56	1	-	0
Gillingham	Dartford	07.57	57	1	-	0

ROSSITER Dudley John
Kingsbridge, 28 October, 1942 (FB)

League Club	Source	Date Signed	Seasons Played	Apps	Subs	Gls
Torquay U		07.61	62-63	24	-	0

ROSTRON John Wilfred (Wilf)
Sunderland, 29 September, 1956 ESch (FB)

League Club	Source	Date Signed	Seasons Played	Apps	Subs	Gls
Arsenal	App	10.73	74-76	12	5	2
Sunderland	Tr	07.77	77-79	75	1	17
Watford	Tr	10.79	79-88	306	11	22
Sheffield Wed	Tr	01.89	88	7	0	0
Sheffield U	Tr	09.89	89-90	33	3	3
Brentford	Tr	01.91	90-92	34	8	2

ROTHWELL Edward (Teddy)
Atherton, 3 September, 1917 Died 2000 (W)

League Club	Source	Date Signed	Seasons Played	Apps	Subs	Gls
Bolton W	Jnrs	02.36	37-48	48	-	2
Southport	Tr	08.49	49-50	40	-	5

ROTHWELL George
Bolton, 22 November, 1923 (WH)

League Club	Source	Date Signed	Seasons Played	Apps	Subs	Gls
Accrington St	Chorley	08.44	46-51	202	-	10

ROTHWELL John (Jack)
Kearsley, 29 March, 1920 Died 1991 (CF)

League Club	Source	Date Signed	Seasons Played	Apps	Subs	Gls
Southport	St Thomas SS	11.38	38-46	18	-	9
Birmingham C	Tr	03.47				
Southport	Tr	08.49				
Crewe Alex	Tr	10.49	49	3	-	1

ROTHWELL Ronald (Ron)
Bury, 10 July, 1920 (FB)

League Club	Source	Date Signed	Seasons Played	Apps	Subs	Gls
Rochdale	Dunfermline Ath	10.46	46-51	48	-	0

ROUGIER Anthony (Tony) Leo
Tobago, 17 July, 1971 Trinidad int (F)

League Club	Source	Date Signed	Seasons Played	Apps	Subs	Gls
Port Vale	Hibernian	01.99	98-99	41	10	8
Reading	Tr	08.00	00-02	47	37	6
Brighton & Hove A	L	02.03	02	5	1	2
Brentford	Tr	08.03	03	29	2	4
Bristol C	Tr	03.04	03	5	1	1

ROUGVIE Douglas (Doug)
Ballingry, 24 May, 1956 S-1 (FB)

League Club	Source	Date Signed	Seasons Played	Apps	Subs	Gls
Chelsea	Aberdeen	08.84	84-86	74	0	3
Brighton & Hove A	Tr	06.87	87	35	0	2
Shrewsbury T	Tr	08.88	88	20	1	3
Fulham	Tr	02.89	88	18	0	1

ROUND Frederick Leonard (Len)
Wallheath, 21 May, 1928 (G)

League Club	Source	Date Signed	Seasons Played	Apps	Subs	Gls
Hull C	Ayr U	06.57	57	17	-	0

ROUND Paul Gordon
Blackburn, 22 June, 1959 (CD)

League Club	Source	Date Signed	Seasons Played	Apps	Subs	Gls
Blackburn Rov	App	08.77	76-80	41	10	5

ROUND Stephen (Steve) Clive
Dudley, 28 February, 1963 (F)

League Club	Source	Date Signed	Seasons Played	Apps	Subs	Gls
Walsall	App	03.80	81-82	5	19	3

ROUND Stephen (Steve) John
Burton-on-Trent, 9 November, 1970 (FB)

League Club	Source	Date Signed	Seasons Played	Apps	Subs	Gls
Derby Co	YT	07.89	91-92	8	1	0

ROUNSEVELL Anthony (Tony) Eldred
Liskeard, 1 April, 1945 (FB)

League Club	Source	Date Signed	Seasons Played	Apps	Subs	Gls
Plymouth Arg	App	12.62	63-67	34	2	0

ROUSE Herbert
Doncaster, 29 November, 1920 (FB)

League Club	Source	Date Signed	Seasons Played	Apps	Subs	Gls
Doncaster Rov		06.48	48-54	35	-	0

ROUSE Shaun
Great Yarmouth, 28 February, 1972 EYth (M)

League Club	Source	Date Signed	Seasons Played	Apps	Subs	Gls
Bristol C	Glasgow Rgrs	06.92				
Carlisle U	Weston-super-Mare	02.94	93	1	4	0

ROUSE Raymond Victor (Vic)
Swansea, 16 March, 1936 WU23-1/W-1 (G)

League Club	Source	Date Signed	Seasons Played	Apps	Subs	Gls
Millwall	Jnrs	03.53				
Crystal Palace	Tr	08.56	56-62	238	-	0
Northampton T	Tr	04.63				
Oxford U	Tr	08.63	63-64	22	-	0
Leyton Orient	Tr	07.65	65-66	40	0	0

ROUSSEL Cedric
Mons, Belgium, 6 January, 1978 Beu21 (F)

League Club	Source	Date Signed	Seasons Played	Apps	Subs	Gls
Coventry C	KAA Ghent (Bel)	10.99	99-00	28	11	8
Wolverhampton W	Tr	02.01	00-01	9	17	2

ROUTLEDGE Thomas Alan
Wallsend, 6 May, 1960 (FB)

League Club	Source	Date Signed	Seasons Played	Apps	Subs	Gls
Bristol Rov	Bath Univ	10.80	80	0	1	0

ROUTLEDGE Ronald (Ron) Wright
Ashington, 14 October, 1937 (G)

League Club	Source	Date Signed	Seasons Played	Apps	Subs	Gls
Sunderland	Jnrs	10.54	56-57	2	-	0
Bradford PA	Tr	05.58	58-61	39	-	0

ROUTLEDGE Wayne Neville
Sidcup, 7 January, 1985 EYth/Eu21-3 (W)

League Club	Source	Date Signed	Seasons Played	Apps	Subs	Gls
Crystal Palace	Sch	07.02	01-04	83	27	10

ROVDE Knut Marius
Trondheim, Norway, 26 June, 1972 (G)

League Club	Source	Date Signed	Seasons Played	Apps	Subs	Gls
Wrexham	Ayr U	01.02	01	12	0	0

ROWAN Barry
Willesden, 24 April, 1942 (W)

League Club	Source	Date Signed	Seasons Played	Apps	Subs	Gls
Brentford	Watford (Am)	10.60				
Millwall	Dover	07.64	64-66	72	0	13
Colchester U	Detroit (USA)	11.68	68	2	0	0
Reading	Durban U (SA)	08.69	69	1	0	0
Plymouth Arg	Tr	09.69	69	10	0	1
Exeter C	Tr	07.70	70-72	76	5	14

ROWAN Brian
Glasgow, 28 June, 1948 (FB)

League Club	Source	Date Signed	Seasons Played	Apps	Subs	Gls
Aston Villa	Baillieston Rov	04.69	69	1	0	0
Watford	Toronto (Can)	10.71	71	8	4	0

ROWAN Jonathan Robert
Grimsby, 29 November, 1981 (F)

League Club	Source	Date Signed	Seasons Played	Apps	Subs	Gls
Grimsby T	YT	07.00	00-03	32	20	6

ROWBOTHAM Darren
Cardiff, 22 October, 1966 WYth (F)

League Club	Source	Date Signed	Seasons Played	Apps	Subs	Gls
Plymouth Arg	Jnrs	11.84	84-87	22	24	2
Exeter C	Tr	10.87	87-91	110	8	47
Torquay U	Tr	09.91	91	14	0	3

League Club	Source	Date Signed	Seasons Played	Apps	Subs	Gls
Birmingham C	Tr	01.92	91-92	31	5	6
Mansfield T	L	12.92	92	4	0	0
Hereford U	L	03.93	92	8	0	2
Crewe Alex	Tr	07.93	93-94	59	2	21
Shrewsbury T	Tr	07.95	95-96	31	9	9
Exeter C	Tr	10.96	96-99	108	10	37
Leyton Orient	L	11.99	99	4	2	0
ROWBOTHAM Jason						
Cardiff, 3 January, 1969 WYth						(FB)
Plymouth Arg	YT	07.87	87-88	8	1	0
Shrewsbury T	Tr	03.92				
Hereford U	Tr	10.92	92	3	2	1
Wycombe W	Raith Rov	09.95	95	27	0	0
Plymouth Arg	Tr	10.96	96-99	42	9	1
Torquay U	Dorchester T	10.00	00	4	1	0
ROWBOTHAM Michael (Mike) Grant						
Sheffield, 2 September, 1965						(M)
Manchester U	App	09.83				
Grimsby T	Tr	08.84	84	3	1	0
ROWDEN Leonard (Len) Albert						
Swansea, 31 May, 1927						(CF)
Swansea T	Clydach	10.53	53	1	-	0
ROWE Benjamin (Ben) Paul						
Hull, 1 October, 1970						(F)
Exeter C	Bristol C (Jnrs)	09.89	89-90	5	7	2
ROWE Brian						
Sunderland, 24 October, 1971						(M)
Doncaster Rov	YT	10.90	90-92	42	12	1
ROWE Colwyn Roger						
Ipswich, 22 March, 1956						(W)
Colchester U	App	01.74	73-74	4	8	2
ROWE Ezekiel (Zeke) Bartholomew						
Stoke Newington, 30 October, 1973						(F)
Chelsea	YT	06.92				
Barnet	L	11.93	93	9	1	2
Brighton & Hove A	L	03.96	95	9	0	3
Peterborough U	Tr	07.96	96-98	13	22	3
Doncaster Rov	L	02.98	97	6	0	2
ROWE Graham Edward						
Southport, 28 August, 1945						(M)
Blackpool	App	07.63	63-70	101	4	12
Tranmere Rov	L	11.70	70	6	1	0
Bolton W	Tr	05.71	71	4	2	0
ROWE James Anthony						
Christchurch, 10 March, 1987						(M)
Bournemouth	Sch	07.04	04	0	2	0
ROWE Mark Terence						
Bodmin, 9 June, 1964 ESch						(M)
Plymouth Arg	App	09.81	81-84	46	9	1
Torquay U	Saltash U	09.86	86	7	0	0
ROWE Norman						
Halesowen, 20 March, 1940						(W)
Walsall	Aston Villa (Am)	03.59	59-60	6	-	0
ROWE Valentine **Norman**						
Shouldham, 14 February, 1926 Died 1988						(FB)
Derby Co	King's Lynn	12.49	51	2	-	0
Walsall	Tr	08.52	52	25	-	0
ROWE Rodney Carl						
Huddersfield, 30 July, 1975						(F)
Huddersfield T	YT	07.93	93-96	14	20	2
Scarborough	L	08.94	94	10	4	1
Bury	L	03.95	94	1	2	0
York C	Tr	02.97	96-99	74	23	20
Halifax T	L	09.99	99	7	2	2
Gillingham	Tr	11.99	99	8	14	4
Hull C	Tr	01.01	00-01	19	16	8
ROWE Edwin **Stanley (Stan)**						
Exeter, 20 August, 1921						(FB)
Exeter C		10.47	47-53	139	-	0
ROWE Norman **Terence (Terry)** Sinclair						
Fulham, 8 June, 1964						(FB)
Brentford	App	06.82	81-84	63	3	1
ROWELL John **Frederick (Fred)**						
Dawdon, 31 December, 1918 Died 1988						(IF)
Bournemouth		09.41	46-47	31	-	11
Wrexham	Tr	07.48	48-49	41	-	5
Aldershot	Tr	08.50	50	5	-	0

League Club	Source	Date Signed	Seasons Played	Apps	Subs	Gls
ROWELL Gary						
Seaham, 6 June, 1957 Eu21-1						(W)
Sunderland	App	07.74	75-83	229	28	88
Norwich C	Tr	08.84	84	2	4	1
Middlesbrough	Tr	08.85	85	27	0	10
Brighton & Hove A	Tr	08.86	86-87	9	3	0
Carlisle U	Dundee	03.88	87	7	0	0
Burnley	Tr	08.88	88-89	8	11	1
ROWETT Gary						
Bromsgrove, 6 March, 1974						(CD)
Cambridge U	YT	09.91	91-93	51	12	9
Everton	Tr	05.94	93-94	2	2	0
Blackpool	L	01.95	94	17	0	0
Derby Co	Tr	07.95	95-97	101	4	2
Birmingham C	Tr	08.98	98-99	87	0	6
Leicester C	Tr	07.00	00-01	47	2	2
Charlton Ath	Tr	05.02	02-03	13	0	1
ROWLAND Alfred (Alf)						
Stokesley, 2 September, 1920 Died 1997						(CD)
Aldershot	Stockton	08.46	46-48	93	-	0
Cardiff C	Tr	02.49	48-49	3	-	0
ROWLAND Andrew (Andy) Arthur						
Derby, 8 September, 1954 EYth						(F)
Derby Co	Jnrs	09.72				
Bury	Tr	08.74	74-78	169	5	59
Swindon T	Tr	09.78	78-85	280	7	80
ROWLAND Andrew (Andy) James						
Taunton, 1 October, 1965 ESch						(F)
Southampton	Exmouth T	11.89				
Torquay U	Tr	03.91	90-91	9	7	1
ROWLAND David Charles						
Stotfold, 12 September, 1940 ESch						(IF)
Luton T	Arlesey T	01.58	57	1	-	0
ROWLAND John Douglas						
Riddings, 7 April, 1941 EYth						(W)
Nottingham F	Ironville Amats	04.61	60-61	26	-	3
Port Vale	Tr	08.62	62-66	147	2	40
Mansfield T	Tr	09.66	66-67	49	0	16
Tranmere Rov	Tr	07.68	68	25	1	3
ROWLAND John Oswald						
Newport, 16 March, 1936 Died 2002 Wu23-1						(CD)
Newport Co	Lovells Ath	06.58	58-68	461	1	11
ROWLAND Keith						
Portadown, 1 September, 1971 NIYth/NIB-3/NI-18						(M)
Bournemouth	YT	10.89	91-92	65	7	2
Coventry C	L	01.93	92	0	2	0
West Ham U	Tr	08.93	93-97	63	17	1
Queens Park Rgrs	Tr	01.98	97-00	32	24	3
Luton T	L	01.01	00	12	0	2
Chesterfield	Tr	08.01	01-02	6	6	0
ROWLAND Leonard (Len) Charles						
Manchester, 23 June, 1925 EAmat						(FB)
Wrexham (Am)	Mansfield T (Am)	05.49	49-50	18	-	0
Stockport Co	Ashton U	12.52	52-56	61	-	0
ROWLAND Stephen (Steve) John						
Wrexham, 2 November, 1981						(FB)
Port Vale	YT	07.01	01-04	90	13	1
ROWLANDS John Henry						
Liverpool, 7 February, 1945						(F)
Mansfield T		10.67	67	12	1	3
Torquay U	Tr	06.68	68	18	0	4
Exeter C	L	01.69	68	1	0	0
Stockport Co	Cape Town C (SA)	08.69	69-70	45	1	11
Barrow	Tr	01.71	70-71	52	2	6
Workington	Tr	07.72	72-73	50	1	11
Crewe Alex	Tr	11.73	73-74	31	4	1
Hartlepool	Seattle (USA)	09.75	75-76	47	2	10
ROWLANDS Martin Charles						
Hammersmith, 8 February, 1979 IRu21-8/IR-3						(M)
Brentford	Farnborough T	08.98	98-02	128	21	20
Queens Park Rgrs	Tr	08.03	03-04	72	5	13
ROWLANDS Trevor Ivor						
Wattstown, 2 February, 1922 Died 1973 WSch						(FB)
Norwich C	Cardiff Nomads	08.46	47-49	10	-	2
Colchester U	Tr	07.50	50-52	46	-	5
ROWLES Albert **Edward (Eddie)** James						
Gosport, 10 March, 1951						(M)
Bournemouth	App	03.68	67-70	58	8	12
York C	Tr	07.71	71-72	61	6	14

League Club	Source	Date Signed	Seasons Played	Apps	Subs	Gls
Torquay U	Tr	06.73	73-74	54	5	13
Darlington	Tr	08.75	75-77	96	7	21
Colchester U	Tr	12.77	77-81	79	12	17

ROWLEY Antonio (Tony) Camilio
Porthcawl, 19 September, 1929 W-1 (CF)

League Club	Source	Date Signed	Seasons Played	Apps	Subs	Gls
Birmingham C	Wellington T	01.49				
Liverpool	Stourbridge	10.53	53-57	60	-	38
Tranmere Rov	Tr	03.58	57-60	100	-	45

ROWLEY Arthur
Liverpool, 9 May, 1933 (IF)

League Club	Source	Date Signed	Seasons Played	Apps	Subs	Gls
Liverpool	Florence Melley BC	05.51	52	11	-	0
Wrexham	Tr	11.54	54-56	54	-	8
Crewe Alex	Tr	02.57	56-57	32	-	8

ROWLEY George **Arthur**
Wolverhampton, 21 April, 1926 Died 2002 EB/FLge-1 (IF)

League Club	Source	Date Signed	Seasons Played	Apps	Subs	Gls
West Bromwich A	Blakenhall St Luke's	05.44	46-48	24	-	4
Fulham	Tr	12.48	48-49	56	-	26
Leicester C	Tr	07.50	50-57	303	-	251
Shrewsbury T	Tr	06.58	58-64	236	-	152

ROWLEY John
Wolverhampton, 23 June, 1944 (FB)

League Club	Source	Date Signed	Seasons Played	Apps	Subs	Gls
Bradford PA	Wellington T	10.67	67	35	0	0

ROWLEY John (Jack) Frederick
Wolverhampton, 7 October, 1918 Died 1998 FLge-3/EB/EWar-1/E-6 (CF)

League Club	Source	Date Signed	Seasons Played	Apps	Subs	Gls
Wolverhampton W	Dudley OB	11.35				
Bournemouth	Tr	02.37	36-37	23	-	12
Manchester U	Tr	10.37	37-54	380	-	182
Plymouth Arg	Tr	02.55	54-56	56	-	14

ROWLEY Kenneth (Ken) Francis
Pelsall, 29 August, 1926 (IF)

League Club	Source	Date Signed	Seasons Played	Apps	Subs	Gls
Wolverhampton W	Elkingtons	10.47	49	1	-	0
Birmingham C	Tr	01.51	50-54	40	-	19
Coventry C	Tr	11.54	54	3	-	0

ROWSON David Andrew
Aberdeen, 14 September, 1976 Scu21-5 (M)

League Club	Source	Date Signed	Seasons Played	Apps	Subs	Gls
Stoke C	Aberdeen	07.01	01	8	5	0
Northampton T	Partick Th	07.04	04	35	2	2

ROXBURGH Alexander (Alex) White
Manchester, 19 September, 1910 Died 1985 EWar-1 (G)

League Club	Source	Date Signed	Seasons Played	Apps	Subs	Gls
Blackpool	Manchester C (Am)	01.31	32-38	57	-	0
Barrow	Tr	08.46	46-47	69	-	0

ROY Andrew (Andy)
Tillicoultry, 14 July, 1928 Died 1999 (IF)

League Club	Source	Date Signed	Seasons Played	Apps	Subs	Gls
Exeter C	Dunfermline Ath	08.49	49	2	-	0

ROY Bryan Edward
Amsterdam, Holland, 12 February, 1970 Holland int (F)

League Club	Source	Date Signed	Seasons Played	Apps	Subs	Gls
Nottingham F	Foggia (It)	08.94	94-96	70	15	24

ROY Eric
Nice, France, 26 September, 1967 (M)

League Club	Source	Date Signed	Seasons Played	Apps	Subs	Gls
Sunderland	Marseille (Fr)	08.99	99-00	20	7	0

ROY John (Jack) Robin
Woolston, 23 March, 1914 Died 1980 (W)

League Club	Source	Date Signed	Seasons Played	Apps	Subs	Gls
Norwich C	Sholing Ath	08.33	34-35	6	-	0
Mansfield T	Tr	04.36	36	25	-	2
Sheffield Wed	Tr	02.37	36-37	15	-	1
Notts Co	Tr	03.38	37-38	15	-	0
Tranmere Rov	Tr	12.38	38	20	-	2
Ipswich T	Aberaman Ath	02.46	46	15	-	2

ROYCE Simon Ernest
Forest Gate, 9 September, 1971 (G)

League Club	Source	Date Signed	Seasons Played	Apps	Subs	Gls
Southend U	Heybridge Swifts	10.91	91-97	147	2	0
Charlton Ath	Tr	07.98	98	8	0	0
Leicester C	Tr	07.00	00	16	3	0
Brighton & Hove A	L	12.01	01	6	0	0
Queens Park Rgrs	L	08.02	02	16	0	0
Charlton Ath	Tr	07.03	03	1	0	0
Luton T	L	10.04	04	2	0	0
Queens Park Rgrs	L	01.05	04	13	0	0

ROYLE Joseph (Joe)
Norris Green, 8 April, 1949 Eu23-10/FLge-1/E-6 (F)

League Club	Source	Date Signed	Seasons Played	Apps	Subs	Gls
Everton	App	08.66	65-74	229	3	102
Manchester C	Tr	12.74	74-77	98	1	23
Bristol C	Tr	11.77	77-79	100	1	18
Norwich C	Tr	08.80	80-81	40	2	9

ROYSTON Robert (Bob)
Gallowgate, 1 December, 1915 Died 1996 (FB)

League Club	Source	Date Signed	Seasons Played	Apps	Subs	Gls
Sunderland	Seaham Colliery	01.35				
Southport	Tr	10.36	37-38	70	-	2
Plymouth Arg	Tr	03.39	38-46	39	-	0

RUARK Anthony (Tony)
West Ham, 23 March, 1933 (CD)

League Club	Source	Date Signed	Seasons Played	Apps	Subs	Gls
Southend U		05.56	56	9	-	0

RUBINS Andrejs
Riga, Latvia, 26 November, 1978 Latvia 42 (M)

League Club	Source	Date Signed	Seasons Played	Apps	Subs	Gls
Crystal Palace	Skonto Riga (Lat)	10.00	00-02	17	14	0

RUDD Edward (Ted)
Wigan, 7 January, 1929 (WH)

League Club	Source	Date Signed	Seasons Played	Apps	Subs	Gls
Bolton W		08.50				
Accrington St	Tr	08.51	51	2	-	0

RUDD John James **(Jimmy)**
Dublin, 25 October, 1919 Died 1985 (W)

League Club	Source	Date Signed	Seasons Played	Apps	Subs	Gls
Manchester C	Terenure Ath	01.38	46	2	-	0
York C	Tr	03.47	46-48	83	-	23
Leeds U	Tr	02.49	48-49	18	-	1
Rotherham U	Tr	10.49	49-51	75	-	11
Scunthorpe U	Tr	10.51	51	32	-	4
Workington	Tr	09.52	52	17	-	1

RUDD William (Billy) Thomas
Manchester, 13 December, 1941 (M)

League Club	Source	Date Signed	Seasons Played	Apps	Subs	Gls
Birmingham C	Stalybridge Celtic	10.59	59-61	24	-	3
York C	Tr	11.61	61-65	193	0	30
Grimsby T	Tr	07.66	66-67	59	1	9
Rochdale	Tr	02.68	67-69	108	0	8
Bury	Tr	06.70	70-76	174	15	19

RUDDOCK Neil
Wandsworth, 9 May, 1968 EYth/Eu21-4/EB-1/E-1 (CD)

League Club	Source	Date Signed	Seasons Played	Apps	Subs	Gls
Millwall	App	03.86				
Tottenham H	Tr	04.86	86-87	7	2	0
Millwall	Tr	06.88	88	0	2	1
Southampton	Tr	02.89	88-91	100	7	9
Tottenham H	Tr	07.92	92	38	0	3
Liverpool	Tr	07.93	93-97	111	4	11
Queens Park Rgrs	L	03.98	97	7	0	0
West Ham U	Tr	07.98	98-99	39	3	2
Crystal Palace	Tr	07.00	00	19	1	2
Swindon T	Tr	08.01	01	14	1	1

RUDDY John Thomas Gordon
St Ives, 24 October, 1986 (G)

League Club	Source	Date Signed	Seasons Played	Apps	Subs	Gls
Cambridge U	Sch	09.04	03-04	39	0	0

RUDGE Dale Anthony
Wolverhampton, 9 June, 1963 (M)

League Club	Source	Date Signed	Seasons Played	Apps	Subs	Gls
Wolverhampton W	App	08.81	82-83	23	4	0
Preston NE	Tr	07.84	84-85	46	1	2

RUDGE David (Dave) Harry
Wolverhampton, 21 January, 1948 (W)

League Club	Source	Date Signed	Seasons Played	Apps	Subs	Gls
Aston Villa	App	05.65	66-69	49	6	10
Hereford U	Tr	08.72	72-75	75	7	8
Torquay U	Tr	12.75	75-77	60	4	4

RUDGE John Robert
Wolverhampton, 21 October, 1944 (F)

League Club	Source	Date Signed	Seasons Played	Apps	Subs	Gls
Huddersfield T	Jnrs	11.61	62-66	5	0	0
Carlisle U	Tr	12.66	66-68	45	5	16
Torquay U	Tr	01.69	68-71	94	2	34
Bristol Rov	Tr	02.72	71-74	50	20	17
Bournemouth	Tr	03.75	74-76	18	3	2

RUDGE Simon James
Warrington, 30 December, 1964 (M)

League Club	Source	Date Signed	Seasons Played	Apps	Subs	Gls
Bolton W	App	12.82	82-85	77	14	14

RUDHAM Keith (Doug) Robert
Johannesburg, South Africa, 3 May, 1926 Died 1991 SAAmat (G)

League Club	Source	Date Signed	Seasons Played	Apps	Subs	Gls
Liverpool	Johannesburg Rgrs (SA)	11.54	54-59	63	-	0

RUDI Petter
Kristiansund, Norway, 17 September, 1973 NoYth/Nou21/No-27 (W)

League Club	Source	Date Signed	Seasons Played	Apps	Subs	Gls
Sheffield Wed	Molde FK (Nor)	10.97	97-00	70	7	8

RUDKIN Thomas (Tommy) William
Peterborough, 17 June, 1919 Died 1969 (W)

League Club	Source	Date Signed	Seasons Played	Apps	Subs	Gls
Wolverhampton W	Creswell	02.38				
Lincoln C	Tr	05.38	38	2	-	1
Arsenal	Peterborough U	01.47	46	5	-	2
Southampton	Tr	08.47	47-48	9	-	0
Bristol C	Tr	05.49	49-50	34	-	4

RUDMAN Harold
Whitworth, 4 November, 1924 (FB)

League Club	Source	Date Signed	Seasons Played	Apps	Subs	Gls
Burnley		12.42	46-56	71	-	0
Rochdale	Tr	07.57	57	21	-	2

League Club	Source	Date Signed	Seasons Played	Career Record Apps	Subs	Gls
RUDONJA Mladen						
Koper, Slovenia, 26 July, 1971 Slovenia 61						(M)
Portsmouth	St Truiden (Bel)	08.00	00-01	4	10	0
RUECROFT Jacob						
Lanchester, 1 May, 1915						(FB)
Halifax T	Goole T	05.38	38-46	60	-	2
Bradford C	Scarborough	01.48	47-48	43	-	0
RUFFETT Raymond (Ray) Douglas						
Luton, 20 July, 1924						(WH)
Luton T	Jnrs	10.41	48	1	-	0
RUFUS Marvin Marcel						
Lewisham, 11 September, 1976						(M)
Leyton Orient	Charlton Ath (YT)	11.94	94	5	2	0
RUFUS Richard Raymond						
Lewisham, 12 January, 1975 Eu21-6						(CD)
Charlton Ath	YT	07.93	94-02	284	4	12
RUGGIERO John Salvatore						
Longton, 26 November, 1954						(M)
Stoke C	App	05.72	76	9	0	2
Workington	L	01.76	75	3	0	0
Brighton & Hove A	Tr	06.77	77	4	4	2
Portsmouth	L	12.77	77	6	0	1
Chester	Tr	04.79	79	9	2	1
RULE Alan Henry						
Southampton, 10 January, 1930						(WH)
Chelsea	Winchester C	11.52				
Norwich C	Tr	09.56	56	8	-	0
Bournemouth	Tr	06.57	57	25	-	0
RUMBLE Paul						
Hemel Hempstead, 14 March, 1969						(FB)
Watford	App	03.87				
Scunthorpe U	L	08.88	88	8	0	1
Maidstone U	Tr	08.89	89-91	48	7	3
RUMBOLD George Arthur						
Alton, 10 July, 1911 Died 1995						(FB)
Crystal Palace	Faringdon	10.34	35	5	-	0
Clapton Orient	Tr	06.37	37-38	52	-	0
Ipswich T	Tr	05.46	46-49	121	-	11
RUMNEY Joseph **Edgar**						
Abberton, 15 September, 1936						(FB)
Colchester U	Jnrs	05.57	57-64	49	-	0
RUNDLE Adam						
Durham, 8 July, 1984						(M)
Darlington	YT	•	01-02	8	9	0
Carlisle U	Tr	12.02	02-03	25	19	1
Mansfield T	Dublin C	01.05	04	18	0	4
RUNDLE Charles (Charlie) Rodney						
Fowey, 17 January, 1923 Died 1997						(IF)
Tottenham H	St Blazey	02.46	46-48	28	-	12
Crystal Palace	Tr	06.50	50-51	38	-	2
RUNDLE Sidney (Sid) Stewart Knight						
Fowey, 19 October, 1921 Died 1987						(WH)
Plymouth Arg	St Blazey	06.45	46-52	53	-	1
RUSH David						
Sunderland, 15 May, 1971						(F)
Sunderland	YT	07.89	90-93	40	19	12
Hartlepool U	L	08.91	91	8	0	2
Peterborough U	L	10.93	93	2	2	1
Cambridge U	L	09.94	94	2	0	0
Oxford U	Tr	09.94	94-96	67	25	21
York C	Tr	01.97	96-97	2	3	0
Hartlepool U	Morpeth T	09.98	98	5	5	0
RUSH Ian James						
St Asaph, 20 October, 1961 WSch/Wu21-2/W-73						(F)
Chester	App	09.79	78-79	33	1	14
Liverpool	Tr	05.80	80-86	224	0	139
Liverpool	Juventus (It)	07.86	88-95	223	22	89
Leeds U	Tr	05.96	96	34	2	3
Newcastle U	Tr	08.97	97	6	4	0
Sheffield U	L	02.98	97	4	0	0
Wrexham	Tr	08.98	98	12	5	0
RUSH Jonathan (Jon)						
Wellington, New Zealand, 13 October, 1961						(G)
Blackpool	(New Zealand)	11.79	80-81	11	0	0
RUSH Matthew James						
Dalston, 6 August, 1971 IRu21-4						(M)
West Ham U	YT	03.90	90-94	29	19	5
Cambridge U	L	03.93	92	4	6	0
Swansea C	L	01.94	93	13	0	0
Norwich C	Tr	08.95	95-96	0	3	0
Northampton T	L	10.96	96	14	0	3
Oldham Ath	Tr	03.97	96-97	17	7	3
RUSHBURY Andrew (Andy) James						
Carlisle, 7 March, 1983						(M)
Chesterfield	Sch	07.02	00-03	23	17	1
RUSHBURY David Graham						
Wolverhampton, 20 February, 1956						(FB)
West Bromwich A	App	02.74	74-75	28	0	0
Sheffield Wed	Tr	11.76	76-78	111	1	7
Swansea C	Tr	07.79	79-80	51	1	0
Carlisle U	Tr	08.81	81-84	120	9	1
Gillingham	Tr	03.85	84	12	0	0
Doncaster Rov	Tr	07.85	85-86	66	0	2
Cambridge U	L	02.87	86	1	0	0
Bristol Rov	Tr	02.87	86	14	2	0
RUSHBY Alan						
Doncaster, 27 December, 1933						(CD)
Doncaster Rov		01.52	53	1	-	0
Mansfield T	Tr	03.57	56-57	20	-	0
Bradford PA	Tr	11.57	57-58	12	-	0
RUSHFELDT Sigurd (Siggi)						
Vadso, Norway, 11 December, 1972 Norway int						(F)
Birmingham C (L)	Tromso (Nor)	10.95	95	3	4	0
RUSHFORTH Peter						
Carlisle, 6 December, 1945						(WH)
Workington (Am)		09.66	66	5	0	0
RUSHTON Brian William Eric						
Sedgley, 21 October, 1943						(FB)
Birmingham C	App	10.60	62-63	12	-	0
Notts Co	Tr	06.67	67	2	1	0
RUSHWORTH Peter John						
Bristol, 12 April, 1927						(WH)
Leicester C	Cheltenham T	11.51				
Bournemouth	Tr	06.53	53-56	88	-	1
RUSK Simon Edward						
Peterborough, 17 December, 1981						(M)
Boston U	Cambridge C	04.01	02-04	50	18	5
RUSLING Graham						
Keadby, 4 April, 1948						(F)
Scunthorpe U		01.67	66-70	71	9	17
RUSSELL Alec						
Bristol, 17 April, 1925						(IF)
Bristol C		11.47	47-48	3	-	0
RUSSELL Alexander (Alex)						
Seaham, 21 February, 1944						(M)
Everton	Marsden CW Jnrs	12.61				
Southport	Tr	11.63	63-69	262	1	63
Blackburn Rov	Tr	08.70	70	22	2	4
Tranmere Rov	Tr	07.71	71-72	54	1	7
Crewe Alex	L	10.72	72	4	0	0
Southport	Tr	11.72	72-74	84	1	12
RUSSELL Alexander (Alex) John						
Crosby, 17 March, 1973						(M)
Rochdale	Burscough	07.94	94-97	83	19	14
Cambridge U	Tr	08.98	98-00	72	9	8
Torquay U	Tr	08.01	01-04	152	1	21
RUSSELL Allan						
Aberdeen, 16 November, 1953						(M)
Peterborough U	Leicester C (App)	08.71	71-72	7	8	1
RUSSELL Colin						
Liverpool, 21 January, 1961						(F)
Liverpool	App	04.78	80	0	1	0
Huddersfield T	Tr	09.82	82-83	64	2	23
Stoke C	L	03.84	83	11	0	2
Bournemouth	Tr	08.84	84-85	65	3	14
Doncaster Rov	Tr	07.86	86-87	43	0	5
Scarborough	Tr	10.87	87	12	1	2
Wigan Ath	Tr	07.88	88	8	0	3
RUSSELL Craig Stewart						
Jarrow, 4 February, 1974						(F)
Sunderland	YT	07.92	91-97	103	47	31

League Club	Source	Date Signed	Seasons Played	Apps	Subs	Gls
Manchester C	Tr	11.97	97-98	22	9	2
Tranmere Rov	L	08.98	98	3	1	0
Port Vale	L	01.99	98	8	0	1
Darlington	L	09.99	99	11	1	2
Oxford U	L	02.00	99	5	1	0
Carlisle U	St Johnstone	01.03	02-03	10	9	1
Darlington	Tr	01.04	03-04	21	19	2

RUSSELL Darel Francis Roy
Mile End, 22 October, 1980 EYth (M)

League Club	Source	Date Signed	Seasons Played	Apps	Subs	Gls
Norwich C	YT	11.97	97-02	99	33	7
Stoke C	Tr	08.03	03-04	91	0	6

RUSSELL Edward (Eddie) Thomas
Cranwell, 15 July, 1928 (WH)

League Club	Source	Date Signed	Seasons Played	Apps	Subs	Gls
Wolverhampton W	St Chad's College	04.46	48-50	30	-	0
Middlesbrough	Tr	12.51	51-52	29	-	1
Leicester C	Tr	10.53	53-57	90	-	5
Notts Co	Tr	08.58	58	9	-	0

RUSSELL Guy Robert
Shirley, 28 September, 1967 (F)

League Club	Source	Date Signed	Seasons Played	Apps	Subs	Gls
Birmingham C	App	05.86	84-87	7	4	0
Carlisle U	L	03.87	86	9	3	2

RUSSELL Hugh (Hughie) William
Redcar, 10 March, 1921 Died 1991 (IF)

League Club	Source	Date Signed	Seasons Played	Apps	Subs	Gls
Gillingham	Bishop Auckland	08.46	50-51	61	-	8

RUSSELL James (Jim) Walker
Edinburgh, 14 September, 1916 Died 1994 SSch (IF)

League Club	Source	Date Signed	Seasons Played	Apps	Subs	Gls
Sunderland	Carrickmuir Jnrs	06.34	35-37	5	-	0
Norwich C	Tr	05.38	38-46	12	-	2
Crystal Palace	Tr	12.46	46-47	43	-	6
New Brighton	Tr	07.48	48	24	-	1

RUSSELL John Matthieson
Plymouth, 22 April, 1938 (W)

League Club	Source	Date Signed	Seasons Played	Apps	Subs	Gls
Plymouth Arg	Jnrs	01.59				
Southport	Tr	07.60	60	1	-	0

RUSSELL Keith David
Aldridge, 31 January, 1974 (F)

League Club	Source	Date Signed	Seasons Played	Apps	Subs	Gls
Blackpool	Hednesford T	04.97	96	0	1	0

RUSSELL Kevin John
Portsmouth, 6 December, 1966 EYth (M)

League Club	Source	Date Signed	Seasons Played	Apps	Subs	Gls
Portsmouth	Brighton & Hove A (App)	10.84	85-86	3	1	0
Wrexham	Tr	07.87	87-88	84	0	43
Leicester C	Tr	06.89	89-91	24	19	10
Peterborough U	L	09.90	90	7	0	3
Cardiff C	L	01.91	90	3	0	0
Hereford U	L	11.91	91	3	0	1
Stoke C	L	01.92	91	5	0	1
Stoke C	Tr	07.92	92	30	10	5
Burnley	Tr	06.93	93	26	2	6
Bournemouth	Tr	03.94	93-94	30	0	1
Notts Co	Tr	02.95	94	9	2	0
Wrexham	Tr	07.95	95-02	172	26	17

RUSSELL Lee Edward
Southampton, 3 September, 1969 (CD)

League Club	Source	Date Signed	Seasons Played	Apps	Subs	Gls
Portsmouth	YT	07.88	88-97	103	20	3
Bournemouth	L	09.94	94	3	0	0
Torquay U	Tr	03.99	98-01	78	4	0

RUSSELL Malcolm
Halifax, 9 November, 1945 (FB)

League Club	Source	Date Signed	Seasons Played	Apps	Subs	Gls
Halifax T	App	03.63	62-68	183	1	0
Southport	Tr	09.68	68-70	92	0	2
Barrow	Tr	12.70	70-71	64	0	2
Stockport Co	Tr	07.72	72	11	0	0

RUSSELL Martin Christopher
Dublin, 27 April, 1967 IRYth/IRu23-1/IRu21-4 (M)

League Club	Source	Date Signed	Seasons Played	Apps	Subs	Gls
Manchester U	App	04.84				
Birmingham C	L	10.86	86	3	2	0
Leicester C	Tr	03.87	86-88	13	7	0
Scarborough	Tr	02.89	88-89	51	0	9
Middlesbrough	Tr	03.90	90	10	1	2

RUSSELL Matthew (Matt) Lee
Dewsbury, 17 January, 1978 (FB)

League Club	Source	Date Signed	Seasons Played	Apps	Subs	Gls
Scarborough	YT	07.96	96-98	21	23	3
Doncaster Rov	L	03.98	97	4	1	0
Halifax T	Tr	07.99	99	3	4	0

RUSSELL William **Peter**
Gornal, 16 January, 1935 (CD)

League Club	Source	Date Signed	Seasons Played	Apps	Subs	Gls
Wolverhampton W	Jnrs	10.52	54-55	3	-	0
Notts Co	Tr	03.56	55-58	106	-	6

RUSSELL Raymond (Ray)
Walsall, 9 March, 1930 (IF)

League Club	Source	Date Signed	Seasons Played	Apps	Subs	Gls
West Bromwich A	Jnrs	05.48				
Shrewsbury T	Burton A	05.54	54-59	168	-	55
Crewe Alex	Tr	03.60	59	13	-	4

RUSSELL Robert (Bobby) Inglis
Aberdour, 27 December, 1919 Died 2004 (WH)

League Club	Source	Date Signed	Seasons Played	Apps	Subs	Gls
Chelsea	Airdrie	12.44	46	2	-	0
Notts Co	Tr	08.48	48	2	-	0

RUSSELL Roger Francis
Corby, 20 November, 1957 (F)

League Club	Source	Date Signed	Seasons Played	Apps	Subs	Gls
Northampton T		09.81	81	0	1	0

RUSSELL Samuel (Sam) Ian
Middlesbrough, 4 October, 1982 (G)

League Club	Source	Date Signed	Seasons Played	Apps	Subs	Gls
Middlesbrough	YT	07.00				
Darlington	L	12.02	02	1	0	0
Scunthorpe U	L	08.03	03	10	0	0
Darlington	Tr	08.04	04	46	0	0

RUSSELL Sidney (Sid) Edward James
Feltham, 4 October, 1937 Died 1994 (FB)

League Club	Source	Date Signed	Seasons Played	Apps	Subs	Gls
Brentford	Jnrs	08.56	56-59	54	-	0

RUSSELL Simon Craig
Hull, 19 March, 1985 (M)

League Club	Source	Date Signed	Seasons Played	Apps	Subs	Gls
Hull C	Sch	●	02	0	1	0
Kidderminster Hrs	Tr	07.04	04	18	10	2

RUSSELL Wayne Leonard
Cardiff, 29 November, 1967 (G)

League Club	Source	Date Signed	Seasons Played	Apps	Subs	Gls
Burnley	Ebbw Vale	10.93	94-96	22	2	0

RUSSELL William (Billy)
Hounslow, 7 July, 1935 (F)

League Club	Source	Date Signed	Seasons Played	Apps	Subs	Gls
Sheffield U	Rhyl	11.57	57-62	144	-	55
Bolton W	Tr	03.63	62-64	22	-	2
Rochdale	Tr	07.66	66-67	60	1	8

RUSSELL William (Bill) Howie
Coatbridge, 19 October, 1919 Died 1989 (IF)

League Club	Source	Date Signed	Seasons Played	Apps	Subs	Gls
Hartlepools U		05.46	46-47	13	-	1

RUSSELL William (Billy) McKnight
Glasgow, 14 September, 1959 SYth (FB)

League Club	Source	Date Signed	Seasons Played	Apps	Subs	Gls
Everton	App	07.77				
Doncaster Rov	Glasgow Celtic	07.79	79-84	241	3	15
Scunthorpe U	Tr	08.85	85-87	113	4	7
Rotherham U	Tr	08.88	88-91	103	2	2

RUSSO Gary
Hemsby, 2 August, 1956 (FB)

League Club	Source	Date Signed	Seasons Played	Apps	Subs	Gls
Ipswich T	App	08.74				
Bournemouth	Tr	07.75	75	1	0	0

RUSSON Ronald (Ron)
Wednesbury, 10 December, 1928 Died 1981 (CD)

League Club	Source	Date Signed	Seasons Played	Apps	Subs	Gls
Wolverhampton W	Jnrs	04.46				
Walsall	Hednesford T	05.48	48-54	145	-	1

RUST Nicholas (Nicky) Charles Irwin
Ely, 25 September, 1974 EYth (G)

League Club	Source	Date Signed	Seasons Played	Apps	Subs	Gls
Brighton & Hove A	Arsenal (YT)	07.93	93-97	177	0	0
Barnet	Tr	08.98	98	2	0	0

RUSTER Sebastien
Marseille, France, 6 September, 1982 (F)

League Club	Source	Date Signed	Seasons Played	Apps	Subs	Gls
Swindon T	AS Cannes (Fr)	10.03	03	0	2	0

RUTHERFORD Colin
Rowlands Gill, 11 July, 1944 (CF)

League Club	Source	Date Signed	Seasons Played	Apps	Subs	Gls
Sunderland	Jnrs	07.61				
Barnsley	Tr	06.63	63	1	-	0

RUTHERFORD Ian Stewart
Hitchin, 24 December, 1972 (F)

League Club	Source	Date Signed	Seasons Played	Apps	Subs	Gls
Crewe Alex	Luton T (YT)	06.91	91	0	1	0

RUTHERFORD Joseph (Joe) Henry Hamilton
Fatfield, 20 September, 1914 Died 1994 (G)

League Club	Source	Date Signed	Seasons Played	Apps	Subs	Gls
Southport	Birtley Colliery	10.36	36-38	88	-	0
Aston Villa	Tr	02.39	38-51	148	-	0

RUTHERFORD Mark Robin
Birmingham, 25 March, 1972 (M)

League Club	Source	Date Signed	Seasons Played	Apps	Subs	Gls
Birmingham C	YT	07.90	89-90	1	4	0
Shrewsbury T (L)	Shelbourne	02.94	93	7	7	0
Shrewsbury T (L)	Shelbourne	09.98	98	0	3	0

League Club	Source	Date Signed	Seasons Played	Career Record Apps	Subs	Gls
RUTHERFORD Michael Alan						
Sidcup, 6 June, 1972						(M)
Queens Park Rgrs	YT	12.89	89	1	1	0
RUTHERFORD Jonathan **Paul**						
Sunderland, 23 February, 1967						(F)
Newcastle U	App	07.85				
Scarborough	Meadowbank Th	09.94	94	6	2	1
RUTHERFORD Robert (Bobby)						
South Shields, 20 April, 1922						(W)
Newcastle U	Wallsend St Luke's	03.44				
Gateshead	Tr	11.45	46-52	9	-	2
RUTHERFORD Robert (Bobby) Alan						
Carlisle, 28 July, 1953 ESch						(M)
Leeds U	App	08.70				
Workington	Tr	11.72	72	1	1	0
RUTHERFORD William (Bill) John						
Bellshill, 23 January, 1930 Died 1980						(WH)
Darlington	Stirling A	07.52	52-58	251	-	3
Southport	Tr	07.59	59-63	176	-	7
RUTLEY Peter						
Exeter, 19 May, 1946						(WH)
Exeter C	App	07.63	62-64	16	-	0
RUTTER David **Brian**						
Poplar, 11 May, 1933						(IF)
Crystal Palace	Cardiff C (Am)	11.54	54	3	-	1
RUTTER Charles (Charlie) Frederick						
Poplar, 22 December, 1927 EB						(FB)
Cardiff C	Taunton T	09.49	50-57	118	-	0
RUTTER Cyril Hutton						
Leeds, 21 February, 1933						(FB)
Portsmouth	Jnrs	07.51	53-62	171	-	0
RUTTER John Thomas						
Warrington, 13 September, 1952						(FB)
Wolverhampton W	App	09.70				
Bournemouth	Tr	08.73	73	2	2	0
Exeter C	Tr	07.74	74-75	31	1	1
Stockport Co	Tr	08.76	76-85	400	4	10
RUTTER Keith Gregg						
Leeds, 10 September, 1931						(CD)
Queens Park Rgrs	Methley U	07.54	54-62	339	-	1
Colchester U	Tr	02.63	62-63	63	-	0
RUTTER Stephen (Steve) John						
Erith, 24 July, 1968						(F)
Maidstone U	(Iceland)	02.92	91	0	1	0
RYALLS Brian						
Hemsworth, 7 July, 1932						(G)
Sheffield Wed	Grimethorpe Colliery	01.53	53-57	41	-	0
RYAN Darragh Joseph						
Cuckfield, 21 May, 1980						(F)
Brighton & Hove A	YT	03.98	97-98	4	5	2
RYAN Darren Thomas						
Oswestry, 3 July, 1972						(W)
Shrewsbury T	YT	10.90	90-91	3	1	0
Chester C	Tr	08.92	92	5	12	2
Stockport Co	Tr	01.93	92-93	29	7	6
Rochdale	Tr	07.94	94-95	19	13	2
Chester C	Tr	03.96	95	2	2	1
RYAN David Peter						
Failsworth, 5 January, 1957						(G)
Manchester U	App	07.74				
Port Vale	L	01.76	75	1	0	0
Southport	Tr	03.76	75-76	23	0	0
RYAN Derek Anthony						
Dublin, 2 January, 1967						(M)
Wolverhampton W	App	10.84	84-86	23	10	5
RYAN Eric William						
Oswestry, 6 January, 1933						(FB)
Mansfield T	Oswestry T	05.51	54-56	20	-	0
RYAN George						
Glasgow, 29 December, 1931						(CF)
Sheffield U	Hull C (Am)	05.51				
Chesterfield	Third Lanark	07.54	54	3	-	0

League Club	Source	Date Signed	Seasons Played	Career Record Apps	Subs	Gls
RYAN Gerard (Gerry) Joseph						
Dublin, 4 October, 1955 IR-16						(W)
Derby Co	Bohemians	09.77	77-78	30	0	4
Brighton & Hove A	Tr	09.78	78-84	131	41	32
RYAN James (Jimmy)						
Stirling, 12 May, 1945						(W)
Manchester U	Corrie Hearts	01.63	65-69	21	3	4
Luton T	Tr	04.70	70-76	172	12	21
RYAN James (Jimmy) Patrick						
Prestatyn, 6 September, 1942 Wu23-1						(CF)
Charlton Ath	Dulwich Hamlet	02.63	62-64	16	-	8
Millwall	Tr	02.65	64-65	12	0	2
Exeter C	Hastings U	01.67	66	20	0	5
RYAN John Bernard						
Failsworth, 18 February, 1962 Eu21-1						(FB)
Oldham Ath	App	02.80	81-82	77	0	8
Newcastle U	Tr	08.83	83-84	28	0	1
Sheffield Wed	Tr	09.84	84	5	3	1
Oldham Ath	Tr	08.85	85-86	20	3	0
Mansfield T	Tr	10.87	87-88	53	9	1
Chesterfield	Tr	06.89	89-90	81	1	6
Rochdale	Tr	06.91	91-93	64	6	2
Bury	Tr	12.93	93	8	1	0
RYAN John Gilbert						
Lewisham, 20 July, 1947						(FB)
Arsenal	Maidstone U	10.64				
Fulham	Tr	07.65	65-68	42	5	1
Luton T	Tr	07.69	69-75	264	2	10
Norwich C	Tr	08.76	76-79	113	3	26
Sheffield U	Seattle (USA)	09.80	80-81	56	0	2
Manchester C	Tr	01.82	81	19	0	0
Stockport Co	Tr	08.83	83	1	1	0
Chester C	Tr	09.83	83	4	0	0
Cambridge U	Tr	10.84	84	5	0	0
RYAN John (Buck) Joseph						
Alloa, 16 October, 1930						(IF)
Charlton Ath	Chippenham T	02.54	54-58	61	-	32
Newcastle U	Tr	03.59				
Bristol C	Tr	07.60	60	3	-	0
RYAN John Oliver						
Liverpool, 28 October, 1944						(W)
Tranmere Rov		08.64				
Luton T	Wigan Ath	10.67	67-68	17	1	1
Notts Co	Tr	05.69	69	22	2	1
RYAN Keith James						
Northampton, 25 June, 1970						(M)
Wycombe W	Berkhamsted T	07.90	93-04	299	52	29
RYAN Kenneth (Ken)						
Accrington, 20 September, 1936						(G)
Accrington St (Am)	Accrington Collieries	04.59	58	1	-	0
RYAN Laurence (Laurie) John						
Watford, 15 October, 1963						(F)
Cambridge U	Dunstable	04.88	87-89	39	12	13
RYAN Leon Michael						
Sunderland, 8 November, 1982						(F)
Scunthorpe U	Kotkan TP (Fin)	09.02	02	0	2	0
RYAN Michael (Mike) Joseph						
Welwyn Garden City, 14 October, 1930						(W)
Arsenal	Chase of Chertsey	07.48				
Lincoln C	Tr	06.52	52	7	-	0
York C	Tr	01.53	52	4	-	0
RYAN Michael (Mike) Stuart						
Stockport, 3 October, 1979						(FB)
Manchester U	YT	07.98				
Wrexham	Tr	03.99	99	4	3	0
RYAN Oliver Paul						
Boston, 26 September, 1985						(F)
Lincoln C	Sch	•	04	0	6	0
RYAN Reginald (Reg) Alphonsus						
Dublin, 30 October, 1925 Died 1997 IR-16/I-1						(IF)
West Bromwich A	Nuneaton Borough	04.45	46-54	234	-	28
Derby Co	Tr	07.55	55-58	133	-	30
Coventry C	Tr	09.58	58-60	65	-	9
RYAN Richard (Richie)						
Kilkenny, 6 January, 1985 IRYth						(M)
Sunderland	YT	01.02	02	0	2	0

League Club	Source	Date Signed	Seasons Played	Apps	Subs	Gls
RYAN Robert (Robbie) Paul						
Dublin, 16 May, 1977 IRSch/IRYth/IRu21-12						(FB)
Huddersfield T	Belvedere	07.94	96-97	12	3	0
Millwall	Tr	01.98	97-03	209	17	2
Bristol Rov	Tr	07.04	04	39	1	0
RYAN Thomas (Tom) Stanley						
Windlesham, 9 July, 1952						(CD)
Reading	App	05.70	70	1	0	0
RYAN Timothy (Tim) James						
Stockport, 10 December, 1974 ESemiPro-14						(FB)
Scunthorpe U	YT	04.93	92-93	1	1	0
Doncaster Rov	Buxton	08.96	96	22	6	0
Doncaster Rov	Southport	05.00	03-04	79	2	6
RYAN Vaughan William						
Westminster, 2 September, 1968 ESch						(M)
Wimbledon	App	08.86	86-91	67	15	3
Sheffield U	L	01.89	88	2	1	0
Leyton Orient	Tr	08.92	92-94	40	4	0
RYDEN Hugh Johnston						
Dumbarton, 7 April, 1943						(F)
Leeds U	Yoker Ath	10.60				
Bristol Rov	Tr	06.62	62	8	-	4
Stockport Co	Morton	07.63	63	38	-	9
Chester	Tr	06.64	64-67	140	1	44
Halifax T	Tr	11.67	67-69	54	1	6
Stockport Co	Tr	12.69	69-72	112	11	15
RYDEN John Johnston						
Dumbarton, 18 February, 1931						(CD)
Accrington St	Alloa Ath	02.54	53-55	80	-	1
Tottenham H	Tr	11.55	55-58	63	-	2
Watford	Tr	06.61	61	24	-	1
RYDER Derek Francis						
Leeds, 18 February, 1947						(FB)
Leeds U	Jnrs	02.64				
Cardiff C	Tr	06.66	66	4	0	0
Rochdale	Tr	07.68	68-71	167	0	1
Southport	Tr	07.72	72-73	80	2	2
RYDER Robert (Bob)						
Bolton, 11 July, 1943 Died 2000						(FB)
Gillingham	Nantwich T	01.65	64-67	8	0	0
RYDER Stuart Henry						
Sutton Coldfield, 6 November, 1973 Eu21-3						(CD)
Walsall	YT	07.92	92-97	86	15	5
Mansfield T	Tr	07.98	98	18	4	2
RYDER Terence (Terry) Roy						
Norwich, 3 June, 1928						(W)
Norwich C	City W	09.46	46-49	46	-	12
Portsmouth	Tr	10.50	50-51	14	-	4
Swindon T	Tr	07.52	52	33	-	13
RYECRAFT Frederick (Fred)						
Southall, 29 August, 1939						(G)
Brentford	Southall	09.59	62-63	33	-	0
RYLANDS David (Dave) Robert						
Liverpool, 7 March, 1953						(CD)
Liverpool	App	03.70				
Hereford U	Tr	09.74	74-75	22	0	0
Newport Co	L	03.75	74	3	0	1
Hartlepool	L	03.76	75	11	0	0
Halifax T	Tr	06.76	76	5	0	0
RYMER George Herbert						
Ardsley, 6 October, 1923						(G)
Barnsley	Ardsley Victoria	12.43	46	3	-	0
Accrington St	Tr	02.47	46	8	-	0

League Club	Source	Date Signed	Seasons Played	Apps	Subs	Gls

S

SAAH Brian Ebo
Hornchurch, 16 December, 1986 (M)

League Club	Source	Date Signed	Seasons Played	Apps	Subs	Gls
Leyton Orient	Sch	•	03-04	13	5	0

SABELLA Alejandro (Alex)
Buenos Aires, Argentina, 5 November, 1954 Argentina int (M)

League Club	Source	Date Signed	Seasons Played	Apps	Subs	Gls
Sheffield U	River Plate (Arg)	08.78	78-79	76	0	8
Leeds U	Tr	06.80	80	22	1	2

SABIN Arthur Henry
Kingstanding, 25 January, 1939 Died 1958 (G)

League Club	Source	Date Signed	Seasons Played	Apps	Subs	Gls
Aston Villa	Jnrs	01.57	56-57	2	-	0

SABIN Eric
Paris, France, 22 January, 1975 (F)

League Club	Source	Date Signed	Seasons Played	Apps	Subs	Gls
Swindon T	Wasquehal (Fr)	07.01	01-02	60	13	9
Queens Park Rgrs	Tr	07.03	03	3	7	1
Boston U	L	03.04	03	2	0	0
Northampton T	Tr	03.04	03-04	37	14	13

SADDINGTON Nigel
Sunderland, 9 December, 1965 (CD)

League Club	Source	Date Signed	Seasons Played	Apps	Subs	Gls
Doncaster Rov	SC Vaux	09.84	84	6	0	0
Sunderland	Roker	01.86	86	3	0	0
Carlisle U	Tr	02.88	87-89	97	0	15

SADLER David
Yalding, 5 February, 1946 EYth/EAmat/Eu23-3/FLge-2/E-4 (CD)

League Club	Source	Date Signed	Seasons Played	Apps	Subs	Gls
Manchester U	Maidstone U	02.63	63-73	266	6	22
Preston NE	Tr	11.73	73-76	104	1	3

SADLER George Handel
Whitwell, 7 May, 1915 (FB)

League Club	Source	Date Signed	Seasons Played	Apps	Subs	Gls
West Ham U	Gainsborough Trinity	12.38	46	1	-	0

SADLER Matthew
Birmingham, 26 February, 1985 EYth (FB)

League Club	Source	Date Signed	Seasons Played	Apps	Subs	Gls
Birmingham C	YT	04.02	02	2	0	0
Northampton T	L	11.03	03	7	0	0

SADLIER Richard Thomas
Dublin, 14 January, 1979 IRYth/IRu21-2/IR-1 (F)

League Club	Source	Date Signed	Seasons Played	Apps	Subs	Gls
Millwall	Belvedere	08.96	96-03	103	42	34

SAFRI Youssef
Casablanca, Morocco, 1 March, 1977 Morocco int (M)

League Club	Source	Date Signed	Seasons Played	Apps	Subs	Gls
Coventry C	Raja Casablanca (Mor)	08.01	01-03	87	4	1
Norwich C	Tr	07.04	04	13	5	1

SAGAR Edward (Ted)
Campsall, 7 February, 1910 Died 1986 NIRL-1/FLge-5/E-4 (G)

League Club	Source	Date Signed	Seasons Played	Apps	Subs	Gls
Everton	Thorne Colliery	03.29	29-52	463	-	0

SAGARE Jake
Yakima, Washington, USA, 5 April, 1980 (F)

League Club	Source	Date Signed	Seasons Played	Apps	Subs	Gls
Grimsby T	Portland (USA)	11.02	02	1	0	0

SAGE Roland **Frank**
Chipping Sodbury, 31 May, 1924 Died 2000 (WH)

League Club	Source	Date Signed	Seasons Played	Apps	Subs	Gls
Cardiff C		02.45				
Newport Co	Tr	04.48	47-48	3	-	0

SAGE Melvyn (Mel)
Gillingham, 24 March, 1964 (FB)

League Club	Source	Date Signed	Seasons Played	Apps	Subs	Gls
Gillingham	App	03.82	81-85	126	6	5
Derby Co	Tr	08.86	86-91	137	3	4

SAHA Louis
Paris, France, 8 August, 1978 FrYth/Fru21/Fr-8 (F)

League Club	Source	Date Signed	Seasons Played	Apps	Subs	Gls
Newcastle U (L)	Metz (Fr)	01.99	98	5	6	1
Fulham	Metz (Fr)	06.00	00-03	100	17	53
Manchester U	Tr	01.04	03-04	16	10	8

SAHLIN Dan
Falun, Sweden, 18 April, 1967 (F)

League Club	Source	Date Signed	Seasons Played	Apps	Subs	Gls
Birmingham C (L)	Hammarby IF (Swe)	11.95	95	0	1	0

SAHNOUN Nicolas Omar Mickael
Bordeaux, France, 3 September, 1980 (M)

League Club	Source	Date Signed	Seasons Played	Apps	Subs	Gls
Fulham (L)	Bordeaux (Fr)	10.00	00	2	5	0

SAIB Moussa
Theniet-el-Had, Algeria, 6 March, 1969 Algeria 43 (M)

League Club	Source	Date Signed	Seasons Played	Apps	Subs	Gls
Tottenham H	Valencia (Sp)	02.98	97-98	3	10	1

SAILE Michael (Mike) Anthony
Heywood, 31 December, 1950 EYth (FB)

League Club	Source	Date Signed	Seasons Played	Apps	Subs	Gls
Bury	App	01.69	68-72	92	1	0

SAINSBURY Kim
Reading, 21 September, 1957 (F)

League Club	Source	Date Signed	Seasons Played	Apps	Subs	Gls
Reading	App	•	74	0	1	0

ST JOHN Ian
Motherwell, 7 June, 1938 Su23-2/SLge-4/S-21 (F)

League Club	Source	Date Signed	Seasons Played	Apps	Subs	Gls
Liverpool	Motherwell	04.61	61-70	334	2	95
Coventry C	Hellenic (SA)	09.71	71	18	0	3
Tranmere Rov	Tr	10.72	72	9	0	1

ST JUSTE Jason Valentine
Leeds, 21 September, 1985 (F)

League Club	Source	Date Signed	Seasons Played	Apps	Subs	Gls
Darlington	Garforth T	09.04	04	9	6	2

ST LEDGER-HALL Sean Patrick
Birmingham, 28 December, 1984 (M)

League Club	Source	Date Signed	Seasons Played	Apps	Subs	Gls
Peterborough U	Sch	07.03	02-04	34	2	0

SAINTY John Albert
Poplar, 24 March, 1946 ESch (F)

League Club	Source	Date Signed	Seasons Played	Apps	Subs	Gls
Tottenham H	App	07.63				
Reading	Tr	08.67	67-69	63	8	19
Bournemouth	Tr	02.70	69-73	111	7	20
Mansfield T	L	11.72	72	3	0	0
Aldershot	Tr	08.74	74-75	26	3	0

SAKHO Lamine
Louga, Senegal, 28 September, 1977 Fru21/Senegal int (M)

League Club	Source	Date Signed	Seasons Played	Apps	Subs	Gls
Leeds U (L)	Marseille (Fr)	08.03	03	9	8	1

SAKIRI Artim
Struga, Macedonia, 23 September, 1973 Macedonia 67 (M)

League Club	Source	Date Signed	Seasons Played	Apps	Subs	Gls
West Bromwich A	CSKA Sofia (Bul)	08.03	03-04	8	20	1

SALAKO Andrew (Andy) Olumide
Lagos, Nigeria, 8 November, 1972 (FB)

League Club	Source	Date Signed	Seasons Played	Apps	Subs	Gls
Charlton Ath	YT	04.91	90	1	0	0

SALAKO John Akin
Lagos, Nigeria, 11 February, 1969 E-5 (W)

League Club	Source	Date Signed	Seasons Played	Apps	Subs	Gls
Crystal Palace	App	11.86	86-94	172	43	22
Swansea C	L	08.89	89	13	0	3
Coventry C	Tr	08.95	95-97	68	4	4
Bolton W	Tr	03.98	97	0	7	0
Fulham	Tr	07.98	98	7	3	1
Charlton Ath	Tr	08.99	99-01	10	37	2
Reading	Tr	11.01	01-03	96	15	13
Brentford	Tr	08.04	04	30	5	4

SALATHIEL David **Neil**
Wrexham, 19 November, 1962 WSch (FB)

League Club	Source	Date Signed	Seasons Played	Apps	Subs	Gls
Wrexham	Sheffield Wed (Jnrs)	05.80	80	4	0	0
Crewe Alex	Tr	06.81	81-82	64	1	0
Wrexham	Arcadia Shepherds (SA)	12.83	83-89	239	1	3

SALE Mark David
Burton-on-Trent, 27 February, 1972 (F)

League Club	Source	Date Signed	Seasons Played	Apps	Subs	Gls
Stoke C	YT	07.90	89	0	2	0
Cambridge U	Tr	05.91				
Birmingham C	Rocester	03.92	91-92	11	10	0
Torquay U	Tr	03.93	92-93	30	14	8
Preston NE	Tr	07.94	94	10	3	7
Mansfield T	Tr	07.95	95-96	36	9	12
Colchester U	Tr	03.97	96-98	69	11	12
Plymouth Arg	L	03.99	98	8	0	1

SALES Ronald (Ronnie) Duncan
South Shields, 19 September, 1920 Died 1995 (CD)

League Club	Source	Date Signed	Seasons Played	Apps	Subs	Gls
Newcastle U	Reyrolles	07.42				
Leyton Orient	Tr	05.47	47-48	46	-	3
Hartlepools U	Colchester U	08.50	50	3	-	0

SALISBURY Gareth
Caernarfon, 11 March, 1941 (IF)

League Club	Source	Date Signed	Seasons Played	Apps	Subs	Gls
Wrexham	Jnrs	05.59	59-61	11	-	0
Norwich C	Tr	07.62				
Luton T	Tr	07.63	63	12	-	2
Colchester U	Tr	07.64	64	15	-	2
Chesterfield	Tr	07.65	65	34	0	9

SALL Abdou Hamed
Dakar, Senegal, 1 November, 1980 (CD)

League Club	Source	Date Signed	Seasons Played	Apps	Subs	Gls
Kidderminster Hrs	Toulouse (Fr)	08.01	01-02	31	0	2
Oxford U	L	11.02	02	0	1	0
Kidderminster Hrs	Revel (Fr)	02.04	03-04	19	2	0

SALLI Janne
Seinajoki, Finland, 14 December, 1977 FiYth/Fiu21/Fi-8 (FB)

League Club	Source	Date Signed	Seasons Played	Apps	Subs	Gls
Barnsley	Haka Valkeakoski (Fin)	11.00	00	6	1	0

SALMAN Danis Mahmut Mehmet
Famagusta, Cyprus, 12 March, 1960 EYth (FB)

League Club	Source	Date Signed	Seasons Played	Apps	Subs	Gls
Brentford	App	08.77	75-85	316	9	8
Millwall	Tr	08.86	86-89	85	8	4
Plymouth Arg	Tr	03.90	89-91	71	3	4
Peterborough U	L	03.92	91	1	0	0
Torquay U	Tr	09.92	92	20	0	0

SALMON Leonard (Len) Alexander
West Kirby, 24 June, 1912 Died 1995 (WH)

League Club	Source	Date Signed	Seasons Played	Apps	Subs	Gls
New Brighton	Hoylake	10.34	34-35	30	-	2
Burnley	South Liverpool	09.41				
Tranmere Rov	Tr	09.46	46-47	30	-	1

SALMON Michael (Mike) Bernard
Leyland, 14 July, 1964 (G)

League Club	Source	Date Signed	Seasons Played	Apps	Subs	Gls
Blackburn Rov	Jnrs	10.81	81	1	0	0
Chester	L	10.82	82	16	0	0
Stockport Co	Tr	08.83	83-85	118	0	0
Bolton W	Tr	07.86	86	26	0	0
Wrexham	Tr	03.87	86-88	100	0	0
Charlton Ath	Tr	07.89	90-97	148	0	0
Oxford U	L	12.98	98	1	0	0

SALMONS Geoffrey (Geoff)
Mexborough, 14 January, 1948 (M)

League Club	Source	Date Signed	Seasons Played	Apps	Subs	Gls
Sheffield U	Jnrs	02.66	67-73	170	10	8
Stoke C	Tr	07.74	74-77	115	3	14
Sheffield U	L	09.77	77	5	0	0
Leicester C	Tr	10.77	77	25	1	4
Chesterfield	Tr	08.78	78-81	119	1	15

SALT Philip (Phil) Thomas
Huddersfield, 2 March, 1979 (M)

League Club	Source	Date Signed	Seasons Played	Apps	Subs	Gls
Oldham Ath	YT	07.97	97-00	12	10	0

SALT Samuel (Sammy) John
Southport, 30 December, 1938 Died 1999 (WH)

League Club	Source	Date Signed	Seasons Played	Apps	Subs	Gls
Blackpool	Jnrs	01.56	60	18	-	0

SALTER Kenneth (Ken)
Cullompton, 16 November, 1933 (G)

League Club	Source	Date Signed	Seasons Played	Apps	Subs	Gls
Exeter C	Cullompton	11.50	50	1	-	0

SALTER Mark Charles
Oxford, 16 March, 1980 (F)

League Club	Source	Date Signed	Seasons Played	Apps	Subs	Gls
Southend U	Frome T	10.02	02	5	8	1

SALTON Darren Brian
Edinburgh, 16 March, 1972 SSch/SYth/Su21-6 (CD)

League Club	Source	Date Signed	Seasons Played	Apps	Subs	Gls
Luton T	YT	03.89	91-92	17	1	0

[SALVA] BALLESTA Vialcho Salvador
Paese, Spain, 22 May, 1975 Spain 3 (F)

League Club	Source	Date Signed	Seasons Played	Apps	Subs	Gls
Bolton W (L)	Valencia (Sp)	01.03	02	1	5	0

SALVAGE Barry John
Bristol, 21 December, 1946 Died 1986 (W)

League Club	Source	Date Signed	Seasons Played	Apps	Subs	Gls
Fulham	Eastbourne U	09.67	67-68	7	0	0
Millwall	Tr	03.69	68	1	1	0
Queens Park Rgrs	Tr	03.71	70-72	16	5	1
Brentford	Tr	02.73	72-74	87	0	8
Millwall	Tr	08.75	75-76	43	12	9

SALVATI Marc Robert
Middlesbrough, 5 March, 1983 (M)

League Club	Source	Date Signed	Seasons Played	Apps	Subs	Gls
York C	YT	●	01	1	7	1

SAM Hector McLeod
Mount Hope, Trinidad, 25 February, 1978 Trinidad 20 (F)

League Club	Source	Date Signed	Seasons Played	Apps	Subs	Gls
Wrexham	CLF San Juan Jab'h (Tr)	08.00	00-04	77	73	35

SAM Lloyd Ekow
Leeds, 27 September, 1984 EYth (F)

League Club	Source	Date Signed	Seasons Played	Apps	Subs	Gls
Charlton Ath	Sch	07.02	04	0	1	0
Leyton Orient	L	01.04	03	5	5	0

SAMBROOK Andrew (Andy) John
Chatham, 13 July, 1979 ESch (FB)

League Club	Source	Date Signed	Seasons Played	Apps	Subs	Gls
Gillingham	Jnrs	●	96	0	1	0
Rushden & Diamonds	Hartwick College (USA)	08.01	01-04	48	21	0

SAMBROOK Raymond (Ray)
Wolverhampton, 31 May, 1933 Died 2000 (W)

League Club	Source	Date Signed	Seasons Played	Apps	Subs	Gls
Coventry C	Wednesfield	09.53	54-57	96	-	26
Manchester C	Tr	01.58	57-61	62	-	13
Doncaster Rov	Tr	06.62	62	8	-	0

SAMMELS Jonathan (Jon) Charles
Ipswich, 23 July, 1945 EYth/Eu23-9/FLge-1 (M)

League Club	Source	Date Signed	Seasons Played	Apps	Subs	Gls
Arsenal	App	08.62	62-70	212	3	39
Leicester C	Tr	07.71	71-77	236	5	21

SAMPLE James (Jim)
Morpeth, 5 November, 1921 Died 1992 (IF)

League Club	Source	Date Signed	Seasons Played	Apps	Subs	Gls
Bradford C	Ashington	08.47	47-48	8	-	2

SAMPSON Ian
Wakefield, 14 November, 1968 (CD)

League Club	Source	Date Signed	Seasons Played	Apps	Subs	Gls
Sunderland	Goole T	11.90	91-93	13	4	1
Northampton T	L	12.93	93	8	0	0
Northampton T	Tr	08.94	94-03	372	10	26

SAMPSON Peter Stanley
Pitsea, 9 July, 1927 (WH)

League Club	Source	Date Signed	Seasons Played	Apps	Subs	Gls
Bristol Rov	Devizes T	06.48	48-60	339	-	4

SAMPSON Raymond (Ray) Victor
Swindon, 6 February, 1935 (IF)

League Club	Source	Date Signed	Seasons Played	Apps	Subs	Gls
Swindon T	Jnrs	05.52	53-58	64	-	10

SAMPSON Thomas (Tommy) William
Southwark, 18 August, 1954 (CD)

League Club	Source	Date Signed	Seasons Played	Apps	Subs	Gls
Millwall	App	06.72	72	0	1	0

SAMUEL JLloyd
Trinidad, 29 March, 1981 EYth/Eu20/Eu21-7 (FB)

League Club	Source	Date Signed	Seasons Played	Apps	Subs	Gls
Aston Villa	YT	02.99	99-04	128	18	2
Gillingham	L	10.01	01	7	1	0

SAMUEL Randolf (Randy) Fitzgerald
Trinidad, 23 December, 1963 Canada int (CD)

League Club	Source	Date Signed	Seasons Played	Apps	Subs	Gls
Port Vale	Fortuna Sittard (Holl)	11.95	95	9	0	1

SAMUELS Dean Walter
Hackney, 29 March, 1973 (F)

League Club	Source	Date Signed	Seasons Played	Apps	Subs	Gls
Barnet	Boreham Wood	12.96	96-97	13	26	4

SAMUELS Leslie (Les)
Oldham, 8 December, 1928 Died 1998 (IF)

League Club	Source	Date Signed	Seasons Played	Apps	Subs	Gls
Burnley		12.49	50	2	-	0
Exeter C	Tr	07.53	53	12	-	1
Wrexham	Tr	03.54	53-54	26	-	11
Crewe Alex	Tr	11.54	54-55	40	-	14
Bradford C	Tr	12.55	55-57	84	-	38
Stockport Co	Tr	03.58	57-58	25	-	5

SAMUELS Robert (Bobby) William Lewis
Aberdeen, 18 May, 1946 (W)

League Club	Source	Date Signed	Seasons Played	Apps	Subs	Gls
Lincoln C	Aberdeen	07.67	67	3	1	0

SAMWAYS Mark
Doncaster, 11 November, 1968 (G)

League Club	Source	Date Signed	Seasons Played	Apps	Subs	Gls
Doncaster Rov	YT	08.87	87-91	121	0	0
Scunthorpe U	Tr	03.92	91-96	180	0	0
York C	Tr	07.97	97	29	0	0
Darlington	Tr	07.98	99	33	1	0

SAMWAYS Vincent (Vinny)
Bethnal Green, 27 October, 1968 EYth/Eu21-5 (M)

League Club	Source	Date Signed	Seasons Played	Apps	Subs	Gls
Tottenham H	App	11.85	86-93	165	28	11
Everton	Tr	08.94	94-95	17	6	2
Wolverhampton W	L	12.95	95	3	0	0
Birmingham C	L	02.96	95	12	0	0
Walsall	Sevilla (Sp)	02.03	02-03	42	0	2

SANAGHAN Joseph (Joe)
Motherwell, 12 December, 1914 Died 1951 (FB)

League Club	Source	Date Signed	Seasons Played	Apps	Subs	Gls
Bradford PA	Blantyre Celtic	08.35	35	4	-	0
Bournemouth	Tr	06.37	37-48	169	-	0
Stockport Co	Tr	08.49	49-50	52	-	0

SANASY Kevin Roy
Leeds, 2 November, 1984 (F)

League Club	Source	Date Signed	Seasons Played	Apps	Subs	Gls
Bradford C	Sch	●	02-04	2	7	1

SANCHEZ John
Paddington, 21 October, 1940 ESch/EYth (WH)

League Club	Source	Date Signed	Seasons Played	Apps	Subs	Gls
Arsenal	Jnrs	10.57				
Watford	Tr	06.59	59-60	19	-	0

SANCHEZ Lawrence (Lawrie) Phillip
Lambeth, 22 October, 1959 ESch/NI-3 (M)

League Club	Source	Date Signed	Seasons Played	Apps	Subs	Gls
Reading	Thatcham T	09.78	77-84	249	13	28
Wimbledon	Tr	12.84	84-93	254	16	33
Swindon T	Tr	03.94	93	6	2	0

SANCHEZ-LOPEZ Carlos
Madrid, Spain, 22 July, 1979 (FB)

League Club	Source	Date Signed	Seasons Played	Apps	Subs	Gls
Bristol Rov	Getafe (Sp)	02.02	01	6	0	0

SAND Peter
Aalborg, Denmark, 19 July, 1972 DeLge (M)

League Club	Source	Date Signed	Seasons Played	Apps	Subs	Gls
Barnsley	Midtjylland (Den)	10.01	01	4	2	1

SANDEMAN Bradley Robert
Northampton, 24 February, 1970 (FB)

League Club	Source	Date Signed	Seasons Played	Apps	Subs	Gls
Northampton T	YT	07.88	87-90	28	30	3
Maidstone U	Tr	09.91	90-91	55	2	8
Port Vale	Tr	09.92	92-95	62	7	1
Rotherham U	Tr	07.96	96	20	1	2
Hereford U	Tr	03.97	96	7	0	0

SANDER Christopher (Chris) Andrew
Swansea, 11 November, 1962 (G)

League Club	Source	Date Signed	Seasons Played	Apps	Subs	Gls
Swansea C	App	11.79	81-83	20	0	0
Wrexham	L	09.84	84	5	0	0
Cardiff C	Tr	08.85	85	8	0	0
Cardiff C	Haverfordwest	03.86	85	5	0	0

SANDERCOCK Kenneth (Ken) Leslie
Plymouth, 31 January, 1951 (M)

League Club	Source	Date Signed	Seasons Played	Apps	Subs	Gls
Torquay U	App	01.69	68-69	42	4	1
Leicester C	Tr	11.69	69	5	4	1
Torquay U	Tr	11.71	71-74	113	6	5

SANDERCOCK Philip (Phil) John
Plymouth, 21 June, 1953 (FB)

League Club	Source	Date Signed	Seasons Played	Apps	Subs	Gls
Torquay U	App	09.71	69-76	199	5	13
Huddersfield T	Tr	06.77	77-78	81	0	1
Northampton T	Tr	09.79	79-80	69	0	3

SANDERS Alan John
Newport, 29 October, 1963 WSch (M)

League Club	Source	Date Signed	Seasons Played	Apps	Subs	Gls
Cardiff C	App	11.81	81	1	1	0

SANDERS Allan
Salford, 31 January, 1934 (FB)

League Club	Source	Date Signed	Seasons Played	Apps	Subs	Gls
Manchester C		08.55				
Everton	Tr	07.56	57-59	56	-	0
Swansea T	Tr	11.59	59-62	92	-	0
Brighton & Hove A	Tr	01.63	62-65	80	0	0

SANDERS James (Jim) Albert
Holborn, 5 July, 1920 Died 2003 (G)

League Club	Source	Date Signed	Seasons Played	Apps	Subs	Gls
Charlton Ath	Longlands	02.44				
West Bromwich A	Tr	11.45	46-57	327	-	0
Coventry C	Tr	07.58	58	10	-	0

SANDERS James (Jim) Charles Frederick
Marlborough, 15 October, 1932 (WH)

League Club	Source	Date Signed	Seasons Played	Apps	Subs	Gls
Bristol C		11.51				
Crystal Palace	Tr	03.55	55-58	46	-	0
Exeter C	Cheltenham T	08.62	62	20	-	1

SANDERS Peter Charles William
Newport, 7 September, 1942 (CF)

League Club	Source	Date Signed	Seasons Played	Apps	Subs	Gls
Newport Co	Jnrs	10.59	60	3	-	0
Gillingham	Tr	07.61	61	2	-	0

SANDERS Roy Joseph
Stepney, 22 September, 1940 (W)

League Club	Source	Date Signed	Seasons Played	Apps	Subs	Gls
Northampton T	Romford	05.62	62	15	-	2

SANDERS Steven (Steve)
Halifax, 2 June, 1978 (FB)

League Club	Source	Date Signed	Seasons Played	Apps	Subs	Gls
Huddersfield T	YT	07.96				
Doncaster Rov	Tr	08.97	97	19	6	0

SANDERSON Eric
Chapeltown, 10 November, 1921 Died 1988 (FB)

League Club	Source	Date Signed	Seasons Played	Apps	Subs	Gls
Rotherham U	Paramore	09.47	47	2	-	1

SANDERSON Ian
Torquay, 26 August, 1956 (F)

League Club	Source	Date Signed	Seasons Played	Apps	Subs	Gls
Torquay U		08.77	77	0	1	0

SANDERSON John Robert McDevitt
Carlisle, 5 February, 1918 Died 1993 (FB)

League Club	Source	Date Signed	Seasons Played	Apps	Subs	Gls
Carlisle U		05.38	38	15	-	0
Wolverhampton W	Tr	02.39				
Luton T	Tr	05.46	46	6	-	0

SANDERSON Keith
Hull, 9 October, 1940 (M)

League Club	Source	Date Signed	Seasons Played	Apps	Subs	Gls
Plymouth Arg	Bath C	08.64	64	29	-	2
Queens Park Rgrs	Tr	06.65	65-68	98	6	10

SANDERSON Michael (Mike)
Germany, 26 October, 1966 (M)

League Club	Source	Date Signed	Seasons Played	Apps	Subs	Gls
Darlington	Hartlepool U (App)	03.86	85	1	0	0

SANDERSON Paul David
Blackpool, 28 July, 1964 (W)

League Club	Source	Date Signed	Seasons Played	Apps	Subs	Gls
Manchester C	Fleetwood T	11.83				
Chester C	Tr	12.83	83	24	0	3
Halifax T	Tr	08.84	84-86	88	16	5
Cardiff C	Tr	07.87	87	8	13	1
Walsall	Tr	03.88	87	0	3	0

SANDERSON Philip (Phil)
Barnsley, 1 November, 1953 (W)

League Club	Source	Date Signed	Seasons Played	Apps	Subs	Gls
Barnsley	Worsborough Bridge	10.74	74	2	0	1

SANDFORD Lee Robert
Lambeth, 22 April, 1968 EYth (FB)

League Club	Source	Date Signed	Seasons Played	Apps	Subs	Gls
Portsmouth	App	12.85	85-89	66	6	1
Stoke C	Tr	12.89	89-95	255	3	8
Sheffield U	Tr	07.96	96-01	142	9	4
Reading	L	09.97	97	5	0	0
Stockport Co	L	10.01	01	7	0	0

SANDIFORD Ian Robert
Chorley, 26 February, 1946 (F)

League Club	Source	Date Signed	Seasons Played	Apps	Subs	Gls
Blackburn Rov	App	02.64				
Stockport Co	Tr	06.64	64-65	47	0	9
Crewe Alex	Tr	01.66	65-66	48	5	17

SANDLANDS Herbert
Nantwich, 9 August, 1931 Died 2005 (CD)

League Club	Source	Date Signed	Seasons Played	Apps	Subs	Gls
Crewe Alex (Am)	Nantwich T	08.54	54	1	-	0

SANDWITH Kevin
Workington, 30 April, 1978 (FB)

League Club	Source	Date Signed	Seasons Played	Apps	Subs	Gls
Carlisle U	YT	07.96	97	2	1	0
Lincoln C	Halifax T	03.04	03-04	35	5	2

SANDY Adam
Peterborough, 22 September, 1958 (M)

League Club	Source	Date Signed	Seasons Played	Apps	Subs	Gls
Northampton T	Wolverton T	02.80	79-82	88	16	7

SANDYS Harold (Harry) Albert
Fulham, 8 October, 1932 (CF)

League Club	Source	Date Signed	Seasons Played	Apps	Subs	Gls
Torquay U	Yeovil T	08.54	54	2	-	0

SANETTI Francesco
Rome, Italy, 11 January, 1979 (F)

League Club	Source	Date Signed	Seasons Played	Apps	Subs	Gls
Sheffield Wed	Genoa (It)	04.98	97-98	1	4	1

SANFORD Mark Alexander
London, 10 September, 1960 (F)

League Club	Source	Date Signed	Seasons Played	Apps	Subs	Gls
Aldershot	Jnrs	06.79	79-82	72	12	23

SANG Neil
Liverpool, 23 May, 1972 (M)

League Club	Source	Date Signed	Seasons Played	Apps	Subs	Gls
Everton	YT	05.90				
Torquay U	Tr	06.91	91	8	6	0

SAN JUAN Jesus
Zaragoza, Spain, 22 August, 1971 (M)

League Club	Source	Date Signed	Seasons Played	Apps	Subs	Gls
Wolverhampton W (L)	Real Zaragoza (Sp)	09.97	97	4	0	0

SANKEY John (Jack)
Winsford, 19 March, 1912 Died 1985 (WH)

League Club	Source	Date Signed	Seasons Played	Apps	Subs	Gls
West Bromwich A	Winsford U	11.30	33-38	144	-	5
Northampton T	Tr	10.45	46-47	42	-	0

SANKEY Martin Andrew
Wellington, 4 May, 1964 (F)

League Club	Source	Date Signed	Seasons Played	Apps	Subs	Gls
Shrewsbury T	App	02.82	82	0	5	0

SANKOFA Osei Omari Kwende
Streatham, 19 March, 1985 EYth (CD)

League Club	Source	Date Signed	Seasons Played	Apps	Subs	Gls
Charlton Ath	Sch	11.02	02	0	1	0

SAN MIGUEL Xavier
Bilbao, Spain, 7 May, 1971 (M)

League Club	Source	Date Signed	Seasons Played	Apps	Subs	Gls
Cambridge U	(Spain)	08.96	96	0	1	0

SANOKHO Amadou
France, 1 September, 1975 (M)

League Club	Source	Date Signed	Seasons Played	Apps	Subs	Gls
Burnley	Sanguistese (It)	09.04	04	0	3	0
Oldham Ath	Tr	03.05	04	0	1	0

SANSAM Christian (Chris)
Hull, 26 December, 1975 (M)

League Club	Source	Date Signed	Seasons Played	Apps	Subs	Gls
Scunthorpe U	YT	12.93	93-95	10	11	1
Scarborough	Halifax T	03.96	95	5	1	0
Bradford C	Tr	08.96	96	0	1	0
Hull C	Tr	11.96	96	2	1	0

SANSBY Clifford (Cliff) Palmer
Peterborough, 24 November, 1934 (FB)

League Club	Source	Date Signed	Seasons Played	Apps	Subs	Gls
Peterborough U	March T	(N/L)	60	1	-	1

SANSOM Kenneth (Kenny) Graham
Camberwell, 26 September, 1958 ESch/EYth/Eu21-8/FLge/E-86 (FB)

League Club	Source	Date Signed	Seasons Played	Apps	Subs	Gls
Crystal Palace	App	12.75	74-79	172	0	3
Arsenal	Tr	08.80	80-87	314	0	6

League Club	Source	Date Signed	Seasons Played	Apps	Subs	Gls
Newcastle U	Tr	12.88	88	20	0	0
Queens Park Rgrs	Tr	06.89	89-90	64	0	0
Coventry C	Tr	03.91	90-92	51	0	0
Everton	Tr	02.93	92	6	1	1
Brentford	Tr	03.93	92	8	0	0
Watford	Chertsey T	08.94	94	1	0	0

SANSOME Paul Eric
New Addington, 6 October, 1961 (G)

League Club	Source	Date Signed	Seasons Played	Apps	Subs	Gls
Millwall	Crystal Palace (App)	04.80	81-87	156	0	0
Southend U	Tr	03.88	87-96	308	0	0
Birmingham C	L	01.96	95	1	0	0

SANTOS Georges
Marseille, France, 15 August, 1970 Cape Verde int (M)

League Club	Source	Date Signed	Seasons Played	Apps	Subs	Gls
Tranmere Rov	Toulon (Fr)	07.98	98-99	46	1	2
West Bromwich A	Tr	03.00	99	8	0	0
Sheffield U	Tr	07.00	00-01	37	24	6
Grimsby T	Tr	09.02	02	24	2	1
Ipswich T	Tr	08.03	03	28	6	1
Queens Park Rgrs	Tr	08.04	04	39	4	5

SANTOS Yazalde (Ali) Damas
New Jersey, USA, 30 July, 1975 (F)

League Club	Source	Date Signed	Seasons Played	Apps	Subs	Gls
Bournemouth	Jersey Scots (USA)	11.95	95	0	3	0

SANTUS Paul Graham
Billinge, 8 September, 1983 (M)

League Club	Source	Date Signed	Seasons Played	Apps	Subs	Gls
Wigan Ath	YT	07.02	01	0	1	0

SAPHIN Reginald (Reg) Francis Edward
Kilburn, 8 August, 1916 (G)

League Club	Source	Date Signed	Seasons Played	Apps	Subs	Gls
Queens Park Rgrs	Walthamstow Ave	06.46	46-50	30	-	0
Watford	Tr	07.51	51-53	57	-	0

SARA Juan Manuel
Ituzaingo, Argentina, 13 October, 1978 (F)

League Club	Source	Date Signed	Seasons Played	Apps	Subs	Gls
Coventry C (L)	Dundee	01.03	02	1	2	1

SARGENT Gary Stewart
Turvey, 11 September, 1952 (F)

League Club	Source	Date Signed	Seasons Played	Apps	Subs	Gls
Norwich C	App	09.70	71	0	1	0
Scunthorpe U	Tr	07.72	72	14	1	1
Peterborough U	Bedford T	07.77	77-78	27	7	5
Northampton T	Tr	06.79	79-80	41	2	4

SAROYA Nevin
Hillingdon, 15 September, 1980 (M)

League Club	Source	Date Signed	Seasons Played	Apps	Subs	Gls
Brentford	YT	06.99	99	0	1	0

SARR Mass
Liberia, 6 February, 1973 Liberia 2 (M)

League Club	Source	Date Signed	Seasons Played	Apps	Subs	Gls
Reading	Hajduk Split (Cro)	07.98	98-99	18	13	3

SARSON Albert
Rossington, 31 December, 1930 (CF)

League Club	Source	Date Signed	Seasons Played	Apps	Subs	Gls
Doncaster Rov	Mansfield T (Am)	08.49	49-50	2	-	0

SARTORI Carlo Domenico
Calderzone, Italy, 10 February, 1948 (M)

League Club	Source	Date Signed	Seasons Played	Apps	Subs	Gls
Manchester U	Jnrs	02.65	68-71	26	13	4

SAS Marco
Vlaardingden, Holland, 16 February, 1971 Hou21 (CD)

League Club	Source	Date Signed	Seasons Played	Apps	Subs	Gls
Bradford C	NAC Breda (Holl)	07.96	96	31	0	3

SATCHWELL Kenneth (Ken) Raymond
Birmingham, 17 January, 1940 (W)

League Club	Source	Date Signed	Seasons Played	Apps	Subs	Gls
Coventry C	US Carburettors	09.58	58-61	68	-	21
Walsall	Nuneaton Borough	01.65	64-66	54	3	7

SAUL Eric Michael
Dublin, 28 October, 1978 (M)

League Club	Source	Date Signed	Seasons Played	Apps	Subs	Gls
Brighton & Hove A	YT	07.97	97	0	4	0

SAUL Frank Lander
Canvey Island, 23 August, 1943 EYth (F)

League Club	Source	Date Signed	Seasons Played	Apps	Subs	Gls
Tottenham H	Jnrs	08.60	60-67	112	4	37
Southampton	Tr	01.68	67-69	47	3	2
Queens Park Rgrs	Tr	05.70	70-71	40	3	4
Millwall	Tr	03.72	71-75	85	11	4

SAUNDERS Carl Stephen
Marston Green, 26 November, 1964 (F)

League Club	Source	Date Signed	Seasons Played	Apps	Subs	Gls
Stoke C		03.83	82-89	130	34	23
Bristol Rov	Tr	02.90	89-93	123	19	42
Oxford U	Tr	12.93	93	2	3	0
Walsall	Tr	02.94	93	1	1	0

SAUNDERS Dean Nicholas
Swansea, 21 June, 1964 FLge/W-75 (F)

League Club	Source	Date Signed	Seasons Played	Apps	Subs	Gls
Swansea C	App	06.82	83-84	42	7	12
Cardiff C	L	03.85	84	3	1	0
Brighton & Hove A	Tr	08.85	85-86	66	6	20
Oxford U	Tr	03.87	86-88	57	2	22
Derby Co	Tr	10.88	88-90	106	0	42
Liverpool	Tr	07.91	91-92	42	0	11
Aston Villa	Tr	09.92	92-94	111	1	38
Nottingham F	Galatasaray (Tu)	07.96	96-97	39	4	5
Sheffield U	Tr	12.97	97-98	42	1	17
Bradford C	Benfica (Por)	08.99	99-00	32	12	3

SAUNDERS Dennis Fowler
Scarborough, 19 December, 1924 Died 2003 EAmat (WH)

League Club	Source	Date Signed	Seasons Played	Apps	Subs	Gls
Newport Co	Huddersfield T (Am)	11.46	46	7	-	0

SAUNDERS Derek William
Ware, 6 January, 1928 EAmat (WH)

League Club	Source	Date Signed	Seasons Played	Apps	Subs	Gls
Chelsea	Walthamstow Ave	07.53	53-58	203	-	9

SAUNDERS George Ernest
Birkenhead, 1 March, 1918 Died 1982 (FB)

League Club	Source	Date Signed	Seasons Played	Apps	Subs	Gls
Everton		02.39	46-51	133	-	0

SAUNDERS Glyn
Nottingham, 16 June, 1956 (FB)

League Club	Source	Date Signed	Seasons Played	Apps	Subs	Gls
Nottingham F	App	06.74	76	4	0	0

SAUNDERS Leonard **James (Jimmy)**
Liverpool, 7 January, 1928 (CF)

League Club	Source	Date Signed	Seasons Played	Apps	Subs	Gls
New Brighton (Am)	Stoneycroft	01.51	50	4	-	2

SAUNDERS Francis **John (Jack)**
Middlesbrough, 24 August, 1924 (CD)

League Club	Source	Date Signed	Seasons Played	Apps	Subs	Gls
Darlington		09.46	46-47	67	-	0
Chelsea	Tr	05.48	49-53	52	-	0
Crystal Palace	Tr	08.54	54-55	59	-	0
Chester	Tr	05.57	57-58	67	-	3

SAUNDERS John George
Worksop, 1 December, 1950 Died 1998 (CD)

League Club	Source	Date Signed	Seasons Played	Apps	Subs	Gls
Mansfield T	App	12.68	69-72	89	0	2
Huddersfield T	Tr	10.72	72-75	121	0	1
Barnsley	L	12.75	75	9	0	0
Barnsley	Tr	03.76	75-78	140	0	7
Lincoln C	Tr	06.79	79	25	1	1
Doncaster Rov	Tr	08.80	80	27	1	2

SAUNDERS John Henry
Maidenhead, 18 December, 1943 (W)

League Club	Source	Date Signed	Seasons Played	Apps	Subs	Gls
Charlton Ath	Jnrs	08.62	62	1	-	0

SAUNDERS John Thomas
Newport, 2 October, 1950 WSch (CD)

League Club	Source	Date Signed	Seasons Played	Apps	Subs	Gls
Newport Co	Birmingham C (App)	08.69	69-70	26	1	0
Leeds U	Tr	07.71				
Walsall	Tr	10.72	72-75	94	5	2

SAUNDERS Mark Philip
Reading, 23 July, 1971 (M)

League Club	Source	Date Signed	Seasons Played	Apps	Subs	Gls
Plymouth Arg	Tiverton T	08.95	95-97	60	12	11
Gillingham	Tr	06.98	98-04	117	55	15

SAUNDERS Paul Brian
Watford, 17 December, 1959 (CD)

League Club	Source	Date Signed	Seasons Played	Apps	Subs	Gls
Watford	App	12.77				
Northampton T	Tr	07.78	78-82	114	12	5

SAUNDERS Robert (Robbie) Charles
Poole, 26 August, 1945 (W)

League Club	Source	Date Signed	Seasons Played	Apps	Subs	Gls
Bournemouth	App	06.63	65	2	1	0

SAUNDERS Ronald (Ron)
Birkenhead, 6 November, 1932 EYth (CF)

League Club	Source	Date Signed	Seasons Played	Apps	Subs	Gls
Everton	Jnrs	02.51	54	3	-	0
Gillingham	Tonbridge	05.57	57-58	49	-	20
Portsmouth	Tr	09.58	58-64	236	-	145
Watford	Tr	09.64	64-65	39	0	18
Charlton Ath	Tr	08.65	65-66	64	1	24

SAUNDERS Ronald (Ron) Albert
Malmesbury, 14 January, 1923 Died 1999 (CD)

League Club	Source	Date Signed	Seasons Played	Apps	Subs	Gls
Swindon T (Am)		04.48	47	1	-	0

SAUNDERS Roy
Salford, 4 September, 1930 EYth (WH)

League Club	Source	Date Signed	Seasons Played	Apps	Subs	Gls
Liverpool	Hull C (Am)	05.48	52-58	132	-	1
Swansea T	Tr	03.59	58-62	94	-	3

SAUNDERS Steven (Steve) John Peter
Warrington, 21 September, 1964 (F)

League Club	Source	Date Signed	Seasons Played	Apps	Subs	Gls
Bolton W	App	09.82	83	3	0	0
Crewe Alex	Tr	07.85	85	15	7	1
Preston NE	Tr	08.86				
Grimsby T	Tr	08.87	87-88	70	6	13
Scarborough	Tr	08.89	89	23	9	1

SAUNDERS Wesley (Wes)
Sunderland, 23 February, 1963 ESch (CD)

League Club	Source	Date Signed	Seasons Played	Apps	Subs	Gls
Newcastle U	Jnrs	06.81	81-84	79	0	0
Bradford C	L	03.85	84	1	3	0
Carlisle U	Tr	08.85	85-87	97	0	11
Torquay U	Dundee	07.90	90-92	60	1	6

SAVA Facundo
Ituzaingo, Argentina, 3 July, 1974 (F)

League Club	Source	Date Signed	Seasons Played	Apps	Subs	Gls
Fulham	Gimnasia Y Esg (Arg)	06.02	02-03	13	13	6

SAVAGE Basir (Bas) Mohammed
Wandsworth, 7 January, 1982 (W)

League Club	Source	Date Signed	Seasons Played	Apps	Subs	Gls
Reading	Walton & Hersham	02.02	01-03	6	10	0
Wycombe W	L	09.04	04	2	2	0
Bury	L	02.05	04	5	0	0

SAVAGE David (Dave) Thomas Patrick
Dublin, 30 July, 1973 IRu21-5/IR-5 (M)

League Club	Source	Date Signed	Seasons Played	Apps	Subs	Gls
Brighton & Hove A	Kilkenny C	03.91				
Millwall	Longford T	05.94	94-98	104	28	6
Northampton T	Tr	10.98	98-00	98	15	18
Oxford U	Tr	08.01	01-02	85	0	5
Bristol Rov	Tr	07.03	03-04	58	7	3

SAVAGE John Alfred
Bromley, 14 December, 1929 (G)

League Club	Source	Date Signed	Seasons Played	Apps	Subs	Gls
Hull C		09.50	50	4	-	0
Halifax T	Tr	03.52	51-53	61	-	1
Manchester C	Tr	11.53	54-57	30	-	0
Walsall	Tr	01.58	57-58	51	-	0

SAVAGE Reginald (Reg)
Eccles, 5 July, 1912 Died 1997 (G)

League Club	Source	Date Signed	Seasons Played	Apps	Subs	Gls
Leeds U	Stalybridge Celtic	02.31	34-38	79	-	0
Nottingham F	Queen of the South	05.46	46	20	-	0

SAVAGE Robert (Robbie) James
Liverpool, 8 January, 1960 (M)

League Club	Source	Date Signed	Seasons Played	Apps	Subs	Gls
Liverpool	App	01.78				
Wrexham	L	10.82	82	27	0	10
Stoke C	Tr	07.83	83	5	2	0
Bournemouth	Tr	12.83	83-86	80	2	18
Bradford C	Tr	12.86	86-87	11	0	0
Bolton W	Tr	09.87	87-89	83	4	11

SAVAGE Robert (Robbie) William
Wrexham, 18 October, 1974 WSch/WYth/Wu21-5/W-39 (M)

League Club	Source	Date Signed	Seasons Played	Apps	Subs	Gls
Manchester U	YT	07.93				
Crewe Alex	Tr	07.94	94-96	74	3	10
Leicester C	Tr	07.97	97-01	160	12	8
Birmingham C	Tr	05.02	02-04	82	0	11
Blackburn Rov	Tr	01.05	04	9	0	0

SAVARESE Giovanni
Caracas, Venezuela, 14 July, 1971 Venezuela 23 (F)

League Club	Source	Date Signed	Seasons Played	Apps	Subs	Gls
Swansea C	San Jose (USA)	10.00	00	28	3	12
Millwall	Tr	08.01	01	0	1	0

SAVILLE Andrew (Andy) Victor
Hull, 12 December, 1964 (F)

League Club	Source	Date Signed	Seasons Played	Apps	Subs	Gls
Hull C		09.83	83-88	74	27	18
Walsall	Tr	03.89	88-89	28	10	5
Barnsley	Tr	03.90	89-91	71	11	21
Hartlepool U	Tr	03.92	91-92	37	0	13
Birmingham C	Tr	03.93	92-94	51	8	17
Burnley	L	12.94	94	3	1	1
Preston NE	Tr	07.95	95-96	56	0	30
Wigan Ath	Tr	10.96	96-97	17	8	4
Cardiff C	Tr	10.97	97-98	34	1	12
Hull C	L	09.98	98	3	0	0
Scarborough	Tr	03.99	98	0	9	0

SAVILLE Peter William
Dalbeattie, 29 August, 1948 (W)

League Club	Source	Date Signed	Seasons Played	Apps	Subs	Gls
Carlisle U		07.66	67	1	0	0
Bradford PA	Hawick Royal Albert	03.69	68-69	31	0	1

SAVIN Keith Anthony
Oxford, 5 June, 1929 Died 1992 (FB)

League Club	Source	Date Signed	Seasons Played	Apps	Subs	Gls
Derby Co	Oxford C	05.50	50-55	65	-	0
Mansfield T	Tr	05.57	57-58	68	-	0

SAVINO Raymond (Ray) John
Norwich, 16 November, 1938 (W)

League Club	Source	Date Signed	Seasons Played	Apps	Subs	Gls
Norwich C	Thorpe Village	02.57	56-61	22	-	3
Bristol C	Tr	07.62	62-67	75	0	2

SAWARD Leonard (Len) Roderick
Aldershot, 6 July, 1927 (CF)

League Club	Source	Date Signed	Seasons Played	Apps	Subs	Gls
Crystal Palace	Beddington	03.49	48-50	9	-	1
Newport Co	Cambridge U	01.54	53-54	25	-	5

SAWARD Patrick (Pat)
Cobh, 17 August, 1928 Died 2002 IR-18 (WH)

League Club	Source	Date Signed	Seasons Played	Apps	Subs	Gls
Millwall	Beckenham	07.51	51-54	118	-	14
Aston Villa	Tr	08.55	55-60	152	-	2
Huddersfield T	Tr	03.61	60-62	59	-	1

SAWBRIDGE John (Jack)
Wigan, 20 September, 1920 Died 1984 (G)

League Club	Source	Date Signed	Seasons Played	Apps	Subs	Gls
Oldham Ath	Crossens	12.45	46-47	8	-	0

SAWYER Brian
Rotherham, 28 January, 1938 (CF)

League Club	Source	Date Signed	Seasons Played	Apps	Subs	Gls
Rotherham U	Rawmarsh Welfare	01.58	57-62	90	-	31
Bradford C	Tr	12.62	62-63	15	-	2

SAWYER Roy
Worsborough Bridge, 29 March, 1940 (CD)

League Club	Source	Date Signed	Seasons Played	Apps	Subs	Gls
Barnsley	Worsborough Bridge	05.58	60-61	2	-	0

SAWYERS Keith Wilson
Banbury, 14 June, 1960 (M)

League Club	Source	Date Signed	Seasons Played	Apps	Subs	Gls
Carlisle U	Carlisle Spartans	01.78	77-79	5	4	0

SAWYERS Robert (Rob)
Dudley, 20 November, 1978 (FB)

League Club	Source	Date Signed	Seasons Played	Apps	Subs	Gls
Barnet	Wolverhampton W (YT)	10.97	97-00	78	6	3

SAXBY Gary Philip
Clipstone, 11 December, 1959 (M)

League Club	Source	Date Signed	Seasons Played	Apps	Subs	Gls
Mansfield T	App	12.77	78	14	2	1
Northampton T	Tr	08.80	80-82	86	10	11

SAXBY Michael (Mick) William
Clipstone, 12 August, 1957 (CD)

League Club	Source	Date Signed	Seasons Played	Apps	Subs	Gls
Mansfield T	App	01.75	75-78	76	3	5
Luton T	Tr	07.79	79-81	82	0	6
Grimsby T	L	03.83	82	10	0	0
Lincoln C	L	11.83	83	10	0	1
Newport Co	Tr	07.84	84	6	0	0
Middlesbrough	Tr	09.84	84	15	0	0

SAXTON Robert (Bobby)
Doncaster, 6 September, 1943 (CD)

League Club	Source	Date Signed	Seasons Played	Apps	Subs	Gls
Derby Co	Denaby U	02.62	64-67	94	2	1
Plymouth Arg	Tr	02.68	67-75	224	6	7
Exeter C	Tr	09.75	75-77	92	0	3

SAYER Andrew (Andy) Clive
Brent, 6 June, 1966 (F)

League Club	Source	Date Signed	Seasons Played	Apps	Subs	Gls
Wimbledon	App	06.84	83-87	46	12	15
Cambridge U	L	02.88	87	2	3	0
Fulham	Tr	08.88	88-89	44	9	15
Leyton Orient	Tr	02.90	89-91	23	7	6
Sheffield U	L	03.91	90	0	3	0

SAYER Peter Anthony
Cardiff, 2 May, 1955 Wu21-2/W-7 (W)

League Club	Source	Date Signed	Seasons Played	Apps	Subs	Gls
Cardiff C	Jnrs	07.73	73-77	70	12	14
Brighton & Hove A	Tr	02.78	77-79	46	9	6
Preston NE	Tr	08.80	80-83	42	3	6
Cardiff C	L	09.81	81	4	0	1
Chester C	Tr	07.84	84	35	1	6

SBRAGIA Richard (Ricky)
Lennoxtown, 26 May, 1956 (CD)

League Club	Source	Date Signed	Seasons Played	Apps	Subs	Gls
Birmingham C	App	05.74	74-77	14	1	1
Walsall	Tr	10.78	78-79	77	0	4
Blackpool	Tr	07.80	80-81	24	2	1
York C	Tr	08.82	82-86	149	0	7
Darlington	L	08.85	85	6	0	0

SCAIFE Nicholas (Nicky) Antony
Middlesbrough, 14 May, 1975 (M)

League Club	Source	Date Signed	Seasons Played	Apps	Subs	Gls
York C	Whitby T	03.95	94-95	0	2	0

SCAIFE Robert (Bobby) Henry
Northallerton, 12 October, 1955 (M)

League Club	Source	Date Signed	Seasons Played	Apps	Subs	Gls
Middlesbrough	App	10.72				
Halifax T	L	01.75	74	5	1	1
Hartlepool	Tr	09.75	75-77	77	3	10
Rochdale	Tr	10.77	77-79	95	3	9

SCALES George
Northwich, 14 March, 1923 Died 1993 (G)

League Club	Source	Date Signed	Seasons Played	Apps	Subs	Gls
Chester	Manchester C (Am)	08.44	46-48	81	-	0

SCALES John Robert
Harrogate, 4 July, 1966 EB-2/E-3 (CD)

League Club	Source	Date Signed	Seasons Played	Apps	Subs	Gls
Bristol Rov	Leeds U (Jnrs)	07.85	85-86	68	4	2
Wimbledon	Tr	07.87	87-94	235	5	11
Liverpool	Tr	09.94	94-96	65	0	2
Tottenham H	Tr	12.96	96-99	29	4	0
Ipswich T	Tr	07.00	00	2	0	0

League Club	Source	Date Signed	Seasons Played	Career Record Apps	Subs	Gls
SCALES Terence (Terry) Albert						
Stratford, 18 November, 1951						(FB)
West Ham U	App	08.69				
Brentford	Tr	07.71	71-76	212	0	5
SCANLON Albert Joseph						
Manchester, 10 October, 1935 Eu23-5/FLge-1						(W)
Manchester U	Jnrs	12.52	54-60	115	-	34
Newcastle U	Tr	11.60	60-61	22	-	5
Lincoln C	Tr	02.62	61-62	47	-	11
Mansfield T	Tr	04.63	62-65	108	0	21
SCANLON John (Ian)						
Birkenshaw, Lanarkshire, 13 July, 1952						(W)
Notts Co	East Stirling	07.72	72-77	99	12	31
SCANNELL Thomas (Tommy)						
Youghal, 3 June, 1925 Died 1992 IR-1						(G)
Southend U	Tilbury	12.49	50-54	98	-	0
SCARBOROUGH Brian						
Ironville, 11 December, 1941						(W)
Derby Co	Jnrs	01.59	58-60	4	-	0
SCARBOROUGH James (Jim) Albert						
Nottingham, 10 June, 1931						(CF)
Darlington	West Bromwich A (Am)	09.51	51-53	49	-	15
SCARGILL Wayne						
Barnsley, 30 April, 1968						(FB)
Bradford C	Frickley Ath	11.93	94	1	0	0
SCARLETT Andre Pierre						
Wembley, 11 January, 1980						(M)
Luton T	YT	07.98	98-00	9	9	1
SCARLETT John Edgar						
Wolverhampton, 1 August, 1934 Died 1960						(IF)
Walsall		03.52	52-53	10	-	2
SCARROTT Alan Richard						
Malmesbury, 22 November, 1944						(W)
West Bromwich A	Chippenham T	12.61				
Bristol Rov	Tr	06.64				
Reading	Tr	04.65	65-67	90	0	7
SCARTH James (Jimmy) William						
North Shields, 26 August, 1926 Died 2000						(W)
Tottenham H	Percy Main Colliery	08.48	49-51	7	-	3
Gillingham	Tr	02.52	51-54	138	-	24
SCATTERGOOD Eric						
Worsborough Bridge, 9 September, 1929 Died 1998						(WH)
Barnsley	Worsborough DST	02.47	49-51	12	-	0
SCHEMMEL Sebastien						
Nancy, France, 2 June, 1975 Fru21						(FB)
West Ham U	Metz (Fr)	01.01	00-02	60	3	1
Portsmouth	Tr	08.03	03	12	2	0
SCHIAVI Mark Antony						
City of London, 1 May, 1964 EYth						(M)
West Ham U	App	11.81				
Bournemouth	L	09.83	83	10	0	0
Bournemouth	Tr	07.84	84	14	5	0
Northampton T	Tr	07.85	85-86	31	4	5
Cambridge U	Tr	09.86	86	24	6	2
SCHMEICHEL Peter Boleslaw						
Gladsaxe, Denmark, 18 November, 1963 Denmark 129						(G)
Manchester U	Brondby (Den)	08.91	91-98	292	0	0
Aston Villa	Sporting Lisbon (Por)	07.01	01	29	0	1
Manchester C	Tr	04.02	02	29	0	0
SCHNOOR Stefan						
Neumunster, Germany, 24 April, 1971						(CD)
Derby Co	SV Hamburg (Ger)	07.98	98-00	48	12	2
SCHOFIELD Daniel (Danny) James						
Doncaster, 10 April, 1980						(W)
Huddersfield T	Brodsworth Welfare	02.99	98-04	124	23	23
SCHOFIELD Ernest (Ernie)						
Sheffield, 29 March, 1921						(IF)
Bradford C		06.45	46	1	-	1
SCHOFIELD Gary						
Eccles, 27 March, 1957						(FB)
Stockport Co		03.78	77	0	1	0
SCHOFIELD Graham						
Manchester, 18 December, 1950						(CD)
Oldham Ath	Brookdale	08.69	69	1	0	0
SCHOFIELD John David						
Barnsley, 16 May, 1965						(M)
Lincoln C	Gainsborough Trinity	11.88	88-94	221	10	11
Doncaster Rov	Tr	11.94	94-96	107	3	12
Mansfield T	Tr	08.97	97-98	81	5	0
Hull C	Tr	07.99	99	13	12	0
Lincoln C	Tr	08.00	00	13	6	0
SCHOFIELD John Reginald						
Atherstone, 8 December, 1931						(G)
Birmingham C	Nuneaton Borough	02.50	52-65	212	0	0
Wrexham	Tr	07.66	66-67	52	0	0
SCHOFIELD Malcolm						
Failsworth, 8 October, 1918 Died 1985						(G)
Oldham Ath		11.37	46	7	-	0
SCHOFIELD Mark Anthony						
Wigan, 10 October, 1966						(FB)
Wigan Ath	App	07.85	83-84	1	1	0
SCHOFIELD Alan **Stewart**						
Blackburn, 24 July, 1933						(IF)
Southport	Blackburn Rov (Am)	07.57	57-58	36	-	9
SCHOFIELD Thomas (Tom)						
Halifax, 22 June, 1926						(G)
Halifax T (Am)	Boothtown	10.52	52	1	-	0
SCHOLES Martin						
Barrow, 28 January, 1954						(CD)
Workington		11.76	76	3	1	0
SCHOLES Paul						
Salford, 16 November, 1974 EYth/E-66						(M)
Manchester U	YT	01.93	94-04	259	62	87
SCHROEDER Nico						
Holland, 19 November, 1947						(G)
Swansea C		07.76	76	1	0	0
SCHUMACHER Steven (Steve) Thomas						
Liverpool, 30 April, 1984 EYth						(M)
Everton	YT	05.01				
Carlisle U	L	10.03	03	4	0	0
Bradford C	Tr	08.04	04	42	1	6
SCHWARZ Stefan Hans						
Malmo, Sweden, 18 April, 1969 Swu21/Sw-69						(M)
Arsenal	Benfica (Por)	05.94	94	34	0	2
Sunderland	Valencia (Sp)	08.99	99-01	62	5	3
SCHWARZER Mark						
Sydney, Australia, 6 October, 1972 AuYth/Auu20/Au-30						(G)
Bradford C	Kaiserslautern (Ger)	11.96	96	13	0	0
Middlesbrough	Tr	02.97	96-04	270	0	0
SCHWINKENDORF Jorn						
Hamburg, Germany, 27 January, 1971						(FB)
Cardiff C	Waldhof Mannheim (Ger)	11.99	99	5	0	0
SCIMECA Riccardo (Riccy)						
Leamington Spa, 13 June, 1975 Eu21-9/EB-1						(CD)
Aston Villa	YT	07.93	95-98	50	23	2
Nottingham F	Tr	07.99	99-02	147	4	7
Leicester C	Tr	07.03	03	28	1	1
West Bromwich A	Tr	05.04	04	27	6	0
SCOFFHAM Stephen (Steve)						
Munster, Germany, 12 July, 1983						(F)
Notts Co	Gedling T	02.04	03-04	7	15	2
SCONCE Mark Allan						
Wrexham, 18 February, 1968						(FB)
Chester C	App	07.86	85	1	1	0
SCOPE David Frederick						
Newcastle, 10 May, 1967						(W)
Northampton T	Blyth Spartans	09.89	89-91	6	13	1
SCOTHERN Ashley John						
Featherstone, 11 September, 1984 EYth						(F)
Barnsley	YT	•	01	0	1	0
SCOTHORN Garry						
Hoyland, 6 June, 1950						(G)
Sheffield Wed	App	06.67	67	1	0	0
SCOTSON Reginald (Reg)						
Stockton, 22 September, 1919 Died 1999						(WH)
Sunderland	Ouston Jnrs	04.39	46-50	61	-	1
Grimsby T	Tr	12.50	50-54	164	-	4

League Club	Source	Date Signed	Seasons Played	Career Record Apps	Subs	Gls
SCOTT Alexander (Sandy) MacNaughton						
Kingsbarns, 17 November, 1922 Died 1995						(FB)
Leicester C	Lochgelly Albert	03.47	47-49	31	-	1
Carlisle U	Tr	01.50	49-55	200	-	4
SCOTT Alexander (Alex) Silcock						
Falkirk, 22 November, 1936 Died 2001 Su23-1/SB/SLge-7/S-16						(W)
Everton	Glasgow Rgrs	02.63	62-66	149	0	23
SCOTT Andrew (Andy)						
Epsom, 2 August, 1972						(F)
Sheffield U	Sutton U	12.92	92-97	39	36	6
Chesterfield	L	10.96	96	4	1	3
Bury	L	03.97	96	2	6	0
Brentford	Tr	11.97	97-00	109	9	28
Oxford U	Tr	01.01	00-03	77	18	24
Leyton Orient	Tr	03.04	03-04	45	2	10
SCOTT Andrew (Andy) Michael						
Manchester, 27 June, 1975						(FB)
Blackburn Rov	YT	01.93				
Cardiff C	Tr	08.94	94-96	14	2	1
Rochdale	Tr	08.97	97	1	2	0
SCOTT Anthony (Tony) James Ernest						
St Neots, 1 April, 1941 EYth						(W)
West Ham U	Jnrs	05.58	59-65	83	0	16
Aston Villa	Tr	10.65	65-67	47	3	3
Torquay U	Tr	09.67	67-69	82	5	4
Bournemouth	Tr	07.70	70-71	60	2	6
Exeter C	Tr	06.72	72-73	51	0	2
SCOTT Augustus (Augie) Fisher						
Sunderland, 19 February, 1921 Died 1998						(IF)
Luton T	Hylton Colliery	03.39				
Southampton	Tr	07.47	47-49	46	-	9
Colchester U	Tr	08.51	51-53	120	-	10
SCOTT Christopher (Chris)						
Wallsend, 11 September, 1963						(CD)
Northampton T	Blyth Spartans	07.87				
Lincoln C	Tr	03.88	88	4	0	0
SCOTT Christopher (Chris) James						
Burnley, 12 February, 1980						(FB)
Burnley	YT	07.98	98	9	5	0
SCOTT Colin George						
Glasgow, 19 May, 1970						(G)
Brentford (L)	Glasgow Rgrs	03.90	89	6	0	0
SCOTT David Perry						
Belfast, 6 June, 1918 Died 1977						(G)
Northampton T	Linfield	05.45	46-47	11	-	0
SCOTT Derek Edward						
Gateshead, 8 February, 1958 ESch						(FB)
Burnley	App	02.75	74-84	277	8	24
Bolton W	Tr	07.85	85-87	119	0	0
SCOTT Dion Elijah						
Warley, 24 December, 1980						(CD)
Walsall	YT	05.99	00-01	0	2	0
Mansfield T	Tr	07.02				
Kidderminster Hrs	Tr	01.03	02	19	0	1
SCOTT Donald (Don)						
Elland, 20 October, 1922 Died 2000						(W)
Halifax T		09.48	48-49	20	-	5
SCOTT Frederick (Freddie) Hind						
Fatfield, 6 October, 1916 Died 1995 ESch						(W)
Bolton W	Fatfield Jnrs	01.35				
Bradford PA	Tr	05.36				
York C	Tr	02.37	36-46	74	-	16
Nottingham F	Tr	09.46	46-56	301	-	40
SCOTT Gary Craig						
Liverpool, 3 February, 1978						(FB)
Tranmere Rov	YT	10.95				
Rotherham U	Tr	08.97	97-98	19	1	0
SCOTT Geoffrey (Geoff) Samuel						
Birmingham, 31 October, 1956						(FB)
Stoke C	Highgate U	04.77	77-79	76	2	3
Leicester C	Tr	02.80	79-81	39	0	0
Birmingham C	Tr	02.82	81-82	18	1	0
Charlton Ath	Tr	10.82	82	2	0	0
Middlesbrough	Tr	06.84	84	2	0	0
Northampton T	Tr	09.84	84	16	1	0
Cambridge U	Tr	07.85	85	19	0	0

League Club	Source	Date Signed	Seasons Played	Career Record Apps	Subs	Gls
SCOTT George William						
Aberdeen, 25 October, 1944						(M)
Liverpool	App	10.61				
Tranmere Rov	Port Elizabeth C (SA)	11.68	68-69	35	1	0
SCOTT Ian						
Radcliffe, 20 September, 1967 ESch						(M)
Manchester C	App	09.85	87-88	20	4	3
Stoke C	Tr	07.89	89-91	21	9	2
Crewe Alex	L	03.91	90	12	0	1
Bury	Tr	08.92	92	7	2	2
SCOTT Ian Richard						
Otley, 4 March, 1969						(FB)
Manchester U	App	03.87				
Stockport Co	Tr	09.87	87-88	23	2	0
SCOTT James (Jim)						
Falkirk, 21 August, 1940 S-1						(W)
Newcastle U	Hibernian	08.67	67-69	70	4	6
Crystal Palace	Tr	02.70	69-71	36	7	5
SCOTT James (Jimmy)						
Hetton-le-Hole, 7 September, 1934 ESch						(WH)
Burnley	Jnrs	09.51	54-60	3	-	0
Oldham Ath	Tr	06.61	61-63	76	-	0
SCOTT James (Jamie) Adamson						
Newcastle, 28 February, 1960						(M)
Newcastle U	App	03.78	77-78	9	1	0
SCOTT James Dennis						
Olney, 5 September, 1945						(IF)
Leyton Orient	Chelsea (Am)	11.62	63-65	22	1	6
SCOTT James John Wedderburn						
Glasgow, 26 December, 1927						(IF)
Workington	Alloa Ath	06.54	54	6	-	1
SCOTT John (Johnny)						
Belfast, 22 December, 1933 Died 1978 NIB/NI-2						(W)
Manchester U	Ormond Star	10.51	52-55	3	-	0
Grimsby T	Tr	06.56	56-62	240	-	51
York C	Tr	06.63	63	21	-	3
SCOTT John						
Normanton, 2 January, 1942						(IF)
Bradford C	Jnrs	08.60	61-62	11	-	2
Chesterfield	Tr	07.63	63	5	-	0
SCOTT John Alfred						
Crosby, Cumberland, 18 July, 1928						(G)
Leeds U	Workington	05.50	50-54	111	-	0
SCOTT John Mather						
Edinburgh, 21 August, 1953						(CD)
Workington	Brechin C	08.75	75	1	1	0
SCOTT Joseph (Joey)						
Plymouth, 11 January, 1953						(F)
Bournemouth	Falmouth T	06.78	78	18	3	4
SCOTT Joseph (Joe) Cumpson						
Fatfield, 9 January, 1930						(IF)
Newcastle U		04.49				
Luton T	Spennymoor U	02.52	52-53	13	-	2
Middlesbrough	Tr	09.54	54-58	93	-	26
Hartlepools U	Tr	01.59	58-59	62	-	8
York C	Tr	06.60	60	17	-	2
SCOTT Keith James						
Westminster, 10 June, 1967						(F)
Lincoln C	Leicester U	03.90	89-90	7	9	2
Wycombe W	Tr	03.91	93	15	0	10
Swindon T	Tr	11.93	93-94	43	8	12
Stoke C	Tr	12.94	94-95	22	3	3
Norwich C	Tr	11.95	95-96	10	14	5
Bournemouth	L	02.96	95	8	0	1
Watford	L	02.97	96	6	0	2
Wycombe W	Tr	03.97	96-98	60	3	20
Reading	Tr	03.99	98-00	20	15	5
Colchester U	Tr	10.00	00	8	1	1
SCOTT Kenneth (Ken)						
Maltby, 13 August, 1931						(W)
Derby Co	Denaby U	08.50	50	2	-	0
Mansfield T	Denaby U	08.52	52	5	-	2
SCOTT Kevin						
Lincoln, 12 November, 1954						(CD)
Lincoln C	Sheffield Polytechnic	02.74	73	1	0	0

League Club	Source	Date Signed	Seasons Played	Career Record Apps	Subs	Gls
SCOTT Kevin Watson						
Easington, 17 December, 1966						(CD)
Newcastle U	App	12.84	86-93	227	0	8
Tottenham H	Tr	02.94	93-95	16	2	1
Port Vale	L	01.95	94	17	0	1
Charlton Ath	L	12.96	96	4	0	0
Norwich C	Tr	01.97	96-97	31	2	0
Darlington	L	01.99	98	4	0	0
SCOTT Lawrence (Laurie)						
Sheffield, 23 April, 1917 Died 1999 FLge-5/EB/EWar-16/E-17						(FB)
Bradford C	Bolton Woods	05.35	35-36	39	-	0
Arsenal	Tr	02.37	46-51	115	-	0
Crystal Palace	Tr	10.51	51-52	28	-	0
SCOTT Lloyd Edward						
Stepney, 13 October, 1961						(G)
Orient	App	10.79				
Blackpool	Tr	07.82	82	2	0	0
SCOTT Malcolm Ernest						
South Shields, 8 May, 1936						(WH)
Newcastle U	Cleadon Jnrs	09.55	56-60	25	-	2
Darlington	Tr	10.61	61-62	47	-	2
York C	Tr	10.63	63	19	-	0
SCOTT Martin						
Sheffield, 7 January, 1968						(FB)
Rotherham U	App	01.86	84-90	93	1	3
Bristol C	Tr	12.90	90-94	171	0	14
Sunderland	Tr	12.94	94-98	104	2	9
SCOTT Melvyn (Mel) Douglas						
Claygate, 26 September, 1939 Died 1997 EYth/Eu23-3						(CD)
Chelsea	Jnrs	11.56	57-61	97	-	0
Brentford	Tr	03.63	62-66	157	0	2
SCOTT Michael (Mike) Ramsey						
Newcastle, 4 December, 1945						(W)
Burnley	App	12.62				
Hartlepools U	Tr	07.64	64	2	-	0
SCOTT Morrys James						
Swansea, 17 December, 1970						(F)
Cardiff C	YT	07.89	89	1	8	0
Southend U	Colchester U	10.90				
Plymouth Arg	Tr	06.91	91	3	3	0
Northampton T	Tr	08.92	92	10	7	2
SCOTT Paul						
Wakefield, 5 November, 1979						(M)
Huddersfield T	YT	07.98	02-03	18	14	2
Bury	Tr	08.04	04	20	3	0
SCOTT Paul David						
Burnley, 29 January, 1985						(FB)
Burnley	Sch	07.04	03	0	2	0
SCOTT Peter Reginald						
Notting Hill, 1 October, 1963						(M)
Fulham	App	10.81	81-91	268	9	27
Bournemouth	Tr	08.92	92	9	1	0
Barnet	Burnham	11.93	93-95	72	6	2
SCOTT Peter William						
Walton, 19 September, 1952 EYth/NI-10						(FB)
Everton	App	07.70	71-74	42	2	1
Southport	L	01.74	73	4	0	0
York C	Tr	12.75	75-78	99	1	3
Aldershot	Tr	03.79	78-82	114	7	2
SCOTT Philip Campbell						
Perth, 14 November, 1974 Su21-4						(M)
Sheffield Wed	St Johnstone	03.99	98-99	2	7	1
SCOTT Richard Paul						
Dudley, 29 September, 1974						(M)
Birmingham C	YT	05.93	92-94	11	1	0
Shrewsbury T	Tr	03.95	94-97	91	14	18
Peterborough U	Tr	07.98	98-00	65	16	7
Peterborough U	Stevenage Borough	12.02	02	13	3	1
SCOTT Richard (Dick) Sydney Arthur						
Thetford, 26 October, 1941						(WH)
Norwich C	Thetford T	11.58	60-62	28	-	1
Cardiff C	Tr	07.63	63-64	37	-	5
Scunthorpe U	Tr	09.64	64-65	47	0	8
Lincoln C	Tr	07.66	66	9	1	1
SCOTT Robert (Bert)						
Bellshill, 20 May, 1930						(W)
Accrington St	Alloa Ath	09.54	54-58	149	-	32

League Club	Source	Date Signed	Seasons Played	Career Record Apps	Subs	Gls
Wrexham	Tr	07.59	59	2	-	0
Oldham Ath	Tr	10.59	59	9	-	1
SCOTT Robert (Bob)						
Broxburn, 13 January, 1964						(F)
Colchester U	Whitburn Jnrs	03.89	88-89	26	11	8
SCOTT Robert (Rob)						
Epsom, 15 August, 1973						(W)
Sheffield U	Sutton U	08.93	94-95	2	4	1
Scarborough	L	03.95	94	8	0	3
Northampton T	L	11.95	95	5	0	0
Fulham	Tr	01.96	95-98	65	19	17
Carlisle U	L	08.98	98	7	0	3
Rotherham U	Tr	11.98	98-04	160	14	9
SCOTT Robert Alexander						
Liverpool, 26 October, 1913 Died 1962 ESch						(G)
Liverpool		05.31				
Burnley	Tr	05.33	33-35	57	-	0
Wolverhampton W	Tr	02.36	35-38	119	-	0
Crewe Alex	Tr	08.47	47-48	44	-	0
SCOTT Robert (Bob) John						
Dundee, 16 March, 1937						(WH)
Cardiff C	Dundee Violet	02.57	57	3	-	0
Swindon T	Tr	06.61				
Newport Co	Tr	11.61	61-62	18	-	0
Southport	Sankey's	07.63	63	3	-	0
SCOTT Robert (Bobby) William						
Liverpool, 22 February, 1953						(CD)
Wrexham	Jnrs	07.71	70-75	15	4	0
Reading	L	01.75	74	5	0	0
Hartlepool	Tr	07.76	76	37	0	0
Rochdale	Tr	07.77	77-78	71	0	3
Crewe Alex	Tr	08.79	79-85	238	1	15
Wrexham	Northwich Vic	01.86	85	2	1	0
SCOTT Stuart **Robin**						
Shrewsbury, 31 March, 1946						(W)
Shrewsbury T	Jnrs	04.64	63-65	18	0	2
SCOTT Ryan						
Saltburn, 20 March, 1976						(G)
Darlington	YT	07.94	93	0	1	0
SCOTT Samuel (Sammy)						
Ashington, 14 June, 1922						(IF)
Hartlepools U	Ashington	02.46	46-47	49	-	17
SCOTT Stephen (Steve) Richard						
Johnstown, 5 November, 1966						(CD)
Wrexham	Oswestry T	03.86	87	0	2	0
SCOTT Walter						
Douglas, 23 June, 1932						(G)
Halifax T	Dumbarton	08.54	54	13	-	0
SCOTT William (Bill) John						
Preston, 14 June, 1921 Died 2002						(FB)
Preston NE	Jnrs	05.39	46-53	208	-	0
SCOTT William (Billy) Reed						
Willington Quay, 6 December, 1907 Died 1969 E-1						(IF)
Middlesbrough	Howden British Legion	05.27	30-31	26	-	5
Brentford	Tr	05.32	32-46	273	-	84
Aldershot	Tr	07.47	47	21	-	0
SCOTTING Allen						
Dartford, 22 April, 1966						(FB)
Gillingham	Charlton Ath (Jnrs)	02.84	83	2	0	0
SCOULAR James (Jimmy)						
Livingston, 11 January, 1925 Died 1998 S-9						(WH)
Portsmouth	Gosport Borough	12.45	46-52	247	-	8
Newcastle U	Tr	06.53	53-60	247	-	6
Bradford PA	Tr	01.61	60-63	108	-	5
SCOWCROFT James (Jamie) Benjamin						
Bury St Edmunds, 15 November, 1975 Eu21-5						(F)
Ipswich T	YT	07.94	95-00	163	39	47
Leicester C	Tr	07.01	01-04	127	6	24
Ipswich T	L	02.05	04	3	6	0
SCREEN Anthony (Tony) Lewis						
Swansea, 9 May, 1952 Wu23-1						(FB)
Swansea T	App	05.70	68-74	125	3	10
SCREEN William (Billy) Robert						
Swansea, 8 November, 1948 Wu23-2						(M)
Swansea T	Jnrs	03.67	67-71	133	9	13
Newport Co	Tr	06.72	72-75	137	5	7

SCRIMGEOUR Brian
Dundee, 11 August, 1959 (FB)

League Club	Source	Date Signed	Seasons Played	Apps	Subs	Gls
Chesterfield	Dundee	07.83	83-86	117	4	16

SCRIMSHAW Stanley (Stan)
Hartlepool, 7 August, 1915 Died 1988 (CD)

League Club	Source	Date Signed	Seasons Played	Apps	Subs	Gls
Hartlepools U	Easington CW	01.36	35-36	17	-	1
Bradford C	Tr	06.37	37-46	20	-	0
Halifax T	Frickley Colliery	10.47	47-49	52	-	0

SCRINE Francis (Frank) Henry
Swansea, 9 January, 1925 Died 2001 W-2 (IF)

League Club	Source	Date Signed	Seasons Played	Apps	Subs	Gls
Swansea T		03.44	47-53	142	-	46
Oldham Ath	Tr	10.53	53-55	78	-	21

SCRINE William Harold
Swansea, 3 December, 1934 (IF)

League Club	Source	Date Signed	Seasons Played	Apps	Subs	Gls
Swansea T	Jnrs	12.51	52	1	-	0

SCRIVENS Stephen (Steve)
Ewell, 11 March, 1957 (W)

League Club	Source	Date Signed	Seasons Played	Apps	Subs	Gls
Fulham	App	03.75	74-75	3	1	1
Brentford	L	12.76	76	5	0	0

SCRIVENS William
Rotherham, 26 May, 1936 (G)

League Club	Source	Date Signed	Seasons Played	Apps	Subs	Gls
Rotherham U		08.56	56	2	-	0

SCRUGHAM Robert
Cleator Moor, 15 May, 1932 (G)

League Club	Source	Date Signed	Seasons Played	Apps	Subs	Gls
Workington	Cleator Moor	08.53	53	3	-	0

SCULLION Stewart McNab Adam
Bo'ness, 18 April, 1946 (W)

League Club	Source	Date Signed	Seasons Played	Apps	Subs	Gls
Charlton Ath	Chesham U	03.65				
Watford	Tr	02.66	65-70	217	8	30
Sheffield U	Tr	05.71	71-73	53	4	7
Watford	Tr	12.73	73-75	87	0	19

SCULLY Anthony (Tony) Derek Thomas
Dublin, 12 June, 1976 IRSch/IRYth/IRu21-10/IRB-1 (W)

League Club	Source	Date Signed	Seasons Played	Apps	Subs	Gls
Crystal Palace	YT	12.93	95-96	0	3	0
Bournemouth	L	10.94	94	6	4	0
Cardiff C	L	01.96	95	13	1	0
Manchester C	Tr	08.97	97	1	8	0
Stoke C	L	01.98	97	7	0	0
Queens Park Rgrs	Tr	03.98	97-00	20	20	2
Cambridge U	Tr	07.01	01-02	20	11	2
Southend U	L	11.02	02	8	0	0
Peterborough U	Tr	03.03	02	0	3	0
Notts Co	Tamworth	02.04	03-04	26	15	5

SCULLY Patrick (Pat) Joseph
Dublin, 23 June, 1970 IRSch/IRYth/IRu23-1/IRu21-9/IRB/IR-1 (CD)

League Club	Source	Date Signed	Seasons Played	Apps	Subs	Gls
Arsenal	YT	09.87				
Preston NE	L	09.89	89	13	0	1
Northampton T	L	08.90	90	15	0	0
Southend U	Tr	01.91	90-93	114	1	6
Huddersfield T	Tr	03.94	93-95	74	0	2

SCURR David William
Netley, 25 September, 1939 Died 1991 (FB)

League Club	Source	Date Signed	Seasons Played	Apps	Subs	Gls
Southampton	Jnrs	04.58	59-60	2	-	0

SCURR John (Jackie) Thomas
North Shields, 30 September, 1940 (IF)

League Club	Source	Date Signed	Seasons Played	Apps	Subs	Gls
Arsenal	North Shields BC	09.59				
Carlisle U	Tr	01.61	60-61	14	-	1

SEABURY Kevin
Shrewsbury, 24 November, 1973 (FB)

League Club	Source	Date Signed	Seasons Played	Apps	Subs	Gls
Shrewsbury T	YT	07.92	92-00	206	23	7

SEACOLE Jason Paul
Oxford, 11 April, 1960 ESch/EYth (F)

League Club	Source	Date Signed	Seasons Played	Apps	Subs	Gls
Oxford U	App	04.77	76-81	104	16	22

SEADEN John Charles
Rochford, 4 June, 1967 (M)

League Club	Source	Date Signed	Seasons Played	Apps	Subs	Gls
Southend U	App	03.85	84-85	18	1	0

SEAGRAVES Christopher (Chris) Anthony
Liverpool, 7 October, 1964 (FB)

League Club	Source	Date Signed	Seasons Played	Apps	Subs	Gls
Liverpool	App	09.82				
Grimsby T	Tr	08.84	84	22	1	0

SEAGRAVES Mark
Bootle, 22 October, 1966 ESch/EYth (CD)

League Club	Source	Date Signed	Seasons Played	Apps	Subs	Gls
Liverpool	App	11.83				
Norwich C	L	11.86	86	3	0	0
Manchester C	Tr	09.87	87-89	36	6	0
Bolton W	Tr	09.90	90-94	152	5	7
Swindon T	Tr	06.95	95-97	57	4	0

SEAL David
Penrith, Australia, 26 January, 1972 (F)

League Club	Source	Date Signed	Seasons Played	Apps	Subs	Gls
Bristol C	Aalst (Bel)	10.94	94-96	24	27	10
Northampton T	Tr	08.97	97-98	35	8	12

SEAL James (Jimmy)
Walton, West Yorkshire, 9 December, 1950 (F)

League Club	Source	Date Signed	Seasons Played	Apps	Subs	Gls
Wolverhampton W	Upton Robins	03.68	68	1	0	0
Walsall	L	01.70	69	17	0	8
Walsall	L	12.70	70	24	0	6
Barnsley	Tr	05.71	71	43	0	12
York C	Tr	07.72	72-76	152	9	43
Darlington	Tr	11.76	76-79	115	7	19
Rochdale	Tr	11.79	79-80	44	9	4

SEALEY Alan William
Canning Town, 24 February, 1942 Died 1996 (F)

League Club	Source	Date Signed	Seasons Played	Apps	Subs	Gls
Leyton Orient	Memorial Sports	08.59	60	4	-	1
West Ham U	Tr	03.61	60-66	107	0	22
Plymouth Arg	Tr	09.67	67	4	0	0

SEALEY Arthur **John**
Wallasey, 27 December, 1945 (W)

League Club	Source	Date Signed	Seasons Played	Apps	Subs	Gls
Liverpool	Warrington T	12.63	64	1	-	1
Chester	Tr	06.66	66-67	3	1	0

SEALEY Leslie (Les) Jesse
Bethnal Green, 29 September, 1957 Died 2001 (G)

League Club	Source	Date Signed	Seasons Played	Apps	Subs	Gls
Coventry C	App	03.76	76-82	158	0	0
Luton T	Tr	08.83	83-88	207	0	0
Plymouth Arg	L	10.84	84	6	0	0
Manchester U	L	03.90	89	2	0	0
Manchester U	Tr	06.90	90	31	0	0
Aston Villa	Tr	07.91	91	18	0	0
Coventry C	L	03.92	91	2	0	0
Birmingham C	L	10.92	92	12	0	0
Manchester U	Tr	01.93				
Blackpool	Tr	07.94	94	7	0	0
West Ham U	Tr	11.94	95	1	1	0
Leyton Orient	Tr	07.96	96	12	0	0
West Ham U	Tr	11.96	96	1	1	0

SEALY Anthony (Tony) John
Hackney, 7 May, 1959 (F)

League Club	Source	Date Signed	Seasons Played	Apps	Subs	Gls
Southampton	App	05.77	77-78	2	5	0
Crystal Palace	Tr	03.79	78-80	16	8	5
Port Vale	L	02.80	79	17	0	6
Queens Park Rgrs	Tr	03.81	80-83	57	6	18
Port Vale	L	02.82	81	6	0	4
Fulham	L	12.83	83	5	0	1
Fulham	Tr	08.84	84-85	17	3	10
Leicester C	Tr	09.85	85-86	28	11	7
Bournemouth	L	03.87	86	8	5	2
Brentford	Braga (Por)	03.89	88	11	1	4
Bristol Rov	Tr	09.89	89-90	21	16	7
Brentford	MyPa (Fin)	10.91	91	9	9	0

SEAMAN David Andrew
Rotherham, 19 September, 1963 Eu21-10/EB-6/E-75 (G)

League Club	Source	Date Signed	Seasons Played	Apps	Subs	Gls
Leeds U	App	09.81				
Peterborough U	Tr	08.82	82-84	91	0	0
Birmingham C	Tr	10.84	84-85	75	0	0
Queens Park Rgrs	Tr	08.86	86-89	141	0	0
Arsenal	Tr	05.90	90-02	405	0	0
Manchester C	Tr	07.03	03	19	0	0

SEAR Reginald **Clifford (Cliff)**
Rhostyllen, 22 September, 1936 Wu23-2/W-1 (FB)

League Club	Source	Date Signed	Seasons Played	Apps	Subs	Gls
Manchester C	Oswestry T	01.57	56-65	248	0	1
Chester	Tr	04.68	68-69	48	1	1

SEARGEANT Steven (Steve) Charles
Liverpool, 2 January, 1951 ESch (FB)

League Club	Source	Date Signed	Seasons Played	Apps	Subs	Gls
Everton	App	07.68	71-77	77	3	1

SEARLE Damon Peter
Cardiff, 26 October, 1971 WSch/WYth/Wu21-6/WB-1 (FB)

League Club	Source	Date Signed	Seasons Played	Apps	Subs	Gls
Cardiff C	YT	08.90	90-95	232	2	3
Stockport Co	Tr	05.96	96-97	34	7	0
Carlisle U	Tr	07.98	98-99	57	9	3
Rochdale	L	09.99	99	13	1	0
Southend U	Tr	07.00	00-02	126	7	3
Chesterfield	Tr	08.03	03	4	1	0

SEARLE Eric Frederick
Guildford, 20 July, 1925 (G)

League Club	Source	Date Signed	Seasons Played	Apps	Subs	Gls
Aldershot		10.47	47-49	14	-	0

SEARLE Stephen (Steve)
Lambeth, 7 March, 1977 (M)

League Club	Source	Date Signed	Seasons Played	Apps	Subs	Gls
Barnet	Sittingbourne	08.97	97-99	67	17	5

SEARS Douglas (Doug) Reginald
Eton, 5 January, 1919 Died 1995 (IF)

League Club	Source	Date Signed	Seasons Played	Apps	Subs	Gls
Grimsby T		10.43				
Reading	Tr	05.46	46	5	-	0
Aldershot	Tr	06.47	47-49	46	-	13

SEARS Gerald (Gerry)
Arkwright Town, 13 January, 1935 (FB)

League Club	Source	Date Signed	Seasons Played	Apps	Subs	Gls
Chesterfield	Jnrs	01.52	52-67	413	0	4

SEARSON Harold (Harry) Vincent
Mansfield, 3 June, 1924 (G)

League Club	Source	Date Signed	Seasons Played	Apps	Subs	Gls
Sheffield Wed	Bilsthorpe Colliery	08.46				
Mansfield T	Tr	06.47	47-48	42	-	0
Leeds U	Tr	01.49	48-51	104	-	0
York C	Tr	11.52	52-53	62	-	0

SEARY Raymond (Ray) Michael
Slough, 18 September, 1952 Died 2001 (FB)

League Club	Source	Date Signed	Seasons Played	Apps	Subs	Gls
Queens Park Rgrs	App	09.70	71	0	1	0
Cambridge U	Tr	03.74	73-75	55	2	0

SEASMAN John
Liverpool, 21 February, 1955 (M)

League Club	Source	Date Signed	Seasons Played	Apps	Subs	Gls
Tranmere Rov	App	02.73	72-74	15	2	0
Luton T	Tr	01.75	74-75	7	1	2
Millwall	Tr	02.76	75-79	157	1	35
Rotherham U	Tr	08.80	80-83	93	7	25
Cardiff C	Tr	08.84	84	10	2	2
Rochdale	L	11.84	84	8	0	0
Chesterfield	Tr	01.85	84	8	2	1
Rochdale	Tr	07.85	85-87	86	1	4

SEATHERTON Raymond (Ray)
Tiverton, 20 May, 1932 (CF)

League Club	Source	Date Signed	Seasons Played	Apps	Subs	Gls
Bristol Rov	Minehead	02.55	55	2	-	2

SEATON Gordon
Wick, 1 September, 1945 (M)

League Club	Source	Date Signed	Seasons Played	Apps	Subs	Gls
Chester	Rhyl	12.66	66-67	46	3	2

SEBA Jesus Hernandez
Zaragoza, Spain, 11 April, 1974 Spu21 (W)

League Club	Source	Date Signed	Seasons Played	Apps	Subs	Gls
Wigan Ath	Real Zaragoza (Sp)	08.95	95-96	8	13	3

SEBOK Vilmos
Budapest, Hungary, 13 June, 1973 Hungary 33 (FB)

League Club	Source	Date Signed	Seasons Played	Apps	Subs	Gls
Bristol C	Ujpest Dosza (Hun)	01.99	98-99	18	5	0

SEDDON Andrew (Andy)
Worsley, 23 November, 1959 (FB)

League Club	Source	Date Signed	Seasons Played	Apps	Subs	Gls
Stockport Co		08.77	78-82	4	3	0

SEDDON Benjamin (Ben) Paul
Liverpool, 5 February, 1952 (CD)

League Club	Source	Date Signed	Seasons Played	Apps	Subs	Gls
Tranmere Rov	Formby	04.73	73	1	0	0

SEDDON David Andrew
Rochdale, 13 April, 1951 (FB)

League Club	Source	Date Signed	Seasons Played	Apps	Subs	Gls
Rochdale	Stafford Rgrs	01.74	73-74	18	2	0

SEDDON Frank Owen
Stockton, 1 May, 1928 (CD)

League Club	Source	Date Signed	Seasons Played	Apps	Subs	Gls
Notts Co		05.46				
Hull C	Tr	05.47	49	3	-	0
Halifax T	Tr	01.51	50-51	4	-	0

SEDDON Gareth Jonathan
Burnley, 23 May, 1980 (F)

League Club	Source	Date Signed	Seasons Played	Apps	Subs	Gls
Bury	RAF Codsall	08.01	01-03	53	26	17

SEDDON Ian Wright
Prestbury, 14 October, 1950 (M)

League Club	Source	Date Signed	Seasons Played	Apps	Subs	Gls
Bolton W	App	06.69	69-72	51	13	4
Chester	Tr	09.73	73-75	62	11	7
Stockport Co	L	11.75	75	4	0	0
Chesterfield	L	01.76	75	2	0	0
Cambridge U	Tr	02.76	75-76	34	3	3
Rochdale	Tr	07.77	77	30	1	3
Wigan Ath	Tr	07.78	78	1	0	0

SEDDON Thomas (Tom)
Rotherham, 25 October, 1935 (FB)

League Club	Source	Date Signed	Seasons Played	Apps	Subs	Gls
Rotherham U		03.54	58	1	-	0

SEDGEMORE Benjamin (Ben) Redwood
Wolverhampton, 5 August, 1975 ESch (M)

League Club	Source	Date Signed	Seasons Played	Apps	Subs	Gls
Birmingham C	YT	05.93				
Northampton T	L	12.94	94	1	0	0
Mansfield T	L	08.95	95	4	5	0
Peterborough U	Tr	01.96	95	13	4	0
Mansfield T	Tr	09.96	96-97	58	9	6
Macclesfield T	Tr	03.98	97-00	84	18	6
Lincoln C	Tr	02.01	00-03	83	25	5

SEDGEMORE Jake Oliver
Wolverhampton, 10 October, 1978 ESemiPro-5 (FB)

League Club	Source	Date Signed	Seasons Played	Apps	Subs	Gls
Shrewsbury T	Northwich Vic	07.03	04	25	6	5

SEDGLEY Stephen (Steve) Philip
Enfield, 26 May, 1968 Eu21-11 (CD)

League Club	Source	Date Signed	Seasons Played	Apps	Subs	Gls
Coventry C	App	06.86	86-88	81	3	3
Tottenham H	Tr	07.89	89-93	147	17	8
Ipswich T	Tr	06.94	94-96	105	0	15
Wolverhampton W	Tr	07.97	97-00	96	10	9

SEDGWICK Christopher (Chris) Edward
Sheffield, 28 April, 1980 (W)

League Club	Source	Date Signed	Seasons Played	Apps	Subs	Gls
Rotherham U	YT	08.97	97-04	195	48	17
Preston NE	Tr	11.04	04	24	0	3

SEDLAN Jason Mark
Peterborough, 5 August, 1979 (M)

League Club	Source	Date Signed	Seasons Played	Apps	Subs	Gls
Mansfield T	YT	07.98	97-98	1	5	0

SEDLOSKI Goce
Golemo Konjari, Macedonia, 10 April, 1974 Macedonia int (CD)

League Club	Source	Date Signed	Seasons Played	Apps	Subs	Gls
Sheffield Wed	Hadjuk Split (Cro)	03.98	97	3	1	0

SEED Trevance (Terry) Frederick
Preston, 3 September, 1923 Died 1994 (CD)

League Club	Source	Date Signed	Seasons Played	Apps	Subs	Gls
Preston NE	Jnrs	07.46				
Carlisle U	Tr	12.46	46-49	81	-	0
Accrington St	Tr	09.50	50	1	-	0

SEEMLEY Ivor John
Sheffield, 30 June, 1929 (FB)

League Club	Source	Date Signed	Seasons Played	Apps	Subs	Gls
Sheffield Wed	Jnrs	07.46	53-54	15	-	0
Stockport Co	Tr	06.55	55-56	81	-	0
Chesterfield	Tr	06.57	57-58	77	-	0

SEGERS Johannes (Hans)
Eindhoven, Holland, 30 October, 1961 (G)

League Club	Source	Date Signed	Seasons Played	Apps	Subs	Gls
Nottingham F	PSV Eindhoven (Holl)	08.84	84-87	58	0	0
Stoke C	L	02.87	86	1	0	0
Sheffield U	L	11.87	87	10	0	0
Wimbledon	Tr	09.88	88-95	265	2	0
Wolverhampton W	Tr	08.96	97	11	0	0
Tottenham H	Tr	08.98	98	1	0	0

SEGURA Victor Abascal
Zaragoza, Spain, 30 March, 1973 Spu21 (FB)

League Club	Source	Date Signed	Seasons Played	Apps	Subs	Gls
Norwich C	Lleida (Sp)	08.97	97-98	24	5	0

SEIGEL Arnold William
Islington, 21 March, 1919 (WH)

League Club	Source	Date Signed	Seasons Played	Apps	Subs	Gls
Leyton Orient	Hendon	06.46	46	9	-	0

SEITH Robert (Bobby)
Coatbridge, 9 March, 1932 (WH)

League Club	Source	Date Signed	Seasons Played	Apps	Subs	Gls
Burnley	Monifieth Tayside	03.49	53-59	211	-	6

SELBY Dennis
Broughton, 15 October, 1920 Died 1969 (W)

League Club	Source	Date Signed	Seasons Played	Apps	Subs	Gls
Chester (Am)		07.46	46	5	-	1

SELF Glenn Walter
Norwich, 4 December, 1953 (F)

League Club	Source	Date Signed	Seasons Played	Apps	Subs	Gls
Norwich C	App	09.70	70-72	4	1	2
Torquay U	L	03.73	72	3	0	0

SELKIRK John (Jack)
Doncaster, 20 January, 1923 Died 1993 (FB)

League Club	Source	Date Signed	Seasons Played	Apps	Subs	Gls
Rotherham U	Edlington CW	10.44	46-56	427	-	13

SELLARS Geoffrey (Geoff)
Stockport, 20 May, 1930 (W)

League Club	Source	Date Signed	Seasons Played	Apps	Subs	Gls
Leeds U	Altrincham	04.50				
Aston Villa	Tr	08.50	50	2	-	0

SELLARS John (Johnny)
Stoke-on-Trent, 28 April, 1924 Died 1985 (WH)

League Club	Source	Date Signed	Seasons Played	Apps	Subs	Gls
Stoke C	Jnrs	10.41	46-57	384	-	14

SELLARS Peter
Market Rasen, 15 March, 1958 (M)

League Club	Source	Date Signed	Seasons Played	Apps	Subs	Gls
Lincoln C	App	•	75	0	1	0

SELLARS Scott
Sheffield, 27 November, 1965 Eu21-3 (W)

League Club	Source	Date Signed	Seasons Played	Apps	Subs	Gls
Leeds U	App	07.83	82-85	72	4	12
Blackburn Rov	Tr	07.86	86-91	194	8	35

League Club	Source	Date Signed	Seasons Played	Apps	Subs	Gls
Leeds U	Tr	07.92	92	6	1	0
Newcastle U	Tr	03.93	92-95	56	5	5
Bolton W	Tr	12.95	95-98	106	5	15
Huddersfield T	Tr	07.99	99-00	29	19	1
Port Vale	Aarhus GF (Den)	01.02				
Mansfield T	Tr	03.02	01-02	17	3	3

SELLEY Ian
Chertsey, 14 June, 1974 EYth/Eu21-3 (M)

League Club	Source	Date Signed	Seasons Played	Apps	Subs	Gls
Arsenal	YT	05.92	92-96	35	6	0
Southend U	L	12.96	96	3	1	0
Fulham	Tr	10.97	97	3	0	0
Wimbledon	Tr	08.00	00	1	3	0
Southend U	L	02.02	01	14	0	0
Southend U	L	08.02	02	11	0	0

SELLS Charles Edward
Paddington, 24 June, 1939 (IF)

League Club	Source	Date Signed	Seasons Played	Apps	Subs	Gls
Exeter C	Wealdstone	08.62	62	14	-	3

SEMARK Robin Harry
Portsmouth, 5 September, 1972 (F)

League Club	Source	Date Signed	Seasons Played	Apps	Subs	Gls
Cardiff C	YT	07.91	91	4	2	0

SEMLEY Alan
Barnsley, 21 February, 1966 (F)

League Club	Source	Date Signed	Seasons Played	Apps	Subs	Gls
Barnsley	App	02.84	83	1	3	0

SEMPLE Ryan
Derry, 2 July, 1977 (M)

League Club	Source	Date Signed	Seasons Played	Apps	Subs	Gls
Peterborough U	YT	●	94	1	1	0

SEMPLE Ryan David
Belfast, 4 July, 1985 (W)

League Club	Source	Date Signed	Seasons Played	Apps	Subs	Gls
Peterborough U	Sch	08.02	02-04	4	9	0

SENDA Daniel (Danny) Luke
Harrow, 17 April, 1981 EYth (FB)

League Club	Source	Date Signed	Seasons Played	Apps	Subs	Gls
Wycombe W	Southampton (Jnrs)	01.99	98-04	173	59	9

SENDALL Richard Adam
Stamford, 10 July, 1967 (F)

League Club	Source	Date Signed	Seasons Played	Apps	Subs	Gls
Blackpool	Watford (App)	07.85	85-86	6	5	0
Carlisle U	Tr	07.88	88-92	48	36	14
Cardiff C	L	09.89	89	3	1	0

SENDEROS Philippe
Geneva, Switzerland, 14 February, 1985 SwitYth/Switu21/Swit-2 (CD)

League Club	Source	Date Signed	Seasons Played	Apps	Subs	Gls
Arsenal	Servette (Swi)	07.03	04	12	1	0

SENIOR Allan Gordon
Dewsbury, 29 September, 1930 (WH)

League Club	Source	Date Signed	Seasons Played	Apps	Subs	Gls
Halifax T		08.52	52	1	-	0

SENIOR Colin
Thornhill, 3 June, 1927 (CD)

League Club	Source	Date Signed	Seasons Played	Apps	Subs	Gls
Huddersfield T	Stocksbridge Works	06.45	50	5	-	1
Accrington St	Tr	06.51	51	27	-	1

SENIOR Karl Robert
Northwich, 3 September, 1972 (M)

League Club	Source	Date Signed	Seasons Played	Apps	Subs	Gls
Chester C	YT	●	89	0	1	0

SENIOR Philip **Malcolm**
Mapplewell, 29 May, 1943 (CF)

League Club	Source	Date Signed	Seasons Played	Apps	Subs	Gls
Barnsley	Jnrs	06.61				
Southport	Tr	07.63	63	2	-	0

SENIOR Michael (Mike) Graham
Huddersfield, 3 March, 1981 (M)

League Club	Source	Date Signed	Seasons Played	Apps	Subs	Gls
Huddersfield T	YT	07.99	00	0	4	0

SENIOR Philip (Phil) Anthony
Huddersfield, 30 October, 1982 (G)

League Club	Source	Date Signed	Seasons Played	Apps	Subs	Gls
Huddersfield T	YT	11.99	02-04	37	3	0

SENIOR Vincent **Roy**
Barnsley, 21 June, 1940 (W)

League Club	Source	Date Signed	Seasons Played	Apps	Subs	Gls
Doncaster Rov		08.60	60	12	-	5
Peterborough U	Tr	07.61	61-63	38	-	11
Millwall	Tr	03.64	63-64	15	-	3
Barnsley	Tr	11.64	64	21	-	4

SENIOR Stephen (Steve)
Sheffield, 15 May, 1963 (FB)

League Club	Source	Date Signed	Seasons Played	Apps	Subs	Gls
York C	App	05.81	80-86	158	10	6
Darlington	L	10.84	84	5	0	0
Northampton T	Tr	06.87	87	1	3	0
Wigan Ath	Tr	10.87	87-89	107	2	3
Preston NE	Tr	07.90	90-91	73	0	3

SENIOR Stuart
Barnsley, 26 October, 1953 (W)

League Club	Source	Date Signed	Seasons Played	Apps	Subs	Gls
Barnsley	App	11.71	72	1	1	0

SENIOR Trevor John
Dorchester, 28 November, 1961 (F)

League Club	Source	Date Signed	Seasons Played	Apps	Subs	Gls
Portsmouth	Dorchester T	12.81	81-82	11	0	2
Aldershot	L	03.83	82	10	0	6
Reading	Tr	08.83	83-86	164	0	102
Watford	Tr	07.87	87	22	2	1
Middlesbrough	Tr	03.88	87-88	9	1	2
Reading	Tr	10.88	88-91	127	10	52

SEOL Ki-Hyeon
South Korea, 8 January, 1979 South Korea int (F)

League Club	Source	Date Signed	Seasons Played	Apps	Subs	Gls
Wolverhampton W	Anderlecht (Bel)	09.04	04	28	9	4

SEPP Dennis
Apeldoorn, Holland, 5 June, 1973 (W)

League Club	Source	Date Signed	Seasons Played	Apps	Subs	Gls
Bradford C	HSC91 (Holl)	06.97	97	0	3	0

SERELLA David (Dave) Edward
King's Lynn, 24 September, 1952 (CD)

League Club	Source	Date Signed	Seasons Played	Apps	Subs	Gls
Nottingham F	App	08.70	71-74	65	3	0
Walsall	Tr	11.74	74-81	265	2	12
Blackpool	Tr	08.82	82-83	34	1	3

SEREMET Dino
Slovenia, 16 August, 1980 (G)

League Club	Source	Date Signed	Seasons Played	Apps	Subs	Gls
Luton T	NK Maribor (Sl)	07.04	04	6	1	0

SERENI Matteo
Parma, Italy, 11 February, 1975 Itu21 (G)

League Club	Source	Date Signed	Seasons Played	Apps	Subs	Gls
Ipswich T	Sampdoria (It)	08.01	01	25	0	0

SERIOUX Adrian Roger
Scarborough, Ontario, Canada, 12 May, 1979 Canada 3 (CD)

League Club	Source	Date Signed	Seasons Played	Apps	Subs	Gls
Millwall	Toronto Lynx (Can)	08.04	04	10	9	0

SERMANNI Thomas (Tommy) Dorby
Glasgow, 1 July, 1954 SSch (M)

League Club	Source	Date Signed	Seasons Played	Apps	Subs	Gls
Blackpool	Albion Rov	03.78	78	6	4	1
Torquay U	Dundee U	08.79	79-82	83	6	12

SERRANT Carl
Bradford, 12 September, 1975 EYth/Eu21-2/EB-1 (FB)

League Club	Source	Date Signed	Seasons Played	Apps	Subs	Gls
Oldham Ath	YT	07.94	95-97	84	6	1
Newcastle U	Tr	07.98	98-99	5	1	0
Bury	L	02.99	98	15	0	0

SERTORI Mark Anthony
Manchester, 1 September, 1967 (CD)

League Club	Source	Date Signed	Seasons Played	Apps	Subs	Gls
Stockport Co	East Manchester	02.87	86-87	3	1	0
Lincoln C	Tr	07.88	88-89	43	7	9
Wrexham	Tr	02.90	89-93	106	4	3
Bury	Tr	07.94	94-95	4	9	1
Scunthorpe U	Tr	07.96	96-97	82	1	2
Halifax T	Tr	07.98	98-99	44	1	0
York C	Tr	09.99	99-00	63	3	2
Shrewsbury T	Tr	03.01	00	0	1	0
Cheltenham T	Tr	03.01	00	10	0	0

SESTANOVICH Ashley Shane
Lambeth, 18 September, 1981 (M)

League Club	Source	Date Signed	Seasons Played	Apps	Subs	Gls
Sheffield U	Hampton & R Borough	02.03	03	0	2	0
Grimsby T	L	06.04	04	17	5	2
Chester C	Tr	02.05	04	3	4	0

SETCHELL Gary John
King's Lynn, 8 May, 1975 (FB)

League Club	Source	Date Signed	Seasons Played	Apps	Subs	Gls
Rushden & Diamonds	Kettering T	06.00	01-02	20	13	1

SETTERS Maurice Edgar
Honiton, 16 December, 1936 ESch/EYth/Eu23-16 (CD)

League Club	Source	Date Signed	Seasons Played	Apps	Subs	Gls
Exeter C	Jnrs	01.54	53-54	10	-	0
West Bromwich A	Tr	01.55	55-59	120	-	10
Manchester U	Tr	01.60	59-64	159	-	12
Stoke C	Tr	11.64	64-67	86	0	5
Coventry C	Tr	11.67	67-69	50	1	3
Charlton Ath	Tr	01.70	69	8	0	1

SEWARD Bruce Walter
Uxbridge, 10 February, 1939 (IF)

League Club	Source	Date Signed	Seasons Played	Apps	Subs	Gls
Brighton & Hove A	Yiewsley	05.57				
Aldershot	Tr	07.59	59	1	-	0

SEWARD Gary
Paddington, 1 October, 1961 (F)

League Club	Source	Date Signed	Seasons Played	Apps	Subs	Gls
Blackpool	App	11.79	79	0	1	0

SEWELL Arthur
Cornforth, 15 July, 1934 (IF)

League Club	Source	Date Signed	Seasons Played	Apps	Subs	Gls
Bradford C (Am)	Bishop Auckland	06.54	54	1	-	0

League Club	Source	Date Signed	Seasons Played	Career Record Apps	Subs	Gls
SEWELL John (Jackie)						
Kells, Cumberland, 24 January, 1927 FLge-5/E-6						(IF)
Notts Co	Whitehaven T	10.44	46-50	178	-	97
Sheffield Wed	Tr	03.51	50-55	164	-	87
Aston Villa	Tr	12.55	55-59	123	-	36
Hull C	Tr	10.59	59-60	44	-	8
SEWELL John David						
Brockley, 7 July, 1936						(FB)
Charlton Ath	Bexleyheath & Welling	01.55	56-63	185	-	5
Crystal Palace	Tr	10.63	63-70	228	3	6
Orient	Tr	08.71	71	5	2	0
SEXTON David (Dave) James						
Islington, 6 April, 1930						(IF)
Luton T	Chelmsford C	06.51	51-52	9	-	1
West Ham U	Tr	04.52	52-55	74	-	27
Leyton Orient	Tr	06.56	56-57	24	-	4
Brighton & Hove A	Tr	10.57	57-58	49	-	26
Crystal Palace	Tr	05.59	59	27	-	11
SEYMOUR Christopher (Chris) David						
Reading, 14 September, 1971						(M)
Reading	YT	07.90	90-91	10	3	0
SEYMOUR Ian Patrick						
Tunbridge Wells, 17 March, 1948						(G)
Fulham	Tonbridge	08.66	66-70	64	0	0
Brighton & Hove A	L	02.71	70	3	0	0
SHAABAN Rami						
Stockholm, Sweden, 30 June, 1975						(G)
Arsenal	Djurgaarden (Swe)	08.02	02	3	0	0
Brighton & Hove A	Tr	02.05	04	6	0	0
SHACKELL Jason Philip						
Stevenage, 27 August, 1983						(FB)
Norwich C	Sch	01.03	02-04	17	2	0
SHACKLETON Alan						
Padiham, 3 February, 1934						(CF)
Burnley		05.54	56-58	31	-	18
Leeds U	Tr	10.58	58-59	30	-	16
Everton	Tr	09.59	59	26	-	10
Oldham Ath	Nelson	08.61	61	10	-	7
SHACKLETON Leonard (Len) Francis						
Bradford, 3 May, 1922 Died 2000 ESch/FLge-2/EB/EWar-1/E-5						(IF)
Bradford PA	Dartford	12.40	46	7	-	4
Newcastle U	Tr	10.46	46-47	57	-	26
Sunderland	Tr	02.48	47-57	320	-	97
SHADBOLT William Henry						
Shrewsbury, 4 August, 1932						(W)
Sheffield Wed	Oswestry T	01.53	52	7	-	0
Halifax T	Tr	03.54	53	3	-	1
SHAIL Mark Edward David						
Sandviken, Sweden, 15 October, 1966 ESemiPro-1						(CD)
Bristol C	Yeovil T	03.93	92-99	117	11	4
Kidderminster Hrs	Tr	07.00	00-01	40	0	1
SHAKES Ricky Ulric						
Brixton, 26 January, 1985						(F)
Bolton W	Sch	07.04				
Bristol Rov	L	02.05	04	0	1	0
Bury	L	03.05	04	4	3	2
SHAKESPEARE Craig Robert						
Birmingham, 26 October, 1963						(M)
Walsall	App	11.81	82-88	276	8	45
Sheffield Wed	Tr	06.89	89	15	2	0
West Bromwich A	Tr	02.90	89-92	104	8	12
Grimsby T	Tr	07.93	93-96	84	22	10
Scunthorpe U	Tr	07.97	97	3	1	0
SHANAHAN Terence (Terry) Christopher						
Paddington, 5 December, 1951						(F)
Ipswich T	Tottenham H (App)	07.69	70	3	1	0
Blackburn Rov	L	09.71	71	6	0	2
Halifax T	Tr	11.71	71-74	88	8	23
Chesterfield	Tr	10.74	74-75	56	4	28
Millwall	Tr	04.76	76	13	7	5
Bournemouth	Tr	07.77	77	14	4	1
Aldershot	Tr	07.78	78-79	16	0	4
SHANDRAN Anthony Mark						
North Shields, 17 September, 1981						(F)
Burnley	YT	11.00	00	0	1	0
York C	Tr	01.03	02	12	6	3

League Club	Source	Date Signed	Seasons Played	Career Record Apps	Subs	Gls
SHANKLAND Andrew (Andy) John						
Stoke-on-Trent, 8 April, 1964						(M)
Port Vale	App	03.82	81-85	15	10	2
SHANKLY William (Bill)						
Glenbuck, 2 September, 1913 Died 1981 SWar-7/S-5						(WH)
Carlisle U	Cronberry	07.32	32	16	-	0
Preston NE	Tr	07.33	33-48	297	-	13
SHANKS Donald (Don)						
Hammersmith, 2 October, 1952 EYth						(FB)
Luton T	Fulham (App)	07.70	71-74	89	1	2
Queens Park Rgrs	Tr	11.74	74-80	176	4	10
Brighton & Hove A	Tr	08.81	81-82	45	1	0
Wimbledon	Eastern Ath (HK)	01.84	83	1	0	0
SHANKS James (Jimmy)						
Barrow, 31 October, 1918						(W)
Barrow	Vickers Sports	10.45	46	23	-	5
SHANKS Robert (Bob)						
Sunniside, 14 December, 1911 Died 1989						(CD)
Swindon T	Leeds U (Am)	05.35	35-36	25	-	1
Crystal Palace	Tr	05.37	37-38	18	-	0
Swindon T	Tr	10.46	46	1	-	0
SHANKS Walter (Wally) George						
Valetta, Malta, 1 May, 1923						(WH)
Chelsea		10.46				
Luton T	Tr	12.46	46-56	264	-	6
SHANNON David Leslie						
Liverpool, 4 May, 1953						(FB)
Sunderland	App	05.70				
Stockport Co	Tr	07.73	73	3	1	1
SHANNON Leslie (Les)						
Liverpool, 12 March, 1926 EB						(WH)
Liverpool	Jnrs	11.44	47-48	11	-	1
Burnley	Tr	11.49	49-58	262	-	39
SHANNON Robert (Rab)						
Bellshill, 20 April, 1966 Su21-7						(M)
Middlesbrough (L)	Dundee U	09.91	91	0	1	0
SHARDLOW Paul Michael						
Stone, 29 April, 1943 Died 1968						(G)
Stoke C	Northwich Vic	05.66	66-67	3	0	0
SHARKEY Dominic (Nick)						
Helensburgh, 4 May, 1943 SSch/Su23-2						(F)
Sunderland	Drumchapel Amats	05.60	59-66	99	0	51
Leicester C	Tr	10.66	66-67	6	0	5
Mansfield T	Tr	03.68	67-69	67	2	17
Hartlepool	Tr	07.70	70-71	55	5	12
SHARKEY Patrick (Pat) George Sharp						
Omagh, 26 August, 1953 NI-1						(M)
Ipswich T	Portadown	09.73	75-76	17	1	1
Millwall	L	11.76	76	7	0	0
Mansfield T	Tr	08.77	77	31	1	5
Colchester U	Tr	06.78	78	5	1	0
Peterborough U	Tr	03.79	78-79	15	0	0
SHARMAN Donald (Joe) William						
Rothwell, 2 February, 1932						(G)
Derby Co	Jnrs	02.49	50	2	-	0
SHARMAN Samuel (Sam) Joseph						
Hull, 7 November, 1977						(FB)
Sheffield Wed	YT	05.96				
Hull C	Tr	03.97	96	2	2	0
SHARP Billy Louis						
Sheffield, 5 February, 1986						(F)
Sheffield U	Sch	07.04	04	0	2	0
Rushden & Diamonds	L	01.05	04	16	0	9
SHARP Duncan						
Barnsley, 16 March, 1933						(CD)
Barnsley	Woolley Colliery	05.50	53-61	213	-	0
SHARP Frank						
Edinburgh, 28 May, 1947						(W)
Carlisle U	Heart of Midlothian	03.67	66-68	32	2	0
Cardiff C	Tr	02.69	68-69	14	1	1
Barnsley	Tr	08.70	70-72	125	0	7
Grimsby T	Tr	07.73	73	26	3	2
Port Vale	Tr	05.74	74	17	7	2

SHARP George Henry
Bedlington, 20 July, 1935 (W)

League Club	Source	Date Signed	Seasons Played	Apps	Subs	Gls
Darlington (Am)		05.57	57	3	-	0
Oldham Ath (Am)	Tr	11.57	57	1	-	0

SHARP Graeme Marshall
Glasgow, 16 October, 1960 Su21-1/S-12 (F)

League Club	Source	Date Signed	Seasons Played	Apps	Subs	Gls
Everton	Dumbarton	04.80	79-90	306	16	111
Oldham Ath	Tr	07.91	91-94	103	6	30

SHARP James
Reading, 2 January, 1976 (CD)

League Club	Source	Date Signed	Seasons Played	Apps	Subs	Gls
Hartlepool U	Andover	08.00	00-01	44	5	2

SHARP John
Knottingley, 25 April, 1937 (W)

League Club	Source	Date Signed	Seasons Played	Apps	Subs	Gls
Halifax T	Fryston Colliery	01.55	54-58	92	-	16

SHARP Kevin Philip
Sarnia, Ontario, Canada, 19 September, 1974 ESch/EYth (FB)

League Club	Source	Date Signed	Seasons Played	Apps	Subs	Gls
Leeds U	Auxerre (Fr)	10.92	92-95	11	6	0
Wigan Ath	Tr	11.95	95-01	156	22	10
Wrexham	Tr	11.01	01	12	3	0
Huddersfield T	Tr	08.02	02	38	1	0
Scunthorpe U	Tr	07.03	03-04	41	5	2

SHARP Neil Anthony
Hemel Hempstead, 19 January, 1978 (CD)

League Club	Source	Date Signed	Seasons Played	Apps	Subs	Gls
Swansea C	Merthyr Tydfil	10.01	01-02	26	6	1

SHARP Norman Winslow
Liverpool, 26 November, 1919 Died 1977 (IF)

League Club	Source	Date Signed	Seasons Played	Apps	Subs	Gls
Everton		11.38				
Wrexham	Tr	09.46	46-49	122	-	16

SHARP Raymond (Ray)
Stirling, 16 November, 1969 Su21-4 (FB)

League Club	Source	Date Signed	Seasons Played	Apps	Subs	Gls
Preston NE	Dunfermline Ath	10.94	94-95	22	0	0

SHARP Ronald (Ronnie)
Montreal, Canada, 22 November, 1932 (W)

League Club	Source	Date Signed	Seasons Played	Apps	Subs	Gls
Doncaster Rov	Arbroath	10.58	58-59	58	-	11

SHARP Thomas (Tom) Alexander
Newmains, 30 July, 1957 (CD)

League Club	Source	Date Signed	Seasons Played	Apps	Subs	Gls
Everton	App	08.75				
Brentford	Tr	01.76	75-76	4	12	1

SHARPE Frederick (Fred) Arthur
Norwich, 26 January, 1924 (IF)

League Club	Source	Date Signed	Seasons Played	Apps	Subs	Gls
Wrexham (Am)		05.48	48	1	-	0

SHARPE Frederick (Freddie) Charles
Brockley, 11 November, 1937 (CD)

League Club	Source	Date Signed	Seasons Played	Apps	Subs	Gls
Tottenham H	Jnrs	05.56	58	2	-	1
Norwich C	Tr	07.63	63-68	107	4	0
Reading	Tr	07.69	69-70	64	0	1

SHARPE Gerald (Gerry) Ralph
Gloucester, 17 March, 1946 (W)

League Club	Source	Date Signed	Seasons Played	Apps	Subs	Gls
Bristol C	App	03.64	64-70	149	4	48

SHARPE John James
Birmingham, 9 August, 1975 (W)

League Club	Source	Date Signed	Seasons Played	Apps	Subs	Gls
Manchester C	YT	07.93				
Exeter C	Tr	02.96	95-96	28	7	2

SHARPE John William Henry
Portsmouth, 9 October, 1957 (FB)

League Club	Source	Date Signed	Seasons Played	Apps	Subs	Gls
Southampton	App	10.75	76-77	21	0	0
Gillingham	Tr	09.78	78-84	192	2	2
Swansea C	Southampton (N/C)	09.85	85	5	0	0

SHARPE Lee Stuart
Halesowen, 27 May, 1971 Eu21-8/EB-1/E-8 (W)

League Club	Source	Date Signed	Seasons Played	Apps	Subs	Gls
Torquay U	YT	05.88	87	9	5	3
Manchester U	Tr	06.88	88-95	160	33	21
Leeds U	Tr	08.96	96-98	28	2	5
Bradford C	Tr	03.99	98-01	36	20	4
Portsmouth	L	02.01	00	17	0	0
Exeter C	Tr	08.02	02	4	0	1

SHARPE Leonard (Len) Thomas
Scunthorpe, 29 November, 1932 (WH)

League Club	Source	Date Signed	Seasons Played	Apps	Subs	Gls
Scunthorpe U	Ashby Institute	05.50	51-61	185	-	6
Hull C	Tr	06.62	62-65	58	0	4

SHARPE Philip (Phil)
Leeds, 26 January, 1968 (F)

League Club	Source	Date Signed	Seasons Played	Apps	Subs	Gls
Halifax T	Doncaster Rov (App)	08.86	86	0	1	0

SHARPE Richard
Wokingham, 14 January, 1967 (F)

League Club	Source	Date Signed	Seasons Played	Apps	Subs	Gls
Rochdale	Coco Expos (USA)	10.94	94	9	7	2

SHARPE Robert
Kirkcaldy, 20 December, 1925 (FB)

League Club	Source	Date Signed	Seasons Played	Apps	Subs	Gls
Darlington	Raith Rov	08.52	52	14	-	0

SHARPLES Brian
Bradford, 6 September, 1944 (CD)

League Club	Source	Date Signed	Seasons Played	Apps	Subs	Gls
Birmingham C	App	12.61	62-68	60	1	2
Exeter C	Tr	12.68	68-70	68	0	4

SHARPLES George Frank Vincent
Ellesmere Port, 20 September, 1943 ESch/EYth (CD)

League Club	Source	Date Signed	Seasons Played	Apps	Subs	Gls
Everton	Jnrs	09.60	60-63	10	-	0
Blackburn Rov	Tr	03.65	64-68	99	4	5
Southport	Tr	07.71	71	23	2	0

SHARPLES John
Wolverhampton, 8 August, 1934 Died 2001 (FB)

League Club	Source	Date Signed	Seasons Played	Apps	Subs	Gls
Aston Villa	Heath T	10.55	58	13	-	0
Walsall	Tr	08.59	59-63	124	-	1

SHARPLES John Benjamin
Bury, 26 January, 1973 (CD)

League Club	Source	Date Signed	Seasons Played	Apps	Subs	Gls
York C	Ayr U	03.96	95-96	38	0	1

SHARPLING Christopher (Chris) Barry
Bromley, 21 April, 1981 (F)

League Club	Source	Date Signed	Seasons Played	Apps	Subs	Gls
Crystal Palace	Jnrs	08.98	99	1	5	0

SHARPS Ian William
Warrington, 23 October, 1980 (CD)

League Club	Source	Date Signed	Seasons Played	Apps	Subs	Gls
Tranmere Rov	YT	07.99	98-04	124	7	5

SHARRATT Christopher (Chris) Michael
West Kirby, 13 August, 1970 (W)

League Club	Source	Date Signed	Seasons Played	Apps	Subs	Gls
Wigan Ath	Stalybridge Celtic	12.91	91-92	11	13	3

SHARRATT Harold (Harry)
Wigan, 16 December, 1929 Died 2002 EAmat (G)

League Club	Source	Date Signed	Seasons Played	Apps	Subs	Gls
Blackpool (Am)	Yorkshire Amats	05.52	52	1	-	0
Oldham Ath (Am)	Bishop Auckland	03.56	55	1	-	0
Nottingham F (Am)	Bishop Auckland	01.58	57	1	-	0

SHARRATT Stuart Edgar
Leek, 26 February, 1942 (G)

League Club	Source	Date Signed	Seasons Played	Apps	Subs	Gls
Port Vale	Oswestry T	03.66	65-71	143	0	0

SHARROCK Anthony (Tony)
Warrington, 8 September, 1955 (G)

League Club	Source	Date Signed	Seasons Played	Apps	Subs	Gls
Southport	Liverpool (Am)	11.73	73	1	0	0

SHAW Adrian
Murton, 13 April, 1966 (M)

League Club	Source	Date Signed	Seasons Played	Apps	Subs	Gls
Nottingham F	App	12.83				
Halifax T	Tr	12.84	84-87	95	5	1
York C	Bridlington T	10.88	88	5	0	0
Chesterfield	Tr	12.88	88-90	40	10	3

SHAW Alan
Preston, 9 October, 1943 (W)

League Club	Source	Date Signed	Seasons Played	Apps	Subs	Gls
Preston NE	Jnrs	10.60				
Hull C	Tr	08.61	61-63	15	-	1

SHAW Alexander (Alex)
(IF)

League Club	Source	Date Signed	Seasons Played	Apps	Subs	Gls
Crewe Alex		12.44	46	14	-	4

SHAW Arthur
Limehouse, 9 April, 1924 (WH)

League Club	Source	Date Signed	Seasons Played	Apps	Subs	Gls
Brentford	Hayes	05.46	46	4	-	0
Arsenal	Tr	04.48	49-54	57	-	0
Watford	Tr	06.55	55	3	-	0

SHAW Barry
Chilton, 31 October, 1948 (W)

League Club	Source	Date Signed	Seasons Played	Apps	Subs	Gls
Darlington (Am)	Crowborough Ath	03.68	67	2	0	0

SHAW Bernard
Selby, 4 September, 1929 (WH)

League Club	Source	Date Signed	Seasons Played	Apps	Subs	Gls
Hull C	Buckley Jnrs	05.48				
Lincoln C	Goole T	10.53	53-54	9	-	1

SHAW Bernard
Sheffield, 14 March, 1945 EYth/Eu23-2 (FB)

League Club	Source	Date Signed	Seasons Played	Apps	Subs	Gls
Sheffield U	App	10.62	62-68	135	1	2
Wolverhampton W	Tr	07.69	69-72	113	3	2
Sheffield Wed	Tr	06.73	73-75	100	4	3

SHAW Cecil Ernest
Mansfield, 22 June, 1911 Died 1977 FLge-1 (FB)

League Club	Source	Date Signed	Seasons Played	Apps	Subs	Gls
Wolverhampton W	Rufford Colliery	02.30	29-36	177	-	8
West Bromwich A	Tr	12.36	36-46	110	-	10

SHAW Christopher (Chris) John
Bournemouth, 23 August, 1965 (M)

League Club	Source	Date Signed	Seasons Played	Apps	Subs	Gls
Bournemouth	Jnrs	06.83	82-85	13	12	2

SHAW Colin Michael
St Albans, 19 June, 1943 EYth (IF)

League Club	Source	Date Signed	Seasons Played	Apps	Subs	Gls
Chelsea	Jnrs	05.60	61	1	-	0
Norwich C	Tr	08.63	63-64	3	-	0
Leyton Orient	Tr	03.65	65	7	0	0

SHAW George David
Huddersfield, 11 October, 1948 (F)

League Club	Source	Date Signed	Seasons Played	Apps	Subs	Gls
Huddersfield T	Jnrs	01.67	66-68	23	3	2
Oldham Ath	Tr	09.69	69-72	155	0	70
West Bromwich A	Tr	03.73	72-74	65	17	17
Oldham Ath	Tr	10.75	75-77	55	4	21

SHAW Eric Lewis
Barnsley, 12 February, 1947 (WH)

League Club	Source	Date Signed	Seasons Played	Apps	Subs	Gls
Barnsley	App	02.65	64	2	-	0

SHAW Gary Robert
Birmingham, 21 January, 1961 EYth/Eu21-7 (F)

League Club	Source	Date Signed	Seasons Played	Apps	Subs	Gls
Aston Villa	App	01.79	78-87	158	7	59
Blackpool	L	02.88	87	4	2	0
Walsall	SK Maxwell Klag (Aut)	02.90	89	4	5	3
Shrewsbury T	Kilmarnock	09.90	90	20	2	5

SHAW Gordon
Bryn, 7 May, 1926 (FB)

League Club	Source	Date Signed	Seasons Played	Apps	Subs	Gls
Southport (Am)	Haydock C & B	07.46	46	2	-	0

SHAW Graham Laurence
Sheffield, 9 July, 1934 Died 1998 Eu23-5/FLge-4/E-5 (FB)

League Club	Source	Date Signed	Seasons Played	Apps	Subs	Gls
Sheffield U	Jnrs	07.51	51-66	439	0	14
Doncaster Rov	Tr	09.67	67	22	0	0

SHAW Graham Paul
Stoke-on-Trent, 7 June, 1967 (F)

League Club	Source	Date Signed	Seasons Played	Apps	Subs	Gls
Stoke C	App	06.85	85-88	83	16	18
Preston NE	Tr	07.89	89-91	113	8	29
Stoke C	Tr	08.92	92-94	23	13	5
Plymouth Arg	L	08.94	94	6	0	0
Rochdale	Tr	03.95	94-95	13	9	0

SHAW Hugh
Clydebank, 29 April, 1929 (WH)

League Club	Source	Date Signed	Seasons Played	Apps	Subs	Gls
Tranmere Rov	Rhyl	06.55	55	3	-	0

SHAW John
Stirling, 4 February, 1954 (G)

League Club	Source	Date Signed	Seasons Played	Apps	Subs	Gls
Leeds U	App	02.71				
Bristol C	Tr	05.74	76-84	295	0	0
Exeter C	Tr	07.85	85-87	109	0	0

SHAW John (Jack) Stephen
Doncaster, 10 April, 1924 (CF)

League Club	Source	Date Signed	Seasons Played	Apps	Subs	Gls
Rotherham U	Yorkshire Main Colliery	04.45	46-52	262	-	122
Sheffield Wed	Tr	06.53	53-57	56	-	21

SHAW Jonathan (Jon) Steven
Sheffield, 10 November, 1983 (F)

League Club	Source	Date Signed	Seasons Played	Apps	Subs	Gls
Sheffield Wed	Sch	07.03	02-04	8	10	2
York C	L	11.03	03	5	3	0

SHAW Joseph (Joe)
Murton, 23 June, 1928 FLge-2 (CD)

League Club	Source	Date Signed	Seasons Played	Apps	Subs	Gls
Sheffield U	Upton Colliery	07.45	48-65	632	0	7

SHAW Kenneth (Ken)
Dukinfield, 15 December, 1920 Died 2004 (CF)

League Club	Source	Date Signed	Seasons Played	Apps	Subs	Gls
Stockport Co	Hyde U	10.42	46-47	41	-	18

SHAW Mark
St Helens, 15 October, 1964 (M)

League Club	Source	Date Signed	Seasons Played	Apps	Subs	Gls
Wigan Ath	Jnrs	11.82	82	3	0	0

SHAW Martin John
Bristol, 14 September, 1960 (M)

League Club	Source	Date Signed	Seasons Played	Apps	Subs	Gls
Bristol Rov	App	09.78	78	1	1	0

SHAW Matthew (Matt) Alan
Blackpool, 17 May, 1984 (F)

League Club	Source	Date Signed	Seasons Played	Apps	Subs	Gls
Sheffield Wed	Stockport Co (YT)	03.02				
Wrexham	Tr	10.04	04	0	1	0
Blackpool	Tr	12.04	04	2	8	0

SHAW Paul
Burnham, 4 September, 1973 EYth (F)

League Club	Source	Date Signed	Seasons Played	Apps	Subs	Gls
Arsenal	YT	09.91	94-96	1	11	2
Burnley	L	03.95	94	8	1	4
Cardiff C	L	08.95	95	6	0	0
Peterborough U	L	10.95	95	12	0	5
Millwall	Tr	09.97	97-99	88	21	26
Gillingham	Tr	07.00	00-03	118	17	26
Sheffield U	Tr	01.04	03-04	20	14	8
Rotherham U	L	08.04	04	9	0	2

SHAW Peter Kevin
Northolt, 9 January, 1956 (CD)

League Club	Source	Date Signed	Seasons Played	Apps	Subs	Gls
Charlton Ath	Staines T	12.77	77-80	100	5	5
Exeter C	L	11.81	81	3	0	0
Gillingham	Tr	02.82	81-85	140	3	2

SHAW Raymond (Ray)
Walsall, 18 May, 1913 Died 1980 (WH)

League Club	Source	Date Signed	Seasons Played	Apps	Subs	Gls
Birmingham	Darlaston	04.37	37-46	12	-	0

SHAW Richard Edward
Brentford, 11 September, 1968 (CD)

League Club	Source	Date Signed	Seasons Played	Apps	Subs	Gls
Crystal Palace	App	09.86	87-95	193	14	3
Hull C	L	12.89	89	4	0	0
Coventry C	Tr	11.95	95-04	272	20	1

SHAW Ronald (Ron)
Bolton-on-Dearne, 1 January, 1924 Died 1991 (W)

League Club	Source	Date Signed	Seasons Played	Apps	Subs	Gls
Torquay U	Harrow T	02.47	46-57	384	-	99

SHAW Samuel (Sam)
Caverswall, 14 September, 1934 (IF)

League Club	Source	Date Signed	Seasons Played	Apps	Subs	Gls
Crewe Alex	Foley	08.56	56	19	-	4

SHAW Simon Robert
Middlesbrough, 21 September, 1973 (FB)

League Club	Source	Date Signed	Seasons Played	Apps	Subs	Gls
Darlington	YT	08.92	91-97	144	32	12

SHAW Steven (Steve)
Manchester, 10 August, 1960 (M)

League Club	Source	Date Signed	Seasons Played	Apps	Subs	Gls
Rochdale	App	●	77	6	0	0

SHAW Stuart
Saltney, 9 October, 1944 (W)

League Club	Source	Date Signed	Seasons Played	Apps	Subs	Gls
Everton	Aintree Villa Colts	12.61	64-65	3	0	0
Crystal Palace	Tr	12.66				
Southport	Tr	03.67	66-68	66	1	6
Port Vale	Tr	07.69	69	1	2	0

SHAWCROSS Francis David
Stretford, 3 July, 1941 EYth/Eu23-1 (M)

League Club	Source	Date Signed	Seasons Played	Apps	Subs	Gls
Manchester C	Jnrs	06.58	58-64	47	-	2
Stockport Co	Tr	06.65	65-66	59	1	14
Halifax T	Tr	03.67	66-69	126	6	21

SHEARD Frank
Spilsby, 29 January, 1922 Died 1990 (CD)

League Club	Source	Date Signed	Seasons Played	Apps	Subs	Gls
Leicester C	Skegness T	08.41				
Southend U	Tr	05.46	46-52	180	-	1

SHEARER Alan
Newcastle, 13 August, 1970 EYth/Eu21-11/EB-1/E-63 (F)

League Club	Source	Date Signed	Seasons Played	Apps	Subs	Gls
Southampton	YT	04.88	87-91	105	13	23
Blackburn Rov	Tr	07.92	92-95	132	6	112
Newcastle U	Tr	07.96	96-04	264	7	138

SHEARER David John
Inverness, 16 October, 1958 (F)

League Club	Source	Date Signed	Seasons Played	Apps	Subs	Gls
Middlesbrough	Clachnacuddin	01.78	77-82	88	9	23
Wigan Ath	L	03.80	79	11	0	9
Grimsby T	Tr	08.83	83	1	3	0
Gillingham	Tr	08.84	84-87	82	11	42
Bournemouth	Tr	10.87	87	8	3	3
Scunthorpe U	Tr	02.88	87-88	16	0	7
Darlington	Tr	12.88	88	6	1	0

SHEARER Duncan Nichol
Fort William, 28 August, 1962 S-7 (F)

League Club	Source	Date Signed	Seasons Played	Apps	Subs	Gls
Chelsea	Clachnacuddin	11.83	85	2	0	1
Huddersfield T	Tr	03.86	85-87	80	3	38
Swindon T	Tr	06.88	88-91	156	3	78
Blackburn Rov	Tr	03.92	91	5	1	1

SHEARER John McMillan
Dunfermline, 8 July, 1917 Died 1979 (IF)

League Club	Source	Date Signed	Seasons Played	Apps	Subs	Gls
Derby Co		03.46				
Bradford C	Tr	10.46	46-48	75	-	17
Grimsby T	Tr	02.49	48-50	34	-	9

SHEARER Lee Sean
Southend-on-Sea, 23 October, 1977 (CD)

League Club	Source	Date Signed	Seasons Played	Apps	Subs	Gls
Leyton Orient	YT	07.95	94-96	14	4	1

SHEARER Peter Andrew
Birmingham, 4 February, 1967 ESemiPro (M)

League Club	Source	Date Signed	Seasons Played	Apps	Subs	Gls
Birmingham C	App	02.85	84	2	2	0
Rochdale	Tr	07.86	86	1	0	0
Bournemouth	Cheltenham T	03.89	88-92	76	9	10
Birmingham C	Tr	01.94	93-94	22	3	7

SHEARER Scott
Glasgow, 15 February, 1981 SB-1 (G)

League Club	Source	Date Signed	Seasons Played	Apps	Subs	Gls
Coventry C	Albion Rov	07.03	03-04	37	1	0
Rushden & Diamonds	L	02.05	04	3	0	0
Rushden & Diamonds	L	03.05	04	10	0	0

SHEARING Peter Fraser
Uxbridge, 26 August, 1938 (G)

League Club	Source	Date Signed	Seasons Played	Apps	Subs	Gls
West Ham U	Hendon	06.60	60	6	-	0
Portsmouth	Tr	07.61	61-63	17	-	0
Exeter C	Tr	06.64	64-65	80	0	0
Plymouth Arg	Tr	06.66	66-67	24	0	0
Exeter C	Tr	07.68	68-70	79	0	0
Bristol Rov	Tr	02.71				
Gillingham	Tr	08.71	71-72	39	0	0

SHEAVILLS James (Jimmy) Edward
Aylesham, 28 July, 1940 Died 2003 (W)

League Club	Source	Date Signed	Seasons Played	Apps	Subs	Gls
Leeds U	Jnrs	09.57				
Peterborough U	Holbeach U	(N/L)	60-62	30	-	8
Barnsley	Tr	06.63	63-64	65	-	6

SHEEDY Kevin Mark
Builth Wells, 21 October, 1959 IRYth/IRu21-5/IR-45 (M)

League Club	Source	Date Signed	Seasons Played	Apps	Subs	Gls
Hereford U	App	10.76	75-77	47	4	4
Liverpool	Tr	07.78	80-81	1	2	0
Everton	Tr	08.82	82-91	263	11	67
Newcastle U	Tr	03.92	91-92	36	1	4
Blackpool	Tr	07.93	93	25	1	1

SHEEHAN Alan Michael Anthony
Athlone, 14 September, 1986 IRYth/IRu21-1 (FB)

League Club	Source	Date Signed	Seasons Played	Apps	Subs	Gls
Leicester C	Sch	09.04	04	1	0	0

SHEEN John (Jock)
Baillieston, 30 August, 1920 Died 1997 (IF)

League Club	Source	Date Signed	Seasons Played	Apps	Subs	Gls
Sheffield U	Baillieston Jnrs	09.37				
Hull C	Tr	07.46	46	5	-	1

SHEERAN Mark John
Newcastle, 9 September, 1982 (F)

League Club	Source	Date Signed	Seasons Played	Apps	Subs	Gls
Darlington	Sch	07.02	01-03	1	31	6

SHEERIN Joseph (Joe) Earnan Raftery
Hammersmith, 1 February, 1979 (F)

League Club	Source	Date Signed	Seasons Played	Apps	Subs	Gls
Chelsea	YT	07.97	96	0	1	0
Bournemouth	Tr	02.00	99	3	3	1

SHEFFIELD Jonathan (Jon)
Bedworth, 1 February, 1969 (G)

League Club	Source	Date Signed	Seasons Played	Apps	Subs	Gls
Norwich C	App	02.87	88	1	0	0
Aldershot	L	09.89	89	11	0	0
Aldershot	L	08.90	90	15	0	0
Cambridge U	Tr	03.91	90-94	56	0	0
Colchester U	L	12.93	93	6	0	0
Swindon T	L	01.94	93	2	0	0
Hereford U	L	09.94	94	8	0	0
Peterborough U	Tr	07.95	95-96	62	0	0
Plymouth Arg	Tr	07.97	97-00	155	0	0

SHEFFIELD Laurence (Laurie) Joseph
Swansea, 27 April, 1939 WSch (F)

League Club	Source	Date Signed	Seasons Played	Apps	Subs	Gls
Bristol Rov	Jnrs	07.56				
Newport Co	Barry T	04.62	61-64	92	-	46
Doncaster Rov	Tr	08.65	65-66	58	0	36
Norwich C	Tr	11.66	66-67	27	0	16
Rotherham U	Tr	08.67	67	19	0	6
Oldham Ath	Tr	12.67	67	18	0	6
Luton T	Tr	07.68	68-69	31	4	12
Doncaster Rov	Tr	10.69	69	13	2	6
Peterborough U	Tr	08.70	70	17	1	6

SHELDON Gareth Richard
Birmingham, 8 May, 1980 (W)

League Club	Source	Date Signed	Seasons Played	Apps	Subs	Gls
Scunthorpe U	YT	02.99	97-01	52	35	6
Exeter C	Tr	08.02	02	7	12	1

SHELDON Kevin John
Cheddleton, 14 June, 1956 (W)

League Club	Source	Date Signed	Seasons Played	Apps	Subs	Gls
Stoke C	App	06.73	75-80	12	3	0
Wigan Ath	Tr	08.81	81-82	29	0	1
Port Vale	L	08.82	82	5	0	0
Crewe Alex	Tr	08.83	83	2	0	0

SHELIA Murtaz
Tbilisi, Georgia, 25 March, 1969 Georgia 27 (FB)

League Club	Source	Date Signed	Seasons Played	Apps	Subs	Gls
Manchester C	Alania Vladikavkas (Lit)	11.97	97-98	15	0	2

SHELL Francis (Frank) Harry
Hackney, 2 January, 1912 Died 1988 (CF)

League Club	Source	Date Signed	Seasons Played	Apps	Subs	Gls
Aston Villa	Ford Sports	05.37	37-38	23	-	8
Birmingham C	Tr	09.46				
Mansfield T	Hereford U	06.47	47	22	-	1

SHELLEY Brian
Dublin, 15 November, 1981 IRu21-4 (FB)

League Club	Source	Date Signed	Seasons Played	Apps	Subs	Gls
Carlisle U	Bohemians	08.02	02-03	60	6	1

SHELLITO Kenneth (Ken) John
East Ham, 18 April, 1940 Eu23-1/E-1 (FB)

League Club	Source	Date Signed	Seasons Played	Apps	Subs	Gls
Chelsea	Jnrs	04.57	58-65	114	0	2

SHELTON Andrew (Andy) Marc
Sutton Coldfield, 19 June, 1980 (M)

League Club	Source	Date Signed	Seasons Played	Apps	Subs	Gls
Chester C	YT	07.98	97-99	14	21	1

SHELTON Gary
Nottingham, 21 March, 1958 Eu21-1 (M)

League Club	Source	Date Signed	Seasons Played	Apps	Subs	Gls
Walsall	App	03.76	75-77	12	12	0
Aston Villa	Tr	01.78	78-81	24	0	7
Notts Co	L	03.80	79	8	0	0
Sheffield Wed	Tr	03.82	81-86	195	3	18
Oxford U	Tr	07.87	87-88	60	5	1
Bristol C	Tr	08.89	89-93	149	1	24
Rochdale	L	02.94	93	3	0	0
Chester C	Tr	07.94	94-97	62	7	6

SHELTON John (Jack) Benjamin Thomas
Wollaston, 9 November, 1912 Died 1992 (FB)

League Club	Source	Date Signed	Seasons Played	Apps	Subs	Gls
Wolverhampton W	Chase Terrace U	12.32				
Walsall	Hednesford T	08.34	34-46	103	-	5

SHEPHEARD Jonathan (Jon) Thomas
Oxford, 31 March, 1981 (CD)

League Club	Source	Date Signed	Seasons Played	Apps	Subs	Gls
Oxford U	YT	06.99	99-00	6	1	0

SHEPHERD Anthony (Tony)
Glasgow, 16 November, 1966 SSch/SYth (M)

League Club	Source	Date Signed	Seasons Played	Apps	Subs	Gls
Bristol C (L)	Glasgow Celtic	12.88	88	2	1	0
Carlisle U	Glasgow Celtic	07.89	89-90	73	2	8

SHEPHERD Arthur Leslie
Liverpool, 11 May, 1922 Died 2002 (W)

League Club	Source	Date Signed	Seasons Played	Apps	Subs	Gls
Liverpool		04.46				
New Brighton	Tr	08.49	49-50	30	-	10

SHEPHERD Brian Albert
Leicester, 29 January, 1935 (FB)

League Club	Source	Date Signed	Seasons Played	Apps	Subs	Gls
Coventry C	Hinckley Ath	10.56	57-59	29	-	0

SHEPHERD Ernest (Ernie)
Wombwell, 14 August, 1919 Died 2001 (W)

League Club	Source	Date Signed	Seasons Played	Apps	Subs	Gls
Fulham	Bradford Rov	04.38	46-48	72	-	13
West Bromwich A	Tr	12.48	48	4	-	0
Hull C	Tr	03.49	48-49	15	-	3
Queens Park Rgrs	Tr	08.50	50-55	219	-	51

SHEPHERD Jamie **Greig**
Edinburgh, 29 September, 1960 (F)

League Club	Source	Date Signed	Seasons Played	Apps	Subs	Gls
Norwich C	Musselburgh Windsor	03.79	79-81	13	3	2
Southend U	Eastern Ath (HK)	08.83	83-84	47	6	11
Peterborough U	Tr	12.84	84-86	53	2	14

SHEPHERD James (Jimmy)
Aspull, 25 June, 1938 (WH)

League Club	Source	Date Signed	Seasons Played	Apps	Subs	Gls
Blackburn Rov	St John Baptist BC	11.55				
Everton	Tr	07.59				
Crewe Alex	Tr	06.60	60-63	49	-	4
Southport	Tr	02.64	63	13	-	6

SHEPHERD John Arthur
Maltby, 20 September, 1945 (M)

League Club	Source	Date Signed	Seasons Played	Apps	Subs	Gls
Rotherham U		04.66	65-67	22	0	2
York C	Tr	09.68	68	5	0	0
Oxford U	Tr	10.69	69	9	2	1

SHEPHERD John Herbert Edwin
Kensington, 29 May, 1932 (IF)

League Club	Source	Date Signed	Seasons Played	Apps	Subs	Gls
Millwall		10.52	52-57	149	-	63
Brighton & Hove A	Tr	06.58	58-59	45	-	19
Gillingham	Tr	02.60	59-60	53	-	23

SHEPHERD Paul David
Leeds, 17 November, 1977 EYth (FB)

League Club	Source	Date Signed	Seasons Played	Apps	Subs	Gls
Leeds U	YT	09.95	96	1	0	0

League Club	Source	Date Signed	Seasons Played	Apps	Subs	Gls
Tranmere Rov	L	02.99	98	0	1	0
Scunthorpe U	Keflavik (Ice)	09.00	00	0	1	0
Luton T	Tr	03.01	00	7	0	0

SHEPHERD Peter
Ivybridge, 27 August, 1965 (G)

League Club	Source	Date Signed	Seasons Played	Apps	Subs	Gls
Exeter C	Jnrs	08.82	82	1	0	0

SHEPHERD Trevor
Sutton-in-Ashfield, 25 December, 1946 (W)

League Club	Source	Date Signed	Seasons Played	Apps	Subs	Gls
Nottingham F	Jnrs	12.63				
Coventry C	Tr	10.66	67-68	12	2	1
Torquay U	L	03.68	67	14	0	6
Plymouth Arg	Tr	06.69	69-70	36	3	4

SHEPHERD John **William (Bill)**
Liverpool, 25 September, 1920 (FB)

League Club	Source	Date Signed	Seasons Played	Apps	Subs	Gls
Liverpool	Elm Park (Liverpool)	12.45	48-51	53	-	0

SHEPHERDSON Harold
Middlesbrough, 28 October, 1918 Died 1995 (CD)

League Club	Source	Date Signed	Seasons Played	Apps	Subs	Gls
Middlesbrough	South Bank East End	05.36	36-46	17	-	0

SHEPPARD Horace **Hedley**
West Ham, 26 November, 1909 (FB)

League Club	Source	Date Signed	Seasons Played	Apps	Subs	Gls
West Ham U	Barking	11.32				
Aldershot	Tr	07.34	34-48	249	-	1

SHEPPARD Richard (Dick) James
Bristol, 14 February, 1945 Died 1998 (G)

League Club	Source	Date Signed	Seasons Played	Apps	Subs	Gls
West Bromwich A	App	02.63	65-68	39	0	0
Bristol Rov	Tr	06.69	69-74	151	0	0
Torquay U	L	12.73	73	2	0	0

SHEPPARD Simon Andrew
Clevedon, 7 August, 1973 ESch/EYth (G)

League Club	Source	Date Signed	Seasons Played	Apps	Subs	Gls
Watford	YT	04.91	92-93	23	0	0
Scarborough	L	03.94	93	9	0	0
Reading	Tr	09.94	95	18	0	0

SHEPPEARD Howard Thomas
Ynysybwl, 31 January, 1933 (IF)

League Club	Source	Date Signed	Seasons Played	Apps	Subs	Gls
Sunderland	Gnasyhard YC	12.51	53	1	-	0
Cardiff C	Tr	05.55				
Newport Co	Tr	06.56	56-57	31	-	5

SHEPSTONE Paul Thomas Adam
Coventry, 8 November, 1970 EYth (M)

League Club	Source	Date Signed	Seasons Played	Apps	Subs	Gls
Coventry C	YT	11.87				
Birmingham C	Tr	07.89				
Blackburn Rov	Atherstone U	05.90	90-91	16	10	1
York C	L	03.92	91	2	0	0

SHERGOLD Wilfred (Wilf) Frederick
Swindon, 18 September, 1943 (WH)

League Club	Source	Date Signed	Seasons Played	Apps	Subs	Gls
Swindon T	Jnrs	10.60	63-65	37	0	0
Bradford C	Tr	06.66	66-67	22	6	2

SHERGOLD William (Billy) Richard
Newport, 22 January, 1923 Died 1968 WAmat/WLge-1 (IF)

League Club	Source	Date Signed	Seasons Played	Apps	Subs	Gls
Newport Co	Bishop Auckland	07.47	47-55	273	-	48

SHERIDAN Alexander (Alex)
Motherwell, 19 July, 1948 (FB)

League Club	Source	Date Signed	Seasons Played	Apps	Subs	Gls
Brighton & Hove A	Queen's Park	08.70	70	12	3	2

SHERIDAN Anthony (Tony) Joseph
Dublin, 21 October, 1974 IRYth/IRu21-5 (W)

League Club	Source	Date Signed	Seasons Played	Apps	Subs	Gls
Coventry C	Jnrs	10.91	92-93	5	4	0

SHERIDAN Darren Stephen
Manchester, 8 December, 1967 (M)

League Club	Source	Date Signed	Seasons Played	Apps	Subs	Gls
Barnsley	Winsford U	08.93	93-98	149	22	5
Wigan Ath	Tr	07.99	99-00	50	8	3
Oldham Ath	Tr	07.01	01-03	72	16	3

SHERIDAN Frank Michael
Stepney, 9 December, 1961 (M)

League Club	Source	Date Signed	Seasons Played	Apps	Subs	Gls
Derby Co	App	07.78	80-81	41	2	5
Torquay U	Tr	08.82	82-83	24	3	3

SHERIDAN George Francis
Wigan, 30 October, 1929 Died 1986 (W)

League Club	Source	Date Signed	Seasons Played	Apps	Subs	Gls
Bolton W		09.50				
Bradford C	Colwyn Bay	01.52	51-52	12	-	1

SHERIDAN John
Ramsgate, 25 May, 1938 (WH)

League Club	Source	Date Signed	Seasons Played	Apps	Subs	Gls
Notts Co	Linby Colliery	07.55	57-65	287	0	9
Hartlepools U	Tr	07.66	66-69	117	3	1

SHERIDAN John Joseph
Stretford, 1 October, 1964 IRYth/IRu23-2/IRu21-2/IRB-1/IR-34 (M)

League Club	Source	Date Signed	Seasons Played	Apps	Subs	Gls
Leeds U	Manchester C (Jnrs)	03.82	82-88	225	5	47
Nottingham F	Tr	08.89				
Sheffield Wed	Tr	11.89	89-96	187	10	25
Birmingham C	L	02.96	95	1	1	0
Bolton W	Tr	11.96	96-97	24	8	2
Oldham Ath	Doncaster Rov	10.98	98-03	132	13	14

SHERINGHAM Edward (Teddy) Paul
Highams Park, 2 April, 1966 EYth/Eu21-1/E-51 (F)

League Club	Source	Date Signed	Seasons Played	Apps	Subs	Gls
Millwall	App	01.84	83-90	205	15	93
Aldershot	L	02.85	84	4	1	0
Nottingham F	Tr	07.91	91-92	42	0	14
Tottenham H	Tr	08.92	92-96	163	3	76
Manchester U	Tr	07.97	97-00	73	31	31
Tottenham H	Tr	07.01	01-02	67	3	22
Portsmouth	Tr	07.03	03	25	7	9
West Ham U	Tr	07.04	04	26	7	20

SHERLOCK Paul Grahame
Wigan, 17 November, 1973 (FB)

League Club	Source	Date Signed	Seasons Played	Apps	Subs	Gls
Notts Co	YT	07.92	93-94	8	4	1
Mansfield T	Tr	03.95	94-96	29	10	2

SHERLOCK Steven (Steve) Edward
Birmingham, 10 May, 1959 (FB)

League Club	Source	Date Signed	Seasons Played	Apps	Subs	Gls
Manchester C	App	05.77				
Luton T	Tr	06.78	78	2	0	0
Stockport Co	Tr	08.79	79-85	236	9	7
Cardiff C	Tr	07.86	86	14	1	0
Newport Co	L	12.86	86	5	0	0
Newport Co	Tr	03.87	86-87	42	2	2

SHERON Michael (Mike) Nigel
St Helens, 11 January, 1972 Eu21-16 (F)

League Club	Source	Date Signed	Seasons Played	Apps	Subs	Gls
Manchester C	YT	07.90	91-93	82	18	24
Bury	L	03.91	90	1	4	1
Norwich C	Tr	08.94	94-95	19	9	2
Stoke C	Tr	11.95	95-96	64	5	34
Queens Park Rgrs	Tr	07.97	97-98	57	6	19
Barnsley	Tr	01.99	98-02	114	38	33
Blackpool	Tr	07.03	03	28	10	8
Macclesfield T	Tr	08.04	04	14	12	3
Shrewsbury T	Tr	03.05	04	6	1	2

SHERRATT Brian
Stoke-on-Trent, 29 March, 1944 (G)

League Club	Source	Date Signed	Seasons Played	Apps	Subs	Gls
Stoke C	App	04.61	61	1	-	0
Oxford U	Tr	08.65	65-67	44	0	0
Nottingham F	L	10.68	68	1	0	0
Barnsley	Tr	06.69	69	15	0	0
Colchester U	Gainsborough Trinity	08.70	70	9	0	0

SHERRATT James (Jimmy) Aaron
Warrington, 24 December, 1921 (FB)

League Club	Source	Date Signed	Seasons Played	Apps	Subs	Gls
Arsenal		12.46				
Hartlepools U	Tr	12.48	48	20	-	4
Leyton Orient	Tr	08.49	49-51	39	-	8
Workington	Tr	08.52	52-53	48	-	3

SHERRATT John Herbert
Stoke-on-Trent, 9 March, 1923 Died 1975 (CF)

League Club	Source	Date Signed	Seasons Played	Apps	Subs	Gls
Port Vale (Am)		03.49	48	2	-	0

SHERWOOD Alfred (Alf) Thomas
Aberaman, 13 November, 1924 Died 1990 WSch/WLge-4/WWar-1/W-41 (FB)

League Club	Source	Date Signed	Seasons Played	Apps	Subs	Gls
Cardiff C	Aberaman Ath	07.42	46-55	354	-	14
Newport Co	Tr	07.56	56-60	205	-	21

SHERWOOD Henry (Jack) William
Reading, 3 September, 1913 Died 1985 (WH)

League Club	Source	Date Signed	Seasons Played	Apps	Subs	Gls
Reading	Islington Corinthians	06.38	38	9	-	1
Aldershot	Tr	09.47	47-48	47	-	5
Crystal Palace	Tr	07.49	49	2	-	0

SHERWOOD Jeffrey (Jeff)
Bristol, 5 October, 1959 (FB)

League Club	Source	Date Signed	Seasons Played	Apps	Subs	Gls
Bristol Rov	Bath C	06.82	82	16	2	0

SHERWOOD Stephen (Steve)
Selby, 10 December, 1953 (G)

League Club	Source	Date Signed	Seasons Played	Apps	Subs	Gls
Chelsea	App	07.71	71-75	16	0	0
Millwall	L	10.73	73	1	0	0
Brentford	L	01.74	73	16	0	0
Brentford	L	08.74	74	46	0	0
Watford	Tr	11.76	76-86	211	0	1
Grimsby T	Tr	07.87	87-92	183	0	0
Northampton T	Tr	08.93	93	15	1	0
Lincoln C	Grimsby T (N/C)	03.95	94	6	1	0

SHERWOOD Timothy (Tim) Alan
St Albans, 6 February, 1969 Eu21-4/EB-1/E-3 (M)

League Club	Source	Date Signed	Seasons Played	Apps	Subs	Gls
Watford	App	02.87	87-88	23	9	2
Norwich C	Tr	07.89	89-91	66	5	10
Blackburn Rov	Tr	02.92	91-98	239	7	25
Tottenham H	Tr	02.99	98-01	81	12	12
Portsmouth	Tr	01.03	02-03	24	6	1
Coventry C	Tr	08.04	04	10	1	0

SHIELDS Anthony (Tony) Gerald
Derry, 4 June, 1980 (M)

League Club	Source	Date Signed	Seasons Played	Apps	Subs	Gls
Peterborough U	YT	07.98	97-03	93	31	3

SHIELDS Duncan
Dumbarton, 6 November, 1949 (CD)

League Club	Source	Date Signed	Seasons Played	Apps	Subs	Gls
Workington	Possilpark YMCA	08.69	69	8	1	0

SHIELDS Greg
Falkirk, 21 August, 1976 SSch/SYth/Su21-2 (FB)

League Club	Source	Date Signed	Seasons Played	Apps	Subs	Gls
Charlton Ath	Dunfermline Ath	08.99	99-00	23	2	2
Walsall	L	02.02	01	7	0	0

SHIELDS James (Jimmy)
Glasgow, 28 November, 1931 Died 2001 (IF)

League Club	Source	Date Signed	Seasons Played	Apps	Subs	Gls
Shrewsbury T	Hibernian	05.56	56	24	-	6

SHIELDS Robert James (Jimmy)
Derry, 26 September, 1931 NIAmat/IrLge-1/NI-1 (CF)

League Club	Source	Date Signed	Seasons Played	Apps	Subs	Gls
Sunderland	Crusaders	03.54				
Southampton	Tr	07.56	56-58	38	-	20

SHIELDS Samuel (Sam) Miller
Denny, 21 March, 1929 (IF)

League Club	Source	Date Signed	Seasons Played	Apps	Subs	Gls
Liverpool	Cowdenbeath	05.49	49	1	-	0
Darlington	Stirling A	06.52	52	21	-	2

SHIELS Dennis Patrick
Belfast, 24 August, 1938 NIB (CF)

League Club	Source	Date Signed	Seasons Played	Apps	Subs	Gls
Sheffield U	Distillery	12.58	58-63	32	-	8
Peterborough U	Tr	07.64	64	12	-	4
Notts Co	Tr	07.65	65	28	1	6

SHIELS James (Jimmy) Matthew
Derry, 24 February, 1938 IrLge-1/NIB (FB)

League Club	Source	Date Signed	Seasons Played	Apps	Subs	Gls
Manchester U	Waterside BC	09.56				
Southend U	Tr	06.61	61	25	-	0

SHILTON Peter Leslie
Leicester, 18 September, 1949 ESch/EYth/Eu23-13/FLge-3/E-125 (G)

League Club	Source	Date Signed	Seasons Played	Apps	Subs	Gls
Leicester C	App	09.66	65-74	286	0	1
Stoke C	Tr	11.74	74-77	110	0	0
Nottingham F	Tr	09.77	77-81	202	0	0
Southampton	Tr	08.82	82-86	188	0	0
Derby Co	Tr	07.87	87-91	175	0	0
Plymouth Arg	Tr	03.92	91-93	34	0	0
Bolton W	Wimbledon (N/C)	03.95	94	0	1	0
Coventry C	Tr	07.95				
West Ham U	Tr	01.96				
Leyton Orient	Tr	11.96	96	9	0	0

SHILTON Samuel (Sam) Roger
Nottingham, 21 July, 1978 (W)

League Club	Source	Date Signed	Seasons Played	Apps	Subs	Gls
Plymouth Arg	YT	•	94-95	1	2	0
Coventry C	Tr	10.95	97-98	3	4	0
Hartlepool U	Tr	07.99	99-00	45	9	7
Kidderminster Hrs	Tr	07.01	01-03	60	19	5

SHIMWELL Edmund (Eddie)
Birchover, 27 February, 1920 Died 1988 E-1 (FB)

League Club	Source	Date Signed	Seasons Played	Apps	Subs	Gls
Sheffield U	Birchover	01.39	46	14	-	0
Blackpool	Tr	12.46	46-56	286	-	5
Oldham Ath	Tr	05.57	57	7	-	0

SHINER Roy Albert James
Seaview, Isle of Wight, 15 November, 1924 Died 1988 (CF)

League Club	Source	Date Signed	Seasons Played	Apps	Subs	Gls
Huddersfield T	Cheltenham T	12.51	51-54	21	-	6
Sheffield Wed	Tr	07.55	55-59	153	-	93
Hull C	Tr	11.59	59	22	-	8

SHINNERS Paul
Westminster, 8 January, 1959 (F)

League Club	Source	Date Signed	Seasons Played	Apps	Subs	Gls
Gillingham	Fisher Ath	10.84	84	1	3	0
Colchester U	L	03.85	84	6	0	1
Orient	Tr	07.85	85-88	73	4	32

SHINTON Robert (Bobby) Thomas
West Bromwich, 6 January, 1952 (F)

League Club	Source	Date Signed	Seasons Played	Apps	Subs	Gls
Walsall	Lye T	03.72	71-73	78	1	20
Cambridge U	Tr	03.74	73-75	99	0	25
Wrexham	Tr	07.76	76-78	128	0	37
Manchester C	Tr	07.79	79	5	0	0
Millwall	L	02.80	79	5	0	3
Newcastle U	Tr	03.80	79-81	41	1	10
Millwall	Tr	03.82	81-82	29	5	4

SHIPLEY George Michael
Newcastle, 7 March, 1959 (M)

League Club	Source	Date Signed	Seasons Played	Apps	Subs	Gls
Southampton	App	03.77	79	2	1	0
Reading	L	03.79	78	11	1	1
Lincoln C	Tr	01.80	79-84	229	1	42
Charlton Ath	Tr	07.85	85-86	61	0	6
Gillingham	Tr	08.87	87-88	27	2	3

SHIPLEY Mark Edward
South Elmsall, 11 February, 1959 (G)

League Club	Source	Date Signed	Seasons Played	Apps	Subs	Gls
Blackburn Rov	App	08.77				
Doncaster Rov	Tr	08.79	79-80	6	0	0

SHIPPERLEY David (Dave) John
Uxbridge, 12 April, 1952 (CD)

League Club	Source	Date Signed	Seasons Played	Apps	Subs	Gls
Charlton Ath	App	04.70	70-73	92	8	8
Plymouth Arg	L	02.74	73	1	0	0
Gillingham	Tr	05.74	74-77	144	0	10
Charlton Ath	Tr	02.78	77-79	53	0	6
Reading	Tr	09.79	79-80	18	1	0

SHIPPERLEY Neil Jason
Chatham, 30 October, 1974 Eu21-7 (F)

League Club	Source	Date Signed	Seasons Played	Apps	Subs	Gls
Chelsea	YT	09.92	92-94	26	11	7
Watford	L	12.94	94	5	1	1
Southampton	Tr	01.95	94-96	65	1	12
Crystal Palace	Tr	10.96	96-98	49	12	20
Nottingham F	Tr	09.98	98	12	8	1
Barnsley	Tr	07.99	99-00	70	8	27
Wimbledon	Tr	07.01	01-02	82	5	32
Crystal Palace	Tr	07.03	03-04	40	1	9

SHIPWRIGHT William (Bill) Kenneth
St Pancras, 22 December, 1932 (CD)

League Club	Source	Date Signed	Seasons Played	Apps	Subs	Gls
Watford	Chesham U	04.53	53-58	146	-	0
Aldershot	Tr	06.59	59-62	123	-	0

SHIRES Alan Jeffrey
Leigh-on-Sea, 29 June, 1948 (W)

League Club	Source	Date Signed	Seasons Played	Apps	Subs	Gls
Southend U	App	•	65	0	1	0
Colchester U	Tr	07.66	66-67	23	0	3

SHIRLEY Alexander (Alex) Gordon
Milngavie, 31 October, 1921 Died 1990 (W)

League Club	Source	Date Signed	Seasons Played	Apps	Subs	Gls
New Brighton	Dundee U	10.46	46	18	-	3
Bradford C	Tr	08.47	47	1	-	0

SHIRTLIFF Paul Robert
Hoyland, 3 November, 1962 ESemiPro (FB)

League Club	Source	Date Signed	Seasons Played	Apps	Subs	Gls
Sheffield Wed	App	11.80	80-82	7	2	0
Northampton T	Tr	07.84	84	27	2	0

SHIRTLIFF Peter Andrew
Hoyland, 6 April, 1961 (CD)

League Club	Source	Date Signed	Seasons Played	Apps	Subs	Gls
Sheffield Wed	App	10.78	78-85	188	0	4
Charlton Ath	Tr	08.86	86-88	102	1	7
Sheffield Wed	Tr	07.89	89-92	104	0	4
Wolverhampton W	Tr	08.93	93-95	67	2	0
Barnsley	Tr	08.95	95-97	48	1	0
Carlisle U	L	10.96	96	5	0	0

SHITTU Daniel (Danny) Olusola
Lagos, Nigeria, 2 September, 1980 Nigeria 1 (CD)

League Club	Source	Date Signed	Seasons Played	Apps	Subs	Gls
Charlton Ath	Carshalton Ath	09.99				
Blackpool	L	02.01	00	15	2	2
Queens Park Rgrs	Tr	10.01	01-04	121	3	13

SHOEMAKE Kevin Paul
Woodford, 28 January, 1965 (G)

League Club	Source	Date Signed	Seasons Played	Apps	Subs	Gls
Orient	App	01.83	83	4	0	0
Peterborough U	Welling U	09.86	86-87	40	0	0

SHONE George Frederick
Runcorn, 15 February, 1922 (CF)

League Club	Source	Date Signed	Seasons Played	Apps	Subs	Gls
Tranmere Rov		12.46	46	4	-	0

SHORE Andrew (Drew) Jonathan
Poole, 8 April, 1982 (M)

League Club	Source	Date Signed	Seasons Played	Apps	Subs	Gls
Bristol Rov	YT	07.01	01	9	0	0

SHORE William Andrew (Andy)
Kirkby-in-Ashfield, 29 December, 1955 (CD)

League Club	Source	Date Signed	Seasons Played	Apps	Subs	Gls
Mansfield T	Jnrs	07.74	74	1	0	0

SHORE Brian
Huddersfield, 1 February, 1935 (CF)

League Club	Source	Date Signed	Seasons Played	Apps	Subs	Gls
Halifax T		10.56	56-57	9	-	3

League Club	Source	Date Signed	Seasons Played	Career Record Apps	Subs	Gls
SHORE Edward (Ted)						
Nuneaton, 18 October, 1927 Died 1976						(W)
Port Vale		10.45	47	3	-	0
Coventry C	Tr	07.48	48-49	2	-	0
SHORE James (Jamie) Andrew						
Bristol, 1 September, 1977 EYth						(M)
Norwich C	YT	09.94				
Bristol Rov	Tr	07.98	98	18	6	2
SHOREY Nicholas (Nicky)						
Romford, 19 February, 1981						(FB)
Leyton Orient	YT	07.99	99-00	12	3	0
Reading	Tr	02.01	01-04	154	0	7
SHORT Alan John Moxley						
Plymouth, 5 July, 1928						(W)
Exeter C	Tamerton	08.50	50	5	-	1
SHORT Christian (Chris) Mark						
Munster, Germany, 9 May, 1970						(FB)
Scarborough	Pickering T	07.88	88-89	42	1	1
Notts Co	Tr	09.90	90-95	77	17	2
Huddersfield T	L	12.94	94	6	0	0
Sheffield U	Tr	12.95	95-97	40	4	0
Stoke C	Tr	07.98	98-99	33	2	0
SHORT Craig Jonathan						
Bridlington, 25 June, 1968 ESch						(CD)
Scarborough	Pickering T	10.87	87-88	61	2	7
Notts Co	Tr	07.89	89-92	128	0	6
Derby Co	Tr	09.92	92-94	118	0	9
Everton	Tr	07.95	95-98	90	9	4
Blackburn Rov	Tr	08.99	99-04	131	3	4
SHORT David						
St Neots, 14 April, 1941						(W)
Lincoln C	St Neots T	11.58	58-59	4	-	0
SHORT John (Jack)						
Great Houghton, 18 February, 1928 Died 1976						(FB)
Wolverhampton W	Wath W	05.48	50-53	98	-	0
Stoke C	Tr	08.54	54-55	55	-	2
Barnsley	Tr	10.56	56-59	109	-	0
SHORT John David						
Gateshead, 25 January, 1921 Died 1986						(WH)
Leeds U	St Hilda's	01.38	46-48	60	-	18
Millwall	Tr	11.48	48-55	245	-	19
SHORT Maurice						
Middlesbrough, 29 December, 1949						(G)
Middlesbrough	App	02.67	67-69	16	0	0
Oldham Ath	Tr	06.70	70	5	0	0
Grimsby T	L	01.71	70	10	0	0
SHORT Russell David Victor						
Ilford, 4 September, 1968						(FB)
Southend U	App	06.87	86	0	1	0
SHORTHOUSE William (Bill) Henry						
Bilston, 27 May, 1922						(CD)
Wolverhampton W	St Mirren OB	04.46	47-56	344	-	1
SHORTT William (Bill) Warren						
Wrexham, 13 October, 1920 Died 2004 WWar-1/W-12						(G)
Chester	Hoole Alex	05.39				
Plymouth Arg	Tr	02.46	46-55	342	-	0
SHOTTON John						
Hartlepool, 17 August, 1971						(M)
Manchester U	YT	05.89				
Hartlepool U	Tr	09.90	90	0	1	0
SHOTTON Malcolm						
Newcastle, 16 February, 1957						(CD)
Leicester C	App	02.75				
Oxford U	Nuneaton Borough	05.80	80-87	262	1	12
Portsmouth	Tr	08.87	87	10	0	0
Huddersfield T	Tr	02.88	87-88	16	0	1
Barnsley	Tr	09.88	88-89	64	2	6
Hull C	Tr	02.90	89-91	58	1	2
Barnsley	Ayr U	07.94	94-95	10	0	1
SHOULDER Alan						
Bishop Auckland, 4 February, 1953						(F)
Newcastle U	Blyth Spartans	12.78	78-81	99	8	35
Carlisle U	Tr	08.82	82-84	110	2	32
Hartlepool U	Tr	06.85	85-87	66	0	24

League Club	Source	Date Signed	Seasons Played	Career Record Apps	Subs	Gls
SHOULDER James (Jimmy)						
Esh Winning, 11 September, 1946						(FB)
Sunderland	Esh Winning Jnrs	02.64	66	3	0	0
Hartlepool	Scarborough	08.73	73-74	62	1	3
SHOWELL George William						
Bilston, 9 February, 1934						(FB)
Wolverhampton W	Jnrs	08.51	54-64	200	-	3
Bristol C	Tr	05.65	65	9	2	0
Wrexham	Tr	11.66	66-67	48	0	1
SHOWERS Derek						
Merthyr Tydfil, 28 January, 1953 WSch/Wu23-6/W-2						(F)
Cardiff C	Jnrs	08.70	70-76	76	7	10
Bournemouth	Tr	07.77	77-78	58	2	19
Portsmouth	Tr	02.79	78-80	36	3	8
Hereford U	Tr	12.80	80-82	87	2	13
SHOWLER Kenneth (Ken)						
Doncaster, 3 February, 1933						(W)
Chesterfield	Bentley Colliery	11.52	53	7	-	0
SHOWLER Paul						
Doncaster, 10 October, 1966 ESemiPro-2						(W)
Barnet	Altrincham	08.91	91-92	69	2	12
Bradford C	Tr	08.93	93-95	72	16	15
Luton T	Tr	08.96	96-98	23	4	6
SHOWUNMI Enoch Olusesan						
Kilburn, 21 April, 1982						(F)
Luton T	Willesden Constantine	09.03	03-04	25	36	13
SHREEVE John (Jack) Thomas Thornton						
Boldon, 18 August, 1917 Died 1966						(FB)
Charlton Ath	Boldon Villa	01.35	36-50	145	-	0
SHREEVES Peter						
Neath, 30 November, 1940						(IF)
Reading	Finchley	01.59	58-65	112	1	17
SHREWSBURY Philip (Phil)						
Langley Mill, 25 March, 1947 EYth						(W)
Notts Co	Jnrs	09.65	66	1	1	0
SHRUBB Paul						
Guildford, 1 August, 1955						(M)
Fulham	App	08.72	72	1	0	0
Brentford	Hellenic (SA)	03.77	76-81	170	12	8
Aldershot	Tr	08.82	82-86	165	9	5
SHTANIUK Sergei						
Minsk, Belarus, 11 January, 1972 Belarus 42						(CD)
Stoke C	Dynamo Moscow (Rus)	08.01	01-02	84	0	5
SHUFFLEBOTTOM Frank						
Chesterfield, 9 October, 1917						(FB)
Ipswich T	Margate	06.38	38	2	-	0
Nottingham F	Tr	09.42	46	2	-	0
Bradford C	Tr	10.46	46-47	56	-	0
SHUKER Christopher (Chris) Alan						
Liverpool, 9 May, 1982						(F)
Manchester C	YT	09.99	01-02	1	4	0
Macclesfield T	L	03.01	00	6	3	1
Walsall	L	02.03	02	3	2	0
Rochdale	L	08.03	03	14	0	1
Hartlepool U	L	12.03	03	14	0	1
Barnsley	Tr	03.04	03-04	48	6	7
SHUKER John						
Eccles, 8 May, 1942						(FB)
Oxford U		12.61	62-76	473	5	46
SHUTE Philip (Phil)						
Darlington, 15 December, 1953						(F)
Darlington	Shildon	03.84	85	2	0	0
SHUTT Carl Steven						
Sheffield, 10 October, 1961						(F)
Sheffield Wed	Spalding U	05.85	85-87	36	4	16
Bristol C	Tr	10.87	87-88	39	7	10
Leeds U	Tr	03.89	88-92	46	33	17
Birmingham C	Tr	08.93	93	18	8	4
Manchester C	L	12.93	93	5	1	0
Bradford C	Tr	08.94	94-96	60	28	15
Darlington	Tr	03.97	96-98	28	25	9
SHUTT Stephen (Steve) James						
Barnsley, 29 November, 1964						(M)
Barnsley	App	11.82	82	1	0	0
Scunthorpe U	Goole T	02.85	84	2	0	1

SHUTTLEWORTH Barry
Accrington, 9 July, 1977 (FB)

League Club	Source	Date Signed	Seasons Played	Apps	Subs	Gls
Bury	YT	07.95				
Rotherham U	Tr	08.97				
Blackpool	Tr	08.98	98-99	16	3	1
Macclesfield T	Scarborough	10.01	01	0	3	0

SHYNE Christopher (Chris)
Rochdale, 10 December, 1950 Died 2004 (G)

League Club	Source	Date Signed	Seasons Played	Apps	Subs	Gls
Rochdale	Dyers Arms	01.77	76-78	20	0	0
Wigan Ath	Tr	08.79	79	10	0	0

SIBBALD Robert (Bobby) Louis
Hebburn, 25 January, 1948 (FB)

League Club	Source	Date Signed	Seasons Played	Apps	Subs	Gls
Leeds U	Jnrs	01.65	66-67	1	1	0
York C	Tr	02.69	68-70	74	5	7
Southport	Tr	07.71	71-76	240	0	13

SIBIERSKI Antoine
Lille, France, 5 August, 1974 FrYth (M)

League Club	Source	Date Signed	Seasons Played	Apps	Subs	Gls
Manchester C	RC Lens (Fr)	08.03	03-04	52	16	9

SIBLEY Albert (Joe)
West Thurrock, 6 October, 1919 (W)

League Club	Source	Date Signed	Seasons Played	Apps	Subs	Gls
Southend U	Jnrs	08.37	46	21	-	3
Newcastle U	Tr	02.47	46-49	31	-	6
Southend U	Tr	07.50	50-55	192	-	36

SIBLEY Eric Seymour
Christchurch, 17 November, 1915 Died 1996 (FB)

League Club	Source	Date Signed	Seasons Played	Apps	Subs	Gls
Tottenham H	Jnrs	05.34				
Bournemouth	Tr	08.37	37	7	-	0
Blackpool	Tr	10.37	37-46	82	-	0
Grimsby T	Tr	12.47	47-48	23	-	0
Chester	Tr	07.49	49	7	-	0

SIBLEY Frank Philip
Uxbridge, 4 December, 1947 EYth (CD)

League Club	Source	Date Signed	Seasons Played	Apps	Subs	Gls
Queens Park Rgrs	App	02.65	63-70	140	3	3

SIBLEY Thomas (Tom) Ivor
Porth, 27 October, 1920 Died 1994 (W)

League Club	Source	Date Signed	Seasons Played	Apps	Subs	Gls
Birmingham C	Ton Pentre	09.43				
Rochdale	Tr	03.47	46-47	23	-	3

SIBON Gerald
Dalen, Holland, 19 April, 1974 (F)

League Club	Source	Date Signed	Seasons Played	Apps	Subs	Gls
Sheffield Wed	Ajax (Holl)	07.99	99-02	98	31	36

SIDDALL Barry Alfred
Ellesmere Port, 12 September, 1954 EYth (G)

League Club	Source	Date Signed	Seasons Played	Apps	Subs	Gls
Bolton W	App	01.72	72-76	137	0	0
Sunderland	Tr	09.76	76-81	167	0	0
Darlington	L	10.80	80	8	0	0
Port Vale	Tr	08.82	82-84	81	0	0
Blackpool	L	10.83	83	7	0	0
Stoke C	Tr	01.85	84-85	20	0	0
Tranmere Rov	L	10.85	85	12	0	0
Manchester C	L	03.86	85	6	0	0
Blackpool	Tr	08.86	86-88	110	0	0
Stockport Co	Tr	06.89	89	21	0	0
Hartlepool U	Tr	03.90	89	11	0	0
West Bromwich A	Tr	08.90				
Carlisle U	Mossley	11.90	90	24	0	0
Chester C	Tr	07.91	91	9	0	0
Preston NE	Northwich Vic	11.92	92	1	0	0

SIDDALL Alfred **Brian**
Northwich, 2 May, 1930 (IF)

League Club	Source	Date Signed	Seasons Played	Apps	Subs	Gls
Stoke C	Northwich Vic	02.51	50-53	59	-	10
Bournemouth	Tr	01.54	53-56	85	-	16
Ipswich T	Tr	05.57	57-60	58	-	6

SIDEBOTTOM Arnold
Barnsley, 1 April, 1954 (CD)

League Club	Source	Date Signed	Seasons Played	Apps	Subs	Gls
Manchester U	Jnrs	02.72	72-74	16	0	0
Huddersfield T	Tr	01.76	75-77	56	5	5
Halifax T	Tr	10.78	78	21	0	2

SIDEBOTTOM Geoffrey (Geoff)
Mapplewell, 29 December, 1936 (G)

League Club	Source	Date Signed	Seasons Played	Apps	Subs	Gls
Wolverhampton W	Jnrs	09.54	58-60	28	-	0
Aston Villa	Tr	02.61	60-64	70	-	0
Scunthorpe U	Tr	01.65	64-66	59	0	0
Brighton & Hove A	NY Generals (USA)	01.69	68-70	40	0	0

SIDIBE Mamady
Mali, 18 December, 1979 Mali 7 (F)

League Club	Source	Date Signed	Seasons Played	Apps	Subs	Gls
Swansea C	CA Paris (Fr)	07.01	01	26	5	7
Gillingham	Tr	08.02	02-04	80	26	10

SIDLOW Cyril
Colwyn Bay, 26 November, 1915 Died 2005 WAmat/WWar-11/W-7 (G)

League Club	Source	Date Signed	Seasons Played	Apps	Subs	Gls
Wolverhampton W	Llandudno T	05.37	37-38	4	-	0
Liverpool	Tr	02.46	46-50	149	-	0

SIDWELL Steven James
Wandsworth, 14 December, 1982 EYth/Eu20/Eu21-2 (M)

League Club	Source	Date Signed	Seasons Played	Apps	Subs	Gls
Arsenal	YT	07.01				
Brentford	L	10.01	01	29	1	4
Brighton & Hove A	L	11.02	02	11	1	5
Reading	Tr	01.03	02-04	100	0	15

SIEVWRIGHT George Edgar Smollett
Broughty Ferry, 10 September, 1937 (WH)

League Club	Source	Date Signed	Seasons Played	Apps	Subs	Gls
Oldham Ath	Dundee U	06.63	63	37	-	4
Tranmere Rov	Tr	06.64				
Rochdale	Tr	07.65	65	31	1	1

SIGERE Jean-Michel Paul
Martinique, 26 January, 1977 Fru21 (F)

League Club	Source	Date Signed	Seasons Played	Apps	Subs	Gls
Rushden & Diamonds	Bordeaux (Fr)	03.00	01	4	3	1

SIGURDSSON Larus Orri
Akureyri, Iceland, 4 June, 1973 IcYth/Icu21-16/Ic-42 (CD)

League Club	Source	Date Signed	Seasons Played	Apps	Subs	Gls
Stoke C	Thor (Ice)	10.94	94-99	199	1	7
West Bromwich A	Tr	09.99	99-03	104	12	1

[SILAS] REBELO FERNANDES Jorge Manuel
Lisbon, Portugal, 1 September, 1976 Portugal 3 (M)

League Club	Source	Date Signed	Seasons Played	Apps	Subs	Gls
Wolverhampton W	Uniao Leiria (Por)	07.03	03	2	7	0

SILENZI Andrea
Rome, Italy, 10 February, 1966 Italy int (F)

League Club	Source	Date Signed	Seasons Played	Apps	Subs	Gls
Nottingham F	Torino (It)	08.95	95-96	4	8	0

SILK Gary Lee
Newport, Isle of Wight, 13 September, 1984 (CD)

League Club	Source	Date Signed	Seasons Played	Apps	Subs	Gls
Portsmouth	Sch	01.04				
Wycombe W	L	07.04	04	19	3	0

SILK George Henry
Orrell Park, 18 October, 1916 Died 1969 (FB)

League Club	Source	Date Signed	Seasons Played	Apps	Subs	Gls
Southport	Miranda	09.35	35-36	14	-	0
Plymouth Arg	Tr	08.37	37-50	86	-	1

SILKMAN Barry
Stepney, 29 June, 1952 (M)

League Club	Source	Date Signed	Seasons Played	Apps	Subs	Gls
Hereford U	Barnet	08.74	74-75	18	19	2
Crystal Palace	Tr	08.76	76-78	40	8	6
Plymouth Arg	Tr	10.78	78	14	0	2
Luton T	L	02.79	78	3	0	0
Manchester C	Tr	03.79	78-79	19	0	3
Brentford	Tr	08.80	80	14	0	1
Queens Park Rgrs	Tr	10.80	80	22	1	2
Orient	Tr	09.81	81-84	133	7	14
Southend U	Tr	07.85	85	38	2	1
Crewe Alex	Tr	09.86	86	1	1	0

SILLE Leslie (Les) Taylor
Liverpool, 12 April, 1928 (W)

League Club	Source	Date Signed	Seasons Played	Apps	Subs	Gls
Bournemouth (Am)	Tranmere Rov (Am)	03.47	46	1	-	0
Crystal Palace (Am)	Ipswich T (Am)	09.48	48	3	-	0
Tranmere Rov (Am)	Tr	02.49	48	1	-	0

SILLETT John Charles
Southampton, 20 July, 1936 FLge-1 (FB)

League Club	Source	Date Signed	Seasons Played	Apps	Subs	Gls
Chelsea	Southampton (Am)	04.54	56-61	93	-	0
Coventry C	Tr	04.62	61-65	108	1	1
Plymouth Arg	Tr	07.66	66-67	37	1	1

SILLETT Richard **Peter** Tudor (FB)
Southampton, 1 February, 1933 Died 1998 EYth/Eu23-3/FLge-1/EB/E-3

League Club	Source	Date Signed	Seasons Played	Apps	Subs	Gls
Southampton	Jnrs	06.50	51-52	59	-	4
Chelsea	Tr	06.53	53-61	260	-	29

SILMAN David Alan
Hampstead, 28 October, 1959 (CD)

League Club	Source	Date Signed	Seasons Played	Apps	Subs	Gls
Brentford	Wolverhampton W (App)	02.78	78	1	0	0

SILMAN Roy
Doncaster, 12 May, 1934 (FB)

League Club	Source	Date Signed	Seasons Played	Apps	Subs	Gls
Rotherham U	Edlington Colliery	04.52	52-59	105	-	2

SILVESTER Peter Dennis
Wokingham, 19 February, 1948 (F)

League Club	Source	Date Signed	Seasons Played	Apps	Subs	Gls
Reading	App	02.66	65-69	76	3	27
Norwich C	Tr	09.69	69-73	99	1	37
Colchester U	L	10.73	73	4	0	0
Southend U	Tr	02.74	73-75	78	2	32
Reading	L	03.75	74	2	0	0
Southend U	Vancouver (Can)	08.76	76	1	0	0
Blackburn Rov	L	10.76	76	5	0	1
Cambridge U	Washington (USA)	08.77	77	2	2	1

SILVESTRE Mikael Samy
Chambray-les-Tours, France, 9 August, 1977 FrYth/Fru21/Fr-36 (FB)

League Club	Source	Date Signed	Seasons Played	Apps	Subs	Gls
Manchester U	Inter Milan (It)	09.99	99-04	186	13	4

[SILVINHO] SILVIO DE CAMPOS Junior
Sao Paulo, Brazil, 30 June, 1974 Brazil 2 (FB)

League Club	Source	Date Signed	Seasons Played	Apps	Subs	Gls
Arsenal	Corinthians (Br)	07.99	99-00	46	9	3

SIM John (Jock)
Glasgow, 4 December, 1922 Died 2000 (CF)

League Club	Source	Date Signed	Seasons Played	Apps	Subs	Gls
Brighton & Hove A	Kirkintilloch Rob Roy	10.46	46-49	32	-	5

SIMB Jean-Pierre
Paris, France, 4 September, 1974 (F)

League Club	Source	Date Signed	Seasons Played	Apps	Subs	Gls
Torquay U	Paris Red Star (Fr)	03.99	98-99	4	16	1

SIMBA Amara Sylla
Dakar, Senegal, 23 December, 1961 France 3 (F)

League Club	Source	Date Signed	Seasons Played	Apps	Subs	Gls
Leyton Orient	Leon (Mex)	10.98	98-99	27	10	13

SIMCOE Kenneth (Ken) Edward
Nottingham, 14 February, 1937 (W)

League Club	Source	Date Signed	Seasons Played	Apps	Subs	Gls
Nottingham F	Jnrs	12.56	57	2	-	1
Coventry C	Tr	05.59	59	8	-	1
Notts Co	Tr	07.60	60	2	-	0

SIMEK Franklin (Frankie) Michael
St Louis, USA, 13 October, 1984 UsYth (CD)

League Club	Source	Date Signed	Seasons Played	Apps	Subs	Gls
Arsenal	Sch	07.02				
Queens Park Rgrs	L	10.04	04	5	0	0
Bournemouth	L	03.05	04	8	0	0

SIMKIN Darren Spencer
Walsall, 24 March, 1970 (FB)

League Club	Source	Date Signed	Seasons Played	Apps	Subs	Gls
Wolverhampton W	Blakenhall	12.91	92-93	14	1	0
Shrewsbury T	Tr	12.94	94	10	2	0

SIMM John (Johnny)
Ashton-in-Makerfield, 24 November, 1929 (W)

League Club	Source	Date Signed	Seasons Played	Apps	Subs	Gls
Bolton W		10.47	47	1	-	0
Bury	Tr	05.51	51-54	47	-	8
Bradford C	Tr	03.55	54-58	95	-	22

SIMMONDS Christopher (Chris) Kenneth
Plymouth, 5 August, 1920 Died 1982 (IF)

League Club	Source	Date Signed	Seasons Played	Apps	Subs	Gls
Millwall	Barry T	05.47	46-49	67	-	14
Leyton Orient	Tr	06.50	50	15	-	1
Workington	Tr	06.51	51-53	119	-	33

SIMMONDS Daniel (Danny) Brian
Eastbourne, 17 December, 1974 (M)

League Club	Source	Date Signed	Seasons Played	Apps	Subs	Gls
Brighton & Hove A	YT	07.93	93-94	8	10	0

SIMMONDS Robert **Lyndon**
Pontypool, 11 November, 1966 WYth (F)

League Club	Source	Date Signed	Seasons Played	Apps	Subs	Gls
Leeds U	App	11.84	84-85	6	3	3
Swansea C	L	10.86	86	7	1	1
Rochdale	Tr	02.87	86-87	65	0	22

SIMMONDS Melvyn (Mel) Robert
Reading, 20 December, 1951 ESch (M)

League Club	Source	Date Signed	Seasons Played	Apps	Subs	Gls
Reading	Manchester U (App)	01.69				
Bournemouth	Tr	07.69	69	4	2	0

SIMMONITE Gordon
Sheffield, 25 April, 1957 ESemiPro (FB)

League Club	Source	Date Signed	Seasons Played	Apps	Subs	Gls
Sheffield Wed	Rotherham (App)	08.75	76	1	0	0
Blackpool	Boston U	09.80	80-82	63	0	1
Lincoln C	Tr	11.82	82-84	71	1	0

SIMMONS Anthony (Tony) John
Stocksbridge, 9 February, 1965 EYth (F)

League Club	Source	Date Signed	Seasons Played	Apps	Subs	Gls
Sheffield Wed	App	02.83	81-82	1	3	0
Queens Park Rgrs	Tr	11.83				
Rotherham U	Tr	03.84	83-86	85	11	27
Lincoln C	Tr	09.86	86	14	5	5
Cardiff C	L	02.87	86	4	1	1

SIMMONS David (Dave) John
Ryde, 24 October, 1948 (F)

League Club	Source	Date Signed	Seasons Played	Apps	Subs	Gls
Arsenal	App	11.65				
Bournemouth	L	11.68	68	7	0	3
Aston Villa	Tr	02.69	68-70	13	4	7
Walsall	L	10.70	70	5	0	2
Colchester U	Tr	12.70	70-72	57	5	11
Cambridge U	Tr	03.73	72-73	19	5	3
Brentford	Tr	03.74	73-75	47	5	17
Cambridge U	Tr	11.75	75	16	1	5

SIMMS Gordon
Leamington Spa, 20 December, 1936 (W)

League Club	Source	Date Signed	Seasons Played	Apps	Subs	Gls
Coventry C (Am)	Flavell's	10.57	57	1	-	0

SIMMS Gordon Henry
Larne, 23 March, 1981 NISch/NIYth/NIu21-14 (CD)

League Club	Source	Date Signed	Seasons Played	Apps	Subs	Gls
Wolverhampton W	YT	04.98				
Hartlepool U	Tr	03.01	01-02	6	5	0

SIMNER Joseph (Joe)
Sedgley, 13 March, 1923 Died 2000 (IF)

League Club	Source	Date Signed	Seasons Played	Apps	Subs	Gls
Chelsea	Folkestone	10.47	47	1	-	0
Swindon T	Tr	07.49	49-50	30	-	12

SIMONS Alan Geoffrey
Wrexham, 2 September, 1968 (G)

League Club	Source	Date Signed	Seasons Played	Apps	Subs	Gls
Port Vale	YT	09.87	87	1	0	0

SIMONSEN Allan Rodenkam
Vejle, Denmark, 15 December, 1952 Denmark int (F)

League Club	Source	Date Signed	Seasons Played	Apps	Subs	Gls
Charlton Ath	Barcelona (Sp)	11.82	82	16	0	9

SIMONSEN Steven (Steve) Preben Arthur
South Shields, 3 April, 1979 EYth/Eu21-4 (G)

League Club	Source	Date Signed	Seasons Played	Apps	Subs	Gls
Tranmere Rov	YT	10.96	97-98	35	0	0
Everton	Tr	09.98	99-03	28	2	0
Stoke C	Tr	08.04	04	29	2	0

SIMPEMBA Ian Frederick
Dublin, 28 March, 1983 IRYth (FB)

League Club	Source	Date Signed	Seasons Played	Apps	Subs	Gls
Wycombe W	YT	07.01	02-03	17	3	2

SIMPKIN Christopher (Chris) John
Hull, 24 April, 1944 (M)

League Club	Source	Date Signed	Seasons Played	Apps	Subs	Gls
Hull C	App	04.62	62-71	284	1	19
Blackpool	Tr	10.71	71-72	31	3	1
Scunthorpe U	Tr	10.73	73-74	61	0	2
Huddersfield T	Tr	08.75	75	25	0	0
Hartlepool	Tr	12.76	76-77	47	0	0

SIMPKIN Joseph (Joe)
Skelmersdale, 26 September, 1921 Died 1969 (WH)

League Club	Source	Date Signed	Seasons Played	Apps	Subs	Gls
Southport	Burscough	04.44	46-47	10	-	2

SIMPKINS Kenneth (Ken)
Wrexham, 21 December, 1943 Wu23-1 (G)

League Club	Source	Date Signed	Seasons Played	Apps	Subs	Gls
Wrexham	Jnrs	05.62	62-63	4	-	0
Hartlepools U	Tr	03.64	63-67	121	0	1

SIMPKINS Michael (Mike) James
Sheffield, 28 November, 1978 (CD)

League Club	Source	Date Signed	Seasons Played	Apps	Subs	Gls
Sheffield Wed	YT	07.97				
Chesterfield	Tr	03.98	98-00	22	4	0
Cardiff C	Tr	05.01	01	13	4	0
Exeter C	L	09.02	02	4	1	0
Cheltenham T	L	12.02	02	2	0	0
Rochdale	Tr	08.03	03	25	2	0

SIMPSON Alexander (Alec)
Glasgow, 24 November, 1924 (WH)

League Club	Source	Date Signed	Seasons Played	Apps	Subs	Gls
Wolverhampton W	Glasgow Benburb	01.47	47-48	2	-	0
Notts Co	Tr	10.49	49-52	74	-	6
Southampton	Tr	11.52	52-54	68	-	1
Shrewsbury T	Tr	07.55	55-57	100	-	4

SIMPSON Archibald (Archie)
Dundee, 8 June, 1933 SSch (FB)

League Club	Source	Date Signed	Seasons Played	Apps	Subs	Gls
Newcastle U	Dundee	07.55				
Barrow	Tr	07.56	56-58	76	-	1

SIMPSON Charles (Charlie) William
Rochdale, 11 July, 1954 (M)

League Club	Source	Date Signed	Seasons Played	Apps	Subs	Gls
Rochdale	App	07.72	72	1	0	1

SIMPSON Colin Robertson
Oxford, 30 April, 1976 (F)

League Club	Source	Date Signed	Seasons Played	Apps	Subs	Gls
Watford	YT	07.94	95	0	1	0
Leyton Orient	Hendon	12.97	97	9	5	3

SIMPSON Cyril
Aylesham, 18 August, 1942 (WH)

League Club	Source	Date Signed	Seasons Played	Apps	Subs	Gls
Gillingham	Jnrs	06.60	59-61	18	-	0

SIMPSON Dennis Ewart
Coventry, 1 November, 1919 Died 2002 (W)

League Club	Source	Date Signed	Seasons Played	Apps	Subs	Gls
Coventry C	Salem Baptist	05.39	46-49	67	-	5
Reading	Tr	05.50	50-54	172	-	32
Exeter C	Tr	05.55	55-56	30	-	4

SIMPSON Elliott David
York, 1 July, 1976 (FB)

League Club	Source	Date Signed	Seasons Played	Apps	Subs	Gls
York C	YT	06.94	94	1	0	0

SIMPSON Fitzroy
Bradford-on-Avon, 26 February, 1970 Jamaica 39 (M)

League Club	Source	Date Signed	Seasons Played	Apps	Subs	Gls
Swindon T	YT	07.88	88-91	78	27	9
Manchester C	Tr	03.92	91-94	58	13	4

League Club	Source	Date Signed	Seasons Played	Career Record Apps	Subs	Gls
Bristol C	L	09.94	94	4	0	0
Portsmouth	Tr	08.95	95-99	139	9	10
Walsall	Heart of Midlothian	03.01	00-02	45	18	4
SIMPSON Gary						
Chesterfield, 10 June, 1959						(F)
Chesterfield	App	07.77	76-80	36	7	8
Chester	Tr	08.81	81-82	57	6	18
SIMPSON Gary John						
Ashford, 14 February, 1976						(CD)
Luton T	YT	07.94				
Fulham	L	03.96	95	5	2	0
SIMPSON George Leonard						
Shirebrook, 3 December, 1933						(IF)
Mansfield T	Jnrs	08.51	52-53	8	-	0
Gillingham	Hereford U	08.56	56	8	-	1
SIMPSON Harold (Harry)						
Ashton-under-Lyne, 2 August, 1927						(W)
Accrington St (Am)	Lytham	04.49	48	1	-	0
SIMPSON James (Jimmy)						
Clay Cross, 8 December, 1923						(IF)
Chesterfield	Parkhouse Colliery	08.45	46	3	-	0
SIMPSON John						
Hedon, 27 October, 1918 Died 2000						(FB)
Huddersfield T	Bridlington T	03.39	46	5	-	0
York C	Tr	03.48	47-53	207	-	0
SIMPSON John Lionel						
Appleby, 5 October, 1933 Died 1993						(G)
Lincoln C	Netherfield	03.57	56	5	-	0
Gillingham	Tr	06.57	57-71	571	0	0
SIMPSON Joshua (Josh)						
Vancouver, Canada, 15 May, 1983 Canada 7						(M)
Millwall	Univ of Portland (USA)	08.04	04	22	8	1
SIMPSON Karl Edward						
Newmarket, 14 October, 1976						(M)
Norwich C	Jnrs	07.95	95-97	4	6	0
SIMPSON Kenneth (Ken)						
Sheffield, 12 June, 1931						(W)
Rotherham U	Ransome & Marles	09.55	55-57	7	-	0
SIMPSON Michael						
Nottingham, 28 February, 1974						(M)
Notts Co	YT	07.92	93-96	39	10	3
Plymouth Arg	L	10.96	96	10	2	0
Wycombe W	Tr	12.96	96-03	267	18	16
Leyton Orient	Tr	07.04	04	45	0	2
SIMPSON Neil						
Hackney, 15 November, 1961 EYth/Su21-11/S-4						(M)
Newcastle U	Aberdeen	07.90	90	1	3	0
SIMPSON Noel Harold						
Mansfield, 23 December, 1922 Died 1987						(WH)
Nottingham F		05.45	46-47	47	-	3
Coventry C	Tr	08.48	48-56	258	-	8
Exeter C	Tr	02.57	56-57	33	-	0
SIMPSON Owen						
Mickley, 18 December, 1943						(FB)
Rotherham U		10.62	64-66	6	0	0
Orient	Tr	09.67	67	36	0	4
Colchester U	Tr	08.68	68	41	2	4
Southend U	Tr	08.69	69-70	64	0	1
Darlington	Tr	03.71	70	11	0	0
Grimsby T	Tr	08.71	71	6	1	0
SIMPSON Paul David						
Carlisle, 26 July, 1966 EYth/Eu21-5						(W)
Manchester C	App	08.83	82-88	99	22	18
Oxford U	Tr	10.88	88-91	138	6	43
Derby Co	Tr	02.92	91-97	134	52	48
Sheffield U	L	12.96	96	2	4	0
Wolverhampton W	Tr	10.97	97-99	32	20	6
Walsall	L	09.98	98	4	0	1
Walsall	L	12.98	98	6	0	0
Blackpool	Tr	08.00	00-01	69	7	13
Rochdale	Tr	03.02	01-02	37	5	15
Carlisle U	Tr	08.03	03	25	0	6
SIMPSON Peter Frederick						
Gorleston, 13 January, 1945						(CD)
Arsenal	App	04.62	63-77	353	17	10

League Club	Source	Date Signed	Seasons Played	Career Record Apps	Subs	Gls
SIMPSON Peter Wilson						
Sunderland, 21 September, 1940 ESch						(IF)
Burnley	Jnrs	11.57	61-62	3	-	0
Bury	Tr	08.63	63	4	-	0
SIMPSON Philip (Phil) Mark						
Lambeth, 19 October, 1969						(M)
Barnet	Stevenage Borough	10.95	95-98	91	9	7
SIMPSON Reginald (Reg)						
Blackburn, 14 June, 1923						(FB)
Preston NE		11.43	46	4	-	0
Carlisle U	Tr	08.48	48	38	-	0
SIMPSON Robert (Bobby)						
Bishop Auckland, 15 September, 1915 Died 1994						(W)
Darlington	West Auckland	08.36	36-46	96	-	14
Hartlepools U	Tr	07.47	47	13	-	1
SIMPSON Robert (Robbie) Anthony						
Luton, 3 March, 1976 EYth						(F)
Tottenham H	YT	11.93				
Portsmouth	Tr	07.96	97	0	2	0
SIMPSON Ronald (Ron)						
Carlisle, 25 February, 1934						(W)
Huddersfield T	Holme Head Works	02.51	51-57	110	-	24
Sheffield U	Tr	05.58	58-64	203	-	44
Carlisle U	Tr	12.64	64-65	46	0	6
SIMPSON Ronald (Ronnie) Campbell						
Glasgow, 11 October, 1930 Died 2004 SAmat/SB/SLge-1/S-5						(G)
Newcastle U	Third Lanark	02.51	51-59	262	-	0
SIMPSON Terence (Terry) John Norman						
Southampton, 8 October, 1938						(WH)
Southampton	Jnrs	06.57	58-61	22	-	1
Peterborough U	Tr	06.62	62	45	-	4
West Bromwich A	Tr	06.63	63-66	71	1	3
Walsall	Tr	03.67	66-67	50	1	4
Gillingham	Tr	07.68	68	35	1	4
SIMPSON Thomas (Tommy)						
Airdrie, 31 July, 1931						(FB)
Darlington	Dundee U	08.56	56-57	4	-	0
SIMPSON William						
Carlisle, 2 October, 1919						(IF)
Carlisle U	Tottenham H (Am)	08.46	46	12	-	2
SIMPSON William George						
Glasgow, 22 May, 1928 Died 2002						(F)
Aston Villa	Trentside Jnrs	05.50				
Crystal Palace	Tr	08.52	52-54	38	-	13
SIMS Harry **Christopher (Chris)**						
Liverpool, 6 December, 1939						(FB)
Blackburn Rov	Clitheroe	04.59	63-64	13	-	0
SIMS Frank						
Lincoln, 12 September, 1931 Died 2001						(CD)
Lincoln C	Ruston Bucyrus	08.51	51-55	3	-	0
SIMS John						
Belper, 14 August, 1952						(F)
Derby Co	App	08.70	72	2	1	0
Luton T	L	11.73	73	3	0	1
Oxford U	L	09.74	74	6	1	1
Colchester U	L	01.75	74	2	0	0
Notts Co	Tr	12.75	75-77	48	13	13
Exeter C	Tr	12.78	78-79	33	1	11
Plymouth Arg	Tr	10.79	79-82	161	2	43
Torquay U	Tr	08.83	83	30	0	8
Exeter C	Tr	02.84	83-84	23	2	6
Torquay U	Tr	11.84	84	15	2	3
SIMS David **Nigel**						
Coton-in-Elms, 9 August, 1931 FLge-2						(G)
Wolverhampton W	Stapenhill	09.48	48-55	38	-	0
Aston Villa	Tr	03.56	55-63	264	-	0
Peterborough U	Tr	09.64	64	16	-	0
SIMS Steven (Steve) Frank						
Lincoln, 2 July, 1957 Eu21-10/EB						(CD)
Leicester C	App	08.74	75-78	78	1	3
Watford	Tr	12.78	78-83	150	2	4
Notts Co	Tr	09.84	84-86	85	0	5
Watford	Tr	10.86	86	19	0	1
Aston Villa	Tr	06.87	87-88	41	0	0
Lincoln C	Burton A	10.90	90	5	0	0

SINAMA-PONGOLLE Florent
Saint-Pierre, Reunion, 20 October, 1984 FrYth/Fru21 (F)

League Club	Source	Date Signed	Seasons Played	Apps	Subs	Gls
Liverpool	Le Havre (Fr)	07.03	03-04	9	22	4

SINCLAIR Brian William
Liverpool, 2 August, 1958 (W)

League Club	Source	Date Signed	Seasons Played	Apps	Subs	Gls
Blackpool	Bury (N/C)	08.77	77	0	2	0
Port Vale	Tr	08.78	78	14	4	2

SINCLAIR Colin MacLean
Edinburgh, 1 December, 1947 SSch/SYth (F)

League Club	Source	Date Signed	Seasons Played	Apps	Subs	Gls
Darlington	Raith Rov	06.71	71-76	201	2	59
Hereford U	Tr	10.76	76-77	20	2	2
Newport Co	Dunfermline Ath	01.78	77-78	29	1	5

SINCLAIR David
Dunfermline, 6 October, 1969 (CD)

League Club	Source	Date Signed	Seasons Played	Apps	Subs	Gls
Millwall	Raith Rov	07.96	96	6	2	0

SINCLAIR Dean Michael
Luton, 17 December, 1984 (M)

League Club	Source	Date Signed	Seasons Played	Apps	Subs	Gls
Norwich C	Sch	05.03	02	1	1	0

SINCLAIR Dennis
Middlesbrough, 20 November, 1931 (W)

League Club	Source	Date Signed	Seasons Played	Apps	Subs	Gls
Derby Co		05.52				
Mansfield T	Tr	07.53	53	1	-	0

SINCLAIR Frank Mohammed
Lambeth, 3 December, 1971 Jamaica 24 (CD)

League Club	Source	Date Signed	Seasons Played	Apps	Subs	Gls
Chelsea	YT	05.90	90-97	163	6	7
West Bromwich A	L	12.91	91	6	0	1
Leicester C	Tr	08.98	98-03	153	11	3
Burnley	Tr	07.04	04	36	0	1

SINCLAIR James **Graeme**
Paisley, 1 July, 1957 SLge-1 (FB)

League Club	Source	Date Signed	Seasons Played	Apps	Subs	Gls
Manchester C (L)	Glasgow Celtic	11.84	84	1	0	0

SINCLAIR Harvey (Harry) Patrick
Bournemouth, 30 November, 1933 (G)

League Club	Source	Date Signed	Seasons Played	Apps	Subs	Gls
Fulham	Bournemouth (Am)	12.50				
Leicester C	Cambridge U	08.56	56	1	-	0
Bristol Rov	Yeovil T	09.58	58	1	-	0

SINCLAIR Jade
Saltburn, 6 November, 1971 (M)

League Club	Source	Date Signed	Seasons Played	Apps	Subs	Gls
Hartlepool U	YT	•	89	4	0	0

SINCLAIR John (Jackie) Evens Wright
Culross, 21 July, 1943 S-1 (W)

League Club	Source	Date Signed	Seasons Played	Apps	Subs	Gls
Leicester C	Dunfermline Ath	05.65	65-67	103	0	50
Newcastle U	Tr	01.68	67-69	42	1	6
Sheffield Wed	Tr	12.69	69-72	97	4	14
Chesterfield	L	03.73	72	10	0	3

SINCLAIR Michael (Mike) John
Grimsby, 13 October, 1938 (CF)

League Club	Source	Date Signed	Seasons Played	Apps	Subs	Gls
Grimsby T	Jnrs	09.57	57-60	6	-	1

SINCLAIR Nicholas (Nick) John Thomas
Manchester, 3 January, 1960 ESch (FB)

League Club	Source	Date Signed	Seasons Played	Apps	Subs	Gls
Oldham Ath	Jnrs	06.78	78-84	73	2	1
Wolverhampton W	L	09.84	84	1	0	0
Tranmere Rov	Tr	10.84	84-85	22	0	1

SINCLAIR Robert Alan
Greenwich, 9 April, 1974 (F)

League Club	Source	Date Signed	Seasons Played	Apps	Subs	Gls
Maidstone U	YT	•	91	1	0	0

SINCLAIR Robert Dunlop
Winchburgh, 29 June, 1915 Died 1993 (W)

League Club	Source	Date Signed	Seasons Played	Apps	Subs	Gls
Chesterfield	Falkirk	05.39				
Darlington	Tr	06.46	46-47	68	-	11

SINCLAIR Ronald (Ronnie) McDonald
Stirling, 19 November, 1964 SSch/SYth (G)

League Club	Source	Date Signed	Seasons Played	Apps	Subs	Gls
Nottingham F	App	10.82				
Wrexham	L	03.84	83	11	0	0
Leeds U	Tr	06.86	86	8	0	0
Halifax T	L	03.87	86	4	0	0
Halifax T	L	12.88	88	10	0	0
Bristol C	Tr	09.89	89-90	44	0	0
Walsall	L	09.91	91	10	0	0
Stoke C	Tr	11.91	91-95	78	2	0
Chester C	Tr	08.96	96-97	70	0	0

SINCLAIR Roy
Liverpool, 10 December, 1944 (M)

League Club	Source	Date Signed	Seasons Played	Apps	Subs	Gls
Tranmere Rov	Liverpool (Am)	10.63	63-68	130	8	17
Watford	Tr	03.69	68-71	32	11	3
Chester	L	12.71	71	5	0	2
Tranmere Rov	Tr	07.72	72	12	0	0

SINCLAIR Scott Andrew
Bath, 26 March, 1989 (F)

League Club	Source	Date Signed	Seasons Played	Apps	Subs	Gls
Bristol Rov	Jnrs	•	04	0	2	0

SINCLAIR Thomas (Tommy)
Ince, 13 October, 1921 (W)

League Club	Source	Date Signed	Seasons Played	Apps	Subs	Gls
Aldershot	Gainsborough Trinity	08.44	46-50	70	-	8
Brentford	Tr	08.50	50	16	-	5
Bradford C	Tr	08.51	51	9	-	0

SINCLAIR Trevor Lloyd
Dulwich, 2 March, 1973 EYth/Eu21-14/EB-1/E-12 (W)

League Club	Source	Date Signed	Seasons Played	Apps	Subs	Gls
Blackpool	YT	08.90	89-92	84	28	15
Queens Park Rgrs	Tr	08.93	93-97	162	5	16
West Ham U	Tr	01.98	97-02	175	2	37
Manchester C	Tr	07.03	03-04	22	11	2

SINCLAIR William (Billy)
High Park, 11 September, 1920 Died 1978 (W)

League Club	Source	Date Signed	Seasons Played	Apps	Subs	Gls
Southport	High Park	09.45	46	15	-	1

SINCLAIR William (Billy) Inglis
Glasgow, 21 March, 1947 (WH)

League Club	Source	Date Signed	Seasons Played	Apps	Subs	Gls
Chelsea	Morton	09.64	64	1	-	0

SINCLAIR William (Willie) Mearns
Blairhall, 14 October, 1934 (IF)

League Club	Source	Date Signed	Seasons Played	Apps	Subs	Gls
Huddersfield T	Falkirk	12.58	58-59	15	-	5
Tranmere Rov	Tr	06.60	60	4	-	0
Halifax T	Tr	10.60	60	21	-	3

SINDALL Mark
Shirebrook, 3 September, 1964 (M)

League Club	Source	Date Signed	Seasons Played	Apps	Subs	Gls
Mansfield T	Notts Co (App)	08.82	82-83	18	3	0

SINGER Dennis **James (Jimmy)**
Fleur-de-Lys, 30 August, 1937 (IF)

League Club	Source	Date Signed	Seasons Played	Apps	Subs	Gls
Newport Co	Hengoed FDL	05.56	57-60	52	-	27
Birmingham C	Tr	09.60	60-61	20	-	8
Bournemouth	Tr	09.62	62-63	59	-	22
Newport Co	Tr	07.64	64	8	-	5

SINGH Harpal
Bradford, 15 September, 1981 (W)

League Club	Source	Date Signed	Seasons Played	Apps	Subs	Gls
Leeds U	YT	09.98				
Bury	L	09.01	01	11	1	2
Bristol C	L	03.02	01	3	0	0
Bradford C	L	11.02	02	3	0	0
Bury	L	08.03	03	20	8	2
Stockport Co	Tr	02.05	04	5	1	0

SINGLETON Anthony (Tony) Joseph
Preston, 30 March, 1936 (CD)

League Club	Source	Date Signed	Seasons Played	Apps	Subs	Gls
Preston NE	Jnrs	05.55	60-67	286	1	0

SINGLETON Bernard (Barney)
Conisbrough, 14 April, 1924 Died 1981 (G)

League Club	Source	Date Signed	Seasons Played	Apps	Subs	Gls
Wolverhampton W	Lincoln C (Am)	05.41				
Exeter C	Tr	01.46	46-53	177	-	1

SINGLETON Martin David
Banbury, 2 August, 1963 EYth (M)

League Club	Source	Date Signed	Seasons Played	Apps	Subs	Gls
Coventry C	App	01.81	81-84	20	3	1
Bradford C	Tr	12.84	84-86	69	2	3
West Bromwich A	Tr	12.86	86-87	15	4	1
Northampton T	Tr	11.87	87-89	45	5	4
Walsall	Tr	09.90	90	20	8	1

SINGLETON Thomas (Tommy) Wilfred
Blackpool, 8 September, 1940 (FB)

League Club	Source	Date Signed	Seasons Played	Apps	Subs	Gls
Blackpool	Jnrs	11.58				
Peterborough U	Tr	06.62	62-64	85	-	1
Chester	Tr	06.65	65-67	87	1	1
Bradford PA	Tr	07.68	68	32	0	1

SINNOTT Lee
Pelsall, 12 July, 1965 EYth/Eu21-1 (CD)

League Club	Source	Date Signed	Seasons Played	Apps	Subs	Gls
Walsall	App	11.82	81-83	40	0	2
Watford	Tr	09.83	83-86	71	7	2
Bradford C	Tr	07.87	87-90	173	0	6
Crystal Palace	Tr	08.91	91-92	53	2	0
Bradford C	Tr	12.93	93-94	34	0	1
Huddersfield T	Tr	12.94	94-96	86	1	1
Oldham Ath	Tr	07.97	97-98	25	6	0
Bradford C	L	03.98	97	7	0	0

SINTON Andrew (Andy)
Cramlington, 19 March, 1966 ESch/EB-3/FLge/E-12 (W)

League Club	Source	Date Signed	Seasons Played	Apps	Subs	Gls
Cambridge U	App	04.83	82-85	90	3	13
Brentford	Tr	12.85	85-88	149	0	28
Queens Park Rgrs	Tr	03.89	88-92	160	0	22

League Club	Source	Date Signed	Seasons Played	Apps	Subs	Gls
Sheffield Wed	Tr	08.93	93-95	54	6	3
Tottenham H	Tr	01.96	95-98	66	17	6
Wolverhampton W	Tr	07.99	99-01	62	10	3

SIRREL James (Jimmy)
Glasgow, 2 February, 1922 (IF)

League Club	Source	Date Signed	Seasons Played	Apps	Subs	Gls
Bradford PA	Glasgow Celtic	05.49	49-50	12	-	2
Brighton & Hove A	Tr	08.51	51-53	55	-	16
Aldershot	Tr	08.54	54-56	31	-	2

SISSOKO Habib
Juvisy-sur-Orge, France, 24 May, 1971 (F)

League Club	Source	Date Signed	Seasons Played	Apps	Subs	Gls
Preston NE	Louhans Cuiseaux (Fr)	02.98	97	4	3	0
Torquay U	R Capellen FC (Bel)	08.00	00	7	7	2

SISSON Michael Anthony
Mansfield, 24 November, 1978 (M)

League Club	Source	Date Signed	Seasons Played	Apps	Subs	Gls
Mansfield T	YT	01.98	97-00	26	5	2

SISSONS John **Graham**
Chester-le-Street, 20 May, 1934 (CD)

League Club	Source	Date Signed	Seasons Played	Apps	Subs	Gls
Birmingham C	Country Girl	07.54	56-62	90	-	0
Peterborough U	Tr	12.61	62-64	68	-	0
Walsall	Tr	11.64	64-67	93	5	1

SISSONS John Leslie
Hayes, 30 September, 1945 ESch/EYth/Eu23-10 (W)

League Club	Source	Date Signed	Seasons Played	Apps	Subs	Gls
West Ham U	App	10.62	62-69	210	3	37
Sheffield Wed	Tr	08.70	70-73	114	1	14
Norwich C	Tr	12.73	73	17	0	2
Chelsea	Tr	08.74	74	10	1	0

SITFORD Jack **Anthony (Tony)**
Crowborough, 28 January, 1940 (FB)

League Club	Source	Date Signed	Seasons Played	Apps	Subs	Gls
Brighton & Hove A		03.59	60-61	22	-	2

SITTON John Edmund
Hackney, 21 October, 1959 (CD)

League Club	Source	Date Signed	Seasons Played	Apps	Subs	Gls
Chelsea	App	10.77	78-79	11	2	0
Millwall	Tr	02.80	79-80	43	2	1
Gillingham	Tr	09.81	81-84	102	5	5
Orient	Tr	07.85	85-90	166	4	7

SIVEBAEK John
Vejle, Denmark, 25 October, 1961 Denmark int (FB)

League Club	Source	Date Signed	Seasons Played	Apps	Subs	Gls
Manchester U	Vejle BK (Den)	02.86	85-86	29	2	1

SIVELL Laurence (Laurie)
Lowestoft, 8 February, 1951 (G)

League Club	Source	Date Signed	Seasons Played	Apps	Subs	Gls
Ipswich T	App	02.69	69-83	141	0	0
Lincoln C	L	01.79	78	2	0	0

SIX Didier
Lille, France, 21 August, 1954 France int (W)

League Club	Source	Date Signed	Seasons Played	Apps	Subs	Gls
Aston Villa	Mulhouse (Fr)	10.84	84	13	3	2

SJOBERG John
Aberdeen, 12 June, 1941 SSch (CD)

League Club	Source	Date Signed	Seasons Played	Apps	Subs	Gls
Leicester C	Banks o' Dee	08.58	60-72	335	1	15
Rotherham U	Tr	06.73	73	6	0	0

SKEDD Anthony (Tony) Stuart
Hartlepool, 19 May, 1975 (M)

League Club	Source	Date Signed	Seasons Played	Apps	Subs	Gls
Hartlepool U	YT	10.93	92-94	39	7	1

SKEECH Henry **Gordon**
Warrington, 15 March, 1934 (FB)

League Club	Source	Date Signed	Seasons Played	Apps	Subs	Gls
Shrewsbury T	Runcorn	11.54	54-62	223	-	2

SKEELS Eric Thomas
Eccles, 27 October, 1939 (CD)

League Club	Source	Date Signed	Seasons Played	Apps	Subs	Gls
Stoke C	Stockport Co (Am)	12.58	59-75	495	12	7
Port Vale	Seattle (USA)	09.76	76	5	0	1

SKEEN George Gray
Gateshead, 4 August, 1920 Died 1984 (WH)

League Club	Source	Date Signed	Seasons Played	Apps	Subs	Gls
Gateshead		10.46	46-49	86	-	3

SKEEN Kenneth (Ken) Albert
Cheltenham, 20 March, 1942 (M)

League Club	Source	Date Signed	Seasons Played	Apps	Subs	Gls
Swindon T	Trowbridge T	09.64	64-66	14	0	4
Oxford U	Tr	07.67	67-73	214	20	27

SKEET Stuart Christopher
Edmonton, 6 July, 1948 (G)

League Club	Source	Date Signed	Seasons Played	Apps	Subs	Gls
Tottenham H	App	12.65				
Northampton T	L	03.69	68	1	0	0

SKEETE Leopold (Leo) Anthony
Liverpool, 3 August, 1949 (F)

League Club	Source	Date Signed	Seasons Played	Apps	Subs	Gls
Rochdale	Ellesmere Port	04.73	72-74	39	1	14

SKELLY Richard Brian
Norwich, 24 March, 1972 (FB)

League Club	Source	Date Signed	Seasons Played	Apps	Subs	Gls
Cambridge U	Newmarket T	01.94	93	2	0	0
Northampton T	Newmarket T	06.94	94	3	0	0

SKELTON Aaron Matthew
Welwyn Garden City, 22 November, 1974 (M)

League Club	Source	Date Signed	Seasons Played	Apps	Subs	Gls
Luton T	YT	12.92	94-96	5	3	0
Colchester U	Tr	07.97	97-00	114	11	17
Luton T	Tr	07.01	01-02	14	3	2

SKELTON Craig Eric
Middlesbrough, 14 September, 1980 (F)

League Club	Source	Date Signed	Seasons Played	Apps	Subs	Gls
Darlington	YT	07.99	00	0	1	0

SKELTON Gavin Richard
Carlisle, 27 March, 1981 (M)

League Club	Source	Date Signed	Seasons Played	Apps	Subs	Gls
Carlisle U	YT	05.99	99	1	6	0

SKELTON George Alfred
Thurcroft, 27 November, 1919 Died 1994 (IF)

League Club	Source	Date Signed	Seasons Played	Apps	Subs	Gls
Huddersfield T	Thurcroft MW	12.45	46	1	-	0
Leyton Orient	Tr	07.47	47	3	-	0

SKIDMORE William (Billy)
Barnsley, 15 March, 1925 Died 2004 (FB)

League Club	Source	Date Signed	Seasons Played	Apps	Subs	Gls
Wolverhampton W	Jnrs	05.42				
Walsall	Tr	05.46	46-50	99	-	10

SKILLEN Keith
Cockermouth, 26 May, 1948 (F)

League Club	Source	Date Signed	Seasons Played	Apps	Subs	Gls
Workington	Netherfield	12.73	73-74	56	8	9
Hartlepool	Tr	07.75	75	4	2	1

SKINGLEY Brian George
Romford, 28 August, 1937 Died 1999 (FB)

League Club	Source	Date Signed	Seasons Played	Apps	Subs	Gls
Bristol Rov	Ilfracombe	01.55				
Crystal Palace	Tr	09.58	58	11	-	0

SKINNER Craig Richard
Bury, 21 October, 1970 (W)

League Club	Source	Date Signed	Seasons Played	Apps	Subs	Gls
Blackburn Rov	YT	06.89	90-91	11	5	0
Plymouth Arg	Tr	08.92	92-94	42	11	4
Wrexham	Tr	07.95	95-98	70	17	10
York C	Tr	03.99	98-99	4	6	0

SKINNER George Edward Henry
Belvedere, 26 June, 1917 Died 2002 (IF)

League Club	Source	Date Signed	Seasons Played	Apps	Subs	Gls
Tottenham H	Callenders	09.38	46	1	-	0

SKINNER Justin
Hounslow, 30 January, 1969 (M)

League Club	Source	Date Signed	Seasons Played	Apps	Subs	Gls
Fulham	App	11.86	86-90	111	24	23
Bristol Rov	Tr	08.91	91-97	174	13	12
Walsall	L	09.97	97	10	0	0

SKINNER Justin James
Dorking, 17 September, 1972 (FB)

League Club	Source	Date Signed	Seasons Played	Apps	Subs	Gls
Wimbledon	YT	07.91	92-95	2	0	0
Bournemouth	L	03.94	93	16	0	0
Wycombe W	L	08.94	94	4	1	0

SKINNER Stephen (Steve) Karl
Whitehaven, 25 November, 1981 (W)

League Club	Source	Date Signed	Seasons Played	Apps	Subs	Gls
Carlisle U	YT	06.00	99	0	2	0
Carlisle U (L)	Gretna	10.01	01	1	5	0

SKIPPER Peter Dennis
Hull, 11 April, 1958 (CD)

League Club	Source	Date Signed	Seasons Played	Apps	Subs	Gls
Hull C	Schultz YC	02.79	78-79	22	1	2
Scunthorpe U	L	02.80	79	0	1	0
Darlington	Tr	05.80	80-81	91	0	4
Hull C	Tr	08.82	82-88	264	1	17
Oldham Ath	Tr	10.88	88	27	0	1
Walsall	Tr	07.89	89-90	81	0	2
Wrexham	Tr	09.91	91	2	0	0
Wigan Ath	Tr	10.91	91	15	3	0
Wigan Ath	Stafford Rgrs	11.92	92-93	73	0	4

SKIRTON Alan Frederick Graham
Bath, 23 January, 1939 (W)

League Club	Source	Date Signed	Seasons Played	Apps	Subs	Gls
Arsenal	Bath C	01.59	60-66	144	1	53
Blackpool	Tr	09.66	66-68	76	1	25
Bristol C	Tr	11.68	68-70	75	3	14
Torquay U	Tr	07.71	71	36	2	7

SKIVERTON Terence (Terry) John
Mile End, 26 June, 1975 ESemiPro-4 (CD)

League Club	Source	Date Signed	Seasons Played	Apps	Subs	Gls
Chelsea	YT	05.93				
Wycombe W	L	02.95	94	8	2	0
Wycombe W	Tr	03.96	95-96	5	5	1
Yeovil T	Welling U	06.99	03-04	61	3	6

SKIVINGTON Glenn
Barrow, 19 January, 1962 (M)

League Club	Source	Date Signed	Seasons Played	Apps	Subs	Gls
Derby Co	Barrow	07.80	80-82	39	7	2
Halifax T	L	03.83	82	4	0	0
Southend U	Tr	08.83	83	2	1	0

SKIVINGTON Michael (Mike) Noel
Glasgow, 24 December, 1921 LoI-1 (CD)

League Club	Source	Date Signed	Seasons Played	Apps	Subs	Gls
Bury	Alloa Ath	06.47				
Rochdale	Tr	01.48	47	1	-	0
Leyton Orient	Dundalk	10.49	49	5	-	0
Gillingham	Tr	07.50	50	8	-	0

SKOPELITIS Giannis Ioannis
Greece, 2 March, 1978 (M)

League Club	Source	Date Signed	Seasons Played	Apps	Subs	Gls
Portsmouth	Aigaleo (Gre)	01.05	04	9	4	0

SKORA Eric
Metz, France, 20 August, 1981 (M)

League Club	Source	Date Signed	Seasons Played	Apps	Subs	Gls
Preston NE	Nancy (Fr)	10.01	01-04	37	14	0

SKOUBO Morten
Struer, Denmark, 30 June, 1980 Deu21-8/De-1 (F)

League Club	Source	Date Signed	Seasons Played	Apps	Subs	Gls
West Bromwich A (L)	B Moenchengl'ch (Ger)	02.04	03	0	2	0

SKOVBJERG Thomas
Esbjerg, Denmark, 25 October, 1974 (M)

League Club	Source	Date Signed	Seasons Played	Apps	Subs	Gls
Kidderminster Hrs	Esbjerg (Den)	08.99	00	7	5	1

SKULL John (Johnny)
Swindon, 25 August, 1932 EYth (W)

League Club	Source	Date Signed	Seasons Played	Apps	Subs	Gls
Wolverhampton W	Swindon T (Am)	06.50				
Swindon T	Banbury Spencer	09.57	57-58	33	-	11

SKUSE Cole
Bristol, 29 March, 1986 (F)

League Club	Source	Date Signed	Seasons Played	Apps	Subs	Gls
Bristol C	Sch	04.05	04	4	3	0

SLABBER Jamie Andrew
Enfield, 31 December, 1984 EYth (F)

League Club	Source	Date Signed	Seasons Played	Apps	Subs	Gls
Tottenham H	YT	01.02	02	0	1	0
Swindon T	L	12.04	04	4	5	0

SLACK Andrew (Andy)
Heywood, 9 June, 1959 (G)

League Club	Source	Date Signed	Seasons Played	Apps	Subs	Gls
Rochdale	Bolton W (App)	01.78	77-78	15	0	0

SLACK Melvyn (Mel)
Bishop Auckland, 7 March, 1944 (WH)

League Club	Source	Date Signed	Seasons Played	Apps	Subs	Gls
Sunderland	Bishop Auckland YC	03.61	64	2	-	1
Southend U	Tr	08.65	65-68	107	4	5
Cambridge U	Tr	01.69	70	33	2	0

SLACK Robert Geoffrey
Morecambe, 13 July, 1934 (W)

League Club	Source	Date Signed	Seasons Played	Apps	Subs	Gls
Stockport Co	Morecambe	11.58	58	8	-	1

SLACK Rodney
Farcet, 11 April, 1940 (G)

League Club	Source	Date Signed	Seasons Played	Apps	Subs	Gls
Leicester C		09.58				
Queens Park Rgrs	Tr	03.61	61	1	-	0

SLACK Trevor Colin
Peterborough, 26 September, 1962 EYth (CD)

League Club	Source	Date Signed	Seasons Played	Apps	Subs	Gls
Peterborough U	App	08.80	80-85	201	1	18
Rotherham U	Tr	08.86	86	14	1	1
Grimsby T	Tr	08.87	87	21	0	0
Northampton T	Tr	02.88	87	13	0	1
Chesterfield	Tr	09.88	88-89	23	0	0

SLADE Robert Frederick
Hounslow, 15 July, 1927 (G)

League Club	Source	Date Signed	Seasons Played	Apps	Subs	Gls
Millwall (Am)	Acton T	10.48	48	1	-	0

SLADE Steven (Steve) Anthony
Hackney, 6 October, 1975 Eu21-4 (F)

League Club	Source	Date Signed	Seasons Played	Apps	Subs	Gls
Tottenham H	YT	07.94	95	1	4	0
Queens Park Rgrs	Tr	07.96	96-99	27	41	6
Brentford	L	02.97	96	4	0	0
Cambridge U	Tr	08.00	00	4	5	1

SLATER John Brian
Sheffield, 20 October, 1932 Died 1999 (IF)

League Club	Source	Date Signed	Seasons Played	Apps	Subs	Gls
Sheffield Wed		05.51	52	3	-	0
Grimsby T	Tr	07.54	54	4	-	0
Rotherham U	Tr	09.55	56	17	-	5
Chesterfield	Tr	06.57	57	15	-	3

SLATER Darren
Bishop Auckland, 4 January, 1979 (M)

League Club	Source	Date Signed	Seasons Played	Apps	Subs	Gls
Hartlepool U	YT	●	95	0	1	0

SLATER Frederick (Fred)
Burton-on-Trent, 25 September, 1925 (CF)

League Club	Source	Date Signed	Seasons Played	Apps	Subs	Gls
Birmingham C	Burton A	11.47	48-49	5	-	1
York C	Tr	06.51	51	13	-	3

SLATER James (Jamie) Jonathan
Wrexham, 27 October, 1968 (F)

League Club	Source	Date Signed	Seasons Played	Apps	Subs	Gls
Wrexham	YT	07.87	87	0	3	0

SLATER John
Heywood, 8 May, 1917 (WH)

League Club	Source	Date Signed	Seasons Played	Apps	Subs	Gls
Rochdale		04.40				
Crewe Alex	Tr	08.46	46	3	-	0

SLATER Malcolm Bruce
Buckie, 22 October, 1939 (W)

League Club	Source	Date Signed	Seasons Played	Apps	Subs	Gls
Southend U	Montrose	11.63	63-66	82	0	6
Leyton Orient	Tr	01.67	66-69	111	0	4
Colchester U	L	10.69	69	4	0	0

SLATER Raymond (Ray)
Seaton Delaval, 22 August, 1931 (CF)

League Club	Source	Date Signed	Seasons Played	Apps	Subs	Gls
Chesterfield	South Shields	06.56	56	2	-	1
Gateshead	Tr	10.56	56	6	-	2

SLATER Robert (Bert)
Musselburgh, 5 May, 1936 Su23-1 (G)

League Club	Source	Date Signed	Seasons Played	Apps	Subs	Gls
Liverpool	Falkirk	05.59	59-61	99	-	0
Watford	Dundee	05.65	65-68	134	0	0

SLATER Robert (Robbie) David
Ormskirk, 22 November, 1964 Australia int (W)

League Club	Source	Date Signed	Seasons Played	Apps	Subs	Gls
Blackburn Rov	RC Lens (Fr)	08.94	94	12	6	0
West Ham U	Tr	08.95	95-96	18	7	2
Southampton	Tr	09.96	96-97	25	16	2
Wolverhampton W	Tr	03.98	97	4	2	0

SLATER Stuart Ian
Sudbury, 27 March, 1969 Eu21-3/EB (W)

League Club	Source	Date Signed	Seasons Played	Apps	Subs	Gls
West Ham U	App	04.87	87-91	134	7	11
Ipswich T	Glasgow Celtic	09.93	93-95	61	11	4
Watford	Leicester C (N/C)	11.96	96-97	22	8	1

SLATER William (Bill) John
Clitheroe, 29 April, 1927 EAmat/E-12 (WH)

League Club	Source	Date Signed	Seasons Played	Apps	Subs	Gls
Blackpool (Am)	Jnrs	05.49	49-51	30	-	9
Brentford (Am)	Tr	12.51	51	7	-	1
Wolverhampton W	Tr	08.52	52-62	310	-	20
Brentford	Tr	07.63	63	5	-	2

SLATTER Leslie (Les) Arthur Heber
Reading, 22 November, 1931 (W)

League Club	Source	Date Signed	Seasons Played	Apps	Subs	Gls
Luton T	Mount Pleasant YC	03.49	49	1	-	0
Aston Villa	Crusaders	08.53				
York C	Tr	07.54	54	13	-	0

SLATTER Neil John
Cardiff, 30 May, 1964 WYth/Wu21-6/W-22 (FB)

League Club	Source	Date Signed	Seasons Played	Apps	Subs	Gls
Bristol Rov	App	05.82	80-84	147	1	4
Oxford U	Tr	07.85	85-89	88	3	6
Bournemouth	L	03.90	89	5	1	0

SLATTERY James Clive
Swansea, 21 July, 1946 (W)

League Club	Source	Date Signed	Seasons Played	Apps	Subs	Gls
Swansea T	North End	10.68	68-71	65	5	10
Hereford U	Tr	07.72	72	3	5	0

SLATTERY Joseph (Joe) William
Newcastle, 3 June, 1926 (CF)

League Club	Source	Date Signed	Seasons Played	Apps	Subs	Gls
Accrington St	Hexham Hearts	06.50	50	13	-	2

SLAVEN Bernard (Bernie) Joseph
Paisley, 13 November, 1960 IR-7 (F)

League Club	Source	Date Signed	Seasons Played	Apps	Subs	Gls
Middlesbrough	Albion Rov	09.85	85-92	286	21	118
Port Vale	Tr	03.93	92-93	29	4	9
Darlington	Tr	02.94	93-94	35	2	7

SLAVEN John
Edinburgh, 8 October, 1985 (F)

League Club	Source	Date Signed	Seasons Played	Apps	Subs	Gls
Carlisle U	Jnrs	11.02	01-02	0	3	0

SLAWSON Stephen (Steve) Michael
Nottingham, 13 November, 1972 (F)

League Club	Source	Date Signed	Seasons Played	Apps	Subs	Gls
Notts Co	YT	07.91	91-94	16	22	4
Burnley	L	02.93	92	5	0	2
Shrewsbury T	L	10.94	94	6	0	0
Mansfield T	Tr	07.95	95	21	8	5
Rotherham U	Tr	07.96	96	2	3	0

SLEE David Carl
Swansea, 30 November, 1947 WSch (FB)

League Club	Source	Date Signed	Seasons Played	Apps	Subs	Gls
Swansea T	Jnrs	01.66	67-70	115	4	0

League Club	Source	Date Signed	Seasons Played	Apps	Subs	Gls
SLEEUWENHOEK John Cornelius						
Wednesfield, 26 February, 1944 Died 1989 ESch/EYthEu23-2/FLge-1 (CD)						
Aston Villa	App	03.61	60-67	226	0	1
Birmingham C	Tr	11.67	67-70	29	1	0
Torquay U	L	03.71	70	11	0	0
Oldham Ath	Tr	07.71	71	2	0	0
SLEIGHT Geoffrey (Geoff)						
Royston, 20 June, 1943 (W)						
Bolton W	Jnrs	08.61	61	2	-	0
SLINGSBY Lee						
Rossington, 27 November, 1970 (M)						
Scarborough	Doncaster Rov (YT)	07.89	89	0	1	0
SLINN Kevin Paul						
Northampton, 2 September, 1974 (F)						
Watford	YT	04.93				
Stockport Co	Tr	07.94	94	2	2	1
SLOAN David						
Lisburn, 28 October, 1941 NIAmat/NIu23-1/NI-2 (W)						
Scunthorpe U	Bangor	11.63	63-67	133	3	42
Oxford U	Tr	02.68	67-72	166	8	28
Walsall	Tr	07.73	73-74	44	5	3
SLOAN James (Jimmy)						
Newcastle, 22 February, 1924 Died 1990 (IF)						
Newcastle U	CA Parsons Ath	01.45				
Hartlepools U	Tr	10.46	46-51	83	-	28
SLOAN Josiah (Paddy) Walter						
Lurgan, 30 April, 1920 Died 1993 IWar-1/IR-2/I-1 (WH)						
Manchester U	Glenavon	09.37				
Tranmere Rov	Tr	05.39				
Arsenal	Tr	05.46	46-47	33	-	1
Sheffield U	Tr	02.48	47	12	-	2
Norwich C	Brescia (It)	12.51	51	6	-	0
SLOAN Mark Scott						
Wallsend, 14 December, 1967 (F)						
Newcastle U	Berwick Rgrs	07.90	90	11	5	1
Cambridge U (L)	Falkirk	02.94	93	4	0	1
Hartlepool U	Falkirk	08.94	94-95	27	8	2
SLOAN Thomas (Tom)						
Ballymena, 10 July, 1959 IrLge-3/NIu21-1/NI-3 (M)						
Manchester U	Ballymena U	08.78	78-80	4	7	0
Chester	Ballymena U	08.82	82	44	0	3
SLOCOMBE Michael (Mike)						
Bristol, 3 May, 1941 (WH)						
Bristol Rov	Jnrs	06.61	61-62	32	-	0
SLOUGH Alan Peter						
Luton, 24 September, 1947 (M)						
Luton T	App	05.65	65-72	265	10	28
Fulham	Tr	08.73	73-76	154	0	13
Peterborough U	Tr	07.77	77-80	104	1	10
Millwall	Tr	06.81	81	14	0	0
SLYNN Frank (Frankie)						
Birmingham, 10 February, 1924 (WH)						
Sheffield Wed	Batchelors Sports	09.46	46-50	44	-	5
Bury	Tr	12.50	50-52	41	-	0
Walsall	Tr	09.53	53	10	-	0
SMALE Thomas Henry (Harry)						
Swansea, 16 July, 1928 (FB)						
Shrewsbury T	Derby Co (Am)	07.50	50-51	14	-	1
Aldershot	Tr	08.52	52	1	-	0
SMALES Kenneth (Ken)						
Hull, 3 May, 1932 (FB)						
Hull C	Brunswick Institute	05.53	56	1	-	0
SMALL Bryan						
Birmingham, 15 November, 1971 EYth/Eu21-12 (FB)						
Aston Villa	YT	07.90	91-94	31	5	0
Birmingham C	L	09.94	94	3	0	0
Bolton W	Tr	03.96	95-96	11	1	0
Luton T	L	09.97	97	15	0	0
Bradford C	L	12.97	97	5	0	0
Bury	Tr	01.98	97	18	0	1
Stoke C	Tr	07.98	98-99	40	5	0
SMALL Colin						
Stockport, 9 November, 1970 ESch (M)						
Rochdale	Manchester C (YT)	07.89	89	5	2	1
SMALL David						
Dundee, 17 July, 1930 (W)						
Watford	Dundee North End	06.50	50-51	5	-	0
SMALL John Hedley						
Billingham, 14 January, 1945 (G)						
Hartlepools U (Am)	Head Wrightson	06.65	65	2	0	0
SMALL Martin Leonard						
Gateshead, 2 February, 1920 (IF)						
Gateshead		08.46	46-51	94	-	29
SMALL Michael (Mike) Anthony						
Birmingham, 2 March, 1962 EYth (F)						
Luton T	Bromsgrove Rov	10.79	81-82	0	4	0
Peterborough U	L	10.82	82	2	2	1
Brighton & Hove A	PAOK Salonika (Gre)	08.90	90	39	0	15
West Ham U	Tr	08.91	91-92	42	7	13
Wolverhampton W	L	09.93	93	2	1	1
Charlton Ath	L	02.94	93	1	1	0
SMALL Peter Victor						
Horsham, 23 October, 1924 (W)						
Luton T	Horsham	08.47	47-49	28	-	5
Leicester C	Tr	02.50	49-54	65	-	16
Nottingham F	Tr	09.54	54-56	87	-	20
Brighton & Hove A	Tr	07.57	57	8	-	3
SMALL Samuel (Sam) John						
Birmingham, 15 May, 1912 Died 1993 (CF)						
Birmingham	Bromsgrove Rov	05.34	34-36	6	-	0
West Ham U	Tr	01.37	36-47	108	-	39
Brighton & Hove A	Tr	03.48	47-49	38	-	0
SMALL Wade Kristopher						
Croydon, 23 February, 1984 (M)						
Wimbledon/MK Dons	Sch	07.03	03-04	64	7	11
SMALLER Paul Andrew						
Scunthorpe, 18 September, 1970 (M)						
Grimsby T	YT	07.89	88-89	1	1	0
SMALLEY Mark Anthony						
Newark, 2 January, 1965 EYth (CD)						
Nottingham F	App	01.83	82-84	1	2	0
Birmingham C	L	03.86	85	7	0	0
Bristol Rov	L	08.86	86	10	0	0
Orient	Tr	02.87	86-89	59	5	4
Mansfield T	Tr	11.89	89-90	49	0	2
Maidstone U	Tr	05.91	91	33	1	2
SMALLEY Paul Thomas						
Nottingham, 17 November, 1966 EYth (FB)						
Notts Co	App	11.84	85-87	112	6	0
Scunthorpe U	Tr	09.88	88-90	84	2	1
Blackpool	L	10.90	90	6	0	0
Leeds U	Tr	12.90				
Doncaster Rov	Tr	03.91	90	14	0	0
SMALLEY Thomas (Tom)						
Kinsley, 13 January, 1912 Died 1984 E-1 (WH)						
Wolverhampton W	South Kirkby Colliery	05.31	31-37	179	-	11
Norwich C	Tr	08.38	38	42	-	1
Northampton T	Tr	10.45	46-50	200	-	2
SMALLMAN David Paul						
Connah's Quay, 22 March, 1953 Wu23-5/W-7 (F)						
Wrexham	Jnrs	11.71	72-74	100	1	38
Everton	Tr	03.75	74-76	19	2	6
SMALLWOOD James (Jim) Wilson						
Bearpark, 1 September, 1925 (WH)						
Chesterfield	Spennymoor U	12.49	49-60	345	-	14
SMALLWOOD Neil						
York, 3 December, 1966 (G)						
York C	Jnrs	06.85	86-87	13	0	0
Darlington	Tr	08.88	88	4	0	0
SMART Allan Andrew Colin						
Perth, 8 July, 1974 (F)						
Preston NE	Inverness CT	11.94	94-95	17	4	6
Carlisle U	L	11.95	95	3	1	0
Northampton T	L	09.96	96	1	0	0
Carlisle U	Tr	10.96	96-97	41	3	16
Watford	Tr	07.98	98-00	48	9	12
Stoke C	L	11.01	01	0	2	0
Oldham Ath	Tr	11.01	01	14	7	6
Crewe Alex	Dundee U	08.03	03	0	6	0
MK Dons	Tr	07.04	04	15	3	4
SMART Gary James						
Totnes, 29 April, 1964 (FB)						
Oxford U	Wokingham T	07.88	88-93	170	5	0

League Club	Source	Date Signed	Seasons Played	Career Record Apps	Subs	Gls
SMART Gary Michael						
Bristol, 8 December, 1963						(M)
Bristol Rov	Mangotsfield U	09.85	85-86	11	8	4
SMART James (Jim)						
Dundee, 9 January, 1947						(W)
Chelsea	Morton	02.65	64	1	-	0
SMART Jason						
Rochdale, 15 February, 1969						(CD)
Rochdale	App	08.86	85-88	116	1	4
Crewe Alex	Tr	07.89	89-91	87	2	2
SMART Kevin Graham						
Newcastle, 17 October, 1958						(FB)
Plymouth Arg	App	10.76	76-77	32	0	0
Wigan Ath	Tr	07.78	78-79	48	1	1
SMART Richard (Dick)						
Bishop Auckland, 19 June, 1921 Died 2003						(IF)
Exeter C	Stanley U	08.46	46-51	103	-	33
SMART Roger William						
Swindon, 25 March, 1943						(M)
Swindon T	Jnrs	05.60	61-72	340	5	43
Charlton Ath	Tr	05.73	73	30	1	1
SMEDLEY Lawrence (Laurie)						
Sheffield, 7 May, 1922						(IF)
Lincoln C		05.45	46-48	11	-	7
SMEE Roger Guy						
Reading, 14 August, 1948						(F)
Chelsea	Jnrs	03.66				
Reading	Tr	01.67	66-69	49	1	16
Reading	KVG Ostend (Bel)	07.73	73	6	3	1
SMEETS Axel						
Karawa, Congo, 12 April, 1974 Beu21						(M)
Sheffield U	AA Ghent (Bel)	07.99	99	2	3	0
SMEETS Jorg						
Bussum, Holland, 5 November, 1970						(M)
Wigan Ath	SC Heracles (Holl)	10.97	97-98	10	14	3
Chester C	L	03.99	98	1	2	0
SMELT Lee Adrian						
Edmonton, 13 March, 1958 ESch						(G)
Colchester U	Jnrs	07.75				
Nottingham F	Gravesend & Northfleet	06.80	80	1	0	0
Peterborough U	L	08.81	81	5	0	0
Halifax T	Tr	10.81	81-83	119	0	0
Cardiff C	Tr	08.84	84-85	37	0	0
Exeter C	L	03.85	84	13	0	0
SMELTZ Shane						
Goppingen, Germany, 29 September, 1981 New Zealand int						(W)
Mansfield T	Adelaide U (Aus)	01.05	04	1	4	0
SMERTIN Alexei						
Barnaul, Russia, 1 May, 1975 Russia 49						(M)
Chelsea	Bordeaux (Fr)	08.03	04	11	5	0
Portsmouth	L	08.03	03	23	3	0
SMETHURST Derek						
Durban, South Africa, 24 October, 1947						(F)
Chelsea	Durban C (SA)	12.68	70-71	14	0	4
Millwall	Tr	09.71	71-74	66	4	9
SMETHURST Edward (Ted)						
Doncaster, 5 March, 1938						(G)
Chesterfield	Denaby U	08.59	59	19	-	0
SMETHURST Peter Joseph						
Durban, South Africa, 8 August, 1940						(IF)
Blackpool	Durban U (SA)	02.60	59	1	-	0
SMEULDERS John						
Hackney, 28 March, 1957 EYth						(G)
Orient	App	07.74				
Bournemouth	Tr	07.79	79-80	14	0	0
Bournemouth	Weymouth	01.84	83-85	75	0	0
Torquay U	Tr	07.86	86	18	0	0
Peterborough U	L	12.86	86	1	0	0
Bournemouth	Poole T	08.87	87	2	0	0
Brentford	Tr	10.88	88	8	0	0
Bournemouth	Tr	03.89	88	7	0	0
SMICER Vladimir (Vlad)						
Degin, Czech Republic, 24 May, 1973 Czu21-7/Cz-1/CzR-74						(M)
Liverpool	RC Lens (Fr)	07.99	99-04	69	52	10

League Club	Source	Date Signed	Seasons Played	Career Record Apps	Subs	Gls
SMILLIE Andrew (Andy) Thomas						
Minster, Sheppey, 15 March, 1941 EYth						(M)
West Ham U	Jnrs	06.58	58-60	20	-	3
Crystal Palace	Tr	06.61	61-62	53	-	23
Scunthorpe U	Tr	07.63	63-64	13	-	2
Southend U	Tr	09.64	64-68	164	0	29
Gillingham	Tr	10.68	68-70	88	6	7
SMILLIE Neil						
Barnsley, 19 July, 1958						(M)
Crystal Palace	App	10.75	76-81	71	12	7
Brentford	L	01.77	76	3	0	0
Brighton & Hove A	Tr	08.82	82-84	62	13	2
Watford	Tr	06.85	85	10	6	3
Reading	Tr	12.86	86-87	38	1	0
Brentford	Tr	08.88	88-92	163	9	18
Gillingham	Tr	07.93	93-94	53	0	3
SMILLIE Ronald (Ron) Drummond						
Grimethorpe, 27 September, 1933						(W)
Barnsley	Jnrs	12.50	51-55	29	-	1
Lincoln C	Tr	06.56	56-59	91	-	15
Barnsley	Tr	07.60	60-61	85	-	16
SMIRK Alfred (Alf) Henry						
Pershore, 14 March, 1917 Died 1996 ESch						(IF)
Southend U	Sunderland Dist Om	05.38	38-47	100	-	26
Gateshead	Tr	03.48	47	11	-	4
SMITH Nathan **Adam**						
Huddersfield, 20 February, 1985						(F)
Chesterfield	Sch	08.04	03-04	6	13	0
SMITH Adrian (Adie) Jonathan						
Birmingham, 11 August, 1973 ESemiPro-3						(CD)
Kidderminster Hrs	Bromsgrove Rov	06.97	00-03	112	10	8
SMITH Alan						
Newcastle, 15 October, 1921						(W)
Arsenal		05.46	46	3	-	0
Brentford	Tr	12.46	46-48	13	-	4
Leyton Orient	Tr	07.49	49	6	-	1
SMITH Alan						
Rothwell, West Yorkshire, 28 October, 1980 EYth/Eu21-10/E-15						(F)
Leeds U	YT	03.98	98-03	148	24	38
Manchester U	Tr	05.04	04	22	9	6
SMITH Charles **Alan**						
Salford, 7 June, 1940						(G)
Stockport Co	Manchester C (Am)	06.60	60	6	-	0
SMITH Alan David						
Sheffield, 7 December, 1966						(CD)
Sheffield Wed	App	12.84				
Darlington	Tr	09.86	86-88	26	5	1
SMITH Alan Frederick						
Newport, 3 September, 1949 WYth						(M)
Newport Co	Cromwell Jnrs	09.66	66-71	89	12	7
SMITH James **Alan**						
Birkenhead, 8 June, 1939						(CD)
Torquay U	Port Sunlight	08.56	57-68	277	1	2
SMITH Alan Martin						
Birmingham, 21 November, 1962 ESemiPro/FLge/EB/E-13						(F)
Leicester C	Alvechurch	06.82	82-86	181	10	73
Arsenal	Tr	03.87	87-94	242	22	87
Leicester C	L	03.87	86	9	0	3
SMITH Alan Michael						
Harrogate, 1 September, 1950						(W)
York C (Am)	Harrogate RI	12.70	70	1	1	0
SMITH Albert Owen Stephen						
Bedwellty, 15 October, 1923 Died 1976						(G)
Cardiff C	Oakdale	04.44				
Newport Co	Tr	05.47	46-47	27	-	0
SMITH Albert William						
Stoke-on-Trent, 27 August, 1918 Died 1992						(WH)
Queens Park Rgrs	Shirley Jnrs	05.39	46-48	62	-	2
SMITH Alexander (Alec)						
Dundee, 4 September, 1927 Died 1991						(FB)
Blackpool		08.46				
Bradford PA	Tr	06.49	49-50	5	-	0
SMITH Alexander (Alex)						
Lancaster, 29 October, 1938						(G)
Accrington St	Weymouth	08.61				

League Club	Source	Date Signed	Seasons Played	Apps	Subs	Gls
Bolton W	Tr	03.62	62-67	19	0	0
Halifax T	Tr	01.68	67-75	341	0	0
Preston NE	Tr	05.76	76	8	0	0

SMITH Alexander (Alex)
Thornhill Lees, 11 May, 1947 (FB)

League Club	Source	Date Signed	Seasons Played	Apps	Subs	Gls
Bradford C	Ossett A	12.64	65-67	91	2	2
Huddersfield T	Tr	03.68	67-68	29	0	0
Southend U	Tr	04.70	70-73	129	1	1
Colchester U	Tr	01.73	73-74	51	0	1
Halifax T	Tr	02.75	74-75	46	1	1

SMITH Alexander (Alex) Philip
Liverpool, 15 February, 1976 (FB)

League Club	Source	Date Signed	Seasons Played	Apps	Subs	Gls
Everton	YT	07.94				
Swindon T	Tr	01.96	95-97	17	14	1
Huddersfield T	Tr	02.98	97	4	2	0
Chester C	Tr	07.98	98	32	0	2
Port Vale	Tr	03.99	98-00	52	6	2
Reading	Tr	07.01	01-02	12	2	2
Shrewsbury T	L	12.02	02	13	0	0
Wrexham	Chester C	07.04	04	17	7	0

SMITH Robert Alexander (Alex)
Billingham, 6 February, 1944 (FB)

League Club	Source	Date Signed	Seasons Played	Apps	Subs	Gls
Middlesbrough	Haverton Hill	12.61	65-71	119	2	1
Darlington	Bangor C	07.74	74-75	43	0	0

SMITH Alfred (Alf)
Wolverhampton (W)

League Club	Source	Date Signed	Seasons Played	Apps	Subs	Gls
Walsall	Bilston	10.53	53	1	-	0

SMITH Allan
(W)

League Club	Source	Date Signed	Seasons Played	Apps	Subs	Gls
Hull C (Am)		09.46	46	1	-	0

SMITH Andrew (Andy) William
Lisburn, 25 September, 1980 NIB-1/NI-18 (F)

League Club	Source	Date Signed	Seasons Played	Apps	Subs	Gls
Sheffield U	Ballyclare Comrades	09.99	00	0	6	0
Bury	L	11.00	00	2	0	0
Preston NE	Glentoran	07.04	04	3	11	0
Stockport Co	L	11.04	04	1	0	0

SMITH Anthony (Tony)
Sunderland, 31 December, 1943 (F)

League Club	Source	Date Signed	Seasons Played	Apps	Subs	Gls
West Ham U	Consett	11.63				
Watford	Tr	06.66	66	3	0	0
Hartlepools U		10.67	67	2	0	1

SMITH Anthony (Tony)
Sunderland, 20 February, 1957 ESch (CD)

League Club	Source	Date Signed	Seasons Played	Apps	Subs	Gls
Newcastle U	Jnrs	07.75	77	1	1	0
Peterborough U	Tr	03.79	78-81	68	0	5
Halifax T	Tr	08.82	82-83	81	2	3
Hartlepool U	Tr	08.84	84-88	200	0	8

SMITH Anthony (Tony)
Sunderland, 21 September, 1971 EYth (FB)

League Club	Source	Date Signed	Seasons Played	Apps	Subs	Gls
Sunderland	YT	07.90	90-94	19	1	0
Hartlepool U	L	01.92	91	4	1	0
Northampton T	Tr	08.95	95	2	0	0

SMITH Archibald (Archie) Nimmo
Larkhall, 23 October, 1924 Died 1995 (CF)

League Club	Source	Date Signed	Seasons Played	Apps	Subs	Gls
Exeter C	Hamilton Academical	05.48	48-51	115	-	43
Carlisle U	Barnstaple T	08.52	52-53	31	-	8

SMITH Arthur Edward
Bourne, 13 February, 1922 Died 1982 (FB)

League Club	Source	Date Signed	Seasons Played	Apps	Subs	Gls
Luton T		05.45				
Aldershot	Tr	08.47	47-48	2	-	0

SMITH Arthur Eric
Whetstone, Leicestershire, 5 September, 1921 (IF)

League Club	Source	Date Signed	Seasons Played	Apps	Subs	Gls
Leicester C	Wolverhampton W (Am)	02.41	46-47	17	-	3
West Bromwich A	Tr	06.48	48-51	49	-	12
Plymouth Arg	Tr	08.52	52-53	28	-	9
Crewe Alex	Tr	06.54	54	5	-	0

SMITH Barry Anthony
Colchester, 3 March, 1953 (G)

League Club	Source	Date Signed	Seasons Played	Apps	Subs	Gls
Colchester U	Jnrs	07.71	71-72	49	0	0

SMITH Joseph Barry
South Kirkby, 15 March, 1934 (CF)

League Club	Source	Date Signed	Seasons Played	Apps	Subs	Gls
Leeds U	Farsley Celtic	10.51	52	2	-	1
Bradford PA	Tr	05.55	55-56	64	-	38
Wrexham	Tr	06.57	57	18	-	10
Stockport Co	Tr	07.58	58	17	-	4
Oldham Ath	Headington U	08.60	60	1	-	0

SMITH Barry Joseph
Ince, 21 September, 1969 (M)

League Club	Source	Date Signed	Seasons Played	Apps	Subs	Gls
Wigan Ath	YT	●	87	0	1	0

SMITH Benjamin (Ben) Peter
Chelmsford, 23 November, 1978 (M)

League Club	Source	Date Signed	Seasons Played	Apps	Subs	Gls
Reading	Arsenal (YT)	04.97	96	0	1	0
Southend U	Yeovil T	06.01	01	0	1	0
Shrewsbury T	Hereford U	06.04	04	10	2	3

SMITH Brian
Bolton, 12 September, 1955 EYth (M)

League Club	Source	Date Signed	Seasons Played	Apps	Subs	Gls
Bolton W	App	09.73	74-78	43	6	3
Bradford C	L	10.77	77	8	0	0
Blackpool	Tulsa (USA)	08.79	79	18	1	1
Bournemouth	Tr	12.80	80-81	40	0	2
Bury	Tr	03.82	81	6	0	0

SMITH Brian
Sheffield, 27 October, 1966 (CD)

League Club	Source	Date Signed	Seasons Played	Apps	Subs	Gls
Sheffield U	App	10.84	84-88	81	3	0
Scunthorpe U	L	03.87	86	6	0	1

SMITH Bryan James
Swindon, 26 August, 1983 (FB)

League Club	Source	Date Signed	Seasons Played	Apps	Subs	Gls
Swindon T	YT	●	99	0	1	0

SMITH Carl Paul
Sheffield, 15 January, 1979 (FB)

League Club	Source	Date Signed	Seasons Played	Apps	Subs	Gls
Burnley	YT	09.97	97-98	5	6	0

SMITH Charles (Charlie)
Oswaldtwistle, 27 June, 1930 (IF)

League Club	Source	Date Signed	Seasons Played	Apps	Subs	Gls
Accrington St (Am)	Oswaldwistlw Imms	06.50	50	1	-	0

SMITH Charles (Charlie) James
Cardiff, 26 August, 1915 Died 1984 (W)

League Club	Source	Date Signed	Seasons Played	Apps	Subs	Gls
Exeter C		08.36	36	5	-	0
Torquay U	Aberdeen	04.46	46	23	-	0

SMITH Christopher (Chris) Alan
Derby, 30 June, 1981 (CD)

League Club	Source	Date Signed	Seasons Played	Apps	Subs	Gls
Reading	YT	06.99				
York C	Tr	07.01	01-03	71	8	0

SMITH Christopher (Chris) Gerald
Birmingham, 3 January, 1977 (M)

League Club	Source	Date Signed	Seasons Played	Apps	Subs	Gls
Walsall	YT	05.95	95	0	1	0

SMITH Christopher (Chris) James
Christchurch, 28 March, 1966 (FB)

League Club	Source	Date Signed	Seasons Played	Apps	Subs	Gls
Bristol Rov	Cheltenham T	05.85	84	1	0	0

SMITH Colin
Bishop Auckland, 30 November, 1951 (CD)

League Club	Source	Date Signed	Seasons Played	Apps	Subs	Gls
Leeds U	App	11.69				
Darlington		09.84	84	2	0	0

SMITH Edwin Colin
Doncaster, 3 March, 1936 (CF)

League Club	Source	Date Signed	Seasons Played	Apps	Subs	Gls
Hull C		01.57	56-59	65	-	39
Rotherham U	Tr	06.60	60	9	-	3

SMITH Colin Richard
Ruddington, 3 November, 1958 ESch (CD)

League Club	Source	Date Signed	Seasons Played	Apps	Subs	Gls
Nottingham F	Jnrs	06.77				
Norwich C	Tr	08.82	82	2	2	0
Cardiff C	See Bee (HK)	10.83	83-84	50	0	3
Aldershot	Tr	12.84	84-89	185	5	4

SMITH William Conway
Huddersfield, 13 July, 1926 Died 1989 (IF)

League Club	Source	Date Signed	Seasons Played	Apps	Subs	Gls
Huddersfield T	Jnrs	05.45	47-50	37	-	5
Queens Park Rgrs	Tr	03.51	50-55	174	-	81
Halifax T	Tr	06.56	56-61	179	-	73

SMITH Craig
Mansfield, 2 August, 1976 (F)

League Club	Source	Date Signed	Seasons Played	Apps	Subs	Gls
Derby Co	YT	08.95				
Rochdale	L	08.97	97	1	2	0

SMITH Craig Mark
Bradford, 8 June, 1984 (M)

League Club	Source	Date Signed	Seasons Played	Apps	Subs	Gls
Halifax T	YT	●	01	0	2	0

SMITH Daniel (Danny)
Armadale, 7 September, 1921 Died 1998 (W)

League Club	Source	Date Signed	Seasons Played	Apps	Subs	Gls
West Bromwich A	Coltness U	05.45	47	7	-	1
Chesterfield	Tr	06.48	48	15	-	4
Crewe Alex	Tr	08.49	49-51	110	-	15

League Club	Source	Date Signed	Seasons Played	Career Record Apps	Subs	Gls
SMITH Daniel (Danny) Lee						
Southampton, 17 August, 1982						(CD)
Bournemouth	YT	04.00	99-01	8	10	0
SMITH David (Dave)						
South Shields, 12 October, 1915 Died 1997						(IF)
Newcastle U	Reyrolles	10.35	35	1	-	0
Northampton T	South Shields	09.43	46-50	128	-	31
SMITH David (Dave)						
Thornaby, 8 December, 1947 ESch						(W)
Middlesbrough	App	12.64	67	1	1	0
Lincoln C	Tr	07.68	68-77	358	13	52
Rotherham U	Tr	07.78	78-79	32	1	3
SMITH David						
Stonehouse, Gloucestershire, 29 March, 1968 Eu21-10						(W)
Coventry C	App	07.86	87-92	144	10	19
Bournemouth	L	01.93	92	1	0	0
Birmingham C	Tr	03.93	92-93	35	3	3
West Bromwich A	Tr	01.94	93-97	82	20	2
Grimsby T	Tr	01.98	97-01	101	11	9
Swansea C	Tr	06.02	02	3	1	1
SMITH David						
Frome, 13 October, 1964						(FB)
Bristol Rov	App	●	81	0	1	0
SMITH David Alan						
Sidcup, 25 June, 1961						(W)
Gillingham	Welling U	08.86	86-88	90	14	10
Bristol C	Tr	08.89	89-91	94	3	10
Plymouth Arg	Tr	12.91	91	14	4	2
Notts Co	Tr	07.92	92	37	0	8
SMITH David Alan						
Stockport, 2 May, 1973						(G)
Doncaster Rov	Bramhall	10.97	97	1	0	0
SMITH David (Dave) Bowman						
Dundee, 22 September, 1933						(FB)
Burnley	East Craigie	09.50	54-60	99	-	1
Brighton & Hove A	Tr	07.61	61	15	-	0
Bristol C	Tr	07.62	62	3	-	0
SMITH David (Dave) Bryan						
Sheffield, 11 December, 1950						(F)
Huddersfield T	Jnrs	04.69	71-73	27	7	7
Stockport Co	L	12.73	73	7	1	0
Halifax T	L	03.74	73	12	1	4
Cambridge U	Tr	07.74	74	15	2	3
Hartlepool	Tr	02.75	74-75	42	0	13
SMITH David (Dave) Christopher						
Liverpool, 26 December, 1970						(M)
Norwich C	YT	07.89	89-93	13	5	0
Oxford U	Tr	07.94	94-98	193	5	2
Stockport Co	Tr	02.99	98-01	64	7	3
Macclesfield T	L	02.02	01	8	0	0
Macclesfield T	Drogheda U	01.03	02-03	10	3	0
SMITH Frank **David (Dave)**						
Holymoorside, 27 July, 1936						(W)
Chesterfield	Jnrs	09.53	53	7	-	0
Mansfield T	Boston U	08.55	55-56	31	-	4
Derby Co	Tr	07.57				
Coventry C	Tr	11.57	57-58	28	-	2
SMITH David (Dave) Frederick						
Nottingham, 11 March, 1956						(M)
Notts Co	App	03.74	75-77	45	5	0
Torquay U	Tr	06.79	79	20	3	1
SMITH David Robert						
Fishponds, 5 October, 1934 Died 2003 EYth						(W)
Bristol C	Jnrs	04.53	55-58	21	-	1
Millwall	Tr	09.59	59	13	-	1
SMITH Dean						
Leicester, 28 November, 1958						(F)
Leicester C	App	12.76	77	8	2	1
Brentford	Tr	10.78	78-80	48	6	16
SMITH Dean						
West Bromwich, 19 March, 1971						(CD)
Walsall	YT	07.89	88-93	137	5	2
Hereford U	Tr	06.94	94-96	116	1	19
Leyton Orient	Tr	06.97	97-02	239	0	32
Sheffield Wed	Tr	02.03	02-03	55	0	1
Port Vale	Tr	08.04	04	12	1	0

League Club	Source	Date Signed	Seasons Played	Career Record Apps	Subs	Gls
SMITH Denis						
Meir, 19 November, 1947 FLge-1						(CD)
Stoke C	Jnrs	09.66	68-81	406	1	29
York C	L	03.82	81	7	0	1
York C	Tr	08.82	82	30	0	4
SMITH Denis Noel						
Grimsby, 23 December, 1932						(FB)
Grimsby T	Jnrs	07.50	52-53	4	-	0
SMITH Dennis						
Nelson, 22 August, 1925						(WH)
Hull C	Frickley Colliery	07.46	46	15	-	0
Accrington St	Tr	10.47	47-53	155	-	15
SMITH Derek Leonard						
Liverpool, 5 July, 1946						(CD/F)
Everton	App	11.63	65-66	3	1	0
Tranmere Rov	Tr	03.68	67-69	77	5	21
SMITH Edmund (Eddie) William Alfred						
Marylebone, 23 March, 1929 Died 1993						(IF)
Chelsea	Wealdstone	05.50				
Bournemouth	Tr	08.52				
Watford	Tr	07.53	53-54	38	-	12
Northampton T	Tr	01.55	54-55	53	-	12
Colchester U	Tr	06.56	56	36	-	13
Queens Park Rgrs	Tr	07.57	57	17	-	1
SMITH Edward (Ted) Ferriday						
Stoke-on-Trent, 19 October, 1920 Died 1982						(CF)
Arsenal		05.38				
Aldershot	Tr	06.47	47	7	-	2
SMITH Edward (Ted) William John						
Grays, 3 September, 1914 Died 1989						(FB)
Millwall	Tilbury	05.35	35-47	143	-	1
SMITH John **Eric**						
Glasgow, 29 July, 1934 Died 1991 S-2						(WH)
Leeds U	Glasgow Celtic	06.60	60-62	65	-	3
SMITH Thomas Henry **Eric**						
Tamworth, 3 November, 1921						(CD)
Leicester C	Castle Bromwich	04.43	46	5	-	0
SMITH Eric Victor						
Reading, 20 March, 1928 Died 1992						(FB)
Reading		04.49	52-55	61	-	1
SMITH Frank Anthony						
Colchester, 30 April, 1936						(G)
Tottenham H	Colchester Casuals	02.54				
Queens Park Rgrs	Tr	05.62	62-65	66	0	0
SMITH Frederick (Fred) Adamson						
Aberdeen, 14 February, 1926						(IF)
Hull C	Aberdeen	10.49	49-50	17	-	1
Sheffield U	Tr	04.51	50-52	40	-	11
Millwall	Tr	01.53	52-55	92	-	20
Chesterfield	Tr	07.56	56	7	-	1
SMITH Frederick (Fred) Edward						
Draycott, 7 May, 1926						(CF)
Derby Co	Draycott	06.47	47	1	-	0
Sheffield U	Tr	03.48	47-51	53	-	18
Manchester C	Tr	05.52	52	2	-	1
Grimsby T	Tr	09.52	52-53	50	-	24
Bradford C	Tr	07.54	54	9	-	3
SMITH Frederick (Fred) Gregg						
West Sleekburn, 25 December, 1942						(FB)
Burnley	Jnrs	12.59	63-69	84	0	1
Portsmouth	Tr	07.70	70-72	82	0	1
Halifax T	Dallas (USA)	09.74	74	3	0	0
SMITH Gary						
Chasetown, 30 December, 1968						(M)
Walsall	App	01.87				
Gillingham	Chasetown	07.89	89	0	1	0
SMITH Gary Anthony						
Trowbridge, 12 November, 1962						(W)
Bristol C	App	11.79	80	7	7	0
SMITH Gary Michael						
Greenford, 4 November, 1955						(CD)
Brentford		01.74	74	3	0	0
SMITH Gary Neil						
Harlow, 3 December, 1968						(M)
Fulham	App	08.86	85	0	1	0

League Club	Source	Date Signed	Seasons Played	Career Record Apps	Subs	Gls
Colchester U	Tr	09.87	87	11	0	0
Barnet	Welling U	08.93	93-94	11	2	0
SMITH Gary Stephen						
Middlesbrough, 30 January, 1984						(M)
Middlesbrough	Sch	07.02				
Wimbledon	L	03.04	03	10	1	3
MK Dons	Tr	08.04	04	20	3	1
SMITH Gavin						
Cambuslang, 25 September, 1917 Died 1992						(W)
Barnsley	Dumbarton	02.39	46-53	257	-	35
SMITH Geoffrey (Geoff)						
Bingley, 14 March, 1928						(G)
Bradford C	Rossendale U	12.52	52-58	253	-	0
SMITH George						
Newcastle, 7 October, 1945						(M)
Newcastle U	App	09.63				
Barrow	Tr	03.65	64-66	91	1	11
Portsmouth	Tr	05.67	67-68	64	0	3
Middlesbrough	Tr	01.69	68-70	74	0	0
Birmingham C	Tr	03.71	70-72	36	3	0
Cardiff C	Tr	06.73	73-74	43	2	1
Swansea C	Tr	05.75	75-77	86	2	8
Hartlepool U	Tr	10.77	77-79	81	4	2
SMITH George						
						(CF)
Walsall (Am)		09.53	53	1	-	0
SMITH George Beacher						
Fleetwood, 7 February, 1921						(IF)
Manchester C	Adelphi LC	05.38	46-51	166	-	75
Chesterfield	Tr	10.51	51-57	250	-	98
SMITH George Casper						
Bromley-by-Bow, 23 April, 1915 Died 1983 EWar-1						(CD)
Charlton Ath	Bexleyheath & Welling	08.38	38	1	-	0
Brentford	Tr	11.45	46	41	-	1
Queens Park Rgrs	Tr	06.47	47-48	75	-	1
Ipswich T	Tr	09.49	49	8	-	0
SMITH George Clarence Bassett						
Portsmouth, 24 March, 1919 Died 2001						(WH)
Southampton	Guernsey Rov	07.38	38-48	95	-	1
Crystal Palace	Tr	05.50	50	7	-	0
SMITH George Henry						
Nottingham, 13 April, 1936						(G)
Notts Co	Dale Rov	07.53	55-66	323	0	0
Hartlepools U	Tr	07.67	67-69	112	0	0
SMITH Gerald (Gerry)						
Huddersfield, 18 November, 1939						(W)
Huddersfield T	Jnrs	05.58				
Bradford C	Tr	07.60	60	7	-	0
SMITH Gordon Duffield						
Kilwinning, 29 December, 1954 Su21-1						(W)
Brighton & Hove A	Glasgow Rgrs	06.80	80-83	97	12	22
Manchester C	Tr	03.84	83-85	40	2	13
Oldham Ath	Tr	01.86	85	14	1	0
SMITH Gordon Melville						
Partick, 3 July, 1954						(FB)
Aston Villa	St Johnstone	08.76	76-78	76	3	0
Tottenham H	Tr	02.79	78-81	34	4	1
Wolverhampton W	Tr	08.82	82-83	35	3	3
SMITH Graham						
Wimbledon, 7 August, 1951						(CD)
Brentford	Wimbledon	08.74	74	7	0	0
SMITH Graham Leslie						
Pudsey, 20 June, 1946						(FB)
Leeds U	Jnrs	02.64				
Rochdale	Tr	06.66	66-73	316	1	3
Stockport Co	Tr	07.74	74-78	147	4	2
SMITH Graham William Charles						
Liverpool, 2 November, 1947						(G)
Notts Co	Loughborough College	08.68	68	10	0	0
Colchester U	Tr	06.69	69-71	95	0	0
West Bromwich A	Tr	12.71	71-72	10	0	0
Cambridge U	Tr	01.73	72-75	85	0	0
SMITH Grant Gordon						
Irvine, 5 May, 1980						(M)
Reading	Wycombe W (YT)	08.98				
Sheffield U	Clydebank	07.01	01-02	2	8	0
Halifax T	L	09.01	01	11	0	0
Plymouth Arg	L	03.03	02	4	1	1
Swindon T	Tr	07.03	03-04	23	14	10
SMITH Granville						
Penrhiwceiber, 4 February, 1937						(W)
Bristol Rov	Jnrs	05.57	58-59	21	-	2
Newport Co	Tr	06.60	60-67	240	0	37
SMITH Harry Arthur						
Wolverhampton, 10 October, 1932						(FB)
Torquay U	West Bromwich A (Am)	01.54	53-60	188	-	1
Bristol C	Tr	07.61	61	1	-	0
SMITH Henry (Harry) Stanley						
Throckley, 11 October, 1908 Died 1993						(CD)
Nottingham F	Throckley Welfare	01.29	29-36	156	-	1
Darlington	Tr	08.37	37-38	65	-	0
Bristol Rov	Tr	08.39	46	3	-	0
SMITH Henry (Harry) Stuart						
Chester, 27 August, 1930						(IF)
Chester	Connah's Quay Nomads	01.53	52-57	73	-	7
SMITH Herbert (Herbie) Henry						
Birmingham, 17 December, 1922 Died 1996						(W)
Aston Villa	Moor Green	05.47	49-53	51	-	8
Southend U	Tr	06.54	54	5	-	0
SMITH (Dr) **Ian** Lennox Taylor						
Edinburgh, 2 April, 1952						(F)
Birmingham C	Queen's Park	03.75	74	0	2	0
SMITH Ian Ralph						
Rotherham, 15 February, 1957 ESch/EYth						(FB)
Tottenham H	App	04.74	75	2	0	0
Rotherham U	Tr	06.76	77	3	1	0
SMITH Jack						
Batley, 17 February, 1915 Died 1975						(CF)
Huddersfield T	Dewsbury Moor Welfare	06.32	32-34	45	-	24
Newcastle U	Tr	09.34	34-37	104	-	69
Manchester U	Tr	02.38	37-38	36	-	14
Blackburn Rov	Tr	03.46	46	30	-	12
Port Vale	Tr	05.47	46-47	29	-	10
SMITH Jack David						
Hemel Hempstead, 14 October, 1983						(FB)
Watford	YT	04.02	02-04	23	2	2
SMITH James (Jim)						
Bolton, 1 January, 1920						(W)
Burnley		03.43				
Leyton Orient	Tr	04.46	46-47	22	-	3
SMITH James (Jim)						
Glasgow, 20 January, 1947 Su23-1/SLge-1/S-4						(M)
Newcastle U	Aberdeen	08.69	69-74	124	5	13
SMITH James (Jim) Alexander Grant						
Arbroath, 16 October, 1937 Died 2002 SSch						(CD)
Preston NE	Arbroath LC	10.55	58-68	314	0	13
Stockport Co	Tr	10.69	69-70	78	0	2
SMITH James Aloysius						
Coatbridge, 9 September, 1925						(W)
Walsall	Coatdyke Jnrs	06.48	48	2	-	0
SMITH James (Jimmy) Harold						
Sheffield, 6 December, 1930						(W)
Chelsea	Shildon	04.51	51-53	19	-	3
Leyton Orient	Tr	07.55	55-57	37	-	3
SMITH James (Jimmy) Hay						
Johnstone, 22 November, 1969						(F)
Torquay U	YT	07.88	87-89	27	17	5
SMITH James (Jamie) Jade Anthony						
Birmingham, 17 September, 1974						(FB)
Wolverhampton W	YT	06.93	94-97	81	6	0
Crystal Palace	Tr	10.97	97-03	136	13	4
Fulham	L	03.99	98	9	0	1
Bristol C	Tr	08.04	04	35	4	2
SMITH James (Jim) Michael						
Sheffield, 17 October, 1940						(M)
Sheffield U	Oaksfield	01.59				
Aldershot	Tr	07.61	61-64	74	-	1
Halifax T	Tr	07.65	65-67	113	1	7
Lincoln C	Tr	03.68	67-68	54	0	0
Colchester U	Boston U	11.72	72	7	1	0

League Club	Source	Date Signed	Seasons Played	Career Record Apps	Subs	Gls
SMITH Jason Leslie						
Bromsgrove, 6 September, 1974 ESch						(CD)
Coventry C	Tiverton T	07.93				
Swansea C	Tiverton T	07.98	98-02	141	1	8
SMITH Jay Alexander						
Lambeth, 24 September, 1981						(M)
Aston Villa	YT	07.00				
Southend U	Tr	08.02	02-03	46	3	6
SMITH Jay Mark						
Hammersmith, 29 December, 1981						(M)
Brentford	YT	07.00	00-04	37	11	0
SMITH Jeffrey (Jeff)						
Middlesbrough, 28 June, 1980						(M)
Hartlepool U	YT	07.98	98	2	1	0
Bolton W	Bishop Auckland	03.01	00-01	1	1	0
Macclesfield T	L	11.01	01	7	1	2
Scunthorpe U	L	01.04	03	1	0	0
Rochdale	L	02.04	03	1	0	0
Preston NE	Tr	03.04	03	0	5	0
Port Vale	Tr	07.04	04	23	11	1
SMITH Jeffrey (Jeff) Edward						
Macclesfield, 8 December, 1935						(FB)
Sheffield U	Jnrs	06.53	56	1	-	0
Lincoln C	Tr	02.58	57-66	315	0	2
SMITH Jeremy						
Leeds, 20 July, 1971						(F)
Wigan Ath	Goole T	08.91	91	0	6	0
SMITH John (Jack)						
Liverpool						(IF)
Ipswich T		12.45	46	2	-	0
SMITH John (Jackie)						
Hartlepool, 24 April, 1936						(F)
Hartlepools U	Jnrs	05.53	53-59	119	-	49
Watford	Tr	07.60	60	20	-	8
Swindon T	Tr	06.61	61-63	97	-	37
Brighton & Hove A	Tr	01.64	63-66	88	0	33
Notts Co	Tr	09.66	66-68	74	4	12
SMITH John						
Shoreditch, 4 January, 1939 Died 1988 EYth/Eu23-1						(M)
West Ham U	Jnrs	01.56	56-59	125	-	20
Tottenham H	Tr	03.60	59-63	21	-	1
Coventry C	Tr	03.64	63-65	34	1	1
Leyton Orient	Tr	10.65	65-66	38	1	3
Torquay U	Tr	10.66	66-67	67	1	8
Swindon T	Tr	06.68	68-70	79	5	9
Walsall	Tr	06.71	71	13	0	1
SMITH John						
Johnstown, 13 September, 1944						(WH)
Wrexham	Burnley (Jnrs)	05.63	64-65	23	1	0
SMITH John						
Liverpool, 14 March, 1953 ESch						(M)
Everton	App	09.70	73	2	0	0
Carlisle U	Tr	06.76	76	4	1	0
Southport	L	02.77	76	17	1	2
SMITH John						
Coatbridge, 27 November, 1956						(F)
Preston NE	App	11.74	73-78	80	11	14
Halifax T	LA Skyhawks (USA)	11.79	79	26	2	6
SMITH John						
Liverpool, 23 July, 1970						(FB)
Tranmere Rov	Jnrs	11.87	88	1	1	0
SMITH John (Jack) Clayton						
Stocksbridge, 15 September, 1910 Died 1986						(G)
Sheffield U	Worksop T	10.30	30-49	347	-	0
SMITH John Edward						
Canning Town, 9 November, 1930 EYth						(FB)
Millwall	Barking	04.56	55-57	64	-	1
SMITH John Owen						
Enderby, 4 September, 1928						(WH)
Northampton T		09.49	50-59	186	-	9
SMITH John (Jack) Thomas						
Birkenhead, 21 December, 1927 Died 2000						(CF)
Liverpool	Bromborough Pool	03.51	51-53	57	-	14
Torquay U	Tr	05.54	54-57	65	-	16

League Club	Source	Date Signed	Seasons Played	Career Record Apps	Subs	Gls
SMITH John Vivian Thomas						
Plymouth, 12 November, 1927						(FB)
Plymouth Arg	Plymouth U	07.50	50-52	3	-	0
Torquay U	Tr	07.54	54-59	164	-	0
SMITH John (Jackie) William						
St Pancras, 27 May, 1920 Died 1991						(W)
Bradford PA	Avro Works	10.43	46-52	204	-	26
SMITH Keith						
Sheffield, 17 October, 1963						(F)
Exeter C	Alfreton T	01.89	88	2	13	2
SMITH Keith Wilson						
Woodville, 15 September, 1940						(F)
West Bromwich A	Jnrs	01.58	59-62	63	-	30
Peterborough U	Tr	06.63	63-64	55	-	28
Crystal Palace	Tr	11.64	64-65	47	3	14
Darlington	Tr	11.66	66	17	0	2
Leyton Orient	Tr	05.67	66	3	0	0
Notts Co	Tr	07.67	67-69	85	4	7
SMITH Kenneth (Ken)						
South Shields, 21 May, 1932						(CF)
Sunderland	Jnrs	08.49	50-52	5	-	2
Blackpool	Headington U	12.54	54-57	6	-	4
Shrewsbury T	Tr	10.57	57-58	44	-	20
Gateshead	Tr	11.58	58-59	45	-	18
Darlington	Tr	12.59	59	24	-	7
Carlisle U	Tr	07.60	60	14	-	12
Halifax T	Toronto Italia (Can)	10.61	61	27	-	6
SMITH Kenneth (Ken)						
Consett, 7 December, 1927						(IF)
Blackpool	Annfield Plain	04.49				
Gateshead	Tr	08.52	52-58	256	-	75
SMITH Kenneth (Ken) George						
Norwich, 22 April, 1936						(CD)
Norwich C	Gothic	09.55	55-56	10	-	0
SMITH Kevan						
Eaglescliffe, 13 December, 1959						(CD)
Darlington	Stockton	09.79	79-84	242	3	11
Rotherham U	Tr	07.85	85-86	59	0	4
Coventry C	Tr	12.86	87	5	1	0
York C	Tr	05.88	88	30	1	5
Darlington	Tr	06.89	90-92	98	0	5
Hereford U	L	10.92	92	6	0	0
Hereford U	Sliema W (Malta)	09.93	93	17	1	0
SMITH Kevin John						
Wallsend, 20 April, 1965						(M)
Cambridge U	App	11.82	82-84	30	8	4
Exeter C	Tr	10.84	84	21	4	2
Torquay U	Tr	07.85	85	20	3	1
SMITH Kevin Paul						
St Pauls Cray, 5 December, 1962						(M)
Charlton Ath	App	08.80	79-83	79	25	14
SMITH Leslie (Les)						
Manchester, 2 October, 1920 Died 2001						(WH)
Huddersfield T	Stockport Co (Am)	03.46	46-47	37	-	0
Oldham Ath	Tr	07.49	49-55	178	-	3
SMITH Leslie (Les)						
Tamworth, 16 November, 1921 Died 1993						(WH)
Mansfield T	Nottingham F (Am)	08.45	46-47	38	-	0
SMITH Leslie George Frederick						
Ealing, 13 May, 1918 Died 1995 EWar-13/E-1						(W)
Brentford	Hayes	03.36	36-38	62	-	6
Aston Villa	Tr	10.45	46-51	181	-	31
Brentford	Tr	06.52	52	14	-	1
SMITH Joseph **Leslie (Les)**						
Halesowen, 24 December, 1927						(W)
Wolverhampton W	Jnrs	04.46	47-55	88	-	22
Aston Villa	Tr	02.56	55-58	115	-	24
SMITH Lindsay James						
Enfield, 18 September, 1954						(CD)
Colchester U	App	03.72	70-76	185	27	16
Charlton Ath	L	08.77	77	1	0	0
Millwall	L	09.77	77	4	1	0
Cambridge U	Tr	10.77	77-82	173	1	7
Lincoln C	L	09.81	81	5	0	0
Plymouth Arg	Tr	07.84	82-83	76	0	5
Millwall	Tr	07.84	84-85	54	1	5
Cambridge U	Tr	07.86	86-88	102	0	16

SMITH Lionel
Mexborough, 23 August, 1920 Died 1980 FLge-3/E-6 (FB)

League Club	Source	Date Signed	Seasons Played	Apps	Subs	Gls
Arsenal	Denaby U	08.39	47-53	162	-	0
Watford	Tr	06.54	54	7	-	0

SMITH Malcolm
Stockton, 21 September, 1953 (F)

League Club	Source	Date Signed	Seasons Played	Apps	Subs	Gls
Middlesbrough	App	10.70	71-75	32	24	11
Bury	L	10.75	75	5	0	1
Blackpool	L	01.76	75	8	0	5
Burnley	Tr	09.76	76-79	82	3	17
York C	Tr	08.80	80-81	28	7	6

SMITH Malcolm Alan
Maidstone, 3 August, 1970 (M)

League Club	Source	Date Signed	Seasons Played	Apps	Subs	Gls
Gillingham	YT	06.88	87	1	1	0

SMITH Mark
Redruth, 21 September, 1963 (FB)

League Club	Source	Date Signed	Seasons Played	Apps	Subs	Gls
Bristol C	App	09.81	81	1	4	0
Plymouth Arg	Exmouth T	03.84	83	3	0	0

SMITH Mark
Torquay, 9 October, 1961 (FB)

League Club	Source	Date Signed	Seasons Played	Apps	Subs	Gls
Torquay U		09.81	81-83	28	2	0

SMITH Mark Alexander
Bellshill, 16 December, 1964 (W)

League Club	Source	Date Signed	Seasons Played	Apps	Subs	Gls
Stoke C (L)	Dunfermline Ath	02.90	89	2	0	0
Nottingham F	Dunfermline Ath	03.90				
Reading	L	12.90	90	3	0	0
Mansfield T	L	03.91	90	6	1	0
Shrewsbury T	Tr	08.91	91-94	64	14	4

SMITH Mark Allen
Birmingham, 2 January, 1973 (G)

League Club	Source	Date Signed	Seasons Played	Apps	Subs	Gls
Nottingham F	YT	02.91				
Crewe Alex	Tr	02.93	92-94	61	2	0

SMITH Mark Craig
Sheffield, 21 March, 1960 Eu21-5 (CD)

League Club	Source	Date Signed	Seasons Played	Apps	Subs	Gls
Sheffield Wed	App	03.78	77-86	281	1	16
Plymouth Arg	Tr	07.87	87-89	82	0	6
Barnsley	Tr	11.89	89-92	101	3	10
Notts Co	Tr	10.92	92	4	1	0
Port Vale	L	01.93	92	6	0	0
Huddersfield T	L	02.93	92	5	0	0
Chesterfield	L	03.93	92	6	0	1
Lincoln C	Tr	08.93	93	20	0	1

SMITH Mark Cyril
Sheffield, 19 December, 1961 (W)

League Club	Source	Date Signed	Seasons Played	Apps	Subs	Gls
Sheffield U	Jnrs	08.80				
Scunthorpe U	Gainsborough Trinity	09.85	85	0	1	0
Rochdale	Kettering T	07.88	88	26	1	7
Huddersfield T	Tr	02.89	88-90	85	11	11
Grimsby T	Tr	03.91	90-92	37	40	4
Scunthorpe U	Tr	08.93	93-94	50	12	8

SMITH Mark Jonathan
Bristol, 13 September, 1979 (CD)

League Club	Source	Date Signed	Seasons Played	Apps	Subs	Gls
Bristol Rov	YT	07.98	98-01	28	5	0

SMITH Mark Leslie
Canning Town, 10 October, 1961 (FB)

League Club	Source	Date Signed	Seasons Played	Apps	Subs	Gls
West Ham U	App	10.79	79	1	0	0

SMITH Mark Stuart
Carlisle, 4 April, 1962 EYth (FB)

League Club	Source	Date Signed	Seasons Played	Apps	Subs	Gls
Orient	App	12.79	78-79	3	0	0

SMITH Martin Geoffrey
Sunderland, 13 November, 1974 ESch/EYth/Eu21-1 (F)

League Club	Source	Date Signed	Seasons Played	Apps	Subs	Gls
Sunderland	YT	09.92	93-98	90	29	25
Sheffield U	Tr	08.99	99	24	2	10
Huddersfield T	Tr	02.00	99-02	72	8	29
Northampton T	Tr	08.03	03-04	74	4	21

SMITH Martyn Christopher
Stoke-on-Trent, 16 September, 1961 (W)

League Club	Source	Date Signed	Seasons Played	Apps	Subs	Gls
Port Vale	Leek T	07.84	84	12	1	1

SMITH Michael (Mike)
Haddington, 15 October, 1923 (CF)

League Club	Source	Date Signed	Seasons Played	Apps	Subs	Gls
Plymouth Arg	Preston Ath	02.48	47	1	-	0

SMITH Michael (Mick)
Sunderland, 28 October, 1958 (CD)

League Club	Source	Date Signed	Seasons Played	Apps	Subs	Gls
Lincoln C	Lambton Star BC	07.77	77-78	20	5	0
Wimbledon	Tr	12.79	79-86	203	2	14
Aldershot	L	10.84	84	7	0	0
Hartlepool U	Seaham Red Star	10.89	89-91	53	2	6

SMITH Michael (Mike) John
Quarndon, 22 September, 1935 ESch (CD)

League Club	Source	Date Signed	Seasons Played	Apps	Subs	Gls
Derby Co	Jnrs	10.52	57-60	22	-	0
Bradford C	Tr	06.61	61-65	134	0	0

SMITH Michael (Mike) Kenneth
Hull, 19 December, 1968 (W)

League Club	Source	Date Signed	Seasons Played	Apps	Subs	Gls
Hull C	App	05.87	88-90	14	5	1

SMITH Michael (Mike) Robert
Liverpool, 28 September, 1973 (W)

League Club	Source	Date Signed	Seasons Played	Apps	Subs	Gls
Tranmere Rov	YT	05.92				
Doncaster Rov	Runcorn	01.96	95-97	33	17	5

SMITH Neil
Warley, 10 February, 1970 (M)

League Club	Source	Date Signed	Seasons Played	Apps	Subs	Gls
Shrewsbury T	YT	07.88	87	0	1	0
Lincoln C	Redditch U	03.90	89-91	13	4	0

SMITH Neil James
Lambeth, 30 September, 1971 (M)

League Club	Source	Date Signed	Seasons Played	Apps	Subs	Gls
Tottenham H	YT	07.90				
Gillingham	Tr	10.91	91-96	204	8	10
Fulham	Tr	07.97	97-98	62	11	1
Reading	Tr	08.99	99-01	33	32	3

SMITH Nicholas (Nicky) Leslie
Berkeley, 28 January, 1969 (W)

League Club	Source	Date Signed	Seasons Played	Apps	Subs	Gls
Southend U	YT	07.87	86-89	49	11	6
Colchester U	Tr	08.90	92-93	71	10	4
Northampton T	Sudbury T	01.95	94	6	0	1

SMITH Nigel Godfrey
Manchester, 22 April, 1959 (CD)

League Club	Source	Date Signed	Seasons Played	Apps	Subs	Gls
Stockport Co	Blackburn Rov (Am)	08.79	80-85	118	5	1

SMITH Nigel Keith
Bath, 12 January, 1966 (M)

League Club	Source	Date Signed	Seasons Played	Apps	Subs	Gls
Bristol C	App	01.84	82	2	0	0
Exeter C	L	11.84	84	1	0	0

SMITH Nigel Paul
Banstead, 3 January, 1958 (CD)

League Club	Source	Date Signed	Seasons Played	Apps	Subs	Gls
Brentford	Banstead Ath	03.75	74-78	81	4	0
Cambridge U	Tr	11.78	78	0	1	0

SMITH Nigel Peter
Leeds, 21 December, 1969 (W)

League Club	Source	Date Signed	Seasons Played	Apps	Subs	Gls
Leeds U	YT	07.88				
Burnley	Tr	07.89	89-90	6	7	0
Bury	Tr	08.91	91	30	4	3
Shrewsbury T	Guiseley	09.92	92	2	0	0

SMITH Norman
Boldon, 23 November, 1919 (CF)

League Club	Source	Date Signed	Seasons Played	Apps	Subs	Gls
Coventry C	Standard Apprentices	05.38	38-47	13	-	0
Millwall	Tr	12.47	47	10	-	0

SMITH Norman
Darwen, 2 January, 1925 Died 1990 (WH)

League Club	Source	Date Signed	Seasons Played	Apps	Subs	Gls
Arsenal	Darwen	07.47				
Barnsley	Tr	10.52	52-58	156	-	14

SMITH Norman Henry
Burton-on-Trent, 27 January, 1924 Died 2000 (IF)

League Club	Source	Date Signed	Seasons Played	Apps	Subs	Gls
Accrington St		02.46	46-47	39	-	6
Oldham Ath	Tr	06.48	48	1	-	0

SMITH Norman Leonard
Carshalton, 2 July, 1928 Died 2003 EAmat (WH)

League Club	Source	Date Signed	Seasons Played	Apps	Subs	Gls
Fulham	Bishop Auckland	07.48	52-56	60	-	0

SMITH Paul Andrew
Bath, 12 September, 1953 (W)

League Club	Source	Date Signed	Seasons Played	Apps	Subs	Gls
Manchester C	Jnrs	09.70				
Portsmouth	Tr	06.73	73	0	1	0

SMITH Paul Antony
Hastings, 25 January, 1976 (W)

League Club	Source	Date Signed	Seasons Played	Apps	Subs	Gls
Nottingham F	Hastings T	01.95				
Lincoln C	Tr	10.97	97-02	122	35	19

SMITH Paul Daniel
Epsom, 17 December, 1979 (G)

League Club	Source	Date Signed	Seasons Played	Apps	Subs	Gls
Charlton Ath	Walton & Hersham	07.98				
Brentford	Carshalton Ath	07.00	00-03	86	1	0
Southampton	Tr	01.04	04	5	1	0

SMITH Paul Elton
Lewisham, 2 November, 1971 (M)

League Club	Source	Date Signed	Seasons Played	Apps	Subs	Gls
Barnet	Horsham	05.95	95	0	1	0

League Club	Source	Date Signed	Seasons Played	Career Record Apps	Subs	Gls
SMITH Ian Paul						
Easington, 22 January, 1976						(W)
Burnley	YT	07.94	93-00	79	33	5
Oldham Ath	L	09.00	00	3	1	0
Hartlepool U	Tr	11.01	01-02	45	10	4
Sheffield Wed	Tr	07.03	03-04	19	8	2
SMITH Paul Michael						
Rotherham, 9 November, 1964						(FB)
Sheffield U	App	11.82	82-85	29	7	1
Stockport Co	L	08.85	85	7	0	5
Port Vale	Tr	07.86	86-87	42	2	7
Lincoln C	Tr	08.87	88-94	219	13	27
SMITH Paul Stepney						
Wembley, 5 October, 1967						(W)
Arsenal	App	07.85				
Brentford	Tr	08.87	87	10	7	1
Bristol Rov	Tr	07.88	88	14	2	1
Torquay U	Tr	03.89	88-91	66	9	12
SMITH Paul William						
Doncaster, 15 October, 1954						(M)
Huddersfield T	App	12.71	72-73	1	1	0
Cambridge U	Tr	09.74	74-75	35	3	3
SMITH Paul William						
East Ham, 18 September, 1971						(M)
Southend U	YT	03.90	89-92	18	2	1
Brentford	Tr	08.93	93-96	159	0	11
Gillingham	Tr	07.97	97-04	338	4	21
SMITH Peter Alec						
Islington, 10 November, 1964						(CD)
Orient	App	11.82	82	8	6	0
SMITH Peter Edward						
Skelmersdale, 30 October, 1980						(M)
Exeter C	YT	07.99	98-99	3	5	0
SMITH Peter John						
Gosport, 6 May, 1932						(FB)
Gillingham	Fleetland	11.54	54-56	6	-	0
SMITH Peter John						
Balham, 27 May, 1935						(WH)
Gillingham	Tunbridge Wells	06.58	58-59	39	-	2
SMITH Peter John						
Cannock, 12 July, 1969						(FB)
Brighton & Hove A	Alma Swanley	08.94	94-98	122	18	5
SMITH Peter Lee						
Rhuddlan, 18 September, 1978 ESch/EYth						(F)
Crewe Alex	YT	07.96	96-00	3	19	0
Macclesfield T	L	09.98	98	12	0	3
SMITH Philip (Phil)						
Fleetwood, 20 November, 1961						(F)
Blackpool	App	11.79	79	1	0	0
SMITH Philip (Phil) Anthony						
Harrow, 14 December, 1979						(G)
Millwall	YT	01.98	98	5	0	0
SMITH Raymond (Ray)						
Portadown, 20 November, 1950						(W)
Oldham Ath	Glenavon	01.68	67	0	2	0
SMITH Harold **Raymond (Ray)**						
Hull, 13 September, 1934						(IF)
Hull C	Jnrs	08.52	54-55	23	-	2
Peterborough U	Tr	07.56	60-62	92	-	33
Northampton T	Tr	10.62	62-63	23	-	7
Luton T	Tr	10.63	63	10	-	1
SMITH Raymond (Ray) James						
Islington, 18 April, 1943						(F)
Southend U	Basildon Minors	12.61	61-66	150	0	55
Wrexham	Tr	07.67	67-71	161	14	60
Peterborough U	Tr	07.72	72	22	0	8
SMITH Raymond (Ray) Scorer						
Evenwood, 14 April, 1929						(WH)
Luton T	Evenwood T	02.50	51-56	12	-	0
Southend U	Tr	08.57	57-59	46	-	1
SMITH Richard Francis						
Reading, 22 October, 1967						(W)
Wolverhampton W	App	07.85	85	0	1	0
Mansfield T	Moor Green Rov	03.87	86	1	1	0

League Club	Source	Date Signed	Seasons Played	Career Record Apps	Subs	Gls
SMITH Richard Geoffrey						
Lutterworth, 3 October, 1970						(CD)
Leicester C	YT	12.88	89-95	82	14	1
Cambridge U	L	09.89	89	4	0	0
Grimsby T	L	09.95	95	8	0	0
Grimsby T	Tr	03.96	95-00	72	7	1
SMITH Robert (Bobby)						
Barnsley, 20 June, 1941						(W)
Barnsley	Jnrs	06.60	62	3	-	0
SMITH Robert (Rob)						
Hull, 25 April, 1950						(FB)
Hull C	App	11.67				
Grimsby T	Tr	09.71	71	10	1	0
Hartlepool	Tr	07.72	72-75	141	11	4
SMITH Robert (Bobby) Alfred						
Lingdale, 22 February, 1933 E-15						(CF)
Chelsea	Jnrs	05.50	50-55	74	-	23
Tottenham H	Tr	12.55	55-63	271	-	176
Brighton & Hove A	Tr	05.64	64	31	-	19
SMITH Robert (Bobby) Gordon John						
Bournemouth, 15 December, 1941						(WH)
Portsmouth	Jnrs	05.59				
Gillingham	Tr	07.62	62	7	-	0
SMITH Robert (Bobby) Nisbet						
Dalkeith, 21 December, 1953						(M)
Leicester C	Hibernian	12.78	78-85	175	6	21
Peterborough U	L	02.82	81	5	0	0
SMITH Robert (Bobby) William						
Prestbury, 14 March, 1944 ESch/EYth						(M)
Manchester U	App	04.61				
Scunthorpe U	Tr	03.65	64-66	82	0	12
Grimsby T	Tr	01.67	66-67	48	4	1
Brighton & Hove A	Tr	06.68	68-70	72	3	2
Chester	Tr	06.71	71	2	0	0
Hartlepool	Tr	10.71	71-72	67	2	7
SMITH Roger Anthony						
Welwyn Garden City, 3 November, 1944						(W)
Tottenham H	App	06.62				
Exeter C	Tr	06.66	66	6	0	3
SMITH Roger William						
Tamworth, 19 February, 1945						(W)
Walsall	App	09.62	62-64	43	-	2
Port Vale	Tr	08.65	65	29	1	6
Walsall	Tr	05.66	66	8	1	0
SMITH Ronald (Ron)						
Aberystwyth, 9 April, 1934						(FB)
Arsenal	Maidenhead U	07.54				
Watford	Tr	08.55	55	2	-	0
SMITH Ronald (Ron)						
Garston, 7 June, 1936						(W)
Liverpool	Stoke C (Am)	12.57				
Bournemouth	Tr	05.59	59-60	36	-	6
Crewe Alex	Tr	07.61	61-63	91	-	11
Port Vale	Tr	10.63	63-64	59	-	6
Southport	Tr	07.65	65-66	77	2	14
SMITH Ronald (Ron) Herbert						
York, 25 November, 1929						(CD)
York C	Harrogate RI	05.54	54	1	-	0
SMITH Roy Harold						
Rawalpindi, India, 19 March, 1936						(IF)
West Ham U	Woodford YC	06.55	55-56	6	-	1
Portsmouth	Hereford U	01.62	61-62	8	-	3
SMITH Roy Peter						
Haydock, 18 June, 1936 Died 1959						(CF)
Southport	Wigan Ath	09.58	58	23	-	4
SMITH Royston (Roy) Leonard						
Shirebrook, 22 September, 1916						(G)
Sheffield Wed	Selby T	02.36	36-47	84	-	0
Notts Co	Tr	12.48	48-52	110	-	0
SMITH Scott David						
Christchurch, New Zealand, 6 March, 1975						(FB)
Rotherham U	YT	10.93	93-96	30	6	0
SMITH Septimus (Sep) Charles						
Whitburn, 15 March, 1912 ESch/FLge-1/E-1						(WH)
Leicester C	Whitburn	03.29	29-48	350	-	35

SMITH Gareth **Shaun**
Leeds, 9 April, 1971 (FB)

League Club	Source	Date Signed	Seasons Played	Apps	Subs	Gls
Halifax T	YT	07.89	88-89	6	1	0
Crewe Alex	Emley	12.91	91-01	380	22	41
Hull C	Tr	07.02	02	17	5	1
Stockport Co	L	09.03	03	3	3	0
Carlisle U	L	10.03	03	4	0	0
Rochdale	Tr	03.04	03	13	0	0

SMITH Stanley (Stan) James
Kidsgrove, 24 February, 1931 (IF)

League Club	Source	Date Signed	Seasons Played	Apps	Subs	Gls
Port Vale		05.50	54-56	60	-	19
Crewe Alex	Tr	07.57	57	28	-	6
Oldham Ath	Tr	03.58	57	4	-	0

SMITH Stanley (Stan) Walter
Coventry, 24 February, 1925 (WH)

League Club	Source	Date Signed	Seasons Played	Apps	Subs	Gls
Coventry C	Nuffield Mechanics	08.46	47-48	29	-	0

SMITH Stephen (Steve)
Huddersfield, 28 April, 1946 (M)

League Club	Source	Date Signed	Seasons Played	Apps	Subs	Gls
Huddersfield T	Jnrs	10.63	64-76	330	12	30
Bolton W	L	12.74	74	3	0	0
Halifax T	Tr	08.77	77-78	78	3	4

SMITH Clifford **Stephen (Steve)**
Birmingham, 13 January, 1961 (F)

League Club	Source	Date Signed	Seasons Played	Apps	Subs	Gls
Walsall	Bromsgrove Rov	08.80	80-81	17	2	3

SMITH Stephen (Steve) James
Lydney, 12 June, 1957 (G)

League Club	Source	Date Signed	Seasons Played	Apps	Subs	Gls
Birmingham C	App	07.75	75	2	0	0
Bradford C	Tr	03.78	78-81	105	0	0
Crewe Alex	Tr	08.82	82-83	54	0	0

SMITH Stephen Martin
Harlow, 19 September, 1986 (M)

League Club	Source	Date Signed	Seasons Played	Apps	Subs	Gls
Cambridge U	Sch	●	03	1	1	0

SMITH Terence (Terry) Peter
Cheltenham, 10 September, 1951 (F)

League Club	Source	Date Signed	Seasons Played	Apps	Subs	Gls
Stoke C	App	12.68	70-71	3	1	1
Shrewsbury T	L	02.73	72	2	0	0

SMITH Terence (Terry) Victor
Rainworth, 10 July, 1942 (WH)

League Club	Source	Date Signed	Seasons Played	Apps	Subs	Gls
Mansfield T	Jnrs	04.60	60	8	-	0

SMITH Thomas (Tot)
Horden, 2 February, 1923 Died 1993 (CD)

League Club	Source	Date Signed	Seasons Played	Apps	Subs	Gls
Newcastle U	Horden CW	03.41	46-49	8	-	0

SMITH Thomas (Tommy)
Liverpool, 5 April, 1945 EYth/Eu23-10/FLge-1/E-1 (CD)

League Club	Source	Date Signed	Seasons Played	Apps	Subs	Gls
Liverpool	App	04.62	62-77	467	0	36
Swansea C	Tr	08.78	78	34	2	2

SMITH Thomas (Tommy) Edgar
Wolverhampton, 30 July, 1959 (F)

League Club	Source	Date Signed	Seasons Played	Apps	Subs	Gls
Sheffield U	Bromsgrove Rov	04.78	78	2	1	1
Huddersfield T	Tr	03.79	78	0	1	0

SMITH Thomas (Tommy) Edward
Northampton, 25 November, 1977 (CD)

League Club	Source	Date Signed	Seasons Played	Apps	Subs	Gls
Manchester U	YT	05.95				
Cambridge U	Tr	04.98	97	0	1	0

SMITH Thomas (Tommy) William
Hemel Hempstead, 22 May, 1980 EYth/Eu21-1 (F)

League Club	Source	Date Signed	Seasons Played	Apps	Subs	Gls
Watford	YT	10.97	97-02	114	35	33
Sunderland	Tr	09.03	03	22	13	4
Derby Co	Tr	07.04	04	41	1	11

SMITH Timothy (Tim) Carl
Gloucester, 19 April, 1959 (M)

League Club	Source	Date Signed	Seasons Played	Apps	Subs	Gls
Luton T	App	05.76	76-77	1	1	0

SMITH Trevor
Brierley Hill, 13 April, 1936 Died 2003 Eu23-15/EB/FLge-2/E-2 (CD)

League Club	Source	Date Signed	Seasons Played	Apps	Subs	Gls
Birmingham C	Jnrs	05.53	53-64	365	-	3
Walsall	Tr	10.64	64-65	12	0	0

SMITH John **Trevor**
Stanley, 8 September, 1910 Died 1997 (IF)

League Club	Source	Date Signed	Seasons Played	Apps	Subs	Gls
Charlton Ath	Annfield Plain	05.33	33-34	23	-	6
Fulham	Tr	03.35	34-37	93	-	19
Crystal Palace	Tr	02.38	37-38	57	-	14
Watford	Yeovil T	06.47	47	10	-	0

SMITH Trevor John
Birmingham, 7 May, 1954 ESch (W)

League Club	Source	Date Signed	Seasons Played	Apps	Subs	Gls
Coventry C	App	05.71				
Walsall	Tr	08.72	72	2	1	0

SMITH Trevor Martin
Middlesbrough, 4 April, 1959 (CD)

League Club	Source	Date Signed	Seasons Played	Apps	Subs	Gls
Hartlepool	Whitby T	07.77	76-78	27	6	1
Hartlepool U	Whitby T	08.82	82	30	2	3

SMITH Trevor Richard
Lowestoft, 12 August, 1946 (FB)

League Club	Source	Date Signed	Seasons Played	Apps	Subs	Gls
Ipswich T	App	08.64	64-65	22	1	0

SMITH Wilfred
Stoke-on-Trent, 18 April, 1917 Died 1995 (WH)

League Club	Source	Date Signed	Seasons Played	Apps	Subs	Gls
Port Vale	Sneyd Colliery	10.36	36-48	87	-	0

SMITH Wilfred (Wilf)
Manchester, 20 January, 1935 (IF)

League Club	Source	Date Signed	Seasons Played	Apps	Subs	Gls
Stockport Co		02.57	57-59	6	-	1

SMITH Wilfred (Wilf) Samuel
Neumunster, Germany, 3 September, 1946 EYth/Eu23-6/FLge-3 (FB)

League Club	Source	Date Signed	Seasons Played	Apps	Subs	Gls
Sheffield Wed	App	09.63	64-70	206	0	4
Coventry C	Tr	08.70	70-74	132	3	1
Brighton & Hove A	L	10.74	74	5	0	0
Millwall	L	01.75	74	5	0	0
Bristol Rov	Tr	03.75	74-76	54	0	2
Chesterfield	Tr	11.76	76	26	1	2

SMITH Wilfred (Wilf) Victor
Pucklechurch, 7 April, 1918 Died 1968 (FB)

League Club	Source	Date Signed	Seasons Played	Apps	Subs	Gls
Bristol Rov	Clevedon T	05.36	37-46	26	-	0
Newport Co	Tr	12.46	46-47	9	-	0

SMITH William (Willie)
Glasgow, 6 December, 1943 (WH)

League Club	Source	Date Signed	Seasons Played	Apps	Subs	Gls
Brentford	Glasgow Celtic	06.63	63-65	25	0	0

SMITH William
Aberdeen, 23 December, 1938 (IF)

League Club	Source	Date Signed	Seasons Played	Apps	Subs	Gls
Darlington	Raith Rov	07.63	63	26	-	7

SMITH William
Cumnock, 12 October, 1942 (IF)

League Club	Source	Date Signed	Seasons Played	Apps	Subs	Gls
Sheffield U	Cumnock Jnrs	07.65	66	2	0	1

SMITH William (Willie)
London, 29 September, 1948 EAmat (FB)

League Club	Source	Date Signed	Seasons Played	Apps	Subs	Gls
Wimbledon	Leatherhead	08.77	77	2	0	0

SMITH William (Bill) Arthur
Lambeth, 2 November, 1938 (G)

League Club	Source	Date Signed	Seasons Played	Apps	Subs	Gls
Crystal Palace	Jnrs	12.56				
Watford	Tr	08.57	58	10	-	0

SMITH William (Bill) Henry
Plymouth, 7 September, 1926 (WH)

League Club	Source	Date Signed	Seasons Played	Apps	Subs	Gls
Plymouth Arg	Plymouth U	08.45				
Reading	Tr	08.47	47	3	-	0
Northampton T	Tr	07.48	48	26	-	6
Birmingham C	Tr	02.50	50-52	55	-	21
Blackburn Rov	Tr	12.52	52-59	119	-	10
Accrington St	Tr	07.60	60	34	-	3

SMITH William (Billy) Roy
Stafford, 20 December, 1930 (FB)

League Club	Source	Date Signed	Seasons Played	Apps	Subs	Gls
Crewe Alex		12.55	55-56	43	-	0

SMITHARD Matthew Philip
Leeds, 13 June, 1976 (M)

League Club	Source	Date Signed	Seasons Played	Apps	Subs	Gls
Leeds U	YT	03.93				
Bradford C	Tr	08.96	96	0	1	0

SMITHERS Timothy (Tim)
Ramsgate, 22 January, 1956 ESemiPro (FB)

League Club	Source	Date Signed	Seasons Played	Apps	Subs	Gls
Oxford U	Nuneaton Borough	05.80	80-82	95	4	6

SMITHIES Michael (Mike) Howard
Hartlepool, 18 September, 1962 (FB)

League Club	Source	Date Signed	Seasons Played	Apps	Subs	Gls
Hartlepool U		12.82	82-86	32	3	0

SMITHSON Rodney George
Leicester, 9 October, 1943 ESch/EYth (CD)

League Club	Source	Date Signed	Seasons Played	Apps	Subs	Gls
Arsenal	App	10.60	62	2	-	0
Oxford U	Tr	07.64	65-74	150	6	6

SMOUT John Richard
Newtown, 30 October, 1941 (G)

League Club	Source	Date Signed	Seasons Played	Apps	Subs	Gls
Crystal Palace		08.65	65	1	0	0
Exeter C	Tr	06.66	66-67	75	0	0

SMYTH Cecil (Cec)
Belfast, 4 May, 1941 (FB)

League Club	Source	Date Signed	Seasons Played	Apps	Subs	Gls
Exeter C	Distillery	08.62	62-68	270	3	1
Torquay U	Tr	08.69	69-70	22	1	0

SMYTH Gerry
Belfast, 5 November, 1931 (W)

League Club	Source	Date Signed	Seasons Played	Apps	Subs	Gls
Cardiff C	Jnrs	08.50				
Chester	Tr	07.51	51	2	-	0

SMYTH John Michael
Dundalk, 28 April, 1970 (FB)

League Club	Source	Date Signed	Seasons Played	Apps	Subs	Gls
Liverpool	Dundalk	05.87				
Burnley	Tr	08.90				
Wigan Ath	Tr	09.91	91	2	6	0

SMYTH Michael (Mike)
Dublin, 13 May, 1940 LoI-1/IR-1 (G)

League Club	Source	Date Signed	Seasons Played	Apps	Subs	Gls
Barrow	Drumcondra	08.62	62-63	8	-	0

SMYTH Peter Rufus Adair
Derry, 3 December, 1924 Died 2001 (IF)

League Club	Source	Date Signed	Seasons Played	Apps	Subs	Gls
Exeter C	Albion Rov	06.50	50	5	-	0
Southport	Tr	07.51	51	5	-	0

SMYTH Herbert Robert (Bob)
Manchester, 28 February, 1921 (WH)

League Club	Source	Date Signed	Seasons Played	Apps	Subs	Gls
Ipswich T	HMS Ganges	12.45	46-47	2	-	0
Halifax T	Tr	08.50	50	2	-	0
Rochdale	Tr	09.50	50	3	-	1
Accrington St	Tr	01.51	50	7	-	0

SMYTH Samuel (Sammy)
Belfast, 25 February, 1925 IrLge-1/I-9 (IF)

League Club	Source	Date Signed	Seasons Played	Apps	Subs	Gls
Wolverhampton W	Linfield	07.47	47-51	102	-	34
Stoke C	Tr	09.51	51-52	40	-	17
Liverpool	Tr	01.53	52-53	45	-	20

SNAPE John (Jack)
Birmingham, 2 July, 1917 Died 2000 (WH)

League Club	Source	Date Signed	Seasons Played	Apps	Subs	Gls
Coventry C	Solihull T	05.36	37-49	106	-	2

SNEDDEN John Duncan
Bonnybridge, 3 February, 1942 SSch (CD)

League Club	Source	Date Signed	Seasons Played	Apps	Subs	Gls
Arsenal	Bonnyvale Star Jnrs	02.59	59-64	83	-	0
Charlton Ath	Tr	03.65	64-65	18	2	0
Leyton Orient	Tr	07.66	66-67	26	1	3
Halifax T	L	11.67	67	5	0	0

SNEDDON Charles (Charlie)
Carriden, 10 June, 1930 Died 1992 (WH)

League Club	Source	Date Signed	Seasons Played	Apps	Subs	Gls
Accrington St	Stenhousemuir	10.53	53-60	213	-	3

SNEDDON David (Dave)
Kilwinning, 24 April, 1936 Su23-1 (IF)

League Club	Source	Date Signed	Seasons Played	Apps	Subs	Gls
Preston NE	Dundee	04.59	58-61	91	-	17

SNEDDON Thomas (Tom)
Livingston, 22 August, 1912 Died 1983 (FB)

League Club	Source	Date Signed	Seasons Played	Apps	Subs	Gls
Rochdale	Queen of the South	07.37	37-46	67	-	0

SNEDDON William (Billy) Cleland
Wishaw, 1 April, 1914 Died 1995 (WH)

League Club	Source	Date Signed	Seasons Played	Apps	Subs	Gls
Brentford	Falkirk	06.37	37-38	66	-	2
Swansea T	Tr	07.39	46	2	-	0
Newport Co	Tr	10.46	46	18	-	0

SNEEKES Richard
Amsterdam, Holland, 30 October, 1968 Hou21 (M)

League Club	Source	Date Signed	Seasons Played	Apps	Subs	Gls
Bolton W	Fortuna Sittard (Holl)	08.94	94-95	51	4	7
West Bromwich A	Tr	03.96	95-00	208	19	30
Stockport Co	Tr	09.01	01	8	1	0
Hull C	Tr	11.01	01	17	5	0

SNELL Albert Edward
Dunscroft, 7 February, 1931 (WH)

League Club	Source	Date Signed	Seasons Played	Apps	Subs	Gls
Sunderland	Doncaster Rov (Am)	08.49	52-54	9	-	1
Halifax T	Tr	11.55	55-56	25	-	0

SNELL Victor (Vic) Derek Robert
Ipswich, 29 October, 1927 (CD)

League Club	Source	Date Signed	Seasons Played	Apps	Subs	Gls
Ipswich T	Jnrs	11.45	49-58	64	-	2

SNIJDERS Mark Werner
Alkmaar, Holland, 12 March, 1972 (CD)

League Club	Source	Date Signed	Seasons Played	Apps	Subs	Gls
Port Vale	AZ67 Alkmaar (Holl)	09.97	97-99	46	9	2

SNODIN Glynn
Rotherham, 14 February, 1960 (FB)

League Club	Source	Date Signed	Seasons Played	Apps	Subs	Gls
Doncaster Rov	App	10.77	76-84	288	21	59
Sheffield Wed	Tr	06.85	85-86	51	8	1
Leeds U	Tr	07.87	87-90	83	11	10
Oldham Ath	L	08.91	91	8	0	1
Rotherham U	L	02.92	91	3	0	0
Barnsley	Heart of Midlothian	07.93	93-94	18	7	0

SNODIN Ian
Thrybergh, 15 August, 1963 EYth/Eu21-4/EB (M)

League Club	Source	Date Signed	Seasons Played	Apps	Subs	Gls
Doncaster Rov	App	08.80	79-84	181	7	27
Leeds U	Tr	05.85	85-86	51	0	6
Everton	Tr	01.87	86-94	142	6	3
Sunderland	L	10.94	94	6	0	0
Oldham Ath	Tr	01.95	94-96	55	2	0
Scarborough	Tr	08.97	97	33	2	0

SNOOKES Eric
Birmingham, 6 March, 1955 (FB)

League Club	Source	Date Signed	Seasons Played	Apps	Subs	Gls
Preston NE	App	03.73	72-73	20	0	0
Crewe Alex	Tr	07.74	74	33	1	0
Southport	Tr	07.75	75-77	106	4	2
Rochdale	Tr	07.78	78-82	183	0	1
Bolton W	Tr	07.83	83	6	0	0

SNOW Simon Gordon
Sheffield, 3 April, 1966 (F)

League Club	Source	Date Signed	Seasons Played	Apps	Subs	Gls
Scunthorpe U	App	08.83	82-83	1	1	0
Preston NE	Sutton T	08.89	89	1	0	0

SNOWBALL Raymond (Ray)
Sunderland, 10 March, 1932 (G)

League Club	Source	Date Signed	Seasons Played	Apps	Subs	Gls
Darlington (Am)	Crook T	10.64	64-66	13	0	0

SNOWDEN Trevor
Sunderland, 4 October, 1973 (W)

League Club	Source	Date Signed	Seasons Played	Apps	Subs	Gls
Rochdale	Seaham Red Star	02.93	92-93	8	6	0

SNOWDON Brian Victor
Bishop Auckland, 1 January, 1935 Died 1995 (CD)

League Club	Source	Date Signed	Seasons Played	Apps	Subs	Gls
Blackpool		09.52	55-59	18	-	1
Portsmouth	Tr	10.59	59-63	114	-	0
Millwall	Tr	10.63	63-66	128	0	0
Crystal Palace	Margate	02.69	68	1	4	0

SOAMES David Michael
Grimsby, 10 December, 1984 (F)

League Club	Source	Date Signed	Seasons Played	Apps	Subs	Gls
Grimsby T	Sch	07.04	02-04	0	24	1

SOARES Louie Pierre
Reading, 8 January, 1985 (M)

League Club	Source	Date Signed	Seasons Played	Apps	Subs	Gls
Reading	Sch	07.04				
Bristol Rov	L	05.05	04	0	1	0

SOARES Thomas (Tom) James
Reading, 10 July, 1986 EYth (M)

League Club	Source	Date Signed	Seasons Played	Apps	Subs	Gls
Crystal Palace	Sch	09.04	03-04	16	9	0

SOBERS Jerrome Roxin
London, 18 April, 1986 (CD)

League Club	Source	Date Signed	Seasons Played	Apps	Subs	Gls
Ipswich T	Ford U	05.04				
Brentford	L	03.05	04	1	0	1

SOBIECH Jorg
Gelsenkirchen, Germany, 15 January, 1969 (FB)

League Club	Source	Date Signed	Seasons Played	Apps	Subs	Gls
Stoke C	NEC Nijmegen (Holl)	03.98	97	3	0	0

SODEN Walter James William
Birmingham, 22 January, 1921 Died 1977 (CF)

League Club	Source	Date Signed	Seasons Played	Apps	Subs	Gls
Coventry C	Boldmere St Michael's	03.48	47-48	2	-	0

SODJE Idoro Akpoeyere (Akpo) Ujoma
Greenwich, 31 January, 1981 (F)

League Club	Source	Date Signed	Seasons Played	Apps	Subs	Gls
Huddersfield T	Erith & Belvedere	09.04	04	1	6	0
Darlington	L	03.05	04	1	6	1

SODJE Efetobore (Efe)
Greenwich, 5 October, 1972 Nigeria 10 (CD)

League Club	Source	Date Signed	Seasons Played	Apps	Subs	Gls
Macclesfield T	Stevenage Borough	07.97	97-98	83	0	6
Luton T	Tr	08.99	99	5	4	0
Colchester U	Tr	03.00	99	3	0	0
Crewe Alex	Tr	07.00	00-02	86	12	3
Huddersfield T	Tr	08.03	03-04	61	6	5
Yeovil T	Tr	03.05	04	6	0	2

SODJE Samuel (Sam) Okeremute
Greenwich, 29 May, 1979 (FB)

League Club	Source	Date Signed	Seasons Played	Apps	Subs	Gls
Brentford	Margate	07.04	04	40	0	7

SOFIANE Youssef
Lyon, France, 8 July, 1984 FrYth (F)

League Club	Source	Date Signed	Seasons Played	Apps	Subs	Gls
West Ham U	Auxerre (Fr)	06.02	03	0	1	0
Notts Co	L	09.04	04	2	2	0

SOLAN Kenneth (Ken)
Middlesbrough, 13 October, 1948 Died 1971 (M)

League Club	Source	Date Signed	Seasons Played	Apps	Subs	Gls
Middlesbrough		11.66				
Hartlepool	L	10.68	68	6	0	1
Darlington	L	03.69	68	6	0	1

SOLANO Nolberto (Nobby) Albino
Lima, Peru, 12 December, 1974 PeruYth/Peru 75 (W)

League Club	Source	Date Signed	Seasons Played	Apps	Subs	Gls
Newcastle U	Boca Juniors (Arg)	08.98	98-03	158	14	29
Aston Villa	Tr	01.04	03-04	42	4	8

SOLBAKKEN Stale
Kongsvinger, Norway, 27 February, 1968 Norway int (M)

League Club	Source	Date Signed	Seasons Played	Apps	Subs	Gls
Wimbledon	Lillestrom (Nor)	10.97	97	4	2	1

SOLEY Stephen (Steve)
Widnes, 22 April, 1971 ESemiPro-1 (M)

League Club	Source	Date Signed	Seasons Played	Apps	Subs	Gls
Portsmouth	Leek T	07.98	98	1	7	0
Macclesfield T	L	03.99	98	5	5	0
Carlisle U	Tr	08.99	99-01	75	8	16

SOLIS Mauricio Mora
Heredia, Costa Rica, 13 December, 1972 Costa Rica int (M)

League Club	Source	Date Signed	Seasons Played	Apps	Subs	Gls
Derby Co	CS Heridiano (CR)	03.97	96-97	3	8	0

SOLKHON Brett Michael
Canvey Island, 12 September, 1982 (CD)

League Club	Source	Date Signed	Seasons Played	Apps	Subs	Gls
Rushden & Diamonds	Arsenal (Jnrs)	07.00	01-02	1	1	0

SOLLITT Adam James
Sheffield, 22 June, 1977 ESemiPro-3 (G)

League Club	Source	Date Signed	Seasons Played	Apps	Subs	Gls
Barnsley	YT	07.95				
Northampton T	Kettering T	07.00	00-01	14	2	0
Rushden & Diamonds	Tr	08.02	02	3	0	0

SOLOMAN Jason Rafael
Welwyn Garden City, 6 October, 1970 EYth (FB)

League Club	Source	Date Signed	Seasons Played	Apps	Subs	Gls
Watford	YT	12.88	90-94	79	21	5
Peterborough U	L	01.95	94	4	0	0
Wycombe W	Tr	03.95	94-95	11	2	1
Wrexham	Tr	08.96	96	2	0	0
Fulham	Tr	11.96	96	1	3	0

SOLSKJAER Ole Gunnar
Kristiansund, Norway, 26 February, 1973 Nou21-19/No-62 (F)

League Club	Source	Date Signed	Seasons Played	Apps	Subs	Gls
Manchester U	Molde FK (Nor)	07.96	96-03	142	71	84

SOLTVEDT Trond Egil
Voss, Norway, 15 February, 1967 Norway 4 (M)

League Club	Source	Date Signed	Seasons Played	Apps	Subs	Gls
Coventry C	Rosenborg (Nor)	07.97	97-98	47	10	3
Southampton	Tr	08.99	99-00	20	10	2
Sheffield Wed	Tr	02.01	00-02	74	0	2

SOMA Ragnvald
Bryne, Norway, 10 November, 1979 NoYth/Nou21-3 (FB)

League Club	Source	Date Signed	Seasons Played	Apps	Subs	Gls
West Ham U	Bryne (Nor)	01.01	00-01	3	4	0

SOMERFIELD Alfred (Alf) George
South Kirkby, 22 March, 1918 Died 1985 (CF)

League Club	Source	Date Signed	Seasons Played	Apps	Subs	Gls
Mansfield T	Frickley Colliery	05.38	38	14	-	6
Wolverhampton W	Tr	03.39				
Wrexham	Tr	06.47	46	2	-	1
Crystal Palace	Tr	09.47	47	10	-	3

SOMERS Michael (Micky) Robert
Mapperley, 27 February, 1945 (W)

League Club	Source	Date Signed	Seasons Played	Apps	Subs	Gls
Chelsea	Nottingham F (Am)	11.62				
Torquay U	Tr	05.64	64-65	39	1	3
Hartlepools U	Tr	07.66	66-68	63	3	3

SOMMEIL David
Point-a-Pitre, Guadeloupe, 10 August, 1974 FrB-1 (CD)

League Club	Source	Date Signed	Seasons Played	Apps	Subs	Gls
Manchester C	Bordeaux (Fr)	01.03	02-04	33	0	2

SOMMER Jurgen Peterson
New York, USA, 27 February, 1969 USA int (G)

League Club	Source	Date Signed	Seasons Played	Apps	Subs	Gls
Luton T	Indiana Univ (USA)	09.91	93-95	82	0	0
Brighton & Hove A	L	11.91	91	1	0	0
Torquay U	L	10.92	92	10	0	0
Queens Park Rgrs	Tr	08.95	95-96	66	0	0

SOMNER Matthew (Matt) James
Isleworth, 8 December, 1982 Wu21-2 (FB)

League Club	Source	Date Signed	Seasons Played	Apps	Subs	Gls
Brentford	YT	07.01	00-04	72	12	1
Cambridge U	Tr	12.04	04	24	0	0

SONG Bahanag Rigobert
Nkenlicock, Cameroon, 1 July, 1976 Cameroon 70 (CD)

League Club	Source	Date Signed	Seasons Played	Apps	Subs	Gls
Liverpool	Salernitana (It)	01.99	98-00	27	7	0
West Ham U	Tr	11.00	00-01	23	1	0

SONKO Ibrahima (Ibu)
Bignola, Senegal, 22 January, 1981 Seu21 (CD)

League Club	Source	Date Signed	Seasons Played	Apps	Subs	Gls
Brentford	Grenoble (Fr)	08.02	02-03	79	1	8
Reading	Tr	07.04	04	35	4	1

SONNER Daniel (Danny) James
Wigan, 9 January, 1972 NIB-4/NI-13 (M)

League Club	Source	Date Signed	Seasons Played	Apps	Subs	Gls
Burnley	Wigan Ath (YT)	08.90	90-92	1	5	0
Bury	L	11.92	92	5	0	3
Ipswich T	Erzgebirge Aue (Ger)	06.96	96-98	28	28	3
Sheffield Wed	Tr	10.98	98-99	42	11	3
Birmingham C	Tr	08.00	00-01	32	9	2
Walsall	Tr	08.02	02	20	4	4
Nottingham F	Tr	08.03	03	19	9	0
Peterborough U	Tr	08.04	04	11	4	0
Port Vale	L	02.05	04	13	0	0

SOO Hong Ying (Frank)
Buxton, 12 March, 1914 Died 1991 EWar-9 (WH)

League Club	Source	Date Signed	Seasons Played	Apps	Subs	Gls
Stoke C	Prescot Cables	01.33	33-38	173	-	5
Leicester C	Tr	09.45				
Luton T	Tr	07.46	46-47	71	-	4

SORENSEN Thomas
Fredericia, Denmark, 12 June, 1976 Deu21-6/DeB-1/De-48 (G)

League Club	Source	Date Signed	Seasons Played	Apps	Subs	Gls
Sunderland	OB Odense (Den)	08.98	98-02	171	0	0
Aston Villa	Tr	08.03	03-04	74	0	0

SORONDO Amaro Gonzalo
Montevideo, Uruguay, 9 October, 1979 Uruguay 26 (CD)

League Club	Source	Date Signed	Seasons Played	Apps	Subs	Gls
Crystal Palace (L)	Inter Milan (It)	09.04	04	16	4	0

SORRELL Anthony (Tony) Charles
Hornchurch, 17 October, 1966 (M)

League Club	Source	Date Signed	Seasons Played	Apps	Subs	Gls
Maidstone U	Bishops Stortford	08.88	89-90	46	9	8
Colchester U	Boston U	11.92	92	4	1	1
Barnet	Tr	02.93	92	8	0	2

SORRELL Dennis James
Lambeth, 7 October, 1940 (WH)

League Club	Source	Date Signed	Seasons Played	Apps	Subs	Gls
Leyton Orient	Woodford T	10.57	58-60	37	-	1
Chelsea	Tr	02.62	61-63	3	-	0
Leyton Orient	Tr	09.64	64-66	74	0	3

SORVEL Neil Simon
Whiston, 2 March, 1973 (M)

League Club	Source	Date Signed	Seasons Played	Apps	Subs	Gls
Crewe Alex	YT	07.91	91	5	4	0
Macclesfield T	Tr	08.92	97-98	79	7	7
Crewe Alex	Tr	06.99	99-04	229	21	13

SOUNESS Graeme James
Edinburgh, 6 May, 1953 SSch/Su23-2/S-54 (M)

League Club	Source	Date Signed	Seasons Played	Apps	Subs	Gls
Tottenham H	App	05.70				
Middlesbrough	Tr	01.73	72-77	174	2	22
Liverpool	Tr	01.78	77-83	246	1	38

SOUTAR Timothy (Tim) John
Oxford, 25 February, 1946 (IF)

League Club	Source	Date Signed	Seasons Played	Apps	Subs	Gls
Brentford	Jnrs	07.63	63	1	-	0

SOUTAR William (Bill)
Dundee, 3 March, 1931 (FB)

League Club	Source	Date Signed	Seasons Played	Apps	Subs	Gls
Burnley	Broughty Ath	12.53				
Chester	Tr	06.57	57-59	51	-	1

SOUTER Donald (Don) Davidson
Hammersmith, 1 December, 1961 (CD)

League Club	Source	Date Signed	Seasons Played	Apps	Subs	Gls
Ipswich T	App	01.79				
Barnsley	Tr	08.82	82	19	2	0
Aldershot	Tr	08.83	83-84	45	0	0

SOUTER Ryan John
Bedford, 5 February, 1978 (CD)

League Club	Source	Date Signed	Seasons Played	Apps	Subs	Gls
Bury	Weston-super-Mare	01.99	98-99	2	3	0

SOUTH Alexander (Alex) William
Brighton, 7 July, 1931 (CD)

League Club	Source	Date Signed	Seasons Played	Apps	Subs	Gls
Brighton & Hove A	Whitehawk BC	03.49	49-54	81	-	4
Liverpool	Tr	12.54	54	6	-	1
Halifax T	Tr	10.56	56-64	301	-	12

SOUTH John Alan
Bow, 30 November, 1952 (CD)

League Club	Source	Date Signed	Seasons Played	Apps	Subs	Gls
Colchester U	Orient (Am)	07.72	72	4	0	0

SOUTH John Edward
Lambeth, 8 April, 1948 (CF)

League Club	Source	Date Signed	Seasons Played	Apps	Subs	Gls
Brentford	Fulham (App)	11.66	66	1	0	0

SOUTHALL Neville
Llandudno, 16 September, 1958 W-92 (G)

League Club	Source	Date Signed	Seasons Played	Apps	Subs	Gls
Bury	Winsford U	06.80	80	39	0	0
Everton	Tr	07.81	81-97	578	0	0
Port Vale	L	01.83	82	9	0	0
Southend U	L	12.97	97	9	0	0
Stoke C	Tr	02.98	97	12	0	0
Torquay U	Doncaster Rov	12.98	98-99	53	0	0
Bradford C	Tr	02.00	99	1	0	0

SOUTHALL Leslie Nicholas (Nicky)
Stockton, 28 January, 1972 (W)

League Club	Source	Date Signed	Seasons Played	Apps	Subs	Gls
Hartlepool U	Darlington (Jnrs)	02.91	91-94	118	20	24
Grimsby T	Tr	07.95	95-97	55	17	6
Gillingham	Tr	12.97	97-00	141	13	17
Bolton W	Tr	07.01	01	10	8	1
Norwich C	L	09.02	02	4	5	0
Gillingham	Tr	12.02	02-04	86	6	2

SOUTHALL Robert
Rotherham, 10 May, 1922 Died 1979 (WH)

League Club	Source	Date Signed	Seasons Played	Apps	Subs	Gls
Chesterfield	Rother Works	12.43	47-52	127	-	11

SOUTHAM James (Jack) Henry
Willenhall, 19 August, 1917 Died 1996 (FB)

League Club	Source	Date Signed	Seasons Played	Apps	Subs	Gls
West Bromwich A	Shornhill Rec	12.42				
Newport Co	Tr	05.46	46	8	-	0
Birmingham C	Tr	11.46	47	1	-	0
Northampton T	Tr	06.49	49-54	145	-	1

SOUTHERN Keith William
Gateshead, 24 April, 1981 (M)

League Club	Source	Date Signed	Seasons Played	Apps	Subs	Gls
Everton	YT	05.99				
Blackpool	Tr	08.02	02-04	78	15	9

SOUTHEY Peter Charles
Parsons Green, 4 January, 1962 Died 1983 (FB)

League Club	Source	Date Signed	Seasons Played	Apps	Subs	Gls
Tottenham H	App	10.79	79	1	0	0

SOUTHGATE Gareth
Watford, 3 September, 1970 E-57 (CD)

League Club	Source	Date Signed	Seasons Played	Apps	Subs	Gls
Crystal Palace	YT	01.89	90-94	148	4	15
Aston Villa	Tr	07.95	95-00	191	0	7
Middlesbrough	Tr	07.01	01-04	136	0	4

SOUTHON Jamie Peter
Dagenham, 13 October, 1974 (M)

League Club	Source	Date Signed	Seasons Played	Apps	Subs	Gls
Southend U	YT	07.93	92	0	1	0

SOUTHREN Thomas (Tommy) Cansfield
Sunderland, 1 August, 1927 Died 2004 (W)

League Club	Source	Date Signed	Seasons Played	Apps	Subs	Gls
West Ham U	Peartree OB	12.49	50-53	64	-	3
Aston Villa	Tr	12.54	54-58	63	-	6
Bournemouth	Tr	10.58	58-59	64	-	11

SOUTHWELL Aubrey Allen
Grantham, 21 August, 1921 Died 2005 (FB)

League Club	Source	Date Signed	Seasons Played	Apps	Subs	Gls
Notts Co	Nottingham F (Am)	12.44	46-56	328	-	2

SOWDEN Maurice
Doncaster, 21 October, 1954 (M)

League Club	Source	Date Signed	Seasons Played	Apps	Subs	Gls
Scunthorpe U	App	10.72	72	3	0	0

SOWDEN Peter (Paddy) Tasker
Bradford, 1 May, 1929 (IF)

League Club	Source	Date Signed	Seasons Played	Apps	Subs	Gls
Blackpool	Jnrs	06.47				
Hull C	Bacup Borough	09.48				
Aldershot	Elgin C	10.50	50	4	-	0
Hull C	Tr	08.51				
Gillingham	Tr	08.52	52-55	134	-	27
Accrington St	Tr	09.56	56-57	54	-	13
Wrexham	Tr	06.58	58-59	38	-	4

SOWDEN William (Billy)
Manchester, 8 December, 1930 (CF)

League Club	Source	Date Signed	Seasons Played	Apps	Subs	Gls
Manchester C	Greenwood Victoria	04.49	52-53	11	-	2
Chesterfield	Tr	11.54	54-56	97	-	59
Stockport Co	Tr	06.57	57	15	-	7

SOWERBY William Henry Roy
Hull, 31 August, 1932 (IF)

League Club	Source	Date Signed	Seasons Played	Apps	Subs	Gls
Wolverhampton W	Pilkington Rec	05.50				
Grimsby T	Tr	01.54	53-54	12	-	1

SPACKMAN Nigel James
Romsey, 2 December, 1960 (M)

League Club	Source	Date Signed	Seasons Played	Apps	Subs	Gls
Bournemouth	Andover	05.80	80-82	118	1	10
Chelsea	Tr	06.83	83-86	139	2	12
Liverpool	Tr	02.87	86-88	39	12	0
Queens Park Rgrs	Tr	02.89	88-89	27	2	1
Chelsea	Glasgow Rgrs	09.92	92-95	60	7	0
Sheffield U	Tr	06.96	96	19	4	0

SPALDING William (Bill)
Glasgow, 24 November, 1926 Died 1999 (W)

League Club	Source	Date Signed	Seasons Played	Apps	Subs	Gls
Bristol C	Ballymena U	01.50	49-50	10	-	0

SPARHAM Sean Ricky
Bexley, 4 December, 1968 (FB)

League Club	Source	Date Signed	Seasons Played	Apps	Subs	Gls
Millwall	Jnrs	05.87	87-89	22	6	0
Brentford	L	03.90	89	5	0	1

SPARK Alexander (Alex) McAlpine
Stenhousemuir, 16 October, 1949 (CD)

League Club	Source	Date Signed	Seasons Played	Apps	Subs	Gls
Preston NE	Jnrs	11.66	67-75	207	18	6
Bradford C	Motherwell	12.76	76-77	32	2	0

SPARKS Christopher (Chris) James
Islington, 22 May, 1960 (FB)

League Club	Source	Date Signed	Seasons Played	Apps	Subs	Gls
Crystal Palace	App	11.77				
Reading	L	08.79	79	3	0	0

SPARROW Brian Edward
Bethnal Green, 24 June, 1962 (FB)

League Club	Source	Date Signed	Seasons Played	Apps	Subs	Gls
Arsenal	App	02.80	83	2	0	0
Wimbledon	L	01.83	82	17	0	1
Millwall	L	12.83	83	5	0	2
Gillingham	L	01.84	83	5	0	1
Crystal Palace	Tr	07.84	84-86	62	1	2

SPARROW John Paul
Bethnal Green, 3 June, 1957 ESch/EYth (FB)

League Club	Source	Date Signed	Seasons Played	Apps	Subs	Gls
Chelsea	App	08.74	73-79	63	6	2
Millwall	L	03.79	78	7	0	0
Exeter C	Tr	01.81	80-82	62	1	3

SPARROW Matthew (Matt) Ronald
Wembley, 3 October, 1981 (M)

League Club	Source	Date Signed	Seasons Played	Apps	Subs	Gls
Scunthorpe U	YT	07.01	99-04	145	25	22

SPARROW Paul
Wandsworth, 24 March, 1975 (FB)

League Club	Source	Date Signed	Seasons Played	Apps	Subs	Gls
Crystal Palace	YT	07.93	95	1	0	0
Preston NE	Tr	03.96	95-97	20	0	0
Rochdale	Tr	07.98	98	21	4	2

SPAVIN Alan
Lancaster, 20 February, 1942 (M)

League Club	Source	Date Signed	Seasons Played	Apps	Subs	Gls
Preston NE	Jnrs	08.59	60-73	411	6	26
Preston NE	Washington (USA)	11.77	77-78	3	4	0

SPEAK Christopher (Chris)
Preston, 20 August, 1973 (FB)

League Club	Source	Date Signed	Seasons Played	Apps	Subs	Gls
Blackpool	Jnrs	07.92	92	0	1	0

SPEAKMAN Robert (Rob)
Swansea, 5 December, 1980 (F)

League Club	Source	Date Signed	Seasons Played	Apps	Subs	Gls
Exeter C	YT	07.99	98-00	4	15	3

SPEAKMAN Samuel (Sammy)
Huyton, 27 January, 1934 (W)

League Club	Source	Date Signed	Seasons Played	Apps	Subs	Gls
Bolton W		09.51				
Middlesbrough	Tr	07.53				
Tranmere Rov	Tr	09.54	54-55	68	-	9

SPEARE James (Jamie) Peter Vincent
Liverpool, 5 November, 1976 (G)

League Club	Source	Date Signed	Seasons Played	Apps	Subs	Gls
Everton	YT	07.95				
Darlington	Tr	03.97	96	3	0	0

SPEARING Anthony (Tony)
Romford, 7 October, 1964 EYth (FB)

League Club	Source	Date Signed	Seasons Played	Apps	Subs	Gls
Norwich C	App	08.82	83-87	67	2	0
Stoke C	L	11.84	84	9	0	0
Oxford U	L	02.85	84	5	0	0
Leicester C	Tr	07.88	88-90	71	2	1
Plymouth Arg	Tr	07.91	91-92	35	0	0
Peterborough U	Tr	01.93	92-96	105	6	2

SPEARRITT Edward (Eddie) Alfred
Lowestoft, 31 January, 1947 (FB)

League Club	Source	Date Signed	Seasons Played	Apps	Subs	Gls
Ipswich T	App	02.65	65-68	62	10	13
Brighton & Hove A	Tr	01.69	68-73	203	7	22
Carlisle U	Tr	06.74	74-75	29	2	1
Gillingham	Tr	08.76	76	19	0	1

SPEARS Alan Frederick
Amble, 27 December, 1938 ESch (W)

League Club	Source	Date Signed	Seasons Played	Apps	Subs	Gls
Newcastle U	Jnrs	02.56				
Millwall	Tr	06.60	60-62	31	-	6
Lincoln C	Tr	07.63	63	2	-	0

SPECTOR Jonathan Michael Paul
Chicago, USA, 1 March, 1986 UsYth (FB)

League Club	Source	Date Signed	Seasons Played	Apps	Subs	Gls
Manchester U	Chicago Sockers (USA)	11.03	04	2	1	0

SPECTOR Miles David
Hendon, 4 August, 1934 EYth/EAmat (W)

League Club	Source	Date Signed	Seasons Played	Apps	Subs	Gls
Chelsea (Am)	Jnrs	05.52	52-53	3	-	0
Millwall (Am)	Hendon	05.56	56	1	-	0

SPEDDING Duncan
Frimley, 7 September, 1977 (FB)

League Club	Source	Date Signed	Seasons Played	Apps	Subs	Gls
Southampton	YT	05.96	97	4	3	0
Northampton T	Tr	07.98	98-02	107	16	2

SPEDDING Thomas (Tom) William
Tynemouth, 8 December, 1925 (CD)

League Club	Source	Date Signed	Seasons Played	Apps	Subs	Gls
Doncaster Rov		03.49	48	1	-	0

SPEED Gary Andrew
Mancot, 8 September, 1969 WYth/Wu21-3/W-85 (M)

League Club	Source	Date Signed	Seasons Played	Apps	Subs	Gls
Leeds U	YT	06.88	88-95	231	17	39
Everton	Tr	07.96	96-97	58	0	16
Newcastle U	Tr	02.98	97-03	206	7	29
Bolton W	Tr	07.04	04	37	1	1

SPEED Leslie (Les)
Caergwrle, 3 October, 1923 (FB)

League Club	Source	Date Signed	Seasons Played	Apps	Subs	Gls
Wrexham	Llandudno	04.45	46-54	211	-	0

SPEEDIE David Robert
Glenrothes, 20 February, 1960 Su21-1/S-10 (F)

League Club	Source	Date Signed	Seasons Played	Apps	Subs	Gls
Barnsley	Jnrs	10.78	78-79	10	13	0
Darlington	Tr	06.80	80-81	88	0	21
Chelsea	Tr	06.82	82-86	155	7	47
Coventry C	Tr	07.87	87-90	121	1	31
Liverpool	Tr	02.91	90	8	4	6
Blackburn Rov	Tr	08.91	91	34	2	23
Southampton	Tr	07.92	92	11	0	0
Birmingham C	L	10.92	92	10	0	2
West Bromwich A	L	01.93	92	7	0	2
West Ham U	L	03.93	92	11	0	4
Leicester C	Tr	07.93	93	37	0	12

SPEIGHT Martyn Stephen
Stockton, 26 July, 1978 (CD)

League Club	Source	Date Signed	Seasons Played	Apps	Subs	Gls
Doncaster Rov	YT	07.96	95	1	0	0

SPEIGHT Michael (Mick)
Upton, 1 November, 1951 EB (M)

League Club	Source	Date Signed	Seasons Played	Apps	Subs	Gls
Sheffield U	App	05.69	71-79	184	15	14
Blackburn Rov	Tr	07.80	80-81	50	1	4
Grimsby T	Tr	08.82	82-83	35	3	2
Chester C	Tr	08.84	84-85	40	0	1

SPEIRS Walter **Gardner**
Airdrie, 14 April, 1963 SYth (M)

League Club	Source	Date Signed	Seasons Played	Apps	Subs	Gls
Hartlepool U	St Mirren	08.89	89	0	1	0

SPELMAN Isaac
Newcastle, 9 March, 1914 Died 2003 (WH)

League Club	Source	Date Signed	Seasons Played	Apps	Subs	Gls
Leeds U	Usworth Colliery	03.33				
Southend U	Tr	05.35	35-36	43	-	3
Tottenham H	Tr	05.37	37-38	28	-	2
Hartlepools U	Tr	05.46	46	25	-	0

SPELMAN Michael (Mike) Thomas
Newcastle, 8 December, 1950 ESch (M)

League Club	Source	Date Signed	Seasons Played	Apps	Subs	Gls
Wolverhampton W	Whitley Bay	11.69				
Watford	Tr	08.71				
Hartlepool	Tr	10.71	71-76	115	6	4
Darlington	L	12.72	72	4	0	0

SPELMAN Ronald (Ron) Edward
Blofield, 22 May, 1938 (W)

League Club	Source	Date Signed	Seasons Played	Apps	Subs	Gls
Norwich C	CNSOBU	08.56	57-60	2	-	0
Northampton T	Tr	11.60	60-61	33	-	3
Bournemouth	Tr	03.62	61-63	28	-	4
Watford	Tr	09.63	63-64	40	-	3
Oxford U	Tr	05.65	65	15	1	1

SPENCE Alan Nicholson
Seaham, 7 February, 1940 EYth (F)

League Club	Source	Date Signed	Seasons Played	Apps	Subs	Gls
Sunderland	Murton Colliery Jnrs	05.57	57	5	-	1
Darlington	Tr	06.60	60-61	24	-	11
Southport	Tr	07.62	62-68	225	5	98
Oldham Ath	Tr	12.68	68-69	26	1	12
Chester	Tr	12.69	69	5	4	2

SPENCE Colin
Glasgow, 7 January, 1960 (F)

League Club	Source	Date Signed	Seasons Played	Apps	Subs	Gls
Crewe Alex	App	02.78	76-78	10	8	1

SPENCE Derek William
Belfast, 18 January, 1952 NI-29 (F)

League Club	Source	Date Signed	Seasons Played	Apps	Subs	Gls
Oldham Ath	Crusaders	09.70	71-72	5	1	0
Bury	Tr	02.73	72-76	140	0	44
Blackpool	Tr	10.76	76	24	3	3
Blackpool	Olympiakos (Gre)	08.78	78-79	58	0	18
Southend U	Tr	12.79	79-81	100	4	32
Bury	HK Rgrs (HK)	08.83	83	9	4	1

SPENCE Joseph (Joe) Louis
Salford, 13 October, 1925 (CD)

League Club	Source	Date Signed	Seasons Played	Apps	Subs	Gls
Chesterfield	Buxton	01.48				
York C	Tr	07.50	50-53	110	-	0

SPENCE Richard (Dickie)
Platts Common, 18 July, 1908 Died 1983 E-2 (W)

League Club	Source	Date Signed	Seasons Played	Apps	Subs	Gls
Barnsley	Platts Common WMC	02.33	32-34	64	-	25
Chelsea	Tr	10.34	34-47	221	-	62

SPENCE Ronald (Ron)
Spennymoor, 7 January, 1927 Died 1996 (WH)

League Club	Source	Date Signed	Seasons Played	Apps	Subs	Gls
York C	Rossington Colliery	03.48	47-58	280	-	25

SPENCE Joseph **William (Bill)**
Hartlepool, 10 January, 1926 (CD)

League Club	Source	Date Signed	Seasons Played	Apps	Subs	Gls
Portsmouth		03.47	49-50	19	-	0
Queens Park Rgrs	Tr	12.51	51-53	56	-	0

SPENCER Anthony (Tony) Raymond
Chiswick, 23 April, 1965 (FB)

League Club	Source	Date Signed	Seasons Played	Apps	Subs	Gls
Brentford	App	04.83	81-83	17	1	0
Aldershot	L	12.84	84	10	0	0

SPENCER Damian Michael
Ascot, 19 September, 1981 (F)

League Club	Source	Date Signed	Seasons Played	Apps	Subs	Gls
Bristol C	YT	06.00	99-00	8	5	1
Exeter C	L	03.01	00	2	4	0
Cheltenham T	Tr	08.02	02-04	53	54	23

SPENCER Derek
Coventry, 10 January, 1931 Died 1989 (G)

League Club	Source	Date Signed	Seasons Played	Apps	Subs	Gls
Coventry C	Lockheed Leamington	12.51	51-52	20	-	0

SPENCER Harold John
Burnley, 30 April, 1919 Died 2003 (WH)

League Club	Source	Date Signed	Seasons Played	Apps	Subs	Gls
Burnley	Jnrs	09.37	46	4	-	1
Wrexham	Tr	07.50	50	11	-	0

SPENCER James Matthew
Stockport, 11 April, 1985 (G)

League Club	Source	Date Signed	Seasons Played	Apps	Subs	Gls
Stockport Co	YT	04.02	01-04	41	1	0

SPENCER John
Glasgow, 11 September, 1970 SSch/SYth/Su21-3/S-14 (F)

League Club	Source	Date Signed	Seasons Played	Apps	Subs	Gls
Chelsea	Glasgow Rgrs	08.92	92-96	75	28	36
Queens Park Rgrs	Tr	11.96	96-97	47	1	22
Everton	Tr	03.98	97-98	5	4	0

SPENCER John Raymond
Bradfield, 20 November, 1934 EYth (IF)

League Club	Source	Date Signed	Seasons Played	Apps	Subs	Gls
Sheffield U	Jnrs	06.54	54-56	24	-	10

SPENCER John (Jack) Shepherd
Bacup, 24 August, 1920 Died 1966 (IF)

League Club	Source	Date Signed	Seasons Played	Apps	Subs	Gls
Burnley	Bacup U	06.48	48-50	37	-	8
Accrington St	Tr	06.51	51	29	-	7

SPENCER Leslie (Les)
Manchester, 16 September, 1936 (IF)

League Club	Source	Date Signed	Seasons Played	Apps	Subs	Gls
Rochdale		01.58	57-59	74	-	17
Luton T	Tr	07.60	60	7	-	1

SPENCER Raymond (Ray)
Birmingham, 25 March, 1933 ESch (WH)

League Club	Source	Date Signed	Seasons Played	Apps	Subs	Gls
Aston Villa	Jnrs	06.50				
Darlington	Tr	03.58	57-60	97	-	5
Torquay U	Tr	06.61	61-63	59	-	1

SPENCER Simon Dean
Islington, 10 September, 1976 (M)

League Club	Source	Date Signed	Seasons Played	Apps	Subs	Gls
Tottenham H	YT	07.95				
Brentford	Tr	07.97	97	1	0	0

SPENCER Thomas (Tommy) Hannah
Glasgow, 28 November, 1945 (CD)

League Club	Source	Date Signed	Seasons Played	Apps	Subs	Gls
Southampton	Glasgow Celtic	07.65	65	3	0	0
York C	Tr	06.66	66-67	54	3	21
Workington	Tr	03.68	67-71	167	0	10
Lincoln C	Tr	01.72	71-73	67	7	10
Rotherham U	Tr	07.74	74-77	137	1	10

SPENDER Simon
Mold, 15 November, 1985 WYth/Wu21-2 (FB)

League Club	Source	Date Signed	Seasons Played	Apps	Subs	Gls
Wrexham	Sch	•	03-04	12	7	0

SPERONI Julian
Buenos Aires, Argentina, 18 May, 1979 (G)

League Club	Source	Date Signed	Seasons Played	Apps	Subs	Gls
Crystal Palace	Dundee	07.04	04	6	0	0

SPERREVIK Tim
Bergen, Norway, 1 January, 1976 (F)

League Club	Source	Date Signed	Seasons Played	Apps	Subs	Gls
Hartlepool U	United Fana (Nor)	08.00	00	4	11	1

SPERRIN Martyn Robin
Edmonton, 6 December, 1956 (F)

League Club	Source	Date Signed	Seasons Played	Apps	Subs	Gls
Luton T	Edgware T	10.77	77	0	1	0

SPERRIN William (Billy) Thomas
Wood Green, 9 April, 1922 Died 2000 (IF)

League Club	Source	Date Signed	Seasons Played	Apps	Subs	Gls
Brentford	Guildford C	09.49	49-55	90	-	27

SPERRING George Burgess
Epsom, 30 April, 1935 (CF)

League Club	Source	Date Signed	Seasons Played	Apps	Subs	Gls
Gillingham (Am)		07.55	55	1	-	0

SPERTI Francesco (Franco)
Italy, 28 January, 1955 (FB)

League Club	Source	Date Signed	Seasons Played	Apps	Subs	Gls
Swindon T	App	01.73	73	1	0	0

SPICER Edwin (Eddie)
Liverpool, 20 September, 1922 Died 2004 ESch (FB)

League Club	Source	Date Signed	Seasons Played	Apps	Subs	Gls
Liverpool	Jnrs	10.39	46-53	158	-	2

SPICER John William
Romford, 13 September, 1983 EYth/Eu20 (M)

League Club	Source	Date Signed	Seasons Played	Apps	Subs	Gls
Arsenal	YT	07.01				
Bournemouth	Tr	09.04	04	39	0	6

SPIERS George Smyth
Belfast, 3 September, 1941 (W)

League Club	Source	Date Signed	Seasons Played	Apps	Subs	Gls
Exeter C	Crusaders	08.63	63	5	-	0

SPIERS Richard (Dick) Alan Jesse
Benson, 27 November, 1937 Died 2000 (CD)

League Club	Source	Date Signed	Seasons Played	Apps	Subs	Gls
Reading	Cholsey U	10.55	55-69	451	2	3

SPILLER Daniel (Danny)
Maidstone, 10 October, 1981 (M)

League Club	Source	Date Signed	Seasons Played	Apps	Subs	Gls
Gillingham	YT	07.00	01-04	56	16	6

SPINK Anthony (Tony) Arthur
Doncaster, 16 November, 1929 (CF)

League Club	Source	Date Signed	Seasons Played	Apps	Subs	Gls
Sheffield Wed		12.49				
Chester	Tr	06.50	51-52	13	-	3
Workington	Weymouth	07.55				
Sunderland	Tr	12.55				
Tranmere Rov	Tr	06.56	56	7	-	3

SPINK Dean Peter
Birmingham, 22 January, 1967 (F)

League Club	Source	Date Signed	Seasons Played	Apps	Subs	Gls
Aston Villa	Halesowen T	07.89				
Scarborough	L	11.89	89	3	0	2
Bury	L	02.90	89	6	0	1
Shrewsbury T	Tr	03.90	89-96	244	29	52
Wrexham	Tr	07.97	97-99	72	13	9
Shrewsbury T	L	11.99	99	1	3	0

SPINK Nigel Philip
Chelmsford, 8 August, 1958 EB-2/FLge/E-1 (G)

League Club	Source	Date Signed	Seasons Played	Apps	Subs	Gls
Aston Villa	Chelmsford C	01.77	79-95	357	4	0
West Bromwich A	Tr	01.96	95-96	19	0	0
Millwall	Tr	09.97	97-99	44	0	0

SPINKS Henry Charles
Great Yarmouth, 1 February, 1920 (CF)

League Club	Source	Date Signed	Seasons Played	Apps	Subs	Gls
Norwich C (Am)	CEYMS	12.46	46	2	-	1

SPINNER Terence (Terry) James
Woking, 6 November, 1953 ESch (F)

League Club	Source	Date Signed	Seasons Played	Apps	Subs	Gls
Southampton	App	07.71	72-73	1	1	0
Walsall	Tr	07.74	74-75	10	6	5

SPIRING Peter John
Glastonbury, 13 December, 1950 EYth (M)

League Club	Source	Date Signed	Seasons Played	Apps	Subs	Gls
Bristol C	Jnrs	06.68	69-72	58	5	16
Liverpool	Tr	03.73				
Luton T	Tr	11.74	74-75	12	3	2
Hereford U	Tr	02.76	75-82	205	22	20

SPITTLE Paul David
Wolverhampton, 16 December, 1964 (M)

League Club	Source	Date Signed	Seasons Played	Apps	Subs	Gls
Oxford U	App	10.82				
Crewe Alex	Tr	08.83	83	4	2	1

SPOFFORTH David John
York, 21 March, 1969 (FB)

League Club	Source	Date Signed	Seasons Played	Apps	Subs	Gls
York C	Jnrs	07.87	87	3	0	0

SPOONER Nicholas (Nick) Michael
Manchester, 5 June, 1971 (FB)

League Club	Source	Date Signed	Seasons Played	Apps	Subs	Gls
Bolton W	YT	07.89	91-94	22	1	2
Oldham Ath	L	10.98	98	2	0	0
Chester C	Charleston (USA)	11.99	99	9	0	0

SPOONER Stephen (Steve) Alan
Sutton, 25 January, 1961 (M)

League Club	Source	Date Signed	Seasons Played	Apps	Subs	Gls
Derby Co	App	12.78	78-81	7	1	0
Halifax T	Tr	12.81	81-82	71	1	13
Chesterfield	Tr	07.83	83-85	89	4	14
Hereford U	Tr	07.86	86-87	84	0	19
York C	Tr	07.88	88-89	72	0	11
Rotherham U	Tr	07.90	90	15	4	1
Mansfield T	Tr	03.91	90-92	55	3	3
Blackpool	Tr	02.93	92	2	0	0
Chesterfield	Tr	10.93	93-94	11	1	0

SPRAGGON Frank
Marley Hill, 27 October, 1945 (CD)

League Club	Source	Date Signed	Seasons Played	Apps	Subs	Gls
Middlesbrough	App	11.62	63-75	277	3	3
Hartlepool	Minnesota (USA)	11.76	76	1	0	0

SPRAGUE Martyn Leslie
Risca, 10 April, 1949 (FB)

League Club	Source	Date Signed	Seasons Played	Apps	Subs	Gls
Newport Co	Lovells Ath	08.68	69-73	155	1	1

SPRAKE Gareth (Gary)
Winch Wen, 3 April, 1945 Wu23-5/W-37 (G)

League Club	Source	Date Signed	Seasons Played	Apps	Subs	Gls
Leeds U	App	05.62	61-72	380	0	0
Birmingham C	Tr	10.73	73-74	16	0	0

SPRATLEY Alan Sidney
Maidenhead, 5 June, 1949 (G)

League Club	Source	Date Signed	Seasons Played	Apps	Subs	Gls
Queens Park Rgrs	App	05.67	68-72	29	0	0
Swindon T	Tr	07.73	73	7	0	0

SPRATT Graham William
Leicester, 17 July, 1939 (G)

League Club	Source	Date Signed	Seasons Played	Apps	Subs	Gls
Coventry C	Oadby T	12.56	57-58	28	-	0

SPRATT Thomas (Tommy)
Cambois, 20 December, 1941 ESch/EYth (M)

League Club	Source	Date Signed	Seasons Played	Apps	Subs	Gls
Manchester U	Jnrs	12.59				
Bradford PA	Tr	02.61	60-63	118	-	45
Torquay U	Weymouth	07.65	65-66	60	1	19
Workington	Tr	01.67	66-67	51	1	14
York C	Tr	03.68	67-68	26	3	1
Workington	Tr	03.69	68-71	141	2	26
Stockport Co	Tr	06.72	72-73	65	0	6

SPRIDGEON Frederick (Fred) Arthur
Swansea, 13 July, 1935 (FB)

League Club	Source	Date Signed	Seasons Played	Apps	Subs	Gls
Leeds U	Jnrs	08.52				
Crewe Alex	Tr	07.56	56	7	-	0

SPRIGGS Stephen (Steve)
Armthorpe, 16 February, 1956 (M)

League Club	Source	Date Signed	Seasons Played	Apps	Subs	Gls
Huddersfield T	App	02.73	74	2	2	0
Cambridge U	Tr	07.75	75-86	411	5	58
Middlesbrough	L	03.87	86	3	0	0

SPRING Andrew (Andy) John
Gateshead, 17 November, 1965 (FB)

League Club	Source	Date Signed	Seasons Played	Apps	Subs	Gls
Coventry C	App	11.83	83-84	3	2	0
Bristol Rov	Tr	07.85	85	18	1	0
Cardiff C	L	10.85	85	1	0	0

SPRING Matthew John
Harlow, 17 November, 1979 (M)

League Club	Source	Date Signed	Seasons Played	Apps	Subs	Gls
Luton T	YT	07.97	97-03	243	7	25
Leeds U	Tr	07.04	04	4	9	1

SPRINGETT Peter John
Fulham, 8 May, 1946 Died 1997 EYth/Eu23-6 (G)

League Club	Source	Date Signed	Seasons Played	Apps	Subs	Gls
Queens Park Rgrs	App	05.63	62-66	137	0	0
Sheffield Wed	Tr	05.67	67-74	180	0	0
Barnsley	Tr	07.75	75-79	191	0	0

SPRINGETT Ronald (Ron) Derrick
Fulham, 22 July, 1935 FLge-9/E-33 (G)

League Club	Source	Date Signed	Seasons Played	Apps	Subs	Gls
Queens Park Rgrs	Victoria U	02.53	55-57	88	-	0
Sheffield Wed	Tr	03.58	57-66	345	0	0
Queens Park Rgrs	Tr	06.67	67-68	45	0	0

SPRINGTHORPE Terence (Terry) Alfred
Draycott, 4 December, 1923 USA int (FB)

League Club	Source	Date Signed	Seasons Played	Apps	Subs	Gls
Wolverhampton W	Jnrs	12.40	47-49	35	-	0
Coventry C	Tr	12.50	50	12	-	0

SPROATES Alan
Houghton-le-Spring, 30 June, 1944 (M)

League Club	Source	Date Signed	Seasons Played	Apps	Subs	Gls
Sunderland	Jnrs	07.61				
Swindon T	Tr	08.63	63-64	3	-	0
Darlington	Tr	09.65	65-73	304	11	17
Scunthorpe U	Tr	08.74	74	19	5	0

SPROATES John
Houghton-le-Spring, 11 April, 1943 Died 2000 (WH)

League Club	Source	Date Signed	Seasons Played	Apps	Subs	Gls
Barnsley	West Auckland T	12.63	63	2	-	0

SPROSON Philip (Phil) Jesse
Stoke-on-Trent, 13 October, 1959 (CD)

League Club	Source	Date Signed	Seasons Played	Apps	Subs	Gls
Port Vale	Jnrs	12.77	77-88	422	4	33
Birmingham C	Tr	07.89	89	12	0	0

SPROSON Roy
Stoke-on-Trent, 23 September, 1930 Died 1997 (CD)

League Club	Source	Date Signed	Seasons Played	Apps	Subs	Gls
Port Vale	Stoke C (Am)	07.49	50-71	755	5	30

SPROSTON Bert
Elworth, 22 June, 1915 Died 2000 FLge-4/EWar-2/E-11 (FB)

League Club	Source	Date Signed	Seasons Played	Apps	Subs	Gls
Leeds U	Sandbach Ramblers	06.33	33-37	130	-	1
Tottenham H	Tr	06.38	38	9	-	0
Manchester C	Tr	11.38	38-49	125	-	5

SPROSTON Neil Robert
Dudley, 20 November, 1970 (CD)

League Club	Source	Date Signed	Seasons Played	Apps	Subs	Gls
Birmingham C	YT	07.89	87	0	1	0

SPRUCE David George
Chester, 3 April, 1923 Died 1998 (CD)

League Club	Source	Date Signed	Seasons Played	Apps	Subs	Gls
Wrexham	Heath Rgrs	10.48	48-51	135	-	3
Barnsley	Tr	05.52	52-56	149	-	0
Chester	Tr	07.58	58-60	63	-	0

SPRUCE Philip (Phil) Thomas
Chester, 16 November, 1929 (WH)

League Club	Source	Date Signed	Seasons Played	Apps	Subs	Gls
Wrexham		11.50	51-55	23	-	0

SPUHLER John (Johnny) Oswald
Sunderland, 18 September, 1917 ESch (W)

League Club	Source	Date Signed	Seasons Played	Apps	Subs	Gls
Sunderland	Jnrs	09.34	36-38	35	-	5
Middlesbrough	Tr	10.45	46-53	216	-	69
Darlington	Tr	06.54	54-55	67	-	19

SPURDLE William (Bill)
St Peter Port, Guernsey, 28 January, 1926 (WH)

League Club	Source	Date Signed	Seasons Played	Apps	Subs	Gls
Oldham Ath	Jnrs	03.48	47-49	56	-	5
Manchester C	Tr	01.50	49-56	160	-	32
Port Vale	Tr	11.56	56	21	-	7
Oldham Ath	Tr	06.57	57-62	144	-	19

SQUIRE Michael (Mike) Richard
Poole, 18 October, 1963 ESch (F)

League Club	Source	Date Signed	Seasons Played	Apps	Subs	Gls
Fulham		07.82				
Torquay U	Dorchester T	03.84	83	12	1	3

SQUIRES Alan
Fleetwood, 26 February, 1923 (FB)

League Club	Source	Date Signed	Seasons Played	Apps	Subs	Gls
Preston NE		12.44				
Carlisle U	Tr	12.46	46-47	24	-	0

SQUIRES Barry
Birmingham, 29 July, 1931 (W)

League Club	Source	Date Signed	Seasons Played	Apps	Subs	Gls
Birmingham C	Lye T	05.53	53	1	-	0
Bradford C	Tr	06.54	54	7	-	0

SQUIRES Frank
Swansea, 8 March, 1921 Died 1988 WWar-2 (IF)

League Club	Source	Date Signed	Seasons Played	Apps	Subs	Gls
Swansea T	Jnrs	05.38	46-47	36	-	5
Plymouth Arg	Tr	10.47	47-49	86	-	13
Grimsby T	Tr	07.50	50	36	-	2

SQUIRES James (Jamie) Alexander
Preston, 15 November, 1975 (CD)

League Club	Source	Date Signed	Seasons Played	Apps	Subs	Gls
Preston NE	YT	04.94	93-96	24	7	0
Mansfield T	L	08.97	97	1	0	0
Carlisle U	Dunfermline Ath	08.00	00	2	3	0

SQUIRES Robert
Selby, 6 April, 1919 (WH)

League Club	Source	Date Signed	Seasons Played	Apps	Subs	Gls
Doncaster Rov	Selby T	09.37	47	21	-	0
Exeter C	Tr	07.49	49	1	-	0

SRNICEK Pavel
Ostrava, Czech Republic, 10 March, 1968 CzR-49 (G)

League Club	Source	Date Signed	Seasons Played	Apps	Subs	Gls
Newcastle U	Banik Ostrava (Cz)	02.91	90-97	148	1	0
Sheffield Wed	Banik Ostrava (Cz)	11.98	98-99	44	0	0
Portsmouth	Brescia (It)	09.03	03	3	0	0
West Ham U	L	02.04	03	2	1	0

STABB Christopher (Chris) John
Bradford, 12 October, 1976 (CD)

League Club	Source	Date Signed	Seasons Played	Apps	Subs	Gls
Bradford C	YT	07.95	94	1	0	0

STABB George Herbert
Paignton, 26 September, 1912 Died 1994 (CF)

League Club	Source	Date Signed	Seasons Played	Apps	Subs	Gls
Torquay U	Dartmouth U	09.31	31-34	93	-	44
Notts Co	Tr	10.34	34	24	-	5
Port Vale	Tr	07.35	35-36	32	-	9
Bradford PA	Tr	09.36	36-46	94	-	4

STACEY Stephen (Steve) Darrow
Bristol, 27 August, 1944 (FB)

League Club	Source	Date Signed	Seasons Played	Apps	Subs	Gls
Bristol C	App	11.61				
Wrexham	Tr	02.66	65-68	101	4	6
Ipswich T	Tr	09.68	68	3	0	0
Chester	L	12.69	69	1	0	0
Charlton Ath	L	01.70	69	1	0	1
Bristol C	Tr	09.70	70	9	0	0
Exeter C	Tr	09.71	71-72	57	2	0

STACEY Steven (Steve) John Anthony
Bristol, 9 June, 1975 (FB)

League Club	Source	Date Signed	Seasons Played	Apps	Subs	Gls
Torquay U	YT	10.93	93	1	0	0

STACEY Terence (Terry) John
Mitcham, 28 September, 1936 EAmat (FB)

League Club	Source	Date Signed	Seasons Played	Apps	Subs	Gls
Plymouth Arg	Carshalton Ath	05.59	59-61	22	-	0
Watford	Tr	07.62				
Gillingham	Tr	08.63	63-64	17	-	0

STACK Graham Christopher
Hampstead, 26 September, 1981 IRYth/IRu21-7 (G)

League Club	Source	Date Signed	Seasons Played	Apps	Subs	Gls
Arsenal	YT	07.00				
Millwall	L	07.04	04	25	1	0

STACK William John
Liverpool, 17 January, 1948 (W)

League Club	Source	Date Signed	Seasons Played	Apps	Subs	Gls
Crystal Palace	Jnrs	01.65	65	2	0	0

STACKMAN Harry Scott
Arizona, USA, 16 November, 1975 (CD)

League Club	Source	Date Signed	Seasons Played	Apps	Subs	Gls
Northampton T	YT	08.94	93	0	1	0

STAFF David Steven
Market Harborough, 8 November, 1979 (F)

League Club	Source	Date Signed	Seasons Played	Apps	Subs	Gls
Boston U	King's Lynn	08.04	04	0	5	0

STAFF Paul
Brancepeth, 30 August, 1962 (W)

League Club	Source	Date Signed	Seasons Played	Apps	Subs	Gls
Hartlepool U	App	08.80	79-83	88	10	14
Aldershot	Tr	08.84	84-85	25	12	11

STAFFORD Andrew (Andy) Grant
Stretford, 28 October, 1960 (W)

League Club	Source	Date Signed	Seasons Played	Apps	Subs	Gls
Halifax T	Blackburn Rov (N/C)	01.79	78-80	33	8	1
Stockport Co	Tr	08.81	81	21	4	1
Rochdale	Tr	08.82	82	1	0	1

STAFFORD Clive Andrew
Ipswich, 4 April, 1963 (FB)

League Club	Source	Date Signed	Seasons Played	Apps	Subs	Gls
Colchester U	Diss T	02.89	88-89	31	2	0
Exeter C	L	02.90	89	2	0	0

STAFFORD Ellis
Sheffield, 17 August, 1929 (FB)

League Club	Source	Date Signed	Seasons Played	Apps	Subs	Gls
Peterborough U	Scarborough	(N/L)	60-62	17	-	0

STAGG William (Billy)
Ealing, 17 October, 1957 (M)

League Club	Source	Date Signed	Seasons Played	Apps	Subs	Gls
Brentford	App	●	74	4	0	0

STAINROD Simon Allan
Sheffield, 1 February, 1959 EYth (F)

League Club	Source	Date Signed	Seasons Played	Apps	Subs	Gls
Sheffield U	App	07.76	75-78	59	8	14
Oldham Ath	Tr	03.79	78-80	69	0	21
Queens Park Rgrs	Tr	11.80	80-84	143	2	48
Sheffield Wed	Tr	02.85	84-85	8	7	2
Aston Villa	Tr	09.85	85-87	58	5	16
Stoke C	Tr	12.87	87-88	27	1	6

STAINSBY John
Stairfoot, 25 September, 1937 Died 2000 (CF)

League Club	Source	Date Signed	Seasons Played	Apps	Subs	Gls
Barnsley	Wath W	12.55	59-60	34	-	12
York C	Tr	07.61	61-62	69	-	21
Stockport Co	Tr	07.63	63	5	-	0

STAINTON Bryan Edward
Scampton, 8 January, 1942 (CD)

League Club	Source	Date Signed	Seasons Played	Apps	Subs	Gls
Lincoln C	Ingham	03.62	61-65	25	1	0

STAINTON James (Jim) Kenneth
Sheffield, 14 December, 1931 (FB)

League Club	Source	Date Signed	Seasons Played	Apps	Subs	Gls
Bradford PA		04.53				
Mansfield T	Tr	08.54	55-56	9	-	0

STAINWRIGHT David (Dave) Peter
Nottingham, 13 June, 1948 (F)

League Club	Source	Date Signed	Seasons Played	Apps	Subs	Gls
Nottingham F	App	08.65	65-66	4	3	1
Doncaster Rov	Tr	07.68	68	1	1	0
York C	Tr	07.69	69	6	2	1

STALKER Alan
Ponteland, 18 March, 1939 (G)

League Club	Source	Date Signed	Seasons Played	Apps	Subs	Gls
Gateshead (Am)	Bishop Auckland	05.58	58	4	-	0

STALKER John Alexander Hastie Inglis
Musselburgh, 12 March, 1959 (F)

League Club	Source	Date Signed	Seasons Played	Apps	Subs	Gls
Leicester C		07.79				
Darlington	Tr	10.79	79-82	107	9	36
Hartlepool U	Tr	01.83	82	3	1	0

STALLARD Mark
Derby, 24 October, 1974 (F)

League Club	Source	Date Signed	Seasons Played	Apps	Subs	Gls
Derby Co	YT	11.91	91-95	19	8	2
Fulham	L	09.94	94	4	0	3
Bradford C	Tr	01.96	95-96	33	10	10
Preston NE	L	02.97	96	4	0	1
Wycombe W	Tr	03.97	96-98	67	3	23
Notts Co	Tr	03.99	98-03	168	17	67
Barnsley	Tr	01.04	03-04	10	5	1
Chesterfield	L	10.04	04	7	2	2
Notts Co	L	02.05	04	16	0	3

STAM Jakob (Jaap)
Kampen, Holland, 17 July, 1972 Holland 45 (CD)

League Club	Source	Date Signed	Seasons Played	Apps	Subs	Gls
Manchester U	PSV Eindhoven (Holl)	07.98	98-01	79	0	1

STAM Stefan
Amersfoort, Holland, 14 September, 1979 Hou21 (CD)

League Club	Source	Date Signed	Seasons Played	Apps	Subs	Gls
Oldham Ath	Huizen (Holl)	02.05	04	11	2	0

STAMP Darryn Michael
Beverley, 21 September, 1978 (F)

League Club	Source	Date Signed	Seasons Played	Apps	Subs	Gls
Scunthorpe U	Hessle	07.97	97-00	18	39	6
Halifax T	L	02.00	99	5	0	0
Northampton T	Scarborough	05.02	02	12	10	4
Chester C	Tr	08.03	04	2	2	0
Kidderminster Hrs	L	11.04	04	4	0	1

STAMP Neville
Reading, 7 July, 1981 (FB)

League Club	Source	Date Signed	Seasons Played	Apps	Subs	Gls
Reading	YT	06.99	98	0	1	0
York C	Tr	10.00	00-01	17	3	0

STAMP Philip (Phil) Lawrence
Middlesbrough, 12 December, 1975 EYth (M)

League Club	Source	Date Signed	Seasons Played	Apps	Subs	Gls
Middlesbrough	YT	02.93	93-01	75	41	6
Millwall	L	09.01	01	0	1	0

STAMPER Frank Fielden Thorpe
Hartlepool, 22 February, 1926 Died 1999 (WH)

League Club	Source	Date Signed	Seasons Played	Apps	Subs	Gls
Hartlepools U	Colchester U	08.49	49-57	301	-	26

STAMPS John (Jackie) David
Thrybergh, 2 December, 1918 Died 1991 (CF)

League Club	Source	Date Signed	Seasons Played	Apps	Subs	Gls
Mansfield T	Silverwood Colliery	10.37	37	1	-	0
New Brighton	Tr	08.38	38	12	-	5
Derby Co	Tr	01.39	38-53	233	-	100
Shrewsbury T	Tr	12.53	53	22	-	4

STAMPS Scott
Edgbaston, 20 March, 1975 (FB)

League Club	Source	Date Signed	Seasons Played	Apps	Subs	Gls
Torquay U	YT	07.93	92-96	80	6	5
Colchester U	Tr	03.97	96-98	52	4	1
Kidderminster Hrs	Tr	09.99	00-03	123	6	0

STANBRIDGE George
Campsall, 28 March, 1920 Died 1973 (FB)

League Club	Source	Date Signed	Seasons Played	Apps	Subs	Gls
Rotherham U		11.38	46-48	36	-	1
Aldershot	Tr	06.49	49	15	-	0

STANCLIFFE Paul Ian
Sheffield, 5 May, 1958 (CD)

League Club	Source	Date Signed	Seasons Played	Apps	Subs	Gls
Rotherham U	App	03.76	75-82	285	0	7
Sheffield U	Tr	08.83	83-90	278	0	12
Rotherham U	L	09.90	90	5	0	0
Wolverhampton W	Tr	11.90	90	17	0	0
York C	Tr	07.91	91-94	89	2	3

STANDEN James (Jim) Alfred
Edmonton, 30 May, 1935 (G)

League Club	Source	Date Signed	Seasons Played	Apps	Subs	Gls
Arsenal	Rickmansworth T	04.53	57-60	35	-	0
Luton T	Tr	10.60	60-62	36	-	0
West Ham U	Tr	11.62	62-67	178	0	0
Millwall	Detroit (USA)	10.68	68-69	8	0	0
Portsmouth	Tr	07.70	70-71	13	0	0

STANDING John Robert
Walberton, 3 September, 1943 (FB)

League Club	Source	Date Signed	Seasons Played	Apps	Subs	Gls
Brighton & Hove A	Bognor Regis T	12.61	61-62	10	-	0

STANDING Michael John
Shoreham, 20 March, 1981 ESch/EYth (M)

League Club	Source	Date Signed	Seasons Played	Apps	Subs	Gls
Aston Villa	YT	03.98				
Bradford C	Tr	03.02	02-03	16	14	2
Walsall	Tr	05.04	04	27	5	4

STANDLEY Thomas (Tommy) Leslie
Poplar, 23 December, 1932 (WH)

League Club	Source	Date Signed	Seasons Played	Apps	Subs	Gls
Queens Park Rgrs	Basildon U	05.57	57	15	-	2
Bournemouth	Tr	11.58	58-64	159	-	5

STANFORD Edward (Eddie) John
Blackburn, 4 February, 1985 (M)

League Club	Source	Date Signed	Seasons Played	Apps	Subs	Gls
Coventry C	Sch	●	02	0	1	0

STANIC Mario
Sarajevo, Bosnia, 10 April, 1972 Croatia 49 (M)

League Club	Source	Date Signed	Seasons Played	Apps	Subs	Gls
Chelsea	Parma (It)	07.00	00-03	39	20	7

STANIFORTH David (Dave) Albry
Chesterfield, 6 October, 1950 (F)

League Club	Source	Date Signed	Seasons Played	Apps	Subs	Gls
Sheffield U	App	05.68	68-73	22	4	3
Bristol Rov	Tr	03.74	73-78	135	18	31
Bradford C	Tr	06.79	79-81	107	8	25
Halifax T	Tr	07.82	82-83	66	3	21

STANIFORTH Gordon
Hull, 23 March, 1957 ESch (F)

League Club	Source	Date Signed	Seasons Played	Apps	Subs	Gls
Hull C	App	04.74	73-76	7	5	2
York C	Tr	12.76	76-79	128	0	33
Carlisle U	Tr	10.79	79-82	118	8	33
Plymouth Arg	Tr	03.83	82-84	87	4	19
Newport Co	Tr	08.85	85-86	84	3	13
York C	Tr	10.87	87	15	4	1

STANIFORTH Ronald (Ron)
Manchester, 13 April, 1924 Died 1988 EB/E-8 (FB)

League Club	Source	Date Signed	Seasons Played	Apps	Subs	Gls
Stockport Co	Newton A	10.46	46-51	223	-	1
Huddersfield T	Tr	05.52	52-54	110	-	0
Sheffield Wed	Tr	07.55	55-58	102	-	2
Barrow	Tr	10.59	59-60	38	-	0

STANISLAUS Roger Edmund Philbert
Hammersmith, 2 November, 1968 (FB)

League Club	Source	Date Signed	Seasons Played	Apps	Subs	Gls
Arsenal	App	07.86				
Brentford	Tr	09.87	87-89	109	2	4
Bury	Tr	07.90	90-94	167	9	5
Leyton Orient	Tr	07.95	95	20	1	0

STANLEY Garry Ernest
Burton-on-Trent, 4 March, 1954 (M)

League Club	Source	Date Signed	Seasons Played	Apps	Subs	Gls
Chelsea	App	03.71	75-78	105	4	15
Everton	Tr	08.79	79-80	52	0	1
Swansea C	Tr	10.81	81-83	60	12	4
Portsmouth	Tr	01.84	83-85	43	4	1
Bristol C	Wichita (USA)	08.88	88	8	2	0

STANLEY Graham
Sheffield, 27 January, 1938 Died 1997 (WH)

League Club	Source	Date Signed	Seasons Played	Apps	Subs	Gls
Bolton W	Jnrs	10.55	56-63	141	-	3
Tranmere Rov	Tr	07.65	65	0	1	1

STANLEY Patrick (Pat) Joseph
Dublin, 9 March, 1938 (FB)

League Club	Source	Date Signed	Seasons Played	Apps	Subs	Gls
Leeds U	Jnrs	03.55				
Halifax T	Tr	05.58	58-62	118	-	1

STANLEY Terence (Terry) James
Brighton, 2 January, 1951 (M)

League Club	Source	Date Signed	Seasons Played	Apps	Subs	Gls
Brighton & Hove A	Lewes	11.69	69-70	16	6	0

STANLEY Thomas (Tommy)
Hemsworth, 7 December, 1962 (M)

League Club	Source	Date Signed	Seasons Played	Apps	Subs	Gls
York C	App	12.80	80-82	14	4	0

STANNARD James (Jim) David
Harold Hill, 6 October, 1962 (G)

League Club	Source	Date Signed	Seasons Played	Apps	Subs	Gls
Fulham	Ford U	06.80	80-84	41	0	0
Southend U	L	09.84	84	6	0	0
Charlton Ath	L	02.85	84	1	0	0
Southend U	Tr	03.85	84-86	103	0	0
Fulham	Tr	08.87	87-94	348	0	1
Gillingham	Tr	08.95	95-98	106	0	0

STANNERS Walter (Wally)
Carriden, 2 January, 1921 (G)

League Club	Source	Date Signed	Seasons Played	Apps	Subs	Gls
Bournemouth	Bo'ness U	07.47	47	3	-	0
Rochdale	Tr	08.49	49	5	-	0

STANSBRIDGE Leonard (Len) Edward Charles
Southampton, 19 February, 1919 Died 1986 (G)

League Club	Source	Date Signed	Seasons Played	Apps	Subs	Gls
Southampton	Jnrs	08.36	37-51	48	-	0

League Club	Source	Date Signed	Seasons Played	Career Record Apps	Subs	Gls
STANSFIELD Adam						
Plymouth, 10 September, 1978 ESemiPro-3						(F)
Yeovil T	Elmore	11.01	03	7	25	6
STANSFIELD Frederick (Fred)						
Cardiff, 12 December, 1917 W-1						(CD)
Cardiff C	Grange Ath	08.43	46-48	106	-	1
Newport Co	Tr	09.49	49	21	-	0
STANSFIELD James Edward						
Dewsbury, 18 September, 1978						(CD)
Huddersfield T	YT	07.97				
Halifax T	Tr	07.98	98-00	24	2	1
STANT Philip (Phil) Richard						
Bolton, 13 October, 1962						(F)
Reading	Camberley	08.82	82	3	1	2
Hereford U	British Army	11.86	86-88	83	6	38
Notts Co	Tr	07.89	89	14	8	6
Blackpool	L	09.90	90	12	0	5
Lincoln C	L	11.90	90	4	0	0
Huddersfield T	L	01.91	90	5	0	1
Fulham	Tr	02.91	90	19	0	5
Mansfield T	Tr	08.91	91-92	56	1	32
Cardiff C	Tr	12.92	92-94	77	2	34
Mansfield T	L	08.93	93	4	0	1
Bury	Tr	01.95	94-96	49	13	23
Northampton T	L	11.96	96	4	1	2
Lincoln C	Tr	12.96	96-99	42	22	20
Brighton & Hove A	Tr	03.01	00	0	7	1
STANTON Brian						
Liverpool, 7 February, 1956						(M)
Bury	New Brighton	10.75	76-78	72	11	13
Huddersfield T	Tr	09.79	79-85	199	10	45
Wrexham	L	03.86	85	8	0	0
Rochdale	Morecambe	12.86	86-87	42	7	4
STANTON Nathan						
Nottingham, 6 May, 1981 EYth						(CD)
Scunthorpe U	YT	03.99	97-04	194	21	0
STANTON Sidney (Sid)						
Dudley, 16 June, 1923						(WH)
Birmingham C		03.46				
Northampton T	Tr	07.46	47-48	7	-	0
STANTON Thomas (Tom)						
Glasgow, 3 May, 1948 SSch						(M)
Liverpool	Jnrs	05.65				
Arsenal	Tr	09.66				
Mansfield T	Tr	09.67	67	37	0	1
Bristol Rov	Tr	07.68	68-75	160	12	7
STAPLES Leonard (Len) Eric						
Leicester, 23 January, 1926 ESch						(FB)
Leicester C	Jnrs	07.47				
Newport Co	Tr	08.49	49-56	164	-	2
STAPLETON Francis (Frank) Anthony						
Dublin, 10 July, 1956 IRYth/IR-71						(F)
Arsenal	App	09.73	74-80	223	2	75
Manchester U	Tr	08.81	81-86	204	19	60
Derby Co	Ajax (Holl)	03.88	87	10	0	1
Blackburn Rov	Le Havre (Fr)	07.89	89-90	80	1	13
Huddersfield T	Aldershot (N/C)	10.91	91	5	0	0
Bradford C	Tr	12.91	91-93	49	19	2
Brighton & Hove A	Tr	11.94	94	1	1	0
STAPLETON John Robert						
Manchester, 30 September, 1969						(FB)
Stockport Co	West Bromwich A (YT)	08.88	88	1	0	0
STAPLETON Joseph (Joe) Edward						
Marylebone, 27 June, 1928						(CD)
Fulham	Uxbridge T	08.52	54-59	97	-	2
STAPLETON Simon John						
Oxford, 10 December, 1968 ESemiPro						(M)
Portsmouth	App	12.86				
Bristol Rov	Tr	07.88	88	4	1	0
Wycombe W	Tr	08.89	93-95	46	3	3
STARBUCK Philip (Phil) Michael						
Nottingham, 24 November, 1968						(F)
Nottingham F	App	08.86	86-90	9	27	2
Birmingham C	L	03.88	87	3	0	0
Hereford U	L	02.90	89	6	0	0
Blackburn Rov	L	09.90	90	5	1	1
Huddersfield T	Tr	08.91	91-94	120	17	36
Sheffield U	Tr	10.94	94-96	26	10	2

League Club	Source	Date Signed	Seasons Played	Career Record Apps	Subs	Gls
Bristol C	L	09.95	95	5	0	1
Oldham Ath	Tr	08.97	97	7	2	1
Plymouth Arg	Tr	03.98	97	6	1	0
STARK Roy Howard						
Nottingham, 28 November, 1953						(CD)
Aston Villa	App	06.69	73	2	0	0
STARK Wayne						
Derby, 14 October, 1976						(M)
Mansfield T	YT	•	93	0	1	0
STARK William (Billy) Reid						
Glasgow, 27 May, 1937						(F)
Crewe Alex	Glasgow Rgrs	08.60	60-61	38	-	13
Carlisle U	Tr	12.61	61-62	35	-	17
Colchester U	Tr	11.62	62-65	95	0	31
Luton T	Tr	09.65	65	8	2	4
Chesterfield	Corby T	07.66	66	30	1	15
Newport Co	Tr	07.67	67	11	0	2
STARKEY Malcolm John						
Bulwell, 25 January, 1936						(IF)
Blackpool		08.54	56-58	3	-	0
Shrewsbury T	Tr	06.59	59-62	121	-	33
Chester	Tr	04.63	62-66	109	0	1
STARLING Alan William						
Barking, 2 April, 1951						(G)
Luton T	App	04.69	69-70	7	0	0
Torquay U	L	02.71	70	1	0	0
Northampton T	Tr	06.71	71-76	238	0	1
Huddersfield T	Tr	03.77	76-79	112	0	0
STARLING Ronald (Ronnie) William						
Pelaw, 11 October, 1909 Died 1991 E-2						(IF)
Hull C	Washington Colliery	10.26	27-29	78	-	13
Newcastle U	Tr	05.30	30-31	51	-	8
Sheffield Wed	Tr	06.32	32-36	176	-	31
Aston Villa	Tr	01.37	36-46	88	-	11
STAROCSIK Felix						
Silesia, Poland, 20 May, 1920						(W)
Northampton T	Third Lanark	07.51	51-54	49	-	19
STATHAM Brian						
Harare, Zimbabwe, 21 May, 1969 Eu21-3						(FB)
Tottenham H	YT	08.87	87-88	20	4	0
Reading	L	03.91	90	8	0	0
Bournemouth	L	11.91	91	2	0	0
Brentford	Tr	01.92	91-96	148	18	1
Gillingham	Tr	08.97	97	16	4	0
STATHAM Derek James						
Wolverhampton, 24 March, 1959 EYth/Eu21-6/EB/E-3						(FB)
West Bromwich A	App	01.77	76-87	298	1	8
Southampton	Tr	08.87	87-88	64	0	2
Stoke C	Tr	08.89	89-90	41	0	1
Walsall	Tr	08.91	91-92	47	3	0
STATHAM Mark Andrew						
Urmston, 11 November, 1975						(G)
Nottingham F	Jnrs	03.93				
Wigan Ath	Tr	07.94	94	1	1	0
STATHAM Terence (Terry)						
Shirebrook, 11 March, 1940						(G)
Mansfield T	Jnrs	03.57	56-59	26	-	0
STATON Barry						
Doncaster, 9 September, 1938 ESch/EYth						(FB)
Doncaster Rov	Jnrs	05.56	55-61	85	-	0
Norwich C	Tr	07.62	62	23	-	1
STAUNTON Stephen (Steve)						
Drogheda, 19 January, 1969 IRYth/IRu21-4/IR-102						(CD)
Liverpool	Dundalk	09.86	88-90	55	10	0
Bradford C	L	11.87	87	7	1	0
Aston Villa	Tr	08.91	91-97	205	3	16
Liverpool	Tr	07.98	98-00	38	6	0
Crystal Palace	L	10.00	00	6	0	1
Aston Villa	Tr	12.00	00-02	65	8	0
Coventry C	Tr	08.03	03-04	66	4	4
STEAD Jonathan (Jon) Graeme						
Huddersfield, 7 April, 1983 Eu21-8						(F)
Huddersfield T	YT	11.01	02-03	54	14	22
Blackburn Rov	Tr	02.04	03-04	32	10	8
STEAD Kevin						
West Ham, 2 October, 1958						(FB)
Tottenham H	App	04.76				
Arsenal	Tr	07.77	78	1	1	0

League Club	Source	Date Signed	Seasons Played	Career Record Apps	Subs	Gls
STEAD Michael (Micky) John						
West Ham, 28 February, 1957						(FB)
Tottenham H	App	11.74	75-77	14	1	0
Swansea C	L	02.77	76	5	0	0
Southend U	Tr	09.78	78-85	297	1	4
Doncaster Rov	Tr	11.85	85-87	83	2	0
STEANE Nigel Brian						
Nottingham, 18 January, 1963						(F)
Sheffield U	App	01.81	79	0	1	0
STEARMAN Richard James						
Wolverhampton, 19 August, 1987						(CD)
Leicester C	Sch	11.04	04	3	5	1
STEBBING Gary Stanley						
Croydon, 11 August, 1965 EYth						(M)
Crystal Palace	App	08.83	83-87	95	7	3
Southend U	L	01.86	85	5	0	0
Maidstone U	KV Ostend (Bel)	07.89	89-91	69	7	4
STEEDMAN Alexander (Alex)						
Edinburgh, 13 May, 1938						(W)
Barrow		09.64	64	9	-	1
STEEDS Cecil						
Bristol, 11 January, 1929						(WH)
Bristol C	Jnrs	03.47	49-51	9	-	0
Bristol Rov	Tr	05.52	56	1	-	0
STEEL Alfred (Alf)						
Glasgow, 15 August, 1925 Died 1997						(G)
Walsall	Petershill	10.47	48-49	2	-	0
Cardiff C	Tr	01.50	49	10	-	0
STEEL Gregory (Greg)						
Clevedon, 11 March, 1959						(FB)
Newport Co	Clevedon T	01.78	77	3	0	0
STEEL William **James (Jim)**						
Dumfries, 4 December, 1959						(F)
Oldham Ath	App	06.78	78-82	101	7	24
Wigan Ath	L	11.82	82	2	0	2
Wrexham	L	01.83	82	9	0	6
Port Vale	Tr	03.83	82-83	27	1	6
Wrexham	Tr	01.84	83-87	164	0	51
Tranmere Rov	Tr	11.87	87-91	161	13	29
STEEL Richard (Dick)						
Sedgefield, 13 March, 1930						(FB)
Bristol C	Ferryhill Ath	06.53	53-55	3	-	0
York C	Tr	07.56	56-57	3	-	0
STEEL Ronald (Ron)						
Newburn, 3 June, 1929						(W)
Darlington	Bishop Auckland	01.50	49-51	66	-	5
STEEL William (Billy)						
Denny, 1 May, 1923 Died 1982 SLge-4/S-30						(IF)
Derby Co	Morton	06.47	47-49	109	-	27
STEELE Bennett John Stanley						
Cramlington, 5 August, 1939						(W)
Everton	Seaton Delaval	05.57				
Chesterfield	Tr	05.58	58	18	-	1
Gateshead	Tr	08.59	59	25	-	5
STEELE Daniel (Danny)						
Southwark, 11 October, 1982						(CD)
Millwall	Jnrs	02.00				
Colchester U	Tr	07.02	02	6	2	0
STEELE Eric Graham						
Wallsend, 14 May, 1954 ESch						(G)
Newcastle U	Jnrs	07.72				
Peterborough U	Tr	12.73	73-76	124	0	0
Brighton & Hove A	Tr	02.77	76-79	87	0	0
Watford	Tr	10.79	79-83	51	0	0
Cardiff C	L	03.83	82	7	0	0
Derby Co	Tr	07.84	84-86	47	0	0
Southend U	Tr	07.87	87	27	0	0
Mansfield T	L	03.88	87	5	0	0
STEELE Frederick (Freddie) Charles						
Hanley, 6 May, 1916 Died 1976 FLge-2/E-6						(CF)
Stoke C	Downings Tileries	08.33	34-48	224	-	140
Mansfield T	Tr	06.49	49-51	53	-	39
Port Vale	Tr	12.51	51-52	25	-	12
STEELE Hedley Verity						
Barnsley, 3 February, 1954						(CD)
Exeter C	Tiverton T	07.74	74	6	1	1

League Club	Source	Date Signed	Seasons Played	Career Record Apps	Subs	Gls
STEELE James (Jim)						
Edinburgh, 11 March, 1950						(CD)
Southampton	Dundee	01.72	71-76	160	1	2
STEELE John (Johnny)						
Glasgow, 24 November, 1916						(IF)
Barnsley	Ayr U	06.38	38-48	49	-	21
STEELE Joseph (Joe) McGuire						
Blackridge, 4 October, 1928 Died 1993						(W)
Newcastle U	Bellshill Ath	12.48				
Bury	Tr	05.50	50	18	-	1
STEELE Lee Anthony James						
Liverpool, 2 December, 1973						(F)
Shrewsbury T	Northwich Vic	07.97	97-99	104	9	37
Brighton & Hove A	Tr	07.00	00-01	24	36	11
Oxford U	Tr	07.02	02-03	6	20	4
Leyton Orient	Tr	07.04	04	37	2	16
STEELE Luke David						
Peterborough, 24 September, 1984 EYth						(G)
Peterborough U	YT	09.01	01	2	0	0
Manchester U	Tr	03.02				
Coventry C	L	09.04	04	32	0	0
STEELE Percival (Percy) Edmund						
Liverpool, 26 December, 1923						(FB)
Tranmere Rov	Carlton	01.44	46-56	311	-	0
STEELE Simon Paul						
Liverpool, 29 February, 1964						(G)
Everton	App	03.82				
Brighton & Hove A	Tr	06.83	83	1	0	0
Blackpool	L	09.83	83	3	0	0
Scunthorpe U	Tr	03.84	83	5	0	0
STEELE Stanley (Stan) Frederick						
Fenton, 5 January, 1937 Died 2005						(M)
Port Vale	Jnrs	05.55	56-60	185	-	66
West Bromwich A	Tr	03.61	60	1	-	0
Port Vale	Tr	08.61	61-64	148	-	22
Port Vale	Port Elizabeth C (SA)	01.68	67	2	0	0
STEELE Timothy (Tim) Wesley						
Coventry, 1 December, 1967						(M)
Shrewsbury T	App	12.85	85-88	41	20	5
Wolverhampton W	Tr	02.89	88-92	53	22	7
Stoke C	L	02.92	91	7	0	1
Bradford C	Tr	07.93	93	8	3	0
Hereford U	Tr	01.94	93-95	24	8	2
Exeter C	Tr	08.96	96	14	14	3
STEELE William (Billy) McCallum						
Kirkmuirhill, 16 June, 1955						(M)
Norwich C	App	06.73	73-76	56	12	3
Bournemouth	L	01.76	75	7	0	2
STEEN Alan William						
Crewe, 26 June, 1922						(W)
Wolverhampton W	Jnrs	03.39	38	1	-	1
Luton T	Tr	05.46	46	10	-	0
Aldershot	Northwich Vic	06.49	49	9	-	0
Rochdale	Tr	06.50	50-51	45	-	8
Carlisle U	Tr	12.51	51	19	-	2
STEEPLES John						
Doncaster, 28 April, 1959						(F)
Grimsby T	Pilkington Rec	05.80	80-81	4	3	0
Torquay U	L	09.82	82	4	1	0
STEFANOVIC Dejan						
Belgrade, Yugoslavia, 28 October, 1974 Serbia 23						(CD)
Sheffield Wed	Red Star Belgrade (Yug)	12.95	95-98	59	7	4
Portsmouth	Vitesse Arnhem (Holl)	07.03	03-04	64	0	3
STEFFEN Willi						
Berne, Switzerland, 17 March, 1925 SwitWar-2						(FB)
Chelsea	(Switzerland)	11.46	46	15	-	0
STEGGLES Kevin Peter						
Ditchingham, 19 March, 1961						(CD)
Ipswich T	App	12.78	80-85	49	1	1
Southend U	L	02.84	83	3	0	1
Fulham	L	08.86	86	3	0	0
West Bromwich A	Tr	02.87	86-87	14	0	0
Port Vale	Tr	11.87	87	20	0	0
STEIN Brian						
Cape Town, South Africa, 19 October, 1957 Eu21-3/E-1						(F)
Luton T	Edgware T	10.77	77-87	378	10	126
Luton T	Annecy (Fr)	07.91	91	32	7	3
Barnet	Tr	08.92	92	17	23	8

STEIN Colin Anderson
Philpstoun, 10 May, 1947 Su23-1/SLge-4/S-21 (F)

League Club	Source	Date Signed	Seasons Played	Apps	Subs	Gls
Coventry C	Glasgow Rgrs	10.72	72-74	83	0	22

STEIN Edwin
Cape Town, South Africa, 28 September, 1955 (M)

League Club	Source	Date Signed	Seasons Played	Apps	Subs	Gls
Barnet	Dagenham	07.82	91	0	1	0

STEIN Earl **Mark** Sean
Cape Town, South Africa, 28 January, 1966 EYth (F)

League Club	Source	Date Signed	Seasons Played	Apps	Subs	Gls
Luton T	Jnrs	01.84	83-87	41	13	19
Aldershot	L	01.86	85	2	0	1
Queens Park Rgrs	Tr	06.88	88-89	20	13	4
Oxford U	Tr	09.89	89-91	72	10	18
Stoke C	L	09.91	91	5	0	0
Stoke C	Tr	11.91	91-93	89	0	50
Chelsea	Tr	10.93	93-95	46	4	21
Stoke C	L	11.96	96	11	0	4
Ipswich T	L	08.97	97	6	1	2
Bournemouth	Tr	03.98	97-99	90	0	30
Luton T	Tr	07.00	00	19	11	3

STEINER Geoffrey (Geoff) Gordon
Hackney, 8 June, 1928 (FB)

League Club	Source	Date Signed	Seasons Played	Apps	Subs	Gls
Watford	Barnet	11.50	51	3	-	0

STEINER Robert (Rob) Herman
Finspang, Sweden, 20 June, 1973 Sweden 3 (F)

League Club	Source	Date Signed	Seasons Played	Apps	Subs	Gls
Bradford C	IFK Norrkoping (Swe)	10.96	96-97	40	12	14
Queens Park Rgrs	L	11.98	98	5	7	3
Walsall	L	03.99	98	10	0	3
Queens Park Rgrs	Tr	07.99	99	24	0	6

STEJSKAL Jan
Prague, Czech Republic, 15 January, 1962 Czechoslavakia int (G)

League Club	Source	Date Signed	Seasons Played	Apps	Subs	Gls
Queens Park Rgrs	Sparta Prague (Cz)	10.90	90-93	107	1	0

STELL Barry
Felling, 3 September, 1961 (M)

League Club	Source	Date Signed	Seasons Played	Apps	Subs	Gls
Sheffield Wed	App	09.79				
Darlington	Tr	10.79	80	7	2	0

STELLING John (Jack) Graham Surtees
Washington, 23 May, 1924 Died 1993 (FB)

League Club	Source	Date Signed	Seasons Played	Apps	Subs	Gls
Sunderland	Usworth High Grange	11.44	46-55	259	-	8

STEMP Wayne Darren
Plymouth, 9 September, 1970 (FB)

League Club	Source	Date Signed	Seasons Played	Apps	Subs	Gls
Brighton & Hove A	YT	10.88	89-90	4	0	0

STENHOUSE Alexander (Alec)
Stirling, 1 January, 1933 (W)

League Club	Source	Date Signed	Seasons Played	Apps	Subs	Gls
Portsmouth	Guildford C	02.57	56-57	4	-	1
Southend U	Tr	11.58	58-60	84	-	7

STENNER Arthur William John
Yeovil, 7 January, 1934 (W)

League Club	Source	Date Signed	Seasons Played	Apps	Subs	Gls
Bristol C	Yeovil	08.54				
Plymouth Arg	Tr	08.55	55	9	-	1
Norwich C	Tr	08.56	56	6	-	0
Oldham Ath	Tr	04.57	56	3	-	0

STENSAAS Stale
Trondheim, Norway, 7 July, 1971 (FB)

League Club	Source	Date Signed	Seasons Played	Apps	Subs	Gls
Nottingham F (L)	Glasgow Rgrs	01.99	98	6	1	0

STENSON Gerard (Ged) Patrick
Bootle, 30 December, 1959 (M)

League Club	Source	Date Signed	Seasons Played	Apps	Subs	Gls
Port Vale	Everton (App)	08.78	78-79	11	1	0

STENSON John Andrew
Catford, 16 December, 1949 ESch/EYth (M)

League Club	Source	Date Signed	Seasons Played	Apps	Subs	Gls
Charlton Ath	App	12.66	67-68	3	8	0
Mansfield T	Tr	06.69	69-71	103	4	21
Peterborough U	L	01.72	71	2	0	0
Aldershot	Tr	07.72	72-73	34	11	4

STEPANOVIC Dragoslav
Rekovac, Yugoslavia, 30 August, 1948 Yugoslavia int (CD)

League Club	Source	Date Signed	Seasons Played	Apps	Subs	Gls
Manchester C	Wormatia (Ger)	08.79	79-80	14	1	0

STEPANOVS Igors
Ogre, Latvia, 21 January, 1976 Latvia 57 (CD)

League Club	Source	Date Signed	Seasons Played	Apps	Subs	Gls
Arsenal	Skonto Riga (Lat)	09.00	00-02	17	0	0

STEPHAN Harold (Harry) William
Farnworth, 24 February, 1924 (WH)

League Club	Source	Date Signed	Seasons Played	Apps	Subs	Gls
Blackburn Rov		09.44	46-47	13	-	1

STEPHEN George Allan
Ellon, 21 September, 1927 (FB)

League Club	Source	Date Signed	Seasons Played	Apps	Subs	Gls
Aldershot		08.48	48	2	-	0

STEPHEN James (Jimmy) Findlay
Fettercairn, 23 August, 1922 SWar-5/S-2 (FB)

League Club	Source	Date Signed	Seasons Played	Apps	Subs	Gls
Bradford PA	Johnshaven Dauntless	08.39	46-48	94	-	1
Portsmouth	Tr	11.49	49-53	100	-	0

STEPHENS Alan
Liverpool, 13 October, 1952 (FB)

League Club	Source	Date Signed	Seasons Played	Apps	Subs	Gls
Wolverhampton W	App	10.70				
Crewe Alex	Tr	07.72	72-73	30	3	0

STEPHENS Alfred (Alf)
Cramlington, 13 June, 1919 Died 1993 (IF)

League Club	Source	Date Signed	Seasons Played	Apps	Subs	Gls
Leeds U	Cramlington BW	09.38				
Swindon T	Tr	08.46	46-47	16	-	2

STEPHENS Arnold Edwin
Ross-on-Wye, 31 January, 1928 Died 1955 (W)

League Club	Source	Date Signed	Seasons Played	Apps	Subs	Gls
Wolverhampton W	Jnrs	04.45				
Bournemouth	Tr	12.48	48-53	70	-	12

STEPHENS Arthur (Archie)
Liverpool, 19 May, 1954 (F)

League Club	Source	Date Signed	Seasons Played	Apps	Subs	Gls
Bristol Rov	Melksham T	08.81	81-84	100	27	40
Middlesbrough	Tr	03.85	84-87	87	5	24
Carlisle U	Tr	12.87	87-88	20	4	3
Darlington	Tr	03.89	88	10	0	4

STEPHENS Herbert (Bert) James
Chatham, 13 May, 1909 Died 1987 (W)

League Club	Source	Date Signed	Seasons Played	Apps	Subs	Gls
Brentford	Ealing Assoc	02.31	31-32	6	-	1
Brighton & Hove A	Tr	06.35	35-47	180	-	86

STEPHENS William **John (Johnny)**
Cardiff, 26 June, 1935 Died 1992 Wu23-1 (W)

League Club	Source	Date Signed	Seasons Played	Apps	Subs	Gls
Hull C	Jnrs	08.53	52-57	94	-	20
Swindon T	Tr	06.58	58-59	18	-	2
Coventry C	Tr	02.60	59	14	-	0

STEPHENS Kenneth (Kenny) John
Bristol, 14 November, 1946 (W)

League Club	Source	Date Signed	Seasons Played	Apps	Subs	Gls
West Bromwich A	App	11.64	66-67	21	1	2
Walsall	Tr	12.68	68-69	6	1	0
Bristol Rov	Tr	10.70	70-77	215	10	13
Hereford U	Tr	10.77	77-79	56	4	2

STEPHENS Kevin Alexander
Enfield, 28 July, 1984 (FB)

League Club	Source	Date Signed	Seasons Played	Apps	Subs	Gls
Leyton Orient	Sch	08.03	02-03	2	2	0

STEPHENS Kirk William
Coventry, 27 February, 1955 (FB)

League Club	Source	Date Signed	Seasons Played	Apps	Subs	Gls
Luton T	Nuneaton Borough	06.78	78-83	226	1	2
Coventry C	Tr	08.84	84-85	33	1	2

STEPHENS Lee Michael
Cardiff, 30 September, 1971 (F)

League Club	Source	Date Signed	Seasons Played	Apps	Subs	Gls
Cardiff C	YT	07.90	90	1	2	0

STEPHENS Malcolm Keith
Doncaster, 17 February, 1930 (IF)

League Club	Source	Date Signed	Seasons Played	Apps	Subs	Gls
Brighton & Hove A		07.54	54-56	29	-	14
Rotherham U	Tr	07.57	57	12	-	3
Doncaster Rov	Tr	07.58	58	10	-	2

STEPHENS Ross
Llanidloes, 28 May, 1985 (M)

League Club	Source	Date Signed	Seasons Played	Apps	Subs	Gls
Shrewsbury T	Sch	•	02-04	0	3	0

STEPHENS Terence (Terry) Guy
Neath, 5 November, 1935 (IF)

League Club	Source	Date Signed	Seasons Played	Apps	Subs	Gls
Tranmere Rov	Everton (Am)	08.55	55-56	15	-	5

STEPHENS William (Bill) John
Cramlington, 13 June, 1919 Died 1974 (CF)

League Club	Source	Date Signed	Seasons Played	Apps	Subs	Gls
Leeds U	Cramlington BW	09.38				
Swindon T	Tr	07.46	46-47	47	-	25
West Ham U	Tr	12.47	47-48	22	-	6

STEPHENSON Alan Charles
Chesham, 26 September, 1944 Eu23-7 (CD)

League Club	Source	Date Signed	Seasons Played	Apps	Subs	Gls
Crystal Palace	Jnrs	02.62	61-67	170	0	13
West Ham U	Tr	03.68	67-71	106	2	0
Fulham	L	10.71	71	10	0	0
Portsmouth	Tr	05.72	72-74	98	0	0

STEPHENSON Ashlyn
South Africa, 6 July, 1974 EYth (G)

League Club	Source	Date Signed	Seasons Played	Apps	Subs	Gls
Darlington	Waterford	09.95	95	1	0	0

STEPHENSON Geoffrey (Geoff)
Tynemouth, 28 April, 1970 (FB)

League Club	Source	Date Signed	Seasons Played	Apps	Subs	Gls
Grimsby T	YT	07.88	88-89	19	2	0

League Club	Source	Date Signed	Seasons Played	Career Record Apps	Subs	Gls
STEPHENSON Robert Leonard (Len)						
Blackpool, 14 July, 1930						(CF)
Blackpool	Highfield YC	11.48	50-54	24	-	10
Port Vale	Tr	03.55	54-56	61	-	16
Oldham Ath	Tr	06.57	57	8	-	0
STEPHENSON Paul						
Wallsend, 2 January, 1968 EYth						(W)
Newcastle U	App	01.86	85-88	58	3	1
Millwall	Tr	11.88	88-92	81	17	6
Gillingham	L	11.92	92	12	0	2
Brentford	Tr	03.93	92-94	70	0	2
York C	Tr	08.95	95-97	91	6	8
Hartlepool U	Tr	03.98	97-01	136	9	9
STEPHENSON Peter						
Ashington, 2 May, 1936 Died 2003						(W)
Middlesbrough		08.55				
Gateshead	Ashington	09.59	59	35	-	6
STEPHENSON George Robert (Bob)						
Derby, 19 November, 1942						(IF)
Derby Co	Derwent Sports	09.60	61-62	11	-	1
Shrewsbury T	Tr	06.64	64	3	-	0
Rochdale	Tr	07.65	65-66	50	1	16
STEPHENSON Ronald (Ron)						
Barrow, 13 April, 1948						(M)
Barrow	App	05.66	66-67	2	0	1
STEPHENSON Roy						
Crook, 27 May, 1932 Died 2000						(W)
Burnley	Crook T	06.49	49-55	78	-	27
Rotherham U	Tr	09.56	56-57	43	-	14
Blackburn Rov	Tr	11.57	57-58	21	-	5
Leicester C	Tr	03.59	58-59	12	-	0
Ipswich T	Tr	07.60	60-64	144	-	21
STEPNEY Alexander (Alex) Cyril						
Mitcham, 18 September, 1942 Eu23-3/FLge-2/E-1						(G)
Millwall	Tooting & Mitcham	05.63	63-65	137	0	0
Chelsea	Tr	05.66	66	1	0	0
Manchester U	Tr	09.66	66-77	433	0	2
STEPNEY Robin (Robbie) Edward						
Horsham, 26 February, 1936						(IF)
Aldershot	Redhill	09.58	58-64	213	-	36
STERGIOPOULOS Marcus						
Melbourne, Australia, 12 June, 1973						(F)
Lincoln C	Auckland Kingz (NZ)	08.00	00	2	5	0
STERLAND Melvyn (Mel)						
Sheffield, 1 October, 1961 Eu21-7/EB/FLge/E-1						(FB)
Sheffield Wed	App	10.79	78-88	271	8	37
Leeds U	Glasgow Rgrs	07.89	89-92	111	3	16
STERLING Worrell Ricardo						
Bethnal Green, 8 June, 1965						(W)
Watford	YT	06.83	82-88	82	12	14
Peterborough U	Tr	03.89	88-92	190	3	29
Bristol Rov	Tr	07.93	93-95	117	2	6
Lincoln C	Tr	07.96	96	15	6	0
STEVEN Trevor McGregor						
Berwick-on-Tweed, 21 September, 1963 ESch/EYth/Eu21-2/E-36						(W)
Burnley	App	09.81	80-82	74	2	11
Everton	Tr	07.83	83-88	210	4	48
STEVENS Arthur						
Battersea, 13 January, 1921						(W)
Fulham	Sutton U	12.43	46-58	386	-	110
STEVENS Brian Edward						
Andover, 13 November, 1933 Died 1980						(G)
Southampton	Andover OB	09.56	56-57	12	-	0
STEVENS Dean William						
Torquay, 7 February, 1986						(W)
Torquay U	Sch	●	02	0	3	0
STEVENS Dennis						
Dudley, 30 November, 1933 Eu23-2/FLge-1						(F)
Bolton W	Jnrs	12.50	53-61	273	-	90
Everton	Tr	03.62	61-65	120	0	20
Oldham Ath	Tr	12.65	65-66	33	0	0
Tranmere Rov	Tr	03.67	66-67	28	4	3
STEVENS Gary Andrew						
Hillingdon, 30 March, 1962 Eu21-8/E-7						(FB)
Brighton & Hove A	App	10.79	79-82	120	13	2
Tottenham H	Tr	06.83	83-89	140	7	6
Portsmouth	Tr	01.90	89-90	52	0	3
STEVENS Gary Martin						
Birmingham, 30 August, 1954						(F)
Cardiff C	Evesham U	09.78	78-81	138	12	44
Shrewsbury T	Tr	09.82	82-85	144	6	30
Brentford	Tr	07.86	86	29	3	10
Hereford U	Tr	03.87	86-89	85	9	10
STEVENS Michael Gary						
Barrow, 27 March, 1963 EB/E-46						(FB)
Everton	App	04.81	81-87	207	1	9
Tranmere Rov	Glasgow Rgrs	09.94	94-97	126	1	2
STEVENS Gregor MacKenzie						
Glasgow, 13 January, 1955 Su21-1						(CD)
Leicester C	Motherwell	05.79	79	4	0	0
STEVENS Ian David						
Malta, 21 October, 1966						(F)
Preston NE	App	11.84	84-85	9	2	2
Stockport Co	Tr	10.86	86	1	1	0
Bolton W	Lancaster C	03.87	86-90	26	21	7
Bury	Tr	07.91	91-93	100	10	38
Shrewsbury T	Tr	08.94	94-96	94	17	37
Carlisle U	Tr	05.97	97-98	64	14	26
Wrexham	Tr	07.99	99	14	2	4
Cheltenham T	L	03.00	99	1	0	0
Carlisle U	Tr	08.00	00-01	64	3	20
Shrewsbury T	Tr	07.02	02	4	14	2
STEVENS John Miles						
Hertford, 21 August, 1941						(CF)
Swindon T	King's Lynn	06.62	62-63	22	-	10
STEVENS Keith Henry						
Merton, 21 June, 1964						(FB)
Millwall	App	03.81	80-98	452	10	9
STEVENS Leslie (Les) William George						
Croydon, 15 August, 1920 Died 1991						(W)
Tottenham H	Jnrs	01.40	46-48	54	-	5
Bradford PA	Tr	02.49	48-49	44	-	4
Crystal Palace	Tr	08.50	50	20	-	3
STEVENS Mark Anthony						
Bristol, 31 January, 1963						(G)
Bristol C	App	02.81				
Swindon T	Tr	06.81	82	1	0	0
STEVENS Mark Richard						
Swindon, 3 December, 1977 ESch						(F)
Oxford U	Jnrs	07.96	97	0	1	0
STEVENS Norman John						
Shoreham, 13 May, 1938						(FB)
Brighton & Hove A	Jnrs	10.55	58	1	-	0
STEVENS Paul David						
Bristol, 4 April, 1960						(FB)
Bristol C	App	04.78	77-84	146	1	3
STEVENS Samuel (Sam) Batson						
Rutherglen, 2 December, 1935						(WH)
Southampton	Airdrie	06.57	58	14	-	0
STEVENSON Alan						
Staveley, 6 November, 1950						(G)
Chesterfield	Jnrs	10.69	69-71	104	0	0
Burnley	Tr	01.72	71-82	438	0	0
Rotherham U	Tr	08.83	83	24	0	0
Hartlepool U	Tr	09.84	84	35	0	0
STEVENSON Alexander (Alex) Ernest						
Dublin, 9 August, 1912 Died 1985 IWar-1/IR-7/I-17						(IF)
Everton	Glasgow Rgrs	01.34	33-48	255	-	82
STEVENSON Andrew (Andy) John						
Scunthorpe, 29 September, 1967						(CD)
Scunthorpe U	Jnrs	01.86	85-92	78	25	4
Doncaster Rov	L	01.92	91	1	0	0
STEVENSON Arthur						
Lanchester, 2 March, 1924 Died 1989						(FB)
Doncaster Rov	Denaby U	11.44	47-48	14	-	0
STEVENSON William Byron						
Llanelli, 7 September, 1956 Wu21-3/W-15						(M)
Leeds U	App	09.73	74-81	88	7	4
Birmingham C	Tr	03.82	81-84	69	5	3
Bristol Rov	Tr	07.85	85	30	1	3

League Club	Source	Date Signed	Seasons Played	Apps	Subs	Gls
STEVENSON Ernest (Ernie)						
Rotherham, 28 December, 1923 Died 1970						(IF)
Wolverhampton W	Jnrs	12.40	47-48	8	-	0
Cardiff C	Tr	10.48	48-49	50	-	15
Southampton	Tr	02.50	49-50	23	-	8
Leeds U	Tr	02.51	50-51	16	-	5
STEVENSON Walter Harry **Horace**						
Derby, 26 June, 1923						(W)
Nottingham F		11.44				
Ipswich T	Tr	02.48	47	3	-	0
STEVENSON James (Jimmy)						
Bellshill, 4 August, 1946 SSch						(CD)
Southend U	Hibernian	07.67	67	33	1	0
STEVENSON Jonathan (Jon) Ashlee						
Leicester, 13 October, 1982						(F)
Leicester C	YT	03.01	01-02	0	12	2
Swindon T	Tr	07.03	03	1	4	0
STEVENSON Morris John						
Tranent, 16 April, 1943						(F)
Luton T	Morton	11.68	68	1	0	0
STEVENSON Nigel Charles Ashley						
Swansea, 2 November, 1958 Wu21-2/W-4						(CD)
Swansea C	App	11.76	75-86	247	12	15
Cardiff C	L	10.85	85	14	0	0
Reading	L	03.86	85	3	0	0
Cardiff C	Tr	08.87	87-88	66	2	2
STEVENSON William (Willie)						
Leith, 26 October, 1939 SLge-1						(M)
Liverpool	Glasgow Rgrs	10.62	62-67	188	0	15
Stoke C	Tr	12.67	67-72	82	12	5
Tranmere Rov	Tr	07.73	73	20	0	0
STEWART Alan Victor						
Newcastle, 24 July, 1922 Died 2004						(CD)
Huddersfield T		04.40	46-48	14	-	0
York C	Tr	08.49	49-56	208	-	1
STEWART Andrew (Andy) Couper						
Methil, 29 October, 1956						(F)
Portsmouth	App	07.74	73-75	14	5	3
STEWART Arthur						
Ballymena, 13 January, 1942 IrLge-5/NI-7						(CD)
Derby Co	Glentoran	12.67	67-69	29	1	1
STEWART Bryan William						
Stockton, 13 September, 1985						(M)
York C	Sch	●	03	2	8	0
STEWART Charles **David (Dave)**						
Belfast, 20 May, 1958 NI-1						(W)
Hull C	App	08.75	74-78	46	5	7
Chelsea	Tr	05.79				
Scunthorpe U	Tr	11.79	79-81	88	9	19
Hartlepool U	Canberra (Den)	03.83	82	6	2	0
STEWART David Steel						
Glasgow, 11 March, 1947 Su23-7/S-1						(G)
Leeds U	Ayr U	10.73	73-78	55	0	0
West Bromwich A	Tr	11.78				
Swansea C	Tr	02.80	79-80	57	0	0
STEWART Edward (Eddie) McDonald						
Dundee, 15 November, 1934						(WH)
Norwich C	Dundee U	07.57	57	13	-	0
STEWART Gareth John						
Preston, 3 February, 1980 ESch/EYth						(G)
Blackburn Rov	YT	02.97				
Bournemouth	Tr	07.99	99-02	83	1	0
STEWART George Gartshone						
Chirnside, 18 October, 1920						(IF)
Brentford	Hamilton Academical	08.46	46-47	24	-	3
Queens Park Rgrs	Tr	03.48	47-52	38	-	5
Shrewsbury T	Tr	01.53	52	10	-	2
STEWART George Scott						
Larkhall, 16 November, 1932						(G)
Bradford C	Stirling A	05.59	59-60	22	-	0
STEWART George Thompson Scott						
Buckie, 17 February, 1927						(CF)
Accrington St	Worcester C	09.54	54-58	182	-	136
Coventry C	Tr	11.58	58-59	40	-	23
Carlisle U	Tr	06.60	60	7	-	2

League Club	Source	Date Signed	Seasons Played	Apps	Subs	Gls
STEWART Gerald (Gerry)						
Dundee, 2 September, 1946						(G)
Preston NE	Jnrs	09.63	66-69	4	0	0
Barnsley	Tr	09.71	71-74	138	0	0
STEWART James **Gordon**						
Durban, South Africa, 7 August, 1927 Died 1980						(IF)
Leeds U	Parkhill (SA)	10.51	51-52	9	-	2
STEWART Graham						
Birkenhead, 8 March, 1938						(CF)
Sheffield U	Everton (Am)	08.58				
Chesterfield	Tr	05.59	59	5	-	2
STEWART Henry						
Wigan, 28 April, 1925 Died 1996						(FB)
Huddersfield T	Thorne Colliery	08.48	48-50	49	-	0
STEWART Ian Edwin						
Belfast, 10 September, 1961 NISch/NI-31						(W)
Queens Park Rgrs	Jnrs	05.80	80-84	55	12	2
Millwall	L	03.83	82	10	1	3
Newcastle U	Tr	08.85	85-86	34	8	3
Portsmouth	Tr	07.87	87	0	1	0
Brentford	L	02.88	87	4	3	0
Aldershot	Tr	01.89	88-90	94	6	0
STEWART James (Jim) Garvin						
Kilwinning, 9 March, 1954 Su23-5/Su21-3/SLge-2/S-2						(G)
Middlesbrough	Kilmarnock	06.78	78-80	34	0	0
STEWART John (Jackie)						
Armadale, 23 January, 1929 Died 2004 SLge-2						(W)
Walsall	East Fife	06.57	57	28	-	4
STEWART John Barry						
Middlesbrough, 28 March, 1937						(W)
York C	Whitby T	09.56	56	1	-	0
STEWART John (Jackie) Gebbie						
Lochgelly, 4 September, 1921 Died 1990						(W)
Birmingham C	Raith Rov	01.48	47-54	203	-	52
STEWART Jordan Barrington						
Birmingham, 3 March, 1982 EYth/Eu21-1						(M)
Leicester C	YT	03.00	99-04	86	24	6
Bristol Rov	L	03.00	99	1	3	0
STEWART William Paul **Marcus**						
Bristol, 7 November, 1972 ESch/FLge						(F)
Bristol Rov	YT	07.91	91-95	137	34	57
Huddersfield T	Tr	07.96	96-99	129	4	58
Ipswich T	Tr	02.00	99-02	65	10	27
Sunderland	Tr	08.02	02-04	77	25	31
STEWART Michael (Mickey) James						
Herne Hill, 16 September, 1932 EAmat						(IF)
Charlton Ath	Corinthian Casuals	10.56	56-58	9	-	3
STEWART Michael James						
Edinburgh, 26 February, 1981 SSch/Su21-7/S-3						(M)
Manchester U	YT	03.98	00-02	5	2	0
Nottingham F	L	07.03	03	11	2	0
STEWART Paul Andrew						
Manchester, 7 October, 1964 EYth/Eu21-1/EB/E-3						(F)
Blackpool	App	10.81	81-86	188	13	55
Manchester C	Tr	03.87	86-87	51	0	26
Tottenham H	Tr	06.88	88-91	126	5	28
Liverpool	Tr	07.92	92-93	28	4	1
Crystal Palace	L	01.94	93	18	0	3
Wolverhampton W	L	09.94	94	5	3	2
Burnley	L	02.95	94	6	0	0
Sunderland	Tr	08.95	95-96	31	5	5
Stoke C	Tr	07.97	97	22	0	3
STEWART Raymond (Ray) Strean McDonald						
Perth, 7 September, 1959 SSch/Su21-12/S-10						(FB)
West Ham U	Dundee U	09.79	79-90	344	1	62
STEWART Reginald (Reg)						
Sheffield, 30 October, 1925						(CD)
Sheffield Wed	Sheffield YMCA	09.44	46	6	-	0
Colchester U	Tr	07.49	50-56	256	-	2
STEWART Robert (Bobby)						
Kirkcaldy, 4 December, 1933 SSch						(IF)
Crewe Alex	Cowdenbeath	08.55	55	22	-	3
STEWART Robert (Robbie) Ashcroft						
Broxburn, 14 June, 1971						(M)
Doncaster Rov	YT	●	88	1	0	0

STEWART Simon Andrew
Leeds, 1 November, 1973 (CD)

League Club	Source	Date Signed	Seasons Played	Apps	Subs	Gls
Sheffield Wed	YT	07.92	92	6	0	0
Shrewsbury T	L	08.95	95	4	0	0
Fulham	Tr	06.96	96	2	1	0

STEWART William (Willie)
Clydebank, 10 March, 1922 Died 1987 (IF)

League Club	Source	Date Signed	Seasons Played	Apps	Subs	Gls
Aldershot	St Mirren	06.51	51-53	27	-	4

STEWART William (Billy) Ian
Liverpool, 1 January, 1965 (G)

League Club	Source	Date Signed	Seasons Played	Apps	Subs	Gls
Liverpool	App	01.83				
Wigan Ath	Tr	07.84	84-85	14	0	0
Chester C	Tr	08.86	86-93	272	0	0
Northampton T	Tr	07.94	94	26	1	0
Chesterfield	L	03.95	94	1	0	0
Chester C	Tr	07.95	95	45	0	0

STIENS Craig
Swansea, 31 July, 1984 WYth (F)

League Club	Source	Date Signed	Seasons Played	Apps	Subs	Gls
Leeds U	YT	08.01				
Swansea C	L	12.02	02	0	3	0

STIFFLE Nelson Everard
India, 30 July, 1928 Died 2005 (W)

League Club	Source	Date Signed	Seasons Played	Apps	Subs	Gls
Chester	Ashton U	12.51	51	7	-	2
Chesterfield	Altrincham	03.54	54	38	-	9
Bournemouth	Tr	05.55	55-57	35	-	7
Exeter C	Tr	03.58	57-59	94	-	17
Coventry C	Tr	07.60	60	15	-	2

STILES John Charles
Manchester, 6 May, 1954 (M)

League Club	Source	Date Signed	Seasons Played	Apps	Subs	Gls
Leeds U	Vancouver (Can)	05.84	84-88	49	16	2
Doncaster Rov	Tr	08.89	89-91	88	1	2
Rochdale	L	03.92	91	2	2	0

STILES Norbert (Nobby) Peter
Manchester, 18 May, 1942 ESch/EYth/Eu23-3/FLge-3/E-28 (M)

League Club	Source	Date Signed	Seasons Played	Apps	Subs	Gls
Manchester U	Jnrs	06.59	60-70	311	0	17
Middlesbrough	Tr	05.71	71-72	57	0	2
Preston NE	Tr	08.73	73-74	44	2	1

STILL John Leonard
West Ham, 24 April, 1950 (CD)

League Club	Source	Date Signed	Seasons Played	Apps	Subs	Gls
Orient (Am)	Jnrs	05.67	67	1	0	0

STILL Robert (Bob) Arthur
Brinscall, 15 December, 1912 Died 1983 (WH)

League Club	Source	Date Signed	Seasons Played	Apps	Subs	Gls
Stockport Co	Chorley	06.34	34-38	155	-	2
Crewe Alex	Tr	08.39	46	1	-	0

STILL Ronald (Ron) George
Aberdeen, 10 June, 1943 (F)

League Club	Source	Date Signed	Seasons Played	Apps	Subs	Gls
Arsenal	Woodside BC	08.61				
Notts Co	Tr	07.65	65-66	46	0	15
Brentford	Tr	07.67	67	1	0	0

STILLE Giles Kevin
Westminster, 10 November, 1958 (M)

League Club	Source	Date Signed	Seasons Played	Apps	Subs	Gls
Brighton & Hove A	Kingstonian	05.79	79-83	20	7	4

STILLIE Derek Daniel
Irvine, 3 December, 1973 Su21-14 (G)

League Club	Source	Date Signed	Seasons Played	Apps	Subs	Gls
Wigan Ath	Aberdeen	08.99	99-01	42	2	0

STILLYARDS George Edward William
Whisby, 29 December, 1918 (FB)

League Club	Source	Date Signed	Seasons Played	Apps	Subs	Gls
Lincoln C	Botolph U	11.42	46-49	100	-	2

STIMAC Igor
Metkovic, Croatia, 6 September, 1967 Croatia 48 (CD)

League Club	Source	Date Signed	Seasons Played	Apps	Subs	Gls
Derby Co	Hajduk Split (Cro)	10.95	95-98	84	0	3
West Ham U	Tr	09.99	99-00	43	0	1

STIMPSON Barrie George
Billingham, 8 February, 1964 (FB)

League Club	Source	Date Signed	Seasons Played	Apps	Subs	Gls
Hartlepool U	App	02.82	80-83	66	2	2
Chesterfield	Tr	11.83	83	27	0	0
Hartlepool U	Tr	11.84	84	18	0	0

STIMSON Mark Nicholas
Plaistow, 27 December, 1967 (FB)

League Club	Source	Date Signed	Seasons Played	Apps	Subs	Gls
Tottenham H	App	07.85	86-88	1	1	0
Leyton Orient	L	03.88	87	10	0	0
Gillingham	L	01.89	88	18	0	0
Newcastle U	Tr	06.89	89-92	82	4	2
Portsmouth	L	12.92	92	3	1	0
Portsmouth	Tr	07.93	93-95	57	1	2
Barnet	L	09.93	95	5	0	0
Southend U	Tr	03.96	95-98	51	5	0
Leyton Orient	Tr	03.99	98	2	0	0

STINSON Hugh Michael John
Waterfoot, 18 May, 1937 (WH)

League Club	Source	Date Signed	Seasons Played	Apps	Subs	Gls
Accrington St	Whitewell Bottom	05.55	58	3	-	0
Gillingham	Tr	07.59	59	1	-	0

STIRK John
Consett, 5 September, 1955 EYth (FB)

League Club	Source	Date Signed	Seasons Played	Apps	Subs	Gls
Ipswich T	App	06.73	77	6	0	0
Watford	Tr	06.78	78	46	0	0
Chesterfield	Tr	03.80	79-82	54	2	0

STIRLAND John **Cecil (Cec)**
Adwick-le-Street, 15 July, 1921 Died 2004 (WH)

League Club	Source	Date Signed	Seasons Played	Apps	Subs	Gls
Doncaster Rov	Jnrs	07.38	46-48	68	-	0
New Brighton	Tr	01.50	49-50	51	-	0
Scunthorpe U	Tr	08.51	51	17	-	0

STIRLING James (Jimmy) Russell
Airdrie, 23 July, 1925 (CD)

League Club	Source	Date Signed	Seasons Played	Apps	Subs	Gls
Bournemouth	Coltness U	07.47	47-49	73	-	1
Birmingham C	Tr	06.50				
Southend U	Tr	12.50	50-59	218	-	2

STIRLING Jude Barrington
Enfield, 29 June, 1982 (CD)

League Club	Source	Date Signed	Seasons Played	Apps	Subs	Gls
Luton T	YT	07.99	00-01	6	4	0

STITFALL Albert Edward
Cardiff, 7 July, 1924 Died 1998 (FB)

League Club	Source	Date Signed	Seasons Played	Apps	Subs	Gls
Cardiff C	Jnrs	11.48	48-50	7	-	1
Torquay U	Tr	03.52	51-52	22	-	1

STITFALL Ronald (Ron) Frederick
Cardiff, 14 December, 1925 WLge-1/W-2 (FB)

League Club	Source	Date Signed	Seasons Played	Apps	Subs	Gls
Cardiff C	Jnrs	09.47	47-63	398	-	8

STOBART Barry Henry
Doncaster, 6 June, 1938 (F)

League Club	Source	Date Signed	Seasons Played	Apps	Subs	Gls
Wolverhampton W	Jnrs	12.55	59-63	49	-	20
Manchester C	Tr	08.64	64	14	-	1
Aston Villa	Tr	11.64	64-67	45	0	18
Shrewsbury T	Tr	10.67	67-68	34	2	9

STOBART Sean Anthony
Wolverhampton, 31 July, 1966 (F)

League Club	Source	Date Signed	Seasons Played	Apps	Subs	Gls
Scunthorpe U	Jnrs	07.84	84	0	2	1

STOBBART George Campbell
Pegswood, 9 January, 1921 Died 1995 (CF)

League Club	Source	Date Signed	Seasons Played	Apps	Subs	Gls
Middlesbrough	Netherton	11.45				
Newcastle U	Tr	09.46	46-48	66	-	21
Luton T	Tr	10.49	49-51	107	-	30
Millwall	Tr	08.52	52-53	68	-	27
Brentford	Tr	05.54	54-55	57	-	17

STOCCO Thomas (Tom) Luca
Westminster, 4 January, 1983 (F)

League Club	Source	Date Signed	Seasons Played	Apps	Subs	Gls
Torquay U	YT	07.01	99-00	2	8	2

STOCK Brian Benjamin
Winchester, 24 December, 1981 Wu21-4 (M)

League Club	Source	Date Signed	Seasons Played	Apps	Subs	Gls
Bournemouth	YT	01.00	99-04	87	32	13

STOCK Harold (Harry)
Stockport, 31 July, 1918 Died 1977 (IF)

League Club	Source	Date Signed	Seasons Played	Apps	Subs	Gls
Stockport Co	Cheadle	07.38	38-47	19	-	5
Oldham Ath	Tr	07.48	48-50	35	-	10

STOCK Russell John
Great Yarmouth, 25 June, 1977 (M)

League Club	Source	Date Signed	Seasons Played	Apps	Subs	Gls
Cambridge U	YT	07.95	95	15	2	1

STOCKDALE David Adam
Leeds, 20 September, 1985 (G)

League Club	Source	Date Signed	Seasons Played	Apps	Subs	Gls
York C	YT	•	02	0	1	0

STOCKDALE Robert (Robbie) Keith
Redcar, 30 November, 1979 Eu21-1/SB-2/S-4 (FB)

League Club	Source	Date Signed	Seasons Played	Apps	Subs	Gls
Middlesbrough	YT	07.98	97-03	62	13	2
Sheffield Wed	L	09.00	00	6	0	0
West Ham U	L	10.03	03	5	2	0
Rotherham U	Tr	02.04	03-04	43	0	1
Hull C	Tr	01.05	04	12	2	0

STOCKIN Ronald (Ron)
Birmingham, 27 June, 1931 (IF)

League Club	Source	Date Signed	Seasons Played	Apps	Subs	Gls
Walsall	West Bromwich A (Am)	01.52	51	6	-	3
Wolverhampton W	Tr	02.52	52-53	21	-	7
Cardiff C	Tr	06.54	54-56	57	-	16
Grimsby T	Tr	06.57	57-59	49	-	14

League Club	Source	Date Signed	Seasons Played	Career Record Apps	Subs	Gls
STOCKLEY Kenneth (Ken) Sidney						
Watford, 24 November, 1926						(WH)
Luton T	Jnrs	02.44				
Watford	Tr	07.48	49	1	-	0
STOCKLEY Samuel (Sam) Joshua						
Tiverton, 5 September, 1977						(FB)
Southampton	YT	07.96				
Barnet	Tr	12.96	96-00	177	5	2
Oxford U	Tr	07.01	01	39	2	0
Colchester U	Tr	08.02	02-04	108	6	2
STOCKS David Henry						
Dulwich, 20 April, 1943						(FB)
Charlton Ath	Jnrs	01.62	61-64	26	-	0
Gillingham	Tr	05.65	65	45	0	0
Bournemouth	Tr	06.66	66-71	220	0	2
Torquay U	Tr	01.72	71-76	150	0	3
STOCKS Joseph (Joe) Ronald						
Hull, 27 November, 1941						(WH)
Hull C	Jnrs	12.58	59-60	9	-	1
Millwall	Tr	08.61	61-63	30	-	1
STOCKWELL Michael (Mick) Thomas						
Chelmsford, 14 February, 1965						(M)
Ipswich T	App	12.82	85-99	464	42	35
Colchester U	Tr	07.00	00-02	121	11	22
STODDART Terence (Terry)						
Newcastle, 28 November, 1931						(WH)
Newcastle U	Jnrs	01.49				
Darlington	Tr	05.54	54-55	9	-	0
York C	Tr	07.56	56	3	-	0
STOKER Gareth						
Bishop Auckland, 22 February, 1973						(M)
Hull C	Leeds U (YT)	09.91	91-92	24	6	2
Hereford U	Bishop Auckland	03.95	94-96	65	5	6
Cardiff C	Tr	01.97	96-97	29	8	4
Rochdale	Tr	02.99	98	11	1	1
STOKES Albert William						
Darnall, 26 January, 1933						(CF)
Grimsby T	Hampton Sports	02.54	54-56	16	-	3
Scunthorpe U	Tr	07.57	57	5	-	2
Southport	Tr	02.59	58	6	-	2
STOKES Alfred (Alfie) Frederick						
Hackney, 3 October, 1932 Died 2002 Eu23-1/FLge-1/EB						(IF)
Tottenham H	Clapton	02.53	52-58	65	-	40
Fulham	Tr	07.59	59	15	-	6
Watford	Cambridge C	04.61	61	14	-	2
STOKES Dean Anthony						
Birmingham, 23 May, 1970						(FB)
Port Vale	Halesowen T	01.93	93-97	53	7	0
Rochdale	Tr	07.98	98-99	28	2	0
STOKES Derek						
Normanton, 13 September, 1939 Eu23-4						(CF)
Bradford C	Snydale Road Ath	04.57	57-59	94	-	44
Huddersfield T	Tr	06.60	60-64	153	-	65
Bradford C	Tr	01.66	65-66	31	1	11
STOKES Robert (Bobby) William Thomas						
Portsmouth, 30 January, 1951 Died 1995 EYth						(F)
Portsmouth	Washington (USA)	08.77	77	23	1	2
STOKES Wayne Darren						
Wolverhampton, 16 February, 1965						(CD)
Gillingham	Coventry C (App)	07.82	82-83	2	1	0
Stockport Co	Gloucester C	10.86	86	17	1	1
Hartlepool U	Tr	07.87	87-89	62	0	1
STOKLE David						
Hartlepool, 1 December, 1969						(CD)
Hartlepool U	YT	07.88	86-89	9	0	0
STOKOE Dennis						
Blyth, 6 June, 1925						(WH)
Chesterfield	North Shields	01.47				
Carlisle U	Tr	07.48	48-53	151	-	2
Workington	Tr	10.53	53-55	107	-	2
Gateshead	Tr	08.56	56	13	-	0
STOKOE Graham Lloyd						
Newcastle, 17 December, 1975						(M)
Stoke C	Newcastle U (YT)	07.94	96	0	2	0
Hartlepool U	L	02.96	95	8	0	0
Hartlepool U	Tr	08.98	98	15	5	0

League Club	Source	Date Signed	Seasons Played	Career Record Apps	Subs	Gls
STOKOE Robert (Bob)						
Mickley, 21 September, 1930 Died 2004						(CD)
Newcastle U	Jnrs	09.47	50-60	261	-	4
Bury	Tr	02.61	60-63	82	-	0
STOLCERS Andrejs						
Latvia, 8 July, 1974 Latvia 79						(M)
Fulham	Shakhtar Donetsk (Ukr)	12.00	00-02	8	17	2
Yeovil T	Tr	09.04	04	23	13	5
STONE Daniel (Danny) John Cooper						
Liverpool, 14 September, 1982						(FB)
Notts Co	Blackburn Rov (YT)	08.01	01-02	16	5	0
STONE David (Dave) Kenneth						
Bristol, 29 December, 1942						(CD)
Bristol Rov	Jnrs	03.60	62-67	145	3	6
Southend U	Tr	07.68	68	6	0	0
STONE Edward Leonard						
Gorleston, 5 January, 1942						(WH)
Charlton Ath	Jnrs	08.59				
Crystal Palace	Tr	05.61	61	1	-	0
STONE Frederick (Fred) William						
Bristol, 5 July, 1925 Died 2002						(FB)
Bristol C		06.47	47-52	64	-	3
STONE Geoffrey (Geoff)						
Mansfield, 10 April, 1924 Died 1993						(CD)
Notts Co	Beeston BC	09.48	48-49	4	-	0
Darlington	Tr	08.50	50-51	31	-	0
STONE John George						
Carlin How, 3 March, 1953						(FB)
Middlesbrough	South Bank	07.70	71	2	0	0
York C	Tr	07.72	72-75	86	0	5
Darlington	Tr	07.76	76-78	120	0	14
Grimsby T	Tr	07.79	79-82	89	5	2
Rotherham U	Tr	09.83	83	10	0	1
STONE Michael (Mick)						
Hucknall, 23 May, 1938						(G)
Notts Co	Linby Colliery	07.58	58	7	-	0
STONE Peter James						
Oxford, 8 October, 1922						(CD)
Luton T (Am)	Oxford C	12.51	51	1	-	0
STONE Steven (Steve) Brian						
Gateshead, 20 August, 1971 E-9						(W)
Nottingham F	YT	05.89	91-98	189	4	23
Aston Villa	Tr	03.99	98-01	66	24	4
Portsmouth	L	10.02	02	5	0	1
Portsmouth	Tr	12.02	02-04	64	4	8
STONEBRIDGE Ian Robert						
Lewisham, 30 August, 1981 EYth						(F)
Plymouth Arg	Tottenham H (YT)	07.99	99-03	124	47	38
Wycombe W	Tr	08.04	04	31	7	4
STONEHOUSE Basil Henry						
Guisborough, 27 October, 1952						(FB)
Middlesbrough	App	12.69				
Halifax T	L	10.72	72	1	1	0
STONEHOUSE Bernard						
Manchester, 23 December, 1934						(W)
Rochdale	Crewe Alex (Am)	08.55	55-56	19	-	1
STONEHOUSE Derek						
Lingdale, 18 November, 1932 Died 2004 EYth						(FB)
Middlesbrough	Lingdale	05.51	53-61	174	-	0
Hartlepools U	Tr	09.63	63-64	34	-	0
STONEHOUSE Kevin						
Bishop Auckland, 20 September, 1959						(F)
Blackburn Rov	Shildon	07.79	79-82	77	8	27
Huddersfield T	Tr	03.83	82-83	20	2	4
Blackpool	Tr	03.84	83-85	53	3	19
Darlington	Tr	07.87	87-88	59	13	20
Carlisle U	L	03.89	88	0	3	0
Rochdale	Tr	07.89	89	13	1	2
STONEMAN Paul						
Whitley Bay, 26 February, 1973						(CD)
Blackpool	YT	07.91	91-94	38	5	0
Colchester U	L	12.94	94	3	0	1
Halifax T	Tr	07.95	98-01	137	2	11
STONES Craig						
Scunthorpe, 31 May, 1980						(M)
Lincoln C	YT	07.97	96-99	10	11	0

STONES Gordon
Kearsley, 18 November, 1934 (CD)

League Club	Source	Date Signed	Seasons Played	Apps	Subs	Gls
Accrington St	Bury (Am)	09.54	55-60	109	-	1

STOPFORD Alan
Sheffield, 20 November, 1946 (W)

League Club	Source	Date Signed	Seasons Played	Apps	Subs	Gls
Chesterfield	Sheffield U (Am)	01.67	66	2	0	0

STOPFORD Leslie (Les)
Manchester, 9 May, 1942 (IF)

League Club	Source	Date Signed	Seasons Played	Apps	Subs	Gls
Chester	Jnrs	06.60	59-61	6	-	1

STORER Peter Russell
Shoreditch, 14 February, 1935 (G)

League Club	Source	Date Signed	Seasons Played	Apps	Subs	Gls
Watford (Am)	Berkhamsted T	03.59	58	9	-	0

STORER Stuart John
Harborough, 16 January, 1967 (W)

League Club	Source	Date Signed	Seasons Played	Apps	Subs	Gls
Mansfield T	Jnrs	●	83	0	1	0
Birmingham C	VS Rugby	07.84	85-86	5	3	0
Everton	Tr	03.87				
Wigan Ath	L	07.87	87	9	3	0
Bolton W	Tr	12.87	87-92	95	28	12
Exeter C	Tr	03.93	92-94	75	2	8
Brighton & Hove A	Tr	03.95	94-98	114	28	11

STOREY Brett Barry
Sheffield, 7 July, 1977 (M)

League Club	Source	Date Signed	Seasons Played	Apps	Subs	Gls
Sheffield U	YT	07.95				
Lincoln C	Tr	03.96	95	0	1	1

STOREY James (Jim)
Rowlands Gill, 30 December, 1929 (FB)

League Club	Source	Date Signed	Seasons Played	Apps	Subs	Gls
Newcastle U	Spen Black & White	05.48				
Exeter C	Tr	06.53	53	9	-	0
Bournemouth	Tr	07.54				
Rochdale	Tr	06.55	55-56	24	-	1
Darlington	Tr	06.57	57	6	-	0

STOREY Luke Dawson
Dawdon, 17 December, 1920 Died 1987 (W)

League Club	Source	Date Signed	Seasons Played	Apps	Subs	Gls
Lincoln C	Blackhall CW	09.47	47-48	11	-	2

STOREY Peter Edwin
Farnham, 7 September, 1945 ESch/FLge-2/E-19 (FB)

League Club	Source	Date Signed	Seasons Played	Apps	Subs	Gls
Arsenal	App	10.62	65-76	387	4	9
Fulham	Tr	03.77	76-77	17	0	0

STOREY Sidney (Sid)
Darfield, 25 December, 1919 (IF)

League Club	Source	Date Signed	Seasons Played	Apps	Subs	Gls
Huddersfield T	Grimethorpe Ath	09.43				
York C	Wombwell Ath	05.47	46-55	330	-	40
Barnsley	Tr	05.56	56	29	-	4
Accrington St	Tr	10.57	57-58	30	-	2
Bradford PA	Tr	07.59	59	2	-	0

STOREY-MOORE Ian
Ipswich, 17 January, 1945 Eu23-2/FLge-2/E-1 (W)

League Club	Source	Date Signed	Seasons Played	Apps	Subs	Gls
Nottingham F	Jnrs	05.62	62-71	235	1	105
Manchester U	Tr	03.72	71-73	39	0	11

STORF David Alan
Sheffield, 4 December, 1943 (W)

League Club	Source	Date Signed	Seasons Played	Apps	Subs	Gls
Sheffield Wed	Jnrs	12.60				
Rochdale	Tr	06.63	63-66	138	0	19
Barrow	Tr	07.67	67-71	154	4	26

STORRAR David McKinnon
Lochgelly, 16 January, 1933 (W)

League Club	Source	Date Signed	Seasons Played	Apps	Subs	Gls
Sheffield Wed		02.51	52	4	-	0

STORRIE James (Jim)
Kirkintilloch, 31 March, 1940 (F)

League Club	Source	Date Signed	Seasons Played	Apps	Subs	Gls
Leeds U	Airdrie	06.62	62-66	123	3	58
Rotherham U	Aberdeen	12.67	67-69	70	1	19
Portsmouth	Tr	12.69	69-71	43	0	12
Aldershot	L	03.72	71	5	0	1

STORTON Stanley (Stan) Eugene
Keighley, 5 January, 1939 (FB)

League Club	Source	Date Signed	Seasons Played	Apps	Subs	Gls
Bradford C	Huddersfield T (Am)	07.57	59-63	111	-	5
Darlington	Tr	01.64	63	15	-	0
Hartlepools U	Tr	07.64	64-65	72	0	0
Tranmere Rov	Tr	07.66	66-69	114	9	2

STORTON Trevor George
Keighley, 26 November, 1949 (CD)

League Club	Source	Date Signed	Seasons Played	Apps	Subs	Gls
Tranmere Rov	Jnrs	10.67	67-71	112	6	8
Liverpool	Tr	08.72	72-73	5	0	0
Chester	Tr	07.74	74-83	396	0	17

STORY Owen Grant
Burton-on-Trent, 3 August, 1984 (F)

League Club	Source	Date Signed	Seasons Played	Apps	Subs	Gls
Rushden & Diamonds	Sch	●	03	0	5	0
Torquay U	Team Bath	12.04	04	0	2	0

STOTT Ian
Wallingford, 17 October, 1955 ESch (CD)

League Club	Source	Date Signed	Seasons Played	Apps	Subs	Gls
Oxford U	West Ham U (N/C)	07.77	77-79	27	0	3

STOTT Keith
Atherton, 12 March, 1944 (CD)

League Club	Source	Date Signed	Seasons Played	Apps	Subs	Gls
Crewe Alex	Manchester C (Am)	10.64	64-69	188	0	11
Chesterfield	Tr	07.70	70-74	141	1	4

STOUTT Stephen (Steve) Paul
Halifax, 5 April, 1964 (FB)

League Club	Source	Date Signed	Seasons Played	Apps	Subs	Gls
Huddersfield T	Bradley Rgrs	01.84	83-84	6	0	0
Wolverhampton W	Tr	04.85	85-87	91	3	5
Grimsby T	Tr	07.88	88-89	3	0	1
Lincoln C	Tr	12.89	89-90	36	10	1

STOWE Dean Desmond
Burnley, 27 March, 1975 (M)

League Club	Source	Date Signed	Seasons Played	Apps	Subs	Gls
Hull C	YT	10.93	92	0	1	0

STOWELL Bruce
Bradford, 20 September, 1941 (M)

League Club	Source	Date Signed	Seasons Played	Apps	Subs	Gls
Bradford C	Leeds U (Am)	12.58	59-71	401	0	16
Rotherham U	Tr	07.72	72	14	2	0

STOWELL Michael (Mike)
Preston, 19 April, 1965 (G)

League Club	Source	Date Signed	Seasons Played	Apps	Subs	Gls
Preston NE	Leyland Motors	02.85				
Everton	Tr	12.85				
Chester C	L	09.87	87	14	0	0
York C	L	12.87	87	6	0	0
Manchester C	L	02.88	87	14	0	0
Port Vale	L	10.88	88	7	0	0
Wolverhampton W	L	03.89	88	7	0	0
Preston NE	L	02.90	89	2	0	0
Wolverhampton W	Tr	06.90	90-00	377	1	0
Bristol C	Tr	07.01	01	25	0	0

STRACHAN Craig Scott
Aberdeen, 19 May, 1982 (F)

League Club	Source	Date Signed	Seasons Played	Apps	Subs	Gls
Coventry C	YT	12.99				
Rochdale	Tr	08.03	03	0	1	0

STRACHAN Gavin David
Aberdeen, 23 December, 1978 SYth/Su21-8 (M)

League Club	Source	Date Signed	Seasons Played	Apps	Subs	Gls
Coventry C	YT	11.96	97-02	5	11	0
Peterborough U	Tr	03.03	02	1	1	0
Southend U	Tr	03.03	02	6	1	0
Hartlepool U	Tr	08.03	03-04	55	10	6

STRACHAN Gordon David
Edinburgh, 9 February, 1957 SSch/SYth/Su21-1/S-50 (M)

League Club	Source	Date Signed	Seasons Played	Apps	Subs	Gls
Manchester U	Aberdeen	08.84	84-88	155	5	33
Leeds U	Tr	03.89	88-94	188	9	37
Coventry C	Tr	03.95	94-96	13	13	0

STRAIN James (Jimmy) Henry
Chesham, 28 November, 1937 (CD)

League Club	Source	Date Signed	Seasons Played	Apps	Subs	Gls
Watford	Chesham U	11.55	56	3	-	0
Millwall	Tr	09.58	58	5	-	0

STRANDLI Frank
Norway, 16 May, 1972 Norway int (F)

League Club	Source	Date Signed	Seasons Played	Apps	Subs	Gls
Leeds U	IK Start (Nor)	01.93	92-93	5	9	2

STRATFORD Paul
Northampton, 4 September, 1955 (F)

League Club	Source	Date Signed	Seasons Played	Apps	Subs	Gls
Northampton T	App	10.72	72-77	169	3	58

STRATHIE William **James**
Falkirk, 12 February, 1913 Died 1976 (CD)

League Club	Source	Date Signed	Seasons Played	Apps	Subs	Gls
Luton T	St Bernard's	05.37	37-38	2	-	0
Northampton T	Tr	07.39	46	6	-	0

STRATTON Reginald (Reg) Malcolm
Kingsley, 10 July, 1939 EYth/EAmat (F)

League Club	Source	Date Signed	Seasons Played	Apps	Subs	Gls
Fulham	Woking	05.59	59-64	21	-	1
Colchester U	Tr	06.65	65-67	112	0	51

STRAUSS William (Bill) Henry
Transvaal, South Africa, 6 January, 1916 Died 1987 (W)

League Club	Source	Date Signed	Seasons Played	Apps	Subs	Gls
Plymouth Arg	Aberdeen	07.46	46-53	158	-	40

STRAW Ian Ernest
Sheffield, 27 May, 1967 (M)

League Club	Source	Date Signed	Seasons Played	Apps	Subs	Gls
Grimsby T	Southampton (App)	08.86	86	7	3	0

League Club	Source	Date Signed	Seasons Played	Apps	Subs	Gls
STRAW Raymond (Ray)						
Ilkeston, 22 May, 1933 Died 2001						(CF)
Derby Co	Ilkeston T	10.51	51-57	94	-	57
Coventry C	Tr	11.57	57-60	143	-	79
Mansfield T	Tr	08.61	61-62	44	-	12
STREET Jeffrey (Jeff) Leslie						
Manchester, 20 April, 1948						(CD)
Manchester C	Jnrs	08.65				
Southport	Tr	08.67	67	9	0	0
Barrow	Altrincham	07.69	69	11	1	1
STREET John						
Rotherham, 19 November, 1926 Died 1988						(G)
Sheffield Wed	Liverpool (Am)	05.45				
Rotherham U		07.47	47	2	-	0
STREET John (Jack)						
West Derby, 30 May, 1928						(WH)
Southport	Tranmere Rov (Am)	01.49	48-49	7	-	1
Reading	Bootle	05.51				
Barrow	Tr	07.53	53-54	30	-	5
STREET John (Jack)						
Sheffield, 27 July, 1934						(W)
Bradford C	Jnrs	11.51	51	1	-	0
STREET Kevin						
Crewe, 25 November, 1977						(M)
Crewe Alex	YT	07.96	97-01	57	58	9
Luton T	L	11.01	01	1	1	0
Bristol Rov	Northwich Vic	11.02	02-03	21	12	2
Shrewsbury T	Tr	10.03	04	15	6	1
STREET Terence (Terry) Edward						
Poplar, 9 December, 1948						(CD)
Leyton Orient	Jnrs	12.66	66	1	0	0
STREETE Floyd Anthony						
Jamaica, 5 May, 1959						(CD)
Cambridge U	Rivet Sports	07.76	76-82	111	14	19
Derby Co	SC Cambuur (Holl)	10.84	84-85	35	0	0
Wolverhampton W	Tr	10.85	85-89	157	2	6
Reading	Tr	07.90	90-91	38	0	0
STREETER Terence (Terry) Stephen						
Brighton, 26 October, 1979						(F)
Brighton & Hove A	YT	06.98	97	0	2	0
STRETEN Bernard Reginald						
Gillingham, 14 January, 1921 Died 1994 EAmat/E-1						(G)
Luton T	Shrewsbury T	01.47	46-56	276	-	0
STRETTON Donald (Don)						
Clowne, 4 September, 1920 Died 1978						(CF)
Halifax T	Thorne Colliery	07.47	47	10	-	5
STREVENS Benjamin (Ben) John						
Edgware, 24 May, 1980						(F)
Barnet	Wingate & Finchley	01.99	99-00	13	21	4
STRICKLAND Derek						
Stoneyburn, 7 November, 1959 SSch						(F)
Leicester C	Glasgow Rgrs	09.79	79	4	3	2
STRIDE David Roy						
Lymington, 14 March, 1958						(FB)
Chelsea	App	01.76	78-79	35	0	0
Millwall	Minnesota (USA)	01.83	82-83	55	0	3
Orient	Tr	07.84	84	29	0	0
STRINGER Christopher (Chris)						
Grimsby, 16 June, 1983						(G)
Sheffield Wed	YT	06.00	00-02	6	3	0
STRINGER David (Dave) Ronald						
Great Yarmouth, 15 October, 1944 EYth						(CD)
Norwich C	Gorleston Minors	05.63	64-76	417	2	18
Cambridge U	Tr	09.76	76-80	153	4	1
STRINGER Edmund						
Sheffield, 6 February, 1925						(IF)
Oldham Ath	Norton Woodseats	07.49	49	1	-	0
STRINGFELLOW Ian Robert						
Nottingham, 8 May, 1969						(F)
Mansfield T	App	04.86	85-93	109	58	28
Blackpool	L	09.92	92	3	0	1
Chesterfield	L	12.93	93	0	1	0

League Club	Source	Date Signed	Seasons Played	Apps	Subs	Gls
STRINGFELLOW Michael (Mike) David						
Kirkby-in-Ashfield, 27 January, 1943						(W)
Mansfield T	Jnrs	02.60	60-61	57	-	10
Leicester C	Tr	01.62	61-74	292	23	82
STRINGFELLOW Peter						
Walkden, 21 February, 1939						(IF)
Oldham Ath	Walkden T	12.58	58-60	54	-	16
Gillingham	Sankey's	12.62	62-63	35	-	2
Chesterfield	Tr	08.64	64	28	-	7
STRODDER Colin John						
Hessle, 23 December, 1941						(FB)
Huddersfield T		04.60				
Halifax T	Tr	07.61	61-62	20	-	0
STRODDER Gary John						
Cleckheaton, 1 April, 1965						(CD)
Lincoln C	App	04.83	82-86	122	10	6
West Ham U	Tr	03.87	86-89	59	6	2
West Bromwich A	Tr	08.90	90-94	123	17	8
Notts Co	Tr	07.95	95-98	116	5	10
Rotherham U	L	01.99	98	3	0	0
Hartlepool U	Tr	02.99	98-00	58	3	0
STRONACH Peter						
Seaham, 1 September, 1956 ESch						(M)
Sunderland	App	09.73	77	2	1	0
York C	Tr	06.78	78-79	30	4	2
STRONG Andrew Forster						
Hartlepool, 17 September, 1966						(FB)
Middlesbrough	App	09.84	84	6	0	0
STRONG Geoffrey (Geoff) Hugh						
Newcastle, 19 September, 1937						(IF)
Arsenal	Stanley U	04.58	60-64	125	-	69
Liverpool	Tr	11.64	64-69	150	5	29
Coventry C	Tr	07.70	70-71	33	0	0
STRONG Gregory (Greg)						
Bolton, 5 September, 1975 ESch/EYth						(CD)
Wigan Ath	YT	10.92	93-94	28	7	3
Bolton W	Tr	09.95	95-99	10	2	1
Blackpool	L	11.97	97	11	0	1
Stoke C	L	03.99	98	5	0	1
Hull C	Motherwell	06.02	02	3	0	0
Cheltenham T	L	02.03	02	3	1	0
Scunthorpe U	L	03.03	02	7	0	0
Bury	L	08.03	03	10	0	0
Boston U	Tr	03.04	04	8	1	0
Macclesfield T	L	12.04	04	4	0	0
STRONG George **James (Jimmy)**						
Morpeth, 7 June, 1916 Died 1989						(G)
Hartlepools U	Pegswood U	02.34	33	1	-	0
Chesterfield	Tr	08.34	34	18	-	0
Portsmouth	Tr	03.35	34-37	59	-	0
Walsall	Gillingham	07.39				
Burnley	Tr	01.46	46-52	264	-	0
STRONG Leslie (Les)						
Streatham, 3 July, 1953						(FB)
Fulham	App	06.71	72-82	369	3	5
Brentford	L	12.82	82	5	0	0
Crystal Palace	Tr	08.83	83	7	0	0
Rochdale	(USA)	10.84	84	1	0	0
STRONG Steven (Steve)						
Bristol, 17 April, 1962						(CD)
Hereford U	App	02.80	78-80	16	0	0
STRONG Steven (Steve) George						
Watford, 15 March, 1978						(CD)
Bournemouth	YT	07.96	94-95	0	2	0
STROUD Derek Neville Lester						
Wimborne, 11 February, 1930						(W)
Bournemouth	Poole T	08.50	50-52	79	-	17
Grimsby T	Tr	06.53	53-54	71	-	12
STROUD Kenneth (Ken) Allan						
Fulham, 1 December, 1953 ESch						(M)
Swindon T	App	03.71	71-81	302	9	16
Newport Co	Tr	08.82	82-83	47	1	0
Bristol C	Tr	10.83	83-84	68	1	4
STROUD Roy William						
Silvertown, 16 March, 1925 ESch/EAmat						(CF)
West Ham U	Hendon	04.52	51-56	13	-	4

STROUD William (Billy) James Alfred
Hammersmith, 7 July, 1919 (WH)

League Club	Source	Date Signed	Seasons Played	Apps	Subs	Gls
Southampton	Jnrs	02.40	46	29	-	4
Leyton Orient	Tr	06.47	47-49	65	-	1
Newport Co	Tr	06.50	50-52	63	-	1
Newport Co	Hastings U	11.53	54	1	-	0

STRUPAR Branko
Zagreb, Croatia, 9 February, 1970 Belgium 17 (F)

League Club	Source	Date Signed	Seasons Played	Apps	Subs	Gls
Derby Co	KRC Genk (Bel)	12.99	99-02	32	9	16

STRUTT Brian John
Malta, 21 September, 1959 (F)

League Club	Source	Date Signed	Seasons Played	Apps	Subs	Gls
Sheffield Wed	App	09.77	79	2	0	0

STUART Edward (Eddie) Albert
Johannesburg, South Africa, 12 May, 1931 (FB)

League Club	Source	Date Signed	Seasons Played	Apps	Subs	Gls
Wolverhampton W	Rangers (SA)	01.51	51-61	287	-	5
Stoke C	Tr	07.62	62-63	63	-	2
Tranmere Rov	Tr	08.64	64-65	83	0	2
Stockport Co	Tr	07.66	66-67	77	0	1

STUART Graham Charles
Tooting, 24 October, 1970 EYth/Eu21-5 (W)

League Club	Source	Date Signed	Seasons Played	Apps	Subs	Gls
Chelsea	YT	06.89	89-92	70	17	14
Everton	Tr	08.93	93-97	116	20	22
Sheffield U	Tr	11.97	97-98	52	1	11
Charlton Ath	Tr	03.99	98-04	136	12	22
Norwich C	Tr	01.05	04	7	1	0

STUART Jamie Christopher
Southwark, 15 October, 1976 EYth/Eu21-4 (FB)

League Club	Source	Date Signed	Seasons Played	Apps	Subs	Gls
Charlton Ath	YT	01.95	94-97	49	1	3
Millwall	Tr	09.98	98-00	42	3	0
Bury	Tr	10.01	01-02	56	5	1
Southend U	Tr	06.03	03	23	3	0

STUART Mark Richard
Chiswick, 15 December, 1966 Esch (W)

League Club	Source	Date Signed	Seasons Played	Apps	Subs	Gls
Charlton Ath	Jnrs	07.84	84-88	89	17	28
Plymouth Arg	Tr	11.88	88-89	55	2	11
Ipswich T	L	03.90	89	5	0	2
Bradford C	Tr	08.90	90-91	22	7	5
Huddersfield T	Tr	10.92	92	9	6	3
Rochdale	Tr	07.93	93-98	166	36	41

STUART Robert (Bobby) William
Middlesbrough, 9 October, 1913 Died 1987 ESch (FB)

League Club	Source	Date Signed	Seasons Played	Apps	Subs	Gls
Middlesbrough	South Bank	01.31	31-47	247	-	2
Plymouth Arg	Tr	10.47	47	20	-	0

STUBBINS Albert
Wallsend, 13 July, 1919 Died 2002 FLge-4/EWar-1 (CF)

League Club	Source	Date Signed	Seasons Played	Apps	Subs	Gls
Newcastle U	Whitley & Monkseaton	04.37	37-46	27	-	5
Liverpool	Tr	09.46	46-52	161	-	75

STUBBS Alan
Kirkby, 6 October, 1971 EB-1 (CD)

League Club	Source	Date Signed	Seasons Played	Apps	Subs	Gls
Bolton W	YT	07.90	90-95	181	21	9
Everton	Glasgow Celtic	07.01	01-04	117	7	3

STUBBS Alfred (Alf) Thomas
West Ham, 18 April, 1922 Died 1986 (WH)

League Club	Source	Date Signed	Seasons Played	Apps	Subs	Gls
Crystal Palace		12.46	47-48	3	-	0

STUBBS Brian Henry
Keyworth, 8 February, 1950 (CD)

League Club	Source	Date Signed	Seasons Played	Apps	Subs	Gls
Notts Co	Loughborough U	09.68	68-79	423	3	21

STUBBS Charles (Charlie) Frederick
West Ham, 22 January, 1920 Died 1984 (IF)

League Club	Source	Date Signed	Seasons Played	Apps	Subs	Gls
Darlington	Bamforths	01.44	46-47	41	-	17

STUBBS Leslie (Les) Levi
Great Wakering, 18 February, 1929 (IF)

League Club	Source	Date Signed	Seasons Played	Apps	Subs	Gls
Southend U	Great Wakering	05.48	49-52	83	-	40
Chelsea	Tr	11.52	52-58	112	-	34
Southend U	Tr	11.58	58-59	22	-	3

STUBBS Robin Gregory
Warley, 22 April, 1941 (F)

League Club	Source	Date Signed	Seasons Played	Apps	Subs	Gls
Birmingham C	Jnrs	04.58	58-62	61	-	17
Torquay U	Tr	08.63	63-68	214	3	120
Bristol Rov	Tr	07.69	69-71	90	3	32
Torquay U	Tr	02.72	71-72	19	2	1

STUBBS William (Billy)
Hartlepool, 1 August, 1966 (F)

League Club	Source	Date Signed	Seasons Played	Apps	Subs	Gls
Nottingham F	Seaham Red Star	04.87				
Doncaster Rov	L	09.87	87	8	1	1
Grimsby T	L	03.88	87	2	5	2

STUCKEY Bruce George
Torquay, 19 February, 1947 (W)

League Club	Source	Date Signed	Seasons Played	Apps	Subs	Gls
Exeter C	App	02.65	65-67	37	2	6
Sunderland	Tr	11.67	67-69	24	2	2
Torquay U	Tr	02.71	70-73	70	18	6
Reading	Tr	11.73	73-76	92	5	7
Torquay U	L	01.75	74	4	0	0
Bournemouth	L	03.77	76	5	0	0

STURGESS Paul Christopher
Dartford, 4 August, 1975 (FB)

League Club	Source	Date Signed	Seasons Played	Apps	Subs	Gls
Charlton Ath	YT	07.93	92-96	43	8	0
Millwall	Tr	07.97	97	12	2	0
Brighton & Hove A	Tr	09.98	98	28	2	0

STURRIDGE Dean Constantine
Birmingham, 27 July, 1973 (F)

League Club	Source	Date Signed	Seasons Played	Apps	Subs	Gls
Derby Co	YT	07.91	91-00	142	48	53
Torquay U	L	12.94	94	10	0	5
Leicester C	Tr	01.01	00-01	20	2	6
Wolverhampton W	Tr	11.01	01-04	51	31	31
Sheffield U	L	01.04	03	2	2	0
Queens Park Rgrs	Tr	03.05	04	0	2	0

STURRIDGE Michael (Mike) Alexander
Birmingham, 18 September, 1962 (F)

League Club	Source	Date Signed	Seasons Played	Apps	Subs	Gls
Birmingham C	App	06.80				
Wrexham	L	12.83	83	3	1	0

STURRIDGE Simon Andrew
Birmingham, 9 December, 1969 (F)

League Club	Source	Date Signed	Seasons Played	Apps	Subs	Gls
Birmingham C	YT	07.88	88-92	129	21	30
Stoke C	Tr	09.93	93-98	43	28	14
Blackpool	L	03.99	98	5	0	1
Northampton T	Tr	08.99	99	10	8	1
Shrewsbury T	L	03.00	99	10	1	1

STURROCK Blair David
Dundee, 25 August, 1981 (F)

League Club	Source	Date Signed	Seasons Played	Apps	Subs	Gls
Plymouth Arg	Dundee U	10.01	01-03	9	54	2
Kidderminster Hrs	Tr	12.04	04	17	5	5

STURROCK David
Dundee, 22 February, 1938 (IF)

League Club	Source	Date Signed	Seasons Played	Apps	Subs	Gls
Accrington St	Dundee U	07.60	60	17	-	5

STUTTARD John Ellis
Padiham, 24 April, 1920 Died 1983 (FB)

League Club	Source	Date Signed	Seasons Played	Apps	Subs	Gls
Plymouth Arg	Burnley (Am)	09.38	38-46	29	-	1
Torquay U	Tr	09.47	47-50	82	-	0

STYLES Arthur (Archie)
Liverpool, 3 September, 1949 ESch/EYth (FB)

League Club	Source	Date Signed	Seasons Played	Apps	Subs	Gls
Everton	App	08.67	72-73	22	1	0
Birmingham C	Tr	02.74	73-77	71	3	4
Peterborough U	Tr	07.78	78	32	0	1
Portsmouth	Tr	07.79	79	28	0	0

STYLES Arthur John
Smethwick, 29 October, 1939 (WH)

League Club	Source	Date Signed	Seasons Played	Apps	Subs	Gls
West Bromwich A	Jnrs	11.56	59	1	-	0
Wrexham	Tr	03.60	59-60	16	-	0

SUART Ronald (Ron)
Kendal, 18 November, 1920 (FB)

League Club	Source	Date Signed	Seasons Played	Apps	Subs	Gls
Blackpool	Netherfield	01.39	46-49	103	-	0
Blackburn Rov	Tr	09.49	49-54	176	-	0

SUCKLING Perry John
Leyton, 12 October, 1965 EYth/Eu21-10 (G)

League Club	Source	Date Signed	Seasons Played	Apps	Subs	Gls
Coventry C	App	10.83	82-83	27	0	0
Manchester C	Tr	06.86	86-87	39	0	0
Crystal Palace	Tr	01.88	87-91	59	0	0
West Ham U	L	12.89	89	6	0	0
Brentford	L	10.91	91	8	0	0
Watford	Tr	07.92	92-93	39	0	0
Doncaster Rov	Tr	07.94	94-95	30	0	0

SUDDABY Peter
Stockport, 23 December, 1947 EAmat (CD)

League Club	Source	Date Signed	Seasons Played	Apps	Subs	Gls
Blackpool	Skelmersdale U	05.70	70-79	330	1	10
Brighton & Hove A	Tr	11.79	79	21	2	0
Wimbledon	Tr	11.81	81	6	0	0

SUDDARDS Jeffrey (Jeff)
Bradford, 17 January, 1929 (FB)

League Club	Source	Date Signed	Seasons Played	Apps	Subs	Gls
Bradford PA	Hull C (Am)	03.49	49-58	327	-	0

SUDDICK Alan
Chester-le-Street, 2 May, 1944 EYth/Eu23-2 (M)

League Club	Source	Date Signed	Seasons Played	Apps	Subs	Gls
Newcastle U	App	10.61	61-66	144	0	41
Blackpool	Tr	12.66	66-76	305	5	65
Stoke C	Tr	12.76	76	9	0	1

League Club	Source	Date Signed	Seasons Played	Apps	Subs	Gls
Southport	L	08.77	77	6	0	0
Bury	Tr	09.77	77	30	4	2

SUFFO Kengne Herve **Patrick**
Ebolowa, Cameroon, 17 January, 1978 Cameroon 29 (F)

League Club	Source	Date Signed	Seasons Played	Apps	Subs	Gls
Sheffield U	Nantes (Fr)	11.00	00-01	16	20	5
Coventry C	Numancia (Sp)	07.03	03-04	22	26	10

SUGDEN Ryan Stephen
Bradford, 26 December, 1980 (F)

League Club	Source	Date Signed	Seasons Played	Apps	Subs	Gls
Oldham Ath	YT	11.98	98-00	4	17	1

SUGGETT Colin
Chester-le-Street, 30 December, 1948 ESch/EYth (M)

League Club	Source	Date Signed	Seasons Played	Apps	Subs	Gls
Sunderland	App	01.66	66-68	83	3	24
West Bromwich A	Tr	07.69	69-72	123	5	20
Norwich C	Tr	02.73	72-77	200	3	21
Newcastle U	Tr	08.78	78	20	3	0

SUGRUE Paul Anthony
Coventry, 6 November, 1960 (M)

League Club	Source	Date Signed	Seasons Played	Apps	Subs	Gls
Manchester C	Nuneaton Borough	02.80	79-80	5	1	0
Cardiff C	Tr	08.81	81	2	3	0
Middlesbrough	Kansas City (USA)	12.82	82-84	66	3	6
Portsmouth	Tr	12.84	84-85	2	2	0
Northampton T	Tr	03.86	85	2	6	2
Newport Co	Tr	08.86	86	1	1	0

SUKER Davor
Osijek, Croatia, 1 January, 1968 YuYth/Yu-2/Cro-63 (F)

League Club	Source	Date Signed	Seasons Played	Apps	Subs	Gls
Arsenal	Real Madrid (Sp)	08.99	99	8	14	8
West Ham U	Tr	07.00	00	7	4	2

SUKUR Hakan
Sakarya, Turkey, 1 September, 1971 Turkey 84 (F)

League Club	Source	Date Signed	Seasons Played	Apps	Subs	Gls
Blackburn Rov	Parma (It)	12.02	02	7	2	2

SULLEY Christopher (Chris) Stephen
Camberwell, 3 December, 1959 (FB)

League Club	Source	Date Signed	Seasons Played	Apps	Subs	Gls
Chelsea	App	08.78				
Bournemouth	Tr	03.81	80-85	205	1	3
Blackburn Rov	Dundee U	03.87	86-91	134	0	3
Port Vale	Tr	07.92	92	40	0	1
Preston NE	Tr	07.93	93	21	0	1

SULLIVAN Alan
Aberdare, 12 November, 1953 WSch (W)

League Club	Source	Date Signed	Seasons Played	Apps	Subs	Gls
Swansea C	App	08.71	70-71	7	0	1

SULLIVAN Brian Anthony John
Edmonton, 30 December, 1941 Died 1985 ESch/EYth (IF)

League Club	Source	Date Signed	Seasons Played	Apps	Subs	Gls
Fulham	Jnrs	05.59	59	2	-	1

SULLIVAN Colin John
Saltash, 24 June, 1951 EYth/Eu23-2 (FB)

League Club	Source	Date Signed	Seasons Played	Apps	Subs	Gls
Plymouth Arg	App	07.68	67-73	225	4	7
Norwich C	Tr	06.74	74-78	154	3	3
Cardiff C	Tr	02.79	78-81	61	2	1
Hereford U	Tr	12.81	81	8	0	0
Portsmouth	Tr	03.82	81-83	94	0	0
Swansea C	Tr	03.85	84-85	53	0	0

SULLIVAN Cornelius (Con) Henry
Bristol, 22 August, 1928 (G)

League Club	Source	Date Signed	Seasons Played	Apps	Subs	Gls
Bristol C	Horfield OB	05.49	50-52	73	-	0
Arsenal	Tr	02.54	53-57	28	-	0

SULLIVAN Derek
Newport, 10 August, 1930 Died 1983 W-17 (WH)

League Club	Source	Date Signed	Seasons Played	Apps	Subs	Gls
Cardiff C	Jnrs	09.47	47-60	275	-	19
Exeter C	Tr	06.61	61	44	-	0
Newport Co	Tr	07.62	62	23	-	0

SULLIVAN Neil
Sutton, 24 February, 1970 S-28 (G)

League Club	Source	Date Signed	Seasons Played	Apps	Subs	Gls
Wimbledon	YT	07.88	90-99	180	1	0
Crystal Palace	L	05.92	91	1	0	0
Tottenham H	Tr	06.00	00-01	64	0	0
Chelsea	Tr	08.03	03	4	0	0
Leeds U	Tr	08.04	04	46	0	0

SUMMERBEE George Michael
Winchester, 22 October, 1914 Died 1955 (WH)

League Club	Source	Date Signed	Seasons Played	Apps	Subs	Gls
Aldershot	Basingstoke T	05.34	33-34	19	-	0
Preston NE	Tr	01.35	37-38	3	-	0
Chester	Tr	05.46	46	9	-	0
Barrow	Tr	06.47	47-49	122	-	0

SUMMERBEE Michael (Mike) George
Cheltenham, 15 December, 1942 Eu23-1/FLge-1/E-8 (W)

League Club	Source	Date Signed	Seasons Played	Apps	Subs	Gls
Swindon T	Cheltenham T	03.60	59-64	218	-	39
Manchester C	Tr	08.65	65-74	355	2	47
Burnley	Tr	06.75	75-76	51	0	0
Blackpool	Tr	12.76	76	3	0	0
Stockport Co	Tr	08.77	77-79	86	1	6

SUMMERBEE Nicholas (Nicky) John
Altrincham, 26 August, 1971 Eu21-3/EB-1 (W)

League Club	Source	Date Signed	Seasons Played	Apps	Subs	Gls
Swindon T	YT	07.89	89-93	89	23	6
Manchester C	Tr	06.94	94-97	119	12	6
Sunderland	Tr	11.97	97-99	87	6	7
Bolton W	Tr	01.01	00	9	3	1
Nottingham F	Tr	11.01	01	17	0	2
Leicester C	Tr	08.02	02	7	22	0
Bradford C	Tr	09.03	03-04	64	4	4

SUMMERBELL Mark
Chester-le-Street, 30 October, 1976 (M)

League Club	Source	Date Signed	Seasons Played	Apps	Subs	Gls
Middlesbrough	YT	07.95	95-00	35	16	1
Bristol C	L	09.01	01	5	0	0
Portsmouth	L	03.02	01	5	0	0
Carlisle U	Tr	08.02	02-03	43	2	1

SUMMERFIELD Kevin
Walsall, 7 January, 1959 EYth (M)

League Club	Source	Date Signed	Seasons Played	Apps	Subs	Gls
West Bromwich A	App	01.77	78-81	5	4	3
Birmingham C	Tr	05.82	82	2	3	1
Walsall	L	12.82	82	4	0	2
Walsall	Tr	02.83	82-83	38	12	15
Cardiff C	Tr	07.84	84	10	0	1
Plymouth Arg	Tr	12.84	84-90	118	21	26
Exeter C	L	03.90	89	4	0	0
Shrewsbury T	Tr	10.90	90-95	140	23	22

SUMMERFIELD Luke John
Ivybridge, 6 December, 1987 (FB)

League Club	Source	Date Signed	Seasons Played	Apps	Subs	Gls
Plymouth Arg	Sch	•	04	0	1	0

SUMMERHAYES David Michael
Cardiff, 21 March, 1947 Wu23-1 (M)

League Club	Source	Date Signed	Seasons Played	Apps	Subs	Gls
Cardiff C	App	03.65	65-67	7	6	0

SUMMERHAYES Robert (Bob) Edward
Cardiff, 8 January, 1951 WSch (M)

League Club	Source	Date Signed	Seasons Played	Apps	Subs	Gls
Cardiff C	App	01.69				
Newport Co	Tr	08.72	72-74	74	6	4

SUMMERHILL Alan
Liss, 25 November, 1950 (CD)

League Club	Source	Date Signed	Seasons Played	Apps	Subs	Gls
Bournemouth	Jnrs	07.68	69	28	0	0
Crewe Alex	Tr	09.70	70-71	46	4	1

SUMMERILL Philip (Phil) Ernest
Erdington, 20 November, 1947 EYth (F)

League Club	Source	Date Signed	Seasons Played	Apps	Subs	Gls
Birmingham C	App	12.64	66-72	108	10	46
Huddersfield T	Tr	01.73	72-74	48	6	11
Millwall	Tr	11.74	74-77	83	4	20
Wimbledon	Tr	09.77	77-78	27	4	4

SUMMERS Christopher (Chris)
Cardiff, 6 January, 1972 WYth (F)

League Club	Source	Date Signed	Seasons Played	Apps	Subs	Gls
Cardiff C	YT	07.90	90	0	3	0

SUMMERS George
Glasgow, 30 July, 1941 (CF)

League Club	Source	Date Signed	Seasons Played	Apps	Subs	Gls
Brentford	Shawfield Jnrs	01.59	60-64	71	-	24

SUMMERS Gerald (Gerry) Thomas Francis
Birmingham, 4 October, 1933 (WH)

League Club	Source	Date Signed	Seasons Played	Apps	Subs	Gls
West Bromwich A	Erdington A	08.51	55-56	22	-	0
Sheffield U	Tr	05.57	57-63	260	-	4
Hull C	Tr	04.64	63-65	59	0	1
Walsall	Tr	10.65	65-66	41	3	1

SUMMERS John (Johnny) Henry
Hammersmith, 10 September, 1927 Died 1962 (CF)

League Club	Source	Date Signed	Seasons Played	Apps	Subs	Gls
Fulham	Jnrs	02.47	49	4	-	0
Norwich C	Tr	06.50	50-53	71	-	33
Millwall	Tr	05.54	54-56	91	-	41
Charlton Ath	Tr	11.56	56-60	171	-	100

SUMMERSBY Roy Donald
Lambeth, 19 March, 1935 (IF)

League Club	Source	Date Signed	Seasons Played	Apps	Subs	Gls
Millwall	Jnrs	03.52	51-58	87	-	13
Crystal Palace	Tr	12.58	58-62	176	-	59
Portsmouth	Tr	06.63	63-64	12	-	1

SUMMERSCALES William (Bill) Charles
Willesden, 4 January, 1949 (CD)

League Club	Source	Date Signed	Seasons Played	Apps	Subs	Gls
Port Vale	Leek T	02.70	69-74	126	3	4
Rochdale	Tr	07.75	75-76	87	0	4

SUMNER Alan
Wrexham, 18 April, 1949 (M)

League Club	Source	Date Signed	Seasons Played	Apps	Subs	Gls
Stockport Co		06.78	78	3	2	0

SUMNER Justin Thomas
Harrogate, 19 October, 1970 (W)

League Club	Source	Date Signed	Seasons Played	Apps	Subs	Gls
Doncaster Rov	Leeds U (YT)	08.89	89	2	0	0

SUMPNER Richard Anthony
Leeds, 12 April, 1947 (CF)

League Club	Source	Date Signed	Seasons Played	Apps	Subs	Gls
Bradford PA	Leeds U (Am)	01.67	66	2	0	1

SUNDERLAND Alan
Conisbrough, 1 July, 1953 Eu23-1/Eu21-1/E-1 (F)

League Club	Source	Date Signed	Seasons Played	Apps	Subs	Gls
Wolverhampton W	App	06.71	71-77	139	19	30
Arsenal	Tr	11.77	77-83	204	2	55
Ipswich T	Tr	02.84	83-85	51	7	11

SUNDERLAND Jonathan (Jon) Paul
Newcastle, 2 November, 1975 (M)

League Club	Source	Date Signed	Seasons Played	Apps	Subs	Gls
Blackpool	YT	07.94	94	0	2	0
Scarborough	Tr	03.96	95-96	3	5	0
Hartlepool U	Tr	12.96	96	6	7	1

SUNDGOT Ole Bjorn
Olsumd, Norway, 21 March, 1972 (F)

League Club	Source	Date Signed	Seasons Played	Apps	Subs	Gls
Bradford C	Molde FK (Nor)	11.96	96-97	11	14	6

SUNLEY David
Skelton, 6 February, 1952 (F)

League Club	Source	Date Signed	Seasons Played	Apps	Subs	Gls
Sheffield Wed	App	01.70	70-75	121	9	21
Nottingham F	L	10.75	75	1	0	0
Hull C	Tr	01.76	75-77	58	11	11
Lincoln C	Tr	07.78	78-79	36	5	6
Stockport Co	Tr	03.80	79-81	79	4	6

SUNLEY Mark
Guisborough, 13 October, 1971 (CD)

League Club	Source	Date Signed	Seasons Played	Apps	Subs	Gls
Middlesbrough	YT	10.89				
Millwall	Tr	02.91				
Darlington	Tr	07.91	91-93	34	1	0
Hartlepool U	Stalybridge Celtic	02.95	94	1	1	0

SURMAN Andrew Ronald Edward
Johannesburg, South Africa, 20 August, 1986 (M)

League Club	Source	Date Signed	Seasons Played	Apps	Subs	Gls
Southampton	Sch	08.03				
Walsall	L	01.05	04	10	4	2

SURMAN Leslie (Les)
Tamworth, 23 November, 1947 Died 1978 (G)

League Club	Source	Date Signed	Seasons Played	Apps	Subs	Gls
Charlton Ath	App	11.65	65	1	0	0
Rotherham U	Tr	06.66	66	1	0	0

SURTEES George **Harrison (Harry)** Hall
Ryhope, 20 December, 1926 (G)

League Club	Source	Date Signed	Seasons Played	Apps	Subs	Gls
Southport	Murton CW	08.46	46	3	-	0

SURTEES Hubert (Hugh)
Durham, 16 July, 1921 Died 1979 (W)

League Club	Source	Date Signed	Seasons Played	Apps	Subs	Gls
Watford	Bushey U	07.46	47-48	13	-	1
Crystal Palace	Tr	08.49	49	5	-	0

SUSSEX Andrew (Andy) Robert
Islington, 23 November, 1964 (M)

League Club	Source	Date Signed	Seasons Played	Apps	Subs	Gls
Orient	App	11.82	81-87	126	18	17
Crewe Alex	Tr	06.88	88-90	86	16	24
Southend U	Tr	07.91	91-95	63	13	14
Brentford	L	12.95	95	3	0	0

SUTCH Daryl
Beccles, 11 September, 1971 EYth/Eu21-4 (FB)

League Club	Source	Date Signed	Seasons Played	Apps	Subs	Gls
Norwich C	YT	07.90	90-01	255	50	9
Southend U	Tr	01.03	02	16	0	1
Boston U	Tr	07.03	03	6	0	0

SUTCLIFFE Frederick (Fred)
Brotherton, 29 May, 1931 (WH)

League Club	Source	Date Signed	Seasons Played	Apps	Subs	Gls
Birmingham C		09.51				
Chester	Tr	06.52	52-54	50	-	2

SUTCLIFFE Frederick (Fred) William Joseph
Fulham, 29 July, 1923 (CF)

League Club	Source	Date Signed	Seasons Played	Apps	Subs	Gls
Millwall		02.47	47-48	12	-	3
Walsall	Tr	07.50	50	4	-	0

SUTCLIFFE Peter David
Manchester, 25 January, 1957 EYth (W)

League Club	Source	Date Signed	Seasons Played	Apps	Subs	Gls
Manchester U	App	07.74				
Stockport Co	Tr	12.75	75-76	19	8	2
Port Vale	Tr	03.77	76-78	44	6	6
Chester	Tr	12.78	78-81	103	6	7
Chester C	Bangor C	11.83	83	11	0	0
Stockport Co	Tr	03.84	83	0	1	0

SUTHERLAND Colin
Glasgow, 15 March, 1975 (FB)

League Club	Source	Date Signed	Seasons Played	Apps	Subs	Gls
Scarborough	Clydebank	12.96	96-97	35	8	0

SUTHERLAND George Burns
Bathgate, 11 September, 1923 Died 1969 (CF)

League Club	Source	Date Signed	Seasons Played	Apps	Subs	Gls
Leyton Orient	Partick Th	08.49	49-50	42	-	22

SUTHERLAND Harry Ross
Salford, 30 July, 1915 (CF)

League Club	Source	Date Signed	Seasons Played	Apps	Subs	Gls
Leeds U	Sedgley Park	07.38	38	3	-	1
Exeter C	Tr	05.47	46-47	14	-	3

SUTHERLAND James (Jimmy) Sinclair
Armadale, 6 August, 1918 Died 1987 (FB)

League Club	Source	Date Signed	Seasons Played	Apps	Subs	Gls
Newport Co	Forth W	07.47	47-48	32	-	0

SUTHERLAND John Francis
Cork, 10 February, 1932 (FB)

League Club	Source	Date Signed	Seasons Played	Apps	Subs	Gls
Everton	Evergreen	05.50	56	6	-	0
Chesterfield	Tr	06.57	57-58	47	-	0
Crewe Alex	Tr	11.58	58-59	46	-	1

SUTTLE Kenneth (Ken) George
Hammersmith, 25 August, 1928 Died 2005 (W)

League Club	Source	Date Signed	Seasons Played	Apps	Subs	Gls
Chelsea	Worthing	08.48				
Brighton & Hove A	Tr	07.49	49	3	-	0

SUTTON Brian
Rochdale, 8 December, 1934 (G)

League Club	Source	Date Signed	Seasons Played	Apps	Subs	Gls
Rochdale	Norden YC	10.52	52-55	13	-	0

SUTTON Christopher (Chris) Roy
Nottingham, 10 March, 1973 Eu21-13/EB-2/E-1 (F)

League Club	Source	Date Signed	Seasons Played	Apps	Subs	Gls
Norwich C	YT	07.91	90-93	89	13	35
Blackburn Rov	Tr	07.94	94-98	125	5	47
Chelsea	Tr	07.99	99	21	7	1

SUTTON David William
Tarleton, 21 January, 1957 (CD)

League Club	Source	Date Signed	Seasons Played	Apps	Subs	Gls
Plymouth Arg	App	07.74	73-77	60	1	0
Reading	L	11.77	77	9	0	0
Huddersfield T	Tr	03.78	77-83	242	0	11
Bolton W	Tr	06.85	85-87	98	0	4
Rochdale	Tr	08.88	88	28	0	2

SUTTON David (Dave) William
Leek, 15 December, 1966 (F)

League Club	Source	Date Signed	Seasons Played	Apps	Subs	Gls
Crewe Alex	Stoke C (App)	07.86	86	0	1	1

SUTTON Gary
Folkestone, 2 February, 1962 (G)

League Club	Source	Date Signed	Seasons Played	Apps	Subs	Gls
Gillingham	App	02.80	80-81	11	0	0

SUTTON James Peter
Glasgow, 6 September, 1949 (M)

League Club	Source	Date Signed	Seasons Played	Apps	Subs	Gls
Newcastle U	St Roch's	06.69				
Mansfield T	Tr	07.70	70	11	2	0

SUTTON John William Michael
Norwich, 26 December, 1983 EYth (F)

League Club	Source	Date Signed	Seasons Played	Apps	Subs	Gls
Tottenham H	YT	07.01				
Carlisle U	L	10.02	02	7	0	1
Swindon T	Tr	12.02	02	0	1	0
Millwall	Raith Rov	01.04	03	2	2	0

SUTTON Melvyn (Mel) Charles
Birmingham, 13 February, 1946 (M)

League Club	Source	Date Signed	Seasons Played	Apps	Subs	Gls
Cardiff C	Aston Villa (Am)	12.67	68-71	135	3	5
Wrexham	Tr	07.72	72-80	355	5	21
Crewe Alex	Tr	08.82	82	13	0	1

SUTTON Michael (Mike) John
Norwich, 5 October, 1944 (M)

League Club	Source	Date Signed	Seasons Played	Apps	Subs	Gls
Norwich C	Jnrs	09.62	62-66	46	5	3
Chester	Tr	05.67	67-69	137	1	9
Carlisle U	Tr	06.70	70-71	51	2	1

SUTTON Richard Melvyn
Gravesend, 21 August, 1965 EYth (CD)

League Club	Source	Date Signed	Seasons Played	Apps	Subs	Gls
Peterborough U	App	•	82	1	0	0

SUTTON Stephen (Steve) John
Hartington, 16 April, 1961 (G)

League Club	Source	Date Signed	Seasons Played	Apps	Subs	Gls
Nottingham F	App	04.79	80-89	199	0	0
Mansfield T	L	03.81	80	8	0	0
Derby Co	L	01.85	84	14	0	0
Coventry C	L	02.91	90	1	0	0
Luton T	L	11.91	91	14	0	0
Derby Co	Tr	03.92	91-95	60	1	0
Reading	L	01.96	95	2	0	0
Birmingham C	Tr	08.96	96	6	0	0

SUTTON Wayne Frank
Derby, 1 October, 1975 (CD)

League Club	Source	Date Signed	Seasons Played	Apps	Subs	Gls
Derby Co	YT	10.92	94-95	4	3	0
Hereford U	L	09.96	96	4	0	0

SVARC Robert (Bobby) Louis
Leicester, 8 February, 1946 (F)

League Club	Source	Date Signed	Seasons Played	Apps	Subs	Gls
Leicester C	App	03.63	64-68	13	0	2
Lincoln C	Tr	12.68	68-71	40	5	16
Barrow	L	09.70	70	15	0	4
Colchester U	Boston U	12.72	72-75	116	0	59
Blackburn Rov	Tr	10.75	75-76	42	8	16
Watford	L	09.77	77	1	0	0

SVARD Sebastian
Hvidovre, Denmark, 15 January, 1983 DeYth/Deu21-9 (FB)

League Club	Source	Date Signed	Seasons Played	Apps	Subs	Gls
Arsenal	FC Copenhagen (Den)	11.00				
Stoke C	L	01.04	03	9	4	1

SVENSSON Anders
Gothenburg, Sweden, 17 July, 1976 Sweden 59 (M)

League Club	Source	Date Signed	Seasons Played	Apps	Subs	Gls
Southampton	Elfsborg (Swe)	07.01	01-04	97	30	9

SVENSSON Mathias
Boras, Sweden, 24 September, 1974 Sweden 3 (F)

League Club	Source	Date Signed	Seasons Played	Apps	Subs	Gls
Portsmouth	Elfsborg (Swe)	12.96	96-97	34	11	10
Crystal Palace	Tirol Innsbruck (Aut)	09.98	98-99	26	6	10
Charlton Ath	Tr	01.00	99-03	42	28	7
Derby Co	L	08.03	03	9	1	3
Norwich C	Tr	12.03	03-04	26	16	11

SVENSSON Michael
Sweden, 25 November, 1975 Sweden 25 (CD)

League Club	Source	Date Signed	Seasons Played	Apps	Subs	Gls
Southampton	Troyes (Fr)	07.02	02-03	59	1	4

SWAILES Christopher (Chris) William
Gateshead, 19 October, 1970 (CD)

League Club	Source	Date Signed	Seasons Played	Apps	Subs	Gls
Ipswich T	YT	05.89				
Peterborough U	Tr	03.91				
Doncaster Rov	Bridlington T	10.93	93-94	49	0	0
Ipswich T	Tr	03.95	94-97	34	3	1
Bury	Tr	11.97	97-00	125	1	10
Rotherham U	Tr	07.01	01-04	167	0	14

SWAILES Daniel (Danny)
Bolton, 1 April, 1979 (CD)

League Club	Source	Date Signed	Seasons Played	Apps	Subs	Gls
Bury	YT	07.97	99-04	154	10	13
Macclesfield T	Tr	01.05	04	17	0	0

SWAIN Kenneth (Kenny)
Birkenhead, 28 January, 1952 (FB)

League Club	Source	Date Signed	Seasons Played	Apps	Subs	Gls
Chelsea	Wycombe W	08.73	73-78	114	5	26
Aston Villa	Tr	12.78	78-82	148	0	4
Nottingham F	Tr	10.82	82-84	112	0	2
Portsmouth	Tr	07.85	85-87	113	0	0
West Bromwich A	L	02.88	87	7	0	1
Crewe Alex	Tr	08.88	88-91	123	3	1

SWAIN Kenneth (Kenny) John
Cardiff, 31 December, 1954 WSch (FB)

League Club	Source	Date Signed	Seasons Played	Apps	Subs	Gls
Newport Co	App	12.72	71-73	7	1	0

SWAIN Malcolm
Hornsey, 2 February, 1952 (M)

League Club	Source	Date Signed	Seasons Played	Apps	Subs	Gls
Reading	App	02.70	70-71	37	4	2

SWAIN Robert
Ripon, 26 March, 1944 (W)

League Club	Source	Date Signed	Seasons Played	Apps	Subs	Gls
Bradford C	Jnrs	09.61	62	7	-	0

SWAIN Sidney (Sid)
Liverpool, 14 October, 1927 Died 1978 (W)

League Club	Source	Date Signed	Seasons Played	Apps	Subs	Gls
Halifax T		07.51	51	8	-	1

SWAINE Mark
Hammersmith, 13 February, 1958 (W)

League Club	Source	Date Signed	Seasons Played	Apps	Subs	Gls
Gillingham	App	●	74	1	0	0

SWALES Stephen (Steve) Colin
Whitby, 26 December, 1973 (FB)

League Club	Source	Date Signed	Seasons Played	Apps	Subs	Gls
Scarborough	YT	08.92	91-94	51	3	1
Reading	Tr	07.95	95-97	33	10	1
Hull C	Tr	12.98	98-00	57	11	0
Halifax T	Tr	08.01	01	20	4	1

SWALLOW Ernest **Barry**
Arksey, 2 July, 1942 (CD)

League Club	Source	Date Signed	Seasons Played	Apps	Subs	Gls
Doncaster Rov	Jnrs	07.59	60-61	51	-	10
Crewe Alex	Tr	08.62	62-63	14	-	0
Barnsley	Tr	07.64	64-66	96	0	1
Bradford C	Tr	02.67	66-69	79	6	7
York C	Tr	10.69	69-75	268	1	21

SWALLOW Ernest (Ernie)
Wheatley Hill, 9 July, 1919 Died 1962 (FB)

League Club	Source	Date Signed	Seasons Played	Apps	Subs	Gls
Doncaster Rov	Bentley Colliery	11.41	46-47	50	-	0
Barnsley	Tr	01.48	47-49	36	-	0
Oldham Ath	Tr	08.50	50	6	-	0

SWALLOW Raymond (Ray)
Southwark, 15 June, 1935 (W)

League Club	Source	Date Signed	Seasons Played	Apps	Subs	Gls
Arsenal	Tooting & Mitcham	12.52	54-57	13	-	4
Derby Co	Tr	09.58	58-63	118	-	21

SWAN Carl
Sheffield, 12 December, 1957 (CD)

League Club	Source	Date Signed	Seasons Played	Apps	Subs	Gls
Doncaster Rov	Burton A	12.80	80-82	14	1	1
Rochdale	L	10.82	82	3	0	0

SWAN Iain
Glasgow, 16 October, 1979 (CD)

League Club	Source	Date Signed	Seasons Played	Apps	Subs	Gls
Oldham Ath	YT	11.96	98	1	0	0

SWAN Maurice Michael George
Dublin, 27 September, 1938 IR-1 (G)

League Club	Source	Date Signed	Seasons Played	Apps	Subs	Gls
Cardiff C	Drumcondra	07.60	60-62	15	-	0
Hull C	Tr	06.63	63-67	103	0	0

SWAN Peter
South Elmsall, 8 October, 1936 EYth/Eu23-3/FLge-6/E-19 (CD)

League Club	Source	Date Signed	Seasons Played	Apps	Subs	Gls
Sheffield Wed	Jnrs	11.53	55-63	260	-	0
Sheffield Wed	(Retired)	07.72	72	13	2	0
Bury	Tr	08.73	73	35	0	2

SWAN Peter Harold
Leeds, 28 September, 1966 (CD)

League Club	Source	Date Signed	Seasons Played	Apps	Subs	Gls
Leeds U	App	08.84	85-88	43	6	11
Hull C	Tr	03.89	88-90	76	4	24
Port Vale	Tr	08.91	91-93	105	6	5
Plymouth Arg	Tr	07.94	94	24	3	2
Burnley	Tr	08.95	95-96	47	2	7
Bury	Tr	08.97	97	26	11	6
Burnley	Tr	08.98	98-99	11	8	0
York C	Tr	03.00	99-00	11	0	0

SWAN Ronald (Ron) McDonald
Plean, 8 January, 1941 (G)

League Club	Source	Date Signed	Seasons Played	Apps	Subs	Gls
Oldham Ath	East Stirling	05.64	64-66	64	0	0
Luton T	Tr	01.67	66	14	0	0

SWANKIE Robert (Bob) Beattie
Arbroath, 25 February, 1932 (WH)

League Club	Source	Date Signed	Seasons Played	Apps	Subs	Gls
Burnley	Arbroath YC	07.50				
Darlington	Gloucester C	01.54	53	1	-	0

SWANN Gary
York, 11 April, 1962 (FB)

League Club	Source	Date Signed	Seasons Played	Apps	Subs	Gls
Hull C	App	04.80	80-86	176	10	9
Preston NE	Tr	11.86	86-91	194	5	37
York C	Tr	06.92	92-93	82	0	4
Scarborough	Tr	08.94	94	24	3	3

SWANN Gordon
Maltby, 7 December, 1937 (W)

League Club	Source	Date Signed	Seasons Played	Apps	Subs	Gls
Rotherham U		07.57	58-60	11	-	1
Barnsley	Tr	07.61	61	2	-	0

SWANNELL John
Walton-on-Thames, 26 January, 1939 EAmat (G)

League Club	Source	Date Signed	Seasons Played	Apps	Subs	Gls
Stockport Co (Am)	Corinthian Casuals	06.59	59	1	-	0

SWEENEY Alan
Paisley, 31 October, 1956 (FB)

League Club	Source	Date Signed	Seasons Played	Apps	Subs	Gls
Huddersfield T	App	11.73	74-77	65	1	0
Hartlepool U	Emley	09.79	79-81	97	0	2

SWEENEY Andrew (Andy)
Chadderton, 15 October, 1951 (W)

League Club	Source	Date Signed	Seasons Played	Apps	Subs	Gls
Oldham Ath	Jnrs	02.71	70-74	37	5	2
Bury	L	03.73	72	2	0	0
Rochdale	Tr	07.75	75	12	5	0

SWEENEY Antony Thomas
Stockton, 5 September, 1983 (M)

League Club	Source	Date Signed	Seasons Played	Apps	Subs	Gls
Hartlepool U	YT	01.02	01-04	54	7	14

SWEENEY Gerald (Gerry)
Renfrew, 10 July, 1945 (FB)

League Club	Source	Date Signed	Seasons Played	Apps	Subs	Gls
Bristol C	Morton	08.71	71-81	396	10	22
York C	Tr	02.82	81	12	0	0

SWEENEY Paul Martin
Glasgow, 10 January, 1965 (FB)

League Club	Source	Date Signed	Seasons Played	Apps	Subs	Gls
Newcastle U	Raith Rov	03.89	88-90	28	8	0
Hartlepool U	Gateshead	08.94	94	1	0	0

League Club	Source	Date Signed	Seasons Played	Career Record Apps	Subs	Gls
SWEENEY Peter Henry						
Glasgow, 25 September, 1984 SYth/Su21-8/SB-1						(F)
Millwall	Jnrs	12.00	01-04	45	14	5
SWEENEY Terry Neil						
Paisley, 26 January, 1979						(M)
Luton T	YT	03.97				
Plymouth Arg	Tr	10.98	98	6	7	1
SWEENEY William Clerihew						
St Andrews, 23 October, 1918						(G)
Carlisle U	Clyde	01.48	47-48	37	-	0
SWEENIE Thomas (Tom) Thornton						
Paisley, 15 July, 1945						(M)
Leicester C	Johnstone Burgh	06.63	63-66	50	1	11
York C	Tr	10.68	68	6	0	1
SWEETZER Gordon Eric Peter						
Toronto, Canada, 27 January, 1957 Canada int						(F)
Brentford		07.75	75-77	68	4	40
Cambridge U	Tr	04.78	77-79	9	0	3
Brentford	Toronto (Can)	01.82	81	8	1	1
SWEETZER James (Jimmy) Edward						
Woking, 8 January, 1960						(F)
Oxford U	App	02.77	78	0	8	1
Millwall	Tr	11.79	79	2	1	1
SWIERCZEWSKI Piotr						
Nowy Sacz, Poland, 8 April, 1972 Poland 92						(M)
Birmingham C	Marseille (Fr)	01.03	02	0	1	0
SWIFT Colin						
Barnsley, 23 December, 1933						(FB)
Barnsley	Jnrs	08.51	55-61	241	-	0
SWIFT Frank Victor						
Blackpool, 26 December, 1913 Died 1958 FLge-3/EWar-14/E-19						(G)
Manchester C	Fleetwood	10.32	33-49	338	-	0
SWIFT Humphrey (Hugh) Mills						
Sheffield, 22 January, 1921 Died 1979 EB						(FB)
Sheffield Wed	Lopham Street Meth	09.42	46-50	181	-	0
SWIFT John Maxwell						
Leeds, 20 September, 1984						(FB)
Bradford C	Sch	08.04	04	2	3	0
SWIFT John **Kenneth (Kenny)**						
Fazakerley, 26 July, 1928						(W)
Liverpool	Jnrs	08.45				
Southport	Tr	07.51	51	5	-	0
SWIFT Trevor						
Rotherham, 14 September, 1948						(CD)
Rotherham U	Jnrs	09.65	67-74	283	4	21
SWIGGS Bradley						
Plymouth, 12 October, 1959						(F)
Plymouth Arg	Liskeard Ath	03.84	83	1	1	0
SWIGGS Robert (Bob)						
Plymouth, 30 March, 1930						(CF)
Plymouth Arg	St Blazey	01.56	55-56	3	-	0
SWINBOURNE Royston (Roy) Harry						
Barnburgh, 25 August, 1929 EB						(CF)
Wolverhampton W	Jnrs	09.46	49-55	211	-	107
SWINBURNE Alan Thomas Anderson						
Houghton-le-Spring, 18 May, 1946						(G)
Oldham Ath	App	09.63	63	4	-	0
SWINBURNE Thomas (Tom) Anderson						
Houghton-le-Spring, 9 August, 1915 Died 1969 EWar-1						(G)
Newcastle U	Herrington Colliery	04.34	34-46	77	-	0
SWINBURNE Trevor						
Houghton-le-Spring, 20 June, 1953						(G)
Sunderland	App	06.70	72-76	10	0	0
Carlisle U	Tr	05.77	77-82	248	0	0
Brentford	Tr	08.83	83-84	45	0	0
Leeds U	Tr	06.85	85	2	0	0
Doncaster Rov	L	09.85	85	4	0	0
Lincoln C	Tr	02.86	85-86	34	0	0
SWINDELLS Jack (Jackie)						
Manchester, 12 April, 1937 EYth						(IF)
Blackburn Rov	Manchester C (Am)	11.57	57-59	9	-	1
Accrington St	Tr	12.59	59-60	65	-	28
Barnsley	Tr	06.61	61	14	-	8
Workington	Tr	02.62	61-62	62	-	19
Torquay U	Tr	07.63	63	18	-	6
Newport Co	Tr	07.64	64	23	-	3
SWINDIN George Hedley						
Campsall, 4 December, 1914						(G)
Bradford C	Rotherham U (Am)	02.33	34-35	26	-	0
Arsenal	Tr	04.36	36-53	271	-	0
SWINDLEHURST David (Dave)						
Edgware, 6 January, 1956 EYth/Eu21-1						(F)
Crystal Palace	App	01.73	73-79	221	16	73
Derby Co	Tr	02.80	79-82	110	0	29
West Ham U	Tr	03.83	82-84	52	9	16
Sunderland	Tr	08.85	85-86	59	0	11
Wimbledon	Anorthosis (Cyp)	03.88	87	2	0	0
Colchester U	Tr	06.88	88	12	0	6
Peterborough U	L	12.88	88	4	0	1
SWINFEN Reginald (Reg)						
Battersea, 4 May, 1915 Died 1996						(FB)
Queens Park Rgrs	Civil Service	03.36	36-46	26	-	5
SWINSCOE Terence (Terry)						
Shirebrook, 31 August, 1934						(FB)
Stockport Co	Spalding U	02.56				
Mansfield T	Tr	11.56	56-58	14	-	0
SWINSCOE Thomas (Tom) William						
Mansfield, 16 October, 1919 Died 1993						(CF)
Chesterfield	Shirebrook Supporters	03.46	46-47	43	-	12
Stockport Co	Tr	02.48	47-49	72	-	31
SWITZER George						
Salford, 13 October, 1973						(FB)
Manchester U	YT	07.92				
Darlington	Tr	08.93	93	12	2	0
SWONNELL Samuel (Sam) Alfred						
Brentwood, 13 September, 1982						(M)
Watford	YT	03.01	02	1	1	0
SWORD Alan						
Newcastle, 5 July, 1934						(CF)
Newcastle U	Jnrs	08.51				
Exeter C	Tr	09.53	55	9	-	4
SWORD Thomas (Tommy) William						
Newcastle, 12 November, 1957						(CD)
Stockport Co	Bishop Auckland	11.79	79-85	236	2	51
Hartlepool U	Tr	07.86	86	18	0	0
Halifax T	L	02.87	86	8	0	2
Stockport Co	Tr	03.87	86-87	6	1	1
SYDENHAM John						
Eastleigh, 15 September, 1939 EYth/Eu23-2						(W)
Southampton	CPC Sports	04.57	56-69	341	2	36
Aldershot	Tr	03.70	69-71	54	5	4
SYKES Alexander (Alex)						
Newcastle-under-Lyme, 2 April, 1974						(W)
Mansfield T	Westfields	06.92	93	1	1	1
SYKES John						
Huddersfield, 2 November, 1950						(F)
Bradford PA	App	11.68	68	1	0	0
Wrexham	Tr	01.69	68	1	0	0
SYKES Kenneth (Ken)						
Darlington, 29 January, 1926						(CF)
Darlington		05.46	46	6	-	2
Middlesbrough	Tr	06.47				
Hartlepools U	Tr	09.49	49	1	-	0
SYKES Norman Albert John						
Bristol, 16 October, 1936 ESch/EYth						(WH)
Bristol Rov	Jnrs	10.53	56-63	214	-	5
Plymouth Arg	Tr	09.64	64	3	-	0
Stockport Co	Tr	09.65	65-66	52	0	7
Doncaster Rov	Tr	02.67	66	15	0	0
SYME Colin						
Rosyth, 23 January, 1924 Died 2001						(W)
Torquay U	Dunfermline Ath	12.46	46	1	-	0
SYMES Michael						
Great Yarmouth, 31 October, 1983						(F)
Everton	YT	02.02				
Crewe Alex	L	03.04	03	1	3	1
Bradford C	Tr	08.04	04	5	7	2

SYMM Colin
Dunston-on-Tyne, 26 November, 1946 (M)

League Club	Source	Date Signed	Seasons Played	Apps	Subs	Gls
Sheffield Wed	Gateshead	05.65	66-68	16	3	1
Sunderland	Tr	06.69	69-71	9	5	0
Lincoln C	Tr	06.72	72-74	60	9	7

SYMMONS Iorwerth
Swansea, 3 February, 1930 (FB)

League Club	Source	Date Signed	Seasons Played	Apps	Subs	Gls
Swansea T	Hafod	05.48	50-51	16	-	0

SYMONDS Anthony (Tony)
Wakefield, 10 November, 1944 Died 2002 (WH)

League Club	Source	Date Signed	Seasons Played	Apps	Subs	Gls
Bradford PA	Great Preston Jnrs	07.62	64-66	28	1	2

SYMONDS Roderick **Calvin** Hilgrove
Bermuda, 29 March, 1932 (CF)

League Club	Source	Date Signed	Seasons Played	Apps	Subs	Gls
Rochdale	Pembroke (Ber)	10.54	55	1	-	0

SYMONDS Richard
Langham, 21 November, 1959 (FB)

League Club	Source	Date Signed	Seasons Played	Apps	Subs	Gls
Norwich C	App	08.78	78-82	55	4	0

SYMONS Christopher (Kit) Jeremiah
Basingstoke, 8 March, 1971 WYth/Wu21-2/WB-1/W-37 (CD)

League Club	Source	Date Signed	Seasons Played	Apps	Subs	Gls
Portsmouth	YT	12.88	88-95	161	0	10
Manchester C	Tr	08.95	95-97	124	0	4
Fulham	Tr	07.98	98-01	96	6	13
Crystal Palace	Tr	12.01	01-03	42	7	0

SYMONS Paul
North Shields, 20 April, 1976 (F)

League Club	Source	Date Signed	Seasons Played	Apps	Subs	Gls
Blackpool	YT	07.94	93	0	1	0

SYRETT David (Dave) Kenneth
Salisbury, 20 January, 1956 EYth (F)

League Club	Source	Date Signed	Seasons Played	Apps	Subs	Gls
Swindon T	App	11.73	73-76	110	12	30
Mansfield T	Tr	08.77	77-78	65	0	20
Walsall	Tr	03.79	78	11	0	3
Peterborough U	Tr	08.79	79-81	75	4	23
Northampton T	Tr	06.82	82-83	42	2	13

SYROS George
Athens, Greece, 8 February, 1976 (CD)

League Club	Source	Date Signed	Seasons Played	Apps	Subs	Gls
Bury	Akratitos (Gre)	08.01	01	9	0	1

SZABO Tibor Lewis
Wibsey, 28 October, 1959 (F)

League Club	Source	Date Signed	Seasons Played	Apps	Subs	Gls
Bradford C	App	10.77	78	8	5	1

SZMID Marek Andrezj
Nuneaton, 2 March, 1982 ESch/EYth (M)

League Club	Source	Date Signed	Seasons Played	Apps	Subs	Gls
Manchester U	YT	09.99				
Southend U	Tr	11.01	01	1	1	0

League Club Source Date Signed Seasons Played Career Record Apps Subs Gls

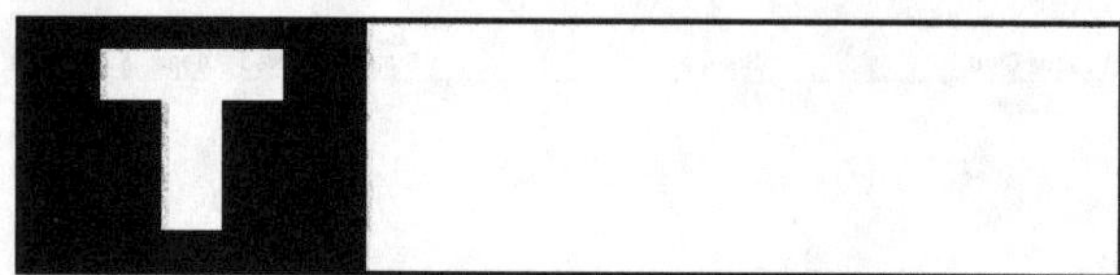

League Club	Source	Date Signed	Seasons Played	Career Record Apps	Subs	Gls
TAAFFE Steven Lee						
Stoke-on-Trent, 10 September, 1979						(F)
Stoke C	YT	08.96	97-99	3	5	0
TABB Jay Anthony						
Tooting, 21 February, 1984 IRu21-7						(M)
Brentford	YT	07.01	00-04	53	33	14
TADMAN Maurice Roy						
Rainham, Kent, 28 June, 1921 Died 1994						(CF)
Charlton Ath	Bexleyheath & Welling	06.38	46	3	-	0
Plymouth Arg	Tr	08.47	47-54	240	-	108
TAFT Douglas (Doug)						
Leicester, 9 March, 1926 Died 1987						(CF)
Derby Co		11.47	48	6	-	1
TAGG Anthony (Tony) Peter						
Epsom, 10 April, 1957						(CD)
Queens Park Rgrs	App	03.75	75	4	0	0
Millwall	Tr	07.77	77-81	130	3	9
Wimbledon	Tr	07.82	82	14	0	0
TAGG Ernest (Ernie)						
Crewe, 15 September, 1917						(WH)
Crewe Alex		10.37	37	19	-	7
Wolverhampton W	Tr	05.38	38	1	-	0
Bournemouth	Tr	05.39	46-48	80	-	8
Carlisle U	Tr	11.48	48	5	-	1
TAGGART Gerald (Gerry) Paul						
Belfast, 18 October, 1970 NISch/NIYth/NIu23-2/NI-51						(CD)
Manchester C	YT	07.89	88-89	10	2	1
Barnsley	Tr	01.90	89-94	209	3	16
Bolton W	Tr	08.95	95-97	68	1	4
Leicester C	Tr	07.98	98-03	105	12	9
Stoke C	L	12.03	03	8	0	2
Stoke C	Tr	02.04	03-04	44	0	2
TAGGART Robert (Bobby)						
Newmains, 10 March, 1927						(IF)
Cardiff C	Coltness U	05.49	49	2	-	0
Torquay U	Tr	06.50	50	14	-	2
Aldershot	Tr	08.51	51	16	-	2
TAIBI Massimo						
Palermo, Italy, 18 February, 1970						(G)
Manchester U	Venezia (It)	09.99	99	4	0	0
TAINTON Trevor Keith						
Bristol, 8 June, 1948 ESch						(M)
Bristol C	App	09.65	67-81	456	30	24
Torquay U	Tr	02.82	81	19	0	1
TAIT Alexander (Alex)						
West Sleekburn, 28 November, 1933 EYth						(CF)
Newcastle U	Jnrs	09.52	54-59	32	-	8
Bristol C	Tr	06.60	60-63	117	-	38
Doncaster Rov	Tr	06.64	64	19	-	7
TAIT Barry Stuart						
York, 17 June, 1938						(IF)
York C	Doncaster Rov (Am)	09.58	58-60	15	-	5
Bradford C	Tr	11.61	61	20	-	10
Halifax T	Tr	07.62	62-63	36	-	23
Crewe Alex	Tr	09.63	63	9	-	2
Notts Co	Tr	07.64	64	3	-	0
TAIT Jordan Alexander						
Berwick-on-Tweed, 27 September, 1979						(FB)
Newcastle U	YT	07.98				
Oldham Ath	Tr	08.99	99	0	1	0
Darlington	Tr	10.00	00	2	1	0
TAIT Michael (Mick) Paul						
Wallsend, 30 September, 1956						(M)
Oxford U	App	10.74	74-76	61	3	23
Carlisle U	Tr	02.77	76-79	101	5	20
Hull C	Tr	09.79	79	29	4	3
Portsmouth	Tr	06.80	80-86	228	12	31
Reading	Tr	09.87	87-89	98	1	9
Darlington	Tr	08.90	90-91	79	0	2
Hartlepool U	Tr	07.92	92-93	60	1	1
Hartlepool U	Gretna	09.94	94-96	74	4	2
TAIT Paul						
Newcastle, 24 October, 1974						(F)
Everton	YT	07.93				
Wigan Ath	Tr	07.94	94	1	4	0
Crewe Alex	Northwich Vic	06.99	99-01	31	32	6
Hull C	L	11.01	01	0	2	0
Bristol Rov	Tr	07.02	02-03	61	13	19
Rochdale	Tr	07.04	04	27	9	2
TAIT Paul Ronald						
Sutton Coldfield, 31 July, 1971						(M)
Birmingham C	YT	08.88	87-96	135	35	14
Northampton T	L	12.97	97	2	1	0
Oxford U	Tr	01.99	98-01	86	5	3
TAIT Peter						
York, 17 October, 1936						(CF)
York C (Am)	Jnrs	08.55	55	3	-	1
TAIT Robert (Bobby) James						
Edinburgh, 4 October, 1938						(IF)
Notts Co	Aberdeen	07.62	62-63	60	-	11
Barrow	Tr	07.64	64-65	78	1	29
Chesterfield	Tr	07.66	66	27	1	2
TAL Idan						
Petach-Tikva, Israel, 13 September, 1975 Israel 38						(M)
Everton	Maccabi Petach T (Isr)	10.00	00-01	13	16	2
TALBOT Andrew (Drew)						
Barnsley, 19 July, 1986						(F)
Sheffield Wed	Dodworth MW	02.04	04	3	18	4
TALBOT Brian Ernest						
Ipswich, 21 July, 1953 Eu21-1/EB/E-6						(M)
Ipswich T	App	07.70	73-78	177	0	25
Arsenal	Tr	01.79	78-84	245	9	40
Watford	Tr	06.85	85-86	46	2	8
Stoke C	Tr	10.86	86-87	51	3	5
West Bromwich A	Tr	01.88	87-89	66	8	5
Fulham	Tr	03.91	90	5	0	1
Aldershot	Tr	03.91	90	10	0	0
TALBOT Daniel (Danny) Brian						
Enfield, 30 January, 1984						(FB)
Rushden & Diamonds	Jnrs	02.01	01-03	10	13	1
TALBOT Ernest (Ernie)						
Workington, 13 November, 1932						(IF)
Workington		08.51	52-57	18	-	7
TALBOT Gary						
Blackburn, 15 December, 1937						(F)
Chester		09.63	63-66	110	1	61
Crewe Alex	Tr	07.67	67	37	0	20
Chester	Tr	06.68	68	43	0	22
TALBOT Jason Christopher						
Irlam, 30 September, 1985						(FB)
Bolton W	Sch	09.04				
Derby Co	L	09.04	04	2	0	0
Mansfield T	L	11.04	04	2	0	0
TALBOT Frank **Leslie (Les)**						
Hednesford, 3 August, 1910						(IF)
Blackburn Rov	Hednesford T	10.30	30-35	90	-	20
Cardiff C	Tr	06.36	36-38	94	-	21
Walsall	Tr	06.39	46	18	-	5
TALBOT Paul Michael						
Gateshead, 11 August, 1979						(FB)
Newcastle U	YT	07.97				
York C	Tr	03.00	99	5	1	0
TALBOT Stewart Dean						
Birmingham, 14 June, 1973						(M)
Port Vale	Moor Green Rov	08.94	94-99	112	25	10
Rotherham U	Tr	07.00	00-03	100	14	8
Shrewsbury T	L	02.03	02	5	0	0
Brentford	Tr	02.04	03-04	50	2	3
TALBOTT Nathan Anthony						
Wolverhampton, 21 October, 1984						(CD)
Yeovil T	Wolverhampton W (Sch)	03.04	03	0	1	0
TALBOYS Steven (Steve) John						
Bristol, 18 September, 1966						(W)
Wimbledon	Gloucester C	01.92	92-95	19	7	1
Watford	Tr	06.96	96-97	2	3	0

League Club	Source	Date Signed	Seasons Played	Career Record Apps	Subs	Gls
TALBUT John						
Headington, 20 October, 1940 ESch/Eu23-7						(CD)
Burnley	Jnrs	10.57	58-66	138	0	0
West Bromwich A	Tr	12.66	66-70	143	1	0
TALIA Francesco (Frank)						
Melbourne, Australia, 20 July, 1972 AuSch/Auu20						(G)
Blackburn Rov	Sunshine GC (Aus)	08.92				
Hartlepool U	L	12.92	92	14	0	0
Swindon T	Tr	09.95	95-99	107	0	0
Sheffield U	Tr	09.00	00	6	0	0
Reading	Royal Antwerp (Bel)	03.02				
Wycombe W	Tr	08.02	02-04	97	0	0
TALKES Wayne Anthony Norman						
Ealing, 2 June, 1952						(M)
Southampton	App	07.69	71-73	7	2	0
Doncaster Rov	L	12.73	73	3	1	0
Bournemouth	Tr	07.74	74	5	0	0
TALLON Darren John Bernard						
Plymouth, 1 June, 1972						(CD)
Plymouth Arg	YT	10.90	90	1	0	0
TALLON Gerrit (Gary) Thomas						
Drogheda, 5 September, 1973						(W)
Blackburn Rov	Drogheda	11.91				
Chester C (L)	Kilmarnock	03.97	96	1	0	0
Mansfield T	Kilmarnock	12.97	97-99	68	7	2
TAMBLING Robert (Bobby) Victor						
Storrington, 18 September, 1941 ESch/Eu23-13/FLge-1/E-3						(F)
Chelsea	Jnrs	09.58	58-69	298	4	164
Crystal Palace	Tr	01.70	69-73	67	1	12
TANKARD Allen John						
Islington, 21 May, 1969 EYth						(FB)
Southampton	App	05.87	85-86	5	0	0
Wigan Ath	Tr	07.88	88-92	205	4	4
Port Vale	Tr	07.93	93-00	261	14	11
Mansfield T	Tr	08.01	01	22	8	2
TANN Adam John						
Fakenham, 12 May, 1982 EYth						(CD)
Cambridge U	YT	09.99	00-04	111	10	4
TANNER Adam David						
Maldon, 25 October, 1973						(M)
Ipswich T	YT	07.92	94-98	49	24	7
Peterborough U	Tr	03.00				
Colchester U	Tr	08.00	00	1	3	0
TANNER Graham George						
Bridgwater, 4 September, 1947						(CD)
Bristol C	App	09.64				
Bradford PA	Tr	10.67	67-68	44	0	2
TANNER John Denys Parkin						
Harrogate, 2 July, 1921 Died 1987 EAmat						(W)
Huddersfield T (Am)	Yorkshire Amats	08.48	48	1	-	1
TANNER Michael (Mike) William						
Bristol, 28 October, 1964						(M)
Bristol C		07.85	85-87	16	3	1
TANNER Nicholas (Nick)						
Kingswood, 24 May, 1965						(CD)
Bristol Rov	Mangotsfield U	06.85	85-87	104	3	3
Liverpool	Tr	07.88	89-92	36	4	1
Norwich C	L	03.90	89	6	0	0
Swindon T	L	09.90	90	7	0	0
TANNER Thomas (Tom)						
Devonport, 24 June, 1922						(W)
Torquay U (Am)	Plymouth U	09.46	46	1	-	0
TANSEY Gerard						
Liverpool, 15 October, 1933						(W)
Everton	Jnrs	10.51				
Tranmere Rov	Tr	07.55	55	3	-	1
TANSEY James (Jim)						
Liverpool, 29 January, 1929						(FB)
Everton		05.48	52-59	133	-	0
Crewe Alex	Tr	06.60	60	9	-	0
TAPKEN Norman						
Wallsend, 21 February, 1913 Died 1996 Lol-2						(G)
Newcastle U	Wallsend Thermal Welf	05.33	34-37	106	-	0
Manchester U	Tr	12.38	38	14	-	0
Darlington	Tr	04.47	46-47	31	-	0

League Club	Source	Date Signed	Seasons Played	Career Record Apps	Subs	Gls
TAPLEY Reginald (Reg)						
Nantwich, 2 November, 1932						(W)
Crewe Alex		09.53				
Rochdale	Tr	10.56	56	1	-	0
TAPLEY Steven (Steve)						
Camberwell, 3 October, 1963						(CD)
Fulham	App	10.81	83-84	2	0	1
Rochdale	L	02.85	84	1	0	0
TAPP Alexander (Alex) Nicholas						
Redhill, 7 June, 1982 ESch						(M)
Wimbledon/MK Dons	YT	01.00	02-04	40	10	4
TAPPING Frederick (Fred) Harold						
Derby, 29 July, 1921						(WH)
Blackpool		10.43				
Chesterfield	Tr	11.47	47	1	-	0
TAPSCOTT Derek Robert						
Barry, 30 June, 1932 W-14						(IF)
Arsenal	Barry T	10.53	53-57	119	-	62
Cardiff C	Tr	09.58	58-64	193	-	79
Newport Co	Tr	07.65	65	12	1	1
TAPSCOTT Eli **John (Johnnie)**						
Falmouth, 29 April, 1928 Died 1981						(WH)
Leeds U		03.50				
Wrexham	Tr	05.50	50-55	172	-	4
TARACHULSKI Bartosz						
Gliwice, Poland, 14 May, 1975						(F)
Yeovil T	Polonia Warsaw (Pol)	07.04	04	27	15	10
TARANTINI Alberto Cesar						
Buenos Aires, Argentina, 3 December, 1955 Argentina int						(FB)
Birmingham C	Boca Juniors (Arg)	10.78	78	23	0	1
TARBUCK Alan David						
Liverpool, 10 October, 1948						(W)
Everton	App	08.66				
Crewe Alex	Tr	06.67	67-69	79	6	18
Chester	Tr	10.69	69-71	69	0	24
Preston NE	Tr	09.71	71-72	42	6	17
Shrewsbury T	Tr	03.73	72-75	107	17	17
Rochdale	Tr	07.76	76-77	48	0	1
TARDIF Christopher (Chris) Luke						
Guernsey, 19 September, 1979						(G)
Portsmouth	YT	07.98	00-01	3	2	0
Bournemouth	L	08.02	02	9	0	0
Oxford U	Tr	07.04	04	40	0	0
TARGETT Haydn **Roy**						
Shepton Mallet, 1 July, 1928						(FB)
Torquay U	Shepton Mallet	10.49	50	1	-	0
TARICCO Mauricio Ricardo						
Buenos Aires, Argentina, 10 March, 1973 Aru23						(FB)
Ipswich T	Argentinos Jnrs (Arg)	09.94	95-98	134	3	4
Tottenham H	Tr	12.98	98-03	125	5	2
West Ham U	Tr	11.04	04	1	0	0
TARNAT Michael						
Hilden, Germany, 27 October, 1969 Germany 19						(FB)
Manchester C	Bayern Munich (Ger)	07.03	03	32	0	3
TARRANT Brian Leslie						
Stainforth, 22 July, 1938						(IF)
Leeds U	Jnrs	08.55				
Mansfield T	Tr	07.60	60	3	-	0
TARRANT John **Edward (Ted)**						
Stainforth, 12 February, 1932						(WH)
Hull C	Jnrs	02.49	50-53	30	-	2
Walsall	Tr	12.53	53-57	102	-	10
TARRANT Neil Kenneth						
Darlington, 24 June, 1979 Su21-5						(F)
Darlington	YT	07.97				
Aston Villa	Ross Co	04.99				
York C	L	10.00	00	6	1	1
TARTT Colin						
Liverpool, 23 November, 1950						(FB)
Port Vale	Alsager College	07.72	72-76	171	4	7
Chesterfield	Tr	03.77	76-81	185	1	7
Port Vale	Tr	10.81	81-84	111	6	9
TATE Alan						
Easington, 2 September, 1982						(CD)
Manchester U	YT	07.00				
Swansea C	L	11.02	02	27	0	0

League Club	Source	Date Signed	Seasons Played	Career Record Apps	Subs	Gls
Swansea C	L	10.03	03	9	0	0
Swansea C	Tr	02.04	03-04	33	7	1
TATE Christopher (Chris) Douglas						
York, 27 December, 1977						(F)
Sunderland	York C (YT)	07.96				
Scarborough	Tr	08.97	97-98	21	28	13
Halifax T	Tr	07.99	99	18	0	4
Leyton Orient	Scarborough	11.00	00-03	34	41	10
Mansfield T	Tr	07.04	04	0	4	0
TATE Craig David						
South Shields, 16 October, 1979						(F)
Shrewsbury T	YT	•	96	0	1	0
TATE Geoffrey (Geoff) Michael						
Leicester, 16 December, 1937 ESch/EYth						(W)
Derby Co	Jnrs	08.55	55	1	-	1
TATE Jeffrey (Jeff)						
Blyth, 11 May, 1959 ESch						(M)
Burnley	Jnrs	08.78	79	5	0	1
TAVENER Colin Raymond						
Trowbridge, 26 June, 1945						(M)
Hereford U	Trowbridge T	06.72	72-73	50	1	3
TAVLARIDIS Eustathis (Stathis)						
Serres, Greece, 25 January, 1980 Gru21						(CD)
Arsenal	Iraklis Salonika (Gre)	09.01	02	0	1	0
Portsmouth	L	01.03	02	3	1	0
TAWSE Brian						
Ellon, 30 July, 1945						(W)
Arsenal	King Street 'A'	04.63	64	5	-	0
Brighton & Hove A	Tr	12.65	65-69	97	5	14
Brentford	Tr	02.70	69-70	19	2	1
TAYLOR Alan						
Thornton-Cleveleys, 17 May, 1943						(G)
Blackpool	Blackpool Rgrs	10.63	65-70	94	0	0
Oldham Ath	L	12.69	69	2	0	0
Stockport Co	L	08.70	70	5	0	0
Southport	Tr	07.71	71-73	102	0	0
TAYLOR Alan						
Derby, 7 March, 1954						(W)
Chelsea	Alfreton T	10.72				
Reading	Tr	05.74	74	13	8	4
TAYLOR Alan David						
Hinckley, 14 November, 1953						(F)
Rochdale	Morecambe	05.73	73-74	55	0	7
West Ham U	Tr	11.74	74-78	88	10	25
Norwich C	Tr	08.79	79	20	4	5
Cambridge U	Vancouver (Can)	10.80	80-81	17	1	4
Hull C	Vancouver (Can)	01.84	83	13	1	3
Burnley	Tr	08.84	84-85	60	4	23
Bury	Tr	06.86	86-87	55	7	10
Norwich C	Tr	09.88	88	1	3	1
TAYLOR Albert (Bert) Herbert						
Worksop, 2 May, 1924						(G)
Bury	Worksop T	10.45	46-47	4	-	0
Sheffield U	Tr	05.48				
Halifax T	Tr	07.51	51	8	-	0
TAYLOR Alexander (Alex)						
Menstrie, 25 December, 1916 Died 1982						(CD)
Carlisle U	King's Park	06.38	38-46	24	-	0
TAYLOR Alexander (Alex)						
Baillieston, 13 June, 1962						(M)
Walsall	Hamilton Academical	08.88	88-89	43	2	6
TAYLOR Andrew (Andy)						
Stratford-on-Avon, 4 April, 1963						(FB)
Northampton T	Aston Villa (App)	06.81	81	17	0	0
TAYLOR Andrew (Andy)						
Chesterfield, 30 December, 1967						(F)
Chesterfield	App	07.86	86-87	7	5	1
TAYLOR Andrew (Andy)						
Rawmarsh, 19 January, 1973						(FB)
Rotherham U	YT	06.91	90-92	17	1	0
TAYLOR Anthony (Tony)						
Glasgow, 6 September, 1946						(FB)
Crystal Palace	Morton	11.68	68-73	192	3	8
Southend U	Tr	08.74	74-75	56	0	1

League Club	Source	Date Signed	Seasons Played	Career Record Apps	Subs	Gls
Swindon T	Tr	08.76	76	20	6	0
Bristol Rov	Athlone T	09.77	77	12	0	0
Portsmouth	Tr	02.78	77	17	0	0
Northampton T	Tr	07.79	79	4	0	0
TAYLOR Archibald (Archie)						
Glasgow, 4 October, 1918 Died 1976						(WH)
Burnley	Cambuslang	05.37	38	3	-	1
Reading	Tr	06.39	46-47	15	-	2
Leyton Orient	Tr	08.48	48-50	46	-	1
TAYLOR Arthur Alexander						
Lambeg, 5 April, 1931						(W)
Luton T	Glentoran	07.50	52-55	8	-	0
TAYLOR Arthur (Archie) Matson						
Dunscroft, 7 November, 1939						(W)
Bristol C	Doncaster Rov (Am)	05.58	59-60	12	-	2
Barnsley	Tr	07.61	61	2	-	0
Hull C	Goole T	05.62	62	1	-	0
Halifax T	Tr	07.63	63-67	174	0	16
Bradford C	Tr	12.67	67	10	1	0
York C	Tr	10.68	68-70	93	3	8
TAYLOR Arthur Sidney						
Birmingham, 14 March, 1925						(CF)
West Bromwich A	Handsworth Wood	03.42	47	4	-	5
TAYLOR Ashley						
Conisbrough, 11 December, 1959						(FB)
Rotherham U	App	12.77	79-81	21	1	0
TAYLOR George **Barry**						
Sheffield, 3 December, 1939 Died 1996						(FB)
Sheffield U	Jnrs	04.59				
Oldham Ath	Tr	06.63	63	40	-	0
Chesterfield	Tr	08.64	64-65	35	0	2
TAYLOR Brian						
Hammersmith, 2 July, 1944						(FB)
Queens Park Rgrs	Jnrs	03.62	62-65	50	0	0
TAYLOR Brian						
Manchester, 29 June, 1942						(WH)
Rochdale	Jnrs	03.62	63-67	131	1	7
TAYLOR Brian						
Hodthorpe, 12 February, 1954						(CD)
Middlesbrough	App	07.71	72-75	14	4	1
Doncaster Rov	Tr	12.75	75-78	118	1	12
Rochdale	Tr	12.78	78-82	152	2	10
TAYLOR Brian John						
Gateshead, 2 July, 1949 Died 1993						(FB)
Coventry C	Durham C	02.68				
Walsall	Tr	05.71	71-77	204	12	25
Plymouth Arg	Tr	10.77	77-78	34	1	5
Preston NE	Tr	10.78	78-81	93	6	1
Wigan Ath	L	03.82	81	7	1	0
TAYLOR John **Brian**						
Rossington, 7 October, 1931						(G)
Doncaster Rov	Sheffield Wed (Am)	03.49				
Leeds U	Worksop T	05.51	51	11	-	0
Bradford PA	King's Lynn	06.54	54-55	66	-	0
TAYLOR Brian Joseph						
Walsall, 24 March, 1937						(W)
Walsall	Jnrs	09.54	54-57	77	-	17
Birmingham C	Tr	06.58	58-61	54	-	7
Rotherham U	Tr	10.61	61-62	42	-	5
Shrewsbury T	Tr	08.63	63-64	73	-	8
Port Vale	Tr	08.65	65-66	44	2	2
Barnsley	Tr	06.67	67	23	1	2
TAYLOR Carl Wilson						
Kirkby Stephen, 20 January, 1937						(W)
Middlesbrough	Penrith	01.56	57-59	11	-	1
Aldershot	Tr	06.60	60-62	78	-	13
Darlington	Tr	09.62	62	19	-	1
TAYLOR Christopher (Chris) James						
Swindon, 30 October, 1985						(FB)
Swindon T	Sch	•	02	0	4	0
TAYLOR Cleveland Ken Wayne						
Leicester, 9 September, 1983						(W)
Bolton W	Sch	08.02				
Exeter C	L	08.02	02	1	2	0
Scunthorpe U	Tr	01.04	03-04	36	28	9

TAYLOR Colin
Stourbridge, 24 August, 1940 Died 2005 (W)

League Club	Source	Date Signed	Seasons Played	Apps	Subs	Gls
Walsall	Stourbridge	02.58	58-62	213	-	94
Newcastle U	Tr	06.63	63-64	33	-	7
Walsall	Tr	10.64	64-67	148	0	52
Crystal Palace	Tr	05.68	68	32	2	8
Walsall	Tr	09.69	69-72	85	11	24

TAYLOR Colin David
Liverpool, 25 December, 1971 EYth (F)

League Club	Source	Date Signed	Seasons Played	Apps	Subs	Gls
Wolverhampton W	YT	03.90	90-92	7	12	2
Wigan Ath	L	01.92	91	7	0	2
Preston NE	L	11.92	92	4	0	0
Doncaster Rov	L	02.93	92	2	0	0

TAYLOR Craig
Plymouth, 24 January, 1974 (CD)

League Club	Source	Date Signed	Seasons Played	Apps	Subs	Gls
Exeter C	YT	06.92	92	2	3	0
Swindon T	Dorchester T	04.97	97-99	47	8	2
Plymouth Arg	L	10.98	98	6	0	1
Plymouth Arg	Tr	08.99	99-02	80	2	6
Torquay U	L	02.03	02	5	0	0
Torquay U	Tr	07.03	03-04	78	1	4

TAYLOR Daniel (Danny) John
Oldham, 28 July, 1982 (FB)

League Club	Source	Date Signed	Seasons Played	Apps	Subs	Gls
Rochdale	YT	●	99	0	1	0

TAYLOR Daryl Shea
Birmingham, 14 November, 1984 (M)

League Club	Source	Date Signed	Seasons Played	Apps	Subs	Gls
Walsall	Sch	07.04	04	10	9	3

TAYLOR David (Dave)
Rochester, 17 September, 1940 (IF)

League Club	Source	Date Signed	Seasons Played	Apps	Subs	Gls
Gillingham	Jnrs	09.57	57-58	21	-	3
Portsmouth	Tr	06.59	59	2	-	0

TAYLOR Derek Milton
Bradford, 6 June, 1927 Died 1984 (W)

League Club	Source	Date Signed	Seasons Played	Apps	Subs	Gls
Halifax T (Am)	Bradford PA (Am)	08.48	48	2	-	0

TAYLOR Douglas (Doug)
Wolverhampton, 20 April, 1931 (CF)

League Club	Source	Date Signed	Seasons Played	Apps	Subs	Gls
Wolverhampton W	West Bromwich A (Am)	10.49	54	3	-	0
Walsall	Tr	11.55	55-56	36	-	8

TAYLOR Ernest (Ernie)
Sunderland, 2 September, 1925 Died 1985 EB/E-1 (IF)

League Club	Source	Date Signed	Seasons Played	Apps	Subs	Gls
Newcastle U	Hylton Colliery	09.42	47-51	107	-	19
Blackpool	Tr	10.51	51-57	217	-	53
Manchester U	Tr	02.58	57-58	22	-	2
Sunderland	Tr	12.58	58-60	68	-	11

TAYLOR Francis (Frank) Gerald
Magherafelt, 2 January, 1923 (W)

League Club	Source	Date Signed	Seasons Played	Apps	Subs	Gls
Leeds U	Bangor	07.49	49	3	-	0

TAYLOR Frederick (Fred)
Burnley, 24 February, 1920 Died 1983 (W)

League Club	Source	Date Signed	Seasons Played	Apps	Subs	Gls
Burnley	Cambuslang	03.37	37-46	49	-	7
New Brighton	Tr	07.48	48-49	55	-	10

TAYLOR Frederick (Freddie) Robert
Doncaster, 28 October, 1943 (W)

League Club	Source	Date Signed	Seasons Played	Apps	Subs	Gls
Doncaster Rov	Jnrs	07.61	61-64	34	-	2

TAYLOR Gareth Keith
Weston-super-Mare, 25 February, 1973 Wu21-7/W-14 (F)

League Club	Source	Date Signed	Seasons Played	Apps	Subs	Gls
Bristol Rov	Southampton (YT)	07.91	91-95	31	16	16
Crystal Palace	Tr	09.95	95	18	2	1
Sheffield U	Tr	03.96	95-98	56	28	25
Manchester C	Tr	11.98	98-99	28	15	9
Port Vale	L	01.00	99	4	0	0
Queens Park Rgrs	L	03.00	99	2	4	1
Burnley	Tr	02.01	00-02	88	7	36
Nottingham F	Tr	08.03	03-04	61	9	15

TAYLOR Geoffrey (Geoff) Arthur
Henstead, 22 January, 1923 (W)

League Club	Source	Date Signed	Seasons Played	Apps	Subs	Gls
Norwich C	CNSOBU	08.46	46	1	-	0
Reading	Tr	03.47	46	1	-	0
Lincoln C	Tr	08.47	47	1	-	0
Brighton & Hove A	Rennes (Fr)	08.48	48	2	-	0
Bristol Rov	Rennes (Fr)	09.51	51	3	-	0
Queens Park Rgrs	SC Bruhl (Swi)	11.53	53	2	-	0

TAYLOR George Alexander
King Edward, Aberdeenshire, 9 June, 1915 Died 1982 (WH)

League Club	Source	Date Signed	Seasons Played	Apps	Subs	Gls
Plymouth Arg	Aberdeen	08.48	48-49	48	-	2

TAYLOR George Edward
Wigan, 21 March, 1920 Died 1983 (G)

League Club	Source	Date Signed	Seasons Played	Apps	Subs	Gls
West Ham U	Gainsborough Trinity	12.38	46-55	115	-	0

TAYLOR George Jack
Dundee, 23 October, 1948 (W)

League Club	Source	Date Signed	Seasons Played	Apps	Subs	Gls
Grimsby T	Jnrs	11.65	65	0	1	0

TAYLOR George Leslie
Edinburgh, 11 May, 1926 (G)

League Club	Source	Date Signed	Seasons Played	Apps	Subs	Gls
Aldershot	Dunfermline Ath	06.53				
Hartlepools U	Tr	11.53	53-54	34	-	0

TAYLOR George McGregor
Edinburgh, 12 December, 1927 (W)

League Club	Source	Date Signed	Seasons Played	Apps	Subs	Gls
Aldershot	Hamilton Academical	07.52	52	8	-	2

TAYLOR Gerald (Gerry) William
Hull, 15 August, 1947 (FB)

League Club	Source	Date Signed	Seasons Played	Apps	Subs	Gls
Wolverhampton W	Jnrs	11.64	66-75	151	3	1
Swindon T	L	10.75	75	19	0	0

TAYLOR Gordon
Ashton-under-Lyne, 28 December, 1944 (W)

League Club	Source	Date Signed	Seasons Played	Apps	Subs	Gls
Bolton W	Curzon Ashton	01.62	62-70	253	5	41
Birmingham C	Tr	12.70	70-75	156	10	9
Blackburn Rov	Tr	03.76	75-77	62	2	3
Bury	Tr	06.78	78-79	58	2	2

TAYLOR Gordon Stanley
Stanley, 10 June, 1936 (G)

League Club	Source	Date Signed	Seasons Played	Apps	Subs	Gls
Gateshead	West Stanley	02.57	57	3	-	0

TAYLOR Graham
Worksop, 15 September, 1944 (FB)

League Club	Source	Date Signed	Seasons Played	Apps	Subs	Gls
Grimsby T	Jnrs	07.62	63-67	189	0	2
Lincoln C	Tr	07.68	68-72	150	1	1

TAYLOR John Henry **(Harry)**
Crawcrook, 5 October, 1935 Died 2002 (W)

League Club	Source	Date Signed	Seasons Played	Apps	Subs	Gls
Newcastle U	Jnrs	11.52	54-59	28	-	5
Fulham	L	02.57	57	4	-	0

TAYLOR Ian
Doncaster, 25 November, 1967 (G)

League Club	Source	Date Signed	Seasons Played	Apps	Subs	Gls
Carlisle U	Bridlington T	08.90				
Scarborough	Tr	02.92	91	1	0	0

TAYLOR Ian Kenneth
Birmingham, 4 June, 1968 (M)

League Club	Source	Date Signed	Seasons Played	Apps	Subs	Gls
Port Vale	Moor Green	07.92	92-93	83	0	28
Sheffield Wed	Tr	07.94	94	9	5	1
Aston Villa	Tr	12.94	94-02	202	31	28
Derby Co	Tr	07.03	03-04	67	14	14

TAYLOR James
Ashton-in-Makerfield, 7 April, 1925 (W)

League Club	Source	Date Signed	Seasons Played	Apps	Subs	Gls
Manchester C		10.44				
Crewe Alex	Tr	06.47	47-48	49	-	8

TAYLOR James (Jim)
Strood, 13 May, 1934 (IF)

League Club	Source	Date Signed	Seasons Played	Apps	Subs	Gls
Charlton Ath	Tonbridge	08.54				
Gillingham	Tr	08.56	56-57	30	-	16

TAYLOR James (Jimmy)
Salford, 2 November, 1936 (W)

League Club	Source	Date Signed	Seasons Played	Apps	Subs	Gls
Bolton W	Jnrs	12.54				
Southport	Tr	07.59	59	29	-	0

TAYLOR James (Jim) Guy
Cowley, Middlesex, 5 November, 1917 Died 2001 FLge-3/E-2 (CD)

League Club	Source	Date Signed	Seasons Played	Apps	Subs	Gls
Fulham	Hillingdon BL	03.38	46-52	261	-	5
Queens Park Rgrs	Tr	04.53	53	41	-	0

TAYLOR Jamie Lee
Bury, 11 January, 1977 (F)

League Club	Source	Date Signed	Seasons Played	Apps	Subs	Gls
Rochdale	YT	01.94	93-96	10	26	4

TAYLOR Jason Lee
Burgess Hill, 12 October, 1985 (F)

League Club	Source	Date Signed	Seasons Played	Apps	Subs	Gls
Rushden & Diamonds	Sch	●	04	4	16	2

TAYLOR Jason Scott
Wrexham, 29 August, 1970 (F)

League Club	Source	Date Signed	Seasons Played	Apps	Subs	Gls
Wrexham	YT	●	88	0	1	0

TAYLOR Jeffrey (Jeff) Neilson
Huddersfield, 20 September, 1930 (CF)

League Club	Source	Date Signed	Seasons Played	Apps	Subs	Gls
Huddersfield T	Huddersfield YMCA	09.49	49-51	68	-	27
Fulham	Tr	11.51	51-53	33	-	14
Brentford	Tr	08.54	54-56	94	-	34

TAYLOR John (Jack)
Barnsley, 15 February, 1914 Died 1978 (FB)

League Club	Source	Date Signed	Seasons Played	Apps	Subs	Gls
Wolverhampton W	Worsborough Bridge	01.34	35-37	79	-	0

League Club	Source	Date Signed	Seasons Played	Apps	Subs	Gls
Norwich C	Tr	06.38	38-46	50	-	0
Hull C	Tr	07.47	47-49	72	-	0

TAYLOR John
Bradford, 24 June, 1924 (IF)

League Club	Source	Date Signed	Seasons Played	Apps	Subs	Gls
Bradford C	Kilmarnock	09.46	46	2	-	2

TAYLOR John
Creswell, 11 January, 1939 (CF)

League Club	Source	Date Signed	Seasons Played	Apps	Subs	Gls
Mansfield T	Chesterfield (Am)	05.57	59	5	-	2
Peterborough U	Tr	07.60	60	1	-	0

TAYLOR John
Durham, 10 July, 1926 (IF)

League Club	Source	Date Signed	Seasons Played	Apps	Subs	Gls
Crystal Palace (Am)	Leytonstone	05.48	48	1	-	0

TAYLOR John (Jack) Ephraim
Chilton, 11 September, 1924 Died 1970 EB (IF)

League Club	Source	Date Signed	Seasons Played	Apps	Subs	Gls
Luton T	Stockton	02.49	48-51	85	-	29
Wolverhampton W	Tr	06.52	52	10	-	1
Notts Co	Tr	02.54	53-56	53	-	19
Bradford PA	Tr	07.57	57	12	-	6

TAYLOR John James
Manchester, 12 October, 1928 (W)

League Club	Source	Date Signed	Seasons Played	Apps	Subs	Gls
Blackpool		09.49				
Accrington St	Tr	07.52	52	16	-	0

TAYLOR John Keith
Manningham, 7 September, 1935 (CF)

League Club	Source	Date Signed	Seasons Played	Apps	Subs	Gls
Bradford C (Am)		02.56	55	1	-	0

TAYLOR John Leslie
Birmingham, 25 June, 1949 (G)

League Club	Source	Date Signed	Seasons Played	Apps	Subs	Gls
Chester	Pwllheli	07.70	70-73	70	0	0
Rochdale	L	10.74	74	3	0	0
Stockport Co	Bangor C	11.75	75	1	0	0

TAYLOR John Patrick
Norwich, 24 October, 1964 (F)

League Club	Source	Date Signed	Seasons Played	Apps	Subs	Gls
Colchester U	Jnrs	12.82				
Cambridge U	Sudbury T	08.88	88-91	139	21	46
Bristol Rov	Tr	03.92	91-93	91	4	44
Bradford C	Tr	07.94	94	35	1	11
Luton T	Tr	03.95	94-95	27	10	3
Lincoln C	L	09.96	96	5	0	2
Colchester U	L	11.96	96	8	0	5
Cambridge U	Tr	01.97	96-03	103	72	40
Northampton T	Tr	03.04	03	3	5	1

TAYLOR Kenneth (Ken)
Huddersfield, 21 August, 1935 (CD)

League Club	Source	Date Signed	Seasons Played	Apps	Subs	Gls
Huddersfield T	Yorkshire Amats	09.52	53-64	250	-	14
Bradford PA	Tr	02.65	64-66	51	0	1

TAYLOR Kenneth (Ken)
Porthmadog, 5 June, 1952 (FB)

League Club	Source	Date Signed	Seasons Played	Apps	Subs	Gls
Wrexham	Jnrs	05.70	70	1	0	0

TAYLOR Edward **Kenneth (Ken)**
Irvine, 17 May, 1956 (M)

League Club	Source	Date Signed	Seasons Played	Apps	Subs	Gls
Scunthorpe U	Ipswich T (App)	08.74	74	7	0	0

TAYLOR Kenneth (Ken) Gordon
South Shields, 15 March, 1931 (FB)

League Club	Source	Date Signed	Seasons Played	Apps	Subs	Gls
Blackburn Rov	North Shields	01.50	54-63	200	-	0

TAYLOR Kenneth (Ken) Victor
Manchester, 18 June, 1936 (CD)

League Club	Source	Date Signed	Seasons Played	Apps	Subs	Gls
Manchester C	Manchester Corp Trans	08.54	57	1	-	0

TAYLOR Kevin
Wakefield, 22 January, 1961 (M)

League Club	Source	Date Signed	Seasons Played	Apps	Subs	Gls
Sheffield Wed	App	10.78	78-83	118	7	21
Derby Co	Tr	07.84	84	22	0	2
Crystal Palace	Tr	03.85	84-87	85	2	14
Scunthorpe U	Tr	10.87	87-90	149	8	25

TAYLOR Kris
Stafford, 12 January, 1984 EYth (M)

League Club	Source	Date Signed	Seasons Played	Apps	Subs	Gls
Manchester U	YT	02.01				
Walsall	Tr	02.03	03-04	16	7	3

TAYLOR Lawrence (Larry) Desmond
Exeter, 23 November, 1947 (G)

League Club	Source	Date Signed	Seasons Played	Apps	Subs	Gls
Bristol Rov	App	12.65	66-69	90	0	0

TAYLOR Lee Vincent
Hammersmith, 24 February, 1976 (CD)

League Club	Source	Date Signed	Seasons Played	Apps	Subs	Gls
Shrewsbury T	Faweh	08.96	96-97	14	3	0

TAYLOR Leslie (Les)
North Shields, 4 December, 1956 (M)

League Club	Source	Date Signed	Seasons Played	Apps	Subs	Gls
Oxford U	App	12.74	74-80	219	0	15
Watford	Tr	11.80	80-85	167	5	13
Reading	Tr	10.86	86-88	69	6	3
Colchester U	Tr	01.89	88-89	44	8	1

TAYLOR Maik Stefan
Hildesheim, Germany, 4 September, 1971 NIu21-1/NIB-1/NI-45 (G)

League Club	Source	Date Signed	Seasons Played	Apps	Subs	Gls
Barnet	Farnborough T	06.95	95-96	70	0	0
Southampton	Tr	01.97	96	18	0	0
Fulham	Tr	11.97	97-02	183	1	0
Birmingham C	Tr	08.03	03-04	72	0	0

TAYLOR Mark
Hartlepool, 5 December, 1962 (FB)

League Club	Source	Date Signed	Seasons Played	Apps	Subs	Gls
Hartlepool U	Henry Smith's BC	08.82	82	1	0	0

TAYLOR Peter **Mark** Richard
Hartlepool, 20 November, 1964 (W)

League Club	Source	Date Signed	Seasons Played	Apps	Subs	Gls
Hartlepool U	Brinkburn Jnrs	08.82	83-85	42	5	4
Crewe Alex	L	12.85	85	3	0	0
Blackpool	Tr	08.86	86-91	104	15	43
Cardiff C	L	12.90	90	6	0	3
Wrexham	Tr	03.92	91-94	50	11	9

TAYLOR Robert **Mark**
Walsall, 22 February, 1966 (M)

League Club	Source	Date Signed	Seasons Played	Apps	Subs	Gls
Walsall	YT	07.84	84-88	101	13	4
Sheffield Wed	Tr	06.89	89	8	1	0
Shrewsbury T	L	02.91	90	19	0	2
Shrewsbury T	Tr	09.91	91-97	244	5	13

TAYLOR Mark Simon
Saltburn, 8 November, 1974 (FB)

League Club	Source	Date Signed	Seasons Played	Apps	Subs	Gls
Middlesbrough	YT	03.93				
Darlington	L	10.94	94	8	0	0
Fulham	Tr	09.95	95	7	0	0
Northampton T	Tr	02.96	95	1	0	0

TAYLOR Martin
Ashington, 9 November, 1979 EYth/Eu21-1 (CD)

League Club	Source	Date Signed	Seasons Played	Apps	Subs	Gls
Blackburn Rov	YT	08.97	98-03	68	20	5
Darlington	L	01.00	99	4	0	0
Stockport Co	L	03.00	99	7	0	0
Birmingham C	Tr	02.04	03-04	15	4	1

TAYLOR Martin James
Tamworth, 9 December, 1966 (G)

League Club	Source	Date Signed	Seasons Played	Apps	Subs	Gls
Derby Co	Mile Oak Rov	07.86	89-96	97	0	0
Carlisle U	L	09.87	87	10	0	0
Scunthorpe U	L	12.87	87	8	0	0
Crewe Alex	L	09.96	96	6	0	0
Wycombe W	L	03.97	96	4	0	0
Wycombe W	Tr	06.97	97-02	234	0	0
Barnsley	L	03.03	02	3	0	0

TAYLOR Matthew Simon
Oxford, 27 November, 1981 Eu21-3 (FB)

League Club	Source	Date Signed	Seasons Played	Apps	Subs	Gls
Luton T	YT	02.99	99-01	127	2	16
Portsmouth	Tr	07.02	02-04	74	23	8

TAYLOR Michael John
Liverpool, 21 November, 1982 (CD)

League Club	Source	Date Signed	Seasons Played	Apps	Subs	Gls
Blackburn Rov	YT	11.99				
Carlisle U	L	09.02	02	10	0	0
Rochdale	L	03.03	02	2	0	0
Cheltenham T	Tr	07.04	04	10	3	0

TAYLOR Paul
Leith, 20 December, 1966 (FB)

League Club	Source	Date Signed	Seasons Played	Apps	Subs	Gls
Mansfield T	App	•	83	3	0	0

TAYLOR Paul Anthony
Ecclesall, 3 December, 1949 (M)

League Club	Source	Date Signed	Seasons Played	Apps	Subs	Gls
Sheffield Wed	Loughborough College	06.71	71-72	5	1	0
York C	Tr	07.73	73	4	0	0
Hereford U	L	01.74	73	0	1	0
Colchester U	Tr	03.74	73	6	3	0
Southport	Tr	07.74	74-76	95	0	16

TAYLOR Peter John
Rochford, 3 January, 1953 ESemiPro/Eu23-4/E-4 (W)

League Club	Source	Date Signed	Seasons Played	Apps	Subs	Gls
Southend U	App	01.71	70-73	57	18	12
Crystal Palace	Tr	10.73	73-76	122	0	33
Tottenham H	Tr	09.76	76-80	116	7	31
Orient	Tr	11.80	80-82	49	7	11
Oldham Ath	L	01.83	82	4	0	0
Exeter C	Maidstone U	10.83	83	8	0	0

TAYLOR Peter Thomas
Nottingham, 2 July, 1928 Died 1990 (G)

League Club	Source	Date Signed	Seasons Played	Apps	Subs	Gls
Coventry C	Nottingham F (Am)	05.46	50-54	86	-	0
Middlesbrough	Tr	08.55	55-59	140	-	0
Port Vale	Tr	06.61	61	1	-	0

TAYLOR Philip (Phil) Anthony
Sheffield, 11 July, 1958 (W)

League Club	Source	Date Signed	Seasons Played	Apps	Subs	Gls
York C	App	07.76	74-77	14	7	1
Darlington	Tr	07.78	78-79	18	8	2

TAYLOR Philip (Phil) Henry
Bristol, 18 September, 1917 ESch/FLge-4/EB/E-3 (WH)

League Club	Source	Date Signed	Seasons Played	Apps	Subs	Gls
Bristol Rov	Bristol St George	05.35	35	21	-	2
Liverpool	Tr	03.36	35-53	312	-	32

TAYLOR Raymond (Ray) Jeffrey
Jump, 1 March, 1930 (W)

League Club	Source	Date Signed	Seasons Played	Apps	Subs	Gls
Huddersfield T	Wath W	09.49	49	2	-	0
Southport	Tr	08.53	53-54	51	-	7

TAYLOR Richard (Dick) Eric
Wolverhampton, 9 April, 1918 Died 1995 (CD)

League Club	Source	Date Signed	Seasons Played	Apps	Subs	Gls
Grimsby T	Wolverhampton W (Am)	05.35	38-47	36	-	0
Scunthorpe U	Tr	05.48	50-53	131	-	2

TAYLOR Richard Herbert
Huddersfield, 24 January, 1957 EYth (G)

League Club	Source	Date Signed	Seasons Played	Apps	Subs	Gls
Huddersfield T	App	01.74	73-81	105	0	0
York C	L	03.80	79	2	0	0

TAYLOR Richard (Dick) Marshall
Hollinwood, 21 August, 1928 (G)

League Club	Source	Date Signed	Seasons Played	Apps	Subs	Gls
Everton	Marine	06.51				
Southport	Formby	08.54	54	1	-	0

TAYLOR Richard (Richie) William
Silksworth, 20 June, 1951 (W)

League Club	Source	Date Signed	Seasons Played	Apps	Subs	Gls
Sunderland	App	10.68	71	0	1	0
York C	Tr	07.72	72	26	2	2

TAYLOR Robert (Bob)
Horden, 3 February, 1967 (F)

League Club	Source	Date Signed	Seasons Played	Apps	Subs	Gls
Leeds U	Horden CW	03.86	85-88	33	9	9
Bristol C	Tr	03.89	88-91	96	10	50
West Bromwich A	Tr	01.92	91-97	211	27	96
Bolton W	L	01.98	97	4	0	1
Bolton W	Tr	03.98	97-99	53	20	20
West Bromwich A	Tr	03.00	99-02	45	41	17
Cheltenham T	Tr	08.03	03	19	9	7

TAYLOR Robert Anthony
Norwich, 30 April, 1971 (F)

League Club	Source	Date Signed	Seasons Played	Apps	Subs	Gls
Norwich C	YT	03.90				
Leyton Orient	L	03.91	90	0	3	1
Birmingham C	Tr	08.91				
Leyton Orient	Tr	10.91	91-93	54	19	20
Brentford	Tr	03.94	93-97	172	1	56
Gillingham	Tr	08.98	98-99	56	2	31
Manchester C	Tr	11.99	99	14	2	5
Wolverhampton W	Tr	08.00	00	5	4	0
Queens Park Rgrs	L	08.01	01	3	1	0
Gillingham	L	10.01	01	3	8	0
Grimsby T	Tr	01.02	01-02	5	0	1
Scunthorpe U	Tr	02.03	02	4	4	0

TAYLOR Robert (Bob) John
Croydon, 16 March, 1936 (WH)

League Club	Source	Date Signed	Seasons Played	Apps	Subs	Gls
Crystal Palace	Fulham (Am)	08.54	54	2	-	0
Gillingham	Tr	09.56	56-58	31	-	5
Millwall	Tr	08.59	59	2	-	1

TAYLOR Robert (Robbie) Shaun
Plymouth, 3 December, 1967 (F)

League Club	Source	Date Signed	Seasons Played	Apps	Subs	Gls
Portsmouth	App	08.86				
Newport Co	Tr	03.87	86-87	38	6	7
Torquay U	Weymouth	09.89	89	11	7	1

TAYLOR Robin Graham
Rinteln, Germany, 14 January, 1971 (M)

League Club	Source	Date Signed	Seasons Played	Apps	Subs	Gls
Wigan Ath	Leicester C (N/C)	10.89	89	0	1	0

TAYLOR Rodney (Rod) Victor
Corfe Castle, 9 September, 1943 (WH)

League Club	Source	Date Signed	Seasons Played	Apps	Subs	Gls
Portsmouth	Jnrs	05.61				
Gillingham	Tr	07.63	63-65	9	2	0
Bournemouth	Tr	02.66	65-66	29	1	0

TAYLOR Roy
Hoyland, 2 April, 1933 (G)

League Club	Source	Date Signed	Seasons Played	Apps	Subs	Gls
Scunthorpe U	Denaby U	01.53	52	2	-	0

TAYLOR Royston (Roy)
Blackpool, 28 September, 1956 (M)

League Club	Source	Date Signed	Seasons Played	Apps	Subs	Gls
Preston NE	App	10.74	75	3	0	0
Blackburn Rov	Sunderland (N/C)	11.76	78	3	0	1

TAYLOR Ryan Anthony
Liverpool, 19 August, 1984 EYth (M)

League Club	Source	Date Signed	Seasons Played	Apps	Subs	Gls
Tranmere Rov	YT	04.02	02-04	82	16	14

TAYLOR Samuel (Sammy) McGregor
Gorbals, 23 September, 1933 (W)

League Club	Source	Date Signed	Seasons Played	Apps	Subs	Gls
Preston NE	Falkirk	06.55	55-60	149	-	41
Carlisle U	Tr	06.61	61-63	93	-	12
Southport	Tr	07.64	64	36	-	3

TAYLOR Scott Dean
Portsmouth, 23 November, 1970 (M)

League Club	Source	Date Signed	Seasons Played	Apps	Subs	Gls
Reading	YT	06.89	88-94	164	43	24
Leicester C	Tr	07.95	95-96	59	5	6
Wolverhampton W	Tr	09.99	99-00	21	11	3
Cambridge U	Tr	11.01	01	0	3	0

TAYLOR Scott James
Chertsey, 5 May, 1976 (F)

League Club	Source	Date Signed	Seasons Played	Apps	Subs	Gls
Millwall	Staines T	02.95	94-95	13	15	0
Bolton W	Tr	03.96	95-96	2	10	1
Rotherham U	L	12.97	97	10	0	3
Blackpool	L	03.98	97	3	2	1
Tranmere Rov	Tr	10.98	98-00	78	30	17
Stockport Co	Tr	08.01	01	19	9	4
Blackpool	Tr	01.02	01-04	97	19	43
Plymouth Arg	Tr	12.04	04	9	7	3

TAYLOR Shaun
Plymouth, 26 March, 1963 (CD)

League Club	Source	Date Signed	Seasons Played	Apps	Subs	Gls
Exeter C	Bideford T	12.86	86-90	200	0	16
Swindon T	Tr	07.91	91-96	212	0	30
Bristol C	Tr	09.96	96-99	105	0	7

TAYLOR Stanley (Stan)
Southport, 17 November, 1932 (W)

League Club	Source	Date Signed	Seasons Played	Apps	Subs	Gls
Southport	Liverpool (Am)	02.56	55	2	-	0

TAYLOR Stephen (Steve) Christopher Edward
Cannock, 7 January, 1970 ESemiPro (F)

League Club	Source	Date Signed	Seasons Played	Apps	Subs	Gls
Crystal Palace	Bromsgrove Rov	06.95				
Northampton T	L	10.95	95	1	1	0

TAYLOR Steven (Steve)
Chesterfield, 18 December, 1973 (F)

League Club	Source	Date Signed	Seasons Played	Apps	Subs	Gls
Chesterfield	Brampton Rov	08.93	93	1	0	0

TAYLOR Steven (Steve) John
Royton, 18 October, 1955 (F)

League Club	Source	Date Signed	Seasons Played	Apps	Subs	Gls
Bolton W	App	10.73	74-77	34	6	16
Port Vale	L	10.75	75	4	0	2
Oldham Ath	Tr	10.77	77-78	45	2	25
Luton T	Tr	01.79	78	15	5	1
Mansfield T	Tr	07.79	79	30	7	7
Burnley	Tr	07.80	80-82	80	6	37
Wigan Ath	Tr	08.83	83	29	1	7
Stockport Co	Tr	03.84	83-84	26	0	8
Rochdale	Tr	11.84	84-86	84	0	42
Preston NE	Tr	10.86	86	5	0	2
Burnley	Tr	08.87	87-88	38	7	6
Rochdale	Tr	03.89	88	16	1	4

TAYLOR Steven Vincent
Greenwich, 23 January, 1986 EYth/Eu21-6 (CD)

League Club	Source	Date Signed	Seasons Played	Apps	Subs	Gls
Newcastle U	Sch	01.03	03-04	12	2	0
Wycombe W	L	12.03	03	6	0	0

TAYLOR Stewart Raymond
Owston Ferry, 6 April, 1946 (FB)

League Club	Source	Date Signed	Seasons Played	Apps	Subs	Gls
Scunthorpe U		08.65	65-68	64	3	0

TAYLOR Stuart
Bristol, 18 April, 1947 (CD)

League Club	Source	Date Signed	Seasons Played	Apps	Subs	Gls
Bristol Rov	Jnrs	01.66	65-79	546	0	28

TAYLOR Stuart James
Romford, 28 November, 1980 EYth/Eu21-3 (G)

League Club	Source	Date Signed	Seasons Played	Apps	Subs	Gls
Arsenal	YT	07.98	01-02	16	2	0
Bristol Rov	L	09.99	99	4	0	0
Crystal Palace	L	08.00	00	10	0	0
Peterborough U	L	02.01	00	6	0	0
Leicester C	L	11.04	04	10	0	0

TAYLOR Thomas (Tommy)
Barnsley, 29 January, 1932 Died 1958 EB/FLge-2/E-19 (CF)

League Club	Source	Date Signed	Seasons Played	Apps	Subs	Gls
Barnsley	Smithies U	07.49	50-52	44	-	26
Manchester U	Tr	03.53	52-57	166	-	112

TAYLOR Thomas (Tommy) Frederick
Hornchurch, 26 September, 1951 ESch/EYth/Eu23-11 (CD)

League Club	Source	Date Signed	Seasons Played	Apps	Subs	Gls
Orient	App	10.68	67-70	112	2	4
West Ham U	Tr	10.70	70-78	340	0	8
Orient	Tr	05.79	79-81	116	0	5

TAYLOR Thomas (Tommy) William James
Wandsworth, 10 September, 1946 (M)

League Club	Source	Date Signed	Seasons Played	Apps	Subs	Gls
Portsmouth		04.64				
Gillingham	Tr	05.65	65	19	1	0
Bournemouth	Tr	06.66	66-67	26	0	8

TAYLOR Walter (Wally) Bingley
Kirton-in-Lindsey, 30 October, 1926 (FB)

League Club	Source	Date Signed	Seasons Played	Apps	Subs	Gls
Grimsby T	Hibaldstow	08.44	49-50	21	-	0
Southport	Tr	07.51	51-57	269	-	1
Oldham Ath	Tr	07.58	58-59	51	-	0

TAYLOR William (Billy)
Edinburgh, 31 July, 1939 Died 1981 (M)

League Club	Source	Date Signed	Seasons Played	Apps	Subs	Gls
Leyton Orient	Bonnyrigg Rose	08.59	60-62	23	-	0
Nottingham F	Tr	10.63	63-68	10	10	1
Lincoln C	Tr	05.69	69-70	74	5	7

TAYLOR William (Billy) Donnachie
Keldholm, 3 June, 1938 (G)

League Club	Source	Date Signed	Seasons Played	Apps	Subs	Gls
Luton T	Partick Th	12.67	67-68	6	0	0

TAYLOR-FLETCHER Gary
Widnes, 4 June, 1981 ESch (F)

League Club	Source	Date Signed	Seasons Played	Apps	Subs	Gls
Hull C (L)	Northwich Vic	03.01	00	1	4	0
Leyton Orient	Northwich Vic	07.01	01-02	10	11	1
Lincoln C	Tr	08.03	03-04	77	3	27

TEAGUE Andrew Harry
Preston, 5 February, 1986 (CD)

League Club	Source	Date Signed	Seasons Played	Apps	Subs	Gls
Macclesfield T	Sch	●	04	5	0	0

TEAGUE William (Bill) Edward
Lydney, 26 September, 1937 Died 1998 (G)

League Club	Source	Date Signed	Seasons Played	Apps	Subs	Gls
Swindon T	Gloucester C	03.61	60-61	3	-	0

TEALE Gary
Glasgow, 21 July, 1978 Su21-6 (W)

League Club	Source	Date Signed	Seasons Played	Apps	Subs	Gls
Wigan Ath	Ayr U	12.01	01-04	94	32	8

TEALE Richard Grant
Millom, 27 February, 1952 (G)

League Club	Source	Date Signed	Seasons Played	Apps	Subs	Gls
Queens Park Rgrs	Slough T	07.73	74	1	0	0
Fulham	Tr	06.76	76	5	0	0
Wimbledon	Tr	08.77	77	15	0	0

TEALE Shaun
Southport, 10 March, 1964 ESemiPro-1 (CD)

League Club	Source	Date Signed	Seasons Played	Apps	Subs	Gls
Bournemouth	Weymouth	01.89	88-90	99	1	4
Aston Villa	Tr	07.91	91-94	146	1	2
Tranmere Rov	Tr	08.95	95-96	54	0	0
Preston NE	L	02.97	96	5	0	0
Carlisle U	Motherwell	02.00	99	18	0	0

TEARSE David (Dave) James
Newcastle, 7 August, 1951 (F)

League Club	Source	Date Signed	Seasons Played	Apps	Subs	Gls
Leicester C	North Kenton BC	10.69	69-70	7	1	1
Torquay U	Tr	11.71	71-74	77	0	23
Reading	L	01.75	74	2	0	0

TEASDALE John (Jack) George
Rossington, 15 March, 1929 (WH)

League Club	Source	Date Signed	Seasons Played	Apps	Subs	Gls
Doncaster Rov		10.49	50-55	113	-	0

TEASDALE John Stewart
Glasgow, 15 October, 1962 (F)

League Club	Source	Date Signed	Seasons Played	Apps	Subs	Gls
Wolverhampton W	Nairn County	12.80	80-81	6	2	0
Walsall	Tr	03.82	81-82	13	0	3
Hereford U	Tr	01.83	82	5	0	1
Blackpool		11.84	84	1	6	1

TEASDALE Thomas (Tommy)
(W)

League Club	Source	Date Signed	Seasons Played	Apps	Subs	Gls
Hull C (Am)		05.47	46	1	-	0

TEATHER Paul
Rotherham, 26 December, 1977 ESch/EYth (M)

League Club	Source	Date Signed	Seasons Played	Apps	Subs	Gls
Manchester U	YT	08.94				
Bournemouth	L	12.97	97	5	5	0

TEBBUTT Robert (Bobby) Stanley
Irchester, 10 November, 1934 (IF)

League Club	Source	Date Signed	Seasons Played	Apps	Subs	Gls
Northampton T		10.56	56-59	57	-	21

TEBILY Olivier
Abidjan, Ivory Coast, 19 December, 1975 Fru21/IvoryC-4 (FB)

League Club	Source	Date Signed	Seasons Played	Apps	Subs	Gls
Sheffield U	Chateauroux (Fr)	03.99	98	7	1	0
Birmingham C	Glasgow Celtic	03.02	01-04	45	16	0

TEDALDI Domenico (Dino) Arch
Aberystwyth, 12 August, 1980 WYth (F)

League Club	Source	Date Signed	Seasons Played	Apps	Subs	Gls
Doncaster Rov	YT	04.97	97	0	2	1

TEDDS William (Bill) Henry
Bedworth, 27 July, 1943 (FB)

League Club	Source	Date Signed	Seasons Played	Apps	Subs	Gls
Coventry C	Jnrs	09.60	61-64	8	-	0

TEDESCO John Joseph
Modbury, 7 March, 1949 (F)

League Club	Source	Date Signed	Seasons Played	Apps	Subs	Gls
Plymouth Arg	App	05.66	66-69	34	8	4

TEECE David Alfred
Rhodes, Lancashire, 1 September, 1927 (G)

League Club	Source	Date Signed	Seasons Played	Apps	Subs	Gls
Hull C	Hyde U	02.52	53-55	25	-	0
Oldham Ath	Tr	06.56	56-58	91	-	0

TEER Kevin Paul
Wood Green, 7 December, 1963 (FB)

League Club	Source	Date Signed	Seasons Played	Apps	Subs	Gls
Brentford	App	12.81	80	0	1	0

TEES Matthew (Matt)
Johnstone, 13 October, 1939 (F)

League Club	Source	Date Signed	Seasons Played	Apps	Subs	Gls
Grimsby T	Airdrie	07.63	63-66	113	0	51
Charlton Ath	Tr	02.67	66-69	88	1	32
Luton T	Tr	08.69	69-70	33	2	13
Grimsby T	Tr	11.70	70-72	83	0	42

TEGGART Neil
Downpatrick, 16 September, 1984 NIYth/NIu21-2 (F)

League Club	Source	Date Signed	Seasons Played	Apps	Subs	Gls
Sunderland	YT	04.02				
Darlington	L	02.04	03	9	6	0
Scunthorpe U	L	12.04	04	1	0	0

TELFER George Andrew
Liverpool, 6 July, 1955 (W)

League Club	Source	Date Signed	Seasons Played	Apps	Subs	Gls
Everton	App	08.72	73-80	81	16	20
Scunthorpe U	San Diego (USA)	12.81	81-82	34	2	11
Preston NE	Altrincham	08.83	83	0	2	0

TELFER Paul Norman
Edinburgh, 21 October, 1971 Su21-3/SB-2/S-1 (W)

League Club	Source	Date Signed	Seasons Played	Apps	Subs	Gls
Luton T	YT	11.88	90-94	136	8	19
Coventry C	Tr	07.95	95-00	178	13	6
Southampton	Tr	11.01	01-04	112	16	1

TELFORD William (Billy) Albert
Carlisle, 5 March, 1956 (F)

League Club	Source	Date Signed	Seasons Played	Apps	Subs	Gls
Manchester C	Tranmere Rov (App)	08.75	75	0	1	0
Peterborough U	Tr	09.75	75	3	1	2
Colchester U	L	01.76	75	1	1	1

TELLING Maurice William
Southwark, 5 August, 1919 Died 1973 (IF)

League Club	Source	Date Signed	Seasons Played	Apps	Subs	Gls
Millwall	Berkhamsted T	10.46	46	1	-	0

TEMBY William (Bill)
Dover, 16 September, 1934 (IF)

League Club	Source	Date Signed	Seasons Played	Apps	Subs	Gls
Queens Park Rgrs	Dover	02.55	55-56	7	-	3

TEMPEST Dale Michael
Leeds, 30 December, 1963 (F)

League Club	Source	Date Signed	Seasons Played	Apps	Subs	Gls
Fulham	App	12.81	80-83	25	9	6
Huddersfield T	Tr	08.84	84-85	63	2	27
Gillingham	L	03.86	85	9	0	4
Colchester U	Lokeren (Bel)	08.87	87-88	69	8	17

TEMPLE Derek William
Liverpool, 13 November, 1938 ESch/EYth/FLge-2/E-1 (W)

League Club	Source	Date Signed	Seasons Played	Apps	Subs	Gls
Everton	Jnrs	08.56	56-67	231	1	72
Preston NE	Tr	09.67	67-69	75	1	14

TEMPLE William (Bill)
Winlaton, 12 December, 1915 (IF)

League Club	Source	Date Signed	Seasons Played	Apps	Subs	Gls
Aldershot	Newbiggin West End	11.34	34-36	14	-	2
Carlisle U	Tr	05.37	37	11	-	4
Grimsby T	Tr	09.38	38	2	-	0
Gateshead	Tr	05.46	46	10	-	1

TEMPLEMAN John Henry
Yapton, 21 September, 1947 (FB)

League Club	Source	Date Signed	Seasons Played	Apps	Subs	Gls
Brighton & Hove A	Arundel T	07.66	66-73	219	7	16
Exeter C	Tr	05.74	74-78	205	1	7
Swindon T	Tr	07.79	79-80	20	1	0

TEN HEUVEL Laurens
Duivendrecht, Holland, 6 June, 1976 (F)

League Club	Source	Date Signed	Seasons Played	Apps	Subs	Gls
Barnsley	FC Den Bosch (Holl)	03.96	95-97	1	7	0
Sheffield U	SC Telstar (Holl)	07.02	02	0	5	0
Bradford C	L	03.03	02	4	1	0
Grimsby T	L	08.03	03	3	1	0

TENNANT Albert
Ilkeston, 29 October, 1917 Died 1986 (FB)

League Club	Source	Date Signed	Seasons Played	Apps	Subs	Gls
Chelsea	Stanton Ironworks	11.34	46-48	2	-	0

TENNANT David
Walsall, 13 June, 1945 (G)

League Club	Source	Date Signed	Seasons Played	Apps	Subs	Gls
Walsall	Jnrs	08.63	63-64	19	-	0
Lincoln C	Worcester C	09.66	66-68	39	0	0
Rochdale	Tr	08.69	70	16	0	0

TENNANT Desmond (Des) Warren
Cardiff, 17 October, 1925 (FB)

League Club	Source	Date Signed	Seasons Played	Apps	Subs	Gls
Cardiff C	Jnrs	08.45				
Brighton & Hove A	Barry T	07.48	48-58	400	-	40

TENNANT John Graham
Darlington, 1 August, 1939 (G)

League Club	Source	Date Signed	Seasons Played	Apps	Subs	Gls
Darlington		05.57	56-57	8	-	0
Chelsea	Tr	08.59				
Southend U	Tr	10.59	60-62	2	-	0

TENNANT Sydney David Keith
Newport, 6 June, 1934 (WH)

League Club	Source	Date Signed	Seasons Played	Apps	Subs	Gls
Newport Co	Jnrs	01.55	55-57	39	-	1

TENNANT Frederick Roy
Durban, South Africa, 12 September, 1936 (CD)

League Club	Source	Date Signed	Seasons Played	Apps	Subs	Gls
Brighton & Hove A		08.57				
Workington	Tr	07.58	58-61	151	-	1

TENNEBO Thomas
Bergen, Norway, 19 March, 1975 (M)

League Club	Source	Date Signed	Seasons Played	Apps	Subs	Gls
Hartlepool U	United Fana (Nor)	08.99	99-00	6	7	0

TENNENT David
Ayr, 22 January, 1930 (W)

League Club	Source	Date Signed	Seasons Played	Apps	Subs	Gls
Ipswich T	Annbank Jnrs	07.52	52	4	-	0

TERESKINAS Andrejus
Telsiai, Lithuania, 10 July, 1970 Lithuania 56 (CD)

League Club	Source	Date Signed	Seasons Played	Apps	Subs	Gls
Macclesfield T (L)	Skonto Riga	11.00	00	0	1	0

TERNENT Raymond (Ray)
Blyth, 9 September, 1948 (FB)

League Club	Source	Date Signed	Seasons Played	Apps	Subs	Gls
Burnley	App	09.65	66-70	13	0	0
Southend U	Tr	06.71	71-72	82	0	1
Doncaster Rov	Tr	08.73	73-76	78	6	3

TERNENT Francis Stanley (Stan)
Gateshead, 16 June, 1946 (M)

League Club	Source	Date Signed	Seasons Played	Apps	Subs	Gls
Burnley	App	06.63	66-67	5	0	0
Carlisle U	Tr	05.68	68-73	187	2	5

TERRIER David
Verdun, France, 4 August, 1973 (FB)

League Club	Source	Date Signed	Seasons Played	Apps	Subs	Gls
West Ham U (L)	Metz (Fr)	06.97	97	0	1	0

TERRIS James
Dunfermline, 25 July, 1933 (FB)

League Club	Source	Date Signed	Seasons Played	Apps	Subs	Gls
Bristol C	Chippenham T	10.55	56-57	4	-	0
Carlisle U	Tr	04.59	59-60	28	-	1

TERRY John George
Barking, 7 December, 1980 Eu21-9/E-16 (CD)

League Club	Source	Date Signed	Seasons Played	Apps	Subs	Gls
Chelsea	YT	03.98	98-04	138	12	10
Nottingham F	L	03.00	99	5	1	0

TERRY Patrick (Pat) Alfred
Lambeth, 2 October, 1933 (F)

League Club	Source	Date Signed	Seasons Played	Apps	Subs	Gls
Charlton Ath	Eastbourne U	03.54	53-54	4	-	1
Newport Co	Tr	05.56	56-57	55	-	30
Swansea T	Tr	02.58	57-58	17	-	9
Gillingham	Tr	10.58	58-60	108	-	60
Northampton T	Tr	07.61	61	24	-	10
Millwall	Tr	02.62	61-63	97	-	41
Reading	Tr	08.64	64-66	99	0	42
Swindon T	Tr	02.67	66-67	60	1	23
Brentford	Tr	06.68	68	29	0	12

TERRY Paul Edward
Barking, 3 April, 1979 ESemiPro-3 (M)

League Club	Source	Date Signed	Seasons Played	Apps	Subs	Gls
Yeovil T	Dagenham & Redbridge	08.03	03-04	57	16	7

TERRY Peter Edward
Edmonton, 11 September, 1972 (M)

League Club	Source	Date Signed	Seasons Played	Apps	Subs	Gls
Aldershot	YT	07.91	90	1	0	0

TERRY Steven (Steve) Graham
Clapton, 14 June, 1962 (CD)

League Club	Source	Date Signed	Seasons Played	Apps	Subs	Gls
Watford	App	01.80	79-87	160	0	14
Hull C	Tr	06.88	88-89	62	0	4
Northampton T	Tr	03.90	89-93	181	0	17

TESSEM Jo
Orlandet, Norway, 28 February, 1972 NoB-1/No-9 (M)

League Club	Source	Date Signed	Seasons Played	Apps	Subs	Gls
Southampton	Molde FK (Nor)	11.99	99-03	67	43	12
Millwall	L	10.04	04	11	1	1

TESTER Paul Leonard
Stroud, 10 March, 1959 (W)

League Club	Source	Date Signed	Seasons Played	Apps	Subs	Gls
Shrewsbury T	Cheltenham T	07.83	83-87	86	12	12
Hereford U	L	11.84	84	4	0	0
Hereford U	Tr	08.88	88-90	105	9	14

TETHER Colin
Halesowen, 11 August, 1939 EYth (FB)

League Club	Source	Date Signed	Seasons Played	Apps	Subs	Gls
Wolverhampton W	Jnrs	08.55	56	1	-	0

TEWLEY Alan Bernard
Leicester, 22 January, 1945 (W)

League Club	Source	Date Signed	Seasons Played	Apps	Subs	Gls
Leicester C	App	03.62	66-68	15	3	5
Bradford PA	Tr	11.69	69	28	0	4
Crewe Alex	Tr	10.70	70-72	57	11	12

THACKERAY Andrew (Andy) John
Huddersfield, 13 February, 1968 (FB)

League Club	Source	Date Signed	Seasons Played	Apps	Subs	Gls
Manchester C	Jnrs	02.86				
Huddersfield T	Tr	08.86	86	2	0	0
Newport Co	Tr	03.87	86-87	53	1	4
Wrexham	Tr	07.88	88-91	139	13	14
Rochdale	Tr	07.92	92-96	161	4	13
Halifax T	Tr	08.97	98	37	1	5

THARME Derek
Brighton, 19 August, 1938 (FB)

League Club	Source	Date Signed	Seasons Played	Apps	Subs	Gls
Tottenham H	Whitehaven	10.56				
Southend U	Tr	05.62	62	7	-	0

THATCHER Benjamin (Ben) David
Swindon, 30 November, 1975 EYth/Eu21-4/W-7 (FB)

League Club	Source	Date Signed	Seasons Played	Apps	Subs	Gls
Millwall	YT	06.92	93-95	87	3	1
Wimbledon	Tr	07.96	96-99	82	4	0
Tottenham H	Tr	07.00	00-02	29	7	0
Leicester C	Tr	07.03	03	28	1	1
Manchester C	Tr	06.04	04	17	1	0

THEAKER Clarence (Cam) Alfred
Spalding, 8 December, 1912 Died 1992 (G)

League Club	Source	Date Signed	Seasons Played	Apps	Subs	Gls
Grimsby T	Spalding T	05.34	35-38	5	-	0
Newcastle U	Tr	11.38	38-46	13	-	0
Hartlepools U	Tr	06.47	47	14	-	0

THEAR Anthony (Tony) Charles
Edmonton, 4 February, 1948 (F)

League Club	Source	Date Signed	Seasons Played	Apps	Subs	Gls
Arsenal	Jnrs	02.65				
Luton T	Tr	07.66	66	12	1	5
Gillingham	Tr	02.67	66-68	7	0	1

THELWELL Alton Anthony
Holloway, 5 September, 1980 Eu21-1 (CD)

League Club	Source	Date Signed	Seasons Played	Apps	Subs	Gls
Tottenham H	YT	01.99	00-01	13	5	0
Hull C	Tr	07.03	03-04	24	5	1

THEOBALD David John
Cambridge, 15 December, 1978 (CD)

League Club	Source	Date Signed	Seasons Played	Apps	Subs	Gls
Ipswich T	YT	06.97				
Brentford	Tr	07.99	99-01	26	5	0
Swansea C	Tr	07.02	02	9	1	0
Cambridge U	Tr	02.03	02	1	3	0

THEODOSIOU Andrew (Andy)
Stoke Newington, 30 October, 1970 (CD)

League Club	Source	Date Signed	Seasons Played	Apps	Subs	Gls
Norwich C	Tottenham H (YT)	07.89				
Hereford U	Tr	07.91	91-92	41	1	2

THEOKLITOS Michael
Melbourne, Australia, 11 February, 1981 (G)

League Club	Source	Date Signed	Seasons Played	Apps	Subs	Gls
Blackpool	Auckland Kingz (NZ)	08.02	02	2	0	0

THETIS Jean-Manuel
Dijon, France, 5 November, 1971 (FB)

League Club	Source	Date Signed	Seasons Played	Apps	Subs	Gls
Ipswich T	Sevilla (Sp)	09.98	98-99	44	3	2
Wolverhampton W	L	08.00	00	3	0	0
Sheffield U	Tr	03.01	00	0	1	0

THEW Lee
Sunderland, 23 October, 1974 (M)

League Club	Source	Date Signed	Seasons Played	Apps	Subs	Gls
Doncaster Rov	YT	08.93	93-94	21	11	2
Scarborough	Tr	08.95	95	9	5	0

THIJSSEN Franciscus (Frans) Johannes
Heumen, Holland, 23 January, 1952 Holland int (M)

League Club	Source	Date Signed	Seasons Played	Apps	Subs	Gls
Ipswich T	Twente Enschede (Holl)	02.79	78-82	123	2	10
Nottingham F	Vancouver (Can)	10.83	83	17	0	3

THIRLBY Anthony Dennis
Berlin, Germany, 4 March, 1976 NIYth (M)

League Club	Source	Date Signed	Seasons Played	Apps	Subs	Gls
Exeter C	YT	07.94	93-95	27	12	2
Torquay U	Tiverton T	02.97	96	1	2	0

THIRLWELL Paul
Washington, 13 February, 1979 Eu21-1 (M)

League Club	Source	Date Signed	Seasons Played	Apps	Subs	Gls
Sunderland	YT	04.97	98-03	55	22	0
Swindon T	L	09.99	99	12	0	0
Sheffield U	Tr	07.04	04	24	6	1

THOGERSEN Thomas
Copenhagen, Denmark, 2 April, 1968 (M)

League Club	Source	Date Signed	Seasons Played	Apps	Subs	Gls
Portsmouth	Brondby (Den)	08.98	98-01	95	13	8
Walsall	L	10.01	01	7	0	2

THOLOT Didier
Feurs, France, 2 April, 1964 (F)

League Club	Source	Date Signed	Seasons Played	Apps	Subs	Gls
Walsall (L)	Sion (Fr)	03.98	97	13	1	4

THOM Lewis McDonald
Stornoway, 10 April, 1944 (W)

League Club	Source	Date Signed	Seasons Played	Apps	Subs	Gls
Shrewsbury T	Dundee U	09.65	65-66	48	1	5
Lincoln C	Tr	05.67	66-68	45	2	4
Bradford PA	Tr	06.69	69	31	0	1

THOM Stuart Paul
Dewsbury, 27 December, 1976 (CD)

League Club	Source	Date Signed	Seasons Played	Apps	Subs	Gls
Nottingham F	YT	01.94				
Mansfield T	L	12.97	97	5	0	0
Oldham Ath	Tr	10.98	98-99	28	6	3
Scunthorpe U	Tr	08.00	00-01	34	7	2

THOMAS Andrew (Andy) Mark
Eynsham, 16 December, 1962 (M)

League Club	Source	Date Signed	Seasons Played	Apps	Subs	Gls
Oxford U	App	12.80	80-85	89	27	32
Fulham	L	12.82	82	3	1	2
Derby Co	L	03.83	82	0	1	0
Newcastle U	Tr	09.86	86-87	24	7	6
Bradford C	Tr	06.88	88	15	8	5
Plymouth Arg	Tr	07.89	89-90	47	3	18

THOMAS Andrew (Andy) Richard
Stockport, 2 December, 1982 (CD)

League Club	Source	Date Signed	Seasons Played	Apps	Subs	Gls
Stockport Co	YT	07.01	01-02	8	4	0

THOMAS Anthony (Tony)
Liverpool, 12 July, 1971 (FB)

League Club	Source	Date Signed	Seasons Played	Apps	Subs	Gls
Tranmere Rov	YT	02.89	88-96	254	3	12
Everton	Tr	08.97	97-98	6	2	0

THOMAS Barrie
Merthyr Tydfil, 27 August, 1954 (M)

League Club	Source	Date Signed	Seasons Played	Apps	Subs	Gls
Swansea C (Am)	Jnrs	08.71	71	2	0	0
Bournemouth	Merthyr Tydfil	08.79	79	3	0	0

THOMAS Ernest **Barrie**
Measham, 19 May, 1937 EYth (F)

League Club	Source	Date Signed	Seasons Played	Apps	Subs	Gls
Leicester C	Measham Imperial	07.54	54-55	7	-	3
Mansfield T	Tr	06.57	57-59	72	-	48
Scunthorpe U	Tr	09.59	59-61	91	-	67
Newcastle U	Tr	01.62	61-64	73	-	48
Scunthorpe U	Tr	11.64	64-66	52	0	26
Barnsley	Tr	11.66	66-67	43	0	19

THOMAS Brian
Neath, 7 June, 1976 (G)

League Club	Source	Date Signed	Seasons Played	Apps	Subs	Gls
Hereford U	YT	●	93	3	0	0

THOMAS Brian Hugh
Carmarthen, 28 June, 1944 (WH)

League Club	Source	Date Signed	Seasons Played	Apps	Subs	Gls
Swansea T	Jnrs	06.62	64	4	-	0

THOMAS Brynley (Bryn)
Coventry, 13 December, 1932 (CF)

League Club	Source	Date Signed	Seasons Played	Apps	Subs	Gls
Coventry C	Longford Rov	09.50	52-53	12	-	1

THOMAS Cedric David
Hebden Bridge, 19 September, 1936 (W)

League Club	Source	Date Signed	Seasons Played	Apps	Subs	Gls
Halifax T	Heptonstall	07.57	57-59	20	-	5

THOMAS Daniel (Danny) Joseph
Worksop, 12 November, 1961 ESch/Eu21-7/E-2 (FB)

League Club	Source	Date Signed	Seasons Played	Apps	Subs	Gls
Coventry C	App	12.78	79-82	103	5	5
Tottenham H	Tr	06.83	83-86	80	7	1

THOMAS Daniel (Danny) Justin
Leamington Spa, 1 May, 1981 (W)

League Club	Source	Date Signed	Seasons Played	Apps	Subs	Gls
Leicester C	Nottingham F (YT)	05.98	99	0	3	0
Bournemouth	Tr	02.02	01-03	35	24	2
Boston U	Tr	03.04	03-04	40	7	6

THOMAS Daniel (Danny) Wayne
Blackwood, 13 May, 1985 WYth (F)

League Club	Source	Date Signed	Seasons Played	Apps	Subs	Gls
Cardiff C	YT	05.02	04	0	1	0

THOMAS David (Dave)
Kirkby-in-Ashfield, 5 October, 1950 EYth/Eu23-11/E-8 (W)

League Club	Source	Date Signed	Seasons Played	Apps	Subs	Gls
Burnley	App	10.67	66-72	153	4	19
Queens Park Rgrs	Tr	10.72	72-76	181	1	27
Everton	Tr	08.77	77-78	71	0	4
Wolverhampton W	Tr	10.79	79	10	0	0
Middlesbrough	Vancouver (Can)	03.82	81	13	0	1
Portsmouth	Tr	07.82	82-84	24	6	0

THOMAS David (Dai)
Abercregan, 1 August, 1926 W-2 (FB)

League Club	Source	Date Signed	Seasons Played	Apps	Subs	Gls
Swansea T	Abercregan Jnrs	08.48	49-59	296	-	15
Newport Co	Tr	07.61	61-62	58	-	1

THOMAS David (Dai) John
Caerphilly, 26 September, 1975 Wu21-2 (F)

League Club	Source	Date Signed	Seasons Played	Apps	Subs	Gls
Swansea C	YT	07.94	94-96	36	20	10
Watford	Tr	07.97	97	8	8	3
Cardiff C	Tr	08.98	98-99	21	10	5

THOMAS David (Dave) Watkin John
Stepney, 6 July, 1917 Died 1991 (CF)

League Club	Source	Date Signed	Seasons Played	Apps	Subs	Gls
Plymouth Arg	Romford	06.38	38-47	74	-	29
Watford	Tr	02.48	47-50	105	-	41
Gillingham	Tr	10.50	50-52	80	-	42

THOMAS Dean Ronald
Bedworth, 19 December, 1961 (FB)

League Club	Source	Date Signed	Seasons Played	Apps	Subs	Gls
Wimbledon	Nuneaton Borough	07.81	81-83	57	0	8
Northampton T	Aachen (Ger)	08.88	88-89	74	0	11
Notts Co	Tr	03.90	89-93	129	5	8

THOMAS Dennis
Hebburn, 2 February, 1926 (W)

League Club	Source	Date Signed	Seasons Played	Apps	Subs	Gls
Bury	Wardley CW	01.49	49	3	-	0
Accrington St	Tr	07.50	50	34	-	5

THOMAS Edward (Eddie)
Newton-le-Willows, 23 October, 1933 Died 2003 (IF)

League Club	Source	Date Signed	Seasons Played	Apps	Subs	Gls
Everton	Jnrs	10.51	56-59	86	-	39
Blackburn Rov	Tr	02.60	59-61	37	-	9
Swansea T	Tr	07.62	62-64	68	-	21
Derby Co	Tr	08.64	64-67	102	3	43
Orient	Tr	09.67	67	11	0	2

THOMAS Edwin Henry Charles
Swindon, 9 November, 1932 (G)

League Club	Source	Date Signed	Seasons Played	Apps	Subs	Gls
Southampton	Swindon BR	05.51	50-51	8	-	0

THOMAS Geoffrey (Geoff)
Swansea, 18 February, 1948 Wu23-3 (M)

League Club	Source	Date Signed	Seasons Played	Apps	Subs	Gls
Swansea T	App	02.66	65-75	345	12	52

THOMAS Geoffrey (Geoff) Paul
Bradford, 12 March, 1946 (FB)

League Club	Source	Date Signed	Seasons Played	Apps	Subs	Gls
Bradford PA	App	03.63	63-65	53	0	0

THOMAS Geoffrey (Geoff) Robert
Manchester, 5 August, 1964 EB-3/E-9 (M)

League Club	Source	Date Signed	Seasons Played	Apps	Subs	Gls
Rochdale	Ashe Labs	08.82	82-83	10	1	1
Crewe Alex	Tr	03.84	83-86	120	5	21
Crystal Palace	Tr	06.87	87-92	192	3	26
Wolverhampton W	Tr	06.93	93-96	36	10	8
Nottingham F	Tr	07.97	97-98	18	7	4
Barnsley	Tr	07.99	99-00	14	24	4
Notts Co	Tr	03.01	00	8	0	1
Crewe Alex	Tr	08.01	01	8	6	2

THOMAS George Vincent
Cardiff, 25 June, 1930 (WH)

League Club	Source	Date Signed	Seasons Played	Apps	Subs	Gls
Cardiff C	Cardiff Nomads	05.49				
Newport Co	Tr	07.53	53-58	137	-	0

THOMAS Gerald (Geoff) Shannon
Derby, 21 February, 1926 (FB)

League Club	Source	Date Signed	Seasons Played	Apps	Subs	Gls
Nottingham F	Jnrs	09.43	46-59	404	-	1

THOMAS Glen Andrew
Hackney, 6 October, 1967 (CD)

League Club	Source	Date Signed	Seasons Played	Apps	Subs	Gls
Fulham	App	10.85	86-94	246	5	6
Peterborough U	Tr	11.94	94	6	2	0

League Club	Source	Date Signed	Seasons Played	Career Record Apps	Subs	Gls
Barnet	Tr	03.95	94-95	22	1	0
Gillingham	Tr	01.96	95-97	20	8	0
Brighton & Hove A	Tr	07.98	98	2	1	0

THOMAS David **Gwyn**
Swansea, 26 September, 1957 WSch/WYth/Wu21-3 (M)

League Club	Source	Date Signed	Seasons Played	Apps	Subs	Gls
Leeds U	App	07.75	74-83	79	10	3
Barnsley	Tr	03.84	83-89	197	4	17
Hull C	Tr	03.90	89-90	21	1	0
Carlisle U	Tr	08.91	91	35	2	1

THOMAS James Alan
Swansea, 16 January, 1979 WYth/Wu21-21 (F)

League Club	Source	Date Signed	Seasons Played	Apps	Subs	Gls
Blackburn Rov	YT	07.96	00	1	3	1
West Bromwich A	L	08.97	97	1	2	0
Blackpool	L	03.00	99	9	0	2
Sheffield U	L	11.00	00	3	7	1
Bristol Rov	L	03.02	01	7	0	1
Swansea C	Tr	07.02	02-04	42	15	16

THOMAS Jeffrey (Jeff)
Newport, 18 May, 1949 WSch/WYth/Wu23-1 (W)

League Club	Source	Date Signed	Seasons Played	Apps	Subs	Gls
Newport Co	Jnrs	05.66	65-72	207	3	31

THOMAS Jerome William
Wembley, 23 March, 1983 ESch/EYth/Eu20 (W)

League Club	Source	Date Signed	Seasons Played	Apps	Subs	Gls
Arsenal	YT	07.01				
Queens Park Rgrs	L	03.02	01	4	0	1
Queens Park Rgrs	L	08.02	02	5	1	2
Charlton Ath	Tr	02.04	03-04	21	4	3

THOMAS John (Jack)
Poole, 28 May, 1936 (G)

League Club	Source	Date Signed	Seasons Played	Apps	Subs	Gls
Bournemouth	Poole T	05.58	58	4	-	0

THOMAS John (Joe) Charles
Great Houghton, 22 September, 1932 (FB)

League Club	Source	Date Signed	Seasons Played	Apps	Subs	Gls
Wolverhampton W	Wath W	08.51				
Barnsley	Tr	06.52	52-57	134	-	0
Mansfield T	Tr	03.58	57-58	41	-	0
Chesterfield	Tr	07.59	59	6	-	0

THOMAS John Ernest
Walsall, 15 July, 1922 Died 1999 (CF)

League Club	Source	Date Signed	Seasons Played	Apps	Subs	Gls
Bournemouth		05.46				
West Bromwich A	Tr	07.46				
Crystal Palace	Tr	10.48	48-51	53	-	17

THOMAS John (Johnny) Wilfred
Liverpool, 23 December, 1926 (W)

League Club	Source	Date Signed	Seasons Played	Apps	Subs	Gls
Everton		12.48				
Swindon T	Tr	02.49	50-51	17	-	3
Chester	Headington U	07.53	53	29	-	5
Stockport Co	Tr	07.54	54	6	-	0

THOMAS John William
Wednesbury, 5 August, 1958 (F)

League Club	Source	Date Signed	Seasons Played	Apps	Subs	Gls
Everton		07.77				
Tranmere Rov	L	03.79	78	10	1	2
Halifax T	L	10.79	79	5	0	0
Bolton W	Tr	06.80	80-81	18	4	6
Chester	Tr	08.82	82	44	0	20
Lincoln C	Tr	08.83	83-84	56	11	17
Preston NE	Tr	06.85	85-86	69	9	38
Bolton W	Tr	07.87	87-88	71	2	31
West Bromwich A	Tr	07.89	89	8	10	1
Preston NE	Tr	02.90	89-91	24	3	6
Hartlepool U	Tr	03.92	91	5	2	1
Halifax T	Tr	07.92	92	10	2	0

THOMAS Walter **Keith**
Oswestry, 28 July, 1929 (W)

League Club	Source	Date Signed	Seasons Played	Apps	Subs	Gls
Sheffield Wed	Oswestry T	09.50	50-51	10	-	1
Cardiff C	Tr	07.52	52-53	9	-	4
Plymouth Arg	Tr	11.53	53-55	35	-	8
Exeter C	Tr	03.56	55-56	43	-	6

THOMAS Kevin Anthony
Whiston, 13 August, 1945 (G)

League Club	Source	Date Signed	Seasons Played	Apps	Subs	Gls
Blackpool	Prescot T	06.66	66-68	12	0	0
Tranmere Rov	Tr	09.69	69-70	18	0	0
Oxford U	Tr	07.71	72	5	0	0
Southport	Tr	07.74	74-75	67	0	0

THOMAS Lee
Tredegar, 1 November, 1970 (FB)

League Club	Source	Date Signed	Seasons Played	Apps	Subs	Gls
Hereford U	Newport Co (YT)	07.89	89	0	1	0

THOMAS David Stuart **Lynne (Lyn)**
Swansea, 19 September, 1920 Died 1993 WSch (CF)

League Club	Source	Date Signed	Seasons Played	Apps	Subs	Gls
Swansea T	Abergregown Jnrs	10.42				
Brighton & Hove A	Tr	06.47	47	13	-	4

THOMAS Martin Richard
Senghenydd, 28 November, 1959 WYth/Wu21-2/W-1 (G)

League Club	Source	Date Signed	Seasons Played	Apps	Subs	Gls
Bristol Rov	App	09.77	76-81	162	0	0
Cardiff C	L	07.82	82	15	0	0
Southend U	L	02.83	82	6	0	0
Newcastle U	Tr	03.83	82-87	118	0	0
Middlesbrough	L	10.84	84	4	0	0
Birmingham C	Tr	10.88	88-92	144	0	0

THOMAS Martin Russell
Lyndhurst, 12 September, 1973 (M)

League Club	Source	Date Signed	Seasons Played	Apps	Subs	Gls
Southampton	YT	06.92				
Leyton Orient	Tr	03.94	93	5	0	2
Fulham	Tr	07.94	94-97	59	31	8
Swansea C	Tr	07.98	98-00	70	21	8
Brighton & Hove A	Tr	03.01	00	1	7	0
Oxford U	Tr	07.01	01	13	1	2
Exeter C	Tr	08.02	02	22	4	3

THOMAS Michael Lauriston
Lambeth, 24 August, 1967 ESch/EYth/Eu21-12/EB-5/E-2 (M)

League Club	Source	Date Signed	Seasons Played	Apps	Subs	Gls
Arsenal	App	12.84	86-91	149	14	24
Portsmouth	L	12.86	86	3	0	0
Liverpool	Tr	12.91	91-97	96	28	9
Middlesbrough	L	02.98	97	10	0	0
Wimbledon	Benfica (Por)	08.00	00	5	3	0

THOMAS Michael (Mickey) Reginald
Mochdre, 7 July, 1954 Wu23-1/Wu21-2/W-51 (M)

League Club	Source	Date Signed	Seasons Played	Apps	Subs	Gls
Wrexham	Jnrs	05.72	71-78	217	13	33
Manchester U	Tr	11.78	78-80	90	0	11
Everton	Tr	08.81	81	10	0	0
Brighton & Hove A	Tr	11.81	81	18	2	0
Stoke C	Tr	08.82	82-83	57	0	14
Chelsea	Tr	01.84	83-84	43	1	9
West Bromwich A	Tr	09.85	85	20	0	0
Derby Co	L	03.86	85	9	0	0
Shrewsbury T	Wichita (USA)	08.88	88	40	0	1
Leeds U	Tr	06.89	89	3	0	0
Stoke C	L	03.90	89	8	0	0
Stoke C	Tr	08.90	90	32	6	7
Wrexham	Tr	07.91	91-92	34	0	2

THOMAS Mitchell Anthony
Luton, 2 October, 1964 EYth/Eu21-3/EB-1 (FB)

League Club	Source	Date Signed	Seasons Played	Apps	Subs	Gls
Luton T	App	08.82	82-85	106	1	1
Tottenham H	Tr	07.86	86-90	136	21	6
West Ham U	Tr	08.91	91-92	37	1	3
Luton T	Tr	11.93	93-98	170	15	5
Burnley	Tr	07.99	99-01	95	4	0

THOMAS Patrick (Pat)
Sidmouth, 7 March, 1965 (M)

League Club	Source	Date Signed	Seasons Played	Apps	Subs	Gls
Exeter C	Sidmouth T	06.82	82	0	1	0

THOMAS Peter John
Treforest, 18 October, 1932 (W)

League Club	Source	Date Signed	Seasons Played	Apps	Subs	Gls
Cardiff C	Jnrs	03.53	53	4	-	1
Exeter C	Tr	12.54	54-55	29	-	4
Newport Co	Tr	07.56	56-57	6	-	1

THOMAS Peter John
Coventry, 20 November, 1944 IR-2 (G)

League Club	Source	Date Signed	Seasons Played	Apps	Subs	Gls
Coventry C	GEC (Coventry)	06.66	66	1	0	0

THOMAS Philip (Phil) Leslie
Sherborne, 14 December, 1952 Died 1998 (M)

League Club	Source	Date Signed	Seasons Played	Apps	Subs	Gls
Bournemouth	App	07.71				
Colchester U	Tr	05.72	72-75	103	5	8

THOMAS Rees
Aberdare, 3 January, 1934 (FB)

League Club	Source	Date Signed	Seasons Played	Apps	Subs	Gls
Cardiff C	Jnrs	01.51				
Torquay U	L	08.53	53	1	-	0
Brighton & Hove A	Tr	09.56	56-57	31	-	1
Bournemouth	Tr	01.58	57-58	48	-	0
Portsmouth	Tr	07.59	59-60	30	-	0
Aldershot	Tr	07.61	61-63	103	-	2

THOMAS Robert (Bob) Albert
Stepney, 2 August, 1919 Died 1990 (IF)

League Club	Source	Date Signed	Seasons Played	Apps	Subs	Gls
Brentford	Hendon	05.39				
Plymouth Arg	Tr	04.46	46	41	-	17
Fulham	Tr	06.47	47-51	167	-	55
Crystal Palace	Tr	09.52	52-54	96	-	31

THOMAS Robert Owen
Redditch, 27 August, 1950 (M)

League Club	Source	Date Signed	Seasons Played	Apps	Subs	Gls
Blackpool		06.69	69	0	1	0

THOMAS Roderick (Rod) Clive
Harlesden, 10 October, 1970 ESch/EYth/Eu21-1 (W)

League Club	Source	Date Signed	Seasons Played	Apps	Subs	Gls
Watford	YT	05.88	87-92	63	21	9

League Club	Source	Date Signed	Seasons Played	Career Record Apps	Subs	Gls
Gillingham	L	03.92	91	8	0	1
Carlisle U	Tr	07.93	93-96	124	22	16
Chester C	Tr	07.97	97-98	28	16	7
Brighton & Hove A	Tr	10.98	98-00	25	23	4
THOMAS Roderick (Rod) John						
Glyncorrwg, 11 January, 1947 Wu23-6/W-50						(FB)
Swindon T	Gloucester C	07.64	65-73	296	0	4
Derby Co	Tr	11.73	73-77	89	0	2
Cardiff C	Tr	11.77	77-81	89	7	0
Newport Co	Gloucester C	03.82	81	3	0	0
THOMAS Scott Lee						
Bury, 30 October, 1974						(M)
Manchester C	YT	03.92	94	0	2	0
Brighton & Hove A	L	03.98	97	7	0	0
THOMAS David **Sidney**						
Machynlleth, 12 November, 1919 W-4						(W)
Fulham	Treharris	08.38	46-49	57	-	4
Bristol C	Tr	06.50	50	13	-	1
THOMAS Stanley (Stan) Herbert						
Birkenhead, 5 September, 1919 Died 1985						(IF)
Tranmere Rov (Am)	Oxford Univ	12.48	48	1	-	0
THOMAS Stephen (Steve)						
Hartlepool, 23 June, 1979 WYth/Wu21-5						(M)
Wrexham	YT	07.97	98-03	85	31	7
Darlington	Tr	08.04	04	11	1	0
THOMAS Steven						
Batley, 29 January, 1957						(FB)
Swansea C (Am)	Jnrs	08.73	73-74	10	0	0
THOMAS Valmore Neville						
Worksop, 30 April, 1958						(FB)
Coventry C	App	03.76				
Hereford U	Tr	03.79	78-80	31	1	1
THOMAS Wayne						
Walsall, 28 August, 1978						(M)
Walsall	YT	07.96	96-99	18	20	0
Mansfield T	L	08.99	99	4	1	0
Shrewsbury T	Tr	01.00	99-00	15	2	1
THOMAS Wayne Junior Robert						
Gloucester, 17 May, 1979						(CD)
Torquay U	YT	07.97	95-99	89	34	5
Stoke C	Tr	06.00	00-04	188	1	7
THOMAS William (Billy) Pryce						
Glyn Neath, 28 October, 1923						(W)
Torquay U	Merthyr Tydfil	09.47	47-54	90	-	17
THOMAS Wilson (Bill) George						
Derby, 18 November, 1918 Died 2001						(IF)
Bristol C	Matlock T	10.44	46-49	77	-	18
THOME Emerson Augusto						
Porto Alegre, Brazil, 30 March, 1972						(CD)
Sheffield Wed	Benfica (Por)	03.98	97-99	60	1	1
Chelsea	Tr	12.99	99-00	19	2	0
Sunderland	Tr	09.00	00-02	43	1	2
Bolton W	Tr	08.03	03	25	1	0
Wigan Ath	Tr	08.04	04	11	4	0
THOMPSON Alan						
Goole, 2 September, 1931						(FB)
Luton T	Westpark Jnrs	12.49	56	1	-	0
THOMPSON Alan						
Newcastle, 22 December, 1973 EYth/Eu21-2						(W)
Newcastle U	YT	03.91	91-92	13	3	0
Bolton W	Tr	07.93	93-97	143	14	33
Aston Villa	Tr	06.98	98-99	36	10	4
THOMPSON William **Alan**						
Liverpool, 20 January, 1952						(CD)
Sheffield Wed	App	01.69	70-75	150	6	3
Stockport Co	Tr	08.76	76-78	93	1	17
Bradford C	Portland (USA)	01.80	79-81	31	0	0
Scunthorpe U	Tr	03.82	81	11	0	0
THOMPSON Alexander (Alex)						
Sheffield, 8 December, 1917 Died 2002						(FB)
Sheffield Wed	Woodhouse Alliance	06.37				
Lincoln C	Tr	03.39	46-47	34	-	1
Tranmere Rov	Tr	06.48	48	1	-	0

League Club	Source	Date Signed	Seasons Played	Career Record Apps	Subs	Gls
THOMPSON Andrew (Andy) Richard						
Cannock, 9 November, 1967						(FB)
West Bromwich A	App	11.85	85-86	18	6	1
Wolverhampton W	Tr	11.86	86-96	356	20	43
Tranmere Rov	Tr	07.97	97-99	91	5	4
Cardiff C	Tr	08.00	00	5	2	0
Shrewsbury T	Tr	01.02	01-02	29	1	0
THOMPSON Arthur						
Dewsbury, 15 June, 1922 Died 1996						(IF)
Huddersfield T	Thornhill Edge	09.41	46-48	25	-	5
THOMPSON Brian						
Kingswinford, 9 February, 1950						(M)
Wolverhampton W	App	02.67				
Oxford U	Tr	10.69	69-72	52	5	4
Torquay U	L	03.73	72	9	0	1
THOMPSON George **Brian**						
Ashington, 7 August, 1952 ESemiPro						(FB)
Sunderland		06.71				
York C	L	03.73	72	4	2	0
Mansfield T	Yeovil T	11.79	79	9	0	0
THOMPSON Charles (Charlie) Maskery						
Chesterfield, 19 July, 1920 Died 1997						(CD)
Sheffield U	Bolsover Colliery	07.37	46	17	-	3
THOMPSON Christopher (Chris) David						
Walsall, 24 January, 1960 EYth						(M)
Bolton W	App	07.77	79-82	66	7	18
Lincoln C	L	03.83	82	5	1	0
Blackburn Rov	Tr	08.83	83-85	81	4	24
Wigan Ath	Tr	07.86	86-87	67	7	12
Blackpool	Tr	07.88	88-89	27	12	8
Cardiff C	Tr	03.90	89	1	1	0
Walsall		02.91	90	3	0	0
THOMPSON Christopher (Chris) Michael						
Warrington, 7 February, 1982						(F)
Grimsby T	Liverpool (YT)	07.01	01-02	7	7	1
THOMPSON Cyril Alfred						
Southend-on-Sea, 18 December, 1918 Died 1972						(CF)
Southend U		07.45	46-47	66	-	36
Derby Co	Tr	07.48	48-49	16	-	3
Brighton & Hove A	Tr	03.50	49-50	41	-	15
Watford	Tr	03.51	50-52	78	-	36
THOMPSON David						
Middlesbrough, 26 February, 1945						(IF)
Lincoln C	Whitby T	06.64	64	3	-	1
THOMPSON David Anthony						
Birkenhead, 12 September, 1977 EYth/Eu21-7						(M)
Liverpool	YT	11.94	96-99	24	24	5
Swindon T	L	11.97	97	10	0	0
Coventry C	Tr	08.00	00-02	61	5	15
Blackburn Rov	Tr	08.02	02-04	44	14	5
THOMPSON David (Dave) George						
Ashington, 20 November, 1968						(CD)
Millwall	App	11.86	87-91	88	9	6
Bristol C	Tr	06.92	92	17	0	0
Brentford	Tr	02.94	93	9	1	1
Blackpool	Tr	09.94	94	17	0	0
Cambridge U	Tr	03.95	94-96	36	8	2
THOMPSON David (Dave) Stanley						
Catterick Camp, 12 March, 1945						(W)
Wolverhampton W	Jnrs	04.62	64	8	-	1
Southampton	Tr	08.66	66-70	21	2	0
Mansfield T	Tr	10.70	70-73	129	2	21
Chesterfield	Tr	12.73	73	14	0	3
THOMPSON David (Dave) Stephen						
Manchester, 27 May, 1962						(W)
Rochdale	New Withington	09.81	81-85	147	8	13
Notts Co	Tr	08.86	86-87	52	3	8
Wigan Ath	Tr	10.87	87-89	107	1	16
Preston NE	Tr	08.90	90-91	39	7	4
Chester C	Tr	08.92	92-93	70	10	9
Rochdale	Tr	08.94	94-96	90	21	11
THOMPSON Dennis						
Whitburn, 10 April, 1924 Died 2001						(CF)
Hull C	Whitburn Welfare	04.47	46-47	9	-	8
THOMPSON Dennis						
Sheffield, 2 June, 1925 Died 1986 ESch						(W)
Sheffield U	Jnrs	08.42	46-50	96	-	20
Southend U	Tr	07.51	51-53	51	-	11

THOMPSON Dennis
Bolsover, 19 July, 1934 (IF)

League Club	Source	Date Signed	Seasons Played	Apps	Subs	Gls
Chesterfield	Jnrs	07.51	50-52	24	-	0
Scunthorpe U	Tr	07.55	55	3	-	0

THOMPSON Desmond (Des)
Southampton, 4 December, 1928 (G)

League Club	Source	Date Signed	Seasons Played	Apps	Subs	Gls
York C	Dinnington	01.51	50-52	80	-	0
Burnley	Tr	11.52	52-54	62	-	0
Sheffield U	Tr	05.55	55-63	25	-	0

THOMPSON Robert **Eric**
Mexborough, 3 December, 1944 (CD)

League Club	Source	Date Signed	Seasons Played	Apps	Subs	Gls
Doncaster Rov	Leeds U (App)	07.62	62	9	-	0

THOMPSON Frederick (Freddie) Norman
Swindon, 24 November, 1937 Died 1998 (WH)

League Club	Source	Date Signed	Seasons Played	Apps	Subs	Gls
Swindon T	Jnrs	09.55	54-60	21	-	1

THOMPSON Garry Lindsey
Birmingham, 7 October, 1959 Eu21-6 (F)

League Club	Source	Date Signed	Seasons Played	Apps	Subs	Gls
Coventry C	App	06.77	77-82	127	7	38
West Bromwich A	Tr	02.83	82-84	91	0	39
Sheffield Wed	Tr	08.85	85	35	1	7
Aston Villa	Tr	06.86	86-88	56	4	17
Watford	Tr	12.88	88-89	24	10	8
Crystal Palace	Tr	03.90	89-90	17	3	3
Queens Park Rgrs	Tr	08.91	91-92	10	9	1
Cardiff C	Tr	07.93	93-94	39	4	5
Northampton T	Tr	02.95	94-96	36	14	6

THOMPSON George
Lisburn, 5 November, 1913 LoI-1 (FB)

League Club	Source	Date Signed	Seasons Played	Apps	Subs	Gls
Huddersfield T	Sligo Rov	12.38				
Exeter C	Tr	06.46	46-47	63	-	4

THOMPSON George Herbert
Maltby, 15 September, 1926 Died 2004 (G)

League Club	Source	Date Signed	Seasons Played	Apps	Subs	Gls
Chesterfield		06.47				
Scunthorpe U	Tr	06.50	50-52	92	-	0
Preston NE	Tr	10.52	52-55	140	-	0
Manchester C	Tr	06.56	56	2	-	0
Carlisle U	Tr	06.57	57-61	204	-	0

THOMPSON Glyn William
Telford, 24 February, 1981 (G)

League Club	Source	Date Signed	Seasons Played	Apps	Subs	Gls
Shrewsbury T	YT	12.98	98	1	0	0
Fulham	Tr	11.99				
Mansfield T	L	01.00	99	16	0	0
Northampton T	Tr	11.02	02-03	18	1	0
Walsall	Tr	08.04				
Chesterfield	Stafford Rgrs	03.05	04	1	0	0

THOMPSON Harold (Harry)
Mansfield, 29 April, 1915 (IF)

League Club	Source	Date Signed	Seasons Played	Apps	Subs	Gls
Mansfield T	Mansfield Invicta	06.32				
Wolverhampton W	Tr	06.33	35-38	69	-	16
Sunderland	Tr	12.38	38	13	-	1
York C	Tr	12.45				
Northampton T	Tr	11.46	46-48	38	-	2

THOMPSON Henry
South Shields, 21 February, 1932 (CF)

League Club	Source	Date Signed	Seasons Played	Apps	Subs	Gls
Gateshead		08.51	51-55	24	-	5

THOMPSON Ian Peter
Dartford, 8 June, 1958 (F)

League Club	Source	Date Signed	Seasons Played	Apps	Subs	Gls
Bournemouth	Salisbury	07.83	83-85	119	2	30

THOMPSON James (Jimmy)
Chadderton, 26 November, 1935 (WH)

League Club	Source	Date Signed	Seasons Played	Apps	Subs	Gls
Oldham Ath	Chadderton	01.54	53-58	110	-	19
Exeter C	Tr	12.58	58-60	105	-	10
Rochdale	Tr	03.61	60-65	199	0	15
Bradford C	Tr	12.65	65	23	1	1

THOMPSON James (Jimmy) Butters
Felling, 7 January, 1943 (FB)

League Club	Source	Date Signed	Seasons Played	Apps	Subs	Gls
Grimsby T	St Mary's BC	09.61	62-66	156	0	2
Cambridge U	Port Elizabeth C (SA)	01.69	70-72	117	1	0

THOMPSON John (Jack)
Cramlington, 21 March, 1915 Died 1996 (IF)

League Club	Source	Date Signed	Seasons Played	Apps	Subs	Gls
Sheffield Wed	Blyth Spartans	06.33	33-38	36	-	9
Doncaster Rov	Tr	05.46	46-47	59	-	17
Chesterfield	Tr	07.48	48-52	82	-	8

THOMPSON John
Dublin, 12 October, 1981 IRYth/IRu21-11/IR-1 (CD)

League Club	Source	Date Signed	Seasons Played	Apps	Subs	Gls
Nottingham F	Home Farm	07.99	01-04	66	14	4

THOMPSON John Henry
Newcastle, 4 July, 1932 (G)

League Club	Source	Date Signed	Seasons Played	Apps	Subs	Gls
Newcastle U	Jnrs	09.50	54-55	8	-	0
Lincoln C	Tr	05.57	57-59	42	-	0

THOMPSON Joseph (Joe) Prudhoe
Seaham, 15 November, 1927 Died 1996 (FB)

League Club	Source	Date Signed	Seasons Played	Apps	Subs	Gls
Luton T	Electrolux	05.46				
Shrewsbury T	Tr	07.51	51	7	-	0

THOMPSON Justin
Prince Rupert, Canada, 9 January, 1981 CaYth/Cau23-7 (F)

League Club	Source	Date Signed	Seasons Played	Apps	Subs	Gls
Bury	Fairfield Univ (Can)	10.03	03	1	0	0

THOMPSON Keith Anthony
Birmingham, 24 April, 1965 EYth (W)

League Club	Source	Date Signed	Seasons Played	Apps	Subs	Gls
Coventry C	App	01.83	82-84	9	3	0
Wimbledon	L	10.83	83	0	3	0
Northampton T	L	03.85	84	10	0	1
Coventry C	Real Oviedo (Sp)	09.88	88-90	2	9	1

THOMPSON Kenneth (Ken) Hurst
Sunderland, 24 April, 1926 (FB)

League Club	Source	Date Signed	Seasons Played	Apps	Subs	Gls
Middlesbrough	Jnrs	11.44				
Gateshead	L	11.46	46	9	-	0
York C	Tr	07.50	50-51	22	-	0

THOMPSON Kenneth (Ken) John
Ipswich, 1 March, 1945 (WH)

League Club	Source	Date Signed	Seasons Played	Apps	Subs	Gls
Ipswich T	Jnrs	03.62	64-65	11	1	0
Exeter C	Tr	06.66	66	38	1	1

THOMPSON Kevan John
Middlesbrough, 8 September, 1948 (F)

League Club	Source	Date Signed	Seasons Played	Apps	Subs	Gls
Hartlepool (Am)	Threadhalls	10.70	69-70	6	0	1

THOMPSON Lee Jonathan
Sheffield, 25 March, 1983 ESch (W)

League Club	Source	Date Signed	Seasons Played	Apps	Subs	Gls
Sheffield U	Jnrs	07.00				
Boston U	Tr	10.02	02-04	40	55	12

THOMPSON Leslie (Les) Allen
Cleethorpes, 23 September, 1968 (FB)

League Club	Source	Date Signed	Seasons Played	Apps	Subs	Gls
Hull C	App	03.87	87-90	31	4	4
Scarborough	L	12.88	88	2	1	1
Maidstone U	Tr	07.91	91	38	0	0
Burnley	Tr	07.92	92-93	38	1	0

THOMPSON Malcolm George
Beverley, 19 October, 1946 (F)

League Club	Source	Date Signed	Seasons Played	Apps	Subs	Gls
Hartlepool	Goole T	11.68	68-69	43	3	9

THOMPSON Marc
York, 15 January, 1982 (F)

League Club	Source	Date Signed	Seasons Played	Apps	Subs	Gls
York C	YT	06.00	99-00	18	4	0

THOMPSON Maxwell (Max) Stewart
Liverpool, 31 December, 1956 (CD)

League Club	Source	Date Signed	Seasons Played	Apps	Subs	Gls
Liverpool	App	01.74	73	1	0	0
Blackpool	Tr	12.77	77-80	92	7	7
Swansea C	Tr	09.81	81-82	25	1	2
Bournemouth	Tr	08.83	83	9	0	0
Port Vale	L	11.83	83	2	0	0

THOMPSON Neil
Beverley, 2 October, 1963 ESemiPro-4 (FB)

League Club	Source	Date Signed	Seasons Played	Apps	Subs	Gls
Hull C	Nottingham F (App)	11.81	81-82	29	2	0
Scarborough	Tr	08.83	87-88	87	0	15
Ipswich T	Tr	06.89	89-95	199	7	19
Barnsley	Tr	06.96	96-97	27	0	5
Oldham Ath	L	12.97	97	8	0	0
York C	Tr	03.98	97-99	42	0	8
Boston U	Scarborough	06.01	02	3	0	0

THOMPSON Neil Philip
Hackney, 30 April, 1978 (FB)

League Club	Source	Date Signed	Seasons Played	Apps	Subs	Gls
Barnet	YT	07.96	95-96	2	1	0

THOMPSON Niall Joseph
Birmingham, 16 April, 1974 Canada 9 (F)

League Club	Source	Date Signed	Seasons Played	Apps	Subs	Gls
Crystal Palace	Jnrs	07.92				
Colchester U	(Hong Kong)	11.94	94	5	8	5
Brentford	Zultse VV (Bel)	02.98	97	6	2	0
Wycombe W	Bay Area Seals (USA)	10.00	00	6	2	0

THOMPSON Nigel David
Leeds, 1 March, 1967 (M)

League Club	Source	Date Signed	Seasons Played	Apps	Subs	Gls
Leeds U	App	12.84	83-86	6	1	0
Rochdale	L	08.87	87	3	2	0
Chesterfield	Tr	03.88	87-89	18	2	1

League Club	Source	Date Signed	Seasons Played	Career Record Apps	Subs	Gls

THOMPSON Patrick (Pat) Alfred
Exeter, 11 February, 1932 (IF)

League Club	Source	Date Signed	Seasons Played	Apps	Subs	Gls
Brighton & Hove A	Topsham	01.51	50	1	-	0

THOMPSON Paul Derek Zetland
Newcastle, 17 April, 1973 (F)

League Club	Source	Date Signed	Seasons Played	Apps	Subs	Gls
Hartlepool U	Redheugh Boys	11.91	92-94	44	12	9

THOMPSON Peter
Blackhall, 16 February, 1936 EAmat (CF)

League Club	Source	Date Signed	Seasons Played	Apps	Subs	Gls
Wrexham (Am)	Blackhall CW	11.55	55-56	42	-	21
Hartlepools U	Tr	07.57	57-58	47	-	22
Derby Co	Tr	11.58	58-61	52	-	19
Bournemouth	Tr	01.62	61-62	39	-	14
Hartlepools U	Tr	09.63	63-65	91	0	34

THOMPSON Peter
Carlisle, 27 November, 1942 ESch/Eu23-4/FLge-5/E-16 (W)

League Club	Source	Date Signed	Seasons Played	Apps	Subs	Gls
Preston NE	Jnrs	11.59	60-62	122	-	20
Liverpool	Tr	08.63	63-71	318	4	41
Bolton W	Tr	11.73	73-77	111	6	2

THOMPSON Peter Colin
Kenya, 25 July, 1942 (M)

League Club	Source	Date Signed	Seasons Played	Apps	Subs	Gls
Peterborough U	Grantham	03.64	63-68	79	6	15

THOMPSON Philip (Phil) Bernard
Liverpool, 21 January, 1954 EYth/Eu23-1/FLge/E-42 (CD)

League Club	Source	Date Signed	Seasons Played	Apps	Subs	Gls
Liverpool	App	02.71	71-82	337	3	7
Sheffield U	Tr	12.84	84-85	36	1	0

THOMPSON Philip (Phil) Paul
Blackpool, 1 April, 1981 (CD)

League Club	Source	Date Signed	Seasons Played	Apps	Subs	Gls
Blackpool	YT	09.98	97-01	37	10	3

THOMPSON Raymond (Ray)
Leeholme, 21 October, 1925 Died 1996 (FB)

League Club	Source	Date Signed	Seasons Played	Apps	Subs	Gls
Sunderland		11.45				
Hartlepools U	Tr	01.47	46-57	396	-	2

THOMPSON Richard John
Hawkesbury, 11 April, 1969 (F)

League Club	Source	Date Signed	Seasons Played	Apps	Subs	Gls
Newport Co	Yate T	01.87	87	10	3	2
Torquay U	Tr	06.88	88	11	4	4

THOMPSON Richard Omar
Balham, 2 May, 1974 (F)

League Club	Source	Date Signed	Seasons Played	Apps	Subs	Gls
Wycombe W	Crawley T	03.99	99	1	5	0

THOMPSON Ronald (Ron)
Sheffield, 24 December, 1921 Died 1988 (IF)

League Club	Source	Date Signed	Seasons Played	Apps	Subs	Gls
Sheffield Wed	Wadsley Colliery	04.45				
Rotherham U	Tr	05.47	47-48	30	-	11
York C	Tr	06.49	49	8	-	0

THOMPSON Ronald (Ron)
Carlisle, 20 January, 1932 (WH)

League Club	Source	Date Signed	Seasons Played	Apps	Subs	Gls
Carlisle U		07.51	51-63	373	-	12

THOMPSON Ryan James Daley
Lambeth, 24 June, 1982 (F)

League Club	Source	Date Signed	Seasons Played	Apps	Subs	Gls
Northampton T	YT	07.00	00	0	2	0

THOMPSON Sidney (Sid)
Bedlington, 14 July, 1928 (IF)

League Club	Source	Date Signed	Seasons Played	Apps	Subs	Gls
Nottingham F		09.47	52-54	22	-	8

THOMPSON Simon Lee
Sheffield, 27 February, 1970 (M)

League Club	Source	Date Signed	Seasons Played	Apps	Subs	Gls
Rotherham U	YT	06.88	88-90	12	16	0
Scarborough	Tr	12.91	91-94	99	9	6

THOMPSON Steven (Steve) Anthony
Manchester, 17 February, 1972 (CD)

League Club	Source	Date Signed	Seasons Played	Apps	Subs	Gls
Gillingham	YT	●	89	1	1	0

THOMPSON Steven (Steve) James
Oldham, 2 November, 1964 (M)

League Club	Source	Date Signed	Seasons Played	Apps	Subs	Gls
Bolton W	App	11.82	82-91	329	6	50
Luton T	Tr	08.91	91	5	0	0
Leicester C	Tr	10.91	91-94	121	6	18
Burnley	Tr	02.95	94-96	44	5	1
Rotherham U	Tr	07.97	97-99	87	16	14
Halifax T	Tr	07.00	00	35	1	2

THOMPSON Steven (Steve) John
Plymouth, 12 January, 1963 ESemiPro (M)

League Club	Source	Date Signed	Seasons Played	Apps	Subs	Gls
Bristol C	Jnrs	07.81	81-82	10	2	1
Torquay U	Tr	02.83	82	0	1	0
Wycombe W	Slough T	02.92	93-94	41	21	3

THOMPSON Steven (Steve) Paul
Sheffield, 28 July, 1955 (CD)

League Club	Source	Date Signed	Seasons Played	Apps	Subs	Gls
Lincoln C	Boston U	04.80	80-84	153	1	8
Charlton Ath	Tr	08.85	85-87	95	0	0
Leicester C	Tr	07.88				
Sheffield U	Tr	11.88	88	20	0	1
Lincoln C	Tr	07.89	89	27	0	0

THOMPSON Stewart Christopher
Littleborough, 2 September, 1964 ESch (F)

League Club	Source	Date Signed	Seasons Played	Apps	Subs	Gls
Rochdale	Blackburn Rov (App)	09.82	82-83	23	8	8

THOMPSON Terence (Terry) William
Barlestone, 25 December, 1946 (FB)

League Club	Source	Date Signed	Seasons Played	Apps	Subs	Gls
Wolverhampton W	App	01.64				
Notts Co	Tr	03.66	65-67	66	0	3

THOMPSON Thomas (Tommy)
Fencehouses, 10 November, 1928 FLge-2/EB/E-2 (IF)

League Club	Source	Date Signed	Seasons Played	Apps	Subs	Gls
Newcastle U	Lumley YMCA	08.46	47-49	20	-	6
Aston Villa	Tr	08.50	50-54	149	-	67
Preston NE	Tr	07.55	55-60	189	-	116
Stoke C	Tr	06.61	61-62	42	-	17
Barrow	Tr	03.63	62-63	44	-	16

THOMPSON Thomas (Tommy) William
Stockton, 9 March, 1938 EAmat (FB)

League Club	Source	Date Signed	Seasons Played	Apps	Subs	Gls
Blackpool	Stockton	08.61	61-68	155	1	1
York C	Tr	07.70	70	4	0	0

THOMPSON John **Trevor**
North Shields, 21 May, 1955 (FB)

League Club	Source	Date Signed	Seasons Played	Apps	Subs	Gls
West Bromwich A	App	01.74	73-75	20	0	0
Newport Co	Washington (USA)	08.78	78-79	32	3	2
Lincoln C	Tr	12.79	79-81	80	0	1

THOMPSON Tyrone I'Yungo
Sheffield, 8 May, 1982 (M)

League Club	Source	Date Signed	Seasons Played	Apps	Subs	Gls
Sheffield U	YT	07.00				
Lincoln C	L	10.02	02	0	1	0
Huddersfield T	Tr	08.03	03	1	1	0

THOMPSON William (Bill)
Berwick-on-Tweed, 31 August, 1916 Died 1989 (G)

League Club	Source	Date Signed	Seasons Played	Apps	Subs	Gls
Leeds U	Ashington	10.35				
Watford		08.46	46	9	-	0

THOMPSON William
Ashington, 23 December, 1921 Died 1986 (W)

League Club	Source	Date Signed	Seasons Played	Apps	Subs	Gls
Gateshead		09.45	46-47	3	-	0

THOMPSON William (Billy)
Bedlington, 5 January, 1940 (CD)

League Club	Source	Date Signed	Seasons Played	Apps	Subs	Gls
Newcastle U	Jnrs	01.57	60-66	79	1	1
Rotherham U	Tr	06.67	67	8	0	0
Darlington	Tr	01.68	67-69	30	0	5

THOMPSON William (Bill) Gordon
Glasgow, 10 August, 1921 Died 1988 (FB)

League Club	Source	Date Signed	Seasons Played	Apps	Subs	Gls
Portsmouth	Carnoustie	03.46	48-52	40	-	2
Bournemouth	Tr	01.53	52-53	46	-	0

THOMPSTONE Ian Philip
Bury, 17 January, 1971 (M)

League Club	Source	Date Signed	Seasons Played	Apps	Subs	Gls
Manchester C	YT	09.89	87	0	1	1
Oldham Ath	Tr	05.90				
Exeter C	Tr	01.92	91	15	0	3
Halifax T	Tr	07.92	92	31	0	9
Scunthorpe U	Tr	03.93	92-94	47	13	8
Rochdale	Tr	07.95	95	11	14	1
Scarborough	Tr	08.96	96	12	7	2

THOMSEN Claus
Aarhus, Denmark, 31 May, 1970 Denmark int (M)

League Club	Source	Date Signed	Seasons Played	Apps	Subs	Gls
Ipswich T	Aarhus GF (Den)	06.94	94-96	77	4	7
Everton	Tr	01.97	96-97	17	7	1

THOMSON Andrew (Andy)
Motherwell, 1 April, 1971 (F)

League Club	Source	Date Signed	Seasons Played	Apps	Subs	Gls
Southend U	Queen of the South	07.94	94-97	87	35	28
Oxford U	Tr	07.98	98	25	13	7
Gillingham	Tr	08.99	99-00	32	20	14
Queens Park Rgrs	Tr	03.01	00-02	43	24	28

THOMSON Andrew (Andy) John
Swindon, 28 March, 1974 (CD)

League Club	Source	Date Signed	Seasons Played	Apps	Subs	Gls
Swindon T	YT	05.93	93-94	21	1	0
Portsmouth	Tr	12.95	95-98	85	8	3
Bristol Rov	Tr	01.99	98-01	124	3	6
Wycombe W	Tr	03.02	01-03	48	2	2

League Club	Source	Date Signed	Seasons Played	Career Record Apps	Subs	Gls
THOMSON Arthur Campbell						
Edinburgh, 2 September, 1948 Died 2002 Su23-3						(CD)
Oldham Ath	Heart of Midlothian	01.70	69-70	27	1	0
THOMSON Bertram (Bert)						
Glasgow, 18 February, 1929						(WH)
Rochdale	Yeovil T	06.58	58-59	55	-	1
THOMSON Brian Lamont						
Paisley, 1 March, 1959						(W)
West Ham U	Morecambe	01.77				
Mansfield T	Tr	08.79	79-81	54	9	1
THOMSON Charles (Chick) Richard						
Perth, 2 March, 1930						(G)
Chelsea	Clyde	10.52	52-55	46	-	0
Nottingham F	Tr	08.57	57-60	121	-	0
THOMSON David Laing						
Bothkennar, 2 February, 1938						(IF)
Leicester C	Dunfermline Ath	08.61	61	1	-	1
THOMSON George Matthewson						
Edinburgh, 19 October, 1936 SLge-2						(FB)
Everton	Heart of Midlothian	11.60	60-62	73	-	1
Brentford	Tr	11.63	63-67	160	2	5
THOMSON Henry (Harry) Watson						
Edinburgh, 25 August, 1940						(G)
Burnley	Bo'ness U	08.59	64-68	117	0	0
Blackpool	Tr	07.69	69-70	60	0	0
Barrow	Tr	08.71	71	40	0	0
THOMSON James (Jimmy) Arnott						
Glasgow, 28 June, 1948						(M)
Newcastle U	Petershill	06.68	69	4	1	0
Barrow	L	12.70	70	2	0	0
Grimsby T	Tr	07.71	71	23	3	4
THOMSON James (Jimmy) Donaldson						
Govan, 17 March, 1931						(IF)
Southend U	Raith Rov	05.56	56-58	40	-	10
THOMSON James (Jim) Shaw						
Provanside, 1 October, 1946						(CD)
Chelsea	Provanside Hibernian	01.65	65-67	33	6	1
Burnley	Tr	09.68	68-80	294	3	3
THOMSON John						
Newcastle, 3 December, 1954						(CD)
Newcastle U	App	12.72				
Bury	Tr	11.73	73-77	92	11	8
THOMSON John Ballantyne						
Muirhead, 22 October, 1934						(FB)
Workington	Heart of Midlothian	05.58	58	11	-	1
THOMSON Kenneth (Kenny) Gordon						
Aberdeen, 25 February, 1930 Died 1969						(CD)
Stoke C	Aberdeen	09.52	52-59	278	-	6
Middlesbrough	Tr	12.59	59-62	84	-	1
Hartlepools U	Tr	10.62	62	28	-	2
THOMSON Lawrence (Lawrie) James						
Menstrie, 26 August, 1936						(W)
Carlisle U	Partick Th	01.60	59	13	-	1
THOMSON Peter David						
Crumpsall, 30 June, 1977						(F)
Bury	Stand Ath	11.95				
Luton T	NAC Breda (Holl)	09.00	00	4	7	2
Rushden & Diamonds	L	11.01	01	1	1	1
THOMSON Richard (Ricky) Blair						
Edinburgh, 26 June, 1957						(F)
Preston NE	App	06.75	74-79	60	11	20
THOMSON Robert (Bobby)						
Menstrie, 21 November, 1939						(FB)
Liverpool	Partick Th	12.62	62-63	6	-	0
Luton T	Tr	08.65	65-66	74	0	0
THOMSON Robert (Bobby)						
Glasgow, 21 March, 1955 SLge-2						(M)
Middlesbrough	Morton	09.81	81	18	2	2
Blackpool	Hibernian	09.85	85-86	50	2	6
Hartlepool U	Tr	08.87	87	2	1	0
THOMSON Robert (Bobby) Anthony						
Smethwick, 5 December, 1943 Eu23-15/FLge-4/E-8						(FB)
Wolverhampton W	App	07.61	61-68	277	1	2
Birmingham C	Tr	03.69	68-70	63	0	0
Walsall	L	11.71	71	9	0	1

League Club	Source	Date Signed	Seasons Played	Career Record Apps	Subs	Gls
Luton T	Tr	07.72	72-75	110	0	1
Port Vale	Hartford (USA)	10.76	76	18	0	0
THOMSON Robert (Bobby) Gillies McKenzie						
Dundee, 21 March, 1937						(IF)
Wolverhampton W	Airdrie	08.54	56	1	-	1
Aston Villa	Tr	06.59	59-63	140	-	56
Birmingham C	Tr	09.63	63-67	109	3	23
Stockport Co	Tr	12.67	67	16	1	0
THOMSON Scott Yuill						
Edinburgh, 8 November, 1966						(G)
Hull C	St Johnstone	08.97	97	9	0	0
THOMSON Steven (Steve)						
Glasgow, 23 January, 1978 SYth						(M)
Crystal Palace	YT	12.95	98-02	68	37	1
Peterborough U	Tr	09.03	03-04	58	8	3
THORBURN James (Jim) Hope Forrest						
Lanark, 10 March, 1938						(G)
Ipswich T	Raith Rov	06.63	63-64	24	-	0
THORDARSON Stefan						
Reykjavik, Iceland, 27 March, 1975 IcYth/Icu21-8/Ic-5						(F)
Stoke C	Bayer Uerdingen (Ger)	06.00	00-01	18	33	8
THORLEY Dennis						
Stoke-on-Trent, 7 November, 1956						(CD)
Stoke C	Jnrs	07.76	76-80	9	4	0
Blackburn Rov	L	03.80	79	2	2	0
THORN Andrew (Andy) Charles						
Carshalton, 12 November, 1966 Eu21-5						(CD)
Wimbledon	App	11.84	84-87	106	1	2
Newcastle U	Tr	08.88	88-89	36	0	2
Crystal Palace	Tr	12.89	89-93	128	0	3
Wimbledon	Tr	10.94	94-95	33	4	1
Tranmere Rov	Heart of Midlothian	09.96	96-97	36	0	1
THORNBER Stephen (Steve) John						
Dewsbury, 11 October, 1965						(M)
Halifax T	Jnrs	01.83	83-87	94	10	4
Swansea C	Tr	08.88	88-91	98	19	5
Blackpool	Tr	08.92	92	21	3	0
Scunthorpe U	Tr	07.93	93-95	71	6	7
THORNE Adrian Ernest						
Brighton, 2 August, 1937						(W)
Brighton & Hove A	Jnrs	08.54	57-60	76	-	38
Plymouth Arg	Tr	06.61	61-63	11	-	2
Exeter C	Tr	12.63	63-64	41	-	8
Leyton Orient	Tr	07.65	65	2	0	0
THORNE Peter Lee						
Manchester, 21 June, 1973						(F)
Blackburn Rov	YT	06.91				
Wigan Ath	L	03.94	93	10	1	0
Swindon T	Tr	01.95	94-96	66	11	27
Stoke C	Tr	07.97	97-01	147	11	65
Cardiff C	Tr	09.01	01-04	116	10	46
THORNE Steven (Steve) Terence						
Hampstead, 15 September, 1968						(M)
Watford	App	07.86				
Brentford	Tr	09.87	87	1	0	1
THORNE Terence (Terry)						
Kirton-in-Lindsey, 2 February, 1947						(IF)
Ipswich T	Lincoln C (Am)	08.64				
Notts Co	Tr	06.66	66	2	0	0
THORNHILL Dennis						
Draycott, 5 July, 1923 Died 1992						(CD)
Wolverhampton W	Jnrs	07.40				
Southend U	Tr	03.48	48-49	11	-	0
THORNHILL Keith Eric						
Crewe, 20 December, 1963						(F)
Crewe Alex	Nantwich T	07.83	83	1	0	0
THORNHILL Rodney (Rod) Derek						
Reading, 24 January, 1942						(CD)
Reading		05.63	63-69	188	4	19
THORNLEY Barry Edward						
Gravesend, 11 February, 1948						(W)
Brentford	Gravesend & Northfleet	09.65	65	7	0	0
Oxford U	Tr	07.67	67-68	22	1	4
THORNLEY Benjamin (Ben) Lindsay						
Bury, 21 April, 1975 ESch/Eu21-3						(W)
Manchester U	YT	01.93	93-97	1	8	0

League Club	Source	Date Signed	Seasons Played	Apps	Subs	Gls
Stockport Co	L	11.95	95	8	2	1
Huddersfield T	L	02.96	95	12	0	2
Huddersfield T	Tr	07.98	98-00	77	22	5
Blackpool	Aberdeen	12.02	02	7	5	0
Bury	Tr	09.03	03	5	0	0

THORNLEY Roderick (Rod) Neil
Bury, 2 August, 1977 (F)

League Club	Source	Date Signed	Seasons Played	Apps	Subs	Gls
Doncaster Rov	Warrington T	09.97	97	1	0	0

THORNLEY Timothy (Tim) James
Leicester, 3 March, 1977 (G)

League Club	Source	Date Signed	Seasons Played	Apps	Subs	Gls
Torquay U	YT	•	94	0	1	0

THORNS John William
Newcastle, 10 July, 1928 Died 1975 (W)

League Club	Source	Date Signed	Seasons Played	Apps	Subs	Gls
Darlington (Am)		08.49	49	1	-	0

THORNTON Sean
Drogheda, 18 May, 1983 IRYth/IRu21-12 (M)

League Club	Source	Date Signed	Seasons Played	Apps	Subs	Gls
Tranmere Rov	YT	•	01	9	2	1
Sunderland	Tr	07.02	02-04	28	21	9
Blackpool	L	11.02	02	1	2	0

THORP Hamilton
Darwin, Australia, 21 August, 1973 (F)

League Club	Source	Date Signed	Seasons Played	Apps	Subs	Gls
Portsmouth	W Adelaide Sharks (Aus)	08.97	97	0	7	0

THORP Michael Stephen
Wallingford, 5 December, 1975 (CD)

League Club	Source	Date Signed	Seasons Played	Apps	Subs	Gls
Reading	YT	01.95	95-97	2	3	0

THORPE Adrian
Chesterfield, 25 November, 1963 (W)

League Club	Source	Date Signed	Seasons Played	Apps	Subs	Gls
Mansfield T	YT	08.82	82	0	2	1
Bradford C	Heanor T	08.85	85-87	9	8	1
Tranmere Rov	L	11.86	86	4	1	3
Notts Co	Tr	11.87	87-88	48	11	9
Walsall	Tr	08.89	89	24	3	1
Northampton T	Tr	03.90	89-91	36	16	6

THORPE Andrew (Andy)
Stockport, 15 September, 1960 (CD)

League Club	Source	Date Signed	Seasons Played	Apps	Subs	Gls
Stockport Co	Jnrs	08.78	77-85	312	2	3
Tranmere Rov	Tr	07.86	86-87	51	2	0
Stockport Co	Tr	01.88	87-91	172	3	0
Doncaster Rov	Chorley	09.97	97	2	0	0

THORPE Anthony (Tony) Lee
Leicester, 10 April, 1974 (F)

League Club	Source	Date Signed	Seasons Played	Apps	Subs	Gls
Luton T	Leicester C (YT)	08.92	93-97	93	27	50
Fulham	Tr	02.98	97	5	8	3
Bristol C	Tr	06.98	98-01	102	26	50
Reading	L	02.99	98	6	0	1
Luton T	L	03.99	98	7	1	4
Luton T	L	11.99	99	3	1	1
Luton T	Tr	07.02	02-03	30	2	15
Queens Park Rgrs	Tr	08.03	03-04	26	15	10
Rotherham U	L	03.05	04	5	0	1

THORPE Arthur William
Lucknow, India, 31 July, 1939 (W)

League Club	Source	Date Signed	Seasons Played	Apps	Subs	Gls
Scunthorpe U	Ossett T	09.60	60-62	27	-	5
Bradford C	Tr	07.63	63-65	81	0	17

THORPE Ian Richard
Blackheath, 3 September, 1953 EAmat (G)

League Club	Source	Date Signed	Seasons Played	Apps	Subs	Gls
Gillingham	Charlton Ath (Am)	09.73	73	5	0	0

THORPE Jeffrey (Jeff) Roger
Whitehaven, 17 November, 1972 (M)

League Club	Source	Date Signed	Seasons Played	Apps	Subs	Gls
Carlisle U	YT	07.91	90-99	104	72	6

THORPE Lee Anthony
Wolverhampton, 14 December, 1975 (F)

League Club	Source	Date Signed	Seasons Played	Apps	Subs	Gls
Blackpool	YT	07.94	93-96	2	10	0
Lincoln C	Tr	08.97	97-01	183	9	58
Leyton Orient	Tr	05.02	02-03	42	13	12
Grimsby T	L	02.04	03	5	1	0
Bristol Rov	Tr	03.04	03-04	25	10	4
Swansea C	L	02.05	04	9	6	3

THORPE Leonard (Len)
Warsop, 7 June, 1924 (WH)

League Club	Source	Date Signed	Seasons Played	Apps	Subs	Gls
Mansfield T	Nottingham F (Am)	08.45	46	5	-	0

THORPE Samuel (Sam)
Sheffield, 2 December, 1920 Died 2002 (WH)

League Club	Source	Date Signed	Seasons Played	Apps	Subs	Gls
Sheffield U	Norton Woodseats	04.45	47-48	2	-	0

THORRINGTON John Gerard
Johannesburg, South Africa, 17 October, 1979 USA 1 (M)

League Club	Source	Date Signed	Seasons Played	Apps	Subs	Gls
Manchester U	Mission Viejos P (USA)	10.97				
Huddersfield T	Bayer Leverkusen (Ger)	03.01	01-03	48	19	7
Grimsby T	Tr	03.04	03	2	1	0

THORSTVEDT Erik
Stavanger, Norway, 28 October, 1962 Norway int (G)

League Club	Source	Date Signed	Seasons Played	Apps	Subs	Gls
Tottenham H	IFK Gothenburg (Swe)	12.88	88-94	171	2	0

THORUP Borge
Copenhagen, Denmark, 4 October, 1943 (FB)

League Club	Source	Date Signed	Seasons Played	Apps	Subs	Gls
Crystal Palace	Morton	03.69	69	0	1	0

THREADGOLD Joseph **Henry (Harry)**
Tattenhall, 6 November, 1924 Died 1996 (G)

League Club	Source	Date Signed	Seasons Played	Apps	Subs	Gls
Chester	Tarvin U	10.47	50-51	83	-	0
Sunderland	Tr	07.52	52	35	-	0
Southend U	Tr	07.53	53-62	320	-	0

THRELFALL Jack
Little Lever, 22 March, 1935 Died 1989 (FB)

League Club	Source	Date Signed	Seasons Played	Apps	Subs	Gls
Bolton W		12.54	55-62	47	-	1
Bury	Tr	11.62	62-64	37	-	1

THRELFALL Joseph **Richard**
Ashton-under-Lyne, 5 March, 1916 Died 1994 (FB)

League Club	Source	Date Signed	Seasons Played	Apps	Subs	Gls
Bolton W		07.45	46	3	-	0
Halifax T	Tr	10.47	47	30	-	0

THRESHER Theodore **Michael (Mike)**
Cullompton, 9 March, 1931 Died 1999 (FB)

League Club	Source	Date Signed	Seasons Played	Apps	Subs	Gls
Bristol C	Chard T	01.54	54-64	379	-	1

THRIPPLETON Allen
Huddersfield, 16 June, 1928 (WH)

League Club	Source	Date Signed	Seasons Played	Apps	Subs	Gls
Millwall	Rainham T	11.50	50-54	26	-	4

THROWER Dennis Alan
Ipswich, 1 August, 1938 (WH)

League Club	Source	Date Signed	Seasons Played	Apps	Subs	Gls
Ipswich T	Landseer OB	08.55	56-64	27	-	2

THROWER Nigel John
Nottingham, 12 March, 1962 (FB)

League Club	Source	Date Signed	Seasons Played	Apps	Subs	Gls
Nottingham F	App	03.80				
Chesterfield	L	02.83	82	4	0	0

THURGOOD Stuart Anthony
Enfield, 4 November, 1981 (M)

League Club	Source	Date Signed	Seasons Played	Apps	Subs	Gls
Southend U	Shimuzu S Pulse (Jap)	01.01	00-02	49	30	1

THURLOW Alec Charles Edward
Depwade, 24 February, 1922 Died 1956 (G)

League Club	Source	Date Signed	Seasons Played	Apps	Subs	Gls
Huddersfield T		09.44				
Manchester C	Tr	09.46	46-48	21	-	0

THURLOW Bryan Alfred
Loddon, 6 June, 1936 Died 2002 (FB)

League Club	Source	Date Signed	Seasons Played	Apps	Subs	Gls
Norwich C	Loddon	07.54	55-63	193	-	1

THURNHAM Roy Thomas
Macclesfield, 17 December, 1942 (CD)

League Club	Source	Date Signed	Seasons Played	Apps	Subs	Gls
Manchester C	Jnrs	06.60				
Wrexham	Tr	06.61	62	2	-	0

THURSTAN Mark Richard
Cockermouth, 10 February, 1980 (M)

League Club	Source	Date Signed	Seasons Played	Apps	Subs	Gls
Carlisle U	Jnrs	07.98	00-01	4	2	0

THWAITES Adam Martin
Kendal, 8 December, 1981 (FB)

League Club	Source	Date Signed	Seasons Played	Apps	Subs	Gls
Carlisle U	YT	06.00	01	0	1	0

THWAITES Dennis
Stockton, 14 December, 1944 ESch/EYth (W)

League Club	Source	Date Signed	Seasons Played	Apps	Subs	Gls
Birmingham C	App	05.62	62-70	83	3	18

THWAITES Peter
Batley, 21 August, 1936 (CF)

League Club	Source	Date Signed	Seasons Played	Apps	Subs	Gls
Halifax T (Am)	Swillington	02.61	60	2	-	0

THYNE Robert (Bob) Brown
Glasgow, 9 January, 1920 Died 1986 SWar-2 (CD)

League Club	Source	Date Signed	Seasons Played	Apps	Subs	Gls
Darlington	Clydebank Jnrs	10.43	46	7	-	0

[TIAGO] MENDES TIAGO Cardoso
Viana do Castelo, Portugal, 2 May, 1981 Portugal 15 (M)

League Club	Source	Date Signed	Seasons Played	Apps	Subs	Gls
Chelsea	Benfica (Por)	08.04	04	21	13	4

TIATTO Daniele (Danny) Amadio
Melbourne, Australia, 22 May, 1973 Auu23/Au-23 (M)

League Club	Source	Date Signed	Seasons Played	Apps	Subs	Gls
Stoke C (L)	FC Baden (Swi)	11.97	97	11	4	1
Manchester C	FC Baden (Swi)	07.98	98-03	112	28	3
Leicester C	Tr	08.04	04	25	5	1

TIBBOTT Leslie (Les)
Oswestry, 25 August, 1955 Wu21-2 (FB)

League Club	Source	Date Signed	Seasons Played	Apps	Subs	Gls
Ipswich T	App	03.73	75-78	52	2	0
Sheffield U	Tr	03.79	78-81	78	0	2

TICKELL Brian Gerard
Carlisle, 15 November, 1939 (CD)

League Club	Source	Date Signed	Seasons Played	Apps	Subs	Gls
Huddersfield T	Raffles U	11.56	58	1	-	0
Carlisle U	Tr	05.59	59	3	-	1

TICKELL Enoch **Roy**
Bootle, 25 April, 1924 (W)

League Club	Source	Date Signed	Seasons Played	Apps	Subs	Gls
Exeter C		12.45				
Southport	Tr	05.47	47	6	-	1

TICKRIDGE Sidney (Sid)
Stepney, 10 April, 1923 Died 1997 ESch (FB)

League Club	Source	Date Signed	Seasons Played	Apps	Subs	Gls
Tottenham H	Jnrs	04.46	46-50	95	-	0
Chelsea	Tr	03.51	50-52	61	-	0
Brentford	Tr	07.55	55-56	62	-	0

TIDDY Michael (Mike) Douglas
Helston, 4 April, 1929 (W)

League Club	Source	Date Signed	Seasons Played	Apps	Subs	Gls
Torquay U	Helston	11.46	46-50	5	-	0
Cardiff C	Tr	11.50	50-54	146	-	20
Arsenal	Tr	09.55	55-57	48	-	8
Brighton & Hove A	Tr	10.58	58-61	133	-	11

TIDMAN Ola
Malmo, Sweden, 11 May, 1979 SwYth/Swu21-2 (G)

League Club	Source	Date Signed	Seasons Played	Apps	Subs	Gls
Stockport Co	La Louviere (Bel)	01.03	02	18	0	0
Sheffield Wed	Tr	07.03	03-04	12	1	0

TIE Li
Liaoning, China, 18 September, 1977 China 79 (M)

League Club	Source	Date Signed	Seasons Played	Apps	Subs	Gls
Everton	Liaoning Bodao (China)	08.02	02-03	32	2	0

TIERLING Lee
Wegburg, Germany, 25 October, 1972 (M)

League Club	Source	Date Signed	Seasons Played	Apps	Subs	Gls
Portsmouth	YT	07.91				
Fulham	Tr	05.92	92-93	7	12	0

TIERNEY Francis
Liverpool, 10 September, 1975 EYth (M)

League Club	Source	Date Signed	Seasons Played	Apps	Subs	Gls
Crewe Alex	YT	03.93	92-97	57	30	10
Notts Co	Tr	07.98	98-99	19	14	4
Exeter C	Witton A	11.00	00	4	3	1
Doncaster Rov	Witton A	03.01	03	10	3	3

TIERNEY James (Jim) McMahon
Ayr, 2 May, 1940 (W)

League Club	Source	Date Signed	Seasons Played	Apps	Subs	Gls
Bradford C	Saltcoats Victoria	01.60	60	2	-	0

TIERNEY Lawrence (Lawrie)
Leith, 4 April, 1959 (M)

League Club	Source	Date Signed	Seasons Played	Apps	Subs	Gls
Wigan Ath	Hibernian	07.80	80	4	3	0

TIERNEY Marc Peter
Prestwich, 23 August, 1985 (CD)

League Club	Source	Date Signed	Seasons Played	Apps	Subs	Gls
Oldham Ath	Jnrs	08.03	03-04	7	6	0

TIERNEY Paul Thomas
Salford, 15 September, 1982 IRu21-7 (FB)

League Club	Source	Date Signed	Seasons Played	Apps	Subs	Gls
Manchester U	YT	07.00				
Crewe Alex	L	11.02	02	14	3	1
Colchester U	L	01.04	03	2	0	0
Bradford C	L	12.04	04	14	2	0

TIGHE John
Aghamore, 13 March, 1923 (G)

League Club	Source	Date Signed	Seasons Played	Apps	Subs	Gls
West Bromwich A	Larkhall Thistle	11.45	46	1	-	0

TIGHE Terence (Terry) William
Edinburgh, 12 August, 1934 Died 2000 (WH)

League Club	Source	Date Signed	Seasons Played	Apps	Subs	Gls
Accrington St	Dunfermline Ath	06.57	57-60	117	-	20
Crewe Alex	Tr	12.60	60-62	81	-	5
Southport	Tr	08.63	63	36	-	3

TIHINEN Hannu
Keminmaa, Finland, 1 July, 1976 Finland int (CD)

League Club	Source	Date Signed	Seasons Played	Apps	Subs	Gls
West Ham U (L)	Viking Stavanger (Nor)	12.00	00	5	3	0

TILER Brian
Rotherham, 15 March, 1943 Died 1990 (CD)

League Club	Source	Date Signed	Seasons Played	Apps	Subs	Gls
Rotherham U	Jnrs	07.62	62-68	213	0	27
Aston Villa	Tr	12.68	68-72	106	1	3
Carlisle U	Tr	10.72	72-73	51	1	1

TILER Carl
Sheffield, 11 February, 1970 Eu21-13 (CD)

League Club	Source	Date Signed	Seasons Played	Apps	Subs	Gls
Barnsley	YT	08.88	87-90	67	4	3
Nottingham F	Tr	05.91	91-94	67	2	1
Swindon T	L	11.94	94	2	0	0
Aston Villa	Tr	10.95	95-96	10	2	1
Sheffield U	Tr	03.97	96-97	23	0	2
Everton	Tr	11.97	97-98	21	0	1
Charlton Ath	Tr	09.98	98-00	38	7	2
Birmingham C	L	02.01	00	1	0	0
Portsmouth	Tr	03.01	00-02	16	3	1

TILER Kenneth (Ken) David
Sheffield, 23 May, 1950 (FB)

League Club	Source	Date Signed	Seasons Played	Apps	Subs	Gls
Chesterfield	Swallownest	09.70	70-74	139	1	1
Brighton & Hove A	Tr	11.74	74-78	130	0	0
Rotherham U	Tr	07.79	79-80	45	1	1

TILLEY Darren John
Bristol, 15 March, 1967 (F)

League Club	Source	Date Signed	Seasons Played	Apps	Subs	Gls
York C	Yate T	01.92	91-92	17	4	0

TILLEY Kevin
Feltham, 6 September, 1957 (FB)

League Club	Source	Date Signed	Seasons Played	Apps	Subs	Gls
Wimbledon	Queens Park Rgrs (App)	09.75	77	11	2	0

TILLEY Peter
Lurgan, 13 January, 1930 (WH)

League Club	Source	Date Signed	Seasons Played	Apps	Subs	Gls
Arsenal	Witton A	05.52	53	1	-	0
Bury	Tr	11.53	53-57	86	-	12
Halifax T	Tr	07.58	58-62	183	-	17

TILLEY Herbert **Rex**
Swindon, 16 February, 1929 (WH)

League Club	Source	Date Signed	Seasons Played	Apps	Subs	Gls
Plymouth Arg	Chippenham T	03.51	52-57	123	-	0
Swindon T	Tr	08.58	58-59	31	-	0

TILLING Harold (Harry) Kynaston
Warrington, 6 January, 1918 Died 1998 (W)

League Club	Source	Date Signed	Seasons Played	Apps	Subs	Gls
Oldham Ath	Whitecross	09.42	47	3	-	0

TILLOTSON Maurice
Silsden, 20 January, 1944 (FB)

League Club	Source	Date Signed	Seasons Played	Apps	Subs	Gls
Huddersfield T	Jnrs	07.62				
Stockport Co	Tr	10.64	64-65	35	0	0

TILLSON Andrew (Andy)
Huntingdon, 30 June, 1966 (CD)

League Club	Source	Date Signed	Seasons Played	Apps	Subs	Gls
Grimsby T	Kettering T	07.88	88-90	104	1	5
Queens Park Rgrs	Tr	12.90	90-91	27	2	2
Grimsby T	L	09.92	92	4	0	0
Bristol Rov	Tr	11.92	92-99	250	3	11
Walsall	Tr	08.00	00-01	50	1	2
Rushden & Diamonds	Tr	02.02	01-02	19	0	0

TILSED Ronald (Ron) William
Weymouth, 6 August, 1952 EYth (G)

League Club	Source	Date Signed	Seasons Played	Apps	Subs	Gls
Bournemouth	App	01.70	69	2	0	0
Chesterfield	Tr	02.72	71	16	0	0
Arsenal	Tr	09.72				
Portsmouth	Tr	03.73	72-73	14	0	0

TILSON Stephen (Steve) Brian
Wickford, 27 July, 1966 (M)

League Club	Source	Date Signed	Seasons Played	Apps	Subs	Gls
Southend U	Witham T	02.89	88-96	199	40	26
Brentford	L	09.93	93	2	0	0
Southend U	Canvey Island	10.02	02-03	2	2	0

TILSTON Thomas (Tommy) Arthur Anthony
Chester, 19 February, 1926 (IF)

League Club	Source	Date Signed	Seasons Played	Apps	Subs	Gls
Chester	Jnrs	09.43	49-50	22	-	7
Tranmere Rov	Tr	06.51	51	25	-	15
Wrexham	Tr	03.52	51-53	78	-	29
Crystal Palace	Tr	02.54	53-55	58	-	13

TILTMAN Richard George
Shoreham, 14 December, 1960 (F)

League Club	Source	Date Signed	Seasons Played	Apps	Subs	Gls
Brighton & Hove A	Maidstone U	11.86	86-87	10	3	1

TIMMINS Arnold
Whitehaven, 29 January, 1940 Died 1994 (IF)

League Club	Source	Date Signed	Seasons Played	Apps	Subs	Gls
Workington	Lowca	09.60	60-63	44	-	10

TIMMINS Charles (Charlie)
Birmingham, 29 May, 1922 (FB)

League Club	Source	Date Signed	Seasons Played	Apps	Subs	Gls
Coventry C	Jack Moulds Ath	09.46	49-57	161	-	5

TIMMINS John
Brierley Hill, 30 May, 1936 (FB)

League Club	Source	Date Signed	Seasons Played	Apps	Subs	Gls
Wolverhampton W	Jnrs	06.53				
Plymouth Arg	Tr	01.58	57	5	-	0
Bristol Rov	Tr	09.58	58	3	-	0

League Club	Source	Date Signed	Seasons Played	Career Record Apps	Subs	Gls
TIMONS Christopher (Chris) Bryan						
Old Langwith, 8 December, 1974						(CD)
Mansfield T	Clipstone CW	02.94	93-95	35	4	2
Leyton Orient	Gainsborough Trinity	03.97	96	6	0	2
TIMSON David Youles						
Syston, 24 August, 1947						(G)
Leicester C	App	09.64	63-66	3	0	0
Newport Co	Tr	08.67	67	22	0	0
TINDALL Jason						
Mile End, 15 November, 1977						(CD)
Charlton Ath	YT	07.96				
Bournemouth	Tr	07.98	98-03	124	36	6
TINDALL Michael (Mike) Chadwick						
Birmingham, 5 April, 1941 EYth						(WH)
Aston Villa	Jnrs	04.58	59-67	118	2	8
Walsall	Tr	06.68	68	7	0	0
TINDALL Ronald (Ron) Albert Ernest						
Streatham, 23 September, 1935 FLge-1						(F)
Chelsea	Jnrs	04.53	55-61	160	-	67
West Ham U	Tr	11.61	61	13	-	3
Reading	Tr	10.62	62-63	36	-	12
Portsmouth	Tr	09.64	64-69	160	2	7
TINDILL Herbert (Bert)						
South Hiendley, 31 December, 1926 Died 1973						(W)
Doncaster Rov	South Hiendley	04.44	46-57	401	-	125
Bristol C	Tr	02.58	57-58	56	-	29
Barnsley	Tr	03.59	59-61	98	-	29
TINGAY Philip (Phil)						
Chesterfield, 2 May, 1950						(G)
Chesterfield	Chesterfield Tube Wks	07.72	71-80	181	0	0
Barnsley	L	03.73	72	8	0	0
TINKLER Eric						
Roodepoort, South Africa, 30 July, 1970 South Africa 46						(M)
Barnsley	Cagliari)lt)	07.97	97-01	78	21	9
TINKLER John						
Trimdon, 24 August, 1968						(M)
Hartlepool U		12.86	86-91	153	17	7
Preston NE	Tr	07.92	92	22	2	2
Walsall	Tr	08.93	93	6	0	0
TINKLER Luke (Lou)						
Chester-le-Street, 4 December, 1923 Died 1995						(W)
Plymouth Arg	West Bromwich A (Am)	10.45	46-47	24	-	4
Walsall	Tr	06.48	48	18	-	0
TINKLER Mark Roland						
Bishop Auckland, 24 October, 1974 ESch/EYth						(M)
Leeds U	YT	11.91	92-96	14	11	0
York C	Tr	03.97	96-98	88	2	8
Southend U	Tr	08.99	99-00	55	1	1
Hartlepool U	Tr	11.00	00-04	185	5	33
TINNEY Hugh Joseph						
Glasgow, 14 May, 1944 Su23-2						(FB)
Bury	Partick Th	03.67	66-72	235	3	3
TINNION Brian						
Workington, 11 June, 1948 EYth						(F)
Workington	Jnrs	03.66	65-68	93	5	25
Wrexham	Tr	01.69	68-75	265	14	54
Chester	L	12.71	71	3	0	0
TINNION Brian						
Stanley, 23 February, 1968						(M)
Newcastle U	App	02.86	86-88	30	2	2
Bradford C	Tr	03.89	88-92	137	8	22
Bristol C	Tr	03.93	92-04	415	43	36
TINSLEY Alan						
Fleetwood, 1 January, 1951						(M)
Preston NE	App	01.69	69	8	1	1
Bury	Tr	08.70	70-74	82	12	15
TINSLEY Colin						
Redcar, 24 October, 1935						(G)
Grimsby T	Redcar BC	09.54	54-57	24	-	0
Darlington	Tr	08.58	58-60	79	-	0
Exeter C	Tr	07.61	61-62	56	-	1
Luton T	Tr	08.63	63-67	55	0	0
TINSON Darren Lee						
Birmingham, 15 November, 1969						(CD)
Macclesfield T	Northwich Vic	02.96	97-02	263	0	5
Shrewsbury T	Tr	07.03	04	42	1	0

League Club	Source	Date Signed	Seasons Played	Career Record Apps	Subs	Gls
TIPPETT Michael Frederick						
Cadbury Heath, 11 June, 1930 Died 2003						(W)
Bristol Rov	Cadbury Heath	04.48	49-51	8	-	2
TIPPETT Thomas (Tommy) John						
Gateshead, 4 August, 1924						(W)
Southend U		05.46	46-51	92	-	20
Bournemouth	Tr	09.51	51-52	37	-	10
TIPTON Matthew John						
Conwy, 29 June, 1980 WYth/Wu21-6						(F)
Oldham Ath	YT	07.97	97-01	51	61	15
Macclesfield T	Tr	02.02	01-04	114	17	41
TISDALE Paul Robert						
Malta, 14 January, 1973 ESch						(M)
Southampton	Jnrs	06.91	94-95	5	11	1
Northampton T	L	03.92	92	5	0	0
Huddersfield T	L	11.96	96	1	1	0
Bristol C	Tr	06.97	97	2	3	0
Exeter C	L	12.97	97	10	0	1
TISTIMETANU Ivan						
Moldova, 27 April, 1974 Moldova 34						(M)
Bristol C	Zimbru Chisinau (Mol)	12.98	98-00	23	12	2
TITTERTON David Stewart John						
Hatton, Warwickshire, 25 September, 1971						(FB)
Coventry C	YT	05.90	89-90	0	2	0
Hereford U	Tr	09.91	91-92	39	12	1
Wycombe W	Tr	08.93	93-94	15	4	1
TIVEY Mark Ronald						
Brent, 10 February, 1971						(W)
Charlton Ath	YT	05.89	91	0	1	0
TOALE Ian						
Liverpool, 28 August, 1967						(FB)
Liverpool	App	05.85				
Grimsby T	Tr	07.87	87	16	4	0
TOASE Donald (Don) Vickers						
Darlington, 31 December, 1929 Died 1992 EYth						(FB)
Newcastle U	Portsmouth (Am)	06.48				
Darlington	Tr	08.51	51	7	-	0
TOBIN Donald (Don) Joseph						
Prescot, 1 November, 1955						(M)
Rochdale	Everton (App)	08.73	73-75	46	2	5
TOBIN Maurice						
Longriggend, 30 July, 1920						(FB)
Norwich C	Longriggend BC	09.38	46-50	102	-	0
TOBIN Robert (Bobby)						
Cardiff, 29 March, 1921						(IF)
Cardiff C	Cardiff Corinthians	08.40	47	2	-	0
TOCKNELL Brian Thomas						
Pretoria, South Africa, 21 May, 1937						(WH)
Charlton Ath	Berea Park (SA)	07.59	60-65	199	0	14
TOD Andrew (Andy)						
Dunfermline, 4 November, 1971						(CD)
Stockport Co (L)	Dunfermline Ath	10.00	00	11	0	3
Bradford C	Dunfermline Ath	08.01	01-02	29	6	5
TODA Kazuyuki						
Tokyo, Japan, 30 December, 1977 Japan 15						(M)
Tottenham H (L)	Shimizu S Pulse (Jap)	01.03	02	2	2	0
TODD Alexander (Alex)						
South Shields, 7 November, 1929						(WH)
Hartlepools U	South Shields Btch	04.50	52-53	4	-	0
TODD Andrew (Andy) John James						
Derby, 21 September, 1974						(CD)
Middlesbrough	YT	03.92	93-94	7	1	0
Swindon T	L	02.95	94	13	0	0
Bolton W	Tr	08.95	95-99	66	18	2
Charlton Ath	Tr	11.99	99-01	27	13	1
Grimsby T	L	02.02	01	12	0	3
Blackburn Rov	Tr	05.02	02-04	52	5	2
Burnley	L	09.03	03	7	0	0
TODD Andrew (Andy) Jonathan						
Nottingham, 22 February, 1979						(M)
Nottingham F	Eastwood T	02.96				
Scarborough	Tr	02.99	98	0	1	0

TODD Christopher (Chris)
Swansea, 22 August, 1981 (CD)

League Club	Source	Date Signed	Seasons Played	Apps	Subs	Gls
Swansea C	YT	07.00	00-01	39	4	4
Exeter C	Drogheda U	01.03	02	12	0	0

TODD Colin
Chester-le-Street, 12 December, 1948 EYth/Eu23-14/FLge-3/E-27 (CD)

League Club	Source	Date Signed	Seasons Played	Apps	Subs	Gls
Sunderland	App	02.66	66-70	170	3	3
Derby Co	Tr	02.71	70-78	293	0	6
Everton	Tr	09.78	78-79	32	0	1
Birmingham C	Tr	09.79	79-81	92	1	0
Nottingham F	Tr	08.82	82-83	36	0	0
Oxford U	Tr	02.84	83	12	0	0
Luton T	Vancouver (Can)	10.84	84	2	0	0

TODD James (Jim)
Belfast, 19 March, 1921 IWar-2 (WH)

League Club	Source	Date Signed	Seasons Played	Apps	Subs	Gls
Blackpool		02.45				
Port Vale	Tr	10.46	46-52	145	-	0

TODD Keith Harris
Clydach, 2 March, 1941 Wu23-1 (F)

League Club	Source	Date Signed	Seasons Played	Apps	Subs	Gls
Swansea T	Clydach	09.59	60-67	196	2	78

TODD Kenneth (Kenny)
Butterknowle, 24 August, 1957 (M)

League Club	Source	Date Signed	Seasons Played	Apps	Subs	Gls
Wolverhampton W	App	08.75	76-77	4	1	1
Port Vale	Tr	08.78	78-79	42	2	9
Portsmouth	Tr	10.79	79	1	2	1

TODD Kevin
Sunderland, 28 February, 1958 (F)

League Club	Source	Date Signed	Seasons Played	Apps	Subs	Gls
Newcastle U	Ryhope Colliery	08.81	81-82	5	2	3
Darlington	Tr	02.83	82-84	99	3	23

TODD Lee
Hartlepool, 7 March, 1972 (FB)

League Club	Source	Date Signed	Seasons Played	Apps	Subs	Gls
Stockport Co	Hartlepool U (YT)	07.90	90-96	214	11	2
Southampton	Tr	07.97	97	9	1	0
Bradford C	Tr	08.98	98	14	1	0
Walsall	L	09.99	99	1	0	0
Rochdale	Tr	08.00	00-01	48	2	3

TODD Mark Kenneth
Belfast, 4 December, 1967 NISch/NIYth/NIu23-1 (M)

League Club	Source	Date Signed	Seasons Played	Apps	Subs	Gls
Manchester U	App	08.85				
Sheffield U	Tr	07.87	87-90	62	8	5
Wolverhampton W	L	03.91	90	6	1	0
Rotherham U	Tr	09.91	91-94	60	4	7
Scarborough	Tr	08.95	95	23	0	1
Mansfield T	Tr	02.96	95	10	2	0

TODD Paul Raymond
Middlesbrough, 8 May, 1920 Died 2000 (IF)

League Club	Source	Date Signed	Seasons Played	Apps	Subs	Gls
Doncaster Rov		09.45	46-49	160	-	49
Blackburn Rov	Tr	07.50	50-51	46	-	12
Hull C	Tr	10.51	51-52	27	-	3

TODD Robert (Bob) Charles
Goole, 11 September, 1949 (W)

League Club	Source	Date Signed	Seasons Played	Apps	Subs	Gls
Liverpool	Scunthorpe U (App)	07.67				
Rotherham U	Tr	03.68	68	2	4	0
Mansfield T	Tr	11.68	68	3	1	0
Workington	Tr	07.69	69	10	6	0

TODD Ronald (Ronnie)
Bellshill, 4 October, 1935 (WH)

League Club	Source	Date Signed	Seasons Played	Apps	Subs	Gls
Accrington St	Lesmahagow	02.56	59	5	-	0

TODD Samuel (Sammy) John
Belfast, 22 September, 1945 NIu23-4/NI-11 (CD)

League Club	Source	Date Signed	Seasons Played	Apps	Subs	Gls
Burnley	Glentoran	09.62	63-69	108	8	1
Sheffield Wed	Tr	05.70	70-72	22	2	1
Mansfield T	L	02.74	73	6	0	0

TODD Thomas (Tommy) Bell
Stonehouse, Lanarkshire, 1 June, 1926 (CF)

League Club	Source	Date Signed	Seasons Played	Apps	Subs	Gls
Crewe Alex	Hamilton Academical	08.55	55	13	-	3
Derby Co	Tr	11.55	55	4	-	3
Rochdale	Tr	05.56	56	5	-	1

TODOROV Svetoslav
Dobrich, Bulgaria, 30 August, 1978 BulgariaYth/Bulgaria-31 (F)

League Club	Source	Date Signed	Seasons Played	Apps	Subs	Gls
West Ham U	Liteks Lovech (Bul)	01.01	00-01	4	10	1
Portsmouth	Tr	03.02	01-03	47	2	27

TOFTING Stig
Aarhus, Denmark, 14 August, 1969 Denmark 41 (M)

League Club	Source	Date Signed	Seasons Played	Apps	Subs	Gls
Bolton W	SV Hamburg (Ger)	02.02	01-02	8	6	0

TOGWELL Samuel (Sam) James
Beaconsfield, 14 October, 1984 (CD)

League Club	Source	Date Signed	Seasons Played	Apps	Subs	Gls
Crystal Palace	Sch	08.04	02	0	1	0
Oxford U	L	10.04	04	3	1	0
Northampton T	L	03.05	04	7	1	0

TOLCHARD Jeffrey (Jeff) Graham
Torquay, 17 March, 1944 (W)

League Club	Source	Date Signed	Seasons Played	Apps	Subs	Gls
Torquay U		03.64	63-64	11	-	4
Exeter C	Tr	07.65	65	1	0	0

TOLLEY Glenn Anthony
Knighton, 24 September, 1984 (M)

League Club	Source	Date Signed	Seasons Played	Apps	Subs	Gls
Shrewsbury T	Sch	●	02	0	1	0

TOLLEY Jamie Christopher
Ludlow, 12 May, 1983 Wu21-12 (M)

League Club	Source	Date Signed	Seasons Played	Apps	Subs	Gls
Shrewsbury T	YT	01.01	99-04	112	12	10

TOLLIDAY Stanley (Stan) Albert
Hackney, 6 August, 1922 Died 1951 (G)

League Club	Source	Date Signed	Seasons Played	Apps	Subs	Gls
Leyton Orient		12.46	46-48	64	-	0

TOLMIE James (Jim)
Glasgow, 20 November, 1960 Su21-1/SLge-1 (W)

League Club	Source	Date Signed	Seasons Played	Apps	Subs	Gls
Manchester C	Lokeren (Bel)	08.83	83-85	46	15	15
Carlisle U	L	03.86	85	7	1	1

TOLSON Maxwell (Max) Norman
Wollongong, Australia, 18 July, 1945 Australia int (CF)

League Club	Source	Date Signed	Seasons Played	Apps	Subs	Gls
Workington	South Coast U (Aus)	02.66	65-66	29	1	6

TOLSON Neil
Wordsley, 25 October, 1973 (F)

League Club	Source	Date Signed	Seasons Played	Apps	Subs	Gls
Walsall	YT	12.91	91	3	6	1
Oldham Ath	Tr	03.92	92	0	3	0
Bradford C	Tr	12.93	93-95	32	31	12
Chester C	L	01.95	94	3	1	0
York C	Tr	07.96	96-98	66	18	18
Southend U	Tr	07.99	99-00	34	2	11

TOLSON William (Bill)
Rochdale, 29 March, 1931 (IF)

League Club	Source	Date Signed	Seasons Played	Apps	Subs	Gls
Rochdale	St Albans BC	10.53	53-54	10	-	0

TOM Steven (Steve)
Ware, 5 February, 1951 (CD)

League Club	Source	Date Signed	Seasons Played	Apps	Subs	Gls
Queens Park Rgrs	App	02.69				
Brentford	Tr	06.71	71	13	5	1

TOMAN James **Andrew (Andy)**
Northallerton, 7 March, 1962 (M)

League Club	Source	Date Signed	Seasons Played	Apps	Subs	Gls
Lincoln C	Bishop Auckland	08.85	85	21	3	4
Hartlepool U	Bishop Auckland	01.87	86-88	112	0	28
Darlington	Tr	08.89	90-92	108	7	10
Scarborough	L	02.93	92	6	0	0
Scunthorpe U	Tr	08.93	93	15	0	5
Scarborough	Tr	12.93	93-95	33	12	3

TOMASSON Jon Dahl
Roskilde, Denmark, 29 August, 1976 Denmark int (F)

League Club	Source	Date Signed	Seasons Played	Apps	Subs	Gls
Newcastle U	SC Heerenveen (Holl)	06.97	97	17	6	3

TOMKIN Cyril John
Barrow, 18 November, 1918 (W)

League Club	Source	Date Signed	Seasons Played	Apps	Subs	Gls
Barrow	Dumbarton	03.48	46-47	3	-	0

TOMKINS Leonard (Len) Anthony
Isleworth, 16 January, 1949 EYth (W)

League Club	Source	Date Signed	Seasons Played	Apps	Subs	Gls
Crystal Palace	App	01.67	67-69	18	2	2

TOMKINSON Derek
Stoke-on-Trent, 6 April, 1931 (IF)

League Club	Source	Date Signed	Seasons Played	Apps	Subs	Gls
Port Vale	Burton A	12.52	52-54	29	-	5
Crewe Alex		08.56	56	17	-	1

TOMKYS Michael (Mike) George
Kensington, 14 December, 1932 EYth (W)

League Club	Source	Date Signed	Seasons Played	Apps	Subs	Gls
Queens Park Rgrs	Fulham (Am)	11.51	51-58	86	-	16

TOMLEY Frederick (Fred) William
Liverpool, 11 July, 1931 Died 1981 (CD)

League Club	Source	Date Signed	Seasons Played	Apps	Subs	Gls
Liverpool	Litherland	09.53	54	2	-	0
Chester	Tr	07.55	55	1	-	0

TOMLIN David (Dave)
Nuneaton, 9 February, 1953 (W)

League Club	Source	Date Signed	Seasons Played	Apps	Subs	Gls
Leicester C	App	02.71	71-75	20	7	2
Torquay U	Tr	04.77	76-77	37	1	2
Aldershot	Tr	08.78	78-80	24	6	2

TOMLINSON Ashley Darrell
Doncaster, 28 September, 1966 (W)

League Club	Source	Date Signed	Seasons Played	Apps	Subs	Gls
Doncaster Rov	App	●	83	2	2	0

TOMLINSON Charles (Charlie) Conway
Sheffield, 2 December, 1919 Died 1971 (W)

League Club	Source	Date Signed	Seasons Played	Apps	Subs	Gls
Bradford PA	Sheffield Wed (Am)	04.39				
Sheffield Wed	Tr	07.44	46-50	68	-	7
Rotherham U	Tr	03.51	50-51	32	-	12

TOMLINSON David Ian
Rotherham, 13 December, 1968 (W)

League Club	Source	Date Signed	Seasons Played	Apps	Subs	Gls
Sheffield Wed	App	12.86	86	0	1	0
Rotherham U	Tr	08.87	87	6	3	0
Barnet	Boston U	12.90	91	0	3	0

TOMLINSON Ezekiel Jeremiah
Birmingham, 9 November, 1985 (M)

League Club	Source	Date Signed	Seasons Played	Apps	Subs	Gls
Stockport Co	West Bromwich A (Sch)	03.05	04	2	3	0

TOMLINSON Francis (Frank)
Manchester, 23 October, 1925 (W)

League Club	Source	Date Signed	Seasons Played	Apps	Subs	Gls
Oldham Ath	Goslings	11.46	46-50	115	-	28
Rochdale	Tr	11.51	51	20	-	2
Chester	Tr	08.52	52	11	-	0

TOMLINSON Francis (Frank)
Manchester, 5 January, 1926 (W)

League Club	Source	Date Signed	Seasons Played	Apps	Subs	Gls
Halifax T	Stalybridge Celtic	11.50	50	14	-	4

TOMLINSON Graeme Murdoch
Watford, 10 December, 1975 (F)

League Club	Source	Date Signed	Seasons Played	Apps	Subs	Gls
Bradford C	YT	●	93	12	5	6
Manchester U	Tr	07.94				
Luton T	L	03.96	95	1	6	0
Bournemouth	L	08.97	97	6	1	1
Millwall	L	03.98	97	2	1	1
Macclesfield T	Tr	07.98	98-99	22	24	6
Exeter C	Tr	07.00	00-01	38	18	6

TOMLINSON Harry
Plymouth, 26 October, 1922 Died 1988 (FB)

League Club	Source	Date Signed	Seasons Played	Apps	Subs	Gls
Doncaster Rov		10.44	46-48	58	-	0

TOMLINSON John
Bebington, 26 June, 1934 EYth (W)

League Club	Source	Date Signed	Seasons Played	Apps	Subs	Gls
Everton	Jnrs	06.52	56	2	-	0
Chesterfield	Tr	06.57	57-58	47	-	5

TOMLINSON Michael (Micky) Lloyd
Lambeth, 15 September, 1972 (W)

League Club	Source	Date Signed	Seasons Played	Apps	Subs	Gls
Leyton Orient	YT	07.91	90-93	7	7	1
Barnet	Tr	03.94	93-96	67	26	4

TOMLINSON Paul
Rotherham, 4 February, 1965 (G)

League Club	Source	Date Signed	Seasons Played	Apps	Subs	Gls
Sheffield U	Middlewood Rov	06.83	83-86	37	0	0
Birmingham C	L	03.87	86	11	0	0
Bradford C	Tr	06.87	87-94	293	0	0

TOMLINSON Robert (Bob) Windle
Blackburn, 4 June, 1924 Died 1996 (FB)

League Club	Source	Date Signed	Seasons Played	Apps	Subs	Gls
Blackburn Rov	Feniscowles	01.43	46-47	25	-	0
Halifax T	Mossley	06.51	51	8	-	0

TOMLINSON Stuart Charles
Ellesmere Port, 10 May, 1985 (G)

League Club	Source	Date Signed	Seasons Played	Apps	Subs	Gls
Crewe Alex	Sch	07.03	02-03	0	2	0

TOMPKIN Maurice
Countesthorpe, 17 February, 1919 Died 1956 (IF)

League Club	Source	Date Signed	Seasons Played	Apps	Subs	Gls
Leicester C	Countesthorpe U	03.38	37	1	-	0
Bury	Tr	12.45				
Huddersfield T	Tr	09.46	46	10	-	1

TOMS Frazer Peter
Ealing, 13 September, 1979 (W)

League Club	Source	Date Signed	Seasons Played	Apps	Subs	Gls
Charlton Ath	YT	07.98				
Barnet	Tr	07.99	99-00	46	19	1

TONER Ciaran
Craigavon, 30 June, 1981 NISch/NIYth/NIu21-17/NI-2 (M)

League Club	Source	Date Signed	Seasons Played	Apps	Subs	Gls
Tottenham H	YT	07.99				
Peterborough U	L	12.01	01	6	0	0
Bristol Rov	Tr	03.02	01	6	0	0
Leyton Orient	Tr	05.02	02-03	41	11	2
Lincoln C	Tr	08.04	04	10	5	2
Cambridge U	L	03.05	04	6	2	0

TONER James (Jimmy)
Shettleston, 23 August, 1924 (W)

League Club	Source	Date Signed	Seasons Played	Apps	Subs	Gls
Leeds U	Dundee	06.54	54	7	-	1

TONER William (Willie)
Glasgow, 18 December, 1929 Died 1999 SLge-5 (WH)

League Club	Source	Date Signed	Seasons Played	Apps	Subs	Gls
Sheffield U	Glasgow Celtic	05.51	51-53	55	-	2

TONES John David
Silksworth, 3 December, 1950 (CD)

League Club	Source	Date Signed	Seasons Played	Apps	Subs	Gls
Sunderland	App	05.68	72	2	4	0
Arsenal	Tr	07.73				
Swansea C	L	09.74	74	7	0	0
Mansfield T	L	10.74	74	3	0	0

TONG David Joseph
Blackpool, 21 September, 1955 (M)

League Club	Source	Date Signed	Seasons Played	Apps	Subs	Gls
Blackpool	App	09.73	74-78	71	8	7
Shrewsbury T	Tr	09.78	78-81	156	4	8
Cardiff C	Tr	08.82	82-85	119	1	3
Rochdale	Tr	09.85	85	0	2	0
Bristol C	Barrow	10.85	85	19	0	0
Gillingham	Tr	03.86	85	5	0	0
Cambridge U	Tr	08.86	86	4	2	0

TONG Raymond (Ray)
Bolton, 3 February, 1942 (W)

League Club	Source	Date Signed	Seasons Played	Apps	Subs	Gls
Blackburn Rov		07.62				
Bradford C	Tr	06.63	63-64	20	-	2

TONGE Alan John
Bury, 25 February, 1972 (M)

League Club	Source	Date Signed	Seasons Played	Apps	Subs	Gls
Manchester U	YT	07.90				
Exeter C	Horwich RMI	12.91	91-93	14	5	1

TONGE Dale
Doncaster, 7 May, 1985 (M)

League Club	Source	Date Signed	Seasons Played	Apps	Subs	Gls
Barnsley	Sch	07.04	03-04	14	1	0

TONGE Jeffrey (Jeff) Alan
Manchester, 5 May, 1942 Died 1996 (W)

League Club	Source	Date Signed	Seasons Played	Apps	Subs	Gls
Bury	Droylsden	03.60	59	1	-	0

TONGE Keith Andrew
Edmonton, 6 November, 1964 (F)

League Club	Source	Date Signed	Seasons Played	Apps	Subs	Gls
Brentford	App	11.82	81	0	1	0

TONGE Michael William
Manchester, 7 April, 1983 EYth/Eu20/Eu21-2 (M)

League Club	Source	Date Signed	Seasons Played	Apps	Subs	Gls
Sheffield U	YT	03.01	00-04	147	9	15

TONKIN Anthony Richard
Newlyn, 17 January, 1980 (FB)

League Club	Source	Date Signed	Seasons Played	Apps	Subs	Gls
Stockport Co	Yeovil T	09.02	02	23	1	0
Crewe Alex	Tr	08.03	03-04	53	8	0

TOON Colin
New Houghton, 26 April, 1940 (FB)

League Club	Source	Date Signed	Seasons Played	Apps	Subs	Gls
Mansfield T	Jnrs	07.57	57-65	213	0	1

TOOTILL George **Albert (Alf)**
Walkden, 20 October, 1913 Died 1984 (CD)

League Club	Source	Date Signed	Seasons Played	Apps	Subs	Gls
Plymouth Arg	Chorley	05.36	36-37	9	-	0
Sheffield U	Tr	01.38	38	12	-	0
Hartlepools U	Tr	07.47	47	18	-	0

TOOZE Dennis George
Swansea, 12 October, 1917 Died 1994 (FB)

League Club	Source	Date Signed	Seasons Played	Apps	Subs	Gls
Coventry C	Redditch T	05.37	46-48	36	-	0

TOOZE Robert (Bob) William
Bristol, 19 December, 1946 (G)

League Club	Source	Date Signed	Seasons Played	Apps	Subs	Gls
Bristol C	Jnrs	07.65				
Shrewsbury T	Tr	03.69	68-72	73	0	0
Gillingham	L	03.72	71	7	0	0

TOPPING Christopher (Chris)
Bubwith, 6 March, 1951 (CD)

League Club	Source	Date Signed	Seasons Played	Apps	Subs	Gls
York C	App	03.69	68-77	410	2	11
Huddersfield T	Tr	05.78	78-80	43	0	1

TOPPING David (Dave)
Shotts, 9 March, 1926 (FB)

League Club	Source	Date Signed	Seasons Played	Apps	Subs	Gls
Torquay U	Clyde	05.48	48-52	151	-	3

TOPPING Henry (Harry) Westby
St Helens, 26 October 1915 (FB)

League Club	Source	Date Signed	Seasons Played	Apps	Subs	Gls
Stockport Co		03.39	38	3	-	0
New Brighton	Tr	08.46	46-47	67	-	0

TORFASON Gudmundur (Gunnar)
Vestmannaeyjar, Iceland, 13 December, 1961 Iceland int (F)

League Club	Source	Date Signed	Seasons Played	Apps	Subs	Gls
Doncaster Rov	St Johnstone	07.94	94	1	3	0

TORGHELLE Sandor
Budapest, Hungary, 5 May, 1982 Hungary 13 (F)

League Club	Source	Date Signed	Seasons Played	Apps	Subs	Gls
Crystal Palace	MTK Hungaria (Hun)	08.04	04	3	9	0

League Club	Source	Date Signed	Seasons Played	Apps	Subs	Gls
TORPEY Stephen (Steve) David James						
Islington, 8 December, 1970						(F)
Millwall	YT	02.89	89	3	4	0
Bradford C	Tr	11.90	90-92	86	10	22
Swansea C	Tr	08.93	93-96	151	11	44
Bristol C	Tr	08.97	97-99	53	17	13
Notts Co	L	08.98	98	4	2	1
Scunthorpe U	Tr	02.00	99-04	193	6	57
TORPEY Stephen (Steve) Robert						
Fazakerley, 16 September, 1981 EYth						(F)
Liverpool	YT	05.99				
Port Vale	Tr	08.01	01	0	1	0
TORRANCE Andrew (Andy)						
Glasgow, 8 April, 1934 Died 2004						(W)
Barrow	Yeovil T	05.58	58	29	-	2
TORRANCE George Clark						
Rothesay, 17 September, 1957						(M)
Brentford	Wokingham T	12.84	84-85	29	5	1
TORRANCE George Syme						
Glasgow, 27 November, 1935						(G)
Leicester C	Thorniewood U	07.54				
Oldham Ath	Tr	08.56	56	4	-	0
Rochdale	Tr	09.57	57	2	-	0
TOSELAND Geoffrey (Geoff)						
Kettering, 31 January, 1931						(W)
Sunderland	Kettering T	12.48	52	6	-	1
TOSER Ernest (Ernie) William						
London, 30 November, 1912 Died 2002 ESch						(CD)
Millwall	Dulwich Hamlet	05.37	37	2	-	0
Notts Co	Tr	09.46	46	2	-	0
TOSH Paul James						
Arbroath, 18 October, 1973						(F)
Exeter C (L)	Hibernian	02.99	98	8	2	2
TOSHACK Jonathan **Cameron**						
Cardiff, 7 March, 1970						(F)
Swansea C	Jnrs	09.88				
Bristol C	Tr	11.89				
Cardiff C	Tr	02.91	90-91	1	4	0
TOSHACK John Benjamin						
Cardiff, 22 March, 1949 WSch/Wu23-3/W-40						(F)
Cardiff C	Jnrs	03.66	65-70	158	4	74
Liverpool	Tr	11.70	70-77	169	3	74
Swansea C	Tr	03.78	77-83	58	5	25
TOTTEN Alexander (Alex) Reginald						
Southampton, 1 October, 1976						(M)
Portsmouth	YT	11.94	94	3	1	0
TOTTOH Melvyn (Mel)						
Manchester, 26 July, 1956						(W)
Preston NE	Lytham	05.85	85	0	1	0
TOULOUSE Cyril Harvey						
Acton, 24 December, 1923 Died 1980						(WH)
Brentford	St Cuthman's	05.46	46-47	13	-	0
Tottenham H	Tr	12.47	48	2	-	0
TOURE Alioune Kissima						
St Brieuc, France, 9 September, 1978 FrYth						(F)
Manchester C	Nantes (Fr)	09.01	01	0	1	0
TOURE Habib **Kolo**						
Ivory Coast, 19 March, 1981 Ivory Coast int						(CD)
Arsenal	ASEC Mimosa (IC)	02.02	02-04	80	18	3
TOVEY Paul William						
Wokingham, 5 December, 1973						(M)
Bristol Rov	YT	07.92	93-95	8	1	0
TOVEY Ronald (Ron) Arthur						
Bristol, 24 September, 1930						(CF)
Bristol C		01.53	52-53	12	-	3
TOVEY William James						
Bristol, 18 October, 1931 Died 2000						(WH)
Bristol C	Jnrs	12.48	48-52	57	-	2
TOWERS Mark **Anthony (Tony)**						
Manchester, 13 April, 1952 ESch/EYth/Eu23-8/E-3						(M)
Manchester C	App	04.69	68-73	117	5	10
Sunderland	Tr	03.74	73-76	108	0	19
Birmingham C	Tr	07.77	77-79	90	2	4
Rochdale	Vancouver (Can)	02.85	84	1	1	0
TOWERS Ian Joseph						
Blackhill, 11 October, 1940						(F)
Burnley	Jnrs	10.57	60-65	43	1	12
Oldham Ath	Tr	01.66	65-67	94	1	45
Bury	Tr	07.68	68-70	43	5	7
TOWERS Edwin **James (Jim)**						
Shepherds Bush, 15 April, 1933						(IF)
Brentford	Jnrs	05.51	54-60	262	-	153
Queens Park Rgrs	Tr	05.61	61	28	-	15
Millwall	Tr	08.62	62	19	-	7
Gillingham	Tr	01.63	62	8	-	6
Aldershot	Tr	07.63	63	28	-	13
TOWERS John						
Willington, 21 December, 1913 Died 1979						(IF)
Darlington (Am)	Willington	09.34	34-38	94	-	22
Darlington	Willington	05.46	46	13	-	0
TOWERS William (Bill) Henry						
Leicester, 13 July, 1920 Died 2000						(WH)
Leicester C	Bentley Engineering	01.45	46	4	-	0
Torquay U	Tr	10.46	46-55	274	-	0
TOWN David Edward						
Bournemouth, 9 December, 1976						(F)
Bournemouth	YT	04.95	93-98	18	38	2
Boston U	Hayes	03.01	02	0	8	0
TOWNEND Gary Alfred						
Kilburn, 1 April, 1940						(IF)
Millwall	Redhill	08.60	60-63	50	-	20
TOWNER Antony (Tony) James						
Brighton, 2 May, 1955						(W)
Brighton & Hove A	App	01.73	72-78	153	9	24
Millwall	Tr	10.78	78-79	68	0	13
Rotherham U	Tr	08.80	80-82	108	0	12
Sheffield U	L	03.83	82	9	1	1
Wolverhampton W	Tr	08.83	83	25	6	2
Charlton Ath	Tr	09.84	84-85	22	5	2
Rochdale	Tr	11.85	85	4	1	0
Cambridge U	Tr	03.86	85-86	8	0	0
TOWNLEY Leon						
Loughton, 16 February, 1976						(CD)
Tottenham H	YT	07.94				
Brentford	Tr	09.97	97	15	1	2
TOWNSEND Andrew (Andy) David						
Maidstone, 23 July, 1963 IRB-1/IR-70						(M)
Southampton	Weymouth	01.85	84-87	77	6	5
Norwich C	Tr	08.88	88-89	66	5	8
Chelsea	Tr	07.90	90-92	110	0	12
Aston Villa	Tr	07.93	93-97	133	1	8
Middlesbrough	Tr	08.97	97-99	73	4	3
West Bromwich A	Tr	09.99	99	15	3	0
TOWNSEND Benjamin (Ben)						
Reading, 8 October, 1981						(FB)
Wycombe W	YT	01.01	99-01	12	1	0
TOWNSEND Christopher (Chris) Gordon						
Caerleon, 30 March, 1966 WSch/WYth						(F)
Cardiff C	Jnrs	07.83	83	2	3	0
TOWNSEND Donald (Don) Edward						
Swindon, 17 September, 1930						(FB)
Charlton Ath	Trowbridge T	07.50	54-61	249	-	1
Crystal Palace	Tr	07.62	62-64	77	-	0
TOWNSEND George Ernest						
Ashton-under-Lyne, 29 July, 1957						(FB)
Rochdale	App	07.75	74-75	31	1	0
TOWNSEND James (Jim) Clabby						
Greenock, 2 February, 1945						(WH)
Middlesbrough	St Johnstone	02.64	63-65	65	2	6
TOWNSEND Leonard (Len) Francis						
Brentford, 31 August, 1917 Died 1997 NIRL-1						(IF)
Brentford	Hayes	05.37	38-46	33	-	12
Bristol C	Tr	06.47	47-48	74	-	45
Millwall	Tr	07.49	49	5	-	1
TOWNSEND Luke Allen						
Guildford, 28 September, 1986						(F)
Queens Park Rgrs	Sch	•	04	0	2	0
TOWNSEND Martin Vincent						
Romford, 15 June, 1946						(G)
Fulham	App	•	63	2	-	0

League Club	Source	Date Signed	Seasons Played	Apps	Subs	Gls
TOWNSEND Neil Royston						
Long Buckby, 1 February, 1950 EYth						(CD)
Northampton T	Jnrs	09.68	68-71	65	2	1
Southend U	Bedford T	07.73	73-78	156	1	7
Bournemouth	Weymouth	07.79	79-80	34	0	2
TOWNSEND Quentin Lee						
Worcester, 13 February, 1977						(CD)
Wolverhampton W	YT	07.95				
Hereford U	Tr	07.96	96	6	1	0
TOWNSEND Russell (Russ) Nelson						
Reading, 17 January, 1960						(M)
Northampton T	Barnet	09.79	79	12	1	0
TOWNSEND Ryan Matthew George						
Ashton-under-Lyne, 2 September, 1985						(FB)
Burnley	Sch	•	03	0	1	0
TOWNSEND William (Billy)						
Bedworth, 27 December, 1922 Died 1988						(G)
Derby Co	Nuneaton Borough	09.42	46-52	79	-	0
TOWNSLEY Derek Johnstone						
Carlisle, 21 March, 1973						(M)
Oxford U	Hibernian	07.03	03	9	2	0
TOWNSON Kevin						
Liverpool, 19 April, 1983 EYth						(F)
Rochdale	Everton (Jnrs)	07.00	00-04	41	61	25
Macclesfield T	L	03.05	04	2	4	0
TOWSE Gary Thomas						
Dover, 14 May, 1952						(G)
Crystal Palace	Folkestone	01.72				
Brentford	Tr	06.73	73	5	0	0
TOZE Edward						
Manchester, 6 March, 1923 Died 1987						(G)
Halifax T	Jnrs	08.50	50	5	-	0
TRACEY Michael (Mike) George						
Blackburn, 14 February, 1935 EAmat						(W)
Luton T	Crook T	11.59	59-60	23	-	3
Lincoln C	Tr	07.61	61	21	-	5
TRACEY Richard Shaun						
Dewsbury, 9 July, 1979						(F)
Sheffield U	YT	06.97				
Rotherham U	Tr	02.98	98	0	3	0
Carlisle U	Tr	03.99	98-00	39	14	11
Macclesfield T	Tr	01.01	00-01	21	12	5
TRACEY Simon Peter						
Woolwich, 9 December, 1967						(G)
Wimbledon	App	02.86	88	1	0	0
Sheffield U	Tr	10.88	88-01	329	3	0
Manchester C	L	10.94	94	3	0	0
Norwich C	L	12.94	94	1	0	0
Wimbledon	L	11.95	95	1	0	0
TRAFFORD Stanley (Stan) John						
Leek, 21 December, 1945						(W)
Port Vale	App	10.64	64	12	-	1
TRAIL Derek John Falconer						
Leith, 2 January, 1946						(W)
Workington	Falkirk	07.67	67-68	39	5	5
Hartlepool	Tr	07.69	69	36	3	2
TRAILOR Cyril Henry						
Merthyr Tydfil, 15 May, 1919 Died 1986 WSch						(WH)
Tottenham H	Jnrs	10.38	46-47	11	-	0
Leyton Orient	Tr	08.49	49-50	39	-	0
TRAIN Raymond (Ray)						
Nuneaton, 10 February, 1951						(M)
Walsall	App	11.68	68-71	67	8	11
Carlisle U	Tr	12.71	71-75	154	1	8
Sunderland	Tr	03.76	75-76	31	1	1
Bolton W	Tr	03.77	76-78	49	2	0
Watford	Tr	11.78	78-80	91	1	3
Oxford U	Tr	03.82	81-83	49	1	0
Bournemouth	L	11.83	83	7	0	0
Northampton T	Tr	03.84	84	46	0	1
Tranmere Rov	Tr	08.85	85	36	0	0
Walsall	Tr	08.86	86	16	0	0
TRAINER John (Jack)						
Glasgow, 14 July, 1952						(CD)
Halifax T	Cork Hibernian	08.76	76-78	101	4	5
Bury	HK Rgrs (HK)	09.80	80	1	0	1
Rochdale	Waterford	08.82	82	7	0	0
TRAINOR Daniel (Danny)						
Belfast, 12 July, 1944 IrLge-2/NIAmat/NIu23-1/NI-1						(F)
Plymouth Arg	Crusaders	08.68	68	16	1	3
TRAINOR Peter						
Cockermouth, 2 March, 1915 Died 1979						(CD)
Preston NE	Workington	08.37				
Brighton & Hove A	Tr	05.38	38-47	71	-	4
TRAMEZZANI Paolo						
Reggio-Emilia, Italy, 30 July, 1970						(FB)
Tottenham H	Piacenza (It)	06.98	98	6	0	0
TRANTER George Henry						
Birmingham, 11 September, 1915 Died 1998						(CD)
West Bromwich A	Rover Works	12.43	46	16	-	0
TRANTER Wilfred (Wilf)						
Pendlebury, 5 March, 1945						(FB)
Manchester U	App	04.62	63	1	-	0
Brighton & Hove A	Tr	05.66	65-67	46	1	1
Fulham	Baltimore (USA)	01.69	68-71	20	3	0
TRAORE Demba						
Stockholm, Sweden, 22 April, 1982						(F)
Cambridge U	Vasulund (Swe)	12.00	00-01	2	6	0
TRAORE Djimi						
St Ouen, France, 1 March, 1980 FrYth/Fru21/Mali int						(FB)
Liverpool	Stade Lavallois (Fr)	02.99	00-04	63	10	0
TRAUTMANN Bernhard (Bert) Carl						
Bremen, Germany, 22 October, 1923 FLge-2						(G)
Manchester C	St Helens T	11.49	49-63	508	-	0
TRAVERS Michael (Mike) Joseph Patrick						
Camberley, 23 June, 1942						(FB)
Reading	Jnrs	10.60	60-66	156	2	34
Portsmouth	Tr	07.67	67-71	74	10	6
Aldershot	Tr	07.72	72	29	1	2
TRAVIS David Alan						
Doncaster, 4 July, 1964						(M)
Doncaster Rov	Hatfield Main Colliery	08.84	84-85	10	2	0
Scunthorpe U	Tr	02.86	85-86	13	0	1
Chesterfield	Gainsborough Trinity	08.87	87	6	5	0
TRAVIS Donald (Don)						
Moston, 21 January, 1924 Died 2002						(CF)
West Ham U	Blackpool (Am)	09.45	46-47	5	-	0
Southend U	Tr	05.48	48	1	-	0
Accrington St	Tr	12.48	48-50	71	-	36
Crewe Alex	Tr	11.50	50-51	36	-	12
Oldham Ath	Tr	10.51	51	5	-	1
Chester	Tr	02.52	51-53	99	-	45
Oldham Ath	Tr	08.54	54-56	109	-	61
TRAVIS Simon Christopher						
Preston, 22 March, 1977						(FB)
Torquay U	YT	•	95	4	4	0
Stockport Co	Holywell T	08.97	97-98	4	18	2
TRAYNOR Gregory (Greg)						
Salford, 17 October, 1984						(M)
Wigan Ath	YT	•	01	0	1	0
TRAYNOR Robert (Bobby) Terence						
Burnham, 1 November, 1983						(W)
Brentford	Sch	07.02	02	0	2	0
TRAYNOR Thomas (Tommy) Joseph						
Dundalk, 22 July, 1933 IR-8						(FB)
Southampton	Dundalk	06.52	52-65	433	0	7
TREACY Darren Paul						
Lambeth, 6 September, 1970						(M)
Millwall	YT	02.89	88-89	7	0	0
Bradford C	Tr	11.90	90	16	0	2
TREACY Francis (Frank)						
Glasgow, 14 July, 1939						(IF)
Ipswich T	Johnstone Burgh	03.61	63-65	17	1	5
TREACY Raymond (Ray) Christopher Patrick						
Dublin, 18 June, 1946 IRu23-1/IR-42						(F)
West Bromwich A	App	06.64	66-67	2	3	1
Charlton Ath	Tr	02.68	67-71	144	5	44
Swindon T	Tr	06.72	72-73	55	0	16
Preston NE	Tr	12.73	73-75	54	4	11
Oldham Ath	L	03.75	74	3	0	1
West Bromwich A	Tr	08.76	76	20	1	6

League Club	Source	Date Signed	Seasons Played	Career Record Apps	Subs	Gls
TREBBLE David **Neil**						
Hitchin, 16 February, 1969						(F)
Scunthorpe U	Stevenage Borough	07.93	93	8	6	2
Preston NE	Tr	07.94	94	8	11	4
Scarborough	Tr	02.95	94-95	40	7	8
TREBILCOCK Michael (Mike)						
Callington, 29 November, 1944						(F)
Plymouth Arg	Tavistock	12.62	62-65	71	0	27
Everton	Tr	12.65	65-67	11	0	3
Portsmouth	Tr	01.68	67-71	100	8	33
Torquay U	Tr	07.72	72	23	1	10
TREES Robert Victor						
Manchester, 18 December, 1977						(M)
Manchester U	YT	07.96				
Bristol Rov	Witton A	06.98	98-99	38	8	1
TREHARNE Colin						
Bridgend, 30 July, 1937						(G)
Mansfield T		12.60	61-65	191	0	0
Lincoln C	Tr	07.66	66	20	0	0
TREHERNE Cyril Albert						
Wellington, 12 March, 1928						(CF)
Shrewsbury T		11.50	50	4	-	1
TREMARCO Carl Philip						
Liverpool, 11 October, 1985						(FB)
Tranmere Rov	Sch	04.04	04	2	1	0
TRENTER Ronald (Ron) Herbert						
Ipswich, 13 December, 1928						(W)
Ipswich T	Jnrs	12.45				
Ipswich T	Clacton T	06.51	51	2	-	0
TRETTON Andrew (Andy) David						
Derby, 9 October, 1976						(CD)
Derby Co	YT	10.93				
Shrewsbury T	Tr	12.97	97-01	105	6	6
TREVIS Derek Alan						
Birmingham, 9 September, 1942 Died 2000						(M)
Aston Villa		06.62				
Colchester U	Tr	03.64	63-68	196	0	13
Walsall	Tr	09.68	68-69	63	2	6
Lincoln C	Tr	07.70	70-72	100	8	18
Stockport Co	Philadelphia (USA)	09.73	73	33	2	2
TREVITT Simon						
Dewsbury, 20 December, 1967						(FB)
Huddersfield T	App	06.86	86-95	216	13	3
Hull C	Tr	11.95	95-97	50	1	1
Swansea C	L	12.97	97	1	0	0
TREWICK Alan						
Blyth, 27 April, 1941 Died 1993						(CF)
Gateshead		06.59	59	10	-	1
TREWICK George						
Stakeford, 15 November, 1933 Died 2003						(CD)
Gateshead	West Sleekburn	04.53	56-59	110	-	0
TREWICK John						
Bedlington, 3 June, 1957 ESch/EYth						(M)
West Bromwich A	App	07.74	74-80	83	13	11
Newcastle U	Tr	12.80	80-83	76	2	8
Oxford U	L	01.84	83	3	0	0
Oxford U	Tr	08.84	84-87	109	2	4
Birmingham C	Tr	09.87	87-88	35	2	0
Hartlepool U	Bromsgrove Rov	10.89	89	8	0	0
TRICK Desmond (Des)						
Swansea, 7 November, 1969						(CD)
Swansea C	YT	07.88	89-90	25	4	0
TRIGG Cyril						
Measham, 8 April, 1917 Died 1993						(CF)
Birmingham	Bedworth T	08.35	35-53	268	-	67
TRIM Reginald (Reg) Frederick						
Portsmouth, 1 October, 1913 Died 1997 ESch						(FB)
Bournemouth	Winton & Moordown	04.31	30-32	22	-	0
Arsenal	Tr	04.33	34	1	-	0
Nottingham F	Tr	07.37	37-38	70	-	0
Derby Co	Tr	12.43				
Swindon T	Tr	07.46	46	15	-	0
TRINDER Jason Lee						
Leicester, 3 March, 1970						(G)
Grimsby T	Oadby T	12.92				
Mansfield T	Oadby T	11.94	94-95	5	3	0

League Club	Source	Date Signed	Seasons Played	Career Record Apps	Subs	Gls
TRINER Donald (Don) Arthur						
Longton, 21 August, 1919 Died 2002						(W)
Port Vale	Downings Tileries	12.38	38-47	25	-	7
TRISE Guy Gavin						
Portsmouth, 22 November, 1933						(IF)
Portsmouth	Jnrs	05.53				
Aldershot	Tr	08.54	54	1	-	0
TROLLOPE Norman **John**						
Wroughton, 14 June, 1943						(FB)
Swindon T	Jnrs	07.60	60-80	767	3	22
TROLLOPE Paul Jonathan						
Swindon, 3 June, 1972 WB-1/W-9						(M)
Swindon T	YT	12.89				
Torquay U	Tr	03.92	91-94	103	3	16
Derby Co	Tr	12.94	94-97	47	18	5
Grimsby T	L	08.96	96	6	1	1
Crystal Palace	L	10.96	96	0	9	0
Fulham	Tr	11.97	97-00	54	22	5
Coventry C	Tr	03.02	01	5	1	0
Northampton T	Tr	07.02	02-03	84	0	8
Bristol Rov	Tr	07.04	04	26	4	2
TROOPS Harold (Harry)						
Sheffield, 10 February, 1926 Died 1963						(FB)
Barnsley	Hadfield Works	12.46	48	3	-	1
Lincoln C	Tr	08.49	49-57	295	-	32
Carlisle U	Tr	06.58	58-59	60	-	1
TROTT Dean						
Barnsley, 13 May, 1967						(F)
Northampton T	Boston U	06.94	94	20	2	4
TROTT Robin Francis						
Orpington, 17 August, 1974						(CD)
Gillingham	YT	05.93	93-94	8	2	0
TROTTER Michael (Mike)						
Hartlepool, 27 October, 1969						(M)
Middlesbrough	YT	11.87				
Doncaster Rov	L	11.88	88	3	0	0
Darlington	Tr	06.90	90-91	16	13	2
Leicester C	Tr	12.91	91-92	1	2	0
Chesterfield	Tr	11.93	93	14	1	1
TROUGHT Michael (Mike) John						
Bristol, 19 October, 1980						(CD)
Bristol Rov	YT	03.99	98-01	25	8	0
TROUGHTON Samuel (Sammy) Edward						
Lisburn, 27 March, 1964 NISch/NIYth						(F)
Wolverhampton W	Glentoran	12.83	83	17	0	2
TRUDGIAN Ryan						
St Austell, 15 September, 1983						(F)
Plymouth Arg	YT	●	00	0	1	0
TRUETT Geoffrey (Geoff) Frederick						
West Ham, 23 May, 1935						(WH)
Crystal Palace	Wycombe W	06.57	57-61	38	-	5
TRUNDLE Lee Christopher						
Liverpool, 10 October, 1976						(F)
Wrexham	Rhyl	02.01	00-02	73	21	27
Swansea C	Tr	07.03	03-04	70	3	38
TRUSLER John (Johnny) William						
Shoreham, 7 June, 1934						(CF)
Brighton & Hove A	Shoreham	08.54	54	1	-	0
TRUSSON Michael (Mike) Sydney						
Northolt, 26 May, 1959						(M)
Plymouth Arg	App	01.77	76-79	65	8	15
Sheffield U	Tr	07.80	80-83	125	1	31
Rotherham U	Tr	12.83	83-86	124	0	19
Brighton & Hove A	Tr	07.87	87-88	34	3	2
Gillingham	Tr	09.89	89-91	69	5	7
TRUSTFULL Orlando						
Amsterdam, Holland, 4 August, 1970 Holland int						(M)
Sheffield Wed	Feyenoord (Holl)	08.96	96	9	10	3
TSKHADADZE Kakhaber						
Rustavi, Georgia, 7 September, 1968 CIS/Georgia 28						(CD)
Manchester C	Alania Vladikav's (Rus)	02.98	97-98	12	0	2
TUCK Peter George						
Plaistow, 14 May, 1932						(IF)
Chelsea	Jnrs	06.51	51	3	-	1

League Club	Source	Date Signed	Seasons Played	Career Record Apps	Subs	Gls
TUCK Stuart Gary						
Brighton, 1 October, 1974						(FB)
Brighton & Hove A	YT	07.93	93-98	78	15	1
TUCKER William **Barrington (Barry)**						
Swansea, 28 August, 1952						(FB)
Northampton T	App	08.70	71-77	209	5	3
Brentford	Tr	02.78	77-82	168	1	5
Northampton T	Tr	10.82	82-83	62	1	5
TUCKER Dexter Calbert						
Pontefract, 22 February, 1979						(F)
Hull C	YT	07.98	97	1	6	0
TUCKER Gordon						
Manchester, 5 January, 1968						(CD)
Huddersfield T	Shepshed Charterhouse	07.87	87-88	30	5	0
Scunthorpe U	Tr	07.89	89	14	1	1
TUCKER Jason James						
Isleworth, 3 February, 1973						(CD)
Aldershot	YT	07.91	90	0	1	0
TUCKER Keith						
Deal, 25 November, 1936						(FB)
Charlton Ath	Betteshanger CW	02.54	54-60	3	-	0
TUCKER Kenneth (Ken)						
Poplar, 2 October, 1925						(W)
West Ham U	Finchley	08.46	47-56	83	-	31
Notts Co	Tr	03.57	56-57	28	-	5
TUCKER Kenneth (Ken) John						
Merthyr Tydfil, 15 July, 1935						(W)
Cardiff C	Aston Villa (Am)	10.55	56-57	13	-	0
Shrewsbury T	Tr	02.58	57-59	46	-	8
Northampton T	Tr	03.60	59-60	10	-	3
TUCKER Lee Antony						
Plymouth, 10 August, 1978						(M)
Torquay U	YT	●	96	0	1	0
TUCKER Lee Derek						
Middlesbrough, 14 September, 1971						(W)
Middlesbrough	YT	10.89				
Darlington	Tr	07.91	91	0	5	0
TUCKER Malcolm						
Cramlington, 12 April, 1933						(CD)
Grimsby T	Newcastle U (Am)	11.50	53-57	40	-	0
TUCKER Mark James						
Woking, 27 April, 1972						(FB)
Fulham	YT	07.90	91-92	3	1	0
TUCKER William (Billy) John						
Kidderminster, 17 May, 1948						(CD)
Hereford U	Kidderminster Hrs	07.72	72-76	135	2	12
Bury	Tr	12.76	76-78	96	0	8
Swindon T	Tr	06.79	79	35	0	4
TUDDENHAM Anthony (Tony) Richard						
Reepham, 28 September, 1956						(FB)
West Ham U	App	09.74				
Cambridge U	Tr	02.76	75-76	11	1	0
TUDGAY Marcus						
Shoreham, 3 February, 1983						(F)
Derby Co	Sch	07.02	02-04	42	29	15
TUDOR Thomas **Edward (Ed)**						
Neston, 15 March, 1935						(IF)
Gillingham	Bolton W (Am)	04.58	58	1	-	0
TUDOR John Arthur						
Ilkeston, 25 June, 1946						(F)
Coventry C	Ilkeston T	01.66	66-68	63	6	13
Sheffield U	Tr	11.68	68-70	64	7	30
Newcastle U	Tr	01.71	70-76	161	3	53
Stoke C	Tr	06.76	76	28	2	3
TUDOR Shane Anthony						
Wolverhampton, 10 February, 1982						(W)
Wolverhampton W	YT	08.99	00	0	1	0
Cambridge U	Tr	11.01	01-04	109	12	21
TUDOR William (Billy) Henry						
Shotton, 14 February, 1918 Died 1965 WSch						(CD)
West Bromwich A	Lavender	05.35	38	31	-	0
Wrexham	Tr	05.46	46-48	56	-	2
TUEART Dennis						
Newcastle, 27 November, 1949 Eu23-1/FLge-2/E-6						(W)
Sunderland	Jnrs	08.67	68-73	173	5	46
Manchester C	Tr	03.74	73-82	216	8	86
Stoke C	Tr	08.83	83	2	1	0
Burnley	Tr	12.83	83	8	7	5
[TUGAY] KERIMOGLU Tugay						
Istanbul, Turkey, 24 August, 1970 Turkey 92						(M)
Blackburn Rov	Glasgow Rgrs	07.01	01-04	107	20	5
TUGMAN James (Jimmy) Robert						
Workington, 14 March, 1945						(FB)
Workington		07.64	65-67	31	12	0
TULIP William (Bill) Edward						
Gateshead, 3 May, 1933						(CF)
Newcastle U		06.51				
Darlington	Tr	05.56	56-57	44	-	34
TULLOCH Roland (Ron)						
South Africa, 15 July, 1932						(WH)
Hull C	(South Africa)	12.53	54	3	-	0
TULLOCH Ronald (Ron) Thomas						
Haddington, 5 June, 1933						(IF)
Southend U	Heart of Midlothian	05.56	56	11	-	3
Carlisle U	Tr	07.57	57-59	73	-	23
TULLY Kevin Francis						
Manchester, 18 December, 1952						(W)
Blackpool	Prestwich Heys	11.72	72-73	10	1	0
Cambridge U	Tr	07.74	74-75	40	4	8
Crewe Alex	Tr	01.76	75-78	81	5	4
Port Vale	Tr	10.78	78-79	7	6	2
Bury	Chorley	08.80	80	7	3	1
TULLY Stephen (Steve) Richard						
Paignton, 10 February, 1980						(FB)
Torquay U	YT	05.98	97-01	90	16	3
TUMBRIDGE Raymond (Ray) Alan						
Hampstead, 6 March, 1955						(FB)
Charlton Ath	App	03.73	72-74	43	3	0
Northampton T	L	02.75	74	11	0	0
TUNE David Barrie						
Reading, 1 November, 1938						(WH)
Reading	Jnrs	11.55	57	1	-	0
TUNE Michael (Mike) Gerard						
Stoke-on-Trent, 28 February, 1962						(M)
Crewe Alex	Stoke C (App)	06.79	79	0	1	0
TUNKS Roy William						
Wuppertall, Germany, 21 January, 1951						(G)
Rotherham U	App	03.68	67-73	138	0	0
York C	L	01.69	68	4	0	0
Preston NE	Tr	11.74	74-80	277	0	0
Wigan Ath	Tr	11.81	81-87	245	0	0
Hartlepool U	Tr	07.88	88	5	0	0
Preston NE	Tr	11.88	88-89	25	0	0
TUNNEY Edward (Eddie) Luton						
Liverpool, 23 September, 1915						(FB)
Everton		08.36				
Wrexham	Tr	09.37	37-51	222	-	0
TUNNICLIFFE William (Billy) Francis						
Stoke-on-Trent, 5 January, 1920 Died 1997						(W)
Port Vale	Jnrs	01.37	36-37	3	-	0
Bournemouth	Tr	05.38	38-46	50	-	7
Wrexham	Tr	06.47	47-52	236	-	74
Bradford C	Tr	01.53	52-54	89	-	20
TUNSTALL Eric Walter						
Hartlepool, 21 November, 1950						(M)
Hartlepool	App	11.68	68	0	1	0
TUOHY Michael (Mickey) Patrick Francis						
West Bromwich, 28 March, 1956						(F)
Southend U	Redditch U	06.79	79	20	1	4
TUOHY William (Liam)						
Dublin, 27 April, 1933 LoI-24/IRB/IR-8						(W)
Newcastle U	Shamrock Rov	05.60	60-62	38	-	9
TUOMELA Marko						
Finland, 3 March, 1972 Finland 21						(CD)
Swindon T (L)	Tromso (Nor)	09.00	00	1	1	0

TUPLING Stephen (Steve)
Wensleydale, 11 July, 1964 (M)

League Club	Source	Date Signed	Seasons Played	Apps	Subs	Gls
Middlesbrough	App	07.82				
Carlisle U	Tr	07.84	84	1	0	0
Darlington	Tr	10.84	84-86	105	6	8
Newport Co	Tr	08.87	87	30	3	2
Cardiff C	Tr	08.88	88-89	3	2	0
Torquay U	L	09.88	88	1	2	0
Exeter C	L	01.89	88	8	1	1
Hartlepool U	Tr	12.89	89-91	83	6	3
Darlington	Tr	08.92	92	8	3	0

TURBITT Peter
Keighley, 1 July, 1951 EYth (W)

League Club	Source	Date Signed	Seasons Played	Apps	Subs	Gls
Bradford C	Keighley Central YC	08.69	69-70	5	3	0

TURLEY James
Manchester, 24 June, 1981 (W)

League Club	Source	Date Signed	Seasons Played	Apps	Subs	Gls
York C	YT	06.99	99-00	14	7	2

TURLEY John William
Bebington, 26 January, 1939 (CF)

League Club	Source	Date Signed	Seasons Played	Apps	Subs	Gls
Sheffield U	Ellesmere Port	05.56	57	5	-	3
Peterborough U	Tr	07.61	61-63	32	-	14
Rochdale	Tr	05.64	64	22	-	5

TURLEY Michael (Mike) Douglas
Rotherham, 14 February, 1936 (WH)

League Club	Source	Date Signed	Seasons Played	Apps	Subs	Gls
Sheffield Wed	Jnrs	03.53	54	3	-	0

TURLEY William (Billy) Lee
Wolverhampton, 15 July, 1973 (G)

League Club	Source	Date Signed	Seasons Played	Apps	Subs	Gls
Northampton T	Evesham U	07.95	95-98	28	0	0
Leyton Orient	L	02.98	97	14	0	0
Rushden & Diamonds	Tr	06.99	01-04	133	1	0

TURNBULL Frederick (Fred)
Wallsend, 28 August, 1946 (CD)

League Club	Source	Date Signed	Seasons Played	Apps	Subs	Gls
Aston Villa	Centre '64 (Blyth)	09.66	67-73	160	1	3
Halifax T	L	10.69	69	7	0	0

TURNBULL George Frederick
Gateshead, 4 February, 1927 Died 2002 (G)

League Club	Source	Date Signed	Seasons Played	Apps	Subs	Gls
Grimsby T	Alnwick T	08.50	50	2	-	0
Accrington St	Tr	09.51	51	33	-	0
Gateshead	Tr	07.52	52	3	-	0

TURNBULL Lee Mark
Stockton, 27 September, 1967 (M)

League Club	Source	Date Signed	Seasons Played	Apps	Subs	Gls
Middlesbrough	App	09.85	85-86	8	8	4
Aston Villa	Tr	08.87				
Doncaster Rov	Tr	11.87	87-90	108	15	21
Chesterfield	Tr	02.91	90-93	80	7	26
Doncaster Rov	Tr	10.93	93	10	1	1
Wycombe W	Tr	01.94	93-94	8	3	1
Scunthorpe U	Tr	03.95	94-96	37	10	7
Darlington	Tr	07.97	97	4	5	0

TURNBULL Paul Daniel
Handforth, 23 January, 1989 (F)

League Club	Source	Date Signed	Seasons Played	Apps	Subs	Gls
Stockport Co	Jnrs	•	04	0	1	0

TURNBULL Ronald (Ron) William
Newbiggin, 18 July, 1922 Died 1966 WLge-1 (CF)

League Club	Source	Date Signed	Seasons Played	Apps	Subs	Gls
Sunderland	Dundee	11.47	47-48	40	-	16
Manchester C	Tr	09.49	49-50	30	-	5
Swansea T	Tr	01.51	50-52	67	-	37

TURNBULL Ross
Bishop Auckland, 4 January, 1985 EYth (G)

League Club	Source	Date Signed	Seasons Played	Apps	Subs	Gls
Middlesbrough	Sch	07.02				
Darlington	L	11.03	03	1	0	0
Barnsley	L	04.04	03	3	0	0
Bradford C	L	08.04	04	2	0	0
Barnsley	L	10.04	04	23	0	0

TURNBULL Roy
Edinburgh, 22 October, 1948 SSch/SYth (M)

League Club	Source	Date Signed	Seasons Played	Apps	Subs	Gls
Lincoln C	Heart of Midlothian	09.69	69	0	2	0

TURNBULL Stephen
South Shields, 7 January, 1987 (M)

League Club	Source	Date Signed	Seasons Played	Apps	Subs	Gls
Hartlepool U	Sch	•	04	0	2	0

TURNBULL Terence (Terry) Michael
Stockton, 18 October, 1945 (F)

League Club	Source	Date Signed	Seasons Played	Apps	Subs	Gls
Hartlepool	Crook T	08.76	76	13	0	3

TURNER Adam Ernest
Glasgow, 13 March, 1934 (WH)

League Club	Source	Date Signed	Seasons Played	Apps	Subs	Gls
Gateshead	Dunfermline Ath	10.58	58	6	-	0

TURNER Alan
Sheffield, 22 September, 1935 (IF)

League Club	Source	Date Signed	Seasons Played	Apps	Subs	Gls
Sheffield U		09.57				
Halifax T	Tr	07.58	58	7	-	0

TURNER Alan
Hull, 5 July, 1943 (M)

League Club	Source	Date Signed	Seasons Played	Apps	Subs	Gls
Coventry C	Scunthorpe U (Am)	03.62	61-65	4	0	0
Shrewsbury T	Tr	07.66	66	14	2	3
Bradford PA	Tr	05.67	67	30	2	4

TURNER Alfred (Alf) Thomas
USA, 26 December, 1929 Died 1987 (CF)

League Club	Source	Date Signed	Seasons Played	Apps	Subs	Gls
New Brighton (Am)	Port Sunlight	02.51	50	4	-	0

TURNER Andrew (Andy) Peter
Woolwich, 23 March, 1975 ESch/EYth/IRu21-7 (W)

League Club	Source	Date Signed	Seasons Played	Apps	Subs	Gls
Tottenham H	YT	04.92	92-94	8	12	3
Wycombe W	L	08.94	94	3	1	0
Doncaster Rov	L	10.94	94	4	0	1
Huddersfield T	L	11.95	95	2	3	1
Southend U	L	03.96	95	4	2	0
Portsmouth	Tr	09.96	96-97	34	6	3
Crystal Palace	Tr	10.98	98	0	2	0
Rotherham U	Tr	07.99	99-00	29	7	1
Rochdale	L	03.01	00	2	2	0
Northampton T	Tamworth	01.03	02	0	3	0

TURNER Arthur Alexander
Poplar, 22 January, 1922 (CF)

League Club	Source	Date Signed	Seasons Played	Apps	Subs	Gls
Colchester U	Charlton Ath (Am)	(N/L)	50-51	45	-	14

TURNER Arthur Owen
Chesterton, 1 April, 1909 Died 1994 (CD)

League Club	Source	Date Signed	Seasons Played	Apps	Subs	Gls
Stoke C	Woolstanton PSA	11.30	30-38	290	-	17
Birmingham	Tr	11.39	38-46	39	-	0
Southport	Tr	02.48	47-48	28	-	0

TURNER Brian
Whittlesey, 27 August, 1925 (CF)

League Club	Source	Date Signed	Seasons Played	Apps	Subs	Gls
Lincoln C (Am)	March T	11.47	47	5	-	0

TURNER Brian
Salford, 23 July, 1936 Died 1999 (WH)

League Club	Source	Date Signed	Seasons Played	Apps	Subs	Gls
Bury	Bury Amats	02.57	57-69	452	3	23
Oldham Ath	Tr	08.70	70	10	1	0

TURNER Brian Alfred
East Ham, 31 July, 1949 New Zealand int (M)

League Club	Source	Date Signed	Seasons Played	Apps	Subs	Gls
Chelsea	Eden (NZ)	05.68				
Portsmouth	Tr	06.69	69	3	1	0
Brentford	Tr	01.70	69-71	88	5	7

TURNER Charles (Charlie) John
Newport, 1 July, 1919 Died 1999 (G)

League Club	Source	Date Signed	Seasons Played	Apps	Subs	Gls
Newport Co	Ebbw Junction	05.38	38-47	37	-	0
Swansea T	Tr	08.48	48	2	-	0

TURNER Christopher (Chris) James
St Neots, 3 April, 1951 (CD)

League Club	Source	Date Signed	Seasons Played	Apps	Subs	Gls
Peterborough U	Jnrs	11.69	69-77	308	6	37
Luton T	Tr	07.78	78	30	0	5
Cambridge U	New England (USA)	09.79	79	15	4	0
Swindon T	New England (USA)	09.80	80	0	3	0
Cambridge U	Tr	10.80	80-83	68	3	3
Southend U	Tr	10.83	83	22	2	2

TURNER Christopher (Chris) Robert
Sheffield, 15 September, 1958 EYth (G)

League Club	Source	Date Signed	Seasons Played	Apps	Subs	Gls
Sheffield Wed	App	08.76	76-78	91	0	0
Lincoln C	L	10.78	78	5	0	0
Sunderland	Tr	07.79	79-84	195	0	0
Manchester U	Tr	08.85	85-87	64	0	0
Sheffield Wed	Tr	09.88	88-90	75	0	0
Leeds U	L	11.89	89	2	0	0
Leyton Orient	Tr	10.91	91-94	58	0	0

TURNER David (Dave)
Derby, 26 December, 1948 (FB)

League Club	Source	Date Signed	Seasons Played	Apps	Subs	Gls
Everton	App	10.66	67	1	0	0
Southport	Tr	05.70	70-72	69	2	0

TURNER David (Dave) John
Retford, 7 September, 1943 (M)

League Club	Source	Date Signed	Seasons Played	Apps	Subs	Gls
Newcastle U	App	10.60	61-62	2	-	0
Brighton & Hove A	Tr	12.63	63-71	292	8	30
Blackburn Rov	Tr	08.72	72-73	23	2	0

TURNER Eric
Huddersfield, 13 January, 1921 Died 1993 (WH)

League Club	Source	Date Signed	Seasons Played	Apps	Subs	Gls
Halifax T	Wooldale W	04.46	46	7	-	0

TURNER Frederick (Fred) Arthur
Southampton, 28 February, 1930 Died 1955 (FB)

League Club	Source	Date Signed	Seasons Played	Apps	Subs	Gls
Southampton	Jnrs	02.50				
Torquay U	Tr	08.51	51	1	-	0
Southampton	Tr	03.53	53-54	19	-	0

TURNER Gordon Reginald
Hull, 7 June, 1930 Died 1976 FLge-1 (IF)

League Club	Source	Date Signed	Seasons Played	Apps	Subs	Gls
Luton T		03.50	50-63	406	-	243

TURNER Graham John
Ellesmere Port, 5 October, 1947 EYth (CD)

League Club	Source	Date Signed	Seasons Played	Apps	Subs	Gls
Wrexham	Jnrs	07.65	64-67	77	0	0
Chester	Tr	01.68	67-72	215	3	5
Shrewsbury T	Tr	01.73	72-83	342	13	22

TURNER Herbert (Bert) Gwyn
Rhymney, 19 June, 1909 Died 1981 WWar-8/W-8 (FB)

League Club	Source	Date Signed	Seasons Played	Apps	Subs	Gls
Charlton Ath	Brithdir	08.33	33-46	176	-	2

TURNER Hugh Peter
Middlesbrough, 12 May, 1917 Died 1992 (FB)

League Club	Source	Date Signed	Seasons Played	Apps	Subs	Gls
Middlesbrough		08.35				
Darlington	Tr	08.39	46	6	-	0

TURNER Iain Ross
Stirling, 26 January, 1984 Su21-2 (G)

League Club	Source	Date Signed	Seasons Played	Apps	Subs	Gls
Everton	Stirling A	01.03				
Doncaster Rov	L	03.05	04	8	0	0

TURNER Ian
Middlesbrough, 17 January, 1953 (G)

League Club	Source	Date Signed	Seasons Played	Apps	Subs	Gls
Huddersfield T	South Bank	10.70				
Grimsby T	Tr	01.72	71-73	26	0	0
Walsall	L	02.73	72	3	0	0
Southampton	Tr	03.74	73-77	77	0	0
Newport Co	L	03.78	77	7	0	0
Lincoln C	L	10.78	78	7	0	0
Walsall	Tr	01.79	78-80	39	0	0
Halifax T	L	01.81	80	5	0	0

TURNER John Andrew James
Harrow, 12 February, 1986 (F)

League Club	Source	Date Signed	Seasons Played	Apps	Subs	Gls
Cambridge U	Sch	12.03	02-04	33	42	10

TURNER John Graham Anthony
Peterlee, 23 December, 1954 (G)

League Club	Source	Date Signed	Seasons Played	Apps	Subs	Gls
Derby Co	App	12.72				
Doncaster Rov	L	02.74	73	4	0	0
Huddersfield T	L	03.75	74	1	0	0
Reading	Tr	05.75	75-77	31	0	0
Torquay U	Tr	08.78	78-79	76	0	0
Chesterfield	Tr	02.80	79-82	132	0	0
Torquay U	Tr	08.83	83	34	0	0
Burnley	Weymouth	08.84				
Peterborough U	Tr	10.84	84-85	60	0	0

TURNER Joseph (Joe)
Barnsley, 21 March, 1931 (G)

League Club	Source	Date Signed	Seasons Played	Apps	Subs	Gls
Stockport Co	Denaby U	07.54	54-56	79	-	0
Darlington	Tr	12.57	57-59	68	-	0
Scunthorpe U	Tr	06.60	60-61	22	-	0
Barnsley	Tr	11.61	61	7	-	0

TURNER Keith John
Coventry, 9 April, 1934 (IF)

League Club	Source	Date Signed	Seasons Played	Apps	Subs	Gls
Nottingham F		06.54	54	1	-	0

TURNER Kenneth (Ken) Gwyn
Great Houghton, 22 April, 1941 (FB)

League Club	Source	Date Signed	Seasons Played	Apps	Subs	Gls
Huddersfield T	Jnrs	10.58	61	5	-	0
Shrewsbury T	Tr	07.63	63-65	64	0	1
York C	Tr	06.66	66-67	88	0	2

TURNER Mark Brendan
Stockport, 19 September, 1956 (FB)

League Club	Source	Date Signed	Seasons Played	Apps	Subs	Gls
Stockport Co	Everton (Am)	08.75	75	8	0	0

TURNER Graham **Mark**
Bebington, 4 October, 1972 (M)

League Club	Source	Date Signed	Seasons Played	Apps	Subs	Gls
Wolverhampton W	Paget Rgrs	07.91	92	1	0	0
Northampton T	Tr	07.94	94	2	2	0
Hereford U (L)	Telford U	03.97	96	6	0	0

TURNER Michael (Mike) Christopher
Stafford, 2 April, 1976 (F)

League Club	Source	Date Signed	Seasons Played	Apps	Subs	Gls
Barnsley	Bilston T	12.98	98	2	11	1

TURNER Michael (Mike) George Elliott
Bridport, 20 September, 1938 EYth (G)

League Club	Source	Date Signed	Seasons Played	Apps	Subs	Gls
Swindon T	Dorchester T	12.61	61-63	75	-	0
Torquay U	Tr	07.64	64-65	14	0	0

TURNER Michael Thomas
Lewisham, 9 November, 1983 (CD)

League Club	Source	Date Signed	Seasons Played	Apps	Subs	Gls
Charlton Ath	YT	03.01				
Leyton Orient	L	03.03	02	7	0	1
Brentford	Tr	08.04	04	45	0	1

TURNER Neil Stuart Thomson
Blackpool, 15 March, 1942 Died 2001 (M)

League Club	Source	Date Signed	Seasons Played	Apps	Subs	Gls
Blackpool	Jnrs	12.59	63-66	10	1	1
Crewe Alex	Tr	07.68	68-71	80	5	4

TURNER Paul
Barnsley, 8 July, 1953 (FB)

League Club	Source	Date Signed	Seasons Played	Apps	Subs	Gls
Barnsley	App	07.71	70-74	27	8	1

TURNER Paul Edward
Cheshunt, 13 November, 1968 (M)

League Club	Source	Date Signed	Seasons Played	Apps	Subs	Gls
Arsenal	App	07.86				
Cambridge U	Tr	09.87	87-88	28	9	0

TURNER Peter Ambrose
Leicester, 14 August, 1931 (IF)

League Club	Source	Date Signed	Seasons Played	Apps	Subs	Gls
Crewe Alex		03.54	54-55	23	-	4

TURNER Philip (Phil)
Frodsham, 20 February, 1927 (IF)

League Club	Source	Date Signed	Seasons Played	Apps	Subs	Gls
Chester	Jnrs	07.46	46-47	27	-	6
Carlisle U	Tr	09.48	48-50	78	-	24
Bradford PA	Tr	06.51	51-53	55	-	24
Scunthorpe U	Tr	06.54	54	5	-	2
Accrington St	Tr	10.55	55-56	14	-	5
Chester	Tr	11.56	56	16	-	3

TURNER Philip (Phil)
Sheffield, 12 February, 1962 (M)

League Club	Source	Date Signed	Seasons Played	Apps	Subs	Gls
Lincoln C	App	02.80	79-85	237	2	18
Grimsby T	Tr	08.86	86-87	62	0	7
Leicester C	Tr	02.88	87-88	18	6	2
Notts Co	Tr	03.89	88-95	223	14	16

TURNER Robert (Robbie) Peter
Littlethorpe, 18 September, 1966 (F)

League Club	Source	Date Signed	Seasons Played	Apps	Subs	Gls
Huddersfield T	App	09.84	84	0	1	0
Cardiff C	Tr	07.85	85-86	34	5	8
Hartlepool U	L	10.86	86	7	0	1
Bristol Rov	Tr	12.86	86-87	19	7	2
Wimbledon	Tr	12.87	87-88	2	8	0
Bristol C	Tr	01.89	88-89	45	7	12
Plymouth Arg	Tr	07.90	90-92	66	0	17
Notts Co	Tr	11.92	92	7	1	1
Shrewsbury T	L	03.93	92	9	0	0
Exeter C	Tr	02.94	93-95	38	7	7
Cambridge U	Tr	12.95	95-96	12	5	4
Hull C	L	10.96	96	5	0	2

TURNER Robin David
Carlisle, 10 September, 1955 EYth (F)

League Club	Source	Date Signed	Seasons Played	Apps	Subs	Gls
Ipswich T	App	04.73	75-83	22	26	2
Swansea C	Tr	03.85	84-85	20	0	8
Colchester U	Tr	11.85	85	6	5	0

TURNER Ross Keith
Sheffield, 17 June, 1979 (G)

League Club	Source	Date Signed	Seasons Played	Apps	Subs	Gls
Scunthorpe U	Worsborough Bridge	03.00	99	1	0	0

TURNER John **Samuel (Sam)**
Pontypool, 9 September, 1980 (G)

League Club	Source	Date Signed	Seasons Played	Apps	Subs	Gls
Charlton Ath	YT	05.99				
Stockport Co	Tr	07.00	01	4	2	0

TURNER Stanley (Stan) Frederick
Wokingham, 31 May, 1941 (W)

League Club	Source	Date Signed	Seasons Played	Apps	Subs	Gls
Reading	Jnrs	12.58	60	3	-	0

TURNER Stanley (Stan) Simpson
Hanley, 21 October, 1926 Died 1991 (FB)

League Club	Source	Date Signed	Seasons Played	Apps	Subs	Gls
Port Vale		03.49	50-56	227	-	0

TURNER Wayne Leslie
Luton, 9 March, 1961 (M)

League Club	Source	Date Signed	Seasons Played	Apps	Subs	Gls
Luton T	App	04.78	78-84	81	3	2
Lincoln C	L	10.81	81	18	0	0
Coventry C	Tr	07.85	85	14	1	1
Brentford	Tr	09.86	86-87	56	0	2

TURNEY James (Jim) Allan
Cramlington, 8 July, 1922 Died 1995 (W)

League Club	Source	Date Signed	Seasons Played	Apps	Subs	Gls
Darlington	Blackhall CW	08.48	48-49	40	-	3

TURPIE Robert (Bob) Paul
Hampstead, 13 November, 1949 (M)

League Club	Source	Date Signed	Seasons Played	Apps	Subs	Gls
Queens Park Rgrs	App	11.67	69	1	1	0
Peterborough U	Tr	07.70	70-71	31	6	3

League Club	Source	Date Signed	Seasons Played	Apps	Subs	Gls
TURTON Cyril						
South Kirkby, 20 September, 1921 Died 2000						(CD)
Sheffield Wed	Frickley Colliery	11.44	46-53	146	-	0
TUTILL Stephen (Steve) Alan						
York, 1 October, 1969 ESch						(CD)
York C	YT	01.88	87-97	293	8	6
Darlington	Tr	02.98	97-99	65	5	0
Chesterfield	Tr	07.00	00	17	2	1
TUTIN Harry						
Sunderland, 6 June, 1919 Died 1994						(W)
Southport (Am)	Houghton Social Club	09.46	46	2	-	0
TUTT Graham Charles						
Deptford, 27 August, 1956						(G)
Charlton Ath	Jnrs	03.74	73-75	65	0	0
Workington	L	09.74	74	4	0	0
TUTTLE David Philip						
Reading, 6 February, 1972 EYth						(CD)
Tottenham H	YT	02.90	90-92	10	3	0
Peterborough U	L	01.93	92	7	0	0
Sheffield U	Tr	08.93	93-95	63	0	1
Crystal Palace	Tr	03.96	95-99	73	8	5
Barnsley	Tr	08.99	99	11	1	0
Millwall	Tr	03.00	99-02	19	4	0
Wycombe W	L	02.02	01	4	0	0
TUTTON Alan						
Bexley, 23 February, 1973						(M)
Maidstone U	Alma Swanley	07.91	91	0	4	0
TUTTY Paul						
Manchester, 22 February, 1952						(CD)
Stockport Co	Manchester U (Am)	07.70	70	1	0	0
TUTTY Wayne Keith						
Oxford, 18 June, 1963						(M)
Reading	Banbury U	08.82	82-83	11	2	4
TWAMLEY Bruce Richardson						
Victoria, Canada, 23 May, 1952 Canada int						(FB)
Ipswich T	Jnrs	10.69	73-74	2	0	0
TWEED Steven						
Edinburgh, 8 August, 1972 Su21-3/SB-2						(CD)
Stoke C	Ionikos (Gre)	08.97	97-98	35	4	0
TWEEDY George Jacob						
Bedlington, 8 January, 1913 Died 1987 E-1						(G)
Grimsby T	Willington	08.31	32-52	347	-	0
TWELL Terence (Terry) Keith						
Doncaster, 21 February, 1947						(G)
Birmingham C	Bourne T	10.64	67	2	0	0
TWENTYMAN Geoffrey (Geoff)						
Brampton, Cumberland, 19 January, 1930 Died 2004 IrLge-9						(WH)
Carlisle U	Swifts Rov	02.47	46-53	149	-	2
Liverpool	Tr	12.53	53-59	170	-	18
Carlisle U	Ballymena U	06.63	63	10	-	0
TWENTYMAN Geoffrey (Geoff)						
Liverpool, 10 March, 1959						(CD)
Preston NE	Chorley	08.83	83-85	95	3	4
Bristol Rov	Tr	08.86	86-92	248	4	6
TWIDDY Christopher (Chris)						
Pontypridd, 19 January, 1976 WYth/Wu21-3						(W)
Plymouth Arg	YT	06.94	94-95	14	3	1
TWIDLE Kenneth (Ken) George						
Brigg, 10 October, 1931						(CF)
Rotherham U	Retford T	12.57	57-58	24	-	6
TWIGG Gary						
Glasgow, 19 March, 1984						(F)
Derby Co	YT	03.01	01-02	1	8	0
Bristol Rov	L	03.04	03	7	1	0
TWIGG Richard (Dick) Lance						
Barry, 10 September, 1939						(G)
Notts Co	Barry T	11.57	58	2	-	0
TWISS Michael John						
Salford, 26 December, 1977						(W)
Manchester U	YT	07.96				
Sheffield U	L	08.98	98	2	10	1
Port Vale	Tr	07.00	00	15	3	3

League Club	Source	Date Signed	Seasons Played	Apps	Subs	Gls
TWISSELL Charles (Charlie) Herbert						
Singapore, 16 December, 1932 EAmat						(W)
Plymouth Arg		04.55	55-57	41	-	9
York C	Tr	11.58	58-60	53	-	8
TWIST Franklin (Frank)						
Liverpool, 2 November, 1940 EYth						(W)
Liverpool	Jnrs	08.58				
Bury	Prescot Cables	10.61	61-62	8	-	0
Halifax T	Tr	07.63	63-64	64	-	10
Tranmere Rov	Tr	07.65	65	7	0	3
TWITCHIN Ian Robert						
Teignmouth, 22 January, 1952 EYth						(FB)
Torquay U	Jnrs	01.70	69-80	374	27	14
TWOMEY James (Jim) Francis						
Newry, 13 April, 1914 Died 1984 IrLge-2/I-2						(G)
Leeds U	Newry T	12.37	37-48	108	-	0
TWYNHAM Gary Steven						
Manchester, 8 February, 1976						(M)
Manchester U	YT	07.94				
Darlington	Tr	03.96	95-96	23	8	3
Macclesfield T	Hednesford T	08.00	00	5	4	0
TYDEMAN Richard (Dick)						
Chatham, 26 May, 1951						(M)
Gillingham	App	05.69	69-76	293	2	13
Charlton Ath	Tr	12.76	76-80	158	0	7
Gillingham	Tr	08.81	81-83	75	1	2
Peterborough U	Tr	10.83	83	29	0	0
TYLER Dudley Hugh John						
Salisbury, 21 September, 1944						(W)
West Ham U	Hereford U	06.72	72-73	29	0	1
Hereford U	Tr	11.73	73-76	97	5	10
TYLER Leonard (Len) Victor						
Rotherhithe, 7 January, 1919 Died 1988						(FB)
Millwall	Redhill	03.43	46-49	90	-	0
Ipswich T	Tr	07.50	50-51	73	-	0
TYLER Mark Richard						
Norwich, 2 April, 1977 EYth						(G)
Peterborough U	YT	12.94	94-04	314	1	0
TYLER Simon						
Pontypool, 1 May, 1962						(F)
Newport Co	Abergavenny Thursday	10.84	84-85	0	4	0
TYNAN Paul						
Whitehaven, 15 July, 1969						(M)
Carlisle U	Ipswich T (App)	08.87	87	2	3	0
TYNAN Robert (Bobby)						
Liverpool, 7 December, 1955 EYth						(M)
Tranmere Rov	App	07.73	72-77	193	2	26
TYNAN Thomas (Tommy) Edward						
Liverpool, 17 November, 1955						(F)
Liverpool	App	11.72				
Swansea C	L	10.75	75	6	0	2
Sheffield Wed	Dallas (USA)	09.76	76-78	89	2	31
Lincoln C	Tr	10.78	78	9	0	1
Newport Co	Tr	02.79	78-82	168	15	66
Plymouth Arg	Tr	08.83	83-84	80	0	43
Rotherham U	Tr	07.85	85-86	32	0	13
Plymouth Arg	L	03.86	85	9	0	9
Plymouth Arg	Tr	09.86	86-89	172	1	73
Torquay U	Tr	05.90	90	34	1	13
Doncaster Rov	Tr	07.91	91	5	6	1
TYNE Thomas (Tommy) Richard						
Lambeth, 2 March, 1981						(F)
Millwall	Slade Green	02.99	00	0	3	0
TYRELL Joseph (Joe) James						
Stepney, 21 January, 1932						(IF)
Aston Villa	Bretforton OB	05.50	53-55	7	-	3
Millwall	Tr	03.56	55-56	37	-	18
Bournemouth	Tr	06.57	57-58	3	-	1
TYRER Alan						
Liverpool, 8 December, 1942						(M)
Everton	Jnrs	12.59	59-61	9	-	2
Mansfield T	Tr	07.63	63-64	41	-	5
Arsenal	Tr	08.65				
Bury	Tr	08.67	67	2	1	0
Workington	Tr	07.68	68-75	228	16	18

League Club	Source	Date Signed	Seasons Played	Career Record Apps	Subs	Gls
TYRER Arthur						
Liverpool, 14 October, 1934						(CF)
Crewe Alex	St Helens	03.58	57	5	-	3
TYRER Arthur Spencer						
Manchester, 25 February, 1931						(WH)
Leeds U	Mossley	09.50	51-53	39	-	4
Shrewsbury T	Peterborough U	06.55	55	24	-	3
Aldershot	Tr	06.56	56-63	234	-	9
TYSON John (Jack)						
Barrow, 19 November, 1935						(W)
Barrow		04.54	53-56	8	-	0
TYSON Nathan						
Reading, 4 May, 1982 EYth/Eu20						(F)
Reading	YT	03.00	99-03	9	24	1
Swansea C	L	08.01	01	7	4	1
Cheltenham T	L	03.02	01	1	7	1
Wycombe W	Tr	01.04	03-04	61	2	31

UDDIN Anwar
Stepney, 1 November, 1981 (CD)

League Club	Source	Date Signed	Seasons Played	Apps	Subs	Gls
West Ham U	YT	07.01				
Sheffield Wed	Tr	02.02				
Bristol Rov	Tr	07.02	02-03	18	1	1

UDEZE Ifeanyi **(Iffy)**
Nigeria, 21 July, 1980 Nigeria 16 (FB)

League Club	Source	Date Signed	Seasons Played	Apps	Subs	Gls
West Bromwich A (L)	PAOK Salonika (Gre)	01.03	02	7	4	0

UFTON Derek Gilbert
Crayford, 31 May, 1928 E-1 (CD)

League Club	Source	Date Signed	Seasons Played	Apps	Subs	Gls
Charlton Ath	Bexleyheath & Welling	09.48	49-59	263	-	0

UGARTE Juan
San Sebastian, Spain, 7 November, 1980 (F)

League Club	Source	Date Signed	Seasons Played	Apps	Subs	Gls
Wrexham	Dorchester T	11.04	04	23	7	17

UGOLINI Rolando
Lucca, Italy, 4 June, 1924 (G)

League Club	Source	Date Signed	Seasons Played	Apps	Subs	Gls
Middlesbrough	Glasgow Celtic	05.48	48-55	320	-	0
Wrexham	Tr	06.57	57-59	83	-	0

UHLENBEEK Gustav (Gus) Reinier
Surinam, 20 August, 1970 (FB)

League Club	Source	Date Signed	Seasons Played	Apps	Subs	Gls
Ipswich T	Tops SV (Holl)	08.95	95-97	77	12	4
Fulham	Tr	07.98	98-99	22	17	1
Sheffield U	Tr	08.00	00-01	47	4	0
Walsall	L	03.02	01	5	0	0
Bradford C	Tr	08.02	02	42	0	1
Chesterfield	Tr	08.03	03	36	1	0
Wycombe W	Tr	07.04	04	36	6	4

ULLATHORNE Robert (Rob)
Wakefield, 11 October, 1971 EYth (FB)

League Club	Source	Date Signed	Seasons Played	Apps	Subs	Gls
Norwich C	YT	07.90	90-95	86	8	7
Leicester C	CA Osasuna (Sp)	02.97	97-98	28	3	1
Sheffield U	Tr	12.00	00-02	39	1	0
Northampton T	Tr	02.04	03	13	0	1
Notts Co	Tr	07.04	04	34	2	0

UNDERHILL Graham Stuart
Bristol, 10 April, 1968 (CD)

League Club	Source	Date Signed	Seasons Played	Apps	Subs	Gls
Bristol C	App	04.86	85	1	0	0

UNDERWOOD Edmund **David (Dave)**
St Pancras, 15 March, 1928 Died 1989 (G)

League Club	Source	Date Signed	Seasons Played	Apps	Subs	Gls
Queens Park Rgrs	Edgware T	12.49	51	2	-	0
Watford	Tr	02.52	51-53	52	-	0
Liverpool	Tr	12.53	53-55	45	-	0
Watford	Tr	06.56	56	16	-	0
Watford	Dartford	04.60	60-62	108	-	0
Fulham	Tr	07.63	63-64	18	-	0

UNDERWOOD George Ronald
Sheffield, 6 September, 1925 (FB)

League Club	Source	Date Signed	Seasons Played	Apps	Subs	Gls
Sheffield U		09.46	49-50	17	-	0
Sheffield Wed	Tr	10.51				
Scunthorpe U	Tr	06.53	53	8	-	0
Rochdale	Tr	06.54	54	19	-	0

UNDERWOOD Paul Victor
Wimbledon, 16 August, 1973 ESemiPro-4 (FB)

League Club	Source	Date Signed	Seasons Played	Apps	Subs	Gls
Rushden & Diamonds	Enfield	06.97	01-03	110	0	1
Luton T	Tr	03.04	03-04	38	0	5

UNDERWOOD William (Bill) Kenneth
Brigg, 28 December, 1921 Died 1993 (W)

League Club	Source	Date Signed	Seasons Played	Apps	Subs	Gls
Hartlepools U (Am)	South Bank	01.48	47	1	-	0

UNGER Lars
Eutin, Germany, 30 September, 1972 Geu21 (M)

League Club	Source	Date Signed	Seasons Played	Apps	Subs	Gls
Southend U (L)	Fortuna Duss'f (Ger)	02.99	98	14	0	0

UNSAL Hakan
Sinop, Turkey, 14 May, 1973 Turkey 29 (FB)

League Club	Source	Date Signed	Seasons Played	Apps	Subs	Gls
Blackburn Rov	Galatasaray (Tu)	03.02	01	7	1	0

UNSWORTH David Gerald
Chorley, 16 October, 1973 EYth/Eu21-6/E-1 (CD)

League Club	Source	Date Signed	Seasons Played	Apps	Subs	Gls
Everton	YT	06.92	91-96	108	8	11
West Ham U	Tr	08.97	97	32	0	2
Aston Villa	Tr	07.98				
Everton	Tr	08.98	98-03	164	24	23
Portsmouth	Tr	07.04	04	15	0	2
Ipswich T	L	01.05	04	16	0	1

UNSWORTH Jamie Jonathan
Bury, 1 May, 1973 (FB)

League Club	Source	Date Signed	Seasons Played	Apps	Subs	Gls
Cardiff C	YT	07.91	90-91	1	3	0

UNSWORTH Lee Peter
Eccles, 25 February, 1973 (FB)

League Club	Source	Date Signed	Seasons Played	Apps	Subs	Gls
Crewe Alex	Ashton U	02.95	95-99	93	33	0
Bury	Tr	08.00	00-04	141	7	6

UPHILL Edward **Dennis** Herbert
Bath, 11 August, 1931 (IF)

League Club	Source	Date Signed	Seasons Played	Apps	Subs	Gls
Tottenham H	Peasedown MW	09.49	50-52	6	-	2
Reading	Tr	02.53	52-55	92	-	42
Coventry C	Tr	10.55	55-56	49	-	16
Mansfield T	Tr	03.57	56-58	83	-	38
Watford	Tr	06.59	59-60	51	-	30
Crystal Palace	Tr	10.60	60-62	63	-	17

UPRICHARD William **Norman** McCourt
Moyraverty, 20 February, 1928 I-7/NI-11 (G)

League Club	Source	Date Signed	Seasons Played	Apps	Subs	Gls
Arsenal	Distillery	06.48				
Swindon T	Tr	11.49	49-52	73	-	0
Portsmouth	Tr	11.52	52-58	182	-	0
Southend U	Tr	07.59	59	12	-	0

UPSON Matthew James
Eye, 18 April, 1979 EYth/Eu21-11/E-7 (CD)

League Club	Source	Date Signed	Seasons Played	Apps	Subs	Gls
Luton T	YT	04.96	96	0	1	0
Arsenal	Tr	05.97	97-01	20	14	0
Nottingham F	L	12.00	00	1	0	0
Crystal Palace	L	03.01	00	7	0	0
Reading	L	09.02	02	13	1	0
Birmingham C	Tr	01.03	02-04	80	0	2

UPTON Colin Clive
Reading, 2 October, 1960 (F)

League Club	Source	Date Signed	Seasons Played	Apps	Subs	Gls
Plymouth Arg	App	10.78	78	2	1	0

UPTON Frank
Ainsley Hill, 18 October, 1934 (CD)

League Club	Source	Date Signed	Seasons Played	Apps	Subs	Gls
Northampton T	Nuneaton Borough	03.53	52-53	17	-	1
Derby Co	Tr	06.54	54-60	224	-	12
Chelsea	Tr	08.61	61-64	74	-	3
Derby Co	Tr	09.65	65-66	35	0	5
Notts Co	Tr	09.66	66	33	1	3
Workington	Worcester C	01.68	67	6	1	0

UPTON James (Jim) Edwin Glen
Coatbridge, 3 June, 1940 (FB)

League Club	Source	Date Signed	Seasons Played	Apps	Subs	Gls
Cardiff C	Tonbridge	08.63	63	5	-	0

UPTON Robin (Nobby) Patrick
Lincoln, 9 November, 1942 (CD)

League Club	Source	Date Signed	Seasons Played	Apps	Subs	Gls
Brighton & Hove A	Jnrs	11.59	62-66	40	0	0

URE John (Ian) Francombe
Ayr, 7 December, 1939 Su23-1/SLge-4/S-11 (CD)

League Club	Source	Date Signed	Seasons Played	Apps	Subs	Gls
Arsenal	Dundee	08.63	63-69	168	0	2
Manchester U	Tr	08.69	69-70	47	0	1

URQUHART George Stuart McWilliam
Glasgow, 22 April, 1950 (M)

League Club	Source	Date Signed	Seasons Played	Apps	Subs	Gls
Wigan Ath	Ross Co	07.79	79-80	63	5	6

URQUHART William (Billy) Murray
Inverness, 22 November, 1956 (F)

League Club	Source	Date Signed	Seasons Played	Apps	Subs	Gls
Wigan Ath	Glasgow Rgrs	11.80	80	5	5	2

URSEM Loek Aloysius Jacobus Maria
Amsterdam, Holland, 7 January, 1958 (W)

League Club	Source	Date Signed	Seasons Played	Apps	Subs	Gls
Stoke C	AZ67 Alkmaar (Holl)	07.79	79-82	32	8	7
Sunderland	L	03.82	81	0	4	0

URWIN Graham Edward
South Shields, 15 February, 1949 (W)

League Club	Source	Date Signed	Seasons Played	Apps	Subs	Gls
Darlington		08.67	67	1	0	0

USHER Brian
Durham, 11 March, 1944 EU23-1 (W)

League Club	Source	Date Signed	Seasons Played	Apps	Subs	Gls
Sunderland	Jnrs	03.61	63-64	61	-	5
Sheffield Wed	Tr	06.65	65-67	55	1	2
Doncaster Rov	Tr	06.68	68-72	164	6	6

USHER John (Johnny) Allison Grey
Hexham, 6 September, 1918 Died 1989 (WH)

League Club	Source	Date Signed	Seasons Played	Apps	Subs	Gls
Watford		05.46	46-47	23	-	3

UTLEY Darren
Barnsley, 28 September, 1977 (CD)

League Club	Source	Date Signed	Seasons Played	Apps	Subs	Gls
Doncaster Rov	YT	12.95	95-97	22	6	1

UYTENBOGAARDT Albert George
Cape Town, South Africa, 5 March, 1930 (G)

League Club	Source	Date Signed	Seasons Played	Apps	Subs	Gls
Charlton Ath	Cape Town Trams (SA)	10.48	48-52	6	-	0

UZELAC Steven (Steve)
Doncaster, 12 March, 1953 (CD)

League Club	Source	Date Signed	Seasons Played	Apps	Subs	Gls
Doncaster Rov	Jnrs	06.71	71-76	182	3	9
Mansfield T	L	02.76	75	2	0	0
Preston NE	Tr	05.77	77-78	9	0	0
Stockport Co	Tr	03.80	79-81	31	0	2

UZZELL John Edward
Plymouth, 31 March, 1959 (FB)

League Club	Source	Date Signed	Seasons Played	Apps	Subs	Gls
Plymouth Arg	App	03.77	77-88	292	10	6
Torquay U	Tr	08.89	89-91	91	1	2

VAESEN Nico Jos-Theodor
Hasselt, Belgium, 28 September, 1969 (G)

League Club	Source	Date Signed	Seasons Played	Apps	Subs	Gls
Huddersfield T	Eendracht Aalst (Bel)	07.98	98-00	134	0	0
Birmingham C	Tr	06.01	01-02	49	1	0
Gillingham	L	12.03	03	5	0	0
Bradford C	L	02.04	03	6	0	0
Crystal Palace	L	03.04	03	10	0	0

VAESSEN Leon Henry
Market Bosworth, 8 November, 1940 ESch (WH)

League Club	Source	Date Signed	Seasons Played	Apps	Subs	Gls
Millwall	Chelsea (Am)	01.58	57-60	26	-	2
Gillingham	Tr	08.61	61-62	29	-	0

VAESSEN Paul Leon
Gillingham, 16 October, 1961 Died 2001 (F)

League Club	Source	Date Signed	Seasons Played	Apps	Subs	Gls
Arsenal	App	07.79	78-81	23	9	6

VAFIADIS Odysseus (Seth) Yickanis
Hammersmith, 8 September, 1945 (W)

League Club	Source	Date Signed	Seasons Played	Apps	Subs	Gls
Queens Park Rgrs	Chelsea (App)	11.62	63	15	-	4
Millwall	Tr	09.64	64	4	-	0

VAIREY Roy Henry
South Elmsall, 10 June, 1932 (G)

League Club	Source	Date Signed	Seasons Played	Apps	Subs	Gls
Stockport Co		09.51	56	5	-	0

VALAKARI Simo Johannes
Helsinki, Finland, 28 April, 1973 Fiu21-1/Fi-32 (M)

League Club	Source	Date Signed	Seasons Played	Apps	Subs	Gls
Derby Co	Motherwell	07.00	00-03	34	12	3

VALENTINE Carl Howard
Clayton, 4 July, 1958 Canada int (W)

League Club	Source	Date Signed	Seasons Played	Apps	Subs	Gls
Oldham Ath	Jnrs	01.76	76-79	75	7	8
West Bromwich A	Vancouver (Can)	10.84	84-85	44	0	6

VALENTINE Peter
Huddersfield, 16 April, 1963 (CD)

League Club	Source	Date Signed	Seasons Played	Apps	Subs	Gls
Huddersfield T	App	04.81	81-82	19	0	1
Bolton W	Tr	07.83	83-84	66	2	1
Bury	Tr	07.85	85-92	314	5	16
Carlisle U	Tr	08.93	93-94	27	2	2
Rochdale	Tr	11.94	94-95	49	1	2

VALENTINE Ryan David
Wrexham, 19 August, 1982 WYth/Wu21-8 (FB)

League Club	Source	Date Signed	Seasons Played	Apps	Subs	Gls
Everton	YT	09.99				
Darlington	Tr	08.02	02-04	108	11	4

VALERO Vincente Xavier
Castellon, Spain, 28 February, 1973 (G)

League Club	Source	Date Signed	Seasons Played	Apps	Subs	Gls
Wrexham	Ciudad Murcia (Sp)	01.05	04	3	0	0

VALERY Patrick Jean Claude
Brignoles, France, 3 July, 1969 (FB)

League Club	Source	Date Signed	Seasons Played	Apps	Subs	Gls
Blackburn Rov	AS Monaco (Fr)	06.97	97	14	1	0

VALLANCE Thomas (Tom) Henshall Wilson
Stoke-on-Trent, 28 March, 1924 Died 1980 (W)

League Club	Source	Date Signed	Seasons Played	Apps	Subs	Gls
Arsenal	Torquay U (Am)	07.47	48-49	15	-	2

VALLARD Leonard (Len) Gerald Harold
Sherborne, 6 July, 1940 (FB)

League Club	Source	Date Signed	Seasons Played	Apps	Subs	Gls
Reading	Yeovil T	05.58	59-61	37	-	2

VALOIS Jean-Louis
Saint-Priest, France, 15 October, 1973 (M)

League Club	Source	Date Signed	Seasons Played	Apps	Subs	Gls
Luton T	OSC Lille (Fr)	09.01	01	32	2	6
Burnley	Clyde	09.04	04	18	12	3

VAN BLERK Jason
Sydney, Australia, 16 March, 1968 AuYth/Au-27 (FB)

League Club	Source	Date Signed	Seasons Played	Apps	Subs	Gls
Millwall	Go Ahead Eagles (Holl)	09.94	94-96	68	5	2
Manchester C	Tr	08.97	97	10	9	0
West Bromwich A	Tr	03.98	97-00	106	3	3
Stockport Co	Tr	08.01	01	13	0	0
Hull C	Tr	01.02	01	10	0	1
Shrewsbury T	Tr	08.02	02	17	6	1

VAN BREUKELEN Johannes (Hans)
Utrecht, Holland, 4 October, 1956 Holland int (G)

League Club	Source	Date Signed	Seasons Played	Apps	Subs	Gls
Nottingham F	FC Utrecht (Holl)	09.82	82-83	61	0	0

VAN BRONCKHORST Giovanni Christiaan
Rotterdam, Holland, 5 February, 1975 Holland 41 (M)

League Club	Source	Date Signed	Seasons Played	Apps	Subs	Gls
Arsenal	Glasgow Rgrs	06.01	01-02	22	19	2

VAN BUYTEN Daniel
Chimay, Belgium, 7 February, 1978 Belgium 21 (CD)

League Club	Source	Date Signed	Seasons Played	Apps	Subs	Gls
Manchester C (L)	Marseille (Fr)	01.04	03	5	0	0

VAN DAMME Jelle
Lokeren, Belgium, 10 October, 1983 Belgium 7 (CD)

League Club	Source	Date Signed	Seasons Played	Apps	Subs	Gls
Southampton	Ajax (Holl)	05.04	04	4	2	0

VAN DEN HAUWE Patrick (Pat) William Roger
Dendermonde, Belgium, 16 December, 1960 W-13 (FB)

League Club	Source	Date Signed	Seasons Played	Apps	Subs	Gls
Birmingham C	App	08.78	78-84	119	4	1
Everton	Tr	09.84	84-88	134	1	2
Tottenham H	Tr	08.89	89-92	110	6	0
Millwall	Tr	09.93	93-94	27	0	0

VAN DER ELST Francois Jean Cecile
Opwyk, Belgium, 1 December, 1954 Belgium int (M)

League Club	Source	Date Signed	Seasons Played	Apps	Subs	Gls
West Ham U	NY Cosmos (USA)	12.81	81-82	61	1	14

VAN DER GEEST Franciscus (Frank) Wilhelmus
Beverwijk, Holland, 30 April, 1973 (G)

League Club	Source	Date Signed	Seasons Played	Apps	Subs	Gls
Darlington	Heracles (Holl)	08.00	00	2	0	0

VAN DER GOUW Raimond
Oldenzaal, Holland, 24 March, 1963 (G)

League Club	Source	Date Signed	Seasons Played	Apps	Subs	Gls
Manchester U	Vitesse Arnhem (Holl)	07.96	96-01	26	11	0

VAN DER KWAAK Peter
Haarlem, Holland, 12 October, 1968 (G)

League Club	Source	Date Signed	Seasons Played	Apps	Subs	Gls
Reading	Ajax (Holl)	08.98	98-99	3	1	0
Carlisle U	L	02.00	99	2	0	0

VAN DER LAAN Robertus (Robin) Petrus
Schiedam, Holland, 5 September, 1968 (M)

League Club	Source	Date Signed	Seasons Played	Apps	Subs	Gls
Port Vale	FC Wageningen (Holl)	02.91	90-94	154	22	24
Derby Co	Tr	08.95	95-97	61	4	8
Wolverhampton W	L	10.96	96	7	0	0
Barnsley	Tr	07.98	98-00	52	15	5

VAN DER LINDEN Antoine
Rotterdam, Holland, 17 March, 1976 (CD)

League Club	Source	Date Signed	Seasons Played	Apps	Subs	Gls
Swindon T	Sparta Rotterdam (Holl)	08.00	00	17	16	1

VANDERMOTTEN William (Willie)
Glasgow, 26 August, 1930 Died 1979 (IF)

League Club	Source	Date Signed	Seasons Played	Apps	Subs	Gls
Bradford PA	Cowdenbeath	03.53	52	1	-	0

VAN DER SAR Edwin
Leiden, Holland, 29 October, 1970 Holland 100 (G)

League Club	Source	Date Signed	Seasons Played	Apps	Subs	Gls
Fulham	Juventus (It)	08.01	01-04	126	1	0

VAN DER VELDEN Carel
Arnhem, Holland, 3 August, 1972 (M)

League Club	Source	Date Signed	Seasons Played	Apps	Subs	Gls
Barnsley	DFC Den Bosch (Holl)	03.96	95-96	7	2	0
Scarborough	Tr	08.97	97	5	3	1

VAN DEURZEN Jurgen
Genk, Belgium, 26 January, 1974 BeYth/Beu21 (M)

League Club	Source	Date Signed	Seasons Played	Apps	Subs	Gls
Stoke C	KFC Turnhout (Bel)	08.01	01-02	44	8	5

VAN DULLEMAN Raymond (Ray) Robert
Gravenhage, Holland, 6 May, 1973 (F)

League Club	Source	Date Signed	Seasons Played	Apps	Subs	Gls
Northampton T	VIOS (Holl)	08.97	97	0	1	0

VAN GOBBEL Ulrich
Surinam, 16 January, 1971 Holland int (FB)

League Club	Source	Date Signed	Seasons Played	Apps	Subs	Gls
Southampton	Galatasaray (Tu)	10.96	96-97	25	2	1

VAN GOOL Roger
Belgium, 1 June, 1950 Belgium int (W)

League Club	Source	Date Signed	Seasons Played	Apps	Subs	Gls
Coventry C	FC Cologne (Ger)	03.80	79-80	17	0	0

VANHALA Jari
Finland, 29 August, 1965 Finland int (F)

League Club	Source	Date Signed	Seasons Played	Apps	Subs	Gls
Bradford C	FF Jaro (Fin)	12.96	96	0	1	0

VAN HEUSDEN Arjan
Alphen, Holland, 11 December, 1972 (G)

League Club	Source	Date Signed	Seasons Played	Apps	Subs	Gls
Port Vale	VV Noordwijk (Holl)	08.94	94-97	27	0	0
Oxford U	L	09.97	97	11	0	0

League Club	Source	Date Signed	Seasons Played	Apps	Subs	Gls
Cambridge U	Tr	08.98	98-99	41	1	0
Exeter C	Tr	07.00	00-01	74	0	0
Mansfield T	Tr	09.02	02	5	0	0
Torquay U	Tr	11.02	02-04	47	0	0

VAN HOOIJDONK Pierre
Steenbergen, Holland, 29 November, 1969 Holland 38 (F)

League Club	Source	Date Signed	Seasons Played	Apps	Subs	Gls
Nottingham F	Glasgow Celtic	03.97	96-98	68	3	36

VAN MIERLO Antonius (Toine) Wilhelmus Matthis
Sorendonk, Holland, 24 August, 1957 Holland int (W)

League Club	Source	Date Signed	Seasons Played	Apps	Subs	Gls
Birmingham C	Willem II Tilburg (Holl)	08.81	81-82	44	0	4

VANNINEN Jukka
Riihimaki, Finland, 31 January, 1977 (M)

League Club	Source	Date Signed	Seasons Played	Apps	Subs	Gls
Exeter C	Rovaniemi Rops (Fin)	12.99	99	3	2	0

VAN NISTELROOY Rutgerus (Ruud) Johannes Martinus
Oss, Holland, 1 July, 1976 Holland 44 (F)

League Club	Source	Date Signed	Seasons Played	Apps	Subs	Gls
Manchester U	PSV Eindhoven (Holl)	07.01	01-04	109	6	74

VAN PERSIE Robin
Rotterdam, Holland, 6 August, 1983 Hou21/Ho-2 (F)

League Club	Source	Date Signed	Seasons Played	Apps	Subs	Gls
Arsenal	Feyenoord (Holl)	04.04	04	12	14	5

VAN ROSSUM Johannes (Erik) Christison
Nijmegen, Holland, 27 March, 1963 (CD)

League Club	Source	Date Signed	Seasons Played	Apps	Subs	Gls
Plymouth Arg	Twente Enschede (Holl)	01.92	91	9	0	0

VANSITTART Thomas (Tom)
Merton, 23 January, 1950 (FB)

League Club	Source	Date Signed	Seasons Played	Apps	Subs	Gls
Crystal Palace	App	04.67	67-69	10	1	2
Wrexham	Tr	02.70	69-74	86	2	1

VAN WIJK Dennis Johannes
Oostzaan, Holland, 16 December, 1962 (FB)

League Club	Source	Date Signed	Seasons Played	Apps	Subs	Gls
Norwich C	Ajax (Holl)	10.82	82-85	109	9	3

VARADI Imre
Paddington, 8 July, 1959 (F)

League Club	Source	Date Signed	Seasons Played	Apps	Subs	Gls
Sheffield U	FC 75 (Hitchin)	04.78	78	6	4	4
Everton	Tr	03.79	79-80	22	4	6
Newcastle U	Tr	08.81	81-82	81	0	39
Sheffield Wed	Tr	08.83	83-84	72	4	33
West Bromwich A	Tr	07.85	85	30	2	9
Manchester C	Tr	10.86	86-88	56	9	26
Sheffield Wed	Tr	09.88	88-89	14	8	3
Leeds U	Tr	02.90	89-92	21	5	5
Luton T	L	03.92	91	5	1	1
Oxford U	L	01.93	92	3	2	0
Rotherham U	Tr	03.93	92-94	55	12	25
Mansfield T	N/C	08.95	95	1	0	0
Scunthorpe U	Boston U	09.95	95	0	2	0

VARGA Stanislav
Lipany, Slovakia, 8 October, 1972 Slovakia 39 (CD)

League Club	Source	Date Signed	Seasons Played	Apps	Subs	Gls
Sunderland	Slovan Bratislava (Slo)	08.00	00-01	18	3	1
West Bromwich A	L	03.02	01	3	1	0

VARNEY John **Francis (Frank)**
Oxford, 27 November, 1929 (FB)

League Club	Source	Date Signed	Seasons Played	Apps	Subs	Gls
Hull C	Oxford C	12.49	50	9	-	0
Lincoln C	Tr	05.51	51-52	20	-	4

VARNEY Luke Ivan
Leicester, 28 September, 1982 (F)

League Club	Source	Date Signed	Seasons Played	Apps	Subs	Gls
Crewe Alex	Quorn	03.03	03-04	22	12	5

VARTY Thomas (Tommy) Heppell
Hetton-le-Hole, 2 December, 1921 (IF)

League Club	Source	Date Signed	Seasons Played	Apps	Subs	Gls
Darlington	Newcastle U (Am)	08.45	46-49	162	-	33
Watford	Tr	09.50	50	34	-	5

VARTY John **William (Will)**
Workington, 1 October, 1976 (CD)

League Club	Source	Date Signed	Seasons Played	Apps	Subs	Gls
Carlisle U	YT	07.95	96-98	79	3	1
Rotherham U	Tr	03.99	98-00	45	2	0

VASPER Peter John
Bromley, 3 September, 1945 (G)

League Club	Source	Date Signed	Seasons Played	Apps	Subs	Gls
Leyton Orient		11.63				
Norwich C	Guildford C	02.68	67-69	31	0	0
Cambridge U	Tr	09.70	70-73	136	0	0

VASS Stephen (Steve)
Leicester, 10 January, 1954 (FB)

League Club	Source	Date Signed	Seasons Played	Apps	Subs	Gls
Hartlepool U	Wycombe W	10.79	79	4	0	0

VASSALLO Barrie Emmanuel
Newport, 3 March, 1956 WSch (M)

League Club	Source	Date Signed	Seasons Played	Apps	Subs	Gls
Arsenal	App	05.73				
Plymouth Arg	Tr	11.74	74-75	6	7	2
Torquay U	Barnstaple T	03.77	76-78	44	2	4

VASSELL Darius
Birmingham, 13 June, 1980 EYth/Eu21-11/E-22 (F)

League Club	Source	Date Signed	Seasons Played	Apps	Subs	Gls
Aston Villa	YT	04.98	98-04	107	55	35

VASSEUR Emmanuel
Calais, France, 3 September, 1976 (M)

League Club	Source	Date Signed	Seasons Played	Apps	Subs	Gls
Leyton Orient	Calais (Fr)	01.01	00	0	2	0

VAUGHAN Anthony (Tony) John
Manchester, 11 October, 1975 ESch/EYth (CD)

League Club	Source	Date Signed	Seasons Played	Apps	Subs	Gls
Ipswich T	YT	07.94	94-96	56	11	3
Manchester C	Tr	07.97	97-99	54	4	2
Cardiff C	L	09.99	99	14	0	0
Nottingham F	Tr	02.00	99-01	38	5	1
Scunthorpe U	L	03.02	01	5	0	0
Mansfield T	L	10.02	02	4	0	0
Mansfield T	Tr	08.03	03	32	0	2
Barnsley	Tr	07.04	04	25	1	4

VAUGHAN Charles (Charlie) John
Bermondsey, 23 April, 1921 Died 1989 EAmat/EB (CF)

League Club	Source	Date Signed	Seasons Played	Apps	Subs	Gls
Charlton Ath	Sutton U	01.47	46-52	227	-	91
Portsmouth	Tr	03.53	52-53	26	-	14

VAUGHAN John **Daniel (Danny)**
Liverpool, 18 February, 1972 (FB)

League Club	Source	Date Signed	Seasons Played	Apps	Subs	Gls
Crewe Alex		09.92	92	3	4	0
Wigan Ath	Tr	07.93	93	2	2	0

VAUGHAN David Owen
Abergele, 18 February, 1983 WYth/Wu21-7/W-2 (M)

League Club	Source	Date Signed	Seasons Played	Apps	Subs	Gls
Crewe Alex	YT	02.01	00-04	112	9	9

VAUGHAN Norman **Glyn**
Llanidloes, 25 August, 1921 Died 2003 (IF)

League Club	Source	Date Signed	Seasons Played	Apps	Subs	Gls
Exeter C	Oldham Ath (Am)	05.46	46-47	6	-	0

VAUGHAN Ian
Sheffield, 3 July, 1961 (CD)

League Club	Source	Date Signed	Seasons Played	Apps	Subs	Gls
Rotherham U	App	07.79	78-80	4	0	0
Stockport Co	L	12.81	81	2	0	1

VAUGHAN James Oliver
Birmingham, 14 July, 1988 EYth (F)

League Club	Source	Date Signed	Seasons Played	Apps	Subs	Gls
Everton	Sch	●	04	0	2	1

VAUGHAN John
Isleworth, 26 June, 1964 (G)

League Club	Source	Date Signed	Seasons Played	Apps	Subs	Gls
West Ham U	App	06.82				
Charlton Ath	L	03.85	84	6	0	0
Bristol Rov	L	09.85	85	6	0	0
Wrexham	L	10.85	85	4	0	0
Bristol C	L	03.86	85	2	0	0
Fulham	Tr	08.86	86	44	0	0
Bristol C	L	01.88	87	3	0	0
Cambridge U	Tr	06.88	88-92	178	0	0
Charlton Ath	Tr	08.93	93	5	1	0
Preston NE	Tr	07.94	94-95	65	1	0
Lincoln C	Tr	08.96	96-99	66	0	0
Colchester U	L	02.97	96	5	0	0
Colchester U	L	11.99	99	6	0	0
Chesterfield	L	01.00	99	3	0	0

VAUGHAN Nigel Mark
Caerleon, 20 May, 1959 WYth/Wu21-2/W-10 (M)

League Club	Source	Date Signed	Seasons Played	Apps	Subs	Gls
Newport Co	App	05.77	76-83	215	9	32
Cardiff C	Tr	09.83	83-86	144	5	41
Reading	L	02.87	86	5	0	1
Wolverhampton W	Tr	08.87	87-89	86	7	10
Hereford U	Tr	08.90	90-91	9	4	1

VAUGHAN Stephen James
Liverpool, 22 January, 1985 (FB)

League Club	Source	Date Signed	Seasons Played	Apps	Subs	Gls
Liverpool	YT	04.02				
Chester C	Tr	06.04	04	14	7	0

VAUGHAN Terence (Terry) Ronald
Ebbw Vale, 22 April, 1938 (IF)

League Club	Source	Date Signed	Seasons Played	Apps	Subs	Gls
Mansfield T	Ollerton Colliery	06.57	58	6	-	2

VAZ TE Ricardo Jorge
Lisbon, Portugal, 1 October, 1986 Portugal Yth (F)

League Club	Source	Date Signed	Seasons Played	Apps	Subs	Gls
Bolton W	YT	10.04	03-04	1	7	0

VEACOCK James (Jimmy)
Liverpool, 5 September, 1919 (CF)

League Club	Source	Date Signed	Seasons Played	Apps	Subs	Gls
Liverpool	Prescot Cables	11.36				
Southport	Marine	11.47	47	10	-	0

League Club	Source	Date Signed	Seasons Played	Career Record Apps	Subs	Gls
VEALL Raymond (Ray) Joseph						
Skegness, 16 March, 1943						(W)
Doncaster Rov	Skegness T	03.61	60-61	19	-	6
Everton	Tr	09.61	62	11	-	1
Preston NE	Tr	05.65	65	10	0	0
Huddersfield T	Tr	12.65	65-66	12	0	1
VEARNCOMBE Graham						
Cardiff, 28 March, 1934 Died 1993 W-2						(G)
Cardiff C	Jnrs	02.52	52-63	207	-	0
VEART Thomas Carl						
Whyalla, Australia, 21 May, 1970 Australia int						(M)
Sheffield U	Adelaide C (Aus)	07.94	94-95	47	19	15
Crystal Palace	Tr	03.96	95-97	41	16	6
Millwall	Tr	12.97	97	7	1	1
VEART Robert (Bobby)						
Hartlepool, 11 August, 1944 EAmat						(F)
Hartlepool	Whitby T	07.70	70-72	59	12	12
VECK Robert (Bobby)						
Titchfield, 1 April, 1920 Died 1999						(W)
Southampton	Jnrs	09.45	46-49	23	-	2
Gillingham	Tr	07.50	50	36	-	12
VEGA Ramon						
Olten, Switzerland, 14 June, 1971 SwitzerlandB-1/Switzerland 24						(CD)
Tottenham H	Cagliari (It)	01.97	96-00	53	11	7
Watford	Tr	07.01	01	23	4	1
VEITCH George Hardy						
Sunderland, 18 January, 1931 Died 2000						(WH)
Hull C	Silksworth Colliery	08.51				
Millwall	Tr	06.52	52-57	93	-	0
VEITCH Thomas (Tommy)						
Edinburgh, 16 October, 1949 Died 1987						(M)
Tranmere Rov	Heart of Midlothian	07.72	72-74	76	3	5
Halifax T	Denver (USA)	08.75	75	20	2	0
Hartlepool	Tr	08.76	76	10	0	0
VENABLES Terence (Terry) Frederick						
Dagenham, 6 January, 1943 ESch/EYth/EAmat/Eu21-4/FLge-1/E-2						(M)
Chelsea	Jnrs	08.60	59-65	202	0	26
Tottenham H	Tr	05.66	65-68	114	1	5
Queens Park Rgrs	Tr	06.69	69-74	176	1	19
Crystal Palace	Tr	09.74	74	14	0	0
VENISON Barry						
Consett, 16 August, 1964 EYth/Eu21-10/E-2						(FB)
Sunderland	App	01.82	81-85	169	4	2
Liverpool	Tr	07.86	86-91	103	7	1
Newcastle U	Tr	07.92	92-94	108	1	1
Southampton	Galatasaray (Tu)	10.95	95-96	23	1	0
VENNARD Walter						
Belfast, 17 October, 1919 Died 1993						(WH)
Stockport Co	Crusaders	09.47	47	5	-	0
VENTERS Alexander (Alec)						
Cowdenbeath, 9 June, 1913 Died 1959 SLge-5/SWar-3/S-3						(IF)
Blackburn Rov	Third Lanark	02.47	46-47	25	-	7
VENTOLA Nicola						
Bari, Italy, 24 May, 1978 Itu21						(F)
Crystal Palace (L)	Inter Milan (It)	09.04	04	0	3	1
VENTOM Eric George						
Hemsworth, 15 February, 1920 Died 1998						(FB)
Brentford		02.46	47	1	-	0
VENUS Mark						
Hartlepool, 6 April, 1967						(FB)
Hartlepool U	Jnrs	03.85	84	4	0	0
Leicester C	Tr	09.85	85-87	58	3	1
Wolverhampton W	Tr	03.88	87-96	271	16	7
Ipswich T	Tr	07.97	97-02	144	4	16
Cambridge U	Tr	08.03	03	21	0	0
VERDE Pedro Andres						
Buenos Aires, Argentina, 12 March, 1952						(F)
Sheffield U	Hercules Alicante (Sp)	08.79	79	9	1	3
VERHOENE Kenny						
Ghent, Belgium, 15 April, 1973						(CD)
Crystal Palace (L)	KRC Harelbeke (Bel)	03.01	00	0	1	0
VERITY Daniel Richard						
Bradford, 19 April, 1980						(CD)
Bradford C	YT	03.98	97	0	1	0
VERITY David (Dave) Anthony						
Halifax, 21 September, 1949						(M)
Scunthorpe U	App	09.67	66-67	3	2	0
Halifax T	Tr	09.68	69-72	64	14	5
VERITY Kevin Patrick						
Halifax, 16 March, 1940						(W)
Halifax T	Jnrs	10.58	58-59	13	-	6
VERNAZZA Paolo Andrea Pietro						
Islington, 1 November, 1979 EYth/Eu21-2						(M)
Arsenal	YT	11.97	97-00	2	3	1
Ipswich T	L	10.98	98	2	0	0
Portsmouth	L	01.00	99	7	0	0
Watford	Tr	12.00	00-03	71	25	2
Rotherham U	Tr	07.04	04	14	13	0
VERNON John Eric						
South Africa, 2 March, 1956						(W)
Stockport Co	Jnrs	04.75	74-75	4	2	0
VERNON John (Jack) Joseph						
Belfast, 26 September, 1918 Died 1981 NIRL-12/IWar-3/IR-2/I-17						(CD)
West Bromwich A	Belfast Celtic	02.47	46-51	190	-	1
VERNON Thomas Royston (Roy)						
Prestatyn, 14 April, 1937 Died 1993 Wu23-2/W-32						(F)
Blackburn Rov	Mostyn YMCA	03.55	55-59	131	-	49
Everton	Tr	02.60	59-64	176	-	101
Stoke C	Tr	03.65	64-68	85	3	22
Halifax T	L	01.70	69	4	0	0
VERNON Scott Malcolm						
Manchester, 13 December, 1983						(F)
Oldham Ath	Sch	07.02	02-04	43	32	20
Blackpool	L	09.04	04	4	0	3
VERON Juan Sebastian						
La Plata, Argentina, 9 March, 1975 Argentina 56						(M)
Manchester U	SS Lazio (It)	07.01	01-02	45	6	7
Chelsea	Tr	08.03	03	5	2	1
VERSCHAVE Matthias						
Lille, France, 24 December, 1977						(F)
Swansea C (L)	Paris St Germain (Fr)	02.01	00	12	0	3
VERTANNES Desmond (Des) Mark Stephen						
Chiswick, 25 April, 1972						(CD)
Fulham	YT	01.89	89	0	2	0
VERVEER Etienne Evert						
Surinam, 22 September, 1967						(M)
Millwall	Nancy (Fr)	12.91	91-93	46	10	7
Bradford C	L	02.95	94	9	0	1
VESEY Kieron Gerard						
Manchester, 24 November, 1965						(G)
Halifax T	Jnrs	02.83	83	2	0	0
VESSEY Anthony (Tony) William						
Derby, 28 November, 1961						(FB)
Brighton & Hove A	App	11.79	80	1	0	0
VEYSEY Kenneth (Ken) John						
Hackney, 8 June, 1967						(G)
Torquay U	Dawlish T	11.87	88-90	72	0	0
Oxford U	Tr	10.90	90-91	57	0	0
Exeter C	Reading (N/C)	10.93	93	11	1	0
Torquay U	Dorchester T	08.97	97-98	37	0	0
Plymouth Arg	Tr	08.99	99	5	1	0
VIALLI Gianluca						
Cremona, Italy, 9 July, 1964 Italy 59						(F)
Chelsea	Juventus (It)	07.96	96-98	46	12	21
VIANA Hugo Miguel Ferreira						
Barcelos, Portugal, 15 January, 1983 PorYth/PorU21-9/PorB-1/Por-12						(M)
Newcastle U	Sporting Lisbon (Por)	07.02	02-03	16	23	2
VICK Leigh						
Cardiff, 8 January, 1978						(M)
Cardiff C	YT	07.96	94-95	2	2	0
VICKERS Ashley James Ward						
Sheffield, 14 June, 1972						(CD)
Peterborough U	Heybridge Swifts	12.97	97	1	0	0
VICKERS Peter						
Kilnhurst, 6 March, 1934 ESch						(IF)
Leeds U	Jnrs	03.51	50-55	20	-	4
Northampton T	Wisbech T	02.60	59	2	-	0

League Club	Source	Date Signed	Seasons Played	Career Record Apps	Subs	Gls
VICKERS Stephen (Steve)						
Bishop Auckland, 13 October, 1967						(CD)
Tranmere Rov	Spennymoor U	09.85	85-93	310	1	11
Middlesbrough	Tr	12.93	93-01	248	11	8
Crystal Palace	L	09.01	01	6	0	0
Birmingham C	Tr	11.01	01-02	18	1	1
VICKERS Wilfred (Wilf)						
Wakefield, 3 August, 1924						(CF)
Brighton & Hove A		09.47	47	5	-	1
West Bromwich A	Tr	05.48				
Aldershot	Tr	06.49	49-51	15	-	1
VICKERY Paul						
Chelmsford, 20 May, 1953						(M)
Southend U	App	•	69	0	1	0
VICTORY Jamie Charles						
Hackney, 14 November, 1975 ESemiPro-1						(FB)
West Ham U	YT	07.94				
Bournemouth	Tr	07.95	95	5	11	1
Cheltenham T	Tr	07.96	99-04	223	3	19
VIDMAR Antony (Tony)						
Adelaide, Australia, 15 April, 1969 AuYth/Au-69						(CD)
Middlesbrough	Glasgow Rgrs	09.02	02	9	3	0
Cardiff C	Tr	07.03	03-04	68	5	2
VIDUKA Mark Anthony						
Melbourne, Australia, 9 October, 1975 AuYth/Auu23/Au-24						(F)
Leeds U	Glasgow Celtic	07.00	00-03	126	4	59
Middlesbrough	Tr	07.04	04	15	1	5
VIEIRA Magno Silva						
Brazil, 13 February, 1985						(M)
Wigan Ath	Jnrs	08.03				
Northampton T	L	01.04	03	7	3	2
VIEIRA Patrick						
Dakar, Senegal, 23 June, 1976 Fru21/Fr-79						(M)
Arsenal	AC Milan (It)	08.96	96-04	272	7	28
VIGNAL Gregory						
Montpellier, France, 19 July, 1981 FrYth/Fru21						(FB)
Liverpool	Montpellier (Fr)	09.00	00-02	7	4	0
VILJANEN Ville						
Helsinki, Finland, 2 February, 1971 Finland 1						(F)
Port Vale	Vastra Frolunda (Swe)	02.99	99-00	26	8	6
VILJOEN Colin						
Johannesburg, South Africa, 20 June, 1948 E-2						(M)
Ipswich T	(South Africa)	03.67	66-77	303	2	45
Manchester C	Tr	08.78	78-79	25	2	0
Chelsea	Tr	03.80	79-81	19	1	0
VILJOEN Nicholas (Nik) Luke						
Auckland, New Zealand, 3 December, 1976						(F)
Rotherham U	YT	06.95	95	5	3	2
VILLA Julio **Ricardo (Ricky)**						
Buenos Aires, Argentina, 18 August, 1952 Argentina int						(M)
Tottenham H	Racing Club (Arg)	07.78	78-82	124	9	18
VILLARS Anthony (Tony) Keith						
Cwmbran, 24 January, 1952 Wu23-2/W-3						(W)
Cardiff C	Cwmbran T	06.71	71-75	66	7	4
Newport Co	Tr	07.76	76	23	6	1
VILLAZAN Rafael						
Montevideo, Uruguay, 19 July, 1956 Uruguay int						(CD)
Wolverhampton W	Huelva (Sp)	05.80	80-81	20	3	0
VILLIS Matthew (Matt)						
Bridgwater, 13 April, 1984						(FB)
Plymouth Arg	Bridgwater T	09.02				
Torquay U	L	07.04	04	12	10	0
VILSTRUP Johnny Pederson						
Copenhagen, Denmark, 27 February, 1969						(M)
Luton T	Lyngby (Den)	09.95	95	6	1	0
VINALL Albert						
Birmingham, 6 March, 1922 Died 1999						(FB)
Aston Villa	Southampton (Am)	07.46	47-53	11	-	1
Walsall	Tr	08.54	54-55	78	-	0
VINALL Edward **John (Jack)**						
Witton, 16 December, 1910 Died 1997						(CF)
Sunderland	Folkestone	10.31	31-32	16	-	3
Norwich C	Tr	06.33	33-37	168	-	72
Luton T	Tr	10.37	37-38	44	-	18
Walsall	Tr	07.46	46	2	-	0

League Club	Source	Date Signed	Seasons Played	Career Record Apps	Subs	Gls
VINCENT Ashley Derek						
Oldbury, 26 May, 1985						(W)
Cheltenham T	Wolverhampton W (Sch)	07.04	04	14	12	1
VINCENT Norman **Edwin (Ned)**						
Prudhoe, 3 March, 1909 Died 1980						(FB)
Stockport Co	Spennymoor U	03.28	28-33	132	-	20
Grimsby T	Tr	06.34	34-46	144	-	2
VINCENT Jamie Roy						
Wimbledon, 18 June, 1975						(FB)
Crystal Palace	YT	07.93	95	19	6	0
Bournemouth	L	11.94	94	8	0	0
Bournemouth	Tr	08.96	96-98	102	3	5
Huddersfield T	Tr	03.99	98-00	54	5	2
Portsmouth	Tr	02.01	00-01	43	5	1
Walsall	L	10.03	03	12	0	0
Derby Co	Tr	01.04	03-04	22	0	2
VINCENT John (Johnny) Victor						
West Bromwich, 8 February, 1947 EYth						(M)
Birmingham C	App	02.64	63-70	168	3	41
Middlesbrough	Tr	03.71	70-72	37	3	7
Cardiff C	Tr	10.72	72-74	58	8	11
VINCENT Robert (Bobby)						
Leicester, 29 May, 1949						(CF)
Notts Co (Am)	Jnrs	01.66	65	1	0	0
VINCENT Robert George						
Newcastle, 23 November, 1962 ESch						(F)
Sunderland	App	11.79	80	1	1	0
Orient	Tr	05.82	81-82	8	1	0
VINDHEIM Rune						
Hoyanguer, Norway, 18 May, 1972						(M)
Burnley	SK Brann Bergen (Nor)	10.98	98	8	0	2
Hartlepool U	Tr	09.99	99	7	0	0
VINE Peter William						
Abingdon, 11 December, 1940 EYth						(IF)
Southampton	Jnrs	12.57	58	1	-	0
VINE Rowan Lewis						
Basingstoke, 21 September, 1982						(F)
Portsmouth	YT	04.01	00-01	3	10	0
Brentford	L	08.02	02	37	5	10
Colchester U	L	08.03	03	30	5	6
Luton T	L	08.04	04	43	2	9
VINEY Keith Brian						
Portsmouth, 26 October, 1957						(FB)
Portsmouth	App	10.75	75-81	160	6	3
Exeter C	Tr	08.82	82-88	270	0	8
Bristol Rov	L	09.88	88	2	1	0
VINNICOMBE Christopher (Chris)						
Exeter, 20 October, 1970 Eu21-12						(FB)
Exeter C	YT	07.89	88-89	35	4	1
Burnley	Glasgow Rgrs	06.94	94-97	90	5	3
Wycombe W	Tr	08.98	98-03	217	4	2
VINTER Michael (Mick)						
Boston, 23 May, 1954						(F)
Notts Co	Boston U	03.72	72-78	135	31	53
Wrexham	Tr	06.79	79-81	89	12	25
Oxford U	Tr	08.82	82-83	67	2	21
Mansfield T	Tr	08.84	84-85	52	2	7
Newport Co	Tr	08.86	86	30	2	7
VIOLLET Dennis Sydney						
Manchester, 20 September, 1933 Died 1999 ESch/FLge-3/E-2						(IF)
Manchester U	Jnrs	09.50	52-61	259	-	159
Stoke C	Tr	01.62	61-66	181	1	59
VIPHAM Peter						
Rawtenstall, 9 September, 1942						(G)
Accrington St	Jnrs	06.61	60	6	-	0
VIRGIN Derek Edward						
South Petherton, 10 February, 1934						(W)
Bristol C		09.55	55-60	21	-	4
VIRGO Adam John						
Brighton, 25 January, 1983 SB-1						(FB)
Brighton & Hove A	Jnrs	07.00	00-04	65	8	10
Exeter C	L	11.02	02	8	1	0
VITTY John (Jack)						
Chilton, 19 January, 1923						(FB)
Charlton Ath	Boldon Villa	11.46	48	2	-	0
Brighton & Hove A	Tr	10.49	49-51	47	-	1
Workington	Tr	07.52	52-56	196	-	3

League Club	Source	Date Signed	Seasons Played	Apps	Subs	Gls
VITTY Ronald (Ron)						
Sedgefield, 18 April, 1927						(FB)
Charlton Ath	Boldon Villa	09.47				
Hartlepools U	Tr	08.49	49	7	-	0
VIVAS Nelson David						
San Nicolas, Argentina, 18 October, 1969 Argentina 34						(FB)
Arsenal	Lugano (Swi)	08.98	98-00	14	26	0
VIVEASH Adrian Lee						
Swindon, 30 September, 1969						(CD)
Swindon T	YT	07.88	90-94	51	3	2
Reading	L	01.93	92	5	0	0
Reading	L	01.95	94	6	0	0
Barnsley	L	08.95	95	2	0	1
Walsall	Tr	10.95	95-99	200	2	13
Reading	Tr	07.00	00-02	62	1	3
Oxford U	L	09.02	02	11	0	0
Swindon T	Tr	07.03	03	14	1	0
Kidderminster Hrs	L	03.04	03	7	0	0
Kidderminster Hrs	L	08.04	04	7	0	0
VIZARD Colin John						
Newton-le-Willows, 18 June, 1933						(W)
Everton	Jnrs	09.51				
Rochdale	Tr	05.57	57-58	41	-	7
VLACHOS Michalis						
Athens, Greece, 20 September, 1967 Greece 10						(M)
Portsmouth	AEK Athens (Gre)	01.98	97-99	55	2	0
Walsall	Tr	02.00	99	11	0	1
VOLMER Joost Gerard Bernard						
Enschede, Holland, 7 March, 1974						(CD)
West Bromwich A	AZ67 Alkmaar (Holl)	08.03	03	10	5	0
VOLZ Moritz						
Siegen, Germany, 21 January, 1983 GeYth/Geu21-10						(FB)
Arsenal	Schalke 04 (Ger)	01.00				
Wimbledon	L	02.03	02	10	0	1
Fulham	Tr	08.03	03-04	63	1	0
VONK Michel Christian						
Alkmaar, Holland, 28 October, 1968						(CD)
Manchester C	SVV Dordrecht (Holl)	03.92	91-94	97	4	4
Oldham Ath	L	11.95	95	5	0	1
Sheffield U	Tr	12.95	95-97	37	0	2
VOWDEN Colin Dean						
Newmarket, 13 September, 1971						(CD)
Cambridge U	Cambridge C	05.95	95-96	27	3	0
VOWDEN Geoffrey (Geoff) Alan						
Barnsley, 27 April, 1941						(F)
Nottingham F	Jersey DM	01.60	59-64	90	-	40
Birmingham C	Tr	10.64	64-70	213	8	79
Aston Villa	Tr	03.71	70-73	93	4	22

WADDELL Robert (Bobby)
Kirkcaldy, 5 September, 1939 (CF)

League Club	Source	Date Signed	Seasons Played	Apps	Subs	Gls
Blackpool	Dundee	03.65	64-66	28	0	5
Bradford PA	Tr	11.66	66	20	0	3

WADDELL William (Willie)
Denny, 16 April, 1950 SSch (F)

League Club	Source	Date Signed	Seasons Played	Apps	Subs	Gls
Leeds U	Jnrs	04.67				
Barnsley	Kilmarnock	05.71	71	17	1	4
Hartlepool	Tr	03.72	71-73	43	5	9
Workington	L	02.73	72	1	2	0

WADDINGTON Anthony (Tony)
Manchester, 9 November, 1924 Died 1994 (WH)

League Club	Source	Date Signed	Seasons Played	Apps	Subs	Gls
Crewe Alex	Manchester U (Am)	01.46	46-52	178	-	8

WADDINGTON John
Darwen, 16 February, 1952 (CD)

League Club	Source	Date Signed	Seasons Played	Apps	Subs	Gls
Liverpool	Darwen	05.70				
Blackburn Rov	Tr	08.73	73-76	99	2	14
Blackburn Rov	Vancouver (Can)	08.77	77-78	40	7	4
Bury	Tr	08.79	79-80	46	1	0

WADDINGTON David **Paul**
Oldbury, 14 February, 1961 ESch (M)

League Club	Source	Date Signed	Seasons Played	Apps	Subs	Gls
Walsall	App	11.78	78-81	14	5	0

WADDINGTON Steven (Steve)
Crewe, 5 February, 1956 (M)

League Club	Source	Date Signed	Seasons Played	Apps	Subs	Gls
Stoke C	App	06.73	76-78	49	3	5
Walsall	Tr	09.78	78-81	122	8	13
Port Vale	Tr	08.82	82	0	1	0
Chesterfield	Tr	07.83	83	14	4	1

WADDLE Alan Robert
Wallsend, 9 June, 1954 (F)

League Club	Source	Date Signed	Seasons Played	Apps	Subs	Gls
Halifax T	Wallsend BC	11.71	71-72	33	6	4
Liverpool	Tr	06.73	73-74	11	5	1
Leicester C	Tr	09.77	77	11	0	1
Swansea C	Tr	05.78	78-80	83	7	34
Newport Co	Tr	12.80	80-81	19	8	8
Mansfield T	Gloucester C	08.82	82	14	0	4
Hartlepool U	(Hong Kong)	08.83	83	12	0	2
Peterborough U	Tr	10.83	83-84	35	1	12
Hartlepool U	Tr	01.85	84	4	0	0
Swansea C	Tr	03.85	84-85	39	1	10

WADDLE Christopher (Chris) Roland
Felling, 14 December, 1960 Eu21-1/E-62 (W)

League Club	Source	Date Signed	Seasons Played	Apps	Subs	Gls
Newcastle U	Tow Law T	07.80	80-84	169	1	46
Tottenham H	Tr	07.85	85-88	137	1	33
Sheffield Wed	Marseille (Fr)	07.92	92-95	94	15	10
Bradford C	Falkirk	10.96	96	25	0	5
Sunderland	Tr	03.97	96	7	0	1
Burnley	Tr	07.97	97	26	5	1
Torquay U	Tr	09.98	98	7	0	0

WADDOCK Gary Patrick
Kingsbury, 17 March, 1962 IRu23-1/IRu21-1/IRB/IR-21 (M)

League Club	Source	Date Signed	Seasons Played	Apps	Subs	Gls
Queens Park Rgrs	App	07.79	79-86	191	12	8
Millwall	RSC Charleroi (Bel)	08.89	89-90	51	7	2
Queens Park Rgrs	Tr	12.91				
Swindon T	L	03.92	91	5	1	0
Bristol Rov	Tr	11.92	92-94	71	0	1
Luton T	Tr	09.94	94-97	146	7	3

WADE Allen
Scunthorpe, 19 July, 1926 (CD)

League Club	Source	Date Signed	Seasons Played	Apps	Subs	Gls
Notts Co		07.52	52-55	9	-	0

WADE Bryan Alexander
Bath, 25 June, 1963 (F)

League Club	Source	Date Signed	Seasons Played	Apps	Subs	Gls
Swindon T	Trowbridge T	05.85	85-87	48	12	18
Swansea C	Tr	08.88	88-89	19	17	5
Brighton & Hove A	Tr	09.90	90-91	12	6	9

WADE Donald (Don) Geoffrey
Tottenham, 5 June, 1926 (IF)

League Club	Source	Date Signed	Seasons Played	Apps	Subs	Gls
West Ham U	Edgware T	12.47	47-49	36	-	5

WADE Samuel **Joseph (Joe)**
Shoreditch, 7 July, 1921 FLge-1 (FB)

League Club	Source	Date Signed	Seasons Played	Apps	Subs	Gls
Arsenal	Hoxton BC	09.45	46-54	86	-	0

WADE Psalms **Meshach**
Bermuda, 23 January, 1973 (M)

League Club	Source	Date Signed	Seasons Played	Apps	Subs	Gls
Hereford U	Pembroke (Ber)	08.91	91-92	13	4	0

WADE Shaun Peter
Stoke-on-Trent, 22 September, 1969 (F)

League Club	Source	Date Signed	Seasons Played	Apps	Subs	Gls
Stoke C	Newcastle T	10.94	94	0	1	0

WADSWORTH Albert William
Heywood, 22 March, 1925 Died 1982 (IF)

League Club	Source	Date Signed	Seasons Played	Apps	Subs	Gls
Oldham Ath	Stalybridge Celtic	08.49	49-51	33	-	8

WADSWORTH Ian Jack
Huddersfield, 24 September, 1966 (F)

League Club	Source	Date Signed	Seasons Played	Apps	Subs	Gls
Huddersfield T	App	09.84	84	0	1	0
Doncaster Rov	Tr	02.86	85	1	1	0

WADSWORTH Michael (Mick)
Barnsley, 3 November, 1950 (W)

League Club	Source	Date Signed	Seasons Played	Apps	Subs	Gls
Scunthorpe U	Gainsborough Trinity	08.76	76	19	9	3

WAGSTAFF Anthony (Tony)
Wombwell, 19 February, 1944 (M)

League Club	Source	Date Signed	Seasons Played	Apps	Subs	Gls
Sheffield U	App	03.61	60-68	138	3	19
Reading	Tr	07.69	69-73	166	7	6

WAGSTAFF Barry
Wombwell, 28 November, 1945 (M)

League Club	Source	Date Signed	Seasons Played	Apps	Subs	Gls
Sheffield U	App	06.63	64-68	107	10	5
Reading	Tr	07.69	69-74	197	6	23
Rotherham U	Tr	03.75	74-76	42	3	1

WAGSTAFF Kenneth (Ken)
Langwith, 24 November, 1942 (F)

League Club	Source	Date Signed	Seasons Played	Apps	Subs	Gls
Mansfield T	Woodland Imperial	05.60	60-64	181	-	93
Hull C	Tr	11.64	64-75	374	4	173

WAGSTAFFE David (Dave)
Manchester, 5 April, 1943 EYth/FLge-1 (W)

League Club	Source	Date Signed	Seasons Played	Apps	Subs	Gls
Manchester C	Jnrs	05.60	60-64	144	-	8
Wolverhampton W	Tr	12.64	64-75	324	0	27
Blackburn Rov	Tr	01.76	75-77	72	3	7
Blackpool	Tr	08.78	78	17	2	1
Blackburn Rov	Tr	03.79	78	2	0	0

WAIN Leslie (Les) John
Crewe, 2 August, 1954 ESch (M)

League Club	Source	Date Signed	Seasons Played	Apps	Subs	Gls
Crewe Alex	App	08.72	70-74	48	5	1
Southport	Tr	07.75	75	3	2	0

WAINE Andrew (Andy) Paul
Manchester, 24 February, 1983 (M)

League Club	Source	Date Signed	Seasons Played	Apps	Subs	Gls
Burnley	Sch	07.02	02	0	2	0

WAINMAN William **Henry (Harry)**
Hull, 22 March, 1947 EYth (G)

League Club	Source	Date Signed	Seasons Played	Apps	Subs	Gls
Grimsby T	Hull C (Am)	07.64	64-77	420	0	0
Rochdale	L	10.72	72	9	0	0

WAINWRIGHT Edward (Eddie) Francis
Southport, 22 June, 1924 FLge-1 (IF)

League Club	Source	Date Signed	Seasons Played	Apps	Subs	Gls
Everton	High Park	03.44	46-55	207	-	68
Rochdale	Tr	06.56	56-58	100	-	27

WAINWRIGHT Lewis
Kirton-in-Lindsey, 15 December, 1930 (FB)

League Club	Source	Date Signed	Seasons Played	Apps	Subs	Gls
Scunthorpe U	Brigg T	05.51	55	2	-	0

WAINWRIGHT Neil
Warrington, 4 November, 1977 (W)

League Club	Source	Date Signed	Seasons Played	Apps	Subs	Gls
Wrexham	YT	07.96	97	7	4	3
Sunderland	Tr	07.98	98	0	2	0
Darlington	L	02.00	99	16	1	4
Halifax T	L	10.00	00	13	0	0
Darlington	Tr	08.01	01-04	109	32	16

WAINWRIGHT Robin Keith
Luton, 9 March, 1951 (M)

League Club	Source	Date Signed	Seasons Played	Apps	Subs	Gls
Luton T	App	12.68	71	15	1	3
Cambridge U	L	03.71	70	1	0	0
Millwall	Tr	11.72	73	2	2	0
Northampton T	Tr	02.74	73-74	23	9	5

WAITE Thomas John **Aldwyn**
Pontllanfraith, 3 August, 1928 (WH)

League Club	Source	Date Signed	Seasons Played	Apps	Subs	Gls
Newport Co		12.51	51-53	56	-	1

WAITE John Aidan
Grimsby, 16 January, 1942 EYth (W)

League Club	Source	Date Signed	Seasons Played	Apps	Subs	Gls
Grimsby T	Jnrs	11.60	61-62	8	-	1

League Club	Source	Date Signed	Seasons Played	Career Record Apps	Subs	Gls
WAITE William (Bill) John						
Newport, 29 November, 1917 Died 1980						(CF)
Oldham Ath	Newport Co (Am)	11.42	46	4	-	4
WAITERS Anthony (Tony) Keith						
Southport, 1 February, 1937 EAmat/FLge-5/E-5						(G)
Blackpool	Bishop Auckland	10.59	59-66	257	0	0
Burnley	Tr	07.70	70-71	38	0	0
WAITES George Edward						
Stepney, 12 March, 1938 Died 2000						(W)
Leyton Orient	Harwich & Parkeston	12.58	58-60	43	-	9
Norwich C	Tr	01.61	60-61	36	-	11
Leyton Orient	Tr	07.62	62	2	-	0
Brighton & Hove A	Tr	12.62	62-63	23	-	1
WAITES Paul						
Hull, 24 January, 1971						(M)
Hull C	YT	07.89	89-90	11	0	0
WAITT Michael (Mick) Hugh						
Hexham, 25 June, 1960						(F)
Notts Co	Keyworth U	12.84	84-86	71	11	27
Lincoln C	Tr	06.87	89	7	1	1
WAKE Brian Christopher						
Stockton, 13 August, 1982						(F)
Carlisle U	Tow Law T	05.02	02-03	12	31	9
WAKE Geoffrey (Geoff) Graham						
Bristol, 25 February, 1954						(G)
Torquay U	Barnstaple T	12.77	77	9	0	0
WAKEFIELD Albert Joseph						
Pudsey, 19 November, 1921						(CF)
Leeds U	Stanningley Works	01.42	47-48	49	-	24
Southend U	Tr	08.49	49-52	109	-	58
WAKEFIELD David (Dave)						
South Shields, 15 January, 1965						(M)
Darlington	App	01.83	82-83	7	15	0
Torquay U	Tr	03.84	83	10	0	1
WAKEHAM Peter Francis						
Kingsbridge, 14 March, 1936						(G)
Torquay U	Kingsbridge	10.53	53-58	58	-	0
Sunderland	Tr	09.58	58-61	134	-	0
Charlton Ath	Tr	07.62	62-64	55	-	0
Lincoln C	Tr	05.65	65	44	0	0
WAKEMAN Alan						
Walsall, 20 November, 1920 Died 2002 ESch						(G)
Aston Villa	Bloxwich Strollers	12.38	38-49	12	-	0
Doncaster Rov	Tr	07.50	50-51	5	-	0
Shrewsbury T	Bloxwich Strollers	02.53	52-53	6	-	0
WAKENSHAW Robert (Robbie) Andrew						
Ponteland, 22 December, 1965 EYth						(F)
Everton	App	12.83	83-84	2	1	1
Carlisle U	Tr	09.85	85	6	2	2
Doncaster Rov	L	03.86	85	8	0	3
Rochdale	Tr	09.86	86	28	1	5
Crewe Alex	Tr	06.87	87-88	18	4	1
WALDEN Harold (Harry) Bertram						
Walgrave, 22 December, 1940						(W)
Luton T	Kettering T	01.61	60-63	96	-	11
Northampton T	Tr	06.64	64-66	76	0	3
WALDEN Richard Frank						
Hereford, 4 May, 1948						(FB)
Aldershot	App	05.65	64-75	400	4	16
Sheffield Wed	Tr	01.76	75-77	100	0	1
Newport Co	Tr	08.78	78-81	151	0	2
WALDOCK Desmond (Des) Haigh						
Northampton, 4 December, 1961						(CD)
Northampton T	App	11.79	78-80	52	2	4
WALDOCK Ronald (Ronnie)						
Heanor, 6 December, 1932						(IF)
Coventry C	Loscoe YC	02.50	52-53	27	-	9
Sheffield U	Tr	05.54	54-56	52	-	10
Scunthorpe U	Tr	02.57	56-59	97	-	45
Plymouth Arg	Tr	09.59	59	18	-	6
Middlesbrough	Tr	01.60	59-61	34	-	7
Gillingham	Tr	10.61	61-63	66	-	14
WALDRON Alan						
Royton, 6 September, 1951						(M)
Bolton W	App	09.69	70-77	127	14	6
Blackpool	Tr	12.77	77-78	22	1	1
Bury	Tr	06.79	79-80	34	0	0
York C	Tr	09.81	81	3	0	1
WALDRON Colin						
Bristol, 22 June, 1948						(CD)
Bury	App	05.66	66	20	0	0
Chelsea	Tr	07.67	67	9	0	0
Burnley	Tr	10.67	67-75	308	0	16
Manchester U	Tr	05.76	76	3	0	0
Sunderland	Tr	02.77	76-77	20	0	1
Rochdale	Atlanta (USA)	10.79	79	19	0	1
WALDRON Ernest (Ernie)						
Birmingham, 3 June, 1913 Died 1994						(IF)
Crystal Palace	Bromsgrove Rov	11.34	34-46	80	-	30
WALDRON Malcolm						
Emsworth, 6 September, 1956 EB						(CD)
Southampton	App	09.74	74-82	177	1	10
Burnley	Tr	09.83	83	16	0	0
Portsmouth	Tr	03.84	83-84	23	0	1
WALES Anthony (Tony)						
Dunscroft, 12 May, 1943 EYth						(FB)
Doncaster Rov	Jnrs	05.60	61-62	25	-	0
WALES Gary						
East Calder, 4 January, 1979 Su21-1						(F)
Walsall (L)	Heart of Midlothian	01.04	03	5	2	1
Gillingham	Heart of Midlothian	03.04	03	3	3	1
WALFORD Stephen (Steve) James						
Highgate, 5 January, 1958 EYth						(CD)
Tottenham H	App	04.75	75	1	1	0
Arsenal	Tr	08.77	77-80	64	13	3
Norwich C	Tr	03.81	80-82	93	0	2
West Ham U	Tr	08.83	83-86	114	1	2
Huddersfield T	L	10.87	87	12	0	0
Gillingham	L	12.88	88	4	0	0
West Bromwich A	L	03.89	88	3	1	0
WALKDEN Francis (Frank)						
Aberdeen, 21 June, 1921 Died 1992						(W)
Rochdale	Bolton W (Am)	11.46	46	1	-	0
WALKER Alan						
Mossley, 17 December, 1959						(CD)
Stockport Co	Mossley	08.78				
Lincoln C	Telford U	10.83	83-84	74	1	4
Millwall	Tr	07.85	85-87	92	0	8
Gillingham	Tr	03.88	87-91	150	1	7
Plymouth Arg	Tr	09.92	92	2	0	1
Mansfield T	Tr	09.92	92	22	0	1
Barnet	Tr	08.93	93-94	59	0	2
WALKER Andrew (Andy) Francis						
Glasgow, 6 April, 1965 Su21-1/S-3						(F)
Newcastle U (L)	Glasgow Celtic	09.91	91	2	0	0
Bolton W	Glasgow Celtic	01.92	91-93	61	6	44
Sheffield U	Glasgow Celtic	02.96	95-97	32	20	20
Carlisle U	Ayr U	08.99	99	3	0	0
WALKER Andrew (Andy) William						
Bexleyheath, 30 September, 1981						(G)
Colchester U	YT	•	98-99	3	0	0
Exeter C	St Albans C	08.01	01	1	0	0
WALKER Arnold						
Haltwhistle, 23 December, 1932						(WH)
Grimsby T	Appleby Frodingham	05.50	50-57	65	-	0
Walsall	Tr	05.58	58-59	7	-	0
WALKER Bruce Alan						
Hungerford, 27 August, 1946						(W)
Swindon T	Jnrs	12.63	65-67	26	3	5
Bradford C	Tr	03.68	67-68	27	1	1
Exeter C	Tr	06.69	69	21	2	2
WALKER Clive						
Oxford, 26 May, 1957 ESch						(W)
Chelsea	App	04.75	76-83	168	30	60
Sunderland	Tr	07.84	84-85	48	2	10
Queens Park Rgrs	Tr	12.85	85-86	16	4	1
Fulham	Tr	10.87	87-89	102	7	29
Brighton & Hove A	Tr	08.90	90-92	104	2	8
WALKER David Clive Allan						
Watford, 24 October, 1945 ESch						(FB)
Leicester C	App	10.62	63-65	17	0	0
Northampton T	Tr	10.66	66-68	72	0	1
Mansfield T	Tr	07.69	69-74	223	6	8

WALKER Colin
Stapleford, 7 July, 1929 (WH)

League Club	Source	Date Signed	Seasons Played	Apps	Subs	Gls
Derby Co	Jnrs	10.46	48-54	25	-	0

WALKER Colin
Rotherham, 1 May, 1958 New Zealand int (F)

League Club	Source	Date Signed	Seasons Played	Apps	Subs	Gls
Barnsley	Gisborne C (NZ)	11.80	80-82	21	3	12
Doncaster Rov	L	02.83	82	12	0	5
Doncaster Rov	Gisborne C (NZ)	11.85	85	3	2	0
Cambridge U	Tr	01.86	85	3	0	1
Sheffield Wed	Harworth CW	08.86	86	2	0	0
Darlington	L	12.86	86	6	1	0
Torquay U	L	10.87	87	3	0	0

WALKER Cyril John
Newport Pagnell, 24 February, 1914 Died 2002 (IF)

League Club	Source	Date Signed	Seasons Played	Apps	Subs	Gls
Watford		11.35				
Gillingham		06.37	37	10	-	3
Sheffield Wed	Tr	10.37	37	4	-	0
Norwich C	Shorts Sports	08.46	46	3	-	2

WALKER David (Dave)
Colne, 15 October, 1941 (CD)

League Club	Source	Date Signed	Seasons Played	Apps	Subs	Gls
Burnley	Jnrs	05.59	60-64	38	-	1
Southampton	Tr	05.65	65-73	189	8	1

WALKER Dean
Newcastle, 18 May, 1962 (CD)

League Club	Source	Date Signed	Seasons Played	Apps	Subs	Gls
Burnley	App	05.80				
Scunthorpe U	Tr	03.82	81	1	0	0

WALKER Dennis Allen
Northwich, 26 October, 1944 Died 2003 ESch (M)

League Club	Source	Date Signed	Seasons Played	Apps	Subs	Gls
Manchester U	App	11.61	62	1	-	0
York C	Tr	04.64	64-67	149	5	19
Cambridge U	Tr	07.68	70-72	48	8	4

WALKER Dennis George
Spennymoor, 5 July, 1948 (F)

League Club	Source	Date Signed	Seasons Played	Apps	Subs	Gls
West Ham U	App	05.66				
Luton T	Tr	08.67	67	0	1	0

WALKER Derek William
Perth, 24 November, 1964 (F)

League Club	Source	Date Signed	Seasons Played	Apps	Subs	Gls
Chesterfield	Falkirk	08.86	86-87	19	4	3

WALKER Desmond (Des) Sinclair
Hackney, 26 November, 1965 Eu21-7/E-59 (CD)

League Club	Source	Date Signed	Seasons Played	Apps	Subs	Gls
Nottingham F	App	12.83	83-91	259	5	1
Sheffield Wed	Sampdoria (It)	07.93	93-00	307	0	0
Nottingham F	Burton A	07.02	02-04	52	5	0

WALKER Donald (Don) Hunter
Edinburgh, 10 September, 1935 (WH)

League Club	Source	Date Signed	Seasons Played	Apps	Subs	Gls
Leicester C	Tranent Jnrs	11.55	57-58	32	-	1
Middlesbrough	Tr	10.59	59-61	23	-	1
Grimsby T	Tr	09.63	63	15	-	1

WALKER (Dr) **Frederick** (Fred)
Stirling, 7 April, 1929 Died 1966 (FB)

League Club	Source	Date Signed	Seasons Played	Apps	Subs	Gls
Southport	Queen's Park	10.51	51-52	5	-	0

WALKER Gary
Manchester, 11 October, 1963 (G)

League Club	Source	Date Signed	Seasons Played	Apps	Subs	Gls
Stockport Co	Oldham T	09.85	85-86	29	0	0

WALKER Robert **Geoffrey (Geoff)**
Bradford, 29 September, 1926 Died 1997 (W)

League Club	Source	Date Signed	Seasons Played	Apps	Subs	Gls
Bradford PA	Jnrs	12.43				
Middlesbrough	Tr	06.46	46-54	240	-	50
Doncaster Rov	Tr	12.54	54-56	77	-	10
Bradford C	Tr	06.57	57	2	-	0

WALKER George William
Sunderland, 30 May, 1934 (IF)

League Club	Source	Date Signed	Seasons Played	Apps	Subs	Gls
Bristol C	Chippenham T	05.56	56-58	15	-	5
Carlisle U	Tr	03.59	58-62	164	-	53

WALKER Glenn Philip
Warrington, 15 March, 1967 (M)

League Club	Source	Date Signed	Seasons Played	Apps	Subs	Gls
Crewe Alex	Burnley (App)	03.85	84	1	1	0

WALKER John **Gordon**
Sheffield, 26 November, 1949 (F)

League Club	Source	Date Signed	Seasons Played	Apps	Subs	Gls
Grimsby T	Stocksbridge Works	11.68	68-69	25	2	5

WALKER Greig George
Dundee, 11 October, 1963 (F)

League Club	Source	Date Signed	Seasons Played	Apps	Subs	Gls
Chesterfield	Broughty Ath	10.83	83	6	0	0

WALKER George **Henry (Harry)**
Aysgarth, 20 May, 1916 Died 1976 (G)

League Club	Source	Date Signed	Seasons Played	Apps	Subs	Gls
Darlington		12.34	35-37	50	-	0
Portsmouth	Tr	03.38	37-46	49	-	0
Nottingham F	Tr	04.47	46-54	293	-	0

WALKER Ian Michael
Watford, 31 October, 1971 EYth/Eu21-9/EB-1/E-4 (G)

League Club	Source	Date Signed	Seasons Played	Apps	Subs	Gls
Tottenham H	YT	12.89	90-00	257	2	0
Oxford U	L	08.90	90	2	0	0
Leicester C	Tr	07.01	01-04	140	0	0

WALKER James (Jimmy)
Belfast, 29 March, 1932 IrLge-3/NI-1 (CF)

League Club	Source	Date Signed	Seasons Played	Apps	Subs	Gls
Doncaster Rov	Linfield	05.54	54-56	47	-	19

WALKER James (Jimmy)
Aberdeen, 25 August, 1933 (FB)

League Club	Source	Date Signed	Seasons Played	Apps	Subs	Gls
Bradford PA	Aberdeen	05.59	59-63	144	-	2

WALKER James (Jimmy) Barry
Sutton-in-Ashfield, 9 July, 1973 (G)

League Club	Source	Date Signed	Seasons Played	Apps	Subs	Gls
Notts Co	YT	07.91				
Walsall	Tr	08.93	93-03	401	2	0
West Ham U	Tr	07.04	04	10	0	0

WALKER James (Jim) Frederick
Sheffield, 1 July, 1931 (FB)

League Club	Source	Date Signed	Seasons Played	Apps	Subs	Gls
Sheffield U	Jnrs	11.48	49-53	4	-	0
Huddersfield T	Tr	08.55				
Peterborough U	Tr	(N/L)	60-64	125	-	0

WALKER James (Jim) McIntyre
Northwich, 10 June, 1947 (FB)

League Club	Source	Date Signed	Seasons Played	Apps	Subs	Gls
Derby Co	Northwich Vic	02.68	67-73	35	7	3
Hartlepool	L	03.70	69	10	0	0
Brighton & Hove A	Tr	09.74	74-75	24	4	4
Peterborough U	Tr	10.75	75-76	20	11	1
Chester	Tr	11.76	76-80	171	1	4

WALKER John
Leigh-on-Sea, 10 December, 1948 (CD)

League Club	Source	Date Signed	Seasons Played	Apps	Subs	Gls
Southend U	App	12.76	77-82	38	13	0

WALKER John (Johnny)
Glasgow, 12 December, 1973 SYth (M)

League Club	Source	Date Signed	Seasons Played	Apps	Subs	Gls
Grimsby T	Clydebank	09.95	95-96	1	2	1
Mansfield T	Tr	09.96	96-98	51	23	4

WALKER John (Johnny) Young Hilley
Glasgow, 17 December, 1928 (IF)

League Club	Source	Date Signed	Seasons Played	Apps	Subs	Gls
Wolverhampton W	Campsie Black Watch	07.47	49-51	37	-	21
Southampton	Tr	10.52	52-57	172	-	48
Reading	Tr	12.57	57-64	287	-	24

WALKER Joshua (Josh) George
Solihull, 20 December, 1981 (M)

League Club	Source	Date Signed	Seasons Played	Apps	Subs	Gls
Manchester U	YT	09.99				
Shrewsbury T	Tr	07.01	01	0	3	0

WALKER Justin Matthew
Nottingham, 6 September, 1975 ESch/EYth (M)

League Club	Source	Date Signed	Seasons Played	Apps	Subs	Gls
Nottingham F	Jnrs	09.92				
Scunthorpe U	Tr	03.97	96-99	126	6	2
Lincoln C	Tr	07.00	00-01	68	8	4
Exeter C	Tr	08.02	02	35	4	5
Cambridge U	Tr	06.03	03-04	59	0	2
York C	L	01.04	03	7	2	0

WALKER Keith Cameron
Edinburgh, 17 April, 1966 (CD)

League Club	Source	Date Signed	Seasons Played	Apps	Subs	Gls
Swansea C	St Mirren	11.89	89-98	262	8	9

WALKER Lee
Pontypool, 27 June, 1976 (M)

League Club	Source	Date Signed	Seasons Played	Apps	Subs	Gls
Cardiff C	YT	07.94	93	1	0	0

WALKER Leonard (Len)
Darlington, 4 March, 1944 (CD)

League Club	Source	Date Signed	Seasons Played	Apps	Subs	Gls
Newcastle U	Spennymoor U	05.63	63	1	-	0
Aldershot	Tr	07.64	64-75	439	10	23
Darlington	Tr	08.76	76-77	10	0	0

WALKER Michael (Mick)
Mexborough, 8 March, 1952 (FB)

League Club	Source	Date Signed	Seasons Played	Apps	Subs	Gls
Bradford PA	App	03.70	68-69	2	2	0

WALKER Michael (Mike) John
Harrogate, 10 April, 1945 (M)

League Club	Source	Date Signed	Seasons Played	Apps	Subs	Gls
Bradford C	Bourne T	10.64	64-65	19	1	1
Mansfield T	Los Angeles (USA)	03.69	68	2	0	0
Stockport Co	Altrincham	08.70	70	1	1	0
Chesterfield	Tr	09.70	70	1	0	0

League Club	Source	Date Signed	Seasons Played	Career Record Apps	Subs	Gls
WALKER Michael (Mike) Stewart Gordon						
Colwyn Bay, 28 November, 1945 Wu23-4						(G)
Reading	Jnrs	01.63				
Shrewsbury T	Tr	06.64	64-65	7	0	0
York C	Tr	06.66	66-68	60	0	0
Watford	Tr	09.68	68-72	137	0	0
Charlton Ath	L	03.73	72	1	0	0
Colchester U	Tr	06.73	73-82	451	0	0
WALKER Joseph **Nicol (Nicky)**						
Aberdeen, 29 September, 1962 SYth/S-2						(G)
Leicester C	Elgin C	08.80	81	6	0	0
Burnley (L)	Heart of Midlothian	02.92	91	6	0	0
WALKER Nigel Stephen						
Gateshead, 7 April, 1959						(M)
Newcastle U	Whickham	07.77	77-81	65	5	3
Crewe Alex	San Diego (USA)	01.83	82	20	0	5
Sunderland	Tr	07.83	83	0	1	0
Blackpool	L	03.84	83	8	2	3
Chester C	Tr	07.84	84	41	0	9
Hartlepool U	Tr	07.85	85-86	77	5	8
WALKER Patrick (Pat) Joseph						
Carlow, 20 December, 1959 IRu21-2						(W)
Gillingham	App	10.77	77-80	34	17	3
WALKER Paul						
Wood Green, 17 December, 1960 ESch						(M)
Brentford	App	01.78	76-82	53	18	5
WALKER Paul Ernest						
Hetton-le-Hole, 26 February, 1958 ESemiPro						(M)
Hull C	Sunderland (App)	05.76				
Doncaster Rov	L	12.76	76	4	0	0
WALKER Paul Graham						
Bradford, 3 April, 1949						(M)
Wolverhampton W	Bradford PA (Am)	10.66	68-71	17	9	0
Watford	L	12.71	71	2	1	0
Swindon T	L	03.73	72	2	3	0
Peterborough U	Tr	07.73	73-74	75	3	3
Barnsley	Tr	07.75	75	11	2	0
Huddersfield T	Ottawa Tigers (Can)	11.76	76	1	0	0
WALKER Peter Martin						
Watford, 31 March, 1933						(W)
Watford	Bushey U	07.54	54-61	172	-	37
WALKER Philip (Phil)						
Sheffield, 27 November, 1956						(G)
Cambridge U	Sheffield U (App)	02.75	74-75	19	0	0
WALKER Philip (Phil) Albert						
Kirkby-in-Ashfield, 27 January, 1957						(F)
Chesterfield	ONRYC Mansfield	12.77	77-82	151	15	38
Rotherham U	Tr	12.82	82-83	20	5	3
Cardiff C	L	09.83	83	2	0	0
Chesterfield	Tr	10.84	84-85	30	8	9
Scarborough	Tr	08.86	87	0	1	0
WALKER Philip (Phil) Leonardus						
Fulham, 24 August, 1954						(M)
Millwall	Epsom & Ewell	10.75	75-78	143	3	17
Charlton Ath	Tr	07.79	79-82	80	9	15
Gillingham	L	11.82	82	1	1	0
WALKER Raymond (Ray)						
North Shields, 28 September, 1963 EYth						(M)
Aston Villa	App	09.81	82-85	15	8	0
Port Vale	L	09.84	84	15	0	1
Port Vale	Tr	08.86	86-96	322	29	33
Cambridge U	L	09.94	94	5	0	0
WALKER Edward **Richard (Dick)** Walter						
Hackney, 22 July, 1913 Died 1988						(CD)
West Ham U	Park Royal	05.34	34-52	292	-	2
WALKER Richard Martin						
Birmingham, 8 November, 1977						(F)
Aston Villa	YT	12.95	97-99	2	4	2
Cambridge U	L	12.98	98	7	14	3
Blackpool	L	02.01	00	6	12	3
Wycombe W	L	09.01	01	10	2	3
Blackpool	Tr	12.01	01-03	38	24	12
Northampton T	L	10.03	03	11	1	4
Oxford U	Tr	03.04	03	3	1	0
Bristol Rov	Tr	08.04	04	20	7	10
WALKER Richard Neil						
Derby, 9 November, 1971						(CD)
Notts Co	YT	07.90	92-96	63	4	4
Mansfield T	L	03.95	94	4	0	0
Cheltenham T	Hereford U	10.98	99-02	67	3	1
WALKER Richard (Ricky) Patrick						
Northampton, 4 April, 1959						(FB)
Coventry C	App	03.77				
Northampton T	Tr	08.78	78-80	50	3	0
WALKER Richard Stuart						
Stafford, 17 September, 1980						(CD)
Crewe Alex	YT	07.99	00-04	65	17	5
WALKER Robert (Bob)						
Wallsend, 23 July, 1942						(CD)
Brighton & Hove A	Gateshead	05.62	62	12	-	1
Bournemouth	Margate	08.65	65-66	10	0	0
Colchester U	Tr	07.67	67	13	4	0
WALKER Robert (Bob) Malcolm						
Glasgow, 15 January, 1935						(W)
Middlesbrough	Redcar	08.52				
Barrow	Tr	08.55	55	10	-	1
WALKER Robert (Rob) Stephen						
Bolton, 20 September, 1985						(CD)
Oldham Ath	Sch	●	03	1	0	0
WALKER Robert Wilson						
Aberdeen, 21 May, 1922 Died 1991						(WH)
Bournemouth	Aberdeen	11.46	46	2	-	2
Wrexham	Tr	06.47	47	2	-	0
WALKER Roger						
Shrewsbury, 17 February, 1944						(W)
Shrewsbury T (Am)	Jnrs	05.60	60	1	-	0
WALKER Roger Anthony						
Bolton, 15 November, 1966						(W)
Bolton W	App	07.85	84-85	7	5	1
WALKER Ronald (Ronnie)						
Sheffield, 4 February, 1932						(W)
Doncaster Rov	Sunderland (Am)	05.50	52-60	240	-	46
WALKER Ronald (Ron)						
Swansea, 24 March, 1933 Died 1989						(CF)
Shrewsbury T		11.55	55	1	-	0
WALKER Ronald (Ronnie) Leslie						
Kingsbury, 2 September, 1952						(CD)
Watford	App	08.70				
Workington	Tr	08.71	71-75	143	10	3
Newport Co	Tr	08.76	76-78	88	1	5
WALKER Ronald (Ron) William						
Westminster, 10 April, 1930 Died 1988						(IF)
Watford	Walthamstow Ave	04.54	54	3	-	0
WALKER Samuel (Sam)						
Eccles, 22 April, 1922						(CD)
Oldham Ath	Darwen	08.47	47	1	-	0
WALKER Scott Edward						
Glasgow, 5 March, 1975						(CD)
Hartlepool U	Alloa Ath	01.04	03	5	1	0
WALKER Shane						
Pontypool, 25 November, 1957						(M)
Hereford U	Arsenal (App)	03.75	74-76	15	2	2
Newport Co	Sligo Rov	08.77	77	27	1	2
WALKER Stephen (Steve)						
Sheffield, 16 October, 1914 Died 1987						(WH)
Sheffield U	Gainsborough Trinity	05.37				
Exeter C	Tr	05.38	38-49	141	-	3
WALKER Steven (Steve)						
Ilkeston, 25 December, 1963						(M)
Halifax T	Ilkeston T	01.82	81	0	1	0
WALKER Steven						
Ashington, 2 November, 1973 ESch						(M)
Doncaster Rov	Blyth Spartans	07.96	96	1	0	0
WALKER Stuart						
Garforth, 9 January, 1951						(G)
York C	Tadcaster A	08.75	76	2	0	0
WALKER Terence (Terry)						
Poppleton, 29 November, 1921						(IF)
York C	Selby T	05.49	49	16	-	9

WALKER Thomas (Tommy) (IF)
Livingston Station, 26 May, 1915 Died 1993 SSch/SLge-5/SWar-11/S-20

League Club	Source	Date Signed	Seasons Played	Apps	Subs	Gls
Chelsea	Heart of Midlothian	09.46	46-48	98	-	23

WALKER Thomas (Tommy) Jackson (W)
Cramlington, 14 November, 1923 Died 2005

League Club	Source	Date Signed	Seasons Played	Apps	Subs	Gls
Newcastle U	Netherton	10.41	46-53	184	-	35
Oldham Ath	Tr	02.54	53-56	120	-	19
Chesterfield	Tr	02.57	56	14	-	1
Oldham Ath	Tr	07.57	57-58	38	-	4

WALKER Thomas (Tom) Jackson (M)
Newcastle, 20 February, 1952

League Club	Source	Date Signed	Seasons Played	Apps	Subs	Gls
Stoke C	App	07.69	71	2	0	0

WALKER Victor (Vic) (WH)
Kirkby-in-Ashfield, 14 April, 1922 Died 1992

League Club	Source	Date Signed	Seasons Played	Apps	Subs	Gls
Nottingham F		08.43				
Stockport Co	Tr	06.46	46-49	94	-	10

WALKLATE Steven (Steve) (M)
Chester-le-Street, 27 September, 1979

League Club	Source	Date Signed	Seasons Played	Apps	Subs	Gls
Middlesbrough	YT	07.98				
Darlington	Tr	02.00	00	2	4	0

WALL Adrian Arthur (W)
Clowne, 25 November, 1949

League Club	Source	Date Signed	Seasons Played	Apps	Subs	Gls
Sheffield Wed	App	05.67	67	3	0	0
Workington	Tr	08.69	69	21	3	2

WALL Thomas **Peter** (FB)
Westbury, Shropshire, 13 September, 1944

League Club	Source	Date Signed	Seasons Played	Apps	Subs	Gls
Shrewsbury T	App	09.62	63-64	18	-	0
Wrexham	Tr	11.65	65-66	15	7	1
Liverpool	Tr	10.66	67-69	31	0	0
Crystal Palace	Tr	06.70	70-77	167	10	4
Orient	L	12.72	72	10	0	0

WALL William (Billy) John (W)
Taunton, 28 October, 1939

League Club	Source	Date Signed	Seasons Played	Apps	Subs	Gls
Chelsea	Jnrs	01.57				
Southend U	Tr	03.60	59-62	56	-	5

WALLACE Adam John (F)
Ashford, Middlesex, 5 October, 1981

League Club	Source	Date Signed	Seasons Played	Apps	Subs	Gls
Southampton	YT	08.01				
Southend U	Tr	03.02	01	0	2	0

WALLACE Barry Danny (M)
Plaistow, 17 April, 1959

League Club	Source	Date Signed	Seasons Played	Apps	Subs	Gls
Queens Park Rgrs	Jnrs	08.76	77-79	17	8	0

WALLACE Clive Low (IF)
Kirriemuir, 6 January, 1932

League Club	Source	Date Signed	Seasons Played	Apps	Subs	Gls
Bury	Montrose	03.59				
Stockport Co	Tr	08.59	59	13	-	4

WALLACE David (Danny) Lloyd (F)
Greenwich, 21 January, 1964 EYth/Eu21-14/E-1

League Club	Source	Date Signed	Seasons Played	Apps	Subs	Gls
Southampton	App	01.82	80-89	238	15	64
Manchester U	Tr	09.89	89-92	36	11	6
Millwall	L	03.93	92	3	0	0
Birmingham C	Tr	10.93	93-94	12	4	2
Wycombe W	L	03.95	94	0	1	0

WALLACE George (IF)
Aberdeen, 18 April, 1920

League Club	Source	Date Signed	Seasons Played	Apps	Subs	Gls
Scunthorpe U		03.46	51-52	33	-	8

WALLACE Gordon Henry (F)
Glasgow, 13 June, 1944

League Club	Source	Date Signed	Seasons Played	Apps	Subs	Gls
Liverpool	App	07.61	62-64	19	-	3
Crewe Alex	Tr	10.67	67-71	90	3	21

WALLACE Ian Andrew (F)
Glasgow, 23 May, 1956 Su21-1/S-3

League Club	Source	Date Signed	Seasons Played	Apps	Subs	Gls
Coventry C	Dumbarton	08.76	76-79	128	2	58
Nottingham F	Tr	07.80	80-83	128	6	36
Sunderland	Brest (Fr)	01.85	84-85	28	6	6

WALLACE Ian Robert (WH)
Wellington, Shropshire, 12 September, 1948

League Club	Source	Date Signed	Seasons Played	Apps	Subs	Gls
Wolverhampton W	App	09.66	66	0	1	0

WALLACE James (CD)
Kirkintilloch, 17 February, 1933 Died 1998

League Club	Source	Date Signed	Seasons Played	Apps	Subs	Gls
Northampton T	Aberdeen	05.55	55	1	-	0

WALLACE James (Jimmy) (W)
Bebington, 13 December, 1937

League Club	Source	Date Signed	Seasons Played	Apps	Subs	Gls
Stoke C		10.55	58-59	8	-	1
Doncaster Rov	Northwich Vic	03.63	62	14	-	1

WALLACE James (Jim) (FB)
Bridge of Allan, 9 June, 1954 Su23-1/SLge-1

League Club	Source	Date Signed	Seasons Played	Apps	Subs	Gls
Aldershot	Dunfermline Ath	07.75	75-76	53	3	0

WALLACE John (Jock) Collins (FB)
Glasgow, 11 January, 1936 Died 1993

League Club	Source	Date Signed	Seasons Played	Apps	Subs	Gls
Rochdale	Falkirk	03.58	57-58	7	-	0

WALLACE John (Jock) Martin (G)
Wallyford, 13 April, 1911 Died 1978

League Club	Source	Date Signed	Seasons Played	Apps	Subs	Gls
Blackpool	Raith Rov	02.34	33-47	240	-	0
Derby Co	Tr	02.48	47	16	-	0

WALLACE John (Jock) Martin Bokas (G)
Wallyford, 6 September, 1935 Died 1996

League Club	Source	Date Signed	Seasons Played	Apps	Subs	Gls
Workington	Blackpool (Am)	09.52	52	6	-	0
West Bromwich A	Airdrie	10.59	59-61	69	-	0

WALLACE Joseph (Joe) Burt (WH)
Glasgow, 28 December, 1933 Died 1993

League Club	Source	Date Signed	Seasons Played	Apps	Subs	Gls
Shrewsbury T	RAOC Donnington	03.54	54-62	337	-	3
Southport	Tr	10.62	62-64	78	-	0

WALLACE Kenneth (Ken) (FB)
Frizington, 14 January, 1932 Died 2005

League Club	Source	Date Signed	Seasons Played	Apps	Subs	Gls
Workington		07.51	51-52	47	-	1

WALLACE Kenneth (Ken) (FB)
Workington, 5 January, 1953

League Club	Source	Date Signed	Seasons Played	Apps	Subs	Gls
Workington	Jnrs	02.74	73-76	6	1	0

WALLACE Kenneth (Kenny) Robert (W)
Islington, 8 June, 1952

League Club	Source	Date Signed	Seasons Played	Apps	Subs	Gls
West Ham U	Jnrs	07.69				
Brentford	L	02.72	71	3	0	0
Hereford U	Tr	07.72	72	26	6	4
Exeter C	Tr	09.73	73	8	2	1

WALLACE Michael (Mick) (FB)
Farnworth, 5 October, 1970 EYth

League Club	Source	Date Signed	Seasons Played	Apps	Subs	Gls
Manchester C	YT	07.89				
Stockport Co	Tr	10.92	92-94	65	5	5

WALLACE Raymond (Ray) George (M)
Greenwich, 2 October, 1969 Eu21-4

League Club	Source	Date Signed	Seasons Played	Apps	Subs	Gls
Southampton	YT	04.88	88-89	33	2	0
Leeds U	Tr	07.91	92-93	5	2	0
Swansea C	L	03.92	91	2	0	0
Reading	L	03.94	93	3	0	0
Stoke C	Tr	08.94	94-98	152	27	15
Hull C	L	12.94	94	7	0	0

WALLACE Robert (Bob) (M)
Huddersfield, 14 February, 1948

League Club	Source	Date Signed	Seasons Played	Apps	Subs	Gls
Huddersfield T	App	05.65	66	4	0	0
Halifax T	Tr	03.67	66-71	190	11	16
Chester	Tr	06.72	72	41	0	9
Aldershot	Tr	07.73	73-76	70	6	1

WALLACE Rodney (Rod) Seymour (F)
Greenwich, 2 October, 1969 Eu21-11/EB-2

League Club	Source	Date Signed	Seasons Played	Apps	Subs	Gls
Southampton	YT	04.88	87-90	111	17	45
Leeds U	Tr	06.91	91-97	187	25	53
Bolton W	Glasgow Rgrs	09.01	01	14	5	3
Gillingham	Tr	08.02	02-03	27	9	12

WALLACE William (Willie) Semple Brown (F)
Kirkintilloch, 23 June, 1941 SLge-4/S-7

League Club	Source	Date Signed	Seasons Played	Apps	Subs	Gls
Crystal Palace	Glasgow Celtic	10.71	71-72	36	3	4

WALLBANK Bernard Frederick (CF)
Preston, 11 November, 1943

League Club	Source	Date Signed	Seasons Played	Apps	Subs	Gls
Southport	St Andrew's (Preston)	08.61	61	1	-	0

WALLBANKS Harold (Harry) (WH)
Chopwell, 27 July, 1921 Died 1993

League Club	Source	Date Signed	Seasons Played	Apps	Subs	Gls
Fulham		10.38	46-47	33	-	1
Southend U	Tr	10.49	49-50	39	-	2
Workington	Tr	08.52	52	26	-	9

WALLBANKS William **Horace** (W)
Chopwell, 4 September, 1918

League Club	Source	Date Signed	Seasons Played	Apps	Subs	Gls
Grimsby T	Aberdeen	11.46	46	9	-	1
Luton T	Tr	05.47	46-47	4	-	1

WALLBANKS James (Jimmy) (CD)
Platt Bridge, 12 September, 1909 Died 1979

League Club	Source	Date Signed	Seasons Played	Apps	Subs	Gls
Barnsley	Annfield Plain	03.29	30	9	-	0
Norwich C	Tr	05.31	31	3	-	0
Northampton T	Tr	08.32	32	2	-	0
Millwall	Wigan Ath	06.34	34-38	88	-	0
Reading	Tr	10.38	38-46	48	-	1

League Club	Source	Date Signed	Seasons Played	Career Record Apps	Subs	Gls
WALLBRIDGE Trevor						
Southampton, 8 February, 1959 (F)						
Bournemouth	Totton	01.78	77	0	1	0
WALLEMME Jean-Guy						
Maubeuge, France, 10 August, 1967 (CD)						
Coventry C	RC Lens (Fr)	07.98	98	4	2	0
WALLER David Harold						
Urmston, 20 December, 1963 (F)						
Crewe Alex		01.82	81-85	165	3	55
Shrewsbury T	Tr	07.86	86	11	0	3
Chesterfield	Tr	03.87	87-89	117	2	53
WALLER Henry (Harry) Harold						
Ashington, 20 August, 1917 Died 1984 (WH)						
Arsenal	Ashington	10.37	46	8	-	0
Leyton Orient	Tr	07.47	47	17	-	0
WALLER Philip (Phil)						
Leeds, 12 April, 1943 (CD)						
Derby Co	Jnrs	05.61	61-67	102	2	5
Mansfield T	Tr	03.68	67-71	153	6	1
WALLEY Ernest (Ernie)						
Caernarfon, 19 April, 1933 (WH)						
Tottenham H	Jnrs	05.51	55-57	5	-	0
Middlesbrough	Tr	05.58	58	8	-	0
WALLEY Keith John						
Weymouth, 19 October, 1954 (M)						
Crystal Palace	App	10.72	73	6	1	1
WALLEY John **Thomas (Tom)**						
Caernarfon, 27 February, 1945 Wu23-4/W-1 (CD)						
Arsenal	Caernarvon T	12.64	65-66	10	4	1
Watford	Tr	03.67	66-71	202	2	17
Orient	Tr	12.71	71-75	155	2	6
Watford	Tr	06.76	76	12	1	0
WALLING Dean Anthony						
Leeds, 17 April, 1969 St Kitts int (CD)						
Rochdale	Leeds U (App)	07.87	87-89	43	22	8
Carlisle U	Guiseley	07.91	91-97	230	6	22
Lincoln C	Tr	09.97	97-98	35	3	5
Cambridge U	Northwich Vic	08.01	01	20	0	0
WALLINGTON Francis **Mark**						
Sleaford, 17 September, 1952 ESch/EYth/Eu23-2 (G)						
Walsall	Heckington U	10.71	71	11	0	0
Leicester C	Tr	03.72	71-84	412	0	0
Derby Co	Tr	07.85	85-86	67	0	0
Lincoln C	Tr	08.88	88-90	87	0	0
WALLIS Derek						
Hartlepool, 6 October, 1937 (CF)						
Hartlepools U (Am)	Durham C	05.63	63	2	-	0
WALLIS Scott Edward						
Enfield, 28 June, 1988 (M)						
Leyton Orient	Sch	●	04	0	3	0
WALLS Arthur Joseph						
Glasgow, 15 January, 1931 (IF)						
Tranmere Rov	Airdrie	06.54	54-55	22	-	6
WALLS David (Dave)						
Leeds, 16 June, 1953 (W)						
Lincoln C	Leeds U (App)	07.71	71-72	9	0	0
WALLS James (Jimmy) Parker						
Dunfermline, 11 March, 1928 Died 1995 (CD)						
Charlton Ath	Crossgates	09.45	49-52	10	-	0
Ipswich T	Tr	05.54	54	1	-	0
WALLS John (Jack)						
Seaham, 8 May, 1932 (G)						
Barnsley	Dawdon Jnrs	05.49	52	7	-	0
Peterborough U	Tr	05.56	60-61	78	-	0
WALLWORK Ronald (Ronnie)						
Manchester, 10 September, 1977 EYth (M)						
Manchester U	YT	03.95	97-01	4	15	0
Carlisle U	L	12.97	97	10	0	1
Stockport Co	L	03.98	97	7	0	0
West Bromwich A	Tr	07.02	02-04	46	6	1
Bradford C	L	01.04	03	7	0	4
WALMSLEY David Geoffrey						
Hull, 23 November, 1972 (F)						
Hull C	YT	07.91	90-91	5	5	4

League Club	Source	Date Signed	Seasons Played	Career Record Apps	Subs	Gls
WALMSLEY Dennis						
Birkdale, 1 May, 1935 (W)						
Southport (Am)	Crossens	05.54	54	4	-	1
WALSCHAERTS Wim						
Antwerp, Belgium, 5 November, 1972 (M)						
Leyton Orient	KFC Tielen (Bel)	07.98	98-00	120	5	9
WALSH Alan						
Hartlepool, 9 December, 1956 (F)						
Middlesbrough	Horden CW	12.76	77	0	3	0
Darlington	Tr	10.78	78-83	245	6	87
Bristol C	Tr	08.84	84-88	215	3	77
Walsall	Besiktas (Tu)	10.91	91	4	0	0
Huddersfield T	Glenavon	12.91	91	0	4	0
Shrewsbury T	Tr	01.92	91	2	0	0
Cardiff C	Southampton (N/C)	03.92	91	1	0	0
Hartlepool U	Backwell U	09.94	94	4	0	1
WALSH Andrew (Andy)						
Blackburn, 15 February, 1970 (CD)						
Bury	Preston NE (N/C)	11.87	87	0	1	0
WALSH John **Brian**						
Aldershot, 26 March, 1932 Died 2001 (W)						
Arsenal	Jnrs	08.49	53-55	17	-	0
Cardiff C	Tr	09.55	55-61	206	-	33
Newport Co	Tr	11.61	61-62	27	-	4
WALSH Colin David						
Hamilton, 22 July, 1962 SSch/SYth/Su21-5 (W)						
Nottingham F	App	08.79	80-85	115	24	32
Charlton Ath	Tr	09.86	86-95	223	19	21
Peterborough U	L	02.89	88	5	0	1
Middlesbrough	L	01.91	90	10	3	1
WALSH Daniel (Danny) Gareth						
Manchester, 23 September, 1979 (M)						
Oldham Ath	YT	07.98	98-99	0	2	0
Chesterfield	Emley	12.01	01	0	1	0
WALSH David (Dave)						
Wrexham, 29 April, 1979 Wu21-8 (G)						
Wrexham	YT	07.97	00-01	12	2	0
WALSH David (Dave) John						
Waterford, 28 April, 1923 NIRL-3/IWar-2/IR-20/I-9 (CF)						
West Bromwich A	Linfield	07.46	46-50	165	-	94
Aston Villa	Tr	12.50	50-54	108	-	37
Walsall	Tr	07.55	55	20	-	6
WALSH Derek						
Hamilton, 24 October, 1967 (M)						
Everton	App	10.84	84	1	0	0
Carlisle U	Hamilton Academical	08.88	88-92	108	13	7
WALSH Francis (Frank)						
Overtown, 15 September, 1923 (CF)						
Southport	Glasgow Celtic	10.49	49	5	-	3
WALSH Gary						
Wigan, 21 March, 1968 Eu21-2 (G)						
Manchester U	Jnrs	04.85	86-94	49	1	0
Oldham Ath	L	11.93	93	6	0	0
Middlesbrough	Tr	08.95	95-96	44	0	0
Bradford C	Tr	09.97	97-02	131	1	0
Middlesbrough	L	09.00	00	3	0	0
Wigan Ath	Tr	07.03	03	1	2	0
WALSH Ian Patrick						
St Davids, 4 September, 1958 WSch/WYth/Wu21-2/W-18 (F)						
Crystal Palace	App	10.75	76-81	101	16	23
Swansea C	Tr	02.82	81-83	32	5	11
Barnsley	Tr	07.84	84-85	45	4	15
Grimsby T	Tr	08.86	86-87	36	5	14
Cardiff C	Tr	01.88	87-88	5	12	4
WALSH James (Jimmy)						
Bellshill, 3 December, 1930 Su23-1 (IF)						
Leicester C	Glasgow Celtic	11.56	56-62	176	-	79
WALSH James (Jimmy) Thomas Patrick						
Paddington, 20 November, 1954 (FB)						
Watford	App	11.72	73-77	60	5	0
York C	Tr	06.78	78-80	91	8	2
WALSH Kevin William						
Rochdale, 11 February, 1928 (WH)						
Oldham Ath	St Patrick's OB	10.49	49-50	3	-	0
Southport	Tr	07.52	52-53	67	-	1
Bradford C	Tr	07.54	54-55	24	-	3
Southport	Tr	08.56	56	3	-	0

League Club	Source	Date Signed	Seasons Played	Career Record Apps	Subs	Gls
WALSH Mario Markus						
Paddington, 19 January, 1966						(F)
Portsmouth	App	01.84				
Torquay U	Tr	01.85	84-86	89	11	18
Colchester U	Tr	08.87	87-88	29	9	12
Southend U	Tr	07.89	89	10	1	2
WALSH Mark						
Preston, 7 October, 1962						(M)
Preston NE	App	10.80	81-83	56	6	2
Exeter C	(New Zealand)	08.85	85	0	1	0
WALSH Michael (Mickey) Anthony						
Chorley, 13 August, 1954 IR-22						(F)
Blackpool	Chorley	11.71	73-77	172	8	72
Everton	Tr	08.78	78	18	3	1
Queens Park Rgrs	Tr	03.79	78-80	13	5	3
WALSH Michael George						
Liverpool, 30 May, 1986						(CD)
Chester C	Rhyl	01.05	04	2	3	1
WALSH Michael Shane						
Rotherham, 5 August, 1977						(CD)
Scunthorpe U	YT	07.95	94-97	94	9	1
Port Vale	Tr	07.98	98-04	144	7	4
WALSH Michael (Mike) Thomas						
Blackley, 20 June, 1956 IR-5						(CD)
Bolton W	Jnrs	07.74	74-80	169	8	4
Everton	Tr	08.81	81-82	20	0	0
Norwich C	L	10.82	82	5	0	0
Burnley	L	12.82	82	3	0	0
Manchester C	Fort Lauderdale (USA)	10.83	83	3	1	0
Blackpool	Tr	02.84	83-88	146	7	6
WALSH Paul Anthony						
Plumstead, 1 October, 1962 EYth/Eu21-4/E-5						(F)
Charlton Ath	App	10.77	79-81	85	2	24
Luton T	Tr	07.82	82-83	80	0	25
Liverpool	Tr	05.84	84-87	63	14	25
Tottenham H	Tr	02.88	87-91	84	44	19
Queens Park Rgrs	L	09.91	91	2	0	0
Portsmouth	Tr	06.92	92-93	67	6	14
Manchester C	Tr	03.94	93-95	53	0	16
Portsmouth	Tr	09.95	95	21	0	5
WALSH Peter						
Dublin, 18 October, 1922 LoI-2						(CF)
Luton T	Dundalk	08.49	49	8	-	2
WALSH Roy						
Belfast, 25 November, 1955 IrLge-1						(CD)
Swindon T	Glentoran	03.80	80	7	0	0
WALSH Roy William						
Dedham, 15 January, 1947						(M)
Ipswich T	App	01.65	65	6	1	0
WALSH Steven (Steve)						
Fulwood, 3 November, 1964						(CD)
Wigan Ath	Jnrs	09.82	82-85	123	3	4
Leicester C	Tr	06.86	86-00	352	17	53
Norwich C	Tr	09.00	00	1	3	0
Coventry C	Tamworth	08.02	02	1	1	0
WALSH Wilfred (Wilf)						
Pontlottyn, 29 July, 1917 Died 1977						(IF)
Arsenal	Jnrs	05.36	38	3	-	0
Derby Co	Tr	06.39	46	1	-	0
Walsall	Tr	03.47	46-47	33	-	4
WALSH William (Billy)						
Dublin, 31 May, 1921 IR-9/I-5						(WH)
Manchester C	Manchester U (Am)	06.38	46-49	109	-	1
WALSH William (Billy)						
Easington, 4 December, 1923						(CD)
Sunderland	Horden CW	09.46	46-52	98	-	1
Northampton T	Tr	07.53	53	19	-	0
Darlington	Tr	06.54	54	28	-	4
WALSHAW Kenneth (Ken)						
Tynemouth, 28 August, 1918 Died 1979						(IF)
Sunderland	North Shields	08.44				
Lincoln C	Tr	08.47	47	17	-	6
Carlisle U	Tr	12.47	47-49	50	-	15
Bradford C	Tr	08.50	50	9	-	3
WALSHAW Lee						
Sheffield, 20 January, 1967						(M)
Sheffield U	App	01.85	84-86	8	1	1

League Club	Source	Date Signed	Seasons Played	Career Record Apps	Subs	Gls
WALSHAW Philip Desmond						
Leeds, 16 April, 1929						(W)
Halifax T (Am)	Jnrs	09.46	46	6	-	1
WALSHE Benjamin (Ben) Matthew						
Hammersmith, 24 May, 1983						(M)
Queens Park Rgrs	YT	07.00	00-02	1	1	0
WALTER William **David**						
Holsworthy, 3 September, 1964						(G)
Exeter C	Bideford T	11.88	88-89	44	0	0
Plymouth Arg	Tr	07.90	90-91	15	0	0
Torquay U	Tr	06.92	92	1	0	0
WALTERS George						
Wolverhampton, 21 June, 1935						(FB)
Shrewsbury T	Jenks & Cattell	02.57	56-62	246	-	3
Newport Co	Tr	09.63	63-65	80	0	2
WALTERS George Archibald						
Glasgow, 30 March, 1939						(W)
Oldham Ath	Clyde	08.59	59	13	-	2
WALTERS Henry						
Wath-on-Dearne, 15 March, 1925 Died 1994						(WH)
Wolverhampton W	Jnrs	06.42				
Walsall	Tr	05.46	46-52	254	-	2
Barnsley	Tr	07.53	53-59	160	-	4
WALTERS Jonathan (Jon) Ronald						
Birkenhead, 20 September, 1983 IRYth/IRu21-1						(F)
Blackburn Rov	YT	08.01				
Bolton W	Tr	04.02	02	0	4	0
Hull C	L	02.03	02	11	0	5
Barnsley	L	11.03	03	7	1	0
Hull C	Tr	02.04	03-04	9	28	2
Scunthorpe U	L	02.05	04	3	0	0
WALTERS Mark Everton						
Birmingham, 2 June, 1964 ESch/EYth/Eu21-9/EB-1/E-1						(W)
Aston Villa	App	05.82	81-87	168	13	39
Liverpool	Glasgow Rgrs	08.91	91-94	58	36	14
Stoke C	L	03.94	93	9	0	2
Wolverhampton W	L	09.94	94	11	0	3
Southampton	Tr	01.96	95	4	1	0
Swindon T	Tr	07.96	96-99	91	21	25
Bristol Rov	Tr	11.99	99-01	46	36	13
WALTERS Michael (Mick)						
Banbury, 17 November, 1939						(WH)
Coventry C	Jnrs	12.56	57	3	-	0
Bradford C	Rugby T	01.62	61-62	19	-	0
WALTERS Peter Louis						
Whickham, 8 June, 1952						(G)
Hull C		08.70	70-71	2	0	0
Darlington	L	03.72	71	16	0	0
WALTERS Robert (Bobby) James						
Glasgow, 9 March, 1944						(CD)
Shrewsbury T	Winsford U	12.62	62	1	-	0
WALTERS Steven (Steve) Paul						
Plymouth, 9 January, 1972 ESch/EYth/ESemiPro						(M)
Crewe Alex	YT	03.89	87-94	135	11	10
WALTERS Trevor Bowen						
Aberdare, 13 January, 1916 Died 1989						(CD)
Chester	Aberaman Ath	05.37	37-48	151	-	1
WALTERS William (Sonny) Edward						
Edmonton, 5 September, 1924 Died 1970 EB						(W)
Tottenham H	Jnrs	08.44	46-55	210	-	66
Aldershot	Tr	07.57	57-58	66	-	11
WALTON David (Dave) Lee						
Bedlington, 10 April, 1973						(CD)
Sheffield U	Ashington	03.92				
Shrewsbury T	Tr	11.93	93-97	127	1	10
Crewe Alex	Tr	10.97	97-02	146	9	3
Derby Co	Tr	07.03	03	3	2	0
Stockport Co	L	02.04	03	7	0	0
Shrewsbury T	Tr	08.04	04	20	2	2
WALTON Frank Hillard						
Southend-on-Sea, 9 April, 1918 Died 1986						(FB)
Southend U	Jnrs	12.37	37-50	144	-	0
WALTON Harold (Harry)						
Manchester, 1 April, 1924 Died 1992						(WH)
Southend U	Leicester C (Am)	05.46	46	1	-	0

WALTON Ian Jeffrey
Goole, 17 April, 1958 (M)

League Club	Source	Date Signed	Seasons Played	Apps	Subs	Gls
Grimsby T	App	•	75	2	0	1
Scunthorpe U	Tr	03.76	76	1	0	0

WALTON John (Johnny) Andrew
Horwich, 21 March, 1928 Died 1979 EAmat (IF)

League Club	Source	Date Signed	Seasons Played	Apps	Subs	Gls
Bury (Am)	Saltash	05.49	49-50	26	-	4
Manchester U (Am)	Tr	07.51	51	2	-	0
Bury (Am)	Tr	07.52	52-53	29	-	2
Burnley	Tr	02.54	54-55	18	-	2
Coventry C	Tr	10.56	56-57	13	-	0
Chester	Kettering T	07.59	59	1	-	0

WALTON Joseph (Joe)
Manchester, 5 June, 1925 FLge-1 (FB)

League Club	Source	Date Signed	Seasons Played	Apps	Subs	Gls
Manchester U	Jnrs	10.43	46-47	21	-	0
Preston NE	Tr	03.48	47-60	401	-	4
Accrington St	Tr	02.61	60	18	-	0

WALTON Mark Andrew
Merthyr Tydfil, 1 June, 1969 Wu21-1 (G)

League Club	Source	Date Signed	Seasons Played	Apps	Subs	Gls
Luton T		02.87				
Colchester U	Tr	11.87	87-88	40	0	0
Norwich C	Tr	08.89	89-91	22	0	0
Wrexham	L	08.93	93	6	0	0
Bolton W	Dundee	03.94	93	3	0	0
Fulham	Fakenham T	08.96	96-97	40	0	0
Gillingham	L	02.98	97	1	0	0
Brighton & Hove A	Tr	07.98	98-99	58	0	0
Cardiff C	Tr	08.00	00	40	0	0

WALTON Paul Anthony
Sunderland, 2 July, 1979 (W)

League Club	Source	Date Signed	Seasons Played	Apps	Subs	Gls
Hartlepool U	YT	07.97	95-96	3	7	0

WALTON Richard (Dick)
Hull, 12 September, 1924 (FB)

League Club	Source	Date Signed	Seasons Played	Apps	Subs	Gls
Leicester C		01.43				
Leyton Orient	Tr	07.48	48-51	63	-	4
Exeter C	Tr	12.51	51-55	135	-	6

WALTON Ronald (Ronnie) Pattern
Plymouth, 12 October, 1945 (W)

League Club	Source	Date Signed	Seasons Played	Apps	Subs	Gls
Northampton T	Rotherham U (Am)	09.63	64	1	-	0
Crewe Alex	Tr	10.65	65	2	0	0
Carlisle U	Tr	01.66	65	1	0	0
Aldershot	Tr	08.66	66-71	190	4	41
Cambridge U	Tr	11.71	71-72	62	0	9
Aldershot	Tr	07.73	73-76	108	5	14

WALTON Roy
Crewe, 19 July, 1928 Died 2003 (WH)

League Club	Source	Date Signed	Seasons Played	Apps	Subs	Gls
Crewe Alex		06.50	50-51	11	-	0

WALTON Simon William
Sherburn-in-Elmet, 13 September, 1987 (M)

League Club	Source	Date Signed	Seasons Played	Apps	Subs	Gls
Leeds U	Sch	09.04	04	23	7	3

WALWYN Kenford Keith Ian
Nevis, 17 February, 1956 Died 2003 (F)

League Club	Source	Date Signed	Seasons Played	Apps	Subs	Gls
Chesterfield	Winterton Rgrs	11.79	80	3	0	2
York C	Tr	07.81	81-86	245	0	117
Blackpool	Tr	06.87	87-88	51	18	16
Carlisle U	Tr	07.89	89-90	59	3	15

WANCHOPE Watson Pablo (Paulo) Cesar
Heredia, Costa Rica, 31 July, 1976 Costa Rica 53 (F)

League Club	Source	Date Signed	Seasons Played	Apps	Subs	Gls
Derby Co	CS Heridiano (CR)	03.97	96-98	65	7	23
West Ham U	Tr	07.99	99	33	2	12
Manchester C	Tr	08.00	00-03	51	13	27

WANDS Alexander (Alex) Mitchell Doig
Cowdenbeath, 5 December, 1922 (WH)

League Club	Source	Date Signed	Seasons Played	Apps	Subs	Gls
Sheffield Wed	Gateshead (Am)	05.45	46	11	-	1
Doncaster Rov	Tr	05.47	47	22	-	0

WANKLYN Edward Wayne
Hull, 21 January, 1960 (M)

League Club	Source	Date Signed	Seasons Played	Apps	Subs	Gls
Reading	App	01.78	77-80	47	7	3
Aldershot	Tr	08.81	81	15	3	2

WANLESS Paul Steven
Banbury, 14 December, 1973 (M)

League Club	Source	Date Signed	Seasons Played	Apps	Subs	Gls
Oxford U	YT	12.91	91-94	12	20	0
Lincoln C	Tr	07.95	95	7	1	0
Cambridge U	Tr	03.96	95-02	264	20	44
Oxford U	Tr	08.03	03-04	56	9	6

WANN Alexander (Sandy) Halley
Stanley, Perthshire, 20 December, 1940 (WH)

League Club	Source	Date Signed	Seasons Played	Apps	Subs	Gls
Manchester C	Luncarty Jnrs	07.58				
Oldham Ath	St Mirren	12.60	60	19	-	0

WANN John Dennis
Blackpool, 17 November, 1950 (W)

League Club	Source	Date Signed	Seasons Played	Apps	Subs	Gls
Blackpool	App	07.67	69-71	11	6	0
York C	Tr	01.72	71-75	65	1	7
Chesterfield	L	11.75	75	3	0	0
Hartlepool	L	01.76	75	2	0	0
Darlington	Tr	07.76	76-78	119	2	13
Rochdale	Tr	06.79	79-80	66	1	7
Blackpool	Tr	10.81	81	13	6	0
Chester C	Workington	10.83	83	2	1	0

WANT Anthony (Tony) George
Shoreditch, 13 December, 1948 EYth (FB)

League Club	Source	Date Signed	Seasons Played	Apps	Subs	Gls
Tottenham H	App	12.65	67-71	46	4	0
Birmingham C	Tr	06.72	72-74	31	2	1
Birmingham C	Philadelphia (USA)	08.75	75-77	67	1	0

WAPENAAR Harald
Vlaardingen, Holland, 10 April, 1970 (G)

League Club	Source	Date Signed	Seasons Played	Apps	Subs	Gls
Portsmouth	FC Utrecht (Holl)	07.03	03	5	0	0

WARBOYS Alan
Goldthorpe, 18 April, 1949 (F)

League Club	Source	Date Signed	Seasons Played	Apps	Subs	Gls
Doncaster Rov	App	04.67	66-67	39	0	11
Sheffield Wed	Tr	06.68	68-70	66	5	13
Cardiff C	Tr	12.70	70-72	57	4	27
Sheffield U	Tr	09.72	72	7	0	0
Bristol Rov	Tr	03.73	72-76	141	3	53
Fulham	Tr	02.77	76-77	19	0	2
Hull C	Tr	09.77	77-78	44	5	9
Doncaster Rov	Tr	07.79	79-81	89	0	21

WARBURTON George
Brymbo, 13 September, 1934 (FB)

League Club	Source	Date Signed	Seasons Played	Apps	Subs	Gls
Wrexham		11.57	58-59	22	-	0
Barrow	Tr	06.60	60	14	-	0

WARBURTON Ian Thomas
Haslingden, 22 March, 1952 (F)

League Club	Source	Date Signed	Seasons Played	Apps	Subs	Gls
Bury	Haslingden	11.72	72	6	0	2
Southport	Tr	07.74	74	5	2	1

WARBURTON Raymond (Ray)
Rotherham, 7 October, 1967 (CD)

League Club	Source	Date Signed	Seasons Played	Apps	Subs	Gls
Rotherham U	App	10.85	84-86	3	1	0
York C	Tr	08.89	89-93	86	4	9
Northampton T	Tr	02.94	93-98	186	0	12
Rushden & Diamonds	Tr	10.98	01	1	0	0
Boston U	Tr	03.02	02	16	0	0

WARD Anthony (Tony)
Warrington, 4 April, 1970 (W)

League Club	Source	Date Signed	Seasons Played	Apps	Subs	Gls
Everton	YT	06.88				
Doncaster Rov	L	12.88	88	4	0	0
Wigan Ath	Tr	06.89	89	8	3	2

WARD Ashley Stuart
Manchester, 24 November, 1970 (F)

League Club	Source	Date Signed	Seasons Played	Apps	Subs	Gls
Manchester C	YT	08.89	89	0	1	0
Wrexham	L	01.91	90	4	0	2
Leicester C	Tr	07.91	91	2	8	0
Blackpool	L	11.92	92	2	0	1
Crewe Alex	Tr	12.92	92-94	58	3	25
Norwich C	Tr	12.94	94-95	53	0	18
Derby Co	Tr	03.96	95-97	32	8	9
Barnsley	Tr	09.97	97-98	45	1	20
Blackburn Rov	Tr	12.98	98-99	52	2	13
Bradford C	Tr	08.00	00-02	75	9	17
Sheffield U	Tr	08.03	03-04	25	8	5

WARD Christopher (Chris)
Preston, 28 April, 1981 (F)

League Club	Source	Date Signed	Seasons Played	Apps	Subs	Gls
Birmingham C	Lancaster C	04.01				
Lincoln C	Leigh RMI	10.02	02	5	1	2

WARD Darren
Worksop, 11 May, 1974 Wu21-2/WB-1/W-5 (G)

League Club	Source	Date Signed	Seasons Played	Apps	Subs	Gls
Mansfield T	YT	07.92	92-94	81	0	0
Notts Co	Tr	07.95	95-00	251	0	0
Nottingham F	Tr	05.01	01-03	123	0	0
Norwich C	Tr	08.04	04	0	1	0

WARD Darren Philip
Harrow, 13 September, 1978 (CD)

League Club	Source	Date Signed	Seasons Played	Apps	Subs	Gls
Watford	YT	02.97	95-01	56	3	2
Queens Park Rgrs	L	12.99	99	14	0	0
Millwall	Tr	10.01	01-04	135	7	4

WARD David (Dai)
Barry, 16 July, 1934 Died 1996 W-2 (IF)

League Club	Source	Date Signed	Seasons Played	Apps	Subs	Gls
Bristol Rov	Barry T	11.54	54-60	175	-	90

League Club	Source	Date Signed	Seasons Played	Apps	Subs	Gls
Cardiff C	Tr	02.61	60-61	34	-	18
Watford	Tr	06.62	62-63	59	-	31
Brentford	Tr	10.63	63-64	47	-	21

WARD David Alan
Crewe, 8 March, 1941 (FB)

League Club	Source	Date Signed	Seasons Played	Apps	Subs	Gls
Swansea T	Taunton T	01.59	60-65	44	0	0

WARD Denis
Burton Joyce, 25 October, 1924 (G)

League Club	Source	Date Signed	Seasons Played	Apps	Subs	Gls
Nottingham F		08.47	47	1	-	0
Stockport Co	Tr	08.49	49-52	52	-	0
Bradford PA	Hastings U	08.55	55-57	50	-	0

WARD Derek
Birkenhead, 17 May, 1972 (FB)

League Club	Source	Date Signed	Seasons Played	Apps	Subs	Gls
Bury	Heswall	08.92	92-93	27	1	0

WARD Derrick
Stoke-on-Trent, 23 December, 1934 (W)

League Club	Source	Date Signed	Seasons Played	Apps	Subs	Gls
Stoke C	Jnrs	08.52	52-60	54	-	9
Stockport Co	Tr	07.61	61-63	81	-	21

WARD Elliott Leslie
Harrow, 19 January, 1985 (CD)

League Club	Source	Date Signed	Seasons Played	Apps	Subs	Gls
West Ham U	YT	01.02	04	10	1	0
Bristol Rov	L	12.04	04	0	3	0

WARD Gavin John
Sutton Coldfield, 30 June, 1970 (G)

League Club	Source	Date Signed	Seasons Played	Apps	Subs	Gls
Shrewsbury T	Aston Villa (YT)	09.88				
West Bromwich A	Tr	09.89				
Cardiff C	Tr	10.89	89-92	58	1	0
Leicester C	Tr	07.93	93-94	38	0	0
Bradford C	Tr	07.95	95	36	0	0
Bolton W	Tr	03.96	95-97	19	3	0
Burnley	L	08.98	98	17	0	0
Stoke C	Tr	02.99	98-01	79	0	0
Walsall	Tr	08.02	02	5	2	0
Coventry C	Tr	08.03	03	12	0	0
Barnsley	L	04.04	03	1	0	0
Preston NE	Tr	08.04	04	6	1	0

WARD Gerald (Gerry)
Stepney, 5 October, 1936 Died 1994 ESch/EYth/EAmat (WH)

League Club	Source	Date Signed	Seasons Played	Apps	Subs	Gls
Arsenal	Jnrs	10.53	53-62	81	-	10
Leyton Orient	Tr	07.63	63-64	44	-	2

WARD Graham William
Dublin, 25 February, 1983 IRYth/IRu21-3 (M)

League Club	Source	Date Signed	Seasons Played	Apps	Subs	Gls
Wolverhampton W	YT	07.00				
Kidderminster Hrs	Tr	08.03	03	17	4	0
Cheltenham T	Tr	08.04	04	0	2	0

WARD Iain Campbell
Cleethorpes, 13 May, 1983 (FB)

League Club	Source	Date Signed	Seasons Played	Apps	Subs	Gls
Grimsby T	Jnrs	11.00	01-02	10	2	0

WARD James (Jim)
Glasgow, 26 July, 1929 Died 1985 (CF)

League Club	Source	Date Signed	Seasons Played	Apps	Subs	Gls
Crewe Alex (Am)	Queen's Park	08.56	56	6	-	0

WARD John
Mansfield, 18 January, 1948 (FB)

League Club	Source	Date Signed	Seasons Played	Apps	Subs	Gls
Notts Co	App	07.65	65	5	0	0

WARD John Patrick
Lincoln, 7 April, 1951 (F)

League Club	Source	Date Signed	Seasons Played	Apps	Subs	Gls
Lincoln C	Adelaide Park	03.71	70-78	223	17	91
Workington	L	09.72	72	9	2	3
Watford	Tr	07.79	79-80	22	5	6
Grimsby T	Tr	06.81	81	2	1	0
Lincoln C	Tr	03.82	81	1	0	0

WARD John Stuart
Frodsham, 15 June, 1933 (W)

League Club	Source	Date Signed	Seasons Played	Apps	Subs	Gls
Crewe Alex (Am)		12.56	56	5	-	1

WARD Joseph (Joe)
Glasgow, 25 November, 1954 (F)

League Club	Source	Date Signed	Seasons Played	Apps	Subs	Gls
Aston Villa	Clyde	12.78	78-79	2	1	0

WARD Mark Steven
Sheffield, 27 January, 1982 ESch (F)

League Club	Source	Date Signed	Seasons Played	Apps	Subs	Gls
Sheffield U	Sheffield Colleges	07.00	00-01	0	2	0

WARD Mark William
Huyton, 10 October, 1962 ESemiPro (W)

League Club	Source	Date Signed	Seasons Played	Apps	Subs	Gls
Everton	App	09.80				
Oldham Ath	Northwich Vic	07.83	83-84	84	0	12
West Ham U	Tr	08.85	85-89	163	2	12
Manchester C	Tr	12.89	89-90	55	0	14
Everton	Tr	08.91	91-93	82	1	6
Birmingham C	Tr	03.94	93-95	63	0	7
Huddersfield T	Tr	03.96	95	7	1	0
Wigan Ath	Tr	09.96	96	5	0	0

WARD Michael (Mike) Henry
Nottingham, 30 August, 1920 (IF)

League Club	Source	Date Signed	Seasons Played	Apps	Subs	Gls
Stockport Co		10.48	48	1	-	0

WARD Mitchum (Mitch) David
Sheffield, 19 June, 1971 (M)

League Club	Source	Date Signed	Seasons Played	Apps	Subs	Gls
Sheffield U	YT	07.89	90-97	135	19	11
Crewe Alex	L	11.90	90	4	0	1
Everton	Tr	11.97	97-99	18	6	0
Barnsley	Tr	07.00	00-02	68	9	0
York C	Tr	08.03	03	27	4	0

WARD Nicholas (Nick) John
Wrexham, 30 November, 1977 (F)

League Club	Source	Date Signed	Seasons Played	Apps	Subs	Gls
Shrewsbury T	YT	07.96	96-97	8	12	1

WARD Noel Gerard
Strabane, 8 December, 1952 (CD)

League Club	Source	Date Signed	Seasons Played	Apps	Subs	Gls
Wigan Ath	Aberdeen	07.76	78-79	47	1	4

WARD Patrick (Pat)
Dumbarton, 28 December, 1926 Died 2003 (WH)

League Club	Source	Date Signed	Seasons Played	Apps	Subs	Gls
Leicester C	Hibernian	09.55	55-57	57	-	0
Crewe Alex	Tr	06.58	58	31	-	1

WARD Paul Terence
Fishburn, 15 September, 1963 (M)

League Club	Source	Date Signed	Seasons Played	Apps	Subs	Gls
Chelsea	App	08.81				
Middlesbrough	Tr	09.82	82-85	69	7	1
Darlington	Tr	09.85	85-87	124	0	9
Leyton Orient	Tr	07.88	88-89	30	1	1
Scunthorpe U	Tr	10.89	89-90	53	2	6
Lincoln C	Tr	03.91	90-92	38	1	0

WARD Peter
Rotherham, 20 October, 1954 (FB)

League Club	Source	Date Signed	Seasons Played	Apps	Subs	Gls
Sheffield U	App	10.72				
Workington	Tr	07.74	74-75	39	4	2

WARD Peter
Durham, 15 October, 1964 (M)

League Club	Source	Date Signed	Seasons Played	Apps	Subs	Gls
Huddersfield T	Chester-le-Street	01.87	86-88	24	13	2
Rochdale	Tr	07.89	89-90	83	1	10
Stockport Co	Tr	06.91	91-94	140	2	10
Wrexham	Tr	07.95	95-98	117	3	14

WARD Peter David
Derby, 27 July, 1955 Eu21-2/E-1 (F)

League Club	Source	Date Signed	Seasons Played	Apps	Subs	Gls
Brighton & Hove A	Burton A	05.75	75-80	172	6	79
Nottingham F	Tr	10.80	80-82	28	5	7
Brighton & Hove A	L	10.82	82	16	0	2

WARD Ralph Arthur
Oadby, 5 February, 1911 ESch (FB)

League Club	Source	Date Signed	Seasons Played	Apps	Subs	Gls
Bradford PA	Hinckley U	11.29	30-35	129	-	0
Tottenham H	Tr	03.36	35-38	115	-	10
Crewe Alex	Tr	08.46	46-48	91	-	7

WARD John **Richard (Richie)**
Scunthorpe, 16 September, 1940 EAmat (IF)

League Club	Source	Date Signed	Seasons Played	Apps	Subs	Gls
Scunthorpe U (Am)	Jnrs	05.58	58	1	-	0
Northampton T (Am)	Tr	06.59	59-61	7	-	0
Millwall	Tooting & Mitcham	07.62	62-63	13	-	3

WARD Robert (Bobby)
Glasgow, 21 October, 1958 (M)

League Club	Source	Date Signed	Seasons Played	Apps	Subs	Gls
Newport Co	Glasgow Celtic	01.80	79-80	2	1	0

WARD Robert (Bob) Andrew
West Bromwich, 4 August, 1953 (G)

League Club	Source	Date Signed	Seasons Played	Apps	Subs	Gls
West Bromwich A	Imperial Star	03.73	74-76	9	0	0
Northampton T	L	02.77	76	8	0	0
Blackpool	Tr	09.77	77-78	41	0	0
Wigan Ath	Tr	07.79	80-81	46	0	0

WARD Ronald (Ron)
Killamarsh, 10 February, 1935 ESch (G)

League Club	Source	Date Signed	Seasons Played	Apps	Subs	Gls
Chesterfield	Jnrs	02.52	51-52	8	-	0

WARD Ronald (Ron)
Altrincham, 17 October, 1932 Died 1998 (IF)

League Club	Source	Date Signed	Seasons Played	Apps	Subs	Gls
Stockport Co		03.54	53-55	17	-	3

WARD Henry **Ronald (Ron)**
Walthamstow, 29 March, 1932 (G)

League Club	Source	Date Signed	Seasons Played	Apps	Subs	Gls
Tottenham H		05.50				
Darlington	Headington U	08.56	56	26	-	0

League Club	Source	Date Signed	Seasons Played	Career Record Apps	Subs	Gls
WARD Scott						
Harrow, 5 October, 1981						(G)
Luton T	YT	10.98	00	0	1	0
WARD Stephen (Steve)						
Chapeltown, 27 December, 1960						(FB)
Lincoln C	App	12.78	79	2	0	0
WARD Stephen (Steve) Charles						
Derby, 21 July, 1959						(W)
Brighton & Hove A	App	10.76				
Northampton T	Tr	08.79	79	13	2	2
Halifax T	Tr	06.80	80-85	233	13	17
WARD Sydney (Syd)						
Dewsbury, 26 November, 1923						(G)
Bradford C	Upton Colliery	09.47	47	2	-	0
WARD Terence (Terry)						
Stoke-on-Trent, 10 December, 1939 Died 1968						(FB)
Stoke C	Jnrs	03.58	59-62	43	-	0
WARD Thomas (Tommy) Alfred						
Wolsingham, 6 August, 1917						(CF)
Sheffield Wed	Crook T	03.37	46-47	35	-	19
Darlington	Tr	08.48	48-53	119	-	32
WARD Timothy (Tim) Victor						
Cheltenham, 17 October, 1918 Died 1993 E-2						(WH)
Derby Co	Cheltenham T	04.37	37-50	238	-	4
Barnsley	Tr	03.51	50-52	33	-	0
WARD Warren						
Plymstock, 25 May, 1962						(F)
York C	Guiseley	03.85	84	4	0	3
Lincoln C	Tr	07.85	85	15	6	8
Exeter C	L	02.86	85	14	0	3
WARD Wayne Walter						
Colchester, 28 April, 1964						(FB)
Colchester U	App	05.82	81-82	17	2	0
WARD Lawrence **Whelan**						
Ovenden, 15 June, 1929						(IF)
Bradford C	Ovenden	10.48	48-53	149	-	37
Bradford PA	King's Lynn	07.55	55-58	108	-	31
WARD William (Billy)						
Chester-le-Street, 30 June, 1949						(W)
Hartlepool (Am)	Spennymoor U	01.72	71-72	8	0	1
Hartlepool	Shildon	01.73	72-74	79	8	9
WARDEN Daniel (Danny)						
Stepney, 11 April, 1973						(M)
Charlton Ath	Arsenal (YT)	07.92	92	1	2	0
WARDLE Ernest (Ernie)						
Stockton, 13 June, 1930 Died 2003						(FB)
Middlesbrough	Billingham Synthonia	05.48				
York C	Tr	01.55	54-58	60	-	2
WARDLE Geoffrey (Geoff)						
Trimdon, 7 January, 1940						(WH)
Sunderland	Houghton Jnrs	01.58				
Lincoln C	Tr	06.61	61	1	-	0
WARDLE George						
Kibblesworth, 24 September, 1919 Died 1991						(WH)
Middlesbrough	Durham BC	05.37	37	1	-	0
Exeter C	Tr	06.39	46	38	-	6
Cardiff C	Tr	05.47	46-48	40	-	11
Queens Park Rgrs	Tr	01.49	48-50	53	-	4
Darlington	Tr	08.51	51-53	95	-	6
WARDLE Ian Spencer						
Doncaster, 27 March, 1970 ESch						(G)
Barnsley	Jnrs	05.88	89	9	0	0
WARDLE Robert (Bob) Ian						
Halifax, 5 March, 1955						(G)
Bristol C	App	11.72				
Shrewsbury T	Tr	07.74	77-81	131	0	0
Liverpool	Tr	08.82				
Wrexham	L	09.83	83	13	0	0
WARDLE William (Billy)						
Houghton-le-Spring, 20 January, 1918 Died 1989						(W)
Southport	Houghton CW	12.36	36-37	14	-	0
Manchester C	Tr	10.37	37	6	-	0
Grimsby T	Tr	07.39	46-47	73	-	11
Blackpool	Tr	05.48	48-50	60	-	1
Birmingham C	Tr	09.51	51-52	60	-	5
Barnsley	Tr	11.53	53-54	28	-	1

League Club	Source	Date Signed	Seasons Played	Career Record Apps	Subs	Gls
WARDLEY Shane David						
Ipswich, 26 February, 1980						(M)
Southend U	Cambridge C	12.00	00	0	2	0
WARDLEY Stuart James						
Cambridge, 10 September, 1975						(M)
Queens Park Rgrs	Saffron Walden T	07.99	99-01	72	15	14
Rushden & Diamonds	Tr	01.02	01-02	54	3	10
Torquay U	Tr	08.04	04	5	2	2
Leyton Orient	Tr	10.04	04	4	2	0
Cambridge U	Tr	01.05	04	1	2	0
WARDROBE Thomas **Barrie**						
Newcastle, 3 July, 1963						(F)
Sunderland	App	04.81				
Hartlepool U	Tr	07.84	84	23	4	2
WARDROBE Michael (Micky)						
Newcastle, 24 March, 1962						(F)
Burnley	App	03.80	80	0	1	0
Stockport Co	Tr	08.81	81-82	19	8	2
WARE Charles (Charlie)						
York, 9 March, 1931						(W)
York C	Jnrs	12.48	53	9	-	0
WARE Paul David						
Congleton, 7 November, 1970						(M)
Stoke C	YT	11.88	87-93	92	23	10
Stockport Co	Tr	09.94	94-96	42	12	4
Cardiff C	L	01.97	96	5	0	0
Macclesfield T	Hednesford T	07.99	99	9	9	2
Rochdale	Tr	07.00	00-01	21	17	2
WARHURST Paul						
Stockport, 26 September, 1969 Eu21-8						(M)
Manchester C	YT	07.88				
Oldham Ath	Tr	10.88	88-90	60	7	2
Sheffield Wed	Tr	07.91	91-93	60	6	6
Blackburn Rov	Tr	08.93	93-96	30	27	4
Crystal Palace	Tr	07.97	97-98	27	0	4
Bolton W	Tr	11.98	98-02	81	10	0
Stoke C	L	03.03	02	4	1	1
Chesterfield	Tr	10.03	03	3	1	0
Barnsley	Tr	12.03	03	3	1	0
Carlisle U	Tr	02.04	03	0	1	0
Grimsby T	Tr	03.04	03	5	2	0
Blackpool	Tr	11.04	04	2	2	0
WARHURST Roy						
Sheffield, 18 September, 1926						(WH)
Sheffield U	Huddersfield T (Am)	09.44	46-49	17	-	2
Birmingham C	Tr	03.50	49-56	213	-	10
Manchester C	Tr	06.57	57-58	40	-	2
Crewe Alex	Tr	03.59	58-59	52	-	1
Oldham Ath	Tr	08.60	60	8	-	0
WARING Thomas **Alan**						
Preston, 3 August, 1929						(CD)
Burnley		08.48				
Halifax T	Tr	07.54	54	12	-	0
WARK John						
Glasgow, 4 August, 1957 SYth/Su21-8/S-29						(M)
Ipswich T	App	08.74	74-83	295	1	94
Liverpool	Tr	03.84	83-87	64	6	28
Ipswich T	Tr	01.88	87-89	87	2	23
Middlesbrough	Tr	08.90	90	31	1	2
Ipswich T	Tr	09.91	91-96	151	3	18
WARK Scott Andrew						
Glasgow, 9 June, 1987						(M)
Rushden & Diamonds	Sch	•	04	0	1	0
WARMAN Philip (Phil) Roy						
Bromley, 18 December, 1950 EYth						(FB)
Charlton Ath	Jnrs	03.68	69-80	313	3	19
Millwall	Tr	08.81	81	27	0	1
WARMINGTON Peter John						
Wythall, 8 April, 1934						(CF)
Birmingham C	Redditch Jnrs	12.51	54-56	8	-	3
WARN Keith Donald						
Watford, 20 March, 1941						(G)
Watford	Croxley BC	04.59	59	3	-	0
WARNE Paul						
Norwich, 8 May, 1973						(M)
Wigan Ath	Wroxham	07.97	97-98	11	25	3
Rotherham U	Tr	01.99	98-04	173	57	28
Mansfield T	L	11.04	04	7	0	1

League Club	Source	Date Signed	Seasons Played	Career Record Apps	Subs	Gls
WARNE Raymond (Ray)						
Ipswich, 16 February, 1929						(CF)
Ipswich T	Leiston	10.50	50-51	30	-	11
WARNE Stephen James						
Sutton-in-Ashfield, 27 February, 1984						(M)
Chesterfield	Sch	07.03	02	2	1	0
WARNER Anthony (Tony) Randolph						
Liverpool, 11 May, 1974						(G)
Liverpool	Jnrs	01.94				
Swindon T	L	11.97	97	2	0	0
Millwall	Tr	07.99	99-03	200	0	0
Cardiff C	Tr	07.04	04	26	0	0
WARNER Dennis Peter Alfred						
Rotherham, 6 December, 1930						(FB)
Rotherham U	Spurley Hey OB	03.50	52-56	64	-	0
Chesterfield	Tr	05.57	57	8	-	0
WARNER John (Jack)						
Tonyrefail, 21 September, 1911 Died 1980 WWar-1/W-2						(WH)
Swansea T	Aberaman Ath	01.34	33-37	135	-	9
Manchester U	Tr	06.38	38-49	102	-	1
Oldham Ath	Tr	06.51	51	34	-	2
Rochdale	Tr	07.52	52	21	-	0
WARNER John						
Ashington, 6 May, 1940						(W)
Luton T		10.59	59	1	-	0
WARNER John						
Paddington, 20 November, 1961						(F)
Colchester U	Burnham Ramblers	02.89	88	7	8	3
Colchester U	Hetbridge Swifts	12.89	89	1	1	0
WARNER Leslie (Les) Horace						
Birmingham, 19 December, 1918 Died 1982						(W)
Coventry C	Jack Moulds Ath	07.37	37-53	199	-	19
WARNER Michael James						
Harrogate, 17 January, 1974						(M)
Northampton T	Tamworth	07.95	96-98	9	19	0
WARNER Philip (Phil)						
Southampton, 2 February, 1979						(FB)
Southampton	YT	05.97	97-98	5	1	0
Brentford	L	07.99	99	1	13	0
Cambridge U	Tr	06.01	01-02	18	2	0
WARNER Reginald (Reg) Owen						
Anstey, 1 March, 1931 Died 1996 EYth						(CD)
Leicester C	Anstey Nomads	04.49	52-53	7	-	0
Mansfield T	Tr	03.55	54-56	33	-	0
WARNER Robert (Rob) Mark						
Stratford-on-Avon, 20 April, 1977						(FB)
Hereford U	YT	01.95	94-96	31	6	0
WARNER Scott John						
Rochdale, 3 December, 1983						(M)
Rochdale	Sch	07.03	02-04	41	8	1
WARNER Vance						
Leeds, 3 September, 1974 EYth						(CD)
Nottingham F	YT	09.91	93-96	4	1	0
Grimsby T	L	02.96	95	3	0	0
Rotherham U	Tr	08.97	97-99	60	2	1
WARNES George						
Worksop, 4 December, 1925						(G)
Rotherham U	Dinnington Colliery	12.44	46-49	98	-	0
Aldershot	Tr	06.50	50-51	32	-	0
WARNOCK Neil						
Sheffield, 1 December, 1948						(W)
Chesterfield	Sheffield FC	07.68	67-68	20	4	2
Rotherham U	Tr	06.69	69-70	46	6	5
Hartlepool	Tr	07.71	71-72	58	2	5
Scunthorpe U	Tr	02.72	72-74	63	9	7
Aldershot	Tr	03.75	74-76	35	2	6
Barnsley	Tr	10.76	76-77	53	4	10
York C	Tr	05.78	78	1	3	0
Crewe Alex	Tr	12.78	78	20	1	1
WARNOCK Stephen						
Ormskirk, 12 December, 1981 ESch/EYth						(W)
Liverpool	YT	04.99	04	11	8	0
Bradford C	L	09.02	02	12	0	1
Coventry C	L	07.03	03	42	2	3

League Club	Source	Date Signed	Seasons Played	Career Record Apps	Subs	Gls
WARREN Christer Simon						
Weymouth, 10 October, 1974						(FB)
Southampton	Cheltenham T	03.95	95-96	1	7	0
Brighton & Hove A	L	10.96	96	3	0	0
Fulham	L	03.97	96	8	3	1
Bournemouth	Tr	10.97	97-99	94	9	13
Queens Park Rgrs	Tr	06.00	00-01	24	12	0
Bristol Rov	Tr	09.02	02	0	2	0
WARREN David John Paul						
Cork, 28 February, 1981 IRYth						(M)
Wrexham	Mayfield U	08.99	99-01	6	0	0
WARREN Derek Bernard						
Colyton, 23 May, 1923						(FB)
Exeter C	Axminster	01.48	48-51	55	-	0
WARREN Lee Anthony						
Manchester, 28 February, 1969						(CD)
Leeds U	YT	08.87				
Rochdale	Tr	10.87	87	31	0	1
Hull C	Tr	08.88	88-93	141	12	1
Lincoln C	L	09.90	90	2	1	1
Doncaster Rov	Tr	07.94	94-97	115	10	3
WARREN Mark Wayne						
Clapton, 12 November, 1974 EYth						(CD)
Leyton Orient	YT	07.92	91-98	134	18	5
Oxford U	L	12.98	98	4	0	0
Notts Co	Tr	01.99	98-01	76	8	1
Colchester U	Tr	08.02	02	20	0	0
Southend U	Tr	06.03	03	27	5	2
WARREN Raymond (Ray) Richard						
Bristol, 23 June, 1918 Died 1988						(CD)
Bristol Rov	Parson Street OB	11.35	35-55	450	-	28
WARREN Robert (Bob)						
Devonport, 8 January, 1927						(CD)
Plymouth Arg	Plymouth U	02.46	46	3	-	0
Chelsea	Tr	07.48	48	1	-	0
Torquay U	Tr	08.51	51	5	-	1
WARRENDER Robert (Bobby)						
Leven, 13 February, 1929 Died 2003						(IF)
York C	East Fife	05.52	52-53	24	-	5
WARRILOW Thomas (Tommy)						
Plumstead, 26 July, 1964						(CD)
Torquay U	Gravesend & N (N/C)	03.87	86	2	0	0
WARRINER Stephen (Steve) William						
Liverpool, 18 December, 1958						(FB)
Liverpool	App	12.76				
Newport Co	Tr	07.78	78-80	28	8	2
Rochdale	Tr	08.81	81-82	11	1	1
Tranmere Rov	Tr	02.83	82	5	4	0
WARRINGTON Andrew (Andy) Clifford						
Sheffield, 10 June, 1976						(G)
York C	YT	06.94	95-98	61	0	0
Doncaster Rov	Tr	06.99	03-04	80	0	0
WARRINGTON Tony						
Ecclesfield, 12 February, 1934						(G)
Lincoln C	Thorncliffe Jnrs	03.54	53-55	2	-	0
WARSAP John (Johnny) William Benjamin						
Leytonstone, 18 May, 1921 Died 1992						(W)
Gillingham		(N/L)	50-52	9	-	1
WARZYCHA Robert						
Wielun, Poland, 20 June, 1963 Poland int						(W)
Everton	Gornik Zabrze (Pol)	03.91	90-93	51	21	6
WASILEWSKI Zdzislaw (Adam)						
Poland, 1925 Died 1956						(CF)
Rochdale		07.53	53	4	-	1
WASS William						
Ryhope, 16 November, 1922						(W)
Middlesbrough		02.45				
Bradford C	Tr	07.46	46	7	-	1
WASSALL Darren Paul James						
Edgbaston, 27 June, 1968						(CD)
Nottingham F	App	06.86	87-91	17	10	0
Hereford U	L	10.87	87	5	0	0
Bury	L	03.89	88	7	0	1
Derby Co	Tr	06.92	92-95	90	8	0
Manchester C	L	09.96	96	14	1	0
Birmingham C	Tr	03.97	96-98	22	3	0

WASSALL John Charles
Erdington, 9 June, 1933 Died 1987 (FB)

League Club	Source	Date Signed	Seasons Played	Apps	Subs	Gls
Coventry C	Jnrs	05.51	55-56	17	-	0
Southport	Tr	08.57	57	4	-	0

WASSALL John Victor
Shrewsbury, 11 February, 1917 Died 1994 (IF)

League Club	Source	Date Signed	Seasons Played	Apps	Subs	Gls
Manchester U	Wellington T	02.35	35-38	45	-	6
Stockport Co	Tr	10.46	46-47	19	-	2

WASSELL Kim
Wolverhampton, 9 June, 1957 (W)

League Club	Source	Date Signed	Seasons Played	Apps	Subs	Gls
West Bromwich A	App	06.75				
Northampton T	Tr	09.77	77-78	13	7	0
Hull C	(Australia)	08.83	83	1	0	0
Swansea C		09.84	84	1	1	0
Wolverhampton W		10.85	85	2	0	0
Shrewsbury T	(Finland)	11.89	89	0	2	0

WATERHOUSE Kenneth (Ken)
Ormskirk, 23 January, 1930 (WH)

League Club	Source	Date Signed	Seasons Played	Apps	Subs	Gls
Preston NE	Burscough	12.48	53-56	20	-	5
Rotherham U	Tr	05.58	58-62	123	-	12
Bristol C	Tr	04.63	62-63	16	-	1
Darlington	Tr	08.64	64	1	-	0

WATERMAN David (Dave) Graham
Guernsey, 16 May, 1977 NIu21-14 (CD)

League Club	Source	Date Signed	Seasons Played	Apps	Subs	Gls
Portsmouth	YT	07.95	96-01	60	20	0
Oxford U	Tr	03.02	01-03	37	10	1

WATERMAN Derek James
Guildford, 12 April, 1939 (WH)

League Club	Source	Date Signed	Seasons Played	Apps	Subs	Gls
Exeter C	Guildford C	06.57	57	4	-	0

WATERS Graham John
St Austell, 5 November, 1971 (FB)

League Club	Source	Date Signed	Seasons Played	Apps	Subs	Gls
Oxford U	YT	05.90				
Exeter C	Tr	07.91	91	1	1	0

WATERS Joseph (Joe) John Wary
Limerick, 20 September, 1953 IR-2 (M)

League Club	Source	Date Signed	Seasons Played	Apps	Subs	Gls
Leicester C	App	10.70	73-74	11	2	1
Grimsby T	Tr	01.76	75-83	356	1	65

WATERS Patrick (Paddy) Mary
Dublin, 31 January, 1922 Died 2004 IWar-1 (CD)

League Club	Source	Date Signed	Seasons Played	Apps	Subs	Gls
Preston NE	Glentoran	06.47	47-49	64	-	0
Carlisle U	Tr	12.50	50-57	252	-	0

WATERS Richard
Gateshead, 18 May, 1945 (G)

League Club	Source	Date Signed	Seasons Played	Apps	Subs	Gls
Darlington (Am)	Blyth Spartans	03.65	64	2	-	0

WATERS Samuel (Sam)
Croy, 31 May, 1917 Died 1975 (W)

League Club	Source	Date Signed	Seasons Played	Apps	Subs	Gls
Halifax T	Third Lanark	07.46	46	25	-	9

WATERS William (Billy) Anthony
Swansea, 19 September, 1931 (G)

League Club	Source	Date Signed	Seasons Played	Apps	Subs	Gls
Blackpool		11.50				
Southend U		11.53				
Swansea T	Tr	08.54				
Wrexham	Tr	06.55	55-59	99	-	0
Millwall	Tr	07.60	60	5	-	0

WATFORD Albert
Chesterfield, 12 February, 1917 Died 1982 (FB)

League Club	Source	Date Signed	Seasons Played	Apps	Subs	Gls
Chester (Am)	Mosborough	08.38	38	1	-	0
Chesterfield		02.44				
Lincoln C	Tr	09.46	46	14	-	0

WATKIN Alan James
Felling, 16 May, 1940 (W)

League Club	Source	Date Signed	Seasons Played	Apps	Subs	Gls
Gateshead (Am)		08.59	59	3	-	0

WATKIN Cyril
Stoke-on-Trent, 21 July, 1926 (FB)

League Club	Source	Date Signed	Seasons Played	Apps	Subs	Gls
Stoke C	Port Vale (Am)	09.44	48-51	86	-	0
Bristol C	Tr	07.52	52	3	-	0

WATKIN George
Chopwell, 14 April, 1944 (CF)

League Club	Source	Date Signed	Seasons Played	Apps	Subs	Gls
Newcastle U	App	04.62	62	1	-	0
Chesterfield	King's Lynn	07.64	64	7	-	1

WATKIN Stephen (Steve)
Wrexham, 16 June, 1971 WSch/WB-2 (F)

League Club	Source	Date Signed	Seasons Played	Apps	Subs	Gls
Wrexham	Jnrs	07.89	90-97	167	33	55
Swansea C	Tr	09.97	97-02	167	39	44

WATKIN Thomas **William** Steel
Grimsby, 21 September, 1932 Died 2001 ESch (W)

League Club	Source	Date Signed	Seasons Played	Apps	Subs	Gls
Grimsby T	Jnrs	10.49				
Gateshead	Tr	12.52	52-53	39	-	14
Middlesbrough	Tr	03.54	53-54	11	-	2
Mansfield T	Tr	06.55	55	25	-	4

WATKINS Albert (Alan) John
Usk, 21 April, 1922 (WH)

League Club	Source	Date Signed	Seasons Played	Apps	Subs	Gls
Plymouth Arg		12.45	46	4	-	1

WATKINS Randall **Burnell (Barry)**
Bedlinog, 30 November, 1921 Died 2004 (FB)

League Club	Source	Date Signed	Seasons Played	Apps	Subs	Gls
Bristol Rov	BAC	10.45	46-54	116	-	7

WATKINS Charles (Charlie)
Glasgow, 14 January, 1921 Died 1998 (WH)

League Club	Source	Date Signed	Seasons Played	Apps	Subs	Gls
Luton T	Glasgow Rgrs	09.48	48-54	218	-	16

WATKINS Dale Allan
Peterborough, 4 November, 1971 ESemiPro-2 (F)

League Club	Source	Date Signed	Seasons Played	Apps	Subs	Gls
Peterborough U	Sheffield U (YT)	08.90	89-90	5	5	0
Cheltenham T	Gloucester C	07.97	99	4	5	0

WATKINS John (Johnny) Vincent
Bristol, 9 April, 1933 EYth (W)

League Club	Source	Date Signed	Seasons Played	Apps	Subs	Gls
Bristol C	Clifton St Vincent's	06.51	53-58	95	-	19
Cardiff C	Tr	06.59	59-60	65	-	17
Bristol Rov	Tr	02.61	60-61	23	-	0

WATKINS Philip (Phil) John
Caerphilly, 2 January, 1945 (WH)

League Club	Source	Date Signed	Seasons Played	Apps	Subs	Gls
Cardiff C	Jnrs	09.62	63	1	-	0

WATKINS Robert (Wally) Stephen
Bristol, 20 December, 1946 (W)

League Club	Source	Date Signed	Seasons Played	Apps	Subs	Gls
Bristol Rov	Bristol C (Am)	07.65	65	1	0	0

WATKINSON Russell (Russ)
Epsom, 3 December, 1977 (W)

League Club	Source	Date Signed	Seasons Played	Apps	Subs	Gls
Southampton	Woking	09.96	96	0	2	0

WATKINSON William (Billy) Wainwright
Prescot, 16 March, 1922 Died 2001 (CF)

League Club	Source	Date Signed	Seasons Played	Apps	Subs	Gls
Liverpool	Prescot Cables	02.46	46-49	24	-	2
Accrington St	Tr	01.51	50-54	105	-	45
Halifax T	Tr	09.54	54-55	60	-	24

WATKISS Stuart Paul
Wolverhampton, 8 May, 1966 (CD)

League Club	Source	Date Signed	Seasons Played	Apps	Subs	Gls
Wolverhampton W	App	07.84	83	2	0	0
Crewe Alex		02.86	85	3	0	0
Walsall	Rushall Olympic	08.93	93-95	60	2	2
Hereford U	Tr	02.96	95	19	0	0
Mansfield T	Tr	07.96	96-97	40	1	1

WATLING Barry John
Walthamstow, 16 July, 1946 (G)

League Club	Source	Date Signed	Seasons Played	Apps	Subs	Gls
Leyton Orient	App	07.64				
Bristol C	Tr	07.65	67-68	2	0	0
Notts Co	Tr	07.69	69-71	65	1	0
Hartlepool	Tr	07.72	72-75	139	0	0
Chester	L	09.75	75	5	0	0
Rotherham U	L	12.75	75	5	0	0
Sheffield Wed	Tr	01.76	75	1	0	0

WATLING John Daniel
Bristol, 11 May, 1925 (W)

League Club	Source	Date Signed	Seasons Played	Apps	Subs	Gls
Bristol Rov	Avonmouth	01.47	47-61	323	-	19

WATSON Albert
Bolton-on-Dearne, 1 June, 1918 (WH)

League Club	Source	Date Signed	Seasons Played	Apps	Subs	Gls
Huddersfield T	Jnrs	12.35	37-47	17	-	0
Oldham Ath	Tr	07.48	48-49	42	-	0

WATSON Alexander (Alex) Francis
Liverpool, 5 April, 1968 EYth (CD)

League Club	Source	Date Signed	Seasons Played	Apps	Subs	Gls
Liverpool	App	05.85	87-88	3	1	0
Derby Co	L	08.90	90	5	0	0
Bournemouth	Tr	01.91	90-94	145	6	5
Gillingham	L	09.95	95	10	0	1
Torquay U	Tr	11.95	95-00	201	1	8
Exeter C	Tr	07.01	01-02	45	1	1

WATSON Andrew (Andy)
Aberdeen, 3 September, 1959 Su21-4 (W)

League Club	Source	Date Signed	Seasons Played	Apps	Subs	Gls
Leeds U	Aberdeen	06.83	83-84	37	1	7

WATSON Andrew (Andy) Anthony
Leeds, 1 April, 1967 (F)

League Club	Source	Date Signed	Seasons Played	Apps	Subs	Gls
Halifax T	Harrogate T	08.88	88-89	75	8	15
Swansea C	Tr	07.90	90	9	5	1

League Club	Source	Date Signed	Seasons Played	Apps	Subs	Gls
Carlisle U	Tr	09.91	91-92	55	1	22
Blackpool	Tr	02.93	92-95	88	27	43
Walsall	Tr	09.96	96-98	57	27	15

WATSON Andrew (Andy) Lyon
Huddersfield, 3 April, 1967 (CD)

League Club	Source	Date Signed	Seasons Played	Apps	Subs	Gls
Huddersfield T	App	04.85				
Exeter C	Tr	07.86	86-87	41	1	1

WATSON Arthur
South Hiendley, 12 July, 1913 Died 1995 (FB)

League Club	Source	Date Signed	Seasons Played	Apps	Subs	Gls
Lincoln C	Monckton CW	05.34	34-35	37	-	0
Chesterfield	Tr	06.36	36-38	10	-	0
Hull C	Tr	06.39	46	35	-	2

WATSON Benjamin (Ben)
Camberwell, 9 July, 1985 Eu21-1 (M)

League Club	Source	Date Signed	Seasons Played	Apps	Subs	Gls
Crystal Palace	Sch	08.04	02-04	27	15	1

WATSON Charles (Charlie) Richard
Newark, 10 March, 1949 (G)

League Club	Source	Date Signed	Seasons Played	Apps	Subs	Gls
Notts Co		02.67	67	1	0	0

WATSON David (Dave)
Liverpool, 20 November, 1961 Eu21-7/E-12 (CD)

League Club	Source	Date Signed	Seasons Played	Apps	Subs	Gls
Liverpool	Jnrs	05.79				
Norwich C	Tr	11.80	80-85	212	0	11
Everton	Tr	08.86	86-99	419	4	22

WATSON David Neil
Barnsley, 10 November, 1973 EYth/Eu21-5 (G)

League Club	Source	Date Signed	Seasons Played	Apps	Subs	Gls
Barnsley	YT	07.92	92-98	178	0	0

WATSON David (Dave) Vernon
Stapleford, 5 October, 1946 E-65 (CD)

League Club	Source	Date Signed	Seasons Played	Apps	Subs	Gls
Notts Co	Stapleford OB	01.67	66-67	24	1	1
Rotherham U	Tr	01.68	67-70	121	0	19
Sunderland	Tr	12.70	70-74	177	0	27
Manchester C	Tr	06.75	75-78	146	0	4
Southampton	Werder Bremen (Ger)	10.79	79-81	73	0	7
Stoke C	Tr	01.82	81-82	59	0	5
Derby Co	Vancouver (Can)	09.83	83	34	0	1
Notts Co	Fort Lauderdale (USA)	09.84	84	23	2	1

WATSON Donald (Don)
Barnsley, 27 August, 1932 (IF)

League Club	Source	Date Signed	Seasons Played	Apps	Subs	Gls
Sheffield Wed	Worsborough Bridge	09.54	54-56	8	-	3
Lincoln C	Tr	12.56	56-57	14	-	2
Bury	Tr	11.57	57-61	172	-	65
Barnsley	Tr	01.62	61	8	-	1
Rochdale	Tr	07.62	62-63	58	-	15
Barrow	Tr	07.64	64	17	-	1

WATSON Garry
Bradford, 7 October, 1955 (FB)

League Club	Source	Date Signed	Seasons Played	Apps	Subs	Gls
Bradford C	App	10.73	72-83	246	17	28
Doncaster Rov	L	10.82	82	13	0	0
Halifax T	Tr	07.84	84	21	0	0

WATSON Gary
Easington, 2 March, 1961 (FB)

League Club	Source	Date Signed	Seasons Played	Apps	Subs	Gls
Oxford U	App	11.78	78-79	24	0	0
Carlisle U	Tr	05.80	80	17	1	0

WATSON Thomas **Gordon**
Wolsingham, 1 March, 1914 Died 2001 (WH)

League Club	Source	Date Signed	Seasons Played	Apps	Subs	Gls
Everton	Blyth Spartans	01.33	36-48	61	-	1

WATSON Gordon William George
Sidcup, 20 March, 1971 Eu21-2 (F)

League Club	Source	Date Signed	Seasons Played	Apps	Subs	Gls
Charlton Ath	YT	04.89	89-90	20	11	7
Sheffield Wed	Tr	02.91	90-94	29	37	15
Southampton	Tr	03.95	94-96	37	15	8
Bradford C	Tr	01.97	96-98	8	13	5
Bournemouth	Tr	08.99	99	2	4	0
Hartlepool U	Tr	09.01	01-02	43	6	23

WATSON Graham Sidney
Doncaster, 3 August, 1949 (M)

League Club	Source	Date Signed	Seasons Played	Apps	Subs	Gls
Doncaster Rov	App	11.66	66-67	47	1	11
Rotherham U	Tr	02.68	67-68	13	0	1
Doncaster Rov	Tr	01.69	68-72	105	4	23
Cambridge U	Tr	09.72	72-78	206	3	24
Lincoln C	Tr	09.78	78-79	43	0	2
Cambridge U	Tr	03.80	79	0	1	0

WATSON Ian
North Shields, 5 February, 1960 (G)

League Club	Source	Date Signed	Seasons Played	Apps	Subs	Gls
Sunderland	App	02.78	78	1	0	0
Rochdale	L	08.79	79	33	0	0

WATSON Ian Lionel
Hammersmith, 7 January, 1944 (FB)

League Club	Source	Date Signed	Seasons Played	Apps	Subs	Gls
Chelsea	Jnrs	02.62	62-64	5	-	1
Queens Park Rgrs	Tr	07.65	65-73	196	6	1

WATSON James (Jimmy)
Cowie, 16 January, 1924 SLge-1/S-2 (IF)

League Club	Source	Date Signed	Seasons Played	Apps	Subs	Gls
Huddersfield T	Motherwell	06.52	52-56	140	-	29

WATSON James
Birmingham, 3 March, 1937 (FB)

League Club	Source	Date Signed	Seasons Played	Apps	Subs	Gls
Walsall		05.55	55	1	-	0

WATSON John
Ruabon, 2 May, 1942 WSch (FB)

League Club	Source	Date Signed	Seasons Played	Apps	Subs	Gls
Everton	Jnrs	05.59				
Chester	Tr	08.60	60-61	25	-	0

WATSON John
Dewsbury, 10 April, 1959 (G)

League Club	Source	Date Signed	Seasons Played	Apps	Subs	Gls
Huddersfield T	Jnrs	03.77				
Hartlepool U	Tr	03.79	78-82	44	0	0

WATSON John (Jack) Fox
Hamilton, 31 December, 1917 Died 1976 (CD)

League Club	Source	Date Signed	Seasons Played	Apps	Subs	Gls
Bury	Douglas Water Thistle	06.36	38	6	-	0
Fulham	Tr	08.46	46-47	71	-	2
Crystal Palace	Real Madrid (Sp)	07.49	49-50	61	-	1

WATSON John Ian
South Shields, 14 April, 1974 (W)

League Club	Source	Date Signed	Seasons Played	Apps	Subs	Gls
Newcastle U	YT	04.92	90	0	1	0
Scunthorpe U	Tr	07.93	93	1	4	0

WATSON John Martin
Edinburgh, 13 February, 1959 (F)

League Club	Source	Date Signed	Seasons Played	Apps	Subs	Gls
Fulham	Dunfermline Ath	08.89	89	12	2	0

WATSON Kenneth (Ken)
Whickham, 8 September, 1934 (WH)

League Club	Source	Date Signed	Seasons Played	Apps	Subs	Gls
Lincoln C		05.52				
Aldershot	Tr	07.55	57-59	29	-	1

WATSON Kevin Edward
Hackney, 3 January, 1974 (M)

League Club	Source	Date Signed	Seasons Played	Apps	Subs	Gls
Tottenham H	YT	05.92	92	4	1	0
Brentford	L	03.94	93	2	1	0
Bristol C	L	12.94	94	1	1	0
Barnet	L	02.95	94	13	0	0
Swindon T	Tr	07.96	96-98	39	24	1
Rotherham U	Tr	07.99	99-01	109	0	7
Reading	L	11.01	01	6	0	0
Reading	Tr	03.02	01-03	40	20	2
Colchester U	Tr	07.04	04	44	0	2

WATSON Liam
Liverpool, 21 May, 1970 (F)

League Club	Source	Date Signed	Seasons Played	Apps	Subs	Gls
Preston NE	Warrington T	03.93	92-93	7	2	3

WATSON Mark Leon
Birmingham, 28 December, 1973 (F)

League Club	Source	Date Signed	Seasons Played	Apps	Subs	Gls
West Ham U	Sutton U	05.95	95	0	1	0
Leyton Orient	L	09.95	95	0	1	1
Cambridge U	L	10.95	95	1	3	1
Shrewsbury T	L	02.96	95	1	0	0
Bournemouth	Tr	05.96	96	6	9	2

WATSON Mark Stewart
Vancouver, Canada, 8 September, 1970 Cau23-13/Ca-58 (CD)

League Club	Source	Date Signed	Seasons Played	Apps	Subs	Gls
Watford	Vancouver 86ers (Can)	11.93	93-94	18	0	0
Oxford U	Osters IF (Swe)	12.98	98-99	57	1	0
Oldham Ath	Tr	09.00	00	1	1	0

WATSON Paul Douglas
Hastings, 4 January, 1975 (FB)

League Club	Source	Date Signed	Seasons Played	Apps	Subs	Gls
Gillingham	YT	12.92	92-95	57	5	2
Fulham	Tr	07.96	96-97	48	2	4
Brentford	Tr	12.97	97-98	37	0	0
Brighton & Hove A	Tr	07.99	99-04	191	6	14

WATSON Peter
Newcastle, 18 March, 1935 (CF)

League Club	Source	Date Signed	Seasons Played	Apps	Subs	Gls
Workington	North Shields	11.62	62-64	45	-	10

WATSON Peter Frederick
Stapleford, 15 April, 1934 (CD)

League Club	Source	Date Signed	Seasons Played	Apps	Subs	Gls
Nottingham F	Jnrs	05.55	55-58	13	-	0
Southend U	Tr	07.59	59-65	247	0	3

WATSON Thomas **Sidney (Sid)**
Mansfield, 12 December, 1927 (WH)

League Club	Source	Date Signed	Seasons Played	Apps	Subs	Gls
Mansfield T	Palterton Welfare	01.49	51-60	292	-	9

League Club	Source	Date Signed	Seasons Played	Career Record Apps	Subs	Gls
WATSON Stanley (Stan)						
Darlington, 17 March, 1937						(CD)
Darlington		11.57	57-58	27	-	0
WATSON Stephen (Steve) Craig						
North Shields, 1 April, 1974 EYth/Eu21-12/EB-1						(FB)
Newcastle U	YT	04.91	90-98	179	29	12
Aston Villa	Tr	10.98	98-99	39	2	0
Everton	Tr	07.00	00-04	106	20	14
WATSON Thomas (Tommy)						
Lesmahagow, 23 August, 1943						(W)
Peterborough U	Stevenage T	05.65	65-67	75	0	20
Walsall	Tr	09.67	67-69	84	2	17
Gillingham	Tr	06.70	70-71	42	7	7
WATSON Thomas Duncan						
Boldon, 3 February, 1936						(W)
West Bromwich A	Boldon CW	11.53				
Gateshead	Tr	06.57	57	21	-	5
WATSON Thomas (Tommy) Robert						
Liverpool, 29 September, 1969						(W)
Grimsby T	YT	07.88	87-95	134	38	24
Hull C	L	10.95	95	4	0	0
WATSON Trevor Peter						
Great Yarmouth, 26 September, 1938						(W)
Fulham	Jnrs	07.56	56-63	17	-	1
WATSON Vaughan						
Mansfield, 5 November, 1931 Died 1984						(CF)
Mansfield T	Mansfield WE	04.52	52-53	14	-	9
Chesterfield	Tr	05.54	54	13	-	5
WATSON William (Bill)						
South Hiendley, 29 May, 1916 Died 1986						(FB)
Lincoln C	Monckton CW	02.35	34-35	9	-	0
Chesterfield	Tr	06.36	46-47	36	-	0
Rochdale	Tr	06.48	48-53	200	-	0
WATSON William (Willie)						
Bolton-on-Dearne, 7 March, 1920 Died 2004 EB/EWar-1/E-4						(WH)
Huddersfield T	Jnrs	10.37	38	11	-	0
Sunderland	Tr	04.46	46-53	211	-	15
Halifax T	Tr	11.54	54-55	33	-	1
WATSON William (Willie)						
New Stevenston, 4 December, 1949						(FB)
Manchester U	Jnrs	12.66	70-72	11	0	0
WATSON William (Willie) Thomas						
Swansea, 11 June, 1918 Died 1978						(FB)
Preston NE		02.46	46	15	-	0
Cardiff C	Tr	10.47	47	1	-	0
WATT John (Johnny)						
Crookedholm, 17 June, 1943						(W)
Blackpool	Saxone Jnrs	08.60	62	5	-	0
Stockport Co	Tr	07.63	63-64	55	-	4
Southport	Tr	03.65	64-65	17	1	2
WATT John Gibson						
Airdrie, 23 November, 1954						(FB)
Watford	App	11.72	71	0	1	0
WATT Michael						
Aberdeen, 27 November, 1970 SSch/Su21-12/SB-1						(G)
Norwich C	Aberdeen	08.98	98	7	1	0
WATT Steven (Steve) Mair						
Aberdeen, 1 May, 1985 Su21-2/SB-1						(CD)
Chelsea	Sch	07.02	04	0	1	0
WATT William (Willie) Douglas						
Aberdeen, 6 June, 1946						(W)
Preston NE	Jnrs	06.63	64-65	7	1	0
WATTERS John						
Glasgow, 24 September, 1913 Died 1989						(IF)
New Brighton	Ayr U	07.36	36	19	-	2
Stockport Co	Cowdenbeath	08.47	47	5	-	1
WATTLEY David Anthony						
Enfield, 5 September, 1983						(CD)
Queens Park Rgrs	YT	09.00				
Lincoln C	Tr	07.03	03	1	2	0
WATTON James (Jimmy)						
Wolverhampton, 1 November, 1936						(FB)
Port Vale	De Graafschap (Holl)	09.62	62	5	-	0
Doncaster Rov	Tr	07.64	64-67	121	2	0

League Club	Source	Date Signed	Seasons Played	Career Record Apps	Subs	Gls
WATTS Derek						
Leicester, 30 October, 1952 ESch						(F)
Leicester C	App	05.70				
Northampton T	L	10.73	73	0	1	0
WATTS Grant Steven						
Croydon, 5 November, 1973						(F)
Crystal Palace	YT	06.92	92	2	2	0
Colchester U	L	01.94	93	8	4	2
Gillingham	Sheffield U (N/C)	09.94	94	2	1	0
WATTS James Alan						
Cowes, 25 October, 1933 Died 2000						(CF)
Gillingham (Am)		12.56	56	12	-	1
WATTS John (Johnny) William						
Birmingham, 13 April, 1931						(WH)
Birmingham C	Saltley OB	08.51	51-62	206	-	3
WATTS Julian						
Sheffield, 17 March, 1971						(CD)
Rotherham U	Frecheville Community	07.90	90-91	17	3	1
Sheffield Wed	Tr	03.92	92-95	12	4	1
Shrewsbury T	L	12.92	92	9	0	0
Leicester C	Tr	03.96	95-97	31	7	1
Crewe Alex	L	08.97	97	5	0	0
Huddersfield T	L	02.98	97	8	0	0
Bristol C	Tr	07.98	98	16	1	1
Lincoln C	L	12.98	98	2	0	0
Blackpool	L	03.99	98	9	0	0
Luton T	Tr	08.99	99-00	71	2	8
WATTS Mark Robert						
Walham Green, 24 September, 1965						(F)
Luton T	App	01.83	82	1	0	0
WATTS Ryan Dale						
Greenford, 18 May, 1988						(F)
Brentford	Sch	●	04	0	1	0
WATTS Steven (Steve)						
Lambeth, 11 July, 1976						(F)
Leyton Orient	Fisher Ath	10.98	98-02	69	63	29
Lincoln C	L	12.02	02	5	0	1
Shrewsbury T	Tr	03.03	02	3	4	0
WAUGH Keith						
Sunderland, 27 October, 1956						(G)
Sunderland	App	07.74				
Peterborough U	Tr	07.76	76-80	195	0	0
Sheffield U	Tr	08.81	81-84	99	0	0
Cambridge U	L	11.84	84	4	0	0
Bristol C	L	12.84	84	3	0	0
Bristol C	Tr	07.85	85-88	167	0	0
Coventry C	Tr	08.89	89	1	0	0
Watford	Tr	01.91	91-92	7	0	0
WAUGH Kenneth (Ken)						
Newcastle, 6 August, 1933						(FB)
Newcastle U	Film Renters	08.52	55	7	-	0
Hartlepools U	Tr	12.56	56-61	195	-	0
WAUGH Warren Anthony						
Harlesden, 9 October, 1980						(F)
Exeter C	YT	07.99	98-99	0	10	0
WAUGH William (Billy) Lindsay						
Edinburgh, 27 November, 1921						(W)
Luton T	Bathgate Thistle	09.44	46-49	135	-	9
Queens Park Rgrs	Tr	07.50	50-52	77	-	6
Bournemouth	Tr	07.53	53	18	-	3
WAY Darren						
Plymouth, 21 November, 1979 ESemiPro-3						(M)
Norwich C	YT	09.98				
Yeovil T	Tr	08.00	03-04	83	1	12
WAY Michael (Mike) Andrew						
Salisbury, 18 May, 1950						(FB)
Oxford U	Thame U	08.69	69-71	14	2	0
WAYMAN Charles (Charlie)						
Bishop Auckland, 16 May, 1922						(CF)
Newcastle U	Spennymoor U	09.41	46-47	47	-	32
Southampton	Tr	10.47	47-49	100	-	73
Preston NE	Tr	09.50	50-54	157	-	105
Middlesbrough	Tr	09.54	54-55	55	-	31
Darlington	Tr	12.56	56-57	23	-	14
WAYMAN Franklyn (Frank)						
Bishop Auckland, 30 December, 1931						(W)
Preston NE		09.53				

League Club	Source	Date Signed	Seasons Played	Career Record Apps	Subs	Gls
Chester	Tr	08.55	55	30	-	2
Darlington	Easington Colliery	06.57	57	1	-	0
WDOWCZYK Dariusz						
Warsaw, Poland, 21 September, 1962 Poland int						(CD)
Reading	Glasgow Celtic	08.94	94-97	77	5	0
WEAH George						
Monrovia, Liberia, 1 October, 1966 Liberia int						(F)
Chelsea (L)	AC Milan (It)	01.00	99	9	2	3
Manchester C	AC Milan (It)	08.00	00	5	2	1
WEAKLEY Bernard						
Rotherham, 20 December, 1932						(W)
Rotherham U		08.55	55	2	-	1
WEALANDS Jeffrey (Jeff) Andrew						
Darlington, 26 August, 1951						(G)
Wolverhampton W	App	10.68				
Darlington	Tr	07.70	71	28	0	0
Hull C	Tr	03.72	71-78	240	0	0
Birmingham C	Tr	07.79	79-81	102	0	0
Manchester U	Tr	02.83	82-83	7	0	0
Oldham Ath	L	03.84	83	10	0	0
Preston NE	L	12.84	84	4	0	0
WEALE Christopher (Chris)						
Chard, 9 February, 1982 ESemiPro-4						(G)
Yeovil T	Jnrs	06.00	03-04	72	1	0
WEALTHALL Barry Arthur						
Nottingham, 1 May, 1942 EYth						(FB)
Nottingham F	Jnrs	06.59	60	2	-	0
Grimsby T	Tr	05.62	61-62	9	-	0
York C	Tr	06.63	63-66	75	0	0
WEARE Arthur **John (Jack)**						
Newport, 21 September, 1912						(G)
Wolverhampton W	Lovells Ath	05.33	33-36	42	-	0
West Ham U	Tr	09.36	36-37	57	-	0
Bristol Rov	St Mirren	11.45	46-49	141	-	0
WEARE Leonard (Len) Nicholas						
Newport, 23 July, 1934						(G)
Newport Co		08.55	55-69	528	0	0
WEARE Ross Michael						
Perivale, 19 March, 1977						(F)
Queens Park Rgrs	East Ham U	03.99	99	0	4	0
Bristol Rov	Tr	07.01	01	9	1	1
WEARMOUTH Michael (Mike)						
Barrow, 16 May, 1944						(CD)
Barrow	Jnrs	06.62	61-63	33	-	0
Preston NE	Tr	03.64	64-66	11	0	0
WEATHERALL Leonard (Len)						
Middlesbrough, 21 May, 1936						(IF)
Grimsby T	Redcar BC	04.55	54-55	10	-	1
WEATHERHEAD Shaun						
Halifax, 3 September, 1970						(CD)
Huddersfield T	YT	07.89				
York C	Tr	09.90	90	6	2	0
WEATHERLY Colin **Mark**						
Ramsgate, 18 January, 1958						(CD)
Gillingham	App	12.75	74-88	408	49	47
WEATHERSPOON Charles (Charlie) William						
Newcastle, 3 October, 1929 Died 1986						(CF)
Sunderland	Jnrs	08.47				
Sheffield U	Annfield Plain	01.51	50	1	-	0
Hartlepools U	Tr	08.52	52	3	-	2
WEATHERSTONE Ross						
Reading, 16 May, 1981						(CD)
Oxford U	YT	10.99	99-00	4	0	0
Boston U	Tr	02.01	02	2	6	0
WEATHERSTONE Simon						
Reading, 26 January, 1980 ESemiPro-3						(M)
Oxford U	YT	03.97	96-00	25	27	3
Boston U	Tr	02.01	02-03	57	5	10
Yeovil T	Tr	01.04	03-04	11	10	1
WEAVER Eric						
Rhymney, 1 July, 1943						(W)
Swindon T	Trowbridge T	12.61	61-66	55	0	6
Notts Co	Tr	08.67	67	16	1	4
Northampton T	Tr	12.67	67-69	61	2	9

League Club	Source	Date Signed	Seasons Played	Career Record Apps	Subs	Gls
WEAVER John Noel						
Wrexham, 26 November, 1924						(FB)
Wrexham	Jnrs	05.46	46	2	-	0
WEAVER Luke Dennis Spencer						
Woolwich, 26 June, 1979 ESch/EYth						(G)
Leyton Orient	YT	06.96	96	9	0	0
Sunderland	Tr	01.98				
Scarborough	L	12.98	98	6	0	0
Carlisle U	Tr	08.99	99-01	53	0	0
WEAVER Nicholas (Nicky) James						
Sheffield, 2 March, 1979 Eu21-10						(G)
Mansfield T	YT	●	95	1	0	0
Manchester C	Tr	05.97	98-04	145	2	0
WEAVER Samuel (Sam)						
Pilsley, 8 February, 1909 Died 1985 FLge-2/E-3						(WH)
Hull C	Sutton T	03.28	28-29	48	-	5
Newcastle U	Tr	11.29	29-35	204	-	41
Chelsea	Tr	08.36	36-38	116	-	4
Stockport Co	Tr	12.45	46	2	-	0
WEAVER Simon Daniel						
Doncaster, 20 December, 1977						(CD)
Sheffield Wed	YT	05.96				
Doncaster Rov	L	02.97	96	2	0	0
Lincoln C	Nuneaton Borough	08.02	02-04	88	0	3
Macclesfield T	L	10.04	04	7	0	0
Kidderminster Hrs	Tr	12.04	04	22	1	0
WEBB Alan Richard						
Wrockwardine Wood, 1 January, 1963						(FB)
West Bromwich A	App	01.80	81-83	23	1	0
Lincoln C	L	03.84	83	11	0	0
Port Vale	Tr	08.84	84-91	187	3	2
WEBB Daniel (Danny) John						
Poole, 2 July, 1983						(F)
Southend U	Southampton (YT)	12.00	00-01	16	15	3
Brighton & Hove A	L	12.01	01	7	5	1
Brighton & Hove A	L	11.02	02	0	3	0
Hull C	Tr	12.02	02-03	4	12	0
Lincoln C	L	03.03	02	4	1	1
Cambridge U	Tr	12.03	03-04	34	9	4
WEBB David (Dave) James						
Stratford, 9 April, 1946						(CD)
Leyton Orient	West Ham U (Am)	05.63	64-65	62	0	3
Southampton	Tr	03.66	65-67	75	0	2
Chelsea	Tr	02.68	67-73	230	0	21
Queens Park Rgrs	Tr	07.74	74-77	116	0	7
Leicester C	Tr	09.77	77-78	32	1	0
Derby Co	Tr	12.78	78-79	25	1	1
Bournemouth	Tr	05.80	80-82	11	0	0
Torquay U	(Manager)	10.84	84	2	0	1
WEBB Douglas (Duggie) John						
Stokenchurch, 10 March, 1939						(IF)
Reading		11.56	56-66	178	2	81
WEBB James Keith						
Warrington, 6 July, 1938						(CF)
Shrewsbury T	Lymm Rov	04.56	55-56	2	-	1
WEBB John						
Liverpool, 10 February, 1952						(FB)
Liverpool	App	02.69				
Plymouth Arg	L	09.73	73	4	0	0
Tranmere Rov	Tr	07.74	74	17	3	0
WEBB Matthew Leslie						
Bristol, 24 September, 1976						(M)
Birmingham C	YT	07.95	94	0	1	0
WEBB Neil John						
Reading, 30 July, 1963 EYth/Eu21-3/EB/FLge/E-26						(M)
Reading	App	11.80	79-81	65	7	22
Portsmouth	Tr	07.82	82-84	123	0	34
Nottingham F	Tr	06.85	85-88	146	0	47
Manchester U	Tr	06.89	89-92	70	5	8
Nottingham F	Tr	11.92	92-93	26	4	3
Swindon T	L	10.94	94	5	1	0
Grimsby T	Tr	08.96	96	3	1	0
WEBB Paul Andrew						
Wolverhampton, 30 November, 1967 ESemiPro-11						(M)
Shrewsbury T	App	11.85				
Kidderminster Hrs	Bromsgrove Rov	07.94	00	23	9	1

League Club	Source	Date Signed	Seasons Played	Career Record Apps	Subs	Gls
WEBB Robert (Bobby)						
Altofts, 29 November, 1933						(W)
Leeds U	Whitwood Tech	04.51	53-54	3	-	0
Walsall	Tr	03.55	54	9	-	3
Bradford C	Tr	07.55	55-61	208	-	59
Torquay U	Tr	07.62	62-63	49	-	12
WEBB Ronald (Ron) Charles Thomas						
Brentford, 13 March, 1925 Died 1999						(WH)
Queens Park Rgrs		10.44				
Crystal Palace	Tr	09.46	46	3	-	0
WEBB Simon						
Ballyhaunis, 19 January, 1978 IRSch/IRYth						(M)
Tottenham H	YT	01.94				
Leyton Orient	Tr	10.99	99	3	1	0
WEBB Stanley (Stan) John						
Middlesbrough, 6 December, 1947						(F)
Middlesbrough		07.67	67-70	20	8	6
Carlisle U	Tr	02.71	70-72	16	10	5
Brentford	Tr	10.72	72-73	37	2	8
Darlington	Tr	07.74	74-75	69	5	21
WEBB William (Billy)						
Mexborough, 7 March, 1932						(FB)
Leicester C	Wath Ath	06.51	51-56	47	-	0
Stockport Co	Tr	06.57	57-62	243	-	0
WEBBER Andrew						
Port Talbot, 15 March, 1963						(F)
Swansea C		11.84	84	0	1	0
Exeter C		09.85	85	1	0	0
WEBBER Damien John						
Rustington, 8 October, 1968						(CD)
Millwall	Bognor Regis T	10.94	94-97	52	13	4
WEBBER Daniel (Danny) Vaughn						
Manchester, 28 December, 1981 EYth/Eu20						(F)
Manchester U	YT	01.99				
Port Vale	L	11.01	01	2	2	0
Watford	L	03.02	01	4	1	2
Watford	L	08.02	02	11	1	2
Watford	Tr	07.03	03-04	48	7	17
Sheffield U	L	03.05	04	6	1	3
WEBBER Eric Victor						
Steyning, 22 December, 1919 Died 1996						(CD)
Southampton	Gosport Ath	03.46	38-50	182	-	0
Torquay U	Tr	10.51	51-54	149	-	2
WEBBER George Marshall						
Abercynon, 28 June, 1925						(G)
Torquay U	Cardiff C (Am)	06.50	50-53	118	-	0
Northampton T	Tr	06.54	54	13	-	0
WEBBER John Vincent						
Blackpool, 2 July, 1918 Died 1989						(IF)
Blackburn Rov	Hyde U	02.47	46-47	8	-	1
WEBBER Keith James						
Cardiff, 5 January, 1943 Died 1983						(F)
Everton	Barry T	02.60	60-61	4	-	0
Brighton & Hove A	Tr	04.63	62-64	35	-	14
Wrexham	Tr	09.64	64-65	73	0	33
Doncaster Rov	Tr	07.66	66-68	63	2	18
Chester	Tr	06.69	69-70	66	8	14
Stockport Co	Tr	07.71	71	36	4	7
WEBBER Trevor						
Bovey Tracey, 5 September, 1968						(W)
Torquay U	App	●	85	5	0	0
WEBER Nicolas						
Metz, France, 28 October, 1970						(CD)
Sheffield U (L)	Le Havre (Fr)	08.00	00	3	1	0
WEBSTER Adam						
Leicester, 3 July, 1980						(F)
Notts Co	Thurmaston	02.99	99	0	1	0
WEBSTER Adrian						
Hawkes Bay, New Zealand, 11 October, 1980						(M)
Darlington	St George (Aus)	10.04	04	16	6	0
WEBSTER Alan John						
Melton Mowbray, 3 July, 1948						(M)
Scunthorpe U		07.66	66-67	4	2	0
WEBSTER Andrew						
Colne, 18 March, 1947						(CF)
Bradford C	Clitheroe	07.65	65-66	10	2	1

League Club	Source	Date Signed	Seasons Played	Career Record Apps	Subs	Gls
WEBSTER John **Barry**						
Sheffield, 3 March, 1935						(W)
Rotherham U	Gainsborough Trinity	05.56	56-61	179	-	37
Bradford C	Tr	06.62	62-63	53	-	9
WEBSTER Colin						
Halifax, 5 March, 1930						(WH)
Halifax T		09.50	50	16	-	1
WEBSTER Colin						
Cardiff, 17 July, 1932 Died 2001 W-4						(IF)
Cardiff C	Cardiff Nomads	05.50				
Manchester U	Tr	05.52	53-58	65	-	26
Swansea T	Tr	09.58	58-62	157	-	66
Newport Co	Tr	03.63	62-63	31	-	4
WEBSTER Eric						
Manchester, 24 June, 1931						(WH)
Manchester C		02.52	52	1	-	0
WEBSTER Harry						
Sheffield, 22 August, 1930						(IF)
Bolton W	Woodburn	10.48	49-56	98	-	38
Chester	Tr	06.58	58-59	34	-	11
WEBSTER Ian Adrian						
Askern, 30 December, 1965						(CD)
Scunthorpe U	App	07.83	82-85	15	3	0
WEBSTER Keith						
Newcastle, 6 November, 1945						(W)
Newcastle U	Stockton	12.62				
Darlington	Tr	11.66	66	8	1	0
WEBSTER Malcolm Walter						
Rossington, 12 November, 1950 ESch/EYth						(G)
Arsenal	App	01.68	69	3	0	0
Fulham	Tr	12.69	69-73	94	0	0
Southend U	Tr	01.74	73-75	96	0	0
Cambridge U	Tr	09.76	76-83	256	0	0
WEBSTER Richard (Dick)						
Accrington, 6 August, 1919 Died 1979						(FB)
Accrington St	Woodnook Amat	11.37	37-38	41	-	0
Sheffield U	Tr	01.39				
Accrington St	Tr	08.45	46-50	186	-	3
WEBSTER Ronald (Ron)						
Belper, 21 June, 1943						(FB)
Derby Co	Jnrs	06.60	61-77	451	4	7
WEBSTER Simon Paul						
Earl Shilton, 20 January, 1964						(CD)
Tottenham H	App	12.81	82-83	2	1	0
Exeter C	L	11.83	83	6	0	0
Exeter C	L	01.84	83	20	0	0
Huddersfield T	Tr	02.85	84-87	118	0	4
Sheffield U	Tr	03.88	87-89	26	11	3
Charlton Ath	Tr	08.90	90-92	127	0	7
West Ham U	Tr	06.93	94	0	5	0
Oldham Ath	L	03.95	94	7	0	0
Derby Co	L	08.95	95	3	0	0
WEBSTER Terence (Terry)						
Retford, 27 September, 1941						(WH)
Sheffield U	Jnrs	10.58				
Accrington St	Tr	11.59				
Barrow	Tr	07.60	60	4	-	0
WEBSTER Terence (Terry) Charles						
Doncaster, 9 July, 1930						(G)
Doncaster Rov	Intake YC	06.48				
Derby Co	Tr	10.48	48-57	172	-	0
WEDDLE Derek Keith						
Newcastle, 27 December, 1935						(IF)
Sunderland	Jnrs	05.53	55-56	2	-	0
Portsmouth	Tr	12.56	56-58	24	-	8
Middlesbrough	Cambridge C	08.61	61	3	-	1
Darlington	Tr	06.62	62-63	37	-	10
York C	Tr	07.64	64-65	44	0	13
WEDDLE George Davison						
Ashington, 24 February, 1919						(IF)
Gateshead		06.46	46-48	46	-	10
WEEKS Graham						
Exeter, 3 March, 1958						(M)
Exeter C	App	03.76	76-77	49	4	1
Bournemouth	Tr	05.78	78	3	0	0

WEETMAN Darren Graham
Oswestry, 7 June, 1968 (W)

League Club	Source	Date Signed	Seasons Played	Apps	Subs	Gls
Wrexham	Jnrs	06.85	85	1	0	0

WEGERLE Roy Connon
Johannesburg, South Africa, 19 March, 1964 USA int (F)

League Club	Source	Date Signed	Seasons Played	Apps	Subs	Gls
Chelsea	Tampa Bay (USA)	06.86	86-87	15	8	3
Swindon T	L	03.88	87	7	0	1
Luton T	Tr	07.88	88-89	39	6	10
Queens Park Rgrs	Tr	12.89	89-91	71	4	29
Blackburn Rov	Tr	03.92	91-92	20	14	6
Coventry C	Tr	03.93	92-94	46	7	9

WEIGH Raymond (Ray) Edward
Flint, 23 June, 1928 (CF)

League Club	Source	Date Signed	Seasons Played	Apps	Subs	Gls
Bournemouth	Shrewsbury T	03.49	49-50	28	-	8
Stockport Co	Tr	07.51	51-53	75	-	29
Shrewsbury T	Tr	06.54	54-56	107	-	43
Aldershot	Tr	07.57	57	11	-	1

WEIR Alan
South Shields, 1 September, 1959 EYth (CD)

League Club	Source	Date Signed	Seasons Played	Apps	Subs	Gls
Sunderland	App	05.77	77	1	0	0
Rochdale	Tr	06.79	79-82	96	10	3
Hartlepool U	Tr	08.83	83	9	1	0

WEIR Alexander (Alex)
Longridge, 20 October, 1916 (W)

League Club	Source	Date Signed	Seasons Played	Apps	Subs	Gls
Preston NE	Stoneyburn Jnrs	02.36				
Watford	Glentoran	12.45	46	1	-	0

WEIR David Gillespie
Falkirk, 10 May, 1970 SSch/S-40 (CD)

League Club	Source	Date Signed	Seasons Played	Apps	Subs	Gls
Everton	Heart of Midlothian	02.99	98-04	189	8	8

WEIR James (Jimmy)
Glasgow, 12 April, 1939 (W)

League Club	Source	Date Signed	Seasons Played	Apps	Subs	Gls
Fulham	Clydebank Jnrs	07.57	57	3	-	0
York C	Tr	06.60	60-62	82	-	38
Mansfield T	Tr	09.62	62	18	-	3
Luton T	Tr	08.63	63	12	-	1
Tranmere Rov	Tr	07.64	64	13	-	3

WEIR John (Jock) Britton
Fauldhouse, 20 October, 1923 Died 2003 (CF)

League Club	Source	Date Signed	Seasons Played	Apps	Subs	Gls
Blackburn Rov	Hibernian	01.47	46-47	23	-	7

WEIR Michael (Micky) Graham
Edinburgh, 16 January, 1966 (W)

League Club	Source	Date Signed	Seasons Played	Apps	Subs	Gls
Luton T	Hibernian	09.87	87	7	1	0
Millwall (L)	Hibernian	03.96	95	8	0	0

WEIR Peter Russell
Johnstone, 18 January, 1958 S-6 (W)

League Club	Source	Date Signed	Seasons Played	Apps	Subs	Gls
Leicester C	Aberdeen	01.88	87-88	26	2	2

WEIR William (Willie) Houston
Baillieston, 11 April, 1968 (W)

League Club	Source	Date Signed	Seasons Played	Apps	Subs	Gls
Shrewsbury T	Baillieston Jnrs	03.90	89-90	4	13	1

WELBOURNE Donald (Don)
Scunthorpe, 12 March, 1949 (CD)

League Club	Source	Date Signed	Seasons Played	Apps	Subs	Gls
Scunthorpe U	App	03.67	66-75	251	3	5

WELBOURNE Duncan
Scunthorpe, 28 July, 1940 (FB)

League Club	Source	Date Signed	Seasons Played	Apps	Subs	Gls
Grimsby T	Scunthorpe U (Am)	08.57	57-63	130	-	3
Watford	Tr	11.63	63-73	404	7	22
Southport	Tr	07.74	74-75	52	1	2

WELCH Keith James
Bolton, 3 October, 1968 (G)

League Club	Source	Date Signed	Seasons Played	Apps	Subs	Gls
Rochdale	Bolton W (Jnrs)	03.87	86-90	205	0	0
Bristol C	Tr	07.91	91-98	271	0	0
Northampton T	Tr	07.99	99-01	117	0	0
Tranmere Rov	Tr	08.02	02	2	0	0
Torquay U	Tr	11.02	02	3	0	0
Mansfield T	Tr	02.03	02	9	0	0

WELCH Michael (Micky)
Barbados, 21 May, 1958 (F)

League Club	Source	Date Signed	Seasons Played	Apps	Subs	Gls
Wimbledon	Grays Ath	11.84	84	2	2	0
Southend U	Grays Ath	02.85	84	4	0	0

WELCH Michael Francis
Winsford, 11 January, 1982 IRYth (CD)

League Club	Source	Date Signed	Seasons Played	Apps	Subs	Gls
Macclesfield T	Barnsley (YT)	08.01	01-04	108	6	5

WELCH Ronald (Ronnie)
Chesterfield, 26 September, 1952 (M)

League Club	Source	Date Signed	Seasons Played	Apps	Subs	Gls
Burnley	App	10.69	70	1	0	0
Brighton & Hove A	Tr	12.73	73-74	35	1	4
Chesterfield	Tr	11.74	74-76	17	7	1

WELFORD William (Bill) Frederick
Newcastle, 14 April, 1934 Died 1999 (WH)

League Club	Source	Date Signed	Seasons Played	Apps	Subs	Gls
Hartlepools U	Crook T	11.58	58	8	-	0

WELLENS Richard Paul
Manchester, 26 March, 1980 EYth (M)

League Club	Source	Date Signed	Seasons Played	Apps	Subs	Gls
Manchester U	YT	05.97				
Blackpool	Tr	03.00	99-04	173	15	16

WELLER Christopher (Chris) William
Reading, 25 December, 1939 (IF)

League Club	Source	Date Signed	Seasons Played	Apps	Subs	Gls
Bournemouth	Reading (Am)	09.59	60-64	74	-	17
Bristol Rov	Tr	07.65	65	2	1	0
Bournemouth	Tr	01.66	65-66	39	2	8

WELLER Keith
Islington, 11 June, 1946 Died 2004 FLge-1/E-4 (W)

League Club	Source	Date Signed	Seasons Played	Apps	Subs	Gls
Tottenham H	App	01.64	64-66	19	2	1
Millwall	Tr	06.67	67-69	121	0	40
Chelsea	Tr	05.70	70-71	34	4	14
Leicester C	Tr	09.71	71-78	260	2	37

WELLER Paul Anthony
Brighton, 6 March, 1975 (M)

League Club	Source	Date Signed	Seasons Played	Apps	Subs	Gls
Burnley	YT	11.93	95-03	199	53	11
Rochdale	Tr	09.04	04	5	0	0

WELLINGS Barry
Liverpool, 10 June, 1958 (F)

League Club	Source	Date Signed	Seasons Played	Apps	Subs	Gls
Everton	App	06.76				
York C	Tr	06.78	78-79	40	7	9
Rochdale	Tr	07.80	80-82	111	5	30
Tranmere Rov	Tr	02.83	82	16	0	3
Tranmere Rov	Northwich Vic	12.83	83	9	0	0
Swansea C	Oswestry T	09.84	84	5	0	3

WELLS Archibald (Archie)
Clydebank, 4 October, 1920 (IF)

League Club	Source	Date Signed	Seasons Played	Apps	Subs	Gls
New Brighton	Alloa Ath	07.46	46-48	37	-	4

WELLS Benjamin (Ben)
Basingstoke, 26 March, 1988 (M)

League Club	Source	Date Signed	Seasons Played	Apps	Subs	Gls
Swindon T	Sch	●	04	0	1	0

WELLS David Peter
Portsmouth, 29 December, 1977 NIYth (G)

League Club	Source	Date Signed	Seasons Played	Apps	Subs	Gls
Bournemouth	YT	07.96	94	0	1	0

WELLS William **David**
Eccleston, Lancashire, 16 December, 1940 (FB)

League Club	Source	Date Signed	Seasons Played	Apps	Subs	Gls
Blackburn Rov	Jnrs	05.58				
Rochdale	Tr	07.63	63	8	-	0

WELLS Dean Thomas
Twickenham, 25 March, 1985 (FB)

League Club	Source	Date Signed	Seasons Played	Apps	Subs	Gls
Brentford	Sch	●	03	0	1	0

WELLS Ian Michael
Wolverhampton, 27 October, 1964 (F)

League Club	Source	Date Signed	Seasons Played	Apps	Subs	Gls
Hereford U	Harrison's	06.85	85-86	47	4	12

WELLS Mark Anthony
Leicester, 15 October, 1971 (W)

League Club	Source	Date Signed	Seasons Played	Apps	Subs	Gls
Notts Co	YT	07.90	91-92	0	2	0
Huddersfield T	Tr	08.93	93	21	1	4
Scarborough	Tr	07.94	94-96	48	14	3

WELLS Peter Alan
Nottingham, 13 August, 1956 (G)

League Club	Source	Date Signed	Seasons Played	Apps	Subs	Gls
Nottingham F	App	10.74	75-76	27	0	0
Southampton	Tr	12.76	76-82	141	0	0
Millwall	Tr	02.83	82-83	33	0	0
Orient	Tr	07.85	85-88	148	0	0

WELSH Alan
Edinburgh, 9 July, 1947 (M)

League Club	Source	Date Signed	Seasons Played	Apps	Subs	Gls
Millwall	Bonnyrigg Rose	07.65	65-67	3	2	0
Torquay U	Tr	11.67	67-71	140	6	45
Plymouth Arg	Tr	07.72	72-73	64	2	14
Bournemouth	Tr	02.74	73-74	33	2	3
Millwall	Tr	08.75	75	5	4	1

WELSH Andrew (Andy)
Manchester, 24 November, 1983 SYth (W)

League Club	Source	Date Signed	Seasons Played	Apps	Subs	Gls
Stockport Co	YT	07.01	01-04	44	31	3
Macclesfield T	L	08.02	02	4	2	2
Sunderland	Tr	11.04	04	3	4	1

WELSH Andrew (Andy) John
Fleetwood, 20 November, 1962 (F)

League Club	Source	Date Signed	Seasons Played	Apps	Subs	Gls
Blackpool	App	08.80	80	1	0	0
Bury		07.84	85	0	1	0

WELSH Colin
Walton, 9 June, 1945 Died 1993 (W)

League Club	Source	Date Signed	Seasons Played	Apps	Subs	Gls
Southport	Everton (Am)	10.63	64	1	-	0

WELSH Donald (Don)
Manchester, 25 February, 1911 Died 1990 FLge-1/EWar-9/E-3 (IF)

League Club	Source	Date Signed	Seasons Played	Apps	Subs	Gls
Torquay U	RN Devonport	02.33	32-34	79	-	4
Charlton Ath	Tr	02.35	34-47	199	-	43

WELSH Eric
Belfast, 1 May, 1942 NIu23-1/NI-4 (W)

League Club	Source	Date Signed	Seasons Played	Apps	Subs	Gls
Exeter C	Distillery	09.59	59-65	105	0	19
Carlisle U	Tr	10.65	65-68	72	5	20
Torquay U	Tr	06.69	69-70	38	1	11
Hartlepool	Tr	07.71	71	13	2	2

WELSH James (Jimmy) Patrick
Edinburgh, 21 December, 1923 Died 2001 (IF)

League Club	Source	Date Signed	Seasons Played	Apps	Subs	Gls
Luton T	Tranent Jnrs	09.46				
Aldershot	Tr	06.48	48	5	-	0

WELSH John Joseph
Liverpool, 10 January, 1984 EYth/Eu20/Eu21-4 (M)

League Club	Source	Date Signed	Seasons Played	Apps	Subs	Gls
Liverpool	YT	01.01	03-04	2	2	0

WELSH Paul William
Liverpool, 10 May, 1966 (CD)

League Club	Source	Date Signed	Seasons Played	Apps	Subs	Gls
Preston NE	Formby	05.84	84-85	13	7	1

WELSH Peter Martin
Coatbridge, 19 July, 1959 ESch (CD)

League Club	Source	Date Signed	Seasons Played	Apps	Subs	Gls
Leicester C	App	08.76	76-81	24	17	4

WELSH Stephen (Steve) George
Glasgow, 19 April, 1968 (CD)

League Club	Source	Date Signed	Seasons Played	Apps	Subs	Gls
Cambridge U	Wimborne T	06.90	90	0	1	0
Peterborough U	Tr	08.91	91-94	146	0	2
Peterborough U (L)	Partick Th	07.96	96	6	0	0
Lincoln C	Ayr U	08.99	99-00	42	1	0

WELTON Roy **Patrick (Pat)**
Eltham, 3 May, 1928 (G)

League Club	Source	Date Signed	Seasons Played	Apps	Subs	Gls
Leyton Orient	Chislehurst	05.49	49-57	263	-	0
Queens Park Rgrs	Tr	03.58	58	3	-	0

WENT Paul Frank
Bromley-by-Bow, 12 October, 1949 ESch/EYth (CD)

League Club	Source	Date Signed	Seasons Played	Apps	Subs	Gls
Leyton Orient	App	10.66	65-66	48	2	5
Charlton Ath	Tr	06.67	67-71	160	3	15
Fulham	Tr	07.72	72-73	58	0	3
Portsmouth	Tr	12.73	73-76	92	0	5
Cardiff C	Tr	10.76	76-78	71	1	11
Orient	Tr	09.78	78-79	45	0	3

WERGE Edwin (Eddie)
Sidcup, 9 September, 1936 (W)

League Club	Source	Date Signed	Seasons Played	Apps	Subs	Gls
Charlton Ath	Bexleyheath	05.55	57-60	44	-	19
Crystal Palace	Tr	05.61	61-64	82	-	6
Leyton Orient	Arcadia Shepherds (SA)	11.66	66-67	30	3	0

WESSON Robert (Bob) William
Thornaby, 15 October, 1940 (G)

League Club	Source	Date Signed	Seasons Played	Apps	Subs	Gls
Coventry C	Thornaby Boys Brigade	11.58	60-65	133	0	0
Walsall	Tr	09.66	66-72	192	0	0
Doncaster Rov	L	02.70	69	5	0	0

WEST Alan
Hyde, 18 December, 1951 Eu23-1 (M)

League Club	Source	Date Signed	Seasons Played	Apps	Subs	Gls
Burnley	App	12.68	69-72	41	4	3
Luton T	Tr	10.73	73-80	272	13	16
Millwall	Tr	07.81	81-82	58	0	4

WEST Colin
Wallsend, 13 November, 1962 (F)

League Club	Source	Date Signed	Seasons Played	Apps	Subs	Gls
Sunderland	App	07.80	81-84	88	14	21
Watford	Tr	03.85	84-85	45	0	20
Sheffield Wed	Glasgow Rgrs	09.87	87-88	40	5	8
West Bromwich A	Tr	02.89	88-91	64	9	22
Port Vale	L	11.91	91	5	0	1
Swansea C	Tr	08.92	92	29	4	12
Leyton Orient	Tr	07.93	93-97	132	10	42
Northampton T	L	09.97	97	1	1	0
Hartlepool U	Northwich Vic	11.99	99	0	1	0

WEST Colin William
Middlesbrough, 19 September, 1967 EYth (F)

League Club	Source	Date Signed	Seasons Played	Apps	Subs	Gls
Chelsea	App	09.85	86-87	8	8	4
Swansea C	L	03.89	88	14	0	3
Hartlepool U	Dundee	08.93	93	29	7	5

WEST David (Dave) Christopher
Dorchester, 16 November, 1964 (W)

League Club	Source	Date Signed	Seasons Played	Apps	Subs	Gls
Liverpool	Dorchester T	03.83				
Torquay U	Tr	09.85	85	19	2	2

WEST Dean
Morley, 5 December, 1972 (FB)

League Club	Source	Date Signed	Seasons Played	Apps	Subs	Gls
Lincoln C	YT	08.91	90-95	93	26	20
Bury	Tr	09.95	95-98	100	10	8
Burnley	Tr	07.99	99-03	145	13	5
Lincoln C	Tr	07.04	04	4	0	0
Boston U	Tr	09.04	04	22	2	0

WEST Edward (Ted)
Parbold, 4 November, 1930 Died 2002 (FB)

League Club	Source	Date Signed	Seasons Played	Apps	Subs	Gls
Doncaster Rov	Eastbourne U	02.53				
Gillingham	Tr	07.54	54-56	98	-	0
Oldham Ath	Tr	07.57	57-60	117	-	0

WEST Gary
Scunthorpe, 25 August, 1964 EYth (CD)

League Club	Source	Date Signed	Seasons Played	Apps	Subs	Gls
Sheffield U	App	08.82	82-84	75	0	1
Lincoln C	Tr	08.85	85-86	83	0	4
Gillingham	Tr	07.87	87-88	51	1	3
Port Vale	Tr	02.89	88-89	14	3	1
Gillingham	L	11.90	90	1	0	0
Lincoln C	L	01.91	90	3	0	0
Lincoln C	Tr	08.91	91	14	4	1
Walsall	L	09.92	92	9	0	1

WEST Gordon
Darfield, 24 April, 1943 Eu23-3/FLge-1/E-3 (G)

League Club	Source	Date Signed	Seasons Played	Apps	Subs	Gls
Blackpool	Jnrs	05.61	60-61	31	-	0
Everton	Tr	03.62	61-72	335	0	0
Tranmere Rov	Tr	10.75	76-78	17	0	0

WEST Paul Darrell
Stafford, 22 June, 1970 (FB)

League Club	Source	Date Signed	Seasons Played	Apps	Subs	Gls
Port Vale	Alcester T	12.91				
Bradford C	Tr	07.92				
Wigan Ath	Tr	08.93	93-94	2	1	0

WEST Taribo
Port Harcourt, Nigeria, 26 March, 1974 Nigeria int (CD)

League Club	Source	Date Signed	Seasons Played	Apps	Subs	Gls
Derby Co (L)	AC Milan (It)	11.00	00	18	0	0

WEST Thomas (Tom)
Salford, 8 December, 1916 (CF)

League Club	Source	Date Signed	Seasons Played	Apps	Subs	Gls
Stockport Co		03.38	37-38	3	-	1
Oldham Ath		10.45				
Rochdale	Tr	06.46	46	4	-	2

WEST Trefor John
Coventry, 14 December, 1944 (FB)

League Club	Source	Date Signed	Seasons Played	Apps	Subs	Gls
West Bromwich A	App	05.62				
Walsall	Tr	05.64	64	12	-	0

WESTAWAY Kevin David
Bristol, 24 November, 1962 (FB)

League Club	Source	Date Signed	Seasons Played	Apps	Subs	Gls
Bristol Rov	App	11.80	80-81	2	0	0

WESTBY Jack Leslie
Aintree, 20 May, 1917 (FB)

League Club	Source	Date Signed	Seasons Played	Apps	Subs	Gls
Blackburn Rov	Burscough	01.37	37	2	-	0
Liverpool	Tr	05.44				
Southport	Tr	08.47	47	13	-	0

WESTCARR Craig Naptali
Nottingham, 29 January, 1985 ESch/EYth (F)

League Club	Source	Date Signed	Seasons Played	Apps	Subs	Gls
Nottingham F	YT	01.02	01-04	2	21	1
Lincoln C	L	12.04	04	5	1	1
MK Dons	L	03.05	04	0	4	0

WESTCOTT Dennis
Wallasey, 2 July, 1917 Died 1960 FLge-1/EWar-4 (CF)

League Club	Source	Date Signed	Seasons Played	Apps	Subs	Gls
New Brighton	Leasowe Road Brickwks	01.36	35	18	-	10
Wolverhampton W	Tr	07.36	36-47	128	-	105
Blackburn Rov	Tr	04.48	48-49	63	-	37
Manchester C	Tr	02.50	49-51	72	-	37
Chesterfield	Tr	06.52	52	40	-	21

WESTCOTT John Peter James
Eastbourne, 31 May, 1979 (W)

League Club	Source	Date Signed	Seasons Played	Apps	Subs	Gls
Brighton & Hove A	YT	07.97	97-98	19	19	0

WESTERVELD Sander
Enschede, Holland, 23 October, 1974 HoYth/Hou21/Ho-6 (G)

League Club	Source	Date Signed	Seasons Played	Apps	Subs	Gls
Liverpool	Vitesse Arnhem (Holl)	06.99	99-01	75	0	0

League Club	Source	Date Signed	Seasons Played	Career Record Apps	Subs	Gls
WESTHEAD Mark Lee						
Blackpool, 19 July, 1975						(G)
Bolton W	Blackpool Mechanics	11.94				
Wycombe W	Telford U	08.98	98-99	3	1	0
WESTLAKE Brian						
Newcastle-under-Lyme, 19 September, 1943						(CF)
Stoke C		09.61				
Doncaster Rov	Tr	06.63	63	5	-	1
Halifax T	Tr	01.64	63-66	100	0	28
Tranmere Rov	Tr	09.66	66	13	1	3
Colchester U	Tr	02.67	66	14	1	5
WESTLAKE Francis (Frank) Arthur						
Bolton-on-Dearne, 11 August, 1915 Died 1999						(FB)
Sheffield Wed	Thurnscoe Victoria	05.37	37-49	110	-	0
Halifax T	Tr	06.50	50	2	-	0
WESTLAKE Ian John						
Clacton, 10 July, 1983						(M)
Ipswich T	Sch	08.02	02-04	71	17	13
WESTLAND James (Jim)						
Aberdeen, 21 July, 1916 Died 1972						(IF)
Stoke C	Aberdeen	09.35	35-38	60	-	16
Mansfield T	Tr	11.46	46	10	-	0
WESTLEY Graham Neil						
Hounslow, 4 March, 1968 EYth						(F)
Gillingham	Queens Park Rgrs (App)	03.86	85-86	1	1	0
WESTLEY Shane Lee Mark						
Canterbury, 16 June, 1965						(CD)
Charlton Ath	App	06.83	83	8	0	0
Southend U	Tr	03.85	84-88	142	2	10
Wolverhampton W	Tr	06.89	89-92	48	2	1
Brentford	Tr	10.92	92-94	61	3	1
Southend U	L	02.95	94	4	1	0
Cambridge U	Tr	08.95	95	3	0	0
Lincoln C	Tr	10.95	95	9	0	1
WESTMORLAND Joseph (Joe) Edward						
Dalston, Cumberland, 30 June, 1937						(FB)
Carlisle U		02.59	58	3	-	0
WESTON Anthony (Tony) Douglas						
Yalding, 3 April, 1945						(FB)
Gillingham	Bromley	11.63	64-69	162	0	3
WESTON Curtis James						
Greenwich, 24 January, 1987						(M)
Millwall	Sch	03.04	03-04	2	2	0
WESTON Donald (Don) Patrick						
New Houghton, 6 March, 1936						(F)
Wrexham	Kinnell Park Barracks	06.59	58-59	42	-	21
Birmingham C	Tr	01.60	59-60	23	-	3
Rotherham U	Tr	12.60	60-62	74	-	23
Leeds U	Tr	12.62	62-65	68	0	24
Huddersfield T	Tr	10.65	65-66	20	2	7
Wrexham	Tr	12.66	66-67	42	0	19
Chester	Tr	06.68	68	1	2	0
WESTON Ian Paul						
Bristol, 6 May, 1968						(M)
Bristol Rov	App	05.86	86-87	13	3	0
Torquay U	Tr	09.88	88-89	57	5	2
WESTON James (Jimmy) John						
Whiston, 16 November, 1955						(M)
Blackpool	Skelmersdale U	01.74	75-79	97	8	8
Torquay U	Tr	06.80	80-81	38	0	1
Wigan Ath	Tr	09.81	81-82	63	3	2
WESTON Reginald (Reg) Harold						
Greenhithe, 16 January, 1918 Died 1998 WLge-1						(CD)
Swansea T	Northfleet	03.45	46-51	229	-	1
WESTON Rhys David						
Kingston, 27 October, 1980 ESch/EYth/Wu21-4/W-7						(CD)
Arsenal	YT	07.99	99	1	0	0
Cardiff C	Tr	11.00	00-04	144	8	2
WESTWELL Simon						
Clitheroe, 12 November, 1961						(FB)
Preston NE	App	10.79	80-82	63	0	1
WESTWOOD Ashley Michael						
Bridgnorth, 31 August, 1976 EYth						(CD)
Manchester U	YT	07.94				
Crewe Alex	Tr	07.95	95-97	93	5	9

League Club	Source	Date Signed	Seasons Played	Career Record Apps	Subs	Gls
Bradford C	Tr	07.98	98-99	18	6	2
Sheffield Wed	Tr	08.00	00-02	79	3	5
Northampton T	Tr	07.03	03-04	27	1	2
WESTWOOD Christopher (Chris) John						
Dudley, 13 February, 1977						(CD)
Wolverhampton W	YT	07.95	97	3	1	1
Hartlepool U	Telford U	03.99	98-04	244	6	7
WESTWOOD Daniel (Danny) Robert						
Dagenham, 25 July, 1953						(F)
Queens Park Rgrs	Billericay T	07.74	74	0	1	1
Gillingham	Tr	11.75	75-81	201	10	74
WESTWOOD Eric						
Manchester, 25 September, 1917 Died 2001 FLge-2/E-B						(FB)
Manchester C	Manchester U (Am)	11.37	38-52	248	-	3
WESTWOOD Gary Michael						
Barrow, 3 April, 1963 EYth						(G)
Ipswich T	App	04.81				
Reading	L	09.83	83	5	0	0
Reading	Tr	07.84	84-87	123	0	0
WESTWOOD William **Raymond (Ray)**						
Kingswinford, 14 April, 1912 Died 1982 FLge-5/E-6						(IF)
Bolton W	Brierley Hill Alliance	03.30	30-47	301	-	127
Chester	Tr	12.47	47-48	38	-	13
WETHERALL David						
Sheffield, 14 March, 1971 ESch						(CD)
Sheffield Wed	YT	07.89				
Leeds U	Tr	07.91	91-98	188	14	12
Bradford C	Tr	07.99	99-04	168	3	10
WETTON Albert (Bert) Smailes						
Winlaton, 23 October, 1928						(CD)
Tottenham H	Cheshunt	10.49				
Brighton & Hove A	Tr	06.51	51-52	3	-	0
Crewe Alex	Tr	10.53	53	2	-	0
WETTON Ralph						
Winlaton, 6 June, 1927						(WH)
Tottenham H	Cheshunt	08.50	51-54	45	-	0
Plymouth Arg	Tr	06.55	55	36	-	1
Aldershot	Tr	11.56	56-57	50	-	1
WHALE Raymond (Ray)						
West Bromwich, 23 February, 1937						(WH)
West Bromwich A	West Bromwich CA	12.54				
Southend U	Tr	04.59	59-60	29	-	0
WHALEY George						
Darlington, 30 July, 1920						(W)
Gateshead	Heart of Midlothian	09.46	46	5	-	0
WHALEY Kenneth (Ken)						
Leeds, 22 June, 1935						(CF)
Bradford PA		06.57	58	1	-	0
WHALEY Simon						
Bolton, 7 June, 1985						(M)
Bury	Sch	10.02	02-04	25	25	4
WHALLEY Gareth						
Manchester, 19 December, 1973						(M)
Crewe Alex	YT	07.92	92-97	174	6	9
Bradford C	Tr	07.98	98-01	99	4	3
Crewe Alex	L	03.02	01	7	0	0
Cardiff C	Tr	07.02	02-03	33	8	2
Wigan Ath	Tr	09.04	04	7	1	0
WHALLEY Harold						
Nelson, 4 April, 1923 Died 1997						(W)
Accrington St	Barnoldswick T	12.46	46	3	-	0
WHALLEY Herbert (Bert)						
Ashton-under-Lyne, 6 August, 1913 Died 1958						(WH)
Manchester U	Stalybridge Celtic	05.34	35-46	32	-	0
WHALLEY Jeffrey (Jeff) Hugh						
Rossendale, 8 February, 1952						(W)
Blackburn Rov	App	02.70	69-70	2	0	0
WHALLEY David **Neil**						
Liverpool, 29 October, 1965						(M)
Preston NE	Warrington T	03.93	92-94	45	5	1
WHALLEY Selwyn Davies						
Stoke-on-Trent, 24 February, 1934						(FB)
Port Vale		08.53	56-65	178	0	7

WHALLEY Shaun James
Prescot, 7 August, 1987 (F)

League Club	Source	Date Signed	Seasons Played	Apps	Subs	Gls
Chester C	Southport	09.04	04	0	3	0

WHARE William (Billy) Frederick
Guernsey, 14 May, 1924 Died 1995 (FB)

League Club	Source	Date Signed	Seasons Played	Apps	Subs	Gls
Nottingham F		05.47	48-59	298	-	2

WHARTON Andrew (Andy)
Bacup, 21 December, 1961 (FB)

League Club	Source	Date Signed	Seasons Played	Apps	Subs	Gls
Burnley	App	12.79	80-83	63	2	6
Torquay U	L	11.83	83	10	0	0
Chester C	Tr	02.84	83-84	19	4	2

WHARTON Guy
Darfield, 5 December, 1916 Died 1990 (WH)

League Club	Source	Date Signed	Seasons Played	Apps	Subs	Gls
Chester	Broomhill	05.34	35	12	-	5
Wolverhampton W	Tr	05.36	36-37	29	-	2
Portsmouth	Tr	11.37	37-47	93	-	4
Darlington	Wellington T	07.48	48-49	39	-	2

WHARTON John (Jackie) Edwin
Bolton, 18 June, 1920 Died 1997 (W)

League Club	Source	Date Signed	Seasons Played	Apps	Subs	Gls
Plymouth Arg	Bolton W (Am)	06.37	38	11	-	2
Preston NE	Tr	07.39	46	25	-	7
Manchester C	Tr	03.47	46-47	23	-	2
Blackburn Rov	Tr	06.48	48-52	129	-	14
Newport Co	Tr	02.53	52-54	72	-	10

WHARTON Kenneth (Ken)
Newcastle, 28 November, 1960 (FB)

League Club	Source	Date Signed	Seasons Played	Apps	Subs	Gls
Newcastle U	Grainger Park BC	01.79	78-88	268	22	26
Carlisle U	Tr	08.89	89	1	0	0
Bradford C	Tr	08.89	89	5	0	0

WHARTON Paul William
Newcastle, 26 June, 1977 EYth (M)

League Club	Source	Date Signed	Seasons Played	Apps	Subs	Gls
Leeds U	YT	06.94				
Hull C	Tr	02.96	95-97	8	3	0

WHARTON Sean Robert
Newport, 31 October, 1968 (F)

League Club	Source	Date Signed	Seasons Played	Apps	Subs	Gls
Sunderland	YT	07.87	88	1	0	0

WHARTON Terence (Terry) John
Bolton, 1 July, 1942 (W)

League Club	Source	Date Signed	Seasons Played	Apps	Subs	Gls
Wolverhampton W	Jnrs	01.59	61-67	223	1	69
Bolton W	Tr	11.67	67-70	101	1	28
Crystal Palace	Tr	01.71	70-71	19	1	1
Walsall	Durban C (SA)	11.73	73	1	0	0

WHATLING Keith Richard
Worlingworth, 1 November, 1947 (W)

League Club	Source	Date Signed	Seasons Played	Apps	Subs	Gls
Ipswich T	Jnrs	03.66				
Exeter C	Tr	07.67	67-68	19	3	3

WHATMORE Neil
Ellesmere Port, 17 May, 1955 (F)

League Club	Source	Date Signed	Seasons Played	Apps	Subs	Gls
Bolton W	App	05.73	72-80	262	15	102
Birmingham C	Tr	08.81	81-82	24	2	6
Oxford U	L	10.82	82	7	0	5
Bolton W	L	12.82	82	10	0	3
Oxford U	Tr	02.83	82-83	26	3	10
Bolton W	L	03.84	83	7	0	2
Burnley	Tr	08.84	84	8	0	1
Mansfield T	Tr	11.84	84-86	71	1	20
Bolton W	Tr	08.87				
Mansfield T	Tr	11.87	87	0	6	0

WHEAT Arthur Bradley
Selston, 26 October, 1921 (WH)

League Club	Source	Date Signed	Seasons Played	Apps	Subs	Gls
Bradford PA	Montrose	12.49	50-51	22	-	3
York C	Tr	08.52	52	4	-	0

WHEATCROFT Paul Michael
Manchester, 22 November, 1980 ESch/EYth (F)

League Club	Source	Date Signed	Seasons Played	Apps	Subs	Gls
Manchester U	YT	07.98				
Bolton W	Tr	07.00				
Rochdale	L	09.01	01	6	0	3
Mansfield T	L	02.02	01	1	1	0
Scunthorpe U	Tr	08.02	02	2	2	0

WHEATLEY Barrie
Sandbach, 21 February, 1938 (IF)

League Club	Source	Date Signed	Seasons Played	Apps	Subs	Gls
Liverpool		03.56				
Crewe Alex	Tr	07.57	57-65	235	0	49
Rochdale	Tr	07.66	66	13	0	4

WHEATLEY Harold **Joseph (Joe)**
Eastham, 9 May, 1920 (WH)

League Club	Source	Date Signed	Seasons Played	Apps	Subs	Gls
Port Vale	Ellesmere Port T	03.38	38	2	-	0
Shrewsbury T	Tr	(N/L)	50	7	-	0

WHEATLEY Roland (Ron)
Nottingham, 20 June, 1924 Died 2003 (WH)

League Club	Source	Date Signed	Seasons Played	Apps	Subs	Gls
Nottingham F	Beeston BC	06.46	47-48	6	-	0
Southampton	Tr	01.49	48-50	10	-	1
Grimsby T	Tr	06.51	51	5	-	0

WHEATLEY Stephen (Steve) John
Bishop Auckland, 12 April, 1959 (G)

League Club	Source	Date Signed	Seasons Played	Apps	Subs	Gls
Gillingham	App	04.77	76-77	4	0	0

WHEATLEY Stephen (Steve) Peter
Hinckley, 26 December, 1929 (W)

League Club	Source	Date Signed	Seasons Played	Apps	Subs	Gls
Derby Co	Hinckley U	12.50	51-52	4	-	0
Chesterfield	Boston U	07.55	55	3	-	0

WHEATLEY Thomas (Tom)
Hebburn, 1 June, 1929 (G)

League Club	Source	Date Signed	Seasons Played	Apps	Subs	Gls
Leeds U	Amble	04.53	53	6	-	0

WHEATLEY William
Mansfield, 5 November, 1920 Died 1965 (W)

League Club	Source	Date Signed	Seasons Played	Apps	Subs	Gls
Mansfield T	Mansfield Colliery	08.48	48-49	38	-	3

WHEATON Gilbert (Gil) John
Mickley, 1 November, 1941 (CD)

League Club	Source	Date Signed	Seasons Played	Apps	Subs	Gls
Grimsby T	Mickley CW	09.60	62	7	-	0
Chester	Tr	06.63	63	1	-	0

WHEELDON Thomas (Tommy) Edward
Whiston, 28 December, 1957 ESch (M)

League Club	Source	Date Signed	Seasons Played	Apps	Subs	Gls
Torquay U	Runcorn	09.81	81	5	3	0
Torquay U	Falmouth T	08.85	85	6	2	0

WHEELER Adam Lawrence
Sheffield, 29 November, 1977 (G)

League Club	Source	Date Signed	Seasons Played	Apps	Subs	Gls
Doncaster Rov	Newcastle U (YT)	04.96	96	1	0	0

WHEELER Alfred (Alf) John
Fareham, 6 April, 1922 (W)

League Club	Source	Date Signed	Seasons Played	Apps	Subs	Gls
Blackburn Rov	Portsmouth (Am)	04.47	47-48	21	-	5
Swindon T	Tr	07.49	49-50	23	-	4

WHEELER Arthur **James (Jimmy)**
Reading, 21 December, 1933 (W)

League Club	Source	Date Signed	Seasons Played	Apps	Subs	Gls
Reading	Huntley & Palmers	08.52	52-66	404	1	143

WHEELER John (Johnny) Edward
Crosby, 26 July, 1928 FLge-2/EB/E-1 (WH)

League Club	Source	Date Signed	Seasons Played	Apps	Subs	Gls
Tranmere Rov	Carlton (Liverpool)	04.46	48-50	101	-	9
Bolton W	Tr	02.51	50-55	189	-	18
Liverpool	Tr	09.56	56-61	164	-	21

WHEELER William **John (Jack)**
North Littleton, 13 July, 1919 (G)

League Club	Source	Date Signed	Seasons Played	Apps	Subs	Gls
Birmingham	Cheltenham T	03.38	38-47	12	-	0
Huddersfield T	Tr	08.48	48-55	166	-	0

WHEELER Paul
Caerphilly, 3 January, 1965 (M)

League Club	Source	Date Signed	Seasons Played	Apps	Subs	Gls
Bristol Rov	App	01.83				
Cardiff C	Aberaman	08.85	85-88	72	29	10
Hull C	Tr	10.89	89	0	5	0
Hereford U	Tr	02.90	89-90	34	20	12
Stockport Co	Tr	08.91	91-92	13	10	5
Scarborough	L	10.92	92	2	5	1
Chester C	Tr	01.93	92-93	34	5	7

WHEELER William Hunter
Carlisle, 27 September, 1920 (WH)

League Club	Source	Date Signed	Seasons Played	Apps	Subs	Gls
Carlisle U		10.46	46	4	-	0

WHELAN Anthony (Tony) Gerard
Dublin, 23 November, 1959 IRu21-1 (FB)

League Club	Source	Date Signed	Seasons Played	Apps	Subs	Gls
Manchester U	Bohemians	08.80	80	0	1	0

WHELAN Anthony (Tony) Michael
Salford, 20 November, 1952 (F)

League Club	Source	Date Signed	Seasons Played	Apps	Subs	Gls
Manchester U	App	12.69				
Manchester C	Tr	03.73	72-73	3	3	0
Rochdale	Tr	07.74	74-76	124	0	20

WHELAN David (Dave)
Bradford, 24 November, 1936 (FB)

League Club	Source	Date Signed	Seasons Played	Apps	Subs	Gls
Blackburn Rov	Wigan BC	12.53	56-59	78	-	3
Crewe Alex	Tr	01.63	62-65	115	0	0

WHELAN Glenn David
Dublin, 13 January, 1984 IRYth/IRu21-13 (CD)

League Club	Source	Date Signed	Seasons Played	Apps	Subs	Gls
Manchester C	YT	01.01				
Bury	L	09.03	03	13	0	0
Sheffield Wed	Tr	07.04	04	36	0	2

League Club	Source	Date Signed	Seasons Played	Career Record Apps	Subs	Gls
WHELAN Noel David						
Leeds, 30 December, 1974 EYth/Eu21-2						(F)
Leeds U	YT	03.93	92-95	28	20	7
Coventry C	Tr	12.95	95-99	127	7	31
Middlesbrough	Tr	08.00	00-02	33	28	6
Crystal Palace	L	03.03	02	7	1	3
Millwall	Tr	08.03	03	8	7	4
Derby Co	Tr	01.04	03	3	5	0
WHELAN Philip (Phil) James						
Reddish, 7 August, 1972 Eu21-3						(CD)
Ipswich T	Jnrs	07.90	91-94	76	6	2
Middlesbrough	Tr	04.95	95-96	18	4	1
Oxford U	Tr	07.97	97-99	51	3	2
Rotherham U	L	03.99	98	13	0	4
Southend U	Tr	07.00	00-02	96	4	6
WHELAN Robert (Bob)						
Salford, 9 November, 1930						(WH)
Manchester C	Salford YC	04.50				
Oldham Ath	Tr	07.52	52	1	-	0
WHELAN Ronald (Ronnie) Andrew						
Dublin, 25 September, 1961 IRSch/IRYth/IRu21-1/IRB/IR-53						(M)
Liverpool	Home Farm	10.79	80-93	351	11	45
Southend U	Tr	09.94	94-95	34	0	1
WHELAN Spencer Randall						
Liverpool, 17 September, 1971						(CD)
Chester C	Liverpool (YT)	04.90	90-97	196	19	8
Shrewsbury T	Tr	11.98	98-99	24	1	0
WHELAN William (Liam) Augustine						
Dublin, 1 April, 1935 Died 1958 IR-4						(IF)
Manchester U	Home Farm	05.53	54-57	79	-	43
WHELLANS Robert (Robbie)						
Harrogate, 14 February, 1969						(F)
Bradford C	App	06.87				
Hartlepool U	L	12.87	87	8	3	1
Rochdale	Tr	07.89	89	5	6	1
WHENT John (Jackie) Richard						
Darlington, 3 May, 1920						(CD)
Brighton & Hove A	Canadian Army	08.47	47-49	101	-	4
Luton T	Tr	08.50	50	11	-	3
WHETTER Gary						
Middlesbrough, 6 September, 1963						(M)
Darlington	Crook T	09.86	86	3	2	1
WHIFFEN Kingsley						
Welshpool, 3 December, 1950						(G)
Chelsea	App	●	66	1	0	0
WHIGHAM William (Willie) Murdoch Morrison						
Airdrie, 9 October, 1939						(G)
Middlesbrough	Falkirk	10.66	66-71	187	0	0
Darlington	Dumbarton	08.74	74	4	0	0
WHING Andrew (Andy) John						
Birmingham, 20 September, 1984						(FB)
Coventry C	Sch	04.03	02-04	48	10	2
WHISTON Donald (Don)						
Chesterton, 4 April, 1930						(FB)
Stoke C	Jnrs	12.49	49-56	30	-	4
Crewe Alex	Tr	02.57	56-57	52	-	8
Rochdale	Tr	05.58	58	14	-	0
WHISTON Joseph (Joe) Rowland						
Stoke-on-Trent, 5 October, 1928						(CF)
Crewe Alex	Johnson Matthey	09.51	51-52	9	-	2
WHISTON Peter Michael						
Widnes, 4 January, 1968						(CD)
Plymouth Arg		12.87	88-89	4	6	0
Torquay U	Tr	03.90	89-91	39	1	1
Exeter C	Tr	09.91	91-93	85	0	7
Southampton	Tr	08.94	94	0	1	0
Shrewsbury T	Tr	09.95	95-96	54	1	3
WHITAKER Colin						
Leeds, 14 June, 1932						(W)
Sheffield Wed	Leeds U (Jnrs)	11.51	51	1	-	0
Bradford PA	Tr	06.53	53-55	49	-	10
Shrewsbury T	Tr	06.56	56-60	152	-	59
Queens Park Rgrs	Tr	02.61	60	8	-	0
Rochdale	Tr	05.61	61-62	54	-	11
Oldham Ath	Tr	10.62	62-63	72	-	29
Barrow	Tr	08.64	64	12	-	0

League Club	Source	Date Signed	Seasons Played	Career Record Apps	Subs	Gls
WHITAKER Daniel (Danny) Philip						
Wilmslow, 14 November, 1980						(M)
Macclesfield T	Wilmslow Sports	07.00	01-04	115	14	19
WHITAKER William (Billy)						
Chesterfield, 7 October, 1923 Died 1995 FLge-1						(CD)
Chesterfield	Tapton School OB	08.42	46	13	-	0
Middlesbrough	Tr	06.47	47-54	177	-	1
WHITBREAD Adrian Richard						
Epping, 22 October, 1971						(CD)
Leyton Orient	YT	11.89	89-92	125	0	2
Swindon T	Tr	07.93	93-94	35	1	1
West Ham U	Tr	08.94	94-95	3	7	0
Portsmouth	L	11.95	95	13	0	0
Portsmouth	Tr	10.96	96-99	133	1	2
Luton T	L	11.00	00	9	0	0
Reading	Tr	02.01	00-01	33	0	0
Exeter C	L	01.03	02	7	0	0
WHITBY Brian Kenneth						
Luton, 21 February, 1939						(W)
Luton T	Vauxhall Motors	05.57	57-58	7	-	1
WHITCHURCH Charles (Charlie) Henry						
Grays, 29 October, 1920 Died 1977 ESch						(W)
West Ham U	Portsmouth (Am)	05.45				
Tottenham H	Tr	01.46	46	8	-	2
Southend U	Tr	07.47	47	17	-	5
WHITE Alan						
Darlington, 22 March, 1976						(CD)
Middlesbrough	YT	07.94				
Luton T	Tr	09.97	97-99	60	20	3
Colchester U	L	11.99	99	4	0	0
Colchester U	Tr	07.00	00-03	128	11	4
Leyton Orient	Tr	07.04	04	26	0	0
Boston U	Tr	03.05	04	11	0	0
WHITE Alexander (Alex)						
Lasswade, 28 January, 1916 Died 1995						(FB)
Chelsea	Bonnyrigg Rose	02.37	46-47	17	-	0
Swindon T	Tr	07.48	48-49	35	-	0
Southport	Tr	07.50	50	3	-	0
WHITE Andrew (Andy)						
Swanwick, 6 November, 1981						(F)
Mansfield T	Hucknall T	07.00	00-03	37	31	10
Crewe Alex	L	10.02	02	0	2	0
Boston U	L	09.03	03	3	3	0
Kidderminster Hrs	L	10.03	03	6	1	1
Crewe Alex	Tr	06.04	04	11	11	4
WHITE Andrew (Andy) Charles John						
Newport, 6 November, 1948						(W)
Newport Co	Caerleon	08.69	69-76	226	28	26
WHITE Antony (Tony) John						
Clacton, 3 November, 1966						(FB)
Bournemouth	Dorchester T	07.85	85	1	0	0
WHITE Archibald (Archie)						
Dumbarton, 16 January, 1959						(M)
Oxford U	App	01.76	76-79	10	14	1
WHITE Arnold (Arnie)						
Bristol, 25 July, 1924						(IF)
Bristol C	Soundwell	03.47	46-50	82	-	12
Millwall	Tr	08.51	51-52	14	-	0
WHITE Barry James						
Beverley, 30 July, 1950						(G)
Hull C	App	08.68				
Halifax T	Tr	11.70	71-74	23	0	0
WHITE Christopher (Chris) Jason						
Chatham, 11 December, 1970						(FB)
Portsmouth	YT	07.89				
Peterborough U	Tr	05.91	91-92	10	3	0
Doncaster Rov	L	01.93	92	6	0	0
Exeter C	Tr	03.93	92-93	18	1	0
WHITE Dale						
Sunderland, 17 March, 1968 ESch						(F)
Sunderland	App	03.86	85	2	2	0
Peterborough U	L	12.87	87	14	0	4
WHITE David						
Urmston, 30 October, 1967 EYth/Eu21-6/EB/E-1						(W)
Manchester C	App	11.85	86-93	273	12	79
Leeds U	Tr	12.93	93-95	28	14	9
Sheffield U	Tr	11.95	95-97	55	11	13

League Club	Source	Date Signed	Seasons Played	Apps	Subs	Gls
WHITE Dean						
Hastings, 4 December, 1958						(M)
Gillingham	Chelsea (App)	07.78	78-82	108	8	26
Millwall	Tr	03.83	82-83	41	0	4
WHITE Dennis						
Hartlepool, 10 November, 1948						(FB)
Hartlepools U		11.67	67-72	55	3	0
WHITE Devon Winston						
Nottingham, 2 March, 1964						(F)
Lincoln C	Arnold T	12.84	84-85	21	8	4
Bristol Rov	Shepshed Charterhouse	08.87	87-91	190	12	53
Cambridge U	Tr	03.92	91-92	15	7	4
Queens Park Rgrs	Tr	01.93	92-94	16	10	9
Notts Co	Tr	12.94	94-95	34	6	15
Watford	Tr	02.96	95-96	28	10	7
Notts Co	Tr	03.97	96-97	11	4	2
Shrewsbury T	Tr	09.97	97-98	37	6	10
WHITE Edward (Ted)						
Crewe, 22 November, 1956						(F)
Crewe Alex		11.78	78	1	0	0
WHITE Edward (Eddie) Richard						
Musselburgh, 13 April, 1935						(CF)
Bradford C	Falkirk	10.59	59	4	-	1
WHITE Frederick (Fred)						
Wolverhampton, 5 December, 1916						(G)
Everton		05.35				
Sheffield U	Tr	05.37	47-49	44	-	0
Lincoln C	Tr	06.50	50	42	-	0
WHITE Gwilym (George) David						
Doncaster, 23 February, 1936						(FB)
Oldham Ath	Plymouth Arg (Am)	08.60	60	1	-	0
WHITE Howard Kenneth						
Timperley, 2 March, 1954						(CD)
Manchester C	App	05.71	70	1	0	0
WHITE Ian Samuel						
Glasgow, 20 December, 1935						(WH)
Leicester C	Glasgow Celtic	05.58	59-61	47	-	1
Southampton	Tr	06.62	62-66	60	1	5
WHITE James (Jimmy)						
Parkstone, 13 June, 1942 EYth						(CD)
Bournemouth (Am)	Jnrs	04.58	57	1	-	0
Portsmouth	Tr	06.59	58-61	34	-	6
Gillingham	Tr	06.63	63-65	65	0	1
Bournemouth	Tr	07.66	66-69	175	0	5
Cambridge U	Tr	12.70	70-71	28	2	2
WHITE Jason Gregory						
Solihull, 19 October, 1971						(F)
Derby Co	YT	07.90				
Scunthorpe U	Tr	09.91	91-93	44	24	16
Darlington	L	08.93	93	4	0	1
Scarborough	Tr	12.93	93-94	60	3	20
Northampton T	Tr	06.95	95-96	55	22	18
Rotherham U	Tr	09.97	97-99	52	21	22
Cheltenham T	Tr	07.00	00-01	8	23	1
Mansfield T	L	09.01	01	6	1	0
WHITE Jason Lee						
Sutton-in-Ashfield, 28 January, 1984						(G)
Mansfield T	Sch	08.02	02-04	4	1	0
WHITE John (Jack)						
Doncaster, 17 March, 1924						(WH)
Aldershot	Sheffield FC	07.44	46-52	209	-	25
Bristol C	Tr	10.52	52-57	216	-	11
WHITE John Alan						
Maldon, 26 July, 1986						(CD)
Colchester U	Sch	02.05	04	16	4	0
WHITE John Anderson						
Musselburgh, 28 April, 1937 Died 1964 Su23-1/SLge-2/FLge-1/S-22						(IF)
Tottenham H	Falkirk	10.59	59-63	183	-	40
WHITE Kenneth (Ken)						
Selby, 15 March, 1922						(WH)
Hull C	Selby T	12.47	48	1	-	0
WHITE Kevin Nicholas						
Poole, 26 June, 1948						(W)
Bournemouth	App	08.66	66-68	46	3	6

League Club	Source	Date Signed	Seasons Played	Apps	Subs	Gls
WHITE Leonard (Len) Roy						
Skellow, 23 March, 1930 Died 1994 FLge-2						(IF)
Rotherham U	Upton Colliery	05.48	50-52	43	-	15
Newcastle U	Tr	02.53	52-61	244	-	142
Huddersfield T	Tr	02.62	61-64	102	-	37
Stockport Co	Tr	01.65	64-65	53	0	24
WHITE Lewis						
Stoke-on-Trent, 2 August, 1927 Died 1982						(W)
Port Vale		10.48	48	1	-	0
WHITE Malcolm						
Wolverhampton, 24 April, 1941						(G)
Grimsby T	Wolverhampton W (Am)	08.58	58-62	65	-	0
Walsall	Tr	08.63	63	28	-	0
Lincoln C	Tr	07.64	64	25	-	0
Bradford C	Tr	07.65	65	9	0	0
Halifax T	Tr	11.65	65-67	100	0	0
WHITE Mark Ivan						
Sheffield, 26 October, 1958						(FB)
Reading	Sheffield U (App)	03.77	77-87	265	13	11
WHITE Maurice Henry						
Keadby, 29 January, 1938						(FB)
Doncaster Rov		04.56	57-60	55	-	0
WHITE Philip (Phil) George John						
Fulham, 29 December, 1930 Died 2000						(W)
Leyton Orient	Wealdstone	07.53	53-63	217	-	28
WHITE Raymond (Ray)						
Ely, 5 February, 1941						(WH)
Millwall	Jnrs	08.58	58	2	-	0
WHITE Raymond (Ray) Bernard William						
Bootle, 13 August, 1918 Died 1988						(WH)
Bradford PA	Tottenham H (Am)	05.46	46-50	151	-	3
WHITE Raymond (Ray) Sidney						
Rochford, 14 January, 1948						(G)
Southend U	App	01.66	63-67	10	0	0
Bristol Rov	Tr	07.68	68	3	0	0
WHITE Richard (Dick)						
Scunthorpe, 18 August, 1931 Died 2002						(CD)
Scunthorpe U	Brumby Amats	(N/L)	50-55	133	-	7
Liverpool	Tr	11.55	55-61	203	-	0
Doncaster Rov	Tr	07.62	62-63	83	-	0
WHITE Ronald (Ron) Thomas						
Bethnal Green, 9 November, 1931 Died 1994						(IF)
Charlton Ath	Maccabi Sports	03.54	53-61	165	-	8
WHITE Stephen (Steve) James						
Chipping Sodbury, 2 January, 1959 ESch						(F)
Bristol Rov	Mangotsfield U	07.77	77-79	46	4	20
Luton T	Tr	12.79	79-81	63	9	25
Charlton Ath	Tr	07.82	82	29	0	12
Lincoln C	L	01.83	82	2	1	0
Luton T	L	02.83	82	4	0	0
Bristol Rov	Tr	08.83	83-85	89	12	24
Swindon T	Tr	07.86	86-93	200	44	83
Hereford U	Tr	08.94	94-95	70	6	44
Cardiff C	Tr	06.96	96-97	44	23	15
WHITE Thomas (Tom)						
High Hold, 10 November, 1924 Died 1998						(IF)
Sunderland	Chester Moor Amat	04.45	46	2	-	1
WHITE Thomas (Tommy)						
Musselburgh, 12 August, 1939						(F)
Crystal Palace	Aberdeen	06.66	66-67	37	2	13
Blackpool	Tr	03.68	67-69	34	0	9
Bury	Tr	06.70	70-71	46	2	13
Crewe Alex	Tr	12.71	71	4	0	0
WHITE Thomas (Tom) Matthew						
Bristol, 26 January, 1976						(CD)
Bristol Rov	YT	07.94	94-99	47	7	1
WHITE William (Willie)						
Clackmannan, 25 September, 1932						(G)
Accrington St	Motherwell	08.53	53	18	-	0
Mansfield T	Tr	05.54	54	3	-	0
Derby Co	L	08.55	55	3	-	0
WHITE William (Billy) Henry						
Liverpool, 13 October, 1936 Died 2000						(IF)
Burnley		01.54	57-59	9	-	4
Wrexham	Tr	03.61	60	8	-	0
Chester	Tr	07.61	61	13	-	3

WHITE Eric Winston
Leicester, 26 October, 1958 (W)

League Club	Source	Date Signed	Seasons Played	Apps	Subs	Gls
Leicester C	App	10.76	76-78	10	2	1
Hereford U	Tr	03.79	78-82	169	6	21
Chesterfield	HK Rgrs (HK)	09.83	83	0	1	0
Port Vale	Tr	10.83	83	0	1	0
Stockport Co	Tr	11.83	83	4	0	0
Bury	Tr	12.83	83-86	125	0	12
Rochdale	L	10.86	86	4	0	0
Colchester U	Tr	02.87	86-88	64	1	8
Burnley	Tr	10.88	88-90	93	11	14
West Bromwich A	Tr	03.91	90-91	13	3	1
Bury	Tr	10.92	92	1	1	0
Doncaster Rov	Tr	01.93	92	4	0	2
Carlisle U	Tr	02.93	92	6	0	0
Wigan Ath	Tr	03.93	92	10	0	2

WHITEAR John Michael
Isleworth, 31 May, 1935 EYth (IF)

League Club	Source	Date Signed	Seasons Played	Apps	Subs	Gls
Aston Villa	Walton & Hersham	04.53				
Crystal Palace	Tr	05.56	56	5	-	1

WHITEFOOT Jeffrey (Jeff)
Cheadle, 31 December, 1933 ESch/Eu23-1 (WH)

League Club	Source	Date Signed	Seasons Played	Apps	Subs	Gls
Manchester U	Jnrs	12.51	49-55	93	-	0
Grimsby T	Tr	11.57	57	26	-	5
Nottingham F	Tr	07.58	58-67	255	0	5

WHITEHALL Steven (Steve) Christopher
Bromborough, 8 December, 1966 (F)

League Club	Source	Date Signed	Seasons Played	Apps	Subs	Gls
Rochdale	Southport	07.91	91-96	212	26	75
Mansfield T	Tr	08.97	97	42	1	24
Oldham Ath	Tr	07.98	98-00	55	21	13

WHITEHEAD Alan
Bury, 20 November, 1956 (CD)

League Club	Source	Date Signed	Seasons Played	Apps	Subs	Gls
Bury	Darwen	12.77	77-80	98	1	13
Brentford	Tr	08.81	81-83	101	1	4
Scunthorpe U	Tr	01.84	83-86	106	2	8
York C	Tr	10.86	86-87	40	1	1
Wigan Ath	L	03.87	86	2	0	0
Halifax T	Tr	08.88	88	10	1	1

WHITEHEAD Alan John
Birmingham, 3 September, 1951 (CD)

League Club	Source	Date Signed	Seasons Played	Apps	Subs	Gls
Birmingham C	App	07.69	71-72	4	0	0

WHITEHEAD Barry
Sheffield, 3 December, 1946 (IF)

League Club	Source	Date Signed	Seasons Played	Apps	Subs	Gls
Chesterfield		07.65	65	5	1	1

WHITEHEAD Clive Robert
Birmingham, 24 November, 1955 EYth (W)

League Club	Source	Date Signed	Seasons Played	Apps	Subs	Gls
Bristol C	Northfield Jnrs	08.73	73-81	209	20	10
West Bromwich A	Tr	11.81	81-86	157	11	6
Wolverhampton W	L	01.86	85	2	0	0
Portsmouth	Tr	06.87	87-88	57	8	2
Exeter C	Tr	07.89	89-90	44	2	5

WHITEHEAD Damien Stephen
St Helens, 24 April, 1979 (F)

League Club	Source	Date Signed	Seasons Played	Apps	Subs	Gls
Macclesfield T	Warrington T	08.99	99-01	20	38	14

WHITEHEAD Dean
Oxford, 12 January, 1982 (M)

League Club	Source	Date Signed	Seasons Played	Apps	Subs	Gls
Oxford U	YT	04.00	00-03	92	30	9
Sunderland	Tr	08.04	04	39	3	5

WHITEHEAD Norman John
Fazakerley, 22 April, 1948 (W)

League Club	Source	Date Signed	Seasons Played	Apps	Subs	Gls
Southport	Skelmersdale U	12.67	67	7	1	0
Rochdale	Tr	07.68	68-71	153	2	11
Rotherham U	Tr	03.72	71-72	29	4	2
Chester	Tr	08.73	73-75	66	8	5
Grimsby T	Tr	08.76	76	3	1	0

WHITEHEAD Philip (Phil) Matthew
Halifax, 17 December, 1969 (G)

League Club	Source	Date Signed	Seasons Played	Apps	Subs	Gls
Halifax T	YT	07.88	86-89	42	0	0
Barnsley	Tr	03.90	91-92	16	0	0
Halifax T	L	03.91	90	9	0	0
Scunthorpe U	L	11.91	91	8	0	0
Scunthorpe U	L	09.92	92	8	0	0
Bradford C	L	11.92	92	6	0	0
Oxford U	Tr	11.93	93-98	207	0	0
West Bromwich A	Tr	12.98	98	26	0	0
Reading	Tr	10.99	99-02	94	0	0
Tranmere Rov	L	09.02	02	2	0	0
York C	L	04.03	02	2	0	0

WHITEHEAD Robert (Bob)
Ashington, 22 September, 1936 (FB)

League Club	Source	Date Signed	Seasons Played	Apps	Subs	Gls
Newcastle U	Fatfield Ath	12.54	57-59	20	-	0
Darlington	Tr	08.62	62-63	53	-	0

WHITEHEAD Scott Anthony
Doncaster, 20 April, 1974 (M)

League Club	Source	Date Signed	Seasons Played	Apps	Subs	Gls
Chesterfield	YT	07.92	91-92	4	5	0

WHITEHEAD Stuart David
Bromsgrove, 17 July, 1976 (CD)

League Club	Source	Date Signed	Seasons Played	Apps	Subs	Gls
Bolton W	Bromsgrove Rov	09.95				
Carlisle U	Tr	07.98	98-02	148	4	2
Darlington	Tr	10.02	02	23	0	0
Shrewsbury T	Telford U	07.04	04	37	3	0

WHITEHEAD William (Billy) George
Maltby, 6 February, 1920 (W)

League Club	Source	Date Signed	Seasons Played	Apps	Subs	Gls
Queens Park Rgrs	Maltby Colliery	08.39				
Aldershot	Tr	08.47	47	6	-	1

WHITEHOUSE Brian
West Bromwich, 8 September, 1935 (IF)

League Club	Source	Date Signed	Seasons Played	Apps	Subs	Gls
West Bromwich A	Vono Sports	10.52	55-59	37	-	13
Norwich C	Tr	03.60	59-61	41	-	14
Wrexham	Tr	03.62	61-63	45	-	19
Crystal Palace	Tr	11.63	63-65	82	0	17
Charlton Ath	Tr	03.66	65	13	0	1
Leyton Orient	Tr	07.66	66-67	52	0	6

WHITEHOUSE Dane Lee
Sheffield, 14 October, 1970 (W)

League Club	Source	Date Signed	Seasons Played	Apps	Subs	Gls
Sheffield U	YT	07.89	88-97	204	27	39

WHITEHOUSE Dean
Mexborough, 30 October, 1963 (M)

League Club	Source	Date Signed	Seasons Played	Apps	Subs	Gls
Barnsley	App	10.81	83	1	1	0
Torquay U	Tr	08.84	84	7	2	0

WHITEHOUSE James (Jimmy)
West Bromwich, 19 September, 1934 (IF)

League Club	Source	Date Signed	Seasons Played	Apps	Subs	Gls
West Bromwich A	Jnrs	11.54				
Reading	Tr	06.56	56-61	203	-	61
Coventry C	Tr	08.62	62-63	46	-	12
Millwall	Tr	03.64	63-64	38	-	13

WHITEHOUSE James (Jimmy) Edward
West Bromwich, 19 September, 1924 (IF)

League Club	Source	Date Signed	Seasons Played	Apps	Subs	Gls
West Bromwich A	Hawthorns	05.48				
Walsall	Tr	06.49	49	20	-	8
Rochdale	Tr	07.50	50-51	46	-	13
Carlisle U	Tr	10.51	51-56	198	-	100

WHITEHOUSE Philip (Phil)
Wolverhampton, 23 March, 1971 (FB)

League Club	Source	Date Signed	Seasons Played	Apps	Subs	Gls
West Bromwich A	YT	07.89				
Walsall	Tr	12.89	89-90	10	2	0

WHITEHURST Walter
Manchester, 7 June, 1934 (WH)

League Club	Source	Date Signed	Seasons Played	Apps	Subs	Gls
Manchester U	Jnrs	05.52	55	1	-	0
Chesterfield	Tr	11.56	56-59	91	-	2
Crewe Alex	Tr	07.60	60	3	-	1

WHITEHURST William (Billy)
Thurnscoe, 10 June, 1959 (F)

League Club	Source	Date Signed	Seasons Played	Apps	Subs	Gls
Hull C	Mexborough T	10.80	80-85	176	17	47
Newcastle U	Tr	12.85	85-86	28	0	7
Oxford U	Tr	10.86	86-87	36	4	4
Reading	Tr	02.88	87-88	17	0	8
Sunderland	Tr	09.88	88	17	0	3
Hull C	Tr	12.88	88-89	36	0	5
Sheffield U	Tr	02.90	89-90	12	10	2
Stoke C	L	11.90	90	3	0	0
Doncaster Rov	Tr	02.91	90-91	22	0	1
Crewe Alex	L	01.92	91	4	6	0

WHITELAW George
Paisley, 1 January, 1937 Died 2004 SAmat (CF)

League Club	Source	Date Signed	Seasons Played	Apps	Subs	Gls
Sunderland	St Johnstone	02.58	57-58	5	-	0
Queens Park Rgrs	Tr	03.59	58-59	26	-	10
Halifax T	Tr	10.59	59-60	52	-	22
Carlisle U	Tr	02.61	60-61	34	-	9
Stockport Co	Tr	01.62	61-62	52	-	18
Barrow	Tr	08.63	63	7	-	0

WHITELEY Albert
Sheffield, 13 July, 1932 Died 2002 (W)

League Club	Source	Date Signed	Seasons Played	Apps	Subs	Gls
Leyton Orient	Sheffield Wed (Am)	11.52	52-53	23	-	3

WHITELEY Andrew (Andy) Mark
Sowerby Bridge, 1 August, 1961 (M)

League Club	Source	Date Signed	Seasons Played	Apps	Subs	Gls
Halifax T		08.79	79-81	20	16	1

League Club	Source	Date Signed	Seasons Played	Career Record Apps	Subs	Gls
WHITELOCK Arthur						
Stockton, 31 July, 1931 (FB)						
Hartlepools U	South Bank	12.50	50	6	-	0
WHITELUM Clifford (Cliff)						
Farnworth, 2 December, 1919 Died 2000 (CF)						
Sunderland	Bentley Colliery	12.38	38-47	43	-	18
Sheffield U	Tr	10.47	47-48	41	-	14
WHITESIDE Arnold						
Garstang, 6 November, 1911 Died 1994 (WH)						
Blackburn Rov	Woodplumpton Jnrs	01.33	32-48	218	-	3
WHITESIDE Charles William Parker						
Liverpool, 16 August, 1927 Died 1988 (IF)						
Swindon T		12.48	49	1	-	0
WHITESIDE Edward **Kenneth (Ken)**						
Liverpool, 11 December, 1929 (IF)						
Preston NE	British Eckna Works	05.52				
Chesterfield	British Eckna Works	05.53	53	9	-	3
York C	Tr	05.54	54	8	-	0
Bournemouth	Tr	07.55	55	1	-	0
WHITESIDE Norman						
Belfast, 7 May, 1965 NISch/NI-38 (M)						
Manchester U	App	07.82	81-88	193	13	47
Everton	Tr	07.89	89-90	27	2	9
WHITESIDE William (Billy) Richard						
Belfast, 24 September, 1935 (W)						
Exeter C	Portadown	11.55	55	3	-	1
Scunthorpe U	Portadown	08.56	56	2	-	0
WHITFIELD George Allan						
Penrith, 10 February, 1934 (FB)						
Carlisle U		11.55	56	1	-	0
WHITFIELD James (Jimmy)						
Hull, 18 May, 1919 Died 1984 (IF)						
Grimsby T	Humber U	05.46	46-48	29	-	7
Scunthorpe U	Tr	04.49	50	16	-	6
Southport	Tr	08.51	51	12	-	0
Scunthorpe U	Tr	02.52	51-54	104	-	25
WHITFIELD John Spoor						
Gateshead, 10 June, 1938 (W)						
Gateshead		07.59	59	1	-	1
WHITFIELD Kenneth (Ken)						
Spennymoor, 24 March, 1930 Died 1995 (CD)						
Wolverhampton W	Shildon	12.47	51-52	9	-	3
Manchester C	Tr	03.53	52-53	13	-	3
Brighton & Hove A	Tr	07.54	54-58	175	-	4
Queens Park Rgrs	Tr	07.59	59-60	19	-	3
WHITFIELD Michael (Mick)						
Sunderland, 17 October, 1962 (M)						
Sunderland	App	10.80	82	3	0	0
Hartlepool U	Tr	08.83	83	15	1	0
WHITFIELD Paul Michael						
St Asaph, 6 May, 1982 WYth/Wu21-1 (G)						
Wrexham	YT	07.01	02-03	7	3	0
WHITFIELD Robert (Bob)						
Bywell, 30 June, 1920 Died 2004 (CD)						
Charlton Ath	Prudhoe	05.39				
Torquay U	Tr	02.47	46-49	11	-	1
WHITFIELD Wilfred (Wilf)						
Chesterfield, 17 November, 1916 (WH)						
Bristol Rov	Worksop T	07.38	38-46	26	-	1
Torquay U		08.49	49-50	47	-	1
WHITHAM Jack						
Burnley, 8 December, 1946 Eu23-1 (F)						
Sheffield Wed	Holy Trinity	11.64	66-69	54	9	27
Liverpool	Tr	05.70	70-71	15	0	7
Cardiff C	Tr	01.74	73-74	12	2	3
Reading	Tr	07.75	75	13	6	3
WHITHAM Terence (Terry)						
Sheffield, 14 August, 1935 (WH)						
Sheffield Wed	Jnrs	09.52	56-58	4	-	0
Chesterfield	Tr	06.61	61-63	66	-	3
WHITINGTON Craig						
Brighton, 3 September, 1970 (F)						
Scarborough	Crawley T	11.93	93	26	1	10
Huddersfield T	Tr	08.94	94	1	0	0
Rochdale	L	11.94	94	1	0	0

League Club	Source	Date Signed	Seasons Played	Career Record Apps	Subs	Gls
WHITINGTON Eric Richard						
Brighton, 18 September, 1946 EYth (M)						
Brighton & Hove A	Chelsea (Am)	10.64	65-67	26	6	8
WHITLEY James (Jim)						
Ndola, Zambia, 14 April, 1975 NIB-1/NI-3 (FB)						
Manchester C	Jnrs	08.94	97-99	27	11	0
Blackpool	L	08.99	99	7	1	0
Norwich C	L	08.00	00	7	1	1
Swindon T	L	12.00	00	2	0	0
Northampton T	L	02.01	00	13	0	0
Wrexham	Tr	10.01	01-04	125	5	1
WHITLEY Jeffrey (Jeff)						
Ndola, Zambia, 28 January, 1979 NIu21-17/NIB-2/NI-19 (M)						
Manchester C	YT	02.96	96-01	96	27	8
Wrexham	L	01.99	98	9	0	2
Notts Co	L	03.02	01	6	0	0
Notts Co	L	10.02	02	12	0	0
Sunderland	Tr	08.03	03-04	65	3	2
WHITLOCK Mark						
Portsmouth, 14 March, 1961 (CD)						
Southampton	App	03.79	81-85	55	6	1
Grimsby T	L	10.82	82	7	1	0
Aldershot	L	03.83	82	14	0	0
Bournemouth	Tr	07.86	86-88	98	1	1
Reading	Tr	12.88	88-89	26	1	0
Aldershot	Tr	08.90	90	28	1	2
WHITLOCK Philip (Phil) John						
Llanhilleth, 1 May, 1930 (WH)						
Cardiff C		02.49				
Chester	Tr	08.50	50-58	142	-	3
WHITLOW Michael (Mike) William						
Northwich, 13 January, 1968 (FB)						
Leeds U	Witton A	11.88	88-91	62	15	4
Leicester C	Tr	03.92	91-96	141	6	8
Bolton W	Tr	09.97	97-02	124	8	2
Sheffield U	Tr	07.03	03	13	4	1
Notts Co	Tr	07.04	04	22	2	0
WHITMARSH Paul						
Beckenham, 18 September, 1973 ESch (F)						
West Ham U	YT	07.92				
Doncaster Rov	Tr	09.93	93	2	4	1
WHITMORE Theodore (Theo) Eccleston						
Montego Bay, Jamaica, 5 August, 1972 Jamaica int (M)						
Hull C	Seba U (Jam)	10.99	99-01	63	14	9
Tranmere Rov	Seba U (Jam)	07.04	04	17	16	5
WHITNALL Brian						
Adwick-le-Street, 25 May, 1933 (FB)						
Hull C	Jnrs	06.50	54	2	-	0
Scunthorpe U	Tr	05.56	56-57	2	-	0
Exeter C	Tr	07.58	58-61	36	-	0
WHITNEY Jonathan (Jon) David						
Nantwich, 23 December, 1970 (FB)						
Huddersfield T	Winsford U	10.93	93-95	17	1	0
Wigan Ath	L	03.95	94	12	0	0
Lincoln C	Tr	10.95	95-98	98	3	8
Hull C	Tr	12.98	98-00	54	3	3
WHITTAKER Frederick (Fred)						
Vancouver, Canada, 12 October, 1923 (CF)						
Notts Co	Vancouver (Can)	08.46	46	10	-	2
WHITTAKER Raymond (Ray) Henry						
Bow, 15 January, 1945 ESch/EYth (W)						
Arsenal	Jnrs	05.62				
Luton T	Tr	03.64	63-68	169	1	40
Colchester U	Tr	07.69	69-70	41	2	7
WHITTAKER Richard (Dick)						
Dublin, 10 October, 1934 Died 1998 IRB/IR-1 (FB)						
Chelsea	St Mary's BC	05.52	55-59	48	-	0
Peterborough U	Tr	09.60	60-62	82	-	0
Queens Park Rgrs	Tr	07.63	63	17	-	0
WHITTAKER Stuart						
Liverpool, 2 January, 1975 (W)						
Bolton W	Liverpool (YT)	05.93	93-94	2	1	0
Wigan Ath	L	08.96	96	2	1	0
Macclesfield T	Tr	08.97	97-99	49	18	5
WHITTAKER William (Bill) Paul						
Charlton, 20 December, 1922 Died 1977 ESch (WH)						
Charlton Ath	Arsenal (Am)	02.40	46-48	28	-	0
Huddersfield T	Tr	11.48	48-49	43	-	0
Crystal Palace	Tr	06.50	50	35	-	1

League Club	Source	Date Signed	Seasons Played	Career Record Apps	Subs	Gls
WHITTAM Ernest (Ernie)						
Thurcroft, 29 October, 1924						(FB)
Rotherham U	Dinnington Ath	04.45	46	1	-	0
WHITTINGHAM Alfred (Alf)						
Altofts, 19 June, 1914 Died 1993						(CF)
Bradford C	Altofts WR Colliery	10.36	36-46	87	-	24
Huddersfield T	Tr	02.47	46-48	67	-	17
Halifax T	Tr	03.49	48-49	39	-	9
WHITTINGHAM Guy						
Evesham, 10 November, 1964						(F)
Portsmouth	Yeovil T	06.89	89-92	149	11	88
Aston Villa	Tr	08.93	93-94	17	8	5
Wolverhampton W	L	02.94	93	13	0	8
Sheffield Wed	Tr	12.94	94-98	90	23	22
Wolverhampton W	L	11.98	98	9	1	1
Portsmouth	L	01.99	98	9	0	7
Watford	L	03.99	98	4	1	0
Portsmouth	Tr	07.99	99-00	15	11	4
Peterborough U	L	08.00	00	1	4	1
Oxford U	L	10.00	00	1	0	1
Wycombe W	Tr	03.01	00	9	3	1
WHITTINGHAM Peter Michael						
Nuneaton, 8 September, 1984 EYth/Eu21-7						(M)
Aston Villa	Sch	11.02	02-04	26	23	1
Burnley	L	02.05	04	7	0	0
WHITTINGHAM Stephen (Steve) Paul						
Wallasey, 4 February, 1962						(F)
Tranmere Rov	App	02.80	78-80	0	2	0
WHITTLE Alan						
Liverpool, 10 March, 1950 ESch/EYth/Eu23-1						(F)
Everton	App	07.65	67-72	72	2	21
Crystal Palace	Tr	12.72	72-75	103	5	19
Orient	Tr	09.76	76	31	2	5
Orient	Persepolis (Iran)	02.78	78-79	16	1	1
Bournemouth		01.81	80	8	1	0
WHITTLE Ernest (Ernie)						
Lanchester, 25 November, 1925 Died 1998						(IF)
Newcastle U	South Moor Jnrs	11.44				
Lincoln C	Seaham Colliery	01.50	49-53	145	-	62
Workington	Tr	03.54	53-56	110	-	44
Chesterfield	Tr	11.56	56	15	-	4
Bradford PA	Tr	08.57	57	18	-	6
WHITTLE Graham						
Liverpool, 30 May, 1953						(F)
Wrexham	Hartshill BC	07.71	70-80	288	18	91
WHITTLE James Archibald						
Hamilton, 5 September, 1929						(CF)
Southampton (L)	Heart of Midlothian	01.54	53	2	-	0
WHITTLE Justin Philip						
Derby, 18 March, 1971						(CD)
Stoke C	Glasgow Celtic	10.94	95-98	66	13	1
Hull C	Tr	11.98	98-03	184	9	2
Grimsby T	Tr	08.04	04	39	1	1
WHITTLE Maurice						
Wigan, 5 July, 1948						(FB)
Blackburn Rov	App	07.66	68	5	2	0
Oldham Ath	Tr	05.69	69-76	307	5	39
Wigan Ath	Barrow	03.80	79-80	21	0	1
WHITTON Stephen (Steve) Paul						
East Ham, 4 December, 1960						(M)
Coventry C	App	09.78	79-82	64	10	21
West Ham U	Tr	07.83	83-84	35	4	6
Birmingham C	L	01.86	85	8	0	3
Birmingham C	Tr	08.86	86-88	94	1	28
Sheffield Wed	Tr	03.89	88-90	22	10	4
Ipswich T	Tr	01.91	90-93	80	8	15
Colchester U	Tr	03.94	93-97	105	11	21
WHITWORTH George Geoffrey						
Eckington, 22 September, 1927						(WH)
Liverpool	Stanton Ironworks	03.50	51	9	-	0
WHITWORTH Harry						
Whitefield, 1 December, 1920 Died 2002						(W)
Bury	Prestwich Central	11.45	46-50	112	-	14
Rochdale	Tr	07.51	51-52	70	-	9
Southport	Northwich Vic	09.53	53	33	-	6
Crewe Alex	Tr	07.54	54	13	-	1
WHITWORTH Neil Anthony						
Ince, 12 April, 1972 EYth						(CD)
Wigan Ath	YT	•	89	1	1	0
Manchester U	Tr	07.90	90	1	0	0
Preston NE	L	01.92	91	6	0	0
Barnsley	L	02.92	91	11	0	0
Rotherham U	L	10.93	93	8	0	1
Blackpool	L	12.93	93	3	0	0
Wigan Ath	Kilmarnock	03.98	97	1	3	0
Hull C	Tr	07.98	98-99	18	1	2
Exeter C	Tr	08.00	00-02	53	4	1
WHITWORTH Stephen (Steve)						
Ellistown, 20 March, 1952 ESch/EYth/Eu23-6/E-7						(FB)
Leicester C	App	11.69	70-78	352	1	0
Sunderland	Tr	03.79	78-81	83	0	0
Bolton W	Tr	10.81	81-82	67	0	0
Mansfield T	Tr	08.83	83-84	80	0	2
WHYKE Peter						
Smithies, 7 September, 1939						(W)
Barnsley	Smithies	01.58	57-60	26	-	1
Rochdale	Tr	07.61	61	5	-	0
WHYMARK Trevor John						
Burston, 4 May, 1950 Eu23-6/E-1						(F)
Ipswich T	Diss T	05.69	69-78	249	12	75
Derby Co	Sparta Rotterdam (Holl)	12.79	79	2	0	0
Grimsby T	Vancouver (Can)	12.80	80-83	83	10	16
Southend U	Tr	01.84	83-84	37	2	6
Peterborough U	Tr	08.85	85	3	0	0
Colchester U	Diss T	10.85	85	2	0	0
WHYTE John **Archibald (Archie)**						
Redding, 17 July, 1919 Died 1973						(CD)
Barnsley	Armadale Thistle	05.38	46-49	91	-	2
Oldham Ath	Tr	08.50	50-55	234	-	0
WHYTE Christopher (Chris) Anderson						
Islington, 2 September, 1961 Eu21-4						(CD)
Arsenal	App	12.79	81-85	86	4	8
Crystal Palace	L	08.84	84	13	0	0
West Bromwich A	Los Angeles (USA)	08.88	88-89	83	1	7
Leeds U	Tr	06.90	90-92	113	0	5
Birmingham C	Tr	08.93	93-95	68	0	1
Coventry C	L	12.95	95	1	0	0
Charlton Ath	Tr	03.96	95	10	1	0
Leyton Orient	Detroit (USA)	01.97	96	1	0	0
Oxford U	Tr	02.97	96	10	0	0
WHYTE David						
Dunfermline, 2 March, 1959						(CD)
Leeds U	App	03.77	76	1	1	0
WHYTE David Antony						
Greenwich, 20 April, 1971						(F)
Crystal Palace	Greenwich Borough	02.89	91-93	17	10	4
Charlton Ath	L	03.92	91	7	1	2
Charlton Ath	Tr	07.94	94-96	65	20	28
Ipswich T	Tr	10.97	97	2	0	0
Bristol Rov	Tr	01.98	97	0	4	0
Southend U	Tr	03.98	97-98	17	9	3
WHYTE Derek						
Glasgow, 31 August, 1968 SSch/SYth/Su21-9/SB/S-12						(CD)
Middlesbrough	Glasgow Celtic	08.92	92-97	160	7	2
WHYTE Francis (Frank)						
Govanhill, 18 April, 1929						(CD)
Swindon T	Glasgow Celtic	06.56	56	7	-	0
WHYTE James (Jimmy) McCreadie						
Glasgow, 19 January, 1930						(IF)
Southend U	Third Lanark	05.54	54-56	33	-	8
WHYTE John (Jock) Nimmo						
West Calder, 7 May, 1921 Died 1998						(FB)
Bradford C	Falkirk	08.50	50-56	236	-	2
WICKS Alan Hayward						
Henley-on-Thames, 8 February, 1933						(WH)
Reading		05.52	55	1	-	0
WICKS Matthew Jonathan						
Reading, 8 September, 1978 EYth						(CD)
Arsenal	Manchester U (YT)	01.96				
Crewe Alex	Tr	06.98	98	4	2	0
Peterborough U	Tr	03.99	98-99	28	3	0
Brighton & Hove A	Tr	09.00	00-01	25	1	3
Hull C	Tr	01.02	01	14	0	0

WICKS Peter
Hemsworth, 14 May, 1948 EYth (G)

League Club	Source	Date Signed	Seasons Played	Apps	Subs	Gls
Sheffield Wed	App	05.65	64-69	13	0	0

WICKS Roger Charles
Warrington, 19 April, 1947 (M)

League Club	Source	Date Signed	Seasons Played	Apps	Subs	Gls
Darlington	Netherfield	02.81	80-82	31	10	4

WICKS Stanley (Stan) Maurice
Reading, 11 July, 1928 Died 1983 EB/FLge-1 (CD)

League Club	Source	Date Signed	Seasons Played	Apps	Subs	Gls
Reading	Castle Street Inst	08.48	49-53	170	-	1
Chelsea	Tr	01.54	54-56	71	-	1

WICKS Stephen (Steve) John
Reading, 3 October, 1956 EYth/Eu21-1 (CD)

League Club	Source	Date Signed	Seasons Played	Apps	Subs	Gls
Chelsea	App	06.74	74-78	117	1	5
Derby Co	Tr	01.79	78-79	24	0	0
Queens Park Rgrs	Tr	09.79	79-80	73	0	0
Crystal Palace	Tr	06.81	81	14	0	1
Queens Park Rgrs	Tr	03.82	81-85	116	0	6
Chelsea	Tr	07.86	86-87	32	0	1

WIDDOP Dennis
Keighley, 14 March, 1931 (W)

League Club	Source	Date Signed	Seasons Played	Apps	Subs	Gls
Bradford C	Portadown	08.54	54	1	-	0

WIDDOWSON John **Robert (Bob)**
Loughborough, 12 September, 1941 (G)

League Club	Source	Date Signed	Seasons Played	Apps	Subs	Gls
Sheffield U	British Ropes	07.59	61-67	7	0	0
York C	Tr	06.68	68-69	30	0	0
Portsmouth	L	11.69	69	4	0	0

WIDDRINGTON Thomas (Tommy)
Newcastle, 1 October, 1971 (M)

League Club	Source	Date Signed	Seasons Played	Apps	Subs	Gls
Southampton	YT	05.90	91-95	67	8	3
Wigan Ath	L	09.91	91	5	1	0
Grimsby T	Tr	07.96	96-98	72	17	8
Port Vale	Tr	03.99	98-00	77	5	8
Hartlepool U	Tr	07.01	01-02	50	6	5
Macclesfield T	Tr	08.03	03-04	55	3	0
Port Vale	Tr	01.05	04	2	4	0

WIEKENS Gerard
Tolhuiswyk, Holland, 25 February, 1973 (CD)

League Club	Source	Date Signed	Seasons Played	Apps	Subs	Gls
Manchester C	SC Vendeem (Holl)	07.97	97-02	167	15	10

WIFFILL David (Dave) Phillip
Bristol, 19 April, 1961 (M)

League Club	Source	Date Signed	Seasons Played	Apps	Subs	Gls
Manchester C	Bath C	04.80				
Bristol Rov	Bath C	08.87	87	2	0	0

WIGG Nathan Marlow
Cardiff, 27 September, 1974 (M)

League Club	Source	Date Signed	Seasons Played	Apps	Subs	Gls
Cardiff C	YT	08.93	93-95	40	18	1

WIGG Ronald (Ron) George
Great Dunmow, 18 May, 1949 Died 1997 (F)

League Club	Source	Date Signed	Seasons Played	Apps	Subs	Gls
Ipswich T	Leyton Orient (App)	04.67	67-69	35	2	14
Watford	Tr	06.70	70-72	91	6	20
Rotherham U	Tr	03.73	72-74	65	0	22
Grimsby T	Tr	01.75	74-76	51	12	12
Barnsley	Tr	03.77	76-77	14	4	5
Scunthorpe U	Tr	10.77	77-78	48	2	7

WIGGAN Trenton Ashton
Jamaica, 20 September, 1962 ESch (W)

League Club	Source	Date Signed	Seasons Played	Apps	Subs	Gls
Sheffield U	App	08.80	79-81	20	4	3

WIGGETT David (Dave) Jonathan
Chapeltown, 25 May, 1957 Died 1978 (FB)

League Club	Source	Date Signed	Seasons Played	Apps	Subs	Gls
Lincoln C	App	06.75	73-75	4	2	0
Hartlepool	Tr	10.76	76-77	54	0	1

WIGGIN Raymond (Ray)
Rushall, 13 September, 1942 (CF)

League Club	Source	Date Signed	Seasons Played	Apps	Subs	Gls
Walsall		09.62	62-63	19	-	6

WIGGINTON Clive Anthony
Sheffield, 18 October, 1950 (CD)

League Club	Source	Date Signed	Seasons Played	Apps	Subs	Gls
Grimsby T	App	10.68	68-74	164	9	6
Scunthorpe U	Tr	07.75	75-76	88	0	7
Lincoln C	Tr	09.77	77-78	60	0	6
Grimsby T	Tr	03.79	78-81	122	0	2
Doncaster Rov	L	03.82	81	13	0	1
Torquay U	Tr	07.82	82	9	0	0
Doncaster Rov	Tr	10.82	82	18	0	0

WIGHTMAN John (Jock) Renton
Duns, 2 November, 1912 Died 1964 (WH)

League Club	Source	Date Signed	Seasons Played	Apps	Subs	Gls
York C	Scarborough	08.33	33	5	-	0
Bradford PA	Tr	09.34	34	17	-	0
Huddersfield T	Tr	01.35	34-36	64	-	0
Blackburn Rov	Tr	01.37	36-46	66	-	2
Carlisle U	Tr	08.47	47	36	-	0

WIGLEY Steven (Steve)
Ashton-under-Lyne, 15 October, 1961 (W)

League Club	Source	Date Signed	Seasons Played	Apps	Subs	Gls
Nottingham F	Curzon Ashton	03.81	82-85	69	13	2
Sheffield U	Tr	10.85	85-86	21	7	1
Birmingham C	Tr	03.87	86-88	87	0	4
Portsmouth	Tr	03.89	88-91	103	17	12
Exeter C	Tr	08.93	93	22	1	1

WIGNALL David Arthur
Wallasey, 3 April, 1959 (M)

League Club	Source	Date Signed	Seasons Played	Apps	Subs	Gls
Doncaster Rov	App	07.76	75-77	35	6	1

WIGNALL Frank
Blackrod, 21 August, 1939 FLge-2/E-2 (F)

League Club	Source	Date Signed	Seasons Played	Apps	Subs	Gls
Everton	Horwich RMI	05.58	59-62	33	-	15
Nottingham F	Tr	06.63	63-67	156	1	47
Wolverhampton W	Tr	03.68	67-68	32	0	15
Derby Co	Tr	02.69	68-71	29	16	15
Mansfield T	Tr	11.71	71-72	50	6	15

WIGNALL Jack David
Liverpool, 26 September, 1981 (CD)

League Club	Source	Date Signed	Seasons Played	Apps	Subs	Gls
Colchester U	YT	•	99	0	1	0

WIGNALL Mark
Preston, 6 December, 1952 (M)

League Club	Source	Date Signed	Seasons Played	Apps	Subs	Gls
Wigan Ath	App	12.80	80-81	34	0	0

WIGNALL Steven (Steve) Leslie
Liverpool, 17 September, 1954 (CD)

League Club	Source	Date Signed	Seasons Played	Apps	Subs	Gls
Doncaster Rov	Liverpool (Jnrs)	03.72	72-76	127	3	1
Colchester U	Tr	09.77	77-83	279	2	21
Brentford	Tr	08.84	84-86	67	0	2
Aldershot	Tr	09.86	86-90	158	3	4

WIJNHARD Clyde
Surinam, 9 November, 1973 (F)

League Club	Source	Date Signed	Seasons Played	Apps	Subs	Gls
Leeds U	Willem II Tilburg (Holl)	07.98	98	11	7	3
Huddersfield T	Tr	07.99	99-01	51	11	16
Preston NE	Tr	03.02	01	6	0	3
Oldham Ath	Tr	08.02	02	24	1	10
Darlington	Beira Mar (Por)	10.04	04	31	0	14

WILBERT George Norman
Dunston-on-Tyne, 11 July, 1924 Died 1993 (CF)

League Club	Source	Date Signed	Seasons Played	Apps	Subs	Gls
Gateshead		08.42	47-54	269	-	95

WILBRAHAM Aaron Thomas
Knutsford, 21 October, 1979 (F)

League Club	Source	Date Signed	Seasons Played	Apps	Subs	Gls
Stockport Co	YT	08.97	97-03	118	54	35
Hull C	Tr	07.04	04	10	9	2
Oldham Ath	L	10.04	04	4	0	2

WILBY Edward
Rotherham, 18 May, 1922 Died 1998 (FB)

League Club	Source	Date Signed	Seasons Played	Apps	Subs	Gls
Wolverhampton W		05.46				
Bradford C	Tr	09.46	46	3	-	0

WILCOCK Roderick (Rod) William
Middlesbrough, 28 February, 1956 (M)

League Club	Source	Date Signed	Seasons Played	Apps	Subs	Gls
Crewe Alex	Southampton (Am)	08.74	74	2	2	0

WILCOCKSON Harold
Sheffield, 23 July, 1943 (FB)

League Club	Source	Date Signed	Seasons Played	Apps	Subs	Gls
Rotherham U		07.63	64-67	109	0	2
Doncaster Rov	Tr	02.68	67-69	75	0	3
Sheffield Wed	Tr	12.69	69-70	40	0	1
Doncaster Rov	Tr	05.71	71-72	36	0	1

WILCOX Anthony (Tony)
Rotherham, 13 June, 1944 (G)

League Club	Source	Date Signed	Seasons Played	Apps	Subs	Gls
Rotherham U		10.62				
Barnsley	Tr	08.64	64	6	-	0

WILCOX Caradoc (Crad)
Treharris, 8 November, 1923 (WH)

League Club	Source	Date Signed	Seasons Played	Apps	Subs	Gls
Cardiff C	Treharris	05.49				
Newport Co	Tr	07.52	52-53	32	-	0

WILCOX Edward Evan
Blaengarw, 24 March, 1927 (IF)

League Club	Source	Date Signed	Seasons Played	Apps	Subs	Gls
West Bromwich A	Oxford C	05.48	48-50	12	-	3

WILCOX Frederick (Fred)
St Helens, 23 October, 1922 (FB)

League Club	Source	Date Signed	Seasons Played	Apps	Subs	Gls
Chester	Everton (Am)	07.47	47	16	-	0

WILCOX George Edwin
Treeton, 23 August, 1917 Died 1991 (FB)

League Club	Source	Date Signed	Seasons Played	Apps	Subs	Gls
Derby Co	Denaby U	10.36	37-46	12	-	0
Rotherham U	Tr	08.48	48	1	-	0

WILCOX Jason Malcolm
Farnworth, 15 July, 1971 EB-2/E-3 (W)

League Club	Source	Date Signed	Seasons Played	Apps	Subs	Gls
Blackburn Rov	YT	06.89	89-99	242	27	31
Leeds U	Tr	12.99	99-03	52	29	4
Leicester C	Tr	08.04	04	11	3	1

WILCOX Raymond (Ray)
Treharris, 12 April, 1921 Died 2003 WLge-2 (CD)

League Club	Source	Date Signed	Seasons Played	Apps	Subs	Gls
Newport Co	Treharris	05.39	46-59	487	-	0

WILCOX Russell (Russ)
Hemsworth, 25 March, 1964 ESemiPro-3 (CD)

League Club	Source	Date Signed	Seasons Played	Apps	Subs	Gls
Doncaster Rov	App	●	80	1	0	0
Northampton T	Frickley Ath	06.86	86-89	137	1	9
Hull C	Tr	08.90	90-92	92	8	7
Doncaster Rov	Tr	07.93	93-95	81	0	6
Preston NE	Tr	09.95	95-96	62	0	1
Scunthorpe U	Tr	07.97	97-01	106	12	4

WILD Peter
Bramhall, 12 October, 1982 (F)

League Club	Source	Date Signed	Seasons Played	Apps	Subs	Gls
Stockport Co	YT	07.01	01-02	1	3	1

WILDE Adam Matthew
Southampton, 22 May, 1979 (W)

League Club	Source	Date Signed	Seasons Played	Apps	Subs	Gls
Cambridge U	YT	02.97	96-98	1	3	0

WILDER Christopher (Chris) John
Wortley, 23 September, 1967 (FB)

League Club	Source	Date Signed	Seasons Played	Apps	Subs	Gls
Southampton	App	09.85				
Sheffield U	Tr	08.86	86-91	89	4	1
Walsall	L	11.89	89	4	0	0
Charlton Ath	L	10.90	90	1	0	0
Charlton Ath	L	11.91	91	2	0	0
Leyton Orient	L	02.92	91	16	0	1
Rotherham U	Tr	07.92	92-95	129	3	11
Notts Co	Tr	01.96	95-96	46	0	0
Bradford C	Tr	03.97	96-97	35	7	0
Sheffield U	Tr	03.98	97-98	11	1	0
Northampton T	L	11.98	98	1	0	0
Lincoln C	L	03.99	98	2	1	0
Brighton & Hove A	Tr	07.99	99	11	0	0
Halifax T	Tr	10.99	99-00	51	0	1

WILDING Craig Anthony
Birmingham, 30 October, 1981 (F)

League Club	Source	Date Signed	Seasons Played	Apps	Subs	Gls
Chesterfield	YT	07.01				
York C	Tr	07.02	02	1	6	0

WILDING Peter John
Shrewsbury, 28 November, 1968 (CD)

League Club	Source	Date Signed	Seasons Played	Apps	Subs	Gls
Shrewsbury T	Telford U	06.97	97-02	170	23	7

WILDON Leslie **Eric**
Middlesbrough, 5 April, 1924 Died 1998 (CF)

League Club	Source	Date Signed	Seasons Played	Apps	Subs	Gls
Hartlepools U	Price's	12.47	47-54	200	-	87

WILE John David
Sherburn, 9 March, 1947 (CD)

League Club	Source	Date Signed	Seasons Played	Apps	Subs	Gls
Sunderland	Durham C	06.66				
Peterborough U	Tr	07.67	67-70	116	2	7
West Bromwich A	Tr	12.70	70-82	499	1	24
Peterborough U	Tr	08.83	83-85	86	1	3

WILEMAN Richard Anthony
Breedon, 4 October, 1947 (W)

League Club	Source	Date Signed	Seasons Played	Apps	Subs	Gls
Notts Co		07.66	66	2	0	0

WILES Ian Robert
Woodford, 28 April, 1980 (CD)

League Club	Source	Date Signed	Seasons Played	Apps	Subs	Gls
Colchester U	YT	07.98	98	0	1	0

WILES Simon Peter
Preston, 22 April, 1985 (M)

League Club	Source	Date Signed	Seasons Played	Apps	Subs	Gls
Blackpool	Sch	05.04	03	0	4	0

WILFORD Aron Leslie
Scarborough, 14 January, 1982 (F)

League Club	Source	Date Signed	Seasons Played	Apps	Subs	Gls
Middlesbrough	Harrogate College	07.99				
York C	Whitby T	07.03	03	4	2	2
Lincoln C	Tr	03.04	03	0	5	1

WILKES David Allan
Worsborough Bridge, 10 March, 1964 (M)

League Club	Source	Date Signed	Seasons Played	Apps	Subs	Gls
Barnsley	App	03.82	81-83	14	3	2
Halifax T	L	03.83	82	4	0	0
Stockport Co	Harps (HK)	08.86	86	8	0	0
Carlisle U	Bridlington T	11.90	90-91	1	4	0

WILKES Stephen (Steve) Brian
Preston, 30 June, 1967 (M)

League Club	Source	Date Signed	Seasons Played	Apps	Subs	Gls
Wigan Ath	App	06.85				
Preston NE	Tr	08.86	87	1	2	0

WILKES Timothy (Tim) Craig
Nottingham, 7 November, 1977 (F)

League Club	Source	Date Signed	Seasons Played	Apps	Subs	Gls
Notts Co	YT	07.96	96	3	0	0

WILKIE Arthur William
Woolwich, 7 October, 1942 (G)

League Club	Source	Date Signed	Seasons Played	Apps	Subs	Gls
Reading	Jnrs	10.59	61-67	169	0	2

WILKIE Derrick
Brandon, 27 July, 1939 (CD)

League Club	Source	Date Signed	Seasons Played	Apps	Subs	Gls
Middlesbrough	Browney Jnrs	03.57	59-60	4	-	0
Hartlepools U	Tr	09.61	61-63	74	-	0

WILKIE Glen Alan
Stepney, 11 January, 1977 (FB)

League Club	Source	Date Signed	Seasons Played	Apps	Subs	Gls
Leyton Orient	YT	03.95	94	10	1	0

WILKIE John Carlin
Dundee, 1 July, 1947 (F)

League Club	Source	Date Signed	Seasons Played	Apps	Subs	Gls
Halifax T	Ross Co	02.73	72-73	29	8	8
Wigan Ath	Elgin C	08.76	78	3	1	0

WILKIE Lee
Dundee, 20 April, 1980 Su21-8/S-11 (FB)

League Club	Source	Date Signed	Seasons Played	Apps	Subs	Gls
Plymouth Arg (L)	Dundee	01.01	00	2	0	0
Notts Co (L)	Dundee	08.01	01	2	0	0

WILKIE Robert (Bob) Mackintosh
Dundee, 7 October, 1935 (W)

League Club	Source	Date Signed	Seasons Played	Apps	Subs	Gls
Tottenham H	Lochee Harp	12.56	56	1	-	0

WILKIN Kevin
Cambridge, 1 October, 1967 (F)

League Club	Source	Date Signed	Seasons Played	Apps	Subs	Gls
Northampton T	Cambridge C	08.90	90-94	67	11	11

WILKINS Alan James
Treherbert, 3 October, 1944 (IF)

League Club	Source	Date Signed	Seasons Played	Apps	Subs	Gls
Swansea T		05.63	63-64	5	-	0

WILKINS Dean Mark
Hillingdon, 12 July, 1962 (M)

League Club	Source	Date Signed	Seasons Played	Apps	Subs	Gls
Queens Park Rgrs	App	05.80	80-82	1	5	0
Brighton & Hove A	Tr	08.83	83	2	0	0
Orient	L	03.84	83	10	0	0
Brighton & Hove A	PEC Zwolle (Holl)	07.87	87-95	295	15	25

WILKINS Ernest **George**
Hackney, 27 October, 1919 Died 1999 (IF)

League Club	Source	Date Signed	Seasons Played	Apps	Subs	Gls
Brentford	Hayes	02.38	38-46	29	-	7
Bradford PA	Tr	02.47	46-47	27	-	6
Nottingham F	Tr	12.47	47-48	24	-	6
Leeds U	Tr	09.49	49	3	-	0

WILKINS Graham George
Hillingdon, 28 June, 1955 (FB)

League Club	Source	Date Signed	Seasons Played	Apps	Subs	Gls
Chelsea	App	07.72	72-81	136	1	1
Brentford	Tr	07.82	82-83	36	2	0
Southend U	L	03.84	83	3	0	0

WILKINS Ian John
Lincoln, 3 April, 1980 (CD)

League Club	Source	Date Signed	Seasons Played	Apps	Subs	Gls
Lincoln C	YT	03.98	97-99	4	2	0

WILKINS Leonard Henry **Jack**
Dublin, 12 August, 1920 (CD)

League Club	Source	Date Signed	Seasons Played	Apps	Subs	Gls
Brighton & Hove A	Guildford C	10.48	48-50	44	-	2

WILKINS Kenneth (Ken)
Salford, 24 October, 1928 Died 1995 (IF)

League Club	Source	Date Signed	Seasons Played	Apps	Subs	Gls
Southampton		10.49	50	2	-	1
Exeter C	Tr	10.51	51	3	-	0
Southampton	Tr	07.52	52	1	-	0

WILKINS Leonard (Len)
Southampton, 20 September, 1925 Died 2003 (FB)

League Club	Source	Date Signed	Seasons Played	Apps	Subs	Gls
Southampton	Cunliffe-Owen	10.45	48-57	260	-	2

WILKINS Michael (Mike) John
Leeds, 6 May, 1942 (CF)

League Club	Source	Date Signed	Seasons Played	Apps	Subs	Gls
Bradford C	Ashley Road Meth	09.59	59	1	-	0

WILKINS Paul
Hackney, 20 March, 1964 (F)

League Club	Source	Date Signed	Seasons Played	Apps	Subs	Gls
Crystal Palace	Tottenham H (App)	01.82	81-83	9	4	3
Preston NE	Tr	06.84	84	3	3	2

WILKINS Raymond (Ray) Colin
Hillingdon, 14 September, 1956 ESch/EYth/Eu23-2/Eu21-1/FLge-1/E-84 (M)

League Club	Source	Date Signed	Seasons Played	Apps	Subs	Gls
Chelsea	App	10.73	73-78	176	3	30
Manchester U	Tr	08.79	79-83	158	2	7
Queens Park Rgrs	Glasgow Rgrs	11.89	89-93	153	1	7
Crystal Palace	Tr	05.94	94	1	0	0
Queens Park Rgrs	Tr	11.94	94-96	16	5	0
Wycombe W	Tr	09.96	96	1	0	0
Millwall	Hibernian	01.97	96	3	0	0
Leyton Orient	Tr	02.97	96	3	0	0

WILKINS Raymond (Ray) John Hamilton
Church Gresley, 16 August, 1928 (CF)

League Club	Source	Date Signed	Seasons Played	Apps	Subs	Gls
Derby Co	Moira U	01.50	49-53	30	-	11
Wrexham	Boston U	05.57	57	3	-	1

WILKINS Richard John
Lambeth, 28 May, 1965 (M)

League Club	Source	Date Signed	Seasons Played	Apps	Subs	Gls
Colchester U	Haverhill Rov	11.86	86-89	150	2	22
Cambridge U	Tr	07.90	90-93	79	2	7
Hereford U	Tr	07.94	94-95	76	1	5
Colchester U	Tr	07.96	96-99	125	2	11

WILKINS Ronald (Ron)
Treherbert, 21 December, 1923 Died 1983 (IF)

League Club	Source	Date Signed	Seasons Played	Apps	Subs	Gls
Newport Co	Gwynfi BC	01.46	46	1	-	0

WILKINSON Alan
Middlewich, 5 June, 1935 (IF)

League Club	Source	Date Signed	Seasons Played	Apps	Subs	Gls
Crewe Alex (Am)	Middlewich	10.55	55	1	-	0

WILKINSON Albert
Barnsley, 3 November, 1928 (W)

League Club	Source	Date Signed	Seasons Played	Apps	Subs	Gls
Bradford C (Am)		03.51	50	2	-	0
Halifax T	Denaby U	07.52	52	14	-	2

WILKINSON Andrew (Andy) Gordon
Stone, 6 August, 1984 (FB)

League Club	Source	Date Signed	Seasons Played	Apps	Subs	Gls
Stoke C	Sch	07.02	03-04	1	3	0
Shrewsbury T	L	03.05	04	9	0	0

WILKINSON George Barry
Bishop Auckland, 16 June, 1935 EYth (WH)

League Club	Source	Date Signed	Seasons Played	Apps	Subs	Gls
Liverpool	West Auckland	06.54	53-59	78	-	0
Tranmere Rov	Bangor C	08.63	63	3	-	0

WILKINSON Barry John
Lincoln, 19 July, 1942 (CF)

League Club	Source	Date Signed	Seasons Played	Apps	Subs	Gls
Lincoln C	Bracebridge Comm C	08.61	62-63	6	-	3

WILKINSON Darron Bromley
Reading, 24 November, 1969 (M)

League Club	Source	Date Signed	Seasons Played	Apps	Subs	Gls
Brighton & Hove A	Wokingham T	08.92	92-93	34	4	3

WILKINSON David
Sunderland, 28 May, 1928 (IF)

League Club	Source	Date Signed	Seasons Played	Apps	Subs	Gls
Blackburn Rov	North Shields	07.48	48	1	-	0
Bournemouth	Tr	06.50	50-51	8	-	3

WILKINSON Derek
Stalybridge, 4 June, 1935 FLge-2 (W)

League Club	Source	Date Signed	Seasons Played	Apps	Subs	Gls
Sheffield Wed	Dukinfield	11.53	54-64	212	-	53

WILKINSON Eric
Sheffield, 6 March, 1931 Died 2002 (IF)

League Club	Source	Date Signed	Seasons Played	Apps	Subs	Gls
Bradford C		01.51				
Sheffield U	Tr	08.53				
Bournemouth	Tr	07.55	55	4	-	0

WILKINSON Eric
Stalybridge, 4 June, 1935 (W)

League Club	Source	Date Signed	Seasons Played	Apps	Subs	Gls
Sheffield Wed	Dukinfield	03.58	58	1	-	0

WILKINSON Ernest (Ernie) Stanley
Chesterfield, 13 February, 1947 (CD)

League Club	Source	Date Signed	Seasons Played	Apps	Subs	Gls
Arsenal	App	02.64				
Exeter C	Tr	06.66	66-67	59	1	0
Rochdale	L	03.68	67	9	0	0

WILKINSON Graham James
Hull, 21 October, 1934 (FB)

League Club	Source	Date Signed	Seasons Played	Apps	Subs	Gls
Hull C	Jnrs	09.52	58-59	3	-	0

WILKINSON Harry Sanderson
Sunderland, 20 March, 1926 (WH)

League Club	Source	Date Signed	Seasons Played	Apps	Subs	Gls
Chelsea		06.46				
Exeter C	Tr	05.50	50	1	-	0
Colchester U	Tr	08.51	52	1	-	0

WILKINSON Herbert (Bert)
Sunderland, 2 August, 1922 (FB)

League Club	Source	Date Signed	Seasons Played	Apps	Subs	Gls
Lincoln C	Murton CW	08.45	46-50	39	-	0

WILKINSON Howard
Sheffield, 13 November, 1943 (W)

League Club	Source	Date Signed	Seasons Played	Apps	Subs	Gls
Sheffield Wed	Sheffield U (Am)	06.62	64-65	22	0	3
Brighton & Hove A	Tr	07.66	66-70	116	13	18

WILKINSON Ian James
North Ferriby, 19 September, 1977 (CD)

League Club	Source	Date Signed	Seasons Played	Apps	Subs	Gls
Hull C	YT	07.96	95	8	0	1

WILKINSON Ian Matthew
Warrington, 2 July, 1973 (G)

League Club	Source	Date Signed	Seasons Played	Apps	Subs	Gls
Manchester U	YT	06.91				
Crewe Alex	Stockport Co (N/C)	10.93	93	2	1	0

WILKINSON Jack
Middlewich, 17 September, 1931 Died 1996 (CF)

League Club	Source	Date Signed	Seasons Played	Apps	Subs	Gls
Arsenal	Witton A	10.53	54	1	-	0
Sheffield U	Tr	03.56	55-56	29	-	16
Port Vale	Tr	06.57	57-59	80	-	39
Exeter C	Poole T	10.59	59-60	48	-	26

WILKINSON Jack Lloyd
Beverley, 12 September, 1985 (F)

League Club	Source	Date Signed	Seasons Played	Apps	Subs	Gls
Hartlepool U	Sch	•	03-04	3	4	2

WILKINSON John
Worksop, 1 April, 1949 (FB)

League Club	Source	Date Signed	Seasons Played	Apps	Subs	Gls
Grimsby T	App	04.66	65-67	8	1	0

WILKINSON John Colbridge
Exeter, 24 August, 1979 (W)

League Club	Source	Date Signed	Seasons Played	Apps	Subs	Gls
Exeter C	YT	07.98	97-00	6	14	2

WILKINSON Joseph (Joe)
Seaham, 8 December, 1934 (G)

League Club	Source	Date Signed	Seasons Played	Apps	Subs	Gls
Burnley	West Auckland	12.55				
Bradford C	Tr	03.59	58-59	17	-	0
Hartlepools U	Tr	02.60	59-61	74	-	0

WILKINSON Kenneth (Ken)
Gateshead, 9 May, 1924 Died 2002 (WH)

League Club	Source	Date Signed	Seasons Played	Apps	Subs	Gls
Huddersfield T	Jnrs	05.42				
Hartlepools U	Tr	04.47	46-48	53	-	5

WILKINSON Neil
Blackburn, 16 February, 1955 (FB)

League Club	Source	Date Signed	Seasons Played	Apps	Subs	Gls
Blackburn Rov	App	02.73	72-76	27	3	0
Port Vale	Great Harwood	07.78	78	7	0	0
Crewe Alex	Tr	10.78	78-80	68	7	0

WILKINSON Norman
Tantobie, 9 June, 1910 Died 1975 (G)

League Club	Source	Date Signed	Seasons Played	Apps	Subs	Gls
Huddersfield T	Tanfield Lea	05.32				
Stoke C	Tr	07.35	35-51	186	-	0

WILKINSON Norman Francis
Alnwick, 16 February, 1931 (CF)

League Club	Source	Date Signed	Seasons Played	Apps	Subs	Gls
Hull C (Am)	Crook T	11.52	53	8	-	3
York C	Tr	05.54	54-65	354	0	127

WILKINSON Paul
Grimoldby, 30 October, 1964 Eu21-4 (F)

League Club	Source	Date Signed	Seasons Played	Apps	Subs	Gls
Grimsby T	App	11.82	82-84	69	2	27
Everton	Tr	03.85	84-86	19	12	6
Nottingham F	Tr	03.87	86-87	32	2	5
Watford	Tr	08.88	88-90	133	1	53
Middlesbrough	Tr	08.91	91-95	161	5	50
Oldham Ath	L	10.95	95	4	0	1
Watford	L	12.95	95	4	0	0
Luton T	L	03.96	95	3	0	0
Barnsley	Tr	07.96	96-97	48	1	9
Millwall	Tr	09.97	97	22	8	3
Northampton T	Tr	07.98	98	12	3	1

WILKINSON Paul Ian
Themelthorpe, 19 April, 1952 (M)

League Club	Source	Date Signed	Seasons Played	Apps	Subs	Gls
Norwich C	App	04.70				
Plymouth Arg	L	01.71	70	2	0	0

WILKINSON Roy Joseph
Hindley, 17 September, 1941 (WH)

League Club	Source	Date Signed	Seasons Played	Apps	Subs	Gls
Bolton W	Jnrs	02.60	60-61	3	-	0

WILKINSON Shaun Frederick
Portsmouth, 12 September, 1981 (M)

League Club	Source	Date Signed	Seasons Played	Apps	Subs	Gls
Brighton & Hove A	YT	08.01	99-03	4	13	0
Chesterfield	L	11.02	02	0	1	0

WILKINSON Stephen (Steve)
Halifax, 6 August, 1946 (G)

League Club	Source	Date Signed	Seasons Played	Apps	Subs	Gls
Halifax T (Am)	Jnrs	08.63	63	2	-	0

League Club	Source	Date Signed	Seasons Played	Career Record Apps	Subs	Gls

WILKINSON Stephen (Steve) John
Lincoln, 1 September, 1968 (F)

League Club	Source	Date Signed	Seasons Played	Apps	Subs	Gls
Leicester C	App	09.86	86-89	5	4	1
Crewe Alex	L	09.88	88	3	2	2
Mansfield T	Tr	10.89	89-94	214	18	83
Preston NE	Tr	06.95	95-96	44	8	13
Chesterfield	Tr	07.97	97-99	57	18	13

WILKINSON Thomas (Tommy)
Wingate, 8 May, 1931 (WH)

League Club	Source	Date Signed	Seasons Played	Apps	Subs	Gls
Hartlepools U	Blackhall Dynamoes	09.52	53-57	22	-	0

WILKINSON Wesley (Wes) Michael
Wythenshawe, 1 May, 1984 (F)

League Club	Source	Date Signed	Seasons Played	Apps	Subs	Gls
Oldham Ath	Nantwich T	03.04	03-04	2	4	0

WILKINSON William (Billy)
Stockton, 24 March, 1943 Died 1996 (M)

League Club	Source	Date Signed	Seasons Played	Apps	Subs	Gls
Hull C	Thornaby Jnrs	05.62	62-72	208	15	34
Rotherham U	Tr	11.72	72-73	25	1	0
Southport	Tacoma (USA)	10.76	76	10	0	0

WILKS Alan
Slough, 5 October, 1946 (F)

League Club	Source	Date Signed	Seasons Played	Apps	Subs	Gls
Chelsea	App	08.64				
Queens Park Rgrs	Tr	05.65	66-70	44	6	14
Gillingham	Tr	07.71	71-75	138	13	29

WILKSHIRE Luke
Wollongong, Australia, 2 October, 1981 AuYth/Auu23-9/Au-4 (M)

League Club	Source	Date Signed	Seasons Played	Apps	Subs	Gls
Middlesbrough	AIOS (Aus)	05.99	01-02	13	8	0
Bristol C	Tr	08.03	03-04	70	4	12

WILLARD Cecil (Jess) Thomas Frederick
Chichester, 16 January, 1924 (WH)

League Club	Source	Date Signed	Seasons Played	Apps	Subs	Gls
Brighton & Hove A	Chichester C	11.46	46-52	190	-	22
Crystal Palace	Tr	07.53	53-54	46	-	5

WILLDER Frederick (Fred)
Lytham St Annes, 20 March, 1944 EYth (IF)

League Club	Source	Date Signed	Seasons Played	Apps	Subs	Gls
Blackpool	Jnrs	05.62				
Chester	Tr	09.63	64-65	1	1	0

WILLDIG Patrick (Pat) Gerald
Stoke-on-Trent, 5 June, 1932 (IF)

League Club	Source	Date Signed	Seasons Played	Apps	Subs	Gls
Port Vale	Stoke C (Am)	05.50	55	2	-	0

WILLEMS Menno
Amsterdam, Holland, 3 October, 1977 (M)

League Club	Source	Date Signed	Seasons Played	Apps	Subs	Gls
Grimsby T	Vitesse Arnhem (Holl)	11.00	00-01	44	10	2

WILLEMS Ron
Epe, Holland, 20 September, 1966 (F)

League Club	Source	Date Signed	Seasons Played	Apps	Subs	Gls
Derby Co	Grasshoppers (Swi)	07.95	95-97	41	18	13

WILLEMSE Stanley (Stan) Bernard
Brighton, 23 August, 1924 ESch/FLge-1/EB (FB)

League Club	Source	Date Signed	Seasons Played	Apps	Subs	Gls
Brighton & Hove A	Jnrs	06.46	46-48	91	-	3
Chelsea	Tr	07.49	49-55	198	-	2
Leyton Orient	Tr	06.56	56-57	59	-	2

WILLER-JENSEN Thomas
Copenhagen, Denmark, 19 September, 1968 (CD)

League Club	Source	Date Signed	Seasons Played	Apps	Subs	Gls
Swansea C	HIK Copenhagen (Den)	03.97	96	7	0	0

WILLETT Ernest (Ernie)
Burslem, 27 July, 1919 Died 1985 (WH)

League Club	Source	Date Signed	Seasons Played	Apps	Subs	Gls
Port Vale	Stoke C (Am)	01.46	46	1	-	0

WILLETT Leonard (Len) William
Ruabon, 17 September, 1940 WSch (WH)

League Club	Source	Date Signed	Seasons Played	Apps	Subs	Gls
Wrexham		05.58	59	1	-	0

WILLETTS Joseph (Joe)
Shotton, 12 July, 1924 Died 1980 (FB)

League Club	Source	Date Signed	Seasons Played	Apps	Subs	Gls
Hartlepools U	Newcastle U (Am)	09.43	46-55	239	-	20

WILLEY Alan
Exeter, 16 September, 1941 (IF)

League Club	Source	Date Signed	Seasons Played	Apps	Subs	Gls
Oxford U	Bridgwater T	12.60	62-65	85	1	23
Millwall	Tr	03.66	65-66	9	1	0

WILLEY Alan Steven
Houghton-le-Spring, 18 October, 1956 (F)

League Club	Source	Date Signed	Seasons Played	Apps	Subs	Gls
Middlesbrough	App	09.74	74-77	27	22	7

WILLGRASS Alexandre (Alex) Paul
Scarborough, 8 April, 1976 (M)

League Club	Source	Date Signed	Seasons Played	Apps	Subs	Gls
Scarborough	Jnrs	07.94	95	2	5	0

WILLIAMS Adrian
Reading, 16 August, 1971 W-13 (CD)

League Club	Source	Date Signed	Seasons Played	Apps	Subs	Gls
Reading	YT	03.89	88-95	191	5	14
Wolverhampton W	Tr	07.96	96-99	26	1	0
Reading	L	02.00	99	5	0	1
Reading	Tr	03.00	99-04	130	2	3
Coventry C	Tr	11.04	04	21	0	2

WILLIAMS Adrian
Bristol, 4 August, 1943 ESch/EYth (IF)

League Club	Source	Date Signed	Seasons Played	Apps	Subs	Gls
Bristol C	Jnrs	08.60	60	4	-	0

WILLIAMS Alan
Bristol, 3 June, 1938 (CD)

League Club	Source	Date Signed	Seasons Played	Apps	Subs	Gls
Bristol C	Jnrs	09.55	56-60	134	-	2
Oldham Ath	Tr	06.61	61-64	172	-	9
Watford	Tr	07.65	65-66	43	0	4
Newport Co	Tr	11.66	66-68	63	0	2
Swansea T	Tr	10.68	68-71	141	2	7

WILLIAMS Alan Clifford
Aberdare, 4 December, 1923 (WH)

League Club	Source	Date Signed	Seasons Played	Apps	Subs	Gls
Norwich C	Fulham (Am)	01.47	46	1	-	0

WILLIAMS Aled Albert
Holywell, 14 June, 1933 (WH)

League Club	Source	Date Signed	Seasons Played	Apps	Subs	Gls
Burnley	Rhyl	10.52				
Chester	Tr	07.57	57	33	-	1

WILLIAMS Alexander (Alex)
Manchester, 13 November, 1961 EYth (G)

League Club	Source	Date Signed	Seasons Played	Apps	Subs	Gls
Manchester C	App	11.79	80-85	114	0	0
Port Vale	Tr	11.86	86-87	35	0	0

WILLIAMS Alvan
Beaumaris, 21 November, 1932 Died 2003 (CD)

League Club	Source	Date Signed	Seasons Played	Apps	Subs	Gls
Bury	Stalybridge Celtic	12.54	55	2	-	1
Wrexham	Tr	06.56	56	13	-	7
Bradford PA	Tr	06.57	57-59	92	-	21
Exeter C	Tr	08.60	60	19	-	1

WILLIAMS Andrew (Andy)
Birmingham, 29 July, 1962 (M)

League Club	Source	Date Signed	Seasons Played	Apps	Subs	Gls
Coventry C	Solihull Borough	07.85	85-86	3	6	0
Rotherham U	Tr	10.86	86-88	87	0	13
Leeds U	Tr	11.88	88-90	25	21	3
Port Vale	L	12.91	91	5	0	0
Notts Co	Tr	02.92	91-93	32	7	2
Huddersfield T	L	09.93	93	4	2	0
Rotherham U	Tr	10.93	93-94	51	0	2
Hull C	Tr	07.95	95	33	1	0
Scarborough	Tr	08.96	96	1	0	0

WILLIAMS Andrew (Andy) Phillip
Bristol, 8 October, 1977 Wu21-9/W-2 (M)

League Club	Source	Date Signed	Seasons Played	Apps	Subs	Gls
Southampton	YT	05.96	97-98	3	18	0
Swindon T	Tr	09.99	99-00	38	6	1

WILLIAMS Anthony Simon
Maesteg, 20 September, 1977 WYth/Wu21-16 (G)

League Club	Source	Date Signed	Seasons Played	Apps	Subs	Gls
Blackburn Rov	YT	07.96				
Macclesfield T	L	10.98	98	4	0	0
Bristol Rov	L	03.99	98	9	0	0
Gillingham	L	08.99	99	2	0	0
Macclesfield T	L	01.00	99	11	0	0
Hartlepool U	Tr	07.00	00-03	131	0	0
Stockport Co	L	01.04	03	15	0	0
Grimsby T	Tr	07.04	04	46	0	0

WILLIAMS Ashley Errol
Wolverhampton, 23 March, 1984 (CD)

League Club	Source	Date Signed	Seasons Played	Apps	Subs	Gls
Stockport Co	Hednesford T	12.03	03-04	54	0	1

WILLIAMS Benjamin (Benny)
Lincoln, 14 April, 1951 (W)

League Club	Source	Date Signed	Seasons Played	Apps	Subs	Gls
Grimsby T	Lincoln U	07.69	69	2	0	0

WILLIAMS Benjamin (Ben) Philip
Manchester, 27 August, 1982 ESch (G)

League Club	Source	Date Signed	Seasons Played	Apps	Subs	Gls
Manchester U	Jnrs	07.01				
Chesterfield	L	12.02	02	14	0	0
Crewe Alex	Tr	03.04	03-04	33	0	0

WILLIAMS Bert Frederick
Bradley, Staffordshire, 31 January, 1920 EB/FLge-5/EWar-4/E-24 (G)

League Club	Source	Date Signed	Seasons Played	Apps	Subs	Gls
Walsall	Thompson's	05.37	37-38	25	-	0
Wolverhampton W	Tr	09.45	46-56	381	-	0

WILLIAMS Brett
Dudley, 19 March, 1968 (FB)

League Club	Source	Date Signed	Seasons Played	Apps	Subs	Gls
Nottingham F	App	12.85	85-92	43	0	0
Stockport Co	L	03.87	86	2	0	0

League Club	Source	Date Signed	Seasons Played	Career Record Apps	Subs	Gls
Northampton T	L	01.88	87	3	1	0
Hereford U	L	09.89	89	14	0	0
Oxford U	L	02.92	91	7	0	0
Stoke C	L	08.93	93	2	0	0
WILLIAMS Brian						
Salford, 5 November, 1955						(FB)
Bury	App	04.73	71-76	149	12	18
Queens Park Rgrs	Tr	07.77	77	9	10	0
Swindon T	Tr	06.78	78-80	89	10	8
Bristol Rov	Tr	07.81	81-84	172	0	21
Bristol C	Tr	07.85	85-86	77	0	3
Shrewsbury T	Tr	07.87	87-88	62	3	1
WILLIAMS Robert **Bryan**						
Liverpool, 4 October, 1927						(WH)
Liverpool	South Liverpool	08.45	48-52	31	-	5
Crewe Alex	South Liverpool	05.54	54-57	140	-	5
WILLIAMS Carl Junior						
Letchworth, 14 January, 1977						(W)
Fulham	YT	07.95	95	2	11	0
WILLIAMS Ceri						
Tonyrefail, 16 October, 1965 WYth						(W)
Newport Co	Jnrs	06.83	82-84	19	8	2
WILLIAMS Charles (Charlie) Adolphus						
Barnsley, 23 December, 1928						(CD)
Doncaster Rov	Upton Colliery	10.48	49-58	157	-	1
WILLIAMS Christopher (Chris) John						
Neath, 21 September, 1976						(F)
Hereford U	YT	09.94	93-94	1	3	0
WILLIAMS Christopher (Chris) Jonathan						
Manchester, 2 February, 1985						(F)
Stockport Co	YT	03.02	01-04	11	20	3
Grimsby T	L	09.04	04	1	2	0
WILLIAMS Christopher (Chris) Robert						
Brecon, 25 December, 1955						(F)
Cardiff C	Talgarth	12.77	77	3	0	0
WILLIAMS Clarence (Clarrie)						
Felling, 13 January, 1933						(G)
Grimsby T	Doncaster Rov (Am)	03.53	52-59	188	-	0
Barnsley	Tr	03.60	60-61	24	-	0
WILLIAMS Corey Dean						
Sheffield, 22 February, 1972						(F)
Rotherham U	Denaby U	08.94	94	0	2	0
WILLIAMS Cyril Edward						
Bristol, 17 November, 1921 Died 1980						(IF)
Bristol C	Jnrs	05.39	46-47	78	-	27
West Bromwich A	Tr	06.48	48-50	71	-	19
Bristol C	Tr	08.51	51-57	218	-	42
WILLIAMS Daniel (Danny)						
Maltby, 20 November, 1924						(WH)
Rotherham U	Silverwood Colliery	10.43	46-59	461	-	22
WILLIAMS Daniel (Danny) Ivor Llewellyn						
Wrexham, 12 July, 1979 Wu21-9						(M)
Liverpool	YT	05.97				
Wrexham	Tr	03.99	99-00	38	1	3
Kidderminster Hrs	Tr	07.01	01-03	108	3	8
Bristol Rov	Tr	03.04	03	6	0	1
Wrexham	Tr	08.04	04	21	0	0
WILLIAMS Daniel (Danny) Josef						
Sheffield, 2 March, 1981						(M)
Chesterfield	YT	07.99	99-01	23	8	0
WILLIAMS Darren						
Birmingham, 15 December, 1968						(M)
Leicester C	App	12.86	88-89	7	3	2
Lincoln C	L	11.89	89	2	0	0
Lincoln C	L	03.90	89	5	2	0
Chesterfield	L	09.90	90	4	1	1
WILLIAMS Darren						
Middlesbrough, 28 April, 1977 Eu21-2/EB-1						(FB)
York C	YT	06.95	94-96	16	4	0
Sunderland	Tr	10.96	96-04	155	44	4
Cardiff C	Tr	09.04	04	17	3	0
WILLIAMS Darwell						
Llanelli, 4 November, 1926 Died 2001						(WH)
Swansea T	Loughor	05.46	50-54	130	-	4

League Club	Source	Date Signed	Seasons Played	Career Record Apps	Subs	Gls
WILLIAMS David						
Sheffield, 7 October, 1931						(WH)
Grimsby T	Beighton MW	03.53	53	5	-	0
WILLIAMS David						
Shafton, 25 February, 1946						(CD)
Doncaster Rov		07.64	64	1	-	0
WILLIAMS David Michael						
Cardiff, 11 March, 1955 WYth/Wu21-1/W-5						(M)
Bristol Rov	Clifton Ath	08.75	75-84	342	10	65
Norwich C	Tr	07.85	85-87	56	4	11
Bournemouth	(Retired)	08.92	92	0	1	0
WILLIAMS David Peter						
Liverpool, 18 September, 1968						(G)
Oldham Ath	YT	08.87				
Burnley	Tr	03.88	88-92	24	0	0
Rochdale	L	09.91	91	6	0	0
Cardiff C	Tr	08.94	94-95	82	0	0
WILLIAMS David Samuel						
Newport, 1 March, 1942						(FB)
Newport Co	Nash U	10.60	60-72	302	4	2
WILLIAMS Dean Anton						
Hemel Hempstead, 14 November, 1970						(F)
Cambridge U	YT	•	87	1	0	0
Brentford	St Albans C	07.93	93	2	1	1
Doncaster Rov	Stevenage Borough	09.94	94	1	0	0
WILLIAMS Dean Paul						
Lichfield, 5 January, 1972						(G)
Birmingham C	YT	07.90	89-90	4	0	0
Brentford	Tamworth	08.93	93	6	1	0
Doncaster Rov	Tr	08.94	94-97	83	2	0
WILLIAMS Derek						
Mold, 15 June, 1934 WAmat						(G)
Manchester C (Am)	Mold Alexandria	05.51	51	1	-	0
Wrexham (Am)	Mold Alexandria	08.54	54	12	-	0
Oldham Ath (Am)	Mold Alexandra	09.56	56	28	-	0
WILLIAMS Derek						
Wardley, 28 January, 1937						(IF)
Grimsby T		01.57	56-61	44	-	19
Bradford PA	Tr	08.62	62	19	-	8
WILLIAMS Herbert **Derek**						
Ellesmere Port, 9 December, 1922						(WH)
Chester	Little Sutton	09.41	46	2	-	0
WILLIAMS Derek Owen						
Chirk, 3 September, 1949						(G)
Shrewsbury T	Oswestry T	10.69	69	1	0	0
WILLIAMS Edgar						
Sheffield, 20 May, 1919 Died 2001						(G)
Rotherham U		05.46				
Nottingham F	Tr	05.47				
Northampton T	Tr	06.48	48	3	-	0
WILLIAMS Edward Mailor Lloyd						
Chester, 28 November, 1935						(W)
Aston Villa	Everton (Am)	08.53				
Wrexham	Tr	08.54	54	1	-	0
WILLIAMS Eifion Wyn						
Anglesey, 15 November, 1975 WB-1						(F)
Torquay U	Barry T	03.99	98-01	84	27	24
Hartlepool U	Tr	03.02	01-04	119	13	37
WILLIAMS Elfyn						
Barmouth, 25 September, 1939 Died 1995						(W)
Wrexham	Portmadoc	03.58	58	1	-	0
WILLIAMS Emlyn						
Maesteg, 15 January, 1912 Died 1989						(FB)
Barnsley	Buxton T	10.36	36-38	88	-	0
Preston NE	Tr	06.39	46-47	62	-	0
Barnsley	Tr	04.48	47-48	17	-	0
Accrington St	Tr	12.48	48	15	-	0
WILLIAMS Eric						
Salford, 10 July, 1921						(FB)
Manchester C	Brindle Heath LC	03.45	46-49	38	-	0
Halifax T	Mossley	10.51	51-53	111	-	0
WILLIAMS Evan Maerdy						
Swansea, 12 October, 1932						(FB)
Cardiff C	Penllegaer	03.50				
Exeter C	Tr	05.54	54	1	-	0

WILLIAMS Evan Samuel
Dumbarton, 15 July, 1943 (G)

League Club	Source	Date Signed	Seasons Played	Apps	Subs	Gls
Wolverhampton W	Third Lanark	03.66	67	13	0	0
Aston Villa	L	08.69	69	12	0	0

WILLIAMS Everton Anthony
Jamaica, 1 February, 1957 (F)

League Club	Source	Date Signed	Seasons Played	Apps	Subs	Gls
Wrexham	Jnrs	07.75	75	1	1	0

WILLIAMS Frank
Halifax, 23 May, 1921 Died 1999 (W)

League Club	Source	Date Signed	Seasons Played	Apps	Subs	Gls
Halifax T (Am)	Boothstown	09.47	47	4	-	0

WILLIAMS Reginald **Frank**
Overton-on-Dee, 12 March, 1917 Died 1978 (G)

League Club	Source	Date Signed	Seasons Played	Apps	Subs	Gls
Wrexham		08.46	46-47	36	-	0

WILLIAMS Gareth Ashley
Cardiff, 10 September, 1982 WYth/Wu21-5 (F)

League Club	Source	Date Signed	Seasons Played	Apps	Subs	Gls
Crystal Palace	Sch	07.02	02	0	5	0
Colchester U	L	01.03	02	6	2	6
Cambridge U	L	10.03	03	4	0	1
Bournemouth	L	02.04	03	0	1	0
Colchester U	L	03.04	03	5	2	2
Colchester U	Tr	09.04	04	12	17	3

WILLIAMS Gareth Cyril
Hendon, 30 October, 1941 (M)

League Club	Source	Date Signed	Seasons Played	Apps	Subs	Gls
Cardiff C	Jnrs	04.59	62-67	161	0	13
Bolton W	Tr	10.67	67-70	108	1	11
Bury	Tr	10.71	71-72	37	2	4

WILLIAMS Gareth James
Cowes, 12 March, 1967 (W)

League Club	Source	Date Signed	Seasons Played	Apps	Subs	Gls
Aston Villa	Gosport Borough	01.88	87-89	6	6	0
Barnsley	Tr	08.91	91-93	23	11	6
Hull C	L	09.92	92	4	0	0
Hull C	L	01.94	93	16	0	2
Bournemouth	Tr	09.94	94	0	1	0
Northampton T	Tr	09.94	94-95	38	12	1
Scarborough	Tr	08.96	96-98	102	3	27
Hull C	Tr	11.98	98-99	36	2	2

WILLIAMS Gareth John
Glasgow, 16 December, 1981 SYth/Su21-9/SB-1/S-5 (M)

League Club	Source	Date Signed	Seasons Played	Apps	Subs	Gls
Nottingham F	YT	12.98	99-03	132	10	9
Leicester C	Tr	08.04	04	25	8	1

WILLIAMS Gary
Birkenhead, 14 May, 1959 (FB)

League Club	Source	Date Signed	Seasons Played	Apps	Subs	Gls
Tranmere Rov	Jnrs	09.76	76	1	0	0
Blackpool	Djurgaarden (Swe)	08.80	80	30	1	2
Swindon T	Tr	08.81	81	37	1	3
Tranmere Rov	Tr	02.83	82-84	82	0	9
Tranmere Rov	Djurgaarden (Swe)	11.85	85-88	81	11	7

WILLIAMS Gary
Wolverhampton, 17 June, 1960 (FB)

League Club	Source	Date Signed	Seasons Played	Apps	Subs	Gls
Aston Villa	App	06.78	78-86	235	5	0
Walsall	L	03.80	79	9	0	0
Leeds U	Tr	07.87	87-88	39	0	3
Watford	Tr	01.90	89-90	39	3	0
Bradford C	Tr	12.91	91-93	84	1	5

WILLIAMS Gary Alan
Bristol, 8 June, 1963 (FB)

League Club	Source	Date Signed	Seasons Played	Apps	Subs	Gls
Bristol C	App	08.80	80-83	98	2	1
Swansea C	Portsmouth (N/C)	01.85	84	6	0	0
Oldham Ath	Bristol Rov (N/C)	08.85	85-90	45	16	12

WILLIAMS Gary Peter
Liverpool, 8 March, 1954 (FB)

League Club	Source	Date Signed	Seasons Played	Apps	Subs	Gls
Preston NE	Marine	04.72	71-76	107	5	2
Brighton & Hove A	Tr	07.77	77-81	158	0	7
Crystal Palace	Tr	07.82	82	10	0	0

WILLIAMS Gavin John
Pontypridd, 20 June, 1980 (W)

League Club	Source	Date Signed	Seasons Played	Apps	Subs	Gls
Yeovil T	Hereford U	05.02	03-04	54	1	11
West Ham U	Tr	12.04	04	7	3	1

WILLIAMS George
Ynysddu, 19 May, 1914 Died 1993 WWar-2 (FB)

League Club	Source	Date Signed	Seasons Played	Apps	Subs	Gls
Charlton Ath		11.34				
Aldershot	Tr	05.36	36-38	68	-	0
Millwall	Tr	11.38	38-46	25	-	0

WILLIAMS David **Geraint**
Treorchy, 5 January, 1962 WYth/Wu21-2/W-13 (M)

League Club	Source	Date Signed	Seasons Played	Apps	Subs	Gls
Bristol Rov	App	01.80	80-84	138	3	8
Derby Co	Tr	03.85	84-91	276	1	9
Ipswich T	Tr	07.92	92-97	217	0	3
Colchester U	Tr	07.98	98	38	1	0

WILLIAMS Gilbert
West Bromwich, 12 January, 1925 Died 1993 (WH)

League Club	Source	Date Signed	Seasons Played	Apps	Subs	Gls
West Bromwich A	Harvills Hawthorn	02.44	47	7	-	0

WILLIAMS Glyndwr (Glyn) James John
Maesteg, 3 November, 1918 WLge-3/W-1 (WH)

League Club	Source	Date Signed	Seasons Played	Apps	Subs	Gls
Cardiff C	Caerau	08.46	46-52	144	-	0

WILLIAMS Gordon
Newcastle, 22 February, 1929 (CF)

League Club	Source	Date Signed	Seasons Played	Apps	Subs	Gls
Sheffield U		09.49	49	5	-	0
Darlington	Tr	06.50	50	5	-	1

WILLIAMS Gordon George
Swindon, 19 June, 1925 Died 1996 (WH)

League Club	Source	Date Signed	Seasons Played	Apps	Subs	Gls
Swindon T	Pinehurst Youth	05.45	46-56	129	-	15

WILLIAMS Graham Evan
Henllan, 2 April, 1938 Wu23-2/W-26 (FB)

League Club	Source	Date Signed	Seasons Played	Apps	Subs	Gls
West Bromwich A	Rhyl Ath	04.55	55-69	308	6	10

WILLIAMS George **Graham**
Wrexham, 31 December, 1936 WSch/Wu23-1/W-5 (W)

League Club	Source	Date Signed	Seasons Played	Apps	Subs	Gls
Bradford C	Oswestry T	08.55	55	8	-	2
Everton	Tr	03.56	55-58	31	-	6
Swansea T	Tr	02.59	58-61	90	-	18
Wrexham	Tr	07.64	64	24	-	6
Tranmere Rov	Wellington T	08.66	66-67	73	1	12
Port Vale	Tr	07.68	68	21	2	1

WILLIAMS Grenville Rees
Swansea, 30 June, 1921 (WH)

League Club	Source	Date Signed	Seasons Played	Apps	Subs	Gls
Arsenal		07.42				
Norwich C	Tr	06.46	46-47	40	-	0
Newport Co	Tr	04.49	49	5	-	0

WILLIAMS Harold
Briton Ferry, 17 June, 1924 W-4 (W)

League Club	Source	Date Signed	Seasons Played	Apps	Subs	Gls
Newport Co	Briton Ferry Ath	11.46	46-48	75	-	17
Leeds U	Tr	06.49	49-55	211	-	32
Newport Co	Tr	03.57	56	10	-	0
Bradford PA	Tr	07.57	57	15	-	0

WILLIAMS Henry (Harry) George
Salford, 24 February, 1929 (IF)

League Club	Source	Date Signed	Seasons Played	Apps	Subs	Gls
Manchester U		05.49				
West Ham U	Witton A	04.51	51	5	-	1
Bury	Tr	06.53	53	2	-	0
Swindon T	Tr	06.54	54	14	-	7

WILLIAMS Herbert (Bert)
Cwmbran, 19 June, 1925 WAmat (IF)

League Club	Source	Date Signed	Seasons Played	Apps	Subs	Gls
Newport Co (Am)	Weston's	09.48	48	2	-	1

WILLIAMS Herbert (Herbie) John
Swansea, 6 October, 1940 WSch/Wu23-5/W-3 (IF)

League Club	Source	Date Signed	Seasons Played	Apps	Subs	Gls
Swansea T	Jnrs	05.58	58-74	491	19	102

WILLIAMS Horace Oswald
Laughton, 4 October, 1921 Died 1978 (CD)

League Club	Source	Date Signed	Seasons Played	Apps	Subs	Gls
Rotherham U	Thurcroft MW	01.43	46-52	206	-	11

WILLIAMS William **Hubert (Bert)**
Manchester, 24 September, 1925 Died 1973 (IF)

League Club	Source	Date Signed	Seasons Played	Apps	Subs	Gls
Bury		01.47	46	1	-	0
Rochdale	Tr	08.49	49	8	-	3
Aldershot	Tr	06.50	50	8	-	4

WILLIAMS Ivor
Scunthorpe, 29 May, 1935 (G)

League Club	Source	Date Signed	Seasons Played	Apps	Subs	Gls
Scunthorpe U		08.59	59	8	-	0

WILLIAMS Jacques
Wallasey, 25 April, 1981 (M)

League Club	Source	Date Signed	Seasons Played	Apps	Subs	Gls
Birmingham C	Bordeaux (Fr)	07.99	00	1	2	0

WILLIAMS James (Jimmy)
Liverpool, 15 July, 1982 (FB)

League Club	Source	Date Signed	Seasons Played	Apps	Subs	Gls
Swindon T	YT	12.99	98-01	21	16	1

WILLIAMS James (Jimmy) Leslie
Wolverhampton, 8 May, 1953 (F)

League Club	Source	Date Signed	Seasons Played	Apps	Subs	Gls
Walsall	Worcester C	03.79	78-79	29	9	2

WILLIAMS Jeffrey (Jeff) Bell
Salford, 1 January, 1933 (IF)

League Club	Source	Date Signed	Seasons Played	Apps	Subs	Gls
Oldham Ath		06.51	51	1	-	0

WILLIAMS Jeremy (Jerry) Simon
Didcot, 24 March, 1960 (M)

League Club	Source	Date Signed	Seasons Played	Apps	Subs	Gls
Reading	App	03.78	76-87	283	26	17
Gillingham	Tr	08.88	88	7	6	0
Aldershot	Tr	07.89	89-90	64	3	7

WILLIAMS John (Johnny)
Greenock, 21 November, 1925 (WH)

League Club	Source	Date Signed	Seasons Played	Apps	Subs	Gls
Blackburn Rov	Port Glasgow Rgrs	06.47				
Southport	Tr	07.48	48	2	-	0

WILLIAMS John
Doncaster, 14 April, 1920 Died 1979 (FB)

League Club	Source	Date Signed	Seasons Played	Apps	Subs	Gls
Leeds U	Denaby U	12.48	48	1	-	0

WILLIAMS John
Pwllheli, 22 August, 1965 (CD)

League Club	Source	Date Signed	Seasons Played	Apps	Subs	Gls
Wrexham	Jnrs	08.82	82	0	1	0

WILLIAMS John Derek
Trelewis, 15 May, 1935 (W)

League Club	Source	Date Signed	Seasons Played	Apps	Subs	Gls
Everton		05.56				
Crewe Alex	Tr	06.57	57	5	-	0

WILLIAMS John Lloyd
Rhymney, 27 January, 1936 (WH)

League Club	Source	Date Signed	Seasons Played	Apps	Subs	Gls
Cardiff C	Jnrs	05.53				
Plymouth Arg	Tr	07.58	58-61	34	-	0
Torquay U	Tr	06.62	62-64	42	-	0

WILLIAMS John Nelson
Birmingham, 11 May, 1968 (W)

League Club	Source	Date Signed	Seasons Played	Apps	Subs	Gls
Swansea C	Cradley T	08.91	91	36	3	11
Coventry C	Tr	07.92	92-94	66	14	11
Notts Co	L	10.94	94	3	2	2
Stoke C	L	12.94	94	1	3	0
Swansea C	L	02.95	94	6	1	2
Wycombe W	Tr	09.95	95-96	34	14	9
Hereford U	Tr	02.97	96	8	3	3
Walsall	Tr	07.97	97	0	1	0
Exeter C	Tr	08.97	97	16	20	4
Cardiff C	Tr	08.98	98	25	18	12
York C	Tr	08.99	99-00	29	13	3
Darlington	Tr	12.00	00	23	1	5
Swansea C	Tr	07.01	01-02	37	31	5
Kidderminster Hrs	Tr	08.03	03	28	16	4

WILLIAMS John (Johnny) Robert
Tottenham, 26 March, 1947 (FB)

League Club	Source	Date Signed	Seasons Played	Apps	Subs	Gls
Watford	App	10.64	64-74	371	3	2
Colchester U	Tr	07.75	75-77	107	1	1

WILLIAMS John (Johnny) Stanley James
Bristol, 16 August, 1935 (M)

League Club	Source	Date Signed	Seasons Played	Apps	Subs	Gls
Plymouth Arg	EEM Department	10.52	55-65	411	1	48
Bristol Rov	Tr	12.66	66-68	66	2	10

WILLIAMS John (Jackie) William
Garston, 1 August, 1929 (W)

League Club	Source	Date Signed	Seasons Played	Apps	Subs	Gls
Tranmere Rov (Am)		08.46	46	1	-	0

WILLIAMS William **John**
Liverpool, 3 October, 1960 (CD)

League Club	Source	Date Signed	Seasons Played	Apps	Subs	Gls
Tranmere Rov	Jnrs	10.79	78-84	167	6	13
Port Vale	Tr	07.85	85-86	50	0	3
Bournemouth	Tr	12.86	86-89	115	2	9
Wigan Ath	L	10.91	91	4	0	0
Cardiff C	Tr	12.91	91-92	5	1	0

WILLIAMS Keith David
Burntwood, 12 April, 1957 (M)

League Club	Source	Date Signed	Seasons Played	Apps	Subs	Gls
Aston Villa	App	04.75				
Northampton T	Tr	02.77	76-80	128	3	6
Bournemouth	Tr	08.81	81-86	99	3	1
Colchester U	Bath C	12.87	87	9	1	0

WILLIAMS Ronald Albert **Keith**
Eastham, 14 January, 1937 (IF)

League Club	Source	Date Signed	Seasons Played	Apps	Subs	Gls
Everton	Jnrs	03.54				
Tranmere Rov	Tr	05.57	57-60	161	-	88
Plymouth Arg	Tr	06.61	61	10	-	4
Bristol Rov	Tr	01.62	61-62	49	-	18

WILLIAMS Kenneth (Ken)
(IF)

League Club	Source	Date Signed	Seasons Played	Apps	Subs	Gls
Watford		01.47	46	2	-	0

WILLIAMS Kenneth (Ken)
Doncaster, 7 January, 1927 (WH)

League Club	Source	Date Signed	Seasons Played	Apps	Subs	Gls
Rotherham U		09.48	49	3	-	0
York C	Tr	07.51	53	1	-	0

WILLIAMS Lee
Birmingham, 3 February, 1973 EYth (M)

League Club	Source	Date Signed	Seasons Played	Apps	Subs	Gls
Aston Villa	YT	01.91				
Shrewsbury T	L	11.92	92	2	1	0
Peterborough U	Tr	03.94	93-95	83	8	1
Mansfield T	Shamrock Rov	03.97	96-01	149	28	9
Cheltenham T	Tr	09.01	01-02	42	9	3

WILLIAMS Lee Charles
Harold Wood, 13 March, 1977 (M)

League Club	Source	Date Signed	Seasons Played	Apps	Subs	Gls
Leyton Orient	Purfleet	07.95	95	1	2	0

WILLIAMS Leroy Daniel
Birmingham, 22 October, 1986 (F)

League Club	Source	Date Signed	Seasons Played	Apps	Subs	Gls
Walsall	Sch	08.04	04	2	5	1

WILLIAMS Leslie (Les)
Thurcroft, 27 March, 1935 (G)

League Club	Source	Date Signed	Seasons Played	Apps	Subs	Gls
Sheffield Wed		07.53	55-56	11	-	0

WILLIAMS Marc Lloyd
Bangor, 8 February, 1973 WSemiPro-1/WB-1 (M)

League Club	Source	Date Signed	Seasons Played	Apps	Subs	Gls
Stockport Co	Bangor C	03.95	94-95	12	6	1
Halifax T	Bangor C	09.98	98	18	6	6
York C	Tr	03.99	98-99	22	11	9

WILLIAMS Marcus Vincent
Doncaster, 8 April, 1986 (W)

League Club	Source	Date Signed	Seasons Played	Apps	Subs	Gls
Scunthorpe U	Sch	●	03-04	0	5	0

WILLIAMS Mark
Hereford, 17 September, 1957 (M)

League Club	Source	Date Signed	Seasons Played	Apps	Subs	Gls
Newport Co	Bromsgrove Rov	08.76	76-78	59	9	9

WILLIAMS Mark
Anglesey, 10 December, 1973 (F)

League Club	Source	Date Signed	Seasons Played	Apps	Subs	Gls
Shrewsbury T	YT	07.92	91-92	0	3	0
Shrewsbury T	Telford U	07.97	97	0	5	0

WILLIAMS Mark Frank
Johannesburg, South Africa, 11 August, 1966 S Africa int (F)

League Club	Source	Date Signed	Seasons Played	Apps	Subs	Gls
Wolverhampton W	RWD Molenbeek (Bel)	09.95	95	5	7	0

WILLIAMS Mark Ross
Chatham, 19 October, 1981 (W)

League Club	Source	Date Signed	Seasons Played	Apps	Subs	Gls
Brentford	YT	11.00	00-02	10	62	4

WILLIAMS Mark Stuart
Stalybridge, 28 September, 1970 NIB-1/NI-36 (CD)

League Club	Source	Date Signed	Seasons Played	Apps	Subs	Gls
Shrewsbury T	Newtown	03.92	91-94	96	6	3
Chesterfield	Tr	08.95	95-98	168	0	12
Watford	Tr	07.99	99	20	2	1
Wimbledon	Tr	07.00	00-02	69	1	7
Stoke C	Tr	03.03	02	5	1	0
Wimbledon/MK Dons	Columbus Crew (USA)	02.04	03-04	22	2	1
Rushden & Diamonds	L	03.05	04	7	0	0

WILLIAMS Mark Thomas
Liverpool, 10 November, 1978 (FB)

League Club	Source	Date Signed	Seasons Played	Apps	Subs	Gls
Rochdale	Barrow	09.98	98	11	3	1
Rotherham U	Tr	03.99	98	10	1	0

WILLIAMS Martin Keith
Luton, 12 July, 1973 (W)

League Club	Source	Date Signed	Seasons Played	Apps	Subs	Gls
Luton T	Leicester C (YT)	09.91	91-94	12	28	2
Colchester U	L	03.95	94	3	0	0
Reading	Tr	07.95	95-99	99	29	26
Swindon T	Tr	08.00	00	17	2	2
Peterborough U	Tr	01.01	00	13	2	2

WILLIAMS Matthew (Matt)
St Asaph, 5 November, 1982 WYth/Wu21-10 (F)

League Club	Source	Date Signed	Seasons Played	Apps	Subs	Gls
Manchester U	YT	02.00				
Notts Co	Tr	03.04	03-04	13	12	1

WILLIAMS Matthew (Matt)
Bury, 21 June, 1988 (CD)

League Club	Source	Date Signed	Seasons Played	Apps	Subs	Gls
Rochdale	Sch	●	04	0	1	0

WILLIAMS Michael (Mike)
Bangor, 1 December, 1956 (M)

League Club	Source	Date Signed	Seasons Played	Apps	Subs	Gls
Wrexham	Jnrs	06.75	74-77	9	0	0

WILLIAMS Michael (Mike)
Mancot, 6 February, 1965 WYth (CD)

League Club	Source	Date Signed	Seasons Played	Apps	Subs	Gls
Chester	App	02.83	81-83	30	4	4
Wrexham	Tr	07.84	84-89	172	6	3

WILLIAMS Michael (Mike) Anthony
Bradford, 21 November, 1969 (M)

League Club	Source	Date Signed	Seasons Played	Apps	Subs	Gls
Sheffield Wed	Maltby Miners Welf	02.91	92-96	16	7	1
Halifax T	L	12.92	92	9	0	1
Huddersfield T	L	10.96	96	2	0	0
Peterborough U	L	03.97	96	6	0	0
Burnley	Tr	07.97	97-98	15	1	1
Oxford U	Tr	03.99	98	0	2	0
Halifax T	Tr	11.99	99	2	1	0

League Club	Source	Date Signed	Seasons Played	Apps	Subs	Gls
WILLIAMS Michael (Mike) John						
Hull, 23 October, 1944						(G)
Hull C	App	10.62	62-65	88	0	0
Aldershot	Tr	07.66				
Workington	Tr	07.68	68-69	15	0	0
Scunthorpe U	Tr	07.70	70-73	28	0	0
WILLIAMS Michael (Mike) John						
Mansfield, 3 November, 1976						(F)
Mansfield T	YT	•	94	0	1	0
WILLIAMS Michael John						
Stepney, 9 October, 1978						(CD)
Leyton Orient	YT	07.97	97	0	1	0
WILLIAMS Mostyn Thomas Webb						
Cwmfelinfach, 2 October, 1928 Died 1990						(FB)
Newport Co	Ynysddu Welfare	12.49	49-51	28	-	0
WILLIAMS Neil John Frederick						
Waltham Abbey, 23 October, 1964						(FB)
Watford	App	08.82				
Hull C	Tr	07.84	84-87	75	16	9
Preston NE	Tr	07.88	88-91	109	12	6
Carlisle U	Tr	08.92	92	19	0	1
WILLIAMS Nigel John						
Canterbury, 29 July, 1954						(FB)
Wolverhampton W	App	08.72	74-75	11	0	0
Gillingham	Tr	07.76	76-78	51	2	1
WILLIAMS Oshor Joseph						
Stockton, 21 April, 1958						(W)
Manchester U	Middlesbrough (App)	08.76				
Southampton	Gateshead	03.78	78-79	5	2	0
Exeter C	L	08.78	78	2	1	0
Stockport Co	Tr	08.79	79-84	192	1	26
Port Vale	Tr	11.84	84-85	47	2	6
Preston NE	Tr	08.86	86-87	38	1	12
WILLIAMS Paul Andrew						
Sheffield, 8 September, 1963 NIYth/NI-1						(F)
Preston NE	Nuneaton Borough	12.86	86	1	0	0
Carlisle U	Tr	07.87				
Newport Co	Tr	08.87	87	26	0	3
Sheffield U	Tr	03.88	87-88	6	2	0
Hartlepool U	Tr	10.89	89	7	1	0
Stockport Co	Tr	08.90	90	24	0	14
West Bromwich A	Tr	03.91	90-91	26	18	5
Coventry C	L	10.92	92	1	1	0
Stockport Co	Tr	01.93	92	6	10	3
Rochdale	Tr	11.93	93-95	22	15	7
Doncaster Rov	L	03.96	95	2	1	1
WILLIAMS Paul Anthony						
Stratford, 16 August, 1965 Eu21-4/EB						(F)
Charlton Ath	Woodford T	02.87	87-89	74	8	23
Brentford	L	10.87	87	7	0	3
Sheffield Wed	Tr	08.90	90-92	78	15	25
Crystal Palace	Tr	09.92	92-94	38	8	7
Sunderland	L	01.95	94	3	0	0
Birmingham C	L	03.95	94	8	3	0
Charlton Ath	Tr	09.95	95	2	7	0
Torquay U	L	03.96	95	9	0	0
Southend U	Tr	08.96	96-97	30	9	7
WILLIAMS Paul Darren						
Burton-on-Trent, 26 March, 1971 Eu21-6						(CD)
Derby Co	YT	07.89	89-94	153	7	26
Lincoln C	L	11.89	89	3	0	0
Coventry C	Tr	08.95	95-01	153	16	5
Southampton	Tr	10.01	01-02	37	2	0
Stoke C	Tr	08.03	03	16	3	0
WILLIAMS Paul John						
Lambeth, 16 November, 1962						(CD)
Chelsea	App	07.80	82	1	0	0
WILLIAMS Paul Leslie						
Liverpool, 25 September, 1970						(FB)
Sunderland	YT	07.89	88-91	6	4	0
Swansea C	L	03.91	90	12	0	0
Doncaster Rov	Tr	07.93	93-94	6	2	0
WILLIAMS Paul Richard Curtis						
Leicester, 11 September, 1969						(FB)
Leicester C	YT	07.88				
Stockport Co	Tr	07.89	89-92	61	9	4
Coventry C	Tr	08.93	93-94	8	6	0
West Bromwich A	L	11.93	93	5	0	0
Huddersfield T	L	11.94	94	2	0	0
Huddersfield T	L	03.95	94	7	0	0
Plymouth Arg	Tr	08.95	95-97	131	0	4
Gillingham	Tr	08.98	98	9	1	1
Bury	Tr	11.98	98-99	36	5	1
WILLIAMS Paul Sylvester						
Newton Abbot, 20 February, 1964						(F)
Bristol C	Ottery St Mary	03.83	82-83	16	3	1
Exeter C	Saltash U	08.85	85-87	8	10	1
WILLIAMS Peter John						
Nottingham, 21 October, 1931						(W)
Derby Co	South Normanton	08.52	52	2	-	0
Chesterfield	Boston U	07.55	55	13	-	4
WILLIAMS Peter Sidney Herbert						
Plymouth, 18 December, 1938						(WH)
Exeter C	Plymouth Arg (Am)	04.60	60	1	-	0
WILLIAMS Peter Wesley						
Deeside, 17 May, 1960						(F)
Wrexham	Jnrs	07.78	78-80	4	6	1
WILLIAMS Philip (Phil) Dean						
Morriston, 24 November, 1966						(W)
Swansea C	App	10.84	83-87	42	16	5
WILLIAMS Philip (Phil) James						
Swansea, 7 February, 1963 WSch						(M)
Blackpool	Arsenal (App)	11.80				
Crewe Alex	(USA)	08.81	81	39	0	3
Wigan Ath	Tr	08.82	82-83	1	2	0
Chester C	L	09.83	83	6	1	0
Crewe Alex	Tr	12.83	83	14	6	3
WILLIAMS Philip (Phil) Leslie						
Birkenhead, 5 April, 1958						(F)
Chester	Jnrs	07.76	76	1	0	0
WILLIAMS Raymond (Ray)						
Wrexham, 1 May, 1931						(FB)
Wrexham	Holyhead	05.51	51	12	-	0
WILLIAMS Raymond (Ray)						
Stoke-on-Trent, 30 August, 1946						(F)
Port Vale	Stafford Rgrs	08.72	72-76	165	8	39
WILLIAMS William **Raymond (Ray)**						
Bebington, 30 December, 1930						(WH)
Tranmere Rov		02.49	51-58	197	-	12
WILLIAMS Reginald (Reg) Frederick						
Watford, 28 January, 1922						(IF)
Chelsea	Watford (Am)	10.45	46-51	58	-	13
WILLIAMS Robert (Bobby) Francis						
Chester, 24 November, 1932						(W)
New Brighton (Am)	Jnrs	08.49	49	1	-	0
Chester (Am)	South Liverpool	10.51	51-53	4	-	0
Chester		05.56	56-59	33	-	3
WILLIAMS George **Robert**						
Felling, 18 November, 1932 Died 2003						(WH)
Rotherham U	Jnrs	07.50	53	4	-	2
Sheffield U	Tr	05.54				
Bradford C	Wisbech T	05.56	56	6	-	0
Mansfield T	Tr	07.57	57-61	154	-	5
WILLIAMS Robert (Bobby) Gordon						
Bristol, 17 February, 1940						(M)
Bristol C	Jnrs	05.58	58-64	187	-	76
Rotherham U	Tr	02.65	64-66	47	0	13
Bristol Rov	Tr	03.67	66-68	28	1	5
Reading	Tr	08.69	69-70	60	5	21
WILLIAMS Robert (Robbie) Ian						
Pontefract, 2 October, 1984						(FB)
Barnsley	Sch	07.04	02-04	23	6	2
WILLIAMS Robert (Bobby) James						
Bridgend, 9 October, 1968						(FB)
Oxford U	YT	08.87				
Hereford U	Tr	08.88	88	5	0	0
WILLIAMS Raymond **Robert**						
Liverpool, 25 October, 1927						(IF)
Liverpool	Jnrs	11.45				
Wrexham	Tr	06.51	51	7	-	0
Shrewsbury T	Tr	10.51	51	5	-	0
WILLIAMS Donald **Rowland (Roley)**						
Swansea, 10 July, 1927 Died 1999 WLge-1						(IF)
Cardiff C	Milford U	02.49	48-55	138	-	19
Northampton T	Tr	03.56	55-56	15	-	0

League Club	Source	Date Signed	Seasons Played	Career Record Apps	Subs	Gls
WILLIAMS Ronald (Ron) Arthur						
Swansea, 12 September, 1949						(F)
Swansea T	Jnrs	09.68	67-68	8	2	1
WILLIAMS Roy Brian						
Hereford, 3 March, 1932						(IF)
Southampton	Hereford U	11.52	52-54	41	-	7
WILLIAMS Ryan Neil						
Sutton-in-Ashfield, 31 August, 1978 EYth						(W)
Mansfield T	YT	•	95-96	9	17	3
Tranmere Rov	Tr	08.97	98	2	3	0
Chesterfield	Tr	11.99	99-00	69	6	13
Hull C	Tr	07.01	01-02	40	12	2
Bristol Rov	Tr	10.03	03-04	24	12	4
WILLIAMS Scott John						
Bangor, 7 August, 1974 WYth/Wu21-5						(FB)
Wrexham	YT	07.93	92-97	26	6	0
WILLIAMS Sidney (Sid) Frederick						
Bristol, 21 December, 1919 Died 2003						(W)
Bristol C		07.46	46-51	100	-	11
WILLIAMS Alfred **Stanley (Stan)**						
South Africa, 1 May, 1919 SWar-1						(W)
Plymouth Arg	Aberdeen	08.49	49	35	-	4
WILLIAMS Stephen (Steve) Michael						
Swansea, 5 November, 1954						(W)
Swansea C		03.76	75	7	3	1
WILLIAMS Steven (Steve)						
Oxford, 21 April, 1983						(G)
Wycombe W	YT	04.02	03-04	19	1	0
WILLIAMS Steven Brian						
Mansfield, 8 July, 1970						(F)
Mansfield T	YT	07.88	86-88	4	5	0
Chesterfield	Eastwood T	10.89	89-92	76	22	12
WILLIAMS Steven (Steve) Charles						
Hammersmith, 12 July, 1958 Eu21-14/EB/E-6						(M)
Southampton	App	07.76	75-84	276	1	18
Arsenal	Tr	12.84	84-87	93	2	4
Luton T	Tr	08.88	88-90	39	1	1
Exeter C	Tr	08.91	91-92	44	4	0
WILLIAMS Steven (Steve) David						
Aberystwyth, 16 October, 1974 WYth						(G)
Cardiff C	Coventry C (YT)	08.93	93-96	33	0	0
WILLIAMS Steven (Steve) John						
Barry, 27 April, 1963 WYth						(F)
Bristol Rov	App	04.81	80	8	0	1
WILLIAMS Steven (Steve) Robert						
Sheffield, 3 November, 1975						(F)
Lincoln C	YT	06.94	93-95	8	9	2
Peterborough U	Tr	02.96	95	0	3	0
WILLIAMS Stuart Grenville						
Wrexham, 9 July, 1930 W-43						(FB)
Wrexham	Victoria YC	06.47	48-49	5	-	0
West Bromwich A	Tr	02.51	51-62	226	-	6
Southampton	Tr	09.62	62-65	148	2	3
WILLIAMS Terence (Terry) John						
Stoke-on-Trent, 23 October, 1966						(M)
Stoke C	App	10.84	84-86	6	5	0
WILLIAMS Thomas (Tommy) Alan						
Garston, 1 August, 1929 Died 1978						(WH)
Tranmere Rov	Jnrs	11.48	46-56	53	-	2
Southport	Tr	08.58	58	17	-	0
WILLIAMS Thomas (Tommy) Andrew						
Carshalton, 8 July, 1980						(FB)
West Ham U	Walton & Hersham	04.00				
Peterborough U	Tr	03.01	00-01	32	4	2
Birmingham C	Tr	03.02	01	4	0	0
Queens Park Rgrs	L	08.02	02	22	4	1
Queens Park Rgrs	L	08.03	03	4	1	0
Peterborough U	Tr	02.04	03	20	1	1
Barnsley	Tr	06.04	04	38	1	0
WILLIAMS Thomas (Tommy) Edward						
Winchburgh, 18 December, 1957						(CD)
Leicester C	App	12.75	77-85	236	5	10
Birmingham C	Tr	08.86	86-87	62	0	1
Grimsby T	Tr	07.88	88-89	19	1	0
WILLIAMS Thomas (Tommy) John						
Battersea, 10 February, 1935 Died 1987						(W)
Colchester U	Carshalton Ath	09.56	56-60	150	-	31
Watford	Tr	06.61	61	12	-	6
WILLIAMS Wayne						
Telford, 17 November, 1963						(FB)
Shrewsbury T	App	11.81	82-88	212	9	7
Northampton T	L	11.88	88	3	0	1
Northampton T	Tr	01.89	88-90	47	5	0
Walsall	Tr	08.91	91-92	56	0	1
WILLIAMS William (Bill) Raymond						
Littleborough, 7 October, 1960						(CD)
Rochdale	Ashe Labs	08.81	81-84	89	6	2
Stockport Co	Tr	07.85	85-88	104	0	1
Manchester C	Tr	10.88	88	0	1	0
Stockport Co	Tr	12.88	88-93	153	3	7
WILLIAMS William (Bill) Thomas						
Esher, 23 August, 1942 ESch/EYth						(CD)
Portsmouth	Jnrs	06.60	60	3	-	0
Queens Park Rgrs	Tr	07.61	61-62	45	-	0
West Bromwich A	Tr	06.63	64	1	-	0
Mansfield T	Tr	01.66	65-67	47	2	0
Gillingham	Tr	09.67	67-71	169	2	8
WILLIAMSON Arthur Hamilton						
Bankfoot, 26 July, 1930						(FB)
Southend U	Clyde	05.55	55-61	269	-	2
WILLIAMSON Brian William						
Blyth, 6 October, 1939						(G)
Gateshead	Seaton Delaval	10.58	58-59	55	-	0
Crewe Alex	Tr	07.60	60-62	54	-	0
Leeds U	Tr	12.62	62-64	5	-	0
Nottingham F	Tr	02.66	67-68	19	0	0
Leicester C	L	08.67	67	6	0	0
Fulham	Tr	11.68	68-69	12	0	0
WILLIAMSON Charles (Charlie)						
Falkirk, 12 April, 1956						(FB)
Bristol C	Jnrs	07.74				
Torquay U	L	03.77	76	5	0	0
WILLIAMSON Charles (Charlie) Harold						
Sheffield, 16 March, 1962						(FB)
Sheffield Wed	App	02.80	79-83	61	1	1
Lincoln C	L	01.84	83	5	0	0
Southend U	L	03.85	84	10	0	0
Chesterfield	Tr	07.85	85-86	47	8	2
WILLIAMSON Colin James						
Gretna, 25 October, 1957						(W)
Workington	Liverpool (N/C)	08.76	76	11	4	2
WILLIAMSON Daniel (Danny) Alan						
West Ham, 5 December, 1973						(M)
West Ham U	YT	07.92	93-96	47	4	5
Doncaster Rov	L	10.93	93	10	3	1
Everton	Tr	08.97	97	15	0	0
WILLIAMSON David (Davey) Francis						
Hong Kong, 15 December, 1975						(M)
Cambridge U	Motherwell	08.96	97	2	4	0
WILLIAMSON Garry Barnes						
Darlington, 24 January, 1982						(F)
Darlington	YT	•	00	1	5	0
WILLIAMSON George						
Newcastle, 13 September, 1925 Died 1994						(CD)
Middlesbrough		12.45				
Chester	Tr	07.47	47-49	75	-	4
Bradford C	Tr	06.50	50-56	223	-	31
WILLIAMSON John **Ian**						
Larbert, 14 March, 1939						(WH)
Norwich C	Falkirk	05.58	58	10	-	1
Bradford PA	Wisbech T	06.62	62	17	-	0
WILLIAMSON James (Jim)						
Birkenhead, 16 June, 1926						(IF)
Tranmere Rov	Jnrs	08.46	46	4	-	3
WILLIAMSON John						
Manchester, 8 May, 1929						(CF)
Manchester C	Newton Heath	08.49	49-54	59	-	18
Blackburn Rov	Tr	03.56	55-56	9	-	3
WILLIAMSON John Barry						
Derby, 3 March, 1981						(FB)
Burnley	YT	07.99	98	0	1	0

League Club	Source	Date Signed	Seasons Played	Career Record Apps	Subs	Gls

WILLIAMSON Kenneth (Ken)
Stockton, 7 August, 1928 (IF)

Darlington (Am)	Bishop Auckland	08.52	52	13	-	3

WILLIAMSON Lee Trevor
Derby, 7 June, 1982 (M)

Mansfield T	YT	07.00	99-04	114	30	3
Northampton T	Tr	09.04	04	31	6	0

WILLIAMSON Michael (Micky)
Ashbourne, 30 May, 1942 (W)

Derby Co	Ashbourne T	08.61	61-63	12	-	0
Gillingham	Tr	07.64	65	1	0	0

WILLIAMSON Michael (Mike) James
Stoke-on-Trent, 8 November, 1983 (CD)

Torquay U	YT	•	01	3	0	0
Southampton	Tr	11.01				
Torquay U	L	09.03	03	9	2	0
Wycombe W	L	07.04	04	32	5	2

WILLIAMSON Philip (Phil) James
Macclesfield, 19 September, 1962 (FB)

Blackburn Rov	App	09.80	81	0	1	0

WILLIAMSON Robert (Bobby)
Edinburgh, 6 December, 1933 Died 1990 (G)

Barnsley	St Mirren	08.63	63-64	46	-	0
Leeds U	Tr	06.65				
Rochdale	Tr	07.66	66-67	36	0	0

WILLIAMSON Robert (Bobby)
Glasgow, 13 August, 1961 (F)

West Bromwich A	Glasgow Rgrs	08.86	86-87	40	13	11
Rotherham U	Tr	07.88	88-90	91	2	49

WILLIAMSON Russell Ian
Loughton, 17 March, 1980 (M)

Wimbledon	YT	06.98				
Southend U	Tr	11.00	00	9	3	0

WILLIAMSON Stewart (Stewie)
Wallasey, 7 April, 1926 (W)

Tranmere Rov	Harrogate Hotspurs	03.44	46-52	92	-	21
Swindon T	Tr	06.53	53-54	17	-	0

WILLIAMSON Thomas (Tommy)
Salford, 16 March, 1913 Died 1992 (WH)

Leeds U	Pendleton Wed	09.32				
Oldham Ath	Northwich Vic	05.35	35-46	157	-	4

WILLIAMSON Thomas (Tom)
Coalville, 24 December, 1984 (M)

Leicester C	YT	09.02	01	0	1	0

WILLINGHAM Charles **Kenneth (Ken)**
Sheffield, 1 December, 1912 Died 1975 FLge-7/EWar-6/E-12 (WH)

Huddersfield T	Worksop T	11.30	32-38	247	-	4
Sunderland	Tr	12.45	46	14	-	0
Leeds U	Tr	03.47	46-47	35	-	0

WILLIS Adam Peter
Nuneaton, 21 September, 1976 (CD)

Coventry C	YT	07.95				
Swindon T	Tr	04.98	98-02	76	16	1
Mansfield T	L	03.99	98	10	0	0
Kidderminster Hrs	Tr	08.03	03	12	0	1

WILLIS Arthur
Denaby, 2 February, 1920 Died 1987 E-1 (FB)

Tottenham H	Finchley	01.44	46-53	144	-	1
Swansea T	Tr	09.54	54-57	98	-	0

WILLIS George
Stanley, 9 November, 1926 (IF)

Wolverhampton W		01.45				
Brighton & Hove A	Tr	02.48	47-48	28	-	13
Plymouth Arg	Tr	05.49	49-55	56	-	14
Exeter C	Tr	03.56	55-56	26	-	3

WILLIS John **George**
Shotton, 25 July, 1933 Died 2002 (W)

Leeds U	Evenwood T	03.53	53	3	-	0
Hartlepools U	Tr	11.54	54-58	25	-	7

WILLIS Graham
Bradwell, Norfolk, 20 October, 1946 (FB)

Norwich C	App	10.64	64	1	-	0

WILLIS James (Jimmy) Anthony
Liverpool, 12 July, 1968 (CD)

Halifax T	Blackburn Rov (App)	08.86				
Stockport Co	Tr	12.87	87	10	0	0
Darlington	Tr	03.88	87-91	90	0	6
Leicester C	Tr	12.91	91-95	58	2	3
Bradford C	L	03.92	91	9	0	1

WILLIS John Johnson
Boldon, 28 May, 1934 (CF)

Blackburn Rov	Boldon CW	08.54	55	1	-	0
Aston Villa	Mossley	08.58	58	1	-	0

WILLIS Paul Edward
Liverpool, 24 January, 1970 (M)

Halifax T	YT	05.88	87-88	1	4	0
Darlington	Tr	03.89	88	1	1	1

WILLIS Roger Christopher
Sheffield, 17 June, 1967 ESemiPro-1 (M)

Grimsby T	Dunkirk (Midland Lge)	07.89	89	1	8	0
Barnet	Tr	08.90	91-92	39	5	13
Watford	Tr	10.92	92-93	30	6	2
Birmingham C	Tr	12.93	93-94	12	7	5
Southend U	Tr	09.94	94-95	30	1	7
Peterborough U	Tr	08.96	96	34	6	6
Chesterfield	Tr	07.97	97-01	68	67	21
Peterborough U	Tr	08.02	02	1	3	0

WILLIS Ronald (Ron) Ian
Romford, 27 December, 1947 EYth (G)

Leyton Orient	Coventry C (Am)	01.66	66-67	45	0	0
Charlton Ath	Tr	10.67	67	1	0	0
Brentford	L	09.68	68	1	0	0
Colchester U	Tr	10.68	68-69	6	0	0

WILLIS Scott Leon
Liverpool, 20 February, 1982 (M)

Mansfield T	Wigan Ath (YT)	03.00				
Carlisle U	Doncaster Rov	08.01	01	0	1	0
Lincoln C	Droylsden	08.02	02-03	23	10	3

WILLMOTT Christopher (Chris) Alan
Bedford, 30 September, 1977 (CD)

Luton T	YT	05.96	98	13	1	0
Wimbledon	Tr	07.99	99-02	50	3	2
Luton T	L	02.03	02	7	1	0
Luton T	L	04.03	02	5	0	0
Northampton T	Tr	07.03	03-04	80	1	1

WILLMOTT Ian Michael
Bristol, 10 July, 1968 (CD)

Bristol Rov	Weston-super-Mare	11.88	89-91	18	4	0

WILLOCK Calum Daniel
Lambeth, 29 October, 1981 ESch/StKitts int (F)

Fulham	ADT College	07.00	00-02	0	5	0
Queens Park Rgrs	L	11.02	02	3	0	0
Bristol Rov	L	08.03	03	0	5	0
Peterborough U	Tr	10.03	03-04	51	13	20

WILLOX Alexander (Sandy)
Lossiemouth, 5 November, 1923 (CF)

Hartlepools U	Alloa Ath	07.51	51	6	-	0

WILLS Gordon Francis
West Bromwich, 24 April, 1934 (W)

Wolverhampton W	West Bromwich A (Am)	12.51				
Notts Co	Tr	08.53	53-57	154	-	45
Leicester C	Tr	05.58	58-61	111	-	30
Walsall	Tr	06.62	62-63	35	-	1

WILLS Kevin Michael
Torquay, 15 October, 1980 (M)

Plymouth Arg	YT	07.99	98-01	17	15	1
Torquay U	Tr	11.02	02-03	12	31	4

WILLS Leonard (Len) Edward
Hackney, 8 November, 1927 (FB)

Arsenal	Eton Manor	10.49	53-60	195	-	4

WILLSHAW George James
Hackney, 18 October, 1912 Died 1993 (W)

Southend U	Walthamstow Ave	02.36	35-37	28	-	6
Bristol C	Tr	06.38	38	34	-	9
Clapton Orient	Tr	07.39	46	12	-	2

WILMOT Rhys James
Newport, 21 February, 1962 WSch/WYth/Wu21-6 (G)

Arsenal	App	02.80	85-86	8	0	0
Hereford U	L	03.83	82	9	0	0
Orient	L	05.84	84	46	0	0
Swansea C	L	08.88	88	16	0	0
Plymouth Arg	L	03.89	88	17	0	0
Plymouth Arg	Tr	07.89	89-91	116	0	0

League Club	Source	Date Signed	Seasons Played	Career Record Apps	Subs	Gls
Grimsby T	Tr	07.92	92	33	0	0
Crystal Palace	Tr	08.94	94	5	1	0
Torquay U	Tr	06.96	96	34	0	0
WILMOT Richard Garry						
Matlock, 29 August, 1969						(G)
Scunthorpe U	Stevenage Borough	03.93	92	3	0	0
WILMOTT Gordon Alfred						
Brinsley, 26 May, 1929 Died 1998						(CD)
Birmingham C		05.47				
Stockport Co	Tr	06.48	48-58	205	-	1
Crewe Alex	Tr	03.59	58-60	52	-	0
WILNIS Fabian						
Surinam, 23 August, 1970						(FB)
Ipswich T	De Graafschap (Holl)	01.99	98-04	194	19	5
WILSHAW Dennis James						
Stoke-on-Trent, 11 March, 1926 Died 2004 EB-2/E-12						(IF)
Wolverhampton W	Packmoor BC	09.43	48-57	211	-	105
Walsall	L	05.46	46	35	-	18
Walsall	L	08.47	47	36	-	8
Walsall	L	08.48	48	3	-	1
Stoke C	Tr	12.57	57-60	95	-	41
WILSHAW Steven (Steve) Edward						
Stoke-on-Trent, 11 January, 1959						(M)
Stoke C	App	01.77				
Crewe Alex	Tr	08.78	78	20	2	1
WILSHIRE Peter John						
Bristol, 15 October, 1934						(CF)
Bristol Rov	Jnrs	01.54	53	1	-	0
WILSON Alan						
Dingle, 17 November, 1952						(M)
Everton	App	07.70	71-72	2	0	0
Southport	Tr	07.75	75-77	134	0	13
Torquay U	Tr	06.78	78	38	4	2
WILSON Albert						
Rotherham, 28 January, 1915 Died 1998						(W)
Derby Co	Stafford Rgrs	05.36	36	1	-	0
Mansfield T	Tr	07.38	38	20	-	2
Crystal Palace	Tr	01.39	38	20	-	6
Rotherham U	Tr	06.46	46	38	-	19
Grimsby T	Tr	07.47	47	17	-	1
WILSON Alexander (Alex)						
Buckie, 29 October, 1933 S-1						(FB)
Portsmouth	Buckie Rov	11.50	51-66	348	2	4
WILSON Alexander (Alex)						
Stenhousemuir, 13 July, 1938						(W)
Rotherham U	Clyde	07.61	61	5	-	0
WILSON Alexander (Alex) Adams						
Wishaw, 29 October, 1908 Died 1971						(G)
Arsenal	Morton	05.33	33-38	82	-	0
Brighton & Hove A	St Mirren	09.47	47	1	-	0
WILSON Allan Armstrong						
Bathgate, 10 January, 1945						(G)
Scunthorpe U	Partick Th	07.64				
Mansfield T	Tr	08.66	66	5	0	0
WILSON Ambrose Maxwell						
Lurgan, 10 October, 1924						(WH)
Swansea T	Glenavon	09.50	50	1	-	0
WILSON Andrew (Andy)						
Rotherham, 27 September, 1940						(W)
Sheffield U		01.60	59-60	4	-	0
Scunthorpe U	Tr	06.61	61-64	112	-	14
Doncaster Rov	Tr	07.65	65	20	1	0
Chesterfield	Tr	07.66	66-67	70	2	13
Aldershot	Tr	07.68	68	19	1	1
WILSON Andrew (Andy) Philip						
Maltby, 13 October, 1947						(W)
Rotherham U		06.67	67	12	2	3
Notts Co	L	08.68	68	1	0	0
Scunthorpe U	Tr	09.68	68	23	0	4
WILSON Andrew (Andy) William						
Ince, 7 January, 1965						(M)
Wigan Ath	Skelmersdale U	08.87	87-88	1	1	0
WILSON Archibald (Archie)						
South Shields, 4 December, 1924 Died 1979						(G)
Gateshead	Tyne Dock Engineers	08.45	46	5	-	0
Lincoln C	South Shields	04.51	50-51	4	-	0

League Club	Source	Date Signed	Seasons Played	Career Record Apps	Subs	Gls
WILSON Beverley (Bev)						
Stockport, 11 April, 1953						(CD)
Stockport Co	App	07.70	69-73	59	2	1
WILSON Bevis (Bev) Alan McLean						
Eccles, 14 May, 1924 Died 1987						(CD)
Wrexham		06.47	47-50	98	-	0
Barrow	Tr	03.51	50-58	307	-	1
WILSON Brian						
Newcastle, 14 April, 1957						(CD)
Blackpool	App	05.74	76-79	21	10	6
Torquay U	Tr	11.79	79-82	129	2	6
WILSON Brian Jason						
Manchester, 9 May, 1983						(FB)
Stoke C	YT	07.01	01-03	1	5	0
Cheltenham T	L	12.03	03	7	0	0
Cheltenham T	Tr	03.04	03-04	42	8	3
WILSON Carl Alan						
Consett, 8 May, 1940						(CF)
Newcastle U	Delves Lane Jnrs	02.58	58	1	-	0
Gateshead	Tr	01.60	59	17	-	4
Doncaster Rov	Tr	07.60	60	15	-	2
Millwall	Tr	07.61	61	5	-	1
WILSON Che Christian Aaron Clay						
Ely, 17 January, 1979						(FB)
Norwich C	YT	07.97	98-99	16	6	0
Bristol Rov	Tr	07.00	00-01	74	1	0
Southend U	Cambridge C	07.03	03-04	51	3	0
WILSON Clive Euclid Aklana						
Manchester, 13 November, 1961						(FB)
Manchester C	Moss Side Amats	12.79	81-86	96	2	9
Chester	L	09.82	82	21	0	2
Chelsea	Tr	03.87	87-89	68	13	5
Manchester C	L	03.87	86	11	0	0
Queens Park Rgrs	Tr	07.90	90-94	170	2	12
Tottenham H	Tr	06.95	95-97	67	3	1
Cambridge U	Tr	08.99	99	27	0	0
WILSON Daniel (Danny) Joseph						
Wigan, 1 January, 1960 NI-24						(M)
Bury	Wigan Ath	09.77	77-79	87	3	9
Chesterfield	Tr	07.80	80-82	100	0	13
Nottingham F	Tr	01.83	82	9	1	1
Scunthorpe U	L	10.83	83	6	0	3
Brighton & Hove A	Tr	11.83	83-86	132	3	33
Luton T	Tr	07.87	87-89	110	0	24
Sheffield Wed	Tr	08.90	90-92	91	7	11
Barnsley	Tr	06.93	93-94	77	0	2
WILSON Darren Anthony						
Manchester, 30 September, 1971						(FB)
Manchester C	YT	07.90				
Bury	Tr	06.91	91	30	3	1
WILSON David						
Glasgow, 21 November, 1923						(W)
Manchester C		07.47				
Bury	Tr	07.48	48	2	-	1
WILSON David (Dave) Charles						
Nelson, 24 December, 1942 ESch/Eu23-7						(W)
Preston NE	Jnrs	04.60	60-66	169	1	29
Liverpool	Tr	02.67	66	0	1	0
Preston NE	Tr	06.68	68-73	99	11	10
Bradford C	L	03.72	71	5	0	0
Southport	L	10.73	73	2	0	0
WILSON David (Dave) Edward Joseph						
Wednesfield, 4 October, 1944						(F)
Nottingham F	Jnrs	10.61	62-65	8	1	1
Carlisle U	Tr	10.65	65-66	55	1	22
Grimsby T	Tr	03.67	66-68	63	0	22
Walsall	Tr	09.68	68-69	33	2	5
Burnley	Tr	09.69	69-70	10	3	0
Chesterfield	Tr	06.71	71-74	125	3	22
WILSON David Graham						
Todmorden, 20 March, 1969 ESch						(M)
Manchester U	App	03.87	88	0	4	0
Lincoln C	L	11.90	90	3	0	0
Charlton Ath	L	03.91	90	6	1	2
Bristol Rov	Tr	07.91	91-92	11	0	0
WILSON Denis						
Bebington, 30 April, 1936						(FB)
Wrexham	Jnrs	07.54				
Stoke C	Rhyl Ath	08.59	59-60	15	-	0

WILSON Dennis Fletcher
Farnham, 6 September, 1929 (FB)

League Club	Source	Date Signed	Seasons Played	Apps	Subs	Gls
Norwich C	Jnrs	09.46				
Aldershot	Tr	06.50	50-51	5	-	0
Crewe Alex		10.55	55	23	-	0

WILSON Donald (Don)
Heywood, 4 June, 1930 Died 2003 (FB)

League Club	Source	Date Signed	Seasons Played	Apps	Subs	Gls
Bury		05.51	52-58	63	-	1

WILSON Eugene (Gene)
Sheffield, 11 September, 1932 (W)

League Club	Source	Date Signed	Seasons Played	Apps	Subs	Gls
Rotherham U	Sheffield Wed (Am)	05.53				
Stockport Co	Tr	05.54	54-61	223	-	42

WILSON Eugene (Gus) Anthony
Manchester, 11 April, 1963 (CD)

League Club	Source	Date Signed	Seasons Played	Apps	Subs	Gls
Crewe Alex	Runcorn	07.91	91-94	112	3	0

WILSON Frederick (Fred) Charles
Nottingham, 10 November, 1918 Died 1994 (CD)

League Club	Source	Date Signed	Seasons Played	Apps	Subs	Gls
Wolverhampton W		05.36				
Bournemouth	Tr	05.37	38-50	98	-	0

WILSON Glenton (Glen) Edward
Winlaton, 2 July, 1929 (WH)

League Club	Source	Date Signed	Seasons Played	Apps	Subs	Gls
Brighton & Hove A	Newcastle U (Am)	09.49	49-59	409	-	25
Exeter C	Tr	06.60	60-61	36	-	2

WILSON Harry
Hetton-le-Hole, 29 November, 1953 ESch/EYth (FB)

League Club	Source	Date Signed	Seasons Played	Apps	Subs	Gls
Burnley	App	12.70	70-71	12	0	0
Brighton & Hove A	Tr	12.73	73-76	130	0	4
Preston NE	Tr	07.77	77-79	38	4	0
Darlington	Tr	09.80	80-82	82	3	0
Hartlepool U	Tr	08.83	83	16	0	0

WILSON Ian William
Aberdeen, 27 March, 1958 S-5 (M)

League Club	Source	Date Signed	Seasons Played	Apps	Subs	Gls
Leicester C	Elgin C	04.79	79-87	276	9	17
Everton	Tr	09.87	87-88	24	10	1
Derby Co	Besiktas (Tu)	02.91	90	11	0	0
Bury	Tr	08.91	91	21	2	1
Wigan Ath	Tr	08.92	92	5	0	0

WILSON James (Jimmy)
Glasgow, 19 December, 1929 (W)

League Club	Source	Date Signed	Seasons Played	Apps	Subs	Gls
Leicester C	Alloa Ath	07.54				
Mansfield T	Tr	03.55	54-55	19	-	1

WILSON James (Jimmy)
Newmains, 20 April, 1942 SLge-1 (W)

League Club	Source	Date Signed	Seasons Played	Apps	Subs	Gls
Newcastle U	Shotts Bon Accord	09.59	60-61	12	-	2

WILSON James (Jim) Allan
Musselburgh, 28 June, 1922 Died 1997 (FB)

League Club	Source	Date Signed	Seasons Played	Apps	Subs	Gls
Luton T	Peterborough U	07.47	47-50	39	-	1
Northampton T	Tr	07.51	51	23	-	0

WILSON James (Jim) Murray
Saltcoats, 19 March, 1923 LoI-1 (IF)

League Club	Source	Date Signed	Seasons Played	Apps	Subs	Gls
Accrington St	Dundalk	07.49	49	4	-	0

WILSON James (Jimmy) Thompson
Middlesbrough, 15 March, 1924 Died 1987 (IF)

League Club	Source	Date Signed	Seasons Played	Apps	Subs	Gls
Chelsea	Gravesend & Northfleet	06.47				
Watford	Tr	11.50	50-56	49	-	12

WILSON Jeffrey (Jeff) Hansel
South Shields, 7 December, 1964 (CD)

League Club	Source	Date Signed	Seasons Played	Apps	Subs	Gls
Darlington	App	12.82	82-83	10	1	0

WILSON John (Jock)
Airdrie, 29 October, 1916 (IF)

League Club	Source	Date Signed	Seasons Played	Apps	Subs	Gls
Chesterfield	Glasgow Celtic	05.39	46	16	-	3
Oldham Ath	Tr	07.47	47-48	29	-	2
Accrington St	Tr	10.48	48-49	27	-	1

WILSON John Allan
Jarrow, 11 April, 1952 (M)

League Club	Source	Date Signed	Seasons Played	Apps	Subs	Gls
Darlington	Consett	09.71	71-72	15	5	1

WILSON John Christopher
Norwich, 28 October, 1934 (FB)

League Club	Source	Date Signed	Seasons Played	Apps	Subs	Gls
Norwich C	Jnrs	08.53	53-58	47	-	0
Chesterfield	Tr	07.59	59	16	-	0

WILSON John (Ian) Grieve
Kennoway, 11 February, 1923 (W)

League Club	Source	Date Signed	Seasons Played	Apps	Subs	Gls
Preston NE	Forfar Ath	11.46	46-47	16	-	6
Burnley	Tr	06.48	48-49	19	-	1
Leicester C	Tr	03.50	49-50	12	-	2
Chesterfield	Tr	10.51	51-52	77	-	18
Rotherham U	Tr	05.53	53-55	108	-	45

WILSON Joseph (Joe)
Workington, 6 July, 1937 (FB)

League Club	Source	Date Signed	Seasons Played	Apps	Subs	Gls
Workington	Jnrs	01.56	55-61	152	-	5
Nottingham F	Tr	03.62	61-64	84	-	1
Wolverhampton W	Tr	03.65	64-66	58	0	0
Newport Co	Tr	05.67	67	43	1	0
Workington	Tr	09.68	68-72	168	1	4

WILSON Joseph (Joe) Alexander
High Spen, 23 March, 1911 Died 1984 (IF)

League Club	Source	Date Signed	Seasons Played	Apps	Subs	Gls
Newcastle U	Tanfield Lea Inst	09.33	34-35	28	-	5
Brighton & Hove A	Tr	05.36	36-46	156	-	15

WILSON Joseph (Joe) Henry
Manchester, 17 May, 1925 (FB)

League Club	Source	Date Signed	Seasons Played	Apps	Subs	Gls
Manchester U	Jnrs	09.44				
Accrington St	Tr	10.46	46-50	109	-	4

WILSON Joseph (Joe) William
West Butsfield, 29 September, 1911 Died 1996 (CD)

League Club	Source	Date Signed	Seasons Played	Apps	Subs	Gls
Newcastle U	Stanley U	09.27	29	1	-	0
Southend U	Tr	08.30	30-34	164	-	4
Brentford	Tr	07.35	35-38	60	-	2
Reading	Tr	08.39				
Barnsley	Tr	05.46	46	20	-	0

WILSON Keith
Beverley, 14 December, 1935 (IF)

League Club	Source	Date Signed	Seasons Played	Apps	Subs	Gls
Southampton	Andover	07.59				
Gillingham	Tr	07.61	61	5	-	2

WILSON Kelvin James
Nottingham, 3 September, 1985 (FB)

League Club	Source	Date Signed	Seasons Played	Apps	Subs	Gls
Notts Co	Sch	07.04	03-04	38	6	2

WILSON Kenneth (Kenny) Malcolm
Dumbarton, 15 September, 1946 (F)

League Club	Source	Date Signed	Seasons Played	Apps	Subs	Gls
Carlisle U	Dumbarton	09.72	72	14	6	1
York C	L	09.73	73	2	0	0
Workington	L	10.73	73	4	1	0

WILSON Kevin James
Banbury, 18 April, 1961 NI-42 (F)

League Club	Source	Date Signed	Seasons Played	Apps	Subs	Gls
Derby Co	Banbury U	12.79	79-84	106	16	30
Ipswich T	Tr	01.85	84-86	94	4	34
Chelsea	Tr	06.87	87-91	124	28	42
Notts Co	Tr	03.92	91-93	58	11	3
Bradford C	L	01.94	93	5	0	0
Walsall	Tr	08.94	94-96	124	1	38
Northampton T	Tr	07.97	97-00	13	18	2

WILSON Lee
Mansfield, 23 May, 1972 (F)

League Club	Source	Date Signed	Seasons Played	Apps	Subs	Gls
Mansfield T	Clipstone CW	02.93	92-93	9	9	1

WILSON Leslie (Les) John
Manchester, 10 July, 1947 (FB)

League Club	Source	Date Signed	Seasons Played	Apps	Subs	Gls
Wolverhampton W	Jnrs	09.64	65-71	90	11	7
Bristol C	L	03.71	70	10	0	0
Bristol C	Tr	11.71	71-72	32	1	1
Norwich C	Tr	09.73	73	6	0	0

WILSON Mark Antony
Scunthorpe, 9 February, 1979 ESch/EYth/Eu21-2 (M)

League Club	Source	Date Signed	Seasons Played	Apps	Subs	Gls
Manchester U	YT	02.96	99	1	2	0
Wrexham	L	02.98	97	12	1	4
Middlesbrough	Tr	08.01	01-02	6	10	0
Stoke C	L	03.03	02	4	0	0
Swansea C	L	09.03	03	12	0	2
Sheffield Wed	L	01.04	03	3	0	0
Doncaster Rov	L	09.04	04	1	2	0

WILSON Patrick (Padi)
Manchester, 9 November, 1971 (F)

League Club	Source	Date Signed	Seasons Played	Apps	Subs	Gls
Plymouth Arg	Ashton U	08.97	97	7	4	1
Doncaster Rov	Tr	01.98	97	10	0	1

WILSON Paul Adam
Maidstone, 22 February, 1977 (F)

League Club	Source	Date Signed	Seasons Played	Apps	Subs	Gls
Gillingham	YT	04.95	94	0	2	0

WILSON Paul Andrew
Norwich, 19 June, 1956 (M)

League Club	Source	Date Signed	Seasons Played	Apps	Subs	Gls
Norwich C	App	07.74	75	0	1	0

WILSON Paul Anthony
Bradford, 2 August, 1968 (FB)

League Club	Source	Date Signed	Seasons Played	Apps	Subs	Gls
Huddersfield T	App	06.86	85-86	15	0	0
Norwich C	Tr	07.87				

League Club	Source	Date Signed	Seasons Played	Apps	Subs	Gls
Northampton T	Tr	02.88	87-91	132	9	6
Halifax T	Tr	12.91	91-92	45	0	7
Burnley	Tr	02.93	92-93	31	0	0
York C	Tr	10.94	94	21	1	0
Scunthorpe U	Tr	08.95	95-96	77	0	2
Cambridge U	Tr	03.97	96-97	38	0	5
WILSON Paul Derek						
Doncaster, 16 November, 1960 ESemiPro (F)						
Scunthorpe U	Yeovil T	02.96	96	0	1	0
WILSON Paul Robert						
Forest Gate, 26 September, 1964 (M)						
Barnet	Barking	03.88	91-99	240	23	24
WILSON Frederick **Peter**						
Newcastle, 15 September, 1947 (FB)						
Middlesbrough		04.66	67	1	0	0
WILSON Philip (Phil)						
Hemsworth, 16 October, 1960 (M)						
Bolton W	App	10.78	79-80	35	4	4
Huddersfield T	Tr	08.81	81-86	229	4	16
York C	Tr	08.87	87-88	38	8	2
Scarborough	Macclesfield T	12.89	89-90	39	4	2
WILSON Philip (Phil) John						
Oxford, 17 October, 1982 (G)						
Oxford U	YT	•	00	1	1	0
WILSON Philip (Phil) Michael						
Billingham, 5 February, 1972 (CD)						
Hartlepool U	YT	•	89	0	1	0
WILSON Ramon (Ray)						
Shirebrook, 17 December, 1934 FLge-10/E-63 (FB)						
Huddersfield T	Langwith Imperial	08.52	55-63	266	-	6
Everton	Tr	07.64	64-68	114	2	0
Oldham Ath	Tr	07.69	69	25	0	0
Bradford C	Tr	07.70	70	2	0	0
WILSON Raymond (Ray) Thomson						
Grangemouth, 8 April, 1947 Su23-1 (FB)						
West Bromwich A	Woodburn Ath	05.64	65-75	230	2	3
WILSON Richard						
Orpington, 8 May, 1960 (F)						
Chelsea	App	08.78				
Charlton Ath	Tr	08.79	79	16	1	1
WILSON Robert						
Motherwell (W)						
Workington	Stirling A	12.52	52	2	-	0
WILSON Robert						
Oxford, 29 May, 1944 (IF)						
Brentford (Am)	Feltham	04.67	66	1	0	1
WILSON Robert James						
Kensington, 5 June, 1961 IRu21-2 (M)						
Fulham	App	06.79	79-84	168	7	33
Millwall	Tr	08.85	85	28	0	12
Luton T	Tr	08.86	86-87	19	5	1
Fulham	Tr	09.87	87-88	43	4	4
Huddersfield T	Tr	07.89	89-90	52	5	8
Rotherham U	Tr	09.91	91	11	3	3
WILSON Robert (Bob) John						
Birmingham, 23 May, 1943 (G)						
Aston Villa	Jnrs	09.61	63	9	-	0
Cardiff C	Tr	08.64	64-67	115	0	0
Bristol C	L	10.69	69	1	0	0
Exeter C	Tr	01.70	69-75	205	0	0
WILSON John **Robert (Bob)**						
Liverpool, 8 September, 1928 (FB)						
Preston NE	Burscough	04.50	52-62	92	-	0
Tranmere Rov	Tr	09.62	62-63	54	-	0
WILSON Robert (Bob) Primrose						
Chesterfield, 30 October, 1941 ESch/S-2 (G)						
Arsenal	Wolverhampton W (Am)	03.64	63-73	234	0	0
WILSON Robert (Bobby) Smail Whitelaw						
Musselburgh, 29 June, 1934 (WH)						
Norwich C	Aberdeen	05.57	57-58	62	-	0
Gillingham	Tr	06.60	60	35	-	0
Accrington St	Tr	07.61				
Chester	Tr	04.62	62	15	-	0
WILSON Ronald (Ron)						
Ellesmere Port, 7 August, 1933 (W)						
Crewe Alex		11.57	57	1	-	0

League Club	Source	Date Signed	Seasons Played	Apps	Subs	Gls
WILSON Ronald (Ron)						
Edinburgh, 6 September, 1941 (FB)						
Stoke C	Musselburgh Ath	08.59	59-63	11	-	0
Port Vale	Tr	11.63	63-70	261	3	5
WILSON Ronald (Ron) Gerard						
Sale, 10 September, 1924 (CF)						
West Ham U		10.44	46-47	3	-	0
WILSON Samuel (Sammy)						
Glasgow, 16 December, 1931 (IF)						
Millwall	Glasgow Celtic	07.59	59	23	-	11
WILSON Scott Andrew						
Farnworth, 25 October, 1980 (M)						
Rochdale	YT	07.99	99	0	1	0
WILSON Scott Peter						
Edinburgh, 19 March, 1977 Su21-7 (CD)						
Portsmouth (L)	Glasgow Rgrs	03.02	01	5	0	0
WILSON Stephen (Steve) Lee						
Hull, 24 April, 1974 (G)						
Hull C	YT	07.92	90-99	180	1	0
Macclesfield T	Tr	03.01	00-04	132	2	0
WILSON Stuart Kevin						
Leicester, 16 September, 1977 (W)						
Leicester C	YT	07.96	96-98	1	21	3
Sheffield U	L	03.00	99	4	2	0
Cambridge U	Tr	12.00	00	3	3	0
WILSON Terence (Terry)						
Broxburn, 8 February, 1969 Su21-4 (CD)						
Nottingham F	App	04.86	87-92	94	11	9
Newcastle U	L	01.92	91	2	0	0
WILSON Thomas (Tommy)						
Bedlington, 15 September, 1930 Died 1992 (CF)						
Nottingham F	Cinderhill Colliery	04.51	51-60	191	-	75
Walsall	Tr	11.60	60-61	53	-	18
WILSON Thomas (Tom)						
Rosewell, 29 November, 1940 (CD)						
Millwall	Falkirk	07.61	61-67	200	1	15
Hull C	Tr	11.67	67-69	60	0	1
WILSON Thomas (Tom) Bastin						
Windygates, 25 July, 1933 (W)						
Reading	Thornton Hibs	03.56	56	8	-	1
Exeter C	Tr	07.57	57	22	-	2
WILSON Thomas (Tommy) Frederick						
Southampton, 3 July, 1930 (FB)						
Fulham	Southampton (Am)	08.50	52-56	45	-	0
Brentford	Tr	07.57	57-61	148	-	0
WILSON Ulrich John						
Surinam, 5 May, 1964 (FB)						
Ipswich T (L)	Twente Enschede (Holl)	12.87	87	5	1	0
WILSON William (Billy)						
Seaton Delaval, 10 July, 1946 (FB)						
Blackburn Rov	Jnrs	09.63	64-71	246	1	0
Portsmouth	Tr	01.72	71-78	188	6	5
WILSON William James Randolph						
Portadown, 23 September, 1936 NIB (WH)						
Burnley	Portadown	09.55	56-57	2	-	0
WILSTERMAN Brian Hank						
Surinam, 19 November, 1966 (CD)						
Oxford U	Beerschot (Bel)	02.97	96-98	28	14	2
Rotherham U	Tr	07.99	99-00	47	5	4
WILTON Graham Ernest						
Chesterfield, 19 October, 1942 (W)						
Chesterfield (Am)	Chesterfield Tube Wks	06.61	61	1	-	0
WILTORD Sylvain						
Neuilly-sur-Marne, France, 10 May, 1974 France 65 (F)						
Arsenal	Bordeaux (Fr)	08.00	00-03	78	28	31
WILTSHIRE David (Dave)						
Folkestone, 8 July, 1954 (FB)						
Gillingham	Canterbury C	01.74	73-75	54	8	2
Aldershot	Tr	07.76	76	5	0	0
WIMBLETON Paul Philip						
Havant, 13 November, 1964 ESch (M)						
Portsmouth	App	02.82	81-83	5	5	0
Cardiff C	Tr	08.86	86-88	118	1	17

League Club	Source	Date Signed	Seasons Played	Apps	Subs	Gls
Bristol C	Tr	05.89	89	10	6	2
Shrewsbury T	Tr	01.90	89-90	25	10	1
Maidstone U	L	01.91	90	2	0	1
Exeter C	Tr	09.91	91	35	1	4
Swansea C	Tr	08.92	92	10	5	1

WIMSHURST Kenneth (Ken) Pinkney
South Shields, 23 March, 1938 (M)

League Club	Source	Date Signed	Seasons Played	Apps	Subs	Gls
Newcastle U	South Shields	07.57				
Gateshead	Tr	11.58	58-59	7	-	0
Wolverhampton W	Tr	11.60				
Southampton	Tr	07.61	61-67	148	4	9
Bristol C	Tr	10.67	67-71	146	3	9

WINDASS Dean
Hull, 1 April, 1969 (F)

League Club	Source	Date Signed	Seasons Played	Apps	Subs	Gls
Hull C	North Ferriby U	10.91	91-95	173	3	57
Oxford U	Aberdeen	08.98	98	33	0	15
Bradford C	Tr	03.99	98-00	64	10	16
Middlesbrough	Tr	03.01	00-02	16	21	3
Sheffield Wed	L	12.01	01	2	0	0
Sheffield U	L	11.02	02	4	0	3
Sheffield U	Tr	01.03	02	16	0	3
Bradford C	Tr	07.03	03-04	73	4	33

WINDER Nathan James
Barnsley, 17 February, 1983 (CD)

League Club	Source	Date Signed	Seasons Played	Apps	Subs	Gls
Halifax T	YT	●	01	0	1	0

WINDLE Charles
Barnsley, 8 January, 1917 Died 1975 (W)

League Club	Source	Date Signed	Seasons Played	Apps	Subs	Gls
Bury		09.38				
Exeter C	Tr	07.39				
Bristol Rov	Tr	12.46	46	7	-	1

WINDLE William (Billy) Henry
Maltby, 9 July, 1920 (W)

League Club	Source	Date Signed	Seasons Played	Apps	Subs	Gls
Leeds U	Denaby U	10.47	47	2	-	0
Lincoln C	Tr	02.48	47-51	91	-	22
Chester	Tr	10.51	51-54	127	-	20

WINDRIDGE David (Dave) Howard
Atherstone, 7 December, 1961 (W)

League Club	Source	Date Signed	Seasons Played	Apps	Subs	Gls
Sheffield U	Jnrs	01.79				
Chesterfield	Tr	03.80	80-82	66	12	14
Blackpool	Tr	08.83	83-86	87	14	18
Bury	(Turkey)	11.88	88	1	0	0
Rochdale	Tr	01.89	88	5	0	0

WINDROSS Dennis
Guisborough, 12 March, 1938 Died 1989 (WH)

League Club	Source	Date Signed	Seasons Played	Apps	Subs	Gls
Middlesbrough	Blackett Hutton	05.56	59-60	4	-	1
Brighton & Hove A	Tr	11.60	60	18	-	2
Darlington	Tr	06.61	61	25	-	4
Doncaster Rov	Tr	06.62	62-63	51	-	4

WINDSOR Robert (Bobby)
Stoke-on-Trent, 31 January, 1926 Died 2000 (W)

League Club	Source	Date Signed	Seasons Played	Apps	Subs	Gls
Stoke C	Jnrs	12.43				
Lincoln C	Tr	02.49	48-49	11	-	1

WINFIELD Bernard John
Draycott, 28 February, 1943 (FB)

League Club	Source	Date Signed	Seasons Played	Apps	Subs	Gls
Nottingham F	Jnrs	05.60	61-73	353	2	4
Peterborough U	Tr	07.74	74	11	0	0

WINFIELD Philip (Phil)
Mexborough, 16 February, 1937 (WH)

League Club	Source	Date Signed	Seasons Played	Apps	Subs	Gls
Lincoln C	Denaby U	10.57	57	1	-	0

WINGATE John Anthony
Budleigh Salterton, 19 December, 1948 (M)

League Club	Source	Date Signed	Seasons Played	Apps	Subs	Gls
Plymouth Arg (Am)	Dawlish T	12.68	68	1	0	0
Exeter C	Dawlish T	02.69	68-73	187	16	32
Bournemouth	Tr	07.74	74	30	3	3
Exeter C	Tr	07.75	75	44	1	2

WINGATE Tony
Islington, 21 March, 1955 (M)

League Club	Source	Date Signed	Seasons Played	Apps	Subs	Gls
Colchester U	App	●	71	0	1	0

WINN Ashley
Stockton, 1 December, 1985 (M)

League Club	Source	Date Signed	Seasons Played	Apps	Subs	Gls
Oldham Ath	Sch	●	04	0	2	0

WINN Stephen (Steve)
Thornaby, 16 September, 1959 (F)

League Club	Source	Date Signed	Seasons Played	Apps	Subs	Gls
Rotherham U		03.78	78-80	17	7	3
Torquay U	Tr	01.82	81	12	2	2
Hartlepool U	Scunthorpe U (N/C)	03.83	82	1	0	0

WINNIE David
Glasgow, 26 October, 1966 SSch/SYth/Su21-1 (FB)

League Club	Source	Date Signed	Seasons Played	Apps	Subs	Gls
Middlesbrough (L)	Aberdeen	03.94	93	1	0	0

WINSPEAR John (Jack)
Leeds, 24 December, 1946 (W)

League Club	Source	Date Signed	Seasons Played	Apps	Subs	Gls
Leeds U	Jnrs	10.64				
Cardiff C	Tr	06.66	66	1	0	0
Rochdale	Tr	07.67	67	15	1	3

WINSTANLEY Craig Jason
Hartlepool, 23 August, 1978 (M)

League Club	Source	Date Signed	Seasons Played	Apps	Subs	Gls
Hartlepool U	YT	12.96	96	0	1	0

WINSTANLEY Eric
Barnsley, 15 November, 1944 EYth (CD)

League Club	Source	Date Signed	Seasons Played	Apps	Subs	Gls
Barnsley	Jnrs	05.62	61-72	410	0	35
Chesterfield	Tr	08.73	73-76	100	1	7

WINSTANLEY Graham
Croxdale, 20 January, 1948 (CD)

League Club	Source	Date Signed	Seasons Played	Apps	Subs	Gls
Newcastle U	App	12.68	66-68	5	2	0
Carlisle U	Tr	08.69	69-74	165	1	8
Brighton & Hove A	Tr	10.74	74-78	63	1	4
Carlisle U	Tr	07.79	79	32	1	1

WINSTANLEY Mark Andrew
St Helens, 22 January, 1968 (CD)

League Club	Source	Date Signed	Seasons Played	Apps	Subs	Gls
Bolton W	App	07.86	85-93	215	5	3
Burnley	Tr	08.94	94-98	151	1	5
Shrewsbury T	L	09.98	98	8	0	0
Wigan Ath	Tr	03.99				
Shrewsbury T	Tr	07.99	99	32	1	1
Carlisle U	Tr	08.00	00-01	70	2	1

WINSTON Samuel (Sammy) Anthony
Islington, 6 August, 1978 (F)

League Club	Source	Date Signed	Seasons Played	Apps	Subs	Gls
Leyton Orient	Norwich C (YT)	08.96	96	3	8	1

WINSTONE Simon John
Bristol, 4 October, 1974 (M)

League Club	Source	Date Signed	Seasons Played	Apps	Subs	Gls
Stoke C	YT	07.93				
Torquay U	Tr	09.94	94	1	1	0

WINTER Daniel (Danny) Thomas
Tonypandy, 14 June, 1918 Died 2004 WWar-2 (FB)

League Club	Source	Date Signed	Seasons Played	Apps	Subs	Gls
Bolton W	Maes-y-Hof	06.35	36-38	34	-	0
Chelsea	Tr	12.45	46-50	131	-	0

WINTER John (Jack) George Adrian
Stoke Newington, 6 March, 1928 (CF)

League Club	Source	Date Signed	Seasons Played	Apps	Subs	Gls
Sheffield U	Gleadless Tel Exch	11.48				
Walsall	Tr	01.51	50-51	41	-	12

WINTER Julian
Huddersfield, 6 September, 1965 (M)

League Club	Source	Date Signed	Seasons Played	Apps	Subs	Gls
Huddersfield T	App	09.83	84-88	89	4	5
Scunthorpe U	L	08.88	88	4	0	0

WINTER Steven (Steve) David
Bristol, 26 October, 1973 (FB)

League Club	Source	Date Signed	Seasons Played	Apps	Subs	Gls
Walsall	YT	03.92	91-92	14	4	0
Torquay U	Taunton T	08.95	95-96	72	1	6

WINTERBOTTOM Dennis Trevor Wilson
Glossop, 23 October, 1928 (CD)

League Club	Source	Date Signed	Seasons Played	Apps	Subs	Gls
Accrington St	Stalybridge Celtic	06.51	51	12	-	0

WINTERBURN Nigel
Nuneaton, 11 December, 1963 EYth/Eu21-1/EB-3/FLge/E-2 (FB)

League Club	Source	Date Signed	Seasons Played	Apps	Subs	Gls
Birmingham C	App	08.81				
Wimbledon	Tr	09.83	83-86	164	1	8
Arsenal	Tr	05.87	87-99	429	11	8
West Ham U	Tr	07.00	00-02	78	4	1

WINTERS Francis (Frank)
Johnstone, 30 October, 1923 (CD)

League Club	Source	Date Signed	Seasons Played	Apps	Subs	Gls
Torquay U	Clyde	05.49	49-51	14	-	0

WINTERS Herbert (Bert) Richard
Coalpit Heath, 14 April, 1920 (CD)

League Club	Source	Date Signed	Seasons Played	Apps	Subs	Gls
Bristol Rov	Westerleigh Sports	09.46	46-47	13	-	0

WINTERS Ian Anderson
Renfrew, 8 February, 1921 Died 1994 (IF)

League Club	Source	Date Signed	Seasons Played	Apps	Subs	Gls
York C	Earswick	08.45	46-47	27	-	10
Gateshead	Boston U	12.48	48-52	152	-	49
Workington	Tr	07.53	53	30	-	3

WINTERS John Mark
Wisbech, 24 October, 1960 (FB)

League Club	Source	Date Signed	Seasons Played	Apps	Subs	Gls
Peterborough U	App	10.78	80-82	60	0	3

League Club	Source	Date Signed	Seasons Played	Apps	Subs	Gls

WINTERS Robert (Robbie)
East Kilbride, 4 November, 1974 S-1 (W)

League Club	Source	Date Signed	Seasons Played	Apps	Subs	Gls
Luton T	Aberdeen	08.02	02	1	0	0

WINTERS Thomas (Tom) Richard
Banbury, 11 December, 1985 (M)

League Club	Source	Date Signed	Seasons Played	Apps	Subs	Gls
Oxford U	Sch	•	03-04	0	5	0

WINTERSGILL David
Northallerton, 19 September, 1965 (M)

League Club	Source	Date Signed	Seasons Played	Apps	Subs	Gls
Wolverhampton W	App	06.83	82-83	3	1	0
Chester C	L	03.84	83	5	0	0
Darlington	(Finland)	11.86	86	15	2	1

WINTLE Frank James
Stoke-on-Trent, 20 December, 1929 Died 2005 (FB)

League Club	Source	Date Signed	Seasons Played	Apps	Subs	Gls
Port Vale		05.49	56	1	-	0

WINTON George (Jock) Douglas
Perth, 6 October, 1929 SB (FB)

League Club	Source	Date Signed	Seasons Played	Apps	Subs	Gls
Burnley	Jeanfield Swifts	09.47	52-58	183	-	1
Aston Villa	Tr	01.59	58-60	37	-	0
Rochdale	Tr	06.61	61-63	119	-	0

WIPFLER Charles (Charlie) John
Trowbridge, 15 July, 1915 Died 1983 (W)

League Club	Source	Date Signed	Seasons Played	Apps	Subs	Gls
Bristol Rov	Trowbridge	09.34	34	18	-	5
Watford	Heart of Midlothian	06.37	37-38	22	-	7
Watford	Canterbury C	09.46	46	13	-	1

WIRMOLA Jonas
Vaxjo, Sweden, 17 July, 1969 (CD)

League Club	Source	Date Signed	Seasons Played	Apps	Subs	Gls
Sheffield U	Sparvagens (Swe)	08.93	93	8	0	0

WISE Dennis Frank
Kensington, 15 December, 1966 Eu21-1/EB-3/E-21 (M)

League Club	Source	Date Signed	Seasons Played	Apps	Subs	Gls
Wimbledon	Southampton (App)	03.85	84-89	127	8	27
Chelsea	Tr	07.90	90-00	322	10	53
Leicester C	Tr	06.01	01	15	2	1
Millwall	Tr	09.02	02-04	70	15	7

WISE Stuart Graeme
Middlesbrough, 4 April, 1984 (CD)

League Club	Source	Date Signed	Seasons Played	Apps	Subs	Gls
York C	Sch	07.03	01-03	24	9	1

WISEMAN George
East Dereham, 23 May, 1921 (G)

League Club	Source	Date Signed	Seasons Played	Apps	Subs	Gls
Notts Co		05.45				
Norwich C	Tr	09.46	46	8	-	0

WISEMAN Scott Nigel Kenneth
Hull, 9 October, 1985 EYth (FB)

League Club	Source	Date Signed	Seasons Played	Apps	Subs	Gls
Hull C	Sch	04.04	03-04	2	3	0
Boston U	L	02.05	04	1	1	0

WISS Jarkko
Tampere, Finland, 17 April, 1972 Finland 36 (M)

League Club	Source	Date Signed	Seasons Played	Apps	Subs	Gls
Stockport Co	Moss FK (Nor)	08.00	00-01	34	7	6

WITCOMB Douglas (Doug) Frank
Cwm, 18 April, 1918 Died 1999 WWar-7/W-3 (WH)

League Club	Source	Date Signed	Seasons Played	Apps	Subs	Gls
West Bromwich A	Enfield	10.37	38-46	55	-	3
Sheffield Wed	Tr	03.47	46-52	224	-	12
Newport Co	Tr	11.53	53	25	-	0

WITHAM Richard (Dick)
Bowburn, 4 May, 1915 Died 1999 (FB)

League Club	Source	Date Signed	Seasons Played	Apps	Subs	Gls
Huddersfield T	Durham C	01.34	33	4	-	0
Blackpool	Tr	02.34	33-37	149	-	0
Oldham Ath	Tr	06.46	46	5	-	0

WITHE Christopher (Chris)
Speke, 25 September, 1962 (FB)

League Club	Source	Date Signed	Seasons Played	Apps	Subs	Gls
Newcastle U	App	10.80	80	2	0	0
Bradford C	Tr	06.83	83-87	141	2	2
Notts Co	Tr	10.87	87-88	80	0	3
Bury	Tr	07.89	89	22	9	1
Chester C	L	10.90	90	2	0	0
Mansfield T	Tr	01.91	90-92	75	1	5
Shrewsbury T	Tr	08.93	93-95	80	9	2

WITHE Peter
Toxteth, 30 August, 1951 E-11 (F)

League Club	Source	Date Signed	Seasons Played	Apps	Subs	Gls
Southport	Smiths Coggins	11.70	70-71	3	0	0
Barrow	Tr	12.71	71	1	0	0
Wolverhampton W	Arcadia Shepherds (SA)	11.73	73-74	12	5	3
Birmingham C	Portland (USA)	08.75	75-76	35	0	9
Nottingham F	Tr	09.76	76-78	74	1	28
Newcastle U	Tr	08.78	78-79	76	0	25
Aston Villa	Tr	05.80	80-84	182	0	74
Sheffield U	Tr	07.85	85-87	70	4	18
Birmingham C	L	09.87	87	8	0	2
Huddersfield T	Tr	07.88	88-89	22	16	1

WITHEFORD James (Jim) Douglas
Ecclesall, 16 April, 1930 (W)

League Club	Source	Date Signed	Seasons Played	Apps	Subs	Gls
Chesterfield (Am)	Norton Woodseats	12.53	53	9	-	0

WITHERS Alan
Bulwell, 20 October, 1930 (W)

League Club	Source	Date Signed	Seasons Played	Apps	Subs	Gls
Blackpool	Aspley BC	07.49	50-54	17	-	6
Lincoln C	Tr	02.55	54-58	97	-	18
Notts Co	Tr	01.59	58-62	121	-	22

WITHERS Charles (Charlie) Francis
Edmonton, 6 September, 1922 Died 2005 EB (FB)

League Club	Source	Date Signed	Seasons Played	Apps	Subs	Gls
Tottenham H	Jnrs	10.47	47-55	153	-	0

WITHERS Colin Charles
Erdington, 21 March, 1940 ESch (G)

League Club	Source	Date Signed	Seasons Played	Apps	Subs	Gls
Birmingham C	West Bromwich A (Am)	05.57	60-64	98	-	0
Aston Villa	Tr	11.64	64-68	146	0	0
Lincoln C	Tr	06.69	69	1	0	0

WITHERS David (Dai) Russell
Llwynypia, 28 April, 1967 (F)

League Club	Source	Date Signed	Seasons Played	Apps	Subs	Gls
Newport Co	Bristol Rov (App)	10.86	86-87	5	4	1
Newport Co	Ton Pentre	04.88	87	2	0	0

WITHEY Graham Alfred
Bristol, 11 June, 1960 (F)

League Club	Source	Date Signed	Seasons Played	Apps	Subs	Gls
Bristol Rov	Bath C	08.82	82	19	3	10
Coventry C	Tr	08.83	83	10	10	4
Coventry C	Seiko (HK)	08.84	84	1	1	0
Cardiff C	Tr	12.84	84-85	27	0	7
Bristol C	Yeovil T	09.86	86	1	1	0
Exeter C	Cheltenham T	07.88	88	5	2	2

WITHINGTON Richard (Dick) Stanley
South Shields, 8 April, 1921 Died 1981 (IF)

League Club	Source	Date Signed	Seasons Played	Apps	Subs	Gls
Blackpool	Jnrs	05.38				
Rochdale	Tr	06.47	47	32	-	6
Chesterfield	Tr	06.48	48	6	-	0

WITSCHGE Richard
Amsterdam, Holland, 20 September, 1969 Holland int (M)

League Club	Source	Date Signed	Seasons Played	Apps	Subs	Gls
Blackburn Rov (L)	Bordeaux (Fr)	03.95	94	1	0	0

WITTER Anthony (Tony) Junior
Jamaica, 12 August, 1965 (CD)

League Club	Source	Date Signed	Seasons Played	Apps	Subs	Gls
Crystal Palace	Grays Ath	10.90				
Queens Park Rgrs	Tr	08.91	93	1	0	0
Plymouth Arg	L	01.92	91	3	0	1
Reading	L	02.94	93	4	0	0
Millwall	Tr	10.94	94-97	99	3	2
Northampton T	Tr	08.98	98	1	3	0
Torquay U	Tr	11.98	98	4	0	0
Scunthorpe U	Welling U	02.99	98	14	0	0

WOAN Alan Esplin
Liverpool, 8 February, 1931 (IF)

League Club	Source	Date Signed	Seasons Played	Apps	Subs	Gls
Norwich C	New Brighton	12.53	53-55	21	-	7
Northampton T	Tr	07.56	56-59	119	-	68
Crystal Palace	Tr	10.59	59-60	41	-	21
Aldershot	Tr	02.61	60-63	108	-	44

WOAN Donald (Don)
Bootle, 7 November, 1927 (W)

League Club	Source	Date Signed	Seasons Played	Apps	Subs	Gls
Liverpool	Bootle	10.50	50	2	-	0
Leyton Orient	Tr	11.51	51-52	25	-	5
Bradford C	Tr	10.52	52-53	21	-	4
Tranmere Rov	Tr	02.54	53-54	27	-	2

WOAN Ian Simon
Heswall, 14 December, 1967 (W)

League Club	Source	Date Signed	Seasons Played	Apps	Subs	Gls
Nottingham F	Runcorn	03.90	90-99	189	32	31
Barnsley	Tr	08.00	00	2	1	0
Swindon T	Tr	10.00	00	21	1	3
Shrewsbury T	Miami (USA)	01.02	01-02	47	3	7

WOFFINDEN Colin
Hove, 6 August, 1947 (F)

League Club	Source	Date Signed	Seasons Played	Apps	Subs	Gls
Brighton & Hove A (Am)	Lewes	11.70	70	0	3	0

WOJTCZAK Edouard Andrew
Poland, 29 April, 1921 Died 1995 (G)

League Club	Source	Date Signed	Seasons Played	Apps	Subs	Gls
York C (Am)	Polish Army	10.46	46	8	-	0

WOLFENDEN Matthew (Matty)
Oldham, 23 July, 1987 (F)

League Club	Source	Date Signed	Seasons Played	Apps	Subs	Gls
Oldham Ath	Sch	•	03-04	0	2	0

League Club	Source	Date Signed	Seasons Played	Apps	Subs	Gls
WOLLEASTON Robert Ainsley						
Perivale, 21 December, 1979						(M)
Chelsea	YT	06.98	99	0	1	0
Bristol Rov	L	03.00	99	0	4	0
Portsmouth	L	03.01	00	5	1	0
Northampton T	L	07.01	01	2	5	0
Bradford C	Tr	07.03	03	6	8	1
Oxford U	Tr	07.04	04	14	6	0
WOLLEN Terence (Terry) Leslie						
Swindon, 30 July, 1943						(FB)
Swindon T	Jnrs	08.60	60-64	84	-	0
WOLSTENHOLME Ian Arthur						
Bradford, 12 January, 1943 EAmat						(G)
York C (Am)	St John's College	10.63	63	2	-	0
WOLSTENHOLME John **Trevor**						
Prestbury, 18 June, 1943						(WH)
Birmingham C	Chloride	09.60				
Torquay U	Tr	08.63	63-65	82	0	2
York C	Tr	07.66	66	11	0	0
WOMACK Albert (Kim) Roy						
Denaby, 20 September, 1934						(W)
Derby Co	Denaby U	10.57	57	2	-	0
Southampton	Tr	05.59				
Workington	Tr	07.60	60	9	-	1
WOMBLE Trevor						
South Shields, 7 June, 1951						(M)
Rotherham U	App	10.68	68-77	185	30	39
Crewe Alex	L	11.71	71	4	0	1
Halifax T	L	03.73	72	9	1	2
WOME Pierre Nlend						
Douala, Cameroon, 26 March, 1979 Cameroon 55						(FB)
Fulham (L)	Bologna (It)	08.02	02	13	1	1
WOMERSLEY Ernest						
Liversedge, 28 August, 1932						(W)
Huddersfield T	Jnrs	09.49	50	2	-	0
WOOD Alan Ernest						
Gravesend, 1 December, 1954						(CD)
Charlton Ath	App	12.72	72	1	0	0
WOOD Alan Herbert						
Newport, 13 January, 1941 WAmat						(CD)
Bristol Rov	Lovells Ath	10.62	62	1	-	0
Newport Co	Merthyr Tydfil	05.65	65-72	149	5	5
WOOD Alfred (Alf) Edward Howson						
Macclesfield, 25 October, 1945 EYth						(F)
Manchester C	App	06.63	62-65	24	1	0
Shrewsbury T	Tr	06.66	66-71	257	1	65
Millwall	Tr	06.72	72-74	99	1	38
Hull C	Tr	11.74	74-76	51	2	10
Middlesbrough	Tr	10.76	76	22	1	2
Walsall	Tr	07.77	77	26	3	2
WOOD Alfred (Alf) Robert						
Aldridge, 14 May, 1915 Died 2001						(G)
Coventry C	Nuneaton T	12.35	37-51	221	-	0
Northampton T	Tr	12.51	51-54	139	-	0
Coventry C	Tr	07.55	55-58	13	-	0
WOOD Archibald (Archie)						
Leven, 18 March, 1926 Died 1986						(W)
Tranmere Rov	Bowhill	08.49	49	31	-	5
WOOD Barrie Wilmot						
Doncaster, 5 December, 1936						(IF)
Doncaster Rov	Wolverhampton W (Am)	08.54	55	2	-	0
Scunthorpe U	Tr	07.58	58	3	-	1
Barnsley	South Shields	03.61	60-61	4	-	2
WOOD Brian Thomas						
Hamworthy, 8 December, 1940						(CD)
West Bromwich A	Hamworthy Ath	01.58				
Crystal Palace	Tr	05.61	61-66	142	1	1
Leyton Orient	Tr	12.66	66-67	58	0	3
Colchester U	Tr	08.68	68-69	71	0	2
Workington	Tr	07.70	70-75	202	2	9
WOOD Charles (Charlie) William						
Poplar, 7 June, 1919 Died 2000						(CD)
Millwall (Am)		05.46	46	3	-	0
WOOD Christopher (Chris) Charles						
Penistone, 18 May, 1955						(G)
Huddersfield T	App	05.72	72	7	0	0
Barnsley	L	02.73	72	1	0	0
Doncaster Rov	L	07.74	74	4	0	0
WOOD Christopher (Chris) Hayden						
Worksop, 24 January, 1987						(F)
Mansfield T	Sch	•	04	0	1	0
WOOD Darren						
Derby, 22 October, 1968						(CD)
Chesterfield	App	06.87	86-88	61	6	3
Reading	Tr	07.89	89	31	1	2
Northampton T	Tr	08.90	90-93	4	0	1
WOOD Darren Terence						
Scarborough, 9 June, 1964 ESch						(FB)
Middlesbrough	App	07.81	81-84	101	0	6
Chelsea	Tr	09.84	84-88	134	10	3
Sheffield Wed	Tr	01.89	88-89	10	1	0
WOOD Eric						
Bolton, 13 March, 1920 Died 2000						(WH)
Rochdale	Bolton W (Am)	08.43	46-50	148	-	15
WOOD Frank						
Manchester, 17 August, 1924						(CD)
Bury	Hulme	10.48	50	1	-	0
Exeter C	Tr	01.53	52	8	-	0
WOOD Gary Terence						
Corby, 2 December, 1955						(FB)
Notts Co	Kettering T	12.77	77-80	7	4	0
WOOD George						
Douglas, 26 September, 1952 S-4						(G)
Blackpool	East Stirling	01.72	71-76	117	0	0
Everton	Tr	08.77	77-79	103	0	0
Arsenal	Tr	08.80	80-82	60	0	0
Crystal Palace	Tr	08.83	83-87	192	0	0
Cardiff C	Tr	01.88	87-89	67	0	0
Blackpool	Tr	03.90	89	15	0	0
Hereford U	Tr	08.90	90	41	0	0
WOOD Graham						
Doncaster, 10 February, 1933						(CF)
Wolverhampton W		09.50				
Halifax T	Tr	06.53	53-54	19	-	3
WOOD Harry						
Barrow, 31 December, 1911 Died 1994						(IF)
Barrow		02.33	32-48	21	-	3
WOOD Henry						
Liverpool, 8 April, 1927						(W)
Chesterfield	South Liverpool	07.53	53	9	-	1
WOOD Hugh Sutherland						
Bellshill, 16 November, 1960						(FB)
Scunthorpe U	Grantham	09.80	80	0	1	0
WOOD Ian Nigel						
Kirkby-in-Ashfield, 24 May, 1958						(FB)
Mansfield T	App	06.76	75-81	135	14	9
Aldershot	Tr	08.82	82	14	0	1
WOOD Ian Thomas						
Radcliffe, 15 January, 1948						(FB)
Oldham Ath	Park Lane Olympic	11.65	65-77	445	6	19
Oldham Ath	San Jose (USA)	08.78	78-79	72	1	3
Burnley	Tr	05.80	80	14	3	0
WOOD Jack						
Royton, 12 February, 1931						(FB)
Aldershot		09.52	52-54	38	-	1
WOOD James (Jimmy) Henry						
Knotty Ash, 25 October, 1938						(G)
Southport	Burscough	04.58	57	1	-	0
WOOD Jamie						
Salford, 21 September, 1978 CaymanIs-2						(F)
Manchester U	YT	07.97				
Hull C	Tr	07.99	99-00	15	32	6
Halifax T	Tr	08.01	01	10	6	0
Swansea C	Tr	07.02	02	13	4	2
WOOD Jeffrey (Jeff) Reginald						
Islington, 4 February, 1954						(G)
Charlton Ath	Harlow T	11.75	75-80	147	0	0
Colchester U	(Denmark)	09.81				
Exeter C	Happy Valley (HK)	08.84	84	33	0	0

League Club	Source	Date Signed	Seasons Played	Career Record Apps	Subs	Gls
WOOD Edward **John (Jackie)**						
Canning Town, 23 October, 1919 Died 1993 EAmat						(IF)
West Ham U	Leytonstone	03.38	37-48	58	-	13
Leyton Orient	Tr	10.49	49	9	-	1
WOOD John Michael						
Walsall Wood, 9 September, 1948						(FB)
Wrexham	Jnrs	07.66	65-67	4	3	0
WOOD Kevin						
Armthorpe, 3 November, 1929						(IF)
Doncaster Rov		10.49				
Grimsby T	Worksop T	03.51	50-51	3	-	2
WOOD Leigh James						
Selby, 21 May, 1983						(CD)
York C	YT	03.02	00-03	44	20	0
WOOD Thomas **Leslie (Les)**						
Helmshore, 20 December, 1932 Died 2005 WSch						(G)
Huddersfield T	Bolton W (Am)	04.52				
Barrow	Tr	08.55	55	31	-	0
Port Vale	Tr	06.56	56	2	-	0
Southport	Tr	01.58	57	1	-	0
WOOD Mark						
Scarborough, 27 June, 1972						(M)
York C	YT	07.90	90	0	1	0
WOOD Michael (Mick)						
Halifax, 9 March, 1962						(F)
Rochdale	Guiseley	08.86	86	5	1	3
WOOD Michael (Mick) James						
Bury, 3 July, 1952						(FB)
Blackburn Rov	App	02.70	69-77	140	8	2
Bradford C	Tr	02.78	77-81	143	3	9
Halifax T	Tr	08.82	82-83	80	1	2
WOOD Neil Anthony						
Manchester, 4 January, 1983 EYth						(F)
Manchester U	YT	01.00				
Peterborough U	L	09.03	03	2	1	1
Burnley	L	01.04	03	8	2	1
Coventry C	Tr	07.04	04	6	7	0
WOOD Nicholas (Nick) Anthony						
Oldham, 6 January, 1966 EYth						(F)
Manchester U	App	06.83	85-86	2	1	0
WOOD Norman						
Chadderton, 20 October, 1921						(W)
Oldham Ath (Am)	Royton Amats	09.46	46	1	-	0
WOOD Norman						
Sunderland, 10 August, 1932						(WH)
Sunderland	Silksworth Jnrs	05.54	54	1	-	0
WOOD Paul						
Uppermill, 20 March, 1970						(M)
Sheffield U	YT	09.88	87	0	1	0
Rochdale	L	11.88	88	2	3	0
WOOD Paul Anthony						
Saltburn, 1 November, 1964						(W)
Portsmouth	App	11.82	83-86	25	22	6
Brighton & Hove A	Tr	08.87	87-89	77	15	8
Sheffield U	Tr	02.90	89-91	19	9	3
Bournemouth	L	01.91	90	20	1	0
Bournemouth	Tr	10.91	91-93	73	5	18
Portsmouth	Tr	02.94	93-95	25	7	3
WOOD Raymond (Ray) Ernest						
Hebburn, 11 June, 1931 Died 2002 Eu23-1/EB/FLge-3/E-3						(G)
Darlington	Newcastle U (Am)	09.49	49	12	-	0
Manchester U	Tr	12.49	49-58	178	-	0
Huddersfield T	Tr	12.58	58-64	207	-	0
Bradford C	Inter Roma (Can)	10.65	65	32	0	0
Barnsley	Tr	08.66	66-67	30	0	0
WOOD Richard Mark						
Ossett, 5 July, 1985						(CD)
Sheffield Wed	Sch	04.03	02-04	45	4	2
WOOD Robert (Bobby)						
Elphinstone, 15 February, 1930 Died 1997						(WH)
Barnsley	Hibernian	07.51	51-64	338	-	41
WOOD William **Ronald (Ron)**						
Manchester, 11 November, 1925						(IF)
Wrexham	Droylsden	11.49	49	16	-	5

League Club	Source	Date Signed	Seasons Played	Career Record Apps	Subs	Gls
WOOD Royden (Roy)						
Wallasey, 16 October, 1930						(G)
Leeds U	Clitheroe	05.52	53-59	196	-	0
WOOD Simon Onward						
Hull, 24 September, 1976						(F)
Coventry C	YT	11.93				
Mansfield T	Tr	03.96	95-96	32	9	4
WOOD Stephen (Steve) Alan						
Bracknell, 2 February, 1963						(CD)
Reading	App	02.81	79-86	216	3	9
Millwall	Tr	06.87	87-91	108	2	0
Southampton	Tr	10.91	91-93	46	0	0
Oxford U	Tr	07.94	94-95	12	1	0
WOOD Steven (Steve) Ronald						
Oldham, 23 June, 1963						(M)
Macclesfield T	Ashton U	07.93	97-00	129	22	19
WOOD Terence (Terry) Laurence						
Newport, 3 September, 1920						(WH)
Cardiff C (Am)	Newport Docks	09.46	46	4	-	0
WOOD Trevor John						
Jersey, 3 November, 1968 NIB/NI-1						(G)
Brighton & Hove A	App	11.86				
Port Vale	Tr	07.88	88-92	42	0	0
Walsall	Tr	07.94	94-96	69	0	0
Hereford U	Tr	01.97	96	19	0	0
WOOD William (Bill)						
Barnsley, 28 December, 1927						(FB)
Sunderland	Spen Jnrs	10.48	49	1	-	0
Hull C	Tr	07.51				
Sheffield U	Tr	06.52	52	5	-	0
WOODALL Arthur John						
Stoke-on-Trent, 4 June, 1930						(W)
Stoke C	Jnrs	05.50	53	1	-	0
WOODALL Brian Harold						
Chester, 6 June, 1948						(W)
Sheffield Wed	App	06.65	67-69	19	3	4
Oldham Ath	L	02.70	69	3	1	1
Chester	Tr	06.70	70	11	2	2
Crewe Alex	L	03.71	70	10	1	3
WOODALL Bertram **John**						
Goole, 16 January, 1949						(F)
York C	Goole T	02.67	67	2	0	0
Rotherham U	Gainsborough Trinity	03.74	73-74	25	1	6
WOODBURN James (Jimmy)						
Rutherglen, 29 January, 1917 Died 1978						(WH)
Newcastle U	Coltness U	02.38	38-47	44	-	4
Gateshead	Tr	09.48	48-51	131	-	10
WOODCOCK Anthony (Tony) Stewart						
Eastwood, 6 December, 1955 Eu21-2/E-42						(F)
Nottingham F	App	01.74	73-79	125	4	36
Lincoln C	L	02.76	75	2	2	1
Doncaster Rov	L	09.76	76	6	0	2
Arsenal	FC Cologne (Ger)	07.82	82-85	129	2	56
WOODCOCK David Keith						
Shardlow, 13 October, 1966						(M)
Sunderland	App	10.84				
Darlington	Tr	08.85	85-86	14	13	2
WOODCOCK Ernest (Ernie)						
Salford, 14 May, 1925						(W)
Bury	Blackburn Rov (Am)	01.47	46-47	18	-	3
Oldham Ath	Tr	06.48	48-49	28	-	4
WOODCOCK Harold (Harry)						
Darlington, 18 September, 1928 Died 2003						(IF)
Darlington		08.52	52-53	5	-	0
WOODCOCK Thomas (Tommy)						
Heapey, 19 March, 1926						(IF)
Southport	Preston NE (Am)	07.46	46	1	-	0
WOODFIELD David						
Leamington Spa, 11 October, 1943						(CD)
Wolverhampton W	Jnrs	10.60	61-69	247	3	13
Watford	Tr	09.71	71-73	14	1	0
WOODFIELD Terry						
Nottingham, 21 January, 1946						(WH)
Notts Co	Jnrs	07.63	63	5	-	0

League Club	Source	Date Signed	Seasons Played	Apps	Subs	Gls
WOODFORD Robert Michael						
Keyworth, 6 December, 1943						(WH)
Notts Co	Jnrs	03.61	61	3	-	0
WOODGATE Jonathan Simon						
Middlesbrough, 22 January, 1980 EYth/Eu21-1/E-5						(CD)
Leeds U	YT	05.97	98-02	100	4	4
Newcastle U	Tr	01.03	02-03	28	0	0
WOODGATE John **Terence (Terry)**						
East Ham, 11 December, 1919 Died 1985						(W)
West Ham U	Beckton	09.38	38-52	259	-	48
WOODHEAD Andrew						
Wallsend, 12 July, 1966						(M)
Gillingham	App	07.82	83	1	1	0
WOODHEAD Dennis						
Hillsborough, 12 June, 1925 Died 1995						(W)
Sheffield Wed	Hillsborough BC	04.45	46-54	213	-	73
Chesterfield	Tr	09.55	55	15	-	6
Derby Co	Tr	01.56	55-58	94	-	24
Southport	L	02.59	58	4	-	1
WOODHEAD Dennis						
Huddersfield, 2 September, 1924 Died 2001						(W)
Bradford C		01.48				
Accrington St	Tr	05.48	48	6	-	0
WOODHEAD Simon Christopher						
Dewsbury, 26 December, 1962						(FB)
Mansfield T	Jnrs	09.80	80-84	108	14	6
WOODHOUSE Curtis						
Driffield, 17 April, 1980 EYth/Eu21-4						(M)
Sheffield U	YT	12.97	97-00	92	12	6
Birmingham C	Tr	02.01	00-02	35	13	2
Rotherham U	L	02.03	02	11	0	0
Peterborough U	Tr	10.03	03-04	58	3	11
WOODHOUSE John						
Middlesbrough, 5 April, 1937						(W)
Leeds U	South Bank	06.55				
Gateshead	Tr	07.57	57	2	-	0
WOODIN Stephen (Steve)						
Birkenhead, 6 January, 1955 New Zealand int						(W)
Tranmere Rov		02.75	74	1	2	0
WOODLEY Derek George						
Isleworth, 2 March, 1942 Died 2002 ESch/EYth						(W)
West Ham U	Jnrs	04.59	59-61	12	-	3
Southend U	Tr	08.62	62-66	160	2	23
Charlton Ath	Tr	06.67	67	2	1	0
Southend U	Tr	10.67	67	7	2	0
Gillingham	Tr	01.68	67-70	99	1	9
WOODLEY Victor (Vic) Robert						
Cippenham, 26 February, 1910 Died 1978 FLge-4/EWar-2/E-19						(G)
Chelsea	Windsor & Eton	05.31	31-38	252	-	0
Derby Co	Bath C	03.46	46	30	-	0
WOODMAN Andrew (Andy) John						
Camberwell, 11 August, 1971						(G)
Crystal Palace	YT	07.89				
Exeter C	Tr	07.94	94	6	0	0
Northampton T	Tr	03.95	94-98	163	0	0
Brentford	Tr	01.99	98-99	61	0	0
Southend U	L	08.00	00	17	0	0
Colchester U	Tr	11.00	00-01	54	0	0
Oxford U	Tr	01.02	01-03	101	0	0
WOODMAN Craig Alan						
Tiverton, 22 December, 1982						(FB)
Bristol C	YT	02.00	00-04	30	12	0
Mansfield T	L	09.04	04	8	0	1
Torquay U	L	12.04	04	20	2	1
WOODROFFE Lewis (Lew) Christopher						
Portsmouth, 29 October, 1921						(W)
Manchester C		10.45	46	9	-	1
Watford	Tr	08.47	47-50	64	-	6
WOODRUFF Arthur						
Barnsley, 12 April, 1913 Died 1983 FLge-2						(FB)
Bradford C		08.34				
Burnley	Tr	07.36	36-51	271	-	0
Workington	Tr	07.52	52	11	-	0
WOODRUFF Robert (Bobby) James						
Wolverhampton, 11 March, 1965 WSch/WYth						(F)
Newport Co	Cardiff C (Jnrs)	08.83	83	9	1	0
Swindon T	L	05.84	83	1	1	0

League Club	Source	Date Signed	Seasons Played	Apps	Subs	Gls
WOODRUFF Robert (Bobby) William						
Highworth, 9 November, 1940						(M)
Swindon T	Jnrs	05.58	58-63	180	-	20
Wolverhampton W	Tr	03.64	63-65	63	0	18
Crystal Palace	Tr	06.66	66-69	123	2	48
Cardiff C	Tr	11.69	69-73	141	9	22
Newport Co	Tr	08.74	74-75	52	0	7
WOODS Alan Edward						
Dinnington, 15 February, 1937 ESch/EYth						(WH)
Tottenham H	Jnrs	02.54	54	6	-	0
Swansea T	Tr	12.56	57-58	30	-	0
York C	Tr	07.60	60-65	227	1	4
WOODS Charles (Charlie) Morgan Parkinson						
Whitehaven, 18 March, 1941						(F)
Newcastle U	Cleator Moor Celtic	05.59	60-61	26	-	7
Bournemouth	Tr	11.62	62-64	70	-	26
Crystal Palace	Tr	11.64	64-65	49	0	5
Ipswich T	Tr	07.66	66-69	65	17	5
Watford	Tr	06.70	70-71	40	2	3
Colchester U	L	11.71	71	3	0	0
WOODS Christopher (Chris) Charles Eric						
Swineshead, 14 November, 1959 EYth/Eu21-6/EB/E-43						(G)
Nottingham F	App	12.76				
Queens Park Rgrs	Tr	07.79	79-80	63	0	0
Norwich C	Tr	03.81	80-85	216	0	0
Sheffield Wed	Glasgow Rgrs	08.91	91-95	106	1	0
Reading	L	10.95	95	5	0	0
Southampton	Colorado (USA)	11.96	96	4	0	0
Burnley	Tr	06.97	97	12	0	0
WOODS Clive Richard						
Norwich, 18 December, 1947						(W)
Ipswich T	Wisbech T	06.69	69-79	217	50	24
Norwich C	Tr	03.80	79-81	29	3	4
WOODS Dennis James						
Norwich, 12 December, 1936						(W)
Watford	Cambridge U	10.62	62	13	-	2
WOODS Derek Edward						
Northampton, 23 March, 1941 EAmat						(W)
Northampton T (Am)	Jnrs	06.59	61	6	-	2
WOODS Edward (Eddie)						
Ton Pentre, 29 July, 1951						(F)
Bristol C	Ton Pentre	09.71	72	1	1	0
Scunthorpe U	L	10.73	73	4	0	2
Newport Co	Tr	09.74	74-78	149	2	54
WOODS Jonathan Paul						
Blackwood, Monmouthshire, 5 October, 1966						(F)
Cardiff C	Jnrs	08.84	84	0	1	0
WOODS Kenneth (Kenny) Stephen						
Liverpool, 15 April, 1974						(M)
Everton	YT	06.92				
Bury	Tr	07.93	93	0	2	0
WOODS Martin Paul						
Airdrie, 1 January, 1986 SYth						(M)
Leeds U	Sch	01.03	04	0	1	0
Hartlepool U	L	09.04	04	3	3	0
WOODS Matthew (Matt) James						
Gosport, 9 September, 1976						(CD)
Everton	YT	07.95				
Chester C	Tr	08.96	96-99	114	21	4
WOODS Maurice (Matt)						
Skelmersdale, 1 November, 1931 FLge-1						(CD)
Everton	Burscough	11.49	52-56	8	-	1
Blackburn Rov	Tr	11.56	56-62	260	-	2
Luton T	Sydney C (Aus)	07.65	65	34	0	0
Stockport Co	Tr	07.66	66-67	85	0	2
WOODS Neil Stephen						
Goole, 30 July, 1966						(F)
Doncaster Rov	App	01.83	82-86	55	10	16
Ipswich T	Glasgow Rgrs	08.87	87-89	15	12	5
Bradford C	Tr	03.90	89	13	1	2
Grimsby T	Tr	08.90	90-97	175	51	42
Wigan Ath	L	11.97	97	1	0	0
Scunthorpe U	L	01.98	97	2	0	0
Mansfield T	L	02.98	97	5	1	0
York C	Tr	07.98	98	5	3	0
WOODS Patrick (Pat) James						
Islington, 29 April, 1933						(FB)
Queens Park Rgrs	Jnrs	06.50	52-60	304	-	15
Colchester U	South Coast U (Aus)	08.63	63	36	-	0

WOODS Peter Anthony
Sale, 21 January, 1950 (M)

League Club	Source	Date Signed	Seasons Played	Apps	Subs	Gls
Manchester U	App	04.67				
Luton T	Tr	04.70				
Southend U	Tr	02.72	71-72	25	0	0
Doncaster Rov	Tr	07.73	73-74	41	8	1

WOODS Raymond (Ray)
Peterborough, 27 April, 1930 (WH)

League Club	Source	Date Signed	Seasons Played	Apps	Subs	Gls
Southend U	Peterborough U	05.48	50-51	3	-	1
Crystal Palace	Tr	06.53	53-54	18	-	0

WOODS Raymond (Ray) Guy
Birkenhead, 7 June, 1965 (W)

League Club	Source	Date Signed	Seasons Played	Apps	Subs	Gls
Tranmere Rov	App	06.83	82-84	9	5	2
Wigan Ath	Colne Dynamoes	03.89	88-90	25	3	3
Coventry C	Tr	01.91	90-91	21	0	1
Wigan Ath	L	01.93	92	12	1	0
Shrewsbury T	Tr	03.94	93-95	40	11	1

WOODS Stephen (Steve) Gerard
Glasgow, 23 February, 1970 (G)

League Club	Source	Date Signed	Seasons Played	Apps	Subs	Gls
Preston NE	Clydebank	10.93	93	19	1	0

WOODS Stephen (Steve) John
Northwich, 15 December, 1976 (CD)

League Club	Source	Date Signed	Seasons Played	Apps	Subs	Gls
Stoke C	YT	08.95	97-98	33	1	0
Plymouth Arg	L	03.98	97	4	0	0
Chesterfield	Tr	07.99	99	22	3	0
Torquay U	Tr	08.01	01-04	125	4	10

WOODS William (Billy)
Farnworth, 12 March, 1926 Died 1980 (IF)

League Club	Source	Date Signed	Seasons Played	Apps	Subs	Gls
Rochdale	Moss Grove	04.45	46	15	-	1
Bradford PA	Tr	01.47	46	5	-	0
Rochdale	Tr	01.49	48-49	13	-	1
Barrow	Tr	11.49	49	16	-	3
Crewe Alex	Tr	07.50				
Accrington St	Tr	11.50	50	3	-	0

WOODS Darragh **William (Billy)**
Cork, 24 October, 1973 IRu21-4 (W)

League Club	Source	Date Signed	Seasons Played	Apps	Subs	Gls
Coventry C	YT	07.92				
Tranmere Rov	Cork C	07.95	96	1	0	0
Blackpool	L	10.96	96	3	0	0

WOODSFORD Jamie Marcus
Ipswich, 9 November, 1976 EYth (F)

League Club	Source	Date Signed	Seasons Played	Apps	Subs	Gls
Luton T	YT	03.95	94-95	2	8	0

WOODTHORPE Colin John
Ellesmere Port, 13 January, 1969 (FB)

League Club	Source	Date Signed	Seasons Played	Apps	Subs	Gls
Chester C	App	08.86	86-89	154	1	6
Norwich C	Tr	07.90	90-93	36	7	1
Stockport Co	Aberdeen	07.97	97-01	114	39	4
Bury	Tr	08.02	02-04	98	3	0

WOODWARD Alan
Chapeltown, 7 September, 1946 EYth/FLge-2 (W)

League Club	Source	Date Signed	Seasons Played	Apps	Subs	Gls
Sheffield U	App	09.63	64-78	536	2	158

WOODWARD Alan
Stanton Hill, 19 June, 1947 (W)

League Club	Source	Date Signed	Seasons Played	Apps	Subs	Gls
Grimsby T	Alfreton T	07.70	70-71	54	0	13

WOODWARD Andrew (Andy) Stephen
Stockport, 23 September, 1973 (FB)

League Club	Source	Date Signed	Seasons Played	Apps	Subs	Gls
Crewe Alex	YT	07.92	92-94	9	11	0
Bury	Tr	03.95	94-99	95	20	1
Sheffield U	Tr	03.00	99	2	1	0
Scunthorpe U	L	09.00	00	12	0	0
Halifax T	Tr	07.01	01	29	1	1

WOODWARD Brian
Leeds, 12 July, 1929 (CF)

League Club	Source	Date Signed	Seasons Played	Apps	Subs	Gls
Leeds U	Jnrs	07.47				
York C	Hereford U	08.50	50	5	-	0

WOODWARD Harry George
Bromley, 29 August, 1919 (CD)

League Club	Source	Date Signed	Seasons Played	Apps	Subs	Gls
Southend U	Chelmsford C	05.46	50-51	14	-	0

WOODWARD John
Stoke-on-Trent, 16 January, 1947 (F)

League Club	Source	Date Signed	Seasons Played	Apps	Subs	Gls
Stoke C	App	03.64	64-66	10	1	1
Aston Villa	Tr	10.66	66-68	22	4	7
Walsall	Tr	05.69	69-72	116	9	23
Port Vale	Tr	02.73	72-74	88	11	30
Scunthorpe U	Tr	07.75	75	16	3	5

WOODWARD John
Glasgow, 10 January, 1949 SYth (M)

League Club	Source	Date Signed	Seasons Played	Apps	Subs	Gls
Arsenal	Possilpark YMCA	01.66	66	2	1	0
York C	Tr	07.71	71-77	152	15	6

WOODWARD Horace **John (Johnny)**
Islington, 16 January, 1924 Died 2002 (CD)

League Club	Source	Date Signed	Seasons Played	Apps	Subs	Gls
Tottenham H	Jnrs	05.46	46-48	63	-	1
Queens Park Rgrs	Tr	06.49	49-50	57	-	0
Walsall	Snowdown CW	07.53	53	5	-	0

WOODWARD Kenneth (Ken) Robert
Battersea, 16 November, 1947 (W)

League Club	Source	Date Signed	Seasons Played	Apps	Subs	Gls
Crystal Palace	App	12.65				
Leyton Orient	Tr	08.66	66	1	0	0

WOODWARD Laurence (Dai)
Troedyrhiw, 5 July, 1918 Died 1997 (WH)

League Club	Source	Date Signed	Seasons Played	Apps	Subs	Gls
Wolverhampton W	Folkestone	05.38				
Walsall	L	11.38	38	29	-	0
Bournemouth	Tr	05.39	46-53	272	-	7

WOODWARD Thomas **Peter**
Birmingham, 6 July, 1934 (G)

League Club	Source	Date Signed	Seasons Played	Apps	Subs	Gls
West Bromwich A	Moor Green Rov	09.54				
Walsall	Tr	08.58	58	13	-	0

WOODWARD Thomas (Tom)
Westhoughton, 8 December, 1917 Died 1994 (W)

League Club	Source	Date Signed	Seasons Played	Apps	Subs	Gls
Bolton W	White Horse Temp	01.35	35-49	152	-	18
Middlesbrough	Tr	10.49	49-50	19	-	6

WOODWARD Vivian
Troedyrhiw, 20 May, 1914 WWar-1 (IF)

League Club	Source	Date Signed	Seasons Played	Apps	Subs	Gls
Fulham	Folkestone	01.36	35-46	92	-	25
Millwall	Tr	02.47	46-47	42	-	13
Brentford	Tr	07.48	48-49	20	-	4
Aldershot	Tr	02.50	49-50	53	-	5

WOODWORTH Anthony (Tony) David
Manchester, 5 March, 1968 (G)

League Club	Source	Date Signed	Seasons Played	Apps	Subs	Gls
Burnley	App	03.86	86	1	0	0

WOOF Clifford (Cliff) Eric
Walton, 20 September, 1956 (F)

League Club	Source	Date Signed	Seasons Played	Apps	Subs	Gls
Liverpool	Jnrs	05.76				
Southport	Jacob's	12.77	77	1	0	0

WOOF William (Billy)
Gateshead, 16 August, 1956 (F)

League Club	Source	Date Signed	Seasons Played	Apps	Subs	Gls
Middlesbrough	App	08.74	74-81	30	16	5
Peterborough U	L	03.77	76	2	1	0
Cardiff C	Blyth Spartans	09.82	82	1	0	1
Hull C	Gateshead	02.83	82	9	2	3

WOOKEY Kenneth (Ken) George
Newport, 30 December, 1946 Died 1992 (W)

League Club	Source	Date Signed	Seasons Played	Apps	Subs	Gls
Newport Co	Jnrs	01.64	64-68	57	6	6
Port Vale	Tr	07.69	69	23	1	4
Workington	Tr	07.70	70	11	6	4

WOOKEY Kenneth (Ken) William
Newport, 23 February, 1922 Died 2003 WSch (W)

League Club	Source	Date Signed	Seasons Played	Apps	Subs	Gls
Newport Co	Jnrs	02.39	46	14	-	2
Bristol Rov	Tr	12.46	46-48	54	-	9
Swansea T	Tr	11.48	48-49	12	-	0
Ipswich T	Hereford U	10.50	50	15	-	1

WOOLCOTT Roy Alfred
Leyton, 29 July, 1946 (F)

League Club	Source	Date Signed	Seasons Played	Apps	Subs	Gls
Tottenham H	Eton Manor	02.68	69	1	0	0
Gillingham	L	02.72	71	13	0	5

WOOLDRIDGE James (Jim)
Rossington, 28 September, 1918 (FB)

League Club	Source	Date Signed	Seasons Played	Apps	Subs	Gls
Doncaster Rov	Glasgow Benburb	12.40	46-47	30	-	0

WOOLDRIDGE Stephen (Steve) Joseph
Chiswick, 18 July, 1950 (FB)

League Club	Source	Date Signed	Seasons Played	Apps	Subs	Gls
Crystal Palace	App	07.67				
Plymouth Arg	L	08.70	70	20	0	0
Colchester U	Tr	06.72	72	3	0	0

WOOLER Alan Thomas
Poole, 17 August, 1953 (FB)

League Club	Source	Date Signed	Seasons Played	Apps	Subs	Gls
Reading	Weymouth	11.71	71-72	38	0	0
West Ham U	Tr	08.73	73-75	3	1	0
Aldershot	Tr	04.76	76-83	264	2	3

WOOLER Michael **Graham**
Huddersfield, 23 October, 1944 (F)

League Club	Source	Date Signed	Seasons Played	Apps	Subs	Gls
Huddersfield T		08.64				
Halifax T	Tr	12.64	64-67	50	7	7

League Club	Source	Date Signed	Seasons Played	Career Record Apps	Subs	Gls
WOOLFALL Alan Francis						
Liverpool, 30 November, 1956						(W)
Bury	Skelmersdale U	10.74	74-78	46	11	11
Port Vale	Tr	08.79	79-80	13	5	3
WOOLFORD Michael (Mike) Elijah George						
Swindon, 29 September, 1939						(IF)
Swindon T	Swindon BR	12.59	59	3	-	0
WOOLGAR Philip (Phil) Robert John						
Worthing, 24 September, 1948						(G)
Brighton & Hove A (Am)	Wigmore Ath	06.66	66	1	0	0
WOOLGAR James **Stewart**						
Chesterfield, 21 September, 1952						(M)
West Bromwich A	App	10.69	72	2	2	0
Doncaster Rov	Tr	07.74	74	2	5	1
WOOLISCROFT Ashley David						
Stoke-on-Trent, 28 December, 1979						(FB)
Stoke C	YT	02.97	98	0	1	0
WOOLLARD Arnold James						
Pembroke, Bermuda, 24 August, 1930						(FB)
Northampton T	Bermuda Ath Ass (Ber)	06.49	50	3	-	0
Newcastle U	Peterborough U	12.52	52-55	8	-	0
Bournemouth	Tr	06.56	56-61	159	-	0
Northampton T	Tr	03.62	61-62	28	-	0
WOOLLETT Alan Howard						
Wigston, 4 March, 1947						(CD)
Leicester C	App	08.64	66-77	212	15	0
Northampton T	Tr	07.78	78	23	0	0
WOOLLETT Charles (Charlie)						
Dawdon, 25 November, 1920						(W)
Newcastle U	Eppleton CW	11.42				
Bradford C	Tr	08.46	46-48	43	-	5
York C	Murton Colliery	02.49	48	4	-	0
WOOLLEY Matthew (Matt) David						
Manchester, 22 February, 1982						(M)
Macclesfield T	Stockport Co (YT)	07.99	00-01	1	4	0
WOOLLEY Robert Alan						
Nottingham, 29 December, 1947 Died 1971						(CF)
Notts Co	App	07.65	63-65	9	0	2
WOOLMER Anthony (Tony) John						
Swardeston, 25 March, 1946						(F)
Norwich C	Jnrs	12.65	66-67	4	1	1
Bradford PA	Tr	10.69	69	30	0	7
Scunthorpe U	Tr	11.70	70-71	35	5	2
WOOLSEY Jeffrey (Jeff) Alexander						
Upminster, 8 November, 1977						(CD)
Arsenal	YT	07.96				
Queens Park Rgrs	Tr	08.97				
Brighton & Hove A	Tr	03.98	97	1	2	0
WOON Andrew (Andy) Geoffrey						
Bognor Regis, 26 June, 1952						(F)
Brentford	Bognor Regis T	10.72	72-74	42	8	12
WOOSNAM Philip (Phil) Abraham						
Caersws, 22 December, 1932 WSch/WAmat/FLge-1/W-17						(IF)
Manchester C (Am)	Bangor C	06.52	52	1	-	0
Leyton Orient	Sutton U	03.55	54-58	108	-	19
West Ham U	Tr	11.58	58-62	138	-	26
Aston Villa	Tr	11.62	62-65	106	0	24
WOOTER Nordin						
Breda, Holland, 24 August, 1976 Hou21-15						(F)
Watford	Real Zaragoza (Sp)	09.99	99-01	37	26	3
WOOTTON Leonard (Len)						
Stoke-on-Trent, 13 June, 1925 Died 1990						(IF)
Port Vale	Everton (Am)	08.45	46	10	-	1
Wrexham	Queen of the South	08.51	51	20	-	2
WOOZLEY David James						
Ascot, 6 December, 1979						(CD)
Crystal Palace	YT	11.97	98-99	21	9	0
Bournemouth	L	09.00	00	6	0	0
Torquay U	L	08.01	01	12	0	0
Torquay U	Tr	03.02	01-03	52	8	3
Oxford U	Tr	07.04	04	11	2	1
Yeovil T	L	03.05	04	0	1	0
WORBOYS Gavin Anthony						
Doncaster, 14 July, 1974						(F)
Doncaster Rov	YT	04.92	91	6	1	2
Notts Co	Tr	05.92				
Exeter C	L	12.93	93	4	0	1
Darlington	Tr	11.94	94-95	30	11	8
Northampton T	Tr	01.96	95	4	9	1
WORDLEY Edward (Ted) Henry						
Stoke-on-Trent, 17 October, 1923 Died 1989						(WH)
Stoke C	Jnrs	10.41	46-49	10	-	0
WORGAN Lee John						
Eastbourne, 1 December, 1983 WYth/Wu21-2						(G)
Wimbledon	Sch	04.03	03	0	3	0
Wycombe W	L	04.04	03	2	0	0
Rushden & Diamonds	Tr	08.04	04	7	0	0
WORKMAN Peter **Ian**						
Liverpool, 13 November, 1962						(M)
Chester	Southport	01.83	82	3	0	0
WORLEY Leonard (Len) Francis						
Amersham, 27 June, 1937 EYth/EAmat						(W)
Charlton Ath (Am)	Wycombe W	10.56	56	1	-	0
Tottenham H (Am)	Wycombe W	05.59	59	1	-	0
WORMLEY Paul						
Leeds, 16 September, 1961						(F)
Barnsley	Yorkshire Amats	10.79	79	1	0	0
WORMULL Simon James						
Crawley, 1 December, 1976						(M)
Tottenham H	YT	07.95				
Brentford	Tr	07.97	97	3	2	0
Brighton & Hove A	Tr	03.98				
Rushden & Diamonds	Dover Ath	03.00	01	4	1	0
WORRALL Benjamin (Ben) Joseph						
Swindon, 7 December, 1975 EYth						(M)
Swindon T	YT	07.94	94	1	2	0
Scarborough	Tr	08.96	96-98	45	22	3
Exeter C	Tr	08.99	99	1	3	0
WORRALL Frederick (Fred)						
Warrington, 8 September, 1910 Died 1979 FLge-2/E-2						(W)
Oldham Ath	Nantwich	12.28	28-31	105	-	21
Portsmouth	Tr	10.31	31-38	313	-	68
Crewe Alex	Tr	04.46	46	6	-	1
WORRALL Gary George						
Salford, 4 November, 1961						(W)
Manchester U	App	11.78				
Peterborough U	Tr	03.84	83-85	93	2	16
Carlisle U	Tr	07.86	86	32	0	0
WORRALL Harold (Harry)						
Northwich, 19 November, 1918 Died 1979						(FB)
Manchester U	Winsford U	10.37	46-47	6	-	0
WORRELL Colin Harvey						
Great Yarmouth, 29 August, 1943						(FB)
Norwich C	Jnrs	11.61	62-64	9	-	0
Leyton Orient	Tr	09.64	64-65	51	0	0
WORRELL David						
Dublin, 12 January, 1978 IRYth/IRu21-17						(FB)
Blackburn Rov	Shelbourne	01.95				
Plymouth Arg	Dundee U	11.00	00-04	147	0	0
WORSDALE Michael **John**						
Stoke-on-Trent, 29 October, 1948						(W)
Stoke C	App	11.65	68	4	0	0
Lincoln C	Tr	05.71	71-73	55	12	9
WORSLEY Graeme						
Liverpool, 4 January, 1969						(FB)
Shrewsbury T	Bootle	03.89	88-92	83	22	4
Bury	Doncaster Rov (N/C)	12.93	93	0	1	0
WORSMAN Reginald (Reg) Herbert						
Bradford, 19 March, 1933						(IF)
Bradford PA	Jnrs	10.53	54-55	22	-	5
Bradford C	Tr	06.56	56	1	-	0
Darlington	Nelson	06.60	60	4	-	1
WORSWICK Michael (Micky) Anthony						
Preston, 14 March, 1945 EAmat						(W)
Wigan Ath	Chorley	08.72	78	0	1	0
WORTHINGTON David (Dave)						
Halifax, 28 March, 1945						(FB)
Halifax T	Jnrs	04.62	61-63	37	-	9
Barrow	Tr	07.64	64-65	60	1	7
Grimsby T	Tr	06.66	66-72	292	1	14
Halifax T	L	10.73	73	5	0	0
Southend U	Tr	12.73	73-75	92	3	0

WORTHINGTON Eric Senior
Sheffield, 29 December, 1925 (IF)

League Club	Source	Date Signed	Seasons Played	Apps	Subs	Gls
Queens Park Rgrs		09.47				
Watford	Tr	08.49	49-50	24	-	4
Bradford C	Dover	09.53	53	2	-	1

WORTHINGTON Frank Stewart
Halifax, 23 November, 1948 Eu23-2/FLge-1/E-8 (F)

League Club	Source	Date Signed	Seasons Played	Apps	Subs	Gls
Huddersfield T	App	11.66	66-71	166	5	41
Leicester C	Tr	08.72	72-77	209	1	72
Bolton W	Tr	09.77	77-79	81	3	35
Birmingham C	Tr	11.79	79-81	71	4	29
Leeds U	Tr	03.82	81-82	32	0	14
Sunderland	Tr	12.82	82	18	1	2
Southampton	Tr	06.83	83	34	0	4
Brighton & Hove A	Tr	05.84	84	27	4	7
Tranmere Rov	Tr	06.85	85-86	51	8	21
Preston NE	Tr	02.87	86-87	10	13	3
Stockport Co	Tr	11.87	87	18	1	6

WORTHINGTON Frederick (Fred)
Manchester, 6 January, 1924 Died 1995 (IF)

League Club	Source	Date Signed	Seasons Played	Apps	Subs	Gls
Bury		07.47	47-50	69	-	14
Leicester C	Tr	03.51	50-54	55	-	9
Exeter C	Tr	07.55	55	16	-	1
Oldham Ath	Tr	06.56	56	10	-	1

WORTHINGTON Gary Lee
Cleethorpes, 10 November, 1966 EYth (F)

League Club	Source	Date Signed	Seasons Played	Apps	Subs	Gls
Manchester U	App	11.84				
Huddersfield T	Tr	07.86				
Darlington	Tr	07.87	87-88	31	9	15
Wrexham	Tr	06.89	89-90	68	4	18
Wigan Ath	Tr	03.91	90-92	51	12	20
Exeter C	Tr	07.93	93	8	7	1
Doncaster Rov	L	03.94	93	8	0	2

WORTHINGTON Jonathan (Jon) Alan
Dewsbury, 16 April, 1983 (M)

League Club	Source	Date Signed	Seasons Played	Apps	Subs	Gls
Huddersfield T	YT	09.01	02-04	85	15	6

WORTHINGTON Martin Paul
Torquay, 25 January, 1981 (F)

League Club	Source	Date Signed	Seasons Played	Apps	Subs	Gls
Torquay U	YT	07.99	98	0	1	0

WORTHINGTON Nigel
Ballymena, 4 November, 1961 IrLge-1/NIYth/NI-66 (FB)

League Club	Source	Date Signed	Seasons Played	Apps	Subs	Gls
Notts Co	Ballymena U	07.81	81-83	67	0	4
Sheffield Wed	Tr	02.84	83-93	334	4	12
Leeds U	Tr	07.94	94-95	33	10	1
Stoke C	Tr	07.96	96	12	0	0
Blackpool	Tr	07.97	97	4	5	0

WORTHINGTON Peter **Robert (Bob)**
Halifax, 22 April, 1947 (FB)

League Club	Source	Date Signed	Seasons Played	Apps	Subs	Gls
Halifax T	App	05.65	64	12	-	0
Middlesbrough	Tr	08.66	67	2	0	0
Notts Co	Tr	09.68	68-73	230	2	1
Southend U	Tr	08.74	74	20	0	1
Hartlepool	L	03.75	74	6	0	0

WOSAHLO Bradley Edward
Ipswich, 14 February, 1975 (W)

League Club	Source	Date Signed	Seasons Played	Apps	Subs	Gls
Brighton & Hove A	YT	07.93	93	1	0	0
Cambridge U	Sudbury T	12.95	95	0	4	0

WOSAHLO Roger Frank
Cambridge, 11 September, 1947 ESch (W)

League Club	Source	Date Signed	Seasons Played	Apps	Subs	Gls
Chelsea	App	12.64	66	0	1	0
Ipswich T	Tr	07.67	67	1	0	0
Peterborough U	Tr	07.68	68	13	2	1
Ipswich T	Tr	07.69	69	0	1	0

WOTTON Paul Anthony
Plymouth, 17 August, 1977 (CD)

League Club	Source	Date Signed	Seasons Played	Apps	Subs	Gls
Plymouth Arg	YT	07.95	94-04	288	31	41

WRACK Darren
Cleethorpes, 5 May, 1976 (W)

League Club	Source	Date Signed	Seasons Played	Apps	Subs	Gls
Derby Co	YT	07.94	94-95	4	22	1
Grimsby T	Tr	07.96	96-97	5	8	1
Shrewsbury T	L	02.97	96	3	1	0
Walsall	Tr	08.98	98-04	240	34	44

WRAGG Douglas (Doug)
Nottingham, 12 September, 1934 ESch (W)

League Club	Source	Date Signed	Seasons Played	Apps	Subs	Gls
West Ham U		06.53	56-59	16	-	0
Mansfield T	Tr	03.60	59-60	46	-	13
Rochdale	Tr	07.61	61-63	103	-	15
Chesterfield	Tr	07.64	64	17	-	4

WRAGG Peter
Rotherham, 12 January, 1931 Died 2004 ESch (IF)

League Club	Source	Date Signed	Seasons Played	Apps	Subs	Gls
Rotherham U	Jnrs	05.48	48-52	31	-	6
Sheffield U	Tr	01.53	52-55	56	-	17
York C	Tr	08.56	56-62	264	-	78
Bradford C	Tr	07.63	63-64	73	-	5

WRAIGHT Gary Paul
Epping, 5 March, 1979 (FB)

League Club	Source	Date Signed	Seasons Played	Apps	Subs	Gls
Wycombe W	YT	07.97	97-98	7	0	0

WRAITH Robert (Bobby)
Largs, 26 April, 1948 (G)

League Club	Source	Date Signed	Seasons Played	Apps	Subs	Gls
Southport	Glasgow Celtic	07.69	69-70	28	0	0

WRATTEN Paul
Middlesbrough, 29 November, 1970 ESch/EYth (M)

League Club	Source	Date Signed	Seasons Played	Apps	Subs	Gls
Manchester U	YT	12.88	90	0	2	0
Hartlepool U	Tr	09.92	92-93	52	5	1

WRAY John Gordon
Mytholmroyd, 7 July, 1941 (G)

League Club	Source	Date Signed	Seasons Played	Apps	Subs	Gls
Halifax T	Stainland A	11.64	64	7	-	0

WRAY Shaun Warren
Birmingham, 14 March, 1978 (W)

League Club	Source	Date Signed	Seasons Played	Apps	Subs	Gls
Shrewsbury T	YT	07.95	95-96	1	3	0

WREH Christopher
Monrovia, Liberia, 14 May, 1975 Liberia 16 (F)

League Club	Source	Date Signed	Seasons Played	Apps	Subs	Gls
Arsenal	Guingamp (Fr)	08.97	97-98	10	18	3
Birmingham C	L	10.99	99	6	1	1

WREN John (Jackie) Mackie
Bonnybridge, 26 April, 1936 (G)

League Club	Source	Date Signed	Seasons Played	Apps	Subs	Gls
Southend U	Hibernian	05.60				
Rotherham U	Tr	08.60	60	1	-	0

WRENCH Mark Nicholas
Warrington, 27 September, 1969 (FB)

League Club	Source	Date Signed	Seasons Played	Apps	Subs	Gls
Wrexham	YT	09.88	88-89	5	1	0

WRIGGLESWORTH John **Lancelot (Lance)**
Halifax, 4 July, 1924 (IF)

League Club	Source	Date Signed	Seasons Played	Apps	Subs	Gls
Halifax T	Watford (Am)	07.46	46	10	-	1

WRIGGLESWORTH William (Billy) Herbert
South Elmsall, 12 November, 1912 Died 1980 (W)

League Club	Source	Date Signed	Seasons Played	Apps	Subs	Gls
Chesterfield	Frickley Colliery	05.32	32-34	34	-	6
Wolverhampton W	Tr	12.34	34-36	50	-	21
Manchester U	Tr	02.37	36-46	27	-	7
Bolton W	Tr	01.47	46-47	13	-	1
Southampton	Tr	10.47	47	12	-	4
Reading	Tr	06.48	48	5	-	0

WRIGHT Alan Geoffrey
Ashton-under-Lyne, 28 September, 1971 ESch/EYth/Eu21-2 (FB)

League Club	Source	Date Signed	Seasons Played	Apps	Subs	Gls
Blackpool	YT	04.89	87-91	91	7	0
Blackburn Rov	Tr	10.91	91-94	67	7	1
Aston Villa	Tr	03.95	94-02	255	5	5
Middlesbrough	Tr	08.03	03	2	0	0
Sheffield U	Tr	10.03	03-04	32	3	1

WRIGHT Alan George
Birmingham, 20 March, 1938 (IF)

League Club	Source	Date Signed	Seasons Played	Apps	Subs	Gls
Walsall		05.58	58	1	-	1

WRIGHT Albert
Clowne, 21 July, 1925 (G)

League Club	Source	Date Signed	Seasons Played	Apps	Subs	Gls
Lincoln C	Ollerton Colliery	10.46	46	1	-	0

WRIGHT Alexander (Alex) Mason
Kirkcaldy, 18 October, 1925 (IF)

League Club	Source	Date Signed	Seasons Played	Apps	Subs	Gls
Barnsley	Hibernian	08.47	47-50	84	-	31
Tottenham H	Tr	09.50	50	2	-	1
Bradford PA	Tr	08.51	51-54	131	-	25

WRIGHT Andrew (Andy) James
Leeds, 21 October, 1978 (W)

League Club	Source	Date Signed	Seasons Played	Apps	Subs	Gls
Leeds U	YT	10.95				
Reading	L	12.98	98	0	2	0

WRIGHT Anthony (Tony) Allan
Swansea, 1 September, 1979 WYth/Wu21-3/WB-1 (M)

League Club	Source	Date Signed	Seasons Played	Apps	Subs	Gls
Oxford U	YT	12.97	97-98	4	3	0

WRIGHT Archibald (Archie) Watson
Glasgow, 23 November, 1924 Died 1990 (IF)

League Club	Source	Date Signed	Seasons Played	Apps	Subs	Gls
Blackburn Rov	Falkirk	05.51	51-52	22	-	10
Grimsby T	Tr	07.53	53	39	-	9
Accrington St	Tr	06.54	54-56	80	-	27

WRIGHT Arthur William Tempest
Burradon, 23 September, 1919 Died 1985 ESch/FLge-2 (WH)

League Club	Source	Date Signed	Seasons Played	Apps	Subs	Gls
Sunderland	Hylton Colliery	09.36	37-54	270	-	13

WRIGHT Barrie
Bradford, 6 November, 1945 ESch/EYth (FB)

League Club	Source	Date Signed	Seasons Played	Apps	Subs	Gls
Leeds U	App	11.62	62-63	5	-	0
Brighton & Hove A	NY Generals (USA)	01.69	68-69	8	2	0

WRIGHT Barry Albert
Wrexham, 23 July, 1939 (FB)

League Club	Source	Date Signed	Seasons Played	Apps	Subs	Gls
Wrexham	Jnrs	05.59	59-61	11	-	0
Chester	Tr	08.62	62	1	-	0

WRIGHT Benjamin (Ben)
Munster, Germany, 1 July, 1980 (F)

League Club	Source	Date Signed	Seasons Played	Apps	Subs	Gls
Bristol C	Kettering T	03.99	99	0	2	0

WRIGHT Bernard
Walthamstow, 19 September, 1923 (G)

League Club	Source	Date Signed	Seasons Played	Apps	Subs	Gls
Notts Co		02.46	46	2	-	0

WRIGHT Bernard Anthony
Derry, 8 June, 1940 (W)

League Club	Source	Date Signed	Seasons Played	Apps	Subs	Gls
Port Vale	Sligo Rov	09.62	62	14	-	2

WRIGHT Bernard (Bernie) Peter
Birmingham, 17 September, 1952 (F)

League Club	Source	Date Signed	Seasons Played	Apps	Subs	Gls
Walsall	Birmingham C (Am)	09.71	71	15	0	2
Everton	Tr	02.72	71-72	10	1	2
Walsall	Tr	01.73	72-76	145	7	38
Bradford C	Tr	02.77	76-77	65	1	13
Port Vale	Tr	06.78	78-79	76	0	23

WRIGHT George **Brian**
Sunderland, 16 September, 1939 (CD)

League Club	Source	Date Signed	Seasons Played	Apps	Subs	Gls
Newcastle U	Jnrs	09.56	59-62	45	-	1
Peterborough U	Tr	05.63	63-71	291	2	9

WRIGHT Brian Raymond
Leicester, 9 January, 1937 EYth (IF)

League Club	Source	Date Signed	Seasons Played	Apps	Subs	Gls
Leicester C	Jnrs	02.54				
Lincoln C	Tr	01.59	58-60	22	-	3

WRIGHT Charles (Charlie) George
Glasgow, 11 December, 1938 (G)

League Club	Source	Date Signed	Seasons Played	Apps	Subs	Gls
Workington	Glasgow Rgrs	06.58	58-62	123	-	0
Grimsby T	Tr	02.63	62-65	129	0	0
Charlton Ath	Tr	03.66	65-70	195	0	0
Bolton W	Tr	06.71	71-72	88	0	0

WRIGHT George **Clifford (Cliff)**
Lingdale, 18 October, 1944 (M)

League Club	Source	Date Signed	Seasons Played	Apps	Subs	Gls
Middlesbrough	App	10.62				
Hartlepools U	Tr	06.64	64-69	179	5	31
Darlington	Tr	02.70	69-70	16	0	4

WRIGHT Darren
Warrington, 7 September, 1979 (F)

League Club	Source	Date Signed	Seasons Played	Apps	Subs	Gls
Chester C	YT	07.98	97-99	24	24	2

WRIGHT Darren James
West Bromwich, 14 March, 1968 (FB)

League Club	Source	Date Signed	Seasons Played	Apps	Subs	Gls
Wolverhampton W	App	07.85	85	1	0	0
Wrexham	Tr	08.86	86-89	105	5	4

WRIGHT David
Warrington, 1 May, 1980 EYth (FB)

League Club	Source	Date Signed	Seasons Played	Apps	Subs	Gls
Crewe Alex	YT	06.97	97-03	206	5	3
Wigan Ath	Tr	06.04	04	19	12	0

WRIGHT Dennis
Boythorpe, 19 December, 1919 Died 1993 (G)

League Club	Source	Date Signed	Seasons Played	Apps	Subs	Gls
Mansfield T	Clay Lane Rgrs	03.39	46-56	379	-	0

WRIGHT Dennis
Royton, 9 January, 1930 Died 2003 (W)

League Club	Source	Date Signed	Seasons Played	Apps	Subs	Gls
Oldham Ath (Am)	Jnrs	05.46	46	3	-	0
Oldham Ath	Glasgow Rgrs	08.51	51	6	-	0

WRIGHT John **Douglas (Doug)**
Rochford, 29 April, 1917 Died 1992 E-1 (WH)

League Club	Source	Date Signed	Seasons Played	Apps	Subs	Gls
Southend U	Chelmsford C	08.36	36-37	31	-	2
Newcastle U	Tr	05.38	38-46	72	-	1
Lincoln C	Tr	12.48	48-54	233	-	2

WRIGHT Evran
Wolverhampton, 17 January, 1965 (F)

League Club	Source	Date Signed	Seasons Played	Apps	Subs	Gls
Walsall	Halesowen T	08.93	93	16	13	5

WRIGHT Gary
Torquay, 21 May, 1966 (FB)

League Club	Source	Date Signed	Seasons Played	Apps	Subs	Gls
Torquay U	Jnrs	08.84	84	2	0	0
Torquay U	Chard T	08.87	87	1	1	0

WRIGHT Gary
Sunderland, 15 September, 1964 (G)

League Club	Source	Date Signed	Seasons Played	Apps	Subs	Gls
Hartlepool U	App	10.82	82	12	0	0

WRIGHT Geoffrey (Geoff) Derrick
Countesthorpe, 1 March, 1930 (IF)

League Club	Source	Date Signed	Seasons Played	Apps	Subs	Gls
Aston Villa		05.49				
Bournemouth	Tr	06.51				
Walsall	Rugby T	03.52	52	16	-	1

WRIGHT George Albert
Sheffield, 4 February, 1920 (IF)

League Club	Source	Date Signed	Seasons Played	Apps	Subs	Gls
Cardiff C		03.42				
Hull C	Tr	06.46	46	4	-	1

WRIGHT George William
Plymouth, 10 October, 1919 (G)

League Club	Source	Date Signed	Seasons Played	Apps	Subs	Gls
Plymouth Arg	Kitto Institute	10.38	38-46	12	-	0
Colchester U	Tr	07.49	50-54	151	-	0

WRIGHT George William
Ramsgate, 19 March, 1930 Died 2000 (FB)

League Club	Source	Date Signed	Seasons Played	Apps	Subs	Gls
West Ham U	Margate	02.51	51-57	161	-	0
Leyton Orient	Tr	05.58	58-61	87	-	1
Gillingham	Tr	07.62	62	4	-	0

WRIGHT Glenn
Liverpool, 27 May, 1956 (M)

League Club	Source	Date Signed	Seasons Played	Apps	Subs	Gls
Blackburn Rov	App	•	73	1	0	0

WRIGHT Ian Edward
Woolwich, 3 November, 1963 EB/E-33 (F)

League Club	Source	Date Signed	Seasons Played	Apps	Subs	Gls
Crystal Palace	Greenwich Borough	08.85	85-91	206	19	90
Arsenal	Tr	09.91	91-97	212	9	128
West Ham U	Tr	08.98	98	20	2	9
Nottingham F	L	08.99	99	10	0	5
Burnley	Glasgow Celtic	02.00	99	4	11	4

WRIGHT Ian Matthew
Lichfield, 10 March, 1972 (CD)

League Club	Source	Date Signed	Seasons Played	Apps	Subs	Gls
Stoke C	YT	07.90	89-92	6	0	0
Bristol Rov	Tr	09.93	93-95	50	4	1
Hull C	Tr	07.96	96-97	65	8	2

WRIGHT James (Jim) Frank
Whitefield, 19 February, 1924 Died 1994 (G)

League Club	Source	Date Signed	Seasons Played	Apps	Subs	Gls
Accrington St (Am)	Bury Amats	09.47	47	1	-	0

WRIGHT Jeffrey (Jeff) Kenneth
Alston, 23 June, 1952 (M)

League Club	Source	Date Signed	Seasons Played	Apps	Subs	Gls
Wigan Ath	Netherfield	03.74	78-81	139	4	19

WRIGHT Jermaine Malaki
Greenwich, 21 October, 1975 EYth (M)

League Club	Source	Date Signed	Seasons Played	Apps	Subs	Gls
Millwall	YT	11.92				
Wolverhampton W	Tr	12.94	94-97	4	16	0
Doncaster Rov	L	03.96	95	13	0	0
Crewe Alex	Tr	02.98	97-98	47	2	5
Ipswich T	Tr	07.99	99-03	147	37	10
Leeds U	Tr	07.04	04	33	2	3

WRIGHT John (Jackie)
Tyldesley, 11 August, 1926 Died 2005 EB (FB)

League Club	Source	Date Signed	Seasons Played	Apps	Subs	Gls
Blackpool	Mossley	06.46	48-58	159	-	1

WRIGHT John Bryant
South Shields, 16 November, 1922 (CD)

League Club	Source	Date Signed	Seasons Played	Apps	Subs	Gls
Hull C	Tyne Dock U	09.47	47	1	-	0

WRIGHT John Francis Dominic
Aldershot, 13 August, 1933 (G)

League Club	Source	Date Signed	Seasons Played	Apps	Subs	Gls
Colchester U		11.54	54-55	4	-	0
Colchester U	Great Bentley	01.61	60	1	-	0

WRIGHT Jonathan (John)
Newburn, 30 January, 1925 (IF)

League Club	Source	Date Signed	Seasons Played	Apps	Subs	Gls
Darlington		01.47	46-48	17	-	0

WRIGHT Jonathan (Johnny)
Belfast, 24 November, 1975 NIYth/NIB (FB)

League Club	Source	Date Signed	Seasons Played	Apps	Subs	Gls
Norwich C	YT	07.94	94-96	5	2	0

WRIGHT Kenneth (Ken) Laurence
Newmarket, 16 May, 1922 Died 1994 (IF)

League Club	Source	Date Signed	Seasons Played	Apps	Subs	Gls
West Ham U	Cambridge T	05.46	46-49	51	-	20

WRIGHT Mark
Dorchester, Oxfordshire, 1 August, 1963 Eu21-4/E-45 (CD)

League Club	Source	Date Signed	Seasons Played	Apps	Subs	Gls
Oxford U	Jnrs	08.80	81	8	2	0
Southampton	Tr	03.82	81-86	170	0	7
Derby Co	Tr	08.87	87-90	144	0	10
Liverpool	Tr	07.91	91-97	156	2	5

WRIGHT Mark Andrew
Manchester, 29 January, 1970 (FB)

League Club	Source	Date Signed	Seasons Played	Apps	Subs	Gls
Everton	YT	06.88	89	1	0	0
Blackpool	L	08.90	90	3	0	0
Huddersfield T	Tr	03.91	90-92	25	7	1
Wigan Ath	Accrington St	11.93	93-94	27	3	1

WRIGHT Mark Anthony
Wolverhampton, 24 February, 1982 (W)

League Club	Source	Date Signed	Seasons Played	Apps	Subs	Gls
Walsall	YT	01.01	00-04	40	17	4

WRIGHT Mark Stephen
Chorley, 4 September, 1981 (F)

League Club	Source	Date Signed	Seasons Played	Apps	Subs	Gls
Preston NE	YT	04.99	98-99	1	2	0

WRIGHT Martin Harold
Chesterfield, 1 April, 1950 (F)

League Club	Source	Date Signed	Seasons Played	Apps	Subs	Gls
Chesterfield	Alfreton T	10.68	68-71	40	3	12
Torquay U	Tr	07.72	72	8	5	3

WRIGHT Matthew Paul
Norwich, 6 January, 1978 (CD)

League Club	Source	Date Signed	Seasons Played	Apps	Subs	Gls
Torquay U	YT	01.97	96	7	2	0

WRIGHT Michael (Mike)
Darlington, 17 February, 1950 (CD)

League Club	Source	Date Signed	Seasons Played	Apps	Subs	Gls
Darlington	Jnrs	06.68	68-72	82	7	0

WRIGHT Michael (Mick) Eric
Newmarket, 16 January, 1942 (IF)

League Club	Source	Date Signed	Seasons Played	Apps	Subs	Gls
Northampton T	Newmarket T	11.59	59-61	26	-	7

WRIGHT Michael (Mike) Howard
Winsford, 22 October, 1948 (IF)

League Club	Source	Date Signed	Seasons Played	Apps	Subs	Gls
Shrewsbury T	App	●	65	0	1	0

WRIGHT John **Michael (Mick)**
Ellesmere Port, 25 September, 1946 EYth (FB)

League Club	Source	Date Signed	Seasons Played	Apps	Subs	Gls
Aston Villa	App	09.63	63-72	280	2	1

WRIGHT Herbert **Montague (Monty)**
Shirebrook, 29 May, 1931 (IF)

League Club	Source	Date Signed	Seasons Played	Apps	Subs	Gls
Leeds U	Bolsover Colliery	10.51				
Stockport Co	Tr	06.53	53	1	-	0
Chester	Tr	07.54	54	21	-	4

WRIGHT Nicholas (Nick) John
Ilkeston, 15 October, 1975 (W)

League Club	Source	Date Signed	Seasons Played	Apps	Subs	Gls
Derby Co	YT	07.94				
Carlisle U	Tr	11.97	97	25	0	5
Watford	Tr	07.98	98-99	32	5	6

WRIGHT Patrick (Pat) Daniel Joseph
Oldbury, 17 November, 1940 (FB)

League Club	Source	Date Signed	Seasons Played	Apps	Subs	Gls
Birmingham C	Brookfield	11.59	59-61	3	-	0
Shrewsbury T	Tr	09.62	62-67	202	0	4
Derby Co	Tr	10.67	67	12	1	0
Southend U	L	03.70	69	11	0	0
Rotherham U	Tr	09.70	70	2	0	0

WRIGHT Paul Antony
Barking, 29 July, 1969 (F)

League Club	Source	Date Signed	Seasons Played	Apps	Subs	Gls
Halifax T	(USA)	10.92	92	1	0	0

WRIGHT Paul Hamilton
East Kilbride, 17 August, 1967 SYth/Su21-3 (F)

League Club	Source	Date Signed	Seasons Played	Apps	Subs	Gls
Queens Park Rgrs	Aberdeen	07.89	89	9	6	5

WRIGHT Peter Brooke
Colchester, 26 January, 1934 (W)

League Club	Source	Date Signed	Seasons Played	Apps	Subs	Gls
Colchester U	Jnrs	11.51	51-63	427	-	90

WRIGHT Peter David
Preston, 15 August, 1982 (F)

League Club	Source	Date Signed	Seasons Played	Apps	Subs	Gls
Halifax T	Newcastle U (YT)	08.01	01	3	11	0

WRIGHT Ralph Lawrence
Newcastle, 3 August, 1947 (M)

League Club	Source	Date Signed	Seasons Played	Apps	Subs	Gls
Norwich C	Spennymoor U	07.68				
Bradford PA	Tr	10.69	69	13	1	1
Hartlepool	Tr	06.70	70	23	1	3
Stockport Co	Tr	07.71	71	19	2	0
Bolton W	Tr	02.72	71-72	25	7	5
Southport	L	12.72	72	6	0	1
Southport	NY Cosmos (USA)	08.73	73	34	3	2

WRIGHT Horace **Raymond (Ray)**
Pontefract, 6 September, 1918 Died 1987 (IF)

League Club	Source	Date Signed	Seasons Played	Apps	Subs	Gls
Wolverhampton W	Woodbourne Ath	05.36	37-38	8	-	1
Exeter C	Tr	03.46	46-47	56	-	11

WRIGHT Richard (Dick)
Mexborough, 5 December, 1931 Died 2003 (G)

League Club	Source	Date Signed	Seasons Played	Apps	Subs	Gls
Leeds U	Hickleton Main Welf	05.49				
Chester	Tr	08.51	52-54	52	-	0

WRIGHT Richard Ian
Ipswich, 5 November, 1977 ESch/EYth/Eu21-15/E-2 (G)

League Club	Source	Date Signed	Seasons Played	Apps	Subs	Gls
Ipswich T	YT	01.95	94-00	240	0	0
Arsenal	Tr	07.01	01	12	0	0
Everton	Tr	07.02	02-04	43	1	0

WRIGHT Robert (Bob) Cooper Allen
Glasgow, 20 February, 1916 Died 1998 (WH)

League Club	Source	Date Signed	Seasons Played	Apps	Subs	Gls
Charlton Ath	Horden CW	05.37	38-46	28	-	0

WRIGHT Ronald (Ronnie) William
Glasgow, 6 December, 1940 (IF)

League Club	Source	Date Signed	Seasons Played	Apps	Subs	Gls
Leeds U	Shettleston Rov	06.59	60	1	-	0

WRIGHT Stephen
Bellshill, 27 August, 1971 Su21-14/SB-2/S-2 (FB)

League Club	Source	Date Signed	Seasons Played	Apps	Subs	Gls
Wolverhampton W (L)	Glasgow Rgrs	03.98	97	3	0	0
Bradford C	Glasgow Rgrs	07.98	98	21	1	0
Scunthorpe U	Dundee U	09.02	02	2	0	0

WRIGHT Stephen John
Liverpool, 8 February, 1980 EYth/Eu21-6 (FB)

League Club	Source	Date Signed	Seasons Played	Apps	Subs	Gls
Liverpool	YT	10.97	00-01	10	4	0
Crewe Alex	L	08.99	99	17	6	0
Sunderland	Tr	08.02	02-04	84	3	2

WRIGHT Stephen (Steve) Peter
Clacton, 16 June, 1959 (CD)

League Club	Source	Date Signed	Seasons Played	Apps	Subs	Gls
Colchester U	Jnrs	06.77	77-81	112	5	3
Wrexham	HJK Helsinki (Fin)	09.83	83-84	76	0	0
Torquay U	Tr	07.85	85	33	0	0
Crewe Alex	Tr	07.86	86-87	67	5	3

WRIGHT Terence (Terry) Ian
Newcastle, 22 June, 1939 (W)

League Club	Source	Date Signed	Seasons Played	Apps	Subs	Gls
Barrow	Nuneaton Borough	11.62	62-64	10	-	0

WRIGHT Thomas (Tommy)
Clackmannan, 20 January, 1928 S-3 (W)

League Club	Source	Date Signed	Seasons Played	Apps	Subs	Gls
Sunderland	Partick Th	03.49	48-54	170	-	51
Oldham Ath	East Fife	03.57	56	7	-	2

WRIGHT Thomas (Tommy) Andrew
Kirby Muxloe, 28 September, 1984 EYth (F)

League Club	Source	Date Signed	Seasons Played	Apps	Subs	Gls
Leicester C	Sch	06.03	01-04	3	18	2
Brentford	L	09.03	03	18	7	3

WRIGHT Thomas (Tom) Birtles
Glossop, 11 January, 1917 Died 1995 (W)

League Club	Source	Date Signed	Seasons Played	Apps	Subs	Gls
Manchester C	Droylsden	06.37				
Hull C	Altrincham	07.47				
Accrington St	Tr	10.47	47-48	20	-	4

WRIGHT Thomas (Tommy) Elliott
Dunfermline, 10 January, 1966 SYth/Su21-1 (W)

League Club	Source	Date Signed	Seasons Played	Apps	Subs	Gls
Leeds U	App	01.83	82-85	73	8	24
Oldham Ath	Tr	10.86	86-88	110	2	23
Leicester C	Tr	08.89	89-91	122	7	22
Middlesbrough	Tr	07.92	92-94	44	9	5
Bradford C	Tr	07.95	95-96	30	15	5
Oldham Ath	Tr	08.97	97	10	2	2

WRIGHT Thomas (Tommy) James
Liverpool, 21 October, 1944 Eu23-7/E-11 (FB)

League Club	Source	Date Signed	Seasons Played	Apps	Subs	Gls
Everton	Jnrs	03.63	64-72	307	1	4

WRIGHT Thomas (Tommy) James
Belfast, 29 August, 1963 FLge/NIu23-1/NI-31 (G)

League Club	Source	Date Signed	Seasons Played	Apps	Subs	Gls
Newcastle U	Linfield	01.88	88-93	72	1	0
Hull C	L	02.91	90	6	0	0
Nottingham F	Tr	09.93	93-96	11	0	0
Reading	L	10.96	96	17	0	0
Manchester C	L	01.97	96	5	0	0
Manchester C	Tr	03.97	96-00	29	0	0
Wrexham	L	02.99	98	16	0	0
Newcastle U	L	08.99	99	3	0	0
Bolton W	L	01.01	00	3	1	0

WRIGHT Thomas (Tommy) Kentigern
Stepps, 11 January, 1925 (W)

League Club	Source	Date Signed	Seasons Played	Apps	Subs	Gls
Aldershot	Dunfermline Ath	07.52	52	14	-	1

WRIGHT Vincent (Vince)
Bradford, 12 April, 1931 EYth (W)

League Club	Source	Date Signed	Seasons Played	Apps	Subs	Gls
Derby Co		09.51				
Mansfield T	Tr	07.52	52	2	-	0

WRIGHT William (Billy)
Liverpool, 28 April, 1958 Eu21-6/EB (CD)

League Club	Source	Date Signed	Seasons Played	Apps	Subs	Gls
Everton	Jnrs	01.77	77-82	164	2	10
Birmingham C	Tr	07.83	83-85	111	0	9
Chester C	L	02.86	85	6	0	1
Carlisle U	Tr	08.86	86-87	87	0	3

WRIGHT William (Billy) Ambrose
Ironbridge, 6 February, 1924 Died 1994 FLge-21/EWar-4/E-105 (WH)

League Club	Source	Date Signed	Seasons Played	Apps	Subs	Gls
Wolverhampton W	Jnrs	02.41	46-58	490	-	13

WRIGHT William (Billy) Hardy Rogers
Corbridge, 4 November, 1962 (F)

League Club	Source	Date Signed	Seasons Played	Apps	Subs	Gls
Burnley		01.81				
Crewe Alex	L	11.82	82	3	0	1

WRIGHT John **William (Billy)**
Blackpool, 4 March, 1931 (W)

League Club	Source	Date Signed	Seasons Played	Apps	Subs	Gls
Blackpool		05.50	51-54	15	-	2
Leicester C	Tr	08.55	55-57	27	-	10
Newcastle U	Tr	08.58	58	5	-	3
Plymouth Arg	Tr	08.59	59-60	42	-	9
Millwall	Tr	08.61	61	15	-	0

WRIGHT William (Billy) Stephen
Wordsley, 26 April, 1959 (FB)

League Club	Source	Date Signed	Seasons Played	Apps	Subs	Gls
Birmingham C	App	04.77				
Lincoln C	Tr	07.78	78	3	0	0

WRIGHT-PHILLIPS Bradley Edward
Lewisham, 12 March, 1985 EYth (F)

League Club	Source	Date Signed	Seasons Played	Apps	Subs	Gls
Manchester C	Sch	07.02	04	0	14	1

WRIGHT-PHILLIPS Shaun Cameron
Greenwich, 25 October, 1981 Eu21-6/E-4 (W)

League Club	Source	Date Signed	Seasons Played	Apps	Subs	Gls
Manchester C	YT	10.98	99-04	130	23	26

WRIGHTSON Jeffrey (Jeff) George
Newcastle, 18 May, 1968 (CD)

League Club	Source	Date Signed	Seasons Played	Apps	Subs	Gls
Newcastle U	App	05.86	86	3	1	0
Preston NE	Tr	07.87	87-91	161	5	4

WRIGLEY Wilfred (Wilf)
Clitheroe, 4 October, 1949 (CD)

League Club	Source	Date Signed	Seasons Played	Apps	Subs	Gls
Burnley	Jnrs	07.68	68-69	6	0	1

WRING Daniel (Danny) Ronald
Portishead, 26 October, 1986 (M)

League Club	Source	Date Signed	Seasons Played	Apps	Subs	Gls
Bristol C	Sch	•	04	0	1	0

WROE Mark
Manchester, 1 June, 1966 (W)

League Club	Source	Date Signed	Seasons Played	Apps	Subs	Gls
Stockport Co	Jnrs	08.85	84-85	26	4	4

WROE Nicholas (Nicky)
Sheffield, 28 September, 1985 (M)

League Club	Source	Date Signed	Seasons Played	Apps	Subs	Gls
Barnsley	Sch	08.04	02-04	28	6	1

WYATT George Albert
Whitechapel, 28 March, 1924 Died 1957 (FB)

League Club	Source	Date Signed	Seasons Played	Apps	Subs	Gls
Crystal Palace		11.47	48	7	-	0

WYATT Michael (Mike) James
Bristol, 12 September, 1974 (W)

League Club	Source	Date Signed	Seasons Played	Apps	Subs	Gls
Bristol C	YT	07.93	93-94	9	4	0
Bristol Rov	Tr	07.95	95	3	1	0

WYATT Reginald (Reg) Gordon
Plymouth, 18 September, 1932 (CD)

League Club	Source	Date Signed	Seasons Played	Apps	Subs	Gls
Plymouth Arg	Oak Villa	08.50	55-64	202	-	2
Torquay U	Tr	10.64	64-66	80	0	6

WYER Peter William
Coventry, 10 February, 1937 (IF)

League Club	Source	Date Signed	Seasons Played	Apps	Subs	Gls
Coventry C		10.55	55	1	-	0
Derby Co	Tr	06.56	56	2	-	1
Coventry C	Tr	07.58	58	4	-	0

WYLDE Rodger James
Sheffield, 8 March, 1954 (F)

League Club	Source	Date Signed	Seasons Played	Apps	Subs	Gls
Sheffield Wed	App	07.71	72-79	157	11	54
Oldham Ath	Tr	02.80	79-82	109	4	51
Sunderland	Sporting Lisbon (Por)	07.84	84	8	3	3
Barnsley	Tr	12.84	84-87	50	2	19
Rotherham U	L	03.88	87	6	0	1
Stockport Co	Tr	07.88	88	24	2	12

WYLDES Robert (Bobby) Jack
Southport, 6 October, 1928 (W)

League Club	Source	Date Signed	Seasons Played	Apps	Subs	Gls
Luton T	Desborough	10.49	49-51	26	-	8

WYLES Thomas **Cecil (Cec)**
Gosberton Clough, 1 November, 1919 Died 1990 (CF)

League Club	Source	Date Signed	Seasons Played	Apps	Subs	Gls
Everton	Peterborough U	02.38				
Blackburn Rov	Tr	10.45				
Bury	Tr	05.46	46	2	-	0
Southport	Tr	11.46	46-49	143	-	53

WYLES Harold
Melton Mowbray, 28 October, 1922 Died 1982 (FB)

League Club	Source	Date Signed	Seasons Played	Apps	Subs	Gls
Leicester C		04.42				
Gateshead	Tr	03.48	47-53	234	-	7

WYLIE John Edward
Newcastle, 25 September, 1936 (WH)

League Club	Source	Date Signed	Seasons Played	Apps	Subs	Gls
Huddersfield T		09.54				
Preston NE	Tr	05.57	58-62	91	-	1
Stockport Co	Tr	11.62	62-63	69	-	2
Doncaster Rov	Tr	08.64	64-67	123	1	2

WYLIE Ronald (Ron) Maurice
Glasgow, 6 August, 1933 SSch (M)

League Club	Source	Date Signed	Seasons Played	Apps	Subs	Gls
Notts Co	Clydesdale Jnrs	09.50	51-58	227	-	36
Aston Villa	Tr	11.58	58-64	196	-	16
Birmingham C	Tr	06.65	65-69	125	3	2

WYLLIE James (Jimmy)
Saltcoats, 15 October, 1927 Died 1992 (IF)

League Club	Source	Date Signed	Seasons Played	Apps	Subs	Gls
Southport	Kilmarnock	07.50	50	15	-	1
Wrexham	Tr	12.50	50	20	-	4

WYLLIE Robinson (Bob) Gourlay Nicholl
Dundee, 4 April, 1929 Died 1981 (G)

League Club	Source	Date Signed	Seasons Played	Apps	Subs	Gls
Blackpool	Dundee U	05.53	53-54	13	-	0
West Ham U	Tr	05.56	56	13	-	0
Plymouth Arg	Tr	07.58	58	5	-	0
Mansfield T	Tr	10.59	59-61	92	-	0

WYNN Walter **Ronald (Ron)**
Wrexham, 2 November, 1923 Died 1983 (CD)

League Club	Source	Date Signed	Seasons Played	Apps	Subs	Gls
Wrexham		04.48	47-55	182	-	12

WYNNE Darren Lee
St Asaph, 12 October, 1970 (M)

League Club	Source	Date Signed	Seasons Played	Apps	Subs	Gls
Chester C	YT	07.89	88-89	0	12	0

XAUSA Davide Antonio
Vancouver, Canada, 10 March, 1976 Canada int (F)

League Club	Source	Date Signed	Seasons Played	Apps	Subs	Gls
Port Vale	Vancouver (Can)	01.98				
Stoke C	Tr	02.98	97	1	0	0

XAVIER Abel
Nampula, Mozambique, 30 November, 1972 PorYth/Poru21/Por-20 (FB)

League Club	Source	Date Signed	Seasons Played	Apps	Subs	Gls
Everton	PSV Eindhoven (Holl)	09.99	99-01	39	4	0
Liverpool	Tr	01.02	01-02	13	1	1

YAKUBU Ayegbeni
Benin City, Nigeria, 22 November, 1982 Nigeria int (F)

League Club	Source	Date Signed	Seasons Played	Apps	Subs	Gls
Portsmouth	Maccabi Haifa (Isr)	01.03	02-04	76	5	35

YALCIN Levent
Middlesbrough, 25 March, 1985 TuYth (F)

League Club	Source	Date Signed	Seasons Played	Apps	Subs	Gls
York C	YT	●	02-03	5	15	0

YALLOP Frank Walter
Watford, 4 April, 1964 EYth (FB)

League Club	Source	Date Signed	Seasons Played	Apps	Subs	Gls
Ipswich T	App	01.82	83-95	289	27	7
Blackpool	L	11.95	95	3	0	0

YANUSHEVSKI Victor
Minsk, Belarus, 23 January, 1960 Died 1993 (CD)

League Club	Source	Date Signed	Seasons Played	Apps	Subs	Gls
Aldershot	CSKA Moscow (Rus)	03.91	90	6	0	1

YARD Ernest (Ernie) John
Stranraer, 3 May, 1941 Died 2004 (M)

League Club	Source	Date Signed	Seasons Played	Apps	Subs	Gls
Bury	Partick Th	12.63	63-64	45	-	13
Crystal Palace	Tr	05.65	65-66	35	2	3
Reading	Tr	11.66	66-68	101	3	6

YARDLEY George McArthur
Kirkcaldy, 8 October, 1942 (F)

League Club	Source	Date Signed	Seasons Played	Apps	Subs	Gls
Luton T	(Australia)	10.66	66	1	0	0
Tranmere Rov	Tr	11.66	66-70	123	0	68

YATES David (Sammy)
Barnsley, 18 March, 1953 (FB)

League Club	Source	Date Signed	Seasons Played	Apps	Subs	Gls
Barnsley	App	03.71	72-77	104	0	2
Grimsby T	L	03.77	76	10	0	0

YATES Dean Richard
Leicester, 26 October, 1967 Eu21-5 (CD)

League Club	Source	Date Signed	Seasons Played	Apps	Subs	Gls
Notts Co	App	06.85	84-94	312	2	33
Derby Co	Tr	01.95	94-97	65	3	3
Watford	Tr	07.98	98	9	0	1

YATES Harry
Huddersfield, 28 September, 1925 Died 1987 (IF)

League Club	Source	Date Signed	Seasons Played	Apps	Subs	Gls
Huddersfield T	Jnrs	10.43	49	1	-	0
Darlington	Tr	05.50	50-51	91	-	29

YATES John
Rotherham, 18 November, 1929 (W)

League Club	Source	Date Signed	Seasons Played	Apps	Subs	Gls
Sheffield U		06.50				
Chester	Tr	08.51	51	2	-	0

YATES Mark Jason
Birmingham, 24 January, 1970 ESemiPro-2 (M)

League Club	Source	Date Signed	Seasons Played	Apps	Subs	Gls
Birmingham C	YT	07.88	87-91	38	16	6
Burnley	Tr	08.91	91-92	9	9	1
Lincoln C	L	02.93	92	10	4	0
Doncaster Rov	Tr	07.93	93	33	1	4
Cheltenham T	Kidderminster Hrs	01.99	99-03	190	4	19
Kidderminster Hrs	Tr	02.04	03	14	0	2

YATES Richard (Dick)
Queensferry, 6 June, 1921 Died 1976 (CF)

League Club	Source	Date Signed	Seasons Played	Apps	Subs	Gls
Chester	Wolverhampton W (Am)	08.39	46-47	52	-	37
Wrexham	Tr	12.47	47-48	31	-	18
Carlisle U	Tr	11.48	48	16	-	9
New Brighton	Tr	08.49	49-50	43	-	14

YATES Stephen (Steve)
Measham, 8 December, 1953 (FB)

League Club	Source	Date Signed	Seasons Played	Apps	Subs	Gls
Leicester C	App	12.71	73-76	12	7	0
Southend U	Tr	11.77	77-83	223	2	8
Doncaster Rov	Tr	12.83	83-84	44	0	1
Darlington	L	01.85	84	4	0	0
Chesterfield	L	03.85	84	1	0	0
Stockport Co	Tr	08.85	85	2	0	0

YATES Stephen (Steve)
Bristol, 29 January, 1970 (CD)

League Club	Source	Date Signed	Seasons Played	Apps	Subs	Gls
Bristol Rov	YT	07.88	86-93	196	1	0
Queens Park Rgrs	Tr	08.93	93-98	122	12	2
Tranmere Rov	Tr	08.99	99-01	109	4	7
Sheffield U	Tr	07.02	02	11	1	0
Huddersfield T	Tr	08.03	03-04	50	2	1

YEATES Mark Stephen
Dublin, 11 January, 1985 IRYth/IRu21-3 (M)

League Club	Source	Date Signed	Seasons Played	Apps	Subs	Gls
Tottenham H	Sch	07.02	03-04	1	2	0
Brighton & Hove A	L	11.03	03	9	0	0
Swindon T	L	08.04	04	3	1	0

YEATS Ronald (Ron)
Aberdeen, 15 November, 1937 SSch/S-2 (CD)

League Club	Source	Date Signed	Seasons Played	Apps	Subs	Gls
Liverpool	Dundee U	07.61	61-70	357	1	13
Tranmere Rov	Tr	12.71	71-73	96	1	5

YEATS Thomas (Tom) Brandon
Newcastle, 30 May, 1935 (W)

League Club	Source	Date Signed	Seasons Played	Apps	Subs	Gls
Sunderland	Jnrs	02.53				
Gateshead	Tr	08.54	54	1	-	0

YEATS William (Billy)
Hebburn, 4 February, 1951 (F)

League Club	Source	Date Signed	Seasons Played	Apps	Subs	Gls
Newcastle U	North Shields	06.71				
York C	Tr	03.72	71-72	8	1	0
Darlington	Tr	08.73	73-74	22	3	7

YEBOAH Anthony (Tony)
Kumasi, Ghana, 6 June, 1966 Ghana int (F)

League Club	Source	Date Signed	Seasons Played	Apps	Subs	Gls
Leeds U	Eintracht Frankfurt (Ger)	01.95	94-96	44	3	24

YELLDELL David Raymond
Stuttgart, Germany, 1 October, 1981 (G)

League Club	Source	Date Signed	Seasons Played	Apps	Subs	Gls
Blackburn Rov	Stuttgart Kickers (Ger)	07.03				
Brighton & Hove A	L	01.05	04	3	0	0

YEO Brian Geoffrey
Worthing, 12 April, 1944 (F)

League Club	Source	Date Signed	Seasons Played	Apps	Subs	Gls
Portsmouth	Jnrs	05.61				
Gillingham	Tr	07.63	63-74	345	11	137

YEO Simon John
Stockport, 20 October, 1973 (F)

League Club	Source	Date Signed	Seasons Played	Apps	Subs	Gls
Lincoln C	Hyde U	08.02	02-04	73	49	37

YEOMAN Ramon (Ray) Irvine
Perth, 13 May, 1934 Died 2004 (WH)

League Club	Source	Date Signed	Seasons Played	Apps	Subs	Gls
Northampton T	St Johnstone	09.53	53-58	169	-	4
Middlesbrough	Tr	11.58	58-63	210	-	3
Darlington	Tr	06.64	64-66	104	0	2

YEOMANS Kelvin
Nottingham, 25 August, 1947 (FB)

League Club	Source	Date Signed	Seasons Played	Apps	Subs	Gls
Notts Co	Beeston	06.67	67	1	0	0

YEOMANSON John (Jack) William
Margate, 3 March, 1920 Died 1997 (FB)

League Club	Source	Date Signed	Seasons Played	Apps	Subs	Gls
West Ham U	Margate	02.47	47-50	106	-	1

YETTON Stewart David
Plymouth, 27 July, 1985 (F)

League Club	Source	Date Signed	Seasons Played	Apps	Subs	Gls
Plymouth Arg	Sch	08.04	02-04	0	3	0

YEUELL Jasper Herbert
Bilston, 23 March, 1925 Died 2003 (FB)

League Club	Source	Date Signed	Seasons Played	Apps	Subs	Gls
Portsmouth	West Bromwich A (Am)	08.46	46-51	30	-	0
Barnsley	Tr	08.52	52	19	-	0

YOBO Joseph
Kano, Nigeria, 6 September, 1980 Nigeria int (CD)

League Club	Source	Date Signed	Seasons Played	Apps	Subs	Gls
Everton	Marseille (Fr)	08.02	02-04	68	11	2

YORATH Terence (Terry) Charles
Cardiff, 27 March, 1950 WSch/Wu23-7/W-59 (M)

League Club	Source	Date Signed	Seasons Played	Apps	Subs	Gls
Leeds U	App	04.67	67-76	121	20	10
Coventry C	Tr	08.76	76-78	99	0	3
Tottenham H	Tr	08.79	79-80	44	4	1
Bradford C	Vancouver (Can)	12.82	82-84	22	5	0
Swansea C	Tr	10.86	86	1	0	0

[YORDI] GONZALEZ DIAZ Jorge
San Fernando, Spain, 14 September, 1974 (F)

League Club	Source	Date Signed	Seasons Played	Apps	Subs	Gls
Blackburn Rov (L)	Real Zaragoza (Sp)	02.02	01	5	3	2

YORK Allan
Newcastle, 13 July, 1941 (FB)

League Club	Source	Date Signed	Seasons Played	Apps	Subs	Gls
Bradford C	Gateshead	02.65	64-66	42	3	2

YORKE Dwight
Canaan, Tobago, 3 November, 1971 Trinidad int (F)

League Club	Source	Date Signed	Seasons Played	Apps	Subs	Gls
Aston Villa	Signal Hill (Tobago)	12.89	89-98	195	36	73
Manchester U	Tr	08.98	98-01	80	16	48
Blackburn Rov	Tr	07.02	02-04	42	18	12
Birmingham C	Tr	08.04	04	4	9	2

YOUDS Edward (Eddie) Paul
Liverpool, 3 May, 1970 (CD)

League Club	Source	Date Signed	Seasons Played	Apps	Subs	Gls
Everton	YT	06.88	90	5	3	0
Cardiff C	L	12.89	89	0	1	0
Wrexham	L	02.90	89	20	0	2
Ipswich T	Tr	11.91	91-94	38	12	1
Bradford C	L	01.95	94	7	0	2
Bradford C	Tr	03.95	94-97	78	0	6
Charlton Ath	Tr	03.98	97-99	52	1	2
Huddersfield T	Tr	07.02	02	25	0	0

YOULDEN Thomas (Tommy) Frederick
Islington, 8 July, 1949 ESch (CD)

League Club	Source	Date Signed	Seasons Played	Apps	Subs	Gls
Arsenal	App	07.66				
Portsmouth	Tr	04.68	68-71	82	7	1
Reading	Tr	07.72	72-76	161	2	3
Aldershot	Tr	04.77	76-80	118	5	1

YOUNG Alan James
Swindon, 12 August, 1983 EYth (F)

League Club	Source	Date Signed	Seasons Played	Apps	Subs	Gls
Swindon T	YT	10.00	00-02	7	22	1

YOUNG Albert Edward
Caerleon, 11 September, 1917 (FB)

League Club	Source	Date Signed	Seasons Played	Apps	Subs	Gls
Arsenal		09.38				
Swindon T	Tr	06.46	46-49	123	-	1

YOUNG Alexander (Alex)
Loanhead, 3 February, 1937 Su23-6/SLge-2/S-8 (F)

League Club	Source	Date Signed	Seasons Played	Apps	Subs	Gls
Everton	Heart of Midlothian	11.60	60-67	227	1	77
Stockport Co	Glentoran	11.68	68	23	0	5

YOUNG Alexander (Alan) Forbes
Kirkcaldy, 26 October, 1955 SSch (F)

League Club	Source	Date Signed	Seasons Played	Apps	Subs	Gls
Oldham Ath	Kirkcaldy YMCA	07.74	74-78	107	15	30
Leicester C	Tr	07.79	79-81	102	2	26
Sheffield U	Tr	08.82	82	23	3	7
Brighton & Hove A	Tr	08.83	83	25	1	12
Notts Co	Tr	09.84	84-85	39	4	13
Rochdale	Tr	08.86	86	19	9	2

YOUNG Allan Robert
Hornsey, 20 January, 1941 (CD)

League Club	Source	Date Signed	Seasons Played	Apps	Subs	Gls
Arsenal	Jnrs	04.59	60	4	-	0
Chelsea	Tr	11.61	61-66	20	0	0
Torquay U	Tr	01.69	68-71	59	0	1

YOUNG Thomas **Anthony (Tony)**
Urmston, 24 December, 1952 (FB)

League Club	Source	Date Signed	Seasons Played	Apps	Subs	Gls
Manchester U	App	12.69	70-75	69	14	1
Charlton Ath	Tr	01.76	75-76	20	0	1
York C	Tr	09.76	76-78	76	2	2

YOUNG Ashley Simon
Stevenage, 9 July, 1985 (F)

League Club	Source	Date Signed	Seasons Played	Apps	Subs	Gls
Watford	Jnrs	07.02	03-04	15	24	3

YOUNG Charles (Charlie) Frederick
Nicosia, Cyprus, 14 February, 1958 (FB)

League Club	Source	Date Signed	Seasons Played	Apps	Subs	Gls
Aston Villa	App	11.75	76	9	1	0
Gillingham	Tr	03.78	77-81	27	1	1

YOUNG Christopher (Chris) William
Manchester, 11 August, 1979 (F)

League Club	Source	Date Signed	Seasons Played	Apps	Subs	Gls
Mansfield T	YT	•	96	0	1	0

YOUNG Clarence (Clarrie) William
Bow, 23 February, 1920 (W)

League Club	Source	Date Signed	Seasons Played	Apps	Subs	Gls
Coventry C	Margate	09.38	46	1	-	0

YOUNG David
Newcastle, 12 November, 1945 (CD)

League Club	Source	Date Signed	Seasons Played	Apps	Subs	Gls
Newcastle U	Jnrs	09.64	69-72	41	2	2
Sunderland	Tr	01.73	72-73	24	6	1
Charlton Ath	Tr	08.74	74-76	76	1	0
Southend U	Tr	09.76	76-77	56	4	0

YOUNG David
Birkenhead, 27 April, 1962 (M)

League Club	Source	Date Signed	Seasons Played	Apps	Subs	Gls
Wigan Ath	Mossley	03.83	82	3	0	0

YOUNG David Alan
Trimdon, 31 January, 1965 (FB)

League Club	Source	Date Signed	Seasons Played	Apps	Subs	Gls
Darlington	App	01.83	82-83	13	5	0

YOUNG Douglas (Doug)
Islington, 2 February, 1927 Died 2001 EAmat (FB)

League Club	Source	Date Signed	Seasons Played	Apps	Subs	Gls
Southend U	Walthamstow Ave	06.53	53-55	38	-	0

YOUNG Eric
Singapore, 25 March, 1960 W-21 (CD)

League Club	Source	Date Signed	Seasons Played	Apps	Subs	Gls
Brighton & Hove A	Slough T	11.82	83-86	126	0	10
Wimbledon	Tr	07.87	87-89	96	3	9
Crystal Palace	Tr	08.90	90-94	161	0	15
Wolverhampton W	Tr	09.95	95-96	31	0	2

YOUNG Eric Royston
Stockton, 26 November, 1952 ESch/EYth (M)

League Club	Source	Date Signed	Seasons Played	Apps	Subs	Gls
Manchester U	App	12.69				
Peterborough U	L	11.72	72	24	1	2
Walsall	L	10.73	73	8	0	0
Stockport Co	L	01.74	73	16	0	0
Darlington	Tr	07.74	74-77	123	7	15

YOUNG George
Dundee, 2 November, 1919 Died 1982 (IF)

League Club	Source	Date Signed	Seasons Played	Apps	Subs	Gls
Watford	Hibernian	07.46	46-48	43	-	5

YOUNG Robert **George**
Newport, 5 January, 1950 Wu23-1 (M)

League Club	Source	Date Signed	Seasons Played	Apps	Subs	Gls
Newport Co	Cromwell Jnrs	07.67	67-71	90	15	6

YOUNG Gerald (Gerry) Morton
Jarrow, 1 October, 1936 E-1 (CD)

League Club	Source	Date Signed	Seasons Played	Apps	Subs	Gls
Sheffield Wed	Hawthorn Leslie	05.55	56-70	308	2	13

YOUNG Gregory (Greg) James
Doncaster, 25 April, 1983 (CD)

League Club	Source	Date Signed	Seasons Played	Apps	Subs	Gls
Grimsby T	Sheffield Wed (YT)	07.02	02-04	13	11	0

YOUNG Jamie Iain
Brisbane, Australia, 25 August, 1985 EYth (G)

League Club	Source	Date Signed	Seasons Played	Apps	Subs	Gls
Reading	Sch	10.03	03	0	1	0

YOUNG John
Hartlepool, 9 November, 1951 (W)

League Club	Source	Date Signed	Seasons Played	Apps	Subs	Gls
Hartlepool	Newcastle U (Am)	08.68	68	3	0	0

YOUNG John Robert
Gateshead, 19 October, 1925 Died 1988 (G)

League Club	Source	Date Signed	Seasons Played	Apps	Subs	Gls
Gateshead (Am)		08.49	49	4	-	0

YOUNG Kenneth (Ken)
Halifax, 11 June, 1930 (IF)

League Club	Source	Date Signed	Seasons Played	Apps	Subs	Gls
Halifax T	Jnrs	11.49	49	1	-	0

YOUNG Kevin
Sunderland, 12 August, 1961 (M)

League Club	Source	Date Signed	Seasons Played	Apps	Subs	Gls
Burnley	App	05.79	78-83	114	6	11
Torquay U	L	11.83	83	3	0	1
Port Vale	L	12.83	83	28	0	4
Bury	Tr	07.84	84-86	85	3	10

YOUNG Leonard (Len) Archibald
West Ham, 23 February, 1912 (CD)

League Club	Source	Date Signed	Seasons Played	Apps	Subs	Gls
West Ham U	Ilford	04.34	33-37	12	-	0
Reading	Tr	11.37	37-47	84	-	0
Brighton & Hove A	Tr	02.48	47-48	8	-	0

YOUNG Luke Paul
Harlow, 19 July, 1979 EYth/Eu21-12/E-2 (FB)

League Club	Source	Date Signed	Seasons Played	Apps	Subs	Gls
Tottenham H	YT	07.97	98-00	44	14	0
Charlton Ath	Tr	07.01	01-04	120	6	2

YOUNG Martin
Grimsby, 9 April, 1955 (CD)

League Club	Source	Date Signed	Seasons Played	Apps	Subs	Gls
Grimsby T	Jnrs	03.74	74-78	87	7	4

YOUNG Michael Samuel
Chester-le-Street, 15 March, 1973 (W)

League Club	Source	Date Signed	Seasons Played	Apps	Subs	Gls
Middlesbrough	Newcastle U (YT)	07.91	91	0	1	0

YOUNG Neil Anthony
Harlow, 31 August, 1973 (FB)

League Club	Source	Date Signed	Seasons Played	Apps	Subs	Gls
Tottenham H	YT	08.91				
Bournemouth	Tr	10.94	94-04	314	18	4

YOUNG Neil James
Manchester, 17 February, 1944 EYth (F)

League Club	Source	Date Signed	Seasons Played	Apps	Subs	Gls
Manchester C	App	02.61	61-71	332	2	86
Preston NE	Tr	01.72	71-73	67	3	16
Rochdale	Tr	07.74	74	8	5	4

YOUNG Noel Johnston
Derry, 22 December, 1932 IrLge-3 (WH)

League Club	Source	Date Signed	Seasons Played	Apps	Subs	Gls
Middlesbrough	Jnrs	04.50				
Doncaster Rov	Tr	01.55	54	3	-	0

YOUNG Quintin
Irvine, 19 September, 1947 Su23-1 (W)

League Club	Source	Date Signed	Seasons Played	Apps	Subs	Gls
Coventry C	Ayr U	07.71	71-72	25	1	2

YOUNG George Raymond (Ray)
Derby, 14 March, 1934 ESch (CD)

League Club	Source	Date Signed	Seasons Played	Apps	Subs	Gls
Derby Co	Jnrs	03.51	53-65	253	1	5

YOUNG Richard (Dick)
Felling, 13 July, 1939 Died 1988 (CF)

League Club	Source	Date Signed	Seasons Played	Apps	Subs	Gls
Newcastle U	Usworth Jnrs	07.57				
Grimsby T	South Shields	03.62	62-64	33	-	13
Stockport Co	Tr	05.65	65	27	0	5

YOUNG Richard Anthony
Nottingham, 18 October, 1968 (F)

League Club	Source	Date Signed	Seasons Played	Apps	Subs	Gls
Notts Co	App	08.86	86	18	17	5
Southend U	Tr	08.87	87-88	5	4	0
Exeter C	Tr	03.89	88-90	32	17	10

YOUNG Richard (Dick) Harter
Gateshead, 17 April, 1918 Died 1989 (FB)

League Club	Source	Date Signed	Seasons Played	Apps	Subs	Gls
Sheffield U	Hebburn St Cuthbert's	11.35	36-48	71	-	0
Lincoln C	Tr	03.49	48-53	100	-	2

YOUNG Robert (Bob) George
Bournemouth, 24 December, 1923 (FB)

League Club	Source	Date Signed	Seasons Played	Apps	Subs	Gls
Bournemouth	Jnrs	01.46	47	1	-	0
Crewe Alex	Tr	06.48	48-51	144	-	2

YOUNG Cecil Rodney (Ron)
Bournemouth, 22 July, 1925 Died 1991 (WH)

League Club	Source	Date Signed	Seasons Played	Apps	Subs	Gls
Bournemouth	Southampton (Am)	06.48	48-49	18	-	0

YOUNG Ronald (Ron)
Dunston-on-Tyne, 31 August, 1945 (W)

League Club	Source	Date Signed	Seasons Played	Apps	Subs	Gls
Hull C		08.63	64-67	24	2	5
Hartlepool	Tr	09.68	68-72	176	10	40

YOUNG Roy
Sheffield, 2 October, 1950 (FB)

League Club	Source	Date Signed	Seasons Played	Apps	Subs	Gls
Doncaster Rov	Sheffield U (Am)	07.70	70	6	1	0

YOUNG Scott
Pontypridd, 14 January, 1976 Wu21-5/WB-1 (CD)

League Club	Source	Date Signed	Seasons Played	Apps	Subs	Gls
Cardiff C	YT	07.94	93-02	257	20	22

YOUNG Charles Stuart Robertson
Falkirk, 23 August, 1929 (G)

League Club	Source	Date Signed	Seasons Played	Apps	Subs	Gls
Sheffield U	Stalybridge Celtic	06.51	51	3	-	0

YOUNG Stuart Rodney
Hull, 16 December, 1972 (F)

League Club	Source	Date Signed	Seasons Played	Apps	Subs	Gls
Hull C	Arsenal (YT)	07.91	91-92	11	8	2
Northampton T	Tr	02.93	92	7	1	2
Scarborough	Tr	08.93	93-94	28	13	10
Scunthorpe U	Tr	12.94	94-95	19	9	3

YOUNG Thomas (Tommy) McIlwaine
Glasgow, 24 December, 1947 (M)

League Club	Source	Date Signed	Seasons Played	Apps	Subs	Gls
Tranmere Rov	Falkirk	06.72	72-76	170	2	27
Rotherham U	Tr	07.77	77-78	11	4	1

YOUNG William (Willie) David
Edinburgh, 25 November, 1951 Su23-5 (CD)

League Club	Source	Date Signed	Seasons Played	Apps	Subs	Gls
Tottenham H	Aberdeen	09.75	75-76	54	0	3
Arsenal	Tr	03.77	76-81	170	0	11
Nottingham F	Tr	12.81	81-82	59	0	5
Norwich C	Tr	08.83	83	5	1	0
Brighton & Hove A	L	03.84	83	4	0	0
Darlington	Tr	09.84	84	4	0	0

YOUNG William (Willie) John
Glasgow, 24 February, 1956 (W)

League Club	Source	Date Signed	Seasons Played	Apps	Subs	Gls
Aston Villa	Arthurlie	07.78	78	3	0	0
Torquay U	Tr	10.81	81-82	35	3	0

YOUNGER Thomas (Tommy)
Edinburgh, 10 April, 1930 Died 1984 SLge-4/S-24 (G)

League Club	Source	Date Signed	Seasons Played	Apps	Subs	Gls
Liverpool	Hibernian	06.56	56-58	120	-	0
Stoke C	Falkirk	03.60	59	10	-	0
Leeds U	Toronto (Can)	09.61	61-62	37	-	0

YOUNGER William (Billy)
Holywell, Northumberland, 22 March, 1940 (IF)

League Club	Source	Date Signed	Seasons Played	Apps	Subs	Gls
Nottingham F	Whitley Bay	05.57	58-60	12	-	2
Lincoln C	L	02.61	60	4	-	0
Walsall	Tr	06.61	61	8	-	5
Doncaster Rov	Tr	12.61	61	18	-	1
Hartlepools U	Tr	08.62	62	37	-	4

YOUNGMAN Stuart Trevor
Beccles, 15 October, 1965 (M)

League Club	Source	Date Signed	Seasons Played	Apps	Subs	Gls
Colchester U	App	07.84	84	0	1	0

YOUNGS Thomas (Tom) Anthony John
Bury St Edmunds, 31 August, 1979 (F)

League Club	Source	Date Signed	Seasons Played	Apps	Subs	Gls
Cambridge U	Jnrs	07.97	97-02	118	32	43
Northampton T	Tr	03.03	02-04	11	15	0
Leyton Orient	Tr	01.05	04	6	4	1

YULU Christian
Kinshasa, DR Congo, 17 August, 1984 (F)

League Club	Source	Date Signed	Seasons Played	Apps	Subs	Gls
Coventry C	Rennes (Fr)	02.03	02	1	2	0

YURAN Sergei
Kiev, Ukraine, 11 June, 1969 Russia int (F)

League Club	Source	Date Signed	Seasons Played	Apps	Subs	Gls
Millwall (L)	FC Porto (Por)	01.96	95	13	0	1

ZABEK Lee Kevin
Bristol, 13 October, 1978 (M)

League Club	Source	Date Signed	Seasons Played	Apps	Subs	Gls
Bristol Rov	YT	07.97	96-99	21	8	1
Exeter C	Tr	08.00	00-01	28	5	0

ZABICA Robert
Perth, Australia, 9 April, 1964 Australia int (G)

League Club	Source	Date Signed	Seasons Played	Apps	Subs	Gls
Bradford C	Perth Glory (Aus)	08.97	97	3	0	0

ZADKOVICH Ruben Anton
Australia, 23 May, 1986 AuYth (M)

League Club	Source	Date Signed	Seasons Played	Apps	Subs	Gls
Queens Park Rgrs	Wollongong Rgrs (Aus)	09.04				
Notts Co	Tr	03.05	04	6	2	1

ZAGORAKIS Theodoros (Theo)
Kavala, Greece, 17 October, 1971 Greece 50 (M)

League Club	Source	Date Signed	Seasons Played	Apps	Subs	Gls
Leicester C	PAOK Salonika (Gre)	02.98	97-99	34	16	3

ZAHANA-ONI Landry
Abidjan, Ivory Coast, 8 August, 1976 (F)

League Club	Source	Date Signed	Seasons Played	Apps	Subs	Gls
Luton T	Bromley	01.99	98-99	4	5	0

ZAKUANI Gabriel (Gaby)
DR Congo, 31 May, 1986 (CD)

League Club	Source	Date Signed	Seasons Played	Apps	Subs	Gls
Leyton Orient	Sch	●	02-04	41	3	2

ZAMORA Robert (Bobby) Lester
Barking, 16 January, 1981 Eu21-6 (F)

League Club	Source	Date Signed	Seasons Played	Apps	Subs	Gls
Bristol Rov	YT	07.99	99	0	4	0
Brighton & Hove A	L	02.00	99	6	0	6
Brighton & Hove A	Tr	08.00	00-02	117	2	70
Tottenham H	Tr	07.03	03	6	10	0
West Ham U	Tr	02.04	03-04	30	21	12

ZAMPERINI Alessandro
Rome, Italy, 15 August, 1982 (CD)

League Club	Source	Date Signed	Seasons Played	Apps	Subs	Gls
Portsmouth	AS Roma (It)	07.01	01	16	0	2

ZAVAGNO Luciano
Rosario, Argentina, 6 August, 1977 (FB)

League Club	Source	Date Signed	Seasons Played	Apps	Subs	Gls
Derby Co	Troyes (Fr)	10.01	01-03	48	4	3

ZDRILIC David
Sydney, Australia, 14 April, 1974 Australia 22 (F)

League Club	Source	Date Signed	Seasons Played	Apps	Subs	Gls
Walsall	Unterhaching (Ger)	08.02	02	9	15	3

ZEGHDANE Lehit
Revin, France, 3 October, 1977 (M)

League Club	Source	Date Signed	Seasons Played	Apps	Subs	Gls
Darlington	Sedan (Fr)	09.00	00	1	2	0

ZELEM Peter Richard
Manchester, 13 February, 1962 (CD)

League Club	Source	Date Signed	Seasons Played	Apps	Subs	Gls
Chester	App	02.80	80-84	124	5	15
Wolverhampton W	Tr	01.85	84-86	45	0	1
Preston NE	Tr	03.87	86	6	0	1
Burnley	Tr	08.87	87-88	17	2	2

ZELIC Nedijeljko (Ned)
Australia, 4 July, 1971 Australia int (M)

League Club	Source	Date Signed	Seasons Played	Apps	Subs	Gls
Queens Park Rgrs	Bor Dortmund (Ger)	08.95	95	3	1	0

ZENCHUK Steven John
Peterborough, 20 November, 1966 (G)

League Club	Source	Date Signed	Seasons Played	Apps	Subs	Gls
Peterborough U	App	08.83	83	1	0	0

ZENDEN Boudewijn (Bolo)
Maastricht, Holland, 15 August, 1976 Holland 54 (M)

League Club	Source	Date Signed	Seasons Played	Apps	Subs	Gls
Chelsea	Barcelona (Sp)	08.01	01-02	24	19	4
Middlesbrough	Tr	08.03	03-04	67	0	9

ZHIYI Fan
Shanghai, China, 22 January, 1970 China 109 (CD)

League Club	Source	Date Signed	Seasons Played	Apps	Subs	Gls
Crystal Palace	Shanghai Shen (China)	09.98	98-01	87	1	4
Cardiff C	Dundee	11.02	02	6	0	0

League Club	Source	Date Signed	Seasons Played	Career Record Apps	Subs	Gls
ZIEGE Christian						
Berlin, Germany, 1 February, 1972 Germany 72						(FB)
Middlesbrough	AC Milan (It)	08.99	99	29	0	6
Liverpool	Tr	08.00	00	11	5	1
Tottenham H	Tr	08.01	01-03	44	3	7
ZIEGLER Reto Pirmin						
Nyon, Switzerland, 16 January, 1986 Switu21/Swit-3						(M)
Tottenham H	Grasshoppers (Swi)	08.04	04	12	11	1
ZIVKOVIC Boris						
Zivinice, Croatia, 15 November, 1975 Croatia 38						(FB)
Portsmouth	Bayer Leverkusen (Ger)	07.03	03	17	1	0
ZOHAR Itzhak (Itzy)						
Tel Aviv, Israel, 31 October, 1970 Israel int						(M)
Crystal Palace	Royal Antwerp (Bel)	08.97	97	2	4	0
ZOIS Peter						
Melbourne, Australia, 21 April, 1978						(G)
Cardiff C	Purfleet	02.98	97	1	0	0
ZOLA Gianfranco						
Oliena, Sardinia, Italy, 5 July, 1966 Italy 35						(F)
Chelsea	Parma (It)	11.96	96-02	185	44	59
ZOLA-MAKONGO Calvin						
Kinshasa, DR Congo, 31 December, 1984						(F)
Newcastle U	YT	01.02				
Oldham Ath	L	08.03	03	21	4	5
Tranmere Rov	Tr	07.04	04	7	8	2
ZONDERVAN Romeo						
Surinam, 4 March, 1959 Holland int						(M)
West Bromwich A	Twente Enschede (Holl)	03.82	81-83	82	2	5
Ipswich T	Tr	03.84	83-91	270	4	13
ZORICICH Christopher (Chris) Vincent						
Auckland, New Zealand, 3 May, 1969 New Zealand int						(FB)
Leyton Orient	Papatoetoe (NZ)	02.90	90-92	53	9	1
ZUNIGA Yanez Herlin **Ysrael**						
Lima, Peru, 27 August, 1976 Peru 17						(F)
Coventry C	FCB Melgar (Peru)	03.00	99-01	11	18	3
ZWIJNENBERG Clemens						
Enschede, Holland, 18 May, 1970						(CD)
Bristol C (L)	Aalborg BK (Den)	09.98	98	1	2	0

League Club	Source	Date Signed	Seasons Played	Career Record Apps	Subs	Gls

THE PROFESSIONAL FOOTBALLERS' ASSOCIATION

Organised professional football began in 1888 with the formation of the Football League. Unsuccessful attempts were made to form a players union, but it was not until 2 December 1907 that the first meeting of the current association took place in Manchester. It was chaired by the famous Welsh international, Billy Meredith of Manchester United. From that early beginning of players joining together to improve their working conditions, the PFA has grown to become the highly respected professional body it is today, not only being involved in all aspects of the game which affect its members but adding to its reputation on the principle of caring for the interests of the game as a whole.

The aim of the PFA has always been to systematically protect and improve the conditions and status of its members. This involves many different aspects, including enforcement of contracts, providing insurance against death and disability, being trustees of contributory and non-contributory pension funds, representing players negotiating contracts, or at disciplinary hearings with the FA Premier League, the Football League or the FA, or in dispute with their clubs over fines or other disciplinary problems. They are represented on the ultimate appeals body for disciplinary measures and are directly involved with matters relating to on field disciplinary offences. Above all we have collective bargaining agreements with the FA, the FA Premier League and the Football League by which no changes can be made to the rules affecting players without our permission.

The PFA has been involved in various disputes during its history. Two of the milestones were the removal of the maximum wage in 1961 and the court ruling that football's retain and transfer system was illegal in 1963. In the 1970s, a commission on industrial relations eventually brought in all the present day procedures that footballers enjoy today. The most important decision was the establishment in 1978 of a player's right to change clubs at the end of his contract. Since the Bosman judgement in the European Court in December 1995, our system has been refined so that all players are free at the end of their contract to join another club but, domestically if a player out of contract is under 24 a compensation fee will still be payable. This is in order to encourage clubs to develop youth systems.

PFA Education Fund provides grants to former and current members wishing to take training courses and qualifications to prepare themselves for a career after their playing days are over. This Fund, which is a registered charity, is the main funder of the two scholarship schemes in football - League Football Education and Premier League Learning - and the Football in the Community Programme, as well as many other initiatives including coaching, anti-racism and drugs awareness programmes and jointly funded medical research projects with the Football Association.

PFA Accident Fund provides money to ensure that all players registered with the Football League and the Premier League are covered for retirement insurance under the Players' Accident Insurance & Sickness Scheme. The amount payable is up to a £20,000 limit. There is also cover for non-league members up to an amount of £5,000. The PFA pays a subsidy to the Premier League and the Football League to make sure every player has private medical insurance and immediate access to the best possible private treatment.

The Accident Fund also provides grants to former members towards the cost of private medical treatment which they require as a result of injuries sustained during their playing career.

PFA Benevolent Fund is a charitable fund which provides grants to former and current members or their dependants who are suffering financial hardship.

PFA Initiatives: The PFA has been at the forefront of all issues which affect not only their membership but also the good of the game in general and it has been and is still currently involved in initiatives that have had a dramatic impact on the game at all levels. The following are a selection of the wide range of such initiatives - Kick It Out, Show Racism the Red Card, Oxfam, National Literacy Trust, Keep your Eye on the Ball (testicular cancer), joint PFA/FA medical initiatives including musculo-skeletal and cardiovascular screening of all scholars and alleged brain injury research.

The PFA continues to work with a host of other charitable organisations offering endorsement and support to the Prince's Trust Football Initiative, National Playing Fields Association, NSPCC Football Full Stop Campaign, Shelter, Scope, Oxfam and Sporting Chance Clinic.

PFA Management Agency: The PFA has formed its own football agency to continue and develop its role of player representation. The Agency provides hands-on representation for players at every stage of their careers and to offer the best advice at all times.

PFA Education Department provides funding for former and current members to gain educational and vocational qualifications and assists players to re-train for a second career.

PFA in the Community: The PFA has been at the forefront of community activity since 1986 when it was instrumental in the launch of the national Football in the Community Programme. The PFA now has its own Community Liaison Officer to raise awareness of the positive impact and pivotal role players have in the success of the Football in the Community Programme.

PFA Coaching Department: The main aim of the Department is to organise coaching courses and provide a coaching service for professional footballers, both current and former, who are interested in developing a structured career in coaching.

PFA Enterprises is the commercial arm of the PFA, generating revenue opportunities for members and charitable funds through a wide variety of activities. PFA Enterprises has developed close relationships with a number of companies who have become official PFA Business Partners, offering products and services to our members.

PFA Financial Management helps and advises members in all areas of their finances, during and after their careers, giving them a full financial planning service which includes advice on mortgages, pensions, savings and other forms of investment.

PFA OFFICE BEARERS 1907-1998

Secretaries/Chief Executives

H C Bloomfield	1907-1910
A J Owen	1910-1913
N J Newbould	1913-1929
J A Fay	1929-1953
C Lloyd OBE	1953-1981
G Taylor BSc (Econ) Hon DArt, Hon MA	1981-

Chairmen

H L Mainman	1907-1910	J W T Neill	1967-1970
E H Lintott	1910-1911	A D Dougan	1970-1978
C Veitch	1911-1918	G Taylor	1978-1980
C Roberts	1919-1921	A Gowling	1980-1982
J Lawrence	1921-1922	S J Coppell	1982-1984
J A Fay	1922-1929	B Talbot	1984-1988
H Matthews	1929-1930	G Crooks	1988-1990
A Wood	1930-1936	B Marwood	1990-1993
A F Barrett	1936-1937	P Nevin	1993-1997
S D Crooks	1937-1946	B Horne	1997-2001
J C Guthrie	1946-1957	N Cusack	2001-2002
J W T Hill	1957-1961	R Jobson	2002-2003
T S Cummings	1961-1963	W Barton	2003-2004
M C Musgrove	1963-1966	D Holdsworth	2004-2005
N Cantwell	1966-1967		

THE PFA AWARDS

Player of the Year: 1974 Norman Hunter (Leeds United); 1975 Colin Todd (Derby County); 1976 Pat Jennings (Tottenham Hotspur); 1977 Andy Gray (Aston Villa); 1978 Peter Shilton (Nottingham Forest); 1979 Liam Brady (Arsenal); 1980 Terry McDermott (Liverpool); 1981 John Wark (Ipswich Town); 1982 Kevin Keegan (Southampton); 1983 Kenny Dalglish (Liverpool); 1984 Ian Rush (Liverpool); 1985 Peter Reid (Everton); 1986 Gary Lineker (Everton); 1987 Clive Allen (Tottenham Hotspur); 1988 John Barnes (Liverpool); 1989 Mark Hughes (Manchester United); 1990 David Platt (Aston Villa); 1991 Mark Hughes (Manchester United); 1992 Gary Pallister (Manchester United); 1993 Paul McGrath (Aston Villa); 1994 Eric Cantona (Manchester United); 1995 Alan Shearer (Blackburn Rovers); 1996 Les Ferdinand (Newcastle United); 1997 Alan Shearer (Newcastle United); 1998 Dennis Bergkamp (Arsenal); 1999 David Ginola (Tottenham Hotspur); 2000 Roy Keane (Manchester United); 2001 Teddy Sheringham (Manchester United); 2002 Ruud van Nistelrooy (Manchester United); 2003 Thierry Henry (Arsenal); 2004 Thierry Henry (Arsenal); 2005 John Terry (Chelsea).

Young Player of the Year: 1974 Kevin Beattie (Ipswich Town); 1975 Mervyn Day (West Ham United); 1976 Peter Barnes (Manchester City); 1977 Andy Gray (Aston Villa); 1978 Tony Woodcock (Nottingham Forest); 1979 Cyrille Regis (West Bromwich Albion); 1980 Glenn Hoddle (Tottenham Hotspur); 1981 Gary Shaw (Aston Villa); 1982 Steve Moran (Southampton); 1983 Ian Rush (Liverpool); 1984 Paul Walsh (Luton Town); 1985 Mark Hughes (Manchester United); 1986 Tony Cottee (West Ham United); 1987 Tony Adams (Arsenal); 1988 Paul Gascoigne (Newcastle United); 1989 Paul Merson (Arsenal); 1990 Matthew le Tissier (Southampton); 1991 Lee Sharpe (Manchester United); 1992 Ryan Giggs (Manchester United); 1993 Ryan Giggs (Manchester United); 1994 Andy Cole (Newcastle United); 1995 Robbie Fowler (Liverpool); 1996 Robbie Fowler (Liverpool); 1997 David Beckham (Manchester United); 1998 Michael Owen (Liverpool); 1999 Nicolas Anelka (Arsenal); 2000 Harry Kewell (Leeds United); 2001 Steven Gerrard (Liverpool); 2002 Craig Bellamy (Newcastle United); 2003 Jermaine Jenas (Newcastle United); 2004 Scott Parker (Chelsea); 2005 Wayne Rooney (Manchester United).

Merit Award: 1974 Bobby Charlton CBE, Cliff Lloyd OBE; 1975 Denis Law; 1976 George Eastham OBE; 1977 Jack Taylor OBE; 1978 Bill Shankly OBE; 1979 Tom Finney OBE; 1980 Sir Matt Busby CBE; 1981 John Trollope MBE; 1982 Joe Mercer OBE; 1983 Bob Paisley OBE; 1984 Bill Nicholson; 1985 Ron Greenwood CBE; 1986 The 1966 England World Cup Team; 1987 Sir Stanley Matthews; 1988 Billy Bonds; 1989 Nat Lofthouse; 1990 Peter Shilton; 1991 Tommy Hutchison; 1992 Brian Clough OBE, MA; 1993 Manchester United 1968 Team; 1994 Billy Bingham CBE; 1995 Gordon Strachan OBE; 1996 Pele; 1997 Peter Beardsley MBE; 1998 Sir Tom Finney CBE; 1999 Tony Ford; 2000 Gary Mabbutt; 2001 Jimmy Hill; 2002 Niall Quinn; 2003 Sir Bobby Robson; 2004 Dario Gradi; 2005 Shaka Hislop.

PFA DIVISIONAL AWARD WINNERS: 2005

FA Barclaycard Premiership: Petr Cech (Chelsea); Gary Neville (Manchester United); John Terry (Chelsea); Rio Ferdinand (Manchester United); Ashley Cole (Arsenal); Frank Lampard (Chelsea); Steven Gerrard (Liverpool); Arjen Robben (Chelsea); Shaun Wright-Phillips (Manchester City); Thierry Henry (Arsenal); Andy Johnson (Crystal Palace).

Coca Cola Championship: Kelvin Davis (Ipswich Town); Graham Alexander (Preston North End); Tom Huddlestone (Derby County); Gary Breen (Sunderland); George McCartney (Sunderland); Jimmy Bullard (Wigan Athletic); Steve Sidwell (Reading); Julio Arca (Sunderland); Inigo Idiakez (Derby County); Nathan Ellington (Wigan Athletic); Jason Roberts (Wigan Athletic).

Coca Cola League Division One: Marlon Beresford (Luton Town); Ryan Taylor (Tranmere Rovers); Curtis Davies (Luton Town); Chris Coyne (Luton Town); Warren Cummings (AFC Bournemouth); Stuart Elliott (Hull City); Paul Merson (Walsall); Ahmet Brkovic (Luton Town); Kevin Nicholls (Luton Town); Steve Howard (Luton Town); Leroy Lita (Bristol City).

Coca Cola League Division Two: Chris Weale (Yeovil Town); Sam Ricketts (Swansea City); Adam Barrett (Southend United); Andy Crosby (Scunthorpe United); Michael Rose (Yeovil Town); Lee Johnson (Yeovil Town); Darren Way (Yeovil Town); Kevin Maher (Southend United); Peter Beagrie (Scunthorpe United); Phil Jevons (Yeovil Town); Lee Trundle (Swansea City).

NOTES

NOTES

NOTES

NOTES

NOTES

NOTES

NOTES

NOTES